UP YOURS!

A GUIDE to UK PUNK, NEW WAVE and early post punk

BY
VeRnon JoYnSoN

Special thanks to Ivor Trueman, Mark Brennan and Steve Whitehouse.

This book is dedicated to rock and pop music collectors everywhere and to Seonaid, Jasmine and Jake for their support. It is also dedicated to my mum Joy who suddenly passed away on 9th June 2000 whilst I was working on this book.

First published in Great Britain in 2001 by Borderline Productions, Print House, Sedgley Street, Wolverhampton, England.
This book is sold subject to the condition that it shall not be lent, resold, hired out or otherwise circulated in any form of binding or cover than it is published in.

ALL RIGHTS RESERVED. ALL CONTENTS COPYRIGHT © 2001.   ISBN 1 899855 13 0

Printed by Craneprint Ltd., Print House, Sedgley Street, Wolverhampton, England.
Front and back cover by Ivor Trueman.

A GUIDE TO U.K. PUNK, NEW WAVE AND EARLY POST PUNK.

CONTENTS

FOREWORD	Page 5
INTRODUCTION	Page 9
A-Z OF PUNK, NEW WAVE AND EARLY POST-PUNK UK BANDS	Page 19
Colour illustrations	(i) - (xii)
VINYL COMPILATIONS	Page 459
CD COMPILATIONS	Page 473
SOME IMPORTANT PUNK, NEW WAVE AND Oi! LABELS	Page 491
INDEX	Page 545

AUTHOR'S NOTE

I have tried to ensure that this book is as accurate as possible, but some of the entries are incomplete, there are bound to be some errors and there are artists omitted who should be in here. A book of this type is never really finished! I'd like to hear from anyone who is able to supply information that is missing in my book, correct errors or add additional entries. Who knows? If enough of you buy it there may be a second volume! If you can do any of these please contact me care of:

BORDERLINE PRODUCTIONS
Print House
Sedgley Street
Wolverhampton
WV2 3AJ
England

or via email: upyours@borderlinebooks.com

Vernon Joynson, September 2001.

X-Ray Spex at The Roundhouse, London 14th May 1978.
Photo: Steven Richards.

FOREWORD

Some of you will be familiar with my earlier works. 'Fuzz, Acid and Flowers' is a guide to American garage, psychedelic and hippie rock between 1964 – 75. 'Tapestry Of Delights' deals with British music of the beat, R&B, psychedelic and progressive eras from 1963 – 76. 'Dreams, Fantasies And Nightmares' is an encylopaedic guide to Canadian, Australian and New Zealand rock and pop between 1963 – 75. It also provides a brief introduction to some of the fantastic sounds that came out of Latin America in this period.

Punk was every bit as exciting as The Beatles and the beat scene or the emergence of psychedelia in the late sixties. By 1976 the rock music industry was becoming self-indulgent and complacent, punk injected the new life, energy and excitement it so badly needed. Any band with enterprise and a little bit of money could put a record out and, if it attracted airplay, who knows they could be destined for a bright future. I was fortunate to live in the heart of London's Camden Town in the late seventies. As a regular at venues like Dingwalls, the Electric Ballroom, the Music Machine, the Marquee, the Vortex, Rock Garden and Hope and Anchor I was fortunate to see many of the acts in this book in their prime.

The Aims of This Book Are:

To provide an encyclopaedic guide for record/CD buyers, collectors and fans to UK punk, new wave and early post-punk, primarily in the 1976-1982 era.

To bring to your attention many artists who didn't attract the publicity and acclaim they deserved first time around. Many of the artists featured have never appeared in music encyclopaedias before. I hope that as a result of this book some of them will receive the recognition they deserve.

The Remit of The Book

As this is a guide to British punk, new wave and early post-punk, entries are mostly confined to British-born artists. To qualify for an entry an artist had to release a record or cassette, appear on a compilation or at very least release some demos. The book is not fully comprehensive, particularly not in the early eighties when there was such a plethora of new indie bands and some quite difficult decisions have been taken about who to include, especially in the early post-punk era.

Whilst the book's time frame is predominantly 1976-82, where artists from that era have recorded beyond 1982 I have continued to document their careers until the mid-eighties. As Oi! or street punk as some prefer to call it and hardcore were attempts to keep the concept of punk alive in the eighties and beyond I have included artists of this genre into the late eighties even though, in some cases, they may not have recorded until after 1982. Oi!, in particular, seems to have been severely underdocumented in music encyclopaedias.

Although this book is largely confined to British-born artists I have taken the liberty of including artists from Ireland and a limited number – such as **Wayne County** (the United States), **Stinky Toys** (France), **Plastic Bertrand** (Belgium) and **The Saints** (Australia) – who weren't British by birth, but were based in Britain when they achieved their success and were an integral part of the punk/new wave scene in this country in the late seventies. A case could probably be made for several others, but constraints of space have made this impossible.

This book concentrates on punk, new wave and early post-punk artists, mainstream pop and rock have been avoided. Deciding who to and who not to include has not been at all easy. Many mainstream artists in the late seventies veered towards punk and new wave if they felt it would help their careers. Some subjective decisions have been made and some quite popish bands like **Altered Images** who had some association with punk in their early days have been included, whilst others like Culture Club (whose first single was in May 1982) haven't. The dividing line has often been a fine one.

For some artists like **Ian Dury**, **Nick Lowe** and **Dave Edmunds**, who'd been around for a while, the punk/new wave scene offered a new lease of life and they've been included because they were an integral part of the

Adam and The Ants at The Roundhouse, London 14th May 1978.
Photo: Steven Richards.

new wave. Others, like David Bowie, continued to prosper in this era, more because he was usually trying new and interesting ideas than because he was an integral part of new wave. I haven't included him, but you can read about his pre-1976 career in my earlier British tome 'The Tapestry Of Delights'.

In the early post-punk era, the mod revival, electronic, doom and gloom, avant-punk, third wave (or hardcore), Oi! and industrial bands are featured, but the ska revival / two-tone bands are not. This would have increased the length of the book considerably and is not a genre I have much knowledge of.

For all artists featured I've tried to include details of reissues, retrospective compilations and collections and appearances on the plethora of various artists compilations, both at the time and retrospectively. It would be a mammoth, almost impossible, task to make this coverage comprehensive and it certainly isn't, but I've tried to make it as full as I can with the resources available to be.

How To Use This Book

1. All bands and solo artists appear in alphabetical order. 'The' is ignored as the first word of a band's name. Individual artists have been alphabetised under surnames e.g. Elvis Costello appears under 'C'.

2. Some entries are very brief, where bands just released one 45 or appeared on a compilation, but for more prolific acts expect to see the following:-

Personnel:	Name	Instrument	Different Line-Up
	MEMBER 1	bs	A
	MEMBER 2	drms	A
	MEMBER 3	gtr	A B
	MEMBER 4	vcls	A B
	MEMBER 5	bs	B
	MEMBER 6	drms	B

The Buzzcocks at The Roundhouse, London 28th May 1978.
Photo: Steven Richards.

ALBUM DISCOGRAPHIES

Where more than one has been released, they are listed in chronological order. Line entries are as follows:-

```
                                                              HCP
ALBUMS: 1(B)   WHEN THE PUNKS GO MARCHING IN
                                    (Riot City CITY 001) 1982 -
        2(B)   BLACK LEATHER GIRL    (Clay CLAYLP 9) 1984 -
         (1)    (2)                   (3)              (4) (5)
```

(1) Line-up on album (where known)
(2) Name
(3) UK label and catalogue number
(4) Year Of Release
(5) Highest chart placing, where applicable

ALBUM / CD REISSUE INFORMATION

Details are given where albums originally issued between 1976 – 1986 have been reissued on vinyl or CD. Details of recordings from this era, which have resurfaced on vinyl or CD compilations, are also given (where known, but as there have been so many compilations they aren't entirely comprehensive).

EP DISCOGRAPHIES (Where applicable)

Where more than one has been released, they are listed chronologically. U.K. label and catalogue number(s), year of release, and where applicable highest chart placings are given. PS indicates that the release was housed in a picture sleeve. They nearly all were in this era. Reissue details are also provided.

SINGLE DISCOGRAPHIES

These are listed chronologically and the same information as for albums and EPs, including details of relevant reissues, and chart placings, is given.

ASSORTED INFORMATION ABOUT THE BAND OR ARTIST

In the text, the name(s) of other bands or artists who are featured in this book appear in bold print to facilitate easy cross-reference. This should enable readers to trace the careers of several musicians, which is often fascinating. Names of songs are identified in italics as are tracks which appear on compilations, which for many will be the only means of accessing the song.

COMPILATION LISTINGS

A list of most compilation albums and CDs referred to, along with label details, catalogue numbers and year of release appears at the end of this book. Both compilations/samplers from the late seventies and early eighties and retrospective compilations are included, though the list is by no means complete as there are so many of them.

PUNK, NEW WAVE AND Oi! LABEL DISCOGRAPHIES

A new feature of this book are the label discographies at the end of the book of some of the key punk, new wave and Oi! labels. Moreso than most previous music genres, punk and Oi!, in particular, were connected with particular labels.

Credits and Acknowledgements

Writing this book has fulfilled one of my dreams and I want to thank the people who've helped me to realise it. I'd particularly like to thank Ivor Trueman (typing/typesetting); Mark Brennan 'Captain Oi!' for promotional copies/label discographies and some compilation listings; Steve Whitehouse (tapes and information); Mike Warth and Nick Walker (45 sleeves); Steve Penfold (information) and Steve Richards for illustrations (which are individually credited) of Steven Richards Photography: 34 Hampden Road, London N8 0HT. www.Rockphotos.i12.com.

I am also grateful to the following sources:- Record Collector magazine; Mojo magazine; Record Collector: Rare Record Price Guide 2000 Millenium Edition; New Musical Express; Sounds; Melody Maker; Terry Hounsome's Rock Record And Single File; Guinness Book Of British Hit Albums And Singles; M.C. Strong's The Great Rock Discography; John Savage's England's Dreaming; Who's New Wave In Music; The New Music Record And Tape Guide; The Virgin Encylopaedia Of Indie And New Wave; R.E.D. Music Master 2001 Catalogue and Deletions; Cherry Red, Captain Oi! and Abraxas Catalogues.

Vernon Joynson.
September 2001.

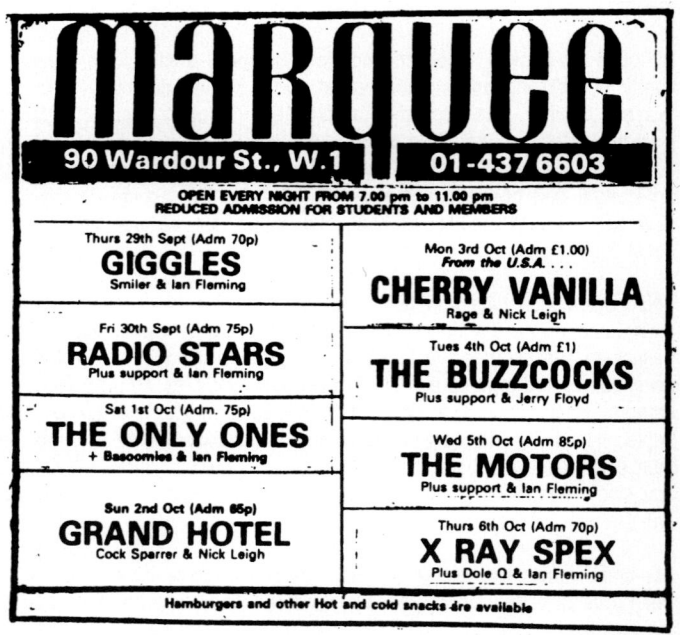

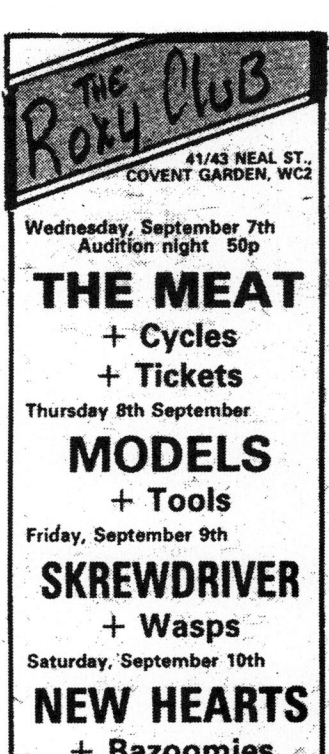

The Ruts at The Electric Ballroom, London 19th October 1979.
Photo: Steven Richards.

Alternative TV at The Roundhouse, London 28th May 1978. Photo: Steven Richards.

Siouxsie and The Banshees at The Roundhouse, London 23rd July 1978. Photo: Steven Richards.

INTRODUCTION

Three key figures in the U.K. punk phenomenon were Steve Jones, Paul Cook and **Malcolm McLaren**. Jones was a West London lad and petty thief who regularly skipped school with his schoolfriend Paul Cook to go round to another schoolmate's Warwick 'Wally' Nightingale's house. It was here, in 1973, that the three of them - formed The Swankers with Steve handling vocals, Paul bashing the skins and Wally playing guitar.

Malcolm McLaren was an art graduate, designer and businessman, who'd opened a clothes shop called 'Let It Rock' on the King's Road in London's fashionable Chelsea, with his partner Vivienne Westwood in 1971. Initially the shop was aimed at Teddy Boys. In 1973, they changed its name to 'Too Fast To Live, Too Young To Die', as it focused more on the rocker market. They renamed it 'Sex' in 1974 by which time it was concentrating on selling their own designs and bondage gear. 'Sex' became a focal point for fashion conscious disaffected youths and Steve Jones was one such person. Jones was aware of **McLaren**'s links with the music industry and continually badgered him to come to a Swankers rehearsal. Eventually **McLaren** agreed probably to get Jones off his back. The crucial link had been made and, although it seems **McLaren** was far from bowled over by the band, it set him thinking. The band lacked a permanent bassist and **McLaren** was instrumental in persuading one of the Saturday helpers in 'Sex', Glen Matlock who he knew could play guitar, to join the band and switch to bass.

The New York Dolls were another important influence on punk. **McLaren** had been fascinated by their raw garage sound and outrageous over-the-top look during an American trip in 1973. Towards the end of 1974 **McLaren** returned to New York to resume his fascination with them. He left his friend Bernie Rhodes to oversee the development of The Swankers. Over in New York, **McLaren** became the New York Dolls' manager in all but name during the winter of 1974/5. He revamped their image and made them even more over-the-top, but their appetite for drugs proved their undoing and, after their virtual disintegration, he returned to London in May 1975.

McLaren's experience in New York had been frustrating and he returned to London determined to translate his ideas into action with The Swankers. His first priority was to find them a striking frontman and vocalist, because Jones didn't really fit the bill. He'd tried and failed to persuade former New York Doll Sylvain Sylvain and Richard Hell of Television to come back to Britain with him to front the band. Again 'Sex' provided the solution, when he spotted a green-haired image-conscious teenager called John Lydon, who was a frequent visitor to the shop with his friends. **McLaren** arranged a hasty audition, with Lydon singing Alice Cooper's *Schools Out* backed by the jukebox in the nearby Roebuck pub and it immediately became apparent that John Lydon (who the other band members soon referred to as Johnny Rotten on account of his rotten teeth) was the man for the job. With founder-member Wally Nightingale ejected because his personality didn't reflect the image **McLaren** envisaged for the band and Jones persuaded to concentrate on playing guitar, the beast was born but they needed a new name to reflect the image **McLaren** envisaged for them. **The Sex Pistols**, a slogan which had once appeared on one of the clothing stall's T-Shirts, seemed ideal. **McLaren** was now determined to do with **The Sex Pistols** what he'd failed to do with The New York Dolls, challenge the establishment. They played their first proper gig on 6th November 1975 at the St. Martin's School of Art. In the following couple of years the increasingly self-indulgent and complacent music industry was turned upside down. Even the British establishment was challenged by disaffected youth.

The burgeoning new music scene in New York became a significant influence on the emerging British punk scene. Patti Smith's *Horses* album had emerged in late 1975 and both its look and content were provocative. A whole new music scene was developing based around CBGB's (a club in New York's downtrodden Bowery district) and spearheaded by talented and innovative groups like Talking Heads, Television (the Grateful Dead of the new wave), The Ramones and Blondie. The word 'punk' also originated in the States. It was used to describe sixties garage bands like The Seeds, Electric Prunes and Thirteenth Floor Elevators, who were being rediscovered in the mid-seventies and again to describe new acts like Patti Smith. By March 1975, Richard Hell (then with an embryonic Television) had written *Blank Generation*, one of the early punk anthems and a magazine called 'Punk' started up in December 1975.

So what was punk? Punk was an attitude and in 1976 the boundaries were clearly drawn. There was the old wave - people like Pink Floyd, Emerson, Lake and Palmer and Bob Dylan and there was punk (or the new wave as some preferred to call it). This not only comprised the first wave of true punk bands like **The Sex Pistols**, **The Clash**, **The Damned** and **The Adverts**, it also embraced artists like **The Count Bishops**, **Eddie and The Hotrods** and **Ian Dury**, who'd been on the pub rock circuit but had the same attitude.

Soon a whole sub-culture would develop. There would be an alternative press of punk fanzines led by Mark P's 'Sniffin' Glue'. There was also punk fashion which was above all designed to shock - multi-coloured peroxided spiky hair and an assortment of safety pins, zips, buckles, chains, bondage belts and more, all designed to offend the passer-by.

Back here in Britain, 1976 was the year punk emerged. On 23rd January, whilst **The Sex Pistols** played at Watford College Union, **The Stranglers** were gigging at the Red Cow in London. The following month **The Sex Pistols** opened for pub-rockers **Eddie and The Hot Rods** at the Marquee. Journalist Neil Spencer was covering the gig for NME. Under a headline of "Don't look over your shoulder but The Sex Pistols are coming" he commented enthusiastically on the rawness and excitement of their "60s styled white punk rock". It was during his interview with the band afterwards that Steve Jones gave him the famous quote "Actually, we're not into music, we're into chaos". Two days later, on Saturday 14th February, The Pistols played at artist/socialite Andrew Logan's Valentine Ball. On 20th February, **The Sex Pistols** turned up to open for Screaming Lord Sutch at High Wycombe College Of Art. Howard Trafford (**Devoto**) and Pete McNiesh (Shelley) drove down from Manchester for the gig and were so enthused by what they saw that night that they returned to Manchester to form **The Buzzcocks**. The same month Geoff Travis opened his Rough Trade record shop in London's Notting Hill. Initially it specialised in reggae and obscure imports, but it soon became one of the focal points of London's punk/new wave/post-punk scene, with its own record label to promote the artists. Among the bands who signed to Rough Trade were **Cabaret Voltaire**, **Stiff Little Fingers**, **Swell Maps**, **The Raincoats**, **Essential Logic**, **The Slits**, **The Monochrome Set**, **The Pop Group**, **Subway Sect**, **Scritti Politti**, **The Fall** and **Spizzenergi**. Many of these recorded just one or two singles for the label before being snapped up by one of the majors. Rough Trade eventually developed into a distributor of smaller independent labels like Mute, Factory, Postcard and Les Disques Du Crepuscule through a network known as 'The Cartel'.

On 30th March, **The Sex Pistols** made their first appearance at Central London's 100 Club with a chaotic gig. Five days later they played the first night of a residency at the El Paradise Strip Club in Soho, London, sandwiched between a strip show in the running order. The night before they'd played the first of three gigs that month at London's Nashville Rooms. The first two, on 3rd and 23rd April, were supporting the **101'ers** (who featured future **Clash** member Joe Strummer). Their second appearance on 23rd attracted a piece in NME after a fight broke out. They returned a third time on 29th April as the headline band.

THE CLASH - The Clash.

On 11th May, **The Sex Pistols** began a Tuesday night residency at the 100 Club. To date they'd only played in and around London, but later in the month they set out on a tour of the north of England playing in places like Sheffield, Middlesbrough and a show at Manchester's Lesser Free Trade Hall, which had been organised by **Howard Devoto** and Pete Shelley. Their own band **The Buzzcocks** had got just three numbers into their debut gig a few weeks earlier at Bolton Institute Of Technology before being forced off stage!

Two days after The Pistols' Manchester gig, Joe Strummer quit the **101'ers** and began rehearsing with a group of musicians who soon became **The Clash**. They made their debut opening for **The Sex Pistols** at the Black Swan in Sheffield on 4th July.

Across in the States, The Ramones had cut their first album back in February, on 4th July they headlined at London's Roundhouse supported by **The Stranglers** and The Flamin' Groovies. **The Stranglers** had also been the support band when Patti Smith made her London debut back on 16th May. Both **The Stranglers** and The Ramones were among the artists to feature in Britain's first punk fanzine 'Sniffin' Glue', when it was launched by Mark P(erry), a former bank clerk that month.

Two days after **The Clash** made their debut, another new name **The Damned** emerged at the 100 Club supporting **The Sex Pistols**. **The Damned** with a bassist and a drummer calling themselves Captain Sensible and Rat Scabies would go on to become one of the era's most durable acts ever.

Later, on 18th July, The Pistols recorded some demos with engineer **Dave Goodman** before returning to Manchester two days later for a second gig at the Lesser Free Trade Hall. Another new band on the bill that night, along with **The Buzzcocks**, were **Slaughter and The Dogs**, who would go on to record the first release (*Cranked Up Really High*) on the new Manchester indie label Rabid, in May 1977. They later became one of the first punk bands to be signed by a major label, Decca.

The Vibrators at The Electric Ballroom, London 19th October 1979.
Photo: Steven Richards.

In August, Jake Riviera and Dave Robinson launched Stiff Records. The first release was **Nick Lowe**'s *Heart Of The City*. Concentrating on one-off deals with new artists Stiff became an important outlet for punk and new wave artists in particular over the next few years. On 7th August, **The Sex Pistols** appeared on the front of Melody Maker ensuring further publicity for the band. The whole London punk scene was now coming together. An early highlight was on Saturday 29th August when **The Sex Pistols**, **The Clash** and **The Buzzcocks** played an all night gig at the Screen On The Green in Islington. Already, though, punk and violence and particularly **The Sex Pistols** and violence were becoming synonymous in many people's minds. This was because of the trouble at their gigs. The organisers of the Mont De Marsan Punk Rock festival in France on 21st August refused to have **The Sex Pistols** on the bill. **The Clash**, who had been invited, withdrew in solidarity. The only punk act to go in the end was **The Damned**. The rest of the roster - The Pink Fairies, **Eddie and The Hot Rods**, **The Count Bishops**, **The Hammersmith Gorrillas** and **The Tyla Gang** - reads more like a roll call of British pub rock as a consequence.

Punk's momentum continued to build during September. **The Sex Pistols** played two consecutive nights at the Club De Chalet Du Lac in Paris on 3rd and 4th. Then back home, the 100 Club Punk Festival, which took place over 20th and 21st September, is usually regarded as a seminal moment in the history of punk. In "England's Dreaming" Jon Savage describes this festival as "the climax of **McLaren**'s campaign to woo the record companies". The line-up for the Monday was **Subway Sect**, **Siouxsie and The Banshees**, **The Clash** and **The Sex Pistols**. On the Tuesday, **The Stinky Toys** (from France), Chris Spedding and **The Vibrators**, **The Damned** and **The Buzzcocks** played. **Siouxsie and The Banshees** fronted by Susan Dallion (or Siouxsie as she soon became known) were making their debut as a spontaneous performance act hastily assembled by **Siouxsie** so they could secure a slot at the gig. **Siouxsie** was part of the now legendary 'Bromley Contingent', who followed **The Sex Pistols** around the London gig circuit in 1976 and accompanied them on their Paris gigs. On drums in this embryonic line-up was **Sid Vicious**, who later joined **The Sex Pistols** on bass when Glen Matlock departed. **The Clash**'s manager Bernie Rhodes wouldn't allow their back-line to support **The Banshees** because he objected to **Siouxsie**'s swastika armband. **The Banshees**' bassist that night Steve Havoc (later Severin) had apparently only picked up a bass guitar once before the performance, which consisted of a 20-minute medley of *The Lord's Prayer* intertwined with *Twist And Shout* and bits of *Knocking On Heaven's Door*. The **Subway Sect**, fronted by **Vic Godard** on vocals, were also making their debut at this gig. With various different line-ups this band became a constant feature on the music scene for the next few decades. **The Clash**, by all accounts, played a great set that night. In the middle of it, Mick Jones broke a guitar string so Joe Strummer put a small transistor radio up to the microphone. It seems he always carried one around with him. **The Sex Pistols** rounded off the first night with a good set and between the songs part of *Spunk*, a bootleg of their early recordings, was played.

The Stinky Toys were moved from the first night to the second to give **Siouxsie and The Banshees** a chance to play and **The Damned** signed a recording contract with Stiff during their soundcheck. During the second night **Sid Vicious** threw a glass tankard which shattered on a pillar injuring several people in the audience and blinding a girl. He was arrested but when the case reached court a year later **Clash** members Joe Strummer and Paul Simonon maintained he was innocent and he got off. The 100 Club's manager Ron Watts, banned all punk bands from appearing at the venue after this incident.

The Vibrators were essentially an R&B-influenced pub-rock band, who first attracted attention from punks after their appearance at this festival. Shortly after, they recorded a 45 *Pogo Dancing* for RAK with Chris Spedding, which was released in November. They later signed to Epic without Spedding. By most accounts the highlight of the second night was **The Buzzcocks**, who went on about midnight and closed the show. Their set included a cover of The Troggs' garage classic *I Can't Control Myself* along with some of their early classic's like *Boredom*, *Breakdown*, *Time's Up*, *Changed My Mind*, *Orgasm Addict* and *Oh Shit*. The 100 Club Punk Festival put punk in the public eye, whereas previously it had been underground. Both 'Melody Maker' and 'Sounds' ran major features on punk afterwards.

In October, **The Sex Pistols** signed a £40,000 contract with EMI. The following day they entered the Landsdowne Studios to record a version of *Anarchy In The UK* with **Dave Goodman**. EMI weren't happy with the end result and four days later the band tried again with EMI staff producer Mike Thorne at the label's Manchester Road studios. **Malcolm McLaren** thought

THE SEX PISTOLS - God Save The Queen 7".

the end result was too raw. The version finally released on 45 was recorded at London's Wessex Studios on 17th October, with Pink Floyd and Roxy Music producer Chris Thomas at the controls.

At the artier end of the spectrum **Throbbing Gristle**, later to become pioneers of industrial music, performed at London's ICA on 18th October. Also playing, but under the name LSD, was **Chelsea**, who were formed by vocalist **Gene October** in the late summer of 1976. **Chelsea** were to prove a very durable second division punk outfit, playing through the eighties with **October** always at the helm supported by various line-ups. Patti Smith returned in October to play at London's Hammersmith Odeon with **The Stranglers** again in support role. The first real U.K. punk single **The Damned**'s *New Rose* was released this month. *Anarchy In The UK* was finally released on 19th November. Two days later **Chelsea**'s vocalist **Gene October** was left to put together a new line-up when the remainder of the band departed to form **Generation X** with Billy Idol handling vocal duties. A week later "The London Weekend Show", hosted by Janet Street-Porter, did a feature on punk rock.

If most household's hadn't heard of punk rock yet they soon were to when **The Sex Pistols** taunted by "Today" show host Bill Grundy to "say something outrageous" unleashed a barrage of four letter words. It all seems rather tame twenty-five years on but at the time it provoked a national outrage fuelled by the press. One TV viewer was apparently so incensed that he kicked in his TV screen! Of nineteen original scheduled dates on their proposed 'Anarchy' tour, only three went ahead. The tour, on which **The Sex Pistols**' were accompanied by **The Damned**, **The Clash** and Johnny Thunders' Heartbreakers finally got going at Leeds Polytechnic on 6th December. They played two gigs at the Electric Circus, Manchester on 9th and 19th December (with **The Buzzcocks**), a gig at Castle Cinema, Caerphilly, after a scheduled gig at the Top Rank, Cardiff was cancelled, and two at the Woods Centre, Plymouth on 21st and 22nd December, before returning to London on 24th December for Christmas.

To get gigs a lot of bands now disassociated themselves with punk, becoming new wave almost overnight.

During the 'Anarchy' tour a new London venue, The Roxy, opened at 41, Neal Street, in Covent Garden. It became London's first live punk venue. **Generation X** played the first night on 21st December and **Siouxsie and The Banshees** were also on the bill. For the next sixteen months most upcoming punk and new wave bands played there. The EMI Harvest label made a number of live recordings there on four nights in March and April 1977 using concealed microphones to capture the ambience of the club and its audience, as well as the music. The end result can be heard on *The Roxy, London, WC2* compilation. The album sold well, reaching No. 24 in the nation's charts. In April 1977, the venue changed hands but it continued to promote punk bands, until its closure in April 1978. In preparation for this, over three nights (31st December 1977, 1st and 2nd January 1978) recordings were made for a *Farewell To The Roxy* album released in May, although in comparison to the earlier album, the bands on this one were second rate.

As 1976 closed, very few punk singles and no genuine U.K. punk album had been released. Pub rock acts who became embroiled on the punk circuit like **Eddie and The Hot Rods**, **The Gorillas**, **The Count Bishops**, **The 101'ers** and **The Vibrators** had all released singles and **Eddie and The Hot Rods** put out their *Teenage Depression* album in November. An early independent release was **The Warm**'s long-forgotten *Teenage Space Queen*. Early punk cash-ins included **Matt Black and The Doodlebugs**' *Punky Xmas* and **The Water Pistols**' now collectable 45 *Gimme That Punk Junk*. Across in the States, meanwhile, The Ramones had released two albums *The Ramones* and *Leave Home*; Blondie released their debut album in December; The Patti Smith Group put out *Radio Ethiopia*; The Modern Lovers had an eponymous album and two popular New York punk/new wave compilations were *Live At CBGB's* (recorded over a weekend in June) and *Max's Kansas City 1976*. Over the next year that would all change as the market was flooded with punk/new wave recordings.

Another significant record label to develop in the punk era was Chiswick. Based in London's Camden Town, it was formed by Ted Carroll, a prominent record collector and dealer in 1976. Early releases on the label included pub rock bands like **The Count Bishops**, **The Gorillas** and the **101'ers**, who became embroiled on the fringes of London's punk/new wave scene. Early punk bands to record on the label included Blackpool's **Screwdriver**, Dublin's **Radiators From Space** and the Scottish band **Johnny and The Self-Abusers**, who later evolved into **Simple Minds**. The label finally reaped the commercial success that eluded it initially when it signed the second incarnation of **The Damned** in 1979, who proceeded to enjoy four hits from *Love Song* onwards. In later years, Chiswick developed into Ace Records, a respected reissue and specialist music outlet and its Big Beat subsidiary continued to carry the punk mantel.

Important punk and new wave venues also opened up outside of London in 1976. Eric's in Matthew Street, Liverpool (just across the road from the site of The Cavern Club where The Beatles had played in the early sixties) became a focal point for punk and new wave on Merseyside. **The Sex Pistols** played there within days of its opening in October 1976. Over the next few years significant Merseyside bands to make their debuts there included **Echo and The Bunnymen**, **The Teardrop Explodes**, **Orchestral Manuvoeures In The Dark**, **Wah! Heat**, **The Yachts** and **Big In Japan**. Later, in 1977, the club started its own record label. The first release was a shared single between **Big In Japan** and **The Chuddy Nuddies**. Over the next two years the label put out releases by **Holly** (this was Holly Johnson later of Frankie Goes To Hollywood), **Pink Military** and **Frantic Elevators** (who featured Mick Hucknall, later with Simply Red).

1977 was the year the punk bands won through but it wasn't always plain sailing. The furore of the Bill Grundy interview failed to die down and EMI sacked **The Sex Pistols** on 12th January as they were preparing for a European tour. Over the next few weeks personality clashes within the band came to a head. Their bassist Glen Matlock departed to form **Rich Kids** and was replaced by **Sid Vicious**. A new recording contract was signed with A&M outside Buckingham Palace on 10th March, but six days later the label had second thoughts and sacked them too! Eventually Virgin had the balls to sign them and three classic singles - *God Save The Queen* (which climbed to No. 2 despite a Radio 1 ban), *Pretty Vacant* and *Holidays In The Sun* - followed. Then, in November, their long-awaited album *Never Mind The Bollocks - Here's The Sex Pistols* entered the charts at No. 1.

By early 1977, **The Clash** were headlining gigs. They soon signed to CBS and proceeded to release a trio of classic punk singles that year, commencing with *White Riot* and an eponymous debut album, which is considered by many to be the definitive U.K. punk album.

The Stranglers, who'd signed to United Artists in December 1976, released their debut 45 *(Get A) Grip (On Yourself)* in February 1977. It was the first of four hits that year. The other three - the double 'A' sides *Peaches / Go Buddy Go*, *Something Better Change / Straighten Out* and *No More Heroes* - all made the Top Ten and their appearances on 'Top Of The Pops' helped to take punk to a wider audience. They also released two classic Top 5 albums - *Stranglers IV (Rattus Norvegicus)* and *No More Heroes*.

The Damned became the first U.K. band to tour the States in April 1977 in an itenary which included an appearance at CBGB's. They were also the first to release an album *Damned Damned Damned* - the first album on Stiff Records, it reached No. 36 in March.

The mod-influenced **Jam** from Woking, Surrey, signed to Polydor in February 1977 and went on to become one of the first punk era's most commercially successful bands, enjoying four No. 1's in the early eighties. In Paul Weller they had one of punk's most prolific and talented songwriters.

SHORT CIRCUIT - LIVE AT THE ELECTRIC CIRCUS 10".

The Tom Robinson Band signed to EMI in 1977, enjoying a No. 5 hit with the anthemic *2-4-6-8 Motorway*. Their *Power In The Darkness* album the following year was one of the era's most powerful political statements.

Sham 69, who were formed by **Jimmy Pursey** in Hersham, Surrey, articulated the consciousness of the working class and are usually heralded as one of the founders of the subsequent Oi! Movement of the early eighties. In 1977, they released a single *I Don't Wanna* for the independent Step Forward label before proceeding to sign for Polydor in October 1977 and enjoy a string of anthemic hits over the next couple of years.

Dublin's **Boomtown Rats** fronted by Bob Geldolf, who would be one of the most influential figures to emerge from punk, signed to Phonogram's Ensign subsidiary and toured the U.K. in the first half of 1977. Their debut single *Looking After No. 1* rose to No. 11 in August 1977 paving the way for a series of subsequent anthemic singles, including two No. 1's *Rat Trap* and *I Don't Like Mondays*.

The Adverts had formed in London early in 1976. Their *One Chord Wonders* 45 for Stiff in 1977 was one of the classic early punk singles and a clever observation on the movement. The band were signed up by the larger Anchor label shortly after and their follow-up release *Gary Gilmore's Eyes*, with its catchy, commercial appeal, became another of punk's early Top 20 hits.

The Fall, one of punk's most durable bands, formed in Manchester in January 1977. One of the city's premier punk/new wave venues was the Electric Circus and **The Fall** went on to make their vinyl debut just a year later, contributing two cuts - *Stepping Out* and *Last Orders* to Virgin's 10" compilation *Short Circuit - Live At The Electric Circus*, which included other seminal Manchester bands like **Joy Division**, **The Drones** and **The Buzzcocks**.

Other significant punk bands to emerge during 1977 included **The Lurkers**, **999** and **Suburban Studs**. From the Fulham area of West London, **The Lurkers** had formed in late 1976. In 1977, they were one of the first signings on a new indie label Beggars Banquet. Their debut single, the catchy *Shadow*, released that July, and the follow-up *Freak Show* in October, were the first two releases on this new label, which was begun as a chain of record stores in London by Mike Stone and Nick Austin who had discovered **The Lurkers** and set about recording them. Over the next few years major new wave artists like **Gary Numan**, **Tubeway Army**, **Bauhaus**, The Heartbreakers and mod revivalists **The Merton Parkas** recorded on this label.

999 were originally from Northampton, but moved down to London early in 1977. In July, they released a debut 45 *I'm Alive* on their own Labritain label. It went down well and helped them secure a major label contract with United Artists. **999** proceeded to go on and produce a series of snappy singles over the next few years like *Nasty Nasty*, *Me And My Desire*, *Emergency* and *Homicide*.

Another of the early punk bands to gain a recording contract was **Suburban Studs**, who formed in Birmingham during 1977, and signed to the Pogo label, which was marketed by WEA. In 1977 and 1978 they became a popular attraction on the punk circuit. Their act included a rampaging cover of The Who's *My Generation*, but their finest moment was their sparky second single *I Hate School*.

During 1977 hundreds of punk bands were forming all over the country. In London, a new punk venue The Vortex opened up at 201, Wardour Street. It had a high profile launch on 11th July 1977 with **Siouxsie and The Banshees**, **Sham 69**, **The Slits** and **Adam and The Ants** on the bill. Things got wild, the Police were called in to investigate a breach of the peace and **Sham 69**'s lead singer **Jimmy Pursey** was later prosecuted and fined £30. Later in the year, a live various artists compilation *Live At The Vortex* was recorded there and released by NEMS in December 1977. It featured a collection of unsigned acts at the time including **The Art Attacks**, **The Maniacs**, **Mean Street**, **Neo**, **The Suspect**, Bernie Tormie and **The Wasps**.

A more important document of live music that year was *Live Stiff Live*, which contained some of the label's artists playing at gigs recorded at the University Of East Anglia, Leicester University and The Lyceum in late 1977. The album did well commercially, reaching No. 28 in the charts. The label occupied the middle ground between punk and new wave and its roster as represented on this budget-priced album included **Elvis Costello**, **Nick Lowe**, **Ian Dury**, **Larry Wallis** and **Wreckless Eric**. The same label also put out another budget collection *Hits Greatest Stiffs* in October 1977, which included 'A' sides of their early 45s by artists like **Nick Lowe**, Pink Fairies, Roogalator, **Tyla Gang**, Lew Lewis, **The Damned**, Richard Hell, **Plummet Airlines** and **Elvis Costello**. The album was accompanied by a free 7", *England's Glory* by Max Wall.

Another seminal live venue in this era was the dingy basement (with its small stage) of the Hope and Anchor Pub in Upper Street, Islington. The venue catered for both emerging punk/new wave bands and the numerous pub rock acts operating on the live circuit at the time. The double album *The Hope And Anchor Front Row Festival* is an eclectic collection of live performances recorded between Tuesday 22nd November and Thursday 15th December 1977. The album features superb performances by artists like **The Stranglers**, **The Only Ones**, **X-Ray Spex**, **The Saints** and **Suburban Studs** alongside staple pub rock acts like Wilko Johnson Band, Steve Gibbons Band and The Pirates. Lots of people bought this and it got to No. 28 in the charts. There was also apparently a second live album *Don't Let The Hope Die* towards the end of the venue's life.

For a while in 1976 and 1977 the terms punk and new wave were largely interchangeable. By 1978, things were beginning to change, although the dividing line between punk and new wave was never very clear. Many of the early punk records had been political and nihilistic in their outlook and bands like **The Ruts** and **Stiff Little Fingers** who emerged subsequently but continued in this tradition always were 'punk' as opposed to 'new wave'. The latter term became used to describe the barrage of melodic punk-inspired records which bombarded the charts during 1978 and 1979. Bands like **The Undertones**, **The Boomtown Rats**, **The Police**, **Squeeze**, **The Skids**, **The Pretenders**, **The Rich Kids**, **Generation X**, **The Rezillos**, **Spizzenergi** and **XTC** typified this new wave which produced some of Britain's finest three minute singles. Many of the most successful 'new wave' performers like **Elvis Costello**, **Nick Lowe**, **Ian Dury**, Wreckless

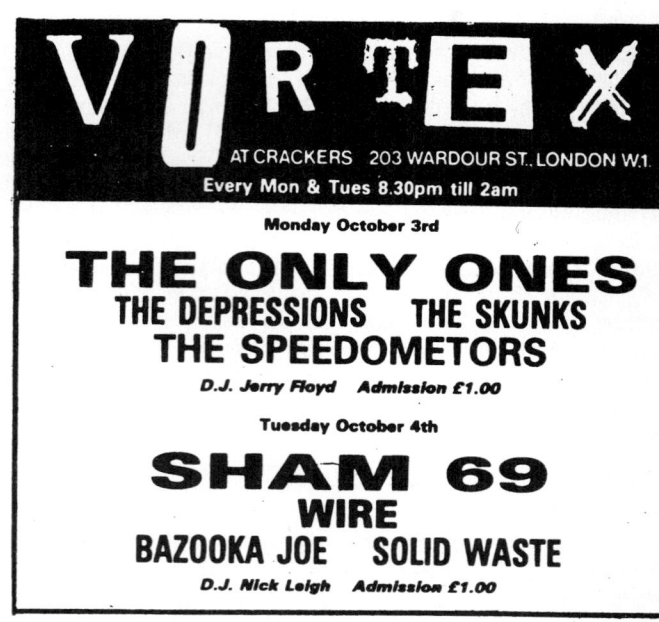

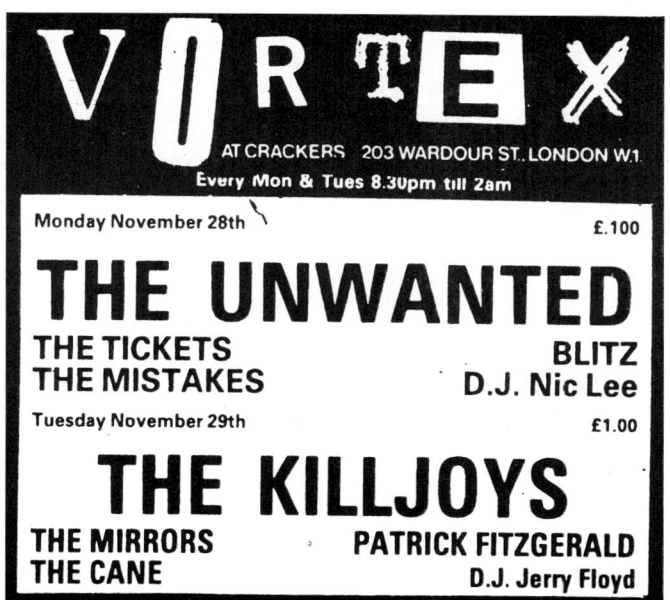

STIFFS LIVE STIFFS - Various Artists.

Eric and **Joe Jackson** never were and never made any attempt to be 'real' punks. However, punk by challenging and redefining the whole value system of the music industry created the climate in which those 'new wave' artists could flourish. Many of these artists had previously been pub-rockers, who'd simply leapfrogged the early months of punk and emerged to establish themselves as credible new wave artists in this era. **Nick Lowe** had been around for years, previously with pub rockers Brinsley Schwarz and Graham Parker. **Ian Dury** had fronted London pub-rockers Kilburn and The High Roads and **Elvis Costello** had been trekking around the pub circuit as a solo performer. **Dave Edmunds**, another cog in the Stiff circus, had been active on the music scene in various groups since the mid-sixties, most notably Love Sculpture. **The Police** were positively OLD (late twenties upwards). Andy Summers was another veteran of the mid-sixties. He'd played extensively with bands and artists like Kevin Ayers, Eric Burdon, Keith Coyne, Soft Machine and Zoot Money (who'd turned psychedelic briefly as Dantalian's Chariot). Gordon Summer (Sting) had been in a jazz outfit called Last Exit and Stewart Copeland had been the drummer in progressive rock combo Curved Air. **Joe Jackson** was previously with a pre-punk combo **Arms and Legs**, who were going nowhere. **The Only Ones** were ageing pubsters who released a 45 *Lovers Of Today* on their own Vengeance label in July 1977. In January 1978, they signed to CBS going on to record one of new wave's defining moments *Another Girl, Another Planet*, which was released in April 1978.

Artists like **Generation X** (*King Rocker* and *Valley Of The Dolls*), **The Stranglers** (*Duchess*) and **X-Ray Spex** (*The Day The World Turned Day-glo* and *Germfree Adolescents*) matured beyond their initial rawness to record new wave classics. **The Jam**, who'd never entirely fitted in the punk scene, went from strength to strength in the new wave era with a series of superb singles. Other classic slices of the new wave included **Jam** protegés **The Vapors**' *Turning Japanese*, **The Jags**' *Back Of My Hand* and **XTC**'s *Making Plans For Nigel*.

Whilst the new wave prospered **The Sex Pistols** split up in 1978 during a U.S. tour. In February, Cook, Jones and **McLaren** went down to Rio to stay with 'great train robber' Ronnie Biggs, which resulted in a new single *No One Is Innocent (A Punk Prayer By Ronald Biggs)* coupled with **Sid Vicious** singing *My Way*. In the months that followed **Vicious** was arrested and charged with the murder of girlfriend Nancy Spungen on 12th October, but died after a heroin overdose the following February.

Johnny Rotten reverted to his real name John Lydon and formed a new band **Public Image Ltd**, who would prove very successful in the post-punk era. **McLaren** concentrated his energies on resolving **The Sex Pistols**' financial affairs and expediting 'The Great Rock 'n' Roll Swindle' movie and accompanying soundtrack, which told the story of punk from **McLaren**'s perspective. Naturally, this depicted him as the driving force behind both **The Sex Pistols** and punk generally. Both the movie and soundtrack were patchy and met with a mixed reception, but *The Great Rock 'n' Roll Swindle* remains the most famous punk-related soundtrack. It was also the most successful commercially, reaching No. 7 during its thirty-three weeks in the charts.

There were two other significant soundtracks from the era. *Jubilee-Cert X*, directed by Derek Jarman, exploited the fact that 1977, the year **The Sex Pistols** and punk broke through, was also the Jubilee year of Queen Elizabeth II. **McLaren** and **The Sex Pistols** also capitalised on this by releasing their controversial *God Save The Queen* so that it would be a hit in Jubilee week and by their Thames river boat celebration, which lead to a rendition of *Anarchy In The UK* alongside the Houses Of Parliament on 7th June. In Jarman's film, Elizabeth I returns from Tudor times to check out her successors' reign into a world dominated by punk. The highlight of the film was its musical content. This included *Deutscher Girls* and *Plastic Surgery* by an early **Adam and The Ants**; **Chelsea**'s *Right To Work* produced by Miles Copeland and **Mark Perry** (which was also issued as a 45); *Nine To Five* by the **Maneaters**, which is rumoured to be **Adam Ant** and **Toyah** (who are both prominent in the cast) under a pseudonym; versions of *Rule Britannia* and *Jerusalem* by **Suzi Pinns**; two ambient Brian Eno cuts and contributions by **Wayne County and The Electric Chairs** and Amilcar.

The second soundtrack *That Summer!*, released in June 1976, comprised previously released material, but from a very impressive musical roster. The New York scene is represented by three of its top artists - The Ramones, The Patti Smith Group and Richard Hell and The Voidoids - alongside Mink DeVille, who were formed in San Francisco by New Yorker Willy De Ville and relocated to New York. The U.K. contributions come from three of Stiff's top artists in the era **Elvis Costello**, **Ian Dury and The Blockheads** and **Wreckless Eric**, along with punkish pub-rockers **Eddie and The Hot Rods**; ace new-wavers **The Boomtown Rats** and **The Only Ones** and the lesser-known **Zones** from Glasgow. Full of quality this must be one of the best soundtracks of the seventies. It sold pretty well, too, reaching No. 36 in the charts. Also released in 1979, was a two volume compilation on

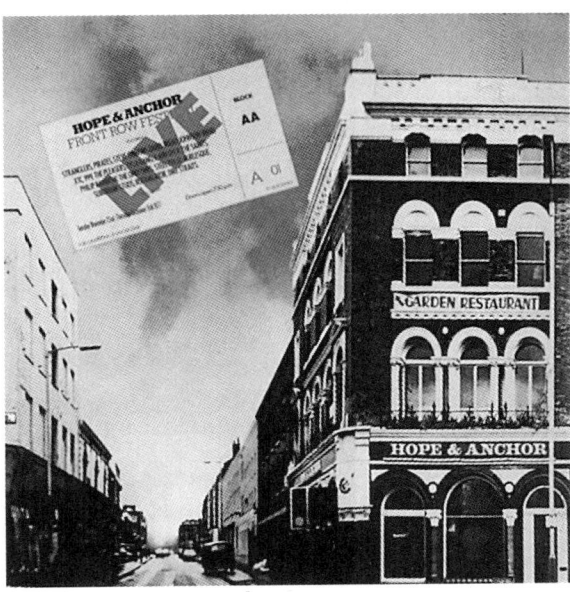

HOPE AND ANCHOR FRONT ROW FESTIVAL - Various Artists.

THAT SUMMER! - Various Artists.

Polydor of punk and new wave's finest moments *20 Of Another Kind*. Of these, the first volume is particularly recommended (see the Compilations section for full details). It got to No. 45 in the charts. Several new labels associated with punk/new wave artists put out samplers in this era. The most prominent were Virgin, Beggars Banquet, Raw, Rough Trade, Fast, Factory, Cherry Red and The Label. Again be sure to check out the compilation section for details.

By the turn of the decade the new music began to break down into a number of different genres. There was the mod revival of 1979, the ska revival, Oi!, a third wave of punk, electronic music, the 'doom and gloom merchants' and industrial music. These genres dominated the early post-punk era and (apart from ska which isn't covered) this book includes their main U.K. proponents.

For those of you too young to remember, the original sixties mods were clean-cut, clothes obsessed youths with a penchant for Italian suits, who rode about on Italian designed scooters, the Vespa or the Lambretta. Top mod bands were The Who and The Small Faces. The enemy was the rockers, with whom they traditionally slugged it out at the seaside over bank holidays. So why a revival a decade and a half later? Two factors seem crucial. Firstly, **The Jam** whose music drew quite heavily from the mid-sixties and never really fitted into punk. Nor did their appearance characterised by black three-button suits, pointy shoes and short, tidy haircuts. **The Jam** were role models for the mod revival and were by now one of the country's top groups. Secondly, the release of 'Quadrophenia' in Autumn 1979, an account of a mod growing up in Shepherds Bush in the golden era, captured the imagination of the nation's youth, many of whom were yearning for a new cause after punk. This fuelled the flames of the mod revival.

20 OF ANOTHER KIND VOL. 1 - Various Artists.

The early part of 1979 witnessed several new mod-influenced bands, although the revival was very much a London-based phenomenon. The most successful would prove to be **Secret Affair**, whose anthemic *Time For Action* (a No. 13 hit) and its follow-up *Let Your Heart Dance* were two of the mod revivals defining moments. **Secret Affair** labelled their fans 'Glory Boys' and gave their first album this title too. Their snazzy vocalist Ian Page was also their self-styled spokesperson during this era. Other key mod revival bands during 1979 were **The Merton Parkas** from Merton Park, **The Purple Hearts** from Romford, South London's **Chords** and Enfield's **Back To Zero**. **The Merton Parkas** were the subject of a feature in 'The Sun' and became the first to appear on 'Top Of The Pops' performing their debut 45 *You Need Wheels*, when it scraped to No. 40. **The Chords** went on to enjoy no less than five minor hits and **The Purple Hearts** had two, of which the first, *Millions Like Us* was another classic.

There was also a succession of mod fanzines. The first and best was 'Maximum Speed', based in North London.

The mod revival mushroomed rapidly. With the new bands came new clubs like Vespas Global Village under the arches at Charing Cross and The Wellington in Waterloo. The best known, though, was the Bridge House in Canning Town. This was because the live *Mods Mayday 79* album was recorded there. The cover sported a photo of a mod of a vespa scooter. Naturally it was recorded on Mayday (7th May 1979) and the album featured live cuts from five of the revival's main proponents - **Secret Affair**, **Beggar**, **Small Hours**, **The Mods** and **Squire**.

MODS MAYDAY VOL. 2 - Various Artists.

Although the mod revival remained predominantly a London phenomenon, the word did spread to the provinces during the year. There were **The Lambrettas** from Lewes in Sussex (who in their revival of The Coasters old R&B hit *Poison Ivy* produced the only mod revival single to reach the Top 10), **The Teenbeats** from Hastings, **The Killimeters** from Huddersfield, **Speedball** from Southend, **Beggar** from Cardiff, **Squire** from Woking and **Sta Prest** from Essex. Other London-based mod revival bands in this era included former pub-rockers **The Crooks**, **Small Hours**, **Long Tall Shorty**, **The Mods** and **The Scooters**. In 'Sounds' Garry Bushell ran a four-page article 'Mod - The Story So Far', which documented the revival scene and listed most of the bands involved so far.

In August 1979, **Secret Affair**, **The Purple Hearts** and **Back To Zero** embarked on a March of The Mods tour. Also on the bill were a couple of 2-Tone acts Madness and The Selector. Over the coming months the mod bands lost out to the emerging 2-Tone bands like The Specials, Madness, The Beat and The Selector. This largely happened because the 2-Tone bands wrote better material. With a few exceptions the mod revival bands were a pale imitation of original greats like The Who and The Small Faces. **The Jam** continued to prosper because they were a quality band, but when Paul Weller broke them up in 1982 even the revival's role models were no more. During the early eighties the mod scene moved into the nightclubs where aspiring mods could dance to R&B and northern soul. Those who hankered after live bands either deserted to 2-Tone or the short-lived 'new-psychedelia' which emerged in London's West End during the spring of 1981. This saw a number of psychedelic venues open up around

London. There was The Groovy Cellar (started by Clive Soloman the manager of **The Mood Six**), The Clinic and Le Kilt in Soho's Wardour Street, which had a psychedelic evening every Tuesday. The fashion focus of this revival lay in two stalls, the Regal and Sweet Charity in Kensington Market. WEA also released a compilation *A Splash Of Colour* containing tracks by the best of the new bands. The pick of the bunch were **The Mood Six**'s *Just Like A Dream* and *Plastic Flowers* and High Tide's excellent *Dancing In My Mind* and *Electric Blue*. Having said this, they were relatively lightweight compared to a band like **The Soft Boys** who'd carried the psychedelic mantle virtually single-hand during the punk/new wave era.

As punk appeared to disintegrate as a musical force at the end of the seventies, there was one post-punk genre Oi! claiming to be 'the sound of the streets' which sought to cling on to what its proponents saw as the 'real' elements of the 1977 punk explosion. Like punk earlier, Oi! was both an attitude and a musical style. Oi! acts played simple four chord tunes with anger and aggression. Band members exuded a tough, no-nonsense, hard-nosed personna. As an attitude Oi! championed the mentality of the football terrace, laddish and anti-authoritarian. It was all about having a good laugh, going to the football with your mates and getting pissed. It was also a reaction against the artier strand of the new wave, bands like **Wire** and **Siouxsie and The Banshees**, who'd emerged during the punk era. Unfortunately, Oi!'s attitude attracted racists, political extremists, football hooligans and young lads just looking for a fight, as well as just fans of the music. So early Oi! gigs were marred by violence in the same way early punk gigs had been.

Unconsciously the Oi! movement existed long before the term was coined with the release of *Oi! - The Album* in 1980. The, then 'Sounds' journalist, Garry Bushell was an early champion of the Oi! cause and 'Sounds', in particular, pushed it hard for a while. The violence associated with Oi! soon undermined these efforts and it found itself with an image problem even worse than punk in its formative period. The catalyst was a **4-Skins** gig at the Harnborough Tavern in Southall in July 1981, when a riot erupted involving the police, people at the concert and a considerable number of local Asians. After this, everyone was queuing up to denounce Oi! and much was made of its right wing associations. These were more by accident than by design and when you listen to the lyrics of these Oi! bands it's apparent that several left-wingers were involved in the movement too. Oi! lyrics were often anti-establishment (**The Oppressed, One-Way System**) and tackled issues like unemployment, street violence and police oppression. Despite this, there was a strong patriotism in some of the lyrics, particularly of groups like **The Last Resort** and this would have appealed to the distasteful right wing elements associated with the movement.

The roots of Oi! are generally traced back to bands like East End pub rockers **Cock Sparrer**, who satirically reproduced the dress of the football terraces and musically despatched solid four-chord anthems; West Ham supporters **Cockney Rejects**, whose praises Garry Bushell was singing as early as 1979; **Sham 69**, whose catchy but sympathetic street anthems became a rallying call to rival skinhead gangs; **The Angelic Upstarts**, whose debut 45 *The Murder Of Liddle Towers* was a stinging attack on police brutality and **Menace**, whose anthemic *GLC* had articulated the frustration of London punk bands at the licensing authority who made it so hard for them to play.

STRENGTH THRU Oi! - Various Artists.

With the release of *Oi! The Album* the movements gained momentum and punk bands like **The Exploited** and **Peter and The Test Tube Babies** who appeared on the album also became associated with it. After promising sales of the debut album, there was strong support for a sequel, which Bushell unwisely titled *Strength Thru' Oi!*, an adaptation of the Nazi slogan 'Strength Through Joy'. Worse still the album - which featured tracks by a new breed of Oi! bands like **Last Resort, Toy Dolls, Infa Riot** and **The Strike** - included a picture of Nicky Crane, a notorious right-wing skinhead on the cover. Then on top of this came the Southall gig - no wonder the movement had a bad image!

After Southall, gigs were banned across the country. Oi! went underground and the **4-Skins** split up for a while, but later reformed with a modified line-up. With few live gigs to go to many of the trouble-makers moved on, only true fans remained and dedicated Oi! labels like Secret kept the movement alive. Secret released *Carry On Oi!*, a third Oi! compilation, in 1981. It included cuts by the re-formed **4-Skins**, earlier bands like **Peter and The Test Tube Babies** and **Infa Riot** as well as showcasing a newer brand of bands like **The Business, The Ejected, The Gonads, Blitz** and **Red Alert**. The fourth Oi! album *Oi! Oi! That's Yer Lot*, released by Secret in 1982, completed the initial series. This introduced more new Oi! bands like **Attak, Crux, Five O, The Oppressed, Sub-Culture** and **The Warriors** as well as street poetry from **Attila The Stockbroker**. The following year Syndicate took over the mantle of Oi! with a new compilation *Son Of Oi!*. This comprised the usual mixture of music (including some live contributions) from old favourites like **The 4-Skins, Angelic Upstarts, Cock Sparrer, The Business** and **The Gonads** and new acts like **Prole, Vicious Rumours** and **Clockwork Destruction**. It also includes two cuts from top Oi! street poet **Garry Johnson**. Syndicate's brace of Oi! compilations was completed in 1984 with *The Oi! Of Sex*. Using the tried and tested format of previous Oi! compilations, this featured Oi! cuts from the likes of **Cock Sparrer, The Gonads, The Burial, Prole** and **ABH** alongside the poetry ranting **Jimmy Mack, Swift Nick** and **Little Dave**.

In the mid-eighties **The Oppressed**'s lead singer Roddy Moreno, who'd done much to counter those who tried to associate Oi! with racism and fascism by forming Sharp (Skinheads Against Racial Prejudice), set up his own Oi! records. They took over from labels like Secret, Syndicate and No Future in carrying the torch of Oi! with albums by bands like **The Oppressed, Section 5, Condemned 84, Vicious Rumours** and **Barbed Wire**.

Just when it seemed Oi! had petered out a new label Link rekindled the flame with *Oi! The Resurrection*, a compilation featuring many new bands. More recently Mark Brennan (former **Business** bassist) and Laurie Pryor (manager, and under the name Ron Rouman **Business**' producer) continue to unearth Oi! classics on their Link, Dojo and Captain Oi! labels. They were responsible for the *Oi! Chartbusters* series on Link and Brennan's phenomenal Captain Oi! label has put out the five volume *Oi! The Rarities* and four volume *Oi! The Singles Collection*, as well as one-offs like *100% British Oi!* and *100% Hardcore Punk Rock*. It has also reissued well over

Oi! THE ALBUM - Various Artists.

BACK ON THE STREETS 7" compilation.

100 classic punk and Oi! albums. Oi! seems guaranteed a cult status. Incidentally, its companion Captain Mod label is busily reissuing many mod and ska recordings from the late seventies and early eighties.

Oi! only slightly pre-dated what 'Sounds' termed 'New Punk' in 1981. In what some have termed punk's third wave, a new generation of punk bands emerged. Acts like **Discharge** (from Stoke-on-Trent), **The Exploited** (from Edinburgh), **Vice Squad** (from Bristol), **Chron Gen** (from Hitchin), **Anti-Nowhere League** (from that most conservative of places Tunbridge Wells), **Anti-Pasti** (from Derby) and **G.B.H.** (from Birmingham) also sought to carry the spirit of punk through the eighties. These groups recorded on labels like Riot City, Clay, No Future, Rondelet, Fresh, Spiderleg and Pax. Their discs sold in quite impressive amounts propelling them into the upper echelons of the indie charts and, in some cases, the national charts too.

Musically, these bands played what would now be termed hardcore punk. Loud, angry, political, no-holes-barred punk thrashes that similarly disadvantaged youths who'd latched onto punk in 1976 and 1977 could identify with. They set a new punk fashion, too, with brightly-coloured Mohican hair styles, studded leather jackets, Doc Martens, Para boots and tattoos.

Radio 1 DJ John Peel, who'd been so influential in championing the first wave of punk, ensured that these new bands got airplay too. New venues like Marples (in Sheffield), the Mayflower (Manchester), Skunx (London) and the Warehouse (Preston) made these bands welcome. In 1981, **The Anti-Nowhere League**, **Anti-Pasti**, **Chron Gen**, **The Discharge** and **The Exploited** came to the attention of a much wider audience by virtue of the 'Apocalypse Now' national one-nighter tour. It was a big success and many similar packages followed culminating in the fifteen-band 'Christmas On Earth' international punk extravaganza at the Leeds' Queens Hall. Top of the bill was **The Damned**, also involved were **Chelsea** and **U.K. Subs** (who got a new lease of life in the eighties as part of punk's third wave), the American hardcore band Black Flag was present and the third wave of U.K. punk was represented by bands like **The Insane** and **Chron Gen**.

Many of the eighties punk bands enjoyed considerable chart success. **Discharge**'s 1982 debut album *Hear Nothing, See Nothing, Say Nothing* climbed to No. 47 in the national charts. **The Anti-Nowhere League**'s debut album *We Are... The League* got to No. 24 and enjoyed eleven weeks in the charts during 1982. A later effort *Live In Yugoslavia* made a brief appearance in the 83 slot. They also enjoyed three minor hit singles in 1982 with their cover of Ralph McTell's *Streets Of London* (No. 48), *I Hate .... People* (No. 46) and *Woman* (No. 72). **Anti-Pasti** narrowly missed the Top 30 when *The Last Call* peaked at No. 31 during a seven week chart sojourn. **The Exploited** enjoyed two Top 20 albums with *Punk's Not Dead* (No. 20) and *Troops Of Tomorrow* (No. 17) during the early eighties and four minor hit singles. The most successful of these was *Dead Cities*, which got to No. 31 and earnt them an appearance on 'Top Of The Pops' - which must have shocked many viewers. They also shared an EP *Don't Let Them Grind You Down* with **Anti-Pasti**, which got to No. 70. **Chron Gen**'s *Chronic Generation* album spent three weeks in the charts peaking at No. 53. **G.B.H.** enjoyed two minor hits in 1982 with *No Survivors* and *Give Me Fire*. **Vice Squad** fronted by the leather clad Queen Of Eighties Punk Beki Bondage enjoyed two hit albums *No Cause For Concern* (No. 32) and *Stand Strong, Stand Proud* (No. 47) and a minor hit single *Out Of Reach* (No. 68).

A separate strand of the third wave of punk were the anarcho-punk bands. The pioneers and most important of these were **Crass**, who'd originally formed as a duo, Steve Ignorant and Penny Rimbaud, back in 1978. **Crass** developed out of an anarchic commune based at Rimbaud's farmhouse in North Weald, Essex. In late 1978 **Crass** had a 12" *Feedling Of The 5,000* issued on Small Wonder, but many pressing plants refused to press the record, mainly on account of the vehemently anti-Christian stance of its track *Reality Asylum*, which still has greater shock value than artists like Eminem. **Crass** linked up with Southern Studios to get round this problem by setting up their own Crass label. They also operated on a not-for-profit basis enabling many more young people to buy their records than otherwise would have. In 1979, their label issued recordings by other bands such as **Conflict** *The House That Jack Built* and **Flux Of Pink Indians** enjoyed a big indie hit with their *Neu Smell* (EP). **Conflict** went on to form and record on their own Mortarhate label and **Flux Of Pink Indians** did the same thing with Spiderleg Head. This label was also an early home to **Subhumans**, who later set up their own Bluurg label. Other bands with similar principles included **Rudimentary Peni**, **Riot Clone**, **Icons Of Filth** and **The Zsounds**.

For these anarcho-punk bands the message was far more important than the music. Their concerns spanned environmental issues, nuclear weapons, vivisection, religion, class and Third World exploitation and capitalism. They usually advocated direct action and developed their own cheaply-produced fanzines as they were largely ignored by the music press.

Punk also had a nihilistic strand which was most pronounced in the stark minimalist music of **Siouxsie and The Banshees** and developed by bands like **The Cure**, **Public Image Limited**, **The Psychedelic Furs** and **Wire**. The Manchester-based Factory label was home to bleak post-punk acts like **Joy Division** (whose music became even more chilling following the suicide of their vocalist Ian Curtis in 1980 and their name change to **New Order**), **A Certain Ratio**, **Durutti Column** and **Orchestral Manoeuvres In The Dark**, whose synth-pop was sombre if not as bleak as the music of some of their label-mates.

Liverpool's doomy post-punk scene was dominated by **Echo and The Bunnymen**, **The Teardrop Explodes** and **Wah Heat!**. Many of you will know that in June 1977 the frontmen of these three groups Ian McCulloch, Julian Cope and Pete Wylie played together in the legendary **Crucial Three**. Their egos and talents were so strong that they weren't together long enough for any vinyl output, which is a shame. Still **Echo and The Bunnymen** produced some of the finest early post-punk recordings with songs like *The Pictures On My Wall* and *Read It In Books* and **The Teardrop Explodes** weren't far behind with songs like *Sleeping Gas*. Liverpool's early post-punk scene is captured brilliantly on Zoo's compilation *To The Shores Of Lake Placid*.

Several of these doomy post-punk acts can be heard on Beggars Banquet offshoot 4AD whose releases included **Mass**'s *You And I*; *Swans On Glass* and *Drowning Man* by **Modern English**; *Controversial Subject* by **The The**; **Cupol**'s *Like This For Ages* (a moody 45 by members of **Wire**); **Dif Juz**'s *Huremics* and **In Camera**'s *Die Laughing*. **Bauhaus**, whose *Bela Lugosi's Dead* 12" and *Dark Entries* 45 are recommended, also recorded a notable

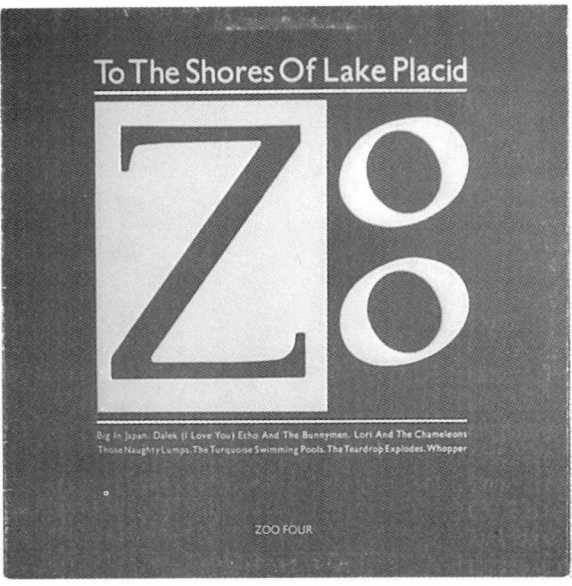

TO THE SHORES OF LAKE PLACID - Various Artists.

album *In The Flat Field* on 4AD. Of course, some of these bands were just going through bleak phases. **The The** and **Modern English**, for example, went on to make much brighter more upbeat music during the eighties. It's also possible to trace the bleak, doomy music of these acts as the precursors of Goth, which became a significant music genre in the eighties.

A distinct, but very much minority genre throughout both the punk and post-punk era was what became known as industrial music. The term seems to have been coined because **Throbbing Gristle**'s debut album *Second Annual Report* contained an Industrial Records imprint. Some have traced the roots of industrial music back to the noise experiments of the Dadaists and Futurists and the music of artists like Kraftwerk, Faust, Eno and David Bowie's electronic experimental phase. The main early U.K. protagonists of industrial music were **Throbbing Gristle** and Sheffield's **Cabaret Voltaire**. The music combined punk, electronic music and the sort of improvisation previously associated with psychedelia. The electronically-treated sound utilised echo, reverb, phasing and tape manipulation to conjure up an 'alien' sound which depicted bleak, urban landscapes. The end result is totally unmelodic and the use of non-musical sounds and recordings have led some to describe it as anti-music.

Although **Throbbing Gristle** formed in Manchester on 3rd September 1975, two of their members Genesis P. Orridge and Cosey Fanni Tutti had, as COUM Transmissions with Arts Council funding, been performing shows such as 'Erection Undress Of Miniprick' (1970), 'Winston Spencer Churchill' (1973), 'Throbbing Gristle' (1974) and 'Rectum As Inner Space' (1976) in art galleries around the world. In 1976, a cassette-only release *The Best Of Throbbing Gristle Volume II* (there is no Volume I) was limited to 50 copies and circulated to friends. In October 1976, COUM Transmissions' 'Prostitution' show opened at the ICA and caused such outrage that they lost their Arts Council grant. The same month **Throbbing Gristle** was launched at the ICA. Much of 1977 was spent setting up Industrial Records and its debut disc *Second Annual Report* was released in November 1977. It was the genre's definitive recording and attracted interest from the music press. The debut 45, *United* issued in July 1978 was, in marked contrast to the album, a synth-pop song and on the flip side they recorded a three-chord punk song *Zyklon B Zombie*! The increasing interest in bands that were 'different' was apparent in November 1978 when 'Sounds' profiled ten of them, including **Throbbing Gristle**, **Robert Rental and Thomas Leer** (whose 1979 album *Bridge* was the first non-**Throbbing Gristle** release on Industrial Records), **Cabaret Voltaire** and **The Normal**, who were all broadly part of the Industrial movement. As early as the mid-seventies **Cabaret Voltaire**, a Sheffield outfit, had been recording electronic sound experiments, inspired by Dada and William Burroughs. Industrial Records released some of these recordings, which captured the band at their most uncompromising, on cassette in 1980. When **Cabaret Voltaire** made their live debut in Sheffield they were physically forced to stop playing and their bassist/vocalist Stephen Mallinder suffered a broken bone in his back in the pandemonium that followed. Along with **Throbbing Gristle** they were the most significant of the early industrial bands and went on to record several albums and 45s. From 1983 onwards their music became more accessible as they transgressed into the electro-dance scene and various strands of dance music.

During 1979 Industrial Records were sent tapes by several other bands including Australians SPK (also known as Surgical Penis Klinik, Socialist Patients Kollectiv and Seppuka), **Clock DVA**, **Rema Rema**, **Section 25**, Metabolist, **Vice Versa**, Glenn Wallis, **Lemon Kittens** and Jonas A. In February 1980, **Throbbing Gristle** headlined at London's Lyceum. Also on the bill were fellow Industrialists **Cabaret Voltaire**, **Clock DVA**, Zev (from San Francisco) and Non (actually Boyd Rice). In October, Sandy Robertson wrote a two page feature in 'Sounds' on Industrial Records. Other artists in the industrial genre worthy of mention are **Come** (who recorded on their own Come Organisation label), **23 Skidoo**, **Nurse With Wound** and William Bennett's notorious **Whitehouse**, the most extreme and uncompromising of all the industrial bands.

If industrial music was the most extreme and weird form of electronic experimentation, there were other groups like **The Human League**, **Tubeway Army** and **Ultravox** experimenting with keyboards and synthesizers in the late seventies. By late 1978, cheap and relatively uncomplicated synthesizers like the Casio and the Wasp were making electronics much more accessible to emerging groups who wanted to be innovative.

The roots of electronic music have been traced back to the early 20th century Italian composers like Pratella and Corra, who used primitive electronic gadgets to make sounds. In the late sixties pioneering American bands like Lothar and The Hand People and Silver Apples had experimented with theremins and moog synthesizers to create (particularly in the latter's case) discordant electronic music. However, it was really 'Krautrock' artists like Kraftwerk (who built their own synthesizers and constructed songs around tape loops and drum machines), Can, Faust, Neu and Tangerine Dream who were the most influential of the pre-punk synthesizer bands. Here in Britain in the wake of their success, artists like David Bowie, Brian Eno and Peter Gabriel began to experiment with synthesizers, vocoders and drum machines. Bowie's 1977 album *Low* (produced by Eno) was particularly significant and influential in this respect. Brian Eno also produced **Ultravox**'s debut album *Ultravox* in 1976. Their awkward rhythms and avant-garde style fell on deaf ears at the time, Island dropped them and their founder **John Foxx** went solo.

Among early **Ultravox** fans was Gary Webb who formed **Tubeway Army**, the first commercially successful electronic post-punk act. After two punkish singles they dispensed with their guitarist and drummer and proceeded to record sci-fi tainted futuristic synth-based singles like *Down In The Park* and *Are 'Friends' Electric?*, which gave them a No. 1. Using the name **Gary Numan** Webb went on to record a series of electronic discs. Further examples of punk era electronic music were the **Human League**'s first single *Being Boiled* and their 12" *Dignity Of Labour* EP, which were issued on Fast Products. In 1979, they were signed by Virgin and recorded two innovative electronic albums *Reproduction* and *Travelogue*. After friction within the band, Martyn Ware and Ian Craig-Marsh decided to quit in October 1980 to form B.E.F (**British Electrical Foundation**), a collective for various dance projects, of which Heaven 17 became the most successful. **Phil Oakey** and Adrian Wright still retained the band's name. With a European tour scheduled they recruited bassist Ian Burden and **Oakey** signed up two teenage dancers Joanne Catherall and Suzanne Sulley, who he'd seen dancing at a Sheffield Club where they were working as cocktail waitresses. **The Human League** Mark 2 played simpler and more pop-orientated synthesized music, but it paid off commercially when they produced a No. 1 album *Dare*, which spawned a No. 1 single *Don't You Want Me*, in 1981.

SOME BIZZARE ALBUM - Various Artists.

By late 1980/early 1981 a whole series of new electronic outfits were emerging. Bands like **Dramatis** (**Numan**'s old backing band), **Dalek I Love You** (who featured former members of **Teardrop Explodes** and **Orchestral Manuvoeuvres In The Dark**), **Fashion**, Interplay, **Landscape** (who played slick, fun-loving and often experimental computer pop), **Modern Eon** (Liverpudlians with a clear **Echo and The Bunnymen** influence), The Passage and **Eric Random** (a talented experimental multi-instrumentalist also involved with **Cabaret Voltaire**) developed.

Two record labels who prompted electronic music in the early eighties deserve special mention. First was Mute, distributed by Rough Trade, the brainchild of Daniel Miller. His studio project **The Silicon Teens** played synthesized versions of old rock 'n' roll classics. Other early exploits included a single he recorded as **The Normal**, the dour **Fad Gadget** and the sober German band D.A.F. (Deutsch Amerikanische Freundschaft). His biggest commercial success, though, came with teenage synth-poppers **Depeche Mode**, who he commandeered from fellow electronic pioneer label Some Bizzare. Their boss Stevo also foresaw the potential for electronic music to move into the mainstream. The label's 1981 sampler *Some Bizzare Album* included contributions from several subsequently successful acts including **Depeche Mode**, **The The**, **B-Movie**, **Blah Blah Blah**, **Blancmange** and **Soft Cell**.

This emerging synthesized pop became popular dance music in the clubs at the start of the eighties. In stark contrast to the scruffy image of punk, these clubsters dressed flamboyantly and often effeminately. The foremost London club for this genre was called Blitz. It was run by Steve Strange, former member of The Photons. In clubs like this the New Romantic movement was born. Its main proponents were 'pretty' groups like North London's **Spandau Ballet** and Birmingham's **Duran Duran**. A revived **Ultravox** also achieved massive success in 1980 with *Vienna*. Along with second string colleagues like **A Flock Of Seagulls**, **Classix Nouveaux**, **Talk Talk** and Strange's own minimalist project **Visage**, these New Romantic groups had a penchant for hair gel and designer gear. The movement was very fashionable for a while but later outfits like Heaven 17 and ABC circumvented New Romanticism to emerge as accomplished dance outfits in their own right, but these fall beyond the time span of this book.

In the 1982-1985 period punk (particularly anarcho-punk) was forced largely underground again and there was a plethora of D.I.Y. cassettes. This book mentions a few of these but doesn't attempt the impossible task of trying to document them all.

Hopefully this overview of punk, new wave and the early post-punk era, the book's hors d'ouvres, has whetted your appetite. Now it's time to get stuck into the meat of the book.

THE SECRET LIFE OF PUNKS - Various Artists.

JUBILEE CERT. X - Soundtrack.

SMALL WONDER PUNK SINGLES COLLECTION, VOL. 2.

Spizz Oil at The Roundhouse, London 23rd July 1978.
Photo: Steven Richards.

A.B.H.

Personnel:			
	NIGEL BOULTON	bs	AB
	CHRIS BRINTON	gtr	A
	PETE CHILVERS	vcls	AB
	TONY CULLINGFORD	drms	AB
	STEVEN CURTIS	gtr	B

A.B.H. formed in early 1981 in Lowestoft, Suffolk. They were originally known as Strecher Case and in those days concentrated on fast, high energy covers of mostly **Sex Pistols** and **Damned** material. Chris Brinton left after a few gigs to be replaced by Steven Curtis. By now the group had changed names to **A.B.H.** and this line-up ('B') remained constant for the remainder of their career.

On 17th July 1982, they recorded a four-track demo tape at Hillside Studios in Ipswich comprising *999*, *Country Boy Rocker*, *Wanna Riot* and *Teenage Aggression*. *Country Boy Rocker* was the only song written by the original line-up ('A'). It was a reference to the intrusion of bikers in the rural villages around Lowestoft. *Wanna Riot* was about the frustration minority groups experienced against an authoritarian government which was manifest in the Brixton and Toxteth riots of 1981. Their first vinyl appearance came when *Country Boy Rocker* and *Wanna Riot* were included on *A Country Fit For Heroes, Vol. 2* (No Future Oi! 23), which was later reissued on one CD with *Vol. 1* (Captain Oi! AHOY CD 15) 1994. You'll also find *Wanna Riot* on *No Future - The Punk Singles Collection* (Captain Oi! AHOY DLP 508) 1996.

In early 1983, **A.B.H.** returned to the same studio to record a second four track demo tape comprising: *Concrete Jungle*, a comment on the London high-rise estates created by misguided planners in the fifties and sixties; *Kids Of The Nation*, which drew on their experiences with the law; *Pissed On Arrival*, which referred to their ardent band of supporters and *Don't Mess With The S.A.S.*, a tribute to their storming of the Iranian Embassy. The latter was by far their strongest song and was later included on *The Oi! Of Sex* (Syndicate SYNLP 4) 1984, also reissued on CD (Captain Oi! AHOY CD 23) 1994. It later got a further airing on *100% British Oi!* (Captain Oi! AHOY DCD 83) 1997.

All of their recorded output was later compiled on *The Oi! Collection* (Captain Oi! AHOY CD 85) 1998, a split CD with **Subculture**.

The Abnormal

ALBUM: 1 SKINS 'N' PUNKS, VOL. 4 (Oi! OIR 010) 198?

NB: This was a split album with **Barbed Wire**.

An Oi! band. *New Generation* from the above album is an Oi! rallying cry with pertinent lyrics for the era and good guitar playing. This recommended song can also be heard on *The Best Of Oi! Records* (CD) (Captain Oi! AHOY CD 38) 1995.

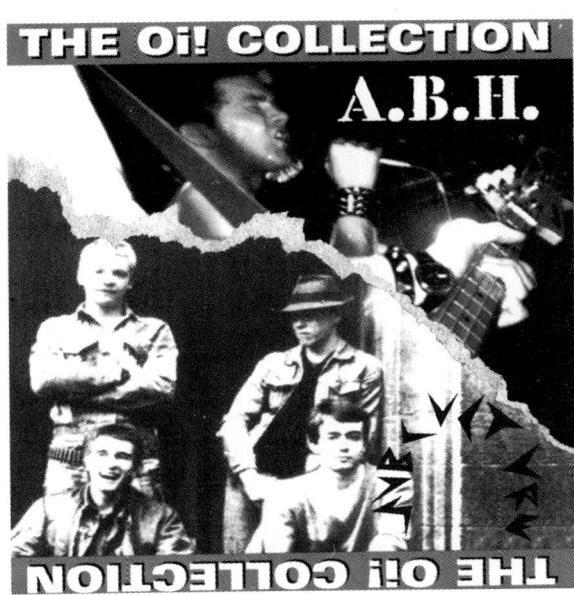

A.B.H. - The Oi! Collection. (CD)

ABRASIVE WHEELS - THE PUNK SINGLES COLLECTION.

Abrasive Wheels

Personnel:			
	DAVE HAWKRIDGE	bs	A
	MARK HOLMES	drms	A
	DAVE RYAN	gtr	AB
	SHONNA	vcls	AB
	'HARRY' HARRISON	bs	B
	'NEV' NEVISON	drms	B

ALBUMS: 1(B) WHEN THE PUNKS GO MARCHING IN
(Riot City CITY 001) 1982
2(B) BLACK LEATHER GIRL (Clay CLAYLP 9) 1984

NB: (1) also issued on CD (Captain Oi! AHOY CD 025) 1994 and again in 1998, also on vinyl (AHOY LP 25) 1996, a limited edition of 1,000. (1) also reissued on vinyl (Get Back GET 17) with five 45 bonus cuts. (2) also issued on CD (Captain Oi! AHOY CD 47) 1995 with five bonus tracks. Also relevant is *Abrasive Wheels - The Punk Singles Collection* (Captain Oi! AHOY CD 51) 1995.

EP: 1(B) VICIOUS CIRCLE (PS) (Vicious Circle / Attack /
Voice Of Youth) (Riot City RIOT 4) 1981

NB: (1) also issued on CD (Abstract AABT 807CD) 1992.

45s:
Army Song/Juvenile/So Low (PS) (Abrasive ABW 1) 1981
* Army Song/Juvenile/So Low (PS) (Riot City RIOT 9) 1982
Burn 'Em Down/Urban Rebels/ (PS) (Riot City RIOT 16) 1982
Jailhouse Rock/Sonic Omen (PS) (Clay CLAY 24) 1983
Banner Of Hope/Law Of The Jungle (PS) (Clay CLAY 28) 1983
The Prisoner/Christianne (PS) (Clay CLAY 33) 1984
The Prisoner/Christianne/
Black Leather Girl (12", PS) (Clay 12 CLAY 33) 1984

* On red vinyl.

Abrasive Wheels formed in Leeds in 1979, but it wasn't until mid-1980 that they released a debut three-cut disc on their own Abrasive label. 3,000 copies were pressed and, with the help of some support slots to **Slaughter and The Dogs**, they soon sold out. Using the money from this record to purchase a transit van, they sought a record contract and the Bristol-based Riot City label duly obliged. Their three track *Vicious Circle* EP made it into the indie Top 20 and regular gigging with bands like **GBH**, **Vice Squad** and **The Partisans** helped establish them on the Oi! circuit. As interest in them grew Riot City reissued *Army Song*, with inital copies coming in red vinyl.

Punk producer Mike Stone oversaw the recordings for *When The Punks Go Marching In*, their first album. This marked a considerable advance on their earlier recordings. It included re-mixes of their earlier *Vicious Circle* EP and included their next 45, *Burn 'Em Down*, which fared well in the indie chart.

Early in 1983, **Abrasive Wheels**' switched to Mike Stone's Clay label for a cover of Elvis Presley's *Jailhouse Rock*. They followed this with a slower-paced but emotional double A-side *Banner Of Hope / Law Of The Jungle*.

By 1984, the music press had lost interest in punk, but in March, again with Stone handling production a new album *Black Leather Girl* and 45 *The Prisoner* were released. *Black Leather Girl* contains twelve classy numbers from the opening cut *Maybe Tomorrow* through to the finale *Devil On My Shoulder*. The title track and songs like *Christianne* and *The Prisoner* are full of class and style. The band split soon after disillusioned by the lack of response to these releases.

The CD reissue of *When The Punks Go Marching In* on Captain Oi! includes all three cuts from their *Army Song* disc and from their *Vicious Circle* EP, *Urban Rebel* (the flip side to *Burn 'Em Down*) and their rare compilation cut *Criminal Youth*. This CD was also available as a colour picture disc as well as on vinyl with a picture insert. There was also a second pressing in green vinyl. The album has also been reissued on Get Back, with new cover artwork and five 45 bonus cuts.

The Captain Oi! CD reissue of *Black Leather Girl* adds five bonus cuts (including their *Banner Of Hope*, *Jailhouse Rock* and *The Prisoner* 45s) to round up all of their releases on Clay.

The Punk Singles Collection contains all of their 'A' and 'B' sides on a full colour picture disc, which was also available on vinyl with a sleeve note insert.

Back in 1982, they contributed *Criminal Youth* to *Riotous Assembly* (Rio City ASSEMBLY 1) and *Vicious Circle* and *Burn 'Em Down* figured on *Life's A Riot And Then You Die* (Riot City CITY 009) in 1985. They also contributed *Vicious Circle*, *Army Song* and *Burn 'Em Down* to *Riot City Singles Collection, Vol. 1* (Anagram CDPUNK 15) 1997 (also on vinyl (Captain Oi! AHOY DLP 503)) and *Voice Of Youth*, *Juvenile* and *Urban Rebel* figured on *Vol. 2* (Anagram CDPUNK 55) 1995 (also on vinyl (Captain Oi! AHOY DLP 511) 1996). Finally, *The Army Song* and *Shout It Out* got a further airing on *100% Hardcore Punk* (Captain Oi! AHOY DCD 84) 1998.

The Accelerators

EP: 1( ) POP GUNS AND GREEN LANTERNS (12")

(Spiv ACCEL EP) 1980

The Accelerators were a Liverpool band. This was a six-track EP.

The Accidents

Personnel:	MARK ROBINS	gtr, vcls	A
	TERRY RUFFLE	gtr, vcls	A
	NICK SMITH	bs, vcls	A
	PAUL SULLIVAN	drms	A

ALBUM: 1(A) KISS ME ON THE APOCALYPSE

(Hook Line 'n' Sinker) 1980

NB: (1) This was unissued but six test pressings existed, some in proof sleeves. It was belatedly issued (Detour CRCD 004) 1996, also on vinyl.

45: Blood Splattered With Guitars/
Curtains For You (PS)
(Hook Line 'n' Sinker HOOK 1) 1980

A punky mod-influenced outfit from Chelmsford, Essex. Their 45 was very promising but their album was scrapped after the test pressing stage. Needless to say these test pressings are now very collectable and expensive.

Eventually, the scrapped album was released by Detour in 1996, dubbed from one of the test pressings in existence. It's clear from this that musically at any rate they were nearer to **Elvis Costello and The Attractions** than mod revival bands like **Secret Affair**.

ABRASIVE WHEELS - Vicious Circle EP.

ABRASIVE WHEELS - Army Song.

ABRASIVE WHEELS - Burn 'Em Down.

ABRASIVE WHEELS - Jailhouse Rock.

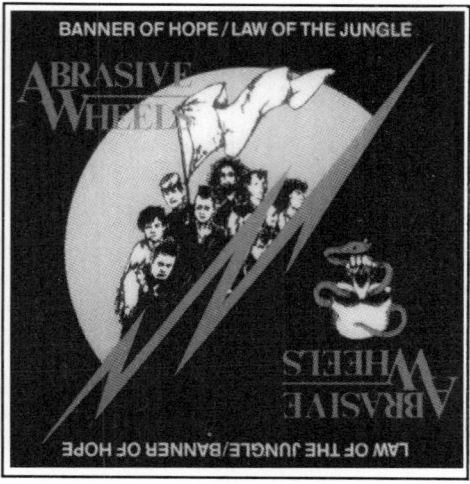
ABRASIVE WHEELS - Banner Of Hope.

ABRASIVE WHEELS - The Prisoner.

You'll also find *Blood Splattered With Guitars* on *100% British Mod* (Captain Mod MODSKA DCD 8) 1998 and on vinyl on *This Is Mod* (dbl) (Get Back GET 39) 1999.

Accidents On East Lancs

45s:	The Back End Of Nature/Rat Race (PS)	(Roach RR 1) 1981
	Tell Me What You Want/	
	We Want It Legalised (PS)	(Roach SPLIFF 001) 1981

A high energy Lancashire band. Their singles, issued on the independent Roach label, were available through Rough Trade.

Accursed

Personnel:	GARY	bs	A
	GLENN	drms	A
	STEVE	gtr, vcls	A

ALBUMS:	1	AGGRESSIVE PUNK	(Wreck 'Em ACC 1) 1983
	2	UP WITH THE PUNKS	(Wreck 'Em ACC 2) 1983
	3(A)	LAUGHING AT YOU	(Wreck 'Em ACC 4) 1984

| 45: | Going Down (PS) | (Wreck 'Em ACC 3) 1979 |

A fast punk band. Their *Up With The Punks* album is badly played and recorded. Cuts include *Nuclear War*, *Hammer Head* and *Off Me Head*. Lots of energy, but that's the best that can be said.

The Aces

Personnel:	CHARLIE CASEY	bs, vcls	A
	NOEL MARTIN	drms	A
	STEVE TANNETT	vcls, gtr	A

| 45: | One Way Street/Why Should It Be Mine (PS) | (Etc ETC 01) 1981 |

This was a later version of **Menace** who'd changed their name to **Vermillion and The Aces** before recording this more moddy effort as **The Aces**. It's already becoming quite collectable.

After this 45 Tannett put his energies into running I.R.S. Records and Casey joined the punk band **The Dark**.

One Way Street can also be heard on *This Is Mod, Vol. 5* (Anagram CDMGRAM 110) 1997 and *100% British Mod* (Captain Mod MODSKA DCD 8) 1998.

Acme Sewage Co

A little known punk era band. They had no 45 or album releases but they did contribute *Smile And Wave Goodbye* to the *Farewell To The Roxy* (Lightning LIP 2) 1978 album, which had quite a jangly instrumental backing and distinctive vocals. This album was later reissued on CD (Captain Oi! AHOY CD 86) 1998. They also contributed two cuts, *I Don't Need You* and *I Can See You* to the *Raw Deal* (Raw RAWLP 1) 1977 compilation. Later Damaged Goods Records unearthed a previously unissued track *I Wish You Dead* and included it on a Raw Records retrospective compilation CD (FNARR CD 009). Later, *I Wish You Dead*, *I Don't Need You* and *I Can't See You* got a further airing on *The Raw Records Punk Collection* (Anagram CDPUNK 14) in 1993.

The Act

Personnel:	DEREK ADAMS	drms, vcls	A
	MARK GILMOUR	lead gtr	A
	NICK LAIRD-CLOWES	lead vcls, gtr	A
	MR. MYSTERY	bs, vcls	A

| ALBUM: | 1(A) | TOO LATE AT 20 | (Hannibal HNBL 1306) 1981 |

| 45s: | Who Let The Flowers Fall/Dance To Despair | (Act ACT 1) 1981 |
| | Too Late At Twenty/Protection (PS) | (Hannibal HNS 701) 1981 |

The Act were also featured playing *Skip The Beat* and *Sure Fire* on the *429 2139* (Rocket DIAL 1) 1979 compilation album of Brighton bands. The former opens with a white reggae beat but then lapses into an ordinary song which suffers from undistinguished vocals. *Sure Fire* is competent instrumentally but again the vocals are weak.

Actifed

Personnel:	JOHN BRISTOW	bs	A
	CLINTON GRACE	gtr	A
	STUART HEMPHILL	drms	A
	DAVID RODGERS	vcls, lead gtr	A

| EP: | 1(A) | DAWN OF LEGION (12", PS) | (Jungle) 1983 |

| 45: | Crucifixion/ | |
| | Black Skinned Blue Eyed Boys (12") | (Jungle JUN 11) 1984 |

From Hounslow in West London, **Actifed** were a popular London club act in 1981 and appeared on the front of 'Sounds' in 1982 without any vinyl output! Unfortunately, contractual complications with their promoter and concern about their name by the drugs company Actifed led to a crucial delay in their recording career. When it finally came in 1983, their 12" *Dawn Of Legion* was well received and they embarked on a national tour to help promote it, but they'd already been written off in the music press. Following a 45 *Crucifixion* they disbanded in late 1984 leaving a projected debut to be shelved.

ABRASIVE WHEELS - Black Leather Girl.

ACCURSED - Laughing At You.

ACTION PACT - Yet Another Dole Queue Song.

ACTION PACT - Heathrow Touchdown EP.

ACTION PACT - Suicide Bag EP.

Action Pact

Personnel:
GEORGE CHEEX	vcls		ABCD
JOE FUNGUS	drms		A
KIM 'DR PHIBES' IGOE	bs		AB
DES 'WILD PLANET'	gtr		ABCD
GRIMLY FIENDISH	drms		BCD
ELVIN PELVIN			
(PHIL LANGHAM)	bs		C
THISTLES	bs		D

ALBUMS: 1(B) MERCURY THEATRE - ON THE AIR
(Fallout FALLLP 013) 1983
2(D) SURVIVAL OF THE FATTEST
(Fallout FALLLP 030) 1984

NB: (1) and (2) reissued on one CD (Captain Oi! AHOY CD 59) 1996, which included their singles *London Bouncers*, *Yet Another Dole Queue Song* and *Cocktail Credibility* plus a full colour eight page lyric booklet. There's also *The Punk Singles Collection* (Captain Oi! AHOY CD 32) 1995, which includes all their 'A', 'B' and EP cuts, including their ultra-rare split single with **Dead Man's Shadow** *Heathrow Touchdown*.

EPs: 1(A) HEATHROW TOUCHDOWN (London Bouncers/
All Purpose Action Footwear) (PS)
(Subversive ANARCHO 1) 1981
2(A) SUICIDE BAG (Suicide Bag/Stanwell/Blue Blood) (PS)
(Fallout FALL 003) 1982
3(B) PEOPLE (People/Times Must Change/Sixties Flix) (PS)
(Fallout FALL 010) 1983
4(C) LONDON BOUNCERS (London Bouncers (Bully Boy Version)/New Kings Girl/Gothic Party Time/
The Cruelist Thief) (12", PS) (Fallout FALL 12 016) 1983
5(D) QUESTION OF CHOICE (Question Of Choice/
Hook Line & Sinker/Suss Of The Swiss) (PS)
(Fallout FALL 019) 1983

NB: (1) One side of this EP is by **Dead Man's Shadow**.

45s: Yet Another Dole Queue Song/
Rockaway Beach (PS) (Fallout FALL 026) 1984
Yet Another Dole Queue Song/Rockaway Beach/
1974/Rock N Roll Part 2 (12", PS) (Fallout FALL 12 026) 1984
Cocktail Credibility/
Consumer Madness (PS) (Fallout FALL 029) 1984

Action Pact were a third wave pop-punk band fronted by a shrieking female vocalist called George Cheex. From Essex, they were originally known as Bad Samaritans. Fungus had been recruited from a local punk band called Savage Upsurge. Their vocalist in these days was a guy called John, who later left and became guitarist for **Dead Man's Shadow**. It was after female guitarist Cheex was recruited that they changed name to **Action Pact**.

After releasing a single by **Dead Man's Shadow** Fresh decided to release a joint EP *Heathrow Touchdown* by both bands. Two of **Action Pact**'s members were still at school when this EP was released. Their two cuts *London Bouncers* and *All Purpose Action Footwear* got a lot of airplay from John Peel and they also did a session for his Radio One show. This session, which was broadcast on 22nd February 1982, comprised *People*, *Suicide Bag*, *Mindless Aggression*, *Losers* and *Cowslick Blues*. Soon after *Suicide Bag*, an anti-glue-sniffing song was put out on 45. This shot to the top of the punk charts and a second Peel session featuring *Times Must Change*, *These Are A Few*, *Fouled On The Footpath*, *Drowning Out The Big Jets*, *Fool's Factions* and *Protest Is Alive* was broadcast on 16th August 1982. Also in 1982, *London Bouncers* was included on *Punk And Disorderly* (Anagram GRAM 001) and *Suicide Bag* turned up on *Punk And Disorderly III* (Anagram GRAM 005) in 1983.

Various line-up changes ensued. Fungus was replaced by someone using the pseudonym of Grimly Fiendish and Kim Igoe departed once their debut album was recorded. His initial replacement was **Dark** guitarist Phil Langham (their producer, who filled in under the alias of Elvin Pelvin).

ACTION PACT - London Bouncers EP.

ACTION PACT - People EP.

The material on *Mercury Theatre - On The Air* is decidely political with songs like *Blue Blood* dealing with Royalty, for example. Unfortunately, the music fails to match the aggression of the vocalist.

Langham appeared with the band playing a May 1983 radio session for Kid Jensen when they performed *Question Of Choice*, *The Cruelist Thief*, *Gothic Party Time* and *New Kings Girl*. He also played on **Action Pact**'s *London Bouncers* EP before being replaced by new bassist Thistles, who like Grimly, hailed originally from Tunbridge Wells.

Thistles made his vinyl debut with the band on *Question Of Choice*, which was released in November 1983 to coincide with their appearance at the Leeds Futurama Festival.

For their next single *Yet Another Dole Queue Song* Steve Drewitt, mainman of **The Newtown Neurotics**, who they often gigged with, was invited to do a duet with George Cheex on a cover of The Ramones' *Rockaway Beach*. There was also a 12" version of this single, released in the summer of 1984, which contained another cover, this time of Gary Glitters' *Rock 'N' Roll Part 2*.

On *Survival Of The Fattest* the music offers more variety and better musicianship and the lyrics are a bit more sophisticated. George's vocals remain unmistakenly unique - and you'll either like or loathe them! As they stand out among the band's music it does tend to mean that their songs all sound similar.

They embarked on a weekend tour to promote *Survival Of The Fattest* and the *Cocktail Credibility* single, which included a gig at the now defunct Hammersmith Clarendon. Unfortunately, it became harder to get gigs and they were attracting little media attention, so they decided to quit in 1985.

Suicide Bag, *People*, *London Bouncers*, *Question Of Choice*, *Yet Another Dole Queue Song* and *Cocktail Credibility* all re-emerged on *The Fallout Punk Singles Collection* (Anagram CDPUNK 30) in 1994.

Action Replay

An obscure sixties influenced band. They have a decent song *Decisions* included as a bonus cut on the CD reissue of *Odd Bods Mods And Sods* (Captain Mod MODSKA CD 2) 1996.

Adam and The Ants

Personnel:
ADAM ANT (STUART GODDARD)	vcls	ABCDEFG HI
ANDY ANT (alias WARREN)	bs	ABCDE
PAUL FLANAGAN	drms	A
LESTER SQUARE	gtr	AB
DAVE BARBE	drms	BCDEF
MARK GAUMONT	gtr	C
JOHNNY BIVOUAC	gtr	D
MATTHEW ASHMAN	gtr	EF

ACTION PACT - Cocktail Credibility.

ACTION PACT - The Punk Singles Collection.

LEE GORMAN	bs		F
MARCO PIRRONI	gtr		G HI
CHRIS "MERRICK" HUGHES	drms		G HI
KEVIN MOONEY	bs		H
TERRY LEE MIALL	drms		HI
GARY TIBBS	bs		I

HCP

ALBUMS:
1(E)	DIRK WEARS WHITE SOX	(Do It RIDE 3) 1979	16
2(H)	KINGS OF THE WILD FRONTIER	(CBS 84549) 1980	1
3(I)	PRINCE CHARMING	(CBS 85268) 1981	2
4(-)	PEEL SESSIONS	(Strange Fruit SFALP 115) 1991	-

NB: (1) also issued on cassette (Do It Ride 3M) 1979. (1) reissued in 1983 (CBS 25361) with a different sleeve and tracks and on cassette (CBS 40-25361). (1) also reissued on CD (Columbia 480 521-2) 1995. Some copies came with the wrong version of *Cartrouble* and were withdrawn. (2) reissued on CD by Sony Europe in 1993 and on (Columbia 477 902-2) 1994. (3) also issued on CD (Columbia 474 606-2) 1996. (4) included the three sessions they recorded for John Peel detailed below:- *Deutscher Girls* / *Puerto-Rican* / *It Doesn't Matter* / *Lou* (30/1/78); *Physical (You're So)* / *Cleopatra* / *Friends* / *Zerox* (17/7/78); and *Table Talk* / *Ligotage* / *Animals And Men* / *Never Trust A Man (With Egg On His Face)* (2/4/79). *B-Side Babies* is accompanied by a 16-page lyric booklet. This is worth getting - he recorded some good 'B' sides, check out *Physical (You're So)* and *Christian D'or*, for example.

HCP

EPs:
1	THE B-SIDES EP (Friends/Kick/Physical)	(Do It DUN 20) 1982	46
2	THE ANT MUSIC EP (PS) (Cartrouble Pt's 1 & 2 / Friends / Kick / Physical)	(Do It DUNIT 20) 1982	-

NB: (1) also issued as a picture disc. (2) issued as a 12".

HCP

45s:
	Young Parisians/Lady (PS)	(Decca F 13803) 1978	9
*	Zerox/Physical (You're So) (PS)	(Do It DUN 8) 1979	-
	Zerox/Whip In My Valise (PS)	(Do It DUN 8) 1979	45
	Cartrouble/Kick!	(Do It DUN 10) 1980	33
	Kings Of The Wild Frontier/ Press Darlings (PS)	(CBS 8877) 1980	2
	Dog Eat Dog/Physical (You're So) (PS)	(CBS 9039) 1980	4
	Antmusic/Fall In (PS)	(CBS 9352) 1980	2
+	A.N.T.S.	(Lyntone LYN 9285) 1981	-
	Stand And Deliver/Beat My Guest (PS)	(CBS A 1065) 1981	1
	Prince Charming/Christian D'or (PS)	(CBS A 1408) 1981	1
	Ant Rap/Friends (picture disc)	(CBS A 1738) 1981	3
	Deutscher Girls/ Plastic Surgery (PS)	(Editions EG EGO 5) 1982	13
	Ant Music/Stand And Deliver (PS)	(Old Gold OG 8739) 1988	-
%	Young Parisians/Lady/ Interview	(Damaged Goods FNARR 7) 1989	-
	Prince Charming/ Goody Two Shoes (PS)	(Old Gold OG 9953) 1990	-

ADAM AND THE ANTS - Kings Of The Wild Frontier.

NB: Their first three singles were reissued with the original catalogue numbers in 1980. * This was a mispressing as the 'B' side was intended to be *Whip In My Valise*. All 3,000 copies were withdrawn. + One-sided blue flexidisc given away free with 'Flexipop' magazine No. 4. % There were two versions of this issue:- (i) 12" in white vinyl with a picture sleeve and numbered fanzine. (ii) 12" as a picture disc with a postcard. Some copies of *Ant Rap* were available as a picture disc (CBS A11 1738) 1981.

Adam Ant's real name was Stuart Goddard. He was born in 1954. He joined his first band, Bazooka Joe and His Rhythm Hot Shots, whilst attending Hornsey School of Art. At one of their concerts at St. Martin's School of Art they were supported by the newly-formed **Sex Pistols**. Their energy and attitude made such an impression on Stuart that he quit Bazooka Joe to form his own outfit, The B-Sides in 1976.

It was in April 1977 that things began to happen. By now Goddard had adopted the stage persona of **Adam Ant**. The B-Sides had become **Adam and The Ants** (line-up 'A') and they played their debut gig at The Roxy on 23rd April 1977.

When **Adam** secured a leading part in Derek Jarman's "Jubilee" film, it also afforded the band the opportunity to perform two songs, *Deutscher Girls* and *Plastic Surgery*. Studio versions of them later appeared on the soundtrack album in 1978, but they did not meet with critical acclaim. Around the same period they appeared as the **Maneaters** on the *Nine To Five* film soundtrack. Later, in 1982, it appeared on a 45. It also featured **Toyah**'s voice and she appeared on the cover of what is now a sought-after rarity. *Deutscher Girls* and *Plastic Surgery* also resurfaced on a compilation *First Edition* (Editions EG EGED 15), which came out in April 1982.

With Matthew Ashman having replaced Johnny Bivouac on guitar (line-up 'E'), they secured a record contract with Decca. Their debut disc appeared in October 1978. Given their punk image, the 'A' side *Young Parisians* was not well received by the band's cult following, many of whom preferred the punchier 'B' side *Lady*. Some copies came with a picture sleeve. When the single was re-promoted in 1980, after the band had broken through it reached No. 9 during a seven week chart stint.

Adam and The Ants had built up a good reputation as a live act but Decca would not finance the promotion they needed. So they quit Decca for a small indie label called Do It, leaving behind with Decca quite a few demos. Most of these have appeared on a bootleg *Decca Sessions* but they remain officially unreleased.

Do It were up for financing an album and, given there was surplus material from the recording sessions, planned a three track EP as well. **Adam Ant** didn't favour this, so the company secretly pressed one of the best tracks, *Physical (You're So)* on the flip to their next 45 *Zerox*. The label was printed with *Whip In My Valise* as the 'B' side, but 3,000 copies were apparently pressed with *Physical*. These are now collectable for **Adam and The Ants** fans. Their fans greeted the savage sound of *Zerox* much more favourably than its predecessor.

Their debut album, released in November 1979, *Dirk Wears White Sox*, was well received too. It certainly contained two of their finest moments *Cartrouble (Parts 1 & 2)* and the atmospheric *Table Talk*, on which **Adam**'s echoing vocal blends perfectly with a hypnotic guitar sound. Shortly after its release Andy Ant departed for the **Monochrome Set** (who also featured Lester Square). His replacement was Lee Gorman.

By late 1979 **Adam** had built up a rapport with **Malcolm McLaren**, who expressed his willingness to manage the band. **Adam** paid him £1,000 to re-vamp their image, but within weeks the two were clashing badly. The end result was that **McLaren** retained the group, who he transformed into **Bow Wow Wow** with the addition of girl vocalist Annabella, but **Adam** retained the rights to the name. He joined forces with Marco Pirroni (ex-**Models** and **Siouxsie and The Banshees**) and drummer/producer Chris "Merrick" Hughes. They recorded *Cartrouble*, backed with *Kick*, which was significant for the double-drumming technique that would become an important element of their sound. Later, in 1981, when re-promoted the single climbed to No. 33. There was also a one-sided 12" promo release of it on (WHAT 1).

Having satisfied their outstanding contractual obligations to Do It, the band signed a new publishing deal with EMI having recruited bassist Kevin Mooney and additional drummer Terry Lee Miall. Their reputation as a live attraction continued to flourish and, after a successful early summer tour, they signed to CBS.

Now sporting a new 'pirate' image their *Kings Of The Wild Frontier* 45 gave them their first hit, albeit only peaking at No. 48. The follow-up *Dog Eat Dog* which featured a re-recording of *Physical* on the 'B' side, was boosted by a 'Top Of The Pops' appearance and climbed to No. 4. It was in the charts for sixteen weeks. The *Kings Of The Wild Frontier* album, released in December 1980, confirmed the band's departure from their earlier punk format. **Adam** had developed a perfect blend of sound and image which helped propel the album to No. 1. It spent sixty-six weeks in the charts overall. It spawned *Antmusic*, their most successful single yet which got to No. 2 and went gold, spending eighteen weeks in the charts. Buoyed on by this new-found popularity Decca and Do It re-promoted earlier material which entered the charts and even the *Kick* single on CBS re-entered the charts, climbing to No. 2, a whole forty-six places higher than first time around.

Kevin Mooney left, a victim of this new found fame. He was replaced by Gary Tibbs, from Roxy Music.

Their fourth CBS single *Stand And Deliver* was released in April 1981 following a U.S. tour. It was catchy, memorable and ideally depicted the band's pirate image. It was also the first of many to be accompanied by an entertaining video. It entered the charts at No. 1 and spent five weeks there.

1981 also saw **Adam** record a flexi-disc called *A.N.T.S.* for the now defunct 'Flexipop' magazine. This lighthearted effort, which is now quite collectable, appeared on blue vinyl and was sung to the melody of Village People's *Y.M.C.A.*.

The title track from their forthcoming album *Prince Charming* was released as a 45 in August 1981. It again topped the charts, which it occupied for twelve weeks. The album followed two months later. It wasn't as strong as

ADAM AND THE ANTS - Stand And Deliver.

ADAM ANT with Jordan at The Roundhouse, London 14th May 1978. Photo: Steven Richards.

THE ADICTS - Sound Of Music.

its predecessor but still sold phenomenally, climbing to No. 2 in the U.K. and bringing further Worldwide success. It also spawned a further Top Three 45 with *Ant Rap*. The album was promoted by the spectacular 'Prince Charming Revue Tour', which played to packed venues across the country.

In February 1982, Editions released two tracks that **Adam and The Ants** had recorded for the *Jubilee* soundtrack. Do-It released a three-track EP *B-Sides*, which got to No. 46. There was also a different version featuring a fourth track, *Cartrouble Pt's 1 & 2*, but probably sensing that his popularity was starting to diminish, **Adam** elected to go solo in 1982 and suddenly the band were no more. **Adam** enjoyed a successful solo career for the rest of the decade, but the details are outside the time-span of this book.

Adam and The Ants suffered initially from emerging at the tail end of punk rock. Their association with S&M images in their early days retarded their progress. In spite of this their excellent value as a live act gradually built them a cult following and then, when **Adam** re-marketed them with a new 'pirate' image and sound to match, they became during 1981 and 1982, a household name. As for **Adam**, well he's certainly been one of the most colourful figures of the late seventies and eighties.

The Peel Sessions album released in 1991 concentrates on their early material - three sessions from January and July 1978 and April 1979 - and is a 'must have' for fans of the band. In 1999, *Young Parisians* was included on the 5-CD box set *1-2-3-4 - A History Of Punk And New Wave 1976 - 1979* (MCA/Universal MCD 60066).

Addix

Personnel:	RONNIE GRIFFIN	A
	GEORGE LLOYD	A
	ALAN OFFER	A
	RICK SMITH	A

45:	Too Blind To See/	
	(No Such Thing As A) Bad Boy (PS)	(Zig Zag ZZ 22002) 1979

This seems to have been a one-off project.

The Adicts

Personnel:	PETE DAVIDSON	gtr	A
	KID DEE (MICHAEL DAVIDSON)	drms	A
	MEL ELLIS	bs	A
	KEITH WARREN	vcls	A

			HCP
ALBUMS:	1(A)	SONGS OF PRAISE	(Dwed SMT 008) 1981 -
	2(A)	SOUND OF MUSIC	(Razor RAZ 2) 1982 99
	3(A)	SMART ALEX	(Razor RAZ 15) 1985 -
	4(A)	THIS IS YOUR LIFE (compilation)	
			(Fallout FALL LP 021) 1985

NB: (1) reissued as a ltd edition of 2,000 copies on yellow vinyl (Fallout FALL LP 006) 1981. There was also a picture disc version (FALL LP 006P). (1) reissued on CD (Great Expectations PIPCD 040) 1993 and again (Cleopatra CLEO 2481CD) 1994. (2) also issued on CD (Cleopatra CLEO 3315CD) 1994. (3) also issued on CD (Great Expectations PIPCD 041) 1993. (2) and (3) reissued on one CD (Captain Oi! AHOY CD 83) 1998. (4) is a compilation which covers their early recordings between 1978-80. It was also issued on CD (FALL CD 021). Also check out *The Complete Adicts Singles Collection* (Anagram CDPUNK 33) 1994, *She's A Rocker* (Laserlight IS 394) 1991 and *Rockers Into Orbit (Live In Alabama)* (Fallout CD 046) 1990. Four more 'best of' collections are:- *Totally Adicted* (Dojo DOJO CD 69) 1992; *The Best Of The Adicts* (Dojo DOJOCD 263) 1996, *Ultimate Adiction (The Best Of The Adicts)* (U.S.) (Cleopatra CLP 9963) 1997, *The Very Best Of The Adicts* (Cherry Red CDPUNK 105) 1998 and an earlier vinyl release *Live & Loud* (Link LP 10) 1987. There's also *The Complete Singles Collection* (dbl) (Captain Oi! AHOY DLP 515) 1997; *27* (Anagram CD PUNK 87) 1987; *Live And Loud* (Japan) (Teichiku TECP 25790) and *Live And Loud* (Split CD with **Vice Squad**) (Step-1 STEP CD 077).

EPs:	1(A)	LUNCH WITH THE ADICTS (This Week/ Easy Way Out/Straight Jacket/ Organised Confusion) (PS)	(Dining Out TUX 1) 1981
	2(A)	BAR ROOM BOP (Champ Elysees/Cowboys/ Who Split My Beer/ Sound Of Music) (12")	(Fallout FALL 12038) 1985

NB: (1) came in a screen-printed picture sleeve.

		HCP
45s:	Viva La Revolution/Steamroller/ Numbers (PS)	(Fallout FALL 002) 1982 -
	Chinese Takeaway/ You'll Never Walk Alone (PS)	(Razor RZS 101) 1982 -
*	Bad Boy/Joker In The Pack/ Shake, Rattle, Bang Your Head (PS)	(Razor RZS 104) 1983 75
	Tokyo/The Odd Couple/Adicts Medley (PS)	(Sire W 9298) 1984 -
	Falling In Love Again/Come Along/It's A Laugh/ Saturday Night (PS)	(Sire UT 9070) 198? -

NB: * Also issued in a shaped picture disc format (Razor RZLP 104) 1983 -.

An interesting later wave punk outfit from Ipswich. They adopted a strong and controversial visual image of face paint and black bowlers, inspired by Stanley Kubrick's movie 'A Clockwork Orange' and adopted an anarchic musical style that won them major indie chart hits with *Chinese Takeaway* and *Bad Boy*, which also spent a week in the national charts at No. 75. Their debut EP *Lunch With The Adicts* on Dining Out is quite inventive with an overall sound texture quite similar to **Wire**. Their sarcastically-named albums also sold well with *Sound Of Music* scraping into the charts for a week at No. 99. *Totally Adicted* features material from each phase of the pop-punk band's career and the emphasis is very much on fun on cuts like *Joker In The Pack* and *Viva La Revolution*.

They continued on the fringe of the indie scene in the late '80s and early '90s. Their later recordings in this period appealed to fans of punk nostalgia.

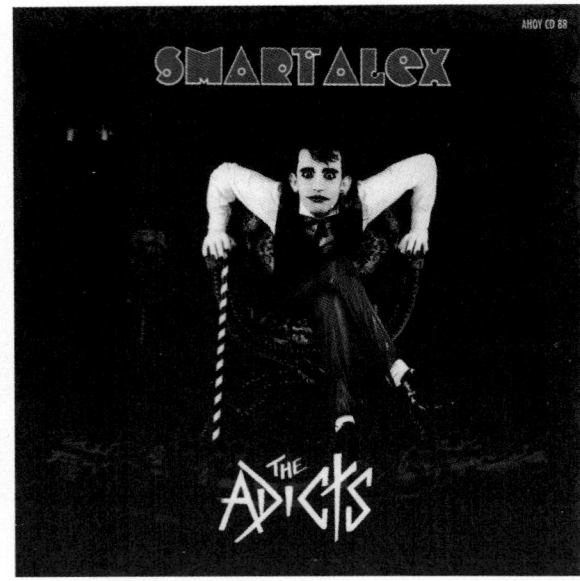

THE ADICTS - Smart Alex.

Live And Loud is very raw and raucous. *The Complete Adicts Singles Collection* is precisely what it purports to be - all their 'A' and 'B' sides arranged in chronological order. *The Best Of The Adicts* (CD) on Dojo in 1996 showcases their spiky, energetic early recordings well. It starts with two cuts from their rare debut EP, *Lunch With The Adicts* and includes their indie hits like *Viva La Revolution*, *Chinese Takaway* and *Bad Boy*. They also figure on *Burning Ambition: A History Of Punk, Vol. 3* (Anagram CD PUNK 98) 1997 with *Viva La Revolution*. The same cut also appeared on *The Fallout Punk Singles Collection* (Anagram CDPUNK 30) in 1994 along with *Champs Elysees*. *Chinese Takeaway* also got a further airing on *Punk, Vol. 2* (Music Club MCCD 027) in 1991, whilst *Love Sucks* featured on *Punk Compilation* (Emporio EMPRCD 550) in 1994.

A.D. 1984 - The Russians Are Coming.

A.D. 1984

Personnel:	JOHN BELL	drms	A
	DAVE FANCOURT	gtr	A
	GLENN HOWARD	gtr	A
	ROB ROSS	vcls	A
	PETER STEVENSON	bs	A
	ADRIAN YORK	keyb'ds	A

45:	The Russians Are Coming/ New Moon Falling (PS)	(Voyage VOY 005) 1979

This 45 was recorded at Surrey Sound Studios. The music format is pretty standard rock but the lyrics on *The Russians Are Coming* are all about stopping the arms race:-

"The enemy is coming, the enemy is coming
the enemy is coming, the Russians are coming!
So mighty was the BOMB
Now all life has gone
Almighty was the BOMB
Now all life has gone
Burned to a cinder, charred to blackened waste
Our planet is dying, atomic war scarred its face
We didn't do a damned thing to STOP THE ARMS RACE
Now it's much too late the Earth has gone without trace
Now it's much too late the Earth has gone without trace"
(from *The Russians Are Coming!*)

Advertising

Personnel:	SIMON BOSWELL	gtr	A
	PAUL BULTITUDE	drms	A
	DENNIS SMITH	bs	A
	TOT TAYLOR	gtr, vcls	A

ALBUM:	1(A)	ADVERTISING JINGLES	(EMI EMC 3253) 1978

45s:	Lipstick/Lonely Guys (PS)	(EMI EMI 2710) 1977
	Stolen Love/Suspender Fun (PS)	(EMI EMI 2754) 1978

A foot-tapping power-pop four-piece who played two-minute jingle songs. *Lipstick* was a punchy single but it didn't get much airplay. The best song by far in their live set was their second single *Stolen Love*, but this failed to breakthrough too and disillusioned they split.

The Adverts

Personnel:	GAYE "ADVERT" BLACK	bs	ABCDE
	HOWARD "PICKUP" BOAK	gtr	ABCD
	LAURIE "DRIVER" MUSCAT	drms	A
	TIM "TV" SMITH	vcls	ABCDE
	JOHN TOWE	drms	B
	ROD LATTER	drms	CD
	TIM CROSS	keyb'ds	DE
	PAUL MARTINEZ	gtr	E
	RICK MARTINEZ	drms	E

HCP

ALBUMS:	1(A)	CROSSING THE RED SEA WITH THE ADVERTS	
		(Bright BRL 2001) 1978	38
	2(D)	CAST OF THOUSANDS	(RCA PL 25246) 1979 -

NB: Some numbered copies of (1) also issued in red vinyl. (1) later reissued in 1981 (Butt ALSO 002), again in 1983 on red vinyl (Butt ALSO 002) and in 1988 on vinyl (Bright BUL 2) and CD (Bright CDBUL 2) 1988, (Link Classics CLINK 001CD) 1990 and (Essential ESMCD 451) 1997. (2) also issued on CD (Anagram CDPUNK 102) 1998. Compilations include *The Punk Singles Collection* (Anagram CDPUNK 95) 1997, *Singles Collection* (LP) (Get Back GET 30) 1998, and *Radio Sessions* (Burning Airlines PILOT 003) 1997. There's also the CD *Live At The Roxy* (Receiver RRCD 136) 1993, *The Complete Peel Sessions* (LP) (Get Back GET 24) 198? and *The Wonders Don't Care: The Complete Radio Recordings* (New Millenium PILOT 3) 1997.

HCP

45s:	One Chord Wonders/Quickstep (PS)	(Stiff BUY 13) 1977 -
	Gary Gilmore's Eyes/ Bored Teenagers (PS)	(Anchor ANC 1043) 1977 18
	Safety In Numbers/ We Who Wait (PS)	(Anchor ANC 1047) 1977 -
	No Time To Be 21/ New Day Dawning (PS)	(Bright BR 1) 1978 38
	Television's Over/ Back From The Dead (PS)	(RCA PB 5128) 1978 -
	My Place/New Church (live) (PS)	(RCA PB 5160) 1979 -
	Cast Of Thousands/ I Will Walk You Home (PS)	(RCA PB 5191) 1979 -
	Gary Gilmore's Eyes/We Who Wait/ New Day Dawning (PS)	(Bright BULB 1) 1983 -
	Peel Session (Metallic PS)	(Strange Fruit SFPS 034) 1987 -
	Peel Session (Grey PS)	(Strange Fruit SFPS 034) 1987 -

Tim 'TV' Smith and Gaye Advert moved to London in the summer of 1976 to form a band. Gaye was new to the business, but Tim 'TV' Smith had worked the West Country circuit for a while and previously led a band called Sleaze, who had been responsible for a limited edition eponymous self-made album of which only 50 were pressed!

As for **The Adverts**, the story goes that they debuted at the Roxy on 23rd January 1977. They were spotted playing there by **Damned** guitarist Brian James. He got the head of Stiff Records to come and hear them and impressed, he later went backstage and signed them.

Their debut 45 *One Chord Wonders*, released in April 1977, became a punk anthem. An immediate club hit, it was also a 'Single of the Week' in 'Sounds'.

"I wonder what we'll play for you tonight
Something heavy or something light
Something to set your soul alight
I wonder how we'll answer when you say
'We don't like you - go away
Come back when you've learnt to play'"
(from *One Chord Wonders*)

An extract from the recording was included on Stiff's promo single *Excerpt's From Stiff's Greatest Hits* and the band were conveniently on hand to promote it as support to **The Damned** on a lengthy tour. It's been reissued on a number of occasions since and appears in the second of Stiff's boxed single sets. Both sides of the 45 also later figured on the *Heroes And Cowards* (Stiff SEE 20) 1978 compilation.

In June 1977, **The Adverts** signed to Anchor Records. Their next single *Gary Gilmore's Eyes* was inspired by executed American murderer Gary Gilmore's desire to donate his eyes to science. It was a punk classic and a commercial success too, climbing to No. 18 during a seven week chart residency to give the band their only Top 20 hit. Indeed, it was one of the earlier punk singles to make the higher echelons of the charts. On the flip was *Bored Teenagers*, a re-recording of another of the band's popular early songs that had previously appeared on the *Live At The Roxy* (Harvest SHSP 4069) 1977 compilation.

Their *Safety In Numbers* single did less well commercially but February 1978 saw them release their classic *Crossing The Red Sea With The Adverts* on the Bright subsidiary label. The album included re-recorded versions of *One Chord Wonders*, *Bored Teenagers* and *Safety In Numbers* as well as *No Time To Be 21*, which had peaked at No. 34 in the charts the previous month. *No Time To Be 21* is a good rock song with a comfortable instrumental challenge. 500 numbered promotional copies of the album were released in red vinyl. These are now sought-after collectables. A later reissue of the album on the Butt label also includes the original version of *Gary Gilmore's Eyes*. The album is a 'must have' for all punk fans. In 1979, *Gary Gilmore's Eyes* resurfaced on *20 Of Another Kind* (Polydor SUPER POLS 1006) and later on *Punk And Disorderly: New Wave 1976 - 1981* (Telstar STAR 2520) 1991 and on *New Wave Archive* (Rialto RMCD 201) 1997.

In the summer of 1978, the band suffered a number of setbacks. Laurie Driver was ousted during an Irish tour and replaced first by ex-**Chelsea**/**Generation X** drummer John Rowe, who then gave way to Rod Latter (ex-**The Maniacs** and **Rings**). Then their record label Bright collapsed.

They finally signed to RCA, in late August 1978, but their next single *Television's Over* failed to make much impact. It was also included on a rather obscure RCA sampler *It's Where Your World Begins* (RCA UK 1) 1978. TV Smith co-wrote its flipside *Back From The Dead* with Richard Strange.

Their next single *My Place* was produced by Tom Newman, who'd worked with Mike Oldfield. It didn't sound like punk at all. Newman also produced their next album, *Cast Of Thousands*, and Oldfield's keyboardist Tim Cross played on this effectively becoming a member of the band. The album was poorly promoted and what proved to be their final single, coupling *Cast Of Thousands* with another album cut *I Will Walk Home*, made very little impression at all.

Following further personnel changes (Howard Pickup and Rod Latter left to be replaced by session man Paul Martinez (of Robert Plant fame) and his brother Rick) **The Adverts**, now in terminal decline, split. Their final gig was at Slough College on 27th October 1979.

TV Smith and Tim Cross formed a new band TV Smith's Explorers. They released an album in 1981 and a few 45s. Cross became a session man and Smith went on to form Cheap before going solo. Gaye 'Advert' Black left the music business altogether and ended up working in local government.

THE ADVERTS - Crossing The Red Sea With.

In 1987 *One Chord Wonders*, *Gary Gilmore's Eyes*, *Bored Teenagers*, *Quickstep* and *New Boys* figured on a Strange Fruit release of the first of their four John Peel sessions. *The Wonders Don't Care: The Complete Radio Recordings* (New Millennium PILOT 3) 1997 presents all four of their Peel sessions recorded between April 1977 and November 1979. The first session contained their three classic early 45 cuts:- *One Chord Wonders*, *Gary Gilmore's Eyes* and *Bored Teenagers*. The second session, from August 1977, was dominated by strong material from their first album. There's the anthemic *New Church*, *Safety In Numbers* and a thumping version of *The Great British Mistake*. This contained the line that became their epitaph, "We couldn't adapt, so we couldn't survive". The session also included a version of *We Who Wait* on which TV Smith's vocals and melody have been likened to Peter Hammill (of **Van der Graaf Generator**). Their two final sessions are less essential. The best way to hear all the Peel sessions is to purchase *The Complete Peel Sessions* (LP) (Get Back GET 24) 199?, which was compiled by T.V. Smith himself. It includes exclusive photos and detailed liner notes. Also relevant from the same label is *Singles Collection* (LP) (Get Back GET 30) 1998, which contains their 'A' and 'B' sides.

The Punk Singles Collection compiles all their 'A' and 'B' sides. Later, in 1999, *One Chord Wonders* got a further airing on the 5-CD box set *1-2-3-4 - A History Of Punk And New Wave 1976-79* (MCA/Universal MCD 60066).

For a few months **The Adverts** were a seminal part of punk rock. Their first album and the *One Chord Wonders* and *Gary Gilmore's Eyes* singles captured the mood perfectly.

Afflicted

ALBUMS:	1	THE AFFLICTED MAN'S MUSICAL BAG	(Bonk AFF 3) 1982
	2	HIGH SPEED AND THE AFFLICTED MAN - GET STONED	(Bonk AFF 6) 1982
45s:	*	I'm Afflicted/Beware	(Bonk AFF 1) 1981
	+	All Right Boy/Who Can Tell (PS)	(Bonk AFF 2) 1982
	#	Afflicted	(Bonk AFF 4) 1982

NB: * This was issued in rubber-stamped white labels in a plain sleeve. Some with an insert. + This was issued in stamped white labels. # This untitled single came in a striped bag.

The Afflicted was really one bloke - a gay right-wing extremist who died of A.I.D.S..

Afraid Of Mice

Personnel incl: PHILIP FRANZ JONES gtr, vcls

ALBUMS:	1(A)	AFRAID OF MICE	(Charisma CAS 1155) 1982
	2(A)	AFRAID OF MICE - THE OFFICIAL BOOTLEG	(Own Label) 1983
45s:		I'm On Fire/Down In The Dark (PS)	(Charisma CB 383) 1981
		Intercontinental/ What Shall We Do? (PS)	(Charisma CB 389) 1981
		Popstar/What I Want (PS)	(Charisma CB 395) 1981
		Transparents/That's Not True (PS)	(Charisma CB 397) 1982
	*	At The Club/I Will Wait (PS)	(Charisma CB 398) 1982

NB: * A free four-track flexi-disc and poster came with this 45.

The pivotal figure in **Afraid Of Mice** was Philip Franz Jones - their remaining members fluctuated over their relatively short history. Before Jones finally decided on **Afraid Of Mice** as a name they had gigged as Beano, The Press and The Jones.

Afraid Of Mice were part of Liverpool's new wave scene fronted by **Echo and The Bunnymen**, **The Teardrop Explodes** and **Orchestral Manuvoeures In The Dark**. They featured on the Liverpool compilation *A Trip To The Dentist* (Skeleton SKL LP 1) 1980. This helped bring them to the attention of a wider audience and secure a deal with Charisma.

Their early singles *I'm On Fire* and *Intercontinental* were enthusiastically received. Their eponymous album, produced by Tony Visconti (who'd earlier worked with David Bowie), was an appealing blend of simple power-pop with an edge provided by angry lyrics and cutting guitars. Despite this, they failed to achieve a breakthrough and *At The Club*, which was accompanied with a free flexidisc was their final vinyl for Charisma. The flexidisc comprised a varied selection of extracts of interesting songs:- *Popstar*, *Bad News*, *Taking It Easy* and *Important Man*, which were taken from their *Afraid Of Mice* album.

They continued to play live and put out *Afraid Of Mice - The Official Bootleg* on their own label in 1985. Their only release after this was a cut on the *Jobs For The Boys* compilation in 1985.

In 1986, Jones disbanded this band and linked up with Alex McKechnie (formerly of Passage and **Modern Eon**) in Two's A Crowd, who later evolved into Up And Running and released an album *Live At Lime Street*.

In 1994, **Afraid Of Mice** played a one-off reunion gig at Liverpool's Royal Court Theatre.

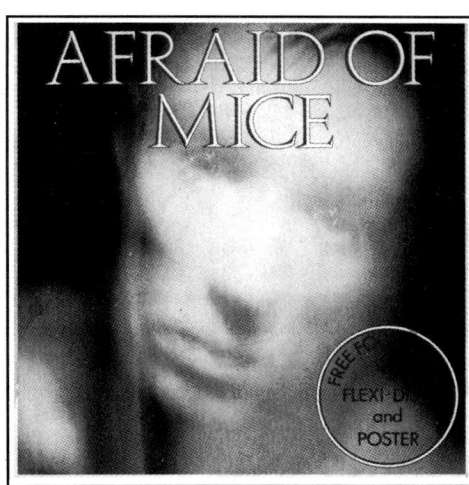

AFRAID OF MICE - At The Club.

After Dark

45s:	Evil Woman/Johnny/Lucy (PS)	(After Dark AD 001)	1981
*	Deathbringer/Call Of The Wild	(Lager PROMO 1)	1983

NB: * This was a promo-only picture disc.

Both of these releases are exceptionally rare.

Airkraft

45:	Move In Rhythm/Pumping Iron	(Square SQS 5)	1980

Airkraft hailed from Halifax in Yorkshire and their new wave number *Move In Rhythm* can also be heard on *Hicks From The Sticks* (Rockburgh Records ROC 111) 1980.

Aka and Charlatans

45:	Heroes Are Losers/Lady Of The Night/ Perhaps One Day (12", PS)	(Vanity VANE 1)	1978

This now scarce 45 came in a screen-printed die-cut picture sleeve.

AK Process

45:	Electronic Music: After All Love/ Post Town (PS)	(Output OPQ 101)	1979

An interesting single - a soundscape of electronic music. Some members had been involved in **File Under Pop**.

AKRYLYKZ - Smart Boy.

Akrylykz

Personnel:	STEVIE B	alto sax, vcls, keyb'ds	A
	ROLAND GIFT	tenor sax, vcls	A
	STEVE PEARS	also sax, vcls	A
	FRED REYNOLDS	bs	A
	PIOTR 'PETE' SWIDERSKI	drms	A
	NIK TOWNEND	gtr	A

45s:	Smart Boy/Spyderman (PS)	(Double R RED 2)	1980
	Smart Boy/Spyderman (PS)	(Polydor POSP 128)	1980
	J.D./Ska'd For Life (PS)	(Polydor 2059 253)	1980

A short-lived group whose records have a reggae/two-tone influence. Both *Smart Boy* and *Spyderman* are quite catchy, but the band made little impression at the time.

The Alarm

Personnel:	EDDIE McDONALD	bs	A
(up to	MIKE PETERS	vcls, gtr	A
1986)	DAVE SHARP	gtr	A
	NIGEL TWIST	drms	A

					HCP
ALBUMS:	1(A)	DECLARATION	(IRS IRSA 204)	1984	6
(up to	2(A)	STRENGTH	(IRS MIRF 1004)	1985	18
1986)					

NB: (1) also issued on CD (IRS CDILP 25887) 1986. (2) also issued on CD (IRS DMIRF 1004) 1987, (IRS DMIRF 1004) 1990 and (IRS IRLD 19006) 1992. Also relevant are *Standards* (IRS EIRSA 1043) 1990 which spent one week at No. 47; also on CD (IRS EIRSACD 1043) 1990, the CD *Compact Hits: The Alarm* (A&M AMCD 906) 1988 and *The Best Of The Alarm And Mike Peters* (EMI 4937512) 1998, which is credited to **The Alarm** and Mike Peters.

				HCP
45s:	Unsafe Buildings/Up For Murder (PS)	(White Cross 001)	1981	-
(up to	Marching On/Across The Border/			
1986)	Lie Of The Land (PS)	(IRS ILS 0032)	1982	-
	The Stand/Third Light (PS)	(IRS PFP 1014)	1983	-
	The Stand/For Freedom/ Reason 41 (12", PS)	(IRS PFPX 1014)	1983	-
	68 Guns (Part 1)/68 Guns (Part 2) (PS)	(IRS PFP 1023)	1983	17
	68 Guns/ Thoughts Of A Young Man (PS)	(IRS PFPX 1023)	1983	-
	Where Were You Hiding When The Storm Broke/ Pavillion Steps (PS)	(IRS IRS 101)	1984	22
	Where Were You Hiding When The Storm Broke/ Pavillion Steps/ What Kind Of Hell (12", PS)	(IRS IRSX 101)	1984	-
*	The Deceiver/Reason 41 (PS)	(IRS IRS 103)	1984	51
	The Deceiver/Reason 41/Lie Of The Land/ Legal Matter (double-pack PS)	(IRS IRSD 103)	1984	-
	The Deceiver/Reason 41/ Second Generation (12", PS)	(IRS IRSX 103)	1984	-

The Chant Has Just Begun/		
The Bells Of Rhymney (PS)	(IRS IRS 114) 1984	48
The Chant Has Just Begun/The Bells Of Rhymney/		
The Stand (12", PS)	(IRS IRSY 114) 1984	-
Absolute Reality/Blaze Of Glory (PS)	(IRS ALARM 1) 1985	35
Absolute Reality/Blaze Of Glory/Room At The Top/		
Reason 36 (double-pack, PS)	(IRS ALARMD 1) 1985	-
Absolute Reality/		
Blaze Of Glory (12", PS)	(IRS ALARM 12) 1985	-
Strength/Majority (PS)	(IRS IPM 104) 1985	40
Strength/Majority (poster bag)	(IRS IPM 104) 1985	-
Strength/Majority/		
Absolute Reality (12", PS)	(IRS IRT 104) 1985	-
Spirit Of '76/Where Were You		
Hiding When The Storm Broke (PS)	(IRS IRM 109) 1986	22
Spirit Of '76/Where Were You Hiding When		
The Storm Broke/Deeside (12", PS)	(IRS IRMT 109) 1986	-
Spirit Of '76/Where Were You Hiding When The Storm		
Broke/Deeside/Knockin' On Heaven's Door (live)/		
68 Guns (live) (12", double-pack)	(IRS IRMTD 109) 1986	-
Knife Edge/Caroline Isenberg (PS)	(IRS IRM 112) 1986	43
Knife Edge/Caroline Isenberg//Howling Wind/		
Unbreak The Promise (double-pack)	(IRS IRMD 112) 1986	-
Knife Edge/Caroline Isenberg/Howling Wind/		
Unbreak The Promise (12", PS)	(IRS IRMT 112) 1986	-

NB: * Some copies also issued on clear vinyl. Other copies also issued on mustard vinyl.

This foursome formed in Rhyl, north Wales in 1977 originally as a punk band called The Toilets. Twist was 19 at the time and the other three were just 18. With the mod revival in 1979 they renamed themselves **17** releasing a now rare 45 on Vendetta, but they failed to achieve a commercial breakthrough.

In 1980, they were kicked off a support slot on a Dexy's Midnight Runners tour for not being good enough. It was after seeing **U2** perform at the Marquee that Mike Peters was inspired to rejuvenate the band. They worked on some new material and the first song to emerge *Alarm Alarm* inspired their new name **The Alarm**. Under this moniker they began gigging during the summer of 1981 locally around the Rhyl area of north Wales.

In September 1981, they cut a 45 in Manchester, *Unsafe Buildings* backed by *Up For Murder*. 2,000 copies were pressed on their own White Cross label. Some were sold at gigs, others sent to record companies and to coincide with this the group relocated to London.

Once in London they got some significant support act gigs to **U2**, **The Jam** and The Beat, which all helped attract press attention. Record companies became interested but **The Alarm** held out until they got the deal they wanted with IRS Records in August 1982.

Their first 45 for IRS *Marching On* appeared in October 1982. It exhibited a clear **Clash** influence with rousing vocals and upfront guitars, although the tight vocal harmonies in the chorus were more melodic than anything **The Clash** could manage. The 45 got some promising reviews but failed to chart. It is now very collectable and hard to find.

ALARM - 68 Guns.

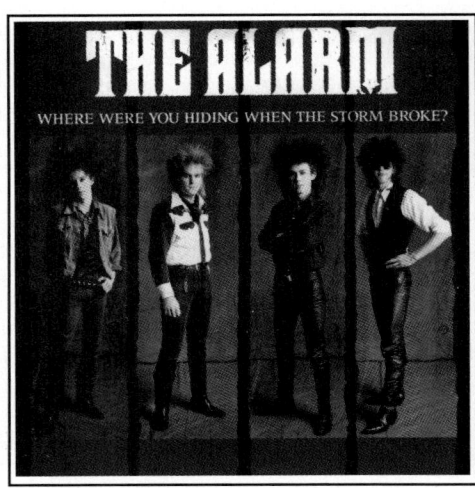

ALARM - Where Were You Hiding When The Storm Broke.

A follow-up *The Stand* appeared in April 1983, produced by Mike Glossop. Again **The Clash** were a clear influence and the single attracted airplay but failed to chart. It was their first to be released in 12" format too and featured different tracks on the flip side.

Their chart breakthrough finally came with their third IRS single *68 Guns*. Again similarities with **The Clash** were evident but unlike *The Stand* it also successfully captured some of the power of their live act. The single soon entered the charts where it spent a total of seven weeks peaking at No. 17. Its success also earnt them an appearance on 'Top Of The Pops', which helped bring them to the attention of a wider audience.

Where Were You Hiding When The Storm Broke proved to be a strong follow-up. Its biting edge helped make it their most powerful single to date and it brought them a second hit, peaking at No. 22 during a six week chart residency after its release in January 1984.

The Alarm's by now long-awaited debut album *Declaration* followed in February. It contained, among its content, newly recorded versions of *The Stand*, *Marching On*, *68 Guns* and *Third Light*, which had all previously been available on 45s. These new versions were mostly less aggressive but more structured than the originals. The album version of *The Stand* for example, comprised a short, acoustic solo by Mike Peters. Among the new material, *The Deceiver*, *Howling Wind*, delivered in the style its title suggested, and *Blaze Of Glory*, particularly catch the ears. Most of the material was penned by Mike Peters and Eddie MacDonald. Dave Sharp contributed a solo composition *Tell Me* and contributed to three others. The album sold well, climbing to No. 6 during its eleven weeks in the charts.

The Deceiver was culled from the album for 45 release in March 1984. A new version of *Reason 41* (originally issued as the live 12" flipside of *The Stand*) was included on the flip. The 12" version included an additional new cut *Second Generation*. *The Deceiver* had clear commercial promise, so the fact it only spent four weeks in the chart peaking at No. 51 was disappointing. Some copies were available in clear and mustard vinyl. It was also available in double-pack format with two additional tracks *Lie Of The Land* and *Legal Matter*.

In the coal dispute of 1984 **The Alarm** made a sizeable financial donation to the National Union Of Mineworkers. They also recorded the old miners' lament *The Bells Of Rhymney* on the flip side to their October 1984 45 *The Chant Has Just Begun*. This may well have fared better had the 'A' side not referred to "gunpowder" and "the fuse" being lit "in the house". The Brighton bomb at the Tory party conference the same month reduced its airplay considerably and it stalled at No. 48 during its four-week chart stay.

Absolute Reality, released in February 1985, was the product of a new session. It featured on its flip side the pulsating *Blaze Of Glory*, which had once been muted as a follow-up to *68 Guns*. The 45 was also issued as a 12" and in double-pack format with two additional cuts; *Room At The Top* and *Reason 36*. This last release was very limited. The 45 enjoyed a six week chart residency peaking at No. 35.

Their second album *Strength* was released in October 1985. The title track was put out as a 45 a few weeks before as a taster in both 7" and 12" format. The 12" release featured a different non-album recording of the flip side *Majority* and a new version of *Absolute Reality*. The 45 continued their series of minor chart successes, climbing to No. 40 during its four weeks in the charts. The album, produced by Mike Howlett, was a diverse collection, which added keyboards to their sound. Their old anthemic style was still there represented by cuts like *Knife Edge* and *Deeside*, but *Walk Forever By My Side* was a romantic acoustic number and *Spirit Of '76* owed more to Bruce Springsteen than **Clash**-influenced punk rock.

Spirit Of '76 was issued as a single in January 1986. In addition to the normal 7" and 12" versions, there was also a 12" double-pack featuring live versions of *68 Guns* and Bob Dylan's *Knockin' On Heaven's Door*. The 45 sold quite well, climbing to No. 22 and spending five weeks in the charts. A second 45 *Knife Edge* followed in April. This had been one of the more dramatic tracks on the *Strength* album. Again, a double-pack was released, in addition to the normal 7" and 12" format. *Knife Edge* spent three weeks in the charts, peaking at No. 43.

Here we must leave **The Alarm** who continued to record until 1991 when Mike Peters went solo. *Standards* released on vinyl and CD in 1990 included most of their finest moments and there's also a four-track cassette *Compact Hits* released in 1988 which contained *68 Guns*, *Blaze Of Glory*, *Shout To The Devil* and *Where Were You Hiding When The Storm Broke*.

The 1998 release *The Best Of The Alarm And Mike Peters* is the most comprehensive collection of their material, containing twenty of their best songs.

Albertos Y Los Trios Paranoias

Personnel:	TONY BOWERS	gtr, vcls, keyb'ds	A
	BOB HARDING	vcls, gtr	A
	JIMMY HIBBERT	vcls, gtr	A
	RAY HUGHES	drms	A
	CHRIS 'C.P.' LEE	vcls, gtr, bs	A
	BRUCE MITCHELL	drms	A
	LES PRIOR	vcls	A
	SIMON WHITE	vcls, gtr	A

ALBUMS:	1(A)	ALBERTOS Y LOS TRIOS PARANOIAS		
			(Transatlantic TRA 316)	1976
	2(A)	ITALIANS FROM OUTER SPACE		
			(Transatlantic TRA 349)	1977
	3(A)	SKITE	(Logo LOGO 1009)	1978
	4(A)	DEATH OF ROCK 'N' ROLL		
			(El Mocambo ELMO 751)	1980

NB: There's also *Snuff Rock: The Best Of The Albertos* (Mau Mau MAU 60) 1990 compilation, which is also on CD (MAUCD 604) 1991 and *Radio Sweat* (Overground OVER 56CD) 1997.

HCP

EPs:	1	SNUFF ROCK (PS) (Kill/Gobbing On Life/Snuffin Like That/Snuffin In A Babylon)	(Stiff LAST 2) 1977 -
	2	DEAD MEAT (PS) (Heads Down No Nonsense Mindless Boogie/Thank You/Fuck You/ Dead Meat Part Two)	(Logo GO(D) 323) 1978 47
	3	CRUISIN' WITH SANTA (PS)	(New Hormones ORG 30) 1982 -

NB: (2) was a double-pack issued in a gatefold picture sleeve.

45s:	Dread Jaws/De Version	(Big T BIG 541) 1976
	Teenage Paradise/Heads Down No Nonsense Mindless Boogie	(EIM ESMO 506) 1980

A talented comedy outfit who rose to acclaim via punk. They released an eponymous debut album in 1976 which made little impact but punk soon changed their fortunes. Chris 'C.P.' Lee wrote the rock musical 'Sleak' and it was performed with much praise in 1977 at the Royal Court Theatre. The main character Norman Sleak is prompted into the ultimate rock 'n' roll act, an on-stage suicide. Lee christened this 'Snuff Rock'. The title was used for their first EP which featured three excellent parodies *Kill*, *Gobbing On Life* and *Snuffin' Like That* as well as a swipe at punk's increasing interest in reggae, *Snuffin' In Babylon*. *Heads Down No Nonsense Mindless Boogie* is also a classic and recommended listening. It spent five weeks in the charts, climbing to No. 47.

On *Italians From Outer Space* the band successfully translate onto vinyl their own brand of satire that came across so successfully at their live gigs.

ALBERTOS Y LOS TRIOS PARANOIAS - Snuff Rock.

In 1999, *Kill* was compiled on the 5-CD box set *1-2-3-4 - A History Of Punk And New Wave 1976 - 1979* (MCA/Universal MCD 60066).

C.P. Lee later formed C.P. Lee and The Mystery Guild. In the late eighties Jimmy Hibbert reappeared as the main voice over and writer of the children's cult character, Count Duckula.

Aliens

45:	When The River Runs Dry	(Alien ALI 001) 1980

Unusually for this era this 45 did not appear in a picture sleeve.

The Allies

45:	Plush Living/Commuter (PS)	(Harp HSP 1025) 1979

A reasonable indie 45 with lots of electric piano to the fore. This proved to be a one-off venture and the record gives no clue as to their origin.

Altered Images

Personnel:	MICHAEL 'TICH' ANDERSON	drms	AB
	CAESAR	gtr	A
	CLARE GROGAN	vcls	ABC
	TONY McDAID	bs	ABC
	JOHNNY Mc ELHONE	gtr	ABC
	JIM McINVEN	gtr	B
	STEPHEN LIRONI	gtr, drms	C

HCP

ALBUMS:	1(B)	HAPPY BIRTHDAY	(Epic EPC 84893) 1981 26
	2(B)	PINKY BLUE	(Epic EPC 85665) 1982 12
	3(C)	BITE	(Epic EPC 25413) 1982 16
	4(-)	COLLECTED IMAGES	(Epic EPC 25973) 1984 -

NB: (1) reissued on vinyl (Epic EPC 32355) 1983. Also issued on CD (Columbia 4805282) 1991 and (Sony Collectors 9329442) 1993. (3) also issued on cassette with five extra tracks; *Bring Me Closer (Dance Mix)*, *Don't Talk To Me About Love (Extended Version)*, *Surprise Me*, *I Don't Want To Know* and *Last Goodbye*. There's also some CD compilations: *The Best Of Altered Images* (Connoisseur Collection VSOP CD 177) 1992 and *Reflected Images (The Best Of Altered Images)* (Epic 4843992) 1996.

EP:	1	GREATEST ORIGINAL HITS (Happy Birthday/ I Could Be Happy/Dead Pop Stars/ A Day's Wait) (PS)	(Epic EPC A 2617) 1982

NB: (1) also issued on cassette (EPC A40-2617) 1982.

HCP

45s:	Dead Pop Stars/Sentimental (PS)	(Epic EPC A 1023) 1981 67
	Dead Pop Stars/Sentimental/ Leave Me Alone (cassette single)	(Epic EPC 40-A 1023) 1981 -
	A Day's Wait/Who Cares? (PS)	(Epic EPC A 1167) 1981 -

Happy Birthday/ So We Go Whispering (PS)	(Epic EPC A 1522)	1981	2
* Happy Birthday (Dance Mix)/So We Go Whispering/ Jeepster (12", PS)	(Epic EPC A 131522)	1981	-
I Could Be Happy/Insects (PS)	(Epic EPC A 1834)	1981	7
I Could Be Happy /Insects (picture disc)	(Epic EPC A 111834)	1981	-
I Could Be Happy (Dance Mix)/Insects/ Disco Pop Stars (12", PS)	(Epic EPC A 131834)	1981	-
See Those Eyes/How About That Then (I've Missed My Train) (PS)	(Epic EPC A 2198)	1982	11
See Those Eyes/How About That Then (I've Missed My Train) (picture disc)	(Epic EPC A 112198)	1982	-
See Those Eyes (Extended Mix)/ See Those Eyes (7" version)/How About That Then (I've Missed My Train) (12", PS)	(Epic EPC A 132198)	1982	-
# Pinky Blue/Think That It Might (Dance Mix) (PS)	(Epic EPC A 2426)	1982	35
Pinky Blue (Dance Mix)/Jump Jump - Think That It Might (Segued Dance Mix) (12", PS)	(Epic EPC A 132426)	1982	-
Don't Talk To Me About Love/ Last Goodbye (PS)	(Epic EPC A 3083)	1983	7
Don't Talk To Me About Love/ Last Goodbye (picture disc)	(Epic WA 3083)	1983	-
Don't Talk To Me About Love (Extended Mix)/ Last Goodbye (12", PS)	(Epic EPC A 133083)	1983	-
Bring Me Closer/Surprise Me (PS)	(Epic EPC A 3398)	1983	29
Bring Me Closer/ Surprise Me (picture disc)	(Epic WA 3398)	1983	-
Bring Me Closer (Extended Mix)/ Surprise Me (12", PS)	(Epic TA 3398)	1983	-
Bring Me Closer (Extended Mix)/ Surprise Me (12", picture disc)	(Epic WTA 3398)	1983	-
Love To Stay/ Another Lost Look (live) (PS)	(Epic EPC A 3582)	1983	46
Love To Stay/Another Lost Look (live) (poster sleeve)	(Epic EPC A 3582)	1982	-
Love To Stay (Extended Version)/ Another Lost Look (live) (12", PS)	(Epic TA 3582)	1983	-
Change Of Heart/ Another Lost Look (PS)	(Epic EPC A 3735)	1983	-
Change Of Heart/Another Lost Look/Happy Birthday/ I Could Be Happy (12", PS)	(Epic TA 3735)	1983	-
Reissue: Happy Birthday/I Could Be Happy	(Old Gold OG 9663)	1987	-

A marginal case for inclusion are post-punk alternative popsters **Altered Images**. Musically, in **The Undertones**' mould their main asset was child-belle Clare Grogan.

Altered Images formed in March 1979 when Johnny McElhone, Michael Anderson and Tony McDaid recruited Clare Grogan as a vocalist. They began rehearsing at Kilmarnock Town Hall and, once Clare had overcome her fear of performing in public, made their debut at a Glasgow pub called The Mars Bar in August 1979. Having recruited a second guitarist Caesar they began to gig regularly around the local pubs and youth clubs. They took their name **Altered Images** from the design company responsible for the sleeve of **The Buzzcocks**' *Promises*, when one of them picked up a copy.

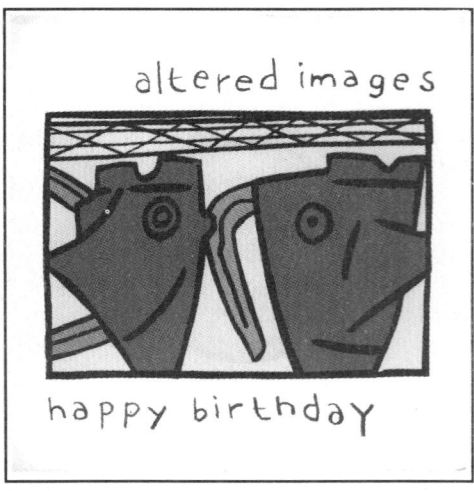

ALTERED IMAGES - Happy Birthday.

The band received a significant boost when Clare Grogan was offered the role of Gregory's Girl by movie-maker Bill Forsyth and the movie became a big success, winning considerable critical acclaim.

Their second break came when a hastily recorded demo tape put together by the band found its way to the **Siouxsie and The Banshees** entourage, who liked what they heard. As a consequence **Altered Images** were given the support slot at Glasgow's Tiffanys on **Siouxsie**'s Scottish tour. It went well and they remained the support band for the rest of **Siouxsie and The Banshees**' tour.

Their next assault was on the airwaves. Firstly, they were filmed for showing on BBC TV playing the 'Futurama' festival in Leeds. Then top radio DJ John Peel carried their mantle by arranging for them to record two sessions for his Radio 1 show. The first in October 1980 featured *Beckoning Strings*, *Legionaire*, *Insects* and *Dead Pop Stars*. The second, broadcast in March 1981, comprised *A Day's Wait*, *Jeepster*, *Idols* and *Midnight*.

They were soon signed to Epic/CBS. Their first 45, the doom-laden *Dead Pop Stars* released in March 1981, confirmed that **Siouxsie and The Banshees** were a definite influence on the band. Despite its release coinciding with the death of John Lennon it sold well enough to spent two weeks in the lower echelons of the chart peaking at No. 67. As well as the 7", the single was also released in cassette format with one additional track *Leave Me Alone*. This format is harder to track down. The 45 was produced by Steve Severin and housed in an elegant picture sleeve designed by David Band. The same pairing was employed for the follow-up *A Day's Wait* in May. The lyrics were submerged beneath a collage of swirling guitar and bass and this one didn't make the lower reaches of the chart.

In early spring 1981, their second guitarist Caesar left to join The Wake. He was replaced by ex-Berlin Blondes member Jim McInven. This new line-up continued to raise the band's profile, guesting on **Adam and The Ants** and **The Cure**'s nationwide tours.

Their big breakthrough came with the release of *Happy Birthday* in August. With Martin Rushent (fresh from working with **The Human League**) now handling production, the end result was an invigorating, vibrant and danceable single, which was ideal for the energetic Grogan to front up. It spent seventeen weeks in the chart, climbing to No. 2. It dominated the *Happy Birthday* album which followed in September, with the remainder of the material produced by Severin unimpressive. Nonetheless, it spent twenty-one weeks in the chart, peaking at No. 26. Fans of the band will want to track down *Happy New Year*, which appeared on a flexidisc which came with the January 1982 issue of 'Flexipop!' magazine. Coming on red, blue or orange vinyl, this freebie also featured *Leave Me Alone* and a remix of the album track *Real Toys*. **Altered Images** are also featured incidentally on a promo-only black vinyl album *Flexipop!* (Lyntone LYN 11966).

Towards the end of 1981, **Altered Images** recorded a third and final Peel session comprising *Little Brown Head*, *Think That It Might*, *Pinky Blue* and *Song Sung Blue*. All four songs would feature on their next album *Pinky Blue*. Two further 45s were released first, as tasters for the forthcoming album. Firstly, *I Could Be Happy* which was ideal for Grogan's exuberant vocal style, was released in December in 7", picture disc and 12" formats. It enjoyed a twelve week chart residency peaking at No. 7. Then, in March 1982, followed *See Those Eyes*, another bouncy dance-pop tune, which rose to No. 11 during its seven week chart sojourn. Originally to have been titled *The Famous Five*, their second album eventually emerged as *Pinky Blue* and the band enjoyed a more minor hit with the title cut. Aside from the singles and an unique version of Neil Diamond's *Song Sung Blue* there is little else of interest on the dance-pop dominated album which saw the band very much focusing on younger audiences. The album enjoyed ten weeks in the chart peaking at No. 12.

Altered Images also contributed to two compilations during 1982. A dance mix of *Happy Birthday* was included on the cassette compilation *Jive Wire* (NME 002) in April and then in December a thowaway cover of Del Shannon's *Little Town Flirt* was included on the original soundtrack to *Party Party* (A&M AMLH 68551), which was a big box office flop.

With the band on a downward spiral things had to change. Anderson and McInven left and ex-Restricted Code and The Cooltones member Stephen Lironi joined the remaining trio to work on a new album *Bite*. The quartet were supplemented for this project by saxophonist Andy Hamilton, keyboards and various session singers. The front cover featured a

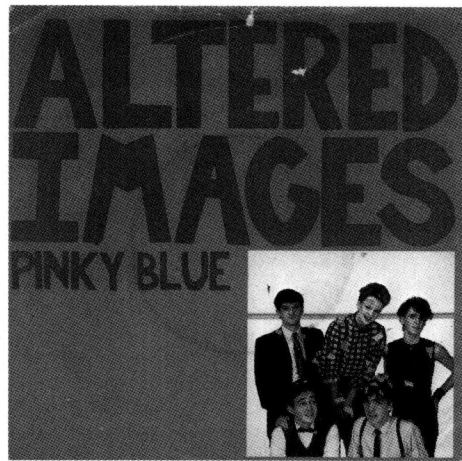

ALTERED IMAGES - Pinky Blue.

sophisticated Clare Grogan clad in an evening dress complete with eyeliner! Production on this album was divided between Tony Visconti and Mike Chapman. The Visconti material was essentially dance-pop, but some of the Chapman-produced songs were attractive pop tunes. Foremost among these was *Don't Talk To Me About Love*, which returned the band to the Top Ten, rising to No. 7 and spending seven weeks in the chart, when released as a taster for *Bite* in March 1983. The album spawned two further hits with *Bring Me Closer* (No. 29) and *Love To Stay* (No. 46), which were issued in various different formats as detailed in the discography. A final 45, comprising more Visconti - produced pop *Change Of Heart* backed by *Another Lost Look*, missed out. *Bite* had fared well, though, climbing to No. 16 during a nine week chart residency. The cassette release of this album features five extra tracks.

By now **Altered Images** had become little more than a launch pad for Clare Grogan's solo ambitions and it came as little surprise that they split before 1983 was out. Their debut album was promptly reissued and *Collected Images*, released in May 1984, compiled their career but was upstaged by *The Best Of Altered Images* in 1992. This collected their hits like *Happy Birthday* and *I Could Be Happy* with some 12" only oddities and album tracks. Then, in 1996, came *Reflected Images: The Best Of Altered Images*, an alternative compilation. Their early material - as evidenced by their *Dead Pop Stars* 45 here - briefly won them the Scottish **Siouxsie** tag, but once CBS got their hands on them their material became more mainstream. You can hear the resulting hits like *Happy Birthday*, *I Could Be Happy*, *See Those Eyes*, *Pinky Blue* and *Don't Talk To Me About Love* here too.

After the band split Clare Grogan revived her acting career, appearing in another Bill Forsyth movie 'Comfort And Joy' and in several BBC dramas, including 'Blott On The Landscape'. Her solo career, when it came in 1986, saw her working with new songwriters Davey Henderson (of Win) and Hilary Morrison (ex-Flowers). Her 1987 45 *Love Bomb (I Love The Way You Beg)* (London LON 134) flopped. She also contributed *Reason Is The Slave* to the compilation *Giant* (London LONLP 35) in 1987. London ended up cancelling her contract due to lack of interest with a further 45 and album in the can. Some CD promos of the later did circulate.

It was Johnny McElhone who went on to greater fame, initially as a member of Hipsway, but much more significantly with Texas.

Altered Images set out as a punk-influenced alternative pop band. Not surprisingly, their early fans soon became disillusioned when they moved into dance-pop territory in a quest for commercial success. Still, Clare Grogan's sheer enthusiasm and energy helped enliven the early eighties for a brief while.

Alternative TV

Personnel:
ALEX FERGUSSON	gtr		A
MARK PERRY	vcls		ABCDEF
TYRONE THOMAS	bs		A
JOHN TOWE	drms		AB
CHRIS BENNETT	drms		C
DENNIS BURNS	bs		BCDE
MICK LINEHAM	gtr		CD
ALAN GRUNER	keyb'ds		E
RAY WESTON	drms		E
ALLISON PHILLIPS			F
STEVE CANNELL			F

ALBUMS:
1(B) THE IMAGE HAS CRACKED (Deptford Fun City DLP 01) 1978
2(C) WHAT YOU SEE IS WHAT YOU ARE (Deptford Fun City DLP 02) 1978
3(D) VIBING UP THE SENILE MAN (PART ONE) (Deptford Fun City DLP 03) 1978
4(-) LIVE AT THE RAT CLUB '77 (Crystal CLP 01) 1979
5(-) ACTION TIME VISION (mid-price compilation) (Deptford Fun City DLP 05) 1980
6(E) STRANGE KICKS (I.R.S. SP 70023) 1981
7( ) PEEP SHOW (Anagram GRAM 32) 1987
8( ) SPLITTING IN TWO (compilation) (Anagram GRAM 40) 1989
9( ) DRAGON LOVE (Chapter 22 CHAPLP 51) 1990

NB: (1) reissued on CD (Anagram CDPUNK 24) 1994 with several bonus tracks and later again on LP (Get Back GET 26) 1998. (2) was a budget price album featuring **ATV** on one side and Here and Now on the other. (3) reissued on CD (Anagram CDMGRAM 102) 1996. (4) was an authorised bootleg. Also issued on CD (Jungle OBSESSED 005) 1993. (7) reissued on CD (Overground OVER 54 CD) 1996. Also relevant is *Live 1978* (Overground/Feel Good All Over FGAO 16/OVER 29) 1993, *Live At The Rat Club '77* (Obsession OBSESS CD 005) 1993 and *The Radio Sessions* (Overground OVER 44CD) 1995.

CASS:
1( ) SCARS ON SUNDAY (Weird Noise WEIRDO 001) 1980
2( ) AN YE AS WELL (Conventional CON 14) 1980

NB: On both of these one side is shared with **Good Missionaries**.

CDs:
1( ) MY LIFE AS A CHILD STAR (Overground OVER 39CD) 1994
2( ) THE RADIO SESSIONS (Overground OVER 44CD) 1995
3( ) THE INDUSTRIAL SESSIONS 1977 (Overground OVER 49CD) 1996
4( ) WATCH 'EM WORK (Overground OVER) 1997
5( ) PUNK LIFE (Overground OVER 70CD) 1998

EPs:
1 SEX/LOVE 12" EP (Victory/Repulsion/You Never Know) (Noiseville VOO 2T) 1986
2 THE SOL 12" EP (Everyday/The World/Affecting People/Pain Barrier) (Chapter 22 12CHAP 46) 1990

45s:
* Love Lies Limp (S.G. Records SG 75 RPS) 1977
How Much Longer/You Bastard (Deptford Fun City DFC 02) 1977
Life After Life/Life After Dub (Deptford Fun City DFC 04) 1978
Action Time Vision/Another Coke (live) (Deptford Fun City DFC 07) 1978
Life/Love Lies Limp (Deptford Fun City DFC 06) 1978
The Force Is Blind/Lost In Room (Deptford Fun City DFC 10) 1979
Knights Of The Future (Deluxe Green)/Alternative To Normal Eating (Nice NICE 2) 1980
The Ancient Rebels/Dub In Bed (I.R.S. DFP 1006) 1981
Communicate/Obsession (I.R.S. DFP 1009) 1981
Welcome To The End Of Fun/Death Time (12") (Noiseville VOO 1T) 1986
My Baby's Laughing (Empty Summer's Dream)/Look At Her Eyes/I Had Love In My Hands (Anagram ANA 36) 1987

NB: * One-sided flexi given away free with "Sniffin' Glue" No. 12.

The driving force behind **Alternative TV** was Deptford-born **Mark Perry**, who first came to notice as editor and writer of the seminal punk fanzine "Sniffin' Glue". Danny Baker, now a famous radio and TV presenter, was an assistant on this fanzine.

By early 1977, **Perry** was becoming restless with his fanzine and itching to form his own band. He teamed up with ex-**Nobody's** guitarist Alex Fergusson and Genesis P. Orridge (then of **Throbbing Gristle**). They first played together in **Throbbing Gristle**'s Industrial Studios. This session was eventually released on CD as *The Industrial Sessions 1977*.

During the spring and summer of 1977, **Perry** put the first **Alternative TV** line-up together (line-up 'A'). Towe had been in **Chelsea** and **Generation X**. They recorded a four song demo (*How Much Longer*, *You Bastard*, *Love Lies Limp* and *Life*), which EMI rejected as too political. So **Perry** set up his own Deptford Fun City label with backing from Miles Copeland.

Alternative TV's first 45 was an excellent punk-reggae song *Love Lies Limp*, which was given away free with the last issue of "Sniffin' Glue". *The Live At The Rat Club '77* album, issued in 1979, brilliantly captures the band's early live set. After their first anti-conformist 45 *How Much Longer*, which dealt with youth culture in a humorous way, was released on Deptford Fun City **Perry** then sacked **Fergusson** and Tyrone Thomas, bringing in Dennis Burns on bass and taking over **Fergusson**'s guitar himself. **Fergusson** went on to form **Cash Pussies**.

The line-up changes did little harm as a couple of classic singles followed. First off, was white reggae *Life After Life* with Jools Holland guesting on piano and Kim Turner on guitar. Better still was *Action Time Vision*, a punk anthem and party favourite, which benefited much from exposure from John Peel. The flip *Another Coke* was a rambling live reggae number.

Their debut *The Image Has Cracked* album mixed live and studio recordings as well as snippets of TV broadcasts about punk. Now an interesting artifact of the era, its best moments included *Viva La Rock 'n' Roll*, *Still Life*, a tribute to an old Mothers of Invention single *Why Don't You Do Me Right?* and, of course, *Action Time Vision*. It challenged much of the punks' ethos not least in its cover on which **Perry** is surrounded by a few classic albums in defiance of punk's philosophy that nothing worthwhile existed prior to 1976.

The CD reissue of *The Image Has Cracked* on Anagram, features eight bonus tracks (including live cuts, alternate takes and 'B' sides) - listen out particularly for *Lost In Room* ('B' side to *The Force Is Blind*). This is one of Anagram's finest releases.

With the addition of new guitarist Mick Lineham the band embarked on a series of free concerts with Here and Now, a sort of hippie type combo. Both bands shared a split album of live material from the tour which captured **Alternative TV** on peak form. Then a row between **Perry** and Bennett about the band's future musical direction led to Bennett's departure and the consequent cancellation of a U.S. tour Miles Copeland had arranged for them.

Forced to change plans, the remaining trio (line-up 'D') set about recording sessions for their next album. Africa provided **Perry** with the inspiration for this and two of the finest cuts were *Release The Natives* and *The Good Missionary*, but much of the record comprised poems and people banging strange instruments. It didn't go down at all well with their fans.

The Force Is Blind was recorded in 1979 with Dave George added to the line-up. An interesting effort with Ann Wombat (of Here and Now) providing space-whisper vocals. *Lost In Room* on the flip was a more raucous effort. Sadly, it was to be their last 45. The band's desire to experiment had

ALTERNATIVE TV & HERE AND NOW - What You See Is What You Are.

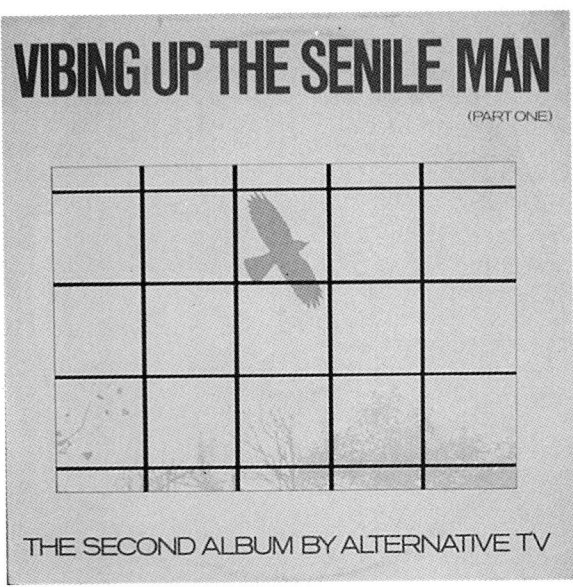

ALTERNATIVE TV - Vibing Up The Senile Man (Part One).

created an ever-widening gulf with their audience. After **Perry** got bottled during a gig at Derby they changed name to **The Good Missionaries**.

You might think this was the end of the story but no. In late 1980, **Perry** resurrected **Alternative TV** with a new line-up ('E'). This recorded the *Strange Kicks* album and two 45s *The Ancient Rebels* and *Communicate*. The album's title track and the first of its 45s can best be described as tuneful pop! The album also featured successful re-recordings of earlier numbers *Sleep In Bed* and *My Hand Was Still Wet* from 1977. It proved to be a one-off venture for Perry had also formed a second project The Reflections. They produced an album (*Slugs And Toad*) and 45 (*4 Countries*) for Cherry Red. After this, the group fell apart and **Perry** had resolved to become a nurse.

But no, there were further re-unions in 1984 (with no vinyl output) and 1986 (line-up 'F'). The latter one spawned two 12" EPs, *Welcome To The End Of Fun* and *Sex/Love* and the *Peep Show* album, which combined pop songs like *Chrissie's Moon* and *My Baby's Laughing* with rawer material, like *Animal*.

Live 1978 includes performances of several well-known songs (*Splitting In Two*, *Fellow Sufferer*, *Love Lies Limp* and *Still Life*), although the sound quality on the final three cuts, recorded at a Westbourne Park Free Festival, is very poor.

Their *Live At The Rat Club* album was recorded by **Throbbing Gristle**'s Genesis P. Orridge on a portable mono recorder and released very much for the band's fans. Its impact suffers from the bootleg-type sound quality but there are some good witty songs on offer including their classic *How Much Longer?* about youth culture, *Alternatives To NATO*, *My Hand Was Still Wet* and a cover of The Mothers Of Invention's *Why Don't You Do Me Right?*.

The Radio Sessions includes their first Peel session. *Love Lies Limp* and *Life After Life* are both good examples of punk/reggae crossovers; *Action Time Vision* was a punchy mod-inspired number and *Still Life* a mayhem of distressed vocals and killer riffs. Their second Peel session featured *The Good Missionary* and *Release The Natives* which both veered much more towards experimental new wave, indeed 'played' running water on the latter track gives the music an eerie, almost psychedelic quality. Also featured are the broody *Nasty Little Lonely* and *Going Round In Circles* with its dizzy riff. There's also three more commercial tracks from 1981 and the collection ends with the previously unknown *Straighten Up* recorded for Radio Bangkok!

They continued to gig during the late '80s and into the '90s, **Perry** also cut a solo CD in 1995 and continued to participate in other projects. There's a lot of life in the old dog yet!

Alternative TV have appeared on several compilations. The cassette *Back To Sing For Free Again Soon* (Fuck Off 1) 1979 includes *Terrified Of Dogs*; *Alive In The Living Room* (Creation CRELP 001) 1984 features their *Lonely Lenny* and an unlabeled mid-80s cassette compilation *Taking This Place Apart* includes a live version of *Splitting In Two*. In 1999, *How Much*

Longer?, one of their finest moments, was included on the lavish 5-CD box set *1-2-3-4 - A History Of Punk And New Wave 1976 - 1979* (MCA/Universal MCD 60066). They also recorded two sessions for John Peel (*Action Time Vision / Still Life / Love Lies Limp / Life After Life*) broadcast on 12th December 1977 and *Nasty Little Lonely / Going Round In Circles / Release The Natives* and *The Good Missionary* went out on air on 27th July 1978.

Setting out as punk idealists and three chord wonders **Perry**'s constant quest for experimentation and creativity made **Alternative TV** a classic example of a band who moved too fast for their audience. **Mark Perry** was undoubtedly one of the more interesting talents to emerge from the punk era.

The Alternators

45:	No Answers/The Kid Don't Know	(Energy NRG 001)	1978

Copies of this one-off punk venture, which unusually did not appear in a picture sleeve, are now quite rare.

Amazorblades

Personnel:	RAY COOPER	bs	A
	STEVE HARRIS	drms	A
	ROB KEYLOCH	vcls, gtr	A
	BENNO MANDELSON	violin	A
	ROBIN WATSON	sax	A

45:	Common Truth/Messaround	(Chiswick NS 20)	1977

This outfit hailed from Brighton. A boogie band in the mould of Chiswick's finest **The Count Bishops**, but not as good. *Common Truth* rattles along nicely with a hook that lodges in the memory and the flip *Messaround* is notable for some stuttering sax which gives it a sleazy feel. *Common Truth* also got an airing on the sampler *Long Shots, Dead Certs And Odds On Favourites* (Chiswick CH 5) in 1978. After their demise, Cooper joined the Oyster Band, Harris went on to Pinksi Zoo and Mandelson did session work for **Magazine** and others.

The Amber Squad

Personnel:	RICHARD BEECHEY	vcls	AB
	PAUL FAIREY	gtr, vcls	AB
	STEPHEN RAWLINGS	bs	AB
	GRAHAM TYERS	drms	AB
	ROBERT MILLER	gtr	B

45s:	I Can't Put My Finger On You/ You Tell A Lie (PS)	(S&T S&T1)	1980
	Can We Go Dancing?/You Should See (What I Do To You In My Dreams) (PS)	(Dead Good DEAD 17)	1980

A Leicester-based mod revival band. The 45 on S&T, 'The Sound Of Leicester' contained a cartoon of a mod on a scooter on the label. With the addition of guitarist Robert Miller, they moved to Dead Good Records for a second 45 later that year. Both 45s are becoming scarce. They also appeared on a local compilation album *Where The Hell Is Leicester?* (S&T) 1980.

Both sides of their first 45 can also be heard on *This Is Mod, Vol. 5* (Anagram CDMGRAM 110) 1997 and *I Can't Put My Fingers On You* also got a further airing on *This Is Mod* (dbl) (Get Back GET 39) 1999. You'll also find both sides of the second 45 on *This Is Mod, Vol. 1 (The Rarities 1979 - 81)* (Anagram CDGRAM 98) 1995. *Can We Go Dancing?* is their best known song. It also crops up on vinyl on *This Is Mod* (dbl) (Get Back GET 39) 1999 and on CD, *100% British Mod* (Captain Mod MODSKA DCD 8) 1998.

American Echoes

45:	Can't Believe It/Las Vegas (PS)	(Blueport BLU 4)	1979
Reissue:	Can't Believe It/Las Vegas (PS)	(Mercury 6007 230)	1979

A Newcastle band whose 45 on Blueport was distributed nationally through Spartan. The 45 was then picked up by Mercury.

Anarcho-Punk Cassette Compilations

Punk went underground in the 1982 - 85 period and a lot of D.I.Y. compilation cassettes were put out which are now very obscure and hard to track down. Very often these had particular themes. Examples include *The Animals Packet* which contains songs remonstrating against testing products on animals, hunting, killing animals to eat, etc. and *Political Piggies* (Anal Probe 001), a benefit tape for Amnesty International. For many of these bands the message they wanted to put across is more important than the music, which is often rudimentary and usually recorded with primitive equipment. The occasional track is a pleasant suprise musically too. Examples include *Screaming Room* by Attrition; frantic but competent assaults on the senses like *Prostitute* by Abductors; the psychedelic *Cronus* by Family Patrol Group; *Butterflys* by Chumbawamba; *Cruise Missiles* by Paramedic Squad and *Winter Of Discontent* by **Political Asylum**. Some of these bands released whole cassettes themselves. See entries by **Karma Sutra, Naked 1981, Nurse With Wound, Political Asylum, The Squat, The Suspects** and **The Throbs** for more details of these.

There were lots of these cassette compilations and the same names crop up on quite a few of them. By way of example details of a few are listed below.

The Animals Packet Side One: A.P.F. Brigade - *Freak*; Instigators - *All Creatures...*; Lost Cherrees - *Please Don't....*; Antidote - *Little By Little*; Andy T - *Vivisection*; Autumn Poison - *Animals Aren't....*; Alternative - *Sick Man's Slaughter*; Chumbawamba - *Animals Song*; Daz - *Untitled*; Snails - *Foxhunts*; Oblivion; **Dave Asgrove/Suspects** - *Animal Population*; A.P.F. Brigade - *Skin*; 2 Mins Of Hate - *Animal's Death*. Side Two: Passion Killers - *What Do They Hide?*; Chumbawamba - *No*; Instigators - *Behind Closed Doors*; Two Way Street - *Animal Liberation*; Antidote - *Spot The Difference*; Attrition - *Monkey In A Bin*; Dave Mills - *Another Test*; Alternative - *Vanity Massacre*; A.P.F. Brigade - *Eat Wheat Not Meat*; Andy T - *Freshly Skinned*.

Political Piggies - A Benefit Tape For Amnesty International (Anal Probe 001) Side One: Nocturnal Emissions - *Rabbit's Don't Cry*; Anarchist Angels - *I Cry With Despair*; Destructors V - *Urban Terrorist*; Do Easy - *Waterside At Twelve*; Epedemic - *Living A Lie*; White Elephants Over Jamaica - *Adverts*; Alternative - *Seen Through Tear Stained Eyes*; Do Easy - *Kick The Dwarf*. Side Two: Epedemic - *No Identity*; Family Patrol Group - *Cronus*; Opera For Infantry - *Untitled*; Destructor V - *Khmer Rouge Boogie*; Cause For Concern - *The Occasional Me And You*; Alternative - *Caroline's Carnival*; **Nurse With Wound** - *The Strange Life Of August Strindberg*; The Apostles - *The Phoenix*.

Standing Upright For No Apparent Reason.... (Concrete Tapes) Side One: Phantoms Of The Underground - *Your Better Off Dead*; Phantoms Of The Underground - *Blood Money*; The Angels - *I Cry With Despair*; The Angels - *You've Created etc.*; Rotten Corpses - *A Rollin' Goofer*; Rotten Corpses - *As They See Us*; Xoset U.K. - *Distraught And Anger*; Xoset U.K. - *Fight For Your Rights*; **Political Asylum** - *Symptom*. Side Two: Distemper - *Violence & Hate*; Distemper - *Living Hell*; Distemper - *Not Missed*; Rotten Corpses - *Hope & Glory*; Rotten Corpses - *Fireball*; Rotten Corpses - *Deluge Song*; The Angels - *Flowers In Full Bloom*; The Angels - *Squat For Peace*; **Political Asylum** - *A Day In The Life*; **Poltical Asylum** - *Tripwire*; **Politcal Asylum** - *The Responsibility.....*

State Of Confusion (Stagnating Body Tapes STAGNANT 1) Side One: Solvent Abuse - *Vigilanti*; Lost Cherrees - *Sexism Sick (Parts 1 & 2)*; **X-Cretas** - *Grim Reaper*; A.P.F. Brigade - *Scared To Die*; Attrition - *Unknown*; Abductors - *Hostage*; Hagar The Womb - *By Force*; **Krondstadt Uprising** - *End Of Part 1*; Commited - *Fuck Conscription*; Glimpo Saucers - *Jock Strap*; **X-Cretas** - *Who Is Mad*; Lost Cherrees - *Society Called Hell*;

A.P.F. Brigade - *Economic League*; Side Two: Committed - *Mental*; Solvent Abuse - *Herion Girls*; **Krondstadt Uprising** - *Divide + Rule*; Hagar The Womb - *For The Ferryman*; Abductors - *Prostitute*; Attrition - *Screaming Room*; **X-Cretas** - *Clone Fashion*; Lost Cherrees - *Freedom*; Committed - *Whose War*; Hagar The Womb - *Routine*; Abductors - *Fascist School*; **Krondstadt Uprising** - *Xenophobia*; Suburban Filth - *Ban The Bomb*; Solvent Abuse - *Glue Kills*; A.P.F. Brigade - *Race To Perfect Death*.

This Is The Squat We Want (1983). This cassette documents a day, the 10th September 1983 to be precise, when a group of people got together in a disused garage, hired a generator, organised bands and held a gig. About 100 people turned up. The sound quality on the tape is very poor, but it is of archival interest. The bands featured include Passion Killers, Alert'd, The Ex, Stagnant Era, Instigators, Ching, 3 Johns, Obesa, 2 Minutes Of Hate, Chumbawamba and Kuffukampf. They were nearly all from the Yorkshire area.

Yours For Autonomy, Vol II (Yours For Autonomy Tapes) Side One: Chumbawamba - *Telly*; Chumbawamba - *Butterflies*; Paramedic Squad - *Cruise Missiles*; **Political Asylum** - *Trust In Me*; **Political Asylum** - *Winter Of Our Discontent*; Acid Attack - *There's Gonna Be Another Acid Attack*; Acid Attack - *Collapse Of A System*; A.P.F. Brigade - *The Government Kills People*; Side Two: Anarchist Angels - *I Cry With Despair*; Chumbawamba - *Work*; The Bored - *What's New*; A.P.F. Brigade - *Surrounded*; A.P.F. Brigade - *Scared To Die*; 4 Minute Warning - *Background*; Anarchist Angels - *Man Destroys, Man Does Not Create*; Dominate Party - *Death Of Thomas*; 4 Minute Warning - *Through The Window*.

The Androids

Personnel:	ROBIN HOLMES	A
	JIM MEGARRY	A
	BILLY McLLAINE	A
	STEVE RAINEY	A

This Northern Irish band recorded just two cuts in the late seventies, which didn't make it onto vinyl at the time. The cuts in question were:- *News Of The World* and *Bondage In Belfast*. The former remains unreleased, but the latter, a punkish number with lots of upfront guitar, later got an airing on *Good Vibrations - The Punk Singles Collection* (Anagram CDPUNK 36). It's certainly worth a listen.

Androids Of Mu

Personnel:	BERSUN	A
	CORRINA	A
	COSMIC	A
	SUZY	A

ALBUM:	1(A)	BLOOD ROBOTS	(Fuck Off FLP 001) 1980

An early eighties punk album which is becoming hard to find.

AND THE NATIVE HIPSTERS - There Goes Concorde Again.

ANGELIC UPSTARTS - Teenage Warning.

And The Native Hipsters

Personnel:	BLATT	vcls

45:	There Goes Concorde Again.... / Stands Still The Building/ I Wanna Be Around	(Heater Volume H.V.R. 003) 1980

This was something of a novelty item of the punk era, although the recording itself was far removed from punk. It was issued from an address in Battersea Rise, London, in a foldaround picture sleeve with an insert (with sheet music on one side and various incomprehensible doodlings on the other) in a polythene bag. The lyrics of the main track comprise a delicate female voice stating 'look, there goes Concorde again'. It benefited from airplay on John Peel's show. An interesting effort!

You can hear *There Goes Concorde Again* in all its glory on the 4-CD box set *25 Years Of Rough Trade Shops* (Mute CDSTUMM 191) 2001.

Angela Rippon's Bum

Personnel incl:	'BOOZY' BARKER	vcls	A
	TONY FITZGERALD	bs	A
	STICKO	gtr	A

This Oi! group came from Tilbury in Essex. They contributed *Fight For Your Lives* to *Back On The Streets* (EP) (Secret SHH 138) 1983, which opens with a great drum roll and advocates street fighting. The cut can also be heard on *Secret Records Punk Singles Collection, Vol. 2* (Anagram CDPUNK 60) in 1995.

Sticko was later in The Chapter.

Angelic Upstarts

Personnel:	DECCA (TAYLOR)	drms	AB
	MENSI (THOMAS MENSFORTH)	vcls	ABCD
	MOND (LOWIE)	gtr	ABCD
	STEVE	bs	A
	KEITH 'STICKS' WARRINGTON	drms	BC
	TONY FEEDBACK	bs	CD
	BRYAN HAYES	gtr	D
	PAUL THOMPSON	drms	D

				HCP
ALBUMS:	1(B)	TEENAGE WARNING	(Warner Bros K 56717) 1979	29
	2(B)	WE GOTTA GET OUT OF THIS PLACE	(Warner Bros K 56806) 1980	54
	3(B)	ANGELIC UPSTARTS LIVE	(Zonophone ZEM 102) 1981	27
	4(B)	2,000,000 VOICES	(Zonophone ZONO 104) 1981	32
	5(C)	STILL FROM THE HEART	(Zonophone ZONO 106) 1982	-
	6(D)	REASON WHY?	(Anagram GRAM 004) 1983	-

7(D)	LAST TANGO IN MOSCOW	(Picasso PIK 004)	1984 -
8(D)	LIVE YUGOSLAVIA	(Picasso HCLP 002M)	1985 -
9(-)	BOOTLEG AND RARITIES (compilation)	(Dojo DOJO LP 7)	1985 -
10(D)	THE POWER OF THE PRESS	(Gas GAS 4012)	1986 -
11(-)	BLOOD ON THE TERRACES	(Link LP 019)	1987 -

NB: Some copies of (3) came with a free live flexi-disc containing *We're Gonna Take The World, Leave Me Alone, The Young Ones* and *White Riot*. (3) also issued on CD (Dojo DOJO CD 169) 1994 with four bonus tracks comprising those given away with the flexi that came free with the album. (4) reissued on Dojo (DOJO CD 81) 1993 with bonus tracks and again (Captain Oi! AHOY CD 158) 2001. (5) also issued on CD (Dojo DOJO CD 144) 1994. (6) also issued on CD (Anagram CD GRAM 004) 1992 and again (Summit SUMCD 4086) 1997. (7) reissued on Great Expectations (PIP 47) 1993. (7) reissued on CD (Captain Oi! AHOY CD 087) 1998 with bonus cuts. (9) reissued on Great Expectations (PIP 49) 1993. (11) issued on CD with a later album *Lost And Found* (Coma COMA CD 11) 1994. (11) also issued on CD (Captain Oi! AHOY CD 116) 1999, with seven bonus tracks comprising their main hits. A recommended CD is *Angel Dust (The Collected Highs 1978 - 83)* (Anagram CDMGRAM 7) 1988. Also of interest is *Alternative Chartbusters* (Plastic Head AOK 102) 1992, *Greatest Hits Live* (Street Link STR CD 027) 1992, *Bombed Out* (Dojo DOJO CD 198) 1994, *The Independent Singles Collection* (Anagram CD PUNK 59) 1995, *Rarities* (Captain Oi! AHOY CD 080) 1997, *The EMI Punk Years* (Captain Oi! AHOY CD 121) 1999 and *The BBC Punk Sessions* (Captain Oi! AHOY CD 138) 2000.

EP:	1	THE BURGLAR	(Anagram ANA 12)	1983

NB: (1) unissued.

HCP

45s:	*	Murder Of Liddle Towers/ Police Oppression (PS)	(Dead Is/Angelic Upstarts 1024)	1978 -
	+	I'm An Upstart/ Leave Me Alone (PS)	(Warner Bros K 17354)	1979 31
		I'm An Upstart/ Leave Me Alone (12", PS)	(Warner Bros K 17354T)	1979 -
	#	Teenage Warning/ The Young Ones (PS)	(Warner Bros K 17426)	1979 29
		Never 'Ad Nothin'/ Nowhere Left To Hide (PS)	(Warner Bros K 17476)	1979 52
		Out Of Control/ Shotgun Solution (PS)	(Warner Bros K 17558)	1980 58
		We Gotta Get Out Of This Place/ Unsung Heroes Pt. 2 (PS)	(Warner Bros K 17576)	1980 65
		I'm An Upstart/ Never 'Ad Nothin' (cassette)	(Warner Bros SPZ 5)	1980 -
		Last Night Another Soldier/The Man Who Came In From The Beano (PS)	(Zonophone Z 7)	1980 51
		England/Stick's Diary (PS)	(Zonophone Z 12)	1980 -
		Kids On The Street/ The Sun Never Shines (PS)	(Zonophone Z 16)	1981 57
		I Understand/Never Come Back (PS)	(Zonophone Z 22)	1981 -
		I Understand/Never Come Back/ Heath's Lament (12", PS)	(Zonophone 12222)	1981 -
		Different Strokes/Different Dub (PS)	(Zonophone Z 25)	1981 -
		Never Say Die/We Defy You (PS)	(Zonophone Z 28)	1982 -
		Woman In Disguise/Lust For Glory (PS)	(Anagram 3)	1982 -
		Woman In Disguise/Lust For Glory/ 42nd Street (12", PS)	(Anagram 12 ANA 3)	1982 -

ANGELIC UPSTARTS - Murder Of Liddle Towers.

ANGELIC UPSTARTS - Last Night Another Soldier.

Solidarity/Five Flew Over (PS)	(Anagram ANA 7)	1983 -
Solidarity/Five Flew Over/Dollars & Pounds/ Don't Stop (12", PS)	(Anagram 12 ANA 7)	1983 -
Not Just A Name/The Leech (PS)	(Anagram ANA 13)	1983 -
Not Just A Name/The Leech/Leave Me Alone/Murder Of Liddle Towers/White Riot (12", PS)	(Anagram 12 ANA 13)	1983 -
Brighton Bomb/Thin Red Line/ Soldier (12", PS)	(Gas GM 30101)	1985 -
Machine Gun Kelly/Paint It In Red/ There's A Drink In It (12", PS)	(Picasso PIK 001)	1985 -
England's Alive	(Link MENSI X1)	1988 -

NB: * This original issue had a pressing of 1,000 only making it their rarest and most collectable artifact. It was reissued the same year in a PS on Rough Trade (RT/SW 001) 1978. + This was also issued in green vnyl without a PS. # This was also issued in red vinyl without a PS.

Far from angelic and (all four original members) from the Brockley Whims Housing Estate in South Shields came the **Angelic Upstarts**, who formed in mid-1977. Clearly influenced by **The Clash** and **Sex Pistols**, both their music and appearance exuded a tough persona. Mensi's vocals were abrasive to the extreme and most of their early material had a strongly anti-establishment stance. Indeed, their political motivations were guided by social justice and their self-financed debut 45, *The Murder Of Liddle Towers* was inspired by an alledged case of police brutality set to a plodding backing. Later picked up and distributed by Small Wonder, it was a powerful and raw punk rendition.

Their lead vocalist and lyricist, Mensi, was also a poet and a trade unionist. This explains the 'politics for the kids' stance of much of their music.

A deal was on the cards with Polydor, but didn't materialise and the band were signed by Warner Bros in early 1979. By this time Steve had been replaced on bass because of drug problems by Ronnie Wooden.

They soon developed a reputation as a popular live band, but their gigs often attracted violence. This was probably partly a response to their tough persona, but increasingly too the result of right wingers who took exception to their left wing political stance.

Line-up 'B' was their most successful, bringing them four hit albums - *Teenage Warning, We Gotta Get Out Of This Place, Angelic Upstarts Live* and *2,000,000 Voices* - and seven (mostly minor) hit singles. *Teenage Warning* was one of their finest. It opened with the blistering line "You wind me up like a clockwork orange, then you hide the key to my destination".

The Teenage Warning album, which was produced by **Sham 69**'s Jimmy Pursey, kicks off with the powerful title track. It's followed by *Student Power*, which dismisses the same as a shower. *Never Again* features a good opening guitar riff and side one concludes with their powerful *Liddle Towers* 45. The second side opens with another of their classics *I'm An Upstart* and concludes with the 45 cut's flip side *Leave Me Alone*. Sandwiched between these is average Oi! fayre such as *Youth Leader, Do Anything* and the frenetic *Let's Speed*.

In the summer of 1980, **The Angelic Upstarts** moved to EMI's re-launched Zonophone label. In July, they released their first single for their new label. *Last Night Another Soldier* was a song about how the media failed to take

ANGELIC UPSTARTS - Last Tango In Moscow.

account of the feelings and impact on soldiers' families of events in Northern Ireland. The song became a 'Sounds' 'Single of the Week' and climbed to No. 51 in the national chart during a four week stint. The flipside, *The Man Who Came In From The Beano*, a piss-take of 'Sounds' journalist Garry Bushell, was the last to feature drummer Keith 'Sticks' Warrington, who left to join **Cockney Rejects** and was later a member of **Red Alert**.

Drummer Paul Thompson, who'd previously been with Roxy Music, joined for their next 45 *England*. This slow-paced patriotic anthem wasn't a hit but has now become a significant collectable. Its flip side *Sticks Diary* was about their former drummer Keith Warrington. An alternate version with different lyrics was also recorded for a late 1980 Peel Radio One session.

Kids On The Street, the follow-up 45 released in January 1981, returned the band to the national charts. It climbed to No. 57 and spent three weeks in the charts.

The title of their third studio album *Two Million Voices* was a reference to the number of registered unemployed in the U.K.. By the time it was released in June 1981 the figure was up to 3 million. The better tracks on the album, aside from the title cut, included *You're Nicked* (this song about Mensi's experience with the police at a Sunderland vs. Arsenal game featured their original drummer Decca Wade, now back in the band); *Jimmy* (about a friend who died in an industrial accident); *Guns From The Afghan Rebels* (a favourite from their live set, which had previously featured on *Oi! The Album*, as did *Last Night Another Soldier*) and *We're Gonna Take The World*. A live version of this last song was included on the flexi disc given away with the *Live* album. The Captain Oi! CD reissue of this album comes with five bonus non-album cuts from this period, lyrics and the usual comprehensive Mark Brennan sleevenotes.

ANGELIC UPSTARTS - Blood On The Terraces.

A new 45 *I Understand* was also released in June 1981. This song told the story of Rastafarian Richard Campbell who died in strange circumstances whilst on remand in Ashford jail. It featured **Stiff Little Fingers** vocalist Jake Burns and ex-**Starjet** singer Terry Sharpe on backing vocals. Despite a good storyline and a cleaned-up version of the lyrics for radio broadcast the single failed to chart.

In late 1981, Tony Feedback replaced Decca, who went solo, and this new line-up 'C' produced *Still From The Heart*, which was less successful than its predecessors. At the request of EMI apparently, *Still From The Heart* saw them discard their punk sound for an insipid synth-pop sound and even tracks like *Flames Of Brixton* and *Black Knights Of The '80s* sound tepid. After this, their line-up was expanded with Mensi, Mond and Feedback being joined by Bryan Hayes on rhythm guitar and Paul Thompson on drums. Success still eluded the revised line-up. Ex-**Splodgenessabounds** vocalist Max Splodge guested on vocals on their *Not Just A Name* 45, but this failed to bring a change in fortunes.

Reason Why? included a few good tunes and the CD reissue includes extra cuts taken from various Anagram 'A' and 'B' sides.

Last Tango In Moscow is considered by many to be the bands last decent punk album. It also contained the 45 *Machine Gun Kelly*. The 1998 CD reissue of this album on Captain Oi! added eight bonus cuts comprised of 'B' sides *Paint It Red* and *There's A Drink In It* as well as six demos; *Listen To The Silence*, *She Don't Cry Anymore*, *I Won't Pay For Liberty*, *Never Return To Hell*, *When Will They Learn* and *No Nukes*.

When *Blood On The Terraces* was released by Link in 1987 it caused a big media controversy due to the title cut. The 1999 CD reissue of this on Captain Oi! also included the seven tracks the band played at their now legendary 'Main Event' gig in 1988. This was a selection of their most popular songs - *Never 'Ad Nothin'*, *Leave Me Alone*, *Teenage Warning*, *Last Night Another Soldier*, *Guns For The Afghan Rebels*, *One More Day* and *Two Million Voices*. The gig ended in a riot and there literally was blood on the dancefloor.

The Independent Punk Singles does what it purports to by compiling their indie label singles. It includes the original version of their debut 45 *The Murder Of Liddle Towers*. *The Rarities*, issued by Captain Oi! in 1997, largely comprises the band's own demos of songs that in quite a few cases were never used.

The EMI Punk Years, put out on Captain Oi! in 1999, is a eighteen-track compilation comprising their best material from their period with EMI, although nothing from their *Live* album is included.

The BBC Punk Sessions compiles their three Peel sessions from 1978, 1980 and 1981. The classic *I'm An Upstart* sounds somewhat subdued on the first session, the material was basically R&B with Mensi's lyrics and vocal style comprising the punk ingredients. The second session captures them at their zenith with three corkers *Guns For The Afghan Rebels*, *Last Night Another Soldier* and *Kids On The Street*. The fourth cut *Sticks Diary* was an ode to their recently departed drummer. The third session kicks off with *2,000,000 Voices* (the title of one of their hit albums), brass is

ANGELIC UPSTARTS - Rarities.

ANGELIC UPSTARTS - The EMI Punk Years.

introduced on *You're Nicked* and the reggae-influenced *I Understand Part 3*. The jewel in the crown is the final cut a superb version of their debut 45 *The Murder Of Liddle Towers*, which was much better than the original.

They eventually disbanded in 1986, but reformed in 1992 for one further unsuccessful album *Bombed Up*. Mensi has also been a member of the Anti Fascist Action Group.

Last Night Another Soldier, *England*, *Kids On The Street*, *I Understand*, *Different Strokes* and *Never Say Die* can all be heard again on *The Zonophone Punk Singles Collection* (Anagram CDPUNK 97) 1997. You can also check out *Woman In Disguise* on *Punk Compilation* (Emporio EMPRCD 550) 1994 and *Teenage Warning* resurfaced on *Punk, Vol. 2* (Music Club MCCD 027) 1991. *Burning Ambitions (A History Of Punk)* (Anagram CDBRED 3) 1996 features *Lust For Glory*, whilst *Vol. 2* (Anagram CDPUNK 81) 1996 includes their classic debut single *Murder Of Liddle Towers*, which also figured on *Oi! Chartbusters, Vol. 1* and *1-2-3-4 - A History Of Punk And New Wave 1976-79* (MCA/Universal MCD 60066) 1999. They also contributed to a number of other compilations. There's a live version of *I Understand* on *Son Of Oi!* (Syndicate SYN LP 3) 1983, later reissued on CD (Captain Oi! AHOY CD 9) 1993. *Blood On The Terraces* got a further airing on *Trouble On The Terraces* (Step-1 STEP LP 91) 1996. A live rendition of *Kids On The Street* can also be heard on *Oi! Against Racism* (Havin' A Laugh HAL LP 004) 1998. *Punk And Disorderly III - The Final Solution* (Anagram GRAM 005) 1983 included *Woman In Disguise*.

Oi! The Singles Collection, Vol. 2 (Captain Oi! AHOY CD 63) 1996 features both sides of their debut 45; *The Murder Of Liddle Towers* and *Police Oppression*. *Vol. 3* of the same series (Captain Oi! AHOY CD 67) 1997 gave a further airing to *Last Night Another Soldier* and *The Man Who Came In From The Beano*. Finally, *Vol. 4* included *England* and *Sticks Diary*. *100% British Oi!* (Captain Oi! AHOY DCD 83) 1997 features *Victory In Poland*, which was specially recorded for the Pax Records compilation *Wargasm* in 1982.

They can also be heard playing *Murder Of Liddle Towers* on *Oi! Fuckin' Oi!* (Harry May MAYO CD 110) in 1999.

Angel Street

45:    Midnight Man/Running Away   (Motor MTR 003) 1979

Unusually in this era this 45 didn't come in a picture sleeve but it was pressed on blue vinyl.

Anihilated

A hardcore punk band whose two belters *Inferno* and *40 Dumb Animals* get an airing on *Punk Lives! - Let's Slam* (Rot SLAM 2) 1986. *Inferno* is about a post-nuclear attack situation. *40 Dumb Animals* is another blistering assault on the senses.

Animal Farm

45:    Model Soldier/John And Julie (PS)   (Rot ASS 7) 1984

A short-lived punk band. *Model Soldier* later resurfaced on *Rot Records Punk Singles Collection* (Anagram CDPUNK 40) in 1994. They earlier contributed *So Sad* and *Who Is The Enemy* to *Have A Rotten Christmas* (Rot ASS 18) 1984.

Anthrax

Personnel:	D	gtr	A
	GARETH	bs	A
	OSKAR	vcls	A
	PETE	drms	A

EPs: 1(A) THEY'VE GOT IT ALL WRONG (P.P.B./ Got It All Wrong/Exploitation/What Will Tomorrow) (PS)
              (Small Wonder SMALL 27) 1983
       2(A) CAPITALISM IS CANNABALISM (EP) (PS)
              (Crass 22 1984/9) 1983

NB: (2) issued in a foldout picture sleeve.

A political four piece from Welwyn Garden City. Their 1983 *They've Got It All Wrong* (EP) on Small Wonder got into the indie Top 10. A fairly routine punk assault, the title cut can also be heard on *Small Wonder Punk Singles Collection, Vol. 1* (Anagram CDPUNK 29) 1994 and on *100% Hardcore Punk* (Captain Oi! AHOY DCD 84) 1998. You can also check out *What Will Tomorrow* on *Vol. 2* (Anagram CDPUNK 70) 1996 of the Small Wonder series. Their second EP on Crass Records also made the indie Top 10 later the same year but nothing seems to have been heard of them since.

Anti-Establishment

Personnel:	NICK FREESTON	drms	ABC
	GAVIN GRITTON	vcls	ABC
	HAGIS	gtr	AB
	COLIN LITTLE	bs	A
	KEVIN READ	bs	BC
	GARY DAWSON	gtr	C

45s: 1980/Mechanical Men (PS)   (Charnel House CADAV 1) 1980
       Future Girl/No Trust (PS)   (Glass GLASS 022) 1982
       Anti Men/Misunderstood (PS)   (Glass GLASS 023) 1983

NB: There's also a CD compilation, *The Oi! Collection* (Captain Oi! AHOY CD 78) 1997.

One of the third wave punk bands. The two mainstays of **Anti-Establishment**, Gavin Gritton and Nick Freeston originally met at a **Saints** / **Chelsea** gig at London's Marquee early in 1978. They formed a band with mates from the Epping and Ongar area, initially called Cardiac Arrest which

ANTI-ESTABLISHMENT - Anti Men.

ANTI-ESTABLISHMENT - The Oi! Collection.

featured future **The The** mainman Matt Johnson. By 1979, they'd changed name to **Anti-Establishment** and stabilised to line-up 'A'. Their debut gig was on 16th November 1979 at Ingatestone Youth Centre. Soon after they persuaded **The Damned**'s Rat Scabies to produce some songs, two of which *1980* and *Mechanical Man*, were released on a 45 by the small Charnel House label. Both cuts later resurfaced on *Oi! The Rarities, Vol. 1* (Captain Oi! AHOY CD 43) 1995. *1980* can also be heard on *100% British Oi!* (Captain Oi! AHOY DCD 83) 1997.

The band then signed to Dave Barker's Glass Records for *Future Girl*, which was again produced by Rat Scabies. Kevin Read had replaced Colin Little on guitar for this recording, both sides of which later got a further airing on *Oi! The Rarities, Vol. 4* (Captain Oi! AHOY CD 58) 1996.

For their third and final single *Anti Men* Gary Dawson came in for Hagis on guitar. Again Rat Scabies handled production and both sides can also be heard on *Oi! The Rarities, Vol. 5* (Captain Oi! AHOY CD 62) 1996.

In addition to these recordings they gigged a lot locally. They also appeared at the Second New Punk convention in early 1981 at Canning Town's Bridge House alongside **Vice Squad** and **The 4-Skins**. They later played at the Acklam Hall Third New Punk Convention (together with **Last Resort** and **Infa Riot**), but it ended in mayhem.

The best guide to their music, which is pretty standard Oi! punk, is the Captain Oi! CD compilation. This includes their singles and twelve previously unreleased demos. Listen out for the pulsating *Front Page News*, *Step Outside*, and *I Feel Hate*. Much of this previously unreleased material is better than their 45s.

The Anti-Nowhere League

Personnel:	ANIMAL	vcls	A B
	MAGOO	gtr	A B
	P.J.	drms	A
	WINSTON	bs	A B
	JOHNATHAN BIRCH	drms	B

				HCP
ALBUMS:	1(A)	WE ARE THE LEAGUE	(WXYZ LMNOP 1)	1982 24
	2(B)	LIVE IN YUGOSLAVIA	(I.D. NOSE 3)	1983 88
	3(B)	THE PERFECT CRIME	(GWR GWLP 12)	1985 -

NB: (1) also issued on CD (Snapper SMMCD 515) 1997. (2) also reissued on CD (I.D. CDOSE 36) 1990. (2) and (3) have been issued on one CD (Loma LOMACD 9) 1992. There have also been several CD compilations, *The Best Of The Anti-Nowhere League* (Street Link STR CD 013) 1991, *The Best Of The Anti-Nowhere League* (Cleopatra CLEO 0729CD) 1994, *Anti-Nowhere League Punk Singles Collection* (Anagram CDPUNK 44) 1995, *The Best Of The Anti-Nowhere League* (Snapper SMMCD 514) 1998 and *Long Live The League* (Dojo DOJO CD 15) 1987. Also relevant are *Live And Loud* (Link LINKCD 120) 1990, *The Horse Is Dead (The Anti-Nowhere League Live)* (Receiver RRCD 219) 1996, *So What (A Tribute To The Anti-Nowhere League)* (various artists) (SPV SPV 08453982) 1997, *Out Of Control* (Receiver RRCD 1872) 2000 and *So What* (Harry May CAN CAN 012) 2001.

				HCP
45s:	*	Streets Of London/So What (PS)	(WXYZ ABCD 1)	1982 48
	*	Streets Of London/So What (12", PS)	(WXYZ ABCD1T)	1982 -
		I Hate.... People/ Let's Break The Law (PS)	(WXYZ ABCD 2)	1982 46
		Woman/Rocker (picture disc)	(WXYZ ABCD 4)	1982 72
	+	Mutant Rock (instr)	(Lyntone LYN 12647)	1982 -
		For You/Ballad Of Decay (PS)	(WXYZ ABCD 6)	1983 -
		Out On The Wasteland/ We Will Survive (picture disc)	(WXYZ ABCS 004P)	1984 -

NB: * These 45s were both withdrawn. + This track appeared on a red flexidisc which came free with 'Flexipop' magazine, issue 26. The other bands on the disc were Defects and Meteors. There were also some white label promo's put out by the **Anti-Nowhere League** of an untitled 45 on GWR (GWR 5) during the early eighties.

Late arrivals on the punk scene, **The Anti-Nowhere League** were formed in that most conservative of places, Tunbridge Wells, in the latter half of 1980. They exuded an archetypal nihilistic punk outlook (rather like **The Angelic Upstarts**), their music was raw and loud.

They played a series of early gigs at London's Lyceum and achieved a national profile as part of the Apocalypse Punk Tour in 1981.

They signed to the indie punk label WXYZ. Their first 45 was something of a novelty for two reasons. First, for its strange choice of material on the 'A' side - a cover of folkie Ralph McTell's hit *Streets Of London*. Secondly, the 'B' side's apparently obscene lyrics led to several copies being seized by the Obscene Publications Squad and both 7" and 12" formats were withdrawn. Not before it had sold several thousand copies, topped the indie chart, and climbed to No. 48 in the national chart, where it spent five weeks, though.

Their subsequent 45s were equally as abrasive as that 'B' side. They sufficiently captured the punk ethos to sell well. Indeed, both *I Hate.... People* and *Woman* scored pretty well in the national charts. Their debut album, too, made the Top 30 with songs that vilified everything in sight. This is a classic punk anthem and tracks like *We're The League*, *Animal*, *Can't Stand Rock 'n' Roll*, *(We Will Not) Remember You* and remixed versions of *I Hate... People* and *Let's Break The Law* were aggressive and abrasive successfully capturing the spirit of punk. It also included their punk rendition of Ralph McTell's *Streets Of London* with its changed lyrics.

In 1985, with Johnathan Birch having replaced P.J. on drums, they recorded a more mainstream rock album for the GWR label, usually associated with heavy rock. The punk era was a few years past by now but their fans, those that were left, had no appetite for this. The album sold poorly and the band members went their separate ways.

They did reform in the early nineties to participate in a punk nostalgia tour.

Of their several punk compilations *The Best Of The Anti-Nowhere League* on Street Link in 1992 features both sides of their debut 45 (although a different 'live' version of *So What* is featured). Otherwise the material with songs like *Let's Break The Law* and *Queen And Country* demonstrates little imagination or originality. Alternatively, *The Complete Punk Singles Collection* is a sixteen-track compilation of all their eighties 'A' and 'B' sides for WYXZ, ABC and Link. *Out Of Control* is a collection of previously

ANTI-ESTABLISHMENT - Future Girl.

ANTI-NOWHERE LEAGUE - We Are The League.

unreleased demos probably from prior to their first 45 and is for diehard fans only. The *So What* compilation on Harry May contains uncensored, previously unreleased and live versions of many of their classic cuts. The title track was later covered by Metallica.

Anti-Pasti

Personnel:	DUGI	gtr	ABC
	MARTIN ROPER	vcls	ABC
	STAN	drms	A
	STU	bs	A
	KEV	bs	BC
	WILL	drms	BC
	OLLY HOON	gtr	C

				HCP
ALBUMS:	1(B)	THE LAST CALL	(Rondelet ABOUT 5) 1981	31
	2(C)	CAUTION IN THE WIND	(Rondelet ABOUT 13) 1982	-

NB: (1) also issued on CD (Anagram Punk Collectors Series CD PUNK 48) 1995 with eight bonus cuts and again on LP (Get Back GET 7) 1996 with seven bonus cuts from their early 45s. (2) also issued on CD (Anagram CD PUNK 53) 1995 and again on LP (Get Back GET 70) 1999. There are also two collections; *The Best Of Anti-Pasti* (Dojo DOJOCD 230) 1996 and *Punk Singles Collection* (Cherry Red CDPUNK 106) 1998.

EP:	1(A)	FOUR SORE POINTS (1980/Something New/ No Government/ Two Years Too Late)	(Rondelet ROUND 2) 1980

				HCP
45s:	*	Let Them Free/Hell/ Another Dead Soldier (PS)	(Rondelet ROUND 5) 1981	-
		Six Guns/Now's The Time/ Call The Army (PS)	(Rondelet ROUND 10) 1981	-
	+	Don't Let Them Grind You Down/	(Superville EXP 1003) 1981	70
		East To The West/ Burn In Your Own Flames (PS)	(Rondelet ROUND 18) 1982	-
		Caution To The Wind/Blind Faith/Last Train To Nowhere (PS with sticker)	(Rondelet ROUND 26) 1982	-

NB: * This was issued in both red and black vinyl. + Recorded with **The Exploited**.

Derbyshire's finest punk band was another which favoured monosyllabic names. They formed in late 1979 and played a very basic punk sound and built up popularity gigging around the Midlands. They were signed up by the Mansfield-based indie label Rondelet.

Their debut disc, a four track EP *Fore Sore Points*, was full of socially-conscious venom and made it into the indie charts.

After a change of personnel in the rhythm section (Kev and Will replacing Stu and Stan), they released a 45 *Let Them Free*, which also brought them further indie chart success.

They were part of the Apocalypse Punk Tour of 1981, which brought them to the attention of music fans nationally. This helped establish their reputation and their debut album *The Last Call* wasn't only a big indie success, it also spent seven weeks in the national album charts, climbing to No. 31. On offer is good powerful punk on cuts like *No Government*, *Brew Your Own*, *Another Dead Soldier* and *Night Of The Warcry*. The title cut *The Last Call* is a frenetic storming number. The album ends with *I Wanna' Be Your Dog* and more great guitar work. Certainly a slab of vinyl worth checking out. It's also been reissued twice on CD with bonus cuts made up from their early 45s; originally as part of Anagram's Punk Collector series and more recently by Get Back.

Their *Six Guns* 45 topped the indie chart. They then collaborated with **The Exploited** on a one-off venture *Don't Let You Grind Them Down*, which spent a week in the national charts at No. 70.

In 1982, another guitarist Olly Hoon was added to their line-up for gigging purposes. Sales of their last two 45s and second album were disappointing, though, and the band split up before the year was out, realising that their time had come and gone!

Caution To The Wind was reissued on CD by Anagram in 1995 and later by Get Back on vinyl. This featured the 45 *East To The West* and three bonus tracks.

Dojo's *The Best Of Anti-Pasti* compilation concentrates on their singles for Rondelet and material from their two albums *The Last Call* and *Caution To The Wind*. **Anti-Pasti** also have six cuts - *No Government*, *Two Years Too Late*, *Another Dead Soldier*, *Six Guns*, *East To The West* and *Caution To The Wind* - included on *Rondelet Punk Singles Collection* (Anagram CDPUNK 49) in 1995. This was also available on vinyl (Captain Oi! AHOY LP 513) 1996.

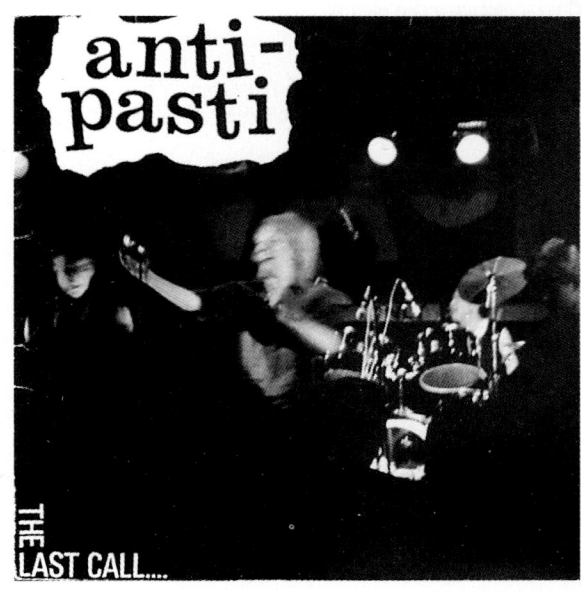

ANTI-PASTI - The Last Call.

Anti-Social

45:	Traffic Lights/Teacher Teacher	(Dynamite DRO 1) 1978

An ultra-rare one-off venture that did not come in a picture sleeve. They are thought to be unconnected to the band who recorded on Lightbeat. *Traffic Lights* is a rock song rather than punk with a flat delivery.

Anti-Social

Personnel:	DAZ	bs	AB
	SID	vcls	A
	SPIG	drms	AB
	WOZ	gtr	AB
	PHIL	vcls	B

EPs:	1(A)	MADE IN ENGLAND (Backstreet Boys/Your Choice/ New Punk/Screw U)	(Lightbeat SOCIAL 1) 1982

	2(A)	OFFICIAL HOOLIGAN (Battle Scarred Skinheads/ Sewer Rat/ Official Hooligan) (PS)	(Beat The System BTS 2) 1982
	3(A)	THE NEW PUNKS (cassette)	(Lightbeat no #) 1982

NB: There's also a compilation CD *Battle Scarred Skinheads* (Captain Oi! AHOY CD 044) 1995.

45:	Too Many People/ Let's Have Some (PS)	(Beat The System FIT 2) 1982

A different and slightly better known band who formed in Blackpool in 1981. Their *Made In England* (EP) was issued in 1982. It comprised four cuts; *Backstreet Boys*, a routine Oi! effort; *Your Choice* which featured some good guitar moments; the anthemic *New Punks* and *Screw U*, which also has a decent guitar sound and seems to be about street fighting. All four cuts later resurfaced on *Oi! The Rarities, Vol. 1* (Captain Oi! AHOY CD 43) 1995.

Their follow-up recording *Too Many People* in late 1982 was credited to **Anti-Social** With Another Punk - the other punk being Mick Crudge of **The Fits**, who shared the vocal role with Sid on this disc. The flip side *Let's Have Some Fun* sounds a mess but you can track down both sides for yourself on *Oi! The Rarities, Vol. 5* (Captain Oi! AHOY CD 62) 1996.

By the time of their third release Sid was replaced on vocals by Phil "Official Hooligan". This release was originally intended as a four-track EP but the fourth track, a cover of **Sham 69**'s *What Have We Got* got omitted at the cutting stage. *Official Hooligan* certainly had a more audible sound than its predecessor. The title cut, which referred to the Police, and *Battle Scarred Skinheads*, are both quite anthemic. These and the third cut *Sewer Rat* later resurfaced on *Oi! The Rarities, Vol. 2* (Captain Oi! AHOY CD 46) 1995. *Official Hooligan* can also be found on *100% British Oi!* (Captain Oi! AHOY DCD 83) 1997.

Official Hooligan, *Backstreet Boys* and *Too Many People* were all included on *Beat The System Punk Singles Collection* (Anagram CDPUNK 61) in 1995.

All of **Anti-Social**'s studio recordings are compiled on *Battle Scarred Skinheads* (Captain Oi! AHOY CD 44) 1995. This CD also features their version of **Sham 69**'s *What Have We Got* and seven cuts from a previously unreleased demo:- *Bollocks, Can't Even Dream, Anti War, New Punks, Union Jack, Live And Let Live* and *Brick War*.

Anti-System

Personnel:	DOM	gtr	A
	GEORGE	bs	A
	NOGSY	vcls	A
	PHIL	drms	A

ALBUMS:	1(A)	NO LAUGHING MATTER	(Reconciliation RECONCILE 1) 1985
	2(A)	A LOOK AT LIFE	(Reconciliation RECONCILE 4) 1986

NB: (1) reissued on vinyl (Anti System SYSTEM 1) 1997 and there's also a CD *Anti-System* (Rebellious Construction REB 1CD) 1992.

EP:	1(A)	DEFENCE OF THE REALM	(Paragon/Pax PAX 11) 1983
45:	Strange Love		(Reconciliation 3) 198?

Anti-System came from the Bradford area. In early 1983 they issued the five track *Defence Of The Realm* EP. Two tracks from this *Government Lies* and *Schoolboy* were later included on *Pax Records Punk Collection* (Anagram CDPUNK 75) 1996. They also contributed *Man's World* and *Breakout* to *Punk Is Dead - Nah The Smell Is Jus Summink In Yer Underpants Innit* (Pax PAX 7) in 1993 and *Schoolboy* also got another airing on *Bollox To The Gonads - Here's The Testicles* (Pax PAX 14) the same year.

They later moved to Reconciliation Records, releasing the single *Strange Love* and two albums *No Laughing Matter* and *A Look At Life*.

Any Trouble

Personnel:	PHIL BARNES	bs, vcls, sax	AB
	CLIVE GREGSON	gtr, vcls	AB
	MEL HARLEY	drms	A
	CHRIS PARKS	gtr, vcls	AB
	MARTIN HUGHES	drms, perc, vcls	B

ALBUMS:	1(A)	LIVE AT THE VENUE	(Stiff TRUBZ 1) 1980
	2(A)	WHERE ARE ALL THE NICE GIRLS?	(Stiff SEEZ 25) 1980
	3(A)	WHEELS IN MOTION	(Stiff SEEZ 27) 1981
	4(B)	ANY TROUBLE	(EMI America 40 1791) 1983
	5(B)	WRONG END OF THE RACE	(EMI 2401 203) 1984

NB: (1) also issued on CD (Line LICD 900099) 1989. (2) also issued on CD (Charly 742462) 1998. (5) also issued on CD (Beat Goes On BGOCD 295) 1995.

45s:	Yesterday's Love/Nice Girls (PS)	(Stiff BUY 74) 1980
	Second Choice/Bible Belt/ The Nice Of The Game (PS)	(Stiff BUY 79) 1980
	No Idea/Girls Are Always Right (PS)	(Stiff BUY 94) 1980
	Trouble With Me/She'll Belong To Me (PS)	(Stiff BUY 119) 1981
	Touch And Go/ Man Of The Moment (PS)	(EMI America EA 154) 1983
	I'll Be Your Man/Human Heart (PS)	(EMI America EA 163) 1983
	Baby Now That I've Found You/ Bricks And Mortar (PS)	(EMI America EA 166) 1984
	Baby Now That I've Found You/ Bricks And Mortar/Does He Call Your Name (12", PS)	(EMI America 12 EA 166) 1984
	Open Fire/Coming Of Age (PS)	(EMI America EA 173) 1984

A Manchester-based quartet whose frontman Clive Gregson penned some quality songs, often about unhapiness in love. The material on their *Where Are All The Nice Guys?* album was pleasant and melodic, somewhat akin to **Elvis Costello**. *The Hurt* and *Second Choice* are arguably the pick of the material on this.

On *Wheels In Motion*, produced by Mike Howlett, they sound more confident as they competently perform some well written material. The

ANTI-SOCIAL - Too Many People.    ANTI-SOCIAL - Official Hooligan EP.    ANTI-SOCIAL - Made In England EP.

ANY TROUBLE - Where Are All The Nice Girls?

stand-out cut is probably *Walking In Chains*, but *Trouble With Love* and *Another Heartache* also catch the ear.

Prior to their next album *Any Trouble* Martin Hughes had replaced Mel Harley on drums and they'd also switched labels to EMI America. The resulting album is more sophisticated than their previous efforts with even stronger melodies and more incisive yet sensitive vocals from Gregson. Its highlights include *Please Don't Stop*, *Man Of The Moment* and *Northern Soul*. Production duties are effectively handled by David Kershenbaum.

Wrong End Of The Race, released a year later, included a pulsating cover of *Baby Now That I've Found You* alongside some interesting new Gregson material and re-recordings of three of their older songs. Billy Bremner, Geoff Muldaur and Richard Thompson guested on this album which featured horns.

After this, having failed to achieve any commercial success, the band petered out.

The Apartment

Personnel:	EMIL	drms	A
	ALAN GRIFFITHS	vcls, gtr	A
	RICHARD WHITE	bs	A

45:	The Car/Winter (PS)	(Heartbeat PULSE 7) 1980

A Bristol band, who prior to this single, made a promising vinyl debut with *The Alternative* on *Avon Calling* (Heartbeat HB 1) 1979.

Architects Of Disaster

45:	Cucumber Sandwich/Friendly Fire	(Neuter NEU 1) 1982

Unusually for this era the 45 didn't come in a picture sleeve but in a polythene bag with a 6" x 6" insert. This band had previously recorded as **Varicose Veins** and **Orange Disaster**.

Arms and Legs

Personnel incl:	MARK ANDREW	lead vcls	A
	JOE JACKSON	piano, electric violin, hrmnca	A
	GRAHAM MABY	bs	A

45s:	Janice/She'll Surprise You	(Mam MAM 140) 1976
	Heat Of The Night/Good Times	(Mam MAM 147) 1976
	Is There Any More Wine/ She'll Surprise You	(Mam MAM 156) 1977

This local Portsmouth band didn't play punk but is significant for including local singer-songwriter **Joe Jackson** who later played a part in new wave.

Originally formed by Andrew and **Jackson** as a Top 40 covers band Edward Bear, they later evolved into **Arms and Legs** and began to write their own material. They released three singles but were swallowed up in the flood of punk and new wave groups. They also had management problems and their failure to make an impression led **Jackson** to quit and the band to split up.

Art Attacks

Personnel:	JD HANEY	drms	A
	M/S	bs	A
	SAVAGE PENCIL	vcls	A
	STEVE SPEAR	gtr	A

45s:	I'm A Dalek/Neutron Bomb (PS)	(Albatross TIT 1) 1978
	First And Last/Punk Rock Stars/ Rat City (PS)	(Fresh FRESH 3) 1979

Savage Pencil in this band was actually cartoonist and journalist Ed Pouncey. Aside from these two 45s, the band can also be heard on a couple of compilations *Live At The Vortex* (NEMS NEL 6013) 1977 features them playing *Animal Bondage* and *Frankenstein's Heartbeat*. They appeared the following year performing *Arabs In 'Arrods* on *Streets* (Beggars Banquet BEGA 1) 1978.

Punk Rock Stars and *Rat City* later resurfaced on *Fresh Records Punk Singles Collection* (Anagram CDPUNK 32) in 1994. *I'm A Dalek* later resurfaced on *Punk Rock Rarities, Vol. 2* (Anagram CD PUNK 83) 1996.

The Art Bears

Personnel:	CHRIS CUTLER	drms, perc	A
	FRED FRITH	gtr, violin, keyb'ds	A
	DAGMAR KRAUSE	vcls	A

ALBUMS:	1(A)	HOPES AND FEARS	(Recommended REC 2188) 1978
	2(A)	WINTER SONGS	(Recommended REC 0618) 1979
	3(A)	THE WORLD AS IT IS TODAY	(Recommended REC 6622) 1981

NB: (1) was issued in a gatefold sleeve with a poster and booklet. (1) also issued on CD (ReR Megacorp RERABCD 2) 1992. (2) was issued with a booklet. (3) played at 45 rpm and issued with a booket. (2) and (3) also issued on one CD (ReR Megacorp RERABCD 1) in 1988.

EP:	1(A)	CODA TO "MAN AND BOY"	(Recommended RE 6622) 1981

NB: (1) This was a live EP on one-sided clear vinyl in a silk-screened picture sleeve only 1,750 were pressed of which 500 were signed and numbered.

45:	Rats And Monkeys/Collapse	(Ralph RR 7904) 1979

Recognise this lot? You might well - they were all former members of Henry Cow. As they sought to extend their musical frontiers they ended up part of the post-punk genre.

Hopes And Fears delightfully showcases Dagmar Krause's voice and Frith and Cutler's inventiveness. The music is pretty cerebral and the term 'progressive' may not be a misplaced description. The CD reissue in 1992 came with three rare bonus tracks.

Winter Songs is lyrically inspired by the medieval era, while the music is gothic and austere, expertly played. *The World As It Is Today* analyses key political concepts; *Democracy, Peace* and *Law*. The music is both inventive and haunting.

Their 45 *Rats And Monkeys* is a frenetic mixture of drums, piano and violin:-

"Rats and monkeys, guard the city as it crumbles into ruins
Walls are loosening but the gates are locked"
(from *Rats And Monkeys*).

After these recordings Cutler founded London's Recommended Records and Frith and Cutler recorded the experimental *Live In Prague And Washington*.

Artery

Personnel:	MICHAEL FIDLER	vcls, gtr	A
	MARK GOULDTHORPE	vcls, gtr	A
	SIMON HINKLER		
	NEIL MACKENZIE	bs	A
	GARY WILSON	drms	A

ALBUMS:	1(A)	ONE AFTERNOON IN A HOT AIR BALLOON	
			(Red Flame) 1983
	2(A)	TERMINAL THE SECOND COMING	
			(Golden Dawn GDLP 1) 1984
	3(A)	LIVE IN AMSTERDAM	(Golden Dawn GDLP 2) 1986

EP:	1(A)	OCEANS ( )	(Red Flame RFM 4) 1982

45s:	Mother Moon/Pretends/Heinz (PS) (Limited Edition TAKE 1) 1979
*	Unbalanced/The Slide (PS) (Aardvark STEAL 3) 1980
	Cars In Motion/Life And Death (PS) (Aardvark AARD 5) 1981
	Afterwards/Into The Garden (PS) (Armageddon AS 026) 1981
	The Clown/The Clown (PS) (Red Flame RF 704) 1982
	Alabama Song/Song For Lena (PS) (Red Flame RF 825) 1983
	Terminal/ (12") (Golden Dawn GD 1202) 1984
	Diamonds/In The Mine Field (7") (Golden Dawn GD 704) 1984
	Diamonds/In The Mine Field (12") (Golden Dawn GD 1202) 1984

NB: * Some copies came with an EP containing *Perhaps*, *Turtle*, *Toytown* and *Heinz*.

Artery were a sort of new wave art rock combo. Hailing from Sheffield they produced a funky post-punk style of music which is worth investigation. Their first slab of vinyl *Mother Moon* appeared on the Limited Edition label in 1979. In 1980, they switched to Aardvark for two further singles, some copies of the first of these, *Unbalanced*, came with a free live EP.

They later recorded more prolifically for Red Flame and Golden Dawn.

ARTERY - Mother Moon.

Art Failure

A Nottingham band who first surfaced when they contributed *Gimmick* to *Hicks From The Sticks* (Rockburgh ROC 111) in 1980. This is electro-pop with unusual vocals. They also recorded a 45 called *Scream Of Pain*.

Article 58

45:	Echoes/Lost And Found/	
	Events To Come (PS)	(Rationale RATE 4) 1981

This 45 was presented in a folded picture sleeve in a zip lock bag.

Art Objects

45:	Hard Objects/Bibliotheque/	
	Fit Of Pique (PS)	(Fried Egg EGG 7) 1981

An arty new wave band from the West Country whose *Hard Objects* can also be heard on *E(gg)clectic* (Fried Egg FRY 2) 1981.

Dave Asgrove Band

CASS:	1	LUCKY DAYS	19??

This is a six-track D.I.Y. cassette by an anarcho-punk artist based in Norwich, who on the opening track *Rebel* fancies himself as a bit of a Jimi Hendrix too. The title cut is somewhat reminiscent of **John Cooper Clarke**, radical poetry set to music. *England Doesn't Care* has a reggae-influenced beat. *Random Relations Part 1 (Eastern Version)* returns to the poetry set to music format. *Night Boat Travellers* is a faster, more punkish number. The final cut *Politicians* is a spoken put down of government and politicians with minimalist backing. This whole cassette is very good. In the 1982 - 85 era lots of anarcho-punk cassettes of a similar ilk to this were released.

Athletico Spizz 80

Personnel:	MARK COALFIELD	keyb'ds	A
	DAVE SCOTT	gtr	A
	G.P. SNARE	drms	A
	JIM SOLAR	bs	A
	SPIZZ	vcls, gtr	A

HCP

ALBUM:	1(A)	DO A RUNNER	(A&M AMLE 68514) 1980 27

NB: Also relevant is *Spizz Not Dead Shock 1978 - 1983* (Cherry Red CDMRED 130) 1996, which includes material from this period.

45s:	*	No Room/Spock's Missing (PS)	(Rough Trade RTSO 5) 1979
		Hot Deserts/Legal Proceedings (PS)	(A&M AMS 7550) 1980
		Central Park/	
		Central Park (alt. version) (PS)	(A&M AMS 7566) 1980

NB: * Credited to **Athletico Spizz Co**.

The dynamic **Spizz** was the key figure behind this outfit. He previously formed **Spizz 77** in October 1977 who'd metamorphised into **Spizz Oil** during 1978. By 1979, with a new group of musicians, he'd formed **Spizzenergi**. Among their recordings was the offbeat 45, *Where's Captain Kirk?* which became the first recording to top the new indie charts. This attracted attention from A&M, but by the time the contract was signed **Spizz** had changed his band's name again to **Athletico Spizz Co.** and then **Athletico Spizz 80**. The *No Room / Spock's Missing* 45 sold well, but

ATHLETICO SPIZZ 80 - Do A Runner.

the *Do A Runner* album became obsessed with science fiction imagery. Without any of the wit or charm of their recent singles tracks like *New Species*, *Rhythmn Inside* and *Effortless* sound robotic and quite repetitive. *European Heroes* is more punkish and one of the better tracks on the album. Also more noteworthy is *Energy Crisis*, which had a clear message to put across:-

"Atomic Energy Authority
Fast breeds in technology
Nuclear scientist producing plutonium
Nasty little substance that we can't controlleum
Council of life impressing on me
Fuel concentration their philosophy"
(from *Energy Crisis*)

The lengthy finale on side two *Airships* has quite an atmospheric introduction, but the appeal of the instrumentation is hindered by repetitive lyrics. The album sold quite well climbing to No. 27 during its five week chart stay.

The romance with A&M was destined to be short-lived, but not before a further name change to **Spizzles**.

ATTAK - Zombies.

Attak

Personnel:	GARY BASNETT	gtr, vcls	A B
	'CHAD' CHADWICK	bs	A B
	LINDSAY McLENNAN	drms	A B
	WOODY	lead gtr	B

ALBUM: 1(B) ZOMBIES (No Future PUNK 6) 1983

NB: (1) also reissued on CD (Captain Oi! AHOY CD 22) 1994 with seven bonus tracks including their two 7" singles for No Future and their compilation contributions.

EP: 1(A) TODAY'S GENERATION (Today's Generation/Murder/No Escape) (PS) (No Future Oi! 7) 1982

45: Murder In The Subway/Future Dream (PS) (No Future Oi! 17) 1982

Attak were formed by Gary Basnett, 'Chad' Chadwick and Lindsay McLennan, (sister of **Blitz** bassist Mackie) in New Mills, Cheshire, in early 1981. Their name was inspired by **Blitz**'s *All Out Attak* 45 and both **Blitz** and **The Violators** were from New Mills too.

Their vinyl debut came when, after much pestering of No Future records with demos, they managed to get a raw, snarling cut called *Blue Patrol* included on *Vol. 1* of *A Country Fit For Heroes* (No Future Oi! 3) in the early eighties, which showcased new unsigned punk talent. This went down well enough to enable them to be offered a recording contract by No Future.

Their first vinyl offering the *Today's Generation* (EP) was a considerable indie hit. The title cut was a blistering assault on the senses, *Hell* was more of the same and the barrage culminated with *No Escape*, which had a great discordant intro. Their indie chart success and growing popularity helped them to secure gigs with **Blitz** and **Peter and The Test Tube Babies**.

A few months later came a 45 *Murder In The Subway*, another fiercely aggressive fast-paced punker with the similarly constructed *Future Dreams* on the flip side. Again this did well in the indie charts and No Future felt the time was right for **Attak** to record an album. At this point they decided to expand to a four-piece and following an advert in 'Sounds', lead guitarist Woody was recruited.

Zombies, the consequent album, contained entirely new material and came out in early 1983. The opening cuts, *Daga 1* and *Daga 2* contain some good melodic guitar passages which were different to anything they'd recorded previously. Otherwise, on offer is snarling, fast-paced punk (oftern with heavy metalish leanings on the title cut, for instance) on cuts like the blistering *This Is The Time*, the raucous *Play The Ace*, the anthemic *Young And Proud* and the album culminated with a typically frantic cover of The Troggs' garage classic *Wild Thing*.

A different version of one cut *Big Brother* was also included on the compilation *Oi! Oi! That's Yer Lot* (Secret SEC 5), the same year.

Zombies turned out to be the band's final release. They became frustrated and quit as it became increasingly hard to get gigs.

Gary Basnett re-emerged several years later as lead vocalist on **Blitz**'s *Killing Dream* album. He also played live gigs with Nidge & Co.

The excellently-packaged Captain Oi! CD *Zombies* includes their earlier album, all three cuts from the *Today's Generation* EP, both sides of the *Murder In The Subway* 45 and their two contributions to the *A Country Fit For Heroes, Vol. 1* and *Oi! Oi! That's Yer Lot* compilations. In addition, *Today's Generation* can also be heard on *100% British Oi!* (Captain Oi! AHOY DCD 83) 1997. Finally, *Today's Generation* and *Murder In The Subway* resurfaced on the *No Future - The Punk Singles Collection* (Captain Oi! AHOY DLP 508) 1996 double album compilation, whilst *Hell*, *No Escape* and *Future Dreams* can be found on the *No Future - The Punk Singles Collection, Vol. 2* (Captain Oi! AHOY DLP 512) 1996 double album compilation.

Attic

EP: 1( ) ALL PLANS EXIST (Brain Booster BB 003) 1980
NB: (1) was issued with stickered white labels.

45: Yes I Want To/We're At War (Attic ATT 1) 1979

An obscure punk era band. Their 45 was issued with white labels in a stamped plain sleeve with an insert.

Attila The Stockbroker

ALBUMS: (up to 1986)	1	RANTING AT THE NATION	(Cherry Red ARED 46) 1983
	2	SAWDUST AND EMPIRE	(Anagram GRAM 13) 1984

EPs:	1	PHASING OUT CAPITALISM (PS)	(No Wonder E 1) 1981
	2	COCKTAILS (Cocktails/Contributory Negligence/Fifth Column/The Oracle/The Night I Slept With Seething Wells) (PS)	(Cherry Red CHERR 46) 1982

This guy's real name was John Blaine. After leaving the University of Kent with a French degree, this performance poet was on the way to becoming a stockbroker, when he set out on the music circuit. Sometimes backed by his own mandolin, he ranted to his audience in a humourous way about the state of the world. He played in two obscure and long-forgotten punk bands English Disease and Brighton Riot Squad prior to joining a new wave band called Contingent who were based in Brussels, Belgium.

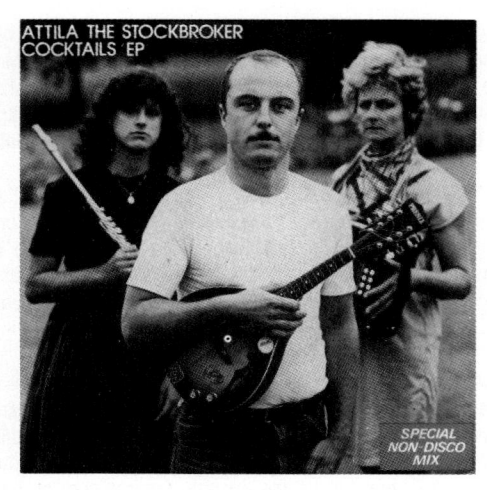

ATTILA THE STOCKBROKER - Cocktails EP.

He secured a session for John Peel, which in turn lead to a contract with Cherry Red. The *Cocktails* EP, released in 1982, captured him near his best, mixing serious pieces like *Contributory Negligence* with the bizarre such as *The Night I Slept With Seething Wells* and *The Oracle*.

A debut album *Ranting At The Nation* followed in 1983. On it he used poems and spoken word to stress the absurdity of British life.

The follow-up album *Sawdust And Empire*, released in 1984, utilised more music and **Attila The Stockbroker** veered more towards folk music as he became a regular fixture on the folk circuit. He often worked with **John Otway** and was involved in staging 'Cheryl The Rock Opera' with **Otway** and Blyth Power, for whom he sometimes played the fiddle.

He also contributed *Willie Whitelaw's Willie* and *Away Day* (a poem about the Law Lords judgement on Fares Fair) to *Oi! Oi! That's Yer Lot!* (Secret SEC 5) 1982. Whilst *Oi! Against Racism* (Havin' A Laugh HAL LP 004) included his *Radio Free Europe*. Earlier he had teamed up with **Newtown Neurotics** to contribute *Andy Is A Corporate / Mindless Version*, an attack on mindless violence and Nazi skinheads, to *Son Of Oi!* (Syndicate SYN LP 3) 1983.

He continued to record into the nineties releasing further albums beyond the timespan of this book:- *Libyan Students From Hell* (Plastic Head PLASLP 009) 1987, *Scornflakes* (Probe Plus PROBE 20) 1988, *Live At The Rivoli* (Musidisc) 1990 and *Donkey's Years* (Musidisc) 1991.

In 1994, he persued his interest in medieval/early music with a new project called Barnstormer. He still remains quite active on the circuit. He is also the resident poet at Brighton and Hove Albion F.C. where he often figures in the pre-match entertainment.

The Attractions

Personnel: STEVE NIEVE (NASON) keyb'ds A
BRUCE THOMAS bs, vcls A
PETE THOMAS drms A

ALBUM: 1(A) MAD ABOUT THE WRONG BOY (F-Beat XXLP 8) 1980
NB: (1) Came with a free EP (COMB 1).

45s: Single Girl/Slow Patience (PS) (F-Beat XX 7) 1980
Arms Race/Lonesome Little Town (PS) (F-Beat XX 10) 1980

These were solo efforts by **Elvis Costello**'s backing band at the time. Bruce Thomas had previously been with Quiver and Pete Thomas had bashed the skins for both Chilli Willy and Wilko Johnson. **The Attractions** were formed in 1977 and their support to **Costello**'s varied compositions in this era was an ingredient in his success.

Their 1980 album was quite a low profile affair, but as **Costello** experimented with various guises their position as his backing band had become increasingly insecure.

Steve Nieve also recorded two solo albums, *Keyboard Jungle* in 1983 and *Playboy* in 1987, both for Demon. Both he and Pete Thomas were in the house band on TV's 'The Jonathan Ross Show' and Bruce Thomas later embarked on a literary career.

Attrix

45s: * Lost Lenore/Hand Timers (PS) (Attrix RB 01) 1978
Procession/11th Hour (PS) (Scoff DT 011) 1981

NB: * Came in a stamped white label picture sleeve.

This group had the first release on the Attrix label.

Auntiepus

Personnel: ROBIN BIBI
CHRIS MILLAR
JIM PAYNE
AUNTIE PUS

45: Half-Way To Venezuela/
Marmalade Freak (PS) (Septic AUNT 1) 1979

This single is most significant for the fact **The Damned**'s Rat Scabies (Chris Millar here) played on it.

The Au Pairs

Personnel: PAUL FOAD gtr, vcls A
PETE HAMMOND drms A
JANE MUNRO bs, vcls A
LESLEY WOODS vcls, gtr A

HCP
ALBUMS: 1(A) PLAYING WITH A DIFFERENT SEX
(Human HUMAN 1) 1981 33
2(A) SENSE AND SENSUALITY (Kamera KAM 010) 1982 79
3(A) EQUALLY DIFFERENT - LIVE IN BERLIN 1981 (live)
(Aka AKA 6) 1983 -

NB: (1) also issued on CD (R.P.M. RPM 107) 1992. (2) also issued on CD (RPM RPM 111) 1993. (3) also issued on CD (RPM RPM 139CD) 1994. Also relevant is *Live In Berlin* (Essential ESMCD 452) 1996. There's also *Shocks To The System - The Very Best Of The Au Pairs* (Cherry Red CDMRED 161) 1999.

45s: You/Domestic Departure/Kerb Crawler (PS) (O2I OTO 2) 1980
It's Obvious/Diet (PS) (O2I OTO 4) 1980
Inconvenience/Pretty Boys (PS) (Human HUM 8) 1981
Inconvenience/Pretty Boys/
Heartache (12") (Human HUM 128) 1981

The Au Pairs were formed by Munro and Woods in Birmingham in late 1978. They first attracted attention supporting UB40 on tour. In 1980 they signed to the indie Human label. They weren't a punk band but prospered as part of the punk/new wave scene, playing their quirky feminist rock.

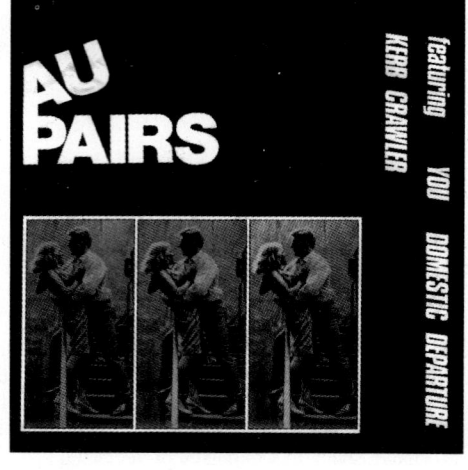

AU PAIRS - You.

Their debut 45 *You* dealt with the police harassment of prostitutes and the provocative lyrics were sung against a background of choppy guitars and a tight rhythm section. Their second single *Diet* was an NME 'Single of the Week' bringing them to the attention of a wider audience. They signed to Human for a further 45 *Inconvenience* before their debut album followed. *Playing With A Different Sex*, was issued in April 1981. It was well received and climbed to No. 33 in the charts. All the compositions were self-penned and it included their three 45s. Much of this is a sort of post-punk funk in a style not dissimilar to **The Gang Of Four** with lyrics which dealt with topics like monogamy and political prisoners. The 1992 CD issue of the album adds another eight cuts and excellent well-illustrated sleeve-notes by Martin Aston.

Sense And Sensuality replaced the hypnotic soundscapes of their debut album with minimalist dance rhythms. **The Pop Group** guested on this album. The later CD issue on RPM also includes six bonus tracks. Two of them are studio demos which have a gentle dub feel; the other four songs are taken from a 1983 session for Radio 1's Janice Long.

Live In Berlin was from a 1981 concert taped during a three-day Womens Festival held in a big circus top in Berlin. This live recording sets out their leftish agenda with songs about Ireland and faking orgasms.

Released in late 1999, *Shocks To The System - The Very Best Of Au Pairs* comprises fifteen cuts compiled by their drummer Pete Hammond and guitarist Paul Foad. This includes their three indie chart singles and cuts from their two albums. It is accompanied by a booklet containing their full discography and a band history.

They disbanded early in 1983. In 1999, *You* got a further airing on the 5-CD box set *1-2-3-4 - A History Of Punk And New Wave 1976 - 1979* (MCA/Universal MCD 60066).

Aural Exciters

| 45: | Spooks In Space '4'/Spooks in Space (PS) | (Ze ZE 700) 1979 |

This one-off 45 came on luminous vinyl in a die-cut picture sleeve.

The Autographs

Personnel:	CHRIS GENT	sax, vcls	A
	RAGGY LEWIS	gtr	A
	DAVE SPICER	bs	A
	PAUL TULLEY	drms	A
	JIM WARD	gtr	A

| 45: | When I'm Still Young/Fabulous | (RAK RAK 281) 1981 |

Lewis had previously been in **The Stukas**. **The Autographs** played catchy R&B in a pop format, with some great sax and competent vocals. Gent was later a member of **The Radio Stars** in 1982.

Avant Gardener(s)

ALBUMS:	1	DIG IT	(Appaloosa AP 013) 1980
	2	THE CHURCH OF THE INNER COSMOS	
			(Appaloosa AP 027) 1984

NB: (1) This was an Italian release, credited to **Avant Gardener**.

| EP: | 1( ) | GOTTA TURN BACK (PS) | (Virgin VEP 1003) 1977 |

NB: (1) Credited to **Avant Gardeners**.

| 45: | Deadwood Stage/ | ( ) 1983 |

A new wave trio who first came to light with a four track EP including cuts such as *Bloodclot Boogie Baby* and *Strange Gurl (sic) In Clothes*. Three years later they had an album released in Italy which included all four tracks from the EP with some other pretty amusing material like *Never Turn Your Back On A Silicon Chip* and a cover of Roky Erikson's *Two Headed Dog*. Fun!

Strange Gurl In Clothes also appeared on *Guillotine 10"* (Virgin VCL 5001) in 1978.

They continued to play live in the early eighties, releasing a 45 *Deadwood Stage* in 1983 and the quasi-psychedelic *The Church Of The Inner Cosmos* in 1984.

Henry Badowski

| ALBUM: | 1 | LIFE IS GRAND | (A&M AMLH 68527) 1981 |

45s:	Making Love With My Wife/	
	Baby Sign Here With Me (PS)	(Deptford Fun City DFC 11) 1979
	Baby Sign Here With Me/	
	Making Love With My Wife	(A&M AMS 7478) 1979
	My Face/Four More Seasons (PS)	(A&M AMS 7503) 1980
	Henry's In Love/Lamb To The Slaughter	(A&M AMS 8135) 1981

Henry Badowski is probably best known for playing with **Wreckless Eric**, **The Good Missionaries** and The Doomed. On his solo efforts, he has an unique style with an almost conversational voice and he plays just about every instrument himself. Many of the songs have a dry sense of humour. *Making Love With My Wife*, a typical effort, can also be heard on *Machines* (Virgin V 2177) 1980.

Back To Zero

Personnel:	BRIAN BETTERIDGE	vcls	A
	SAM BURNETT	gtr, vcls	A
	MAL	bs	A
	ANDY MOORE	drms, vcls	A

| 45: | Your Side Of Heaven/ | |
| | Back To Back (PS) | (Fiction FICS 004) 1979 |

From Enfield in North London **Back To Zero** were one of the earlier and better mod revival acts of 1979. *Your Side Of Heaven* had clout. They also figured on the 'March Of The Mods' tour along with **Secret Affair** and **Purple Hearts**.

The Balloons

Personnel:	BILL LAWSON	drms, vcls	AB
	CHRIS PROUD	gtr, vcls	ABCD
	DAVE SWIFT	bs	BCD
	CHRIS WEBSTER	vcls	BCD
	STEPHEN PENFOLD	drms	C
	DOMINIC LUCKMAN	drms	D

| ALBUM: | 1(C) | (LOVE RUNS) THROUGH YOUR ELBOW | |
| | | | (Earwacks WAK 003) 1981 |

45s:	Calling All Human Beings/(Love Runs) Through	
	Your Elbow (PS)	(Earwacks WAK 001) 1978
	Jean-Paul's Wife/The Slope (PS)	(Earwacks WAK 002) 1980

The Balloons originated out of Jezandwell's Train Set in 1977. Originally comprised of just Chris Proud and Bill Lawson, the band never gigged in this form but recorded a single for their own Earwacks record label in early 1978, *Calling All Human Beings/(Love Runs) Through Your Elbow*. shortly afterwards, the line-up was expanded, with Dave Swift and Chris Webster being added. However, in the summer of 1978, Bill Lawson quit and was replaced by Stephen Penfold on drums. In this format the band gigged in and around London in the late seventies. They also recorded another single on Earwacks in 1980. This was the double 'B' side *Jean-Paul's Wife/The Slope*. The single got great reviews, including 'Single of the Week' by Mark Ellen at New Music News - the short-lived replacement to NME and Melody Maker, when journalists from the latter two went on strike and formed their own paper. Despite favourable press, the band could never achieve any degree of success as the music was simply too way-out for most people's tastes. Proud, in particular, was inspired by *Trout Mask Replica*-period Beefheart and **The Balloons**, unlike other leftfield bands of the period (for instance, **Cabaret Voltaire**, **The Pop Group** etc), warped the rhythm as well as the melody. A **Balloons**' song was a combination of "cells", each cell complementing but totally separate from the others. Key changes and rhythm changes abounded. As a consequence, **The Balloons** were something of an acquired taste. In 1981, partly financed by a publishing advance from Cherry Red Records, **The Balloons** recorded their own album on Earwacks, *(Love Runs) Through Your Elbow*. By this time, such press interest as there was had waned and the album sold poorly. Shortly afterwards Penfold quit to concentrate on **To The Finland Station** full-time and was replaced by Dominic Luckman (drums), who, in turn, quit in 1982 and found some success with The Cardiacs. The core of Proud and Swift (with various others) continue as **The Balloons** to this day, still terrifying unsuspecting punters in South-east London.

Honey Bane

EP:	1	YOU CAN BE YOU	(Crass 521984/1) 1981

HCP

45s:	Turn Me On Turn Me Off/In Dreams/T'aint Nobody's Business/Negative Exposure (gatefold PS) (double-pack)	(Zonophone Z 15) 1981 37
	Baby Love/Mass Production (PS)	(Zonophone Z 19) 1981 58
	Jimmy (Listen To Me)/Negative Exposure/ Jimmy (Listen To Me) (PS)	(Zonophone Z 23) 1982 -
	Wish I Could Be Me/ Childhood Prince (PS)	(Zonophone Z 32) 1982 -
	Dizzy Dreamers/I O's Burning/ Ongoing Situation	(Zonophone Z 36) 1982 -

Honey Bane (whose real name was Donna Boylan) was just fourteen when **The Fatal Microbes**, who she fronted up, formed. Her distinctive punky vocals made the band but in 1981 she went solo. Her first solo venture was a three track EP *You Can Be You*, which she recorded with **Crass** as her backing band. She then signed to EMI's Zonophone label and enjoyed hits with her first two singles. During 1981 *Turn Me On Turn Me Off* spent five weeks in the charts climbing to No. 37 and *Baby Love* achieved a best position of No. 58 during its three week chart residency. After three further less successful 45s she faded from the scene but returned to prominence while appearing in a London fringe theatre production by virtue of acting out an explicit sex scene with ex-**Skids** lead vocalist Richard Jobson.

Two of her singles, *Turn Me On Turn Me Off* and *Jimmy (Listen To Me)*, later resurfaced on *The Zonophone Punk Singles Collection* (Anagram CDPUNK 97) 1997.

Ed Banger

ALBUM:	1	FROM BANGOR TO BASKERVILLE (compilation)	(Clay) 1993

45s:	*	Kinnel Tommy/Baby Was A Baby (PS)	(Rabid TOSH 104) 1978
	+	I've Just Had My Car Nicked/ P.C. Plod/Sponge (PS)	(Spiv DIV 1) 1981
		Poor People/Vicars In The Dark (PS)	(Cloud Nine CNS 01) 1983

NB: * This was reissued with numbered picture sleeves (EMI International INT 570) 1978. + This came with a photo insert.

THE BANNED - Little Girl.

BARBED WIRE - The Age That Didn't Care.

This guy was also known as Eddie Baskerville, who'd been vocalist Ed Garrity in **The Nosebleeds** and who was later a guitarist in **Slaughter and The Dogs**. On *Kinnel Tommy* Ed assumes the persona of an exasperated football fan screaming out all the right moves to his local team. This is accompanied by spiralling synthesiser and Garson-like piano. The end result worked quite well.

Kinnel Tommy later resurfaced on *Rabid / TJM Singles Collection* (Receiver RRCD 227) in 1996.

Bankrobbers

Personnel:	LIAM CARVILLE	keyb'ds, vcls	A
	JOBY FOX	bs	A
	JOHN McDONALD	gtr	A
	SEAMUS O'NEIL	drms	A

45s:	On My Mind/All Night (PS)	(Good Vibrations GOT 18) 1979
	Jenny/Please Come Back (PS)	(EMI KNAB 1) 1983
	Jenny/Please Come Back/ Oh No I've Got That Feeling (12")	(EMI 12KNAB 1) 1983
	Problem Page/ Problem Page (alt. version) (PS)	(EMI KNAB 2) 1984
	Problem Page/ Problem Page (alt. version) (12")	(EMI 12KNAB 2) 1984
*	Jenny/The Interview/ Over The Edge (PS)	(Good Vibrations TUBE 1) 1984

NB: * Special 'Tube' issue.

A bright energetic pop/punk combo. *On My Mind* penned by bassist Joby Fox is lively with some glimpses of good guitar and keyboards which blend in nicely. You'll also find it on *Good Vibrations - The Punk Singles Collection* (Anagram CDPUNK 36). Their promising debut led to the band being snapped up by EMI for whom they cut two further singles *Jenny* and *Problem Page* without breaking through commercially. A publicity stunt involving fake pound notes embossed with their logo became the subject of a police investigation!

The Banned

Personnel:	PETE FRESH	gtr	A B
	RICK MANSWORTH	gtr, vcls	A
	PAUL SORDID	drms, vcls	A B
	JOHN THOMAS	bs	A
	BEN DOVER	gtr, vcls	B
	TOMMY STEELE	bs	B

HCP

45:	Little Girl/CPGJ's (PS)	(Can't Eat EAT 1 UP) 1977 -
	Little Girl/CPCJ's (PS)	(Harvest HAR 5145) 1977 36
	Him Or Me/You Dirty Rat	(Harvest HAR 5149) 1978 -

A garage band from Croydon. Their first 45 was self-financed and a few copies were produced in hand made sleeves. This is now very collectable. Back in 1966 *Little Girl* had been an American hit for a pioneer punk outfit from San Jose, California, called The Syndicate Of Sound. On the strength of this release they were signed up by Harvest who reissued their first 45 and with the help of a major label's promotion it made the singles charts, peaking at No. 36, spending six weeks in all in the charts.

Musically we're talking nice ringing guitars with snappy drums, cute vocals and lyrics. All four of their 45 cuts can be heard on *Business Unusual* (Cherry Red ARED 2) 1979.

Barbed Wire

Personnel:	CAMERON	gtr	A
	HENDO	vcls	A
	IAN	drms	A
	RALPH	bs	A

ALBUM: 1(A) THE AGE THAT DIDN'T CARE (Oi! 006) 1986

NB: (1) later issued on CD (Captain Oi! AHOY CD 39) 1995 with eight bonus tracks.

A fast 'n' furious four piece Oi! band from Livingston, Scotland. They also toured with **The Exploited** and **Conflict**. They finally split up in early 1988. *The Age That Didn't Care*, the title track to their album, can also be heard on *100% British Oi!* (Captain Oi! AHOY DCD 83) 1997. It's a wholehearted punk thrash. You'll also find *No Hope* and *Nazi Briton (Fuck Off)* on *This Is Oi!* (Oi OIR 004) 1986, which was subsequently reissued (Captain Oi! AHOY CD 6) 1993.

The 1995 Captain Oi! CD reissue of *The Age That Didn't Care* also included their two cuts from the *This Is Oi!* compilation and their six cuts - *Stealin' Babiez*, *Face Don't Fit*, *Killing Time*, *Don't Let The Bastards Beat U*, *Hark (I Hear No Angels Sing)* and *The Christmas Song* - from their split *Skins 'N' Punks, Vol. 4* (Oi OIR 010) album with The Abnormal.

They are still playing today under new moniker Chinese Burn.

Wild Willy Barrett

ALBUMS:	1	CALL OF THE WILD	(Polydor 2383541) 1979
(up to	2	KRAZY KONG ALBUM	(Black Eyes EYE 001) 1981
1986)	3	ORGANIC BONDAGE	(Galvanised DIP 1) 1986

NB: Also relevant is a CD *Open Toed And Flapping* (Park PRKD 29) 1995.

45s:	Return Of Kong/	
	Nice To Know You're My Friend (PS)	(Logo GO 105) 1977
	Let's Play Schools/I Did It Otway (PS)	(Polydor 2059 067) 1979
	We've Gotta Get Out Of This Place/	
	Barrett's Blues (PS)	(Blackeye DARK 3) 1981
	Tales Of The Raj/	
	Drunks That Pass In The Night	(Blackeye DARK 4) 1981
	Shot Of Red Eye/I'm A Dog	(Redeye RED 1) 1981
	Old Joe Clarke/Rabbit In Boston	(Carrere CAR 266) 1983
	Rapping On A Mountain/Soundhog	(Carrere CAR 281) 1983

Wild Willy Barrett is best known as one half of a duo with **John Otway**. **Barrett** was the guitar and fiddle playing half of the partnership and they were renowned for their entertaining stage act. They enjoyed a No. 27 hit with *Really Free*, which spent eight weeks in the charts and a more minor hit with *DK 50-80*, which climbed to No. 45 during a four week chart stint. The 'B' side of *Really Free*, *Beware Of The Flowers (Cos I'm Sure They're Going To Get You Yeh)* also had lots of character and eccentricity and was included on *20 Of Another Kind* (Polydor POLS 1006) in 1979. As a solo artist **Wild Willy Barrett** made less impact.

Bauhaus

Personnel:	DANIEL ASH	gtr, vcls	A
	KEVIN HASKINS	drms, perc	A
	DAVID JAY (HASKINS)	bs, vcls	A
	PETER MURPHY	vcls	A

HCP

ALBUMS:	1(A)	IN THE FLAT FIELD	(4 AD CAD 13) 1980 72
	2(A)	MASK	(Beggars Banquet BEGA 29) 1981 30
	3(A)	THE SKY'S GONE OUT	(Beggars Banquet BEGA 42) 1982 4
	4(A)	PRESS THE EJECT AND GIVE ME THE TAPE	(Beggars Banquet BEGA 38) 1982 -
	5(A)	BURNING FROM THE INSIDE	(Beggars Banquet BEGA 45) 1983 13
	6(A)	1979-1983 (compilation)	(Beggars Banquet BEGA 64) 1985 36

NB: (1) reissued on CD (4AD GAD 13CD) 1988 and again 1998. (2) was reissued in 1982 with a new sleeve and a collage of stills from the video inside. (2) reissued on CD (Lowdown BBL 29CD) 1988. (3) was issued with the free LP (4), although (4) was later issued separately in December 1982 with a free 45 and poster. (3) reissued on CD (Lowdown BBL 42CD) 1989. (4) reissued on CD (Beggars Banquet BEGA 38 CD) 1988 and (Lowdown BBL 38 CD) 1989. (5) also issued as a picture disc (BEGA 45P) 1983. (5) reissued on CD (Beggars Banquet BEGA 45 CD) 1988 and (Lowdown BBL 45 CD) 1989. Extra tracks were added to (6) to make two CDs available separately:- *1979-1983 Volume One* (Beggars Banquet BEGA 64CD1) 1985 and *1979-1983 Volume Two* (Beggars Banquet BEGA 64CD2) 1985. Also relevant is *Swing The Heartache (The BBC Sessions)* (Beggars Banquet BEGA 103CD) 1989, also on double album, *Singles 1981 - 1983* (Beggars Banquet BBP 4CD) 1988, *Tribute To Bauhaus* (various artists) (Cleopatra CLEO 9861 CD) 1996, *Bela (A Tribute To Bauhaus)* (various artists) (Doppelganger DOP 51) 1998; *The Very Best Of Bauhaus* (Beggars Banquet) 1998 and *Gotham - Live 1998* (2-CD) (Cargo/KK 7281822 0025) 1999.

HCP

45s:	*	Bela Lugosi's Dead/Boys/	
		Dark Entries (12", PS)	(Small Wonder TEENY 2) 1979 -
		Dark Entries/Untitled (PS)	(Axis AXIS 3) 1980 -
		Dark Entries/Untitled (PS)	(Beggars Banquet BEG 37) 1980 -
		Dark Entries/Untitled (PS)	(4AD AD3) 1980 -

BAUHAUS - Bela Lugosi's Dead.

BAUHAUS - Dark Entries.

+	Terror Couple Kill Colonel/Scopes/		
	Terror Couple Kill Colonel (PS)	(4AD AD7) 1980	-
	Telegram Sam/Crowds (PS)	(4AD AD17) 1980	-
	Telegram Sam/Crowds/Rose Garden/		
	Funeral Of Sores (12", PS)	(4AD AD17T) 1980	-
	Kick In The Eye/Satori (PS)	(Beggars Banquet BEG 54) 1981	59
	Kick In The Eye/Satori (12")	(Beggars Banquet BEG 54T) 1981	-
	The Passions Of Lovers/David J: Peter Murphy: Kevin Haskins:		
	Daniel Ash (PS)	(Beggars Banquet BEG 59) 1981	56
	Kick In The Eye/Harry/		
	Earwax (PS)	(Beggars Banquet BEG 74) 1982	45
	Kick In The Eye/In Fear Of Dub/Harry/		
	Earwax (12", PS)	(Beggars Banquet BEG 74T) 1982	-
	Kick In The Eye/Poison Pen/Harry/Earwax		
	(12" misspressing) (PS)	(Beggars Banquet BEG 74TAI) 1982	-
	Spirit/Terror Couple Kill Colonel (live in Paris) (PS)		
		(Beggars Banquet BEG 79) 1982	42
	Spirit/Terror Couple (picture disc)		
		(Beggars Banquet BEG 79P) 1982	-
	Ziggy Stardust/		
	Third Uncle (PS)	(Beggars Banquet BEG 83) 1982	15
	Ziggy Stardust/Party Of The First Part/Third Uncle/		
	Waiting For The Man (12", PS)		
		(Beggars Banquet BEG 83 T) 1982	-
&	A God In An Alcove (Early Version)	(Lyntone LYN 12106) 1982	-
	Lagartija Nick/		
	Paranoia! Paranoia!	(Beggars Banquet BEG 88) 1983	44
	Lagartija Nick/Watch That Grandad Go/Paranoia! Paranoia!/		
	In The Flat Field		
	(live in Paris) (12", PS)	(Beggars Banquet BEG 88T) 1983	-
	She's In Parties/		
	Departure (PS)	(Beggars Banquet BEG 91) 1983	26
	She's In Parties/		
	Departure (picture disc)	(Beggars Banquet BEG 91P) 1983	-
	She's In Parties (extended)/Here's The Dub/		
	Departure (12", PS)	(Beggars Banquet BEG 91T) 1983	-
#	The Passion Of Lovers/Kick In The Eye/Spirit/Ziggy		
	Stardust/Lagartija Nick/She's In Parties (12", PS)		
		(Beggars Banquet BEG 100E) 1983	52
	The Sanity Assassin/		
	Spirit In The Sky (Fan Club single)	(Lyntone 13777/8) 1983	-
$	Dark Entries/Terror Couple Kill Colonel/Telegram Sam/		
	Terror Couple Kill Colonel (alt. version) (12", PS)		
		(4AD BAD 312) 1984	-

NB: * Also issued as a 12" on white vinyl and then later in 1986 on blue vinyl. + Originally issued in June 1980, a remixed version was issued in October of that year. & A blue flexidisc given away free with 'Flexipop' magazine, issue 23. There was also a hard vinyl test pressing. # There was also a test pressing of the above with the wrong version of *Terror Couple Kill Colonel*. $ Also issued as 3" picture CD in 1988.

Taking their name in recognition of the German school of art whose aims they sought to emulate **Bauhaus** formed in late 1978. Their debut gig was on New Years Eve 1978 at a Wellingborough pub.

BAUHAUS - Mask.

BAUHAUS - Ziggy Stardust.

Within a few months the now legendary Small Wonder label had offered them a recording session. The outcome was a stunning 12" *Bela Lugosi's Dead*, which sounded quite unlike anything that had gone before. I remember the impact it first made on me when I first heard it on the John Peel show. Although originally issued on black vinyl, there was a slightly later white vinyl pressing, which is rare and more sought-after.

There were five different versions of their punkish follow-up *Dark Entries*, which had figured uncredited on their previous release. By now they had signed to the 4AD label. This 45 is also recommended.

By now they had built up a large cult following. Their live shows were an experience, utilising white lights, videos and a strobe light. A John Peel Radio One session, first broadcast in 1979 but repeated a number of times subsequently helped develop their reputation further. The *Terror Couple Kill Colonel* 45, inspired by a newspaper headline, was a further progression. Their final 4AD single, a frantic rework of T. Rex's *Telegram Sam* came in 12" format as well as the usual 7" and with a promotional video.

Their debut album, released in October 1980, contained none of their 45s. Artistically important, with Daniel Ash's guitar style having considerable appeal, it veered towards psychedelia, which was unusual for the period. With none of their better known songs included it wasn't particularly accessible at the time, but retrospectively many recognise it as one of the year's most important albums.

In March 1981, they switched to the Beggars Banquet label. The ensuing 45 *Kick In The Eye* was more commercial with a dance rhythm. A clear attempt to breakthrough to a wider audience, though it didn't succeed, it did give them their first hit single climbing to No. 59, during its three week chart residency.

Mask, their second album, was more melodic, though still sought to experiment. Months after its release, the inner gatefold sleeve was altered, a collage of stills from the video of the title track being substituted for the previous group photo.

A remix of *Kick In The Eye* was released in February 1982 along with two previously unissued songs (*Harry* and *Earwax*) from their 1979 *Bela Lugosi* sessions. The 12" included an additional track *In Fear Of Dub*. However, in error, another unreleased song *Poison Pen* was included on test pressings. The masters of this version weren't destroyed and were erroneously used for a further run of 1,500 copies the following year. By the time the further error was discovered and the release withdrawn a few hundred copies had gone into the shops, mostly in the U.S.. Given *Poison Pen* has had no official release, these copies are now collectable.

In an almost desperate attempt for mainstream success for their next 45 they covered Norman Greenbaum's party classic *Spirit In The Sky*. Original sleeves had silver type and the usual Beggars Banquet label on the record, but on later pressings this was changed to grey type with a 'Bauhaus' label. The arrangement of the song wasn't particularly strong and only just made the Top 50. They re-recorded a longer and better version for their next album.

Shortly after, **Bauhaus** performed *Bela Lugosi's Dead* in 'The Hunger', a modern version of the Dracula story set in New York. For their next single they surprisingly decided to cover David Bowie's classic *Ziggy Stardust*. Perhaps chosing an already well-known song gave them the tonic to get a Top 20 hit. It climbed to No. 15 and was their biggest hit by far, spending seven weeks in the charts.

Free with the first 30,000 copies of their new album *The Sky's Gone Out* came a live album recorded from shows in late 1981 and the Old Vic, London in February 1982. It was also released separately with a free live single recorded in Paris and a poster of group photos donated by the public. *Press The Eject And Give Me The Tape* took its name from the last words on a bootleg tape that a security man had confiscated during the Old Vic concert *The Sky's Gone Out*.

Early in 1983, they scored another Top 40 hit with their *Lagaritija Nick* 45. Work on their next album *Burning From The Inside* was disrupted when Peter Murphy went down with viral pneumonia. This caused him to miss quite a few recording sessions and he only sang on five of the nine tracks. One of the strongest, the atmospheric *She's In Parties*, was quickly released as a 45 and, climbing to No. 26, became their second biggest hit single. Overall it was a very diverse album. Well received, it entered the charts at No. 13 and climbed into the Top 10, but it was the product of individuals rather than a group and sure enough it was soon confirmed that the band had decided to go their separate ways.

After they split there was one final release for their fan club members. A track omitted from their albums, *The Sanity Assassin* was coupled with a cover version of Norman Greenbaum's *Spirit In The Sky* and 325 copies were sent free to their fan club members.

Swing The Heartache compiles all their BBC recordings (two Peel sessions and three David Jensen ones) plus five previously released recordings. Some of their Peel recordings like *Party Of The First Part* and *Swing Your Heartache* sound quite experimental, whilst the Bowie influence is evident on *Ziggy Stardust* (their surprise hit) and *A God In An Alcove* and *She's In Parties* shows them straying into New Romantic territory.

Kick In The Eye can also be heard on *Gothic Rock 2* (Jungle FREUD CD 051) 1995 and *Rose Garden Funeral Of Sores* was included on *Natures Mortes* (4AD CAD 117CD) in 1997.

When the band went their separate ways, Daniel Ash and Kevin Haskins turned their hitherto part-time band Tones On Tail into a full-time one. David J. went solo, but later turned up again with the other two in Love and Rockets. Peter Murphy had an unsuccessful venture named **Dali's Car** with **Mick Karn** of **Japan**, but then launched a pretty successful solo career.

Bauhaus reformed in 1998 and all their shows were sold out. In the 'States they were welcomed with open arms. The live double-CD *Gotham-Live 1998* (there was also a 500-copies only vinyl version) was recorded on their re-union tour. Versions of many of their most popular songs are included like *Kick In The Eye*, *She's In Parties*, *Hollow Hills*, *The Passion Of Lovers* etc. The CD format includes one new cut *Severance* that is not on the vinyl.

Bauhaus' brooding music and imagery and their sense of experimentation

BAUHAUS - THE SKY'S GONE OUT.

make them an interesting act for collectors, though they never achieved quite the success they deserved at the time.

The Bears

Personnel:	CALLY CAMERON	drms	AB
	GEORGE GILL	gtr	ABC
	CHRIS KERSHAW	sax	A
	MICK NORTH	vcls	A
	RON WEST	bs	AB
	JOHN ENTRIALS	vcls	BC
	RICHIE	drms	C
	TIM	bs	C

ALBUM: 1(A/B) INSANE (Tigerbeat GROWL 001) 1986

45s:	On Me/Wot's Up Mate (PS)	(Waldo's JS 001) 1979
	Insane/Decisions (PS)	(Good Vibrations Int. GVI 1) 1979
	Spain/Artist	(Release RL 970) 1979

The Bears came fom Watford and were formed by ex-**Wire** guitarist George Gill. Line-up 'A' didn't record because vocalist Mick North was tragically killed in a car accident. He was replaced by John Entrials (formerly of Paper Dollies). Their debut disc on Waldo's came in various differently designed sleeves with an insert. It later resurfaced on *Punk Rock Rarities, Vol. 1* (Anagram CD PUNK 63) in 1995. They also had a cut *Fun Fun Fun* included on the *Farewell To The Roxy* (Lightning LIP 2) 1978 compilation, which is also available on CD (Captain Oi! AHOY CD 86) 1998. These were the work of line-up 'B'. Line-up 'C' had the distinction of recording the first single on Good Vibrations. The opening chords of *Decisions* sound very similar to **Sham 69**'s *If The Kids Are United* but it's a good raucous punker whatever. You'll also find it on *Good Vibrations, The Punk Singles Collection* (Anagram CDPUNK 36) 1994. By this time, Cally and Ron West had left to form **The Tea Set** and they'd recruited a new drummer called Richie and a bassist called Tim. They continued gigging until mid-1979 and later reformed in 1986 whilst Tigerbeat released their posthumous live collection *Insane*. They were an underrated band.

The Bearz

45s:	She's My Girl/Girls Will Do (PS)	(Axis AXIS 2) 1980
	Darwin/Julie (PS)	(Occult OCC 1) 1984

A different act spelt with a z. I've no other data on these.

Bee Bee Cee

Personnel:	BLACKIE	keyb'ds	A
	BOB GILHOOLEY	bs	A
	DAVE GILHOOLEY	vcls	A
	CALLUM McNAIR	gtr	A
	ZOKKO	drms	A

45:	You Got To Know The Girl/ We Ain't Listening (PS)	(Rel RE 48-S) 1977

This single was an amalgam of poppy punk which didn't sell well at the time. Twenty years on there was a resurgence of interest in it and nowadays it's a very rare and sought-after punk artefact.

Mark Beer

ALBUM:	1 DUST ON THE ROAD	(My China TAO 001) 1981
EP:	1 ISOLATIONS (PS)	(Waste WAS 001) 1980
45:	Pretty/Per (Version) (PS)	(Rough Trade RT 70) 1981

Isolations is a D-I-Y four-track EP, which was quite interesting.

B.E.F. (British Electric Foundation)

Personnel:
- GLENN GREGORY — vcls — A
- IAN CRAIG MARSH — A
- MARTYN WARE — A

ALBUMS:
- 1(A) MUSIC FOR STOWAWAYS (Virgin V 2888) 1980 - HCP
- 2(A) MUSIC FOR LISTENING TO (Virgin BEF 1) 1981 -
- 3(A) MUSIC OF QUALITY AND DISTINCTION VOL. 1 (Virgin VV 2219) 1982 25

NB: (1) was a cassette, but there was also an unissued test pressing album version which is quite collectable now. (2) was a Canadian EP, which included much of the material from (1). (2) also issued on CD (Caroline 11242) 1997. There was also a 5 x 7" box set version of (3) plus an insert.

45s:
- * Anyone Who Had A Heart/(inst. version) (PS) (Virgin VS 484) 1982
- # These Boots Are Made For Walking/(alt. version) (PS) (Virgin VS 493) 1982
- x It's Over/(alt. version) (Virgin VS 498) 1982
- + Ball Of Confusion/(alt. version) (PS) (Virgin VS 500) 1982

NB: * As **B.E.F. Present Sandie Shaw**. # As **B.E.F. with Paula Yates**. x As **B.E.F. with Billy McKenzie**. + As **B.E.F. with Tina Turner**.

B.E.F. (also known as **British Electric Foundation**) was an experimental part-time project for former **Human League** members Marsh and Ware when they were with the electronic dance/funk rock outfit Heaven 17. As **B.E.F.** the duo added singer Glenn Gregory and pursued a variety of concept projects with a variety of other people.

Music For Stowaways only released on tape (although test pressings of an album version exist) comprised a wide variety of moody instrumentals and sound experiments. Much of the material from this tape was later reissued on a Canadian EP, *Music For Listening To* which included an extra track *A Baby Called Billy*.

For *Music Of Quality And Distinction* they brought a variety of top performers like Sandie Shaw, Tina Turner, Billy McKenzie, **John Foxx** and Gary Glitter to perform cover versions of oldies. After this, the experiment petered out.

Beggar

Personnel:
- NEIL GREGORY — lead vcls, harp — A
- JEFF JOHN — gtr, vcls — A
- MIKE SLOCOMBE — drms — A
- MARK WILLIAMS — bs, vcls — A

A rough-edged mod revival band. Originally from Cardiff, they moved to Leyton in East London and figured on the live compilation *Mods Mayday '79* (Bridge House BHLP 003) 1979 playing *Don't Throw Your Life Away*, *Broadway Show* and *All Night*. They later figured on *Mod's Mayday 2 - Modnight At The Bridge* (Receiver RRCD 228) 1997, which comprises outtakes from the original night.

Neil Gregory was later in the Co-Stars.

BETHNAL - The Fiddler.

Berlin Blondes

45s:
- Science/Mannequin (PS) (EMI EMI 5031) 1980
- Marseille/The Poet (Scratch SCR 005) 1980

A Glasgow band.

Bethnal

Personnel:
- GEORGE CSAPO — vcls, violin — A
- PETE DOWLING — drms — A
- NICK MICHAELS — gtr — A
- EVERTON WILLIAMS — bs — A

ALBUMS:
- 1(A) DANGEROUS TIMES (Vertigo 9102 020) 1978
- 2(A) CRASH LANDING (Vertigo 9102 029) 1978

45s:
- * The Fiddler/This Ain't Just Another Love Song (PS) (Bethnal VIOL 1) 1977
- We've Gotta Get Out Of This Place/Outcome (PS) (Vertigo BET 1) 1978
- + Don't Do It/Where Do We Stand (PS) (Vertigo BET 2) 1978
- Nothing New/Summer Wine (PS, blue vinyl) (Vertigo 6059 213) 1978

NB: * This 45 was given away free at gigs. + There was also a 12" PS version of this release.

This multi-ethnic London-based band, who emanated from Bethnal Green (hence their name), built up a strong reputation as a live band during 1976. Everton Williams is black, George Csapo and Nick Michaels are Greek Cypriots. Only drummer Pete Dowling is English. They were also unusual in that George Csapo played keyboards and violin, not instruments usually associated with the 'back to basics' punk format. The Who seem to have been a strong influence on their hard-driving sound. Their repertoire included the Townshend classic *Baba O'Riley*, but they were far from carbon-copies of The Who largely because Csapo's imaginative and spectacular violin playing and writing made them unique.

Their initial self-financed 45, which bore more than a passing resemblence to The Who's *The Seeker*, was given away free at gigs during 1977. They attracted major label attention and signed to Vertigo. Their debut 45, a cover of The Animals' *We've Gotta Get Out Of This Place* was fine but added nothing new to the original interpretation. Their debut album *Dangerous Times* highlighted their energy and good musicianship, but suffered from poor production and didn't really succeed in translating their live sound onto vinyl.

Crash Landing, which was produced by Jon Astley (Pete Townsend's brother-in-law) and Phil Chapman, saw the band moving towards a stadium style rock which alienated their original fans and won few new converts.

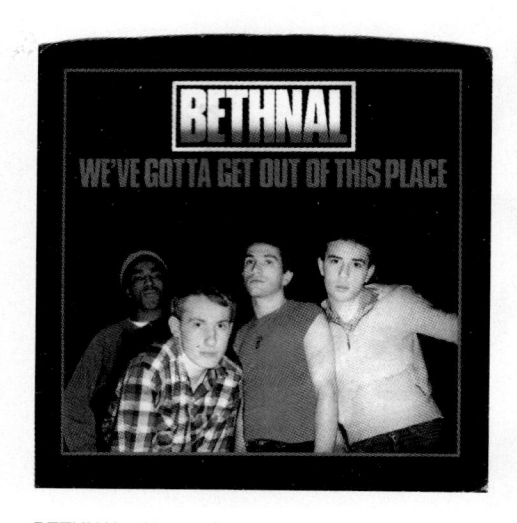

BETHNAL - We've Gotta Get Out Of This Place.

Bet Lynch's Legs

45s: Riders In The Sky/High Noon (PS) (Absurd ABSURD 10) 1980
Some Like It Hot/Some Don't (PS) (Absurd ABSURD 11) 1980

This was a pseudonym for Absurd recording artist John Scott. Bet Lynch was of course the well-endowed barmaid of the Rovers Return in 'Coronation Street'! Scott later described *Riders In The Sky* as "a Jonathan Richmond-type version of 'High Noon'". The follow-up *Some Like It Hot / Some Don't* featured both tunes all at once over each other with a dub version of the end result on the flip side!

The Betrayed

ALBUM: 1 SKINS 'N' PUNKS, VOLUME 2 (Oi OIR 008) 1987

NB: (1) this was a split album with **Oi! Polloi**.

A rudimentary Oi! band whose *United Oi!* from the above recording later resurfaced on *The Best Of Oi! Records* (Captain Oi! AHOY CD 38) 1995.

SKINS 'N' PUNKS Vol. 2.

Big In Japan

Personnel:
PHIL ALLEN drms AB
BILL DRUMMOND vcls, gtr ABCD
KEVIN WARD vcls, bs AB
IAN BROUDIE gtr BCD
JAYNE CASEY vcls BCD
PETER 'BUDGIE' CLARK drms CD
HOLLY JOHNSON bs C
DAVID BALFE bs D

EP: 1( ) FROM Y TO Z AND NEVER AGAIN
(Nothing Special/Cindi And The Barbi Dolls/
Suicide A Go Go/Taxi) (Zoo CAGE 01) 1978

45s: * Big In Japan/ (Eric's 0001) 1977
Kizza Me/Dream Lover (Aura AUS 103) 1979

NB: * Other side by **Chuddy Nuddies**.

An historically significant Merseyside band. Many of them went on to greater things. They formed, initially, in Liverpool in May 1977 as a trio (line-up 'A'). All three were mad about **The Clash**. After a few gigs Broudie and Casey were added to the line-up and Clive Langer (of Deaf School fame) played a few gigs for them too. He was also on their debut single on the Eric's label (this was launched by a local club of that name). It was a strange affair shared with a combo called **The Chuddy Nuddies** (actually **The Yachts** under a pseudonym). The lyrics on the *Big In Japan* 45 were virtually inaudible.

Almost immediately after the 45's release Ward and Allen departed. They were replaced by Holly Johnson and Peter 'Budgie' Clark, who'd previously been in a short-lived outfit **Nova Mob**, which also contained Julian Cope. This line-up gigged extensively for six months and with their visually striking, theatrical set, they were attracting the interest of some of the major labels. At this point Johnson left to go solo and David Balfe (formerly with **Dalek I Love You**) replaced him.

Ironically, they were on the brink of bigger things - having passed an audition for Stiff, when they decided to split. They played a farewell concert at Eric's in late August 1978.

They nearly all went on to greater things. In the short term Drummond formed his own label, Zoo Records. Its first release was a **Big In Japan** EP *From Y To Z And Never Again*, which included four of their previously unissued songs. The superb sampler *To The Shores Of Lake Placid* (Zoo FOUR) 1982 included *Suicide A Go Go*, a highly distinctive song (which had previously appeared on *From Y To Z And Never Again*) and the previously unreleased *Society For Cutting Up Men*, which had some pleasing guitar moments and was quite an original sound at the time. Drummond later joined up with Balfe as **Lori and The Chameleons** and, of course, Balfe was later in **The Teardrop Explodes** and went on to launch Food Records (Blur's label). Drummond became half of the commercially successful KLF. Holly Johnson became lead singer of Frankie Goes To Hollywood. Broudie was later in The Lightning Seeds. Jayne Casey became lead singer with **Pink Military**. Finally Peter 'Budgie' Clark went on to **The Slits** and **Siouxsie and The Banshees**. So there you have it!

The Bishops

Personnel:
PAUL BALBI drms A
ZENON DE FLEUR gtr, vcls A
JOHNNY GUITAR gtr A
STEVE LEWINS bs A
DAVE TICE vcls A

ALBUMS: 1(A) LIVE AT THE ROUNDHOUSE (10" mini LP)
(Chiswick CH 7) 1978
2(A) CROSSCUTS (Chiswick CWK 3009) 1979

NB: (1) was also issued in 12" format. There's also a compilation *The Best Of The Bishops* (Chiswick CDWIKD 150) 1995.

45s: I Take What I Want/No Lies (PS) (Chiswick NS 33) 1978
* Mr. Jones/Human Bean/Route 66/
Too Much Too Soon (Chiswick NS 35) 1978
+ I Want Candy/See That Woman (PS) (Chiswick NS 37) 1978
I Want Candy/See That Woman (6" PS) (Chiswick NS 376) 1978
I Want Candy/
See That Woman (10", PS) (Chiswick NS 3710) 1978
I Want Candy/See That Woman (PS) (Chiswick CH1S 101) 1978
I Want Candy/
See That Woman (6", PS) (Chiswick CH1S 1016) 1978
I Want Candy/
See That Woman (10", PS) (Chiswick CH1S 10110) 1978
Mr. Jones/Human Bean/Route 66/
Too Much Too Soon (Chiswick CH1S 111) 1979

NB: * This was only available as a test pressing. + This was also available as a picture sleeve in 6" and 10" format. # This and the following two 45s were reissues of the earlier one.

This was a later version of **The Count Bishops** with an abbreviated name. The **Count Bishops** also recorded as **Mike Spenser and The Cannibals**.

Their *Mr. Jones* 45 on Chiswick 37 was never issued, but was a test pressing. This is their rarest and most collectable item.

The Bishops were doubtless a good live band but their repertoire, relying largely on covers of classic rock 'n' rollers and R&B from the sixties, was found wanting when translated onto vinyl. Their self-penned material lacked originality or indeed any real distinction and this more than anything limited their appeal to a cult following on the pub circuit. Still, they remain an important part of the early pub scene.

They split in 1979, following Zenon De Fleur's death in March in a motor accident, shortly before the release of *Crosscuts*.

Bitch

Personnel incl: GABY GAWIN

| 45: | Big City/Wild Kids (PS) | (Hurricane FIRE 5) 1979 |

On this 45 Bitch sound like a third division **Penetration**.

Blah Blah Blah

Personnel:
CHRIS ANDREWS	bs	A
MARTIN CROXFORD	synth, piano	A
VICKY JONES	synth	A
IAN SMITH	vcls	A
PETER WIGGINS	gtr	A

ALBUM: 1(A) BLAH BLAH BLAH   (Trans Universal TV 1) 1982

NB: There was also an unreleased album on Some Bizzare for which test pressings exist in 1981.

45s:
- In The Army/Why Diddle (PS)   (Absurd ABSURD 1) 1979
- * Heavenly View/(plus track by St Vitus' Dance)   (Lyntone LYN 17627) 198?

NB: * One sided 33 r.p.m. flexidisc with 'Helden' fanzine.

Blah Blah Blah's *In The Army* was mastered straight from the low grade supermarket cassette on which it arrived in the office. They also contributed the decidely strange *Central Park* to the *Some Bizzare Album* (Some Bizzare BZLP 1) in 1981. They also recorded an album's worth of material for Some Bizzare, for which test pressing exist, but they eventually had an album's worth of material released by Trans Universal in 1982.

Blancmange

Personnel:
NEIL ARTHUR	vcls	AB
STEPHEN LUSCOMBE	keyb'ds, synth	AB
LAURENCE STEVENS	drms	A

HCP
ALBUMS: 1(B) HAPPY FAMILIES   (London SH 8552) 1982 30
(up to 2(B) MANGE TOUT   (London SH 8554) 1982 8
1986)   3(B) BELIEVE YOU ME   (London LONLP 10) 1985 54

NB: (2) also issued on CD (London 81023502) 1984, but deleted in 1991. Later reissued (Spectrum 5521082) 1996. (3) also issued on CD (London 8203012) 1985. Also relevant are:- *Second Helpings (Best Of Blancmange)* (London 8280432) 1990; *Heaven Knows (Best Of Blancmange)* (Elite ELITE 024 MCD) 1992; *The Third Course* (Spectrum 550 1942) 1994; and *The Best Of Blamange* (Connoisseur Collection VSOPCD 226) 1996.

EP: 1(A)   IRENE AND MAVIS (Disco-A-Bomb-Bomb/
(up to   Holiday Camp/Overspreading/Art Genius/
1986)   Modichy In Aneration/Concentration Baby/
               Just Another Spectre) (PS)   (Blash Music MFT 1) 1980

HCP
45s: * Living On The Ceiling/Sad Day (excerpt)/
(up to   (track by Passage) (flexidisc)   (Lyntone LYN 1183/4) 1982 -
1986)   I've Seen The World/
           God's Kitchen (PS)   (London BLANC 1) 1982 65
           I've Seen The World (Extended)/God's Kitchen
           (Extended) (12", PS)   (London BLANCX 1) 1982 -
           Feel Me/Feel Me (instrumental) (PS) (London BLANC 2) 1982 46
           Feel Me/Feel Me
           (instrumental) (picture disc)   (London BLAPD 2) 1982 -
           Feel Me (Extended)/Feel Me
           (instrumental) (12", PS)   (London BLANCX 2) 1982 -
           Living On The Ceiling/
           Running Thin (PS)   (London BLANC 3) 1982 7
           Living On The Ceiling/
           Running Thin (12", PS)   (London BLANCX 3) 1982 -
           Waves/Games Above My Head (PS)   (London BLANC 4) 1983 19
           Waves/
           Games Above My Head (12", PS)   (London BLANCX 4) 1983 -
        # Blind Vision/Heaven Knows
           Where Heaven Is (PS)   (London BLANC 5) 1983 10
           Blind Vision/Heaven Knows Where
           Heaven Is/Blind Vision
           (alternate version) (12", PS)   (London BLANCX 5) 1983 -
           That's Love, That It Is/Vishnu (PS) (London BLANC 6) 1983 33
           That's Love, That It Is/
           Vishnu (picture disc)   (London BLAPD 6) 1983 -
           That's Love, That It Is/
           Vishnu (12", PS)   (London BLANCX 6) 1983 -
           Don't Tell Me/Get Out Of That (PS) (London BLANC 7) 1984 8
           Don't Tell Me/
           Get Out Of That (picture disc)   (London BLAPD 7) 1984 -
           Don't Tell Me/
           Get Out Of That (12", PS)   (London BLANCX 7) 1984 -
           (The) Day Before You Came/
           All Things Are Nice (PS)   (London BLANC 8) 1984 22
           (The) Day Before You Came/
           All Things Are Nice (picture disc) (London BLAPD 8) 1984 -
        + (The) Day Before You Came/All Things Are Nice/
           Feel Me (live) (12", PS)   (London BLANCX 8) 1984 -
           What's Your Problem?/
           Side Two (PS)   (London BLANC 9) 1985 40
           What's Your Problem?/Side Two/
           Living On The Ceiling (12", PS)   (London BLANCX 9) 1985 -
           What's Your Problem?/Side Two/Living On The Ceiling/
           Feel Me (12" picture disc)   (London BLAPD 9) 1985 -
           Lose Your Love/John (PS)   (London BLANC 10) 1985 -
           Lose Your Love/John/
           Mixing On The Ceiling (12", PS)   (London BLANCX 10) 1985 -
           Lose Your Love/John/That's Love That It Is/Games Above
           My Head (double 12" picture disc) (London BLAPD 10) 1985 -
           I Can See It/
           Scream Down The House (PS)   (London BLANC 11) 1986 71
           I Can See It/
           Scream Down The House (12", PS)   (London BLANCX 11) 1986 -
Reissues: Blind Vision/Living On The Ceiling (Old Gold OG) 1988 -
           Living On The Ceiling/Don't Tell Me (Old Gold OG) 1988 -

NB: * This was a 33 rpm flexidisc which came free with 'Melody Maker' magazine. # There was also a version issued on clear vinyl with a pic sleeve and insert (BLATP 5). + There may also have been a 12" picture disc version.

Blancmange was formed in London in 1980 by Neil Arthur, who was born on 15th June 1958 in Darwen, Lancashire and Stephen Luscombe, who was born on 29th October 1954. Initially they gigged as a trio, the third member being Laurence Stevens on drums. They released a debut 45 *Irene And Mavis* on their own label in 1980.

Their initial break came when they were invited to perform an instrumental number *Sad Day* on *The Some Bizzare Album* (Some Bizzare BZLP 1) in 1981. This featured other up-and-coming early eighties bands like **Depeche Mode**, **Soft Cell** and **The The**. This exposure helped secure them a contract with London Records early in 1982. The same year an excerpt of *Sad Day* along with what would become their most successful commercial number *Living On The Ceiling* appeared on the flexidisc, which also

BLANCMANGE - Happy Families.

featured a track by **The Passage**, and came free with 'Melody Maker' magazine. This helped bring them to the attention of a wider audience.

Their debut 45 for London *I've Seen The Word* was released in March 1982 in both 7" and 12" formats. It was a delicate somewhat reserved electro-pop composition which brought them some early commercial success, climbing to No. 65 during its two week chart stay. *God's Kitchen* on the reverse side was rather eccentric lyrically and more upbeat musically. Prior to this Neil and Stephen had reverted to a duo utilising a drum machine instead of Laurence Stevens.

Their next single, released in July 1982, comprised both a vocal and instrumental version of the same song *Feel Me*. There's quite a pronounced Talking Heads influence on this cut, which has appealing instrumentation but perhaps suffered from being a little monotonous. Still it consolidated on their earlier success peaking at No. 46 during its five week chart stay.

For their debut album, *Happy Families*, David Rhodes guested on guitar on six of the ten tracks. James Lane was guest drummer on two tracks. Stevie Lange was brought in to share backing vocals with Joy Gates on *I Can't Explain* and *Kind* and with Madeline Bell on *Feel Me* and *Waves*. The album was recorded at CBS and Battery Studios, London, between February and August 1982. *I've Seen The Word*, *God's Kitchen* and *Feel Me* were all featured, but the stand-out cut was the eastern-influenced *Living On A Ceiling*, which became **Blancmange**'s best known song. Released as a 45 in October, one month after the album came out, it climbed to No. 7 becoming their best-selling single and enjoying a total chart stay of fourteen weeks. The album spent a massive thirty-eight weeks in the charts, although it didn't climb above No. 30. Whilst comparisons with bands like Talking Heads, **Soft Cell** and **Orchestral Manoeouvres In The Dark** were inevitable, **Blancmange** did have their own unique sound and certainly *Happy Families* was among the best albums of 1982. It spawned one further hit when *Waves* climbed to No. 19 during a nine week chart residency in February 1983.

More guest musicians - Pandit Dimesh (tablas) and Deepak Khazanchi (sitar) - were brought in for their second album *Mange Tout*, released in May 1984. Overall, this represented an enhancement on their earlier effort. The material was generally beatier with more strings, woodwind and horns, making for a more melodious and less monotonous sound. Three of its finest moments *Blind Vision* (No. 10), *That's Love, That It Is* (No. 33) and *Don't Tell Me* (No. 8) were released as 45s prior to the album's release, with *Don't Tell Me* performing particularly well spending ten weeks in the charts in all. All three 45s were released in both 7" and 12" formats and there were also picture disc releases of *That's Love That Is* and *Don't Tell Me*. The album itself performed very solidly climbing to No. 8 during a seventeen week chart residency. It also spawned one final hit when *(The) Day Before You Came*, an Abba cover, rose to No. 22 and spent a total of eight weeks in the charts in the summer of 1984.

During 1985 David Rhoades was added to their line-up as a session guitarist. Their third album *Believe You Me*, released in October, was their most ambitious. It utilised a plethora of guest musicians, four producers and was recorded in seven different studios. The album had its moments with *What's Your Problem?* (an earlier 45 which had enjoyed five weeks in the charts peaking at No. 40), *Why Don't They Leave Things Alone* and *Don't You Love It All* (which featured Hugh Masekela on flugelhorn), but its disappointing commercial performance - just two weeks in the charts with a best position of No. 54 - was an indication that their days may be numbered. Indeed they were, when they decided to split up in 1986 after just two further singles; *Lose Your Love* and *I Can See*.

After **Blancmange**'s demise Stephen Luscombe tried his hand at writing film scores with East India Company. Neil Arthur tried his luck (unsuccessfully) as a solo artist. In September 1992, he recorded *One Day, One Time* with help from Carol Kenyon. He also contributed to a Channel 4 documentary.

Compilation appearances by the band have included *Living On The Celing* on *The Model* (Spectrum 5529 182) 1997.

To access **Blancmange**'s music now, try one of the compilations listed in the discography. *Heaven Knows* compiles all their hits like *Living On The Ceiling*, *Waves* and *Don't Tell Me*, along with many other fine tracks which emphasised Neil Arthur and Steven Luscombe's ability to indulge in accomplished musicianship and rhythmic interplay. Alternatively, *Third Course (Best Of Blancmange)* is a solid compilation of their material.

Blanks

Personnel:	ALLEN ADAMS	vcls	A
	PHIL ATTERSON	gtr	A
	ANDY BUTLER	drms	A
	ANDY JACKSON	gtr	A

45:	The Northern Ripper/ Understand (PS)	(Void SRTS/79/CUS/560) 1979

The Blanks formed out of the personnel of **The Destructors**, a third generation Peterborough punk band. They achieved notoriety with their *Northern Ripper* 45, which was released at the time the Yorkshire Ripper was on the prowl. Adams even ended up being interviewed by the task force the police set up to find the murderer.

They dissolved after a disastrous tour when they were support band to **Discharge** and Adams then rejuvenated **The Destructors**.

BLITZ - Razors In The Night.

Blitz

Personnel:	CARL	vcls	A
	CHARLIE	drms	A
	MACKIE	bs	A
	NIDGE	gtr	A

HCP

ALBUMS:	1(A)	VOICE OF A GENERATION	(No Future PUNK 1) 1982 27
	2( )	SECOND EMPIRE JUSTICE	(Future FL 1) 1983 -

NB: (1) also issued on CD (No Future CDPUNK 1) 1992. There's also a number of CD compilations, *The Complete Blitz Singles Collection* (Anagram CD PUNK 25) 1994, *The Best Of Blitz* (Dojo DOJOCD 123) 1993, *Blitz On All Out Attack* (Dojo DOJOCD 93) 1993, *The Very Best Of Blitz* (Anagram CDPUNK 104) 1998, *Warriors* (Harry MAY MAYO CD 102) 1999 and *All Out Attack* (LP) (Get Back GET 14) 1997, which includes many cuts from *Voice Of A Generation*, their *All Out Attack* (EP) and first two 45s. Also relevant are a seventeen-track vinyl compilation *The Complete Singles Collection* (Get Back GET 71) 1999, *Voice Of A Generation (The No Future Years)* (2-CD set) (Anagram CDPUNK 114) 2000 and *Punk Singles & Rarities 1980 - 83* (Captain Oi! AHOY CD 161) 2001.

EP:	1(A)	ALL OUT ATTACK (Someone's Gonna Die/Attack/ Fight To Live/45 Revolutions)	(No Future Oi! 1) 1981

45s:	Razors In The Night/ Never Surrender (PS)	(No Future Oi! 6) 1982
	Warriors/Youth (PS)	(No Future Oi! 16) 1982
	New Age/Fatigue (PS)	(Future FS 1) 1983
	Telecommunication/Teletron (PS)	(Future FS 3) 1983
	Solar (Extended Remix)/ Husk (Dance Mix) (12", PS)	(Future 12 FS 6) 1983

An early eighties punk quartet from New Mills, Manchester who were an important flagship of the Oi! Movement. Carl, Nidge and Mackie had all previously played in XS Rhythm, a band formed by future popster Lloyd Cole. They were also significant as the first act signed to the No Future label in late 1981.

Their debut EP in December 1981 comprised four 'smash the establishment' style songs. The first 500 copies came with rubber stamped labels and sold out within a few days. They are now very collectable. The EP made a big impression in the indie chart, as did their follow-up singles *Never Surrender* and *Warriors*. They also contributed *Voice Of A Generation* to an EP *Total Noise* (Total Noise TOT 1) in 1982 which comprised other Oi! Bands. This cut can also be heard on *Oi! The Rarities, Vol. 5* (Captain Oi! AHOY CD 62) 1996.

In February 1982, **Blitz** released a double 'A' side 45 *Razors In The Night/Never Surrender*, which many consider the finest punk single of the year. *Razors In The Night*, despite its title, is an anti-violence song with a strong chorus and powerful guitar work. *Never Surrender* is a blistering, fast-paced tribute to all the punks who kept going despite changes in fashion. Both these songs later resurfaced on *Oi! The Singles Collection, Vol. 1* (Captain Oi! AHOY CD 60) 1996.

Warriors, the last of the band's recordings by the original line-up, followed in August 1982. Like their previous 45, this featured more pulsating guitar and a good vocal performance by Carl. On the flip side was a re-recording of *Youth* (one of two songs **Blitz** had contributed to the *Carry On Oi!* (Secret SEC 2) 1981 compilation, later reissued on CD (Captain Oi! AHOY CD 119) 1999, the other cut being *Nation On Fire*. Both sides of the *Warriors* 45 can also be heard on *Oi! The Singles Collection, Vol. 3* (Captain Oi! AHOY CD) 1997. *Warriors* can also be found on *100% British Oi!* (Captain Oi! AHOY DCD 83) 1997 and *Youth* also figured on *The Secret Life Of Punks* (LP) (Secret SEC 10) 1982.

When their debut album was released in October 1982, not only did *Voice Of A Generation* climb to No. 2 in the indie charts for several weeks, it also climbed to No. 27 in the national charts, in which it enjoyed a toal of three weeks.

After this the band split in two factions. Nidge and Mackie formed **Rose Of Victory**, whilst Carl and Charlie retained the name and veered more towards a **New Order** sound. Subsequent records issued under the **Blitz** name bore little resemblance to these early Oi! classics.

The Complete Blitz Singles Collection is a seventeen-track 'hits' compilation of fast 'n' furious, metallic, aggressive punk with titles like *Never Surrender*, *Warriors* and *Someone's Gonna Die*. There's lots of fuzzy guitar work here and lyrics which are vaguely anti-everything.

As one would expect for a band of this stature **Blitz**'s material has also resurfaced on other compilations. *No Future - The Punk Singles Collection* (Captain Oi! AHOY DLP 508) 1996 features *Someone's Gonna Die Tonight*, *Attack*, *Never Surrender* and *Warriors*. *Vol. 2* (Captain Oi! AHOY DLP 512) 1996 of the same series includes *Fight To Live*, *45 Revolutions*, *Razors In The Night* and *Youth*. They also contributed *Never Surrender* to *100% Hardcore Punk Rock* (Captain Oi! AHOY DCD 84) 1997.

Warriors a 1999 CD kicks off with two cuts *Youth* and *Nation On Fire* which originally appeared on the *Carry On Oi!* compilation. There are also three cuts - *Time Bomb*, *4Q* and *Criminal Damage* - from an EP recorded for No Future which remained in the can. The title track is included together with six cuts recorded live at the Lyceum. These are all worth a spin but the final four cuts are poor and date from 1989 when their guitarist Nidge reformed the band. He handled all the instruments himself and brought in Garry Basnett from **Attak** on vocals. This duo recorded a well-below-par album *The Killing Dream* for Skunk records. **Blitz** also resurfaced on the 1999 CD compilation *Oi! Fuckin' Oi!* (Harry May MAYO CD 110) with *Warriors*.

Punk Singles & Rarities 1980 - 83 comprises all of **Blitz**'s singles, compilation cuts and demos up to their *New Age* single in 1983. As with all Captain Oi!'s reissues it is nicely presented and includes sleevenotes by Mark Brennan.

BLITZ - Warriors.

Blitz

This five-piece was distinctive for their female vocalist and her unusual voice. They supported **Adam and The Ants** among others, but split in mid-1978 after all their equipment was stolen after a gig with **Open Sore**. Their sole vinyl legacy is the unusual opening cut *Strange Boy* to *Farewell To The Roxy* (Lightning LIP 2) 1978, on which the unique female vocals catch the ear. The album is now available on CD (Captain Oi! AHOY CD 86) 1998.

The Blitz Brothers

45s:	Gloria/Songs/Records (PS)	(Vertigo BLIT 21) 1979
	The Rose Tattoo/Walking Alone (PS)	(Vertigo BLIT 22) 1980

The Blitz Brothers were **Dalek I** and friends in disguise. Their version of *Gloria* is void of much of the excitement of the original, though.

Blitzkrieg

Personnel:	PHIL DIN	drms	A
	CHRIS HIND	bs	ABC
	MIC ROPHONE	vcls	ABC
	GARY 'GAZ' SUMNER	gtr	ABC
	JOHN McCALLUM	drms	B
	BAMBI	drms	C

EPs: 1(B) LEST WE FORGET (The Future Must Be Ours/
              Abuse Of Power/Destruction/Lest We Forget/
              Warfares Heroes)   (No Future Oi! 8) 1982
         2(C) ANIMAL LIPSTICK (Conscious Prayer/
              Land Of Failure/No Compromise)
                                    (Sexual Phonograph SPH 3) 1983

NB: All the above cuts and a few more besides are compiled on a split CD with **Insane** *The Punk Collection* (Captain Oi! AHOY CD 126) 1999.

Blitzkrieg were formed in Southport, Merseyside, in 1979 by line-up 'A'. They gigged quite extensively around the north of England during 1980 and their vinyl debut came in January 1981 when *The Future Must Be Ours*, which remains one of their finest songs, was included on *A Country Fit For Heroes* (No Future Oi! 3). This was later issued on CD with *Vol. 2* of the same series, *A Country Fit For Heroes Volume 1 & 2* (Captain Oi! AHOY CD 15) 1994.

By the time they signed a singles deal with No Future they had a new drummer John McCallum. The *Lest We Forget* (EP) contained five cuts including *The Future Must Be Ours* and was well received. It reached No. 11 in the indie chart and they embarked on a national tour with **The Varukers** and Mayhem in support.

In 1983, John McCallum was replaced on drums by Bambi and they released the *Animal Lipstick* (EP) on Illuminated Records subsidiary Sexual Phonograph. This got to No. 30 in the indie chart. By now there were quite a few personality clashes in the band and they split shortly after. Bambi and Gary Sumner went on to form a later version of **The Insane**. Chris Hind joined Mayhem.

In 1986, Bambi linked with Spike in his band The Parasites and toured the U.K.. They also released a split album with The Sanity Assassins. At the end of 1987 Spike and Bambi reformed **Blitzkrieg** with original member Gary Sumner and Trev from Bambi's later version of **The Insane**. That's

BLITZKRIEG/INSANE - The Punk Collection.

not the end of the story either.... there were two subsequent incarnations of **Blitzkrieg** in 1988 and 1990 (the later one recorded an album *The Future Must Be Ours* for the Retch label), but these exploits really are outside this book's timeframe. Most of their songs were fast-paced and frantic. Three of their best have later resurfaced on compilations. *Lest We Forget* and *The Future Must Be Ours* can both be heard on *No Future - The Punk Singles Collection* (Captain Oi! AHOY DLP 508) 1996. *Abuse Of Power*, with its screaming guitar intro resurfaced on *No Future - The Punk Singles Collection, Vol. 2* (Captain Oi! AHOY DLP 512) 1996.

Check out the split Captain Oi! CD with **Insane** for a complete rundown on their career. You'll also find *The Future Must Be Ours* on *100% Hardcore Punk Rock* (Captain Oi! AHOY DCD 84) 1997.

Blitzkrieg Bop

Personnel:	MICKY DUNN	gtr	A
	BLANK FRANK	vcls, keyb'ds	AB
	GLORIA	gtr	AB
	NICKY KNOXX	drms	AB
	MICK SICK	bs	AB
	TELLY SETTNEITHER	gtr	B

45s:	Let's Go/Nine Till Five/	
	Bugger Off (PS)	(Morton Sound MTN 3172/3) 1977
	Let's Go/Life Is Just So-So/	
	Mental Case (PS)	(Lightning GTL 504) 1977
	U.F.O./Bobby Joe (PS)	(Lightning GTL 543) 1978

Blitzkrieg Bop were the first punk band from the north-east of England. Their main influence was The Ramones, as their name suggests. They are affectionately remembered for their rare debut 45 released on Morton Sound in 1977. Only 500 copies were pressed and it's now a collectors'

BLOOD - Megalomania.

item, although it was re-recorded for their follow-up 45 - their first for Lightning.

In fact they'd been playing on the youth club circuit a while before the emergence of punk. *Top Of The Pops*, a 28-track CD compilation has all you'll want to hear of them and more including *Let's Go*, *Bugger Off* and *Police State* and it comes with copious sleevenotes. There's also a CD compilation *Top Of The Pops* (Overground OVER 69 CD) 1998.

U.F.O. later resurfaced on *Lightning Records Punk Collection* (Anagram CDPUNK 79) 1996.

Blood

Personnel:	J.J. BEDSORE	gtr	AB
	CARDINAL JESUS HATE	vcls	AB
	MUTLEY	bs	AB
	DR. WILDTHING	drms	A
	EVO TANKHEAD	drms	B

ALBUMS:	1(B)	FALSE GESTURES FOR A DEVIOUS PUBLIC	
			(Noise NOYZLP 1) 1982
	2( )	SICK KICKS FOR SHOCK ROCKERS	
			(Conquest QUEST 3) 1985

NB: (1) reissued on red vinyl (Link Classics CLINK 5) in the 1980s and also issued on CD (Mog MOGCD 008) 1998.

45s:	Megalomania/Calling The Shots/	
	Parasite In Paradise (PS)	(No Future Oi! 22) 1983
	Stark Raving Normal/Mesrine (PS)	(Noise NOYZ 1) 1983

Discovered by **Cockney Rejects'** Stinky Turner, **The Blood** were originally known as Coming Blood and came from Charlton in South-east London. As Coming Blood they made their vinyl debut contributing *Such Fun* to *Oi! Oi! That's Yer Lot* (Secret SEC 5) 1982. This is a very raw recording with growling vocals from Cardinal Jesus Hate. The song resurfaced again later on *100% British Oi!* (Captain Oi! AHOY DCD 83) 1997.

They signed to No Future for the *Megalomania* (EP) with **Frankie Flame**, who also played piano on the opening cut, handling production. They were championed by Oi! founder Garry Bushell. There was quite a metal as well as a punk influence on these three tracks. *Parasite In Paradise* is a stomping song with rampaging guitar and *Calling The Shots* was similar in style but is not quite as good. All three cuts later resurfaced on *Oi! The Singles Collection, Vol. 2* (Captain Oi! AHOY CD 63) 1996. *Megalomania* can also be heard on *No Future - The Punk Singles Collection* (Captain Oi! AHOY DLP 508) 1996.

They then moved to Noise Records for the *Stark Raving Normal* 45, which was the first release on Noise, a subsidiary of Syndicate Records. For this release Evo Tankhead, formerly of **Major Accident** and later in **Warfare**, took over on drums from Dr. Wildthing. The flipside *Mesrine* is excellent. The 45 made it to the Top 10 of the indie chart. *Stark Raving Normal* and *Mesrine* both later resurfaced on *Oi! The Singles Collection, Vol. 4* (Captain Oi! AHOY CD 71) 1997. *Stark Raving Normal* can also be heard on *Oi! Fuckin' Oi!* (Harry May MAYO CD 110) in 1999.

BLOOD - Stark Raving Normal.

They went on to record two albums *False Gestures For A Devious Public* and *Sick Kicks For Shock Rockers*. Later, in December 1987, they shared a split album with **The Gonads** *Full Time Result* (Link LP 024). There is still a version of the band on the road today.

The Blood were one of the first bands to mix punk with metal.

The Bloodclots

The Bloodclots contribute a punk rendition of *Louie Louie* to *Raw Deal* (Raw RAWLP 1) in 1977, but don't appear to have released any other vinyl output.

The Bloomsbury Set

45s:	This Year Next Year/		
	The Other Side Of You (PS)	(Graduate GRAD 13)	1980
	Hangin' Around With The Big Boys/		
	Getting Away From It All (PS)	(Stiletto STL 13)	1983
	Dress Parade/Serenade (PS)	(Stiletto STL 15)	1983

A band who were around for a while without attracting much attention. Both the lyrics and production on *Hangin' Around With The Big Boys* give a nod and a wink in the direction of flower-power.

Blue Movies

45:	Mary Jane/(this side by The Noise)	(Rok ROK IX/X) 1980

An obscure mod revival band. *Mary Jane* has a great intro and instrumentation but the vocals lack distinction. Nothing is known about the band, although you can also check out *Mary Jane* on *100% British Mod* (Captain Mod MODSKA DCD 8) 1998 or on *Odd Bods Mods And Sods* (Captain Mod MODSKA CD 2) 1996, on which it appears as a bonus track.

Blue Nile

Personnel:	ROBERT BELL	bs, synth	AB
(up to	PAUL BUCHANAN	vcls, gtr, synth	AB
1986)	PAUL JOSEPH MOORE	keyb'ds, synth	AB
	(CALUM MALCOLM	keyb'ds, vcls	B)
	(NIGEL THOMAS	drms	B)

HCP

ALBUM:	1(A)	A WALK ACROSS THE ROOFTOPS	
(up to			(Linn LKH 1) 1984 80
1986)			

NB: (1) Also issued on CD (Linn/Virgin LKHCD 1) 1988.

45s:	I Love This Life/The Second Act (PS)	(RSO RSO 84) 1981
(up to	Stay/Saddle The Horses (white PS)	(Linn LKS 1) 1984
1986)	Stay/Saddle The Horses (12", white PS)	(Linn LKS 1-12) 1984
	Stay (Remix)/Saddle The Horses (PS)	(Linn LKS 1) 1984
*	Stay (Remix)/Saddle The Horses/Tinsel Town	
	In The Rain/Heatwave (instrumental) (PS)	(Linn LKSD 1) 1984
	Stay (Extended Remix)/	
	Saddle The Horses (12", PS)	(Linn LKS 1-12) 1984
	Tinsel Town In The Rain/	
	Heatwave (instrumental) (PS)	(Linn LKS 2) 1984
	Tinsel Town In The Rain (Extended)/Regret/	
	Heatwave (instrumental) (12", PS)	(Linn LKS 2-12) 1984

NB: * Doublepack.

This unique Scottish trio formed in Glasgow in 1981. After a 45 on RSO, which is now very hard to find, they were offered a record contract by East Lothian label Linn. Part of the deal was that their sound was tested for hi-fi equipment. *A Walk Across The Rooftops*, their debut album released in April 1984, showed them to be capable of sophisticated, emotional and

BLUE ORCHIDS - The Greatest Hits (Money Mountain).

atmospheric music notable for Paul Buchanan's appealing voice. Highlights included the title cut, *Stay* which was released in no fewer than five different formats the same month and the exquisite *Tinsel Town In The Rain*, also later a 45. The album spent two weeks in the charts, peaking at No. 80. They were essentially a studio band, but later returned to tour the 'States in spring 1990 and also guested on Robbie Robertson's 1991 album *Storyville*. They made further recordings and achieved some commercial success in the nineties.

Blue Orchids

Personnel:	UNA BAINES	keyb'ds	A
	MARTIN BRAMAH	gtr, vcls	A
	RICK GOLDSHAW	gtr, bs	A
	I.F. ROGERS	drms	A

ALBUM:	1(A)	THE GREATEST HITS (MONEY MOUNTAIN)
		(Rough Trade ROUGH 37) 1982
EP:	1(A)	AGENTS OF CHANGE (12")
		(Rough Trade ROUGH 117 T) 1982

NB: (1) This was issued in a carrier bag.

45s:	Disney Boys/The Flood (PS)	(Rough Trade RT 065) 1981
	Work/	
	The House That Faded Out (PS)	(Rough Trade RT 067) 1981

A short-lived Manchester quartet. Both Baines and Bramah had previously played in **The Fall**. They produced a unique sound characterised by Baines' organ, jangling guitar and distinct, often flat, vocals. The EP was their strongest output. They also had a song *Low Profile* on *C-81* (Rough Tapes COPY 1), a 1981 NME-Rough Trade cassette compilation.

Blunt Instrument

Personnel:	BILL BENFIELD	gtr	A
	ROB SANDALL	vcls, gtr	A
	ED SHAW	bs	A
	DAVID SINCLAIR	drms	A

45:	No Excuse/Interrogation (PS)	(Diesel DCL 01) 1978

This late seventies punk combo changed names to **London Zoo**, when Benfield left in July 1978.

David Sinclair was later in **TV Smith's Explorers**.

Blurt

Personnel:	PETE CREESE	gtr, trombone	A
	JAKE MILTON	drms, vcls	A
	TED MILTON	vcls, sax	A

ALBUMS: (up to 1986)	1(A)	IN BERLIN	(Armageddon ARM 6) 1981
	2(A)	BLURT	(Red Flame) 1982
	3(A)	BULLETS FOR YOU	(Divine) 1984
	4(A)	FRIDAY THE 12TH	(Another Side) 1985
	5(A)	POPPYCOCK	(Toeblock TBL 002) 1986

NB: They also contributed one side to *Factory Quartet* (dble) (Factory FACT 24) in 1981.

45s:	My Mother Was A Friend Of The Enemy/ Get (PS)	(Test Pressing TB 1) 1980
	The Fish Needs A Bike/This Is My Royal Wedding Souvenir (PS)	(Armageddon AS 013) 1981
	White Line Fever (12")	(Another Side SIDE 8418) 1982

Blurt played minimalist music characterised by the sound of Ted Milton's alto sax and largely incoherent echoed vocals, Jake Milton's pulsating and monotonous drumbeat and Pete Creese's minimal guitar contributions.

Of their albums, *In Berlin* is one of the best. The vocals are clearer on *Bullets For You* recorded live in a wine cellar and *Friday The 12th* was another live album - recorded in Belgium.

Ted Milton also recorded a solo album *Love Is Like A Violence* in 1984.

B-Movie

Personnel: (up to 1986)	GRAHAM BOFFREY	drms	ABCDE
	PAUL STATHAM	gtr	ABCDEF
	STEVE HOVINGTON	vcls, bs	BCDE
	RICK HOLLIDAY	keyb'ds	CDEF
	LUCIANO CODEMO	bs	D
	MIKE PEDHAM	bs	E
	ANDY JOHNSON		F
	MARTIN SMEDLEY		F

ALBUM: (up to 1986)	1(F)	FOREVER RUNNING	(Sire 9252721) 1985

NB: Also relevant is *Dead Good Tapes* (Discussion WAXLP 1/WAXCD 1) 1988 and there was also a picture disc version of the album (WAXLP 1P).

EPs:	1(C)	TAKE THREE	(Dead Good DEAD 9) 1980
	2(C)	NOWHERE GIRL (12", EP)	(Dead Good BIG DEAD 12) 1980

HCP

45s: (up to 1986)	*	Remembrance Day/ (other side by **Soft Cell**) Remembrance Day/	(Lyntone LYN 10410) 1981 -
		Institution Walls (PS)	(Deram DM 437) 1981 61
		Marilyn Dreams/ Film Music (Part 1) (PS)	(Deram DM 443) 1981 -
		Marilyn Dreams/ Film Music (Part 1) (12", PS)	(Deram DMX 443) 1981 -
		Nowhere Girl/ Scare Some Life into Me (PS)	(Some Bizarre BZS 8) 1982 67

NB: * This red or green flexidisc came with issue 12 of 'Flexipop' magazine.

This post-punk combo was originally from Mansfield. They played a form of guitar and keyboard-orientated music, but were also linked by some with the New Romantic movement when Steve became their manager.

Boffrey and Statham had both originally been in a punk band The Aborted. Steve Hovington was added to the duo and they also played as Studio 10 before they finally decided on the name **B-Movie**. After sending a demo to the Lincoln-based Dead Good label they were invited to contribute two cuts to the compilation *East* (Dead Good GOOD 1) in 1980. Keyboardist Rick Holliday joined soon after. Their *Take Three* EP also came out in 1980 and was warmly received. A six track 12" EP *Nowhere Girl* was released a little while later.

In 1981, they switched to Deram for *Remembrance Day*, which again was quite well received by the critics. It also became their first hit spending three weeks in the charts and rising to No. 61. The follow-up *Marilyn Dreams* later that year was less successful. *Moles* was included on *Some Bizzare Album* (Some Bizzare BZLP 1) in 1981. They embarked on an European tour. Bassist Luciando Codemo came in for this tour, which meant Hovington only had to handle vocals.

After this, the line-up changes became more rapid. Codemo being replaced by Mike Pedham (ex-Everest The Hard Way). Boffrey left to join Soft As Ghosts and Holliday departed soon after for Six Sed Red. They were replaced by Andy Johnson and Martin Smedley. The new line-up recorded an album *Forever Running*, but by now the band was disintegrating.

Statham went on to play with Pete Murphy and Then Jericho. Hovington was later with One although he later re-united with Holliday.

Posthumously a lot of their material was issued on Wax and Dead Good, including *The Dead Good Tapes* (Wax WAXLP 1) 1988 (also available as a picture disc) and CD (Wax WAXCD 1) 1988 and *Remembrance Days* (Dead Good GOOD 3) 1991, which came with a 7" *The Fool/Swinging Lights* (CHEAP 1) 1991.

Bodies

Personnel:	MARK ADAMS	vcls, synth	A
	TONY COBLEY	drms	A
	MICK TONSLEY	gtr, bs	A
	LEON THOMPSON	gtr	A

45:	Art Nouveau/Machinery (PS)	(Waldo's HS 007) 1979

This came in a poster picture sleeve in five different colours, but later in a standard picture sleeve.

The Bollock Brothers

Personnel incl:	JOCK McDONALD	vcls	A

ALBUMS: (up to 1986)	1(A)	THE LAST SUPPER (dble)	(Charly BOLL 100) 1983
	2(A)	NEVER MIND THE BOLLOCKS '83	(Charly BOLL 101) 1983
	3(A)	LIVE PERFORMANCES (OFFICIAL BOOTLEG) (dble)	(Charly BOLL 102) 1983
	4(A)	'77 '78 '79	(Mausoleum KOMA 788011) 1985
	5(A)	THE 4 HORSEMAN OF THE APOCALYPSE	(Charly BOLL 103) 1985
	6(A)	ROCK 'N' ROLL SUICIDE	(Junk Rock JUNK 788010) 1986

NB: (1) also issued on CD (Charly CDCHARLY 175) 1989 and again (Charly CDCRH 103) 1997. (2) also issued on CD (Charly CDCHARLY 178) 1989 and again (Charly CDCRH 104) 1997. (3) also issued on CD (Charly CDCHARLY 174)

B-MOVIE - Nowhere Girl.

1989 and again (Charly CDCRH 102) 1997. (5) also issued on CD (Charly CDCHARLY 72) 1987 and (Charly CDCRH 109) 1997. There's also *The Best Of The Bollocks* (Charly CDCRM 1011) 1993 and *What A Load Of Bollocks* (Metrodome METRO 287) 2000.

45s:	Horror Movies/Enchantment (PS)	(Charly CTD 130)	1981
(up to	Slow Removal Of Van Gogh's Ear/		
1986)	Scream And Shout (12", PS)	(Charly BOLL 3)	1982
	The Bunker/The Boot Leg Man (12", PS)	(Charly BOLL 4)	1983
	Prince And The Showgirl/		
	Showgirls (12", PS)	(Disc DID 127700)	1984
	Drac's Back/Horror Movies (12")	(Charly BOLL 6)	1986
	Drac's Back/Horror Movies (7")	(Charly BOLL 7)	1986
	Harley Davidson (12")	(Play It Again Sam BIAS 36)	1986

Fronted by Jock McDonald **The Bollock Brothers** were only a half serious outfit. *The Last Supper* was a musically inept double studio album notable for including *Horror Movies*, a Munster-type dance tune which was probably their best known song.

Never Mind The Bollocks '83 was an amusing novelty record on which the band cover the whole of the **Sex Pistols**' debut album (including the cover design) but add their own lyrics too and employ a synthesizer with the result that many of the tunes sound more akin to a second division **New Order**. The album even features a guest vocal appearance from Michael Fagin (who was arrested for transversing security at Buckingham Palace) on *Pretty Vacant* and *God Save The Queen*.

Fagin crops up again on one side of *Live Performances*, which is a two record set of concert appearances. The material features most of the band's material and much of **The Sex Pistols'**.

The 4 Horseman contains material penned by McDonald, Alex Harvey and Vangelis, but it was produced by the band! A truely bizarre band!

The recent *What A Load Of Bollocks* (CD) is a good overall guide to their music.

The Bombers

Personnel:	EDDIE PARPWORTH	vcls, gtr	A
	RICHARD ROBERTS	gtr	A
	CLIFFORD SHIPMAN	drms	A
	PETE TOYE	bs	A

45:	I'm A Liar Baby/2230 AD (PS)	(The Label TLR 006)	1978

An ageing trio (two have beards and one is bald). An inoffensive punk record with a *Statue Of Liberty* riff.

Books

Personnel incl:	STEPHEN BETTS	vcls, synth	A

ALBUM:	1(A)	EXPERTISE	(Logo VOLUME 1) 1980

45s:	Broadcast/Hirohito	(Logo BOOK 1)	1980
	Photomaton/Take Us To Your Leader (PS)	(Logo BOOK 2)	1980
	Expertise/Fowie Church Clock (PS)	(Logo BOOK 3)	1980

A new wave electro-pop outfit centered around Stephen Betts. The album is well-produced by Colin Thurston. The music is flash but lacking in originality.

The Boomtown Rats

Personnel:	PETE BRIQUETTE	bs	AB
	GERRY COTT	gtr	A
	SIMON CROWE	drms	AB
	JOHNNY FINGERS	keyb'ds	AB
	BOB GELDOF	vcls	AB
	GARRY ROBERTS	gtr	AB

HCP

ALBUMS:	1(A)	THE BOOMTOWN RATS	(Ensign ENVY 1)	1977	18
	2(A)	TONIC FOR THE TROOPS	(Ensign ENVY 3)	1978	8
	3(A)	THE FINE ART OF SURFACING	(Ensign ENROX 11)	1979	7
	4(A)	MONDO BONGO	(Mercury 6359 042)	1980	6
	5(B)	V DEEP	(Mercury 6359 082)	1982	64
	6(B)	IN THE LONG GRASS	(Mercury MERL 38)	1985	-

NB: (1) reissued (Mercury PRICE 57) 1983. (2) reissued (Mercury PRICE 58) 1983 and also on CD (Mercury 5140532) 1993. (3) reissued (Mercury PRICE 73) 1984. (5) reissued on CD (Mercury 800 042-2) 1983.

HCP

45s:		Looking After # 1/Born To Burn/		
		Barefootin' (PS)	(Ensign ENY 4)	1977 11
		Looking After # 1/Born To Burn/		
		Barefootin' (12", PS)	(Ensign ENY 4)	1977 -
		Mary Of The 4th Form/Do The Rat (PS)	(Ensign ENY 9)	1977 15
		She's So Modern/Lying Again (PS)	(Ensign ENY 13)	1978 12
		Like Clockwork/How Do You Do? (PS)	(Ensign ENY 14)	1978 6
		Rat Trap/So Strange (PS)	(Ensign ENY 16)	1978 1
	*	Rat Pack	(Ensign)	1978 -
		I Don't Like Mondays/		
		It's All The Rage (PS)	(Ensign ENY 30)	1979 1
		Diamond Smiles/Late Last Night (PS)	(Ensign ENY 33)	1979 13
		Someone's Looking At You/		
		When The Night Comes (PS)	(Ensign ENY 34)	1980 4
		Banana Republic/		
		Man At The Top (PS)	(Ensign BONGO 1)	1980 3
		The Elephants Graveyard (Guilty)/		
		Real Difference (PS)	(Ensign BONGO 2)	1981 26
		Never In A Million Years/		
		Don't Talk To Me (PS)	(Mercury MER 87)	1981 62
	+	Dun Laoghaire	(Flexipop 003)	1981 -
		House On Fire/		
		Europe Looked Ugly (PS)	(Mercury MER 91)	1982 24
		House On Fire/Dub/		
		Europe Looked Ugly (12")	(Mercury MER 91)	1982 -
		Charmed Lives/No Hiding Place (PS)	(Mercury MER 106)	1982 -
		Charmed Lives/No Hiding Place/		
		Nothing Happened Today/		
		Storm Breaks (double-pack)	(Mercury MER 106)	1982 -
		Tonight/Precious Time (PS)	(Mercury MER 154)	1984 73
		Tonight/Precious Time/		
		Walking Downtown (12")	(Mercury MERX 154)	1984 -
		Drag Me Down/		
		An Icicle In The Sun (PS)	(Mercury MER 163)	1984 50
		Drag Me Down/		
		An Icicle In The Sun (12")	(Mercury MERX 163)	1984 -
		Dave/Hard Times (PS)	(Mercury MER 179)	1984 -
		Dave/Hard Times (picture disc)	(Mercury MER 179)	1984 -
		Dave/Hard Times/Live Side (12")	(Mercury MERX 179)	1984 -
		Hold Of Me/Never In A Million Years	(Mercury MER 184)	1985 -
		Hold Of Me/Say Hi To Mick/		
		Never In A Million Years (12")	(Mercury MERX 184)	1985 -
Reissue:		I Don't Like Mondays/Rat Trap	(Old Gold OG 9790)	1987 -

NB: * The first six singles in a plastic wallet. + A one-sided flexi disc issued in clear, red, green and yellow vinyl and given away free with 'Flexipop No. 3'.

BOOMTOWN RATS - Mary Of The 4th Form.

The Boomtown Rats came together in Dun Laoghaire, near Dublin in the second half of 1975. Bob Geldof, who'd been born in Dublin on 5th October 1954, had previously worked as a music journalist, for NME amongst others. Most of the band were former students and they were originally known as The Nightlife Thugs. Apparently Geldof chose the name **The Boomtown Rats** in a book he was reading about the American folk singer Woody Guthrie on the night of their first public gig at a Dublin high school in November 1975. As a kid Guthrie had been in a gang called The Boomtown Rats.

Their early months were spent gigging around Ireland. In October 1976, they moved to England and attracted attention from a handful of labels. They signed to Phonogram's Ensign subsidiary.

They toured the U.K. incessantly in the first half of 1977 and also played as a support act to the U.S. combo Tom Petty and The Heartbreakers. Their debut 45, *Looking After No. 1* was a high-energy punker. It climbed to No. 11 in the U.K. charts. The follow-up, *Mary Of The Fourth Form* was a similar anthemic pulsating punker which brought them a further Top 20 hit, peaking at No. 15.

Although the band rose to prominence on the crest of 1977's punk rock explosion, their debut album demonstrated their musical diversity. If *Looking After No. 1* was symptomatic of their punk credentials, lots more traditional rock influences are there too. *I Can Make It If You Can*, a ballad has been likened to Mott The Hoople, whilst *Joey's On The Street Again* was quite Springsteen-ish and *Never Bite The Hand That Feeds* recalls Dr. Feelgood. The album made the U.K. Top 20, climbing to No. 18 and enjoying eleven weeks in the charts.

Their next 45, *She's So Modern* climbed to No. 12 in May 1978 and *Like Clockwork* gave them their first Top 10 hit, peaking at No. 6 in July 1978. Both 45s previewed the more inventive and sophisticated sound of their second album *Tonic For The Troops*, which they both figured on. This spent forty-four weeks in the U.K. charts, peaking at No. 8. *Don't Believe What You Read* and *Me And Howard Hughes* are slick and catch the ears, but in *Rat Trap*, the album spawned an accessible No. 1 with wide appeal to rock as well as punk audiences. It topped the U.K. charts for two weeks.

The band's biggest selling single was inspired by a devastating event that took place on 29th January 1979 in San Diego, California. A schoolgirl named Brenda Spencer shot and killed several school pupils. When asked what lead her to do it she said "I don't like Mondays"! It was this sick tragedy which inspired Geldof to write the song. Prior to its release, they embarked on an American tour, which included an appearance at the California Music Festival, and ended at the New York Palladium. When it was released as a 45, *I Don't Like Mondays*, climbed to No. 1 in its second week and spent four weeks at the pinnacle of the charts. It was also their most controversial recording, Spencer's parents tried to have it banned in the U.S., where many radio stations refused to play it. Nonetheless, it gave them their only U.S. hit, climbing to No. 73 in March 1980.

Their next album, *The Fine Art Of Surfacing*, was patchy in comparison with previous efforts. On the positive side, it included the epic *I Don't Like Mondays*, the melodic *Someone's Looking At You* and the showstopper *When The Night Comes*, which is resplendent with some gorgeous Latin American acoustic guitar. The remainder, whilst technically fine is lacklustre and the material below par compared with previous efforts. Still by now the

BOOMTOWN RATS - Tonic For The Troops.

band could do little wrong and they made it to No. 7 in the album charts. It spawned further U.K. 45 hits too with *Diamond Smiles* (a No. 13) and *Someone's Looking At You* returned them to the Top 5 again (peaking at No. 4). Shortly after its release they set off on a World Tour which took them to Europe, the United States, Australia and Japan.

In December 1980, their next 45, *Banana Republic* bounced them back into the U.K. Top 5, peaking at No. 3, but in retrospect it sounds second rate to these ears, compared to their earlier 45s.

Their *Mondo Bongo* album, released in February 1981, continued their commercial success, rising to No. 6. Again, in retrospect, the verdict on the music must be inconclusive. There are fine moments, particularly the African-Caribbean style *Elephants Graveyard (Guilty)*, (which spawned a further 45 hit (No. 26)), *Don't Talk To Me* and *Up All Night*. There's some pleasing percussion on these but their rewrite of a Rolling Stones' tune (*Under Their Thumb... Is Under My Thumb*) was pretty disasterous and, like a few others, added little to the album.

Fans of the band may also be interested in a 5-track, Canadian-only EP *Rat Tracks*, released on Vertigo in 1981. It featured a remix of *Up All Night*, a live cut and a few other obscurities.

Never In A Million Years became their first 45 to fail to make the U.K. Top 30 but this was rectified by their next release *House On Fire*.

Another item of interest to collectors is the one-sided flexi-disc *Dun Laoghaire*, which was given away free with issue No. 3 of 'Flexipop' magazine in 1981. It came in clear, yellow, red or green vinyl.

Gerry Cott left the band early in 1981 and they persevered as a quintet. The fact they were now a quintet and their next album was their fifth influenced the choice of its title *V Deep*. Cott, incidentally, went on to release a couple of solo 45s. This album was better, but less successful

BOOMTOWN RATS - She's So Modern.

BOOMTOWN RATS - I Don't Like Mondays.

BOOMTOWN RATS - Someone's Looking At You.

commercially, only making the No. 64 slot. Their next 45, *Charmed Lives*, failed to chart at all. The highlight for Geldof in 1982 was arguably his starring role in Pink Floyd's 'The Wall'. There were signs he was looking to diversify and, after the final minor U.K. hits in 1984, *Tonight* and *Drag Me Down*, he concentrated on ventures new.

Geldof was taking an increasing interest in world humanitarian issues, particularly strarvation in Africa. In November 1984, he wrote with **Midge Ure** and organsied the recording of Band Aid's *Do They Know It's Christmas?* The galaxy of stars on this recording included the other **Boomtown Rats** members and from this point the band effectively ceased to exist. *Do They Know It's Christmas?* became the best-selling record of all time.

On 28th January 1985, he contributed to the equivalent U.S. humanitarian recording - U.S.A. for Africa's *We Are The World*. He organised Live Aid the same year and the band reformed to participate in this. He was knighted by the Queen, in acknowledgement of his humanitarian activities in 1986 and also married long-time girlfriend Paula Yates, but as you'll all know it later ended in tears.

The story was not quite over on the vinyl front. There's a U.S.-only *Retrospective* EP, released in 1983. Its six tracks included *Rat Trap*, *I Don't Like Mondays* and *Up All Night*.

The Boomtown Rats reformed for a final album *In The Long Grass*. They certainly looked wasted on the cover of what was a bitter and aggressive album. Some people rate it, but it failed to chart at all, so it was little suprise when Geldof launched a moderately successful solo recording career in November 1986. Geldof and Fingers also occasionally worked with Greedy Bastards.

Inevitably, **The Boomtown Rats** have been featured on several compilations. Appearances include *Looking After No. 1* on *New Wave* (Vertigo 6300 902) in 1977 and *The Best Punk Album In The World... Ever, Vol. 1* (2-CD) (Virgin VTDCD 42) 1995; *She's So Modern* on *That Summer!* (soundtrack) (Spartan/Arista SPART 1088) 1979, along with *Kicks*; *She's So Modern* on *Punk And Disorderly: New Wave 1976 - 1981* (Telstar STAR 2520) 1991 (also on CD) and *Rat Trap* on *The Best Punk Album... Ever, Vol. 2* (2-CD) (Virgin VTDCD 79) 1996. In 1999, *Looking After No. 1* was included on the 5-CD box set *1-2-3-4 - A History Of Punk And New Wave 1976 - 1979* (MCA/Universal 60066).

The Boomtown Rats rose to fame under the punk rock banner, but had the artistic independence and creativity to transcend punk into rock. They made some classic recordings along the way, especially in the late seventies/early eighties.

Bow Wow Wow

Personnel:	MATTHEW ASHMAN	gtr	A
	DAVE BARBEROSSA	drms	A
	LEROY GORMAN	bs	A
	ANNABELLA LWIN		
	(MYANT MYANT AYE)	vcls	A

HCP

ALBUMS: 1(A) SEE JUNGLE! SEE JUNGLE! GO JOIN YOUR GANG YEAH! CITY ALL OVER, GO APE CRAZY
(RCA RCALP 0027 3000) 1981 26
2(A) I WANT CANDY (compilation) (EMI EMC 3416) 1982 26
3(A) WHEN THE GOING GETS TOUGH, THE TOUGH GET GOING (RCA RCALP 6068) 1983 -

NB: (1) reissued in 1989 and also on CD (Great Expectations PIPCD 022) 1990 and (One Way OW 34502) 1997. (2) reissued in 1990 and also on CD (Great Expectations PIPCD 021) 1990. (3) reissued in 1990 and also on CD (Great Expectations PIPCD 022) 1990 and (One Way OW 34503) 1997. There's also some compilations:- *The Best Of Bow Wow Wow* (Receiver RRCD 116) 1989, also on vinyl; *Aphrodisiac (The Best Of Bow Wow Wow)* (Camden 74321419672) 1996 and *Girl Bites Dog - Your Compact Disc Pet* (EMI U.S.A. 7243 827223 2 8) 1994 and a live set, *Live In Japan* (Receiver RRCD 233) 1997.

HCP

CASS: 1(A) BOW WOW WOW - YOUR CASSETTE PET
(EMI WOW 1) 1980 58

BOW WOW WOW - I Want Candy.

HCP

45s/Cassettes:
* C-30 C-60 C-90 Go!/
Sun Sea And Piracy (EMI EMI 5088) 1980 34
+ W.O.R.K. (N.O. NAH NO NO MY DADDY DON'T)/
C-30.... Anda! (EMI TCEMI 5153) 1981 62
Prince Of Darkness/
Orang Utang (poster PS) (RCA RCA 100) 1981 58
Prince Of Darkness/Orang Utang/
Sinner Sinner Sinner (12", PS) (RCA RCA 12100) 1981 -
The Mile High Club/
C-30 C-60 C-90 Go! (Tour D'Eiffel TE 001) 1981 -
Chihuahua/Golly Golly Go Buddy (PS) (RCA RCA 144) 1981 51
Go Wild In The Country/
El Boss Dicho (PS) (RCA RCA 175) 1982 7
See Jungle (Jungle Boy)/
T.V. Savage (PS) (RCA RCA 220) 1982 45
I Want Candy
 (PS, one-sided etched 'B' side) (RCA RCA 238) 1982 -
I Want Candy/King Kong (PS) (RCA RCA 238) 1982 9
I Want Candy/See Jungle/Go Wild In The Country/
Chiuahua (cassette) (RCA RCXK 004) 1982 -
Louis Quatorze (re-recorded)/
Mile High Club (PS) (RCA RCA 263) 1982 66
Fools Rush In/
Uomo Sex Al Apache (inst) (PS) (EMI EMI 5344) 1982 -
% Elimination Dancing (New Version)/
King Kong (New Version) (Lyntone LYN 11358) 1982 -
$ Do You Wanna Hold Me?/
What's The Time (Hey Buddy) (PS) (RCA RCA 314) 1983 47
Reissue: Go Wild In The Country/
I Want Candy (Old Gold OG 9638) 1987 -

NB: * Some of these cassettes were issued in promo 'dog food' can with inserts. + A cassette-only release. # Also issued in 12" format. % This was a green or clear one-sided 33 r.p.m. flexidisc given away free with 'Flexipop' issue 18. $ There was also a picture disc version of this release.

Bow Wow Wow were put together in London in 1979 by entrepreneur **Malcolm McLaren**. He teamed up 15-year old singer Annabella Lwin with three former members of **Adam and The Ants**.

With **McLaren** publicising them they inevitably attracted controversy, particularly when their debut 45 *C-30 C-60 C-90 Go!*, which gave them a No. 34 hit, extolled the virtues of home taping. They followed this with *Your Cassette Pet*, a unique cassette-only collection of eight songs. Aside from a cover of Brook Benton's *Fool's Rush In*, the remaining seven were penned by the band and are notable for Annabella's breathless vocal style. Also of note was the drumming, which originated from the African Burundi tribe.

Two additional female backing vocalists were added during 1981. Their next two singles - *W.O.R.K.* and *Prince Of Darkness* - were minor hits and *Chihuahua* climbed to No. 51 in October 1981.

The same month their debut album was released with Annabella in an artistic nude pose on the cover. Her mother was furious at **McLaren**'s management of her and apparently he nearly replaced her with Boy George late in 1981! The debut album, was released with a different title, *Wild In*

The Country, in the 'States. Certainly the album, which climbed to No. 26, was a good one containing several of their 45 sides including *Prince Of Darkness*, *Chihuahua*, *Go Wild In The Country* and *See Jungle (Jungle Boy)*. The last two cuts climbed to No. 7 and 45 respectively when issued as 45s the following year. On the 1990 CD issue of this album the ordinary versions of several tracks are replaced by 12" versions.

They achieved a further Top Ten Hit in May 1982 with what possibly became their best known song, *I Want Candy*. A highly commercial number with a great beat, it was originally a hit for The Strangeloves in the 'States in June 1965. It was covered here by Brian Poole and The Tremeloes, who enjoyed a Top 30 hit with it the following month.

In 1982, **Bow Wow Wow** also had a four track EP *Last Of The Mohicans* released in the 'States, which included *I Want Candy*.

I Want Candy, presumably because of its commercial appeal, was also chosen as the title for a 1982 compilation. However, the content of the album here and Stateside was noticeably different. Here it included all the tracks from *Your Cassette Pet* (EP) (except *Louis Quatorze*), a few single cuts and the material from the earlier *Last Of The Mohicans* (EP), which included a re-recorded version of *Louis Quatorze*. Meanwhile the U.S. version of the album featured the four tracks from the *Last Of The Mohicans* (EP), four cuts from their debut album and two new ones. To complicate matters further a U.S.-only compilation album was released on Harvest in 1982 called *Twelve Original Recordings*. This featured an abridged version of the British *I Want Candy* release!

Bow Wow Wow's final 45 hit was *Do You Wanna Hold Me?*, which got to No. 47 in March 1983. February of that year saw the release of their final album *When The Going Get Tough, The Tough Get Going*. Well **Bow Wow Wow** disbanded after it! Annabella embarked on what proved to be a short and unsuccessful solo career and then retired from the music scene, although she returned in 1994. Matthew Ashman formed Chiefs Of Relief.

That final album was pretty good. It was made after they had parted company with **Malcolm McLaren**. It stuck pretty much to their earlier music format but they missed the level of publicity they enjoyed when **McLaren** was behind them pulling the strings.

An interesting band, well worth checking out - buy the U.K. *I Want Candy* compilation or the more recent *The Best Of Bow Wow Wow*, which came out on CD and vinyl in 1989.

I Want Candy benefitted from the inclusion of the *My Cassette Pet* tape-only release. *The Best Of Bow Wow Wow* includes *Go Wild In The Country*, *King Kong* and an alternate take of *Elimination Dancing* (not the album or 'Flexipop' version) which were all missing from *I Want Candy*, but it only includes an edited version of *W.O.R.K.* and like *I Want Candy* omits *Chihuahua*. So both are a good introduction to the band but neither is the definitive compilation.

Girl Bites Dog - Your Compact Disc Pet is a collection of non-album singles and one previously unissued cut *Cast Iron Cut*.

Aphrodisiac (The Best Of Bow Wow Wow), issued on BMG/Camden in 1996 includes their hit singles but there's a lot of dross on here too. It's hardly the most consistent of compilations.

The Box

Personnel incl:			
CHARLIE COLLINS	sax		A
PETER HOPE	vcls		A
PAUL WIDGER	gtr		A

ALBUMS:	1(A)	SECRETS OUT	(Go Disc VFM 4) 1983
	2(A)	GREAT MOMENTS IN BIG SLAM	(Go Disc VFM 5) 1984
	3(A)	MUSCLE OUT	(Double Vision DVR P3) 1985
EPs:	1(A)	NO TIME FOR TALK	(Go Disc VFM 1) 1983
	2(A)	THE MUSCLE IN	(Double Vision DVR 10) 1984

Hailing from Sheffield this band comprised former members of Sheffield funk outfit **Clock DVA**. Musically they combined the spontaneity of jazz with hard-edged rock to conjure up a frantic and quite unique end result. It works best on *Secrets Out*. *Muscle Out* released after they split was recorded live at the Leadmill in Sheffield.

The Boyfriends

Personnel:			
STEVE BRAY	drms		A
PAT COLLIER	vcls, gtr		A
MARK HENRY	bs		A
CHRIS SKORNIA	keyb'ds		A

45s:	I'm In Love Today/Saturday Night	(United Artists UP 36424) 1977
	Don't Ask Me To Explain/Jenny	(United Artists UP 36442) 1978
	Last Bus Home/Romance	(United Artists UP 36478) 1978

Led by Pat Collier who had earlier been in **The Vibrators**, **The Boyfriends** had a clean, youthful image with short hair, clean clothes and happy smiles. Musically, they played fast and melodic power-pop and they were one of the best bands of this ilk on the late seventies London gig circuit.

THE BOYFRIENDS - Last Bus Home.

The Boys

Personnel:			
JACK BLACK	drms		ABC
MATT DANGERFIELD	bs		ABC
JOHN PLAIN	gtr		ABC
DUNCAN 'KID' REID	vcls, gtr		ABC
CASINO STEEL	keyb'ds		A
RUDI	keyb'ds		C

				HCP
ALBUMS:	1(A)	THE BOYS	(NEMS NES 6001) 1977	50
	2(A)	ALTERNATIVE CHARTBUSTERS	(NEMS NEL 6015) 1978	-
	3(A)	TO HELL WITH THE BOYS	(Safari 12 BOYS) 1979	-
	4(B)	BOYS ONLY	(Safari BOYS 4) 1980	-

NB: (1) and (2) later reissued on coloured vinyl (Link CLINK 2) and (Link CLINK 3) respectively in the original sleeve artwork. (1) and (2) also issued on one CD (Loma LOMACD 12) 1994. (1) reissued on CD (Captain Oi! AHOY CD 101) 1999 with eight bonus cuts. (2) also reissued on vinyl (Get Back GET 53) 1999 with two 7" bonus tracks *Teacher's Pet* and *Schooldays*. (2) reissued on CD (Captain Oi! AHOY CD 104) 1999 with six bonus cuts. (3) and (4) also issued on one CD (Loma LOMACD 20) 1994. (3) reissued on vinyl (Get Back GET 51) 2000 in a gatefold sleeve with five bonus cuts. (3) reissued on CD (Captain Oi! AHOY CD 113) 1999 with five bonus cuts. (4) reissued on vinyl (Get Back GET 52) 2000 in a gatefold sleeve with three bonus cuts. (4) reissued on CD (Captain Oi! AHOY CD 117) 1999 with three bonus cuts. There have also been a number of interesting retrospective releases; *Odds And Sods* (Rough Trade RTD CD34-910) 1989 was a German release of previously unreleased songs from the 1977-81 era compiled by Die Toten Hosen's Campino; *Live At The Roxy* (Link CLINK 4) 1991, also on CD (Receiver RRCD 135) 1990 and *Learning English Vol. 1* (Charisma 91823) 1991, which includes a guest appearance from the band playing *Brickfield Nights*. They also shared a split disc with **The Vibrators** *BBC Radio One In Concert* (Windsong WINCD 036) 1993. More recent CD compilations are *The Best Of The Boys* (Dojo DOJOCD 137) 1995, *Complete Punk Singles Collection* (Anagram CDPUNK 85) 1996, *Punk Rock Rarities* (Captain Oi! AHOY CD 120) 1999 and *To Original Hell With / Odds And Sods* (Captain Oi! AHOY CD 144) 2000.

45s:	I Don't Care/Soda Pressing (PS)	(NEMS NES 102) 1977
	First Time/Whatcha Gonna Do/Tuning Grey (PS)	(NEMS NES 111) 1977

Brickfield Nights/Teacher's Pet (PS)	(NES NEW 116)	1978
* Kamikaze/Bad Days (PS)	(Safari SAFE 21)	1979
Terminal Love/I Love Me (PS)	(Safari SAFE 23)	1980
You Better Move On/Schoolgirls (PS)	(Safari SAFE 27)	1980
Weekend/Cool (PS)	(Safari SAFE 31)	1980
Let It Rain/Lucy (PS)	(Safari SAFE 33)	1980
Woch Woch Woch/One Way	(Parole)	1981

NB: * Some copies of this 45 came with a booklet.

Solid rather than exceptional, **The Boys** were actually much better received in Europe (the Belenux and Scandinavian countries in particular) than the U.K.. Casino Steel, their keyboard player and co-writer of much of the material on their first three albums was Norwegian. He'd been with The Hollywood Brats previously.

They formed in London in June 1976 and signed to NEMS Records early in 1977. Their debut single *I Don't Care* and the follow-up *The First Time* charted in a number of Benelux and Scandinavian countries. Like their eponymous debut album we're talking high energy power-pop, with pop and Beatlesque influences on some tracks, and more standard punk format. Their debut album made No. 50 in the U.K. charts for one week and was to give them their only chart success. The opening cut *Sick On You* had a glorious mock-malevolence that made it one of the ultimate punk-rock records:-

"I'm gonna be, gonna be sick on you!
I'm gonna be, gonna be sick on you!
And if I'm gonna puke, you betcha life I'll puke on you!
(from *Sick On You*)

Other powerful numbers include *Tumble With Me*, *Tonight*, *No Money*, *Box Number* and *Cop Cars* and the final cut *Living In The City*:-

"Living in the city under traffic control
It's just enough to make you believe
There's a subway to heaven and an underground to kingdom come
Living in the city under shadows of things to come
Everywhere I turn there's lights like a midnight sun!"
(from *Living In The City*)

Their debut album has had various reissues since. The Captain Oi! CD reissue came with a total of eight bonus cuts, including their alter ego **The Yobs**' Xmas ditty *Run Rudolph Run* and *The Worm Song*. The bonus **Boys**' cuts comprise *Whatcha Gonna Do* and *Turning Grey*; a long version of *The First Time*, demo versions of *Lonely Schooldays* and *Take A Heart* and an alternative version of *I Don't Care*. The package also comes with a twelve-page booklet containing liner notes and lyrics to classics like *The First Time*, *I Don't Care* and *Sick On You*. There was also a Japanese-only vinyl release of this set.

Strangely, *Alternative Chartbusters* seemed better, complete with two fine pop-punk singles *Brickfield Nights* and the previously released *First Time*, alongside a number of engaging tunes and often humourous lyrics. *Sway (Quien Sera)*, though, was a rather strange amalgam of samba and punk. There's an hilarious ballad *Backstage Pass* and a lush ballad *Heroine*, whilst *Do The Contract Hustle* appeared to be a comment on the state of the music industry. This album was re-released on Link in 1990, with a slightly different track listing. In 1999, Captain Oi! reissued it in its original format plus six bonus cuts, including the deliberately naff *Silent Night* (under their alter ego **The Yobs**). The other five bonus cuts are *Teacher's Pet*, *Schooldays*, *Lies*, *She's No Angel* and *You're The Other Man*. The lyrics to all songs and a detailed history of the album all figure in a twelve-page deluxe booklet which accompanied the CD. There was also a Japanese-only vinyl version of this release and there's an Italian reissue on Get Back, which came with two 7" bonus cuts *Teacher's Pet* and *Schooldays*.

After this **The Boys** switched to the independent Safari label. They released five 45s and two albums on this label. Their *To Hell With The Boys* album featured organ for the first time and more dual guitar work than previously. This made for a more rounded, fuller sound but didn't capture the imagination of the British record buying public. The album featured their singles *Terminal Love* and *Kamikaze*. The CD reissue on Captain Oi! comes with five bonus cuts; the single *You Better Move On* and its flip side *Schoolgirls*; *I Love Me* (the flip side to *Terminal Love*) and two more **Yobs** songs *Rub A Dum Dum* and *Another Christmas*. Alternatively, if you're into vinyl, the Get Back reissue of the album also contains five bonus cuts, lyrics and detailed liner notes by Mark Brennan.

The downward spiral accelerated when Steel was deported. They soldiered on as a four-piece but the resulting *Boys Only* album was disappointing. It included their version of the Sam Cooke classic *Wonderful World* and their last two Safari singles *Weekend* and *Let It Rain*. The Captain Oi! CD reissue of this comes with three bonus cuts; the single version of *Terminal Love*, *Cool* (the flip side to *Weekend*) and *Lucy* (flip side to *Let It Rain*). It also contains a booklet with full lyrics and the story of the album. Again there's a vinyl alternative on Get Back with three bonus cuts, liner notes from Mark Brennan and lyrics. They split up after a final 45 for the Parole label.

Ah yes, the story isn't quite over... They also recorded two sessions for John Peel. The first featured *Sick On You*, *First Time*, *Rock Relic*, *Living In The City* and *Cop Cars* went out on 8th August 1977. The second featuring *TCP*, *Boys*, *Classified Suzie* and *Brickfield Nights* on 15th May 1978. The *Odds and Sods* album put out by Rough Trade in 1989, includes previously unreleased material by the band. They also shared a *BBC Radio One In Concert* album with **The Vibrators** in 1993.

Their *Live At The Roxy Club* set from 1977 veered towards power pop and sounded relatively melodic for early punk rockers. It displayed, however, little originality, which offered early insight into why they were always destined to remain minor league punk-rockers. On their split BBC *Radio 1 Live In Concert* CD with **The Vibrators** they show up quite well with their fairly melodic pop-punk contributions like *First Time* and *Cop Cars*.

The *Punk Rock Rarities* CD in 1999 compiles their demos, unreleased mixes and unreleased material like *Little Runaround*, which was intended for the *Boys Only* album. There's plenty to interest the band's fans here, as well as guitarist Matt Dangerfield's funny sleevenotes.

To Original Hell With comprises demos of songs on their *To Hell With The Boys* album, except for *Independent Girl*. The material was originally released by Casino Steel on his Revolution imprint in 1989. The same year *Odds And Sods*, a collection of previously unreleased tracks recorded between 1977 and 1981, was compiled by Die Toten Hosen vocalist Campino and put out on the German label Totenkopf. This two on one CD collection will be welcomed by **The Boys**' fans.

As explained earlier **The Boys** also had an alter-ego, **The Yobs**. See that entry for details.

'Honest' John Plain, their guitarist, later recorded an album called *New Guitars In Town* with **Lurker** Pete Stride. Both bands played in support and indeed, became quite closely associated over time.

The First Time was also included on the *20 Of Another Kind* (Polydor SUPER POLS 1006) compilation in 1979 and again on the 5-CD set *1-2-3-4 - A History Of Punk And New Wave 1976 - 1979* (MCA/Universal 60066) in 1999.

Brakes

Personnel:	JOHN BROWN	drms	A
	JOE FADIL	gtr, vcls	A
	BOB PENNY	bs	A
	KEITH WILSON	gtr, vcls	A

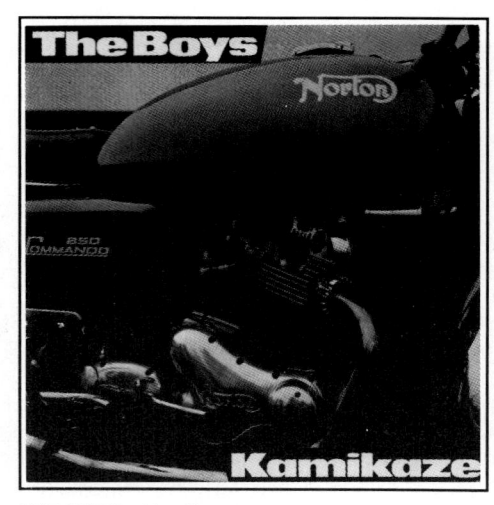

THE BOYS - Kamikaze.

ALBUM: 1(A) FOR WHY YOU KICKA MY DONKEY
(Magnet MAGL 5029) 1979

45s: The Way I See It/
Never Making Love (PS) (Magnet MAG 154) 1979
Blame It On The Brakes/
Doing Life (PS) (Magnet MAG 161) 1980

Brakes sounded similar to bands like **The Gas** - a sort of more aggressive version of bands like **The Vapors**.

Breakout

A hardcore punk band whose *Waste Away* on the compilation *Wet Dreams* articulated the frustration skinheads faced because of their appearance:-

"Skinhead on the dole with nothing to do
An ordinary kid like me and you
He has no job his life was wasting away
Waiting for the weekend everyday
Waste away wasting away
Waste away wasting away
Waste away wasting away
Wasting away can't face another day
He wanted a future, wanted any sort of job
But because he had short hair they called him a yob
He tried and tried, couldn't get anywhere
Because of his appearance, I'd call that unfair"
(from *Waste Away*)

This is an excellent punchy song with great guitar.

Brent Ford and The Nylons

45: 19th Nervous Breakdown/
Big Rock Candy Mountain (Brumbeat) 1978

Issued on the Brumbeat label with no catalogue number and no picture sleeve. The latter was unusual in the punk era. Who were they?

BRIAN BRAIN - Another Million Miles.

Brian Brain

Personnel: MARTIN ATKINS   A

EP: 1(A) CULTURE (Fun People/At Home He's A Tourist/
Working In A Farmyard In A White Suit/
Careeing (Secret SHH 109) 1980

45s: They've Got Me In The Bottle/I Get Pain (Secret SHH 101) 1978
Another Million Miles/
Personality Counts (PS) (Secret SHH 105) 1979
Jive Jive/
Hello To The Working Classes (PS) (Secret SHH 119) 1981
Funky Zoo/Flies (PS) (Secret SHH 142) 1982

This guy (Martin Atkins) is better known for his spells as drummer in **Public Image Ltd** (briefly in 1980 and again from May 1982 - mid-1984). He was born in Coventry in August 1959.

His EP, which is anarchic and lighthearted, is hampered by poor recording quality and consequently a rather flat sound. *Another Million Miles* and its flipside *Personality Counts* are offbeat and a bit messy

There was a fast medium bowler called Brian Brain who played cricket for Worcestershire and Gloucestershire in the sixties and seventies! Not a name I imagine too many people have!

Brick Wall Band

Personnel: MARTIN FOSTER   gtr   A
IAN GODDARD   drms   A
CHRIS IRELAND   vcls   A
PETE MALLINSON   lead gtr   A
JOHN MURRAY   bs   A
(TONY NAYLOR   keyb'ds   A)

This band can be heard playing *Distant Drums* on *499 2139* (Rocket DIAL 1) 1979, with Tony Naylor guesting on keyboards. It is a pop-punkish rendition of Jimmy Reeves' 1966 No. 1 hit, which picks up pace and is quite catchy after a slow intro.

Brilliant

Personnel: PAUL FERGUSON   drms   A
PAUL RAVEN   bs   A
MARTIN GLOVER YOUTH   gtr, bs   ABC
MARCUS   B
STEPHAN   B
TIN TIN   B
JIMMY CAUTY   gtr   C
JUNE LAWRENCE   vcls   C

ALBUM: 1( ) KISS THE LIPS OF LIFE (Food BRILL 1) 1986

EP: 1( ) Soul Murder/Growler/
Soul Murder (12") (Food SNAK 001) 1984

HCP

45s: That's What Friends Are For/
(up to   Push (PS) (Limelight LIME 7001) 1981 -
1986)   Colours/Colours (Monster
Mix) (12", PS) (Rough Trade RTT 105) 1983 -
* It's A Man's Man's World/
Crash The Car (PS) (Food FOOD 5) 1985 -
It's A Man's Man's World/Crash The Car/It's A Dub
Dub Dub World (12", PS) (Food FOODT 5) 1985 58
Love Is War/The Red Red Groovy (PS) (Food FOOD 6) 1986 64
Love Is War/The Red Red Groovy/
Ruby Fruit Juice (12", PS) (Food FOODT 6) 1986 -
Love Is War (pic. disc) (Food FOOD 6PT) 1986 -
Somebody/The Burning Necklace (PS) (Food FOOD 7) 1986 67
Somebody/The Burning Necklace/
Love Is War (12", PS) (Food FOODT 7) 1986 -
The End Of The World/
How High Is The Sun (PS) (Food FOOD 8) 1986 -
The End Of The World/
How High Is The Sun (12", PS) (Food FOODT 8) 1986 -

NB: * Also issued as a picture disc.

Brilliant was formed by ex-**Killing Joke** bassist Martin Glover Youth. The original line-up also featured former **Killing Joke** members Paul Ferguson and Paul Raven, although they soon returned to **Killing Joke**. They underwent further changes and the line-up eventually stabilised at 'C'. They were critically acclaimed, particularly for their gorgeous cover version of James Brown's *It's A Man's Man's World*, which spent five weeks in the charts in 1985. They enjoyed two further minor hits with *Love Is War* and *Somebody* the following year and released an album *Kiss The Lips Of Life*, but they failed to build on their earlier promise in commercial terms.

Broken Bones

Personnel:	BAZ	drms	A
	BONES	gtr	A
	NOBBY	vcls	A
	TEZZ	bs	A

ALBUMS:	1( )	DEM BONES	(Fallout FALLLP 028P) 1984
(up to	2( )	F.O.A.D.	(Fallout FALLLP 041) 1987
1987)	3( )	DECAPITATED	(Fallout FALLLP 043) 1987

NB: (1) is a picture disc album. It was also issued on CD (Fallout FALLCD 028) 1990. (3) also issued as a picture disc (043P).

45s:	Decapitated/Problem/	
(up to	Liquidated Brains (PS)	(Fallout FALL 020) 1985
1986)	Cruxifix/Fight The Good Fight/	
	I.O.U. (PS)	(Fallout FALL 025) 1985
*	Seeing Through My Eyes/The Point Of Agony/	
	It's Like (PS)	(Fallout FALL 034P) 1985
	Seeing Through My Eyes/The Point Of Agony/It's Like/	
	Decapitated Part 2/	
	Death Is Imminent (10", PS)	(Fallout FALL 10034) 1985
	Never Say Die/10,s Or A Dime/	
	Gotta Get Out Of Here (12", PS)	(Fallout FALL 039) 1986

NB: * Picture disc release.

Broken Bones were formed by ex-**Discharge** members Bones and Tezz. Line-up 'A' above is the initial one but they subsequently underwent many changes. Briefly, in the mid-eighties they were at the forefront of U.K. hardcore punk along with **Discharge**. In addition to the above releases, they also had a video *Live At Leeds* (Visionary/Jettisoundz JE 129) in October 1984.

They continued to record long after the time frame of this book, moving in a more metal direction for albums like *Losing Control* (Heavy Metal HMRLP 133) 1989, *Trader In Death* (Heavy Metal HMRLP 141) 1990, *Stitched Up* (Rough Justice JUST 18) 1991 and *Brain Death* (Rough Justice JUST 19) 1992.

Four of their finest moments - *Decapitated, Cruxifix, Through My Eyes* and *Never Say Die* - were later included on *The Fallout Punk Singles Collection* (Anagram CDPUNK 30) in 1994. The blistering *Decapitated* with its striking opening has also resurfaced on *100% Hardcore Punk* (Captain Oi! AHOY DCD 84) 1998.

Tezz was playing with Battalion Of Saints and **The Business** in the late nineties.

The Brothers Gonad

Personnel:	GAL GONAD	A
	MAX SPLODGE	A

EP:	1(A)	DELILAH (Delilah/Lager Top/Sandra/	
		My Grandma) (PS)	(Razor RAZ 103) 198?

This was a spin-off project from **The Gonads** and **Splodgenessabounds**. The result was a comedy punk EP! Some tracks later resurfaced on *Razor Records Punk Collection* (Anagram CDPUNK 45) 1995.

B-Team

45:	All I Ever Wanted/Bad Day	(Diamond DIA 8) 1985

A little known mod revival band. You'll also find both sides of their 45 on *This Is Mod, Vol. 4 (Modities)* (Anagram CDMGRAM 107) 1996.

Bullets

45:	Girl On Page 3/Grammar School Girls	(Big Bear BB 16) 1978

A five-piece Birmingham band. They ran into legal difficulties with 'The Sun' newspaper as a result of *Girl On Page 3*.

THE BUSINESS - Suburban Rebels.

The Burial

This five-piece from Scarborough in the north-east of England blended Oi! with ska. They made their vinyl debut with their two contributions, *Friday Night* and *Old Man's Poison* to *Oi! Of Sex* (Syndicate SYNLP 4) in 1984. This was later reissued on CD (Captain Oi! AHOY CD 23) 1994. *Friday Night* later resurfaced on *100% British Oi!* (Captain Oi! AHOY DCD 83) 1997. Not one of the stronger Oi! bands.

They later remodelled themselves as a pop band in the mould of The Housemartins and recorded an album *A Day On The Town* for Skank Records.

Burial were also the backing band for Nick Toczeck.

Jean-Jacques Burnel

HCP

ALBUMS:	1	EUROMAN COMETH	(United Artists UAG 30214) 1979	40
	2	FIRE AND WATER	(Epic EPC 25707) 1983	-

NB: (1) reissued on Mau Mau (P MAU 601) 1988 as a picture disc and also issued on CD (EMI CDEMC 3615) 1992 and again (Eastworld EW 002CD) 1998. (2) credited to **Jean-Jacques Burnel and Dave Greenfield**. There's also a second CD *Un Jour Parfact* (CBS 4624242) 1986 which was available on import and eventually released on CD (SIS SISCD 002) 1994.

45s:	Freddie Laker (Concorde And Eurobus)/	
	Ozymandias (PS)	(United Artists UP 36500) 1979
+	Girl From The Snow Country/Ode To Joy (live)/	
	Do The European (live) (PS)	(United Artists BP 361) 1980
*	Rain And Dole And Tea/	
	Consequences (PS)	(Epic EPCA 4076) 1984

NB: + Unissued. * Credited to **Jean-Jacques Burnel** and Dave Greenfield.

These were solo projects for **The Stranglers'** Jean-Jacques Burnel some of which were made with Dave Greenfield. As his name suggests, he was French, and he was also a keen biker and a former skinhead. He secured an economics degree from Bradford University, but was working as a van driver in Guidford, Surrey, when he met Hugh Cornwell, which led to him joining **The Stranglers**.

His first solo album *Euroman Cometh* spent five weeks in the charts peaking at No. 40. Released in 1979 the album's concept of a united Europe seemed a long-way off but less so today. Of the eleven original cuts, some were sung in French and some in German. On the album he was assisted by Carey Fortune (ex-**Chelsea**), Pete Howells (ex-**Drones**), Brian James (gtr) (ex-**Damned**) and Lew Lewis (hrmnca) (ex-**Eddie and The Hot Rods**). He also embarked on a short, unsuccessful tour to help promote the album. His touring band comprised Howells, Lewis, John Ellis (ex-**Vibrators**), who also played for the support band Rapid Eye Movement and Penny Tobin (keyb'ds). The 1992 CD reissue features nine bonus live tracks recorded at Hemel Hempstead. Whilst the instrumentation is interesting and atmospheric, the vocals suffer from being monotonous at times, rendering this some way short of a classic.

In 1980, *Girl From The Snow Country* was scheduled for solo release and then withdrawn. The copies that did get into circulation are now among the most collectable new wave releases. Expect to pay in excess of £400, but beware the 45 has been bootlegged.

Burnel later teamed up with Dave Greenfield on a soundtrack for the Vince Coudanne film 'Ecoutez Vos Mars'. Then in 1986, he formed a sixties covers band called the Purple Helmets with John Ellis, Alex Gifford and Laurent Sinclair. Although he assembled the band for a one-off gig at the 'Trans Musicale Avant Festival' in France, initially, he kept it together with Greenfield replacing Sinclair. Former Tears For Fears drummer Manny Elias later joined.

Un Jour Parfait was originally a European-only release just available here on import. However, it was eventually released here on CD by Stranglers Information Service in 1994. Much of the material is acoustic, recalling **The Stranglers**' *Feline* period but *Weekend* and *Tristeville Le Soir* are rockier. The CD reissue contained three previously unreleased tracks and came in a new sleeve.

The Business

Personnel:	NICK CUNNINGHAM	drms	A
	MICKY FITZ	vcls	ABCD
	STEVE KENT	gtr	A D
	MARTIN SMITH	bs	A
	KEV BOYCE	drms	B
	MARK BRENNAN	bs	BCD
	STEVE WHALE	gtr	BCD
	MICKY FAIRBAIRN	drms	CD

ALBUMS:	1(B)	SUBURBAN REBELS	(Secret SEC 11) 1983
	2(B)	1980-81 OFFICIAL BOOTLEG	(Syndicate SYNLP 2) 1983
	3(B)	LOUD, PROUD 'N' PUNK LIVE	(Syndicate SYNLP 6) 1984
	4(C)	SATURDAY HEROES	(Harry May SE 13) 1985
	5(-)	SINGALONEABUSINESS	(Dojo DOJO LP 35) 1986
	6(D)	WELCOME TO THE REAL WORLD	(Link LINK LP 035) 1988
	7(D)	SMASH THE DISCOS	(Link LINK LP 046) 1988
	8( )	IN AND OUT OF BUSINESS	(Link LRMO 1) 1990

NB: (1) also issued on CD (Captain Oi! AHOY CD 7) 1993 with four bonus tracks. (1) and (6) also reissued on one CD (Loma LOMACD 32) 1994. (2) also issued on CD (Mog MOGCD 002) 1998. (3) also issued on CD (Step STEP CD 024) 1998. (4) also issued on CD (Captain Oi! AHOY CD 013) 1994 with five bonus tracks and again in 1998. (5) also issued on CD (Captain Oi! AHOY CD 19) 1994. (6) also issued on CD (Captain Oi! AHOY CD 2) 1993 and again in 1998. (7) also issued on CD (Mog MOG CD 001) 1998. (8) was available mail-order only. They also had three tracks on *The Secret Punk Singles Collection.* (Anagram CD PUNK 13). Other relevant releases include *Keep The Faith* (Century Media CM 770832) 1998, *Truth The Whole Truth And Nothing But The Truth* (Burning Heart BHR 067 CD) 1997, *The Best Of The Business* (Link LINK CD 156) 1992, *The Best Of The Business* (Dojo DOJOCD 124) 1993, *The Complete Singles Collection* (Anagram CDPUNK 57) 1995, *The Best Of The Business* (Snapper SMMCD 539) 1998 and *Harry May* (Harry May CAN CAN 011) 2001.

EP:	1(B)	OUT OF BUSINESS (H-Bomb/Tell Us The Truth/ Last Train To Clapham Junction/Do They Owe Us A Living/Law And Order)	(Secret SHH 150) 1983

NB: (1) promotional only white label release.

45s: (up to 1986)	Harry May/ National Insurance Blacklist (PS)	(Secret SHH 123) 1981
	Smash The Discos/Disco Girls/Dayo (The Banana Boat Song) (PS)	(Secret SHH 132) 1982
	Get Out Of My House/All Out Tonight/Foreign Girl/ Outlaw (12" PS)	(Wonderful World Of... 121) 1985
	Drinking N Driving/H-Bomb (live) (PS)	(Diamond DIA 001) 1985
	Drinking N Driving/H-Bomb (live)/Hurry Up Harry/ Drinking N Driving (orig. version)	(Diamond DIA 001T) 1985

A four-piece formed in Lewisham, South London during 1979. They were closely associated with the Oi! Movement which grew up in the early eighties. They were part of a package that described itself as Oi! Against Racism And Political Extremism But Still Against The System. Line-up 'A' recorded *Product* and *Suburban Rebels* for the *Carry On Oi!* (Secret SEC 2) 1981 compilation, which was later reissued on CD (Captain Oi! AHOY CD 119) 1999. *Product* can also be heard on *100% British Oi!* (Captain Oi! AHOY DCD 83) 1997. *Suburban Rebels* is one of their finest moments with great guitar riffs and an anthemic chorus which articulated the feelings of the early Oi! movement:-

"They're the sons and daughters
Of well off bankers
Tom Robinson's army of trendy wankers
Flared blue jeans and anoraks
With yellow streaks all down their backs
Who act so tough when they're on TV
But trendy wankers don't scare me

Oi Oi Oi the chosen few
This is what we think of you
Oi Oi Oi the chosen few
This is what we think of you

Suburban rebels playing at reds
You would be urban terrorists
You don't scare us with your badges and banners
You know fuck all about heavy manners"
(from *Suburban Rebels*)

They were the support act at the **4-Skins** calamitious gig at the Hamborough Tavern, but they split just before Secret Records released their first 45 *Harry May* in November 1981. *Harry May* mixed punk with raucous pop and also benefitted from a rousing chorus and pulsating guitar work. The song was originally formulated as a naff version of a **Sham 69** song with Micky Fitz shouting "Harry May" frequently throughout. The flip side *National Insurance Blacklist* drew attention to the unofficial blacklist operated by the building trade on anyone considered too conversant with Trade Union rights. Again, the guitar playing on this catches the ear. Both

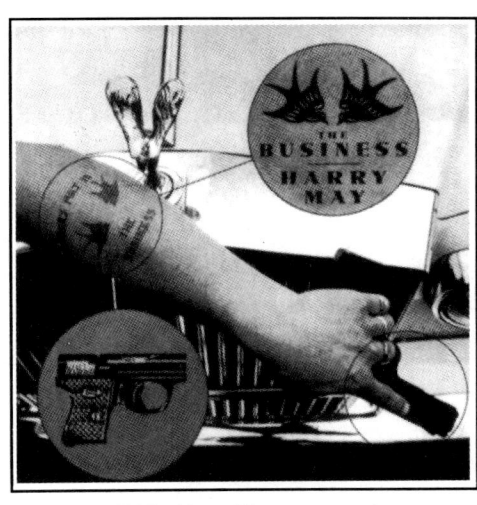

THE BUSINESS - Harry May.

THE BUSINESS - Smash The Discos.

sides of this 45 can also be heard on *Oi! The Singles Collection, Vol. 1* (Captain Oi! AHOY CD 60) 1996. To keep interest in the band alive the label released a version of *Step Into Christmas* on its compilation EP *Bollocks To Christmas* (Secret SHH 126) in 1981.

The band reformed in the summer of 1982 with a modified line-up ('B'). Brennan, Boyce and Whale all joined from a South-east London band called The Blackout. *Smash The Discos* again had a strong chorus and catchy guitar segments. The flip side *Disco Girls* had a strong rhythm backing and was about girls who went out without spending any money on their drinks. The third cut *Dayo* was an Oi! arrangement of the traditional Negro spiritual. Their *Smash The Discos* single was well received and spent five weeks at No. 2 in the indie chart. It lead to the formation of 'The Anti Disco League'. All three of these tracks later resurfaced on *Oi! The Singles Collection, Vol. 3* (Captain Oi! AHOY CD 67) 1997.

Their early punk albums were well received. *Suburban Rebels*, produced by **Cockney Rejects** Micky Geggus, was a barnstorming set released in 1983. Dominated by the superb title cut, it also included their *Harry May* 45 and the original version of live favourite *Drinking And Driving*. The 1993 CD reissue of this album on Captain Oi! comes with four bonus tracks - the three cuts from their *Smash The Disco* single and *Loud Proud 'N' Punk*, which they'd contributed to the *Total Noise* (EP) (Total Noise TOT 1) in 1982. The Secret label closed in 1983 and they continued to record on various labels including Syndicate, Wonderful World Of, Diamond and Link before splitting at the end of the eighties.

Their *Out Of Business* 12" white label EP featured five songs from their unreleased debut album that weren't re-recorded for their *Suburban Rebels* album. Secret, who were going bust, planned to release it as their parting shot but went under before they could, leaving just a handful of test pressings behind, making this one of the most valuable and collectable Oi! artefacts.

A second studio album *Saturday's Heroes* followed on Harry May Records in 1985. By now Micky Fairbairn had replaced Kev Boyce on drums. Its eleven cuts were in the same barnstorming style as *Suburban Rebels*. The title cut articulated the Oi! philosophy:-

"There's a handy little firm at the game today
Having a laugh causing trouble on the way
Rucking on the terrace, bundles in the street
Fighting for glory in half lit streets
Gonna take away my I.D. card
But you'll never get me down Scotland Yard
We're Saturday's Heroes'"
(from *Saturday's Heroes*')

You'll also find *Saturday's Heroes*, along with *Handball* (from the later *Welcome To The Real World*) album, on *Trouble On The Terraces - 16 Classic Football Anthems* (Step-1 STEP LP 91) 1996. The *Saturday's Heroes*' album also included a new version of their live favourite *Drinking 'N' Driving*, a remix of *All Out Tonight* and other stand-out cuts were *Freedom* and *Nothing Can Stop Us*. The Captain Oi! CD reissue of this album came with five bonus cuts. First there's their version of **Sham 69**'s

THE BUSINESS - Saturday Heroes.

THE BUSINESS - Welcome To The Real World.

Hurry Up Harry, then three of the four tracks from their *Get Out Of My House* (12") (*Foreign Girl* is already on the album) and finally a compilation cut *Coventry*. The *Saturday's Heroes*' album was a U.K. indie chart Top 10 album.

Singalongabusiness issued by Dojo in 1986 was a 'best of' from the band's early years including their indie hit singles *Harry May*, *Smash The Discos*, *Get Out Of My House* and *Loud Proud 'N' Punk* plus other of their classic tracks like *Suburban Rebels*, *Real Enemy* and *Product*. The Captain Oi! 1994 CD reissue of this adds two bonus cuts, a 1989 45 *Do A Runner* and the ultra-rare *Get Your Tits Out*.

By the time of their third 'proper' studio album released by Link in 1989 **The Business** had expanded to a five-piece with original guitarist Steve Kent rejoining. This includes their *Do A Runner* single from the same year and the anti-Maradonna football ode *Hand Ball*:-

"Three thousand miles is a long way to go
To be beaten by a dwarf in Mexico
He was a cheat who didn't give a damn
Couldn't use his head so he used his hand
The ref gave a goal the blind ol' sod
And Maradonna claimed it's the hand of God
So out of the cup but what do you expect
From a poxy little country and a circus reject"
(from *Hand Ball*)

Of the other cuts *Ten Years* celebrates the band's achievement - still going strong ten years on, the title cut *Welcome To The Real World*, *Fear In Your Heart*, *We'll Take 'Em On* and *We Gotta Go* are the more powerful. The Captain Oi! CD reissue includes four bonus cuts, including a 12" version of the title song, to round up their late eighties recordings. The original reissue was limited to 750 copies and only available by mail-order.

Smash The Discos as the title track suggests and *Disco Girls* articulate their hatred of discos. Other highlights include *National Insurance Blacklist*, *Blind Justice* and *Last Train To Clapham Junction*. The material was formerly half of *Back To Back, Vol. 2* but in this package was expanded by the addition of the original version of *Suburban Rebels* and an extended version of the title track.

The Best Of The Business on Link in 1992 (their bassist Mark Brennan owned the label) is a twenty-eight track compilation which demonstrates the band to be intelligent, humorous and musically competent - a cut above many of their Oi! compatriots. Indeed, there's some fine guitar work on cuts like *Do A Runner* and *Welcome To The Real World*.

The Complete Singles Collection is a 26-track compilation which features all the tracks on their rare *Out Of Business* EP, as well as their singles including their finest moments like *Harry May* and *Smash The Discos*.

Harry May is a twenty-four track collection of many of their favourites and includes an excellent **Crass** cover *Do They Owe Us A Living?* and a re-work of **Sham 69**'s nugget *Tell Us The Truth*.

Other compilation contributions by **The Business** include *Employers Black List* and *Harry May* which can also be heard on *The Secret Life Of Punk* (Secret SEC 10) 1982 and *Real Enemy* on *Oi! Oi! That's Yer Lot!* (Secret SEC 5) 1982. *Secret Records Punk Singles Collection, Vol. 1* (Anagram CDPUNK 13) 1993 includes *Harry May* and *Smash The Discos, Vol. 2* (Anagram CDPUNK 60) 1995 gave further exposure to *Employers Blacklist* and *Disco Girls*. A total of seven songs - *Harry May, National Insurance Blacklist, Smash The Discos, Last Train To Clapham Junction, Tell Us The Truth* and *Do They Owe Us A Living?* - figure on *Secret Records (The Best And The Rest)* (Get Back GET 12) 1999, which simply underscores their significance as one of the very best Oi! bands of the eighties.

Buzzards

See **The Leighton Buzzards**.

THE BUZZCOCKS - Spiral Scratch EP.

The Buzzcocks

Personnel:
HOWARD DEVOTO	vcls		A
STEVE DIGGLE	vcls, gtr		ABCD
JOHN MAHER	drms		ABCD
PETE SHELLEY	vcls, gtr		ABCD
GARTH SMITH	bs		B
STEVE GARVEY	bs		CD
MIKE JOYCE	drms		D

HCP

ALBUMS:
1(C) ANOTHER MUSIC IN A DIFFERENT KITCHEN
    (United Artists UAG 30159) 1978 15
2(C) LOVE BITES (United Artists UAG 30197) 1978 13
3(C) A DIFFERENT KIND OF TENSION
    (United Artists UAG 30260) 1979 26
4(C) SINGLES - GOING STEADY (Liberty LBR 1043) 1981 -
5(C) TOTAL POP (Weird Systems WS 021) 1987 -
6(-) LIVE AT THE ROXY CLUB, 2ND APRIL 1977
    (Absolutely Free LP 002) 1989 -
7(-) PRODUCT 5LP BOXED SET (EMI PROD 1) 1989 -
8(-) TIME'S UP (Document DLP 2) 1990 -
9(-) SPIRAL SCRATCH (Document DVIT) 1990 -
10(-) OPERATORS MANUAL - BUZZCOCKS BEST
    (EMI 797534) 1991 -
11(-) THE PEEL SESSIONS (Strange Fruit SFRCD 104) 1991 -

NB: (1) originally issued with a limited edition printed carrier bag and black inner sleeve. Most copies just had the inner sleeve. (1) reissued at budget price (Liberty ATAK 51) 1985 and on CD (EMI CD FA 3199) 1988 and (EMI/Premier PRDFCD 3) 1996. (2) reissued at budget price (Fame FA 3174) 1987 and on CD (EMI CD FA 3174) 1988 and (EMI/Premier PRDFCD 4) 1996. (1) and (2) also reissued on one CD (EMI CDP 7931092) 1994. (3) originally issued with some copies containing a free single *You Say You Don't Love Me/Raison D'etre* and reissued on CD (EMI CZ 93) 1988. (4) reissued at budget price (Liberty ATAK 52) 1985 and on CD (EMI CDP 7 464492) 1987 and (Fame CDFA 3241) 1990. (1), (2) and (3) all reissued on blue vinyl by Fan Club (FC 021, 022 and 023 respectively) in 1987. (6) reissued (Receiver RR 131) 1989. (6) also issued on CD (Receiver RRCD 131) 1996. (7) also issued as a 3-CD set (EMI/Premier PRODUCT 1) 1995. (8) comprises of outtakes and live material also on CD. (8) also issued on CD again (Mute Scratch 2CD) 2000. (9) consists of outtakes and demos also on CD. (10) also issued on CD (EMI Premier CDP 7975342) 1996. Other relevent releases are *French* (Dojo DOJOCD 237) 1995, reissued (Snapper SMMCD 541) 1998; *The Peel Sessions Album* (Strange Fruit SFRCD 104) 1994; *Entertaining Friends (Live At Hammersmith Odeon - March 1979)* (EMI CDP 7987292) 1992 and again on (EMI Gold CD GOLD 1029) 1996 at mid-price; *I Don't Mind* (EMI Gold CDGOLD 1093) 1997; *Lest We Forget* (Danceteria RE 158 CD) 1993 and (ROIR RE 158 CD) 1994; *Chronology* (EMI Gold CDGO 2073) 1997; *Modern / A Different Kind Of Product* (EMI CD LRL 013) 1999 and *Small Songs With Big Hearts/Beating Hearts* (2-CD) (New Millenium Communications PILOT 78) 2000.

HCP

EPs:
1(A) SPIRAL SCRATCH (Breakdown/Time's Up/Boredom/
    Friends Of Mine) (PS) (New Horizons ORG 1) 1977 31
2( ) THE PEEL SESSION 7/9/77
    (Strange Fruit SFPS 044) 1988 -

NB: (1) reissued in August 1979 with an altered picture sleeve and a paper label.

HCP

45s:
Orgasm Addict/Whatever Happened To...? (PS)
    (United Artists UP 36316) 1977 -
What Do I Get?/Oh Shit (PS) (United Artists UP 36348) 1978 37
I Don't Mind/Autonomy (PS) (United Artists UP 36386) 1978 55
Love You More/
Noise Annoys (PS) (United Artists UP 36433) 1978 34
Ever Fallen In Love (With Someone You Shouldn't 've?)/
Just Lust (PS) (United Artists UP 36455) 1978 12
Promises/Lipstick (PS) (United Artists UP 36471) 1978 20
* Everybody's Happy Nowadays/
Why Can't I Touch It? (PS) (United Artists UP 36499) 1979 29
+ Harmony In My Head/Something's Gone Wrong
Again (PS) (United Artists UP 36541) 1979 32
You Say You Don't Love Me/
Raison D'etre (PS) (United Artists BP 316) 1979 -
Why She's A Girl From The Chainstore/
Are Everything (PS) (United Artists BP 365) 1980 61
Strange Thing/
Airwaves Dream (PS) (United Artists BP 371) 1980 -
Running Free/
What Do You Know (PS) (United Artits BP 392) 1980 -

NB: * Came in three different coloured picture sleeves. + Issued in red or blue picture sleeve.

Howard Devoto and Pete Shelley met by chance at Bolton Institute of Higher Education in October 1975. Shelley was initially making his own experimental music and performing with his own group the Jets Of Air. In February 1976, they drove down to High Wycombe together to see **The Sex Pistols** perform. Two months later **Howard Devoto** promoted **The Sex Pistols** first gig in Manchester.

The story goes that on one of their trips to London to watch **The Sex Pistols**, they were reading a copy of 'Time Out' when they came across the phrase "getting a buzz, cocks!". This inspired the name of the band they were in the process of forming. The band became a reality in June 1976. Their first gig was supporting **The Sex Pistols** and then **The Damned** at two Manchester gigs on 20th July 1976. They followed this with gigs supporting **The Sex Pistols** and **The Clash** at the Screen On The Green Cinema in Islington, London, in August and then appeared at the 100 Club Punk Festival in September 1976.

Surprisingly, perhaps, there was still no interest from record companies so **The Buzzcocks** became one of the first punk bands to self-finance and release their own record. This became an increasing occurrence in the punk era. The first run of between 700 - 1,000 of the now legendary *Spiral Scratch* EP sold quickly and, by the time production of the record ceased in September 1977, 16,000 copies had been sold. The stand-out song on the EP was *Boredom*, which probably came closest to capturing their energy and style best on vinyl. The two-note guitar solo was a classic moment in the history of new wave. When the EP was reissued in August 1979, it missed a Top 30 slot by just one place and spent six weeks in the charts.

Just two weeks after the release of *Spiral Scratch* **Howard Devoto** decided to quit. Tiredness and ill health were among the reasons he gave, but he returned in 1978 with his own band **Magazine**. Garth Smith (who'd been in Shelley's Jets Of Air) came in on bass and, with Steve Diggle moving across to guitar, Pete Shelley took over the vocal role as well as his guitar duties.

With a new line-up 'B' the band continued business as usual, supporting **The Clash**, at the Harlesden Coliseum in March and then on their 'White Riot' tour. *The Roxy London WC2* album, which documents punk in early 1977, included two tracks by this line-up, *Breakdown* (from *Spiral Scratch*) and *Love Battery* (previously unreleased).

In August 1977, they were finally signed by a major label, United Artists. Their early singles were good but in the case of the first two the titles plunged them into controversy. *Orgasm Addict* suffered predicable difficulties securing daytime airplay and, at first, EMI refused to press *What Do I Get?* because of the title of its 'B' side *Oh Shit*, which caused offence to some. Eventually, they had a change of heart and, after about a months delay, the classic *What Do I Get?* was released in February 1978. The driving, snappy pop-punk ditty was one of their finest moments. It gave them the first in a series of Top 40 hits. Meanwhile Garth Smith had been sacked from the band for unreliability. His replacement was Steve Garvey and the band's classic line-up was now in place.

Their debut album, *Another Music In A Different Kitchen* was a stunner. Released in March 1978, it commences with the riff from *Boredom* and contained songs like *You Tear Me Up* and *Love Battery* from **Howard Devoto**'s days with the band, two Diggle numbers *Autonomy* and *Fast Cars* (which are wrongly credited on the album to Shelley/**Devoto**) and a good number of Shelley's compositions. On one of these *Sixteen* he spoke for many of us in the lyrics "How I hate modern music. Disco, boogie and pop". Due to a mix-up one cut *I Need* got missed off of some early pressings of the album.

To promote the record they toured with **The Slits**. Two of its best tracks *I Don't Mind* and *Autonomy* were released on a 45, which got to No. 55 during a two week chart tenure. They then embarked on the 'Entertaining Friends' tour with **Penetration** and released a further 45. The overtly pop *Love You More* at 1'45" was one of the shortest singles ever. Despite the poor value for money in terms of quantity, it climbed to No. 34 and spent six weeks in the charts.

Their magnum opus commercially was *Ever Fallen In Love (With Someone You Shouldn't 've)*. The chorus was so catchy and for a while many fans would sing or hum it. Although their biggest hit, in retrospect it's perhaps surprising that it didn't climb above the No. 12 slot. It spent eleven weeks in the charts in all.

Their second album *Love Bites*, released in September 1978, wasn't as good as its predecessor. The Diggle/Shelley composition *Promises*, a classic snappy, catchy number is arguably the pick of the bunch. It was culled for 45 release and gave them their second Top 20 hit. The album also included three old Shelley songs, *ESP*, *Sixteen Again* and *Lipstick*. The latter is of interest as originally containing the riff that made **Magazine**'s *Shot By Both Sides* so famous. It also contained two instrumentals, *Walking Distance*, which was the first song penned by Steve Garvey, and *Late For The Train*. To promote the album they undertook the 'Beating Hearts' tour in October and November 1978 supported by **Subway Sect**. The album's sales seemed to benefit from their recent 45 successes and it reached No. 13 in the album charts, where it spent a total of nine weeks.

At the start of 1979 the band took a brief break. During this time Shelley undertook production duties for **Albertos Y Los Trios Paranoias**. They regrouped in February to record the *Everybody's Happy Nowadays* 45. This just made the U.K. Top 30. They undertook a few European gigs and a five-day U.K. tour in March 1979. They also started to pursue solo projects. Shelley also played with the Tiller Boys for a while and Garvey guested with **Teardrop Explodes**.

In March 1979, United Artists reissued all the band's 7" back catalogue. They did their first of four John Peel sessions in May. These can be heard in their entirety on *The Peel Sessions* (Strange Fruit SFRCD 104) 1991. The first one included *Harmony In My Head* penned by Steve Diggle, it was chosen for their next 45. His aggressive vocal style contrasted notably with Shelley's more sensitive delivery. This was issued in a red or blue picture sleeve and peaked at No. 32 in the charts in which it spent six weeks in all.

Their third album *A Different Kind Of Tension* was released in September 1979. Two of the best cuts on side one, Pete Shelley's typically catchy love-pop number *You Say You Don't Love Me* and the fast-paced punkish *Raison D'etre*, were put out as a 45, but surprisingly it became their first since *Orgasm Addict* to fail to chart. The 45 came free with a limited number of the albums, when it was first released. The rest of Side One was dominated by three up-tempo, punkish Diggle compositions:- *Sitting Round At Home*, *You Know You Can't Help It* and *Mad Mad Judy*. On Side Two some of Pete Shelley's best compositions with the band can be found. *I Don't Know What To Do With My Life* opens the side in his typical catchy style. *Money* has a good instrumental opening and features some good guitar work. *Hollow Inside* spawned another classic guitar riff. The title track is a classic, too, with more excellent ringing and fuzzy guitar work. The snappy and simple *I Believe* was another of Shelley's finest songs and culminated in the repeated phrase "There is no love in this world anymore".

In August 1979, with the band trying to break into the lucrative U.S. market, a compilation was issued in the U.S.A.. Entitled *Going Steady* it contained the 'A' and 'B' sides of their first eight 45s. It was imported into the U.K. because it was such an important chronicle of U.K. punk, but didn't get a U.K. release until 1981. It's a good introduction to the band's material and was reissued in 1985 at budget price.

Returning to the U.K., the band toured with **Joy Division** but hesitated over their next move. Their May 1980 Manchester Polytechnic gig was subsequently broadcast live on the Mike Read Show. Included in this were Diggle's *Why She's A Girl From The Chainstore* and *Strange Thing*, which became the band's next two 45s. The first, climbed to No. 61. It would be their last 45 hit. Their final 45, another Diggle composition, *Running Free*, came out in December 1980.

After this, with Shelley in particular clearly losing interest in and enthusiasm for the project, things fell apart fast. Their 'Tour By Instalments' disintegrated after a few gigs. Then EMI took over United Artists and refused to pay them an advance. In the spring of 1981 Shelley walked out on them. He turned solo and Diggle formed Flag Of Convenience.

A late song *I Look Alone* can be found on *C 81*, a NME/Rough Trade tape. They also had *Times Up* on the *Short Circuit / Live At The Electric Circus* 10", which came out on a choice of blue, yellow, or orange vinyl. More of this concert appeared on a bootleg called *The Best In Good Food*.

Lest We Forget - Buzzcocks Live was a live tape issued by ROIR tapes in 1983. The late eighties saw the release of a five LP box set. The band reformed the same year, 1989, with Mike Joyce (ex-Smiths) added on drums. Their gigs included an appearance at the Brixton Academy which saw them clad in white suits. Joyce, incidentally, was later in **Public Image Ltd**.

A U.S. only album *Ten ROIR Years* (Roir A 125) 1991 included a live version of *Ever Fallen In Love*. The same year EMI issued a 'best of' *Operators Manual Buzzcocks Best*. Also in 1991, *Live At The Roxy, WC2* (Receiver RR 132) included *Boredom*. The CD version of *Live At The Roxy Club April '77* on Absolutely Free included one cut not included on the album called *Love Battery*.

Lest We Forget is a CD reissue of a ROIR cassette-only release recorded during the band's 1979-80 U.S. tour. As such it's an excellent retrospective set.

BUZZCOCKS - A Different Kind Of Tension.

Product released in 1989 is a 5-LP box set comprising their first four albums and *Many Parts* (a previously unreleased collection). This comprised a live set they did for Capital records in 1978, their last three singles and *I Look Alone* (previously only available on the NME/Rough Trade 'C81' cassette). The live material includes competent versions of old favourites like *Fiction Romance, What Do I Get?, Noise Annoys* and *Times Up*. Accompanying the box set is a sixteen-page colour booklet full of photos and text by Jon Savage. The later three CD set is also accompanied by lengthy sleevenotes from Jon Savage and is full of perfect pop-punk hooks and witty poignant lyrics. A reminder of just what a good band **The Buzzcocks** were.

As well as the Peel sessions the **Buzzcocks** also recorded two for the David Jenson Show. On 29th May 1978, they recorded *I Don't Mind, Love You More* and *Noise Annoys*, followed on 4th December 1978, by *16 Again,. What Do I Get?* and *Promises*.

The Peel Sessions Album, also from 1989, includes songs like *Pulsebeat, Late For The Train, Lipstick* (which featured the original *Shot By Both Sides* riff), Pete Shelley's *I Don't Know, What To Do With My Life* and *Hollow Inside* and Steve Diggle's *Mad Mad July*.

Time's Up, released in 1991, will be of particular interest to **Buzzcocks**' fans who don't already own it. Taken from a recording session in October 1976 (two months before the one which produced *Spiral Scratch*) it never gained an official release, although it was bootlegged back in 1977. That **The Buzzcocks** formed after watching **The Sex Pistols** play is evident from hearing this disc. The aggressive simplicity of the backing and **Devoto**'s voice are evidence of this. There's a fine cover of The Troggs' *I Can't Control Myself* and rather less predictably a cover of Captain Beefheart's *I Love You You Big Dummy*. The fact that they would quickly progress beyond a few chords was evident on tracks like *You Tear Me Up, Lester Sands (Drop In The Ocean)* and *Don't Mess Me 'Round*. Essentially for fans of the band, it should also be of interest to many others.

The 12" pressing of the *Spiral Scratch* EP, also released in 1991, was a limited numbered edition of 5,000 issued in its original sleeve. The wide grooves of the 12" format ensure the four songs contained therein - *Breakdown, Time's Up, Boredom* and *Friends Of Mine* - are louder and clearer than ever.

Operator's Manual from 1991 is a double album's or CD's worth of classic pop-punk from arguably the most melodic of the early punk bands.

Entertaining Friends from 1992 is compiled from a live concert at the Hammersmith Odeon in March 1979 and is a very accurate portrayal of the group in concert. It contains their hits and album highlights and is a worthwhile acquisition for **Buzzcocks**' fans.

In 1996 EMI reissued *Another Music In A Different Kitchen* on CD along with a bonus CD comprising the effervescent *Orgasm Addict* and their classic *What Do I Get?* (along with their 'B' sides).

Love Bites, their second album was also reissued on CD in 1996. The accompanying bonus CD added the *Love You More* and *Noise Annoys* 45s.

A new **Buzzcocks** CD *Modern* appeared in 1999 along with a second disc *A Different Kind Of Product*. This compiles their 'A' sides from *Orgasm Addict* through *Promises* to *What Do You Know*. For those punters with computer facilities three videos are thrown in of *What Do I Get?, Promises* and *Why She's A Girl From The Chainstore* in an expanded selection along with photos and memorabilia.

Mute's 2000 reissue of *Time's Up* includes a fine selection of memorabilia from **Howard Devoto**'s archive and a few minutes of Super-8 footage from Manchester's Lesser Free Trade Hall in 1976.

Small Songs With Big Hearts / Beating Hearts is a 2-CD live set. *Small Songs* is from the Rainbow in 1979, the climax to their tour to support their third album *A Different Kind Of Tension*. The highlight of this set is the encores:- *Breakdown, Love You More, What Do I Get?* and *Boredom*. *Breaking Hearts* is taken from a Manchester gig on the 1978 *Love Bites* tour. The band are on better form throughout here.

Inevitably, they have figured on several various artists retrospective compilations too. *Ever Fallen In Love* can also be heard on *The Best Punk Album In The World... Ever, Vol. 1* (Virgin VTDCD 42) 1995, *The Best*

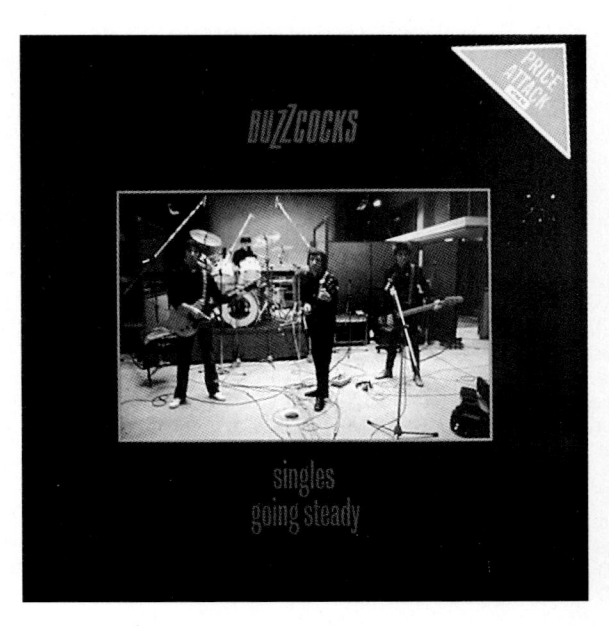

THE BUZZCOCKS - Singles Going Steady.

Punk Anthems.... Ever (2-CD) (Virgin VTDCD 198) 1998, *A History Of Punk, Vol. 1* (Virgin CDOVD 486) 1997, *Punk - The Worst Of Total Anarchy* (2-CD) (Disky SP 871952) 1996, *The Sound Of The Suburbs* (Columbia 488252) 1997, *Spiked* (EMI Gold CDGOLD 1057) 1996, *Teenage Kicks* (PolyGram TV 5253382) 1995 and *Something Better Change (Punk Junk)* (EMI OP 5237 7824) 2000. *Orgasm Addict* resurfaced on *Punk And Disorderly: 1976 - 1981* (Telstar STAR 2520) 1991 (also on CD), *The Best Punk Album In The World.... Ever, Vol. 2* (2-CD) (Virgin VTDCD 79) 1996, *The Best Punk Anthems... Ever* (2-CD) (Virgin VTDCD 198) 1998 and on the 5-CD box set *1-2-3-4 - A History Of Punk And New Wave 1976 - 1979* (MCA/Universal 60066). You can also check out *Boredom* on *25 Years Of Rough Trade Shops* (4-CD Box Set) (Mute CDSTUMM 191) 2001, *Burning Ambitions (A History Of Punk)* (Anagram CDBRED 3) 1996 and *New Wave Archive* (Rialto RMCD 201) 1997. *What Do I Get?* got further exposure on *The Best Punk Album In The World.... Ever, Vol. 1* (Virgin VTDCD 42) 1995, *Punk* (Music Club MCCD 015) 1991, *Spiked* (EMI Gold CDGOLD 1057) 1996 and *Punk - Live And Nasty* (Emporio EMPRCD 586) in 1995. Other compilation appearances have included *I Love You More* on *Punk - The Worst Of Total Anarchy* (2-CD) (Disky SP 871952) 1996; *I Don't Mind* on *The Best Punk Album In The World.... Ever, Vol. 2* (2-CD) (Virgin VTDCD 79) 1996 and *Everybody's Happy Nowadays* on *God Save The Punks* (2-CD) (Disky DOU 882552) 1998 and *Time's Up* on *Punk* (Music Club MCCD 015) 1991.

The Buzzcocks were really a singles band and they produced some of the finest of the punk/new wave era.

Cabaret Voltaire

Personnel:	RICHARD H. KIRK	gtr, woodwind	AB
	STEPHEN MALLINDER	bs, vcls	AB
	CHRIS WATSON	electronics, tapes	A

HCP

ALBUMS:
1(A) LIMITED EDITION (cassette only) (Cabaret Voltaire) 1976 -
2(A) MIX-UP (Rough Trade ROUGH 4) 1979 -
3(A) LIVE AT THE Y.M.C.A. 27.10.79 (Rough Trade ROUGH 7) 1980 -
4(A) THE VOICE OF AMERICA (Rough Trade ROUGH 11) 1980 -
5(A) CABARET VOLTAIRE 1974-76 (cassette only) (Industrial IRC 35) 1981 -
6(A) RED MECCA (Rough Trade ROUGH 27) 1981-
7(A) LIVE AT THE LYCEUM (Rough Tapes COPY 002) 1981-
8(A) THE PRESSURE COMPANY - BENEFIT FOR SOLIDARITY (Paradox Product SOLID 1) 1982 -
9(A) 2x45 (Rough Trade ROUGH 42) 1982 98
10(A) JOHNNY YESNO (Doublevision DVR 1) 1983 -
11(A) CRACKDOWN (Virgin/Some Bizarre CV1) 1983 31
12(A) MICRO-PHONIES (Virgin/Some Bizarre CV2) 1984 69
13(A) THE COVENANT, THE SWORD AND THE ARM OF THE LAW (Virgin/Some Bizarre CV3) 1985 57

	14( )	CODE	(Parlophone PCS 7312) 1987 -
	15( )	GROOVY, LAID BACK AND NASTY	
			(Parlophone PCS 7338) 1990 -
	16(-)	LISTEN UP WITH CABARET VOLTAIRE (dbl)	
			(Mute CABS 5) 1990 -
	17(-)	THE LIVING LEGENDS CABARET VOLTAIRE (dbl)	
			(Mute CABS 6) 1990 -
	18( )	THE DRAIN TRAIN	(Mute CABS 12) 1990 -

NB: (1) was a cassette-only release limited to 25 copies. (2) reissued on vinyl (Mute CABS 8) 1990 and on CD (Mute CABS 8) CD 1990. (3) reissued at budget price on vinyl (Mute CABS 4) 1990 and at budget price on CD (Mute CABS 4 CD) 1990. (4) reissued on vinyl (Mute CABS 2) 1990 and on CD (Mute CABS 2 CD) 1990. (5) was a cassette only release later issued on CD (Mute CABS 15CD) 1992. (6) reissued on vinyl (Mute CABS 3) 1990 and on CD (Mute CABS 3 CD) 1990. (7) reissued on CD (Mute CABS 13 CD) 1990. (9) was originally issued in a 2x12" format with a gatefold sleeve. It was reissued in a 2x12" format on vinyl (Mute CABS 9) 1990 and on CD (Mute CABS 9 CD) 1990. (10) reissued on vinyl (Mute CABS 10) 1990 and on CD (Mute CABS 10 CD) 1990. Initial copies of (11) came with a bonus *Doublevision* 12" EP containing *Diskono, Doublevision, Moscow* and *Badge Of Evil* (CV DV 1). The album was reissued on CD (Virgin/Some Bizarre CVCD 1) 1984 with some bonus tracks. (12) reissued on CD (Virgin/Some Bizzare CVCD 2) 1984 with extended versions of *Sensoria* and *Blue Heat* and again in 1991. (13) reissued on CD (Virgin/Some Bizzare CVCD 3) 1985 with *Sleepwalking* and *Big Funk* added and again in 1991. (14) reissued on CD (Parlophone CDPCS 7312) 1987 with *Hey Hey* and *Here To Go (Little Dub)* added. (15) reissued on CD (Parlophone CDPCS 7338) 1990. (16) reissued on CD (Mute CABS 5CD) 1990. (17) reissued on CD (Mute CABS 6CD) 1990. (18) reissued on CD (Mute CABS 12 CD) 1990. There's also on CD *The Golden Moments Of Cabaret Voltaire* (Rough Trade RUF CD 6001) 1987, *Drinking Gasoline* (Virgin CVMCD 1) 1991, *8 Crepuscule Tracks* (Les Disques Du Crepuscule TWI 7492) 1996, *Plasticity* (Les Disques Du Crepuscule TWI 9752) 1996 and *Radiation: BBC Recordings 84-86* (Burning Airlines PILOT 039) 1998.

MINI CD/12" MAXI:
    1   THREE MANTRAS (Western Mantra/Eastern Mantra)
                              (Rough Trade RT 038) 1980

NB: (1) reissued on vinyl (Mute CABS 7) 1990 and on CD at mid-price (Mute CABS 7 CD) 1990.

EP: 1   Talkover/Here She Comes Now/Do The Mussolini
          (Headkick)/The Set Up (PS)   (Rough Trade RT 003) 1978

HCP

45s:		'Nag Nag Nag'/Is That Me (Finding Someone	
(up to		At The Door Again)? (PS)	(Rough Trade RT 018) 1979 -
1990)		Silent Command/	
		Chance Versus Causality (PS)	(Rough Trade RT 035) 1979 -
		Seconds Too Late/	
		Control Addict (PS)	(Rough Trade RT 060) 1980 -
		Jazz The Glass/	
		Burnt To The Ground	(Rough Trade RT 095) 1981 -
	*	Eddie's Out/Walls Of Jericho (12")	(Rough Trade RT 096) 1981 -
	+	Gut Level (live)	(Masterbag BAG 4) 1982 -
		Just Fascination/	
		Empty Walls (PS)	(Virgin/Some Bizzare CVS 1) 1983 -
		Yashar (5'00")/	
		Yashar (7'20") (12", PS)	(Factory Benelux FBN 25) 1983 -
	#	Just Fascination/	
		The Crackdown (12")	(Virgin/Some Bizzare CVS 112) 1983 -
		The Dream Ticket/	
		Safety Zone (PS)	(Virgin/Some Bizzare CVS 2) 1983 -
		The Dream Ticket/	
		Safety Zone (12")	(Virgin/Some Bizzare CVS 212) 1983 -
		Sensoria/Cut The Damn Camera (PS)	
			(Virgin/Some Bizzare CVS 3) 1984 -
		Sensoria/Cut The Damn Camera (12")	
			(Virgin/Some Bizzare CVS 312) 1984 -
		James Brown/	
		Bad Self Part 1 (PS)	(Virgin/Some Bizzare CVS 4) 1985 -
		James Brown/	
		Bad Self Part 1 (12")	(Virgin/Some Bizzare CVS 412) 1985 -
		Drinking Gasoline: Record 1 - Kino/Sleepwalking.	
		Record 2 - Big Funk/Ghost Talking (2x 12")	
			(Virgin CVM 1) 1985 71
		I Want You/	
		Drink Your Poison (PS)	(Virgin/Some Bizzare CVS 5) 1985 -
		I Want You/Drink Your Poison/	
		C.O.M.A. (12")	(Virgin/Some Bizzare CVS 512) 1985 -
	%	The Drain Train: Shakedown (The Whole Thing)/Menace/	
		Electro-Motive	(Doublevision DVR 121) 1986 -
		Don't Argue/	
		Don't Argue (Whose Arguing)	(Parlophone R 6157) 1987 69
		Don't Argue (Ext. Mix)/Don't Argue (Hate	
		And Destroy Mix) (12")	(Parlophone 12R 6157) 1987 -
		Don't Argue (Dance Mix)/	
		Don't Argue (Dub) (12")	(Parlophone 12RX 6157) 1987 -
		Here To Go/Here To Go (Dub) (PS)	(Parlophone R 6166) 1987 -
		Here To Go (Ext Mix)/Here To Go (Space Dub Mix) (12")	
			(Parlophone 12R 6166) 1987 -
		Here To Go (Linn Drum Mix)/Here To Go (Eleven	
		Eleven Mix) (12")	(Parlophone 12RX 6166) 1987 -
	$	Hypnotised (Daniel Miller Mix)/	
		Hypnotised (Gerald's Vocal Mix)	(Parlophone RS 6227) 1989 66
	&	Hypnotised (Fon Fence Mix)/Hypnotised (Fon Force Dub)/	
		Hypnotised (Daniel Miller Dub Mix)/Hypnotised (Robert Gordon	
		Mix) (12")	(Parlophone 12RS 6227) 1989 -
		Hypnotised (A Guy Called Gerald's Music Mix)/Hypnotised	
		(Fon Force Mix)/Hypnotised (Western Works Mix)/Hypnotised	
		(Gerald's Vocal Mix) (12")	(Parlophone 12X 6227) 1989 -
		Hypnotised (Fon Force Mix)/Hypnotised (Gerald's	
		Vocal Mix) (CD)	(Parlophone CD CDR 6227) 1989 -
		Keep On/Keep On (Les Dub)	(Parlophone R 6250) 1990 55
		Keep On (Sweet Exorcist Mix)/Keep On (Sleazy Dog Mix)/	
		Keep On (Mayday Mix) (12")	(Parlophone 12R 6250) 1990 -
		Keep On (Western Works Mix)/	
		Keep On (Clubbing) (CD)	(Parlophone CD CDR 6250) 1990 -
		'Nag Nag Nag'/Yashar/Yashar (The John Robie	
		Remixes) (CD)	(Mute CABS 1 CD) 1990 -
		Easy Life/	
		Easy Life (Robert Gordon Mix)	(Parlophone R 6261) 1990 61
		Easy Life/Fluid/Positive I.D. (12")	(Parlophone 12R 6261) 1990 -
		Easy Life (Vocal)/Easy Life (Strange)/Easy Life (Very Strange)	
		(Mixed by Robert Gordon	
		and Fon Force) (12")	(Parlophone 12RX 6261) 1990 -

NB: * The initial 12" release included *Jazz The Glass* and *Burnt To The Ground*. + This was a flexidisc which came free with 'Masterbag' magazine. # This was a double 'A' side. % Early copies included a 12" *Shakedown (The Whole Thing) (Version)/Shakedown (The Whole Thing) (Dub)* (2x12") (Doublevision DVR D4) 1986. $ This was a limited edition postcard pack. & The first 5,000 copies of this came with a fold-out sleeve and poster.

This Sheffield trio emerged during the late seventies punk era although their music was very different from that of their contemporaries. Their name derives from the Dadaist club set up by Hugo Ball in Zurich in May 1917. The anarchic spirit of Dada, it seems was to undermine the stale, bourgeois character of western art.

Originally seven, though the numbers soon dwindled to three, they formed in 1973/74 to record experimental tapes rather than to become a band as such. In 1976, they duplicated 25 copies of one of their cassettes and called it "Limited Edition". It remains their rarest and most sought-after release. However, you can check out some of the material from this on their 1981 cassette-only release *Cabaret Voltaire 1974-1976*. Be warned - the material is highly experimental. Indeed, a large number of music fans would find it a major ordeal to sit and listen to their music at all!

Their uniqueness did win them a cult following and they were signed by Rough Trade. They released *Extended Play*, designing the cover themselves. Their radical, electronic music and the inclusion of Lou Reed's *Here She Comes Now* led some to place them in the Velvet Underground, Can, electronic avant-garde tradition, but their music was less accessible than the bands mentioned. The inclusion of two of their tracks, *Baader Meinhof* and *Sex In Secret* on the legendary *A Factory Sample* (Factory FAC 2) 1978 EP brought them to the attention of a wider audience. Along with **Throbbing Gristle** they became pioneers of what is now termed industrial music.

The debut 45 *'Nag Nag Nag'* can best be described as a monotonous barrage of noise, but it won them acclaim in radical new wave circles and among some critics. On the flip was a live recording, dating from June 1975.

Their first album *Mix-Up* was basically a mix of electronics and tape loops. Their unnerving *Silent Command* single made the indie chart, as did their next venture, a double 'A'-sided 12" single *Three Mantras*, which had a playing time of over 40 minutes of what was essentially a tapestry of noises, sounds and percussion, venturing into non-Western musical styles.

Their budget album *Live At The Y.M.C.A. 27.10.79*, released in January 1980, sold in considerable quantities and their *Seconds Too Late* single, whose picture sleeve attempted to express the band's music in a visual format, was also well received.

Some consider *The Voice Of America* to be their best album. It combined older material with newer works like the political *Voice Of America / Damage Is Done* which used tapes and sparse electronics to represent the repressive and libertarian elements of American life.

In 1981, they were commissioned to make videos for Factory Records. They were also engaged by the BBC to help produce records by **23 Skidoo**, **Eric Random** and others for a Peter Care film 'Johnny Yesno'.

Their *Red Mecca* album was an uncompromising recording with a decidedly sombre, gloomy aura. It included a reworked version of Henry Mancini's score for Orson Welles' *Touch Of Evil*, titles like *Spread The Virus* and *Black Mask* helped conjure up the record's almost death-like feel.

September 1981 saw the cassette-only release *Live At The Lyceum*, which had been recorded the previous February. The *Eddie's Out* 12" single was very strange. Following its release Chris Watson suddenly decided to leave the band. He disliked the increased travelling and concert appearances which came from the band's increased popularity.

Kirk and Mallinder continued as a duo. Their first engagement was a benefit gig for the Polish Solidarity Movement at Sheffield University, under the banner of the Pressure Company. **Eric Random** guested on guitar and percussion for this. The concert was recorded and later released in Spring 1982. All the royalties from *The Pressure Company - Benefit For Solidarity* went to Solidarity.

Their fourth studio album, a two-12" set called *2x45* consisted of one 12" containing three tracks all recorded at Western Works Studio by the original three members. The second 45, which had a heavier percussive feel, was taped in Manchester with help from **Eric Random**.

In 1982 **Cabaret Voltaire** toured Japan. Drummer Alan Fish was added to their touring line-up. One of their concerts at Tsubaki House, Tokyo, was recorded and issued as *Ha!*. The same year they released a video/film compilation "Doublevision". The soundtrack included previously unissued titles like *Trash Pt. 1* and *Trash Pt. 2*. The video was reissued in 1990 as "Mute Film Presents Cabaret Voltaire".

1983 saw the group in search of better equipment and a wider audience. They ended their relationship with Rough Trade and issued a 45 *Yashar* on the independent Factory Benelux label. Recorded by the original trio, it was drastically remixed by John Robie in New York. Long-term, however, they signed a deal with Virgin through the independent Some Bizzare organisation. Their first release for the label was the *Just Fascination* 45. It varied quite considerably from their previous work by adding a rhythmic, disco-like pattern to their music. **Soft Cell**'s keyboardist Dave Bell assisted on the disc which was recorded at Trident Studios.

Their *Crackdown* album was released in August 1983. Dominated by a throbbing bass/drum beat it was much more mainstream than anything they had done previously and didn't go down well with their fans. Early copies contained a bonus album of soundtrack music from the previous year's "Doublevision" video. The four atmospheric songs featured were *Diskono*, *Doublevision*, *Moscow* and *Badge Of Evil*. The songs on *Crackdown* tend mostly to a funk format and a wide array of high-tech electronic textures. A wide variety of instrumentation is evident too.

The soundtrack to "Johnny Yesno" - Peter Care's film about a junkie, was released on the band's own Doublevision label in November 1983. The material on it was recorded back in 1981 by the original trio. It had a sort of eerie electronic feel to the music and was welcomed by the band's fans who'd been disappointed by *Crackdown*.

Some consider *Sensoria*, released in September 1984, to be the best of their 12" recordings. On it the band attempt a brand of high-tech beat music. It utilises incessant phrases over a collage of drums, percussion, synthesisers, voices and wind instruments.

Their next album *Micro-Phonies* carried on where *The Crackdown* left off, except that it was sparser but with greater emphasis on rhythm. On cuts like *The Operative* and *James Brown* they appeared to be moving into hip-hop territory.

At the start of 1985 came their *James Brown* 45 - a tribute to the soul singer. Much of their remaining time was spent making a film/video "Gasoline In Your Eye". Four tracks from it were issued on a double 12" 45 entitled *Drinking Gasoline*.

Their eleventh album, *The Covenant, The Sword And The Arm Of The Lord*, which was named after an American neo-Nazi religious organisation, mixed voices, conversations and extracts from U.S. media documentaries with unpredictable instrumentals and vocals, successfully many think. A tape of a U.S. marksman explaining how to fire a gun preceded one track *Kickback*.

As band members were increasingly concentrating on solo ventures, their only new record in 1986 was *The Drain Train*, a double 12". Merging hip-hop and funk, it confirmed just how far the band had moved musically from their early days.

In early 1986, they parted company with Virgin/Some Bizzare and signed to EMI's Parlophone label. The subsequent albums *Code* and *Groovy Laid Back And Nasty* are irrelevant to this book, comprising a dance orientated sound aimed at the disco market. Full details of these and subsequent 12" and 45 releases appear in the discography at the start of this article.

More relevant to readers is the CD compilation *The Golden Moments Of Cabaret Voltaire* put out by Rough Trade in 1987 and *Radiation: BBC Recordings 84-86*, which covers their slightly more accessible period, and was released on Burning Airlines in 1998.

In 1990, Mute reissued most of the band's early material. Full details are given in the discography. Also of interest will be two compilations. *The Living Legends* include all the Rough Trade 'A' and 'B' sides. *Listen Up With Cabaret Voltaire* compiled a number of previously unissued cuts, compilation recordings and NME cassette tracks from the same era. Much of this is inaccessible material and is recommended only to loyal followers of the band.

Aside from *A Factory Sample*, referred to early in this article, **Cabaret Voltaire** have appeared on a number of other compilations. *Business Unusual* (Cherry Red ARED 2) 1979 included *Do The Mussolini (Headkick)*. *Wanna Buy A Bridge?* (Rough Trade US 3) 1979 featured *Nag Nag Nag*. *Factory Benelux Greatest Hits* (Factory Benelux FBN 27) 1983 included the John Robie mix of *Yasyar*. *The Industrial Records Story* (Illuminated JAMS 39) 1984 gave an airing to *Saturday Night In Biot*. *A Diamond Hidden In The Mouth Of A Corpse* (JGPS 035) 1985 included *Dead Man's Shoes*. The cassette compilation *Magnetic North* (Touch TSC) 1985 included *Diffusion*. *If You Can't Please Yourself, You Can't Please Your Soul* (Some Bizzare ET 260663-1) 1985 featured *Product Patrol*. *Underground*, a cassette which came free with copies of 'Underground' magazine included *Seconds Too Late*. *Funky Alternatives Two* (Concrete Productions CPROD LP 2) 1987 included *Doom Doom* and the CD *Salvation Soundtrack* (Interphon CD IPCD 20022-26) 1988 gave an airing to *Twanky Party* and *Jesus Saves*. They also contributed to the background music of *Smack My Crack* (JGPS) 1987. Finally, in 2001, *Nag Nag Nag* was included on *25 Years Of Rough Trade Shops* (4-CD Box Set) (Mute CDSTUMM 191).

Then there are the NME freebies. All three were cassette-only compilations. *Mighty Reel* (NME 004) 1982 included *Loosen The Clamp*. *Mad Mix 2* (NME 008) 1983 contained *Why Kill Time (When You Can Kill Yourself)*. *High Voltage* (NME 028) 1987 featured *Baader Meinhof*.

Stephen Mallinder and Richard H. Kirk both recorded quite extensively as solo artists during the eighties. Chris Watson recorded with the Hafler Trio.

So early **Cabaret Voltaire**'s irreverence to musical convention made them inaccessible to many, though to some they were significant as one of the first electronic/industrial bands. Their later transgression to the electro-dance scene and various strands of dance music won them a wider audience but would doubtless have reviled many of their fans from their Rough Trade days.

Jo Callis

45:   Woah Yeah/Sinistrale/Dodo Boys (PS) (Pop: Aural POP 12) 1981

This was a solo venture for **Jo Callis** who was also with **The Rezillos**, **Human League**, **Shake** and Boots For Dancing.

Camera Obscura

45:   Destitution/Race In Athens (PS) (Small Wonder SMALL 28) 1980

One of the lesser known acts to record on Small Wonder.

Andy Cameron

45:   Ally's Tartan Army/
      I Want To Be A Punk Rocker   (Klub KLUB 5) 1978
      We'll Be There Over There/
      Don't Cry For Us Argentina   (Klub KLUB 6) 1979

These humorous punk era 45s did not appear in picture sleeves.

Cardiac Arrest

EP: 1( ) A BUS FOR A BUS ON A BUS (Bus For A Bus On A Bus/Cake For Bertie's Party/Food On The Wall) (PS)   (Tortch TOR 2) 1979

A four piece from Morecombe in Lancashire.

The Cardiacs

Personnel: (up to 1986)			
MICK PUGH	vcls	ABC	
JIM SMITH	bs	ABCD	
TIM SMITH	gtr, vcls	ABCD	
PETER TAGG	drms	AB	
COLVIN MYERS	keyb'ds	B	
MARK CAWTHRA	drms	CD	
WILLIAM D DRAKE	keyb'ds	D	
DOMINIC LUCKMAN	drms	D	
TIM QUY	perc	D	
SARA SMITH	sax	D	

CASS: 1 THE OBVIOUS IDENTITY   (Alphabet) 1980
      2 TOY WORLD   (Alphabet) 1981
      3 ARCHIVE CARDIACS   (Alphabet) 1983
      4 THE SEASIDE   (Alphabet) 1983
      5 MR & MRS SMITH & MR DRAKE   (Alphabet) 1984

NB: (3) also issued on CD (Alphabet Business Concern ALPHCD 000) 1995. (4) also issued on CD (Alphabet Business Concern ALPHCD 013) 1995.

ALBUMS: 1 BIG SHIP   (Alphabet ALPH 004) 1987
        2 RUDE BOOTLEG (LIVE AT THE READING FESTIVAL, 1986)   (Alphabet ALPH 005) 1987

NB: There's also a compilation *Cardiacs Sampler* (Alphabet Business Concern ALPHCD 019) 1995. (2) also issued on CD (Alphabet Business Concern ALPH CD 005) 1995.

45:   + Running In The Street/TV Friends (PS)   (Another AN 1) 1981
NB: + Credited to **Cardiac Arrest**.

This band started life in 1978 in Surrey as Philip Pilf and The Filth, but when Colvin Myers joined on keyboards they changed name to **Cardiac Arrest**.

In 1979, Tagg left to form Trudy. His replacement on drums was Mark Cawthra. Mike Pugh and Colvin Myers departed too soon after but new personnel were recruited and line-up 'D' stabilised for a few years. With their name abbreviated to **The Cardiacs** they recorded a series of cassettes and built up a cult live following with their theatrical stage act. Eventually some vinyl followed and by the late eighties their music was more mainstream. Much of it was quite strange and unlike anything heard before.

In 1995, their whole back catalogue was reissued and there was also a specially priced CD sampler featuring a track from each of their earlier albums and one each from planned new projects by Tim Smith, William Drake and Sara Smith.

THE CARPETTES - Radio Wunderbar EP.

The Carpettes

Personnel:	KEVIN HEARD	drms	A
	GEORGE MADDISON	bs	AB
	NEIL THOMPSON	gtr, vcls	AB
	TIM WILDER	drms	B

ALBUMS: 1( ) FRUSTRATION PARADISE   (Beggars Banquet BEGA 14) 1979
        2( ) FIGHT AMONG YOURSELVES (Beggars Banquet BEGA 21) 1980

NB: There are also two CD compilations, *The Best Of The Carpettes* (Anagram CDPUNK 80) 1996 and *The Early Years* (Overground OVER 68CD) 1997.

EP: 1( ) RADIO WUNDERBAR: (How About Me And You/Help I'm Trapped/Radio Wunderbar/Cream Of The Youth)   (Small Wonder SMALL 3) 1977

45s: Small Wonder?/2 Ne 1 (PS)   (Small Wonder SMALL 9) 1978
      I Don't Mean It/
      Easy Way Out (PS)   (Beggars Banquet BEG 27) 1979
      Johnny Won't Hurt You/Frustration Paradise
      (double-pack)   (Beggars Banquet BEG 32) 1980
      Total Insecurity/Keys To Your Heart (free with BEGA 32)
                                   (Beggars Banquet SAM 119) 1980
      Nothing Ever Changes/You Never Realised/
      Frustration Paradise (live) (PS) (Beggars Banquet BEG 47) 1980
      The Last Lone Ranger/Love So Strong/
      Fan Club (PS)   (Beggars Banquet BEG 49) 1980

The Carpettes were formed in mid-1977 by line-up 'A'. They also recorded two sessions for John Peel. The first on 24th July 1978 featured *Reach The Bottom, I Don't Mean It, Away From It All* and *Indo-China*. The second on 21st December 1978 included *Cruel Honesty, What Can I Do, Double Platinum, It Don't Make Sense* and *Routine*.

They'd made their debut with the *Radio Wunderbar* (EP) on Small Wonder in 1977 but after one further 45 signed to new indie label Beggars Banquet. Their 1979 album *Frustration Paradise*, produced by Bob Sargeant, was no-frills rock 'n' roll with bright tunes, which were better than average but in no way exceptional. Typical of this was *Lost Love*, which was brought to the attention of a wider audience by virtue of its inclusion of *20 Of Another Kind, Vol. 2* (Polydor POLX 1) in 1979.

Colin Thurston handled production on their 1980 album *Fight Among Yourselves*, which was in similar mould but not quite as good as its predecessor and, by the end of the year, they had fizzled out.

Retrospective compilation appearances include *Radio Wunderbar* and *Small Wonder* on *Small Wonder Punk Singles Collection, Vol. 1* (Anagram CDPUNK 29) 1994 and *Vol. 2* (Anagram CDPUNK 70) 1996 of the same series featured *How About Me And You* and *2NEl*.

They subsequently contributed four tracks, *I Don't Mean It, Johnny Won't Hurt Me, Nothing Ever Changes* and *Last Lone Ranger* to *Beggars Banquet - The Punk Singles Collection* (Anagram CD PUNK 73) 1996.

The Early Years compilation features nineteen above-average cuts from this Geordie punk band.

Chris Carter

| CASSETTE: | 1 | THE SPACE BETWEEN | 1980 |

NB: (1) Edited and digitally remastered for CD release (Mute ICCICD) 1992

Chris Carter was probably the most influential and interesting member of **Throbbing Gristle** who were arguably the most significant of the post-punk era Industrial bands. Back in 1980 **Carter**, who was a technical whizz-kid, released a C90 cassette, as part of the band's collectable tape series. Musically, there's lots of swirling synthesised sounds which had much in common with the synthesised rock of German bands like Tangerine Dream. The CD reissue of this tape is edited and digitally remastered and features an extended version of *Walkabout*.

Carter went on to record during the eighties with Cosey Fanni Tutti as **Chris and Cosey**.

Case

Personnel:	MARC ADAMS	bs	A
	ROB BROOK	gtr	A
	DERWENT	drms	A
	MICKY DONNELLY	sax	A
	MATTHEW NEWMAN	vcls	A
	NEIL PYZER	sax	A

| EP: | 1(A) | WHEAT FROM THE CHAFF (Smiling My Life Away/Oh/Criminal Ways) (PS) | (SUS SUS 1) 1984 |

A South-east London Oi! band managed by Dave Long and supported by Oi! creator Garry Bushell. Their sole vinyl epitaph was this three track EP. *Smiling My Life Away* is a frenetic rant but the horn section was unusual for an Oi! group. This is even more prominent on *Oh*, which is quite dancey and veered towards 2-Tone. *Criminal Ways* has an unusual instrumental intro which gives way to growling vocals. It is a really original song. The group could have been big, but it didn't happen.

Aside from this EP, which was subsequently included in its entirety on *Oi! The Rarities, Vol. 1* (Captain Oi! AHOY CD 43) in 1995, they did record a number of demos. **Case** also performed a session for Radio One's Kid Jensen which comprised *I Ain't Gonna Dance*, *You'll Be My Fool*, *Let That One Go* and *You Know What's Good For You*.

Micky Donnelly and Neil Pyzer went on to play for **Spear Of Destiny**. Derwent went on to play in various mod bands like **Long Tall Shorty**, **Joe Public**, **The Rage** and in **The Angelic Upstarts**.

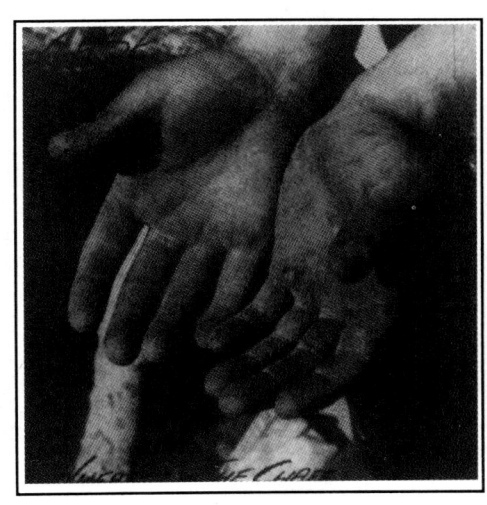

CASE - Wheat From The Chaff EP.

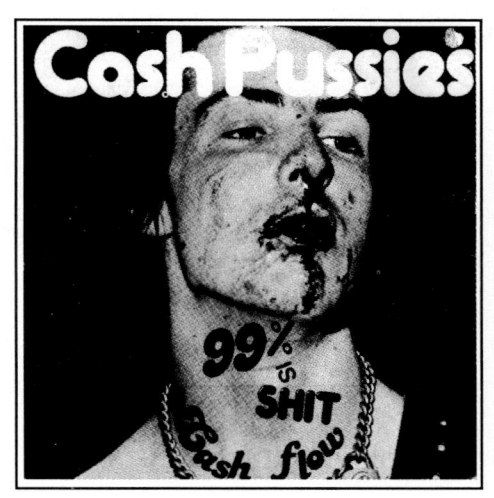

THE CASH PUSSIES - 99% Is Shit.

The Cash Pussies

Personnel:	ALEX FERGUSSON	gtr	A
	ALAN GRUNER		
	DIANA RICH		
	RAY WESTON		

| 45: | 99% Is Shit/Cash Flow | (The Label TLR 010) 1979 |

Alex Fergusson had previously been in **Alternative TV**. The 'A' side starts with the voice of **Sid Vicious** mumbling about how the general public were scum. The record was apparently a parody of **The Sex Pistols**' *Belsen Was A Gas*.

The Catch

Personnel:	PEET COOMBES	gtr, vcls	A
	ANNIE LENNOX	vcls, keyb'ds, flute	A
	DAVE STEWART	gtr, keyb'ds	A

| 45: | Borderline/Black Blood | (Logo GO 103) 1977 |

This short-lived venture was formed by Annie Lennox, Dave Stewart and his best friend guitarist and vocalist Peet Coombes. Lennox and Stewart had met whilst working at Pippins restaurant in North London. Stewart had previously played in Longdancer (see my earlier book 'Tapestry Of Delights' for details of them).

The Catch's sole 45 was a minor hit in Holland. U.K. pressings are now very rare and expensive, but expect to pay even more for European pressings.

With the addition of drummer Jim Tooney and bassist Eddie Chin, **The Catch** soon became **The Tourists** and Lennox and Stewart later went on to find fame and fortune in Eurythmics.

Celia and The Mutations

Personnel:	CELIA	vcls	A
	JJ BRUNEL	bs	A
	JET BLACK	drms	A
	HUGH CORNWELL	gtr	A
	DAVE GREENFIELD	keyb'ds	A

45s:	Mony Mony/Mean To Me (PS)	(United Artists UP 36262) 1977
	You Better Believe Me/Round And Round (PS)	(United Artists UP 36318) 1977
	Mony Mony/Mean To Me (promo only)	(S.I.S./Liberty FREE 18) 1981

The Mutations were actually **The Stranglers**. Celia was luscious-looking and that's the best that can be said. Their debut 45, a cover of the Tommy James and The Shondells' classic *Mony Mony* pales alongside the original. Its flip side *Mean To Me* is better.

A Certain Ratio

Personnel: (up to 1986)

JEREMY KERR	bs, vcls	ABCDEFG	H
MARTIN MOSCROP	gtr, vcls	ABCDEFG	H
PETER TERRELL	gtr	ABCD	
SIMON TOPPING	vcls, trumpet	ABCDE	
DONALD JOHNSON	drms, perc	BCDEFG	H
MARTHA TILSON	vcls	C	
ANDY CONNELL	keyb'ds, vcls	EFG	H
CAROL MacKENZIE	guest vcls	E	
TONY QUIGLEY	sax	G	H
TOM BARRISH	guest trombone		H
CORRINE DREWERY	guest vcls		H
PAUL HARRISON	guest bs programme		H

ALBUMS: (up to 1986)

				HCP
1(B)	THE GRAVEYARD AND THE BALLROOM	(Factory FACT 16C)	1980	-
2(C)	TO EACH....	(Factory FACT 35)	1981	-
3(C)	SEXTET	(Factory FACT 55)	1982	53
4(D)	I'D LIKE TO SEE YOU AGAIN	(Factory FACT 65)	1982	-
5(-)	THE OLD AND THE NEW (comp)	(Factory FACT 135)	1986	-
6(H)	FORCE	(Factory FACT 166)	1986	-

NB: (1) originally issued as a cassette (one side live; one side studio) with an insert inside a plastic pouch. The first 400 copies came in orange, but it was later available in blue, green, red and grey. (1) reissued in cassette format in 1985 in a blue linen effect box with inserts. (1) also issued on CD (Creation CREV 022CD) 1994. (2) originally issued in a gatefold sleeve and later issued on CD (Creation CREV 023CD) 1994. (3) also issued on CD (Creation CREV 024CD) 1994. (4) also issued on CD (Creation CREV 025CD) 1994. (5) was issued with a free 7" *Shack Up/The Thin Boys* (7 FAC 135) stuck on the front. (5) also issued on CD (Creation CREV 026CD) 1994. (6) also issued on CD (Factory FACD 166) 1986 with three bonus cuts; *Si Fermi Ogrido*, *Inside* and *Nostromo A Go-Go* and reissued (Creation CREV 027CD) 1994. Also of interest is *A Certain Ratio Live In America* (private cassette) 1985, which was sold at gigs. It was later issued on vinyl (Dojo DOJOLP 47) 1987 and CD (Dojo DOJOCD 47) 1987. There's also a budget compilation *Sampler* (Creation CREV 013LP) 1994 of which just 1,000 copies were pressed.

45s: (up to 1986)

*	All Night Party/The Thin Boys (PS)	(Factory FAC 5)	1979
+	Shack Up/And Then Again Live	(Factory Benelux/Les Disques Du Crépuscule FAC BN 1-004)	1980
	Flight/Blown Away/And Then Again (12", PS)	(Factory FAC 22)	1980
x	The Double 12": Flight/And Then Again/Blown Away/Do The Du (Casse)/The Fox/Shack Up/Son's Heir (PS)	(Factory FACT 42)	1981
	Waterline/Funaezekea (12", PS)	(Factory FAC 52)	1981
#	Guess Who?/Guess Who? (Part Two) (12", PS)	(Factory Benelux FBN 17)	1982
	Knife Slits Water/Tumba Rumba (PS)	(Factory FAC 62-7)	1982
	Knife Slits Water/Kether - Hot Knives Mix - In Special (12", PS)	(Factory FAC 62-T)	1982
	I Need Someone Tonite (Edit)/Don't You Worry 'Bout A Thing (Edit) (promo-only)	(Factory FAC 72/7)	1983
	I Need Someone Tonite/Don't You Worry 'Bout A Thing (12", PS)	(Factory FAC 72)	1983
	Life's A Scream/There's Only This (12", PS)	(Factory FAC 112)	1984
@	Life's A Scream (Edit)/There's Only This (Edit)	(Factory FAC 112P)	1984
α	Brazilia/Brazilia (Extended Mix) (12", PS)	(Factory Benelux FBN 32)	1985
	Wild Party (Edit)/Sounds Like Something Dirty (Edit) (promo-only)	(Factory FAC 1287)	1985
	Wild Party/Sounds Like Something Dirty (12", PS)	(Factory FAC 128)	1985
	Wild Party/Sounds Like Something Dirty/Life's A Scream (live)/Force (live)/Wild Party (live) (cassette)	(Factory FAC 128C)	1985
	Mickey Way (The Candy Bar)/Inside/Si Fermi Ogrido (12", PS)	(Factory FAC 168)	1986

NB: * Only 5,000 copies were pressed. Of these 1,000 came with a sticker on the back saying 'ltd. edition on poor quality vinyl'. + Belgian 7". x Italian 12" double pack came in a picture sleeve. The last three cuts had previously been issued on a U.S. 45 (FACUS 4) in 1981. # Belgian 12", issued in a die-cut sleeve. @ This was a promo-only 7" pack which came with a photo, special envelope and biography. α Belgian 12".

A Certain Ratio formed in 1978 in Manchester when Jeremy Kerr, Martin Moscrop, Peter Terrell and Simon Topping decided to form a band. Their name was taken from a line in Brian Eno's *Talking Tiger Mountain.....* album, although some later speculated that it was taken from a remark by Adolf Hitler. By 1979 they were writing their own material - a sort of brooding punk-funk, which was also influenced by avant-garde jazz. Later, they became influenced by salsa and dance material.

Their first break came when **Joy Division**'s manager Rob Gretton linked them with the Manchester-based indie label Factory. May 1979 saw the release of their debut 45 *All Night Party*, produced by the late Martin Hannett. Just 5,000 copies were pressed, 1,000 of them featured a sticker on the reverse side saying "ltd edition on poor quality vinyl". It was a typically dark, brooding, Factory effort and sold well. It's not easy to track down now.

After its release their line-up was supplemented by drummer Donald Johnson. Their next product was a cassette-only release (though it was later issued on CD in 1994) *The Graveyard And The Ballroom*. This initially came in an orange-coloured plastic pouch, but was later available in blue, green, red or grey vinyl. One side was recorded at a live gig at London's Electric Ballroom in October 1979 when they were the support band to Talking Heads. The other side was recorded over two days in the studio.

October 1979 also saw them record their first of three John Peel sessions. The four songs featured were *All Night Party*, *Flight*, *Do The Du (Casse)* and *Choir*. They also enjoyed a 25-minute slot on Radio 1's 'In Concert' series in April 1980.

Alongside their interest in post-punk of the new rock left, the band were also into black/dance music, particularly Northern Soul. For their next 45 they covered Bankbarra's mid-seventies funk classic *Shack Up*, which with Hannett handling production, they delivered in an uniquely English way. This was probably their best known release, but it wasn't released in the U.K. originally. Instead it was selected as the first release on Factory's Brussels-based subsidiary Factory Benelux. It got such good reviews that it was soon made available on import here. It also made an impact in the 'States, where it figured in Billboard's dance chart and got released as part of a special four-track 12" for the U.S. market.

A Certain Ratio live at The Electric Ballroom, London 26th October 1979. Photo: Steven Richards.

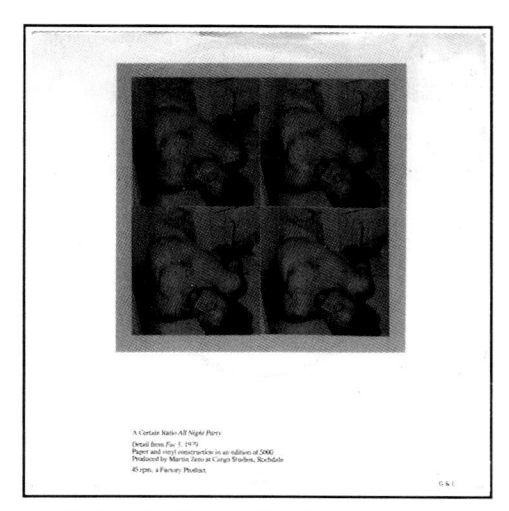

A CERTAIN RATIO - All Night Party.

Their October 1980 45 *Flight*, a percussion-dominated number, was heralded a masterpiece by NME's Paul Morley. They ended the year appearing with SPK and **Throbbing Gristle** just before Christmas in a 'Psychic Youth Rally In Heaven'.

Their eagerly awaited debut album *To Each.....* emerged in May 1981. Recorded in New York, it featured their new vocalist Martha Tilson who they'd met in the 'States. She had previously played with Occult Chemistry. Her strange vocal style quickly became an important ingredient of their sound. It contained *Winter Hill*, a lengthy percussion-dominated track which in many respects pre-dated the trance movement. *The Fox* was notable for Simon Topping's free-form trumpet. Other tracks like *Felch* and *Forced Laugh* developed their funkier elements. The album was their last output produced by Martin Hannett.

On 2nd July 1981, they recorded a superb second Peel session. Comprising *Skipscada*, *Day One* and *Knife Slits Water* many fans consider this as the best thing they ever did. Different versions of all their songs eventually appeared on their *Sextet* album.

Their December 1981 45 *Waterline* was a bizarre effort but in many respects one of the best. Then, in January 1982, they reverted to a pseudonym Sir Horatio to record a 12" reggae instrumental single *Abracadabra / Sommadub* (Rock Steady 666 MIX IT).

Their second album *Sextet* released the same month was their most successful record commercially. Not only did it top the indie charts, it spent three weeks in the national charts climbing to No. 53. The album is dominated by Martha Tilson's wailing vocals and disco dance rhythms.

A further Factory Benelux single appeared in July. *Guess Who?* was released in 12" format in Belgium in a die-cut sleeve. They followed this with *Knife Slits Water* in September. After this Martha Tilson departed and the band reverted back to a quintet.

Their third album *I'd Like To See You Again*, released in October, suffered from the absence of Tilson's vocals. Only two cuts *Touch* and *Showcase* stand out on this album, which is dominated by largely uninspired, jazz funk, percussion dominated material. *Touch* was also featured on their third and final John Peel session broadcast on 1st December 1982 along with *Piu Lento* and *Who's To Say?*

1982 ended on a downward spiral which continued into 1983. Peter Terrell quit to go to India at the start of the year. A few months later Simon Topping left too. He later re-emerged in Manchester dance groups Quando Quango and T-Coy. Andy Connell came in as a permanent replacement on keyboards and vocal for a while and Carol MacKenzie guested on vocals for the remainder of the year. Their only vinyl product was a bland jazz-funk record *I Need Someone Tonite* backed by a straight cover of Stevie Wonder's *Don't You Worry 'Bout A Thing*. A promo-only 7" release contained edited versions of both songs. The official release was in 12" format. *I Need Someone Tonite* and *Don't You Worry 'Bout A Thing* were both earlier previewed in a 2nd April 1983 Janice Long session along with *Shack Up* and *Si Fermi O Grido*. When this made little impact changes were inevitable in what had been a bad year. Carol MacKenzie was replaced and Tony Quigley, who'd previously played in Kalima (a Factory label band who Kerr and Moscrop often played with), came in on saxophone. The new line-up made their debut at Hammersmith in August. It was sharper than before, particularly with Quigley's sax contributions. A new single *Life's A Scream* was released in various 12" formats and as an edited 7" promo with a photograph and a special envelope containing a biography.

Two months later they experimented with Brazilian music on a Factory Benelux single *Brasilia*. Their next 45 *Wild Party/Sounds Like Something Dirty* featured a much more metallic sound. Along with the promo-only 7" and 12" format there was also a limited cassette release which featured three tracks *Life's A Scream*, *Force* and *Wild Party* recorded for Radio One's 'Saturday Live' programme.

In 1985, they gigged intensively and some of their live material was captured on a cassette *Live In America* which was sold at their gigs.

In 1986, a single compilation was released of their material. *The Old And The New* came with a bonus 7" 45 *Shack Up* and *The Thin Boys* on the front.

The year concluded with a further album *Force*. The CD version came with three bonus cuts; *Inside*, *Nostromo A Go-Go* and *Si Fermi O Grido*.

The remainder of **A Certain Ratio**'s story falls outside the time span of this book. They signed for a major label A&M in 1987 but things went wrong and in 1990 their contract with A&M wasn't renewed. In 1991, they signed to Rob Gretton's post-Factory venture Rob's Records and remained with them during the nineties.

A Certain Ratio have also appeared on a number of compilations. Back in 1980 a live version of *Fech* appeared on the cassette *From Brussels With Love* (Les Disques Dú Crépuscle TWI 007) 1989. This was originally issued in a pouch with a booklet, but was later reissued in 1982, then in 1986 as a double album. *Touch Meridians 2* (Touch M2) 1983, another cassette release in a pouch with inserts contained *Si Fermi Ogrido*. *The Factory Benelux Greatest Hits* (Factory Benelux FBN 27) 1983 album gave a further airing to *Guess Who? (Remix)*. In 1985, *Sounds Like Something Dirty (Remix)* figured on *Audio Visual - Abstract Magazine 6* (Sweatbox SAM 006). Finally, *Manchester - So Much To Answer For* (Strange Fruit SFRLP 20) 1990 included *Do The Du (Casse)*, which was originally recorded for the John Peel show. It was also available on CD.

A Certain Ratio were certainy interesting and definitely pioneering. They pioneered a new funk-punk sound which was ahead of its time and soon incorporated jazz into the equation too.

A CERTAIN RATIO - Shack Up.

Chaos UK

Personnel incl:	CHAOS	vcls	A
	ANDY FARRIER		A
	SIMON GREENHAM		A
	POTTS		A

ALBUMS: 1(A) CHAOS UK LP (Riot City CITY 002) 1983
        2(A) SHORT SHARP SHOCK
              (Children Of The Revolution GURT 1) 1986

NB: (1) also issued on CD (Anagram CDGRAM 48) 1991. (2) also issued on CD

(Anagram CDPUNK 71) 1996. *Total Chaos* (Get Back GET 48) 1999 compiles their early eighties singles for Riot City and more.

EPs:	1(A)	BURNING BRITAIN (Four Minute Warning/ Kill You Baby/Army/Victimize) (PS) (Riot City RIOT 6) 1982
	2(A)	LOUD, POLITICAL AND UNCOMPROMISING (No Security/Hypocrite/ What About A Future) (PS) (Riot City RIOT 12) 1982
	3(A)	THE SINGLES (12", PS) (Riot City 12 RIOT 32) 1984

NB: (3) comprised their two earlier EPs plus a track from *Riotous Assembly* called *Senseless Conflict*. There's also some CD collections: *The Best Of Chaos U.K.* (Anagram CDPUNK 108) 1998, *Total Chaos (The Singles Collection)* (Anagram CD MGRAM 48) 1992 and *Floggin' The Corpse* (Anagram CD PUNK 65) 1995. *Earslaughter/100% 2 Fingers In The Air Punk Rock* (Anagram CD PUNK 103) 1998 couples 1985's *Radioactive Earslaughter* with *100% 2 Fingers...* from 1991.

Chaos UK were one of the first U.K. hardcore punk acts to win widespread acceptance abroad as well as here in Britain. Their totally 'in yer face' sound heralded by their *Burning Britain* (EP), released on the Bristol-based Riot City label in 1982, took punk in a more non-musical direction.

If you want to check out **Chaos UK** you can do no worse than track down their *Total Chaos* singles collection. This mid-price compilation runs through their energetic, anti-authoritan rantings.

Alternatively, you could try their sixteen-track collection of outtakes and live tracks, *Floggin' The Corpse*, which also includes material from the 'U.K./O.K.' film. The main targets of their high octance rantings were Thatcher, the police and parents.

Chaos UK also figured on a couple of Riot City label compilations. *Senseless Conflict* can also be heard on *Riotous Assembly* (Riot City ASSEMBLY 1) 1982 and *Four Minute Warning* got further exposure on *Life's A Riot And Then You Die* (Riot City CITY 009) 1985. You'll also find *Four Minute Warning* and *No Security* on *Riot City Singles Collection, Vol. 1* (Anagram CDPUNK 15) 1997 or on vinyl (Captain Oi! AHOY DLP 503), whilst *Kill Your Baby* and *What About A Future* can be heard on *Vol. 2* (Anagram CDPUNK 55) 1995 or (Captain Oi! AHOY DLP 511) 1996 of the same series.

Chaos UK also resurfaced on *100% Hardcore Punk* (Captain Oi! AHOY DCD 84) 1998, playing the frenetic *Four Minute Warning* and *No Security*.

Their *Radioactive Earslaughter* opens with *Hope You Got A Fuckin' Headache* which sounds 100% pure thrash metal with screaming vocals and raging guitars.

Chaos UK continued well beyond this book's time frame with album releases like *Chipping Sodbury Bonfire Tapes* (Slap Up SLAPLP 1) 1989, *Ear Slaughter* (**Chaos UK** and Extreme Noise Terror) (Manic Ears ACHE 001) 1990, *Raw Noise* (Discipline DISC 6/DISCCD 6) 1992 and *100% Fingers In The Air Punk Rock* (Slap Up SLPLP 002) 1993.

They still tour regularly although vocalist Chaos is their only remaining original member.

CHAOS UK - The Singles.

Chaotic Dischord

ALBUMS:	1	FUCK POLITICS FUCK RELIGION FUCK THE LOT OF YOU (Riot City CITY 004) 1983
	2	LIVE IN NEW YORK (Riot City CITY 008) 1984
	3	F*UCK OFF YOU C*NT WHAT A LOAD OF BOLLOCKS (Syndicate SYNLP 12) 1984
	4	NOW THAT'S WHAT I CALL A FUCKING RACKET VOL. 1 (Not Very Nice GRR 1) 1985
	5	GOAT FUCKING VIRGIN KILLERZ FROM HELL (Not Very Nice GRR 2) 1986
	6	VERY FUCKING BAD (Not Very Nice GRR 3) 1988

NB: (1) also issued on CD (Anagram CDPUNK 72) 1996 with their *Don't Throw It All Away* 12" single. (5) also issued on CD (Anagram CDPUNK 84) 1996. There's also a CD compilation *Their Greatest Fuckin' Hits* (Anagram CDPUNK 27) 1994.

EPs:	1( )	FUCK THE WORLD (Fuck The World/ Sold Out To The GPO/ You're Gonna Die) (PS) (Riot City RIOT 10) 1982
	2( )	NEVER TRUST A FRIEND (Never Trust A Friend/ Popstars/Are Students Safe) (PS) (Riot City RIOT 22) 1983
12" Single:		DON'T THROW IT ALL AWAY (Great Rock 'n' Roll Swindle/Don't Throw It All Away/Stab Your Back/ Sausage, Beans And Chips/Who Killed ET (I Killed The Fucker!)/22 Hole Doc. Martens/Anarchy In Woolworths/Batcave Benders Meet The Alien Durex Machine) (Riot City 12 RIOT 30) 1983

With pseudonyms like Ampex, E Stix, Ransid and Pox **Chaotic Dischord** were actually members of **The Vice Squad** and their roadies. Their records were deliberately over-the-top and offensive as they took the piss out of the early eighties punk scene. They sold in considerable quantities and were as good as the more serious efforts around at the time.

Back in 1982 they contributed *Accident* to *Riotous Assembly* (Riot City ASSEMBLY 1) and *Never Trust A Friend*, *Don't Throw It All Away* and *Cliff* were included on *Life's A Riot And Then You Die* (Riot City CITY 009) in 1985. More recently, *Fuck The World* and *Never Trust A Friend* have resurfaced on *Riot City Singles Collection, Vol. 1* (Anagram CDPUNK 15) 1997 or on vinyl (Captain Oi! AHOYDLP 503) 199?. *Vol. 2* (Anagram CDPUNK 55) 1995 or on vinyl (Captain Oi! AHOYDLP 511) 1996 of the same series feature *Too Late* and *Pop Stars*.

Fuck Religion Fuck Politics can also be heard in all its glory on *100% Hardcore Punk* (Captain Oi! AHOY DCD 84) 1998. It is excessively over-the-top.

If you want to investiate **Chaotic Dischord** further, try Anagram's 1994 compilation *Their Greatest Fuckin' Hits*.

Chaotic Youth

Personnel:	IAN	gtr	A
	JOHN	drms	A
	RICKY	bs	A
	TOMMY	vcls	A

EP:	1(A)	SAD SOCIETY (Sad Society/No Future U.K./ Tip Off/ Arms Race) (PS) (Beat The System YOUTH 1) 1982

From Scotland this was one of the lesser known hardcore punk bands. *Sad Society*, *No Future U.K.* and *Arms Race* later resurfaced on *Beat The System Punk Singles Collection* (Anagram CDPUNK 61) in 1995. Their bassist Ricky McGuire was later in **The Fits** and **The UK Subs**.

Charge

Personnel:	DAVE	bs	A
	STU P. DIDIOT	gtr	A
	MARTYN	drms	A
	MOOSE	vcls	A

ALBUM:	1(A)	PERFECTION	(Kamera KAM 013) 1982

EP:	1(A)	DESTROY THE YOUTH (Destroy The Youth/ No One Knows/Can I Go To Heaven Now/ Absolution) (PS)	(Kamera ERA 003) 1982

45s:	Kings Cross/Brave New World/ God's Kids (PS)	(Test Pressing TP 3) 1981
*	Fashion/Ugly Shadows (PS)	(Kamera ERA 007) 1982
	Luxury/Madman In The North (PS)	(Kamera ERA 015) 1982

NB: * Pressed on red vinyl.

An early eighties punk band. All three tracks on the Test Pressing 45 were later included on *Punk Rock Rarities* (Anagram CDPUNK 63) 1995.

Charlie Parkas

45:	The Ballad Of Robin Hood/ Space Invaders (PS)	(Paranoid Plastics PPS 1) 1980

This 45 featured members of **Alberto Y Los Trios Paranoias**.

The Chefs

Personnel:	CARL EVANS	gtr, vcls	A
	RUSS GREENWOOD	drms	A
	BRUV McCALLUM	gtr	A
	HELEN McCOOKERYBOOK	bs, vcls	A

45s:	Sweetie/Thrush/Records & Tea/ Someone I Know (PS)	(Attrix RB 10) 1980
	24 Hours/Thrush (PS)	(Graduate GRAD 11) 1980
	24 Hours/Let's Make Up/ Someone I Know	(Attrix RB 13) 1981

A south coast band. In addition to these 45s, they contributed *You Get Everywhere* and *Food* to the sampler *Vaultage '79 (Another Two Sides Of Brighton)* (Attrix RB 08) 1979. Both cuts are quite good. Four more - *Sweetie*, *24 Hours* and *Let's Make U* - subsequently resurfaced on *Vaultage Punk Collection* (Anagram CDPUNK 101) 1997.

The Cheetahs

45:	Radio Active/The Only One/Minefield (PS)	(Zoom ZUM 14) 1979

Radio Active is a dull pun on wanting to listen to the radio but not wanting to be radio-active because of the energy source of the radio.

Chelsea

Personnel:	JOHN TOWE	drms	A
	BILLY IDOL	gtr	A
	TONY JAMES	bs	A
	GENE OCTOBER	vcls	ABC
	HENRY BADOWSKI	bs	B
	CAREY FORTUNE	drms	B
	JAMES STEVENSON	gtr	BC
	CHRIS BASHFORD	drms	C
	DAVE MARTIN	gtr	C
	GEOFF MYLES	bs	C

ALBUMS:	1(C)	CHELSEA	(Step Forward SFLP 2) 1979
	2(C)	ALTERNATIVE HITS	(Step Forward SFLP 5) 1982
	3(C)	EVACUATE	(Step Forward SFLP 7) 1982
	4( )	LIVE AND WELL	(Picasso PIK 003) 1984
	5( )	UNRELEASED STUFF	(Clay CLAY 101) 1988
	6( )	LIVE AT THE MUSIC MACHINE 1978	(Released Emotions REM 016) 1992

NB: (1), (2) and (3) also issued on CD (Captain Oi! AHOY 91, 92 and 94 respectively) 1998. (5) also issued on CD (Clay CLAYCD 101) 1993. (6) issued on CD (Released Emotions REM 016 CD) 1992. Also relevant are *Underwraps* (I.R.S. (Illegal) EIRSACD 1011) 1989; *Fools And Soldiers* (Receiver RRCD 242) 1997; *The BBC Punk Sessions* (Captain Oi! AHOY CD 159) 2001 and the compilation *Punk Rock Rarities* (Captain Oi! AHOY CD 106) 1999.

45s:	Right To Work/The Loser (PS)	(Step Forward SF 2) 1977
	High Rise Living/No Admission (PS)	(Step Forward SF 5) 1977
	Urban Kids/No Flowers (PS)	(Step Forward SF 8) 1978
	No-one's Coming Outside/ What Would You Do? (PS)	(Step Forward SF 14) 1980
	Look At The Outside/ Don't Get Me Wrong (PS)	(Step Forward SF 15) 1980
	No Escape/Decide (PS)	(Step Forward SF 16) 1980
	Rockin' Horse/Years Away (PS)	(Step Forward SF 17) 1981
	Freemans/ID Parade/ How Do You Know (PS)	(Step Forward SF 18) 1981
	Evacuate/New Era (PS)	(Step Forward SF 20) 1981
	War Across The Nation/ High Rise Living (Remix)	(Step Forward SF 21) 1982
*	Stand Out/Last Drink (PS)	(Step Forward SF 22) 1982
	Give Me More/Sympathy For The Devil	(Chelsea CH 001) 1984

NB: * This was also released as a picture disc.

Gene October was the driving force behind **Chelsea**. He placed an advert in 'Melody Maker'. This enabled him to recruit John Towe (drms) and Tony James (bs), who brought with him guitarist Billy Idol (whose real name was William Broad). Broad had been part of the 'Bromley contingent' of **Sex Pistols** fans. With his new line-up assembled October got the band rehearsing and they played some gigs (including one as support to **The Stranglers**). Somehow, though, the chemisty wasn't right and the three instrumentalists quit to form **Generation X** within a few weeks. October, meanwhile, was left to put together a new band.

By March 1977 October had assembled a new line-up 'B' and sorted a deal with the Step Forward label. This line-up recorded *Right To Work* and *High Rise Living*. In terms of lyrics and style of delivery theirs was the music of the working class. The raw and punchy *Right To Work* was assumed to be a rallying cry for full employment, although in retrospect it seems it was anti-union. *High Rise Living* dealt with the depressive nature of concrete jungles but lacked the punch of its predecessor musically. However, this line-up only lasted until September 1977, when it disintegrated. **Badowski** joined **Wreckless Eric** as saxophonist.

Still October was nothing if not resilient and he and Stevenson, who was later in **Generation X**, assembled another new line-up 'C'. This recorded their debut album *Chelsea*, which had some good moments. Stevenson's guitar work is worth hearing on tracks like *I'm On Fire* and October's vocal style is a little unusual and at its best on their cover of Jimmy Cliff's *Many Rivers To Cross*.

Alternative Hits, their second album comprised mainly tracks which had previously been on 45s. It does include their debut 45, *Right To Work*, which was not on their first album.

Evacuate was a less aggressive album, arguably an attempt to court a wider rock audience, but it doesn't really come off.

By rights by 1982 **Chelsea**'s time had come and gone and they should

CHELSEA - High Rise Living.

have gone the way of other punk bands, but they didn't. Resilient as ever October soldiered on, making more records with various different line-ups throughout the eighties and into the nineties.

Chelsea also recorded two sessions for John Peel. The first broadcast on 27th June 1977 included *No Admission*, *High Rise Living*, *Right To Work*, *Pretty Vacant* and *Blind Date*. The second was on 3rd July 1978 and featured *No Flowers*, *Urban Kids*, *Come On* and *I'm On Fire*. Finally, they played a session for Mike Read on 7th September 1979 comprising *Fools And Soldiers*, *Don't Get Me Wrong* and *Trouble Is The Day*.

Unreleased Stuff contains twelve rare recordings which date from 1978. It is pretty raw and ragged.

Live At The Music Machine conveys a sense of urgency and aggression as the band rattle through *High Rise Living* and *Come On*.

In 1999, one of their finest moments *Right To Work* was included on the 5-CD box set *1-2-3-4 - A History Of Punk And New Wave 1976-1979* (MCA/Universal 60066). The same year Captain Oi! put out *Punk Rock Rarities*, a 19-track compilation of rare demos and remixes. Finished versions of all but one of these songs appeared on official releases. The odd cut out is a demo version of *Blind Date*, which was otherwise only heard on a June '77 Peel session. There are also versions of their *Right To Work*, *Urban Kids* and *High Rise Living* singles and a cover of **The Sex Pistols'** *Pretty Vacant*. The collection also contains versions of eight songs from their 1979 debut album and five from the follow-up, *Alternative Hits*.

Captain Oi!'s *BBC Punk Sessions* (CD) comprises material from four Radio One sessions and an 'In Concert' performance. Their June 1977 Peel Session helped promote their debut 45, *Right To Work*. The second session in July 1978 was centred around their third single *Urban Kids*, which also figured in their third session for Kid Jensen in October 1978. The final session was for Mike Read and broadcast in September 1979. This comprised two cuts - *Fools And Soldiers* and *Trouble Is The Day* - from their debut album and two more - *Don't Get Me Wrong* and *Look At The Outside* - which later turned up on the second *Alternative Hits* album. The 'In Concert' set, from a gig at the Paris Theatre on Regent Street, included nine of their best known songs. It was originally broadcast on 29th September 1979. The twenty-six track collection is accompanied by sleevenotes from guitarist James Stevenson.

The Chords

Personnel:	BRETT ASCOTT	drms	A
	BILLY HASSETT	gtr, ld vcls	A
	MARTIN MASON	bs, vcls	A
	CHRIS ROPE	gtr, vcls	A
	MICK TALBOT	piano	A

HCP

ALBUM: 1(A) SO FAR AWAY (Polydor Super POLS 1019) 1980 30

NB: (1) above came with a free 7" (*Now It's Gone/Things We Said* (KRODS 1). The German release (Metronome 60 312) 1980 has some different cuts. (1) reissued on CD (MODSKA CD 10) 2000 with eleven bonus cuts. Also relevant are:- *No One Is Listening Anymore* (Unicorn PHZA 1) 1986 which was actually recorded live at the Rainbow, Finsbury Park, London in 1980 and the CD release *Live At The Rainbow* (Dojo DOJOCD 178) 1994. Compilations include *This Is What They Want* (Polydor 5493932) (2-CD) 2000.

HCP

45s:	Now It's Gone/Don't Go Back (PS)	(Polydor 2059 141) 1979 63
	Maybe Tomorrow/	
	I Don't Wanna Know/Hey Girl (PS)	(Polydor POSP 101) 1980 40
	Something's Missing/	
	This Is What They Want (PS)	(Polydor POSP 146) 1980 55
	The British Way Of Life/	
	The Way It's Got To Be (PS)	(Polydor 2059 258) 1980 54
	In My Street/	
	I'll Keep Holding On (PS)	(Polydor POSP 185) 1980 50
	One More Minute/	
	Who's Killing Who (PS)	(Polydor POSP 270) 1981 -
	Turn Away Again/	
	Turn Away Again (Again) (PS)	(Polydor POSP 288) 1981 -

A bunch of **Jam** clones from South London. Their debut 45 *Now It's Gone* was full of excitement and enthusiasm. It can also be heard on *20 Of Another Kind, Vol. 2* (Polydor POLX 1) in 1979. Their best song (and also the strongest on their album *So Far Away*, which spent three weeks in the charts peaking at No. 30) was *Maybe Tomorrow*. It was also their most successful commercially, climbing to No. 40 during a five week chart stay. In addition to this they had four other minor hits. Their album included competent covers of *She Said, She Said* and *Hold On, I'm Coming*.

They were originally called The Action and in 1980 covered *I'll Keep Holding On* on a 'B' side - the song was a popular part of the '60s Action's live act. They auditioned unsuccessfully for 'Quadrophenia' and spent a while working with **Sham 69**'s Jimmy Pursey on his abortive J.P. label.

In their final days lead vocalist Billy Hassett quit and Kip from **The Vibrators** came in as a replacement, but they disintegrated soon afterwards.

In 2000, Captain Mod reissued their *So Far Away* album on CD. This featured their *Maybe Tomorrow* and *Something's Missing* hits and their remaining hits appear as bonus cuts.

This Is What They Want is a digitally remastered 2-CD compilation with a lavish booklet and seventeen previously unreleased tracks. It's an ideal introduction to the band.

Chris and Cosey/Creative Technology Institute

Personnel:	CHRIS CARTER	synth, gtr, vcls	A
	COSEY FANNI TUTTI	synth, vcls	A

ALBUMS:	1(A)	HEARTBEAT	(Rough Trade ROUGH 34) 1981
(up to	2(A)	TRANCE	(Rough Trade ROUGH 44) 1982
1986)	3(A)	SONGS OF LOVE AND LUST	
			(Rough Trade ROUGH 64) 1984
	4(A)	ELEMENTAL 7 - THE ORIGINAL SOUNDTRACK	
			(Doublevision DVR) 1984
	5(A)	EUROPEAN RENDEZVOUS	(Doublevision DVR 8) 1984
	6(A)	TECHNO PRIMITIV	(Rough Trade ROUGH 84) 1985

NB: (1) also issued as a cassette with two additional cuts, *Pressure Drop* and *Tight Fit* (Rough Trade COPY 008) 1981 and later on CD (CTICD 004) 1988. (2) also issued on CD (Conspiracy CTICD 005) 1988. (3) also issued on CD (Conspiracy CTICD 006) 1988. (6) also issued on CD (CTICD 003) 1986. Also relevant is *Best Of Chris And Cosey* (Conspiracy CTICD 002) 1989, *Collectiv, Vol. 1* (Conspiracy CTICD 001) 1989, *Vol. 2* (Conspiracy CTICD 002) 1989, *Vol. 3* (Conspiracy CTICD 007) 1989 and *Vol. 4* (Conspiracy CTICD 008) 1989.

EPs:	1(A)	HAMMER HOUSE (12")	(Conspiracy C.T.I. CTI 1) 1984
(up to	2(A)	GIFT OF TONGUES (12")	(Conspiracy C.T.I. CTI 2) 1984
1986)			

45s:		October (Love Song)/	
(up to		Little Houses (PS)	(Rough Trade RT 078) 1981
1986)		October (Love Song)/	
		Little Houses (12", PS)	(Rough Trade RTT 078) 1981
	*	Sweet Surprise	(Electronic Sound Maker no #) 198?
		Conspiracy International/The Gift Of Tongues/	
		The Need (PS)	(International One CTI 002) 1984
	+	Sweet Surprise 1 (1984)/	
		2 (1985) (12", PS)	(Rough Trade RTT 148) 1985

NB: * This was a magazine with a free cassette. + With Annie Lennox and Dave Stewart.

Chris Carter and Cosey Fani Tutti both first played together in industrial music pioneers **Throbbing Gristle**. When they disbanded in 1981, the pair continued to record first as **Chris and Cosey** and later as CTI (Creative Technology Institute).

Their debut album *Heartbeat* was similar in style to **Throbbing Gristle**'s earlier material. There's lots of pulsating synthesizer sounds, but other bits recall Kraftwerk style electro-pop.

The material on *Trance* is mostly moody and dark as the title suggests. Its marketing was disrupted by a disagreement with Rough Trade about the price of the album.

They released two singles in 1983. A Japanese-only collaboration with John Duncan called *Nikki* and the more mainstream *October (Love Song)*.

Songs Of Love And Lust, released in 1984, was cold and disappointing in comparison to their earlier work, with repetitive and weak material.

CTI's *Elemental 7* was dominated by synthesizers, often recalling spacey seventies rock. It was recorded with **Cabaret Voltaire**'s John Lacey. *European Rendezvous* was a live set recorded across the continent in 1983.

Their relationship with Rough Trade broke down after *Techno Primitiv*. They embarked on the *Sweet Surprise* project with Eurythmics. Originally it came as a free cassette with the 'Electronic Sound Maker' magazine. In Europe their material was handled by Play It Again Sam, who reissued most of their output.

Christian Death

ALBUMS:	1	ONLY THEATRE OF PAIN	(No Future FL 2) 1983
(up to	2	DEATHWISE	(Invitation SD 4) 1984
1986)	3	CATASTROPHE BALLET	(Invitation SD 5) 1984
	4	OFFICIAL ANTHOLOGY OF LIVE BOOTLEGS	(Jungle Nos 006) 1986

NB: (4) issued in a black and yellow sleeve, some copies came on pink vinyl.

A gothicy/industrial crossover band. Much of their music is dark and disturbing.

Christianity B.C.

An eighties punk band. They contributed *What A Shame*, a competent number with some decent guitar playing, to *Wet Dream* (Rot ASS 4) 1984.

CHRON GEN - Chronic Generation.

Chron Gen

Personnel:	GLYNN BARBER	vcls, gtr	A
	PETE DIMMOCK	bs	A
	JOHN JOHNSON	drms	A
	JOHN THURLOW	gtr	A

			HCP
ALBUM:	1(A)	CHRONIC GENERATION Oi, No. 1	
		(Secret SEC 3) 1983	53

NB: (1) reissued (Razor RAZ 20) 19?? and again on vinyl (Get Back GET 9) 19?? with four bonus tracks taken from early singles. Also relevant are *Nowhere To Run* (Picasso PIK 002) 1985, *Apocalypse Live Tour* (Chaos APOCA 1) 1984 and *Live At The Waldorf, San Francisco* (Picasso HCLP 001M) 1993 and (Punx PUNXCD 3) 1995.

EPs:	1(A)	PUPPETS OF WAR (Puppets Of War/Mindless Few/ Lies/Chronic Generation)	(Gargoyle GRGL 780) 1981
	2(A)	LIVING NEXT DOOR TO ALICE (Living Next Door To Alice/Ripper/Puppets Of War)	(Secret SEC 3) 1982

NB: (1) was also reissued later in the year with the same catalogue number but with a silver and black label. Some copies of (2) came free with *Chronic Generation Oi* magazine No. 1 but it also came with their album. There's also a few compilations *Best Of Chron Gen* (Captain Oi! AHOY CD 18) 1994; *Live At The Old Wardorf, San Francisco* (Great Expectations PIP CD 046) 1993; *Nowhere To Run* (Great Expectations PIP CD 045) 1993 and *Chronic Generation* (Great Expectations PIPCD 044) 1993.

45s:	Reality/Subway Sadist (PS)	(Step Forward SF 19) 1981
	Jet Boy Jet Girl/Abortions (Live)/ Subway Sadist (Live) (PS)	(Secret SHH 129) 1982
	Outlaw/Behind Closed Doors/ Disco Tech (PS)	(Secret SHH 139) 1982

Chron Gen first formed in January 1978, but their recording career didn't take off until the Oi! wave of British punk in the early eighties.

In summer 1981, they put out an EP *Puppets Of War* on their own Gargoyle label. Among its cuts was *Chronic Generation*, a song from which they had taken their own name in abbreviated form. Their follow-up 45 *Reality* was an indie hit. They were able to promote it and gain further national exposure as members of the Apocalypse Punk package tour. This helped them gain a deal with Secret Records. They recorded an album which spent three weeks in the Album Charts peaking at No. 53 and a couple of 45s for Secret, including a cover of Captain Sensible's *Jet Boy, Jet Girl*. They also contributed one cut, *Clouded Eyes* to the label's *Britannia Waives The Rules* (EP) (Secret SHH 136).

Live At The Old Waldorf, San Francisco is taken from a live concert in 1985. The band had a larger following in the 'States than in Britain. This is really U.K. hardcore, but the material including renditions of *Lies*, *Nowhere To Run*, *Wasted Love* and *Living Next Door To Alice* is marred by poor sound quality.

Nowhere To Run is a CD reissue of six mid-eighties tracks by the band.

The Best Of Chron Gen, put out on Captain Oi! in 1994 is a twenty-six track compilation by this third generation punk band. Energetic, well meaning, low-fi and very early eighties in terms of material.

Other compilation appearances by the band have included *Jet Boy Jet Girl* on *The Secret Life Of Punk* (Secret SEC 10) 1982, *Outlaw* on *Punk And Disorderly III - The Final Solution* (Anagram GRAM 005) 1983, *Puppets Of War* on *Fresh Records Punk Singles Collection* (Anagram CDPUNK 32) 1994 and *Jet Boy Jet Girl* and *Abortions* on *Secret Records (The Best And The Rest)* (Get Back GET 12) 1999. *Jet Boy Jet Girl*, *Attack Exploited*, *Clouded Eyes* and *Outlaw* to *Secret Records Punk Singles Collection, Vol. 1* (Anagram CDPUNK 13) 1993, whilst *Vol. 2* includes *Subway Sadist*, *Behind Closed Doors* and *Disco Tech*.

Chron Gen's music was fun and all of their recordings are recommended.

Chuddy Nuddies

Personnel:	BOB BELLIS	drms	A
	MARTIN DEMPSEY	bs	A
	HENRY PRIESTMAN	piano	A
	MARTIN WATSON	gtr, vcls	A

45:	Do The Chudd/(flip by **Big In Japan**)	(Eric's 001) 1977

The Chuddy Nuddies were actually **The Yachts** playing under a pseudonym.

The Cigarettes

Personnel:	ADRIAN PALMER	drms	A
	ROB SMITH	vcls, gtr	A
	STEVE TAYLOR	vcls, bs	A

EP:	1(A)	THE CIGARETTES (Stay Inside/Looking At You/ Frivolous Disguise)	(Dead Good KEVIN 1) 1978

NB: (1) Although this album was unissued these tracks later appeared on the now rare compilation *East* (Dead Good GOOD 1) 1980.

| 45s: | * | They're Back Again, Here They Come/I've Forgot My Number/All We Want Is Your Money (gatefold PS) | (Company CIGCO 008) 1979 |
| | | Can't Sleep At Night/It's The Only Way To Live (Die) (PS) | (Dead Good DEAD 10) 1980 |

NB: * Initially on burgundy label, later on black label.

The Cigarettes were a mod-influenced band who formed as early as 1978 in Lincolnshire. Although their rare EP was never released, all three of its cuts appeared on the rare mod revival compilation EP *East* in 1980.

The Cigarettes went on to record two 45s which are now rare and sought-after.

Both of their 45s can also be heard on *This Is Mod, Vol. 1: The Rarities 1979-81* (CDM GRAM 98) 1995. You'll also find *Can't Sleep At Night* on *This Is Mod* (dbl) (Get Back GET 39) 1999, whilst *They're Back Again*, which commences with a gentle piano introduction which soon gives way to a driving guitar backing, gets further exposure on *100% British Mod* (Captain Mod MODSKA DCD 8) 1998. The soothing piano returns at the end.

The Circles

Personnel:	KEITH ALLEN	drms	A
	TONY HOWELLS	gtr	A
	GLEN TRANTER	bs	A
	MICK WALKER	vcls, gtr	A

45s:	Opening Up/Billy (PS)	(Graduate GRAD 4) 1979
	Opening Up/Billy (PS)	(Chrysalis CHS 2418) 1980
	Angry Voices/Summer Nights (PS)	(Vertigo ANGRY 1) 1980
	Circles / Summer Nights (PS)	(Graduate GRAD 17) 1985

This West Midlands mod revival band came together in mid-1979. Mick Waller had previously been in Injectors and Allen in **Neon Hearts**. They issued a demo tape and on the strength of this were signed to a local Graduate label who released their debut 45 *Opening Up* in November 1979. Both this and the flip side *Billy* were group compositions. Certainly *Opening Up* is one of the strongest songs the mod revival produced. It got to No. 15 in the indie charts and was soon picked up for reissue by Chrysalis in early 1980. They switched to Vertigo for *Angry Voices* the same year, but split following a U.K. tour in September 1980.

Later, in 1985, Graduate unearthed *Circles* which had actually been recorded back in 1979. Both sides of this were later included on *This Is Mod, Vol. 1: The Rarities 1979-81* (CDM GRAM 98) 1995.

Opening Up later resurfaced on vinyl on *This Is Mod* (dbl) (Get Back GET 39) 1999, whilst *Circles*, a catchy group composition, can also be found on *100% British Mod* (Captain Mod MODSKA DCD 8) 1998.

THE CLASH - Give 'Em Enough Rope.

THE CLASH - Remote Control.

Clapham South Escalators

| 45: | Get Me To The World On Time/Leave Me Alone/ Cardboard Cut Outs (PS) | (Upright UP YOUR 1) 1981 |

The Meteors recording under the pseudonym of **Clapham South Escalators** covered The Electric Prunes' psychedelic classic *Get Me To The World On Time*. The Meteors were a Cramps - influenced combo who made a series of albums during the eighties but with only limited commercial success.

The Clash

Personnel:	TERRY CHIMES	drms	AB D
	MICK JONES	gtr	ABCDE
	KEITH LEVENE	gtr	A
	PAUL SIMONON	bs	ABCDEF
	JOE STRUMMER	vcls, gtr	ABCDEF
	NICKY 'TOPPER' HEADON	drms	C
	PETE HOWARD	drms	EF
	NICK SHEPPARD	gtr	F
	VINCE WHITE	gtr	F

			HCP
ALBUMS:	1(B)	THE CLASH	(CBS 82000) 1977 12
	2(C)	GIVE 'EM ENOUGH ROPE	(CBS 82431) 1978 2
	3(C)	LONDON CALLING (dbl)	(CBS CLASH 3) 1979 9
	4(C)	SANDINISTA! (triple)	(CBS FSLN 1) 1980 19
	5(C)	COMBAT ROCK	(CBS FMLN 2) 1982 2
	6(F)	CUT THE CRAP	(CBS 26601) 1985 16
	7(-)	THE STORY OF THE CLASH VOL. ONE (compilation)	(CBS 460244) 1988 7
	8(-)	THE SINGLES (compilation)	(CBS 4689461) 1991 68
	9(-)	THE TWELVE INCH MIXES (CD) (compilation)	(CBS 450123) 1992 -
	10(-)	THE CLASH ON BROADWAY (compilation)	(CBS 4284) 1992 -
	11(-)	SUPER BLACK MARKET CLASH (3x10" LP) (compilation)	(Columbia 474546-1) 1993

NB: (1) reissued on CBS (32232) in 1982. (2) also reissued on CBS (32444) 1984. (1) issued on CD (Columbia 4687832) 1991. (2) issued on CD (CBS CD 32444) 1991. (3) issued on CD (CBS 4601142) 1991. (4) issued on CD (Columbia 4633642) 1989. (5) issued on CD (CBS CD 32787) 1991. (6) issued on CD (CBS 465 1102) 1991 and again (Columbia 495 3502) 2000 with *Do It Now* as a bonus track. (7) issued on CD (Columbia 4602442) 1991 and again in 1995. (7) reissued as a 2-CD set (Columbia 495351 2) 1999. (8) issued on CD (Columbia 4689462) 1991 and again (Columbia 495353 2) 1999 with lyric sheets. (10) also issued on CD (Legacy 4689462) 1994. (10) reissued as a 3-CD set (Epic/Legacy EPC 497453 2) 2000. (11) reissued on CD (Columbia 4687632) 1991 and (Columbia 4745462) 1996 and again (Sony 474546-2) 1996 with bonus tracks. (11) reissued on CD (Columbia 495352) 1999 with additional cuts comprising 'B' sides and 45 only cuts. There's also a CD set of (1), (2) and (5) (CBS 4673832) 1990. In October 1999, (1) - (8) and (10) - (11) were all reissued on vinyl and CD, along with the U.S. version of their debut album. There's also a retrospective live CD *From Here To Eternity* (Columbia 4961832) 1999, also available as a double album (Columbia 4961831) 1999.

				HCP
EPs:	1( )	CAPITOL RADIO (Interview With Tony Parsons/ Listen)	(CBS/NME CL-1)	1977 -
	2( )	THE COST OF LIVING (I Fought The Law/Groovy Times/Gates Of The West/Capitol Radio)	(CBS 7324)	1979 22
	3( )	Complete Control/London Calling/Bank Robber/ Clash City Rocker	(CBS A 40 2907)	1982 -

NB: (1) came free with New Musical Express. (2) was issued in a gatefold sleeve with a special inner sleeve. (3) was a cassette-only EP.

			HCP
45s:	White Riot/1977 (PS)	(CBS S CBS 5058)	1977 38
	Remote Control/ London's Burning (live) (PS)	(CBS S CBS 5293)	1977 -
	Complete Control/ The City Of The Dead (PS)	(CBS S CBS 5664)	1977 28
	Clash City Rockers/ Jail Guitar Doors (PS)	(CBS S CBS 5834)	1978 35
	(White Man) In Hammersmith Palais/ The Prisoner (PS)	(CBS S CBS 6383)	1978 32
	Tommy Gun/ 1,2, Crush On You (PS)	(CBS S CBS 6788)	1978 19
	English Civil War/ Pressure Drop (PS)	(CBS S CBS 7082)	1979 25
	London Calling/ Armagideon Time (PS)	(CBS S CBS 8087)	1979 11
	London Calling/Armagideon Time/Justice Tonight (alt. version)/ Kick It Over (alt. version) (12" PS)	(CBS S CBS 128087)	1979 -
	Bankrobber/ (flip side by Mikey Dread) (PS)	(CBS S CBS 8323)	1980 12
	The Call-Up/Stop The World (PS)	(CBS S CBS 9339)	1980 40
	Hipsville U.K./ Radio One (die-cut PS)	(CBS S CBS 9480)	1981 56
	The Magnificent Seven/ The Magnificent Dance (PS)	(CBS A 1133)	1981 34
	The Magnificent Seven/ The Magnificent Dance (12", PS)	(CBS 12A 1133)	1981 -
	This Is Radio Clash/Radio Clash	(CBS A 1797)	1981 47
	This Is Radio Clash/Radio Clash/Radio Five/ Outside Broadcast (12" PS)	(CBS A 12 1797)	1981 -
	Know Your Rights/ First Night Back In London (PS)	(CBS A 2309)	1982 43
	Rock The Casbah/Long Time Jerk (PS)	(CBS A 2479)	1982 30
	Rock The Casbah/ Long Time Jerk (pic disc)	(CBS A 11 2479)	1982 -
	Rock The Casbah/Long Time Jerk/ Mustapha Dance (12" PS)	(CBS A 13 2479)	1982 -
*	Should I Stay Or Should I Go/ Straight To Hell (PS)	(CBS A 2646)	1982 17
	Should I Stay Or Should I Go/ Straight To Hell (pic disc)	(CBS A 11 2646)	1982 -
	Should I Stay Or Should I Go/ Straight To Hell (12" PS)	(CBS A 13 2646)	1982 -

THE CLASH - Combat Rock.

THE CLASH - London Calling.

This Is England/Do It Now (PS)	(CBS A 6122)	1985 24
This Is England/Do It Now/ Sex Mad Roar (12" PS)	(CBS TA 6122)	1985 -
I Fought The Law/City Of The Dead/Police On My Back/ 48 Hours (PS)	(CBS CLASH 1)	1988 29
+ London Calling/Brand New Cadillac/ Rudy Can't Fail (PS)	(CBS CLASH 2)	1988 46
London Calling/Brand New Cadillac/Rudy Can't Fail/ Street Parade (12" PS)	(CBS CLASH T2)	1988 -
This Is Radio Clash/ Radio Clash (PS)	(CBS CBS 6516533)	1988 -
Return To Brixton/ Guns Of Brixton (PS)	(CBS CBS 6560727)	1990 57
Return To Brixton/SW 2 Dub/ Guns Of Brixton (12" PS)	(CBS CBS 656072 6)	1990 -
x Should I Stay Or Should I Go/London Calling/ Train In Vain/I Fought The Law	(Columbia 656 667-7)	1991 1
x Rock The Casbah/Tommy Gun/ (White Man) In Hammersmith Palais/ Straight To Hell	(Columbia 656 814-7)	1991 15
x London Calling/Clampdown/The Call Up/ London's Burning	(Columbia 656 946-7)	1991 64
London Calling/Brand New Cadillac/ Return To Brixton (12" poster PS)	(Columbia 656 946-6)	1991 -

NB: * Some limited edition copies had a laser-etched on one side. + Some copies of this release came in a box set (CLASHB 2) in 1988. x These were reissues. Some appeared as CDs in tins.

The Clash are always regarded as one of the seminal bands of U.K. punk. They were formed in Shepherds Bush, London, in June 1976. Their founding members were Mick Jones (gtr), who was born in Brixton on 26th June 1955 and Paul Simonon, also a London lad born in Brixton on 15th December 1955. Whereas Jones had been in a London punk outfit London SS for nine months prior to this, Simonon had never even played an instrument before, but he took up bass guitar. The line-up was completed by Joe Strummer (gtr, vcls), who was persuaded to leave R&B outfit **101ers**, Terry Chimes (drms) and Keith Levene (gtr), who left after just five shows but was later in **Public Image Ltd.**.

Their first gig was an unannounced support to **The Sex Pistols** in Sheffield, but their first publicised appearance was at Islington's Screen On The Green on 29th August 1976. In those early days, particularly with the potential for violence at punk concerts, gigs were hard to come by. They did play at the 100 Club Punk Festival, London, on 20th September 1976, but not long after Levene left. In December 1976, they played on **The Sex Pistols** controversial 'Anarchy In The U.K.' tour, which certainly brought them publicity. However, most of the gigs on the tour were cancelled due to venue bans.

By January 1977, with record companies now racing to sign up punk bands and with a successful gig at Covent Garden's Roxy, which was fast becoming one of London's premier punk venues, beneath their belt. Bernie Rhodes who'd been their manager from the outset, negotiated a contract for them with CBS.

Their debut 45 *White Riot* epitomised what punk was all about in 1977. An angry appeal for social anarchy. Lyrically the flip side said it all "no Elvis, Beatles or Rolling Stones in 1977". *White Riot* became a minor U.K. hit.

Their debut album *The Clash*, issued in April 1977, is considered by many to be punk's finest album. A claim supported by its performance in various rock polls over the years. The format was very simple. Strummer's anguished vocals cut across a simple rhythmic backing. The lyrics were full of anger and aggression and they used the tried and tested sixties verse-and-chorus song structure to convey their messages. The songs were short, usually between 2-3 minutes. *I'm So Bored With The U.S.A.* articulated punk's alienation from mainstream American culture. *London's Burning* voiced the riotous spirit of 1977. *Career Opportunities* exposed the dead-end jobs teenagers were being forced into. It also included their first effort at reggae, a cover of Junior Murvin's *Police And Thieves*. Chimes left shortly after this album was recorded. He was replaced by Nicky 'Topper' Headon, who'd been born on 30th May 1955 in Bromley, Kent.

To promote their debut album they embarked in May 1977 on the 'White Riot' U.K. tour with two other emerging and promising punk acts, **The Jam** and **The Buzzcocks** as support. However, **The Jam** withdrew from the tour at the end of the first month. The album got to No. 12 in the charts and it also sold over 100,000 copies on import to the 'States, where it was deemed unsuitable for airplay. The album was only belatedly released in the U.S.A. during their second U.S. tour in September 1979, when it climbed to No. 126 in the album charts. The U.S. issue included a bonus 45 with *Groovy Times* and *Gates Of The West*, two songs recorded after its original U.K. release.

Meanwhile back in the U.K., *Remote Control* was released as the band's second 45 with a live version of *London's Burning* on the flip. It did not chart. There was also a 12" promo version, which is now quite rare and collectable.

Around this time NME issued vouchers for a free cassette single by the band. This featured two new cuts, *Listen* and *Capitol Radio*, which was a no-holes-barred attack on the unadventurous programming of the London-based commercial radio station. Also on the cassette was a recording of an interview Tony Parsons had conducted with the band. 10,000 copies were issued in all, but this is the rarest and most collectable **Clash** item.

During the summer of 1977 they had a couple of brushes with the law, which recalled comparison with the rebellious Rolling Stones, and served only to enhance their punk credibility. Strummer and Headon were both fined £5 for spray-painting "Clash" on a wall. The following evening the pair spent an evening in Newcastle jail as a result of failing to respond to a charge arising from the theft of a pillow case from a Holiday Inn. They were fined £100. They dubbed the new tour they embarked on shortly after "Out On Parole".

Their next single *Complete Control* had a fuller sound and brought them their biggest hit to date, but it lacked a memorable melody or riff. The flip, *City Of The Dead*, showed a little more musical ambition.

Their progress was halted in February 1978 when Strummer fell ill with hepatitis and was hospitalised. When he was restored to full fitness they returned in March 1978 with their fourth 45, *Clash City Rockers*. This

THE CLASH - Cost Of Living EP.

THE CLASH - Complete Control.

featured an incisive guitar riff and climbed to No. 35 in the U.K.. The flip side *Jail Guitar Doors* helped cement their rebel image.

They brushed against the law again in March 1978. Simonon and Headon were arrested and fined in London's Camden Town for shooting down racing pigeons. They were fined a total of £800.

June 1978, saw the issue of *(White Man) In Hammersmith Palais*. This climbed to No. 32 in the U.K. and was a little more accessible and restrained than some of their earlier work. The flip side paid homage to cult TV series "The Prisoner".

Work was also underway on their second album during the summer of 1978 when they met U.S. producer Sandy Pearlman (who'd worked with Blue Oyster Cult and The Dictators) who took over its production. In *Tommy Gun*, *English Civil War*, *All The Young Punks*, *Safe European Home* and *Last Gang In Town* it contained some of Strummer and Jones' best material. Whether Pearlman's heavier rock production worked is more controversial. Certainly some critics felt the songs were at times indecipherable beneath the wall of sound. Still, with the band better known, it rose to No. 2 in the U.K., where promo copies contained a special poster, mapping out the world's trouble spots. It was their first album to be released in the 'States, though it only got to No. 128 there. *Tommy Gun* and *English Civil War* were both issued as 45s, with non-album 'B' sides. This continued their run of U.K. hits, but *Tommy Gun* also gave them their first U.S. Top 20 hit, where it peaked at No. 19.

Their *Cost Of Living* EP was issued in May 1979. It included a cover of Sonny Curtis' *I Fought The Law* (which was a Transatlantic hit in the mid-sixties for The Bobby Fuller Four), a remake of *Capitol Radio*, which had previously appeared on the NME freebie EP, and two songs which seemed aimed at the U.S. market, *Gates Of The West* and the acoustic *Groovy Times*. The poppier direction went down like a lead balloon with **Clash** die-hards, but it climbed to No. 22 in the charts. It was warning of their desire to diversify and seek out new directions, which would later become apparent in their love of reggae. Of course, if they'd continued in this direction they'd have probably achieved really big commercial success, which eluded them throughout their career.

In September 1979, they embarked on their second U.S. tour which became known as "The Clash Take The Fifth" referring to the presence of a temporary fifth member **Ian Dury and The Blockheads'** Mickey Gallagher on keyboards. **The Undertones** were the main support act on this tour, but psychobilly band The Cramps, R&B stalwarts Sam and Dave, Screamin' Jay Hawkins and Lee Dorsey and country singer Joe Ely also figured. It was during this tour that their debut album was belatedly issued in the 'States.

The Clash also worked on their third album in the second half of 1979. This time veteran R&B/soul producer Guy Stevens was at the helm. The end product *London Calling*, a double album which was sold for the price of a single one, was finally released at Christmas 1979. This was much more diverse than their previous efforts, transending punk, rock, reggae, rockabilly and R&B. The title track *London Calling* was released as a 45. It enjoyed ten weeks in the charts and climbed to No. 11 giving them their biggest U.K. hit. One of the album's reggae tracks, *Armagideon Time* was put on the flip and the 12" release contained extra dub material. In the

'States, a R&B cut (not listed on the album's sleeve or label) *Train In Vain (Stand By Me)* was released as a 45. It brought them their first U.S. hit, reaching No. 23 in May the following year. The album marked a significant move away from punk/new wave with ska (*Rudie Can't Fail*), and rockabilly (*Brand New Cadillac*) featured, as well as more sophisticated rock and reggae. The album which originally was to be titled *The New Testament*, climbed to No. 9 in the U.K. and No. 27 in the U.S..

On 27th December 1979, they co-starred with **Ian Dury** at the second of four concerts staged at the Hammersmith Odeon for the people of Kampuchea.

On 15th March 1980, the Jack Hazan/David Mingay documentary film "Rude Boy" opened in London. It was about a **Clash** roadie and much of it had been filmed on the road with the band over the previous 18 months.

In June 1980, **The Clash** toured the U.S. again and Europe. The Jamaican deejay Mickey Dread guested on some of their European gigs and they recorded *Bankrobber* with him. It was eventually released as a 45 in the U.K. (after initially only being available on Dutch import). It got to No. 12 occupying the charts for ten weeks. Meanwhile in the 'States, a mini-album *Black Market Clash* which had been tailored for the U.S. market, was released. It included flipsides like *The Prisoner*, *City Of The Dead* and a remix of *Pressure Drop*, as well as the original version of *Capitol Radio*, *Bankrobber*, an edited version of *Armagideon* and a previously unreleased cover of Booker T & The MG's instrumental *Time Is Tight*.

The band, meanwhile, had started work at the Electric Ladyland studios in New York in August 1980. During their visits to the 'States they had been getting heavily into black music. This became apparent when the 36 track triple album *Sandinista!* was released in December 1980, in the week John Lennon was murdered. The title was taken from that of the left wing Nicaraguan freedom movement. At the band's insistence the triple album was sold for the price of a double. Like most triple albums, some of the material was a bit rambling. In the 'States, Epic reduced it to twelve tracks *Sandinista Now* for promo purposes. They also released *If Music Could Talk*, an interview album, which is now quite collectable and pricey. The album's stronger cuts included *The Call Up*, a gentle anti-draft song, which brought them another minor U.K. hit; *Hitsville U.K.*, a weaker rather twee song, which failed to make the Top 50 (peaking at No. 56) and the disco-rap *The Magnificent Seven*, which climbed to No. 34. In the U.K. *Sandinista!* peaked at No. 19. In the U.S. it climbed to No. 24.

December 1981 closed with the release of *This Is Radio Clash*, which was played in the same disco-style as *The Magnificent Seven*. It reached No. 47 in the U.K. and they beagan work on a new album. The album was left uncompleted as, in January 1982, as they headed east for the first time. Their tour took in Japan, New Zealand, Australia, Hong Kong and Thailand. When they returned to Britain, in March, to finish recording Glyn Johns was at the controls.

By now, though, the chemistry behind the band was decidedly wobbly. During 1981, Mick Jones had opted out for several weeks to produce an album for his girlfriend Ellen Foley. Then, on the verge of the "Know Your Rights" tour to promte their new *Combat Rock* album, Joe Strummer disappeared and gigs had to be cancelled. He eventually re-emerged in Paris, where he'd gone to flee from the stresses of rock stardom. The album itself was patchy, but it had its moments. One of these was *Know Your Rights*, a high octane and raw rendition, which charted at No. 43. Another was the disco-orientated *Rock The Casbah*, which later got to No. 30, when issued as a 45 in the U.K. and No. 8 in the U.S.. Mick Jones' cover of *Should I Stay Or Should I Go*, a beat-orientated number, got to No. 17 in the U.K. and No. 45 in the U.S.. This may have been aided by clever marketing, which saw the album issued in four different formats. *Straight To Hell* which was put on the flip of this 45, was quite an emotional and appealing song. Despite its patchiness, *Combat Rock* was extremely successful commercially. In Britain it rose to No. 2, spending a total of 23 weeks in the charts. In the 'States, it became a million-selling album and their biggest, climbing to No. 7.

Behind the facade of their commercial success, the group dynamics were in trouble. 'Topper' Headon left the band the day Strummer returned. He was replaced by their original drummer Terry Chimes as they embarked on their biggest U.S. tour to date. Undoubtedly this aided the sales of *Combat Rock* in the Staes. In February 1983, Chimes left again. He went on to play in Gem and Cowboys International. His replacement was Pete Howard (ex-Cold Fish), who joined in May. Then, in September, it was announced that Joe Strummer and Paul Simonon had decided that Mick Jones should leave the group because he had drifted apart from the original idea of **The Clash**. So off Jones went to Woolwich, reportedly to make demos with a band called Sigue Sigue Sputnik and back U.S. graffiti artist **Futura 2000** on a rap 45, though he later re-emerged with Big Audio Dynamite. In December 1983, members of **The Clash** appeared on Janie Jones and The Lash single *House Of The Ju-Ju Queen* / *Sex Machine*. Janie Jones' exploits had been celebrated on **The Clash**'s first album.

In January 1984, guitarists Vince White and Nick Sheppard were added as **The Clash** re-emerged as a five-piece. Sheppard had previously been in **The Cortinas**.

When *Cut The Crap*, their next album was released it was savaged by the critics and rightly so. It sold far lower quantities than any previous **Clash** album and had few memorable moments. The football choir vocals of songs like *We Are The Clash* and similar shouters sounded like out-takes from a 1977 album, but times had moved on. The band's name carried the album to No. 16 in the U.K., but it could only scrape to No. 171 in the U.S.. In Britain, the *This Is England* 45, culled from it, brought them a Top 30 hit. After their "Busking Tour" of the U.K. failed to revive their fortunes they split in late 1985.

For the next couple of years Strummer concentrated on acting, notably in Alex Cox's "Straight To Hell". Headon's emerging solo career for Mercury collapsed, when he was jailed for possession of heroin in November 1987.

In 1988, the release of the double retrospective compilation *The Story Of The Clash* revived interest in the band. It rose to No. 7 in the U.K.. The 45, *I Fought The Law* was released as a trailblazer and peaked at No. 29 and later another cut *London Calling* was reissued and climbed to No. 46.

The *Twelve Inch Mixes* is basically a five track CD. The problem is that apart from *The Magnificent Dance* which is basically a 'B' side reworking of *The Magnificent Seven*, the other four tracks featured are basically the same versions as the 7" 'A' sides.

THE CLASH - From Here To Eternity.

The Story Of The Clash, Vol. 1 is a double CD set that features all their singalong hits.

Super Black Market Clash, originally issued on vinyl as 3 x 10" in 1993 was originally issued on CD in 1991 and again at mid-price on Sony in 1996. This collection also includes all their flip sides from *1977* to *Mustapha*. *Dance* alongside gems like *Time Is Tight* and *Rubber Dub* as well as *Listen*, which was the backing track to their Tony Parsons interview on the *Capital Radio* EP.

In 1999 *Complete Control* was the opening track on the 5-CD box set *1-2-3-4 - A History Of Punk And New Wave 1976-79* (MCA/Universal MCD 60066).

In 1994, *Clash On Broadway*, originally issued for the U.S. market, was digitally remastered and issued as a 3-CD set here in Britain. It's a perfect **Clash** artefact. It also came with a sixty-three-page booklet containing lots of previously unpublished Pennie Smith photos, including funny ones of

Mick Jones and Paul Simonon standing outside their squat in Davis Road, Acton, in early 1976 in their flares. There are also features by Lenny Kaye and the late Lester Bangs and quotes relating to each track from Joe Strummer, Mick Jones, Paul Simonon and 'Topper' Headon, as well as Keith Levine, their manager Bernie Rhodes and a few more besides. The sixty-three-track, 3-CD package included eight previously unreleased tracks. These comprise spirited live versions of *English Civil War*, *I Fought The Law* and *Lightning Strikes*; two first album demos (*Janie Jones* and *Career Opportunities*) produced by Guy Stevens and three previously unissued cuts. The first, *One Emotion* dates from the *Give 'Em Enough Rope* sessions and is OK but unexciting; the second, *Every Little Bit Hurts* is a cover of an Ed Cobb number, notable for soulful vocals from Jones and an accomplished piano backing from Mickey Gallagher and, finally, *Midnight To Stevens* (a tribute to one of their producers), which sounds pretty lacklustre.

In 1999, *From Here To Eternity*, a retrospective live album, was released. The majority of the material is taken from the early eighties. Its release was accompanied by the re-promotion of **The Clash**'s entire back catalogue suitably remastered and a limited box set combining their 1977-82 studio recordings with the live album. There was also a TV documentary "Westway To The World" about the band, which was made available as a video.

Strummer later embarked on a restricted solo career and Simonon formed the short-lived Havana 3A.M.. Jones subsequently enjoyed considerable success utilising sampling and keyboard technology in the dance-orientated Big Audio Dynamite (later known as simply BAD) with his friend Don Letts, who was also a film-maker and reggae DJ.

For many **The Clash** were the classic U.K. punk band. They were certainly one of the most ambitious and diverse. Their desire to experiment and move on musically enabled them to outlive the punk era and survive until 1985.

The Classics

Personnel:
PAUL BAVERSTOCK	lead gtr, vcls	A
JAMES HONEYWOOD	drms	A
JULIE SUFFIELD	lead vcls	A
MARK THURSFIELD	bs, vcls	A
JOHN WOOTTEN	gtr, vcls	A

45: Audio Audio/Carscape (PS)   (Rocket XPRES 29) 1980

You can also hear *Audio Audio* on *499 2139* (Rocket DIAL 1) 1979. It's quite a catchy number.

Classix Nouveaux

Personnel:
JAK AIRPORT	gtr, synth	A
B.P. HURDING	drms	ABC
SAL SOLO	vcls	ABC
MIK SWEENEY	bs	ABC
GARY STEADMAN	gtr, synth	B
JIMI SUMAN	gtr	C

                                                                   HCP

ALBUMS:
1(B)	NIGHT PEOPLE	(Liberty LBG 30325)	1981	66
2(C)	LA VERITE	(Liberty LBG 30346)	1982	44
3(C)	SECRET	(Liberty KBG 1834241)	1983	-

NB: There's also a CD, *The Very Best Of Classix Nouveau* (EMI Gold CDGOLD 1104) 1997.

                                                                   HCP

45s:
	The Robot's Dance/623 (PS)	(ESP ES 1)	1980 -
	Nasty Little Green Men/Test Tube Babies (PS)	(United Artists BP 378)	1980 -
*	Guilty/Night People (PS)	(Liberty BP 388)	1981 43
*	Tokyo/Old World For Sale (PS)	(Liberty BP 397)	1981 67
	Inside Outside/We Don't Bite (PS)	(Liberty BP 403)	1981 45
	Inside Outside/We Don't Bite/Every Home Should Have One (12", PS)	(Liberty BP 12403)	1981 -
*	Never Again/627 (PS)	(Liberty BP 406)	1981 44
*	Is It A Dream?/Where To Go (PS)	(Liberty BP 409)	1982 11
*	Because You're Young/It's Not Too Late (PS)	(Liberty BP 411)	1982 43
*+	The End... Or The Beginning/Chemin Chagrin (PS)	(Liberty BP 414)	1982 60
*	Forever And A Day/Switch (PS)	(Liberty BP 419)	1983 -
	Never Never Comes/Manitou (PS)	(Liberty BP)	1983 -
	Never Never Comes/Manitou/No Other Way (12")	(Liberty BP)	1983 -

NB: * Also issued as a 12". + Also issued as a picture disc.

Classix Nouveaux were one of the electro-rock/pop bands that grew out of the post-punk era. They veered towards the new romantic movement of the early eighties.

The band was formed in London in 1979 by Sal Solo and Mick Sweeney. The totally bald Solo gave them a distinctive visual impression. He was also a talented vocalist and multi-instrumentalist. They utilised synthesizers as well as guitars, bass, drums and sax to produce reasonably appealing dance rock.

Jak Airport left to form Airport and Dean before their first 45 *The Robot's Dance* on the indie ESP label. He was replaced by Gary Steadman. They attracted sufficient attention to be signed by United Artists during the Autumn of 1980.

Their first album *Night People* (titled *Classix Nouveaux* in the 'States) has its moments with some melodic songs. It spent two weeks in the charts, peaking at No. 66. It also produced three hit singles - *Guilty* (its stand out track), *Tokyo* and *Inside Outside*.

In late 1981, Steadman departed to join **A Flock Of Seagulls** and was replaced by Finish-born Jimi Suman. The new line-up recorded *La Verite* which was more complicated than its predecessor. It fared better commercially, this time enjoying a four week chart residency and a best position of No. 44. It also spawned three more hits *Never Again*, *Is It A Dream?* and *Because You're Young*.

Classix Nouveau live at the Polytechnic of Central London, 12th October 1979. Photo: Steven Richards.

CLASSIX NOUVEAUX - Nasty Little Green Men.

Their third album *Secret*, produced by Alex Sadgin, utilised guest musicians and horns. More rhythmic than their two earlier albums it contained some loud, energetic dance numbers best exemplified by *No Other Way* and *All Around The World* as well as an enticing pop song in *Forever And A Day*. Despite obvious quality the album surprisingly didn't chart.

The band, which won a large European following and also toured Eastern Block countries, finally split in 1984. Compilation appearances included *Is It A Dream* on *The Model* (Spectrum 5529182) 1997 and on *New Romantics* (EMI Gold CDGOLD 1041) 1996. Sal Solo did what his name suggested with some initial commercial success. B.P. Hurding, who'd once been in **X-Ray Spex**, joined Two Minds Crack.

Alan Clayson and The Argonauts

Personnel:	ALAN BARWISE	drms	A
	ALAN CLAYSON	vcls	A
	MIC DOVER	gtr	A
	HAYDN AMADEUS MEDDICK	keyb'ds	A
	SANDY MONTIETH	bs	A
	ALAN WHETTON	sax	A

ALBUM:	1( )	WHAT A DIFFERENCE A DECADE MADE	(Butt 005) 1985
EP:	1( )	LAST RESPECTS	(Rackets ARG 36) 1982
45:		The Taster/Landwaiser (live) (PS)	(Virgin VS 215) 1978

Alan Clayson is better known as a rock author on the beat music era. This band played light boogie-rock.

The Clerks

Personnel incl: MARTIN PAUL   vcls

45s:	No Good For Me/	
	(other side by **The Hazard**)	(Rok ROK VIII VII) 1979
	Dancing With My Girl/On The Telephone/	
	All I Want Is You (PS)	(Puddisc SRT 8 KS 1538) 1984

A London-based band led by vocalist Martin Paul who were signed to Rok Records, a label formed by Caruso Fuller and Tony Matthias in Fulham, West London in late 1979 to expose new bands. Rok issued *No Good For Me* on a shared single with **The Hazard** in 1979 and, the following year, this track and *When The Lights Go Out* featured on the now legendary and rare *Odd Bods Mods And Sods* (Rok ROK LP 1) 1980 compilation. This is now more accessible thanks to its recent CD reissue (Captain Mod MODSKA CD 2) 1996 with several bonus cuts.

The Clerks also issued a second 45 on Puddisc in 1984.

When The Lights Go Out isn't one of the stronger mod revival discs, but you can also check it out on *100% British Mod* (Captain Mod MODSKA DCD 8) 1998.

Clock DVA

Personnel:	CHARLIE COLLINS	sax, flute, perc	AB
	DAVID J. HAMMOND	gtr	A
	ADI NEWTON (ADOLPHUS NEWTON)	vcls, clarinet, synth	ABCD
	ROGER QUAIL	drms, perc	AB
	STEVE 'JUDD' TURNER	bs, treated gtr	AB
	PAUL WIDLER	gtr	B
	PAUL BROWSE	sax	CD
	NICK SANDERSON	drms	CD
	JOHN VALENTINE-CARRUTHERS	gtr, bs	CD
	DEAN DENNIS	bs	D

ALBUMS/CASS:	1(A)	DEEP FLOOR	(Private Cassette) 1980
	2(A)	FRAGMENT OVATION	(Private Cassette) 1980
	3(A)	WHITE SOULS IN BLACK SUITS	(Industrial IRC 31) 1981
	4(B)	THRIST	(Fetish FR 2002) 1981
	5(D)	ADVANTAGE	(Polydor POLS 1082) 1983

NB: (3) originally issued as a cassette, available as an album in 1983 and on CD (Contempo CONTECD 157) 1992 in Italy. (4) also issued on CD (Contempo CONTEDISC 192) 1992 in Italy. (5) also issued on CD (Interfisch EFA 1706CD) 1989. There's also a compilation *Collective* (Hyperium HY 39100) 1994.

EP:	1(C)	PASSION STILL A FLAME (Son Of Song/Theme From I.M.D./Don't (It's Taboo)/Noise In Limbo) (PS)	(Polydor POSP 437) 1982
45s:		4 Hours/Sensorium (PS)	(Fetish FET 008) 1981
	x	High Holy Disco Mass/The Voice That Speaks From Within (Triumph Over Will) (PS)	(Polydor) 1982
	*	Resistance/The Secret Life Of The Blacksuit (PS)	(Polydor POSP 578) 1983
	*	Breakdown/Black Angel's Death Song (PS)	(Polydor POSP 627) 1983

NB: x 'A' side credited to **DVA**. * Also available in 12" format.

Formed in Sheffield in 1979 by Adi Newton (real name Adolphus Newton) **Clock DVA** were another of the post-punk industrial bands of this era. Adi had initially fronted **The Future** who went on to become **The Human League**. The following year **Clock DVA** released two private cassettes. They also had a cut *You're Without Sound* included on *Hicks From The Sticks* (Rockburgh ROC 111) in 1980. Then, in 1981, an indie 45 on Fetish and a cassette *White Souls In Black Suits* on Industrial Records followed. This was actually available on vinyl in Italy. The music on this recording is both soulful and permeated by an urban metal noise to create an altogether eerie atmosphere.

With Paul Widler replacing David J. Hammond on guitar *Thirst* maintained dancey rhythms, but the soulfulness of its predecessor gave way to electro machine-type noises and chants.

In 1981, Steve 'Judd' Turner died and the remaining members formed The Box. Adi put together an entirely new line-up 'C' to record the *Passion Still*

ALAN CLAYSON AND THE ARGONAUTS - Last Respects EP.

Aflame EP in 1982 and then Dean Dennis supplemented the line-up on bass for the funky, more dance-orientated *Advantage*, which is generally considered to be their best album in this era. There are some effective splatterings of sax and trumpet amongst the driving drum/bass rhythms and Adi Newton's emotional vocals. This produced two strong 45s *Resistance* and *Breakdown* but still commercial success eluded them. On the flip side of *Breakdown* they recorded their only cover version - of Velvet Underground's *Black Angel's Death Song*.

Despite their atmospheric and usually exciting music **Clock DVA** failed to achieve any commercial success and disbanded early in 1984.

Valentine-Carruthers rejoined **Siouxsie and The Banshees**, whilst Sanderson and Dennis worked with Gun Club's Jeffrey Lee Pierce on his solo projects. Adi formed Anti-Group in 1985 and later reformed **Clock DVA** with Paul Browse and Dean Dennis in 1988. This second incarnation recorded well into the nineties.

Clockwork Soldiers

45:	Wet Dreams/Suicide/ In The Name Of Science (PS)	(Rot ASS 5)	1984

A mid-eighties punk band. In addition to the above **Clockwork Soldiers** contributed the title cut and *Hit And Run* to *Wet Dreams* (Rot ASS 4) in 1984 and *Wet Dreams* resurfaced again on *Rot Records Punk Singles Collection* (Anagram CDPUNK 40) in 1994.

"Speeding along nearly doing a ton
A bit pissed up and my sights nearly gone
Someone steps right in my way
Stood no chance, couldn't get away
Hit and run, hit and run, hit and run, run
Draw the car straight to a halt
He's lying there dead and it's all my fault
But I can't stay I'm over the limit
So I hide the body and step right on it
Hit and run, hit and run, hit and run, run"
(from *Hit And Run*)

The Clues

Personnel:	IAN COOK	gtr	A
	JOHN GRIFFIN	drms	A
	ANDREW SCOTT	bs	A
	PAUL SMITH	vcls, hrmnca	A

45:	No Vacancies (6 tracks)	(Clues Records)	1981

An obscure mod combo. Cook and Griffin co-wrote *No Vacancies*, which came out on their own label in 1981 complete with a lyric insert. This contains nice guitar work and melodic vocals. It got further exposure on *100% British Mod* (Captain Mod MODSKA DCD 8) 1998.

Ian Cook was later in **Crush**.

THE COCKNEY REJECTS - Flares 'N' Slippers.

Cobra

Personnel:	NIGEL BOYD	vcls	A
	GLEN CRAWFORD	gtr	A
	NIGEL HAMILTON	drms	A
	K. SEWELL	gtr	A
	M. THOMPSON	bs	A

45:	Graveyard Boogie/Looking For A Lady (PS)	(Rip Off RIP 3)	1978

A rare and expensive 45 to track down now. **Nigel Hamilton** also played with **The Speed** and was later in **The Tearjerkers**.

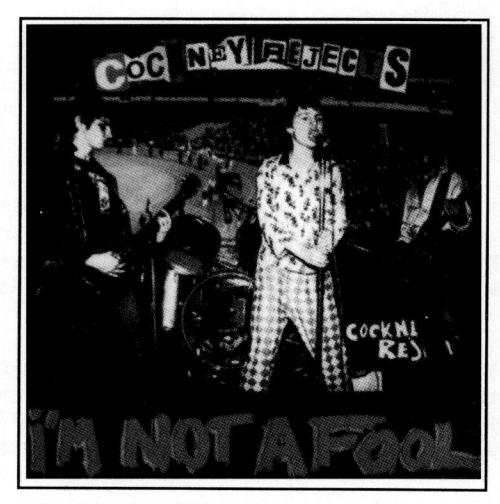

THE COCKNEY REJECTS - I'm Not A Fool.

Cockney 'n' Westerns

45:	She's No Angel/ Had A Real Good Time (PS)	(Beggars Banquet BEG 39)	1980

This one-off project included members of **The Boys** and **The Roadies**.

The Cockney Rejects

Personnel:	MICKY GEGGUS	gtr	AB
	PAUL HARVEY	drms	A
	CHRIS MURREL	bs	A
	JEFFERSON 'STINKY' TURNER	vcls	AB
	VANCE RIORDAN	bs	B
	ANDY SCOTT	drms	B

ALBUMS:	1(B)	GREATEST HITS VOLUME 1		HCP
		(Zonophone ZONO 101)	1980	22
	2(B)	GREATEST HITS VOLUME 2		
		(Zonophone ZONO 102)	1980	23
	3(B)	GREATEST HITS VOLUME 3 (LIVE AND LOUD)		
		(Zonophone ZEM 101)	1981	27
	4(B)	THE POWER AND THE GLORY		
		(Zonophone ZONO 105)	1981	-
	5(B)	WILD ONES (Zonophone AKA 1)	1982	-

NB: (1) and (2) reissued on one CD (Slogan SLOG CD 4) 1992. (1) also issued on CD (Dojo DOJOCD 136) 1994 with four bonus tracks. (1) issued on CD again (Rhythm Vicar PREACH 011CD) 1999. (2) also issued on CD (Dojo DOJOCD 138) 1994 with four bonus tracks. (2) issued on CD again (Rhythm Vicar PREACH 012 CD) 1999. (3) also issued on CD (Dojo DOJOCD 168) 1993 with four bonus tracks. (4) also issued on CD (Dojo DOJOCD 174) 1993 with four bonus tracks. (4) also issued on CD (Captain Oi! AHOYCD 122) 1999, with five bonus tracks. (5) also issued on one CD with *Lethal* (Loma LOMACD 38) 1994. *Lethal* has been issued as a single CD (Neat NEATCD 1049) 1996. Also relevant are *Unheard Rejects / Flares 'N' Slippers* (Step-1 STEPCD 020) 1998; *Oi! Oi! Oi!* (Can Can CAN CAN 005CD) 1997; *The Best Of The Cockney Rejects* (Dojo DOJO CD 82) 1992 (now deleted); *We Are The Firm* (Dojo DOJOCD) 1986; *Punk Singles Collection* (Anagram CDPUNK 90) 1997; *The Greatest Cockney Rip-Off* (Harry May MAYO CD 102) 1999; *The Very Best Of The Cockney Rejects* (Anagram CDPUNK 113); and *Greatest Hits Vol. 4* (Rhythm Vicar PREACH 021 CD) 2000.

45s:	Flares 'N' Slippers/Police Car/		
	I Wanna Be A Star (PS)	(Small Wonder SW19)	1979 -
	I'm Not A Fool/East End (PS)	(EMI EMI 5008)	1979 65
	Bad Man/The New Song (PS)	(EMI EMI 5035)	1980 65
*	The Greatest Cockney Rip-Off/ Hate Of The City (PS)	(Zonophone Z 2)	1980 21
	I'm Forever Blowing Bubbles/ West Side Boys (PS)	(Zonophone Z 4)	1980 35
	We Can Do Anything/15 Nights (PS)	(Zonophone Z 6)	1980 65
	We Are The Firm/ War On The Terraces (PS)	(Zonophone Z 10)	1980 54
	Easy Life/Motorhead/ Hang 'Em High (PS)	(Zonophone Z 20)	1981 -
	On The Streets Again/London (PS)	(Zonophone Z 21)	1981 -
	Till The End Of The Day/ Rock 'n' Roll Dreams (PS)	(A.K.A. AKS 102)	1982 -

NB: * issued on yellow vinyl.

Avid West Ham fans, **The Cockney Rejects** formed in East London in 1978. They carried the mantel of bands like **Cock Sparrer** and **Sham 69**. Micky Geggus was vocalist Jefferson 'Stinky' Turner's brother.

Their mentor was **Sham 69**'s Jimmy Pursey and they were initially managed by 'Sounds' journalist Garry Bushell. After submitting a demo tape to Small Wonder Records, who offered them a one-single deal, they persuaded Pursey to produce it. The resulting three track *Flares 'N' Slippers* sold its initial pressing briskly during the summer of 1979. *Flares 'N' Slippers* was a frenetic punk offering. The second cut *Police Car* had a spoken intro of "Freedom there ain't no fucking freedom", which was later sampled and released by The Heavy Metal Outlaws. This cut was also frantic and the 45 culminated with *I Wanna Be A Star*. All three cuts subsequently resurfaced on *Oi! The Singles Collection, Vol. 2* (Captain Oi! AHOY CD 63) 1996. This helped win them a deal with EMI which led to five albums and a string of 45s (including half a dozen consecutive hits). By the time of *I'm Not A Fool*, their debut single for EMI which was again produced by Jimmy Pursey, Paul Harvey and Chris Murrel had left to be replaced by Vance Riordan (bs), (previously of **Dead Flowers**) and Andy Scott (drms), who was once with The Ticket. *I'm Not A Fool*, released on 26th October 1979, actually reached No. 65 in the U.K. charts. Both this and the flip side *East End* were brash and raucous punkers. The 'thanks John' vocal at the end of *East End* was in appreciation of Radio 1 DJ John Peel who'd had them in for a couple of sessions. Both *I'm Not A Fool* and *East End* were included on the band's debut album *Greatest Hits Vol. 1* and they later resurfaced on *Oi! The Singles Collection, Vol. 3* (Captain Oi! AHOY CD 67) 1997. The follow-up *Bad Man* contained one of Oi!'s finest riffs and was also one of the best **Cockney Rejects**' songs. The flip side *New Song* was a real barnstormer too. Both these cuts also appeared on their debut album *Greatest Hits, Vol. 1* and subsequently on *Oi! The Singles Collection, Vol. 4* (Captain Oi! AHOY CD 71) 1997. Ironically, *Bad Man* also climbed to No. 65, but spent three as opposed to two weeks in the charts. Although their first three albums were called *Greatest Hits, Vol.'s 1, 2* and *3*, they weren't compilations at all. All three, the third was a live one, made the lowest third of the Top 30.

Their next 45, *The Greatest Cockney Rip-Off*, fared much better rising to No. 21.

THE COCKNEY REJECTS - Bad Man.

The Power And The Glory, the band's fourth album included the single *On The Streets Again*. The Captain Oi! reissue of this comes with five rare bonus tracks:- *Lomdob, Beginning Of The End, Motorhead, Francine* and *T.N.T.*. It also contains complete lyrics for each song and a detailed history of the album. There's a tinge of punk on tracks like *On The Run* and *Teenage Fantasy* but this is mostly a metal album.

After this **The Cockney Rejects** turned into a metal band in the mid-eighties and severed their connection with Oi!.

Most of the material musically combined the chants of the football terrace with an anti-establishment stance. They were early heroes for the Oi! Movement of the early eighties but were gradually edged out in terms of popularity by the newer Oi! bands whose often violent gigs won them more publicity.

Inevitably **The Cockney Rejects** have figured on a number of compilations. Their appearances include the opening cut *Oi, Oi, Oi* and *Here We Go Again* on the seminal *Oi! The Album* (EMI ZIT 1) 1980, later reissued on CD (Captain Oi! AHOY CD 72) 1997; *Beginning Of The End* on *100% British Oi!* (Captain Oi! AHOY DCD 83) 1997; *The Greatest Cockney Rip-Off* on *Burning Ambition: A History Of Punk, Vol. 3* (Anagram CD PUNK 98) 1997 and *Police Car* on *Oi! Chartbusters, Vol. 1* (Link LP 03) 1987. *The Greatest Cockney Rip Off, I'm Forever Blowing Bubbles, We Can Do Anything, We Are The Firm, Easy Life* and *On The Streets Again* were all included on *The Zonophone Punk Singles Collection* (Anagram CDPUNK 97) in 1997. *Budman* figured on *Punk - The Worst Of Total Anarchy* (2-CD) (Disky SP 871952) in 1996 and *Flares 'N' Slippers* got a further airing on *Punk, Vol. 2* (Music Club MCCD 027) 1991. Finally, *Flares 'N' Slippers* can also be found on *Small Wonder Punk Singles Collection, Vol. 1* (Anagram CDPUNK 29) 1994 and *Vol. 2* (Anagram CDPUNK 70) 1996 of the same series showcased their version of *Police Car*.

The Best Of The Cockney Rejects features twenty-two of their terrace-style anthems, including *Flares 'N' Slippers* and *The Greatest Cockney Rip-Off* and captures the band at their best. *The Greatest Cockney Rip-Off* CD, released in 1999, commences with the title cut, followed by all three cuts from their debut *Flares 'N' Slippers* EP for Small Wonder. Much of the other material is from their metal years and eminently forgettable although this patchy collection concludes with a pulsating and raw live version of *Bad Man*. The same year they contributed to the *Oi! Fuckin' Oi!* (Harry May MAYO CD 110) 1999 CD compilation.

The Very Best Of Cockney Rejects is a twenty-two track compilation put out by Anagram in 1999. All their best 'A' sides are included together with many of their better 'B' sides and album tracks in a digipak sleeve with a full discography of the band.

Greatest Hits, Vol. 4 is the work of a reformed **Cockney Rejects**. Lead vocalist Stinky Turner and guitarist Mickey Geggins are ably assisted by Tony Van Frater and Andrew Laing (of **Red Alert**) as they re-record a mixture of their early Oi! anthems and their later more metal orientated material.

Cock Sparrer

Personnel:	MICKY BEAUFOY	gtr	AB
	STEVE BRUCE	drms	AB
	STEVE BURGESS	bs	AB
	GARRIE LAMMIN	gtr	A
	COLIN McFAULL	vcls	AB

ALBUMS:	1( )	SHOCK TROOPS	(Razor RAZ 9) 1983
	2( )	RUNNIN' RIOT IN '84	(Syndicate SYNLP 7) 1984
	3( )	TRUE GRIT	(Razor RAZ 26) 1986
	4( )	LIVE AND LOUD	(Link LINKLP 05) 1987
	5( )	RUNNIN' RIOT IN '84	(Link LINKLP 032) 1988

NB: (1) also issued on CD (Captain Oi! AHOY CD 004) 1997, with bonus tracks. (1) and (2) also issued on one CD (Step-1 STEP CD 028) 1998. (4) also issued on CD (Pin Head PINCD 103) 1998. Other relevant releases are *Rarities* (Captain Oi! AHOY CD 36) 1994; *Bloody Minded (The Best Of Cock Sparrer)* (Dr. Strange DSR 73) 1997; *The Best Of Cock Sparrer* (Step-1 STEP CD 014) 1998; *Two Monkeys* (Blitzcore BC 1710CD) 1997; *England Belongs To Me* (Can Can CANCAN 007CD) 1997; *Diamonds And Pearls* (DDS DDS 003) 2000; and they also contributed to a CD *Live And Loud* (Step-1 STEP CD 004) 1998 shared with **The Business**.

45s:
	Runnin' Riot/Sister Suzie	(Decca FR 13710) 1977
	We Love You/Chip On My Shoulder	(Decca FR 13732) 1977
*	We Love You/Chip On My Shoulder (12" PS)	(Decca LFR 13732) 1977
	England Belongs To Me/ Argy Bargy (PS)	(Carrerre CAR 225) 1982

NB: * Only 7,500 copies of this were pressed.

From London's East End **Cock Sparrer** formed in 1974 as a pub rock band, attracting a mostly skinhead audience. With the emergence of **The Sex Pistols** and punk rock in 1976, they latched onto this movement and were signed by Decca in 1977.

Apparently they were approached by **Malcolm McLaren** before he discovered **The Sex Pistols** but his offer of management was refused because he didn't buy a round of drinks!

Like **Sham 69** and **Cockney Rejects**, **Cock Sparrer** set out to use punk as a medium for expressing working class sentiments. Unfortunately, **Cock Sparrer**'s attempts at this were more pedestrian than those of their colleagues. They dealt in solid four-chord anthems. They wore the clothing of the football terraces of the time - 'Clockwork Orange' - style boots and braces.

Their debut 45, Runnin' Riot was basically a skinhead boot-boy anthem, dealing with the issue of street violence. Demo copies, which are now very rare and expensive, came with a picture sleeve depicting a photo of a West Ham pitch invasion. Unusually, though, for the punk era the main release didn't have a picture sleeve. For the follow-up, the band covered The Rolling Stones' We Love You. Again the 7" came without a picture sleeve, but there was also a 7,500 limited edition 12" version of this release with a picture sleeve and a photo insert. Again chart success eluded them. With the onset of Oi! in the early eighties they celebrated a resurgence in their popularity after Garry Bushell included Running Riot and a new cut Taken For A Ride on Strength Thru' Oi! (Decca) in 1981.

In 1982, they switched to Carrere for England Belongs To Me. The original 'B' side the tongue in cheek Colonel Bogey was replaced at the last moment by Argy Bargy, a good Cockney anthem. They might have known a patriotic title like this would mean trouble in the Oi! era but apparently not. The song was adopted as the anthem of right-wing, racist, neo-Nazi skins and the basically non-political band recoiled in horror and withdrew from the music scene for a while. This led to a loss of momentum so when they returned with a series of later albums for Razor, Syndicate and Link the writing was on the wall.

True Grit includes their two Decca singles, Running Riot and a cover of The Rolling Stones' We Love You, but the bulk of the material comprises previously unreleased Decca demos.

Rarities is a sixteen-track CD which includes their seminal terrace anthems like Runnin' Riot and Trouble On The Terraces as well as three cuts taken from the sought-after series of eighties Oi! compilations.

In 1999, they contributed England Belongs To Me to Oi! Fuckin' Oi! (Harry May MAYO CD 110), a CD compilation. Both sides of the England Belongs To Me 45 had earlier resurfaced on Oi! The Singles, Vol. 1 (Captain Oi! AHOY CD 60) 1996. Chip On My Shoulder can also be heard on 100% British Oi! (Captain Oi! AHOY DCD 83) 1997. They'd earlier recorded a live version of this song for Son Of Oi! (Syndicate SYN LP 3) 1983, later reissued on CD (Captain Oi! AHOY CD 9) 1993. They also supplied the title track and Runnin' Riot to Trouble On The Terraces - 16 Classic Football Anthems (Step-1 STEP LP 19) 1986. The Oi! Of Sex (Syndicate SYN LP 4) 1994, later reissued on CD (Captain Oi! AHOY CD 23) 1994, included The Sun Says. Back in 1980, they'd supplied Sunday Stripper for Oi! The Album (EMI ZIT 1), which has also been reissued on CD (Captain Oi! AHOY CD 72) 1997.

Diamonds And Pearls is a set of demos, originally issued in Spain which later resurfaced on Razor as True Grit. The content is described earlier in this entry, but this CD issue has no bonus tracks and is re-packaged with no sleevenotes or photos, which is disappointing.

COCK SPARRER - England Belongs To Me.

The Cocteau Twins

Personnel: (up to 1986)	ELIZABETH FRASER	vcls	ABCDEF
	ROBIN GUTHRIE	gtr, drms programming, keyb'ds	ABCDEF
	WILL HEGGIE	bs	A
	SIMON RAYMONDE	bs, keyb'ds, gtr	C EF
	RICHARD THOMAS	sax	D
	HAROLD BUDD	piano	F

HCP

ALBUMS: (up to 1986)	1(A)	GARLANDS	(4AD CAD 211) 1982 -
	2(B)	HEAD OVER HEELS	(4AD CAD 313) 1983 51
	3(C)	TREASURE	(4AD CAD 412) 1984 29
	4(D)	VICTORIALAND	(4AD CAD 602) 1986 10
	5(F)	THE MOON AND THE MELODIES	(4AD CAD 611) 1986 46

NB: (1) also issued on CD (4AD CAD 211) 1986 with six additional cuts, Dear Heart, Blind Dumb Deaf, Hearsay Please, Hazel, Speak No Evil and Perhaps Some Other Acon. (2) also issued on CD (4AD CAD 313) 1986 with the Sunburst And Snowblind EP added. (3) also issued on CD (4AD CAD 412) 1986. (4) also issued on CD (4AD CAD 602) 1986. (5) credited to Harold Budd, Elizabeth Fraser, Robin Guthrie and Simon Raymonde. Also issued on CD (4AD CAD 611) 1986. There's also a CD compilation The Pink Opaque (4AD CAD 513) 1985 and The Singles Collection (Capitol) 1991. This CD box set featured their nine previous singles and a new one and from March 1992 all ten were sold as CD singles individually.

HCP

EPs: (up to 1986)	1(A)	LULLABIES (It's All But An Ark Lark/ Alas Dies Laughing/ Feathers-Oar-Blades) (12", PS)	(4AD) 1982 -
	2(B)	SUNBURST AND SNOWBLIND (Sugar Hiccup/ From The Flagstones/Because Of Whirl-Jack/ Hitherto)	(4AD) 1983 -
	3(C)	TINY DYNAMITE (Pink Orange Red/Ribbed And Veined/Sultitan Iban/ Plain Tiger) (12", PS)	(4AD BAD 510) 1985 52
	4(C)	ECHOES IN A SHALLOW BAY (Pale Clouded White /Great Spangled Fritillary/Melonella/ Eggs In Their Shells) (12", PS)	(4AD CAD 511) 1985 65

NB: (3) and (4) also issued on CD (BAD 510/511 CD) 1986.

HCP

45s: (up to 1986)	Peppermint Pig/Hazel (PS)	(4AD AD 303) 1983 -
	Peppermint Pig/Hazel/ Laugh Lines (12", PS)	(4AD BAD 303) 1983 -
	Sugar Hiccup (one-sided, promo only)	(4AD AD 314) 1984
	Pearly-Dewdrops Drop/Pepper Tree (PS)	(4AD AD 405) 1984 29
	Pearly-Dewdrops Drop/Pepper Tree/ The Spangle Maker (12", PS)	(4AD BAD 405) 1984 -
	Aikea - Guinea/Kookaburra (PS)	(4AD AD 501) 1985 41
	Aikea - Guinea/Kookaburra/Rococo/ Quiquose (12", PS)	(4AD BAD 501) 1985 -
	Love's Easy Tears/ Those Eyes, That Mouth (PS)	(4AD AD 610) 1986 53
	Love's Easy Tears/Those Eyes, That Mouth/ Sigh's Smell Of Farewell (12", PS)	(4AD BAD 610) 1986 -

The Cocteau Twins formed in Grangemouth, Scotland, in 1981. Actually a trio comprising Elizabeth Fraser, Robin Guthrie and Will Heggie, they travelled down to London in November 1981 armed with two demo tapes. The first was given to Radio One DJ John Peel, who they went on to record two sessions for. The second was given to Simon Raymonde, who was the son of the sixties producer/arranger Ivor Raymonde. Simon was working as a shop assistant at the time beneath the company offices of 4AD Records. He played the tape to the label's manager Ivo Watts-Russell who, after hearing it, offered to help.

Their first album *Garlands* was released in June 1982. It cost just £900 to record in nine days but was a big indie chart hit. The band had successfully created a sound that was unique. It was based around Fraser's almost tuneless vocals, treated guitars and bass with a drum synthesizer. The end result was a richly textured, somewhat arty atmospheric sound which won them much critical acclaim. The cassette version contained four additional cuts. They soon attracted major label interest but elected to release material as and when they were ready through 4AD. Much of the remainder of 1982 and the early part of 1983 was spent supporting **Orchestral Manuvoeures In The Dark** on a fifty-date tour. In October 1982 *Lullabies* a 12" EP was released and brought them considerable indie chart success without managing to break into the mainstream chart. The band slimmed down to a duo when Heggie left during the summer of 1983 to form Lowlife.

The Cocteau Twins finally achieved mainstream commercial success with their second album *Head Over Heels* released in October 1983. Fraser's vocals are better on this album and the songriting is more sophisticated and varied. *In Our Anglehood* is quite rocky and Fraser's soaring vocals on cuts like *Musette And Drums* and *In The Gold Dust Rush* are very appealing, whilst *Sugar Hiccup* displays a more melodic side to their music. The album spent a very credible fifteen weeks in the charts despite never rising above No. 51. The same month a strong four song EP was released titled *Sunburst And Snowblind*. This included a different version of *Sugar Hiccup*. The subsequent CD issue of this album in 1986 included the content of the EP.

Simon Raymonde, who'd been playing in an outfit called Drowning Craze, joined on bass, guitar and keyboards as the band reverted back to a trio. The enlarged line-up achieved singles chart success when their April 1984 single *Pearly - Dewdrops! Drop* climbed to No. 29 during its five weeks in the charts. This was really their first pop crossover hit, but they turned down the chance to appear on 'Top Of The Pops' to help promote it.

Treasure released in November 1984 was their finest work. From the opening track *Ivo* a meticulous blend of Fraser's powerful vocals, guitars and increased use of keyboards and drums is achieved to produce an intriguing and fascinating sound. It's hard to single out individual tracks because a consistent standard is maintained throughout. The album spent eight weeks in the charts rising to No. 29. A brilliant effort.

In March 1985 they released three four song EPs. The first *Aikea - Guinea* sounded very similar to previous albums. It spent three weeks in the singles chart, peaking at No. 41. This was followed by two 12" - only EPs *Tiny Dynamite* and *Echoes In A Shallow Bay*. These were very similar in sound and sustained the group's recently-found commercial success spending two weeks and one week in the chart and climbing to No. 52 and 65 respectively. 1985 also saw the release of *The Pink Opaque* a CD-only compilation, which documented their career to date.

Prior to the release of their fourth album *Victorialand* in April 1986 Richard Thomas (of **Dif Juz**) came in to replace Simon Raymonde who fell ill. *Victorialand* continued the band's tradition of pleasant mood music. Fraser is given possibly more vocal freedom than on previous efforts and the instrumental backing was largely psychedelic-tinged treated acoustic guitar. The public liked it and the album became their most successful in commercial terms, climbing to No. 10 during its seven weeks in the charts. Simon Raymonde returned to the fold during the summer to replace Richard Thomas who returned to **Dif Juz**.

Love's Easy Tears, a 45 of new material (the 12" version contained an additional cut *Sigh's Smell Of Farewell*), brought them a further hit when it spent one week in the charts at No. 53 in October 1986. It would be their last single for nearly two years. In November, they completed a sell-out tour and collaborated with 4AD's latest signing Harold Budd on *The Moon And The Melodies*, which was credited to Budd and all three **Cocteau Twins** individually. After this the band took a rest but returned in 1988 and continued to record into the nineties.

THE COCTEAU TWINS - Treasure.

Elizabeth Faser and Robin Guthrie guested as part of **This Mortal Coil**, which was a conglomeration of 4AD musicians on the *Song To The Siren* 45, which was a revival of a Tim Buckley song. It spent over a year in the indie charts as well as climbing to No. 66 in the U.K.. Robin Guthrie went on to produce for several 4AD artists as well as Gun Club in 1987. Liz and Robin became parents in 1989.

In 2001, *Sugar Hiccup* got a further airing on the 4-CD box set *25 Years Of Rough Trade Shops* (Mute CDSTUMM 191).

The Cocteau Twins were responsible for some of the most interesting and rewarding mood music of the eighties. Their sound was unique and is strongly recommended if you haven't heard any of their music.

Color Tapes

45:    Cold Anger/Leaves Of China (PS)   (Wavelength HURT 4) 1979

A one-off venture by a Bristol band. *Cold Anger* lacks any real energy or excitement, which is probably why. The 45 was produced by Mark Stewart of **The Pop Group**.

COMBAT 84 - Orders Of The Day EP.

Combat 84

Personnel:	BROWNIE	drms	A
	DEPTFORD JOHN	bs	A
	CHRIS HENDERSON	vcls	A
	JIM MONCUR	gtr	A

EP:	1(A)	ORDERS OF THE DAY (Poseur/Skinhead/Violence Combat 84) (PS) (Victory VIC 1) 1984

45:    Rapist/The Right To Choose/
       Baryy Prudom (PS)   (Victory VIC 2) 1984

An Oi! band. Their best known song *Rapist* appeared to advocate a stronger government and capital punishment. You'll also find it on *Oi! Chartbusters, Vol. 1* (Link LP 03) 1987.

Prior to this they recorded the four track *Orders Of The Day* (EP), which was released in a wraparound sleeve by Victory Records in 1984. Most of the songs *Poseur*, *Skinhead*, *Voilence* and *Combat 84* are a rallying call to skinheads and glorify their lifestyle.

On account of its name the band encountered a lot of hostile media coverage. They lost a record deal with Secret Records and starred in a BBC 'Arena' documentary. The band finally split in late 1984. Both Deptford John and Jim Moncur later joined **UK Subs** and Deptford John later played for a while in **The Exploited**.

All four cuts from the *Orders Of The Day* (EP) later resurfaced on *Oi! The Rarities, Vol. 5* (Captain Oi! AHOY CD 62) 1996 and *Poseur* can also be heard on *100% British Oi* (Captain Oi! AHOY DCD 83) 1997.

Coming Shortly

45:    Doing The Flail/(other side by **The Squire**) (Rok ROK 1/11) 1979

A Milton Keynes band. *Doing The Flail* wasn't one of the label's finest offerings, but it can also be heard as a bonus cut on Captain Mod's CD reissue of *Odds Bods Mods And Sods* (MODSKA CD 2) 1996.

Comsat Angels

Personnel:			
(up to 1986)	KEVIN BACON	bs	AB
	MIC GLAISHER	drms	AB
	STEVEN FELLOWS	vcls, gtr	AB
	ANDY PEAKE	keyb'ds, synth	AB
	(PAUL ROBERTSON	keyb'ds	B)

HCP

ALBUMS:	1(A)	WAITING FOR A MIRACLE	(Polydor 2383 578) 1980 -
(up to	2(A)	SLEEP NO MORE	(Polydor POLS 1038) 1981 51
1986)	3(A)	FICTION	(Polydor POLS 1075) 1982 94
	4(A)	LAND	(Jive HIP 8) 1983 91
	5(B)	7 DAY WEEKEND	(Jive HIP 29) 1985 -

NB: (1) also issued on CD (RPM RPM 155) 1996. (2) also issued on CD (RPM RPM 156) 1996. (3) also issued on CD (RPM RPM 157) 1996. (4) also issued on CD (Connoisseur Collection VSOPCD 329) 2001 with additional tracks. (5) also issued on CD (Connoisseur Collection VSOPCD 330) 2001 with additional tracks. There are also a couple of CD compilations *Time Considered (BBC Sessions)* (RPM RPM 106) 1992 and *Unravelled (Dutch Radio Sessions No. 1)* (RPM RPM 123) 1994.

HCP

45s: x Red Planet/I Get Excited/
(up to   Specimen No. 2 (PS)   (Junta JUNTA 1) 1979 -
1986)   Total War/Waiting For A Miracle (PS) (Polydor 2059 227) 1980 -
         Total War/Waiting For A Miracle/
         Home On The Range (12", PS)   (Polydor 2059 227) 1980 -
         Independence Day/We Were (PS)   (Polydor 2059 257) 1980 -
         Eye Of The Lens/At Sea (PS)   (Polydor POSP 242) 1981 -
         Eye Of The Lens/At Sea/Another World/
         Gone (12", PS)   (Polydor POSP 12242) 1981 -
         Do The Empty House/Now I Know/Red Planet
         Revisited (double pack 7")   (Polydor POSP 359) 1981 -
         It's History/Zinger (PS)   (Polydor POSP 432) 1982 -
         After The Rain/Private Party (PS) (Polydor POSP 513) 1982 -
         Will You Stay Tonight/Shining Hour (PS) (Jive JIVE 46) 1983 -
         Will You Stay Tonight/Shining Hour/
         A World Away (12", PS)   (Jive JIVET 46) 1983 -
         Island Heart/Scissors And Stones (PS) (Jive JIVE 51) 1983 -
         Island Heat/
         Scissors And Stones (12", PS)   (Jive JIVET 51) 1983 -
         Independence Day/Mister Memory (PS) (Jive JIVE 54) 1984 75
         Independence Day/Mister Memory/
         Intelligence (12", PS)   (Jive JIVET 54) 1984 -
       * Independence Day/Mister Memory/Total War/
         After The Rain (double-pack 7") (Jive JIVE 54) 1984 -
         You Move Me/
         Escape From Willesden (PS)   (Jive JIVE 65) 1984 -
         You Move Me/Land/
         Eye Of The Lens (live) (12", PS) (Jive JIVET 65) 1984 -
         Day One/Will You Stay Tonight (7") (Jive JIVE 73) 1984 -
         Day One/Will You Stay Tonight/
         Independence Day (12", PS)   (Jive JIVET 73) 1984 -
         I'm Falling/New Heart And Mind (PS) (Jive JIVE 87) 1985 -
       + I'm Falling (Extended)/New Heart And Mind/
         Citadel (12", PS)   (Jive JIVET 87) 1985 -
         Forever Young/Still It's Not Enough (PS) (Jive JIVE 111) 1985 -
         Forever Young/Still It's Not Enough/
         Sign (12", PS)   (Jive JIVET 111) 1985 -

NB: x Later reissued on red vinyl. * Also available as a 12". + In blue vinyl.

Comsat Angels formed in Sheffield in 1978. They were initially known as Radio Earth but for contractual reasons they didn't record until the change of name to **Comsat Angels**. They sought to create atmospheric, haunting mood music from the outset. In this pursuit they tended to conjure up melancholic melodies with hushed vocals and firm beat to great effect on their early recordings.

After a three track release *Red Planet* on the independent Junta label they signed to Polydor in late 1979. Their musical formula works to near perfection on their 1980 album *Waiting For A Miracle*. The stand-out cuts are *Total War* and *Independence Day*, which were both issued as singles earlier in 1980. They deserved commercial success with these, which remain among their finest moments, but they were still getting known.

Following a 45 *Eye Of The Lens* in March 1981, a second album *Sleep No More* was released in August. This was a more sombre affair, which suffered from a lack of variety, although it contained some good tracks such as *Dark Parade* and *Our Secret*. It was also their most successful album commercially. It climbed to No. 51 during its five weeks in the charts.

Any 45 success continued to elude them as a double 7", coupling *Do The Empty House* and *Now I Know* on one disc with *Red Planet Revisited* on another, missed out.

Their 1982 album *Fiction* enjoyed two weeks in the album charts with a best position of No. 94. It proved they would continue to produce intelligent unnerving music on tracks like *Zinger* and *Ju-Ju Money*, whilst *It's History* another of its stronger songs had been selected for 45 release to preview the album and another cut *After The Rain* was culled for subsequent release.

In 1983, they switched labels and attempted to break into the American market. This led to a number of contractual problems and they had to be promoted as C.S. Angels in the U.S. after the communications conglomorate Comsat threatened legal action. Their fourth album *Land* was

COMSAT ANGELS - Sleep No More.

CONDEMNED 84 - Oi! Ain't Dead.

produced by Mike Howlett. It contains a number of more memorable, poppier tunes, which were among the best things they did. There is less anger in Steve Fellow's guitar work on this album and with Andy Peake's synthesizer more prominent, they achieved the more commercial sound their new label Jive desired. *Alicia* is arguably the stand out track. Again it registered in the lower echelons of the album charts, climbing to No. 91 during its two week stay. The album included a re-recorded version of *Independence Day* and they eventually made an incursion into the singles chart when this and *Mister Memory* from *Land* were included on the *Independence Day EP* which spent one week at No. 75 in January 1984. In April, a Dutch compilation was issued which comprised material from their Polydor days.

Paul Robertson guested on keyboards for their 1985 recordings including their *7 Day Weekend* album produced by Mtume, Chris Tsangurides and Mike Howlett. It spawned two further singles *I'm Falling* and *Forever Young* but neither they or the album reached the charts and commercially the group was in decline. When Robertson departed in the Autumn of 1985 they reverted back to a quartet.

They broke up in 1987 after one further album *Chasing Shadows* which was produced by Robert Palmer, who also guested on it. They reformed in 1992 and went on to release two albums in the nineties; *My Minds Eye* (1992) and *The Glamour* (1995).

Time Considered is a nineteen-cut album of their BBC Radio Sessions of their gloomy, moody brand of rock. The collection features Peel sessions from back in 1979, their 'Janice Long Show' version of The Rolling Stones' *Citadel* and the most recent material was taken from a Bruno Brookes Show in 1984. The sound quality is very good - on a par with their studio albums.

CONDEMNED 84 - Battle Scarred.

The CD reissues of *Land* and *7 Day Weekend* on Connoisseur Collection come with extensive sleevenotes and additional tracks.

The Condemned

45:	Soldier Boy/Endless Revolution/	
	(cuts by **The Proles**)	(Rock Against Racism RAR 1) 1979

The Condemned are much more obscure than **The Proles** who they shared this four track 45 with.

Condemned 84

Personnel:	CLIFF	drms	A
	GUNK	bs	AB
	MICK	gtr	AB
	KEV PARKER	vcls	AB
	NIALL	drms	B

ALBUM: (up to 1986)	1(A)	BATTLE SCARRED (mini LP)	(Oi! OIR 003) 1986

EPs: (up to 1987)	1(A)	Oi! AIN'T DEAD (Oi! Ain't Dead/Under Her Thumb/ Follow The Leader/The Nutter) (12", PS)	(RFB SIN 2) 1986
	2(B)	IN SEARCH OF THE NEW BREED (Boots Go Marching In/Up Yours/We Will Never Die/ Kick Down The Doors) (12", PS)	(RFB SIN 3) 1987

An Ipswich-based Oi! band who first emerged with the *Battle Scarred* mini-album in 1986. They also appeared on *This Is Oi!* (Oi! OIR 004) the same year. *This Is Oi!* was later reissued on CD (Captain Oi! AHOY CD 6) 1993. Kev's growling vocals are the distinctive feature on their two contributions *Jimmy Davey* and *Teenage Slag*.

They followed this with the *Oi! Ain't Dead* (EP) later that year. Again, the main distinguishing feature was Kev Parker's growling voice. You can also check out the title track on *100% British Oi!* (Captain Oi! AHOY DCD 83) 1997.

A further EP *In Search Of The New Breed* followed in 1987. For this, Niall replaced the previous drummer Cliff. All four of these Oi! classics later resurfaced on *Oi! The Rarities, Vol. 3* (Captain Oi! AHOY CD 53) 1995.

They went on to record a further album *Face The Aggression* and have remained active on the Oi! scene ever since.

A cut from their *Battle Scarred* album was later included on *The Best Of Oi! Records* (Captain Oi! AHOY CD 38) 1995.

CONDEMNED 84 - In Search Of The New Breed.

Conflict

Personnel:	JOHN CLIFFORD	bs	ABC
	GRAHAM	gtr	A
	COLIN JERWOOD	vcls	ABC
	KEN	drms	A
	STEVE	gtr	BC
	PACO	drms	BC
	PAULINE BECK	vcls	C

ALBUMS: (up to 1986)
1(B) IT'S TIME TO SEE WHO'S WHO NOW (Corpus Christi CHRIST 3) 1981
2(B) INCREASE THE PRESSURE (Mortarhate MORTLP 6) 1984
3(B) THE UNGOVERNABLE FORCE (Mortarhate MORTLP 20) 1985
4(B) ONLY STUPID BASTARDS USE EMI (Model Army THIS NOT 599) 1986

NB: (1) reissued on vinyl (Mortarhate MORTLP 110) 1994, also on CD (MORTCD 110) 1994. (3) also issued on CD (Mortarhate MORTCD 020) 1998. There's also two compilations, *Standard Issue Vol. 1 1982 - 87* (Mortarhate MORT 40) 1989 and *There Must Be Another Way - The Singles* (Jungle FREUD CD 068) 2001, which rounds up their singles for Mortarhate.

EPs: (up to 1986)
1(C) A HOUSE THAT MAN BUILT (Crass 221984/1) 1982
2(A) LIVE AT THE CENTRE IBERICO (Xntrix XN 2001) 1982

NB: (2) reissued on Mortarhate (MORT 7) 1984.

45s: (up to 1986)
A Nation Of Animal Lovers/ Liberate (poster PS) (Corpus Christi CHRIST IT'S 4) 1983
The Serenade Is Dead (both sides) (PS) (Mortarhate MORT 1) 1983
This Is Not Enough (both sides) (PS) (Mortarhate MORT 8) 1985
The Battle Continues (both sides) (PS) (Mortarhate MORT 15) 1985

An anarcho-punk band who formed in Eltham, South-east London in 1979. They'd also played under a variety of names including Splattered Rock Stars. They were very influenced by **Crass** and shared their concerns about animal welfare and pacifism. Like **Crass** their's was also basically an anarchic agenda. They made their live debut in Eltham during April 1981. Their early line-ups were fluid but solidified into line-up 'A', although Steve and Paco soon took over from Graham and Ken on guitar and drums respectively.

Pauline Beck came in on vocals for their debut EP *A House That Man Built* on the Crass label. They advocated direct action for many causes which brought them into frequent conflict with the police. The studio material on *Increase The Pressure* and *The Ungovernable Force* is generally thought to capture them at their best.

They organised a massive benefit for the Animal Liberation Front's anti-whaling team at the Brixton Ace on 26th May 1983.

They set up their own Mortarhate label, which enabled them to release material throughout the eighties.

Crass' Steve Ignorant had guested on their *A Nation Of Animal Lovers* in 1983 - the cover to which lead to incitement charges against them incidentally. After Colin Jerwood was badly assaulted in an Eltham pub, Ignorant had a two year tenure as their joint vocalist between 1987 and 1989.

They continued to record well beyond the timeframe of this book. Subsequent albums on Mortarhate were *Turning Rebellion Into Money* (1987) (which documented the rioting that occured after their 1987 Brixton Academy gig), *The Final Conflict* (1988), *From Protest To Resistance* (1988), *Against All Odds* (1989), *Conclusion* (1993) *We Won't Take No More* (CD) (1995) and *In The Venue* (1997).

If you're curious to hear **Conflict** the recent CD compilation *There Must Be Another Way - The Singles*, which rounds up their singles on Mortarhate, could be a good place to start.

John Cooper Clarke

ALBUMS:
1 DISGUISE IN LOVE (CBS 83132) 1978
2 WALKING BACK TO HAPPINESS 'LIVE' (10") (CBS JEC 1) 1979
3 SNAP CRACKLE AND BOP (CBS 84083) 1980
4 OU EST LA MAISON DU FROMAGE (Rabid NOTE 1) 1980
5 ME AND MY BIG MOUTH (Epic 84979) 1981
6 ZIP STYLE METHOD (Epic 85667) 1982

NB: (1) also issued on CD (Epic 4805302) 1995. (3) also issued on CD (Epic 4773802) 1994. (4) also issued on CD with extra cuts (Receiver RRCD 110) 1996.

EP: 1 PSYCLE SLUTS (EP) (Psycle Sluts Pt's 1 and 2/ Suspended Sentence/Innocents) (PS) (Rabid TOSH 103) 1977

NB: (1) some copies pressed in yellow or blue vinyl.

HCP

45s:
Post-war Glamour Girls/ Kung Fu International (PS) (CBS CBS 6541) 1978
* Gimmix/I Married A Monster From Outer Space (PS) (Epic EPC 7009) 1979
Splat/Twat/Sleepwalk (PS) (Epic EPC 7982) 1979
It Man/36 Hours (PS) (Epic EPC 8655) 1980
The Day My Dad Went Mad/ A Distant Relation (PS) (Epic A 2077) 1982
Night People/ The Face Behind The Scream (PS) (Epic A 2521) 1982

NB: * Also issued in triangular shaped orange vinyl.

Along with **Patrick Fitzgerald**, **John Cooper-Clarke** was one of two great poets of the punk era. He is extremely long-sighted and his dark glasses gave him a distinct visual image. Leaving school at fifteen, he had a succession of jobs including apprentice motor mechanic and window cleaner culminating in a two year stint as a laboratory technician at Salford Tech. He played bass in obscure psychedelic bands in the late sixties. Like so many others involved in new wave, he'd become bored by the state of rock by the mid-seventies. He began his poetry readings in the early seventies in local folk clubs around the Salford area of Manchester where he grew up. For a while he teamed up with a Manchester band called The Ferretts, who added music to his slots.

In October 1977, he was the support act for a **Buzzcocks** gig at Manchester's Electric Circus. The gig was recorded for Virgin's *Short Circuit At The Electric Circus* (Virgin VCL 5003), released in 1978, which included two of his efforts *You Never See A Nipple In The Daily Express* and *I Married A Monster From Outer Space*. In December 1977, he recorded an EP for Tosh Ryan's local indie label Rabid, which was centred around the two part, decidedly odd and very amusing *Psycle Sluts*. Another poem from this, *Innocents* was featured on the 1978 compilation *Streets* (Beggars Banquet BEGA 1).

JOHN COOPER CLARKE - Disguise In Love.

In February 1978, he was signed to Epic and his *Disguise In Love* album was released. Like his earlier EP it was produced by Martin Hannett, but this featured guest appearances from **Buzzcocks**' Pete Shelley and **Be-Bop Deluxe**'s Bill Nelson. The album is full of 100mph punk (or post-punk) poems, hilarious jokes and the odd obscenity. Its masterpieces include *I Don't Want To Be Nice* (the opening cut), the near danceable *Teenage Werewolf*, *Valley Of The Long Lost Women* and *Reader's Wives*. There are also a couple of live cuts - *Psycle Sluts* and *Salome Maloney*. This was followed by a live 10" album, *Walking Back To Happiness* in mid-1979. A little earlier that year he released his second 45 *Gimmix*. To help live up to its name there was a limited edition pressing in triangular shaped orange vinyl.

In 1980, he represented Britain in the first World Poetry Olympics held at Poet's Corner in Westminster Abbey. Two of his poems, *Psycle Sluts 1 & 2* and *Bronze Adonis* appeared on *The Crap Stops Here* (Absurd LAST 1) 1980 compilation.

On his next album *Snap Crackle And Bop* he was supported by former **Penetration** lead singer **Pauline Murray**'s new band **Invisible Girls**. This was his most successful effort commercially. It also contained his best-known effort *Beasley Street*. His half-sung, half-spoken, fast-paced lyrics dealt with issues of urban decay, VD, insomnia, drugs and the uncomfortable situation of enforced family get togethers. One track *Evidently Chickentown* is more electronic and on *36 Hours* he rages about life behind bars where the daily routine is "shave, shit, shower and a shoe shine". After his *Zip Style Method* album in 1982, he wound down his recording career.

In addition to the above discography, he recorded two sessions for John Peel. The first on 6th November 1978 featured *I Married A Monster From Outer Space*, *Readers' Wives*, *Health Fanatic* and *Split Beans*. The second on 15th March 1982 comprised *Midnight Shift*, *The Day My Dad Went Mad*, *The New Assasin* and *Night People*. The following year, he did a session for the Janice Long show which consisted of *Health Fanatic*, *The Day My Dad Went Mad* and *I Wanna Be Yours*.

Innocents, *Suspended Sentence* and *Psycle Sluts* can all be found on *Rabid/TJM Punk Singles Collection* (Receiver RRCD 227) in 1996. He also contributed *Kung Fu International* to *The Best Punk Album In The World.... Ever, Vol. 1* (2-CD) (Virgin VTPCD 42) in 1995 and *The Best Punk Anthems.... Ever* (2-CD) (Virgin VTDCD 198) in 1998; and *Beasley Street* to *The Best Punk Album In The World.... Ever Vol. 2* (2-CD) (Virgin VTDCD 79) 1996. His very funny *Psycle Sluts* can also be heard on *1-2-3-4 - A History Of Punk And New Wave 1976 - 1979* (MCA/Universal 60066) (5-CD) box set.

Clarke also wrote two books of poetry 'The Cooper Clarke Directory' and 'Ten Years In A Open-Neck Shirt'. In the late eighties he shacked up with Nico of Velvet Underground fame. After her death he re-emerged with a lower profile on the alternative club circuit, although he didn't record and nowadays only performs very occasionally.

Hugh Cornwell

ALBUMS: (up to 1986)	1	NOSFERATU	(United Artists UAG 30251) 1979

NB: (1) credited to **Hugh Cornwell** and Robert Williams. It was later issued on CD (EMI CDP 799 104 2) 1992 and again (Eastworld EW 0001 CD) 1998.

45s: (up to 1986)	* White Room/ Losers In A Lost Land (PS)	(United Artists BP 320) 1979
	One In A Million/Siren Song (PS)	(Portrait PRT A 6509) 1985
	One In A Million/ Siren Song (12", PS)	(Portrait PRT TX 6509) 1985

NB: * Credited to **Hugh Cornwell** and Robert Williams.

Hugh Cornwell was born in North London on 28th August 1948. He later attended the same grammar school as future guitar virtuoso Richard Thompson, who taught him to play bass. They were in a school group together called Emil and The Detectives along with Nick Jones (the son of Max Jones - the 'Melody Maker' jazz critic). They mostly played Buddy Holly and Everly Brothers' covers.

Cornwell played in various local groups - during spells at Bristol University studying Chemistry and two and a half years in Sweden pursuing 'research'. Returning to England, he took a job teaching biology in an 'A' level grammer in Guildford, but lost the job for becoming over-friendly with the pupils. Whilst he was in Guildford he met **J.J. Burnel**. By now **Cornwell** was playing lead guitar and he gave **J.J. Burnel** a bass guitar, which he soon mastered. **The Stranglers** were soon born and the rest is history, as they say.

Whilst with **The Stranglers** in 1979 **Hugh Cornwell** recorded an album *Nosferatu* with Captain Beefheart's drummer Robert Williams, who played bass, moog and percussion on the album. Two members of Devo guested on this album too, which accounts for the Devo-like effects. The project is of interest to **Stranglers**' fans largely because it previewed some of the lyrical and musical concerns of the band during the eighties. It is quite a demanding album for the listener, but a cover of Cream's *White Room*, which was released as a 45, provided some light relief. By this time **Cornwell**'s extra-curricular activities also included producing an unreleased album for Leila and The Snakes and a five-cut demo for **The Pop Group**.

During the eighties with **The Stranglers Cornwell** had to endure a jail term for heroin possession.

In the post-1986 period, **Cornwell** concentrated on seriously trying to launch a solo career. In 1987, his *Facts And Figures* single was a minor hit and featured on the soundtrack of the animated film 'When The Wind Blows'. However, his *Wolf* album the same year was disappointing. He teamed up with Robert Cook and Andy West for the *CCW* album in 1992. Then, in 1993, he collaborated with Alex Gifford (bs), Chris Goulstone (gtr), Ted Mason (gtr) and Robert Williams (drms) for a much better album *Wired*. *Guilty* (in 1997) continued to enhance the development of his mainstream solo career.

The Cortinas

Personnel:			
	DEXTER DALWOOD	bs	A
	MIKE FEWINS	gtr	A
	NICK SHEPPARD	gtr	A
	DANIEL SWAN	drms	A
	JEREMY VALENTINE	vcls	A

ALBUM:	1(A)	TRUE ROMANCES	(CBS 82831) 1978

45s:	Fascist Dictator/ Television Families (PS)	(Step Forward SF 1) 1977
	Defiant Pose/Independence (PS)	(Step Forward SF 6) 1978
*	Defiant Pose/Independence (12" PS)	(Step Forward SF 6) 1978
	Heartache/Ask Mr. Waverley (PS)	(CBS CBS 6759) 1978

NB: * This was issued in a pink die-cut sleeve.

The Cortinas were a teenage garage-band from Bristol. They started out playing R&B in the summer of 1976. Their first break came when they got a gig supporting **The Stranglers** at The Roxy. Their first two 45s were typical belting punk offerings. On the strength of these they were signed up to a major label. The resulting album *True Romances* is much more mainstream in style and delivery - rock 'n' roll, R&B and pop-rock. The two best cuts, *Heartache* and *Ask Mr. Waverley* were also put out on a 45.

In addition to the above discogarphy, **The Cortinas** recorded one session for John Peel on 26th July 1977. It comprised *Defiant Pose*, *Television Families*, *Having It* and *Further Education*.

Nick Sheppard later joined **The Clash**.

Elvis Costello and The Attractions

Personnel:			
	ELVIS COSTELLO	gtr, vcls	A
	STEVE NASON	keyb'ds	A
	BRUCE THOMAS	bs	A
	PETE THOMAS	drms	A

				HCP
ALBUMS: (up to 1986)	1(-)	MY AIM IS TRUE	(Stiff SEEZ 3) 1977	14
	2(A)	THIS YEAR'S MODEL	(Radar RAD 3) 1978	4
	3(A)	ARMED FORCES	(Radar ADA 14) 1979	2

4(A)	GET HAPPY!!	(F-Beat XXLP 1)	1980	2
5(-)	TEN BLOODY MARY'S & TEN HOW'S YOUR FATHERS			
		(F-Beat XXC 6)	1980	-
6(A)	TRUST	(F-Beat XXLP 11)	1981	9
7(A)	ALMOST BLUE	(F-Beat XXLP 13)	1981	7
8(A)	IMPERIAL BEDROOM	(F-Beat XXLP 17)	1982	6
9(-)	PUNCH THE CLOCK	(F-Beat XXLP 19)	1983	3
10(A)	GOODBYE CRUEL WORLD	(F-Beat 7L 70317)	1984	10
11(A)	THE BEST OF ELVIS COSTELLO - THE MAN			
		(Telstar STAR 2247)	1985	8
12(-)	KING OF AMERICA	(F-Beat ZL 70496)	1986	11
13( )	BLOOD AND CHOCOLATE	(IMP XFIEND 80)	1986	16

NB: (2) was originally issued with a free single, *Stranger In The House / Neat, Neat, Neat* (SAM 83) 1978. (5) was a cassette-only release in a gold case. (7) was issued in four different coloured sleeves. (12) credited to The Costello Show. (13) also issued as a cassette. (1) reissued (IMP FIEND 13) 1986 and on CD (IMP FIEND CD 13) 1986. (2) reissued (F-Beat XXLP 4) 1980 and (IMP FIEND 18) 1984 and on CD (IMP FIEND CD 18) 1984. (3) reissued (IMP FIEND 21) 1984 and on CD (IMP FIEND CD 21) 1986 and as an extended reissue (Demon DPAM 3) 1993. (4) reissued (IMP FIEND 24) 1984 and on CD (IMP FIEND CD 24) 1986 and as an extended reissue (Demon DPAM 5) 1994. (5) reissued (IMP FIEND 27) 1984 and on CD (IMP FIEND CD 27) 1986. (6) reissued (IMP FIEND 30) 1984 and on CD (IMP FIEND CD 30) 1986 and as an extended reissue (Demon DPAM 6) 1994. (7) reissued (IMP FIEND 33) 1984 and on CD (IMP FIEND CD 33) 1986 and on extended reissue (Demon DPAM 7) 1994. (8) reissued (IMP FIEND 36) 1984 and on CD (IMP FIEND CD 36) 1986 and as an extended reissue (Demon DPAM 8) 1994. (9) also issued on CD (Demon FIEND 72) 1987 and again (Demon DPAM 9) 1995. (10) reissued on vinyl (Demon FIEND 75) 1987 and on CD (F-Beat ZD 70317) 1986 and as an extended reissue (Demon DPAM 10) 1995. (11) reissued (IMP FIEND 52) 1986 and on CD (IMP FIEND CD 52) 1986 and as an extended reissue (Demon DPAM 13) 1995. (12) reissued on vinyl (Demon FIEND 78) 1987 and CD (F-Beat ZD 70946) 1986 and as an extended reissue (Demon DPAM 11) 1986, initial copies came with a bonus CD, *Live On Broadway, 1986*. (13) reissued on CD (IMP FIEND CD 80) 1986. There was also an *Interview Picture Disc* (Baktabak BAK 2001) 1987. *Out Of Our Idiot* (Demon FIEND 67) 1987 and on CD (Demon FIEND CD 67) 1987 was a 'B' sides, rarities compilation. *Girls, Girls, Girls* (Demon FIEND 160) 1981 was a double LP compilation also issued on cassette (Demon FIEND CASS 160) with a different track listing in 1989 and *Vol. 2* (Demon FIENDCASS 161) 1989 as a second cassette compilation. There's also *The Very Best Of Elvis Costello And The Attractions* (2LP) (Demon DPAM LP 13) 1994 and on CD (Demon DPAM 13) 1994. Also of interest will be a 4-CD box set *The First 12 ½ Years* (Demon DPAM BOX 1) 1993 which includes reissues of *My Aim Is True*, *This Year's Model* and *Armed Forces* plus a fourth CD *Live At The El Mocambo* (DPAM 4). All CDs issued on Demon were remastered and reissued in 1997. Also check out *Girls, Girls, Girls* (2-CD set) (Demon DFIEND 160) 1996 and (1), (2) and (3) issued with one *Live* (CD) on a 4-CD set *Two And A Half Years* (Demon DPAMBOX 1) 1998.

HCP

45s:	Less Than Zero/Radio Sweetheart (PS)	(Stiff BUY 11)	1977	-
(up to	Alison/			
1986)	Welcome To The Working Week (PS)	(Stiff BUY 14)	1977	-
	Red Shoes/Mystery Dance (PS)	(Stiff BUY 15)	1977	-
	Watching The Detectives/Blame It On Cain (live)/			
	Mystery Dance (live) (PS)	(Stiff BUY 20)	1977	15
	(I Don't Want To Go To) Chelsea/			
	You Belong To Me (PS)	(Radar ADA 3)	1978	16
	Pump It Up/Big Tears (PS)	(Radar ADA 10)	1978	24

ELVIS COSTELLO - Armed Forces.

	Radio Radio/Tiny Steps (PS)	(Radar ADA 24)	1978	29
	Oliver's Army/My Funny Valentine (PS)	(Radar ADA 31)	1979	2
	Accidents Will Happen/Talking In The Dark/			
	Wednesday Week (PS)	(Radar ADA 35)	1979	28
	I Can't Stand Up (For Falling Down)/			
	Girls Talk (PS)	(F-Beat XX1)	1980	4
*	Stranger In The House/(flip side by George Jones) (PS)			
		(Epic EPC 8560)	1980	-
	High Fidelity/			
	Getting Mighty Crowded (PS)	(F-Beat XX 3)	1980	30
	High Fidelity/Getting Mighty Crowded/			
	Clowntime Is Over (Version 2) (PS)	(F-Beat XX3T)	1980	-
	New Amsterdam/			
	Dr. Luther's Assistant (PS)	(F-Beat XX5)	1980	36
	New Amsterdam/Luther's Assistant/Ghost Train			
	/Just A Memory (EP) (PS)	(F-Beat XX 5E)	1980	-
	New Amsterdam/Luther's Assistant/Ghost Train/			
	Just A Memory (pic disc) (PS)	(F-Beat XX 5P)	1980	-
	Clubland/Clean Money/			
	Hoover Factory (PS)	(F-Beat XX12)	1980	60
	From A Whisper To A Scream/			
	Luxembourg (PS)	(F-Beat XX14)	1981	-
	Good Year For The Roses/			
	Your Angel Steps Out Of Heaven (PS)	(F-Beat XX17)	1981	6
	Sweet Dreams/Psycho (live) (PS)	(F-Beat XX19)	1981	42
	I'm Your Toy (live)/Cry Cry Cry/			
	Wondering (PS)	(F-Beat XX21)	1982	51
	I'm Your Toy (live)/My Shoes Keep Walking Back To You/			
	Blues Keep Calling/			
	Honky Tonk Girl (12" PS)	(F-Beat XX21T)	1982	-
	You Little Fool/Big Sister/			
	The Stamping Ground (PS)	(F-Beat XX 26)	1982	52
	Man Out Of Time/Town Cryer (PS)	(F-Beat XX 28)	1982	58
	Man Out Of Time/Town Cryer/			
	Imperial Bedroom (12" PS)	(F-Beat XX28T)	1982	-
	From Head To Toe/			
	The World Of Broken Hearts (PS)	(F-Beat XX30)	1982	43
	Party Party/Imperial Bedroom (PS)	(A&M AMS 8257)	1982	48
+	Pills And Soap/			
	Pills And Soap (Extended Version) (PS)	(Imp IMP 001)	1983	16
	Everyday I Write The Book/			
	Heathen Town (PS)	(F-Beat XX 32)	1983	28
	Everyday I Write The Book/Heathen Town/			
	Night Time (12" PS)	(F-Beat XX 32T)	1983	-
	Let Them All Talk/The Flirting Kind (PS)	(F-Beat XX33)	1983	59
	Let Them All Talk (Extended Remix)/			
	The Flirting Kind (12" PS)	(F-Beat XX33T)	1983	-
+	Peace In Our Time/			
	Withered And Died	(Imposter TRUCE 1)	1984	48
	I Wanna Be Loved/			
	Turning The Town Red (PS)	(F-Beat XX35)	1984	25
	I Wanna Be Loved (Radio Version)/Turning The Town Red/			
	I Wanna Be Loved (Extended Version) (12" PS)			
		(F-Beat XX35T)	1984	-
	I Wanna Be Loved (Radio Version)/Turning The Town Red/			
	I Wanna Be Loved (Disco Version) (12" PS)			
		(F-Beat XX352)	1984	-
	The Only Flame In Town/			
	The Comedians (PS)	(F-Beat XX 37)	1984	71
	The Only Flame In Town (Disco Version)/			
	Pump It Up (Dance Mix)/The Comedians (12" PS)			
		(F-Beat XX372)	1984	-
#	Green Shirt/Beyond Belief (PS)	(F-Beat 2B 40086)	1985	68
#	Green Shirt/Beyond Belief/Oliver's Army/			
	A Good Year For The Roses (PS)	(F-Beat 2B 40085/7)	1985	
#	Green Shirt/Beyond Belief/			
	Green Shirt (Extended Mix) (12" PS)	(F-Beat 2T 40086)	1985	
$	Living A Little, Laughing A Little/			
	(flip side by John Hiatt) (PS)	(CBS A 6121)	1985	-
&	The People's Limousine/They'll Never Take Her			
	Love Away From Me (PS)	(IMP IMP 006)	1985	
£	Green Shirt/Beyond Belief/The People's Limousine/			
	They'll Never Take Her Love Away From Me (PS)			
		(F-Beat 2B 40085/7)	1985	
@	Less Than Zero/Radio Sweetheart/Alison/			
	Watching The Detectives (12" PS)	(Stiff BUYIT 239)	1985	
@	Don't Let Me Be Misunderstood/Baby's Got A			
	Brand New Hairdo (PS)	(F-Beat 2B 40555)	1986	33

@	Don't Let Me Be Misunderstood/Baby's Got A Brand New Hairdo/Get Yourself	
	Another Fool (12" PS)	(F-Beat 2T 40556) 1986 -
	Tokyo Storm Warning Parts 1 & 2 (PS)	(IMP IMP 007) 1986 73
	Tokyo Storm Warning Parts 1 & 2/	
	Black Sails In The Sunset (12" PS)	(IMP IMP 007T) 1986 -
	I Want You Parts 1 & 2 (PS)	(IMP IMP 008) 1986 -
	I Want You Parts 1 & 2/	
	I Hope You're Happy Now (12" PS)	(IMP IMP 008T) 1986 -

NB: * with George Jones. Flip side by George Jones. + credited to The Imposter, not issued in a picture sleeve. # also issued in green vinyl in a clear PVC sleeve. $ with John Hiatt. Flip side by John Hiatt. Also 12" version with three other songs by John Hiatt. & credited to The Coward Brothers in a die-cut sleeve. £ issued in a shrinkwrapped double pack. @ credited to The Costello Show.

Elvis Costello's real name is Declan McManus. He was born on 25th August 1955. His father Ross was a bandleader, so he was born into a musical family. He grew up in Liverpool and began writing songs in his early teens. He left school at sixteen and got work as a computer operator. He developed his music career playing as a solo artist in local folk clubs using the name D.P. Costello (Costello was his mother's maiden name).

In 1976, he became vocalist in a country-rock band Flip City. They circulated some demos around record companies and this eventually led to a deal with Stiff Records, who suggested that he renamed himself as **Elvis Costello**. Although he didn't play punk, largely because of the timing of his career, he became marketed as part of the punk movement.

Late in 1976 Stiff funded his first recording sessions at Pathway studios in Islington. The U.S. band Clover was recruited as a temporary backing band.

His debut 45, *Less Than Zero*, was released in April 1977, but failed to chart. The follow-up *Alison*, a fine ballad and arguably one of the best things he ever wrote, came out the following month, but also failed to chart. Despite this lack of early commercial success, **Costello** went full-time in the music business in July 1977. He assembled a new band, **The Attractions**, Steve Nason (aka Steve Nieve) (keyb'ds), Bruce Thomas (bs) (who'd previously been with The Sutherland Brothers and Quiver) and Peter Thomas (drms) (who'd been with Chilli and The Red Hot Peppers). They played their first gig at the Nashville Pub in London.

Through a timely coincidence **Costello**'s debut album *My Aim Is True* was released to widespread critical acclaim the week Elvis Presley died. The U.S. edition of the album also included *Watching The Detectives*. The stand-out song was the heart-rendering tearjerker *Alison*.

"Oh, it's so funny to be seeing you after so long girl,
And with the way you look I can understand you were not impressed
I heard that you let that little friend of mine take off your party dress"
(from *Alison*)

It was a powerful and emotional debut album, which showcased his talent and promise as a songwriter.

ELVIS COSTELLO - Trust.

ELVIS COSTELLO - Goodbye Cruel World.

In October 1977, **Elvis Costello and The Attractions** joined the 'Stiff Live' tour. It also featured **Ian Dury**, **Nick Lowe**, **Wreckless Eric** and **Larry Wallis**. With **The Attractions** he contributed two cuts, a fine version of Dusty Springfield's 1964 U.K. No. 3 hit *I Just Don't Know What To Do With Myself* and *Miracle Man* to the *Stiff Live Stiffs* (Stiff GET 1) 1978 tour album. Then in November, his manager Jake Riviera formed a new label, Radar Records, and **Costello** became their first artist. His final 45 for Stiff was *Watching The Detectives*. This highly accessible song with its catchy beat brought him his first hit, climbing to No. 15. Meanwhile he toured the 'States for the first time, performing *Radio Radio* on TV's 'Saturday Night Live' against record company instructions.

In March 1978, he returned to the 'States for a further tour which helped secure *My Aim Is True* a peak position of 32. During the tour, a show at the El Mocambo, in Toronto was recorded for a promotional album.

In April 1978, *This Years Model* **Costello**'s first album with **The Attractions** was released. It combined sixties pop influences with punk energy and spawned two of his finest singles, *I Don't Want To Go To Chelsea* and *Pump It Up*. Again both songs were accessible with memorable beats. They peaked at No. 16 and 24 respectively in the U.K. and the album rose to No. 4. *Radio Radio* dealing with the state of the nation's airwaves climbed to No. 29 in November of that year.

He followed it in January 1979 with his highly successful *Armed Forces* album. This was originally to be titled *Emotional Facism* but the name wasn't used to maximise its marketability. It made No. 2 in the U.K. charts, and later, spurred on by a successful U.S. tour, No. 30 there. The excellent *Oliver's Army* 45 culled from the album also made No. 2. This album really marked the highpoint of his career, but this was damaged a little later when, during a U.S. tour, he became embroiled in a drunken argument and brawl with Stephen Stills and Bonnie Bramlett in Columbus, Ohio. **Costello** later apologised for his behaviour in a 'Rolling Stone' interview and it didn't do irreputable damage. In May 1979, he enjoyed a further U.K. hit with *Accidents Will Happen*. He also produced the first Specials album in June.

With the collapse of Radar Records, Riviera set up a new label F-Beat. **Costello**'s *I Can't Stand Up For Falling Down* brought him a No. 4 hit. A cover of an old Sam and Dave song it marked a change of direction towards soul, which was confirmed by his next *Get Happy!!* album. Produced by **Nick Lowe**, this secured him further chart success peaking at No. 2 in the U.K. and No. 11 in the U.S.. His talents as a songwriter were now widely acknowledged. Linda Rondstadt covered *Alison* on her *Living In The U.S.A.* (1978) album and *Party Girl*, *Girls Talk* and *Mad Love* on *Mad Love* (1980).

Hi Fidelity and *New Amsterdam* brought him further U.K. hits in April and June respectively. Then in November 1980, a U.S. compilation of outtakes, demos and unreleased U.K. 45s was put out called *Taking Liberties*. It included *Hoover Factory* a song **Costello** had written to help save the historic Hoover factory site in Northolt, West London. The compilation climbed to No. 28 in the 'States. Meanwhile, in Britain, a similar project but with a different track listing was released in cassette-only format and called *Ten Bloody Mary's And Ten How's Your Fathers*.

ELVIS COSTELLO - Spike.

Trust, released in January 1981, signalled a further change in direction. It tried to capture the rhythmic elements of *Get Happy!!* without referring so obviously to soul influences. Wordplay was an important element on the album, with many songs being a parade of puns and metaphors. Another of the album's themes was a distaste for the press, which was most overt on *Fish And Chip Papers*. *Trust* included *Clubland*, a 45 dealing with corruption which had been a minor U.K. hit in December 1980. *Trust* was another successful album commercially, climbing to No. 9 in the U.K. and 28 in the U.S.. To hep promote *Trust* he toured the U.S. again in January 1981 with **Squeeze** as his support band.

When **Costello** returned from the 'States he and **The Attractions** recorded an album of country covers *Almost Blue* with producer Billy Sterrill in Nashville. The 'South Bank Show' TV programme did a special show about the recording sessions for the album. The album sold well here in the U.K. peaking at No. 7, but it flopped in the 'States where they didn't know how to market it and it only got to No. 50. The 45, *A Good Year For Roses*, culled from it made No. 6 in the U.K., where a cover of Patsy Cline's *Sweet Dreams* later climbed to No. 42. More chart success followed with **Squeeze**'s *Eastside Story*, which was co-produced by **Costello**.

In January 1982, **Elvis Costello and The Attractions** played at London's Royal Albert Hall with The Royal Philharmonic Orchestra. *I'm Your Toy*, recorded live with the Royal Philharmonic Orchestra got to No. 51 in April and *You Little Fool* made No. 52 in June.

Imperial Bedroom, released in July 1982 and co-produced with former Beatles engineer Geoff Emerick, was his most ambitious album yet. It failed to produce a significant hit single but did have some fine tracks, like *Almost Blue*, a heartfelt ballad and *Beyond Belief*. In commercial terms, it made No. 6 in the U.K. and No. 30 in the 'States. The year closed with *Patsy Patsy*, from an A&M soundtrack, climbing to 45 in the U.K.

In May 1983, with F-Beat negotiating a change of distribution, **Costello** recorded on his own Imp label *Pills And Soap* using the name The Imposter. His next hit, *Everyday I Write The Book* (No. 28) was written in ten minutes as a spoof. **Costello** explained in a 'Record Collector' interview in September 1995 that he'd originally intended it as a lovers' rock song, but later added a more modern rhythmic treatment. It was culled, like *Pills And Soap* from his next album *Punch The Clock*, which featured backing vocals from Afrodiziak. In contrast to his previous work, this album produced by Clive Langer and Alan Winstanley (who produced Madness), marked a clear shift towards a glossy pop format. The album had its moments, though, *Shipbuilding* was a beautiful piece and *King Of Thieves* was a long, more complex effort.

His next album *Goodbye Cruel World*, using the same producers, was universally slated. **Costello** was getting divorced at the time it was recorded and on a low. In retrospect he hated the record, which contained a number of pop songs clearly aimed at the charts. It contained another Imposter 45, *Peace In Our Time*, which had reached No. 48 and *I Wanna Be Loved*, which made No. 25 assisted by a Godley and Creme video. *The Only Flame In Town*, recorded with Darryl Hall only reached No. 71 here in Britain and No. 56 in the U.S.. The album peaked at No. 10 in the U.K. and No. 35 in the U.S..

Costello became aware of the album's faults whilst performing many of its songs during his first U.S. solo tour in Spring 1984. His support act, T-Bone Burnette, soon joined him in the Coward Brothers, a slice of light relief which the two songwriters enjoyed from the strain of performing alone. He also toured with **The Attractions** in what was a busy year.

Early in 1985 **Costello** played a small acting role in Alan Bleasdale's TV Series 'Scully', which he wrote the theme *Turning The Town Red* for. He also produced *Rum, Sodomy And The Lash* for The Pogues. In April *The Best Of Elvis Costello - The Man* was released and promoted on TV. It climbed to No. 8 in the U.K., and one of his early tracks culled from it, *Green Shirt* reached No. 68. However, his only new release of the year was his recording with Burnette (as The Coward Brothers) of *The People's Limousine*. He appeared solo in Live Aid playing *All You Need Is Love*.

In February 1986, he released a cover of The Animals' 1965 hit *Don't Let Me Be Misunderstood* credited to The Costello Show. He was backed on the disc by a group of U.S. musicians The Confederates. It climbed to No. 33. His next album, in March 1986, was recorded under his real name. Produced by T-Bone Burnette *The King Of America* was musically very diverse covering country, cajun, Tex Mex and Irish music. It was the first album he'd recorded without **The Attractions**. Originally it was supposed to be recorded half with them and half without but it didn't work out that way. In the end they just played on one track. Instead he drew on a range of U.S. session players from the James Burton/Jerry Scheff/Ron Tutt stable, which had backed Elvis Presley in the late sixties, as well as Tom Waites, Los Lobos and Hall and Oates. The album made No. 11 in the U.K. and No. 39 in the U.S.. On 16th May **Costello** married The Pogues' bassist Caitlin O'Riordan in Dublin, Ireland. In August 1986, he made another film appearance, this time as a bungling musician in 'No Surrender'. The same month he was re-united with **The Attractions** on the tempestous *Tokyo Storm Warning* 45, a protest song about the end of the world. Issued on the Imp label it peaked at No. 73 in Britain. It also figured on his next album *Blood And Chocolate*, which also featured **The Attractions**. The album reached No. 16 in the U.K. and No. 84 in the 'States.

During 1987, Paul McCartney invited **Costello** to help write songs on his next album and this partnership flickered on and off sporadically over the next eight years. In September the MacManus Gang released *A Town Called The Big Nothing* from the soundtrack of Alex Cox's *Straight To Hell* mock western movie in which **Elvis Costello** played a minor role. **Costello** also wrote *The Courier* in which his wife starred. In November, he signed a worldwide deal with Warner Bros (excluding the U.K.). He insisted on the clause preventing the company releasing his recordings in South Africa, until apartheid ended. His debut on Warner Bros was *Spike*, trailed by *Veronica*, a 45 co-written with McCartney. He continued to record until the present day and there are a number of retrospective and compilation releases listed in the discography which are worth investigation.

The Very Best Of Elvis Costello issued on CD in 1994 concentrates on singles from his catalogue in the period from *My Aim Is True* to *Blood And Chocolate* but it also includes some of his better album cuts, notably the epic *I Want You, Beyond Belief* and *Watch Your Step*.

Significant compilation appearances have included:- *Less Than Zero* on *A Bunch Of Stiff Records* (Stiff SEE 2) 1977, *Radio Sweetheart* on *Hits Greatest Stiffs*, *I Just Don't Know What To Do With Myself*, *Miracle Man* and *Sex And Drugs And Rock And Roll* (all live) on *Stiff Live Stiff* (Stiff GET 1) 1978 (later reissued on Music For Pleasure (MFP 50445). *(I Don't Want To Go To) Chelsea* and *Watching The Detectives* were both included on *That Summer!* (soundtrack) (Spartan/Arista SPART 1088) in 1979. The film soundtrack to *Americathon* (Lorimar CBS 70172) 1979 included *I Don't Want To Go To Chelsea* and *Crawling To The U.S.A.*, whilst *Concert For The People Of Kampuchea* (dbl) (Atlantic 60153) 1981 included a live version of *The Imposter*. A live version of *Psyche Song* figured on *Fundamental Frolics* (BBC REB 435) 1981. He contributed *Party Party* to the film soundtrack of the same name (A&M AMLH 68551) 1982. *Every Man Needs A Woman* (Polydor POLH 13) 1984 included *Walking On Thin Ice*. *Sometimes A Great Notion* (EMI TOP CAT 1) 1984 included *Really Mystified* and *The End Of The Rainbow* figured on *It's A Live-In World* (dbl) (EMI AHPLP 1) 1986. *Pump It Up* appeared on *Punk And Disorderly: New wave 1976-1981* (Telstar STAR 2520) in 1991 (also on CD). Finally, he's appeared on a couple of freebie NME cassettes - *Dancin' Master* (NME NME 001) 1981 featured *Big Sister* and *Pogo A Gogo* (NME 021) 1986 included a demo version of *Watching The Detectives*.

As a talent, particularly as a songwriter, **Costello** shone out in the punk/new wave era so it's absolutely no surprise that he has long survived it until the present day.

The Count Bishops

Personnel:
PAUL BALBI	drms		AB
ZENON DE FLEUR	gtr, vcls		AB
JOHNNY GUITAR	gtr		AB
STEVE LEWINS	bs		AB
MIKE SPENCER	vcls		A
DAVE TICE	vcls		B

ALBUM: 1(A) THE COUNT BISHOPS   (Chiswick WIK 1) 1977

NB: There's also two CD compilations *Speedball + 11* (Chiswick CDWIKM 161) 1995 and *The Best Of The Count Bishops* (Chiswick CDWIKD 150) 1995.

EP: 1(A) SPEEDBALL (Route 66/Ain't Got You/
Beautiful Delilah/Teenage Letter)   (Chiswick SW1) 1975

NB: (1) The first 1,000 copies were issued in a glossy picture sleeve.

45s: Train Train/Taking It Easy (PS)   (Chiswick S5) 1976
Baby You're Wrong/Stay Free (PS)   (Chiswick S12) 1977
I Need You/Talk To You/Good Guys Don't Wear White/
Taste And Try (PS)   (Chiswick PROMO 1) 1977

The Count Bishops are significant for two reasons. Firstly, their *Speedball* EP in early 1976 was the first release by an independent punk/new wave label in Britain. The London-based Chiswick label preceding Stiff by a few months. Secondly, they were an important link between the R&B pub rock scene of the mid-seventies typified by bands like Dr. Feelgood and the early punk scene.

The *Speedball* EP was their only recording to feature Mike Spencer, a Brooklyn-born gravel throated singer. It captured the rawness and energy of the rock 'n' roll and R&B of the mid-sixties. Spencer later formed the durable garage band The Cannibals.

The Count Bishops also recorded two sessions for John Peel. The first on 17th May 1976 featured *Takin' It Easy, Confessin' The Blues, Wang Dang Doodle* and *Dust My Blues*. The second on 27th July 1977 comprised *Till The End Of The Day, Don't Start Me Talking, I Want Candy* and *Hands On The Wheel*.

Their debut 45 *Train Train* was released in 1976. The follow-up *Baby You're Wrong*, was a powerful number which was given further exposure through its inclusion on the sampler *Long Shots Dead Certs And Odds On Favourites* (Chiswick CH5) in 1978.

Their eponymous 1977 album, the first on Chiswick, blended their Chicago blues / Beat Boom covers repertoire with five originals. Three, penned by bassist Steve Lewins were in the Ruff Tuff Boogie style and two - *Baby You're Wrong* and *Stay Free* - written by rhythm / slide guitarist Zenon de Fleur had been put out on a 45 earlier in the year. The covers were diverse: The Standells' *Good Guys Don't Wear White*, The Kinks' *I Need You*, Savoy Brown *Taste And Try*, Howlin' Wolf's *Meet Me In The Bottom*, Chuck Berry's *Down The Road Apiece* (which featured Jools Holland of **Squeeze** playing some fine pumping roadhouse piano), Slim Harpo *Don't Start Crying Now* and Elmore James *Shake Your Money Maker*. Overall, a decent album blending traditional rock, blues and their own individual flair.

The Best Of The Count Bishops will appeal to fans of pub rock rather than punk and new wave. It confirms that musically they were far closer to bands like Dr. Feelgood and **Eddie and The Hot Rods** with their cranked up covers of sixties R&B, soul and garage standards plus a few originals, than to bands like **The Sex Pistols**. This compilation includes several finest moments from their 1977 debut album, early singles like *Train Train* (which are difficult to find) and three previously unreleased out-takes (*Good Times*, a cover of The Kinks' *Till The End Of The Day* and a throwaway cut *Paul's Blues*) along with seven live cuts from a February 1978 gig at the Roundhouse with an early incarnation of Motorhead.

The Count Bishops with two competent guitarists and an excellent rhythm section were a good live band but their eponymous debut album demonstrated their limitations - a lack of strong original material and any any additional dimension to translate onto vinyl. After this they changed names to **The Bishops**.

Wayne County and The Electric Chairs

Personnel:
WAYNE COUNTY	vcls		AB
VAN HALLER	bs		A
J.J. JOHNSON	drms		A
ELLIOT MICHAELS	gtr		AB
HENRY PADOVANI	keyb'ds, gtr		A
PETER JORDAN	bs		B
SAMMY MINELLI	drms		B

ALBUMS: 1(A) ELECTRIC CHAIRS   (Safari LONG 1) 1978
2(A) STORM THE GATES OF HEAVEN (Safari GOOD 1) 1978
3(A) THINGS YOUR MOTHER NEVER TOLD YOU
(Safari GOOD 2) 1979
4(B) ROCK 'N' ROLL RESURRECTION   (Safari LIVE 1) 1980
5(A) BEST OF THE ELECTRIC CHAIRS   (Safari NEN 1) 1981

NB: There's also a CD compilation, *Rock 'N' Roll Cleopatra (From Sneakers To Stilettos)* (RPM RPM 119) 1993.

EPs: 1( ) THE ELECTRIC CHAIRS (Stuck On You/
Paranoia Paradise/The Last Time)   (Illegal IL 002) 1977
2( ) BLATENTLY OFFENZIVE (Fuck Off/Toilet Love/
Night Time/Mean Mutha Fuckin' Man) (PS)
(Safari WC 2) 1978

45s: * Max's Kansas City 1976/Flip Your Wig/
Cream In My Jeans (PS)   (Max's Kansas City MAX 1213) 1976
Fuck Off/On The Crest   (Sweet F.A. WC 1) 1977
+ Eddie and Sheena/
Rock And Roll Cleopatra (PS)   (Safari SAFE 1) 1978
I Had Too Much To Dream Last Night/
Fuck Off   (Safari SAFE 6) 1978
Trying To Get On The Radio/
Evil Minded Woman (PS)   (Safari SAFE 9) 1978
Thunder When She Walks/
What You Got (PS)   (Illegal IL 005) 1979
Berlin/Waiting For The Marines (PS)   (Safari SAFE 13) 1979
% Berlin (Long Version)/Waiting For The Marines/
Midnight Pal (12" PS)   (Safari SAFE LS 13) 1979
$ So Many Ways/
J'Attends Les Marines (PS)   (Safari SAFE 18) 1979
Fuck Off/Toilet Love (pic disc)   (Safari WCP 3) 1983

NB: * U.S.-only release. + Early copies of this 45 came with a cartoon strip insert. # Unissued. % Issued on pink vinyl. $ by **The Electric Chairs**.

Ok so **Wayne County** was an American, but because the band were mostly based in Britain, made most of their records here and hardly any of them were released in the 'States I've decided to include them here.

Transexual **County** grew up in Dallas, but split for Atlanta, Georgia as soon as he was old enough. It was there that he made his first stage

WAYNE COUNTY - Blatently Offenzive EP.

appearances at underground parties and the like. In 1968, he hopped on a Greyhound bus one day and headed for New York. Hanging out at the Stonewall bar, he soon became part of the Big Apple's emerging new wave scene. He met underground photographer Leee Black Childers who introduced him to many of the city's 'superstars' and the VIPs-only backroom of Max's Kansas City, the Big Apple's hippest night spot. Influenced by one of the celebs **Wayne County** wrote a play 'World'. In a Record Collector interview he recalled 'It was about sexual geography, using historical characters and ridiculous sexual situations. I played Florence Nightingale and her twin sister Ethel'. The play also featured **Cherry Vanilla**. Andy Warhol spotted **Wayne County** and **Cherry Vanilla** and offered them both a role in 'Pork', a play written from his phone conversations. Leee Black Childers was appointed the play's stage manager. After a successful spell at New York's La Mamma theatre, it transferred to London's Roadhouse. Back in New York, he played a transvestite revolutionary in a play entitled 'Island', which also featured Patti Smith and **Cherry Vanilla**. He then teamed up with the Marcus brothers and put his theatrics to rock 'n' roll in the form of his first band Queen Elizabeth. They did produce a live demo comprising *Stuck On You*, *Max's*, *Confusion* and *Wonder Woman*. It was later re-recorded with a different backing band, Mainman.

Queen Elizabeth fell apart and, in 1973, **Wayne County** formed a new Anglophile-inspired band, the Backstreet Boys. They had their setbacks, particularly when underground label ESP declared an album they'd funded to be too commercial for release. However, in 1976, they did contribute three cuts; *Cream In My Jeans*, *Max's* and *Flip Your Wig* to the *Max's Kansas City* compilation album, which was originally on Max's label but was later reissued on CBS. They were also issued on a U.S.-only 45.

With the band failing to breakthrough at the forefront of the emerging New York new wave spearheaded by the New York Dolls, Ramones, Patti Smith and Blondie, it was Miles Copeland, then running Illegal Records, who persuaded **County** that the future would be rosier for him in Britain. Once there, he put together a new backing band **The Electric Chairs**.

The band immediately made an impact over here and encouraged by this Illegal Records put out a three track EP comprising a cover of The Rolling Stones' *The Last Time*, *Stuck On You* and *Paranoia Paradise* (a sanitised version of one of **County**'s early songs, *Fucked By The Devil*). A further 45, *Thunder When She Walks / What You Got* was also planned, but then held back until 1979.

During 1977 **Wayne County and The Electric Chairs** signed to the emerging Safari Records. Their first 45 for the label *Fuck Off* appeared in November 1977. Its lyrics "If you don't want to fuck me baby, fuck off" gelled beautifully into the punk scene. The same year they performed *Paranoia Paradise* in Derek Jarman's 'Jubilee' and it was included on the resulting soundtrack album (Polydor EG 2302 079) the following year.

In 1978, Safari released *Eddie And Sheena*. Early copies came with a cartoon-strip insert. The song recounted a love story between a Ted and a punk. They followed this with an eponymous album. This contained much of their early material and some numbers originally performed by **Wayne County** with The Backstreet Boys. Highlights included *Max's Kansas City*

WAYNE COUNTY - Blatently Offensive LP.

CRACK - Going Out.

and *Bad In Bed*. The album was slickly produced by Deep Purple's producer Martin Bush who smoothed out the rougher edges from their basic rock 'n' roll cum punk sound.

Storm The Gates Of Heaven, their second album, was their most commercially successful. It came in a great cover and on a spew-coloured lavender vinyl. It captured many of their finest musical moments significantly the title cut, *Man Enough To Be A Woman*, a steaming version of *I Had Too Much To Dream Last Night* and the fiercesome *Speed Demon*.

After a spell in Berlin, the band returned to the studio in early 1979 to record, *Things Your Mother Never Told You* with producer and **Flying Lizard** mainman David Cunningham. The end product was more experimental than anything preceding it. Much of side one like *Wonder Woman*, *Baby With A Stolen Face* and *Un-con-troll-able* was in their usual rock 'n' roll vein, but the title cut with its striking, discordant intro and superb ending and *About A Murdered Woman*, with its nearly spoken lyrics, were a pointer to the experimentation developed further on side two. This is notable for a strong Velvet Underground influence, particularly on *Midnight Pal* (which recalls *I'm Waiting For The Man*) and experimentation and sound effects on songs like *Berlin* and *C3*. However, it displeased their label who wanted commercial not experimental rock.

After this **Wayne County** returned to the 'States with Elliot Michaels and put together a new line-up 'B'. This line-up was captured well below par on a New Year's Eve concert in 1979, which was issued on Safari in 1980, *Rock 'n' Roll Resurrection*.

However, their *Best Of The Electric Chairs* is a well-balanced collection of their finest moments on white vinyl, which can be recommended. More recently, *Rock 'N' Roll Cleopatra*, released on RPM in 1993, is a twenty-track compilation from Safari's back catalogue - all the live favourites are there and the compilation is accomplished by a fold-out describing the band's history.

In 1999, *(If You Don't Want To Fuck Me) Fuck Off* resurfaced on the lavish 5-CD box set *1-2-3-4 - A History Of Punk And New Wave 1976 - 1979* (MCA/Universal MCD 60066).

Wayne County carried on recording as Jayne County, spending most of the early eighties in Berlin, but that's another story.

Court Martial

Personnel:	RICHARD BRAYBROOK	A
	IAN BURROUGH	A
	SIMON BURROUGH	A
	ALEX McPHERSON	A

EPs:	1(A)	GOTTA GET OUT (Gotta Get Out/Fight For Your Life/ Young Offender) (PS)	(Riot City RIOT 5) 1982
	2(A)	NO SOLUTION (No Solution/Too Late/ Take Control) (PS)	(Riot City RIOT 11) 1982

A punk group from Bristol. They formed in 1979, whilst still at school and worked with **Vice Squad** on local gigs. In addition to these two 45s, they contributed *Your War* to *Riotous Assembly* (Riot City ASSEMBLY 1) in 1982 and *Gotta Get Out* to *Punk And Disorderly* (Anagram GRAM 001) in 1982 and *Life's A Riot And Then You Die* (Riot City CITY 009) in 1985. *Gotta Get Out* and *No Solution* can also be found on *Riot City Singles Collection, Vol. 1* (Anagram CDPUNK 15) 1997 or on vinyl (Captain Oi! AHOY DLP 503). *Vol. 2* (Anagram CDPUNK 55) 1995 or (Captain Oi! AHOY DLP 511) included *Fight For Your Life* and *Too Late*.

The Coventry Automatics

Personnel:			
	JERRY DAMMERS (GERALD DANKIN)	vcls, keyb'ds	ABC
	LYNUAL GOLDING	gtr	ABC
	HORACE PANTER	bs	ABC
	TERRY HALL	vcls	BC
	ROD BYERS	gtr	BC
	NEVILLE STAPLES	vcls, perc	BC
	SILVERTON HUTCHINSON	drms	B

ALBUM: 1(C) THE COVENTRY AUTOMATICS (Receiver RRLP 178) 1993

NB: (1) was recorded in 1978. It was also issued on CD (RRCD 178) 1993.

This band formed in July 1977 as **The Coventry Automatics** (line-up 'A'). Initially they strove to achieve a fusion of punk and reggae but with only limited success. The line-up was expanded to included Byers, Hall, Staples and Silverton early in 1978 and they veered more towards ska with better results. To avoid confusion with another Automatics they became known as The Coventry Specials for a while but later settles for Specials a.k.a. and the rest is history (as they say). The above album will interest archivists who want to know what **The Coventry Automatics** sounded like back in 1978.

The tracks sound boisterous and fresh. Eight of them - including *Stupid Marriage*, *Nite Club*, *Concrete Jungle* and *It's Up To You* - reappeared re-worked on the Specials first album. The five which weren't - *Look But Don't Touch*, *Rachel*, *Rock 'N' Roll Nightmare*, *Wake* and *Jay Walker* - were more variable in quality. The transition from the punk/ska/reggae of **The Coventry Automatics** to the ska/reggae of The Specials really wasn't that great.

The Crabs

Personnel:			
	TONY DIGGINES	vcls, gtr	A
	ASHLEY MORSE	bs	A
	RICK NEWSON	gtr	A
	RICCI TITCOMBE	drms	A

The Crabs sole vinyl legacy is to have contributed one cut *Lullabies Lie* to the *Farewell To The Roxy* (Lightning LIP 2) 1978 album. In addition, they did record a session for John Peel on 3rd May 1978. It comprised *Victim*, *Under Pressure* and *Don't Want Your Love*, in addition to *Lullabies Lie*. You'll also find *Lullabies Lie* on *Lightning Records Punk Collection* (Anagram CDPUNK 79) 1996.

Crack

Personnel:			
	DEAN GIFFORD	bs	A
	STEVE JONES	vcls, gtr	AB
	ANDY KING	drms	A
	SHANE WOOLRIDGE	gtr	A
	DAVE BEALE	bs, vcls	B
	MAZ	gtr, vcls	B
	MARK MOBLEY	drms, vcls	B

ALBUM: 1(B) IN SEARCH OF THE CRACK (Link LP 073) 1989

NB: (1) reissued on CD (Captain Oi! AHOY CD 11) 1993 with six bonus cuts.

45s:	*	Don't You Ever Let Me Down/ I Can't Take It	(RCA RCA 214) 1982
		Going Out/The Troops Have Landed (PS)	(RCA RCA 255) 1982
		All Or Nothing/I Caught You Out (PS)	(RCA CRACK 1) 1983

NB: * Came in a die-cut 'Battle Of The Bands' sleeve. There's also two CD compilations *All Cracked Up: Demos And Rarities* (Captain Oi! AHOY CD 69) 1997 and *Best Of The Crack* (Captain Oi! AHOY CD 109) 1999.

The Crack came from Cheltenham in Gloucestershire. In 1982 they won a televised 'Battle Of The Bands' competition and their reward was a major record label deal with RCA, which was unusual for an Oi! band. The resulting 45, *Don't You Ever Let Me Down* was a strong debut, but despite quite a lot of airplay the accessible recording failed to chart. This and its guitar driven flipside *I Can't Take It Anymore* have both resurfaced on *Oi! The Rarities, Vol. 4* (Captain Oi! AHOY CD 58) 1996. The follow-up *Going Out* was more abrasive in sound and style. It again featured competent guitar playing. Its flip side *The Troops Have Landed* was similar in style. Again, the single failed to sell significantly. Their third and final effort was their own, quite different, interpretation of The Small Faces' classic *All Or Nothing* backed by the energetic *I Caught You Out*. Both sides of these last two 45s can also be heard on *Oi! The Rarities, Vol. 5* (Captain Oi! AHOY CD 62) 1996. The fact that all three singles were good but failed to sell in quantities has lead to them becoming significant Oi! collectors' items. The original line-up also recorded eight other demos - *We've Got A Right To Know*, *That's Me Away*, *Wait Till The Day Arrives*, *The Battle Song*, *Take Me Away*, *Nag Nag Nag*, *My World* and *Hard Road*, which were broadly in the same style as their 45. These never saw the light of day at the time because RCA decided to drop the band, presumably because of the lack of commercial success. These can now be heard on *All Cracked Up - The Demos And Rarities* (CD) (Captain Oi! AHOY CD 69) 1997 along with two cuts from the mid-eighties (when the band were known as Gun Shy and featured line-up 'B' above) and three songs recorded under the name of The Guv'nors. The Guv'nors featured Steve Jones (vcls), ex-**Business** members Mark Brennan (bs) and Steve Kent (gtr) and ex-Tank/**Blood** drummer Mark Brabbs. With the backing of Link records this was intended to be the band to take Oi!/Street punk into the nineties but the various band

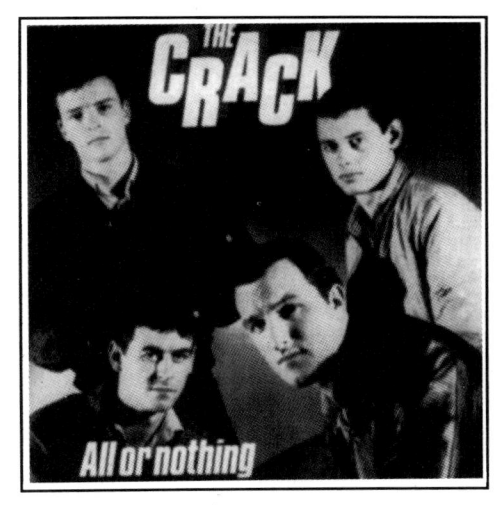

CRACK - All Or Nothing.

CRACK - In Search Of.

members had too many other commitments to devote the time this project would have needed.

In 1987, Jones had launched a new version of **The Crack** (line-up 'B'). This released the *In Search Of The Crack* album in 1988, which is also available on CD (Captain Oi! AHOY CD 11) 1993 with six bonus cuts, including a rousing version of Slade's *Cum On Feel The Noize*. **The Crack** were still gigging and recording at the end of the twentieth century.

Other compilation appearances by the band have included *Going Out* on *100% British Oi!* (Captain Oi! AHOY DCD 83) 1997 and a cut on *Oi! Fuckin' Oi!* (CD) (Harry May MAYO CD 110) in 1999.

The Best Of The Crack (CD) compilation put out by Captain Oi! in 1999, includes their 45 cuts (except for *All Or Nothing*), tracks from *The Crack Wants You* EP, the Link album *In Search Of The Crack*, rare compilation cuts, oddities like *I Need Ya* (an early recording released on 10" in Germany in 1997) and other previously unreleased material.

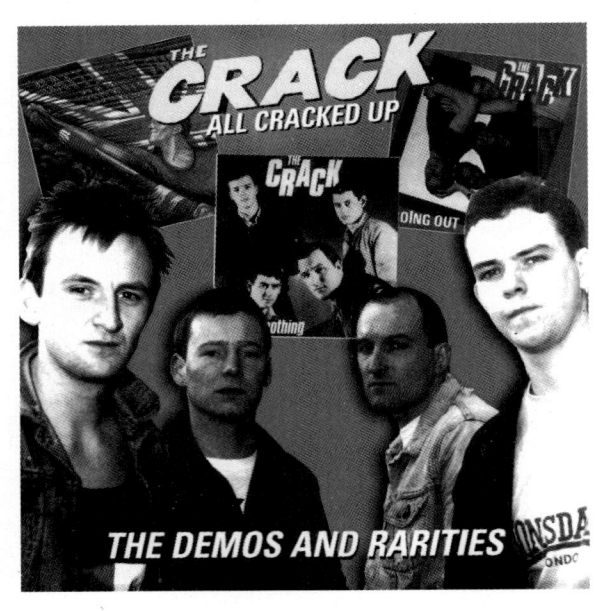

CRACK - All Cracked Up.

Crash

Personnel:	ANDY	gtr	A
	DUNCAN	drms	A
	IAN	bs	A
	NIDGE	vcls	A

EP: 1(A) FIGHT FOR YOUR LIFE (Fight For Your Life/Religion/ Kill The Cow/TV Times) (Crash no #) 1981

NB: (1) this was reissued on a split 12" with **Crux** (No Future Oi! 18) 1982.

This South Yorkshire band released the *Fight For Your Life* (EP) on their own label in late 1981, but they couldn't afford to finance a picture sleeve to go with it. It was later reissued by No Future on a split 45 with **Crux**.

All four songs on this EP are fast, no-holes-barred punk, *Kill The Cow* was a reference to Maggie Thatcher. They can all be heard on *Oi! The Rarities, Vol. 2* (Captain Oi! AHOY CD 46) 1995.

Crass

Personnel:	STEVE IGNORANT	vcls	AB
	PENNY RIMBAUD	drms	AB
	JOHN DE VIVRE	vcls, gtr, keyb'ds	B
	PHIL FREE	gtr, vcls	B
	EVE LIBERTINE	vcls	B
	ANDY PALMER	gtr	B
	PETE WRIGHT	bs, vcls	B

HCP

ALBUMS: 1( ) STATIONS OF THE CRASS (dbl) (Crass 52 1984) 1979 -
2( ) PENIS ENVY (Crass 32 1984/1) 1981 -
3( ) CHRIST THE ALBUM (dbl) (Crass BOLLOX 2U2) 1982 26
4( ) YES SIR I WILL (Crass 12 1984/2) 1983 -

NB: (1) reissued in 1981 and 1987 and on CD (Crass 521984) 1990. (2) reissued in 1987 and on CD (Crass 321984) 1990. (3) reissued on CD (Crass BOLLOX 2U2 CD) 1990. (4) reissued on CD (Crass 121984/2) 1990. There's also a compilation, *Best Before 1984* (Crass CRASS 5CD) 1990, also issued on vinyl. Other relevant CDs are *Christ The Bootleg* (Allied ALLIED 76CD) 1996, *Ten Notes On A Summers Day* (Crass CATN 06CD) 1998 and *You'll Ruin It For Everyone* (Pomona ONA 002CD) 1994.

EP: 1( ) THE FEEDING OF THE 5,000 (Small Wonder WEENY 2) 1978

NB: (1) reissued with the addition of *Reality Asylum* (Crass 62194) 1978. Then reissued in 1980 as *Feeding Of The 5,000 EP (2nd Sitting)*, reissued again in 1981 and 1987 on Crass and on CD (Crass 621984) 1990.

45s: Reality Asylum/Shaved Women (PS) (Crass 521984/1) 1979
Bloody Revolutions/(other side by **Poison Girls**) (PS) (Crass Xntrix 421984/1) 1980
Nagasaki Nightmare/Big A Little A (PS) (Crass 421984/5) 1980
* Rival Tribal Rebel Revel/Bully Boys Go Out Fighting (PS) (Crass 421984/6) 1981
Merry Crassmass/Merry Crassmass - Have Fun (PS) (Crass COLD TURKEY 1) 1982
+ Who Dunnit? Parts 1 & 2 (PS) (Crass 121984/4) 1982
How Does It Feel (To Be Mother Of 1,000 Dead?)/The Immortal Death/Don't Tell Me You Care (PS) (Crass 121984/6) 1982
Sheep Farming In The Falklands/Gotcha! (live) (Crass 121984/3) 1983
Gotcha! (no label) 1983

NB: * This was initially available as a flexi-disc with 'Toxic Graffiti' fanzine. It was later issued in a hard vinyl picture sleeve. + Some copies were issued on brown vinyl and some in black. # This was issued as a clear flexidisc.

This was the product of an anarchic commune who were based at Penny Rimbaud's farmhouse in North Weald, Essex.

They originally formed as a duo in 1978, but soon expanded their ranks. Their first live appearance was at a squatters free festival. This helped them secure a one-off deal with Small Wonder. A 12" EP with no less than 17 tracks *The Feeding Of The 5,000* resulted. One of the tracks became a two minutes silence they called *Free Speech*, after the opening cut *Reality Asylum* was offensive to some and no pressing plant would manufacture the EP with it on.

After this brush with the establishment, the commune resolved to release all subsequent product on their own label. Their debut 45, *Reality Asylum* was designed to shock with its venomous anti-religious lyrics. Much of their material was highly political, often with titles like *Penis Envy* or *Christ The Album* unlikely to be marketed in the local high street.

Their first album *Stations Of The Crass* featured three studio sides and one live side. Deploying an unnerving church-organ aura *Penis Envy* paralleled rampant sexism with man's rape of nature and society. *Christ The Album*, a boxed two record studio and live set sported a 28-page booklet about

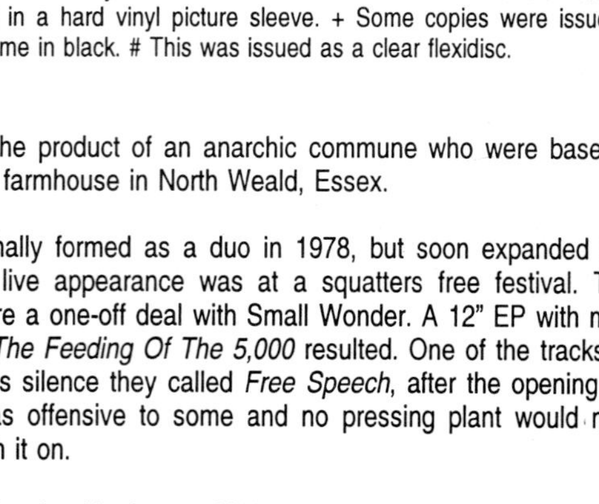

CRASS - Reality Asylum.

revolution and one man who died for it. This actually spent two weeks in the Album charts peaking at No. 26. Their final effort, *Yes Sir I Will* was their response to the Falklands' War, which blamed Thatcher for the deaths.

You'll Ruin It For Everyone is a seventeen-track live affair taped at a gig disrupted by the National Front in Perth in July 1981.

In their desire to sell albums at low prices they omitted to charge VAT on them and the band folded when faced with an Inland Revenue bill of some magnitude! Still in their heyday **Crass** were one of the most extreme and minimalist of the punk bands.

Their classic *Reality Asylum* was included on the 4-CD box set *25 Years Of Rough Trade Shops* (Mute CDSTUMM 191) in 2001.

The Cravats

Personnel:	DAVE BENNETT	drms	A
	ROB DALLAWAY	gtr, vcls	A
	THE SHEND	bs, vcls	A
	YEHUDI STORAGEHEATER	sax, clarinet	A

ALBUM:	1(A)	THE CRAVATS IN TOYTOWN	(Small Wonder CRAVAT 1) 1980

EPs:	1( )	RUB ME OUT	(Crass 221984/2) 1982
	2( )	THE LAND OF GIANTS	(Reflex 12RE 10) 1985

45s:	Gordon/Situations (PS)	(The Cravats CH 004) 1978
	The End/Burning Bridges/ I Hate The Universe (PS)	(Small Wonder SMALL 15) 1979
*	Precinct/ Who's In Here With Me? (PS)	(Small Wonder SMALL 24) 1980
	You're Driving Me Mad/ I Am The Dreg (PS)	(Small Wonder SMALL 25) 1980
	Off The Beach/ And The Sun Shone On (PS)	(Small Wonder SMALL 26) 1981
	Terminus/Little Yellow Froggy (PS)	(Glass GLASS 21) 1982
	D.C.L. (Laboratory Server No. 1) (flexidisc)	(Lyntone) 198?

NB: * Some copies came with a free flexidisc *Fireman*, the flip side to which was *Divide* by A Flux In 3D.

This band were offered a deal by Small Wonder after releasing a 45 on their own label. Their stand-out song is *The End*, an unnervingly discordant instrumental, but the other two tracks on this 45, *Burning Bridges* and *The Universe* are less distinguished.

The End, *Precinct*, *You're Driving Me* and *Off The Beach* can all be heard on *Small Wonder Punk Singles Collection, Vol. 1* (Anagram CDPUNK 29) 1994, whilst *Burning Bridges* and *I Am The Dreg* figured on *Vol. 2* (Anagram CDPUNK 70) 1996 of the same series.

THE CRAVATS - The End.

Craze

Personnel incl: HUGH ASHTON

ALBUM:	1( )	SPARTANS	(Harvest SHSP 4114) 1980

45s:	Motions/Spartans (PS)	(Cobra COB 3) 1979
*	Motions/Spartans (PS)	(Harvest HAR 5200) 1980
	Lucy/Stop Living In The Past (PS)	(Harvest HAR 5205) 1980

NB: * This reissue had a different picture sleeve.

Previously known as **Skunks** this band later became Hard Corps, recording several 45s.

THE CREATURES - Feast.

The Creatures

Personnel:	PETER CLARK (BUDGIE)	drms	A
	SIOUXSIE SIOUX	vcls	A

				HCP
ALBUM: (up to 1986)	1(A)	FEAST	(Wonderland SHELP 1) 1983	17

				HCP
EP:1(A)	WILD THINGS (Mad Eyed Screamer/So Unreal/ Not Not Them/Wild Thing/ Thumb)	(Polydor POSPG 354) 1981	24

NB: (1) This was a 2 x 7" double-pack EP. 5,000 copies came in a gatefold sleeve.

			HCP
45s: (up to 1986) *	Miss The Girl/ Hot Springs In The Snow (PS)	(Wonderland SHE 1) 1983	21
	Right Now/Weathercade (PS)	(Wonderland SHE 2) 1983	14
	Right Now/Weathercade (12", PS)	(Wonderland SHEX 2) 1983	-

NB: * Early copies came in a gatefold picture sleeve.

The Creatures were an occasional sideline project for Siouxsie Sioux and drummer Peter 'Budgie' Clark for much of **Siouxsie and The Banshees'** career. They formed the project whilst spending time together in Hawaii after recording their *Juju* album. The *Wild Thing* EP, which got to No. 24 and spent seven weeks in the charts, was recorded there using Hawaiian artists in the background. The result was five voice and percussion pieces and a re-work of The Troggs' classic *Wild Thing*.

The *Feast* album incorporated the marimba and a Hawaiian choir as it explores Hawaiian style music. The novelty helped it sell well as it became a Top 20 album climbing to No. 17 and spending nine weeks in the charts.

In this first period **The Creatures** also produced two hit singles, of which the second *Right Now* was excellent.

The project was then put on ice but re-emerged again during 1989 and 1990 when there was a lull in **Siouxsie and The Banshees**' recording activity. An album *Boomerang* and two 45s resulted from this second incarnation.

Criminal Class

Personnel:	CRAIG ST. LEON	vcls	A
	DANNY	gtr	A
	JIM	bs	A
	JOHN	drms	A

45:	Fighting The System/Soldier (PS)	(Inferno HELL 7) 1982

One of the lesser-known Oi! bands, from Coventry. Their vinyl debut came when they contributed two cuts *Blood On The Streets* and *Running Away* to the legendary *Strength Thru Oi!* (Decca) 1981 compilation. They also appeared at the first 'New Punk Convention', along with **The Angelic Upstarts** and **Infa Riot**. *Fighting The System* was a promising debut 45 and they had the potential to become one of the best Oi! bands on the circuit, but they split soon after the single was released. Both sides of the 45 can also be heard on *Oi! The Rarities, Vol. 1* (Captain Oi! AHOY CD 43) 1995 and *Fighting The System* has also been given another airing on *100% Bristish Oi!* (Captain Oi! AHOY DCD 83) 1997. If you're curious to hear more of this band go no further than *Blood On The Streets - The Criminal Class Oi! Collection* (Captain Oi! AHOY CD 155) 2000. This fourteen track collection includes the outfit's two contributons to *Strength Thru Oi!*, both sides of their *Fighting The System* 45 and ten previously unreleased studio demos from 1981 and 1982. The accompanying booklet also contains liner notes from their vocalist Craig St. Leon.

CRIMINAL CLASS - Fighting The System.

Crisis

Personnel:	CLEANER	A
	DOUGLAS P	AB
	LESTER JONES	AB
	PHRAZER	A
	TONY WAKEFORD	AB
	DEXTER	B
	LUKE RENDALL	B

EPs:	1(A)	HYMNS OF FAITH (12", PS)	(Ardkor CR1 003) 1980
	2(B)	HOLOCAUST UK (12", PS)	(Crisis NOTH 1/CRI 002) 1982

45s:	No Town Hall (Southwark)/Holocaust/P.C. One Nine Eight Four (PS)	(Peckham Action NOTH 1) 1979
	UK '79/White Youth (PS)	(Ardkor CRI 002) 1979
	Alienation/Brückwood Hospital (PS)	(Ardkor CRI 004) 1981

A very stark experimental left wing punk band. The 45s were left wing and sloganist. *UK '79* is quite stark and experimental, with catchy guitar. The flip side *White Youth* was more derivative of the early seventies in the playing if not the vocals, but attracted unwanted interest from the National Front. *Alienation* reverted more to the style of their debut 45.

Luke Rendall was later in **Theatre Of Hate**.

CRISIS - UK '79.

Crispy Ambulance

Personnel:	KEITH DARBYSHIRE	bs	A
	ROBERT DAVENPORT	gtr	A
	ALAN HEMPSTALL	vcls	A
	GARY MADELEY	drms	A

CASS:	1(A)	THE BLUE AND YELLOW OF THE YACHT CLUB	(CBST 7) 1983
	2(A)	OPEN GATES OF FIRE	(CBST 8) 1983

ALBUM:	1(A)	THE PLATEAU PHASE	(Factory) 1982

NB: (1) also issued on CD (Factory Benelux FBN 12 CD) 1990.

45s:	*	From The Cradle To The Grave/4 Minutes From The Frontline (PS)	(Aural Assault AAR 001) 1979
		Unsightly And Serene: Not What I Expected/Deaf (10", PS)	(Factory FAC 32) 1981

NB: * Available in both a matt and gloss picture sleeve.

Crispy Ambulance formed in Manchester in 1978. They started out playing Hawkwind and **Magazine** covers. In 1979, they released a 45 *From The Cradle To The Grave* on their own label. It came to the attention of Rob Gretton (manager of **Joy Division** and later **New Order**). He arranged for their 10" single *Unsightly And Serene* to come out on Factory and they came very near to sounding like **Joy Division**. Indeed Alan Hempstall once stood in for Ian Curtis at a **Joy Division** gig when he was sidelined by an epileptic attack.

Subsequent releases appeared on Factory Benelux, but the group disbanded in 1981, although they later re-appeared with more members as Ram Ram Kino.

The Crooks

Personnel:	CHRIS BRODERICK	bs	A
	CHRIS 'DING' DEAN	vcls, gtr	A
	TIM PARRY	vcls, gtr	A
	MICKY SPARROW	drms	A

ALBUM:	1(A)	JUST RELEASED	(Blueprint BLUP 5002) 1980

NB: (1) also issued on CD (Captain Mod MODSKA CD 1) 1996 with two bonus cuts.

45s:	Modern Boys/The Beat Goes On (die-cut PS)	(Blueprint BLU 2002) 1979
	All The Time In The World/Bangin' My Head (PS)	(Blueprint BLU 2006) 1980

The Crooks formed in North London in late 1977. They soon became part of the burgeoning mod revival scene. The sharp dressers, in their sharply pressed high collar button downs and toniks, secured a residency at The Pegasus, Stoke Newington, and were touted as the next **Jam** for a while.

They played with top mod bands like **Back To Zero**, **The Chords**, **Secret Affair** and **Small Hours**, as well as supporting **The Police** at The Nashville on one occasion (the pairing obviously appealing to the promoter's humour).

They signed to Blueprint and their debut single *Modern Boys* came out in October 1979. This successfully recaptured the spirit off 1966. They followed it up with *All The Time In The World* in January 1980, which also featured on their album *Just Released* in April 1980. The album confirmed that their roots were very much in the mid-sixties sounds of bands of The Who, Kinks and Small Faces era, particularly on cuts like *Thousand Faces*, *I Don't Love You Any More* and a superb version of The Small Faces' *Understanding*. In 1996, Captain Mod reissued this album on CD, adding their first 'A' side *Modern Boys* and second 'B' side *Bangin' My Head*, to compile all their recorded output on one release. **The Crooks** embarked on a U.K. tour with **The Merton Parkas** to help promote this album.

By mid-1980 **The Crooks** ran out of steam. Broderick and Dean quit the music scene, whilst Parry and Sparrow formed Modern Jazz, who released two singles *In My Sleep* and *Ivory Towers* for Magnet. They later became Blue Zoo, enjoying U.K. hits with *I'm Your Man* (No. 55) and *Cry Boy Cry* (No. 13) in 1982 and *I Just Can't (Forgive And Forget)* (No. 60) in 1983. Parry went on to co-write Yazz's 1988 No. 2 hit *Stand Up For Your Love Rights* and now works as an A&R man, whilst Sparrow bangs the skins for Nenah Cherry.

All four of their 45 cuts later resurfaced on *This Is Mod, Vol. 2* (Anagram CDMGRAM 101) 1996, whilst *Modern Boys* can also be found on *100% British Mod* (Captain Mod MODSKA DCD 8) 1998.

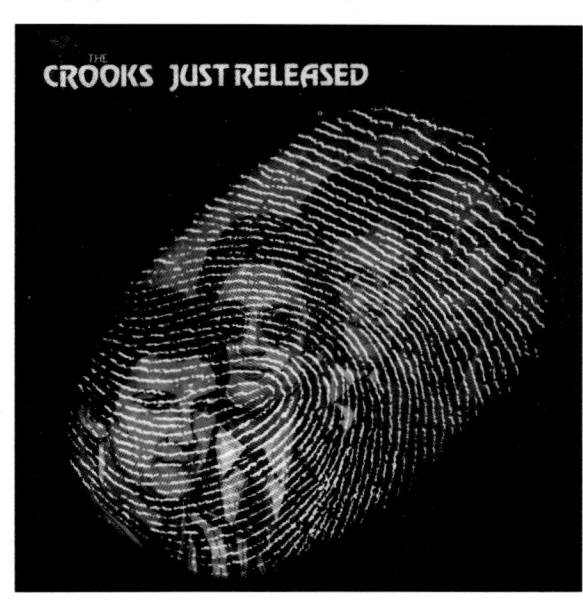

THE CROOKS - Just Released.

Crossed Hammers

Personnel:	J.J. BEDSORE	bs	A
	STEVE KENT	vcls, gtr	A
	D. WILDTHING (EARL BARKHOUSE)	drms	A

A short-lived Oi! combo featuring ex-**Business** guitarist Steve Kent, **Blood** guitarist J.J. Bedsore and **Blood**'s drummer D. Wildthing (whose real name was Earl Barkhouse). Bedsore and Kent were also in a part-time project called **Prole**. **Crossed Hammers** contributed *Here We Go*, an unmemorable effort to *The Oi! Of Sex* (Syndicate SYNLP 4) 1984, which was later reissued on CD (Captain Oi! AHOY CD 23) 1994.

Crowbar

45:	Hippie Punks/White Riot (PS)	(Skinhead SKIN 1) 1984

One of the rarest and most collectable Oi! singles. Nothing is known about the band. *Hippie Punks* is distinctive for extremely throaty vocals and the lyrics seem to attack anarcho-punks. The flip side is a reasonable cover of **The Clash** classic *White Riot*. Thanks to *Oi! The Rarities, Vol. 3* (Captain Oi! AHOY CD 53) 1995 you can hear both sides of this previously obscure single, if you want.

CROWBAR - Hippie Punks.

Crux

Personnel:	ANDY GARNER	drms	A
	HIGGY	bs	A
	ANDY McGRATH	vcls	A
	MICK McGRATH	gtr	A

EP:	1(A)	KEEP ON RUNNING (Keep On Running/Streets At Night/Brighton Front/I'll Die With My Boots On) (12", PS)	(No Future Oi! 18) 1982

NB: (1) this EP formed one side of a split 12" EP. The other side contained four tracks from **Crash**. Later, they figured on a split CD with **The Samples** *The Oi! Collection* (Captain Oi! AHOY CD 79) 1997.

Crux formed in Nuneaton in 1978 and were originally known as Rough Treatment. Their vinyl debut came when they contributed *C.I.A.* to *A Country Fit For Heroes, Vol. 1* (No Future Oi! 3). This compilation album and *Vol. 2* of the same series has since been reissued on one CD (Captain Oi! AHOY CD 15) 1994. *C.I.A.* was taken from a six-track demo which remained unreleased until the other five tracks - *Give Us Work*, *Brighton Front*, *Riot*, *War* and *Skinhead* - were included on a split CD with **The Samples** *The Oi! Collection* (Captain Oi! AHOY CD 79) 1997. You'll also find *C.I.A.* on *100% British Oi!* (Captain Oi! AHOY DCD 83) 1997.

In 1982, **Crux** recorded the *Keep On Running* EP, which was released on one side of a split 12" on No Future Records. *Keep On Running* is *not* a cover of the Spencer Davis Group hit but their own mediocre fast-paced punk composition. *Streets At Night* is a stronger track with some decent guitar moments. *Brighton Front* (which had originally figured on their six-track demo) opens with guitar mayhem, which gives way to another frantic rant. *I'll Die With My Boots On* is in a similar style. All four cuts can also be heard on *Oi! The Rarities, Vol. 1* (Captain Oi! AHOY CD 43) 1995.

Crux also contributed a version of **The Angelic Upstarts'** *Liddle Towers* to *Oi! Oi! That's Yer Lot* (Secret SEC 5) 1983.

Cuban Heels

Personnel:	PAUL ARMOUR	bs	A
	LAURIE CUFFE	gtr	A B
	DAVIE DUNCAN	drms	A
	JOHN MALARKY	vcls	A B
	NICK CLARKE	bs	B
	ALI McKENZIE	drms	B

ALBUM:	1(A)	WALK OUR WAY TO HEAVEN	(Virgin V 2210) 1981

45s:	Downtown/	
	Do The Smoke Walk (PS)	(Housewife's Choice JY ½) 1978
	Little Girl/Fast Living Friend (PS)	(Greville GR 1) 1980
	Walk On Water/Take A Look (PS)	(Cuba Libre DRINK 1) 1981
	Sweet Charity/Day As You Go (PS)	(Virgin VS 413) 1981
	My Colours Fly (PS)	(Virgin VS 439) 1981
*	Walk On Water/Hard Times (PS)	(Virgin VS 440) 1981

NB: * This came with a free flexidisc.

A quirky and witty Glaswegian pop quartet formed in 1978. They were fronted by John Malarky who'd been in **Johnny and The Self-Abusers**, a Scottish punk band some of whose members were later in **Simple Minds**. Initially, their musical repertoire was R&B with the occasional punk song, but they also attracted a lot of mod revivalists. On the road they combined the right blend of originals with covers of songs like Cat Stevens' *Matthew And Son*. For their debut 45 they selected a pop-punk cover of Petula Clarke's early sixties hit *Downtown*.

In 1979, Armour and Duncan left. Nick Clarke and Ali McKenzie came in as replacements. Further indie singles *Little Girl* and *Walk On Water* followed, but when they signed to Virgin for *Walk Our Way To Heaven* and further singles their material became more commercial. Despite this, commercial success continued to elude them and they called it a day in 1982.

Cuddly Toys

Personnel:	TONY BAGGETT	bs	A
	PADDY PHIELD	drms	A
	SEAN PURCELL	vcls	AB
	FAEBHEAN KWEST	gtr	A
	BILLY SURGEONER	gtr	A
	TERRY NOAKES	gtr	B
	ROBERT PARKER	drms	B

ALBUMS:	1(A)	GUILLOTINE THEATRE	(Fresh FRESH LP 1) 1981
	2(B)	TRAILS AND CROSSES	(Fresh FRESH LP 6) 1982

45s:	Madman/Join The Girls (PS)	(Parole PURL 7) 1981
	Astral Joe/Slow Down (PS)	(Parole PURL 9) 1981
	Madman/Join The Girls (PS)	(Fresh FRESH 10) 1981
	Astral Joe/Slow Down (PS)	(Fresh FRESH 20) 1981
	Someone's Crying/ Bring On The Ravers (PS)	(Fresh FRESH 25) 1981
	It's A Shame/Fall Down (PS)	(Fresh FRESH 39) 1981

Cuddly Toys evolved out of Irish-based glam-punk band **Raped**. For their debut 45 they covered *Madman* - the only song co-written by David Bowie and Marc Bolan. Indeed, Bolan in particular seems to have been a strong influence. Their debut album *Guillotine Theatre* was very derivative of Bowie in his *Ziggy Stardust* days. Their first two singles were released by both Parole (**Raped**'s old label) and Fresh.

Terry Noakes and Robert Parker joined vocalist Sean Purcell in a revamped line-up for *Trails And Crosses*, which added keyboards and eighties rhythms. After this failed to make much impact the group faded from the scene. Their four 'A' sides - *Madman, Astral Joe, Someone's Crying* and *It's A Shame* - later resurfaced on *Fresh Records Punk Singles Collection* (Anagram CDPUNK 32) in 1994.

The Cult

Personnel:	IAN ASTBURY	vcls	ABC
	BILLY DUFFY	lead gtr	ABC
	NIGEL PRESTON	drms	A
	JAMIE STUART	bs	ABC
	MARK BRZEZICKI	drms	B
	LES WARNER	drms	C

ALBUMS: (up to 1986)	1(A)	DREAMTIME	(Beggars Banquet BEGA 57) 1984 21
	2(B)	LOVE	(Beggars Banquet BEGA 65) 1985 4

NB: (1) originally issued with a free album *Dreamtime Live At The Lyceum*. *Dreamtime/Dreamtime Live At The Lyceum* (Beggars Banquet BEGC 57) 1984 also issued as a doubleplay cassette. (1) also issued as a picture disc (BEGA 57P) and on CD with three extra cuts, *Bonebag, Sea And Sky* and *Resurrection Joe* (BEGA 57CD) 1984 and again (Beggars Banquet BBL 2009 CD) 1996. (2) also issued on CD (Beggars Banquet BEGA 65CD) 1986 with two extra cuts, *Little Face* and *Judith*. (2) reissued on CD again (Beggars Banquet BBL 65 CD) 1997. *Pure Cult - For Rockers, Ravers, Lovers And Sinners* (Beggars Banquet BEGA 130 B) 1992, also on CD. Fans of the band will want *Rare Cult* (6-CD) (Beggars Banquet RCBOX 1 CD) 2000 and there's also a 15-track sampler.

45s: (up to 1986)	Spiritwalker/ Flower In The Desert (PS)	(Situation 2 SIT 33) 1984 -
	Spiritwalker/Flower In The Desert/ Bonebag (12", PS)	(Situation 2 SIT 33T) 1984 -
	Go West/Sea And Sky (PS)	(Beggars Banquet BEG 115) 1984 -
	Go West/Sea And Sky (poster sleeve)	(Beggars Banquet BEG 115P) 1984 -
	Go West/Sea And Sky/Brothers Grimm (live) (12", PS)	(Beggars Banquet BEG 115T) 1984 -
*	Resurrection Joe/Resurrection Joe (Hep Cat Mix) (PS)	(Beggars Banquet BEG 122) 1984 74
*	Resurrection Joe (Long Version)/Resurrection Joe/ Resurrection Joe (Hep Cat Long Version) (12", PS)	(Beggars Banquet BEG 122T) 1984 -
	She Sells Sanctuary/ No. 13 (PS)	(Beggars Banquet BEG 135) 1985 15
x	She Sells Sanctuary (Long Version)/ (Howling Mix)/ The Snake/ Assault On Sanctuary	(Beggars Banquet BEG 135C) 1985 -
	She Sells Sanctuary (Long Version)/No. 13/ The Snake (12", PS)	(Beggars Banquet BEG 135T) 1985 -
	She Sells Sanctuary (Howling Mix)/Assault On Sanctuary (12", PS)	(Beggars Banquet BEG 135TP) 1985 -
	Rain/Little Face (PS)	(Beggars Banquet BEG 147) 1985 17
+	Rain/Little Face/(Here Comes The) Rain (12", PS)	(Beggars Banquet BEG 147T) 1985 -
	Revolution (Re-Mix)/ All Souls Avenue (PS)	(Beggars Banquet BEG 152) 1985 -
	Revolution (Full Length Remix)/All Souls Avenue/Judith/ Sunrise (12", PS)	(Beggars Banquet BEG 152T) 1985
#	Revolution/All Souls Avenue/Judith/ Sunrise (7" double-pack)	(Beggars Banquet BEG 152D) 1985
	Revolution (Full Length Re-mix)/All Souls Avenue/Judith/ Sunrise (cassingle)	(Beggars Banquet BEG 152C) 1985

NB: * Also issued in a die-cut or textured sleeve. x Cassette. + Came with or without silhouette effect on the picture sleeve. # Gatefold sleeve.

Previously known as **Death Cult**, they had decided to drop 'death' from their name early in 1984 feeling it may limit their potential audience. Their first appearance as **The Cult** was on 'The Tube' in January.

Whereas Astbury's former bands **Southern Death Cult** and **Death Cult** were associated with 'positive punk' and 'gothic rock' **The Cult**'s music veered towards a sort of bombastic heavy metal which makes them of only marginal relevance here.

Spiritwalker, **The Cult**'s first 45 in May 1984 turned out to be their last on Situation 2. It topped the indie charts. After this they signed a long-term deal with Beggars Banquet. The same month a show of theirs at the Lyceum was filmed and taped.

In August, *Go West* their first 45 for Beggars Banquet was released in three different formats:- 7", 12" and as a limited fold-out poster bag 7".

Their first album *Dreamtime* came out the following month. It was originally to be titled *A Flower In The Desert*. The first 20,000 copies came with a

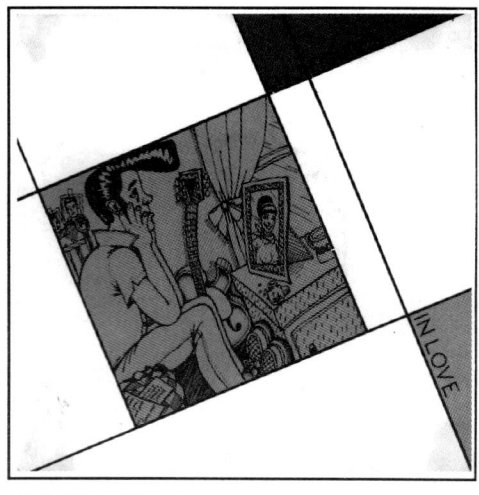

CULT FIGURES - In Love.

free live album of recordings from the Lyceum. Both albums were also issued as a double play cassette and the CD release in 1986 included three extra 45 cuts. *Dreamtime* was well-produced, blending domineering drums with layered lead guitar work and Astbury's dramatic vocal style. It enhanced their reputation in terms of sales too, spending eight weeks in the charts and peaking at No. 21. Collectors may be interested in the original test pressings of *Dreamtime* from when it was scheduled for release on Situation 2. These featured a different version of *Go West* with a psychedelic 'phased' ending.

The remainder of 1984 was spent touring and in November they appeared on "The Old Grey Whistle Test". The year ended with the release of another single *Resurrection Joe* (various versions of the song were featured). This got to No. 74, during a two week chart stay. They were voted best group by readers of 'Zig Zag' that year.

In 1985, Steve Brown (who'd worked with Wham and ABC) took over their production. A new single *She Sells Sanctuary* was released in four different formats - these are detailed in the discography. This catchy number was probably their best song of this period. It certainly sold well, spending seventeen weeks in the charts and peaking at No. 15. To help promote it, they toured Europe and then the U.K..

Nigel Preston departed (again due to musical differences) during the recording of a new album. Big Country's Mark Brzezicki was brought in to help complete it. Prior to the album's release a further 45 *Rain* was released in September. There were limited edition versions of the 7" and 12" copies that came with semi-visible patterns spot-varnished on the front and back of the cover. Again the 45 sold well, peaking at No. 17 in an eight week chart stay.

Their second album *Love*, released in October 1985, took much of its inspiration from sixties hard-rock and garage-punk bands. Inevitably, then it featured hard-rockers and pulsating boogie but there were a few slower cuts too. Despite a slating in some sections of the rock press it improved on their previous commercial performances rising to No. 4 and spending a massive twenty-two weeks in the charts. Most of the second half of 1985 was spent touring intensively, first in the Far East, then nationwide during October culminating in a gig on 24th November at Hammersmith Palais. After this they headed out to tour the U.S. and promote the album. For these live gigs Les Warner, who'd worked with Johnny Thunders, Julian Lennon and Randy California, was recruited to the drum slot and he became a permanent menber.

One further 45 *Revolution* was released in a range of formats in November and climbed to No. 30 during a seven week chart residency. This was a remixed version from the one on their *Love* album. Another cut from the album *Nirvana* featured on the sampler *One Pound Ninety-Nine* (Beggars Banquet BBB 1) 1985, which was quickly deleted and is now hard to find.

The Cult went on to enjoy considerable success throughout the eighties and into the nineties but that's another story that falls beyond the remit of this book.

Pure Cult - For Rockers, Ravers, Lovers And Sinners is an 18-track collection of their better moments. There was also a four album, 2-CD box set version of *Pure Cult* available which included seventeen extra live tracks, recorded at a 'secret' Marquee gig in late 1991.

Rare Cult is a 6-CD set comprising ninety-tracks, including radio sessions, 'B' sides, remixes, and loads of unreleased material, including the abandoned *Peace* album. There's also a fifteen-track sampler CD, *Rare Cult*.

Dreamtime was reissued again on CD in 1996 with copious sleevenotes, rare photos in a sixteen page colour booklet and expert remastering, but none of the Lyceum live material from the original free album is included.

Cult Figures

Personnel:	GARY	lead vcls, gtr	A
	JOCK	drms, vcls	A
	JONNY	gtr, vcls	A
	MARTIN	bs, vcls	A

EP:	1(A)	IN LOVE (I Remember/Laura Kate/ Almost A Love Song) (PS)	(Rather GEAR 8) 1980

45:	Zip Nolan (Highway Patrolman)/Playing With Toys/ Zip Dub (folded PS)(Rather GEAR 4/Rough Trade RT 020) 1979

These recordings are most significant for the fact **The Swell Maps** helped out on them. *I Remember* is nothing special. *Laura Kate* is a Shadows-style instrumental. *Almost A Love Song* does have quite a snappy beat.

Cult Hero

Personnel:	FRANK BELL	vcls	A
	MICHAEL DEMPSEY	bs	A
	ROBERT SMITH	gtr	A
	LOL TOLHURST	drms	A

45:	I'm A Cult Hero/I Dig You (PS)	(Friction FICS 006) 1979

The **Cult Hero** were essentially members of **The Cure** with postman Frank Bell on vocals. In 1993, their 45 was reissued free with an Italian lyric book (SIAE SCONC 004). *I'm A Cult Hero* was a disco-tinged song, which Smith had written for Bell, who used to walk around Crawley wearing a T-shirt sporting the lettering "I'm A Cult Hero". The 45 is now an established **Cure** rarity.

CULT MANIAX - Where Do We All Go.

Cult Maniax

Personnel:	BIG AL	vcls	A
	FOX	bs	A
	MIL	drms	A
	PAUL	lead gtr	A

EPs:	1(A)	FULL OF SPUNK (PS)	(Xcentric Noise SIXTH 1) 1984
	2(A)	WHERE DO WE ALL GO (12", PS)	(Xcentric Noise TENTH 1) 1985

NB: (1) came in a wraparound picture sleeve.

45s:	Blitz/Lucy Looe (PS)	(Elephant Rock ER 1) 1982
	Frenzie/The Russians Are Coming/Black Horse/ Death March (PS)	(Next Wave NXT 2/BAK 1) 1982
	Frontier/I Always Lose My Temper/ It'll Take Time (PS)	(Anti-Hype DL 001) 198?
	The Amazing Adventures Of Johnny The Duck And The Bath Time Blues/Freedom/Maniax (PS)	(Xcentric Noise EIGHT 1) 1984
	The Amazing Adventures Of Johnny The Duck And The Bath Time Blues/Freedom/ Maniax (12", PS)	(Xcentric Noise EIGHT IT) 1984

A mid-eighties Devon band. *Where Do We All Go* is a six-track 12" mini-album recorded live at the Adam & Eve's in Leeds. On offer is pretty mundane punk/new wave. Not recommended.

They also have a cut *Cities* on *Rot Records Punk Singles Collection* (Anagram CDPUNK 40) 1994.

Cupol

45: Like This For Ages/Kluba Cupol (12", PS) (4AD BAD 9) 1980

This excellent moody 45 was the product of an offshoot project by members of **Wire**. The 'A' side played at 45 rpm and the flip side at 33 rpm. *Like This For Ages* later resurfaced on *Natures Mortes* (4AD CAD 117CD) 1997.

The Cure

Personnel:
MICHAEL DEMPSEY	bs	A	
ROBERT SMITH	gtr, vcls	ABCDEFG	
LOL TOLHURST	drms	ABCDEFG	
SIMON GALLUP	bs	BC G	
MATHIEU HARTLEY	keyb'ds	B	
ANDY ANDERSON	drms	DE	
PHIL THORNALLEY	bs	D	
PORL THOMPSON	gtr	EFG	
VINCE ELY	drms	F	
BORIS WILLIAMS	drms	G	

HCP

ALBUMS: (up to 1986)
1(A)	THREE IMAGINARY BOYS	(Fiction FIX 1)	1979	44
2(B)	17 SECONDS	(Fiction FIX 004)	1980	20
3(C)	FAITH	(Fiction FIX 6)	1981	14
4(C)	PORNOGRAPHY	(Fiction FIXD 7)	1982	8
5(-)	BOYS DON'T CRY	(Fiction SPELP 26)	1983	71
6(-)	JAPANESE WHISPERS (mini-LP)	(Fiction FIXM 8)	1983	26
7(E)	THE TOP	(Fiction FIXS 9)	1984	10
8( )	CONCERT - THE CURE LIVE	(Fiction FIXH 10)	1984	26
9(E)	THE HEAD ON THE DOOR	(Fiction FIXH 11)	1985	7
10(-)	STANDING ON THE BEACH - THE SINGLES	(Fiction FIXH 12)	1986	4

NB: (1) also issued on cassette (Fiction FIXC 1) 1979 and CD (Fiction 827 686-2) 1990 and again in 1992. (2) also issued on cassette (Fiction FIXC 4) 1980 and CD (Fiction 827 354-2) 1985 and again in 1992. (3) also issued on cassette with *Carnage Visors* (Fiction FIXC 6) 1981, originally with a black and white cover and paper labels then subsequently in a red 2-for-1 cover and on CD (Fiction 827 687-2) 1985 and again in 1992. (4) also issued on cassette (FIXDC 7) 1982 and CD (Fiction 827 688-2) 1986 and again in 1992. (5) also issued on cassette (Fiction SPEMC 36) 1983, on CD (Fiction 815 011-2) 1986 and again in 1992. The CD version omits *Object* and *World War*, but adds *So What*. (6) also issued on cassette (Fiction FIXMC 8) 1983, on CD (Fiction 817 470-2) 1987 and again in 1992. (7) also issued on cassette (Fiction FIXSC 9) 1984, on CD (Fiction 821 136-2) 1984 and again in 1992. (8) also issued on cassette (Fiction FIXHC 11) 1985, on CD (Fiction 827 231-2) 1985 and again in 1992. (9) also issued on a double cassette *Concert - The Cure Live / Curiosity: Cure Anomalies 1977 - 1984* (Fiction FIXHC 10) 1984, on CD (Fiction 823 682-2) 1984 and again in 1992. (10) also issued on a doubleplay cassette *Standing On The Beach / All The Hits / Unavailable B-Sides* (Fiction FIXHC 12) 1986 and on CD as *Staring At The Sea - The Singles* (Fiction 829 239-2) 1986, which got to No. 4 in the charts. Other relevant releases are *Cure: Interview Picture Disc* (Baktabak CBAK 4003) 1988, *Cure (Interview Disc)* (Network 3D 003) 1996, *The Interview* (Talking Music SPEEK 015) 1998 and *Into A Sea Of Cure* (Misternacban MMBCD 1) 1999.

HCP

45s: (up to 1986)
Killing An Arab/10.15 Saturday Night (PS)	(Small Wonder SMALL 11)	1978	-
Killing An Arab/10.15 Saturday Night (PS)	(Fiction FICS 001)	1979	-
Boys Don't Cry/Plastic Passion (PS)	(Fiction FICS 002)	1979	-
Jumping Someone Else's Train/I'm Cold (PS)	(Fiction FICS 005)	1979	-
A Forest/Another Journey By Train (PS)	(Fiction FICS 10)	1980	31
A Forest (extended version)/Another Journey By Train (12" PS)	(Fiction FICSX 10)	1980	-
Primary/Descent (PS)	(Fiction FICS 12)	1981	43
Primary (extended)/Descent (12" PS)	(Fiction FICSX 12)	1981	-
Charlotte Sometimes/Splintered In Her Head (PS)	(Fiction FICS 14)	1981	44
Charlotte Sometimes/Splintered In Her Head/Faith (live) (12" PS)	(Fiction FICSX 14)	1981	-
The Hanging Garden/Killing An Arab (live)	(Fiction FICS 15)	1982	34
The Hanging Garden/One Hundred Years/A Forest (live)/Killing An Arab (live) (7" double pack) (PS)	(Fiction FICG 15)	1982	-
Let's Go To Bed/Just One Kiss (PS)	(Fiction FICS 17)	1982	44
Let's Go To Bed (extended)/Just One Kiss (extended) (12" PS)	(Fiction FICSX 17)	1982	-
The Walk/The Dream (PS)	(Fiction FICS 18)	1983	12
The Walk/The Dream (picture disc)	(Fiction FICSP 18)	1983	-
* Upstairs/The Dream/The Walk/Lament (12" PS)	(Fiction FICSX 18)	1983	-
The Lovecats/Speak My Language (PS)	(Fiction FICS 19)	1983	7
The Lovecats/Speak My Language (pic disc)	(Fiction FICSP 19)	1983	-
The Lovecats (extended)/Speak My Language (extended) (12" PS)	(Fiction FICSX 19)	1983	-
The Caterpillar/Happy The Man (PS)	(Fiction FICS 20)	1984	14
The Caterpillar/Happy The Man/Throw Your Foot (12" PS)	(Fiction FICSX 20)	1984	-
In Between Days/The Exploding Boy (PS)	(Fiction FICS 22)	1985	15
In Between Days/The Exploding Boy/A Few Hours After This (12" PS)	(Fiction FICSX 22)	1985	-
+ Close To Me (remix)/A Man Inside My Mouth (PS)	(Fiction FICS 23)	1985	24
Close To Me (extended remix)/A Man Inside My Mouth/Stop Dead (12" PS)	(Fiction FICSX 23)	1985	-
Half An Octopus: Close To Me (remix)/A Man Inside My Mouth/New Day/Stop Dead (10" PS)	(Fiction FICST 23)	1985	-
Boys Don't Cry (New Voice New Mix)/Pill Box Tales (PS)	(Fiction FICS 24)	1986	22
Boys Don't Cry (New Voice Club Mix)/Pill Box Tales/Do The Hansa (12", PS)	(Fiction FICSX 24)	1986	-

NB: * Some copies were also issued in 12" format whrinkwrapped with *Let's Go To Bed* 12" (FICSX 17) sticker on cellophane. + Some copies were also issued with a poster sleeve of which some had a blue-and-white *Head On The Door* sticker.

Robert Smith, Michael Dempsey and Lol Tolhurst began playing music together as long ago as 1972. They were attending a progressive Catholic school Notre Dame Middle School which encouraged its pupils to pursue their vocations at the time. Their first band was called Obelisk and at the end of the school year they performed for their class as a quintet with the addition of boys called Alan Hill on bass and Marc Ceccagno playing on guitar. They all progressed onto St. Wilfrid's Comprehensive but after 'O' levels Robert and Michael went on to the sixth form whilst Lol (Laurence) went on to study chemistry at Crawley College.

By early 1976, with a modified line-up (Paul Thompson replacing Cecagno on guitar), the band were billing themselves as Malice and playing cover versions. Then, with the onset of punk in 1977, a change of moniker to Easy Cure (after the title of one of Lol's songs) was felt desirable. In April they responded to an advert placed in 'Melody Maker' by Ariola Hansa, a

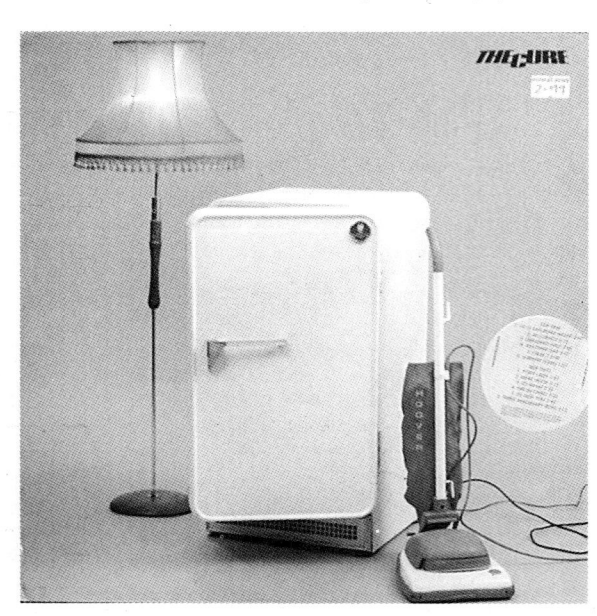

THE CURE - Three Imaginary Boys.

THE CURE - 17 Seconds.

German indie label, seeking artists who wanted to be recording stars. After sending off a tape and a photo, they were invited to a video recording session after which they were offered a recording contract. However, they soon realised it wasn't all it appeared when, after reading the contract they realised that each member only received an advance of 50p and they weren't called in to record for another six months. They were itching to get started and did their first serious gig at The Rocket, Crawley on 6th May 1977. They also played at an open-air peace concert in Crawley in June 1977 (which was filmed by Robert's dad) and later at a Jubilee Day party in the Surrey village of Earlswood.

At the first recording session for Hansa on 11th October 1977 they recorded *See The Children*, *I Just Need Myself*, *I Want To Be Old*, *Pillbox Tales* and *Meathook*. A later session on 15th November produced *Rebel Rebel*, *I Saw Her Standing There*, *I'm Cold*, *Little Girl* and an extremely slow version of *Killing An Arab*. After one further session in January 1978 when *Plastic Passion*, *I Just Need Myself*, *Rebel Rebel* and *Smashed Up* were recorded, Hansa decided they weren't going to get what they wanted out of the Easy Cure and let them go in March 1978. Shortly after the band parted company with Porl Thompson shortly after because his lead guitar breaks were out of step with the times.

To mark a new chapter in their history the band now truncated their name to **The Cure**. Financed by a benevolent friend the band recorded a demo tape of four self-penned songs, *10.15*, *Fire In Cairo*, *Boys Don't Cry* and *It's Not You*, which they duly sent to all the major record companies. The only positive response came from Polydor A&R man Chris Parry, which eventually resulted in them being signed to a new subsidiary label called Fiction. Their music was different to anything before - stark, melancholic and minimalist. It also featured some catchy hooks and had a popish appeal. They began to gig extensively and on 12th November 1978 recorded a session for John Peel's late night show comprising *Killing An Arab*, *10.15 Saturday Night*, *Boys Don't Cry* and *Fire In Cairo*. The four tracks were subsequently put out on an EP on the Strange Fruit label in July 1982.

In December 1978, their debut 45 *Killing An Arab* was released. It seems Parry wanted to test the waters before putting it out on his own label, so he licensed the first 15,000 copies to the now legendary Walthamstow-based Small Wonder label. The stark single based around its distinctive eastern-sounding guitar riff was critically acclaimed and sold rapidly, though it failed to chart when reissued the following February on Parry's Fiction label. It was inspired by a passage in Albert Camus' novel 'The Stranger'. However, the title attracted unwanted interest by the National Front, which marred several of their gigs. In 1979, *Killing An Arab* resurfaced on the *20 Of Another Kind* (Polydor SUPER POLS 1006) compilation.

An extensive tour during the spring of 1979 coincided with the release of their debut album *Three Imaginary Boys*. The cover artwork was unusual featuring a picture of a lamp, fridge and hoover against a pink background on the front and no track listing on the back. An interesting debut, it featured a somewhat bizarre version of Hendrix' *Foxy Lady* and eleven innovative originals. *10.15 Saturday Night* and *Accuracy* were basically good pop tunes. *Another Day* had a highly original discordant intro. *Object*, *Grinding Halt* and *Fire In Cairo* were all up-tempo but melodic too. *Subway Song* is minimalist but catchy and once again very original. *It's Not You* is punkish. The title cut and finale conjured up a feeling of desolation. The album made it to No. 44 in the charts, in which it spent three weeks in all.

On 16th May 1979 **The Cure** recorded their second John Peel session:- *Desparate Journalist*, *Grinding Halt*, *Subway Song*, *Plastic Passion* and *Accuracy*. A later David Jenson session on 29th August comprised *Boys Don't Cry*, *Do The Hansa* and *Three Imaginary Boys*.

In June 1979, a further 45 *Boys Don't Cry* was released to excellent reviews but surprisingly failed to chart. It got a further airing on *20 Of Another kind, Vol. 2* (Polydor POLX 1) in 1979. In September, they supported **Siouxsie and The Banshees** on a U.K. tour and Robert Smith joined them on stage when their guitarist John McKay withdrew. In November, a further 45, *Jumping Someone Else's Train* was critically acclaimed yet also failed to chart. The single was deriding kids who latch onto a certain type of music because it's the latest fashion.

Towards the end of 1979 the band took a break and Robert Smith embarked on the first two of what would be a number of side projects. He issued an EP on the Dance Fools Dance label, which he formed with Simon Gallup, an old colleague from Crawley who would shortly replace Michael Dempsey on bass. One side featured The Obtainers - two 11 year old boys bashing on pots and pans and playing *Yeh Yeh Yeh* and *Pussy Wussy*. The other side comprised Gallup's new group The Mag-Spys playing *Lifeblood* and *Bombs*. Just 100 copies were pressed and sold for 50p each. Largely on account of the small pressing, today it is an expensive collectors item. Smith then issued the **Cult Hero** single. See that entry for details.

Michael's final departure from the band was triggered by his cool reaction to the darker material Robert Smith was writing for a second **Cure** album. So Simon Gallup became a permanent member of the band and keyboardist Mathieu Hartley was also drafted in from Mag-Spys. The new line-up set off on a British and European tour. Upon their return in the New Year, they set about recording their second album *17 Seconds*. One cut *A Forest* was released as a taster 45. It reached No. 31 in the U.K. as the band toured America and later Australia to promote the album. *17 Seconds* meet with a mixed reception from fans and reviewers alike. Its minimalist and rather dour soundscapes on cuts like *Three* and the title track certainly don't have wide appeal, although songs like *A Forest* and *Play For Today* are faster and tighter and would do. It reached No. 20 in the U.K., this time enjoying a ten week chart residency,

On 10th March 1980, they recorded their third John Peel session. It comprised *A Forest*, *17 Seconds*, *Play For Today* and *M*. A fourth session - comprising *Holy Hour*, *Forever*, *Primary* and *All Cats Are Grey* followed on 15th January 1982. They also did a session for Richard Skinner - *Funeral Party*, *A Drowning Man* and *Faith* on 2nd March 1981.

It became apparent during the Australasian tour that Mathieu wasn't fitting into the band and he left, leaving them to continue as a trio. Their third album *Faith* was eventually completed, after a number of abortive recording sessions, in April 1981. Two cuts *Primary* and *Descent* were put out on a

THE CURE - A Forest 12".

single in late March. *Primary* had a certain urgency about it and backed by a driving, measured drum-beats made No. 43. It was one of the more appealing tracks on the album. The other significant cut was *Doubt*. Elsewhere, the mood of the music was one of despair. The instrumentation is built around slow, repetitive bass lines and faint, atmospheric guitars. Some regarded it as an understated classic. Others found it simply dull. The U.K. cassette version included the instrumental soundtrack to a short film *Carnage Visors*, an animated film made by Simon's brother Ric Gallup in his garage in just three days. Considering the inaccessibility of much of the material the album did well to climb to No. 14 in the U.K. album charts. In the 'States, the sarcastically titled *Happily Ever After* coupled *17 Seconds* and *Faith* into a double album for release.

In the summer 1981 tour the band used the 'Carnage Visors' film to prelude their own performance. Around this time Robert's mother was ill and his grandmother died. Then, during the European leg of the tour, Laurence's mother died. The band returned to England for the funeral, but resumed the tour immediately afterwards on Lol's insistence. Still, the intensive touring and these personal disasters left the band emotionally and physically drained when they returned to England in September.

A non-album 45, *Charlotte Sometimes* was released in October 1981. A doomy pop song with a sombre keyboard arrangement, it only reached No. 48 in the U.K., whilst many expected it to do better.

They commenced 1982 with a fifth session for John Peel. This comprised *Figurehead*, *A Hundred Years*, *Siamese Twins* and *A Hanging Garden* on 4th January.

The Cure finally made the U.K. Top 10 with their *Pornography* album in May 1982. The end result was a messy amalgam of clattering drums, unnerving guitars and anguished vocals. There seems little variety or diversity between the tracks and the overall mood of the album, which is certainly not for the suicidal, is one of desolation. *The Hanging Garden* was selected for 45 release and reached No. 34 in the charts, whilst the band was touring the U.K. to help promote the album.

During the European leg of the tour, after a fist-fight in a Strasbourg nightclub between Robert Smith and Simon Gallup, they disbanded temporarily and returned to Britain. Robert decided to try his hand at a solo career. He recorded a solo version of *Lament* for a flexi-disc to be given away with 'Flexipop' magazine. Lol Tolhurst started piano sessions with a woman in Maida Vale and their manager Chris Parry became worried that the band was finished for good. So he persuaded Robert and Lol to record a 'pure' pop record without Simon (now 'sacked' from the group) to challenge the presumption that all the group's music was about doom and gloom. With sessionman Steve Goudling on drums they recorded an inane pop number called *Let's Go To Bed*. Released in November 1982, it only climbed to No. 44 in the U.K. but was a surprise hit in California.

With Gallup going on to form a band called The Cry with former **Cure** keyboardist Mathieu Hartley, Robert Smith stepped in to play guitar for **Siouxsie and The Banshees** again, following John McGeoch's departure. He stayed with them for most of 1983 between **The Cure**'s commitments. He also arranged for a Crawley band Animation to put out a 45 on his

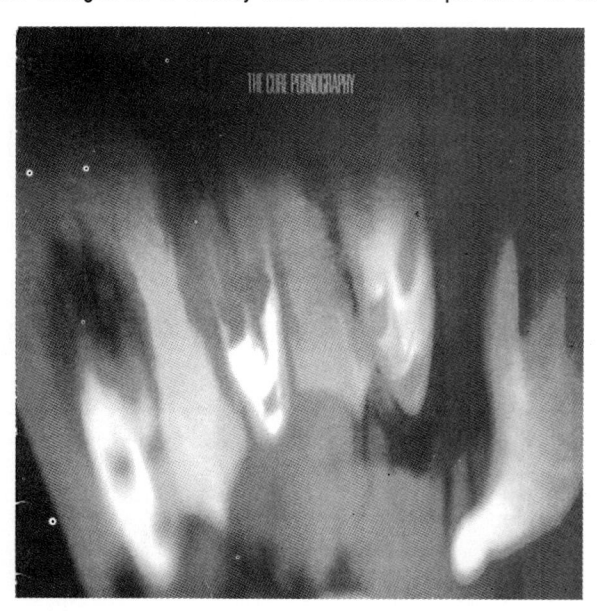

THE CURE - Pornography.

THE CURE - In Between Days.

Dance Fools Dance label, but it made little impression. Neither did the eponymous album that Lol Tolhurst produced for And Also The Trees, on which he played keyboards.

In early spring 1983, they performed a version of *Siamese Twins* on BBC 2's 'Riverside' arts programme. Steve Severin had played bass on this and during March and April Smith and Severin established a project called **The Glove**, a psychedelic, dance-orientated project whose output - an album *Blue Sunshine* and two 45s, *Like An Animal* and *Punish Me With Kisses*, were well received.

After an enjoyable performance on BBC 2's 'The Oxford Road Show' in April 1983, Smith and Tolhurst felt ready to start serious recording again. With ex-**Japan** producer Steve Nye, they recorded *The Walk* 45. This merged their previous doom and gloom sound with a new pop sound and charted comfortably, peaking at No. 12 here in the U.K.. The duo was supplemented by Phil Thornalley (bs) and ex-Brilliant drummer Andy Anderson and they stabilised into a foursome.

They starred at The Elephant Fayre festival in Cornwall and toured the 'States briefly before heading for Paris, where they recorded their next 45 *The Lovecats*. Inspired by the film 'The Aristocats', it became their biggest U.K. hit climbing to No. 7. *Boys Don't Cry* a U.S. budget-priced compilation of material from their early days was released here in August 1983. It entered the U.K. album charts at No. 93 and re-entered at No. 77 a month later. Meanwhile, in the 'States, a mini-album *The Walk*, was compiled by Sire and climbed to No. 179. This was their first album to make the charts there. Meanwhile, here in England, in December 1983, the 'A' and 'B' sides of *Let's Go To Bed*, *The Walk* and *The Lovecats* were compiled on a mini-album *Japanse Whispers*. This climbed to No. 26 and there was now a resurgence of public interest in the band. An expanded version of the U.K. release reached No. 181 in the 'States in March 1984.

Phil Thornalley departed to produce for **Duran Duran** before the band began work on their sixth album *The Top* early in 1984. Robert played bass on this album, but during the sessions Porl Thompson played sax and soon found himself back in the band. Robert was still playing with **Siouxsie and The Banshees** and helped record their *Hyaena* album alongside *The Top*. The *Caterpillar*, a likeable, upbeat and catchy number, was selected from the next album for 45 release. It made it to No. 14 spending seven weeks in the charts as the group toured the U.K. to promote their new album. A popular show opener during this tour was *Shake Dog Shake*, a slow, surging metallic gem from the album. The wailing *Piggy In The Mirror* and pleading *Give It To Me* were other strong numbers on an album that only went some way to advance the band's recent revival. By the end of the European tour to promote the album, which reached No. 10 in the U.K. and No. 180 in the U.S., Smith was exhausted and had to miss a scheduled **Siouxsie and The Banshees** tour.

The group relaxed that summer and a live album *Concert* (the cassette version of which also featured a compilation of early rarities) was released in October 1984. It reached No. 26 in the U.K. the following month. The group now to some degree revitalised, embarked on a tour of New Zealand, Australia, Japan, Canada and the U.S.. Sadly, Anderson, now the worse for drink went completely off the rails after a show in Tokyo and had to return home, leaving the band drummer-less. Vince Ely (who'd played with **The Psychedelic Furs**) filled in briefly before being replaced by former

Thompson Twins drummer Boris Williams. In the autumn of 1984 Robert Smith and Simon Gallup were brought together by former **Cure** roadie Gary Biddles to patch up their differences. This culminated in Smith inviting Gallup to rejoin the band.

So, in April 1985, with Thompson (from their Easy Cure days) and Gallup back on board, they set about recording their next album, *The Head On The Door*. In July 1985, *In Between Days* was released as a foretaste of what was to come. Assisted by a Tim Pope video the popish tune, with its gentle keyboard riff and upbeat bass line breezed into the Top 20, peaking at No. 15. It enjoyed a ten week chart residency. The album, which met with favourable reviews, marked a return to a simpler, more pop-orientated sound. A second track, *Close To Me*, provided a second U.K. hit from the album (No. 24) and *A Night Like This*, a slow rock song built around a major chord prgression and a light Latin-tinged number *The Blood*, about a Portuguese wine purported to induce horrifying visions when consumed in large quantites, were other notable tracks. Climbing to No. 7 in spending thirteen weeks in the charts, it was their most successful album to date. This was soon bettered the following year when *Standing On A Beach - The Singles* reached No. 4 and spent a massive thirty-five weeks in the charts.

In 1999, *10:15 Saturday Night* was included on the 5-CD box set *1-2-3-4 - A History Of Punk And New Wave 1976 - 1979* (MCA/Universal MCD 60066). The same year on a various artists **Cure** tribute album *Into A Sea Of Cure*, a series of Argentinian indie bands tackle **The Cure**'s back catalogue!

The Cure continued to record well into the nineties, which is a measure of their creativity, resilience and diversity. They were undoubtedly one of the most interesting products of the punk era.

Cyanide

Personnel:	BOB DeVRIES	vcls	A
	DAVE STEWARD	gtr	A
	MICK STEWART	drms	A
	DAVE THOMPSON	bs	A

ALBUM:	1(A)	CYANIDE	(Pye NSPL 18554) 1978

45s:	I'm A Boy/Do It	(Pye 7N 46048) 1978
	Mac The Flash/Hate The State	(Pye 7N 46094) 1978
	Fireball/Your Old Man	(Pinnacle PIN 23) 1979

Cyanide's album is full of aggression and speed but is almost totally devoid of any originality or creativity. Despite this, their records are now rare and collectable.

They also contributed *Fireball* and *Mess I'm In* to the *Backstage Pass* (Supermusic SUP 2001) 1977 compilation.

DAGABAND - Second Time Around.

The Cybermen

EP:	1( )	THE CYBERMEN (Cybernetic Surgery/
		Where's The New Wave?/Hanging Around/
		I Can't Help It)	(Rockaway AERE 101) 1978

45:	You're To Blame/It's You I Want	(Rockaway LUV 002) 1979

These records are hard to find and now collectable.

Dagaband

Personnel:	GREG BOYNTON	keyb'ds	A
	PHIL BOYNTON	perc, vcls	A
	STEVE FIDLER	lead gtr, bs	A

45s:	Test Flight/Images (PS)	(Rutland RX 100) 1980
	Second Time Around/Reds Under The Bed/
	I Can See For Miles (PS)	(MHM A-M 094) 1983

Chesterfield was this band's home. The vocalist seems to be doing an imitation of David Surkamp (of Pavlov's Dog) and musically there's strong progressive rock influences with lots of guitar and keyboard histrionics on *Second Time Around* and *Reds Under The Beds*. The other cut is a keyboard-driven, unusual cover of The Who's *I Can See For Miles*.

DALEK I - Dalek I Love You.

Dalek I (Dalek I Love You)

Personnel:	DAVID BATES	vcls	A
	ALAN GILL	vcls, synth	A
	CHRIS HUGHES	bs	A
	DAVE HUGHES	keyb'ds	A
	HUGH JOES	drms	A

ALBUMS:	1(A)	COMPASS KUM'PAS	(Back Door OPEN 1) 1980
	2( )	DALEK I LOVE YOU	(Korova KODE 7) 1983

NB: (1) also issued on CD (Fontana 8368944) 1989. (2) credited to **Dalek I Love You**.

45s:	Freedom Fighters/
	Two Chameleons (PS)	(Vertigo DALEK 1) 1980
	The World/We're All Actors	(Vertigo DALEK 2) 1980
	Dalek I Love You (Destiny)/Happy/
	This Is My Uniform (PS)	(Back Door DOOR 5) 1980
*	Dalek I Love You/Eight Track (PS)	(Back Door CLOSE 1) 1980
*	Heartbeat/Astronauts (PS)	(Back Door DOOR 10) 1981
*	Holiday In Disneyland/
	Masks And Licenses (PS)	(Korova KOW 25) 1982
*	Ambition/Hot Person (PS)	(Korova KOW 29) 1983
*	Horrorscope/These Walls We Build (PS)	(Korova KOW 31) 1983

NB: * Credited to **Dalek I Love You**.

Dalek I Love You evolved out of a Liverpool punk band Radio Blank. Alan Gill and David Balfe formed them in November 1977. The story goes that Balfe wanted to call them The Daleks, whilst Gill favoured Darling I Love You - hence the compromise **Dalek I Love You**.

Balfe left in 1978 to join **Big In Japan** before **Dalek I Love You** made it onto vinyl. From 1980 onwards, though, a series of highly-regarded synthesizer-pop singles were put out.

On *Compass Kum'Pas*, Alan Gill (later of **Teardrop Explodes**) and Dave Hughes (later of **Orchestral Manuvoeuvres In The Dark**) produced a very Eno-influenced electronic sound with a wide range of synthesizers, guitars and percussion. *Dalek I Love You (Destiny)* was also included on *Machines* (Virgin V 2177) in 1980. It's a pleasant electro-pop single. On the flip side *Happy* opens with some freeform jazzy piano but soon develops into synthesizer-driven electro-pop and *Uniform* is very similar ro early **Orchestral Manuvoeuvres In The Dark**.

In 1982 they had a cut from 1979 *A Suicide* included on *To The Shores Of lake Placid* (Zoo FOUR). It's a sensitive and interesting number with distinctive keyboards.

The band underwent several line-up changes during its relatively short life and the 1983 album was recorded by a reformed line-up. This featured layered synthesizers with taints of psychedelia and excellent vocals and harmonies.

Compass Kum'Pas was later reissued by Fontana in 1989.

Dalek O.K.

45:	This Life/Rejected/ Man Of The World (PS)	(Experimental Products EXPS 1) 1980

A different band about whom I've no other info.

Dali's Car

Personnel:	MICK KARN	bs		A
	PETER MURPHY	vcls		A

			HCP
ALBUM: 1(A)	WAKING HOUR	(Paradox DOXLP 1)	1984 84

45s:	*	The Judgement Is The Mirror/ High Places (PS)	(Paradox DOX 1) 1984
		The Judgement Is The Mirror/High Places/ Lifelong Moment (12, PS)	(Paradox DOX DOX 112) 1984

NB: * This was also available as a picture disc (DOXY 1).

This was a short-lived collaboration between **Bauhaus** frontman Peter Murphy and **Japan**'s bassist Mick Karn. They contributed two cuts to the cassette compilation *Jobs Not Yobs* in 1982. Two years later they signed to Virgin for this electro-pop 45 and the *Waking Hour* followed a month later. Neither met with much acclaim although *Waking Hour* did spend a week in the album charts at No. 84. They soon parted to pursue other projects.

The Damned

Personnel:	RAY BURNS (CAPTAIN SENSIBLE)	bs	ABCDE
	BRIAN JAMES	gtr	AB
	CHRIS MILLER (RAT SCABIES)	drms	ABCDEF
	DAVE VANIAN	vcls	ABCDEF
	ROBERT 'LU' EDMUNDS	gtr	B
	ALISTAIR WARD	bs	C
	PAUL GRAY	bs	DE
	ROMAN JUGG	keyb'ds, gtr	EF
	BRYAN MERRICK	bs	F

THE DAMNED - New Rose.

				HCP
ALBUMS:	1(A)	DAMNED DAMNED DAMNED	(Stiff SEEZ 1)	1977 36
(up to	2(B)	MUSIC FOR PLEASURE	(Stiff SEEZ 5)	1977 -
1986)	3(C)	MACHINE GUN ETIQUETTE	(Chiswick CWK 3011)	1979 31
	4(D)	THE BLACK ALBUM (dbl)	(Chiswick CWK 3015)	1980 29
	5(-)	THE BEST OF THE DAMNED	(Big Beat DAM 1)	1981 43
	6(E)	STRAWBERRIES	(Bronze BRON 542)	1982 15
	7(E)	LIVE SHEPPERTON 1980	(Big Beat NED 1)	1982 -
	8(E)	LIVE IN NEWCASTLE	(Damned DAMU 2)	1983 -
	9(F)	PHANTASMAGORIA	(MCA MCFW 3275)	1985 11
	10(-)	DAMNED BUT NOT FORGOTTEN	(Dojo DOJO LP 21)	1986 42

NB: 2,000 copies of (1) came with an **Eddie and The Hot Rods** photo on the rear sleeve, some shrinkwrapped with title sticker. (1) and (2) reissued as a double pack, 5,000 copies only available by mail order (Stiff MAIL 2) 1983. (1) reissued as a picture disc (Demon FIEND 91) 1987 and on CD (Demon FIENDCD 91) 1987, again (Frontier 310332) 1997 and again (Edsel EDCD 677) 2000. (2) reissued on orange vinyl (Demon FIEND 108) 1987 and on CD (Demon FIEND CD 108) 1988. (3) reissued on blue, white or clear vinyl (Ace DAM 2) 1982 and on CD (Big Beat CDWIK 905) 1988. (4) reissued as a single album with lyrics and poster (Ace DAM 3) 1982 and a double album (Chiswick WIKMZ 91) 1990 and on CD (Big Beat CDWIK 906) 1987. (5) issued on red or blue vinyl and on CD (Big Beat CD DAM 1) 1987. (6) issued originally with a scented lyric sheet and reissued as a picture disc (Dojo DOJOPD 46) 1986 and on CD (Dojo DOJOCD 46) 1986 and again (Dojo ESMCD 472) 1997, (Cleopatra CLEO 10292) 1993 and (Essential ESMCD 473) 1997. Only 5,000 of (7) issued with a 'Collectors Catalogue'. It was later issued on CD (Big Beat CDWIKM 27) 1988. 5,000 of (8) issued, by mail order only and a further 5,000 as a picture disc. (9) issued on white vinyl, but was also available as a picture disc (MCFP 3275) with a free blue vinyl 12" *Eloise* (MCG9 3275) and there's a mispressing with different tracks from label or sleeve; some on white vinyl (MCF 3275), also issued on CD (MCA DMCF 3275) 1985. More 1987 releases were *The Light At The End Of The Tunnel* (MCA MCSP 312) 1987 and *Live At The Lyceum 1981* (IPNOSE 18) 1987. From 1988 came *The Best Of Vol. 1 1/2 The Long Lost Weekend* (Big Beat WIK 80) 1988. Also of relevance are *Not The Captain's Birthday Party - Live At The Roundhouse* (Stiff GET 4) 1986, a mini-LP on blue vinyl at 45 rpm reissued in 1991 on Demon and on CD (VEXCD 7) 1991, *Final Damnation* (Essential ESSLP 008) 1989 and on CD (ESSCD 008) 1989 and *Live At The Lyceum* (Revolver RRLP 159) 1992 which came on clear vinyl. There are also a number of CD compilations, *Collection: The Damned* (Castle Collector Series CCSCD 278) 1990, also issued as a double album on the same label; *Mindless, Directionless Energy (Live)* (I.D. CDOSE 18) 1987 and again (I.D. CDOSE 18X) 1989 also on vinyl; *MCA Singles A's And B's* (Connoisseur Collection VSOPCD 174) 1992; *Alternative Chartbusters* (Plastic Head AOK 101) 1992 and *The Light At The End Of The Tunnel* issued as a double album and CD set (MCA DMCSP 312) 1991 and reissued (MCA MCLOD 19007) 1992. This got to No. 87 when it was first released on vinyl (MCA MCSP 312) in 1987. Although CD catalogue numbers are given for these compilations they were all originally issued on vinyl. More recent compilations include: *Skip Off School To See The Damned (The Stiff Singles A's + B's)* (Demon VEXCD 12) 1992; *The MCA Singles A's & B's* (Connoisseur Collection VSOP CD 174) 1992; *Ballroom Blitz - Live* (Receiver RRCD 159) 1993, *Born To Kill (2-CD set)* (Snapper SMDCD 143) 1997, *The Chaos Years* (Cleopatra CLP 9960) 1997, *Damned But Not Forgotten* (Essential ESMCD 472) 1997, *Eternally Damned (The Very Best Of The Damned)* (MCI Music MUSCD 017) 1994; *Fiendish Shadows* (Cleopatra CLP 9804) 1996; *I'm Alright Jack And The Beanstalk* (The Record Label MOCDR 1) 1997; *Noise (The Best Of The Damned Live)* (Emporio EMPRCD 592) 1995, *The Sessions Of The Damned* (Strange Fruit SFR CD 121) 1994 and (Strange Fruit SFRSCD 070) 1998; *Tales From The Damned* (Cleopatra CLEO 71392) 1993; *From The Beginning* (Spectrum 550747-2) 1995; *The Radio One Sessions* (Nightracks CDNT 011) 1996; *Neat Neat Neat* (Demon FBOOK 14) 1997; *The Pleasure And The Pain: Selected Highlights 1982 - 1991* (2-CD) (Castle Music ESACD 901) 2000 and *Marvellous* (Big Beat CDWIKK 198) 2001.

EPs:	1(D)	FRIDAY THE 13TH EP (Disco Man/The Limit Club/ Billy Bad Breaks/Citadel) (PS)	(NEMS TRY 1)	1981 50
	2(-)	THE DAMNED (Sick Of Being Sick/Stretcher Case Baby/ Help/New Rose/ Problem Child) (12", PS)	(Stiff BUY IT 238)	1986 -
	3(A)	PEEL SESSIONS (Stab Your Back/Neat Neat Neat/ New Rose/So Messed Up/I Fall) (12" metallic finish PS)	(Strange Fruit SFPS 040)	1987 -

HCP

45s: (up to 1986)

	New Rose/Help (PS)	(Stiff BUY 6)	1976 -
	Neat Neat Neat/Stab Your Back/ Singalongascabies (PS)	(Stiff BUY 10)	1977 -
*	Stretcher Case Baby/ Sick Of Being Sick (PS)	(Stiff DAMNED 1)	1977 -
	Problem Child/You Take My Money (PS)	(Stiff BUY 18)	1977 -
+	Don't Cry Wolf/One Way Love (PS)	(Stiff BUY 24)	1977 -
#	Love Song/Burglar	(Dodgy Demo Co.)	1978 -
%	Love Song/Noise Noise Noise/ Suicide (PS)	(Chiswick CHIS 112)	1979 20
	Smash It Up/Burglar (PS)	(Chiswick CHIS 116)	1979 35
	I Just Can't Be Happy Today/Ballroom Blitz/ The Turkey Song (PS)	(Chiswick CHIS 120)	1979 46
	History Of The World Part 1/I Believe The Impossible/ Sugar And Spite (PS)	(Chiswick CHIS 135)	1980 51
	History Of The World Part 1/I Believe The Impossible/ Sugar And Spite (12" PS)	(Chiswick CHIS 12 135)	1980 -
	There Ain't No Sanity Clause/Hit Or Miss/ Looking At You (live) (PS)	(Chiswick CHIS 139)	1980 -
	Four Pack (Stiff BUY 6, 10, 18 & 24 in a plastic wallet)	(Stiff GRAB 2)	1981 -
$	Love Song/Noise Noise Noise	(Big Beat NS 75)	1982 -
^	Smash It Up/Burglar (PS)	(Big Beat NS 76)	1982 -
**	Wait For The Blackout/ (other side by Captain Sensible)	(Big Beat NS 77)	1982 -
++	Lovely Money/Lovely Money (Disco Mix)/ I Think I'm Wonderful (PS)	(Bronze BRO 149)	1982 42
	Dozen Girls/Take That/Mine's A Large One, Landlord/ Torture Me (PS)	(Bronze BRO 158)	1982 -
##	Lively Arts/Teenage Dream (PS)	(Big Beat BS 80)	1982 -
	Lively Arts/Teenage Dream/ I'm So Bored (10" PS)	(Big Beat NST 80)	1982 -
	Generals/Disguise/ Citadel Zombies (PS)	(Bronze BRO 159)	1982 -
	White Rabbit/Rabid Over You/ Seagulls (PS)	(Big Beat NS 85)	1983 -
	White Rabbit/Curtain Call (12" PS)	(Big Beat NST 85)	1983 -
%%	Thanks For The Night/ Nasty (PS)	(Plus One DAMNED 1)	1984 43
$$	Thanks For The Night/Nasty/ Do The Blitz (12")	(Plus One DAMNED 1T)	1984 -
η	Grimly Fiendish/Edward The Bear (PS)	(MCA GRIM 1)	1985 21
φ	Grimly Fiendish (Spic 'n' Span Mix)/ Edward The Bear (12" PS)	(MCA GRIMT 1)	1985 -
	Grimly Fiendish (Bad Trip Mix)/Grimly Fiendish/ Edward The Bear (12")	(MCA GRIMX 1)	1985 -
	The Shadow Of Love/Ten Inches Of Hell Mix/ Nightshift/Would You (10" PS)	(MCA GRIMX 2)	1985 25
	Edition Premier: The Shadow Of Love/Nightshift/Let There Be Rats/Wiped Out (double pack)	(MCA GRIM 2/GRIM Y 2)	1985 -
κ	Is It A Dream (Wild West End Mix)/ Street Of Dreams (live) (PS)	(MCA GRIM 3)	1985 34
λ	Is It A Dream (Wild West Express Mix)/ Street Of Dreams (live)/Curtain Call (live)/Pretty Vacant (live)/Wild Thing (live) (12" PS)	(MCA GRIMT 3)	1985 -
	An Interview With The Damned 1985 Part 1 - Rat & Bryn (pic disc)	(TALK 1)	1985 -
	An Interview With The Damned 1985 Part 2 - Dave & Roman (pic disc)	(TALK 2)	1985 -
μ	Thanks For The Night/Nasty	(Plus One DAMNED 1P)	1986 -
	Eloise/Temptation (PS)	(MCA GRIM 4)	1986 2
ν	Eloise (Extended)/Temptation/ Beat Girl (12", PS)	(MCA GRIMT 4)	1986 -
o	Eloise (Extravagant Mix)/Temptation/ Beat Girl (12", PS)	(MCA GRIMX 4)	1986 -
Reissue:	Lively Arts/Teenage Dream/ I'm So Bored (12" PS)	(Big Beat NST 80)	1985 -
π	Thanks For The Night/ Nasty (12", PS)	(Plus One DAMNED P1)	1986 -

NB: * Limited edition freebie. + Some copies in pink vinyl. # Limited edition mail-order only as The Doomed. % Some copies in red vinyl with four different picture sleeves. $ Some on blue vinyl and in three different sleeves. ^ Initially on red vinyl. ** There was also a picture disc release (NSP 77). ++ There was also a picture disc release (BROP 149). ## Some copies on green vinyl. %% 1,000 each on red, white and blue vinyl. There was also a picture disc release (DAMNED 1P). η In a gatefold picture sleeve. The first 1,000 copies were autographed. There was also a picture disc release. φ Came with an autographed picture sleeve. κ Came with 5 badges. λ Came with five **Damned** badges. μ This was a collector's edition of 1,000 "Woman Shaped" picture disc with a plinth. Fifty copies were also produced as uncut shaped picture discs which are more collectable. ν There was also a limited edition 12" version of 2,000 on blue vinyl. o This was also a limited edition of 2,000. π This was a 12" reissue picture disc.

The Damned were significant in the early days of U.K. punk as the first punk band to release a single, an album, tour the 'States and appear on TV. In retrospect, they are perhaps even more significant for their staying power - still going strong in 1987 when they disbanded, although there have been various re-union gigs since.

They started out as a trio. Ray Burns, born on 23rd April 1955 and later known as Captain Sensible, had been playing in various bands since 1970 and also featured in an early line-up of **Johnny Moped**. He figured on *Basically, The Original Johnny Moped Tape*, which was later released by Chiswick as a 7" promo in 1978. Brian James had been a member of seminal London punk band **London SS** along with Chris Miller (alias Rat Scabies), who'd earlier played in an outfit called Riot. Miller had been born in Kingston-upon-Thames, a London suburb, on 30th July 1957. They teamed up with rock journalist Nick Kent to play two gigs as The Subterraneans, but then recruited Dave Vanian (real name Letts) as vocalist to form **The Damned**. Vanian, who'd been working as a gravedigger would have looked in place as part of a Dracula movie. He gave the band a distinctive visual presence.

The Damned made their debut on 6th July 1976 supporting **The Sex Pistols** at London's 100 Club. Their music was fast and furious. They soon established themselves as one of London's most exciting live bands. On 21st August they appeared at the Mont de Marsan, the first European Punk Rock Festival in the south of France. Soon after, they parted company with their original manager Andy Czezowski and signed to Stiff Records. Stiff's Jake Riviera became their new manager.

Their debut 45 *New Rose*, produced by **Nick Lowe**, was released in November 1976. It typified their fast and furious style and soon became Stiff's biggest seller to date. Without doubt it was one of the finest moments of U.K. punk and no collection of this genre can be complete without it. The flip side featured a rapid version of Lennon/McCartney's *Help*. Stiff quickly signed a one-off distributon deal with United Artists to help cater for the increased demand, although the 45 wasn't a hit and it certainly deserved to be. *Help* also figured on *Hits - Greatest Stiffs* (Stiff FIST 1) in 1977.

In December 1976, they supported **The Sex Pistols** on the 'Anarchy In The U.K.' tour, but they were subsequently slung off it for trying to play a gig without **The Sex Pistols**. Returning to London, they played at the Hope

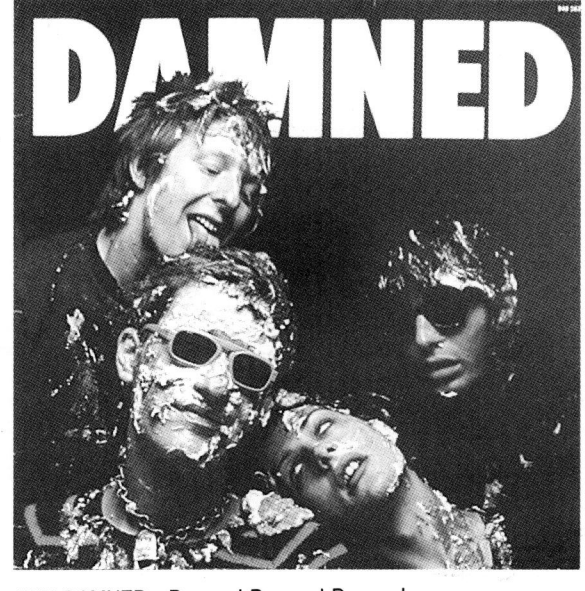

THE DAMNED - Damned Damned Damned.

and Anchor in Islington, a legendary punk venue, but in the wake of the Bill Grundy interview and reaction against punk found it difficult securing gigs.

Damned Damned Damned, produced by **Nick Lowe** like their debut single, was the first punk album released in the U.K. in February 1977. Most of its songs were written by Brian James, including *New Rose* and its follow-up 45 *Neat Neat Neat*. Also on the album was the flip side to their second single, the manic *Stab Your Back* penned by Scabies. There was also a third cut *Singalongascabies*, which was unavailable elsewhere. The picture sleeve version of this 45 captured the band wearing plastic bags on their heads. Other highlights of their debut album were *One Of The 2* and *See Her Tonight*. The album, which was critically acclaimed and climbed to No. 36 in the U.K. charts, in which it spent a total of ten weeks, concluded with a barnstorming version of The Stooges' *I Feel Alright*. Indeed, there was no doubting the influence of acts like The MC5, Iggy Pop and The Stooges on their music. Around 2,000 copies of the album were issued with a picture of **Eddie and The Hotrods** on the reverse of the sleeve. A publicity stunt or an error as the red record company sticker asserted? Views are divided, but these copies which also sported a large **Damned** sticker on the original shrink wrap are now collectable.

On 8th April 1977, **The Damned** became the first U.K. punk group to tour the 'States with The Dead Boys. The tour opened at New York's top punk venue CBGB's. On their return home, they embarked on a major U.K. tour with **The Adverts** in May. They also did three nights at the Marquee Club in London in July. At these gigs copies of what has subsequently become one of the most collectable punk records, *Stretcher Case Baby* were given away. Around 5,000 of these were produced in all, 250 of which were given away in an NME competition. It was produced by Shel Talmy.

In August, on James' insistence a second guitarist, the previously unemployed Robert 'Lu' Edmunds was recruited. Pink Floyd's drummer Nick Mason was recruited to produced the follow-up album, in preference to Shel Talmy, and Lol Coxhill guested on sax in a few places. The bulk of the material was again written by James. This caused resentment with the other members amongst whom tensions were increasing. Side one had some fine cuts, including *Problem Child*, selected for 45 release in September as a prelude to the album, and *Don't Cry Wolf*, a follow-up 45 a month after the album's release in November. Neither these or the album, which sought to experiment unsuccessfully on side two, charted. Desite its great cover the album didn't deliver what its title promised. (Stiff later reissued both **The Damned**'s first two albums as a mail-order only package in 1986).

By the time the album was released Rat Scabies had quit. Future Culture Club and ex-**London** drummer Jon Moss was hastily recruited for a November tour with U.S. combo The Dead Boys, which failed to stem their decline. In January 1978, they parted company with Stiff.

Later that year Stiff released two boxed sets containing ten singles in each (the label's first 20 7" issues in all). The black box featured *New Rose* and *Neat Neat Neat*. The brown box contained *Problem Child*. With just 5,000 copies of the boxes released these too are collectable.

In February 1978 the group split. James went on to form his own band **Tanz Der Youth** and later did a couple of low-key solo singles as Brian James and The Brains. Vanian joined The Doctors Of Madness for a few live gigs. Moss and Edmunds went on to **The Edge**. Captain Sensible

THE DAMNED - White Rabbit.

joined **The Softies** on guitar. He played on their Dutch-only 45 *Jet Boy Jet Girl* (Roker POS 15077). He also worked with **Johnny Moped** and later formed his own outfit **King**. Meanwhile Rab Scabies put together his own band White Cats too. **The Damned** played a farewell gig at the Rainbow, which ended with a frenzied version of *I Feel Alright* after which everything on stage was wrecked!

At this point, like many subsequent punk bands, **The Damned** could easily have become a relatively small but significant thread in the tapestry of U.K. rock but the unpredicatable happened. On 5th September, Scabies, Vanian and Sensible played a re-union gig at London's Electric Ballroom as Les Punks, with Motorhead's Lemmy on bass. They decided to reform, gigging for a couple of months as The Doomed (now with ex-**Chelsea** guitarist Henry Badowski temporarily on bass), Captain Sensible having switched to guitar, whilst they sought to acquire the rights to "The Damned" name from its owner James. This line-up recorded six tracks in November 1978, two of them *Love Song* and *Burglar* were available as a mail-order 45 on Dodgy Demo.

In early 1979, Alistair Ward (ex-**Saints**) had replaced **Badowski** on bass and The Doomed had become **The Damned**. This new line-up's debut gig was at Croydon's Greyhound and they signed to Chiswick Records. Three hit singles followed as *Love Song*, *Smash It Up* and *I Just Can't Be Happy Today* peaked at No's 20, 35 and 46 respectively. All three contained non-album 'B' sides. *Love Song*, was issued on red vinyl in four different, picture covers each featuring one of the band's members. *Smash It Up* was backed by a new recording of *Burglar*, whilst a live version of The Sweet's *Ballroom Blitz* (with Lemmy on bass) and *The Turkey Song* (which wasn't mentioned on the label or cover) appeared on the reverse of *I Just Can't Be Happy Today*.

A new album *Machine Gun Etiquette* was released in November 1978. Containing their three hit single 'A' sides, the anthemic *Noise Noise Noise*, *Plan 9 Channel 7* and a fine cover of MC5's *Looking At You*, it climbed to No. 31 in the album charts during a five week residency underscoring their increasing popularity. Make no mistake, this was a good record. The band had also re-established itself as a popular live attraction.

In February 1980, Ward left for Tank (a heavy metal outfit as its name suggests). Former **Eddie and The Hotrods** bassist Paul Gray was recruited in his place. They returned with *The Black Album* - a double album set in the U.K. and single record in the U.S.. The first two sides marked a definate new direction for the band, comprising melodic rock with acoustic guitar, vocal harmonies, synthesizers and mellotron. Cuts like *Wait For The Blackout* and *Dr. Jeckyll And Mr. Hyde* epitomized this new dimension to their sound beautifully. Side three is a single composition, the 17-minute *Curtain Call* and side four is a live 'best of' recorded at Shepperton Studios. The 1982 reissue of this album omitted *Curtain Call* and the live side, but, released as a single album, had a lyric sheet and the first 12,000 copies came with a psychedelic poster.

Their next single was a remix of a cut *The History Of The World Part 1* which had appeared on *The Black Album*. Two new songs, *I Believe The Impossible* and *Sugar And Spite* appeared on the flip. In addition to the normal 7", Chiswick also released it as a 12" against the band's wishes. They publicly pledged to autograph any copies fans brought along to gigs as a gesture of good will, though it's not known how many copies were actually autographed. The 45 got to No. 51 in the U.K. and their album reached No. 29, spending three weeks in the charts. As a result of their dispute with Chiswick *There Ain't No Sanity Clause*, their next 45 was the last for the company and it failed to chart at all.

In March 1981, the band toured the 'States to help promote the U.S. version of *The Black Album* although it failed to chart there. They then toured Europe in June, returning to London for a fifth anniversary concert at the Lyceum in July. That November they signed to NEMS. The following month the label released their *Friday The 13th* EP, which included *Disco Man* and a version of The Rolling Stones' *Citadel*. It just made the Top 50. *The Best Of The Damned*, which included live versions of their Stiff singles, was put out on Chiswick's Big Beat label and peaked at No. 43. The album also gave a first U.K. release to *Rabid (Over You)*, which would be the 'B' side of their cover of Jefferson Airplane's psychedelic classic *White Rabbit*, when it was eventually released in the U.K. in 1983. Collectors will be interested in the limited number of *The Best Of The Damned*, which were released on both red and blue vinyl.

During 1981 Stiff made **The Damned**'s first four singles available once again as a limited edition four pack in a plastic wallet.

Having drafted temporary keyboard player Tosh for live gigs, **The Damned** closed 1981 by appearing at the 'Christmas On Earth' festival in Leeds alongside a new generation of 'punk' bands like **Anti-Pasti**, **GBH** and **Chron Gen**.

In May 1982, they signed a new deal with Bronze Records. Captain Sensible also struck up a solo contract with A&M. In July, Sensible's first solo release *Happy Talk* (from the 'South Pacific' musical) topped the charts for two weeks to give him the first in a series of solo hits. **The Damned**, meanwhile, returned to the charts with *Lovely Money*, which climbed to No. 42. A follow-up single, in September *Dozen Girls* failed to chart at all.

Strawberries, their first album of new material for nearly two years, was released in October 1982. It's more memorable for the strawberry-smelling lyric sheet it was packaged in than its musical content. For this album Roman Jugg was added to the line-up on keyboards. He also played on the subsequent tour. The album rose to No. 15 but only spent four weeks in the charts. *Generals* culled from it for 45 release failed to chart at all. The following April the band were dropped by Bronze and Gray quit the band. A 45 release with Captain Sensible's *Glad It's All Over* backed by a medley of **Damned** oldies on the flip *Damned On 45* kept interest alive in the band by climbing to No. 6 in the singles charts.

The next eighteen months was a very quiet period for the band. Their only recording was a one-off 45 release for Plus One, *Thanks For The Night*, which peaked at No. 43. They suffered what many felt at the time might be a killer blow in August 1984, when Sensible quit to concentrate on his solo career and acting. Jugg switched from keyboards to guitar, whilst Bryn Merrick came in on bass.

In October 1984, their new line-up ('F') signed a worldwide deal with MCA and proceeded to enjoy considerable chart success in the remainder of the decade in a more mainstream pop vein. This included covers of Barry Ryan's 1968 hit *Eloise* and Love's *Alone Again Or*.

Significant compilation appearances in the band's early days included *New Rose* on *New Wave* (Vertigo 6300 902) 1977 and *The Punk Of 1976* (Abstract ABS 004) 1981, whilst their cover of *Help* figured on *Hits Greatest Stiffs* (Stiff FIST 1) 1977. *Excerpts From Stiff's Greatest Hits* features extracts of *Problem Child* and *Don't Cry Wolf*, sandwiched between DJ talk. They also appeared on *The Moonlight Tapes* (Danceville DANCE 1) 1980 credited as The School Bullies for contractual reasons playing the version of *Teenage Dream* used as the 'B' side to *Lively Arts*. *Grimly Fiendish* also featured on *Out Now* (dbl) (Chrysalis-MCA OUTV 1) 1985 and *The Shadow Of Love* figured on *Now That's What I Call Music* (dbl) (EMI NOW 5) 1985. *Eloise* resurfaced on *Hits 4* (CBS) 1986, *Stretcher Case Baby* can also be heard on NME's cassette-only *Pogo A Go Go*. They also appeared on a couple of film soundtracks. *UK/DK - The Original Soundtrack* (Anagram GRAMM 006) 1983 included *Ignite*, whilst the previously unreleased *Dead Beat Dance* got an airing on *The Return Of The Living Dead* (Big Beat WIK 38) 1985. More recently, *Smash It Up* figured on *Punk Lost And Found* (Shanachie SH 5705) in 1996 and *New Rose* appeared on *1-2-3-4 - A History Of Punk And New Wave* (MCA/Universal MCD 60066) 1999.

The Light At The End Of The Tunnel, released in 1987, is nicely packaged with tinted photos and a Pete Frame family tree. Unfortunately the musical content is far from comprehensive omitting songs like *Stretcher Case Baby*, *White Rabbit* and *Don't Cry Wolf*. There are a few rarities and alternate mixes of some of their lesser known songs but overall the musical selections don't do the band justice. The *Live At The Lyceum* 1981 album doesn't boast wonderful sound quality but it contains pretty decent versions of *I Feel Alright*, *Love Song* and *Drinking About My Baby*.

Best Of Vol. 1½: The Long Lost Weekend is an attractively-packaged rarities set. It features one new cut *Over The Top*, which they recorded with Motorhead, several rock tracks from the *Strawberries* and *Friday The 13th* albums, a frantic cover of Sweet's *Ballroom Blitz* along with their covers of Jefferson Airplane's *White Rabbit* and The Rolling Stones' *Citadel*.

The CD version of *The Final Damnation* (a live recording of their 1988 Town and Country Club reunion) was a limited edition (3,000) picture disc which reproduced the flowery front cover artwork.

Not The Captain's Birthday Party taped from a Roundhouse gig in November 1977 contains nine tracks of total mayhem, from early songs like *New Rose* and *Fan Club* through to classics off their second album like *Problem Child* and *You Take My Money*.

Skip Off School To See The Damned (The Stiff Singles A's & B's) is exactly what it says - many of their finest moments like *New Rose*, *Neat Neat Neat*, *Stretcher Case Baby*, *Problem Child* and *Sick Of Being Sick* are packed together on one short CD. Unfortunately by the time they moved to MCA in 1985 **The Damned** were well past their best and so *The MCA Singles A's & B's* pales into insignificance by comparison.

The School Bullies is a set featuring eight live tracks recorded in late 1978 at the Moonlight Club in West Hampstead. The set opens with *Teenage Dream* and among the other material is two cuts, *Melody Lea* and a cover of MC5's *Looking At You* from their *Machine Gun Etiquette* album. Added to the end is an interview with Rat Scabies by Mark Brennan which accounts for at least half of the total running time. Scabies talks lucidly and honestly about many aspects of the band's career, making this essential for **Damned** fans.

Tales From The Damned is a fifteen-track rarities compilation comprising material from the early eighties. 'B' sides including *Burglar*, the ethereal *Sugar And Spite* are included along with *Over The Top*, which saw **The Damned** linking up with Motorhead and the atmospheric *Sea Gulls*, which figured on the 'B' side to **The Damned**'s version of *White Rabbit*.

Sessions Of The Damned is a high quality twenty-two cut set comprising all six of the sessions they recorded for John Peel over eight years making this a very welcome release.

Eternally Damned - The Very Best Of The Damned is a twenty-track compilation of mostly singles. For some reason it kicks off with *Neat Neat Neat* (not *New Rose*) which is track number two. It includes many of their early punk gems on a collection which spans their career and is a good starting point if you haven't any of their other material.

Be wary of *From The Beginning* issued by Spectrum in 1995. The earliest material on the sixteen-track collection dates from their 1982 album *Strawberries* and the latest stuff is from a 1989 live gig.

The 1996 CD *The Radio One Sessions* is the companion to the earlier Peel-orientated *Sessions Of The Damned*. *The Radio One Sessions* concentrates on the band's appearances for Mike Read, Janice Long and 'Saturday Live'. Despite this, the album kicks off with *Liar* (from a stray Peel session). *I Just Can't Be Happy Today* (which commences with the riff to King Crimson's *21st Century Schizoid Man*) is further evidence of their prog-rock influence. All but five of the songs on this seventeen-track collection date from 1980 onward so it's not recommended if like most of us you prefer their early works.

Neat Neat Neat put out by Demon in 1997 compiles the cream of **The Damned**'s early work into a mammoth book-shaped three-CD pack. However, on the downside it jumbles up tracks from their first four albums all over the place. It's unlikely to appeal to die-hard **Damned** fans who will have all the material anyway, whilst the casual fan may not bother with such an expensive set.

Damned But Not Forgotten, originally from 1986, compiled twelve unissued songs and demos from their era with Bronze. Reissued again at mid-price

THE DAMNED - Phantasmagoria.

by Dojo in 1997 it includes a far superior version of *Disco Man* to the original, an early version of *Dozen Girls* with different lyrics which actually list twelve girls' names, a burst of *Purple Haze* and the end of *I Think I'm Wonderful*.

The 1998 reissue of *Sessions Of The Damned* on Strange Fruit includes the 1978 session, the masters of which vanished from the BBC some time ago, but which were dubbed from a copy Rat Scabies taped off air at the time.

The 2-CD collection *The Pleasure And The Pain: Selected Highlights 1982 - 1991* seems a fairly random selection of material. It includes five cuts from their *Strawberries* album, a selection of their 45s between 1982-91 and a seven-cut unmixed live set from The Town and Country Club in 1988. This is a disappointing, rather pointless compilation with poor sleevenotes.

The latest 'best of' CD *Marvellous* commences with *Love Song* and also includes all of their Chiswick U.K. 'A' sides, a 'B' side *Ballroom Blitz*, *White Rabbit*, a radio edit of *I Just Can't Be Happy Today* (with a different speech over the middle eight) by Dave Vanian and a great live version of *Looking At You*. At just over thirty-eight minutes this a good but disappointingly short collection.

The Dancing Did

45s: Dancing Did/Corny Pirates (PS) (Fruit & Veg F&V 1) 1979
The Haunted Tearooms/Squashed Things On The Road (PS) (Fruit & Veg F&V 2) 1980

The Dancing Did's punky-folk debut 45 came with a smudge of genuine soil from the Vale of Evesham!

Danse Society

Personnel:			
	PAUL GILMARTIN	drms	ABC
	PATRIC HERTZ	gtr	A
	PAUL HAMPSHIRE	bs	A
	PAUL NASH	lead gtr	ABC
	STEVE RAWLINGS	vcls	ABC
	LYNDON SCARFE	keyb'ds	AB
	TIM WRIGHT	bs	BC
	DAVID WHITAKER	keyb'ds	C

HCP
ALBUMS: 1(B) SEDUCTION (mini-album) (Society SOC 882) 1982 -
2(B) HEAVEN IS WAITING (Society 205 972) 1984 39
NB: (2) also issued on CD (Great Expectations DIPCD 024) 1991.

EP: 1(A) DANSE SOCIETY (There Is No Shame In Death/ Dolphins/These Frayed Edges) (12", PS)(Pax PAX 2) 1981
NB: (1) Originally issued on black or blue vinyl.

HCP
45s: * The Clock/Continent (PS) (Society SOC 3-81) 1981 -
(up to Woman's Own/We're So Happy (PS) (Pax SOC 5) 1982 -
1986) + Woman's Own/Continent/We're So Happy/ Belief (12", PS) (Pax PAX 5) 1982 -
Hide/Somewhere (PS) (Society SOC 4) 1983 -
Hide/Somewhere/ The Theme (12", PS) (Society SOC 124) 1983 -
x Wake Up/Seduction (PS) (Society SOC 5) 1983 61
Heaven Is Waiting/Lizard Man (PS) (Society SOC 6) 1983 60
Heaven Is Waiting (Extended)/ Lizard Man (12", PS) (Society SOC 126) 1983 -
2,000 Light Years From Home/ Seen The Light (PS) (Arista SOC 7) 1984 -
α 2,000 Light Years From Home/Seen The Light/ Angel (dub) (12", PS) (Arista SOC 127) 1984 -
2,000 Light Years From Home/Seen The Light/Sway/ Endless (7", double-pack) (Arista DFS 77) 1984 -
Say It Again/ Fade Away (She's In My Dreams) (PS) (Arista SOC 8) 1985 -
Say It Again/Fade Away

DANSE SOCIETY - Danse Society EP.

(She's In My Dreams) (12", PS) (Arista SOC 128) 1985 -
Say It Again/Fade Away (She's In My Dreams)/Sensimilia/ Treat Me Right (7", double-pack) (Arista SOC 228) 1985 -
Hold On (To What You've Got)/Danse: Move/ Heaven Is Waiting/Dance Mix (12"" PS) (Arista SOC 229) 1986 -

NB: * Originally issued in a brown, black and white fold-out picture sleeve. Later pressings came in a black and white fold-out picture sleeve. + Issued in a spined picture sleeve. x Also issued as a 12". # Also issued as a picture disc. α Came on light blue vinyl.

Danse Society formed in Barnsley in 1980. They were originally and briefly known as Danse Crazy. Steve Rawlings and Paul Nash had both been in Y? and Paul Gilmartin and Lyndon Scarfe had played together in Lips-X. Both were local Barnsley groups. A successful appearance at the Leeds Futurama Festival helped secure them a deal with the indie label Pax. The resulting EP is now hard to find. They then formed their own Society label for subsequent efforts. Musically they played a dark and deep sort of 'Gothic punk' with synthesizers, with some similarities to **Joy Division**.

After *The Clock* 45 Tim Wright came in on bass to replace Paul Hampshire and Patric Hertz when they left to join 4BE 2.

In August 1982, they released a mini-album *Seduction* which gave them some profile among what was labelled by some as 'positive punk' with its dark brooding sound. Commercially success came when Arista co-issued some of their releases. *Wake Up* and *Heaven Is Waiting* spent three and two weeks respectively in the 45 charts peaking at No's 61 and 60. The latter, in particular, was much more dance-orientated rock music with Stock Aitken Waterman producing, but this left their original fans cold. It became the title cut to their subsequent album released in February 1984. Also of note on the album was a weird interpretation of The Rolling Stones' *2,000 Light Years From Home*, which was also released as a 45 the following month.

After this Lyndon Scarfe quit. Former Music For Pleasure keyboardist David Whitaker came in as a replacement.

In 1986, Steve Rawlings went solo using the monicker Danse Society International. He released an album *Looking Through* on Society in 1986. The following year he released a 45 *Saturn Girl/Love It* as Society. The remaining members of **Danse Society** formed Johnny and The Clouds.

Dark

Personnel:			
	JIM BRYSON	gtr, synth	A
	PHIL LANGHAM	vcls, bs	A
	JIM KANE	drms	A
	ANDY RIFF	gtr	A

ALBUMS: 1(A) CHEMICAL WARFARE (Fresh FRESH LP 9) 1982
2(A) THE LIVING END (mini-album) (Fallout FALL LIVE 005) 1982

NB: There's also a CD compilation, *The Best Of The Dark* (Captain Oi! AHOY CD 40) 1995.

45s:	My Friends/John Wayne (PS)	(Fresh FRESH 2) 1981
	Hawaii Five O/Don't Look Now (PS)	(Fresh FRESH 13) 1981
	Einstein's Brain/Shattered Glass (PS)	(Fresh FRESH 24) 1981
	In The Wires/Shattered Glass (PS)	(Fresh FRESH 35) 1981
	The Masque/War Zone (PS)	(Fresh FRESH 46) 1982

A raw and aggressive Oi! band from Islington in North London whose sound is captured in all its glory on *Chemical Warfare*. Unfortunately Fresh who were going out of business at the time the album was released, were unable to promote it effectively and it sank without trace.

Their final offering *The Living End* contains eight songs from their final concert and the sound quality could be better, but it captures their energy.

My Friends, *John Wayne*, *Einstein's Brain*, *On The Wires*, *Masque* and *Hawaii Five-O* all got fresh exposure on *Fresh Records Punk Singles Collection* (Anagram CDPUNK 32) in 1994.

The Dazzlers

45s:	Phonies/Kick Out (PS)	(Charisma CB 325) 1978
	Lovely Crash/	
	Feeling In Your Heart (PS)	(Charisma CD 380) 1979
	Feeling Free/No One Ever Knows (PS)	(Charisma CB 838) 1979

A very young looking band, whose music is geared much towards the pop end of the spectrum, but there's nothing to make them stand out from the pack.

The D.C. 10's

45:	Bermuda/	
	I Can See Through Walls (PS)	(Certain Euphoria ACE 451) 1980

A short-lived mod revival band.

The Deadbeats

Personnel:	STEVE DURKIN	vcls	A
	NICK JACKSON	vcls	A
	MEL JEFFERSON	bs	A
	KELV	drms	A
	ADRAIN RIGGS	gtr	A

45:	Choose You/Julie's New Boyfriend/	
	Oh No	(Red Rhino RED 3) 1980

A mod revival combo. All three cuts can also be heard on *This Is Mod, Vol. 1: The Rarities 1979 - 81* (CDM GRAM 98) 1995. Their finest moment *Choose You*, which sounds firmly rooted in the mod style of the mid-sixties, can also be found on vinyl on *This Is Mod* (dbl) (Get Back GET 39) 1999 and on CD *100% British Mod* (Captain Mod MODSKA DCD 8) 1998.

Dead Generation

This was actually the **Cockney Rejects** playing under a pseudonym. They contributed one cut, *Francine*, an old ZZ Top track to the *Total Noise* (EP) (Total Noise TOT 1) in 1983. The EP was originally intended to be the first in a series showcasing Oi! Punk and Punk metal. This song later resurfaced on *Oi! The Rarities, Vol. 5* (Captain Oi! AHOY CD 62) 1996.

Dead Fingers Talk

Personnel:	TONY CARTER	drms	A
	ANDY LINKLATER	bs	A
	JEFF PARSONS	gtr	A
	BOB PHOENIX	vcls	A

ALBUM:	1(A)	STORM THE REALITY STUDIOS	(Pye NSPH 24) 1978

NB: (1) also issued on CD as *Storm The Reality Studios - Plus* (Essential ESMCD 929) 2000 plus eight bonus tracks.

45s:	Can't Think Straight/	
	Hold On To Rock 'n' Roll	(Pye 7N 46069) 1978
	This Crazy World/The Boyfriend (PS)	(Pye 7N 46156) 1978
Reissue:	This Crazy World/The Boyfriend (PS)	(Pye 7P 156) 1980

Not a well known band, but this Hull outfit were ahead of their time for Bob Phoenix's lyrics which dealt with gay issues. Their sole, Mick Ronson-produced album, was later cited by **Tom Robinson** as a significant influence on his own subsequent efforts. Its highlights include *Nobody Loves You When You're Old And Gay* and *Fight Our Way Out Of Here*. The new wave, hard rock outfit employed lots of Hendrixy guitar.

The CD issue of their album on Essential in 2000 came with eight bonus cuts, including both sides of their *Crazy World* single.

Dead Man's Shadow

Personnel:	MATT DAGNUT	vcls, bs	A
	IAN FISHER	drms	A
	JOHN IGOE	gtr	A

ALBUM:	1(A)	TO MOHAMMED.... A MOUNTAIN	
			(Criminal Damage CRILP 110) 1984

NB: There's also a CD compilation *The 4P's* (Get Back GET 22 CD) 1987

EPs:	1(A)	HEATHROW TOUCHDOWN (PS)	
			(Subversive ANARCHO 1) 1981
	2(A)	BOMB SCARE (Bomb Scare/Another Hiroshima/	
		Fighting For Reality) (PS)	(Rondelet ROUND 16) 1982

NB: (1) one side was by **Action Pact**.

45s:	Neighbours/Poxy Politics/War Ploys/	
	Morons (PS)	(Hog HOG 1) 1980
	Flower In The Gun/	
	The Last Cowboy (PS)	(Rondelet ROUND 16) 1982
	Toleration Street/In My Dreams (PS)	(Expulsion OUT 4) 1983
	Another Year/	
	One Man's Crusade (PS)	(Criminal Damage CRI 106) 1983

A punk band. *Flower In The Gun* is mid-paced, which is quite unusual for this type of band, and has an anti-violence message. It was also included on *Wet Dream* (Rot ASS 4) 1984. Three of their songs - *Bomb Scare*, *Another Hiroshima* and *Flower In The Gun* - got a further airing on *Rondelet Punk Singles Collection* (Anagram CDPUNK 49) 1995, which was also issued on vinyl (Captain Oi! AHOY LP 513) 1996. *Flower In The Gun* can also be found on *Rot Records Punk Singles Collection* (Anagram CDPUNK 40) 1994.

Deadly Toys

EP:	1	EP (Nice Weather/Roll On Doomsday/I'm Logical/	
		Don't Mess Around) (PS)	(Bonnaud/Hunt DT 1) 1979

A low profile EP which came with no writing credits and no fancy cover.

DEATH CULT - Gods Zoo.

Roll On Doomsday is restrained psychedelia that links evocative lyrics about London during impending floods to an unassuming tune. *Don't Mess Around* is equally engaging and flirts with dub. Promising, but they never appear to have followed it up.

Death Cult

Personnel:	IAN ASTBURY	vcls	AB
	BILLY DUFFY	lead gtr	AB
	RAY MONDO	drms	A
	JAMIE STUART	bs	AB
	NIGEL PRESTON	drms	B

EP: 1(A) DEATH CULT (Brothers Grimm/Ghost Dance/Horse Nation/Christians) (12", PS) (Situation 2 SIT 23T) 1983

NB: (1) This 12" was issued with an A3 insert. There's also a CD *Ghost Dance* (Beggars Banquet BBL 2008CD) 1996.

45s: Gods Zoo/
Gods Zoo (These Times) (PS) (Situation 2 SIT 29) 1983
Gods Zoo/
Gods Zoo (These Times) (12", PS) (Situation 2 SIT 29T) 1983

This new band was formed by Ian Astbury (who'd been Ian Lindsay in his former band **Southern Death Cult**) a couple of weeks after he left them disillusioned about their future music direction. Other members included Billy Duffy (who'd been in **Theatre Of Hate** and with **Ed Banger and The Nosebleeds**), Jamie Stewart (who'd played in Ritual and Crisis) and Ray Mondo (also previously in Ritual).

In July 1983, the new outfit released a four-track 12" called *Death Cult*. Early copies of this contained an A3 interview sheet with data on the band's recent activities. The same month the band played their first live gig in Oslo, Norway. They went on to play other European gigs including a couple of festivals. In September, they embarked on a U.K. tour in Swansea, which culminated in an appearance at the Futurama 5 festival in Leeds on 18th September. Three days later Ray Mondo left citing 'musical differences'. He was replaced by Nigel Preston who'd previously been with **Theatre Of Hate**, The Red Lights and Sex Gang Children. He remained for their second 45 *Gods Zoo*, which is rather ordinary.

Early in 1984 the group decided to drop 'death' from their name, feeling that it may restrict their audience. They became known as simply **The Cult**.

Ghost Dance released by Beggars Banquet in 1996 compiles a superb 1983 Radio One session with the tracks from their critically acclaimed EP.

Death Sentence

Personnel:	DAVE	vcls	A
	GLENN	bs	A
	MICK	gtr	A
	STEVE	drms	A

EP: 1 DEATH AND PURE DESTRUCTION (Death And Pure Destruction/Die A Hero/Victims Of War/Death Sentence) (PS) (Beat The System DEATH 1) 1982

An eighties punk band from Nottingham. *Death Sentence* and *Victims Of War* got a further airing on *Beat The System Punk Singles Collection* (Anagram CDPUNK 61) in 1995. They were one of the first multi-racial punk bands.

Debutantes

45: Man In The Street/(other side by **Innocent Bystanders**) (Rok ROK XVII/XVIII) 1980

This was another of those obscure bands who recorded for Rok Records. *Man In The Street* has quite an interesting and unusual guitar introduction which gives way to a fairly routine modish offering. The cut also appears as a bonus track on the Captain Mod reissue of *Odds Bods Mods And Sods* (Captain Mod MODSKA CD 2) 1996.

Defects

Personnel:	BUCK	vcls	A
	DUKIE	gtr	A
	GARY	bs	A
	GLENN	drms	A

ALBUM: 1(A) DEFECTIVE BREAKDOWN (WXYZ LMNOP 2) 1983

NB: (1) later issued on CD (Captain Oi! AHOY CD 29) 1994 with eight bonus tracks including their *Suspicious Minds* single.

45s: Dance Till You Drop/Guilty Conscience/
Brutality (PS) (Casualty CR 001) 1981
Survival/Brutality (PS) (WXYZ ABCD 3) 1982
* Dance
Suspicious Minds/Song For Mark Walker/
Know 'Bout You (PS) (I.D. EYE 2) 1983

NB: * This also features tracks by **The Anti-Nowhere League** and Meteors and came free with 'Flexipop' Issue 26 on a red vinyl flexidisc.

An Oi! band from Belfast, who supported **The Clash** when they toured there. Their album is a good example of the genre and they created quite a stir on the early eighties punk scene.

The CD reissue of their sole album *Defective Breakdown* includes eight bonus cuts including the 45 versions of *Dance* and *Survival* (which also appeared on the album in different formats), the original 45 version of *Brutality* (as well as a later alternative version of the song) together with their other 45 cuts; *Guilty Conscience, Song For Mark Walker, Suspicious Minds* and *Know About You*, thereby rounding up all the band's recordings.

DEFECTS - Survival.

Delta 5

Personnel:	ROZ ALLEN	bs	A
	KELVIN KNIGHT	drms	A
	BETHAN PETERS	vcls, bs	A
	ALAN RIGS	gtr	A
	JUIZ RIGS	gtr	A

ALBUM: 1(A) SEE THE WHIRL (Pre PREX 6) 1981

45s: Mind Your Own Business/
Now That You've Gone (PS) (Rough Trade RT 31) 1979
Anticipation/You (PS) (Rough Trade RT 41) 1980
Try/Colour (PS) (Rough Trade RT 61) 1981

Delta 5, a three girl, two boy band, formed in Leeds in September 1978 as part of that city's 'funk/punk' scene. They were quite closely linked to **The Mekons** in their early days. Indeed Roz Allen played on **The Mekons** first 45.

They signed to Rough Trade in 1979. On *Mind Your Own Business* there is a sparse funk backdrop behind staggered feminist vocal interplay and

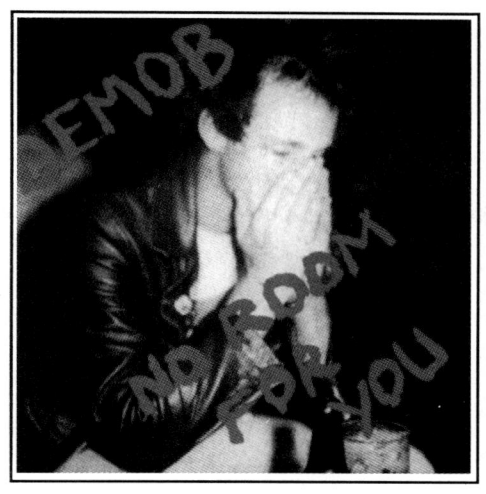

DEMOB - No Room For You EP.

Gang Of Four style guitar. The overall effect is simple and catchy. The follow-up *Anticipation* was their most successful 45 in terms of sales and took them into the indie charts.

In 1981, many of the original band left and with them went their punk consciousness. They switched to the Pre label for their album, *See The Whirl*. Unfortunately it attracted minimal interest and before the year was out the revised line-up called it quits.

Demob

Personnel:	BARRY	bs	A
	JOHN	drms	A
	MIFF	vcls	A
	TERRY	gtr	A

EP:	1(A)	NO ROOM FOR YOU (No Room For You/ Think Straight/New Breed) (PS)	(Round Ear EAR 3) 1981
45:	*	Anti Police/ Teenage Adolescent (PS)	(Round Ear ROUND 1) 1981

NB: * Was originally issued in a foldout picture sleeve, but later copies came in a standard picture sleeve.

Demob were a popular early eighties band on the Oi!/punk circuit, although not strictly of these genres. Round Ear released their *Anti Police* 45 in late 1981. The song was pretty much what one would expect and bombasted the police for victimising people who looked different. i.e. punks 'n' skins. The flip side *Teenage Adolescence* doesn't stand out in any way. You'll also find both sides of this 45 on *Oi! The Rarities, Vol. 5* (Captain Oi! AHOY CD 62) 1996.

Later, in 1981, Round Ear released their *No Room For You* (EP). The title cut is disappointing, but *Think Straight* and *New Breed* are pretty typical fast-paced punkers. All three cuts have resurfaced on *Oi! The Rarities, Vol. 4* (Captain Oi! AHOY CD 58) 1996.

Demob gigged as a support band with some of the top Oi! acts of the early eighties like **The Angelic Upstarts** and **Vice Squad**.

Their drummer John later boxed professionally for England and their guitarist Terry was in a later line-up of **Screaming Dead**.

Demon Preachers

Personnel:	CAMILLA ARMSTRONG	bs	A
	NICK EWADE	vcls	A
	GERRY HEALY	drms	A
	TONY WARD	gtr	A

45s:	Royal Northern/Laughing At Me/ Steal Your Love/Dead End Kidz	(Illegal SRTS 78110) 1978
	Little Miss Perfect/ Perfect Dub (PS)	(Small Wonder SMALL TEN) 1978

This band is most notable for including Nick Ewade who was later Nick Fiend in Alien Sex Fiend. You'll also find *Little Miss Perfect* on *Small Wonder Punk Singles Collection, Vol. 1* (Anagram CDPUNK 29) in 1994.

Depeche Mode

Personnel:	VINCE CLARKE	synth	A
	ANDY FLETCHER	synth	ABC
	DAVID GAHAN	vcls	ABC
	MARTIN GORE	synth	ABC
	ALAN WILDER	synth	C

ALBUMS: HCP

(up to	1(A)	SPEAK AND SPELL	(Mute STUMM 5) 1981 10
1986)	2(B)	A BROKEN FRAME	(Mute STUMM 9) 1982 8
	3(C)	CONSTRUCTION TIME AGAIN	(Mute STUMM 13) 1983 6
	4(C)	SOME GREAT REWARD	(Mute STUMM 19) 1984 5
	5(-)	SINGLES 1981-85	(Mute MUTEL 1) 1985 6
	6(C)	BLACK CELEBRATION	(Mute STUMM 26) 1986 4

NB: (1) also issued on CD (Mute CDSTUMM 5) 1988 with four extra tracks *Dreaming Of Me, New Life (Extended), Shout! (Rio Mix)* and *Any Seconds Now (Altered)*. (2) also issued on CD (Mute CDSTUMM 9) 1988. (3) also issued on CD (Mute CDSTUMM 13) 1988. (4) also issued on CD (Mute CDSTUMM 19) 1987. (5) also issued on CD (Mute CDMUTEL 1) 1987. (6) also issued on CD (Mute CDSTUMM 26) 1987 with three extra tracks, *Breathing In Fumes, But Not Tonight (Extended)* and *Black Day*. There are also three box sets:- *Singles 1-6* (Mute DMBX 1) 1991, *Singles 7-12* (Mute DBMX 2) 1991 and *Singles 13-18* (Mute DMBX 3) 1991.

HCP

45s:	Dreaming Of Me/Ice Machine (PS)	(Mute MUTE 013) 1981 57
(up to	New Life/Shout! (PS)	(Mute 7MUTE 014) 1981 11
1986)	New Life (Remix)/ Shout! (12", PS)	(Mute 12MUTE 014) 1981 -
	Just Can't Get Enough/ Any Second Now (PS)	(Mute 7MUTE 016) 1981 8
	Just Can't Get Enough (Schizo Mix)/ Any Second Now (Altered) (12", PS)	(Mute 12MUTE 016) 1981 -
	See You/Now This Is Fun (PS)	(Mute 7MUTE 018) 1982 6
	See You (Extended)/Now This Is Fun (Extended) (12", PS)	(Mute 12MUTE 018) 1982 -
	The Meaning Of Love/ Oberkorn (It's A Small Town) (PS)	(Mute 7MUTE 22) 182 12
	The Meaning Of Love (Fairly Odd Mix)/ Oberkorn (Development Mix) (12", PS)	(Mute 12MUTE 22) 1982 -

DEMOB - Anti Police.

DEPECHE MODE - Dreaming Of Me.

Leave In Silence/Excerpts From My Secret Garden (PS)	(Mute 7BONG 1)	1982 18
Leave In Silence (Longer)/Further Excerpts From My Secret Garden (12", PS)	(Mute 12BONG 1)	1982 -
Get The Balance Right/ The Great Outdoors (PS)	(Mute 7BONG 2)	1983 13
Get The Balance Right (Combination Mix)/ The Great Outdoors/ Tora! Tora! Tora! (live) (12", PS)	(Mute 12BONG 2)	1983 -
Get The Balance Right (Original)/ My Secret Garden/See You/Satellite/Tora! Tora! Tora! (live 'B' sides) (Ltd 12", blue PS)	(Mute L12BONG 2)	1983 -
Everything Counts/Work Hard (PS)	(Mute 7BONG 3)	1983 6
Everything Counts (In Larger Amounts)/Work Hard (East End Remix) (12", PS)	(Mute 12BONG 3)	1983 -
Everything Counts (Original 7" mix)/New Life/ Boys Say Go/Nothing To Fear/The Meaning Of Love (live 'B' sides) (Ltd 12", red PS)	(Mute L12BONG 3)	1983 -
Love In Itself/Fools (PS)	(Mute 7BONG 4)	1983 21
Love In Itself 3/Fools (Bigger)/ Love In Itself 4 (12", PS)	(Mute 12BONG 4)	1983 -
Love In Itself 2/Just Can't Get Enough/A Photograph Of You/ Shout/Photographic (live 'B' Sides) (Ltd 12", green PS)	(Mute L12BONG 4)	1983 -
People Are People/ In Your Memory 2 (PS)	(Mute 7BONG 5)	1984 4
People Are People (Different Mix)/ In Your Memory 2 (Slik Mix) (12", PS)	(Mute 12BONG 5)	1984 -
People Are People (Adrian Sherwood On U-Sound Remix)/ (7" mix)/In Your Memory (7" mix) (Ltd 12", PS)	(Mute L12BONG 5)	1984 -
Master And Servant/(Set Me Free) Remotivate Me (PS)	(Mute 7BONG 6)	1984 9
Master And Servant (Slavery Whip Mix)/ (Set Me Free) Remotivate Me (Release Me) (12", PS)	(Mute 12 BONG 6)	1984 -
Master And Servant (On U-Sound Sci-Fi Classic)/ Are People People?/(Set Me Free) Remotivate Me (7" mix) (Ltd 12", PS)	(Mute L12BONG 6)	1984 -
Blasphemous Rumours/ Somebody (Remix) (PS)	(Mute 7BONG 7)	1984 16
Blasphemous Rumours/I Told You So/ Everything Counts (Live 'B' sides) (PS)	(Mute 7BONG 7T)	1984 -
Blasphemous Rumours/Somebody/Two Minute Warning/ Ice Machine/Everything Counts (live 'B' sides) (12", PS)	(Mute 12BONG 7)	1984 -
Shake The Disease/Flexible (PS)	(Mute 7BONG 8)	1985 18
Shake The Disease (Remix Extended)/ Flexible (Remixed Extended Version) (12", PS)	(Mute 12BONG 8)	1985 -
Shake The Disease (Edit The Shake)/ Master And Slave (live)/Flexible (Pre-Deportation Mix)/ Something (Gareth Jones Metal Mix) (12", PS)	(Mute L12BONG 8)	1985 -
* It's Called A Heart/ Fly On The Windscreen (PS)	(Mute 7BONG 9)	1985 18
It's Called A Heart (Extended)/Fly On The Windscreen (Extended) (12", PS)	(Mute 12BONG 9)	1985 -
It's Called A Heart (Extended)/(Slowmix)/Fly On The Windscreen (Extended)/ (Death Mix) (12", double pack)	(Mute D12BONG 9)	1985 -
Stripped/But Not Tonight (PS)	(Mute 7BONG 10)	1986 15
Stripped (Highland Mix)/But Not Tonight (Extended Remix)/ Breathing In The Fumes/Fly On The Windscreen (Quiet)/ Black Day (12", PS)	(Mute 12BONG 10)	1986 -
A Question Of Lust/ Christmas Island (PS)	(Mute 7BONG 11)	1986 28
A Question Of Lust/Christmas Island (Extended)/ People Are People (live)/It Doesn't Matter Two (Instr.)/ A Question Of Lust (Minimal) (12", PS)	(Mute 12BONG 11)	1986 -
+ A Question Of Lust (Flood Mix)/Christmas Island/ If You Want (live)/Shame (live)/ Blasphemous Rumours (live) (cass.)	(Mute CBONG 11)	1986 -
A Question Of Time/ Black Celebration (live) (PS)	(Mute 7BONG 12)	1986 17
A Question Of Time (Extended Remix)/Black Celebration/ Something To Do/ Stripped (live 'B' sides) (12", PS)	(Mute 12BONG 12)	1986 -
A Question Of Time (Newtown Mix)/(Live Remix)/ Black Celebration (Black Tulip Mix)/More Than A Party (Live Remix) (Ltd 12", PS)	(Mute L12BONG 12)	1986 -

NB: * Initial copies came with a poster. + This cassette was marketed in a special 7" pack with a book and badge.

Depeche Mode formed in Basildon, Essex, during the summer of 1980. Clarke, Fletcher and Gore had all previously played in a trio called Composition Of Sound, which was a guitar-based band. They switched names to **Depeche Mode** around the same time they swapped to synthesizer-based music and recruited vocalist David Gahan.

Their vinyl debut came when Some Bizzare label supremo Stevo included *Photographic* from their first ever recording session on the *Some Bizarre Album* (Some Bizzare BZLP 1) in early 1981. The album included bands signed to the label or which the label was trying to sign. Many of them went on to be closely associated with the New Romantic movement as were **Depeche Mode** at the time of their early gigs, which largely comprised covers of songs like *Then I Kissed Her*, *The Price Of Love* and *Mouldy Old Dough*.

Despite their inclusion on this compilation, **Depeche Mode** actually opted to sign to Daniel Miller's Mute Records. He had spotted them supporting **Fad Gadget** at the Bridge House in East London. Their debut single *Dreaming Of Me* climbed to No. 57, spending four weeks in the charts, but it marked the start of an incredible run of hit singles that totalled twenty-three by the turn of the decade. *Dreaming Of Me* topped the indie chart as did their follow-up *New Life*, three months later. Helped by a 12" release this climbed to No. 11 in the national charts, in which it spent a total of fifteen weeks. Their third single, another Vince Clarke composition *Just Can't Get Enough* took them into the Top 10. It peaked at No. 8 during a ten week chart stay.

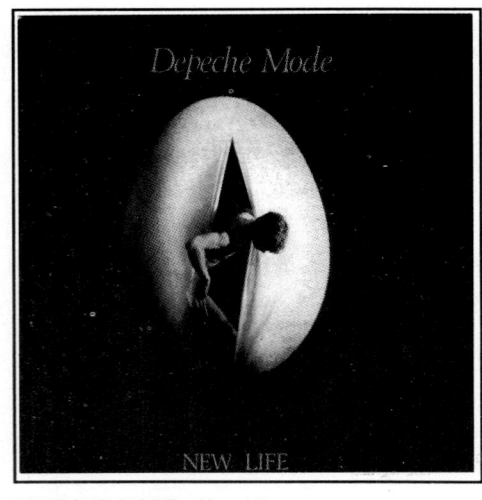

DEPECHE MODE - New Life.

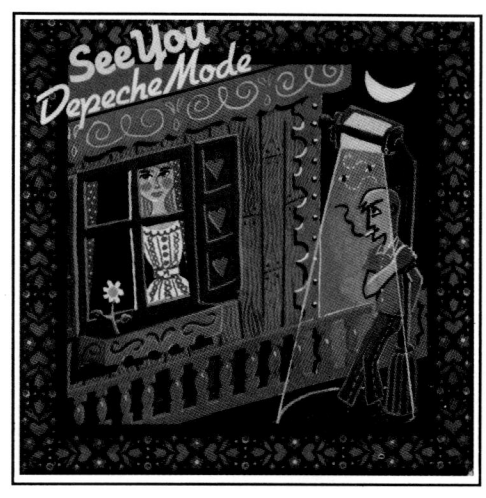

DEPECHE MODE - See You.

Their debut album *Speak And Spell* was released in autumn 1981. It met with critical acclaim and considerable commercial success, spending an incredible thirty-three weeks in the chart with a best position of No. 10. It was a good collection of modern dance tunes, although arguably the best tracks on it were their earlier hit singles *Dreaming Of Me*, *New Life* and *I Can't Get Enough*.

At this point some were predicting a grim future for the band when their songwriter Vince Clarke left in November 1981, thoroughly fed up with the constant touring. He teamed up with Alison Moyet to form Yazoo and was later half of Erasure. When Clarke left Martin Gore took over his role as songwriter and proceeded to write a series of good, melodic songs. Musically Clarke was replaced by ex-Hitman Alan Wilder (initially only for live work). Their next single *See You* was recorded by a trio. It was also one of the first songs Gore ever wrote. It demonstrated his flair for melody and climbed to No. 6 during a ten week chart stay. The follow-up *The Meaning Of Love* had a respectable showing, too, peaking at No. 12. After this, they departed for what proved a successful U.S. tour before returning to London to begin work on a second album.

Their sixth single *Leave In Silence* was released in August 1982. It marked the introduction of the BONG prefix, which subsequently became standard for all their singles. Also, whereas previously their 12" releases had simply been extended versions of their 7" releases, this 12" included an alternate quieter mix of the 'A' side, as well as the usual extensions. The single enjoyed ten weeks in the charts with a best position of No. 18.

A Broken Frame, released in October 1982, maintained the dance-based music of their earlier work but also experimented a little. *My Secret Garden* had a funky base, *Satellite* was moulded around a ska beat and *Monument* had a Japanses slant. All ten tracks were penned by Martin Gore and, although the album was only in the charts a third of the time of its predecessor it actually got two places higher to No. 8. Soon after its release, **Depeche Mode** embarked on an extremely successful two month European tour.

Alan Wilder made his studio debut on *Get The Balance Right*, released in January 1983. It shot to No. 13, spending eight weeks in the charts. As well as the usual 7" and 12" singles, a second 12" in a specially designed and individually numbered sleeve up to 5,000 may interest collectors. On this *Get The Balance Right* was accompanied by four tracks recorded live at the Hammersmith Odeon in October 1982. The tracks in question were *My Secret Garden*, *Tora! Tora! Tora!*, *See You* and *Satellite*.

During the spring **Depeche Mode** embarked on a successful Worldwide tour, taking in the United States, Canada, Japan and Hong Kong.

Their July 1983 single *Everything Counts*, which brought them another Top 10 hit, coming to rest at No. 6 during its eleven week chart sojourn, also had a deluxe 12" version. This included four more live cuts from the Hammersmith Odeon concert - *Boys Say Go*, *New Life*, *Nothing To Fear* and *The Meaning Of Love*.

Their third album *Construction Time Again*, released in August, marked a significant change in direction. They ditched synthesizers for computers and sampling methods. Alan Wilder played on the album. He also wrote *Two Minute Warning* and co-wrote *Work Hard*, with Gore which had included on the flip side of *Everything Counts* a month earlier. For another cut *Pipeline*, the band had sampled underground train sounds in London's Brick Lane. The album was a big hit, climbing to No. 6, during a twelve week chart residency. It also achieved their first European success, climbing to No. 7 in Germany. *Love In Itself*, released in September, missed the Top 20 by just one slot. The 12" deluxe release included the final four live releases from the Hammersmith Odeon concert:- *Just Can't Get Enough*, *Photograph Of You*, *Photographic* and *Shout*.

If in commercial terms *Love In Itself* had performed disappointingly this was more than offset by their March 1984 *People Are People* single. Not only did it register at No. 4 - their highest U.K. chart position to date - it also gave them their first U.S. hit. In the 'States it peaked at No. 13 and spent an impressive eighteen weeks in the charts.

Master And Servant, released in August 1984, brought **Depeche Mode** a further Top 10 hit, but their next album *Some Great Reward* marked a further milestone in their career. It marked their transgression towards industrial music incorporating a sort of unsettling synthesized factory din. In Britain, the album climbed to No. 5 and spent a total of twelve weeks in the charts. More significantly, in America, it got to No. 51, giving an early indication of the considerable international success they would later go on to achieve. The album also spawned a furher double 'A' side hit single coupling *Blasphemous Rumours* alongside *Somebody*.

In 1985, two more hit singles - *Shake The Disease* (No. 18) and *It's Called A Heart* (No. 18) - sustained their chart success. Here in Britain, a compilation *The Singles 1981 - 85* was released in October. It comprised their thirteen 'A' sides to date. The fine collection rose to No. 6 during its twenty-two weeks in the charts. In the 'States, a compilation of similar material *Catching Up*, was put out. This excluded some cuts which had appeared on an earlier U.S.-only release *People Are People* but included *Fly On The Windscreen* (which appeared on their next U.K. studio album) and *Flexible*.

In 1986, they embarked on a punishing concert schedule to support their new album *Black Celebration*. As the title suggests, this was a depressive bleak album, indicative of their interest in conjuring up monotonous urban soundscapes. There was less variety in the material, but it achieved their highest chart placing to date No. 4. By contrast their three singles that year - *Stripped* (No. 15), *A Question Of Lust* (No. 28) and *A Question Of Time* (No. 17) - all failed to reach the Top Ten.

Depeche Mode had transgressed from a singles to an album-orientated audience. Indeed, they went on to phenomenal international success and are still playing today.

DEPECHE MODE - People Are People.

THE DEPRESSIONS - Living On Dreams.

The Depressions

Personnel:	DAVE BARNARD	bs, vcls	A B
	OZZY 'CROWBAR' GARVEY	drms	A B
	FRANK 'HAMMER' SMITH	gtr	A
	ERIC 'RICO THE KNIFE' WRIGHT	gtr, vcls	A
	TONY MAYBERRY	gtr, vcls	B

ALBUMS:	1(A)	THE DEPRESSIONS	(Barn 2314 105) 1978
	2(B)	IF YOU KNOW WHAT I MEAN	(Barn 2314 107) 1978

NB: (2) as The DPs. There's also *The Punk Rock Collection* (Captain Oi! AHOY CD 66) 1997.

45s:	Living On Dreams/Family Planning (PS)	(Barn 2014 112) 1977
	Messing With Your Heart/Street Kid (PS)	(Barn 2014 119) 1978
	Get Out Of This Town/Basement Daze (PS)	(Barn 2014 122) 1978
*	If You Know What I Mean/Running Away (PS)	(Barn 2014 126) 1978
*	Television Romeo/Born To Win (PS)	(Barn 2014 129) 1978

NB: * Credited to The DPs.

The Depressions came from Brighton where they started life as a pub-rock band called Tonge, but when the 'punk explosion' of 1977 came along they transformed themselves into a flown-blown peroxided punk band, changing their name to **The Depressions** and signing to Chas Chandler's Barn label. Their debut 45 *Living On Dreams* was a joint 'Sounds' 'Single of the Week' along with **The Sex Pistols**' *Holidays In The Sun*. They embarked on a U.K. tour supporting Steve Gibbons and followed this up with support tours to **The Motors** and Slade. They also headlined a few gigs themselves. *Living On Dreams* and their next two 45s *Messing With Your Heart* and *Get Out Of This Town*, which were both taken from their debut album, all showed up well in the indie charts. Their first album is very much fourth division pseudo-punk. Soon after its release they switched names to The

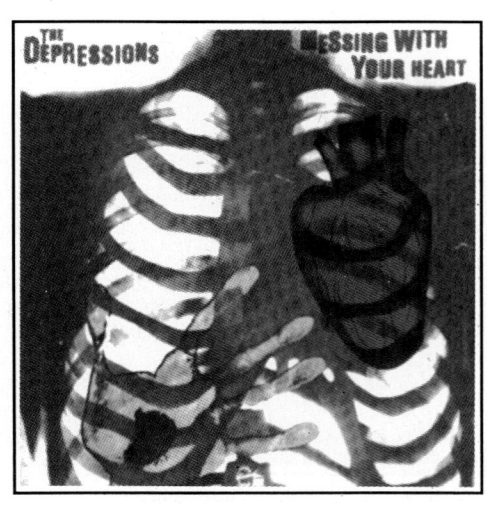

THE DEPRESSIONS - Messing With Your Heart.

DPs and recorded a second pseudo-power pop effort. Certainly an improvement on this first it's still none too memorable. Earlier their guitarist Frank Smith had quit when a fan was tragically beaten to death at the end of their set at Preston Poly when a fight broke out between two groups of football supporters, whilst they were supporting **The Vibrators** on a U.K. tour. His replacement was ex-Joe Cool and The Killers guitarist Tony Mayberry. They finally split in early 1979 when there was a disappointing response to their second album.

Dave Barnard went on to form the mod-flavoured **Vandells** and also toured with Steve Ellis Love Affair for a while. Later in 1983, he teamed up with Eric Wright to compose *The Goldstone Rap* (Energy Records 12 NRG 2), a single written to commemorate Brighton and Hove Albion's run to the 1983 FA Cup final!

The 1997 Captain Oi! CD *The Punk Rock Collection* is the best means of accessing their music. The twenty-four track collection includes their first album, their three singles and a whole batch of previously unreleased demos.

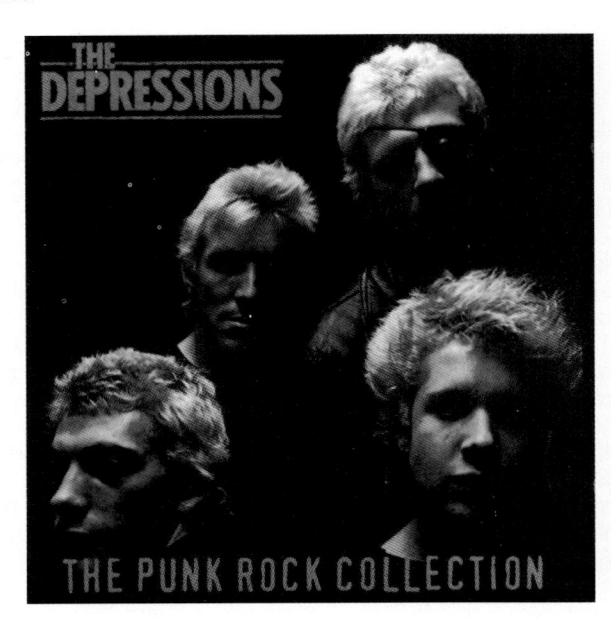

THE DEPRESSIONS - The Punk Rock Collection.

The Desperate Bicycles

Personnel:	DAVE PAPWORTH	drms	A
	NICKY STEVENS	gtr	A
	ROGER STEVENS	bs	A
	DANNY WIGLEY	vcls	A B
	DAN ELECTRO	gtr	B
	JEFF TITLEY	drms	B

ALBUM:	1(B)	REMORSE CODE	(Refill RR 6) 1980

EP:	1( )	NEW CROSS NEW CROSS (Product/Paradise Lost/Advice On Arrest/Holidays/The Housewife Song/Cars)	(Refill RR 3) 1978

45s:	*	Smokescreen/Handlebars (PS)	(Refill RR 1) 1977
	*	The Medium Was Tedium/Don't Back The Front (PS)	(Refill RR 2) 1977
		Occupied Territory/Skill (PS)	(Refill RR 4) 1978
		Grief Is Very Private/Obstructive/Conundrum (PS)	(Refill RR 7) 1978

NB: * Both songs appeared on each side of the 45.

This band was formed in Dalston, London in March 1977 as an experiment. They wanted to see how much it would cost to record and distribute their own record. Obviously the cost wasn't prohibitive because they made a few others. Their first D.I.Y. effort was unusual for containing the same two songs on each side, so it was really a sort of EP. 500 copies of their first release were pressed - it cost just £153 to record! They pressed 1,000 copies of the follow-up, which also repeated the same unusual two songs on each side format. On *Smokescreen* the lyricist has more words than he can cram onto the melody and the vocals are a bit breathless.

The second pressing of 1,000 sold out in a fortnight. The Refill label became self-financing, the money from the second pressing going to finance 1,000 copies of their second single *The Medium Was Tedium* - a record in praise of amateurism, which sold out in a week! The flip side, *Don't Back The Front* was a reaction against the right wing National Front, which tried to shanghai punk for its own dubious political ends.

New Cross, New Cross their third sngle was a six-tracker.

Although they were associated by timing with the punk movement they were one of a very limited number of bands (the other most significant one being **The Soft Boys**) experimenting with psychedelia in this era. As such they pre-dated the neo-psychedelic movement by some years. Their album was a successful amalgam of guitar interplay and tape and sound effects. Interesting.

By 1980 they had become a trio with Wigley the only surviving original member, but by 1981 this trio had split.

The Destructors (V)

Personnel:			
ALLEN ADAMS	vcls		ABCD
PHIL ATTERSON	gtr		AB
DIP	bs		ABC
ANDY JACKSON	gtr		B
ANDY BUTLER	drms		C
ANDY McDONALD	drms		D
DAVE ITHERMEE	lead gtr		D
DAVE	gtr		D

ALBUM: 1(D) BOMB HANOI, BOMB SAIGON, BOMB DISNEYLAND
(Carnage Benelux KILL 666) 1984

EPs: 1( ) JAILBAIT (Jailbait/Kalgsnocov/Sewage Worker/
Image) (PS) (Illuminated ILL 14) 1982
2( ) FORCES OF LAW (Wild Thing/Forces Of Law/
Neutron Bomb) (PS) (Illuminated ILL 19) 1983
3( ) CRY HAVOC AND UNLEASH THE
DOGS OF WAR (12", PS) (Criminal Damage 12104) 1983
4( ) TV EYE (TV Eye/The Fatal Kiss/
Love Like Glass) (PS) (Criminal Damage CRI 108) 1984

NB: (4) credited to **Destructors V**.

45s: Meaningless Names/AK 47/Police State/Dachau/
Death Squad (PS) (Carnage Book 2) 1982
Religion/Soldier Boy/Agent Orange/
Corpse Gas (PS) (Carnage Benelux KILL 2) 982

The Destructors were a third generation punk band from Peterborough whose songs dealt with issues of pacifism, human rights and anarchy. They formed in 1977, initially as a trio. Andy Jackson joined soon after but before long he and Atterson quit to form **The Blanks** and they were soon joined by Adams and Butler. **The Blanks** achieved notoriety with their *Northern Ripper* 45. When **The Blanks** disbanded, Adams rejuvenated **The Destructors** (line-up 'D') who proceeded to release a series of sloganistic punk records.

The Details

45s: Keep On Running/Run'ins (PS) (Energy NRG 2) 1980
 * Keep On Running/Run'ins (12") (Energy NRG 002) 1980
 + London Marathon (Keep On Running)/
Run'ins (instr) (PS) (Energy NRG 6) 1981

NB: * Promo-only, appeared in a stickered plain sleeve. + Reissued to help promote the 1981 London Marathon.

It seems this modish bands cover of *Keep On Running* was used to help promote the London marathon.

The Detonators

Personnel:			
PAT BYARS	keyb'ds		A
JEFF FINLIN	drms		A
TED LUCKTENBERG	bs		A
LANE PETTIGREW	vcls		A
BRAD WORDEN	gtr		A

EPs: 1(A) THE DETONATORS (Need Your Love Tonight/
Great Big Ghetto/Shoob Shooby Do/
Give Me A Helping Hand) (Big Blast no #) 1978
2(A) THE DANCE (Don't Talk/Opening A Modern Art/
Restless Kids/Passe/Need Love Tonight/
Great Biog Ghetto/Give Me A Helping Hand/
Shoob Shooby Do) (Local LR 1) 1978

This Belfast punk band also contributed a couple of tracks *Light At Your Window* and *Cruisin'* to the *Belfast Rock* (Rip Off ROLP 1) 1978 compilation, but they were a relatively short-lived outfit.

Devil's Dykes

This Brighton outfit contributed two cuts *Fruitless* and *Plastic Flowers* to the *Vaultage '78 (Two Sides Of Brighton)* (Attrix RB 3) 1978 compilation. Both songs are quite unusual.

Howard Devoto

HCP

ALBUM: 1 JERKY VERSIONS OF THE DREAM
(Virgin V 2272) 1983 57

NB: (1) later reissued on vinyl (Virgin OVED 129) 1988 and also issued on CD (CDV 2272) 1990.

45s: Rainy Season/Rain Forest (PS) (Virgin VS 598) 1983
Cold Imagination/
Out Of Shape With Me (PS) (Virgin VS 624) 1984

Inspired by **The Sex Pistols** Howard Devoto is probably best remembered as co-founder of **The Buzzcocks** in Manchester in 1975, with **Pete Shelley**. After the seminal *Spiral Scratch* (EP) **Devoto** left to form **Magazine**, who were one of the finest new wave bands, as **Devoto** sought to develop beyond punk and power pop.

After he broke up **Magazine Devoto** embarked on a solo career. Barry Adamson and Dave Formula from **Magazine** among others helped out on this solo album. The ten tracks explored a variety of musical styles and it is worth a spin. It met with some commercial success too, climbing to No. 57 during its two weeks in the album charts.

Cold Imagination was later included on *A Post Punk Primer* (Virgin CDOVD 498) in 1997.

Diagram Brothers

Personnel:			
FRASER	vcls, gtr		A
JASON	bs		A
LAWRENCE	gtr		A
SIMON	gtr		A
ANDY	bs		B

ALBUM: 1( ) SOME MARVELS OF MODERN SCIENCE
(New Hormones) 1981

45s: We Are All Animals/There Is No Shower/
I Would Like To Live In Prison (PS) (Diagram Bros CON 1) 1980
Bricks/Postal Bargains (PS) (New Hormones ORG 9) 1981

Diagram Brothers were a part of the Manchester art-new wave circuit encircling New Hormones. Their lyrics dealt with current events and their music was pretty weird with some similarity to early **XTC**.

On *There Is No Shower* there is discordant guitar backing:-

"David's mother has written to the council. David has no legs he needs a downstairs shower. This is a bad thing. There is no shower. The letter is passed from office to office. The reply says 'Sorry we have no money left'" (from *There Is No Shower*)

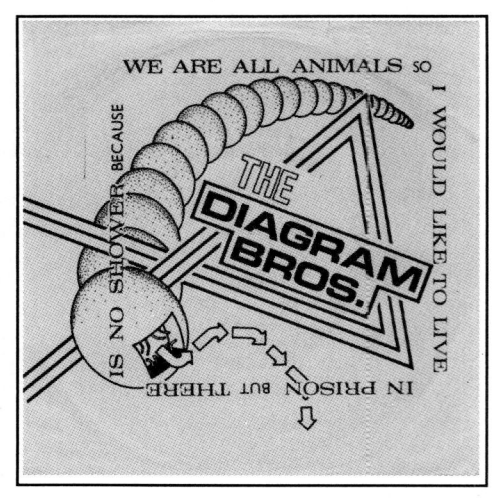

DIAGRAM BROTHERS - We Are All Animals.

Dials

Personnel:	JAMIE BOLSTAR	bs	A
	NEIL CLARKE	sax, vcls	A
	JEFF HEMSLEY	drms	A
	NEIL HOWES	gtr, vcls	A
	MATT STOKES	vcls	A

45s:	All I Hear/Running (PS)	(Scere Records ACT 1) 1976
	She Thought Her Nose Was Bleeding But It's Snot	(Scene Records) 197?

The Dials came from the Sunbury area of South-west London and were a very popular band locally for a while. They were great mates with **The Members** and toured with them nationally. They'd evolved out of an earlier group called Jerry Walter and The Pedestrians. *All I Hear* is a very rare single now. It's notable for the use of brass, which was unusual on punk recordings. It also contains some great guitar work. The flip side *Running* is similar in style to **The Members** vocally. The single's picture sleeve features the record label's symbol on the cover. A second single *She Thought Her Nose Was Bleeding But It's Snot* was also released but withdrawn the same day when the record label owner didn't like what he was hearing - a few copies got out.

Sadly, their vocalist Matt Stokes died very rapidly of cancer.

Die Electric Eels

45:	Agitated/Cyclotron (PS)	(Rough Trade RT 008) 1979

An experimental indie single. *Agitated* is full of snarling vocals, a few trebly bursts of guitar, an amplified vacuum cleaner and the end result is a repugnant noise. A record to shock your friends with. Unorthodox and far from easy on the ear.

Dif Juz

Personnel:	GARY BROMLEY	bs	A
	ALAN CURTIS	gtr	A
	DAVE CURTIS	gtr	A
	RICHIE THOMAS	drms, sax	A

ALBUMS:	1(A)	EXTRACTIONS	(4AD GAD 505) 1985
	2(A)	OUT OF THE TREES (mini-album)	(4AD CAD 612) 1986

NB: (1) also issued on CD (4AD CAD 505CD) 1998. They also had a cassette release *Time Clock Turns* (Pleasantly Surprised PS 9) 1985.

EPs:	1(A)	HU/RE/MI/C/S (12")	(4AD BAD 109) 1981
	2(A)	VIBRATING AIR (Heset/Diselt/Gumet/Soarn)	(4AD BAD 116) 1981
	3(A)	WHO SAYS SO	(Red Flame RFM 24) 1983

Dif Juz were one of the gloom and doom merchants that evolved in the post-punk era. Their debut EP *Huremics* comprised four moody and improvisational instrumentals utilising the guitar, drums and bass format. The sleeve offers no information whatever about the band. The follow-up *Vibrating Air* continued in much the same format - instrumental atmospheric mood music.

Their first full length album *Extractions* was the first to feature vocals courtesy of Liz Fraser. **The Cocteau Twins** also helped out on the record and Robin Guthrie handled the production. With lots of keyboards and sax this was less atmospheric than their previous efforts but still very enjoyable.

Re: later resurfaced on *Natures Mortes* (4AD CAD 117CD) in 1997.

Thomas later played drums for Jesus and Mary Chain and Butterfly Child and Dave Curtis went on to play for **Wolfgang Press**. Alan Curtis moved to New York and Gary Bromley was last heard of working as an electrician.

The Direct Hits

ALBUMS:	1	BLOW UP	(Whaam! BIG 7) 1984
	2	THE HOUSE OF SECRETS	(Make MAKE 1P) 1986

NB: There's also a compilation *The Magic Attack* (Tangerine TANG CD 9) 1995.

45s:	Modesty Blaise/ Sunny Honey Girl (PS)	(Whaam! WHAAM 007) 1982
	Christopher Cooper/ She Didn't Really Care (PS)	(Direct POP 001) 1985

Hailing from Tooting in South London this mod revival combo had previously been known as **The Exits** until late 1980. They were signed by **Television Personalities**' Whaam! label.

The Magic Attack is a 'best of' compilation comprising all their U.K. singles and some of the stronger cuts from their two albums. The music is an amalgam of late sixties whimsical Britpop á la Kinks and post-mod revival power-pop. This is reinforced by song titles like *Modesty Blaise*, *What Killed Aleister Crowley* and *English Girls*. A worthwhile purchase.

The Directions

Personne:	JOHN BURKE	keyb'ds	A
	TONY BURKE	gtr, vcls	A
	STEVE MARTINEZ	drms	A
	MARTIN WILSON	bs	A

45:	Three Bands Tonite/On The Train (PS)	(Tortch TOR 004) 1979

Hailing from the Shepherds Bush area of London, where they formed in late 1978, **The Directions** were a popular attraction at the Fulham Greyhound and 101 Club. Their sole 45 is the jewel in the crown of many mod collections as many of the 2,000 copies pressed were ruined when their manager's basement was flooded. This means it is now extremely hard to find and very expensive. *Three Bands Tonite* tells the story of a disastrous gig where only **The Directions** were prepared to go on with the show. **The Teenbeats** and **The Sta-prest** 'wanna take their money and go', so the song goes.

The Directions recorded an unreleased album at the time.

The Directions also contributed a couple of tracks, *It May Be Too Late* and *Weekend Dancers* to the later compilation of mod rarities, *The Beat Generation And The Angry Young Men* (Well Suspect SUSS 1) 1984, which has been reissued on CD (Captain Mod MODSKA CD 3) 1997. They also appear on *This Is Mod, Vol. 4* (Anagram CDM GRAM 107) 1996. Their finest moment, the stylish *Three Bands Tonite* can also be heard on *100% British Mod* (Captain Mod MODSKA DCD 8) 1998.

They later evolved into Big Sound Authority, a soul/pop outfit who made several 45s in the mid-eighties for MCA, having initially signed to Paul Weller's Respond label. Big Sound Authority had two hits in 1985 with *This House* (No. 21) and *A Bad Town* (No. 54).

The Directors

Personnel:	RICHARD JACOBS	lead gtr, vcls	A
	DAVE MASTERS	gtr, vcls	A
	MARK ROBERTS	bs	A
	JOHN SIMPSON	drms	A

The Directors sole vinyl offering seems to have been a promising cut called *What You've Got* which appear on *Avon Calling - The Bristol Compilation* (Heartbeat HB 1) in 1979.

Discharge

Personnel incl:	CAL (KEVIN) MORRIS	vcls	A
	BONES (A. ROBERTS)	gtr	A
	GARRY MALONEY	drms	A
	RAINY WAINWRIGHT	bs	A

HCP

ALBUMS:	1(A)	HEAR NOTHING, SEE NOTHING, SAY NOTHING		
			(Clay CLAYLP 3)	1982 40
	2(A)	NEVER AGAIN	(Clay CLAYLP 12)	1984 -
	3(A)	GRAVE NEW WORLD	(Clay CLAYLP 19)	1986 -

NB: (1) reissued on CD (Clay CLAYCD 3) 1990 and (Receiver RRCD 255) 1998. (2) was issued on red vinyl and reissued on CD (Clay CLAYCD 12) 1990 and (Receiver RRCD 256) 1998. There was also a compilation album *Discharge 1980 - 1986* (Clay CLAYLP 24) 1987 and *Live At City Garden* (Clay CLAYCD 103) 1990, also on vinyl and in 1993. Also relevant are *Protest And Survive* (Clay CLAYCD 113) 1994; *Protest And Survive* (2-CD) (Snapper SMDCD 131) 1997; *The Singles Collection* (Clay CLAYCD 120) 1995; *Discharged (A Tribute To Discharge)* (various artists) (Rhythm Vicar PREACH 001 CD) 1992 and *Free Speech For The Dumb* (2-CD) (Essential ESACD 798) 1999.

EP:	1(A)	REALITIES OF WAR (Realities Of War/		
		They Declare It/But After The Gig/		
		Society's A Victim) (PS)	(Clay CLAY 1)	1980 -
	2(A)	WHY (12" EP)	(Clay PLATE 2)	1981 -

NB: (2) reissued on CD with additional tracks (Clay PLATE 002 CD) 1990 and 1993 and (Reciever RRCD 259) 1998.

HCP

45s:	Fight Back/War's No Fairy Tale/Always Restrictions/		
	You Take Part In Creating This System/		
	Religion Instigates (PS)	(Clay CLAY 3)	1980 -
	Decontrol/It's No TV Sketch/		
	Tomorrow Belongs To Us (PS)	(Clay CLAY 5)	1980 -
	Never Again/Death Dealers/		
	Two Monstrous Nuclear Stock-Piles (PS)	(Clay CLAY 6)	1981 64
	State Violence, State Control/		
	Doomsday (PS)	(Clay CLAY 14)	1982 -
	Price Of Silence/		
	Born To Die In The Gutter (PS)	(Clay CLAY 29)	1983 -
	The More I See/		
	Protest And Survive (PS)	(Clay CLAY 34)	1984 -
	The More I See (Extended Version)/		
	Protest And Survive (12" PS)	(Clay 12CLAY 34)	1984 -
	Ignorance/No Compromise (PS)	(Clay CLAY 43)	1985 -
	Ignorance (Extended Version)/		
	No Compromise (PS)	(Clay 12 CLAY 43)	1985 -

Formed in Stoke-on-Trent at the end of the seventies **Discharge** were part of the wave of angry working class punk bands that emerged in Britain in the early eighties.

Aggressive vocalist Cal (Kevin) Morris and bassist Rainy Wainwright were the everpresents among a very flexible line-up. In 1980, the band became the first to sign to local potteries indie label Clay Records. It was run by former Beggars Banquet employee Mike Stone.

Despite their aggressive image epitomised by Cal's vocal style and their appearance (leathers, bovver boots etc.), their recorded output was characterised by a strong anti-war theme. Their brutal debut EP *Realities Of War* was a steady seller, re-pressed many times, and made an impression on the indie chart. The following year their *Why* EP actually topped the indie chart and their *Never Again* 45 got to No. 64 in the national charts later that year, during a three week residency.

Of their albums *Hear Nothing, See Nothing, Say Nothing* displayed all the energy and power of the early **Sex Pistols** or **Clash**. It is well played, high speed and powerful, although the lyrics are largely inaudible. No wonder they were an important live attraction in the early eighties. They co-headlined the Apocalypse Now Tour along with **Anti-Pasti**, **Anti-Nowhere League**, **Chron Gen** and **The Exploited**.

Bones left to form **Broken Bones** in the mid-eighties.

As interest in this movement waned in the mid-eighties they modified their musical style into a thrash metal sound, which cost them what was left of their original punk following. Still they soldiered on until 1987 when the compilation *Discharge 1980-86* was released. A further live compilation *Live At City Garden* appeared in 1990.

Discharge reformed in 1991 with Cal from the original line-up. *Live At The Garden New Jersey* is compiled from the group's 1983-84 U.S. tour. **Discharge** are also included on *100% Hardcore Punk* (Captain Oi! AHOY DCD 84) 1998 playing *Decontrol*. They recorded a CD/album *Massacre Divine* in 1991 and CD *Shootin' Up The World* in 1993.

Free Speech For The Dumb is a double-CD forty-track collection which includes all their most significant cuts up to and including their 1982 45 *State Violence* when their founding member Bones left the band, making it a pretty comprehensive 'best of'. The CD set is lavishly packaged with a colour foldout booklet containing sleevenotes, a discography and lots of photos.

Disco Zombies

Personnel:	DODD	bs	A
	DAVE HENDERSON	vcls	A
	MARK SUTHERLAND	gtr	A
	ANDY ROSS	gtr	A

EP:	1(A)	THE INVISIBLE (Top Of The Pops/Time Will Tell/	
		Punk A-Go-Go/	
		Disco Zombies)	(Uptown/Wizzo WIZZO 1) 1979

45s:	*	Drums Over London/	
		Heartbeats Love (PS)	(South Circular SGS 106) 1979
		Here Comes The Birds/	
		Mary Millington (PS)	(Dining Out TUX 2) 1981

NB: * Issued in a three-sided black, white and pink or black, white and green wraparound handmade picture sleeve.

A Leicester new wave band whose four-track EP was released on Uptown, a small new wave label operating out of Marblethorpe, Lincolnshire. It retailed for just 99p.

Drums Over London is ill-disciplined, loosely structured pop, but with quite a strong chorus. They also issued a cassette entitled *From Spit To Skewer* (Corporation CORP 2 C30).

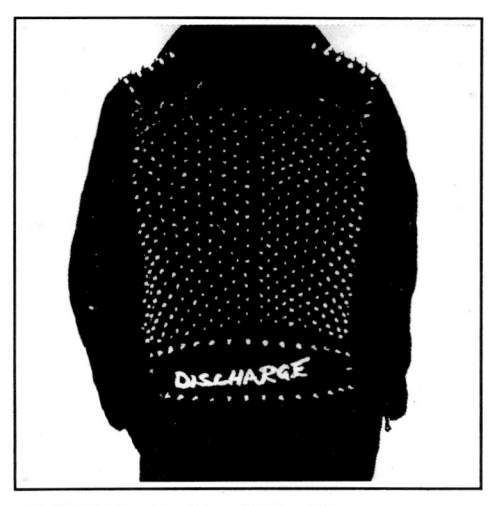

DISCHARGE - Realities Of War EP.

When the group disbanded in 1980, Andy Ross worked as a solo artist using the name Fifty Fantastic. This was also the same band as the mod/psychedelic group **The Steppes**.

Disorder

Personnel:
DEAN	vcls	ABC
MICK	bs	A
STEVE	gtr	ABCDE
VIRUS	drms	ABCD
STEVE ROBINSON	bs	B
TAFF	bs	CDE
BOOBS	vcls	DE
GLENN	drms	E

ALBUMS:
1( ) UNDER THE SCALPEL BLADE (Disorder AARGH 1) 1984
2( ) LIVE IN OSLO (Disorder AARGH 2) 1985
3( ) ONE DAY SON, ALL THIS WILL BE YOURS (Disorder AARGH 3) 1986

NB: (1) also issued on CD (Anagram CDPUNK 19) 1996. (2) also issued on one CD with their 1989 album *Violent World* (Anagram CDPUNK 39) 1994. (3) credited to **Disorder** and Kaska Process. *The Complete Disorder* is also available on vinyl (Get Back GET 37LP) 1998. An alternative compilation is *The Best Of Disorder* (Anagram CDPUNK 109) 1998. There's also a CD compilation *The Complete Disorder* (Anagram CDMGRAM 49) 1991 and also relevant is *The Rest Home For Senile Old Punks Proudly Presents Disorder* (Anagram CD PUNK 88) 1997 and *Tapes From The Attic* (Overground OVER 60CD) 1997.

EPs:
1( ) PERDITION (Stagnation/Life/Out Of Order/Condemned/ Media/Suicide Children/Preachers/ Rembrance Day) (12") (Disorder 12ORDER 3) 1982
2( ) MENTAL DISORDER (Bullshit Everyone/Rampton Song/ Provocated War/3 Blind Mice/ Buy I Gurt Pint) (Disorder ORDER 4) 1983
3( ) THE SINGLES COLLECTION (12") (Disorder 12ORDER 5) 1984

NB: (3) comprised (1) and (2).

45s: Complete Disorder/Insane Youth/Today's World/ Violent Crime (PS) (Disorder ORDER 1) 1981
Distortion To Deafness/More Than Fights/Daily Life/ You've Got To Be Someone (PS) (Disorder ORDER 2) 1981

This punk combo formed in Bristol in 1980. Like many of their contemporaries their music exuded a strong protest theme. When they were unsuccessful in getting signed by the city's local Riot City indie label they simply formed their own Disorder label and then got their records distributed by Riot City.

Their line-up fluctuated over the years. The *Complete Disorder* CD is the best guide to their music, which is full of energy, aggression and rantings on cuts like *Insane Youth*. It compiles all their singles and EPs for Riot City. An alternative compilation utilising album cuts too is *The Best Of Disorder*.

In 1997 Anagram released *The Rest Home For Senile Old Punks Proudly Presents Disorder* (Anagram CD PUNK 88) 1997. The mid-price twenty-four cut collection of anti-establishment speed punk had been lying in the can for some years.

Their *Rampton Song* can also be heard on *Burning Ambition: A History Of Punk, Vol. 3* (Anagram CD PUNK 98) 1997 and the band also contributed *Rampton Song* and *Complete Disorder* to *100% Hardcore Punk* (Captain Oi! AHOY DCD 84) 1998.

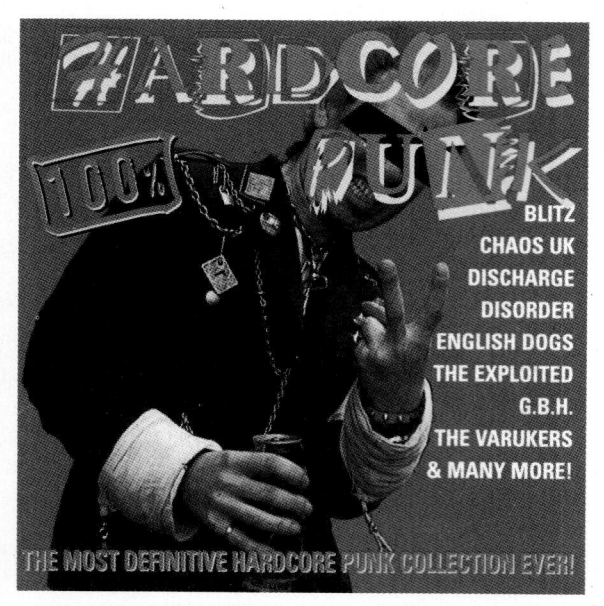

100% HARDCORE PUNK compilation featuring Disorder.

Distractions

Personnel:
MIKE FINNEY	vcls	AB
STEVE PERRIN-BROWN	gtr	AB
LAWRENCE TICKLE	bs	A
TONY TRAP	drms	A
PIP NICHOLLS	bs	B
ALEC SIDEBOTTOM	drms	B
ADRIAN WRIGHT	gtr	B

ALBUM: 1(B) NOBODY'S PERFECT (Island ILPS 9604) 1980

EP: 1(B) YOU'RE NOT GOING OUT DRESSED LIKE THAT (12" EP) (TJM TJM 2) 1979
2(B) AND THEN THERE'S (Island) 1981

45s: Time Goes By So Slow/Pillow Fight (PS) (Factory FAC 12) 1979
It Doesn't Bother Me/ One Way Love (PS) (Island WIP 6533) 1979
Boys Cry/Paracetomal Paralysis (PS) (Island WIP 6568) 1980
Something For The Weekend/ What's The Use (PS) (Island WIP 6650) 1980

This new wave band from Manchester was originally formed by Finney and Perrin-Brown whilst they were at college in 1975. With the onset of punk and the influence of **The Buzzcocks** in particular the line-up was revised in late 1977 with the addition of Nicholls, Sidebottom and Wright, who'd all been with The Purple Gang in the sixties. They soon became a popular live attraction around Manchester with their own brand of sixties-influenced punk. After an EP *You're Not Going Out Dressed Like That*, which comprised four melodic and sharp tunes, stridently delivered, they secured a contract with Terry Wilson's Factory label. *Time Goes By So Slow* has a steady, almost serene arrangement with a sweet guitar sound and sorrowful lyrics. A sad, but invigorating pop song in **The Undertones**' mould. Although it had chart potential it failed to get sufficient airplay to breakthrough. Their sound was characterised by the jangly, guitar quarrelling of Steve Perrin and Adrian Wright.

In September 1979, **The Distractions** signed to Island and re-recorded a version of *It Doesn't Bother Me*. In 1980, an album *Nobody's Perfect* was released. This contained material from their earlier days with some new songs. A cover of the Eden Kane hit *Boys Cry* and *Something For The Weekend* followed. Like their final EP *And Then There's* they were warmly received but failed to breakthrough commercially and they split in 1981. *It Doesn't Bother Me* was later included on *Rabid / TJM Punk Singles Collection* (Receiver RRCD 227) in 1996.

The Distributors

Personnel: TONY STEPHENS (possibly)
MICK SWITZERLAND (possibly)

45s: TV Me/Wireless (foldover PS) (Tap TAP 1) 1980
Lean On Me/Never Never (PS) (Red Rhino RED 5) 1981
Hold/Get Rid Of These Things (Red Rhino RED 009) 1981
Hold/Get Rid Of These Things/ Wages For Lovers (12", PS) (Red Rhino REDT 009) 1981

An experimental electro-pop outfit from Wakefield in Yorkshire. *TV Me* was an interesting debut and was also included on *Hicks From The Sticks* (Rockburgh ROC 111) in 1980.

Disruptors

Personnel:	KEV	A
	PAUL	A
	STEVE	A
	TIM	A

EP: 1(A) ALIVE IN THE ELECTRIC CHAIR (EP)
(Radical Change RC 8) 1985

NB: (1) also issued as a 12" (RC 128) 1985.

45s: Young Offender/U.K. Soldier/
No Place For You (PS) (Radical Change RC 1) 1982
Shelters For The Rich/Animal Farm/
Self Rule (PS) (Radical Change RC 2) 1982
Bomb Heaven/Die With Mother/
Poem (PS) (Radical Change RC 6) 1984

An anarcho-punk band whose lyrics were more important than the music. A very **Crass**-like band.

The Disturbed

Personnel incl: JOSI MUNNS   vcls

45: Betrayed/I Don't Believe (PS)   (Parole PURL 3) 1979

A one-off, but Munns' deliberate, sulky vocals have some appeal.

The Dodgems

Personnel:	DOUG POTTER	gtr, vcls	A
	GARY TURNER	bs, vcls	A
	CHARLIE ZUBER	drms	A

45s: Science/Fiction/Hard Shoulder (PS) (Attrix RB 7) 1980
Lord Lucan Is Missing/
Gotta Give It Up (PS) (Criminal SWAG 12) 1980

This Brighton band also featured on that town's compilation album *Vaultage '78 (Two Sides Of Birghton)* (Attrix RB 03) 1978 playing *I Don't Care* and *Lord Lucan Is Missing*, which both capture the amateurism of the period and were produced by Jonathan King. You can also check out *Lord Lucan Is Missing* on *Vaultage Punk Collection* (Anagram CDPUNK 101) 1997.

Dogsbody

Personnel:	BROWNIE	drms	A
	COILY	vcls	A
	SNAGGER	gtr	A
	ZEB	bs	A

Dogsbody hailed from Middlesborough and often supported **Major Accident** at gigs. They contributed a cut called *Murder*, which was produced by Brian Collison who looked after **Accidents**, to *The Oi! Of Sex* (Syndicate SYNLP 4) 1984, also reissued on CD (Captain Oi! AHOY CD 23) 1994. *Murder* is a half-decent, fast-paced, punk song.

Zeb later emerged as Zlaughter in the heavy metal outfit Warfare, which was formed by former **Accidents**, **Blood** and **Angelic Upstarts**' drummer Evo.

The Doodlebugs

45: Nightmare/Punky Xmas   (Punk BCS 0005) 1977

A novelty cash-in release.

VAULTAGE PUNK SINGLES COLLECTION includes The Dodgems.

The Dole

Personnel:	MATTHEW GILLAT	bs	A
	PETE HOWSAM	keyb'ds	A
	IAN NEEVE	vcls	A
	SIMON PAGE	gtr	A
	PAUL VJESTICA	drms	A

45: New Wave Love/Hungry Men No Longer Steal Sheep But Are There Hanging Judges? (die-cut PS) (Ultimate ULT 402) 1978

Drummer Paul Vjestica was still at school when **The Dole** formed in Peterborough with an average age of seventeen in late 1977. They did local support slots for **999** and **The Radiators** before releasing their sole 45. They conjured up an appealing sound on *New Wave Love*, with catchy keyboards, good guitar and competent vocals. It was also given an airing on the compilation *Business Unusual* (Cherry Red ARED 2) in 1979. The 'A' side was about a girl who followed the band. It can also heard on *Punk Rock Rarities, Vol. 2* (Anagram CDPUNK 83) 1996.

The Dole split up the same year. Howsam later resurfaced in Dancing Mirage. Vocalist Ian Neeve then formed The Name and guitarist Simon Page formed The Point.

The Doll

Personnel:	MARION VALENTINE	vcls, gtr	AB
	MARIO WATTS	drms	A
	ADONIS YIANNI	keyb'ds	A
	CHRISTOS YIANNI	bs	AB
	DENNIS HAYES	keyb'ds	B
	PAUL TURNER	drms	B
	JAMES WEST-ORAM	gtr	B

ALBUM: 1(B) LISTEN TO THE SILENCE
(Beggars Banquet BEGA 12) 1979
HCP

45s: Don't Tango On My Heart/
Trash (Beggars Banquet BEG 4) 1978 -
Desire Me/TV Addict/Burning Up Like A Fire/
Desire Me (double pack) (Beggars Banquet BEG 11) 1978 28
Desire Me/TV Addict (12") (Beggars Banquet BEG 11T) 1978 -
Cinderella With A Husky Voize/
Because Now (Beggars Banquet BEG 26) 1979 -
Used To Be A Hero/Heroes (Beggars Banquet BEG 31) 1980 -
Burning Up Like A Fire/
Frozen Fire (Beggars Banquet BEG 38) 1980 -

Doll's recording debut came in 1977 when they contributed *Trash* to the *Streets* (Beggars Banquet BEGA 1) compilation. Their second 45 *Desire*

Me, released in December 1978, took them into the Top 30. It spent eight weeks in all in the charts.

Five of their tracks - *Don't Tango On My Heart, Trash, Desire, Cinderella With A Husky Smile* and *You Used To Be My Hero* - were included on *The Beggars Banquet Punk Collection* (Anagram CDPUNK 73) in 1996.

Dome

Personnel:	BRUCE GILBERT	gtr, vcls, synth	A
	GRAHAM LEWIS	bs, vcls, synth	A

ALBUMS:	1(A)	DOME ONE	(Dome DOME 1) 1980
	2(A)	DOME 2	(Dome DOME 2) 1980
	3(A)	DOME 3	(Dome DOME 3) 1981
	4(A)	MZUI (WATERLOO GALLERY)	(Cherry Red BRED 27) 1982
	5(A)	WILL YOU SPEAK THIS WORLD: DOME IV	(Uniton U 011) 1983

NB: (1) and (2) issued on one CD (Grey Area DOME 12CD) 1992. (3) and (5) issued on one CD (Grey Area DOME 34 CD) 1992.

EP:	1(A)	3R4 (Barge Claim/3,4/Barge Claim/R) (12", PS)	(4AD CAD 16) 1980

45s:	So/Drop (PS)	(Dome DOM 45) 1980
	Ends With The Sea/Hung Up To Dry While Building An Arch (PS)	(4AD AD 106) 1981

When **Wire** disbanded in 1980 Gilbert and Lewis contributed to work as a duo exploring a wide range of experimental music as **Dome**. On *MZUI (Waterloo Gallery)*, in conjunction with Russell Mills, they placed microphones around a London Art Gallery. They also recorded an album *Whilst Climbing Thieves Vie For Attention* (Court COURT 1) 1983 as P10 and collaborated with Mute label boss Daniel Miller in Duet Emmo (an anagram of Mute and Dome) for an album *Or So It Seems* (Mute STUMM 11) 1983 and 45, *Or So It Seems/Heart Of Hearts (Or So It Seems)* (12") (Mute MUTE 025) 1983. They were both in the re-formed **Wire** in 1984.

The Donkees

Personnel incl: N. FERGUSON

45:	Listen To Your Radio/ Watched By Everyone (PS)	(MCA MCA 737) 1981

This was a later version of **The Donkeys**. See that entry for more details.

The Donkeys

Personnel incl: N. FERGUSON

45s:	*	What I Want/Four Letters (PS)	(Rhesus GO APE 102) 1980
		No Way/You Jane (PS)	(Rhesus GO APE 3) 1980
		Don't Go/Living Legends (PS)	(Rhesus GO APE 105) 1980
		Let's Float/Watched By Everyone (PS)	(MCA MCA 721) 1981
Reissues:		No Way/You Jane (PS)	(Back Door DOOR 006) 1980
		What I Want/Four Letters (PS)	(Deram DM-R 431) 1980
		Don't Go/Living Legends (PS)	(MCA MCA 682) 1981

NB: * This release came with a yellow or orange label.

Originally a power pop act, this Wakefield combo soon became identified with the mod revival movement but also supported **Stiff Little Fingers** on one of their tours. Their first three singles for Rhesus Go attracted sufficient interest to get reissued on their different labels. In 1981, they also recorded a new 45 for MCA. After an agreement with MCA, they changed name to **The Donkees** for a final release.

The Door and The Window

Personnel:	BENDLE	A
	NAG	A
	MARK PERRY	A

ALBUMS:	1(A)	DETAILED TWANG	(NB Records NB 5) 1980
	2(A)	MUSIC AND MOVEMENT	(NB Records NB 9) 1980

NB: (2) was a live cassette.

EPs:	1(A)	FIRST (Subculture/Fashion Slaves/Nostradamus/ Don't Kill Colin/Worst Band)	(NB Records NB 1) 1979
	2(A)	SECOND (Production Line/He Feels Like A Doris/ Innocent/ Dig/I Like Sound)	(NB Records NB 3) 1979

NB: (2) appeared with a white label with stickers and an insert in picture sleeve in a polythene bag.

The Door and The Window was a sideline **Alternative TV** project involving **Mark Perry**. Musically, these records are extremely experimental and consist of a jumble of different sounds and effects. In addition to the above, the band made three compilation appearances; the *Deleted Fun Time* (Deleted DEC 009) cassette included *Human Torch*, the *Mother Of A Punk* (Conventional CON 013) 1980 cassette aired two more of their songs *Pokerville* and *Swinger* and, finally, the double EP *Ankst In My Pants* (Dep DEP 002) 1981 featured *C.C.H.* and came in a foldover card picture sleeve with a polythene bag.

Double Vision

Personnel:	ED ASH	gtr	A
	HILDA ASH	bs	A
	MELANIE DICKS	vcls	A
	PADDY GIGG	drms	A
	NEIL McDOUGALL	perc	A
	DAN STEVENS	lead gtr	A

This group contributed *My Dead Mother* to *Avon Calling - The Bristol Compilation* (Heartbeat HB 1) in 1979. Melanie Dicks' vocals are distinctive. The overall sound is very **Police**-influenced.

Dregs

EP:	1( )	THE DREGS: (The Dregs Of Humanity/I Am Insane/ Fatal Attraction/Schoolgirls)	(Disturbing DRO 1) 1979

This is an unimpressive EP of formless punk/heavy metal which will only interest a small number of people.

Drinking Electricity

Personnel incl: A. MacFARLANE

ALBUM:	1(A)	OVERLOAD	(Survival SURLP 1) 1982

THE DOOR AND THE WINDOW - Second.

45s:	Shaking All Over/China (PS)	(Pop Aural POP 4) 1980
	Shake Some Action/	
	Shake Some Action (alt version) (PS)	(Pop Aural POP 5) 1980
	Cruising Missiles/	
	Shaking All Over (Dub) (PS)	(Pop Aural POP 8) 1980
	Subliminal/Random Particles (PS)	(Survival SUR 1) 1981
	Good Times/Colour Coding (PS)	(Survival SUR 5) 1982

A London-based duo supplemented by a guest bassist. They played synthesized rock with a strong electronic bent but not as well as bands like **Blancmange** and **Soft Cell**.

Drive

45:	Jerkin'/Push 'N' Shove	(NRG NE 467) 1978

An obscure punk band, whose sole 45 was unusual for not coming in a picture sleeve in this era. It is now rare and expensive if you succeed in tracking a copy down. *Jerkin'* was also included on *Streets* (Beggars Banquet BEGA 1) in late 1977.

THE DRONES - Bone Idle.

The Drones

Personnel:	MJ DRONE	vcls, gtr	A
	GUG 'GANGRENE' CALLENDAR	lead gtr	A
	PETE HOWELLS	drms	A
	WHISPER (STEVE CUNDELL)	bs	A

ALBUM:	1(A)	FURTHER TEMPTATIONS	(Valer VLRP 1) 1977

NB: (1) reissued on CD with seven bonus 45 tracks (Anagram CD PUNK 20) 1993. Also relevant is *Tapes From The Attic* (Overground OVER 60CD) 1997 and *The Attic Tapes 75-82* (Get Back GET 25) on vinyl. Also relevant is *Further Temptations* (dbl) (Get Back GET 6), a double album set.

EP:	1(A)	TEMPTATIONS OF A WHITE COLLAR WORKER	
		(Lookalikes/Corgi Crap/Hand On Me/	
		You'll Lose)	(Ohms GOOD MIX 1) 1977

45s:	*	Be My Baby/Lift Off The Bans (12")	(Valer VRSP 1) 1977
		Bone Idle/I Just Wanna Be Myself (PS)	(Valer VRS 1) 1977
	+	Bone Idle/I Just Wanna Be Myself (Fifth Avenue CAS 107) 1977	
		Can't See/Fooled Today (PS)	(Fabulous JC4) 1980

NB: * Unreleased. + This was a cassette with a flip open 'cigarette box' sleeve.

Forming in late 1976 **The Drones** were one of Manchester's earliest punk bands having evolved out of a R&B-influenced band Rockslide. **The Drones** were a leading attraction at the city's Electric Circus Club in the early days. They soon became one of the first Manchunian bands to move down to London where they were a frequent attraction at the Roxy among other venues.

In May 1977, they released an EP, *Temptations Of A White Collar Worker* on the tiny Ohms label. They then switched to Valer (another small label). Initially they recorded a 12" single *Be My Baby*, which was not released.

Then, in October 1977, *Bone Idle* was available in both vinyl and cassette format, but it sold poorly. It has a fast-paced guitar riff and quite a catchy chorus:-

"Somewhere you'll find somethin' to do
Somethin' you really want to
Want to do a lot of things that are new
That nobody needs to explain to you!
Explain to you!
'Cos you're bone idol! bone idol!
Why think about things you won't do
You're a bone idol, bone idol
Simple/You want to be"
(from *Bone Idol*)

The following month they contributed *Lookalikes* (from their earlier EP) to the *Streets* (Beggars Banquet BEGA 1) 1977 compilation. On 13th December 1977, they recorded a session for John Peel comprising *Be My Baby*, *The Change*, *Clique* and *Movement*. The same month, their *Further Temptations* album hit the shops. It exhibited the typical enthusiasm of many of the early punk bands but was poorly produced and contained nothing to single it out from the crowd. Sales were poor and it is now difficult to find in its original format. Readers wanting to hear more of their music should seek out the CD reissue on Anagram, which also contains some of their 45 cuts.

Persecution Complex, included on Virgin's *Short Circuit - Live At The Electric Circus* (VCL 5003) compilation in June 1978, was probably their best known song. By now, though, **The Drones** were on the point of splitting, having found it difficult to progress beyond the early punk format. There was a brief reformation in 1980, which produced a further 45.

They returned in 1999 with a new twelve-track studio album *Sorted* (CD) (Captain Oi! AHOY CD 111), which included a remix of *Johnny Go Home* and the scathing *Dirty Bastards*.

Expectations - Tapes From The Attic 75 - 82 is a worthwhile collection of unreleased studio cuts, alternate takes and live material. The first cut *Expectations* is a cover of Iggy Pop and The Stooges' *Search And Destroy* and it dates from 6th November 1975. Drone's vocals are good 'n' snotty but sadly the guitars need fleshing out! The remaining twenty-one tracks include a cover of *Be My Baby* (a rejected 45 back in '77), glam-punk (*The Clique*); two cuts from their last recording session in May 1979; an outtake from their contribution to the legendary *Live At The Electric Circus* 10" and six cuts from a 1996 reunion. The sound quality is varied but Overground went to a lot of trouble with this compilation and also provided a breakdown of the CD's various sources. *Bone Idol* can also be heard on the 5-CD set *1-2-3-4 - A History Of Punk And New Wave 1976-1979* (MCA/Universal 60066) 1999. The double album *Further Temptations* is a complete discography of **The Drones'** late seventies and early eighties output.

The Drug Addix

Personnel:	RON GRIFFIN	drms	A
	KIRSTY 'MANDY DOUBT' MacCOLL	vcls	A
	ART NOUVEAU	vcls, gtr	A
	ALAN OFFER	bs	A
	STERLING STERLING	vcls	A

EP:	1(A)	MAKE A RECORD (Gay Boys In Bondage/	
		Addington Struggle/Special Clinic/	
		Glutton For Punishment)	(Chiswick SW 39) 1978

A five-piece from Surrey. Vocalist Stirling Silver sings in the sordid masochistic melodrama *Gay Boys In Bondage*:-

"Got some smack in the heel of my leather thigh boot
Got some valium in the pocket of my rubber suit!"
(from *Gay Boys In Bondage*)

In Art Nouveau they had had a pretty good guitarist too. They are most notable for being the first outlet for Kirsty MacColl, who later launched a successful solo career and was later tragically killed when hit by a jet ski whilst holidaying with her family.

Dry Rib

EP: 1 THE DRY SEASON (Alaska/Cruelty Of The Victim/
Quailseed) (PS) (Clockwork COR 001) 1979

NB: (1) This EP played at 33 r.p.m. It was issued in a wraparound photocopied sleeve with screen-printed labels.

This group got their break when Ed Ball, better-known for his spells in **Television Personalities**, and his own band **The Times**, saw them playing live and was knocked out by their performance. Their music and arrangements were complex, like an orchestrated piece for three instruments. They were an 'interesting' new wave act. Ed Ball paid to have 2,500 copies of their EP pressed, but only 400 sold, leaving him in dire financial straits! The record came out on an orange label and Ball had wanted to call it Clockwork Orange Records, but this was felt to have fascist implications.

The Duplicates

45: I Want To Make You Very Happy/
Call Of The Faithful (Stiff BUY 54) 1979

This is a synthesized power pop 45. It didn't come in a picture sleeve.

Duran Duran

Personnel:
SIMON CULLEY	bs, clarinet	A	
STEPHEN DUFFY	vcls	A	
NICK RHODES	keyb'ds	ABCDEFG	
JOHN TAYLOR	gtr, bs	ABCDEFG	
ROGER TAYLOR	drms	BCDEFG	
ANDY WICKETT	vcls	BCD	
JOHN CURTIS	gtr	C	
ANDY TAYLOR	gtr	DEF	
SIMON LE BON	vcls	FG	

HCP
ALBUMS: 1(F) DURAN DURAN (EMI EMC 3372) 1981 3
(up to 2(F) RIO (EMI EMC 3411) 1982 2
1986) 3(F) SEVEN AND THE RAGGED TIGER
  (EMI EMC 1654541) 1983 1
 4(F) ARENA (EMI EX26 0308 1 DD 2) 1984 6
 5(G) NOTORIOUS (EMI DDN 331) 1986 16

NB: (1) also issued on CD (Parlophone CDPRG 1003) 1995. (2) also issued on CD (Parlophone CDPRG 1004) 1993. (3) also issued on CD (Parlophone CDPRG 1005) 1993. (4) issued in a gatefold sleeve in vinyl and on CD (EMI CDP 7460422 DD 2) 1984. (5) also issued on CD (EMI CDP 7464152) 1986. There are also a number of compilations and collections including *Decade* (EMI DDX 10) 1989 on vinyl and (EMI CDDX 10) 1989 on CD, *Greatest* (CD) (EMI 496 23 92) 1998, *Strange Behaviour* (2-CD) (EMI 493 9722) 1999 and *Original Gold* (2-CD) (Disky HR 857722) 1999.

HCP
45s: Planet Earth/Late Bar (PS) (EMI EMI 5137) 1981 12
(up to Planet Earth (Night Version)/Planet Earth/
1986) Late Bar (12", PS) (EMI 12EMI 5137) 1981 -
 Careless Memories/Khanada (PS) (EMI EMI 5168) 1981 37
 Careless Memories/Fame/
 Khanada (12", PS) (EMI 12EMI 5168) 1981 -
 Girls On Film/Faster Than Light (PS) (EMI EMI 5206) 1981 5
 Girls On Film (Night Version)/Girls On Film/
 Faster Than Light (12", PS) (EMI 12EMI 5206) 1981 -
 My Own Way/Like An Angel (PS) (EMI EMI 5254) 1981 14
 My Own Way (Night Version)/Like An Angel/
 My Own Way (Short Version) (EMI EMI 5254) 1981 -
 Hungry Like The Wolf/
 Careless Memories (live) (PS) (EMI EMI 5295) 1982 5
 Hungry Like The Wolf (Night Version)/
 Careless Memories (Live) (12", PS) (EMI 12EMI 5295) 1982 -
 Save A Prayer/
 Hold Back The Rain (Remix) (PS) (EMI EMI 5327) 1982 2
 Save A Prayer/Hold Back The
 Rain (12" Remix) (12", PS) (EMI 12EMI 5327) 1982 -
 Rio/The Chauffeur (Blue Silver) (PS) (EMI EMI 5346) 1982 9
 Rio (Part 2)/Rio (Part 1)/
 My Own Way (12", PS) (EMI 12EMI 5346) 1982 -
 Is There Something I Should Know?/
 Faith In This Colour (Slow Mix) (PS) (EMI EMI 5371) 1983 1
 Is There Something I Should Know? (Monster Mix)/
 Faith In This Colour (12", PS) (EMI 12EMI 5371) 1983 -
 Union Of The Snake/
 Secret Oktober (PS) (EMI EMI 5429) 1983 3
 Union Of The Snake (Monkey Mix)/
 Secret Oktober (12", PS) (EMI 12EMI 5429) 1983 -
 New Moon On Monday/
 Tiger Tiger (PS) (EMI DURAN 1) 1984 9
 New Moon On Monday (Extended)/
 Tiger Tiger (12", PS) (EMI 12DURAN 1) 1984 -
 The Reflex/Make Me Smile (Come Up
 And See Me) (live) (PS) (EMI DURAN 2) 1984 1
 The Reflex/Make Me Smile (Come Up And See
 Me) (live) (poster PS) (EMI DURAN P2) 1984 -
 The Reflex (Dance Mix)/The Reflex/Make Me Smile (Come
 Up And See Me) (live) (12", PS) (EMI 12DURAN 2) 1984 -
 The Reflex (Dance Mix)/The Reflex/Make Me Smile (Come
 Up And See Me) (live) (12", pic disc) (EMI 12DURAN P2) 1984 -
 The Wild Boys/(I'm Looking For) Cracks In The
 Pavement (live) (PS) (EMI DURAN 3) 1984 2
* The Wild Boys/(I'm Looking For) Cracks In The
 Pavement (PS) (EMI DURAN (A-E) 3) 1984 -
 The Wild Boys (Wilder Than Wild Boys) (Extended)/
 The Wild Boys 45/(I'm Looking For) Cracks In The
 Pavement (Live) (12", PS) (EMI 12DURAN 3) 1984 -
+ A View To A Kill/A View To A Kill (That
 Fatal Kiss) (PS) (Parlophone DURAN 007) 1985 2
 Notorious/
 Winter Marches On (PS) (Parlophone DON 45) 1986 7
x Notorious (Latin Rascals Mix)/Winter Marches On/
 Notorious (Parlophone TCD DNX 45) 1986 -
 Notorious (Extended)/Notorious 45/
 Winter Marches On (12", PS) (Parlophone 12DDN 45) 1986 -
 Notorious (Latin Rascals Mix)/
 Winter Marches On (12", PS) (Parlophone 12DDNX 45) 1986 -

NB: * This was released in five different picture sleeves. + This was also released on white vinyl with a gatefold picture sleeve. x A cassette release.

Duran Duran along with groups like **Spandau Ballet**, **Ultravox** and **Visage**, spearheaded the "New Romantic" movement in the early eighties, which was a backlash against punk and new wave.

The group was formed in 1978 in Birmingham by Nick Rhodes (whose real name was Nick Bates), a Birmingham lad, and John Taylor, from Solihull, Stephen Duffy was their original vocalist and the line-up was completed by Simon Culley on bass and a drum machine.

Their name came from the character played by Milo O'Shea in the Jane Fonda science fiction movie 'Barbarella'. It was at Barbarella's club in Birmingham that they played several early gigs.

Colley and Duffey left during 1979 and Andy Wickett (ex-TV Eye) came in on vocals. Their new drummer was Roger Taylor, who'd been with a Birmingham punk band called The Scent Organs. With John Taylor switching to bass, John Curtis had a brief spell as their guitarist. When he left, they placed an advert in Melody Maker for a 'live wire guitarist'. Andy Taylor from Cullercoats, Newcastle, was recruited to fill the slot. At this stage, they were still unable to achieve a stable line-up. When Wicketts left, they utilised a number of temporary vocalists.

Their next break came when the owners of Birmingham's newly opened Rum Runner club (Paul and Michael Berrow) gave them a residency at the club and a management contract. They still had to crack the lead vocalist slot. The man for the moment was Simon Le Bon, who'd been born in Bushey, Hertfordshire, but was studying drama at Birmingham University at the time. He was recommended by an old girlfriend who was working at the Rum Runner as a barmaid at the time. He secured the vocal slot in April but didn't join the band full-time until he'd completed his university course in July. The definitive **Duran Duran** line-up was now in place. None of the Taylor's are related. That summer **Duran Duran** played succcessfully at Edinburgh Festival in Scotland. In November, they embarked on the first major U.K. tour supporting Hazel O'Connor. Before the year was out, the Berrow brothers secured them a worldwide recording contract with EMI.

Roxy Music seem to have been a significant influence on these photogenic dandies who created a lush but powerful rock sound using pretty elementary electronics. With producer Colin Thurston they proceeded to record some classic material. *Planet Earth* (No. 12) and *Careless Memories* (No. 37) brought early 45 successes. Their eponymous debut album contained both these singles and spawned a third *Girls On Film* (No. 5), which was promoted with the assistance of a striking Godley and Creme directed video. Musically, they successfully blended elements of seventies disco (beat, repetition and gimmickery) with an updated form of rock. The album was a big success. It climbed to No. 3 and spent a staggering one hundred and eighteen weeks in the charts.

Following a further hit *My Own Way* (No. 14) in December 1981, **Duran Duran** embarked on a worldwide tour the following April which lasted most of 1982. Their second album *Rio* showcased their songwriting and increasingly intricate arrangements. Le Bon's vocal performance is superb and cuts like *Last Chance On The Stairway*, *New Religion* and the title track are particularly strong on melody. The album provided three further U.K. hit singles *Hungry Like The Wolf* (No. 5), *Save A Prayer* (No. 2) and *Rio* (No. 9) on which Andy Hamilton guested on saxophone. All three made an impact in the 'States, where they reached No's 3, 16 and 14 respectively, although *Save A Prayer* was not a hit until 1985. *Rio* not only climbed to No. 2 in Britain where it spent a staggering one hundred and nine weeks in the charts, it also climbed slowly but surely up the U.S. charts, peaking at No. 6 and becoming a million-selling album.

In recognition of their rising commercial appeal in the United States their American label Harvest released remixes of four of their best songs *Hungry Like The Wolf*, *Girls On Film*, *Hold Back The Rain* and *My Own Way* on an EP called *Carnival* in 1982. It climbed to No. 98.

The group was now phenomenally popular. On 26th March 1983, a visit to a New York video shop attracted 5,000 fans and mounted police had to be deployed to control them. *Is There Something I Should Know?*, their next single, a non-album track, entered the U.K. charts at No. 1 the same month - a feat only a limited number of artists have ever managed to achieve. By August it had reached No. 4 in the 'States and went on to become a million-seller.

On 20th July 1983, **Duran Duran** headlined a MENCAP charity concert attended by the Prince and Princess of Wales. In November, they embarked on a five month World Tour taking in Britain, Japan, Australia, Canada and the U.S.A.

Prior to their next album *Seven And The Ragged Tiger*, they severed their relationship with producer Colin Thurston as they sought to develop a more jerky rhythmic music style. Alex Sadkin, Ian Little and the band themselves handled production on this next venture. The change of direction was successful commercially. In Briatin the album reached No. 1 during a forty-seven week chart stint. It also produced three more U.K. hit singles - *Union Of The Snake* (No. 3), *New Moon On Monday* (No. 9) and *The Reflex* (No. 1). The latter was actually remixed for 45 release by Nile Rodgers, formerly of Chic. It topped the U.K. charts for four weeks and the U.S. charts for two weeks to give the band another worldwide million-seller. *Union Of The Snake* got to No. 3 in the 'States, where *New Moon On Monday* reached No. 10 and the album peaked at No. 8. Despite the commercial success, whether the album was an artistic success is much more debatable. The songwriting and melodies are certainly weaker than on previous efforts.

Romance was clearly in the air for Roger Taylor, who married Giovanni Cantonne in Naples, Italy on 27th July 1984 and, under a month later, Nick Rhodes married U.S. model Julie Anne in London on 18th August.

After the success of *The Reflex*, **Duran Duran** secured the services of Nile Rodgers on what would be another massive hit - *The Wild Boys* (No. 2 on both sides of the Atlantic). It was kept off the top slot by Paul Hardcastle's *Nineteen*. As a quid pro quo Simon Le Bon and Andy Taylor sang backing vocals on the Sister Sledge single *Lost In Music*, which Rodgers produced.

The band's next project was a feature-length concert film. Structured around an eight-minute promo video for *The Wild Boys* (which was based on the concept of the William S. Burroughs novel of the same name), *Arena* ended up one hour long. In the film the band save the earth from the evil Dr. Duran (whose played by Milo O'Shea, who had played the same character in the film 'Barbarella'). The accompanying live album *Arena* climbed to No. 6 in the U.K. album charts in which it spent a total of 31 weeks. In the 'States, *Arena* got to No. 4 becoming their fourth million-selling album.

Duran Duran also participated in the all-star recording session for *Do They Know It's Christmas?* with Simon Le Bon handling one of the lead vocal lines. This raised the band's profile further and it was enhanced yet again when a chance meeting at a party between Nick Rhodes and the late Cubby Brocolli, led to the band being chosen to sing the soundtrack to the next Bond movie *A View To A Kill*. This is generally accepted as being one of the best Bond theme tunes. It climbed to No. 2 in Britain, where it spent sixteen weeks in the chart, whilst in the 'States it topped the charts for two weeks to give them a sixth million-selling single. With everything they touched seeming to turn to gold, suddenly things went wrong. Le Bon's voice broke disastrously halfway through a performance of *A View To A Kill*, in July 1985, during the Live Aid concert in Philadelphia. The media were preparing the band's obituary when **Duran Duran** disbanded for a while to pursue other projects. These were primarily a hard rock band Power Station and a similar sounding group Arcadia. In August 1985, Le Bon was involved in another disaster when the yacht he and the other crewmen were competing in during the gruelling Fastnet race capsized after being hit by a Force 9 gale.

When **Duran Duran** regrouped in 1986 only three of the original members remained. Roger Taylor had left Arcadia after their album had been completed due to a nervous breakdown and Andy Taylor departed to pursue a largely unsuccessful solo project. Before leaving permanently, Andy did produce some guitar parts to the *Notorious* album. The band never replaced Roger with a permanent drummer. Nile Rodgers acted as a part-time guitarist and producer on the album, which marked a further change in direction for the band. Although remaining synth-based the music was much funkier and this alienated many of their original fans. The album's title cut was released as a single. It climbed to No. 7 here in Britain but only spent six weeks in the charts overall. The album itself got to No. 16 and enjoyed a similar number of weeks in the charts overall. In the 'States both fared somewhat better, the single peaked at No. 2 and the album at No. 12.

Girls On Film later resurfaced on *New Wave Classics* (2-CD) (Disky DOU 878282) in 1998.

Duran Duran continued to record and make various comebacks in the remainder of the eighties and throughout the nineties, but their most successful days were behind them. In the early eighties, though at the helm of the New Romantics their achievements and significance were enormous. Compilations like *Decade*, *Greatest* and *Original Gold* capture this effectively.

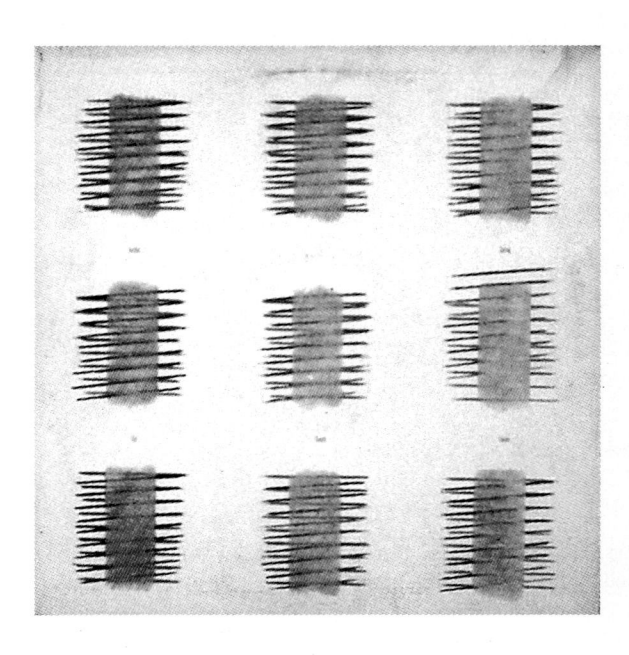

DURUTTI COLUMN - Another Setting.

Durutti Column

Personnel:
TONY BOWERS	bs	AB	
CHRIS JOYCE	drms	AB	
BRUCE MITCHELL	perc	AB	EFG HI
PHIL RAINFORD	vcls	A	
VINI REILLY	vcls	A	
DAVE ROWBOTHAM	gtr	AB	
PETER CROOKS	bs	C	
GAMMER	melody	C	
MARTIN HANNETT	switches	C	
TOBY (PHILIP TOMANOV)	drms	C	
PHIL RAYNHAM	vcls	D	
MAUNAGH FLEMING	cor anglais	FG H	
SIMON TOPPING	trumpet	F	
RICHARD HENRY	trombone	G	
TIM KELLETT	trumpet	G H	
MERVYN FLETCHER	sax	G	
CAROLINE LAVELLE	cello	G	
JOHN METCALFE	viola	HI	
ELEANOR	cello	H	

ALBUMS: (up to 1986)
- 1(C) THE RETURN OF THE DURUTTI COLUMN (Factory FACT 14) 1980
- 2(E) L C (Factory FACT 44) 1981
- 3(A) ANOTHER SETTING (Factory FACT 74) 1983
- 4(F) LIVE AT THE VENUE LONDON (VU VINI 1) 1983
- 5(G) WITHOUT MERCY (Factory FACT 84) 1984
- 6(H) CIRCUSES AND BREAD (Factory Benelux FBN 36) 1986

NB: (1) originally issued in January with a sandpaper sleeve and Martin Hannett's 'Testcard' flexi containing *First Aspect Of The Same Thing/Second Aspect Of The Same Thing* (Fact 14C). Later reissued in July without the flexi. (1) also issued on CD (Factory Too 8288292) 1996. (2) also issued on CD (Factory Too 8288272) 1996. (3) was initially issued with a perfumed cut-out insert. (4) was a limited edition release of 4,000 only. (5) was issued with stuck-on prints on the sleeve. (6) was also issued on CD (Factory FACD 1504) 1986. Also relevant are *Amigos Em Portugal (Dedications For Jacqueline)* (Fundacao Atlantica 1652071) 1983, a compilation released in Portugal; *Dome Arigato* (Factory FACD 144) 1985, a CD-only release recorded live in Japan; *Valuable Passages* (Factory FACD 164) 1986, a CD compilation; *The Durutti Column - The First Four Albums* (Factory FACD 224) 1988, a 4-CD set; and *The Sporadic Recordings* (Spore CD 1) 1989, a numbered limited edition of 4,000 compilation. There's also an interesting cassette, *The Durutti Column Live At The Bottom Line, New York* (Reach-Out International A-152) 1987, later issued on CD (Danceteria RE 152CD) 1993.

EPs: (up to 1986)
- 1(E) DEUX TRIANGLES (Favourite Painting/Zinni/Piece For Out Of Tune Grand Piano) (PS) (Factory Benelux FBN 10) 1982
- 2(E) SAY WHAT YOU MEAN, MEAN WHAT YOU SAY (Goodbye/The Room/A Little Mercy/Silence/E.E./Hello) (12", PS) (Factory FAC 114) 1986
- 3(I) GREETINGS THREE (Florence Sunset/All That Love And Maths Can Do/San Giovanni Dawn/For Friends In Italy) (12", PS) (Materialii Sonori MASO 700003) 1986

45s: (up to 1986)
- Lips That Would Kiss (From Prayers To Broken Stone)/Madeleine (12", PS) (Factory Benelux FAC BN 2) 1980
- *Enigma/Danny (PS) (Sordide Sentimentale SS 45005) 1981
- Lips That Would Kiss (From Prayers To Broken Stone)/Madeleine (PS) (Factory Benelux FAC BN 2-005) 1981
- +For Patti/Weariness And Fever (PS) (Factory Benelux FBN 100) 1982
- I Get Along Without You Pretty Well/Prayer (PS) (Factory FAC 64) 1983
- Tomorrow/Tomorrow (Live In Japan) (PS) (Factory Benelux FBN 51) 1986
- Tomorrow/Tomorrow (Live In Japan)/All That Love And Maths Can Do (12", PS) (Factory Benelux FBN 51) 1986

NB: * Only 2,730 numbered copies of this 45 were produced with a fold-out picture sleeve with inserts. + Only 100 copies of this were printed.

Along with **Joy Division**, **The Durutti Column** was one of Manchester-based Factory Records big successes of the post-punk era. Little is known about the act because its lynch pin, Manchester-born virtuoso guitarist Vini (Vincent) Reilly, has always shunned the attention of the press and little information is ever made available about the group.

Vini Reilly started playing piano as a child and then aged 10, bought and quickly learnt his first guitar. It was whilst punk rock was taking the nation by storm in 1977 that Vini joined his first group **The Nosebleeds**, who recorded a rare 45 for Rabid Records and then disbanded.

Reilly was a mate of Tony Wilson, who was hosting alternative music shows for Granada Television at the time. In January 1978, Reilly accepted an invitation from Wilson to join a group called **Durutti Column** which he was managing in his spare time. The remaining members Chris Joyce (drms), and Dave Rowbotham (gtr) had been in two earlier groups called Flashback and Fastbreeder. Shortly after Reilly joined, vocalist Phil Rainford and bassist Tony Bowers were added to the line-up. The group soon gigged at The Factory Club which Wilson had opened up in Manchester. Things didn't really work out with Rainford, who was sacked in July 1978. Then in August, the remaining members recorded two tracks; *No Communication* and *Thin Ice (Detail)* for the legendary *A Factory Sampler* (EP), with Martin Hannett producing. However, it proved to be the original line-ups only recording session as they split shortly after due to musical differences. This could well have been the end of **The Durutti Column** but wasn't because Vini Reilly decided to carry on alone. Bowers, Joyce and Rowbotham, meanwhile, formed The Moth Men.

It was January 1980 when the fruits of Reilly's labours in the recording studio with Tony Wilson during the spring and summer of 1979 were consigned to vinyl with the release of *The Return Of Durutti Column*. Housed in a sandpaper sleeve and with occasional assistance from Peter Crooks (bs) and Toby (drms) the album comprised nine classically-structured guitar pieces put through echoplex. The best of these is *Conduct*, which featured emotional electric guitar playing with peaks and troughs. Unfortunately the sandpaper sleeve had to be withdrawn because it scratched other records on the shelves, but these early copies also contained Martin Hannett's 'Testcard' flexi, which featured *First Aspect Of The Same Thing* and *Second Aspect Of The Same Thing*. The album was later reissued in a black sleeve in July 1980. The idea of the sandpaper cover seems to have come from the activities of an anarchic group in Europe called Situationist Internationale, who published a book in a sandpaper cover so that it would detroy the other books on the shelf. It seems they also used the title 'The Return Of The Durutti Column' quite frequently in their manifestos, but they also papered the walls of Strasbourg with a comic strip called 'The Return Of Durutti Column'. The name Durutti was probably after the revolutionary anarchist Buenaventura Durrutti (but it had two r's), who tried to liberate Spain in the 1930's.

In November 1980, Reilly recorded a now very rare single *Lips That Would Kiss (From Prayers To Broken Stone)*. This comprised, on both sides, simple electric guitar put through an echo unit and backed by a drum machine. Aside from his work with **Durutti Column** Reilly was also a member of **Pauline Murray**'s backing group **The Invisible Girls** during the 1980s. Before the year was out **Durutti Column** had also contributed three cuts *For Mimi*, *For Belgian Friends* and *Self-Portrait* to a Factory double 12" compilation called *A Factory Quartet*. The musical menu on offer this time was tough and strident, in marked contrast to their earlier efforts. Donald Johnson sat in on drums for these recordings.

In March 1981, a second single *Enigma/Danny* was released by the Rouen-based Sordide Sentimentale label. Just 2,730 copies were produced and lavishly packaged. Then, in April, they contributed two cuts *Sleep Will Come* (about **Joy Division**'s Ian Curtis) and *Piece For An Ideal* to the compilation cassette *From Brussels With Love* (Disques Du Crepuscule TW 1 007). This was later issued as a double album in October 1982. A second compilation appearance came on the double album *The Fruit Of Original Sin* (Disques Du Crepuscule TWI 035) 1981. The three tracks featured were a song titled *Party* and two instrumentals, *Experiment In Fifth* and *The Eye And The Hand*.

Vini recorded the second **Durutti Column** album *LC* in five hours after he'd bought a four-track Teac tape machine from guitarist Bill Nelson. It seems the title came from the Italian anarchist slogan 'Lutte Continuum' ('The Struggle Continues'). On offer here is tranquil ambient music. He sings with echoplex electric guitar and Bruce Mitchell's tranquil percussion. After its release their fans had a rare opportunity to see them on the road in quite extensive tours of Europe and North America. One reason why they didn't tour more often was that Vini, who suffered from anorexia nervosa, was often ill. **Durutti Column** were included on a cassette recording of the European package tour *Some Of The Interesting Things You See On A Long Distance Flight* (Disques Du Crepuscule TWI 081) 1982, to which they contributed *Party*. This was subsequently reissued on vinyl (TWI 082) 1983 and later on CD. As 1981 drew to a close, a tasty Vini guitar track *One*

Christmas For Our Thoughts was included on the sampler *Chantons Noel: The Ghosts Of Christmas Past* (Disques Du Crepuscule TWI 058) 1981. A re-make of this was later issued on vinyl (TWI 158) in December 1982.

With **Durutti Column** on the road much more 1982 was a quieter year on the recording front. *The Deux Triangles* 12" EP in October comprised three strange piano-dominated and somewhat avant-garde meanderings; *Favourite Painting*, *Zinni* and *Piece For Out Of Tune Grande Piano*.

By 1983 Vini was moving **Durutti Column** towards chamber music. If the 'A' side of their June single *I Get Along Without You Now* was pretty poppy, the flip side *Prayer* veered towards traditional classical music. Their third album *Another Setting*, released in August, also had a classical bent but was underminded by poor production and being badly pressed.

A rare live album *Live At The Venue London* was recorded in 1983 and released as an official bootleg on the Vu label in June. Apparently, 4,000 copies were pressed. Now a popular cult band, they toured Japan, Australasia and Eastern Europe. Vini also guested on a single by **The Wake** playing on the 'B' side *Everybody Works So Hard*.

The 1984 album *Without Mercy* was an orchestral one which put music to a Keats poem. Tony Wilson handled production and the line-up expanded to include Richard Henry (tombone), Tim Kellett (trumpet), Mervyn Fletcher (sax), Caroline Lavelle (cello) and Blaine Reininger (violin, viola). A companion EP *Say What You Mean, Mean What You Say* followed in a rough grey sleeve in January 1985. Its six tracks were quite diverse ranging from orchestral to guitar/drum machine format. Of particular note is the eerie unnerving vocal recording *The Room* about a guy waiting to be executed.

During an April 1985 tour of Japan **Durutti Column** recorded material for *Demo Arigato*, a live CD-only release. An obscure outtake of *Prayer* was also included on a Norwegian new music compilation *Sense Of Beauty*.

A new studio album *Circuses And Bread* was released in May 1986 (and available on CD a month later). It seemed to span all their musical styles and went down well with their fans. The 7" version of *Tomorrow* culled from the album was backed by a live version of the track recorded in Japan. The 12" also featured an extra cut *All That Love And Maths Can Do*. A modified line-up of Vini Reilly, Bruce Mitchell, Tim Kellett, John Metcalfe (viola), Eleanor (cello) and Manaugh Fleming were responsible for these recordings. By the Autumn of 1986, though, Kellett had departed to join former band members Chris Joyce and Tony Bowers in Simply Red and **Durutti Column** had slimmed down to a trio of Reilly, Mitchell and Metcalfe. They recorded the *Greetings Three* 12" EP, which was released in Italy but available as an import in the U.K..

As we leave the unfolding story of **The Durutti Column** in December 1986 Factory released *Valuable Passages*, a boxed cassette containing many of their finest moments and the previously unreleased *C.F.O. M.O.D.* (recorded in May of that year).

Certainly, **The Durutti Column** were one of the more interesting bands to emerge out of the new wave. The fact they survived into the nineties is testamony to their quality. Along the way they made many esoteric and collectable recordings.

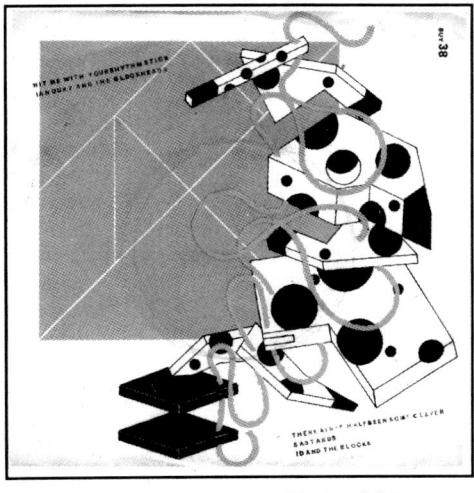

IAN DURY - Hit Me With Your Rhythm Stick.

Ian Dury (and The Blockheads)

Personnel:
IAN DURY	vcls	ABCD
CHARLIE CHARLES	drms	AB
MICKY GALLAGHER	keyb'ds	AB
CHAZ JANKEL	gtr, keyb'ds	A CD
DAVEY PAYNE	sax	AB D
JOHN TURNBALL	gtr	AB
NORMAN WATT-ROY	bs	AB
WILKO JOHNSON	gtr	B
SLY DUNBAR	drms	C
ROBBIE SHAKESPEARE	bs	C
TYRONE DOWNIE	keyb'ds	C
RAY COOPER		D

ALBUMS:
				HCP
1(A)	NEW BOOTS AND PANTIES	(Stiff SEEZ 4)	1977	5
2(A)	DO IT YOURSELF	(Stiff SEEZ 14)	1979	2
3(B)	LAUGHTER	(Stiff SEEZ 30)	1981	48
4(C)	LORD UPMINSTER	(Polydor 5042)	1981	53
5(-)	JUKE BOX DURY	(Stiff SEEZ 41)	1981	-
6(-)	GREATEST HITS	(Fame FA 3031)	1981	-
7( )	4,000 WEEKS HOLIDAY	(Polydor POLD 5112)	1984	54

NB: (7) credited to **Ian Dury** and The Music Students. (1) reissued in 1986, also on CD (Demon FIENDCD 63) 1986 and (Hit AHL CD 57) 1998. (2) reissued in 1990, also on CD (Demon FIENDCD 133) 1990 and (Hit AHL CD 58) 1998. (3) also issued on CD (Hit AHL CD 59) 1998. (4) reissued in 1989 and on CD (Great Expectations PIPCD 005) 1990. (7) reissued and on CD (Great Expectations PIPCD 004) 1990. There are also some compilations *Ian Dury And The Blockheads* (Demon FIENDCD 777) 1991; *Sex And Drugs And Rock And Roll* (Demon FIENDCD 69) 1987, also on vinyl; and *The Best Of Ian Dury* (Disky DC 869752) 1996.

45s:
Sex And Drugs And Rock And Roll/Razzle In My Pocket (PS)	(Stiff BUY 17)	1977 -
Sex And Drugs And Rock And Roll/Razzle In My Pocket (PS orange vinyl)	(Stiff BUY 17)	1977 -
Sweet Gene Vincent/You're More Than Fair (PS)	(Stiff BUY 23)	1977 -
Sex And Drugs And Rock And Roll/England's Glory/Two Steep Hills (PS)	(Stiff FREEBIE 1)	1978 -
What A Waste/Wake Up And Make Love To Me (PS)	(Stiff BUY 27)	1978 9
What A Waste/Wake Up And Make Love To Me (12" PS)	(Stiff BUY 2712)	1978 -
Hit Me With Your Rhythm Stick/Clever Bastards (PS)	(Stiff BUY 38)	1978 1
Hit Me With Your Rhythm Stick/Clever Bastards (12" PS)	(Stiff BUY 3812)	1978 -
Reasons To Be Cheerful Pt. 3/Common As Muck (PS)	(Stiff BUY 50)	1979 3
Reasons To Be Cheerful Pt. 3/Common As Muck (12" PS)	(Stiff BUY 5012)	1979 -
I Want To Be Straight/That's Not All (PS)	(Stiff BUY 90)	1980 22
I Want To Be Straight/That's Not All (12" PS)	(Stiff BUY 9012)	1980 -
Sueperman's Big Sister/You'll See Glimpses (PS)	(Stiff BUY 100)	1980 51
Spasticus Autisticus (2 versions) (PS)	(Polydor POSP 285)	1981 -
* Really Glad You Came/Inspiration (PS)	(Polydor POSP 646)	1983 -
* Very Personal/Ban The Bomb (PS)	(Polydor POSP 673)	1984 -
Very Personal/Ban The Bomb/The Sky Is The Limit	(Polydor POSPX 673)	1984 -
Profoundly In Love With Pandora/Eugenios (PS)	(EMI EMI 5534)	1985 45
Profoundly In Love With Pandora/Eugenios (pic disc)	(EMI EMIP 5534)	1985 -

Reissues:
What A Waste/Wake Up And Make Love To Me (PS)	(Stiff BUY 135)	1981 -
Hit Me With Your Rhythm Stick/Sex And Drugs And Rock And Roll (PS)	(Stiff BUY 214)	1984 55
Hit Me With Your Rhythm Stick/Sex And Drugs And Rock And Roll (PS)	(Stiff BUY 214)	1985 -
Reasons To Be Cheerful Pt. 3/Wake Up And Make Love To Me (PS)	(Stiff BUYIT 214)	1985 -
Hit Me With Your Rhythm Stick (2nd remix)/	(Flying FLYR 1)	1991 73

Ian Dury was born on 12th May 1942 in Upminster, Essex. He contracted polio at the age of seven, probably after a visit to a Southend swimming pool. This had a profound effect on his life leaving him partially crippled. He entered the music business in November 1970, forming Kilburn and The High Roads, initially as a part-time band, whilst he was lecturing at Canterbury College Of Art. In December 1971, they played their first gigs at Croydon School Of Art and Canterbury College Of Art.

They started out playing the London pub circuit in January 1973. The openings were initially instigated by Dave Robinson, who later became the managing director of Stiff Records. They were spotted playing the London pub circuit by Charlie Gillett, who briefly became their manager. He was soon succeeded by Dave Robinson. Those early days were hard. At one stage their transit van more or less fell to pieces. It was only thanks to the comradeship of three fellow pub-rockers on the London circuit (Bees Make Honey, Ducks Deluxe and Brinsley Schwarz) playing a benefit show at Camden Town Hall to raise money to pay the repair bill that they were able to continue gigging. Later that year their support slot to The Who brought them wider exposure.

In January 1974, Kilburn and The High Roads signed to WEA's Raft label. They recorded an album, produced by Tony Ashton, which wasn't issued when the label closed down, but was given an airing in the U.K. in 1978 after Dury became famous. They went on to record an album *Handsome* and a couple of 45s for Dawn, before splitting in the summer of 1975, disillusioned at their lack of success.

In November 1975, Dury bounced back with a new six-piece group Ian Dury and The Kilburns. In March 1976, Chaz Jankel (ex-Byzantium) joined on keyboards and started a songwriting partnership with Ian Dury. When the group split in June, (largely because Dury's doctor ordered him off the road for health reasons) he continued writing with Jankel material, for what later become his first solo album.

Back on the road Dury signed to Dave Robinson's Stiff Records in August 1977. Punk rock was now in full swing, but Dury who'd been on the scene since the start of the decade, should by rights have been one of the old farts punk was committed to blowing away. Far from it, like **Elvis Costello**, Ian Dury became something of a role model for the punk movement. His use of working class idiom and the humour of his lyrics made him acceptable to the punk audience, although his sort of jazzy style of music was some way wide of the normal punk format.

On 12th December 1977, the band recorded their only session for John Peel. This featured four of their best songs: *Sex And Drugs And Rock And Roll*, *Clever Trevor*, *Sweet Gene Vincent* and *Blockheads*.

His first single, *Sex And Drugs And Rock And Roll*, in August 1978, epitomised what life was all about for large numbers of people. It was one of his finest moments but surprisingly did not chart. Then Ian Dury and The Blockheads was put together for the 'Stiff Live Stiffs' U.K. promotional tour in September 1977. This line-up utilised several of the session men Dury and Jankel had used to record his debut album *New Boots And Panties*. Watt-Roy, Charles, Gallagher and Turnball had all previously played in Loving Awareness. Watt-Roy and Charles had also been part of Glencoe, whilst Gallagher had figured in Frampton's Camel too and Payne had been **Wreckless Eric**'s saxophonist. The promotional album that followed contains Ian Dury and The Blockheads playing *Billericay Dickie* and *Wake Up And Make Love To Me*, whilst all the artists on the tour join together for a rendition of *Sex Drugs Rock & Roll & Chaos* on the final cut of the *Stiff Live Stiffs* (Stiff GET 1) 1978 tour album.

New Boots And Panties is one of the masterpieces of the punk era. A brilliant album - originality, energy, wit and humour. It had it all and was unlike anything heard before. Aside from *Sex And Drugs And Rock And Roll*, which wasn't listed on the cover, it had several other highs. Outrageous numbers like *Plaistow Patricia*, *Billericay Dickie*, *Clever Trevor* and *Blockheads* deal with characters from working class life in their lyrics. Other songs like *Sweet Gene Vincent*, *My Old Man* and *If I Was With A Woman* display a more sensitive side, whilst *Wake Up And Make Love To Me!* demonstrated that this sensitivity could extend to the music too. Although a second solo 45 culled from the album *Sweet Gene Vincent* failed to chart, the album itself enjoyed something of the success it deserved. It climbed to No. 5, here in the U.K., where it spent in total of 90 weeks in the charts.

In March 1978, the band toured the 'States supporting Lou Reed. As a result *New Boots And Panties* climbed to No. 168 in the U.S. charts in May. The same month Dury enjoyed his first U.K. hit with *What A Waste*, which made the Top Ten. To help promote the 45, they toured the U.K. with comedian Max Wall as support act. Wall recorded a version of Dury's *England's Glory*, which was put out on Stiff. The following month, Humphrey Ocean, a friend from Dury's art school days, covered Dury's *Whoops A Daisy*. The result was released by Stiff. During 1978 'Sounds' collaborated with Stiff to produce *Can't Start Dancin'* (Stiff/Sounds 3) and both *Sex Drugs And Rock And Roll* and *Razzle In My Pocket* were included on it. *Sex And Drugs And Rock And Roll* and *What A Waste* were both included on the soundtrack *That Summer!* (Spartan/Arista SPART 1088) in 1979.

In January 1979, Dury's 45 magnum opus *Hit Me With Your Rhythm Stick* topped the U.K. charts for a week. A superb single and great dance number, it simply exuded raw drive and energy. This was one of the finest 45s of the punk era.

The *Do It Yourself* album, released in June 1979 in a variety of "wallpaper pattern" sleeve designs, marked a move away from the coarse music of *New Boots And Panties* to a more sophisticated sound which trangressed both rock 'n' roll and disco. Notable cuts included the upbeat *Dance Of The Screamers* and *Sink My Boats* and the more relaxed *Inbetweenies*. The album reached No. 2 here in the U.K. and No. 126 in the U.S.A.. Unusually none of the cuts were released as 45s, although *Hit Me With Your Rhythm Stick* was added as a bonus 45.

The band's next 45 was the unusual *Reasons To Be Cheerful Pt. 3*, which embraced both R&B and disco flavours, to make the U.K. Top 3 in August 1979. In December Dury played at the People Of Kampuchea concert at London's Hammersmith Odeon.

In July 1980, Wilko Johnson, formerly of Dr. Feelgood and The Solid Senders, joined on guitar. He replaced Chas Jankel, who left to go solo. This marked a decline for the band whose material was seldom as strong again. In September, *I Want To Be Straight*, the band's first recording with Johnson, was decent enough and reached No. 22. It was followed by *Sueperman's Big Sister* in November. A taster from their next album, this couldn't quite make the Top 50. The wrong spelling was deliberate to avoid copyright problems. The album *Laughter* is disappointing. It contains a perponderance of rather lacklustre funk-rock tracks like *Take Your Elbow Out Of The Soup You're Sitting On Chicken* and *Superman's Big Sister*, but there's also more whimsical material which doesn't really work.

In December 1980, the band embarked on a U.K. "Soft As A Baby's Bottom" tour to help promote *Laughter*, which climbed to No. 48 here and No. 159 in the 'States. After this Dury disbanded The Blockheads and quit Stiff. He signed to Polydor Worldwide and recorded a new 45, *Spasticus Autisticus* for 'Year Of The Disabled'. It failed to chart, when radio stations refused to play it and was deleted within a month.

In October 1981, he re-united with Dankel and put together a new band (line-up 'C') to record *Lord Upminster* at Nassau in the Bahamas. The album was funky but the material was weak compared to his earlier efforts. Only one cut on *Lord Upminster* is noteworthy and that's *Spasticus (Autisticus)* which got banned by the BBC by referring to physically handicapped people (of which Dury was one) in a mildy humorous way.

If you don't have any other Ian Dury releases you may be interested in *Juke Box Dury*, a compilation released by Stiff in November 1981. It contains their best Stiff 45s and a few select album cuts. Surprisingly, though, it didn't chart.

The Blockheads continued to record unsuccessfully for a while without Dury, for whom 1982 and 1983 were quiet years in musical terms. He returned, eventually, in early 1984 with *4,000 Weeks Holiday*. This was credited to Ian Dury and The Music Students. In fact the album had been scheduled for release the previous year but Polydor refused to until a song about holiday tycoon Billy Butlin and another titled *Fuck Off Noddy* were removed. The album's cover had a homemade look but the music on offer was pretty slickly produced soul, though delivered in Dury's speak-singing style. The album reached No. 54 in the U.K., but the two cuts chosen for 45 release, *Very Personal* and the political *Ban The Bomb*, did not chart. This 45 ended his relatively unsuccessful period with Polydor.

In 1985, Dury teamed up again with The Blockheads for live work. He returned to the charts in November when *Profoundly In Love With Pandora*, his theme, from the TV series 'The Secret Diary Of Adrian Mole' reached No. 45 in the singles charts. Over the coming years he went solo but reformed The Blockheads for two reunion gigs during 1990. As his recording career waned, he concentrated more on acting, writing songs and painting. Jankel also went solo, whilst Watt-Roy and Turnbull were later in the Captains Of Industry with **Wreckless Eric**.

Sex And Drugs And Rock And Roll released on Demon in 1987 was a re-work of Stiff's *Juke Box Dury* compilation (which itself was later reissued on Fame as *Greatest Hits*), which omitted *Wake Up* and *Sweet Gene Vincent* in favour of two more obscure tracks. Side one is consistently good and includes two of their finest moments *Hit Me With Your Rhythm Stick* and *Reasons To Be Cheerful Pt. 3* (the 7" version), but by comparison side two is rather patchy.

In 1991, *Sex And Drugs And Rock & Roll* figured on *Punk And Disorderly: New Wave 1976 - 81* (Telstar STAR 2520) and again, in 1995, on *The Best Punk Album In The World.... Ever, Vol. 1* (2-CD) (Virgin VTDCD 42); *Vol. 2* (2-CD) (Virgin VTDCD 79) included *Sweet Gene Vincent*, whilst *The Best Punk Anthems.... Ever* (2-CD) (Virgin VTDCD 198) 1998 also included *Sex And Drugs And Rock & Roll*. In 1999, one of his finest *Sex And Drugs And Rock And Roll* was included on *1-2-3-4 - A History Of Punk And New Wave 1976 - 1979* (MCA/universal MCD 60066), a 5-CD box set compilation.

Films **Dury** appeared in include 'Number One' (1987), 'Pirates' (1986) and 'Hearts Of Fire' (1987). TV plays have included 'King Of The Ghettos' (1986), 'Talk Of The Devil' (1986) and 'Night Moves' (1987). He also worked on many commercials.

Sadly, in recent years, he became engaged in a battle against cancer, which he finally succumbed to on 27th March 2000, aged 57. In April 2001, he was honoured by a tribute album, a new version of his 1977 album *New Boots And Panties*. Available as a CD, cassette and limited edition gold vinyl release it includes the following stars performing its original tracks:- *Wake Up And Make Love With Me* (Sinead O'Connor), *Sweet Gene Vincent* (Robbie Williams), *I'm Partial To Your Abracadabra* (Paul McCartney), *My Old Man* (Madness), *Billericay Dickie* (Billy Bragg and The Blokes), *Clevor Trevor* (**Wreckless Eric**), *If I Was With A Woman* (Cerys Matthews of Catatonia), *Blockheads* (Grant Nicholas of Feeder), *Plaistow Patricia* (Shane McGowan) and *Blackmail Man* (Keith Allen).

IAN DURY - NEW BOOTS AND PANTIES.

Dyaks

Personnel:	GROLL EVANS	bs	A
	BRIAN NEVILL	drms	A
	CHRIS REEVES	gtr, vcls	A

45: Gutter Kids/It's A Game (PS) (Bonaparte BONE 2) 1978

This seems to have been a one-off effort. *It's A Game* can also be heard on *Punk Rock Rarities, Vol. 2* (Anagram CDPUNK 83) 1996.

Earthbound

Personnel incl: JUTTA NEINHAUS vcls

EP: 1 Liberated Lady/The Robot/
Song For South Kensington (12") (Archway CHS 308) 1979

45: Liberated Lady/The Robot (PS) (Archway CHS 308) 1979

The 12" EP came in a laminated cover, with lyrics and was produced by the group with ex-White Noise member David Vorhaus. It's an attempt at erotica-rock with absurdly contorted vocals. Very hard to listen to.

East End Badoes

Personnel incl: TERRY HAYES
ANDY RUSSELL

One of the more obscure Oi! Bands, they contributed one track *The Way It's Gonna Be* to the *Back On The Street* (EP) (Secret SHH 138), which was originally given away with *Oi! Oi! That's Yer Lot* (Secret SEC 5) in 1983. It can also be heard on *Secret Records Punk Singles Collection, Vol. 2* (Anagram CDPUNK 60) 1995.

They included DJ Terry Hayes, who along with Terry Adams ran the infamous Oi! The Disco at the Ancient Brit - the subject matter of **Cock Sparrer**'s *Argy Bargy*.

Eater

Personnel:	ANDY BLADE	vcls	ABC
	BRIAN CHEVETTE	gtr	ABC
	PHIL ROWLAND	drms	A
	IAN WOODCOCK	bs	ABC
	SOCIAL DEMISE	drms	B
	ROGER "DEE GENERATE" BULLEN	drms	C

ALBUMS: 1(C) THE ALBUM (The Label LP 001) 1977
2(-) THE HISTORY OF EATER (De Lorean EAT 1) 1985

NB: (1) later reissued on vinyl (Get Back GET 27 LP) 1998 with four bonus cuts. (2) 1,000 copies were issued in either red, white or blue vinyl. Each came with a free 45 (EAT FREEBIE 1) which did not have a picture sleeve. Other copies came on green vinyl without the 45. There's also a CD compilation, *The Compleat Eater* (Anagram CD PUNK 10) 1993. An alternative collection is *All Of Eater* (Creativeman Disc CMD 024) 1998.

EP: 1( ) GET YOUR YO-YO'S OUT (Debutantes' Ball/No More/
Thinking Of The U.S.A./
Holland (PS) (The Label TLR 007) 1978

NB: (1) issued in both 7" and 12" formats on white vinyl with blue, green or red picture sleeves.

45s: Outside View/You (PS) (The Label TLR 001) 1977
Thinking Of The U.S.A./Space Dreamin'/
Michael's Monetary System (PS) (The Label TLR 003) 1977
Lock It Up/Jeepster (PS) (The Label TLR 004) 1977
Lock It Up/Jeepster (12", PS) (The Label TLR 004/12) 1977
What She Wants She Needs/
Reaching For The Sky (PS) (The Label TLR 009) 1978

Eater were the youngest punk band around when they formed in 1976. The 14 and 15 year olds were still at school! Their youth perhaps went some way to explain their yobbish behaviour, which attracted some press attention in their early days but did more harm in the long run.

Their first live gig was in November 1976 in Manchester, when they had **The Buzzcocks** as their support! Their recording debut came when they contributed two cuts, *15* and *Don't Need It* to the *Live At The Roxy* (Harvest SHSP 4069) compilation. This was originally released in June 1977. It was later re-released on Receiver (RR 132) in 1991.

They were signed by The Label, a new London indie, and their debut 45, *Outside View*, came out in March 1977. Much of their music comprised cover versions. They were particularly partial to Velvet Underground material (*I'm Waiting For The Man* and *Sweet Jane*). They also revived Alice Cooper's *15*. None of their material - several singles, an EP (*Get Your Yo-Yo's Out* was an oblique reference to The Rolling Stones) and one album - made much impact. They were basically young kids, striving to master their instruments and out to shock.

Most of the material on *The Compleat Eater* compilation was taken from their debut album. It's okay punk with some decent **Buzzcocks**-style guitar work at times. Alternatively, *The Album* was reissued in 1998 on Get Back with extensive liner notes from former **Eater** member Andy Blade and four extra cuts that weren't on the original release.

Waiting For The Man later resurfaced on *Punk Lost And Found* (Shanachie SH 5705) 1996. You can also hear *Thinking Of The U.S.A.*, arguably their finest moment, on the 5-CD compilation box set *1-2-3-4 - A History Of Punk And New Wave 1976 - 1979* (MCA/Universal MCD 60066) 1999. It had previously appeared on *Burning Ambitions, Vol. 2 (A History Of Punk)* (Anagram CDPUNK 81) in 1996.

They split at the end of the seventies. Andy Blade went solo but with little success. Dee Generate ended up as a social worker! An earlier drummer for the band was Phil Rowland, who was later with **Studio Sweethearts** and **Slaughter and The Dogs**.

Echo and The Bunnymen

Personnel:
IAN McCULLOCH	vcls, gtr		AB
LES PATTINSON	bs		AB
WILL SERGEANT	lead gtr		AB
'ECHO'	(a drum machine)		A
PETE DE FREITAS	drms		B

ALBUMS: (up to 1986)
				HCP
1(B)	CROCODILES	(Korova KODE 1)	1980	17
2(B)	HEAVEN UP HERE	(Korova KODE 3)	1981	10
3(B)	PORCUPINE	(Korova KODE 6)	1983	2
4(B)	OCEAN RAIN	(Korova KODE 8)	1984	4
5(B)	SONGS TO LEARN AND SING	(Korova KODE 13)	1985	6

NB: (1) Early pressings came with a free single *Do It Clean/Read It In Books* (Sam 128). (1) also issued on CD (Korova 2423162) 1989. (2) also issued on CD (Korova 2423172) 1988. (3) Early pressings included a free cassette of the group's sessions on the John Peel Show. (3) also issued on CD (Korova 2400272) 1988. (4) also issued on CD (Korova 2403882) 1984. (5) issued with a free 7" reissue of *The Pictures On My Wall* plus a lyric booklet, some copies were signed. There was also a picture disc release (KODE 13P), which came without the lyric sheet or free 7". A later singles compilation is *The Cutter* (WEA 4509-91886-2) 1993. Fans will also want to check out *The Peel Sessions* (Strange Fruit SFPSD 060) 1994 and the CD *Ballyhoo (The Best Of Echo And The Bunnymen)* (Korova TEN 0630191032) 1997.

EP:
				HCP
1(B)	SHINE SO HARD (Crocodiles/Zimbo/Over The Wall/ All That Jazz) (live) (12", PS)	(Korova ECHOZ 1)	1981	37

NB: (1) also issued as a cassette (Korova ECHO 1M) 1981.

45s: (up to 1986)
			HCP
*	The Pictures On My Wall/ Read It In Books (PS)	(Zoo CAGE 004) 1979	-
+	Rescue/Simple Stuff (PS)	(Korova KOW 1) 1980	-
	Rescue/Simple Stuff/Pride (12", PS)	(Korova KOW 1T) 1980	-
	The Puppet/Do It Clean (PS)	(Korova KOW 11) 1980	-
	A Promise/Broke My Neck (PS)	(Korova KOW 15) 1981	49
	A Promise/Broke My Neck (Long Version) (12", PS)	(Korova KOW 15T) 1981	-
	The Back Of Love/The Subject (PS)	(Korova KOW 24) 1982	19
	The Back Of Love/The Subject/Fuel (12", PS)	(Korova KOW 24T) 1982	-
x	The Cutter/Way Out And Up We Go (PS)	(Korova KOW 26) 1983	8
#	The Cutter/Way Out And Up We Go/Zimbo (live) (12", PS)	(Korova KOW 26T) 1983	-
	Never Stop/Heads Will Roll (PS)	(Korova KOW 28) 1983	15
	Never Stop (Discotheque)/Heads Will Roll (Summer Version)/ The Original Cutter (A Drop In The Ocean) (12", PS)	(Korova KOW 28T) 1983	-
	The Killing Moon/Do It Clean (PS)	(Korova KOW 32) 1984	9
%	The Killing Moon (All Night Version)/The Killing Moon/Do It Clean (live) (12", PS)	(Korova KOW 32T) 1984	-
	Silver/Angels And Devils (PS)	(Korova KOW 34) 1984	30
	Silver (Tidal Wave)/Silver/Angels And Devils (12", PS)	(Korova KOW 34T) 1984	-
	Seven Seas/All You Need Is Love (PS)	(Korova KOW 35) 1984	16
α	Seven Seas/All You Need Is Love/The Killing Moon/Stars Are Stars (Acoustic Version)/Villiers Terrace (Acoustic Version) (7" double-pack)	(Korova KOW 35F/SAM 202) 1984	-
β	Seven Seas/All You Need Is Love/The Killing Moon/Stars Are Stars (Acoustic Version)/Villiers Terrace (Acoustic Version) (12", PS)	(Korova KOW 35T) 1984	-
χ	Bring On The Dancing Horses/Over Your Shoulder (PS)	(Korova KOW 43) 1985	21
	Bring On The Dancing Horses/Over Your Shoulder/Villiers Terrace/Monkeys (7" double-pack)	(Korova KOW 43 F/SAM 269) 1985	-
	Bring On The Dancing Horses (Extended)/Over Your Shoulder/Red Bugs And Ballyhoo (12", PS)	(Korova KOW 43 T) 1985	-

NB: * Only 4,000 copies were issued with *The Revenge Of Voodoo Billy* scratched in the 'B' side. There were two different colour combinations:- blue lettering on yellow and green on light grey. + The 7" version came in two different picture sleeves. x Some copies came with a free cassette which featured *The Cutter, Villiers Terrace, Ashes To Ashes (Stars Are Stars), Monkeys* and *Read It In Books* (KOW 26C). # Some copies came with a poster. % Some copies came with a free songsheet. α This numbered limited edition came in a gatefold sleeve with a booklet. β The 12" version came in two different sleeves. χ There was also a picture disc version which was cow-shaped and housed in a stickered PVC sleeve.

In the spring of 1977, Julian Cope, Ian McCulloch and Pete Wylie formed The Crucial Three. The group never advanced beyond the rehearsal stage, although its three members would go onto far greater fame. In the summer of 1978, Cope and McCulloch came together again for a new venture, A Shallow Madness, but again mostly musical differences rendered this short-lived.

Eventually McCulloch got his group together with chef **Will Sergeant** and initially a drum machine they christened Echo. Shortly before their live debut at Eric's in Liverpool Les Pattison joined as bassist and **Echo and The Bunnymen** were born. They performed a 15-minute version of *Monkeys*.

Their first single *The Pictures On My Wall / Read It In Books* came out on the local Zoo label in March 1979 produced by David Balfe and Bill Drummond. It became an NME 'Single of the Week'. *The Pictures On My Wall* was essentially an acoustic version, although it was re-recorded in a more complex format for their debut album. *Read It In Books* was a song McCulloch wrote about Julian Cope. The red Bunnymen on the picture sleeve soon became the group's insignia.

In August 1979, the band recorded their first session for John Peel. David Balfe stood in on keyboards. With a number of record companies interested the band eventually signed to Sire, but their releases were out out on their own Korova subsidiary. This was named after the milk bar in 'Clockwork Orange'! In October, the band replaced 'Echo' (their drum machine) with Pete De Freitas, a friend of David Balfe's brother who was born in Trinidad. De Freitas turned his back on the opportunity of a University education to join them.

Their second single *Rescue* was the first to appear on Korova. A more confident effort than their first, it appeared in April 1980 in both 7" and 12" formats, the latter also featured an additional track *Pride*. It was enthusiastically received by the critics. When their first album arrived in July its many reviews compared it to sixties outfits like The Doors, Velvet Underground and 13th Floor Elevators, but everyone acknowledged that **Echo and The Bunnymen** were far more than mere copyists and added their own unique interpretation to the music. As a marketing ploy a free single, *Do It Clean / Read It In Books* was available with a copy of the album, but you had to write to the record company to get a copy. This single is now one of the rarest **Echo and The Bunnymen** artefacts. The album, which included *Pictures On My Wall* and *Rescue*, sold well climbing to No. 17 in the charts during a six week residency. It established McCulloch as a heavyweight vocalist and heralded the band as one of the most exciting acts around.

In comparison to previous efforts their next 45, a non-album effort released in September 1980 *The Puppet* was disappointing. It had an interesting raga section in the middle but lacked the melody of their earlier efforts and it didn't make the charts.

The band's stage act in this era was quite a spectacle, with McCulloch clad in army clothing amidst a camouflage background and liberal use of dry ice. During this period they played a 'secret' gig at the Winter Gardens, Buxton. To get a free ticket you had to apply to Zoo. Their next vinyl release in April *Shine So Hard* was an EP that had been recorded at Buxton. It was released without the group's full blessing but brought them further commercial success spending four weeks in the charts and climbing to No. 37. It was also available as a cassette.

Their second album *Heaven Up Here* followed in May. It was a denser, less accessible work than *Crocodiles*, characterised by scratching guitars and a plethora of drums. The disc was voted 'Album Of The Year' by NME readers. It improved on the performance of its predecessor, climbing to No. 10 and spending sixteen weeks in the charts. *A Promise* was the only cut with much commercial potential and this was remixed and issued as a 45 in July. A previously unissued edited live cut, recorded in Sweden, *Broke My Neck* was put on the flip side, but the 12" release featured the full unedited version. *A Promise* became a minor hit, working its way to No. 49 during its four week chart sojourn.

1982 saw the band release just one 45. *The Back Of Love* in May. It became their first Top Twenty hit climbing to No. 19 and spending seven weeks in the chart. It also helped to introduce the band to a younger audience. Earlier in February, **Will Sergeant** released a solo album *Themes For Grind* on his own 92 Happy Customers label. This was a weird, experimental, instrumental effort.

The remainder of the year was spent writing new materal which eventually appeared on their third album *Porcupine*, released in January 1983. The cover pictured the band in the snow-covered mountains of Iceland, reflecting their obsession with rugged scenery at that time. The album was a fine collection of bizarre, challenging songs on which their earlier 45 *The Back Of Love* and their contemporary 45 *The Cutter* stood out. The latter brought them their biggest hit to date, climbing to No. 8 during its eight week chart stay. It was a superb song, featuring a startling raga-like use of bagpipes. It appeared in three different formats. The 7" had the otherwise unavailable *Way Out And Up We Go* on the flip; the 12" added an additional track *Zimbo* and there was also a five-track cassette-only single featuring *The Cutter, Villiers Terrace, Ashes To Ashes, Monkeys* and *Read It In Books*. Added interest was given to the album by Ravi Shankar's offbeat violin insertions and this too brought them much success. It rose to No. 2 and spent seventeen weeks in the chart in all.

In the summer of 1983, **Echo and The Bunnymen** embarked on a tour which encompassed several remote Scottish Isles. A new single *Never Stop* was released to coincide with the tour. The tour culminated with some gigs at the Royal Albert Hall.

The Killing Moon, released in January 1984, was possibly their best 45 yet. It again experimented successfully with raga elements and rose to No. 9 during its six week chart stay. Their fourth album *Ocean Rain* followed in April. Again McCulloch's strong vocals and Sergeants' varied guitar playing stand out and there are a number of fine tracks *The Killing Moon, Seven Seas, Crystal Days* and *Silver*. The latter was culled for 45 release and, although less successful than its recent predecessors still made the Top 30. *Seven Seas* was later released as a single in July and fared better, peaking at No. 16 during its seven week chart stay. Overall the fully orchestrated *Ocean Rain* is usually considered the band's masterpiece. It certainly spent the largest time in the charts - a massive twenty-six weeks but with the best position of No. 4 - two lower than *Porcupine*.

In December 1984, McCulloch released a solo 45, a cover of the Kurt Weill/Maxwell Anderson composition *September Song*, but it failed to sell in significant quantities.

During 1985, **Echo and The Bunnymen** toured Scandinavia in April and released a compilation *Songs To Learn And Sing* in November. This was preceded by a new single *Bring On The Dancing Horses* in October. This spent seven weeks in the charts, missing the Top 20 by just one place. The compilation featured all their singles from *Rescue* onwards, which guaranteed it was superb. The CD version featured four extra cuts; *Pride, Simple Stuff, Read It In Books* and *Angels And Devils*. For those people who weren't diehard fans and didn't have all the singles already it was just what was needed. It gave the band another Top Ten Album, enjoying fifteen weeks in the chart and a best position of No. 6.

As we leave the band in 1986 they were undergoing their first personnel upheaval since Pete De Freitas joined them in October 1979. De Freitas now left to play with The Sex Gods, a band of friends and Bunnymen roadies. In his place ex-Haircut 100 drummer Blair Cunningham was recruited for a U.S. tour, with Dave Palmer (ex-ABC) and Stephen Morris (of **New Order**) being pulled in to work on a new album. In the event De Freitas rejoined the band in August and the album was re-recorded with him. The band would survive until the summer of 1992 (without McCulloch for much of 1986 and 1989) and Pete De Freitas from June 1989 onwards, as he was tragically killed in a motorcycle accident.

Up to 1986 the group made a few compilation appearances. The first was the inclusion of *Monkeys* on *Street To Street: A Liverpool Album* (Open Eye OE LP 501) 1979, which is long deleted. A live version of *The Puppet*, not issued elsewhere was included on the double compilation *Urgh! A Music War* (A&M) 1981. Finally, the original version of *The Pictures On My Wall* was included on the cherished *To The Shores Of Lake Placid* (Zoo ZOO 4) 1982 compilation, which came in a gatefold sleeve with a four page booklet.

The Cutter (subtitled *12 Classic Tracks*) includes *Crocodiles, A Promise* and *Kingdom*, a live version of *Paint It Black* and Julian Cope and Ian McCulloch's *Read It In Books*. Also included is a cover of *All You Need Is Love* that they did for Channel 4's 'Playing At Home' series, which turned up originally on the flip side to the *Seven Seas* 45.

The Peel Sessions CD is taken from a late night session taped in August 1979 after the appearance of the band's debut 45, *Pictures On My Wall* but before the release of their first album. It was shortly before drummer Pete De Freitas joined the group and David Balfe (later keyboardist for **Teardrop Explodes** and co-founder of Food Records) handled percussion on this session. The featured songs were *Read It In Books* (co-written with Julian Cope), *Stars Are Stars* and *Bagsy Yours* (an early version of *Monkeys*). The session is a worthwhile artefact but only just under thirteen minutes long. The latest 'best of' collection to their material is *Ballyhoo (The Best Of Echo And The Bunnymen)*.

Echo and The Bunnymen were one of the finest groups out of Liverpool since The Beatles and as part of the 'new wave' produced some of the most interesting and imaginative music of the early eighties.

ECHO AND THE BUNNYMEN - Crocodiles.

Eddie and The Hot Rods

Personnel:			
	PAUL GRAY	bs	AB
	DAVE HIGGS	gtr	ABC
	LEW LEWIS	mouth harp	A
	BARRIE MASTERS	vcls	ABC
	STEVE NICOL	drms	AB
	GRAEME DOUGLAS	gtr	BC
	T.C.	bs	C

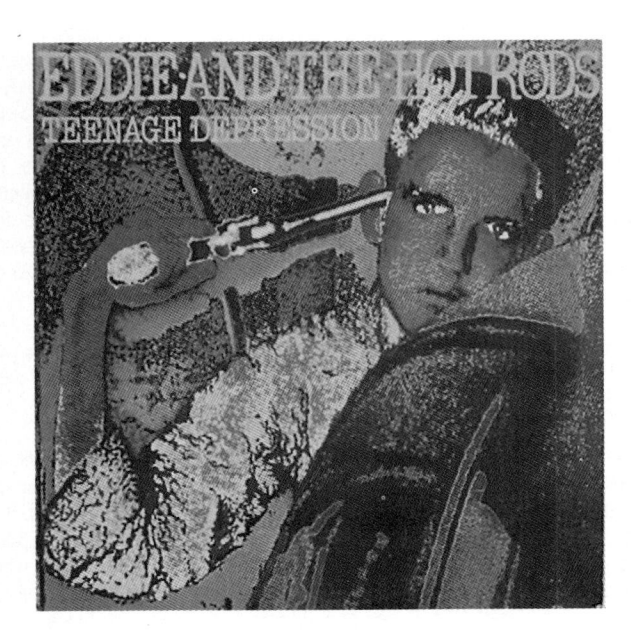

EDDIE AND THE HOT RODS - Teenage Depression.

				HCP
ALBUMS:	1(A)	TEENAGE DEPRESSION	(Island ILPS 9457)	1976 43
	2(B)	LIFE ON THE LINE	(Island ILPS 9509)	1977 27
	3(B)	THRILLER	(Island ILPS 9563)	1979 50
	4(C)	FISH AND CHIPS	(EMI EMI 3344)	1980 -

NB: (1) also issued on CD (Edsel EDCD 563) 1998 and again (Captain Oi! AHOY CD 132) 2000 with twelve bonus cuts. (2) reissued on CD (Captain Oi! AHOY CD 133) 2000 with nine bonus cuts. There are also a few relevant compilations, *Curse Of The Hot Rods* (Hound Dog BUT 002) 1990, also on CD (Link LINK CD 157) 1992, *Live And Rare* (CD) (live) (Receiver RRCD 177) 1993, *The End Of The Beginning (The Best Of)* (CD) (Island IMCD 156) 1994, *Doing Anything They Wanna Do....* (Anagram CDMGRAM 108) 1996, *Gasoline Days* (Creative Man CMCD 008) 1996, *Get Your Balls Off* (Skydog 622412) 1996 and *Ties That Bind* (Dojo DOJOCD 173) 1994 have also been paired on one CD. Also of interest is *BBC Radio One Live In Concert* (Windsong WINDCD 062) 1994.

				HCP
EPs:	1(A)	LIVE AT THE MARQUEE (96 Tears/ Get Out Of Denver/ Medley: Gloria-Satisfaction) (PS)	(Island IEP 2)	1976 43
	2(B)	LIVE AT THE SPEED OF SOUND (Hard Drivin' Man/ Horseplay/Double Checkin' Woman/All I Need Is Money/On The Run) (PS)	(Island IEP 5)	1977 -

NB: (2) was issued in 7" format with a picture sleeve and as a 12" with a plain sleeve.

			HCP
45s:	*	Writing On The Wall/ Cruisin' (In The Lincoln) (some PS)	(Island WIP 6270) 1976 -
		Wooly Bully/Horseplay (Weary Of The Schmaltz) (PS)	(Island WIP 6306) 1976 -
		Teenage Depression/Shake (PS)	(Island WIP 6354) 1976 35
		I Might Be Lying/Ignore Them (PS)	(Island WIP 6388) 1977 44
	+	Do Anything You Wanna Do/ Schoolgirl Love (PS)	(Island WIP 6401) 1977 9
	+	Do Anything You Wanna Do/Schoolgirl Love (12", white stickered sleeve)	(Island 12WIP 6401) 1977 -
		Quit This Town/ Distortion May Be Expected (PS)	(Island WIP 6411) 1977 36
	#	Till The Night Is Gone/Flipside Rock	(Island WIP 6418) 1977 -
		Life On The Line/Do Anything You Wanna Do (live) (PS)	(Island WIP 6438) 1977 -
		Life On The Line/Do Anything You Wanna Do/ (I Don't Know) What's Really Going On/ Why Can't It Be (live) (12", PS)	(Island 12 WIP 6438) 1977 -
		Media Messiahs/ Horror Through The Straighness	(Island WIP 6464) 1978 -
		Power And The Glory/ Highlands One, Hopefuls Two	(Island WIP 6474) 1979 -
		At Night/You'd Better Run/ Looking Around (PS)	(EMI EMI 5052) 1980 -
		Wide Eyed Kids/Leave Us Alone	(EMI EMI 5110) 1980 -
		Farther On Down The Road/ Fish 'n' Chips	(EMI EMI 5160) 1981 -
		Fought For You/Hey Tonight (PS)	(Waterfront WP 59) 1984 -

NB: * There were some promo copies of this 45 in generic title picture sleeves (WIP 6270 DJ). Some copies of the release came in black and white picture sleeves. + Credited to The Rods. # Featured ex-MC5 member Rob Tyner on vocals and credited to Rob Tyner and The Hotrods.

Eddie and The Hotrods were formed in the Canvey Island and Southend area in 1975 by amateur boxer Barrie Masters. In their early days they played a high energy form of R&B, very similar to Dr. Feelgood. Their manager, lyricist and producer Ed Hollis got them a contract with Island Records and they became a regular attraction on the London pub circuit. Before long, the punky persona of their vocalist Barrie Masters and their youthful image, saw them being lumped together with the growing punk rock wave, in the music press at least.

Their early 45s included a zippy rendition of Sam The Sham and The Pharoah's *Wooly Bully*. They reached the Top 50 with their third release, *Live At The Marquee* (EP). They were a great live band and this captured them at their best. However, it comprised four high energy cover versions; *96 Tears* (? and The Mysterians), *Get Out Of Denver* (Bob Seger), *Gloria* (Them) and *Satisfaction* (The Rolling Stones).

They built on this success with *Teenage Depression*, their first album, released in December 1976. Musically, fairly simple R&B-influenced rock was on offer, but the high energy format fitted ideally with the emerging punk scene and the album made considerable impact at the time of its release. It climbed to No. 43 in the album charts and the title cut, its finest moment, peaked at No. 35 in the singles chart. On the U.S. release two soul covers are omitted to make way for the four live cuts from their earlier EP.

Lew Lewis left after this to go solo. He was later jailed for 7 years in 1987 for his part in a post office robbery. Former Kursaal Flyers' guitarist Graham Douglas came in to replace him.

Eddie and The Hotrods recorded two sessions for John Peel during 1977. The first broadcast on 21st February 1977 comprised *Keep On Keeping On*, *Why Can't It Be*, *Teenage Depression* and *On The Run*. The second hit the airwaves on 17th October 1977 and featured *Life On The Line*, *I Don't Know What's Going On*, *Telephone Girl* and *Beginning Of The End*.

With this new line-up the band ascended to its commercial peak during 1977 with the release of *I Might Be Lying* and *Do Anything You Wanna Do* (on this last one they were credited simply as 'The Rods'). They rose to No. 44 and No. 9, respectively in the U.K. charts. Both were driving, high-energy rockers. They helped pave the way for *Life On The Line*, their second and commercially most successful album, which contained strong songs and enthusiastic and competent musicianship. It peaked at No. 27 in the charts. The album also spawned another hit single. *Quit This Town*, another fine, high energy driving rocker, which got to No. 36. Surprisingly perhaps, the album's title track failed to chart when put out as a 45. Indeed *Quit This Town* was to be their last hit single. Things had looked so

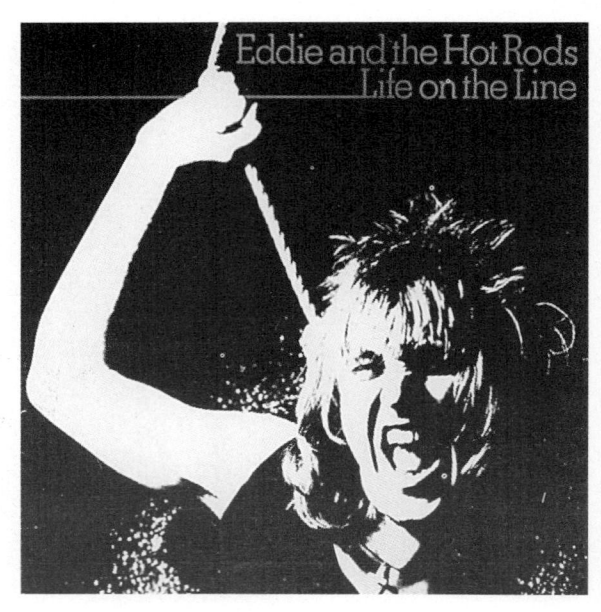

EDDIE AND THE HOTRODS - Life On The Line.

EDDIE AND THE HOTRODS - Thriller.

promising for the band but then they all went wrong. Why? Well, it seems to be a case of their inability to keep apace with the changing mood of music. Their high energy, driving rock was enthusiastically received by punk audiences of the late seventies but this approach seemed out of step with early eighties new wave.

Their inability to keep pace with changing times became apparent on *Thriller*. The musicianship is competent but the material is uninteresting. The late Linda McCartney sang some backup parts on this album.

Shortly after *Thriller*, Gray left to join **The Damned** and T.C. came in on bass. Rufus Jenkins (accordian) and Al Kooper (keyb'ds, gtr, vcls) guested on their April 1981 album *Fish 'n' Chips*. This was also a commercial failure and the band split before the year was out.

Barrie Masters joined The Inmates. He reformed **Eddie and The Hotrods** in 1984 with Tex Axile (drms). This new line-up recorded the *Fought For You* 45 and *One Story Town* (live) mini-album. They finally split towards the end of 1985. Axile was later in Transvision Vamp.

Additional to the two John Peel sessions already mentioned there was a third on 5th March 1979 featuring *Strangers On The Payphone*, *Power And Glory*, *Breathless* and *Living Dangerously*. 14 days later they also recorded *Power And Glory*, *Out To Lunch* and *He Does It With Mirrors*.

In 1979, *Do Anything You Wanna Do* was included on the soundtrack *That Summer!* (Spartan/Arista SPART 1088). Later, in 1998, it resurfaced on *The Best Punk Anthems.... Ever* (2-CD) (Virgin VTDCD 198).

The band's drummer Steve Nicol also featuring in **The Snivelling Shits**, which mainly comprised three 'Sounds' newspaper journalists.

In 1991, *Do Anything You Wanna Do* was included on the compilation *Learning English Vol. 1* by Die Toten Hosen (Charisma 91823) and on *The Sound Of The Suburbs* (Columbia 488825 2) 1997. In 1990, Hound Dog issued *The Curse Of The Hot Rods*, a collection of previously unissued material compiled from the left-overs of their last sessions for Island in the summer of 1979. As well as their own material the album includes covers of The Young Rascals' *You Better Run* and The Small Faces' *I Got Mine*. There's also a track produced by Al Kooper. This was also issued on CD by Link in 1992.

In 1999, *Teenage Depression* re-emerged on the 5-CD box set *1-2-3-4 - A History Of Punk And New Wave 1976 - 1979* (MCA/Universal MCD 60066).

Both their first albums were reissued again on CD in 2000. *Teenage Depression* comes with twelve bonus cuts including the whole of the *Live At The Marquee* (EP). *Life On The Line* has nine bonus cuts including their rare *'Till The Night Is Gone (Let's Rock)*, on which they collaborated with MC5's Rob Tyler. Both come with loads of photos, rare sleeves and the band's Island discography.

Even now many late seventies music fans will hold fond memories of those **Eddie and The Hotrods** gigs.

The Edge

Personnel:	ROBERT LU EDMONDS	gtr, vcls	A
	GLYN HAVARD	bs	A
	JON MOSS	drms	A
	GAVIN POVEY	keyb'ds	A

ALBUM:	1(A)	SQUARE ONE	(Hurricane FLAK 102) 1980

45s:	Macho Man/I'm Cold (PS)	(Albion ION 4) 1978
*	Downhill/American Express (PS)	(Hurricane FIRE 3) 1979
	Watching You/Overtaking (PS)	(Hurricane FIRE 6) 1979

NB: * Some copies were also issued on white vinyl.

The Edge were formed in 1978. Robert Lu Edmonds and John Moss had previously been in an unrecorded line-up of **The Damned**. Prior to this John Moss had been with punk band **London**. Keyboardist Gavin Povey had played for Lew Lewis and Glyn Havard had spells in Jade Warrior and **The Yachts**.

The Edge's debut single *Macho Man* that attacked the karate, biker, stud image was interpreted by some as a critique against **The Stranglers'** J.J. Burnel, which the band denied.

Musically **The Edge** played a diverse, melodic rock with amusing lyrics. In addition to their own output they backed U.S. new wavers Jane Aire and The Belvederes on their first album and Kirsty MacColl on hers.

John Moss went on to achieve fame with Culture Club, whilst Lu Edmond's later bands included **Spizzles** and Shriekback.

Dave Edmunds

Personnel:	BILLY BREMNER	gtr	A
(1977 -	DAVE EDMUNDS	vcls, bs	ABCD
1985)	NICK LOWE	bs	A
	TERRY WILLIAMS	drms	A D
	DAVID CHARLES	drms	BC
	JOHN DAVID	bs	BCD
	MICKEY GEE	gtr	BC
	JEFF LENNY	bs, synth	C
	RICHARD TANDY	keyb'ds	D

HCP

ALBUMS:	1(A)	GET IT	(Swansong SSK 59404) 1977 -
(1977 -	2(A)	TRACKS ON WAX	(Swansong SSK 59407) 1978 -
1985)	3(A)	REPEAT WHEN NECESSARY	
			(Swansong SSK 59409) 1979 39
	4(A)	SECONDS OF PLEASURE	(F-Beat XXLP 7) 1980 34
	5(-)	TWANGIN'	(Swansong SSK 59411) 1981 37
	6(A)	THE BEST OF DAVE EDMUNDS	
			(Swansong SSK 59413) 1981 -
	7(B)	DE 7TH	(Arista SPART 11841) 1982 60
	8(C)	INFORMATION	(Arista 205 348) 1983 92
	9(D)	RIFF RAFF	(Arista 206 396) 1984 -

NB: (4) also issued on vinyl and CD (Line LICD 0005) 1989 and (Demon FIENDCD 28) 1990. (7) came with a bonus EP *Live At The Venue* (Juke 1). There are also various compilations:- *The Dave Edmunds Anthology (1968 - 90)* (Rhino R2 71191) 1993; *The Best Of Dave Edmunds* (Warner Bros 7567903382) 1997; *Chronicles* (Connoisseur Collection VSOPCD 209) 1994; *The Collection* (Disky DC 878622) 1997; *I Hear You Knocking* (EMI Gold CDGOLD 1083) 1997; and *Rockin' (The Best Of Dave Edmunds)* (Camden 74321451922) 1997.

EP:	1	BABY I LOVE YOU (PS)	(RCA PE 5243) 1980

HCP

45s:	Here Comes The Weekend/	
(1976-	As Lovers Do	(Swan Song SSK 19408) 1976 -
1986)	Where Or When/	
	New York's A Lonely Town	(Swan Song SSK 19409) 1976 -
	Ju Ju Man/	
	What Did I Do Last Night?	(Swan Song SSK 19410) 1977 -
	I Knew The Bride/	
	Back To Schooldays	(Swan Song SSK 19411) 1977 26
	Deborah/	
	What Looks Best On You	(Swan Song SSK 19413) 1978 -

	Television/ Never Been In Love (PS)	(Swan Song SSK 19414)	1978 -
	A-1 On The Jukebox/ It's My Own Business (PS)	(Swan Song SSK 19417)	1979 -
*	Girls Talk/Bad To Bad (PS)	(Swan Song SSK 19418)	1979 4
	Queen Of Hearts/Creature From The Black Lagoon (PS)	(Swan Song SSK 19419)	1979 11
	Crawling From The Wreckage/ As Lovers Do (PS)	(Swan Song SSK 19420)	1979 59
	Singin' The Blues/ Boys Talk (PS)	(Swan Song SSK 19422)	1979 28
x	Baby Ride Easy/Too Bad About Sandy (PS)	(F-Beat XX8)	1980 -
+	Wrong Way/Now And Always	(F-Beat)	1980 -
	Almost Saturday Night/ You'll Never Get Me Up (PS)	(Swan Song K 19424)	1981 58
#	The Race Is On/(I'm Gonna Start) Living Again If It Kills Me (PS)	(Swan Song K 19425)	1981 34
	Warmed Over Kisses (Left Over Love)/ Louisiana Man (PS)	(Arista ARIST 439)	1981 -
	Me And The Boys/ Queen Of Hearts (live) (PS)	(Arista ARIST 471)	1982 -
	Baby I Love You/Born To Be With You	(RCA GOLD 548)	1982 -
	From Small Things Big Things Come/ Your True Love (live) (PS)	(Arista ARIST 478)	1982 -
	Slipping Away/ Don't Call Me Tonight (PS)	(Arista ARIST 522)	1983 60
	Slipping Away/ Don't Call Me Tonight (12", PS)	(Arista ARIST 522)	1983 -
	Information/ What Have I Got To Do To Win (PS)	(Arista ARIST 532)	1983 -
	Information/What Have I Got To Do To Win (12", PS)	(Arista ARIST 12532)	1983 -
	Something About You/ Can't Get Enough (PS)	(Arista ARIST 562)	1984 -
	Something About You/Can't Get Enough/ Slipping Away/Warmed Over Kisses (Left Over Love)/ From Small Things Big Things Come (12", PS)	(Arista ARIST 562)	1984 60
	Steel Claw/ How Could I Be So Wrong (PS)	(Arista ARIST 583)	1984 -
	High School Nights/Porky's Revenge (PS)	(CBS A 6177)	1985 -

NB: * Some copies also issued on clear vinyl. x 'A' side credited to Carlene Carter and **Dave Edmunds**. + Some copies on yellow vinyl. # Credited to **Dave Edmunds** and Stray Cats.

Dave Edmunds was born on 15th April 1944 in Cardiff, Wales. He was still at school when he formed his first band The 99'ers and he also played in a local group called The Raiders in the mid-sixties before moving up to London in 1966 to join The Image. He and their drummer left the following year to join a new group The Human Beans. After one 45 they changed names to Love Sculpture. You can read about them and **Edmunds**' next band (the first incarnation of Rockpile) in my earlier book 'The Tapestry Of Delights'.

Having reverted to a solo career in 1972 **Dave Edmunds** seemed to get a second wind in the punk/new wave era. In September 1976, he signed to Led Zeppelin's Swan Song label, although his first two 45s *Here Comes The Weekend* and *Where And When* for them failed to chart. He fared better as a producer when The Flaming Groovies' album *Shake Some Action*, which he'd done the honours on, climbed to No. 142 in the U.S..

In February 1977, he put together a new version of Rockpile (line-up 'A'), which soon embarked on a short tour of Britain and Europe. His next album *Get It*, released in April 1977, was his best for years and included a version of **Nick Lowe**'s re-write of Chuck Berry's *I Knew The Bride*. It also included an **Edmunds/Lowe** ode to The Everly Brothers *Here Comes The Weekend*. Whilst the album failed to chart *I Knew The Bride* spent eight weeks in the chart peaking at No. 26 when released as a 45 in June. Having toured the 'States as support to Bad Company back in April, Rockpile embarked on an extensive U.K. tour in October. Then, in November, **Edmunds** played on **Nick Lowe**'s first Stiff Records tour package.

Lowe co-wrote much of the material on **Edmunds** next album *Trax On Wax*. Although neither the album nor any of the three 45s from it (*Deborah, Television* and *A-1 On The Jukebox*) failed to chart, the band's live reputation in this era was enhanced considerably. They played at the Knebworth Festival that summer. **Edmunds** himself appeared with Emmylou Harris and The Hot Band at London's Hammersmith Odeon. Then, in October, he toured the 'States as part of a package with **Elvis Costello** and **Mink De Ville**.

1979 was the year **Edmunds** made a significant commercial breakthrough. His *Repeat When Necessary* album, released in June, included some fine moments; notably a cover of **Elvis Costello**'s *Girls Talk* which got to No. 4 in the U.K. spending eleven weeks in the charts, and No. 56 in the U.S.; *Queen Of Hearts* which spent nine weeks in the charts with a best position of No. 11 and the sultry *The Creature From The Black Lagoon*. It also spawned one further hit, *Crawling From The Wreckage*, written by Graham Parker. This got to No. 59 during a four week chart residency. The album, too, brought chart success, climbing to No. 39 and spending a credible twelve weeks in the charts. Rockpile concluded the year playing a benefit concert for Kampuchea, now freed from the stranglehold of the Khymer Rouge, with Wings and **Elvis Costello**.

Rockpile started 1980 with a U.S. tour supported by the U.S. band Fabulous Thunderbirds, who **Edmunds** would later go on to produce a couple of albums for. **Edmunds** enjoyed a further U.K. hit with *Singing The Blues*, which got to No. 28 spending eight weeks in the charts, in February. The song had originally been a fifties hit for Tommy Steele and Guy Mitchell. In October Rockpile released their sole album *Seconds Of Pleasure*. On this guitarist Billy Bremner delivers vocals on no-holes - barred *Heat* and *(You Ain't Nothing But) Fine Fine Fine*. There's a cover of Chuck Berry's *Oh What A Thrill*, the Everly Brothers' *Now And Always* and the bluesy *A Knife And A Fork*. Most of the material is rock 'n' roll, with the emphasis on the roll. The album originally came with a 7" single *Nick Lowe And Dave Edmunds Sing The Everly Brothers*. This featured versions of *When Will I Be Loved, Take A Message To Mary* and a couple of other classics. In Britain Rockpile's album spent five weeks in the charts, climbing to No. 34, but neither of the 45s taken from it *Teacher Teacher* or *Wrong Way* charted. The album fared better in the 'States where it got to No. 27 and *Teacher Teacher* was a hit there rising to No. 51.

At the start of 1981 Rockpile disbanded. **Nick Lowe** concentrated on his solo career and Terry Williams joined Dire Straits. **Edmunds** now used old friends and session musicians on his recordings. He made the mistake of rushing out a new album *Twangin'*. This sounded like a mish-mash of odds and sods and marked a regression to the 'one-man band' sound of his early days. Still, it had a few good songs to carry it home commercially. His cover of a John Fogerty song *Almost Saturday Night* got to No. 58 during a three week chart stint here in Britain and No. 54 in the U.S.. A follow-up 45 *The Race Is On* fared better, rising to No. 34 in the U.K. during a six week chart stint. This featured a U.S. rockabilly band called The Stray Cats whose album **Edmunds** had produced. At the end of the year Swan Song put out a compilation album *The Best Of Dave Edmunds*. This documented his career from *Sabre Dance* (with Love Sculpture) onwards, drawing thirteen cuts from his Swan Song albums. Despite containing a lot of his best music it didn't chart in Britain. In the 'States it made a modest No. 163.

Having put together a new band (line-up 'B') and signed a new deal with Arista, **Edmunds** returned in 1982 with a fine album *De 7th*. Among its better moments were a rendition of Bruce Springsteen's *From Small Things*

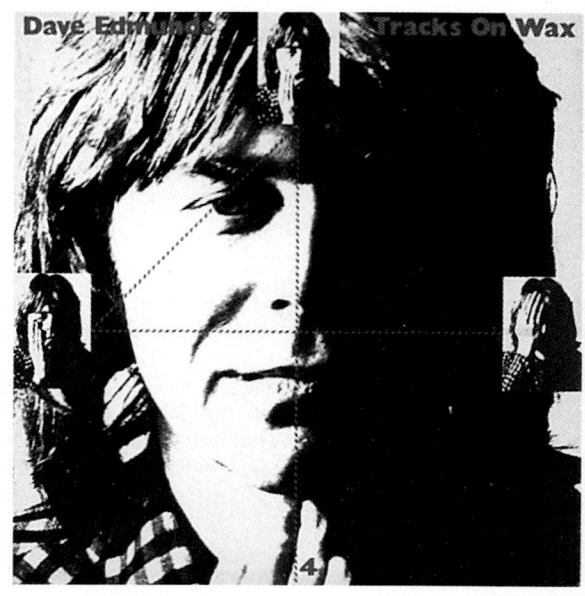

DAVE EDMUNDS - Tracks On Wax.

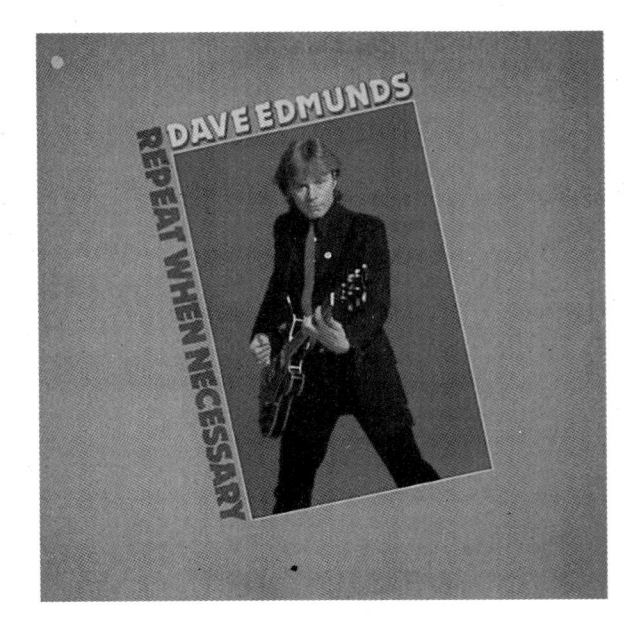

DAVE EDMUNDS - Repeat When Necessary.

(Big Things One Day Come) and a ripping version of New Rhythm and Blues Quintet (N.R.B.Q's) *Me And The Boys*. The album spent three weeks in the charts here in Britain climbing to No. 60, whilst in common with much of his work, it fared rather better in the 'States reaching No. 46. However, neither *Warmed Over Kisses (Left Over Love)* or *Me And The Boys* enjoyed much commercial success when released as 45s and a summer nationwide tour was interrupted when he was hospitalised with internal bleeding after constant touring. He recovered in August to play at the Reading Festival and then took part in the U.S. Festival at San Bernadino, California between 3-5th September.

During 1983 and 1984 **Edmunds** struck up a collaboration with Jeff Lynne, which was really an attempt to produce slicker, more commercial music. The collaboration produced two albums. The first of these was *Information*, which spent two weeks in the U.K. charts but failed to get higher than No. 92. It also produced a hit single *Slipping Away*. This rose to No. 60 during its four week chart sojourn, but it would prove to be his last U.K. hit. Again both album and single fared better in the U.S.A. where they climbed to No. 51 and 34 respectively. **Edmunds'** second collaboration with Jeff Lynne *Riff Raff* fared less well, missing out completely in Britain and only crawling to No. 140 in the 'States. Lynne produced six cuts on this album. **Edmunds** continued his production work - his latest credited being The Everly Brothers' comeback single *On The Wings Of A Nightingale*, which was written by Paul McCartney. This fulfilled a lifelong ambition of working with them. As the eighties unfolded it was really **Edmunds'** career as a producer which flourished, most significantly as he guided The Stray Cats to the top of the charts.

The Dave Edmunds Anthology (1968 - 90) is a 2-CD set which covers his time from Love Sculpture to his first solo album of the nineties. Most of what you need to hear of his music in this era is on here.

The Ejected

Personnel:	JIM BROOKS	vcls, gtr	AB
	DAVE OWERS	drms	A
	MICK ROBINSON	drms	B
	GARY SANDBROOK	vcls, bs	AB

ALBUMS:	1(B)	A TOUCH OF CLASS	(Riot City CITY 003) 1983
	2(B)	SPIRIT OF REBELLION	(Riot City CITY 007) 1984

NB: (1) also issued on CD (Captain Oi! AHOY CD 24) 1994 with eight bonus tracks, also on vinyl. (2) also issued on CD (Captain Oi! AHOY CD 34) 1998 with six bonus tracks. There's also a compilation *The Best Of The Ejected* (Captain Oi! AHOY CD 112) 1999.

EPs:	1(A)	HAVE YOU GOT 10p? (Have You Got 10p?/Class Of '82/One Of The Boys) (PS)	(Riot City 14) 1982
	2(A)	NOISE FOR THE BOYS! (Fast 'N' Loud/Don't Care/What Happened In Brighton) (PS)	(Riot City 19) 1983
	3(A)	PRESS THE BUTTON (Russians/24 Years/In The City) (PS)	(Riot City 28) 1983

Another Oi! band from Dagenham in Essex. They made their vinyl debut on the *Carry On Oi!* (Secret SEC 2) 1981 compilation with line-up 'A' contributing *East End Kids* and *What Am I Gonna Do?*. Then in 1982, **The Ejected** signed to Riot City for whom their debut disc was the *Have You Got 10p?* EP. The title cut was promising but *Class Of '82* was quite a working class punk anthem and *One Of The Boys* expressed similar sentiments, but was a less convincing song. All three cuts later resurfaced on *Oi! The Singles Collection, Vol. 2* (Captain Oi! AHOY CD 63) 1996. *Have You Got 10p?* can also be heard on *100% British Oi!* (CD) (Captain Oi! AHOY DCD 83) 1997. This EP was their only recording to feature Mick Robinson and a re-recorded version of the title cut later appeared on their first album.

The *Noise For The Boys!* EP followed in 1983 along with a patchy debut album *A Touch Of Class*. After a third EP, *Press The Button*, **The Ejected** released a second album *Spirit Of Rebellion*. This was a big improvement on their debut, with a much fuller sound and strong material including the frantic *Hang 'Em High*, a version of **The Stranglers'** *Go Buddy Go* and the amusing *Dirty Schoolgirls*. The production for this album was handles by former **UK Subs'** guitarist Nicky Garrett. Work commenced on a follow-up EP *Public Animals* but this was shelved when Riot City went under and the band broke up shortly after. There was a short-lived reformation in 1997.

The Best Of The Ejected compilation on Captain Oi! was put together by their only constant member vocalist/guitarist Jim Brooks, who witnessed a whole series of line-up changes. It includes all their singles, tracks from both albums, *East End Kids* and four new songs.

The Captain Oi! reissue of *A Touch Of Class* came with eight bonus tracks comprising the complete content of their *Have You Got 10p?* and *Noise For The Boys!* EPs and their two contributions to *Carry On Oi!* which were *East End Kids* and *What Am I Gonna Do?*. This release was available as a full picture disc CD and on vinyl with a lyric sheet. There was also a second pressing in red vinyl.

Captain Oi! also reissued their second album *Spirit Of Rebellion* on CD. The six bonus tracks featured all three cuts from their non-album *Press The Button* (EP) and three previously unreleased demos - *Public Animals No. 1, Generation Landslide* and *Rock Star*.

Other compilation appearances include *Have You Got 10p?* on *Life's A Riot And Then You Die* (Riot City CITY 009) 1985; *Have You Got 10p?, Fast 'n' Loud* and *Russians* on *Riot City Singles Collection, Vol. 1* (Anagram CDPUNK 15) 1997 and *Class Of '82, I Don't Care* and *Twenty Four Years* on *Vol. 2* (Anagram CDPUNK 55) 1995 of the same series. These last two compilations were also issued on vinyl by Captain Oi! (AHOY DLP 503 and 511).

Electric Guitars

45s:	The Continental Shelf/Health (PS)	(Fried Egg EGG 12) 1981
	Language Problems/Night Bears (PS)	(Stiff BUY 148) 1982
	Beat Me Hollow/Genghis Khan	(Stiff BUY 161) 1982

A West Country band. Originally signed to Fried Egg, they were later picked up by Stiff. Their debut 45 is melodic guitar driven power-pop. *The Continental Shelf* can also be heard on the sampler *E(gg)clectic* (Fried Egg FRY 2) 1981.

THE EJECTED - HAVE YOU GOT 10p? EP.

THE ENEMY - 50,000 Dead.

Electro Tunes

Personnel incl:	ADRIAN COOK	vcls, gtr	A
	TONY HANNAFORD	gtr	A

45:	If This Ain't Love/Bodywork (PS)	(Cobra COS 5) 1979

Adrian Cook had previously been lead singer in Dirty Tricks and Wally, whilst Tony Hannaford had been a sideman for G.T. Moore.

Embryo

Personnel:	STEVE BREWER	drms	A
	SIMON HART	vcls	A
	PETER LEY	gtr	A
	PHILLIP LEY	bs	A

45:	I'm Different/You Know He Did (PS)	(Rampant RAM 001) 1980

Formed in mid-1979 by the Ley Brothers, **Embryo** were an excellent live act on the London circuit. They released one 45 on their own Rampant label, but it suffered from poor distribution. Both sides can also be heard on *Punk Rock Rarities, Vol. 1* (Anagram CDPUNK 63) 1995. This band was later known as **Jump Squad**.

Emergency

Personnel:	AKY		A
	CHRIS		A
	DENNIS		A
	FLANNEL		A

EP:	1(A)	EMERGENCY (Points Of View/City Fun/Does Anybody Realise) (PS)	(Riot City RIOT 21) 1983

THE ENEMY - Fallen Hero.

An eighties punk band from Manchester. It's rumoured that **Blitz** were involved with their EP. As well as recording this EP they also contributed *Points Of View* to *Life's A Riot Anf Then You Die* (Riot City CITY 009) in 1985. The track also resurfaced on *Riot City Singles Collection, Vol. 1* (Anagram CDPUNK 15) 1997 and *Vol. 2* (Anagram CDPUNK 55) 1995 gave a further airing to *City Fun*. Both of these last two compilations were also issued on vinyl by Captain Oi! (AHOY DLP 503 and 511).

Empire

Personnel:	BOB ANDREWS	gtr	A
	SIMON BERNAL		A
	MARK LAFF	drms	A

ALBUM:	1(A)	EXPENSIVE SOUND	(White Line DE 001) 1980
45:		Hot Seat/ All These Things (PS)	(Dinosaur/White Line D/E 004) 1981

Bob Andrews and Mark Laff formed this relatively short-lived venture after they left **Generation X** early in 1980 after an argument about that band's future musical direction.

THE ENEMY - Punk's Alive.

The Enemy

Personnel:	MARK HERRINGTON	drms	AB
	STEVE MELLORS	gtr	A
	STEVE O'DONNELL	bs	AB
	MARK WOODHOUSE	vcls	AB
	KEVIN LAMB	gtr	B

ALBUMS:	1(B)	GATEWAY TO HELL	(Fallout FALL LP 015) 1983
	2(B)	LAST BUT NOT	(Rot ASS 12) 1984

NB: The CD *Gateway To Hell* (Captain Oi! AHOY CD 33) 1995 is a reissue of their 1983 album but it also includes a round up of all their other recordings for Fallout and Tin Tin.

45s:	50,000 Dead/Societies Fools/ Neutral Ground (PS)	(Tin Tin NM 1) 1981
	Fallen Hero/Tomorrow's Warning/ Prisoner Of War (PS)	(Fallout FALL 001) 1982
*	Punk's Alive/Piccadilly Sidetracks/ Twist And Turn (PS)	(Fallout FALL 004) 1982
	Last Rites/Why Not (PS)	(Fallout FALL 014) 1983
	Last But Not Least/Images (live) (PS)	(Rot ASS 9) 1984

NB: * This was issued on orange vinyl.

The Enemy formed in Derby in early 1980 and stabilised into the above line-up in mid-1981. They got together sufficient funds to produce a DIY single *50,000 Dead / Societies Fools / Neutral Ground*, which they put out on their own Tin Tin label. The first two tracks, in particular, were very credible punk songs. The 45 was recorded at Derby's Old Cottage studios and distributed by Fresh Records. The 45 attracted the attention of the newly-formed Fallout label, who offered them a one album and three singles contract!

THE ENEMY - Last Rites.

After becoming the first band to sign to Fallout, they released another 45 *Fallen Hero / Tomorrow's Warning / Prisoner Of War* early in 1982, which came with a free lyric sheet. This trio of competent punk songs was followed by three more *Punk's Alive / Piccadilly Sidetracks / Twist And Turn* later that year. This 45 came on orange vinyl. *Punk's Alive* was a blistering punk assault with a catchy intro, which was undoubtedly one of the best songs they ever recorded. *Piccadilly Sidetracks* was similar but lacked that cutting edge and *Twist And Turn* was a credible cover of the old **Slaughter and The Dogs** classic.

Kevin Lamb replaced Steve Mellors on guitar prior to the release of their third Fallout 45 *Last Rites* in 1983. This was another fast-paced punker with a snappy guitar intro. An album *Gateway To Hell* followed shortly after. This featured thirteen powerful punk songs, including new versions of *50,000 Dead* and *Societies Fools*, as well as their earlier 45 cuts *Last Rites* and *Prisoner Of War*. For a punk album it was also notable for the orchestrated opening cut *Intro* and there was a clear anti-war protest theme to many of the cuts like *Warcry*. The album concludes with the powerful *Murder On The Streets*.

In 1984, *Enemy* switched to the Mansfield-based Rot Records for whom they recorded a half-live/half-studio album *Last But Not Least*, the title cut of which was also released on 45. The album proved to be their final vinyl.

In 1994, *Fallen Hero*, *Punks Alive* and *Last Rites* were all included on *The Fallout Punk Singles Collection* (Anagram CDPUNK 30). The same year *Last But Not Least* was compiled on *Rot Records Punk Singles Collection* (Anagram CDPUNK 40).

The welcome Captain Oi! CD compilation draws together their *Gateway To Hell* album, all their 45 recordings for Fallout and their first single on Tin Tin.

THE ENEMY - Gateway To Hell.

English Dogs

Personnel:	JON	gtr	A
	PINCH	drms	A
	WAKEY	vcls	A
	WATTIE	bs	A

ALBUMS: 1(A) MAD PUNX AND ENGLISH DOGS (mini-LP) (Clay PLATE 6) 1983
2(A) INVASION OF THE PORKY MEN (Clay CLAYLP 10) 1984
3(A) FORWARD INTO BATTLE (Rot ASS 20) 1985
4(A) WHERE LEGEND BEGAN (Under One Flag FLAG 4) 1986

NB: (1) reissued on vinyl (Sewage Co. EDMP 01) 1997. (1) and (2) also issued on one CD (Captain Oi! AHOY CD 048) 1998. (4) also issued on CD (Powerage PRAGE 003CD) 1997.

EP: 1(A) TO THE ENDS OF THE EARTH (Ambassador Of Fire/ The Chase Is On/Incisor/ Survival Of The Fittest) (12", PS) (Rot ASS 17) 1984

A punk band from Grantham in Lincolnshire. On *Invasion Of The Porky Men*, tracks like *Fall Of Max*, *Ghost Of The Past* and *Carol* they successfully blend melody with power. Other winners among the album's fourteen cuts include *Astroph's Waiting*, *Mercenary* and *Newsflash*. It also includes a version of **Slaughter and The Dogs** *Cranked Up Really High*.

Like many hardcore punk bands **The English Dogs** underwent several personnel changes and in the mid-eighties veered towards a metal sound. They continued playing and recording way beyond the time frame of this book and are still a regular attraction at European punk festivals.

As a taster to their sound check out two of their finest moments the superb *Psycho Killer* and *Ultimate Sacrifice* on *100% Hardcore Punk* (Captain Oi! AHOY DCD 84) 1998. Alternatively you could try *Incisor* and *Forward Into Battle* on *Rot Records Punk Singles Collection* (Anagram CDPUNK 40) in 1994.

The Prodigy's Giz Butt has also been a member of this band.

English Sub-Titles

ALBUM: 1 ORIGINAL DIALOGUE (Glass GLASS LP 013) 1982

45s: Time Tunnel/Sweat/ Reconstruction (PS) (Small Wonder SMALL 22) 1979
* Tannoy/Cars On Fire (PS) (Glass 007/10 SEC 21) 1982

NB: * This release came in a folded picture sleeve in a bag with an insert.

One of the lesser known bands to have recorded on Small Wonder. *Time Tunnel* later resurfaced on *Small Wonder Punk Singles Collection, Vol. 1* (Anagram CDPUNK 29) 1994 and *Sweat* was included on *Vol. 2* (Anagram CDPUNK 70) 1996. They later recorded an album and 45 for Glass.

The Escalators

Personnel:	MARK GULLICK	vcls	A
	MIKE JOHNSON	drms	A
	STEVE MUSHAM	gtr	A
	TIM SALES	bs	A

The Escalators can be heard playing *Carscape* on the compilation *499 2139* (Rocket DIAL 1) 1979. The backing on this sounds strongly influenced by **The Police**.

Essential Bop

Personnel:	STEVE BUSH	vcls	A
	DANNY	gtr	A
	NICK	drms	A
	SNAKE ROBINSON	bs	A
	WOODY TINDER	keyb'ds	A

CD:- 1(-) CHRONICLES (Sugar Shack FOD 021) 2000

This group's vinyl debut came with *Chronicle* on *Avon Calling - The Bristol Compilation* (Heartbeat HB 1) in 1979. The keyboards on this conjured up a sort of psych/progressive atmosphere, but the track didn't have enough quality to distinguish it from the 'also-rans'.

They went on to record a few indie singles, were interviewed by Paul Morley and toured the 'States before deciding to split.

The *Chronicles* (CD), which comes with amusing self-depreciating sleevenotes by their vocalist Steve Bush, compiles their career which did produce some decent songs.

Essential Logic

Personnel:	LORA LOGIC (aka SUSAN WHITBY)	sax, vcls	AB
	PHILIP LEGG (aka ASHLEY BUFF)	gtr, vcls	AB
	JOHN OLIVER	bs	A
	RICH TEA (aka RICH THOMPSON)	drms	AB
	DAVE WRIGHT (aka DAVE FLASH)	sax	AB
	MARK TURNER	bs	B

ALBUM:	1(B)	BEAT RHYTHM NEWS - WADDLE YA PAY?	(Rough Trade ROUGH 5) 1979
EP:	1(B)	ESSENTIAL LOGIC (Wake Up/Eagle Bird/ Quality Crayon Wax OK/Bod's Message) (12", PS)	(Virgin VS 261) 1979
45s:		Aerosol Burns/World Friction (PS)	(Rough Trade SELL 1) 1978
		Flora Force/Popcorn Boy (PS)	(Rough Trade RT 029) 1979
		Eugene/Tame The Neighbours (PS)	(Rough Trade RT 050) 1979
		Music Is A Better Noise/ Moontown (PS)	(Rough Trade RT 053) 1980
		Fanfare In The Garden/ The Captain (PS)	(Rough Trade RT 074) 1980

Laura Logic had been an original member of **X-Ray Spex** at the age of 15, when she should have been at school. In 1978, she formed her own band **Essential Logic**, when she was just out of art school.

Their first 45 on their own label attracted some attention and they later worked out a deal with Rough Trade. In the interim they recorded an eponymous EP for Virgin, based around two guitars, two saxes and Logic's distinctive vocal style. It was a pretty chaotic recording.

On their subsequent album *Beat Rhythm News* there's a tighter sound and her vocals are pretty vivacious, though the album is undermined in places by tinny production.

None of **Essential Logic**'s discs had met with significant commercial success and by the end of 1980 they disintegrated.

Lora went on to a solo career. Her first solo effort was *Pedigree Charm* for Rough Trade in 1980. This was a clear progression on previous efforts. Her vocals were better produced, the sax was less meandering and the rhythms were tighter. Surprisingly, though, she didn't persevere and guested with Red Crayola, **The Raincoats** and **The Swell Maps**, among others. She then took to Hare Krishna and played in a religious cult band (as did her former band leader **Poly Styrene**).

Ethel The Frog

Personnel incl:	TERRY HOPKINSON	A
	DOUG SHEPPARD	A

ALBUM:	1(A)	ETHEL THE FROG	(EMI EMC 3329) 1980

NB: (1) also issued on CD (Anagram CDMETAL 11) 1997.

45:	Eleanor Rigby/Fight Back	(EMI EMI 5041) 1980

Unusually for this period **Ethel The Frog**'s 45 - a cover of The Beatles' classic - did not come in a picture sleeve.

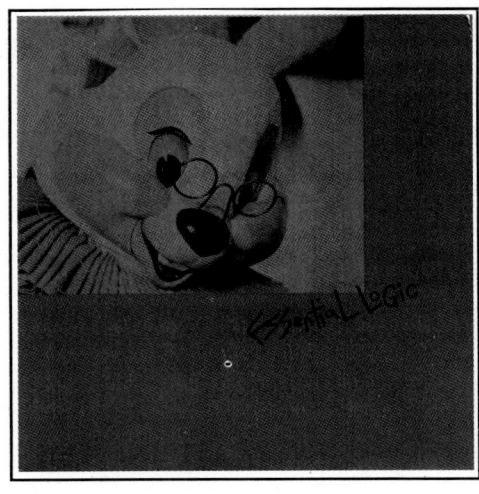

ESSENTIAL LOGIC - Essential Logic EP.

Europeans

Personnel:	JAMES COLE	drms	A
	JONATHAN COLE	vcls, synth, gtr	A
	JON KLEIN	lead gtr	A
	STEVE STREET	vcls, bs	A

45:	Europeans/Voices (PS)	(Heartbeat PULSE 2) 1979
	Europeans/It Wasn't Me (PS)	(Rialto TREB 105) 1979

This quartet made their vinyl debut playing *On The Continent* on *Avon Calling - The Bristol Compilation* (Heartbeat HB 1) in 1979. This was a promising new wave effort. Their *Europeans* 45 that year was picked up by Rialto, but there seems to have been no subsequent vinyl output.

The Exile

Personnel:	DOUGIE B	drms	A
	ROBERT KIRK	bs	A
	GARY SOTT	vcls, gtr	A
	STAN WORKMAN	gtr	A

EP:	1(A)	DON'T TAX ME (Jubilee '77/ Fascist DJ) (PS)	(Boring Records BO 1) 1977
45:		The Real People/Tomorrow Today/ Disaster Movie (PS)	(Charly CYS 1033) 1978

A Glasgow new wave band whose *Don't Tax Me* (EP) is hampered by poor sound quality as one would expect from a home-made product. The material is lively, but predictable. *Jubilee '77* slags off the monarchy but not with the vigour of **The Sex Pistols**. *Fascist DJ* is closer to the mark, though.

The Exits

Personnel:	GENO BUCKMASTER	gtr	A
	JOHN CLARKSON	keyb'ds	A
	GARY HURLEY	drms	A
	COLIN SWAN	vcls, bs	A

EP:	1(A)	YODELLING EP (Apathy/Glandular Angela/ Going Places/Fuck The Weekend/ I Love The Dole) (PS)	(Way Out WOO 1) 1978
45:		The Fashion Plague/Cheam	(Lightning GIL 519) 1978

The Exits formed in South London in 1978. The label's on their 45 were on the wrong sides of the record and it's now quite collectable. **The Exits'** *Yodelling EP* was self-made and is now very hard to find and expensive when you do. It was issued on their own Way Out label with a gatefold picture sleeve and hand-stamped labels. A limited edition release, each copy was numbered.

Both sides of their Lightning 45 later resurfaced on *This Is Mod 2* (Anagram CDMGRAM 101) 1996. You'll also find *The Fashion Plague*, a group composition, on *100% British Mod* (Captain Mod MODSKA DCD 8) 1998. The *Fashion Plague* has attractive vocals and really conjures up Carnaby Street circa 1966.

They recorded an album of material which remained in the can as Swan and Buckmaster quit in 1980 to form **The Direct Hits**.

Expelaires

Personnel incl: CRAIG ADAMS

45s:	To See You/Frequency (PS)	(Zoo CAGE 007) 1979
	Sympathy (Don't Be Taken In)/ Kicks (PS)	(Rockburgh ROCS 222) 1980

The Expelaires came from Leeds. Their main claim to fame must now be the inclusion of Craig Adams, who went on to play in **Sisters Of Mercy** and **The Mission**. Their debut 45 *To See You* had a strong Doors and Talking Heads influence. Their dancey *Sympathy (Don't Be Taken In)* can also be heard on *Hicks From The Sticks* (Rockburgh Records ROC 111) 1980.

THE EXPELLED - No Life, No Future EP.

The Expelled

Personnel:	JOANNE 'JO!' BALL	vcls	A
	RICKY FOX	drms	ABCD
	CRAIG 'MACCA' McEVOY	bs	ABCD
	TIM RAMSDEN	gtr	ABCD
	JEWELIE	vcls	B
	PENNY	vcls	C

EP:	1(A)	THE SINGLES (Dreaming/No Life, No Future/ What Justice/Government City/ Make It Alone) (PS)	(Riot City 12 RIOT 33) 1984

NB: There's also a CD *The Expelled: A Punk Rock Collection* (Captain Oi! AHOY CD 105) 1999.

45s:	No Life, No Future/Dreaming/ What Justice (PS)	(Riot City RIOT 8) 1982
	Government Policy/Make It Alone (PS)	(Riot City RIOT 17) 1982

The Expelled formed in Rothwell near Leeds in West Yorkshire in 1982 inspired by the Oi! scene. They recorded a five track demo at nearby Normanton. Three of them - *What Justice?*, *Blown Away* and *Dreaming* - were later re-recorded, but the other two *Army Song* and *Teenage Expectations* remained unreleased until their later inclusion on the Captain Oi! *Punk Rock Collection*. On the strength of this tape they were signed to the Riot City label. They recorded four songs *No Life, No Future, Dreaming, What Justice?* and *Blown Away* on 1st February 1982 at Cave Studios in Bristol. The first three cuts were released as the *No Life, No Future* (EP), on which *Dreaming* was easily the strongest song, whilst *Blown Away* was included on the *Riotous Assembly* (Riot City ASSEMBLY 1) 1982 compilation. The EP got to spend ten weeks in the indie chart and the band played a series of live gigs supporting the likes of **The Business**, **The Exploited**, **Infa Riot**, **Abrasive Wheels** and **Vice Squad**. *Dreaming* was also included on *Punk And Disorderly* (Anagram GRAM 001) in 1982. On 11th July 1982, they returned to the studio to record a double 'A' side single *Government Policy / Make It Alone*. This again fared well in the indie chart and also attracted a lot of airplay from John Peel. At the end of 1982, after they'd been offered a Peel session, Jo announced that she was leaving the band to get married. They recruited a local girl Jewelie and the session broadcast on 10th January 1983 was a long, long way from one of Peel's best. A series of live gigs followed in early 1983 but Jewelie left the band and for a short while a new singer Penny came in. This line-up ('C') didn't play live but they did record two new songs - *Cider* and *Violent Minds*. They weren't released at the time, but after the band's demise Rot Records used both of them on their *A Kick Up The Arse - Vol. 1* compilation in 1985 and on their farewell double album *The End Of An Era* in 1988. They also included *Cider* on the *Religious As Hell* compilation in 1986.

By September 1983 **The Expelled** had given up the search for another female vocalist and Craig 'Macca' McEvoy took over this role, as the band remained a trio. They returned to the studio for other recordings, which for various reasons never saw the light of day, but after poor audiences McEvoy departed to **The Underdogs** in March 1984 and the band called it a day in April.

The previous year *Government Policy* had been included on *Punk And Disorderly III - The Final Solution* (Anagram GRAM 005) 1983. *Make It Alone* figured on *Life's A Riot And Then You Die* (Riot City CITY 009) in 1985. More recently, *Dreaming* and *Make It Alone* have resurfaced on *Riot City Singles Collection, Vol. 1* (Anagram CDPUNK 15) 1994 or on vinyl (Captain Oi! AHOY DLP 503) 1996. *Vol. 2* (Anagram CDPUNK 55) 1995 or on vinyl (Captain Oi! AHOY DLP 511) 1996 includes *What Justice* and *Government Policy*. You can check out *Cider* on *Rot Records Punk Singles Collection* (Anagram CDPUNK 40) 1994.

The Captain Oi! CD compilation includes their fine 45 cuts and three from compilations, *Blown Away*, *Cider* and *Violent Minds*. The compilation also includes nine previously unreleased tracks. Of these five were from a 1981 demo. The other four - *Don't Wanna See You*, *Waiting For Tomorrow*, *Got No Cider* and *Three To Twelve* - were recorded for a Riot City mini-album which never appeared because the label went under. These are actually pretty good and considerably more accomplished than their earlier issued product for Riot City. Attractively packaged and with extensive sleeve notes this CD is recommended.

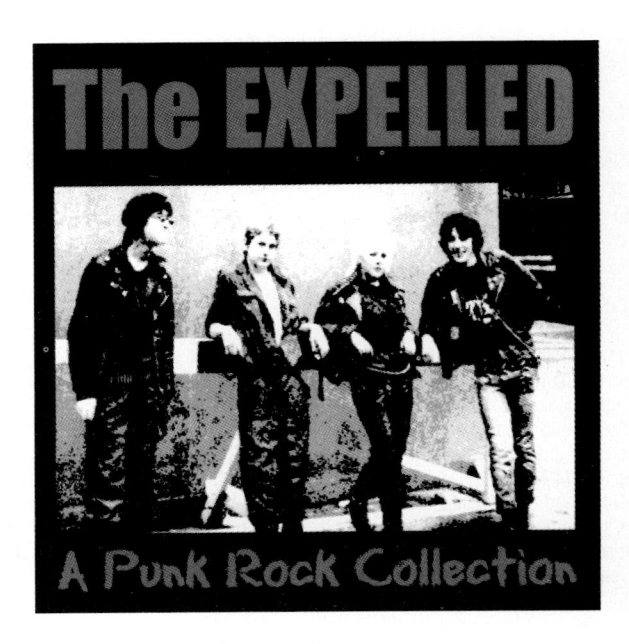

THE EXPELLED - Punk Rock Collection.

The Ex-Pistols

Personnel: DAVE SPIERS   vcls   A

HCP

45: Land Of Hope And Glory/
Flowers Of Romance (PS)   (Virginia PISTOL 76) 1984 69

Although not released until the mid-eighties, when it climbed to No. 69 in the national singles charts, this record was actually recorded back in 1978. Spiers was joined by former members of **The Users** for this recording.

Exploding Seagulls

45: Johnny Runs For Paregoric/
Take Me To The Cinema (PS)   (Fried Egg EGG 8) 1981

Some members of Bristol's Blue Aeroplanes were involved in this band. *Johnny Runs For Paregoric* is a rather lighthearted song, which also got an airing on the compilation *E(gg)clectic* (Fried Egg FRY 2) 1981.

THE EXPLOITED - Horror Epics.

The Exploited

Personnel:			
WATTIE BUCHAN	vcls		AB
DRU STIX CAMPBELL	drms, vcls		AB
'BIG' JOHN DUNCAN	gtr, vcls		A
GARY McCORMICK	bs, vcls		AB
BILLY	gtr		B

HCP

ALBUMS: 1(A) PUNK'S NOT DEAD   (Secret SEC 1) 1981 20
(up to   2(A) EXPLOITED LIVE - ON STAGE
1985)   (Superville EXPLP 2001) 1981 52
         3(A) TROOPS OF TOMORROW   (Secret SEC 8) 1982 17
         4(B) LET'S START A WAR (SAID MAGGIE ONE DAY)
                                 (Pax PAX 18) 1983 -
         5( ) HORROR EPICS   (Dojo DOJOLP 37) 1986 -

NB: (1) reissued in June 1982 and again in 1989 (Link LINK LP 065). (1) also issued on CD (Snapper SMMCD 530) 1998. (2) issued on CD (Continium 10001 2) 1992 and again on vinyl (Dojo DOJOLP 9) 1989. (3) reissued (Link LINK LP 066) 1989 and also issued on CD (Snapper SMMCD 529) 1998. (1) and (3) were reissued as a double cassette (Roadrunner RR 49651) 1989. (4) also issued on CD (Snapper SMMCD 531) 1994 and (4) and (5) on one CD (Loma LOMACD 3) 1994. (5) also issued on CD (Dojo DOJOCD 184) 1994 and (Snapper SMMCD 532) 1998. There's also a compilation, *Totally Exploited* (Dojo DOJOLP 1) 1984, which was reissued in 1986 (also on CD) (Dojo DOJOCD 1) 1986. There are also a number of live releases; *Live On Stage 1981 / Live At The Whitehouse 1985* (CD) (Loma LOMACD 2) 1994, *Live On The Apocalypse Now Tour '81* (cassette) (Chess) 1985, which was issued on vinyl in 1987 (Chaos APOCA 2), *Live At The Whitehouse* (Suck SDLP 2) 1986 also on CD (Pin Head PINCD 104) 1998, *Live And Loud* (Link LP 018) 1987 and which was later reissued on CD (Anagram CDPUNK 18) 1996. Also of interest are *The Singles* (CD) (Cleopatra CLEO 5000CD) 1994 and *The Singles Collection* (Dojo DOJOLP 118) 1993, also on CD (DOJOCD 118) 1993 and (Street Link STRCD 018) 1992. They also contributed eight cuts to *The Punk Singles Collection* (Anagram CDPUNK 13) 199?. *Live On Stage 1981* has been reissued on one CD together with *Live At The Whitehouse 1985* (Loma LOMACD 2) 1991 and 1994, but a lot of rawness and excitement of their live show gets lost on CD format. Another relevant live set is *Live In Japan* (Dojo DOJOCD 109) 1994 and this is also available as a 2-CD set with *Totally Exploited* (Snapper SMDCD 136) 1997. Recent compilations include *Punk Singles & Rarities 1980 - 83* (Captain Oi! AHOY CD 160) 2001 and *Dead Cities* (Harry May CAN CAN 008) 2001.

HCP

EPs: 1(A)   EXTRACTS FROM EDINBURGH NITE CLUB
(up to   (Exploited EXP 003) 1981 -
1986)   2(A)   Don't Let Them Grind You Down/
               (other 2 songs by
               Anti-Pasti) (12" EP)   (Superville EXP 1003) 1981 70
        3( )   Jesus Is Dead/Politicians/Drug Squad/Privacy/
               Invasion (12" EP)   (Rough Justice) 1986 -
        4( )   Dead Cities/Punk's Not Dead/Army Life/
               Exploited Barmy Life (12" EP)   (Archive 4) 1986 -

HCP

45s: Army Life/Fuck The Mods/
(up to   Crashed Out (PS)   (Exploited EXP 001) 1980 -
1985)   Exploited Barmy Army/I Believe In Anarchy/
        What You Gonna Do? (PS)   (Exploited EXP 002) 1980 -
        Dogs Of War/
        Blown To Bits (live) (PS)   (Secret SHH 110) 1981 63
        Dead Cities/Hitler's In The Charts Again/
        Class War (PS)   (Secret SHH 120) 1981 31
        Attack/Alternatives (PS)   (Secret SHH 130) 1982 50
        Computers Don't Blunder/
        Addiction (PS)   (Secret SHH 140) 1982 -
        Rival Leaders/Army Style/
        Singalongabushell (PS)   (Blurg Pax PAX 15) 1983 -
Reissues: Army Life/Fuck The Mods/
             Crashed Out (PS)   (Secret SHH 112) 1981 -
             Exploited Barmy Army/I Believe In Anarchy/
             What You Gonna Do (PS)   (Secret SHH 113) 1981 -

Formed in East Kilbride, Scotland in 1980, **The Exploited**, who later moved to Edinburgh, were part of the third wave of U.K. punk in the early eighties. This was a very aggressive and wild brand of punk closely associated with the Oi! movement. Their lead vocalist Wattie Buchan sported a wonderful mohican haircut. This along with the band's studs and leather style clothing reinforced their aggressive persona superbly.

Their first single emerged in October 1980. It contained three tracks - *Army Life*, *Crashed Out* and *Fuck The Mods*. Both this and the follow up, *Exploited Barmy Army*, *I Believe In Anarchy* and *What You Gonna Do?*, were released on their own Exploited label. They both met with success in the indie charts which led to their being signed to Secret Records in 1981. The titles of their early 45 tracks offered considerable insight into their music, which was strongly anti-establishment and anti-authority and pro-anarchy and 'leave me to do my own thing'.

Their debut 45 for Secret, *Dogs Of War* actually made the national charts, climbing to No. 63. Their debut album *Punk's Not Dead* fared even better, making No. 20 in the album charts in which it spent eleven weeks in all. Predictably, it was full of rants and chanting choruses against the authorities. This album also topped the indie charts for a couple of weeks.

In 1981 they were part of the high profile 'Apocalypse Now' tour along with **The Anti-Nowhere League**, **Anti-Pasti**, **Chron Gen** and **Discharge**. This introduced them to a wider audience and another hit single *Dead Cities*, which only missed the Top 30 by one place. Their appearance on 'Top Of The Pops' to help promote it was improbable, but it did actually happen. The other two cuts on the 45 were titled *Hitler's In The Charts Again* and *Class War!*

Their second live album suffered from poor sound quality, but still people bought it in sufficient quantities for it to make the No. 52 slot, though its chart residency was confined to three weeks.

They enjoyed further success in the singles charts too, first with *Attack* (No. 50) and then with a joint EP with **Anti-Pasti**, to which **The Exploited** contributed *Don't Let Them Grind You Down*.

Their highest chart placing, though, was achieved with their *Troops Of Tomorrow* album in 1982. It spent nearly three months in them peaking at No. 17. The lyrics are more audible and the production is clearer on this than their previous efforts. After this Billy (formerly with Screetel replaced 'Big' John Duncan, who later formed Blood Uncles, on guitar). Their bassist Gary McCormick, incidentally, had previously been with **Josef K**.

By 1983, the Oi! movement had become passe and understandably their popularity declined. Had they been able to move with the times things might have been different, but they continued to put out recordings on a variety of different labels throughout the eighties with modified line-ups. Although the sales declined considerably they still enjoyed a loyal cult following.

Live And Loud released on Link in 1987 utilises tapes from 1981, 1985 and 1986 and includes a cover of **The Sex Pistols'** *Belsen Was A Gas*, a collection of songs about sex and violence and an unflattering song about Maggie Thatcher.

The Exploited also contributed a cut to *Pax Records Punk Collection* (Anagram CDPUNK 75) 1997. *Dogs Of War, Army Life, Exploited Barmy Army, Top, Computers Don't Blunder* and *Troops Of Tomorrow* were all included on *Secret Records Punk Singles Collection, Vol. 1* (Anagram CDPUNK 13) 1993. *Vol. 2* (Anagram CDPUNK 60) 1995 featured *Blown To Bits, Fuck The Mods, I Believe In Anarchy, Hitler's In The Charts Again, Alternative* and *Addiction*. The following year two of their finest moments *Dead Cities* and *Rival Leaders* were compiled on *100% Hardcore Punk* (Captain Oi! AHOY DCD 84). Then, in 1999, *Dead Cities, Class War, Alternative, Crashed Out* and *What You Gonna Go?* were all included on *Secret Records (The Best And The Rest)* (Get Back GET 12).

Captain Oi!'s *Punk Singles & Rarities 1980 - 83* includes all their singles and EP tracks from this era along with cuts from *Oi! - The Album, Apocalypse Tour 1981, Britannia Waives The Rules* and a DJ-only promo 12" of *Troops Of Tomorrow*. The *Totally Exploited* double CD on Recall/Snapper comprises unsourced live material, including apparently nineteen cuts from Japan. There is some duplication between the two CDs but all their favourites are featured.

The eighteen track *Dead Cities* picture disc CD compilation on Harry May includes some of their classic tracks like the title cut, *Barmy Army, Punk's Not Dead*, and *Alternative* along with a few 'B' sides, notably the amazing *Hitler's In The Charts Again* and a few album cuts.

For readers wanting to explore their music the *Totally Exploited* compilation on Dojo (issued on vinyl and CD) or *The Singles Collection* (CD) on Streetlink are recommended. They also contributed eight cuts to *The Punk Singles Collection* (Anagram CDPUNK 13).

Wattie still fronts a line-up of **The Exploited** today. They still tour around the world and recent recordings confirm that they've lost none of the anger and energy of their early years.

Ex-Producers

Personnel:	TOM CONDON	gtr, vcls	A
	JOHN CULLEN	drms, vcls	A
	DAVIE MOORE	bs	A

Ex-Producers hailed from Belfast. They contributed *The System Is Here* and *Behind The Door* to the *Belfast* (Shock Rock SLR 007) 1980 compilation. Both suffer from being weak compositions and rather muffled production.

External Menace

Personnel:	DEREK	drms	A
	SNAZ	bs	A
	SNEDDY	gtr	A
	WULLIE	vcls	A

EPs:	1(A)	YOUTH OF TODAY (Youth Of Today/Don't Conform/Main St. Riot/Someday)	(Beat The System MENACE 1) 1982
	2(A)	NO VIEWS (No Views/We Wanna Know/Poor Excuse/Escape From Hell)	(Beat The System MENACE 2) 1982

NB: There's also a CD *Pure Punk Rock* (Captain Oi! AHOY CD 52) 1995 which compiles the above EPs, their compilation appearances on the Rot label and six previously unreleased cuts.

External Menace formed in 1980 in Coatbridge, Scotland. By 1982 their line-up had stabilised to 'A' above and they were signed by Beat The System Records for whom they recorded the above two EPs. Four tracks from these - *Youth Of Today, Someday, No Views* and *Poor Excuse* - were included on *Beat The System Punk Singles Collection* (Anagram CDPUNK 61) in 1995. They also figured on quite a few compilations released on the Rot label. All of these recordings, plus six previously unissued cuts were compiled on Captain Oi!'s 1995 compilation. You'll also find one of their best songs *No Views* on *100% Hardcore Punk* (Captain Oi! AHOY DCD 84) 1998.

The group continued to play under various line-ups and names years beyond the time frame of this book. In 1994, they reverted back to the **External Menace** monicker. They recently released an EP.

Ezy Meat

Personnel:	IVAN LAVERY	gtr, vcls	A
	PAUL LAVERY	bs	A
	RAY McKENNA	drms	A
	DERMOT O'KANE	vcls	A

Ezy Meat came from Belfast. Their sole vinyl output seems to have been two tracks, *Sexy Lady* and *Soho Escapade*, on the compilation *Belfast* (Shock Rock SLR 007) in 1980. *Sexy Lady* features some decent guitar work and clocking in at five and a half minutes *Soho Escapade* is more adventurous than most material by bands of this ilk.

The 4-Skins

Personnel:	GARY HODGES	vcls	A
	TOM HOXTON	bs	AB
	JOHN JACOBS	drms	AB
	STEVE PEAR	gtr	A
	PANTHER	vcls	B
	ROI PEARCE	vcls	C

HCP

ALBUMS:	1(B)	THE GOOD, THE BAD AND THE 4-SKINS	(Secret SEC 4) 1982 80
	2(C)	A FISTFUL OF... 4-SKINS	(Syndicate SYN 1) 1983 -
	3( )	FROM CHAOS TO 1984	(Syndicate SYN LP 5) 1984 -

NB: (1) also issued on CD (Captain Oi! AHOY CD 003) 1993 with bonus cuts. In 1994 the label put out a special picture disc edition of this release with the same catalogue number. (2) also issued on CD (Captain Oi! AHOY CD 008) 1994 with two bonus tracks and again in 1998. (1) and (2) reissued as a double set and retitled *A Few 4-Skins More* (Link LP 015) 1987. There are also four compilations *A Few 4-Skins More Vol. 2* (Link LP 021) 1987 and (Step-1 STEPCD 016) 1998, *The Wonderful World Of (The Best Of The 4-Skins)* (Link LP 02) 1987 and (Step-1 STEPCD 027) 1998, *One Law For Them* (Can Can CAN CAN 006 CD) 1997 and *Singalong-A-4-Skins* (Pin Head PINCD 102) 1998. Also relevant is *Live And Loud* (Link LP 090) 1989; *Clockwork Skinhead* (Harry May MAYO CD 103) 1999; and *Singles & Rarities* (Captain Oi! AHOY CD 128) 1999.

THE 4-SKINS - One Law For Them.

45s:	One Law For Them/	
	Brave New World (PS)	(Clockwork Fun CF 101) 1981
	Yesterday's Heroes/Justice/	
	Get Out Of My Life (PS)	(Secret SHH 125) 1981
	Lowlife/Bread Or Blood (PS)	(Secret SHH 141) 1982

This East End quartet formed in 1979. They chose a new name designed to attract attention with its sexual and skinhead connotations. They were among the first of the early eighties wave of punk Oi! bands to attract national exposure when their lead vocalist Gary Hodges appeared on the front cover of the 1st November 1980 edition of 'Sounds'. They contributed two cuts, *Chaos* and *Wonderful World* to the 'Sounds'-sponsored *Oi! - The Album* (EMI ZIT 1) 1980 compilation, which was initially sold through mail-order by the magazine. It has since been reissued on vinyl and CD by Captain Oi! *Chaos* was the stronger song of the two. Given their aggressive persona it's no suprise they attracted among others a violent core of fans out to make trouble at Oi! gigs.

They put out a debut 45 *One Law For Them* on their own Clockwork Fun indie label. They also contributed two cuts *1984* and *Sorry* to *Strength Thru' Oi!* (Decca) 1981. Shortly after came the notorious riot at the Hamborough Tavern in Southall, London, in July 1981 at which **The 4-Skins** and a number of Oi! bands were playing. There was basically a pitched battle between the police and some of those at the gig. Their guitarist Steve was hurt inadvertently in the ensuing melee and the band quit (Gary Hodges and Steve quit for good).

The remaining members reformed later that year, when things had settled and signed to Secret Records. They contributed *Evil* to the *Carry On Oi!* (Secret SEC 2) 1981 compilation, released a 45 *Yesterday's Heroes* and appeared on a second compilation *Bollocks To Christmas* (Secret SHH 126) during 1981 playing a version of Slade's *Merry Christmas Everybody*. The following year their storming debut *One Law For Them* appeared on *The Secret Life Of Punk* (Secret SEC 10) 1982.

In April 1982, they put out an album *The Good, The Bad And The 4-Skins*, which climbed to No. 80 in the U.K. album charts, in which it spent four weeks in all. The opening cut on the studio side *Plastic Gangsters* is Cockney-ish but far from typical Oi! It was later put out on a 45. The Oi! mantel is carried by *Jeaulousy*. Their earlier 45, *Yesterdays Heroes*, which has quite a melodic guitar passage, and *Justice* are also included. The final track on the studio side *Manifesto* is an attack on the egocentricity of politicians. The live side includes many of their old favourites like *Wonderful World*, *Evil*, *A.C.A.B.*, *Chaos* and *One Law For Them*.

They then contemplated a move into 2-Tone recording a 45, *Plastic Gangsters / Sretsgnag Citsalp* (Secret SHH 144) 1983 under the name Plastic Gangsters. They then experienced a change of mind and the 45 remained unissued. A few DJ copies did circulate making these among the rarest artifacts of the punk era. Copies now go for in excess of £100.

The Secret label shut down leaving a further projected single *Seems To Me* unissued even in promo form.

1983 and 1984 did see two further albums of their material issued on Syndicate. They also contributed *On The Streets*, a raucous Oi! anthem, to *Son Of Oi!* (Syndicate SYNLP 3) in 1983, which has since been reissued on CD by Captain Oi!. Later another pulsating song *Saturday* and *ACAB*

THE 4-SKINS - Yesterday's Heroes.

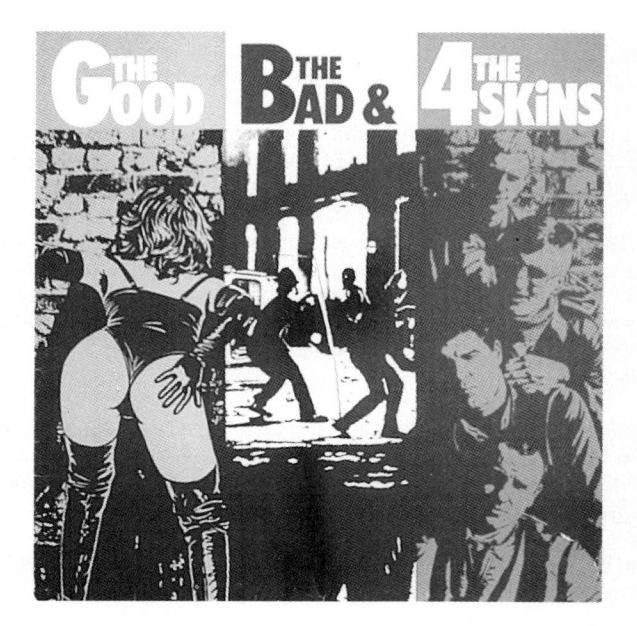

THE 4-SKINS - The Good, The Bad And The 4-Skins.

were included on *Trouble On The Terraces - 16 Classic Football Anthems* (Step-1 STEP LP 91) in 1996.

The Wonderful World Of is a compilation comprising material from the Gary Hodges era as well as from his replacement Panther. It comprises typical fast-paced punk.

A Few 4-Skins More is a reissue of their first two albums repackaged as one double album set. By contrast *A Few 4-Skins More, Vol. 2* is also a double set concentrating on rarities, with live and studio tracks, some old 'B' sides and demos. The end of Side 4 veers towards novelty material with a cover of the *Dambusters March*, Slade's *Merry Xmas Everybody* and *Plastic Gangsters* played backwards! *Live And Loud* features a set recorded live at the Bridgehouse in the early eighties and includes their popular numbers like *Wonderful World*, *Chaos*, *1984* and *Evil*.

The CD reissue of their second album *A Fistful Of 4-Skins* on Captain Oi! includes two bonus tracks *On The Streets* and *Saturday*. In 1996 they contributed *One Law For Them* and *Brave New World* to *Oi! The Singles Collection, Vol. 1* (Captain Oi! AHOY CD 60).

Singalong-A-4-Skins, from 1998, compiles various live cuts. *Clockwork Skinhead*, from 1999, provides a good analysis of their career. It features five tracks with Gary Hodges on vocals including their debut 'A' side on Clockwork Fun *One Law For Them*, *Sorry* and *Evil*. It also includes tracks such as their *Low Life* 45 for Secret and the previously unreleased *Seems To Me* alongside other cuts from the era of their second vocalist (former roadie Panther). The remaining material is from the period of their third singer (ex-**Last Resort**'s) Roi Pearce. The same year *One Law For Them* was included on *Oi! Fuckin' Oi!* (Harry May MAYO CD 110), an excellent Oi! compilation. *One Law For Them*, *Yesterday's Heroes*, *Low Life* and *Seems To Me* all resurfaced on *Secret Records Punk Singles Collection, Vol. 1* (Anagram CDPUNK 13) 1993. *Vol. 2* (Anagram CDPUNK 60) 1995 included *Brave New World* and *Justice*. Later, *One Law For Them*, *Justice*,

FAD GADGET - Make Room.

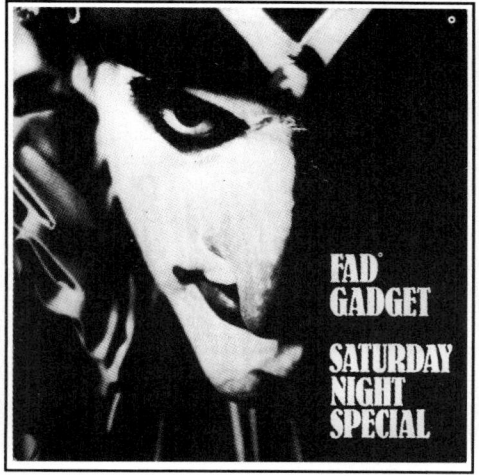

FAD GADGET - Saturday Night Special.  FAD GADGET - King Of The Flies.  FAD GADGET - Life On The Line.

Get Out Of My Life and *Norman* all got a further airing on *Secret Records (The Best And The Rest)* (Get Back GET 12) in 1999.

As its title suggests the 1999 *Singles & Rarities* CD compiles all their singles and contributions to Oi! compilations, but there are extra bonuses. Firstly, both sides of the band's unreleased 45 for Secret, *Seems To Me / Norman* plus five demo tracks recorded with their original vocalist Gary Hodges.

Fad Gadget

ALBUMS:			
1	FIRESIDE FAVOURITES	(Mute STUMM 3)	1980
2	INCONTINENT	(Mute STUMM 6)	1981
3	UNDER THE FLAG	(Mute STUMM 8)	1982
4	GAG	(Mute STUMM 15)	1984

NB: (1) also issued on CD (Mute CDSTUMM 3) 1991. (2) also issued on CD (Mute CDSTUMM 6) 1991. (3) also issued on CD (Mute CDSTUMM 8) 1991. (4) also issued on CD (Mute CDSTUMM 15) 1991.

45s:		
	Back To Nature/The Box (PS)	(Mute MUTE 2) 1979
	Ricky's Hand/Handshake (PS)	(Mute MUTE 6) 1980
	Fireside Favourite/Insecticide (PS)	(Mute MUTE 9) 1980
	Make Room/Lady Shave (PS)	(Mute MUTE 12) 1981
	Saturday Night Special/ Swallow It Live (PS)	(Mute MUTE 17) 1981
*	King Of The Flies (flexi)	(Lyntone LYN 10209) 1981
	King Of The Flies/Plain Clothes (PS)	(Mute MUTE 21) 1982
	Life On The Line/4M (PS)	(Mute MUTE 24) 1982
	For Whom The Bells Toll II/ Love Parasite (PS)	(Mute MUTE 26) 1983
	I Discover Love/ Lemmings On Lovers Rock (PS)	(Mute MUTE 28) 1983
	Collapsing New People/ Spoil The Child (PS)	(Mute MUTE 30) 1984
	Collapsing New People/ Spoil The Child (12", PS)	(Mute 12 MUTE 30) 1984
	One Man's Meat/ Sleep, Ricky's Hand (PS)	(Mute MUTE 33) 1984
	One Man's Meat/ Sleep, Ricky's Hand (12", PS)	(Mute 12MUTE 33) 1984

NB: * This red vinyl flexidisc came free with 'flexipop' magazine, issue 11. The reverse side featured a track by **Depeche Mode**.

Fad Gadget was actually Frank Tovey, who was assisted by a variety of people on his very varied range of vinyl output. Tovey was creative and unpredictable - the sort of person one would expect to blossom under the banner of the new wave, when a lot of traditional music values were challenged.

On his second 45 *Ricky's Hand* he can be heard playing a Black & Decker V8 double speed electric drill - get the picture? This also got an airing on *Machines* (Virgin V 2177) in 1980. Relying a lot on synthesizers, his first album sounds similar to early **Human League**. The second effort *Incontinent* was better produced and experimented with a wide variety of instruments.

Under The Flag veered more towards dance music with a mild soul influence. Alison Moyet, who was also recording on Mute at the time sings on a few tracks and even plays saxophone on one of them!

Tovey also recorded under his own name an album with Boyd Rice *Easy Listening For The Hard Of Hearing* (Mute STUMM 20) 1984 and later cut a solo album on Mute in 1986.

The Fall

Personnel:			
UNA BAINES	electric piano	A	
MARTIN BRAMAH	gtr	A B	
KARL BURNS	drms, bs	A B	F G H I J K
TONY FRIEL	bs	A	
MARK E. SMITH	vcls	A B C D E F	G H I J K
YVONNE PAWLETT	keyb'ds	B C	
MARC RILEY	bs, gtr	B C D E F	
STEVE HANLEY	bs	C D E F G H I K	
MIKE LEIGH	drms	C D	
CRAIG SCANLON	gtr	D E F G H I J K	
PAUL HANLEY	drms, keyb'ds	E F G H I	
BRIX E. SMITH	gtr, vcls	H I J K	
GAVIN FRIDAY	vcls	I	
SIMON ROGERS	bs, keyb'ds	J K	

				HCP
ALBUMS:	1(B)	LIVE AT THE WITCH TRIALS		
(up to			(Step Forward SFLP 1) 1979	-
1985)	2(D)	DRAGNET	(Step Forward SFLP 4) 1979	-
	3(D)	TOTALE'S TURNS (IT'S NOW OR NEVER)		
			(Rough Trade ROUGH 10) 1980	-
	4(C)	GROTESQUE (AFTER THE GRAMME)		
			(Rough Trade ROUGH 18) 1980	-
	5(-)	THE EARY YEARS 1977-79		
			(Step Forward SFLP 6) 1981	-
	6(F)	HEX ENDUCTION HOUR	(Kamera KAM 005) 1982	71
	7(F)	ROOM TO LIVE (UNDILUTABLE SLANG TRUTH)		
			(Kamera KAM 011) 1982	-
	8(H)	PERVERTED BY LANGUAGE		
			(Rough Trade ROUGH 62) 1983	-
	9(I)	THE WONDERFUL AND FRIGHTENING WORLD OF THE FALL	(Beggars Banquet BEGA 58) 1984	62
	10(-)	HIP PRIESTS AND KAMERADS		
			(Situation 2 SITU 13) 1985	-
	11(K)	THIS NATION'S SAVING GRACE		
			(Beggars Banquet BEGA 67) 1985	54

NB: (1) also issued on CD (Cog Sinister COGYP 103CD) 1997. (2) reissued on I.R.S. (SFAL 4), also on CD (I.R.S. Illegal SFLPCD 4) 1990. (3) also issued on CD (Dojo DOJOCD 83) 1992 and again (Essential ESM CD 638) 1998. (4) reissued on CD (Castle CLACD 391) 1993 and again (Essential ESMCD 640) 1998. (6) reissued on Line in 1987 and on CD (Line LICD 9000126) 1989; and again in 1998; and (Cog Sinister COGVP 119 CD) 1999. (7) reissued on Line (LILP 400109) 1987 and on CD (Cog Sinister COGVP 105 CD) 1998. (8) reissued on CD (Line LICP 900116) 1989; (Essential ESMCD 639) 1998 and (Cog Sinister COGVP 104 CD) 1999. (9) reissued in 1988 on vinyl and on CD (Beggars Banquet BEGA 58 CD) 1985 and (Lowdown BBL 58 CD) 1988. CD version has seven extra tracks. The cassette version of (10) had four extra cuts which were also included on the CD reissue (Lowdown SITL 13 CD) in 1988. (11) reissued on vinyl and CD (Beggars Banquet BEGA 67 CD) 1985 and (Lowdown BBL 67 CD) 1990. Other compilations of interest are: *In The Palace Of Swords Revisited ('80-'83)* (Cog Sinister COG 1) 1987 also on CD (CDCOG 1); *458489 (A Sides 1984-89)* (Cog Sinister) 1990. The CD release (Beggars Banquet BEGA 111 CD) 1990 had three extra cuts and this release charted at No. 47; *458489 (B Sides 1984 - 89)* (Cog Sinister) 1990 also on CD (Beggars Banquet BEGA 116CD) 1990; *The Collection* (CD) (Castle CCDCD 365) 1993; *BBC Radio 1 Live In Concert* (CD) (Windsong WIN CD 038) 1993; *The Fall Archives* (Rialto RMCD 214) 1997; *Live On Air In Melbourne 1982* (Cog Sinister COGYP 108CD) 1998; *Live Various Years* (Cog Sinister COGYP 111CD) 1998; *The Peel Sessions* (Strange Fruit SFRSCD 048) 1998; *Slates / Part Of America Therein 1981* (Loma LOMACD 10) 1994 and again (Essential ESM CD 637) 1998; *Smile.... It's The Best Of The Fall* (Castle CCSCD 823) 1998; *Northern Attitude* (Music Club MCCD 350) 1998; *Early Fall 77-79* (Cog Sinister COGVP 123 CD) 2000; *Austurbaejarbio* (Cog Sinister COGVP 125 CD) 2001, which was recorded in Iceland in 1983; *Live In Cambridge, 1988* (Cog Sinister COGVP 115 CD) 2001 and *Backdrop* (Cog Sinister COGVP 127 CD) 2001, gives an official release to this bootleg assortment of freebie, live and compilation material from the seventies and eighties.

EPs: 1(A) BINGO-MASTERS BREAKOUT! (Psycho Mafia/
(up to Bingo-Masters/Repitition) (PS) (Step Forward SF 7) 1978
1985) 2(E) SLATES (An Old Lover etc./Leave The Capital/
Middle Mass/Fit And Working Again/Slates, Slags etc./
Proll Art Threat) (10" six track maxi-single) (PS)
(Rough Trade RT 071) 1981
3(I) CALL FOR ESCAPE ROUTE (12") (Draygo's Guilt/
Clear Off/No Bulbs; 7" Slang King/
No Bulbs) (PS) (Beggars Banquet BEG 120E) 1984

NB: Also of interest is *The Peel Sessions* (28/11/78) (Strange Fruit SFPS 028) 1987. (2) repackaged on CD with *A Part Of America Therein 1981* (Dojo LOMA CD 10) 1993.

45s: It's The New Thing/
(up to Various Times (PS) (Step Forward SF 9) 1978
1985) Rowche Rumble/In My Area (PS) (Step Forward SF 11) 1979
Fiery Jack/Second Dark Age/
Psykick Dancehall No. 2 (PS) (Step Forward SF 13) 1980
How I Wrote 'Elastic Man'/
City Hobgoblins (PS) (Rough Trade RT 048) 1980
Totally Wired/Putta Block (PS) (Rough Trade RT 056) 1980
Lie, Dream Of A Casino Soul/
Fantastic Life (PS) (Kamera ERA 001) 1981
Look, Know/I'm Into C.B. (PS) (Kamera ERA 004) 1982
The Man Whose Head Expanded/
Ludd Gang (PS) (Rough Trade RT 133) 1983
Kicker Conspiracy/Wings/Container Drivers/
New Puritan (double single PS) (Rough Trade RT 143) 1983
Marquis Cha Cha/Room To Live (Kamera ERA 014) 1983
Oh Brother/Godbox (PS) (Beggars Banquet BEG 110) 1984
Oh Brother/(Instrumental)/
Godbox (12", PS) (Beggars Banquet BEG 110T) 1984
C.R.E.E.P./
Pat-Trip Dispenser (PS) (Beggars Banquet BEG 116) 1984
* C.R.E.E.P. (Extended Version)/
Pat-Trip Dispenser (12", PS) (Beggars Banquet BEG 116T) 1984
Rollin' Dany/
Couldn't Get Ahead (PS) (Beggars Banquet BEG 134) 1985
Rollin' Dany/Couldn't Get Ahead/
Petty Thief Lout (12", PS) (Beggars Banquet BEG 134T) 1985
Cruisers Creek/L.A. (PS) (Beggars Banquet BEG 150) 1985
Cruisers Creek/
L.A./Vixen (12", PS) (Beggars Banquet BEG 150T) 1985

NB: * This was issued in two formats, as a 12" on green vinyl and as a 12" with a free art print picture sleeve.

The Fall play their own unique brand of music, often termed anti-rock, which is unpleasant, challenging, respected in some musical circles and reviled in many others. Developing during the punk era they have attained a very loyal cult following around the world.

They formed in Prestwich, Manchester in January 1977, making their live debut in May on what was already a blossoming music scene.

In June 1978, they contributed two cuts, *Stepping Out* and *Last Orders* to the 10" mini-album Manchester compilation *Short Circuit - Live At The Electric Circus* (Virgin VCL 5003) 1978, which came out in blue vinyl. Not an easy compilation to track down it was later reissued, as a double 10" set, along with the *Guillotine* sampler.

Shortly after these recordings, the band were signed by indie label Step Forward. This was a London-based label owned by Miles Copeland. Their debut release for the label was the three-track *Bingo Master's Break-Out* EP. It's lyrical strangeness laid down the gauntlet for the band's style and what was to come.

By the time of **The Fall**'s first 45 *It's The New Thing*, original bassist Tony Friel had been replaced by Marc Riley and Yvonne Pawlett had relieved Una Baines on keyboards. Their debut album in January 1979 *Live At The Witch Trials*, despite its title was made in the studio in two days. More poppy material was interspersed on this including *Rebellious Jukebox*, which later appeared in the 'States on the double album *IRS Greatest Hits Volume 2 and 3* (SP 70800) in January 1981. The album, produced by Bob Sargeant, was well received, despite the inaccessibility of much of the music. On the American release *Various Times* was added and *Mother / Sister* and *Industrial Estate* excluded.

To help promote their recordings they embarked on a series of live gigs. The band was never harmonious and early in 1979 Martin Bramah left to team up with Una Baines to form **Blue Orchids**. Marc Riley moved across to guitar with Steve Hanley coming in on bass. Drummer Karl Burns departed too, first for a stint in Passage with Tony Friel, but he later had a stint in **PiL**. Mike Leigh came in on drums. This new line-up released a 45, *Rowche Rumble*, which exuded a denser sound than its predecessors. It was their last with a permanent keyboard player. Shortly after Yvonne Pawlett was replaced by Craig Scanlon, as a second guitarist.

Their second album *Dragnet* came out in October 1979. Scanlon's scratchy guitar style was distinctive and helped create a rougher sound (or more correctly noise). *Spectre Vs Rector* and *A Figure Walks* on this album are usually considered to be among their finer moments on what was a diverse collection of songs which followed few of rocks conventions.

Their final new release on Step Forward was *Fiery Jack* taken from *Dragnet*. A typically unpredictable 45.

FALL - It's The New Thing.

FALL - Bingo Masters Breakout! EP.

FALL - Fiery Jack.

In Spring 1980, they signed to leading indie label Rough Trade, which was from their viewpoint an obvious vehicle to help promote the band. Their first release for them was a budget priced album *Totale's Turns (It's Now Or Never)*. Recorded live between October 1979 and February 1980, the majority of its material was from *Dragnet* and recent 45s. It did, however, contain two new cuts *That Man* and *Cary Grant's Wedding*.

Prior to their next 45, *How I Wrote 'Elastic Man'* Mike Leigh was replaced on drums by Paul Hanley. It was vintage **Fall** 'noise' superimposed over a rockabilly beat. The follow-up *Totally Wired* sounded very unappealing, but then this was partly what the band were about.

Grotesque (After The Gramme) released in December 1980 comprised mostly one or two chord jams with sociopolitical lyrics whose message was hampered by this background noise. Among their cult fans *Pay Your Rates* and *Container Drivers* from this album became particularly popular. The following month came a 4,000 limited edition cassette-only release *Live At The Acklam Hall* (Chaos Tapes LIVE 006), that will interest fans of the band who don't already have it. It included cuts from *Grotesque*, but also material like *Slates*, which hadn't yet been recorded for release.

They went to the 'States for a short tour in the Winter of 1980. Upon their return, they set about recording the six-track 10" maxi single *Slates*, which was released in April 1981. This is considered to be one of their best recordings and was certainly better produced than most of the others. *Leave The Capitol* and *Fit And Working Again* were quite accessible rock tracks and this particular recording had appeal beyond their cult fans. It also proved to be the final release of their first period with Rough Trade. Most of the rest of the year was spent touring Iceland, the 'States and Britain.

Towards the end of 1981 their first single for Camera was released, *Lie, Dream Of A Casino Soul*. A couple of months earlier Step Forward put out a compilation *The Early Years 1977-79*. This confirmed both sides of their three Step Forward 45s and their *Bingo-Masters Breakout* EP.

Part of their *Hex Enduction Hour* album, released in March 1982, was recorded in Iceland, where their music was relatively popular. The album was notable for its two drummer line-up, Karl Burns having rejoined for their earlier *Lie, Dream Of A Casino Soul* 45. The subsequent *Room To Love* mini-LP was disappointing.

Around this time the band was disrupted by internal strife. A 26-date summer tour of Australia ended with Smith and Riley coming to blows in a disco. Riley left soon after and enjoyed some success with his own creation Marc Riley and The Creepers.

Their *Marquis Cha Cha / Papal Visit* 45, which dealt with the Falklands War and the Pope's visit wasn't distributed after its release in Autumn 1982, because Kamera went bankrupt. The original catalogue number KAM 013 was later blacked out and replaced with KAM 014 to tie in with what appeared on the label. Some copies eventually made it into the shops in November 1983, but with *Room To Live* on the 'B'-side. This 45 is one of **The Fall**'s most collectable items. Around this time, two live discs were released. *A Part Of America Therein 1981* (Cottage Records LP 1) 1982 was recorded during the band's U.S. tour. It was imported into Britain by Rough Trade. The sound quality was variable but it contained many of their familiar songs plus *Cash 'n' Carry*, a remake of *Stop Mithering* from their *Grotesque* album. The second live disc was *Fall In The Hole*, an authorised double bootleg album put out only in New Zealand. Its sound quality was good as was its selection of material, mostly from their *Hex* and *Room To Live* albums.

1983 was an eventful year for the band. Mark Smith met and soon married Californian Laura Elise, who was soon integrated into the band as Brix E. Smith. With Kamera bankrupt their next 45, *The Man Whose Head Expanded* was put out on Rough Trade in June. This was followed in October by a double single release. This comprised two new songs *Kicker Conspiracy* and *Wings*, as well as *Container Drivers* and a new version of *New Puritan*. These last two were both from an earlier John Peel session. In December came their final Rough Trade release, the album *Perverted By Language*, which featured his new American wife as co-guitarist. *Smile* was the stand-out track on this album which also included the live cut *Tempo House*.

In 1984, **The Fall** signed to Beggars Banquet, who proceeded to issue their singles in both 7" and 12" format. Their *The Wonderful And Frightening World Of The Fall* album was a little more polished than most of its predecessors. Controversially it also featured flamboyant **Virgin Prunes** vocalist Gavin Friday on a couple of tracks, *Copped It* and *Skeleton's Song*. Brix also co-wrote several of the songs on it. The cassette version contained seven extra tracks, both sides of their recent *Oh Brother* and *C.R.E.E.P.* 45s for Beggars Banquet and all three songs from their forthcoming *Call For Escape Route* EP. The American vinyl release of the album contained two extra tracks *C.R.E.E.P.* and *No Bulbs*.

Call For Escape Route was also released in October 1984. It came out as a 12" (*Draygo's Guilt*, *No Bulbs* and *Clear Off*), which again featured Gavin Friday as co-vocalist. With it was a free 7" with different takes of *Slang King* (from that on the album) and *No Bulbs*.

In March 1985, Beggars Banquet subsidiary label Situation 2 issued a compilation of their material for Kamera plus a live version of the previously unreleased *Mere Pseud Mag. Ed.* from 1983. The cassette version, however, featured an additional four unreleased live cuts, *Jawbone And The Air Rifle*, *Who Makes The Nazis?*, *And This Day* and *Just Step Sideways*.

In late 1984, Simon Rogers came in on bass and keyboards for second drummer Paul Hanley. Steve Hanley also took a holiday for much of 1985.

Their next 45, released in July 1985, was a cover of *Rollin' Dany* a little known Gene Vincent song. This was a double 'A' side and the other side, *Couldn't Get Ahead*, co-written by Mark Smith's American wife proved more popular. That summer they toured the 'States again and appeared at the WOMAD festival. They ended the year releasing one of their most acclaimed albums *This Nation's Saving Grace* in October. Steve Hanley returned to the line-up on bass for this, whilst Simon Rogers remained, helping out on keyboards, acoustic guitar and bass. There are signs of commercialism on this album on *Cruiser's Creek* and the synthesized (even danceable) *L.A.*. Both cuts were put out on a double 'A' side 45 the same month. The 12" release contained an extended version of *L.A.* and a new song *Vixen*. Also of note are the guitar assault of *Bombast* and the decidedly strange *I Am Damo Suzuki* (a song about Can's ex-lead vocalist). The cassette version of the album had three extra cuts, *Couldn't Get Ahead*

FALL - Rowche Rumble.

and *Petty Thief Lout* from their previous 45 and *Vixen*. The U.S. vinyl release included *Cruiser's Creek* in place of *Barmy*.

Other compilation appearances by **The Fall** in the pre-1985 era were *C.R.E.E.P.* and *Lay Of The Land* on the budget priced £1.99 (Beggars Banquet BBB 1) 1985. They also figured on the *Rough Trade Compilation* (Phonogram 6435 086) 1981, released for the German market and the Cherry Red cassette sampler *Pillows And Prayers* (Cherry Red PZRED 41) 1982. They did several sessions for John Peel over the years.

The Fall's *Peel Sessions* EP dates from 1978. The four tracks featured *Put Away*, *Mess Of My*, *No Xmas For John Key* and *Like To Blow* capture **The Fall** at their rawest and most uncompromising.

The Fall Collection on Castle in 1993 offers a cut-price selection of material from the band's two spells with Rough Trade in the early eighties. It includes two of their classic 45s:- *Totally Wired* and *How I Wrote 'Elastic Man'* together with many of their better album cuts from this era. Also featured are the previously unissued *Medical Acceptance Gate* and their cover of The Beatles' *A Day In The Life* which appeared on NME's *Sgt Pepper Knew My Father* compilation.

Around the same time Dojo repackaged **The Fall**'s *Slates* mini-LP together with *A Part Of America Therein 1981*, which was recorded in the 'States and originally issued on Cottage in 1982. This is a well-balanced, sensitively compiled CD which fans of the band should like.

BBC Radio 1 Live In Concert is taken from a rather haphazardly-recorded May 1987 concert and doesn't capture the band at their best as a live act.

Smile.... It's The Best Of The Fall, released on CD by Castle Communications in 1998 is a rather misleading title. It's really an arbitary collection of bits and pieces. There's a studio version of *Smile* from *Perverted By Language*, a live *Totally Wired* (from 1981) and a live *Lie Dreams Of A Casino Soul* as well as oldies like *Rowche Rumble*.

Cog Sinister's 1998 *Live On Air / In Melbourne '82* captures the band live in Australia and also comes with a bonus EP for which the record information lists only three tracks when there are in fact six.

Northern Attitude put out by Music Club in 1998, is a **Fall** compilation which draws on worthwhile alternative versions of premier cuts like *Telephone Thing*, *The Man Whose Head Expanded*, *I Feel Voxish* and *Edinburgh Man*. It comes with an excellent career overview by Pat Gilbert and with its lively sound is a worthwhile addition to their voluminous catalogue.

Early Fall 77 - 79 is as its title suggests a collection of early 45s, album cuts and two live tracks from their "Electric Circus" 10".

In 2001, *How I Wrote 'Elephant Man'* was included on *25 Years Of Rough Trade Shops* (Mute CD STUMM 191), a 4-CD box set. The same year saw a CD release of *Austurbaejarbio*, which was recorded in Iceland back in 1983, along with *Live In Cambridge, 1988*. More interesting is the official release of their *Backdrop* bootleg on CD. It comprises a collection of freebies, live and compilation material from the seventies and eighties.

The Fall are certainly not for everyone - you'll either like them or loath them, but they were one of relatively few punk bands to survive into the nineties and in doing so they've compromised few of their principles.

Fallen Angels

ALBUMS:	1	FALLEN ANGELS	(Fallout FALLLP 023) 1984
	2	SIX POINT SIX	(Wishbone HB 2001) 1984

NB: (1) also issued on cassette with an extra track (FALL CLP 23) 1984 and on CD (Cleopatra CLP 501) 1999. Other relevant releases are *In Lovng Memory* (Jungle FREUD 12) 1988 and *Wheel Of Fortune* (Jungle FREUD 23) 1988.

45s:	Amphetamine Blues/He's A Rebel (PS)	(Fallout FALL 022) 1984
	Inner Planet Love/Precious Heart (PS)	(Fallout FALL 027) 1984
	Inner Planet Love/	
	Precious Heart (12", PS)	(Fallout FALL 12027) 1984

An eighties punk band. You can also hear *Amphetamine Blues* and *Inner Planet Love* on *The Fallout Punk Singles Collection* (Anagram CDPUNK 30) 1994.

FASHION - Fabrique.

Fan Club

Personnel:	REINER LOWRY	bs	A
	KAREL SILVA	keyb'ds	A
	NICK CHRISTIAN SLAYER	gtr	A
	JOHN TEETA	gtr, drms, vcls	A

45:	Avenue/Night Caller (PS)	(M&S SJP 791B) 1978

The **Fan Club** 45 came in a wraparound photocopied picture sleeve. It is now quite collectable.

Nick Christian Slayer was later in Plastics UK and Transvision Vamp.

The Fans

45s:	Givin' Me That Look/Stay The Night/	
	He'll Have To Go (PS)	(Fried Egg EGG 3) 1979
	Cars And Explosions/	
	Dangerous Goodbyes (PS)	(Albion FAN 1) 1980
	You Don't Live Here Anymore/	
	Following You (PS)	(Fried Egg EGG 10) 1981

A new wave band whose rhythm section sounds very much like **The Police** on *Following You*, which can also be heard on *E(gg)clectic* (Fried Egg FRY 2) 1981.

Fashion (Music)

Personnel:	DIK DAVIES	drms	ABCDEF
	LUKE	gtr, vcls	A
	JOHN MULLIGAN	bs	ABCDEF
	MARTIN DEE HARRIS	vcls, gtr	BCD
	MARTIN RECCI	bs, vcls	CDEF
	MARTIN STOKER	drms	C
	TONY	vcls	C
	TROY TATE	vcls, gtr	E
	ALAN DARBY	vcls, gtr	F

HCP

ALBUMS:	1(A)	PRODUCT PERFECT	(Fashion FML 1) 1979 -
	2(D)	FABRIQUE	(Arista SPART 1185) 1982 10
	3(F)	TWILIGHT OF IDOLS	(De Stijl EPC 25909) 1984 69

NB: There was also a CD compilation *The Height Of Fashion* (Arista 260626) 1990. It was basically a reissue of their *Fabrique* album with additional tracks.

HCP

45s:	*	Steady Eddie Steady/	
		Killing Time (PS)	(Fashion Music FM 001) 1978 -
		Citinite/Wastelife (PS)	(Fashion Music FM 002) 1979 -
		Silver Blades/Silver Blades (A Deeper Cut) (PS)	

		(Fashion Music FM 003)	1980 -
+	Move On/Mutant Move (PS)	(Arista ARIST 440)	1981 -
+	Streetplayer (Mechanik)/Streetplayer (Mechanik) (alt version) (PS)	(Arista ARIST 456)	1981 46
	Something In Your Picture/Something In Your Picture (alt version) (7", PS)	(Arista ARIST 472)	1982 -
	Something In Your Picture/Something In Your Picture (alt version)/Motor Drive/ Smokey Dialogue (12", PS)	(Arista ARIST 472)	1982 -
	Love Shadow/Let's Play Dirty (PS)	(Arista ARIST 483)	1982 51
+	Eye Talk/Slow Down	(Epic A 4106)	1984 69
+	Dreaming/White Line Fever (PS)	(CBS A 4327)	1984 -
	You In The Night/Yamashata Theme	(De Stijl A 4502)	1984 -
	You In The Night/Yamashata Theme/Hurricane/ White Stuff (double pack)	(CBS DA 4502)	1984 -

NB: * Initially issued in a green picture sleeve. Later copies came in a black and white one. + Issued in both 7" and 12" formats.

Originally formed as **Fashion Music** in Birmingham as a trio in 1977. Growing up in the punk era they played a clever form of pop that drew on elements of reggae, punk and electronic music but translated them into their own music brand. Their debut 45 *Steady Eddie* was a great record, synthesized and crisp, slow and moody, with a dash of evil. Their first three 45s and album were recorded by the trio on their own label but distributed by Miles Copeland's 'Faulty' products. Prior to the *Silver Blades* 45, Dee Harris replaced Luke on vocals and guitar. Luke went to France.

In many respects their debut album *Product Perfect* is unremarkable. Most of the material was penned by Mulligan and Davis. It did feature some subtle hooks and effects, though.

In 1980, they abbreviated their name to **Fashion** and expanded briefly to a sextet (line-up 'C'). Vocalist Tony in this line-up had previously been in **Neon Hearts**) but they reverted to a quartet (line-up 'D') for their next four 45s and the *Fabrique* album, having been signed by Arista. This was much funkier and dancey, with immediate appeal. It actually made it to No. 10 in the album charts. All four of their 45s in this era were culled from the album and two of them *Streetplayer (Mechanik)* and *Love Shadow* charted at No. 46 and 51 respectively.

In October 1982, former **Teardrop Explodes** member Troy Tate replaced Dee Harris, who formed Zee with Pink Floyd's Richard Wright. Later, in 1983, Tate, who went solo was replaced by ex-Cado Belle member Alan Darby on vocals and guitar.

In late 1983, they switched to Epic for three further 45s and an album. Their first 45 *Eye Talk* became their last hit single, peaking at No. 69. Their *Twilight Of Idols* album continued in the style of *Fabrique* - dancey with solid rhythms. Most of the material on this album was written by their new wild guitarist Alan Darby. It charted at No. 69.

When they split in 1984, Darby went on to do session work for Bonnie Tyler, Paul Young and Robert Palmer among others. Mulligan also made videos for **The Stranglers**.

The 1990 compilation CD *The Height Of Fashion* is the best introduction to their music now.

Fast Cars

Personnel:	TONY DYSON	drms	A
	CRAIG HILTON	gtr	A
	STEVE MURRAY	vcls	A
	STUART MURRAY	bs	A

45:	The Kids Just Wanna Dance/ You're So Funny (PS)	(Streets Ahead SA 3) 1979

Fast Cars came from Manchester and once supported **The Jam**. *The Kids Just Wanna Dance*, which came out in October 1979, was certainly likely to get the kids dancing and had considerable commercial appeal. Sadly, it didn't sell in quantity and is now rare and collectable. So it's inclusion on *100% British Mod* (Captain Mod MODSKA DCD) 1998 is particularly welcome.

In 1996, the original line-up reformed for a one-off gig with **Salford Jets**.

Fast Set

Personnel:	PETER FARRUGIA	gtr, synth	A
	DAVID KNIGHT	synth, programming	A
	MARK SEBASTIAN JONES	voice	A

45:	Junction One/ Children Of The Revolution (PS)	(Axis AXIS 1) 1980

The Fast Set were clearly fans of Marc Bolan. They covered *Children Of The Revolution* on the 'B' side of their sole 45 and also had another Bolan composition *King Of The Rumbling Spires* included on *Some Bizzare Album* (Some Bizzarre BZLP 1) in 1981.

The Fatal Microbes

Personnel incl:	HONEY BANE (DONNA BOYLAN)	vcls	A
	PETE FENDER	gtr	A

EP:	1(A)	FATAL MICROBES MEET THE POISON GIRLS (includes *Violence Grows* and *Beautiful Pictures*) (12" EP) (Small Wonder WEENY 3) 1979

45:	Violence Grows/Beautiful Pictures/ Cry Baby (PS)	(Small Wonder SMALL 20) 1979

A short-lived punk band. Vocalist **Honey Bane** (real name Donna Boylan was just 14 when they formed. She was residing in a home for wayward teenagers. Their guitarist Pete Fender was the son of **Poison Girls'** lead singer Vi Subversa and through this connection **The Fatal Microbes** got two of their songs, *Violence Grows* and *Beautiful Pictures*, included on an EP *Fatal Microbes Meet The Poison Girls*, which featured two **Poison Girls'** tracks on the other side. When the EP sold out, but demand for the record didn't go away Small Wonder put out the two **Fatal Microbes** tracks on a single with a third song, *Cry Baby* added. *Violence Grows* is an excellent song distinguished by **Honey Bane**'s distinctive vocals and a slow backing influenced by Velvet Underground at times. *Beautiful Pictures* is a much faster and more typical punker. *Cry Baby* is an interesting interpretation of 'Cry baby bunting, daddy's gone a-hunting', but it's **Honey Bane**'s vocals that really make this disc.

After this 45 **Honey Bane** went solo (see entry for details).

Violence Grows later resurfaced on *Small Wonder Punk Singles Collection, Vol.1* (Anagram CDPUNK 29) 1994 and *Vol. 2* (Anagram CDPUNK 70) 1996 gave a further airing to *Beautiful Picture*.

Pete Fender was later in **Omega Tribe**.

The Feckin' Ejits

Personnel incl: AIDAN STERLING

The Feckin' Ejits came from Aylesbury in Buckinghamshire. They were a humorous and energetic band with a popular, anthemic live set. Their sole

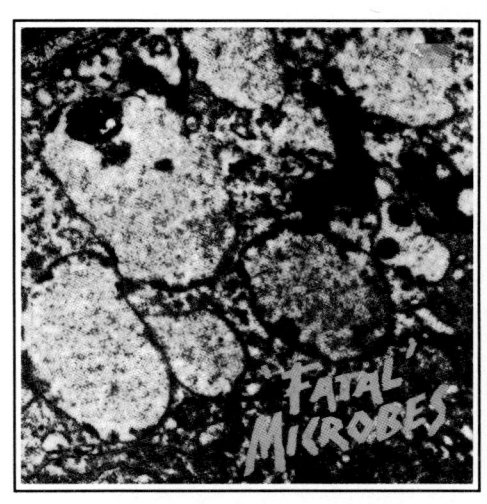

THE FATAL MICROBES - Violence Grows.

vinyl epitaph was *The Picket Song* and *Ejits Party* on *This Is Oi!* (Oi! OIR 004) 1986, which was later reissued on CD (Captain Oi! AHOY CD 6) 1993.

The Feelies

Personnel incl: MERCER
MILLION

45s:	Raised Eyebrows/Facé La (PS)	(Rough Trade RT 024) 1979
+	Facé La/The Boy With Perpetual Nervousness/ Everybody's Got Something To Hide (Except Me And My Monkey)	(Stiff no #) 1979
*	Everybody's Got Something To Hide/ Original Love	(Stiff BUY 65) 1980

NB: + A promotional flexi-disc free with 'Be Stiff' fanzine. Only 5,000 copies were produced. * Unreleased.

A four-piece band. *Raised Eyebrows* was an instrumental single. They then signed to Stiff to record their own different interpretation of Lennon and McCartney's *Everybody's Got Something To Hide (Except Me And My Monkey)*.

Graham Fellows

45:	*	Men Of Oats And Creosote/Rebecca	(EMI INT 598) 1979

NB: * 'B' side credited to **Jilted John**.

Graham Fellows was the man who conceived **Jilted John** and on the 'B' side of this 45 he reverts to his alter ego. The 'A' side, recorded under his own name, was a bizarre cloth-cap tribute to traditionalists from the north, backed by a brass band and lavish orchestration, on which **Fellows** sounds like a cross between **John Cooper-Clarke** and Clive Dunn.

Fenzyx

Personnel:	TONY GIALANZE	A
	LYONS	A
	O'CONNELL	A
	RUTTER	A

45:	Angels Of Mercy/Soldiers	(Ellie Jay EJSP 9655) 1981

This release is noticeable for the demo version being pressed by mistake and not the proper recording.

Alex Fergusson

45:	Stay With Me Tonight/Brushing Your Hair	(Red RR 003) 1980

This as a one-off solo outing by **Alternative TV**'s Scottish-born guitarist. Much later in 1994, he released an eponymous album on his own label (500 copies were pressed and the album was only available by mail order) followed by a CD *Perverse Ballad* (Overground OVER 51CD) 1996 in a numbered limited edition of 500, which displays his songwriting credentials for all to see.

Eddie Fiction

45:	UFO Part 2/UFO Part 1 (PS)	(Absurd ABSURD 2) 1979

This was actually former **Nosebleeds** member **Eddie Banger** recording under a pseudonym.

File Under Pop

45:	Heathrow/Corrugate/ Heathrow SLB (PS)	(Rough Trade RT 011) 1979

A one-off experimental indie single. Some members were also involved in **AK Process**.

Fingerprintz

Personnel incl:	KENNY ALTON	bs, vcls	AB
	CHA BURNZ	gtr, vcls	AB
	JIMME O'NEILL	gtr, vcls	AB
	BOB SCHILLING	drms	A
	DOGDAN WICZLING	drms	B

ALBUMS:	1(A)	THE VERY DAB	(Virgin V 2119) 1979
	2(A)	DISTINGUISHING MARKS	(Virgin V 2170) 1980
	3(B)	BEAT NOIR	(Virgin V 2201) 1981

EP:	1(A)	DANCING WITH MYSELF (12", PS) (Dancing With Myself/Sean's New Shoes)	(Virgin 12 23512) 1979

45s:	Do You Want To Know A Secret/ Who's Your Friend (PS)	(Virgin VDJ 28) 1977
	Dancing With Myself/ Sean's New Shoes (PS)	(Virgin VS 235) 1978
	Who's Your Friend/Do You Want To Know A Secret/ Nervz/Night Nurse (PS)	(Virgin VS 252) 1979
	Tough Luck/Detonator (PS)	(Virgin VS 278) 1979
	Bullet Proof Heart/Hide And Seek (PS)	(Virgin VS 358) 1980
	Houdini Love/All About You (PS)	(Virgin VS 375) 1980
	Shadowed/Madame X (PS)	(Virgin VS 420) 1981
	Bohemian Dance/Coffee & Screams (PS)	(Virgin VS 432) 1981
	The Beat Escape/Disorient Express (PS)	(Virgin VS 452) 1981

A Scottish new wave group lead by Jimme O'Neill. In 1979, they toured as support to Rachel Sweet and **The Skids** among others. Their lead vocalist Jimme O'Neill also penned *Say When* for Lene Plaits.

Their debut album *The Very Dab* featured eleven more of O'Neill's dark tales. It shows the band specialising in elaborate, multi-layered guitar rhythms alongside powerful reggae-influenced bass lines. The end result is a variable album but it works quite well on tracks like *Fingerprince* and *Wet Job*.

Their second album *Distinguishing Marks* was produced by **Nick Garvey** of **The Motors**. In 1980, they contributed *Yes Eyes* to the *Cash Cows* (Virgin MILK 1) sampler. The third, *Beat Noir*, experimented with rock/funk fusion, but none of the albums broke the band commercially.

They also acted as **Lene Lovich**'s backing band for a while. O'Neill penned her hit single *Say When*.

FINGERPRINTZ - The Very Dab

O'Neill and Wiczling went on to play on Jacqui Brooke's solo album *Sob Stories*. Wiczling also recorded with **Adam Ant** and played on some of his tours.

Fire Engines

Personnel: RUSSELL BURN   gtr   A
            DAVID HENDERSON   gtr, vcls   A
            GRAHAM MAIN   bs   A
            MURRAY SLADE   gtr   A

ALBUM: 1(A) LUBRICATE YOUR LIVING ROOM
                                  (Pop: Aural ACC 001) 1980

NB: They also had an album *Aufgeladen und Bereit fur Action und Spass* (Fast America) 1981 released in the U.S.A..

45s: Get Up And Use Me/
          Everything Roses (PS)   (Codex Comms. CDX 01) 1980
      *   Candyskin/Meat Whiplash (PS)   (Pop: Aural POP 010) 1981
          Big Gold Dream/
          Sympathetic Anaesthetic (PS)   (Pop: Aural POP 013) 1981
      x   Big Gold Dream/Sympathetic Anaesthetic/
          New Things In Cartons (12", PS)   (Pop: Aural POP 01312) 1981

NB: * This came with a fold-out picture sleeve in a poly bag. x Some copies came in a gatefold picture sleeve.

A Scottish quartet who were full of punk energy with rugged electric guitars and aggressive vocals. There is a lot of overlap between their U.K. and U.S. albums, but if you can track down the U.S. one do. It includes two of their finest moments not on the British one, *Candyskin* and *Everything Roses*. It also substitutes *Meat Whiplash* for the less exciting *Lubricate Your Living Room Pt. 2*.

The First Steps

45s: The Beat Is Back/She Ain't In Love/
          Let's Go Cuboids (PS)   (English Rose ER 1) 1979
          Anywhere Else But Here/Airplay/
          I Got The News (PS)   (English Rose ER 111) 1981

From Mildenhall in Suffolk, **The First Steps** were the county's leading 'mod revival' band. They recorded two 45s on their own English Rose label, which was named after **The Jam** track on *All Mod Cons*.

Fischer Z

Personnel: DAVID GRAHAM   bs   AB
            STEVE LIDDLE   drms, perc   AB
            STEVE SKOLNIK   keyb'ds, vcls   A
            JOHN WATTS   gtr, vcls   AB

                                                       HCP
ALBUMS: 1(A) WORD SALAD   (United Artists UAG 30232) 1979 66
(up to 2(A) GOING DEAF FOR A LIVING
1986)   (United Artists UAG 30295) 1980 -
        3(B) RED SKIES OVER PARADISE
                                  (United Artists UAG 30326) 1981 -
        4(-) ONE MORE TWIST   (EMI EMC 3402) 1982 -
        5(-) THE ICEBERG MODEL   (EMI EMC 3427) 1983 -

NB: (1) also issued on CD (Liberty CDP 746 684 2) 1987. (2) also issued on CD (Liberty CDP 746 685 2) 1987. (3) also issued on CD (Liberty CDP 746 683 2) 1987. (4) and (5) are solo efforts by John Watts. There's also a compilation *Going Red For A Salad (UA Years 1979 - 1982)* (Capitol Greenlight Series GO 2030) 1990, also on CD (Capitol CZ 295) 1990. The CD has four additional cuts, *One Voice*, *Involuntary Movement*, *Mayday Mayday* and *I Smelt Roses (In The Underground)*.

                                                       HCP
45s: Wax Dolls/
(up to   Angry Brigade (PS)   (United Artists UP 36458) (PS) 1978 -
1986)   Remember Russia/

FISCHER Z - The Worker.

          Bigger Since Now (PS)   (United Artists UP 36486) 1979 -
          The Worker/Kitten Curry (PS) (United Artists UP 36509) 1979 53
          First Impressions/
          High Wire Walker (PS)   (United Artists BP 305) 1979 -
          So Long/Hiding (PS)   (United Artists BP 342) 1979 72
          Limbo/The Rat Man (PS)   (United Artists BP 360) 1980 -
          Marliese/Right Hand Man (PS) (United Artists BP 387) 1981 -
          Cutters Lullaby/
          You'll Never Find Brian Here (PS) (United Artists BP 398) 1981 -
      *   Speaking A Different Language/
          Ha Ha Ha (PS)   (EMI EMI 5239) 1981 -
      *   One Voice/Holiday In France (PS) (EMI EMI 5266) 1982 -
      *   Your Fault/Sarawego (PS)   (EMI EMI 5298) 1982 -
      *   I Smelt Roses/I Need Action (PS) (EMI EMI 5361) 1982 -
      *   Mayday Mayday/
          Turn The Lights On (PS)   (EMI EMI 5387) 1983 -

NB: * These were solo singles by John Watts.

The talent behind **Fischer Z** was the songwriter and musician John Watts. The band were a significant link between new wave pop and the synthesized music of the early eighties.

Their first two singles *Wax Dolls* and *December Russia* met with some acclaim. The sleeve to *Remember Russia* contained a Ralph Steadman cartoon illustration. Their third single *The Worker* actually broke into the charts, where it spent five weeks and climbed to No. 53.

Their debut album *Word Salad* also made an impression in the album charts, spending a week at No. 66. Subsequent efforts failed to build on or even sustain this early commercial success.

In 1981, Watts started recording under his own name, but his solo efforts made little impact.

FISCHER Z - Red Skies Over Paradise.

Red Skies Over Paradise is a pleasant, but in no way special album. *In England* is fast and punchy, *Battalions Of Strangers* is one of the strongest and most melodic songs and *Cruise Missiles* has a clear message to get across:-

"We share a common destination
Each person has their time to die
But men are speeding up our journey
By seeing what they can destroy with their
Cruise missiles (we're living near those)
Cruise missiles (we're looking for those)
Cruise missiles (they're not five years away)"
(from *Cruise Missiles*)

He reformed **Fischer Z** in 1988 and they recorded further albums - *Reveal* (1988), *Destination Paradise* (1992) and *Kamikaze Shirt* (1994) - and 45s, but those fall outside this book's timespan.

Fish Turned Human

Personnel:	ADRIAN COLE	piano, vcls	A
	PHILIP FURIE	vcls	A
	MICHAEL IKON	gtr	A
	JULIAN TREASURE	drms, vcls	A

EP:	1(A)	TURKEYS IN CHINA (The International/ Porky's Minion/Here Come The Nuns/ 24 Hour Shop) (PS)	(Sequel PART 1) 1979
45:		Drinking Milk In Cars/ (track by Animal Transport)	(Detour DEEP 2) 1981

Their EP was recorded at Spaceward Studio on 24th August 1978, with Andy Metcalfe (of **The Soft Boys**) guesting on bass, and released the following year. On offer is experimental guitar-based indie music which works best on *The International* and *24 Hour Shop*.

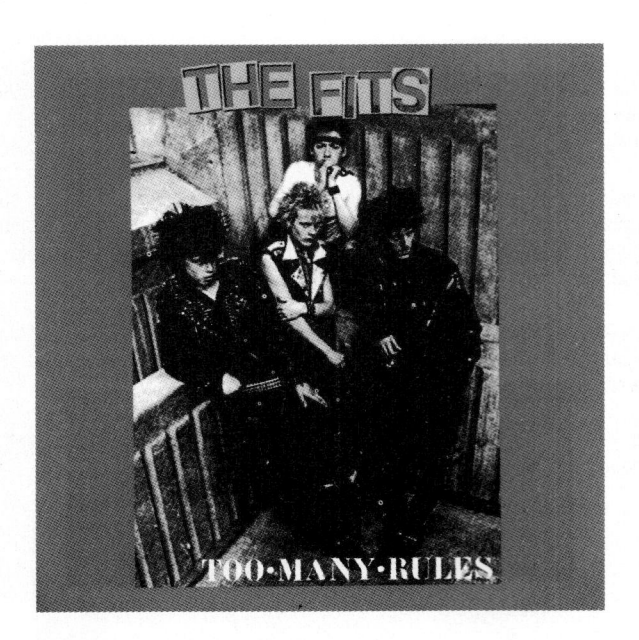

THE FITS - Too Many Rules.

The Fits

Personnel:	ANDY BARON	bs	ABCDE
	BILL	gtr	A
	MICK CRUDGE	vcls	ABCDE
	KEV HALLIDAY	drms	AB
	STEVE WITHERS	gtr	BCDE
	PAUL	drms	C
	TEZ McDONALD	drms	D
	RICKY McGUIRE	bs	E

ALBUMS:	1(B)	NOTHING AND NOWHERE	(Rondelet ABOUT 6) 1982
	2( )	FACT OR FICTION (mini-LP)	(Trapper FIT 3) 1985

NB: There's also two CDs: *The Punk Collection* (Captain Oi! AHOY CD 41) 1995 and *Too Many Rules* (Get Back GET 18CD) 1997.

FISH TURNED HUMAN - Turkeys In China.

EPs:	1(B)	YOU SAID WE'D NEVER MAKE IT (Odd Bod Mod/ Bad Dream/Listen To Me) (PS)	(Lightbeat/Beat The System FIT 1) 1980
	2(E)	THE LAST LAUGH (Last Laugh/Different Ways/ Nothing To Prove) (PS)	(Rondelet ROUND 30) 1982

NB: (1) came in a wraparound picture sleeve. (2) was also issued as a picture disc.

45s:	Think For Yourself: Burial/ Straps (PS)	(Rondelet ROUND 13) 1982
	Tears Of A Nation/Bravado/ Breaking Point (PS)	(Corpus Christi ITS 9) 1983
	Action/Achilles Heel (PS)	(Trapper FIT 1) 1984
	Action/Achilles Heel/ Peace And Quiet (12", PS)	(Trapper EARFIT 1) 1985
	Fact Or Fiction/Give Away (PS)	(Trapper FIT 2) 1985

The Fits formed in Blackpool in October 1979. By the end of the year the punk band's original guitarist Bill was replaced by Steve Withers. In 1980, they moved to Manchester to record their three track EP *You Said We'd Never Make It*. The first 1,500 copies were released on Beat The System and the rest on Lightbeat. It sold over 3,000 copies in all and got to No. 2 in the punk charts. 'Ignore politics, ignore religion'... the stand out track *Listen To Me* was a fine slice of punk nihilism. *Odd Bod Mod* was a rant against the mod revivalists of 1979.

By the Autumn of 1981, **The Fits** were touring quite extensively as a support act and playing at major venues. On 2nd November, they entered Ric Rak Studios in Leeds where they recorded *Burial* and *Straps*. Six days later they signed to Rondelet, who released both tracks on a 45 in January 1983. Both songs were the business and the release was well received. In March, they returned to Ric Rak studios to record an album's worth of material, which was released as *Nothing And Nowhere* in June. Possibly not as good as their earlier EP and 45, it still had its moments with some fine lyrics. The title track stands out, *Prostitute* and *Make Me Wanna* feature fine guitar work, *I Don't Need It* is a 100 m.p.h. rant and there's also a punk version of Rolling Stones' classic *Jumping Jack Flash*, though it pales in comparison to the original. Kev Halliday had left the band in May and was replaced by a guy called Paul for one gig, who in June made way for ex-**One Way System** member Tez McDonald. Then Andy Baron departed in August, with Ricky McGuire (previously of **Chaotic Youth**) coming in to replace him. This new line-up ('E') recorded the *Last Laugh* (EP) in October 1982, with **Knox** of **The Vibrators** handling production.

Unfortunately, Rondelet was on the way out, a tour to coincide with the EP's release was cut back from thirteen to three dates and a European tour cancelled. This affected sales, which was a pity because musically this EP was an improvement on their album.

In 1983, a new line-up recorded *Tears Of A Nation* for Corpus Christi. The title cut was arguably their finest moment and met with deserved critical acclaim. It topped the punk chart and got to No. 3 in the indie chart. **The Fits** then switched to **Peter and The Test Tube Babies**' Trapper Records for the *Action* and *Fact Or Fiction* singles and a mini-album, before going their separate ways in March 1986.

In 1995, *I Hate*, *Time Is Right* and *Listen To Me* were included on *Beat The System Punk Singles Collection* (Anagram CDPUNK 61). The same year *Burial* and *Last Laugh* figured on *Rondelet Punk Singles Collection* (Anagram CDPUNK 49) 1995, which is also available on vinyl (Captain Oi! AHOY LP 513) 1996.

All of their recordings are compiled on the twenty-seven track *Fits Punk Collection* (Captain Oi! AHOY CD 41) 1995 which comes with an eight page booklet and full sleeve notes by vocalist Mick Crudge which are summarised here. Alternatively, *Too Many Rules* (Get Back GET 18) includes their recordings for Rondelet and their first EP on Beat The System/Lightbeat on the nineteen track vinyl collection. The CD release includes the three additional cuts from their classic 1983 7" released on Corpus Christi. *Too Many Rules* can also be heard on *100% Hardcore Punk* (Captain Oi! AHOY DCD 84) 1998.

PATRICK FITZGERALD - Backstreet Boys.

Patrick Fitzgerald

ALBUMS:
1. GRUBBY STORIES (Small Wonder/Polydor 2383 533) 1979
2. GIFTS AND TELEGRAMS (Red Flame RF 8) 1982
3. DRIFTING TOWARDS VIOLENCE (Himilaya HIM 009) 1984

NB: There's also a CD compilation *The Very Best Of Patrick Fitzgerald: Safety-Pin In My Heart* (Anagram CD PUNK 31) 1994.

EPs:
1. SAFETY-PIN STUCK IN MY HEART (Banging And Shouting/Safety Pin Stuck In My Heart/Work Rest Play Reggae/Set We Free/Optimism/Reggae) (Small Wonder SMALL 4) 1977
2. THE PARANOID WARD/THE BEDROOM TAPES (Babysitter/Irrelevant Battles/Cruellest Crime/Paranoid Ward/Bingo Crowd) (mono/stereo) (Small Wonder WEENY 1) 1978
3. THE PARANOID WARD/THE BEDROOM TAPES (12") (Babysitter/Irrelevant Battles/Cruellest Crime/Paranoid Ward/Bingo Crowd/Ragged Generation/Live Out My Stars/George) (mono/stereo) (Small Wonder WEENY 1) 1978

45s:
Buy Me Sell Me/Little Dippers/Trendy/Backstreet Boys (PS) (Small Wonder SMALL 6) 1977
All Sewn Up/Hammersmith Odeon (Polydor 2059 091) 1979
Improve Myself/The Bingo Crowd/My New Family (Polydor 2059 135) 1979
Tonight (Red Flame FSEP 1) 1980
Personal Loss/Straight Boy (Red Flame RF 708) 1982

Patrick Fitzgerald was unique on the British punk scene - an acoustic poet, who couldn't really sing but could just about master an acoustic guitar. Some people considered him 'the Bob Dylan of punk'. A true London East Ender. He was born in Stratford, grew up in Leytonstone and went to school in Forest Gate. He left school with six 'O' Levels and worked in an office for a couple of years whilst learning to play acoustic guitar. A long period on the dole and abortive attempts to get a band together followed. He auditioned unsuccessfully for **London SS** (which never got off the ground) in 1976. Then he worked with a theatrical group for a few months, during which time he sent a demo tape to the Walthamstowe-based Small Wonder label, who offered him a deal. He also wrote 'Babytalk' one of two one-act plays presented by The Activists Youth Theatre Group for a ten day London season. It ran at The Garage, Holbein Place, SW1.

His first release, *Safety Pin Stuck In My Heart* EP, released in December 1977, attracted some attention in the rock press. The follow-up four track 45 featuring *Backstreet Boys* built on this. *Backstreet Boys*, in which he articulates the fear of being beaten up by thugs was arguably his finest moment. *The Paranoid Ward* (EP), issued in October 1978 in both 7" and 12" formats (the latter with three additional cuts), helped further to establish his style. His strength was in his lyrics - often angry or sad and sometimes strange - they mostly dealt with the punk lifestyle and life in late seventies Britain for young people.

He also recorded three sessions for John Peel. The first broadcast on 15th February 1978 featured *Don't Tell Me*, *Bingo Crowd*, *Little Dippers*, *Safety Pin* and *Back Street Boys*. A second followed on 31st July with *No Fun Football*, *Little Fishes*, *A Missed Kid*, *Sound Of My Street* and *Jarvis*. The final one on 17th April 1979, comprised *Suicidal Wreck*, *Improve Myself*, *Tonight*, *All The Splattered Children* and *Dance Music - Late Night*.

His Small Wonder releases secured him quite a bit of live work in punk venues around the country. He also supported **The Jam** on a national tour. He attracted the attention of Polydor, who offered him a deal. The 45s and the *Grubby Stories* album resulted.

On *Grubby Stories* some tracks were just acoustic. Others utilised a full backing band with Peter Wilson (his producer) on guitar and keyboards, **Buzzcocks**' drummer John Maher and **Penetration** bassist Robert Blamire. The album had its moments, but didn't sell significantly and **Fitzgerald**'s relationship with Polydor became short-term.

In the early eighties, **Fitzgerald** continued to record and perform on the 'alternative' music circuit. *The Moonlight Tapes* (Armageddon MOON 1) 1981 included *Breathing Painful* and he recorded a few more 45s and two further albums on Red Flame and Himalaya.

Irrelevant Battles can also be heard on the *20 Of Another Kind* (Polydor SUPER POLS 1006) 1979 compilation, whilst *All Sewn Up* and *Improve Myself* figured on *Vol. 2* (Polydor POLX 1) of the same series, *Safety Pin Stuck In My Heart* and *Buy Me Sell Me* can both be heard on *Small Wonder Punk Singles Collection, Vol. 1* (Anagram CDPUNK 29) 1994, whilst *Vol. 2* (Anagram CDPUNK 70) 1996 includes *Set Me Free*, *Little Dippers* and *Irrelevant Battles*. Later, in 1999, *Safety-Pin Stuck In My Heart* got a further outing on the 5-CD box set *1-2-3-4 - A History Of Punk And New Wave 1976 - 1979* (MCA/Universal MCD 60066).

The Anagram CD *Safety-Pin Stuck In My Heart* compilation contains 31 tracks and compiles the best of his material from his days with Small Wonder and then with Polydor. It's well worth listening to.

In retrospect, **Fitzgerald** is of significance as a minor cult figure of the punk era and a genuine talent.

Five O

Personnel:
SI GIBSON	vcls	A
JAKE	drms	A
JIM	bs	A
KAF McKEE	gtr	A

Five O hailed from Bromley in Kent. Their vinyl debut was *Dr. Crippins*, a song about the notorious Victorian murderer, which appeared on *Oi! Oi! That's Yer Lot* (Secret SEC 5) in 1983. It was a promising effort but they split in 1984 before this promise was fulfilled. *Dr. Crippins* got a further airing on *Sound Of Oi!* in 1988 and they did reform but no new recordings were released.

Five Or Six

Personnel:	GRAHAM CASSIE	bs, vcls	A
	DAVID HARPER	gtr, vcls	A
	SIMON HARPER	drms	A
	DANIEL WHITTOCK	gtr, vcls	A
	DAVID KNIGHT	drm machine, synth	A

ALBUM:	1(A)	THRIVING AND HAPPY LAND	
			(Cherry Red FRIZBEE 2) 1982

EPs:	1(A)	POLAR EXPOSURE (12", PS) (Nine tracks in all)	(Cherry Red 12CHERRY 23) 1981
	2(A)	FOUR FROM FIVE OR SIX (12", PS)	(Cherry Red 12CHERRY 43) 1982

45:	Another Reason/The Trial (PS)	(Cherry Red CHERRY 19) 1981

An indie band whose music unfortunately sounds like a dirge of nothingness. The 45 was produced by Kevin Coyne. They also contributed *Portrait* to *Pillows And Prayers* (Cherry Red 2RED 41) 1982, also on CD (CDMRED 41) 1996.

The Fix

Personnel:	CHARLIE BARRETT	bs	A
	CY CURNIN	vcls	A
	RUPERT GREENNALL	keyb'ds	A
	JAMIE WEST	lead gtr	A
	ADAM WOODS	drms	A

45:	Lost Planes/I've Been Here Before (PS)	(101 Club 101) 1981

A synthesized pop 45. This band later became **The Fixx**.

THE FIX - Lost Planes.

The Fixx

Personnel:	ALFIE AGIES	bs	A
	CY CURNIN	vcls	A
	RUPERT GREENNALL	keyb'ds	A
	JAMIE WEST	gtr	A
	ADAM WOODS	drms, perc	A

ALBUMS: (up to 1986)	1(A)	SHUTTERED ROOM	(Fixx FX 1001) 1982
	2(A)	REACH THE BEACH	(Fixx FX 1002) 1983
	3(A)	PHANTOMS	(Fixx FX 1003) 1984
	4(A)	WALKABOUT	(Fixx FX 1004) 1986

NB: (2) also issued on CD (MCA MCAD 5419) 1986. (3) also issued on CD (MCA DIDX 127) 1984. (4) also issued on CD (MCA MCAD 5705) 1986.

HCP

45s: (up to 1986) *	Some People/I've Found You (PS)	(MCA FIXX 1) 1982	-
	Stand Or Fall/The Strain (PS)	(MCA FIXX 2) 1982	54
	Red Skies/Is It By Instinct (PS)	(MCA FIXX 3) 1982	57
	Saved By Zero/Overboard The Fool (PS)	(MCA FIXX 4) 1983	-
	One Thing Leads To Another/Opinions/Red Skies/Stand Or Fall (double-pack, PS)	(MCA FIXX 4) 1983	-
	One Thing Leads To Another/Reach The Beach (PS)	(MCA FIXX 5) 1983	-
	Are We Ourselves/Questions (PS)	(MCA FIXX 6) 1984	-
	Less Cities More Moving People/Deeper And Deeper (PS)	(MCA FIXX 7) 1984	-
	Less Cities More Moving People/Deeper And Deeper (12", PS)	(MCA FIXX 17) 1984	-
	I Will/Questions (PS)	(MCA FIXX 9) 1985	-
	I Will/Questions (12", PS)	(MCA FIXX 19) 1985	-
	Secret Separation/Sense The Adventure	(MCA FIXX 10) 1986	-
	Secret Separation/Rediscover/Sense The Adventure (12", PS)	(MCA FIXXT 10) 1986	-

NB: * This was also available as a picture disc.

An atmospheric synthesizer dance combo whose records were produced by Rupert Hine. They were originally known as **The Fix** adding an 'x' after their first 45. There was also a change of bassist with Alfie Agies replacing Charlie Barnett.

Their first album *Shuttered Room* produced two minor hits with *Stand Or Fall* and *Red Skies*. They climbed to No. 54 and 57 respectively and each spent a total of four weeks in the charts.

Rupert Hine's production possibly gave them the edge over several other bands around of this ilk.

Flag Of Convenience

Personnel incl:	STEVE DIGGLE	bs, vcls	ABC
	DAVE FARROW	bs	A
	JOHN MAHER	drms	AB
	D.P.	keyb'ds	A
	GARY HAMER	bs	BC
	MARK	keyb'ds	B
	JOHN CAINE	drms	C

45s:	Life On The Telephone/The Other Man's Sin	(Sire SIR 4057) 1982
	Change/Longest Life (PS)	(Weird Systems WEIRD 1) 1984
	New House/Keep On Pushing	(M.C.M MCM 186) 1986
	Last Train To Safety (12")	(Flag Of Convenience FOC 1) 1987

Flag Of Convenience was formed in 1982 by former **Buzzcocks** Steve Diggle and John Maher. *Life On The Telephone*, released in September 1982, was pleasant enough and featured some sharp guitar work from Diggle, but it certainly wasn't in the same class as **The Buzzcocks**. There was a two year wait and some regrouping until line-up 'B' recorded *Change* in December 1984. Some time after John Caine came in on drums with both John Maher and Mark departing. This latest line-up 'C' made two further 45s. In 1987 they abbreviated heir name to F.O.C. and went on to record two further 12" EPs under this moniker.

THE FIXX - Saved By Zero.

The Flirts

45: The Kind Of Boy You Can't Forget/
Give Him A Great Big Kiss (PS) (Magnet) 1979

A well produced 45 with good drums, although it sounded a bit dated in 1979.

A Flock Of Seagulls

Personnel:
FRANK MAUDSLEY	bs		AB
PAUL REYNOLDS	gtr		A
ALI SCORE	drms		AB
MIKE SCORE	vcls, keyb'ds		AB
GARY STEADMAN	gtr		B

HCP
ALBUMS:	1(A)	A FLOCK OF SEAGULLS	(Jive HOP 201) 1982 32
	2(A)	LISTEN	(Jive HIP 4) 1983 16
	3(A)	THE STORY OF A YOUNG HEART	(Jive HIP 14) 1984 30
	4(B)	DREAM COME TRUE	(Jive HIP 32) 1986 -

NB: (1) also issued as a picture disc (Jive HOPX 201) 1983. (1) reissued in 1986. (2) also issued as a picture disc (Jive HIPX 4) 1983. (3) also issued on CD (Jive CHIP 14) 1984. There are also a number of compilations:- *The Best Of A Flock Of Seagulls* (Jive HIP 41) 1986 reissued in 1988 and also on CD (Jive CHIP 41) 1991; *The Best Of A Flock Of Seagulls* (Music Club MCCD 114) 1993; *The Best Of A Flock Of Seagulls* (Tring QED 082) 1996; *20 Classics Of The '80s* (Emporio EMPRCD 562) 1995; and *Telecommunications* (Elite ELITE 024 CD) 1992.

HCP
45s:	It's Not Me Talking/ Factory Music (PS)	(Cocteau COQ 23) 1981 -
	Telecommunication/Intro (PS)	(Jive JIVE 4) 1981 -
	Telecommunication/Intro (12", PS)	(Jive JIVET 4) 1981 -
	Modern Love Is Automatic/Windows (PS)	(Jive JIVE 8) 1981 -
*	Modern Love Is Automatic/Windows/You Can Run/ D.N.A.	(Jive JIVET 8) 1981 -
	Telecommunication/ Modern Love Is Automatic	(Jive JIVE 12) 1981 -
	Telecommunication/ Modern Love Is Automatic (12", PS)	(Jive JIVET 12) 1981 -
+	I Ran/Pick Me Up (PS)	(Jive JIVE 14) 1982 43
	I Ran/Pick Me Up/Messages (12", PS)	(Jive JIVET 14) 1982 -
+	Space Age Love Song/Windows (PS)	(Jive JIVE 17) 1982 34
	Space Age Love Song/ Windows (12", PS)	(Jive JIVET 17) 1982 -
	Wishing (I Had A Photograph Of You)/ Committed (PS)	(Jive JIVE 25) 1982 10
	Wishing (I Had A Photograph Of You)/ Committed (12", PS)	(Jive JIVET 25) 1982 -
+	Nightmares/Rosen Montag (PS)	(Jive JIVE 33) 1983 53
	Nightmares/Rosen Montag/ Last Flight (12", PS)	(Jive JIVET 33) 1983 -
+	Transfer Affection/I Ran (live) (PS)	(Jive JIVE 41) 1983 38
	Transfer Affection/I Ran (live) (12", PS)	(Jive JIVET 41) 1983 -
	(It's Not Me) Talking/Tanglimara (PS)	(Jive JIVE 47) 1983 -
	(It's Not Me) Talking/ Tanglimara (12", PS)	(Jive JIVET 47) 1983 -
#	The More You Live, The More You Love/ Lost Control (PS)	(Jive JIVE 62) 1984 26
	The More You Live, The More You Love/ Lost Control (12", PS)	(Jive JIVET 62) 1984 -
	Never Again (The Dancer)/ Living In Heaven (PS)	(Jive JIVE 78) 1984 -
	Never Again (The Dancer)/Living In Heaven/The More You Live, The More You Love (12", PS)	(Jive JIVET 78) 1984 -
	Who's That Girl (She's Got It)/Wishing (I Had A Photograph Of You) (PS)	(Jive JIVE 106) 1985 66
	Who's That Girl (She's Got It)/Wishing (I Had A Photograph Of You)/(Hits Medley) (12", PS)	(Jive JIVET 106) 1985 -
	Heartbeat Like A Drum/Heartbeat Like A Drum (inst) (PS)	(Jive JIVE 113) 1986 -
	Heartbeat Like A Drum/Heartbeat Like A Drum (inst.)/Heartbeat Like A Drum (alt version) (12", PS)	(Jive JIVET 113) 1986 -

NB: * Doublepack. + Also issued as a picture disc (JIVEP 14, 17, 33, 41). # Also issued as a square picture disc (JIVEP 62). Also relevant is *Collection* (Jive AFOS 1) 1985, a collection of their first ten 7" singles on Jive. The same *Collection* (Jive AFLOCK 1) 1985 was also available in 12" format.

A Flock Of Seagulls were formed in Liverpool in 1980 by hairdresser Mike Score and his brother Ali. They were part of the techno rock-pop movement that developed in the post-punk era. Their first break came when Bill Nelson released a 45 for them on his own Cocteau label. They then moved down to London where they were signed by CBS subsidiary Jive. They were the first of the second wave of Liverpool bands to achieve success in the 'States, where their videos were frequently shown on MTV.

With Mike Howlett producing their debut album *A Flock Of Seagulls* they began to develop their own style of futuristic techno rock-pop. Their other main distinctive trait was Mike Score's cockatoo hair style. Although it only climbed to No. 32, their debut album spent a very credible forty-four weeks in the charts. It did even better in the 'States, peaking at No. 10. It also spawned two minor hit singles; *I Ran* (No. 43), which actually got to No. 9 in the 'States and *Space Age Love Song*.

Their second album *Listen* was similar in style and reached greater heights commercially (No. 16) although chart success was sustained over a shorter period (ten weeks). The understated *Nightmares* only made it to No. 53 when issued as a 45 but *Transfer Affection* (No. 38) gave them a further hit when selected for 45 release.

For their third album *The Story Of A Young Heart* the group dispensed with Howlett's services and the album suffers as a consequence. The first side consisted largely of bland romantic ballads with dull vocals. The second side is rockier and an improvement with *Suicide Day* catching the ear. It also spawned one hit single *The More You Live, The More You Love* (No. 26). Sales were relatively disappointing and, although it climbed to No. 30, the album only spent five weeks in the charts.

Reynolds left after this album with ex-**Classix Nouveaux** guitarist Gary Steadman coming in as a replacement. With Mike Score handling production a further album *Dream Come True* comprising rather simplistic romantic numbers was released. Neither the album nor its pre-taster *Heartbeat Like A Drum* achieved any commercial success and Steadman joined The Roytes in late 1986. Mike Score soldiered on with various Philadelphia musicians for a while before the band disintegrated.

Compilation appearances by the band have included *I Ran* and *Wishing* on *New Wave Classics* (2-CD) (Disky DOU 878282) 1998, whilst *I Ran* and *Wishing If I Had A Photograph Of You* can also be found on *Wave (The Biggest New Wave Hits)* (3-CD set) (Disky HR 868442) 1996.

Flux Of Pink Indians

Personnel incl:
DEREK BIRKETT	bs		AB
COLIN LATTER	vcls		AB
ANDY SMITH	gtr		A
KEVIN HUNTER	gtr		B
MARTIN WILSON	drms		B

HCP
ALBUMS:	1(B)	STRIVE TO SURVIVE CAUSING THE LEAST SUFFERING POSSIBLE	(Spiderleg SDL 8) 1982 79
(up to 1987)	2(B)	THE FUCKING CUNTS TREAT US LIKE PRICKS	(Spiderleg SDL) 1984 -
	3(B)	UNCARVED BLOCK	(One Little Indian TPLP 1) 1987 -
	4(B)	TREAT	(One Little Indian TPLP 3) 1987 -

NB: (1) came with a 12-page booklet housed in a gatefold jacket, and later issued on vinyl (One Little Indian TRLP 2) 1987 and CD (One Little Indian TPCD 2) 1983 with their *Neu Smell* EP added. (3) credited to **Flux** and also issued on CD (TPLP 1CD) 1988 with their *Neu Smell* EP added. There's also a CD compilation *Not So Brave* (Overground OVER 67CD) 1997 and *Live Statement* (Overground OVER 87VP CD) 2000.

EPs:	1(B)	NEU SMELL (Neu Smell/Tube Disaster/Poem/ Sick Butchers/ Background Of Malfunction) (PS)	(Crass 321984/2) 1981
	2(B)	TAKING A LIBERTY	(Spiderleg SDL 16) 1985

NB: (1) also issued in various formats on One Little Indian in 1987.

A quasi-intellectual quartet who were formed by singer Colin Latter and bassist Derek Birkett after the demise of The Epileptics in 1979. They used punkish rock as a medium to express their far left political views. The musical menu is militaryistic with tuneless vocals but crisp drumming. Their brand of anarcho-punk was one of few rivals to **Crass** at the time. Their first album actually spent two weeks in the charts, peaking at No. 79.

Their debut EP *Neu Smell* sold around 40,000 copies. On the 'Pig-Side', the title cut and *Poem* are both narratives. *Tube Disaster* and both cuts on the 'Bacon-Side' are sung within a punkish rock format. The follow-up *Strive To Survive* sold around 20,000 copies with no promotion whatsoever. Their second album was extremely experimental testing the premise that if the music was virtually unlistenable punters would check out the lyrics instead.

Their third album *The Fucking Cunts Treat Us Like Pricks* was banned by HMV and removed from one shop by the Police. After that they veered more towards dance music and formed their own label One Little !ndian on which some of their records were subsequently reissued.

Not So Brave is a twenty-five cut compilation of (all bar one) unissued tracks and alternate takes. There's an album's worth of material from 1982 which eventually evolved into their debut album *Strive To Survive Causing The Least Suffering Possible*; their first demo from the summer of 1980; their contribution (*Tapioca Sunrise*) to the *Wargasm* album and live tracks taped at the Triad in their home town of Bishop's Stortford in 1982.

Live Statement (CD) captures the band at their uncompromising best during a concert in Nottingham in November 1982 with former Epileptics Kevin Hunter and Martin Wilson in the line-up.

They continued to record after 1986.

FLUX OF PINK INDIANS - Neu Smell EP.

The Flying Lizards

Personnel:
- STEVE BERESFORD — keyb'ds, bs, gtr — A
- DAVID CUNNINGHAM — gtr, violin, keyb'ds, vcls — AB
- RORY ACLAM — keyb'ds — B
- ANNE BARNARD — horns — B

ALBUMS:
- 1(A) FLYING LIZARDS (Virgin V 2150) 1980 60
- 2(A) FOURTH WALL (Virgin V 2190) 1981 -
- 3( ) TOP TEN (Statik STATLP 20) 1984 -

NB: (3) also issued on CD (Statik CDST 20) 1986.

45s:
- Summertime Blues/All Guitars (Virgin VS 230) 1978 -
- Money/Money (alt version) (Virgin VS 276) 1979 5
- T.V./Tube (PS) (Virgin VS 325) 1980 43
- Move On Up/Portugal (PS) (Virgin VS 381) 1980 -
- Hands 2 Take/Continuity (PS) (Virgin VS 392) 1981 -
- Sex Machine/Flesh And Steel (PS) (Statik TAK 19) 1984 -
- Sex Machine/Flesh And Steel/Machine Sex (12", PS) (Statik TAK 1912) 1984 -
- Dizzy Miss Lizzie/Dizzy (PS) (Statik TAK 25) 1984 -
- Dizzy Miss Lizzie/Dizzy (12", PS) (Statik TAK 2512) 1984 -

FLYING LIZARDS - Summertime Blues.

Fronted by pianist David Cunningham, **The Flying Lizards** were a novelty group in the new wave era. They developed their own unique sound by striping down classic rock songs to a slowed down minimalist synthesized level and adding robotic expressionless vocals. The end result was cover versions that sounded really different. It worked a treat on Eddie Cochrane's *Summertime Blues* and brought them a Top 5 hit with the follow-up *Money*, which enjoyed ten weeks in all in the charts. Both were also featured on their debut album, which also enjoyed a three week residency in the charts, peaking at No. 60.

Their second album *Fourth Wall* saw the band's sound veering between electro-pop and trance. It lacked overall consistency but had some interesting moments. The novelty of their sound soon wore off and after one further minor hit *T.V.* the hits dried up, but by now **The Flying Lizards** had earnt their place in rock history.

They weren't finished just yet either. They returned in 1984 with *Top Ten*, another album of bizarre rock 'n' roll covers of classics by Jimi Hendrix, James Brown, Little Richard, Leonard Cohen etc. In fact it's not bad and showcases Cunningham's skills in dissecting and then reconstructing classic rock songs in his own image.

David Cunningham also recorded a more serious solo effort *Grey Scale* (Piano PIANO 001) in 1980. In 1998, they contributed *Money* to *The Best Punk Anthems.... Ever!* (Virgin VTDCD 198) CD compilation. Earlier, in 1980, *Hands 2 Take* had figured on the sampler *Cash Cows* (Virgin MILK 1).

Fly On The Wall

Personnel:
- BUNKER BRAZIER — A
- LYNTON GARNER — A
- TONY MARTIN — A
- TUG — A

EP: 1(A) DEVON DUMB (In The News Today/Educated/Lucky Ones) (PS) (Next Wave NEXT 1) 1979

A very sought-after EP, which is reputedly very good. It was issued in a black and white photocopied cover. An indie-punkish band.

The Flys

Personnel:
- DAVE FREEMAN — gtr — AB
- JOE HUGHES — bs — AB
- PETE KING — drms — A
- NEIL O'CONNOR — gtr, vcls, keyb'ds — AB
- GRAHAM DEAKIN — drms — B

ALBUMS:
- 1(A) WAIKIKI BEACH REFUGEES (EMI EMC 3249) 1978
- 2(B) FLY'S OWN (EMI EMC 3316) 1979

NB: There's also a compilation *Flys Buzz Back* (See For Miles 304) 1990, also on CD (SEECD 304) 1990.

THE FLYS - Love And A Molotov Cocktail.

EPs:	1(A)	BUNCH OF FIVE (Saturday Sunrise/ Love And A Molotov Cocktail/Can I Crash You/ Me And My Buddies/Just For Your Sex) (PS)	(Zama ZA 10 EP) 1977
	2(B)	FOUR FROM THE SQUARE (Night Creatures/ Lois Lane/16 Down) (PS)	(Parlophone R 6063) 1980

45s:	Love And A Molotov Cocktail/Can I Crash Here?/ Civilization (PS)	(EMI EMI 2747) 1978
	Fun City/E.C. 4 (PS)	(EMI EMI 2795) 1978
	Waikiki Beach Refugees/We Don't Mind The Rave (yellow vinyl) (PS)	(EMI EMI 2867) 1978
	Beverley/Don't Moonlight On Me (PS)	(EMI EMI 2907) 1979
*	Name Dropping/Fly v Fly (PS)	(EMI EMI 2936) 1979
	Living In The Sticks/ We Are The Lucky Ones (PS)	(EMI EMI 2979) 1980
	What Will Mother Say?/ Undercover Agent Zero (PS)	(Parlophone R 6036) 1980

NB: * Some copies issued on green vinyl.

A Coventry-based mod-influenced band who started out as Midnight Circus in the mid-seventies. **The Flys** main plus was the rather individual songwriting talents of Neil O'Connor (he was singer Hazel O'Connor's brother). These are showcased on *Love And A Molotov Cocktail*, which is probably their best known song. Originally included on their debut *Bunch Of Five* EP, released in November 1977, it was also chosen for their first 45 in January 1978.

Their other recording of note was their first album. *Waikiki Beach Refugees*, released in November 1978. Unfortunately, appearing a few months in advance of the mod revival spearheaded by bands like **The Merton Parkas** and **Secret Affair**, it attracted little attention. Still, it contained many fine moments of power-punk expressed in songs like *Don't Moonlight On Me*, *Don't Mind The Rave* and *I Don't Know*.

FLYING LIZARDS - Money.

Their second album *Fly's Own* was bland in comparison. Much of the material, like the opening three cuts, *Let's Drive*, *Energy Boy* and *Fascinate Me*, is guitar-driven but suffers from weak vocals. *Talking To The Wall* has a lively chorus with handclaps and sharp lyrics. *16 Down* and *Fortunes* is similar in style. *Own* has an almost psychedelic texture. These are the better moments. New drummer Graham Deakin got a lead vocal on *Freezing*, which is a Cockney/Scaffold throwaway and overall, despite some good cuts, the album failed to fulfill the promise of its predecessor.

They also recorded three sessions for John Peel. The first on 23rd March 1978 featured *New Hearts*, *Fun City*, *We Don't Mind The Rave* and *Living In The Sticks*. A second session on 21st November 1978 consisted of *Love And A Molotov Cocktail*, *Name Dropping*, *I Don't Know* and *Waikiki Beach Refugees*. Their final session in 1979 comprised *Let's Dance*, *Energy Boy*, *Frenzy Is 23* and *I'll Survive*.

The band split in 1980. King later played in After The Fire and briefly for Emerson, Lake and Palmer. He sadly died of cancer, aged just 26. His replacement in **The Flys** Graham Deakin had previously been with John Entwistle's Ox.

Hughes and Freeman became The Lover Speaks and signed to A&M. They failed to break through commercially, but almost ten years after its release Annie Lennox celebrated a massive worldwide hit with their delightful ballad *No More I Love You's*.

The best introduction to their music is *Flys Buzz Barck*. It's evident from this that they weren't a punk band. Had they come three years earlier they could have been big but they eventually fell apart disillusioned with their lack of success. *Love And A Molotov Cocktail* can also be heard on *Learning English Vol. 1 By Die Toten Hosen* (Charisma 91823) 1991. It re-emerged again on *1-2-3-4 - A History Of Punk And New Wave 1976 - 1979* (MCA/Universal MCD 60066), a lavish 5-CD box set, issued in 1999. Back in 1979 *The Rare Stuff* (EMI SHSM 2028) included four cuts by the band:- *E.C. 4*, *Love And A Molotov Cocktail*, *Can I Crash Here?* and *Civilization*.

Ford Workers On Strike

45:	The Ford Strike Song	(Ford U.K. Workers Combine) 1978

This was a bit of fun and propoganda from the strikers at the Ford car plant in Dagenham, Essex, based on the famous Vietnam War anthem by Country Joe and The Fish:-

"And it's one-two-three, what are we fighting for?
You can stuff your five per cent
Cos it won't pay the rent
And it's five-six-seven, kicking in the factory gate
It's one in the eye for Sunny Jim
Whoopee, we're gonna win"

(from *The Ford Strike Song*)

THE FLYS - Beverley.

FOREIGN LEGION - Foreign Legion EP.

Foreign Legion

Personnel:	HELEN	bs, vcls	A
	LYNNE	gtr	A
	MARCUS	vcls	A
	MARSHON	drms	A

EP:	1(A)	FOREIGN LEGION (Message From Nowhere/		
(up to		Trenchline/National Affairs/		
1986)		Lots Of Fun) (PS)	(Rent A Rocket)	1986

NB: They also contributed six tracks to *The Cry Of The Legion* (DSS DSS 024) 2001, a split album with **Major Accident**.

Foreign Legion came from Merthyr Tydfil. After this EP, they changed to an all male line-up. They went on to release a further EP *Surf City* (Schlawiner Records S 805), which came on green vinyl and a now ultra-rare album *Welcome To Fort Zindernauf*, but both these recordings fell outside the time span of this book.

On the *Foreign Legion* (EP), *Message From Nowhere* features some decent guitar work, whilst *Trenchline* has some poignant lyrics about the futility of war. These two cuts subsequently resurfaced on *Oi! The Rarities, Vol. 2* (CD) (Captain Oi! AHOY CD 46) 1995.

Most recently they have contributed six cuts of melodic punk to a split album with **Major Accident**.

Foreign Press

45:	Downpour/Crossfire/		
	Behind The Glass (PS)	(Streets Ahead SA 1)	1979

Foreign Press were one of Manchester's bright new hopes in 1979. **Joy Division**'s manager Rob Gretton helped the group produce the disc. Musically, they managed a sort of '79 psychedelia with choppy, spiralling music and edgy guitars. Sadly, they never made it.

FOREIGN PRESS - Set Your Love In Motion.

Foreign Press

45:	Set Your Love In Motion/The Spell (PS)	(EMI EMI 5488) 1984

This synthesized pop-soul 45 is probably by a different combo. There's quite a New Romantic influence on this.

48 Chairs

Personnel incl:	CHRIS SCOTT		A

ALBUM:	1(A)	70% PARANOID	(Relentless R 102) 1981

45:	Snap It Around/Psycle Sluts (PS)	(Absurd ABSURD 3) 1979

The man behind this band was Chris Scott who played with **Alberto Y Los Trios Paranoias** and was also featured on many of the discs released on Absurd Records during 1979 and 1980.

48 Chairs were actually his band. *Snap It Around* is experimental and largely instrumental with occasional high-pitched vocals. The flip side on their Absurd 45 was an avant-garde instrumental version of **John Cooper Clarke**'s *Psycle Sluts*.

48 Chairs were one of a number of Absurd acts later to end up on the Relentless Records imprint.

48 CHAIRS - Snap It Around.

48 Hours

Personnel:	ANGE	vcls	A
	BLUE	drms	A
	BOB	bs	A
	SHAUN HARVEY	gtr	A

This group's sole vinyl offering appears to have been *Back To Ireland* on the *4 Alternatives* (EP) (Hartbeat PULSE 4) in 1979.

John Foxx

HCP

ALBUMS:	1	METAMATIC	(Metal Beat V 2146) 1980	18
(up to	2	THE GARDEN	(Virgin V 2194) 1981	24
1986)	3	THE GOLDEN SECTION	(Virgin V 2233) 1983	27
	4	IN MYSTERIOUS WAYS	(Virgin V 2355) 1985	85

NB: (1) also issued on CD (Virgin CDV 2146) 1993. (2) also issued on CD (Virgin CDV 2194) 1993. (4) also issued on CD (Virgin CDV 2355) 1987, but deleted in 1991.

HCP

45s:	Underpass/Film One (PS)	(Virgin VS 318) 1979	31
(up to *	My Face (flexi)	(Island Music/Smash Hits) 1980	-
1986) +	No-One Driving/Glimmer/This City/		
	Mr. No (double pack, gatefold PS)	(Virgin VS 338) 1980	32

Burning Car/20th Century (PS)	(Virgin VS 360)	1980 35
Burning Car/20th Century (picture disc)	(Virgin VS 360)	1980 -
Miles Away/Long Time (PS)	(Virgin VS 382)	1980 51
Europe (After The Rain)/ The Jungle (PS)	(Virgin VS 393)	1981 40
Dancing Like A Gun/Swimmer II (PS)	(Virgin VS 459)	1981 -
Endlessly/Young Man (PS)	(Virgin VS 513)	1982 66
Endlessly/Young Man (picture disc)	(Virgin VS 513)	1982 -
Endlessly/Ghosts On Water/Dance With Me/ A Kind Of Love (double pack 7")	(Virgin VSY 513)	1982 -
Your Dress/Woman On A Stairway (PS)	(Virgin VS 615)	1984 61
Your Dress/Woman On A Stairway/Lifting Sky/ Annexe (double pack 7")	(Virgin VSY 615)	1984 -
Like A Miracle/Wings And A Wind (PS)	(Virgin VS 645)	1984 -
Like A Miracle/Wings And A Wind (shaped picture disc)	(Virgin VSP 645)	1984 -
The Stars On Fire What Kind Of A Girl (PS)	(Virgin VS 771)	1985 -
The Stars On Fire/ What Kind Of Girl (12", PS)	(Virgin VS 77112)	1985 -

NB: * This was a one-sided yellow vinyl flexidisc which came free with 'Smash Hits' magazine. + Some copies also came in a stickered gatefold picture sleeve.

John Foxx was a stage name for Dennis Leigh, who'd been born in Chorley, Lancashire. He first entered the music business as a member of Tiger Lily who eventually evolved into the much better known **Ultravox**. He was their lead vocalist for three albums but left to go solo in 1979.

Having sent up his own Metal Beat label **Foxx** released his first solo effort - a 45 *Underpass* at the very end of 1979. It brought him his first U.K. hit climbing to No. 31 and spending eight weeks in the charts. *Underpass* was also included on *Machines* (Virgin V 2177) in 1980. Its parent album *Metamatic* also climbed to No. 18. On this album, with Conny Plank handling production, he deployed minimalist electronic sounds and a vocal style that sounded rather distant. Fans of this may also be interested in a Canadian compilation called *John Foxx*, which re-arranged a number of songs on this first album.

Collectors will also want to track down one of his rarest releases, which came out in 1980. A one-sided yellow vinyl flexidisc version of *My Face* which came free with 'Smash Hits' magazine. **Foxx** returned to the charts with his four-track 45 *No-One Driving* and then on both sides of the Atlantic later in the year when *Burning Car* reached No. 37 in the U.K. and No. 51 in the U.S..

In 1981, **Foxx** achieved two further U.K. hits with *Miles Away* and *Europe (After The Rain)*. Both featured on his next album *The Garden* which conjured up a lusher more pastoral sound than its predecessor utilising acoustic instruments to help balance the use of synthesizers. Again sales were good. The album spent six weeks in the charts peaking at No. 24.

1982 was a quieter year for **Foxx** but his next 45 was released in three different formats (see the discography) and spent three weeks in the lower reaches of the charts, peaking at No. 66.

Foxx's third album *The Golden Section* came out in 1983 and Zeus B. Held co-produced it with **Foxx**. The album's highlight was the earlier 45 *Endlessly*, but some reviewers likened several of the tracks to the Beatles in their psychedelic phase. Certainly his music is inventive and interesting and his vocals are dramatic. The cassette version of the album contained six additional cuts. Although it only spent three weeks in the charts it did climb to No. 27 in the U.K. to give him a third consecutive Top 30 album.

Although his fortunes declined commercially **Foxx** continued to record and make music of quality and inventiveness well beyond the time span of this book. He later worked as a computer art designer.

Bruce Foxton

HCP

ALBUM: (up to 1986)	1	TOUCH SENSITIVE	(Arista 206251) 1984 68

HCP

45s: (up to 1986)	*	Freak/Writing On The Wall (PS)	(Arista BFOX 1) 1983 23
		This Is The Way/ Sign Of The Times (PS)	(Arista BFOX 2) 1983 56
		It Makes Me Wonder/ Trying To Forget You (PS)	(Arista BFOX 3) 1984 74
		It Makes Me Wonder/ Trying To Forget You (12", PS)	(Arista BFOX 123) 1984 -
		SOS My Imagination/ 25 Or 6 To 4 (PS)	(Arista BFOX 4) 1984 -
		SOS My Imagination/ 25 Or 6 To 4 (12", PS)	(Arista BFOX 124) 1984 -
		Play The Game To Win/ Welcome To The Hero (PS)	(Harvest HAR 5239) 1986 -
		Play The Game To Win/Welcome To The Hero/ Living In A Dream World (12", PS)	(Harvest 12HAR 5239) 1986 -

NB: * Also issued as a picture disc.

Bruce Foxton, born on 1st September 1955, will always be best remembered as bassist in **The Jam**. When they split in late 1982, **Foxton** went solo, recording the *Touch Sensitive* album in 1984. With a four-piece band and a number of guests he produced ten self-penned songs which explored a variety of styles from dance-rock through to pop. It was a promising effort and brought him some commercial success too, climbing to No. 68 during a four week chart stint.

Foxton also enjoyed three hit singles with *Freak* (No. 23), *This Is The Way* (No. 56) and *It Makes Me Wonder* (No. 74), which spent five, three and one week in the charts respectively. However, rather than pursuing his solo career further, **Foxton** went on to join the reformed **Stiff Little Fingers**.

Frankie Flame

Personnel:	FRANKIE 'BOY' FLAME	vcls, piano	A
	STEVE FORWARD	gtr	A
	MARTIN O'NEAL	drms	A
	BILL PICKARD	bs	A

45:	Dick Barton/Bloodshot Eyes (PS)	(Falcon FLA 001) 1986	

A colourful character from South-east London **Frankie Flame** was originally a member of Woody Woodmansey's U Boat. In 1983 he contributed *On Yer Bike* to the *Oi! Oi! That's Yer Lot* (Secret SEC 5) compilation. He was a popular live artist in the eighties performing several Oi! classics at the Firkin chain of pubs. The same year he appeared as Oi! The Robot performing *Manifesto!!* on *Son Of Oi!* (Syndicate SYNLP 2) 1983, which was later issued on CD (Captain Oi AHOY CD 9) 1993. This is a synth-pop style recording.

Both sides of the *Dick Barton* 45 later resurfaced on *Oi! The Rarities, Vol. 2* (Captain Oi! AHOY CD 43) 1995, but this particular Cockney style recording was a long way from Oi!'s finest moment.

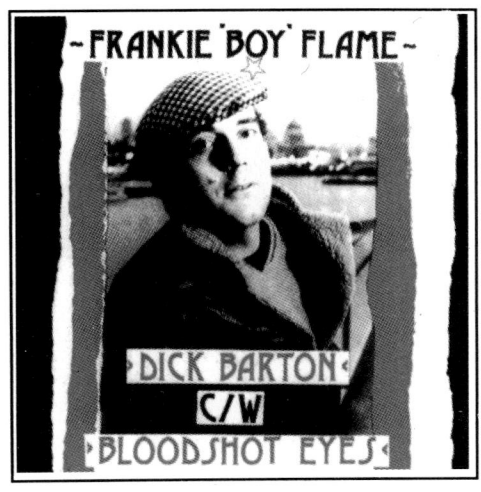

FRANKIE FLAME - Dick Barton.

The Frantic Elevators

Personnel:
MICK HUCKNALL	vcls, gtr		A
NEIL SMITH	gtr		A
BRIAN TURNER	bs, keyb'ds		A
KEV WILLIAMS	drms		A

ALBUM: 1(A) THE EARLY YEARS (mini-LP) (TJM TJM 101) 1987

NB: This was reissued on Receiver (KNOB 2) 1988 with a new sleeve and free interview disc as *Mick Hucknall And The Frantic Elevators*. There's also a compilation *Singles* (Essential ESMCD 797) 2000.

45s:
- Voice In The Dark/Passion/Every Day I Die (PS) (TJM TJM 5) 1979
- * Hunchback Of Notre Dame/See Nothing And Everything/Don't Judge Me (demo only) (TJM TJM 6) 1980
- You Know What You Told Me/Production Prevention (PS) (Eric's ERIC'S 6) 1980
- Searching For The Only One/Hunchback Of Notre Dame (PS) (Crackin' Up CRACK 1) 1981
- Holding Back The Years/Pistols In My Brain (PS) (No Waiting WAIT 1) 1982

NB: * unreleased, demo only.

Formed in Manchester by Mick Hucknall during 1978 **The Frantic Elevators** had a reputation for a kickin' ass stage act. They played an energetic punkish mode of music and cut four 45s on four different labels over nearly as many years. Their main claim to fame was having future Simply Red member Mick Hucknall as a founding member. Indeed, as their final 45, they cut the first version of *Holding Back The Years*, which would later become Simply Red's biggest international hit. As a result of his subsequent fame their unreleased *Hunchback Of Notre Dame* is one of the rarest artefacts of the punk era and a copy would set back any fans in excess of £100.

Some members also figured on the 45 by **The Mothmen**, released on Absurd Records in 1979.

Singles (CD) released by Essential in 2000 comprises six tracks from their first two TJM releases from 1979/80 and an interview with Mick Hucknall from an uncredited source. Unfortunately it's badly recorded and doesn't even mention **The Frantic Elevators**.

Voice In The Park later got a further airing on *Rabid/TJM Punk Singles Collection* (Receiver RRCD 227) in 1996.

The Freshmen

45: Never Heard Anything Like It/Bombing Run (PS) (Release RL 975) 1979

This 'A' side about a youth writing for advice on how to cope with his parents' constant moaning and nagging, was an NME 'Single of the Week'. 'Dear Judith' writes back:-

"Dear mixed up, there's not much I can do
You seem to be somewhat immature
Your family sound a well adjusted crew
And I can only recommend that you
Shut up! You aggravating pup!
I swear that I never heard anything like it"

(from *Never Heard Anything Like It*).

The musicianship is good and there's a powerful horn section and raucous delivery, but it never made it!

The Freshies

Personnel:
EDDIE CARTER	gtr		AB
BOB DIXON	drms		A
CHRIS SIEVEY	vcls, gtr		AB
BARRY SPENCER	bs		A
MIKE DOHERTY	drms		B
RICK SARKO	bs		B

CASS:
- 1( ) ALL SLEEP'S SECRETS (Razz RAZZC 1) 1978
- 2( ) MANCHESTER PLAYS (Razz RAZZCS-2) 1979
- 3( ) SING THE GIRLS FROM BANANA ISLAND (Razz RAZZCS-3) 1979
- 4(B) ROUGH AND READY (Razz CS-4) 1980
- 5(B) LONDON PLAYS (Razz CS-5) 1981
- 6( ) JOHNNY RADAR STORY (ETS 1) 1985
- 7( ) JOHNNY RADAR STORY (ETS 1) 1985
- 8( ) EARLY RAZZ (ETS 3) 1985
- 9( ) STUDIO OUT-TAKES (ETS 4) 1985

NB: (1) is a 12-track cassette. (2) is a cassette, radio session and interview, only 1,000 were released. (3) is a 16-track cassette, only 1,000 were released. (4) is a 12-track cassette, only 1,000 were released. (5) is a cassette with live and radio sessions, only 1,000 released. (6) is a 20-track cassette, some came with a free Frank Sidebottom 8-track *Firm Favourites*. (7) was a vinyl test pressing of (6). (8) and (9) were cassettes. There's also a CD compilation, *The Very Very Best Of The Freshies* (Cherry Red CDMRED 129) 1996.

EPs:
- 1( ) BAISER (Baiser (Taste Of A Boy)/Two Of The Same Girl/Washed Up/Moon Midsummer/Plus **Chris Sievey** solo cuts) (Razz RAZZ EP 1) 1978
- 2( ) STRAIGHT IN AT No. 2 (Johnny Radar/U-Boat/Skid Room/Last) (Razz RAZZ EP 2) 1979
- 3( ) THE MEN FROM BANANA ISLAND WHOSE STUPID IDEAS NEVER CAUGHT ON IN THE WESTERN WORLD AS WE KNOW IT (Amoca Cadiz/Children Of The World/Octopus) (Razz RAZZ 3) 1979
- 4( ) RED INDIAN MUSIC (Razz RAZZ 8) 1980
- 5( ) THE BIZ (I'm In Love With The Girl On The Virgin Manchester Megastore Checkout Desk/Wrap Up The Rockets/Buy Me A Shirt/Tell Me I'm Ill/Frank Talks To Chris (conversation))(12") (Virgin HANNAH 1) 1984

NB: (1) Copies were numbered with handwritten labels. (2) copies were numbered with handwritten labels in green or orange PS. Only 1,000 pressed. (3) issued in black and white PS or numbered blue PS. (4) with **Chris Sievey**. (5) on white label with stickered sleeve.

HCP

45s:
- Octopus/Sheet Music (PS) (Absurd 9) 1980 -
- My Tape's Gone/Moon Midsummer (PS) (Razz RAZZ 4) 1980 -
- We're Like You/(flip side by **Chris Sievey**) (PS) (Razz RAZZ 5) 1980 -
- Yellow Spot/If It's News (PS) (Razz RAZZ 6) 1980 -
- No Money/Oh Girl (PS) (Razz RAZZ 7) 1980 -
- Ship The Fight, Jim/Baiser (PS) (Razz RAZZ 9) 1980 -
- * I'm In Love With The Girl On The Virgin Manchester Megastore Check-out Desk/Singalong Version (PS, some with free lyric book) (Razz RAZZ 11) 1980 54
- I'm In Love With The Girl On The Virgin Manchester Megastore Check-out Desk (Radio version)/Singalong Version ('bleeped') (white label radio issue, 200 pressed) (Razz RAZZ 12) 1980 -
- \+ One To One/House Beautiful (Razz RAZZ 13) 1980 -
- Wrap Up The Rockets/It's Gonna Get Better (MCA MCAS 693) 1981 -
- Wrap Up The Rockets/It's Gonna Get Better/

THE FRESHIES - Wrap Up The Rockets 12".

Tell Her I'm Ill (12", PS)	(MCA MCAS 693)	1981 -
I Can't Get Bouncing Babies By The Teardrop Explodes/		
Tell Her I'm Ill	(MCA MCAS 725)	1981 -
Dancin' Doctors/One To One	(Razz RP 508)	1981 -
Fasten Your Seat Belts/Best We Can Do	(Stiff BUY 158)	1982 -
If You Really Love Me... Buy Me A Shirt/		
I Am The Walrus (PS)	(CV CVS 1)	1983 -

NB: * Reissued on MCA (MCA 670) 1981. + unreleased.

Chris Sievey also worked as a solo artist. **Sievey** linked up with a stream of artists in this band but the most consistent line-up was 'B' between 1980-82. Bassist Rick Sarko had previously been with **Ed Banger and The Nosebleeds** and drummer Mike Doherty was previously in **The Smirks**. Their *Straight In At No. 2* (EP) is an alive, alert record but **The Freshies** are best remembered for *I'm In Love With The Girl On The Virgin Manchester Megastore Check-out Desk*, which when it was reissued on MCA actually made No. 54 in the national charts in February 1981. The song spent three weeks in the charts in all. It can also be found on *Punk Lost And Found* (Shanachie SH ST05) 1996.

The Very Very Best Of The Freshies Some Long And Some Short Titles is a twenty-three track collection which includes *I'm In Love With The Girl On The Virgin Manchester Megastore Check-out Desk* and *I Can't Get Bouncing Babies By The Teardrop Explodes* along with various other singles, album cuts and unreleased demos. It contains all you should need by the band.

The Front

Personnel:	DREW BLOOD	gtr	A
	GRAHAM BROAD	drms	A
	JP PORTER	gtr	A
	TOMMY TROUBLE	vcls, bs	A

45:	System/Queen's Mafia (PS)	(The Label TLR 005)	1978

Trouble (aka Ben Brierly) and Blood (aka Andrew Lipscombe) formed **The Front** in late 1977. They were based in the Chelsea area of London. Brierly married Marianne Faithful and played in a later line-up of **The Vibrators** and Lipscombe married Angie Bowie. JP went on to play with Eric Clapton and produced The Smiths among others. Broad had a spell with Dollar before becoming an in-demand session musician. In addition to this 45, **The Front** also contributed two cuts *Hospital Case* and *Queen's Mafia* to the compilation *The Label Sofa* (The Label TLRLP 002) 1978.

Fruit Eating Bears

Personnel:	CHRIS CRASH	drms	A
	GARY CROUDANCE	bs, vcls	A
	NEVILLE CROZIER	vcls, gtr	A

CD:	1(A)	GENTLE CREATURES, DESPITE THEIR FIERCE APPEARANCE (Overground OVER 83CD) 1999	
45s:	Door In My Face/		
	Going Through The Motions	(DJM DJS 857)	1978
	Cherie Heavy/Fifties Cowboy	(Lightning GIL 509)	1978

The Fruit Eating Bears formed in June 1977 and played around the London punk circuit supporting bands like **The Clash**, **The Damned** and **The Adverts**. When they played at a punk festival in Chelmsford City football ground they even got to appear on 'News At Ten'. Unbeknown to them their publisher entered *Door In My Face* (later selected for 45 release) for the Eurovision Song Contest as a joke and to everyone's amazement it made the final twelve in the 'Song For Europe' heats! When *Door In My Face* was released as a 45, in April 1978, it sold poorly. However, one of their songs *1.30, 2.30, 3.35* was later covered by The Pirates on their *Happy Birthday Rock And Roll* album. They also backed Hazel O'Connor for a recording session which produced five tracks, two of which comprised her *Eee - I - Adio* debut on Albion. They split soon after though.

If you want to know more, check out Overground's superbly compiled 33-track CD retrospective *Gentle Creatures, Despite Their Fierce Appearance*. The title is a quote from Terry Wogan's introduction of them for their Eurovision Song Contest appearance at the Royal Albert Hall on primetime TV in 1978. This appears unlisted complete with the introduction as track 33 on the compilation. The remaining 32 tracks feature almost all their studio work and 13 live cuts from a gig at the Highcliffe, Margate in 1977. The CD is accompanied by a 12-page booklet with many photos and press cuttings, relating the story of the band as told by them.

Cheavy Heavy can also be heard on *Lightning Records Punk Collection* (Anagram CDPUNK 79) 1996.

Fun Four

Personnel incl: STEVEN DALY
JAMES KING

45:	Singing In The Shadows/By Products/ Elevator Crush (PS)	(NMC NMC 010)	1980

This Glasgow band's 45 is now rare and quite sought-after because Orange Juice's Steven Daly played on it. It also featured James King, who later recorded with the Lone Wolves. They also recorded on Swamplands and Thrash. It's a good guitar sound too.

Futura 2000 With The Clash

45s:	The Escapades Of Futura 2000/ Instrumental (PS)	(Celluloid CYZ 104)	1983
	The Escapades Of Futura 2000/ Instrumental (12", PS)	(Celluloid CYZ 104)	1983

Futura 2000 was an American graffiti artist. Although on this rap 45 he's credited as being backed by **The Clash** it appears that the backing band comprised just Mick Jones, who'd just developed a liking of rap.

Johnny G

ALBUMS:	1	SHARP AND NATURAL	(Beggars Banquet BEGA 6)	1978
	2	G-BEAT	(Beggars Banquet BEGA 16)	1979
	3	WATER INTO WINE	(Beggars Banquet BEGA 30)	1981

EP:	1	MONOPHENIA (Monophenia/Highway Shoes/ Can't Catch Every Train) (Beggars Banquet BEG 13) 1978

45s:	Call Me Bwana/Suzi Was A Girl From Greenford	(Beggars Banquet BEG 3)	1978
	Hippy's Graveyard/ Miles And Miles	(Beggars Banquet BEG 7)	1978
	Everybody's Gone Cruisin' On A/ Sick 'n' Tired	(Beggars Banquet BEG 13)	1978
	The Golden Year/ The Permanent Stranger (PS)	(Beggars Banquet BEG 16)	1979
	Night After Night/ Old Soldiers (PS)	(Beggars Banquet BEG 40)	1980
	Blue Suede Shoes Leave Me Alone/ Highway Shoes (PS)	(Beggars Banquet BEG 44)	1980
	Alone With Her Tonight/I Just Want To Sing The Blues (PS)	(Beggars Banquet BEG 65)	1981
	G Beat/Leave Me Alone (PS)	(Beggars Banquet BEG 67)	1981

Johnny G was quite an eccentric one man band that came out of the pub-rock scene in this era. His records had wit and humour and covered a very diverse range of musical styles incorporating reggae, R&B, folk, country blues etc. His debut single *Call Me Bwana* was an unusual, funny and compassionate song about the positions of black and white in late seventies Britain. *The Hippy's (sic) Graveyard* was disappointing by comparison.

On *Sharp And Natural* Steve Lillywhite helped out on bass, along with skiffle outfit Brett Marvin and The Thunderbolts and Mark Hollis handled production. A fun record. However, it was overshadowed by his second album *G-Beat*. This was a low-budget recording utilising voice, guitar, a few drums, keyboards and mostly acoustic bass. Free with it came a bonus album *G-Beat 2 (Leave Me Alone)* which comprises singles, outtakes and alternative versions.

Water Into Wine was a much more sophisticated product produced by Bob Andrews (who'd been with The Rumour) with many pub-rock figures playing on it. It includes an eccentric slide-guitar version of King Crimson's *21st Century Schizoid Man* and a bizarre tribute *Johnny G Fan Club* sung by label-mate Ivor Biggun. It also came with a bonus album *Pure Beaujolais*, which comprised part live material and some outtakes and projected 45s that never got an official release.

The Gadgets

Personnel:	JOHN HYDE	synths	AB
	MATT JOHNSON	synths	AB
	COLIN LLOYD TUCKER	synths	AB
	PETE ASHWORTH	drms	B
	TIM BROUGHTON	drms	B

ALBUMS:	1(A)	GADGETREE	(Final Solution FSLP 001) 1980
	2(A)	LOVE, CURIOSITY, FRECKLES AND DOUBT	(Final Solution FSLP 002) 1981
	3(B)	THE BLUE ALBUM	(Glass GLALP 006) 1982

NB: (1) reissued with a different sleeve (Plastic Head PLAS LP 013) 1989 and on CD (PLAS CD 013) 1989. (2) reissued (Plastic Head PLAS LP 014) 1989 and on CD (PLAS CD 014) 1989. (3) reissued (Plastic Head PLAS LP 016) 1989 and on CD (PLAS CD 016) 1989. There was also a cassette release of (3) (Glass GLAMC 006) 1983.

45:	We Had No Way Of Knowing/	
	Acid Bath	(Glass GLASS 026) unissued
	We Had No Way Of Knowing/	
	Acid Bath (12")	(Glass GLASS 12026) unissued

This was primarily a studio-based outfit made up of former members of **Plain Characters** whose music was centered around a drum machine and a Wasp synthesizer. The initial sessions resulted in the *Gadgetree* album which was finished by Hyde. They also contributed a cut to the 1980 Some Bizzare compilation which got lost and has never seen the light of day.

Just 2,000 copies were recorded of their second album *Love, Curiosity, Freckless And Doubt*. Although Matt Johnson was still a member of the group, he was now concentrating on his main group **The The**.

For **The Gadgets** final album *The Blue Album* Tucker and Hyde were assisted by a 'guest members' Peter Ashworth and Tim Broughton. On *We Had No Way Of Knowing* Craig Whipsnade guested on guitar. This was a live album recorded in the studio with Matt Johnson's contributions dubbed in later.

All three **Gadgets** albums were later reissued by Plastic Head and the second and third ones featured the original artwork.

Only recommended if you like experimental synthesizer-led music.

Gaffa

Personnel:	MICK BARRATT	drms	A
	WAYNE EVANS	vcls, bs	A
	JOHN MASLEN	gtr	A
	EDDIE SMITH	gtr	A

ALBUMS:	1(A)	HISS & HZ	(Gaffa 'n' Product NC 001) 1979
	2(A)	LIVE AT THE IMPERIAL	(Gaffa 'n' Product NPC 1) 1980
	3(A)	NEITHER USE NOR ORNAMENT	(Gaffa 'n' Product ZZZZ 001) 1980

EPs:	1(A)	NORMAL SERVICE WILL NEVER BE RESUMED	(Cleverley Bros CBM 2) 1977
	2(A)	FIRM FAVOURITES	(Next SMALL 2) 1978
	3(A)	FRIENDS AND ENEMIES (Big Fight Nerves/ Target Practice/I Am Not Your Friend)	(Gaffa 'n' Product NC 001) 1979

45s:	Hearts Of Stone/ You Know I Love You	(Gaffa 'n' Product ZZZZ 5001) 1979
	Attitude Dancing/ Long Weekend	(Gaffa 'n' Product ZZZZ 5002) 1979
	Man With A Motive/ Your Side My Side	(Gaffa 'n' Product ZZZZ 5003) 1980

A Nottingham band.

Gang Of Four

Personnel:	DAVE ALLEN	bs	A
	HUGO BURNHAM	drms	ABCD
	ANDY GILL	gtr	ABCDE
	JON KING	vcls, keyb'ds	ABCDE
	BUSTA CHERRY JONES	bs	B
	SARA LEE	bs, vcls	C
	JON ASTROP	vcls	DE
	CHUCK KIRKPATRICK	vcls	DE
	JOHN SOMBATERO	bs	DE
	ALFA ANDERSON	backing vcls	DE
	BRENDA WHITE	backing vcls	DE
	STEVE GOULDING	drms	E

HCP

ALBUMS:	1(A)	ENTERTAINMENT	(EMI EMC 3313) 1979 45
	2(A)	SOLID GOLD	(EMI EMC 3364) 1981 52
	3(C)	SONGS OF THE FREE	(EMI EMC 3412) 1982 61
	4(D)	HARD	(EMI 1652191) 1983 -
	5(E)	AT THE PALACE (live)	(Mercury MERL 51) 1984 -

NB: (1) also issued on CD (EMI CZ 541) 1995 with extra tracks. The following will also be of interest *The Peel Sessions (1979-81)* (strange Fruit SFRLP 107), also on CD (Strange Fruit SFRCD 107) 1990; the compilation *A Brief History Of The 20th Century* (Warner Brothers WB 26448) 1990, also on CD (EMI CDEMO 3583) 1990; *You Can Catch Up With History (1978-83)* (Capitol Greenlight GO 2028) 1990, also on CD (CDP 795 051 2) 1990; *Shrinkwrapped* (Wen WENCD 003) 1995, *Solid Gold* (EMI EMC 3364) 1981, later on CD (Premier CZ 561) 1996 and *100 Flowers Bloom* (2-CD set) (Rhino R2 75479) 1999.

EP:	1(A)	DAMAGED GOODS (Damaged Goods/ Love Like Anthrax/Armalite Rifle)	(Fast Products 5) 1978

NB: Also relevant is *The Peel Session* (12") (16/1/89) (I Found That Essence Rare/Return The Gift/5-45/At Home He's A Tourist) (Strange Fruit SFPSC 8) 1986.

HCP

45s:	At Home He's A Tourist/ It's Her Factory (PS)	(EMI EMI 2956) 1979 58
	Outside The Trains Don't Run On Time/ He'd Send In The Army (PS)	(Zonophone Z1) 1980 -
*	What We All Want/History's Bunk (PS)	(EMI EMI 5146) 1981 -
*	Cheeseburger/Paralysed (PS)	(EMI EMI 5177) 1981 -

the Gadgets. Blue Album
the gadgets are Matt Johnson
Colin Lloyd Tucker and John
Hyde. drums Tim Broughton
and Pete Ashworth.
guitar on we had no way of knowing.
Craig Whipsnade. recorded at
De Wolfe studios. engineers
Les Sanders and Rob Poole
The third Gadgets long playing record
This is pop music Play it loud

THE GADGETS - The Blue Album.

*	To Hell With Poverty/ Capital (It Fails Us Now) (PS)	(EMI EMI 5193)	1981 -
*	I Love A Man In Uniform/ World At Fault (PS)	(EMI EMI 5299)	1982 65
	Call Me Up (If I'm Home)/ I Will Be A Good Boy (PS)	(EMI EMI 5320)	1982 -
*	Is It Love/Man With A Good Car (PS)	(EMI EMI 5418)	1983 -
	Silver Lining/Independence (PS)	(EMI EMI 5440)	1983 -
	I Will Be A Good Boy (live)/Is It Love (live)/ Call Me Up (live) (12")	(Mercury GANG 12)	1984 -

NB: * Also released in 12" format.

The Gang Of Four were formed in Leeds in 1977 by journalist Andy Gill, Jon King and Hugo Burnham. Dave Allen was added to the line-up a few months later in early 1978 to complete the fourth member of 'the gang'. The name was after the political faction associated with Mao Tse-Tung's widow. It was apparently suggested by **The Mekon**'s Andy Corrigan.

The debut EP *Damaged Goods* recorded by Bob Last's Fast label was a challenging disc. It set the style for the energetic brand of alternative rock/funk with a political stance, which their two debut albums for EMI *Entertainment* and *Solid Gold* delved further into achieving considerable chart success in the process. The four tracks featured on the Strange Fruit EP from 1986 date from a popular session the band did for Peel in January 1979. All four tracks included turned up on their *Entertainment* album released later that year.

Damaged Goods, *Love Like Anthrax* and *Armalite Rifle* (in other words all their tracks from their debut EP) were all included on the label sampler *Fast Product* (Fast EMC 3312) in 1979.

After the *Cheeseburger* 45 Buster Cherry Jones formerly with Sharks came in on bass for Dave Allen who joined Shriekback. This new line-up recorded just one 45. *To Hell With Poverty*, in July 1981, which was released in both a 7" and 12" format. After this Buster's brief stint with the band ended. Sarah Lee, who'd previously played with Jane Aire and Robert Fripp, came in on bass and vocals as a replacement.

This new line-up ('C') recorded *I Love A Man In Uniform*, which was also released in 7" and 12" formats. Although it climbed to No. 65 in the charts it was destined to go higher had it not been removed from the BBC's playlist at the time because of the Falklands war.

Their *Songs Of The Free* album, released in May 1982, included a number of 'deep from the heart' onslaughts on many of society's ills aside from the anti-militarism which had been the target of *I Love A Man In Uniform*, which was also on the album. This is recognised to be both innovative and stirring. Two further tracks *Call Me Up (If I'm Home)* and *I Will Be A Good Boy* were also culled for 45 release, but they failed to build on the band's earlier modest comercial success.

There was also a U.S.-only EP, *Another Day / Another Dollar*, issued in June 1982. This comprised both sides of the *To Hell With Poverty* 45, *History's Bunk* (the non-album flip side to *What We All Want* - an early 45 from March 1981) and two live versions of *Solid Gold*, which showcased their appeal as a live band.

At this point a number of backing singers were added (see line-up 'D'). The band shifted further into the dance sound for their next album *Hard*. Two 45s, *Is It Love* and *Silver Lining* were released from this album. Drummer Hugo Burnham left a few months prior to its release and no drummer is credited on the album. Burnham went on to join Illustrated Man. Prior to this, he did some session work with ABC. He later became Shriekback's manager. Former Rumour member Steve Goulding eventually replaced him and was present on the live *At The Palace* album, which was a souvenir of their final tour. The album included many of their finer moments, but by now the band were a spent force. They split in mid-1984 and Jon King went on to form King Butcher. Andy Gill went solo but only had one 45 *Dispossession*, released in August 1987, to show for it.

One track off *Entertainment* which caused a few ripples at the BBC was *At Home He's A Tourist* because it makes a reference to contraceptives. The introduction to the song featured distinctive and discordant guitar work with which the band are associated.

In 1999, *Damaged Goods* was included on the 5-CD box set *1-2-3-4 - A History Of Punk And New Wave 1976 - 1979* (MCA/Universal MCD 60066).

King and Gill later reformed **The Gang Of Four** in 1990. One disappointing album *Mall* and two 45s resulted. There was a further reformation in 1995.

The best retrospective release is *A Brief History Of The 20th Century*, available in both CD and vinyl format. *The Peel Sessions (1979 - 81)* captures their three sessions during that period. They also recorded a session for David Jensen on 12th August 1982 comprising *We Live As We Dream Alone*, *World At Fault*, *Good Boy* and *History Of The World*.

100 Flowers Bloom is a 2-CD compilation put out by Rhino in 1999. It contains cuts from all their albums and hard-to-find and unreleased material and is accompanied by a fifty-page booklet full of rare pictures, memorabilia and interviews.

Gill later went into producing. His credits included Red Hot Chilli Peppers. Allen later became co-president of the World Domination label and a respected producer. Burnham later worked as a record company executive.

The Gang Of Four were among the most interesting and influential post-punk bands.

Gangsters

ALBUM:	1( ) THE GANGSTERS	(Storybeat BEAT 2) 1979

45s:	Record Company/Harlow Town	(Storybeat BEAT 1) 1979
	Best Friend/Best Friend (Dub)	(Storybeat BEAT 3) 1979
	Rudi The Red Noised Reindeer/ White Christmas	(Big Bear BB 25) 1980
	Wooly Bully/We Are The Gangsters	(Big Bear BB 26) 1980

A pop-punk band from Harlow in Essex. Their music was energetic and sixties influenced. The album was distributed by Spartan.

GANG OF FOUR - Is It Love.

GARDEZ DARKX - Freeze.

Gardez Darkx

Personnel:	PAUL DARKX	trumpet	A
	LATIF GARDEZ	gtr	A

45s:	Freeze/Heartbeat (PS)	(New Bristol NBR 02) 1978
	Bliss/Winter Scene (PS)	(Bristol/Wavelength HURT 2) 1978

Freeze is full of studio gimmickry and sounds messy, but on the flip side *Heartbeat* Paul Darkx's trumpet adds a disquieting tone to Latif Gardez's chunky guitar work.

Paul Gardiner

HCP

45s:	Stormtrooper In Drag/		
	Night Talk (PS)	(Beggars Banquet BEG 61) 1981	49
*	Stormtrooper In Drag/		
	Night Talk (12")	(Beggars Banquet BEG 61T) 1981	-
	Venus In Furs/No Sense (PS)	(Numa NU 1) 1984	-
	Venus In Furs (Extended Mix)/No Sense/		
	Venus In Furs (7" mix) (12", PS)	(Numa NUM 1) 1984	-

NB: * Unreleased, but pressed as white label promos.

These were solo efforts by **Paul Gardiner**, the bassist with **Tubeway Army**, **Gary Numan** and **Dramatis** (a short-lived early eighties **Numan** project). **Numan** guested as the uncredited vocalist on *Stormtrooper In Drag*, which got to No 49 and spent four weeks in the charts.

Nick Garvey

ALBUM:	1 BLUE SKIES	(Virgin V 2231) 1982

45:	Take A Look Over My Shoulder/	
	The Lion And Me (PS)	(Virgin VS 504) 1982

These were solo ventures for the former Ducks Deluxe and **Motors** guitarist, bassist and producer. He's supported on these projects by various members of **The Motors**, **Tyla Gang** and **Bram Tchaikovsky**. The album has its moments on cuts like *Skin*, *Think (Tough)* and *Take A Look Over My Shoulder*. He's got a good voice and offers up some decent music on these ventures. *The Lion And Me* is a non-album cut.

The Gas

Personnel:	BURKE	A
	SAMPSON	A
	VICKERS	A

ALBUM:	1(A)	EMOTIONAL WARFARE	(Polydor POLE 152) 1981

45s:	It Shows Your Face/Tomorrow	(Polydor POSP 192) 1980
	Ignore Me/Do It, Don't Tell Me	(Polydor POSP 264) 1981
	Treatment/That's It (PS)	(Polydor POSP 296) 1981
	The Finger/Knock It Down (PS)	(Polydor POSP 344) 1981
	Breathless/Heartache/Hostage	(Polydor POSP 411) 1982

Many of these releases are very sought-after. The band were like a more aggressive **Vapors**.

GBH

Personnel:	COLIN	vcls	A
	JOCK	gtr	A
	ROSS	bs	A
	WILF	drms	A

ALBUMS:	1(A)	CITY BABY ATTACKED BY RATS	(Clay CLAYLP 4) 1982
(up to	2(A)	CITY BABIES REVENGE	(Clay CLAYLP 8) 1983
1986)			

NB: (1) reissued on vinyl (Roadrunner RR 9949) 1989 and also issued on CD (Clay CLAYCD 4) 1990 and (Receiver RRCD 257) 1988. (2) reissued on vinyl (Roadrunner RR 9877) 1989 and also on CD (Clay CLAYCD 8) 1990 and (Receiver RRCD 258) 1998. Also relevant are: *The Clay Years 1981-1984* (Clay CLAYCD 21) 1987 and 1993; *Diplomatic Immunity* (Clay CLAY 106) 1990; *The Clay Recordings* (2-CD set) (Clay CLAYCD 112) 1993; *The Singles Collection* (Clay CLAYCD 119) 1995; *Punk Junkies* (We Bite WB 1151CD) 1996; and *Live In Los Angeles* (Anagram CD PUNK 82) 1996.

EP:	1(A)	LEATHER, BRISTLES, STUDS AND ACNE (Necrophilia/ D.O.A./State Executioner/Lycanthropy)	
			(Clay PLATE 3) 1981

NB: (1) reissued on CD (Clay PLATECD 3) 1993.

HCP

45s:	No Survivors/Self Destruct/		
(up to	Big Women (PS)	(Clay CLAY 8) 1982	63
1986)	Sick Boy/Slit Your Own Throat/		
	Am I Dead Yet (PS)	(Clay CLAY 11) 1982	-
	Give Me Fire/Mantrap (PS)	(Clay CLAY 16) 1982	69
	Give Me Fire/Mantrap (picture disc)	(Clay CLAY 16P) 1982	-
	Catch 22/Hellhole (PS)	(Clay CLAY 22) 1983	-
	Do What You Do/Four Men (PS)	(Clay CLAY 36) 1984	-
	Do What You Do/Four Men/		
	Children Of Dust (12", PS)	(Clay CLAY 1236) 1984	-

Formed in 1980, this yobbish quartet (originally known as Charged GBH) from Birmingham are said to have played their first gig as a benefit for prostitutes on the same day as the 1980 cup final. They soon followed fellow Stoke-On-Trent punksters **Discharge** in signing to the city's indie label Clay Records. Both bands were at the helm of the British hardcore movement in the early eighties.

Their debut EP *Leather, Bristles, Studs And Acne* - a good description of the band's visual image - brought them indie chart success. Then, in December 1981, they supported **The Damned**, **UK Subs** and several other

G.B.H. - City Baby Attacked By Rats.

top bands at the 'Christmas On Earth' punk bonanza at the Queens Hall, Leeds. This helped win them wider public exposure and was probably a factor in two of their three 1982 45s, *No Survivors* and *Give Me Fire* enjoying modest success in the national charts. They spent two and three weeks respectively in the charts.

Their albums *City Baby Attacked By Rats* and *City Baby's Revenge* are generally recognised to be two of the best of this musical genre. Both typify their frantic 100 m.p.h. rantings with songs like *Time Bomb*, *Wardogs*, *Slut*, *Maniac*, *Valley Of Death* and *High Octane Fuel*.

They continued gigging and recording with later releases (not included in the discography as they were post-1986) on the Rough Justice label.

A good introduction to their recordings for Clay is *The Clay Years '81-'84* (Clay CLAYCD 21) 1987. Alternatively *Diplomatic Immunity* compiles many of their old singles and some of their more popular album cuts to form a sort of 'Best Of' collection.

Live In Los Angeles, released by Anagram in 1996, was recorded at L.A.'s Celebrity Theatre in 1988, so strictly-speaking is outside this book's timeframe. Still highlights include *Freak Of Nature* and *City Attacked By Rats*. **GBH** also contributed *Sick Boy* to *100% Hardcore Punk* (Captain Oi! AHOY DCD 84) 1998.

GBH continue to tour and record. They remain a major force on the punk scene.

Gene Loves Jezebel

Personnel:	MICHAEL ASTON	vcls	ABC
(up to	JAY (JOHN) ASTON	gtr, vcls	ABC
1986)	DICK HAWKINS	drms	A
	STEVE MARSHALL	bs	A
	MARCUS GILVEAR	drms	BC
	I.C. HUDSON	gtr	B
	PETER RIZZO	bs	BC
	JAMES STEVENSON	gtr	C

				HCP
ALBUMS:	1(A)	PROMISE	(Situation 2 SITU 7) 1983	-
(up to	2(B)	IMMIGRANTS	(Situation 2 SITU 14) 1985	-
1986)	3(C)	DISCOVER	(Beggars Banquet BEGA 73) 1986	32

NB: (1) also issued on CD (Situation 2 SITL 7CD) 1988. (2) also issued on CD (Situation 2 SITU 14CD) 1988. (3) was issued with a live bonus album *Glad To Be Alive* and also issued on CD (Beggars Banquet BEGA 73CD) 1986.

		HCP
45s:	Shaving My Neck/	
(up to	Sun And Insanity (PS) (Situation 2 SIT 18) 1982	-
1986)	Shaving My Neck/Sun And Insanity/Machismo/	
	Glad To Be Alive (12", PS) (Situation 2 SIT 18T) 1982	-
	Screaming (For Emmalene)/So Young (Heave	
	Hard Heaven Ho) (PS) (Situation 2 SIT 20) 1982	-
	Screaming (For Emmalene)/So Young	
	(Heave Hard Heaven Ho)/	
	No Voodoo Dollies (12", PS) (Situation 2 SIT 20T) 1982	-
	Bruises/Punch Drunk (PS) (Situation 2 SIT 24) 1983	-
	Bruises/Punch Drunk/	
	Brando Bruises (12", PS) (Situation 2 SIT 24T) 1983	-
	Influenza (Relapse)/	
	Walking In The Park (PS) (Situation 2 SIT 31) 1984	-
	Influenza (Relapse)/Walking In The Park/	
	Stephen (12", PS) (Situation 2 SIT 31T) 1984	-
	Shame (Whole Hearted Howl)/Georgeous	
	Thin Things (PS) (Situation 2 SIT 35) 1984	-
	Shame (Whole Hearted Howl)/	
	Georgeous Thin Things (12", PS) (Situation 2 SIT 35T) 1984	-
	Cow/One Someone (PS) (Situation 2 SIT 36) 1985	-
	Cow/One Someone/Cow (extended)/	
	Weep For Her (Cow) (12", PS) (Situation 2 SIT 36T) 1985	-
	Desire/Flame (S. Harley Mix) (PS) (Situation 2 SIT 41) 1985	-
	The Sweetest Thing/	
	Psycho II (PS) (Beggars Banquet BEGA 156) 1986	75
	The Sweetest Thing/Psycho II/Sweetest	
	Jezebel (12", PS) (Beggars Banquet BEGT 156) 1986	-
	Heartache/Beyond (PS) (Beggars Banquet BEGA 161) 1986	71
	Heartache/Beyond Debt/Heartache (alt. version)/	
	Deli Babies (12", PS) (Beggars Banquet BEGT 161) 1986	-
	Desire/Message (PS) (Beggars Banquet BEGA 173) 1986	-
	Desire (U.S. Club Mix)/Heartache	
	(U.K. Club Mix) (Beggars Banquet BEGA 173TC) 1986	-
	Desire/Message/Sapphire Scavenger/	
	New Horizons (12", PS) (Beggars Banquet BEGT 173) 1986	-

GENE LOVES JEZEBEL - Promise.

Gene Loves Jezebel were formed in Porthcawl, Wales in 1981 by two identical twins Jay and Michael Aston. By 1982, they had moved up to London and, after supporting The Higsons on tour, they were signed up by Situation 2.

Their debut 45 *Shaving My Neck* was a big indie hit. For a while they utilised additional guests Steve Goulding (sax), and John Murphy (drms), who'd previously played with SPK and The Associates. On tour, during 1983, they used Albio De Luca (gtr) (later of Furyo) and Julienne Regan (bs) (who was later in All About Eve).

Their 1983 *Bruises* single reached No. 7 in the indie charts. They also recorded successful radio sessions with Radio One's John Peel and David Jensen and completed a successful headlining U.K. tour.

Their debut album *Promise* is powerful with a full sound, roughly produced with rich guitars and a drifting beat and aggressive but rather tuneless vocals. *Bruises* is included and another cut *Influenza* was culled for release as a single, but the sensitive *Bread From Heaven* particularly catches the ear. Well worth checking out.

The U2 influence is also evident on the follow-up *Immigrant*, produced by John Leckie. By now the line-up had been modified. Peter Rizzo came in on bass for Steve Marshall. Marcus Gilvear, came on board from Glaxon 5 when Hawkins departed to join **Skeletal Family**. Finally, I.C. Hudson, who'd sometimes participated on earlier tours, was added to complete the new five piece line-up. Stand out tracks included *Shame*, which boasted a pulsating beat and catchy chorus and *Always A Flame* a dancey rocker with an appealing melody. The American version of the album added another U2 - influenced number *Bruises*.

In the Autumn of 1985, former **Chelsea** and **Generation X** member James Stevenson replaced I.C. Hudson. After being signed up by Beggars Banquet **Gene Loves Jezebel** achieved a significant commercial breakthrough when *The Sweetest Thing* and *Heartache* entered the singles chart, peaking at No's 75 and 71 respectively, whilst their next album *Discover* climbed to No. 32 during its four week chart tenure. A live bonus album *Glad To Be Alive* came with it. In this period they also toured the 'States quite successfully.

This punk influenced gothic-rock outfit recorded well into the nineties and is definitely worth checking out. Michael Aston emigrated to the 'States at the end of the eighties, but Jay kept the band going.

Generation X

Personnel:	BOB 'DERWOOD' ANDREWS	gtr	A B
	BILLY IDOL	vcls	A B C
	TONY JAMES	bs, vcls	A B C
	JOHN TOWE	drms	A
	MARK LAFF	drms	B
	TERRY CHIMES	drms	C
	JAMES STEPHENSON	gtr	C

HCP

ALBUMS:	1(B)	GENERATION X	(Chrysalis CHR 1169) 1978 29
	2(B)	VALLEY OF THE DOLLS	(Chrysalis CHR 1193) 1979 51
	3(C)	KISS ME DEADLY	(Chrysalis CHR 1327) 1981 -
	4(-)	BEST OF GENERATION X	(Chrysalis CHM 1521) 1985 -

NB: (3) credited to **Gen X**. (1) reissued on CD (Chrysalis CCD 1169) 1986 and again (EMI Gold 7243 8 52957-2) in 1996. (2) reissued on CD (Chrysalis CCD 1193) 1986. (3) reissued on CD (Chrysalis CCD 1327) 1987. Also of interest is *The Original Generation X* (M.B.C. JOCK LP 9), *Generation X Live* (M.B.C. JOCK LP 11) and *Perfect Hits (1975-81)* (Chrysalis CCD 1854) 1991, also on vinyl. Two later CD compilations are:- *Sweet Revenge* (Mutiny MUTINY 14) 1998 and *Generation X* (EMI Gold CDGOLD 1039) 1996. Also relevant is *Live At The Paris Theatre '78 & '81* (EMI 7243 4 99402 2) 1999.

HCP

45s:	Your Generation/Day By Day (PS)	(Chrysalis CHS 2165) 1977 36
	Wild Youth/Wild Dub (PS)	(Chrysalis CHS 2189) 1977 -
*	Wild Youth/No No No (PS)	(Chrysalis CHS 2189) 1977 -
	Ready Steady Go/No No No (PS)	(Chrysalis CHS 2207) 1978 47
+	King Rocker/Gimme Some Truth	(Chrysalis CHS 2261) 1978 11
#	Valley Of The Dolls/Shakin' All Over (PS)	(Chrysalis CHS 2310) 1979 23
%	Friday's Angels/Trying For Kicks/This Heat (PS)	(Chrysalis CHS 2330) 1979 62
$	Dancing With Myself/Ugly Rash (PS)	(Chrysalis CHS 2444) 1980 62
$	Dancing With Myself/Ugly Dub/Loopy Dub (12", PS)	(Chrysalis CHS 12 2444) 1980 -
**	Dancing With Myself/Untouchables/King Rocker/Rock On (PS)	(Chrysalis CHS 2488) 1981 60
$	Dancing With Myself/Untouchables/King Rocker/Rock On (12", PS)	(Chrysalis CHS 12 2488) 1981 -

NB: * Misspress B-side. + This was also reissued in four different coloured picture sleeves: Red (Idol); Pink (James); Orange (Derwood); Yellow (Laff) in January 1980. # initial copies came in brown vinyl. % Initial copies came in pink vinyl. $ credited to **Gen X**. ** Credited to **Gen X**, initial copies came in clear vinyl.

Generation X were formed in London in 1976 by Billy Idol (whose real name was William Broad; born in Middlesex on 30th November 1955) and Tony James. The pair met when James, pissed off with the inability of **London SS** whom he was rehearsing with, to form a stable line-up, answered an advert Idol had placed in 'Melody Maker'. Idol, James and Towe were all involved in an embryonic **Chelsea** line-up with that bands founder **Gene October**. Within a couple of months, though, Idol, James and Towe had left **Chelsea** to form their own band, **Generation X**. The title for the band was borrowed from a sixties paperback on Billy's mothers bookshelf. The new band was completed with the addition of Bob 'Derwood' Andrews on guitar, leaving Billy to concentrate on vocals. Billy and Tony had met him at the Fulham Greyhound.

Generation X played their first gig on 10th December 1976 at the Central College of Art and Design in London. They followed this on 21st December with an appearance at the Roxy Club in Covent Garden.

John Towe left **Generation X** in April 1977. He went on to join **Alternative TV** and then **The Adverts**. His replacement was Mark Laff from **Subway Sect**. The same month they recorded the first of three sessions for John Peel. The 20th April 1977 session comprised *Day By Day, Listen, Youth Youth Youth* and *Your Generation*. Within weeks of the broadcast various bootlegs of the concert were in circulation and the band hadn't even signed to a record label. The second Peel session followed on 21st July and featured *From The Heart, Rock On, Gimme Some Truth* and *No No No*. The same month the band signed to Chrysalis.

On 22nd August 1977 they recorded a session for Dave Lee Travis. This featured *Day By Day, No No No, Your Generation* and *Rock On*. The same month a bootleg EP featuring *Your Generation, Save My Life* and *Ready Steady Go* entered circulation.

Their debut single *Your Generation*, released in September 1977, was generally well received, although peaking at only No. 36 and spending four weeks in the charts, the sales were disappointing considering their reputation on the London live circuit prior to securing a contract. The follow-up *Wild Youth*, a spirited number and key part of their live set, failed to chart at all. It's worth noting that there was a white label pressing of *Your Generation* backed by an instrumental version of *Listen* and a misspressing of *Wild Youth* coupled with *No No No* instead of the intended dub mix of the 'A' side. These are both very scarce and important collectables for fans of the band now.

The eponymous debut album, recorded in just seven days, was released in March 1978. It included many of their classic songs from the previous year; *From The Heart, Day By Day, Ready Steady Go* (culled for 45 release), *Listen, Youth Youth Youth, One Hundred Punks* etc. Three new songs - *Kiss Me Deadly, Promises Promises* and *Invisible Man* were added. It was a classic album, there's not a naff track on it and for American fans the U.S. release had the bonus of including *Your Generation* and *Wild Youth* as well as covers of John Lennon's *Gimme Some Truth* and Johnny Kidd's *Shakin' All Over*. Despite the album's commercial leanings (which most punk bands avoided) in Britain the band only reached a disappointing No. 29 with this album, which spent four weks in the charts overall. The *Ready Steady Go* 45, a fitting tribute to the classic TV show, also scored poorly in commercial terms barely making the Top 50. Later, in 1979, it resurfaced on the *20 Of Another Kind* (Polydor SUPER POLS 1006) compilation.

The remainder of 1978 was a quiet period for the band. On 27th June, they did a session for David Jensen consisting of *King Rocker* (as then unreleased), *One Hundred Punks* and a cover of Johnny Kidd's *Shakin' All Over*. They were also busy working on a new album with former Mott The Hoople man Ian Hunter handling production. It was released in January 1979 but sadly wasn't worth the long wait. Except that is for the superb *King Rocker*. This was the obvious candidate for 45 release, backed by a version of John Lennon's *Gimme Some Truth* (taken from a Peel session on 21st July 1977). Peaking at No. 11 it gave them their biggest hit by some way and was released in four different colour vinyls. The album climbed only to No. 51 in the charts in which it spent five weeks overall. Two further cuts - *Valley Of The Dolls* (No. 23) and *Friday's Angels* (No. 62) - were released as 45s with some success but the overall sound on the album is rather flat.

On 14th February 1979, they played their last of three John Peel sessions. It featured four songs - *Paradise West, Love Like Fire, Night Of The Cadillacs* and *English Dream* - from the *Valley Of The Dolls* album.

The band were now at a crossroads. Billy was getting into dub music but Mark Laff and Bob Andrews weren't and left, after a disagreement about their future direction. Former **Clash** drummer Terry Chimes came in for Laff and James Stephenson was enticed away from **Chelsea** to play guitar.

This new line-up became known as **Gen X**. Their first recording *Dancing With Myself*, released in September 1980, was inspired by a visit to Japan "where all the discos have mirrors and people danced with their own

GENERATION X - Generation X.

reflections" Tony James explained in a Record Collector interview in 1987. The band also issued this as its first 12" single, replacing the 7" 'B'-side *Ugly Rash* by a dub mix, *Ugly Dub* and an additional track *Loopy Dub*. An alternative version of *Dancing With Myself* was used as the 'A' side. Then, in the New Year following its warm reception in the music press, Chrysalis repackaged it with a new catalogue number. They then released it on clear vinyl, in both 7" and 12" format backed by *The Untouchables*, *King Rocker* and *Rock On*. This alternate version did make it to No. 60 in the charts. *Dancing With Myself* really was the only outstanding track on an otherwise disappointing album *Kiss Me Deadly*, which like the re-packaged single, was released in January 1981. Overall, this was a pale imitation of how they sounded on their debut album. The band knew this, too, and split the same month when Billy Idol moved to New York.

Billy wasted no time in launching a solo career which is another story in itself. Several **Generation X** tracks re-appeared, either in original or re-recorded formats, on subsequent Billy Idol 45s. Tony James went on to form Sigue Sigue Sputnik. He was later in **Sisters Of Mercy**. Laff formed 20 Flight Rockers. Stevenson later worked with Henry Padovani, Kim Wilde and **Gene Loves Jezebel**.

Like many other bands **Generation X** did reform, but just for one night in September 1993.

Compilation appearances have included *Shakin' All Over* and *New Order* on *Punk Lost And Found* (Shanachie SH 5705) 1996; *Ready Steady Go* on *The Best Punk Anthem In The World.... Ever, Vol. 1* (2-CD) (Virgin VTDCD 42) 1995; *King Rocker* on *Vol. 2* (Virgin VTDCD 79) 1996 of the above and on *Teenage Kicks* (PolyGram TV 5253382) 1995, *Spiked* (EMI Gold CDGOLD 1057) 1996, and *Punk - The Worst Of Total Anarchy* (2-CD) (Disky SP 871952) 1996; and *Valley Of The Dolls* on *God Save The Punks* (2-CD) (Disky DOU 882552) 1998.

Their punk pedigree was confirmed when *Your Generation* was included on the 5-CD set *1-2-3-4 - A History Of Punk and New Wave 1976 - 1979* (MCA/Universal 60066) in 1999. The same year EMI issued a *Live At The Paris Theatre '78 & '81* on CD. The '78 concert captures the band at their punk best, by the '81 gig they sound past this but still sound accomplished. Unfortunately, the CD is poorly packaged with no photos or sleeve-notes.

Genocide

EP: 1 IMAGES OF DELUSION (Images Of Delusion/
Pre Set Future/Last Days On Earth/
Plastic People In Stereo) (PS)   (Safari SAP 2) 1979

The picture sleeve shows them in stern uniforms gazing wistfully into the distance. So it's no suprise that musically this sounds like third rate **Gary Numan** with loads of moog.

The Gents

Personnel:	MARTIN BOURTON	bs, vcls	A
	STEVE CHAMBERS	gtr	A
	GLYN REES DAVIES	drms, vcls	A
	STEPHEN KENDELL	keyb'ds	A

45s: (up to 1986)		
The Faker/The Pink Panther	(Posh POSH 001)	1981
Schooldays/True Stories (some PS)	(Kosmic KOS 6886)	1982
Revenge/Girl (PS)	(Posh POSH 007)	1983
The Gent/Revenge/Over Me (PS)	(Posh MEGA 1)	198?
Shout/The Faker (PS)	(Lambs To The Slaughter GN 7)	1985
New Direction/ You Are The Sun (PS)	(Lambs To The Slaughter GN 8)	1985
Stay With Me/Heat Of The Sun (PS)	(Prism GN 9)	1985
Stay With Me/Heat Of The Sun/Don't Turn Away/ Tomorrow Ne'ercome (12", PS)	(Prism GN 9)	1985
Give It To Me/At The Dance	(Prism GN 1)	1986
Give It To Me/At The Dance (12")	(Prism GN 11)	1986
Friday On My Mind	(Lambs To The Slaughter GN 12)	1986
Friday On My Mind (12")	(Lambs To The Slaughter GN 12)	1986

A Yorkshire-based mod revival band from Doncaster, who continued to record into the mid-eighties whilst at the same time earning a living playing all the latest hits of the times in local night clubs. *The Faker* was also included on *The Countdown Compilation* (Countdown) 1985, which has been reissued on CD (Captain Mod MODSKA CD 6) 1997.

THE GENTS - The Gent.

Gerry and The Holograms

Personnel:	C.P. LEE
	JOHN SCOTT

45s:	Gerry and The Holograms/ Increased Resistance (PS)	(Absurd ABSURD 4)	1979
	The Emperor's New Music	(Absurd ABSURD 5)	1979

This was an interesting collaboration between Absurd label recording artist John Scott and C.P. Lee of **Alberto Y Los Trios Paranoias** (who Scott also played with). Their debut 45 sounded similar to The Residents using distortion and repetition to conjure up a sound that was both 'industrial' and futuristic.

The second disc *The Emperor's New Music* - was a punk gimmick 45, which was literally unplayable because the disc was glued into the sleeve so it couldn't be played! Some copies had 'Rough Trade' stickers on the picture sleeves, which actually said 'Do Not Play This Record' on it. Despite this quite a few copies were sold. It seems that this gimmick was created out of badly pressed **Slaughter and The Dogs** records they didn't know what to do with!

The Gifted Children

Personnel:	BERNARD COOPER	bs	A
	MARK 'EMPIRE' SHEPPARD	drms	A
	DAN TREACY	vcls	A

GERRY AND THE HOLOGRAMS - Gerry And The Holograms.

45:	Painting By Numbers/		
	Lichtenstein Girl (PS)	(Whaam! WHAAM 001)	1981

This was basically a **Television Personalities**' project featuring Dan and Empire with a little-known bassist. They recorded under a different name because they wanted to experiment. This 45 is now rare and collectable. An album of material was muted but scrapped when Bernard Cooper disappeared.

Girls At Our Best

Personnel:	JAMES ALAN (JEZ)	gtr	A
	JUDY EVANS (JO)	vcls	A
	CARL HARPER (TITCH)	drms	A
	GERARD SWIFT (TERRY)	bs	A

HCP

ALBUM:	1(A)	PLEASURE	(Happy Birthday RVLP 1) 1981 60

NB: (1) also issued on CD (Vinyl Japan ASKCD 047) 1994, with extra tracks.

45s:	Getting Nowhere Fast/Warm Girls (PS)	(Records RR 001) 1980
	Politics/It's Fashion (PS)	(Rough trade RT 055) 1981
	Go For Gold/I'm Beautiful Now (PS)	(Happy Birthday UR 4) 1981
	Fast Boyfriends/This Train (PS)	(Happy Birthday UR 6) 1981

A misleading name. The only girl amongst them was vocalist Judy Evans. They formed in Leeds during 1980. The band members had previously been in The Butterflies and The Expelaires.

Their musical menu combined punk with a brand of alternative rock. Their sound was distinguished by Judy's shrill vocal style.

Their debut 45 *Getting Nowhere Fast* was released in April 1980 on a small label but distributed by Rough Trade. It sold reasonably well and *Politics* was issued as a follow-up six months later. They courted a radical feminist image on account of their name and this last song in particular, which was ironic in view of their gender make up - only one woman in the band.

They switched to the Happy Birthday label for two further 45s; *Go For Gold* and *Fast Boyfriends* and the *Pleasure* album in 1981. The 45 sales were disappointing. The first 10,000 copies of the album came with a free 'pleasure bag' containing two postcards, a sticker and a stencil as well as a lyric insert. Judy's distinctive vocals and some witty lyrics make it a worthwhile listen. It sold quite well too, spending three weeks in the album charts and peaking at No. 60.

Girlschool

Personnel:	DENISE DUFORT	drms	ABC
(up to	KELLY JOHNSON	lead gtr, vcls	AB
1985)	KIM McAULIFFE	vcls, gtr	ABC
	ENID WILLIAMS	bs, vcls	A
	GIL WESTON	bs, vcls	BC
	CHRIS BONACCI	gtr	C
	JACKIE BONIMEAD	vcls, gtr	C

HCP

ALBUMS:	1(A)	DEMOLITION	(Bronze BRON 525) 1980 28
(up to	2(A)	HIT AND RUN	(Bronze BRON 534) 1981 5
1985)	3(B)	SCREAMING BLUE MURDER	(Bronze BRON 541) 1982 27
	4(B)	PLAY DIRTY	(Bronze BRON 548) 1983 66

NB: (1) and (2) reissued on one CD (Loma LOMACD 1) 1991. (3) and (4) reissued on one CD (Loma LOMA CD 4) 1992. There are also some relevant compilations, *Race With The Devil* (Raw Power RAWLP 013) 1986 on vinyl, also on CD (Receiver RRCD 254) 1998; *Cheers You Lot* (Metal Masters METALMCD 127) 1991, also on vinyl (METALPM 127) 1989; *Collection* (Castle CCSCD 314) 1991, also on vinyl; *The Best Of Girlschool* (Dojo DOJOCD 103) 1994; *From The Vaults* (Sequel NEMCD 642) 1994; *Nightmare At Maple Cross / Take A Bite* (Loma LOMA CD 8) 1992; *Emergency* (2-CD set) (Snapper SMDCD 126) 1997; *Live* (Communique CMGCD 013) 1995; *King Biscuit Presents....* (King Biscuit KBFHCD 007) 1998; and *The Collection* (2-CD set) (Essential CM DDD 014) 2000.

HCP

EPs:	1(A)	ST. VALENTINE'S DAY MASSACRE (Please Don't Touch/Emergency/Bomber)	(Bronze BRO 116) 1981 5
	2(B)	WILDLIFE (Wildlife/Don't Call It Love/ Don't Stop)	(Bronze BRO 144) 1982 58

NB: (1) Motorhead and **Girlschool** (also known as Headgirl).

HCP

45s:	*	Take It All Away/It Could Be Better (PS)	(City NIK 6) 1979 -
(up to	+	Take It All Away/It Could Be Better	(Mulligan LUNS 723) 1979 -
1985)		Emergency/Furniture Fire (PS)	(Bronze BRO 89) 1980 -
		Nothing To Lose/Baby Doll (PS)	(Bronze BRO 95) 1980 -
		Race With The Devil/ Take It All Away (PS)	(Bronze BRO 100) 1980 49
		Yeah Right/The Hunter (PS)	(Bronze BRO 110) 1980 -
		Hit And Run/Tonight (PS)	(Bronze BRO 118) 1981 32
		Hit And Run/Tonight/Tush (10", PS)	(Bronze BROX 118) 1981 -
		C'mon Let's Go/Tonight (live) (PS)	(Bronze BRO 126) 1981 42
		C'mon Let's Go/Tonight (live)/ Demolition (live) (10", PS)	(Bronze BROX 126) 1981 -
		1-2-3-4 Rock And Roll/Tush (PS)	(Bronze BRO 169) 1983 -
		1-2-3-4 Rock And Roll (Extended)/Tush (New Version)/ Don't Call It Love (New Version)/ Emergency (12", PS)	(Bronze BROX 169) 1983 -
		20th Century Boy/ Breaking All The Rules (PS)	(Bronze BRO 171) 1983 -
		20th Century Boy/Breaking All The Rules/ Like It Like That (12", PS)	(Bronze BROX 171) 1983 -
		Burning In The Heat/Surrender (PS)	(Bronze BRO 176) 1984 -
		Burning In The Heat/ Surrender (12", PS and booklet)	(Bronze BROX 176) 1984 -

NB: * There were two versions of this 45. One came in red vinyl with a pink picture sleeve and black and white front cover picture. The other was on black vinyl with an orange picture sleeve. + This Irish version was on red vinyl and not in a picture sleeve.

Girlschool are a marginal case for inclusion in this book. Essentially a heavy metal rock/pop combo, they were influenced by their punkish counterparts The Runaways and rose to prominence in the punk era and during its aftermath as a leather clad girl band.

They formed in South London in March 1978. Their founder members Kim McAuliffe and Enid Williams had both previously been in a group called Painted Lady. Denise Dufort was the sister of Dave Dufort, who was the drummer of Angel Witch. Their debut 45 was released on the indie label City in November 1979. It was later reissued in 1981, after it had done well enough to get them a deal with Bronze towards the end of 1979.

They were managed by Doug Smith, who was Motorhead's manager. Their early 45s for Bronze *Emergency* and *Nothing To Lose* did quite well, but didn't make the charts. They really attracted national attention through the success of their debut album *Demolition*, which rose to No. 28 in the album charts. It enjoyed a ten week chart residency in all. *Demolition* included their first two singles as well as their very credible cover of *Race With The Devil*. This song was originally written by Adrian Gurvitz for his band The Gun, who had a Top Ten hit with it back in Autumn 1968. **Girlschool**'s version got to No. 49 and helped raise their profile.

GIRLSCHOOL - Race With The Devil.

Their next big break came when they teamed forces with Motorhead on the *St. Valentine's Day Massacre* (EP) the following year. It included *Emergency* (their first 45), a cover of Johnny Kidd's *Please Don't Touch*, which had been his first hit back in 1959, and a new song *Bomber*. With the extra clout of Motorhead and their fans behind it the EP got to No. 5 and spent eight weeks in the charts in all.

They consolidated on this success, when their second album *Hit And Run* also climbed to No. 5, this time in the album charts, during a residency of six weeks. It spawned two more hit singles, the title track (No. 32) and a cover of The McCoys' *C'mon Let's Go* (No. 42). Other tracks featured included *Yeah Right* (a single from November 1980 that had missed the charts) and a cover of ZZ Top's *Tush*.

In late 1981, Enid Williams left and joined Framed. Former **Killjoys**' member Gil Weston came in as a replacement. The modified line-up put out a third album *Screaming Blue Murder*, in June 1982. This included a cover a The Rolling Stones' *Live With Me* and a collection of originals, mostly penned by McAuliffe and Johnson. The album sold well, peaking at No. 27 and spending six weeks in all in the charts, but unlike its predecessors it failed to produce any hit singles. Indeed only one 'A' side *Wildlife* was issued from the album and it missed out in that respect.

From 1983 onwards their record sales declined. Their fourth album *Hit And Run* became their first not to chart. Although comprised largely of self-penned material it was its one cover version, T Rex's *20th Century Boy* which was selected for 45 release and it didn't chart. A second 45 *Burning In The Heat* also flopped. After this Kelly Johnson left. Former She members Chris Bonacci (gtr) and Jackie Bonimead (vcls, gtr) came in as the band expanded to a quintet. A U.S.-only album *Running Wild* was released in 1985. The following year they teamed up with Gary Glitter to record a new version of *I'm The Leader Of The Gang (I Am)*. After this unsuccessful venture Jackie Bonimead left and they reverted to a quartet. Two further albums were recorded - *Nightmare At Maple Cross* (1986) and *Take A Bite* (1988) - but after little success they called it quits. They did reform in 1992, though and the same year these albums were reissued on one CD.

Girlschool are certainly worth checking out, although much of their stronger material was covers of other people's songs. The best introduction to their material is *The Collection*, which includes most of their finer moments and more. Other alternative compilations of their material include *Race With The Devil* and *Cheers You Lot*.

Girl Skwadd

| Personnel incl: | JENNINGS | A |
| | O'DONNELL | A |

45: Sweet Talk/Love Condition (PS)   (Ariola AHA 551) 1979

An NME review described this one-off as "accompanied by ping-pong Euro electronics... sounding like a legless Siouxsie doing a wicked send-up of El Duce Ferrara". Perhaps it's no suprise there was no follow-up.

Gist

Personnel: STUART MOXHAM   vcls, instr   A

ALBUM: 1(A)   EMBRACE THE HERD   (Rough Trade ROUGH 25) 1983

NB: (1) later issued on CD (Rykodisc RCD 10465) 1999.

45s:	This Is Love/Yanks (PS)	(Rough Trade RT 058) 1981
	Love At First Sight/ Light Aircraft (PS)	(Rough Trade RT 085) 1981
	Fool For A Valentine/ Food For A Person (PS)	(Rough Trade RT 125) 1983

Stuart Moxham with his brother Phil comprised two-thirds of Cardiff band **Young Marble Giants**. On *This Is Love* he is assisted by his brother Phil on bass. On *Yanks* Lewis Mottram helps out on bass. Both songs are quite appealing. On *Embrace The Herd* Stuart (who is **Gist**) is helped by Phil on three tracks and various other friends and colleagues on some of the others. The end result is delicate new wave-influenced pop songs and strange instrumentals.

GIST - This Is Love.

Glass Torpedoes

Personnel incl: BABRA DONOVAN   vcls

45:   Someone Different/ Morning Noon & Night (PS)   (Teen Beat TDR 1) 1979

A briefly promising Liverpool band who never made it. This 45 showcased Barbra Donovan's vocals, lashings of wild guitar and some catchy pop tunes but all to no avail.

Glaxo Babies

Personnel:	GEOFF ALSOPP	drms	A
	DAN CATSIS	gtr, vcls	A
	ROB CHAPMAN	vcls	A
	TOMMY NICHOLS	bs, vcls	A
	TONY WRAFTERS	sax	A

| ALBUMS: | 1(A) | NINE MONTHS TO THE DISCO | (Heartbeat HB 2) 1980 |
| | 2(A) | PUT ME ON THE GUEST LIST | (Heartbeat HB 3) 1980 |

EP: 1(A)   THIS IS YOUR LIFE (This Is Your Life/Stay Away/ Because Of You/ Who Killed Bruce Lee)   (Heartbeat 12 PULSE 3) 1979

| 45s: | Christine Keeler/ Nova Bossanova (PS) | (Heartbeat PULSE 5) 1979 |
| | Limited Entertainment/Dahij/ There Is Room For You In The | (Y LP 6) 1981 |

A Bristol combo whose vinyl debut came when they contributed *It's Irrational* to *Avon Calling - The Bristol Compilation* (Heartbeat HB 1) in

GLAXO BABIES - Put Me On The Guest List.

1979, which set the tone for what followed. They deploy a wide array of noises, disjointed voices and sonic sounds on their first album. Most of the cuts are not in a rock format at all but the band are a good example of the type of sound the 'new wave' produced.

Their second album *Put Me On The Guest List* is basically a compilation of previously unreleased studio efforts from 1978-79. The content is inconsistent and unpredictable, ranging from fragile pop to complex underground and much in between.

Rob Chapman went on to form his own group **The Transmitters** who cut an album in 1981.

The Glory

ALBUM: 1   SKINS 'N' PUNKS, VOLUME 3   (Oi! OIR 009) 198?

NB: (1) this was a split album with The Magnificent.

An Oi! band whose powerful *Clockwork Land* from the above album was later included on *The Best Of Oi! Records* (CD) (Captain Oi! AHOY CD 38) 1995.

SKINS 'N' PUNKS VOL. 3, a split album with The Glory.

The Glove

Personnel:
ANDY ANDERSON	drms	A
GINNY HEWES	strings	A
JEANETTE LANDRAY	vcls	A
MARTIN McCARRICK	cello	A
STEVEN SEVERIN	bs	A
ROBERT SMITH	vcls	A
ANNE STEPHENSON	strings	A

HCP
ALBUM: 1(A)   BLUE SUNSHINE   (Wonderland SHELP 2) 1983   35

NB: (1) some copies were mispressings with double printed sleeve. (1) reissued on Polydor in 1990, also issued on CD (Polydor 8150192) 1990.

45s: Like An Animal/Mouth To Mouth (PS) (Wonderland SHE 3) 1983
Like An Animal (Club, What Club? Mix)/Like An Animal/
Mouth To Mouth (12", PS)   (Wonderland SHEX 3) 1983
Punish Me With Kisses/
The Tightrope (PS)   (Wonderland SHE 5) 1983

This project was put together by **The Cure**'s Robert Smith (who was playing with **Siouxsie and The Banshees** at the time) and the latter's bassist Steven Severin. The band were named after the villain in 'Yellow Submarine' and the cover to their album *Blue Sunshine* is plastered with sixties memorabilia. So you can get the picture, eighties new wave playing pseudo psychedelic pop ditties and it's all good fun. *Like An Animal*,

featuring Jeanette Landray on vocals, stands out and was also released as a 45, as was another cut *Punish Me With Kisses*. The album also sold pretty well climbing to No. 35 during a three week chart stay.

Vic Godard and The Subway Sect

See **The Subway Sect**.

Golinski Brothers

Personnel:
TOM BEATTIE	drms	A
OLLIE CROOK	bs	A
DARRIS	vcls	A
WILL GIBBS	sax	A
BOB GOLINSKI	gtr	A

45:    Bloody/Toy   (Badger BAD 6) 1980

A short-lived south coast project. In addition to this 45 **The Golinski Brothers** also contributed two of the best cuts to *Vaultage '79 (Another Two Sides Of Brighton)* (Attrix RB 08) 1979. *Bloody* is a lighthearted love song:-

"What am I bloody well supposed to do
Get my bloody well self
Bloody stuck on you"
(from *Bloody*)

Their second track *Too Scared* is an excellent new wave composition. *Bloody* can also be found on *Vaultage Punk Collection* (Anagram CDPUNK 101) 1997.

The Gonads

Personnel:
GARRY BUSHELL	vcls	ABC
NICK CUNNINGHAM	drms	A
MICKY FITZ		AB
STEVE KENT	gtr	A C
MARTIN SMITH	bs	A
KEV BOYCE	drms	B
MARK BRENNAN	bs	B
STEVE WHALE	gtr	B
J.J. BEDSORE		C
MARK BRABBS		C

ALBUM: 1( )   LIVE THE OFFICIAL BOOTLEG
(Red Robin SYNDLP 8) 1984

NB: There's also a CD compilation, *Punk Rock Will Never Die* (Mog MOGCD 007) 1998 and also relevant are: *Live And Loud* (Street Link LINK LP 049) 1988 and *The Revenge Of The Gonads* (Street Link LINK LP 085) 1989.

THE GLOVE - Blue Sunshine.

EPs:	1( )	PURE PUNK FOR NOW PEOPLE (Punk Rock Will Never Die/Got Any Wrigleys John?/Sandra Bigg (Really Big)/I Lost My Love (To A U.K. Sub)/ Annie's Song)	(Secret SHH 131) 1982
	2( )	PEACE ARTISTS (She Can't Whip Me/ Punk City Rockers/Gonads Anthem/ SLAG)	(Secret SHH 134) 1982
	3( )	DELILAH (THE PUNK EPIC)	(Razor RZS 103) 1983

This was journalist and major Oi! publicist Garry Bushell's old pub rock band rejuvenated. Their vinyl debut came when *Tuckers Ruckers Ain't No Suckers* appeared on *Carry On Oi!* (Secret SEC 2) 1981, which was reissued on CD (Captain Oi! AHOY CD 119) 1999. The song can also be heard on *Trouble On The Terraces - 16 Classic Football Anthems* (Step-1 STEP LP 91) 1996. They also contributed *White Christmas* to *Bollocks To Christmas* (EP) (Secret 126) in 1981.

In 1982 came the hilarious *Pure Punk For Now People* (EP) and the equally funny *Peace Artists* (EP). The amusing *I Lost My Love (To A U.K. Sub)*, which appeared on the first of these EPs, also got a further airing on *The Secret Life Of Punk* (Secret SEC 10). The same year they contributed *TNT* to the *Total Noise* (EP) (Total Noise TOT 1) 1982.

Jobs Not Jails appeared on *Son Of Oi!* (Syndicate SYNLP 3) in 1983. On this recording Bushell was backed by Steve Kent, J.J. Bedsore (**The Blood**) and Mark Brabbs (**Tank**), whereas on previous efforts he'd been backed by the first two incarnations of **The Business**. *Son Of Oi!* has also been reissued on CD (Captain Oi! AHOY CD 9) 1993. They also recorded a third EP on Razor in 1983.

On *Live And Loud* they transform *The Monkees Theme* into *Go Mad with The Gonads* and *Pleasant Valley Sunday* into *SE7 Dole Day*. The remainder of the album comprises the band's originals like *I Lost My Love To A U.K. Sub*, *Punk Rock Will Never Die* and *Tuckers Ruckers Ain't No Suckers*. *The Revenge Of The Gonads* is a compilation of their better moments.

Compilation appearances included *I Lost My Love To A UK Sub* and *Punk City Rockers* on *Secret Records Punk Singles Collection, Vol. 1* (Anagram CDPUNK 13) 1993, whilst *Vol. 2* (Anagram CDPUNK 60) 1995 included *Punk Rock Will Never Die*, *Got Any Wriggly's John* and *She Can't Whip Me*.

They returned in 1999 with a brand new CD *Oi!... Back And Barking* (Captain Oi! AHOY CD 115). This was actually their first ever studio album. It contained thirteen brand new tracks, including the double 'A' side 45 *Oi! Nutter/England's Glory* and a new version of the Oi! classic *Dead End Yobs*, which featured **Garry Johnson**, the original Oi! poet. The same year, they contributed *Tuckers Ruckers Ain't No Suckers* to *Oi! Fuckin' Oi!* (Harry May MAYO CD 110).

Dave Goodman and Friends

Personnel:	PAUL COOK	drms	A
	DAVE GOODMAN	vcls	A
	STEVE JONES	gtr	A
	IAN WOODCOCK	bs	A

45s:	Justifiable Homicide/ Take Down Your Fences (PS)	(The Label TLR 8) 1978

Dave Goodman produced several of the early **Sex Pistols** recordings and he linked up with former **Sex Pistols** Paul Cook and Steve Jones for these recordings. 15,000 copies of the 45 were pressed on red vinyl, a number of additional copies emerged on usual black vinyl. A few copies were printed with a 'Steve Jones and Paul Cook' credit and these now fetch in excess of £50.

Justifiable Homicide was about the murder of Liddle Towers, an alledged case of police brutality. This song was re-adapted the same year by **The Angelic Upstarts** as *The Murder Of Liddle Towers*. *Justifiable Homicide* can also be heard on *Business Unusual* (Cherry Red ARED 2) in 1979. The band also featured on *The Label Sofa* (The Label TLRLP 002) compilation in 1978.

BOLLOCKS TO CHRISTMAS featuring The Gonads.

The Good Missionaries

Personnel:	HENRY BADOWSKI	drms	A
	DENNIS BURNS	bs	A
	DAVE GEORGE	gtr	A
	GILLIAN HANNA	recorder	A
	MARK PERRY	vcls, gtr	A

ALBUM:	1(A)	FIRE FROM HEAVEN	(Deptford Fun City DLP 04) 1979

NB: There's also *Spontaneous Emissions* (Conventional no #), which is a studio/live cassette.

EPs:	1(A)	VIBING UP THE SENILE (The Good Missionary Part 1 (live)/The Good Missionary Part 2 (live)/Kif Kif's Free Freakout (live)	(Unnormality NORM 001) 1980
	2(A)	DERANGED IN HASTINGS (Keep Going Backwards/ Attitudes)	(Unnormality NORM 002) 1981

NB: (1) only 1,000 copies pressed. (2) came with a printed insert in a poly bag.

By the spring of 1979 **Alternative TV** were moving away from their original punk format and playing more experimental and cerebral material. Songs like *Release The Natives* didn't go down well with what were still predominantly punk audiences. After **Mark Perry** got knocked out by a bottle at Derby, **Alternative TV** decided to re-group and re-name themselves as **The Good Missionaries**. The line-up still comprised **Mark Perry** and Dennis Burns, supplemented by Mark's girlfriend Gillian Hanna on recorder, Dave George on bass and former **Chelsea** and **Damned** bassist **Henry Badowski**. In a final wild summer the band catapulted head-long into the avant-punk wilderness on the 'pay no more than £2.50' live album *Fire From Heaven*. They also recorded a couple of EPs on the Unnormality label but things didn't really work out too well and this line-up split.

Mark Perry made a few solo recordings and after a six month spell in the **Lemon Kittens** became a sideman in an **Alternative TV** spin-off project **The Door and The Window**. Dave George moved down to Hastings and continued **The Good Missionaries** down there with different personnel. **Henry Badowski** went solo, enjoying a minor hit with *Baby Sign Here With Me*. In 1981, **Badowski** recorded a whimsical pop album *Life Is A Grand*.

In the final judgement **The Good Missionaries** were a failed experiment with their meandering, rather formless, music resulting from over self-indulgence.

Gordon and Julie

Personnel:	GORDON	vcls
	JULIE	vcls

45s:	Gordon's Not A Moron/ I'm So Happy To Know You (PS)	(Dog 003) 1978
	J-J-Julie (Yippee Yula)/Gettin' It Together (PS)	(Dog 004) 1979

These were spin-off 45s from **Jilted John**.

Gordon The Moron

Personnel: GORDON — vcls

45s:	* De Do Dough Don't Be Dough/?	(Rabid TOSH 107) 1978
	Fit For Nothing/Sold On You (PS)	(Rabid TOSH 111) 1979

NB: * Scheduled for release, but it never actually appeared.

Another project linked to **Jilted John**.

The Gorillas

Personnel:	GARY ANDERSON	drms	A
	ALAN BUTLER	bs	A
	JESSE HECTOR	vcls, gtr	A

ALBUM: 1(A) MESSAGE TO THE WORLD (Raw RWLP 103) 1978

NB: (1) also issued on CD (Damaged Goods DAMGOOD 49) 1994.

45s:	She's My Gal/Wait Till Tomorrow (PS)	(Chiswick S4) 1976
	Gatecrasher/Gorilla Got Me (PS)	(Chiswick S8) 1976
	It's My Life/My Son's Alive (PS)	(Raw RAW 14) 1978
	Message To The World/ Outta My Brain (PS)	(Raw RAW 26) 1978
	Move It/Song For Rita (PS)	(Chiswick CHIS 151) 1981

This was a later version of **The Hammersmith Gorillas**. Their early 45s showcased Jesse Hector's strained vocal style effectively over a mod-inspired, tight rhythm section. *It's My Life* was his own composition, which owed much to Bo Diddley and the phaser dial *not* The Animals song. The album is less convincing, but it has its moments. Their cover of Jimi Hendrix's *Foxy Lady* isn't one of them! Their live repertoire also included The Kinks' *You Really Got Me* and the band were rivals to **The Vibrators** in terms of being an elderly punk band.

It's My Life and *My Son's Alive* can also be heard on *The Raw Records Punk Collection* (Anagram CDPUNK 14) in 1993. *Gatecrasher* got a further airing on *The Chiswick Sampler (Good Clean Fun)* (Chiswick CDWIKX 162) 1995 and *She's My Gal* and *Gorilla Got Me* resurfaced on *The Chiswick Story* (2-CD) (Chiswick CDWIK 2 100) in 1992.

The Graduate

Personnel:	JOHN BAKER	vcls, gtr	A
	STEVE BUCK	keyb'ds, flute	A
	ANDY MARSDEN	drms	A
	ROLAND ORZABAL	vcls, gtr	A
	CURT SMITH	vcls, bs	A

ALBUM: 1(A) ACTING MY AGE (Precision PART 001) 1980

45s:	Elvis Should Play Ska/Julie Julie (PS)	(Precision PAR 100) 1980
	Ever Met A Day/Shut Up (PS)	(Precision PAR 104) 1980
	Ambition/Bad Dreams (PS)	(Precision PAR 111) 1980
	Mad One/Somebody Put Out The Fire	(Blue Hats BHR) 198?
Reissue:	Shut Up/Ever Met A Day	(Precision PAR 117) 1981

Graduate were formed in Bath by Curt Smith, who was born on 24th June 1961 and Roland Orzabal (real name Roland Orzabal De La Quintana), who was born on 22nd August 1961 in Portsmouth. They played ska-pop, one of the strands of the post-punk era which we won't be concentrating on in this book. In 1981, Smith and Orzabal both left **Graduate** to form Tears For Fears, who became one of the top soulful rock outfits of the eighties.

The Graduates

Personnel:	NICK LYNE	A
	KEVIN PARSONS	A
	BEN RUST	A
	GARY STOREY	A

45: If You Want It/Hey Young Girl (PS) (Graduate GRAD 1) 1979

An obscure mod revival band who released this 45 on their own label. Both sides can also be heard on *This Is Mod, Vol. 5* (Anagram CDMGRAM 110) 1997.

Grow-Up

Personnel:	ROGER BLACKBURN	bs	A
	JOHN BLISSETT-SMITH	gtr, vcls	A
	TONY KING	bs	A
	HARRY VAN ROOIJ		

ALBUM: 1(A) WITHOUT WINGS (Up Records GROW 1) 1981

EP: 1(A) GROW-UP (Stay Alive/10 Mins/Photo/Lake/ River/So Long) (PS) (Object Music OM 5) 1979

A five-piece from Manchester fronted by **Spherical Objects**' guitarist John Blisset-Smith who also handles vocals and also wrote each of the six short pieces on the EP. The music is strange, characterised by his vivid guitar style. Better still are the two cuts, *You Are The One* and *Night Rally*, which they contributed to *A Manchester Collection* (Object Music OBJ 003) 1979.

The G.T.'s

An obscure punk band who contributed two cuts to *Raw Deal* (Raw RAWLP 1) in 1977 *Millionaire* and *Move On*, but they don't appear to have recorded any other vinyl. *Millionaire* later appeared on *The Raw Records Punk Collection* (Anagram CDPUNK 14) in 1993.

The Gymslips

Personnel:	PAULA RICHARDS	vcls, gtr	ABC
	SUZANNE SCOTT	bs, vcls	AB
	KAREN YARNELL	drms, vcls	AB
	(KATHY BARNES	keyb'ds	B)
	MICHELLE CHOWRIMOOTOO	drms	C
	KAREN KAY	bs	C
	SUE VICKERS	keyb'ds	C

ALBUM: 1(B) ROCKIN' WITH THE RENEES (Abstract ABT 006) 1983

NB: (1) came with a free 4 track EP featuring *Silly Egg*, *Take Away*, *Pie N Mash* and *Multi-Coloured Sugar*. It was also released for export as *Drink Problem*, but with a different sleeve and the same track listening. There's also a CD compilation *Rocking With The Renees* (Captain Oi! AHOY CD 124) 1999.

45s:	48 Crash/Miss Nunsweeta (PS)	(Abstract ABS 011) 1982
	Big Sister/Yo Yo/Pie And Mash (PS)	(Abstract ABS 014) 1983
	Robot Man/Multi-Coloured Sugar/ Take Away (PS)	(Abstract ABS 015) 1983
	Evil Eye/Wonderland (PS)	(Abstract ABS 033) 1985

THE GRADUATE - Elvis Should Play Ska.

Evil Eye/Wonderland/
Don't Lead Me On (12", PS) (Abstract ABS 12033) 1985

This East London post-punk all female trio who formed in 1981 was about as near as one could get to a female Oi! band and many of their earlier recordings were of that ilk. Initially sporting schoolgirls clothing, **The Gymslips** supported The Dolly Mixtures on a U.K. tour and their first vinyl excursion was *Midnight City*, which they contributed to the *Making Waves* compilation on Girlfriends Records.

John Peel saw one of their gigs at London's ICA and invited them to play what would prove to be the first of five sessions for him. Broadcast on 20th May 1982, it comprised *Erika (With A K)*, *Renees*, *Big Sister*, *48 Crash* and *You'll Never Walk Alone*. A second session followed on 16th September 1982 - *Barbara Cartland*, *Pie & Mash*, *Drink Problem*, *Thinking Of You* and *Robot Man*. This led to a deal with Abstract Records and their debut single in October 1982, a cover of Susi Quatro's hit *48 Crash*, climbed to No. 17 in the indie chart. On 20th December 1982, they returned for a third Radio One session - this time for Kid Jensen. It comprised *Miss Nunsweeta*, *Yo Yo*, *Some Girls* and *Dear Marje*.

Early in 1983 a three track 45 *Big Sister* was released and an album *Rockin' With The Renees* followed in April. For this they expanded to a four-piece with the addition of Kathy Barnes on keyboards. The album got rave reviews in the music press and contained some of their best material. There's *Barbara Cartland* (a song about the writer who misinterprets the meaning of love in her books), *Wandering Stars* (which takes a look back to the '70s, the era of flares and platforms, to see how silly they would look in the early '80s), *Dear Marje* (a song about problems sent to agony aunt Marje Proops, who after a while has enough and clears off to Hawaii), *Complications* (a song about someone two timing their boyfriend who doesn't think they'll get caught), *Big Sister* (about having a friend you're very fond of who after a while starts forgetting about you and thinking only of her boyfriend) and there's even a love song, *Thinking Of You*. The album opens with *Renees*, which is really about them:

"See us walking down the street
Monkey boots upon our feet
In our red tag Levi jeans
Can't miss us cos we're the Reens
Get drunk get smashed get pissed get fat

We're the Renees here we come
One two three and up yer bum
We're the Renees here we come

Double chin and short cropped hair
Always take the piss we really don't care
George's pie 'n' mash is what we like to eat
We go to Chans for a special treat"
(*Renees*)

Musically, the album is full of variety - they also incorporated quite a lot of glam rock influences into their music.

They played two further Peel sessions on 30th May (*Silly Egg*, *Wandering Star*, *Up The Wall* and *More Tea Vicar?*) and 7th December 1983 (*Whirlwind Flings*, *Loves Not The Answer*, *Valley Girl* and *Call Again*). The next 45 *Robot Man* was well received and their earlier album was re-titled *Drink Problem* and released in a different sleeve for the U.S. market. They seemed poised for greater things, but nothing happened!

It seems that 'personnel and contractual' problems led to Paula recruiting a new line-up 'C'. This recorded a final Peel session on 6th June 1984 (*Leave Me, Soldier*, *On The Line* and *We're Gonna Bring Your Empire Down*) and their last single, the ambitious *Evil Eye*, produced by **Angelic Upstart** Mond Cowrie. By now, their music was veering more towards synth-pop and was miles away from how they sounded in 1982.

The recent Captain Oi! compilation is a twenty-seven-track collection spanning their entire output from 1981 - 85. Nicely packaged it comes with a history by label owner Mark Brennan, lyrics and sleevenotes by the band's vocalist/guitarist Paula Richards from which part of this entry is based.

48 Crash, *Big Sister*, *Robot Man*, *Evil Eye* and *Drink Problem* can all be heard on *Abstract Punk Singles Collection* (Anagram CDPUNK 52) in 1995.

When **The Gymslips** split in 1985 Yarnell went on to play for the Norwich-based band Serious Drinking and The Blueberry Hellbellies. She later re-united with Richards (who'd been working with The Deltones and Potato 5) in The Renees in 1987.

Gyro

45:	Central Detention Centre/	
	Purple And Red	(Rabid TOSH 104) 1978

A one-off 45. You can also check out *Central Detention Centre* on *Rabid/TJM Punk Singles Collection* (Receiver RRCD 227) in 1996.

Paul Haig

HCP

ALBUMS:	1	RHYTHM OF LIFE	(Island ILPS 9742)	1984 82
(up to	2	THE WARP OF PURE FUN		
1986)			(Operation Afterglow OPA 3) 1985 -	

NB: He also issued a cassette *Drama* (Rational) 1981. (2) also issued on CD (Crepuscule TWICD 669) 1987.

45s:	Running Away/Time (PS)	(Operation Twilight OPT 03) 1982
(up to	Heaven Sent/Running Away (PS)	(Island IS 111) 1983
1986)	Justice/On This Night Of Decision (PS)	(Island IS 138) 1984
	The Only Truth/Ghost Rider (PS)	(Crepuscle IS 198) 1984
	The Only Truth/Ghost Rider (12", PS)	(Crepuscle 12IS 198) 1984
	The Only Truth (U.S. Remix)/	
	Ghost Rider/Instr.	(Crepuscule ISX 198) 1984
	Big Blue World (2 Versions) (PS)	(Factory TWI 230) 1984
	Big Blue World (2 Versions) (12", PS)	(Factory TWI 231) 1984
	Heaven Help You Now (2 Versions)/	
	World Raw/Chance (PS)	(Operation OPA 2) 1985
	Heaven Help You Now (2 Versions)/	
	World Raw/Chance (12", PS)	(Operation 12OPA 2) 1985
	Love Eternal (PS)	(Operation 12 OPA 2) 1985
	Love Eternal (12", PS)	(Operation 12 OPA 6) 1986

Singer and guitarist **Paul Haig** had been with Scotland's **Josef K** prior to going solo. For his solo efforts **Haig** enlisted some distinguished sessionmen including Tom Bailey, Anton Fier and Bernie Worrell. Alex Sadkin handled the production. *Rhythm Of Life* was a pleasant synthesizer-driven album with plenty of dancey music. Similar to bands like **Human League** and **New Order**, but more lightweight in style. Its finer moments included *Heaven Sent* (an earlier single) and a further track *Justice* culled from the album. The 45s weren't hits but the album sold well enough to spend two weeks in the charts rising to No. 82.

For his second album *The Warp Of Pure Fun* he teamed up with ex-Associate Alan Rankine (lead gtr), Mike McCann (bs) and James Lock (drms). The result was a more enterprising and slicker album which featured Bernard Sumner on guitar on *Love And War*. Other notable cuts on an appealing album are *Heaven Help You Now*, a folkier form of synthesized rock, and *Love And War*.

Hambi and The Dance

Personnel incl:	HAMBI HARAMBOLDUS	vcls	A

ALBUM:	1(A)	HEARTACHE	(Virgin V 2211) 1982

45s:	Too Late To Fly The Flag/	
	She Doesn't Talk (PS)	(Virgin VS 414) 1981
	L'image Craque/	
	L'image Craque (alt-version) (PS)	(Virgin VS 437) 1981
	Living In A Heartache/Radio America (PS)	(Virgin VS 474) 1982
	I Don't Want To Lose You/Julie (PS)	(Pink Pop HAMB 1) 1986
	I Don't Want To Lose You/	
	Julie (12", PS)	(Harry Barter HAMB 121) 1986

A Liverpool band whose music attempted to combine good old rock 'n' roll with synthesized art rock with varying degrees of success.

The Hammersmith Gorillas

Personnel:	GARY ANDERSON	drms	A
	ALAN BUTLER	bs	A
	JESSE HECTOR	vcls, gtr	A

45:	* You Really Got Me/		
	Leaving Home	(Penny Farthing PEN 849)	1974

NB: * Reissued with PS (Raw RAW 2) 1977.

A mod-inspired London trio who never got the recognition they deserved. They later changed name to **The Gorillas**. In 1999, Big Beat issued a retrospective CD *Gorilla Got Me* (Big Beat CDWIKD 198) which includes both sides of their 45, unissued tracks and live material.

Happy Family

Personnel incl:	NICHOLAS CURRY	vcls	A

ALBUM:	1(A) THE MAN ON YOUR STREET	(4AD CAD 214) 1982

NB: (1) also issued on CD (4AD GAD 214CD) 1998.

45:	Puritans/Innermost Thoughts/	
	The Mistake (PS)	(4AD AD 204) 1982

Subtitled "Songs From The Career Of Dictator Hall" *The Man On Your Street* is a failed attempt at a story album. The music lacks anything of real interest as does the material and delivery.

Charlie Harper

ALBUM:	1 STOLEN PROPERTY	(Flicknife SHARP 100) 1981

NB: There's also a compilation *The Best Of Charlie Harper & The Urban Dogs* (Captain Oi! AHOY CD 108) 1999.

45s:	* Barmy London Army/Talk Is Cheap (PS)	(Gem GEMS 35) 1980
	Freaked/Jo (PS)	(Ramkup CAC 005) 1981

NB: * Issued on green or yellow vinyl.

Charlie Harper is best-known as the "old man of punk" and vocalist of the hardy annuals **UK Subs**. He also formed the garage-influenced **Urban Dogs** with fellow **UK Sub** Alvin Gibbs, **Knox** from **The Vibrators** and drummer Matthew Best of Psychic TV.

In the early eighties **Harper**'s extra-curricular activities from **The Urban Dogs** included solo 45s, *Barmy London Army* in 1980 and the strange Doors'-like *Freaked* in 1981. He also recorded a solo album *Stolen Property* the same year.

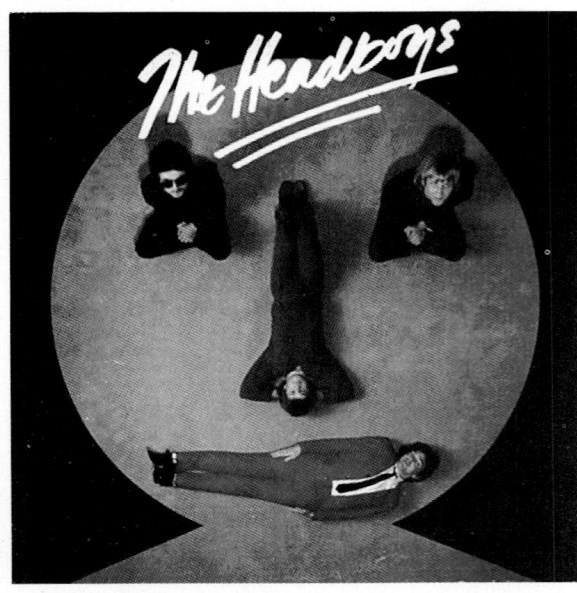

THE HEADBOYS - The Headboys.

All his best solo material (including both 45s) is compiled on Captain Oi's 1999 CD compilation along with the best material from his **Urban Dogs** period.

Hazard

45:	Gotta Change My Life/	
	(other side by **The Clerks**)	(Rok ROK VIII/VII) 1979

A Cambridge band. *Gotta Change My Life* is a melodic song with pleasing vocals and twangy guitar. You can also find it among the bonus cuts on Captain Mod's CD reissue of Rok's 1979 compilation *Odds Bods Mods And Sods* (Captain Mod MODSKA CD 2) 1996.

Headache

Personnel:	COLIN CHEW	drms	A
	PAUL CREMONA	bs	A
	DANNY DRUMMOND	vcls	A
	STEVE LAMBERT	gtr	A

45:	Can't Stand Still/	
	No Reason For Your Call (PS)	(Lout LOUT 001) 1977

A now rare and one-off punk 45. Musically this was an amalgam of **Eddie and The Hot Rods** - style R&B and The Velvet Underground.

The Headboys

Personnel:	GEORGE BOYTER	bs, vcls	A
	LOU LEWIS	gtr, vcls	A
	CALUM MALCOLM	keyb'ds, vcls	A
	DAVY ROSS	drms, vcls	A

ALBUM:	1(A) HEADBOYS	(RSO RS-1-3068) 1979

45s:	The Shape Of Things To Come/	
	The Mood I'm In (PS)	(RSO RSO 40) 1979
	Stepping Stones/Before Tonight (PS)	(RSO RSO 49) 1979
	Kicking The Kans/Double Vision/	
	My Favourite D.J. (PS)	(RSO RSO 56) 1980

One of those now forgotten popish new wave bands like **The Invaders**. There's little reason to remember them really. You'll also find *The Shape Of Things To Come* on *20 Of Another Kind, Vol. 2* (Polydor POLX 1) 1979. All three of their 'A' sides can also be heard on their album, which was produced, engineered and mixed by Peter Kerr and the band at Castle Sound Studios, Pencaitland, Scotland. They are among the stronger tracks on an album which is pleasant-enough but has no special ingredient to elevate it above the also-rans.

Headhunters

Personnel incl: JOWE HEAD

45:	Wipe Out The Funk/Decline/	
	Land (12", PS)	(Shout XW 1201) 1982
	Impossible/Straitjacket (PS)	(Shout XS 005) 1983

Ex-**Swell Map** Jowe Head recorded with this band before joining **Television Personalities** on bass.

The Heartbeats

45s:	Talk To Me/	
	Don't Want Romance (PS)	(Red Shadow REDS 2) 1980
	* Go/One Of The People (PS)	(Nothing Shaking SHAD 1) 1981

NB: * Came on blue vinyl.

An obscure early eighties band whose second 45 was modish and is the more sought-after of the two.

ROBYN HITCHCOCK - Black Snake Diamond Role.

Helsinki 5 Below

45: Jennifer Darling/Women In Love   (Future Earth FER 1) 1979

A Sheffield band whose 45 was issued by the Doncaster indie label Future Earth.

Heroes

Personnel incl: CHRIS BRADFORD   vcls   A

ALBUM: 1(A) BORDER RANGERS   (Polydor 2442 171) 1980
NB: (1) A Dutch release.

45: Some Kind Of Women/10% Will Do   (Polydor POSP 105) 1980

A short-lived pop combo whose music gave you a nod and a wink in the direction of bands like The Knack and **The Jam**. Their album was released in Holland.

Robyn Hitchcock (and The Egyptians)

Personnel: (up to 1986)			
ROBYN HITCHCOCK	vcls, gtr	ABC
MATTHEW SELIGMAN	bs	AB
ROD JOHNSON	drms	B
SARA LEE	bs	B
ANTHONY THISTLEWAITE	sax	B
OTIS FLETCHER	horns	C
ROGER JACKSON	keyb'ds	C
ANDY METCALFE	bs	C
MORRIS WINDSOR	drms	C

ROBYN HITCHCOCK - Bells Of Rhymney.

ROBYN HITCHCOCK - Groovy Decay.

ALBUMS: (up to 1986)			
1(A)	BLACK SNAKE DIAMOND ROLE	(Armageddon ARM 4) 1981
2(B)	GROOVY DECAY	(Albion ALB 110) 1982
3(C)	I OFTEN DREAM OF TRAINS	(Midnight Music CHIME 0005) 1984
4(C)	FEGMANIA!	(Midnight Music CHIME 0008) 1985
5(C)	GOTTA LET THIS HEN OUT!	(Midnight Music CHIME 0015) 1985
6(C)	EXPLODING IN SILENCE	(Black Mountain BM 80) 1986

NB: (3), (4), (5) and (6) credited to **Robyn Hitchcock** and The Egyptians. (1) also issued on vinyl (Aftermath AFT 1) 1986 and CD (Aftermath ASTCD 1) 1988 and again (Sequel RSACD 819) 1995 with bonus tracks. (2) also issued in Holland (Midnight CHIME 019) 1985 with a new cover, two new non-album tracks *It Was The Night* and *How Do You Work This Thing?* but minus *Grooving From An Inner Plane* from the 1982 release and on CD (Line ALCD 9000008) 1989, (Midnight Music CHIME 019CD) 1990 and (Sequel RSACD 820) 1995 with bonus tracks. (3) also issued on CD (Midnight Music CHIME 0005CD) 1986 and (Sequel RSACD 821) 1995 with bonus tracks. (4) also issued on CD (Midnight Music CHIME 0008CD) 1986 and (Sequel RSA CD 822) 1995 with bonus tracks. (5) also issued on CD (Midnight Music CHIME 0015CD) 1986 and (Sequel RSACD 823) 1995 with three extra tracks, *The Fly*, *Only The Stones Remain* and *Egyptian Cream*. (6) also issued as a picture disc album. Also relevant is *Invisible Hitchcock* (Glass Fish MOIST 2CD) 1990 and (Sequel RSACD 825) 1995, *The Collection (Uncorrected Personality Traits)* (Sequel RSACD 957) 1998 and *The Kershaw Sessions* (ROOTCD 001) 1994.

EP: 1(C) ROBYN HITCHCOCK (Eaten By Her Own Dinner/Happy The Golden Prince/ Grooving On An Inner Plane/Messages Of Dark/ The Abandoned Brain) (PS)   (Midnight Music) 1986

ROBYN HITCHCOCK - Man Who Invented Himself.

ROBYN HITCHCOCK - I Often Dream Of Trains.

ROBYN HITCHCOCK - Fegmania.

45s:
* The Man Who Invented Himself/
  Dancing On God's Thumb (PS)   (Armageddon AS 008) 1981
  America/It Was The Night/
  How Do You Work This Thing? (PS)   (Albion ION 103) 1982
+ 52 Stations/COSMOPOLITANS: How To Keep Your Husband Happy/MOTOR BOYS MOTOR: Little Boy And Fat Man/
  dB's: Amplifier   (Albion FREEBIE 1) 1982
  Eaten By Her Own Dinner/Listening To The Higsons/
  Dr. Sticky (PS)   (Midnight Music DING 2) 1982
  Eaten By Her Own Dinner/Grooving On An Inner Plane/
  Message Of The Dark/The Abandoned Brain/Happy The
  Golden Prince (12", PS)   (Midnight Music DONG 2) 1982
  Nightride To Trinidad (Long Version)/Kingdom Of Love/
  Midnight Fish (12", PS)   (Albion 12 ION 1036) 1983
x Happy The Golden Priest   (Bucketfull Of Brains BOB 8) 1984
  The Bells Of Rhymney/Falling Leaves/Winter Love/The
  Bones In The Ground (12", PS)   (Midnight Music DONG 8) 1984
  Heaven/Dwarfbeat/
  Some Body (12", PS)   (Midnight Music DONG 12) 1985
  Brenda's Iron Sledge (live)/Only The Stones Remain/The Pit
  Of Souls (Parts 1-IV) (12", PS)   (Midnight Music DONG 17) 1985
  If You Were A Priest/
  The Crawling (PS)   (Glass Fish OOZE 1) 1986

NB: * Some copies came with a flexidisc *It's A Mystic Trip/Grooving On An Inner Plane* (4 SPURT 1). + This was a flexidisc which came free with the *Groovy Decay* album or at gigs. x This was a flexidisc which came free with 'Bucketfull Of Brains' magazine. There were also 20 copies produced as a hard vinyl white label test pressing.

Robyn Hitchcock was one of the most interesting and underrated figures to emerge out of the new wave era both as a solo artist and with his earlier band **The Soft Boys**.

This very talented songwriter has his roots in the psychedelic pop of the sixties but in his melodic and emotional compositions he doesn't simply re-create it, he adds his own personality and interpretation to take the music a step further.

Black Snake Diamond Role commences with two music hall ditties, then explores emotion with *Meat* and *Love*, which close each side, ballads *Acid Bird* and the bizzare *Do Policemen Sing?*, which is his swipe at authority.

Groovy Decay, produced by Steve Hillage, has a smoother sound. Among its finest moments are *St Petersburg*, which deals with the dark side of life, *52 Stations*, which addresses the failure of love and *Groovin' On An Inner Plane*, which features a rap style vocal. This album was later repackaged and released in Holland in 1985 with slightly different tracks. See the discography for details.

I Often Dream Of Trains is a largely acoustic album and one of his weirdest. There's an heart-rendering ballad *Flavours Of Night* whilst the stranger side to his music is represented by *Uncorrected Personality Traits*, a track about difficult children when they grow up and *Furry Green Atom*

Bowl. He was assisted on some cuts by several ex-**Soft Boys**.

In 1985, he put together a new support band The Egyptians, which featured ex-**Soft Boys** Andy Metcalfe and Morris Windsor alongside two newcomers Roger Jackson and Otis Fletcher. The lyrics are as witty as ever and the instrumentation on tracks like *Glass* and *My Wife And My Dead Wife* create a rich texture into which his superb electric guitar playing and Metcalfe's moody bass blend beautifully.

Gotta Let This Hen Out! is basically a live album recorded at the Marquee in April 1985. It includes a selection of his best tracks including *Brenda's Iron Sledge*, *Kingdom Of Love*, *My Wife And My Dead Wife*, *I Often Dream Of Trains* and a non-album 45 cut *Listening To The Higsons*. The CD release includes three extra tracks *The Fly*, *Only The Stones Remain* and *Egyptian Cream*.

Exploding In Silence is a live picture disc which includes some of the same songs as the above. *Invisible Hitchcock* is comprised of unreleased outtakes.

The Kershaw Sessions is a nineteen-track CD compiled from sessions recorded between 1985 and 1991, so mostly outside this book's timeframe. Highlights include pop-psych numbers like *Tropical Flesh Mandala*, *Brenda's Iron Sledge* and *Lady Waters And The Hooded One*. He's even included a cover of Harry Belfonte's *Banana Boat Song*, which didn't get any radio play at the time.

If you're into guitar-driven rock with clever lyrics and strong melodies all a bit offbeat, investigate **Hitchcock**, if you're not already familiar with his work.

ROBYN HITCHCOCK - Groovy Decoy.

Holly

45s:	Yankee Rose/Treasure Island/	
	Desperate Dan	(Eric's ERIC'S 003) 1979
	Hobo Joe/Stars Of The Bars (PS)	(Eric's ERIC'S 007) 1979

These were early solo recordings by Holly Johnson formerly of **Big In Japan** and later of the stunningly successful Frankie Goes To Hollywood.

The Hollywood Brats

Personnel:	EUNON BRADY	gtr	A
	WAYNE MANOR	bs	A
	ANDREW MATHESON	vcls	A
	LOUIS SPARKS	drms	A
	CASINO STEELE	keyb'ds	A

ALBUM: 1(A) THE HOLLYWOOD BRATS   (Cherry Red ARED 6) 1980

NB: (1) also issued on CD (Cherry Red CDRED 106) 1993. There's also a CD release, *Growing Up Wrong* (Episode LUSCD 6) 1990.

45:	Then He Kissed Me/	
	Sick On You (PS)	(Cherry Red CHERRY 6) 1979

Not from Hollywood at all.

The material on the album was actually recorded during 1974-75. Steele was later in **The Boys** and Brady re-emerged in **The Tools**.

Homosexuals

ALBUM: 1( ) THE HOMOSEXUALS' RECORD
                    (Recommended RR# 18) 1984

EP: 1( ) BIGGER THAN THE NUMBER YET MISSING THE DOT
                    (Black Noise BN 1) 1981

NB: (1) This came on clear vinyl with a fold-around, hand-painted sleeve.

45s:	* Divorce Proceedings/	
	Mecho Madness (12")	(Black Noise F 12 No. 2) 1979
	Hearts In Exile/	
	Soft South Africans (PS)	(L'Orelei PF 151) 1979

NB: * Issued in a plain sleeve with a sticker.

An above average punk band whose songs offer intelligence and sense to simple raw energy and the tunes are often quite catchy in a **Buzzcocks** sort of way.

Their retrospective album plays at 45 r.p.m. It's a sixteen track collection of singles and rough mixes done at low cost - hence a few rough edges.

ROBYN HITCHCOCK - Heaven.

HUMAN LEAGUE - Dignity Of Labour EP.

Horrorcomic

Personnel:	WALLY BANTAM	drms	A
	ROY BOGHART	bs	A
	FRANKIE DEAN	gtr	A
	ROGER REP	vcls	A

45s:	I'm All Hung Up On Pierrepoint/The Exorcist/	
	Sex In The Afternoon (PS)	(Lightning/B&C BVZ 0007) 1977
	I Don't Mind/England 77 (PS)	(Lightning GIL 512) 1978
	Jesus Christ/Cut Your Throat (PS)	(B&C BCS 18) 1979

An obscure punk band whose *I Don't Mind* can also be heard on *Lightning Records Punk Collection* (Anagram CDPUNK 79) 1996.

Hot Water

45s:	Different Morning/Premium Bondage (PS)	(Duff) 1978
	Get Lost!/Bird's Eye View (PS)	(Duff DWR 101) 1979

Hot Water hailed from Rochdale. *Get Lost* is helped by dual female vocals and saxophone, which make it stand out from the rest.

Human League

Personnel:	PHIL OAKEY	vcls	ABCDE
	IAN CRAIG-MARSH	synth	AB
	MARTIN WARE	synth	AB
	ADRIAN WRIGHT	synth, visuals	BCDE
	IAN BURDEN	bs, synth	CD
	JO CATHERALL	vcls	CDE
	SUSANNE SULLY	bs, vcls	CDE
	JO CALLIS	gtr	D
	JIM RUSSELL	synth	E

				HCP
ALBUMS:	1(B)	REPRODUCTION	(Virgin V 2133) 1979	49
(up to	2(B)	TRAVELOGUE	(Virgin V 2160) 1980	16
1986)	3(D)	DARE!	(Virgin V 2192) 1981	1
	4(D)	LOVE AND DANCING	(Virgin OVED 6) 1982	3
	5(D)	HYSTERIA	(Virgin V 2315) 1984	3
	6(E)	CRASH	(Virgin V 2391) 1986	7

NB: (1) was originally released with a picture inner sleeve. It was later reissued at mid-price (Virgin OVED 114) 1988 and on CD (Virgin CDV 2133) 1988, also at mid-price. (2) later reissued at mid-price (Virgin OVED 115) 1988 and on CD (Virgin CDV 2160) 1988, also at mid-price. (3) originally issued in a gatefold sleeve, but some copies were also produced with a white or black vinyl picture disc, die-cut with a sleeve insert. (3) later reissued at mid-price (Virgin OVED 333) 1990 and on CD (Virgin CDV 2192) 1983. (4) was an instrumental album credited to League Unlimited Orchestra. It was also issued on CD (Virgin CDOVED 6) 1986. (5) later reissued at mid-price (Virgin OVED 177) 1988 and also issued on CD (Virgin CDV

2315) 1984. (6) later reissued at mid-price (Virgin OVED 253) 1990 and also issued on CD (Virgin CDV 2391) 1986. *Dare! / Hysteria / Crash* (Virgin TPAK 3) 1990 also issued as a limited edition 3-CD set on picture discs. Also relevant is *Greatest Hits* (Virgin HLTV 1) 1988, which got to No. 3. It was also issued on CD, minidisc and DCC (Virgin HLCD 1) 1988 and as a picture disc (Virgin HLCDP 1) 1989. There's also *Trance League Express (A Tribute To The Human League) (Various Artists)* (Hypnotic CLP 9934) 1997.

HCP

EPs: (up to 1986)	1(B)	THE DIGNITY OF LABOUR PARTS 1-4 (12", PS) (Fast Products FAST 10/Virgin VF 1) 1979 -
	2(B)	HOLIDAY '80 (Marianne/Dancevision/Being Boiled/Rock 'N' Roll/Nightclubbing) (12") (Virgin SV 105) 1980 56

NB: (1) Some copies came with a spoken-word flexidisc (F10X/VF 1). (2) was originally released as a double-pack on purple and blue labels, 10,000 copies only. It was later reissued in 1981 as a double pack with green/red labels and a gatefold picture sleeve. It was also available as a three track EP (Dancevision/Being Boiled/Rock 'n' Roll) with magenta/blue labels. It was also reissued as a 5-track EP with magenta/blue labels (Virgin SV 105-12) 1981, but soon withdrawn. In 1992 *Holiday '80* re-entered the chart and climbed to No. 46.

HCP

45s: (up to 1986)	*	Being Boiled/Circus Of Death (PS) (Fast Product FAST 4) 1978 -
		Empire State Human/Introducing (PS) (Virgin VS 294) 1979 -
	x	Empire State Human/Introducing/Only After Dark/Toyota City (double-pack PS) (Virgin VS 351) 1980 62
		Only After Dark/Toyota City (Long Version) (PS) (Virgin VS 351) 1980 -
		Empire State Human/Introducing (12", PS) (Virgin VS 351-12) 1980 -
	α	Being Boiled/Circus Of Death (PS) (EMI/Fast Product FAST 4) 1980 6
	β	Boys And Girls/Tom Baker (PS) (Virgin VS 395) 1981 48
	χ	The Sound Of The Crowd/The Sound Of The Crowd (Add Your Voice) (PS) (Virgin VS 416) 1981 12
	χδ	The Sound Of The Crowd (Complete)/(Instrumental) (Virgin VS 416-12) 1981 -
	χδ	Love Action (I Believe In Love)/Hard Times (Virgin VS 435) 1981 3
	χ	Hard Times/Love Action (I Believe In Love)/Hard Times (instr)/Love Action (instr.) (12", PS) (Virgin VS 435-12) 1981 -
	ε	Open Your Heart/Non-Stop (PS) (Virgin VS 453) 1981 6
	ε	Open Your Heart/Non-Stop/Open Your Heart (instr.)/Non-Stop (instr.) (12", PS) (Virgin VS 453-12) 1981 -
	φ	Don't You Want Me?/Seconds (PS) (Virgin VS 466) 1981 1
		Don't You Want Me?/Seconds/Don't You Want Me? (Extended Dance Mix) (12", PS) (Virgin VS 466-12) 1981 -
		Mirror Man/(You Remind Me Of) Gold (PS) (Virgin VS 522) 1982 2
		Mirror Man/(You Remind Me Of) Gold (picture disc) (Virgin VSY 522) 1982 -
		Mirror Man (Extended)/(You Remind Me Of) Gold/Gold (instr.) (12", PS) (Virgin VS 522-12) 1982 -
	χ	(Keep Feeling) Fascination/Total Panic (PS) (Virgin VS 569) 1983 2
	χ	(Keep Feeling) Fascination (Extended)/(Keep Feeling) Fascination (Improvisation)/Total Panic (12", PS) (Virgin VS 569-12) 1983 -
		The Lebanon/Thirteen (PS) (Virgin VS 672) 1984 11
		The Lebanon (Extended)/Thirteen/The Lebanon (instr.) (12", PS) (Virgin VS 672-12) 1984 -
		Life On Your Own/The World Tonight (PS) (Virgin VS 688) 1984 16
		Life On Your Own/The World Tonight/Life On Your Own (Extended) (12", PS) (Virgin VS 688-12) 1984 -
		Louise/The Sign (Remix) (PS) (Virgin VS 723) 1984 13
		Louise/The Sign (Remix) (picture disc) (Virgin VSY 723) 1984 -
	η	Louise/The Sign (Extended Remix) (12", PS) (Virgin VS 723-12) 1984 -
		Human/Human (instr.) (Virgin VS 880) 1986 8
		Human (Extended)/(Accapella)/(Instr.) (12", PS) (Virgin VS 880-12) 1986 -
		I Need Your Loving/I Need Your Loving (instr.) (PS) (Virgin VS 900) 1986 72
		I Need Your Loving (Extended)/(Dub)/(Instr.) (12", PS) (Virgin VS 900-12) 1986 -
	φ	I Need Your Loving (Extended)/(Dub)/(Accapella)/(Instr.) (12" double pack) (Virgin VS 900 12DJ) 1986 -

NB: * The original issue came with black and white picture labels. x Came in a stickered and shrinkwrapped double pack. α Reissued on red and yellow labels and again in 1982. β Came in a gatefold picture sleeve. χ Credited to **Human League Red**. χδ came in a stickered picture sleeve. ε Credited to **Human League Blue**. Some copies as the 7" possible came on coloured vinyl. φ Credited to **Human League 100**. Some copies of the 7" came with a poster. η Some copies of the 12" came with a poster. φ This was a 12" double pack, promo-only release.

The Human League formed in Sheffield in January 1978 when hospital porter **Phil Oakey** teamed up with his old friends Ian Craig-Marsh and Martin Ware. These two had previously played in an outfit called Dead Daughters, but had abandoned their guitars to concentrate on playing purely electronic music in an outfit called The Future. In June 1977, they were joined by Adi Newton and it was when he left six months later to join another Sheffield electronic band **Clock DVA** that the remaining two members of The Future recruited **Oakey** as their vocalist.

The new trio got the inspiration from a sci-fi boardgame called Starforce for their new name the **Human League**. Then, in January 1978, they recorded a three track demo at Sheffield's Devonshire Lane Studios - *Being Boiled*, *Circus Of Death* and *Toyota City* - which was sent to independent British labels. It came to the attention of Bob Last, who ran Fast Products. Within a couple of weeks Last had issued two of the tracks and later became their manager. *Being Boiled* was **Oakey**'s first composition. On hearing it Johnny Rotten described them as 'trendy hippies'! Both sides of the *Being Boiled* 45 were included on *Fast Product* (Fast EMC 3312) in 1979. *Being Boiled* was also included on *Machines* (Virgin V 2177) in 1980. The same year *The Black Hits Of Space* featured on *Cash Cows* (Virgin MILK 1).

In November 1978, they embarked on their first national tour supporting **Siouxsie and The Banshees** along with **Spizz Oil**. Then, in April 1979, the group signed a long-term deal with Virgin, who licensed *The Dignity Of Labour EP* to Fast Products to preserve their indie status. The EP was instrumental and featured what might be termed 'industrial' music. It became pretty monotonous after a while!

By now the trio had become a quartet with the addition of Philip Adrian Wright as their 'visual director' responsible for onstage slides and films. This enlarged line-up supported Iggy Pop on a European tour. The band's first single for Virgin was a disco effort *I Don't Depend On You / Cruel* (VS 269), which was also available as a 12" (VS 269-12). Credited to **The Men** it was released in July and flopped badly.

Their first album *Reproduction* emerged in October. A month earlier one of the cuts *Empire State Human* had been issued as a 45. This eventually spent two weeks in the charts with No. 62 its highest position but not until its reissue in June 1980. Still it stood out on an album that otherwise comprised rather cold hi-tech synthesized music with deadpan vocals. The album also contained a new recording of their original demo of *Circus Of Death* and a cover of The Righteous Brothers' *You've Lost That Loving Feeling*. Although it was well-received in some quarters sales from the album weren't great. Later, when they became famous it entered the charts in August 1981, eventually climbing to No. 49 during a twenty-three week chart duration. For now, though, they still had a lot of people to win over.

HUMAN LEAGUE - Holiday 80.

This was underscored when they were dropped from a supporting slot on a Talking Heads U.K. tour because their "remote-controlled entertainment" went down badly with audiences.

They returned in April 1980 with the two-single EP package *Holiday '80*, which included a new recording of *Being Boiled*. The most interesting track was *Marianne*, which was one of the best things they did in their early days. Virgin planned it as a single and even allocated it a number (VS 371), but in the event it only came out in Australia. On a more commercial tact the EP included their interpretation of Gary Glitter's *Rock 'n' Roll* and Iggy Pop's *Nightclubbin'*. The EP spent five weeks in the charts, peaking at No. 56.

A new album *Travelogue* followed in May. This was a warmer more fun-loving album than its robotic predecessor. The material it contained was much stronger. The synthesizers were subtler and the lyrics more sophisticated, dealing with issues such as kitsch culture and science fiction. It spent a staggering forty-two weeks in the charts, climbing to No. 16. It also spawned a further 45, a cover of Mick Ronson's *Only After Dark*, which came with a free 7" single coupling *Empire State Human* with *Introducing*, but it did not chart. The band was vast becoming a household name, though, and appeared in the new wave rock movie 'Urgh! A Music War'.

As their popularity increased so did friction within the band. In October 1980, Martyn Ware and Ian Craig-Marsh decided to quit to concentrate on the **British Electrical Foundation**. This was an umbrella organisation for various dance projects of which Heaven 17 was the most successful. **Oakey** and Wright still retained the rights to the band's name and with a European tour planned bassist Ian Burden was recruited from a local band called Graf and **Oakey** recruited two Sheffield-born teenage dancers Joanne Catherall and Suzanne Sulley whom he had seen dancing at a local Sheffield club where they were working as cocktail waitresses. So, with contractual obligations to fulfil, the new line-up set off on a European tour in November 1980.

The new line-up, produced by Martin Rushent, played simpler and poppier music, which is of less relevance to this book. *Boys And Girls*, a 45 released in February 1981, brought them a minor hit. It enjoyed a four week chart stay, climbing to No. 48. *The Sound Of The Crowd*, released in April in both 7" and 12" formats, fared much better climbing to No. 12 during a ten week chart residency. Then, with the addition of former **Shake**, Boots For Dancing and **Rezillos** member Jo Callis added on guitar, their trio of hits was completed with *Love Action* (credited to **Human League Red**), released in July, which actually climbed to No. 3 during its thirteen weeks in the charts.

In October 1981, they issued a new album *Dare!* which came in a gatefold sleeve and shot to No. 1, spending a staggering seventy-one weeks in the chart. There was also a picture disc version of the album, which came on white or black vinyl in a die-cut sleeve, but which omitted one track. The album featured their previous hit *Love Action* and two other tracks which were culled for 45 release. The musical menu was now danceable pop music and *Open Your Heart* (credited to **Human League Blue**) and *Don't You Want Me* (credited to **Human League 100**) brought them further commercial success climbing to No. 6 and No. 1 respectively. It wasn't just the most popular songs on the album that were good, though. Check out *Seconds*, a subtle cut about the JFK assassination. They also achieved considerable success in the U.S.A., where *Dare!* climbed to No. 3 and *Don't You Want Me* spent three weeks at No. 1, becoming a million-seller.

In June 1982, the **Human League** issued an instrumental version of seven of the tracks on *Dare*, along with one new tune under the pseudonym The League Unlimited Orchestra. This also climbed to No. 3. It largely contained dance material, some of which was annoyingly repetitive. It only got to No. 135 in the 'States, though.

November 1982 saw the release of another pop ditty *Mirror Man*, which was available in 7" and 12" format and as a picture disc. This rose to No. 2 and enjoyed ten weeks in the charts. *(Keep Feeling) Fascination*, which was available in 7" and 12" formats and credited to **Human League Red**, achieved similar dizzy heights, following its release in April 1983, but only managed nine weeks in all in the charts. The two singles climbed to No's 30 and 8 respectively in the 'States where a mini-album *Fascination* was released.

It wasn't until June 1984, just four months short of three years after *Dare!*, that the **Human League** came up with a new album *Hysteria*. By now they had parted company with Rushent, choosing to produce the album themselves with help from Chris Thomas and Hugh Padgham. To their credit they decided to omit their earlier non-album hit singles and concentrate on new material. If *Don't You Know I Want You* sounded like an attempt to recycle the sound of their biggest hit, the album also contained some tender ballads in the form of *Louise* and *Life On Your Own*. Perhaps most interestingly of all the synthesizers were dumped in favour of a simple pop/rock format on *The Lebanon*, which also took a political stance. Commercially, the verdict on the album was favourable. It climbed to No. 3, spending eighteen weeks in the charts, here in the U.K. and reached No. 62 in the 'States. This was in spite of the fact the band refused to tour or do any promotional work for the album. It seems they thought they were so popular they didn't have to! The album produced some further hit singles; *The Lebanon* (U.K. No. 11, U.S. No. 64), *Life On Your Own* (U.K. No. 16) and *Louise* (U.K. No. 13). They were all released in 7" and 12" formats and *Louise* was available as a picture disc as well. Sandwiched between *Life On Your Own* and *Louise* in October 1984, **Phil Oakey** linked up with disco producer Giorgio Moroder to record *Together In Electric Dreams*, which also featured a Peter Frampton guitar solo. It climbed to No. 3 in Britain and became more successful than the film.

In 1985 the band retired to **Oakey**'s home studio and began working with Colin Thurston, who'd produced their first LP, on a new album. Callis left during this period to work with Feargal Sharkey and Burden went too. The band were trimmed down to a trio of **Phil Oakey**, Joanne Catherall and Susanne Sulley, but then supplemented by Associates' drummer Jim Russell and members of **Comsat Angels** in the sessions. At the same time, **Oakey** continued to collaborate with Giorgio Moroder, releasing a 45, *Goodbye Bad Times* in June, which climbed to No. 44 in the U.K. and an album *Chrome* in July, which only got to No. 52. As for the **Human League**'s projected new album - it simply didn't appear on its scheduled release date in September. A decision had been taken to ditch the sessions with Thurston. Instead, the following year, **Oakey**, Catherall, Sulley and Russell headed for Minneapolis, Minnesota, where they worked with Jimmy Jam and Terry Lewis (who'd been the men behind Janet Jackson's successful *Control* album) and spent four months recording a new album. The sessions ended in acrimony with Jam and Lewis bringing in session singers and players to get the album as they wanted. Despite all the pain the end result was worth it in that the subsequent vinyl output re-established the band's profile. The 45 *Human* spent eight weeks in the U.K. charts peaking at No. 8, but also topped the U.S. charts. When the parent album *Crash* emerged it made No. 7 in the U.K. (although it dropped out of the charts after just six weeks) and climbed to No. 24 in the U.S.. However, the other 45 culled from the album *I Need Your Loving* spent only a week at No. 72.

The Human League continued to record into the nineties, but their output became more erratic. Their *Greatest Hits* album, released in 1988, is exactly what its title suggests and includes all their finest commercial moments. However, if you've more into the experimentation that the new wave was initially all about you'd want to check out their early output up to the *Holiday 80* EP.

HUMAN LEAGUE - Dare.

Icon A.D.

Personnel:	C	A
	DICKY	A
	M. HOLMES	A
	P. SMITH	A

EPs: 1(A) DON'T FEED US SHIT (Face The Facts/
What's Your Name?/Fight For Peace/
You Fight To Kill) (PS)   (Radical Change RC 3) 1983
2(A) LET THE VULTURES FLY (Say No/Medals/
Tridents 1 & 2) (PS)   (Radical Change RC 4) 1983

An anarcho-punk band similar to **Crass**.

Icons Of Filth

ALBUM: 1( ) ONWARDS CHRISTIAN SOLDIERS
(Mortarhate MORT 5) 1984

EPs: 1( ) USED ABUSED AND UNAMUSED (Used Abused
And Unamused/Measure Of Insecurity/
Asking Too Much/
Virus) (PS)   (Corpus Christi CHRISTITS 7) 1983
2( ) BRAINDEATH (PS)   (Mortarhate MORT 10) 1985
3( ) THE FILTH AND THE FURY   (Mortarhate MORT 18) 1986

A London band whose records are characterised by raw punk guitar, political lyrics and shouted vocals. Their lyrics deal with issues like class, nuclear war and vivisection.

The Idiots

Personnel:	BILLY JOHNSON	A
	GARY THOMPSON	A
	DEE WILSON	A
	BARRY YOUNG	A

This band had one cut *Parents* included on the *Battle Of The Bands* (Good Vibrations GOT 7) 1978 EP which also featured cuts by **Rudi**, **Spider** and **Outcasts**. They were regulars at the Harp Bar in Belfast and also appeared in the movie 'Shellshock Rock' performing a version of *Teenager In Love*. Barry Young's younger brother Brian was a guitarist with **Rudi**.

Ijax All Stars

A very marginal case for inclusion, but they're in because they appeared on *Vaultage '79 (Another Two Sides Of Brighton)* (Attrix RB 08) in 1979. Their two contributions, the instrumental *Sounchek* and *Reggaed Rumble* are, as the second title suggests, basically reggae.

Illustration

Personnel:	JULIA ADAMSON	keyb'ds, piano	A
	TONY HARRISON	vcls	A
	TIM JOHNSON	synth, piano	A
	PAUL LANCASTER	bs	A
	GEORGE TERRY	drms	A

An electro-pop combo. Their sole vinyl offering seems to have been *Tidal Flow* on *Some Bizzare Album* (Some Bizzare BZLP 1) in 1981, which features some soothing piano.

I'm So Hollow

Personnel incl:	ROD LEIGH	vcls	A
	JANE WILSON	vcls	A

ALBUM: 1(A) EMOTION/SOUND/EMOTION
(Illuminated/Vital JAMS 5) 1981

45: Dreams To Fill The Vacuum/
Distraction   (Hologram ISH 002) 1981

An early eighties dance quartet from Sheffield. Their vinyl debut came with the inclusion of *I Don't Know* on *Hicks From The Sticks* (Rockburgh Records ROC 111) in 1980. This was noteworthy for Jane Wilson's distinctive vocals which you'll either love or hate and their tendency to utilise odd noises and treatments. They built on this sound on subsequent recordings, but never rose to much prominence. Their *Dreams To Fill The Vaccuum* 45 didn't come in a picture sleeve but was presented in a PVC sleeve and came on clear vinyl.

In Camera

Personnel incl: ANDREW GRAY   gtr, keyb'ds

EPs: 1( ) IV SONGS (The Conversation/The Attic/
Fragment Of Fear/Legion) (12", PS)   (4AD BAD 19) 1980
2( ) FIN (12", PS)   (4AD BAD 205) 1982

NB: There's also a CD *13 (Unlucky For Some)* (4AD GAD 205CD) 1998.

45: Die Laughing/Final Achievement (PS)   (4AD AD 8) 1980

These post-punk merchants of doom were of a similar ilk to other 4AD label-mates like **Modern English**, **Dif Juz**, **The The**, **Cupol** and **Mass**. *13 (Lucky For Some)* includes all of their recorded output, together with four unreleased recordings from a brief 1991 reformation. Whilst the earlier material is post-punk discordant rock, the later songs veer much more towards the low-key experimental/dance vibe which their keyboardist and guitarist Andrew Gray developed when he left to form **Wolfgang Press**.

Die Laughing also resurfaced on *Natures Mortes* (4AD CAD 117CD) in 1997.

The Incredible Kidda Band

Personnel:

45: Everybody Knows/No Nerve (some PS)   (Psycho P 2608) 1978

NB: There's also a vinyl 2-LP compilation *Too Much, Too Little, Too Late* (Detour DRLP 023) 2000, also on CD.

A melodic pop-punk band in the mould of groups like **The Jam** and **The Jags**. **The Incredible Kidda Band** utilised two singers and harmony vocals. A few copies of their *Everybody Knows* 45 on Psycho came in a picture sleeve. The single is now rare and collectable. Detour's 29-track compilation spanning 1977-81 does them justice and it's a shame some of their songs weren't issued whilst they were still gigging.

Indecent Exposure

Personnel:	GRAHAM BACON	gtr	A
	TOM BRENNAN	bs	A
	STEVE 'MILKY' REEVE	vcls	A
	SEDGE SWOTTON	drms	A

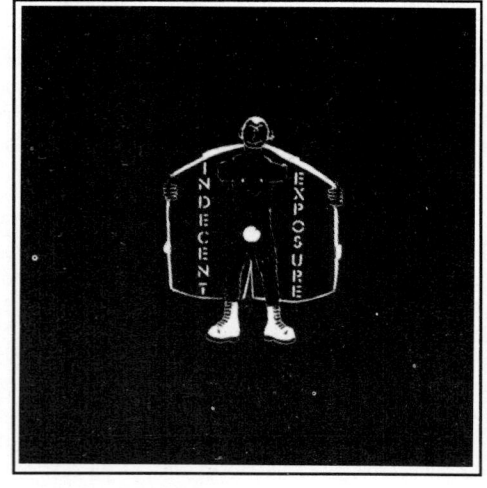

INDECENT EXPOSURE - Riots.

45: Riots/A Matter Of Time   (Index no #) 1984

Indecent Exposure were out of Hemel Hempstead in Hertfordshire. They financed this 45, which unusually for the genre and era didn't come in a picture sleeve. *Riots* was a typical Oi! offering and *A Matter Of Time* opens with some good guitar work and the lyrics explain how Thatcher would be stopped in the end 'it was just a matter of time' - six years to be precise! You can hear both sides of this 45 on *Oi! The Rarities, Vol. 5* (Captain Oi! AHOY CD 62) 1996.

The band supported groups like **The Business**, **Section 5** and **Vicious Rumours** on the Oi! circuit. They also contributed a cut *Bank Holidays* to *Oi! Glorious Oi!* (Link LINK LP 023) 1987.

Tom Brennan and Sedge Swotton were both later in Ska band Ska'd For Life and Steve Reeve became a Formula 3 racing driver.

The Industrials

Personnel:	MIKE BOLT	vcls, gtr, keyb'ds	A
	CYCLOPS	drms	A
	J.B. FRANK	vcls, gtr, keyb'ds, drms	A
	JAN MACKENZIE	vcls	A
	DANNY STAG	vcls, gtr, keyb'ds, bs	A
	CALVIN TEARDROP	bs	A

ALBUM: 1(A) INDUSTRIALS   (Epic 84399) 1980

A bland synthesizer-based pop album, which is technically well-produced, but contains little to grab the ear.

INFA-RIOT - Kids Of The '80s.

Infa-Riot

Personnel:	BARRY DAMERY	gtr	A
	MARK REYNOLDS	drms	A
	FLOYD WILSON	bs	A
	LEE WILSON	vcls	A

                                                               HCP
ALBUM: 1(A) STILL OUT OF ORDER   (Secret SEC 7) 1982 42
NB: (1) also issued on CD (Captain Oi! AHOYCD 010) 1993. See also *Live And Loud* (Link LINK LP 052) 1988 and *In For A Riot* (Harry May MAYOCD 104) 1999.

45s: Kids Of The '80s/Still Out Of Order (PS) (Secret SHH 117) 1981
     The Winner/School's Out (PS)   (Secret SHH 133) 1982

Formed in 1979 as part of the second wave of U.K. punk bands, **Infa-Riot**, a four-piece from Wood Green in North London, were closely associated with the Oi! movement and their gigs were disrupted by all the violence that went with it.

After recording a 45, *Five Minute Fashions* in 1980 which remained unissued until its inclusion on a Captain Oi! CD in 1993, their wilting career was rescued when they appeared at the first 'New Punk Convention'

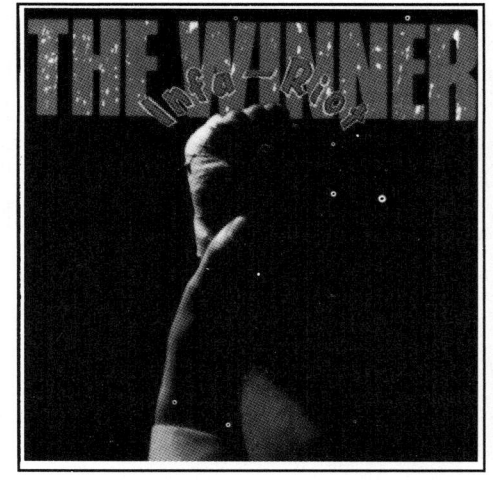

INFA-RIOT - The Winner.

concert in Southgate, North London. This was promoted by 'Sounds' writer and apologist for the Oi! movement Garry Bushell. They then contributed two tracks *We Outnumber You* and *Riot Riot* (no wonder their gigs were disrupted by violence) to Sounds' *Strength Through Oi!* album in 1981. Later in 1981, they were signed by Secret for whom they released an album, which climbed to No. 42 in the charts, and two 45s. This was a pretty typical Oi! album. The title track (also the flip side to their first Secret 45) is above average and the opening cut *Emergency* (a **Girlschool** composition) catches the ear. Of the remaining material, *Power* is quite anthemic; *The Winner* (their second Secret 45) sounds quite accessible with some decent guitar work; and the final cut *In For A Riot* is one of the strongest. The CD reissue on Captain Oi! comes with five bonus cuts *Kids Of The Eighties* (their first Secret 45), *Schools Out* (not the Alice Cooper song and the flip side to *The Winner*), *Feel The Rage* (their contribution to *Britannia Waives The Rules* (Secret 136-12) 1982) and demo versions of *Five Minute Fashions* and *Riot Riot*. There's also a vinyl version of this release which comes complete with picture inserts and a biography of the band.

Both sides of their first 45 can also be heard on *Oi! The Singles Collection, Vol. 1* (Captain Oi! AHOY CD 60) 1996. *Vol. 4* (Captain Oi! AHOY CD 71) 1997 of the same series features both sides of their second 45. You'll also find *Riot Riot* on *100% British Oi!* (Captain Oi! AHOY DCD 83) 1997. *Kids Of The 80's* and *Feel The Rage* both resurfaced on *Secret Records Punk Singles Collection, Vol. 1* (Anagram CDPUNK 13) 1993, whilst *Vol. 2* (Anagram CDPUNK 60) 1995 featured *School's Out*. They also contributed *Power* to *Pax Records Punk Collection* (Anagram CDPUNK 75) 1997, whilst *Secret Records (The Best And The Rest)* (Get Back GET 12) 1999 features *Kids Of The 80's*.

The 1988 *Live And Loud* album was taken from a 1985 reunion concert. The 1999 CD compilation *In For A Riot* comprises ten cuts from their debut album *Still Out Of Order*, demo versions of *Riot Riot* and *Five Minute Fashion* produced by **Angelic Upstarts**' Mensi (whose band was clearly a

INFA-RIOT - Still Out Of Order.

big influence on **Infa-Riot**), their two 45s *Kids Of The '80s* and *The Winner* and two cuts from their *Live And Loud* album on Link. The same year **Infa-Riot**'s *Kids Of The 80's* was included on *Oi! Fuckin' Oi!* (Harry May MAYO CD 110), an excellent compilation.

They later changed name to The Infa's recording an album *Sound And Fury* (Panache PANLP 501) 1984 and 45, *Sound And Fury / Triffic Spiff Ya O.K.* (PS) (Panache PAN 101) 1984, under this monicker. They split later in the same year disillusioned by their lack of gigs and the media backlash against Oi!.

Inner City Unit

Personnel:
- DEAD FRED — vcls, keyb'ds — A B
- BAZ MAGNETO — bs, vcls — A
- MICK STUPP — drms — A
- TREN THOMAS — gtr, vcls — A B
- NIK TURNER — sax, vcls — A B
- RAY BURNS (CAPTAIN SENSIBLE) — gtr — B
- DON FERARI — drms — B
- BILL BOSTON — horns — B
- MAX WALL — vcls — B

ALBUMS:
- 1(A) PASS OUT (THE 360° PSYCHO DELERIA SOUND) (Riddle RID 002) 1980
- 2(B) THE MAXIMUM EFFECT (Avatar AALP 5004) 1981
- 3(B) PUNKADELIC (Flicknife SHARP 103) 1982
- 4(B) NEW ANATOMY (Demi Monde) 1984
- 5(B) THE PRESIDENT'S TAPES (Flicknife SHARP 031) 1985

NB: (4) also issued on CD (Spalax 14845) 1997.

EPs:
- 1(B) BEER, BACCY, BINGO, BENIDORM (Beer, Baccy, Bingo, Benidorm/ In The Mood (Nude)) (Avator AAA 113) 1981
- 2(B) BLOOD AND BONES (Blood And Bones/ Little Black Egg/Paint Your Windows White/ Help Sharks) (Jettisoundz JZ5) 1985

45s:
- Solitary Ashtray/ So Try As I Did (Dub Version) (Riddle RID 001/ICU 45) 1979
- Paradise Beach/ Amyl Nitrate (die-cut sleeve) (Riddle RID 003) 1979
- Bones Of Elvis/Sid's Song (Avator AAA 119) 1982

This London-based five-piece fronted by Nik Turner (formerly of Hawkwind) were an important part of the city's music scene in the late seventies and early eighties. They updated Hawkwind's sound in a way that was acceptable in the 'new wave' era. At the end of 1980 Don Ferrari replaced Mike Stupp on drums and Ray Burns (Captain Sensible) came in for Baz Magneto. Bill Boston and Max Wall were added to the line-up.

Innocent Bystanders

45: Where Is Johnny?/(other side by **Debutantes**) (Rok ROK XVII/XVIII) 1980

Another of those obscure acts who recorded on the Fulham-based Rok label. *Where Is Johnny?* is quite a beaty number which was included among the bonus cuts on Captain Mod's CD reissue of *Odds Bods Mods And Sods* (Captain Mod MODSKA CD 2) 1996.

Insane

Personnel:
- DAVID ELLESMERE — drms — ABCD1 E
- SIMON MIDDLEHURST — gtr — ABCD2 E
- DEAN PORTER — bs — A
- BARRY TABERNER — vcls — AB D2 E
- TINA WALSH — gtr — A
- JULIAN BERRIMAN — bs — B
- DR. DEAN MITCHELL — vcls — CD1
- STEVE PRESCOTT — bs — CD2
- PHIL — gtr — D1
- TREV — bs — D1
- KEITH FINCH — drms — D2
- GARY SUMNER — bs — E

CD: 1(-) THE PUNK COLLECTION (Captain Oi! AHOY CD 126) 1999

NB: (1) was a split CD with **Blitzkrieg**.

EP: 1(C) EL SALVADOR (El Salvador/Nuclear War/ Chinese Rock) (PS) (No Future Oi 10) 1982

45s:
- Politics/Dead And Gone/Last Day (PS) (Riot City RIOT 3) 1981
- Why Die?/War And Violence (PS) (Insane INSANE 1) 1983
- Berlin Wall/(other side by **The Skeptix**) (White Rose BD 1) 1984

A punk band, **The Insane** formed in Wigan in 1979 (line-up 'A'). By 1980 their rhythm guitarist Tina Walsh had left reducing them to a four-piece. Bassist Dean Porter had gone with Julian Berriman coming in as a replacement. The new line-up ('B') was by now a regular attraction on Lancashire's live circuit. In 1981, they also contributed *Nuclear War* to the *Ten From The Madhouse* compilation. This was a promising effort with effective vocals and a tight rhythm section.

In May 1981, the project was frozen as Dave Ellesmere joined **Discharge** playing on their *Why?* album and on the 'Apocalypse Punk Tour'. He left **Discharge** after the tour to join **Flux Of Pink Indians** along with **Insane**'s guitarist Simon Middlehurst, but this was a touring not a recording line-up. When the tour was over **The Insane** was taken off ice. Dave Ellesmere was going out with **Vice Squad**'s Beki Bondage at the time, who introduced them to the Riot City label. The *Politics* 45 was released. All three tracks were above average full-blooded assaults on the senses and the disc was well received eventually climbing to No. 18 in the indie chart in December 1981. A year which had seen the band raise its profile through live appearances at venues like the "Woodstock Revisited" festival at London's Rainbow and the "Christmas On Earth" at Leeds Queens Hall ended on a high note.

By 1982, **The Insane**'s line-up had changed again with Ellesmere and Middlehurst joined by Dean Mitchell on vocals and Steve Prescott on bass. This line-up ('C') recored an EP *El Salvador* for No Future in spring 1982. The title track about the conflict then taking place in El Salvador was one of their finest moments and featured some fine guitar work. The EP also featured a re-recorded version of *Nuclear War*. The third cut *Chinese Rocks* had an authentic chorus. This EP was their most successful recording, climbing to No. 6 in the indie chart.

By 1983 things get complicated. Ellesmere and Middlehurst had a disagreement and each of them had a version of the band in existence for a while. Ellesmere's line-up ('D1') enjoyed plenty of live work supporting **The English Dogs** and **Varukers** among other. Middlehurst's version released a self-financed 45 *Why Die?* in 1983. The production on this is messy but it pursued the anti-violence theme which ran through many of their songs and is typical 100 m.p.h. hardcore punk. Similar themes were pursued on the flip side *War And Violence*. The single met with some success, climbing to No. 38 in the indie chart in October 1983. Ellesmere joined **Blitzkrieg** for a while, but by the end of 1983, he and Middlehurst

INTENSIVE CARE - Cowards EP.

INTENSIVE CARE - Rebels, Rockets And Rubbermen.

had settled their differences and a new **Insane** line-up ('E') was in place again. This toured Europe extensively covering Germany, Belgium, Holland, Switzerland and Australia. In 1984, it contributed another fine cut *Berlin War* to a split 7" with **The Skeptix** on White Rose records. That ends the complex history of **The Insane**.

El Salvador later resurfaced on *Punk And Disorderly, Vol. 2 (Further Charges)* (Anagram CDPUNK 22) 1993, whilst you can also check out *Dead And Gone* on *100% Hardcore Punk* (Captain Oi! AHOY DCD 84) 1998. All of the band's recordings are rounded up on the excellent split CD with **Blitzkrieg** *The Punk Collection* released by Captain Oi! in 1999. This is well worth investigating and comes with informative sleevenotes by Mark Brennan on which this entry is based.

Instant Automations

EP:	1( )	PETER PAINTS HIS FENCE (Peter Paints His Fence/ Nice Job For The Lad/Laburnam Walk/New Musak/ People Laugh At Me (Coz I Like Weird Music)/ John's Vacuum Cleaner) (PS)	(Deleted DEP 001) 1980

Some members of this group had been in **The Tronics**. Their EP played at 33 r.p.m. and came in a poly bag with an insert and numbered copies.

Intensive Care

Personnel:	GAV HILLS	gtr	A
	IAIN KILGALLON	vcls	AB
	LIAM KNIGHT	gtr	A
	SPIKE	bs	A
	WEE LEE	drms	A
	ASH	gtrs	B
	GLEN	bs	B
	MARK	drms	B

EPs:	1(A)	COWARDS (Cowards/Class Of 84/ Organised Crime) (PS)	(Punishment Block CELL 1) 1984
	2(B)	REBELS, ROCKETS & RUBBERMEN (The Hypocrite/ As Sober As A Judge/Points Of View/Rebels/ Exocet U.K./Rubberman) (12", PS)	(Back To Back BTB 001) 1987

NB: There's also a compilation *The Oi! Collection* (Captain Oi! AHOY CD 110) 1999.

Intensive Care formed in Scotland in 1980. By the time of their vinyl debut, two cuts *Fight And Die* and *Ghost Town* on *A Country Fit For Heroes, Vol. 2* (No Future Oi 3) 1983, their original vocalist Iain Kilgallon had relocated to West Sussex.

In 1984, a three-track EP *Cowards* emerged via Punishment Block. Sales were good but a follow-up didn't emerge largely due to problems with distributors. They recorded for Link in 1987 and then released a six-cut 12" *Rebels, Rockets & Rubbermen* on their own Back To Back imprint in 1987. They began work on an album *They Came They Saw They Conquered*. Eight tracks were laid down but the album was never completed.

The 1999 Captain Oi! compilation re-assembles all their recorded output. All three cuts on the *Cowards* EP can also be heard on *Oi! The Rarities, Vol. 3* (Captain Oi! AHOY CD 53) 1995 and *Oi! The Rarities, Vol. 4* (Captain Oi! AHOY CD 58) 1996 contains all six songs from *Rebels, Rockets & Rubbermen*.

Ghost Town also got a further airing on *100% British Oi!* (CD) (Captain Oi! AHOY DCD 83) 1997.

Intra Vein

45:	Speed Of The City/Sick	(Bum FP 001) 1979

This 45 appeared in a printed PVC sleeve or a stamped plain sleeve. Both versions are rare and collectable, particularly the former. The band were also known as simply Vein.

Intro

45s:	Haunted Cocktails/Departures (PS)	(MCA MCA 794) 1982
	Lost Without Your Love/Epic (PS)	(MCA MCA 819) 1982

A short-lived dance-orientated pop combo.

Invaders

ALBUM:	1	TESTCARD	(Polydor 2383589) 1980

45s:	Girls In Action/No Secrets (PS)	(Polydor 2059 111) 1979
	Best Thing I Ever Did/ Much Closer Still (PS)	(Polydor 2059 157) 1979
	Magic Mirror/Shirley You're Wrong (PS)	(Polydor 2059 263) 1980
	Backstreet Romeo/Rock Methodology/ Invasion Of Privacy (PS)	(Polydor POSP 180) 1980

A somewhat forgotten popish new wave band. The 'A' side of their first two 45s both got a further airing on *20 Of Another Kind, Vol. 2* (Polydor POLX 1) in 1979 and both are eminently forgettable.

I.Q. Zero

45s:	Insects/Electromotion/ Quirky Pop Music (PS)	(Object Music OM 9) 1979
	She's So Rare/Crazy Dolls (PS)	(Logo GO 374) 1979
	She's So Rare/Crazy Dolls (PS)	(SRT SRT 80623) 1979

From Blackburn in Lanashire. *Insects* is very much in the mould of early **XTC**.

INTRO - Haunted Cocktails.

INVADERS - Girls In Action.

Joe Jackson

				HCP
ALBUMS:	1	LOOK SHARP!	(A&M AMLH 64743) 1979	40
(New wave	2	I'M THE MAN	(A&M AMLH 64794) 1979	12
only)	3	BEAT CRAZY	(A&M AMLH 64837) 1980	42

NB: (1) Some copies came on white vinyl. (1) later reissued at mid-price (A&M AMID 120) 1982 and at budget price (Hallmark SHM 3154) 1985. (1) also issued on CD (A&M CDA 64743) 1984 and again (A&M CDMID 115) 1992. (2) later issued on CD (A&M CDA 3221) 1988 and again (A&M CDMID 117) 1992. (3) also issued on CD (A&M CDA 3241) 1985. There are also a couple of CD compilations which include material from the period Steppin' Out (The Very Best Of Joe Jackson) (A&M 3970522) 1990 and This Is It (Anthology/2 CD Set) (A&M 5404022) 1997.

			HCP
45s:	Is She Really Going Out With Him?/		
(New wave	You Got The Fever (PS)	(A&M AMS 7392) 1978	-
only)	Sunday Papers/Look Sharp! (PS)	(A&M AMS 7413) 1979	-
	One More Time/Don't Ask Me (PS)	(A&M AMS 7433) 1979	-
*	One More Time/		
	Don't Ask Me (10", PS)	(A&M AMSP 7433) 1979	-
	Is She Really Going Out With Him?/		
	You Got The Fever (PS)	(A&M AMS 7459) 1979	13
	I'm The Man/Come On (live) (PS)	(A&M AMS 7479) 1979	-
	It's Different For Girls/Friday (PS)	(A&M AMS 7493) 1979	5
	Kinda Kute/Geraldine And John (PS)	(A&M AMS 7513) 1980	-
	The Harder They Come/		
	Out Of Style/Tilt (PS)	(A&M AMS 7536) 1980	-
	The Harder They Come/		
	Out Of Style/Tilt (12", PS)	(A&M AMSP 7536) 1980	-
	Mad At You/		
	Enough Is Not Enough (PS)	(A&M AMS 7563) 1980	-
	Beat Crazy/Is She Really		
	Going Out With Him (live) (PS)	(A&M AMS 8100) 1981	-

NB: * These came on white vinyl with a free badge.

Like **Nick Lowe**, **Dave Edmunds**, **Ian Dury**, **Larry Wallis** and others **Joe Jackson** was not a newcomer to music at the onset of new wave. He was born on 11th August 1954 in Burton-on-Trent, but the following year his family moved to Portsmouth, where he lived until January 1978. By the age of eleven he was receiving violin lessons. Then, having persuaded his parents to buy him a piano, he taught himself how to play and composed his own music. He secured an S-Level in music and between 1971 - 74 studied for a three year piano scholarship at the Royal Academy. When he left, he formed his first group Edward Bear, a Top 40 covers band who evolved into **Arms and Legs**. Under this latter moniker they started writing their own material and signed a deal with MAM, who got them some London gigs. **Jackson** wasn't the lead vocalist in this band but played piano, electric violin and harmonica and sang on the occassional number. Despite releasing three 45s for MAM they failed to make any impact and, when **Jackson** decided to quit, they split up.

Jackson now decided to pursue a solo career, but rather than employ the usual method of circulating a demo tape around the record companies, he decided to record a demo album and have it pressed and distributed in a properly designed sleeve. To finance this he took a job as an occasional cabaret artist at the Playboy Club in Portsmouth. When his demo was complete, he took it first to United Artists who passed it over, but they did alert Albion Music, a publishing company. They gave Joe a songwriting contract, got him a manager and sent it to American A&M producer David Kershenbaum. He loved the demo and arranged for **Joe Jackson** to record a debut album. A backing band was put together, comprising Graham Maby (bs) (ex-**Arms and Legs**) and Dave Houghton (drms) and Gary Sanford (gtr), who'd both helped on his demo sessions. Their debut gig was on 30th August 1978 at St. Mark's Park, Notting Hill. Shortly after they embarked on a five week tour with **The Pleasers**.

With a debut album in the can A&M decided to issue a single first, starting out with Is She Really Going Out With Him?. The song highlighted his writing skills with sharp, clever lyrics, allied to a memorable hook. It was well received by the music press but not by the public, initially, and it sank without trace. His debut album Look Sharp! was released in January 1979, again to enthusiastic reviews. **Jackson** refused to overdub any of the instrumentation on the album which gave it a live feel. Aside from the 45 'A' side, other standout cuts included Sunday Papers, a witty attack on trashy tabloids, and the crushing Fools In Love. Musically, the material ranged from ballads to power pop. In the first few months of 1979, he toured the U.K. which helped to get the album into the charts. It climbed to No. 40. He then toured North America in April and May and was very enthusiastically received on account on his witty, intelligent songs. With the album in the U.S. Top 20 A&M decided to reissue Is She Really Going Out With Him?. This time it got to No. 13 here and No. 21 in the 'States. He was now a force to be reckoned with on both sides of the Atlantic. Is She Really Going Out With Him? and Sunday Papers were also included on the sampler No Wave (A&M AMLE 68505) in 1979.

The cover of his second album I'm The Man depicted him posing as an Oxford Street wide-boy, looking very sharp indeed! As well as the title cut, stand-out tracks included Geraldine And John, On The Radio and a very original number It's Different For Girls, dealing with a reverse of the macho man / subservient woman roles. Its release coincided with a further U.K. tour and helped it climb to No. 5 to give him his biggest hit.

For his third album Beat Crazy, which was credited to the **Joe Jackson Band**, **Jackson** handled the production himself, but it didn't receive the same critical acclaim as its two predecessors and **Joe Jackson** disbanded his group keeping only Graham Maby, his bassist for future projects.

His 1980 single The Harder They Come (a cover of the Jimmy Cliff hit) was a pointer that he was considering a change of direction. He went on in the early eighties to a complete stylistic shift reviving old jazz classics on Jumpin' Jive his homage to Cab Calloway and Louis Jordan and put together a new band specifically just for this project. Around the same time he relocated to New York and enjoyed Worldwide success with his lush and accomplished pop album Night And Day, which was split into a 'Night' side of upbeat songs and a 'Day' side of slow songs. Surprisingly it only climbed to No. 44 in the U.K. and the first three singles from it failed to chart at all. It wasn't until A&M remarketed Steppin' Out six months after its release and it climbed to No. 6, which in turn helped boost sales of the album again so that it got the success it deserved, re-entering the chart and climbing to No. 3.

JOE JACKSON - Look Sharp!

Since then, **Jackson** has continued to release the occasional pop album and experiment with soundtracks and classical projects but without ever enjoying the same success.

His importance to new wave is underscored by the inclusion of *Is She Really Going Out with Him?* on the 5-CD box set compilation *1-2-3-4 - A History Of Punk And New Wave 1976 - 1979* (MCA/Univeral MCD 60066) in 1999.

The Jags

Personnel:			
	ALEX BAIRD	drms	AB
	STEVE PRUDENCE	bs, vcls	A
	TWINK	gtr, vcls	AB
	NICK WATKINSON	gtr, vcls	AB
	MICHAEL COTTON	bs, vcls	B
	PADDY O'TOOLE	keyb'ds	B

ALBUMS:
1(A) EVENING STANDARD (Island ILPS 9603) 1980
2(B) NO TIE LIKE A PRESENT (Island ILPS 9655) 1981

NB: There's also a compilation *The Best Of The Jags* (Spectrum 55 48602) 1999.

EP: 1(A) BACK OF MY HAND (Back Of My Hand/Double Vision/Single Vision/What Can I Do?)
(Island I2SWIP 6501) 1979

HCP
45s: Back Of My Hand/Double Vision (PS) (Island WIP 6501) 1979 17
Woman's World/Dumb Blonde (PS) (Island WIP 6531) 1979 75
Party Games/
She's So Considerate (PS) (Island WIP 6587) 1980 -
I Never Was A Beach Boy/
Tune Into Heaven (PS) (Island WIP 6666) 1980 -
The Sound Of G.O.O.D.B.Y.E./
The Hurt (Island WIP 6683) 1981 -

The Jags rose to brief prominence in the punk era playing a sort of fast-paced pop which was just about acceptable to punk audiences. Given that *Woman's World* only spent a week in the charts, the catchy *Back Of My Hand* on which many likened their sound to **Elvis Costello**, can be regarded as a 'one hit wonder'. Don't be put off by this, all the songs on their debut EP are pretty good fun and their first album, in particular, is full of enthusiasm and energy. Still, they did fail to fulfill their early promise.

Back Of My Hand later resurfaced on *Teenage Kicks* (PolyGram TV 5253382) in 1995.

THE JAGS - Back Of My Hand 12" EP.

THE JAGS - Evening Standards.

The Jam

Personnel:			
	RICK BUCKLER		
	(PAUL RICHARD BUCKLER)	drms	A
	BRUCE FOXTON	bs, vcls	A
	PAUL WELLER	vcls, gtr	A

HCP
ALBUMS: 1(A) IN THE CITY (Polydor 2383 447) 1977 20
2(A) THIS IS THE MODERN WORLD
(Polydor 2383 475) 1977 22
3(A) ALL MOD CONS (Polydor POLD 5008) 1978 6
4(A) SETTING SONS (Polydor POLD 5028) 1979 4
5(A) SOUND AFFECTS (Polydor POLD 5035) 1980 2
6(A) THE GIFT (Polydor POLD 5055) 1982 1
7(A) DIG THE NEW BREED (Polydor POLD 5075) 1982 2
8(A) SNAP! (dbl LP compilation) (Polydor SNAP 1) 1983 2
9(A) GREATEST HITS (Polydor 8495541) 1991 2

NB: (1) reissued (Polydor SPELP 27) 1983 (No. 100) and in 1990 on vinyl and CD (Polydor 817 1242). (1) reissued on digitally remastered CD (Polydor 537 417-2) 1997. Test pressings also exist of (1) which are very rare. (2) reissued (Polydor SPELP 66) 1984 and in 1990 on vinyl and CD (Polydor 823 2812). (2) reissued on digitally remastered CD (Polydor 537 418-2) 1997. (3) reissued (Polydor) 1980 and in 1989 on vinyl and CD (Polydor 823 2822). (3) reissued on digitally remastered CD (Polydor 537 419-2) 1997. (4) reissued on CD (Polydor 8313142) 1983 and again on vinyl and CD (Polydor 823 2842) 1988. (4) reissued on digitally remastered CD (Polydor 537 420-2) 1997 and on vinyl (Simply Vinyl SVLP 209) 2000. (5) reissued on digitally remastered CD (Polydor 537 421-2) 1997. (6) reissued in 1990 on vinyl and CD (Polydor 823 2852). (6) reissued on digitally remastered CD (Polydor 537 422-2) 1997. (7) reissued (Polydor SPELP 107) 1987 and on CD (Polydor 8100412) 1990. There was also a limited edition version of comprising (8) and *Live At Wembley* EP (SNAP 45) with *Move On Up*, *Get Yourself Together*, *The Great Depression* and *But I'm Different Now*. This was available on vinyl (Polydor SNAP 1) and CD (Polydor SNAP C 1). (1) and (2) reissued as a double LP with a gatefold sleeve (Polydor 2683 074) 1980 and on CD (Polydor 847 7302) 1991. (3) and (4) reissued as a double LP with a gatefold sleeve (Polydor 10574098) 1983. (5) and (6) reissued as a double LP wirh a gatefold sleeve (Polydor TWO MCI) 1983. (9) also issued on CD (Polydor 849554-2) 1991. There's also a CD version of (8) *Compact Snap* (Polydor 821 712-2) 1984. Also relevant are: a double album *Extras* (Polydor POL 900) 1992 also on CD (Polydor 5131772) 1992 which was available to fan club members; two BBC Transcription *In Concert* discs from Paris Theatre, London on 10th June 1978 and Golders Green Hippodrome, London on 2nd February 1982; *Live Jam* (Polydor 519 667) 1993 contains most of their classics and reached No. 28 in the U.K. charts; *Wasteland* (Pickwick PWKS 4129 P) 1992 is a CD compilation; *Beat Surrender* (Carousel 5500062) 1993; *The Jam Collection* (2-CD set) (Polydor 5314932) 1996; *The Very Best Of The Jam* (Polydor 537 4232) 1997; *Direction Reaction Creation* (5-CD set) (Polydor 537 1432) 1997 and *Extras* (Polydor 5131772) 1992. There are also two tribute albums, *Fire And Skill (The Songs Of The Jam)* (Ignition IGNLP 3 / IGNCD 3) 1999 and *A Jam Tribute (Various Artists)* (Rhythm Vicar PREACH 008CD) 1998.

EP: 1(A) PEEL SESSION (In The City/Art School/
I've Changed My Address/Modern World)
(Strange Fruit SFPS 80) 1990 -

NB: (1) also issued on CD (Strange Fruit SFPSCD 080) 1990 and reissued again in 1996.

HCP

45s:	In The City/Takin' My Love (PS)	(Polydor 2058 866)	1977 40
	All Around The World/		
	Carnaby Street (PS)	(Polydor 2058 903)	1977 13
	The Modern World/Sweet Soul Music (live)/Back In My Arms		
	Again (live)/Bricks And Mortar (part live) (PS)		
		(Polydor 2058 945)	1977 36
	News Of The World/Aunties And Uncles (Impulsive Youths)/		
	Innocent Man (PS)	(Polydor 2058 995)	1978 27
	David Watts/		
	'A' Bomb In Wardour Street (PS)	(Polydor 2059 054)	1978 25
	Down In The Tube Station At Midnight/So Sad About Us/		
	The Night (PS)	(Polydor POSP 8)	1978 15
	Strange Town/		
	The Butterfly Collector (PS)	(Polydor POSP 34)	1979 15
	When You're Young/		
	Smithers-Jones (PS)	(Polydor POSP 69)	1979 17
	The Eton Rifles/		
	See-Saw (laminated PS)	(Polydor POSP 83)	1979 3
	Going Underground/The Dreams Of		
	Children (laminated PS)	(Polydor POSP 113)	1980 1
*	Going Underground/The Dreams Of Children/		
	The Modern World (live)/Away From The Numbers (live)/		
	Down In The Tube Station At Midnight (live) (PS, double pack)		
		(Polydor POSPJ 113/2816024)	1980 -
	Start!/Lisa Radley (PS)	(Polydor 2059 266)	1980 1
+	Pop Art Poem/		
	Boy About Town	(Flexipop 2/Lyntone LYN 9048)	1980 -
B	That's Entertainment/Down In The Tube Station		
	At Midnight (live) (embossed PS)	(Metronome 0030 364)	1981 21
	Funeral Pyre/Disguises (PS)	(Polydor POSP 257)	1981 4
0	Absolute Beginners/		
	Tales From The Riverbank (PS)	(Polydor POSP 350)	1981 4
Ξ	When You're Young (live)	(Lyntone)	1981 -
A	Tales From The Riverbank	(Fan Club no #)	1982 -
	Town Called Malice/Precious (PS)	(Polydor POSP 400)	1982 1
	Town Called Malice (live)/		
	Precious (extended) (12", PS)	(Polydor POSPX 400)	1982 -
	Just Who Is The Five O'Clock Hero/		
	The Great Depression (PS)	(Polydor 2229254)	1982 8
	Just Who Is The Five O'Clock Hero/The Great Depression/		
	War (12", PS)	(Polydor)	1982 -
	The Bitterest Pill/Pity Poor Alfie/		
	Fever (PS)	(Polydor POSP 505)	1982 2
	Beat Surrender/Shopping (PS)	(Polydor POSP 540)	1982 1
Δ	Beat Surrender/Shopping/Move On Up/		
	Stoned Out Of My Mind/		
	War (PS, double pack)	(Polydor POSPJ 540/JAM 1)	1982 -
X	Move On Up (live)	(MM PAULO 100)	1982 -

NB: In April 1980 the following 45s were reissued in their picture sleeves and many as shown below re-entered the charts. Early originals had curved edges on sleeve openings whereas the reissues are straight with fatter lettering on the labels.

	In The City/Takin' My Love (PS)	(Polydor 2058 866)	1980 40
	All Around The World/		
	Carnaby Street (PS)	(Polydor 2058 903)	1980 43
	The Modern World/Sweet Soul Music (live)/		
	Back In My Arms Again (live)/		
	Bricks And Mortar (part live) (PS)	(Polydor 2058 945)	1980 52
	News Of The World/Aunties And Uncles (Impulsive Youths)/		
	Innocent Man (PS)	(Polydor 2058 955)	1980 53
	David Watts/		
	'A' Bomb In Wardour Street (PS)	(Polydor 2059 054)	1980 54
x	Down In The Tube Station At Midnight/So Bad About Us/		
	The Night (PS)	(Polydor POSP 8)	1980 -
	Strange Town/		
	The Butterfly Collector (PS)	(Polydor POSP 34)	1980 44

NB: In January 1983 after the band split all of its regular 45s up to and including Town Called Malice were reissued and re-entered the charts as detailed below:-

	In The City/Takin' My Love (PS)	(Polydor 2058 866)	1983 47
	All Around The World/		
	Carnaby Street (PS)	(Polydor 2058 903)	1983 38
	The Modern World/Sweet Soul Music (live)/		
	Back In My Arms Again (live)/		
	Bricks And Mortar (part live) (PS)	(Polydor 2058 945)	1983 51
	News Of The World/Aunties And Uncles (Impulsive Youths)/		
	Innocent Man (PS)	(Polydor 2058 955)	1983 39
	David Watts/		
	'A' Bomb In Wardour Street (PS)	(Polydor 2059 054)	1983 50
	Down In The Tube Station At Midnight/So Bad About Us/		
	The Night (PS)	(Polydor POSP 8)	1983 30
	Strange Town/		
	The Butterfly Collector (PS)	(Polydor POSP 34)	1983 42
	When You're Young/		
	Smithers-Jones (PS)	(Polydor POSP 69)	1983 53
	The Eton Rifles/See-Saw (PS)	(Polydor POSP 83)	1983 54
	Going Underground/		
	Dreams Of Children (PS)	(Polydor POSP 113)	1983 21
	Start!/Liza Radley (PS)	(Polydor 2059 266)	1983 62
	Funeral Pyre/Disguises (PS)	(Polydor POSP 257)	1983 -
	Absolute Beginners/		
	Tales From The Riverbank (PS)	(Polydor POSP 350)	1983 -
	Town Called Malice/		
	Precious (PS)	(Polydor POSP 400)	1983 73
	That's Entertainment/Down In The Tube Station		
	At Midnight (embossed PS)	(Polydor POSP 482)	1983 60
E	Interview with Paul Weller and		
	Bruce Foxton (picture disc)	(PJAM 1)	1983 -
	That's Entertainment/Down In The Tube Station		
	At Midnight (live)	(Polydor)	1991 -
	That's Entertainment/Down In The Tube Station		
	At Midnight (live)	(Polydor)	1991 -
	Town Called Malice (live) (12")	(Polydor)	1991 -
	The Dreams Of Children/		
	Away From The Numbers (live)	(Polydor)	1992 -
	The Dreams Of Children/Away From The Numbers (live)/		
	This Is The Modern World (live) (12")	(Polydor)	1992 -
Other Reissues:	Beat Surrender/The Bitterest Pill	(Old Gold OG)	1989 -
	Town Called Malice/Absolute Beginners	(Old Gold OG)	1990 -
	Going Underground/Start!	(Old Gold OG)	1990 -
	The Eton Rifles/Down In The Tube Station		
	At Midnight	(Old Gold OG)	1990 -

NB: * This was a 100,000 pressing. + There are two versions of this release. One

THE JAM - Beat Surrender.

THE JAM - Going Underground.

THE JAM - Town Called Malice.

THE JAM - The Bitterest Pill.

appeared as a blue, yellow or green one-sided flexi with 'Flexipop' magazine Issue 2. Another version had the same tracks on both sides on a hard white vinyl label in a picture sleeve. This pressing of 300 was available by mail order only. O This was a 100,000 pressing. Ξ This was a one-sided fan club flexidisc. Λ This was a one-sided fan club flexi-disc. X This was a flexi-disc which came free with 'Melody Maker'. B This was a German release, available here on import. Δ This was a double pack release. E This was a numbered limited edition release of 1,200. Be sure to check out two CD single compilations:- *45 r.p.m.: The Singles 1977-79* (Polydor 587 610-9) 2001 and *45 r.p.m.: The Singles 1980-82* (Polydor 587 978-2) 2001.

The Jam were undoubtedly one of the punk era's premier and most commercially successful bands. Paul Weller was born on 25th May 1958. He met Rick Buckler (real name Paul Richard Buckler), who entered the world on 6th December 1955 at school in Woking, Surrey, where together with several classmates they used to jam together in the school music room at lunchtimes during 1973-74. When they left school Weller and Buckler teamed up with bassist **Bruce Foxton**, born on 1st September 1955, and second guitarist Steve Brookes. Taking the school jamming sessions as the inspiration for the group's name, they started playing around the youth and social clubs. Brookes soon left when they started to venture out into the club circuit and they stabilised into the now seminal trio.

By mid-1976, they had become a regular live attraction in London. They gigged at venues like The Marquee and 100 Club and were a regular attraction at the Red Cow pub, where in early 1977, they secured a residency. During this period they were eyed over by a number of record companies, but it was eventually Polydor who won the race to sign them for a reputed advance of £6,000.

With their sports mohair suits and Rickenbacker guitars the band were in many repects a mod revival band (Weller's favourite band was The Who), but the media linked them closely with the bourgeoning punk movement, which they soon became a very important part of.

Although their debut 45 *In The City* released in April 1977 had the same title as a Who 'B'-side, it was actually penned by Weller. It was produced by A&R man Chris Parry who had been responsible for signing them. The punchy song rose to No. 40 in the charts where it enjoyed a six week stay.

"And I know what you're thinking
You still think I'm crap
But you'd better listen man
Because the kids know where it's at"
(from *In The City*)

They played their first John Peel session on 2nd May 1977. The four songs it featured - *In The City, Art School, I've Changed My Address* and *Modern World* - were later issued on an EP, *Peel Session* EP (Strange Fruit SFPS 80) in 1990.

Their first album *In The City* came out the same month. Recorded in 11 days, all the songs were penned by Paul Weller except for the jokey *Batman* theme and their pulsating cover of Laurie Williams' oldie *Slow Down*. They launched into their first headlining U.K. tour to help promote it and it climbed to No. 20 in the U.K. charts. It spent eighteen weeks in the charts in all.

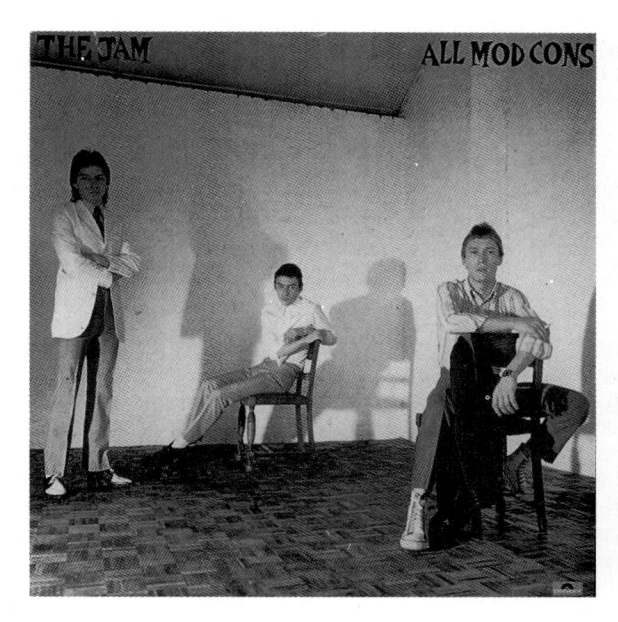

THE JAM - All Mod Cons.

All Around The World, released in June 1977, gave them their first Top 20 hit, peaking at No. 13 and enjoying eight weeks in the charts. They also made their first 'Top Of The Pops' appearance to help promote it. A further John Peel session on 25th July 1977 comprised *All Around The World, London Girl, Bricks And Mortar* and *Carnaby Street*. Following tours of Europe and the 'States. *The Modern World*, released in November 1977, gave them another (if smaller) hit single. The album it was from *This Is The Modern World* also appeared the same month. Musically, it represented little progression on *In The City* but it benefitted from better production. The U.S. release included *All Around The World* which was omitted from the British version. Aside from the title track the other stand-out cut was *Standards*. *This Is The Modern World* spent five weeks in the charts, peaking at No. 22.

In December 1977, they set off on a major U.K. tour to help promote the album. It soon hit the headlines when the band became involved in a brawl with a group of rugby players at a Leeds hotel.

They seemed to like to have 'world' in their titles. Their next 45, released in February 1978, *News Of The World* brought them a further Top 30 hit, while they supported Blue Oyster Cult on a U.S. tour. On their return they played *News Of The World, The Night* and *'A' Bomb In Wardour Street* on a David Jensen session on 12th June 1978. It was followed in August by the only cover version they ever recorded as an 'A' side - a Kinks album cut *David Watts*. *David Watts* is a song about the schoolboy who had everything. The kid whose good at sport, passes his exams, wins the fights and gets the girl. Gradually they diversified from their early Who influence and The Kinks (and Ray Davies their vocalist and major songwriter) became one of their other influences. It was coupled with a popular original *'A' Bomb In Wardour Street*. It climbed to No. 25 and the same month they made a successful appearance at the Reading Festival. Then in October, the excellent *Down In The Tube Station At Midnight* gave them their second Top 20 hit, climbing to No. 15 during a seven week chart residency.

It also featured, along with *David Watts* and *'A' Bomb In Wardour Street* on their superb *All Mod Cons* album, released in November 1978. The biting social commentary on another cut *Mr. Clean* was evidence of Weller's increasing political interest and awareness. Quite a few songs originally intended for the album, like *On Sunday Morning* and *I Want To Paint*, were scraped on the advice of producer Chris Parry, a decision which clearly paid off. On another cut *In The Crowd* Weller was able to display his full range of talents as a guitarist. It became their most successful album to date, climbing to No. 6 during a stay of seventeen weeks in the charts. They embarked on a European tour to help promote it.

In 1979, they achieved further Top 20 hits with *Strange Town* and *When You're Young* before the powerful punkish anthem *Eton Rifles* became their best selling single yet, peaking at No. 3 during a twelve week chart tenure. It previewed their *Setting Sons* album, released the following month. This included five songs from a scrapped concept album about three friends who meet after most of England has been destroyed by atomic war. If this isn't somber, the other material (aside from a cover of *Heatwave*) is even bleaker. Many regard this as their finest album and certainly it contains some of Weller's most beautiful melodies. On 5th November 1979, **The Jam** played their final session for John Peel. It featured *Thick As Thieves*, *The Eton Rifles*, *Saturday's Kids* and *When You're Young*.

The Jam were now at the zenith of their career. *Going Underground* in March 1980 became the first single of the eighties to go straight to No. 1 in its week of release. It was an immediately accessible and powerful recording which spent nine weeks in the charts in all. They followed this with another excellent 45 *Start!*, which also made No. 1 during an eight week chart stay. It was based on an adaptation of The Beatles' *Taxman* riff.

Sound Affects, released in November 1980, included *Start!* and also their following 45 *That's Entertainment*, which reached No. 21, despite only being available as an import here, having been released on the German Metronome label. After the sombre mood of *Setting Sons*, the music on *Sound Affects* is more danceable and the lyrics a little lighter. The fans still liked it because it reached No. 2 and again spent nineteen weeks in the chart. In December they embarked on a major U.K. tour culminating in sell-out concerts at the Rainbow. Weller was also busily setting up his own publishing company Riot Stories with his royalties.

1981 was a quieter year for the band. They enjoyed two U.K. No. 4 hit singles with *Funeral Pyre* and *Absolute Beginners*. Paul Weller, meanwhile, was beginning to branch out into other areas. In August 1981, he made a programme for BBC TV's 'Something Else' on class awareness. Then, in October, he set up 'Jamming' magazine, which was run by fan Tony Fletcher as well as his own Respond record label. **The Jam** ended the year playing a number of sell-out Christmas dates in London.

The strenuous schedule began to take its toll on Paul Weller. He suffered a breakdown whilst beginning work on new recordings in January. The same month an EP was released in the 'States containing five cuts previously released on singles, including *Funeral Pyre* and *Absolute Beginners*. It climbed to No. 176, but this was really evidence of their failure to crack the U.S. market where they enjoyed little more than cult status. This clearly troubled Weller over the next few years. He began to attribute their inability to translate their phenomenal success in the U.K. internationally to the tight rock format of their music. This lead him to begin to explore other influences like R&B and soul, although the challenge was how to change their musical style without losing the roots that made them the band they were.

This conundrum explains *The Gift*, released in March 1982, which entered new musical territory for **The Jam** with songs like *Trans-Global Express* and *Precious*. These utilised lots of percussion and strong funk/Latin rhythms. In February *Precious* was included on a double 'A' 45 with another cut from the album, the Motownish *Town Called Malice* and released as a 12" single. It topped the charts during an eight week residency and **The Jam** became the first band since The Beatles to perform two numbers on the same edition of 'Top Of The Pops' when they played both sides of the record.

The *Gift* album also topped the charts which it was in for a total of twenty-four weeks and achieved No. 82 (which would prove to be their best position in the 'States). Aside from the two cuts on the double 'A' side 45,

THE JAM - Setting Sons.

THE JAM - Sound Affects.

other highlights were *Happy Together*, *Ghosts* and *Just Who Is The Five O'Clock Hero*. The last track was chosen as their next 45 and reached No. 8. The same month the album came out **The Jam** embarked on a four month "Trans Global Unity Express" tour which took in the U.K., Europe, Canada, U.S. and Japan.

When they returned from the tour Weller took a two week vacation in Italy. Whilst there, tired and disillusioned with its musical format, he decided to disband **The Jam**. However, this decision wasn't made public until 28th October 1982. Meanwhile, in September, a further 45 *The Bitterest Pill (I Ever Had To Swallow)*, on which Weller duetted with Jenny McKeowen (of The Belle Stars), was released. It climbed to No. 2 here in Britain, spending seven weeks in the charts.

After **The Jam** announced their split they certainly went out in style. *Beat Surrender*, their final 45, was an instant No. 1 in Britain, where it spent a total of nine weeks in the charts, but sadly failed in the 'States, where it was censored by U.S. radio. *Dig The New Breed* (live), a retrospective live album comprising 14-tracks from various gigs in the 1977-82 era, made No. 2. A U.S.-only compilation of their U.K. hits, *The Bitterest Pill (I Ever Had To Swallow)*, reached No. 135 in the 'States. **The Jam** played a final U.K. tour which was a great success. It included six sold-out nights at Wembley Arena and a final gig in Brighton, the mod's symbolic centre.

Shortly after **The Jam** split in late 1982, Paul Weller formed the hugely successful Style Council, which enabled him to explore soul and funk-based musical territories over a number of years. **Foxton** and Buckler both went solo, initially, and **Foxton** released an album *Touch Sensitive* on Arista. Buckler then formed Time U.K. and both of them were later together in Sharp. By the nineties Rick Buckler was running his own recording studio and **Bruce Foxton** joined the reformed **Stiff Little Fingers**.

As one would expect **The Jam** have featured on a number of compilations. Taking the cassette compilations first, a live version of *When You're Young* featured on *Dancin' Master* (NME 001) 1981; *Beat Surrender* was included on *Top Trax* (Weetabix CRUNCH 4) and *In The City* figured on *Pogo A-Go-Go* (NME 021) 1986. *SFX 6* (1982) includes Paul Weller talking about *The Gift*. Moving swiftly on to vinyl, *20 Of A Different Kind* (Polydor POLS 1006) 1979 includes *In The City* and *'A' Bomb In Wardour Street*, whilst *Vol. 2* (Polydor POLX 1) 1979 of the same series features *Strange Town* and *Butterfly Collector*. *Little Boy Soldiers* can be heard on *Life In The European Theatre* (WEA K 58412) 1982 and finally *In The City* appears on the 5-CD set *1-2-3-4 - A History Of Punk And New Wave 1976 - 1979* (MCA/Universal 60066) 1999.

The Jam's legacy has seldom been far away. In January 1983, Polydor reissued all 16 of **The Jam**'s singles and virtually all of them re-entered the charts simultaneously. This was unprecedented. Later that year Polydor put out a double-album greatest hits compilation *Snap* which reached No. 2 and spent 30 weeks in the charts. Eight years later, in 1991, a *Greatest Hits* album again rose to No. 2 and two years later *Live Jam* climbed to No. 28.

THE JAM - Down In The Tube Station At Midnight.

Avoid Pickwick's compilation *Wasteland* which is an arbitrary cross-section of their recordings between 1977 and 1979 which has very few points to commend it.

The Beat Surrender compilation from 1993 leans pretty heavily on their bigger hits like *When You're Young*, *Town Called Malice*, *Beat Surrender* and *Funeral Pyre*, but there are some good album tracks like *Pretty Green* and *Private Hell* thrown in and one 'B' side *Carnaby Street*.

The tracks on *Live Jam*, released in 1993, are taken from the Rainbow (1979), Newcastle City Hall (1980), Hammersmith Palais (1981), the Appollo Glasgow, Wembley Arena and the Edinburgh Playhouse (1982).

Extras is an authoritative collection of 'B' sides, demos and outtakes which Paul Weller described to Record Collector magazine in 1995 as "the best Jam compilation so far, for the real Jam fan".

The Jam Collection, is a two-CD set issued in 1996, which often omits 'A' sides of singles in favour of album tracks (there's the upfront *Burning Sky* and *Private Hell* and the sentimental *English Rose*, for example) and 'B' sides. The collection ends with the wonderfully laid back *Shopping*.

The same year Strange Fruit put a new cover on the four song *Peel Session* set they issued back in 1990. On the down side the version of *In The City* is a bit limp, but the version of *The Modern World* featured here was recorded some months before the album appeared. Also featured are *Art School* (with its Kinks-style ending) and *I've Changed My Address* (with country-rock style guitar licks).

In 1997, Polydor put out a 5-CD set *Direction Reaction Creation*, which was accompanied by an eighty-eight page colour booklet with gig lists, liner notes and rare photos. A few months later they reissued their first six albums digitally remastered and with extensive sleevenotes. Before the year was out *Precious* was included on *Just Can't Get Enough: New Wave Dance Hits Of The 80s* (Rhino R2 72586) 1997; *The Eton Rifles* got a further airing on *The Sound Of The Suburbs* (Columbia 488825 2) 1997 and *All Around The World* resurfaced on *A History Of Punk, Vol. 2* (Virgin CDOVD 487) 1997.

It's worth remembering that by the time **The Jam** disbanded in 1982 they had been far more successful than any of their contemporaries. Indeed, they had become the U.K.'s top band with eighteen Top 40 singles (including four No. 1's) and five Top 10 albums.

After Style Council's demise in 1990, Weller embarked on a successful solo career, discarding dance music for more soulful vocals and a guitar driven sound. His third studio album exceeded one million U.K. sales becoming the best selling album of his career.

Jam fans will be excited by Polydor's two box set of CD singles covering their 1977-79 and 1980-82 output. The box sets came with extras comprising CD-Roms of selected singles, limited edition Pennie Smith prints and sleevenotes from Paolo Hewitt.

The Jam successfully combined the power and energy of punk rock with mid-sixties mod fashion and were undoubtedly one of the finest bands of the punk/new wave era.

Japan

Personnel:
RICHARD BARBIERI	keyb'ds, synthesizer	AB
ROB DEAN	gtr, mandolin	A
STEVE JANSEN (STEVE BATT)	drms, perc	AB
MICK KARN (ANTHONY MICHAELIDES)	bs	AB
DAVID SYLVIAN (DAVID BATT)	vcls, gtr, keyb'ds	AB

HCP

ALBUMS:
1(A)	ADOLESCENT SEX	(Ariola AHAL 8004)	1978	-
2(A)	OBSCURE ALTERNATIVES	(Ariola AHAL 8007)	1978	-
3(A)	QUIET LIFE	(Ariola AHAL 5011)	1980	53
4(B)	GENTLEMEN TAKE POLAROIDS	(Virgin V 2180)	1980	45
5(A/B)	ASSEMBLAGE (comp.)	(Hansa HANLP 1)	1981	26
6(B)	TIN DRUM	(Virgin V 2209)	1981	12
7(A/B)	OIL ON CANVAS (live, dbl)	(Virgin VD 2513)	1983	5
8(A/B)	EXORCISING GHOSTS (dbl, comp)	(Virgin VED 3510)	1984	45

NB: (1) reissued in September 1982, then again on Fame (FA 41 3108) 1984 and on CD (Hansa) 1989. (2) reissued in September 1982, then again on Fame (FA 4130981) 1984 and on CD (Hansa) 1989. (1) and (2) reissued on cassette (Ariola XTWO 24) 1983. (3) reissued in 1981, then again on Fame (FA 3037) 1982 and on CD (Arista 251 261) 1993. (4) reissued in 1985 also on CD and then on CD (Virgin CDV 2180) 1988. (5) reissued on vinyl (Fame FA 3136) 1985. (6) reissued on vinyl (Virgin OVED 158) 1986, on CD (Virgin CDV 2209) 1988 and again on vinyl (Virgin LPCENT 41) 1997. (7) also issued on CD (Virgin CDVD 2513) 1992. (8) also issued on CD (Virgin VGDCD 3510) 1985, but with two tracks omitted. Later compilations included *Souvenir From Japan* (Ariola 410 360) 1989 also on CD (RCA 260.360) 1989, *The Other Side Of* (Receiver RR 150), also on CD (Receiver RRCD 150) 1991 and *In Vogue* (Camden 74321393382) 1996.

HCP

45s:
	Don't Rain On My Parade/ Stateline	(Ariola Hansa AHA 510)	1978 -
	The Unconventional / Adolescent Sex (some PS)	(Ariola Hansa AHA 525)	1978 -
*	Sometimes I Feel So Low/ Love's Infectious (PS)	(Ariola Hansa AHA 529)	1978 -
+	Life In Tokyo Pt. 1/Pt.2 (PS)	(Ariola Hansa AHA 540)	1979 -
+	Life In Tokyo (long)/ Life In Tokyo (short) (12", PS)	(Ariola Hansa AHAD 540)	1979 -
x	I Second That Emotion/ Quiet Life (PS)	(Ariola Hansa AHA 559)	1980 -
	Gentlemen Take Polaroids/The Experience Of Swimming (autographed PS)	(Virgin VS 379)	1980 60
	Gentlemen Take Polaroids/The Experience Of Swimming/ The Width Of A Room/ Burning Bridges (double pack, PS)	(Virgin VS 379)	1980 -
α	The Art Of Parties/ Life Without Buildings (PS)	(Virgin VS 409)	1981 48
α	Visions Of China/ Taking Islands In Africa	(Virgin VS 436)	1981 32

THE JAM - Beat Surrender (Compilation).

JAPAN - Oil On Canvas.

- α Ghosts/The Art Of
  Parties (alt. version) (picture disc)   (Virgin VS 472) 1982 5
- α Cantonese Boy/Burning Bridges/Gentlemen Take
  Polaroids/The Experience Of Swimming (double pack, PS)
      (Virgin VS 502) 1982 24

Reissues:
- α Life In Tokyo/
  European Son (PS)   (Ariola Hansa HANSA 4) 1981 -
- α Quiet Life/A Foreign Place/
  Fall In Love With Me (PS)   (Ariola Hansa HANSA 6) 1981 19
- α European Song/Alien (PS)   (Ariola Hansa HANSA 10) 1982 31
- α Live In Tokyo/Theme (PS)   (Ariola Hansa HANSA 17) 1982 28

Night Porter/Ain't That Peculiar (PS)   (Virgin VS 554) 1982 29
Night Porter/Ain't That Peculiar/
Methods Of Dance (12", PS)   (Virgin VS 55412) 1982 -
I Second That Emotion/   (Hansa HANSA 12) 1982 9
All Tomorrow's Parties/   (Hansa HANSA 18) 1983 38
Canton (live)/
Visions Of China (live) (PS)   (Virgin VS 581) 1983 42
Visions Of China/
Taking Islands In Africa (PS)   (Virgin VS 436) 1984 -
Visions Of China/Taking Islands In Africa/
Swing (12", PS)   (Virgin VS 43612) 1984 -
Ghosts/The Art Of Parties/
Visions Of China (3" CD EP)   (Virgin CDT 11) 1983 -
Gentlemen Take Polaroids/
Cantonese Boy (12" version)/Methods Of Dance
(12" version) (3" CD EP)   (Virgin CDT 32) 1988 -
I Second That Emotion/
All Tomorrow's Parties   (Old Gold OG 9666) 1987 -
I Second That Emotion/All Tomorrow's Parties/
Life In Tokyo (12")   (Old Gold OG 4020) 1987 -
Quiet Life/Life In Tokyo   (Old Gold OG 4031) 1987 -
Ghosts/Cantonese Boy   (Old Gold OG) 1987 -
I Second That Emotion/Quiet Life/
Life In Tokyo (CD EP)   (Old Gold OG) 1992 -

NB: * Initially issued on blue vinyl. + Released on red vinyl. x This was issued both in dull red vinyl with a card or paper picture sleeve and in black vinyl. α Also issued in 12" format.

Japan were formed in the Catford/Lewisham area of South London in the mid-seventies. The founding members were David Batt (later known as **David Sylvian**) who was born in Lewisham on 23rd February 1958, his brother Steve Batt (later known as Steve Jansen) who was also born in Lewisham on 1st December 1959 and school friends Richard Barbieri, born on 30th November 1957 and Anthony Michaelides (who later adopted the stage name **Mick Karn**), another Londoner born on 24th July 1958. An early influence on their music was Roxy Music. A second guitarist Rob Dean was recruited in response to a music press advert. Their initial big break came when they won a talent contest staged by the German label Ariola-Hansa, which had recently opened a London office. The label repsponded by offering the band a contract, which it duly accepted. At this point the Batt brothers and Michaelides adopted the stage names by which they became known.

Japan grew and developed during the punk era but the music they played was very much at the new wave end of the spectrum and in many ways far removed from the power and energy of punk. However, in appearance they looked every bit an over-the-top glam-punk band on the lines of The New York Dolls and recalling some of the theatrical style of Alice Cooper.

Their debut 45, in March 1978, was the Rogers-Hammerstein penned *Don't Rain On My Parade* from the musical 'Funny Girl'. It didn't chart but set them on their way. It was included on their debut album *Adolescent Sex*, on which the band played a form of guitar rock influenced by the likes of David Bowie and Roxy Music. It sold only moderately, as did the next 45 which culled two tracks *The Unconventional* and *Adolescent Sex* from the album. The 'A' side is a heavyish slab of rock funk. The flip side is promising too:-

"We're just another hype
But the pressure's getting harder"
(from *Adolescent Sex*)

In November 1978, a second album *Obscure Alternatives* was issued. The sound was still guitar dominated with **Sylvian**'s sneering vocals but it did utilise more keyboards and also delved, none too convincingly, into reggae and funk territory. One cut *Sometimes I Feel So Low* was selected for 45 release the same month, but neither the 45 or album were warmly received.

In May 1979, they enjoyed their debut hit, not here in Britain but in Japan with *Life In Tokyo*, which was produced by Giorgio Moroder.

Their British breakthrough came in early 1980 with their next album *Quiet Life*. The producer on this album was John Punter, who'd previously worked with Roxy Music. He was able to conjure up a sort of suave but decadent sound which moved them on from the glam-rock/punk of their early days and anticipated the sound of the New Romantic movement, which was just around the corner. The whole album is recommended but the stand-out track is a superb cover version of Velvet Underground's *All Tomorrow's Parties*, which allowed the group to display its full talents. It deservedly brought them their first chart success in the U.K., climbing to No. 53. The following month they produced a superb cover of Smokey Robinson's *I Second That Emotion*, which deserved to chart too but didn't at that time. It proved to be their last recording for Ariola-Hansa. In July 1980, they signed to Virgin and maintained their working relationship with producer John Punter. The same year *Ain't That Peculiar* was included on the *Cash Cows* (Virgin MILK 1) sampler.

Their new musical direction meant that Dean's guitar playing was superfluous. He departed, moving to L.A., but he later formed the disappointing Illustrated Man. The remaining quartet recorded the excellent *Gentlemen Take Polaroids* album. On this Barbieri's diverse keyboard playing incorporated oriental traditions which gave the music new adventure. The album peaked at No. 45 and spent ten weeks in the charts. It undoubtedly benefitted from the growing interest in the New Romantic movement, which the band's music was ideally suited to and in some respects anticipated. The title cut was issued with *Burning Bridges* (from the album) and two none album cuts *The Experience Of Swimming* and *The Width Of A Room* as a twin single package for the price of one.

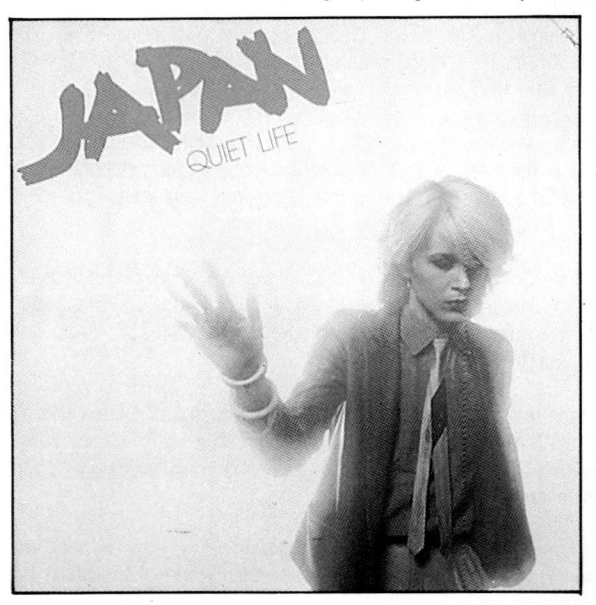

JAPAN - Quiet Life.

JAPAN - Tin Drum (CD).

Everyone likes a bargain and this was another factor in growing public interest in the band. The double pack 45 rose to No. 60, during its two week chart stay.

Highlighting this growing association with the New Romantic movement **Gary Numan** guested on their next 45 *The Art Of Parties*, which consolidated on their earlier chart success climbing to No. 48 in May 1981. As the band began work on a new album, their previous label Ariola-Hansa set out to exploit their growing success. In August 1981, *Life In Tokyo* was reissued on 45, along with the title cut from their earlier *Quiet Life* album which reached No. 19. They also put out a compilation of their earlier material *Assemblage*, which spent a staggering forty-six weeks in the chart peaking at No. 26. The cassette version of this release included remixes, three previously unreleased live recordings and an extra studio track.

Their new album *Tin Drum*, released in November 1981, was worth waiting for. Indeed it was their magnum opus. The standard was set by the superb and strongly oriental influenced opening cut *Visions Of China*, which was arguably the finest song they ever recorded. There is such diversity of musical styles here, ranging from Middle Eastern to Oriental to funk. The music exudes subtlety and is full of intricate rhythms and strong drumming. Technically excellent, in addition to *Visions Of China* many of their finest songs *Canton*, *Cantonese Boy* and *Ghosts* are on this album as well as their earlier single *The Art Of Parties*. Deservedly the album climbed to No. 12 and *Ghosts* (No. 5) and *Cantonese Boy* (No. 24) both enjoyed considerable chart success when released as 45s the following year.

By now though disagreements within the band, particularly between **Sylvian** and **Karn**, were beginning to disrupt what had previously been a united band. Fuel was added to the fire when band members started to concentrate on solo projects. In June 1982, **Karn** issued a 45 *Sensitive* for Virgin, which failed to chart; later, in November, his album *Titles* climbed to No. 74. Jansen and Barbieri guested on the album, along with Ricky Wilde and many others. It featured good bass, woodwind and keyboards. In July 1982, Hansa reissued their cover of *I Second That Emotion* and it climbed to No. 9 spending a total of eleven weeks in the charts. The following month, **Karn** and Jansen played on Japanese combo Akiko Yano's album whilst Barbieri produced Swedish band Lustans Lakejar. **Sylvian**, meanwhile, recorded *Bamboo Houses* with Yellow Magic Orchestra's Ryiuchi Sakamoto. The album was credited to Sylvian Sakamoto and climbed to No. 30.

As the band toured Britain, Hansa continued its reissue programme with *Life In Tokyo*, which made the No. 28 slot. The by now inevitable announcement of their split was made on 22nd November 1982, following a final Hammersmith Odeon concert. The following month, *Night Porter* got to No. 29 in the singles chart in which it spent a total of nine weeks.

As with so many bands, after they split, a number of exploitation releases followed. Hansa's final release in March 1983 was **Japan**'s revival of Velvet Underground's *All Tomorrow's Parties*. This made it to No. 38 during a four week chart residency. In May, a live version of *Canton* was released and became their final hit single in the U.K.

The double live LP *Oil On Canvas* recorded during their final U.K. tour was a fitting tribute to the band. It contained a good range of their material and most of their finest moments like *Gentlemen Take Polaroids*, *Visions Of China*, *Ghosts*, *Quiet Life*, *The Art Of Parties* and *Canton*. It also included a few songs like *Voices Raised In Welcome Hands Held In Prayer* and *Temple Of Dawn* not previously committed to vinyl. Guitarist Masami Tsuchiya from Ippu-Do assisted on this tour and therefore figured on the album too. It climbed to No. 5 in the charts, in which it spent a total of fourteen weeks.

Also of interest will be *Exorcising Ghosts*, a double album compilation of their later work issued by Virgin in November 1984. This peaked at No. 45 in the charts. Even after this, further exploitation 45 releases followed, but none of them sold significantly.

Following their split in 1982, **Sylvian** went solo. Just prior to this, a significant and highly recommended recording by him was *Forbidden Colours*, on which he teamed up with Ryuichi Sakamoto. Sakamoto also starred in the David Bowie/Tom Conti movie that 'Merry Christmas Mr. Lawrence' was the theme to. It rose to *No. 16* in the charts. **Karn** joined forces with former **Bauhaus** vocalist Pete Murphy to form the short-lived **Dali's Car**. Barbieri and Jansen formed Dolphin Bros. In the nineties **Sylvian** worked with Robert Fripp, whilst Jansen, Barbieri and **Karn** teamed up together again, releasing numerous albums on their own Medium label. Barbieri currently plays keyboards for Porcupine Tree.

In Vogue (CD) was a budget collection of their late seventies material for Ariola-Hansa. It includes awful cover versions of *I Second That Emotion* and *All Tomorrows Parties*. *Quiet Life* later resurfaced on *New Romantics* (EMI Gold CDGOLD 1041) in 1996, whilst *Gentlemen Take Polaroids* got a further airing on *A Post Punk Primer* (Virgin CDOVD 498) in 1997.

Japan remain a very unique band in the history of U.K. new wave. If you haven't heard them, they are definitely worth checking out.

J-C's Mainmen

Personnel: ARTURO BASSICK
  J-C CARROLL
  ED CASE
  ADRIAN LILLYWHITE
  CHRIS PAYNE

45: Casual Trousers/Earbending (PS) (Fresh FRESH 28) 1981

J-C's Mainmen comprised **The Members** J-C Carroll and other band members and **The Lurkers** Arturo Bassick. *Earbending* can also be heard on *Fresh Records Punk Singles Collection* (Anagram CDPUNK 32) in 1994.

JAPAN - Gentlemen Take Polaroids (CD).

Jell

Personnel:	LISA LISA	clarinet	A
	ERIC RANDOM	gtr, bs, drms	A
	LYNN SEED	melodica, voice	A

Jell were most notable for the involvement of **Eric Random**, who'd worked closely with **Cabaret Voltaire** among others and recorded several solo albums and singles in the eighties in his own right. He also fronted Eric Random and The Bedlamites. Jell's only vinyl outing seems to have been *I Dare Say It Will Hurt A Little*, a strange, offbeat, electronic composition which they contributed to *Some Bizzare Album* (Some Bizzare BZLP 1) in 1981.

The Jerks

Personnel:	CHARLES ACID	bs	A
	JOHNNY BEST	keyb'ds	A
	PAUL GILBERT	gtr	A
	KELV ISSUE	drms	A
	SIMON SNAKKE	vcls	A

45s:	Get Your Woofing Dog Off Me/		
	Hold My Hand (PS)	(Underground URA 1)	1978
	Cool/Cruisin' (Again) (PS)	(Lightning GIL 549)	1978
	Come Back Bogart/Are You Strong Enough?/		
	The Strangest Man Of All (PS)	(Laser LAS 25)	1980

NB: There's also a CD compilation *Jerk Off* (Overground OVER 65 CD) 1997.

The Jerks were a West Yorkshire combo. Their debut 45 *Get Your Woofing Dog Off Me* (a punk update of The Stooges' *I Wanna Be Your Dog*) was released on their own Underground label. Its cover shows the five-piece protecting their privates in a public loo as a policeman restrains his vicious-looking alsation. The session was funded by Phonogram.

If you want to know more go straight for Overground's chronological fifteen-track compilation which shows them to be a **Clash**-influenced club punk combo.

Get Your Woofing Dog Off Me and *Cool* later resurfaced on *Lightning Records Punk Collection* (Anagram CDPUNK 79) 1996.

The Jets

A punk quartet from London. They are not the same band who recorded on Soho Records, Good Vibrations, Rebel Records or EMI. They supported Steel Pulse at the Vortex and got to play on *Farewell To The Roxy* (Lightning LIP 2) 1978, which has been reissued on CD (Captain Oi! AHOY CD 86) 1998. Their contribution *TV Drink* is very rudimentary.

Joe Public

Personnel:	KEVIN LEADBETTER	vcls	A
	ROBB MARCHE	gtr	A
	SHAUN McLUSKEY	drms	A
	MIKE SMITH	bs	A

45:	Herman's Back/Travelling With Raymond/		
	Like It (PS)	(Wavelength HURT 3)	197?

This group also contributed one cut *Hotel Rooms* to the *4 Alternatives* (EP) (Heartbeat PULSE 4) in 1979.

Jilted John

ALBUM:	1	TRUE LOVE STORIES		
			(EMI International INS 3024)	1978

NB: (1) reissued with the addition of the **Gordon The Moron** 45, (Essential ESMCD 771) 1999.

HCP

45s:	Jilted John/Going Steady (PS)	(Rabid TOSH 105)	1978	-
	Jilted John/ Going Steady (PS)	(EMI International INT 567)	1978	4
	True Love/ I Was A Pre-Pubescent (PS)	(EMI Internatonal INT 577)	1978	-
	The Birthday Kiss/ Baz's Party (PS)	(EMI International INT 587)	1978	-

The man behind **Jilted John** was Graham Fellows. From Yorkshire originally he was a drama student in Manchester when he recorded this novelty punk disc for Rabid Records. Produced by Factory's Martin Hannett, the lyrics dealt with the angst of being jilted for a better looking guy. This was sung in a sort of downbeat monologue over a breakneck instrumental track. Word of the record soon got around and it came to EMI's attention. They reissued it and it became a classic 'one hit wonder' of the punk era. Spending twelve weeks in the charts, it peaked at No. 4.

The album is fun and full of similar tales like *I Was A Pre-Pubescent*, *Baz's Party* and *In The Bus Shelter*. The project also lead to a couple of less successful follow-ups from **Gordon The Moron** and **Julie and Gordon**.

Fellows wisely realised a project like this would be strictly time-limited and returned to acting. He was later in Coronation Street. In the nineties, he created a more resilient musical/comedy character in the form of John Shuttleworth.

Jilten John has resurfaced on several compilations including *20 Of A Different Kind* (Polydor POLS 1006) 1979, *Rabid/TJM Punk Singles Collection* (Receiver RRCD 227) 1996, *Punk And Disorderly: New Wave 1976 - 1981* (Telstar STAR 2520) 1991, *The Best Punk Album In The World.... Ever, Vol. 1* (2-CD) (Virgin VTDCD 42) 1995, *The Best Punk Anthems.... Ever* (2-CD) (Virgin VTDCD 198) 1998, *A History Of Punk, Vol. 1* (Virgin CDOVD 486) 1997, *New Wave Archive* (CD) (Rialto RMCD 201) 1997 and *1-2-3-4 - A History Of Punk And New Wave 1976 - 1979* (MCA/Universal MCD 60066) (5-CD Box set) 1999. *Seventeen* can also be found on *New Wave Archive* (Rialto RMCD 201) 1997.

Johnny and The Self-Abusers

Personnel:	CHARLIE BURCHILL	gtr	A
	TONY DONALD	bs	A
	JIM KERR	vcls	A
	ALI MACKENZIE	gtr	A
	BRIAN McGEE	drms	A
	ALLAN McNELL	keyb'ds	A
	JOHN MILARKY	gtr	A

45:	Saints And Sinners/Dead Vandals (PS)	(Chiswick NS 22)	1977

One of the shortest lived of punk outfits **Johnny and The Self-Abusers** went their separate ways the day after their 45 was released.

Kevin Burchill and McGee formed **Simple Minds** and rest is history as they say. For these two reasons the 45 is quite collectable.

Saints And Sinners later resurfaced on *Punk Lost And Found* (Shanachie SH 5705) 1996. A year later *Dead Vandals* was included on *The Chiswick Sampler (Good Clean Fun)* (Chiswick CDWIKX 162).

Garry Johnson

Garry Johnson was probably the best known of the Oi! poets whose proliferations were included on various Oi! albums. He made his debut on *Strength Thru Oi!* (Decca) 1981 with *National Service*, *Dead End Yobs* and *The New Face Of Rock 'n' Roll*. He then contributed *If Looks Could Kill* on *The Oi! Of Sex* (Syndicate SYNLP 4) 1984, also reissued on CD (Captain Oi! AHOY CD 23) 1994, he is backed by **Frankie Flame**. His verbal rants *The Young Conservatives* and *Boy About Town* had earlier appeared on *Son Of Oi!* (Syndicate SYNLP 3) 1983, also reissued on CD (Captain Oi! AHOY CD 9) 1993. *Carry On Oi!!* (Secret SEC 2) 1981 opens with his Oi! rallying call to punks 'n' skins *United*. This compilation was also reissued on CD (Captain Oi! AHOY CD 119) 1999.

The Jolt

Personnel:	ROB COLLINS	vcls, gtr	A
	JIM DOAK	bs	A
	KEVIN KEY	vcls	A
	IAIN SHEDDEN	drms	A

ALBUM:	1(A)	THE JOLT	(Polydor 2383 504) 1978
45s:		You're Cold/All I Can Do (PS)	(Polydor 2058 936) 1977
		What'cha Gonna Do About It/ Again And Again (die-cut PS)	(Polydor 2059 008) 1978
		I Can't Wait/Route 66 (PS)	(Polydor 2059 039) 1978
		Maybe Tonight/I'm In Tears/See Saw/ Stop Look (PS)	(Poydor 2229 215) 1979
		Maybe Tonight/ See Saw (promo only)	(Polydor 2229 215 DJ) 1979

A Scottish mod-influenced punk band from Glasgow who were very much in the mould of **The Jam** though not in the same class. The covered The Small Faces' *What'cha Gonna Do 'Bout It* and Paul Weller gave them *See Saw* to record.

Their best known song is probably *No Excuses* by virtue of its inclusion on *20 Of Another Kind* (Polydor SUPER POLS 1006) in 1979.

Josef K

Personnel incl:	PAUL HAIG	vcls		A

ALBUM:	1(A)	THE ONLY FUN IN TOWN	(Postcard 811) 1981

(up to 1986)

NB: (1) also issued on CD as part of *The Only Fun In Town/Sorry For Laughing* (Les Temps Moderne LTMCD 2305) 1990. Also relevant is *Young And Stupid* (Les Temps Moderne LTMCD 2307) 1989 and *Crazy To Exist (Live)* (LTMCD 2319)

45s:	*	Chance Meeting/Romance (PS)	(Absolute ABS 1) 1979
(up to 1986)	+	Radio Drill Time/Crazy To Exist (live) (PS)	(Postcard 80-3) 1980
	#	It's Kinda Funny/Final Request (PS)	(Postcard 80-5) 1980
	α	Chance Meeting/Pictures	(Postcard 81-5) 1981
		Sorry For Laughing/ Revelation (PS)	(Postcard 81-4/TWI 023) 1981

NB: * 1,000 copies only produced. + Came in hand-coloured fold around picture sleeves with blue labels. # Came with a picture sleeve in a polythene bag. Some copies had a picture insert. α Came in a die-cut sleeve. Some contained a postcard.

A Scottish band who produced a series of melancholic dark, brooding singles, which are all contained on their album.

Radio Drill Time was a manic but classic 45. Their planned debut album (which would have been the first for Postcard) was shrouded in doubt and the disc *Sorry For Laughing* was abandoned although twenty or so test pressings got out and were selling for considerable sums on the collectors market. The band returned to the studio and later emerged with an album, *The Only Fun In Town*. They broke up soon after the album was released and **Haig** went on to produce solo product which sounded similar to **New Order**. The later CD release on Les Temps Moderne combined both these albums on one CD. The CD suggests that the material on *Sorry For Laughing* benefited from cleaner production and possibly was the better of the two. Les Temps Moderne also put out a second CD *Young And Stupid*, which comprised the 'A' and 'B' sides of all their singles, BBC session material, their compilation appearances and two unreleased demo tracks; *Torn Mentor* and *Night Ritual*, which were recorded prior to their first single. There's also a strange cover of Alice Cooper's *Applebush*. Both CDs came with comprehensive liner notes.

Crazy To Exist (Live) features two live sets and in-depth sleevenotes. The first ten-cut show was recorded in 1981 in Scotland and was previously issued in Japan as the *Rare Live* album. The sound quality is good, but the band aren't on top form. The second set is from the Venue in London later the same year. Its ten songs duplicate five from the earlier show. Overall, it's an archival release.

Joy De Vivre

45:	Our Wedding	(Crass CR & SS ENVY 1) 1981

This flexidisc involving members of **Crass** is now rare. Issued on white vinyl it did not come in a picture sleeve, which was unusual for the times, though perhaps not for flexidiscs.

Joy Division

Personnel:	BERNARD ALBRECHT (BERNARD DICKEN)	gtr, vcls	A
	IAN CURTIS	vcls	A
	PETER HOOK	bs	A
	STEPHEN MORRIS	drms	A

				HCP
ALBUMS:	1(A)	UNKNOWN PLEASURES	(Factory FACT 10) 1979	71
	2(A)	CLOSER	(Factory FACT 25) 1980	6
	3(A)	STILL (live and rare) (dbl)	(Factory FACT 40) 1981	5
	4(A)	SUBSTANCE: 1977-1980	(Factory FACT 250) 1988	7

NB: (1) reissued 1982 and on CD (Factory FACD 10) 1986. It was issued again on CD (London 520016) 1994 and (Factory Too TEN 3894282232) 2000. (2) reissued 1982 and on CD (Factory FACD 25) 1986. It was issued again on CD (London 52 0015) 1994 and (London TEN 3894282192) 1999. (3) reissued on CD (Factory FACD 40) 1987, again (London 52 0017) 1994 and again (Factory Too TEN 3894282222) 2000. (4) reissued on CD with seven bonus tracks (Factory FACD 250) 1988 and again (London 52 0014) 1994. Also of relevance is *The Peel Sessions* (Strange Fruit SFR LP/CD 11) 1990, on vinyl and CD; *Preston - The Warehouse 28/2/80* (Fractured FACD 260) 2000; and *Closer Still (A Tribute To Joy Division) (Various Artists)* (Dressed To Kill FUCT 354) 2000. There's also a compilation *Permanent: The Best Of Joy Division* (London 828 624-1) 1995 also on CD, which got to No. 16 and *Heart And Soul* (4-CD box set) (London 828 968-2) 1997. Also of relevance are two various artists tributes to the band, *A Means To An End (The Music Of Joy Division)* (Hut CDHUT 29) 1995, *Ceremonial (A Tribute To Joy Division)* (Tess EFA 064982) 1996 and *The Complete BBC Recordings* (Strange Fruit SFRSCD 094) 2000.

EPs:	1(A)	AN IDEAL FOR LIVING (An Ideal For Living/Warsaw/

JOY DIVISION live at The Electric Ballroom, London 26th October 1979.
Photo: Steven Richards.

JOY DIVISION - Live at The Electric Ballroom, London 26th October 1979. Photo: Steven Richards.

	Leaders Of Men/No Love Lost/ Failures) (10", PS)	(Enigma PSS 139) 1978
2(A)	THE PEEL SESSIONS (31/1/79) (Exercise One/ Insight/She's Lost Control/ Transmission) (12", PS)	(Strange Fruit SFPS 013) 1986
3(A)	THE PEEL SESSIONS 2 (26/11/79) (Love Will Tear Us Apart/24 Hours/Colony/ Sound Of Music) (12", PS)	(Strange Fruit) 1987

NB: (1) only 1,000 issued originally. (1) reissued as a 12" EP, 1,200 pressed (Anonymous ANON 1) 1978, then reissued and retitled *The Ideal Beginning* (Enigma) 1985. (2) reissued on CD (Strange Fruit SFPSCD 013) 1988. (3) reissued on CD (Strange Fruit SFPSCD 033) 1988. (2) and (3) later issued on one album *The Peel Sessions* (Strange Fruit SFRLP 111) 1990, also on CD (SFRCD 111) 1990.

			HCP
45s:	Transmission/Novelty (PS)	(Factory FAC 13) 1979	-
*	Komakino/Incubation/(As You Said)	(Factory FAC 28) 1980	-
	Love Will Tear Us Apart/These Days/Love Will Tear Us Apart (alt. version) (PS)	(Factory FAC 23) 1980	13
	Love Will Tear Us Apart/These Days/Love Will Tear Us Apart (alt. version) (12", PS)	(Factory FAC 23-12) 1980	-
	Transmission/Novelty (12", PS)	(Factory FAC 13-12) 1981	-
	Atmosphere/The Only Mistake (PS)	(Factory FAC 2137) 1988	34
	Atmosphere/The Only Mistake/The Sound Of Music/Love Will Tear Us Apart (12", PS)	(Factory FAC 213) 1988	-
	Atmosphere/Love Will Tear Us Apart/ Transmission (live) (CD)	(Factory FACD 213) 1988	-
	Love Will Tear Us Apart (Radio Version) (Arthur Baker Remix)/Atmosphere (12")	(London UK YOJX 1) 1995	-
	Love Will Tear Us Apart (Radio Version)/Love Will Tear Us Apart/These Days/ Transmission (live) (CD)	(London UK YOJCD 1) 1995	-

NB: * Flexidisc, only 10,000 pressed.

Joy Division, now a legendary band of this era, were formed as Warsaw by Ian Curtis, Bernard Albrecht (who was born as Bernard Dickens), Peter Hook and Stephen Morris in mid-1977 in Salford, Manchester. The name Warsaw was taken from a cut on David Bowie's *Low* album. Curtis and Morris were both from Macclesfield originally. The band originally came together six months previously as The Stiff Kittens, but didn't get to the stage of gigging.

Warsaw made their debut on 29th May 1977 at Manchester's Electric Circus. They were first support act on a bill that included **The Buzzcocks** and **Penetration**. On 18th July 1977, they entered the Pennine Sound Studios in Oldham and recorded a five song demo. The songs - *Inside The Line*, *Gutz*, *At A Later Date*, *The Kill* and *You're No Good For Me* - were all later included on a bootleg 12" *The Ideal Beginning* (Enigma PSS 138) 1981. Significantly though, they weren't considered sufficiently worthwhile to include on their 1997 4-CD box set *Heart And Soul*.

In December 1977, Warsaw changed their name to **Joy Division** to avoid comparison with **Warsaw Pakt**, a London-based punk band who had just issued their first album. The name **Joy Division** was taken from Nazi concentration camp novel 'House Of Dolls'. Inevitably this caused them some media problems with a few unfairly branding them as little Nazis.

On 14th April 1978, they played at an audition night at Manchester Rafters Club, which was organised by Stiff and Chiswick, two of the top indie labels. They were the last band to come on stage, at about 2 a.m. in the morning, but they made a lasting impression on a number of people. Most important of all journalist Tony Wilson, who'd just set up his Factory Records label was there and so was club DJ and their future manager Rob Gretton.

In June 1978, they issued *An Ideal For Living* (EP) on their own Enigma label. The record is now extremely rare. Expect to pay in excess of £100 for a copy. Its fold-out sleeve stated "this is not a record - it is an enigma". A later release on Anonymous is also very hard to find and expensive to purchase now. The same month they contributed *At A Later Date* to the 10" compilation *Short Circuit - Live At The Electric Circus* (Virgin VCL 5003) 1978. Some copies of this compilation were issued in orange and yellow vinyl and these are now very collectable.

Later in January 1979, having signed to Factory, they contributed two tracks *Digital* and *Glass* to the label's double-pack compilation EP *A*

JOY DIVISION - Closer.

Factory Sample (Factory FAC 2) 1979. Both tracks were produced by Martin Hannett. This EP is also very rare and has been counterfeited. Originals have stickers and very loose shrinkwrap.

In June 1979, they contributed two further tracks to the 12" EP *Earcom 2* (Fast Products FAST 9B) 1979. The tracks in question were *Auto-suggestion* and *From Safety To Where?*.

Factory owner put his life savings £8,000 into the recording of their debut album *Unknown Pleasures*, which was again produced by Martin Hannett. It enabled 10,000 copies to be produced. The album was stunning and highly original. They conjured up a chilling, despondent and dark sound upon which sounds of ambulance sirens and breaking glass interject. It is unreservedly recommended. At the time it topped the indie chart and climbed to No. 71 nationally after it was redistributed in July 1980. As they became more popular and in demand, they increased their live performances. This put greater pressure on vocalist Ian Curtis' health. He was an epileptic. Eventually this had disastrous consequences.

In October 1979, their classic 45 *Transmission* was released. Although it didn't chart it was critically acclaimed. Their rapidly growing reputation was enhanced still further by *Love Will Tear Us Apart* in April 1980. Initially, it made the indie charts, but a couple of months after Curtis' suicide it gave them a Top 20 hit, peaking at No. 13 during a nine week chart residency. The same month Factory took the very unusual step of providing record stalls with a three track flexidisc containing *Komakino*, *Incubation* and *As You Said* to be given away free to fans. The band completed a second album *Closer* and played a number of live gigs in Britain. Unfortunately, some had to be cancelled due to Curtis' ill health.

The devastating blow came when Curtis hung himself in the early hours of 18th May - a few days before they were due to fly to the 'States for a tour.

As with so many bands their greatest commercial success came after the death of their star, but who knows how big they might have become if he'd have lived!

Closer was another superb album. Tracks like *Isolation*, *Heart And Soul*, *Twenty Four Hours* and *Decades* conjured up a distant and empty sound with somewhat distorted synthesizers and Curtis' meandering and gloomy vocals, whilst *Atrocity Exhibition* conveyed a situation of sheer chaos and despair. This is also strongly recommended. In the wake of Curtis' death this climbed to No. 6, spending eight weeks in the charts.

Curtis was such a central figure it was clear the band couldn't continue without him and, in January 1979, the remaining three re-launched as **New Order**, with Albrecht taking over the vocal role.

It was of course, inevitable that any **Joy Division** material still in the can would quickly find its way onto vinyl. Much of this material was collected on *Still* and released in October 1981. The double album comprised studio outtakes, including a version of the Velvet Underground's *Sister Ray*, the only cover version they ever recorded and a live disc. A good representative collection of their material, it climbed to No. 5 in the U.K.,

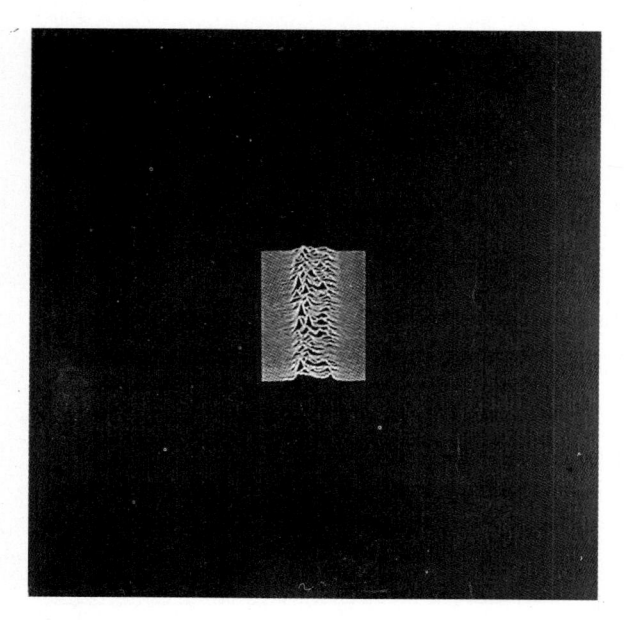

JOY DIVISION - Unknown Pleasures.

spending a total of twelve weeks in the charts. Later, in August 1982, Factory's video division Ikon issued 'Here Are The Young Men', a 60-minute live video of the band, which was later re-released in 1988.

In November 1983, *Love Will Tear Us Apart* re-entered the charts, climbing to No. 19. Later in 1988, *Atmosphere* was reissued and reached No. 34. The same year Factory released a new compilation album of the band's material, *Substance 1977-80*. It included some, but not all of their finest moments, and climbed to No. 7 in the charts. The CD version contained seven extra tracks so is better value. It was reissued again in 1993.

Joy Division recorded two sessions for John Peel in all on 31st January and 26th November 1979. They are shown in the EP discography above, as both were issued initially on 12" EPs in November 1986 and September 1987 respectively. Both were later reissued on separate CD EPs in July 1988. Alternatively, the two sessions can be heard together on album or CD on Strange Fruit (1990).

Any real fan of the band will want *Heart And Soul*, a four-CD box set, issued by London in 1997. This covers the band's musical history from the sessions which produced its first single in December 1977. It contains their two classic studio albums, *Unknown Pleasures* and *Closer*, several 45 cuts and contributions to compilations, radio session recordings, a few studio demos, one disc of previously unissued live recordings and, finally, two previously unreleased recordings taped at their final rehearsal session. The sleeve notes are penned by Paul Morley.

It was a very unrepresentative track of theirs *Warsaw* which was included on the 5-CD box set compilation *1-2-3-4 - A History Of Punk And New Wave 1976 - 1979* (MCA/Universal MCD 60066) in 1999. However, their classic *Transmission* figured on the 4-CD set *25 Years Of Rough Trade Shops* (Mute CDSTUMM 191) in 2001.

The Complete BBC Recordings, issued on Strange Fruit in 2000, not only comprises their two Peel sessions (which have been issued before and include early versions of classic songs like *Transmission*, *Love Will Tear Us Apart* and *She's Lost Control*), but also versions of *Transmission* and *She's Lost Control* which they performed on BBC's 'Something Else' show in September 1979 and a brief off-air interview with Ian Curtis and Steve Morris on Radio One's 'Rock On' show from August 1979. Well worth purchasing for fans of the band.

Joy Division were one of the really great indie alternative rock bands. Their unsettling and slightly sinister, dark music was original and exceptional. An essential band for new wave fans.

The Jump

45s:	Shake Up/All In Vain (PS)	(Caveman CLUB 1)	1980
	Tomorrow's Mine/Love In The Park	(Rewind REWIND 4)	1981

An obscure mod band. Their singles have attracted little interest from collectors to date.

Jump Squad

Personnel:	STEVE BREWER	drms	A
	SIMON HART	vcls	A
	PETER LEY	gtr	A
	PHILLIP LEY	bs	A

45:	Lord Of The Dance/Debt (PS)	(101 UR 2) 1981

This band was earlier known as **Embryo**. Both sides of the 45 were later included on *Punk Rock Rarities, Vol. 1* (Anagram CDPUNK 63) 1995. The highlight of their career was a successful tour of Malta. They later changed names to The Untouchables, releasing a white label 45 *Protect Your Love*. Then, in 1985, they became Under The Gun, releasing 45s on Wizz and Rampant. In 1989, the Ley brothers and Steve Brewer became The Guitar Gangsters, whose albums included *Prohibition* (Link LINK LP 105) 1989, *Money With Menace* (Vice HABIT 001) and *Power Chords For England* (Anagram CDMGRAM 78) 1994.

The Junco Partners

45s:	Swinging Sixties Boys/Peepin 'N' Hidin'	(Rigid JUNK 1028) 1979
	Tall Windows/Noizez In My Head (PS)	(Energy NRG 4) 1981
*	Tall Windows (Extended)/Noizez In My Head (Extended) (12", promo-only)	(Energy NRGX 4) 1981

NB: * This came in a plain sleeve with a stickered white label.

A sixties band who recorded a 45 for Columbia in 1965 and an album for Philips in 1971. They returned to include a sixties photo for the cover of their mod-style *Swinging Sixties Boys* 45.

Just Frank

45:	You/(other side by **Split Screens**)	(Rok ROK III/IV) 1980

A Leeds band, whose melodic *You* was also included on *Odds Bods Mods And Sods* (Rok ROK LP 1). Its roots lie in British beat circa 1964 as much as in the mid-sixties mod sound. *Odds Bods Mods And Sods*, incidentally, has been reissued on CD (Captain Mod MODSKA CD 2) 1996, with several bonus cuts. You'll also find *You* on *100% British Mod* (Captain Mod MODSKA DCD 8) 1998.

Justin Case

45:	TV/(other side by **Straight Up**)	(Rok ROK XIX/XX) 1980

Little is known about this band. *TV* is pretty ordinary. It can also be heard as a bonus cut on the Captain Mod CD reissue of *Odds Bods Mods And Sods* (MODSKA CD 2) 1996, which originally included their only other known recording *Staik Motion*, which with some catchy guitar flashes, is the stronger of the two. This was later included on *100% British Mod* (Captain Mod MODSKA DCD 8) 1998

Harry Kakoulli

ALBUM:	1	EVEN WHEN I'M NOT	(Oval OVLP 505) 1980

45s:	I'm On A Rocket/I Wanna Stay	(Oval HARRY 18) 1980
	Baby Don't Like/Jealous Mind	(Strut STRUT 1) 1983
	Sugar Daddy (2 Versions) (PS)	(Strut STRUT 3) 1985
	Sugar Daddy (2 Versions) (12", PS)	(Strut STRUT X3) 1985

This album is a respectable popish effort from this former member of **Squeeze**. He's assisted by Garrell Redfearn (synthesizer), Nick Robbins (drms) and Nigel Sharpe (gtr).

Billy Karloff

Personnel:	GLEN BUGLASS	bs	A
	NEIL HAY	gtr	A
	PAUL JELLIMAN	gtr	A

	BILLY KARLOFF	vcls	A
	BRIAN 'DOLPHIN' TAYLOR	drms	A

ALBUM: 1(A)   THE MANIAC   (White) 1978

45s: Back Street Billy/Crazy Paving (PS) (Wanted CULT-45-001) 1978
       Summer Holiday/It's Too Hot (PS)   (Warner Bros K 17818) 1981
    * Headbangers/
       Don't Keep Me Down (PS)   (Warner Bros K 17753) 1981

NB: * Credited to **Billy Karloff** and The Extremes.

Billy Karloff and his colleagues operated under a number of different names in this era, including The Punks, Scum Of The Earth, **Billy Karloff** and The Goats, **Billy Karloff** Band, **Billy Karloff** and The Supremes and **Billy Karloff** and The Extremes, who recorded the *Headbangers* 45.

Of his band, Brian Taylor had previously been with **The Tom Robinson Band** and Hay and Jelliman had come from Somme.

Musically, we're talking **Sham 69** style punk. They were a popular live attraction at London's Roxy Club in those halycon days.

In their final incarnation, the band got a deal with U.S. label Warner Brothers and put out a U.S.-only album of punk shouters, *Let Your Fingers Do The Talking*, in 1981.

Aside from these albums and 45s, they contributed one cut, *Relics From The Past* to the *Farewell To The Roxy* (Lightning LIP 2) 1978 compilation album. Both sides of the *Back Street Billy* 45 can also be found on *Punk Rock Rarities, Vol. 1* (Anagram CDPUNK 63) 1995.

Karma Sutra

Personnel:	BUNGLE	A
	GEOFFREY	A
	GEORGE	A
	ZIPPY	A

CASS: 1(A)   IF YOU ENVY THE DESIRABLE

The above is a six-track cassette notable for some driving guitar work delivered within a punk format. The material is varied, utilising sound effects in places, and is worth seeking out. There were probably other cassettes.

Mick Karn

                                                                          HCP
ALBUMS: 1   TITLES   (Virgin V 2249) 1982 74
(up to
1986)

NB: (1) also issued on CD (Virgin CDV 2249) 1990.

                                                                          HCP
45s: It Doesn't Matter Anymore/
(up to   Wide Boy (PS)   (RPM RPM 5118) 1981 -
1986)   Sensitive/   (Virgin V) 1982 -
       *   After A Fashion/Textures   (Musicfest FEST 1) 1983 39
       *   After A Fashion/Textures (12", PS) (Musicfest FESTX 1) 1983 -

NB: * Credited to **Midge Ure** and **Mick Karn**.

This guy's real name was Anthony Michaelides and he was born in London on 24th July 1958. In the early eighties **Karn** was bassist with **Japan**. He released the above solo album when they split up in 1982. In addition to **Karn**, it featured several session musicians and it climbed to No. 74, spending a total of three weeks in all in the album charts. It featured good bass, woodwind and keyboards.

In June 1983, he teamed up with **Ultravox**'s **Midge Ure** for a one-off 45 *After A Fashion*. This spent four weeks in the charts, peaking at No. 39. *After A Fashion* later resurfaced on *New Romantics* (EMI Gold CDGOLD 1041) in 1996.

In 1984, he formed **Dali's Car** wiith ex-**Bauhaus** singer Pete Murphy, but he returned to concentrate on his solo career in 1986 recording a 45 *Buoy* in 1987, which was credited to **Mick Karn** featuring David Sylvian. He recorded further albums *Dreams Of Reasons Produce Monsters* (1987), *Bestial Cluster* (1993), *Beginning To Melt* (1994), with former **Japan** colleagues Steve Jansen and Richard Barbieri, *Polytown* (1994) with David Torn and Terry Bozio and *Tooth Mother* (1995).

Karn is also an accomplished sculptor and his work has been exhibited in galleries around the world.

Klark Kent

ALBUM: 1   KLARK KENT (10")   (A&M AMLE 68511) 1980

NB: (1) issued on green vinyl.

                                                                          HCP
45s: *   Don't Care/Thrills/Office Girls (PS)   (Kryptone KK 1) 1978 -
      +   Don't Care/Thrills/Office Girls (PS)   (A&M AMS 7376) 1978 48
      x   Too Kool To Kalypso/
          Theme For Kinetic Ritual (PS)   (Kryptone KMS 7390) 1978 -
      x   Away From Home/Office Talk (PS)   (A&M AMS 7532) 1980 -
      x   Rich In A Ditch/Grandelinquent (PS)   (A&M AMS 7554) 1980 -

NB: * Most on green vinyl, some on black. + Issued on green or black vinyl. x Issued on green vinyl.

This was a pseudonym for former Curved Air drummer Stewart Copeland, who was banging the skins for **The Police** in this era. American-born Copeland arrived in Britain in the early seventies to join his rock manager brother Miles and his other brother Ian, who was a booking agent.

Don't Care was released on the indie label Kryptone in May 1978 and Copeland played all the instruments on the accomplished power-pop single. When A&M picked it up and re-released it in August it sneaked into the Top 50. The follow-up *Too Kool To Kalypso*, released in November 1978, wasn't in the same class and failed to chart. With **The Police**'s success at the end of the seventies Copeland put this sideline on hold until 1980 when he returned with a mini-album and more singles.

The 10" album was basically a compilation of his 45s. The 10" release came on green vinyl in a K-shaped jacket. The standout tracks are the instrumental *Theme For Kinetic Ritual* and *Don't Care*, a clever sort of pop-punk amalgam, which spent four weeks in the charts, peaking at No. 48 when issued as a 45. Back in 1979 *Don't Care* and *Office Girls* were included on the *No Wave* (A&M AMLE 68505) 1979 sampler. *Don't Care* later resurfaced on *1-2-3-4 - A History Of Punk And New Wave 1976 - 1979* (MCA/Universal MCD 60066), a lavish 5-CD box set issued in 1999.

Since the disbandment of **The Police** in 1984 Copeland has branched into TV and film projects including 'Wall Street', 'Talk Radio', 'Rapa Nui' and 'The Equaliser'. He also composed a full opera for the Cleveland Opera called 'Holy Blood and The Crescent Moon'.

The Kidz Next Door

Personnel:	GRANT FLEMMING	bs	A
	ANGUS HOPE (TOOTHPASTE)	gtr	A
	ROBBIE PURSEY	vcls	A
	PETER WOODLEY	drms	A

45:   What's It All About?/
      The Kidz Next Door (PS)   (Warner Bros K 17492) 1979

Sham 69's **Jimmy Pursey** handled production on this mod revival band's 45 and his younger brother Robbie was in the band! Consequently this 45 is now quite collectable.

The Killermeters

Personnel:	GRAHAM JESSOP	drms	A
	MICK MOORE	gtr	AB
	SID RUTTLE	bs	AB

	TONY RUTTLE	gtr	AB
	VIC VESPA (SZCZESNOWICZ)	vcls	AB
	GARY WESTWELL	drms	B

45s:	Why Should It Happen To Me?/		
	Cardiac Arrest (Some PS)	(Psycho P 2620)	1979
	Twisted Wheel/SX 225 (PS)	(Gem GEMS 22)	1980

NB: There's also a compilation, *Metric Noise* (Detour DRCD 013) 1997, also on a double album.

Fronted by Vic Vespa (he'd been known as Vic Vomit and his real name was Szczesnowicz) in his earlier days as a punk. **The Killermeters** out of Huddersfield were the north's top mod act. As such they supported the big 'mod revival' acts like **The Purple Hearts** and **Secret Affair** as well as touring with pop-punk outfits like **The Undertones** and **Eddie and The Hotrods**.

A mix-up at the printers meant that only the last batch of their debut 45 *Why Should It Happen To Me?* came in picture sleeves. As a result they later gave some sleeves away at gigs. The single was a melodic mod-pop offering. *Twisted Wheel*, their second 45 was a tribute to the Northern Soul venue. By now, Gary Westwell had replaced Graham Jessop on drums. The track on the reverse side titled *SX 225* was a reference to a brand of customised Lambretta.

A third 45 got to the demo stage but was shelved as they renamed themselves Soldiers Are Dreamers and latched onto the psychedelic revival scene.

The Metric Noise compilation kicks off with their Psycho 45 and also includes their 45 for Gem and their remaining output and six demos. Also included are covers of The Nazz's *Open My Eyes* and The Byrds' *Eight Miles High*. It's a primitive but enjoyable collection of their material.

The Killermeters have also featured on a number of compilations. *Twisted Wheel* and *SX 225* can also be heard on *This Is Mod, Vol. 2* (Anagram CDMGRAM 101) 1996, whilst *Why Should It Happen To Me* and *Cardiac Arrest* can also be found on *This Is Mod, Vol. 5* (Anagram CDMGRAM 110) 1997. Their finest moment, *Why Should It Happen To Me* also got a further airing on *This Is Mod* (dbl) (Get Back GET 39) 1999 and *100% British Mod* (Captain Mod MODSKA DCD 8) 1998.

Killing Joke

Personnel:	JAZ COLEMAN	vcls	ABC
(up to	MARTIN 'YOUTH' GLOVER	bs, vcls	A
1986)	PAUL FERGUSON	drms	ABC
	GEORDIE WALKER	gtr, synthesizer	ABC
	GUY PRATT	bs	B
	PAUL RAVEN	bs	C

				HCP
ALBUMS:	1(A)	KILLING JOKE	(Polydor EGMD 545) 1980	39
(up to	2(A)	WHAT'S THIS FOR?		
1986)			(Malicious Damage EGMD 550) 1981	42
	3(B)	REVELATIONS	(Malicious Damage EGMD 3) 1982	12
	4(B)	HA-KILLING JOKE LIVE	(E.G. EGMDT 4) 1982	66
	5(C)	FIRE DANCES	(E.G. EGMD 5) 1983	29
	6(C)	NIGHT TIME	(E.G. EGLP 61) 1985	11
	7(C)	BRIGHTER THAN A THOUSAND SUNS		
			(E.G. EGLP 66) 1986	-

NB: (1) later reissued and on CD (E.G. EGCD 57) 1987. (2) later reissued and on CD (E.G. EGCD 58) 1987. (3) later reissued and on CD (E.G. EGCD 59) 1987. (4) was a 10" mini-album. (5) later reissued and on CD (E.G. EGCD 60) 1987. (6) later reissued and on CD (E.G. EGCD 61) 1987. (7) also issued on CD (E.G. EGCD 66) 1986. There's also a compilation on vinyl and CD, *Laugh, I Nearly Bought One* (Virgin EG CDV 2693) 1992.

EP:	1(A)	Nervous System/Turn To Red/		
(up to		Are You Receiving	(Malicious Damage MD 410) 1979	
1986)				

NB: (1) This 10" EP came in a bag. Some copies had pictures and four cards.

			HCP
45s:	Turn To Red/Nervous System (PS)	(Island WIP 6550) 1980	-
(up to	Almost Red/Nervous System/Are You Receiving?/		
1986)	Turn To Red (12", PS)	(Island 12 WIP 6550) 1980	-
	Wardance/Psyche (PS)	(Malicious Damage MD 540) 1980	-
	Requiem/Changes (PS)	(E.G. EGMD 1.00) 1980	-
	Requiem/Change/Change/		
	Requiem (12")	(E.G. EGMX 1.00) 1980	-
	Follow The Leaders/Tension (PS)	(E.G. EGMDS 1.01) 1981	55
	Follow The Leaders/Follow The Leaders - Dub/		
	Tension (10", PS)	(E.G. EGMDX 1.01) 1981	-
	Empire Song/Brilliant (PS)	(E.G. EGO 4) 1982	43
	Chop Chop/Good Samaritan (PS)	(E.G. EGO 7) 1982	-
	Birds Of A Feather/		
	Flock-The B Side (PS)	(E.G. EGO 10) 1982	64
	Birds Of A Feather/		
	Flock-The B Side (12", PS)	(E.G. EGOX 10) 1982	-
	Let's All Go (To The Fire Dances)/		
	Dominator (PS)	(E.G. EGO 11) 1983	51
	Let's All Go (To The Fire Dances)/		
	The Fall Of Because (live)/		
	Dominator (alt version) (12", PS)	(E.G. EGOX 11) 1983	-
	Me Or You/Wilful Days/		
	Feast Of Blaze (double pack, gatefold PS)		
		(E.G. EGOD 14/KILL ½) 1983	57
	Me Or You/Feast Of Blaze/Let's All Go (To The Fire		
	Dances)/The Full Of Because (live)/Dominator		
	(alt version) (12", sealed double pack)	(E.G. EGOXD 14) 1983	-
	Eighties/Eighties (Coming Mix) (PS)	(E.G. EGO 16) 1984	60
	Eighties (Serious Dance Mix)/Eighties/		
	Eighties (Coming Mix) (12", PS)	(E.G. EGOX 16) 1984	-
	A New Day/Dance Day (PS)	(E.G. EGO 17) 1984	56
	A New Day (Dub Mix)/		
	A New Day (12", PS)	(E.G. EGOX 17) 1984	-
	Love Like Blood/Blue Feather (PS)	(E.G. EGO 20) 1985	16
	Love Like Blood (Gestalt Mix)/Love Like Blood/		
	Blue Feather (12", PS)	(E.G. EGOY 20) 1985	-
	Kings And Queens		
	(Knave Mix) (12", PS)	(E.G. EGOY 21) 1985	58
+	Kings And Queens (The Right Royal Mix)/The Madding Crowd/		
	Kings And Queens (12", PS with poster)	(E.G. EGOX 21) 1985	-
	Adorations/Exile (PS)	(E.G. EGO 27) 1986	42
	Adorations/Exile/Ecstacy (12", PS)	(E.G. EGOY 27) 1986	-
	Adorations/Exile/Ecstacy/		
	Adorations (instr. mix) (double-pack)	(E.G. EGOD 27) 1986	-
	Sanity/Goodbye To The Village (PS)	(E.G. EGO 30) 1986	70
	Sanity/Goodbye To The Village/		
	Victory (12", PS)	(E.G. EGOY 30) 1986	-
	Sanity/Goodbye To The Village (Stickered PS and		
	'Wardance' remix cassette)	(E.G. EGO 30) 1986	-

NB: + There was also a version with a different and withdrawn picture sleeve.

KILLING JOKE - A New Day.

Killing Joke were formed in London by Jaz Coleman and Paul Ferguson, although they soon moved to Cheltenham. They weren't part of the original punk explosion and its early eighties revival, but they were an important part of the U.K. new wave and without punk, their blistering guitar assault probably wouldn't have caught on.

KILLING JOKE - Killing Joke.

Jaz Coleman had actually been born in Egypt and Martin 'Youth' Glover had begun his life in Africa too.

Their muical style was quite unique, mixing post-punk angst with experiemental rock and occult lyrics. Jaz Coleman wrote most of their material, often assisted by the other group members.

They played some early gigs supporting **Joy Division** and **The Ruts** before signing to Island-E.G. and starting their own label Malicious Damage. They released a three track single on it in October 1979. Three singles - *Nervous System*, *Wardance* and *Requiem* - followed, which got quite a lot of exposure over the airwaves from DJ John Peel. They then released their eponymous debut album. This spanned both heavy metal and the new wave. It's basically a guitar, bass and drums assault filtered through distortion and tone modulation, but some use is made of synthesizers. Most of the music is delivered at breakneck speed and enough people bought it to propel it to No. 39 in the charts, in which it spent a total of four weeks in all.

Released in May 1981, *Follow The Leaders* gave them their first U.K. hit single, climbing to No. 55. *What's This For?* was a more funk and dance-orientated album. It again sold quite well, peaking at No. 42, during its five week chart residency.

After this Martin 'Youth' Glover left to form **Brilliant**. He was replaced by Guy Pratt on bass. The new line-up released *Revelations*, which marked a return to the brutal guitar, bass and drum assault on the senses. Their best selling album to date, it peaked at No. 12 spending six weeks in the charts. It spawned two 45s - *Empire Song*, which came out a month before and got to No. 43 and *Chop-Chop*, which failed to chart. It seems Ferguson and Coleman disappeared to Iceland before the album was released, alledgedly because they thought the apocalypse was coming. They worked there with various local bands.

When they returned their next 45 *Birds Of A Feather* was more accessible and tuneful than some of their previous work, although this wasn't particularly reflected in sales as it only reached No. 64 and spent just two weeks in the charts. The same year they recorded a live 10" album in Toronto, Canada. This made the lower reaches of the album charts.

At this point Guy Pratt departed to join Icehouse and Paul Raven, formerly with **Neon Hearts**, took over on bass. The new line-up recorded the excellent *Fire Dances*, which was released in July 1983. This contained many of their finest songs *Rejuvenation*, *Feast Of Blaze* and *Frenzy* and took them into the Top 30 for the second time. The title cut, *Let's All Go (To The Dances)* was released as a 45 the previous month and brought them a No. 51 hit.

After a break of nearly two years, during which they enjoyed more minor hits with *Me Or You*, *Eighties* and *A New Day*, they returned with a new album *Night Time* in February 1985. Rising to No. 11 during a nine week chart tenure this proved to be their most successful album of all and it contained their magnum opus *Love Like Blood*, which became their biggest hit, peaking at No. 16. It epitomised all that was best about their music - a scorching guitar assault on the senses, with pounding rhythms and hard-hitting lyrics.

After the success of *Night Time* their next album *Brighter Than A Thousand Suns* was relatively disappointing, spending just one week in the charts at No. 54. Two cuts *Adorations* and *Sanity* were culled for 45 release and each of them met with modest success. *Adorations* spent six weeks in the charts in all climbing to No. 42 and *Sanity* occupied the No. 70 slot for one week.

They continued into the nineties with line-up changes, but that's beyond the time-span of this book and besides their finest hours were in the early and mid-eighties.

Most of their finest songs can be heard on the 1992 compilation, *Laugh, I Nearly Bought One*.

They also appeared on a number of compilations, including *Eighties* on *The Best Punk Album In The World... Ever, Vol. 1* (2-CD) (Virgin VTDCD 42) 1995, *Wait* on *Burning Ambitions (A History Of Punk)* (Anagram CDBRED 3) 1996, *Love Like Blood* re-emerged on *New Wave Classics* (dbl) (Disky DOU 878282) 1998 and *Requiem* resurfaced on *A Post Punk Primer* (Virgin CDOVD 498) 1997.

The Killjoys

Personnel:			
	LEE BURTON	drms	A
	MARK PHILLIPS	gtr	A B
	KEVIN ROWLAND	vcls	A B
	HEATHER TONGE	backing vcls	A
	GHISLAINE WESTON	bs	A B
	BOB PEACH	drms	B

ALBUM: 1(-) NAIVE (Damaged Goods FNARR 10) 1991

NB: (1) issued on green vinyl. There's also a CD compilation *A Million Songs* (Mushroom D 30930) 1993.

45: Johnny Won't Get To Heaven/Naive (PS) (Raw RAW 3) 1977

This group is most significant for containing Kevin Rowland who formed Dexy's Midnight Runners in Birmingham in July 1978. Like so many of the crop of '77 they modelled themselves on **The Sex Pistols**.

They signed to new indie label Raw in 1977, releasing their debut 45 in September that year. The following month they played their first of two sessions for John Peel on 18th October 1977. It featured four of their best songs; *Recognition, At Night, Back To Front* and *Naive*. *At Night* also figured on the compilation *Raw Deal* (Raw RAWLP 1) 1977. Later, in 1993, *Johnny Won't Get To Heaven, Naive* and *At Night* resurfaced on *The Raw Records Punk Collection* (Anagram CDPUNK 14).

A second Peel session followed on 13th February 1978. This time they recorded *All The Way, Smoke Your Own, Spit On Me* and *Ghislaine*.

With Rowland's subsequent fame and success in Dexy's Midnight Runners there was inevitable interest in his earlier ventures. This led to the release of a compilation album *Naive* in 1991. The compilation has a studio side which features both sides of their Raw 45, *Johnny Won't Get To Heaven* and *Naive*, alongside the previously unreleased *At Night* and *Recognition*. This is fine but the live side is really rudimentary featuring very imperfect versions of *Johnny Won't Get To Heaven, At Night, Trevors Sob* and an acappella version of *Moon River*, on which they sound rather the worse for booze. Two years earlier, one of their finest cuts *Recognition* was included on an EP on Scrotum (201). The other material came from **The Sex Pistols**, **Sick Things** and **The Users**.

Johnny Won't Get To Heaven resurfaced on *Punk Lost And Found* (Shanachie SH 5705) 1996 and on the 5-CD box set *1-2-3-4 - A History Of Punk And New Wave 1976 - 1979* (MCA/Universal 60066) 1999.

In 1982 Ghislaine Weston joined leather clad girl band **Girlschool**.

King

Personnel:	HENRY BADOIWSKI	vcls, keyb'ds	A
	DAVE BERK	drms	A
	KIM BRADSHAW	bs	A
	CAPTAIN SENSIBLE	gtr	A

A short-lived punk era group. Captain Sensible had been with **The Damned** and Dave Berk had played with **Johnny Moped**. Their only recorded output was a session for John Peel on 20th July 1978. It comprised *Antidope, Jet Boy Jet Girl, My Baby Don't Care* and *Baby Sign Here With Me*. *Antipope* was later included on the *Winters Of Discontent* (CD) (Strange Fruit SFRCD 204) 19?? compilation.

Kleenex

Personnel:	LISCOT HA	drms	AB
	MARLENE MARDER	gtr	AB
	KLAUDIA SCHIFF	bs	AB
	REGULA SING	vcls	A
	CRIGEL FREUND	vcls	B

ALBUM: 1(A/B) DIE KLEENEX SPIELEN   (Rough Trade C 40) 1979

NB: (1) cassette only live album.

EP: 1(A)   BERI BERI (Beri Beri/Ain't You/Heidi's Head/ Nice)   (Sunrise 078 51964) 1978

45s: Ain't You/Heidi's Head (poster PS)   (Rough Trade RT 9) 1978
     You/U (PS)   (Rough Trade RT 14) 1979
*   Split/Die Matrosen (PS)   (Rough Trade RT 47) 1980
*   Elsinger Wind/When The Cat's Away The Mice Play (PS)   (Rough Trade RT 62) 1981

NB: * As Liliput.

This all-girl quartet was actually Swiss, but I've included them here since they came to Britain and recorded on the London-based Rough Trade label.

Their first release was a 500 limited edition EP *Beri Beri* on Sunrise. Comparisons with better known girl outfits like **Siouxsie and The Banshees** were inevitably made.

After they signed to Rough Trade Sing left and was replaced by Crigel Freund from a European punk act Chaos. They recorded three reasonably successful 45s for Rough Trade and a cassette-only live album and gigged regularly in the U.K..

Later in 1980, they changed name to Liliput and recorded two further 45s and an album.

KLEENEX - You.

THE K9's - Idi Amin.

The K9's

Personnel:	IAIN 'SPROGG' AIRD	bs, vcls	A
	RICK DELLAR	vcls, perc	A
	KEV DRAIN	drms, perc, vcls	A
	GREG MUDEN	gtr, synth, vcls	A

45:    Idi Amin/Sweeney Todd/ The K9 Hassle (PS)   (Dog Breath Records WOOF 1) 1979

This is now a rare 45. Just 1,000 were issued initially with numbered picture sleeves. It was later reissued with different labels and a limited pressing of 500. The content ensured no airplay, but this is a good example of DIY punk with lyrics like:

"Sweeney Todd,
Sweeney Todd,
Sweeney Todd,
You're a fucking old sod"
(from *Sweeney Todd*)

and

"Sitting in jungle in the long tall grass
Six foot Idi on his big black arse
Round about eleven he's got nothing to do
So he kills a few people like me and you!"

(from *Idi Armin*).

Knox

ALBUM: 1   PLUTONIUM EXPRESS   (Razor RAZ 7) 1983

45:    Gigolo Aunt/Alligator Man   (Armageddon AS 003) 1980

Knox was the founding figure, frontman and songwriter for **The Vibrators**. This solo album featured various members of Hanoi Rocks. Some tracks were also included on *Razor Records Punk Collection* (Anagram CDPUNK 45) 1995. *Gigolo Aunt* was a cover of the Syd Barrett song and featured **The Soft Boys'** Matthew Seligman, with **Robyn Hitchcock** also appearing on the 'B' side.

Kronstadt Uprising

Personnel:	FILF	gtr	A
	ANDY FISHER	bs	A
	PAUL LAWSON	gtr	A
	STEVE PEGRUM	drms	A

EPs: 1(A)   THE UNKNOWN REVOLUTION (EP) (Blind People/ Dreamers Of Peace/Kronstadt Uprising/ Why The Black Flag/End Of Part One/ Xenophobia (PS)   (Spiderleg 12) 1983

	2(A)	PART OF THE GAME (EP) (Part Of The Game/		
		The Horseman) (PS)	(Dog Rock SD 108)	1985

NB: There's also a CD compilation, *Insurrection* (Underground OVER 85VP CD) 2000.

Krondstadt Uprising were an anarcho-punk band who formed in Southend-On-Sea in 1981. Their name was derived from an uprising at the Krondstadt naval base in 1921. They appeared on a number of cassette tapes. For example, they supplied three cuts *End Of Part 1*, *Divide + Rule* and *Xenophobia* to *States Of Confusion* (Stagnating Body Tapes). In 1982, they contributed *Receiver Deceiver* to the compilation *Bullshit Detector Vol. 2* (Crass 1984/3) 1982. Following this they went on to record *The Unknown Revolution* EP for Spiderleg in 1983 followed by the *Part Of The Game* EP for Dog Rock in 1985. By this stage they'd moved away from their anarcho-punk musical format to one influenced by Johnny Thunders and the Lords Of The New Church. They finally split in 1987. During their eight year life they underwent many line-up changes and drummer Steve Pegrum was their only ever-present member.

Insurrection is a 23-track compilation mostly comprised of demos which Pegrum, who also wrote the sleevenotes for this CD, had put together.

Krypton Tunes

Personnel:	DAVE BASS	gtr	A
	JANUARY	gtr	A
	BOB LACKI	drms	A
	JOHN WADLOW	vcls, gtr	A

EP:	1(A)	EXTENDED PLAY (Underhand/Heavy Breathing/		
		My Night To Moan) (PS)	(Secret SR 0059)	1979

45s:	Behind Your Smile/		
	Coming To See You (PS)	(Black And Red FIRE 1)	1978
	Limited Vision/All In Jail (PS)	(Lightning GIL 546)	1978

A Welsh fluoride punk combo. *Behind Your Smile* sounds like it was recorded with primitive equipment! The EP was produced by David Cunningham. You can also check out *All In Jail* on *Lightning Records Punk Collection* (Anagram CDPUNK 79) 1996.

The Lambrettas

Personnel:	JEZ BIRD	lead vcls, gtr	A
	MARK ELLIS	bs	A
	DOUG SANDERS	lead gtr, vcls	A
	PAUL WINCER	perc	A

ALBUMS:	1(A)	BEATBOYS IN THE JET AGE	(Rocket TRAIN 10)	1980
	2(A)	AMBIENCE	(Rocket TRAIN 14)	1981

NB: (1) also issued on CD (Dojo DOJOCD 187) 1994. (2) also issued on CD (Dojo DOJOCD 219) 1996 with four bonus cuts. Also relevant *The Best Of The Lambrettas* (Dojo DOJOCD 195) 1995 and *The Definitive Collection (Beat Boys In The Jet Age)* (Castle CCSCD 828) 1998. The latter was updated to a 2-CD set *Definitive Collection / Beat-Boys In The Jet Age* (Essential ESACD 934) 2000.

KNOX - Gigolo Aunt.

45s:	+	Go Steady/Listen Listen/		HCP
		Cortinas (PS)	(Rocket XPRES 23)	1979 -
	*	Poison Ivy/Runaround	(Rocket XPRES 25)	1980 7
		Da-A-A-Ance/		
		(Can't You) Feel The Beat	(Rocket XPRES 33)	1980 12
	x	Da-A-A-Ance/(Can't You) Feel The		
		Beat (picture disc)	(Rocket XPRES 333)	1980
	#	Page 3/Steppin' Out Of Line	(Rocket XPRES 36)	1980
	α	Another Day (Another Girl)/		
		Steppin' Out (Of Line)	(Rocket XPRES 36)	1980 49
		Good Times/Lamba Samba	(Rocket XPRES 48)	1981 -
		Decent Town/		
		Da-A-A-Ance (live in Europe)	(Rocket XPRES 62)	1981 -
		Decent Town/Da-A-A-Ance (live in Europe)/Total Strangers/		
		Young Girls (12", PS)	(Rocket XPRES 6212)	1981 -
	β	Somebody To Love/		
		Nobody's Watching Me (PS)	(Rocket XPRES 74)	1982 -

NB: + Later copies came in an art sleeve. * Some copies came in a withdrawn '2-Stroke' label and sleeve. x This release came in two different shades; red, white and blue or pink, white and blue. # Withdrawn, some picture sleeves are rumoured to exist. α Came in 'emergency' picture sleeve. β There were some mispressings of this release which credited *Leap Before You Look* on the label and sleeve.

Although **The Lambrettas** were originally from Lewes in Sussex, the group is usually associated with Brighton, which with all its 'mod' credentials was appropriate for a mod revival band.

They made their vinyl debut playing *Go Steady*, which skips along quite nicely, on the sampler *499 2139* (Rocket DIAL 1) 1979, the title was the number to ring if your band sounded like any of the ones on the record. They first came to wider attention when their cover of *Poison Ivy* made it into the Top 10, climbing to No. 7 during a twelve week chart residency. However, the 'Two Strokes' sleeve it came in didn't go down at all well with 2-Tone. They followed this with *Da-A-A-Ance*, one of Jez Bird's own compositions, which climbed to No. 12 and spent eight weeks in the charts. Both songs featured on their debut album *Beat Boys In The Jet Age*. This showed they had humour, some good hooks and confirmed Bird's ability as a songwriter. The tunes are full of comments about teenage life and the music is tuneful mod-pop. The album ends with a reprise of the three cuts on their debut 45 (*Go Steady*, *Listen Listen* and *Cortinas*).

There was more controversy when 'The Sun' took exception to their next release *Page 3* and it had to be retitled *Another Day (Another Girl)*. This also enjoyed four weeks in the charts, climbing to No. 49.

Their second album *Ambience* lacked the same catchy hooks which made their first one worthwhile as they seemed to search in vain for a new focus. Their final 45 was a cover of a Jefferson Airplane U.S. hit.

The Dojo CD reissue of *Ambience* in 1996 added four bonus cuts; two 'B' sides - *Lamba Samba* and *Anything You Want* plus their pedestrian cover of Jefferson Airplane's *Somebody To Love* and its flip side *Nobody's Watching Me*.

The Lambrettas made a worthwhile contribution to the mod revival and if you want to check them out any of the compilations listed in the discography do them justice.

Landscape

Personnel:	RICHARD BURGESS	vcls, drms	ABC
	ANDY PASK	bs	ABC
	PETER THOMS	trombone	ABC
	JOHN WALTERS	woodwind, keyb'ds	ABC
	CHRIS HEATON	keyb'ds	BC
	STEVE LOVE	gtr	C
	STEPHEN ROBBINS	synth	C

				HCP
ALBUMS:	1(A)	LANDSCAPE	(RCA RCALP 5248)	1980 -
	2(B)	FROM THE TEA-ROOMS OF MARS.... TO THE		
		HELL-HOLES OF URANUS	(RCA RCALP 5003)	1981 13
	3(C)	MANHATTEN BOOGIE WOOGIE		
			(RCA RCALP 6037)	1982

NB: (1) and (2) later issued on one CD (Mau Mau MAUCD 618) 1992, which took the title of their second album.

LANDSCAPE - Workers Playtime.

LANDSCAPE - U2MEIX2MUCH.

45s:	U2XMEIX2MUCH/Don't Give Me No Rebop/		
	Sixteen (PS)	(Event Horizon EVE 137)	1978 -
	Workers Playtime/Nearly Normal/		
	Too Many Questions (PS)	(Event Horizon EVE 139)	1978 -
	Japan/Gotham City (PS)	(RCA PB 5183)	1979 -
	Sonja Henje/Neddy Sindrum (PS)	(RCA PB 5259)	1980 -
	European Man/Mechanical Bride (PS)	(RCA EDM 1)	1980 -
	European Man/		
	Mechanical Bride (12", PS)	(RCA EDMT 1)	1980 -
	Einstein A Go-Go/New Religion (PS)	(RCA RCA 22)	1981 5
	Einstein A Go-Go/New Religion/		
	Japan (12", PS)	(RCA RCA 22)	1981 -
*	Norman Bates/From The Tea-Rooms Of Mars....		
	To The Hell-Holes Of Uranus (PS)	(RCA RCA 60)	1981 40
*	It's Not My Name/Mistaken Identity (PS)	(RCA RCA 186)	1982 -
*	Eastern Girls/Back Of Your Hands (PS)	(RCA RCA 219)	1982 -
*+	So Good So Pure So Kind/		
	The Fabulous Neutrons (PS)	(RCA RCA 311)	1983 -
*+	You Know How To Hurt Me/		
	Feel So Right	(RCA RCA 333)	1983 -
Reissue:	Einstein A Go-Go/Norman Bates	(Old Gold OG ?)	1989 -

NB: * Also issued as a 12". + Credited to **Landscape III**.

Landscape was formed in London in 1977 by Richard Burgess, Andy Pask, Peter Thoms and John Walters. After releasing two 45s for the Event Horizon indie label, they were signed by RCA in 1979. Burgess had once been in soft-rock outfit Easy Street. He also worked as a producer for **Visage**, King and **Spandau Ballet**. He was the vocalist and handled the drums for **Landscape** who played a form of slick, fun-loving and often experimental computer-keyboard pop. This was one of the main genres that developed in the post-punk era. All of their material was group compositions.

Their debut eponymous album made only a limited impression, as did their earlier singles which included *Sonja Henje* about the Finnish ice-skater who appeared in forties films.

LANDSCAPE - So Good, So Pure, So Kind.

Chris Heaton was added to their line-up on keyboards prior to their second album *From The Tea Rooms Of Mars...*. This included a witty ode to Japanese industry *Shake The West Awake* and a song about the killer in the sixties Hitchcock film 'Psycho', *Norman Bates*. This was a No. 40 hit and spent seven weeks in the charts, but it was another track *Einstein A Go-Go* which gave them their commercial break. The electronic novelty song took them to No. 5 early in 1981 and enjoyed a fifteen week chart residency. The parent album also sold well, climbing to No. 13 during its twelve weeks in the charts.

After this their line-up was supplemented again by the addition of Steve Love (gtr) and Stephen Robbins (synth). This new line-up set about recording a more disco-orientated album *Manhatten Boogie-Woogie*, but neither this or subsequent singles could revive their brief flirtation with commercial success. They even tried a change of name to **Landscape III** in 1983. *So Good, So Pure, So Kind* was a powerful ballad with clear, strong vocals from Richard Burgess. A Sounds 'Single of the Week', it could easily have been a hit, but it wasn't. With the change of name doing little to reverse their slide they split up later that year.

Richard Burgess concentrated on production work for **Spandau Ballet**. He also recorded a self-produced solo album *Richard James Burgess* in 1984 which comprised six long commercial dance tracks.

Andy Pask made a living writing theme tunes for TV programmes like 'The Bill'.

Last Resort

Personnel:	ANDY 'LONGFELLOW' BENFIELD	drms	A B
	CHARLIE DUGGAN	gtr	A B
	ROI PEARCE	bs, vcls	A B
	SAXBY	vcls	A
	ARTHUR 'BILKO' KITCHENER	bs	B

ALBUM: 1(B) A WAY OF LIFE: SKINHEAD ANTHEMS
(Last Resort 1) 1982

NB: (1) reissued on CD (Captain Oi! AHOYCD 1) 1993 with four bonus cuts. Also available on record in both black and clear vinyl complete with lyric insert. There are also a couple of compilations, *The Best Of The Last Resort* (Step-1 STEPCD 010) 1998 and *Violence In Our Minds* (Can Can CANCAN 003CD) 1997.

Cass Single:
Violence In Our Minds/Held Hostage/
Soul Boys   (Last Resort LAST 1) 1981

NB: Some copies came with a fourth track, a cover of **The Squad**'s *Eight Pound A Week*.

Last Resort were an Oi! band. Based in Herne Bay, Kent, they were managed and named after the infamous Last Resort shop. They had a self-financed cassette single in 1981. The same year they contributed *Working Class Kids*, a rallying call to working class youth and *Johnny Barden* to *Strength Thru' Oi!* (Decca). Then, later that year another of their songs *King Of The Jungle* was included on *Carry On Oi!* (Secret SEC 2), which was later reissued on CD (Captain Oi! AHOY CD 119) in 1999.

If you want to hear more of their music you need go no further than the *A Way Of Life: Skinhead Anthems* CD, which was the first release on Link owner Mark Brennan's new Captain Oi! label. It contains 15 of their better songs many of which have incredibly xenophobic titles like *Red White And Blue*, *Lionheart* and *Rose Of England*.

"Walking down the road with a dozen pals of mine
Looking for some aggro just to pass the time
We met a stupid hippie who tried to run away
I punched him in the nose just to pass the time of day"
(from *Violence In Our Minds*)

"Another day another night
Another drink another fight
It's a shame we get the blame
Always wrong and never right
We're the new generation
Searching for an explanation
Football matches and rock n roll
Makes us a little out of control"
(from *Rebels With A Cause*)

"The government polices are out of hand
They ain't got a clue how to run this land
Margaret Thatcher the stupid old bitch
Takes from the poor and gives to the rich

She thinks we can't see her plan
To kill the spirit of the working class man
Make us redundant put us on the dole
Put us in prisons without parole

They're a bunch of stuck-up snobs
They think the kids are mindless yobs
But we'll stop them in the end
And they will find out we are their friends"
(from *We Rule OK*)

In addition to the whole of their original 1982 album the Captain Oi! reissue features four bonus tracks:- *Stormtroopers In Stapress*, *King Of The Jungle*, *Resort Boot Boys* and *Oi! Oi! Skinhead*. Of these *King Of The Jungle* had previously appeared on the *Carry On Oi!* (Secret SEC 2) 1982 compilation, which was later reissued (Captain Oi! AHOY CD 119) 1999. The lyrics on all their cuts are very audible and a crucial element of their music, which is not as fast-paced as that of most of their contemporaries. There's lots of working class consciousness here.

Last Resort have three tracks: *Violence In Our Minds*, *Held Hostage* and *Soul Boys* on *Oi! The Singles Collection, Vol. 2* (Captain Oi! AHOY CD 63) 1996, whilst *100% British Oi!* (Captain Oi! AHOY DCD 83) 1997 includes them playing *Resort Bootboys*, which was earlier included on *Trouble On The Terraces - 16 Classic Football Anthems* (Step-1 STEP LP 91) in 1996.

LAST RESORT - Way Of Life.

LAST ROUGH CAUSE - The Violent Few EP.

With the backlash against Oi! it became difficult for the band to get gigs. They mutated into **The Warriors** but then Roi Pearce, who'd switched from bass to vocals in **Last Resort**'s second line-up, left to become the **4-Skins** third lead vocalist. That spelt the death knell for the band.

Roi Pearce formed a heavier version of the band, The Resort, in 1989 and they put out one album *1989* and then evolved into Heavy Metal Outlaws.

Aside from the Captain Oi! CD, both Step-1 and Can Can have issued compilations of the band's material. They were certainly one of the better Oi! bands.

Last Resort

45:	Having Fun/F.U. 2	(Red Meat RMRS 01)	1978

A different punk era band. The 45 was issued in a die-cut printed paper sleeve and is now rare, but nothing else is known about them.

Last Rough Cause

Personnel:	ANDY	vcls, bs	A
	MAX	drms	A
	STE	gtr	A

ALBUMS:	1(A)	SKINS 'N' PUNKS, VOL. 1	(Oi! OIR 007) 1986
	2(A)	SOFT LIGHTS AND LOUD GUITARS, VOL. 2	(Released Emotions REM 003) 198?

NB: (1) was a split album with **Society's Rejects**. (2) was a split album with Anhrefen.

EP:	1(A)	THE VIOLENT FEW (The Violent Few/My Life/ No Real Reason/Let Them Know)	(L.R.C. LRC 001) 1986

Last Rough Cause hailed from Darlington in the north-east of England. In addition to appearing on the two above split albums, they recorded an EP which was produced by **Major Accidents**' Con Larkin and put out on their own L.R.C. label. This was a competent and relatively melodic effort. Two of the cuts *The Violent Few* and *My Life* later resurfaced on *Oi! The Rarities, Vol. 1* (Captain Oi! AHOY CD 43) 1995. You can also hear *My Life* on *The Best Of Oi! Records* (Captain Oi! AHOY CD 38) 1995.

The Last Stand

45:	Just A Number/Caviare (PS)	(Silly Symbol SJP 825) 1981

An obscure mod-influenced 45.

The Last Words

Personnel:
- MALCOLM BAXTER — vcls — A
- STEVE BERESFORD — keyb'ds — A
- JOHN DUNN — drms — A
- ANDY GROOME — gtr — A
- RICKY LEE KANDALL — bs — A
- DICK NIGHTDOCTOR — sax — A

ALBUM: 1(A) THE LAST WORDS (Armageddon ARM 2) 1980

45s:
- Animal World/ No Music In The World Today (PS) (Rough Trade RT 022) 1979
- Todays Kidz/ There's Something Wrong (PS) (Remand REMAND 2) 1979
- Todays Kidz/Walk Away (PS) (Armageddon AS 1) 1980

An indie punk type band.

Thomas Leer

ALBUMS:
1. THE BRIDGE (Industrial IR 0007) 1979
2. CONTRADICTIONS (Cherry Red ERED 26) 1982
3. SCALE OF TEN (Arista 207208) 1985

NB: (1) credited to **Thomas Leer and Robert Rental**. Later issued on CD (Grey Area BRIDGE 10CD) 1992. (2) issued as a 12" double pack and later issued on CD (Cherry Red CDBDRED 105) 1993.

EP:
1. FOUR MOVEMENTS (Don't/Letter From America/ Tight As A Drum/ West End) (12", PS) (Cherry Red 12CHERRY 28) 1981

45s:
- * Private Plane/International (PS) (Oblique ER 101) 1978
- + Private Plane/ International (PS) (Company/Oblique OBCD 1) 1978
- All About You/ Saving Grace (PS) (Cherry Red CHERRY 52) 1982
- All About You/ Saving Grace (12", PS) (Cherry Red 12CHERRY 52) 1982
- International/Easy Way (PS) (Arista LEER 1) 1984
- x International/Easy Way (12", PS) (Arista LEER 121) 1984
- Heartbeat/Control Yourself (Arista LEER 2) 1985
- x Heartbeat/Control Yourself (12", PS) (Arista LEER 122) 1985
- No. 1/Chasing The Dragon (PS) (Arista LEER 3) 1985
- No. 1/Chasing The Dragon/ Trust Me (12", PS) (Arista LEER 123) 1985

NB: * This was issued in a folded photocopied picture sleeve with hand stamped labels. + This reissue came in a printed picture sleeve. x These releases were also available as 12" picture discs (LERPD 121 and LERPD 122) respectively.

Thomas Leer was one of the most creative synthesizer artists of this era. Most of his recordings were made in his home studio utilising synthesizers and tape machines.

THOMAS LEER - Four Movements EP.

He first attracted attention with a privately-pressed 45 *Private Plan* in 1978. This was given wider exposure by virtue of its inclusion on *Business Unusual* (Cherry Red ARED 2) in 1979 and *Machines* (Virgin V 2177) in 1980. Then in 1979 he teamed up with **Robert Rental** to record *The Bridge*. This synthesized-pop album was quite a pivotal moment in pop. Financed by Industrial Records, the album utilised rhythms driven by tape loops and quirky keyboard patterns overlaid by a barrage of sound effects and improvised voices. Some of the later tracks were more ambient. It pointed the way to the later electro-pop which bands like **The Human League** and **Blancmange** took into the mainstream.

The *4 Movements* EP and *Contradictions* demonstrated new synthsizer music could have energy and soul. Highlights of *4 Movements* include *Don't* and *Letter From America*. The later was also selected as the title track for a 1982 U.S. album on Cachalot which compiled both *4 Movements* and *Contradictions*. The CD reissue of *Contradiction* included as bonus tracks both sides of their *Private Plane* 45 and their Cherry Red singles.

If you're into synthesizer music you'll find **Thomas Leer** one of its better exponents.

Lemon Kittens

Personnel:
- KARL BLAKE — gtr, vcls — A
- DANIELLE DAX — sax — A
- PETE FALLOWELL — drms — A
- IAN STURGESS — bs — A

ALBUMS:
1(A) WE BUY A HAMMER FOR DADDY (United Dairies UD 02) 1980
2(A) THE BIG DENTIST (Illuminated JAMS 131) 1982

NB: (1) also issued on CD (Biter Of Thorpe 131-03 CD) 1993. (2) also issued on CD (Biter Of Thorpe BOT 131 O5 CD) 1996.

EPs:
1(A) SPOONFED AND WRITHING (Shakin' All Over/ This Kind Of Dying/Morbotalk/Whom Do I Have To Ask?/Chalet D'amour/...Nor A Mirror) (PS) (Step Forward SF 10) 1979
2(A) CAKE BEAST (Kites/Only A Rose/Popsykle) (12", PS) (United Dairies UD 07) 1981

NB: (1) later issued on CD (Biter Of Thorpe BOT 131-08 CD) 1996 with bonus cuts. (2) came with an inner sleeve and insert.

The Lemon Kittens were one of the earliest of a number of experimental avant-punk bands who sprang up at the end of the 1970s. Karl Blake a Reading office worker was already determined to put out his own record under this name and was trying to set up an arts centre in Reading with some friends when he was looking for someone to do the artwork for his EP and Danielle Dax volunteered. Southend-born Dax was living in Kenya at the time of the punk explosion and missed it completely. She told Blake she could play saxophone (which she couldn't at all) and was soon invited into the band. *The Spoonfed And Writhing* EP put out by **Mark Perry** on his Step Forward label was mostly recorded by Karl on a couple of Akai two-track machines. Ian Sturgess and Pete Fallowell were used for infrequent live appearances, but before long Dax and Blake were playing up to 20 different instruments between them. Some of the songs on that first EP - like *Whom Do I Have To Ask?* and *Chalet D'amour* were pretty offbeat - as they set out to create avant-garde music. The 1996 CD reissue is also bolstered by additional material from the same sessions.

Their debut album *We Buy A Hammer For Daddy* utilised a wide array of instruments, vocal styles and abstract noise to create a disturbed album. Song titles like *(Afraid Of Being) Bled By Leeches* and *False Alarm (Malicious)* only served to reinforce the atmosphere. The album was received with critical acclaim at the time.

They soon relocated from Reading to Richmond in South-west London linking up with John Fothergill who released their next EP, a 12" titled *Cake Beast*, on his expanding United Dairies label. On offer was a cover of Simon Dupree and The Big Sound's *Kites*, the popish *Popsykle* and post-punkish *Only A Rose*. The same month they contribute *Funky 7*, a collection of tape loops and weird vocal lines to *Hoisting The Black Flag* (United Dairies UD 05) 1981, which is now an extremely collectable compilation. Other compilation appearances were... *In Wooden Brackets* on

Perspectives And Distortion (Cherry Red BRED 15) 1981 and *What The Cat Brought In* on *The Wonderful World Of Glass* (Glass GLASS 010) 1981.

They split after a disappointing second album *The Big Dentist* in 1982. If you do track down a copy the highlight is a cut called *Mylmus*. As for the rest, the opening cut *They Are Both Dirty* features a lone sax over a myriad of pulsating synthesizers and Karl Blake exercises his vocal chords on *Nudies*, which also features regular rhythms undercut by the whine of a child's voice on tape loop.

Both Dax and Blake went on to record solo projects. Blake was also later in Shock Head Peters.

The Leopards

Personnel:			
	CLAIRE MACAULEY	bs	A
	JEANNIE MACAULEY	vcls	AB
	ROD MACAULEY	gtr	AB
	KEVIN WIREMU	drms	AB
	RICHARD PHETHEAN	bs	B

45: Strange Rhythmical Music/Veronica (PS)   (Warped W 103) 1979

The Leopards were formed by Rod Macauley in 1977. Rod came from York, but moved down to London to form the band. It also featured his sister Claire Macauley and his wife Jeannie Macauley. The band were completed by Kevin Wiremu. The band gigged around London in the late 1970s and early 1980s. They recorded a single for Warped Records in 1979. The single got good reviews, although Gary Bushell in 'Sounds' compared Jeannie to Robert Plant! Their style was spiky, post-punk pop. The 'A' side was a peculiar mixture of **The Stranglers** and The B52s. At times the record is danceable at others quite strange, but the vocals stand out.

The band had attracted major label interest by 1980. Eventually, Logo Records financed them to do a one-off single with an option on further releases. The band went to the ultra-hip Cargo Studios in Rochdale to record one of their best songs, *The Big Heat*, as a single. The finished item was of Spectoresque proportions with over-dubs galore, reverb, backwards guitar - a psychedelic classic. Logo, absolutely appalled at what they heard, ripped up the contract there and then and the single was never released. After this, the band lost heart: Claire Macauley quit and later joined **To The Finland Station**. She was replaced by Richard Phethean. The band limped on for a few more months, changing its name to Spin Red, before disbanding in 1981.

Le Ritz

Personnel:			
	BERNIE BOLT	keyb'ds	A
	LOFTY BROOKS	drms	A
	CHUCK KEY	gtr	A
	STEVE MIDNIGHT	vcls	A
	DICK TATER	bs	A
	BUSS WHITE	gtr	A

45: Punker/What A Sucker (PS)   (Breakers BS 2001) 1977

A hard to find and collectable punk 45.

Les Elite

Personnel:			
	DAVID CROSSLEY	drms	A
	CHRIS GRIERSON	vcls	A
	JOHN KIELY	bs	A
	ALLICK LETORT	gtr	A

Les Elite appeared on *499 2139* (Rocket DIAL 1) 1979 playing *Career Girls*, which is quite a riffy number.

THE LEYTON BUZZARDS - Saturday Night Beneath The Plastic Palm Trees.

The Letters

Personnel:			
	MIKE LODGE	bs, vcls	A
	STEVE MARSH	gtr	A
	KEVIN REED	drms	A

45: Nobody Loves Me/
Don't Want You Back (PS)   (Heartbeat PULSE 9) 1979

This Bath-based band formed in 1978 and was associated with the 'mod revival'. Their sole 45 *Nobody Love Me*, a pleasant mod-pop number, is now hard to find and collectable. They also contributed *Don't Want You Back* to *This Is Mod, Vol. 1: The Rarities 1979 - 81* (CDM GRAM 98) 1995, whilst *Nobody Loves Me* later resurfaced on *This Is Mod* (dbl) (Get Back GET 39) 1999 and *100% British Mod* (Captain Mod MODSKA DCD 8) 1998.

The Leyton Buzzards

Personnel:			
	GEOFF DEANE	vcls	ABC
	DAVID JAYMES	bs	ABC
	DAVE MONK	gtr	A
	KEVIN STEPTOE	drms	AB
	VERNON AUSTIN	gtr	BC
	TONY GAINSBOROUGH	drms	C

ALBUM: 1(-) FROM JELLIED EELS TO RECORD DEALS
                                    (Chrysalis CHR 1213) 1979

HCP

45s: 19 And Mad/Villain/
Youthanasia (PS)   (Small Wonder SMALL 7) 1978
Saturday Night Beneath The Plastic Palm Trees/
Through With You (PS)   (Chrysalis CHS 2288) 1979 53
I'm Hanging Around/Don't Want To Go To Art School/
No Dry Ice Or Flying Pigs (PS)   (Chrysalis CHS 2328) 1979 -
* We Make A Noise/
Disco Romeo (PS)   (Chrysalis CHS 2360) 1979 -
Can't Get Used To Losing You/
Weird Frenz (PS)   (WEA K 18284) 1980 -

NB: * credited to The Buzzards.

As their name hints, **The Leyton Buzzards** were formed in Leyton in East London. They formed in 1976, initially as a R&B pub rock band but soon switched over to the emerging punk rock sound and became regulars at The Roxy.

Indeed their debut three track 45 contains a forgotten classic *19 And Mad*. The lyrics capture the punk ethos superbly.

"I am 19 going out of my head
I am 19 getting on for dead
I won't make 20 and I don't want to"
(from *19 And Mad*).

THE LEYTON BUZZARDS - 19 And Mad.

The band members adopted various pseudonyms for their single, which was included on the compilation *Business Unusual* (Cherry Red ARED 2) in 1979.

The following month they played their first of four sessions for John Peel. It featured *Through With You*, *Art School*, *Can't Get Used To Loving You* and their finest moment *19 And Mad*.

Dave Monk left after this, but with new guitarist Vernon Austin drafted in as a replacement, they won a Radio One competition for unsigned bands. Their prize was a contract with Chrysalis and their first single on their new label was *Saturday Night (Beneath The Plastic Palm Tree)* all about riotous living but with a more reggae-influenced beat. A distinct change of style from its predecessor this bought them their one and only hit, climbing to No. 53 during a five week stay. This was previewed as part of their second John Peel session on 22nd January 1979, along with *Baby, If You Love Me Say Yes*, *The Greatest Story Ever Told* and *Love Is Just A Dream*.

It was all downhill thereafter. Subsequent singles for Chrysalis weren't quite as good and an attempt to rebrand themselves as The Buzzards for *We Make A Noise* failed. This is a shame because it should have been a hit:-

"The music climate's turned against us it seems
We're full of East End promise but we've lost our dreams
Now everybody says we're a noisy band
We've got a one way ticket back to garageland'
(from *We Make A Noise*)

They did do two further Peel sessions. The first, on 27th June 1979 featured *Sharp Young Men*, *Last Tango In Leyton*, *People In The Street* and *Sweet Dreams*. The final one on 21st January 1980 featured *When You Walk In The Room*, *Telephone*, *Jeaulousy* and *Swanky Pop*. They split very shortly after.

From Jellied Eels To Record Deals was cheaply packaged. Comprising their singles like frantic punk anthem *19 And Mad*, their lightly-reggaed *Saturday Night Beneath The Plastic Palm Tree*, the poppy *Hanging Around*

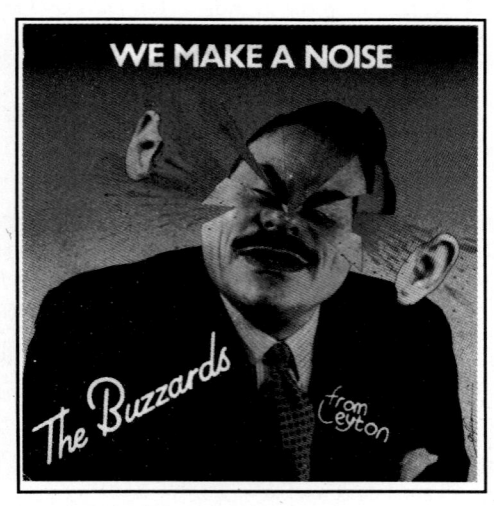

THE BUZZARDS - We Make A Noise.

and the raucous Slade-like *We Make A Noise*; some Peel session material and demos, it retailed for just £4. Among these are frantic punkers like *Mixed Marriages* and *No Dry Ice And Flying Pigs*; sharp pop like *Land Of The Free* and *Sharp Young Men*; silly covers like *Can't Get Used To Losing You* (a future 45) and *The Greatest Story Ever Told*, a kind of account of punk's rise and fall.

Within a year Deane and Jaymes returned with a new team of supporting musicians as Modern Romance, having got into Latin dance-orientated music. Modern Romance enjoyed a number of hits between 1981-83.

19 And Mad later resurfaced on *Small Wonder Punk Singles Collection, Vol. 1* (Anagram CDPUNK 29) 1994 and *Youthanasia* figured on *Vol. 2* (Anagram CDPUNK 70) 1996 of the same series. You can also check out *19 And Mad* on the 5-CD set *1-2-3-4 - A History Of Punk And New Wave 1976 - 1979* (MCA/Universal MCD 60066), released in 1999.

Ligotage

Personnel incl:	BEKI BONDAGE	vcls	A
	LINC	bs	A
	STEVE ROBERTS	drms	A

ALBUM: 1(A) FORGIVE AND FORGET-LIVE (Picasso PIK 005) 1984

Ligotage was formed by Beki Bondage after her split with **Vice Squad**. It also included ex-**Chelsea** bassist Linc and ex-**UK Subs** drummer Steve Roberts. This live album, recorded at the Marquee Club in the summer of 1984 was their only vinyl outing. A cut also features on *Razor Records Punk Collection* (Anagram CDPUNK 45) 1995.

The Lillettes

Personnel:	ROBYN BANKS	keyb'ds	A
	BARB DWYER	vcls	A
	PHIL PERFECT	gtr, vcls	A
	MICK PERRIN	bs	A
	DAVE ROBSON	gtr, vcls	A
	TIM VICIOUS	drms	A

The Lillettes, from the Brighton area, contributed *Hey Operator* and *Nervous Wreck* (not the **Radio Stars** hit) to the *Vaultage '79 (Another Two Sides Of Brighton)* (Attrix RB 08) 1979 sampler. Both were quite promising contributions but there seem to have been no subsequent vinyl outings. They were both compiled again on *Vaultage Punk Collection* (Anagram CDPUNK 101) 1997.

Lip Moves

45: Guest/What Is (Tichonderoga HP 1) 1979

A punky band from Southampton who named their record label after the street where they lived. Most copies of their 45 were autographed and it came in a wraparound sleeve with an insert and stickered white labels.

Musically, though, we're talking third division buzzsaw punk.

Little Dave

An Oi! ranter whose *Being Short* included on *The Oi! Of Sex* (Syndicate SYNLP 4) 1984, also reissued on CD (Captain Oi! AHOY CD 23) 1994, is about precisely what the title suggests.

Llygod Ffyrnig

Personnel:	GARY BEARD	gtr	A
	JULIAN LEWIS	drms	A
	HYWEL PECKHAM	gtr	A
	DAFYDD RHYS	vcls	A
	PETE WILLIAMS	bs	A

45: N.C.B./Sais/Cariad Y Bus Stop (PS) (Pwdwr PWDWR 1) 1978

A short-lived Welsh punk band whose name means The Ferocious Mine in English. Their sole 45 is now very rare, expect to pay towards £100 for a copy. *N.C.B.* was also included on the *Labels Unlimited* (Cherry Red ARED 4) 1979 compilation.

Local Heroes SW9

Personnel: KEVIN ARMSTRONG gtr, vcls A
            KIM BARTI drms A
            MATTHEW SELIGMAN bs A

ALBUMS: 1(A) DRIP DRY ZONE (Oval OVLP 504) 1980
         2(A) NEW OPIUM/HOW THE WEST WAS WON
                               (Oval OVLP 302) 1982

A London-based trio whose music offered radical political perspectives within a sort of rhythm 'n' pop format. *Drip Dry Zone* is very listenable. Tom Bailey of The Thompson Twins helped out on clarinet and alto sax. The title cut veers towards white reggae, as does *Bluebottle*, whilst *Bad Acting*, *Stabbed In The Heart Again* and *Another Modern Romance* are among the better of the pop/rock material. Certainly worth a spin. The second album was partly a solo effort by Kevin Armstrong who later worked with Thomas Dolby. Matthew Seligman is probably better known as a member of **The Soft Boys**.

Lockjaw

Personnel incl: RIC GALLUP vcls
                 SIMON GALLUP bs

45s: Radio Call Sign/The Young Ones (PS) (Raw RAW 6) 1977
      Journalist Jive/I'm A Virgin/
      A Doonga Doonga (PS) (Raw RAW 19) 1978

Simon Gallup was later in **The Cure** and Ric paid for **The Cure**'s very first demo. Very much a third division punk outfit. *Radio Call Sign* was poor and the flip side *was* a badly played rehash of the title song from a 1961 Cliff Richard movie! Both cuts later resurfaced on *The Raw Records Punk Collection* (Anagram CDPUNK 14) in 1993. Simon Gallup has been quoted in 'Record Collector' as saying that he thinks this first 45 is complete rubbish.

London

Personnel incl: JON MOSS drms A
                 RIFF REGAN vcls A

ALBUM: 1(A) ANIMAL GAMES (MCA MCF 2823) 1978
NB: There's also a CD compilation *Punk Rock Collection* (Captain Oi! AHOY CD 077) 1997.

EP: 1(A) SUMMER OF LOVE (No Time/Siouxsie Sue/
           Summer Of Love/
           Friday On My Mind) (PS) (MCA MCA 319) 1977
NB: There was also a 12" version (MCA 12 MCA 319) 1977.

45s: Everyone's A Winner/Handcuffed (MCA MCA 305) 1977
      Animal Games/Us Kids Cold (MCA MCA 336) 1977

London were part of the first wave of punk bands but not one of the best. Unusually for this era their 45s did not come with picture sleeves. They probably suffered from recording without a proper producer. Their music was rather a mish-mash between an all-out punk assault on the one hand and pop on the other.

In retrospect, their main claim to fame was the inclusion of drummer Jon Moss, who later played for **The Damned** and Culture Club.

LOCAL HEROES SW9 - Drip Dry Zone.

London SS

Personnel incl: TONY JAMES bs
                 MICK JONES gtr
                 BRYAN JAMES gtr
                 ROLAND HOT drms

Many key players on London's punk scene were involved in trying to get this project together, although it never did end up with a settled line-up, play a single live gig or record any records.

Guitarist Mick Jones and bassist Tony James spent from March 1975 to the end of 1976 trying to put together a punk band. They did recruit guitarist Bryan James and made a demo tape with drummer Roland Hot, but James became impatient at the lack of progress and left in January 1976 to form **The Damned** with Rat Scabies. Mick Jones then departed, teaming up with Joe Strummer (of the **101ers**) to form **The Clash**. Tony James then departed to form **Chelsea** with Billy Idol and **Gene October**. James and Idol later formed **Generation X**. Nicky Headon, who had turned down the drummer's role, replaced Terry Chimes in **The Clash** in 1977.

Long Tall Shorty

Personnel incl: JIMMY GRANT bs A
                 KEITH MONO vcls AB
                 TONY PERFECT vcls, gtr AB
                 MARK REYNOLDS drms A

45s: # By Your Love/1970's Boy (PS) (Warner Bros K 17491) 1979
(up to * If I Was You/
1986)   That's What I Want (D.R.C./Lyntone LYN 9904) 1981
         Win Or Lose/Ain't Done Wrong (PS) (Ramkup CAC 007) 1981
      + On The Street Again/I Fought The Law/
         Promises (PS) (Diamond DIA 002) 1985
         What's Going On/Steppin' Stone/Win Or Lose/
         England (PS) (Diamond DIA 005) 1986

NB: # This disc was withdrawn. * Flexidisc. + Some copies came with a poster. There's also a CD *1970's Boys* (Captain Mod MODSKA CD 5) 1997.

This London band started life as Ben E. Dorm and The Tourists and The Indicators. Their first single was produced by **Sham 69**'s **Jimmy Pursey**, but when his J.P. label fell through Warners Bros. released it only to withdraw it after a week. It is rumoured that only 200-300 copies got out so naturally it's quite collectable now. A whole album's worth of material titled *1970's Boy* was recorded with **Pursey** but then scrapped. *1970's Boy* is an aggressive, sixties-influenced song. **Pursey** helped **Long Tall Shorty** secure a U.K. tour with **The Chords**, but **Long Tall Shorty** split up after the first night.

Perfect and Mono then put together a new line-up. In 1981, they recorded a flexidisc which was donated to 'Direction Reaction Creation' fanzine. A third 45 was then recorded on the obscure Ramkup label, which they helped promote by an appearance at the Reading festival. This is now hard to find and collectable.

Musically they were closest to punk but with some mod revival tendencies. Perfect quit to join **The Angelic Upstarts** for a while and **UK Subs'** **Charlie Harper** played on harmonica on one of their cuts.

They reformed on several occasions, recording *Anti CND* (Capitol CLA 55) 1985 as Joe Public. This 45 is hard to find now. They also recorded two 45s on Diamond in the mid-eighties as **Long Tall Shorty**.

In 1988 Backs planned to issue their earlier abandoned album from their days with **Jimmy Pursey**, but again the project was shelved at the last minute. Apparently some test pressings do exist *1970's Boy* (Re-Elect The President NIXON 6) 1988 and would be valued at £100 upwards. 1988 also saw the release of an official bootleg album *Rockin' At The Savoy* (Lambs To The Slaughter LTS 7) 1988.

They also contributed seven cuts, *On The Streets Again*, *I Fought The Law*, *Promises*, *What's Going On*, *Steppin' Stone*, *Win Or Lose* and *England* to *This Is Mod, Vol. 3* (Anagram CDMGRAM 106) 1996. *Win Or Lose* later resurfaced again on *This Is Mod, Vol. 5* (Anagram CDMGRAM 110) 1997, whilst *What's Going On* and *On The Streets Again* can also be found on *This Is Mod* (dbl) (Get Back GET 39) 1999 and *100% British Mod* (MODSKA DCD 8) 1998 gave fresh exposure to *1970's Boy*.

The 1997 CD *1970's Boy* is a twenty-track compilation comprising three early demos, their 45s for Warner Bros and Ramkup, a Luton-based indie label. There's also the *Anti-CND* single that a 1985 re-union line-up recorded as Joe Public. A worthwhile collection.

One of their members Derwent was later in **The Case** and **The Rage**.

Lori and The Chameleons

Personnel:	DAVID BALFE	keyb'ds	A
	BILL DRUMMOND	gtr, vcls	A
	GARY DWYER		
	LORI LARTEY	vcls	A
	RAY MARTINEZ		
	TIM WHITTAKER		

45s:	Touch/Love On The Ganges (PS)	(Zoo CAGE 006) 1978
	The Lonely Spy/Peru (PS)	(Korova KOW 5) 1980
Reissues:	Touch/Love On The Ganges (PS)	(Sire SIR 4025) 1979
	Touch/The Lonely Spy/ Love On The Ganges (12", PS)	(Korova KOW 20T) 1979
	Touch/The Lonely Spy (PS)	(Korova KOW 20) 1981

For this project David Balfe of **The Teardrop Explodes** teamed up with his business partner Bill Drummond, an art student Lori Lartey, Gary Dwyer (also of **Teardrop Explodes**), former Deaf School drummer Tim Whittaker and Ray Martinez. *Touch* is an excellent electro-pop 45, originally issued on Zoo in 1978, then on Sire and a year later its Korova subsidiary with a different flip side. In the lyrics Lori tells of her love for a pretty Japanese boy in a seductive voice. The record features an ear-catching oriental guitar solo and evokes the mysteries of the East as well as the mysteries of adolescence, love and the thrill of holiday romances. The follow-up *The Lonely Spy* was another fine effort in a similar style. This was also included on the compilation *To The Shores Of Lake Placid* (Zoo ZOO FOUR) in 1982. It also appeared on the 'B' side to a third issue of *Touch* in 7" and 12" formats in 1981.

LORI AND THE CHAMELEONS - Touch.

The Loved One

Personnel:	DRYDEN HAWKINS	voice, audio induction units, sonics, period indication	A
	ZEB	gtrs, produced organ, bs	A

45:	Telstar/Sunday Morning Fever (PS)	(Polydor POSP 295) 1981

An experimental electronics outfit. As well as this 45 they contributed *Observations* to *Some Bizzare Album* (Some Bizzare BZLP 1) in 1981.

Lene Lovich

HCP

ALBUMS:	1 STATELESS	(Stiff SEEZ 7) 1979 35
	2 FLEX	(Stiff SEEZ 19) 1980 19
	3 NO MAN'S LAND	(Stiff SEEZ 44) 1982 -

NB: (1) also issued on CD (Line LICD 901066) 1994 and again with extra tracks (Disky STIFFCD 20) 1994. (2) also issued on CD (Line LICD 901071) 1991 and again (Disky STIFFCD 21) 1994. (3) also issued on CD (Disky STIFFCD 22) 1994. There are also a number of compilations, *The Stiff Years Vol. 1* (Great Expectations PIPCD 007) 1990, *The Stiff Years Vol. 2* (Great Expectations PIPCD 008) 1990, *The Stiff Years* (Disky HRCD 8035) 1994 and *The Very Best Of Lene Lovich* (Disky DC 878582) 1997. There was also a promo-only album *Lene Lovich Interview* (Stiff LENE 1) 1978.

HCP

45s:	I Saw Mommy Kissing Santa Claus/The Christmas Song (Merry Christmas To You)/ Happy Christmas	(Polydor 2058 812) 1976 -
*	I Think We're Alone Now/ Lucky Number (PS)	(Stiff BUY 32) 1978 -
+	I Think We're Alone Now (Japanese)/ Lucky Number	(Stiff BUY J32) 1978 -
	Lucky Number/Home (PS)	(Stiff BUY 42) 1979 3
	Lucky Number/Home/ Lucky Number (alt. version) (12", PS)	(Stiff BUYIT 42) 1979 -
	Say When/One Lonely Heart (PS)	(Stiff BUY 46) 1979 19
	Say When/One Lonely Heart (12", PS)	(Stiff BUYIT 46) 1979 -
	Bird Song/Trixi (PS)	(Stiff BUY 53) 1979 39
	Bird Song/Trixi/Too Tender (12", PS)	(Stiff BUYIT 53) 1979 -
	Angels/The Fly (PS)	(Stiff BUY 63) 1980 -
	Angels/The Fly (12", PS)	(Stiff BUYIT 63) 1980 -
	What Will I Do Without You?/Joan/Monkey Talk/ The Night/Too Tender (To Touch)/You Can't Kill Me (double 45 set)	(Stiff BUY 69) 1980 58
	New Toy/Cat's Away (PS)	(Stiff BUY 97) 1981 53
	New Toy/Cat's Away (12", PS)	(Stiff BUYIT 97) 1981 -
	Lucky Number/New Toy (PS)	(Stiff BUY 149) 1982 -
	It's You, Only You/Blue (PS)	(Stiff BUY 164) 1982 68
	It's You, Only You/Blue (picture disc)	(Stiff BUY 164) 1982 -

NB: * 5,000 copies only were pressed. + Mail order promo only.

Although American-born **Lene Lovich** was an important part of the Stiff entourage launched in 1978. She had previously worked on horror film soundtracks. Her vocal eccentricities and warbled intonation made a decided impression on the 'Be Stiff' tour. She also contributed two tracks, *Money Talk* and *Momentary Breakdown* to *Can't Start Dancin'* (Stiff SOUNDS 3) in 1978. She could also play the sax and was partnered by her shaven-headed husband guitarist Les Chappell.

Her debut album *Stateless* was in truth patchy, but distinctive for her chirpy vocal style. It contained her classic *Lucky Number* single, which climbed to No. 3 and spent eleven weeks in the chart. A second hit *Say When* was culled from the album and this peaked at No. 19 during a respectable ten week chart stint. The songs are performed to keyboard-dominated arrangements and despite the variable material, it rose to No. 35 during its eleven weeks in the chart. The track order was reshuffled and the content remixed on the U.S. version.

LENA LOVICH - Flex EP.

Flex utilises synthesizers to conjure up a more modern sound although the better material, which brought her two further hits - *Bird Song* (No. 39) and *What Will I Do Without You?* (No. 58), as well as one miss *Angels* - can't outshine the best songs on *Stateless*. By now she was better-known and *Flex* made the Top Twenty, although it was only in the charts for six weeks.

She went on to enjoy further minor hits with *New Toy* (No. 53) and *It's You, Only You* (No. 68) and a third, less successful album *No Man's Land*. There was an eight year gap before **Lovich** and Chappell teamed up for a further album *March* in 1990.

Compilation appearances, in addition to ones on the Stiff label, include *Lucky Number* on *New Wave Classics* (2-CD) (Disky DOU 878282) 1998. There are also retrospective compilations like *The Stiff Years* and *The Very Best Of Lene Lovich*.

Lene Lovich will be remembered for her distinctive vocal style and eccentricities, which paved the way for others in the future.

Nick Lowe

Personnel: (up to 1986)			
BILLY BREMNER	gtr		A
DAVE EDMUNDS	gtr		A
NICK LOWE	vcls, bs, gtr		ABC
TERRY WILLIAMS	drms		A
MARTIN BELMONT	gtr		BC
PAUL CARRACK	keyb'ds		BC
BOBBY IRWIN	drms		BC
JAMES ELLER	bs		C

				HCP
ALBUMS: (up to 1986)	1(A)	THE JESUS OF COOL	(Radar RAD 1)	1978 22
	2(A)	LABOUR OF LUST	(Radar RAD 21)	1979 43
	3(B)	NICK THE KNIFE	(F-Beat XXLP 14)	1982 99
	4(C)	THE ABOMINABLE SNOWMAN	(F-Beat XXLP 18)	1983 -
	5(C)	NICK LOWE AND HIS COWBOY OUTFIT	(RCA 79338)	1984 -
	6(C)	ROSE OF ENGLAND	(F-Beat 70765)	1985 -

NB: (1) also issued on CD (Demon FIENDCD 131) 1988 and again on vinyl. (2) also issued on CD (Collectors Choice CK 36087) 1988 and (Demon FIENDCD 182) 1990 and again on vinyl. (3) reissued (Demon FIEND 183) 1986 and on CD (Demon FIENDCD 183) 1990. (4) also issued on CD (Demon FIENDCD 184) 1990. (5) also issued on CD (Demon FIENDCD 185) 1990. (6) also issued on CD (Demon FIENDCD 73) 1988. There are also a number of compilations; *16 All-Time Lowe's* (Demon FIEND 20) 1984 and later on CD (Demon FIENDCD 20) although it contained four extra tracks and again (Diablo DIAB 801) 1993. *Nick's Nack* (Demon FIENDCD 59) 1986, also on vinyl; *Basher: The Best Of Nick Lowe* (Demon FIENDCD 142) 1989, also released on vinyl as a double album; *Boxed* (4-CD set) (Demon NICK 1) 1994 and *The Doings* (4-CD set) (Demon LOWE 50) 1999.

EP:	1(-)	BOWI (PS)	(Stiff LAST 1) 1977

			HCP
45s: (up to 1986)	So It Goes/Heart Of The City (PS)	(Stiff BUY 1)	1976 -
	Halfway To Paradise/ I Don't Want The Night To End (PS)	(Stiff BUY 21)	1977 -
	I Love The Sound Of Breaking Glass/ They Called It Rock (PS)	(Radar ADA 1)	1978 7
	Little Hitler/Cruel To Be Kind (PS)	(Radar ADA 12)	1978 -
	American Squirm/(What's So Funny 'Bout) Peace, Love And Understanding (PS)	(Radar ADA 26)	1978 -
	Crackin' Up/Basing Street (PS)	(Radar ADA 34)	1979 34
	Cruel To Be Kind/ Endless Grey Ribbon (PS)	(Radar ADA 43)	1979 12
	Burning/Zulu Kiss (PS)	(F-Beat XX 20)	1982 -
	My Heart Hurts/ Pet You And Hold You (PS)	(F-Beat XX 23)	1982 -
	My Heart Hurts/Pet You And Hold You/Cracking Up/ (What's So Funny 'Bout) Peace, Love And Understanding (double 7", PS)	(F-Beat XX 23)	1982 -
	Ragin' Eyes/Tangue-Rae (PS)	(F-Beat XX 31)	1983 -
	Ragin' Eyes/Tangue-Rae/ Cool Reaction (12", PS)	(F-Beat XXT 31)	1983 -
	Half A Man And Half A Boy/Awesome	(F-Beat XX 34)	1984 53
	Half A Man And Half A Boy/Awesome/ Cool Reaction (12", PS)	(F-Beat XXT 34)	1984 -
	L.A.F.S. (Love At First Sight)/(Hey Big Mouth) Stand Up And Say That (PS)	(F-Beat XX 36)	1984 -
	L.A.F.S. (Love At First Sight)/(Hey Big Mouth) Stand Up And Say That/Baby It's You (12", PS)	(F-Beat XXT 36)	1984 -
	I Knew The Bride (When She Used To Rock 'n' Roll)/ Darlin' Angel Eyes	(F-Beat 2B 40303)	1985 -
	I Knew The Bride (When She Used To Rock 'n' Roll)/ Darlin' Angel Eyes/ Seven Nights To Rock (12", PS)	(F-Beat 2B 40304)	1985 -

Although **Nick Lowe** had been around in the music business a long time before the late seventies, he is one of those whose career gained considerable impetus with the onset of 'new wave' in the late seventies and early eighties.

Lowe was born on 24th March 1949 in Woodchurch, Suffolk. He formed a school band with Brinsley Schwarz in 1963 called Sound Plus 1. They evolved into Kippington Lodge in 1967 and, after a series of singles, were relaunched as Brinsley Schwarz in 1969 and over the next few years established themselves as an important part of the pub-rock scene in London. They finally disbanded in 1975. A year earlier **Lowe** had made a brief appearance in 'Stardust'. Now with his careeer as a rock star in abeyance, he became a producer in July 1975. The albums he worked on inlcuded The Kursaal Flyers' *Chocs Away*, Dr. Feelgood's second album *Malpractice* and Graham Parker's *Howling Wind*. He also recorded a couple of glam-rock singles under pseudonyms. First there was the Tartan Horde's *Bay City Rollers, We Love You / Rollers Theme* (United Artists UP 35891) 1975, which was a parody of the then current teenyboppers The Bay City Rollers. The second credited to The Disco Brothers was *Let's Go To The Disco / Everybody Dance* (United Artists UP 36057) 1976 which parodied the disco craze sweeping the music world in this era. The two singles were even combined on one album *The Disco Brothers / Tartan Horde* EP in 1976.

NICK LOWE - I Love The Sound Of Breaking Glass.

In 1976, **Lowe** signed to Jake Riviera's new Stiff label, which became a Vanguard for punk and new wave. His first single *So It Goes* was the first release on the new label. He also became the label's in-house producer responsible for **The Damned**'s first album *Damned Damned Damned* and **Elvis Costello**'s first single *Less Than Zero* among others. Outside of Stiff he also produced **Dave Edmunds**' *Get It* album and Clover's *Chicken Funk*.

In May 1977, he released a four track EP for Stiff called *Bowi*. The title was a tongue-in-cheek response to David Bowie's *Low* album. In July, having written **Edmunds**' *I Knew The Bride*, he joined **Edmunds**' group Rockpile, but he still continued his solo career and working as a producer. He handled production on **Costello**'s debut album *My Aim Is True* and The Rumour's *Max*. In October **Lowe** released what would turn out to be his last single on Stiff, a cover of Billy Fury's *Halfway To Paradise*. **Lowe** was also a key performer on the 'live Stiffs' tour with labelmates **Elvis Costello**, **Wreckless Eric** and **Ian Dury**. With his backing band he contributed *I Knew The Bride* and *Let's Eat* to the *Stiff Live Stiffs* (Stiff GET 1) 1978 tour album. In 1977, *Heart Of The City* was included on *Hits - Greatest Stiffs* (Stiff FIST 1). At the end of the year, like **Costello** he left Stiff for Riviera's new Radar Records.

1978 was the year **Lowe** broke through into the mainstream. In February his *Jesus Of Cool* album was released. It's full of well-crafted, intelligent 'new wave' pop tunes. One of its strongest tracks *I Love The Sound Of Breaking Glass* was released as a 45 and became a smash Top 10 hit. It climbed to No. 7 during its eight weeks in the charts. It also gained more exposure from its inclusion on the soundtrack to *That Summer!* (Spartan/Arista SPART 1088) in 1979. Another cut *Little Hitler*, co-written with **Dave Edmunds**, was released on 45 in May but missed out. A non-album 45 *American Squirm* released in November met with the same fate. It featured on its flip side *(What's So Funny 'Bout) Peace, Love And Understanding*, which had been penned by Brinsley Schwarz.

The *Jesus Of Cool* album had done well. Here in Britain it spent nine weeks in the charts, peaking at No. 22. It also got to No. 127 in the U.S. charts which so many British new wave artists had difficulty breaking into. For U.S. release the album had been retitled *Pure Pop For Now People*. On this album the stompy *Shake And Pop* was given a different much smoother arrangement and retitled *They Call It Rock*. The scorching live version of *Hearts Of The City* was replaced with a studio recording and **Lowe**'s parody of The Bay City Rollers', *Roller Show* was added. Mickey Jupp's *Juppanese*, which **Lowe** co-produced in May, was his last production assignment for Stiff, although he continued his production work. **The Pretenders**' *Stop Your Sobbing* and **Elvis Costello**'s *Armed Forces* were further production credits in early 1979.

In May 1979, he released a new 45 *Crackin' Up*. It spent five weeks in the charts, peaking at No. 34. *Crackin' Up* had been taken from his next album *Labour Of Lust*, which had been recorded in London and Helsinki with Rockpile (**Dave Edmunds**, Terry Williams (drms) and Billy Bremner (gtr)). This was a less frenetic effort than his debut album. It mostly comprised mid-tempo rockers and love songs. These ranged from the sincere (*You Make Me* and *Without Love*) to the lighthearted (*Switch Board Susan* and *American Squirm*, an earlier unsuccessful single). It also included *Cruel To Be Kind*, which he'd co-written with an old Brinsley Schwarz friend Ian Gomm. The punters liked *Labour Of Lust* on both sides of the Atlantic. It spent six weeks in the charts in Britain peaking at No. 43 and climbed to No. 31 in the 'States.

It was a hectic summer for **Lowe**. On U.S. Independence Day Rockpile commenced a U.S. tour supporting Blondie. Then on 15th August the film 'Americathon', which **Lowe** had contributed to the soundtrack of, enjoyed its premier. Three days later he married Carlene Carter (Johnny Cash's stepdaughter in LA). **Lowe** was now at the height of his popularity and on 1st September 'Born Fighters', a documentary about **Nick Lowe** and **Dave Edmunds** was shown on TV in Britain. The same month he achieved a No. 12 hit with *Cruel To Be Kind* (a re-recording of the 'B'-side to *Little Hitler*) on both sides of the Atlantic. After this **Lowe** put his solo career on hold whilst he concentrated during 1980 on working on the road and in the studio with Rockpile. Their only album *Seconds Of Pleasure* was released in October 1980. He still found time for his production work on **Elvis Costello**'s *Get Happy*, although **Costello**'s *Trust* in January 1981 would prove to be the last album he produced for **Costello** for five years.

In February 1981, Rockpile split and **Lowe** formed his own outfit Nick Lowe and The Chaps. He also produced Carlene's *Blue Nun* album in September. In February 1982, Nick Lowe and The Chaps changed name to Noise To Go. This outfit was responsible for the *Nick The Knife* album. It featured some danceable love songs like *Queen Of Sheba* and *Couldn't You Love More Than I Do* as well as more melancholic material like *Raining Raining*, *Too Many Teardrops* and *My Heart Hurts*. In Britain it spent a disappointing two weeks in the charts at No. 99, but in the 'States it got to No. 50. Two 45s - *Burning* and *My Heart Hurts* - were culled from the album but neither charted. In October, **Lowe** produced The Fabulous Thunderbirds album *Rhythm*.

After this James Eller was added to the line-up on bass. The modified line-up worked on *The Abominable Snowman*, which hit the shops in June 1983. It was co-produced by Roger Bechirian and marked another good performance by **Lowe**. *We Want Action* and *Raging Eyes* were lively upbeat numbers. The latter had been released as a 45 to preview the album in April but it did not chart. In some ways the album was less typical for **Lowe**. There's the use of strings on *How Do You Talk To An Angel* and a more serious side of **Lowe** is apparent on *Wish You Were Here*. The album missed out commercially in Britain but got to No. 129 in the 'States.

In January 1984, **Lowe** co-produced John Hiatt's album *Riding With The Kings*. Nick returned to his own band, releasing a new album *Nick Lowe And His Cowboy Outfit* in May 1984. Again this featured a variety of styles. The Tex-Mex track *Half A Boy And Half A Man* was selected for 45 release. This gave him his first hit single for almost five years, climbing to No. 53 during its three weeks in the charts. The album also featured *L.A.F.S. (Love At First Sight)* (which was released as a follow-up 45 but failed to chart), *Baby It's You* (a duet with **Elvis Costello**) and *Awesome*, a fifties instrumental. The album didn't make the U.K. charts but got to No. 113 in the U.S..

In September 1984, a compilation *Sixteen All-Time Hits* was released on Demon. Concentrating very much on his earlier material (almost half of the songs were from his first album) it included material from his debut 45 *So It Goes* onwards. However, it didn't chart.

His late 1985 album *Rose Of England* was again varied. Alongside some of **Lowe**'s first compositions like the title cut, *Lucky Dog* and *(Hope To God) I'm Right*, was a cover of **Elvis Costello**'s *Indoor Fireworks*, John Hiatt's *She Don't Love Nobody* and a new, rather unnerving version of *I Knew The Bride*, which is produced by Huey Lewis, who performs it with his band, The News. The album would prove to be his last for F-Beat and his last recording with The Cowboy Outfit, which had featured on the previous two albums.

I Knew The Bride was released as a 45 in the 'States, where it climbed to No. 77, but neither the album or 45 made the charts in Britain. The 45's success in the 'States was probably more due to the involvement of Huey Lewis and The News, who were enormously popular there at the time.

Lowe bowed out of any further recordings until February 1988 when he returned with a new album *Pinker And Prouder Than Precious*. Demon records released a second **Lowe** compilation *Nick's Knack* in March 1986. This features Rockpile's *Now And Always*, *Basing Street* (the 'B' side to *Crackin' Up*) and a selection of mostly weaker material from all his albums up to *The Abominable Snowman*. As we leave the time span of this book, **Lowe** continued his close association with **Elvis Costello** handling production of his *Blood And Chocolate* album.

Lowe's production credits in the seventies and eighties included Richard Hell, **The Pretenders**, Carlene Carter and **Wreckless Eric**. He continued other low profile recordings in the nineties and early in the decade teamed up with Ry Cooder, John Hiatt and Jim Kellner to form Little Village, a sort of roots supergroup.

Lowe's credentials in the history of punk and new wave were underscored when *So It Goes* was included on *1-2-3-4 - A History Of Punk And New Wave 1976 - 1979* (MCA/Universal MCD 60066), a 5-CD box set issued in 1999.

The Low Numbers

Personnel incl: PHIL PAYNE

45:        Keep In Touch/Nine All Out (PS)   (Warner Bros K 17493) 1979

Jimmy Pursey handled the production on this mod revival band's single, which was originally scheduled for release on the J.P. label. Still, it got to see the light of day when it was picked up by Warner Brothers.

Ludus

Personnel:
- ARTHUR CADMON (PETER SADLER) gtr — A
- LINDER (LINDA MULVEY) vcls — ABC
- PHIL 'TOBY' TOLMAN drms — ABC
- WILLIE TROTTER bs — AB
- IAN DEVINE (IAN PINCOMBE) bs — C

ALBUM: 1( ) DANGER CAME SMILING (New Hormones ORG 20) 1982

NB: There was also a cassette *Linder Sings Bardot*.

EP: 1( ) THE SEDUCTION (2 x 12", each in PS) (New Hormones ORG 16) 1981

45s:
- The Visit/Lullaby Cheat/Unveil (12", PS) (New Hormones ORG 4) 1980
- My Cherry Is In Sherry/Anatomy Is Not Destiny (PS) (New Hormones ORG 8) 1981
- * PICKPOCKET (New Hormones CAT 1) 1981
- + Mother's Hour/Patient (PS) (New Hormones ORG 12) 1981

NB: * C-30 casette pack with A4 book and button in PVC bag. + Came with a poster.

Ludus was one of the more interesting bands to emerge from Manchester's new wave in the late seventies. They formed in 1978 and were fronted by Linder, a former girlfriend of **Howard Devoto** whose real name was Linda Mulvey. Linda designed the stern and decadent covers of **The Buzzcocks'** *Orgasm Addict* 45 and **Magazine**'s *Real Life* album. A pamphlet of fatalistic collages she produced with trainee lawyer Jon Savage was published by New Hormones (ORG 2 to *Spiral Scratch*'s ORG 1). She'd been born in Liverpool in 1954. Her sloganistic and feministic lyrics gave them a distinctive sound. Of their original backing band Arthur Cadmon (real name Peter Sadler) had been in Manicured Noise and drummer Phil 'Toby' Tolman was previously in **Ed Banger and The Nosebleeds**.

Trotter was later replaced by Ian Devine (real name Ian Pincombe) soon after Cadmon had also left. They always avoided the mainstream - their music being largely improvisational.

Later in 1989, Ian Devine linked up with Alison Statton (formerly of Weekend) to form Devine and Statton.

The Lurkers

Personnel (up to 1986):
- ARTURO BASSICK bs — A
- MANIC ESSO drms — ABC
- PETE STRIDE gtr — ABCD
- HOWARD WALL vcls — ABC
- KYM BRADSHAW bs — B
- NIGEL MOORE bs — CD
- MARK FINCHAM vcls — D
- PETE HAYNES drms — D

HCP

ALBUMS (up to 1986):
- 1(C) FULHAM FALLOUT (Beggars Banquet BEGA 2) 1978 57
- 2(C) GOD'S LONELY MEN (Beggars Banquet BEGA 8) 1979 -
- 3(C) LAST WILL AND TESTAMENT (compilation) (Beggars Banquet BOPA 2) 1980 -
- 4(D) THIS DIRTY TOWN (Clay CLAY 104) 1982 -

NB: (1) reissued on CD (Captain Oi! AHOY CD 073) 1997. (2) reissued on CD (Captain Oi! AHOY CD 074) 1997. (3) reissued also on CD (Lowdown BBL 2CD) 1988. (4) reissued (CLAYLP 104) 1989 and on CD (Clay CLAYCD 104) 1993. They reformed in late 1989 and released a number of further albums, *King Of The Mountain* (Street Link LINKLP 087) 1989, *Live And Loud* (live) (Link LINKLP 103) 1989, *Powerlive* (Released Emotions) 1990 and *Live In Berlin* (Released Emotions REM 015CD) 1991. There were also further CD compilations, *Totally Lurked* (Dojo DOJO CD 74) 1992, *The Beggars Banquet Punk Singles* (Anagram CDPUNK 94) 1997 and *Take Me Back To Babylon* (Receiver RRCD 243) 1997. Also *Powerjive* and *King Of The Mountain* have been coupled on one CD (Anagram CDPUNK 69) 1995 and *The BBC Punk Sessions* (Captain Oi! AHOY CD 137) 2000 compiles all four of their Peel Radio One sessions.

THE LURKERS - Fulham Fallout.

EP: 1(D) FINAL VINYL (12", EP) (Let's Dance Now (No Time To Be Strangers)/Midnight Hour/By The Heart/Frankenstein Again) (Clay PLATE 7) 1984

HCP

45s:
- * Free Admission Single: Shadow/Love Story (PS) (Beggars Banquet BEG 1) 1977 -
- Freak Show/Mass Media Believer (PS) (Beggars Banquet BEG 2) 1977 -
- + Ain't Got A Clue/Ooh Ooh I Love You (PS) (Beggars Banquet BEG 6) 1978 45
- (15,000 came with gold free flexi-disc below) Chaos Bros Fulham Fallout Forty-Free (BEG 6 ½)
- I Don't Need To Tell Her/Pills (PS) (Beggars Banquet BEG 9) 1978 49
- Just 13/Countdown (PS) (Beggars Banquet BEG 14) 1979 66
- Shadow/Love Story/Freak Show/Mass Media Believer (reissue double pack) (Beggars Banquet BACK 1) 1979 -
- I Don't Need To Tell Her/Pills//Just 13/Countdown (reissue double pack) (Beggars Banquet BACK 3) 1979 -
- Out In The Dark/Cyanide (PS) (Beggars Banquet BEG 19) 1979 72
- New Guitar In Town/Pick Me Up/Little Ol' Wine Drinker Me (PS) (Beggars Banquet BEG 28) 1979 72
- This Dirty Town (I Can't Find Myself)/Wolf At The Door (Clay CLAY 12) 1982 -
- o Drag You Out/Heroin (It's All Over) (PS) (Clay CLAY 17) 1982 -
- Frankenstein Again/One Man's Meat (Clay CLAY) 1983 -
- Let's Dance Now/Midnight Hour (Clay CLAY 32) 1984 -

NB: * This was originally issued on black vinyl, but was reissued on red, blue or white vinyl in 1978. + This 45 was also reissued with a different picture sleeve and a clear vinyl picture flexi-disc. o Some copies were issued as a picture disc (Clay CLAY 17P) 1982.

From West London, **The Lurkers** were a minimalist punk quartet, who formed in late 1976. **The Lurkers** played a sort of bouncy pub-punk that owed far more to a band like **Eddie and The Hot Rods** than to **The Clash** and **The Jam**. They were one of the first signings of new indie label Beggars Banquet. After an inital 45, the no-nonsense *Shadow* in July 1977 Arturo Bassick left and ex-**Saint** Kym Bradshaw replaced him on bass for a second 45, *Freak Show* in October 1977. On 27th October, they also showcased five of their songs - *Freakshow*, *Total War*, *I'm On Heat*, *Then I Kissed Her* and *Be My Prisoner* - on the first of four sessions for John Peel.

Bradshaw didn't settle and was replaced on bass before their next 45, *Ain't Got A Clue*, released in May 1978, by Nigel Moore. Beggars Banquet came up with the shrewd marketing ploy of giving away a flexidisc with the 45 which helped give the band their first hit. It climbed to No. 45. Most of their songs were raw punk-rock delivered at breakneck speed, a bit like The Ramones. A month earlier they previewed the disc's release in a second John Peel session on 24th April, along with *Pills*, *I Don't Need To Tell Her* and *Jenny*.

Their debut album *Fulham Fallout*, released in April 1978 was produced by Mick Glossop to achieve a good clear sound. Its better songs included the two 45s *Shadows* and *Ain't Got A Clue*, but like much of their music it sounds rather pedestrian overall. With a hit 45 already under their belts this made it to No. 57 and a further 45 from the album *I Don't Need To Tell Her* gave them a second Top 50 hit, just squeezing up to No. 49 in the Summer of 1978.

On 7th August 1978, they recorded a third session for John Peel comprising *Here Come The Bad Times*, *God's Lonely Men*, *In Room 309* and *Countdown*. Their final session, which came five weeks later on 30th January 1979, consisted of *Whatever Happened To Mary*, *Take Me Back To Babylon*, *Out Of The Dark* and *See The World*. All but the last song later turned up on their *God's Lonely Men* album. *Out In The Dark* brought them another minor hit, spending a week in the charts at No. 72, as did its follow-up *New Guitar In Town*. You can also find *Out In The Dark* on *20 Of Another Kind, Vol. 2* (Polydor POLX 1) in 1979.

Unlike some of their better quality punk counterparts **The Lurkers** didn't progress musically and so they paid the price commercially. A second album, released in April 1979, *God's Lonely Men* sounds rather plodding and short of diversity.

They split up for a while in late 1979. **Pete Stride** collaborated on an album with 'Honest' John Plain (of **The Boys**) *New Guitars In Town* (Beggars Banquet BEGA 17) 1980. On this they were backed by Tony Bateman (bs) and Jack Black (drms). It showed promise.

In 1982, **Stride** and Moore got back together again bringing in two new members Mark Fincham on vocals for Howard Wall and Pete Haynes came in for Manic Esso on drums. The new line-up ('D') signed to Clay and released an album *This Dirty Town*, an EP *Final Vinyl* and four 45s before splitting again.

This Dirty Town features several unreleased tracks recorded around the same time as the band released *Dirty Town* as a 45 on Clay in 1982. It should interest their fans but the material isn't up to the quality of their earlier recordings for Beggars Banquet.

Live In Berlin is a limited edition issue drawing material from the (reformed) **Lurkers** in Berlin. The sound quality and playing is adequate and the album does include some new material.

Totally Lurkered, released by Dojo in 1992, is a fifteen-track collection which contains all their best-known Beggars Banquet recordings. The album's first track *Love Story* was the first release for the label and also featured are their minor classics like *New Guitar In Town*, *God's Lonely Men* and *Ain't Got A Clue*.

The Beggars Banquet Singles Collection as its title suggests runs through their 45 'A' and 'B' sides - a few minor classics here like *Shadow*, *Ain't Got A Clue* and *Cyanide* - but overall it tends to confirm why they were only ever a second division punk band.

The BBC Punk Sessions compiles all four of their sessions for John Peel's 'Radio 1' show. The first session, from October 1977, comprising songs like *Freak Show* and *Then I Kissed Her* (retitled as *Then I Kicked Her*) is crude. The second one, from '78 included early versions of their minor hit *Ain't Got A Clue* and its excellent follow-up *I Don't Need To Tell Her*. The third session comprised early versions of songs from their second album *God's Lonely Men*, including the title cut, *Whatever Happened To Mary* and *Out In The Dark*, which are better than the album versions. The final session was never broadcast for some unknown reason. John Plain (ex-**Boys**) is on guitar and their influence is evident. This CD is an essential purchase for **Lurkers**' fans.

There was a further reformation in 1988, which released quite a lot of live material.

If you want to explore **The Lurkers**' music further try the *Totally Lurkered* CD compilation on Dojo in 1992 or *Last Will And Testament - Greatest Hits*, originally released in 1980 and reissued on CD in 1988. In 1991, *Just 13* was included on the compilation *Learning English Vol. 1 By Die Toten Hosen* (Charisma 91823). Earlier in 1979, *I'm On Heat* had figured on *20 Of Another Kind* (Polydor SUPER POLS 1006). Later in 1996, *Shadow* and *Freak Show* got a further airing on *Beggars Banquet - The Punk Singles Collection* (Anagram CDPUNK 73). It also featured a post-**Lurkers** Pete Stride/John Plain duet *Laugh At Me* along with *Just 13* and *Out In The Dark*. Other compilation appearances by the band included *Ain't Got A Clue* on *Punk, Vol. 2* (Music Club MCCD 027) 1991, *Wolf At The Door* on *Live And Nasty* (Emporio EMPRCD 586) 1995 and *Heroin It's All Over* on *Punk - The Worst Of Total Anarchy* (2-CD) (Disky SP 871952) 1996. You'll also find *Ain't Got A Clue* and *Solitaire* on *Spiked* (Summit SUMCD 4094) 1997.

In 1999 *Shadow* got a further airing on *1-2-3-4 - A History Of Punk And New Wave 1976 - 1979* (5-CD set) (MCA/Universal MCD 60066).

Machines

Personnel:	JOHN DEE	drms	A
	DUF	bs, vcls	A
	NICK PAUL	vcls, gtr	A

45:	True Life/Everything's Technical/You Better Hear/ Evening Radio (PS)	(Wax EAR 1) 1978

A one-off punk 45, which came with a stamped picture sleeve and white labels. It is now hard to find and quite an expensive purchase. Not bad considering it was recorded in half an hour in a studio charging £8 an hour in Basildon, Essex! Under these circumstances, the mix is naturally weak and the songs don't stand out either, but they do feature some beautifully crazed guitar playing.

Jimmy Mack

This guy's real name was Paul Wellings and the ranter later ended up working for 'The Sun'. Now that figures if you hear his verbal tirade against social workers entitled *Zombie Mind Eaters* which got an airing on *The Oi! Of Sex* (Syndicate SYNLP 4) 1984, also reissued on CD (Captain Oi! AHOY CD 23) 1994. If you hate social workers (and there is some poignancy in his lyrics), you'll love this!

Mad Virgins

Personnel:	BRAD BRAT	bs	A
	CRACKER JACK	vcls	A
	GARY LEGO	drms	A
	BRIAN TEEN	gtr	A
	TOMMY	gtr	A

45:	Fuck And Suck/I Am A Computer	(Romantic EDE 5) 1978

Given the 'A' side's title airplay was non-existent and this remains unheard by most punk fans.

Magazine

Personnel:	BARRY ADAMSON	bs	ABCDEF
	HOWARD DEVOTO	vcls	ABCDEF
	BOB DICKINSON	keyb'ds	A
	MARTIN JACKSON	drms	ABC
	JOHN McGEOGH	gtr	ABCD
	DAVE FORMULA	keyb'ds	CDEF
	JOHN DOYLE	drms	DEF
	ROBIN SIMON	gtr	E
	BEN MANDELSON	gtr	F

				HCP
ALBUMS:	1(C)	REAL LIFE	(Virgin V 2100) 1978	29
	2(D)	SECONDHAND DAYLIGHT	(Virgin V 2121) 1979	38
	3(D)	THE CORRECT USE OF SOAP	(Virgin V 2156) 1980	28
	4(E)	PLAY LIVE	(Virgin V 2184) 1980	69
	5(F)	MAGIC, MURDER AND THE WEATHER	(Virgin V 2200) 1981	39
	6(-)	AFTER THE FACT (compilation)	(Virgin VM 1) 1982	-

NB: (1) reissued in March 1984 and on CD (Virgin CDV 2100) 1988. (2) reissued and also on CD (Virgin CDV 2121) 1988. (3) reissued and also on CD (Virgin CDV 2156) 1988. (4) reissued and also on CD (Virgin CDV 2184) 1988. (5) reissued and also on CD (Virgin CDV 2200) 1988. There's also a CD 'best of' *Rays And Hail 1978-81* (Virgin COMCD 5) 1987, which was reissued in 1993. Also relevant are

Scree (Rarities 1976-81) (Virgin CDOVID 312) 1990, *BBC Radio 1 Live In London (1978)* (CD) (Windsong 040) 1993 and *Maybe It's Right To Be Nervous Now* (3-CD) (Virgin MAGBOX 1) 2000 and the set is accompanied by *Magazine.... (Where The Power Is)* (Virgin CDV 2924) 2000, a single CD compilation that overhauls *Rays And Hail 1978 - 81*.

EP:	1(-) SHOT BY BOTH SIDES (12", EP) (Shot By Both Sides/Goldfinger/Give Me Everything/Song From Under The Floorboards)	(Virgin VS 592-12)	1983

HCP

45s: +	Shot By Both Sides/My Mind Ain't So Open (PS)	(Virgin VS 200)	1978 41
	Touch And Go/Goldfinger (PS)	(Virgin VS 207)	1978 -
	Give Me Everything/You Big Dummy (PS)	(Virgin VS 237)	1978 -
	Rhythm Of Cruelty/TV Baby (PS)	(Virgin VS 251)	1979 -
	A Song From Under The Floorboards/Twenty Years Ago (PS)	(Virgin VS 321)	1980 -
	Thank You (Falettinme Be Mice Elf Again)/The Book (PS)	(Virgin VS 328)	1980 -
	Upside Down/Light Pours Out Of Me (PS)	(Virgin VS 334)	1980 -
	Sweetheart Contract/Feed The Enemy (PS)	(Virgin VS 368)	1980 54
*	Sweetheart Contract/Feed The Enemy/Twenty Years Ago/Shot By Both Sides (all live) (7" double-pack)	(Virgin VS 368)	1980 -
	About The Weather/In The Dark (PS)	(Virgin VS 412)	1981 -
	About The Weather/In The Dark/The Operative (12", PS)	(Virgin VS 412-12)	1981 -

NB: + This was also released with a card or paper picture sleeve. * Also issued as a 12" (Virgin VS 368-12) 1980.

Magazine were formed in 1977 by **Howard Devoto**, who'd previously been vocalist with **The Buzzcocks**. Although a stated reason for leaving **The Buzzcocks** was to return to college, he also wanted to experiment with a more complex and sophisticated form of rock music, which still retained the new found energy of punk. The musicians that made up **Magazine** (line-up 'A') were previously unknowns and Bob Dickinson left after only four months.

They played their first live gig in October 1977 on the final night of Manchester's Electric Circus club alongside **The Buzzcocks**. They were quickly snapped up by Virgin in January 1978 and that month their stunning debut 45 *Shot By Both Sides* was released. This was one of their finest moments, epitomising all that was best about their futuristic music. A lush, multi-layered web of driving bass and keyboards mixed with **Devoto**'s somewhat unnerving vocals. It climbed to No. 41 and would probably have got higher had they not sacrificed an appearance on 'Top Of The Pops' by refusing to mime to it.

On 20th February 1978, they recorded the first of four sessions for John Peel. It featured two cuts from their *Real Life* album (the title cut and the

MAGAZINE - Real Life.

MAGAZINE - Secondhand Daylight.

superb *Light Pours Out Of Me*, the 'B' side of their debut 45, *My Mind Ain't So Open* and *Touch And Go*, which would be released as their next 45. This didn't fare as well commercially following its release in April 1978. The 'B' side included a cover of John Barry's *Goldfinger* (theme to the early James Bond classic). After this Dave Formula was added on keyboards.

Their debut album *Real Life* was released in June 1978 to enthusiastic reviews. Aside from their earlier hit single, it contained other tracks like *The Light Pours Out Of Me*, *Motorcade* and *Recoil*, which came near to capturing the band at their best. All the material on the album was penned by **Devoto** and it climbed to No. 29 during its eight week chart stay.

Martin Jackson quit the band after *Real Life*. He joined Chameleons and was later in Swing Out Sister. John Doyle came in as a replacement.

They returned for a second John Peel session comprising *Give Me Everything*, *Burst*, *Big Dummy* and *Boredom* on 31st July 1978.

Two further 45s were released - *Give Me Everything* (backed by a cover of Captain Beefheart's *I Love You, You Big Dummy*) and *Rhythm Of Cruelty* - but failed commercially.

Their second album, *Secondhand Daylight* was released in March 1979. It wasn't met with universal acclaim and contained very few 45 cuts (only *Rhythm Of Cruelty* their last 'A' side released the previous month). *I Wanted Your Body*, *Back To Nature* and *Permafrost* are the album's three relative masterpieces. The former has a gripping melody provided by keyboardist David Formula and bassist Barry Adamson. *Back To Nature* is arguably one of the band's finest songs with floods of imagery and **Devoto** on tip-top form vocally. *Permafrost*, the final cut, exhibits an Iggy Pop influence lyrically and vocally to provide a chilling end to what was a strong closing number:-

"As the day stops dead
At the place where we've stopped
I will drug you and fuck you
On the permafrost"
(from *Permafrost*)

Whilst not as innovative as *Real Life*, *Secondhand Daylight* sold quite wel climbing to No. 38 and spending a further eight weeks in the charts.

On 14th May 1979, they played a third Peel session. This time *TV Baby* (flip side to their earlier *Rhythm Of Cruelty* 45), *Thank You Falettinme* a cover of a Sly and The Family Stone song, (later released as a 45 in March 1980) and *Permafrost* (which had appeared on *Secondhand Daylight*) were on offer.

The second half of 1979 was a quiet period for the band. Following *Secondhand Daylight* in March 1979, they had no further recorded output until the 45 *A Song From Under The Floorboards* was released in February 1980. They recorded their fourth and final Peel session on 14th January 1980. This featured *A Song From Under The Floorboards*, *20 Years Ago* (its flip side), *Look What Fear Has Done* (not hitherto released on vinyl) and *Model Worker* (which later appeared on their *Correct Use Of Soap* album).

In April 1980, a further 45 *Upside Down* was issued with a live version of the classic *The Light Pours Out Of Me* on the flip side. Like all their 45s since their superb debut *Shot By Both Sides*, this also failed to chart.

The Correct Use Of Soap, released in May 1980, proved to be their best selling album of all, climbing to No. 28 in the album charts in which it spent a total of four weeks. It did indeed include some of their best songs like *A Song From Under The Floorboards*, *Philadelphia* and *Sweetheart Contract*. Capturing the band back at its best again, it is recommended.

In July 1980, live versions of four of their finest songs - *Sweetheart Contract*, *Feed The Enemy*, *Twenty Years Ago* and *Shot By Both Sides* - were issued in both 12" and double-pack 7" formats. Fans of the band will want these in their collection.

During the summer John McGeogh departed to join **Siouxsie and The Banshees**. He was later in **Public Image Ltd**. He was replaced on guitar by former **Ultravox** member Robin Simon.

The new line-up recorded *Play* live during an Australian concert at Melbourne Festival Hall. It includes many of their best songs, although Robin Simon didn't sound fully integrated into the band and the production could have been better. Robin Simon didn't hang around and was replaced by Ben Mandleson, formerly of **Amazorblades** for what would prove to be the final **Magazine** line-up. Initially he was hired to play on the sessions for the next album *Magic, Murder And The Weather*, but he remained as a full-time member.

This final album was preceded in May 1981 by the release of one of its cuts *About The Weather* as a 45. Again, it was a 45 that didn't do well commercially. **Devoto**, meanwhile, was tiring from the pressures of constant touring as he had with **The Buzzcocks** earlier. Three weeks before the album's release, he announced he was unwilling to tour to promote it. The album itself reached No. 39 in the charts during a three week residency. Compared with previous efforts Dave Formula's keyboards were very much to the fore. Whilst it was not **Devoto**'s intention to disband the group through his announcement, given how key he was to the line-up, the other members felt there was little value in carrying on the band without him.

There have been a number of compilations which readers wanting an introduction to the band's music for the first time may want to investigate. *After The Fact* released in 1982 was essentially a 'best of', including their singles and a number of 'B' sides. The U.S. version contained three additional cuts *Goldfinger*, *My Mind Ain't So Open* and *The Book*.

Rays And Hail 1978-81 (The Best Of Magazine) was a later compilation, again with similar material but greater emphasis on album material. It includes *Shot By Both Sides* and most of their best songs along with a good biographical booklet.

MAJOR ACCIDENT - Massacred Melodies.

There's also a CD collection of rarities *Scree*, released in 1990. *Scree* includes the band's harder to find 'B' sides and non-album singles. Arguably their two finest moments were *Shot By Both Sides* (a live version of the song is featured on this CD) and *The Light Pours Out Of Me* (the CD features an alternate take). Also of interest is a cranked up version of Captain Beefheart's *I Love You You Big Dummy*.

After their split in mid-1981 **Howard Devoto** went solo and set up a new band, which included Dave Formula on keyboards. His album *Jerky Versions Of The Dream* climbed to No. 57 in the album charts in August 1983.

The *BBC Radio 1 Live In London* CD is a six-track set released in 1993 but taped in 1978. It features compelling versions of *Shot By Both Sides* and *My Tulpa*, although *Back To Nature* is a bit dull and *Great Beautician In The Sky* goes on a bit.

Inevitably their classic *Shot By Both Sides* has appeared on a number of compilations including *The Best Punk Album In The World.... Ever, Vol. 1* (2-CD) (Virgin VTDCD 42) 1995, *The Best Punk Anthems.... Ever* (Virgin VTDCD 198) 1998, *God Save The Punks* (2-CD) (Disky DOU 882552) 1998, *A History Of Punk, Vol. 1* (Virgin CDOVD 486) 1997, *Spiked* (EMI Gold CDGOLD 1057) 1996 and on the 5-CD box set *1-2-3-4 - A History Of Punk And New Wave 1976 - 1979* (MCA/Universal MCD 60066) 1999. In addition, *Song From The Floorboards* was featured on *A Post Punk Primer* (Virgin CDOVD 498) in 1997.

Maybe It's Right To Be Nervous Now is a 3-CD set. The first two CDs contain every non-album **Magazine** track and a few from albums sequenced chronologically over the two CDs, but interspersed between them are ten live cuts from their 1980 album *Play Live* and five differently-mixed tracks that aren't too different from the originals. The third CD contains all their John Peel sessions recorded for the BBC between 1978-80. *Magazine... (Where The Power Is)*, the single compilation CD that came with it, is a revised version of the previously-issued *Rays And Hail 1978-81*. It deletes one cut *I Want To Burn Again* but includes three additional ones.

Barry Adamson joined Pete Shelley and later played for Nick Cave and The Bad Seeds. John Doyle later joined Armour Show and Ben Mandelson joined **The Mekons**. Dave Formula and Barry Adamson were also later in **Visage**.

Magazine were one of the best new wave bands. Their *Real Life* album, in particular, is essential and if you haven't heard it, you should.

Magic Michael

Personnel:	M.G. COUSINS (MICHAEL)	A
	RAT SCABIES	A
	CAPTAIN SENSIBLE	A
	ALGY WARD	A

45: Millionaire/My Friend And I (PS) (Atomic MAGIC 1) 1980

This 45 featured Rat Scabies and Captain Sensible of **The Damned**.

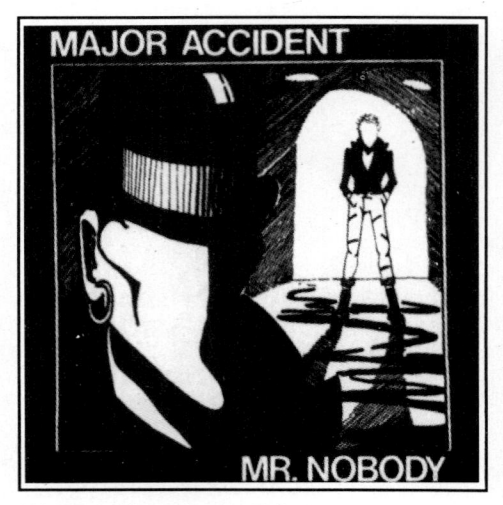

MAJOR ACCIDENT - Mr. Nobody.

MAJOR ACCIDENT - A Clockwork Legion.

Major Accident

Personnel:
DAVE HAMMOND	gtr	ABCDEF	
CON LARKIN	bs	ABCDEFG H I	
PAUL LARKIN	vcls	ABCDEFG H I	
COL STEPHENSON	drms	A	
PORKY STEPHENSON	drms	B	
STU LEE	drms	C	
EVO	drms	DE H	
ANDY HARDING	gtr	EF	
GARY JONES	drms	FG	
STAPS	gtr	G H I	
RICH	drms	I	

ALBUMS:
1(C)	MASSACRED MELODIES	(Step Forward SFLP 9)	1982
2(F)	A CLOCKWORK LEGION	(Flicknife SHARP 016)	1984
3(H)	PNEUMATIC PNEUROSIS	(Flicknife SHARP 027)	1984
4(H)	TORTURED TUNES LIVE	(Syndicate SYNLP 9)	1984
5(H)	CRAZY	(Link LINKLP 012)	1985

NB: (1) and (2) also coupled on one CD (Captain Oi! AHOY CD 027) 1994 and again in 1998. Other CD releases comprised: *Crazy/Tortured Tunes* (Loma LOMACD 43) 1996 (reissues of (2) their live offering from Syndicate and *Crazy*, which was recorded in 1985. Both had previously appeared on Link) and *Clockwork Heroes* (Captain Oi! AHOY CD 16) 1994 and again in 1998. They also contributed six cuts to *The Cry Of The Legion* (DSS DSS 024) 2001, a split CD released with **Foreign Legion**.

45s:
*	Warboots/Terrorist Gang	(Massacred Melodies MAME 1001)	1982
	Mr. Nobody/That's You (PS)	(Step Forward SF 23)	1983
	Fight To Win/Free Man (PS)	(Flicknife FLS 216)	1983
	Leaders Of Tomorrow/Dayo/ Breakaway (PS)	(Flicknife FLS 023)	1983
	Respectable/Man On The Wall (PS)	(Flicknife FLS 026)	1984

NB: * Test pressings only.

Major Accident formed in Darlington in late 1977, although it took the best part of a year for their line-up to stabilise to 'A' above. By then, the band were playing a mixture of punk covers and originals and had become quite a popular attraction on the small north-east England punk circuit. Col Stephenson's brother Porky had taken over on drums by early 1980 when they entered the studio to record a three track EP which included *Terrorist Gang* but remains unreleased because of a row with the recording studio. Line-up 'B' also recorded the original version of what was to become their debut album *Massacred Melodies*, but an incompetent engineer ruined the master tapes so the recordings remain unreleased. Two songs from the session *Warboots* and *Terrorist Gang* did, however, reach the test pressing and artwork stage. By the time they did win a contract with Step Forward Records Stu Lee had replaced Porky Stephenson on drums. It was this line-up ('C') that re-recorded a version of *Massacred Melodies*, which was released in late 1982. To help promote the album the group toured with **Chelsea** and built up quite a good following in the process. The album included *Warboots* and *Terrorist Gang* and is brim full of standard fast-paced Oi!:-

"When you've got them on your feet
And you are cruising in the street
No one dare stand in your way
If they do they're going to pay"
(from *Warboots*)

"Terrorist gang always seems to make the news
Terrorist gang using murder to show their views
Terrorist gang bullethole through the head
Terrorist gang shoot the bastards dead"
(from *Terrorist Gang*)

The stand-out cuts on the album are *Mr. Nobody* (a later 45), which has an excellent guitar intro, *Brides Of The Beast* with its melodramatic opening and more good guitar work, whilst *Psycho* has a noticeable opening drum roll.

In early 1983, Step Forward released *Mr. Nobody* as a 45 with another album cut *That's You* on the flip. They gigged with **Infa-Riot** to help promote it and it made the lower reaches of the indie Top 30. The band were then signed by Flicknife, with Evo having replaced Stu Lee on drums. A non-album 45 *Fight To Win* was released in April 1983, which made No. 23 in the indie chart. The band were expanded to a five-piece with the addition of Andy Harding for the follow-up *Leaders Of Tomorrow* in late 1983, which fared better still climbing to No. 18 in the indie chart.

Soon after its release Evo left. He went on to play with **The Blood**, **Angelic Upstarts** and **Warfare**. His replacement was former Seizure drummer Gary Jones. This new line-up ('F') recorded the *A Clockwork Legion* album and one of its cuts *Respectable* was released as a 45. This featured a distinctive guitar intro and cuts more melodic than most of the earlier work. The album found them in mellower mood. There were still some frantic Oi! numbers, like *Middle Class Entertainment*, *Clockwork Toys*, their earlier 45 *Leaders Of Tomorrow* and *Sorry (We Can't Help You)*. Other cuts showed far more diversity, particularly the ambitious instrumental title cut, the melodic guitar sound of *Affliction* and the child's vocals and spoken passages on *Twisted Mind*.

They also appeared on BBC TV's 'Off The Peg' programme. Soon after Harding and Hammond both left and with just former Blind Attack guitarist Staps joining they reverted back to a four-piece. At the same time they shortened their name to Accident.

During 1984 Syndicate released a 1983 **Major Accident** gig as *Tortured Tunes Live* and Flicknife compiled their 45 releases on a further album *Pneumatic Pneurosis*.

Crazy, released by Link in 1985, featured six new songs and seven re-recorded cuts from their *A Clockwork Legion* album. With Evo installed behind the drums again, they embarked on a successful U.S. tour to help promote it. Another new drummer Rich was featured on a final recording

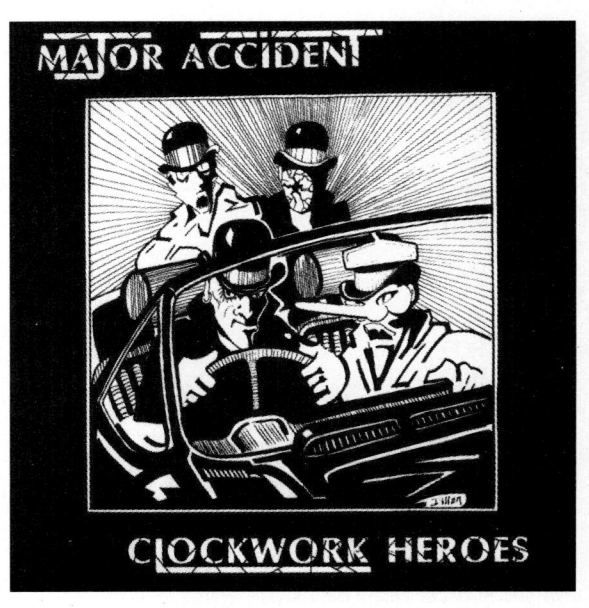

MAJOR ACCIDENT - Clockwork Heroes.

session which produced *Sherwood Rangers*, which featured on the U.K. version of the *Crazy* album. They finally split in 1997 after a short French tour.

Both their first two albums are coupled on one Captain Oi! CD, which is good value. The same label's *Clockwork Heroes* (CD) is a 'best of', which includes the 'A' and 'B' sides of all their singles. There was an album version of this release in both black and white vinyl. Both sides of their *Mr. Nobody* single also resurfaced on *Oi! The Singles Collection, Vol. 1* (Captain Oi! AHOY CD 60) 1996.

Despite frequent personnel changes, this 'Clockwork Orange'-inspired mob and leaders of the Clockwork punk movement recorded some exciting streetpunk and at times diverse music. They were possibly underrated.

Malcolm Practice

Personnel:	ROSS BAILLIE	keyb'ds, vcls	A
	DAVE PITT	lead vcls, bs	A

This duo can be heard playing *Sex Object* and *Kicking Up A Fuss* on *499 2139* (Rocket DIAL 1) 1979.

"Sex object, I'm a sex object
Dirty sex object, dirty sex object
I'm getting sex object"
(from *Sex Object*)

Sex Object is in yer face and *Kicking Up A Fuss* is a tinny keyboard-orientated number, which wouldn't have been out of place in the mid-sixties.

The Man-Eaters

Personnel:	ADAM ANT	vcls	A
	DAVE BARBE	drms	A
	MARK GAUMONT	gtr	A
	ANDY 'ANT' WARREN	bs	A
	TOYAH WILCOX	vcls	A

45: Nine To Five/(flipside by Suzi Pinns) (E.G. Editions EGO 8) 1982

This was a one-off collaboration between **Adam and The Ants** who teamed up with **Toyah** to record the title cut to the soundtrack for 'Nine To Five'!

Mania

Personnel:	GARY	vcls	A
	MACK	gtr	A
	SEAN	bs	A
	SPOT	drms	A

This Sheffield-based band never actually issued their own 45. They did contribute *Power To The People* and *Stick Together* to *Punk's Dead - Nah Mate The Smell Is Jus Summink In Yer Underpants* 12" (Pax PAX 7) 1982 and *Stick Together* got a further airing on *Pax Records Punk Collection* (Anagram CDPUNK 75) 1996. They also recorded for Rot Records, contributing *We Don't Need You* and *Shoulder To Shoulder* to *Two Ninety Nine* (Rot ASS 10) 1984.

The Maniacs

Personnel:	ROB CRASH	bs	A
	ROD LATTER	drms	A
	ALAN LEE SHAW	vcls, gtr	A

ALBUM: 1(A) AIN'T NO LEGEND (Released Emotions REM 006) 1991

45: Chelsea '77/
Ain't No Legend (PS) (United Artists UP 36327) 1977

Rod Latter and Alan Lee Shaw were in **The Rings** together prior to forming this band with Rob Crash. They contributed two cuts, *Break My Heart* and *History* to the *Live At The Vortex* (NEMS 6013) 1978 compilation, the year after this 45 was released.

Latter joined The Monotones when the band split up and was later in **The Adverts**. Shaw formed **The Physicals**, while Crash formed The Psychotic Tanks.

The Maniacs reformed for a while in 1991 and the above album of outtakes was issued. In 1993, Shaw resurfaced again in a **Damned** reunion.

Bob Manton

45: There's No Trees In Brixton Prison/
Brixton Walkabout (PS) (Mainstreet MS 101) 1981

The sole solo outing from the former vocalist of **The Purple Hearts**.

Manufactured Romance

Personnel:	MARK CHAPMAN	gtr	A
	BENNY DI MASSA	drms	A
	NICK MEDLIN	bs	A
	BOB MOORE	gtr	A
	NINA SPENCER	vcls	A

45: I've Had The Time Of My Life/
Room To Breathe (Fresh FRESH 16) 1981

This 45 was issued in various different colour picture sleeves. The 'A' side can also be heard on *Fresh Records Punk Singles Collection* (Anagram CDPUNK 32) in 1994.

Martin and The Brownshirts

Personnel incl:	GRAVENEY
	URMSTON

45: Taxi Driver/Boring (Lightning GIL 507) 1978

A one-off 45 which is hard to find now. The band came from Cleveland and the single was also issued on the Belgian Tabatha label in a different sleeve. *Taxi Driver* later resurfaced on *Lightning Records Punk Collection* (Anagram CDPUNK 79) 1996.

Mass

ALBUM: 1( ) LABOUR OF LOVE (4AD CAD 107) 1981

45: * You And I/Cabbage (PS) (4AD AD 14) 1980

NB: * Some copies came with a poster insert in a die-cut sleeve.

A slightly doomy post-punk act of a similar ilk to **The The**, **Modern English**, **Dif Jaz** and **In Camera**. They were an early incarnation of **Wolfgang Press** and *You And I* can also be heard on *Natures Mortes - Still Lives* (4AD CAD 117CD) 1997.

Mau Maus

Personnel:	PAUL BARKER	drms	A
	ANDY LEVICK	gtr	A
	CHRIS TAYLOR	vcls	A
	KEVIN WARREN	bs	A

ALBUMS:	1(A)	LIVE AT THE MARPLES	(Pax PAX 16) 1983
	2(A)	RUNNING WITH THE PACK	(Pax PAX 20) 1984
	3(A)	MY JUDGE AND JURY	(Rebellion REBLP 1) 1984
	4(A)	FEAR NO EVIL	(Rebellion REBLP 001) 1985

NB: There's also a compilation *The Mau Maus Punk Singles Collection* (Captain Oi! AHOY CD 61) 1998.

The Punk Singles Collection

FRESH RECORDS PUNK SINGLES COLLECTION featuring Manufactured Romance.

EPs:	1(A)	SOCIETY'S REJECTS (Society's Rejects/Secret Society/Images/Social System/The Kill/Leaders/Crisis/The Oath) (PS)	(Pax PAX 6) 1982
	2(A)	FACTS OF WAR (Facts Of War/Just Another Day/Unforgotten/Religious Rights/Running With The Pack) (PS)	(Pax/Paragon PAX 12) 1983
	3(A)	TEAR DOWN THE WARS (PS)	(Rebellion REBEL 01) 1985
	4(A)	SCARRED FOR LIFE (12", PS)	(Rebellion REBEL 1202) 1985
45:		No Concern/Clampdown/Who Do We Suffer (PS)	(Pax PAX 8) 1982

The **Mau Maus** were formed in Sheffield in 1979. They became regulars on the city's live circuit and this led to a deal with Pax Records. A debut EP *Society's Rejects*, released in August 1982, made the indie Top 30. The title cut is a pulsating hardcore punker, which can also be heard on *100% Hardcore Punk* (Captain Oi! AHOY DCD 84) 1998. They followed this with the *No Concern* 7", produced by **Infa Riot**'s Lee Wilson, which also made the indie Top 30.

In July 1983, the **Mau Maus** released a further EP *Facts Of War*, which was their most successful recording commercially. Its highlight was another full-blooded number *Just Another Day*, which can also be heard on *100% Hardcore Punk*. They completed a successful tour with **The Exploited**, but following this, the project was put on ice when Kevin Warren fell ill with cancer.

In this first phase they also appeared on a number of Pax Records compilations:- *Wargasm* (Pax PAX 4) 1982, *Punk's Dead - Nah Mate The Smell Is Jus Summink In Yer Underpants* (12") (Pax PAX 7) 1982, *Bollox To The Gonad's Here's The Testicles* (Pax PAX 14) 1983 and *Daffodils To The Daffodils, Here's The Daffodils* (Pax PAX 19).

They returned in the mid-eighties with a series of self-financed albums and 45s on their own Rebellion label, but found themselves out of step with the times and finally split in late 1985.

The best way of getting to hear them now is to buy the Captain Oi! CD *Mau Maus Punk Singles Collection*, which contains all their EPs and their 45.

Maxim's Trash

Personnel:	DAVE BERK	drms	A
	RAY BURNS	bs, keyb'ds	A
	JOHNNY MOPED	vcls	A
	XERXES	vcls	A
45:	Disco Girls/Blu Shus (PS)		(Gimp GIMP 1) 1979

This was an early version of the **Johnny Moped** band. Although not released until after they had split in 1979, the 45 was recorded in 1975. It was released in a plastic picture sleeve and with hand-stamped white labels. It is now very collectable and expensive to purchase.

Mayhem

Personnel:	COLLO	drms	A
	DEADCAT	bs	A
	JOHNNY	gtr	A
	MICK McGEE	vcls	A
EPs:	1(A)	GENTLE MURDER (Dogsbody/Street Fight/Patriots/Blood Money)	(Riot City RIOT 13) 1982
	2(A)	PULLING PUPPET STRINGS (Gentle Murder/Your Face Fits/Clean Cut)	(Riot City RIOT 24) 1983

This punk band formed in Southport in late 1979. They played regularly with **Vice Squad** who recommended them to Riot City Records. As well as these two EPs, they contributed a storming cut called *Psycho* to *Riotous Assembly* (Riot City ASSEMBLY 1) in 1982, but they split before recording an album. Later, in 1985, *Gentle Murder* figured on *Life's A Riot And Then You Die* (Riot City CITY 009). More recently, *Dogsbody* and *Gentle Murder* have featured on *Riot City Singles Collection, Vol. 1* (Anagram CDPUNK 15) in 1993 and *Vol. 2* (Anagram CDPUNK 55) 1995 gave a further airing to *Street Fight* and *Your Face Fits (Lie And Die)*. Both these last two compilations were also issued on vinyl by Captain Oi!.

Finally, *Psycho* later resurfaced on *100% Hardcore Punk* (Captain Oi! AHOY DCD 84) in 1998.

Malcolm McLaren

Malcolm McLaren was arguably the most important figure in the rise of U.K. punk as he was the man who manipulated **The Sex Pistols** to stardom and without them it's unlikely that punk would have come into being at all.

McLaren had been born in London on 20th January 1947. He came from a middle class background but not from a stable family unit. By the second half of 1965 he had become an art student. He studied at Harrow Art School and then Croydon Art College and later studied film and photography at Goldsmith's College. In 1967, he formed a professional and personal relationship with fellow art student Vivienne Westwood which would prove very significant in the next few years. In this era he also became interested in radical politics, not for political ends, it was the relationship between radical politics and art and culture that interested **McLaren**. He became involved in an anarchic outfit called King Mob for a while. They hijacked Selfridges to give away presents dressed as Santa Claus on one occasion.

Late in 1971, **McLaren** and Westwood acquired an old boutique at 430, Kings Road and turned it into 'Let It Rock', a fifties revival shop. As well as selling rare records and memorabilia from the era, they sold custom-made 'T' shirts, leather jackets and the like, much of which was actually made by fashion designer Vivienne Westwood. The shop was also commissioned to provide costumes for the film 'That'll Be The Day', which was set in the fifties and starred David Essex and Ringo Starr.

In the Spring of 1973, to attract a more diverse audience, they re-christened the shop 'Too Fast To Live, Too Young To Die'. As well as stocking fifties gear, they broadened their costume base and also got the opportunity to display their range of styles at the National Boutique show in New York. Whilst there **McLaren** met The New York Dolls, the glam-punk band who were big on the Manhattan Club scene and about to break nationally having just secured a record contract with Mercury. **McLaren** and The New York Dolls developed a mutual fascination with one another. They were gripped by his way out gear and he was intrigued by their attitude and energy. He linked up with them again during their U.K. and European tour in late 1973.

In April 1974, **McLaren** and Westwood decided to refocus their Kings Road shop once more. They closed 'Too Fast To Live, Too Young To Die' and converted it into a new shop 'Sex', which would concentrate on bondage, rubber and fetish wear but in a style in which it could be widely worn by adventurous young people. **McLaren** also agreed to let Steve Jones (one of his customers) who was trying to form a band with Paul Cook and Warwick Nightingale have some rehearsal space, leaving his friend Bernie Rhodes to oversee them.

In late 1974, **McLaren** returned to the 'States to find The New York Dolls the worse for booze and drugs and in some disarray. He loosely became their manager and got them clad in visually striking red leather and back on the road. However, things backfired badly when their new hammer and sickle logo provoked hostility from America's very strong anti-communist forces. The New York Dolls broke up in 1975 and **McLaren**'s attempts to form a new band with The Dolls' Sylvian Sylvian proved in vain. So **McLaren** returned to London and transferred his musical interest to Steve Jones' band. He decided to take them and groom them as Britain's answer to The New York Dolls. The story appears in **The Sex Pistols** entry. It effectively closed with the 1979 film 'The Great Rock 'n' Roll Swindle' by which time **McLaren** and **The Sex Pistols** had made lots and lots of money. In October 1979, he became manager of **Adam and The Ants**. After helping to create the 'Borundi' style double drumming, he fired **Adam** and took the remaining Ants and fashioned them into a new but similar band **Bow Wow Wow**. To front it he used a 14 year old exotic schoolgirl Annabella L'win who he met in a launderette! **Bow Wow Wow** became hot property in the early eighties.

In 1982, **McLaren** signed to Charisma. He began working with scratchers, rappers and break-dancers, who featured on his debut Top 10 hit *Buffalo Gals*. This was credited to **Malcolm McLaren** and The World Famous Supreme Team.

In 1985, he split somewhat acrimoniously with Vivienne Westwood, but by now he'd launched a new career. He'd become not just a singer and musician but also an organiser, marketeer and front man for such diverse styles as African tribal music, New York style street dance and the like. These recordings were a regular feature in the charts of the 1980s. On his 1984 album *Fans* he even combined hip-hop with opera.

Never one to stand still **McLaren** was one of the really adventurous and provocative figures of the punk/new wave era.

The Meanies

45:	Waiting For You/It's True (PS)	(Vendetta VD 002) 1979	

This band was associated with the 'mod revival' of 1979.

Mean Street

Personnel:	KENNY BISHOP	drms	AB
	CHRIS GORGIER	gtr	AB
	JEREMY HARRINGTON	vcls	AB
	GARY NUMAN (WEBB)	bs	A

Gary Numan formed this punk group in early 1977 and they played at all the major punk venues of the day. Harrington had previously been in the 'B' sides. **Numan** left by the time they recorded *Bunch Of Stiffs* for *Live At The Vortex* (NEMS NEL 6013) 1978, later on CD (Anagram CDPUNK 68) 1995. **Mean Street** continued as a three-piece until splitting in April 1978. They did reform briefly in 1980.

Numan, of course, went on to front **Tubeway Army** and then enjoyed an extremely successful solo career. Bishop and Gorgier were later in **Action Replay**, whilst Harrington went on to play with Gloria Mundi and **The Monochrome Set**.

The Media

Personnel:	MARTIN JACKS	vcls	A
	BRIAN LEE	drms	A
	PETER ROSSIE	gtr	A
	MICHAEL WHICHELLO	bs	A

45:	South Coast Rockers/		
	Back On The Beach Again (PS)	(Brain Booster Music 4) 1980	

A mod revival band from Portsmouth. This 45 came in a very rare picture sleeve. *Back On The Beach Again* is a fairly typical effort with good Who-influenced guitar work which can also be heard on *100% British Mod* (Captain Mod MODSKA DCD 8) 1998.

Medium Medium

Personnel:	STEVE HARVEY	drms	A
	JOHN LEWIS	vcls, sax	A
	ANDY RYDER	gtr	A
	GRAHAM SPINK		A
	ALLAN TURTON	bs	A

ALBUM:	1(A)	THE GLITTERHOUSE	(Cherry Red BRED 19) 1981

45s:	Them Or Me/Freeze (PS)	(Apt. SAP 01) 1980
	Hungry, So Angry/	
	Nadsat Dream	(Cherry Red CHERRY 18) 1981

From the Nottingham area, **Medium Medium** played a sort of heavy funk.

The Glitterhouse album featured a couple of strong cuts *Hungry, So Angry* and *Further Than Funk Dream* but a good standard wasn't maintained throughout. *Them Or Me* can also be found on *Hicks From The Sticks* (Rockburgh Records ROC 111) 1980.

The Mekons

Personnel:	ROSS ALLEN	bs	A
(up to	ANDY CARRIGAN	vcls	A
1981)	TOM GREENHALGH	gtr	A
	JON LANGFORD	drms	A
	KEVIN LYCETT	gtr	A
	MARK WHITE	vcls	A

ALBUMS:	1(A)	THE QUALITY OF MERCY IS NOT STRNEN	
(up to			(Virgin V 2143) 1979
1986)	2(A)	THE MEKONS	(Red Rhino REDMEK 1) 1981
	3(-)	THE MEKONS STORY (compilation)	(CNT CNT 009) 1982
	4(-)	FEAR AND WHISKEY	(Sin SIN 001) 1985
	5(-)	THE EDGE OF THE WORLD	(Sin SIN 003) 1986

NB: (1) also issued on CD (Virgin CDV 2143) 1990. (2) also issued on CD (Cherry Red CDMGRAM 76) 1994. Also relevant is *New York On The Road 86-87* (Roir RUSCD 8269) 2001 on import!

EP:	1(-)	THE ENGLISH DANCING MASTER (12", EP)	
			(CNT CNT 014) 1982

45s:	Never Been In A Riot/32 Weeks/	
(up to	Heart And Soul (PS)	(Fast Products FAST 1) 1978
1986)	Where Were You?/I'll Have To Dance Then	
	On My Own (PS)	(Fast Products FAST 7) 1978
	Work All Week/Unknown Wrecks (PS)	(Virgin VS 300) 1979
	Teeth/Guardian/Kill/	
	Stay Cool (double-pack, gatefold PS)	(Virgin SV 101) 1980

THE MEKONS - Where Were You?

THE MEKONS - The Quality Of Mercy Is Not Strnen.

Snow/Another One	(Red Rhino RED 7)	1980
This Sporting Life/Frustration (PS)	(CNT CNT 001)	1981
This Sporting Life/Frustration/ Never Been In A Riot (PS)	(CNT CNT 001)	1981
This Sporting Life/Fight The Cuts (PS)	(CNT CNT 008)	1982
Crime And Punishment	(Sin SIN 1)	1986
Beaten And Broken/Chop That Child In Half/Hey Susan/ Deep End	(Sin SIN 2)	1986
Hello Cuel World	(Sin SIN 4)	1986
Slightly South Of The Border	(Sin SIN 5)	1986

The Mekons (the name was adapted from one of Dr. Who's enemies) were one of Leeds finest punk bands. They originally signed to the Edinburgh-based indie label Fast Products and both their first two 45s were enthusiastically received. *Where Were You?* is a particularly good single. All five 45 cuts were included on the sampler *Fast Product* (Fast EMC 3312) in 1979. They also played two Peel sessions in 1978. The first, on 14th March 1978, featured *Garden Fence Of Sound, Where Were You, Letters In The Post, Lonely And Wet, Dance And Drink The Mekons* and *Dan Dare Out Of Space*. A second session followed on 2nd October comprising *Like Spoons No More, Treviora Trousers, What Are We Going To Do Tonight* and *I'll Have To Dance Then*.

The positive reception given to their first two 45s lead to a deal with Virgin. This resulted in two 45s - *Work All Week* and *Teeth* (as part of a double pack) and an album, *The Quality Of Mercy Is Not Strnen*. Musically, this visited the guitar funk genre for which fellow Leeds outfit **The Gang Of Four** were better known. Somehow, though, the screaming vocals didn't gell with the backing music and although some critics welcomed the album, it didn't sell in quantites. Its better moments included *I Saw You Dance*, a tale of teenage lust; *After Six*, a telephone-love pop number and *Rosanne*, a song about affection and tolerance, which has some delicate piano buried deep in the mix.

1979 saw them record a further Peel session comprising *I See You Dance, Watch The Film, After 6* and *Beetroot*.

At the start of 1981, they issued a second album *The Mekons* on the independent Red Rhino label. This veered more towards synthesized pop with a danceable beat. The same month, January 1981, saw their final Peel session on which they played *East Is Red, Weak Chain, The Building* and *English White Boy Engineer*.

The Mekons Story was a compilation on which tracks were interspersed by narrative. They split in 1981 but reformed in the mid-eighties and recorded a number of further discs into the nineties.

The Roir import was originally a cassette-only release in 1987. Primitively recorded it comprises live cuts interspersed with verbals from their tour. Two of their classic songs *Where Were You?* and *Never Been In A Riot* have been added to the content of the original cassette release and some attempt has been made to improve the sound quality.

In the mid-eighties Langford was in the post-punk trio the Three Johns.

In 1999, *Where Were You?* was included on *1-2-3-4 - A History Of Punk And New Wave 1976 - 1979* (MCA/Universal MCD 60066), which is a 5-CD box set.

The Mekons still have a sizeable cult following, especially in the U.S.A..

The Members

Personnel:			
	GARY BAKER	lead gtr	A
	ADRIAN LILLYWHITE	drms	ABC
	J.C. MAINMAN (JEAN-MARIE CARROLL)	gtr, vcls	ABC
	CHRIS PAYNE	bs, vcls	ABC
	NICKY TESCO	vcls	AB
	NIGEL BENNETT	lead gtr	BC

HCP

ALBUMS:	1(B)	AT THE CHELSEA NIGHTCLUB	(Virgin V 2120)	1979	45
	2(B)	1980-THE CHOICE IS YOURS	(Virgin V 2153)	1980	-
	3(C)	GOING WEST	(Albion ALB 115)	1983	-

NB: (1) reissued in 1980 and again (Virgin OVED 44) 1990. (2) reissued in 1991 and on CD (Virgin CDOVD 310). (1) and (2) reissued as a double album in 1988 and on one CD (Virgin CDOVD 310) 1990. There's also a CD compilation *Sound Of The Suburbs - A Collection Of The Members' Finest Moments* (Virgin CDOVD 455) 1995.

EP:	1(C)	RADIO	(Genetic-Island)	1982

HCP

45s:			
	Solitary Confinement/ Rat Up A Drainpipe (PS)	(Stiff ONE 3)	1978 -
	The Sound Of The Suburbs/ Handling The Big Jets (PS)	(Virgin VS 242)	1979 12
+	Offshore Banking Business/ Solitary Confinement (PS)	(Virgin VS 248)	1979 31
+	Killing Time/G.L.C. (PS)	(Virgin VS 292)	1979 -
+	Romance/ Ballad Of John And Martin (PS)	(Virgin VS 333)	1980 -
	Flying Again/Disco Oui Oui/Love In A Lift/ Rat Up A Drainpipe (double-pack PS)	(Virgin VS 352)	1980 -
	Working Girl/Holiday In Tanganika (PS)	(Albion 1012)	1981 -
	Working Girl/Holiday In Tanganika/ Everybody's A Holiday (12", PS)	(Albion 12 1012)	1981 -
+	Radio/If You Can't Stand Up (PS)	(Island WIP 6773)	1982 -
+	The Sound Of The Suburbs/ Offshore Banking Business (PS)	(Virgin 58412)	1983 -
+	Working Girl/The Family (PS)	(Albion 1050)	1983 -
+	Going West/Membership (PS)	(Albion 1053)	1983 -

NB: + Also issued as a 12".

The Members were formed in the commuter belt to the south of London - Camberley, Surrey to be precise, in 1977. Their vocalist Nicky Tesco was a

FAST PRODUCT - featuring The Mekons.

THE MEMBERS - The Sound Of The Suburbs.

graduate currently working as an insurance salesman. They played their first gig at London's Roxy club in July 1977. Their recording debut came with *Fear On The Streets*, which was included on the compilation *Streets* (Beggars Banquet BEGA 1) in 1977. This helped them achieve a one-off deal with Stiff on their appropriately named 1-Off subsidiary label. It produced an excellent punk debut *Solitary Confinement*. This set the store for much of their music to follow - simple tunes with good guitar riffs and rough-edged vocals. They have been decribed by some as the intelligent bloke's **Sham 69**. The lyrics dealt with the issues of boredom and loneliness. It was produced by ex-Pink Fairy and fellow Stiff artiste **Larry Wallis**. It featured an accomplished arrangement with a number of subtle time changes and Tesco's coarse, sometimes spoken, vocals were distinctive too.

After this 45 Gary Baker left and was replaced on lead guitar by Nigel Bennett. They spent a year without a recording contract until signing to Virgin in late 1978. They played their first of three sessions for John Peel on 23rd January 1979. On offer were *Love In A Lift*, *Phone-In Show*, *At The Chelsea Nightclub* and *Sound Of The Suburbs*. The first three songs would later figure on their debut album when it was released in April 1979, the final one was released as their follow-up 45 to *Solitary Confinement* in January 1979. *Sound Of The Suburbs* was their finest moment. Simple tune, powerful vocals, good guitar riffs and slightly humorous lyrics about the banality of suburban life. They had produced a punk classic and it got the sales it deserved, climbing to No. 12 in the charts, in which it spent a total of nine weeks.

On 19th February 1979, they did a session for Andy Pebbles comprising *Soho A Go-Go*, *Physical Love*, *Solitary Confinement* and *Handling The Big Jets*. The first and third of these were also included on their debut album and the last was on the flip side to their *Sound Of The Suburbs* 45.

Their third 45, released in March 1979, *Offshore Banking Business* was also significant as one of the first and best sorties into reggae by a white punk band. It also sold pretty well, climbing to No. 31 in the charts, in which it enjoyed a five week residency.

Their debut album *At The Chelsea Nightclub*, when it was released in April 1979, included their first and third 45s (but not *Sound Of The Suburbs*) and most of their best songs. It is unreservedly recommended, a shame it didn't feature their classic 45, though. It was also effectively produced by Adrian Lillywhite's brother Steve and the album reached No. 45 in the charts.

Sadly, their career was all downhill from here. Their next 45 *Killing Time*, released in September 1979, failed to impress but it is of interest for including *G.L.C.* on the flip, which had been an earlier 'A' side for **Menace**. On 1st October 1979, they played a second session for John Peel featuring *Muzak Machine*, *Killing Time*, *Romance* and *Gang War*. A further 45, *Romance* released in March 1980 failed to impress, but along with *Killing Time* and a later May 1980 45 cut *Flying Time*, was included on their second album *1980 - The Choice Is Yours*. The material on this was decidedly inferior to that of their debut. Only their cover of ex-Pink Fairy **Larry Wallis**' *Police Car* really stands out and record sales were disappointing. The band may have realised it wasn't one of their best records because in session for Mike Read the same month it was released they played four cuts, *Muzak Machine*, *Physical Love*, *Brian Was* and *The Gean Men*, which weren't on the album at all.

In spring 1980, Nicky Tesco left the band to go solo. They became a quartet with Jean Carroll and Chris Bayne taking over vocal duties.

In their later days they switched between a number of different record labels. A final Peel session, on 13th April 1981, featured *Boys Like Us*, *Chairman Of The Board*, *Working Girl* and *Birmingham*. They also played a couple of sessions for Richard Skinner on 4th May and 24th September 1981 respectively. The first featured *Going West*, *At The Arcade*, *Nobody* and *Everyday's A Holiday*. The second comprised *Family*, *Boys Like Us*, *Radio* and *Against The World*. Of these, *Radio*, *Boys Like Us* and *Go West* were all released as 45s, as were two versions of *Working Girl*, but all to no avail chartwise.

With new producer Martin Rushent the band attempted a comeback in 1982 with the *Radio* EP. The U.S. version of this contained an extra cut. They had a U.S. album on Arista *Uprhytmn, Downbeat*, the same year. Now adding two horns to make them a sextet, they explored funk and rap, as well as reggae and punk on this crisply produced album. Lyrically, their songs had changed too, losing their humour for social commentary. In 1983, *Uprhythm Downbeat* was released in Britain as *Going West*. The album also included their final four 45s, but it didn't chart and they split in the spring of 1983. This prompted a reissue of their finest monent *The Sound Of The Suburbs* backed by *Offshore Banking Business* in both 7" and 12" format.

In 1988, their first two albums were reissued as a double album set.

Sound Of The Suburbs can also be heard on *The Best Punk Album In The World.... Ever, Vol. 1* (2-CD) (Virgin VTDCD 42) 1995, *The Best Punk Anthems.... Ever* (2-CD) (Virgin VTDCD 198) 1998, *Punk - The Worst Of Total Anarchy* (2-CD) (Disky SP 871952) 1996 and *The Sound Of The Suburbs* (Columbia 4888252) in 1997. In 1999, their punk credentials were confirmed when *Solitary Confinement* was included on *1-2-3-4 - A History Of Punk And New Wave 1976 - 1979* (MCA/Universal MCD 60066), which is a lavishly packaged 5-CD box set.

The Membranes

Personnel:			
(up to 1986)	MARTIN CRITCHLEY	vcls	ABC
	MARTIN KELLY	drms	AB
	JOHN ROBB	bs	ABCDE
	MARK TILTON	gtr	ABCD
	'GOOFY SID' COULTHART	drms	BCDE
	STEVE FARMERY	gtr	C
	STAN	bs	E

ALBUMS:				
(up to 1986)	1(A)	CRACK HOUSE	(Criminal Damage CRIMLP 105)	1985
	2(E)	THE GIFT OF LIFE	(Creation CRELP 006)	1985
	3( )	PULP BEATING 1984 AND ALL THAT	(Criminal Damage CRIMLP 130)	1986
	4(-)	GIANT	(Constrictor CON 00004)	1986
	5( )	SONGS OF LOVE AND FURY	(In Tape IT 038)	1986

NB: There's also two CD compilations: *The Best Of The Membranes* (Anagram CDMGRAM 112) 1997 and *Kiss Ass Godhead* (Overground 66VPCD) 2001.

THE MEMBERS - At The Chelsea Nightclub.

THE MEMBRANES - Muscles.

EP:	1(E) DEATH IN TRAD ROCK (12" EP)	
	(Criminal Damage CR1 12125)	1984

45s:	* Flexible Membrane: Fashionable Junkies/		
(up to	Almost China (PS)	(Vinyl Drip VD 005)	1980
1986)	Muscles/Entertaining Friends/		
	All Roads Lead To Norway (PS)	(Vinyl Drip VD 007)	1982
	Muscles/Entertaining Friends/		
	All Roads Lead To Norway (PS)	(Rondelet ROUND 19)	1982
	Pin Strip Hype/Funny Old World/The Hitch/		
	Man From Moscow (PS)	(Rondelet ROUND 28)	1982
	Spike Milligan's Tape Recorder/		
	All Skin And Bones (PS)	(Criminal Damage CRI 115)	1984
	Spike Milligan's Tape Recorder/		
	All Skin And Bones (12", PS)	(Constrictor CON 9)	1986
	Everything's Brilliant	(In Tape IT 29)	1986
	Everything's Brilliant (12")	(In Tape ITT 129)	1986

NB: * Flexidisc.

This punk band formed in Preston, Lancashire, in 1977 but was actually based in Blackpool. Robb was also the instigator of the 'Blackpool Rox' fanzine. Their *Muscles* 45 got a lot of airplay from John Peel and is generally regarded as among the best DIY efforts of the era. Steve Farmery came in on guitar shortly after its release and they joined Rondelet, who reissued it and then put out *Pin Stripe Hype*, but unfortunately closed down soon after. They switched to the Criminal Damage label and relocated to Manchester for the guitar assault of *Spike Milligan's Tape Recorder*, which was critically acclaimed and could have broken through with good distribution, which it didn't have. The same fate befell their 12" release *Death To Trad Rock*.

When in 1985 they signed to a label with better distribution the resulting album was disappointing. They remained together until the end of the decade through, undergoing further line-up changes with more releases.

Muscles and *High Street Yanks* later resurfaced on *Rondelet Punk Singles Collection* (Anagram CDPUNK 49) 1995, which was also issued on vinyl.

Kiss Ass Godhead is a twenty-track 'best of', which traces their development from a garage punk band to a more mature electro-tinged melodic pop-sounding outfit.

The Men

Personnel:	IAN CRAIG-MARSH	synth	A
	PHIL OAKEY	vcls	A
	MARTYN WARE	synth	A
	ADRIAN WRIGHT	synth, visuals	A

45s:	I Don't Depend On You/Cruel (PS)	(Virgin VS 269)	1979
	I Don't Depend On You/Cruel (12", PS)	(Virgin VS 269-12)	1979

Yes, this is **The Human League**. After signing to Virgin their first 45, a disco effort, for their new label was credited to **The Men**.

MENACE - Screwed Up.

Menace

Personnel:	CHARLIE CASEY	bs	A
	NOEL MARTIN	drms	A
	STEVE TANNETT	gtr	A
	MORGAN WEBSTER	vcls	A

45s:	Screwed Up/Insane Society (PS)	(Illegal IL 004)	1977
	Screwed Up/Insane Society (12", PS)	(Illegal IL 004)	1977
	I Need Nothing/Electrocutioner (PS)	(Illegal IL 008)	1978
	G.L.C./I'm Civilized (PS)	(Small Wonder SMALL 5)	1978
	Final Vinyl: Last Year's Youth/		
	Carry No Banners (PS)	(Small Wonder SMALL 16)	1979
	The Young Ones/Tomorrow's World/		
	Live For Today (PS)	(Fresh FRESH 14)	1980

NB: There's also a CD compilation *GLC-RIP* (Captain Oi! AHOY CD 17) 1994, which was later issued on vinyl (AHOYLP 17) 1994 as a limited edition release of 1,000.

This punk band formed in 1977 and had two singles released on Miles Copeland's Illegal label. The first was *Screwed Up*, which was released in both 7" and 12" formats on 27th August 1977. Both sides of this record later turned up on *Oi! The Singles Collection, Vol. 2* (Captain Oi! AHOY CD 63) 1996. You can also hear *Screwed Up* on *100% British Oi!* (Captain Oi! AHOY DCD 83) 1997. Also recorded in June 1977 and produced by Velvet Underground's John Cale was *I Need Nothing*, although it wasn't released by Illegal Records until March 1979 by which time the band were on their way to splitting up. Competent, but not on a par with their finest moment *GLC*, both sides of this 45 also re-emerged on *Oi! The Singles Collection, Vol. 4* (Captain Oi! AHOY CD 71) 1997. Their most interesting effort was *G.L.C.* - a powerful tirade against the licensing controls being imposed by the Conservative-controlled authority under Sir Horace Cutler in an attempt to make it hard for punk bands to get gigs, A great punk anthem.

"G.L.C. G.L.C. You're full of shit shit shit shit shit shit"

MENACE - G.L.C.

A group composition, it was one of the best releases on Small Wonder. It later figured on *Oi! Chartbusters, Vol. 1* (Link LP 03) 1987 and the 5-CD set *1-2-3-4 - A History Of Punk And New Wave 1976 - 1979* (MCA/Universal MCD 60066) 1999. The flip side, *I'm Civilised* can also be heard on *Oi! Fuckin' Oi!* (Harry May MAYO CD 110) in 1999. *GLC* and *Last Year's Youth* resurfaced on *Small Wonder Punk Singles Collection, Vol. 1* (Anagram CDPUNK 29) 1994 and *I'm Civilised* and *Carry No Banners* can be found on *Vol. 2* (Anagram CDPUNK 70) 1996. Their final 45 *Young Ones* was later included on *Fresh Records Punk Singles Collection* (Anagram CDPUNK 32) in 1994.

GLC-RIP is an eleven-track compilation of anthemic choruses and four chord verses. Very much what you'd expect from this yobbish band, it collects all their 'B' sides together on a picture disc CD. There's also a vinyl version available in both black and blue. This contains a photo insert of all the band's collectable singles sleeves.

When **Menace** split up, Casey, Martin and Tannett became **The Aces** releasing two singles on Vermillion and the Mod-ish *One Way Street* on ETC Records.

Tannett later worked for Illegal in the U.K. and reformed the band for a gig in 1998.

Menace were very influential on the Oi! bands of the early eighties. One of their roadies was Roi Pearce, who was later vocalist with **Last Resort** and the **4-Skins**.

MENACE - I Need Nothing.

The Merton Parkas

Personnel:	NEIL HURRELL	bs, vcls	A
	SIMON SMITH	drms	A
	DANNY TALBOT	gtr, vcls	A
	MICK TALBOT	piano, vcls	A

ALBUM: 1(A) FACE IN THE CROWD (Beggars Banquet BEGA 11) 1979

NB: (1) also issued on CD (Lowdown BBC 11 CD) 1988. Also relevant is *The Complete Mod Collection* (Anagram CDM GRAM 111) 1997.

EP: 1(A) THE SINGLES (You Need Wheels/Man With The Disguise/Give It To Me Now/Put Me In The Picture/Plastic Smile/In The Midnight Hour) (Beggars Banquet BEG 93E) 1983

HCP

45s: * You Need Wheels/I Don't Want To Know You (PS) (Beggars Banquet BEG 22) 1979 40
Plastic Smile/The Man With The Disguise (PS) (Beggars Banquet BEG 25) 1979 -
Give It To Me Now/Gi's It (PS) (Beggars Banquet BEG 30) 1979 -
Put Me In The Picture/In The Midnight Hour (PS) (Beggars Banquet BEG 43) 1980 -
Flat 19/Band Of Gold (PS) (Well Suspect BLAM 002) 1983 -
+ You Need Wheels/I Don't Want To Know You (PS) (Beggars Banquet BEG 22) 198? -

NB: * Came in a coloured picture sleeve, with red paper labels, some with a free patch. + Reissued in a black and white picture sleeve and plastic silver labels.

Originally called The Sneakers they latched onto **Merton Parkas** a pun combining the area of London they were from with the name of the essential garment of mod fashion. They were one of the mod revival bands to achieve chart success when *You Need Wheels* climbed to No. 40 during a six week chart tenure. Its release coincided with an album whose cover captured them besuited on Brighton beach. It included a cover of *Tears Of A Clown* and more of their 45 cuts, but in truth the playing was tame and the material uninteresting.

Their further 45s failed to enjoy the commercial success of *You Need Wheels*. One of the best is *The Man With The Disguise*. *Give It To Me Now* is quite ska-influenced. *Put Me In The Picture* and *Plastic Smile* are pretty ordinary and their cover of *In The Midnight Hour* is tame, one of the worst I've heard. They disbanded in the early eighties. In 1983, two of their previously unissued tracks were put out on a 45 on the Well Suspect label. The same year Beggars Banquet released an EP *The Singles* containing most of their earlier singles tracks.

Mick Talbot also guested on **The Jams'** *Setting Sons* and on **The Chords'** album. He went on first to The Bureau (a spin-off band from Dexy's Midnight Runners) before finding fame with Paul Weller as a member of Style Council.

They also contributed two Beggars Banquet outtakes *Flat 19* and *Band Of Gold* to *This Is Mod, Vol. 4* (Anagram CDMGRAM 107) 1996.

Mods Mayday 2 - Modnight At The Bridge (Receiver RRCD 228) 1997 kicks off with six of their songs which didn't appear on the original *Mods Mayday '79* live album because they'd signed to Beggars Banquet.

Simon Smith was later with **The Mood Six**, **The Times**, **The Direct Hits** and, more recently, Small Town Parade.

Metrophase

Personnel:	STEEV BURGESS	
	NIKKI MAPP	vcls, gtr
	EPIC SOUNDTRACKS	

45s: * In Black/Neobeauty/Cold Rebellion (PS) (Neo London PHASE 1) 1979
+ New Age/Frames Of Life (Neo London MS 02) 1980
Reissue: x In Black/Neobeauty/Cold Rebellion (PS) (Fresh FRESH 6) 1980

NB: * Issued in a photocopied picture sleeve with a lyric insert. + issued in a fold-out picture sleeve with stamped white labels. x This reissue came in a better quality picture sleeve.

Metrophase is a certain Steev Burgess. He recorded *In Black* with help from **Nikki Sudden** (aka Nikki Mapp) and **Epic Soundtracks** (of **Swell Maps**). The music is unexciting, though.

THE MERTON PARKAS - The Singles EP.

MIGHTY WAH - A Word To The Wise Guy.

Midnight Rags

Personnel incl: PAUL ROLAND

45s:	Public Enemy/Alcatraz/Mamma Said (PS)	(Ace ACE 005) 1980
*	The Cars That Ate New York/ Oscar Automobile (PS)	(Velvet Moon VM 1) 1980

NB: * This 45 was withdrawn.

Midnight Rags are most notable for including Paul Roland.

Mighty Wah

Personnel:	CHARLIE GRIFFITHS	synth	A
	CHRIS JOYCE	drms	A
	JAY NAUGHTON	piano	A
	THE SAPPHIRES	backing vcls	A
	CARL WASHINGTON	bs	A
	PETE WYLIE	vcls, gtr	A

HCP

ALBUMS:	1(A)	A WORD TO THE WISE GUY	(Beggars Banquet BEGA 54) 1984 28
	2(-)	THE WAY WE WAH! (compilation)	(WEA WX11) 1984 -

NB: (1) also issued on CD (Lowdown BBL 54CD) 1989. There's also *The Maverick Years 1980 - 81 (The Official Bootleg)* (WEA) 1983 on vinyl and an EP *The Peel Sessions (22.8.84)* (Strange Fruit SFS) 1987.

HCP

45s:	* Come Back (The Story Of The Reds)/The Devil In Miss Jones (PS)	(Beggars Banquet BEG 111) 1984 20
	Weekends/Shambeko (The Lost Generation) (PS)	(Beggars Banquet BEG 117) 1984 -
	Weekends/Shambeko (The Lost Generation)/ Body And Soul (Acoustic)/Something Wrong With Eddie (12", PS)	(Beggars Banquet BEG 117T) 1984 -

NB: * Also available as a 12".

This was a later incarnation of **Wah! Heat** and **Wah!** Read those entries first before proceeding with this one. *A Word To The Wise Guy* is a pleasant collecion of wide-ranging material covering pop, soul, funk and more. Again it went down well with the punters climbing to No. 28 during its six weeks in the charts. The accompanying single *Come Back* also sold well bringing them a Top 20 hit.

The Mighty Wah! spit in 1984 when Chris Joyce left to join Simply Red. In November of that year *The Way We Wah!* compiled most of their best singles moments. Also of interest will be an EP released on Strange Fruit in 1987 which featured a Peel session from August 1984.

Steve Miro and Eyes

Personnel:	FREDERICK BURROWS	trumpet	A
	JIMMY CARTER	bs, vcls	A
	BRIAN MARTIN	drms, vcls	A
	STEVE MIRO	gtr, vcls	A
	DUNCAN PRESTBURY	keyb'ds, vcls	A
	STEVE SOLAMAR	hrmnca	A

ALBUMS:	1(A)	RUDE INTRUSIONS	(Object Music OBF 008) 1980
	2(A)	SECOND SENTENCE	(Object Music OBJ 015) 1981
	3(A)	TRILEMNA	(Glass GLALP 001) 1983

45s:	I Like It/Once Ain't Enough (PS)	(Raw RAW 16) 1978
	Once Upon A Lifetime (PS)	(Raw RAW 29) 1978
	Up And About/ Smiling In Reverse (PS)	(Object Music OM 03) 1978
	Dreams Of Desire/ Queens Of The Sea (PS)	(Object Music OM 10) 1979

A Manchester band. *Dreams Of Desire* is a bright new pop number with a delightfully understated melody, whinning sax part and an appealing guitar solo.

The Mirrors

Personnel:	ALAN JONES	bs	AB
	GARY LLOYD	lead vcls, gtr	AB
	ANDY SMITH	lead gtr	AB
	TREVOR TARLING	drms	A
	BREE DANIELS	lead gtr	B

45s:	Cure For Cancer/Nice Vice (PS)	(Lightning GIL 503) 1978
	Dark Glasses/999 (PS)	(Lightning GIL 540) 1979

A Welsh band. There are shades of rockabilly in Andy Smith's frenetic guitar likely to appeal to Dr. Feelgood and Pirates fans. Gary Lloyd, their songwriter, lead vocalist and rhythm guitarist could write good rock songs like *Risk* and *Viper* and he was a good rock singer with an emotive, somewhat anguished voice. Their most popular live number was *Terrorist*, an ultra-fast punk blast. *Cure For Cancer* and *Dark Glasses* later resurfaced on *Lightning Records Punk Collection* (Anagram CDPUNK 79) 1996.

Missing Presumed Dead

ALBUMS:	1( )	HOW'S YOUR BUM	(Sequel PART 4) 1979
	2( )	REVENGE	(Sequel PART 5) 198?

45:	Say It With Flowers/Double Life/Driving Home/ Family Tree (PS)	(Sequel PART 2) 1979

Missing Presumed Dead was a six-piece whose music was rather mundane. Paul Harknett's lyrics are sometimes worth a listen, though.

Missing Scientists

Personnel:	JOE FOSTER	lead vcls, synth, bs	A
	MARK 'EMPIRE' SHEPPARD	perc, backing vcls	A
	DAN TREACY	gtr, synth, backing vcls	A
	JACKI	synth	A

45:	Big City, Bright Lights/ Discotheque X (PS)	(Rough Trade RT 057) 1980

This was really a solo project by **Television Personalities'** member Joe Foster, shortly before he left the band. The 'A' side was a cover of a Dandy Livingstone song. He was assisted on it by fellow **Television Personalities** members Dan Treacy and Mark 'Empire' Sheppard. It also featured Daniel Miller (the man behind the Mute label). *Big City Bright Lights* is experimental electro-pop with a reggae influence. It's an excellent single. On the flip is another reggae-influenced song *Discotheque X*, another Joe Foster composition.

Collectors will also be interested in a rare Japanese picture sleeve release of the 45.

The Mob

Personnel:	CURTIS		A
	MARK		A
	JOSEF PORTAR		A

45s:	Youth/Crying Again (PS)	(All The Madmen MAD 001) 1980
	Witch Hunt/Shuffling Souls/ What's Going On (PS)	(All The Madmen MAD 002) 1980
	No Doves Fly Here/ I Hear You Laughing (PS)	(Crass 321984/7) 1982
	The Mirror Breaks/Stay	(All The Madmen MAD 6) 1983
	MAD PACK (3 x 7" in 12" pack)	(All Madmen MADPACK 1) 198?

An anarcho-punk band in the **Crass** mould. They are still gigging today under the name Blythe Power.

M.O.D.

45:	M.O.D./M.O.D. (PS)	(Vertigo 6059 233) 1979

David Essex was responsible for this novelty 45 featuring a mod on a scooter on the cover. Some copies of the single were misspressed with a 2-Tone label design not used by that label until 1983.

Mod '79

45:	Green Onions/High On Your Love	(Casino Classics CC 13) 1979

This band covered *Green Onions*, Booker T & The MG's classic R&B instrumental which became a hit again when it was reissued in 1979 on the back of the wave of interest in 'Quadrophenia'. This version, which wasn't as good, came out on a Northern Soul label.

The Models

Personnel:	MICK ALLEN	bs	A
	TERRY DAY (aka TERRY LEE MIALL)	drms	A
	CLIFF FOX	gtr, vcls	A
	MARCO PIRRONI	gtr	A

THE MISSING SCIENTISTS - Big City, Bright Lights.

ALBUMS:	1(A)	ALPHA BRAVO etc.	(A&M AMLH 68529) 1981
	2(A)	LOCAL AND/OR GENERAL	(A&M AMLH 68536) 1982

45:	Freeze/Man Of The Year (PS)	(Step Forward SF 3) 1977

The Models were a short-lived punk band. They recorded a session for John Peel on 13th July 1977 comprising *Man Of The Year*, *Censorship*, *Brainwash* and *Freeze*. The following month two of these songs appeared on their sole vinyl offering. *Freeze* is a high energy, fast and loud rocker, more in the mould of **Eddie and The Hot Rods** than **The Sex Pistols**.

After their demise Pirroni, who'd been with **Siouxsie and The Banshees**, and Day both later joined **Adam and The Ants**.

The Modernaires

Personnel:	PHILIP BRADLEY	gtr, vcls, synth	A
	HUGH HUGHES	bs, keyb'ds, vcls	A
	LEA WINSHULL WINS	vcls	A
	DAVID BAYNTON POWER	drms, vcls	A

ALBUM:	1(A)	WAY OF LIVING	(Illuminated JAMS 3) 1980

45s:	Life In Our Times/Barbed Up (PS)	(Illuminated ILL 2) 1980
*	We Did It Again/And Again (PS)	(Illuminated ILL 4) 1981

NB: * Red vinyl.

A poor popish new wave band.

MODERN ENGLISH - Drowning Man.

Modern English

Personnel:	RICHARD BROWN	drms	AB
	MICK CONROY	bs, vcls	ABC
	ROBBIE GREY	vcls	ABC
	GARY McDOWELL	gtr, vcls	A
	STEPHEN WALKER	keyb'ds	AB
	AARON DAVIDSON	keyb'ds, gtr	C

ALBUMS:	1(A)	MESH AND LACE	(4AD CAD 105) 1981
	2(B)	AFTER THE SNOW	(4AD CAD 206) 1982
	3(B)	RICHOCHET DAYS	(4AD CAD 402) 1984
	4(C)	STOP START	(Sire 9253431) 1986

NB: (1) reissued on CD (4AD CAD 105CD) 1993 and again (4AD GAD 105CD) 1998. (2) reissued on CD (4AD 206CD) 1993 and again (4AD CAD 206CD) 1998. (3) reissued on CD (4AD 402CD) 1993 and again (4AD CAD 402CD) 1998.

EP:	1(B)	GATHERING DUST (Gathering Dust/Mesh And Lace/Smiles And Laughter/ Swans On Glass/Home) (12", PS)	(4AD AD 306) 1983

45s:	Drowning Man/Silent World (PS)	(Limp LMP 2) 1979
	Swans On Glass/Incident (PS)	(4AD AD 6) 1980
	Gathering Dust/ Tranquility Of A Summer Moment (PS)	(4AD AD 15) 1980

Smiles And Laughter/Mesh And Lace (PS)	(4AD AD 110)	1981
Life In The Gladhouse/ The Choicest View (12", PS)	(4AD BAD 208)	1982
I Melt With You/The Prize (PS)	(4AD AD 212)	1982
Someone's Calling/ Life In The Gladhouse (PS)	(4AD AD 309)	1983
Chapter 12/Ringing In The Changes (PS)	(4AD AD 401)	1984
Chapter 12/Ringing In The Changes/ Reflection (12", PS)	(4AD BAD 401)	1984
Breaking Away (PS)	(4AD AD 406)	1984
Breaking Away (12", PS)	(4AD BAD 406)	1984

Formed in Colchester, Essex, in 1979, **Modern English** were very much part of the doom and gloom post-punk genre. Their debut 45 on the indie Limp label is quite ear-catching. The 'A' side *Drowning Man* is decidedly bleak:-

"I'm swimming to my destiny
No need for reality
No one can see me
No one can touch me
See me round my ankle
Water in my brain
I'm drowing, going under
I'm drowning, going under
Going under, going under"

(from *Drowning Man*).

The flip side *Silent World* is even gloomier, visualising a post nuclear situation and sung to a very sparse backing:-

"Dusty streets of misty dew
Bounds of metal rusted through
Crumbling buildings, plaster and stone
No one hear to echo on
It's a silent world
It's a silent world
It's a silent world
It's a silent world

Shutters creek and windows gap
Weeds grow on their wild estate
Computerset world has fallen down
Yet another empty town
It's a silent world
It's a silent world
It's a silent world
It's a silent world

Nothing moves and nothing stares
Everything's dead who ever cared
It's no use crying or talking now
Someone somewhere pressed the button
It's a silent world
It's a silent world
It's a silent world
Someone somewhere pressed the button"

(from *Silent World*).

On the strength of this 45 they were signed up by 4AD and released an album *Mesh And Lesh* of similarly gloomy material. There's a strong **Joy Division** influence here. The musical soundscapes are emotional but there aren't many memorable melodies or riffs, which is probably why it was largely overlooked at the time.

Their second album *After The Snow* moved completely away from their earlier gloominess to strongly melodic dance material. Their jagged guitars and dull bass lines are supplemented here by flutes and acoustic guitars and some compared their sound on this album to **A Flock Of Seagulls**. The band became popular on the college radio circuit in the U.S.A. where the album was warmly received and they relocated to New York.

The *Gathering Dust* EP compiles five atmospheric non-album tracks from their 1980 and 1981 era.

Their third effort *Richochet Days* was well produced and included some catchy tunes like *Rainbow's End* and *Hands Across The Sea* as they attempted to consolidate their appeal to U.S. audiences. However, its bland feel and glossy production would turn off their earlier new wave fans.

By the time *Stop Start* was recorded Stephen Walker and Richard Brown had departed whilst Aaron Davidson had joined on keyboards and guitar. Unfortunately in their quest for commercial approval *Stop Start* veered towards anonymous pop/rock and they disbanded soon after. Robbie Grey returned to England to form a new group.

Compilation appearances have included *Gathering Dust* on *Natures Mortes* (4AD CAD 117CD) 1997.

Modern English later reformed in 1990 for an album called *Pillow-Lips* but it aroused little interest.

Their three albums for 4AD have been reissued on CD and each contains extra tracks culled from later singles and, in the case of *Richochet Days*, an unreleased demo. Taken together, the three CDs contain all the material they recorded for 4AD.

MODERN ENGLISH - Mesh And Lace.

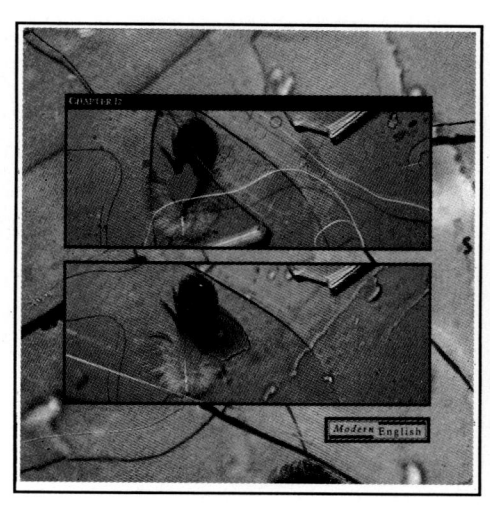

MODERN ENGLISH - Chapter 12.

Modern Eon

Personnel:	ALIX	gtr, vcls, keyb'ds, horns	A
	DANNY HAMPSON	bs	A
	CLIFF HEWITT	drms, perc	A
	TIM LEVER	gtr, sax	A
	BOB WAKELIN	synth, vcls, perc	A

ALBUM: 1(A) FICTION TALES (Din Disc DID 11) 1981

MODERN EON - Fiction Tales.

EP: 1(A) PIECES (Choreography/The Look Of Smack/
Second Still/Special Patrol)   (Modern Eon EON 001) 1980

45s: Euthenics/Waiting For The Cavalry (PS) (Inevitably INEV 3) 1980
  * Euthenics/Choreography/Waiting For The Cavalry/
   The Real Hymn (12")   (Dinsales 2) 1981
  + Euthenics (New Version)/
   Cardinal Signs (PS)   (Din Disc DIN 30) 1981
   Child's Play/Visionary (PS)   (Din Disc DIN 31) 1981

NB: * This was a white label album sampler. + Issued in a tri-gatefold folder picture sleeve.

A Liverpudlian band and there is a clear **Echo and The Bunnymen** influence in their music. Their rather insecure rock music has flashes of originality, moments of odd instrumentation and good drumming. Worth checking out. You'll also find *Choreography* on *Hicks From The Sticks* (Rockburgh Records ROC 111) 1980.

Modern Man

Personnel:
JIM COOK	vcls	A
COLIN KING	drms, vcls	A
ALI McLEOD	gtr	A
DAN MITCHELL	gtr, synth	A
MIKE MORAN	bs	A

ALBUM: 1(A) CONCRETE SCHEME   (MAM LP 5001) 1980

45s: All The Little Idiots/Advance (PS)   (Mam MAM 204) 1980
   Body Music/I Couldn't Stop   (Mam MAM 206) 1980
   Things Could Be Better/Wastelands   (Mam MAM 207) 1980

Produced by **Midge Ure**, this Scottish band are often likened to a second division **Rich Kids**. Still the music whatever it lacks in originality is pleasant and often catchy.

The Mo-dettes

Personnel:
RAMONA CARLIER	vcls	A
KATE CORRIS	gtr	AB
JANE CROCKFORD	bs	AB
JUNE MILES-KINGSTON	drms	AB
SUE SLACK	vcls	B

ALBUM: 1(A) THE STORY SO FAR   (Deram SML 1120) 1980

HCP

45s: White Mice/
   Masochistic Opposite (PS) (Mode/Rough Trade MODE 1) 1979 -
  + Twist And Shout
   (freebie flexidisc)   (S.F.I. SFI 550/MODE ½) 1980 -

THE MO-DETTES - White Mice.

 x Paint It Black/
   Bitta Truth (PS)   (Deram DET-R-1/MODE ½) 1980 42
   Tonight/Waltz In Blue Minor (PS)   (Deram DET 3) 1981 68
   White Mice/Kray Twins (live) (PS)   (Human HUM 10) 1981 -

NB: + This was given away free at gigs. x This came with the free flexidisc *Twist And Shout* and inset in a black and white or blue and white picture sleeve.

The Mo-dettes were a multi-national group from a variety of backgrounds. I've included them here since two of them were British. Jane Crockford had once shared a squat with **Sid Vicious** and Johnny Rotten and had briefly been in Bank Of Dresden before joining **The Mo-dettes**. June Miles-Kingston had been employed as a background musician on the set of **The Sex Pistols**' film *The Great Rock'n' Roll Swindle*, which is where she first met their third member, American guitarist Kate Corris. Kate had moved to London in 1974 and was briefly in one of the earliest **Slits** line-ups in 1977. The quartet was completed by Swiss vocalist Ramona Carlier, a former ballet student from Geneva, who moved to London because there was no punk scene in Switzerland.

They formed in early 1979 and their debut 45, *White Mice*, released on their own Mode label and distributed by Rough Trade, made quite an impression. It made the upper echelons of the indie chart. Its good showing helped the band secure a deal with Decca's Deram subsidiary. An unusual choice because this label was very much associated with progressive rock in the early seventies.

Their first disc for Deram was a very credible cover of The Rolling Stones' *Paint It Black*, which had been a popular part of their live act. It was marketed with a free flexi *Twist And Shout*, which had been given away at gigs. It climbed to No. 42 in the charts but after this the band began to loose their way. Their album *The Story So Far*, was competent but rather bland and poorly produced. They enjoyed just one more minor hit with *Tonight*. Then, in mid-1981, Carlier left. Sue Slack was recruited to replace her on vocals and they veered towards a more commercial sound, but when Corris left a few months later the group fell apart.

Jane Crockford later married Dan Woodgate of Madness. In the late eighties, June Miles-Kingston re-emerged as drummer in The Communards.

The Mods

ALBUM: 1 LOST TOUCH   (Bootlegged Records 007) 1980

This rare bootleg was only sold at Portabello Market.

The Mods

Personnel:
MARK CASSON	lead vcls	A
IAN GUTHRIE	drms	A
ALAN ROBSON	gtr, vcls	A
DAVE ROSS	bs, vcls	A

THE MOLESTERS - Disco Love.

THE MOLESTERS - End Of Civilisation.

This band appeared on the now legendary *Mods Mayday '79* (Bridge House BHLP 0038) live album playing three average cuts *Tonight's The Night*, *Let Me Be The One* and *Love Only Me*.

The Molesters

Personnel:

45s:	Disco Love/		
	Commuter Man (PS)	(Small Wonder SMALL 14)	1978
	End Of Civilisation/		
	Girl Behind The Curtain (PS)	(Small Wonder SMALL 18)	1979

Not one of the better known acts to feature on the Walthamstow-based Small Wonder label. *Small Wonder Punk Singles Collection, Vol. 1* (Anagram CDPUNK 29) 1994 features *Disco Love* and *End Of Civilisation*, whilst *Commuter Man* and *Girl Behind The Curtain* turn up on *Vol. 2* (Anagram CDPUNK 70) 1996. *Disco Love* is very ordinary. *Commuter Man* on the reverse features good guitar work, but suffers from weak vocals. *End Of Civilisation* comes in a striking crucifix picture sleeve but the music is ordinary. Again the flip side *Girl Behind The Curtain* is slightly better with more pleasing guitar moments.

Moment

ALBUM:	1 THE WORK GETS DONE	(Rave RAVEUP 1)	1986

NB: This was issued on coloured vinyl. There's also a CD compilation *Mod Gods* (Tangerine TANGCD 10) 1996.

45s:	In This Town/Just Once	(Diamond DIA 004)	1985
(up to	One, Two, They Fly/Karl's New Haircut	(Diamond DIA 008)	1985
1986) *	Poor Mr. Diamond (Part's 1 & 2)	(Tenth Floor)	198?

NB: * Promo only.

THE MO-DETTES - Paint It Black.

The Moment were a mid-eighties mod revival band. You'll also find *In This Town* and *One, Two, They Fly* on *This Is Mod, Vol. 3 (Diamond Collection)* (Anagram CDMGRAM 106) 1996, but the best source to hear their material is the Tangerine CD compilation *Mod Gods*.

The Monitors

45:	Telegram/Compulsory Fun (PS)	(Monitor MON 1)	1979
Reissue:	Telegram/Compulsory Fun (PS)	(RSO 39)	1979

Telegram is a nicely-constructed song around a jangly two-note guitar riff and a crisp sound. It was picked up by RSO and attracted a lot of airplay from John Peel, but didn't make it.

The Monochrome Set

Personnel:	BID	gtr, vcls	ABCDEF
	J.D. HANEY	drms, vcls	ABC
	JEREMY HANNINGTON	bs	AB
	BOB SARGEANT	keyb'ds, vcls	C
	LESTER SQUARE	gtr, vcls	ABCDEF
	TONY	film projection	BCDEF
	ANDREW WARREN	bs, vcls	CDEF
	LES CRANE	drms	D
	MORRIS WINDSOR	drms	E
	CARRIE BOOTH	keyb'ds	EF
	FOZ	gtr	F
	NICK WESOLOWSKI	drms	F

				HCP
ALBUMS:	1(C)	STRANGE BOUTIQUE	(Din Disc DID 4)	1980 62
	2(D)	LOVE ZOMBIES	(Din Disc DID 8)	1980 -
	3(E)	ELIGIBLE BACHELORS	(Cherry Red BRED 34)	1982 -
	4(-)	VOLUME! BRILLIANCE! CONTRAST! (compilation)		
			(Cherry Red MRED 47)	1983 -
	5( )	THE LOST WEEKEND	(Blanco y Negro BYN 5)	1985 -

NB: (1) reissued (Virgin OVED 53) 1984. (2) reissued (Virgin OVED 56) 1984. (1) and (2) reissued on one CD as *Colour Transmission* (Virgin CDVM 9021) 1993. (3) reissued on CD (Cherry Red CDBRED 34) 1991 and again on (Summit SUMCD 4096) 1997. (4) reissued on CD (Cherry Red CDBRED 47) 1993. There are also some compilations: *Fin! Live* (El ACME 1) 1986, *Colour Transmission* (Virgin COM CD 9) 1988, *Westminster Affair* (Cherry Red ACME 17CD) 1988, *What A Whopper!* (Richmond MONDE 2CD) 1992, *Black And White Minstrels 1975 - 1979* (Cherry Red CDMRED 118) 1995, *Tomorrow Will Be Too Long: The Best Of The Monochrome Set* (Virgin CDOVD 458) 1995, *History 1978 - 1996* (Cherry Red CDBRED 128) 1996 and *Chaps* (2-CD set) (Recall/Snapper SMDCD 134) 1997.

EP:	1( )	Jacob's Ladder (EP) (Jacob's Ladder/Andiano/	
		La Boom Boom/Starry Nowhere/Yo Ho Ho/	
		Three Bottles Of Wine) (Blanco Y Negro NECT 4)	1984

45s:	Alphaville/He's Frank (PS)	(Rough Trade RT 005)	1979
	Eine Symphonie Des Graunes/		
	Lester Leaps In (PS)	(Rough Trade RT 019)	1979

The Monochrome Set/		
Mr. Bizarro (PS)	(Rough Trade RT 028)	1979
He's Frank (Slight Return)/Silicone Carne/		
Fallout (all cuts live)	(Disque Bleu BL 1)	1980
Strange Boutique/		
Surfing SW 12 (PS)	(Din Disc DIN 18)	1980
405 Lines/Goodbye Joe (PS)	(Din Disc DIN 23)	1980
Apocalypso/Fiasco Bongo (PS)	(Din Disc DIN 26)	1980
The Mating Game/		
J.D. Haney (PS)	(Cherry Red CHERR 42)	1982
Cast A Long Shadow/		
The Bridge (PS)	(Cherry Red CHERR 51)	1982
The Jet Set Junta/Love Goes Down		
The Drain/Noise	(Cherry Red CHERR 60)	1983
Jacobs Ladder/Andiano (PS)	(Blanco y Negro NEG 4)	1984
Wallflower/Big Ben Bongo	(Blanco y Negro NEG 12)	1985

The history of **The Monochrome Set** is quite closely linked to that of **Adam and The Ants**. From early 1976 until February 1977 **Adam Ant** (gtr, vcls), Bid (vcls), Lester Square (gtr), Andy Warren (bs) and a variety of drummers rehearsed as The B-Sides. They couldn't get any live work and eventually Lester Square and Andy Warren went off to join the recently formed **Adam and The Ants**. Bid meanwhile spent most of 1977 trying to put together a line-up for his new band **The Monochrome Set**, which he eventually formed in January 1978. This soon included Lester Square who only spent a month in **Adam and The Ants**. After appearing on the first **Adam and The Ants** album, Andy Warren was back in the fold too. The line-up circa 1979 was completed by ex-**Art Attacks** drummer J.D. Haney and former Gloria Mundi and Mean Street bassist Jeremy Hannington.

During 1979 the band issued a trio of singles for Rough Trade - *Alphaville*, *Eine Symphonie Des Graunes* and *The Monochrome Set* - which all differed in style. The third of these was really their sort of theme tune. Early in 1979, the band recruited film maker Tony whose work was projected at the back of the stage whilst the band performed.

They toured America and Hannington decided to remain there which opened the way for old B-Sides member Andrew Warren to re-unite with Bid and Lester Square again. This new line-up signed to the Virgin subsidiary Din Disc and began work on their debut album *Strange Boutique*, which was much more popish than their singles for Rough Trade. The material veered towards cabaret on tracks like *Love Goes Down The Drain*, *Goodbye Joe* and the title track. There's also a new version of their earlier 45 *The Monochrome Set*. The album was quite well received. It spent four weeks in the charts, peaking at No. 62. It would prove to be their only chart album. The title track was culled for 45 release but didn't enjoy similar commercial success and nor did subsequent 45s *405 Lines* and *Apocalypso*.

Their second album *Love Zombies* continued with the cabaret-style material but with more melodic and less bizarre content. Bid's vocals were sharper and overall the album was more accessible. Despite all this it didn't achieve the commercial success of its predecessor and **The Monochrome Set** never elevated themselves beyond 'cult band' status.

THE MONOCHROME SET - Strange Boutique.

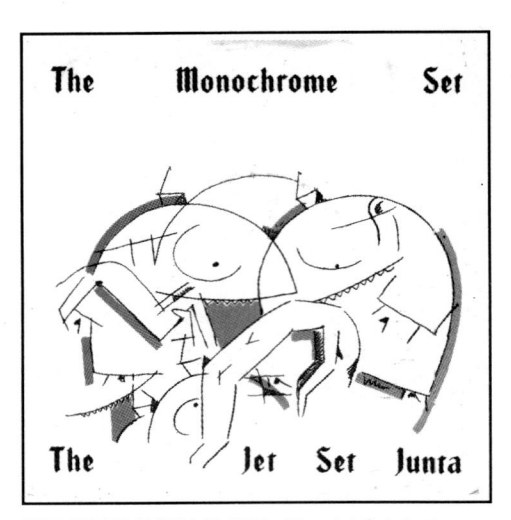

THE MONOCHROME SET - The Jet Set Junta.

Les Crane took over briefly on drums from J.D. Haney before ex-**Soft Boys** member Morris Windsor took over on drums for the sex satire 45 *The Mating Game* and their credible third album *Eligible Batchelors*, which also featured Carrie Booth on keyboards. The album had a clean production and some bouncy melodies but it didn't take off. Shortly after came further line-up changes with Nick Wesolowski taking over from Morris Windsor on drums and Foz joining on guitar.

In 1983, Cherry Red put out a compilation of their recordings for Rough Trade and some of their Radio 1 Sessions entitled *Volume! Brlliance! Contrast!*. The same year they enjoyed an indie hit with *Jet Set Junta*, a none-too-serious indictment of dodgy South American politics.

In 1984, their *Jacob's Ladder* EP was well received as was their fourth studio album *The Lost Weekend*. Clever and entertaining this drew on '30s, '50s and '60s influences for much of the material. Like their 45 *Wallflower* later that year it failed to chart and the band became disheartened and split in 1985.

There have been several compilations of their material. The first of these *Fin! Live* came on the Cherry Red subsidiary El label in 1986. *Colour Transmission* released two years later by Virgin repackaged their first two albums that they had recorded for Din Disc. This was later issued on CD in 1993. The same year Cherry Red put out *Westminster Affair* which focussed on their early material. *Black And White Minstrels* concentrated on the 1975 - 1979 era. Probably their best overall compilation was Virgin's *Tomorrow Will Be Too Long: The Best Of The Monochrome Set* in 1995.

The story doesn't end here. **The Monochrome Set** reformed in December 1989. Bid, Lester and Warren were now joined by Orson Presence (gtr, keyb"s). They recorded a series of albums during the nineties --*Dante's Casine*, *Charade*, *Misere* and *Trinity Road* - and spent a lot of time touring the Far East where they have a particularly strong cult following.

What A Whopper! is a rarities set. It includes some of their recordings for Virgin's Din Disc label in 1980, their one-off 1981 45 *Ten Don'ts For Honeymooners* for Charisma's Pre subsidiary, *Strange Boutique*, *Goodbye Joe*, *The Man With The Black Moustache*, *Sugar Plum* and *Black Are The Flowers*, which displays a psychedelic influence. It certainly showcases their unique blend of pop and art and there's lots of creativity here.

Black And White Minstrels is a sixteen-track compilation comprising of material they recorded between 1975 and 1978. It also includes reworkings of their early Rough Trade material.

Chaps is a classy 2-CD set compiling material from various phases of their career, including their 1990 comeback album *Dangerous Casino*, which is outside the timespan of this book. Overall this is an interesting collection of brisk and superior indie-pop.

Back in 1980 *405 Lines* and *Apocalypso* were included on *Dindisc 1980* (DinDisc DONE 1). Later in 1982, *Eine Symphonie Des Grauns* was included on *Pillows And Prayers* (Cherry Red 2RED 41), also on CD (CDMRED 41) 1996. In 1999, *The Monochrome Set* resurfaced on *1-2-3-4 - A History Of Punk And New Wave 1976 - 1979* (MCA/Universal MCD 60066), which was a definitive 5-CD box set. It had also figured earlier on *A Post Punk Primer* (Virgin CDOVD 498) 1997.

A difficult band to classify musically because they utilised many different styles **The Monochrome Set** are best remembered as an interesting cult band.

The Mood

45s:	Is There A Reason/Waves In Motion (PS)	(RCA RCA 129) 1981
	Don't Stop/Watching Time (PS)	(RCA RCA 171) 1982
*	Paris Is One Day Away/ No One Left To Blame (PS)	(RCA RCA 211) 1982
+	Passion In Dark Rooms/ The Munich Thing (PS)	(RCA RCA 276) 1982
	I Don't Need Your Love Now/ She's Got Me (PS)	(RCA RCA 420) 1984
	I Don't Need Your Love Now/ She's Got Me (12", PS)	(RCA RCAT 420) 1984

NB: * Also issued as a picture disc. + Some copies come in a poster sleeve.

This New Romantic trio played synthesizer dominated pop very much in the mould of groups like **Spandau Ballet**. It's pleasant enough but wouldn't set the world alight. *Passion In Dark Rooms* was also issued in a fold out poster picture sleeve.

THE MOOD - Passion In Dark Rooms.

The Moodists

ALBUMS:	1	ENGINE SHUDDER	(Red Flame RFM 21) 1983
(up to	2	THRISTY'S CALLING	(Red Flame RFA 39) 1984
1986)	3	DOUBLE LIFE	(Red Flame RFM 44) 1985

45s:	The Disciples Know/She Cackles (PS)	(Red Flame RF 721) 1983
(up to	Runaway/Chevolet Rise (PS)	(Red Flame RFB 39) 1984
1986)	Runaway/Chevolet Rise/ Bury Splinters (12", PS)	(Red Flame RSB 3912) 1984
	Justice And Money Too	(Creation CRET 22) 1985
	Take The Red Carpet Out Of Town/ Jack Of Diamonds/Everybody Don't Tell Her	(TIM 12 MTI) 1986

An early eighties band who failed to achieve much prominence. *Runaway* is full of searing, see-sawing, razor blade guitars and certainly showed promise.

Mood Six

Personnel:	TONY CONWAY	lead gtr	ABCD
	ANDY GODFREY	bs	ABCD
	GUY MORLEY	gtr	A
	PAUL SHUREY	keyb'ds	A
	SIMON SMITH	drms	ABCD
	PHIL WARD	vcls	ABC
	CHRIS O'CONNOR	keyb'ds	B
	SIMON TAYLOR	keyb'ds	CD
	GERRY O'SULLIVAN	vcls	D

THE MOOD SIX - The Difference Is....

ALBUMS:	1(B)	THE DIFFERENCE IS...	(Psycho PSYCHO 33) 1985
(up to 1986)	2(B)	A MATTER OF	(Cherry Red BRED 71) 1986

NB: There's also a CD compilation *Songs From The Lost Boutique - The Best Of Mood Six* (Cherry Red CDMRED 141) 1997.

EP:	1(B)	PLASTIC FLOWERS (Plastic Flowers/) (12")	(Psycho PSYCHO 4001) 1985

45s:	Hanging Around/Mood Music (PS)	(EMI EMI 5300) 1982
(up to*	She's Too Far (Out)/Venus (PS)	(EMI EMI 5336) 1982
1986)	Plastic Flowers/It's Your Life (PS)	(Psycho PSYCHO 2001) 1985

NB: * Unreleased, although white label copies with picture sleeves do exist.

The Mood Six first came to attention in the London-based mini-psychedelic revival of the Spring of 1981 playing venues like The Groovy Cellar (the club Phil and Tony started with Clive Soloman, who was then their manager), The Clinic and Le Kilt at Soho's Wardour Street. Their drummer Simon Smith, born on 3rd December 1958 in Merton Park, London had previously been with mod revivalists **The Merton Parkas**, Tony Conway and Andy Godfrey had also been with the modish Security Risk, whilst Paul Shurey and Guy Morley came from the **VIPs**.

The Mood Six's first vinyl offering was two tracks on WEA's 1981 new psychedelia compilation *A Splash Of Colour*. Both contributions, the catchy *Plastic Flowers* and *Just Like A Dream*, were highly derivative of sixties pop psychedelia. These were two of the best cuts on what at the time was an important compilation. The band got to be interviewed on BBC TV's 'Nationwide' and this helped them secure a recording contract with EMI.

Their debut 45 *Hanging Around* was not as good as the two tracks they had contributed to *A Splash Of Colour* and didn't sell well. The follow-up *She's Too Far (Out)* was shelved at the last moment (although some white label copies with picture sleeves do exist), when they were dropped by EMI.

A dormant period followed during which Guy Morley and Paul Shurey left and Chris O'Connor came in on keyboards. This new line-up recorded *The Difference Is*, an album of well-crafted, melodious pop songs written by Tony Conway. The material, particularly tracks like *Victim*, *Plastic Flowers* and *Brief Encounter*, is excellently suited to Chris O'Connor's superb keyboard playing and string arrangements and Phil Ward's crystal clear vocals. Both this and a 12" EP *Plastic Flowers*, which contained a re-recording of the title cut and three previously unreleased cuts, are well worth obtaining.

The band switched to Cherry Red for the 1986 album *A Matter Of*. This was another collection of pleasing pop with *What Have You Ever Done?* probably the stand-out track.

They continued to operate but with a very low profile well beyond the timeframe of this book. Simon Taylor replaced Chris O'Connor on keyboards for a 1987 45 *I Saw The Light*. This would prove to be their last recording for Cherry Red. Later Phil Ward was replaced on vocals by Gerry O'Sullivan, and in 1993, they released an album *And This Is It* (Lost Recording Company) on their own label.

Songs From The Last Boutique is a nicely put together collection of their material and much of it is impressive enough to suggest that if events had unfolded differently they could have done quite well.

Simon Smith and Simon Taylor both subsequently re-emerged in another modish band Small Town Parade.

The Moors Murderers

| Personnel incl: | STEVE STRANGE | vcls |
| | CHRISSIE HYNDE | gtr |

| 45: | * Free Hindley/The Ten Commandments (PS) | (Popcorn) 1978 |

NB: * Unissued.

This was a one-off project by punk icon **Steve Strange** and is notable for featuring Chrissie Hynde on guitar. The 45 was withdrawn before release.

Strange was later in **Visage**.

Johnny Moped

Personnel:	DAVE BERK	drms	AB
	FRED BERK	bs	AB
	RAY BURNS	gtr	A
	JOHNNY MOPED	vcls	AB
	SLIMY TOAD	gtr	B

| ALBUM: | 1(B) CYCLEDELIC | (Chiswick WIK 8) 1978 |

NB: There's also a CD *Basically (Studio Recordings Live At The Roundhouse 19th Feb 78) - The Best Of Johnny Moped* (Chiswick CDWIKD 144) 1995.

45s:	No-One/Incendiary Device	(Chiswick 515) 1977
	Darling, Let's Have Another Baby/Something Else/	
	It Really Digs	(Chiswick NS 27) 1978
	Little Queenie/Hard Lovin' Man (live)	(Chiswick NS 41) 1978
	Basically The Original Johnny Moped Tape	
	(2 versions)	(Chiswick PROMO 3) 1978

This Croydon band is now most notable for containing Ray Burns who became Captain Sensible in **The Damned**. He appeared on the live version of *Hard Lovin' Man* and on the *Basically The Original Johnny Moped Tape*, which were recorded in 1976.

Their break came when *Hard Lovin' Man* was included on *Live At The Roxy WC2* (Harvest SHSP 4069) 1977, which was later reissued on Receiver in 1991. This helped secure them a contract with Chiswick. Their debut single *No One* is propelled by a manic rhythm section courtesy of Fred and Dave Berk. We're talking fast 'n' flashy rock. *No One* also got an airing on *Long Shots Dead Certs And Odds On Favourites* (Chiswick CH 5) in 1978. Their album was a drunken slapstick rendition of songs, including an inept falsetto version of Chuck Berry's *Little Queenie*.

They were one of Chiswick's top bands because they bridged the gap between mid-seventies pub rock and the beery end of punk. What set them apart from some of their contemporaries was that they drew on progressive rock influences. Captain Sensible and **Johnny Moped** had both played together in a pre-punk era band Genetic Breakdown, so they weren't constrained from spinning up the occasional meandering alley. On *Basically - The Best Of Johnny Moped* Ace combine eighteen studio cuts with eleven previously unissued live cuts from a Roundhouse Concert on 19th February 1978.

Later in 1992, *No One*, *Darling Let's Have Another Baby* and *Little Queenie* all resurfaced on *This Chiswick Story* (2-CD) (Chiswick CDWIK 2 100) and three years later *Groovy Ruby* got more exposure by virtue of its inclusion on *The Chiswick Sampler (Good Clean Fun)* (Chiswick CDWIKX 162). *Hard*

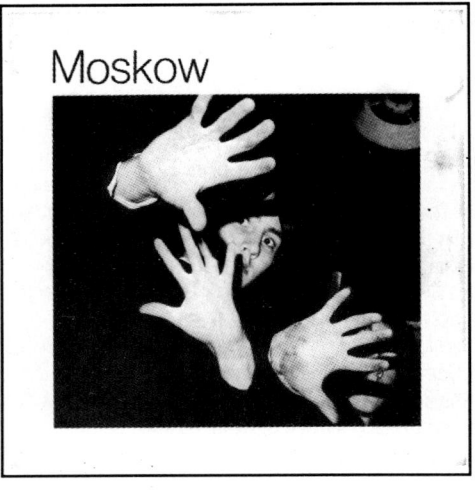

MOSKOW - Man From U.N.C.L.E.

Lovin' Man later resurfaced on *Punk - Live And Nasty* (Emporio EMPRCD 586) 1995 and on *1-2-3-4 - A History Of Punk And New Wave 1976 - 1979* (MCA/Universal MCD 60066), a 5-CD box set issued in 1999. The song was recorded live at The Roundhouse in London's Chalk Farm. Originally the 'B' side of their *Little Queenie* 45, it became a big live favourite.

The band split in late 1978 after incessant gigging. There were subsequent occasional re-unions, once as a twelve member band (including five guitarists), The Johnny Moped Big Band.

Moped, Toad and Dave Berk re-grouped in 1991 for the *Search For Xerxes* album (Xerxes was a former band member), although most of the material on the album was recorded back in 1978.

Moskow

Personnel:	DAVID ASHMORE	vcls	A
	DAVID COLE	gtr	A
	TREVOR FLYNN	bs	A
	JAN KALICKI	drms	A
	MICHAEL MATHEWS	keyb'ds	A

45s:	Man From U.N.C.L.E./	
	White Black (PS)	(Moskow SRS 2103) 1978
	Man From U.N.C.L.E./	
	Too Much Commotion	(Rialto TREB 107) 1979
	Man From U.N.C.L.E./White Black (PS)	(T.W. HIT 103) 1981
	Man From U.N.C.L.E./White Black	(Moskow SRT 3) 1982

A west country outfit who released a D-I-Y 45 in 1978. It was picked up by Rialto in 1979 and its new 'B' side, an interesting and innovative cut *Too Much Commotion* was included on *Avon Calling - The Bristol Compilation* (Heartbeat HB 1) in 1979. Their *Man From U.N.C.L.E.* 45 did attract some attention at the time for its unusual synthesized intro and siren sound effects. 'The Man From U.N.C.L.E.' of course was a top TV series and the 45 is worth hearing but **Moskow** soon vanished from the scene.

The Most

| 45: | Carefree/In And Out | (SRT SRTS/CUS 570) 1979 |

This band was part of the mod revival wave of 1979. Their single didn't come in a picture sleeve which was unusual for the era but it contained a stamped lyric insert.

Elton Motello

| ALBUMS: | 1 VICTIM OF TIME | (Pinball 6.23650) 1978 |
| | 2 POP ART | (Edge HOG 1) 1980 |

NB: (1) was a German release.

45s:	Pogo Pogo/Jet Girl	(Pinball 6.12186) 1977
	Jet Boy Jet Girl/Pogo Pogo	(Lightning LIG 508) 1978
	Pop Art/20th Century Fox	(Passport PS 7920) 1980

Elton Motello, who had worked in the studio with Belgium **Plastic Bertrand**, is best known for an annoying 1978 45 *Jet Boy Jet Girl*, which used the backing track of **Plastic Bertrand**'s *Ca Plane Pour Moi* with vocals about fellatio. His *Victim Of Time* album featured a seven minute version of this. A collection of singles and other recordings circa 1977 and 1978 also included a good cover of The Small Faces' *Sha La La La Lee* (again using the Bertrand backing track of the song) and a version of *Pipeline*. There's quite a bit of humour in the album too.

The follow-up *Pop Art* marked a complete change of direction towards synthesizer style pop with lots of weird experimentation, which doesn't always work. However, the cover of The Who's *I Can't Explain* sounds good.

Jet Boy Jet Girl later resurfaced on *Lightning Records Punk Collection* (Anagram CDPUNK 79) 1996.

The Mothmen

Personnel:	TONY BOWERS	gtr, bs	A
	BOB HARDING	bs, organ, gtr	A
	CHRIS JOYCE	drms	A
	DAVID ROWBOTHAM	gtr, bs	A

| ALBUMS: | 1(A) PAY ATTENTION | (On-U-Sounds LP 2) 1981 |
| | 2(A) ONE BLACK DOT | (Do It RIDE 9) 1982 |

45s:	Does It Matter Irene?/	
	Please Let Go (PS)	(Absurd ABSURD 6) 1979
*	Show Me Your House And Car/	
	People People (PS)	(Do It DUN 12) 1981
*	Show Me Your House And Car/	
	People People (12", PS)	(Do It DUNNIT 12) 1981
	Temptation/People People (PS)	(Do It DUN 14) 1981
	Wadadu/As They Are (PS)	(Do It DUN 19) 1982

NB: * Both versions were deleted after one day.

Their albums are slightly psychedelic, strange, experimental and a little danceable but not distinctive enough to make much lasting impression.

Motor Boys Motor

| Personnel incl: | BILL CARTER | vcls, gtr | A |

| ALBUM: | 1(A) MOTOR BOYS MOTOR | (Albion ALB 111) 1982 |

| 45: | Drive Friendly/Fast 'n' Bulbous/ | |
| | Grow Fins (PS) | (Silent SSH 4) 1980 |

This short-lived London outfit is most significant for including the talented Bill Carter who went on to front up hard driving R&B band Screaming Blue Messiahs.

Their album cover and enclosed poster featured a black man's face with lots of snakes crawling out of his mouth! The general musical format was an amalgam of energetic punk and boogie rock, but it's certainly nothing special.

The Motors

Personnel:	NICK GARVEY	gtr, vcls	AB
	ANDY McMASTERS	bs, vcls	AB
	RICK SLAUGHTER		
	(WERNHAM)	drms	A
	BRAM TCHAIKOVSKY		
	(PETER BRAMALL)	gtr	A
	MARTIN ACE	bs	B
	TERRY WILLIAMS	drms	B

HCP

ALBUMS:	1(A) THE MOTORS	(Virgin V 2089) 1977 46
	2(A) APPROVED BY THE MOTORS	(Virgin V 2101) 1978 60
	3(B) TENEMENT STEPS	(Virgin V 2151) 1980 -
	4(-) GREATEST HITS (compilation)	(Virgin V 2204) 1981 -

NB: (1) reissued in 1990 and on CD (Virgin CDV 2089) 1990. (2) reissued in 1990 and on CD (Virgin CDV 2101) 1990. There's also *Airport (The Motors' Greatest Hits)* (Virgin CDVM 9032) 1995.

HCP

45s:	+	Dancing The Night Away/	
		Whiskey And Wine (PS)	(Virgin VS 186) 1977 42
		Be What You Wanna Be/	
		Beat The Hell Out Of Me (PS)	(Virgin VS 194) 1977 -
		Sensation/The Day I Found A Fiver (PS)	(Virgin VS 206) 1978 -
	+	Airport/Cold Love (PS)	(Virgin VS 219) 1978 4
		Forget About You/Picturama (PS)	(Virgin VS 222) 1978 13
		Forget About You/Picturama /The Middle Bit/	
		Soul Surrender (12")	(Virgin VS 222-12) 1978 -
		Today/Here Comes The Hustler (PS)	(Virgin VS 236) 1978 -
	x	Love And Loneliness/	
		Time For Make-Up (PS)	(Virgin VS 263) 1980 58
		That's What John Said/Crazy Alice (PS)	(Virgin VS 349) 1980 -
		Metropolis/Love Round The Corner (PS)	(Virgin VS 363) 1980 -
		Dancing The Night Away (Remix)/	
		Be What You Gotta Be (PS)	(Virgin VS 427) 1981 -
Reissue:		Airport/Forget About You	(Old Gold OG) 1988 -

NB: + Also released as a 12". The 12" version of *Airport* came in blue vinyl. x There was also a 10" version of this on red, green, blue or yellow vinyl in a die-cut picture sleeve.

The Motors were formed in London in early 1977 by **Nick Garvey**, who was born in Stoke-On-Trent in 1951, and Ricky Wernham, who adoped the name Ricky Slaughter in this band. Wernham had been in earlier bands - Bazooka Joe and The Snakes, who made one 45, *Lights Out / Teenage Head* for Dynamite Records in 1976. They teamed up with Andy McMasters, a Glaswegian who **Garvey** had played with in Ducks Deluxe, and **Bram Tchaikovsky**, whose real name was Peter Bramall.

Their debut gig was at the Marquee in March 1977. They were soon signed to Virgin. Their debut disc, released in September 1977, was a great guitar driven power-popper *Dancing The Night Away*. A superbly arranged and energetic 45 it took them into the Top 50, peaking at No. 42, greatly aided by repeated airplay from John Peel. It spent four weeks in the charts in all.

A six-minute version kicked off their eponymous album released the same month. Nothing else on it was quite as good but *Cold Love*, *Phoney Heaven* and *Emergency* all provided greater evidence of their energetic, full blown guitar assault. It proved to be their most successful album, climbing to No. 46 during its five week chart residency. The CD issue in 1990 includes bonus cuts.

There next two 45s - *Be What You Wanna Be* and *Sensation* - missed out on any chart action. *Sensation* was also included on their next album, *Approved By The Motors*, which was released in the same month in April

THE MOTHMEN - Pay Attention.

THE MOTORS - The Motors.

1978. Overall, this was an improvement on their first effort, although some of the energy and gusto was sacrificed, it demonstrated their ability to write superbly arranged and catchy melodies supported by energetic instrumentation. Aside from *Sensation*, the album spawned three other singles. The next two *Airport* and *Forget About You* were big hits, climbing to No's 4 and 13 respectively. They illustrated perfectly the melodic side to their music. The album also had some arse-kicking numbers epitomised by *You Beat The Hell Outta Me*, which had originally appeared on the flip side of *Be What You Wanna Be*. The final 45 from the album *Today* missed the charts but the album spent one week in the Top 100 at No. 60. This was a disappointing performance given it was a more consistent effort than the debut, which had made the Top 50. The CD issue of *Approved By The Motors* came with bonus cuts.

Bram Tchaikovsky left **The Motors** in August 1978 to form Battleaxe and Ricky Slaughter also split. Their replacements Martin Ace and Terry Williams had both played together previously in Welsh group Man. Tired of touring **Garvey** and McMasters took a break for a while and then got Jimmy Iovine to produce their next album *Tenement Steps* in New York. Its best known track *Love And Loneliness* was released as a 45 in February 1980, a month before the album appeared. Its chorus was very derivative of Steve Stills' *Love The One You're With* and overall the album was disappointing. Two further cuts, *That's What John Said* and *Metropolis* were issued as 45s and after they flopped, the band split up.

Nick Garvey went solo, releasing an album and 45 *Blue Skies* for Virgin in 1982. Terry Williams joined Dire Straits.

A good starting point for people wanting to discover **The Motors** is their *Greatest Hits* album, released in 1981. Compilation appearances have included *You Beat The Hell Outta Me* on *Guillotine 10"* (Virgin VCL 5001) in 1978 and *Dancing The Night Away* on *The Best Punk Album In The World.... Ever, Vol. 1* (2-CD) (Virgin VTDCD 42) 1995 and *The Best Punk Anthems.... Ever!* (Virgin VTDCD 198) 1998. Meanwhile, you'll also find *Airport* on *A History Of Punk, Vol. 2* (Virgin CDOVD 487) 1997 and *Teenage Kicks* (PolyGram TV 5253382) 1985.

MP's

| 45: | Housewives Choice/ | | |
| | Life On The Dole | (Moving Plastic WSP 006) 1980 |

Unusually for the period this record was not housed in a picture sleeve.

Murder Inc.

Personnel:	KEV BOYCE	drms	A
	STEIV BREED	gtr	A
	JOHN DAVIDSON	vcls	A
	GYPO EVANS	lead gtr	A
	PAUL GREBER	bs	A

| EP: | 1(A) | SOUNDS SO FALSE (Sounds So False/Polythene Dream/ Nobody Cares) | (MIL MIL 1) 1980 |

Murder Inc. formed in late 1979 in West Kingsdown, Kent. They released this EP on their own MIL label the following year. The EP can also be heard in its entirety on *Punk Rock Rarities, Vol. 1* (Anagram CDPUNK 63) 1995. They later became Another Episode. Then, in 1981, Boyce joined The Blackout. Along with Blackout members Mark Brehnan and Steve Whale he joined **The Business** in 1982. He later left them in 1984 teaming up with ex-**Chelsea** guitarist Nick Austin in Bandits At 4 O'Clock.

Murder The Disturbed

Personnel:	JOHN FARRER	vcls	A
	CHRIS MORDAY	bs	A
	FOSTER NEVANS	drms	A
	STEVE ZODIAC	gtr	A

| EP: | 1(A) | GENETIC DISRUPTION (D.N.A./Walking Corpses/ The Ultimate System) (PS) | (Small Wonder SMALL 17) 1979 |

The picture sleeve to this three track EP shows a diagram of a human brain. Recorded at Spectro Arts Workshop, Newcastle, their home town, the best track is *D.N.A.* which has a relentless rhythm and exudes a slightly unnerving feel. *Walking Corpses* is a zombie-like number as its title indicates. *The Ultimate System* on the flip side is less distinctive.

D.N.A. later resurfaced on *Small Wonder Punk Singles Collection, Vol. 1* (Anagram CDPUNK 29) 1994 and *Vol. 2* (Anagram CDPUNK 70) 1996 includes *Walking Corpses*.

Pauline Murray and The Invisible Girls

Personnel:	ROBERT BLAMIRE	bs	A
	MARTIN HANNETT	keyb'ds	A
	STEVE HOPKINS	keyb'ds	A
	JOHN MAHER	drms	A
	PAULINE MURRAY	vcls	A

HCP

| ALBUM: | 1(A) | PAULINE MURRAY AND THE INVISIBLE GIRLS | (Illusive/RSO 2934 277) 1980 25 |

NB: (1) also issued on CD (Polestar/Trident PSTRCD 01) 1993 and later (Burning Airlines PILOT 002) 1997.

HCP

45s:	Dream Sequences (One)/		
	Dream Sequences (Two) (PS)	(Illusive IVE 1) 1980 67
	Dream Sequences (One)/		
	Dream Sequences (Two) (10" PS)	(Illusive IVEX 1) 1980 -
	Mr. X/Two Shots	(Illusive IVE 2) 1980 -
	Searching For Heaven/Animal Crazy (PS)	(Illusive IVE 3) 1981 -

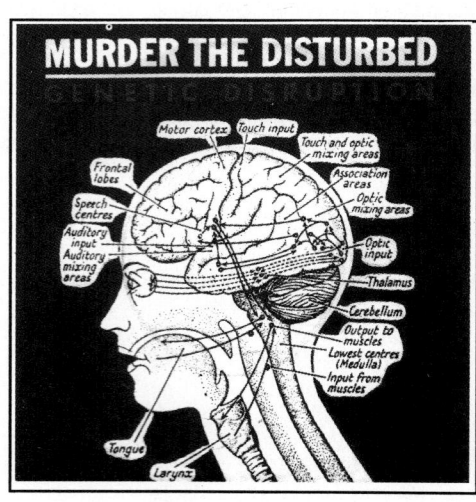

MURDER THE DISTURBED - Genetic Disruption EP.

Searching For Heaven/Animal Crazy/
The Visitor (10" PS)   (Illusive IVEX 3) 1981 -

Pauline Murray put the band together with husband Robert Blamire and producer Martin Hannett after the demise of **Murray** and Blamire's earlier punk band **Penetration**. John Maher was previously drummer with **The Buzzcocks**. Their eponymous album, released in October 1980, included a lively, passionate performance from **Murray** supported by competent musicianship using material which veered more towards folk-rock than punk. The album made it to No. 25 during its four weeks in the charts and with *Dream Sequences* the band even enjoyed a minor hit single, something she never did with **Penetration**. Musically on this album Pauline had moved on from **Penetration** - the fayre on offer was more melodic and sophisticated, but of course Pauline's vocals were unmistakable. The later CD reissue of the album featured three bonus cuts - the three tracks on the spring 1981 *Searching For Heaven* 10", which had been recorded with assistance from **New Order**'s Bernard Sumner and The Mission's Wayne Hussey. All of their singles were non-album tracks - *Animal Crazy* on their final effort saw them move towards a dance music beat.

The band toured the U.K. with **John Cooper Clarke** and then Europe, but split when **Pauline Murray** ran off with Robert Blamire.

Pauline's later ventures included **Pauline Murray and The Storm**, **Pauline Murray and The Saints** and some solo recordings.

Pauline Murray and The Storm

Personnel incl: ROBERT BLAMIRE
               PAULINE MURRAY

45s: Holocaust/Don't Give Up (PS)   (Polestar PSTR 001) 1984
Holocaust/Don't Give Up/
Aversion (12", PS)   (Polestar PSTR 12-001) 1984
New Age/Body Music (PS)   (Polestar PSTR 003) 1986
New Age/Archangel/
Body Music (12, PS)   (Polestar PSTR 12-003) 1986

This was a later project for **Pauline Murray** who'd previously fronted **Pauline Murray and The Invisible Girls** and prior to that **Penetration**.

Music For Pleasure

ALBUMS: 1 INTO THE RAIN   (Polydor POLS 1070) 1982
               2 BLACKLANDS   (Whirlpool WHLS 6) 1985

45s: The Human Factor/
Madness At The Mission (PS)   (Rage RAGE 1) 1981
Fuel To The Fire/Debris (PS)   (Rage RAGE 2) 1981
Switchback/I Recall (PS)   (Polydor POSP 464) 1982
Light/Malefice (PS)   (Polydor POSP 533) 1982
Time/Slide (PS)   (Polydor POSP 553) 1983
Dark Crash/Urban Poison (PS)   (Polydor POSP 594) 1983

MYSTERE FIVE'S - Shake Some Action.

Disconnection/Whiplash Caress (PS)   (Whirlpool WH1) 1984
Chrome Hit Corrosion (12")   (Whirlpool WH4) 1984

An electro-pop band from Leeds. They made their vinyl debut when *The Human Factor* was included on *Hicks From The Sticks* (Rockburgh Records ROC 111) in 1980. The song was issued on Rage the following year. **Music For Pleasure** were signed by Polydor for whom they recorded an album *Into The Rain* and four 45s, but without any commercial breakthrough.

The Mutants

Personnel: PAUL PLEASANT   drms   AB
               RODDIE RODENT   gtr   AB
               AL SATION   bs   AB
               KEITH 'KID' STEELE   gtr   A
               SWEET WILLIAM   vcls   AB

45s: Boss Man/Back Yard Boys (PS)   (Rox ROX 002) 1977
    * Hard Time/School Teacher/Lady (PS)   (Rox ROX 005) 1978
NB: * Released on red vinyl.

A Liverpool band who blended heavy metal with new wave. Decent guitars and affected vocals, quite well produced. Both sides of the second 45 can also be heard on *Punk Rock Rarities, Vol. 1* (Anagram CDPUNK 63) in 1995.

MYSTERE FIVE'S - Never Say Thank You.

Mystere Five's

45s: Shake Some Action/No Message (PS)   (Flicknife FLS 001) 1980
Never Say Thank You/
Heart Rules The Head (PS)   (Flicknife FLS 002) 1981

This little known band had a connection with **Wayne County and The Electric Chairs**. They have the distinction of producing the first two 45s on Flicknife. *Shake Some Action* is quite beaty with some good guitar passages.

Their second 45 *Never Say Thank You* is quite unusual, but the flip side is dreadful.

Mystery Girls

EP: 1( )   SOUNDS LIKE (Famous Men/Baby Baby/
                   X-Ray-Eyes/Love)   (Strange HAM 001) 1980

45:     I'm A Believer/Modern Mystery Pop/
Walking Backwards (PS)   (Strange HAM 002) 1981

A Slough band.

NAAFI Sandwich

45:	Slice One/Slice Two (PS)	(Absurd ABSURD 8)	1980

One of the more obscure discs to be released on Absurd records.

Naked 1981

Personnel:
BASHER	drms	A
CHRIS	gtr	A
MIDGE	bs	A
TONE	vcls	A

CASS:	1(A)	NAKED 1	1981

An anarcho-punk band who produced this D.I.Y. cassette, which was recorded at Rochester, Kent, in 1981. Given that the contact address for information about the band was Gillingham, also in Kent, it's a fair bet that this was a Medway area band. It's not a bad effort either - guitar-led punk. *Sick Again*, *Frightened* and *Mid 1930's/Pre-War Germany* are the better cuts on side one. The second side isn't as good, but *Boys In Blue* certainly caught my ears.

Naked Lunch

Personnel:
CLIFF	synth	A
MICK	synth, sequencer	A
PAUL	gtr, bs, synth	A
TONY	vcls	A

45s:	Rabies/Slipping Again (PS)	(Ramkup CAC 003)	1981

An electro-pop combo very much in the mould of early **Human League**. They also contributed *La Femme* to *Some Bizzare Album* (Some Bizzare BZLP 1) in 1981.

The Name

Personnel:
DAVE COTTON	bs	A
IAN GRAHAM	gtr	A
JOE MACCOLL	drms	A
BEN McKNIGHT	vcls	A

45:	Forget Art, Let's Dance/Misfits (PS)	(Din Disc DIN 14)	1980

One of the leading mod revival acts from north of Watford (Peterborough to be precise). They were unusual in that they had a black vocalist, which gave their single (originally to have been titled *Fuck Art, Let's Dance* before the record company put its foot down) a different dimension.

Maccoll had previously been in **The Now**. The original un-censored version of *Fuck Art Let's Dance* can also be heard on *100% British Mod* (Captain Mod MODSKA DCD 8) 1998. After **The Name** split up in late 1981 Maccoll later emerged in Shopping For Girls, **Destructors V** (along with Dave Cotton), Five Go Mad In Europe and The Pleasureheads. He was last heard of playing with Plastic Hip.

Nash The Slash

ALBUMS:	1( )	CHILDREN OF THE NIGHT	(Din Disc DID 9)	1980
	2( )	AND YOU THOUGHT YOU WERE NORMAL		
			(Shanghai HAI 104)	1984

45s:	Dead Man's Curve/Reactor No. 2 (PS)	(Din Disc DIN 28)	1981
	19th Nervous Breakdown/		
	Danger Zone (PS)	(Din Disc DIN 29)	1981
	Novel Romance/In A Glass Eye (PS)	(Din Disc DIN 33)	1981
*	Swing-Shift (flexi-version)	(Smash Hits no #)	1981

NB: * This was one side of a blue flexidisc which came free with 'Smash Hits' magazine. The other side featured **Orchestral Manoeuvres In The Dark**.

Nash The Slash played electro-pop similar in style to **Fad Gadget**.

Nasty Media

45:	Spiked Copy/Winter/The Ripper/		
	John Peel	(Lightning GIL 542)	1979

Little is known about this band, but you'll also find *Spiked Copy* on *Lightning Records Punk Collection* (Anagram CDPUNK 79) 1996.

Naughtiest Girl Was A Monitor

45s:	All The Naked Heroes/Wax Museum/		
	West Street (PS)	(Aardvark STEEL 4)	1980
	Front/Sensation - No Sensation/Synthesizer, The		
	Story So Far (PS)	(Illuminating KSU NGWAM 1)	1981
	Is All I Need	(Dining Out TUX 22)	1982

One of the lesser-known synth-pop bands in the mould of **The Human League**, **Gary Numan** and **Orchestral Manuvoeures In The Dark**. *All The Naked Heroes* is a pleasant enough song. *Wax Museum* and *West Street* are instrumentals, which soon become monotonous.

Nazis Against Facism

45:	Sid Did It (Intelligible)/		
	Sid Did It (Radio Version) (PS)	(Stage STAGE 1)	1979
Reissue:	Sid Did It (Intelligible)/		
	Sid Did It (Radio Version) (PS)	(Truth TRUTH 1)	1979

There were different picture sleeve versions of this release which featured members of **The Vibrators**. The original version is now very collectable and quite expensive.

"The white blood was squirting
And Nancy was hurting
But Sid did it
All the pistols of sex
Had blanks up their spout
Shit and piss and vomit
Was all they could get out
So Sid did it"
(from *Sid Did It*)

The lyrics get much cruder after this!

The Negatives

45s:	Electric Waltz/Money Talsk (PS)	(Aardvark STEAL 1)	1980
	Scene Of The Crime (PS)	(Aardvark STEAL 3)	1981

Out of Bradford, this modish band also contributed to the label's compilation *Bouquet Of Steel* (Aardvark STEAL 2) in 1980.

NAUGHTIEST GIRL WAS A MONITOR -

NAZIS AGAINST FACISM - Sid Did It.

Neo

Personnel:	MARTIN GORDON	bs	A
	IAN NORTH	vcls, gtr	AB
	PAUL SIMON	drms	AB
	ROBIN SIMON	gtr	AB
	GEORGE DYNER	bs	B

45:	Trans-sister/Failed Pop Song	(Jet 130) 1978

Formed by Ian North, this group originally known as Ian's Radio. North had previously played in Milk 'n' Cookies and Gordon had been with Sparks and Jet. He left during the lifetime of the band to join **Radio Stars**. His replacement on bass was George Dyner. As well as this 45, they contributed to *Live At The Vortex* (NEMS NEL 6013) in 1977.

When they split, Robin Simon joined **Magazine**.

Neon

45s:	Bottles/I'm Only Little/	
	Anytime Anyplace Anywhere (PS)	(Sellout FAB 3) 1978
	Don't Eat Bricks/Hanging Off An O	(Radar ADA 27) 1979
	Making Waves/Me I See In You (PS)	(3D 3D 1) 1980

Apart from these three 45s on indie labels **Neon** recorded a session for John Peel on 22nd March 1979. This is of interest because none of its four songs - *Confuse The News, Eyeing Up Diddies, Plum Plum Crazy* and *Exterminate* - were featured on their 45s.

Neon Hearts

Personnel:	TONY DEARY	gtr, vcls	A
	MARK FULLER	drms	A
	STEVE HEART	sax	A
	PAUL RAVEN	bs	A

ALBUM:	1(A)	POPULAR MUSIC	(Sabril SATL 4012) 1980

NB: There's also a CD compilation, *Ball And Chain* (Overground OVER 64CD) 1997.

45s:	Venus/Eccentric/	
	Regulations (8", PS)	(Neon Hearts NEON 1) 1977
	Answers/Armchair Thriller (PS)	(Satril SAT 133) 1978
	Popular Music/Pretty As A Picture (PS)	(Satril SAT 139) 1979

Neon Hearts were formed in Wolverhampton in spring 1977 by saxophonist Steve Heart. He'd been forced out of the **Suburban Studs** after they'd been told that punk bands didn't have sax players. The **Neon Hearts** started up their own club which soon became a magnet for punk bands across the country. They issued an 8" single on their own label, which is now collectable and hard to track down. It's a classic slice of early punk. They then signed to Satril, who proceeded to remodel them into a glam pop outfit. Their disappointing album didn't arrive until 1980.

Soon after **Neon Hearts** split up disillusioned. Tony Dial joined **Fashion**. Paul Raven went on to play with **Killing Joke** and then Prong. Steve Heart formed 21C.

They also recorded a John Peel session on 5th April 1979 comprising *The Other Great Sex Prose, Roll-On Deodorant, Body Language* and *Rings Of Confidence*.

The twenty-seven track *Ball And Chain* CD compilation includes fifteen previously unheard songs from five studio recordings and their sole Peel session. Their debut 45 kicks off the collection of quirky, energetic punk, albeit not premier league punk. It's still worth a spin and it avoids their Satril era recordings, aside from a few demos.

The Nerves

Personnel:	PAUL CASSON	A
	GORDON GLOVER	A
	MARTIN HEATH	A

45:	TV Adverts/Sex Education	(Lightning GIL 520) 1978

This is not the same band that released an album on Good Vibrations. *TV Adverts* can also be heard on *Lightning Records Punk Collection* (Anagram CDPUNK 79) 1996.

The New Hearts

Personnel:	DAVE CAIRNS	gtr	AB
	JAMIE CROMPTON	drms	A
	JOHN HARTY	bs	AB
	IAN PAINE	vcls	AB
	MATT MacKINTYRE	drms	B

45s:	Just Another Teenage Anthem/	
	Blood On The Knife (PS)	(CBS 5800) 1977
	Plain Jane/My Young Teacher (PS)	(CBS 6381) 1978

The New Hearts recorded one session for John Peel on 14th October 1977, in addition to releasing these 45s. Comprising *Revolution - What Revolution?, Love's Just A Word, Here Come The Ordinaries* and *Just Another Teenage Dream*, it included three songs not released on vinyl.

Their second 45 was produced by **Radio Stars**' bassist Martin Gordon. Indeed, Jamie Crompton, who was replaced on drums by Matt MacKintyre, later joined them.

Dave Cairns and Ian Paine were later in **Secret Affair**.

Colin Newman

ALBUMS: (up to 1986)	1	A-Z	(Beggars Banquet BEGA 20) 1980
	2	PROVISIONALLY ENTITLED THE SINGING FISH	(4AD CAD 108) 1981
	3	NOTTO	(4AD CAD 201) 1982
	4	COMMERCIAL SUICIDE	(Crammed Discs CRAM 045) 1986

NB: (1) also issued on CD (Lowdown BBL 20 CD) 1988. (2) and (3) also issued on CD (4AD GAD 108 2 CD) 1988. (4) also issued on CD (Crammed Discs CRAM 045 CD) 1986.

45s:	B/Classic Remains/	
	Alone On Piano (PS)	(Beggars Banquet BEG 48) 1980
	Inventory/This Picture (PS)	(Beggars Banquet BEG 52) 1981
	We Means We Starts/Not To (Remix) (PS)	(4AD AD 209) 1982
	Feigned Hearing/	
	I Can't Hear Your	(Crammed Discs CRAM 13457) 1986

Colin Newman had been a founder member of **Wire**. Upon the initial demise of **Wire** in 1980 **Newman** embarked on a solo career assisted initially by former colleagues Bruce Gilbert (gtr), Robert Gotobed (drms) and Mike Thorne (keyb'ds) and Desmond Simmonds (bs).

His first album *A-Z* (which had initially been intended as **Wire**'s fourth album) explored similar territory to his former band, successfully but possibly with an over-excess of keyboards in some places.

Newman played everything on his next solo effort *Provisionally Entitled The Singing Fish* embracing a wide array of different instruments. The ten tracks were titled *Fish 1*, *Fish 2* etc. Far from monotonous as one might have expected the music is both interesting and thoughtful.

A few months later followed *Not To*, which was much more in the style of his debut. He reassembled Desmond Simmonds (bs), Simon Gillham (bs) and Robert Gotobed (drms) for this, but Mike Thorne's keyboards were noticeably missing. *Not To* comprised a challenging blend of often minimalistic material. Some of it was left over from *A-Z* and some was new material.

Newman then took a long sabbatical from music, obtaining a grant to travel to India where he undertook a series of recordings. He returned in 1984 and **Wire** reformed. In 1985, he produced Minimal Impact's album *Raging Souls* and two of the band - Malka Spiegal and Sean Bonnar - helped out on is next solo album *Commercial Suicide*.

NEW MODEL ARMY - Vengeance.

New Model Army

Personnel:	ROBB HEATON	drms	AB
	STUART MORROW	bs	A
	SLADE THE LEVELLER		
	(JUSTIN SULLIVAN)	vcls, gtr	AB
	JASON 'MOORE' HARRIS	bs	B

HCP
ALBUMS: 1(A) VENGEANCE (Abstract ABT 006) 1984 73
(up to 2(A) NO REST FOR THE WICKED (EMI NMA LP 1) 1985 22
1986) 3(B) THE GHOST OF CAIN (EMI EMC 3516) 1986 45

NB: (1) also reissued in 1987 as part of a six-box set of Abstract label records *Six Disques Bleu*. (2) also reissued on Fame in 1988 and on CD (Fame CDFA 3198/CDM 792 686 Z) 1989 and again (EMI Gold CDGOLD 1019) 1996. (3) also issued on CD (EMI CDEMC 3516) 1987, (EMI CDP 746 695 2) 1989, (EMI CZ 215) 1989 and (Fame CDFA 3237) 1990 and again in 1994. Also relevant is *Radio Sessions (1983 - 84)* (Abstract ABT 017) 1988, also on CD (ABT 017CD) 1988, *Vengeance - The Independent Story* (Abstract ABT 008CD) 1987 was a CD compilation containing the *Vengeance* album and CD issued on Shout and Abstract, *B-Sides And Abandoned Tracks* (EMI 7243 8 30374 2) 1994 and *BBC Radio 1 Live In Concert* (Windsong CD 051) 1993.

HCP
45s:	*	Bittersweet/Betcha/Tension (PS)	(Shout QS 002) 1983 -
(up to	+	Bittersweet/Betcha//Tension/Fashion/	
1986)		The Cause	(Shout QS 002) 1983 -
		Great Expectations/Waiting (PS)	(Abstract ABS 0020) 1983 -
		The Price/1984 (PS)	(Abstract ABS 0028) 1984 -
		The Price/1984/No Man's Land/Great Expectations/	
		Notice Me (12", PS)	(Abstract 12ABS 0028) 1984 -
		No Rest/Heroin (PS)	(EMI NMA 1) 1985 28
		No Rest/Heroin (cassingle)	(EMI TC NMA 1) 1985 -
		No Rest/Heroin//Vengeance/The Price/	
		No Greater Love (12", double-pack)	(EMI 12NMA 1) 1985 -
		Better Than Them/No Sense//Adrenalin/	
		Trust (double-pack, gatefold sleeve)	(EMI NMAD 2) 1985 49
		Better Than Them/No Sense/Adrenalin/	
		Trust (PS)	(EMI NMA 2) 1985 -
		Better Than Them/No Sense/Adrenalin/	
		Trust (12", PS)	(EMI 12NMA) 1985 -
		Brave New World/R.I.P. (PS)	(EMI NMA 3) 1985 57
		Brave New World (Extended)/R.I.P. (Alt. mix)/	
		Brave New World 2 (12", PS)	(EMI 12NMA 3) 1985 -
		Brave New World/R.I.P./Brave New World 2//	
		Young Gifted And Skint/Sex (The Black	
		Angel) (12" double-pack)	(EMI 12NMAD 3) 1985 -
		51st State/Ten Commandments (PS)	(EMI NMA 4) 1986 71
		51st State/Ten Commandments (12", PS)	(EMI 12NMA 4) 1986 -
		51st State/Ten Commandments//Liberal Education/No Rest/	
		No Man's Land (12", double-pack)	(EMI 12NMAD 4) 1986 -

NB: * Reissued in 1986. + This single came with a free flexi.

New Model Army was formed in 1980 in Bradford, Yorkshire by singer/writer/guitarist Justin Sullivan (who became known as Slade The Leveller) and bassist Stuart Morrow. Sullivan had been born back in 1956. In their early days as part of Bradford's small independent music community they formed a close relationship with punk poetress Joolz, which continued throughout their career.

After a series of live gigs around Britain they secured a one-single deal with Shout Records. This resulted in the release of *Bittersweet* in May 1983. Early copies came with a free flexi containing two live cuts *Fashion* and *The Cause*. Six months later they signed to Abstract issuing a further 45 *Great Expectations*. Both 45s showcased their unique blend of protest punk and 'political' (in the broadest sense) lyrics. Both made the indie Top 20. Their lyrics often looked back to a golden age for Britain that modern technology had destroyed. Sullivan (by now known as Slade The Leveller, which like their name was a clear nod in the direction of Civil War politics) adopted a vocal style that was very 'English'.

Their debut album *Vengeance* issued in April 1984 contained cuts like *Spirit Of The Falklands* (an ironic comment on the country's latest colonial adventure), *Smalltown England* (an almost talkin' punk blues about middle class conformity) and *Liberal Education*. As well as being a big indie success topping the indie charts the album made some impact on the mainstream charts, where it spent five weeks and climbed to No. 73.

Their final indie label release was *The Price* in October 1984. Like the preceding album this also topped the indie charts. The 12" version added three cuts to the 7" listing: *No Man's Land*, *Great Expectations* and *Notice Me*.

The following month the band surprisingly signed to EMI, but under an arrangement whereby their artistic freedom was unaffected. They benefited almost immediately when their next single *No Rest* took them into the national charts, climbing to No. 28 during a five-week stay. The sales were probably helped by a 12" double-pack release which included a bonus record of live material. These have an interesting history. They were from a bootleg tape of the band performing at Brixton GLC festival in mid-1984 which they had removed from a bootleg stall in Camden Market in London. A month later EMI released a video of the band performing at the Marquee in London. Described as "Live 21.04.85" the 30-minute tape included *Ambition*, *Heroin*, *No Rest*, *Better Than Them*, *Christian Militia*, *No Greater Love* and *Young, Gifted And Skint*.

Their first album for EMI *No Rest For The Wicked* was released in May 1985. The back cover included an extract of the Magna Carta - evidence of the band's continuing pursuit of ideals. Morrow left prior to the release of this album, although he played on it.

The album lacked some of the punch and aggression of its predecessor but still contained some stronger tracks as evidenced by *My Country*, *Better Than Them*, *Grandmother's Footsteps* and *No Rest*. The album climbed to No. 22 but could only manage three weeks in the charts.

In June *Better Than Them* was culled for inclusion on an acoustic EP. The first 10,000 copies were issued as a double-pack single rather than a single-record EP. This record also charted for two weeks with No. 49 its best position.

With a new 17 year old bassist Jason 'Moore' Harris added to their line-up in place of Morrow the band applied for visas to visit the U.S.A.. Remarkably they were refused on artistic grounds although most people suspect the band's politics were the real reason for the decision. It wasn't until after four further attempts that they finally gained entry to the U.S.A. in 1986.

Their next 45 *Brave New World* was released in November 1985. It spent one week in the charts at No. 57. The 12" release included both extended and alternate versions of the flip. Collectors again should be interested in the 12" double-pack version of this release since the extra live recordings of *Young, Gifted And Skint* and *Sex* were recorded illegally from a gig in Lyon and liberated from a market in Paris where the band found them being sold.

During 1985 Sullivan co-wrote a single with their old friend Joolz called *Love Is* (Columbia JLZ 1), which Sullivan and Heaton also played on. Two years later Sullivan and Heaton played the backing music on her album *Hex* (Columbia SLX 6711) whilst Joolz recited her poetry.

In September 1986, **New Model Army** released their third album *The Ghost Of Cain* with Glyn Johns handling production. His production values were evident on tracks like *Poison Street* and *Ballad*, which both featured Mark Feltham's bluesy mouth-harp. In the 'States it later became their first full length album release having been preceded by a mini-album *New Model Army* which compiled tracks from their 45 releases. Whilst the album sold well, climbing to No. 45 during its five weeks in the charts, the 45 culled from it *51st State* (how the band viewed Britain's relationship with America) could only manage a disappointing peak position of No. 71 during two weeks in the charts.

As we leave the remit of this book Abstract issued a compilation CD *Vengeance - The Independent Story*, which featured the *Vengeance* album and their non-album tracks issued as 45s on Shout and Abstract. The following year Abstract returned to release *Radio Sessions*, a collection of their 1983/1984 recordings all but one of which were broadcast by the BBC.

BBC Radio One - Live In Concert is a thirteen-track release from a concert at Berlin's Eissporthalle in May 1980 which captures them performing with their usual energy numbers like *51st State*, *Purity* and *Ambition*.

B Sides And Abandoned Tracks, released by EMI in 1994 is a slightly misleading title. There are certainly plenty of 'B' sides on this eighteen-track compilation but the 'abandoned' tracks are simply those originally on EPs. One rarity is included, though, the 'U.S. Remix' of *Lights Go Out*, originally issued on the U.S. version of their *Poison Street* EP.

You can also check out *Vengeance, Great Expectations* and *Price* on *Abstract Punk Singles Collection* (Anagram CDPUNK 52) 1995. *Vengeance* resurfaced again, along with *You'll Never Know*, on *Burning Ambitions, Vol. 2 (A History Of Punk)* (Anagram CDPUNK 81) 1996 and *No Rest* featured on *New Wave Classics* (2-CD) (Disky DOU 878282) 1998.

As we leave them **New Model Army** to their credit had achieved a cult following, signed to a major label without compromising their artistic freedom and they continue to be one of interest to record collectors. They'd also enjoyed and would go on to enjoy considerable commercial success. No mean achievement!

New Order

Personnel: (up to 1986)	GILLIAN GILBERT	keyb'ds, synth	A
	PETER HOOK	bs	A
	STEPHEN MORRIS	drms	A
	BERNARD SUMNER (BERNARD DICKEN)	vcls, gtr	A

HCP

ALBUMS: (up to 1986)	1(A)	MOVEMENT	(Factory FACT 50) 1981 30
	2(A)	POWER, CORRUPTION AND LIES	(Factory FACT 75) 1983 4
	3(A)	LOW-LIFE	(Factory FACT 100) 1985 7
	4(A)	BROTHERHOOD	(Factory FACT 150) 1986 9

NB: (4) There was also a version which came in a metallic sleeve two months after the original release. In the U.S.A. a mini-LP compilation *New Order 1981 - 82* (Factory FACTUS 8) 1982 was released. (1) also issued on CD (Factory FACD 50) 1986. (2) also issued on CD (Factory FACD 75) 1986. (3) also issued on CD (Factory FACD 100) 1986. There was also a cassette edition of (3) (Factory FACT 100C) 1985 in a presentation pack with three extra tracks, *The Perfect Kiss, The Kiss Of Death* and *Perfect Pit*. (4) also issued on CD (Factory FACD 150) 1986. There are also a number of relevant compilations, *Substance* (Factory FACT 200) 1987 got to No. 2. There was also a numbered limited edition of 1,000 which came in a different sleeve. The cassette version of this release (Factory FACT 200 C) 1987 included an extra cassette of B-sides and Benelux editions. The compilation was also available on CD (Factory FACD 2000) 1987. Also of relevance is *Complete Peel Sessions: New Order* (Strange Fruit SFRCD 110) 1990, *BBC Radio 1 Live In Concert* (Windsong WINCD 011) 1992, *The Best Of New Order* (Factory 8285802) 1995, *The Rest Of New Order* (Factory 8286612) 1995, *Substance 1987* (Factory 5200082) 1998 and *The John Peel Sessions* (BBC/Strange Fruit SFRCD 095) 2000.

HCP

EPs:	1(A)	THE PEEL SESSIONS (1.6.82) (Turn The Heater On/ We All Stand/Too Late/ 5-8-6) (12", PS)	(Strange Fruit SFPS 001) 1986 54
	2(A)	THE PEEL SESSIONS (26.1.81) (Truth/Senses/I.C.B./ Dreams Never End) (12", PS)	(Strange Fruit SFPS 001) 1987 -

NB: (1) also issued on cassette (SFPSC 001) 1987 and (2) also on CD (SFPSCD 001) 1988.

HCP

45s: (up to 1986)		Ceremony/In A Lonely Place (PS)	(Factory FAC 33) 1981 34
	+	Ceremony/In A Lonely Place (Extended Remix) (12", PS)	(Factory FAC 33-12) 1981 -
	*	Ceremony (Re-recording)/In A Lonely Place (Extended) (12", PS)	(Factory FAC 33-12) 1981 -
	o	Everything's Gone Green/ Procession (PS)	(Factory FAC 53) 1981 38
	x	Everything's Gone Green (Extended)/Mesh/ Cries And Whispers (12", PS)	(Factory Benelux FBN 8) 1981 -
	#	Temptation/Hurt (PS)	(Factory FAC 63) 1982 29
		Temptation (Extended)/ Hurt (Extended) (12", PS)	(Factory FAC 63-12) 1982 -
	++	THE HACIENDA CHRISTMAS FLEXI: We Will Rock You/ Ode To Joy	(Factory FAC 51B) 1982 -
	α	Blue Monday/The Beach (12", PS)	(Factory FAC 73) 1983 9
		Confusion/Confusion Beats/Confused (instr.)/ Confusion (Rough Mix) (12", PS)	(Factory FAC 93) 1983 12
		Confusion/Confusion (Rough Mix) (PS) (DJ only)	(Factory 7 FAC 93) 1983 -
		Thieves Like Us/ Lonesome Tonight (12", PS)	(Factory FAC 103) 1984 18
		Thieves Like Us (Edit)/ Lonesome Tonight (Edit) (PS)	(Factory 7 FAC 103) 1984 -
	β	Murder/Thieves Like Us (instr.)	(Factory Benelux FBN 22) 1984 -
		The Perfect Kiss/	

NEW ORDER - Movement.

Kiss Of Death (PS)	(Factory 7 FAC 123) 1985	46
χ The Perfect Kiss/Kiss Of Death/ The Perfect Pit (12", PS)	(Factory FAC 123) 1985	-
Sub-Culture/Dub-Vulture (12", PS)	(Factory FAC 133) 1985	63
Sub-Culture (Edit)/ Dub-Vulture (Edit) (PS)	(Factory 7 FAC 133) 1986	-
Shellshock (Edit)/ Thieves Like Us (instr.) (PS)	(Factory FAC 143-7) 1986	28
Shellshock/Shellcock (12", PS)	(Factory FAC 143-12) 1986	-
State Of The Nation (Edit)/ Shame Of The Nation (Edit) (PS)	(Factory FAC 153-7) 1986	30
State Of The Nation/ Shame Of The Nation (12", PS)	(Factory FAC 153-12) 1986	-
Bizarre Love Triangle (Edit)/ Bizarre Dub Triangle (PS)	(Factory FAC 163-7) 1986	56
Bizarre Love Triangle/ Bizarre Dub Triangle (12", PS)	(Factory FAC 163-12) 1986	-

NB: + Came in a cream and blue picture sleeve.* Copies came in a green picture sleeve. o Came in several different colour sleeves. x A Belgian pressing. # Plays at 33 r.p.m. ++ A limited edition of 4,400 given away free at the Hacienda Club. α Various picture sleeves. β This was a Belgian pressing. There was also a 12" PS version (FBNL 22) 1984. χ Came with pink or blue inner sleeve.

After **Joy Division**'s lead singer Ian Curtis committed suicide in May 1980 Bernard Dicken was determined to keep the band together under a new name. Dicken had been born in 1956 in Salford, Machester, but when his mother remarried in 1968 he became known as Sumner. Whilst he was in **Joy Division** he called himself Albrecht but in **New Order** he became known as Barnie Sumner. Before joining **Joy Division** he'd worked in a supermarket, an accounts office and in advertising.

Peter Hook, born in Salford, Manchester, had been at school with Sumner and was just a month younger. He started his working life in the war office but then passed through various minor jobs before forming **Warsaw**. He utilised a lot of effects in his bass style.

Steve Morris, born in Macclesfield, Cheshire on 28th October 1957, had been a wild kid, expelled from school before he got involved in the music scene.

Along with these three former members of **Joy Division**, a fourth member Gillian Gilbert was added in November 1980. Born on 27th January 1961 in Manchester, she became interested in punk music while at school in Macclesfield. She played acoustic guitar in an all-girl punk group The Inadequates, which also featured her sister. When that collapsed she became a close friend of Steve Morris and she was studying at Stockport College of Technology when she heard of Ian Curtis' death. When Morris invited her to join **New Order** she terminated her academic career to become keyboard/synthesizer player and occasional second guitarist in the band.

Prior to Gilbert joining, **New Order** operated as a trio. They made their live debut at The Beach Club in Manchester on 29th July 1980. Then, between 20—30th September 1980, they played four gigs on the U.S. East Coast, which **Joy Division** had been booked to play back in May. The trio also

NEW ORDER - Thieves Like Us 12".

NEW ORDER - Everything's Gone Green.

recorded a 45 *Ceremony* backed by *In A Lonely Place* in September 1980. Both were produced by Martin Hannett. The songs were written whilst Ian Curtis was still alive and the vocals on *Ceremony* featured an emotional style that was very similar to Curtis' and the rhythm section blended in perfectly. The flip side was a slow, brooding number with a haunting singing style. The single was originally issued as a 7" with a gold-coloured embossed sleeve in February 1981. It came out a month later on 12" with a green cover. Then, in July 1981, a different version came out in a cream sleeve with a blue stripe border. This had been recorded back in November 1980 just after Gillian Gilbert had joined the group. This version wasn't as good and was quickly withdrawn but is now an extremely sought-after disc. It was replaced by the original version of the song but the new cream sleeve was retained. *Ceremony* brought them a minor hit, climbing to No. 34 during its five weeks in the charts.

New Order also played their first London gig on 9th February 1981 at the Heaven Club. It was supposed to be a 'secret' gig, but news soon leaked out and the 1,000 tickets sold 'very quickly. They were supported by **Section 25** and The Stockholm Monsters.

Early in 1981, the four-piece recorded a session for John Peel, which was broadcast in February. It comprised *Dreams Never End*, *Truth*, *ICB* and *Senses*. The first three appeared again in a Granada TV Special broadcast in June 1981 along with three more cuts *Death Rattle*, *Little Death* and *Ceremony*.

In May 1981, **New Order** underwent a short European tour encompassing France, Belgium, West Germany, Denmark, Sweden and Norway. Later on 20th June, they played at the Glastonbury Fayre CND benefit.

A second single released in September 1981 marked a distinct change of style. The 'A' side *Everything's Gone Green* utilised a dance-orientated synthesized beat, which along with Sumner's softer vocals and Gilbert's synthesizer, gave the song a decidedly disco feel. The flip side *Procession* did return to their usual rock format, though. Collectors may be interested in a Factory Benelux import version of the 45 which featured the full-length version of the 'A' side and two new songs, *Mesh* and *Cries And Whispers* on the flip. *Everything's Gone Green* spent five weeks in the charts but couldn't advance beyond No. 38.

Their debut album *Movement* was issued in November 1981. Dominated by electronics, it was produced by Martin Hannett and contained some excellent guitar and synthesizer playing with the vocals less prominent in the mix. The material was variable, though, with *Dreams Never End* and *Doubts Even Here* the two most memorable tracks on it. It spent ten weeks in the charts, peaking at No. 30, which was a respectable debut performance. However, the group was unhappy with how the album sounded and severed their relationship with Martin Hannett. Their next single *Temptation* (which was previewed on BBC's 'Riverside' programme and released in April 1982) was produced by the band themselves and the first time they used a sequencer. It took them into the Top 30 for the first time, climbing to No. 29 during its seven weeks in the charts.

On 1st June 1982, **New Order** played a second John Peel session which included an unrecorded version of *Turn The Heater On* penned by reggae artist Keith Hudson. They toured Italy later that month returning to Manchester to play at a free members' evening at the city's Hacienda Club on 26th June.

On 11th September, they headlined the first day of the fourth Futurama festival in Leeds. Then eight days later they played at the first festival of Independent Rock 'n' Roll in a basketball stadium in Athens, Greece.

In November 1982, a mini-album *New Order 1981 - 82* was released in the United States and Canada. It contained *Temptation, Everything's Gone Green, Hurt, Procession* and *Mesh* and became a popular purchase on import over here. In late November, they embarked on a 10-day tour of Australia. The following month a 7" flexidisc featuring *We Will Rock You* and *Ode To Joy* was given away free to Hacienda club members at the venue's Christmas Eve Party.

In the next few months **New Order** underwent a drastic change of musical style that would see them develop from a cult band to a household name over the coming months. They unveiled this on *Blue Monday*, which was released in March 1983 on 12" format only. By 1987 it had become the best selling 12" to date. Back in 1983 it rose to No. 9 and spent seventeen weeks in the charts. The new style comprised state-of-the-art dance music with Sumner's vocals superimposed over high-tech disco beats. Production was now handled by U.S. dance producer/mixer Arthur Baker. The 45 was also issued in a variety of different picture sleeves, which should interest collectors.

Their second album *Power, Corruption And Lies* also came out in March 1983 packaged in a beautiful sleeve featuring a full-colour reproduction of a painting by Fantin Latour. This was their masterpiece combining old rock base with new technology. Sumner's vocals were clearer on this album than previously and there was a good variety of material. Fast, uptempo, punkish numbers were represented by *Age Of Consent* and *Ultraviolence*. The synthetic sound previewed on *Blue Monday* was continued on *The Village* and *Ecstacy*, which utilised an Apple Computer speech synthesizer. Meloncholic ballads were represented by *Your Silent Face* and *Leave Me Alone*. The only weaker number was the meandering *We All Stand*. The album spent an impressive twenty-nine weeks in the charts peaking at No. 4. It contained no 45 releases, although *Blue Monday* was later added to the cassette version of the album.

In August 1983, a new single *Confusion* was released. Musically this was their worst effort yet, a clear sop to the U.S. dance floor fans among whom *Blue Monday* had become a firm favourite following its U.S. release on Arthur Baker's dance-based Streetwise label. However, *Confusion* was a decidely inferior version of the concept, although this didn't prevent it climbing to No. 12 in Britain where it spent seven weeks in the charts.

In April 1984, **New Order** visited Japan for the first time, playing sell-out concerts in Tokyo and Osaka. They also had a brief recording session whilst in Tokyo which produced *State Of The Nation*, which was subsequently put out as a 45 in 1986. In Britain their next 45 *Thieves Like Us* was released the same month. The 'A' side, co-written with Arthur Baker was a heavy organ dominated number with lots of synthesizers too and good vocals. The flip side was a strong more rock-based number. The single brought **New Order** a further Top 20 hit rising to No. 18 during its five week stay in the charts. In Europe Factory Benelux put out *Thieves Like Us* as a flip side to a special 12" single. On the 'A' side was a **Joy Division** - style track called *Murder* with Steve Morris really letting fly on acoustic drums. Collectors will also be interested in a Polish 7" version of *Blue Monday* in circulation around European radio stations during Spring 1985, which includes *Thieves Like Us* on the flip side. This is a real ultra-rarity.

In August 1984, **New Order** were featured in BBC's "Rock Around The Clock". Their session was also broadcast on Radio 1 at the same time.

In May 1985, though, the band contravened their unwritten policy of not issuing tracks from albums. Their next single release was *The Perfect Kiss*, a simple, happy, disco-based song which was fine, but the drum programming used was the same as on *Blue Monday*. Moreover the flip side *Kiss Of Death* was a regigged dub version of the 'A' side. The 12" version of this release also included a version of their American 7", *The Perfect Pit*. *The Perfect Kiss* managed only a four week stay in the charts in Britain with a highest position of No. 46, a definate downturn in fortunes. In the 'States it became the first release on Quincy Jones' Quest label.

The parent album to *The Perfect Kiss*, *Low Life* was also released in May 1985. This was a fine effort, though not up to the standard of its predecessor. It opens with *Love Vigilantes*, a fine rock number on which Sumner sings as the ghost of a fighter pilot flying home to see his wife and family yet realising he is dead. It is followed by **The Perfect Kiss**. Other highlights include *Subculture*, which is very much in the *Blue Monday* mode with drum drones and cleverly presented lyrics and *Elegia*, a Bernard Sumner instrumental composition on which some piercing guitar playing and simple synthesizer builds up into a climatic sixties style fuzz-sounding ending. *Low-Life* made it to No. 7 here in Britain and spent ten weeks in the charts. It also became their first hit album in the 'States, peaking at No. 94.

In August 1985, Factory put out on 12" a remix of *Sub-Culture* with another version *Dub-Vulture* on the flip. This was against the wishes of the group but the label were spurred on by the demands of the American market. Like its preceeding 45 *Sub-Culture* spent four weeks in the chart but the highest position it could manage was No. 63.

In March 1986, a further 45 was released; *Shellshock* was backed by *Shellcock* in both 7" and 12" formats. The 7" was an edited version of a song which was constructed through electronic sampling methods. *Shellshock* was also featured on the soundtrack to the 'Pretty In Pink' movie and this helped it climb to No. 28 during its five week chart stay. In April Factory's Ikon label released **New Order**'s controversially-titled live home video "Pumped Full Of Drugs".

State Of The Nation, which **New Order** had recorded on their visit to Tokyo in April 1985, was released in both 7" and 12" format with a re-arrangement of the 'A' side *Shame Of The Nation* on the reverse side. This spent just three weeks in the charts with a peak position of No. 30.

In September 1986, a Peel session containing *Turn The Heater On, We All Stand, Too Late* and *5-8-6* was released on vinyl. The songs were recorded in Revolution Studios in Cheadle without a producer. Their cover of Keith Hudson's *Turn The Heater On* had been their first attempt at a reggae number. The sombre *Too Late* sounded like something out of their **Joy Division** days and *We All Stand* and *5-8-6* were reworked for their *Power, Corruption And Lies* album (with *5-8-6* renamed *The Village*). Unusually for archival projects of this type it aroused sufficient interest to spend a week in the charts at No. 54.

Their fourth album *Brotherhood*, released in September 1986, marked a further change of direction in their career. It was divided into two distinct sides. The first had 'acoustic' drum/bass sounds, whilst the second utilised synthetically-programmed bass/drum patterns. Overall, this was an extremely consistent album. Most tracks contained particular features guaranteed to catch the listener's attention. *Weirdo* had a great guitar intro. There was some appealing acoustic guitar on *As It Was When It Was*, some great fuzz guitar playing on *Broken Promise*, a fine keyboard solo on *All Day Long* and some inventive bass playing from Hook on *Way Of Life*. *Bizarre Love Triangle* was notable for its futuristic use of technology and another fine, emotive vocal performance from Sumner. A remixed version of this track by Shep Pettibone was culled for 45 release in November and spent two weeks in the charts with a best position of No. 56. The parent album got to No. 9 but only spent five weeks in the chart. A metalic sleeved version of *Brotherhood* appeared on the collectors market in November.

Although **New Order**'s subsequent exploits extend beyond the remit of this book mention must be made of their 1987 compilation album *Substance*, which was released in August 1987. There was also a limited edition release of *Substance* with a pressing of 1,000 which came in a different sleeve. The vinyl version of *Substance* only contains the 'A' sides of their 12" singles and only the British releases. The CD and double cassette formats do include the Factory Benelux bonus tracks, *Cries And Whispers*, *Mesh, Murder* and the *Thieves Like Us* instrumental. On all formats the versions of *Temptation* and *Confusion* were the re-done film soundtrack recordings (explained later) from May 1987 not the original 45 versions. There was also a tracking error on early copies of the double cassette release whereby *Murder* was listed on Tape Two but appeared on Tape One. *Substance* became their biggest hit to date climbing to No. 3 and enjoying a thirty-seven week chart stay.

The Rest Of New Order is an album of remixes which successfuly leave most of the original songs in place despite the extended instrumental passages and beefed up techno and house grooves. So it actually works quite well. Initial copies also came with a free album of eight *Blue Monday* remixes!!

In addition to appearing on the "Pretty In Pink" soundtrack and the accompanying album on A&M, the original recording of *Temptation* was used for the film "Something Wild" and *Touched By The Hand Of God*,

Sputnik, *Skullcrusher*, *Salvation Theme* and *Confusion* appeared on the soundtrack album of "Salvation", released by Disques du Crepescule.

New Order have also appeared on a number of compilations. *Haystack* can be heard on *From Brussels With Love* (Les Disques Du Crepuscule TW 1 007) 1980, a cassette in a pouch with a booklet which was later reissued in 1982. *Prime 5-8-6-Pts 1&2* was included on *Featuremist* (Touch TO 1) 1982, another cassette in a pouch with a booklet format release. An edited version of *Sunrise* was included on *Debut 11* (Debut DEBUT 011) 1985, a 10" album and magazine package. Finally *New Order I/V* and *Thieves Like Us* appeared in *Soundwave 5* (Soundwave SOS-SWOS) 1984, a cassette magazine.

The John Peel Sessions have been reissued on a new BBC CD. The 1981 session is very **Joy Division** influenced. The 1982 session is a pointer to their later musical formula.

New Order were a group that let their music do the talking. Completely disinterested in celebrity status and, by all accounts, very ordinary people, they isolated themselves from the press. Their avoidance of interviews, their name and their Peter Saville-designed record sleeves with typography borrowed from posters of the Third Reich fuelled speculation in their early days that they were a group of neo-Nazis, but this thoery lost credibility over time. Whilst little is known about the band members their music can be seen as one of the final links between punk rock and the new post-industrial angst of the early eighties.

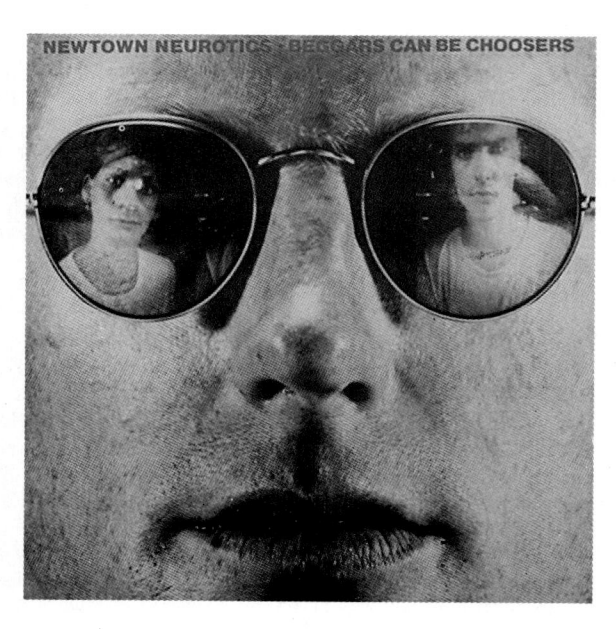

NEWTOWN NEUROTICS - Beggars Can Be Choosers.

Newtown Neurotics

Personnel:	TONY 'TIGGY' BARBER	drms	A
	COLIN DREDD	bs, vcls	AB
	STEVE DREWETT	vcls, gtr	AB
	SIMON LOMOND	drms	B

ALBUM: 1(B) BEGGARS CAN BE CHOOSERS (Razor RAZ 6) 1983
NB: (1) also issued on CD (Dojo DOLECD 111) 1995. There's also a singles compilation *45 Revolutions Per Minute Singles 1979 - 1984* (Jungle FREUD LP 31) 1990, also on CD (Jungle FREUD CD 31) 1994 as well as the more recent compilation *Punk Singles Collection* (Anagram CD PUNK 91) 1997.

45s:	Hypocrite/You Said No	(No Wonder A 45) 1979
	When The Oil Runs Out/Oh No	(No Wonder NOW 4) 1980
	Kick Out The Tories!/	
	Mindless Violence! (PS)	(CNT 4/No Wonder Now 56) 1982
	Licensing Hours/No Sanctuary (PS)	(CNT CNT 010) 1982
	Blitzkrieg Bop/Hypocrite (New Version)/	
	I Remember You (PS)	(Razor RZS 107) 1983
	Susie Is A Heartbreaker	(No Wonder) 1984

The Newtown Neurotics formed in Harlow, Essex, in the spring of 1978. They played a blend of leftist pop-punk. The first two releases on their own No Wonder label are now hard to find. After these, Simon Lomond replaced Tony Barber on drums. In the eighties they were a popular attraction on the festival circuit. They switched to the short-lived CNT label for the overtly political *Kick Out The Tories!* and an attack on Britain's licensing hours. When CNT folded, they signed to Razor records for their album *Beggars Can't Be Choosers*, a powerful enough effort with scathing lyrics.

"It all begins at school when they tell you you're useless
And the jobs you get offered make this conclusive
For years and years they've been telling you lies
Your full potential's never been realised
And then you slip into the attitude of
'I make a mess of everything I do'

chorus: Don't sit around, you've got to wake up and live
Don't piss around, you've got to wake up and live"
(from *Wake Up*)

There's also a song called *Living With Unemployment* which is sung to the tune of **The Members**' *Solitary Confinement* but with altered lyrics:-

"I was living in a newtown
I had problems with my parents
So I moved on up to London town
Where they said things were happening, going down

Chorus: Living in a bedsit
Bunking the tube trains
Sleeping all day long
And you know no-one, 'cos you don't go out
'cos you're out of work
You just watch television
Living with unemployment"
(from *Living With Unemployment*)

A cover of The Ramones' *Bltzkrieg Bop* was culled from the album for 45 release to help promote it. After one final 45 *Susie Is A Heartbreaker* (suggesting more Ramones' influence) they deleted the Newtown from their name and recorded for Jungle as The Neurotics.

You'll also find *Kick Out The Tories* on *Punk And Disorderly III - The Final Solution* (Anagram GRAM 005) 1983, also on CD (CDPUNK 23) 1993. The same year they teamed up with **Attila The Stockbroker** to record *Andy Is A Corporate / Mindless Version*, an attack on mindless violence and Nazi skinheads, which you can hear on *Son Of Oi!* (Syndicate SYN LP 3) 1983, which was later reissued (Captain Oi! AHOY CD 9) 1993. *Kick Out The Tories* and *Mindless Violence* later resurfaced on *Abstract Punk Singles Collection* (Anagram CDPUNK 52) in 1995.

Nicky and The Dots

| Personnel incl: | DOUSELEY |
| | DWYER |

| 45: | Never Been So Stuck/ | |
| | Linoleum Walk (PS) | (Small Wonder SMALL 12) 1979 |

A tasty popish single by a Brighton band. Musically it veers in the direction of **XTC**. They also contributed three cuts *Girl Gets Nervous*, *I Find That Really Surprises Me* and *Wrong Street* to *Vaultage '78 (Two Sides Of Brighton)* (Attrix RB 03) in 1978. The second cut, in particular, is quite competent pop. *Wrong Street* and *Girls Get Nervous* resurfaced again on *Vaultage Punk Collection* (Anagram CDPUNK 101) 1997. You'll also find *Never Been So Stuck* on *Small Wonder Punk Singles Collection, Vol. 1* (Anagram CDPUNK 29) 1994 and *Linoleum Walk* can also be heard on *Vol. 2* (Anagram CDPUNK 70) 1996.

Nightingales

Personnel:	ALAN APPLEBY	AB
	PAUL APPLEBY	AB
	JOE CROW	A
	EAMONN DUFFY	AB
	ROBERT LLOYD	AB
	NICK BEALES	B
	ANDY LLOYD	B

ALBUMS: 1(B) PIGS ON PURPOSE   (Cherry Red BRED 39) 1982
(up to   2(B) HYSTERICS   (Ink INK 1) 1983
1986)   3(-) JUST THE JOB (compilation) (Vindaloo VILP 1) 1984
         4( ) IN THE GOOD OLD COUNTRY WAY
                                       (Vindaloo YUS 7) 1986

NB: Also of relevance is *The Peel Sessions* (EP) (Stange Fruit SFPS 052) 1988 and a compilation *What A Scream 1980-86* (Mau Mau MAU 607) 1991, also on CD (MAUCD 607) 1991.

EPs: 1(B) USE YOUR LOAF (Use Your Loaf/Inside Out/
              Under The Lash) (PS)   (Cherry Red CHERRY 34) 1982
         2(B) THE NIGHTINGALES (Which Hi-Fi?/Give 'Em Time/
              My Brilliant Career/The Son Of
              God's Mate) (12", PS) (Cherry Red 12CHERRY 44) 1982

45s: Idiot Strength/Seconds (PS)   (Rough Trade RT 075) 1981
(up to   Paraffin Brain/
1986)   Elvis Last Ten Days (PS)   (Cherry Red CHERR 38) 1983
         Urban Ospreys/Cakehole (PS)   (Cherry Red CHERR 56) 1983
         Crafty Fag/How To Age (PS)   (Ink INK 71) 1983
         The Crunch (12")   (Vindaloo YUS 1) 1984
         It's A Cracker (12")   (Vindaloo UGH 9) 1985
         What A Carry On (12")   (Vindaloo YUS 4) 1985

The focal force behind Birmingham's **Nightingales** was Robert Lloyd, who'd been born at Cannock, Staffordshire in 1959. He was the founder of The Prefects, one of the earliest punk bands who toured with **The Clash** in those halycon days. After The Prefects split up, he formed **The Nightingales** utilising many of the personnel who'd previously been with him in The Prefects.

They released their debut 45 *Idiot Strength* on their own Vindaloo label in 1981 in association with Rough Trade. After this Crow departed and Andy Lloyd and Nick Beales came in as replacements. They were then signed up by Cherry Red and, with the weight of a bigger label behind them, enjoyed some success in the indie chart.

The *Use Your Loaf* EP was quite melodic and had its moments. *Pigs On Purpose*, their first album was an advancement on this, with some abrasive guitar playing and Robert Lloyd's interesting lyrics and vocal tirades.

The self-titled 1982 12" is quite adventurous.

In 1983, they changed labels again to Ink. This next album *Hysterics* featured a wider range of instrumentation, now incorporating banjo, trombone and viola and a wider range of musical styles. The *Happy Medium*, for example, veered towards country and western.

Unhappy with how record companies were handling his band's career, Lloyd decided to re-launch the Vindaloo label. The release of *The Crunch* coincided with more personnel changes in the band. It's quite a powerful effort capturing Lloyd's vocals in a more melodic mood. The *Just The Job* compilation also featured *The Crunch*, some non-album 45s and a cut from their earlier *Hysterics* album.

NIGHTINGALES - The Nightingales 12" EP.

Their first studio album *In The Good Old Country Way* added elements of country and bluegrass to their own musical style. Lloyd's lyrics are at their cleverest on tracks like *Part Time Moral England* and *I Spit In Your Gravy* and the *Heartache Collector* is also an outstanding track. This was probably **Nightingales**' best album but as Lloyd devoted more time to a fairly successful roster of artists like We've Got A Fuzzboz And We're Gonna Use It on his own label he had less time for **The Nightingales**. The end came when their keyboardist went to tour the 'States with Fuzzbox.

Their story ended with a 1991 compilation *What A Scream* on Mau Mau. The sleevenotes were penned by John Peel, who'd championed them throughout their career, especially in their early days. Talking of John Peel, their October 1980 session for him, which exhibited strong **Joy Division** and **Wire** ambitions, was issued on an EP by Strange Fruit in 1988. *What A Scream* is made more interesting by the inclusion of various demos, live material and rarities, rather than simply rehasing their better-known songs. This is an intelligently compiled set which certainly does justice to a band who never had a distinctive enough musical identity to advance beyond the second division of post-punk bands.

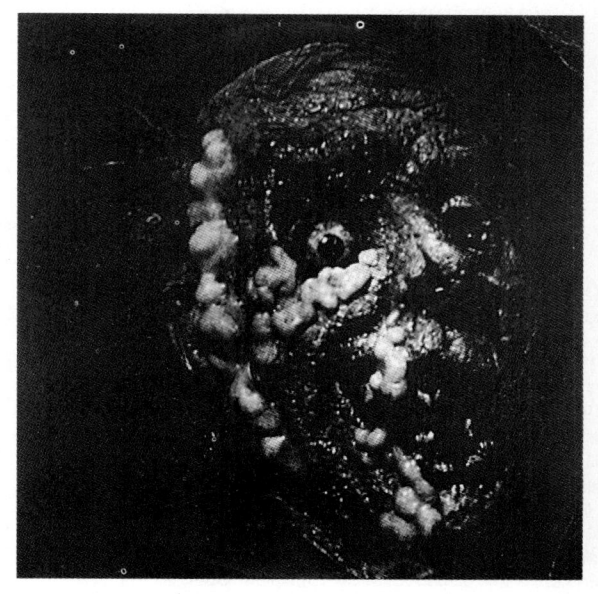

NIGHTMARES IN WAX - Black Leather 12".

Nightmares In Wax

Personnel incl: PETE BURNS   A

EP: 1(A) BIRTH OF A NATION (PS)   (Inevitable INEV 0002) 1979

45s: Black Leather/Shangri-La (12", PS)   (KY KY 9) 1984
     * Black Leather/Shangri-La/Girls Song (12", PS) (KY KY 9 ½) 1985

NB: * Only 3,000 copies of this disc were released in a different picture sleeve.

Nightmares In Wax are notable for including Pete Burns, who briefly played in a Liverpool band with Julian Cope and Pete Wylie of **Wah!** before forming this band. He went on to form Dead Or Alive. Their EP is now rare and quite collectable. *Black Leather* is an ode to leather clad bikers which suffers from being too repetitive. It lapses into a rendition of K.C. and The Sunshine Band's *That's The Way I Like It* at one point. Their strange and superb *Shangri-La* can also be heard on *Hicks From The Sticks* (Rockburgh Records ROC 111) 1980.

The Nightriders

Personnel: ANDREW CLARKE   drms   A
             PETER MACKENDER   bs   A
             STEPHEN PEEL   gtr   A
             STEPHEN SEYMOUR   vcls   A

45:    I Saw Her With Another Guy/
       London Town (PS)   (Stardust STR 1001) 1979

The Nightriders hailed from the Cambridge/Ely area. They replaced **The Squires** as support band to **The Purple Hearts** on the 'March Of The

Mods' tour of 1979. Their 45 came with a picture insert and is now quite scarce. It was released on the Stardust label owned by former Honeycomb Martin Murray.

I Saw Her With Another Guy veers very much in the mod-pop direction. You can also check it out on *100% British Mod* (Captain Mod MODSKA DCD 8) 1998.

999

Personnel:
NICK CASH			
(KEITH LUCAS)	vcls, gtr		ABC
GUY DAYS	gtr		ABC
PABLO LABRITAIN	drms		A C
JON WATSON	bs		ABC
(ED CASE	drms		B)

ALBUMS:
				HCP
1(A)	999	(United Artists UAG 30199)	1978	53
2(A)	SEPARATES	(United Artists UAG 30209)	1978	-
3(C)	THE BIGGEST PRIZE IN SPORT	(Polydor POLS 1013)	1980	-
4(A)	THE BIGGEST TOUR IN SPORT (live)	(Polydor PD 16307)	1980	-
5(A)	CONCRETE	(Albion ITS 999)	1981	-
6(A)	THE SINGLES ALBUM	(SOS SOS 999)	1981	-
7(A)	THE EARLY STUFF (compilation)	(EMI 7986022)	1981	-
8(A)	13TH FLOOR MADNESS	(Albion AS 8502)	1983	-
9(A)	FACE TO FACE	(Labritain LABLP 1000)	1985	-

NB: (1) later reissued (Fan Club FC 026) 1987, also on CD (026 CD) 1990. (1) also issued on CD (Dojo DOJOCD 149) 1993 and again (Captain Oi! AHOY CD 147) 2000 with bonus cuts. (2) later reissued (Fan Club FC 027) 1987, also on CD (027 CD) 1991. (2) also issued on CD (Dojo DOJOCD 150) 1993 and again (Captain Oi! AHOY CD 148) 2000 with bonus cuts. (3) also issued on CD (Anagram CDPUNK 67) 1995. (4) was a six track mini-album. (4) also issued on CD (Anagram CDPUNK 67) with extra tracks. (5) reissued (Line ALLP 400017) 1987, also on CD (Line LICD 900017) 1991. (7) also on CD (EMI CDGO 2031) 1992. (9) also issued on CD (Obsession OBSESS CD 003) 1993. Also relevant are the compilations, *Lust, Power And Money* (ABCLP 11) 1987, also on CD (ABCD 11) 1989 and again (Castle Music DOJOCD 129) 1993; *The Early Stuff* (EMI CPP 7986022) 1992, also on CD (CDGO 2031) 1992; *Greatest Hits Live* (Street Link STR CD 026) 1992; *Independent Punk Singles Collection* (Anagram CDPUNK 78) 1996; *Live At The Nashville 1979* (Anagram CDPUNK 93) 1997; *You Us It* (Anagram CDPUNK 92) 1997; *Emergency* (Receiver RRCD 245) 1997, *Takeover* (Get Back GBR 010) 1998 and *English Wipeout* (Overground OVER 90 VPCD) 2001.

45s:
				HCP
	I'm Alive/Quite Disappointing (PS)	(Labritain LAB 999)	1977	-
*	Nasty Nasty/No Pity (PS)	(United Artists UP 36299)	1977	-
	Nasty Nasty/No Pity (78 rpm promo)	(United Artists FREE 7)	1977	-
	Waiting/Action (12", mail-order freebie)	(Labritain 12 FREE 10)	1978	-
	Me And My Desire/Crazy (PS)	(United Artists UP 36376)	1978	-
	Emergency/My Street Stinks (PS)	(United Artists UP 36399)	1978	-
	Feelin' Alright With The Crew/Titanic (My Over) Reaction	(United Artists UP 36435)	1978	-
+	Homicide/Soldier (PS)	(United Artists UP 36467)	1978	40
	I'm Alive/Quite Disappointing (PS)	(United Artists UP 36519)	1979	-
	Found Out Too Late/Lie Lie Lie (PS)	(Radar ADA 46)	1979	69
	Trouble/Love Made A Fool Of You (PS)	(Polydor POSP 99)	1980	-
x	Obsessed/Change/Lie Lie Lie (PS)	(Albion ION 1011)	1981	71
α	Li'l Red Riding Hood/Waiting For Your Number To Be Called/I Ain't Gonna Tell Ya (live) (PS)	(Albion ION 1017)	1981	59
χ	Indian Reservation/So Greedy (Remixed)/Taboo (Remix) (PS)	(Albion ION 1023)	1981	51
δ	Wild Sun/Scandal In The City/Bongos On The Nile (PS)	(Albion ION 1033)	1982	-
ε	Wild Sun/Scandal In The City/Don't You Know I Need You (12", PS)	(Albion ION 121033)	1982	-
	13th Floor Madness/Night Shift/Arabesque (PS)	(Albion ION 1055)	1983	-
	13th Floor Madness/Night Shift/Arabesque (12", PS)	(Albion ION 121055)	1983	-

NB: * On green vinyl. + Some copies on green vinyl. x PS with patch, some were shrinkwrapped. α PS with stencil, some were shrinkwrapped. χ PS with sticker, some copies in clear vinyl. δ On yellow vinyl. Also issued on cassette (Albion CION 1033) 1982. ε Some issued in red or yellow vinyl.

Originally from Northampton and known as 48 Hours, they changed their name to **999** in May 1977, having already moved down to London. Nick Cash (real name Keith Lucas) had previously been with **Ian Dury**'s band Kilburn and The High Roads. In July 1977, they released a debut 45 *I'm Alive* on their own Labritain label. It was well received and this lead to them being signed by United Artists.

They produced a series of snappy singles sung with urgency - *Nasty Nasty*, *Me And My Desire* and *Emergency* - which received favourable reviews but didn't sell in sufficient quantities to make the charts. During 1978 they contributed two cuts, *Quite Disappointing* and *Crazy* to the *Front Row Festival* (Warner Bros WBK 46077) 1978 compilation. *Emergency*, arguably the best thing they did, also turned up subsequently on *20 Of Another Kind* (Polydor SUPER POLS 1006) in 1979, along with *Homicide*, another of their songs which gave them their first hit. It climbed to No. 40 during a three week stay in the charts following its release in October 1978. The following month, on 1st November 1978, the band recorded their only session for John Peel. Aside from *Homicide*, it comprised *Subterfuge*, *Soldier* and *Let's Face It*.

Their debut album *999* was released in March 1978. Spending just one week in the charts at No. 53 it would prove to be their only hit album. Produced by power-pop producer Andy Arthurs, it demonstrated their limitations as well as their strengths. The 45 cuts like *Me And My Desire* and *Emergency* demonstrated the latter, but the album lacked that special ingredient, uniqueness or originality to make it stand out from the crowd.

Separates, the follow-up album released in Autumn 1978, was a progression on their debut. With Martin Rushent producing they achieved a tighter sound. Its high points included the cleverly-arranged *Homicide*, a no-holes-barred rocker *High Energy Plan* and a tightly arranged 45 cut *Feelin' Alright With The Crew*, which was released just before their initial chart success with *Homicide*. Had it been released after *Homicide* it probably would have charted too.

999 worked hard to establish themselves as a live band, touring Europe and the U.S. extensively, as well as Britain. In 1979, *Separates* was retitled as *High Energy Plan* and released in the 'States with a different track listing. A couple of tracks were removed with two more 45 cuts substituted in their place.

Their progress was disrupted in the spring of 1979, when Labritain was involved in a car crash. Ed Case took over on drums for a while. They moved briefly to Radar Records and enjoyed a minor hit with *Found Out Too Late*.

In January 1980, they signed a new deal with Polydor. They retained Ed as a second drummer on their next album *Biggest Prize In Sport*. A new producer Vic Maile took the controls on this one, which saw them moving away from their early punk roots. Only the poppy title track really engages the ears.

999 - 999.

In an attempt to rekindle interest in the band Polydor released a six track live mini-album recorded in the 'States during 1980. The recording quality on *Biggest Tour In Sport* is good and it included most of their best known and popular songs like *Emergency*, *Homicide* and *Feelin' Alright With The Crewe*. However, despite this, it did not become a hit album.

Switching labels again to Albion in 1981 they released an album of new material *Concrete*. This veered more towards guitar rock and covered some songs from the sixties like *Fortune Teller* and *Li'l Red Riding Hood*. The latter was a minor hit in 1981 and so was the follow-up *Indian Reservation*, another oldie, this one had been a hit for Don Fardon back in 1970. *Concrete* further confirmed their move away from punk.

Perhaps the release of *The Singles Album* in 1981 was a recognition by the record company that the end was near. In fact of all their releases it is the most essential, containing both sides of their first seven singles from *I'm Alive* onwards - all their 45s released on United Artists.

Indeed they split up in 1982, but later reformed with their original line-up to record two further albums - *13th Floor Madness* in 1983 veered towards disco and wasn't well received but *Face To Face*, released on their own label, was quite engaging melodic rock.

Other compilation appearances have included in 1991, *Nasty Nasty* an early 45, on the compilation *Learning English, Vol. 1 By Die Toten Hosen* (Charisma 91823). EMI also released a compilation, *The Early Stuff*. This comprises twenty-three tracks including the band's first six singles, some of their best early album cuts and a couple of rarities *Action* and *Waiting*, which were previously only available on a limited edition 12" given away with inital copies of their second album *Separates*, released back in 1978.

Greatest Hits Live is a rather ragged collection - the playing is competent but for a live set it conveys little excitement.

More recently, their finest moment *Emergency* has figured on the lavish 5-CD box set *1-2-3-4 - A History Of Punk And New Wave 1976 - 1979* (MCA/Universal MCD 60066) in 1999. Then in 2000, Captain Oi! reissued their first two albums again on CD with bonus cuts. *999* comes with three, including the punk classic *Nasty Nasty*. Their second album *Separates* came with four bonus cuts, including *Waiting* and *Action*, which were available originally on an exclusive 12" to the first 10,000 people who bought the album. There's also a CD compilation, *Lust, Power And Money* on ABC.

English Wipeout is a twenty-seven cut live set comprising gigs from Manchester in 1977 and Leicester in 1980. The quality of the former is not good but it does capture them very early in their career and includes a live rendition of *Emergency* which is very different from the studio version. The sound quality of the Leicester gig is much better and the content concentrated on their then current album *The Biggest Prize In Sport* and had Pablo Labritain back on drums having recovered from a road accident. The CD comes with a booklet full of photos, memorabilia and sleevenotes from Steve Harnett.

They certainly had staying power and lasted many years beyond most of their punk era compatriots. They toured throughout the U.K. and Europe during the eighties and nineties and are one of the few first wave U.K. punk bands playing today with three original members still in the line-up.

Nipple Erectors

Personnel:	JERRY ARCANE	drms	A
	SHANNE BRADLEY	bs	A
	SHANE MacGOWAN	vcls	A
	ROGER TOWNDROW	gtr	A

45:	King Of The Bop/Nervous Wreck (PS)	(Soho SH ½) 1978

NB: (1) The first 50 copies had a glossy picture sleeve which is more collectable than later copies which came in a matt sleeve.

This outfit formed in London in late 1977. Their name got them press coverage but made live gigs hard to come by. Their sole release under this moniker was a sort of punk and rockabilly amalgam. After this they decided to shorten their name to **The Nips** to get more gigs.

999 - Trouble.

The Nips

Personnel:	JERRY ARCANE	drms	A
	SHANNE BRADLEY	bs	AB
	SHANE MacGOWAN	vcls	AB
	ROGER TOWNDROW	gtr	A
	STAN BRENNAN	gtr	B
	GAVIN DOUGLAS	drms	B

ALBUMS:	1(B)	ONLY AT THE END OF THE BEGINNING	
			(Soho HOHO 1) 1980
	2(-)	BOPS, BABES, BOOZE & BOVVER	
			(Big Beat WIK 66) 1987

45s:	All The Time In The World/	
	Private Eyes (foldover PS)	(Soho SH 4) 1978
*	Gabrielle/Vengeance	(Soho SH 9) 1980
	Gabrielle/Vengeance (PS)	(Chswick CHIS 119) 1980
	Happy Song/Nobody To Love (PS)	(Test Pressing TP 5) 1981

NB: * Originally issued with no picture sleeve, there was also a tour copy of this which sported a 'licensed to cool' stamp.

Formerly **The Nipple Erectors**, the London-based quartet's debut single under their truncated name was *All The Time In The World*. It made little impression and it was over a year later and with a changed line-up ('B') that they returned in 1980 with *Gabrielle*, a much more commercial rockabilly/punk song which made quite an impression in the indie chart and proved to be their best-selling single. Originally issued on Soho without a picture sleeve, which was very unusual for this era, the single was later reissued in a picture sleeve by Chiswick. Vocalist Shane MacGowan was a big **Jam** fan and *Gabrielle* may have been inspired by **The Jam**'s *Strange Town*.

Meanwhile Soho put out their *Only At The End Of The Beginning* album, which only sold in small quantities and is now very hard to track down.

A further period elapsed before they returned with their final release on Burning Rome's Test Pressing label produced by Paul Weller. With little promotion, the 45 was destined to remain obscure and the band decided to call it a day, but what of its lyrics:-

"Ian Page says wear a suit,
Keep your pockets full of loot
The mods are gonna dance through the night
- Sing a happy song"
(from *Happy Song*)

Three of their rarities *Gabrielle*, *Happy Song* and *Nobody To Love* later resurfaced on *This Is Mod, Vol. 1: The Rarities 1979 - 81* (Anagram CDM GRAM 98) 1995. *Gabrielle* can also be heard on *Punk Lost And Found* (Shanachie SH 5705) 1996 and on *1-2-3-4 - A History Of Punk And New Wave 1976 - 1979* (MCA/Universal MCD 60066) 1999. *Happy Song* and *Nobody To Love* can both be heard on *This Is Mod, Vol. 1 (Rarities 1979-81)* (Anagram CDMGRAM 98) 1995 or alternatively on vinyl on *This Is Mod* (dbl) (Get Back GET 39) in 1999.

MacGowan briefly joined an outfit called The Chainsaw but later found fame and fortune as lead singer in The Pogues, who were enormously successful in the late eighties and early nineties.

No Choice

Personnel:	CID	vcls	A
	GAGZEE	vcls	A
	MARTIN OWEN	lead gtr	A
	SPIKE	drms	A
	SVEND	bs	A

EP: 1(A) SADIST DREAM (Sadist Dream/Nuclear Disaster/ Cream Of The Crop) (PS) (Riot City RIOT 20) 1983

A Welsh band. They formed in Cardiff and played as a support act to **Conflict** and **Infa-Riot** before releasing this EP. The title cut views life through the eyes of a sadist. The lyrics are almost spoken and accompanied predominantly by guitar. After a slow introduction *Nuclear Disaster* is much faster-paced and *Cream Of The Crop* is a typical no-holes-barred punk-rocker.

Cream Of The Crop can also be heard on *Riot City Singles Collection* (Anagram CDPUNK 15) 1997 and *Sadist Dream* featured on *Vol. 2* (Anagram CDPUNK 55) 1995 of the series. Both of these compilations were also issued on vinyl by Captain Oi! (AHOY DLP 503 and 511).

NO CHOICE - Sadist Dream EP.

No Entry Band

Personnel:	DOUGIE BURNS	drms	A
	ROBERT KIRK	bs	A
	KEN LITTLE	vcls, gtr	A
	ILONA TURLEWICZ	vcls, gtr	A
	KEN TURLEWICZ	vcls	A

EP: 1(A) COLD AND LONELY LIVES (Everytime/Manoeuvre/ I'd Like To Think/ Cold And Lonely Life) (Kube Arts KA 1) 1978

A Glasgow band was responsible for this four song EP. In 1978 this record, which drew on influences mid-way between Fairport Convention and Dire Straits with a grey autumnal '73 feel, sounded a tad dated as it dealt with the much-covered subject of modern love. Still, the title cut in particular had a certain charm.

The Normal

Personnel:	DANIEL MILLER	synth, vcls

45: T.V.O.D./Warm Leatherette (PS) (Mute MUTE 001) 1978

The Normal was actually future Mute Records boss Daniel Miller. He also teamed up with **Robert Rental** (see entry for details) for a one-sided album as **Robert Rental and The Normal**. In May 1978, the London-based **Normal** produced one of the first singles from the new electronic-based school of music.

T.V.O.D. can also be heard on *25 Years Of Rough Trade Shops* (4-CD box set) (Mute CDSTUMM 191) in 2001.

Norman and The Hooligans

45: I'm A Punk/Re-Entry (President PT 461) 1977

Unusually for the era this 45 wasn't housed in a picture sleeve.

The Normil Hawaiians

Personnel:	BRIAN KEELEY	drms	A
	JIM LUSTED	gtr	A
	NICK ROSE	bs	A
	GUY SMITH	vcls, gtr	AB
	JANET ARMSTRONG	vcls	B
	NOEL BLANDEN	gtr	B
	SIMON MARCHANT	gtr	B
	WILF WILLIAMS	bs	B

ALBUMS: 1(B) MORE WEALTH THAN MONEY (Illuminated JAMS 23) 1983
2(B) WHAT'S GOING ON? (Illuminated JAMS 38) 1984

EP: 1(A) GALA FAILED (Party Party/Levels Of Water/Obedience/ The Return/Sang Sang) (12", PS) (Red Rhino RED 8) 1981

45s: The Beat Goes On/Ventilation/ Heaven (PS) (Dining Out TUX 13) 1981
Still Obedient/Should You Forget (PS) (Illuminated ILL 7) 1981

Don't be mislead by the name, this mob were actually from Kent. They recorded on a variety of labels, releasing their first single on Dining Out in 1981. The same year they put out a five track EP *Gala Failed* on Red Rhino and a further single *Still Obedient* on Illuminated. The music on these is experimental and interesting, certainly worth a twirl.

None of these singles sold particularly well and the initial line-up split up in early 1982. Janet Armstrong went off to do session work and later handled the female vocals on David Bowie's *Absolute Beginners* single.

Guy Smith proceeded to assemble a new line-up ('B'). They rarely gigged but recorded two albums for Illuminated before taking very much a back seat for the remainder of the decade. There was a further album *Return Of The Levellers* (Demi-Monde DMLP 1012) 1989.

THE NORMIL HAWAIIANS - Gala Failed EP.

The Nosebleeds

Personnel incl:	ED BANGER (aka ED GARRITY)	vcls	A
	PETER CROOKES	bs	AB
	VINI REILLY	gtr	A
	TOBY ROMANOV	drms	AB
	STEVEN MORRISSEY	vcls	B
	BILLY DUFFY	gtr	B

45:	Ain't Bin To No Music School/ Fascist Pigs (PS)	(Rabid TOSH 12) 1977

This band, who started life as Wild Ram, became **Ed Banger and The Nosebleeds** in 1977. Originally from Wythenshawe in Manchester, line-up 'A' recorded *Ain't Bin To No Music School*, which was credited to **The Nosebleeds** and only the second release on the Manchester-based Rabid label. It's a simple and direct punk song - typical of this period.

Early in 1978, **Ed Banger** (Ed Garrity) left to join **Slaughter and The Dogs** whilst Vini Reilly, a skilled guitarist and pianist joined **The Durutti Column**. He effectively became the lynch-pin of the band continuing well into the nineties.

Romanov and Crooks then recruited Billy Duffy (gtr) and Steven Morissey (vcls). This second line-up revised the band's material but only managed two live appearances (one as support to **Magazine**) and then split in May 1978.

As most of you will know Morissey later formed The Smiths, with Marr, Joyce and Rourke. They were one of the top post-punk outfits in the 1982 - 87 period. Thereafter Morrisey embarked on an erratic and sometimes controversial solo career.

Duffy went on to **Theatre Of Hate** and later joined **Death Cult** who soon became **The Cult**, who enjoyed huge success in the late eighties, in particular.

Both sides of **The Nosebleeds**' 45 can be found on *Rabid/TJM Punk Singles Collection* (Receiver RRCD 227) in 1996 and their finest moment, *Ain't Bin To No Music School* got a further airing on the 5-CD box set, *1-2-3-4 - A History Of Punk And New Wave 1976 - 1979* (MCA/Universal 60066) 1999.

Notsensibles

Personnel:	GARY	bs	A
	HAGGIS	vcls	A
	SAGE HARTLEY	gtr	A
	KEVIN 'PLOPPY' HEMMINGWAY	drms	A
	ROGER ROWLINSON	keyb'ds	A

ALBUM: 1(A) INSTANT CLASSIC (Bent) 1980

NB: (1) reissued (Snotty Snail SSLP 1) 1980 and again later on CD *Instant Punk Classics* (Anagram CD PUNK 38) 1994, with additional tracks.

45s:	(I'm In Love With) Margaret Thatcher/Little Boxes/ Gary Bushell's Band Of The Week (PS)	(Redball RR 02) 1979
	Death To Disco/Coronation Street Hustle/ Lying On The Sofa (PS)	(Bent SMALL BENT 5) 1980
	(I'm In Love With) Margaret Thatcher/Little Boxes/ Gary Bushell's Band Of The Week (PS)	(Snotty Snail NELCOL 1) 1980
	I Thought You Were Dead/I Make A Balls Of Everything I Do/Teenage Revolution (PS)	(Snotty Snail NELCOL 3) 1980
	I Am The Bishop/ The Telephone Rings Again (PS)	(Snotty Snail NELCOL 6) 1981

This somewhat lighthearted shambolic band hailed from Burnley in Lancashire. They were one of the punk era's great pisstakes. Their bizzare and eccentric style was best exemplified by their *(I'm In Love With) Margaret Thatcher*, which was understandably their most successful venture. After all records that take the piss out of politicians are always good for a laugh. The song is belted out in a lighthearted sort of singalong punk format and attracted enough attention by virtue of its novelty to reach the higher echelons of the indie chart in 1980. On the flip side *Little Boxes*

NOTSENSIBLES - (I'm In Love With) Margaret Thatcher.

is a lighthearted snip at the growing materialism of the times delivered in a similar singalong punk format. The final cut *Gary Bushell's Band Of The Week* is complete slapstick. Originally issued on the small Redball label with a pressing of just 1,000 its reissue on Snotty Snail the following year brought it to the attention of a slightly larger audience. Who knows what would have happened if it had been picked up by a major label? The picture sleeve features a sickly picture of her with her right hand gesticulating a V sign. This was their finest moment, but they had some other highly original, humorous, but musically shambolic, releases like *Death To Disco* and *I Make A Balls Of Everything I Do*. In 1980 their *Instant Classic* album rounded up many of their songs and this has subsequently been reissued on CD format if you want to hear what they sounded like.

Their finest moment, *I'm In Love With Margaret Thatcher*, later resurfaced on the 5-CD set *1-2-3-4 - A History Of Punk And New Wave 1976 - 1979* (MCA/Universal MCD 60066) 1999.

The Now

Personnel:	PAUL FARRER	bs	A
	JOHN MacCOLL	drms	A
	MIKE McGUIRE	vcls	A
	STEVE ROLLS	gtr	A

45s:	* Development Corporations/Why (PS)	(Ultimate ULT 401) 1977
	+ Into The 1980s/Nine O'Clock (PS)	(Raw RAW 31) 1979

NB: * Some on blue vinyl. + Only 800 copies of this were pressed.

Both 45s by this Peterborough band are now rare and quite expensive to purchase. Only 800 copies of *Into The 1980's* were pressed. *Development Corporations* was well-intentioned identi-punk, but with nothing to make it stand out from the crowd. Consequently, it's only likely to appeal to specialist collectors. *Into The 1980's* was actually cut back in 1977 but not released until 1979.

Gary Numan

HCP

ALBUMS: (up to 1986)	1	THE PLEASURE PRINCIPLE	(Beggars Banquet BEGA 10) 1979	1
	2	TELEKON	(Beggars Banquet BEGA 19) 1980	1
	3	LIVING ORNAMENTS '79	(Beggars Banquet BEGA 24) 1981	47
	4	LIVING ORNAMENTS '80	(Beggars Banquet BEGA 25) 1981	39
	5	LIVING ORNAMENTS '79/'80	(Beggars Banquet BOX 1) 1981	2
	6	DANCE	(Beggars Banquet BEGA 28) 1981	3
	7	I, ASSASSIN	(Beggars Banquet BEGA 40) 1982	8
	8	WARRIORS	(Beggars Banquet BEGA 47) 1983	12
	9	THE PLAN	(Beggars Banquet BEGA 55) 1984	29

10	BESERKER	(Numa NUMA 1001) 1984	45
11	WHITE NOISE (live) (dbl)	(Numa NUMAD 1002) 1985	29
12	THE FURY	(Numa NUMA 1003) 1985	24
13	STRANGE CHARM	(Numa NUMA 1005) 1986	59

NB: (1) reissued (Beggars Banquet BBLC 4) 1988 and also issued on CD (Beggars Banquet BBL 10CD) 1998 (remastered). (2) initially issued with a free single, *Remember I Was Vapour/On Broadway* and a poster, reissued (Beggars Banquet BBLC 19) 1988 and also issued on CD (Beggars Banquet BBL 19CD) 1998 (remastered). (3) reissued (Beggars Banquet BBLC 24) 1988. (4) reissued (Beggars Banquet BBLC 25) 1988. (5) issued as a boxed set, but also available as a doubleplay cassette (Beggars Banquet BOXC1) 1981. (6) originally issued in a gatefold sleeve with a free poster, reissued (Beggars Banquet BBLC 28) 1988 and on CD (Lowdown BBL 28CD) 1988. (7) originally issued with a free poster and reissued (Beggars Banquet BBLC 40) 1988. (8) reissued (Beggars Banquet BBLC 47) 1988. (12) also issued as a picture disc (NUMAP 1003) 1985 and issued on CD (Numa CDNUMA 1004) 1986. (13) also issued on CD (Numa CDNUMA 1005) 1987. Some of **Numan**'s albums were also paired and issued on one CD but with some tracks missing *Pleasure Principal / Warriors* (Beggars Banquet BEGA 10CD) 1987 and again (BEGA 153 CD) 1994, *Replicas / The Plan* (Beggars Banquet BEGA 7CD) 1987 and again (BEGA 152 CD) 1994, *Telekon / I Assassin* (Beggars Banquet BEGA 19CD) 1987 and again (BEGA 154 CD) 1994; and *Tubeway Army / Dance* (Beggars Banquet BEGA 4CD) 1987 and again (BEGA 151 CD) 1994. There are also a number of relevant compilations, *Collection: Gary Numan* (Castle Collector Series CCSCD 229) 1989, also available as a double album (CCSLP 229) 1989; *Double Peel Session* (12" mini album) (Strange Fruit SFPMA 202) 1989, also on CD (SFPMACD 202) 1989; *Images 1 / 2* (Fan Club GNFCDA 1 / 2) (double album with interviews and music, 1977 - 79), *Images 3 / 4* (Fan Club GNFCDA 3 / 4) (double album with interviews and music, 1980 - 81), *Images 5 / 6* (Fan Club GNFCDA 5 / 6) (double album with interviews and music, 1982 - 83), *Images 7 / 8* (Fan Club GNFCDA 7 / 8) (double album with interviews and music, 1984 - 86); *Exhibition* (compilation) (dbl) (Beggars Banquet BEGA 88) 1987, which got to No. 43, also on double CD (BEGA 88CD) 1987; *The Best Of Gary Numan* (Beggars Banquet BEGA 150 CD) 1993 is a double CD; *The Best Of Gary Numan 1984 - 1992* (Emporio EMPRCD 666) 1996; *Gary Numan Archive Vol. 1* (Rialto RMCD 205) 1997, *Gary Numan Archive Vol. 2* (Rialto RMCD 225) 1997, *The Numan Years* (5CD set) (Eagle EAGBX 025) 1998; *Random 2* (Beggars Banquet BBQCD 197) 1998 and *The Story So Far* (3CD Set) (Receiver RRXCD 505) 1996.

HCP

EPs: (up to 1986)	1	THE LIVE EP (Are Friends Electric/Beserker/Cars/ We Are Glass) (PS)	(Numa NU 7) 1985	27

NB: (1) came in black, white or blue vinyl and was also available as a 12" (Numa NUM 7) 1985.

HCP

45s: (up to 1986)	*	This Is My Live	(Beggars Banquet TUB 1) 1979	-
	+	Cars/Asylum (PS)	(Beggars Banquet BEG 23) 1979	1
		Complex/Bombers (live) (PS)	(Beggars Banquet BEG 29) 1979	6
		Complex/Bombers (live)/Me I Disconnect From You (live) (12", PS)	(Beggars Banquet BEG 29T) 1979	-
		We Are Glass/Trois Gymnopedies 1st Movement (PS)	(Beggars Banquet BEG 35) 1980	5
	x	I Die: You Die/ Down In The Park (PS)	(Beggars Banquet BEG 46) 1980	6
		This Wreckage/ Photograph (PS)	(Beggars Banquet BEG 50) 1980	20

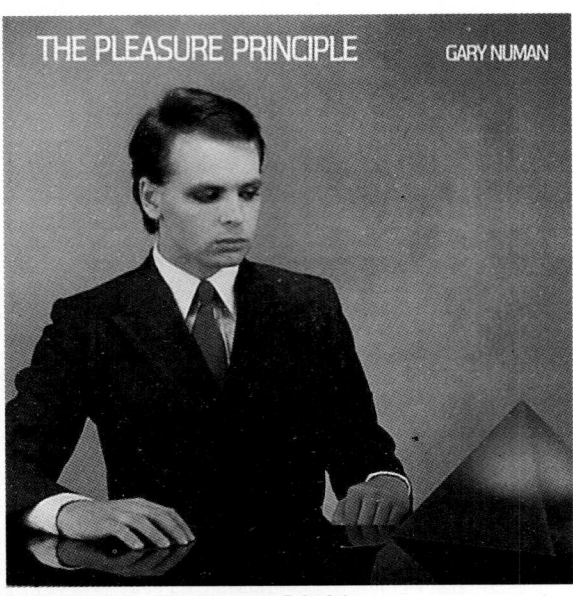

GARY NUMAN - The Pleasure Principle.

GARY NUMAN - Telekon.

α	Stormtrooper In Drag/ Night Talk (PS)	(Beggars Banquet BEG 61) 1981	49
β	Stormtrooper In Drag/ Night Talk (12" promo)	(Beggars Banquet BEG 61T) 1981	-
	She's Got Claws/ I Sing Rain (PS)	(Beggars Banquet BEG 62) 1981	6
	She's Got Claws/I Sing Rain/ Exhibition (12", PS)	(Beggars Banquet BEG 62T) 1981	-
	Love Needs No Disguise/ Take Me Home (PS)	(Beggars Banquet BEG 68) 1981	33
	Love Needs No Disguise/Night Talk/ Face To Face (12", PS)	(Beggars Banquet BEG 68T) 1981	-
	Music For Chameleons/ Noise Noise (PS)	(Beggars Banquet BEG 70) 1982	19
	Music For Chameleons (Extended)/Noise Noise/Bridge? What Bridge (12", PS)	(Beggars Banquet BEG 70T) 1982	-
	We Take Mystery (To Bed)/ The Image Is (PS)	(Beggars Banquet BEG 77) 1982	9
	We Take Mystery (To Bed) (Extended)/ The Image Is/We Take Mystery (early version) (12", PS)	(Beggars Banquet BEG 77T) 1982	-
	White Boys And Heroes/ War Games (PS)	(Beggars Banquet BEG 81) 1982	20
	White Boys And Heroes (Extended)/War Games/ Glitter And Ash (12", PS)	(Beggars Banquet BEG 81T) 1982	-
	That's Too Bad/Oh Didn't I Say/Bombers/ O.D. Receiver/Blue Eyes/Do You Need The Service (12", PS)	(Beggars Banquet BEG 92E) 1983	-
	Warriors/ My Car Slides (1) (PS)	(Beggars Banquet BEG 95) 1983	20
	Warriors (extended)/My Car Slides Parts 1 & 2 (12", PS)	(Beggars Banquet BEG 95T) 1983	-
χ	Warriors/My Car Slides (1)	(Beggars Banquet BEG 95P) 1983	-
	Sister Surprise/ Poetry And Power (PS)	(Beggars Banquet BEG 101) 1983	32
δ	Sister Surprise/Poetry And Power/ Letter (12", PS)	(Beggars Banquet BEG 101T) 1983	-
	Beserker/Empty Bed Empty Heart (PS)	(Numa NU 4) 1984	32
	Beserker (extended)/Empty Heart Empty Bed/ Beserker (7" mix) (12", PS)	(Numa NUM 4) 1984	-
ε	Beserker/Empty Bed Empty Heart	(Numa NUP 4) 1984	
	My Dying Machine/Here Am I (PS)	(Numa NU 6) 1984	66
	My Dying Machine (extended)/Here Am I/ She Cries (12", PS)	(Numa NUM 6) 1984	-
ϕ	Change Your Mind/Remix Remake Remodel (PS)	(Polydor POSP 722) 1985	17
γ	Change Your Mind (extended)/Remix Remake Remodel/ Fools In A World Of Fire (12", PS)	(Polydor POSPX 722) 1985	-
η	Your Fascination/We Need It (PS)	(Numa NU 9) 1985	46
ι	Your Fascination (extended)/We Need It/ Anthem (12", PS)	(Numa NUM 9) 1985	-
	Call Out The Dogs/ The Ship Comes Apart (PS)	(Numa NU 11) 1985	49
	Call Out The Dogs (Extended)/This Ship Comes Apart/		

	No Shelter (12", PS)	(Numa NUM 11) 1985 -
φ	Miracles/The Fear (PS)	(Numa NU 13) 1985 49
κ	Miracles (Extended)/ The Fear (Extended) (12", PS)	(Numa NUM 13) 1985 -
λ	This Is Love/Survival (PS)	(Numa NU 16) 1986 28
μ	This Is Love (extended)/ Survival (12", PS)	(Numa NUM 16) 1986 -
ν	I Can't Stop/Faces (PS)	(Numa NU 17) 1986 27
o	I Can't Stop (extended)/Faces (12", PS)	(Numa NUM 17) 1986 -
π	New Thing From London Town/ Time To Die (PS)	(Numa NU 19) 1986 52
θ	New Thing From London Town (Extended)/ Time To Die (Extended) (12", PS)	(Numa NUM 19) 1986 -
ρ	I Still Remember/Puppets (PS)	(Numa NU 21) 1986 74
σ	I Still Remember (Extended remix)/ Puppets (extended) (12", PS)	(Numa NUM 21) 1986 -

NB: * This was a double-sided white label promo for *The Plan*. Only 300 were pressed. + There was also a German 12" version of this release in a picture sleeve (INT 126.501). Some copies of the 7" were mispressed on dark red vinyl. The 45 was also released on cassette in a cigarette-pack style box (SPC 7). x The flip side contained the piano version of *Down In The Park*. Six white label copies were also produced of this 45 with an alternate version of the 'A' side. α By **Paul Gardiner** with **Gary Numan** on vocals. β This was a white label promo version. χ There was also a plane-shaped picture disc version of this release (BEG 95P). δ *Letter* on this disc is an identical song to *Face To Face*. ε This was a shaped picture disc. φ Credited to Sharpe and **Numan**. The Sharpe was Bill Sharpe of Shakatak. There was also a shaped picture version of this release (POSPP 722). γ Credited to Sharpe and **Numan**, this was a picture disc release. η There was also a picture disc release (NUP 9). ι There was also a picture disc release (NUMP 9). φ Some copies came on red or white vinyl. κ Some copies of this also came on red or white vinyl. φ and κ both came with a free flexi. λ There was also a picture disc release (NUP 16). μ There was also a picture disc release (NUMP 16). ν There was also a plane-shaped picture disc release (NUP 17). o There were also different releases with a Picture Mix (NUMP 17) and Club Mix (NUDJ 17) of *I Can't Stop*. ν and o both came with a free flexi. π There was also a picture disc release (NUP 19). θ There was also a picture disc release (NUMP 19). ρ There was also a picture disc release (NUP 21). σ There was also a picture disc release (NUMP 21).

This entry picks up **Gary Numan**'s career in 1979 after **Tubeway Army** and runs through until 1986 where the remit of this book ends. For details of his early days see **The Tubeway Army** entry.

After the release of *Replicas* in June 1979 **Gary Numan** went solo, but retained Billy Currie (keyb'ds), Paul Gardiner (bs), Chris Payne (synth, viola) and Cedric Sharpley (drms) to work with. A double-sided white label promo *This Is My Life* was available in limited quantities for *The Plan* project, just 300 were pressed, but his first widely available release was *Cars*, which previewed his purely electronic album *The Pleasure Principle*, which was released the following month in September 1979. *Cars* went to No. 1 where it spent eleven weeks and also went on to become a big international hit. The album also topped the charts, where it spent a massively impressive twenty-one weeks. The album was a testimony to **Numan**'s increasing interest in technology in both the lyrics and the music. In 1979, one of his songs *Tracks* was also included on *20 Of Another Kind, Vol. 2* (Polydor POLX1). **Numan** also commenced a sell-out U.K. tour for which he designed two massive columns of light housing the band and remote control pyramids. He decided to have his Hammersmith Odeon show videoed and when it was released in 1980 it became the first ever music video on general release. He also played a second show there, after the first sold out, with the proceeds going to the Save The Whale fund.

In November 1979 **Numan** released a further single *Complex*. This was an electronic ballad which he used a superb video with animated graphics to promote. It proved another big hit, climbing to No. 6 and spending nine weeks in the charts.

1980 was a hectic year for **Numan**. He embarked on an extensive tour of the world, taking the massive Touring Principle light show to Europe, Japan and The United States. *Cars* climbed to No. 9 becoming the first electronic hit in the 'States. Indeed, *Replicas*, *The Pleasure Principle* and *Are Friends Electric?* all became worldwide hits that year. When he returned home Gary was voted the best male singer in the British Rock and Pop Awards. With Dennis Haines (keyb'ds) replacing Billy Currie who had returned to **Ultravox** and **Visage**, Russell Bell had also been added to the touring band on guitar.

In May 1980 a new single *We Are Glass* was released. This combined guitars with **Numan**'s familiar electronic sound and spent seven weeks in the charts, peaking at No. 5. On the flip side was a version of Eric Satie's *Trio Gymnopediers*. He followed this success with *I Die You Die*, released in August. This climbed to No. 6 spending seven weeks in the charts.

His next album *Telekon* also got to No. 1, though this one only spent eleven weeks in the charts. Initial copies came with a free single containing two live cuts *Remember I Was Vapour* and The Drifters' *On Broadway*. He resisted the temptation of including recent hits on the album to concentrate on new material. It included more guitar than his recent efforts. A number of coloured vinyl versions of the album were put out on Intercord. To help promote it Numan embarked on a twenty-date U.K. tour with a new light show as part of a new futuristic stage act. In December, after his return to England, *This Wreckage* a slow synthesized dominated song was culled from *Telekon*. It spent seven weeks in the chart and just made No. 20. He also had *Aircrash Bureau* included on the electro compilation *Machines* (Virgin V 2177) in 1980.

GARY NUMAN - Dance.

In 1981 in Germany Intercord issued an authorised compilation album *Photograph*, which came in a fine gatefold sleeve. It caused controversy and was quickly withdrawn. By now Gary had taken the big decision to retire completely from live work. He played three sell-out shows in April at London's Wembley Arena which were the largest he had ever done. The stage was extended especially and additional panels of light and coloured lamps were fitted. **Gary Numan** used a remote-controlled car to drive himself across the stage and the light crew were accommodated in a space-type capsule in what was regarded as one of the best exhibitions of lights in British rock history. It was on the final night that **Numan** announced his retirement from the stage to concentrate on videos and recordings. The show was videoed and released as "Micromusic" topping the video charts. Shortly after, a double-album boxed set *Living Ornament 1979 - 80*, was released. It climbed to No. 2 in the charts, though only spent four weeks there. The two records, which included tracks from his 1979 and 1980 tours, were also made available as individual albums. Each spent three weeks in the charts, climbing to No's 47 and 39 respectively. The 1979 one is the stronger of the two, with synthesizer work with **Ultravox**'s Billie Currie.

In July **Numan** sang lead vocals on Paul Gardiner's 45 *Stormtrooper In Drag*, which was also briefly available as a 12" white label promo, as well as a 7". It climbed to No. 49 in the charts.

A new **Gary Numan** single *She's Got Claws* was released in August. For this he sported a 1930s style gangster look. Musically, it blended jazz and electronic influences. It was promoted by a new video directed by Julian Temple. It sold well, spending six weeks in the charts and climbing to No. 6. It also featured one of his strangest recordings on the flip side *I Sing Rain*.

His next album *Dance* was released in September. Written about the aftermath of his first real love it featured prominent saxophone and guests appearances from Queen's Roger Taylor and **Japan**'s **Mick Karn**. The tunes were much less danceable than some of his earlier output but displayed his flair for ironic lyrics. Again the album sold well, spending eight weeks in the charts and climbing to No. 3.

1981 had been a successful year for **Numan** during which the readers of 'Smash Hits' magazine had voted him the Best Male Singer of 1981. He also returned to the charts at the end of December singing vocals on his old backing band's single Love Needs No Disguise, which got to No. 33 in the charts. The band had named themselves Dramatis.

In January 1982, **Numan** hit the headlines when the plane he was returning from the Milden Pop Festival in lost height because of fuel pump failure and had to crash land on the A 3051 in Hampshire. Some in the media accused him of doing this deliberately as a publicity-seeking stunt, although **Numan**, whose now a respected pilot, wasn't even piloting the plane at the time.

Numan was forced to spend much of 1982 in the 'States as a tax exile. He released a new single Music For Chameleons which featured Pino Pallidino on bass. It spent seven weeks in the charts, peaking at No. 19 and a further single We Take Mystery (To Bed) fared better climbing to No. 9 during a four week residency. Whilst in the 'States **Numan** decided to embark on a short tour of live concerts to see if he had any appetite for stage work again. It seems he had - within a year of announcing his retirement from touring.

His 1982 album I Assassin, released in September was another big success commercially. A more nostalgic album than his recent efforts it veered back towards his earlier hits. It reached No. 8 in the charts during a six-week stay. It contained his earlier hits, Music For Chameleons and We Take Mystery (To Bed), whilst a third song White Boys And Heroes written about the way we perceive old movie stars, was released as a 45 in August and climbed to No. 20. In the 'States a hits album Newman Numan compiled all his singles to date. There was also a special U.S. 12" promo release which comprised a new 8'20" mix of White Boys And Heroes with We Take Mystery (To Bed) on the flip.

Gary flew back to Britain in April 1983. He was greeted by thousands of his loyal fans when he landed at Blackbush Airfield. This time it was a leather clad **Numan** - the new image coming from an idea in the "Mad Max" films. He used it to good effect on the sleeve on his next 45 Warriors, released in September 1983. It also appeared as a plane-shaped picture disc. Like its predecessor it got to No. 20, but enjoyed an additional week in the charts. To help promote the single and album of the same name he embarked on a lavish 40-date comeback tour. The set featured a futuristic city skyline and ruins with hundreds of lights (some of which were triggered by **Numan**'s voice) amongst which **Numan** and his backing band (Dramatis plus **Numan**'s brother John Webb) were based.

The Warriors album blended electronics with guitar and haunting saxophone. Sister Sister was culled for 45 release and spent three weeks in the charts peaking at No. 32. The 12" version of this release contained a pressing error whereby the 'B' side featured a previously released song Face To Face mistitled as Letters. The album, partly produced by Bill Nelson, rose to No. 12 during a six-week chart stint.

Numan ended his British tour at London's Dominion Theatre in November. A book was issued containing photo's of the tour which is now hard to come by. Sister Sister proved to be **Numan**'s last release for Beggar's Banquet. Early in 1984 he formed his own Numa label, to which he also signed his brother John Webb, Steve Braun, Hohokam and model Caroline Munro. Beggars Banquet meanwhile, issued some previously unreleased **Tubeway Army** material.

Numan returned in 1984 with a new 'Berserker' image - comprising white face make-up and blue hair it was one of his most eccentric. However, his first release wasn't one on his newly-formed Numa label, but an album on Beggars Banquet The Plan in October 1984, which compiled a number of **Numan**'s early demos which led to him being signed by the label. **Numan** was fully supportive of this project and even wrote the sleeve-notes. On the musical menu here is guitar-based music, which was quite punky without being aggressive. The album was credited to **Gary Numan and Tubeway Army** and some of these early demos later resurfaced re-recorded with additional keyboards on the Tubeway Army album. The Plan, which was also available as a picture disc spent four weeks in the album charts climbing to No. 29.

Numan's first Numa release the same month was his Berserker 45. He appeared on 'Top Of The Pops' and 'Razzmatazz' to help promote it, but it suffered from poor distribution and only climbed to No. 32 during its five week chart residency. It was also the title track to his next album. This marked his move into computer synthesizers. The album also included This

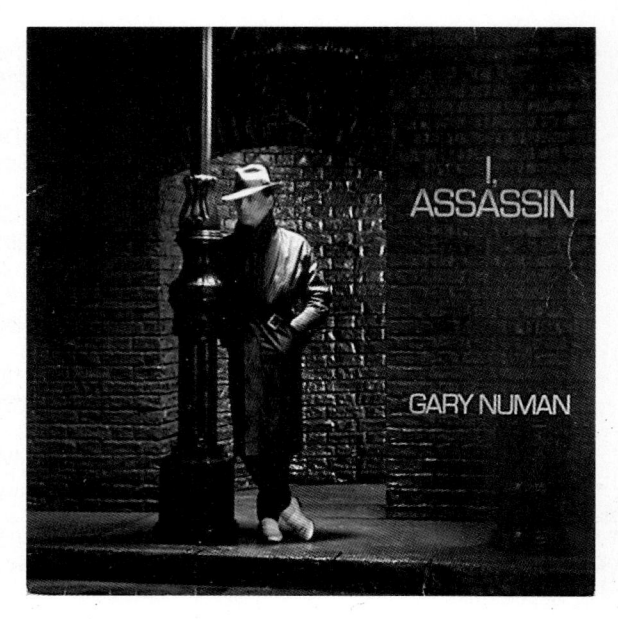

GARY NUMAN - I, Assassin.

Is New Love, which he'd sung an embryonic version of earlier in the year on "The Leo Sayer Show" and "The Main Attraction" and My Dying Machine, which was culled for 45 release in December. The album, which in its cassette format, included six extended tracks spent three weeks in the chart, peaking at No. 45 whilst My Dying Machine only managed a disappointing No. 66.

In March 1985, **Numan** linked up with Shakatak's Bill Sharpe whilst recording at Stepperton's Rock City Studios to record which was presumed at the time to be a one-off single, Change Your Mind. It ended up a Top 20 hit, spending eight weeks in the charts. It was also included on Bill Sharpe's album Famous People, which got to No. 17 and the CD release of this included the 12" mix of the 45.

In May 1985, **Numan** released the double album White Noise, which contained live material spanning his career to date. A live EP was also released in both 7" and 12" format and on black, white or blue vinyl containing Are Friends Electric?, Berserker, Cars and We Are Glass. Here in Britain the EP sold surprisingly well considering it contained old material, spending four weeks in the charts and peaking at No. 27. In Belgium it even made the Top 10!

With **Numan**'s next 45 Your Fascination, released in August 1985, came another new image. This time a red bow tie and James Bond - type white suit. To help promote the single a video was made of **Numan** and his girlfriend Tracy Adams. The title track was put out on a 45, in 7" and 12" formats, both were also available as picture discs and the 12" had an extended version of the 'A' side and an additional cut Anthem. It spent five weeks in the charts but failed to advance beyond No. 46. In September a follow-up single Call Out The Dogs was released. This included sound effects from the "Blade Runner" film. The flip side No Shelter was also an excellent noteworthy instrumental. The promotional video for this single featured **Numan** performing in front of huge blocks of moving light. However, it spent just two weeks in the charts failing to advance beyond No. 49. The same month **Numan**'s next album The Fury appeared. This included both Your Fascination and Call Out The Dogs and in November, a sad synthesizer ballad Miracles, which also climbed to No. 49 but spent three weeks in the charts, was released. This was available in white or red in 7" or 12" formats (the 12" has an extended version of Miracles). It came in a picture sleeve featuring **Numan** and his girlfriend.

The Fury album contained mostly computer synthesizer music devoid of any real emotion or passion. **Numan** embarked on a seventeen-date tour to help promote it. It climbed to No. 24 during its five-week chart residency. The cassette version featured extended versions of all tracks, whilst the album was also available as a picture disc. It also became his first album to receive a full CD release.

In October, inspired by the success of Change Your Mind, Sharpe and **Numan** returned with a new single New Thing From London Town, which was in the hard dance mode. The 45 again earnt good reviews and got to No. 52 in the charts. A remixed version of the song was later featured on **Numan**'s Strange Charm album.

Needless to say when **Numan** returned in April 1986 with his next single he also launched another new image - this time sporting a black suit, winged collar and bow tie. **Numan** appeared on 'Top Of The Pops' to promote the mournful, slow ballad *This Is Love*, which came in the now usual formats but also with a free flexi. *This Is Love* spent three weeks in the charts, peaking at No. 28. Two promotional videos were made to promote the follow-up 45, *I Can't Stop* which emerged in June again with a free flexi. One featured **Numan** pursuing his other big passion apart from music, which was flying. The disc spent four weeks in the chart peaking at No. 27. Its various formats included a plane-shaped picture disc. Both of these singles figured on his *Strange Charm* album, released in November 1986. However, the album only managed two weeks in the charts peaking disappointingly at No. 59.

The same month, after seeing the 'Animal Squad' TV series **Numan** put out a 45 *I Still Remember* to help the RSPCA. This wasn't a new song - the track was taken from *The Fury* but remixed with new vocals and lyrics. **Numan** used footage of himself with his pet dog interspersed with photos provided by the RSPCA for the promotional video. Despite the 'good cause' it was his least successful single to date just spending a week at No. 74.

Numan continued to record as a solo artist as well as building on his fruitful relationship with Bill Sharpe. In 1987, he also linked up to become vocalist with Radio Heart although the material met with a mixed reception from his fans.

The Best Of Gary Numan on Beggars Banquet in 1993 is a double CD compilation, comprising thirty-four reasonably compiled tracks. It includes *Are Friends Electric?* and *Cars* as well as many other 'A' sides, one 'B' side (*We Are So Fragile*) and several album tracks.

The Best Of Gary Numan on Emporio in 1996 is a spartanly packaged compilation which concentrates on his mid-eighties material, which was certainly not among his best. Approach with caution.

Archive, Vol. 1 on Rialto in 1997 is an eighties mixture of in-concert and studio recordings. It includes live recordings of **Numan**'s synth-pop smashes like *Are Friends Electric?*, *Cars* and *We Are Glass*.

Random 1 is a tribute album featuring versions of his material by acts like St. Etienne, Jimi Tenor, Matt Sharp and Damon Albarn, Moloko and Jesus Jones. *Random 2* comprises remixes of original **Numan** material, with cutting edge dance producers at the controls. There was also a 4 x 12" coloured vinyl edition of just 2,500 copies which sold out on its day of release.

Love him or loathe him there's no denying **Gary Numan**'s commercial success and his significance as a pioneer in the development of electro-pop.

The Numbers

Personnel:	NICK McAULEY	gtr, vcls	A
	ANGELO BRUSCHINI	gtr	A
	LEE GARDENER	drms	A
	WAYNE KINGSTON	bs	A

EP:	1(A)	ROCK STARS (Rock Stars/Fines/ I Don't Know What I Want/ Leather Jacket) (PS)	(Blasto SRTS 79/CUS 358) 1979
45s:		Alternative Suicide/Blue Movies/Hotel Rooms/ Back In Ireland (PS)	(Heartbeat PULSE 4) 1979
		Five Letter Word/Alone (PS)	(RCA RCA 74) 1981
		I Don't Know/Mr. President (PS)	(RCA RCA 169) 1981

The Numbers made their vinyl debut with *Cross-Slide* on *Avon Calling - The Bristol Compilation* (Heartbeat HB 1) in 1979, on which they achieved quite a tight sound with some useful guitar. They released further recordings for Heartbeat and Blasto that year before being signed to RCA for two further 45s, but they failed to break through commercially. *Alternative Suicide* also appeared on *4 Alternatives* (Heartbeat PULSE 4) in 1979.

Nurse With Wound

Personnel incl: STEVE STAPLETON

ALBUMS: (up to 1986)	1	CHANCE MEETING ON A DISSECTING TABLE OF A SEWING MACHINE AND UMBRELLA	
			(United Dairies UD 01) 1979
	2	TO THE QUIET MEN FROM A TINY GIRL	
			(United Dairies UD 03) 1980
	3	MERZBILD SCHWET	(United Dairies UD 04) 1980
	4	INSECT AND INDIVIDUAL SILENCED	
			(United Dairies UD 08) 1981
	5	OSTRANENIE 1913	(Third Mind TMR 03) 1984
	6	HOMOTOPY TO MARIE	(United Dairies UD 012) 1985
	7	AUTOMATING VOL. 1	(United Dairies UD 019) 1986
	8	A MISSING SENSE	(United Dairies UD 020) 1986

NB: (1) - (3) originally pressed in quantities of just 500. (4) had a pressing of 1,000. (5) and (7) had pressings of 3,000. (6) had a pressing of 5,000. (8) had a pressing of 2,000 and **Nurse With Wound** appear on one side only. Organum are on the reverse side. (1) also issued on CD (United Dairies UD 01 CD) 1992. (6) also issued on CD (United Dairies UD 013 CD) 1992.

Nurse With Wound were a low profile experimental project led by Steve Stapleton, which was part of the **Throbbing Gristle** stable. Their debut album *Chance Meeting...* (and expect to pay well over £100 for an original copy) was full of highly improvised music, featured very trebly guitar and an extremely doctored drum machine. The third and final track fetaures weird piano with random snippets of spoken French language. It concludes with what sounds like a vacuum cleaner.

In parts *Homotopy To Marie* recalls early Zappa/Mothers Of Invention chaos and mayhem. Highly avant-garde and certainly an acquired taste. If you're curious go for the CD reissue 'cos the original will set you back approaching £50.

Phil Oakey and Giorgio Moroder

			HCP
ALBUM: (up to 1986)	1	CHROME	(Virgin V 2351) 1985 52

NB: (1) also issued on CD (Virgin CDV 2351) 1985 and reissued at mid-price (Virgin OVED 187) in 1987.

		HCP
45s: (up to 1986)	Together In Electric Dreams/ (Instrumental) (PS)	(Virgin VS 713) 1984 3
	Together In Electric Dreams/ (Instrumental) (pic disc)	(Virgin VSY 713) 1984 -
	Together In Electric Dreams/ (Instrumental) (12", PS)	(Virgin VS 713-12) 1984 -
	Goodbye Bad Times/(Instrumental) (PS)	(Virgin VS 772) 1985 44
	Be My Lover Now/(Instrumental) (PS)	(Virgin VS 800) 1985 -
	Be My Lover Now/ (Instrumental) (12", PS)	(Virgin VS 800-12) 1985 -
Reissue:	Together In Electric Dreams/ Goodbye Bad Times	(Old Gold OG 9825) 1988 -

Phil Oakey is best known as a founder member and inspiration behind **The Human League**. He was born on 2nd October 1955 in Sheffield, where he was working as a hospital porter when the band was formed. In October 1984, he teamed up with disco producer Giorgio Moroder to record *Together In Electric Dreams*, which was also notable for a Peter Frampton guitar solo. They found themselves with a No. 3 hit and continued to collaborate during 1985, when they enjoyed further chart success with *Goodbye Bad Times*, released in June, which got to No. 44 and an album *Chrome*, which came out the following month and got to No. 52 during a five week chart residency. The collaboration ended when their next 45, *Be My Lover Now* flopped.

The Obtainers/Mag-Spys

45:	Yeh Yeh Yeh/Pussy Wussy/ (two cuts by Mag-Spys)	(Dance Fools Dance no #) 1979

Only 100 copies of this were issued in a stickered plain sleeve. It is extremely rare and sought-after because the Mag-Spys tracks featured **The Cure**'s Simon Gallup.

Occasionally David

Personnel incl:	RAY BATE		A
	CLIVE WHITLOCK		A

EP:	1(A)	TWIST AND SHOUT (Spectacles/The Beaver/ The Deco Paranoia/Girl You're A Happening Thing) (PS)	(Oven Ready OD 77901) 1979
CASS:	1(A)	FOREVER CHANGES	(Oven Ready no #) 1980
45:		I Can't Get Used To Losing You (So I'm Coming Back)/ Will You Miss Me Tonight? (PS)	(Oven Ready OD 1/98002) 1980

Occasionally David stopped playing live in 1980. Ray Bate and Clive Whitlock then ousted all the other members to concentrate on writing and recording. Among these subsequent ventures was a complete, track for track, pastiche of Love's classic 1967 album *Forever Changes*, which they released on cassette.

Occult Chemistry

Personnel incl:	THOMAS DIXON	bs
	MARTHA TILSON	lead vcls

45s:	*	Water Earth Fire Air (Rough Version)	(Bikini Girl no #) 1980
	+	Water Earth Fire Air/ Fire Air Water Earth (PS)	(Dining Out TUX 4) 1981

NB: * This was a 5" ckear flexi-disc in a stamped envelope which came with 'Bikini Girl' magazine. + This had a handmade picture sleeve.

Occult Chemistry included Martha Tilson on lead vocals, who was later with **A Certain Ratio**. Thomas Dixon was also a member on bass before joining Funkapolitan.

Gene October

45s:	Suffering In The Land/Suffering Dub (PS)	(Illegal ILS 034) 1983
	Don't Quit/Burning Sounds (PS)	(Slipped Discs SPLAT 001) 1984

These were solo efforts by the **Chelsea** frontman.

The Odds

Personnel:	COLIN BROCKWELL	drms	AB
	STUART MATTHEWMAN	sax, gtr	AB
	SAM LEYLAND	vcls	AB
	BILL McKEOWN	bs	AB
	KEIRON MOSES	gtr	B

45s:	Saturday Night/ Not Another Love Song (PS)	(Double R RED 001) 1980
	Yesterday Man/So You Think (PS)	(JSO EAT 1) 1981
*	Dread In My Bed/Spare Rib	(JSO EAT 7) 1981

NB: * Came with a press release.

A mod revival band from Hull. Their best known song was a mod-pop offering *Saturday Night* which you can also hear, along with its flip side *Not Another Love Song*, on *This Is Mod, Vol. 1 (Rarities 1979 - 81)* (Anagram CDMGRAM 98) 1995. Indeed, more recently *Saturday Night* has resurfaced on *100% British Mod* (Captain Mod MODSKA DCD 8) 1998 and on vinyl on *This Is Mod* (dbl) (Get Back GET 39) 1999.

Then, with the addition of Kieron Moses they recorded two more ska orientated 45s on JSO. Matthewman later played in Sade's backing band.

The Offs

45:	Johnny Too Bad/624803	(Crack In The World OFFS 0) 1979

The 'A' side of this single is a rockability reggae version of The Slickers' *Johnny Too Bad*.

Oi! Polloi

ALBUM:	1	UNITE AND WIN	(Oi! OIR 011) 198?

This Edinburgh band have proved one of the most durable Oi!/protest punk outfits, appearing on numerous benefit singles and albums over the years to raise funds for many good causes. They have recorded on many different labels. The *This Is Oi!* (Oi OIR 004) 1986 compilation, which was later reissued on CD (Captain Oi! AHOY CD 6) 1993, showcased their frantic and enthusiastic *Minority Authority* and their excellent version of the Oi! punk classic *Skinhead*. The latter can also be heard on *The Best Of Oi! Records* (Captain Oi! AHOY CD 38) 1995, whilst *Boot Down The Door* has resurfaced on *Rot Records Punk Singles Collection* (Anagram CDPUNK 40) in 1994.

Finally, you'll find their raucous *Thugs In Uniform* on *100% Hardcore Punk Rock* (CD) (Captain Oi! AHOY DCD 84) 1997.

O-Level

Personnel incl:	ED BALL		A
	DANIEL TREACY		A

EP:	1(A)	THE MALCOLM EP (We Love Malcolm MacLaren/ Leave Me/Everybody's On Revolver/ Stairway To Boredom) (PS)	(Kings Road KR 002) 1978
45:		East Sheen/Pseudo Punk (PS)	(Psycho PSYCHO 2) 1978

This was essentially a spin-off project from **Television Personalities**. Ed Ball was also involved in **The Times** and **Teenage Film Stars**. O-Level also contributed to the compilation album *Day In The Life Of Gilbert And George* (Rev-Ola CREV 005) in 1993, also on CD. Their sole 45 came in a 'map' or 'schoolboy' picture sleeve. Both, particularly the latter, are now quite collectable. The EP, also, is quite hard to find now and came in two versions too. The photocopied wraparound picture sleeve is rarer and more collectable than the printed picture sleeve.

Adrian Thrills writing in NME described *We Love Malcolm* as 'their tongue in safety-pinned cheek hymn of praise to Brian Epstein of the blank generaton'. On the flip side *Everybody's On Revolver Tonight* was their response to **The Rezillos**' *Top Of The Pops*:-

"They've all gone to see the Banshees
They're on next after X Ray Spex
Think I'll have a cup of cocoa
While my friends are out, and pogo
Revolver, Revolver
Everybody's on Revolver
Part-time punks
Pseudo-punks
Everybody's on Revolver tonight"
(from *Everybody's On Revolver Tonight*)

On *Stairway To Boredom* a falsetto vocal tries to come to terms with rock steady.

The compilation *1977 - 1980 - A Day In The Life Of Gilbert And George* contains **O Level**'s two 45s, **Teenage Filmstars** three 45s and four previously unreleased cuts by each artist.

Omega Tribe

Personnel:	PETEROLEUM YORKIE		
	BIGM'N	drms, vcls	A
	RADLY HARDMAN	bs, vcls	A
	PETE FENDER	drms, vcls	A

| | PETE LOUDM'N | gtr, vcls | A |
| | HUGH TWITM'N | vcls, gtr | A |

| EP: | 1(A) | ANGRY SONGS | (Crass 221984/10) 1983 |

45: It's A Hard Life/Young John (PS) (Corpus Christ CHRIS 12) 1984
NB: Also issued as a 12" (ITIS 12) 1984.

This band included Pete Fender, who also played with **Fatal Microbes**. Aside from the opening cut *Another Bloody Day* the pace on their four-track EP is fast and furious. Lyrically their stance is uncompromising, excluding virtually everyone without spiky hair and a leather jacket.

101'ers

Personnel:	RICHARD DUDANSKI	drms	A
	DAN KELLECHER	bs	A
	JOE STRUMMER	vcls, gtr	A
	CLIVE TIMPERLEY	gtr	A

| ALBUM: | 1(A) | ELGIN AVENUE BREAKDOWN | (Andalucia AND 101) 1981 |

45s:	Keys To Your Heart/	
	5 Star R'n'R Petrol (PS)	(Chiswick (N)S 3) 1976
	Keys To Your Heart/	
	5 Star R 'n' R Petrol (PS)	(Big Beat NS 3) 1979
	Sweet Revenge/	
	Rabies (From The Dogs Of Love)	(Big Beat NS 63) 1981

This was a gritty R&B style London-based pub-rock band. In their short career they released just one 45, *Keys To Your Heart*. Joe Strummer then went off to join **The Clash** and Richard Dudanski was later in **Public Image Ltd**.

In view of Strummer's involvement the **101'ers** are obviously of considerable interest to fans of **The Clash**. *Keys To Your Heart* was reissued on Big Beat in 1979 and then in 1981 a retrospective album, *Elgin Avenue Breakdown* was released. As well as including *Keys To Your Heart* it contained three previously unreleased 1975/76 demo sessions and a live performance. Two tracks were put out on 45 the same year. On the musical menu was high energy raucous rock 'n' roll and, of course, the group is an important artefact in the history of **The Clash**.

Keys To Your Heart can also be heard on *Punk Lost And Found* (Shanachie SH 5705) 1996.

One Way System

Personnel:	GAZ BUCKLEY	bs	A
	TOM COUCH	drms	A
	DAVID ROSS	gtr	A
	GAV WHITE	vcls	A

| ALBUMS: | 1(A) | ALL SYSTEMS GO | (Anagram GRAM 003) 1982 |
| | 2(A) | WRITING ON THE WALL | (Anagram GRAM 008) 1983 |

ONE WAY SYSTEM - Give Us A Future.

ONE WAY SYSTEM - Jerusalem.

NB: (1) also issued on CD (Captain Oi! AHOYCD 014) 1994 with nine bonus cuts and again in 1998. (2) also issued on CD (Captain Oi! AHOYCD 021) 1994 and again in 1998 with ten bonus cuts. Also relevant is *Best Of One Way System* (Anagram CDPUNK 50) 1995, *Gutterbox* (2 CD set) (Get Back GET 21 CD) 1997 and *Return To Breizh* (Visionary Jettisoundz OWS 4CD) 1997.

| EP: | 1(A) | VISIONS OF ANGELS (Children Of The Night/Down/ | |
| | | Shine Again/Out Of Mind) (PS) | (Anagram ANA 19) 1984 |

45s:	Stab The Judge/Riot Torn City/	
	Me And You (PS)	(Lightbeat WAY 1) 1982
	Give Us A Future/	
	Just Another Hero (PS)	(Anagram ANA 1) 1982
	Jerusalem/Jackie Was A Junkie (PS)	(Anagram ANA 5) 1983
	Breakin' In/Cum On Feel The Noise (PS)	(Anagram ANA 9) 1983
	This Is The Age/Into Fires (PS)	(Anagram ANA 14) 1983

An Oi! band from Fleetwood in Lancashire. They were managed by the legendary 'Lord' John Bentham, who also ran Jettisoundz Video. After the promising *Stab The Judge* 45 on Lightbeat in 1982 they were signed by Anagram, for whom they proceeded to record an EP, four 45s and an album. *Stab The Judge* was included on the *Punk And Disorderly* (Anagram GRAM 001) 1982 compilation.

Their first album *All Systems Go* is a succession of fast-paced, no-holes-barred punk. Aside from the final cut, *Your Ready Now*, the band wrote the remaining twelve tracks and the lyrics concentrated on the hopelessness and frustration experienced by many youths in early eighties Britain.

"One more year and nothing's changed
Government policies still the same
The future's bleak and life's a bore
So what the fuck are we living for

Chorus:
Give us a future don't you let us down
Give us a future show us some concern
Give us a future don't you watch us drown
Give us a future or we will put you down"
(from *Give Us A Future*)

Give Us A Future was their debut 45 for Anagram. It also had the distinction of being the first 45 released on this prolific punk label. It was later included on *Punk And Disorderly III - The Final Solution* (Anagram GRAM 005) 1983. Their second 45 for Anagram *Jerusalem* is also on this album.

The Captain Oi! CD reissue on this album includes all three cuts from their debut release: *Stab The Judge*, *Just Another Hero* (the 'B' side to *Give Us A Future*), *Jackie Was A Junkie* (the 'B' side to *Jerusalem*) and four previously unreleased demos:- *Jerusalem*, *1980's*, *Spokesmen For The Teenagers* and *All You Kids*.

There's also a vinyl version (AHOY LP 14) of this CD reissue (without the bonus tracks) with a full lyric insert and some pressings came on clear vinyl.

ONE WAY SYSTEM - All Systems Go.

One Way System's second and final studio album *Writing On The Wall* was issued by Anagram in 1983. The musical format is unchanged from the first album. The lyrics tackle issues like drug addiction (*This Is The Age* and *On Line*), corruption (*Corrupted World*) and the futility of life (*One Day Soon*).

"Livin' in a riot torn burnt out part of the city
Ain't got no one around who's gonna show you no pity
Livin' in a sewer where only rats dare to roam
Ain't got no one tryin' to make you feel at home"
(from *One Day Soon*)

One of the best cuts on this album is *Neurotix* - a plea not to judge gangs of kids at first sight. *Into The Fires* features a guitar section which is a welcome break from the rather rigid musical format. All the cuts on the album were penned by the band.

The CD reissue of this album on Captain Oi! includes a non-album 'B' side their cover of Slade's *Cum On Feel The Noize*, all four cuts from their *Visions Of Angels* (EP), which would prove to be their final recording and no less than six previously unreleased demos:- *Stab The Judge*, *Me And You*, *Jackie Was A Junkie*, *Jerusalem*, *Give Us A Future* and *Magic Roundabout*. The CD reissue is also available on vinyl (AHOY LP 21) with a lyric insert, but without the bonus tracks.

Give Us A Future, *Just Another Hero*, *Jerusalem*, *Cum On Feel The Noize*, *Breakin' In* and *Children Of The Night* all later resurfaced on *Anagram Punk Singles Collection* (Anagram CDPUNK 52) 1995. *Jerusalem* and *Jackie Was A Junkie* can also be heard on *Oi! The Singles Collection, Vol. 4* (Captain Oi! AHOY CD 71) 1997. You'll also find *Give Us A Future* and *Just Another Hero* on *Oi! The Singles Collection, Vol. 1* (Captain Oi! AHOY CD 60) 1996. *Stab The Judge*, *Riot Torn City* and *Me And You* all got a further airing on *Beat The System Punk Singles Collection* (Anagram CDPUNK 61) in 1995. Finally, *Give Us A Future* and *Police Story* resurfaced on *100% Hardcore Punk* (Captain Oi! AHOY DCD 84) in 1998.

One Way System returned in 1996, though only drummer Tom Couch and guitarist Dave Crabtree survived from the original line-up. They remain one of the most powerful acts on the punk scene.

The Onlookers

45:	You And I/Understand/Julia (PS)	(Demon D 1012) 1982

This Slough-based band were a neo-psychedelic act with a liking for Small Faces covers. They contributed to *Subway* (Chick CHR 001) 1981, a rare compilation of Slough bands which came on clear vinyl. They'd actually split by the time this 45 was released. *You And I* and *Understand* later resurfaced on *This Is Mod, Vol. 4* (Anagram CDMGRAM 107) 1996.

The Only Ones

Personnel:
MIKE KELLIE	drms	A
ALAN MAIR	bs	A
PETER PERRETT	vcls, gtr	A
JOHN PERRY	gtr	A

ALBUMS:
				HCP
1(A)	THE ONLY ONES	(CBS 82830)	1978	56
2(A)	EVEN SERPENTS SHINE	(CBS 83451)	1979	42
3(A)	BABY'S GOT A GUN	(CBS 84089)	1980	37

NB: (1) reissued (CBS 32077) in 1984 and on CD (Columbia 4773792) 1994. (2) reissued (CBS 83451) in 1985 and on CD (Columbia 4785032) 1995. (3) reissued (CBS 84089) in 1985 and on CD (Columbia 4836622) 1996. There are also a number of compilations to choose from:- *Alone In The Night* (Dojo DOJO 43) 1986; *The Only Ones Live* (Mau Mau MAUCD 603) 1981, reissued 1989, also on vinyl; *Peel Sessions: Only Ones* (Strange Fruit SFRCD 102) 1989, also on vinyl and again in 1994; *The Immortal Story* (Columbia 471267 2) 1992 also issued as a double album and *The Big Sleep* (live) (CD) (Jungle FREUD 45) 1993. *The Immortal Story* was later reissued on CD by Sony in 1999 at 'a nice price' of £6. There's also a mini-album *Remains* (Closer CL 0012) 1984 of out-takes from their last album which was issued in France. It was later issued on CD (Closer CLCD 12) 1988 with extra cuts from a promo EP which accompanied review copies of the album. Then again (Anagram CD GRAM 67) 1993 and 1996. There's also a U.S.-only compilation *Special View* (CBS 36119) 1979, which was available here on import.

			HCP
45s:	Lovers Of Today/ Peter And The Pets (PS)	(Vengeance VEN 001) 1977	-
	Lovers Of Today/ Peter And The Pets (12")	(Vengeance VEN 001) 1977	-
	Another Girl, Another Planet/ Special View (PS)	(CBS S CBS 6228) 1978	57
*	Another Girl, Another Planet/ As My Wife Says (12" PS)	(CBS S CBS 12-6576) 1978	-
	You've Got To Pay/This Ain't All (It's Made Out To Be) (PS)	(CBS S CBS 7086) 1979	-
	Out There In The Night/ Lovers Of Today	(CBS S CBS 7285) 1979	-
+	Out There In The Night/Lovers Of Today/ Peter And The Pets (12" PS)	(CBS S CBS 12-7285) 1979	-
x	Trouble In The World/ Your Chosen Life (black and red PS)	(CBS S CBS 7963) 1979	-
	Trouble In The World/ Your Chosen Life (PS)	(CBS S CBS 7963) 1979	-
α	Fools/Castle Built On Sand (PS)	(CBS S CBS 8535) 1980	-
β	Baby's Got A Gun/Silent Night	(Vengeance VEN 002) 1983	-

NB: * There was also a promo-only release in this format which did not come in a picture sleeve. + This came in blue vinyl and two slight sleeve variations exist. x This release was withdrawn. α The 'A' side was credited to **The Only Ones** with Pauline Murray. β The 'B' side was by Peter Perrett.

The Only Ones were formed in South London in 1976 by singer and guitarist Peter Perrett. Perrett had previously fronted up England's Glory, whose other members were Harry Kakoulli (bs), Michael Kemp (keyb'ds)

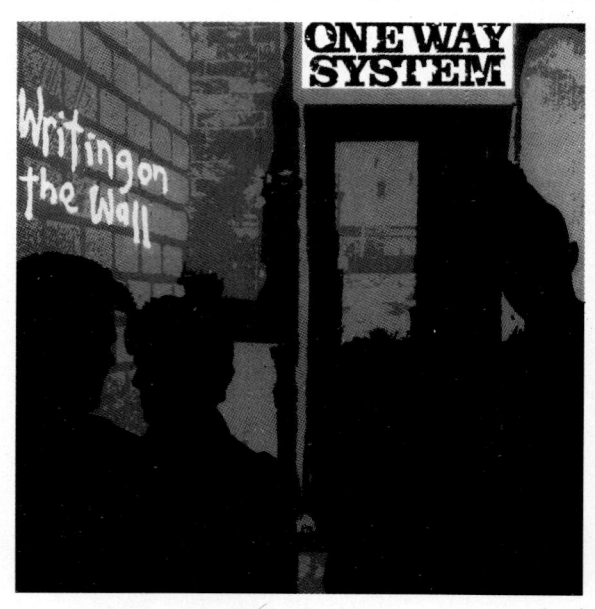

ONE WAY SYSTEM - Writing On The Wall.

and Jon Newey (drms), who now works as a music journalist. Harry's sister Zena managed the band and also helped out on backing vocals. Harry left to join **Squeeze** in 1974 and Peter Perrett recruited Mike Kellie, who'd been born in Birmingham on 24th March 1947 (previously with Spooky Tooth and Frampton's Camel), John Perry (ex-Rabbites From Hell) and veteran bassist Alan Mair (previously with Beatstalkers) who'd been playing since the sixties. This line-up made these veterans one of the oldest bands on the punk circuit.

They released their first 45, *Lovers Of Today*, in the summer of 1977 on the Vengeance label, which Zena and Peter set up themselves. It impressed enough to attract CBS to sign them. Their first major label release, in spring 1978, was the superb new wave classic *Another Girl, Another Planet*. Despite only reaching No. 57 during its two weeks in the charts, this showcased Perrett's songwriting and vocal style superbly and was in all respects an excellent song. It was also one of the stand-out cuts on their eponymous excellent debut, which made it to No. 56 in the album charts but deserved to do much better. Also gracing side one was *City Of Fun* another fast-paced number, *The Whole Of The Law*, a slow, lazy love song, *Breathing Down*, which had a distinctive bass line, backing female vocals and some jazzy keyboards and the six minute finale and despairing drug song *The Beast*. The highlight of side two were a studio version of *Creature Of Doom* and *No Peace For The Wicked*.

Originally issued in 7" format, shortly before the album in Spring 1978, *Another Girl, Another Planet* was reissued again that summer in 12" format with the original flip side *Special View* replaced by *As My Wife Says*. Neither of these tracks were included on their debut album. There was also a promo-only release of this 12" single, which did not come in a picture sleeve.

Creatures Of Doom from their debut album was included on the *Hope And Anchor Front Row Festival* (Warner Brothers WBK 66077) 1978 compilation.

You've Got To Pay, a catchy number, was released as a 45 to preview their *Even Serpents Shine* album in spring 1979. The album was very similar to its predecessor in style. It didn't contain any cuts quite of the stature of *Another Girl, Another Planet* but a very consistent standard, both in terms of songwriting and playing, is maintained throughout the album, which deservedly climbed to No. 42 during its two week stay in the charts. Unfortunately, a second 45 release culled from it, *Out There In The Night* which featured a strong chorus with female backing vocals courtesy of Koulla Kakoulli, didn't sell in sufficient quantities to chart.

In the 'States, a compilation *Special View* was released in the summer of 1979. Taking the flip side of the original 7" release of *Another Girl, Another Planet* as its title track, it concentrates on a selection of tracks from their first two albums plus the two Vengeance recordings. The compilation was also issued in Europe and New Zealand.

Trouble In The World was another unsuccessful 45 for the band in Autumn 1979. The original black and red 'group' picture sleeve was withdrawn soon after its release and this is now very rare and certainly the most collectable and expensive **Only Ones** artefact.

Both tracks from this 45 later figured on *Baby's Got A Gun*, which proved to be the **Only Ones** final studio album. Although it was their most successful album commercially, rising to No. 37 and spending five weeks in the charts, they disbanded in March 1981 disillusioned with the level of success they had achieved. The better material on that album included a different mix of *Trouble In The World* (minus the backing chorus, with less keyboards and a lengthier fadeout), *Why Don't You Kill Yourself* and the Bo Diddleyish *Me And My Shadow*. Just prior to this they'd teamed up with former **Penetration** lead vocalist **Pauline Murray** to record a cover of Johnny Duncan's *Fools* which was included on the album. *Live*, drawing on material from more than one of their studio albums, dates from quite late in their career. It's full of their gritty, raw guitar sound, but Perrett's vocals sound over-stretched in contrast to his studio work and the lasting impression is that they weren't on top form for this project.

Perrett formed a new band Decline and Fall, with Nick Howell on drums and Douglas Bruce (ex-**Snatch**) on bass, but that wasn't around for long at all.

Later, in 1983, a new 45 *Baby's Got A Gun* was released with a solo Peter Perrett rendition of the traditional carol *Silent Night* on the 'B' side. It came without a picture sleeve and is now hard to find, despite a reissue in 1985.

THE ONLY ONES - The Only Ones.

The Only Ones recorded four sessions for John Peel in all. These were all included on an album originally released on Strange Fruit in 1989, and later on CD in 1992. The same year Columbia reissued *Another Girl, Another Planet* on 45 with a track by **The Psychedelic Furs** on the reverse side. The 12" version also includes **The Only Ones'** *Lovers Of Today*.

An album of Perrett's material with his original band *England's Glory - The Legendary Lost Recordings* was released by 5 Hours Back in 1987.

There are various **Only Ones** compilation releases of which *The Immortal Story* is the most comprehensive and was originally available on double album and CD format. The compilation includes twenty-one tracks from the band's three CBS albums. As well as gems like *Another Girl, Another Planet, Covers Of Today, In Betweens* and *Peter And The Pets*, there are previously unavailable mixes of *Baby's Got A Gun, Oh Lucinda (Love Becomes A Habit)* and *No Solution*, as well as the obscure 'B' side to *Obscene, Your Chosen Life*.

Remains is a varied compilation of their material ranging from the bluesy *River Of No Return*, the country-tinged *I Only Wanna Be Your Friend*, intricate songs like *My Rejection* and world-weary, looser material like *Flowers* and *Prisoners*. A worthwhile collection.

The Big Sleep is a live album from a European concert, but at the time of its release all but five of the songs were already available on other live albums, making this release of interest to serious fans of the band only.

The Peel Sessions Album content is culled from songs off their four late seventies albums and their old favourites like *Oh Lucinda* and *Another Girl, Another Planet* are here too and with the band playing on its top form it's perhaps no wonder that guitarist John Perry claims in the sleevenotes he prefers this compilation to the original studio albums.

Back in 1979, *Another Girl, Another Planet* figured on the soundtrack *That Summer!* (Spartan/Arista SPART 1088). In 1995, it was included on *The Best Punk Album In The World.... Ever, Vol. 1* (2-CD) (Virgin VTDCD 42) 1995 and included on *The Best Punk Anthems... Ever* (2-CD) (Virgin VTDCD 198) 1998. Their finest moment, *Another Girl, Another Planet* is also captured on the 5-CD box set *1-2-3-4 - A History Of Punk And New Wave 1976 - 1979* (MCA/Universal MCD 60066) 1999.

Perrett finally made his much rumoured comeback as The One in 1994 and released a solo album, *Wake Up Sticky*, in 1996.

The Only Ones were one of the best and most talented bands to emerge from the new wave. They actually had the talent to achieve more than they did.

Open Sore

An obscure punk combo who formed in the summer of 1977. They were regulars on the punk circuit - until their equipment was stolen at the same time as **Blitz**'s during a "Farewell To The Roxy" tour in the summer of

1978. Their sole vinyl epitaph is *Vertigo*, which appeared on the *Farewell To The Roxy* (Lightning LIP 2) 1978 compilation. This has been reissued on CD (Captain Oi! AHOY CD 86) 1998. It's a fast-paced punker with great vocals and a few promising guitar moments. *Vertigo* was also included on *Lightning Records Punk Collection* (Anagram CDPUNK 79) 1996.

The Oppressed

Personnel:			
LEE JENKINS	drms		A
DOM MORENO	bs		AB
RODDY MORENO	vcls		AB
RUSSELL 'DUCKY' PAYNE	gtr		ABC
MARTIN BRENNAN	vcls		BC
GARY TIER	drms		BC
RONNIE PAYNE	bs		C

ALBUMS:
1(A) OI! OI! MUSIC (Oppressed OPLP 1) 1984
2(B) FATAL BLOW (Skinhead CREW 1) 1985
3(C) DEAD AND BURIED (Oi! OIR 012) 1988

NB: (1) also issued on CD (Captain Oi! AHOY CD 5) 1993 with bonus tracks and again in 1997. (2) and (3) reissued together on one CD (Captain Oi! AHOY CD 42) 1994 and again in 1998. Also relevant is *Live 1984* (Step-1 STEPCD 107) 1998 and *The Best Of The Oppressed* (Dojo DOJOCD 227) 1996, later reissued (Step-1 STEPCD 122) 2000.

EP: 1(A) NEVER SAY DIE (Urban Soldiers/Ultra Violence/ Run From You) (PS) (Firm NICK 1) 1983

45: Work Together/Victims (Oppressed OPPO 1) 1983

The Oppressed hailed from Cardiff. They are infamous for their rare *Work Together* single. Their debut album *Oi! Oi! Music* comprises 15 cuts taped at a live gig in Cardiff in January 1984. It opens with *We're The Oppressed*:

"Born to fight, born to win
We were all born to be skin
Born with Marten's on our feet
Facing truth there's no retreat"
(from *We're The Oppressed*)

As Roddy Moreno says on the liner notes of the Captain Oi! CD reissue: "All we tried to do back then was have a laugh and have a say... To sum up we were just four working class skinheads who hated racism and voted Labour". Their aggression was ever present in the lyrics of songs like *Violent Society*, *Gun Law* (which challenged the right of 'the boys in blue' to carry guns), *Ultra Violence* and *Riot*. On songs like *Fight For Your Life* and *Government Out* the lyrics get political:-

"The Tory Party got no soul
Three and a half million on the dole
Maggie's boys don't give a damn
About the plight of the working man"
(from *Fight For Your Life*)

"You listen to the stories, you listen to their lives

THE OPPRESSED - Never Say Die.

THE OPPRESSED - Work Together.

You listen to their propaganda, they're the bastards you despise

Here the people scream and shout
We want government, government out

Labour cuts the dole queue's, the Tories cut your throat
Neither party gives a shit, all they're after is your vote"
(from *Government Out*)

The Captain Oi! CD reissue of *Oi! Oi! Music* features both sides of their *Work Together* 45 plus the legendary *Never Say Die* (EP) among a total of eight bonus cuts. It's also available on vinyl (AHOY LP 5) with a full lyric insert.

Dead And Buried also featured the band's *Never Say Die* (EP), both sides of their *Work Together* 45 and their *Oi The Tape* cuts (*Riot*, *Leave Me Alone*, *Joe Hawkins*, *Government* and *It Ain't Right*).

Fatal Blow featured three Oi! covers on side one. Their versions of **Sham 69**'s *Angels With Dirty Faces* along with *Bad Man* and *ACAB* comprise side one, whilst side two is taken up with demos from 1981 and 1982.

Dead And Buried and *Fatal Blow* are also combined on a Captain Oi! CD and the same package is also available on vinyl with a lyric and picture insert.

Their frontman Roddy Moreno fought back against those who tarred Oi! with the brush of facism by forming Sharp (Skinheads Against Racial Prejudice). He was the force behind Oi! Records who lead the wave of street punk in the mid-eighties. Cuts like *B-N-P (Full Of Shit)*, *Nazi Nightmares* and *Nazi Skinhead* on *The Best Of The Oppressed* were attempts to distance Oi! from right wing extremists. Originally issued by Dojo in 1996, it was reissued again by Step-1 in 2000.

THE OPPRESSED - Oi! Oi! Music.

THE OPPRESSED - Fatal Blow.

They've appeared on several compilations. *Work Together* and *Victims* later resurfaced on *Oi! The Singles Collection, Vol. 1* (Captain Oi! AHOY CD 60) 1996. You'll also find *Urban Soldiers*, *Ultra Violence* and *Run From You* on *Oi! The Singles Collection, Vol. 3* (Captain Oi! AHOY CD 67) 1997. *White Flag* can be heard on *100% British Oi!* (Captain Oi! AHOY DCD 83) 1997. It had originally appeared on *Oi! Oi! That's Yer Lot!* (Secret SEC 5) 1982. *Oi! Against Racism* (Havin' A Laugh HAL LP 004) includes *Sleeping With The Enemy*. They contributed *We're The Hooligans* to *Trouble On The Terraces - 16 Classic Football Anthems* (Step-1 STEP LP 91) 1986 and *Work Together* to *This Is Oi!* (Oi! OIR 004) in 1986, which was subsequently reissued on CD (Captain Oi! AHOY CD 6) 1993. Two more of their songs *Joe Hawkins* and *Victims* can also be heard on *The Best Of Oi! Records* (Captain Oi! AHOY CD 38) 1995. Later, in 1999, *White Flag* got further exposure on *Oi! Fuckin' Oi!* (Harry May MAYOCD 110).

The Optimists

45:	Mull Of Kintyre/	
	The Plumber's Song	(Armageddon AS 018) 1981

The Optimists probably weren't a real group but a pseudonym for a group who wanted to record a pretty dreadful version of the Paul McCartney song which ends with bagpipes. The flip side is terrible too. Both cuts got a further airing on *Oi! The Rarities, Vol.3* (Captain Oi! AHOY CD 53) 1995.

Orange Disaster

45:	Something's Got To Give/Out Of The Room/	
	Hiding From Frank	(Neuter OD 1) 198?

This band previously recorded as **Varicose Veins** and were later known as **Architects Of Disaster**. Unusually for the period this 45 wasn't housed in a picture sleeve.

Orchestral Manoeuvres In The Dark (O.M.D.)

Personnel:	PAUL HUMPHREYS	keyb'ds, synthesizers	ABC
	ANDREW McCLUSKEY	vcls, bs	ABC
	DAVID HUGHES	keyb'ds	B
	MALCOLM HOLMES	drms	BC
	MALCOLM COOPER	sax, keyb'ds	C

HCP

ALBUMS:	1(A)	ORCHESTRAL MANOEUVRES IN THE DARK		
(up to			(Din Disc DID 2)	1980 27
1986)	2(B)	ORGANISATION	(Din Disc DID 6)	1980 6
	3(C)	ARCHITECTURE AND MORALITY		
			(Din Disc DID 12)	1981 3
	4(C)	DAZZLE SHIPS	(Virgin V 2261)	1983 5
	5(C)	JUNK CULTURE	(Virgin V 2310)	1984 9
	6(C)	CRUSH	(Virgin V 2349)	1985 13
	7(C)	THE PACIFIC AGE	(Virgin V 2398)	1986 15

NB: (1) was originally released in a total of six different sleeves. It was reissued on vinyl (Virgin OVED 96) 1984 and on CD (Virgin DIDCD 2) 1987, (2) was originally released in two different sleeves, one included an insert and free 7" *(Introducing Radios, Distance Fades Between Us, Progress* and *Once When I Was Six)* (DEP 2). It was reissued on vinyl (Virgin OVED 147) 1988 and on CD (Virgin DIDCD 6) 1987. (3) was originally issued in four different sleeves. It was reissued on vinyl (Virgin OVED 276) 1990 and on CD (Virgin CDID 12) 1988. (4) came in a gatefold sleeve originally. It was reissued on vinyl (Virgin OVED 106) 1987 and on CD (Virgin CDV 2261) 1985. Initial copies of (5) came with a free 7" (JUNK 1). It was reissued on vinyl (Virgin OVED 215) 1989 and on CD (Virgin CDV 2310) 1986. (6) reissued on vinyl (Virgin OVED 244) 1990 and on CD (Virgin CDV 2349) 1986. (7) reissued on vinyl (Virgin OVED 255) 1990 and on CD (Virgin CDV 2398) 1986. There's also one vinyl compilation *The Best Of O.M.D.* (Virgin LPOMD 1) 1988, which got to No. 2. This is also available on CD (CD/P OMD 1) 1988. The CD release came with four extra tracks, *Telegraph*, *We Love You* (12"), *La Femme Accident* (12") and *Genetic Engineering*. There was also a picture disc version of this release. There's the *CD Boxed Set* (Virgin TPAK 7) 1990 which included picture discs of *Orchestral Manoeuvres In The Dark*, *Architecture And Morality* and *Organisation* and *Navigation - The OMD B Sides* (Virgin CDV 2938) 2001.

HCP

45s:	++	Electricity/Almost (PS)	(Factory FAC 6) 1979 -
(up to		Electricity/Almost (PS)	(Din Disc DIN 2) 1979 -
1986)		Red Frame - White Light/	
		I Betray My Friends (PS)	(Din Disc DIN 6) 1980 67
		Red Frame - White Light/	
		I Betray My Friends (12", PS)	(Din Disc DIN 6-12) 1980 -
		Messages/Taking Sides Again (PS)	(Din Disc DIN 15) 1980 13
		Messages (Extended)/Waiting For The Man/	
		Taking Sides Again (10", PS)	(Din Disc DIN 15-10) 1980 -
		Enola Gay/Annex (PS)	(Din Disc DIN 22) 1980 8
	*	Enola Gay/Annex (12", PS)	(Din Disc DIN 22-12) 1980 -
		Souvenir/Motion And Heart (Amazon Version)/	
		Sacred Heart (no PS)	(Din Disc DIN 24) 1981 3
		Souvenir (Extended)/Motion And Heart (Amazon Version)/	
		Sacred Heart (10", PS)	(Din Disc DIN 24-10) 1981 -
		Joan Of Arc/The Romance Of The	
		Telescope (Unfinished) (PS)	(Din Disc DIN 36) 1981 5
		Joan Of Arc/The Romance Of The	
		Telescope (Unfinished) (12", PS)	(Din Disc DIN 36-12) 1981 -
	+	Pretending To See The Future (live)	
		/Nash The Slash track	(Smash Hits) 1981 -
		Maid Of Orleans (The Waltz Joan Of Arc)/	
		Navigation (PS)	(Din Disc DIN 40) 1982 4
	x	Maid Of Orleans (The Waltz Joan Of Arc)/	
		Navigation (12", PS)	(Din Disc DIN 40-12) 1982 -
	o	Maid Of Orleans (The Waltz Of Joan Of Arc)/	
		Navigation/Of All The Things	
		We've Made (12", PS)	(Din Disc DIN 40-12) 1982 -
		Genetic Engineering/4-Neu (PS)	(Virgin VS 527) 1983 20
		Genetic Engineering/4-Neu (picture disc)	(Virgin VSY 527) 1983 -
		Genetic Engineering (312mm Version)/	
		4-Neu (12", PS)	(Virgin VS 527-12) 1983 -
		Telegraph/66 And Fading (PS)	(Virgin VS 580) 1983 42
		Telegraph/66 And Fading (picture disc)	(Virgin SY 580) 1983 -
		Telegraph (Extended)/	
		66 And Fading (12", PS)	(Virgin VS 58-172) 1983 -
		Locomotion/Her Body In My Soul (PS)	(Virgin VS 660) 1984 5
		Locomotion/Her Body In	
		My Soul (shaped picture disc)	(Virgin VSS 660) 1984 -
		Locomotion (5.20)/Her Body In My Soul/	
		The Avenue (12", PS)	(Virgin VS 660-12) 1984 -
		Talking Loud And Clear/	
		Julia's Song (PS)	(Virgin VS 685) 1984 11
		Talking Loud And Clear/	
		Julia's Song (picture disc)	(Virgin VSY 685) 1984 -
		Talking Loud And Clear (Extended)/	
		Julia's Song (Extended) (12", PS)	(Virgin VS 685-12) 1984 -
		Telsa Girls/Telegraph (live) (PS)	(Virgin VS 705) 1984 21
		Telsa Girls (Different Mix)/	
		Telegraph (live) (cassette)	(Virgin TV 5705-12) 1984 -
		Telsa Girls (Remix)/Garden City/	
		Telegraph (live) (12", PS)	(Virgin VS 705-12) 1984 -
		Never Turn Away/Wrappup (PS)	(Virgin VS 727) 1984 70
		Never Turn Away/	
		Wrappup (picture disc)	(Virgin VSY 727) 1984 -

O.M.D. - Electricity.

Never Turn Away (Extended)/Wrap Up/
Waiting For The Man (live) (12", PS)   (Virgin VS 727-12) 1984 -
So In Love/Concrete Hands (PS)   (Virgin VS 766) 1985 27
So In Love/Concrete Hands/Maria Gallante/
White Trash (live) (double pack, PS)   (Virgin VS 766) 1985 -
So In Love/Concrete Hands (Extended)/
Maria Gallente   (12", PS) (Virgin VS 766-12) 1985 -
So In Love (Extended Remix)/Concrete Hands (Extended)/
Maria Gallante (12", picture disc)   (Virgin VS 766-14) 1985 -
Secret/Drift (PS)   (Virgin VS 796) 1985 34
Secret/Drift (poster sleeve)   (Virgin VS 796) 1985 -
Secret (Extended)/Drift (12", PS)   (Virgin VS 796-12) 1985 -
Secret (Extended)/Drift/Red Frame-White Light/
I Betray My Friends
(12", double pack, PS)   (Virgin VS 796-12) 1985 -
La Femme Accident/Firegun   (Virgin VS 811) 1985 42
La Femme Accident/
Firegun (shaped picture disc)   (Virgin VSS 811) 1985 -
La Femme Accident/Firegun/La Femme
Accident (12" Mix) (12", PS)   (Virgin VS 811-12) 1985 -
La Femme Accident/Firegun/La Femme
Accident (12" Mix)/Locomotion (live)/
Enola Gay (12", double-pack, PS)   (Virgin VSD 811-12) 1985 -
If You Leave/
88 Seconds In Greensboro' (PS)   (Virgin VS 843) 1986 48
If You Leave (Extended)/88 Seconds In Greensboro'/
Locomotion (live) (12", PS)   (Virgin VS 843-12) 1986 -
(Forever) Live And Die/This Town (PS)   (Virgin VS 888) 1986 11
(Forever) Live And Die/
This Town (picture disc)   (Virgin VSY 888) 1986 -
α (Forever) Live And Die (Extended)/(Forever) Live And Die/
This Town (12", PS)   (Virgin VS 888-13) 1986 -
We Love You/We Love You (Dub) (PS)   (Virgin VS 911) 1986 54
We Love You/We Love You (Dub)/If You Leave/
88 Seconds In Greensboro'
(double pack, PS)   (Virgin VSD 911) 1986 -
We Love You/We Love You (Dub)/Souvenir/Electricity/
Enola Gay/Joan Of Arc/We Love You/
We Love You (Dub) (7" plus cassette)   (Virgin VSC 911) 1986 -
We Love You (Extended)/We Love You/
We Love You (Dub) (12", PS)   (Virgin VS 911-12) 1986 -

NB: ++ This came in a braille cover. * Some copies of his release were shrinkwrapped. + Issued free with "Smash Hits" on blue flexi vinyl. x 'Glass' cover. o 'Coin' cover. Some initial copies incorrectly list *Experiment In Vertical Take Off*. α Early copies of the sleeve listed the catalogue number as Virgin VS 888-12.

Orchestral Manoeuvres In The Dark (O.M.D.) rose to prominence on the crest of the new wave of music which emerged in the wake of the punk rock explosion. The origins of the band go back to when Paul Humphreys, born on 27th February 1960, became a roadie for Equinox, a band containing some of his school friends. The band approached Andy McCluskey, born on 24th June 1959 to become their bassist and he also became their vocalist. Paul and Andy soon realised that they shared an interest in experimental electronic music. Heavily influenced by Kraftwerk they hung around together after gigs conducting various sound experiments. During this time Paul became increasingly proficient on keyboards and they called themselves VCL XI. They both made a one-off live appearance in a band called Hitlerz Underpants which a friend of theirs Andy Pratt had formed.

Then, in December 1977, they formed an eight-piece group called The Id, which also included former Equinox drummer Malcolm Holmes. The Id became an important part of Liverpool's new wave scene at this time, along with **The Teardrop Explodes** and **Echo and The Bunnymen**, who were just starting up.

In June 1978, The Id recorded three cuts at the Open Eye Gallery. One of these was *Julia's Song*, co-written by Julia Kneale, who sang with The Id and was an ex-girlfriend of Andy's. The track brought The Id to the attention of a wider audience by virtue of its inclusion on the *Street To Street - A Liverpool Album* (Open Eye OE LP 501) 1979 compilation.

The Id didn't survive beyond the summer of 1978 and Andy also had a brief spell with another band **Dalek I Love You**.

Their first big break came when Andy and Paul met a guy called Paul Collister later that summer. He owned a TEAC A 344 four-track recorder called Winston. **O.M.D.** were in business. With Paul doing the mixing they made their debut at Eric's on 12th October 1978. Their set included *Electricity*, *Julia's Song* and *Red Frame / White Light*. Roger Earle, Eric's owner, put them in contact with Tony Wilson. Having heard a two-song tape they sent him featuring *Electricity* and *Almost* he offered to put them out on the new Factory label he'd set up with Alan Erasmus. 5,000 copies of the resultant single were pressed. It was produced by Martin Hannett (using the pseudonym Martin Zero). Released in a black-on-black braille cover the 45 received much airplay from DJ John Peel. Their innovative sound attracted much attention and the original pressing quickly sold out. To help promote it **O.M.D.** had participated in a tour with other Factory acts **Joy Division** and **A Certain Ratio**.

O.M.D.'s next big break came when Carol Wilson, who'd set up Virgin subsidiary Din Disc, got to hear the 45. She signed them up and reissued the 45 in a different sleeve. Although it wasn't a hit the 45 certainly got them better known and helped secure them a slot on the **Gary Numan** tour in Autumn 1979.

Using their advance from Din Disc **O.M.D.** built their own studio, the Gramophone Studio. They soon repaid John Peel's faith in them by recording a four song session for him comprising *Red Frame / White Light* (about a telephone box), *Messages*, *Julia's Song* and *Bunker Soldiers*.

In February 1980, *Red Frame / White Light* was issued as a single in both 7" and 12" format. It climbed to No. 67 in the charts. It previewed their eponymous debut album released the same month. This included all of their good early songs and is recommended. In addition to Humphries, McCluskey and, of course Winston, three musicians made guest appearances. David Fairbairn played guitar on *Messages* and *Julia's Song*. Malcolm Holmes played drums on *Julia's Song*. Malcolm Cooper added saxophone on *Mystereality*. The stand-out tracks were *Electricity* and *Messages*, which climbed to No. 13 during its eleven weeks in the charts when it was released as a 45 in May 1980. The album was warmly welcomed and rose to No. 27 in the charts in which it spent twenty-nine weeks in all. Their success with *Messages* secured them a 'Top Of The Pops' appearance. A 10" edition of this 45 in a slightly different cover included an interesting cover of Velvet Underground's *I'm Waiting For The Man*.

The inclusion of *Messages*, *Waiting For The Man* and a new version of *Electricity* on the sampler *Din Disc 1980* (Din Disc DONE 1) 1980, which came with a free 20" by 20" game, brought them to the attention of a wider audience. They also recorded a second session for John Peel featuring *Dancing*, *Pretending To See The Future*, *Motion And Heat* and *Enola Gay*.

Enola Gay, a song inspired by the plane that dropped the first nucleur bomb on Hiroshima in 1945, was an appealing song and an obvious choice for their next 45. It was released in September 1980. Some 12" copies were shrink-wrapped adding to their value. The single became their first Top 10 hit, peaking at No. 8 during its fifteen week chart stint. It also broke through internationally. It did very well in Japan and topped the charts in four European countries:- Italy, France, Spain and Portugal.

The following month *Organisation*, **O.M.D.**'s second album was released. *Enola Gay* was the stand-out cut but the material on this was more varied than on its predecessor. There are many beautiful melodies on this album on tracks like *2nd Thought*, *VCL XI*, *Motion And Heat* and *Promise*, whilst segments of *The Misunderstanding* and the final cut *Stanlow* showcase their more experimental side. Malcolm Holmes guested on this album on drums and acoustic percussion. It sold well, peaking at No. 6 and this time spending twenty-five weeks in the charts. Two different sleeve designs were issued. Initial copies came in a grey sleeve with a merchandising insert and included a bonus single of early tape experiments and live tracks. The 7" also surfaced in France as a white label promo. Later copies of the album simply came in a black cover.

In the 'States *O.M.D.*, a U.S.-only album was issued, containing a selection of the better tracks from both albums, including both *Electricity* and *Enola Gay*. Paul married his girlfriend Maureen , whilst in New York in September 1981. Paul Collister, who became their first manager, was replaced by Gordian Troeller.

Their next single *Souvenir*, released in August 1981, was their first to feature Paul on vocals. It also utilised tape-loops based on choral music. It continued their chart success here in England, rising to No. 3 during a twelve week residency, but also topped the charts in France and Spain. On the flip was *Motion And Heat* and a non-album cut *Sacred Heart*. There was also a 10" version of the single, which included an extended version of *Souvenir*. Some copies came with a Din Disc price sticker and 40 were mispressed onto the 'A' side of Human League's *Love Action*. These are highly collectable and expensive, but the majority of them were withdrawn at the time. **O.M.D.** enjoyed a further Top five hit with *Joan Of Arc*, a song Andy wrote on the 500th anniversary of her death. Peaking at No. 5, this spent fourteen weeks in the charts.

Their third album followed in November 1981. Both Malcolm Holmes and Martin Cooper, who'd only guested on previous albums, appeared fully on these. Mike Douglas, who later joined **Human League**, guested on the album as an additional keyboard player. The album is innovative as it experiments further with technology. Its highlights were their two previous hit singles *Souvenirs* and *Joan Of Arc* and *Maid Of Orleans (The Waltz Of Joan Of Arc)*, which brought them another Top 5 single after its release in January 1982. It also topped the charts in eight European countries. The album was released in four different colour sleeves - white, blue, green and yellow, each with a cut-out cover revealing the inner sleeve. It was later reissued in a plain sleeve. With the band increasingly well-known, this proved to be **O.M.D.**'s most successful album. It spent 39 weeks in the charts going platinum and peaked at No. 3. They toured the U.K. and U.S. extensively to promote the album.

Collectors may be interested in a couple of **O.M.D.** flexidiscs from this period. One free with the American "Trouser Press" magazine featured *The New Stone Age* and *Bunker Soldiers*. The other free with "Smash Hits" included a live version of *Pretending To See The Future*. In the 'States a promotional interview album *Interchords* was released. Aside from Paul and Andy being interviewed by Richard Skinner, it features eight tracks from their first three albums.

With Din Disc folding during 1982, **O.M.D.** switched to its parent label Virgin for their next album *Dazzle Ships*, with Rhett Davies as co-producer. Prior to its release one of the tracks *Genetic Engineering* was issued as a 45 in February 1983. It just made the Top 20 in the U.K.. A non-album cut *4-Neu* was on the flip side. The 12" release included a 312mm version of the 'A' side.

O.M.D. - Red Frame White Light.

O.M.D. - Organisation.

Compared to their previous efforts *Dazzle Ships* was an inconsistent album. It was slated in some quarters of the press. It had some highpoints like *Telegraph*, *Silent Running* and *International*, but the title track and songs like *Time Zones* were weak. This was reflected in the way the album only spent 13 weeks in the chart, although it still climbed to No. 5. It came in an interesting gatefold sleeve originally. This had cut-holes with a geometric map of the world revealing the different time zones. *Telegraph* was culled for 45 release in April 1983, but only made it to No. 42 during its four week chart tenure. After this they embarked on a European tour supported by **The Cocteau Twins**.

Soon after they returned *Locomotion* was issued as a 45 in April 1984. They continued the practice of a non-album cut *Her Body In My Soul* on the flip. The 12" version had an extended version of the 'A' side and a new song *The Avenue*. There was a train-shaped version of the 7" which is quite collectable. The single made No. 5 spending eleven weeks in the charts in the U.K. and reaching the Top 5 in six countries. A CD version of the 12" tracks was later released.

Locomotion featured on their next album *Junk Culture*, again released to mixed reviews. In fact it was a much stronger album than *Dazzle Ships*. It featured fine melodies, an **O.M.D.** strength, interspersed with more dance-based styles. Stand-out tracks included *Telsa Girls*, *Locomotion* and *Talking Loud And Clear*. Initial copies of the album contained a one-sided freebie *(The Angels Keep Turning) The Wheels Of The Universe*. The album climbed to No. 9 spending twenty-seven weeks in the charts. The band embarked on a world tour to help promote it. Aside from including their earlier single *Locomotion*, it went on to produce three further ones. *Talking Loud And Clear* (backed by a re-recorded version of *Julia's Song*) made it to No. 11. An edited version of *Telsa Girls* (backed by a live version of *Telegraph*, the 12" had an extra cut *Garden City* and a remix of the 'A' side) got to No. 21. *Never Turn Away*, notable for one of Paul's few vocal performances, failed to climb beyond the No. 70 slot.

O.M.D. began work on a new album in Spring 1985. It was produced by Stephen Hague. *Crush*, eventually released in June, was their most mainstream album. It spawned further hit singles *So In Love* (No. 27), *Secret* (No. 34) and *La Femme Accident* (No. 42), which were issued in various different formats detailed in the discography. *So In Love* became their first U.S. hit (No. 26) whilst they were on tour there and *La Femme Accident* featured a stunning track *Firegun* on the flip. The final cut *If You Leave*, a rather ordinary ballad was used on the soundtrack to "Pretty In Pink" and spent thirteen weeks in the U.S. charts peaking at No. 4. Of more interest is *Women III*, dealing with feminism and *88 Seconds In Greensboro*, which was inspired by a 'World In Action' programme about 88 seconds of madness when Ku Klux Klan members shot dead five people participating in a peaceful anti-Klan march.

In November 1985, **O.M.D.** embarked on an extensive tour of the United States and Canada supporting the Thompson Twins, returning home in January 1986. Early that year they replaced Gordon Troeller as their manager with Steve Jensen and Martin Kirkup. Stephen Hague, who'd produced *Crush*, was retained in this role as they began work on their next album *The Pacific Age*. In their time-honoured fashion a 45 cut *(Forever)*

Live And Die was issued in advance of the album. It narrowly missed the Top 10, stalling at No. 11. *The Pacific Age* met with mixed reviews. It's fair to say it wasn't one of their best albums, but it still made it to No. 15 in the album charts and continued their success Stateside, where it got to No. 47. Rather than the usual U.S. and European tour to promote it, **O.M.D.** staged the much more ambitious and lengthy Pacific Age International Tour which took in New Zealand, Australia, Hong Kong and Japan as well as Canada, the 'States and the U.K. A further 45 *We Love You* was culled from the album with a dub version of the song on the flip. There was also a 7" double-pack featuring *If You Leave* and *88 Seconds In Greensboro* on the second disc, which came in a gatefold sleeve. Of more interest to collectors will be the 7" edition that came with a free six-track cassette entitled *Retro* which included four early singles; *Electricity, Enola Gay, Souvenir* and *Joan Of Arc*, as well as the two versions of *We Love You*. For all the different versions the 45 didn't get beyond No. 54 and a re-recorded version of *Shame*, which originally appeared on *The Pacific Age* only climbed two places higher to No. 52. *Shame* was issued in three different formats but collectors will probably be most interested in the 5" CD version featuring an extended mix of *Shame, Goddess Of Love, (Forever) Live And Die* (12" mix) and *Messages*.

We must leave the band's history here as they continued into the nineties, but I must draw attention to *The Best Of O.M.D.*, issued in March 1988. It went platinum and was their highest charting album in the U.K. climbing to No. 2 and spending a total of thirty-two weeks in the charts. It rose to No. 46 in the 'States as well. It's a good selection of their best material. The CD version came with four extra cuts, which are detailed in the discography.

Navigation - The OMD B Sides traces the progression of this band, which veered between pop and experimental electronic music. Their 'B' sides were often quite bleak so this collection veers a lot towards the melancholic.

Orchestral Manoeuvres In The Dark were one of those groups at the helm of electro-pop in this era and their place in music history seems assured.

The Orgasm Guerrillas

Personnel:	J.J BEDSORE	bs	A
	MARK BRABBS	gtr	A
	STEVE KENT	vcls, gtr	A

This was a pseudonym used by part-time Oi! project **Prole**. They had two vinyl offerings. First up is their piss-take of Syndicate label boss Dave Long

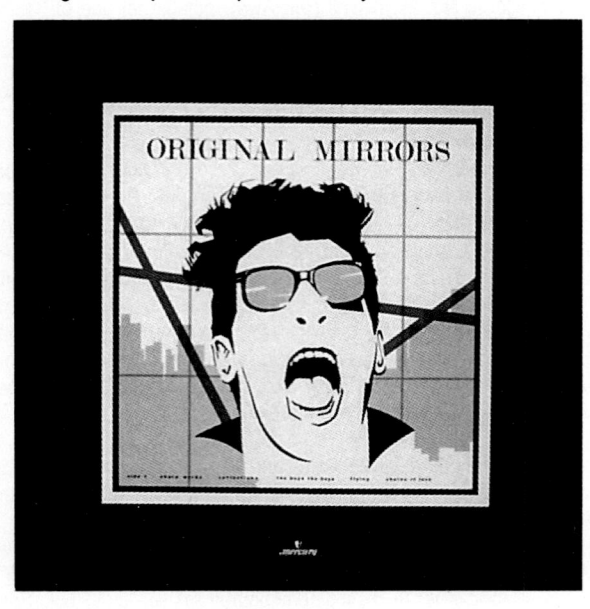

ORIGINAL MIRRORS - Original Mirrors.

JOHN OTWAY AND WILD WILLY BARRETT- Deep And Meaningless.

Sing Something Swindle, which was included on *Son Of Oi!* (Syndicate SYNLP 3) 1983, which was later reissued on CD (Captain Oi! AHOY CD 9) 1993. Their second was a send up of Syndicate's other boss Ron Rouman *Frankie Goes To Pot*, which is amusing and can be found on *The Oi! Of Sex* (Syndicate SYNLP 4) 1984, also reissued on CD (Captain Oi! AHOY CD 23) 1994.

Original Mirrors

Personnel:	STEVE ALLEN	vcls	AB
	IAN BROUDIE	gtr	AB
	JIMMY HUGHES	bs	AB
	PETE KIRCHER	drms	AB
	JONATHAN PERKINS	keyb'ds	AB
	PHIL SPALDING	bs	B

ALBUMS: 1(A) ORIGINAL MIRRORS (Mercury 9102 1039) 1980
2(B) HEART-TWANGO AND RAW BEAT
(Vertigo 6359 046) 1981

NB: There's also a CD *Heartbeat (The Best Of The Original Mirrors)* (Mercury 5325942) 1996.

45s: Could This Be Heaven/
Night Of The Angels (PS) (Mercury 6007 245) 1979
Boys Cry/Chain Of Love (PS) (Mercury 6007 251) 1979
20,000 Dreamers/
The Time Has Come (PS) (Mercury DREAM 1) 1981
Dancing With The Rebels/
Sure Yeah (PS) (Mercury MER 65) 1981

Fronted by former Deaf School member Steve Allen this was a rather self-indulgent project whose bombastic pop-rock lacked self-discipline and consequently had a tendency to sprawl and meander. The better tracks on the first album are *Chains Of Love, Boys Cry* and *Feel Like A Train*, but there's a dreadful cover of The Supremes' *Reflections*.

John Otway and Wild Willy Barrett

Personnel:	WILD WILLY BARRETT	A
	JOHN OTWAY	A

HCP
ALBUMS: 1(A) JOHN OTWAY AND WILD WILLY BARRETT
(Extracted EXLP 1) 1977 -
2(A) OTWAY AND BARRETT LIVE AT THE ROUNDHOUSE
(White Label OBL 1) 1977 -

	3(A)	DEEP AND MEANINGLESS	(Polydor Super 2383 501)	1978 44
	4(-)	WHERE DID I GO RIGHT?	(Polydor Super 2383 532)	1979 -
	5(A)	WAY/BAR	(Polydor Super 2383 581)	1980 -
	6(A)	GONE WITH THE BIN (THE BEST OF OTWAY-BARRETT)	(Polydor POLS 1039)	1981 -
	7(-)	ALL BALLS AND NO WILLY	(Empire HAMLP 1)	1982 -
	8(-)	GREATEST HITS	(Strikeback)	1986 -

NB: (4), (7) and (8) credited to **John Otway**. (1) came in an handmade stickered sleeve. It was later reissued (Polydor Super 2383 453) 1977. (2) was a privately-pressed freebie with handwritten labels in a plain sleeve. Only 250 numbered copies were pressed. (3) came in a stickered sleeve with a free 7" *Racing Cars (Jet Spotter On The Track) / Down The Road (live)* (OT 1). (1) and (3) reissued on one CD (Music Corporation TMC 9302) 1996. (4) and (7) reissued on one CD (Music Corporation TMC 9605) 1996. Also relevant are *Live* (Amazing Feet OTCD 4001) 1995 and *Cor, Baby That's Really Me* (Strike Back SBR 004 CD) 1995, which is a 'best of' collection.

EPs:	1(A)	I DID IT OTWAY	(Stiff)	1981
	2(A)	HEAD BUTTS	(Empire)	1982
	3(A)	12 STITCH EP	(Empire HAM 5T)	1982

NB: (3) came in a polythene bag with a jay-card. (1) was released in Canada as a full length album comprising four additional tracks to the six original ones. It came in the same cover but in red rather than green.

HCP

45s: (1)*	Gypsy/Misty Mountain	(County COUN 215)	1972 -
(up to	Murder Man/If I Did	(Track 2094 111)	1973 -
1985)	Louisa On A Horse/Misty Mountain	(Track 2094 133)	1976 -
(1)o	Louisa On A Horse/Beware Of The Flowers	(Viking YRS CF 01)	1976 -
	Racing Cars (Jet Spotter On The Track)/Running From The Law (PS)	(Polydor 2058 916)	1977 -
+	Really Free/Beware Of The Flowers (Cos I'm Sure They're Going To Get You Yeh) (PS)	(Polydor 2058 951)	1977 27
(1)	Geneve/It's A Long Time Since I Heard Homestead On The Farm (PS)	(Polydor 2059 001)	1978 -
(1)	Baby's In The Club/Julie Julie Julie (PS)	(Polydor 2059 060)	1978 -
(1)	Frightened And Scared/Are You On My Side? (PS)	(Polydor 2059 105)	1979 -
(1)x	Frightened And Scared (instrumental)/Are You On My Side? (PS)	(Polydor 2059 105)	1979 -
	Birthday Boy/Wow, What A Woman (PS)	(Polydor POSP 143)	1980 -
α	DK 50-80/It's A Long Time Since I Heard Homestead On The Farm/Homestead On The Farm (PS)	(Polydor 2059 250)	1980 45
(1)	Green Green Grass Of Home/Wednesday Club (PS)	(Stiff BUY 101)	1980 -
(1)	Turning Point/Too Much Air, Not Enough Oxygen (die-cut PS)	(Stiff BUY 115)	1981 -
	Headbutts/Live Version Headbutts (PS)	(Stiff Indie STIN 1)	1982 -
(1)x	In Dreams/		
	You Ain't Seen Nothing Yet (PS)	(Empire HAM 3)	1982 -
(1)β	Mass Communication/Baby It's The Real Thing (PS)	(Empire HAM 6)	1983 -
(1)	Middle Of The Winter/It Makes Me See Red (PS)	(Strike Back SBR 1)	1983 -

NB: (1) **John Otway** solo releases. * This was a private pressing with a duplicated lyric sheet. o Private pressing. + This was issued in a picture sleeve or die-cut review sleeve. x Only three copies were pressed making this an extremely expensive (in excess of £100) and collectable item. α The second song is credited to **John Otway** and the third one to **Wild Willy Barrett**. x Credited to **John Otway** Sweat. β Released on green vinyl.

John Otway was a loveable eccentric from Aylesbury, Buckinghamshire. Most of his better musical moments were in the company of multi-instrumentalist **Wild Willy Barrett** and by far his best known song is the extremely catchy and accessible *Really Free*. It captured much of the punk ethos and along with *Beware Of The Flowers (Cos I'm Sure They'e Going To Get You Yeh)* turned up on the *20 Of Another Kind* (Polydor POLS 1006) 1979 compilation.

The pair of them were really better live than on vinyl but their first album, originally a private pressing which was picked up by Polydor, is a good starting point. His third album *Deep And Meaningless* actually spent one week in the charts at No. 44. This included *Beware Of The Flowers* and a number of story songs of which the lengthy *Josephine*, *Riders In The Sky* and *Running From The Law* are the best.

Gone With The Bin is a reasonable compilation, but is probably surpassed by the 1995 CD collection *Cor, Baby That's Really Me*.

Ouida and The Numbers

45:	Runaway/Yeah, Yeah, Yeah, Yeah (PS)	(Modern STP 1)	1980

This 45 was produced by **Strangler** Hugh Cornwell.

The Out

Personnel:	DAVE BASSNET	keyb'ds	A
	GEORGE BOROWSKI	gtr	A
	CHRIS DANIELS	bs	A
	LYNDSEY FROST	drms	A
	JO ROBERTS	vcls	A

45s:	Who Is Innocent?/Linda's Just A Statue (PS)	(Rabid TOSH 113)	1979
	Who Is Innocent/Linda's Just A Statue (PS)	(Virgin VS 308)	1979
	Better The Devil/It's Not Enough (PS)	(Cargo CRS 14)	1980

The Out released a handful of singles on different labels. *Who Is Innocent?* is a catchy song, produced by Andy MacPherson at Revolution Studios, Cheadle Hulme, Cheshire and released on the Manchester-based Rabid Records. *Linda's Just A Statue* is similar but more lighthearted. Both songs were penned by guitarist **George Borowski**.

Who Is Innocent? later re-emerged on *Rabid/TJM Punk Singles Collection* (Receiver RRCD 227) in 1996.

The Outcasts

Personnel:	COLIN COWAN	drms	A
	GREG COWAN	vcls, bs	ABC
	MARTIN (MARTY) COWAN	gtr	ABC
	COLIN GETGOOD	gtr	ABC
	ROSS GRAHAM	drms	B
	RAYMOND FALLS	drms	C

ALBUMS:	1(A)	SELF CONSCIOUS OVER YOU	(Good Vibrations BIG 1)	1979
	2( )	BLOOD AND THUNDER	(Abstract ABT 004)	1983
	3( )	SEVEN DEADLY SINS	(New Rose NEW 40)	1984

NB: (1) issued on CD (Dojo DOJOCD 182) 1994. (2) issued on CD (New Rose ROSE 16CD) 1984. (2) and (3) also issued on one CD *Blood And Thunder / Seven*

THE OUT - Who Is Innocent?

Deadly Sins (Captain Oi! AHOY CD 68) 1997. Also relevant is *Outcasts Punk Singles Collection* (Anagram CDPUNK 62) 1995.

EP:	1(A)	FROM PROGRAMME LOVE TO MANIA VIA BEATING AND SCREAMING, PARTS 1 AND 2 (Programme Love/Beating And Screaming Pt's 1 And 2/Mania) (PS) (Outcasts Only 001) 1981

45s:	+	Frustration/Don't Wanna Be No Adult/ You're A Disease (PS)	(It Records IT 4) 1978
	*	Just Another Teenage Rebel/ Love Is For Sops (PS)	(Good Vibrations GOT 3) 1978
		Self Conscious Over You/ Love You For Never (PS)	(Good Vibrations GOT 17) 1979
		Magnum Force/Gangland Warfare (PS)	(GBH GBH 001) 1981
		Angel Face/Gangland Warfare (PS)	(Outcasts Only 002) 1982
		Nowhere Left To Run/The Running's Over/ Time To Run (PS)	(Anagram ANA 12) 1983
		Nowhere Left To Run/Instrumental/The Running's Over/ Ruby (12" PS)	(Anagram ANA 1212) 1983
		Seven Deadly Sins/Swamp Fever	(New Rose NEW 38) 1984
		1969/Psychotic Shakedown/ Blue Murder	(New Rose NEW 52) 1984

NB: + This was later reissued (Combat Rock CRO 20). * This was issued in various picture sleeves, some featured the band, others had 'type' on the front.

The Outcasts were arguably the rawest and roughest of the Northern Irish punk bands, who seemed pre-occupied with tough poses. They have also proved the most durable.

They were formed in June 1977 and were centred around the three Cowan brothers - Marty (gtr), Greg (bs, vcls) and Colin (drms). The quartet was made up by guitarist, Colin 'Getty' Getgood. Marty was an ex-teacher, Colin and Greg worked for their father's painting and decorating business and 'Getty' worked in Good Vibrations. They played their first gig in August 1977 and received a one-off recording contract with It records (based in Portadown) that Autumn. The result, *You're A Disease*, may have sold as many as 5,000 copies. It is a song about scorning religion - a lethal disease in Ireland. At this time they were managed by Jake Burns' girlfriend Tara Winters.

Early 1978 marked the start of the benificial association with Good Vibrations. Their first single for the label *Love Is For Sops / Just Another Teenage Rebel* was released in the late summer of 1978. It became one of the label's biggest sellers. They formed a close relationship with Terri Hooley, who became their manager, and grew to be the label's major band and one of the few big name bands to remain in Belfast. Indeed throughout this period they gigged regularly and persistently at The Harp Bar and other venues around the province.

1979 saw them issue their debut album, *Self Conscious Over You*, which was the first album issued on Hooley's label. The title track was the best - a touching story of a childhood crush delivered affectionately, despite the rough guitar sound. Other tracks of note on the album, were *Cyborg* - a tale about a super-human generation - and *Clinical Love*, a futuristic science fiction number about the replacement of orthodox sexual relationships by something more impersonal. The title cut was also issued as a 45.

THE OUTCASTS - Blood And Thunder.

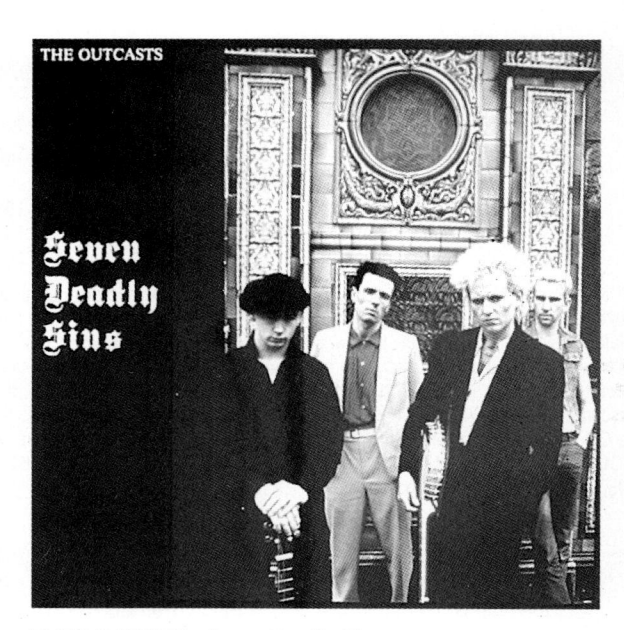

THE OUTCASTS - Seven Deadly Sins.

During 1981, the band formed their own Outcasts label. With distribution through Spartan, they issued a 4-track EP in early October, *From Programme Love To Mania Via Beating And Screaming, Parts 1 And 2*. It was a captivating number with nosediving, stabbing guitars. The band ended 1981, which had been a year of consolidation for them, playing at the 'Christmas On Earth' festival, held at Leed's Queens Hall on 20th December 1981.

Sadly, May 1982 brought tragedy when their drummer, Colin Cowan, was killed in a road crash. It had been Colin who had instigated and co-ordinated the Outcasts Only label. Ironically two years earlier his brother, Greg, had nearly been killed in a car crash and, more recently, Getty Getgood had spent three months in hospital with severe stomach poisoning. However, the group survived this setback demonstrating their determination by going ahead with a planned June tour as a trio. They also dedicated their next single, *Angel Face*, an old Glitter Band number, which was a coalition of traditional rock and new technology, to Colin.

The flip side, *Gangland Warfare* related a nasty incident which occurred one evening when Greg and Martin Cowan were returning from The Harp Bar. The record ends with the sound of smashing bottles and heavy bike chain lashes.

In November 1982, they signed to Abstract Records for their *Blood And Thunder* album, which was released later that month.

In late October 1983, a new **Outcasts** 45, *Nowhere Left To Run* appeared on Anagram Records in 7" and 12" form.

By 1984 they had signed to New Rose, who issued their next mini-album, *Seven Deadly Sins*, and its title track as a 45. This marked a change in musical direction away from punk towards rockabilly on *Seven Deadly Sins* and *Swamp Fever*. The other three cuts were an instrumental *The Chase*, a re-hash of Bowie's *5 Years* little-changed from the original and *Waiting For The Rain*, a mainstream rock number.

The Outcasts also featured on a number of compilations. You'll also find *Cops Are Coming* on *Battle Of The Bands* (EP) (Good Vibrations GOT 7) 1978. *Cyborg* also figured on the limited edition *Room To Move* (EP) (Energy NRG 1) 1980. You can also check out *Just Another Teenage Rebel* on *Business Unusual* (Cherry Red A-RED 2) 1979 and *Mania* resurfaced on *Punk And Disorderly* (Abstract AABT 100) 1982.

More recently *The Cops Are Comin'*, *Self Conscious Over You* and *Love You For Never* have resurfaced on *Good Vibrations - The Punk Singles Collection* (Anagram CD PUNK 36) 1994; *Nowhere To Run* can be found on *Abstract Punk Singles Collection* (Anagram CDPUNK 52) 1995 and on *Anagram Punk Singles Collection* (Anagram CDPUNK 37) 1994; whilst *Just Another Teenage Rebel* got a further airing on the lavish 5-CD box set compilation *1-2-3-4 - A History Of Punk And New Wave 1976 - 1979* (MCA/Universal MCD 60066) in 1999.

After **The Undertones** and **Stiff Little Fingers**, **The Outcasts** (along with groups like **Protex**, **Rudi** and **Ruefrex**) were among the best bands to come out of Northern Ireland in this era.

The Outpatients

Personnel:	NICK BURT	gtr	A
	TONY DOUGHTY	vcls	A
	TOM NEWTON	bs	A
	JENTS OTZEN	drms	A
	PADDY CARROL	gtr	A

45: New Japanese Hairstyles/Children (PS) (Albion ION 1014) 1981

The Outpatients formed in West London in 1976. They spent several months writing and rehearsing, then, in 1978, they went through a period of experimenting with bizarre theatrics, from which they emerged unscathed. They developed their own unique style which can be heard on this single. The group were managed by Nicky Tesco of **The Members**, who shared the production credits with John Brand (ex-**Ruts**, **Holly and The Italians** and **XTC** kingpin).

The Outsiders

Personnel:	ADRIAN BORLAND	vcls, gtr	A
	GRAHAM GREEN	gtr	A
	ADRIAN JANES	drms	A
	BOB LAWRENCE	bs	A

ALBUMS:	1(A)	CALLING ON YOUTH	(Raw Edge RER 1) 1978
	2(A)	CLOSE UP	(Raw Edge RER 3) 1978

NB: There's also a compilation *Vital Years* (Three Lines LINE 4) 1994.

EP:	1(A)	ONE TO INFINITY (One To Infinity/New Uniform/ Freeway/Consequences) (Raw Edge RER 2) 1977

45:	*	Vital Hours/Take Up	(Xciting Plastic) 1978

NB: * This was unissued.

This was a Liverpool punk combo fronted by Adrian Borland, who later formed **The Sound** and a more experimental combo **Second Layer**, who he ran as a parallel project. They received further exposure by virtue of the inclusion of *Consequences* on the compilation *Business Unusual* (Cherry Red ARED 2) in 1979, although the track confirms them as very much third division punk.

Vital Years is a CD compilation which appeared in a cardboard box with a booklet. Clearly Iggy Pop and The Stooges were an influence.

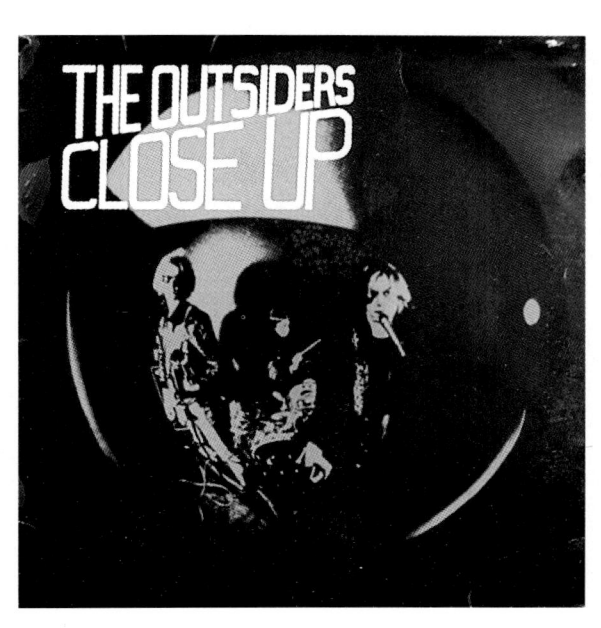

THE OUTSIDERS - Close Up.

The Pack live at The Electric Ballroom, London 19th October 1979. Photo: Steven Richards.

The Pack

Personnel:	KIRK BRANDON	vcls	AB
	JIM WALKER	drms	A
	JONATHON WERNER	bs	AB
	SIMON WERNER	gtr	AB
	RAB FAB BEITH	drms	B

CASS:	1( )	THE PACK LIVE 1979	(Donut DONUT 2) 1982

NB: *Dead Ronin* (Yeaah! YEAAH 25) 2001 is a compilation CD.

EPs:	1( )	KIRK BRANDON AND THE PACK OF LIES (Brave New Soldiers/Heathen/King Of Kings/Number 12) (SS SS IN2/SS 2N1) 1980
	2( )	LONG LIVE THE PAST (Thalidomide/King Of Kings/ St. Teresa/Abattoir) (Cyclops CYCLOPS 1) 1982

45s:	Brave New Soldiers/Heathen (PS)	(SS PAK 1) 1979
	King Of Kings/Number 12 (PS)	(Rough Trade RT 025) 1979

The Pack formed in South London. Only 2,500 copies of their debut 45 *Brave New Soldiers* were pressed, making it a collectable nowadays. After a second 45, *Kings Of Kings* for Rough Trade, they went on to record a couple of EPs and an in-concert cassette. Jim Walker was later in **Public Image Ltd.**, Kirk Brandon joined **Theatre Of Hate** and was later in **Spear Of Destiny**. The Werner brothers went on to **Straps** and Jonathon Werner was later in **Theatre Of Hate**.

The recent *Dead Ronin* collection includes the rare *Brave New Soldiers*, two versions of the 'B' side *Heathen* and no less than three different versions of the follow-up 45 *King Of Kings*. It comes with biographical notes courtesy of their founder member Kirk Brandon.

THE PACK - Muchas Gracias.

The Pack

45:	Muchas Gracias/Limelight (PS)	(Escape ESC 102)	1981

This was a separate outfit unconnected to **The Pack** which featured Kirk Brandon. *Muchas Gracias* has a Latin flavour as the title suggests.

Pale Fountains

Personnel:	ANDY DIAGRAM	vcls	A
	MICHAEL HEAD	gtr, vcls	A
	CHRIS McCAFFREY	bs	A
	THOMAS WHELAN	drms	A

HCP

ALBUMS:	1(A)	PACIFIC STREET	(Virgin V 2274) 1984	85
	2(A)	FROM ACROSS THE KITCHEN TABLE	(Virgin V 2333) 1985	94

NB: (1) also issued on CD (Virgin CDV 2274) 1989. (2) also issued on CD (Virgin CDV 2333) 1989.

HCP

45s:	Just A Girl/(There's Always) Something On My Mind (PS)	(Operation Twilight OPT 09) 1982	-
	Thank You/Meadow Of Love	(Virgin VS 557) 1983	48
	Palm Of My Hand/ Love's A Beautiful Place (PS)	(Virgin VS 568) 1983	-
	Unless/Natural (PS)	(Virgin VS 614) 1984	-
	Unless/Natural (12", PS)	(Virgin VS 61412) 1984	-
	Don't Let Your Love Start A War/ Love Situation (PS)	(Virgin VS 668) 1984	-
	Don't Let Your Love Start A War/ Love Situation (12", PS)	(Virgin VS 66812) 1984	-
	Jean's Not Happening/ Bicycle Thieves (PS)	(Virgin VS 735) 1984	-
	Jean's Not Happening/ Bicycle Thieves (12", PS)	(Virgin VS 73512) 1984	-
	From Across The Kitchen Table/Thank You/ Bicycle Thieves (12", PS)	(Virgin VS 75012) 1985	-
*	From Across The Kitchen Table/Bicycle Thieves/ Thank You/Just A Girl (PS)	(Virgin VS 750) 1985	-

NB: * Double pack 7".

Pale Fountains were formed in Liverpool in the early eighties by songwriter Michael Head and Chris McCaffrey. Andy Diagram had previously been in Dislocation Dance and **The Diagram Brothers**.

Pale Fountains will be remembered for wearing short baggy trousers visually. Musically, they draw on influences like soft pop and 'bossa nova', but also earlier acts like The Beatles and Love.

Originally recording on Operation Twilight, they were signed to Virgin and attempted to make it big. Their first album *Pacific Street* did spend two weeks in the charts peaking at No. 85. The most appealing track was possibly *Reach* but overall the album was very derivative of other styles and lacked any originality to make it big.

In 1983, **Pale Fountains** enjoyed their only hit single when *Thank You* climbed to No. 48 during its six week chart stay.

Commercially their follow-up album *From Across The Kitchen Table* fared worse than *Pacific Street* managing just one week at No. 94. Produced by Ian Broudie, in many respects it was a stonger effort overall with *Shelter*, *27 Ways To Get Back Home* and *Jean's Not Happening* particularly catching the ear.

Having failed in their quest for stardom they split after the second album. Michael Head went on to form Shack with his brother John.

The Panik

Personnel:	B. DALE	drms	A
	HILTON	bs	A
	IAN NANCE	vcls, gtr	A
	ERIC RANDOM	gtr	A

EP:	1(A)	IT WON'T SELL (Modern Politcs/Urban Damnation/ Murder)	(Rainy City SHOT 1) 1977

Musically nihilistic, this disc did sport an excellent picture sleeve, reprinted courtesy of 'Life' magazine in 1964. It depicts a group of Peppermint Lounge Lizards on the look out for action.

The group came from Manchester. Their EP was the only release on Rainy City, a label formed by future **Joy Division** and **New Order** manager Rob Gretton. Indeed **Panik** vocalist Ian Nance is rumoured to have auditioned for the vocal slot when **Joy Division** first formed! **Panik**'s whole EP later resurfaced on *Punk Rock Rarities, Vol. 1* (Anagram CDPUNK 63) 1995.

Paranoia

ALBUM:	1	SHATTERED GLASS	(Rot ASS 1) 1984

45:	Dead Man's Dreams/Man In Black (PS)	(Rot ASS 8) 1984

An obscure punk band. The title cut to their album can also be found on *Wet Dreams* (Rot ASS 4) 1984 and on *Rot Records Punk Singles Collection* (Anagram CDPUNK 40) 1994. It's an excellent song with great female vocals and lyrics set in a post-nuclear attack scenario:

"The nuclear age has begun
Soldiers roam the streets in gas marks
Space like men in white suits
Your chance of survival none"
(from *Shattered Glass*)

Also on *Wet Dreams* is *Dissilusion*, another better than average offering with more powerful female vocals and pace changes:

PARTISANS - Police Story.

"Things are never what they seem
Much more like a nightmare dream
They just want to make you scream
And you call it dissillusion"
(from *Disillusion*)

The Parrots

EP: 1 THE PARROTS (Photography Song/Home Sweet Home/Serious Thing/Breaking Up Now Song) (PS)   (Attrix RB 14) 1980

In addition to this EP **The Parrots** contributed two cuts to *Vaultage '78 (Two Sides Of Brighton)* (Attrix RB 03) in 1978. The first *Larger Than Life* is all about Brighton and *Vicious Circles* is a promising popish effort.

The Partisans

Personnel:
- BOB 'SPIKE' HARRINGTON — vcls — ABCD
- MARK 'SHARK' HARRIS — drms — ABCD
- ANDY LEALAND — gtr — ABC
- LOUISE WRIGHT — bs — A
- DAVE PARSONS — bs — B

ALBUMS:
1(A) THE PARTISANS (No Future PUNK 4) 1983 94 HCP
2(B/C) TIME WAS RIGHT (Cloak And Dagger PART LP 1) 1984 -

NB: (1) was repressed in 1990 in red vinyl. *Police Story* (Anagram CD PUNK 4) 1992 and later reissued on LP and CD (Get Back GET 15) 1997 comprises their first album with their first two 45s as bonus cuts. The CD is a strictly limited edition of 300. (2) was later reissued in a new sleeve (Link LINK LP 033) 1998 and later again on CD (Captain Oi! AHOY CD 70) 1997 with four bonus tracks. Also relevant is *The Best Of The Partisans* (Captain Oi! AHOY CD 103) 1999, which includes cuts from both their albums, 45s and two previously unissued cuts from 1989.

45s:
- Police Story/Killing Machine (No Future Oi! 2) 1981
- 17 Years Of Hell/The Power And The Greed/Bastards In Blue (PS) (No Future Oi! 12) 1982
- Blind Ambition/Come Clean/Change (PS) (Cloak And Dagger PART 1) 1983

Reissue: 17 Years Of Hell/The Power And The Greed/Bastards In Blue (Visionary V 702) 198?

The Partisans formed in the summer of 1979 in Bridge End in south Wales. The four members were just 14 at the time! Initially they covered punk classics of the era but they soon set about writing some of their own material and sent a demo to Chris Berry, who'd founded No Future Records. The demo included originals like *Killing Machine*, *No Time* and *Arms Race* and covers of punk classics like **Stiff Little Fingers'** *Wasted Life*, **UK Subs'** *C.I.D.*, **The Sex Pistols'** *Pretty Vacant* and **The Cockney Rejects'** *Flares 'N' Slippers*. On the strength of this Berry signed the band. Their double 'A' side single *Police Story* and *Killing Machine* was issued on 28th September 1981. The abrasive anti-authoritarian, anti-police disc became a big indie hit, climbing to No. 5 during a twenty-two week chart stay. *Police Story* starts with a tune to the old TV series 'Dixon Of Dock Green' followed by the lyrics 'Dixon - you're gone forever'. To help promote the disc they gigged with **Blitz** at Manchester's Mayflower Club. The 45 attracted the attention of 'Sounds' Garry Bushell, who invited **The Partisans** to appear on *Carry On Oi!* (Secret SEC 2) in 1981. This was later issued on CD (Captain Oi! AHOY CD 119) 1999. Their contributions *Arms Race* and *No U Turns* are normally considered two of the album's stronger cuts. As the album cuts helped raise their profile they undertook further gigs with **Blitz**, **Peter and The Test Tube Babies** and **The Ejected**, who also figured on the compilation. They also played at London's Zig Zag club in a No Future label night along with **Red Alert**, **Blitz** and **Peter and The Test Tube Babies**.

Their second 45 *17 Years Of Hell* followed on 27th May 1982. The disc comprised three more, no nonsense full-blooded Oi! assaults and their anti-police stance was further enforced by one of them *Bastards In Blue*. This also spent weeks in the indie chart, eventually climbing to No. 2. All three cuts can now be heard on *The Oi! Singles Collection, Vol. 4* (Captain Oi! AHOY CD 71) 1997. *17 Years Of Hell* has also resurfaced on *100% British Oi!* (Captain Oi! AHOY DCD 83), also released in 1997.

PARTISANS - Blind Ambition.

If you prefer vinyl then their No Future 45s have also been reissued on this too. *No Future - The Punk Singles Collection* (Captain Oi! AHOY DLP 508) 1996 features *Police Story*, *17 Years Of Hell* and *The Power And The Greed*. *Vol. 2* (Captain Oi! AHOY DLP 512) 1996 of the same series contains *Killing Machine* and *Bastards In Blue*.

February 1983 saw the release of their self-titled debut album. This contained new versions of *Arms Race* and *No U Turns* (which had earlier appeared on *Carry On Oi!*) and their earlier 45 *17 Years Of Hell* along with nine other no-nonsense, fast-paced punkers. Some of these were re-recordings of cuts which had appeared on their early demo.

In October 1983, the new Cloak and Dagger label issued a new three track 45 *Blind Ambition* by the band. The title cut was one of their strongest songs. By now Louise Wright had been replaced on bass by Dave Parsons and the band had relocated to Bayswater in West London. It attracted a rave review in 'Punk Lives', got quite a lot of airplay and rose to No. 23 during a seven week stay in the indie charts.

In summer 1984, a second album *Time Was Right* was released. This was a half live, half studio effort which got to No. 20 in the indie chart. The live cuts were recorded at Brixton Ace during a predominantly anarcho event. The studio cuts, recorded after this gig, were the work of a three piece with Andy handling bass duties. This was because Dave Parsons had left. He later achieved chart success with Transvision Vamp and is now in Bush.

Both **The Partisans** albums have been reissued. The first retitled *Police Story* with their first two 45s as bonus tracks is available on both vinyl and CD. The second has been reissued on CD by Captain Oi!. The thirteen original cuts are supplemented by *Change* and *Come Clean* (from their *Blind Ambition* 45) and two previously unreleased demos *I Never Needed You* and *Time Was Right*.

The Best Of The Partisans (CD) features their classic singles *Police Story*, *17 Years Of Hell* and *Blind Ambition* as well as tracks from both their

PARTISANS - 17 Years Of Hell.

PARTISANS - Best Of (CD).

albums. The booklet also includes a band history on which these notes are based.

In late 1989, Harris and Harrington got in touch with Link Records and recorded two cuts *Run Go Grab* and *Eyes Shut*. These are also included on Captain Oi!'s 1999 'best of' CD.

Police Story and *No U Turns* both got a further airing on *100% Hardcore Punk* (Captain Oi! AHOY DCD 84) in 1998. *17 Years Of Hell* earlier resurfaced on *Punk Compilation* (Emporio EMPRCD 550) in 1994 and on *Burning Ambitions, Vol. 2 (A History Of Punk)* (Anagram CDPUNK 81) 1996. Back in 1988 *Blind Ambitions* was featured on *Oi! Chartbusters Volume 2* (Link LP 016), which has now been reissued on CD (Harry May MAYO CD 502) 2001. *Blind Ambitions* has also resurfaced on the *Oi! Fuckin' Oi!* (Harry May MAYO CD 110) 1999 compilation.

The Passengers

Personnel incl:	GARY FINCH	bs	A
	JULIAN MACQUEEN	vcls, gtr	A
	GRAHAM PAINTING	gtr, vcls	A

45s:	Two Lovers/Something About You (I Don't Like)	(Epic EPC 7830) 1979
	Something About You (I Don't Like)/ Two Lovers	(Epic EPC 7967) 1979
	In The Goodnight Hour/Calling On Moscow	(Index) 1980

The Passengers were formed in London in early 1978. They featured the considerable song-writing talents of Julian MacQueen, as well as Graham Painting, Gary Finch, and assorted drummers. The band were a new wave/power pop band. In 1978, they had a management contract with Bluebird Music. Through the management company, the band got a deal with Epic in 1979. Their first single *Two Lovers / Something About You (I Don't Like)* got considerable airplay but didn't chart. Epic re-released the single later in 1979, simply swapping the 'A' and 'B' side around, but the single again failed to chart. **The Passengers** recorded an album for Epic at the end of 1979, which was never released on Epic.

By late 1980, MacQueen and Finch had had enough. MacQueen, in particular, wanted the band to be more radical - a kind of poppier version of the **Gang Of Four** - whereas Epic wanted a cuddly pop band, which is what they thought they had signed. After renaming the band Propaganda, MacQueen, along with Finch, left and formed **To The Finland Station** and, shortly afterwards, Epic dropped the band. However, as it was technically Bluebird that had been signed to Epic and not **The Passengers**, Bluebird owned the tapes of the album. This was to be released on Index Records, although it is believed that only test pressings exist. However, a single taken from the album, *In The Goodnight Hour* was released on Index in 1980.

PARTISANS - Time Was Right.

The Passions

Personnel:	CLAIRE BIDWELL	bs	A
	BARBARA GOGAN	gtr, vcls	A B
	CLIVE TIMPERLEY	keyb'ds, vcls, violin	A B
	RICHARD WILLIAMS	drms	A
	DAVE AGAR	bs	B

HCP

ALBUMS:	1(A)	MICHAEL AND MIRANDA	(Fiction FIX 003) 1980 -
	2(B)	30,000 FEET OVER CHINA	(Polydor 2383 616) 1981 92
	3(B)	SANCTUARY	(Polydor POLS 1066) 1982 -

NB: (2) also issued on CD (Great Expectations PIPCD 028) 1991. There's also a CD compilation *Passion Plays* (Polydor S 298602) 1996.

EP:	1(B)	SQUARE (Square/Why Me?/The Snow/I'm In Love With A German Film Star) (PS) (Polydor CRUSH 1) 1982

HCP

45s:	Needles And Pills/Body And Soul (PS)	(Soho SH 5) 1978 -
	Hunted/Oh No It's You (PS)	(Fiction FICS 8) 1979 -
	The Swimmer/War Song (PS)	(Polydor POSP 184) 1980 -
	I'm In Love With A German Film Star/ I'm Shy (PS)	(Polydor POSP 222) 1981 25
	Skin Deep/Radiate (PS)	(Polydor POSP 256) 1981 -
	The Swimmer/Some Fun (PS)	(Polydor POSP 325) 1981 -
	Africa Mine/I Feel Cheap (PS)	(Polydor POSP 384) 1982 -
	Jump For Joy/The Story (PS)	(Polydor POSP 435) 1982 -
	Sanctuary/Tempting Fate (PS)	(Polydor POSP 487) 1982 -

THE PASSIONS - Michael And Miranda.

The Passions were part of the post-punk movement. After a debut 45 *Needles And Pills* on the indie Soho label they got a one-off deal with Fiction to record *Hunted*. Both these 45s met with favourable reviews and helped them secure a long-term deal with an U.K. major label, Polydor. **The Passions** sound was characterised by fragile guitars (particularly aided by ex-**101**er Clive Timperley), catchy melodies and Barbara Gogan's worried vocal style.

Their debut album *Michael And Miranda* is fairly unmelodic with minimalist arrangements and stark vocals. The lyrics tackle issues like neuroses on *Absentee*, unhappy love on *Oh No, It's You* and suspicion and fear *Man On The Tube*.

30,000 Feet Over China, their follow-up is less bleak in style and content. It was made with a new producer Nigel Gray and with Dave Agar replacing Claire Bidwell on bass. It did better commercially, possibly because of the more melodic sound on songs like *Runaway*, *Someone Special* and the pop sensibility of *Bachelor Girls*. It spawned their only hit single, the tongue-in-cheek *I'm In Love With A German Film Star*, which climbed to No. 25 during an eight week chart stay. This song later resurfaced on *A History Of Punk, Vol. 2* (Virgin CDOVD 487) 1997.

In January 1982, they released *Africa Mine*, which was a haunting condemnation of colonial exploitation, which deserved to do better.

The highlight of their final album *Sanctuary* was the soaring title track, which was also released as a single but did not chart. With Barbara Grogan's vocals growing in stature and the addition of a synthesizer this conjured up a smooth sound which represented a marked departure from the starkness of their earlier efforts.

The Pathetix

EP:	1( )	THE PATHETIX	(TJM TJM 12) 1979
45:		Aleister Crowley/Don't Touch My Machine/ Snuffed It (PS)	(No Records No 001) 1978

Hailing from Nelson in Lancashire came **The Pathetix**. *Aleister Crowley* is a five minute composition centred around a seance where The Devil makes an unwelcome appearance and snuffs the lot of them! *Love In Decay* from their EP, can also be heard on *Rabid/TJM Punk Singles Collection* (Receiver RRCD 227) 1996.

Penetration

Personnel:

ROBERT BLAMIRE	bs	AB
GARY CHAPLIN	gtr	A
PAULINE MURRAY	vcls	AB
GARY SMALLMAN	drms	AB
NEALE FLOYD	gtr	B
FRED PURSER	keyb'ds	B

				HCP
ALBUMS:	1(B)	MOVING TARGETS	(Virgin V 2109) 1978	22
	2(B)	COMING UP FOR AIR	(Virgin V 2131) 1979	36
	3(B)	RACE AGAINST TIME	(Virgin/Clifdayn PEN 1) 1979	-

NB: (1) First 15,000 copies were issued on luminous vinyl. (1) reissued on vinyl (Virgin OVED 40) 1984 at budget price and on CD (Virgin CDV 2109) 1990. There are also some CD compilations, *Don't Dictate (The Best Of Penetration)* (Virgin CDOVD 450) 1995; *Penetration* (Burning Airlines PILOT 001) 1993 is a compilation of demos and live material and they shared the following CD with **The Ruts** and *BBC Radio 1 Live In Concert* (Windsong WIN CD 009) 1991. A later vinyl compilation is *The Early Years* (Get Back GET 13) 1997.

45s:	Don't Dictate/Money Talks (PS)	(Virgin VS 192) 1977
	Firing Squad/Never (PS)	(Virgin VS 213) 1978
	Life's A Gamble/V.I.P. (PS)	(Virgin VS 226) 1978
	Danger Signs/Stone Heroes (live)	(Virgin VS 257) 1979
	Danger Signs/Stone Heroes (live)/ Vision (live) (12" PS)	(Virgin VS 257-12) 1979
	Come Into The Open/Lifeline (PS)	(Virgin VS 268) 1979
	Don't Dictate/Free Money/Life's A Gamble/ Danger Signs (12" PS)	(Virgin VS 593-12) 1983

PENETRATION - Don't Dictate.

Penetration (who took their name from the Iggy Pop song of that title) were one of the finest punk bands of the late seventies to come from northern England. They were formed in the small mining village of Ferryhill in County Durham by 18 year old former art student **Pauline Murray** and her friend Robert Blamire, after going to see a **Sex Pistols** gig in Manchester. They played their first gig at the Rock Garden, Middlesborough in October 1976 and made their London debut at the Roxy Club early the following year supporting **Generation X** and **The Adverts**.

They were invited to record some demos for Virgin, which were later released in the latter days of their career. On the strength of these and one song in particular, *Don't Dictate*, they were offered a one-single contract with Virgin. Released in November 1977, *Don't Dictate* was a pulsating punk song. One of the best in a year of many gems. It's anti-authoritarian message was ideal for 1977. However, despite making a favourable impression the 45 did not chart. The flip side *Money Talks* was briefer and less distinctive.

Early in 1978 their main songwriter Gary Chaplin quit the band. He was tired of relentless gigging and all the pressures that went with it. He was replaced by Neale Floyd on rhythm guitar and a little later, second guitarist Fred Purser was added giving the band an altogether heavier sound.

The new line-up recorded a second 45 *Firing Squad* backed by *Never*, released in May 1978. This was another powerful 45 showcasing Pauline's vocals superbly. Like their next effort, the more melodic *Life's A Gamble*, which came out in October 1978, it achieved good reviews but didn't make the charts. Indeed **Penetration** surprisingly never did achieve a hit single, which was a complete travesty.

The first 15,000 copies of their debut album *Moving Targets*, issued in October 1978, came on luminous vinyl. Whilst from a gimmicky viewpoint it shined in the dark, the sound quality was very crackly so if you're seeking one out now you may want to go for an ordinary copy. In terms of content the album was a delight - a pot pouri of high-powered pulsating post-punk with **Murray**'s piercing vocals and plenty of guitar thrills from Fred Purser. By the time of its release Pauline and bassist Robert Blamire had got married. Pauline sounded so much like Patti Smith but even better on their cover of Patti's *Free Money* and the album also contained a good cover of **The Buzzcocks**' *Nostalgia*. Otherwise the album contained appealing originals. Aside from the pop-punk 45 cut, *Life's A Gamble*, other stand-out tracks include *Movement*, which is full of meandering melodies and changing rhythms, the punkish *Silent Community* and songs like *Vision* and *Future Daze*, which veered towards the new wave.

Penetration toured Europe and America early in 1979, returning to Britain for another major tour in the spring. Their next 45 *Danger Signs* was originally recorded at Wessex Studios but the following weekend they re-recorded the song, along with *Last Saving Grace* and *Coming Up For Air* for a John Peel session eventually broadcast on 7th March 1979. They took the Peel sessions to Virgin and convinced them to let them re-record *Danger Signs* they way they wanted to. The 7" was backed by a non-album cut *Stone Heroes* and the 12" by two non-album cuts *Stone Heroes* and *Vision*. In fact both the 7" and 12" listed a 6.42 minute version of *Vision* on the sleeves. It didn't appear on the 7" at all and only appeared on the 12" in its usual three minute version. 15,000 copies were distributed with this wrong sleeve information which didn't help. Again it failed to chart. The

Penetration live at The Roundhouse, London 28th May 1978. Photo: Steven Richards.

PENETRATION - Firing Squad.

discarded version of *Danger Signs*, which is less dynamic, resurfaced with early demos and some later live material on the *Race Against Time* album.

In May 1979, **Penetration** returned to the 'States for a gruelling thirty-four-date, five-week tour, which started to nurture disharmony within the band. They returned home exhausted and with their two guitarists not speaking to one another to begin to work on their next album *Coming Up For Air*.

Despite this the album, released in September 1979, fared quite well commercially, peaking at No. 36 during its four week stay in the charts. This may have been helped by Virgin putting it out at a special introductory price of £3.99, though as a work of quality this demeaned the album somewhat. It also left the band in debt due to high recording costs. In reality, whereas *Moving Targets* had contained strong and exciting material throughout, on *Coming Up For Air* only *Lifeline*, *On Reflection* and *Shout About The Noise* really catch the ear. On 15th October 1979 **Penetration** recorded these three tracks along with *Your Saving Grace* (also from the album) for a Mike Read session. The production on the album by Steve Lillywhite didn't help much either resulting in a rather muffled sound.

Penetration had decided to split before the album appeared in the shops. The split was announced at a Newcastle City Hall gig, which was recorded and later issued as an 'official bootleg' album *Race Against Time*. The record comprised a live side containing this energetic concert and a studio side of early demos. This was later re-released in 1993 and retitled *Penetration* (Burning Airlines PILOT 1), in addition seven bonus tracks were added from Peel sessions including the excellent *Movement* which demonstrated their potential way beyond a three chord punk band. The set comes with a twelve-page full-colour booklet including a career history penned by journalist Phil Sutcliffe.

In 1999, their finest moment *Don't Dictate* figured on the 5-CD set *1-2-3-4 - A History Of Punk And New Wave 1976 - 1979* (MCA/Universal MCD 60066). It had figured on *Guillotine 10"* (Virgin VCL 5001) back in 1978, on *The Best Punk Album In The World.... Ever, Vol. 2* (2-CD) (Virgin VTCD 79) in 1996, again on *The Best Punk Anthems.... Ever* (2-CD) (Virgin VTDCD 198) in 1998, on *Spiked* (EMI Gold CDGOLD 1057) 1996, *Wave (The Biggest New Wave Hits)* (3-CD set) (Disky HR 868442) 1996 and *A History Of Punk, Vol. 1* (Virgin CDOVD 486) in 1997. *Danger Signs* got fresh exposure on *God Save The Punks* (2-CD) (Disky DOU 882552) 1998.

Not long after the split Pauline was invited to sing on **The Only Ones**' final album *Baby's Got A Gun* and duet with Peter Perrett on the countryish *Fools* single.

A few months later **Murray** and Blamire teamed up with producer Martin Hannett and session players to form **Pauline Murray and The Invisible Girls**.

Subsequent ventures included **Pauline Murray and The Storm**, **Pauline Murray and The Saint** and some solo ventures. She was one of the finest female vocalists of British punk and new wave and deserved greater success.

Perfect Zebras

| ALBUM: | 1 | MIXING WITH WILDLIFE | (Focus FOLP 1) 1982 |

45s:	Running With Zebras/Man Or Machine (PS)	(Focus FOS 1) 1982
	Touching My Heart Again/	
	In For The Kill (PS)	(Focus FOS 2) 1982
	Fascination/Why Underestimate (PS)	(Focus FOS 9) 1982

A synthesized pop outfit. *Fascination* is certainly a pretty good song.

Mark Perry

| ALBUM: | 1 | SNAPPY TURNS | (Deptford Fun City DLP 06) 1980 |

NB: (1) also issued on CD (Borrowers Rec Co TBRCD 01) 1993 and again in 1995 with the addition of four bonus tracks *Whole World's Down On Me*, *I Live - He Dies*, *You Cry Your Tears* and *Music Death?*

45s:	Whole World's Down On Me/	
	I Live - He Dies	(Deptford Fun City DFC 12) 1980
+*	You Cry Your Tears/	
	Music Death?	(Deptford Fun City DFC 09) 1980
+	You Cry Your Tears/Music Death?	(NB NB 7) 1980

NB: + Credited to **Mark Perry** and Dennis Burn. * Unissued. The later release on NB Records was housed in a polythene bag.

Mark Perry is better known as a member of **Alternative TV**. He was working as a bank clerk when he was inspired by The Ramones to start the 'Sniffin' Glue (And Other Rock 'N' Roll Habits)' fanzine. He quit his job, shortened his name to Mark P and, along with a group of friends who included Danny Baker (later to become a TV and radio presenter), became the unofficial media spokespersons for punk in those halycon days. By the time he stopped producing 'Sniffin' Glue' in August 1977, **Perry** (who'd previously been in a trio called The New Beatles with Steve Walsh and Tyrone Thomas) had formed **Alternative TV** with **Alex Fergusson**.

His mid-1980 solo album *Snappy Turns* included Dennis Burns, Anno Wombat, Nag and Bendle among the credits. It's a pretty bleak album mirroring **Perry**'s rather introspective mood at that time. Among its better tracks are *Death Looks Down* and *Inside*. From the same sessions came a rather amateurish but exhuberant cover of Ken Boothe's hit *The Whole World's Down On Me*. The flip *I Live - He Dies* was inspired (not sure that's the right word) by **Perry**'s memories of bullying in his school days. The record does have the distinction of being the last on the Deptford Fun City label. A second 45 recorded with Dennis Burn was eventually put out on NB Records.

In addition to the above discography some **Mark Perry** songs have featured on compilations. *The Four EPs* (Con no #) 1980 cassette includes three live cuts *Death Looks Down*, *The Sound Of Music* and *Sorrow Cried Blood*. *Tapezine 2* (Fuck Off no#) 1980 cassette includes *Cold Rain* (a demo by **Perry** and **Alternative TV** member **Alex Fergusson**), an interview

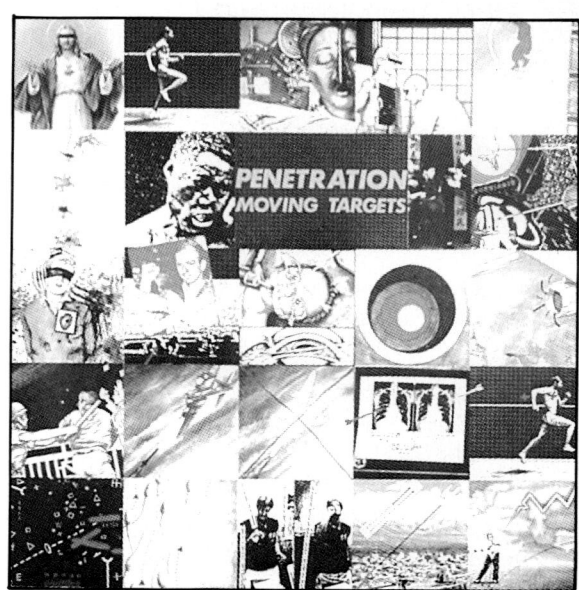

PENETRATION - Moving Targets.

with **Perry** and *Snappy Turn*. *Room Noise* (Rapid Eye Movement) 1980 cassette included **Perry**'s *Bold Chance*. *Miniatures* (Pipe PIPE 2) 1980, a limited edition album of 500 which contained a poster, included **Perry**'s *Talking World War III Blues*. *Folk In Hell* (Fuck Off no #) 1982 contained **Perry**'s *Take It Easy, Persepectives And Distortion* (Cherry Red BRED 15) included **Perry**'s *Dear Dear* and finally *Communicate!!!! Live At Thames Poly* (Thames Poly Students Union TPSU 0001) 1985, a double album with a booklet, included **Perry**'s *Crazy Crazy* and *Release The Natives - Spanish Heaven*.

Perry was also involved in **The Good Missionaries**, **The Reflection** and **The Door and The Window**. In the nineties, he was involved in a band called Baby Ice Dog.

PETER AND THE TEST TUBE BABIES - Banned From The Pubs.

Peter and The Test Tube Babies

Personnel:
	PETER BYWATERS	vcls	A
	DEREK GREENING	gtr	A
	NICHOLAS LOIZIDES	drms	A
	CHRIS MARCHANT	bs	A

ALBUMS: (up to 1986)
1(A)	THE MATING SOUNDS OF SOUTH AMERICAN FROGS		(Trapper THIN 1) 1983
2(A)	PISSED AND PROUD		(No Future PUNK 3) 1982
3(A)	ANOTHER LOUD, NOISY, BLARING PUNK ROCK LP		(Hairy Pie HP 1) 1985
4(A)	SOBERPHOBIA		(Hairy Pie HP 002) 1986

NB: (1) reissued (Trapper CHIN 001) 1985 and on CD (We Bite 3123 CD) 1995. (2) reissued (Roadrunner RR 9938) 1988 and on CD (Dojo DOJO CD 70) 1992 and (No Future CDPUNK 3) 1995. (3) reissued on CD (Dojo DOJO CD 67) 1992 and (We Bite WB 3125 CD) 1995. (4) reissued on CD (We Bite WB 3128 CD) 1995. (5) also issued on CD (Dojo DOJOCD 67) 1994. Their singles are compiled on *The Punk Singles Collection* (Anagram CDPUNK 64) 1995 and also of interest is *Live And Loud* (Street Link LINKCD 108) 1992, *Totally Test Tubed* (Dojo DOJOCD 62) 1992 and again (We Bite WB 3126 CD) 1995 and *The Best Of Peter And The Test Tube Babies* (Dojo DOJOCD 57) 1988, also on vinyl (DOJOLP 57) 1988.

EP:
1(A)	ROTTING IN THE FART-SACK (12")	(Jungle JUNG 21T) 1985

NB: (1) came on white vinyl.

45s:
Banned From The Pubs/Moped Lads/ Peacehaven Wild Lads (PS)	(No Future Oi! 4) 1982
Run Like Hell/Up Yer Bum (PS)	(No Future Oi! 15) 1982
Zombie Creeping Flesh/No Invitation/ Smash And Grab (PS)	(Trapper EARS 1) 1983
Zombie Creeping Flesh/No Invitation/ Smash And Grab (12" PS)	(Trapper 12 EARS 1) 1983
The Jinx/Trapper Ain't Got A Bird (PS)	(Trapper EARS 2) 1983
The Jinx/ Trapper Ain't Got A Bird (12" PS)	(Traper 12 EARS 2) 1983
Pressed For Cash/Blown Out Again (Blender Version)/ Peace And Quiet But Never Dreamed It Was Going To Be Like This * (12" PS)	(Trapper EARFIT 1) 1984
Blown Out Again/ Peace And Quiet (12" PS)	(Trapper ARFITS 1) 1984
Whimpeez/Never Made It (PS)	(Trapper EARS 3) 1985
Keys To The City/Keith Moon (PS)	(Hairy Pie TTB 1) 1986
Keys To The City/Keith Moon/ Work Hard (12" PS)	(Hairy Pie TTB 121) 1986

NB: * This track was credited to Fits.

Peter and The Test Tube Babies hailed from Brighton in 1978. That year their first vinyl excursion came from contributing a track *Elvis Is Dead* to *Vaultage '78 (Two Sides Of Brighton)* (Attrix RB 03) 1978, a compilation of South Coast punk bands. This was later included on *Vaultage Punk Collection* (Anagram CDPUNK 101) 1997.

They gigged solidly around the South Coast circuit but their career only really took off when the onset of Oi! in 1981 gave them a second wind. They contributed two cuts *Rob A Bank (Wanna)* and *Intensive Care* to *Oi! The Album* (EMI ZIT 1) in 1980. It was initially only available by mail order from 'Sounds'. This gave them wider public exposure and helped secure them a John Peel session and a deal with No Future which produced two 45s *Banned From The Pubs* and *Run Like Hell*. *Banned From The Pubs* is certainly one of their finest moments. *Moped Lads* is a bit wilder whilst *Peacehaven Wild Kids* has a punkish beat but quite melodic guitar. All three cuts can also be heard on *Oi! The Singles Collection, Vol. 2* (Captain Oi! AHOY CD 63) 1996. *Banned From The Pubs*, *Peacehaven Wild Kids* and their second 'A' side *Run Like Hell* can also be heard on *No Future - The Punk Singles Collection* (Captain Oi AHOY DLP 512) 1996. *Vol. 2* of the same series (Captain Oi! AHOY DLP 512) 1996 featured *Moped Lads* and their very basic *Up Yer Bum*, which can also be heard on *100% British Oi!* (Captain Oi! AHOY DCD 83) 1997. There was also a live album *Pissed And Proud*, containing many favourites from their stage act like *Keep Britain Untidy* and *Up Yer Bum*, which in common with their early 45s showed up well in the indie charts.

They also contributed *Transvestite* and *Maniac* to *Carry On Oi!* (Secret SEC 2) 1981, which was reissued on CD (Captain Oi! AHOY CD 119) in 1999.

They then set up their own label Trapper Records and released several singles like *Jinx, Zombie Creeping Flesh, Blown Out Again* and *Keys To The City*.

The Punk Singles Collection is a twenty-three track compilation of lowest common denominator punk. Later in 1999, *Maniac* got a further airing on the *Oi! Fuckin' Oi!* (Harry May MAYO CD 110) compilation.

They continued to record throughout the eighties on Jungle and Hairy Pie and were still plying their yobbish and slightly humourous brand of Oi! punk at the end of the nineties.

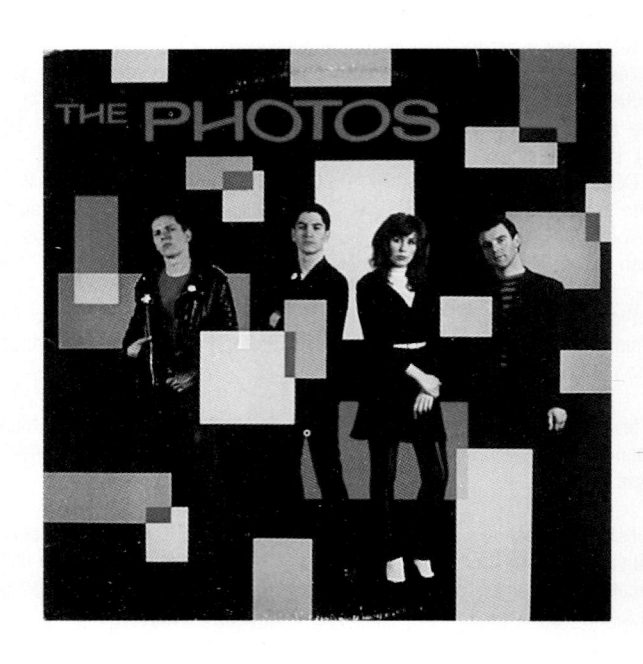

THE PHOTOS - The Photos.

The Photos

Personnel:
STEVE EAGLES	gtr, vcls		AB
OLLY HARRISON	drms		A
DAVE SPARROW	bs, vcls		AB
WENDY WU (WENDY CRUISE)	vcls		A
ANGUS HINES	drms		B

				HCP
ALBUM:	1(A)	THE PHOTOS	(Epic PHOTO 5) 1980	4

NB: (1) came with a free album *The Blackmail Tapes*. There's also a CD (Epic 4916972) 1998.

			HCP
45s:	I'm So Attractive/Guitar Hero (PS)	(CBS CBS 7984) 1979	-
*	Friends/Je T'Aime	(CBS CBS 8785) 1980	-
	Irene/Cridsilla/Barbarells/Shy	(Epic EPC 8517) 1980	56
	Now You Tell Me That We're Through/ Je T'Aime	(Epic EPC 8872) 1980	-
	Life In A Day/ More Than A Friend (PS)	(Epic EPCA 1010) 1981	-
	We'll Win/You Won't Get To Me (PS)	(Epic EPCA 1369) 1981	-
	There's Always Work/Work Phrase (PS)	(Rialto RIA 16) 1983	-

NB: * This 45 was withdrawn soon after release.

The Photos came from Evesham in Worcestershire and comprised a male trio centred around vocalist Wendy Wu and her voice. Steve Eagles, Olly Harrison and Dave Sparrow were previously in an outfit called **Satan's Rats**, who cut three 45s for DJM. They tried originally to attract Jane Casey of **Big In Japan** as their vocalist but later settled for Wendy, whose real name was Wendy Cruise. She'd been born on 29th November 1959 in Winston Green.

Despite the punkish exterior, musically they dished up inane lyrics and likeable but largely unmemorable tunes. Early U.K. pressings of their album came with a bonus disc of their *Blackmail Tapes* from a slightly earlier phase. They are perhaps best remembered for their punkish interpretation of Bacharach/David's *I Just Don't Know What To Do With Myself*.

They fared quite well commercially. Their album made the Top 5 during a nine week stay and they had a minor hit with *Irene*, which peaked at No. 56.

Wendy later embarked on a brief and unsuccessful solo career (three 45s for Epic). Meanwhile **The Photos** reformed briefly in 1983 as a trio with Angus Hines replacing Olly Harrison on drums. It proved a brief reformation, just producing the *There's Always Work* 45 for Rialto. They split again for the last time later in 1983. Wendy formed Strange Cruise and Steve Eagles joined Blurt. Later, in the early nineties, he formed Bang Bang Machine.

The Physicals

Personnel:
STEVE BYE	drms		A
ALEX LEE SHAW	gtr, vcls		AB
STEVE SCHMIDT	gtr		A
CHRISTER SOL	bs		A
ALVIN GIBBS	gtr		B
JOHN TOWE	drms		B

EP:	1(A) ALL SEXED UP (All Sexed Up/Breakdown On Stage/ No Life In The City/You Do Me In) (PS)	(Physical PR 001) 1978

NB: There's also a CD retrospective *Skullduggery* (Overground OVER 80CD) 1999.

45:	Pain In Love/Be Like Me (PS)	(Big Beat NS 58) 1980

The Physicals were put together by Alex Lee Shaw, who'd previously been in **The Rings** and **The Maniacs**. Their *All Sexed Up* EP was released on their own label in 1978. It sold 5,000 copies, which aroused interest from ex-**Sex Pistols** Paul Cook and Steve Jones who offered to produce their next single *Pain In Love / Be Like Me*. Although Jones withdrew at the eleventh hour, Cook not only produced it, he also played drums on it.

By 1980, they had run out of ideas and **Damned** guitarist Brian James invited Shaw to join The Brains along with Alvin Gibbs (ex-**Users**, later of **UK Subs**) and John Towe (ex-**Chelsea** and **Generation X**). when James played with Iggy Pop's band briefly, the remaining Brains reconvened as **The Physicals** to record five new Shaw songs which remained in the can.

The 1999 Overground seventeen-track CD retrospective includes the original line-up's EP and other studio cuts, several good quality studio recordings and the unreleased tracks by the later incarnation.

Shaw was later involved in The Hellions, which was one of Brian James' post-**Damned** ventures. Then, in 1993 Shaw joined a **Damned** reunion.

The Pigs

Personnel:
RICKY GALLI	drms		A
KIT GOULD	gtr		A
EAMONN McANDREW	vcls		A
NIGEL ROBINSON	bs		A

45:	Youthanasia/They Say/Psychopath/ National Front	(Recorder NBR 01) 1977

The Pigs were one of the early punk bands who didn't last the course, despite *National Front* (an anti-National Front song) receiving quite a lot of airplay from John Peel at the time.

THE PIGS - Youthanasia.

Pink Industry

Personnel:
JAYNE CASEY	vcls		A
AMBROSE REYNOLDS	bs, keyb'ds		A

ALBUMS:	1(A)	LOW TECHNOLOGY	(Zulu ZULU 2) 1983
	2(A)	WHO TOLD YOU - YOU WERE NAKED	(Zulu ZULU 4) 1984
	3(A)	NEW BEGINNINGS	(Zulu ZULU 7) 1985

NB: There's also a compilation *Pink Industry* (Cathexis CRL 18) 1988 and a CD *Retrospective* (Parade Amourese CONCATH 001 CD) 1989.

45s:	Is This The End?/47/Don't Let Go/ Final Cry (12, PS)	(Zulu ZULU 1) 1982
	What I Wouldn't Give/	(Zulu RA 8) 1985

After Liverpool-based **Pink Military** split, vocalist Jayne Casey, who'd also been with **Big In Japan** back in the late seventies, teamed up with Ambrose Reynolds (who'd later be in an early Frankie Goes To Hollywood line-up) in **Pink Industry**. Their debut 45 *Is This The End?* was extremely promising and the band produced music that was ethereal, haunting and at times original. Their reputation was consolidated further through their *Low Technology* and *Who Told You - You Were Naked* albums. The later introduced new studio techniques, a wider range of instruments and was quite eastern-influenced.

They returned in 1985 with *New Beginnings* and an accompanying 45 *What I Wouldn't Give*, which had a photograph of Morissey on the picture sleeve.

After this they faded from attention but there are a couple of retrospective compilations outlined in the discography and they are certainly worth investigating if you're not familiar with their music.

Pink Military

Personnel:
CHARLIE	keyb'ds	A
JAYNE CASEY	vcls	A
CHRIS JOYCE	drms	A
MARTIN	gtr, bs	A
NEIL	perc	A
NICKY	gtr, synth	A

ALBUM:	1(A)	DO ANIMALS BELIEVE IN GOD	(Virgin/ERIC'S 004) 1980
EP:	1(A)	BUDDHA WALKING DISNEY SLEEPING (Degenerated Man/Sanjo Kantara/Clown Town/Heaven Hell) (fold-out sleeve)	(Last Trumpet LT 001) 1979
	2(A)	BLOOD AND LIPSTICK (12" die-cut PS)	(Eric's ERIC'S 002) 1979
45:		Did You See Her?/Everyday	(Eric's ERIC'S 005) 1980

Pink Military were part of the new wave of Liverpool bands in the late seventies and early eighties. They were formed by Jayne Casey after **Big In Japan** split in 1978. The following year they cut a couple of EPs. Their album covered a range of different styles and is reasonable but not essential listening. *I Cry* is a soft haunting song. *Did You See Her?* also released as a 45, is commercial but less interesting. Side Two is much more experimental with tracks like *Living In A Jungle*, *Dreamtime*, *War Games*, *Heaven/Hell* and it culminates with the haunting title track, which is really quite enticing.

Suzi Pinns

45s:	Rule Britannia/Jerusalem (PS)	(Polydor 2001 770) 1978
	Jerusalem/(flip by **The Man-eaters**)	(E.G. Editions EGO 8) 1982

Suzi Pinns is best remembered for contributing *Rule Britannia* and *Jerusalem* to the *Jubilee* (Polydor/E.G. 2302 079) original soundtrack album in 1977.

Pin Point

Personnel:
DAVID ALLEN	bs	A
ARTURO BASSICK (A.P. BILLINGSLEY)	gtr, vcls	A
HUGH GRIFFITHS	drms	A
I.P. HARTNELL	keyb'ds	A
MOSLEY	keyb'ds	A
MARTIN RUSHENT	keyb'ds	A

ALBUM:	1(A)	THIRD STATE	(Albion ALB 103) 1980

NB: (1) came with a free EP.

45s:	Richmond/Love Substitute (PS)	(Albion DEL 8) 1979
	Waking Up To Morning/ Floods And Trickles (PS)	(Albion ION 1002) 1980
	Yo Yo/ Drowning In The Wave Of Life (PS)	(Albion ION 1007) 1981

A three-piece outfit from Fulham. They featured ex-**Lurker** Arturo on guitar.

The Piranhas

Personnel:
MIKE COOK	violin	A
JOHNNY HELMER	gtr	A
RICHARD MYHILL	keyb'ds	A
GRAHAM PRESKETT	violin	A
DICK SLEXIA	drms	A
ZOOT	sax	A

ALBUM:	1(A)	THE PIRANHAS	HCP (Sire SRK 6098) 1980 69

NB: (1) originally recorded for Attrix (RB 09) 1979, but unreleased. Also relevant is *The Attrix* CD (Anagram CDMGRAM 115) 1997.

45s:	Jilly/Coloured Music (PS)	HCP (Attrix RB 4) 1980 -
	Yap Yap Yap/Happy Families (PS)	(Attrix RB 6) 1980 -
	Tom Hark/Getting Beaten Up/ Boyfriend (PS)	(Sire SIR 4044) 1980 6
	I Don't Want My Body/Well Away (PS)	(Sire SIR 4046) 1980 -
	Viglegele/Nobody (PS)	(Dakota DAK 2) 1981 -
*	Zambezi/Who Needs You/ Darabukkus (PS)	(Dakota DAK 6) 1982 17
	Easy Come, Easy Go/ Waste Of Space (PS)	(Dakota DAK 9) 1983 -

NB: * **The Piranhas** featuring Boring Bob Grover.

A marginal case for inclusion are **The Piranhas** from the south coast of England. They rose to a degree of prominence as part of the punk/new wave movement but musically they veered more towards light-hearted ska in the vein of early Madness and Bad Manners, who you won't read about in this book. Their vinyl debut came when they contributed three cuts; *Tension*, *Virginity* and *I Don't Want My Body* to *Vaultage '78 (Two Sides Of Brighton)* (Attrix RB 03) in 1978. The use of saxophone on these cuts sets them appart from the other material on the compilation. *Virginity* is quite an amusing diatribe about the vocalist desperate to lose his and *I Don't Want My Body* developed their lighthearted ska vein. They recorded an unreleased album for Attrix in 1979, but the material was later put out on Sire in 1980. Some of their songs were rooted in the instrumental sound of the sixties. Their album sold quite well climbing to No. 69 during a three week stay. They spent twelve weeks in the singles charts peaking at No. 6 with *Tom Hark*, whilst a later effort *Zambesi* credited to **The Piranhas** featuring Boring Bob Grover made No. 17 during a nine week stay. Their lyrics were quite humourous and their songs addressed slightly offbeat subjects with titles like *Getting Beaten Up* and *I Don't Want My Body*.

Four of their songs *Jilly*, *Virginity*, *Tension* and *Happy Families* later resurfaced on *Vaultage Punk Collection* (Anagram CDPUNK 101) in 1997.

The Attrix CD comprises demos for their self-titled 1980 album for Sire.

Placebo

Personnel:
GARY WILD	A
MICHELLE WILD	A

ALBUMS:	1(A)	ENGLAND'S TRANCE	(Aura AUL 721) 1982
	2(A)	SHELLS	(Aura AUL 725) 1982

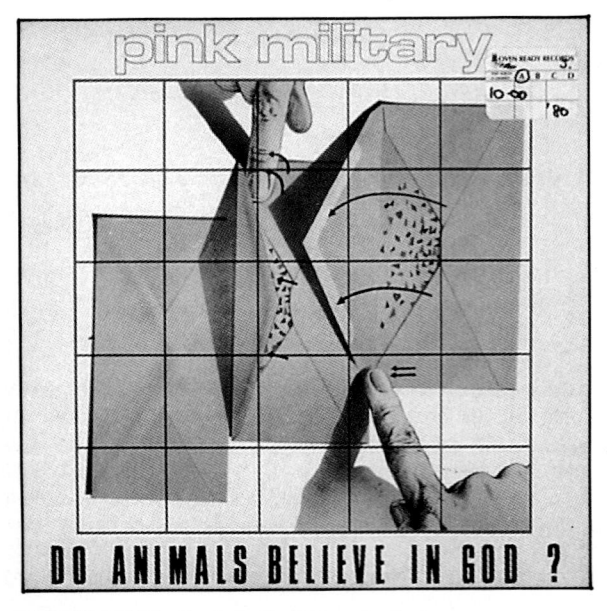

PINK MILITARY - Do Animals Believe In God.

THE PIRANHAS live at The Camden Palace, London 22nd July 1980.

NB: (1) also issued on CD (See For Miles SEEECD 488) 1998. (2) also issued on CD (See For Miles SEECD 489) 1998.

| 45: | Poppy Dance/Punishing Pierrot (PS) | (Aura AUS 33) 1982 |

An early eighties indie band, critically acclaimed at the time who included elements of **Siouxsie and The Banshees**, **Cocteau Twins** and **Gary Numan** in their cold, gently mysterious 'New Romantic' sound.

Plain Characters

Personnel: JOHN HYDE
MATT JOHNSON
COLIN TUCKER

| ALBUM: | 1(A) | INVISIBLE YEARNINGS | (Abstract Sounds ABT 001) 1983 |

45s:	I Am A/Very Peculiar Julia	(Rouge RMSPC 1) 1977
	Man In The Railings/O (PS)	(Final Solution FS 001) 1979
	Menial Tasks/	
	Conversation Piece (PS)	(Abstract Sounds ABS 5) 1981

This band, which never progressed beyond minor label releases was linked to **The Gadgets**. Matt Johnson also later fronted **The The**.

Plastic Bertrand

Personnel: ELTON MOTELLO vcls A

ALBUMS:	1(A)	AN I	(Sire 9103 258) 1978
	2(A)	CA PLANE POUR MOI (compilation)	
			(Repulic REPL 4331) 1993

HCP

45s:	Ca Plane Pour Moi/Pogo Pogo	(Sire 6078 616) 1978 8
	Sha La La La Lee/Naif Song	(Vertigo 6059 209) 1978 39
	C'est Le Rock 'n' Roll/Affection	(Vertigo 6059 215) 1978 -
*	Tout Petite La Planete/Je Fait Un Plan/	
	Hit 78	(Sire SIR 4012) 1979 -

NB: * Also issued in 12" format.

Plastic Bertrand's real name was Roger Jouret. The pretty blonde Belgian is included here because his records became a part of the U.K. punk scene. With producer and songwriter Lou Deprijck, he conjured up the persona of **Plastic Bertrand** very much in the safety-pin image of punk. Jouret had previously been drummer in a Belgian punk trio called Hubble Bubble, who had specialised in doing offbeat versions of old classics.

Plastic Bertrand will always be best remembered for *Ca Plane Pour Moi (This Life's For Me)*. The song featured **Bertrand** singing nonsensical French lyrics over a classic punkish three-chord drone with wailing saxes and falsetto "ooh-wee-ooh". It worked perfectly taking the 45 to No. 8 during an eight week chart stay in spring 1978. The song got a further airing on *20 Of Another Kind* (Polydor SUPER POLS 1006) in 1979. The catchy song which becomes irritating after a few plays was included on his debut album, which also included a lively cover of The Small Faces' *Sha La La La Lee*. This was culled for a follow-up 45 and also climbed to No. 39 during a five week stay.

He went on to put out other albums in Belgium and Canada which aren't really relevant here. The best introduction to his music is the *Greatest Hits* collection which compiles all his European hits, but don't get excited 'cos it's mostly pop.

Plastix

Personnel:	MARK HOGGINS	drms	A
	HUGGY LEAVER	vcls	A
	NICK SAYER	gtr	A
	MARK WILMSHURST	bs	A

From the Brighton and Hastings areas **Plastix** formed in mid-1977. They are best known for *Tough On You*, their contribution to *Farewell To The Roxy* (Lightning LIP 2) 1978, which was recently reissued on CD (Captain Oi! AHOY CD 86) 1998. *Tough On You* is a snarling garage-punker. They appeared with **The Crabs** at London's Marquee but then disappeared from the scene.

In 1978, Sayer and Wilmshurst resurfaced in Fan Club. Sayer went on to play with The Kempton Rockers and Midnight & The Lemon Boys, before achieving success in Transvision Vamp. Leaver went on to play in the mod combo **The Teenbeats**, whilst Mark Hoggins joined **Peter and The Test Tube Babies**, whom he stayed with for several years.

Play Dead

Personnel:	STEVE GREEN	A
	ROB HICKSON	A
	WIFF SMITH	A
	PETE WADDLETON	A

ALBUMS:	1(A)	THE FIRST FLOWER	(Jungle FREUD 3) 1984
	2(A)	FROM THE PROMISED LAND	(Clay CLAYLP 11) 198?
	3(A)	INTO THE FIRE	(Clay CLAYLP 16) 1985
	4(A)	COMPANY OF JUSTICE	(Tanz TANZLP 1) 1985
	5(A)	SINGLES '82 - '85	(Clay CLAYLP 20) 1986
	6(A)	CAUGHT FROM BEHIND	(Dojo DOJOLP 34) 1986
	7(A)	FINAL EPITAPH	(Jungle FREUD 15) 1987

NB: (4) also issued on CD (Jungle FREUDCD 041) 1993. There are also two CD compilations *First Flower* (Cleopatra CLEO 7519CD) 1994 and *Resurrection* (Clay CLAYCD 111) 1994.

45s:	Poison Takes A Hold/Introduction (PS)	(Fresh FRESH 29) 1981
	TV Eye/Final Epitaph (PS)	(Fresh FRESH 38) 1981
	Propaganda/Propaganda (Mix) (PS)	(Jungle JUNGLE 002) 1983
	Shine/Promise (PS)	(Situation 2 SIT 28) 1983
	Shine/Promise/Gaze (12", PS)	(Situation 2 SIT 28T) 1983

Break/Blood Stains (PS)	(Clay CLAY 31)	1984
Break/Blood Stains/Pleasure (12", PS)	(Clay 12 CLAY 31)	1984
Isabel/Solace (PS)	(Clay CLAY 35)	1984
Isabel/Solace (12", PS)	(Clay 12CLAY 35)	1984
* This Side Of Heaven	(Tanz TANZ 1)	1985

NB: * Unissued, but some white label promotional copies did get into circulation.

A new wave combo from Banbury, Oxfordshire, whose synthesizer-dominated music is worth a listen. After two 45s for Fresh, they switched to Jungle for the *Propaganda* 45 (probably their best known song) and a six track album *The First Flower*, which included *Propaganda*. Musically, this is quite interesting and challenging. They made further albums for Clay in particular and 45s for Situation 2 and Clay but never broke big.

One of their songs *Poison Takes A Hold* can also be heard on *Fresh Records Punk Singles Collection* (Anagram CDPUNK 32) 1994, whilst *Tenant* got a further airing on *In Goth Daze* (Anagram CDGRAM 89) 1998.

The Pleasers

Personnel:	BO BENHAM	bs	A
	STEVE McNERNEY	vcls, gtr	A
	NICK POWELL	gtr	A
	DAVE ROTSHELLE	drms	A

45s:	You Know What I'm Thinking/ Hello Little Girl	(Solid Gold SGR 104) 1977
	A Girl I Know/ Don't Go Breaking My Heart (PS)	(Arista ARIST 21) 1977
	You Keep Tellin' Lies/I'm In Love/ Who Are You (PS)	(Arista ARIST 180) 1978
	You Don't Know/Billy (PS)	(Arista ARIST 209) 1978

The Pleasers were one of a handful of early 1978 'beat boom' bands who replicated pre-*Rubber Soul* Beatles music on the London pub circuit. Fun for a short while. When the novelty wore off they went onto the cabaret circuit.

Plugs

EPs:	1( )	PLUGROCK (Too Late/UFO/Sally) (PS)	(Cathedral CATH 1) 1979
	2( )	CRACKIN' UP (Crackin' Up/Watching The Box/ Hard Work Never Hurt Anybody)	(Plug Pop POP 1) 1981

NB: (1) was issued in a gatefold picture sleeve.

45:	Indoor Shopping Centre/ High Society (PS)	(Gargoyle GRGL 782) 1981

A Lincoln band, who specialised in what they called Plug Rock. These EPs were released independently. Even the label and sleeve of the first was all their own work.

Plummet Airlines

Personnel:	RICHARD BOOTH	gtr	A
	KEITH GOTHERIDGE	drms	A
	DARYL HUNT	bs	A
	DUNCAN KERR	gtr	A
	HARRY STEVENSON	vcls, gtr	A

45s:	Silver Shirt/This Is The World (PS)	(Stiff BUY 8) 1976
	It's Hard/My Time In A While (PS)	(State STAT 66) 1977

In addition to these 45s, **Plummet Airlines** also recorded two sessions for John Peel. The first, on 14th September 1976, comprised *Don't Give A Damn*, *You're Keeping Us Talking*, *Water To Wine* and *Stars Will Shine*. The second, on 28th February 1977, featured *Our Last Dance*, *Call Out The Engine Driver*, *Since I Left You* and *Dr. Boogie*.

POISON GIRLS - Fatal Microbes Meet The Poison Girls EP.

Pneumonia

Personnel:	NIGEL PORKE	perc	A
	STEVE SPON	gtr	A
	STEVE VOICE	bs	A
	SNO WHITE (GAYNOR)	vcls	A

EP:	1(A)	Exhibition/Coming Attack/(2 cuts by **U.K. Decay**) (PS)	(Plastic PLAS 001) 1979

A Luton punk band. They and another local band **U.K. Decay** both contributed two cuts to this EP, which was issued in a folded picture sleeve. Steve Spon was also in **U.K. Decay**.

Poems

EP:	1( )	ACHIEVING UNITY (2 versions)	(Polka DOT 1) 1981

The Poems hailed from Glasgow and contained half of what would become the female duo Strawberry Switchblade. In addition to this EP, they released a C15 cassette on Life Like Comfort and contributed *Posters On The Wall* to the compilation *Spectacular Commodity* (Groucho Marxist WH 1).

Poison Girls

Personnel:	LANCE D'BOYLE	drms	A
	RICHARD FAMOUS	gtr	A
	BERNHARDT REBOURS	bs	A
	VI SUBVERSA	vcls	A

ALBUMS:	1(A)	CHAPPAQUIDICK BRIDGE	(Crass 421984/2) 1980
	2(A)	TOTAL EXPOSURE (live)	(Xntrix XN) 1981
	3(A)	WHERE'S THE PLEASURE	(Xntrix XN 2006) 1982
	4(A)	7 YEAR SCRATCH	(Xntrix RM 101) 1984

NB: (1) was issued with a free flexidisc *Statement* (421984/7). (2) was pressed on clear vinyl in a transparent sleeve. There were also three important CD compilations; *Poisonous* (2 CD set) (Snapper SMDCD 137) 1998, *Statement (The Complete Recordings 1977-89)* (2 CD set) (Cooking Vinyl COOKCD 087) 1997 and *Their Finest Moments* (Nectar NTMCD 541) 1997 and (Reactive REMCD 503) 1998.

EPs:	1(A)	FATAL MICROBES MEET THE POISON GIRLS (Closed Shop/Piano Lessons)	(Small Wonder WEENY 3) 1979
	2(A)	HEX	(Small Wonder WEENY 4) 1979

45s:	+	Persons Unknown/ (other side by **Crass**) (PS)	(Crass/Xntrix 421984/1) 1980
	*	Pretty Polly/Bully Boys (live)	(Crass 421984/10) 1981
		All Systems Go/Promenade Immortelle/ Dirty Work (PS with lyrics)	(Crass 421984/8) 1981
		One Good Reason/	

Cinnamon Gardens (PS)	(Illuminated ILL 23)	1983
Are You Happy Now?/ Cream Dream (PS)	(Illuminated ILL 25)	1983
Are You Happy Now?/Cream Dream	(Reekus RKS 11)	1984
Are You Happy Now?/ Toys For The Boys (12")	(Illuminated ILL 312)	1984
I'm Not A Real Woman/ Take The Toys From The Boys (PS)	(Xntrix XN 2009)	1984
I'm Not A Real Woman/Take The Toys From The Boys/ Tension/Perfect Crime (12")	(Xntrix 12XN 2009)	1984
Are You Happy Now?/Menage Abatoir And Whiskey Voice (12")	(Illuminated ILL 312)	1985
The Price Of Grain	(Upright UPT 12)	1985

NB: + This 45 came in a folded 21" by 14" poster picture sleeve. The reverse side featured *Bloody Revolutions* by **Crass**. * This item appeared in a square red or clear flexidisc free with 'In The City' fanzine.

The Poison Girls were one of the more politicized bands of the punk era. They used their music to get across their social and sexual points in an intelligent and subtle as opposed to sloganist way. Their name bordered on the ironic as their sole female, vocalist Vi Subversa, was a middle-aged woman and the other three members were men.

Forming in 1977, their first vinyl offering came in May 1979. They contributed two cuts - *Closed Shop* and *Piano Lessons* - to a Small Wonder EP shared with **The Fatal Microbes**. In fact the Microbes' guitarist Pete Fender was Subversa's son!

They followed this with a 12" eight-cut EP for Small Wonder.

In 1980, they developed a close association with another highly politicised band, the anarchic **Crass**. **The Poison Girls** provided *Persons Unknown* on the reverse of **Crass'** *Bloody Revolutions* 45. Their debut album *Chappaquidick Bridge* came out on Crass' label in 1981 accompanied by a free flexi disc entitled *Statement*. The music on the album is abrasive, inaccessible and often unnerving but it won much acclaim among alternative music circles. It showed up well in the indie charts as did a further 45 *All Systems Go*.

In 1981, the band established their own label Xntrix. They released a live album *Total Exposure* which appeared on clear vinyl inside a transparent plastic sleeve. This live album included some of the songs from their earlier studio effort, but in an even less accessible format.

Where's The Pleasure, in 1982, was less political and more accessible musically as Subversa turned her attention to more sexual matters. The album also served to showcase her vocal talents, which were developed further on their final effort *Songs Of Praise*.

In the mid-nineties the box CD set *Statement* was released to document their output. They also played a one-off re-formation gig in London in June 1995.

The Police

Personnel:	STEWART COPELAND	drms, vcls	AB
	HENRY PADOVANI	gtr, vcls	A
	STING (GORDON SUMNER)	vcls, bs	AB
	ANDREW SUMMERS (SOMERS)	gtr	B

					HCP
ALBUMS:	1(B)	OUTLANDOS D'AMOUR	(A&M AMLH 86502)	1978	6
(up to	2(B)	REGGATTA DE BLANC	(A&M AMLH 64792)	1979	1
1986)	3(B)	ZENYATTA MONDATTA	(A&M AMLH 64831)	1980	1
	4(B)	GHOST IN THE MACHINE	(A&M AMLK 63730)	1981	1
	5(B)	SYNCHRONICITY	(A&M AMLX 63735)	1983	1
	6(B)	EVERY BREATH YOU TAKE - THE SINGLES	(A&M EVERY 1)	1986	1

NB: (1) early copies came on blue vinyl. (1) reissued on CD (A&M CDA 68502) 1989, but deleted in 1990. Reissued again (A&M CDMID 126) 1991 and on vinyl (Vivante VPLP 003) 1999. (2) reissued on CD (A&M CDA 64792) 1979, but deleted in 1990. Reissued again (A&M CDMID 127) 1992. (3) reissued on CD (A&M CDA 64831) 1986 but deleted in 1990. Reissued again (A&M CDMID 128) 1992. (4) reissued on CD (A&M CDA 63730) 1983, but deleted in 1991. Reissued again (A&M CDMID 162) 1992. (5) reissued on CD (A&M CDA 63735) 1983, but later deleted. Reissued again (A&M CDMID 186) 1993. (6) reissued on CD (A&M EVECD 1) 1986, but deleted in 1992. (6) reissued again on CD (Vivante 1053-DTS)

THE POLICE - Can't Stand Losing You.

2000. There are also two significant compilations *Message In A Box* (4-CD set) (A&M 5401502) 1993 and *The Police Live* (2-CD set) (A&M 5402222) 1995. Finally, there are three Various Artists CD tributes to the band *Outlandos D'Americas (A Rock En Espanol Tribute To The Police)* (Ark 21 1539112) 2000, *Regatta Mondatta* (Virgin VTCD 147) 1997 and *The Very Best Of Regatta Mondatta* (Ark 21 1539082) 2000.

				HCP
45s:		Fall Out/Nothing Achieving (PS)	(Illegal IL 001)	1977 -
(up to	*	Roxanne/Peanuts (PS)	(A&M AMS 7348)	1978 -
1986)	o	Can't Stand Losing You/ Dead End Job (PS)	(A&M AMS 7381)	1978 42
	o	So Lonely/Time This Time (PS)	(A&M AMS 7402)	1978 6
	+	Roxanne/Peanuts (PS)	(A&M AMS 7348)	1979 12
	#	Can't Stand Losing You/ Dead End Job (PS)	(A&M AMS 7381)	1979 2
	x	Message In A Bottle/Landlord (PS)	(A&M AMS 7474)	1979 1
	χ*	Walking On The Moon/ Visions Of The Night (PS)	(A&M AMS 7494)	1979 1
		Fall Out/Nothing Achieving	(Illegal IL 001)	1979 47
	α	POLICE PACK	(A&M AMPP 6001)	1980 17
	##	SIX-TRACK RADIO SAMPLER (PS)	(A&M SAMP 5)	1980 -
	o	Don't Stand So Close To Me/ Friends (poster PS)	(A&M AMS 7564)	1980 1
	o	De Do Do Do, De Da Da Da/A Sermon	(A&M AMS 7578)	1980 5
		Invisible Sun/Shamelle (PS)	(A&M AMS 8164)	1981 2
		Every Little Thing She Does Is Magic/ Flexible Strategies (PS)	(A&M AMS 8174)	1981 1
		Spirits (In The Material World)/Low Life (poster PS, some with badge)	(A&M AMS 8194)	1981 12
		Every Breath You Take/Murder By Numbers (PS, with free badge)	(A&M AM 117)	1983 1
		Every Breath You Take/Murder By Numbers/ Truth Hits Everybody/Man In A Suitcase (double pack, gatefold PS)	(A&M AM 117/AM 01)	1983
		Every Breath You Take/Murder By Numbers (picture disc)	(A&M AM 117)	1983 -
	β	Wrapped Around Your Fingers/ Someone To Talk To	(A&M AM 127)	1983 7
		Synchronicity II/Once Upon A Dream	(A&M AM 153)	1983 17
		King Of Pain/Tea In The Sahara	(A&M AM 176)	1984 17
		Don't Stand So Close To Me/ (live version)	(A&M AM 354)	1986 24
		Roxanne '86/Synchronicty II	(A&M)	1986 -

NB: * 7" issued in 'telephone' picture sleeve. Also issued as a 12" with 'telephone' picture sleeve. o Also issued as a 7" shaped picture disc. + Reissue with a 'group' picture sleeve. # Reissue in red, yellow, green or white vinyl - some copies had a mispressed 'B'-side which played *No Time This Time*. x Issued on green vinyl and also as a 7" shaped picture disc. χ Also issued as a 12". α This comprised a 6x7" printed PVC featuring AMS 7348, AMS 7381, AMS 7402, AMS 7474, AMS 7494 and *The Bed's Too Big Without You/Truth Hits Everybody*. ## This was a promotional radio sampler which appeared in a custom picture sleeve. β Versions of this were issued with a 'Sting' picture disc, and 1,000 copies each were done with Andy Summers and Stewart Copeland picture discs.

Like **Elvis Costello** and others **The Police**'s association with the punk scene at the start of their career helped them model their image, sound and musical direction. It helped propel them to the megastars they later became.

The Police were formed in London early in 1977 by Stewart Copeland, Sting (real name Gordon Sumner) and Henry Padovani. Copeland was actually a U.S. citizen. He'd been born in Alexandria, Egypt, on 16th July 1952. He was previously the drummer in U.K. progressive rock combo Curved Air. Gordon Sumner was born on 2nd October 1951 at Wallsend, Northumberland. He'd previously worked as a primary school teacher and had played in a jazz outfit called Last Exit. The third member Henry Padovani had been born in Corsica.

Stewart Copeland's brother Miles was the manager of Curved Air at the time. He had lots of connections in the music industry and this worked out to **The Police**'s advantage. They began rehearsing at Copeland's Mayfair studio on 12th January 1977. A month later they recorded their debut 45 *Fall Out* at Pathway Studios. The two sides cost just £150 to record. Miles Copeland put it out on his indie label Illegal in May 1977. This disc had a strong punk influence and got into the indie chart. Miles Copeland ensured too that with their spiky blonde-haired image they had a punkish image as a band which identified them clearly as part of the new wave. This was a crucial factor in their rapid rise to fame.

In late February 1977 they went to New York to rehearse with U.S. singer **Cherry Vanilla** with a view to backing her on a forthcoming U.K. tour. The tour kicked off on 3rd March at the Roxy Club in London's Covent Garden. Also on the bill were Johnny Thunders and The Heartbreakers. The tour helped promote the band to a wider audience. They followed it with a tour of Holland on 19th March supporting **Wayne County and The Electric Chairs**.

THE POLICE - Outlandos D'Amour.

Shortly after the release of their *Fall Out* single in May, Stewart Copeland and Sting were invited by Gong member Mike Howlett to join veteran guitarist Andy Summers in a live band called Strontium 90. Andy Summers was a decade older than the others. His name at birth, on 31st December, 1942 in Poulton Le Fylde, Lancashire was Andrew Somers, but he had changed the surname during his musical career. He had played extensively with bands and artists like Kevin Ayers, Eric Burdon, Keith Coyne, Soft Machine and Zoot Money who turned psychedelic for a while as Dantalian's Chariot. Summers brought an echo unit to the band which combined effectively with Copeland's inverted reggae drum style to provide a very distinctive and powerful rhythm section to supplement Sting's vocal style.

The Police gigged briefly as a foursome when, after playing at London's Marquee Club in June 1977, Andy Summers was added to the line-up. However, two days after a recording session on 10th August with John Cale handling the production Henry Padovani decided to leave the band. He went on to form The Flying Padovani Brothers. The new trio's first gig was at Rebecca's in Birmingham on 18th August. Four days later they headed off to Munich in Germany, where they recorded and played with Eberhand Schoener who was working on his *Video Flashback* album for EMI.

THE POLICE - Roxanne.

In January 1978, the band started recording their debut album. Then in March Miles Copeland arranged for them to support Spirit on a U.K. tour he was organising for them.

By now they were sporting the spiky dyed blonde hair image, which had first surfaced in an advert for Wrigley's chewing gum the previous month. This ensured they became associated with U.K. punk.

The band signed to A&M in March 1978. Their debut 45 *Roxanne* showcased their unique rhythm sound. It was full of clever riffs and rhythms. Arguably, it was one of the best things they did. It was well received in the music press, but didn't chart largely because they were working with Schoener's Laser Theatre in Germany and weren't here in the U.K. to help promote it.

In July 1978, Copeland recorded *Don't Care* under the name **Klark Kent** along with a 10" album on green vinyl. This also failed to make the charts.

With Sting, who'd previously appeared in many TV commercials, taking part in the filming of The Who's 'Quadrophenia' in which he played Ace, a second **Police** 45 was issued. *I Can't Stand Losing You* took the band into the charts climbing to No. 42 during a five week stay. In many respects, particularly the catchy rhythm sound, it was similar to *Roxanne*.

After appearing on Radio 1's "Kid Jensen Show" on 16th October 1978, **The Police** set off on their first U.S. tour. It commenced with an appearance at New York prestigious new wave venue CBGB's.

Soon after their return to England their debut album *Outlandos D'amour* was released and one of its tracks *So Lonely* was released as a 45. The album was a fair start. The stand-out tracks were their earlier 45s *Roxanne* (whose flip side *Peanuts* was also included), *Can't Stand Losing You* and *So Lonely*. The opening cut *Next To You* was quite punkish. *Hole In My Life* was punchy with quite catchy rhythms. The final cut *Masoko Tanga* confirmed their interest in white reggae, but *Be My Girl-Sally* with its spoken section was an unfortunate inclusion which certainly didn't enhance the album, which got to No. 6 and went on to spend an incredible ninety-six weeks in the charts.

In February 1979, they started work on a second album. This was interrupted in early March when they set off on a twenty-nine-date U.S. tour, which commenced at L.A.'s 'Whisky A Go Go'. Whilst they were away their first two A&M singles were re-released to cash-in on their growing popularity. With *Roxanne* climbing up the charts, to No. 12 this time during a nine week stay, they made their first appearance on 'Top Of The Pops' on 25th April. They returned to the U.S. for a third tour where *Roxanne* had reached No. 32 and the *Outlandos D'amour* album peaked at No. 23.

In June **The Police** embarked on their first headlining U.K. tour and they were a prime attraction at the Reading Rock Festival that year. Encouraged by the success of *Roxanne* after its reissue, A&M decided to re-release *Can't Stand Losing You*. This time it climbed to No. 2 during August 1979, as part of a new eleven week stay. With 'Quadrophenia' being premiered the same month Sting was much in demand as an actor. He turned down a number of film offers, including to play the villain in the James Bond 'For Your Eyes Only', to concentrate on the band, which was now on the brink of stardom.

In September 1979, *Message In A Bottle* was released as their next 45. Broadly similar in style to its predecessors it was extremely catchy and very accessible. Within two weeks of release it was topping the charts, in which it spent eleven weeks. Surprisingly it only got to No. 74 when released in the 'States. During September the group played an eleven date U.K. tour and then crossed to the 'States for a two month tour, commencing at New York's Diplomat Hotel. Whilst on the tour **The Police** recorded a video, for their forthcoming single *Walking On The Moon*, at the Kennedy Space Center in Houston, Texas.

Their second album, *Reggatta De Blanc*, which they co-produced with Nigel Gray, was dominated by *Message In A Bottle*. Overall, the material on this album wasn't as strong as its predecessor, but it did include *Walking On The Moon* which gave them another U.K. No. 1 when released as 45. With **The Police** now at the height of their popularity the album's sales were very good. It spent four weeks at No. 1 in Britain during a total stay of seventy-four weeks. In the 'States the album was released as a double 10" album and climbed to No. 25. In Britain, *Fall Out*, originally released by Illegal back in 1977, was reissued. This time it made it into the charts, though only as high as No. 47.

In January 1980, **The Police** embarked on their first World Tour. Opening in Buffalo, New York State, it covered nineteen countires in all, ending in Newcastle where they played two charity gigs for the Northumberland Association Of Boys Clubs.

So Lonely, a cut from their first album originally issued as a 45 in October 1978, was reissued in February 1980. This time it climbed to No. 6 in the charts in which it spent ten weeks in all.

In June, a collection of the first five **Police** singles were issued on blue vinyl as part of a *Six Pack*. The sixth disc featured *The Bed's Too Big Without You* (from their *Regatta De Blanc* album) and *Truth Hits Everybody*.

With Sting and Summers now living in Eire as tax exiles **The Police** began work on their third album in Hilversum, Holland. They returned to Britain to headline the "Regatta De Bowl" charity gig held at Milton Keynes in Bedfordshire. On 8th August, they set off on a months tour of Europe. It kicked off at the Wechter Festival in Belgium.

In September, their next 45 *Don't Stand So Close To Me* was issued. Another of their direct and instantly accessible songs it spent four weeks at No. 1 during a ten week chart stay. In April 1981, it also reached No. 10 in the 'States. The song was one of the highlights of their *Zenyatta Mondatta* album, released in October 1980. Produced by the band and Nigel Gray, the album featured some excellent instrumentation and musicianship. However, some of the lyrics were becoming a little too sugary and inane as evidenced by *De Do Do Do, De Da Da Da*. The album was another big success commercially, topping the charts for four weeks during a thirty-one week stay. It also became their first to make the U.S. Top Ten, peaking at No. 5. The title cut was later voted the Best Rock Instrumental Performance at the 23rd Grammy Awards the following February.

The Police continued to tour extensively - a thirty-three date tour of North America in October/November 1980 was followed by three concerts in Argentina in December. Then, in January 1981, they set off on a two-month World Tour taking in North America, Japan, Australia and New Zealand.

THE POLICE - Spirits (In The Material World).

Because of its accessibility *De Do Do Do, De Da Da Da* was put out as a 45 in December 1980. It is the type of song one could tire of quickly and it's worth noticing that it wasn't the usual No. 1. It did still reach No. 5 in the U.K. and No. 10 in the United States, though.

They changed producers for their fourth album with Hugh Padgham replacing Nigel Gray as co-producer. It was recorded at AIR studios in the Caribbean island of Montserrat. The project was filmed by the BBC, presented by **Squeeze**'s Jools Holland and shown on air the forthcoming Christmas.

Invisible Sun, about the Northern Irish troubles, was selected for 45 release in September to preview the album. It stalled at No. 2 in Britain, but only because it was kept off the top spot by **Adam and The Ants**' *Prince Charming*. The 45 spent eight weeks in the charts overall. When the *Ghost In The Machine* was released in October it spent three weeks at No. 1 in the U.K. during a twenty-seven week stay. In January 1982, it started a six week stint at No. 2 in the 'States. **The Police** were now megastars and this was very much a mainstream rock album. It spawned two further hit singles; *Every Little Thing She Does Is Magic* (U.K. No. 1, U.S. No. 3) and *Spirits In The Material World* (U.K. No. 12, U.S. No. 11). A fourth cut, *Secret Journey* was released as 45 in the 'States only, where it climbed to No. 46.

1982 was generally a quiter year for the band. At the 24th Grammy Awards on 29th February, they won Best Rock Vocal Performance For A Duo Or Group for *Don't Stand So Close To Me* and Best Rock Instrumental Performance for *Behind My Camel*, a track on *Zenyatta Mondatta*. They played alongside Fleetwood Mac, Talking Heads and others at the U.S. Festival in San Bernadino, California. Generally, though, with a lull in proceedings, members concentrated on solo projects. In September Sting released his first solo single, a new version of *Spread A Little Happiness* from the soundtrack of 'Brimstone And Treacle'. It got into the U.K. Top 20. Andy Summers teamed up with Robert Fripp (of King Crimson) to release an instrumental album *I Advanced Mask* in October.

In May 1983, *Every Breath You Take*, was released as a 45 from their forthcoming album *Synchronicity II*. The Sting song about obsessive love was an absolute classic. It spent four weeks on top of the charts in Britain, during an eleven week stay. In the 'States, it topped the charts for no less than eight weeks. The song had numerous awards heaped on it. It was named Billboard's Top Single Of The Year and awarded Best Group Video at the Second Annual American Video Awards. At the Grammy's it was named Song Of The Year and Best Pop Performance By A Duo Or Group With Vocal. *Synchronicity II* was an enormous commercial success. It topped the album charts here for two weeks in a forty-eight week stay, but in the 'States topped the charts for an incredible seventeen weeks. It also spawned three further hit singles:-- *Wrapped Around Your Finger* (U.K. No. 7, U.S. No. 8), the title cut (U.K. No. 17, U.S. No. 16) and *King Of Pain* (U.K. No. 17, U.S. No. 3). It also proved to be their last new album. Although they didn't officially split up until 1986, the three members concenrated on their solo projects hereafter. An attempt to record a follow-up to *Synchronicity II* in 1986 was abandoned.

In October 1986, a revised version of *Don't Stand So Close To Me '86* was released as a precursor to the inevitable greatest hits package that followed in November. *Every Breath You Take - The Singles* brought them a final U.K. No. 1 and U.S. No. 7.

Roxanne and *I Can't Stand Losing You* were both included on the sampler *No Wave* (A&M AMLE 68505) back in 1979.

Political Asylum

Personnel:	CHEESY	gtr, bs	A
	RAMSEY	vcls	A
	SPIKE	drms	A

CASS:	1(A)	FRESH HATE	1983
45:		Winter Of Our Discontent (Children Of Revolution COR 5)	1985

An anarcho-punk band from Stirling in Scotland with a strong nuclear disarmament message. The above cassette was recorded at Black Gold Studio, Blanefield in April 1983, and released as a D.I.Y. demo. The songs have titles like *Disarm Or Die, Nothing Left, Carnage, Winter Of Our Discontent, The Slaughter, Play No Part* and *System Of War*. Although the prime concern is to get the message across the playing is quite competent for this type of release. There's some good guitar work and the vocals are adequate. I believe they issued three cassettes in all.

This was by no means their only cassette appearance. They also appeared on *Standing Upright For No Apparent Reason....* (Concrete Tapes) contributing, *Symptom, A Day In The Life, Tripwire, The Responsability....* and *Yours For Autonomy, Vol. II* (Yours For Autonomy Tapes) includes *Winter Of Our Discontent* and *Trust In Me*.

Their message is clear and summarised on the cassette's sleevenotes:-

"One cannot expect to achieve peace through violence. Violence breeds violence, reaction begs counter-reaction. Freedom lies in the emancipation of the mind, not coercion. From the Sunday roast to the dead hero, we are led to believe that violence and brutality is a natural existence, an inetgral, essential part of human life. Until this fallacy can be dispelled, when violence will not be blandly accepted, but abhorred, a true society based on trust will prove impossible. To expect to bring about this utopia by force is truly a fantasy. The state, with its army, police and well established hierachies, can easily suppress any overt dissent. Subversion must come from within, and stem from the individual. For anarchy is the only "system" which offers oneself as the basic institution. The frailties and cruelties of the present system cannot be torn down - but they can be exposed through propaganda. To force someone to become an anarchist is a contradiction in terms, however you can convince them. Anarchy will never work on a national scale at this moment in time, yet it can become a reality for those who desire it. Anarchy is anti-authority not anti-organisation. Organise and participate.... Together we are stronger than they think!"

It comes across clearly on their songs as you can see from the example below:-

"The fields have turned grey and the trees have lost their leaves
There's no-one to be seen, only crosses and wreaths
Row upon row of graves, lying there
They died for their country but it doesn't seem to care
Chorus:- And I don't wanna die
As the harsh wind whips up and the rain turns to snow
The priest said they died for God but how were they to know
That when they joined up, their heads held high
That in the next 6 months they were gonna die?
Chorus:- The widow enters the field, dressed in black
Trying to come to terms with what's happened to her Jack
She holds in her hand a model from the state
But her mind is empty, she can't even hate
Chorus:- I've had enough of fighting, for them, their war
I'm sick of it now, I don't want it no more
If they want to maim let them get on with it
But leave me out of their self made shit!
Chorus
(from *Winter Of Our Discontent*)

The cassette's final cut *White Poppies* was recorded live at The Guidhall, Stirling on 20th February 1983 and is predominantly instrumental.

Punk Lives - Let's Slam compilation featuring Political Asylum.

Political Asylum also appeared a number of compilations on Rot Records. For example, they contributed *Flight Of Fancy* and *Cats Eyes* to *Punk Lives - Let's Slam* (Rot SLAM 2) 1986. In the post-1986 era they went on to record albums.

The Pop Group

Personnel:			
	SEAN OLIVER	bs	A
	BRUCE SMITH	drms, perc	ABC
	MARK STEWART	vcls	ABCD
	JOHN WADDINGTON	gtr	ABCD
	DAVID WRIGHT	sax	A
	GARETH SAGER	gtr, sax	BCD
	SIMON UNDERWOOD	bs	B
	DAN KATSIS	bs	CD
	TRISTAN HONSINGER	cello	CD
	PAUL STUART	drms	D

ALBUMS: 1(B) Y   (Radar RAD 20) 1979
        2(D) FOR HOW MUCH LONGER DO WE TOLERATE
              MASS MURDER?   (Rough Trade ROUGH 9/Y Y2) 1980
        3(D) WE ARE TIME   (Rough Trade ROUGH 12/Y Y5) 1980

NB: (1) came with a large fold-out poster. It was reissued (Radar SCAN LP 14) in 1996 in a gatefold sleeve with one bonus track, *She Is Beyond Good And Evil*. The reissue was also available on CD (Radar SCAN CD 14) 1996. (2) was issued with four large black and white posters. (3) was issued in a plain black sleeve. There's also a compilation, *We Are All Prostitutes* (Radarscope SCAN CD 31) 1998, also on vinyl (SCAN LP 31).

45s: She Is Beyond Good And Evil/3.38 (PS)   (Radar ADA 29) 1979
        She Is Beyond Good And Evil/
        3.38 (12" PS)   (Radar ADA 1229) 1979
        We Are Prostitutes/Amnesty International Report On
        British Army Torture Of Prisoners   (Rough Trade RT 023) 1979
        Where's There's A Will There's A Way/
        (flip side by **The Slits**)   (Rough Trade RT 039/YY1) 1980

The Pop Group were one of a number of interesting bands to come from Bristol over the years - others included Massive Attack, Portishead and Tricky, but these were part of a later era. They formed in mid-1977 and their name, which Stewart, Smith and Sager had agreed upon during an evening out up in London, was ironic. Their unstructured, anarchistic punk-angst was about as far removed from commercial pop music as one can get.

After eighteen months they secured a recording contract with the major-backed indie label Radar. A debut 45, *She Is Beyond Good And Evil* emerged in March 1979. For both this and their album *Y*, they used producer Dennis 'Blackbeard' Bovell, a member of U.K. dub band Matumbi, as producer. The single was more structured than most of what followed, but didn't sell well. Their album, which followed in April 1979, came with a large fold-out coloured poster, was quite unlike anything issued before or since. Comparisons are often made with Beefheart in terms of lack of structure and tribal dance beats are also in evidence. Synthesizing these two main ingredients **The Pop Group** offered their own unique musical interpretation. The album's unusual cover sported a photo of the mud people of Papua New Guinea. Inside the sleeve was a huge free colour poster with a photomontage of scenes of human misery. If the opening cut *Thief Of Fire* had some semblence of structure most of what followed was highly experimental - full of unnerving and minimalist soundscapes. Tracks like *Snowgirl* and *Blood Money*, in particular, are extremely improvisational and, as such, inaccessible to the majority of the record buying public. Needless to say it didn't sell well, but in time it will become an interesting collectors' item. In 1996, it was reissued on vinyl and CD with their first 45 'A' side added.

The band suffered considerable financial problems - they even held a 'Bankrupcy Benefit' to generate enough cash for them to continue. Their relationship with Radar became increasingly strained. Towards the end of 1979, it was announced that their next records would go through Rough Trade. At the same time Simon Underwood departed to join Pigbag and Dan Katsis (also of **Glaxo Babies**) replaced him on bass. Tristan Honsinger was added on cello. The new line-up released a new 45, *We Are All Prostitutes* in October 1979. The savage attack on capitalism made the indie Top 10 and was one of the finest examples of avant-garde punk. You'll also find it on the 5-CD box set *1-2-3-4 - A History Of Punk And New Wave 1976 - 1979* (MCA/Universal MCD 60066) 1999.

(i)

Replay Adam and The Ants Addix The Adicts A.D. 1984 Advertising The Adverts Afflicted Afraid Of Mice After Dark Airkraft Aka and Charlatans AK kz The Alarm Albertos Y Los Trios Paranoias Aliens The Allies Altered Images Alternative TV The Alternators Amazorblades The Amber Squad American cho-Punk Cassette Compilations The Androids Andy W Of Mu And The Native Hipsters Angela Rippon's Bum Angelic Upstarts Angel Street Anihilated Anthrax Anti-Establishment Th Pasti Anti-Social Anti-Social Anti System Art Failure Any Trouble The Apartment Architects Of and L Objects Dave ve Band Athletico Spizz 80 Attak Atti Attila The Stockbroker The Attraction pus T ardener(s) Back To Zero The Balloons Hr Danger Bankrobbers The d Wire Bee Bee Ce British Electric Found Bet Betna The Betn Blanc Blitz Brothers Blo nsbury S ment Blu The Box ord and Jues Burn Vol A C Case Ti A Ch Cheetahs C Clapha a Cockney mned 84 Martial Th ners Crow Dag rmen Generation Depressions Dif Juz The body The Dor okies The D Double Vision Drug Addicts uran Duran Durutti Column Ian Dury (and Th thbound East End Badc and The Hot Rods Empty The Enemy English Escalators Essential M e Exile The Exits Ex s Fatal Micro roducers External M lien Angels Fan Clu er Z Fish Turned n' Ejits The Feelies Cl tion File Under Pop Kn Lizards Fly On its Patrick Fitzgerald ience The Flirts A F lators The Freshm lys Ford Workers On 48 Hours John Foxx The Gas GBH G les The Front Fruit E e Gang Of Four Gan Ko Gedd Glass Ton Loves Jezebel Gen rograms The Gifted Ko Missionaries Gor Babies The Glory T ki Brothers The G Tho Hammersmith Gordon The Moron to The G.T.'s The Gyn The Egyptians) Hi y Family Charlie Ha s The Heartbeats H in Camera The He wood Brats Homose A.D. Icons Of Filth T Insp Intro I.Q. Zero In Band Indecent Exp ent Bystanders Insa n The Jolt Josef K jackson The Jags Th Joe Public Jilted Jo Killermeters Killing Ch Krypton Last Resort Kent The Kidz Ne e The Last Stand T Lovich Nick Lowe Dave Llygod Flyrnig s The Lillettes Lite bers Ludus The Lurke dent Malcolm Man-Eaters The I Manton Manufactured Romance Martin and The Brownsh alcolm McLaren The Meanies The Media Medium N Mekons The Men Th ight Rags Mighty Wah S and Eyes The Mo ng Prece sh Modern Eon in Mo-dettes lods T Mods The N ow The Me Sure The m The Storm Mo Ingales T utor Nazis tiians gans T fionaly Bez It Quick st Ouic assen iltlens non P ator TI e Ltd P tors The ys T u y R sts Rea Red London Red L ctions Reflex Action Rema-Rema Rob and The Nor e Revo ouse The R nge The Revillos Kimberley Rew ids The Rezilos ch Kids Riff Raff Rikki R Of Earth Rikki and The Num one Riot Squad Robert and The Remoulds Tom Robins Of Victory The Rowdi ubble Rudi Rus Sabre Jets Sad Lovers and Gia s Salford Jets The Sats The Sco Scrit Layer Se Chame Bitch k Tre Will Se Things Sc Im dly Ske Smice erity Sr Spea Cal Q Squad T In Stop s The p and Joh Suddi Su w Take On ets The Tal Bd Russians T Those Helicopters Those Naughty Lumps The Th s The Tigers Ti tchists Terry Tonk The Tools Too Much Totally Outra Toy Dolls The T smitters Trax Steve Treatment The Trend The Trokkoids ming Pool's TV 2 nk and The Fairies Twist 2.3 (Children) Sean Tyla (Gang) Typhoons U K S gs Th dogs The Unde h The Untouchables The Unwanted Upbar The Upset Urban Disturbance Urban Dogs Midge Ure andells Cherry Vanil Varicose Veins Various Artists The Varukers V.D.U.'s Vermilion (and The Aces) The Vibrators Vice Cream Sid Vicious Vicious Rumours Victim The Violators Vipers V.I.P.'s The Virgin Prunes Visage The Visitors Vivabeat Von Trapp Family V2 Vye Want Wall Milk Manderas Wasted Youth The Warm Way jets The Waspo Wasteland Weekend Sports Steve Ignorant Michel Lies White Robe

(ii)

(iii)

Replay Adam and The Ants Addix The Adicts A.D. 1984 Advertising The Adverts Afflicted Afraid Of Mice After Dark Airkraft Aka and Charlatans AK
kz The Alarm Albertos Y Los Trios Paranoias Aliens The Allies Altered Images Alternative TV The Alternators Amazorblades The Amber Squad American
cho-Punk Cassette Compilations ... is Of Mu And The Native Hipsters Angela Rippo... lic Upstarts Angel Street Anihilated
Anth... ... Anti-Pasti Anti-Social Anti-Social Anti System Ar... ...artment Architects Of D
and L... ...rt Objects Dave Asgrove Band Athletico Spizz ... Attraction
epus ... ...Gardener(s) Henry Badowski Back To Zero The
d Wir... ...z Bee Bee Cee Mark Beer B.E.F. (British Elec...
The B... ...Blah Blancmange Blanks Blitz Blitz The Blitz
nsbury... ...Bo
The Bo... ...uri
es Bur... ...ette
r Case... ...ret
Cheetah... ... Th
s Claph... ...a Cockn... ...Conc
emned ... ...ectric
Martial ... ...ooks C
ners Cr... ...Cyan
rmen Da... ...he Dea
Generat... ...Depech
Depress... ...rals Die
Dif Juz T... ...ad The
body The Doodlebugs The Dole The Doll Dome The D... ...Double Vision Dregs Dri... ...rive The
... Dry Rib The Duplicates Duran Duran Durutti ... ...thbound East End Badoes Eate... ...nd The Bu
and The Hot R... ...he Edge Dave Edmunds The Ej... ...ency Empire The Enemy English Dogs English Su
...caters Essen... Essential Logic Ethel The Fro... ...xpelled The F... ...elody S... ...The E...
... Elits The Fe... ...Alex Ferg... ...Engines The First Steps Fisch... ...
its Patrick Fizz... ...alls Flux Of Pink Indians T...
ys Ford Wo... ...
ies The Proh... ...
Loves Jez... ...
Babies T... ...
Gordon ... ...
y Family ... ...
ood Bre... ...
Band In... ...
ckson ... ...
oy Di... ...
Killem... ...
The... ...
Dav... ...
ers ... ...
Ma... ...
Mekons... ...
g Presumed Dead ... ...
ods The... ...
lo The M... ...
re The M... ...urray a... ...ry Nash... ...en Today The Story N...A Monitor Naz...
m Th No ... ...
ingales N... ...
iens. Th... ...
sionally O... ...
The Opp... ...
t Ouida a... ...
assenger... ...
Indust... ...
monia Po... ...
ator The P... ...
e Ltd. Pub... ...
ators The R... ...
sts Reality ... ...
ctions Refl... ...
nge The R... ...izz... ...ythm C
Of Earth R... ...Sq... ...e The Rivals
Of Victory ... ...udi ...errex Run 229 R.U.1
s Salford Jets The Sc... ...e Satel... ...Scars The Scene The Sc...
and Lay... ...will ...Sex Aids The Sex Pistols Shake Sham ...
k Trea... ...Sileen Teens S...
rhood T... ...er and Th
The Sl... ...Disease
rity Soc... ...Cult S
Spear ... ...he Ca
rical Ob... ...nd The
Squad Th... ...ky T
The Sto... ...Stree
e and Joh... ...
Sudden S... ...
he Take O... ...
beats The... ...
Be Russia... ...
ts The Tige... ...
Toy Dolls ... ...Tru
ming Pool... ...Typh... ...travox! Und...
rdogs The ... ...rban... ...re The Users U2 T...
Vandells Ch... ... Vapors Varicose Veins Variou... ...ators Vice Creems Vice Squ
s Sid Vicious Vicious Rumours Victim The Violators Vipers V.I.P.'s The Virgin Pr... ...vice Vegeta... ...on Trapp Family V2 Vye Wah! Wah! H
arry Wallis Wanderers The Wardens The Warm Warm Jets The Warriors Warsaw Pakt The Wasps Wasteland Water Pistols Where's Lisse White Boy WI

Replay Adam and The Ants Addix The Adicts A.D. 1984 Advertising The Adverts Afflicted Afraid Of Mice After Dark Alkratti Alka and Charlatans AK-H
kz The Alarm Albertos Y Los Trios Paranoias Aliens The Allies Altered Images Alternative TV The Alternators Amazonblades The Amber Squad American C
ho-Punk Cassette Compilations The Androids Androids Of Mu And The Native Hipsters Angelica Rippon's Bum Angelic Upstarts Angel Street Annihilated
Anthrax Anti-Establish   gue Anti-Pasti Anti-Social Anti-Social Anti System Art Failure Any Trouble The Apartment Architects Of D
                                             5   bjects Dave Asgrove Band Athletico Spizz 80 Attak Attic Attila The Stockbroker The Attractio
                                                                                                            ic Foundation) Beggar Berlin Blondes Bethnal Bet I
                                                                                                                                                         Rats Bo
                                                                                                                                                         e Buria
                                                                                                                                                          rpente
                                                                                                                                                          cky T
                                                                                                                                                         Cigaret
                                                                                                                                                         e Cond
                                                                                                                                                         Electric
                                                                                                                                                         rooks C
                                                                                                                                                         e Cyan
                                                                                                                                                         Deani
                                                                                                                                                         Depech
                                                                                                                                                         ls Die L
                                                                                                                                                          e Dol
              The Doll Dome T   Bun
ug Addix Dry Rib The Duplicates Duran Duran D   ish Su
The Hot Rods The Edge Dave Edmunds The Ejected Electric Guitars   Even
                                                                       The Frog Europeans The Exile T   pelaires The E   Pistols Exploding Seagulls The Ex
                                                       Fan   ub The Fans   st Cars Fast Set The Fatal Microb
                                                                                                                         Fingerprintz   Steps Fischer Z Fish Turned I
                                                                                                                        Flock Of S   e Flying Lizards Fly On T
                                                                                                                            Bruce F   levators The Freshm
                                                                                                                            psters   The Gas GBH G
                                                                                                                           Child   ist Glass Torp
                                                                                                                                                               smith G
                                                                                                                                                            Josef K
                                                                                                                                                          Kidz Ne
                                                                                                                                                         esort Last
                                                                                                                                                         Lillettes Lip
                                                                                                                                                         Nick Lowe T
                                                                                                                                                            n-Eaters M
anton Manufactured Romance M   Media Medium M
ekons The Mamba   diro and Eyes The
                                                                                                   Mod   th The Mo-dettes M
                                                                                                 ton Parkas The Method Metrop
                                                                                                                                                      ped Moskow The Mos
                                                                                                                                                     rray and The Storm Mu
                                                                                                                                                The S   Girl Was A Monitor Nazis A
                                                                                                                                                             New Or   wn Neurotics Nicky and Th
                                                                                                                                                          oed The Norm   man and The Hooligans Th
                                                                                                                                                        key and Giorgio Moroder The Obtainers/Ma
                                                                                                                                                     One Way System The Onlookers The Only Ones
                                                                                                                                                  Original Mirrors The Others John Otway and Wi
                                                                                                                                              untains The Panik Paranoia The Parrots The Pa
                                                                                                                                         Test Tube Babies The Photos The Physicals Th
                                                                                                                                   tix Play Dead The Pleasers Plugs Plumme
                                                                                                                                Signs Pork Dukes The Portraits Post Mortem Po
                                                                                                                             ors The Psychedelic Furs Psychos Psykyk Volts
                                                                                                                             Pursey PVC 2 The Quar   The Questions Ra
                                                                                                                            Patrol Reacta The Re   on The Reactors Rea
                                                                                                                                     rry Red Rage Redskins The Reduc
                                                                                                                                  ators Restricted Hours The R
                                                                                                                                                                                     Rikki and TI
                                                                                            os Rhabstallion Rhesus Ne   Rh   b
                                                  ples Satan's   Giant
                                                  mples Satan's   Dis
                                                  Mo   Cult S
                                                                                                                                                      The
                                                                                                                                                        Band Th
                                                                                                                                                         Stinky To
                                                                                                                                                        The Stree
                                                                                                                                                        Disease
                                                                                                                                                    uda Subwa
                                                                                                                                                      emics Mich
                                                                                                                                                    age Filmsta
                                                                                                                                                    eatre Of Hat
                                                                                                                                                    Gristle The
                                                                                                                                                         The Touris
                                                                                                                                              Outta Hand Band T   The Tu
                                                                                                                                               kkoids Troops Of Tomorrow
ning Pools TV 2   nk and The Tatties Twist 2.9 (Children) Sean Tyla (Gang) Typhoons U.K. Subs Ultra-Violent Ultravox! Und
dogs The Undertones Uniations   Untouchables The Unwanted Uproar The Upset Urban Disturbance Urban Dogs Midge Ure The Users U2 The
andells Cherry Vanilla The Vapors Varicose Veins Various Artists The Varukers V.D.U.'s Vermillion (and The Aces) The Vibrators Vice Creems Vicious Squad
Sid Vicious Vicious Rumours Victim The Violators Vipers V.I.P.'s The Virgin Prunes Visage The Visitors Vivabeat Von Trapp Family V2 Vye Wah! Wh
ary Wallis Wanderers The Wardens The Warm Warm Jets The Warriors Warsaw Pakt The Wasps Wasteland Water Pistols Where's Lisse White Boy Whon

[vi]

(vii)

Replay Adam and The Ants Addix The Adicts A.D. 1984 Advertising The Adverts Afflicted Afraid Of Mice After Dark Airkraft Aka and Charlatans AK Akz The Alarm Albertos Y Los Trios Paranoias Aliens The Allies Altered Images Alternative TV The Alternators Amazorblades The Amber Squad American ho-Punk Cassette Compilations The Androids Androids Of Mu And The Native Hipsters Angela Rippon's Bum Angelic Upstarts Angel Street Anihilated Anthrax Anti-Establishment The Anti-No... ...the Anti-Pasti Anti-Social Anti-Social Anti System Art F... ...Trouble The Apartment Architects Of E and legs Art Attacks The ... ...Art Objects Dave Asgrove Band Athletico Spizz 80 ... ...Stockbroker The Attraction pus The Au Pa... ...nt Gardener(s) Henry Badowski Back To Zero The Ba... ...rz Bee Bee Cee Marx Beer B.E.F. (British Electric ... Bela Blanomange Blanks Blitz Blitz The Blitz Br... ...sbu... ...Duruttti... ...steve Edmunds The Eje... ...elators... ... ...Patrick... ... Ford... ...ies The... Loves... ... ...orden... y Family... oped... Berldt... phor... Joy Di... ma... Tag... Dave J... uts J... acktor... kets Th... ng Rosenrose Des... dots The Monocri... To The Meatmen ...re The Mutants... The Negati... gates Ni... ntens The N... sonally Devi... he Copper... to The Cram... bosentor... endersic... ony... ...for The... ...Ltd. P... ...tors Th... ts Reality... tions Reflex Actio... ...nge The Revillos Kimberly... Of Earth Rikki and The Numbers The... Of Victory... Salford... ...d Layer... Treatment... hood Th... The Slits... ly Societ... Spear Of... ical Object... quad The... The Stope... and John... Sudden... he Take O... eals The... Be Russ... s The Tig... Toy Dolls... ming Poo... dogs The... ...andells Cherry Vanilla The Vapors Varicose Veins Various Artists The Varukers V.D.U.'s Vermillion (and The... the Vibrators Vice Creems Vice Sq Sid Vicious Vicious Rumours Victim The Violators Vipers V.I.P.'s The Virgin W... Visage The Visitors Vivabeat Von Trapp Family V2 Vye Wah!...

(ix)

JAM
SOUND AFFECTS
NO.80
POW!
REPLICAS
tubeway army
The MEKONS
WHERE WERE YOU?
I'LL HAVE TO DANCE THEN (ON MY OWN)
a double A side
FAST
ADAM AND THE ANTS
"Stand & Deliver!"
TROUBLE
AS8502
999
THE CLASH
GIVE 'EM ENOUGH ROPE
"IF YOU REALLY LOVE ME """" BUY ME A SHIRT"
CHRIS SIEVEY AND THE FRESHIES
MYSTERE FIVE'S
NEVER SAY THANK YOU
c/w
HEART RULES THE HEAD
anti-pasti
THE LAST CALL...
BACK ON THE STREETS
KIDNAPPED
The Resistance

(xi)

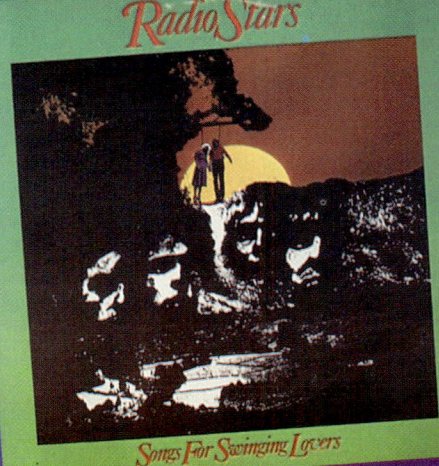

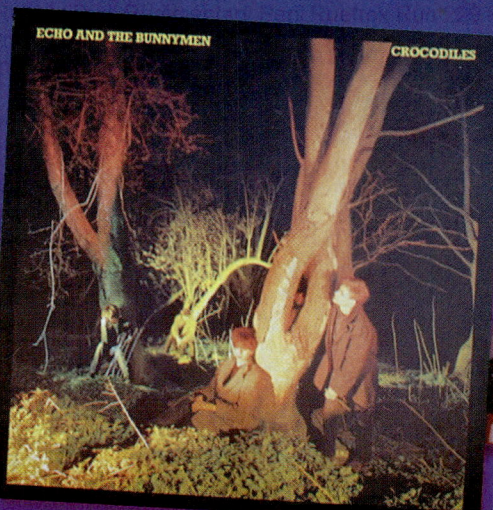

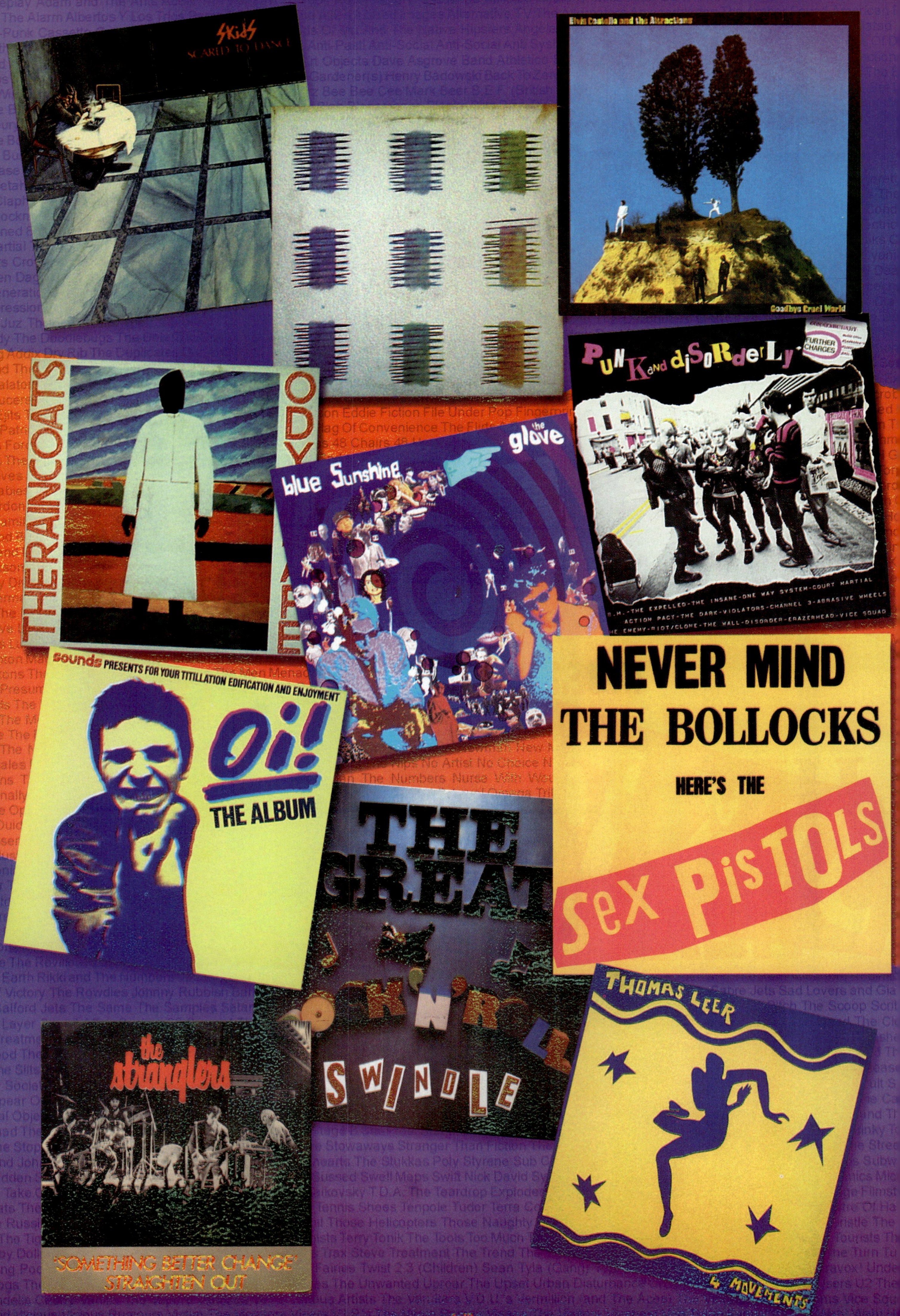
Skids
SCARED TO DANCE
Elvis Costello and the Attractions
Goodbye Cruel World
THE RAINCOATS
ODYSHAPE
PUNK and disORderLy
FURTHER CHARGES
blue Sunshine
the glove
sounds PRESENTS FOR YOUR TITILLATION EDIFICATION AND ENJOYMENT
Oi!
THE ALBUM
NEVER MIND
THE BOLLOCKS
HERE'S THE
Sex PisTOLs
THE GREAT
ROCK 'N' ROLL
SWINDLE
the stranglers
'SOMETHING BETTER CHANGE'
STRAIGHTEN OUT
THOMAS LEER
4 MOVEMENTS

THE POP GROUP - Y.

"We are all prostitutes
Everyone has their price
And you too will learn to live the lie
Aggression, competition, ambition
Consumer fascism

Capitalism is the most barbant of all religions

Department stores are our new cathedrals
Our cars are martyrs to the cause

We are all prostitutes
Our children shall rise up against us
Because we are the ones to blame
We are the ones they'll blame
They will give us a new name
We shall be

Hypocrites, hypocrites, hypocrites
(*We Are All Prostitutes*)

After this Bruce Smith left to join **The Slits**. Paul Stuart replaced him on drums. The new line-up released a 45 *Where There's A Will There's A Way*, which was released as a double 'A' side for just 70p alongside with **The Silts'** *In The Beginning There Was A Rhythm*. It was released in March 1980 - the same month as their new album *For How Much Longer Do We Tolerate Mass Murder?*. The music on this, full of rage and anger, was a revolutionary tirade against imperialism and the establishment. It actually topped the indie charts for a few weeks in 1980.

By now, though, more unpaid bills were piling up so it was decided to release another budget-priced album *We Are Time*. It was a collection of out-takes, Peel recordings, poor live recordings and some good previously unreleased studio recordings like *Trap* and *Amnesty Report*.

As friction grew within the band between Stewart and Sager, they decided to split in 1980. Stewart recorded an excellent version of *Jerusalem* to kick off a long standing solo career. Sager and Bruce Smith joined up with original **Pop Group** bassist Sean Oliver, **Slits'** backing vocalist Neneh Cherry and Bristol-based pianist Mark Springer to form Rip, Rig and Panic. They cut three albums for Virgin and then re-grouped as Float Up C.P. Smith and Cherry also married. After Float Up C.P.'s demise, Sagar formed a band called Head, who released two albums.

John Waddington formed Maximum Joy, whilst afer a year's break Simon Underwood joined Pigbag. In 1982, they had a Top 3 hit with *Papa's Got A Brand New Pigbag*.

In the final analysis, **The Pop Group** were avant-garde punk revolutionaries who flexed their muscles but weren't around for long enought to make a major impact. Interesting, though. The adventurous among you must hear those first two albums and the *We Are All Prostitutes* 45.

The Pop Rivets

Personnel:
BILLY CHILDISH	vcls		AB
VALENTINE LAX	drms, vcls		AB
WILL POWER	gtr, vcls		AB
LI'P RUSS	drms		A
RUSSELL SQUARE	bs, vcls		B

ALBUMS: 1(A) EMPTY SOUNDS FROM ANARCHY RANCH
(Hypocrite HIP-0) 1979
2(B) THE POP RIVETS GREATEST HITS
(Hypocrite HIP 007) 1980

NB: There's also *Chatham's Burning - Live 1977 & 1978 Demos* (Damaged Goods DAMGOOD 142) 1997, vinyl only.

EPs: 1(A) POP RIVETS (Hypocrite HEP 001) 1979
2(A) FUN IN THE U.K. (Hypocrite JIM 1) 1979

45: Pop Rivets/Sulphate (PS) (Hypocrite HEP 002) 1979

A garage punk band from Canterbury fronted by a fresh-faced Billy Childish, who later evolved into The Milkshakes. The latter became one of the standard bearer's of the trash/garage movement in the U.K. during the eighties. Back in October 1977, they recorded a gig at Detling Village Hall which Damaged Goods have issued as *Chatham's Burning - Live 1977 & 1978 Demos* on brown vinyl along with some of their 1978 demos. The best cuts are the cover versions of *White Riot*, *My Generation*, *Boredom*, *Stingray*, *Wotcha Gonna Do About It* etc., but the sound quality is rough to say the least.

THE POP RIVETS - Chatham's Burning - Live 1977 & 1978.

A Popular History Of Signs

Personnel incl:
ANDY JARMAN	vcls, bs		A
PETE SCAMMELL	gtr, keyb'ds		A

45s:
Justice Not Vengeance/Possession (PS) (Melodia M1) 1980
Crowds/Crossing The Border (PS) (Melodia M2) 1981
Dancing With Ideas/The Traveller (PS) (Melodia M4) 1982

Along with **To The Finland Station**, **A Popular History Of Signs** (PHOS) were founder members of Melodia. The mainstays of the group were Andy Jarman and Pete Scammell. Andy and Pete had been in new wave band Prime Movers at the end of the 1970s. After becoming inspired by the synth sounds of bands such as **Orchestral Manoeuvres In The Dark** and the repetition/drone effects used by the Velvet Underground and **Joy Division**, they formed **PHOS**. Their first single for Melodia was *Justice Not Vengeance* in 1980. The single got rave reviews and was followed by further singles, *Crowds* in 1981 and *Dancing With Ideas* in 1982. Apart from Jarman and Scammell, various other members came and went, Scammell himself leaving in the mid-1980s. The band continued until the late 1980s when Jarman relocated to Spain. Jungle and Melodia put out a compilation album *England In The Rain* (Jungle FREUD 21) in 1988.

Pork Dukes

Personnel:	GERMUN LE PIG	drms	A
	HARRENDUS STYLES	gtr	A
	MARK E. VALLEY	keyb'ds	A
	VILAS STYLES	vcls	A

ALBUMS:	1(A)	PIG 'N A POKE	(Wood PORK 001) 1979
	2(A)	PIG OUT OF HELL	(Wood PORK 2) 1980

NB: (1) originally issued on pink vinyl with a warning sticker and post card. (1) reissued on Butt (PORK 1) in 1982. There's also a compilation *All The Filth* (Vinyl Japan ASKLP 98) 2000 also on CD (ASKCD 98) 2000 with additional tracks. There's also a retrospective EP *Telephone Masturbator* (Vinyl Japan TASK 66) 2000 containing *Telephone Masturbator, Melody Makers, Bend And Flush* and *Throbbing Gristle*.

45s:	Bend And Flush/Throbbing Gristle (PS)	(Wood WOOD 9) 1977
	Making Bacon/Tight Pussy (12" PS)	(Wood BRANCH 9) 1978
	Telephone Masturbator/ Melody Makers (PS)	(Wood WOOD 56) 1978

The Pork Dukes were one of the early bands on the London punk scene, but they never advanced beyond being a lower division band. They were competent musicians but their material was offensive and purile. They played under pseudonyms, perhaps they didn't want to be embarrassed by these records for the rest of their lives.

If you do want to hear what they sounded like, check out the recent *All The Filth* compilation, which is available on both vinyl and CD (with extra tracks).

The Portraits

Personnel:	CY CURNN	vcls	A
	RUPERT GREENALL	keyb'ds	A
	ADAM WOODS	drms	A

45s:	Little Women/Easy (PS)	(Ariola ARO 194) 1979
	Hazard In The Home/Never Let Go (PS)	(Ariola ARO 206) 1980

This band later beacme **The Fix**. Under that name they recorded a 45 on the 101 Club's own label:- *Lost Planes / I've Been Here Before* (PS) (101 Club 101) 1981. They then extended their name to **The Fixx** and released more. See their entry for details.

Post Mortem

Personnel:	CHRIS	bs	A
	LORRAINE	vcls	A
	MARTIN	gtr	A
	MICK	drms	A

EPs:	1(A)	POST MORTEM (Day By Day/48 Crash/ Can The Can) (PS)	(Beat The System POST 1) 1983
	2(A)	AGAINST ALL ODDS (Better Off Dead/Asylum/ Nuclear Game/A Mental Scar You Won't Forget) (PS)	(Regime RM 006) 1984

An eighties punk band from the Skegness and Hull area, who released the last recording on Beat The System. You can also check out *IRA* and *Day By Day* on *Beat The System Punk Singles Collection* (Anagram CDPUNK 61) 1995.

Pragvec

Personnel:	DAVID BOYD	bs	A
	NICK CASH	drms	A
	SUSAN GOGAN	vcls	A
	JOHN STUDHOLME	gtr	A

ALBUM:	1(A)	NO COWBOYS	(Spec RESPECT 1) 1981
EP:	1(A)	EXISTENTIAL (Existential/Bits//Wolf/ Cigarette) (PS)	(Spec SP 001) 1978
45:		Expert/Follower (PS)	(Spec SP 002) 1979

Centred around vocalist Susan Gogan **Pragvec** formed in London during 1978. Gogan and Studholme had previously played together in an R&B band The Derelicts. Their debut disc, a four track EP *Existential* was released in December 1978 on their own Spec label and marketed through Rough Trade. Prior to this they had recorded a session for John Peel comprising *Nervous, Bits, Ruby* and *Stay* on 29th August 1978. A second session followed on 7th February 1979. This consisted of *Toast, Expert, Follower* and *Hijack*. They went for brief song titles, didn't they?

The *Existential* EP is unnerving 'noisy' music. Interesting but not accessible. The words and music are penned by Gogan and Studholme.

In July 1979, *Expert* was released as a 45 and they embarked on a ten-day tour with two other Rough Trade bands **The Monochrome Set** and **Manicured Noise**. Despite this, the 45 failed to sell in significant quantities.

In 1981, they recorded an album, which was eventually released in October of that year. The album, in a sort of pop-punk format, was well-packaged with a free poster and badge. It sank without trace, probably partly as a result of under-promotion. People's eyes were turning more towards the second wave of punk, based around Oi!, for new excitement by then.

Predator

ALBUM:	1( )	PREDATOR	(Roadrunner RR 9714) 1986

45s:	Punk Man/Paperboy Song	(Burst SOL ½) 1978
	Predators Don't Mess Around/Do You Wanna Dance/ Plastic Surgeon	(Rock JKM no#) 1981

Released with an insert but not in a picture sleeve, the *Punk Man* 45 is now one of the most expensive artefacts of the punk era.

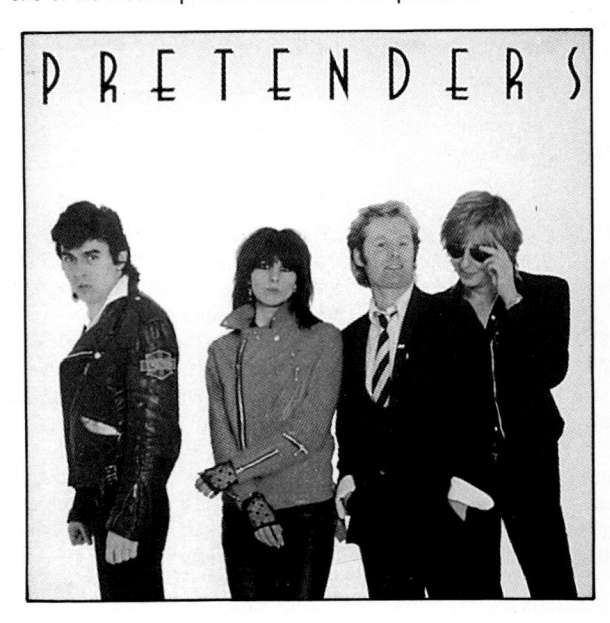

THE PRETENDERS - Pretenders.

The Pretenders

Personnel: (up to 1986)	PETE FARNDON	bs	ABC
	JAMES HONEYMAN-SCOTT	gtr, keyb'ds	AB
	CHRISSIE HYNDE	vcls, gtr	ABCDEFG
	GERRY MACKLEDUFF	drms	A
	MARTIN CHAMBERS	drms	BCDEFG
	BILLY BREMNER	gtr	CD
	TONY BUTLER	bs	D
	MALCOLM FOSTER	bs	EF
	ROBBIE McINTOSH	gtr	EFG
	PAUL CARRACK	keyb'ds	F
	BLAIR CUNNINGHAM	drms	G
	TIM STEVENS	bs	G

THE PRETENDERS - Pretenders II.

BERNIE WORRELL   keyb'ds   G

			HCP
ALBUMS:	1(A)	PRETENDERS (Real RAL 3)	1979 1
(up to	2(A)	PRETENDERS II (Real SRK 3572)	1981 7
1986)	3(E)	LEARNING TO CRAWL (Real WX 2)	1984 11
	4(G)	GET CLOSE (WEA WX 64)	1986 6

NB: (1) also issued on CD (WEA 256774) 1983. (2) also issued on CD (WEA 256924 2) 1986. (3) also issued on CD (WEA 923980 2) 1984. (4) also issued on CD (WEA 240976 2) 1986. There's also some compilations *The Singles* (WEA WX 135) 1987, also on CD (WEA 242229 2) 1987, which got to No. 6, *Packed!* (WEA WX 346) 1990, also on CD (WX 346 CD) 1990, which got to No. 19, reissued again on CD (East West 9031714032) 1994, *Last Of The Independents* (WEA 4509958221) 1994, *Don't Get Me Wrong - 14 Classic Tracks* (Carlton 4509918852) 1993 and *Greatest Hits* (WEA 8573846074) 2000.

			HCP
45s:	Stop Your Sobbing/The Wait	(Real ARE 6)	1979 34
(up to	Kid/Tattoed Love Boys (PS)	(Real ARE 9)	1979 33
1986)	Brass In Pocket/Swinging London (PS)	(Real ARE 11)	1979 1
	Brass In Pocket/Swinging London/ Nervous But Shy (12", PS)	(Real ARE 11)	1979 -
	Talk Of The Town/Cuban Slide (PS)	(Real ARE 12)	1980 8
	Message Of Love/Porcelain (PS)	(Real ARE 15)	1981 11
	Day After Day/In The Sticks (PS)	(Real ARE 17)	1981 45
	Day After Day/In The Sticks/ The Adultress (12", PS)	(Real ARET 17)	1981 -
	I Go To Sleep/The English Rose (PS)	(Real ARE 18)	1981 7
	I Go To Sleep/The English Rose/ Waste Not Want Not (12", PS)	(Real ARET 18)	1981 -
	Back On The Chain Gang/(Part 2) (PS)	(Real ARE 19)	1982 17
	Back On The Chain Gang/(Part 2)/ My City Was Gone (12", PS)	(Real ARET 19)	1982 -
	2,000 Miles/The Law Is The Law (PS)	(Real ARE 20)	1983 15
	2,000 Miles/The Law Is The Law/ Money (live) (12", PS)	(Real ARET 20)	1983 -
*	Middle Of The Road/ Watching The Clothes (PS)	(Real ARE 21)	1984 -
	The Thin Line Between Love And Hate/ Time The Avenger (PS)	(Real ARE 22)	1984 49
	The Thin Line Between Love And Hate/Bad Boys Get Spanked/ Time The Avenger (12", PS)	(Real ARET 22)	1984 -
	Don't Get Me Wrong/Dance (7", PS)	(Real YZ 85)	1986 10
	Don't Get Me Wrong (Extended)/ Dance (12", PS)	(Real YZT 85)	1986 -
	Hymn To Her/Roomful Of Mirrors (PS)	(Real YZ 93)	1986 8
	Hymn To Her/Roomful Of Mirrors/ Stop Your Sobbing (demo) (12", PS)	(Real YZT 93)	1986 -

NB: * Also issued as a 12" (Real ARET 21).

The Pretenders were formed by American Chrissie Hynde and Hereford-based musicians Peter Farndon on bass, James Honeyman-Scott on guitar and Gerry Mackleduff on drums (who was replaced by Martin Chambers after the recording of their first single). At the time they recorded Ray Davies' *Stop Your Sobbing*, for which **Nick Lowe** handled production, they didn't have a name. It seems Chrissie eventually chose **The Pretenders** after The Platters' hit *The Great Pretender*.

Chrissie's main musical influences had been various American soul stars. She'd begun to play guitar back in 1967 and joined a band called Sat.Sun.Mat, which included Mark Mothesbaugh, who went on to become keyboardist with Devo. After spending three years at Kent State University studying, she headed for London in 1973. Whilst working as a model at St. Martins School Of Art and selling leather handbags in Oxford Street, she met NME journalist Nick Kent who invited her to write for the music paper. She worked briefly at **Malcolm McLaren**'s clothes shop 'Sex' in 1974 before moving to Paris to join The Frenchies. In 1975, she returned to the 'States joining R&B group Jack Rabbit in Cleveland, Ohio. The following year she returned to London to join The Berk Brothers (Dave and Fred) but before long they replaced her as vocalist with **Johnny Moped**. In February 1977, she sang backing vocals on Chris Spedding's *Hurt* album - she'd first met Spedding whilst in Paris in 1974. She recorded a demo tape of *The Phone Call* and aroused interest from Dave Hill (of Anchor Records) who was busy forming Real Records. He funded further demo sessions for her.

The foundations were therefore made for Chrissie's new band **The Pretenders** to record for Real Records.

They soon developed a style, which was essentially an amalgam of new wave and power pop. Their debut 45, released in January 1979, showcased Chrissie's vocal talents superbly and was a superb new wave pop song with immediate appeal. It enjoyed a credible nine weeks in the chart peaking at No. 34. The new band began to tour the club circuit taking in venues like The Marquee and The Moonlight Club in West Hampstead. In June 1979, a follow-up 45 *Kid* produced by Chris Thomas made it to No. 33 during a seven week chart residency and **The Pretenders** embarked on a month's tour of the U.K., which included a headlining gig at the Lyceum. Later, on 22nd October, they commenced the first of four consecutive Monday night gigs at the Marquee Club.

Their trio of three excellent opening singles was completed by *Brass In My Pocket*, the best of the three penned by Chrissie and Honeyman-Scott. It took them to the top of the charts and enjoyed a seventeen-week chart residency overall. As 1979 ended the band played two Christmas gigs at London's Marquee and participated in the Concert for Kampuchea at London's Hammersmith Odeon.

The Pretenders were now hot property. As Real Records were bought by U.S. label Sire, Dave Hill left Real to become the band's full-time manager. The band embarked on a thirty-date U.K. tour and their long-awaited debut album *Pretenders* entered the charts, in which it went on to spend a staggering thirty-five weeks, at No. 1. This was one of *the* classic albums of the era, which also went on to reach No. 9 in the 'States.

Hynde's husky voice helped distinguish them from other bands and her sex appeal contributed greatly to their popularity. Their debut album, which included all three of their earlier singles, was also notable for Honeyman-Scott's inventive guitar work on cuts like *Mystery Achievement* and *Tattooed Love Boys*.

In April 1980, as their latest 45 *Talk Of The Town* rose to No. 8 and spent a similar number of weeks in the chart, **The Pretenders** embarked on their first American tour. Chrissie Hynde met one of her music idols Ray Davies at a New York club and they quickly became embroiled in a three year relationship. The mini-tour had its highs and its lows. A gig at the 3,500-seater Santa Monica Civic Auditorium sold out in two hours, but towards the end of the tour Chrissie was involved in a fight with a bouncer and got to sample an American jail for a night. **The Pretenders** returned to North America for a further tour in August including an appearance at the New Wave festival in Toronto, Canada. In October, they embarked on a new fifteen-date U.K. tour, but with all this touring they produced only one new 45 during the year and their fans and the music world were hungry for more new material.

In February 1981, a new 45 *Message Of Love* just missed the Top 10. To keep interest alive an EP *Extended Play* comprising both sides of their *Talk Of The Town* and *Message Of Love* 45s and a live version of *Precious* (another excellent cut from their debut album) was released in April. This made it to No. 27 in the 'States, but wasn't released here in Britain. The same month Honeyman-Scott married model Peggy Sue Fender and in May Chambers tied the knot with Tracey Atkinson.

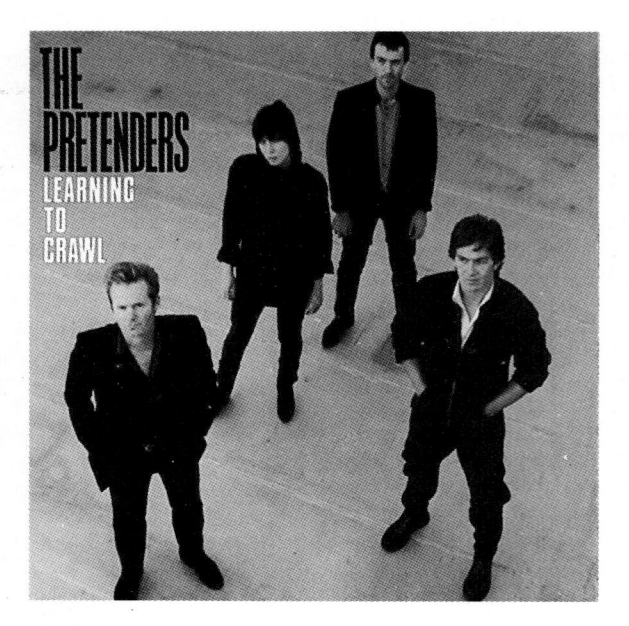

THE PRETENDERS - Learning To Crawl.

After a long wait *Pretenders II* was released in August. The stand-out cuts on this were their earlier 45s and *I Go To Sleep* (later selected for 45 release in November). Little of the remaining material was of the standard of their debut. *Day After Day* was culled for 45 release but only managed four weeks in the chart and a peak position of No. 45. *I Go To Sleep* improved on this taking them back into the Top 10 later in the year. Despite all this their reputation and popularity carried them through and the album's sales were impressive. In Britain it enjoyed twenty-seven weeks in the chart and a best position of No. 7 and it climbed to No. 10 in the 'States. The same month they embarked on a new U.S. tour, but it had to be cancelled when Chambers injured his fist smashing a lamp in his hotel room. In December, some Christmas gigs were being planned, but these too had to be cancelled when he damaged his other hand. They finally got back on the road in January 1982 touring initially in the 'States, and then went on to play in Japan, Hong Kong and Australia.

The remainder of the year was disasterous for at least two of their members. On 14th June Farndon was fired by the band. On 16th June Honeyman-Scott, who'd become addicted to cocaine and heroin, died. Later, on 14th April 1983, Farndon overdosed and died in the bath. He'd been in the process of forming a band with Rob Stoner and ex-**Clash** member Topper Headon at the time. To keep the band going Big Country's Tony Butler came in on bass temporarily (he later rejoined Big Country) and former Rockpile member Billy Bremner came in on lead guitar. This new line-up recorded the superb *Back On The Chain Gang*. This catchy song was arguably one of the best things they ever did. Here it spent nine weeks in the chart rising to No. 17. In the 'States, where it was included in Robert DeNiro's film 'King Of Comedy', it did even better rising to No. 10.

The deaths and Chrissie Hynde's pregnancy meant that 1982 and most of 1983 were quiet years for the band. In February 1983, Chrissie Hynde's and Ray Davies' daughter Natalie was born and after this work got underway to shore-up the band. Former Manfred Mann's Earth Band and Night guitarist Robbie McIntosh was brought in to replace Billy Bremner and on his recommendation Malcolm Foster was brought in on bass paving the way for Butler to rejoin Big Country. The new line-up appeared in the three-day U.S. festival at San Bernadino, California from 28-30th May. Later, in November, the festive *2,000 Miles* climbed to No. 15, spending nine weeks in all in the charts.

January 1984 heralded the release of a new album *Learning To Crawl* which marked a return to form for a revitalised band. Alongside *Back On The Chain Gang* and *2,000 Miles* were stunning new songs like *Middle Of The Road* (which surprisingly missed out when released as a 45 here after it had made the U.S. Top 20) and *Time The Avenger*. Spending sixteen weeks in the chart the album narrowly missed the Top 10, peaking at No. 11. To coincide with its release the band embarked on 'The Pretenders World Tour'.

After her relationship with Ray Davies broke down Chrissie had a whirlwind romance with Jim Kerr of **Simple Minds** and married him on 5th May 1985. Their U.S.-only single *Show Me* peaked at No. 28 in March 1984. In April they released a revival of The Persuaders' early seventies hit *The Thin Line Between Love Or Hate*, having recruited ex-Ace, Roxy Music and former solo artist Paul Carrack on keyboards. Sales were disappointing, though. In Britain, it stiffed at No. 49 and only managed three weeks in the chart. In the 'States it only got to No. 83.

1985 was another very quiet year for the band though they did appear at the Live Aid Spectacular in Philadelphia on 13th July, following **Simple Minds** on stage. In September UB40 invited Chrissie to share the vocals on their cover of Sonny and Cher's *I Got You Babe*. It topped the charts and also got to No. 28 in the 'States.

After this **The Pretenders** regrouped. Chrissie Hynde still used Robbie McIntosh but brought in Tim Stevens on bass, Bernie Worrell on keyboards and former Haircut 100 member Blair Cunningham replaced Chambers on drums for some numbers in lengthy recording sessions which eventually led to an excellent new album *Get Close*, which spawned two further hit singles; *Don't Get Me Wrong* and *Hymn To Her*, which rose to No. 10 and 8 and spent nine and twelve weeks in the charts respectively. *Get Close* showed the new line-up had again rejuvenated the band and all the indications were that **The Pretenders** would be superstars for some years to come. *The Singles* (compilation), released in 1987 on both vinyl and CD is a good introduction to their music.

Compilation appearances have included *Stop Your Sobbing* on *The Best Punk Album In The World.... Ever, Vol. 1* (2-CD) (Virgin VTDCD 42) 1995, *Brass In My Pocket* on *Vol. 2* (Virgin VTDCD 79) 1996 of the same series and on *Teenage Kicks* (PolyGram TV 5253382) 1995.

Be wary of *Don't Get Me Wrong - 14 Classic Tracks* as apart from the title track and *Brass In My Pocket* the remaining material on this mid-price compilation is taken from either albums or 'B' sides. Of course, they were still good but they weren't the best. The best compilation is now the *Greatest Hits* CD released in 2000.

Private Dicks

Personnel:			
	HUW DAVIES	bs	A
	PAUL GUIVER	gtr	A
	GAVIN KING	vcls	A
	MARK SEABRIGHT	drms	A

45s:	She Said Go/Private Dicks (PS)	(Heartbeat PULSE 6) 1979
	Follow My Lead/	
	You Want It You Got It (PS)	(Heartbeat PULSE 9) 1980

In addition to their two 45s, **Private Dicks** contributed the accessible and rather polished *Green Is In The Red*, to *Avon Calling - The Bristol Compilation* (Heartbeat HB 1) in 1979.

Private Sector

Personnel:		
	JOHN McSTEA	A
	MARK McSTEA	A
	ERIC WATERS	A

45s:	Just Just (Wanna) Stay Free/	
	Things Get Worse (PS)	(TJM TJM 8) 1978
	Like A Ton Of Bricks (It's Hit Me)/	
	Mix (12", PS)	(Food For Thought YUMT 103) 1983

This is very run-of-the-mill fayre.

The Professionals

Personnel:			
	PAUL COOK	drms, vcls	A
	STEVE JONES	gtr, vcls	A
	RAY McVEIGH	gtr, vcls	A
	PAUL MYERS	bs	A

ALBUM:	1(A)	I DIDN'T SEE IT COMING	(Virgin V 2220) 1981

NB: (1) also issued on CD (Virgin VJCP 68059) 1999. There's also a CD compilation *The Professionals* (Virgin CDOVD 459) 1997.

			HCP
45s:	Just Another Dream/Action Man (PS)	(Virgin VS 353) 1980	-
*	1-2-3/White Light White Heat/Baby I Don't Care (PS)	(Virgin VS 376) 1980	43
	Join The Professionals/Has Anyone Got An Alibi (PS)	(Virgin VS 426) 1981	-
	The Magnificent/Just Another Dream (PS)	(Virgin VS 456) 1981	-
+	Little Boys In Blue (extract)/(other cut is an extract by Gillan)	(Sounds FREEBIE No 2) 1981	-

NB: * Most copies came with a giant poster in a stickered PVC sleeve, but some were signed by Steve Jones and Paul Cook and sold via Red Rhino. + This was a one-sided flexi playing at 33 rpm with a printed die-cut sleeve which was given away free with copies of 'Sounds'.

This was an offshoot from **The Sex Pistols** and due to the involvement of Paul Cook and Steve Jones **The Professionals** initially enjoyed a high media profile. The music on offer is basically rock-based. Their better moments including the rousing *Kick Down The Door*, *Payola* and *The Management*, which came with **Public Image Ltd** - style guitar.

Kick Down The Doors also figured on the sampler *Cash Cows* (Virgin MILK 1) in 1980, whilst *Justifiable Homicide* resurfaced on *Punk Lost And Found* (Shanachie SH 5705) 1996.

Prole

Personnel:	J.J. BEDSORE	bs	A
	STEVE KENT	vcls, gtr	A
	MARTIN NEAL	drms	A

This was a part-time project which was the creation of 'Sounds' Garry Bushell. It was fronted by ex-**Business** guitarist Steve Kent, who co-wrote their material with Bushell. Of the other two members Martin Neal also played for **Frankie and The Flames** and bassist J.J. Bedsore was in **The Blood**. **Prole**'s *Generation Landslide* can be heard on *100% British Oi!* (Captain Oi! AHOY DCD 83) 1997. Certainly this suggests that they'd have prospered as a full-time project.

Prole also appeared on *The Oi! Of Sex* (Syndicate SYNLP 4) in 1984 playing *We'll Never Say Die* and *Destination Room 101*. Of these, the latter with its mildly discordant guitar playing (in places) is by far the most interesting. This album was later reissued on CD (Captain Oi! AHOY CD 23) 1994.

Steve Kent and J.J. Bedsore also operated under the pseudonyms of **Orgasm Guerillas** and **The Crossed Hammers**.

The Proles

Personnel:	JOHN BLACK	vcls, bs. hrmnca	A
	PETER SHORT	gtr, vcls	A
	KEVIN WILLIS	gtr	A
	KEVIN WILSON	drms	A

45s:	Soft Ground/SMK	(Small Wonder SMALL 23) 1978
	Stereo Love/Thought Crime/(other two cuts by **The Condemned**)	(Rock Against Racism T.RARI 1) 1979

This act appears to be unconnected to the **Proles** who recorded an EP *The Proles Go To The Seaside* (Can't Play) 1978. *Soft Ground* later resurfaced on *Small Wonder Punk Singles Collection, Vol. 1* (Anagram CDPUNK 29) 1994 and *Vol. 2* (Anagram CDPUNK 70) 1996 includes *SMK*.

Protex

Personnel:	PAUL MAXWELL	bs	A
	OWEN McFADDEN	drms	A
	DAVID McMASTER	gtr	A
	AIDAN MURTAGH	vcls	A

ALBUM:	1(A)	STRANGE OBSESSIONS	(Polydor) 1980

NB: (1) a Dutch release.

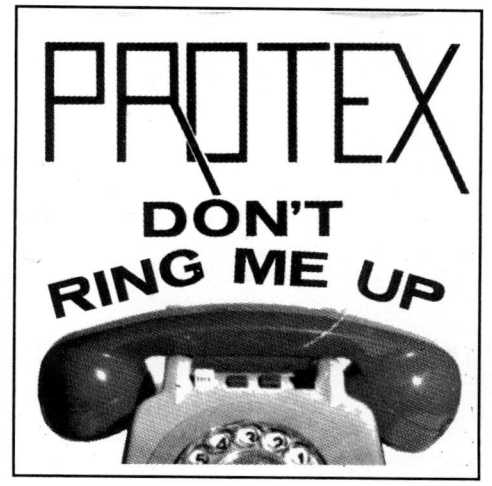

PROTEX - Don't Ring Me Up.

45s:	Don't Ring Me Up/(Just Want) Your Attention/Listening In (Wraparound PS)	(Good Vibrations GOT 6) 1978
	Don't Ring Me Up/(Just Want) Your Attention/Listening In (PS)	(Rough Trade GOT 1) 1979
	I Can't Cope/Popularity (PS)	(Polydor 2059 124) 1979
	I Can Only Dream/Heartache (PS)	(Polydor 2059 167) 1979
	A Place In Your Heart/Jeepster (PS)	(Polydor 2059 245) 1980

Protex were formed in January 1978, originally as Protex Blue (a well-known condom brand). Guitarist Aidan Murtagh and drummer Owen MacFadden had previously played together in an outfit called The Incredibly Boring Band. The other half of the quartet was completed by Paul Maxwell (bs) and David MacMaster (rhythm gtr), who shared vocals with Murtagh. Like **Ruefrex**, **Protex** were a Belfast band who gigged regularly at the city's Harp bar and also attracted the attention of Terri Hooley. Good Vibrations once again offered them a platform and they recorded an EP *Don't Ring Me Up*. By now the band had a pool of a dozen or so original numbers, like *I Can't Cope*, *Strange Obsessions*, *Smile And Say Goodbye* and *Popularity*, which pondered the pitfalls of fame.

In 1979, **Protex** signed to Polydor, who also snapped up **The Xdreamists**. Polydor immediately issued *I Can't Cope / Popularity* as a single. It did not meet with wide acclaim although later, it was voted by NME Readers the best 1979 single by an Ulster band. In July, of the same year, they supported **Adam and The Ants** on a nationwide tour and also headlined gigs in their own right at Deptford's Albany Empire on 24th July and Islington's Hope And Anchor on 8th August. Their second Polydor single, released in November 1979 *I Can Only Dream*, produced by Chas Chandler, was stronger than the first, and exhibited a strong Pete Shelley influence. However, it lacked the originality or individuality to provide a breakthrough.

By now **Protex** had built up a loyal following on the U.K. mainland and after touring with **The Boomtown Rats**, **Protex** headlined a series of gigs in December at The Bridge House, Canning Town (15th Dec.), the Hope And Anchor (17th Dec.), Dundee Maryat Hall (19th Dec.), Aberdeen College Of Commerce (20th Dec.), Cumbernauld (21st Dec.), and The Bungalow, Glasgow (22nd Dec.). They visited Belfast's Pound on 2nd January 1980 before returning to England for the release of their debut album *Strange Obsessions*. This was an amalgam of punk and power pop but didn't sell well.

A further single, *A Place In Your Heart*, followed, but like the earlier ones it met with little success. They were dropped by Polydor in 1980 and split up soon after.

They have also figured on a number of compilations. *I Can't Cope* got a further airing on *20 Of Another Kind, Vol. 2* (Polydor POLX-1) 1979. *I Can Only Dream* also figured on a Polydor Sampler U.S. promo-only 12" EP in 1980. *A Place In Your Heart*, *I Can Only Dream*, *I Can't Cope* and *All I Wanna Do (Is Rock 'n' Roll)* all resurfaced on *Made In Britain* (Polydor PDI 6295) 19??.

More recently, *Don't Ring Me Up* and *Listening In* have re-appeared on *Good Vibrations - The Punk Singles Collection* (Anagram CDPUNK 36) 1994 and *Don't Ring Me Up* also got an airing on *1-2-3-4 - A History Of*

Punk And New Wave 1976 - 1979 (MCA/Universal MCD 60066) 1999, which is a 5-CD box set.

Pseudo Existors

45s: Pseudo Existence/Coming Up For Air/
        Now Modern Warfare (PS)   (Dead Good DEAD 2) 1979

NB: This appeared in a rubber-stamped folded picture sleeve with a pink and white label. Later copies had a white and black label and came in a stamped white sleeve.

This single is now had to find in either format and is sought-after by some collectors.

THE PSYCHEDELIC FURS - The Psychedelic Furs.

The Psychedelic Furs

Personnel: (up to 1986)	JOHN ASHTON	lead gtr	ABCD
	RICHARD BUTLER	vcls	ABCD
	TIM BUTLER	bs	ABCD
	VINCE ELY	drms	A
	DUNCAN KILBURN	sax, vcls	AB
	ROGER MORRIS	gtr	AB
	PHIL CALVERT	drms	B
	KEITH FORSEY	drms	C
	MARS WILLIAMS	sax	CD
	PAUL GARISTO	drms	D

				HCP
ALBUMS: (up to 1986)	1(A)	THE PSYCHEDELIC FURS	(CBS 84084) 1980	18
	2(A)	TALK TALK TALK	(CBS 84892) 1981	30
	3(B)	FOREVER NOW	(CBS 85909) 1982	20
	4(C)	MIRROR MOVES	(CBS 25950) 1984	15

NB: (1) also issued on CD (Columbia 4933432) 1999. (2) also issued on CD (CBS 32539) 1989 and again (Columbia 4873892) 1996. (3) also issued on CD (CBS 85909) 1986. (4) also issued on CD (CBS 25950) 1987. There have also been a number of compilations: *Collection: The Psychedelic Furs* (Castle CCSCD 308) 1991; *All Of This And Nothing* (CBS 4611102) 1991, also on vinyl (CBS 461101) 1983, which got to No. 67, but the CD has extra tracks; and *Should God Forget (A Retrospective 2 CD Set)* (Columbia 4873892) 1997. Also of relevance is *The BBC Radio One Sessions* (Strange Fruit SFRSCD 003) 1997.

			HCP
45s: (up to 1986)	*	We Love You/Pulse (PS)	(Epic EPC 8005) 1979 -
		Sister Europe/(Untitled) (PS)	(CBS 8179) 1980 -
		Mr. Jones/Susan's Strange (PS)	(CBS 9059) 1980 -
	o	Dumb Waiters/Dash (PS)	(CBS A 1166) 1981 59
	+	Pretty In Pink/Mack The Knife (PS)	(CBS A 1327) 1981 43
	x	Pretty In Pink/Mack The Knife/ Soap Commercial (12")	(CBS A 13 1327) 1981 -
	#	Love My Way/ Aeroplane (dance mix) (some PS)	(CBS A 2549) 1982 42
		Danger/I Don't Want To Be Your Shadow	(CBS A) 1982 -
		Danger/I Don't Want To Be Your shadow/ Goodbye (Mix)	(CBS 13 A) 1982 -
	α	Heaven (Pt's 1 & 2)	(CBS A 4300) 1984 29
		Heaven/Heartbeat (Remix) (12", PS)	(CBS TA 4300) 1984 -
		The Ghost In You/Another Edge (PS)	(CBS A 4470) 1984 68
		The Ghost In You/Calypso Dub/ President Gas (live) (12", PS)	(CBS TA 4470) 1984 -
	β	Heartbeat (Mendelssohn Mix)/My Time	(CBS A 4654) 1984 -
	χ	Heartbeat (Mendelssohn Mix)/My Time/ Here Comes Cowboys (U.S. Remx)/ Heaven (U.S. Remix)	(CBS DA 4654) 1984 -
	δ	Pretty In Pink (Film Version)/ Love My Way	(CBS A 7342) 1986 18
	ε	Pretty In Pink (Film Version)/Love My Way/ Heaven/Heartbeat	(CBS DA 7242) 1986
		Heartbeat Beat/New Dream (PS)	(CBS 6501837) 1986 -
		Heartbeat Beat/New Dream/ Heartbeat Beat (Alt. Version) (12", PS)	(CBS 6501866T) 1986 -
	φ	Heartbeat Beat/New Dream//Sister Europe/ Into You Like A Train/President Gas	(CBS 6501830) 1986 -

NB: * This came in a green, pink or orange picture sleeve. o The first 5,000 copies came with a playable picture sleeve. + Also issued as a picture disc (CBS WA 1327). x This did not come in a picture sleeve but shrinkwrapped with a free T-Shirt. # The first 5,000 came in a gatefold picture sleeve. α This was housed in a plastic wrap and came with a poster. β This was also available as a 12" (CBS TA 4300). χ This was a 7" double pack release. δ This was a re-recorded version of CBS A 1327. ε This was a 7" double pack release. φ The original 7" was shrinkwrapped with a free cassette containing the other three tracks.

The Psychedelic Furs were formed in London in 1977 by Richard and Tim Butler and colleagues. After a session for Radio 1's John Peel they signed to Epic-CBS in 1978. A debut 45 *We Love You* was released in October 1979 and attracted some attention without charting. It was notable for Richard Butler's rather bored vocal style and a drone-laden wall of noise based around two guitars and Duncan Kilburn's saxophone or keyboards which characterised their early sound. They followed this with the haunting *Sister Europe* in February 1980, which sounded strongly influenced by New York's seminal Velvet Underground.

Both these 45s were included on their eponymous debut album, released in March 1980, which many likened to an adaptation of David Bowie's sound around the time of his *Low* album. Whilst their vocalist Richard Butler often appeared in psychedelic gear on stage their name was misleading as the beat of their music, particularly on tracks like *Fall*, *Pulse* and *Wedding Song*, was cleverly contrived to appeal to new wave audiences. Also worth hearing on their first album is the opening cut *India*, another of their haunting songs. All the material was written and arranged by the band and the album made the Top 20, spending six weeks in the charts with a best position of No. 18.

They soon moved to New York and became enormously popular in the 'States after a series of successful tours. Their first inroad into the Singles Chart came with *Dumb Waitress*, released in April 1981, although it only got to No. 59 during its two week stay. This was included on their second album *Talk Talk Talk*, released the following month. This spent nine weeks in the charts (three more than its predecessor although it only climbed to No. 30. With Steve Lillywhite handling production, the dronish 'wall of noise' of their previous album gives way to a sharper, crisper and more melodious sound. The stand-out cut was the catchy *Pretty In Pink*, which climbed to No. 43 when it was later released as a single. It went on to serve as the inspiration for a 1986 film and soundtrack album of the same name and the single was later re-recorded and re-released that year for that purpose. The singles' flip side, a cover of Bobby Darin's *Mack The Knife* was one of the few non-originals they recorded. Also recommended on the *Talk Talk Talk* album are *Into You Like A Train*, *No Tears* and *All Of This And Nothing*.

After the *Pretty In Pink* 45 Vince Ely, who'd been in **The Unwanted** prior to joining the band, left to play with ex-**Soft Boy** Robyn Hitchcock, ex-**Birthday Party** drummer Phil Calvert came in as his replacement. The new line-up set to work on a new album *Forever Now* with Todd Rundgren handling production. The end reult was a more sophisticated sound, utilising carefully selected session players and orchestration. This was best illustrated by the superb *Love My Way*, which got to No. 42 and spent six weeks in the charts when released in July as a taster for the album which followed a month later. The album enjoyed the same chart duration and just made the Top 20. A further 45 *Danger* was culled for 45 release but didn't trouble the charts.

THE PSYCHEDELIC FURS - Talk Talk Talk.

Further personnel changes ensued when Calvert departed for Crime and The City Solution. He was replaced by Keith Forsey. Kilburn and Morris also left and Mars Williams (formerly with The Waitresses) came in on saxophone. Forsey helped with the production of their next album *Mirror Moves*, which took a more commercial slant than their previous work. The end result was a well organised and well produced album which contained in *The Ghost In You*, *Here Come The Cowboys*, *Heaven* and *Heartbeat* a number of good rockers. Soon after this album Paul Garisto replaced Keith Forsey on drums.

As you'd expect **The Psychedelic Furs** have figured on a number of compilations including the following:- *Pretty In Pink* on *The Sounds Of The Suburbs* (Columbia 4888252) 1997, *Teenage Kicks* (PolyGram TV 5253382) 1995 and *Wave Party* (Columbia 4758322) 1995, which also included *Heaven*.

The Psychedelic Furs continued to flourish well beyond the time-span of this book and into the nineties. There are some compilations of their earlier years that may well be of interest *Collection: The Psychedelic Furs*, *All Of This And Nothing* (the CD version has extra tracks) and *Should God Forget*, which is a retrospective 2-CD set covering the whole of their career.

The Radio One Sessions is worth hearing for their first Peel session in August 1979 which aroused considerable excitement in the press at the time.

Psychos

The Psychos sound pure 1977 punk judging by their two contributions - *Young British And White* and *Soul Train* - to the *Raw Deal* (Raw RAWLP 1) 1977 sampler. *Young British And White* can also be heard on *The Raw Records Punk Collection* (Anagram CDPUNK 14) 1993 along with *So Young* and *Straight Jacket*.

Psykyk Volts

| 45: | Totally Useless/ | | |
| | Horror Story No. 5 (PS) | (Ellie Jay EJPS 9262) 1979 |

NB: Also listed as (MHG GHM 109).

A rare and collectable 45 from the end of the decade. **Psykyk Volts** were a three-piece from Dewsbury near Leeds. Musically, this was somewhere between heavy metal and ghoul pop.

Public Image Ltd. (P.I.L.)

Personnel:	KEITH LEVENE	gtr	ABCDEF
(up to	JOHN LYDON	vcls	ABCDEF
mid-1984)	JIM WALKER	drms	A
	JAH WOBBLE		
	(JOHN WORDIE)	bs	ABC
	DAVE CROWE	drms	B
	JEANETTE LEE	keyb'ds, synth	BCDE
	RICHARD DUDANSKI	drms	C
	MARTIN ATKINS	drms	D
	KEN LOCKE	keyb'ds	F

PiL - Public Image.

HCP

ALBUMS:	1(A)	PUBLIC IMAGE	(Virgin V 2114) 1978	22
(up to	2(B)	METAL BOX 1	(Virgin METAL 1) 1979	18
1985)	3(C)	SECOND EDITION (dble)	(Virgin VD 2512) 1980	46
	4(C)	PARIS AU PRINTEMPS (live)	(Virgin V 2183) 1980	61
	5(D)	FLOWERS OF ROMANCE	(Virgin V 2189) 1981	11
	6(E)	LIVE IN TOKYO	(Virgin VGD 3508) 1983	28
	7(F)	THIS IS WHAT YOU WANT...		
		THIS IS WHAT YOU GET	(Virgin V 2309) 1984	56

NB: (1) reissued at budget price (Virgin OVED 160) 1986, also on CD (Virgin CPV 2114) 1986. (2) comprised three 12" discs separated by circles of paper plus an inner sheet packaged in a box with the PiL logo embossed on the lid. It was reissued on CD (Virgin MTLCD 1) 1990. (3) reissued on CD (Virgin CDVD 2512) 1987. (4) reissued on vinyl (Virgin OVED 50) 1984 at budget price and on CD (Virgin CDV 2183) 1990. (5) reissued on vinyl (Virgin OVED 51) 1984 at budget price and on CD (Virgin CDV 2189) 1990. (6) comprised two 12" discs plus a poster. It was reissued on CD (Virgin CDV 2366) 1986 and again (Virgin VGDCD 3508) in 1992. (7) reissued on vinyl at budget price (Virgin OVED 176) 1986 and on CD (Virgin CDV 2309) 1990. There's also a hits compilation, *The Greatest Hits... So Far* (CD) (Virgin CDV 2644) 1990, also on vinyl, which got to No. 20, *PiL - Interview Picture Disc* (Baktabak BAK 2045) 1986, a picture disc album and, most significantly, *Plastic Box* (4-CD set) (Virgin PILBOX 1) 1999.

HCP

45s:	*	Public Image/The Cowboy Song	(Virgin VS 228) 1978	9
(up to		Death Disco/And No Birds Do Sing (PS)	(Virgin VS 274) 1979	20
1985)	+	Death Disco (½ Mix)/		
		Megamix (12 Ltd ed. PS)	(Virgin VS 27412) 1979	-
		Memories/Another (PS)	(Virgin VS 299) 1979	60
		Memories (extended version)/		
		Another (12" PS)	(Virgin VS 29912) 1979	-
	x	Flowers Of Romance/		
		Home Is Where The Heart Is (PS)	(Virgin VS 397) 1981	24
		Flowers Of Romance (Instrumental)/		
		Home Is Where The Heart Is (12" PS)	(Virgin VS 39712) 1981	-
		This Is Not A Love Song/		
		Public Image (PS)	(Virgin VS 529) 1983	5
	α	This Is Not A Love Song/Blue Water/		
		This Is Not A Love Song (Remix)/		
		Public Image (12" ltd ed.)	(Virgin VS 52912) 1983	
	α	Bad Life/Question Mark	(Virgin VS 675) 1984	71
		Bad Life (Extended)/		
		Question Mark (12" PS)	(Virgin VS 67512) 1984	-

NB: * This was released in a newspaper sleeve. + This was a limited edition release of 5,000. The 'B' side was *Fodderstomp* from their first album remixed. x The 'B' side plays at 33 r.p.m. α This was a limited edition release in an embossed sleeve.

Public Image Ltd. are significant in the context of this book as probably the first major post-punk band whose music took account of the punk sound and ethos but strived hard to produce something completely different to punk.

After **The Sex Pistols** split in January 1978 Johnny Rotten, who reverted to his real name of John Lydon, formed a new band **Public Image Ltd.**. He recruited Keith Levene, who'd been in the original **Clash** line-up and Jah Wobble (real name John Wordle), who were both friends of his. Canadian drummer Jim Walker, who'd been in a band called Furies, was added following auditions. An early joke name for the band was Carnivorous Butterflies.

Lydon re-signed to Virgin and their debut 45 *Public Image* was released in September 1978. Marketed in a newspaper sleeve the disc sold well and made it into the Top 10, though much of this was due to Lydon's involvement. The 'A' side was dominated by a heavy bass which sounds too prominent in the mix thereby obscuring the lyrics. The flip was self-indulgent - a disco backing track superimosed by verbal rantings.

"You never listened to a word that I said
You only see me for the clothes that I wear
Or did the interest go so much deeper
It must have been the colour of my hair
Public image public image"
(from *Public Image*)

In this era the band deliberately kept live performances to a minimum. Their debut gig was in Paris on 14th December 1978. They also played two Christmas 1978 gigs at London's Rainbow Theatre.

The original producer for their debut album *Public Image* (also known as *First Issue*) John Leckie was sacked by the band who ended up producing it themselves. It marked a complete break from the three-minute song format which had been an important ingredient of punk. The opening cut *Theme* was nine minutes long for a start with the lyrics 'I wish I could die' repeated to such an extent as to become irritating. *Fodderstomp* was similarly annoying and self-indulgent. Many of their fans didn't know quite what to make of it. Their live shows at this stage were often barracked and on at least one occasion the band's response was to walk off stage. Their original drummer Jim Walker left after this album to join **The Pack**. Dave Crowe came in as a replacement and Jeanette Lee was added to the line-up on keyboards as the band expanded to a quintet.

They responded with the *Death Disco* 45, usually considered one of their finest moments. It got to No. 20 and spent a total of seven weeks in the charts. A 12" version was also put out with a vastly extended 'A' side and a different flip side, *Megamix*. This was disappointing, though, being a remixed version of *Fodderstomp* from their first album with rambling synthesizers replacing the earlier vocals. They followed this with *Memories* in September 1979. This 12" version had an extended 'A' side but no additional tracks. *Memories* peaked at No. 60 in the charts.

Their next 'album' *Metal Box* had been a year in the making but was well worth the wait. Released in November 1979, it comprised three 12" discs,

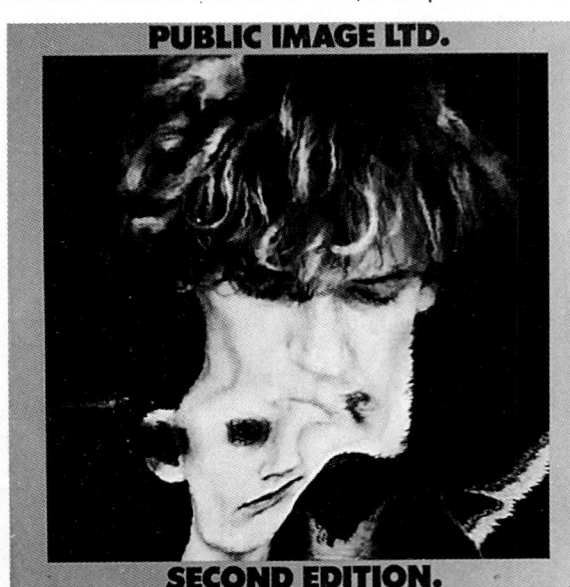

PiL - Second Edition.

PiL - Paris Au Printemps.

each separated by a sheet of paper and a page of A5-size track listings and times. These were presented inside a circular metal tin embossed with the PiL logo. Initially 20,000 copies were produced and these sold very quickly. A further 40,000 were then pressed. The musical menu was impressive. Jah Wobble's throbbing bass lines provided a pounding rhythm around which Levene's guitar and keyboards flickered. Lydon's wails and moans, reminiscent of Captain Beefheart, gell effectively with the instrumentation to produce music that is both engaging and unnerving. The band originally envisaged no song titles for the project, but they were added later at Virgin's insistence. Some of their earlier material was remixed on this album. A remixed version of *Death Disco* appeared as *Swanlake* and *Another* (the flip of their *Memories* 45) appeared as *Graveyard*, *Memories* was remixed and then joined together with a second version. *Poptones* and *Careering* were the most accessible songs in the project, which included a repetitive but somehow compelling cut called *Socialist*. The metal tin format was expensive to produce so in the 'States the package was issued as a short double album *Second Edition*, with lyrics on the inner sleeve. After a few months the same format and title was marketed here in a gatefold sleeve, where it sold for just £5.49.

By the time the band recorded a session for John Peel on 17th December 1979 and appeared on 'The Old Grey Whistle Test', performing *Poptunes* and *Careering* on both occasions, Crowe had been replaced on drums first by ex-**101ers** and Basement S member Richard Dundanski. He recorded and played live with the band between April - September 1979. Then ex-**Fall** drummer Karl Burns stood in briefly before Martin Atkins (also known as **Brian Brain**) joined in the Autumn. Dudanski, meanwhile joined **The Raincoats**.

In January 1980, the rather lacklustre *Paris Au Printemps* live album was issued. It contained many of their better songs but the sound quality was poor. Still it was released to counter bootlegs on which the sound quality would probably have been even worse.

Suffering from continual police harassment John Lydon switched the whole **PiL** outfit to New York and kept a low profile in the U.K.. They embarked on a ten-date U.S. tour which resulted in Atkins being sacked and Jah Wobble leaving to go solo.

With this trimmed down line-up they recorded *Flowers Of Romance*. The title track was released on 45 in March 1981, backed by *Home Is Where The Heart Is*, which featured Jim Walker on drums and had been left over from the first album sessions. The album followed in April. Without Jah Wobble's throbbing bass, the band based its sound around drums, which were mostly played by Keith Levene and John Lydon. The better tracks, aside from the title cut, were the Middle-Eastern-influenced *Four Enclosed Walls* and *Banging The Door*, but this was an extremely stark and uncommercial album, which ironically became their highest-charting album of all peaking at No. 11, although it only spent five weeks in the charts.

Around January 1982 Jeanette left but Ken Locke, who'd previously worked solo and been a member of Cowboys International, came in on keyboards. A new bassist Peter Jones was recruited and PiL made a number of live appearances between September 1982 and March 1983. Meanwhile a new album, *You Are Now Entering The Commercial Zone* was promised but never emerged. Instead came more upheaval with first Jones and then Levene quitting the band. Levene did little after leaving the band and Jones never again experienced such limelight.

Lydon and Atkins arrived in Britain in November 1983 to embark on an extensive tour with a new line-up of New Jersey-based musicians. The *Live In Tokyo* album, released in September 1983, consisted of two 12" discs, a poster and a rather lacklustre performance of old and new material was contained on the vinyl therein. A U.S. promo-only issue of *Live In Tokyo* included all the tracks on one album in an unique sleeve. A month earlier, in August, a studio recording of one of the tracks from the live album *This Is Not A Love Song* became their biggest selling 45 thus far reaching No. 5 and spending ten weeks in the charts. There was also a 12" version with a limited edition embossed logo sleeve, an additional non-album cut, *Blue Water* and a remixed 'A' side.

Their next album, *This Is What You Want... This Is What You Get* included both *Love Song* and its follow-up 45 *Bad Life*, which only got to No. 71. This was disappointing after the success of *Love Song*, but so was the album's final chart placing of 56. **PiL** started work on this album before Levene's departure but his guitar contributions were removed from the finished product. He therefore released his own version of the album a month later called *The Commercial Zone*. Five songs from *This Is What You Want...* appear on this (some with changed titles) alongside some solo cuts.

PiL - Flowers Of Romance.

Lydon disbanded the outfit in mid-1984, which for the purposes of this book is where we leave them. Of course, he went on to reform them in 1985 and they went on to enjoy considerable further success.

The Greatest Hits So Far includes all of their singles and more of a nicely balanced collection which charted their career up to 1990.

Back in 1980 *Pied Piper* was included on *Machines* (Virgin V 2177) and *Attack* on *Cash Cows* (Virgin MILK 1). Other compilation appearances have included *Death Disco* on *The Best Punk Album In The World... Ever, Vol. 2* (2-CD) (Virgin VTDCD 79) 1996; *Public Image* on *The Best Punk Anthems.... Ever* (2-CD) (Virgin VTDCD 198) 1998 and on *God Save The Punks* (2-CD) (Disky DOU 882552) 1998, *This Is Not A Love Song* on *New Wave Classics* (2-CD) (Disky DOU 878282) 1998 and *Albatross* on *A Post Punk Primer* (Virgin CDOVD 498) 1997. In 1999, *Public Image* also was included on the 5-CD box set compilation *1-2-3-4 - A History Of Punk And New Wave 1976 - 1979* (MCA/Universal MCD 60066).

Earlier in 1996, Lydon revived the original **Sex Pistols** line-up for the 'Filthy Lucre' tour which spawned a live album.

If you want chapter and verse on **Public Image Ltd** you need the 4-CD set *Plastic Box* released by Virgin in 1999.

PiL - Live In Tokyo.

Public Zone

45:	Naive/Innocent (PS)	(Logo GO 104) 1977

This one-off venture came in a striking red and black sleeve, which is the best thing about this offering from these would-be punks:-

"So naive! Your offer's always on your sleeve! Too easy to deceive! So naive!"
(from *Naive*).

Pulp

Personnel:	ANNE BEAN	vcls	A
	PAUL BURWELL	drms	A
	SIMON HINCKLER	gtr	A

45s:	* Low-Flying Aircraft/Something Just Behind My Back/ So Lo	(Pulp Music PB 1) 1979

This is a completely different **Pulp** from the later and much better known one fronted by Jarvis Cocker.

The labels on this now rare and collectable 45 are blank, some copies are numbered up to 2,000 and signed. Some also had handmade sleeves.

Musically *Low-Flying Aircraft* is wonderfully delerious amalgam of punk and avant-garde. A mix of Burwell's manic percussion and Bean's vocal grunts and screams laced with a garnish of distortion and feedback.

Simon Hinckler was later with The Mission.

Puncture

Personnel:	PAUL CALLUM	vcls, gtr	A
	STEVE COUNSEL	bs	A
	ANTHONY KEEN	keyb'ds	A
	MARTY TRUSS	drms	A

45:	Mucky Pup/You Can't Rock 'n' Roll (In A Council Flat) (PS)	(Small Wonder SMALL 1) 1977

This band has the distinction of providing the first release on the Walthamstow-based Small Wonder label, but little else to commend them. This Cockney combo's *Mucky Pup* largely consists of the phrase "I'm a mucky pup" bellowed over and over again. There are also lines about nose-picking!

Mucky Pup later resurfaced in all its glory on *Small Wonder Punk Singles Collection, Vol. 1* (Anagram CDPUNK 29) 1994 and *Vol. 2* (Anagram CDPUNK 70) 1996 includes *Can't Play Rock 'n' Roll*.

Punishment Of Luxury

Personnel:	BRIAN BOND	vcls	AB
	MALLA CABALLA	gtr	A
	JIMMY GIRO	bs	AB
	NEVILLE LUXURY	gtr	AB
	JEFF THWAITE	drms	A
	STEVE SECRET	drms	B

ALBUM: 1(B) LAUGHING ACADEMY (United Artists UAG 30258) 1979

NB: (1) issued on CD (Dojo DOJOCD 147) 1993 with one bonus cut. There's also a further CD *Revolution By Numbers* (Overground OVER 66 CD) 1997, also on vinyl (OVER 66 LP) 1997.

45s:
	Puppet Life/The Demon (PS)	(Small Wonder SMALL 8) 1978
	Engine Of Excess/Jellyfish (PS)	(United Artists UP 36507) 1979
	Secrets/Brain Bomb (PS)	(United Artists UP 36537) 1979
	Laughing Academy/ Baby Don't Jump (PS)	(United Artists BP 317) 1979
*	Hold Me/Golden Corsets (PS)	(Red Rhino RED 33) 1983

NB: * as Punilux.

Newcastle's **Punishment Of Luxury** made some impression with their debut single *Puppet Life*, released on Small Wonder in July 1978. It stands out among some variable material on their *Laughing Academy* album, released in September 1979.

On 30th August 1978, they recorded their first of two John Peel sessions. It featured *Funk Me* and *Babalon* (both later featured on their *Laughing Academy* album) and *Let's Get Married*, which wasn't committed to vinyl.

A second John Peel session on 30th May 1979 comprised *Radar Buy - Metropolis* and *British Baboon* (also both on their album) and *Secrets*, which was selected for 45 release in August 1979.

Aside from the superb, punchy *Puppet Life*, their album suffers from rather synthesized heavy metal riffing on many tracks. The title track sounds an attempt at something more melodic but suffers from poor production. *Radar Bug / Metropolis* features some engaging and urgent guitar work. It also has some interesting changes of pace. *Funk Me* has quite a striking guitar intro and is pretty riffy throughout with powerful vocals. *All White Jack* features good guitar, keyboard and drum interplay in places. *Obsession* has some good moments but most of the other cuts fall some way short of being noteworthy. To help promote it they appeared at the Reading Festival, but their performance wasn't well received and they split soon after.

The band later reformed in 1983 as Punilux (their name was often abbreviated to this in any case). They recorded one 45 under this moniker.

The CD reissue of *Laughing Academy* adds *Baby Don't Jump*, a 1979 'B' side.

Revolution By Numbers comprises material for a second album (which was never released when United Artists were bought by EMI who decided to drop them) and bonus cuts from when they soldiered on with Red Rhino, the north-east's premier indie label in 1983.

Punishment Of Luxury - Puppet Life.

Small Wonder Punk Singles Collection, Vol. 1 (Anagram CDPUNK 29) 1994 gave a further airing to *Puppet Life*, whilst *Vol. 2* (Anagram CDPUNK 70) 1996 included *Demon*. In 1999, their magnum opus *Puppet Life* was also captured on *1-2-3-4 - A History Of Punk And New Wave 1976 - 1979* (MCA/Universal MCD 60066), a 5-CD box set.

Punishment Of Luxury - Laughing Academy.

The Punkettes

45: Goin' Out Wiv A Punk/Polythene (Response SR 511) 1977

Unusually this 45 did not appear in a picture sleeve. It was one of the early 'cash-in' releases.

Pure Hell

Personnel:	SPIDER	A
	LENNY STILL	A
	STINKER	A
	CHIP WRECK	A

45: These Boots Are Made For Walking/ No Rules (PS) (Golden Sphinx GSX 002) 1978

A punk era cover of the Nancy Sinatra hit.

The Purple Hearts

Personnel:	ROBERT MANTON	vcls	A
	JEFF SHADBOLT	bs, vcls	A
	GARY SPARKS	drms	A
	SIMON STEBBING	gtr, vcls	A
	CHRIS TSANGARIDES	keyb'ds	A

ALBUMS:
1(A)	BEAT THAT!	(Fiction FIX 2) 1980
2(B)	HEAD ON COLLISION TIME	(Razor RAZS 13) 1985
3(B)	POP-ISH FRENZY	(Razor RAZS 19) 1986

NB: (2) also issued on CD (Great Expectations PIPCD 042) 1993. (3) also issued on CD (Great Expectations PIPCD 043) 1994. *Head On Time Collision* (2-CD) (Yeaah YEAAH 9) 1999 combines (2) and (3) on a double set.

HCP

45s:
	Millions Like Us/Beat That! (PS)	(Fiction FICS 003) 1979	57
	Frustration/ Extraordinary Sensation (PS)	(Fiction FICS 007) 1979	-
	Jimmy/What Am I Gonna Do (PS)	(Fiction FICS 9) 1980	60
*	My Life's A Jigsaw/The Guy Who Made Her A Star/ Just To Please You (PS)	(Safari SAFE 30) 1980	-
	Plane Crash/Scooby Doo/ Gun Of Life (PS)	(Road Runner RR 1) 1982	-

NB: * This was initially issued in a fold-out picture sleeve.

A very authentic 1966/68 Who style neo mod outfit who are worth a mention here as they became part of the live new wave scene. They were originally known as Jack Plug and The Sockets. From Romford in Essex, they were at the forefront of the East London/Essex neo-mod revival. They were good at what they did! They also achieved minor hits with *Millions Like Us* and *Jimmy*, which spent three and two weeks in the charts respectively and were part of the 'March Of The Mods' tour in 1979!

Manton also issued a solo 45 before the band returned in the mid-eighties for a live album, recorded at the 100 Club in December 1984 and issued by Razor the following year. It was later reissued on CD by Great Expectations in 1993. Compared to their earlier studio album *Beat That!* this is a disappointing collection. They do offer enthusiastic renditions of their early 45s like *Jimmy*, *Frustration* and *Millions Like Us*, but their later singles like *Gun Of Life*, *Plane Crash* and *My Life's A Jigsaw* come across less well and there's a ramshackle version of Them's *Gloria*. They also recorded a disappointing second album *Pop-Ish Frenzy*, which lacked the excitement and quality of material of their debut.

They have reformed for the occasional gig since their demise. They've also figured on a number of compilations. You'll find *Millions Like Us* on *20 Of Another Kind, Vol. 2* (Polydor POLX-1) 1979; *Scooby Doo* and *Gun Of Life* on *This Is Mod, Vol. 2* (Anagram CDMGRAM 101) 1996; *My Life's A Jigsaw*, *Guy Who Made Her A Star* and *Just To Please You* on *This Is Mod, Vol. 5* (Anagram CDMGRAM 110) 1997; *Gun Of Life* on *This Is Mod* (dbl) (Get Back GET 39) 1999 and *Plane Crash* on *100% British Mod* (Captain Mod MODSKA DCD 8) 1998.

In 1999, Yeaah released *Heads On Collision Time* (a riotous live set originally released in 1985) and *Popish Frenzy* (a less impressive 1986 studio album) on a double CD set, *Head On Time Collision Again*.

Jimmy Pursey

ALBUMS:	1	IMAGINATION CAMOFLAGE	(Polydor 2442180) 1980
(up to	2	ALIEN ORPHAN	(Epic EPC 85235) 1982
1986)	3	REVENGE IS NOT THE PASSWORD	(Turbo) 1983
	4	THE LORD DIVIDES	(Eskimo Green) 1983

NB: (3) and (4) credited to James. T. Pursey. (3) also issued on CD (Arcade 3012832) 1997.

45s:	Lucky Man/	
(up to	Black And White Rock Reggae (PS)	(Polydor POSP 154) 1980
1986)	Animals Have More Fun/Sus (PS)	(Epic EPCA 1336) 1981
	Naughty Boys Like Naughty Girls/	
	Who's Making You Happy? (PS)	(Epic EPCA 1830) 1981
	Alien Orphan/Conversation (PS)	(Epic EPCA 2118) 1982
*	If Only Before/	
	Above And Beyond (12")	(Eskimo Green CODE 2) 1984
*	If Only Before/Revenge Is Not	
	The Password (PS)	(Stage One CODE 27) 1985
	Zapp Pow/Bass Camp Mix	(Videocat JIMM 1) 1986
	Zapp Pow/Bass Camp Mix (12")	(Videocat JIMMYT 1) 1986

NB: * credited to James T. Pursey.

Jimmy Pursey will always be best remembered as the leader and vocalist with **Sham 69**. He'd formed the band in 1976 and saw punk as a medium through which he could channel his working class consciousness. Unfortunately, it all turned sour when their gigs were increasingly disrupted through violence. By the summer of 1980 **Pursey** and the lads decided to disband. **Pursey** decided to embark on a solo career. He also used this to take a change in direction musically.

On his debut album *Imagination Camouflage* he utilises a wider range of musical instruments, incorporating slide guitar, sax and synthesizers to produce more diverse and emotional material. None of the songs are classics, but a good level of consistency is maintained throughout.

Alien Orphan developed these ideas further introducing jazz, funk and electro-rock with riffy bass, guitar and keyboards into an elaborate soundscape. Unfortunately, devoid of much lyrical poignancy or song structure, it fails to capture one's attention and blends into the background.

Overall, **Pursey**'s solo career was none-too-successful, but he worked as a producer, too, even during his years with **Sham 69**, when he also worked with a number of mod revival bands.

PVC 2

Personnel:	WILLY GARDNER	gtr	A
	KENNY HYSLOP	drms	A
	BILLY McISAAK	vcls, gtr	A
	MIDGE URE	gtr, vcls	A
	RUSSELL WEBB	bs	A

45:	Gonna Put You In The Picture/Pain/	
	Deranged, Demented And Free	(Zoom ZUM 2) 1977

This was the mid-seventies pop group Slik experimenting in punk and operating under a pseudonym.

Ure went on to join **The Rich Kids** and the remainder of the band became **The Zones**. Ure was also later in **Ultravox**.

The Quads

Personnel:	J. DOHERTY	A
	C. JONES	A
	S. JONES	A
	T. JONES	A

HCP

45s:	There Must Be Thousands/	
	You've Gotta Jive (PS)	(Big Bear BB 23) 1979 66
	There's Never Been A Night/	
	Take It (PS)	(Big Bear BB 24) 1979 -
	U.F.O./Astronaughts Journey (PS)	(Big Bear BB 29) 1980 -

The Quads formed in Birmingham in 1979. They quickly established themselves as a live act and got signed by the city's main indie label Big Bear Records. Their debut disc got plenty of airplay. It was heavily plugged by John Peel and was also a Paul Burnett record of the week. It featured tough vocals, a cranked up lead guitar motif and other extravagant guitar passages, which took it into the national charts, peaking at No. 66. They also contributed two live cuts to the double album compilation *Brum Beat - Live At The Barrel Organ* (Big Bear BRUM 1) 1979. In terms of records sales their subsequent 45s failed to build on their earlier success and they faded from attention. They went their separate ways in the early eighties.

The Questions

45s:	Some Other Guy/	
	Rock 'n' Roll Ain't Dead (PS)	(Zoom ZUM 6) 1978
	Can't Get Over You/Answers (PS)	(Zoom ZUM 8) 1979

A 'modish' band whose two singles have aroused little interest among collectors to date.

THE PURPLE HEARTS - Head On Collision Time.

Rabid

Personnel: NICK EDWARDS   A
             DEAN GRANT   A
             KEITH PENNY   A
             PAUL RAYNER   A

ALBUM: 1(A) BRING OUT YOUR DEAD (mini-LP)
                                        (Fallout FALL 009) 1982

EP: 1(A) BLOODY ROAD TO GLORY (Jubilee/Glory Of War/
              Police Victim/Crisis 82) (PS)   (Fallout FALL 007) 1982

One of the lesser known early eighties punk bands from Leicester. In addition to the above one of their songs *Jubilee* also got a further airing on *The Fallout Punk Singles Collection* (Anagram CDPUNK 30) in 1994. Earlier, in 1986, they contributed *Black Cat* and *Bloody Road To Glory* to *Punk Lives - Let's Slam* (Rot SLAM 2). Both tracks are very guitar-orientated.

The Radiators

Personnel: PHIL CHEVRON   vcls, gtr   A
             JAMES CRASHE   drms   A
             PETER HOLIDAI   gtr   A
             MARK MEGARAY   bs   A

ALBUM: 1(A) GHOST TOWN   (Chiswick CWK 3003) 1979

NB: (1) reissued (Big Beat WIK 85) 1989 and also issued on CD (Big Beat CD WIK 85) 1989. There are also two other CD releases, *Cockles And Mussels (The Best Of The Radiators From Space)* (Chiswick CDWIKS 156) 1995 and *Alive-Alive-O (Live In London 1978) Rare Studio Tracks* (Chiswick CDWIKD 164) 1996.

45s: Million Dollar Hero/
        Blitzin' At The Ritz (PS)   (Chiswick NS 29) 1978
        Walkin' Home Alone/Try And Stop Me/
        Hucklebuck (PS)   (Chiswick NS 45) 1978
        Million Dollar Hero (Remix)/
        Blitzin' At The Ritz (PS)   (Chiswick CHIS 106) 1978
        Let's Talk About The Weather/Try And Stop Me/
        Hucklebuck (PS)   (Chiswick CHIS 113) 1979
        Kitty Ricketts/Ballad Of The Faithful
        Departed (PS)   (Chiswick CHIS 115) 1979
        Stranger Than Fiction/Prison Bars/
        Who Are The Strangers? (PS)   (Chiswick CHIS 126) 1980
        The Dancing Years/
        (Instrumental Mix) (PS)   (Chiswick CHIS 133) 1980
        Song Of The Faithful Departed/
        Looting (PS)   (Chiswick CHIS 144) 1981

This was a later version of **The Radiators From Space**. Linking up with veteran producer Tony Visconti, they recorded a number of further singles and an album *Ghost Town*, in July 1979. This also had its moments but veered more towards power pop. The material is again strong confirming their potential which sadly remained unfulfilled.

Cockles And Mussels - The Best Of The Radiators is a pretty good collection of the Irish punk band's amalgam of rock 'n' roll, doo wop and high-octane pub rock. It also showcases Phil Chevron's early singer-songwriter skills (he was later with The Pogues) and suggests that the band really under-achieved.

Alive - Alive O! is a punky live set recorded at the Roundhouse in February 1978 in the transitional period between their *TV Tube Heart* album (in their **Radiators From Space** era) and their under-rated follow-up *Ghost Town*. The CD release includes ten bonus tracks and among them are several rare demos. The band's live reputation is underscored by their versions of *Television Screen* and *Prison Bars*.

They split up in the early eighties. In 1985, Phil Chevron re-emerged to produce The Pogues' *Dirty Old Town* album in 1985. He later joined them on guitar - so he eventually attained the commercial success he deserved.

Back in 1992, *Million Dollar Hero* and *Dancing Years* resurfaced on *The Chiswick Story* (2-CD) (Chiswick CDWIK 2 100) 1992, whilst *Let's Talk About The Weather* got a further airing on *The Chiswick Sampler (Good Clean Fun)* (Chiswick CDWIKX 162) 1995.

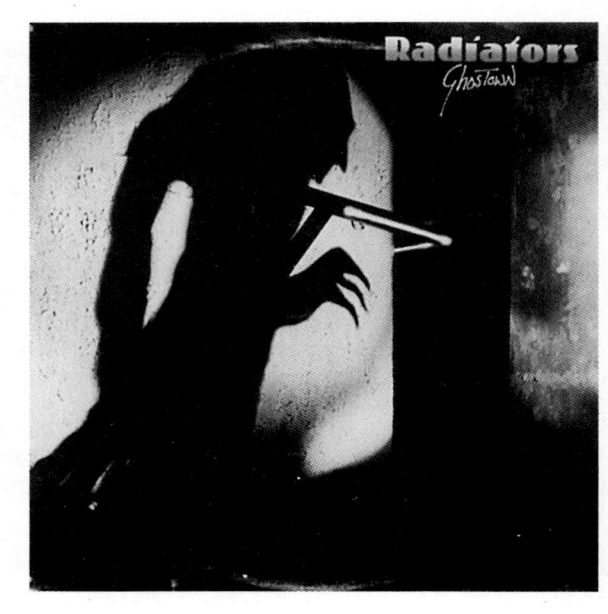

THE RADIATORS - Ghost Town.

The Radiators From Space

Personnel: PHIL CHEVRON   vcls, gtr   A B
             JAMES CRASH   drms   A B
             PETER HOLIDAI   gtr   A B
             MARK MEGARAY   bs   A B
             STEPHEN RAPID   vcls   A

ALBUM: 1(B) TV TUBE HEART   (Chiswick WIK 4) 1977

EP: 1(A) FOUR ON THE FLOOR (EP) (Enemies/Teenager In
              Love/Television Screen/
              Psychotic Reaction) (PS)   (Big Beat SW 57) 1980

45s: Television Screen/Love Detective (PS) (Chiswick S 10) 1977
       *   Television Screen/Love Detective (PS) (Chiswick NS 10) 1977
            Enemies/Psychotic Reaction (PS)   (Chiswick NS 19) 1977
       +   Prison Bars/
            (Why Can't I Be) A Teenager In Love   (Chiswick NS 24) 1978

NB: * This is a late repressing. + A promo-only white label release in a stamped white sleeve and loose printed labels.

The Radiators From Space were originally from Dublin, where they formed in 1975. Initially they used the name Greta Garbage and The Trash Cans. They were signed by Chiswick in spring 1977 and, whilst they never achieved commercial success, they were a talented and significant find.

Television Screen was a powerful debut single. It was also significant as the first punk single released by Chiswick. Indeed they were one of the earliest punk bands. It was also included on their sampler *Long Shots Dead Certs And Odds On Favourites* (Chiswick CH 5) in 1978, along with *Enemies*. The influence of U.S. garage bands on punk (there were many similarities between the two phenomenons) was evident again when they covered U.S. garage band The Count Five's *Psychotic Reaction* on the flip side of the follow-up *Enemies*.

Their vocalist Steve Rapid quit on the brink of the recording sessions for their debut album. Phil Chevron took over vocal duties for *T.V. Tube Heart*, which was released in late 1977. The music on the album was clever and melodic. The band were clearly a quality outfit. They were frequent visitors to mainland U.K. after its release, gigging to help promote it.

In early 1978, feeling **The Radiators From Space** to be a bit of a mouthful, they shortened their name to **The Radiators**.

Back in 1992 *Television Screen* figured on *The Chiswick Story* (2-CD) (Chiswick CDWIK 2 100) 1992 and *Enemies* got a further airing on *The Chiswick Sampler (Good Clean Fun)* (Chiswick CDWIKX 162) 1995. *Television Screen* resurfaced on *Punk Lost And Found* (Shanachie SH 5705) 1996 and on the 5-CD box set *1-2-3-4 - A History Of Punk And New Wave 1976 - 1979* (MCA/Universal MCD 60066) in 1999.

Radio 5

45:	True Colours/		
	Animal Connections (PS)	(Rockburgh ROCS 225)	1980

Radio 5 hailed from Bradford in Yorkshire and were relatively short-lived. *True Colours* was an indie pop song, which was also included on *Hicks From The Sticks* (Rockburgh Records ROC 111) in 1980.

Radio Stars

Personnel:

ANDY ELLISON	vcls	ABCDEFG	
MARTIN GORDON	bs	ABCDE G	
IAN McLEOD	gtr	ABCDEFG	
CHRIS TOWNSON	drms	A	
GARY THOMPSON	drms	B	
STEVE PARRY	drms	C FG	
JAMIE CROMPTON	drms	DE	
TREVOR WHITE	vcls, bs	EF	
CHRIS GENT	sax	G	
HUGH McDOWELL	cello	G	
TOMMY WILLIS	gtr	G	

ALBUMS:	1(C)	SONGS FOR SWINGING LOVERS	(Chiswick WIK 5)	1977
	2(D)	THE HOLIDAY ALBUM	(Chiswick CWK 3001)	1978
	3(-)	TWO MINUTES MR. SMITH	(Moonlight MNA 001)	1982

NB: (1) was shrinkwrapped with a free single *No Russians In Russia / Dirty Pictures* (Promo 2). There was also a cassette version, released after the album, which included both free single tracks. There's also a 29 track compilation CD, *Somewhere There's A Place For Us* (Ace CDWIKD 107) 1992.

EP:	1(B)	STOP IT! (No Russians In Russia//Box 29/Johnny		
		Mekon/Sorry I'm Tied Up) (PS)	(Chiswick SW 17)	1977

HCP

45s:	Dirty Pictures/Sail Away (PS)	(Chiswick S 9)	1977 -
	Nervous Wreck/Horrible Breath (PS)	(Chiswick NS 23)	1977 39
	Nervous Wreck/		
	Horrible Breath (12" PS)	(Chiswick NST 23)	1977 -
*	From A Rabbit/The Beast No. 2 (PS)	(Chiswick NS 36)	1978 -
+	From A Rabbit/To A Beast (PS)	(Chiswick NS 36)	1978 -
	Radio Stars/		
	Accountancy Blues (PS)	(Chiswick CHIS 102)	1978 -
	The Real Me/Good Personality (PS)	(Chiswick CHIS 109)	1979 -
	My Mother Said/		
	Two Minutes Mr. Smith (PS)	(Snap ECG 1)	1982 -
	Good Personality/		
	Talking 'Bout You (PS)	(Moonlight MNS 001)	1982 -

NB: * There were two different mixes of the 'B' side, with matrix no's 5288-IT and 5288-27, in a generic Chiswick sleeve. Some copies came in a clear plastic outer sleeve with green **Radio Stars** logo. + 6" 'hip-pocket' issue.

RADIO STARS - Songs For Swinging Lovers.

Radio Stars formed in early 1977. Andy Ellison, Martin Gordon, Ian McLeod and Chris Townson had all previously been in Jet, who recorded one album for CBS in 1975. Indeed, back in May 1966 Ellison and Townson had been members of the Leatherhead-based Silence, who in September 1966 became the legendary John's Children. As most of you will know they included Marc Bolan for a while.

Radio Stars were born when Andy Ellison, who also cut three solo 45s in the late sixties, passed Chiswick records' supremo Ted Carroll a tape of four final Jet songs. Carroll liked *Dirty Pictures* so the four former Jet members came together to remix it. After its release on 8th April 1977 it made the indie charts and became an NME 'Single of the Week'.

For their first live appearance on 30th April Gary Thompson replaced Chris Townson on drums, in Karsuhe, Germany. They proceded to tour Germany with UFO for a fortnight.

On 20th May 1977, they recorded the first of three John Peel sessions comprising *Horrible Breath, Dirty Pictures, Dear Prudence* and *No Russians In Russia*. A second on 18th November 1977, consisted of *Good Personality, Beast Of Barnsley, Don't Waste My Time* and *Is It Really Necessary?*.

Their next release was the *Stop It!* (EP), which included an old Jet song, *Johnny Mekon* and *No Russians In Russia*, which was inspired by President Ford's comment that the Eastern Block was not influenced by the Soviet Union. They made their TV debut playing *No Russians In Russia* on Marc Bolan's show. The song was also included on the sampler *Long Shots Dead Certs And Odds On Favourites* (Chiswick CH 5) in 1978.

By the time they set to work recording their debut album *Songs For Swinging Lovers* Gary Thompson had been replaced on drums by Steve Parry. The original title *Bowels Stuffed With Spleen* was vetoed by Chiswick Records. The album was preceded by the release of its most commercial cut *Nervous Wreck* as a 45 in October 1977. It had a catchy melody but was pop rather than punk or new wave. It became their only hit peaking at No. 39 during its three week chart stint.

The album followed on 25th November. It was not without controversy including a song about Reg Chapman, rapist and self-styled beast in *Beast Of Barnsley*. The song *Elvis Is Dead Boring* had to be changed to *Arthur Is Dead Boring* after an engineer at Olympic studios refused to work on the song. The album even featured a little jingle to plug the group's label *Buy Chiswick Records*. Overall, though, the quality of material on the album is too inconsistent to make for a good record. Despite the marketing ploy of including *Dirty Pictures* and *No Russians In Russia* on a freebie 7" which came with the album, it didn't trouble the charts.

Their next 45, *From A Rabbit* dealt with the pluses and minuses of body building. It got a lot of airplay from BBC's Kid Jensen and a new marketing ploy - the release of a novelty 'hip-pocket' 6" issue was used. Despite all this, it failed to move sufficient quantities to chart.

The band returned from a winter tour to start work on a second album. Halfway through Parry was replaced on drums by Jamie Crompton (from **New Hearts**). However, their manager placed an embargo on his face and he appeared on the subsequent *Holiday Album* cover wearing a rubber Mickey Mouse head. John Mackie stood in for a few gigs when Crompton rejoined his old band for a few gigs.

They appeared at the 1978 Reading Festival and embarked on a forty-two-date tour to promote their new album. By now the **New Hearts** had split and Jamie Crompton was back in **Radio Stars** again alongside new vocalist Trevor White. They also played two more radio sessions during October 1978. The first on 4th October was their final Peel session and featured four cuts from their forthcoming album; *Boy Meets Girl, Radio Stars* (their 45), *Sex In Chains Blues (Again Mama)* and *Sitting In The Rain*. Two weeks later, on 17th October, they recorded four more cuts - *Radio Stars, Baffin Ireland, Norwegian Wood* and *Rock 'n' Roll For The Time Being* - for David Jensen. These were also from their forthcoming album.

Their *Holiday Album* was eventually released in November 1978, by which time their tour was over. One cut, *Radio Stars* was culled for 45 release in September. Originally running at just one minute six seconds it was considered too short for radio airplay - so the band recorded two new versions. One simply repeated the song twice, with Andy's impersonation of a DJ saying "Well, there we are, the fabulous new single from Radio Stars, let's hear it again" linking the two segments. The other version joined them via a new middle passage. When the album came out, it received mixed reviews and registered poor sales. The real problem was it didn't contain material of a consistently high quality.

Martin Gordon left and went into hospital to have his wisdom teeth removed. Trevor White switched to bass and Steve Parry rejoined, replacing Jamie Crompton on drums. They cut a new 45 *The Real Me* in January 1979. It received favourable reviews but didn't chart. They embarked on a new tour in February, but their lack of commercial success forced them to split that summer.

In 1982, Moonlight Records released *Two Minutes Mr. Smith*, an obscure compilation by the band and to help promote it two cuts, *Good Personality* and *Talkin' 'Bout You* (originally on their first album), were put out on a 45. Both the compilation and 45 passed largely unnoticed.

In 1983, Andy Ellison and Martin Gordon reformed **Radio Stars** as a seven piece, but it was only ever intended as a short-term venture. The three additional players were Hugh McDowell (ex-Electric Light Orchestra) on cello, Chris Gent on sax and Tommy Willis (ex-Blue Meanies) on guitar. The new line-up recorded three new songs, including *Two Minutes Mr. Smith* before splitting.

In 1991, German band Die Toten Hosen recorded a version of *Dirty Pictures* on their album *Learning English Vol. 1* and asked Andy Ellison to sing on it.

The following year Ace released a twenty-nine track CD compilation of their material, *Somewhere There's A Place For Us*. As well as featuring their best songs it had a number of unreleased songs and oddities. These included *Dear Prudence* recorded for the *Stop It!* (EP) but not eventually used on it; *My Mother Said* (an obscure 1982 45 'A' side featuring the seven-piece line-up) and an edited version of *It's All Over* (from their second album). It was intended for a 45 release, which never was.

Martin Gordon went on to Blue Meanies and production work. Andy Ellison kept the band's name alive throughout the eighties and nineties and, in 1997, a **Radio Stars** song *Blame It On The Youth* was included on the CD compilation *Holidays In The Sun 2* (Visionary HITS 02) 1997.

Four of their songs, *Dirty Pictures*, *No Russians In Russia*, *Nervous Wreck* and *Real Me* got fresh exposure on *The Chiswick Story* (2-CD) (Chiswick CDWIK 2 100) in 1992. Later, in 1995, *Radio Stars* and *Buy Chiswick Records* re-emerged on *The Chiswick Sampler (Good Clean Fun)* (Chiswick CDWIKD 162). Then, in 1999, *Nervous Wreck* got a further airing on the 5-CD box set *1-2-3-4 - A History Of Punk And New Wave 1976 - 1979* (MCA/Universal 60066).

Radio Stars were a significant, but not essential, new wave band. They had a few good songs, but all their albums lacked sufficient consistency to become real classics.

THE RAINCOATS - Odyshape.

The Rage

45s: Looking For You/Come On Now (PS)   (Diamond RAGE 1) 1986
 * Looking For You/Come On Now/Great Balls Of Fire/
  Hallelujah I Love Her So (12")   (Diamond RAGE 112) 1986

NB: * This was unissued but test pressings do exist.

A mod revival combo. *Looking For You*, *Come On Now* and *Hallelujah I Love Her So* can also be found on *This Is Mod, Vol. 3 (Diamond Collection)* (Anagram CDMGRAM 106) 1996 and you can also check out *Looking For You* again on vinyl on *This Is Mod* (dbl) (Get Back GET 39) 1999.

The Raincoats

Personnel:			
ANA DA SILVA	gtr, vcls	ABCDEFG
GINA BIRCH	bs	ABCDEFG
ROSS CRIGHTON	violin, gtr	ABC
NICK TURNER	drms	AB
JEREMIE FRANK	gtr	BC
RICHARD DUDANSKI	drms	C G
VICKY ASPINALL	violin, gtr	DEFG
PALMOLIVE	drms	D
INGRID WEISS	drms	E
CHARLES HAYWARD	drms	F
DEREK GODARD	perc	G
PADDY O'CONNELL	sax	G

ALBUMS:
1(A) THE RAINCOATS (Rough Trade ROUGH 3) 1979
2(D) ODYSHAPE (Rough Trade ROUGH 13) 1981
3(G) MOVING (Rough Trade ROUGH 66) 1984

NB: (1) reissued on CD (Rough Trade R 3022) 1993. (2) reissued on CD (Rough Trade R 3042) 1994. (3) reissued on CD (Rough Trade R 3062) 1994. They also had a U.S.-only cassette *The Kitchen Tapes* (ROIR A 120) 1983, which has been reissued on CD (Roir RUSCD 8238) 1998. There's also a CD compilation, *Looking In The Shadows* (Rough Trade R 4032) 1996.

45s: Fairytale In The Supermarkets/In Love/
 Adventures Close To Home (PS)   (Rough Trade RT 013) 1979
 No-One's Little Girl/
 Running Away (PS)   (Rough Trade RT 093) 1982
 Animal Rhapsody/No-one's Little Girl/
 Honey Mad Woman (12" PS)   (Rough Trade RT 153) 1983

The Raincoats were a punk-inspired all girl group. They formed in October 1977 when two Hornsey Art College students Ana Da Silva and Gina Birch from Ladbrook Grove in London teamed up with guitarist Ross Crighton and drummer Nick Turner. They soon began writing songs and rehearsing. Their first live appearance followed in December of that year. They supported Doll by Doll at the Tabernacle in West London.

Crighton soon left to concentrate on his work for Rough Trade. His replacement was a dynamic young guitarist called Jeremie Frank. Then drummer Nick Turner left to be replaced by Richard Dudanski, who'd previously been with **101'ers** and was later with **PiL**. Turner was later in The Barracudas and Lords of The New Church.

By the end of 1978 their line-up stabilised into a four piece Ana Da Silva, Gina Birch, ex-York University music graduate Vicky Aspinall (previously with feminist band Jam Today) and former **Slits'** drummer Palmolive. Their first gig was at Acklam Hall supporting **The Passions** in January 1979. On 5th January, they recorded a four track session for John Peel. This comprised *In Love*, based on simple chord changes and distorted violin, *You're A Million*, *Adventures Close To Home* and *Fairytale In The Supermarket*, a spirited song and again utilising distorted violin, which was selected as the 'A' side of their debut 45, released in April 1979. It featured three of the four songs in their first Peel session, the omission being *You're A Million*. Gina Birch's *In Love* on the 'B' side, was also included on the sampler *Wanna Buy A Bridge?* (Rough Trade ROUGH US-3), which was targetted at the U.S. market.

Their debut album *The Raincoats* followed in November 1979. It was recorded in just two weeks and certainly bordered on the unconventional. It deployed esoteric, philosophical lyrics and songs like *The Void*, *Off Duty Trip* and *You're A Million* were full of stop-start rhythms. *Adventures Close*

To Home and In Love are on there too and the distorted violin hints at a Velvet Underground influence. There's also a cover version of Ray Davies' Lola, which performed by an all girl band played havoc with the song's lyrics. By now they were being heralded as one of the great hopes for the future. They had successfully completed a U.K. tour with **Kleenex** and **Spizzenergi**. They'd also appeared on a 'South Bank Show' TV documentary about Rough Trade recording Fairytale....

In September 1979, there was an important line-up change that had an enormous impact on the future direction of the band. Palmolive departed to return to her Spanish homeland. Ingrid Weiss was recruited as a replacement in January 1980 but it was 18 months before any new recorded output was released. In the interim the new line-up gigged spasmodically. The new line-up's debut was at Portsmouth in February 1980. They also played in Paris (with **The Slits**), Italy, Holland, Germany and on the Eastern Seaboard of the U.S.A. that spring. In June, they played an avant-garde set at the Communist Party benefit at Alexandra Palace.

Although no new vinyl appeared in 1980, the band did produce a thirty-two-page, pocket-sized publication 'The Raincoats Booklet'. Comprising photos, lyrics (including ones to a number of new songs which would eventually appear on their second album), illustrations and details of their history, it was available free at selected outlets. On 18th December 1980, they recorded their second and final session for John Peel. It comprised Using My Eyes, Family Treat and Baby Song.

Their long-awaited second album Odyshape eventually appeared in June 1981. Still not particularly accessible, their sound had expanded - the distorted violin had given way to poignant acoustic and jangly electric guitar. It was an original and provocative album and one of its cuts, Shouting Out Loud was also included on C-81 (Rough Tapes COPY 1) 1981, a mail-order cassette, the result of a collaboration between NME and Rough Trade, which was available from NME.

Ingrid Weiss left before the album was completed and other band members pursued their own directions at this point. Bassist Gina Birch became an important part of Mayo Thompson's new Red Crayola line-up and Vicky Aspinall appeared playing violin on The New Steppers debut album.

In late 1981, **The Raincoats** regrouped for a series of European gigs. They performed a poignant song from Odyshape about a girl who's Only Loved At Night and Baby Song.

In May 1982, an old live favourite No-One's Little Girl was paired with a cover of Sly and The Family Stone's Running Away on a 45, but sadly it attracted only limited airplay. Later that year one of their performances in New York was released as The Kitchen Tapes on a U.S. Reach Out International cassette. This veered towards folk and jazz, even utilising dance beats. On 17th August 1982, they recorded three cuts for a David Jensen session:- Dance Of Hopping Mad, Honey-Mad Woman and Ooh Ooh La La.

In late 1983 an enlarged line-up 'G' set about recording their third and final album Moving. Eventually released in February 1984 Moving included more sophisticated versions of songs that originally featured on The Kitchen Tapes.

By the time Moving appeared in the shops the band had split. Gina Birch and Vicki Aspinall re-emerged several years later as a duo called Dorothy. They recorded three singles during 1988-89, but none of them sold particularly well or made much impression.

Their classic debut album was reissued by Rough Trade in 1993 with one additional cut Fairytale In The Supermarket and sleevenotes by Kurt Cobain.

A year later the same label reissued Moving with one additional cut No One's Little Girl (their second single).

The Raincoats have figured on a number of other Rough Trade compilations in addition to Wanna Buy A Bridge?, but most of them were released abroad. Running Away appeared on Selezione (Rough Trade/Base RT 011) in Italy, In Love appeared on Clear Cut (Rough Trade/Japam RTL 5) 1980 in Japan and No-one's Little Girl has resurfaced on Compilation (Rough Trade Deutschland RTD 5) in Germany and Rough Trade Records - MNW (MNW X 3) in Scandinavia. The track also appeared on the CD compilation A Constant Sense Of Interruption (Rough Trade CCD 6004) over here. In 2001, Fairytale In The Supermarket got fresh exposure on the 4-CD box set 25 Years Of Rough Trade Shops (Mute CDSTUMM 191).

The Raincoats may not be easy on the ears but they challenged the musical limits of their times and are certainly worth investigating.

Eric Random

ALBUMS:	1	EARTHBOUND GHOST NEED	
			(New Hormones ORG 18) 1982
	2	TIME-SPLICE	(Doublevision DVR 11) 1985

NB: (1) credited to **Eric Random** meets Bedlamites. There was also an earlier cassette Live In Europe (New Hormones CAT 4) 1980.

EP:	1	THAT'S WHAT I LIKE ABOUT ME (12")	
			(New Hormones ORG 6) 1980

45s:	23 Skidoo/	
	Subliminal (PS)	(Disque De Crepescule TW 1029) 1981
	Dow Chemical Company/	
	Skin Deep (PS)	(New Hormones ORG 11) 1981
*	Mad As Mankind (radio version)/	
	Dream Web Of Maya (12", PS)	(Doublevision DVR 7) 1984

NB: * **Eric Random** with The Bedlamites.

Eric Random is a talented, experimental multi-instrumentalist perhaps best known for his involvement with **Cabaret Voltaire**. On these experimental recordings **Random** covers a wide range of musical styles incorporating art-noise, jazz and reggae. He gives the music unusual arrangements and often adds odd and eerie instrumentation. Earthbound Ghost Need even features a version of Ravel's Bolero.

The Raped

Personnel:	TONY BAGGETT	bs	A
	FABIAN KWEST	gtr	A
	PADDY	drms	A
	SEAN PURCELL	vcls	A

ALBUM:	1(A)	PHILES AND SMILES	(Iguana PILAGED 1) 1984

NB: (1) was an official bootleg with booklet. There's also a compilation The Complete Raped Singles Collection (Anagram PUNK CD 35) 1994.

EP:	1(A)	PRETTY PAEDOPHILES (Moving Target/Raped/	
		Escalator Hater/Normal) (PS)	(Parole KNIT 1) 1978

45:	Cheap Night Out/	
	Foreplay Playground (PS)	(Parole PURL 1) 1978

An early punk band who later became **Cuddly Toys**. Under this later incarnation they dyed their hair and proceeded to play Bowie-influenced glam-rock, which lacked any new dimension or interpretation whatsoever.

The Complete Raped Punk Collection is a nineteen-track compilation of studio material, live recordings, demos and outtakes of their amateurish punk boogie fayre. Moving Target (the opening cut of their 1978 Pretty Paedophiles EP) stands out a bit against the rest.

Rat Patrol

Rat Patrol were discovered by **Attila The Stockbroker** and came from the West Country. Their sole appearance on vinyl was Rat Trap on The Oi! Of Sex (Syndicate SYNLP 4) 1984. This compilation was later reissued on CD (Captain Oi! AHOY CD 23) 1994. This Rat Trap has no connection to **The Boomtown Rats** but stylistically did bear some comparison to **Ian Dury**. Lyrically they represented the socialist side of Oi!.

THE REACTION - I Can't Resist.

Reacta

45:   Stop The World/SUS (PS)   (Battery Operated WAC 1) 1979

A rare and collectable punk-era artefact (reputedly only 300 copies were pressed) which had involvement from members of **Television Personalities**. Both Dan Treacy and Ed Ball produced it and various band members also played on it.

The Reaction

Personnel:	BRUCE DOUGLAS	bs	A
	MARK HOLLIS	vcls, gtr	A
	GEORGE PAGE	gtr	A
	GINO P. WILLIAMS	drms	A

45:   I Can't Resist/I Am A Case (PS)   (Island WIP 6437) 1978

A mod-pop outing produced by Ed Hollis and recorded at Island Studios. The cover has a picture of an irresistable strawberry and cream desert. The 'A' side penned by Mark Hollis is unexceptional but the flip side written by their guitarist George Page is pretty beaty with some good guitar work and a great psychedelic ending straight out of 1967.

The Reactors

45:   I Want Sex/I'm A Reactor   (Sabotage) 1979

An obscure indie single and the lyrics weren't exactly stunning:-

"I've got my neutrons, I've got my protons
I've got my electrons
I've got my.... 'er.... shoes on!"

Reafer

Personnel:	MICK HAYS	gtr	A
	HUW JONES	bs	A
	NICK MASTERSON	drms	A
	IMRAN RAHMAN	lead vcls, gtr	A

Reafer's sole vinyl offering is playing *Green Glass Green* on the compilation *499 2139* (Rocket DIAL 1) 1979. This is quite derivative of the sixties with some melodic guitar work.

The Realists

Personnel:	PAUL ASTLES	gtr	A
	JOHN CONROY	drms	A
	ALAN DUNN	bs	A
	RALPH HOLDEN	gtr	A

REALITY - Who Killed The Golden Goose?

45:   I've Got A Heart/Living In The City (PS)   (Stiff OFF 4) 1978

A northern four-piece who relocated to Deptford in South London. Full of enthusiasm and fun their *I've Got A Heart* was met with some acclaim but they failed to follow it up.

Reality

Personnel:	PETE	bs	A
	GULLET	drms	A
	VENG	gtr, vcls	A

45s: Blind To The Truth/Acceptable Death Loss/
      Death Of Morality (PS)   (Subversive SUB 6) 1982
      Who Killed The Golden Goose?/
      Lonely Shadow (PS)   (Jungle/Fight Back FIGHT 3) 1984

NB: There's also a compilation CD *Young Drunk Punks* (Overground OVER 79CD) 1999.

A popular punk band on the East Anglian circuit in the early eighties. Their debut 45 *Blind To The Truth* had an issue of just 1,000 copies on Subversive in 1982 and is now collectable. They released a second 45 on Fight Back in 1984 before splitting up the following year. The song in question *Who Killed The Golden Goose?* features some good guitar segments but isn't a strong enough composition to leave much lasting impression. The same is true of the flip side.

The Overground CD compilation supplements the band's five 45 cuts with 12 tracks of demos, rehearsals and live cuts along with an eight page booklet.

The Record Players

EP: 1( ) DOUBLE C SIDE (MOR/Don't Go Backwards/
      Wrong Song/Ignore Us)   (Wreckord WRECK 001) 1978

NB: (1) also listed as Aerco (AERO 1104) 1978.

45:   Give An Inch/Squirming In The Vermin By The Bonny Banks
      Of Clyde/67/Parasite (PS)   (Wreckord WRECK 002) 1980

One of the 'also-rans' of the era, **The Record Players** came from Kent. Their best known song is probably the promising *M.O.R.* by virtue of its inclusion on *Business Unusual* (Cherry Red ARED 2) 1979.

The Records

Personnel:	WILL BIRCH	drms	ABCD
	PHIL BROWN	bs, vcls	ABCD
	HUW GOWER	gtr, vcls	AB
	JOHN WICKS	gtr, vcls	ABCD
	IAN GIBBONS	keyb'ds	B

JUDE COLE	gtr, vcls		C
CHRIS GENT	vcls		D
DAVE WHELAN	gtr		D

ALBUMS: 1(B) SHADES IN BED aka THE RECORDS
(up to (Virgin V 2122) 1979
1986) 2(C) CRASHES (Virgin V 2155) 1980
3(D) MUSIC ON BOTH SIDES (Virgin V 2206) 1982

NB: (1) came with a bonus 12" EP *High Heels*. There are also two compilations: *Smashes, Crashes And Near Misses* (Virgin COMCD 13) 1988 and *The Best Of The Records* (Virgin CDOVD 456) 1995. Also relevant is *Paying For The Summer Of Love* (Skyclad Records CD78) 1990 on vinyl and CD (Angel Air SJPCD 078) 2001.

45s: Starry Eyes/Paint Her Face (PS) (NB NB 2) 1978
Rock 'n' Roll Love Letter/
Wives & Mothers Of Tomorrow (PS) (Virgin VS 247) 1979
Teenarama/Held Up High (PS) (Virgin VS 250) 1979
Hearts In Her Eyes/So Sorry (PS) (Virgin VS 330) 1980
Imitation Jewellery/
Your Own Soundtrack (PS) (Virgin VS 442) 1981

The Records were old pub-rockers who received a new lease of life in the new wave era with a highly accessible blend of power-pop. They were led by drummer Will Birch. He was born around 1950 in Essex and began his drumming career in a Southend band called The Geezenstacks back in the sixties. He proceeded to progress through a series of little known bands over the next few years - The Flowerpots (who included Wilko Johnson), Surly Bird, Glory, Cow Pie, the Hot Jets and he even had a few gigs with Dr. Feelgood. In late 1973, he joined Southend's prime pub-rockers The Kursaal Flyers. When they split in November 1977 he teamed up with John Winks (who'd been The Kursaal Flyers' lead singer in their final months). **The Records** were completed when they recruited Phil Brock (of The Janets) and Huw Gower (who Birch had seen playing a one off gig with The Ratbites From Hell, an old **Peter Perrett** band).

The Records made their live debut at Bristol Granary Club in March 1978. In November they released a promising debut single *Starry Eyes*, which was well received. They got themselves onto the 'Be Stiff' tour (the only non-Stiff act on it) to back Rachel Sweet but ended up opening the show too.

In 1979, they signed to Virgin and continued to release high quality, accessible, tuneful Anglo-pop recordings with pleasing harmonies and ringing guitars. Many of these were collected on their debut album *Shades In Bed* (which was retitled *The Records* for U.S. release and given a different cover and track running order). Whilst *Starry Eyes* and *Teenarama* had been released as singles several of the other cuts like, *Girls That Don't Exist* (an older song dating from their Kursaal Flyer days), *Affection Rejected* and *Girl*, could easily have been culled for 45 release too. It really is an excellent disc and comes strongly recommended. Early copies of the album also came with a free 12" single containing **Records**' covers of classic songs, including The Kinks' *See My Friends* and Spirit's *1984*. In the 'States, initial copies of the album came with a bonus untitled 7" disc. Ian Gibbons was pulled in to play keyboards on this album.

THE RECORDS - Shades In Bed.

THE RECORDS - Paying For The Summer Of Love.

Huw Gower left prior to the second album. He joined David Johannson's band and went on to release two solo albums in the late eighties. Jude Cole came in as his replacement. *Crashes*, their second album, was mostly produced by Craig Leon. It wasn't a great follow-up but did have two notable cuts (both produced by Mick Glossop) - *Man With A Girl Proof Heart*, which Birch had written in his days as a Kursaal Flyer, and *Hearts In Her Eyes*, which The Searchers did on their comeback album later that year.

After a two year gap, they returned in 1982 as a five-piece with *Music On Both Sides*, a pleasant enough album hampered by poor vocals - it was their swansong although they did return later with albums in 1988 (*A Sunny Afternoon In Waterloo*) and 1990 (*Paying For The Summer Of Love*).

In 1995 Virgin released *The Best Of The Records*.

The 2001 CD *Paying For The Summer Of Love* comprised the original versions of songs which were later re-recorded for their *Shades In Bed* album and two previously unissued tracks, *Coin Machine* and *If I Write Your Number In My Book*. It comes with sleevenotes by their vocalist John Wicks.

Red Alert

Personnel:			
TONY VAN FRATER	gtr		ABC
STEVE SMITH	vcls		ABC
KID STOKER	gtr		A C
GAZ STUART	bs		AB
MITCH	drms		A
NOBBY	drms		B
KEITH 'STICKS' WARRINGTON	drms		C

ALBUM: 1(B) WE'VE GOT THE POWER (No Future PUNK 5) 1983
(up to
1986)

NB: (1) also issued on CD (Captain Oi! AHOY CD 12) 1993 with fourteen bonus tracks. There's also four compilations: *Red Alert - The Oi! Singles Collection* (Captain Oi! AHOY CD 45) 1995; *The Rarities* (Captain Oi! AHOY CD 107) 1999; *The Best Of Red Alert* (Captain Oi! AHOY CD 146) 2000 and *Border Guards* (Harry May MAYO CD 121) 2001.

EPs: 1(A) BORDER GUARDS (Border Guards/Third And Final/
(up to Sell Out) (PS) (Guardian GM-RA/B 61) 1980
1986) 2(B) THERE'S A GUITAR BURNING (There's A Guitar
Burning/The Dust Has Settled/Tranquility/
All The Way To Glory/The Revolution Will Come/
Cast Iron's Crusade) (No Future 12Oi! 27) 1983

NB: (1) reissued by Combat Rock in 1994.

45s: In Britain/Screaming At The Nation/
(up to Murder Missile (PS) (No Future Oi! 5) 1982
1986) Take No Prisoners/Empire Of Crime/

RED ALERT - Border Guards EP.

Sell Out (PS)	(No Future Oi! 13) 1982
City Invasion/Negative Reaction (PS)	(No Future Oi! 20) 1983

An Oi! punk band from Sunderland. Their *Border Guards* EP is one of Oi's rarest records. Only 250 copies were ever made and the band glued all the sleeves themselves. Recorded on 24th May 1980, copies of the EP were sold by the band at gigs and helped to secure them a deal with No Future for whom they released three singles, two EP's and an album. They also contributed a cut called *SPG* to the seminal *Carry On Oi!* (Secret SEC 2) 1981 compilation, which was reissued again (Captain Oi! AHOY CD 119) in 1999.

The three tracks on the *Border Guards* EP are pretty standard Oi! fayre. *Third And Final* had some distinctive guitar parts. *District Border* is a frenetic assault on the senses. A weakness in the EP is that in many places the lyrics are inaudible. It was reissued on the French Combat Rock label in 1994. Two years later all three tracks were compiled on *Oi! Rarities, Vol. 1* (Captain Oi! AHOY CD 43) 1996.

By 1982, **Red Alert** had slimmed to a four-piece with the departure of original drummer Mitch and Kid Stoker, who'd gone to join **Red London**. With new drummer Nobby *In Britain* was released in February 1982. It contained three more high energy Oi! tracks, which are also captured on *Oi! The Singles Collection, Vol. 1* (Captain Oi! AHOY CD 60) 1996. It shot up the indie chart at the time and a follow-up *Take No Prisoners* in mid-1982 consolidated on their success with the band establishing themselves as a leading act on the Oi! live circuit. The title cut can also be heard on *100% British Oi!* (Captain Oi! AHOY DCD 83) 1997. A further 45 *The City Invasion* followed in 1983 along with their debut album *We've Got The Power*. This featured a different version of the superb *S.P.G.* from that which had appeared on the *Carry On Oi!* compilation and to offer good value for money contained none of their singles at the time. However, the CD reissue on Captain Oi! includes as bonus cuts all of their singles for the No Future label. On CD it is available as a full colour picture disc with an eight page booklet, but it was also released on both black and red vinyl with a lyric insert. The album was quite well received and a Top 5 indie chart entry.

RED ALERT - In Britain.

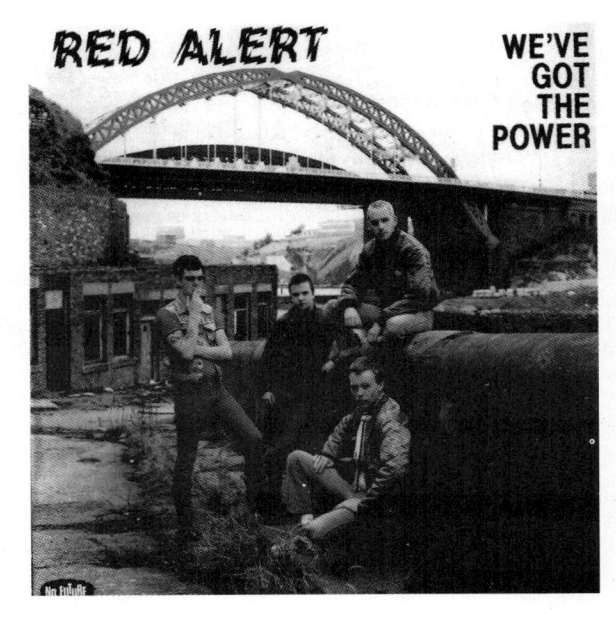

RED ALERT - We've Got The Power.

A six-track 12" single *There's A Guitar Burning* followed the album but the band split in 1984 after the No Future label folded.

There was a reformation in mid-1989 (line-up 'C') featuring ex-**Angelic Upstarts** and **Cockney Rejects'** drummer Keith 'Sticks' Warrington. After several gigs across Europe they signed to Knockout Records in Germany which resulted in the *Blood Sweat And Beers* album in 1992. A second album *Beyond The Cut* followed with **The Toy Dolls'** Dicka on drums. Then, in 1994, ex-**Red London** drummer Matty Forster was hitting the skins for the double 7" *Drinking With Red Alert/Street Survivors*. In 1996, they issued another album *Breaking All The Rules* on Dojo followed by *Wearside* on Rhythm Vicar in 1999.

No Future - The Punk Singles Collection (Captain Oi! AHOY DLP 508) 1996 includes *In Britain*, *Murder Missile*, *Take No Prisoners*, *City Invasion* and *There's A Guitar Burning*. *Vol. 2* (Captain Oi! AHOY DLP 512) 1996 of the same series features *Screaming At The Nation*, *Empire Of Crime*, *Sell Out*, *Negative Reaction* and *All The Way To Glory*.

Red Alert - The Oi! Singles Collection (CD) (Captain Oi! AHOY CD 45) 1995 features every 'A' and 'B' side the band released on a twenty-seven track set. This includes their ultra-rare *Border Guards* (EP) and the obscure *Drinking With The Red Alert* 7" which includes a rousing version of **The Cockney Rejects'** *Beginning Of The End*.

The Rarities CD is a twenty-two track compilation of demos and previously unreleased material. The opening cut *We've Got The Power* was recorded in 1981, at the same time as *SPG* their contribution to the *Carry On Oi!* (Secret SEC 2) 1981 compilation, later reissued on CD (Captain Oi! AHOY CD 119) 1999. The next four cuts are from a 1982 demo for their *We've Got The Power* album. Next up is a seven-track demo they recorded at the

RED ALERT - Best Of.

RED ALERT - The Oi! Singles Collection.

Bullseye Studios in County Durham in 1984, after No Future had folded. This included a cover of **The Clash**'s *White Man In Hammersmith Palais*. The next session is from 1990 after the band reformed and included the previously unreleased *The Light Has Gone* and *No Good Or Bad Days*, which was covered by **Red London** on their *Tumbling Dice* album. The remaining material is also from the nineties and less relevant to this book, although the cuts include covers of **Sham 69**'s *If The Kids Are United* and **The Angelic Upstarts**' *England*. The CD is a good appraisal of the band's twenty-year career and they're still going strong today. *SPG* resurfaced on the *Oi! Fuckin' Oi!* (Harry May MAYO CD 110) compilation in 1999.

The Best Of Red Alert (CD) opens with *Third And Final*, from their very rare debut EP. It also includes their classic eighties cuts *In Britain*, *S.P.G.*, *We've Got The Power*, *City Invasion*, *It's Me Boys* and *There's A Guitar Burning*. This compilation also draws considerable material from their nineties output and three new cuts with **Charlie Harper** guesting on vocals. There are also sleevenotes by Tony Van Frater.

The *Border Guards* compilation on Harry May concentrates mostly on material recorded since their reformation in 1989 and particularly from their 1996 *Breaking All The Rules* album for Dojo. It does include, though, the original version of *SPG* and a previously unreleased version of the **UK Subs**' *CID*.

Red Balune

45:   Capitalist Kid/Spider In Love   (MCCB 001) 1978

A strange record. An NME review described it as "Music of the revolution, like Kraftwerk falling down a lift-shaft with somebody elses instruments." The flip side is equally weird. The end result is a jumbled collage of noise and sounds which doesn't really work. The flip side is also marred by repetitve lyrics.

REDBEAT - Survival.

REDBEAT - Redbeat 12".

Redbeat

45:   Red Beat/Machines In Motion/
       More Or Less Cut (12", PS) (Malicious Damage MD 4940) 1980
       Survival/See (PS)   (Manic Machine RB 2) 198?

Red Beat veers towards reggae, whilst *Machines In Motion* leans more towards dance music. *Survival* is a bleak song about surviving a nuclear war. The flip side *See* is similar in style, but not as good. It was distributed by Rough Trade.

Their first 45 was housed in a PVC bag as opposed to a picture sleeve.

Red Lights

45:   Never Wanna Leave/Seventeen (PS)   (Free Range PF 5) 1978

This is a sought-after 45. **Red Lights** were a punk band notable for good guitar work.

Red London

Personnel: RAICH CARTER   drms   A
              PATTY SMITH   vcls   A
              GAZ STOKER   bs   A
              KID STOKER   gtr   A

ALBUMS: 1(A) THIS IS ENGLAND   (Razor RAZ 10) 1983
        2(-) A LOOK BACK IN ANGER
                               (Released Emotions REM 013) 1992

EP: 1(A) STEN GUNS IN SUNDERLAND (This Is England/
              Soul Train/Revolution Times) (PS) (Razor RZS 105) 1983

Red London were a punk-inspired band who set about breathing life back into new wave. They released an album for Razor and then went on to a succession of French labels.

They were formed by the Stoker brothers in 1980 and took their name from a **Sham '69** 'B' side. Gaz Stoker had previously been in The Rebels and his brother Kid had been in **Red Alert**.

On their *Sten Guns In Sunderland* (EP), *Soul Train* is quite catchy with melodic guitar work and certainly not typical Oi! punk. *Revolution Times* is much more in that mould and the EP also features *This Is England*, the title cut to their Razor album. All three cuts have resurfaced on *Oi! The Rarities, Vol. 4* (Captain Oi! AHOY CD 58) 1996. They also contributed *Children Of War* to *Oi! Against Racism* (Havin' A Laugh HAL LP 004).

A Look Back In Anger, released in 1992 on red vinyl, contains their favourite material recorded live in the studio. It includes original numbers

RED LONDON - Sten Guns In Sunderland EP.

like *To Kill A King* and *Revolution Times* as well as covers of the punk classics *Complete Control* and *I Fought The Law* by **The Clash**.

The Stokers' still have a version of the band on the road today with Marty Clark on vocals and Matty Forster on drums. They tour Europe frequently and still release albums. Recent examples have been *Tumbling Dice* and *Last Orders Please*.

Red Lorry Yellow Lorry

Personnel:			
	MICK BROWN	drms	AB
	MARTIN FAGEN	lead gtr	A
	CHRIS REED	vcls, gtr	AB
	STEVE SMITH	bs	A
	PAUL SOUTHERN	bs	B
	WOLFIE (DANE WOLFENDEN)	lead gtr	B

ALBUMS: 1(B) TALK ABOUT THE WEATHER (Red Rhino REDLP 50) 1985
(up to 1986) 2(B) PAINT YOUR WAGON (Red Rhino REDLP 65) 1986

NB: (2) originally came with a free 7" *Paint Your Wagon/More Jipp* (REDF 65). 5,000 copies only came with this 7" which was stamped and numbered in a plain sleeve. (2) also issued on CD (REDCD 65) 1986. (1) and (2) coupled on one CD (Cherry Red CDMRED 115) 1994. Also relevant are two compilations, *Smashed Hits* (Red Rhino REDLP 86) 1988, also issued on CD (REDCD 86) and again (Dojo DOJOCD 210) 1995; *The Singles 1982 - 1987* (Cherry Red REDLP 109/CDMRED 109) 1994, *The Best Of Red Lorry Yellow Lorry* (Cleopatra CLEO 9404) 1994 and *The Very Best Of Red Lorry Yellow Lorry* (Cherry Red CDMRED 167) 2000.

EP: 1(B) THIS TODAY (PS) (Red Rhino RED 48) 1984

45s: Beating My Head/
(up to I'm Still Waiting (PS) (Red Rhino RED 20) 1982
1986) Take It All/Happy (PS) (Red Rhino RED 28) 1983
He's Read/See The Fire (PS) (Red Rhino RED 39) 1983
Monkeys On Juice/Push (PS) (Red Rhino RED 49) 1984
Monkeys On Juice/Push/
Silence (12", PS) (Red Rhino REDT 49) 1984
Hollow Eyes/Feel A Piece (PS) (Red Rhino RED 50) 1984
Hollow Eyes/Feel A Piece (12", PS) (Red Rhino REDT 52) 1984
Change/Generation (PS) (Red Rhino RED 55) 1984
Change/Generation (12", PS) (Red Rhino REDT 55) 1984
Spinning Around/
Hold Yourself Down (PS) (Red Rhino RED 60) 1985
Spinning Around/
Hold Yourself Down (12", PS) (Red Rhino REDT 60) 1985
Walking On Your Hands (PS) (Red Rhino RED 66) 1986
Walking On Your Hands (12", PS) (Red Rhino REDT 66) 1986
Cut Down/Running Fever (PS) (Red Rhino RED 73) 1986
Cut Down/Running Fever/
Pushed Me (12", PS) (Red Rhino REDT 73) 1986

Part of the post-punk gothic genre, this band formed in Leeds in July 1982 and were soon signed by the Red Rhino label. They carried the mantle of **Joy Division** through the eighties and into the nineties. *Take It All* their second 45 was a full frontal wall of sound interspersed with equally uncompromising vocals.

By the time of their debut album Paul Southern had replaced Steve Smith on bass and Wolfie (Dane Wolfenden) had come in for Martin Fagen on guitar. The music on *Talk About The Weather* is at times tuneless and mostly murky, but the swirling guitar sound is appealing and some of their lyrics are memorable. One of the tracks *Hollow Eyes* proved particularly popular in gothic circles and was championed by Radio 1 DJ John Peel, which brought their music into many more homes.

"I've seen that look I know those eyes
I think this is a thin disguise
Alone at last but no surprise
I'd seen it in those hollow eyes"
(from *Hollow Eyes*)

Their minimalist lyrics are demonstrated by one of the other cuts *Strange Dream*:-

"It was a strange dream
He stood and stared
Those shining faces
Those darkened eyes
And alone he ran
Alone he ran"

(*Strange Dream*)

Hollow Eyes was culled for 45 release and they followed this with another excellent effort *Chance*, which featured some distinctive droning organ.

The first 5,000 copies of their second album *Paint Your Wagon* came with a free 7" single which included the title cut. This is even more derivative of **Joy Division** than their debut, particularly on cuts like *Save My Soul* and *Head All Fire*.

After this the band switched to Beggars Banquet subsidiary Situation 2 and there were further line-up changes. They made a number of further albums in this phase but they are beyond the time span of the book.

Red Lorry Yellow Lorry were an interesting band. Try checking out one of their singles compilations for starters. *The Singles 1982 - 87* features 26 tracks in all, including all their early eighties material for Red Rhino (including the 'B' sides) and there are also lots of later cuts from their period with Situation 2. An alternative compilation is *Smashed Hits*, which comprises fourteen of their indie hits and near misses.

They also contributed *Beating My Head* and *Hollow Eyes* to *In Goth Daze* (Anagram CDMGRAM 89) in 1998.

Steve Smith and Paul Southern were later in Ghost Dance, which was something of a youth supergroup, since it also featured Anne Marie Hurst when she left **Skeletal Family**.

The recent CD compilation *The Very Best Of Red Lorry Yellow Lorry* on Cherry Red is now the best introduction to this interesting band's music.

Red Rage

Personnel:		
	JAMES EDMUNDS	A
	NOGGIN	A
	DAVE PELLING	A

45: Total Control/I Give You This (PS) (Flicknife FLS 203) 1980

This is a very rare and sought-after punk 45 which is notable for its good rock style guitar work.

Redskins

Personnel:			
	CHRIS DEAN (X. MOORE)	vcls, gtr	AB
	MARTIN HEWES	bs	AB
	NICK KING	drms	A
	PAUL HOOKHAM	drms	B

			HCP
ALBUM:	1(B)	NEITHER WASHINGTON NOR MOSCOW	
		(Decca FLP 1) 1986	31

NB: (1) later issued on CD (London 828642) 1997. There's also *Live* (Dojo DOJOCD 188) 1994.

EPs:	1(B)	THE POWER IS YOURS.... THE BOOTLEG EXCERPTS PROPAGANDA (The Power Is Yours/Take The Goods And Buy Them/99 ½ Won't Do/ Take 3) (10")	(Decca FXT 3) 1986
	2(B)	IT CAN BE DONE (It Can Be Done/Let's Make It Work! (live)/K.O.! K.O.! (live)/A Plateful Of Hateful (10")	(Decca FXT 4) 1986
	3(A)	THE PEEL SESSIONS (12") (Strange Fruit SFPS 30) 1987	

NB: (1) played at 33 r.p.m. and was issued in a stickered plain black die-cut sleeve. (2) was issued with numbered copies in a stickered plain white die-cut sleeve.

			HCP
45s:	The Peasant Army/Leu Bronstein (PS)	(CNT CNT 007) 1982	-
	Lean On Me!/Unionise! (PS)	(CNT CNT 016) 1983	-
	Lean On Me! (Northern Mix)/ Unionise! (Break Mix) (12", PS)	(CNT CNTX 016) 1983	-
	Keep On Keepin' On!/ Red Strike The Blues! (PS)	(Decca F 1) 1984	43
*	Keep On Keepin' On! (Die On Your Feet Mix)!/ 16 Tons (Coal Not Dole)/ Reds Strike The Blues! (12")	(Decca FX 1) 1984	-
	I Kick Over The Statues!/ Young And Proud (PS)	(Abstract Dance AD 6) 1985	-
	Bring It Down (This Insane Thing)/You Want It They've Got It	(Decca F 2) 1985	33
	Bring It Down (This Insane Thing)/You Want It They've Got It/ Burn It Up (12")	(Decca FX 2) 1985	-
	Bring It Down! (This Insane Thing)/You Want It They've Got It/ Turnin' Loose (The Furious Flames)/Take No Heroes (live)/ Go Get Organised (live) (double pack, stickered gatefold PS)	(Decca FDP 2) 1985	-
	The Power Is Yours	(Decca F 3) 1986	59
	The Power Is Yours (12")	(Decca FX 3) 1986	-
	It Can Be Done/ K.O. K.O. (Kick Over Apartheid)	(Decca F 4) 1986	-

NB: * Some copies came shrinkwrapped with a free 7".

Redskins were a political trio who carried the mantle of the left wing of the skinhead movement. Along with people like Billy Bragg they were for a while at the forefront of rock's Socialist movement. They originally formed in York as No Swastikas but soon moved down to London. Their singer and guitarist Chris Dean was also a writer for 'New Musical Express'. In this band he assumed the identity of X. Moore. The trio were all members of The Socialist Workers Party. In the studio and live they were often supplemented by a brass section.

RED LORRY YELLOW LORRY - Talk About The Weather.

Their song titles often ended with an exclamation mark! The lyrics and delivery were invariably strident. The lyrics enticed the oppressed to rise up and were of greater importance than the music, which was normally a simple and catchy R&B-influenced sound supplemented by keyboards and horns.

Initially they signed to the Leeds-based CNT label in 1982. Their debut 45 *The Peasant Army* attracted enough attention to secure them a Radio 1 Peel session.

This was repeated on a number of occasions and helped bring them to a wider audience. The follow-up *Lean On Me!* was later voted 'Single of the Year' by 'Sounds' Garry Bushell.

Around 1984 King was replaced by Paul Hookham on drums. Hookham was formerly with English Subtitles, Lemons and Woodentops. **Redskins** strongly allied themselves to the cause of the striking mineworkers in the mid-eighties, playing a number of benefits on their behalf. They were also signed up to a major label and enjoyed their first of three hits when *Keep On Keepin' On* climbed to No. 43 and spent five weeks in the chart. The following year *Bring It Down (This Insane Thing)* went five places better over a similar period.

They failed to maintain the standard of their earlier material and their third and final hit *The Power Is Yours* could only rise to No. 59 during its two weeks in the chart.

Their debut album *Neither Washington Nor Moscow* in 1986 was promising and met with some acclaim. It achieved quite good sales too, climbing to No. 31 during a four week chart residency. The band failed to capitalise on this, splitting up the same year.

In addition to the above discography **Redskins** contributed one cut *Kick Over The Statues (The Ramsey McKinnock Mix)* to a freebie EP which came with 'The Hit' (The Hits HOT 001) 1985 magazine, issue 1. The EP also featured cuts by Style Council, Jesus and Mary Chain and Simply Red.

The following year they supplied *You Want It They've Got It (Red Soul & Fury Unreleased Mix)* to a free EP with 'Jamming!' (Jamming/London J 1) 1986. Also featured on the EP were cuts by Then Jericho, Daintees and Communards.

The Reducers

Personnel:	GRAHAM BARSTOW	drms	A
	STUART LYONS	bs	A
	RAGGY F.C.	vcls	A
	ROB TYNAN	gtr	A

45s:	Things Go Wrong/ We Are Normal (PS)	(Vibes XP 1/VR 001) 1978
	Man With A Gun/Vengeance/ Can't Stop Now (PS)	(Vibes VR 003) 1979

The Reducers came from Bury but recorded in Manchester. Their first 45 was sharp rock with neat echo touches. Both of these 45s are now expensive to purchase.

The Reflections

Personnel:	DENNIS BURNS	A
	NAG	A
	MARK PERRY	A

ALBUM:	1(A)	SLUGS AND TOADS	(Cherry Red BRED 22) 1982

45:	4 Countries/ The Coroner And The Inquest	(Cherry Red CHERRY 33) 1982

The Reflections were a short-lived project which **Mark Perry** formed with Dennis Burns and Nag alongside a reincarnation of **Alternative TV**. The album had its moments notably an excellent version of ex-13th Floor Elevators vocalist Roky Erikson's *The Interpreter* and *Tightrope Walker*, a driving duet featuring **Perry** and Nag.

Reflex Action

Personnel:
- MARK BRADLEY — drms — A
- PAUL BRADLEY — bs — A
- DAVID JOHNSTON — vcls — A
- HENRY LUKE — gtr — A
- CHRIS McLAVERTY — vcls, lead gtr — A

A Belfast band who contributed two cuts: *Spies* and *Recession* to the compilation *Belfast* (Shock Rock SLR 007) in 1980. *Spies* has a white reggae beat and *Recession* features dead pan vocals which somehow don't work with the instrumentation.

Rema-Rema

Personnel:
- GARY ASQUITH — A
- MARCO PERRONI — A

EP: 1(A) WHEEL IN THE ROSES (Feedback Song/Rema-Ream/Instrumental/Fond Affections) (12") (4AD BAD 5) 1980

This EP was a collaboration between **Adam and The Ants'** guitarist Marco Perroni and future Renegade Soundwave member Gary Asquith. **Rema - Rema** can also be heard on the compilation *Natures Mortes - Still Lives* (4AD CAD 117CD) 1997.

Robert Rental (and The Normal)

Personnel:
- ROBERT RENTAL — AB
- DANIEL MILLER — B

ALBUMS:
- 1(A) THE BRIDGE (Industrial IR 0007) 1979
- 2(B) ROBERT RENTAL AND THE NORMAL (Rough Trade ROUGH 17) 1980

NB: (1) was recorded with **Thomas Leer** and later issued on CD (Grey Area BRIDGE 10CD) 1992. (2) was a one-sided album in a plain red sleeve credited to **Robert Rental and The Normal**.

45s:
- * Paralysis/A.C.C. (PS) (Regular ER 102) 1978
- + Paralysis/A.C.C. (PS) (Company/Regular RECO 2) 1978
- Double Heart/On Location (PS) (Mute MUTE 10) 1980

NB: * This was originally issued in a black and white photocopied, foldover picture sleeve. + This later reissue was in a different colour picture sleeve.

Robert Rental was a self-taught synthesizer player. *The Bridge* recorded with **Thomas Leer** comprised gloomy electro-pop songs with repetitive sounds and various effects. *Monochrome Days* is one of an inconsistent album's finest moments. However, it is of significance in that it pointed the way for bands like **The Human League** and **Blancmange** in the eighties. He teamed up with **The Normal** (aka future Mute Records boss **Daniel Miller**) for a one-off album which carried on from where sixties live electronics, tape loops and devices left off. The resulting one-sided album is a one-sided experiment in live electronics, tape loops and other devices. Only for fans of this type of music!

A.C.C. was also included on *Business Unusual* (Cherry Red ARED 2) in 1979.

The Reputations

Personnel:
- MARTIN BROAD — drms — A
- RICHARD BULL — gtr — A
- JOHN HOLLIDAY — bs — A
- PAUL LEWIS — vcls — A
- PAUL WICKENS — keyb'ds — A

45: I Believe You/Breaking Communications/All Day And All Night/They Think (double pack) (Blueprint BLUX 101) 1979

This mod revival band was originally known as **The Young Ones**. *I Believe You* has prominent keyboards and strong vocals. You'll also find it on *100% British Mod* (Captain Mod MODSKA DCD 8) 1998.

THE RESISTANCE - Kidnapped.

When **The Reputations** split in late 1980 Holliday formed Escape Club, Bull joined Incognito and Wickens became a much in demand session player for Paul McCartney among others.

The Resistance

Personnel:
- MARK DAMRON — vcls, gtr — A
- JOHN O'LEARY — bs — A
- IAIN REID — keyb'ds — A
- MARTIN SAUNDERS — drms — A

45: Kidnapped/Say No To The Macho (PS) (Marquis GAT 413) 1979

Both sides of this popish 45 were penned by Mark Damron and certainly his vocals are delicious on *Kidnapped*. The 45 was distributed and marketed by Faulty Products.

Resistance 77

Personnel:
- KEIRON EGAN — bs — ABC
- IAN 'ODY' HODSON — vcls — ABC
- GARY NAYLOR — drms — AB
- GUY NAYLOR — gtr — A
- LUGGY — gtr — BC
- PAUL MARSHALL — drms — C

ALBUM: 1(B) THOROUGHBRED MEN (Rot ASS 14) 1984

NB: (1) reissued on CD (Captain Oi! AHOY CD 31) 1994 along with all their other recordings, including rare compilation cuts to make a total of twelve bonus cuts in all.

RESISTANCE 77 - Thoroughbred Men.

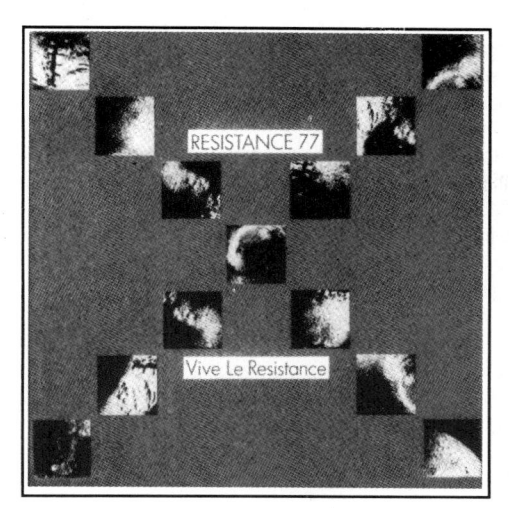

RESISTANCE 77 - Vive Le Resistance EP.

RESISTANCE 77 - You Reds.

EPs:
1(A) NOWHERE TO PLAY (Nottingham Problem/ Join The Army/Collars And Ties/ Nucelar Attack) (PS)   (Riot City RIOT 18) 1983
2(B) VIVE LE RESISTANCE (Enemy/Will They Survive/ Russia/Advance Factory Units/ Banned From The Welfare)   (Rot ASS 6) 1983

45: You Reds/Young And Wrong (PS)   (Resistance RESIST 1) 1990

Resistance 77 formed in South Normanton, Derbyshire in 1980. They were originally known as The Anti Heroes but decided to change their name because of the number of bands with Anti in their name at the time (**The Anti-Nowhere League**, **Anti-Social**, **Anti-Establishment** and **Anti-Pasti**). In their early days they played support slots to **The 4-Skins**, **The Exploited** and **Flux of Pink Indians** among others.

Their first vinyl excursion came when they contributed *Bricks In Brixton*, a fast-paced punker about the Brixton riots, to the *Riotous Assembly* (Riot City ASSEMBLY 1) compilation. They followed this in early 1983 with the *Nowhere To Play* EP, which brought their fast-paced Oi! punk with often intelligent lyrics to some prominence. The EP got to No. 5 in the 'Sounds' Punk chart and made the lower reaches of the indie chart. The EP included an early version of *Nuclear Attack*, later featured on their sole album:

"I don't wanna die
I don't wanna meet my maker
Someone's gonna push the button
But don't ring the undertaker
It's a one way trip and everyone's invited
It's gonna be too late, once the fuse has been ignited"
(from *Nuclear Attack*)

Guy Naylor departed soon after and was replaced by Luggy on guitar for their five cut EP *Vive Le Resistance*, which was put out by the Mansfield-based Rot Records. They also contributed two cuts *Send In The SAS*, with its catchy guitar intro and *Communist Cunt* to the compilation *Wet Dreams* (Rot ASS 4).

At the suggestion of Rot Records' supremo Dunk they set to work on an album with two and a half days studio time and a budget of just £150! The result *Thoroughbred Men* is now one of punk's rarest albums and it's also something of an overlooked classic. The title cut stands out with a great guitar intro, *Love Song* is slow-paced and different from the fast-paced assault of the other material. There's a punk version of Clive Dunn's No. 1 hit *Grandad* and the lyrics of songs like *Brains Of The Nation* were certainly pertinent:-

"Maggies in, Labour's out but I don't give a fuck
They're all a bunch of hypocrites if you take a closer look
We'll keep inflation down
We'll create more jobs
We'll look after pensioners
We'll sort out the yobs
If you're our friends we don't need enemies

Sitting on your brains talking out your arse
Another resolution another fucking farce

Spoil the workers fun to give another kid a gun

Maggie lies, Labour tries to make her look a twat
Pass an act but it's a fact they don't know what they're on about"
(*Brains Of The Nation*)

This album is recommended but sadly it got precious little exposure or publicity at the time. Demoralised by this and a lack of music labels interested in this type of material they entered a period of inactivity. They re-emerged in 1988 with a new drummer Paul Marshall. They got to the final of a 'Battle Of The Bands' competition held in Bradford and then, in 1990, a tribute single *You Reds / Young And Wrong* was released on their own label to celebrate Kieron's beloved Nottingham Forest's achievement in reaching the Littlewoods Cup Final that year. They were still gigging occasionally during the nineties.

Aside from their 1990 45, all of their recorded output is compiled on the Captain Oi! 1994 CD and you really should buy it 'cos this band was an overlooked punk gem.

Both sides of their 1990 single *You Reds / Young And Wrong* can also be heard on *Oi! The Rarities, Vol. 2* (Captain Oi! AHOY CD 46) 1995. You'll also find *Nuclear Attack* on *100% Hardcore Punk Rock* (Captain Oi! AHOY DCD 84) 1997. It had earlier been included on *Life's A Riot And Then You Die* (Riot City CITY 009) in 1985. Other compilation appearances include *Nottingham Problem* on *Riot City Singles Collection, Vol. 1* (Anagram CDPUNK 15) 1997 and *Join The Army* on *Vol. 2* (Anagram CDPUNK 55) 1995 of the same series. Both these last two compilations were also issued on vinyl by Captain Oi! (AHOY DLP 503 and 511). Two further cuts, *Enemy* and *Russia* appeared on *Rot Records Punk Singles Collection* (Anagram CDPUNK 40) in 1994.

The Resistors

45: For Jeannie/Takeaway Love/ End Of The Line (PS)   (Break SMASH 1) 1980

A mod revivalist combo.

Restricted Hours

EP: 1( ) Getting Things Done/Still Living Out The Car Crash/ (2 cuts by **Syndicate**)   (Stevenage) 1979

The label gives a strong clue to this band's location. Some members later played for **The Astronauts**.

The Retreads

45: Would You Listen Girl/One After 909/ You Said You Knew (PS)   (Eddie Osmo EO 101) 1981

Out of Spratton in Northampton **The Retreads** were a Beatlesque-sounding combo whose three track 45 is now rare and collectable. It includes a cover of *One After 909* and came with a mini-poster insert.

Revenge

45s:	Our Generation	(Loony LOO 1) 1978
	We're Not Gonna Take It/Pornography (PS)	(Loony LOO 2) 1978

Both these 45s are horrendously rare and expensive to acquire now.

The Revillos

Personnel:	FAY FIFE	vcls	A
	HI-FI HARRIS	gtr	A
	KID KUPKA	gtr	A
	WILLIAM MYSTERIOUS	bs	A
	EUGENE REYNOLDS	keyb'ds, vcls	A
	ROCKY RHYTHM	drms	A
	D.K. SMYTHE	bs	

ALBUMS:	1(A)	REV UP	(Snatzo/Dindisc DID X 3) 1980
	2(-)	ATTACK	(Superville SV 4001) 1982

NB: (1) came with green or pink titles. (1) reissued on vinyl (Virgin OVED 53) 1984. (2) was withdrawn and is now becoming collectable. There are also a number of CD releases:- *Attack Of The Giant Revillos* (Receiver RRCD 204) 1995, *Live And On Fire In Japan* (Vinyl Japan ASKCD 046) 1995 also on vinyl (ASKLP 046) 1995, *Motorbike Beat* (Mau Mau MAUCD 643) 1995, *From The Freezer* (Damaged Goods DAMGOOD 97CD) 1996 and *BBC Radio Sessions* (Vinyl Japan ASKCD 80) 1998.

HCP

45s:	Where's The Boy For Me/	
	The Fiend (PS)	(Snatzo/Dindisc DIN 1) 1979 -
	Motor Bike Beat/	
	No Such Luck (PS)	(Snatzo/Dindisc DIN 5) 1979 45
	Scuba Scuba/	
	Scuba Boy Bop (PS)	(Snatzo/Dindisc DINZ 16) 1980 -
	Hungry For Love/	
	Voodoo 2 (PS)	(Snatzo/Dindisc DINZ 20) 1980 -
	She's Fallen In Love With A Monster Man/	
	Mind Bending Cutie Doll (PS)	(Superville SV 1001) 1982 -
	Bongo Brain/Hip City - You Were Meant For Me (PS)	
		(Superville SV 2001) 1982 -
	Tell Him/Graveyard And Groove (PS)	(Aura AUS 135) 1982 -
	Bitten By A Love Bug/Cat Call (PS)	(EMI RVL 1) 1983 -
	Bitten By A Love Bug (Extended Version)/	
	Cat Call (12" PS)	(EMI 12 RVL 1) 1983 -
	Midnight/Z-X-Y (PS)	(EMI RVL 2) 1984 -
	Midnight (Extended Version)/	
	Midnight (7" Version) (12" PS)	(EMI 12 RVL 2) 1984 -

The Revillos were formed by Reynolds and Fife on the breakup of **The Rezillos**. The were signed by Virgin's Dindisc subsidiary label. They recorded several singles and the *Rev Up* album, which was full of a number of sixties derived songs including *On The Beach*, *Secret Of The Shadow*, *Motorbike Beat* (which brought them a minor hit when released as a 45), *Hungry For Love*, *Cool Jerk* etc.. It really was a lot of fun, but failed to chart. Both *Hungry For Love* and *On The Beach* can also be heard on *Dindisc 1980* (Din Disc DONE 1) 1980.

After this they recorded further releases on their own Superville label. A second album *Attack* was released but then withdrawn. Consequently it is now hard to find and collectable. Their progress was also hampered by line-up changes. Fife, Reynolds and Rhythm were constant factors, but various guitarists, bassists and back-up singers came and went. After further singles on Aura and EMI, they decided to call it a day.

Motorbike Beat is a compilation of their rocky thrash-trash sound which recalls The Cramps but without the same horror. Their earlier material like *Rev Up!*, *Where's The Boy For Me* and *Motorbike Beat* is the best.

From The Freezer is a rarities collection, which includes demo recordings of *Motorbike Beat* and *Where's The Boy For Me* and a load of live takes, 'B' sides and rehearsal versions.

Graveyard Groove later resurfaced on *New Wave Archive* (Rialto RMCD 201) in 1997.

KIMBERLEY REW - My Baby Does Her Hairdo Long.

Kimberley Rew

45s:	Stomping All Over The World/Nothing's Going To	
	Change Your Life/	
	Fighting Someone's War	(Armageddon AS 004) 1980
*	My Baby Does Her Hairdo Long/	
	Fishing (PS)	(Armageddon AS 012) 1981

NB: * With the dB's.

These were solo efforts by superb **Soft Boys** guitarist **Kimberley Rew**, who was later with Katrina and The Waves.

Reward System

Personnel:	MARK BENJAMIN	gtr	A
	SUE BRADLEY	vcls	A
	TIM FALLA	drms	A
	MICK PERRIN	bs	A
	ULRICH D.	vcls, keyb'ds	A

A Brighton band in **The Poison Girls** vein whose sole vinyl offering was *Extradition* on *Vaultage '80* (Attrix RB 11) 1980. It was later included on *Vaultage Punk Collection* (Anagram CDPUNK 101) 1987.

Ambrose Reynolds

ALBUMS:	1	WORLD'S GREATEST HITS (New Hormones CAT 4) 1982
	2	GREATEST HITS (Zulu ZULU 3) 1983

NB: (1) was a cassette.

KIMBERLEY REW - Stomping All Over The World.

These were solo projects by **Ambrose Reynolds** who later teamed up with Jayne Casey (formerly of **Big In Japan** and **Pink Military**) in **Pink Industry**.

The Rezillos

Personnel:
JO CALLIS (LUKE WARM)	gtr	ABC	
FAY FIFE (SHEILA HYNDE)	vcls	ABC	
HI-FI HARRIS (ALAN HARRIS)	gtr	A	
WILLIAM MYSTERIOUS (WILLIAM DONALDSON)	sax, bs	AB	
ANGEL PATERSON (ALAN HARRISON)	drms	ABC	
EUGENE REYNOLDS	vcls	ABC	
D.K. SMYTHE	bs	A	
GALE WARNING	backing vcls	A	
SIMON TEMPLAR	bs	C	

HCP
ALBUMS:
1(B) CAN'T STAND THE REZILLOS (Sire K 56530) 1978 16
2(C) MISSION ACCOMPLISHED.... BUT THE BEAT GOES ON (Sire SRK 6069) 1978 30

NB: (1) also issued on CD (Receiver RRCD 204) 1995. Also relevant is Can't Stand The Rezillos: The (Almost) Complete Rezillos (Sire 7599-26942-2) 1996.

HCP
45s:
o Can't Stand My Baby/ I Wanna Be Your Man (PS) (Sensible FAB 1) 1977 -
* Flying Saucer Attack/ (My Baby Does) Good Sculptures (PS) (Sensible FAB 2) 1977 -
Flying Saucer Attack/ (My Baby Does) Good Sculptures (PS) (Sire 6078 612) 1977 -
* Cold Wars/William Mysterious Overture (Sire 6198 215) 1978 -
Top Of The Pops/ 2,000 Rezillos Under The Sea (PS) (Sire SIR 4001) 1978 17
Destination Venus/Mystery Attack (PS) (Sire SIR 4008) 1978 43
+ Can't Stand My Baby/ I Wanna Be Your Man (PS) (Sensible FAB 1 (Mark 2)) 1979 71
x Top Of The Pops/Destination Venus (Sire SPC 3) 1981 -

NB: o Limited edition of 15,000, the first 5,000 numbered. * Unissued. + This was a reissue with a new picture sleeve. The run out groove reads "Come Back John Lennon". 4,000 copies comprised a mispressing with the 'B' side playing *(My Baby Does) Good Sculptures* (live). The run out groove on this reads "De-sire-able product?".

The Rezillos formed at Edinburgh Art College in March 1976. The original line-up was an eight-piece. Musically they drew on influences like R&B, sixties pop and glam but delivered them in a punk style.

They began gigging around Scotland in the Autumn of 1977 and very unique they looked too in their Thunderbirds/comic book outfits. They took their name from a comic book called 'The Revilo Cafe'. Their debut single *I Can't Stand My Baby* was released in July 1977 on the new indie label Sensible Records. It previewed their fast-paced punkish musical format and abrupt ending perfectly, but didn't chart. However, it did make sufficient impression to secure them a deal with the major Sire label in November 1977. At this point, Harris, Smythe and Warning quit the band. The remaining five members moved down to London. On 3rd December 1977, they recorded their first of two sessions for John Peel. It comprised *Good Sculptures*, *No* and *Top Of The Pops* (all later recorded for their debut album) and *Fight Amongst Yourselves*.

Their next single, the superb *Flying Saucer Attack*, another fast-paced punkish bundle of fun, had originally been scheduled for release on the Sensible label, but that was cancelled and instead it was issued on Sire. The flip side *(My Baby Does) Good Sculptures* had a catchy guitar riff delivered in their distinctive style. With a pounding beat, it was potentially a great dance record and really deserved to break through into the national charts. Unfortunately, it didn't. *(My Baby Does) Good Sculptures* was also included on *The Sire Machine Turns You Up* (Sire SMP 1) in 1978.

Sire despatched the band to New York early in 1978 to record their debut album *Can't Stand The Rezillos*. This was another of the finest moments of British punk. It included their first 'A' side *I Can't Stand My Baby*, both sides of their first Sire 45 *Flying Saucer Attack* and *(My Baby Does) Good Sculptures*, and real fun-loving thrashing covers of *Glad All Over* (originally

THE REZILLOS - Can't Stand The Rezillos.

by Dave Clarke Five) and *I Like It* (of Freddie and The Dreamers fame). It also featured a number of other superb originals delivered at breakneck speed in **The Rezillos**' highly individualistic style. Of these *Somebody's Gonna Get Their Head Kicked In Tonight* about violence on the dance floor and *Top Of The Pops*, which gave them a Top 20 hit when released as a 45 one month after the album, stand out. Of the others, *Getting Me Down* featured some good guitar moments; *Bad Guy Reaction* is another frantic thrash attack; *No* has quite a catchy call and retort style with some good guitar moments and throaty vocals; *2,000 A.D.* contains a catchy intro, leaving *It Gets Me* and *Cold Wars* as possibly the two weaker cuts on the album. Still both are worth a listen on what was a very consistent debut album. The only real criticism is possibly a lack of variety - there are no slower numbers, no let up in the fast-paced high energy punk-rock. *Can't Stand The Rezillos* briefly brought them the commercial success they deserved. It climbed to No. 17 in the U.K. album charts during a ten week stay in the Top 100. The album spawned the 45 *Top Of The Pops*, which indeed made it onto the show, climbing to No. 17 and spending nine weeks in the charts. *Can't Stand The Rezillos* is recommended listening.

The month before the album's release, in July 1978, **The Rezillos** played their second and final John Peel session on 8th June 1978. It comprised *Cold Wars*, *Destination Venus*, *Somebody's Gonna Get Their Head Kicked In Tonight* and *Can't Stand My Baby*.

A month after the album's release they played a session for David Jensen on 22nd August 1978. This featured *Top Of The Pops*, *Glad All Over* and *It Gets Me* (all from the album) and the previously unreleased *Getting Me Down*.

Fuelled by the success of their album they embarked on a national tour with label-mates **The Undertones** and enjoyed a further hit with their next 45 *Destination Venus*. This spent four weeks in the charts peaking at No. 43.

They could have been on the brink of stardom, but sadly they fell apart having decided to split before the year was out. Their farewell gig at Glasgow's Apollo on 23rd December 1978 was recorded and released the following April as *Mission Accomplished... But The Beat Goes On*. It was a typical fun-loving **Rezillos** rave up but was undermined by poor sound quality. For fans and others who'd purchased their first album it also duplicated six of those tracks. Still, there were five new tunes, as well as typically energetic covers of *I Need You* (The Kinks), *Ballroom Blitz* (Sweet) and *Land Of 1,000 Dances* (Cannibal and The Headhunters).

Sire's 1996 CD *Can't Stand The Rezillos: The (Almost) Complete Rezillos* is a repro of the one issued in the 'States in 1993. As well as their first album there are thirteen live bonus cuts, including reworking of Sweet's *Ballroom Blitz* and The Kinks' *I Need You*.

Top Of The Pops later resurfaced on *The Best Punk Album In The World.... Ever, Vol. 1* (2-CD) (Virgin VTDCD 42) 1995 and on *The Best Punk Anthems.... Ever* (2-CD) (Virgin VTDCD 198) 1998. In 1999, *I Can't Stand My Baby* got a further airing on the 5-CD box set *1-2-3-4 - A History Of Punk And New Wave 1976 - 1979* (MCA/Universal MCD 60066).

When the parting of the waves came, the vocalists went one way and the instrumentalists the other. Reynolds and Fife teamed up with drummer Rocky Rhythm and three girl backing vocalists to join **The Revillos** (see entry for more details). They achieved modest success. Callis, Templar and Paterson (who'd replaced Mysterious on bass after he walked out when Sire had delayed the release of their debut album for three months whilst they were sorting a distribution deal) linked up with former Index member Troy Tate to form **Shake**, who gigged for 18 months but with limited success. Callis later joined **The Human League**.

Rhabstallion

| 45: | Day To Day/Breadline (PS) | (Rhab RHAB 001) 1981 |

Some of these 45s came with a badge. Both formats are now rare and quite expensive to purchase.

Rhesus Negative

Rhesus Negative were for a short while the house band at Harp Bar in Belfast. Their music contrasted with the other Northern Irish bands of this era. Their material typified by numbers such as *Rhesus Babies*, *My Baby Left Me* and *Contact Radiation* was weak and unattractive. They soon vanished into oblivion.

Rhythm Of Life

Personnel incl: PAUL HAIG

| 45s: | * Soon/Summertime (PS) | (Rational RATE 6) 1981 |
| | + Uncle Sam/Portrait Of The Heart (PS) | (Rational RATE 7) 1982 |

NB: * Also listed on label as Rhythm RHYTHM 1. + Also listed on label as Rhythm RHYTHM 2.

This group included **Paul Haig** who was also with **Josef K**.

The Ribs

Personnel:	IAN BALCHIN	vcls, gtr	A
	BUTCH BEAGLEY	lead vcls, gtr	A
	TAFF EVANS	drms	A
	DUNCAN REDPATH	bs	A

| 45: | Man With No Brain/ Long Time Coming (PS) | (Aerco AERS 101) 1978 |

The record label Aerco was based in Woking, Surrey. Unfortunately, both sides of this 45 are pretty nondescript.

THE RIBS - Man With No Brain.

The Rich Kids

Personnel:	RUSTY EGAN	drms	A
	GLEN MATLOCK	bs	A
	STEVE NEW	gtr	A
	MIDGE URE	gtr, vcls	A

HCP

ALBUM: 1(A) GHOSTS OF PRINCES IN TOWERS (EMI EMC 3263) 1978 51

NB: (1) later reissued on EMI (Fame FA 4130771) 1983 series. (1) also issued on CD (Dojo DOJOCD 151) 1993 with an additional track *Here Comes The Nice* (live) and again (Cherry Red CDMRED 157) 1999 with three additional tracks. There's also a CD compilation of unreleased rarities, demos and live material, *Burning Sounds* (Rev-Ola CREV 051 CD) 1998.

HCP

45s:	* Rich Kids/Empty Words (PS)	(EMI EMI 2738) 1978 24
	Marching Men/ Here Comes The Nice (PS)	(EMI EMI 2803) 1978 -
	Ghosts Of Princess Tower/Only Arsenic	(EMI EMI 2848) 1978 -

NB: * Issued on red vinyl.

Glen Matlock formed **The Rich Kids** after he'd parted company with **The Sex Pistols** in February 1977. His dream was to get together a band of like-minded individuals who shared his passion for music. His first recruit was 17-year old Londoner Steve New, who'd unsuccessfully auditioned for **The Sex Pistols** when they'd placed an advert in Melody Maker a year or so earlier for a second guitarist. New recommended Rusty Egan, who'd taken over his job as a delivery boy at Warner Brothers, to fill the vacant drum slot. The new trio began rehearsing at **The Clash**'s rehearsal facility in Camden and a Stoke Newington squat during the early summer of 1977. It soon became apparent that they lacked a decent vocalist. The quest to find one took several twists and turns. First, they placed an advert in the music papers, but this didn't produced the desired result. They tried Jeff Deaf (later of The Smart) but it seems they decided his voice wasn't what they required. Paul Weller (of **The Jam**), Mick Jones (of **The Clash**) and **Howard Devoto** (formerly of **The Buzzcocks** and later **Magazine**) were all approached, but declined. It later transpired that future **Dexy Midnight Runners**' mainman Kevin Rowland had travelled down from Birmingham to audition, only to find a note pinned on the door to say the slot had already been filled. The slot finally went to **Midge Ure**, who was lured away from ailing Scottish band Slik. However, in the interim Mick Jones played several gigs with them on a temporary basis in August 1977.

The Rich Kids finally signed with EMI in November 1977 and set about recording with Mike Thorne at the Abbey Road Recording Studio. Both Matlock and **Ure** were influenced by sixties and seventies pop. This really dictated that the group's music was going to be more sophisticated than the primal punk thrash of many of their contemporaries. Indeed, they can now be viewed as early exponents of what became known as power pop.

Their debut single issued on red vinyl and simply titled *Rich Kids* climbed to No. 24 in the charts in January 1978, during a five week stay. The track was generally acknowledged to be their best song of the era. It had also formed part of their first of two John Peel sessions on 7th November 1977. This lead to its later inclusion on *Winters Of Discontent* (Strange Fruit SFRCD 204) in 1991, which compiled various cuts from Peel sessions. The other three tracks featured in this **Rich Kids** session were *Young Girls*, *Burnin' Sounds* and *Bullet Proof Lover*.

A second Peel session was recorded on 3rd April 1978. It comprised *Ghosts Of Princes*, *Lovers And Fools*, *Empty Words* and *Here Comes The Nice*. The later had been a sixties hit for The Small Faces. For one gig at the Lyceum in London on 26th April 1978 the band were joined by Ian MacLagan, organist with The Small Faces (who'd recently reformed). Indeed MacLagan later contributed to **The Rich Kids**' first album and even contemplated joining them at one stage.

Surprisingly, a second **Rich Kids**' single, *Marching Men* written by Midge Ure, failed to follow-up on their earlier chart success. The anthemic song was one of their finest moments. Along with the title track, *Ghosts Of Princes Of Towers*, it was one of the stand-out tracks on their album, recorded in a tiny recording studio in Barnes, South-west London, owned by South African singer John Kongos. Mike Thorne was replaced on the controls by the late Mick Ronson, former guitarist with David Bowie's backing band The Spiders From Mars.

THE RICH KIDS - Ghosts Of Princes In Towers.

By now though, tensions were beginning to emerge between band members about the musical content of the album. Both Matlock and New were uncomfortable with **Ure**'s poppier contributions like *Young Girls, Lovers And Fools* and his earlier single with PVC-2 *Put You In The Picture*. Matlock wanted more of his material on the album, but **Midge Ure** had been in the business longer and argued strongly for his material.

A month before the album's release Matlock and New took time out to rehearse in a 'fun' grop called **Vicious White Kids**, which also featured **Sid Vicious** and Rat Scabies. They played a one-off gig on 15th August 1978 at the Electric Ballroom in London's Camden Town, as a leaving present to Sid, who was due to fly to New York with girlfriend Nancy Spungen the next day.

When the *Ghost Of Princes In Towers* album was eventually released in October 1978, it was met with restrained acclaim. Some blame Ronson for the rather muffled production. Certainly, New produced some inventive, and at times futuristic guitar riffs, on an album of variable material. It spent just one week at No. 51 in the album charts. The melodic title track was released as a 45 but failed to chart at all. Somehow the band seemed out of time with the post-punk consciousness.

By now a split was inevitable. Rusty Egan and **Midge Ure** were beginning to get into the New Romantic scene whilst Glen Matlock and Steve New became increasingly detached from the band, but also wanted to stick to a rock format. It seems the band decided to split soon after their album made the charts, but they kept it a secret from the wider world, whilst they were planning their next career moves and fulfilling any outstanding contractual obligations.

Some previously unreleased material from this later stage can be heard on the CD compilation *Burning Sounds* on Rev-Ola. Certainly cuts like *Tomorrow's Zone*, *Precious* and *Point It To Your Head* sound worthwhile. It's worth noting that the 1999 reissue of their *Ghosts Of Princes Tower* on Cherry Red comes with three extra cuts; *Empty Words*, *Here Comes The Nice* (live) and *Only Arsenic*.

Their final concert was at Wembley Arena supporting David Essex.

Back in 1979, their are 'B' side *Only Arsenic* was included on *The Rare Stuff* (EMI SHSM 2028) 1979. Later *Rich Kids* got a further airing on *Teenage Kicks* (PolyGram TV 5253382) in 1995 and on *1-2-3-4 - A History Of Punk And New Wave 1976 - 1979* (MCA/Universal MCD 6006) 1999, a box 5-CD set.

Rusty Egan and **Midge Ure** went on to join New Romantic electronics outfit **Visage**. Within six months Ure had left **Visage** and, after a brief stint with Thin Lizzy, joined **Ultravox**. New briefly worked in one of Johnny Thunder's bands and he and Matlock later worked with Iggy Pop. Then New went on to **Generation X** before fronting a new band called Lewd. Matlock also wrote his biography and appeared on **The Sex Pistols**' 'Filthy Lucre' tour of 1996.

Riff Raff

Personnel:			
STEPHEN 'BILLY' BRAGG	vcls, gtr	ABCDEF
ROBERT HANDLEY	drms	ABCDEF
STEVEN 'RICEY' RICE	keyb'ds	AB
PHILLIP 'WIGGY' WIGG	gtr	ABCDEF
JOHN WAUGH	bs	B
RYAN O'LOCHLAINN	bs, gtr	CDE
PETE WATKINS	bs	D
'LITTLE' KEVIN BEECH	bs	E
MARK EARWOOD	gtr	F
OSCAR O'LOCHLAINN	drms	F

EP: 1(C) I WANNA BE A COSMONAUT (Cosmonaut/ Romford Girls/What's The Latest/ Sweet As Pie) (Chiswick SW 34) 1978

45s:	Barking Park Lake/Ruan O'Lochlain	(Albion DEL 6) 1979
	Every Girl/You Shared House	(Geezer GZ 1) 1980
	Kitten/Fantocide	(Geezer GZ 2) 1980
	Little Girls Know/She Don't Matter	(Geezer GZ 3) 1980
	New Home Town/Richard	(Geezer GZ 4) 1980

This outfit was most significant for including Billy Bragg, who formed the band with fellow Barking boy Philip 'Wiggy' Wigg in 1976. The duo soon teamed up with Robert Handley and Steven 'Ricey' Rice and entered a talent competition in Hornchurch that November as The Flying Tigers. They recruited a fifth member Johnny Waugh on bass soon after and moved up to Oundle, near Peterborough. Up there they met Ryan O'Lochlainn (who'd been with London pub-rockers Bees Make Honey) and it was his wife who gave them their new name **Riff Raff**.

In 1978, they signed a deal with Chiswick. By now Rice had left the band and O'Lochlainn had taken over on bass from Waugh, who'd also left. In June, Chiswick put out 4,000 copies of the *Cosmonaut* EP. The best track and probably their finest moment was the amusing *Romford Girls*. However, they failed to attract any interest from the major labels.

Ryan O'Lochlainn switched to guitar and Pete Watkins joined on bass. He was soon replaced on bass by 'Little' Kevin Beech. In 1979, a 45 was released on Albion. The following year, in desperation to attract attention, they released four singles with pressings of 1,000 each on their own Geezer label. They obviously weren't aware of the disasterous effect this had on Moby Grape when Columbia/CBS released all ten of their debut album's tracks as the 'A' or 'B' sides of five singles simultaenously back in 1967! Line-up 'F' played on these releases and Oscar O'Lochlainn was just twelve at the time. Predictably no big breakthrough came!

After **Riff Raff** disbanded Billy Bragg briefly joined the army! He returned as a folk-punk solo act in 1982 which he called Spy vs Spy. After signing to Charisma a mini-album *Life's A Riot With Spy vs Spy* was released in July 1983 and it was the start of a successful career for Bragg, who became one of the country's best songwriters of the eighties and nineties. His material often had a political edge and he fronted the group of musicians known as Red Wedge who played for the Labour Party during the 1992 general election campaign. Philip 'Wiggy' Wigg was Bragg's roadie, producer and guitarist during his solo years and in the late nineties had his own band Click. Rice and Handley joined Bragg and Wigg for a couple of **Riff Raff** reunions over the years.

Cosmonaut can also be heard on *The Chiswick Story* (2-CD) (Chiswick CDWIK 2) 1992, whilst *Romford Girls* got further exposure on *The Chiswick Sampler (Good Clean Fun)* (Chiswick CDWIKX 162) in 1995 and on the 5-CD box set *1-2-3-4 - A History Of Punk And New Wave 1976 - 1979* (MCA/Universal MCD 60066) in 1999.

Rikki and The Last Days Of Earth

Personnel incl: RIKKI SYLVAN A

ALBUM: 1(A) FOUR MINUTE WARNING (DJM DJF 20526) 1978

45s:	Oundle 29/5/77 (1-sided)	(Own label) 1977
	City Of The Damned/Victimized (PS)	(DJM DJS 10814) 1977
	Loaded/Street Fighting Man (PS)	(DJM DJS 10822) 1978
	Twilight Jack/No Wave (PS)	(DJM DJS 10860) 1978

RIKKI AND THE LAST DAYS OF EARTH - City Of The Damned.

After beginning with a self-made one-sided 45 *Oundle 29/5/77* which is now quite rare and collectable, the five-piece **Rikki and The Last Days Of Earth** were signed by DJM later in 1977. *City Of The Damned*, produced by Rikki Sylvan, is quite promising and eventful. *Loaded* is also quite a good song about a businessman. The flip side is a contrived version of The Rolling Stones' *Street Fighting Man*. Their appropriately titled *Four Minute Warning* album, which gives the impression of overblown pomp rock and three 45s attracted little attention and Rikki Sylvan tried his hands at a solo career. The resulting album *The Silent Hours* (Kaleidoscope 851 98) 1981 comprised rather dull predominently synthesizer music.

Rikka and The Numbers

45:	The Heartbreak Kid/Headlines	(Rainbow RAIS 1) 1977

A one-off venture. *The Heartbreak Kid* is a headbanger but with a 'sanitized' attempted chart chorus. The attempt at commercial glory didn't succeed and the group remained in obscurity.

The Rings

Personnel:	ROD LATTER	drms	A
	ALAN LEE SHAW	gtr, vcls	A
	DENNIS STOW	bs	A
	TWINK	vcls	A

45:	I Wanna Be Free/Automobile (PS)	(Chiswick S 14) 1977

The Rings were notable for including former Pink Fairies member Twink, who went solo after this short-lived project. Their sole 45 was produced by **Radio Stars**' bassist Martin Gordon and does include some good guitar work. *I Wanna Be Free* was also included on the sampler *Long Shots Dead Certs And Odds On Favourites* (Chiswick CH 5) in 1978 and *The Chiswick Story* (2-CD) (Chiswick CDWIK 2 100) in 1992. Shaw and Latter went on to form **Maniacs**.

Riot/Clone

Personnel:	D. FLOYD	vcls	A
	ROO	lead gtr	A

EPs: (up to 1986)	1( )	THERE'S NO GOVERNMENT LIKE NO GOVERNMENT	(Riot Clone RCR 001) 1982
	2( )	DESTROY THE MYTH OF MUSICAL DESTRUCTION	(Riot Clone RCR 002) 1982
	3(A)	BLOOD ON YOUR HANDS (Why Do You Have To Eat Me?/ Running/Society)	(Riot Clone RCR 004) 1983

Riot/Clone were an early eighties band whose songs had a strong message, but whose music was extremely empty. One cut on their *Blood On Your Hands* 45 *Society* was recorded at The Swan, Kingston, in November 1982. The sound quality is extremely poor, as is the playing. The remaining two tracks were recorded at Fair Deal Recording Studios in Hayes, Middlesex. The 'A' side *Why Do You Have To Eat Me?* is unusual. The first few minutes include extracts of speakers making the case against animal slaughter. The song lyrics then take up the case but within a very pedestrian musical format:-

"I stand my feet slipping through the slats
I'm fed powered milk to make me fat
My only scenery's metal bars
Not for me the sky or the stars
Apparently I will soon be veal
Nobody bothered to ask me how I feel
I will be hung up by my feet
To yield expensive lighter meat"
(from *Why Do You Have To Eat Me?*)

An earlier cut *Death To Humanity* was included on *Punk And Disorderly* (Anagram GRAM 001) 1982.

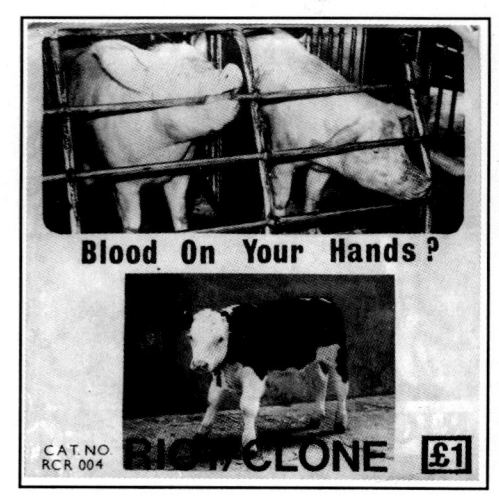

RIOT/CLONE - Blood On Your Hands.

Riot Squad

Personnel:	DUNK	vcls	A
	NELLO	gtr	A
	POMIE	drms	A
	WAYNE	bs, vcls	A

ALBUM:	1(A)	NO POTENTIAL THREAT	(Rot ASS 13) 1984

NB: There's also a CD *Complete Riot Squad Punk Collection* (Anagram CDPUNK 41) 1995.

EPs:	1(A)	DON'T BE DENIED (Lost Cause/Suspicion/ Unite And Fight/Police Power)	(Rot ASS 1) 1983
	2(A)	THERE AIN'T NO SOLUTION (There Ain't No Solution/ Government Schemes)	(Rot ASS 3) 1984

45s:	Fuck The Tories/We Are The Riot Squad/ Civil Destruction (PS)	(Rondelet ROUND 23) 1982
	Riot In The City/Religion (PS)	(Rondelet ROUND 25) 1982
	I'm OK Fuck You/In The Future/Societies Fodder/ Friday Night Hero (PS)	(Rot ASS 2) 1983

An Oi! band from Mansfield. Their half punk half skin line-up ensured they won a good following from both cults. When they moved on to Rot Records from Rondelet their sound veered more towards hardcore punk. *Don't Be Denied*, *I'm OK - Fuck You* and *No Solutions* were all indie chart hits. They disbanded in late 1984 and their records are now pricey collectables.

Twenty-one of their raucous songs are compiled on *Riot Squad Punk Singles Collection*. *Fuck The Tories*, *We Are The Riot Squad* and *Civil Destruction* are very rauxous and tuneless punk thrashes, but the 45 came in a great picture sleeve.

They've also figured on a few compilations. *Unite And Fight* and *Friday Night Hero* were both included on *Wet Dream* (Rot ASS 4) 1984. *Fuck The*

Tories, We Are The Riot Squad and Riot In The City can also be found on Rondelet Punk Singles Collection (Anagram CDPUNK 49) 1995, which was also issued on vinyl (Captain Oi! AHOY LP 513) 1996. You can also check out Lost Cause, I'm OK Fuck You, There Ain't No Solution and Hate The Law on Rot Records Punk Singles Collection (Anagram CDPUNK 40) in 1994 and Police Power on Pax Records Punk Collection (Anagram CDPUNK 75) 1996. Finally, Society's Fodder and Lost Cause resurfaced on 100% Hardcore Punk Rock (Captain Oi! AHOY DCD 84) 1997.

Riot Squad

45:	Total Onslaught (PS)	(The THE 001) 1982

This a different band to the outfit from Mansfield, but this is also a bit Oi!-like.

The Rip Chords

Personnel:	SEAN DROMGOOLE	vcls	A
	MORRIS GOULD	bs	A
	JOHNATHAN JETLAG	gtr	A
	MICHAEL TREI	drms	A

EP:	1(A)	TELEVISION (Ringing In The Streets/Music's/ Peace Artist/Television Television)	(Cells SELL 1) 1979

A Lincoln band whose EP had some great lyrics:-

"Music is a giant biz
The record kings pull all the strings
The dinosaurs are music's whores
Irrelevant white elephants
They don't relate
They're not so great
They're all too vain to entertain
Their sets are filled with overkill
Pretentiousness in vast excess!"
(from Music's)

The Rivals

Personnel:	MARK EDWARDS	gtr, vcls	A
	MARC HEBDEN	drms	A
	PAUL LENSTER	bs, vcls	A

45s:	Future Rights/Flowers (PS)	(Ace ACE 007) 1980
	Here Comes The Night/ Both Sides (PS)	(Oakwood/Ace ACE 011) 1980

These recordings were by a different **Rivals** from the one on Sound On Sound. Here Comes The Night and Both Sides later resurfaced on Punk Rock Rarities, Vol. 1 (Anagram CDPUNK 63) in 1995.

RIOT SQUAD - Fuck The Tories.

THE RIVITS - Multiplay.

The Rivits

Personnel:	STEVE DWIRE	bs	A
	DOANE PERRY	drms	A
	JESS RODEN	drms, vcls	A
	PETER WOOD	keyb'ds, vcls	A
	(LEE GOODALL	sax	A)

ALBUM:	1(A)	MULTIPLAY	(Island ILPS 9617) 1980

45s:	Saturday Night At The Dance/ Girl Next Door (PS)	(Alien ALIX 001) 1978
	Alright On The Night (flexidisc)	(Alien no #) 1978
	Never/Boy Meets Girl (PS)	(Alien ALIX 002) 1979

A third division new wave band. They are most notable for including Jess Roden, who fronted his own band in the mid-seventies. The Multiplay album was produced by Roden and Peter Wood and the title cut is one of the strongest, along with the finale Red Light On. Nail It Down and Lookin' typified their U.S.-influenced sound. Old Broadway is a slower song. Overall, this is an undistinguished album.

Robert and Remoulds

45:	X No. 1/Do Eyes Ever Meet?	(Black And White BW 1) 1979

An obscure mod-influenced disc.

Tom Robinson Band

Personnel:	MARK AMBLER	keyb'ds	AB
	MARK GRIFFITHS	bs	A
	ANTON MAUVE	gtr	A
	TOM ROBINSON	vcls, bs	ABCDEF
	BRETT SINCLAIR	gtr	A
	MICK TREVISICK	drms	A E
	DANNY KUSTOW	gtr	BCDE
	BRIAN 'DOLPHIN' TAYLOR	drms	BC
	NICK PLYTAS	keyb'ds	C
	PRESTON HEYMAN	drms, vcls	D
	IAN PARKER	keyb'ds, vcls	DEF
	CHARLIE MORGAN	drms	F
	GEOFF DALY	sax	F
	GRAHAM COLLIER	double bs	F
	GEOFF SHARKEY	gtr	F

				HCP
ALBUMS:	1(B)	POWER IN THE DARKNESS	(EMI EMI 3226) 1978	4
	2(D)	TRB 2	(EMI EMI 3296) 1979	18
	3(-)	TOM ROBINSON BAND (compilation)	(Fame FA 3028) 1982	-

NB: (1) reissued in 1983 (EMI EMS 106681) 1983, also issued on CD (Cooking Vinyl COOKCD 076) 1994 and (Razor And Tie RE 2018) 1996. (2) reissued in 1983, also issued on CD (Cooking Vinyl COOKCD 077) 1994 and (Razor And Tie RE 2019) 1996. There are also various CD compilations: *The Collection 1977 - 87* (EMI CDP 7 48543 2) 1987, also on vinyl, *Back In The Old Country* (Connoisseur Collection VSOPCD 138) 1989 (also on vinyl VSOPLP 138), *Glad To Be Gay Cabaret '79* (live) (Panic ROBBO 2) 1992, (Teldec 625304) 1984 and on CD (Line LICD 900261) 1989 and (Castaway Northwest CNWVP 003 CD) 2000, *Last Tango* (Line LICD 900508) 1989, *Glad To Be Gay Cabaret / Last Tango* (Line LICD 921215) 1992, *The Gold Collection* (EMI CD GOLD 1015) 1996 and *Rising Free (The Best Of Tom Robinson)* (EMI Gold CDGOLD 1098) 1997.

EPs:				
	1(-)	GOOD TO BE GAY	(Chebel SRT/CUS 015)	1975 -
	2(B)	RISING FREE (Don't Take No For An Answer/ Glad To Be Gay/Martin/ Right On Sister)	(EMI EMI 2749)	1978 18

NB: (1) credited to Bradford Gay Liberation Front.

				HCP
45s:		2-4-6-8 Motorway/I Shall Be Released	(EMI EMI 2715)	1977 5
	*	Don't Take No For An Answer/ Glad To Be Gay	(EMI EMI 2749)	1978 18
		Up Against The Wall/I'm Alright Jack	(EMI EMI 2787)	1978 33
		Too Good To Be True/ Power In The Darkness	(EMI EMI 2847)	1978 -
		Bully For You/Our People	(EMI EMI 2916)	1979 68
	+	All Right All Night/Black Angel	(EMI EMI 2946)	1979 -
		Never Gonna Fall In Love/ Getting Tighter	(EMI EMI 2967)	1979 -
	x	Stand Together/A Dyke's Gotta Do	(Deviant DEVIANT 1)	1979 -
		Now Martin's Gone (live)/ Atmospherics (live) (flexidisc)	(Panic PROMO 2)	1982 -

NB: * 2-track jukebox issue. + Withdrawn, demo only. x With Gay Pride.

Tom Robinson, like **Elvis Costello** and **Ian Dury**, was another example of a musician whose music was pre-dated and outlasted the punk era but who was swept up and invigorated by its momentum.

Tom Robinson was born on 1st June 1950 in Cambridge. He developed an interest in music during his youth, learning to play oboe, clarinet and bass guitar. It was during a spell in Finchden Manor, a readjustment centre in Kent, that he met Danny Kustow, with whom he later formed his first group, Davanq in 1971. They didn't make it onto vinyl.

Then, in 1973, he formed an acoustic trio Cafe Society with Ray Doyle and Hereward Kaye. They were signed to The Kinks' Konk label and their eponymous 1975 album was recorded with help from Ray Davies and Mick Avory. During 1975, **Robinson** recorded the *Good To Be Gay* (EP) using the moniker the Bradford Gay Liberation Front. Fans of the band and collectors may want to track this down - it is now rare and hard to find.

An embryonic **Tom Robinson Band** was formed in November 1976, after **Robinson** had left Cafe Society. It's line-up ('A') proved unstable and it never made it onto vinyl. Out of its demise **Robinson** formed a tighter four-piece outfit in January 1977. Overtly homosexual, **Robinson** sought to allay his band to a range of radical causes, most notably Gay Liberation and Rock Against Racism. In this era he penned a series of stunning

TOM ROBINSON Band - 2-4-6-8 Motorway.

songs. Music of the street whose lyrics were designed to break down people's fear of one another. The enemy was identified as both the establishment and the National Front. After six months of constant gigging, the band were signed to EMI, after that label's disastrous episode with **The Sex Pistols**. Like the 'Pistols, the **Tom Robinson Band (T.R.B.)** played snappy, high energy songs, but in the case of **T.R.B.** with a strong politically radical slant.

Ironically perhaps their debut 45 in October 1977, *2-4-6-8 Motorway* was totally apolitical. It was a stomping anthemic number and an almost timeless party number. An ideal first record to make an impression with to a wide audience, which is exactly what it did. It brought them a No. 5 hit (a position they never bettered) during a nine week stay. The following month they played their first of two John Peel sessions on 7th November. It featured *Don't Take No For An Answer* and *Martin* (later on their *Rising Free* (EP)) and *Long Hot Summer* and *Ain't Gonna Take It* (which were later included on their debut album).

TOM ROBINSON Band - Rising Free.

They followed this in February 1978 with the much more challenging live *Rising Free* EP. This reached No. 18 early in 1978. The stand-out track *Glad To Be Gay*, on which **Robinson** proudly proclaimed his homosexuality and shocked much of middle England. The EP contained some other good cuts, notable the storysong *Martin* and the beaty rock 'n' roller *Right On Sister*, which stated his support for Women's Lib. *Don't Take No For An Answer* was simply a solid rock 'n' roller.

Up Against The Wall, released in May 1978, gave them a third Top 40 single, peaking at No. 33 during a six week chart stay. It typified their heartfelt passion and political anger, which was so prevalent on their superb debut album.

"Look out, listen can you hear it
Panic in the county hall
Look out, listen can you hear it
Whitehall, ...up against the wall"
(from *Up Against The Wall*)

This was one of the definitive albums of the seventies and *Up Against The Wall* was its opening cut. The same fervently anti-racist and anti-establishment messages came across on other anthemic numbers fuelled on by Danny Kustow's raging guitar playing on tracks like *Ain't Gonna Take It; Long Hot Summer* (a possible reference to the earlier Stonewall riots); *The Winter Of '79; Man You Never Saw, Better Decide Which Side You're On, You Gotta Survive* and the crowning finale *Power In The Darkness*, which mocked false conservative values of freedom. The lyrics were always intelligent and related to the struggle as they perceived it:-

"Have you heard an ugly whisper?
Is the rumour really true?
Just in time we're next in line
They're really after me and you
Since the demonstration
They've been down on every side
Rounding up the kids at random
On the curfew every night

Don't repeat this conversation
Don't let on we've met before
Try and make out I'm a stranger
I'm a man you never saw

Church police were round this morning
And the army's on our track
Took away my books and papers
Only just got out the back
I just don't need to tell you
That your place is being watched
Don't go into work tomorrow
Try to make it down the docks

Don't repeat this conversation
Don't let on we've met before
Try and make out I'm a stranger
I'm the man you never saw

Dump your car and burn your letters
Smash your glasses, cut your hair
Buy a suit and take a raincoat
When you go, don't tell us where...."
(from *Man You Never Saw* by Ambler/Robinson)

The clear message of their lyrics was that it was time to stand up and be counted:-

"Power in the darkness
Stand up and fight for your rights"
(from *Power In The Darkness* by Ambler/Robinson)

were the concluding lyrics on the album.

Robinson had spelt out his philosophy in New Musical Express and part of it was reproduced on the album's sleevenotes:-

"Politics isn't party broadcasts and general elections, it's yer kid sister who can't get an abortion, yer best mate getting paki-bashed, or sent down for possessing one joint of marijuana, the GLC deciding which bands we can't see... it's everyday life for rock fans, for everyone who hasn't got a cushy job or rich parents."

"I got no illusions about the political left any more than the right: just a shrewd idea which of the two side's gonna stomp on us first. All of us - you, me, rock 'n' rollers, punks, longhairs, dope smokers, squatters, students, unmarried mothers, prisoners, gays, the jobless, immigrants, gypsies.... to stand aside is to take sides. If music can ease even a tiny fraction of the prejudice and intolerance in this world, then it's worth trying. I don't call that 'unnecessary overtones of violence'. I call it standing up for your rights. And if we fail, if we all get swallowed up by big biznis before we achieve a thing, then we'll have ta face the scorn of tomorrow's generation. But we're gonna have a good try. Fancy joining us?"
(Tom Robinson in New Musical Express).

After *Power In The Darkness* the band underwent the first of numerous personnel changes. First Ambler and then Taylor departed. A succession of keyboard players and drummers came and went - all of which destabilised the band. Ex-Roogalator member Nick Plytas (who'd also played with **Lene Lovich**) was Ambler's original replacement on keyboards in spring 1978. By summer, he, in turn had been relaced by Ian Parker. When 'Dolphin' Taylor went off to **Stiff Little Fingers**, he was replaced by ex-Brand X member Preston Heyman in December 1978.

His second Peel session, recorded on 12th March 1979, comprised five tracks - *All Right All Night*, *Black Angel*, *Blue Murder*, *Crossing Over The Road* and *Law And Order* - which later appeared on *TRB 2*.

TRB 2, their second album, was released in April 1979. Produced by Todd Rundgren, it echoed the music and message of its predecessor but with a more mainstream sound. It was savaged by the critics for its sloganeering and considered unimaginative after the band's pulsating debut. Not surprisingly it didn't fare as well as its predecessor, stalling at No. 18 in a six week chart stay. The 45 culled from it, *Bully For You* crawled to No. 68. The flip-side was a non-album cut.

Two further cuts from *TRB 2*, *Alright All Night* and *Black Angel*, were released on a May 1979 45, but soon withdrawn.

Further line-up changes ensued. Preston Hayman departed to play with Kate Bush. He was replaced briefly on drums by the returning Nick Trevisick, but he was soon relieved by Charlie Morgan. Kustow quit, he would later reappear in Glen Matlock's **Spectres**. Geoff Sharkey came in as his replacement on guitar and Graham Collier and Geoff Daly were added to the line-up on double bass and saxophone respectively. This new line-up ('F') released one further 45 *Never Gonna Fall In Love (Again)*, which flopped. After this **Tom Robinson** realised a complete re-think was needed. He disbanded the outfit in the late summer of 1979 and suffered a nervous breakdown as the strain of it all began to tell.

He returned to form a new band called Sector 27 in 1980, who recorded on the new Panic label which he set up. He moved to Hamburg in Germany in 1982, going solo again and adopting a more mainstream musical style during the eighties - particularly for his 1983 No. 6 hit *War Baby* - which is not really relevant here. He briefly reformed the **Tom Robinson Band** in 1990.

There are a number of relevant compilations:- *The Collection, 1977-87*, which spans the whole of his career. Side One concentrates on his material with **The Tom Robinson Band** and inevitably includes *2-4-6-8 Motorway*, *Grey Cortina* and *Martin*. Side Two concentrates on his later solo career but includes new live versions of *Old Friend* and *Glad To Be Gay*. *Back In The Old Country* is probably the only **Robinson** compilation not to include *Glad To Be Gay*. Otherwise this double set (priced at £4.99 originally) includes nearly all his finest moments. It's also available as one CD. *Tom Robinson Band* released as early as 1982 is a good compilation of the band's material whereas the later compilations tend to draw on material spanning his whole career. With notes by **Tom Robinson**, it includes 45 and EP tracks as well as many of their better album tracks. Other relevant compilations are *The Gold Collection* and *Rising Free (The Best Of Tom Robinson)*. *Cabaret '79* was a live recording made shortly after **Tom Robinson Band** disbanded. As well as the inevitable rendition of *Glad To Be Gay*, it included a reading of Noel Coward's *Mad About The Boy*, which caused **Robinson** some problems with his estate.

The first **Tom Robinson Band** album is a powerful political and musical statement. Lyrics are always more commanding when the writer has something important to say. For a short while **Robinson** certainly did. In 1978, he helped organise a "Rock Against Fascism" rally in East London and his work for Gay radical activist movements is well-known. His music and his politics mellowed somewhat in the eighties, when he also acknowledged he was bi-sexual as opposed to homosexual.

2-4-6-8 Motorway later resurfaced on *The Best Punk Album In The World.... Ever, Vol. 1* (2-CD) (Virgin VTDCD 42) 1995, *The Best Punk Anthems.... Ever!* (Virgin VTDCD 198) 1998, *The Sound Of The Suburbs* (Columbia 4888252) 1997 and *Teenage Kicks* (PolyGram TV 5253382) 1995 and *Up Against The Wall* got a further airing on *1-2-3-4 - A History Of Punk And New Wave 1976 - 1979* (MCA/Universal MCD 60066), a lavish 5-CD box set issued in 1999.

TOM ROBINSON BAND - Power In The Darkness.

Rose Of Victory

Personnel:	NIGEL BEVERLEY	vcls	A
	GARY BOWLER	drms	A
	MACKIE	bs	A
	NIDGE	gtr	A

45:	Suffragette City/Overdrive (PS)	(No Future Oi 24) 1983

This 45 came about when Nidge and Mackie from **Blitz** spent a weekend in a Stockport studio and covered David Bowie's *Suffragette City*. This decent cover version later resurfaced on *No Future - The Punk Singles Collection* (Captain Oi! AHOY DLP 508) 1996. You can also hear the flip side, an instrumental called *Overdrive* on *No Future - The Punk Singles Collection, Vol. 2* (Captain Oi! AHOY DLP 512) 1996.

The Rowdies

Personnel:	ALAN EMMS	vcls	A
	ROB EMMS	gtr	A
	KEVIN ELLISON	bs	A
	RICHARD LARSHAW	drms	A
	STEVE SHARP	gtr	A

45s:	A.C.A.B. (All Coppers Are Bastards)/ Negative Malfunction/Freeze Out	(Birds Nest BN 109) 1978
	She's No Angel/Had Me A Real Good Time (PS)	(Teenage Depression TD ½) 1979

A punk band from Worcester. In 1980 Steve Sharp went on to front a group called **Steve Sharp and The Cleancuts**, who were clearly a mod revival band judging by their 45, *We Are The Mods / He Wants To Be A Mod* (Happy Face MM 122) 1980. Expect to pay a lot of money for this 45 now, which, unusually for the times, was not released in a picture sleeve.

Johnny Rubbish

45s:	Living In NW3 4JR/ The Other Side	(United Artists UP 36405) 1978
	Santa's Alive/Policeman	(United Artists UP 36479) 1978

Neither of **Rubbish**'s 45s came in picture sleeves and neither are at all collectable. On *Living In NW3 4JR* to the tune of *Anarchy In The UK*, Johnny Rubbish does a fair Lydon imitation:-

"I am a capitaLIST
I am a profitEER....
Because 'I want to live/In NW3/Retire to Jersey'"
(from *Living In NW3 4JR*)

The flipside is a puerile set of bad jokes and dead sketches which are supposed to be a 'News At Ten' pastiche.

RUDIMENTARY PENI - Death Church.

Barney Rubble

An Oi! poet who in his rantings extolled the virtues of skinhead culture in a similar mould to **Garry Johnson**. He first appeared backed by The Rubbles singing *Bootboys*, which glorified skinhead culture on *Oi! The Album* (EMI ZIT 1) 1980, which was later issued on CD by Captain Oi! on *Strength Thru' Oi!* (Decca) 1981 he turns to poetry to get his message across on *Best Years Of Our Lives* and *Beans* which consists of:

"I like beans
I like sauce
I like sexual intercourse"
(from *Beans*)

Rudi

Personnel:	GRAHAM MARSHALL	drms	A
	RONNIE MATHEWS	vcls, gtr	AB
	JOHNNY STEWART	bs	AB
	BRIAN YOUNG	gtr, vcls	AB
	GORDON BLAIR	bs, vcls	B

EP:	1(A)	I SPY (I Spy/Genuine Reply/Sometimes/ Ripped In Two) (PS)	(Good Vibrations GOT 12) 1979

45s:	*	Big Time/Number 1 (folded PS)	(Good Vibrations GOT 1) 1978
		When I Was Dead/Bewerewolf/ The Pressure's On (PS)	(Jam CREATE 1) 1981
		Crimson/14 Steps (PS)	(Jam CREATE 3) 1982

NB: * Only 3,000 copies were issued. There is now a retrospective CD, *Big Time (The Best Of Rudi)* (Anagram CDPUNK 77) 1996.

One of the best of the Northern Irish punk bands **Rudi** had formed in Belfast in 1975. Prior to their first single Graham Marshall was replaced by ex-**Stiff Little Finger** Gordon Blair. In their early days **Rudi** played high energy versions of songs by Bowie, the New York Dolls and T. Rex. They took their name from a 45 by proto-punks The Jook (see 'The Tapestry Of Delights' for details of them). It was after seeing **Rudi** and **The Outcats** at a concert in early 1978 that Terri Hooley had the inspiration to form his Good Vibrations label. Indeed **Rudi**'s single *Big Time* was the first record released on the label. One of their early songs, *We Hate The Cops*, which dealt with the sad saga of the cancelled **Clash** concert, and whose chorus recited *SS-RUC*, was to have been their debut single for Good Vibrations, although it was subsequently withdrawn as the more popular **Stiff Little Fingers** took up the political banner. But neither their *I Spy* EP or their Good Vibrations 45 won them national acclaim. They remained popular in Belfast and soldiered on as a trio, after Gordon Blair left to play briefly with **The Outcasts**, before forming his own band. They later switched to Jamming Records, for whom they recorded two further 45s, *When I Was Dead* in 1981 and *Crimson* in 1982.

Even as late as August 1982 they captured the limelight at The Lady Of The Lake Festival in Fermanagh, which featured a handful of Ulster bands.

Rudi also contributed one cut, *Overcome By Fumes*, to the *Battle Of The Bands* EP (Good Vibrations GOT 7) 1978. Released as a double-pack, without a picture sleeve, the other bands featured were **Idiots**, **Outcasts** and **Spider**.

Brian Young's elder brother Barry played in **The Idiots**.

More recently *Big Time*, *Overcome By Fumes* and *I Spy* have all resurfaced on *Good Vibrations - The Punk Singles Collection* (Anagram CDPUNK 36) 1994. *Big Time* has also resurfaed on the 5-CD box set *1-2-3-4 - A History Of Punk And New Wave 1976 - 1979* (MCA/Universal MCD 60066) 1999.

Rudimentary Peni

Personnel:	NICK BLINKO	vcls	A
	GRANT	bs	A
	JON	drms	A

ALBUM:	1(A)	DEATH CHURCH	(Corpus Christi CHRISTITS 6) 1983

NB: (1) also issued on CD (Outer Himalayan BOOB 004CD) 1994.

EPs:	1(A)	RUDIMENTARY PENI	(Outer Himalayan OH 003) 1981
	2(A)	FARCE	(Crass 211984/2) 1982

NB: (1) initially issued in an A4 foldout picture sleeve with a booklet. It was later issued in a 14" by 7" picture sleeve. (2) initially issued in a 21" by 14" foldout black and white picture sleeve. There's also a CD *EPs Of RP* (Outer Himalayan BOOB 003CD) 1994.

This London-based hardcore trio were part of the anarchic **Crass** family. Their 1981 eponymous EP is very raw. Characterised by Nick Blinko's screaming, piercing vocals, the end result is pretty tuneless mayhem. Their second EP *Farce* was a definite improvement, but it's on their debut album *Death Church* that they really win through. There's a clear **Sex Pistols** influence here, the guitar assault and lyrics have gusto and purpose and the end reult is far from tuneless, but still very inaccessible.

Ruefrex

Personnel:	PAUL BURGESS	drms	ABC
	ALLAN CLARKE	vcls	A
	TOM COULTER	bs	ABC
	HEPBURN FORGIE	gtr	ABC
	GORDY BLAIR	bs	C
	GARY FERRIS	gtr	C

ALBUM:	1(C)	FLOWERS FOR ALL OCCASIONS	
(up to 1986)			(Kasper KATLP 1) 1985

EP:	1(A)	ONE BY ONE (One By One/Cross The Line/ Don't Panic) (PS)	(Good Vibrations GOT 8) 1979

NB: (1) came in a fold-over picture sleeve, with two different designs.

45s:	Capital Letters/April Fool (PS)	(Kabuki KAR 7) 1983
	Paid In Kind/The Perfect Crime (PS)	(One By One 1x1) 1984
	The Wild Colonial Boy/ Even In The Dark Hours (PS)	(Kasper KAS 2) 1986
	In The Traps/ Leaders Of The Last Resort (PS)	(Kasper KAS 3) 1986

Ruefrex was a Belfast band which had grown up in the Protestant stronghold around The Shankhill Road, where they played most of their gigs. Good Vibrations provided the platform for them to record a superb EP *One By One* in 1979. The band made a point of playing to both Catholic and Protestant audiences in Belfast, a fact related in *Cross The Line*, a cut on their debut EP. The melodramatic title cut was excellent in its day.

Ruefrex failed to achieve greater popularity because the collapse of Good Vibrations left them without a record company before they had achieved enough to attract a major company. Had they not been in limbo when BBC Northern Ireland broadcast a half hour documentary *Cross The Line* about their motivations and problems, the story might have been different. As it was their April 1983 45 *Capital Letters*, an angry punk groan, made little impression.

Ruefrex split for a while in 1983. Lyricist Paul Burgess took up a teaching job, whilst Coulter and Forgie joined separate groups. However, realising that the group was an important vehicle for their self-expression, they reformed and issued a further 45 *Paid In Kind* in 1984. A friend in London paid for them to record *The Wild Colonial Boy*, which was only their fourth single in seven years. It's a vigorous attack on those Americans giving money to terrorist organisations in Northern Ireland, delivered from a Loyalist standpoint, but from the middle ground in which **Ruefrex** had always stood. Indeed, in May 1985, they played a benefit gig for Lagan College the first project in Northern Ireland to provide integrated secondary education for comparable numbers of Catholics and Protestants under the one roof.

Musically **Ruefrex** changed little throughout their career - catchy tunes, anti-violence lyrics and a guitar-orientated sound. They were later based in London. Their songs still dealt with the troubles in Ulster and took an anti-extremist stance. Aside from *Wild Colonial Boy*, other politico/pop tracks on their 1985 album *Flowers For All Occasions* include *Paid In Kind* (a 1984 single) which deals with the loss of innocent lives in pursuit of a terrorist mission and *By The Shadow-Line* a strong number, which deals with the British military presence in Ulster.

RUEFREX - Flowers For All Occasions.

The title track is a sensitive song about a pregnant woman who is widowed through sectarian violence.

"There are flowers for all occasions,
Floral tributes to the dead.
Orange lilies, shamrock greens,
Bloody scarlet, poppy red"
(from *Flowers For All Occasions*)

This, and *Even In The Darkest Hours*, a song about a despairing man whose woman has left him, highlighted the increasing sensitivity of Paul Burgess' songwriting talents. Overall, the second side of this album is by far the strongest.

Aside from the persistent **Outcasts**, **Ruefrex** were the only significant Ulster band from the late '70s still gigging by the late '80s, albeit from the comparative safety of the mainland. They did release a second album *Playing Cards With Dead Man* (Flicknife BLUNT 041) 1987.

Cross The Line was later included on *Good Vibrations - The Punk Singles Collection* (CD) (Anagram CDPUNK 36) 1994.

Run 229

Personnel:	MARK ALLEN	vcls	A
	RAY BIBBY	drms	A
	NICK CARR	bs	A
	JOHN JONES	gtr	A
	STEPHEN JONES	gtr	A

45:	Soho/Dance/In This Day And Age	(MM JR 7040S) 1980

From the Deeside area, this modish outfit took their name from the number plate of their tour van (well as good a place as any I suppose) and put out this rare one-off single, which unusually for the times didn't come in a picture sleeve.

Soho is a straight forward mod-pop song, penned by John Jones, which can also be heard on *100% British Mod* (Captain Mod MODSKA DCD 8) in 1998. They also recorded a second single *Emily*, which remains unreleased because they split up immediately afterwards.

Rus

45:	Pop-Stars/Patterns (PS)	(Adventure AD 001) 198?

A solo artist with an appealing voice. *Pop-Stars* is very popish but pleasant.

RUS - Pop-Stars.

The Ruts

Personnel:
PAUL FOX	gtr	ABCD
PAUL MATTOCKS	drms	A
MALCOLM OWEN	vcls	AB
DAVE RUFFY	bs, drms	ABCD
JOHN JENNINGS	bs, vcls	BCD
GARY BARNACLE	sax, keyb'ds, vcls	C
DAVE WINTHORP	sax	D

ALBUMS:
				HCP
1(B)	THE CRACK	(Virgin V 2132)	1979	16
2(B)	GRIN AND BEAR IT (compilation)	(Virgin V 2188)	1980	28
3(C)	ANIMAL NOW	(Virgin V 2193)	1981	-
4(C)	RHYTHM COLLISON	(Bohemian BOLP 4)	1982	-

NB: (1) reissued (Virgin OVED 80) 1988 as part of its mid-price series and on CD (Virgin CDV 2132) 1990. (2) reissued (Virgin OVED 57) 1984 as part of its mid-price series. (3) and (4) credited to Ruts D.C.. There are also two live albums, *Live: Ruts* (Dojo DOJO LP 52) 1987 and *Live And Loud* (Link LINK LP 013) 1987, also on CD (Street Link LINK CD 013) 1992. Their three Peel sessions were also released on one album, *Peel Sessions* (Strange Fruit SFRLP 109) 1990. This was also available on CD, *Peel Sessions - Complete Sessions 1979 - 1981* (Strange Fruit SFRCD 109) 1990. Other CD collections include *You Gotta Get Out Of It* (Virgin COM CD 7) 1981, *BBC Radio One Live In Concert* (Windsong WIN CD 009) 1991 (this is a shared disc with **Penetration**), *Demolition Dancing* (Receiver RRCD 182) 1994, *Something That I Said - The Best Of The Ruts* (Virgin CDOVD 454) 1995; some **Ruts** fans may be interested in a limited edition German CD, *Ruts Rules* (Vince Lombardy EFA 12303-2) 1994 and most recently, there's *In A Can* (Harry May CAN CAN 009) 2001. There's also *A Tribute To The Ruts (Various Artists)* (Rejected REJ 100022) 1999.

EPs:
1(B)	Babylon's Burning/West One (Shine On Me)/ Something That I Said/ Staring At The Rude Boys	(Virgin VS 583-12)	1983
2(A)	PEEL SESSION 14.5.79 (Sus/Society/You're Just A.../ It Was Cold/Something That I Said)	(Strange Fruit SFPS 011)	1986
3(B)	THE SKIDS VS THE RUTS	(Virgin VSCDT 1411)	1992

NB: (2) was later available on cassette too (Strange Fruit SFPSC 011) 1987.

45s:
				HCP
*	In A Rut/H-Eyes	(People Unite SJP 795)	1979	-
	In A Rut/H-Eyes	(People Unite RUT 1)	1979	-
	Babylon's Burning/Society (PS)	(Virgin VS 271)	1979	7
	Babylon's Burning/Society (12" PS)	(Virgin VS 271-12)	1979	-
	Something That I Said/ Give Youth A Chance (PS)	(Virgin VS 285)	1979	29
	Jah War/I Ain't Sofisticated (PS)	(Virgin VS 298)	1979	-
+	Staring At The Rude Boys/ Love In Vain (PS)	(Virgin VS 327)	1980	22
	West One (Shine On Me)/The Crack	(Virgin VS 370)	1980	43
	Babylon's Burning/(other side by **XTC**)	(RSO RSO 71)	1980	-
o	Different View/Formula Eyes (PS)	(Virgin VS 396)	1981	-
o	Whatever We Do/ Push Yourself Make It Work (PS)	(Bohemian B 02)	1982	-
o	Stepping Bondage/Lobotomy/Rich Bitch	(Bohemian BO 4)	1983	-

Reissue:
	Babylon's Burning/ Staring At The Rude Boys	(Old Gold OG 9829) 1988 -

NB: * 1,000 copies only, with a black-ringed label, no picture sleeve. + Some copies came with a gatefold picture sleeve and competition stickers. o Credited to Ruts D.C..

The roots of **The Ruts** go back to the schoolboy friendship of Paul Fox and Malcolm Owen. They grew up in Hayes, Middlesex, and both shared a love of music. In the early seventies they spent several years living in a commune on the Isle of Angelsey in Wales. Whilst there they became friendly with Paul Mattocks, who'd been a school friend of Paul Fox. Mattocks played flute, guitar and keyboards, but he'd eventually end up as **The Ruts'** drummer.

Back at the commune the trio formed a group Aslan who played at various hippie gatherings. Their music spanned rock, celtic folk and soul. They never made it onto vinyl, though.

In 1975, the commune broke up. Fox and Owen returned to London. Fox and Mattocks joined Hit and Run, a commercial funk band. In August 1977, inspired by attending a recent **Sex Pistols** gig, Malcolm Owen 'phoned Paul Fox and suggested they form a punk band. **The Ruts** were born. The original line-up comprised Owen, Fox, Dave Ruffy (bs) and Paul Mattocks (drms). After their first rehearsal on 18th August they'd penned *Lobotomy* and *Go Go Go* (which later became *Stepping Bondage*). *I Ain't Sofisticated* was written soon after.

Their live debut came on 16th September 1977 when they played three songs at the Target, Hayes. Shortly after Fox and Ruffy quit Hit and Run and the band recorded four songs on 1st October. Parts of this session later emerged on the *Stepping Bondage* 3-track release six years later in 1983. They now began gigging seriously and extensively. Their programme included an appearance at the Roxy Club in early December 1977. It soon became apparent that Mattocks was uncomfortable doing the fast-paced drumming that punk required so Dave Ruffy switched to drums with John 'Segs' Jennings coming in on bass. The new line-up supported **Wayne County and The Electric Chairs** at High Wycombe Town Hall on 25th January 1978.

Much of the remainder of 1978 was spent touring with reggae band Misty In Roots. Some of these gigs were part of Rock Against Racism and Anti-Nazi League events.

On 9th March 1979, **The Ruts** recorded three of their finest for a David Jensen radio show. The songs in question were *In A Rut*, *Babylon's Burning* and *Something That I Said*.

Misty In Roots had their own record label People Unite. A deal was struck for **The Ruts** to record their debut single on the label. Just 1,000 copies of *In A Rut* were pressed after the song was recorded at Fairdeal Studios, a small eight track studio in Hayes. The original pressing is distinguished by a black rim around the label. It did not (unusually for punk singles in this era) come in a picture sleeve, when released in May 1979. The flip side *H-Eyes* was a warning song against hard drug use.

The 45 came to the attention of deejay John Peel, who played it frequently on his Radio One show. This attracted attention from Virgin, who signed **The Ruts** in spring 1979. Their first release for Virgin, in July 1979, *Babylon's Burning* was one of the definitive punk singles of 1979. It brought them to national attention as it soared to No. 7 in the charts, during an eleven week stay. The flip side, *Society* was a high speed assault on the senses - the result of producer Mick Glossop telling Paul Fox to play as fast as he could! *Babylon's Burning* was also included on the *Times Square* (dbl) (RSO 2685 145) 1980 movie soundtrack.

Capitalising on the success of *Babylon's Burning*, a second Virgin single *Something That I Said* was released the following month. This spent five weeks in the charts, peaking at No. 29. On the flip side was a Peel session recording of *Give Youth A Chance*.

The Ruts debut album *The Crack* was released in September 1979 with a sticker stating '£3.99 pay no more!'. This marketing ploy obviously helped album sales. **The Ruts'** affinity with reggae and the fruits of their association with Misty In Roots (during which John Jennings learnt to play bass) becomes very apparent on this album. The album's jewel in the crown was a version of *Jah Wars*. Members of Misty In Roots and Malcolm Owen's wife Rocky played on this. It was very unusual for white bands to play reggae at this time and this met with a mixed reaction from their predominantly punk audience. An edited version of *Jah Wars* was culled for 45 release, but it failed to chart largely because the BBC felt it too political and refused to give it airplay. Also included on the album were *Babylon's Burning* and *Something That I Said*, but not *In A Rut*. *The Crack* was well-received, despite being an unusual mixture of punk-rock flavoured with reggae and politics. It spent six weeks in the Top 100, peaking at No. 16.

Hot on the heels of the success of their album and failure of the *Jah Wars* single **The Ruts** took off on a forty-date 'Grin And Bear It' tour. Early in 1980 they played a further Peel session and embarked on a new 'Back To Blighty' tour. A further 45, *Staring At The Rude Boys* was released and took them back into the Top 30 in May 1980. Although outwardly all seemed fine, inwardly the strain of stardom and touring had taken its toll on Owen, in particular, who'd become addicted to heroin. His poor health caused throat nodes and the 'Back To Blighty' tour had to be abandoned. His vocal part for the next single *West One (Shine On Me)* had to be shelved and the band put on hold. Owen took time out from the band and moved into his parents house to try to kick the habit. Whilst there he tragically died of an accidental heroin overdose, aged just 26, on 14th July 1980.

Virgin decided to go ahead and release *West One* with out-takes from *The Crack* on the flip in September 1980. The 45 got to No. 43, spending four weeks in the charts, but the band declined an opportunity to appear on 'Top Of The Pops' because it would have involved miming to Owen's vocal part. *West One (Shine On Me)* can also be heard on the 1980 sampler *Cash Cows* (Virgin MILK 1) 1980.

In November 1980, Virgin released a live album *Grin And Bear It*. It comprised a number of live tracks from a French TV show recorded at the Chorus Theatre in Paris and various odds and ends, including both sides of their debut 45 for People Unite, which hadn't been included on *The Crack*. *Grin And Bear It* also charted. During a four week chart stay it rose to No. 28. A four page photo insert accompanied original copies of the album.

With Owen's death many expected **The Ruts** to die a death or simply disband. In fact Jennings handled most of the vocals and they carried on under the new name Ruts D.C.. They added long-time friend Gary Barnacle to their line-up and played from August 1980 to late 1983. They released several well-received singles but met with little commercial success. During 1982 Barnacle was replaced by ex-**Secret Affairs**' Dave Winthorp.

Ruts D.C. finally folded in mid-1983 when Ruffy joined Aztec Camera. Barnacle had earlier departed to **Visage**. Ruffy and Jennings both went on to do lots of session work. Fox later linked up with Rat Scabies.

To mark the 15th anniversary of Malcolm Owen's death the band reformed to record a new album *Rhythm Collision II*. By the time of this recording, later issued on CD in 1994 (Roir Europe/Danceteria RE 151 CD), they'd become a dub-funk outfit. They were also featured on a Greek compilation *Rock '80s, Vol. 3* (Virgin PolyGram 2473 822) 1981. The track included was *No Time To Kill*, which hadn't been committed to vinyl previously.

There have been a plethora of retrospective **Ruts** releases, including their complete Peel sessions, two live albums and two recommended CD compilations *You Gotta Get Out Of It* and *Something That I Said - The Best Of The Ruts*.

Their *Peel Sessions* EP from a May 1979 session includes strong versions of *Sus* and *Something That I Said*.

Live And Loud! released on Link in 1987 captures the band near to their best. It features some of their best-known tracks like *Babylon's Burning*, *Something That I Said*, *Jah Wars* and an extended version of *In A Rut*. Alongside these are less serious offerings like *Ditty Pt's 1 & 2* and a version of *Blue Suede Shoes*.

The CD reissue of *The Crack* in 1990 adds three 'B' sides; *Give Youth A Chance*, *I Ain't Sofisticated* and *The Crack* to the band's sole album recorded with their original singer Malcolm Owen.

In A Can is a sixteen-track collection compiled from three different studio sessions, which includes four very different versions of *Babylon's Burning*, different takes of *H-Eyes* and *Black Man's Pinch*.

The Ruts have also appeared on several compilations. *Babylon's Burning* can also be found on *The Best Punk Album In The World.... Ever, Vol. 1* (2-CD) (Virgin VTDCD 42) 1995, *The Best Punk Anthems.... Ever* (2-CD) (Virgin VTDCD 198) 1998, *A History Of Punk, Vol. 1* (Virgin CDOVD 486) 1997, *Punk, Vol. 2* (Music Club MCCD 027) 1991, *Punk - Live And Nasty* (Emporio EMPRCD 586) 1995, *Punk - The Worst Of Total Anarchy* (2-CD) (Disky SP 871952) 1996, *Spiked* (EMI Gold CDGOLD 1057) 1996 and *New Wave Archive* (Rialto RMCD 201) 1997 features a live version of the song. *Staring At The Rude Boys* got a further airing on *The Best Punk Album In The World.... Ever, Vol. 2* (2-CD) (Virgin VTDCD 79) 1996 and *God Save The Punks* (2-CD) (Disky DOU 882552) 1998. You'll also find *Something That I Said* on *Punk, Vol. 2* (Music Club MCCD 027) 1991. Finally, *In A Rut* has resurfaced on *Burning Ambitions (A History Of Punk)* (Anagram CDBRED 3) 1996 and, more recently, on *1-2-3-4 - A History Of Punk And New Wave 1976 - 1979* (MCA/Universal MCD 60066) 1999, which was a 5-CD box set.

The Ruts had a short but successful career and would figure in most people's Top 20 punk rock bands.

Sabre Jets

45s:	Radioland/Rockin' At The Ace Cafe/	
	Caledonia (PS)	(Blueport BLU 2) 1979
	Voodoo Cave/At The Quayside (PS)	(Blueport BLU 5) 1980

A Newcastle band whose 45s were available nationally with distribution through Spartan.

Sad Lovers and Giants

Personnel:	GRACE ALLARD	vcls	A
	TRISTAN GAREL FUNK	gtr	A
	NIGEL POLLARD	drms	A
	CLIFF SILVER	bs	A
	DAVID WOOD	keyb'ds	A

ALBUMS:	1(A)	EPIC GARDEN MUSIC	
(up to			(Midnight Music CHIME 0001) 1982
1986)	2(A)	FEEDING THE FLAME	
			(Midnight Music CHIME 0003) 1983
	3(A)	IN THE BREEZE	(Midnight Music CHIME 0007) 1984
	4(A)	TOTAL SOUND (mini-album)	
			(Midnight Music CHIME 0022) 1986

NB: (1) also issued on CD (Midnight Music CHIME 0001CD) 1988. (2) also issued on CD (Midnight Music CHIME 0003CD) 1988.

EP:	1(A)	CLE	(Last Movement LM 003) 1981

45s:	Colourless Dream/	
(up to	Things We Never Did (PS)	(Last Movements LM 005) 1981
1986)	Lost In A Moment/	
	The Tightrope Touch (PS)	(Midnight Music DING 1) 1982

THE RUTS - The Crack.

Man Of Straw/Cowboys (PS)	(Midnight Music DING 5)	1983
Man Of Straw/Cowboys (alt. version)/ Close To The Sea (12", PS)	(Midnight Music DONG 5)	1983

Sad Lovers and Giants hailed from Watford in Hertfordshire. Their sound was characterised by Garel-Funk's jangling guitar and Woods' rather sophisticated sax and keyboards. The post-punk combo at times sound new wave and much of their music is moody and brooding. Their early singles *Colourless Dream* and *Lost In A Moment* were well received. One of their best efforts was *Man Of Straw* which was culled from the *Feeding The Flame* album. Overall, though, this album is much quieter and has a less immediate appeal.

In The Breeze comprised alternative versions of tracks from their first two albums recorded for BBC DJ John Peel's show, some previously unreleased tracks and some live tracks. It is worth investigating, but by late 1983 the group had disbanded. The *Total Sound* mini-album, which had been recorded live for a Dutch radio broadcast in 1983, was released (after they had split) in 1986.

The group did reform in 1987 releasing a further 45 *White Russains* and two subsequent albums - *The Mirror Test* and *Les Annes Veries* - in 1988. Only Pollard and Allard from the original line-up were still involved by this time. Two further albums - *Headland* and *Treehouse Poetry* - followed in 1991.

The Saints

Personnel: (up to 1985)	CHRIS BAILEY	vcls	ABCD
	KIM BRADSHAW	bs	A
	IVOR HAY	drms	AB
	ED KUEPPER	gtr	AB
	ALGY WARD	bs	B
	CHRIS BARRINGTON	gtr	CD
	MARK BIRMINGHAM	drms	CD
	JANINE HALL	bs	C
	TRACEY PEW	bs	D

ALBUMS: (up to 1985)				
1(A)	I'M STRANDED	(Harvest SHSP 4065)	1977
2(B)	ETERNALLY YOURS	(Harvest SHSP 4078)	1978
3(B)	PREHISTORIC SOUNDS	(Harvest SHSP 4094)	1978
4(C)	MONKEY PUZZLE	(New Rose ROSE 1)	1981
5(C)	OUT IN THE JUNGLE	(New Rose ROSE 11)	1982
6(D)	A LITTLE MADNESS TO BE FREE	(New Rose ROSE 38)	1984
7(D)	LIVE IN A MUD HUT	(New Rose ROSE 55)	1985

NB: (1) also issued on CD (Triple XXX TX 51243 CD) 1987 and again on CD (Captain Oi! AHOY CD 129) 1999, with bonus cuts. (2) reissued (Fan Club 035) 1987; on CD (Fan Club FC 035) 1990 (now deleted); (New Rose 422309) 1994; (Triple XXX TX 5124 CD) 1997; and (Captain Oi! AHOYCD 127) 1999, with bonus cuts. (3) reissued on Fan Club in 1987 and also on CD (New Rose 422312) 1994. (4) also issued on CD (New Rose ROSE 1CD) 1981, but now deleted. (5) later reissued on vinyl (Flicknife SHARP 106) 1990 and also issued on CD (New Rose ROSE 11CD) 1988. (6) also issued on CD (New Rose ROSE 38CD) 1984. There are also a number of compilations, on vinyl *The Best Of The Saints (1977-78)* (Razor RAZ 21) 1986, *Scarce Saints* (Raven RV 04) 1989 (also on CD RVCD-04), on vinyl and CD *The New Rose Years (Greatest Hits)* (Fan Club FC 060), also on CD (Fan Club FC 060CD) 1990 (the CD issue has five extra cuts) and CD only *Out In The Jungle* (New Rose ROSE 11 CD) 1988 (now deleted), *Songs Of Salvation 1976 - 88* (Raven) 1991; *The Most Primitive Band In The World* (Hot HOT 1053 CD) 1995; *7799: Big Hits On The Underground* (2-CD) (Last Call 305 1512) 1999; *Know Your Product (The Best Of The Saints)* (EMI GOLD CDGO 2069) 1996 and *7799: Big Hits On The Underground* (2-CD) (Last Call 305 1512) 1999.

EPs: (up to 1985)			
1(B)	ONE TWO THREE FOUR (Lipstick On Your Collar/ One Way Street/Demolition Girl/ River Deep Mountain High)	(Harvest 5137)	1977
2(C)	PARALYTIC TONIGHT DUBLIN TOMORROW (12")	(New Rose)	1982

NB: (1) was issued as an EP with a picture sleeve and also as a double-pack with a gatefold picture sleeve. (2) was a French-only release.

HCP

45s: (up to 1985)		
I'm Stranded/No Time (PS)	(Power Exchange PX 242)	1976 -
I'm Stranded/(other side by Chuck Stanley)	(Power Exchange PXE 101)	1977 -
Erotic Neurotic/One Way Street	(Harvest HAR 5123)	1977 -
This Perfect Day/LIES	(Harvest HAR 5130)	1977 34
This Perfect Day/LIES/ Do The Robot (12" PS)	(Harvest HAR 125130)	1977 -
Know Your Product/Run Down Security/	(Harvest HAR 5148)	1978 -
All Times Through Paradise (PS)	(Harvest HAR 5166)	1978 -
In The Mirror/Always (PS)	(New Rose)	1980 -
Follow The Leader/Animal (PS)	(Flicknife FLS 15)	1983 -
Imagination/Prisoner (live)	(New Rose NEW 43)	1984 -
Ghost Ship/Wrapped Up And Blue	(New Rose NEW 37)	1985 -
x I Dreamed Of Marie Antoinette/ (other side by The Mock Turtles)	(Bucketfull Of Brains Mag No. 32)	1988 -

NB: x Freebie, which came free with 'Bucketfull Of Brains', issue 32.

The Saints are a marginal case for inclusion as they originated from Australia. They formed in Brisbane in 1975. They first come to notice here in Britain when *I'm Stranded*, which had been issued by Fatal in Australia, was issued here in Britain by Power Exchange. **The Saints** soon became the first Aussie punk band to achieve any international success. *I'm Stranded* was enthusiastically acclaimed in the rock press. With Chris Bailey's snarling vocals and the raw garage style backing it was something of a punk classic. On the strength of *I'm Stranded* the band were signed up by EMI Harvest and relocated to London. In May 1977 an album, named after their debut 45, was released. Two cuts, *Erotic Neurotic* and *One Way Street* were selected for 45 release the same month to help promote the album, but they didn't chart. However, a second 45 *This Perfect Day* was selected for release in July 1977. It gave them what would prove to be their only U.K. hit. During a four week chart residency, it rose to No. 34.

After this Kim Bradshaw left to join **The Lurkers**. The replacement was Alisdair Ward. The new line-up recorded an EP *One Two Three Four*, which included *One Way Street* and *Demolition Girl* (from their debut album) and covers of *Lipstick On Your Collar* and Ike and Tina Turner's *River Deep Mountain High*.

In March 1978, a second album *Eternally Yours* was released. This utilised a horn section for the first time and, although the sound was a little less frenetic than on the debut album, the playing was arguably tighter. The album had been premiered by the release of two of the finest tracks, *Know Your Product* backed by *Run Down* on a 45 the previous month. Neither the album or the 45 sold in sufficient quantities to chart though.

The band began working on a third album *Prehistoric Sounds* almost as soon as their second album had been released. Again the album was previewed in August 1978 by the release of two of its cuts on a 45, *Security* backed by *All Times Through Paradise*. When the album followed in September, their earlier R&B and soul influences became evident. An increasing problem had been friction with their record company and this was quoted as the reason for their decision to split, which was announced soon after *Prehistoric Sounds* was released.

THE SAINTS - I'm Stranded.

In 1979, a dire cover of Ike and Tina Turner's *River Deep, Mountain High* was included on *The Rare Stuff* (EMI SHSM 2028), along with the other three cuts from their *One Two Three Four* (EP) - *One Way Street, Lipstick On Your Collar* and *Demolition Girl*. The previous year **The Saints** were captured live playing *Demolition Girl* on *Hope And Anchor Front Row Festival* (dbl) (Warner Bros K 66077).

Hay and Kuepper headed back to Australia, where Kuepper went on to form The Laughing Clowns. Ward joined **The Damned**. Bailley held on to **The Saints** name and in 1980 put the band together again with a new line-up ('C'). Their *Monkey Puzzle* album, released in January 1981, had been preceded by a non-album 'A' side *In The Mirror* in October 1980. (The flip side *Always* was from *Monkey Puzzle*). The album came with a free live 7" containing earlier classics - *I'm Stranded, Security* and *This Perfect Day*. The later CD release also included the content of their 12" French-only EP *Paralytic Tonight Dublin Tomorrow*. This featured horn work on many of its five cuts. The end result being a sort of amalgam of punk and Chicago blues. *Monkey Puzzle* itself contained lots of basic rock 'n' roll including a rip-roaring cover of *Dizzy Miss Lizzy*. After one further 45, *Follow The Leader* **The Saints** took a sabbatical whilst their leader Chris Bailey concentrated on producing two solo albums. The first *Casablanca* was recorded in Paris. Just an acoustic or electric guitar backing is used on predominantly folk/blues material. He followed this, in 1984, with *What We Did On Our Holidays*. This featured various cover versions including *In The Midnight Hour, Bring It On Home To Me, I Heard It Through The Grapevine* and *Another Saturday Night*.

The Saints returned towards the end of 1984. By the time Tracy Pew (ex-Birthday Party) had replaced Janine Hall on bass. This line-up produced two further albums which were put out by the French New Rose label *A Little Madness To Be Free* (1984) and *Live In A Mud Hut* (1985). At this point we must leave them but they soldiered on throughout the eighties. Tragically, Pew died of cancer in November 1986 necessitating further line-up changes. The later albums and line-up never recaptured the impact they briefly enjoyed during their punk heyday.

There are a number of worthwhile compilations to choose from including *The Best Of The Saints 1977 - 78, The New Rose Years (Greatest Hits)* and *Know Your Product (The Best Of The Saints)*.

The Scarce Saints album blends B-sides, EP tracks and unissued live material. The CD version has three additional live cuts; *Security* and the frenetic *I'm Stranded* from a Paris performance in 1981 and the previously unissued *Prisoner* from a 1984 Scandinavian tour. Alongside these are two additional studio cuts of B-sides - *Heavy Metal* and a different version of *Don't Send Me Roses*.

The New Rose Years is a twelve cut album or seventeen-track CD which compiles rare B-sides and album cuts that were mostly overlooked in Britain. It's a good blend of punk, fiery rock, folk-rock, pure wierdness and even glimpses of psychedelia on cuts like *Ghostships* and *Let's Pretend*.

The Most Primitive Band In The World is a raucous lo-fi recording from 1974 done in a Brisbane garage on a mono cassette-deck at guitarist Ed Kuepper's parents' home. You can hear items like *Erotic Neurotic, (I'm) Stranded* and *Wild About You*, which pre-date anything comparable by at least two years. However, bearing in mind the sound quality, this is predominantly of archival value.

The Saints have also appeared on a few compilations. You can also check out *This Perfect Day* on *The Best Punk Album In The World.... Ever, Vol. 2* (2-CD) (Virgin VTDCD 79) 1996 and on *God Save The Punks* (2-CD) (Disky DOU 882552) 1998. *The Punk Compilation* (Emporio EMPRCD 550) 1994 includes *Follow The Leader*. Finally, you'll also find *I'm Stranded* on *Burning Ambitions (A History Of Punk)* (Anagram CDBRED 3) 1996 and on the 5-CD box set *1-2-3-4 - A History Of Punk And New Wave 1976 - 1979* (MCA/Universal MCD 60066) in 1999.

7799: Big Hits On The Underground comes with sleevenotes from singer and second guitarist Chris Bailey who took over control of the band when founding member and seminal guitarist Ed Kuepper left in 1978. His notes give details of the numerous musicians who passed through the band.

In 1999, Captain Oi! reissued their first two albums. Each now had bonus tracks and a twelve-page booklet with detailed sleevenotes, lyrics and record sleeve illustrations.

SALFORD JETS - Gina EP.

Salford Jets

Personnel: GERRARD — A
HUBBARD — A
KERRY — A
MORRIS — A
SWEENEY — A

EP:	1(A)	GINA (Gina/Steady With You/ I Want You/Hey) (PS)	(RCA PE 5210) 1979	
				HCP
45s:		Looking At The Squares/Dancing School	(WEA K 18088) 1978	-
		Manchester Boys/Last Bus	(EMI INT 590) 1979	-
		Who You Looking At?/Don't Start Trouble	(RCA 5239) 1980	72
		She's Gonna Break Your Heart/ Bright City Lights (some PS)	(RCA 5271) 1980	-
		City Youth/ Keep Away From My Baby (PS)	(Lunar SAL 1) 1980	-
		Soldiers Of Fortune/Young Bugs	(Polydor POSP 248) 1981	-
	+	Pain In My Heart/(alt version) (PS)	(Ka KA 17) 1983	-

NB: + Also issued as a 12".

The Salford Jets were a Manchester band. Their debut EP was issued in a 3D picture bag and sold for the price of a 45. All four cuts are love songs and basically popish. They actually managed a minor hit. *Who You Looking At?* spent two weeks in the charts peaking at No. 72.

The Same

Personnel incl: STEVE ROSE

45s:	Movements/Wild About You (PS)	(Wessex WEX 267) 1980	
	Wild About You/Movements (PS)	(Blueprint BLU 2008) 1980	

A Worthing mod-influenced trio whose 45 was later reissued on the Blueprint label. This reissue also has blue print on the sleeve. It made 'Single of the Week' on Radio One. Both sides of their 45 resurfaced on *This Is Mod, Vol. 2* (Anagram CDMGRAM 101) 1996 and *Wild About You*, their finest moment, also got fresh exposure on *100% British Mod* (Captain Mod MODSKA DCD 9) in 1998.

There were a number of bands operating with this name in the early eighties.

The Samples

Personnel: TONY ALLEN — drms — A
DAVE EVANS — lead gtr — A
DAVE SAUNDERS — gtr — A
PASCAL SMITH — bs — A
SEAN TAYLOR — vcls — A

EPs: 1(A) VENDETTA (Vendetta/Computer Future/
Rabies) (Sample no #) 1980
2(A) DEAD HERO (Dead Hero/Fire Another Round/
Suspicion) (PS) (No Future Oi! 14) 1984

NB: They also shared a split CD with **Crux** The Oi! Collection (Captain Oi! AHOY CD 79) 1997.

The Samples came from Worcester and were managed by Chris Berry, who owned No Future Records. They first emerged in 1980 with a now ultra-rare EP released on their own label. The disc was stuck inside an A4 four page sleeve, each copy numbered, and then put into a PVC bag!! Vendetta deals with Police vendettas. As its title suggests Computer Future addresses the issue of computerisation. The best of the three cuts is the more varied Rabies with its highly audible lyrics. All three songs were later captured on Oi! The Rarities, Vol. 3 (Captain Oi! AHOY CD 53) 1995.

They returned in 1984 with the Dead Hero (EP). The title cut is a pulsating punk number, which can also be heard on the No Future - The Punk Singles Collection (Captain Oi! AHOY DLP 508) 1996 double album and was earlier included on Punk And Disorderly, Vol. 3 The Final Solution (Anagram CD PUNK 23) 1993. Fire Another Round, which appears to draw parallels with the 'troubles' in Ireland, got a further airing on the No Future - The Punk Singles Collection, Vol. 2 (Captain Oi! AHOY DLP 512) 1996 double album.

The Samples also contributed Government Downfall to A Country Fit For Heroes, Vol. 1 (12") (No Future Oi! 3) in the early eighties. This compilation has been paired with Vol. 2 of the series and reissued on one CD (Captain Oi! AHOY CD 15) 1994.

They did record a third disc but it never saw the light of day when No Future went to the wall.

More recently, in 1997 the excellent Captain Oi! label included **The Samples** on a split CD with **Crux** (Captain Oi! AHOY CD 79). **The Samples'** contribution comprised the Vendetta and Dead Hero EPs in their entirety and five previously unreleased cuts; Government Downfall, 1984, Nobody Cares, Fight For Your Life and Running Down The World.

Satan's Rats

Personnel:	STEVE EAGLES	gtr, vcls	AB
	OLLY HARRISON	drms, perc	AB
	DAVE SPARROW	bs, gtr, vcls	A
	PAUL RENCHER	vcls	B
	ROY WILKES	bs	B

45s:	In My Love For You (PS)	(DJM DJS 10819) 1977
	Year Of The Rats/Façade (PS)	(DJM DJS 10821) 1977
	You Make Me Sick/Louise (PS)	(DJM DJS 10840) 1978
Reissues:	*Year Of The Rat/Louise (PS)	(Overground OVER 01) 1989
*	In My Love For You/Façade (PS)	(Overground OVER 02) 1989
o	You Make Me Sick	(Overground OVER 14) 1991

NB: * 600 copies on yellow vinyl, 400 on white vinyl, 25 on gold vinyl and some numbered test pressings. o Issued on clear vinyl, 567 copies only.

THE SATELITES - Human Being.

Satan's Rats played fast-paced punk. They were a more serious version of a band like **The Jerks**. You Make Me Sick and Louise can both be heard on Punk Rock Rarities, Vol. 2 (Anagram CDPUNK 83) 1996.

They later joined up with Wendy Wu and came back as **The Photos**.

The Satelites

Personnel:	AMANDA DE GREY	vcks, keyb'ds	A
	SNEAK DEAKON	gtr	A
	DANNY HEATLEY (DEWDROP)	drms	A
	JOHNNY MRZ	bs	A
	DR. STRANGELOVE	vcls	A

45s:	Urban Guerilla/High Rise Hillbilly's (PS)	(Rewind REWIN 2) 1980
	Human Being/Windscale Boy (PS)	(Rewind REWIN 7) 1981
	Nightmare/Holy War/ Danse Macabre (PS)	(Kamera ERA 16) 1982
	Vietnam/Lucy Is A Prostitute/I Fell In Love With A Lesbian (PS)	(Brickyard EOR 1) 1983

An interesting early eighties indie combo. Human Being was produced by **The Damned**'s Rat Scabies. The 'B' side is notable for its lyrics:-

"The dim distant future's looking bleak
My brain is numb and I can't speak
Atomic fall-out made me so weak
Radiation leak made me a freak"

"I'm a mutation, 'cos of radiation
I am the windscale boy"
(from Windscale Boy)

All three cuts from their final 45 can also be heard on Punk Rock Rarities, Vol. 2 (Anagram CDPUNK 83) 1996.

The Scabs

EP: 1 THE SCABS (Amory Building/Leave Me Alone/
Don't Just Sit There/U.R.E.) (Clubland) 1979

45: Among Building/Leave Me Alone (Clubland) 1979

The Scabs were from Exeter and both their EP and 45 were available by mail-order from Clubland Records.

Scars

Personnel:	BOBBY KING	vcls	A
	CALUNN MACKAY	drms	A
	JOHN MACKIE	bs	A
	PAUL RESEARCH	gtr	A

ALBUM: 1(A) AUTHOR! AUTHOR! (Pre PREX 5) 1981

45s:	Horrowshow/Adult/ery (PS)	(Fast Product FAST 8) 1979
*	Your Attention Please	(I.D. ID-1) 1981

NB: * This was a gold vinyl flexidisc that came with 'ID' magazine, Issue 3.

Scars formed in Edinburgh, Scotland, where they emerged out of that city's late seventies punk scene. They released a 45 on the city's Fast Products label which showcased their highly melodic style and both sides were also included on Fast Product (Fast EMC 3312) in 1979. In 1981, they had been sufficiently well received to be signed by Charisma Records' short-lived Pre subsidiary. Author! Author! had rather pompous production of their melodic seventies guitar sound but they split up soon after its release and consequently never had the opportunity to fullfill their early promise.

In the 'States, an EP was released comprising three cuts from the album and one additional song.

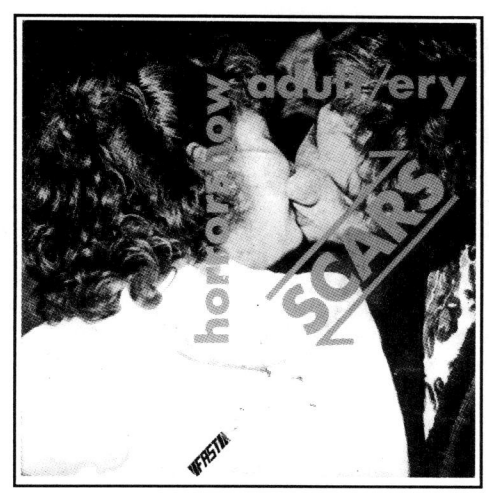

SCARS - Horrorshow.

The Scene

Personnel:	COLIN BANKS	bs, vcls	A
	GARY CORBETT	vcls, gtr	A
	KEERON McGEE	drms	A
	JOHN WRIGHT	gtr, vcls	A

45:	I've Had Enough/Show 'Em Now	(Inferno BEAT 2) 1980

A Midlands-based neo-mod band.

The Scene

Personnel:	DAVE GREEN	gtr	A
	IAN HARDING	vcls, gtr	A
	IAN JAMES	bs	A
	GEORGE MAZUR	drms	A

45:	Hey Girl/Reach The Top (PS)	(Hole In The Wall HS 1) 1980

A different outfit formed in Yorkshire in September 1978. Their sole 45 is a sixties-influenced mod composition penned by Ian Harding. You'll also find *Hey Girl* on *100% British Mod* (Captain Mod MODSKA DCD 9) 1998.

The Scene

Personnel:	ANDY ORR	drms	A
	GARY WOOD	gtr	A
	RUSSELL WOOD	bs	A
	ANDREW WELSH	vcls	A

45s:	Looking For A Love/Let Me Know (PS)	(Diamond DIA 001) 1983
	Something That You Said/Stop-Go (PS)	(Diamond DIA 003) 1985

Yet a third **Scene** who evolved out of **The Diplomats**. Like the reformed **Long Tall Shorty**, this **Scene** signed to the mid-eighties mod revival label Diamond.

Something That You Said is a fast-paced sixties-influenced song. This band has no less than six cuts - *Looking For Love, Let Me Know, Something That You Said, Good Lovin'* and *2 Plus 2 What's Music* - on *This Is Mod, Vol. 3 (Diamond Collection)* (Anagram CDMGRAM 106) 1996 and *Looking For Love* later resurfaced on vinyl on *This Is Mod* (dbl) (Get Back GET 39) in 1999.

There was also a fourth Scene - a soul revival band, rumoured to include Mari Wilson's brother who recorded on GTO.

Schoolgirl Bitch

45:	Abusing The Rules/	
	Think For Yourself	(Garage!/Aerco AERS 102) 1978

A now rare and collectable punk single which did not come in a picture sleeve.

The Scoop

Personnel:	MARTYN CLAPSON	gtr	A
	SAM HODGKIN	vcls	A
	JAMES MORRIS	bs	A
	JOHN TURNER	drms	A

EP:	You Can Do It/Disco/My Friend Tony/	
	Anonymity ('PS)	(Sharp POINT 1) 1980

A short-lived mod-influenced outfit from London, who later splintered into King Trigger and Dance Chapter. *You Can Do It*, a group composition with harmony vocals and catchy guitar moments, can also be found on *100% British Mod* (Captain Mod MODSKA DCD 9) 1998.

Scritti Politti

Personnel:	GREEN GARTSIDE	vcls	ABCDEFG
(up to	NIAL JINKS	bs	AB
1986)	TOM MORLEY	drms	ABC
	MATTHEW 'K'	programme organiser	ABC
	MIKE MacEVOY	synth, vocoder	BC
	MGOTSE	double bs	B
	JOE CANG	bs	C
	STEVE SIDWELL	trumpet	C
	JAMIE TALBOT	sax	C
	STEVE FERRONE	drms	D
	PAUL JACKSON Jnr.	gtr	D
	MARCUS MILLER	bs	D
	ROBBIE BUCHANAN	keyb'ds	E
	DAVID FRANK	keyb'ds	E
	FRED MAHER	drms	E
	DAVID GAMSON	keyb'ds	FG
	ALLAN MURPHY	gtr	FG
	NICK MOROCH	gtr	G

HCP

ALBUMS:	1(C)	SONGS TO REMEMBER		
			(Rough Trade ROUGH 20) 1982	12
	2(G)	CUPID AND PSYCHE '85	(Virgin V 2350) 1985	5

NB: (1) also issued on CD (Rough Trade ROUGHCD 20) 1987. (2) also issued on CD (Virgin CDV 2350) 1985.

EPs:	1(A)	FOUR 'A' SIDES (Doubt Beat/Confidences/	
		Bibbly O'tek/P.A.'s)	(Rough Trade RT 027 T) 1979
	2(A)	WORK IN PROGRESS (John Peel Session) (Hegamony/	
		Scritlocks Door/Opec-Immac/	
		Messthetics)	(Rough Trade SCRIT 2/RT 034) 1979

NB: (2) was released with photocopied inserts.

HCP

45s:	*	Skank Blog Bologna/Is And Ought Of		
(up to		The Western World (28/8/78) (PS)		
1986)			(St. Pancras SCRIT 1) 1978	-
	x	Songs To Remember/		
		The Cassette Interview	(Rough Trade) 1979	-
		The Sweetest Girl/		
		Lions After Slumber (PS)	(Rough Trade RT 091) 1981	64
		The Sweetest Girl/		
		Lions After Slumber (12" PS)	(Rough Trade RT 091T) 1981	-
		Faithless/		
		Faithless Part II (inst.) (PS)	(Rough Trade RT 101) 1982	56
		Faithless/		
		Faithless Part II (inst.) (12" PS)	(Rough Trade RT 101T) 1982	-
	+	Asylums In Jerusalem/		
		Jacques Derrida (PS)	(Rough Trade RT 111) 1982	43
		Asylums In Jerusalem (extended)/		
		Jacques Derrida (12" PS)	(Rough Trade RT 111T) 1982	-
	+	Wood Beez (Play Like Aretha Franklin)/		
		('A' dub version) (PS)	(Virgin VS 657) 1984	-
		Wood Beez (Play Like Aretha Franklin) (extended)/		
		('A' dub version) (12" PS)	(Virgin VS 65712) 1984	-
	+	Absolute/('A' version) (PS)	(Virgin VS 680) 1984	17

	Absolute (extended)/		
	('A' version) (12" PS)	(Virgin VSY 680)	1984 -
+	Hypnotise/('A' version) (PS)	(Virgin VS 725)	1984 68
	Hypnotise (extended)/		
	('A' version) (12" PS)	(Virgin VS 72512)	1984 -
α+	The Word Girl/Flesh And Blood (PS)	(Virgin VS 747)	1985 6
	The Word Girl (extended)/		
	Flesh And Blood (extended)	(Virgin VS 74712)	1985 -
+	Perfect Way/('A' version) (PS)	(Virgin VS 780)	1985 48
	Perfect Way (extended)/		
	('A' version) (12" PS)	(Virgin VS 78012)	1985 -

NB: * This came in a photocopied stapled fold-out picture sleeve, with hand stamped white labels. x This was a promo-only cassette release with a 12-page booklet and two photos. + There were also shaped picture disc versions of these 7" singles. α Credited to **Scritti Politti** featuring Ranking Ann.

Scritti Politti were formed by Leeds art school student Green Gartside in late 1977. Originally they were a punk band with a clear left wing message and a name taken from the tome 'Scritto's Republic'.

Their debut 45 *Skank Blog Bologna* in 1978 came out on their own St. Pancras label - a classic homemade punk debut. Musically it combined punkish rock and sparse electronics but evident as well were jazz and reggae influences. This gave them quite an unique sound.

In 1979, they linked their St. Pancras label with Rough Trade thereby securing wider distribution for their records. The EP *Four A-Sides* was the first output from this partnership. It sold sufficiently to make it into the indie charts. It also helped secure them a John Peel session. This consisted of four songs - *Hegamony, Scritlocks Door, Opec-Immac* and *Messthetics*. These also made their way onto an EP titled *Work In Progress*, which followed their earlier EP into the indie chart.

The first of several line-up changes followed. The band was expanded into a sextet with Mike MacEvoy coming in on synthesizer and vocoder and Mgotse on double bass. Robert Wyatt also guested on piano for their next 45 *The Sweetest Girl* - a jazzy ballad. Available in both 7" and 12" formats it was well received. It also brought them their first hit, peaking at No. 64 during a three week chart stay.

After this, Nial Jinks left. He was replaced on bass by Joe Cang. Jamie Talbot came in on saxophone and Steve Sidwell was added on trumpet. Mgotse also left. This new line-up achieved further chart success with *Faithless* (No. 56) and the double A-side *Asylums In Jerusalem / Jacques Derrida* (No. 43). They also recorded their debut album *Songs To Remember*, which climbed to No. 12 in September 1982 during a seven week chart stay. It was full of catchy tunes and a more soul-based sound. The highlights, though, were really their earlier singles *Asylums In Jerusalem, The Sweetest Girl* and *Faithless*. Gartside's affected vocal style made all the songs appealing.

Scritti Politti had increasingly become a vehicle for Gartside's musical ambitions and after the debut album he disbanded the rest of the 'band' and moved to New York. There he worked with producer Arif Mardin to produce a polished soul sound which was far removed from **Scritti Politti**'s punk beginnings. With Tom Morley having gone solo, Gartside now worked with entirely new U.S. musicians. Marcus Miller (who'd played with Miles Davis) came in on bass. On drums was Steve Perrone (who'd played with Brian Auger). Paul Jackson junior was the new guitarist. Gartside switched to a major label Virgin and released a Top 10 U.K. hit single *Wood Beez (Play Like Aretha Franklin)*. It later climbed to No. 91 in the U.S. too, in February 1986.

Fuelled on by this success Gartside enlisted a new trio of guest musicians, Robbie Buchanan and David Frank on keyboards and Fred Maher on drums to record *Absolute*. This climbed to No. 17 during a nine week chart stay.

Gartside then worked with David Gamson on keyboards and Allan Murphy on guitar to record *Hypnotise*. This spent just two weeks in the charts in November 1984, peaking at No. 68.

Nick Moroch was added to the above trio for the 45s *The Word Girl* and *Perfect Way* and for the *Cupid And Psyche '85* album, which were all released during 1985. Credited to **Scritti Politti** featuring Ranking Ann *The Word Girl* climbed to No. 6 here in the U.K. during a twelve week chart reign. *Perfect Way*, by contrast only reached No. 48 here, spending five weeks in the charts. It was a different story in the U.S.A., where it was a much bigger hit. It peaked at No. 11 during a twenty-five week stay. Both featured on the *Cupid And Psyche '85* album along with *Wood Beez, Absolute* and *Hypnotise*. This ensured the album was a pleasant record, full of well-crafted songs. It spent nineteen weeks in the U.K. charts, where it peaked at No. 5.

Scritti Politti (Gartside and various session musicians) went on to play well into the nineties and enjoyed further hits. Madness also had a minor hit with *Sweetest Girl* in 1986. In 2001, **Scritti Politti**'s version was included on the 4-CD box set *25 Years Of Rough Trade Shops* (Mute CDSTUMM 191). Earlier *Asylum In Jerusalem* had figured on *Wave (The Biggest New Wave Hits)* (3-CD set) (Disky HR 868442) in 1996.

Second Layer

Personnel incl:	ADRIAN BORLAND	gtr, vcls	A
	GRAHAM GREEŃ	gtr	A

ALBUM:	1(A)	WORLD OF RUBBER	(Cherry Red BRED 14) 1982

EP:	1(A)	FLESH AS PROPERTY (Court And Wars/	
		Metal Sheet/Germany) (PS)	(Tortch-r TOR 001) 1979

NB: (1) Originally issued in a white picture sleeve with black printed labels. (1) reissued (Tortch/Fresh FRESH 5) 1981 in a yellow picture sleeve with white labels. (1) projected for release again (Cherry Red CHERRY 21) 1981, but remained unreleased.

45:		State Of Emergency/I Need Noise/	
		The Cutting Motion (PS)	(Tortch TOR 006) 1980

Adrian Borland had fronted Liverpool's punksters **The Outsiders** between 1977-78. In late 1979, with a modified line-up, they evolved into a new wave outfit **The Sound**, but parallel to them Borland created **Second Layer** as a more experimental and harder project.

Secret Affair

Personnel:	DAVID CAIRNS	gtr, vcls	ABC
	IAN PAGE	vcls, trumpet, keyb'ds	ABC
	SEB SHELTON	drms	AB
	DENNIS SMITH	bs, vcls	ABC
	DAVE WINTHROP	sax	BC
	PAUL BULTITUDE	drms	C

				HCP
ALBUMS:	1(B)	GLORY BOYS	(I-Spy I SPY 1)	1979 41
	2(B)	BEHIND CLOSED DOORS	(I-Spy I SPY 2)	1980 48
	3(C)	BUSINESS AS USUAL	(I-Spy I SPY 3)	1982 84

NB: (1) issued with two inserts. (1) also issued on CD (Captain Mod MODSKA CD 14) 2001 with two bonus cuts. (2) also issued on CD (Captain Mod MODSKA CD 19) 2001. (3) issued with stickered sleeve. (3) also issued on CD (Captain Mod MODSKA CD 16) 2001. There's also *City Of Dreams* (1988), a semi-official bootleg recorded live at the Bridge House in 1979. There are also three relevant CD releases *Glory Boys Behind Closed Doors* (RCA 74321276182) 1995, *Live At The Bridge* (Receiver RRCD 250) 1997 and *The Very Best Of Secret Affair (Time For Action)* (Camden 74321487322) 1997.

SECRET AFFAIR - Time For Action.

			HCP
45s:	* Time For Action/Soho Strut (PS)	(I-Spy SEE 1) 1979	13
	Let Your Heart Dance/ Sorry Wrong Number (PS)	(I-Spy SEE 3) 1979	32
	+ My World/So Cool	(I-Spy SEE 5) 1980	16
	Sound Of Confusion/ Take It Or Leave It (PS)	(I-Spy SEE 8) 1980	45
	Do You Know?/Dance Master	(I-Spy SEE 10) 1981	57
	Lost In The Night (Mack The Knife)/ The Big Beat	(I-Spy SEE 11) 1982	-

NB: * Initially in a brown 'paper bag' picture sleeve with black print. Later copies came in a black sleeve with white print. + Initially with paper labels. Later with silver labels.

Secret Affair were a 'new wave with soul' band formed by Ian Page (ex-**New Hearts**) and David Cairns. They were at the very forefront of the mod revival in 1979. They were influenced by The Who and **The Jam** and the like but they weren't simply copyists. **Secret Affair**'s music had its own style and above all boundless enthusiasm. They appeared on the now legendary *Mods Mayday '79* (Bridge House BHLP 0038) playing what would prove to be their first two hits, *Time For Action* and *Let Your Heart Dance* and a third song *I'm Not Free (But I'm Cheap)*. They then set up their own I-Spy label. Their debut 45 *Time For Action* was simply electric, one of those records that sounds like a breath of fresh air and wonderful for parties. Who can stand still to a record like this? It sold 6,000 copies in a day and not surprisingly became a Top 20 hit, spending ten weeks in the charts and peaking at No. 13. Chris Gent of **The Autographs** was guest saxophonist on this 45. They followed it in October 1979 with another superb effort *Let Your Heart Dance*. This spent six weeks in the charts, climbing to No. 32. It deserved to do better, but possibly suffered from being too similar in style to their debut. Both were on the *Glory Boys* album, released in November 1979. This featured above average tunes spiced up with the occasional use of horns and all delivered with the band's characteristic enthusiasm. Aside from a cover of Smokey Robinson's *Going To A Go-Go*, it featured all originals. It enjoyed commercial success, too, climbing to No. 41 and spending eight weeks in the charts. Prior to the release of *Glory Boys* Dave Winthorp, formerly of Supertramp and Juicy Lucy, was added to their line-up as a permanent fixture. The superb Captain Mod CD reissue of this contains two bonus cuts, lyrics, singles covers and excellent sleevenotes.

In 1980 **Secret Affair** enjoyed further hit singles with *My World* (No. 16) and *Sound Of Confusion* (No. 45).

In September, *Behind Closed Doors* their second album, was released. Again, this is a good album with tighter instrumentation and more meaningful lyrics. It featured the 'A' sides of their two previous singles *My World* and *Sound Of Confusion*. It sold quite well, climbing to No. 48 and spending four weeks in the charts, but it didn't improve on the performance of *Glory Boys*. Seb Shelton, who'd joined **Secret Affair** from **Young Bucks**, left at this point for Dexy's Midnight Runners and Paul Bulitude came in as replacement drummer.

1981 was a quiet year for the band in terms of vinyl output. Just one 45 *Do You Know?* was released. Spending four weeks in the charts and peaking

SECRET AFFAIR - Glory Boys.

SECRET AFFAIR - Lost In The Night.

at No. 57 it would prove to be their final hit. It also figured on their third album *Business As Usual*, released in February 1982. This had been preceeded by the release of one of the few cover versions the band ever did, Bobby Darin's *Lost In The Night (Mack The Knife)*, as a 45. It flopped. Indeed by early 1982 the whole mod revivalist movement was evaporating. **Secret Affair**, who'd been at the helm of the movement, couldn't maintain their profile, *Business As Usual* contains *Do You Know?* and *Lost In The Night*, but lacked the creative spark of their first two efforts. When it could only climb to No. 84 the writing was on the wall for the band, which disbanded in mid-1982.

Both *Behind Closed Doors* and *Business As Usual* are now available on CD, courtesy of Captain Mod. The nicely-packaged sets are accompanied by sleevenotes, lyrics and single covers.

Bultitude joined Mari Wilson and The Wilsations. Smith became part of Nik Kershaw's backing act. Ian Page formed The Bop, who released a 45 *Too Young To Know* (Parlophone PAGE 1) in 1984, which flopped. Cairns later formed The Flag.

In 1997, Receiver issued the *Live At The Bridge* (CD), which comprised **Secret Affair**'s material from the famous *Mods Mayday '79* album concert. The CD comprises Page/Cairns originals from their *Glory Days* album and respectable covers of Motown classics (*Get Ready*, *Going To A Go-Go*, *Road Runner* and *Dancing In The Streets*). A worthwhile, fresh souding album.

Their classic single *Time For Action* later resurfaced on *Teenage Kicks* (PolyGram TV 5253382) in 1995. **Secret Affair**'s significance as one of the very best mod revival bands was considerable and they should have secured their place in rock history.

Section 25

Personnel:	LARRY CASSIDY	gtr, vcls	ABCDE
	VINCENT CASSIDY	electronics, drum machine	ABCDE
	PHIL	gtr	A
	PAUL WIGGIN	gtr	BCDE
	JOHN	drms	C
	LEE SHALLCROSS	drms	D
	ANGELA FLOWERS	vcls, keyb'ds	E
	JENNY ROSS	vcls, keybds	E

ALBUMS:	1(C)	ALWAYS NOW	(Factory FACT 45) 1981
(up to	2(D)	THE KEY OF DREAMS	(Factory Benelux) 1982
1986)	3(E)	FROM THE HIP	(Factory FACT 90) 1984
	4(E)	LOVE AND HATE	(Factory FACT 160) 1986

NB: (1) was released in an envelope folder and later reissued on CD (Les Temps Modernes LTMCD 2308) 1992. (2) also issued on CD (Les Temps Modernes LTMCD 2310) 1992. (3) also issued on CD (Les Temps Modernes LTMCD 2314) 1992. Also relevant are *Live In America And Europe 1982* (Les Temps Modernes LTMCD 2312) 1988 and *Deus Ex Machina - Archive Recordings 1983 - 1985* (Les Tempes Modernes LTMCD 2316) 1998.

45s: (up to 1986)	Girl's Don't Count/New Noise/ Up To You (PS)		(Factory FAC 18) 1980
	The Beast/Sakura Sakura/ Trident (12", PS)		(Factory FAC 66) 1983
	Back To Wonder/Beating Heart (PS)		(Factory FAC 68) 1983
	Looking From A Hilltop (2 versions) (PS)		(Factoy FAC 108) 1984
	Looking From A Hilltop (2 versions) (12", PS)		(Factory FAC 108) 1984
	Crazy Wisdom (2 versions)		(Factory FBN 45) 1985

From Blackpool, Lancashire, **Section 25** (named after a provision in the Mental Health Act) is centered around the Cassidy brothers who formed them in November 1977, initially as a duo utilising a drum machine. In April 1978, a third member guitarist Phil was added and they made their live debut that June. In November Paul Wiggin replaced Phil on guitar and a second drummer John was recruited. Musically they were in the mould of **Joy Division** with flat, depressing vocals, upfront drums and a guitar/synthesizer backing. Initially they were unable to recruit a suitable keyboardist and they used pre-recorded tapes.

They contributed a song called *After-Image* to *Hicks From The Sticks* (Rockburgh Records ROC 111) in 1980. Their debut 45, *Girls Don't Count*, was well received the same year. *Always Now* and *The Key Of Dreams* both display quite a strong Doors influence but overall their music exudes anxiety and insecurity. The CD reissue of *Always Now* on Les Temps Modernes was boosted by the inclusion of their rare Ian Curtis/Rob Gretton - produced debut 45 *Girls Don't Count*, along with *After Image* and *Red Voice*, which were recorded for 1980 compilation albums and not previously included on **Section 25** compilations. The magnum opus on their self-produced second album *The Key Of Dreams* is *Surtra*, a fifteen-minute Can and Pink Floyd influenced jam. The eventual album was edited down from over five hours worth of improvised music. They toured Europe extensively in this era, often as support to **New Order**.

Wiggin left soon after their first album was released and a new drummer Lee Shallcross was recruited. He toured with them in the 'States. After the release of *The Key Of Dreams* the Cassidy's decided to cancel further live gigs from February 1983 and go back to the drawing board. They re-emerged in August as a five-piece (line-up 'E'), playing their first live gig in December.

From The Hip ranged from driving electronic dance music to ambient mood segments - clearly evidence of **New Order**'s influence on them. Hardly surprising when you consider the album was produced by **New Order** guitarist Bernard Sumner. When one cut *Looking From A Hilltop* was remixed for 45 release it became a club hit in New York. This can be seen as an attempt to make electro-rock commercially viable which had been attempted by **Cabaret Voltaire** a year or so earlier. A further album *Love And Hate* followed in 1986, but somehow despite their undoubted talent they fell out of favour and eventually disbanded.

In 1998, Les Temps Modernes issued *Live In America And Europe 1982*, which also sounds influenced by **New Order**'s experiments with electronics at the time.

Deus Ex Machina is another collection of live tracks and demos. *Tchiako* (from 1984) was a moody and minimalist instrumental and *4tmi*, a melodic Kraftwerk-influenced instrumental. The live cuts utilise plenty of freeform electronics, but there are also some more traditional song structures. The extended remix of *Beating Heart* (from June 1983) utilised a TB-303 bass line machine and is one of the earliest examples of this. Cuts like *Sweet Forgiveness* and *Slinky* (from 1985) were heavily sequenced.

Sema 4

Personnel:	STEVE GIBSON	gtr	A
	GEOFF HARDAKER	drms	A
	DAVID 'JOCK' MARSTON	vcls, bs	A

EPs:	1(A)	4 FROM SEMA 4 (Even If I Know/Sema 4 Messages/Actors All/ Do You Know Your Friends) (PS)	(Pollen PBM 022) 1979
	2(A)	UP DOWN AROUND	(Pollen PBM 024) 1979

NB: (1) came in two different coloured sleeves. Only 500 numbered copies were issued. (2) was a limited edition of 1,000. There's also a CD compilation *In Memory Of* (Detour DRCD 015) 1997, also on vinyl (DRLP 015).

This mod revival band from York formed after David 'Jock' Marston had left punk band Cyanide. *Sema 4 Messages* is one of the more underrated neo-mod songs which deserved greater success. All four cuts from their *4 From Sema 4* (EP) can also be heard on *This Is Mod, Vol. 5* (Anagram CDMGRAM 110) 1997. You'll also find *Even If I Know* on *This Is Mod* (dbl) (Get Back GET 39) 1999, whilst the excellent *Sema 4 Messages* resurfaced on *100% British Mod* (Captain Mod MODSKA DCD 8) 1998. All of their recordings are rounded up on *In Memory Of* (Detour DRLP/CD 015) 1997.

The Senate

Personnel:	KIRK BRANDON
	RUSTY EVAN

45:	Original Sin/Do You Believe In The Westworld? (PS)	(Burning Rome BRR 7) 1984
	Original Sin/Do You Believe In The Westworld? (Live) (PS)	(War WAR 1) 1984
	Original Sin (Extended)/Original Sin (Alt. Version)/ Do You Believe In The Westworld? (Live) (12", PS)	(War 12WAR 1) 1984

This was a one-off collaboration between **Spear Of Destiny** member Kirk Brandon and former **Skids** and **Visage** man Rusty Egan. They recorded two versions of the first 45 by Brandon's previous band **Theatre Of Hate** *Original Sin* and put another **Theatre Of Hate** classic *Do You Believe In Westworld?* on the flip. Whilst all three songs only made it onto the 12" released on Egan's War label, the 7" (containing the shorter version of *Original Sin*) was released both on Brandon's Burning Rome label and Egan's War label.

Will Sergeant

ALBUM: (up to 1986)	1	THEMES FROM GRIND	(Ninety-Two Happy Customers HAPLP 1) 1983

NB: (1) also issued on CD (Ninety-Two Happy Customers HAPSCD 001) 1997, with a bonus cut.

45: (up to 1986)	Favourite Branches/(Other side by Ravi Shankar & Bill Loveday) (PS)	(WEA K 19238) 1982
CASS:	1 WEIRD AS FISH	(no label or cat #) 1978

NB: (1) only seven copies of this were issued, each with a different cover.

Will Sergeant is best known as guitarist with **Echo and The Bunnymen**. *Weird As Fish* was a bedroom tape and is now very collectable as only seven copies were made each with a different cover. *Favourite Branches* is also rare now.

THE SEX PISTOLS - Pretty Vacant.

Themes From Grind, his solo album, was an offbeat experiment in instrumental space-rock and ambient soundscapes. The later CD also includes *Favourite Branches* as a bonus cut.

17

Personnel:	EDDIE McDONALD	bs	A
	MIKE PETERS	vcls, gtr	A
	DAVE SHARP	gtr	A
	NIGEL TWIST	drms	A

45:	Don't Let Go/		
	Bank Holiday Weekend (PS)	(Vendetta VD 001)	1980

17 formed in Rhyl, north Wales in 1977 as a punk band called The Toilets. They changed name to **17** in 1979 to coincide with the mod revival and issued this one 45, which is a standard mod-pop offering. They were very young at the time. The flip side *Bank Holiday Weekend* glorified one of the important events in the mod life style. This 45 is now very rare and collectable.

17 didn't achieve a commercial breakthrough but emerged rejuvenated in 1980 as **The Alarm**. In 1991, Mike Peters went solo.

Sex Aids

Personnel:	THRUSH BREEDER	A
	CHRIS T. CRUST	A
	CROW MAN	A
	KIRK	A

EP:	1(A)	BACK ON THE PISS AGAIN (Back On The Piss Again/		
		The Amazing Mr. Michael Hogarth/We Are		
		The Road Crew) (PS)	(Riot City RIOT 23)	1983

This light-hearted eighties punk project involved the roadies of **Vice Squad** and **Chaotic Dischord**. *Back On The Piss Again* was later included on *Riot City Singles Collection, Vol. 1* (Anagram CDPUNK 15) 1997 and *We Are The Road Crew* figured on *Riot City Singles Collection, Vol. 2* (Anagram CDPUNK 55) 1995. Both of these compilations were also issued on vinyl by Captain Oi! (AHOY DLP 503 and 511).

The Sex Pistols

Personnel:	PAUL COOK	drms	AB
	STEVE JONES	gtr	AB
	GLEN MATLOCK	bs	A
	JOHNNY ROTTEN (JOHN LYDON)	vcls	AB
	SID VICIOUS (JOHN RITCHIE)	bs, vcls	B

HCP

ALBUMS:	1(B)	NEVER MIND THE BOLLOCKS, HERE'S THE SEX			
		PISTOLS	(Virgin V 2086)	1978	1
	2(-)	THE GREAT ROCK 'N' ROLL SWINDLE (dbl)			
			(Virgin VD 2510)	1979	7
	3(-)	SOME PRODUCT: CARRY ON SEX PISTOLS			
			(Virgin VR 2)	1979	6
	4(-)	FLOGGING A DEAD HORSE (compilation)			
			(Virgin V 2142)	1980	23
	5(-)	THE GREAT ROCK 'N' ROLL SWINDLE (single album)			
			(Virgin V 2168)	1980	-
	6(-)	KISS THIS (dbl)	(Virgin V 2702)	1992	-

NB: (1) was issued in four different formats. Firstly, with a track listing on the rear sleeve and including *Submission*; secondly with a poster (SPOTS 001) and one-sided 45 *Submission* (VDJ 24), sealed with an orange sticker; thirdly 1,000 copies were pressed in a pink rear sleeve with no track listing; and finally in January 1978 a picture disc was released (VP 2086). (1) was reissued in 1985 at budget price (Virgin OVED 136) and again on vinyl (Virgin VP 2086) 1998. (1) later issued on CD (Virgin CDV 2086) 1986, reissued (Virgin CDVX 2086) 1993 and also on CD (Virgin VJCP 68050) 1999. (2) issued in a gatefold sleeve. The first 50,000 copies included *Watcha Gonna Do About It*, the rest didn't. Some copies had spoken overdubs on *God Save The Queen Symphony*. (2) later issued on CD (Virgin CDVD 2510) 1986, reissued (Virgin CDVDX 2510) 1993 and again on CD (Virgin VJCP 68057) 1999. (3) later issued on CD (Virgin CDVR 2) 1993. (4) reissued at a budget price (Virgin OVED 165) 1986 and as a mid-price CD (Virgin CDV 2142) 1986. (5) reissued at mid-price (Virgin OVED 234) 1989. (6) also issued on CD (Virgin CDV 2702) 1992 and some copies came with a live bonus CD (Virgin CDVX 2702) 1992. Another relevant budget issue was *The Original Pistols Live* (Fame FA 41 31491) 1986, later issued on CD (Fame CDFA 3149) 1989.

OTHER SEX PISTOLS ALBUMS:

1( )	THE MINI ALBUM	(Chaos MINI 1) 1985
2( )	THE ORIGINAL PISTOLS LIVE	(Receiver RRLP 101) 1985
3( )	AFTER THE STORM (mini-LP)	(Receiver RRLP 102) 1985
4( )	LAST SHOW ON EARTH	
		(McDonald Brothers JOCK 1) 1986
5( )	THE SEX PISTOLS' 10TH ANNIVERSARY ALBUM	
		(McDonald Brothers JOCK LP 3) 1986
6( )	THE FILTH AND THE FURY (6 album box set)	
		(McDonald Brothers JOCK BOX 1) 1987
7( )	INTERVIEW PICTURE DISC	
		(Music And Media SP 1001) 1988
8( )	IT SEEMED TO BE THE END UNTIL THE BEGINNING	
		(MBC JOCK LP 12) 1988
9( )	ANARCHY WORLDWIDE	(Specific SPAW 101) 1988
10( )	ORIGINAL PISTOLS	(Counterpoint CDEP 13 C) 1988
11( )	LIVE AND LOUD	(Link LINKLP 063) 1989
12( )	NO FUTURE U.K.?	(Receiver RRLP 117) 1989
13( )	PRETTY VACANT	(Receiver RRLD 004) 1991
14( )	INTROSPECTIVE: SEX PISTOLS	
		(Baktabak MINT 5008) 1992
15(-)	INTERVIEW DISC	(Total SEX 1LP) 1996

NB: (1) reissued as a picture disc (Chaos AMPL 37) 1986 and issued on CD (Chaos APOCA 3) 1989. (2) reissued as a picture disc (American Phonogram APKPD 13) 1986 and on CD (Receiver RRCD 101) 1989, then again with *Submission* (Dojo DOJOLP 45) 1989 and on CD (Dojo DOJO CD 45) 1990. (3) also included four cuts by The New York Dolls. Later issued on CD (Receiver RRCD 102) 1991. (8) also issued on CD (MCB JOCK 12) 1988. (11) 1,000 copies were issued on pink 'marbled' vinyl and a numbered edition of 500 copies were issued on green vinyl. It was also issued on CD (Link LINK CD 063) 1992. (12) also issued on CD and 1,000 were a limited edition picture disc format (Receiver RRCD 117) 1989. There was also a 2-CD repackage of RRCD 101 and RRCD 117 titled *Pretty Vacant* (RRDCD 004) 1993. (14) also issued on CD (Baktabak CINT 5008) 1992. (15) also issued on CD (Total SEX 1CD) 1996. The following were CD-only retrospectives:- *The Best And The Rest Of* (Action Replay CDAR 1008) 1989, *The Sex Pistols Conversation Disc* (TCDS ABCD 019) 1991, this was a limited edition of 2,500, *Better Live Than Dead* (Restless 722 522) 1988, (Dojo DOJO CD 73) 1992 and (Essential ESMCD 321) 1995, *Live At Chelmsford Prison* (Dojo DOJO CD 66) 1993 and *Early Daze - The Studio Collection* (Street Link STR CD 019) 1992, which was later reissued (Dojo DOJO CD 119) 1993. Other CD releases include *The 78 Club (Live In Burton On Trent) 1976* (Yeaah YEAAH 10) 1999, *Early Daze (The Studio Collection)* (Dojo DOJOCD 119) 1993, *Early Daze* (Essential ESMCD 925) 2000, *Filthy Lucre Live* (Virgin CDVUS 116) 1996, again (Virgin EMI CDVUS 116) and again (Virgin VJCP 68051) 1999, *Live At Winterland* (When WENCD 008) 1996, *Live At The Longhorn* (Castle Music Pictures CMP 1004) 2000, *Never Mind The Bollocks/Spunk* (Virgin SPUNK 1) 1996, *Pirates Of Destiny* (Dojo DOJOCD 222) 1996 and (Essential ESMCD 609) 1998, *Raw* (Emporio EMPRCD 716) 1997, *Sex Pistols Archive* (Rialto RMCD 218) 1997, *Wanted (The Goodman Tapes)* (Dojo DOJOCD 216) 1995 and again (Essential ESMCD 608) 1998 and *There Is No Future* (Essential ESMCD 783) 1999.

There was also a cassette release *The Heyday* (Factory FACT 30) 1980, which contained documentary material. It was released in a satin pouch with a Christmas card.

HCP

45s:	*	Anarchy In The U.K./I Wanna Be Me	(EMI EMI 2566) 1976	38
(up to	+	God Save The Queen/No Feelings	(A&M AMS 7284) 1977	-
1992)		God Save The Queen/		
		Did You No Wrong (PS)	(Virgin VS 181) 1977	2
		Pretty Vacant/No Fun (PS)	(Virgin VS 184) 1977	6
		Holidays In The Sun/Satellite (PS)	(Virgin VS 191) 1977	8
	x	Lentilmas - A Seasonal Offering To You		
		From Virgin Records	(Virgin/Lyntone LYN 3261) 1977	-
		No-one Is Innocent (A Punk Prayer By Ronald Biggs)/		
		My Way (PS)	(Virgin VS 220) 1978	7
	α	The Biggest Blow (A Punk Prayer By Ronald Biggs)/		
		My Way (12" PS)	(Virgin VS 22012) 1978	-
		Something Else/Friggin' In The Riggin'	(Virgin VS 240) 1979	3
	β	Silly Thing/Who Killed Bambi? (PS)	(Virgin VS 256) 1979	6
		C'mon Everybody/The God Save The Queen Symphony/		
		Watcha Gonna Do About It (PS)	(Virgin VS 272) 1979	3
	χ	The Great Rock 'n' Roll Swindle/		

	Rock Around The Clock (PS)	(Virgin VS 290)	1979 21
	(I'm Not Your) Steppin' Stone/		
	Pistol's Propaganda (PS)	(Virgin VS 339)	1980 21
	Pistols Pack (6x45s in 'accordion' plastic wallet: God Save The Queen/Pretty Vacant; Holidays In The Sun/My Way; Something Else/Silly Thing; Steppin' Stone/Anarchy In The U.K.; Black Leather/Here We Go Again; C'mon Everybody/ The Great Rock 'n' Roll Swindle)	(Virgin SEX 1)	1980 -
δ	Who Killed Bambi?/		
	Rock Around The Clock (PS)	(Virgin VS 443)	1981 -
	Anarchy In The U.K./No Fun (PS)	(Virgin VS 609)	1983 -
	Anarchy In The U.K./No Fun/ EMI (12" PS)	(Virgin VS 609-12)	1983 -
	Interview (12" picture disc)	(Pig Dog PD 1)	1984 -
	Anarchy In The U.K./EMI/No Fun (3" CD)	(Virgin CDT 3)	1985 -
ε	Submission/No Feelings (PS)	(Chaos DICK 1)	1985 -
φ	Submission/ Anarchy In The U.K. (12" PS)	(Chaos EXPORT 1)	1985 -
	Anarchy In The U.K. (live)/Flogging A Dead Horse (12" PS)	(McDonald Brothers JOCK 1201)	1986 -
γ	The Original Sex Pistols Live (Anarchy In The U.K./ I'm A Lazy Sod/Pretty Vacant/ Substitute) (live) (12")	(Archive 4 TOF 104)	1986 -
	The Original Pistols (Anarchy In The U.K. (live)/ Pretty Vacant (live)/No Fun (live)/ Substitute (live)) (CD)	(Classic Tracks CDEP 13 C)	1988 -
	God Save The Queen/Did You No Wrong/ Don't Give Me No Lip Child (3" CD)	(Virgin CDT 37)	1988 -
	Cash For Chaos (Submission (live)/God Save The Queen/ Liar) (PS)	(Specific SPCFC 102)	1988 -
η	Pretty Vacant/ I Wanna Be Me (PS)	(Spiral Scratch SCRATCH 4)	1988 -
	The Early Years Live (Anarchy In The U.K. (live)/ Pretty Vacant (live)/Liar (live)/Dolls (alias "New York") (live) (12" PS)	(Receiver REPLAY 3012)	1990 -
j	Anarchy In The U.K./ I Wanna Be Me (PS)	(Virgin VS 1431)	1992 33
k	Pretty Vacant/No Feelings (PS)	(Virgin VS 1448)	1992 56

NB: * The first 5,000 copies were housed in a black sleeve and miscredited Chris Thomas as producer of the 'B' side *I Wanna Be Me*. Later copies came in an EMI sleeve with a Dave Goodman production credit on the 'B' side. + This release which came without a picture sleeve is one of the rarest all time U.K. singles. All A&M copies of this 45 were allegedly destroyed, but some survive. x This was a Christmas freebie flexidisc, some came with a Christmas card. α Some copies of this 12" also contained an interview. β The 'B' side was with **Tenpole Tudor**. χ The 'B' side was with **Tenpole Tudor**. δ Both sides were credited to **Tenpole Tudor** with **The Sex Pistols**. ε Only 5,000 copies were released in blue, pink and yellow vinyl. φ These came in pink or yellow vinyl. γ This was a limited edition of 5,000. η This came with 'Spiral Scratch' magazine issue 4, the 'B' side actually plays *Seventeen*. φ There was also a cassette version (VSC 1431), a CD version which included an additional demo version of *Anarchy* (VSCDT 1431) and a CD digipack version of the latter with a poster (VSCDX 1431). κ There was also a 12" version comprising *Pretty Vacant* and demo versions of *Satellite*, *No Feelings* and *Submission* (VST 1448) and a CD digipack which substituted a demo version of *EMI* for *Satelitte* (VSCDG 1448) and a CD release comprising *Pretty Vacant*, a demo version of *Seventeen*, a second demo version of *Submission* and *Watcha Gonna Do 'Bout It?* (VSCDT 1448) 1992.

The Sex Pistols were the founders of punk rock, the band who started it all and turned the U.K. music industry inside out. **Malcolm McLaren** is the man credited with making them the success they were but the concept of the band dates back to 1972 and Steve Jones. He would regularly bunk off school and spend time at his friend Warwick Nightingale's house, along with another truant schoolboy Paul Cook. Jones gradually stole various instruments, including part of a drum kit and Cook bought the rest of it on HP. Cook fancied himself as a bit of a vocalist. Aside from Jones, the other two members in this four-piece band were two schoolmates Jimmy Mackin (organ) and Steve Hayes (bs). They initially called themselves The Strand after The Roxy Music cut *Do The Strand*, but later renamed themselves The Swankers.

In the early seventies **Malcolm McLaren** ran a fifties gear shop with Vivienne Westwood on the Kings Road called Let It Rock. In early 1973 Jones was a frequent visitor to the shop and aware that **McLaren** had customers connected with the music business tried to arouse his interest in the band. The Swankers also needed rehearsal space and probably to get Jones off his back **McLaren** got them a suitable space in Covent Garden Community Centre. Inevitably Jones pestered **McLaren** to go and hear them play but by now Steve Hayes had left and they were without a bass player. **McLaren** wasn't particularly grabbed by what he heard but he was aware that Glen Matlock, an art student who helped out at Let It Rock on Saturdays, could play guitar. After a while, **McLaren** introduced Matlock, who he'd persuaded to switch to bass, to the band and by mid-1974 their line-up had stabilised into Steve Jones (vcls), Glen Matlock (bs), Paul Cook (drms) and Wally Nightingale (gtr). Throughout 1974 - 1975, this line-up rehearsed a series of classic sixties songs.

During 1973 **McLaren** had visited New York and been fascinated by the city's emerging punk scene focused around The New York Dolls and Richard Hell. Towards the end of 1974 **McLaren** returned to New York largely to continue his interest in The New York Dolls. Whilst there **McLaren** revamped The Dolls' image and became their unofficial manager over the winter of 1974-75. He hyped them with a tacky image contrived with heavy make-up and all-red fetishistic stage outfits, but none of their records sold particularly well and they failed to capture the record buying public's imagination outside of their New York club heartland. Their vocalist and guitarist Johnny Thunders and drummer Jerry Nolan left disillusioned in May 1975 (although David Johansen kept a revised line-up together until January 1977). Malcolm McLaren returned to London in May 1975 having seen his dream band crumble before his eyes. He'd also tried but failed to persuade New York Doll Sylvain Sylvain and Richard Hell to come with him to front the band he'd left his friend Bernie Rhodes to oversee whilst he was in the 'States. Frustrated by his failure to recruit an American frontman, **McLaren** persuaded Steve Jones to shift to doing what he did best, playing guitar and founder member Wally Nightingale, a more reserved character than the others who didn't really fit the image **McLaren** was conjuring up for the band, to leave altogether. **McLaren** now focused on finding a Brit to front the band. Steve New and NME writer Nick Kent were both tried out as vocalists and **Midge Ure** later claimed that he was offered a job as guitarist in the band.

McLaren's imagination was aroused by a green-haired image-conscious teenager called John Lydon, who along with his friends was a frequent visitor to his Kings Road shop (which by now had been re-named Sex). Recognising Lydon's potential to front the band from an image perspective, he persuaded Lydon to sing along to the Alice Cooper classic *Schools Out* backed by the juke box in the Roebuck pub near to his shop Sex. Although the other three members took a dislike to him at first sight it was apparent from this 'audition' that Lydon was the right man to front the band. Ever conscious of image **McLaren** renamed the band **The Sex Pistols**. This name had been a slogan on one of his shop's controversial T-Shirts. Lydon, conspicious for how rotten his teeth were, was soon given the nick-name Johnny Rotten by the other band members and it stuck.

McLaren's dream was alive again and the band rehearsed with a new panasche. Their repertoire comprised cover versions of Who, Dave Berry and Small Faces numbers and they began working on a few originals like *No Feelings*, *Problem* and *Submission*. They played their first gig at St. Martin's School Of Art in London's Charing Cross Road on 6th November 1975 supporting Bazooka Joe. The plug was pulled on them after just five songs but they made enough impression to get a second booking the following night at Central London Polytechnic. **McLaren** deliberately kept them out of the traditional pub rock venues because he wanted them to stand out as different from other bands. Instead he had them gate crashing college gigs and claiming to be the official support band - a ploy that normally worked and although it earnt them no money it brought them plenty of stage practice. A gig at Ravensbourne Art College at Bromley in

THE SEX PISTOLS - Holidays In The Sun.

Kent was attended by Simon Barker who soon spread the word of this unconventional band to his friends - the 'Bromley Contingent' of ardent **'Pistols** fans was born out of this moment.

The Sex Pistols gigged steadily over the coming months. Appearances included Watford College on 23rd January 1976 and London's Marquee on 12th February 1976, where they were top of the bill for **Eddie and The Hot Rods**, who were showcasing for a record company. When NME journalist Neil Spencer spoke to them afterwards they gave him the famous quote "We're not into music, we're into chaos", which they'd clearly been primed to trot out by **McLaren**. **McLaren** was also persuading them to drop most of the sixties and R&B covers from their stage act and to concentrate on performing their own material, however rudimentary some of it might be. This was all part of his ploy of emphasising their uniqueness and originality.

On Saturday 14th February, they courted the art world elite with a performance at Andrew Logan's Valentine's Ball at London's Butlers Wharf. On hearing that someone from NME had arrived for their impromptu gig **McLaren** persuaded one of his aide's Pamela Rooke to get up on stage so Johnny Rotten could in the middle of Iggy Pop's *No Fun* break all the zips on her leotard to ensure the band got publicity.

On Friday 20th February 1976, they arrived at High Wycombe College Of Art to open for Screaming Lord Sutch. They weren't booked. They just turned up, said they were the support band, set up their equipment and played. Ron Watts, then manager of the 100 Club on Oxford Street was at the gig, thought they were great and began to book them on a regular basis, whereas other venues and promoters didn't want anything to do with them. Their 100 Club debut on 30th March 1976 ended in chaos when Rotten was either pushed or jumped off stage and left the club with **McLaren** running off to try to retrieve him. He returned fifteen minutes later to find Steve Jones had ripped the strings off his guitar in frustration so the band couldn't play anymore. On 3rd and 23rd April, they supported the **101'ers** at the Nashville Rooms in West London and on 29th they headlined their own gig there. When, on 11th May 1976, they commenced a Tuesday night residency at the 100 Club punk rock as a serious musical phenomena was born because the venue became a place where punk bands started up.

During the first half of 1976 **The Sex Pistols** also started gigging outside of London. They played at places like Manchester, Sheffield, Middlesborough and Birmingham. The punters and the music press were about equally divided on their merits and because of the extreme reactions their whole personna generated their gigs were often associated with violence. Their fan base was expanding, though, and on 7th August 'Melody Maker' put **The Sex Pistols** on its front cover. An all-night concert at The Screen On The Green in Islington, North London on 29th August with **The Clash** and **The Buzzcocks** was a sell-out.

After seeing **The Sex Pistols** at Barbarella's in Birmingham on 14th August Polydor A&R man Chris Parry tried to persuade the label to sign the band, but was thwarted.

Their TV debut came playing *Anarchy In The U.K.* on 'So It Goes', which was broadcast on 4th September, whilst the band played the second of a two night gig at the Club De Chalet Du Lac in Paris. The first night was packed but it turned out there was no admission charge. The second night the punters had to pay and the place was almost deserted!

On 20th September, **The Sex Pistols** played on the first day of the 100 Club Punk Festival alongside **The Clash, Siouxsie and The Banshees** and **Subway Sect**. That afternoon they'd signed a management contract with Glitterbest Ltd., owned by **Malcolm McLaren**. The second day of the highly successful festival, which was one of the highlights of the U.K. punk scene, featured **The Damned, The Vibrators, The Buzzcocks** and **Stinky Toys**. However, **Sid Vicious** who was in the audience threw a bottle, for which someone else was blamed, leading the 100 Club to ban punk bands for the future. Whilst all this was happening **The 'Pistols** were playing at the Top Rank in Cardiff.

Following rival interest from Polydor, Chrysalis and RAK, **The Sex Pistols** signed a £40,000 two year contract with EMI on 8th October 1976. Since May 1976 the band had recorded several demos in various studios some of which later resurfaced on the legendary *Spunk* bootleg. The group initially used Chris Spedding as a producer then worked with Dave Goodman, who produced the demo of *Anarchy In The U.K.* and *Pretty Vacant* which was sent to EMI and others. After the EMI deal in October, ex-Roxy Music producer Chris Thomas took over production duties. *Anarchy In The U.K.*

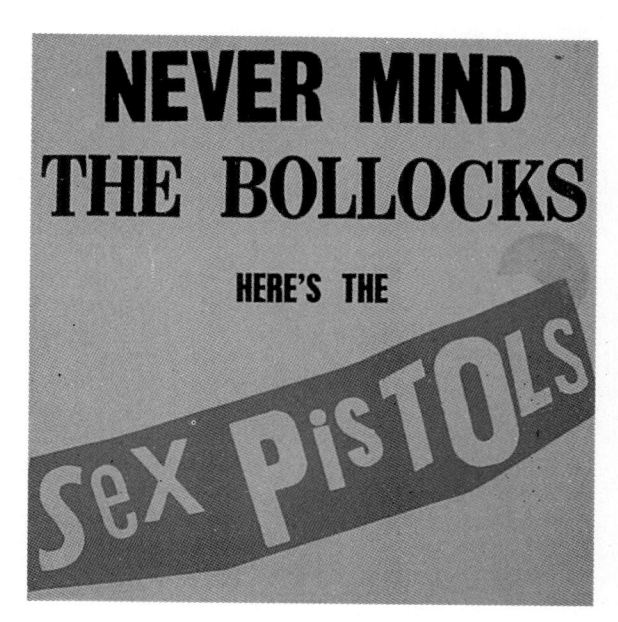

THE SEX PISTOLS - Never Mind The Bollocks.

was released on 19th November 1976. A first pressing came in a black picture sleeve crediting Thomas with production of both sides. Others came in the usual EMI sleeve and correctly credited Dave Goodman on the 'B' side *I Wanna Be Me*. A few demo copies came in a white sleeve with a note that the production credit for the 'B' side should go to Goodman and not Thomas. These are very collectable now. Even rarer are a handful of one-sided white label releases.

On 1st December 1976 came their now notorious appearance on LWT's 'Today At Six' programme. Egged on by host Bill Grundy (who was later suspended for two weeks as a result), the group's use of several everyday swear words provoked an outcry amongst the British public fuelled by sensationalist tabloid headlines the next day. **McLaren** couldn't have planned a better publicity coup himself. The band and punk rock generally rapidly became a magnet for disaffected youth all over the country. But problems lie ahead with the 'Anarchy In The U.K.' national tour, which was projected to last for all of December, as successive local authorities and venues rushed to cancel their gigs. The tour was decimated to the extent that only three of the nineteen planned gigs went ahead at Leeds, Manchester and Plymouth plus a few hastily-arranged replacements. On 4th December EMI's record packers went on strike refusing to handle the *Anarchy* single. It entered the charts at No. 38 just before Christmas but then had to be withdrawn.

On 6th January 1977, EMI capitulated to external pressures and their own doubts by cancelling **The Sex Pistols** contract and paying them off with the second half of their £40,000 advance. If the disrupted tour had cost **McLaren** and the band an estimated £10,000, the pay off had put them back in credit and press coverage remained high.

McLaren was back at AA&M touting for a new contract within days playing a different take of *Anarchy* and a rough take of *No Future*, which would later become *God Save The Queen*. Nonetheless the band spent the rest of January and February without a recording contract. Personality clashes within the band, particularly between Matlock and Rotten, had been apparent for several months. There were also musical differences between Matlock and the rest of the band. Matlock left in February 1977, whether he quit as he claimed or was fired as they claimed is not entirely clear, but **McLaren** had been grooming **Sid Vicious** as a replacement and even arranged for him to learn how to play bass guitar! Certainly Matlock's desire to write more melodic material wasn't in line with what the rest of the group and, more importantly, **McLaren** had in mind. After Glen's departure, though, the band wrote just three more songs, which suggests he was probably the main musical inspiration within the band. Still, Matlock, who went on to form **Rich Kids** with **Midge Ure** on vocals, wrote little more of consequence himself and **Rich Kids** became not much more than a footnote in punk history.

Sid Vicious was actually born John Simon Ritchie on 10th May 1957. His parents separated two years later and he was brought up by his mother Anne, who was somewhat unstable. He also used her maiden name, Beverly. The turmoil of his early life may have accounted for the self-destructive streak in his personality which would ultimately prove literally fatal.

THE SEX PISTOLS - Live In Trondeheim.

Vicious had previously been in Flowers Of Romance with Viv and Palmolive (later of **The Slits**) and Keith Levine, who later linked with Rotten in **PiL** in 1978. Johnny Rotten had almost certainly been instrumental in getting Sid into the band in which he had felt isolated. Jones and Cook had been friends since their schooldays and Sid was a mate of Rotten's so it helped restore a balance. The fact that Sid, who drummed for **Siouxsie and The Banshees** at their debut gig at the 100 Club Punk Rock Festival, could barely play didn't matter. He had the right attitude and a reputation for aggression which gave an edge to their live performances.

On 10th March 1977, the band signed a new £75,000 recording contract with A&M, after **McLaren** weighed up offers from both CBS and A&M. The deal was celebrated by a ceremony outside Buckingham Palace, although the real contracts were signed the previous day. Copies of a second single *God Save The Queen* were pressed for a 25th March release, but on 16th March the band were fired again! It seems a number of events in those six days led to A&M having second thoughts. They arrived at the signing party drunk. Paul Cook had a black eye where Sid had punched him, Steve Jones had made a nuisance of himself to A&M employees in the ladies toilet and Sid also destroyed a toilet bowl whilst trying to wash his feet. Later in the week Lydon had scuffled with 'Old Grey Whistle Test' presenter Bob Harris outside The Speakeasy in London who sent his lawyers round to A&M after alledgedly receiving a death threat from one of Lydon's colleagues. It's also thought that some of A&M's existing artists had complained about the signing. All the copies of *God Save The Queen* A&M had pressed were allegedly destroyed but a few survived and these (which were not in picture sleeves) are among the rarest and most collectable U.K. singles of all. Collectors should watch out for fakes, which are simply later Virgin copies with A&M labels stuck on either side.

The Sex Pistols found themselves in the strange situation of being the highest profile rock band in the land but they had no records in the shops to sell and it was virtually impossible for them to get a gig. **Vicious** was by now hooked on heroin, which musicians from the New York punk scene had introduced to the U.K. scene a few months earlier. They played a one-off gig at Islington's Screen On The Green on 3rd April, but it didn't go well and three days later **Vicious** was hospitalised with hepatitis, brought about by his heroin addiction. This effectively put the band off the road for a further month.

McLaren used this lay off to good effect to negotiate another record deal. By now labels were very wary of paying large advances to a band with just one single and lots of bad publicity. Decca, Pye and Polydor weren't interested and **McLaren** turned down CBS who were willing to sign the band but wouldn't pay an advance. The impasse was finally solved when the band signed to Virgin on 13th May for an advance of £15,000. They'd earlier signed to Barclay in France. Still things weren't plain sailing when the pressing plant staff, aware of the forthcoming Jubilee celebrations threatened to strike and the platemaking company refused to make the plates for the single's sleeve. These problems were eventually resolved and the single was officially released on 27th May. With special royal blue labels and a picture sleeve showing a defaced image of the Queen with a punk style safety-pin added, it attracted considerable publicity and controversy. More ensued from the song's reference to Queen and country as 'a fascist regime'. It was banned by most radio and TV stations and major retail chains like W.H. Smith, Boots and Woolworth's refused to stock it. Despite this, it entered the singles chart at No. 11 and reached No. 2 in Jubilee Week, during a nine week chart residency. With gigs still hard to come by **McLaren** organised for the band to have a commemorative cruise down the River Thames on a riverboat called the Queen Elizabeth. As the boat passed the Houses Of Parliament **The Sex Pistols** let rip with a version of *Anarchy In The U.K.*. After one of the band's drunken entourage attacked a cameraman the captain decided to turn back, calling the authorities in the process. The police were waiting when the boat returned and arrested and charged **McLaren**, his partner Vivienne Westwood and a number of others with a range of relatively minor offences.

After this the press were out to get the band and incited their readers into physical action. Within a week Johnny Rotten (twice) and Paul Cook were attacked by Teddy Boys and the whole band was forced into hiding.

A third single *Pretty Vacant* was released on 2nd July. A simple, catchy single, it featured a witty picture sleeve. The rear illustration depicted two coaches whose destinations were 'Boredom' and 'Nowhere'. This time the single attracted airplay. There was a promotional film, directed by Mike Mansfield, shown on 'Top Of The Pops' and Lydon was interviewed by Tommy Vance on 'Capital Radio'. *Pretty Vacant* climbed to No. 6 and spent a total of eight weeks in the charts. The 'B' side was a version of Iggy and The Stooges' *No Fun* produced by Dave Goodman a year earlier.

Whilst *Pretty Vacant* had been taking the U.K. charts by storm **McLaren**, keen to maintain the momentum, had been in the 'States talking to shlock-movie director Russ Meyer about a possible movie. On 13th July, **The Sex Pistols** began a tour of Scandinavia. All fourteen gigs went ahead as scheduled and they performed *Anarchy In The U.K.* on Swedish TV.

When they returned to Britain gigs were still hard to come by but they were keen to continue touring. So S.P.O.T.S. (Sex Pistols On Tour Secretly) was devised. They played six gigs under assumed names at The Lafayette Club in Wolverhampton (as The Spots), in Doncaster (as The Tax Exiles), in Scarborough (as Special Guests), the Rock Garden Middlesborough (as Acne Rabble), in Plymouth (as The Hampsters) and finally on 1st September at Penzance's Winter Gardens where they were simply billed as 'a mystery band of international repute'. Only four new songs were added to their repertoire *Bodies*, *EMI*, *Holidays In The Sun* and *Belsen Was A Gas*.

On 15th October their fourth single *Holidays In The Sun*, one of their few post-Matlock compositions, was released. Again they hit problems. The cartoon picture sleeve was withdrawn after it was discovered that it infringed the copyright of a Belgian Travel Service brochure, but a number of copies leaked out. All subsequent copies were sold in plain white bags. The single was also banned by Capital Radio for alledgedly comparing Belsen with a holiday camp. Despite these hiccups sales were quite good and the single which opened with the line "A cheap holiday in other people's misery" climbed to No. 8, spending six weeks in the charts. The 'B' side *Satellite* featured one of Jones' classic guitar solos.

On 28th October 1977, their long-awaited debut album *Never Mind The Bollocks - Here's The Sex Pistols* was released in an eye-catching yellow and pink sleeve. Some took offence at the title and a court ruling was necessary to establish that it was not an offence for shops to display an album sleeve in public with the word 'bollocks' on it. With advance orders of 125,000 it qualified for a gold disc and immediately topped the album chart in which it spent a total of fourty-eight weeks. It included little by way of new material and all four of their singles, which was disappointing for their fans who already had them. The first 50,000 copies of the album contained a poster collage and a one-sided single *Submission*. There was a second slightly rarer pressing which included *Submission* on the album and came with a totally white back sleeve and no track listing. Most later pressings included *Submission* on the album and a track listing on the rear sleeve. A budget reissue of this album on Virgin in 1985 boasts an additional cut *Belsen Was A Gas* on the sleeve but it isn't on the album. A limited edition picture disc version of the album was also released in January 1978.

Aside from their four singles, which account for a third of the album, also on offer are several live favourites. There's *Submission*:-

"Submission
Going down, down, dragging her down
Submission

I can't tell you what I've found"
(from *Submission*)

No Feelings is a good fast-paced dance tune:-

"I got no emotion for anybody else
You better understand I'm in love with myself
My self
My beautiful self"
(from *No Feelings*)

Many of the songs *Liar*, *Problems*, *Seventeen* (which rambles at times) and *EMI* (which predictably bitches about the label) are similar in pace and style. *EMI* is one of three post-Matlock songs on the album - the other two being *Holidays In The Sun* and *Bodies*:-

"She was a girl from Birmingham
She had just had an abortion
She was a case of obscenity
Her name was Pauline, she lived in a tree
She was a no-one who killed her baby
She was an animal
She was a bloody disgrace"
(from *Bodies*)

There's quite a discordant opening to this song which turns out to be one of the highlights of the album. Not entirely sure what the song's supposed to be about, though.

On 1st December 1977, **Vicious** and Spungen were arrested for drug possession, but no charges resulted and the band headed to Holland for a nine gig tour. Returning to Britain on 15th December they played a handful of U.K. gigs culminating in a Christmas Day concert at Huddersfield's Ivanhoe's club. This charity performance proved to be this incarnation's last ever U.K. concert.

With U.K. gigs hard to come by and visa problems overcome, they headed for the 'States (where their album had been well received) on 3rd January 1978. A U.S. tour places strain on all bands and for **The Sex Pistols** it proved their undoing. Relationships within the band were so strained that Cook and Jones wouldn't travel with Rotten, whose relationship with **McLaren** was also poor. **Vicious**, meanwhile, was increasingly succumbing to heroin. Their opening gig at Atlanta had been a poor performance by their own admission and by the time of their fifth gig at San Francisco's Winterland **Vicious** was so drugged out that he was incapable of playing. The P.A. system was inadequate and the gig (which was captured on the *Gun Control* bootleg and later released officially as *Last Concert On Earth*) was a shambles. Lydon, who'd said in a radio interview earlier in the day "I don't like rock music, I don't know why I'm in it. I just want to destroy everything" turned to the audience at the end of the concert and said "Ever get the feeling you've been cheated?". Rotten then quit the band or was sacked depending on whose version you believe. **Vicious** overdosed on heroin and was hospitalised. **McLaren**, meanwhile, cancelled a scheduled European tour and flew down to Rio with Cook and Jones to record with Great Train Robber Ronald Biggs, who was living there in exile. The result

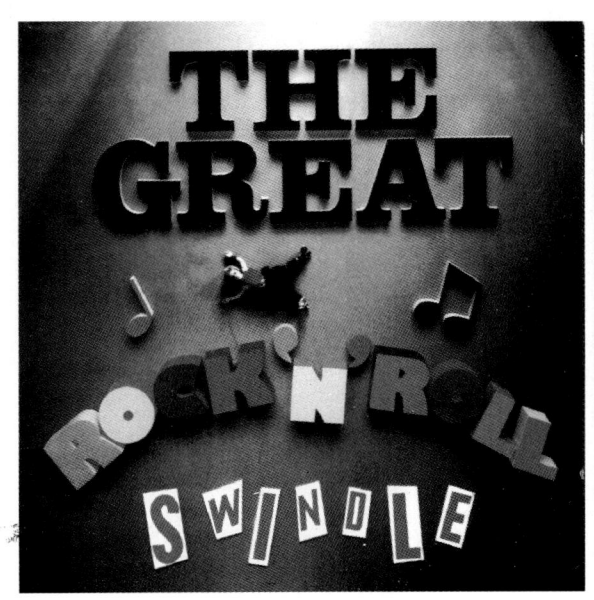

THE SEX PISTOLS - The Great Rock 'n' Roll Swindle.

THE SEX PISTOLS - C'mon Everybody.

was *No One Is Innocent (A Punk Prayer By Ronald Biggs)*, which reached No. 7 and spent ten weeks in the charts, after its release in June 1978. The flip side contained a punk version of *My Way* with **Sid Vicious** on lead vocals. The 12" version gave the 'A' side a different title *The Biggest Blow* and the first 20,000 copies were mispressed and contained a bonus Cook, Jones and Biggs interview. Some copies of *My Way* were wrongly coupled with **The Motors'** *Airport* - a most unusual item. After this **Vicious** effectively ceased to function as a band member. He played a 'Sid Sods Off' farewell gig in London with various punks before moving to New York with his American girlfriend Nancy Spungen, who was also a heroin addict, as well as a former groupie and prostitute. What happened next has been well documented in Alex Cox's 'Sid And Nancy' movie. On 11th October, Spungen was found stabbed to death with Sid's hunting knife in their hotel room. Sid was arrested for her murder and jailed. **McLaren** bailed him on 17th October with money from Virgin. After a failed suicide attempt on 21st October, he finally O.D'd on heroin on 2nd February 1979.

'The Great Rock 'n' Roll Swindle' movie was released in October 1979. It depicts **McLaren** as the driving force behind the band and the whole punk rock phenomenon. Both the film and the accompanying soundtrack album were held up by a court battle between **McLaren** and Rotten (who on 27th May had formed a new band **Public Image Ltd**) about the use of **The Sex Pistols** name. The double album contained studio outtakes from the 'Anarchy' sessions, including covers of songs like *Johnny B. Goode* and *Road Runner*, two versions of *Belsen Was A Gas* (one from their final San Francisco Winterland concert with **Vicious'** bass practically absent and the other with Biggs on lead vocals); **McLaren** singing *You Need Hands* and there were also a number of songs recorded by Cook, Jones and **Vicious** in 1978 with **Eddie 'Tenpole' Tudor** standing in on vocals. Musically, the album was extremely mediocre but ironically it got to No. 7, spending a massive thirty-three weeks in the U.K. album charts. In the 'States, where *Never Mind The Bollocks...* had got to No. 106, it didn't figure in the charts at all. The first 50,000 copies featured an awful version of The Small Faces' *Watcha Gonna Do 'Bout It*, which didn't appear on later pressings. Several singles were lifted from the album and they all did well resulting in a late flurry of chart activity. Their covers of Eddie Cochran's rockers *Something Else* and *C'mon Everybody* both made it to No. 3, spending twelve and nine weeks in the charts respectively. Also from the soundtrack, *Silly Thing* climbed to No. 6 during an eight week chart residency. The title cut narrowly missed the Top 20, stalling at No. 21 in the Autumn of 1979. The following summer another album cut *(I"m Not Your) Stepping Stone* reached No. 21 during an eight week chart stay.

Johnny Rotten refused to play any part in 'The Great Rock 'n' Roll Swindle' and only appears in the live footage of old gigs. The project marked the demise of **The Sex Pistols**. Lydon was concentrating on his new band **Public Image Ltd**. Jones and Cook, for their part, initially played with Ronald Biggs and subsequently as **The Professionals** although they were soon out of the public eye. Jones later moved to the 'States where he played in various heavy metal outfits. Cook was out of the public eye for much longer, but resurfaced in the mid-nineties as Edwyn Collins' drummer.

During the late seventies Virgin released two further **Sex Pistols** albums. The first, *Some Product: Carri On Sex Pistols* was a budget-priced collection of radio interviews and commercials. It did include the notorious Bill Grundy interview, but despite being largely dispensible, reached a staggering No. 6 and managed ten weeks in the charts. The second,

Flogging A Dead Horse, was a collection of 'A' and 'B' sides which also charted, peaking at No. 23. Then, in December 1980, Virgin released a collection of their first eight 'A' sides *The Pistols Pack* (*My Way* was preferred to *No One Is Innocent*) along with two Cook and Jones songs from 1978, *Black Leather* and *Here We Go Again*, which had only previously been available on a Japanese compilation.

There has since been a plethora of material which adds little of interest to their recording output. One record worth purchasing is the 1985 six-track *Mini Album*, which comprised raw versions of songs that had been included on the *Spunk* bootleg. A later picture disc version in 1986 substituted *Pretty Vacant* for *I Wanna Be Me*. This release also spawned a 45 *Submission* backed by *No Feelings* on the 7" in a limited edition of 5,000 in pink or yellow vinyl. The 12" version featured *Anarchy In The U.K.* on the flip side and was pressed on six different colours.

The Original Pistols Live, released in February 1985, is essentially an official issue of the *Indecent Exposure* bootleg taken from a live recording at Burton-on-Trent in September 1976, minus two songs, *Submission* and *(I'm Not Your) Stepping Stone*. The same year Receiver released a mini-album *After The Storm*. This showcased four '**Pistols** cuts *New York*, *Anarchy*, *Pretty Vacant* and *Liar*, alongside four New York Dolls' cuts.

Many of the dubious mid-eighties live releases suffer from very poor sound quality. Be particularly wary of *Where Were You In '77?*. The track listing on the cover is wrong listing *Substitute* when *I Wanna Be Me* features instead and *Looking For A Kiss* is announced on the record as *New York*.

In 1992, Virgin released *Kiss This* a two-CD set. One disc is basically an enlarged *Never Mind The Bollocks* plus important 'B' sides, **Sid Vicious** *My Way* and Steve Jones' *Silly Thing*. The second disc features material from their July 1977 Scandinavian tour.

In 1996, to the surprise of many **The Sex Pistols**' original line-up (Cook, Jones, Lydon and Matlock) reformed for the 'Filthy Lucre Tour'. Their first live appearance for fifteen years at Finland's Messila Festival on 21st June was well received. On 23rd June they played and presented a remarkably unified image to a euphoric audience at London's Finsbury Park. Further gigs followed at Glasgow, Belfast, a 'secret' gig at Shepherd's Bush Empire and an appearance at the Phoenix Festival. A *Filthy Lucre Live* album (containing most of their old favourites) got to No. 26 in August 1996 and a live version of *Pretty Vacant* made No. 18 in the singles chart. It was strictly a one-off reunion, though. Glen Matlock recorded a solo album *Who's He When He's At Home?* for Creation just prior to the 'Filthy Lucre Tour', Paul Cook continued to play with Edwyn Collins and Lydon had signed a solo artist contract with Virgin. In 1997, Steve Jones became Guns 'N' Roses new bass player, having previously played with L.A. band The Neurotic Outsiders (who'd featured two Guns 'N' Roses members).

In November 1996, came *Live At Winterland*, the first official release of their final U.S. gig. Don't get excited. This is their hits played badly with dodgy sound quality and will be dispensible unless you're a completist. More relevant was the double-pack reissue of *Never Mind The Bollocks...* with the legendary *Spunk* bootleg.

In late 1999, Essential released *There Is No Future* on CD. This originally appeared as the *No Future U.K.?* bootleg in 1977 at the same time as the '**Pistols**' debut album. It contains recordings of demos produced by Dave Goodman in July 1976 and January 1977. They are raw and rough 'n' ready but this suits most of their early material and the version of *Anarchy In The U.K.* is probably their best ever. The fifteen cuts, in a different order from the original *No Future U.K.?* release, are supplemented by a cover of *Substitute*.

In summer 2000, the Italian label Get Back released *Burton-On-Trent Recordings*, their 1976 gig in its entirety and correct running order. It includes frantic, raucous versions of *Anarchy In The U.K.*, *Pretty Vacant* and *Problems*. Whilst the sound quality could be better, this is essential for **Sex Pistols** collectors.

Later in the year, Essential put out a trio of CDs containing **Sex Pistols**' material. *Live In Chelmsford Prison* is pretty raw. *Better Live Than Dead*, originally titled *Indecent Exposure*, is recognised to be one of their best live recordings, and *Early Daze* gives another outing to their seven July 1976 demos recorded with Dave Goodman at their rehearsal studio in Denmark Street.

Inevitably, **The Sex Pistols** classic singles have appeared on numerous retrospective punk collections over the years, including the following. *Anarchy In The U.K.* on *1-2-3-4 - A History Of Punk And New Wave* (5-CD set) (MCA/Universal MCD 60066) 1999, *The Best Punk Album In The World Ever... Vol. 1* (2-CD set) (Virgin VTDCD 42) 1995, *The Best Punk Anthems.... Ever* (2-CD set) (Virgin VTDCD 198) 1998, *Punk - The Worst Of Total Anarchy* (2-CD set) (Disky SP 871952) 1996 and *Punk, Vol. 2* (Music Club MCCD 027) 1991. *God Save The Queen* has resurfaced on *The Best Punk Album In The World... Ever, Vol. 1* (2-CD set) (Virgin VTDCD 42) 1995, *The Best Punk Anthems... Ever* (2-CD set) (Virgin VTDCD 198) 1998, *A History Of Punk, Vol. 1* (Virgin CDOVD 486) 1997, *New Wave Archive* (Rialto RMCD 201) 1997 and *Punk - The Worst Of Total Anarchy* (2-CD set) (Disky SP 871952) 1996. You'll also find *Pretty Vacant* on *The Best Punk Album In The World... Ever, Vol. 2* (2-CD set) (Virgin VTDCD 79) 1996, *God Save The Punks* (2-CD set) (Disky DOU 882552) 1998, *Punk* (Music Club MCCD 015) 1991 and *Teenage Kicks* (PolyGram TV 5253382) 1995. *Holidays In The Sun* got a further airing on *The Best Punk Album In The World... Ever, Vol. 2* (2-CD set) (Virgin VTDCD 79) 1996 and *Punk, Vol. 2* (Music Club MCCD 027) 1991. Other compilation appearances have included *No One Is Innocent* on *God Save The Punks* (2-CD set) (Disky DOU 882552) 1998; *EMI* on *Punk* (Music Club MCCD 015) and *Submission* on *Punk - Live And Nasty* (Emporio EMPRCD 586) 1995.

With the twenty-five year anniversary of punk approaching you can expect the plethora of **Sex Pistols** releases to continue.

The Sex Pistols will always be a legend - they gave the increasingly complacent and self-indulgent music industry a good kick up the arse. Manipulated and manufactured as they were by **McLaren**, they spearheaded punk rock which became a magnet for disaffected youth in an era of high unemployment. Their first four singles are classics and always will be, as is their first album, and in Johnny Rotten they had one of punks very best vocalists.

Shake

Personnel:	JO CALLIS	gtr	A
	ANGEL PATTERSON	drms	A
	TROY TATE	gtr	A
	SIMON TEMPLAR	bs	A

EP:	1(A)	CULTURE SHOCK (Culture Shock/Glass House/ Dream On/ (But) Not Mine) (10", PS)	(Sire SIR 4016-10) 1979
45s:		Culture Shock/Dream On	(Sire SIR 4016) 1979
		Invasion Of The Gamma Men/ Night By Night (PS)	(Sire SIR 4035) 1980

Jo Callis, Angel Paterson and Simon Templar formed Tate when **The Rezillos** split up. Surprisingly, since Callis had written most of **The Rezillos**' material he allowed Patterson and Templar to write too for **Shake** and the end result was this EP. *Culture Shock* displayed Callis' strange and

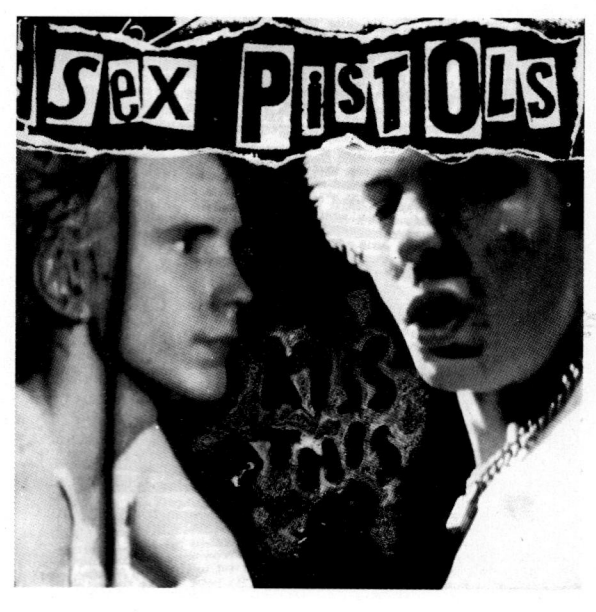

THE SEX PISTOLS - Kiss This.

screetching guitar style and his clever songwriting, being a song about the language gap facing a Brit abroad:-

"The food is funny and the weather is strange
I'm losing all my money on the rate of exchange
I say, excuse me please mister how much is this
Very sorry sir, no speak Engleesh!"
(from *Culture Shock*)

Still, before long, Callis was off to join **The Human League**.

SHAM 69 - Borstal Breakout.

Sham 69

Personnel:
BILLY BOSTIK	drms		A
JOHNNY GOODFORNOTHING	gtr		A
NEIL HARRIS	gtr		A
JIMMY PURSEY	vcls		ABCD
ALBIE SLIDER (ALBERT MASKAIL)	bs		AB
MARK CAIN	drms		BC
DAVE PARSONS	gtr		BCD
DAVE TREGANNA	bs, vcls		CD
RICK GOLDSTEIN	drms		D

HCP

ALBUMS:
1(C)	TELL US THE TRUTH	(Polydor 2383 491)	1978	25
2(C)	THAT'S LIFE	(Polydor POLD 5010)	1978	27
3(C)	THE ADVENTURES OF THE HERSHAM BOYS	(Polydor POLD 5025)	1979	8
4(D)	THE GAME	(Polydor POLD 5033)	1979	-
5(-)	FIRST, THE BEST AND THE LAST (compilation)	(Polydor 2383 596)	1980	-

NB: (1) reissued (Receiver RRD 001) 1989 and on CD (Dojo DOJOCD 256) 1996, (Essential ESMCD 513) 1997 and (Sanctuary CMRCD 020) 2001, with bonus tracks. (2) reissued (Skunx SHAMX 1) 1988 and also on CD (Dojo DOJOCD 257) 1996. (1) and (2) also issued as a double album set (Receiver RRLD 001) 1993. (3) came with a 12" EP (2812 045) with a stickered sleeve. (3) also issued on CD (Dojo DOJOCD 258) 1996, (Essential ESMCD 515) 1997 and (Sanctuary CMRCD 021) 2001 with bonus tacks. (4) reissued (Receiver RRLD 002) 1989 and on CD (Dojo DOJOCD 259) 1996 and also (Essential ESMCD 516) 1977. (5) came with a live EP (Riot 1/2816 028). (5) also issued on CD (Polydor 5134292) 1994. There have also been a number of retrospective live and compilation releases:- *Angels With Dirty Faces - The Best Of Sham 69* (Receiver RRLP 104) 1986; *Live And Loud* (Link LINKLP 004) 1987 also on CD (LINKCD 004) 1991; *Live And Loud, Vol. 2* (Link LINKLP 025) 1988 also on CD (LINKCD 025) 1992; *The Best Of The Rest Of Sham 69* (Receiver RRCD/LP 112) 1989; *Live At The Roxy* (live tapes '77) (Receiver RRCD/LP 133) 1990; *Complete Live* (Castle Classics CLACD/LP 153) 1989; *Sham 69 Live* (Action Replay CDAR 1011) 1990 and (Emporio EMPRCD 582) 1995; *BBC Radio 1 Live In Concert* (Windsong WIN 049) 1993; *Rare And Unreleased* (Limited Edition CD 5) 1991; *The Best Of Sham 69* (2-CD set) (Essential ESDCD 350) 1995; *The Best Of Sham 69* (Essential ESMCD 512) 1997; *Borstal Breakout* (2-CD set) (Snapper SMDCD 141) 1998; *Live In Japan* (Dojo DOJOCD 105) 1994; *Sham's Last Stand* (Street Link LINKCD 075) 1992; (Dojo DOJOCD 95) 1993 and (Snapper SMMCD 540) 1999; *The First, The Best And The Last* (Polydor 2383596) 1981 and on CD (Polydor 5134292) 1994; *United* (Hallmark 304462) 1997; *The Very Best Of The Hersham Boys* (Castle Select SELCD 504) 1998; *Angels With Dirty Faces* (2-CD) (Essential ESDCD 780) 1999; *Rarities 1977 - 80* (Captain Oi! AHOY CD 139) 2000 and *Laced Up Boots And Corduroys* (Delta 47 036) 2000.

EPs:
1(C)	Angels With Dirty Faces/Borstal Breakout/ Hurry Up Harry/ If The Kids Are United	(Polydor POSP 602)	1982	
2(-)	LIVE EP (Borstal Breakout/If The Kids Are United/ Angels With Dirty Faces/Rip Off)	(Receiver 3016)	1991	

HCP

45s: (up to 1986)
+	I Don't Wanna/Ulster/Red London (black and white photo PS)	(Step Forward SF 4)	1977 -
+	I Don't Wanna/Ulster/Red London (12" black and white photo PS)	(Step Forward SF 412)	1977 -
*	Songs Of The Streets/Fanx	(Polydor no #)	1977 -
	Borstal Breakout/ Hey Little Rich Boy (PS)	(Polydor 2058 966)	1978 -
	Angels With Dirty Faces/The Cockney Kids Are Innocent (PS)	(Polydor 2059 023)	1978 19
	If The Kids Are United/Sunday Morning Nightmare (PS)	(Polydor 2059 050)	1978 9
	Hurry Up Harry/No Entry (PS)	(Polydor POSP 7)	1978 10
	Questions And Answers/I Gotta Survive (live)/With A Little Help From My Friends (PS)	(Polydor POSP 27)	1979 18
	Hersham Boys/I Don't Wanna (live)/Tell Us The Truth (live) (PS)	(Polydor POSP 64)	1979 6
	Hersham Boys/I Don't Wanna (live)/Rip Off (live)/ I'm A Man, I'm A Boy (live)/Tell Us The Truth (live) (12" PS)	(Polydor POSPX 64)	1979 -
	You're A Better Man Than I/ Give A Dog A Bone (PS)	(Polydor POSP 82)	1979 49
	Tell The Children/Jack (PS)	(Polydor POSP 136)	1980 45
	Unite And Win/I'm A Man (PS)	(Polydor 2059 259)	1980 -

NB: + Later reissued in 1979 in a yellow picture sleeve. * This was a one-sided concert freebie with a red brick-wall label. It was later counterfeited, but the counterfeits have white labels.

Sham 69 were formed in Hersham, Surrey, by **Jimmy Pursey** in 1976. They took their name from the last four letters of Hersham and the fact 1969 was considered a classic skinhead year. **Pursey** was a man of considerable energy who saw punk as an ideal medium through which to channel his class consciousness. The original line-up also comprised Billy Bostik (drms), Johnny Goodfornothing (gtr), Neil Harris (gtr) and Albie Slider (bs), but in June 1977 **Pursey** off-loaded all but Slider feeling that they lacked sufficient commitment to the band. In came Mark Cain (drms) and Dave Parsons (gtr) and with the leaner, meaner four-piece band he recorded *I Don't Wanna* for Step Forward in October 1977. It was released in both 7" and 12" formats and was later reissued in both, but in yellow picture sleeves in 1979, after they'd become famous.

Sham 69 fans will also want to seek out a one-sided concert freebie *Songs Of The Streets / Fanx* from 1977, which is the rarest vinyl offering from the band, but beware - it has been counterfeited!

I Don't Wanna attracted enough attention to secure them a major label contract with Polydor. With Dave Treganna having replaced Albie Slider on bass, they recorded their one and only Peel session on 6th December 1977. It comprised *Borstal Breakout*, *Hey Little Rich Boy*, *They Don't Understand*, *Rip Off* and *What 'Av We Got?*.

SHAM 69 - Hersham Boys.

Borstal Breakout was selected as their first 45 for Polydor in January 1978. It typified their forthright, no-holes-barred style of delivery, but didn't chart - possibly because they weren't that well known at the time. This was soon rectified by subsequent releases, though.

Tell Us The Truth, their debut album, followed in February 1978. It included both sides of their debut 45 for Poydor as well as *Ulster* from their earlier Step Forward 45. With one live side and very loose production it set the style of their chanted populist slogans. What's more the punters seemed to like it. The album climbed to No. 25 in the charts during an eight week stay.

They followed this album with a trio of their finest singles. First, in April 1978, came *Angels With Dirty Faces*, which gave them their first U.K. hit single, peaking at No. 19 and spending ten weeks in the U.K. charts. Their decidedly British appeal to predominantly working class kids never did make much headway in the 'States. The follow-up in July, *If The Kids Are United*, fared even better. Highly anthemic, it had immediate appeal and was tailor-made to be chanted like football chants, particularly as it culminated with chants of 'united', 'united'. A great party piece of the era, too, this took them into the Top 10, peaking at No. 9 during a nine week chart stay. The trio was rounded off with the laddish *Hurry Up Harry* in October which appeared to be about the importance of going down 'a pub'. This spent eight weeks in the chart peaking at No. 10.

Their vinyl offerings for 1978 concluded in November with their second album *That's Life*. Of their previous three 45s, it included *Angels With Dirty Faces* and *Hurry Up Harry*, but not the anthemic *If The Kids Are United*. The remaining tracks often use 'life extract' type dialogues to deal with issues between boys and girls, kids and their parents and so on... only with limited success. The band were at their height of their popularity and the album attained No. 27 in the charts.

Given this forthright, anthemic style of delivery, **Sham 69** had always been an exciting, energetic live act. Unfortunately, their gigs increasingly attracted riotous skinhead fans and more unsavoury yobbish right wing and racist elements. Their concerts were increasingly interrupted by violence. The band often cancelled them when they got wind of threatened trouble in advance. Things came to a head after a riot at a Hendon gig in January 1979, when **Pursey** announced they would not perform live again. A few farewell concerts were attempted during the early half of 1979. One, at London's Rainbow Theatre, descended into a mass of fighting after just 20 minutes. Again the curtain was lowered on further live performances.

On vinyl, they enjoyed further success in 1979. In March, *Questions And Answers* brought them a further Top 20 hit, rising to No. 18 in a nine week chart stay. The three-track 45 also included a live version of *I Gotta Survive* and one of their very few cover versions - of The Beatles' *With A Little Help From My Friends*.

Hersham Boys, released in both 7" and 12" format in July, gave them their biggest hit of all. It got to No. 6 and spent nine weeks in the charts. A classic sloganistic anthem which glorified the skinhead culture that was an important core of their following. The three track 45 this time contained two live numbers - *I Don't Wanna* and *Tell Us The Truth*.

SHAM 69 - That's Life.

SHAM 69 - Angels With Dirty Faces.

Their third album, *The Adventures Of The Hersham Boys*, followed in September. Marking some change in direction it featured more keyboards then their previous efforts (courtesy of Peter Wilson, who was **Pursey**'s co-producer) and, in places, more poetic lyrics. It came with a free 12" single featuring two of their earlier classics, *If The Kids Are United* and *Borstal Breakout*. Naturally, too, the album featured their earlier hit *Hersham Boys* along with *Questions And Answers*. It also included another of their rare cover versions - of The Yardbirds' *You're A Better Man Than I*. This proved to be their best-selling album, climbing to No. 8 and spending eight weeks in the charts. In October, *You're A Better Man Than I* was released as a 45 and climbed to No. 49.

They were persuaded due to the success of *The Adventures Of The Hersham Boys* to play some live gigs again. Rick Goldstein replaced Mark Cain on drums. This new line-up carried on gigging until the summer of 1980. In March, another 45 *Tell The Children* brought them a further hit. It climbed to No. 45, during a brief three week stay. It would also prove to be their last. *The Game*, their fourth album released in May, failed to chart at all. However, their songwriting and musicianship had improved considerably, but the tide was turning against them. Their reputation had also been tarnished by a series of attacks on their credibility in the press. Their final 45, *Unite And Win*, released in June, failed to chart at all and they called it a day.

In November, Polydor put out a compilation *The First, The Best And The Last*. This included the 'A' and 'B' sides of their first three Polydor 45s and all their other 45 'A' sides, except for *You're A Better Man Than I*. The 'B' side *Give A Dog A Bone* was substituted in its place.

Tregenna, Parsons and Goldstein all teamed up with former Dead Boys member Stiv Bators to form **The Wanderers**. They recorded an album, *The Only Lovers Left Alive* and a couple of 45s. The second of these was a cover of Bob Dylan's *The Times They Are A-Changin'*. When **The Wanderers** split, in August 1981, first Bators and later Tregenna joined Lords Of The New Church. Later, in 1982, Parsons formed Framed. He also appeared in Time U.K., with ex-**Jam** drummer Rick Buckler and in the late 1980s was in the punk-influenced pop band Transvision X.

In the summer of 1980, **Jimmy Pursey** embarked on a none-too-successful solo career. Later in 1987 **Pursey** and Parsons reformed **Sham 69**. An album *Volunteer* and a series of 45s were released, but they never recaptured their previous chart success.

Borstal Breakout and *If The Kids Are United* both resurfaced on the *20 Of A Different Kind* (Polydor POLS 1006) in 1977, whilst *Hersham Boys* and *No Entry* (the flip side to *Hurry Up Harry*), which dealt with the fact that **Pursey**'s criminal record meant they couldn't tour the 'States, were included on *20 Of Another Kind, Vol. 2* (Polydor POLX-1) 1979. There's a live version of *If The Kids Are United* on *New Wave Archive* (Rialto RMCD 201) 1997. You can also check it out on *Burning Ambitions, Vol. 3* (Anagram CDPUNK 98) 1997, *The Best Punk Album In The World.... Ever, Vol. 2* (2-CD) (Virgin VTDCD 79) 1996 and *The Best Punk Anthems.... Ever* (2-CD) (Virgin VTDCD 198) 1998. *Hersham Boys* got a further airing on *A History Of Punk, Vol. 1* (Virgin CDOVD 486) 1997 and *Punk - The Worst Of Total Anarchy* (2-CD) (Disky SP 871952) 1996. *Punk* (Music Club MCCD 015) 1991 includes *Angels With Dirty Faces* and *Rip Off*, whilst *Punk - Live And Nasty* (Emporio EMPRCD 586) 1995 features them playing

SHAM 69 - If The Kids Are United.

a live version of **The Clash**'s *White Riot*. *If The Kids...* also made a guest appearance on *Learning Engish Vol. 1* by Die Toten Hosen. You'll also find *Borstal Breakout* on *Punk, Vol. 2* (Music Club MCCD 027) 1991, *Oi! The Singles Collection, Vol. 2* (Captain Oi! AHOY CD 63) and on *1-2-3-4 - A History OF Punk And New Wave 1976 - 1979* (MCA/Universal MCD 60066) 1999.

Live And Loud! from 1987 probably dates from after their second album. The recording quality and choice of material is not up to the live side of *Tell Us The Truth* but some of their finest anthems - *Angels With Dirty Faces*, *Borstal Breakout*, *If The Kids Are United*, *They Don't Understand* and *Red London* are included, as well as a cover of **The Clash**'s *White Riot*.

The Best Of, also from 1987, on Receiver includes their five Top 20 hits from the late seventies, *Borstal Breakout* and live versions of *I Don't Wanna* and *What Have We Got*.

Live And Loud! Vol. 2 suffers from poor recording quality. Side One is from the era when 'Dodie' Cain was their drummer. Side Two dates from later - their last Scottish gig - and the material is weaker.

On *BBC Radio 1 Live In Concert* from 1979, **Sham 69** run through many of their favourites, although it does include an embarrassing cover of The Beatles' *Day Tripper*.

The Best Of Sham 69 is a double CD comprising a hits disc and a 'Live At The Roundhouse' disc, which is a reminder of their in-concert energy. Then in 1996, Dojo reissued their first four albums on CD and each came with additional bonus tracks culled from 'B' sides.

Angels With Dirty Faces is a 2-CD set issued by Essential in 1999. It compiles their seven chart singles, along with cuts from their four Polydor albums. The double-CD also comes in a slipcase with a nice fold-out booklet. For some reason, though, live versions of their three tracks from their Step Forward debut *I Don't Wanna* are used in preference to the original and superior studio versions. Otherwise it's an excellent compilation.

Rarities 1977 - 80 (CD) commences with three demos of *Borstal Breakout*, *George Davis Is Innocent* and *They Don't Understand*. Also featured are two demos that emerged on their *Unite And Win* 45, six redone for their final Polydor album *The Game* and three originally intended for the *Quadrophenia* soundtrack. This is really one for **Sham 69** fans.

Laced Up Boots And Courduroys is a good twenty-track 'best of'. It comprises their singles *If The Kids Are United*, *Borstal Breakout* and *Hersham Boys*, tracks from all four of their Polydor albums and 'B' sides like *No Entry* and cuts including *We Gotta Fight*, *Rip Off* and *They Don't Understand* from the live side of *Tell Us The Truth* (their debut album). The CD comes with extensive sleevenotes. The only real downside is that it closes with iffey live versions of *Hurry Up Harry* and *Angels With Dirty Faces*. Sanctuary, who own **Sham 69**'s Polydor back catalogue are currently reissuing their Polydor albums, remastered with contemporary bonus tracks, along with fold-out booklets containing sleevenotes, rare photos and quotes from **Sham 69** guitarist Dave Parsons.

Sham 69 were lots of fun at the time and it's a pity their career was marred by the violence at their gigs. There is a plethora of retrospective compilations and live recordings of their material still available.

The Shapes

Personnel:	SEYMOUR BYBUSS	vcls	A
	DAVE GEE	drms	A
	BRIAN HELICOPTER	bs	A
	TIM JEE	gtr	A
	STEVE RICHARDS	gtr	A

EP:	1(A)	THE SHAPES (WOT'S FOR LUNCH MUM)
		(Sofa SEAT 1/FRR 004) 1979

NB: (1) This had an insert but no picture sleeve.

45:	Blast Off/Airline Disaster (PS)	(Good Vibrations GOT 13) 1979

The Shapes were from Leamington Spa. They first released an EP for Sofa Records, but then became one of the few non-Northern Irish bands to sign to Terri Hooley's Good Vibrations label. They also recorded a session for John Peel.

Airline Disaster, as its title suggests about an unpleasant and finally aborted flight, is played in a typical fast-paced punk style. More recently, it has resurfaced on *Good Vibrations --The Punk Singles Collection* (Anagram CDPUNK 36) 1994.

Steve Sharp and The Cleancuts

45:	We Are The Mods/	
	He Wants To Be A Mod	(Happy Face MM 122) 1980

This is one of the most collectable mod revival recordings. The group emerged out of another Worcester band, a punk act called **The Rowdies**. Only between 300-500 copies of this 45 were pressed and copies change hands for over £100.

Shock Treatment

Personnel:	PAUL KELLY	drms	A
	BASIL McCAUSLAND	bs	A
	BILLY McIlHENNY	vcls	A
	DAVY McLARON	gtr	A

Shock Treatment were a short-lived Belfast band, circa 1980, whose *Belfast Telegraph* was featured on *The Room To Move* (Energy NRG 1) 1980 compilation EP. It also later resurfaced on *Good Vibrations - The Punk Singles Collection* (Anagram CD PUNK 36) 1994. They were originally supposed to release *Belfast Telegraph* on a compilation entitled *Belfast On A Thin Wire*, but when that didn't become a reality they released a self-financed EP called *Big Checked Shirts*.

McIlhenny later became editor of 'Smash hits' magazine!

SHAM 69 - Hurry Up Harry.

Shoes For Industry

Personnel:	ANDY BOOT	gtr	A
	BASSETT DAVIES	vcls, sax	A
	LAZIO	keyb'ds, vcls	A
	STEVE LONNEN	bs	A
	TIM NORFOLK	gtr	A
	JOHN SCHOFIELD	drms	A

ALBUM: 1(A) TALK LIKE A WHELK (Fried Egg FRY 1) 1981

45s: Falling In Love Again (Can't Help It)/
Laughing Song (Laughbeat) (PS) (Fried Egg EGG 001) 1979
Spend/Sheepdog Trials Inna
Babylon (PS) (Fried Egg EGG 004) 1981

A short-lived Bristol band whose lyrics were full of angst and whose music was dominated by a pounding rhythm section. *Jerusalem*, a cut from the album was also included on the compilation *E(gg)clectic, Vol. 1* (Fried Egg FRY 2) 1981, along with *Invasion Of The French Boyfriends*, which has a spoken intro. and sounds quite theatrical. File under doom and gloom.

The Shove

Personnel:	MICK	bs	A
	SNAZ	drms	A
	STEVE	vcls	A
	STRAW	gtr	A

EP: 1(A) THE SHOVE (Raise The Roof Tonite/Violence/Pigs/
Nutters Of York) (Shove Off Records) 1981

This four-piece formed in York in 1981, releasing this EP on their own label, although it never actually came with a sleeve. Mark Brennan reveals that some of their fans made up a sleeve with a copy of a poster used to advertise the EP locally! **The Shove** were heavily into football. The track *Nutters Of York* was about York City F.C.'s away 'firm'. The whole EP can also be heard on *Punk Rock Rarities, Vol. 2* (Anagram CDPUNK 83) 1996.

Shox

Personnel:	MIKE ATKINSON		A
	JACQUI BROOKES		A
	JOHN PETHERS		A

45: No Turning Back/Lying Here (PS) (Axis AXIS 4) 1980
Reissue: No Turning Back/
Lying Here (PS) (Beggars Banquet BEG 33) 1980

Shox played synthesizer-orientated music.

Shrink

45s: Valid Or Void/You Chaffeur Me (Oval AMS 7409) 1979
I Am A Doll/Mr. Caz (A&M AMS 7434) 1979
Wibble Wobble/Prisoner (RCA RCA 70) 1981

Shrink hailed from Morecombe in Lancashire and was a quietly eccentric figure prone to shave his head and paint his skin gold. His best known song was *Valid Or Void* by virtue of its inclusion on the sampler *No Wave* (A&M AMLE 68505) in 1979.

The Sick Things

EP: 1 THE LEGENDARY SICK THINGS (EP) (Anti-Social Disease/Sleeping With The Dead/Street Kids/
Bondage Boy) (Chaos CH 3) 1983

A punk group with a distinctive girl vocalist. The above EP was actually recorded back in 1977 at the zenith of the punk era, although it was not released until 1983. Their best known song *Bondage Boy* was also included on an EP (Spiral Scratch 201) 1989, alongside cuts by the better-known **Sex Pistols**, **The Users** and **The Killjoys**. It was also included, along with *Kids On The Street*, on *Raw Deal* (Raw RAWLP 1) in 1977.

Chris Sievey

ALBUMS: 1 ALL SLEEP'S SECRETS (Razz CS 1) 1978
2 CHRIS SIEVEY'S BIG RECORD
(Cordelia ERICAT 015) 1986

NB: (2) came with a free 7" copy of his first 45. *Baiser / Last* (TOSH 109).

CASS: 1 GIRL IN MY BLUE JEANS (Hey Boss no #) 1975
2 ALL SLEEP'S SECRETS (Razz CS-1) 1976
3 NO GO DEMOS (Razz no #) 1980
4 DENIGRATION NOW (Razz RAZZ 4) 1982

NB: (1) was a 16-track cassette. Only 250 were issued. Only 1,000 of (2) were issued. (3) came with a "Complete Book Of Rejection Slips" booklet. Only 400 copies were released. (4) came with a booklet and originally had a release of 500. It was later reissued (just 250 copies) with two extra tracks (11.37 ETS-S) in 1985.

EPs: 1 BAISER (Baiser/Two Of The Same/
(Cuts by **The Freshies**) (Razz RAZZX EP 1) 1977
2 RED INDIAN MUSIC (Razz RAZZ 8) 1980

NB: (1) played at 33 rpm and included two tracks each by **Chris Sievey** and **The Freshies**. The EP had handwritten labels.

45s: Baiser/Last (PS) (Rabid TOSH 109) 1979
+ My Tape's Gone/Moon Midsummer (Razz RAZZ 4) 1980
Hey/(cut by **The Freshies**) (PS) (Razz RAZZ 5) 1980
Skip The Flight/Jim Basier (Razz RAZZ 9) 1982
x Camouflage (ZX 81 Programme "Camouflage")/
Flying Train/F.T. (PS) (Random RND 1) 1983
o If You Really Love Me, Buy My Shirt/
I Am The Walrus (CV CVS 1) 198?

NB: + Some copies of this 45 came with 'True Life Revealing Confessions Of Romance And Love' fanzine. x This was a computer single. Only 2,000 copies were issued and the 'B' side played at 33 rpm. o With **The Freshies**.

Chris Sievey is best known as the vocalist with **The Freshies**, but he also had some solo outings, on which he was often backed by various members of **The Freshies**. These are detailed above. A number of his releases, particularly some of the cassettes are quite collectable now.

Silent Noise

45: I've Been Hurt (Too Many Times Before)/
Heart To Heart (Silent Noise/Easy ER 02) 1979

This Norwich band were part of the mod revival of 1979.

CHRIS SIEVEY - If You Really Love Me, Buy Me A Shirt.

THE SILICON TEENS - Judy In Disguise.

The Silicon Teens

Personnel:	DARRYL	vcls	A
	DIANE	synth	A
	JACKI	synth	A
	PAUL	electro drums	A

ALBUM: 1(A) MUSIC FOR PARTIES   (Mute STUMM 2) 1981

NB: (1) also issued on CD (Mute CDSTUMM 2) 1996.

45s:	Let's Dance/Memphis Tennessee (PS)	(Mute MUTE 3) 1979
	Judy In Disguise/Chip 'n' Roll (PS)	(Mute MUTE 4) 1980
	Just Like Eddie/Sun Sight (PS)	(Mute MUTE 8) 1980
	Red River Rock/Chip 'n' Roll (PS)	(Mute SIL 1) 1988

This was basically a studio project for Daniel Miller, who through his Mute Records, released a single as **The Normal** and in his work as a producer played a pioneering role in the emergence of the synthesizer in modern rock music. The *Music For Parties* album features synthesizer versions of old rock 'n' roll classics like *Memphis Tennessee*, *Judy In Disguise* and *You Really Got Me*, with vocals added, alongside a number of new songs. Some of these tracks were also issued as 45s. Easily accessible, it's all good fun. I've mentioned the project here because it was also caught up with the "new wave".

You'll also find *Memphis Tennessee* on *Machines* (Virgin V 2177) 1980.

Simple Minds

Personnel:	CHARLIE BURCHILL	gtr	ABCDE
(up to	DEREK FORBES	bs	ABCD
1986)	JIM KERR	vcls	ABCDE
	BRIAN McGEE	drms	A
	MICK McNEILL	keyb'ds	ABCDE
	KENNY HYSLOP	drms	B
	MIKE OGLETREE	drms	C
	MEL GAYNOR	drms	DE
	JOHN GIBLING	bs	E

				HCP
ALBUMS:	1(A)	LIFE IN A DAY	(Zoom ZULP 1) 1979	30
(up to	2(A)	REAL TO REAL (CACOPHONY)		
1986)			(Arista SPART 1109) 1980	-
	3(A)	EMPIRES AND DANCE	(Arista SPART 1140) 1980	41
	4(B)	SONS AND FASCINATION/SISTER FEELINGS CALL		
		(dbl)	(Virgin V 2207) 1981	11
	5(B)	SONS AND FASCINATION	(Virgin V 2207) 1981	-
	6(B)	SISTER FEELINGS CALL	(Virgin OVED 2) 1981	-
	7(-)	CELEBRATION	(Arista SPART 1183) 1982	45
	8(D)	NEW GOLD DREAM (81-82-83-84)		
			(Virgin V 2230) 1982	3
	9(D)	SPARKLE IN THE RAIN	(Virgin V 2300) 1984	1
	10(E)	ONCE UPON A TIME	(Virgin V 2364) 1985	1

NB: (1) reissued on vinyl (Virgin VM 6) 1982 and at mid-price (Virgin OVED 95) 1985 and also issued on CD (Virgin VMCD 6) 1986. (2) reissued on vinyl (Virgin V 2246) 1982 and at mid-price (Virgin OVED 124) 1985 and also issued on CD (Virgin CDV 2246) 1988 and again (Virgin VIP CDVIP 157) 1996. (3) reissued on Virgin (Virgin V 2247) 1982 and at mid-price (Virgin OVED 211) 1988 and also reissued on CD (Virgin CDV 2247) 1988. (4) also issued on CD (Virgin CDV 2207) 1986. (7) reissued on vinyl (Virgin V 2248) 1982 and again at mid-price (Virgin OVED 275) 1989. (8) also issued on CD (Virgin CDV 2230) 1983. Some copies of (9) also came on white vinyl. (9) also issued on CD (Virgin CDV 2300) 1984 and again in 1992. Some copies of (10) were picture discs in gatefold sleeves. (10) also issued on CD (Virgin CDV 2364) 1985. There's also a compilation *Glittering Prize - Simple Minds 81 - 92* (Virgin SMTVD 1) 1992 and a 3-CD set of their first three albums; *Life In A Day / Real To Real (Cacophony) / Empires And Dance* (Virgin TPAK 2) 1990.

			HCP
45s:	Life In A Day/Special View (PS)	(Zoom ZUM 10) 1979	62
(up to	Chelsea Girl/Garden Of Hate (PS)	(Zoom ZUM 11) 1979	-
1986)	Changeling/Premonition (Live) (PS)	(Arista ARIST 325) 1979	-
*	I Travel/New Warm Skin (PS)	(Arista ARIST 372) 1980	-
	I Travel (Alt. Mix)/		
	Film Theme (12", PS)	(Arista ARIST 12372) 1980	-
	Celebrate/Changeling (PS)	(Arista ARIST 394) 1981	-
	Celebrate (Alt. Mix)/Changeling/		
	I Travel (12", PS)	(Arista ARIST 12394) 1981	-
	The American/League Of Nations (PS)	(Virgin VS 410) 1981	59
	The American (Alt. Mix)/		
	League Of Nations (12", PS)	(Virgin VS 410-12) 1981	-
	Love Song/The Earth That You Walk		
	Upon (Instr.) (PS)	(Virgin VS 434) 1981	47
	Love Song/The Earth That You Walk		
	Upon (12", PS)	(Virgin VS 434-12) 1981	-
	Sweat In Bullet/20th Century Promised		
	Land (PS)	(Virgin VS 451) 1981	52
+	Sweat In Bullet/20th Century Promised Land/		
	Premonition (Live)/		
	League Of Nations (Live) (PS)	(Virgin VS 451) 1981	-
	Sweat In Bullet (Alt. Mix)/20th Century Promised Land/		
	League Of Nations (Live)/In Trance As		
	Mission (Live) (12", PS)	(Virgin VS 451-12) 1981	-
	I Travel/		
	30 Frames A Second (Live) (PS)	(Arista ARIST 448) 1982	-
	I Travel (Alt. Mix)/30 Frames A Second (Live)/		
	I Travel (Live) (12", PS)	(Arista ARIST 12448) 1982	-
	Promised You A Miracle/		
	Theme For Great Cities (PS)	(Virgin VS 488) 1982	13
	Promised You A Miracle/Theme For Great Cities/Seeing		
	Out The Angel (Instr. Mix) (12", PS)	(Virgin 488-12) 1982	-
	Glittering Prize/		
	Glittering Theme (Instr.) (PS)	(Virgin VS 511) 1982	16
	Glittering Prize (Alt. Mix)/		
	Glittering Theme (Instr.) (12", PS)	(Virgin VS 511-12) 1982	-
α	Someone, Somewhere In Summertime/		
	King Is White And In The Crowd (PS)	(Virgin VS 538) 1982	36
	Someone, Somewhere In Summertime/		
	King Is White And In The Crowd/Soundtrack For		
	Every Heaven (12", PS)	(Virgin VS 538-12) 1982	-
	I Travel (Alt. Mix)/		
	Film Theme (12", PS)	(Virgin VS 578-12) 1983	-
	Waterfront/		
	Hunter And The Hunted (Live) (PS)	(Virgin VS 636) 1983	13
	Waterfront (Alt. Mix)/Hunter And		
	The Hunted (Live) (12", PS)	(Virgin VS 636-12) 1983	-
β	Speed Your Love To Me/Bass Line (PS)	(Virgin VS 649) 1984	20
	Speed Your Love To Me (Alt. Mix)/Speed Your		
	Love To Me/Bass Line (12", PS)	(Virgin VS 649-12) 1984	-
β	Up On The Catwalk/		
	A Brass Band In Africa (PS)	(Virgin VS 661) 1984	27
	Up On The Catwalk (Alt. Mix)/A Brass Band In		
	African Chimes (12", PS)	(Virgin VS 661-12) 1984	-
χ	Don't You (Forget About Me)/A Brass Band In		
	African Chimes (PS)	(Virgin VS 749) 1985	7
	Don't You (Forget About Me)/A Brass Band In		
	African Chimes (12", PS)	(Virgin VS 749-12) 1985	-
	Alive And Kicking/		
	Alive And Kicking (Instr.) (PS)	(Virgin VS 817) 1985	7
	Alive And Kicking/		
	Alive And Kicking (Instr.) (12", PS)	(Virgin VS 817-12) 1985	-
δ	Alive And Kicking/Alive And kicking (Instr.)/		
	Up On The Catwalk (Live) (12")	(Virgin VS 817-13) 1985	-

	Sanctify Yourself/Sanctify Yourself (Instr.)	(Virgin SM 1) 1986	10
ε	Sanctify Yourself/Sanctify Yourself (Instr.)/Love Song (Live)/Street Hassle (Live) (PS)	(Virgin SMP 1) 1986	-
	Sanctify Yourself (Alt. Mix)/Sanctify Yourself (Instr. Alt. Mix) (12", PS)	(Virgin SM 1-12) 1986	-
	All The Things She Said/Don't You (Forget About Me) (Live)	(Virgin VS 860) 1986	9
	All The Things She Said (Alt. Mix)/Promised You A Miracle (Alt. Mix)/Don't You (Forget About Me) (Live) (12", PS)	(Virgin VS 860-12) 1986	-
	Ghostdancing/Jungleland (Instr.)	(Virgin VS 907) 1986	13
	Ghostdancing (Alt. Mix)/Ghostdancing (Instr.)/Jingleland (Alt. Mix)/Jingleland (Instr. Mix) (CD Single)	(Virgin MIKE 907-12) 1986	-
	Ghostdancing (Alt. Mix)/Ghostdancing (Instr.)/Jingleland (Alt. Mix)/Jingleland (Instr. Mix) (12". PS)	(Virgin VS 907-12) 1986	-

NB: * This came with a free blue flexi *Kaleidoscope / Film Theme Dub*. + Doublepack. α Some copies also came in a poster sleeve and some (VSY 538) were issued as a picture disc. β Some copies (VSY 649) were issued as a picture disc. χ Some copies issued as a shaped picture disc. δ These were issued in a limited edition gold sleeve. ε Double-pack.

Simple Minds were formed in early 1978 in the Gorbals area of Glasgow, Scotland by Jim Kerr, Charlie Burchill and Duncan Barnwell following the demise of the punk outfit **Johnny and The Self Abusers** of whom they were all members. Their name was taken from a line in a David Bowie song. They made their debut in February as a trio at Glasgow's Satellite Club and then became a regular attraction at Glasgow's Mars Bar. By May they had recruited keyboardist Mike McNeill who'd played with various local bands and Derek Forbes on bass. They soon recorded a six-song demo at Glasgow's Ca Va studio which eventually found its way to Ian Cranna who was contributing to the New Musical Express at the time and he went on to manage jangly Scottish pop-rock outfit Orange Juice. Later, in November, a further demo was recorded and subsequently released via the Edinburgh independent label Zoom, which was a subsidiary of Arista. The tie in with Arista ensured that their Zoom releases were pressed in large quantities. By now Duncan Barnwell had been axed.

Simple Minds now secured the production services of John Leckie, who had worked successfully in the capacity with **Magazine**. In April 1979, they released their debut album and the title track was issued as a 45, with a non-album flip side *Special View*. The album entered the charts at No. 30 and spent five more weeks falling down the charts. The 45 also spent two weeks in the singles chart peaking at No. 62. *Life In A Day* was the only album issued by Zoom, although some **Simple Minds** later releases on Arista carried the Zoom logo on their sleeve. It was by far their most commercial album. There's a definite sixties feel on tracks like the modish *Sad Affair* and the orchestrated pop of *Chelsea Girl* (this was issued as the follow-up 45 to *Life In A Day* but didn't chart). Others like *All For You* recall early psychedelia ála Doors and Jefferson Airplane. The album was subsequently reissued twice as part of Virgin's 'VM' series in 1982 and then in their budget 'OVED' series in 1985. A year later it was available on CD.

The group spent most of the remainder of 1979 gigging extensively in Britan and Europe. They made two appearances on the 'Old Grey Whistle Test', including a session shot in New York's Hurrah club during the band's first visit to the 'States in October. They also set to work on a second and much more experimental album. The end product *Real To Real Cacophony* was released in January 1980. One reviewer originally described it as "probably the most uncommercial album ever released by Arista". Aside from the sole single it produced *Changeling*, (which failed to chart) it certainly lacked the pop appeal of *Live In A Day* but it contained in *Carnival (Shelter In A Suitcase)* and a haunting instrumental *Film Theme* some of their finest moments and an altogether denser sound. Originally issued on Arista this album was reissued twice by Virgin in 1982 and 1985 and twice on CD in 1988 and 1996. Probably on account of its lack of commercialism, it failed to chart. This led to tensions between Zoom and Arista which resulted in Zoom requesting to be removed from Arista's roster. However, under the terms of the original deal Arista held the rights to **Simple Minds** and without their main asset Zoom soon collapsed. However, Findlay who'd ran Zoom, formed Schoolhouse Management with Robert White and they handled the band's future affairs.

Empires And Dance, released September 1980, marked a complete change of direction with **Simple Minds** moving towards synthesizer work, which was beginning to dominate music at the time. The result was an atmospheric album which had its moments. Two singles were released *I Travel* and *Celebrate* but neither charted. Capturing prevalent music trends, as it did, the album did manage No. 41 during a three-week chart stay. Together with the rest of the Arista releases *Empires And Dance* was reissued on Virgin in 1982 and again at mid-price in 1988, when it was also issued on CD. One further song from the album *30 Frames A Second* was issued on 45, but only in a live form different to the album take.

Shortly before Arista passed their **Simple Minds** catalogue onto Virgin, they released a compilation album *Celebration* in February 1982. The compilation comprised two tracks from *Life In A Day* (the title cut and *Chelsea Girl*); four from *Real To Real Cacophony* (*Premonition*, *Factory*, *Calling Your Name* and *Changeling*), three from *Empires And Dance* (*I Travel*, *Celebrate* and *30 Frames A Second*) and the previously non-album rarity *Kaleidoscope*, which had only appeared on the free flexi disc that came with early copies of the original 1980 *I Travel* single. The album, which rose to No. 45 and enjoyed seven weeks in the charts, was also reissued (along with the other **Simple Minds** Arista albums) in October 1982.

Having renounced their rights to any back royalties and signed a new deal with Virgin **Simple Minds** returned to the studio with renewed energy. Their first recording for Virgin *The American* 45, released in May 1981, spent three weeks in the lower reaches of the charts climbing to No. 59. Soon after Brian McGee left to get married and was replaced by former Silk member Kenny Hyslop. A further 45 *Love Song* gave them another minor hit peaking at No. 47. The same month two albums *Sons And Fascinations* and *Sister Feelings Call* were released, initially as a limited edition double album, although they were subsequently released separately too. On cassette, the two albums were packaged together under the collective title of *Sons And Fascinations*, with the track order changed from the vinyl version. The two albums were also combined on the CD release titled *Sons And Fascination (Sister Feelings Call)*. The album became their most successful to date, spending weeks in the charts and missing the Top 10 by just one place. It also spawned a further minor hit in *Sweat In Bullet*. Again the music of this double package marked a change of direction towards semi-funky modern dance music. *Theme For Geat Cities* on the *Sister Feelings Call* album continued their tradition of fine instrumentals.

1982 proved a year of progress and consolidation for the band. In April, the strong and soulful dance tune *Promised You A Miracle* won them a host of new fans, reaching No. 13 during an eleven-week chart stay. The 12" version featured an extended mix of the 'A' side and a bonus instrumental mix of *Seeing Out The Angel*. At this point Hyslop departed to form Set The Tones and Mike Ogletree came in as a replacement. The new line-up released a further 45 *Glittering Prize* in August. This emotional, pretty ballad secured them a further hit, again spending eleven weeks in the charts and rising to No. 16. The 12" version was another extended mix, while on the flip of the 7" and 12" were different remixes of the track under the title *Glittering Theme*.

Mike Ogletree did not stop long with **Simple Minds**. By the time their next album *New Gold Dream (81-82-83-84)* was released, he'd gone off to join Fiction Factory. Former session drummer Mel Gaynor came in as his replacement. The album (despite the suggestion of the sub-title) was not a compilation, but another significant step forward. Aside from the stand-out title track, its highlights included their two earlier singles, *Promised You A*

SIMPLE MINDS - Life In A Day.

SIMPLE MINDS - I Travel.

Miracle and *Glittering Prize* as well as a future one *Someone Somewhere*. *New Gold Dream* was the album which really broke **Simple Minds** into the big time. It climbed to No. 3 and spent a staggering fifty-two weeks in the chart. The band embarked on a sell-out U.K. tour and it was also their first record to make any impression in the 'States when it climbed to No. 69 during a nineteen-week chart stay during 1983. Back here in Britain *Someone Somewhere* gave them a third hit single from the album, spending five weeks in the chart and peaking at No. 36. Besides the 7", which contained a version of *King Is White And In The Crowd* recorded for a BBC Radio David Jensen show on the flip, there was also a 7" picture disc and a 7" black vinyl version with a fold-out poster sleeve. The 12" version contained an extra track *Every Heaven*.

Simple Minds returned to the charts in November 1983 when *Waterfront* reached No. 13 during a ten week stay. This was a taster for the next album *Sparkle In The Rain*. It had a live version of *The Hunter And The Hunted*, originally on their previous album, on the flipside.

A second taster from their new album *Speed Your Love To Me* followed in January 1984 and it is generally considered to be one of their best songs. In adition to the usual 7" and 12" format there was 7" picture disc release. The flip side *Bass Line* didn't appear on the forthcoming album and the 12" version also included a longer version of the 'A' side. *Speed Your Love To Me* made No. 20 and spent four weeks in the charts.

The following month *Sparkle In The Rain* (their next album made with producer Steve Lillywhite) was released. It was another fine album with intricate rock rhythms and Kerr's appealing vocals. The highlights included their two previous singles *Waterfront* and *Speed Your Love To Me* and a later one *Up On The Catwalk* (a No. 27), *Book Of Brilliant Things* and a cover of Lou Reed's *Street Hassle*. The album emphatically established the band as one of Britain's leading acts when it reached No. 1. It also spent a remarkable fifty-seven weeks in the charts.

In March 1984, the band set off on a U.K. tour but it had to be cancelled when Jim Kerr was taken ill at the end of the opening night in Birmingham on 13th March. Still, he soon recovered and married **Pretenders**' lead vocalist Chrissie Hynde on 5th May. Shortly after **Simple Minds** played eight consecutive nights at Hammersmith Odeon.

Nearly a year elapsed until their next record. This was *Don't You Forget About Me*, which got to No. 7 during an eleven-week chart residency, following its April 1985 release here in Britain. More important, the song which was taken from the soundtrack album of the film *The Breakfast Club* (A&M AMA 5045) 1985, was the one that broke the band in the 'States. This was largely due to the extra publicity they received from the link to the film. Ironically this No. 1 U.S. single which spent twenty-two weeks in the charts over there wasn't written by the band. In fact the film-makers offered it to Billy Idol and Bryan Ferry, who both turned it down.

Their next 45 *Alive And Kicking* included an instrumental version of the song on the flipside. The 12" version also added a live version of *Up On The Catwalk* and was originally available in a collectable gold cover. *Alive And Kicking* again climbed to No. 7 and featured on their October 1985 album *Once Upon A Time*. This repeated the achievement of its predecessor when it topped the U.K. album charts in which it spent a staggering eighty-three weeks in all! By the time of its release they'd appeared in Live Aid at Philadelphia and their song *Ghostdancing* had been credited to Amnesty International for whom they toured. Later in the year Jim and Chrissie had given birth to a baby. The album, which was produced by Jimmy Iovine and Bob Clearmountain, suffered from being made for American radio. Of course that didn't stop it producing more hit singles in the form of *Sanctify Yourself* (No. 10), *All The Things She Said* (No. 9) and *Ghostdancing* (No. 13).

1986 was a momentus year for **Simple Minds** as a live act. On 22nd June they topped the bill at Milton Keynes Bowl Pop Festival and they also embarked on a World Tour. As we leave them in 1986 they had become stadium stars but it didn't end there. They went on to build on this success and record successfully for many years to come.

Aside from *Don't You Forget About Me* on *The Breakfast Club* their other compilation appearances have included *Chelsea Girl* on *The Old Grey Whistle Test* (BBC BELP 017); *Love Song* on *Methods Of Dance, Vol. One* (Virgin OVED 5) and *Every Heaven* (previously only available on the 12" version of *Someone Somewhere In Summertime*) on *Methods Of Dance, Vol. Two* (Virgin OVED 7). In addition many of their hits have turned up on chart compilations. *Life In A Day* later resurfaced on *A History Of Punk, Vol. 2* (Virgin CDOVD 487) 1997.

Sinister

Personnel:			
	STEVE LACE	keyb'ds	A
	STEVE LEONARD	drms	A
	CARL MORRIS	bs, vcls	A
	DAVE MORRIS	gtr, vcls	A
	MIKE SMITH	lead vcls	A

Sinister's sole vinyl epitaph seems to have been *Alice In Wonderland* on the compilation *499 2139* (Rocket DIAL 1) 1979, which is a pretty decent popish effort.

Siouxsie and The Banshees

Personnel:	MARCO PIRRONI	gtr	A
(up to	STEVE SEVERIN		
1986)	(STEVEN BAILEY)	bs, keyb'ds, synth	ABCDEF
	SIOUXSIE SIOUX		
	(SUSAN DALLION)	vcls	ABCDEF
	SID VICIOUS	drms	A
	P. FENTON	gtr	B
	KENNY MORRIS	drms	BC
	JOHN McKAY	gtr	C
	BUDGIE (PETER CLARK)	drms	DEF
	JOHN McGEOGH	gtr	D
	JOHN CARRUTHERS	gtr	D F
	ROBERT SMITH	gtr	E

				HCP
ALBUMS:	1(C)	THE SCREAM	(Polydor POLD 5009)	1978 12
(up to	2(C)	JOIN HANDS	(Polydor POLD 5024)	1979 13
1986)	3(D)	KALEIDOSCOPE	(Polydor 2442 177)	1980 5
	4(D)	JUJU	(Polydor POLS 1034)	1981 7
	5(-)	ONCE UPON A TIME - THE SINGLES		
			(Polydor POLS 1056)	1981 21
	6(D)	A KISS IN THE DREAMHOUSE		
			(Polydor POLP 5064)	1982 11
	7(E)	NOCTURNE (dbl)	(Wonderland SHAH 1)	1983 29
	8(E)	HYAENA	(Wonderland SHEHP 1)	1984 15
	9(F)	TINDERBOX	(Wonderland SHEHP 3)	1986 13

NB: (1) issued on CD (Wonderland 839 008 2) 1989 and reissued at mid-price in 1995. (2) issued on CD (Wonderland 839 004 2) 1989 and reissued at mid-price in 1995. (3) issued on CD (Wonderland 839 006 2) 1989 and reissued at mid-price in 1995. (4) issued on CD (Poydor 839005-2) 1989 and reissued at mid-price in 1995. (5) issued on CD (Polydor 831 542-2) 1989. (6) issued on CD (Polydor 839 007-2) 1989 and reissued at mid-price in 1995. (7) issued on CD (Polydor 839 009-2) and reissued at mid-price in 1995. (8) issued on CD (Wonderland 821 510-2) 1984 and reissued at mid-price in 1995. (9) issued on CD (Wonderland 829 145-2) 1986 with five extra cuts:- *Cities In Dust* (Extended Eruption Mix)/*An Execution / Quarterdrawing Of The Dog / Lullaby / Umbrella*) and reissued at mid-price in 1995. There's also a limited edition box pack of their singles *Twice Upon A Time/The Singles* (Wonderland/Polydor 517 160-2) 1992.

SIOUXSIE AND THE BANSHEES - Hong Kong Garden.

EPs:
                                                                HCP
1(F) THE THORN (12" PS) (Overground/Voices/
      Placebo Effect/Red Over White)
                            (Wonderland SHEEP 8) 1984 47
2(C) PEEL SESSION 5.12.77 (12" PS) (Love In A Void/
      Mirage/Metal Postcard/Suburban Relapse)
                            (Strange Fruit SFPS 012) 1987 -
3(C) PEEL SESSIONS Feb 78 (12", PS)
                            (Strange Fruit SFPS 066) 1989 -

NB: (2) was also available as a cassette EP four months later in June 1987 (Strange Fruit SFPSC 012) 1987.

                                                                HCP
45s: * Hong Kong Garden/Voices (PS)   (Polydor 2059 052) 1978 7
(up to   The Staircase (Mystery)/
1986)   20th Century Boy (PS)   (Polydor POSP 9) 1979   24
            Playground Twist/Pull To Bits (PS) (Polydor POSP 59) 1979 28
         x Mittageisen (Metal Postcard)/
            Love In A Void (PS)   (Polydor 2059 151) 1979 47
            Happy House/
            Drop Dead - Celebration (PS)   (Polydor POSP 117) 1980 17
            Christine/Eve White, Eve Black (PS) (Polydor 2059 249) 1980 24
            Israel/Red Over White (PS)   (Polydor POSP 205) 1980 41
            Israel (Extended)/
            Red Over White (Extended) (12") (Polydor POSPX 205) 1980 -
            Spellbound/Follow The Sun (PS) (Polydor POSP 273) 1981 22
            Spellbound/Follow The Sun/
            Slap Dash Snap (12" PS)   (Polydor POSPX 273) 1981 -
            Arabian Knights/
            Supernatural Thing (PS)   (Polydor POSP 309) 1981 32
            Arabian Knights/Supernatural Thing/
            Congo Conga (12" PS)   (Polydor POSPX 309) 1981 -
         o Fireworks/Coal Mind (PS)   (Polydor POSP 450) 1982 22
            Fireworks/Coal Mind/
            We Fall (12" PS)   (Polydor POSPX 450) 1982 -
            Slowdive/Cannibal Roses (PS)   (Polydor POSP 510) 1982 41
            Slowdive/Cannibal Roses/
            Obsession II (12" PS)   (Polydor POSPX 510) 1982 -
            Melt/Il Est Ne Le Divin Enfant (PS) (Polydor POSP 539) 1982 49
            Melt/Il Est Ne Le Divin Enfant/
            A Sleeping Rain (12" PS)   (Polydor POSPX 539) 1982 -
         α Dear Prudence/Tattoo (PS)   (Wonderland SHE 4) 1983   3
            Dear Prudence/Tattoo/There's A Planet In
            My Kitchen (12" PS)   (Wonderland SHEX 4) 1983 -
            Swimming Horses/Let Go (PS)   (Wonderland SHE 6) 1984 28
         δ Swimming Horses/Let Go/
            The Humming Wires (12", PS)   (Wonderland SHEX 6) 1984 -
            Dazzle/I Promise (PS)   (Wonderland SHE 7) 1984 33
            Dazzle/I Promise/Throw Them To
            The Lions (12", PS)   (Wonderland SHEX 7) 1984 -
            Overground/Placebo Effect (PS) (Wonderland SHE 8) 1985 -
         β Cities In Dust/An Execution (PS) (Wonderland SHE 9) 1985 21
            Cities In Dust (Extended Eruption Mix)/An Execution/
            Quarterdrawing Of The Dog (12" PS)
                                            (Wonderland SHEX 9) 1985 -
         χ Candyman/Lullaby (PS)   (Wonderland SHE 10) 1986 34
            Candyman/Lullaby/
            Umbrella (12" PS)   (Wonderland SHEX 10) 1986 -

NB: * The first 10,000 copies came in a gatefold sleeve. x This was a double 'A' side release. o Some copies came in a gatefold picture sleeve (POSPG 450). α A limited edition of 30,000 came in a fold-out PS. β Some copies came in a limited edition poster sleeve. χ A limited edition double-pack of 2,000 came in a gatefold picture sleeve and a free second one-sided 7" *Umbrella*. δ The picture sleeve came with a poster.

The roots of **Siouxsie and The Banshees** go back to late 1975, when Susan Dallion met Steve Bailey at a **Sex Pistols** gig. Thereafter they quickly entered what became known as the Bromley Contingent, a small rather elite group of fans who followed **The Sex Pistols** around the London Club circuit in 1976. With their highly experimental dress styles the Bromley contingent soon became a very important influence on bourgeoning punk fashion.

Siouxsie (as Susan was now calling herself) went a step further when, on 20th September 1976, at the opening night of the 100 Club Punk Festival she and a hastily assembled group of friends stepped up onto stage for an impromptu performance. The friends concerned were Steve Severin (bs), Marco Pirroni (gtr) and John Beverly (**Sid Vicious**) (drms). Their original intention was to remain on stage until they were thrown off. Their name **Siouxsie and The Banshees** was inspired by a Vincent Price horror film 'Cry Of The Banshee', which had recently appeared on TV. After rehearsing for about three hours, they launched into a medley which incorporated elements of *The Lord's Prayer*, *Knocking On Heaven's Door* and *Twist And Shout*. They kept this medley going for 20 minutes and then abruptly stopped, due to a misunderstanding between Severin and Pirroni. After the festival this line-up disintegrated. **Sid Vicious** joined Flowers Of Romance and then, of course, joined the seminal **Sex Pistols**. Pirroni formed **The Models** and had a brief stint with **Rema Rema**. He finished up as a key man in **Adam and The Ants**.

Siouxsie and Severin were left to their own devices and spent the following six months trying out various musicians with the aim of establishing a permanent rehearsing and performing band. By February 1977, the embryonic band had stabilised to consist of **Siouxsie**, Severin, Peter Fenton (gtr) and Kenny Morris (drms). They made their live debut at Croydon's Red Deer the same month supporting **The Heartbreakers**. They performed six of their own songs and a cover of Marc Bolan's *20th Century Boy*.

On 12th March 1977, Track Records paid for them to record a session. It comprised *Captain Scarlet*, *Scrapheap*, *Psychic* and *Bad Shape*, along with early versions of *Love In A Void* and *The Lord's Prayer* merged into one song. This session subsequently turned up on the *Track Rehearsals* bootleg EP, which didn't secure them a recording contract.

It has been rumoured that they recorded a demo for EMI in June, but these rumours seem unfounded. Indeed, record companies were wary about **Siouxsie**'s penchant for swastikas, which saw the band labelled as fascists.

In July 1977, Fenton left and a former fan John McKay replaced him on guitar. This modified line-up first performed at an Andrew Logan/Derek Jarman party at Shad Thames, Butler's Wharf, London. Their first public performance was at the recently opened Vortex on 11th July.

SIOUXSIE AND THE BANSHEES - The Staircase (Mystery).

SIOUXSIE AND THE BANSHEES - Playground Twist.

Later, in November 1977, the band was filmed for Granada's "So It Goes" broadcast performing *Make Up To Break Up*. They also figured in Don Lett's "The Punk Rock Movie" performing *Bad Shape* and *Carcass* during their tour supporting The Heartbreakers in July, as well as backstage scenes at the Roxy in April. They also recorded a version of T. Rex's *20th Century Boy* and *Captain Scarlett* for inclusion on *The Roxy, London WC 1* album in 1977, but then vetoed their inclusion - presumably because they weren't enamoured with the results!

In November 1977, they recorded their first Peel session. Comprising *Love In A Void*, *Mirage*, *Metal Postcard* and *Suburban Relapse*, it was broadcast on 5th December 1977. They toyed with the idea of putting this session out on a self-distributed EP, but the idea was eventually thwarted by BBC bureaucracy. The session eventually made its way onto vinyl on a Strange Fruit EP in 1987.

A second session was broadcast on 23rd February 1978. The four numbers performed were *Hong Kong Garden*, *Overground*, *Carcass* and *Helter Skelter*. This session also eventually made it onto vinyl on a second Strange Fruit EP in 1988.

After being rejected by a number of labels, including EMI, Decca, Chrysalis and Anchor, **Siouxsie and The Banshees** returned from a self-financed sixteen-date U.K. tour, to sign a favourable deal with Polydor in June 1978.

In August 1978, they made their official vinyl debut with the stunning, oriental sounding *Hong Kong Garden*. The 10,000 initial copies appeared in a gatefold sleeve, but with a successful two TV appearances on 'Revolver' (on which the song was premiered) and 'Top of The Pops', it stormed the charts. The original edition rapidly sold out and the song - one of *the* classics of the punk movement climbed to No. 7 during a ten week chart stay - a very high position for a punk single.

The Scream, their debut album, appeared in October 1978. It was produced by Steve Lillywhite and the band. Neither side of their first 45 featured on this album. The music was brooding, abrasive and grim. **Souxsie**'s icy wailing accompanied by a brutal instrumental backing. Aside from their own unique interpretation of Lennon and McCartney's *Helter Skelter*, their songs were all originals. With its sparse, unnerving introduction, its frenetic delivery and abrupt ending *Helter Skelter* is arguably the album's highlight, the sparse instrumentation of opening cut *Pure* is interesting and leads into *Jigsaw Feeling*, which perfectly showcases **Siouxsie**'s wailing vocals and the band's stark punk thrash.

"Send me forwards - say my feelings
But all the signals - send me reeling
Jigsaw feeling"
(from *Jigsaw Feeling*)

A similar formula was successfully repeated on *Overground* and *Carcass*, *Mirage* is more upbeat in the style of *Hong Kong Garden*.

"My limbs are like palm trees
Swaying in no breeze
My body's an oasis
To drink from as you please
I'm not seeing what I'm meant to believe in
Your non excuse for human being."
(from *Mirage*)

The introduction to *Metal Postcard* captures McKay's guitar work at its most abrasive and **Siouxsie**'s vocals at their most dexterous. *Nicotine Stain* addresses the issue of nicotine addiction:-

"It's just a habit
When I reach to the packet
For my last cigarrette
Until the day breaks
And then my hand shakes
But it's just driving me insane
When the smoke gets in my brain
I can't resist it"

and later...

"I'm so congested
Cos north, south, east and west
Catarrh rests on my chest
Congealed and twisted
Cough up and shift it
But I can feel my lungs collapse
Sinking deep into my lap
I'm so useless"
(from *Nicotine Stain*)

Suburban Relapse deals with some of the frustrations and futility of life in suburbia.

"I'm sorry that I hit you
But my string snapped
I'm sorry I disturbed your cot-nap
But whilst finishing a chore
I asked myself "what for"
Then something snapped
I had a relapse...
A suburban relapse."
(from *Suburban Relapse*)

Concluding with the equally excellent *Switch*, *The Scream* was one of punk's Top 10 albums by one of punk's finest bands. They'd equal and surpasse it with some of their subsequent singles but they never attained this standard on album again. It sold well, too, climbing to No. 12 during an eleven week chart stay.

In March 1979, a follow-up 45 *The Staircase (Mystery)* was released. With its swirling guitar topped by **Siouxsie**'s strident vocals it typified the Banshees' sound. On the flip was a frenetic version of Marc Bolan's *20th Century Boy*. The chart placing, No. 24 in an eight week stay, was disappointing though.

On 16th April 1979 they recorded a third Peel session. It featured four cuts from the forthcoming album *Join Hands* - *Placebo Effect*, *Playground Twist*, *Regal Zone* and *Poppies*.

In July 1979, *Playground Twist* was released as a taster for the forthcoming *Join Hands* album. Sales were again disappointing - the 45 barely made it into the Top 30 and spent only six weeks in the charts.

Join Hands, their second album, followed in August. It was produced by Mike Stavrou. Early copies of the album included a sticker stating that it 'contains their hit single *Playgound Twist*'. The album is perhaps most notable for including their version of *The Lord's Prayer*. The stand out cuts on what some could find a depressive album are *Playground Twist*, *Premature Burial*, which has a great choppy guitar intro, and *Mother* with its music box style accompaniment is unusual.

"This catacomb compels me
Corroding and inert
It weighs and tries to pull me
Must I resist or re-assert?

The unchanged and the unchangeable
Doing the zombierama
Singing oh come and be like me
We're all sisters and brothers

SIOUXSIE AND THE BANSHEES - Once Upon A Time.

Ejected to this state of being
Don't bury me with this
I'm in a state of catalepsy
Can I really exist?
(from *Premature Burial*)

The album climbed to No. 13, just one place lower than *The Scream*, but only spent five weeks in the charts, as against *The Scream*'s eleven. It's fair to say that although *Join Hands* included some strong material it wasn't in any way a progression on *The Scream*.

A huge U.K. tour to promote the album sold out, but halfway through it Morris and McKay abruptly left. The evening's concert at the Aberdeen Capitol, went ahead with **The Cure** (who'd been the support band) playing two sets. **Siouxsie** and Severin joined them on stage for a 10 minute rendition of *The Lord's Prayer* at the end and the audience had their money refunded. After unsuccessfully trying to persuade ex-**Sex Pistols** Paul Cook and Steve Jones to join the band, the tour continued after a nine day break with **The Cure**'s Robert Smith standing in on guitar and ex-**Slits** drummer Peter 'Budgie' Clark added on drums, following Cook's recommendation.

In mid-September, doubtless fuelled by greed, Polydor arranged for the band's German single (*Mittageisen*), a German language version of *Metal Postcard* to be available on import. It never got a full U.K. release but climbed to No. 47 during a three week stay on import sales alone.

By January 1980, Smith had decided not to join **Siouxsie and The Banshees** on a full-time basis. Marco Pirroni was considered for the guitar slot but it eventually went to **Magazine**'s John McGeoch. The modified line-up's first vinyl offering was *Happy House*, released the following month. More melodic than their previous efforts, this propelled them back into the Top 20 (for the first time since *Hong Kong Garden*). It climbed to No. 17, spending eight weeks in all in the charts.

In May 1980, came the haunting, flower-powery *Christine*. This continued their recent more melodic vein and was another of their finest moments. It again enjoyed an eight week chart stay, but didn't advance beyond No. 24. Original quantities stated incorrectly that the 'B' side, *Eve White, Eve Black* was produced by the group and Nigel Gray. Later copies corrected this by saying that it was a band production. The 'A' side was about Christine Sizemal, an American woman diagnosed as having 22 personalities.

Kaleidoscope, released in August 1980, marked the end of their original 'wall of noise' sound with the inclusion of softer and more melodic numbers like *Happy House* and *Christine*. It got to No. 5 and yet only spent six weeks in the charts. Although it did contain some fine songs, the album didn't hang together well overall.

In December a further 45 *Israel* was released. Co-written by the band, neither the 'A' or 'B' side appeared on an album (apart from compilations). It was also the first of their singles to be issued in 12" format. The 12" version also included a bonus track. It's now one of their harder 45s to find. It was their least successful 45 to date, only reaching No. 41 in an eight week chart residency. Some have speculated that, given the band's early 'fascist' label some radio programmers may have been wary of any political messages the song may have been construed as delivering.

On 18th February 1981, the band recorded a fourth Peel session. This featured *Halloween, Voodoo Dolly, But Not Them* and *Into The Light*. Aside from *But Not Them* all these tracks later appeared on their forthcoming *Juju* album.

A new single *Spellbound* followed in May 1981. This and the follow-up *Arabian Knights* were both quite complex. They benefited from the technical prowess of recent recruits 'Budgie' and McGeoh and reached No. 22 and 32 respectively during eight and seven week chart-stays. Both were available in 7" and 12" formats, with the 12" versions each containing one additional track.

Both *Spellbound* and *Arabian Knights* were among the highlights of their fourth album *Juju*, released in June 1981. Originally conceived as a double-set, it was heralded by many as their strongest album to date. It spent seventeen weeks in the charts peaking at No. 7. As part of the album's promotion **Siouxsie and The Banshees** did a session for the Richard Skinner show, which included a reworking of *Red Over White, Arabian Knights, Supernatural Things* and an alternate version of *Head Cut*, one of the high points of the album.

In July 1981, the band embarked on a thirty-date U.K. tour - their biggest yet. It would prove to be their last with subsequent live appearances being very much one-offs.

In October, **Siouxsie and The Banshees** toured the U.S. extensively. An U.S.-only EP *Arabian Knights* (the U.K. 12" plus one extra cut) was made available. Meanwhile, in the U.K., a five-cut EP *Wild Things* was released using a pseudonym **The Creatures**. It had been recorded as part of the *Juju* sessions by **Siouxsie** and Budgie alone. In November, the 'A' side *Mad Eyed Screamer*, a drum solo with words, became an unlikely Top 30 hit. The original 5,000 copies were released as two separate discs in a gatefold sleeve, but later repressings reverted to the two records in one sleeve format.

They rounded off 1981 by releasing *One Upon A Time - The Singles*. This included all their 'A' sides to date (including *Staircase Mystery* and *Israel*, which weren't included on any previous albums) plus *Mirage*, a track from *The Scream*, which was nearly selected as a follow-up 45 to *Hong Kong Garden*. Although, somehat surprisingly their singles album only climbed to No. 21 in the charts it did spend six months in them. Original copies came with sleeve notes by Paul Morley and an inner lyric sleeve and initial copies contained a colour print of **Siouxsie**. It was also issued as a video, with *Red Light* substituted for *Mirage* and *Love In A Void*.

A further single *Fireworks*, released in May 1982, had originally been intended for inclusion on the compilation, but delays in securing a producer prevented this. Again available in 7" and 12" formats, the original picture sleeve is now very collectable. *Fireworks* got to No. 22 during a brief six week chart stay. During the summer, the band headlined at the Elephant Fayre festival in Cornwall.

Their next single *Slowdive* followed in August 1982. This spent only four weeks in the charts, peaking at No. 41. It previewed their next album *A*

SIOUXSIE AND THE BANSHEES - Christine.

Kiss In The Dream House, released in September. The title was apparently inspired by a TV programme about a Hollywood dream house, where in the 1930s one could go and spend a night with a moviestar look-a-like of your choice. This was quite an esoteric album with tracks like *Obsession* (an interesting continuation of this *Obsession II* was added to the 12" version of *Slowdive*), the medieval recorder flavour of *Green Fingers* and *Melt*, a spaghetti Western ballad, which was selected as their next 45. *A Kiss In The Dreamhouse* sold well, climbing to No. 11 in an eleven week chart stay. By contrast, *Melt* met a similar fate to *Slowdive*. Indeed, the best position it could manage during its five week chart stay was No. 49.

On the eve of a new U.K. tour in December 1982 John McGeoch was diagnosed as suffering from depression. Robert Smith of **The Cure** again stood in and McGeoch was edged out.

For most of 1983 the band kept a low profile. **Siouxsie** and Budgie spent the New Year in Hawaii recording **The Creatures**' debut album *The Feast*. Smith and Severin linked with Jeanette Landray (of Zoo) to become **The Glove** and record an album *Blue Sunshine*. Severin also helped out on Marc Almond's Mambas album *Torment And Toreadors*.

In March, though, **Siouxsie and The Banshees** embarked on an extensive tour of Australia, New Zealand and Japan. They also formed their own Wonderland label, which was distributed through Polydor. After this members returned to their own projects like **The Creatures** and **The Glove**. In September, they re-united to play isolated gigs, including one at the Royal Albert Hall.

Their recording lay off did them good, because when they returned to the studio the first vinyl output was a superb cover of *Dear Prudence* (from The Beatles' *White Album*), which was lushly arranged with phased guitars and vocals. It actually added something to the original and (despite some critical derision in the music press) got the chart success it deserved. It became their biggest hit single, peaking at No. 3 during its eight week stay. The first 30,000 copies came in a green triple fold-out sleeve.

In December 1983, they released *Nocturne*, a double live set of their Royal Albert Hall gigs with no overdubs. It contained an interesting selection of material from previous albums, but the idea of a new wave band releasing a double live album was derided in many parts of the music press. Still the album climbed to No. 29 and enjoyed ten weeks in the charts.

In April 1984, they enjoyed a No. 28 hit with the moody *Swimming Horses* and then *Dazzle*, released in June (to coincide with their next album *Hyaena*) reached No. 33. It was the opening and one of the more interesting tracks on *Hyaena* (which also included *Swimming Horses*). Another cut *Belladonna* also appeared on the German *Debut* album/magazine. As *Hyaena* was released Robert Smith was forced to leave the band (being in two bands had ground down his health). His replacement was ex-**Clock DVA** guitarist John 'Valentine' Carruthers. The new line-up completed U.S. and U.K. tours.

Their next recording project was *The Thorn* (EP) released in 12" format-only in October 1984. For this they re-recorded four of their old songs - *Red Over White*, *Placebo Effect*, *Overground* and *Voices* - with an orchestra! None of the cuts unnerving qualities were lost. Two tracks *Voices* and *Overground* were coupled as a 7" promo (SHEDJ 8).

In October 1985, they embarked on a thirty-date U.K. tour but there was no new album because of problems finding the right producer (Bob Ezrin and Hugh Jones were both dropped). A 45 *Cities In Dust* was released and climbed to No. 21 during a six week chart stay. The band received a further set back when **Siouxsie** dislocated a kneecap at the Hammersmith Odeon. Later, Capitol Radio broadcast four songs - *Arabian Knights*, *Happy House*, *Cities In Dust* and *Candyman* from this concert. During the tour the band previewed material that eventually appeared on their next album *Tinderbox*.

Tinderbox was eventually released in April 1986. It was arguably their most consistent album since *The Scream*. **Siouxsie**'s voice sounded great on tracks like *The Sweetest Chill* and *Cannons* and in *Candyman* it spawned one of their finest singles for years, with its vigorous on-beat drum. In addition to the usual 7" and 12" formats, *Candyman* was also released as a double-pack featuring *Umbrella* on a one-sided 7". This format was a limited edition of 2,000. *Candyman* didn't get the chart success it merited - peaking at No. 34 during a five week residency. *Tinderbox* fared better - No. 13 during a six week stay. The album also rekindled interest in the band - they appeared twice on 'The Tube'. First for an interview and showing of the *Candyman* video, then later on the show's 100th edition

SIOUXSIE AND THE BANSHEES - Dear Prudence.

performing *Candyman* and *92 Degrees* (also from the album). They also recorded a new Peel session.

In 1996, **Siouxsie** and Budgie dissolved The Banshees and resumed working as **The Creatures**. An album was released in 1998 and they embarked on a tour later that year.

Twice Upon A Time/The Singles is a limited edition CD box pack of singles which is deceptive. It contains only one volume of hits. The double-pack-sized box is fleshed out by a CD-shaped piece of polystyrene foam which you're meant to throw away and put your own *Once Upon A Time* CD inside. This volume maintains the excellence of their first *Once Upon A Time* hits volume throughout with songs like *Cities In Dust*, their excellent cover of The Beatles' *Dear Prudence*, *Melt!*, *Peek-A-Boo*, *The Killing Jar* and *Kiss Them For Me*. It only serves as a reminder of what a quality band they were.

Inevitably the band have appeared on a number of compilations, most notably *Christine* on *The Best Punk Album In The World.... Ever, Vol. 1* (2-CD) (Virgin VTDCD 42) 1995 and *Hong Kong Garden* on *Vol. 2* (2-CD) (Virgin VTDCD 79) 1996 of the same series. In 1999, *(The Staircase) Mystery* got further exposure on the lavish 5-CD box set, *1-2-3-4 - A History Of Punk And New Wave 1976 - 1979* (MCA/Universal MCD 60066).

Siouxsie and The Banshees subsequent exploits fall outside the remit of this book. Suffice it to say that they continued to enjoy considerable success in the second half of the eighties and well into the nineties. Considering their amateurish beginnings --their inital intention had been to annoy the crowd sufficiently at their 1976 debut to get thrown off stage - they not only survived the punk era that had created them, but their increasing musical sophistication and experimentation put them on a pedestal compared to almost all other surviving punk bands. They truly were one of punk's finest.

The Sisterhood

Personnel:	ANDREW ELDRITCH	vcls	A
	LUCAS FOX	drms	A
	PATRICIA MORRISON	bs, vcls	A
	JAMES RAY	gtr	A
	ALAN VEGA	synth	A

ALBUM: 1(A) GIFT (Merciful Release SIS 020) 1986
NB: (1) also issued on CD (Merciful Release SIS 020CD) 1994. (1) later reissued on vinyl (Merciful Release 11316841) and CD (Merciful Release 11316842).

45: Giving Ground (Remix)/Giving
Ground (Album Version) (PS) (Merciful Release SIS 010) 1986

A short-lived act formed by **Sisters Of Mercy** frontman Andrew Eldritch after the band disbanded in mid-1985 and whilst the former members were squabbling about the future rights to the name. The band had pedigree. Patricia Morrison, who later worked with Eldritch in a reformed **Sisters Of Mercy**, had been in Far Bible and Gun Club, whilst Alan Vega had fronted the New York-based experimental electronic duo Suicide.

339

The Sisters Of Mercy

Personnel:	ANDREW ELDRITCH	vcls	ABC
	GARRY MARX	gtr	ABC
	(DOKTOR AVALANCHE)	(drum machine)	ABC
	CRAIG ADAMS	bs	BC
	BEN GUNN	gtr	B
	WAYNE HUSSEY	gtr	C

HCP

ALBUM:	1(C)	FIRST AND LAST AND ALWAYS		
(up to 1986)			(Merciful Release MR 337L) 1985	14

NB: (1) also issued on CD (Merciful Release 240 616 2) 1988 and again re-mastered (Merciful Release 9031773792) 1992.

EP:	1(B)	THE REPTILE HOUSE (Kiss The Carpet/Lights/	
(up to 1986)		Valentine/Burn/ Fix) (12", PS)	(Merciful Release MR 023) 1983

HCP

45s:	*	The Damage Done/Watch/		
(up to 1986)		Home Of The Hitmen (PS)	(Merciful Release MR 007) 1980	-
		Body Electric/Adrenochrome (PS)	(CNT CNT 002) 1982	-
	+	Alice/Floorshow (PS)	(Merciful Release MR 015) 1982	-
		Anaconda/Phantom (PS)	(Merciful Release MR 019) 1983	-
		Alice/Floorshow/1969/ Phantom (12", PS)	(Meciful Release MR 021) 1983	-
		Temple Of Love/ Heartland (PS)	(Merciful Release MR 027) 1983	-
		Temple Of Love (Extended)/Heartland/ Gimme Shelter (12", PS)	(Merciful Release MRX 027) 1983	-
		Body And Soul/Train (PS)	(Merciful Release MR 029) 1984	46
		Body And Soul/Body Electric/Train/ Afterhours (12", PS)	(Merciful Release MR 029T) 1984	-
	x	Alice/Temple Of Love/Reptile House/ Body And Soul	(Merciful Release WEA) 1984	-
	α	Walk Away/ Poison Door (PS)	(Merciful Release MR 033) 1984	45
	β	Walk Away/Poison Door/ On The Wire (12", PS)	(Merciful Release MR 033T) 1984	-
		No Time To Cry/ Blood Money (PS)	(Merciful Release MR 035) 1985	63
		No Time To Cry/Blood Money/ Bury Me Deep (12", PS)	(Merciful Release MR 035T) 1985	-

NB: * Only 1,000 copies were pressed. This disc has been counterfeited, but they don't have the MR7 matrix number. + Issued in a white background picture sleeve. x This was a promo only 4 x 12" box set. α Some copies came with a flexidisc *Long Train* (Sam 218). β Came with a flexidisc *Long Train*.

Sister Of Mercy were formed in Leeds in 1980 by Andrew Eldritch and Garry Marx. In fact Eldritch's name by birth was Andrew Taylot and he was born in May 1959 in East Anglia, England. They formed their own Merciful record label and with the addition of a drum machine which they called Doktor Avalanche proceeded to release *The Damage Done*. Only 1,000 copies were pressed. It is an excellent example of atmospheric goth-punk and is consequently very sought-after. Should you be fortunate enough to locate a copy it could set you back in excess of £100. Beware, too, of counterfeits! They toured in support of Aussie avant-garde gothic/new wave combo Birthday Party and **The Psychedelic Furs** and then appeared at the Leeds Futurama Festival in the early eighties. Prior to their next 45 ex-Expelaires bassist Craig Adams and guitarist Ben Gunn were added to the line-up.

By the time of their 1983 release *Temple Of Love* they had perfected a sort of danceable doom rock sound and former Dead Or Alive and **Hambi and The Dance** man Wayne Hussey had replaced Ben Gunn. Then, in 1984, their label got national distribution from WEA and *Body And Soul* spent three weeks in the lower reaches of the charts peaking at No. 46. This feat was slightly improved upon by their next 45 *Walk Away*, which also enjoyed a three week chart residency but went one place better to No. 45.

Their album *First And Last And Always* included just two of their earlier singles, although they had recorded enough material to fill a whole album in itself prior to its release. Aside from *Walk Away*, the other 45 cut was its successor 45 *No Time To Cry*, which managed two weeks in the charts and a best position of No. 63. Produced by Dave Allen, the album blended power-pop style guitar and dancier rhythms with Eldritch's gloomy vocals to produce one of the defining moments of post-punk doom and gloom.

Sisters Of Mercy disbanded in mid-1985. Hussey and Adams went on to form The Mission and Gary Marx helped to form Ghost Dance. Whilst squabbles took place about the future use of the band's name Eldritch put together a new outfit **The Sisterhood** and moved to Berlin. This included Patricia Morrison who worked again with Eldritch as **Sisters Of Mercy** after they acquired rights to the name from 1987 onwards. They achieved much commercial success with a format which incorporated glam to their earlier disco-goth sound... but that's another story.

Six Minute War

Personnel:	CHAZ	gtr, vcls	A
	DAVE	drms	A
	DOG	bs, vcls	A
	EGG	vcls, bs	A

EPs:	1(A)	SIX MINUTE WAR (Big Week/Giles Hall/Camera/ Strontium 90/Strike/Progress/Man From Uncle/ Labelled/He's Dead/Marker Pens/ MRS P)	(Private Pressing) 198?
	2( )	SIX MINUTE WAR - SLIGHTLY LONGER SONGS (The Weathermen/Rod Of Iron/Kung Fu Killers/ Last Prop)	(Private Pressing) 198?
	3( )	SIX MINUTE WAR - MORE SHORT SONGS (Nurses/ Youth Culture/Protect & Survive/So Sad/ Sell Out)	(Private Pressing) 198?

An anarcho-punk band who usually hung around the Hackney area of London. They put out their own records on a not-for-profit basis retailing them at either 50p or 75p. The first EP is punkish. The music on the second one is more experimental.

Skeletal Family

Personnel:	STEVE CRANE	drms	A
	KARL HEINZ	synth	ABCDE
	ANNE-MARIE HURST	lead vcls	ABCD
	STAN GREENWOOD	gtr	ABCDE
	TROTWOOD		
	(ROGER NOWELL)	bs	ABCDE
	HOWARD DANIELS	drms	B
	MARTIN HENDERSON	drms	CD
	GRAHAM PLEETH	synth	D
	KATRINA	vcls	E
	KEVIN PHILLIPS	drms	E

ALBUMS:	1(C)	BURNING OIL	(Red Rhino REDLP 44) 1984
(up to 1986)	2(D)	FUTILE COMBAT	(Red Rhino REDLP 57) 1985
	3(E)	GHOSTS	(Onsala International ONS 1) 1986

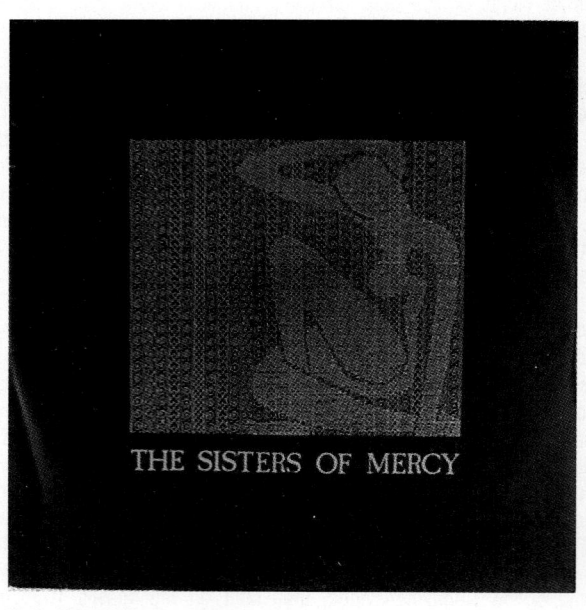

THE SISTERS OF MERCY - Alice 12".

NB: (1) and (2) later issued on one CD (Loma LOMACD 40) 1995. There's also a CD compilation, *The Singles Plus: 1983 - 85* (Anagram CDGRAM 75) 1994.

EP:	1(C)	RECOLLECT (Waiting Here/The Wind Blows/Lies/ She Cries Alone/The Night/ Eternal)	(Red Rhino REDS T42) 1984
45s: (up to 1986)		Trees/Just A Friend (PS)	(Luggage RRP 00724) 1983
		The Night/Waiting Here (PS)	(Red Rhino RED 36) 1983
		She Cries Alone/ The Wind Blows (PS)	(Red Rhino RED 41) 1984
		She Cries Alone/The Wind Blows/ Ashes (12", PS)	(Red Rhino REDT 41) 1984
		So Sure/Batman (PS)	(Red Rhino RED 43) 1984
		So Sure/Batman/Trees (12", PS)	(Red Rhino REDT 43) 1984
		Promised Land/Stand By Me (PS)	(Red Rhino RED 54) 1985
		Promised Land/Stand By Me/ Just A Friend (12", PS)	(Red Rhino REDT 54) 1985
		Restless/What Goes Up (PS)	(Chrysalis CHS 2970) 1986
		Restless/What Goes Up (12", PS)	(Chrysalis CHS 122970) 1986
		Just A Minute/Big Love (PS)	(Chrysalis CHS 3015) 1986
		Just A Minute/Big Love (12", PS)	(Chrysalis CHS 123015) 1986

The **Skeletal Family** came from Bingley in Yorkshire, where they formed in late 1982. They were clearly influenced by the emergence of gothic punk but took their name from a cut on David Bowie's 1974 *Diamond Dogs* album (*Chant Of The Circling Skeletal Family*).

After a debut single on the Luggage label, in March 1983, they signed to the Yorkshire-based indie label Red Rhino. With Howard Daniels now on drums they recorded *The Night*, another goth-influenced disc similar to what bands like **Bauhaus** were doing at the time. By their next 45 *She Cries Alone* in January 1984 Martin Henderson had taken over on drums. The flip side *The Wind Blows* was taken from a Peel session. This line-up also released *So Sure* in June and *Recollect*, a 12" EP comprising early demos. This featured the original demo of *Lies* from September 1982 and different versions of *Waiting Here* and *The Night* from May 1983. They supported **The Sisters Of Mercy** on tour prior to the release of their debut album *Burning Oil*, by which time they had quite a sizeable following.

For their *Promised Land* 45, in February 1985, Graham Pleeth came in on synthesizer. The flip side contained a cover version of Ben E. King's *Stand By Me*. Their second album *Futile Combat* did quite well in the indie charts helping to secure them a contract with Chrysalis.

After their singer Anne Marie Hurst departed to join Ghost Dance, (who were something akin to a 'goth' supergroup also featuring Steve Smith and Paul Southern from **Red Lorry Yellow Lorry**) it was a revised line-up with Kevin Phillips on drums and Katrina on vocals that issued their album *Ghosts* and two 45s for Chrysalis, deploying a more commercial sound probably at the behest of the record company. When they made little impact, the band were dropped.

Alone She Cries and *So Sure* later re-emerged on *In Goth Daze* (Anagrm CDMGRAM 89) in 1998. The 7" version of *She Cries Alone*, along with *Wind Blows* and *Eternal*, date from December 1983. An interesting and recommended disc.

The Singles Plus: 1983 - 85 is a seventeen-track collection of their material for Red Rhino with Anne Marie's melodramatic vocals, lots of brooding bass lines and tom-toms.

Skeptix

Personnel:	CHIG	drms	A
	FISH	gtr	A
	SNOTTY	vcls	A
	USHER	bs	A

ALBUM:	1(A)	SO THE YOUTH	(Rok O Rama RRR 17) 1983

NB: There's also a CD compilation, *Pure Punk Rock* (Captain Oi! AHOY CD 96) 1998.

EP:	1(A)	RETURN TO HELL (Return To Hell/War Drum/ Another Day) (PS)	(Zenon SKEP 003) 1983

SKELETAL FAMILY - Recollect EP.

45s:		Routine Machine/Curfew (PS)	(Zenon SKEP 001) 1982
		Scarred For Life/Born To Lose/ Peace Force (PS)	(Zenon SKEP 002) 1983
	*	Vendetta/Berlin Wall (PS)	(White Rose BD 1) 1994

NB: * *Berlin Wall* was by **The Insane**.

A hardcore punk band from Stoke, who were a significant force on that scene for a while in the early eighties. Their debut 45 *Routine Machine* came out in late 1982. They finally went their separate ways in 1986. If you want to know more check out the Captain Oi! compilation which includes their *So The Youth* album, their ultra-rare EPs and their compilation album cuts. It also comes with a nice booklet. They've also appeared on a few compilations. *Legion Of The Damned* and *Traitor* figured on *Bollox To The Gonads Here's The Testicles* (Pax PAX 14) 1983. They also figure on *Vol.'s 1* and *2* of Rot's *Have A Rotten Christmas*. *Return To Hell* can be found on *Rot Records Punk Singles Collection* (Anagram CDPUNK 40) 1994 and *Traitor* was given fresh exposure on *100% Hardcore Punk* (Captain Oi! AHOY DCD 84) in 1998.

Their guitarist Fish was later in **Discharge**.

The Skids

Personnel:	STUART ADAMSON (WILLIAM STUART ADAMSON)	lead gtr	ABCD
	RICHARD JOBSON	vcls, gtr	ABCDE
	TOM KELLICHAN	drms	A
	BILL SIMPSON	bs	AB
	RUSTY EGAN	drms	B
	RUSSELL WEBB	bs, vcls	CDE
	MIKE BAILLIE	drms	C
	KENNY HYSLOP	drms	D
	PAUL WISHART	sax, flute	E
	J.J. JOHNSON	drms	E

				HCP
ALBUMS:	1(A)	SCARED TO DANCE	(Virgin V 2116) 1979	19
	2(B)	DAYS IN EUROPA	(Virgin V 2138) 1979	32
	3(C)	THE ABSOLUTE GAME	(Virgin V 2174) 1980	9
	4(E)	JOY	(Virgin V 2217) 1981	-
	5(-)	FANFARE (compilation)	(Virgin VM 2) 1982	-

NB: (1) There were some blue vinyl copies of this which were quickly withdrawn. They are now very collectable. (1) reissued (Virgin OVED 41) 1984 and also on CD (Virgin CDV 2116) 1990. The withdrawn first pressings of (2) featured German 'gothic' lettering and a 1936 olympics picture. (2) reissued (Virgin OVED 42) 1984 and on CD (Captain Oi! AHOY CD 172) 2001 with seven bonus tracks. (3) came with a free album *Strength Through Joy* (Virgin VDJ 33) 1980 and reissued (Virgin OVED 43) 1984. (4) reissued (Virgin OVED 200) 1988. There have also been two other compilations; *Dunfermline* (Virgin V 9022) 1993 and also on CD (Virgin COMCD 10) 1987, later reissued (Virgin CDVM 9022) 1993 and *Sweet Suburbia (The Best Of The Skids)* (Virgin CDOVD 457) 1995. Also relevant is *BBC Radio 1 Live In Concert* (Windsong WIN 008) 1992.

EPs:	1(A)	WIDE OPEN (The Saints Are Coming/ Of One Skin/Confusion/Night And Day) (7" and 12" red vinyl)	(Virgin VS 232-12) 1978 -
	2(-)	INTO THE VALLEY (Into The Valley/Masquerade/ Scared To Dance/Working For The Yankee Dollar) (12")	(Virgin VS 241-12) 1983 -
	3(-)	THE SKIDS VS THE RUTS	(Virgin VSCDT 1411) 1992 -

HCP

45s:		Charles/Reasons/Test-Tube Babies (PS)	(No Bad NB 1) 1978 -
	*	Sweet Suburbia/Open Sound (PS)	(Virgin VS 227) 1978 70
		The Saints Are Coming/ Of One Skin (PS)	(Virgin VS 232) 1978 48
	*	Into The Valley/T.V. Stars (PS)	(Virgin VS 241) 1979 10
		Masquerade/Out Of Town (PS)	(Virgin VS 262) 1979 14
	+	Masquerade/Out Of Town/Another Emotion/ Aftermath Dub	(Virgin VS 262) 1979 -
		Charade/Grey Parade (PS)	(Virgin VS 288) 1979 31
		Working For The Yankee Dollar/ Vanguard's Crusade (PS)	(Virgin VS 306) 1979 20
	+	Working For The Yankee Dollar/Vanguard's Crusade/ All The Young Dudes/Hymns For A Haunted Ballroom	(Virgin VS 306) 1979 -
	o	The Olympian/(cut by **XTC**)	(Smash Hits HIT 002) 1979 -
		Animation/Pros And Cons (PS)	(Virgin VS 323) 1980 56
		Circus Games/One Decree (PS)	(Virgin VS 359) 1980 32
	x	Goodbye Civilian/Monkey McGuire Meets Specky Potter Behind The Lochore Institute (PS)	(Virgin VS 373) 1980 52
		A Woman In Winter/Working For The Yankee Dollar (live) (PS with comic booklet)	(Virgin VSK 101) 1981 49
	α	Fields/Brave Man (PS)	(Virgin VS 401) 1981 -
		Iona/Blood And Soul (PS)	(Virgin VS 449) 1981 -

NB: * Some copies came on white vinyl. + 7" double pack. o This 33 rpm red flexidisc came free with 'Smash Hits' magazine. x This was released in two formats. One had a poster picture sleeve and came in a polythene bag. There was also a picture disc version (VSP 373) 1980.

The Skids were one of Scotland's premier punk bands. They formed in Dunfermline as a quartet in 1977, very much centered around Richard Jobson, their singer, songwriter and creative force.

Their first break came when their local record shop owner Sandy Muir became their manager. He released their debut *Charles* 45 on his own No Bad label. This attracted sufficient attention to persuade Virgin to sign the band in May 1978. For the next couple of years **The Skids** didn't look back.

Modelling themselves as a clever punk/new wave combo with an engaging visual image based around Jobson's ultra-combed hair and kick-dance, they soon achieved success. On 19th May 1978, they recorded their first of five sessions for John Peel. It comprised *Of One Skin, Open Sound, Confusion, Night And Day* and *TV Stars*. *Of One Skin* was later featured on the *Winters Of Discontent* (Strange Fruit SFRCD 204) 1990 compilation.

THE SKIDS - Scared To Dance.

The anthemic pop-punker *Sweet Suburbia* released in September 1978 gave them a minor hit, spending one week at No. 70 on 23rd September. It later re-entered the charts for a further two weeks in October, but its highest position this time was 71. Earlier on 1st September, **The Skids** had recorded a second Peel session comprising *Dossier Of Fallibility, Hope And Glory, Six Times* and *The Saints Are Coming*. It was *The Saints Are Coming*, which was chosen as their next 45 with *Of One Skin*, originally recorded for their first Peel session, on the flip side. This got to No. 43 during November, during a three week chart stay. Both songs were also included on their *Wide Open* (EP) along with *Confusion* and *Night And Day*, which had also originally both been recorded for their first Peel session.

In February 1979, **The Skids** reached the Top 10 with the fast-paced, anthemic *Into The Valley*. Peaking at No. 10, it spent eight weeks in the charts. Early copies were also available on white vinyl.

On 26th February 1979, they recorded a third Peel session featuring *Summer, Hang On To The Shadows, Zit* and *Walk On The Wild Side*. The same month their debut album *Scared To Dance* was released. This included *Into The Valley, Charles* (their debut indie 'A' side) and *The Saints Are Coming*, but not *Sweet Suburbia*. The other stand-out cut on the album is *Hope And Glory*. The musical format relies on Jobson's forthright, heavy vocal style and an instrumental section driven by Adamson's loud guitar playing and Kellichan's semi-martial drumming. Apparently there were major disagreements between Adamson and producer David Batchelor during the recording sessions for this album. Adamson threatened to quit, but eventually decided to stay. The album sold quite well. Spending ten weeks in the charts, it climbed to No. 19.

In March 1979, a non-album cut, *Masquerade* gave them their second Top 20 hit. It climbed to No. 14 during a nine week chart stay. A version of *Masquerade* was also recorded during their fourth Peel session on 7th May 1979 along with *War Poets, Withdrawal Symptoms* and *Hymns For A Haunted Ballroom*.

After *Masquerade* was released, drummer Tom Kellichan quit. His replacement was former **Rich Kids** member Rusty Egan. *Charade* released in September 1979, reached No. 31, spending six weeks in the charts. It previewed their second album *Days In Europa*. Former Be Bop Deluxe guitarist Bill Nelson handled the production on this and also contributed the keyboards. The end result was a more polished, refined sound, but with the punkish edge removed with it went much of the band's appeal. Aside from *Charade, Working For The Yankee Dollar* and *Animation* catch the ear. The album fared less well than their debut commercially. It spent just five weeks in the charts, climbing to No. 32. The 2001 CD reissue of this on Captain Oi! comes with seven bonus tracks, including the hit single *Masquerade* and many non-album 'B' sides. It also comes with deluxe packaging, including lyrics.

Not surprisingly *Working For The Yankee Dollar* and *Animation* were released as 45s in November 1979 and February 1980 respectively. The first peaked at No. 20 and spent eleven weeks in the charts. The second climbed to No. 56 during a three week stay.

Sandwiched between these two releases were further personnel changes. Russell Webb, previously with **The Zones** and Slik replaced Bill Simpson on bass. Rusty Egan departed to **Visage** and was replaced on drums by Mike Baillie, who'd been with Insect Bites.

The new line-up enjoyed further success with *Circus Games*, released in July 1980 to preview their forthcoming album. It spent seven weeks in the charts, peaking at No. 32. *The Absolute Game*, which followed in September, proved to be their most successful album of all. It spawned two further hit singles in *Goodbye Civilian* (No. 52) and *A Woman In Winter* (No. 49). The latter featured a live version of their earlier hit *Working For The Yankee Dollar* on the flip side. *The Absolute Game* was produced by Mick Glossop. His semi-grandoise arrangements worked well as Jobson's material became more arty and far-removed from their earlier forthright style. Arguably, it demonstrated the band could keep pace with the changing times. It only spent five weeks in the charts but reached No. 9. A bonus album, *Strength Through Joy* of completed studio outtakes, came with early pressings. It's not essential, but hard-core fans of the band will want a copy.

On 15th September 1980, **The Skids** recorded their fifth and final Peel session. Aside from *Circus Games*, the other three songs *Filming In Africa, Incident In Algiers* and *Snakes And Ladders* did not feature on any of their albums or 45s at the time.

THE SKIDS - Charade.

Adamson, whose contribution to the band was considerable, finally left in June 1981 to set up a new guitar-driven band. This was Big Country, who emerged the following year. Baillie departed to join Epsilon around the same time. He was replaced on drums briefly by ex-**Zones** and Slik member Kenny Hyslop. After an unsuccessful 45 *Fields*, Hyslop joined **Simple Minds**. **The Skids** were now Jobson and Webb. They recruited Paul Wishart on saxophone and flute and worked on a failed concept album called *Joy* (about Scotland) with drummer J.J. Johnson, The Associates, Virginia Astley, Tim Cross (gtr), Alan Darby (gtr), Ken Lockie and Mike Oldfield (gtr). By now, Jobson was showing less interest in music as he pursued his other interests of acting and writing. He appeared on stage and published a collection of poetry called 'A Man For All Seasons' in 1981. It was perhaps inevitable that he should decide to dismantle the band early in 1982.

In May 1982, Virgin released *Fanfare*, an excellent compilation of **The Skids**' singles and essential album tracks. A year later to the month Virgin put out four of the band's finest moments - *Into The Valley*, *Masquerade*, *Scared To Death* and *Working For The Yankee Dollar* - on one 12" EP. *Dunfermline* superceded *Fanfare* as the best compilation of their material and again it contained most of their best songs making it an excellent introduction to their material. More recently Virgin have released *Sweet Suburbia (The Best Of The Skids)* which contains much the same material.

Inevitably **The Skids** have also appeared on a number of compilations. Back in 1980 *Arena* was included on the sampler *Cash Cows* (Virgin MILK 1). You can also check out *Into The Valley* on *The Best Punk Album In The World.... Ever, Vol. 1* (2-CD) (Virgin VTDCD 42) 1995, *The Best Punk Anthems.... Ever* (2-CD) (Virgin VTDCD 198) 1998 and *A History Of Punk, Vol. 1* (Virgin CDOVD 486) 1997. *Saints Are Coming* can also be found on *The Best Punk Album In The World.... Ever, Vol. 2* (2-CD) (Virgin VTDCD 79) 1996, *The Best Punk Anthems.... Ever* (2-CD) (Virgin VTDCD 198) and *God Save The Punks* (2-CD) (Disky DOU 882552) 1998. *Working For The Yankee Dollar* resurfaced on *Teenage Kicks* (PolyGram TV 5253382) 1995. Finally, *Sweet Suburbia*, can also be heard on *20 Of A Different Kind* (Polydor POLS 1006) 1979, *Spiked* (EMI Gold CDGOLD 1057) 1996 and on the lavish 5-CD box set *1-2-3-4 - A History Of Punk And New Wave 1976 - 1979* (MCA/Universal MCD 60066) in 1999.

The 1990 CD reissue of their first album *Scared To Dance* boasts seven extra tracks:- *Sweet Suburbia*, *Open Sound*, *TV Stars*, *Night And Day*, *Confusion*, *Reasons* and *Test Tube Babies*.

The *BBC Radio 1 Live In Concert* CD includes live versions of some of their old favourites including *Into The Valley* and *The Saints Are Coming*.

Dunfermline - A Collection Of The Skids Finest Moments was a compilation originally issued on vinyl in 1987 and then re-released on CD in 1993 through Virgin Universal. It includes their three big hits - *Into The Valley*, *Masquerade* and *Working For The Yankee Dollar* - as well as quite a few more minor hits like *Charade* and *Circus Games*. It does justice to one of the better pop-punk bands of the era.

Alongside his acting and writing career Jobson made two attempts to unsuccessfully launch a solo career and also worked again with Webb and others in a band called Armoury Show. These efforts produced several further albums and 45s, but little comercial success. He also conquered epilepsy and alcohol additction, but in the late eighties his marriage to TV presenter Mariella Frostup folded.

Skin Deep

Personnel:	RITCHIE BROWN	bs	A
	BOB CLAMP	gtr	A
	STUART GARDNER	vcls	A
	RUSSEL 'JOAB' HALL	vcls	A
	NEIL	drms	A

EP:	1(A)	FOOTBALL VIOLENCE (Football Violence/ Boots On His Feet/ Count The Dead) (PS)	(Enemy ENEMY 1) 1985

Skin Deep formed in West Lothian, Scotland, in 1983. They gigged frequently in and around Falkirk, Bathgate and Stenhousemuir, often gigging with local punk band Possessed Images. Their *Football Violence* (EP), released on the Enemy Records in 1985, was hampered by poor distribution and this is now one of the rarest and hardest Oi! recordings to find in its original format. The title track is quite amusing and well worth a spin. It was later included on *100% British Oi!* (CD) (Captain Oi! AHOY DCD 83) 1997. The other two cuts aren't as good, but all three got a further airing on *Oi! The Rarities, Vol. 3* (Captain Oi! AHOY CD 53) 1995.

SKIN DEEP - Football Violence EP.

Skin Disease

This was apparently Chumbawamba taking the piss out of Oi! in contributing *I'm Thick* to *Back On The Streets* (EP) (Secret SHH 138) in 1983. Not many people got the joke but it got another airing on *Secret Records Punk Singles Collection, Vol. 2* (Anagram CDPUNK 60) 1995.

Ski Patrol

Personnel incl:	IAN LOWERY	vcls

45s:	Everything Is Temporary/ Silent Screams (PS)	(Clever Metal VIN 1) 1980
	Agent Orange/Driving Through The City At Night (PS)	(Malicious Damage MD 2) 1980
	Cut/Faith In Transition (PS)	(Malicious Damage MD 3) 1981

NB: There's also a CD EP *Agent Orange* (Three Lines LINE 1) 1994.

Ian Lowery had fronted punk band **The Wall** in the late seventies. After their demise he led this new wave outfit, who, after a debut 45 on Clever Metal, signed to **Killing Joke**'s Malicious Damage label. They recorded *Agent Orange* (the title refers to the chemical defoliant and weapon of murder the Americans used in the Vietnam war) with a throbbing, repetitive bassline, to produce a chilling record. The follow-up *Cut* seems to have been inspired by **Public Image**.

The CD EP features both sides of the *Agent Orange* 45, *Cut* and a 1992 re-recording of *Agent Orange* by Lowery and three new musicians who weren't in the band.

Skrewdriver

Personnel:			
	GRINNY	drms	A
	RON HARTLEY	gtr	A
	KEITH McKAY	bs	A
	IAN STUART	vcls	A

ALBUM: 1(A) ALL SKREWED UP (Chiswick CH 3) 1977

NB: (1) This was a 12-track mini-LP which played at 45 rpm, It came in three different colour sleeves. There was also a 15-track full length album *All Skrewed Up* (Chiswick WIK 3) 1977 released in Germany.

45s:
* You're So Dumb/Better Off Crazy (PS) (Chiswick S 11) 1977
  Anti-Social/19th Nervous Breakdown (PS) (Chiswick NS 18) 1977
+ Streetfight/Unbeliever (Chiswick NS 28) 1978
  Built Up, Knocked Down/Case Of Pride/
  Breakout (PS) (TJM TJM 4) 1980
  Back With A Bang (12" PS) (Skrewdriver SKREW IT) 1982
  White Power/Smash The I.R.A./
  Shove The Dove (PS) (White Noise WN 1) 1983
  Voice Of Britain/Sick Society (PS) (White Noise WN 2) 1983

NB: * There were orange and green versions of this picture sleeve. + This was unissued, but white label acetates do exist and are extremely rare.

A primitive skinhead punk band from Blackpool, although they were an early signing for the London-based Chiswick label. Very white working class in outlook and style, they were also reputedly National Front supporters. Their 12-track mini-album *All Skrewed Up* played at 45 rpm and contained a very basic, primal punk noise. Tucked away among these was a cover of The Who's *Won't Get Fooled Again*. They did have a full length fifteen-track version of the album released in Germany.

The 'A' sides of their first two singles (*Anti-Social* and *You're So Dumb*) were included on the sampler *Long Shots Dead Certs And Odds On Favourites* (Chiswick CH 5) in 1978.

They officially split in 1979 but there were subsequent reformations in the eighties. They were also known as Racist Agitators for a while.

The Skunks

Personnel incl: HUGH ASHTON
FRANK CORNELLI

45: Good From The Bad/
Back Street Fightin' (Eel Pie EPS 001) 1978

Members of this band were later in Craze and Hard Corps. Just 2,000 copies of *Good From The Bad* were pressed and it came in a die-cut 'swirl' sleeve. There's some decent guitar, but it's an unexceptional effort, which can also be heard on *Business Unusual* (Cherry Red ARED 2) 1979.

Slaughter and The Dogs

Personnel:			
	WAYNE BARRETT	vcls	A D
	HOWARD 'ZIP' BATES	bs	ABCDE
	ERIC 'THE MAD MUFFET' GRANTHAM	drms	A DE
	MIKE ROSSI	gtr, vcls	ABCDE
	BILLY DUFFY	gtr	BC
	PHIL ROWLAND	drms	BC
	STEVE MORRISSEY	vcls	B
	ED BANGER	vcls	E

ALBUMS:
1(A) DO IT DOG STYLE (Decca SKL 5292) 1978
2(A) LIVE SLAUGHTER RABID DOGS (Rabid HAT 23) 1978
3(A) LIVE AT THE FACTORY (Thrush 1) 1978
4(D) BITE BACK (DJM DJF 20566) 1980

NB: (1) later reissued on multicoloured vinyl as a numbered limited edition 1,000 copy release with two multi-coloured stickers (Damaged Goods FNARRLP 2) 1989. (1) also issued on CD (Captain Oi! AHOY CD 131) 2000 with two bonus cuts. (2) was issued in a plain white sleeve with a large sticker. (3) reissued (Receiver RRLP 114) 1989. (4) was credited to Slaughter and later issued on CD (Captain Oi! AHOY CD 142) 2000. Also relevant is *The Slaughterhouse Tapes* (Link LP 092) 1989 and *Cranked Up Really High* (Captain Oi! AHOY CD 50) 1995.

EPs:
1(C) BUILD UP NOT DOWN (It's Alright/Edgar Allan Poe/
Twist and Turn/UFO) (12" PS) (TJM TJM 3) 1979
2(D) HALF ALIVE (Twist And Turn/Cranked Up Really
High/Where Have All The Boot Boys Gone) (12" PS)
 (Thrush THRUSH 1) 1982

45s:
* Cranked Up Really High/The Bitch (PS) (Rabid TOSH 101) 1977
+ Where Have All The Boot Boys Gone?/
  You're A Bore (PS) (Decca FR 13723) 1977
  Where Have All The Boot Boys Gone?/
  You're A Bore (12" PS) (Decca LF 13723) 1977
  Dame To Blame/Johnny T (Decca FR 13743) 1977
x Quick Joey Small/Come On Back (Decca FR 13758) 1978
  You're Ready Now/Runaway (PS) (DJM DJS 10927) 1979
o East Side Of Town/One By One (PS) (DJM DJS 10936) 1980
o I'm The One/What's Wrong Boy? (live)/
  Hell In New York (PS) (DJM DJS 10945) 1980
α Where Have All The Boot Boys Gone?/You're A Bore/
  Johnny T (PS) (Damaged Goods FNARR 1) 1988

NB: * Originals came with blue and later cream plastic labels. There was also a later pressing with a black and white paper label. + This came in a paper or plastic label. x With Mick Ronson. o credited to Slaughter. α 1,000 copies only were released, 500 on green vinyl and 500 on red vinyl.

The four original members of **Slaughter and The Dogs** - Wayne Barrett, Howard 'Zip' Bates, Eric Grantham and Mike Rossi - all attended Sharston High School together in Wythenshawe in south Manchester. When they originally formed in early 1976 their stage act was unique. They scattered large amounts of talcum powder to achieve a 'smoky' stage effect. Musically, they paid homage to both glam-rock and the garage punk of U.S. bands like The MC5 and The Stooges. They took their name from two of their biggest influences - Mick Ronson's *Slaughter On Tenth Avenue* and David Bowie's *Diamond Dogs*.

During 1976 they established themselves as a popular attraction on the Manchester pub circuit. They also managed to convince **Malcolm McLaren** they had 'a huge following', which secured them a support slot to **The Sex Pistols** at their legendary Manchester Lesser Free Trade Hall gig on 20th July 1976.

Their first vinyl excursion came in 1977 when two of their live recordings from late 1976, *Runaway* and *Boston Babies*, were featured on *Live At The Roxy, WC2* (Harvest SHSP 4069). This collection was later reissued (Receiver RR 132) in 1991. They also appeared in a punk documentary which Don Letts filmed at The Roxy Club, where they were a regular attraction. Then, in May 1977 they became the first act to record on Manchester indie label Rabid Records when *Cranked Up Really High* was released as a 45. Now very much associated with the punk scene they became one of the very first major label signings of a punk band when Decca snapped them up later that year.

SLAUGHTER AND THE DOGS - Cranked Up Really High.

SLAUGHTER AND THE DOGS - Do It Dog Style.

From thereon, instead of things only getting better, they went downhill! Their first album *Do It Dog Style* was produced by Mick Ronson, who also helped out on the last of their three Decca 45s, an aggressive rendition of the old Kasenatz-Katz Singing Orchestral Circus hit *Quick Joey Small*. *Do It Dog Style* kicks off with their now seminal single *Where Have All The Bootboys Gone?*, which had significant influence on the subsequent Oi!/street punk movement. Its cover versions include earlier Kasenatz Katz bubblegum hit *Quick Joey Small*, which **Slaughter and The Dogs** later released as a 45 (Mick Ronson made a guest appearance on this) and The New York Dolls' *Where Are The Mystery Girls?*. Their cover of Velvet Underground's *I'm Waiting For The Man* was less successful, but the album also has another good original in *Since You Went Away* which ends with an extended guitar section. Neither the album or the 45s sold well and disillusioned, they decided to split up in mid-1978.

In many cases that would have been that, but in this case it wasn't! Rossi and Bates decided to reform the band as a live act. They recruited ex-**Eater** drummer Phil Rowland, guitarist Billy Duffy and briefly his friend Steve Morrisey on vocals (though Morrisey left when they failed an audition and Rossi assumed vocal duties). In 1979 the new line-up recorded the *Build Up Not Down* (EP) for TJM Records, but it made little impression and they changed name to **Studio Sweethearts** for a while. After one 45 for DJM under this moniker the original line-up (with Barrett and Grantham back in the fold) recorded an album *Bite Back* and a further three 45s for DJM (apart from the first of these 45s all of their DJM recordings were now credited simply to **Slaughter**). *Bite Back* was produced by former Mott The Hoople drummer Dale Griffin. Musically, though, the band's guitar driven noisy rock sound had little to distinguish it from the rest of the pack and they faded away overshadowed by Oi! bands in the early eighties.

Ex-**Nosebleeds** vocalist **Ed Banger** took over the vocal slot from Wayne Barrett in their twilight days.

Mike Rossi was later in The Duellists, but Duffy and Morrisey went on to achieve real fame in **The Cult** and The Smiths respectively.

The Slaughterhouse Tapes comprise a mixture of demos, live recordings and studio outtakes in lo-fi stereo. Included here are versions (but not the most familiar ones) of songs like *Where Have All The Bootboys Gone?*, *Runaway*, *Boston Babies* and *White Light White Heat*. The collection really highlights that **Slaughter** had their moment on *The Roxy, London WC2* album but had little to offer subsequently.

Cranked Up Really High, released by Captain Oi! in 1995 is a collection of rarities, demos and live cuts. The title cut was one of their raucous early singles and the collection tends to steer clear of their better known Decca material for cuts like *Boston Babies* and *I'm Mad (Demo)*. Also included are some of their later-era recordings like *The Flight* and *Situations*.

Cranked Up Really High, *Bitch*, *It's Alright*, *Edgar Allen Poe*, *Twist And Turn* and *UFO* all got fresh exposure on *Rabid / TJM Punk Singles Collection* (Receiver RRCD 227) 1996. You'll also find *Where Have All The Boot Boys Gone* on *New Wave Archive* (Rialto RMCD 201) 1997, *Runaway* on *Punk - Live And Nasty* (Emporio EMPRCD 586) 1995, whilst both sides of their debut 45 *Cranked Up Really High* and *The Bitch* also got a further airing on *Oi! The Singles Collection, Vol. 4* (Captain Oi! AHOY CD 71) 1997. You can also check out *Where Have All The Boot Boys Gone?* on *1-2-3-4 - A History Of Punk And New Wave 1976 - 1979* (MCA/Universal 60066) 1999, which is a 5-CD box set.

Amazingly their debut album wasn't given a CD release until the year 2000 courtesy of the prolific Captain Oi! label. The reissue comes with two bonus tracks (*Johnny T*, a Thunders tribute, and *Come On Back*), a band history, illustrations of foreign releases and a Decca discography which all go to help make this an exceptional CD reissue.

Slime

Personnel:	JOCK SAYERS	bs, vcls	A
	JOCK TATE	drms	A
	'SLIMEY' TOAD	gtr	A

45:	Controversial/Loony (PS)	(Toadstool GOOD 1) 1978

'Slimey' Toad was also in **Johnny Moped**.

The Slits

Personnel:	VIV ALBERTINE	gtr	ABCD
	ADRIANNA FOSTER (ARI UP)	vcls	ABCD
	SUZY GUTSY	bs	A
	KATE KORUS	gtr	A
	PALMOLIVE	drms	AB
	TESSA POLLITT	bs	BCD
	BUDGIE (PETER CLARK)	perc, drms	C
	BRUCE SMITH	drms	D

HCP
ALBUMS:	1(C)	CUT	(Island ILPS 9573) 1979	30
	2(-)	BOOTLEG RETROSPECTIVE	(Rough Trade YY 3) 1980	-
	3(D)	RETURN OF THE GIANT SLITS	(CBS 85269) 1981	-
	4(B)	THE PEEL SESSIONS (mini-LP)	(Strange Fruit SFPMA 207) 1988	-

NB: (1) also issued on CD (Island IMCD 89) 1990. (2) was a budget price release. Early versions of (3) came with a free 7" 45, *American Radio Interviewer / Face Place (Dub)* (XPS 125). (4) also issued on CD (Strange Fruit SFPMACD 207) 1988 and again (Strange Fruit SFRSCD 052) 1998. There's also a CD only collection *In The Beginning (An Anthology)* (Jungle FREUDCD 057) 1997.

EP:	1(B)	THE PEEL SESSIONS (Love And Romance/Shoplifting/ New Town/Vindictive)	(Strange Fruit SFPS 021) 1987

HCP
45s:	Typical Girls/ I Heard It Through The Grapevine	(Island WIP 6505) 1979	60
	Typical Girls/(Brink Style)/I Heard It Through The Grapevine/ Leibe And Romanze (12" PS)	(Island 12WIP 6505) 1979	-
*	In The Beginning There Was Rhythm/(cut by **The Pop Group**) (PS)	(Rough Trade/Y RT 039/Y-1) 1980	-
	Man Next Door/ Man Next Door (dub) (PS)	(Rough Trade/Y RT 044/Y-4) 1980	-
	Animal Space/Animal Spacier (PS)	(Human HUM 4) 1980	-
+	Earthbeat/Begin Again Rhythm (PS)	(CBS A 1498) 1981	-
	Earthbeat/Earthdub/ Begin Again Rhythm (12" PS)	(CBS A 131498) 1981	-

NB: * Demo copies featured two one-sided singles in a pack. + There was a 7" promo version in an envelope sleeve together with two promotional photos.

The Slits' origins go back to the punk fan scene which grew up around London in 1976. Viv Albertine was a student at Hornsey Art College and along with Spanish-born drummer Palmolive had rehearsed with **Sid Vicious**' embryonic band The Flowers Of Romance, alongside Keith Levine. After Sid sacked them from his band they teamed up with guitarist Kate Korus and bassist Suzy Gutsy. The latter also recruited fourteen-year old friend Arianna Foster (who soon shortened her name to Ari Up) as vocalist. **The Slits** were born, but the original line-up only survived a few gigs. Suzi Gutsy soon left to form The Flicks, although they never got beyond the rehearsal room. Kate Korus lasted only three gigs before going off to form **The Modettes**. She had previously been in a band called The Castrators and **The Slits** returned to that band to recruit Tessa Pollitt as a replacement for Suzy Gutsy.

The definitive **Slits** line-up Albertine, Ari Up, Palmolive and Pollitt was now in place. In April 1977 they went out on the road, supporting **The Clash** on the 'White Riot' tour. The band soon got a violent image, which was reinforced by their appearance in Derek Jarman's 'Jubilee' film trashing cars and generally raising hell.

On 19th September 1977, they recorded the first of two Peel sessions. It featured *Love And Romance*, *Vindictive* (alias *Let's Do The Split*), *New Town* and *Shoplifting*. All four songs were passionate and frantic punkers. Another musical remnant of the band's sound in 1977 was a bootleg set recorded live at Dingwalls. Although more amateurish than the Peel session, it confirmed their passion and commitment.

Their wayward reputation made record companies wary of them and they remained unsigned during 1978. In March they supported **The Buzzcocks** on tour. Then in May they recorded their second Peel session, which is usually considered to be their finest moment. This comprised a trio of their finest songs - the riffy *So Tough*, *Instant Hit* a general mayhem within which a near-spoken vocal and awesome guitar compete and the session was rounded off with Palmolive's *FM* (alias *Frequent Mutilation*). After a summer tour with **The Rich Kids**, they went abroad for a series of concerts, playing in Berlin and France. Then, in October 1978, something happened that would change the future direction of the band. Palmolive was forced out by the band's management who were seeking someone more professional. Budgie, a mate who'd been with Liverpool bands **The Spitfire Boys** and **Big In Japan**, was drafted in as a replacement as **The Slits** were invited as special guests of **The Clash** on the 'Sort It Out' tour in November.

In April 1979, came the rather surprising announcement that **The Slits** had been signed to Island. Shortly after BBC's 'Grapevine' series used the band's version of Marvin Gaye's hit *I Heard It Through The Grapevine* as its theme. The cut was also featured on the *We Did 'Em Our Way* compilation of punk re-works and on NME's *Pogo A Go Go* (NME 021) 1986 retrospective punk cassette, which was available by mail-order from NME.

I Heard It Through The Grapevine was also on the flip of the band's long awaited debut 45 *Typical Girls*, released in September 1979. This got to No. 60 during a three week chart stay, but it would prove to be their only hit single. A 12" version was released too, but the two additional cuts on it were of little interest.

The *Cut* album appeared the same month. At Island **The Slits** had been assigned to reggae producer and musician Dennis Bovell. The front cover was notable for the band appearing bare breasted but muddy. The production was controversial. As Mark Paytress put it writing in 'Record Collector', 'Bovell had stripped the songs bare, and rebuilt a highly polished studio-orientated sound which fused dub production techniques with the group's unconventional musical structures'. Writing in 'Melody Maker' John Orme peceptively described the album as 'Pere Ubu playing ring-a-ring-a-roses with Captain Beefheart somewhere in Jamaica'. Most of their early classics were there - *Instant Hit*, *So Tough*, *Shoplifting*, *Love And Romance*, *FM* and, of course, *Typical Girls*, but they sounded different and in the process some fans felt they had lost their potency. The album attracted considerable attention - to help market it a 60" x 40" poster of the muddy **Slits** image was produced and it is now quite collectable. The album climbed to No. 30 spending five weeks in the charts.

After *Cut*'s release Budgie went off to replace Kenny Morris in **Siouxsie and The Banshees**. Bruce Smith came in from **The Pop Group** as a replacement. The new line-up ('D') embarked on a short tour to help promote the album and engaged jazz trumpeter Don Cherry and a keyboardist known simply as Penny to help support them.

On New Year's Eve 1979, **The Slits** made their U.S. debut at Hurrah in New York. Keith Levine came on stage with them for the encore. They played The Electric Ballroom, London early in 1980 together with Palmolive's first post-**Slits** band **The Raincoats** and **This Heat**. A little later they performed at the 'Rock Au Feminin' night at the Bataclan in Paris. They also appeared later in the year at the 'Beating The Blues' festival at London's Alexandra Palace in aid of the Communist Party.

THE SLITS - Cut.

Their next 45 *In The Beginning There Was Rhythm* marked a change of style to a simpler, repetitive funk sound and their break with Island. They teamed up with **The Pop Group** to form the Y label (distributed through Rough Trade). On the other side of this double 'A' side was **The Pop Group**'s *Where There's A Will There's A Way*. Unfortunately, the single captures neither band at their best and the one redeeming feature was the 70p price. Demo copies feature two one-sided singles in a pack and are more collectable.

Despite its budget price their *Retrospective - Official Bootleg* album, which came in a plain white sleeve with song titles randomly scrawled on the label was a big disappointment. It comprised poorly recorded live material and a poor selection of demos and is best forgotten.

Their next two singles were *Man Next Door*, a reggae cover of a John Holt song and *Animal Space*, a band original notable for a haunting, high-pitched guitar motif. Steve Beresford, **The Flying Lizards**' keyboardist guested on the latter.

CBS signed the group in June 1981 and the main product of that association was their final album *Return Of The Giant Slits*. Early pressings came with a free 7", which featured an excerpt from a U.S. radio interview backed by a dub version of *Face Place*, one of the album's stronger cuts. The main musical influence now seemed to be African tribalism but the attempt to make the band more commercially successful was hampered by inconsistent material. *Earthbeat* was culled for 45 release and there is a 7" promo-only release issued in an envelope sleeve together with two promotional photos, which is now an extremely rare item.

With Viv Albertine wanting to concentrate on dance and Tessa Pollitt's ambitions as an artist, there seemed little desire to keep the band together. They announced that they would be splitting in December 1981.

Bruce Smith joined Rip, Rig and Panic. Viv Albertine ended up as an independent film producer. She had an examination of the impact of punk on women rock musicians broadcast on Channel 4 in 1990 and it included brief **Slits** footage. Tessa Pollitt had her art exhibited in a Bristol gallery and then was part of the backing band for Brion Gysin at the 'Final Academy' series of concerts organised by Genesis P. Orridge. She then quit the music scene. Ari Up appeared on the first two New Age Steppes albums. In 1997, Palmolive was playing drums in a Christian rock band in Massachusetts!

Strange Fruit's release of their two Peel sessions has plugged an important gap in their discography. The Strange Fruit EP released in 1987 contains three of the four songs that later turned up on the debut album *Cut*. However, they are virtually unrecognisable from the versions on their album. On *Cut* they adopted a predominantly reggae sound but on this EP you can hear raw, rough and punkish versions of *Love And Romance*, *Shoplifting* and their live favourite *New Town* as they were originally performed. The fourth cut *Vindictive* wasn't included on *Cut* but did later appear as *Let's Do The Split* on *Bootleg Retrospective*. The later *Peel Sessions* mini-album from 1989 included their original session featured on the earlier EP and three tracks from a later spring 1978 session. The cuts in question; *So Tough*, *Instant Hit* and *FM* capture the band at its finest and the album is recommended. More recently *In The Beginning (A Live Anthology)* comprises concert material from 1977 and 1981. It starts with a set recorded at London's Dingwalls in September 1977 and concludes with a version of *In The Beginning* (featuring Neneh Cherry) recorded at the band's farewell show at Hammersmith Palais in December 1981.

Typical Girls got further exposure on *A History Of Punk, Vol. 1* (Virgin CDOVD 486) 1997 and again on the 5-CD box set *1-2-3-4 - A History Of Punk And New Wave 1976 - 1979* (MCA/Universal MCD 60066) in 1999.

The Slits were part of a new generation of punk bands who helped establish women as a serious force in rock. For a brief while, in 1978, they threatened to take a hitherto male dominated scene by storm. They were unpredictable, exciting, passionate and sometimes shocking. They were certainly a good band but they could have been sensational - they never fulfilled their early promise.

Smack

Personnel:	GEOFF CRANE		A
	JOHN HARRISON		A
	GED McNULTY		A
	STEVE SPICER		A

| 45: | Edward Fox/Come Again (PS) | (4-Spin 001) 1978 |

Smack's *Edward Fox* is a poppy-punk 45, which is rather underrated.

Small Hours

Personnel:	DAVE BURKE	drms	AB
	KYM BRADSHAW	bs	A
	RIMOND HAND	gtr, vcls	AB
	CAROL ISAACS	organ, piano	AB
	NEIL THOMPSON	lead vcls	AB

45s:	The Kid/Business In Town/Midnight To Six/		
	End Of The Night (PS)	(Automatic K 17708) 1980
	The Kid/Business In Town/Midnight To Six/		
	End Of The Night (10", PS)	(Automatic K 17708X) 1980

Originally known as Street Cleaners, **The Small Hours** were a popular live attraction in this era. Prior to releasing their now rare and collectable 45 they had teamed up with Kym Bradshaw from **The Saints** to appear on *Mods Mayday '79* (Bridge House BHLP 003) 1979 playing *Hanging In The Balance*, *Midnight To Six* and *End Of The Night*. They also figured on *Mods Mayday 2 - Modnight At The Bridge* (Receiver RRCD 228) 1997, which comprises outtakes from the night.

THE SMIRKS - O.K. U.K.

Small World

Personnel:	MICK COHEN	bs	A
	PAUL GUIDOTTI	drms	A
	CHRIS PHILPOTT	vcls	A
	JOHN WRATTEN	gtr	A

45:	Love Is Dead/Liberty (PS)	(Whaam! WHAAM 003) 1981
	First Impressions/Stupidity Street/	
	Tomorrow Never Comes (PS)	(Valid VC 001) 1983

A mod revival outfit from Barking in East London. In addition to these two rare and collectable 45s, **Small World** recorded two demo tapes in 1981 which were available through mail-order. Their drummer Paul Guidotti had previously played with **The Stripes**. *First Impressions*, *Stupidity Street* and *Tomorrow Never Comes* can also be investigated on *This Is Mod, Vol. 5* (Anagram CDMGRAM 110) in 1997. The brassy *First Impressions*, which features strong vocals and a good melody, later resurfaced on *100% British Mod* (Captain Mod MODSKA DCD 8) 1998. Finally, *Stupidity Street* later turned up on vinyl on *This Is Mod* (dbl) (Get Back GET 39) in 1999.

Smart Alec

| 45: | Scooter Boys/Soho (PS) | (B&C BCS 20) 1980 |

The title *Scooter Boys* suggests this rare single was probably the work of a mod revival outfit.

The Smirks

Personnel incl:	MIKE DOHERTY	drms	A
	NEIL FITZPATRICK	lead gtr, vcls	A
	SIMON MILNER	vcls, gtr	A
	IAN 'MOG' MORRIS	bs, vcls	A

45s:	O.K. U.K./Streets (PS)	(Beserkley BZZ 17) 1978
	Rosemary/Up Eh Up (PS)	(Beserkley BZZ 23) 1978
	American Patriots/Angry With Myself/	
	Penetration (PS)	(Smirksongs DHSS 1) 1979
	To You/New Music (PS)	(Smirksongs DHSS 2) 1979

This band was initially signed up by the Californian Beserkley label, but then dropped after two singles. After this they put out two releases on their own label. The lead vocals were pretty brain-damaged.

Their *O.K. U.K.* single is a melodic power-pop composition, which argues the merits of Britain as against California. *Angry With Myself* features a melodic break **The Buzzcocks** would have been envious of. *Penetration* sees Milner at his most strung out and *American Patriots* is sheer unadulterated rock 'n' roll. For their final 45 *To You* they signed a distribution deal with Virgin. Both sides of this single featured imaginative guitars, harmonies and changes of pace.

Mike Doherty went on to play in **The Freshies**.

Snatch

Personnel:	JUDY NYLON	vcls	AB
	PATTI PALLADIN	vcls	AB
	BRUCE DOUGLAS	bs	B
	JERRY NOLAN	drms	B
	KEETH PAUL	gtr	B
	NICK PLYTAS	keyb'ds	B

| ALBUM: | 1(B) | SNATCH | (Pandemonium WITCH 1) 1983 |

45s:	Stanley/I.R.T. (PS)	(Lightning LIG 502) 1978
	All I Want/When I'm Bored (foil PS)	(Lightning LIG 505) 1978
	Shopping For Clothes/Joey/	
	Red Army (12" die-cut PS)	(Fetish FET 004) 1980

Judy Nylon was originally part of the New York new wave scene before coming to London and teaming up with Patti Palladin to form **Snatch**. They played a German style electronic music. Their debut single *Stanley/ I.R.T.* was recorded as a duo in Palladin's Maida Vale living room and released in the U.K. via Greg Shaw's Bomp label. For the rockier *All I Want* they were joined by four others including The Heartbreakers' Jerry Nolan and Roogalators' Nick Plytas. Between their first two singles the duo collaborated with Brian Eno on *RAF*, the 'B' side of *The King's Lead Hat* (Polydor 2001 762) 1978. *Joey* and *Red Army* on their 12" release for Fetish were both softish electronic ballads. *Shopping For Clothes* was more blues-inspired.

Judy Nylon went on to record a solo album *Pal Judy* (On-U-Sound LP 16) in 1982. She later worked with John Cale and sang the vocals on John Cale's live album *Even Cowgirls Get The Blues*. Palladin went on to provide backing vocals on a number of Johnny Thunders' albums. In 1978, they recorded an album of duets together called *Copy Cats*, which she produced. It was a compilation of swamp-rock/R&B covers. After Johnny Thunders' died she recorded a tribute album *I Only Wrote This Song For You* for him.

All I Want can also be heard on *1-2-3-4 - A History Of Punk And New Wave 1976 - 1979* (MCA/Universal MCD 60066), a 5-CD box set issued in 1999.

Sneak Preview

Personnel:	EMBRAIN	keyb'ds	A
	JIMMER	drms	A
	LYNDON PARRY	bs, vcls	A
	NEIL TAYLOR	vcls, gtr	A

This band's sole vinyl offering seems to have been the promising pop-punkish *Slugweird* on *Avon Calling - The Bristol Compilation* (Heartbeat HB 1) in 1979. It suggested that better things were on the horizon but they didn't materialise.

Sniff 'N' The Tears

Personnel:	LES DAVIDSON	gtr, vcls	A
	JAMIE LANE	drms	A
	LOZ NETTO	gtr	A
	PAUL ROBERTS	gtr, vcls	A
	NICK SOUTH	bs	A
	MIKE TAYLOR	keyb'ds	A

ALBUMS:	1(A)	FICKLE HEART	(Chiswick WIK 9) 1978
	2(A)	THE GAMES UP	(Chiswick CWK 3014) 1980
	3(A)	LOVE ACTION	(Chiswick 2018) 1981
	4(A)	RIDE BLUE DIVIDE	(Chiswick 3020) 1982
	5(A)	RETROSPECTIVE	(Chiswick TONE 1) 1983

NB: (1) reissued (Chiswick CWD 3002) 1978, and again (Chiswick SNIP 1) 1982 and also issued on CD (Chiswick CDWIKM 9) 1991. (2) reissued (Chiswick SNIP 2) 1982 and also issued on CD (Chiswick CDWIKM 92) 1990. (3) reissued (Chiswick CDWIKM 96) 1991 and also issued on CD (Chiswick CDWIKM 96) 1991. (4) reissued (Chiswick 97) 1991. (5) also issued on CD (Chiswick 813 1272) 1988. There's also a *Best Of Sniff 'n' The Tears* (Chiswick CDWIK 102) 1991, *No Damage Done* (Provogue PRD 70482) 1992 and *The Best Of Sniff 'n' The Tears (Driver's Seat)* (Chiswick CDWIKK 199) 1999.

HCP

45s:	Driver's Seat/Slide Away	(Chiswick NS 40) 1978 -
	Driver's Seat/Slide Away	(Chiswick CHIS 105) 1978 42
*	Driver's Seat/Slide Away	(Chiswick CHISP 105) 1978 -
	One Love/5 & Zero (PS)	(Chiswick CHIS 129) 1980 -
	Poison Pen Mail/	
	What Can Daddy Do? (PS)	(Chiswick CHIS 131) 1980 -
	That Final Love/	
	Like My Fantasy (PS)	(Chiswick CHIS 146) 1981 -
	Hungry Eyes/Bagatelle (PS)	(Chiswick DICE 10) 1982 -
Reissue:	Drivers Seat/Slide Away (PS)	(Chiswick DICE 11) 1982 -

NB: * This was a picture disc.

A soul-influenced pop-rock band who are worth a passing mention but who were closer to the pub-rock circuit than early eighties new wave.

Sniff 'n' The Tears' first 45 was cancelled, but some test pressings do exist. When it was reissued a little later *Driver's Seat* was a minor hit, climbing to No. 42 and spending five weeks in all in the charts. Paul Roberts was a fine vocalist who sounded a little like Robert Palmer. The disc had obvious commercial appeal.

The Snivelling Shits

Personnel:	GIOVANNI DADOMO	vcls	A
	DAVE FUDGER	bs	A
	PETE MAKOWSKI	gtr	A
	STEVE NICOL	drms	A

ALBUM:	1(A)	I CAN'T COME	(Damaged Goods FNARR LP 3) 1989

45s:	Terminal Stupid/I Can't Come (PS)	(Ghetto Rockers PRE 2) 1977
	Isgodaman?/Terminal Stupid/	
	I Can't Come (PS)	(Damaged Goods FNARR 4) 1989
*	Isgodaman?/Terminal Stupid/	
	I Can't Come	(Damaged Goods FNARR 48) 1989

NB: * This version comprised a box set with a badge and inserts. It came on pink vinyl in a stamped plain white sleeve.

Apart from Steve Nicol who was a member of **Eddie and The Hot Rods** this band comprised a trio of journalists from 'Sounds' newspaper having a bit of fun. The 1977 45 is now scarce. *Terminal Stupid* is one minute and thirty-two seconds of breakneck bop-rock about a guy who gets plastered, meets a girl, wakes up beside her the next morning and can't believe his misfortune:-

"Terminal stupid
Your head's in a mess
Could count all your brain cells
On one finger or less"
(from *Terminal Stupid*)

SNIFF 'N' THE TEARS - Driver's Seat.

THE SNIVELLING SHITS - Terminal Stupid.

I Can't Come on the flip side is a lighthearted ditty about a guy who can't ejaculate.

In 1989, Damaged Goods released a whole album's worth of outtakes by the band on brown vinyl. Three of the cuts were also put out on 45 and the material is worth investigating. *Terminal Stupid* can also be heard on *Punk Lost And Found* (Shanachie SH 5705) 1996.

Social Disease

A Bristol punk band who released a four-track cassette *The World At Ransom* on Rot in 1983.

THE SOFT BOYS - Near The Soft Boys EP.

Social Security

Personnel:	SIMON BLACKMORE	gtr	A
	SIMON CARTLEDGE	bs	A
	PAUL HARRISON	vcls	A
	BILL SARGENT	drms	A
	DOMINIC WHITE	gtr	A

45:	I Don't Want My Heart To Rule My Head/Stella's Got A Fella/Cider/Choc Ice (PS)	(Heartbeat PULSE 1) 1978

A West Country band whose 45 was the first release on the Bristol-based Heartbeat label.

Society's Rejects

Personnel:	CARL	bs	A
	KIZZ	drms	A
	MARK	vcls	A
	SCON	gtr	A

ALBUM:	1(A)	SKINS 'N' PUNKS VOL. 1	(Oi OIR 007) 198?

NB: (1) was a split album with **Last Rough Cause**.

An Oi! band from Cardiff, Wales, whose recordings were produced by **The Oppressed**'s Roddy Moreno. They recorded a split album with **Last Rough Cause** for Oi! Records. You can also hear their fast 'n' frantic *It's Your Life* and *Politician* on *This Is Oi!* (Oi! OIR 004) 1986, which was later reissued on CD (Captain Oi! AHOY CD 6) 1993. They also turn up playing *United We Stand* on *The Best Of Oi! Records* (Captain Oi! AHOY CD 38) 1995.

The Soft Boys

Personnel:	ALAN DAVIS	gtr	A
	ROBYN HITCHCOCK	vcls, gtr	ABC
	ANDY METCALFE	bs	AB
	JIM MELTON	hrmnca	AB
	MORRIS WINDSOR	drms	ABC

THE SOFT BOYS - I Wanna Destroy You.

	KIMBERLEY REW	gtr, hrmnca, vcls	BC
	MATTHEW SELIGMAN	bs, keyb'ds	C

ALBUMS:	1(B)	A CAN OF BEES	(Two Crabs CLAW 1001) 1979
	2(C)	UNDERWATER MOONLIGHT	(Armageddon ARM 1) 1980
	3(C)	ONLY THE STONES REMAIN/TWO HALVES FOR THE PRICE OF ONE (part live)	(Armageddon BYE 1) 1982
	4(-)	INVISIBLE HITS (compilation)	(M.Music CHIME 0002) 1983
	5(-)	THE SOFT BOYS 1976-81 (dble CD compilation)	(Rykodisc RCD 10234/35) 1993

NB: (1) originally issued on black and white labels. It was reissued on Aura (AUL 709) 1980, with slightly different tracks and later the original Two Crabs release was was issued again in 1984. It was also issued on CD (Rykodisc RCD 20231) 1992. (2) also issued on CD (Rykodisc RCD 20232) 1992 and (Matador OLE 500-2V) 2001. (3) featured one side studio, one side live. (4) also issued on CD (Rykodisc RCD 20233) 1992. Also relevant is *Raw Cuts* (Overground OVER 05) 1990.

EPs:	1(A)	GIVE IT TO THE SOFT BOYS (Wading Through A Ventilator/The Face Of Death/Hear My Brane) (PS)	(Raw RAW 5) 1977
	2(C)	NEAR THE SOFT BOYS (Kingdom Of Love/Vegetable Man/Strange) (PS)	(Armageddon AEP 002) 1980
	3(A)	WADING THROUGH A VENTILATOR (The Yodelling Hoover/Give It To The Soft Boys/Vyrna Knowl Is A Headbanger/Wading Through A Ventilator/The Face Of Death/Hear My Brane) (12" PS)	(Delorean SOFT 1P) 1985

NB: There was also a test pressing of (1) which has a withdrawn track *Vyrna Knowl Is A Headbanger* in place of *Wading Through A Ventilator*. Only two copies were produced and these change hands for in excess of £100. (2) was reissued in 1982. Some picture disc copies of (3) were also produced.

45s:	(I Want To Be An) Angelpoise Lamp/Fat Man's Son (PS)	(Radar ADA 8) 1978
	I Wanna Destroy You/I'm An Old Pervert (Disco) (PS)	(Armageddon AS 005) 1980
	Only The Stones Remain/The Asking Tree (PS)	(Armageddon AS 029) 1981

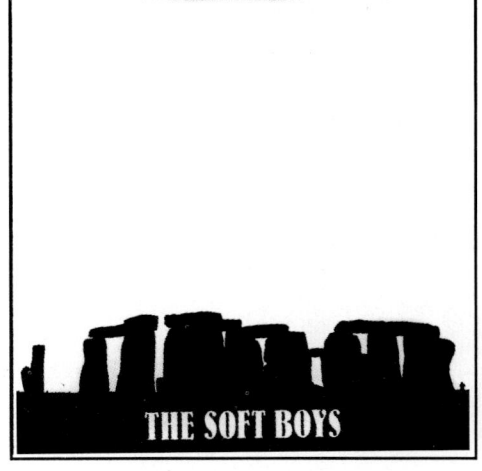

THE SOFT BOYS - Only The Stones Remain.

THE SOFT BOYS - Can Of Bees.

THE SOFT BOYS - Underwater Moonlight.

THE SOFT BOYS - Only The Stones Remain/Two For The Price Of One.

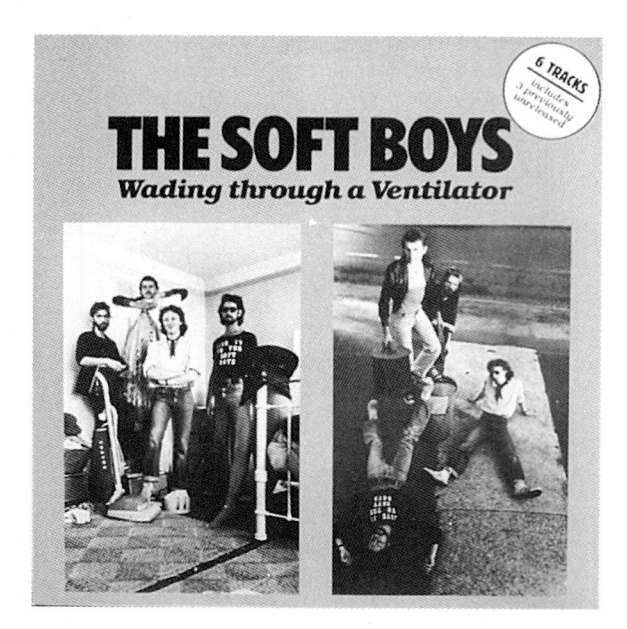

THE SOFT BOYS - Invisible Hits.

THE SOFT BOYS - Wading Through A Ventilator EP.

THE SOFT BOYS - Love Poisoning.

x   Love Poisoning/
    When I Was A Kid (PS)   (Bucketfull Of Brains BOB 1) 1982
o   He's A Reptile/Song No. 4 (PS)   (Midnight Music DING 4) 1983
α   Deck Of Cards/(cut by **Robyn Hitchcock** and Peter Buck)
                                  (Bucketfull Of Brains BOB 17) 1987
β   The Face Of Death/
    The Yodelling Hoover (PS)   (Overground OVER 4) 1989

NB: x This originally appeared in a picture sleeve both with and without copies of "Bucketfull Of Brains" fanzine. o There were two different picture sleeve designs for this release. α This flexidisc came with "Bucketfull Of Brains" fanzine, issue 23. β 600 copies were pressed on yellow vinyl, 400 on white vinyl and there were also fifteen gold test pressings.

The Soft Boys hailed from Cambridge, as Syd Barrett had a decade or so earlier. Barrett was a clear influence on this innovative new wave band as was West Coast psychedelia. They played an exciting amalgam of punk and psychedelia ('punkadelia') which has only retrospectively received the true acclaim it really deserved.

Formed by **Robyn Hitchcock**, who was born in East Grinstead and had once worked as a busker, in 1976, **The Soft Boys** first emerged with the *Give It To The Soft Boys* (EP) in November 1977. It's 'A' side *Wading Through A Ventilator* is a discordant but powerful assault on the listener's senses, with strong psychedelic overtones. There was an early test pressing of this EP which didn't include this song. In its place was *Vyrna Knowl Is A Headbanger*. Only two copies were produced making this one of the most expensive collectable items of the punk era. Whatever, it's really the two psychedelic cuts on the 'B' side of this EP that stand out. The guitar work on *Hear My Brane* creates an unnerving sense of insecurity and *The Face Of Death* relayed the story of a Cambridge dosser with a sickly pallid face who had subsequently died. A song entitled *Where Are The Prawns* was also recorded at the same recording session.

After this **Kimberley Rew**, a highly talented guitarist, joined the band on guitar, harmonica and vocals in place of Alan Davis. The new line-up's first disc *(I Want To Be) An Anglepoise Lamp* was issued on Radar in May 1978, but in comparison to their debut EP it was a great disappointment. It later resurfaced on *Punk Lost And Found* (Shanachie SH 5705) 1996. Yet as a live attraction the band was a devastating spectacle, dominated by **Kimberley Rew**'s discordant yet incisive guitar work and **Hitchcock**'s unique voice and wry humour. In October 1979, Raw withdrew plans to release *Where Are The Prawns* from the band's first recording session. Radar refused to release any more of their records, so the band set up their own company, Two Crabs.

In April 1979, they released their debut album *A Can Of Bees*. It had its moments, particularly *The Pigworker*, a swirling song about a strange holiday camp and *Human Music*, a slower, softer, number and the excellent *Do The Chisel*, a classic piece of late seventies psychedelia. The CD reissue on Rykodisc includes several bonus tracks. After a lengthy tour to promote this album harmonicist Jim Melton left to form his own band and the original bassist, Andy Metcalfe, joined Telephone Bill and The Smooth Operators to be replaced by Matthew Seligman.

In 1980, the new line-up released the *Near The Soft Boys* (EP), which featured two **Hitchcock** compositions, *Kingdom Of Love*, from their second *Underwater Moonlight* album and *Strange*, a haunting little song, together with a superb cover of a Syd Barrett song, *Vegetable Man*. Another Barrett number, *Astronomie Domine* was one of their popular live encores.

Their *Underwater Moonlight* album was a considerable improvement on the first, with **Kimberley Rew**'s guitar work growing in stature all the time and particularly on one track, *The Kingdom Of Love*. It is surprising the album failed to produce a hit when many tracks, notable the title track, *Queen Of Eyes* and *Positive Vibrations* had such immediate appeal. Their less commercial side was in evidence, too, particularly in *I'm An Old Pervert*, notable for its unusual guitar intro and unconventional rhythms and *I'm Insanely Jealous*, one of the high spots of their live act, which featured a paranoid vocal tirade from **Hitchcock** backed by throbbing bass feedback and climatic drum rolls. **Robyn Hitchcock**'s lyrics are among the best, full of wit and eccentricity:-

"They say disinfectant is the only thing I drink
But cleanliness of the soul is more important don't you think?"
(from *Old Pervert*)

The more punkish *I Wanna Destroy You* a rant against war, was the cut selected for 45 release with *I'm An Old Pervert* on its reverse. The CD reissue of *Underwater Moonlight* on Rykodisc includes several bonus tracks, including *Vegetable Man* and the **Fall**-meets-Stooges single *Only The Stones Remain*. In 2001, their original 1980 *Underwater Moonlight* album was reissued on CD by Matador with ten extra tracks and a live disc too. After a further 45 in 1981 the band split. It was a sad case of an excellent band playing in the wrong era. Seligman joined The Thompson Twins and **Kimberley Rew** went on to form Katrina and The Waves. **Robyn Hitchcock** went on to a fairly successful solo career and then fronted his own band The Egyptians, which comprised the original **Soft Boys**' rhythm section of Andy Metcalfe and Morris Windsor plus Roger Jackson on keyboards. They made a string of albums and 45s throughout the eighties, many of which almost rivalled **The Soft Boys**' classic works.

There have been a number of posthumous **Soft Boys** releases. *Only The Stones Remain/Two Halves For The Price Of One* contains half studio and half live recordings. It gave a first airing to *Where Are The Prawns?*, from their 1977 recording session; *Only The Stones Remain*, their final 45; their cover of Barrett's *Astronomie Domine*, *Underwater Moonlight* and *Black Snake Diamond Role*, which **Hitchcock** later used as the title of his first solo album.

Inexplicably *Invisible Hits* (recorded in 1979) was not released until 1983, some time after they'd split. Five of the eleven tracks were previously unissued songs. Cuts like *Let Me Put It Next To You*, *Empty Girl* and *Blues In The Dark* captured **Hitchcock**'s songwriting at its best. Of the remaining six tracks, two were different versions from the originals and four were final mixes of previously roughly mixed songs. Initial copies included an order form for a cassette *Live At The Portland Arms*. This was an all acoustic live tape which included a bizarre collection of cover versions. The CD reissue of *Invisible Hits* on Rykodisc includes five different versions (either alternative mixes or live performances) of songs like *Love Poisoning* and *Have A Heart Betty (I'm Not Fireproof)*.

In August 1985, *Wading Through A Ventilator* issued on Delorean featured the three original tracks from the *Give It To The Soft Boys* EP on Side Two and *The Yodelling Hoover*, *Give It To The Soft Boys* and *Vyrna Knowl Is A Headbanger* on Side One. Like the *Wading Through A Ventilator* 12" single on Delorean, the six-track CD set *Raw Cuts* put out by Overground in 1990 compiles all but one of the recordings from the first **Soft Boys**' session in 1977, from which Raw released the seminal *Give It To The Soft Boys* EP that summer. Aside from the three tracks which comprise that EP, this CD features the original version of *Ventilator* when it was known as *Vyrna Knowl Is A Headbanger*, *Give It To The Soft Boys* itself and *The Yodelling Hoover*. All of this material could be described as punkadelic - early Pink Floyd-influenced psychedelia tinged with punk.

The definitive compilation, though is the 2-CD set, *The Soft Boys 1976-81*, which includes most of their finest moments. Disc one contains three cuts recorded in **Hitchcock**'s living room (March 1977); four tracks from the sessions for their debut EP *Give It To The Soft Boys* (June 1977); the 1978 *Anglepoise Lamp* 45 plus three cuts (*Fatman's Son*, *Where Are The Prawns!* and *Salamander*) from their aborted 1978 Radar album; six previously unreleased live cuts from late 1978 and three other tracks from a Cambridge gig the same year. Disc two features three cuts from their *A Can Of Bees* album, three outtakes from the album's sessions (November 1978); three cuts from *Invisible Hits*; early versions of *Insanely Jealous* and *Underwater Moonlight* (1979); three tracks from the resulting *Underwater Moonlight* album; four live Hope and Anchor cuts (March 1980) and *Only The Stones Remain*.

THE SOFT BOYS - He's A Reptile.

SOFT CELL - Non-Stop Ecstatic Dancing.

Soft Cell

Personnel: MARC ALMOND   vcls   A
            DAVID BALL   keyb'ds A

HCP

ALBUMS: 1(A) NON-STOP EROTIC CABARET
(up to   (Some Bizarre BZLP 2) 1981 5
1986)   2(A) NON-STOP ECSTATIC DANCING (mini-album)
                          (Some Bizarre BZX 1012) 1982 6
        3(A) THE ART OF FALLING APART
                          (Some Bizarre BIZL 3) 1983 5
        4(A) THIS LAST NIGHT IN SODOM
                          (Some Bizarre BIZL 6) 1984 12
        5(A) SOFT CELL - THE SINGLES
                          (Some Bizarre BZLP 3) 1986 58

NB: (1) also issued on CD (remastered) (Some Bizarre 5325952) 1996. (2) also issued on CD (Some Bizarre 5582652) 1998. (3) was originally accompanied by a free 12" Martin/Hendrix medley containing *Hey Joe*, *Purple Haze* and *Voodoo Chile* (APART 12). (3) also issued on CD (Some Bizarre 5582662) 1998. (4) also issued on CD (Some Bizarre 5582672) 1998. CD compilations have included *Their Greatest Hits* (Some Bizarre 830 708-2) 1986, *Memorabilia - The Singles (Soft Cell and Marc Almond)* (Some Bizarre 8485122) 1991 and *Say Hello To Soft Cell* (Spectrum 5520862) 1996.

EP: 1(A) MUTANT MOMENTS (Potential/L.O.V.E. Feelings/Metro MRX/Frustration)(Big Frock AFB 1) 1980

HCP

45s: * Memorabilia/
         A Man Can Get Lost (PS)   (Some Bizarre HARD 1) 1981 -
         Memorabilia (Extended)/
         Persuasion (Extended) (12") (Some Bizarre HARD 12) 1981 -
         Tainted Love/
         Where Did Our Love Go? (PS) (Some Bizarre BZS 2) 1981 1
         Tainted Love/Tainted Dub/
         Where Did Our Love Go? (12") (Some Bizarre BZS 212) 1981 -
         Tainted Love/Memorabilia (12") (Some Bizarre BZS 212) 1981 -
         Bedsitter/Facility Girls (PS) (Some Bizarre BZS 6) 1981 4
         Bedsitter (Extended)/Facility
         Girls (Extended) (12", PS)   (Some Bizarre BZS 612) 1981 -
      + Metro Mr. X/
         (other side by **B-Movie**)   (Lyntone LYN 10410) 1981 -
         Say Hello, Wave Goodbye/
         Instrumental (PS)   (Some Bizarre BZS 7) 1982 3
         Say Hello, Wave Goodbye (Extended)/
         Fun City (12", PS)   (Some Bizarre BZS 712) 1982 -
         Torch/Secure Me (PS)   (Some Bizarre BZS 9) 1982 2
         Torch (Extended)/
         Secure Me (Extended) (12", PS) (Some Bizarre BZS 912) 1982 -
         What!/..... So (PS)   (Some Bizarre BZS 11) 1982 3
         What! (Extended)/
         ..... So (Remix) (12", PS)   (Some Bizarre BZS 112) 1982 -
         Where The Heart Is/
         It's A Mug's Game (PS)   (Some Bizarre BZS 16) 1982 21
         Where The Heart Is (Extended)/It's A Mug's
         Game (Extended) (12", PS)   (Some Bizarre BZS 1612) 1982 -
         The 12" Singles (Boxed set of six 12" singles)
                                      (Some Bizarre CELBX 1) 1982 -
         Numbers/Barriers (PS)   (Some Bizarre BZS 17) 1983 25
         Numbers (Extended)/
         Barriers (Extended) (12", PS) (Some Bizarre BZS 1712) 1983 -
         Soul Inside/
         You Only Live Twice (PS)   (Some Bizarre BZS 20) 1983 16
         Soul Inside/Loving You, Hating Me (Extended Remix)/
         You Only Live Twice/
         007 Theme (double pack)   (Some Bizarre BZS 2020) 1983 -
         Soul Inside/You Only Live Twice/
         007 Theme/Loving You, Hating Me (Extended
         Remix) (12", PS)   (Some Bizarre BZS 2012) 1983 -
         Down In The Subway/
         Disease And Desire (PS)   (Some Bizarre BZS 22) 1984 24
         Down In The Subway (Extended)/Disease And Desire/
         Born To Lose (12")   (Some Bizarre BZS 2212) 1984 -
      x Down In The Subway (Remix)/
         Disease And Desire/
         Born To Lose (12", PS)   (Some Bizarre BZSR 2212) 1984 -

NB: * Limited pressing of 10,000. + This green vinyl flexi came free with 'Flexipop' 12. x This 12" release came in gold and red picture sleeves.

Marc Almond, from Southport, Lancashire was into the punk scene in the late seventies. Dave Ball was a Northern Soul fan, who had a two-track tape recorder he enjoyed playing electronic pieces on. The two Fine Art students first met at Leeds Polytechnic in 1978. In the early days Ball wrote soundtrack music for Almond to sing to. Their first live gig was at Leeds Poly in December 1979. These early gigs tended to be mutli-media events utilising slides and films.

The duo released just 2,000 copies of their debut recording, an EP *Mutant Moments* financed by Ball in the summer of 1980. Today, it is the rarest and most collectable **Soft Cell** release. Watch out for a 'Japanese Fan Club' bootleg reissue of this disc which is identical to the original, except that the matrix number has been printed on, whereas on the original release it was scratched on. A strike at the pressing plant delayed its release and they appeared at the prestigious 'Leeds Futurama 2' concert with no record to promote. Despite this, they were well received. Their next break came when Some Bizzare label supremo Stevo, who'd heard and been impressed by their *Mutant Moments* (EP), invited them to record a song for his new label's first release, a compilation *Some Bizzare Album* (Some Bizzare BZLP 1) in 1981, which contained many bright hopes for the future. The track in question *The Girl With The Patent Leather Face* cost £20 to record.

After an initial 45 *Memorabilia* was released in March 1981, they teamed up with producer Mike Thorne (who'd worked with **Wire**) to record an Ed Cobb composition called *Tainted Love*. It was a big favourite on the Northern Soul circuit and had previously been recorded by Gloria Jones. It is the

SOFT CELL - The Art Of Falling Apart.

song everyone associates **Soft Cell** with. Not only was it a U.K. No. 1, spending sixteen weeks in the charts, it was also a worldwide smash. It got to No. 8 in the 'States, where it spent an incredible forty-three weeks in the charts, and topped the charts in almost twenty countries around the world. Two months later, a further Top 5 hit *Bedsitter* proved that their earlier success was no fluke. The same month **Soft Cell** contributed a re-recorded version of *Metro MRX* (from their debut EP) to a green vinyl flexidisc which came free with issue 12 of 'Flexipop' magazine. On the flip side was a track by **B-Movie**.

In December 1981, a debut album *Non-Stop Erotic Cabaret* was released. It revealed Almond's fascination for the seedier side of life. The album included their earlier hits *Tainted Love* and *Bedsitter* and also spawned a future No. 3 with the slower *Say Hello, Wave Goodbye*. Other notable cuts were *Sex Dwarf, Entertain Me, Youth* and *Seedy Films*. The album was a big success, peaking at No. 5 and spending an incredible forty-six weeks in the charts.

During 1982 **Soft Cell** enjoyed further big hits with *Torch* and the Northern Soul favourite *What!*. To keep the momentum going, in June 1982, a mini-album *Non-Stop Ecstatic Dancing* was released. It featured the rapping voice of Cindy Ecstacy. Again, it fared well commercially, climbing to No. 6 during an eighteen week chart stay. Collectors will also be interested in *The 12" Singles*, a boxed set containing all of their 12" singles up to and including *What!*, in their original sleeves.

Soft Cell recorded their next studio album, *The Art Of Falling Apart* in New York. The album was still reliant on synthesizer and rhythms but they also achieved a sort of psychedelic sound on this album. It came with a free 12", which contained a medley of Hendrix songs:- *Hey Joe, Purple Haze* and *Voodoo Chile*. The album peaked at No. 5 but only spent nine weeks in the chart.

From hereon, though, in commercial terms the band was in decline. Subsequent singles *Where The Heart Is* and *Numbers* failed to crack the Top 20. The latter dealt very candidly with the subject of one night stands, which made some radio stations reluctant to give it airplay. Phonogram had so little confidence in *Numbers* that it was initially marketed shrink-wrapped together with a free copy of *Tainted Love*. Marc Almond and Steve successfully persuaded Phonogram to withdraw this ploy, but the ones that got out are quite collectable now. **Soft Cell** completed a successful U.K. tour in this period but increasingly Marc Almond and David Ball were concentrating on solo projects.

Back in early 1982 Marc Almond had formed various associates to be the Mambas (a name which dates from his pre-**Soft Cell** days) on two solo albums *Untitled* (which comprised an album and a 12") and *Torment And Toreros*. Credited to Marc and The Mambas these were both issued along with three 45s - *Big Louise* (1982), *Black Heart* (1983) (a No. 49 hit) and *Torment* (1983) - on Stevo's Some Bizzare label. Prior to these, a three track 12" single containing *Fun City, Sleaze* and *Taking It And Shaking It* had been issued to **Soft Cell**'s 'Gutterhearts' fan club using the Marc and The Mambas moniker. Later that year, Marc Almond and Friends had recorded a free flexidisc with 'Flexipop' Issue 23. The featured song was a cover of **Throbbing Gristle**'s *Discipline*. Marc Almond and David Ball also appeared on Vicious Pink Phenomena's *My Private Tokyo / Promises* single in return for them performing the backing vocals on **Soft Cell**'s debut album.

Dave Ball, meanwhile, had scored music for a Virgin theatre production of Tennessee Williams' "Suddenly Last Summer" and worked on a solo album *In Strict Tempo*, which was released in November 1983. Psychic TV's Genesis P. Orridge sang on two of the tracks *Man In The Man* and *Sincerity*, but it wasn't well received.

With so much concentration on solo projects **Soft Cell**'s lifespan looked limited. The split was announced in December 1983, but they had to fullfill some contractual commitments. This comprised some pre-booked U.S. dates and the band then returned to the U.K. for some farewell performances at Hammersmith Palais in January 1984. The final **Soft Cell** album *This Last Night In Sodom* was issued posthumously in March 1984. The previous September, *Soul Inside*, an uptempo, almost rock sounding, single had been released as a taster. It proved their most successful for a while reaching No. 16, but only spending a total of five weeks in the chart. The 12" version contained a remix of *Loving You, Hating Me* from their second album. It is one of their more sought-after 12" releases. In the U.S. *Soul Inside* was issued as a 12" EP, containing both sides of the *Numbers* 12" and a new song *Her Imagination*. *This Last Night In Sodom* didn't capture **Soft Cell** at their best and was slated by some critics. A further single was culled from it and released in February 1984. *Down In The Subway*, penned by Jack Hammer, gave the band a final hit, peaking at No. 24 during its six week chart sojourn. Despite being relatively disappointing *This Last Night In Sodom* still got to No. 12 in the album charts.

Inevitably, a compilation of **Soft Cell**'s singles followed the split. Dave Ball's subsequent involvement in the music industry was spasmodic largely comprising guest appearances on other people's albums. Marc Almond went on to release a number of records. Initially supported by a new backing group The Willing Singers he recorded two further albums - *Vermin In Ermine* (1984) and *Stories Of Johnny* (1985) - and several singles. He has continued to record well beyond the time frame of this book.

The best guides to **Soft Cell**'s music retrospectively are *Say Hello To Soft Cell*, which concentrates more on their album cuts and *Memorabilia (The Singles) (Soft Cell and Marc Almond)*. They were a very significant part of the synthetic-pop scene in the early eighties with their catchy soul-flavoured songs.

The Softies

Personnel:	JACK BOOTHE	bs, gtr, keyb'ds, violin, vcls	A
	KEITH LINE	drms	A
	MICHAEL SMITH	gtr, vcls	A
	(SUSAN BOOTH		A)
	(SALLY COOPER		A)
	(COLLEEN DUFFY-SMITH		A)
	(HUGH JONES	12-strings	A)

ALBUM:	1(A)	NICE AND NASTY	(Charly CRL 5012) 1979

45s:	Suicide Pilot/C.I. Angel (PS)	(Charly CYS 1037) 1977
*	Jet Boy Jet Girl/ Children Of The Damned (PS)	(Poker POS 15077) 1978
	Suicide Pilot/C.I. Angel (PS)	(Charly CYS 1036) 1978
	Killing Time/Whiskey Man/ Somethings Gonna Change (PS)	(Charly CYS 1047) 1980

NB: * A Dutch-only release.

The *Nice And Nasty* album was very diverse musically. The core of the group were Jack Boothe, Keith Line and Michael Smith, but they're also assisted by three girls Susan Booth, Sally Cooper and Colleen Duffy-Smith, as well as Hugh Jones on 12-strings. The album was arranged and conducted by Jack Boothe. Keith Line looks a bit like Michael of **Magic Michael** - there could have been some connection. Captain Sensible (of **The Damned**) teamed up with **The Softies** for their earlier *Jet Boy Jet Girl* 45, a Dutch-only release, which is now quite collectable. Their 1980 *Killing Time* 45 is quite accessible.

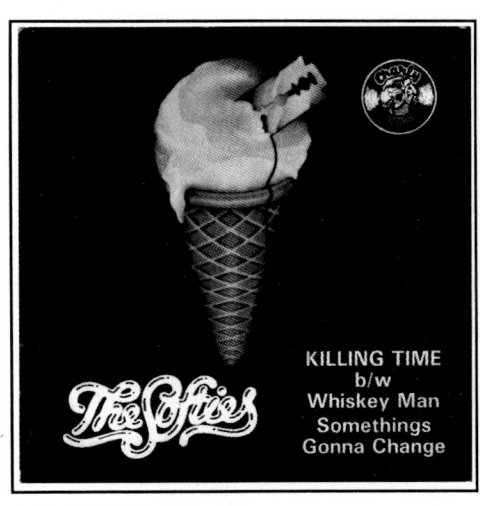

THE SOFTIES - Killing Time.

Some Chicken

Personnel:	IVOR BADCOCK	vcls	A
	TERRY BULL	bs	A
	JESS CHICKEN	gtr	A
	GALWAY KINNELL	drms	A

45s:	New Religion/Blood On The Wall (PS)	(Raw RAW 7) 1977
	Arabian Daze/No. 7 (PS)	(Raw RAW 13) 1978
*	Arabian Daze/No. 7 (12")	(Raw RAWT 13) 1978

NB: * This was later reissued (Raw RAWT 17) 1978 for superstitious people who didn't like buying the record with the catalogue number 13.

A lower division punk combo. *New Religion* was an obscure but run-of-the-mill example of the genre. All four cuts later resurfaced on *The Raw Records Punk Collection* (Anagram CDPUNK 14) in 1993.

Sonic Git

45:	Ain't Nuffink In My Pants	(Cider GIT 001) 1977

This was a one-sided sewage colour flexi-disc. Some copies came with the 'My School's A Cunt' fanzine.

SORE THROAT - Sooner Than You Think.

Sore Throat

Personnel:	DAN FLOWERS	bs	A
	MATT FLOWERS	keyb'ds	A
	CLIVE KIRBY	drms	A
	GREGORY MASON	alto sax	A
	REID SAVAGE	gtr	A
	JUSTIN WARD	vcls	A

ALBUM:	1(A)	SOONER THAN YOU THINK	(Hurricane FLAK 101) 1979

45s:	Complex/I Dunno (PS)	(Hub Cap SPIN 1) 1978
	Flak Jacket/Kamikaze Kid (PS)	(Fast Bucks 102) 1978
	Zombie Rock/I Don't Wanna Go Home (PS)	(Albion 3) 1978
	Kamikaze Kid/Crackdown (PS)	(Hurricane FIRE 2) 1979
	Seventh Heaven/Off The Hook (PS)	(Hurricane FIRE 10) 1979
	Diggin' A Dream/Stocker Stomp (PS)	(Hurricane FIRE 13) 1980

Sore Throat set out as a punk band but later utilised horns and dance rhythms, before they became fashionable. Their sole album was diverse in style, ranging from slow ballads to fast-paced rockers, but their songwriting was limited. The title cut and the slower *Mr. Right* are the best tracks, but inoffensive it might be, essential it certainly isn't.

The Sound

Personnel:	ADRIAN BORLAND	gtr, vcls	A B
	BOB LAWRENCE	bs	A
	JAN	perc	A B
	GRAHAM GREEN	bs	B
	MICHAEL DUDLEY	drms	B

ALBUMS:	1(B)	THE SOUND	(Tortch TOR 008) 1979
(up to	2(B)	JEOPARDY	(Korova KODE 2) 1980
1986)	3(B)	FROM THE LION'S MOUTH	(Korova KODE 5) 1981
	4(B)	ALL FALL DOWN	(WEA 240010/1) 1982
	5(B)	HEADS AND HEARTS	(Statik STAT LP 24) 1985
	6(B)	IN THE HOTHOUSE	(Statik STAT DLP 1) 1985

NB: (5) also issued on CD (Statik CDST 24) 1986 with several additional tracks.

EPs:	1(B)	PHYSICAL WORLD (Cold Beat/Physical World/	
(up to		Unwritten Law) (PS)	(Tortch TOR 003) 1979
1986)	2(B)	SHOCK OF DAYLIGHT (PS)	(Statik STAB 1) 1984

NB: (2) also issued on CD (Warzone RENCD 1) 1996.

45s:	Heyday/Brute Force (PS)	(Korova KOW 10) 1980
(up to	Sense Of Purpose/Point Of No Return	(Korova KOW 21) 1981
1986)	Hot House/New Dark Age (PS)	(Korova KOW 23) 1982
	Counting The Days/	
	Dreams Then Plans (PS)	(Statik TAK 16) 1984
	One Thousand Reasons/	
	Blood And Poison (PS)	(Statik TAK 28) 1984
	One Thousand Reasons/Blood And Poison/	
	Steal Your Air (12")	(Statik TAK 28) 1984
	Temperature Drop/Oiled	(Statik TAK 34) 1985

Prior to forming Liverpool's **Sound** Adrian Borland had fronted **The Outsiders** between 1977-78. When Graham Green and Michael Dudley were recruited to play alongside percussionist Jan they changed name to **Sound** just prior to recording the *Physical World* EP for Tortch in December 1979. Whilst **The Outsiders** had been a punk combo **The Sound** adopted a new style more in the mould of **The Psychedelic Furs** and Liverpool compatriots **Echo and The Bunnymen**. Their debut EP attracted enough favourable attention for them to be signed by Korova, for whom they released a couple of albums and three singles. *Jeopardy* showcased Adrian Borland's gripping vocals and these contained attractive music. *From The Lion's Mouth* consolidated the promise of their debut with a fuller sound. These albums helped to establish Borland as one of the most creative writers of post-punk Britain. Alongside all this Borland and Green had created a more experimental project called **Second Layer**.

One **Sound** album to avoid is their one effort for WEA *All Fall Down* which lacked much flair or interest, but with a switch to Statik came a return to form with the six-song EP *Shock Of Daylight* with some melodic and spirited material and performances. However, their two subsequent albums for Statik weren't as good.

In 1983, the band split, although Borland recorded a further album *Alexandria* as Adrian Borland and The Citizens for Play It Again Sam in 1989.

Epic Soundtracks

EP:	1	POPULAR, CLASSICAL (Jelly Babies/A 3-Acre Floor/	
		Pop In Packets) (PS)	(Rough Trade RT 084) 1981

45:	*	Rain, Rain Rain/	
		Ghost Train (12" PS)	(Rough Trade RT 104) 1982

NB: * Recorded with Jowe Head.

These were solo ventures by **Epic Soundtracks**, who was a member of **Swell Maps** as was Jowe Head. There's also a collection of outtakes called *Debris* (Return To Sender RTS 20) 1995. The release had a pressing of 2,000 and was sold by mail order.

SOUTHERN DEATH CULT - Southern Death Cult.

The Southern Death Cult

Personnel:	AKY (NAWAZ QUERESHI)	drms	A
	BUZZ BURROWS	gtr	A
	BARRY JEPSON	bs	A
	IAN LINDSAY (ASTBURY)	vcls	A

HCP
ALBUM: 1(A) SOUTHERN DEATH CULT
(Beggars Banquet BEGA 46) 1983 43

NB: (1) also issued on CD (Lowdon BBL 46CD) 1988 and again in 1996. Also relevant is a CD *Complete Recordings* (Situation 2 SITU 2329 CD) 1991.

45s:	* Fatman/Moya	(Situation 2 SIT 19) 1982
	Fatman/Moya/The Girl (12", PS)	(Situation 2 SIT 19T) 1982

NB: * Issued in a poster bag.

By 1982 the original thrust of punk had been lost. With fashion-orientated dance groups from the night clubs dominating the music scene many pundits were craving for new rock saviours. **Southern Death Cult** from Bradford were one of a number of groups to emerge as part of what was termed 'positive punk'. They were fronted by Ian Lindsay. Originally from the north west of England Lindsay's family had spent part of his childhood in Scotland before returning to Merseyside and then emigrating to Canada. He returned to Britain in 1978 at the height of the punk explosion. He spent a while singing with groups in Liverpool and Ireland before settling in Bradford, where he provided the family piece in the jigsaw of a new group **Southern Death Cult**. Word about the band spread fast and their early live gigs were well attended. They decided to sign to the independent label Situation 2 and in December 1982 released a double 'A' sided 45 *Moya/Fatman*, which came as a 7" with a fold-out poster bag and later as a 12" with an additional cut *The Girl*. Although this release didn't live up to all the hype, it topped the indie chart and climbed to No. 43 in the national chart during a three week stay.

In early 1983 the band supported **Bauhaus** on a national tour, which led to them being linked with 'goth rock'. However, by mid-March Ian Lindsay was dissatisfied with his colleagues' future direction and decided to leave. Within just two weeks he had formed a new group **Death Cult**.

An album of the band's material was issued retrospectively in June to fulfil contractual obligations. The album comprised three songs recorded live on a cassette at Rafters in Manchester during December 1982, four songs from Radio One sessions and early demos of *Fatman*, *Moya* and *The Crypt*. It didn't really capture them at their best. The CD version compiles the three cuts from their debut 12", six from BBC sessions (four Jensen and two Peel and these have the worst sound quality), one *The Crypt* from an EMI studio session, three tracks taped live in Manchester and two studio cuts (*Moya* and *Fatman*) which close the CD.

The remaining **Southern Death Cult** members formed an outfit called Getting The Fear.

Spandau Ballet

Personnel:	TONY HADLEY	vcls, synth	A
	JOHN KEEBLE	drms	A
	GARY KEMP	keyb'ds, gtr	A
	MARTIN KEMP	bs	A
	STEVE NORMAN	sax, gtr	A

HCP
ALBUMS: 1(A) JOURNEY TO GLORY (Reformation CHR 1331) 1981 5
(up to 2(A) DIAMOND (Reformation CDL 1353) 1982 15
1986) 3(A) TRUE (Reformation CDL 1403) 1983 1
4(A) PARADE (Reformation CDL 1473) 1984 2
5(A) THE SINGLES COLLECTION (Chrysalis SBTV 1) 1985 3
6(A) THROUGH THE BARRICADES
(Reformation CBS 450 259-1) 1986 7

NB: (1) also issued on CD (Chrysalis CCD 1331) 1982, (EMI Gold CDGOLD 1046) 1996 and (Disky DC 875512) 1997. (2) also issued as a box set of 4 x 12" singles with posters and lyric sheet (Chrysalis CBOX 1353) 1982. (3) also issued on CD (Chrysalis CCD 1403) 1986 and again in 1990. (4) also issued on CD (Chrysalis CPCD 1473) 1987 and (EMI Gold CDGOLD 1010) 1996. (5) also issued on CD (Chrysalis CCD 1498) 1986. (6) also issued on CD (CBS 4502592) 1986, 1990 and 1994. There's also a number of compilations and collections *The Best Of Spandau Ballet* (Chrysalis CCD 1894) 1991, *The Best Of Spandau Ballet (18 Original Hits/3-CD set)* (Disky LAD 873262) 1996, *Twelve Inch Mixes* (Chrysalis CCD 1574) 1987 and again in 1994, *The Collection* (EMI Gold CDGOLD 1081) 1997, *Gold (The Best Of Spandau Ballet)* (Chrysalis 5267002) 2000 and *Original Gold* (2-CD set) (Disky HR 857732) 1999.

HCP
45s: To Cut A Long Story Short/To Cut A Long
(up to Story Short (Instr.) (PS) (Reformation CHS 2473) 1980 5
1986) To Cut A Long Story Short/To Cut A Long Story
Short (instr.) (12", PS) (Reformation CHS 122473) 1980 -
The Freeze/
The Freeze (instr.) (PS) (Reformation CHS 2486) 1981 17
The Freeze/
The Freeze (instr.) (12", PS) (Reformation CHS 122486) 1989 -
Musclebound/Glow (PS) (Reformation CHS 2509) 1981 10
Musclebound/Glow (12", PS) (Reformation CHS 122509) 1981 -
+ Chant No. 1 (I Don't Need This Pressure On)/
Feel The Chant (PS) (Reformation CHS 2528) 1981 3
+ Chant No. 1 (I Don't Need This Pressure On)/
Feel The Chant (12", PS) (Reformation CHS 122528) 1981 -
Paint Me Down/
Man With Guitar (Re-Paint) (PS) (Chrysalis CHS 2560) 1981 30
Paint Me Down/Man With
Guitar (Re-Paint) (12", PS) (Chrysalis CHS 122560) 1981 -
She Loved Like Diamond/She Loved
Like Diamond (alt. version) (PS) (Chrysalis CHS 2585) 1982 49
She Loved Like Diamond/She Loved Like
Diamond (alt. version) (12", PS) (Chrysalis CHS 122585) 1982 -
Instinction/Gently (PS) (Chrysalis CHS 2602) 1982 10
Instinction/Gently (picture disc) (Chrysalis CHSP 2602) 1982 -
Instinction/Gently/

SPANDAU BALLET - Chant No. 1 12".

	Chant No. 1 (Remix)	(Chrysalis CHS 122602) 1982	-
	Lifeline/Live And Let Live (PS)	(Chrysalis CHS 2642) 1982	7
	Lifeline/ Live And Let Live (picture disc)	(Chrysalis CHSP 2642) 1982	-
	Lifeline/ Live And Let Live (12", PS)	(Chrysalis CHS 122642) 1982	-
	Communication (Parts 1 & 2) (PS)	(Reformation CHS 2662) 1983	12
	Communication (Parts 1 & 2) (picture disc)	(Reformation CHSP 2662) 1983	-
	Communication (Parts 1 & 2) (12", PS)	(Reformation CHS 12262) 1983	-
	True/Lifeline (PS)	(Reformation SPAN 1) 1983	1
	True/Lifeline (picture disc)	(Reformation SPANP 1) 1983	-
	True/Lifeline (12", PS)	(Reformation SPANX 1) 1983	-
	Gold (Parts 1 & 2) (PS)	(Reformation SPAN 2) 1983	2
	Gold (Parts 1& 2) (picture disc)	(Reformation SPANP 2) 1983	-
	Gold (Extended)/ Foundation (12", PS)	(Reformation SPANX 2) 1983	-
	Only When You Leave/ Paint Me Down (PS)	(Reformation SPAN 3) 1984	3
	Only When You Leave/ Paint Me Down (picture disc)	(Reformation SPANP 3) 1984	-
	Only When You Leave (Extended)/Only When You Leave/ Paint Me Down (12", PS)	(Reformation SPANX 3) 1984	-
	I'll Fly For You/To Cut A Long Story Short (live) (PS)	(Reformation SPAN 4) 1984	9
*	I'll Fly For You/To Cut A long Story Short (live) (picture disc)	(Reformation SPANP 4) 1984	-
	I'll Fly For You (Extended)/I'll Fly For You (live)/ To Cut A Long Story Short (live) (12", PS)	(Reformation SPANX 4) 1984	-
x	Highly Strung (Parts 1 & 2)	(Reformation SPAN 5) 1984	15
	Round And Round/ True (gatefold PS)	(Reformation SPAN 6) 1984	18
α	Round And Round/True (live)/ Gold (live) (12", PS)	(Reformation SPANX 6) 1984	-
	Fight For Ourselves/Fight... The Heartache (PS)	(Reformation A 7264) 1986	15
	Fight For Ourselves (Extended)/Fight For Ourselves/ Fight.... The Heartbeat (12", PS)	(Reformation TA 7264) 1986	-
	Through The Barricades/ With The Pride (PS)	(Reformation SPANS 1) 1986	6
	Through The Barricades/ With The Pride (picture disc)	(Reformation SPANSP 1) 1986	-
	Through The Barricades (Extended)/Through The Barricades/ With The Pride (12", PS)	(Reformation PANDST 1) 1986	-
Reissues:	Communication/Lifeline	(Old Gold OG 4037) 1987	-
	To Cut A Long Story Short/Chant No. 1 (I Don't Need This Pressure On)	(Old Gold OG 9677) 1987	-
	True/Gold	(Old Gold OG 9679) 1987	-

NB: + Assisted by Beggar & Co. * This came in five different picture discs. x Some copies came on silver vinyl. α Some copies came on gold vinyl, others came with a poster, sticker, postcard and five photos.

Along with **Duran Duran** and a rejuvenated **Ultravox**, **Spandau Ballet** were at the forefront of the New Romantic movement of the early eighties.

Spandau Ballet members all showed talent at a young age. Gary Kemp was just nine when he was given his first guitar by his parents. He later performed at a school prize-giving day in front of the Bishop of Stepney, who was so impressed he gave Kemp a tape recorder which he used over the coming years when writing songs. With his brother Martin he went on to attend Owens Grammar in Islington, where he met Tony Hadley (born Anthony Patrick Hadley), John Keeble and Steve Norman, who like the Kemps were born and grew up locally in Islington, North London. Hadley had received vocal lessons as a child and won a talent contest in 1974 singing a version of Gary Puckett and The Union Gap's *Young Girl*. Martin Kemp showed promise at football and trained with Arsenal Football Club for a while in his teens.

After failing his 'A' levels Gary Kemp started a power pop group called The Makers with Hadley, Keeble, Norman and Richard Miller, but it petered out. He later revived the group in 1979 with another old school mate Steve Dagger. In this revised line-up, his brother Martin Kemp featured on bass (although he couldn't actually play it at the outset) and Richard Miller wasn't involved. This second incarnation of The Makers changed their name to **Spandau Ballet** and got heavily into the clubbing scene in places like The Blitz and Billy's Le Kilt at the end of the decade. During a Steve Strange party at The Blitz in December 1979, Island Records boss Chris Blackwell attempted to sign the band. However, Steve Dagger had other ideas and wasn't interested in Blackwell's offer. Instead, with the help of a lawyer, he set up the band's own Reformation label and subsequent;y signed a deal to license its releases to Chrysalis Records.

SPANDAU BALLET - Gold 12".

By March 1980, **Spandau Ballet** had successfully modelled themselves in the 'New Romantic' image with fashionable clothing, hair gel and make-up. They were a frequent attraction in London's clubs but to attract publicity also performed a number of unusual one-off concerts. This included a gig at the Scala Cinema, which was filmed for inclusion in a documentary about the current club scene. They also did a gig on board the H.M.S. Belfast, a Second World War cruiser moored on London's River Thames.

In December 1980, their debut release *To Cut A Long Story Short* appeared. This tight, riffy dance tune made quite an impact and sold well enough to take them to No. 5 during an eleven week chart stint. It established their style which was heavily rhythmic, quite funky and characterised by lots of synthesizers and powerful vocals. It also glistened like a jewel on their debut album *Journey To Glory*, produced by Richard James Burgess, which also got to No. 5. The album spent an impressive twenty-nine weeks in the charts. It also contained two other successful singles *The Freeze* (No. 17) and *Musclebound* (No. 10).

Fuelled on by their success here in Britain **Spandau Ballet** visited the 'States in April 1981 playing at New York's Underground Club. To help spread 'New Romanticism', they took with them a number of British fashion designers.

Back in Britain in the summer of 1981, they released one of their finest slabs of vinyl. Assisted by U.K. funk outfit Beggar & Co., their *Chant No. 1 (I Don't Need This Pressure On)* added a funky-soul feel to their rock base to sound very distinctive and different at the time. The single got to No. 3 and enjoyed a ten week run in the charts. It figured on their 1982 album *Diamond*, which utilised horns. This album also included two earlier 45s *Paint Me Down* (No. 30) and *She Loved Like Diamond* (No. 49). A further cut, *Instinction* was later remixed by Trevor Horn for 45 release and just made the Top 10. The 12" release also added a remixed version of *Chant No. 1*. Overall, though, the *Diamond* album performed less favourably than their debut, only managing to climb to No. 15 during its eighteen weeks in the chart.

Spandau Ballet now changed direction. Working with a new production team of Tony Swain and Steve Jolley, they discarded their synthesizers and rhythmic funk for a form of soul-influenced schmaltzy rock. It produced some memorable melodies with cuts like *True* (the title cut of their next album, which when issued as a 45 topped the U.K. charts in its second week of release and went on to spend four weeks at No. 1), *Lifeline* (No. 7), *Communication* (No. 12) and *Gold*, which were all hit singles in their own right. *Gold* was arguably their magnum opus, a superb song which had both drama and melody. It was kept off the top spot in Britain by K.C. and The Sunshine Band's *Give It Up*, but BBC TV used it as the theme for its Olympic coverage that year. In July 1983, at the peak of their popularity,

Spandau Ballet performed at prestigious London venues like the Royal Albert Hall, Sadler's Wells Theatre and the Royal Festival Hall. In Britain the *True* album topped the charts for a week and spent a staggering ninety weeks in the charts in all. It was also the album which cracked the U.S. market, climbing to No. 19. The *True* and *Gold* singles were also U.S. hits, reaching No's 4 and 29 respectively.

Their fourth album *Parade*, released in the summer of 1984, was similar in style. *Only When You Leave*, one of the tracks, was selected for 45 release as a taster, a month earlier. A mellow song, it brought them another big hit, peaking at No. 3 in Britain and spending nine weeks in the charts. It subsequently got to No. 34 in the 'States. *Parade* climbed to No. 2 here in Britain and spent thirty-nine weeks in the chart. It was kept off the top by Bob Marley's *Legend* album. In the 'States, **Spandau Ballet** were failing to capitalise on their earlier successes and the album only climbed to No. 50. Whilst in Britain three subsequent hits were culled from the album - *I'll Fly For You* (no. 9), (which was also issued in five different picture disc formats, as part of a marketing ploy), *Highly Strung* (No. 15) (some copies came in silver vinyl) and *Round And Round* (No. 18) (the 12" version was released in various formats) - none of these charted in the 'States. **Spandau Ballet** became increasingly bitter about this and the following year sued Chrysalis, blaming the label's inefficient marketing of them in the 'States for their disappointing commercial performance.

The band's legal dispute with Chrysalis prevented them from releasing any new material until it was resolved. Despite this, they were never far away from the public eye for long. In late November 1984, they participated in the recording sessions for Band Aid's *Do They Know It's Christmas?* and Tony Hadley sang one of the lead lines in the song, which predictably became a Christmas No. 1. They also played six nights at Wembley Arena, London, that December. The following July, they appeared on the Live Aid bill at Wembley.

During the recording hiatus Chrysalis released the worthwhile compilation *The Singles Collection*, against the band's wishes. It sold well, with the aid of a TV promotion campaign, peaking at No. 3 and spending forty-nine weeks in the charts. By 1986, the legal dispute was resolved. Freed from Chrysalis, **Spandau Ballet** signed a new contract with CBS and made it a condition that none of their records were released in South Africa because of apartheid. Gary Kemp had performed solo on the Labour Party's Red Wedge U.K. tour that year.

Their new album *Through The Barricades* was recorded in France. In the usual tradition it was preceded by a taster single *Fight For Ourselves*, which reached No. 15 in the U.K. The album got to No. 7, but enjoyed a relatively short nineteen week chart stint by the band's standards. The title cut, a ballad, got to No. 6 in the singles chart to give them their biggest hit since *Only When You Leave* over two years earlier. In January 1987, *How Many Lies*, a third single from the album reached No. 34.

As we leave **Spandau Ballet** at the end of 1986 their best years were over. It's worth reflecting that between 1980 - 89 they enjoyed a run of twenty consecutive U.K. Top 50 hits. Their original line-up had stayed intact throughout. In their later years, they branched out. Most notably, the Kemp brothers played the notorious twin gangsters in 'The Krays', a 1988 film.

SPANDAU BALLET - Only When You Leave 12".

Inevitably, there are still plenty of compilations and collections of their songs on the market. Appearances on compilations have included *Chant No. 1* on *The Model* (Spectrum 5529182) 1997 and *New Romantics* (EMI Gold CDGOLD 1041) 1996. You'll also find *To Cut A Long Story Short* on *Wave (The Biggest New Wave Hits)* (3-CD set) (Disky HR 868442) 1996 and *Be Free With Your Love* on *Wave Party* (Columbia 4758322) 1995. **Spandau Ballet**'s place in rock and pop history as one of the bands at the helm of the 'New Romantic' movement, who went on to become one of the most successful acts of the eighties, is assured.

Spear Of Destiny

Personnel:			
	CHRIS BELL	drms	A
	KIRK BRANDON	vcls, gtr	ABC
	LASCELLES JAMES	sax	A
	STAN STAMMERS	bs	ABC
	JOHN LENNARD	sax	B
	NEIL PYZER	keyb'ds, sax	BC
	DOLPHIN TAYLOR	drms	BC
	MICKEY DONNELLY	sax	C
	ALAN ST. CLAIRE	gtr	C

HCP

ALBUMS:	1(A)	GRAPES OF WRATH	(Epic EPC 25318) 1983 62
(up to	2(C)	ONE-EYED JACKS	(Epic EPC 25836) 1984 22
1986)	3(C)	WORLD SERVICE	(Epic EPC 26514) 1985 11

NB: (1) reissued at mid-price (Epic EPC 32779) 1986. There are also some relevant compilations, *S.O.D. - The Epic Years* (Epic EPC 4508721) 1987, which got to No. 53 and was also issued on CD (Epic CDEPC 4508722) 1987; *Collection: Spear Of Destiny* (Castle Collector CCSCD 297) 1991; and *Time Of Our Lives (The Best Of Spear Of Destiny)* (Virgin CDOVD 449) 1995. There are also a couple of live releases *BBC Radio One Live In Concert* (Windsong WINCD 055) 1994 and *Live At The Lyceum 22.12.85* (Mau Mau MAUCD 638) 1993.

HCP

45s:	Flying Scotsman/The Man Who Tunes		
(up to	The Drums (PS)	(Epic SPEAR 1) 1983 -	
1986) *	Flying Scotsman (Extended)/Africa/The Man Who		
	Tunes The Drums (12", PS)	(Epic SPEAR 13-1) 1983 -	
	The Wheel/The Hop (PS)	(Epic A 3372) 1983 59	
	The Wheel/The Hop (Picture disc)	(Epic WA 3372) 1983 -	
	The Wheel/The Hop/Grapes Of Wrath (Live)/		
	The Preacher (Live) (Double pack PS)	(Epic DA 3372) 1983 -	
	The Wheel/The Hop/Solution (Live)/Roof Of The World		
	(Live)/Love Is A Ghost (Live) (12", PS)	(Epic TA 3372) 1983 -	
	Prisoner Of Love/Rosie (PS)	(Epic A 4068) 1984 59	
	Prisoner Of Love/Rosie/Rainmaker (Live)/		
	Don't Turn Away (Live) (Doublepack, PS)	(Epic DA 4068) 1984 -	
	Prisoner Of Love/Rosie/Grapes Of		
	Wrath (1984 Version) (12", PS)	(Epic TA 4068) 1984 -	
	Liberator/Forbidden Planet (PS)	(Epic A 4310) 1984 67	
	Liberator (Extended Remix)/Liberator (Dub Mix)/		
	Forbidden Planet (12", PS)	(Epic TA 4310) 1984 -	
	All My Love (Ask Nothing)/		
	Last Card (PS)	(Epic A 6333) 1985 61	
	All My Love (Ask Nothing) (Extended)/Last Card/		
	Walk In My Shadow (12", PS)	(Epic TA 6333) 1985 -	
	All My Love (Ask Nothing) (Extended)/Last Card/		
	The Wheel (Live)/Prisoner Of Love (Live)/		
	Liberator (Live) (12", PS)	(Epic QTA 6333) 1985 -	
	Come Back/Cole Younger (PS)	(Epic A 6445) 1985 55	
	Come Back (Dub Mix)/Cole Younger/		
	Young Men (Return Of) (12", PS)	(Epic TA 6445) 1985 -	
	Come Back (Dub Mix)/Cole Younger/		
	Young Men (Return Of)/Come Back (WL Remix)		
	(12", double-pack)	(Epic DTA 6445) 1985 -	
	The Wheel/Flying Scotsman (Extended)/		
	Prisoner Of Love/		
	Liberator (Extended Remix) (12")	(Old Gold OG 4007) 1986 -	

NB: * The first 5,000 copies of the 12" came with a free poster.

After winding up his previous band **Theatre Of Hate** in September 1982, Kirk Brandon regrouped with Stan Stammers as **Spear Of Destiny** in December 1982. They were joined by Chris Bell (previously with King Trigger and Thompson Twins) on drums and former Mighty Diamonds

SPEAR OF DESTINY - Grapes Of Wrath.

member Lascelles James on sax. The same month they embarked on a national tour playing mostly old **Theatre Of Hate** material.

Their debut single *Flying Scotsman* appeared in record outlets in February 1983. It sported a traditional tune somewhat similar to *The Bonnie Banks Of Loch Lomond*. The 12" version of the release contained a bonus track *Africa* (taken from an earlier Radio One session), an extended version of the 'A' side and the first 5,000 copies came with a free poster. Despite some commercial potential the single failed to chart.

The band played a punk-influenced form of power rock, which often had an anthemic feel. Their debut album *Grapes Of Wrath* utilised material originally projected for a second **Theatre Of Hate** album. The guitar-based sound of their earlier work was most evident on *Solution*, but much of the album was dominated by James' sax playing. Nick Launay handled production, but the album managed only two weeks in the charts, peaking at No. 62. From April to June the band toured Europe extensively to promote the album. In May *The Wheel*, one of the tracks on it, was selected for 45 release. The 7" was also available as a picture disc, whilst the 12" contained three tracks from a live gig in Aberdeen. There was also a 7" double-pack which contained two different numbers from the Aberdeen gig. *The Wheel* was a live favourite from the band and it did better commercially than its predecessor, spending five weeks in the charts and climbing to No. 59.

In August 1983, Brandon decided to modify the line-up to give the band more commitment. John Boy Lennard (who previously been in **Theatre Of Hate**) came back into the fold, along with himself and Stammers and two entirely new recruits Dolphin Taylor (drms) (previously with **Stiff Little Fingers** and **Tom Robinson Band**) and Neil Pyzer (sax and keyb'ds) (previously with **Howard Devoto** Band, Dexy's Midnight Runners and **The Case**). Of the two departeees Chris Bell joined The Specimen and **Gene Loves Jezebel** and Lascelles James appeared to drift out of the music business.

This new line-up recorded the *Prisoner Of Love* single, which spent three weeks in the charts, peaking at No. 59, and had their own arrangement of a traditional number *Rosie* on the flip. By the time the 45 was in the shops in January 1984 Lennard had departed and Mickey Donnelly (ex-**The Case**) and additional guitarist Alan St. Claire had joined up.

A further 45 *Liberator* followed in April, but its commercial performance - two weeks in the chart and a peak position of 67 - was disappointing. This is surprising because it was one of their most powerful numbers with a blistering opening drum/guitar assault, wailing sax and an arse-kicking chorus. It was the stand-out track on their second album *One-Eyed Jacks*, which emerged before the end of the month. They went on tour during April and May to promote the album, on which Nick Tauber handled production. The album was characterised by Brandon's all-out vocal assault, which is at its most pronounced on *Liberator* and *Rainmaker*. The album was well received, going on to spend seven weeks in the chart with a best position of No. 22. They also appeared at the York Rock Festival in September 1984 along with **Echo and The Bunnymen** and **The Sisters Of Mercy**.

Prior to their third album Brandon recorded a one-off single with Rusty Egan as **The Senate** (see entry for details). In May 1985, a much more mainstream single *All My Love (Ask For Nothing)* appeared, which wasn't well received by the band's fans. Sales were possibly added by the band's appearance at Milton Keynes Bowl in late June as support to **U2** and the disc reached No. 61. A live favourite *Come Back* was selected for the follow-up but lost much of its hard-edge through the transition to vinyl. Despite this sales were reasonably good. The single climbed to No. 55, spending three weeks in the chart. *All My Love* and *Come Back* both figured on their *World Service* album released the following month. This featured some of their strongest material yet. Highlights included the title track dealing with world starvation; *I Can See* which dealt with drug abuse and the magnum opus *Mickey*, an emotional story of a young man who leaves a dead end job to join the army and is sent to the Falklands where he loses his sight after treading on a mine and yearns to return home to his mum. The album concludes with *Harlan Country*, which deals with an oppressed American mining community. The band's most successful album to date, this entered the chart at No. 11 and enjoyed seven weeks in all in the charts. Just when they seemed on the brink of even greater success Brandon decided to disassemble the band.

Live At The Lyceum 22/12/85, which actually dates from 1984, does quite a good job at capturing some of the excitement of their concerts.

BBC Radio One Live In Concert features a Kilburn concert from April 1987. The band certainly aren't on top form here and even their live favourites like *Liberator* and *Rocket Ship* lack excitement.

The only release in 1986 was an Old Gold 12" EP which featured extended versions of *Flying Scotsman* and *Liberator* along with *The Wheel* and *Prisoner Of Love*.

Here we leave **Spear Of Destiny** but it was not the end because Brandon returned in December 1986 with a new line-up and the band continued to be a musical force well into the nineties.

The band have also appeared on some retrospective compilations. *Never Take Me Alive* can also be heard on *A Post Punk Primer* (Virgin CDOVD 498) 1997 and *Wheel* has resurfaced on *Wave Party* (Columbia 4758322) 1995.

Special Duties

Personnel:	STEVE ARROGANT	vcls	AB
	BART	gtr	AB
	STEVE DUTY	bs	AB
	MARK GREGORY	drms	A
	STU CRASSHATER	drms	B

ALBUM: 1(B) '77 IN '82   (Rondelet ABOUT 9) 1982
(up to 1986)

NB: (1) also reissued on CD (Captain Oi! AHOY CD 35) 1995 with eleven bonus tracks. Also on vinyl (AHOY LP 35) 1995. There's also three CDs: *'77 In '97* (Captain Oi! AHOY CD 75) 1997; *Live At GBGB's* (Special Duties SD 1977) 1999 and *The Punk Singles Collection* (Captain Oi! AHOY CD 118) 1999.

SPECIAL DUTIES - Violent Society.

SPECIAL DUTIES - Police State.

SPECIAL DUTIES - '77 In '82.

| EPs:
(up to
1986) | 1(B) | VIOLENT SOCIETY (Violent Society/
It Ain't Our Fault/
Colchester Council) (PS) | (Rondelet ROUND 15) 1982 |
| | 2(B) | POLICE STATE (Police State/We Gotta Fight/
It Just Ain't Me/
Special Duties) (PS) | (Rondelet ROUND 20) 1982 |

45s: (up to 1986)	Violent Society/ Colchester Council (PS)	(Charnel House SARCOPHAGI 2) 1980
	Bullshit Crass/You're Doing Yourself No Good (PS)	(Rondelet ROUND 24) 1982
	Punk Rocker/Too Much Talking (PS)	(Expulsion OUT 1) 1983

An Oi! band from Colchester in Essex. They first came to prominence on account of vocalist Steve Arrogant's war of words with **Crass** in the letter pages of 'Sounds'. Their vinyl debut, issued by Charnel House Records in late 1980, was produced by **Lurkers'** vocalist Howard Wall. It was also their only 45 to feature their original drummer Mark Gregory, who later played for **Condemned 84**. The 'A' side *Violent Society* became one of their live favourites and sounds very similar to **Stiff Little Fingers'** *Alternative Ulster* and on the flip *Colchester Council*'s main lyrics "Colchester Council... full of shit" was another of their finest moments, despite obvious connections with **The Clash**'s *London's Burning* and **Menace**'s *GLC*. In January 1982, Rondelet Records released both songs again on an EP along with *It Ain't Our Fault*, the lyrics to which were really a continuation of *Colchester Council*. All three cuts were later re-recorded for their debut album *'77 In '82*.

Their May 1982 EP *Police State* brought them their first indie chart success, climbing to No. 23. The title cut is a brief rant about the police wasting time harassing people because of the way they were dressed, *We Gotta Fight* was a rant about high unemployment in Britain at the time and how further education wasn't the answer to keeping the jobless figures down. *It Just Ain't Me* was written to express the frustration Steve Arrogant felt whilst working as a trainee for a print company and *Special Duties* craved for the magic of 1977.

SPECIAL DUTIES - Bullshit Crass.

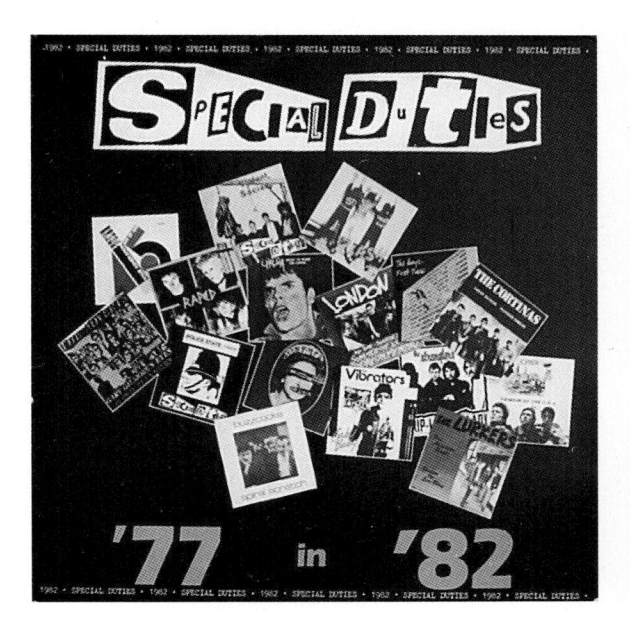

Along with *Violent Society*, *Bullshit Crass* released in October 1982 was probably their best-known song. It reached No. 7 in the indie charts and attracted considerable attention. **Crass** had said "Punk Is Dead" as early as 1979 and **Special Duties** were trying to keep it alive in 1982 - hence the war of words.

Special Duties' debut album *'77 In '82* was aptly titled. All their songs sounded straight out of '77 - fast-paced punk rants. Lyrically, they had plenty to say:-

"Cheap labour in disguise
Youth opportunities, government lies
Keeps young kids off the dole
Future sealed or so they're told

Government policies cause of recession
Government policies too much aggression
Government policies working class enemy
Government policies a change there's gotta be"
(from *Government Policies*)

"Why do you blame youth for what's happening today
Who got us in this mess anyway
Does it make you feel better to pass the blame
Of course it does because you're all the same

Too much talking but you get no results
Too much talking always look for faults
Too much talking that's what you do
And that's why we've got no faith in you"
(from *Too Much Talking*)

This latter song, the opening cut on their *'77 in '82* album was re-recorded for the 'B' side of *Punk Rocker*, their final 45 of the eighties put out on Expulsion Records. The song was about a stereotypical punk who tarted himself up hours before the gig and was then afraid to dance in case he ruined his image. It reached No. 37 in the indie charts but proved to be their final eighties vinyl.

The superb Captain Oi! label reissued their *'77 in '82* album in 1995 with eleven bonus cuts, which included their two EPs and 45 for Rondelet and their rare Charnel House 45. This was also available on vinyl with a lyric insert.

They reformed in 1986, releasing a 45 *Mutt* on One Stop. In 1997, when Colchester United reached the final of the Auto Windscreen Shield, they bizarrely released *Wembley! Wembley!* as their official single.

'77 In '97 comprised new recordings. Eighteen cuts on CD (Captain Oi! AHOY CD 75) and twelve on vinyl (AHOY LP 75).

The *Live At CBGB's* CD features a concert from July 1998. It's a good quality recording comprising mostly old material with some new songs interspersed. It's nicely packaged too, with lots of photos.

SPECIAL DUTIES - Punk Rocker.

The *Punk Singles Collection* CD, released in 1999 by Captain Oi!, includes tracks from all their ten singles to date. Some of these are outside the time span of this book but their Colchester United tribute *Wembley! Wembley!* should not be missed if you're a football fan in the lower divisions of the Nationwide Football League. Also of note are covers of **The Lurkers**' *Shadow* (the '77 band who were most influential on them), **The Clash**'s *Tommy Gun*, **The Adverts**' *Gary Gillmore's Eyes* and **The Killjoy**'s *Johnny Won't Go To Heaven*. These last two had appeared on a three-track EP released by Data Records in June 1999 and their version of *Johnny Won't Go To Heaven* was also included on *Punk Rock Jukebox Vol. 2* on Blackout Records.

Violent Society, *Colchester Council*, *Police State* and *Bullshit Crass* all resurfaced on *Rondelet Punk Singles Collection* (Anagram CDPUNK 49) 1995, which was also released on vinyl (Captain Oi! AHOY LP 513) 1996. *Punk Rocker* and *Too Much Talkin'* can also be heard on *Oi! The Rarities, Vol. 2* (Captain Oi! AHOY CD 46) 1995, whilst *Violent Society* and *Colchester Council* get a further airing on *Oi! The Rarities, Vol. 4* (Captain Oi! AHOY CD 58) 1996. Finally, a later hardcore song *Violent Youth* resurfaced on *100% Hardcore Punk* (Captain Oi! AHOY DCD 84) in 1998.

The Spectres

Personnel:			
PAUL COOK	drms		A
DANNY KUSTOW	gtr		ABC
GLEN MATLOCK	bs, vcls		ABCD
STEVE NEW	gtr		AB
BUDGIE	drms		B
MARK AMBLER	keyb'ds		C
ART COLLINS	sax		CD
GRAEME POTTER	drms		CD
C.C. SMITH			
DOLPHIN TAYLOR	drms		
MICK HANSON	gtr		D

45s:		
This Strange Effect/ Getting Away With Murder (PS)	(Direct Hit DH 1)	1980
Stories/Things (PS)	(Demon D 1002)	1980

The Spectres began in the spring of 1979 as an attempt by Matlock and New to relaunch **The Rich Kids**, which they had previously played in together. Former **Sex Pistol** Paul Cook was soon replaced on drums by Budgie. At the end of July they recorded a session for John Peel billed as Jimmy Nortons's Explosion (Norton was an old art school buddy of Glen's). The session comprised three Matlock compositions, *Getting Away With Murder*, *Just Like Lazarus* and *Ambition* along with Kustow's *Lost In A Landslide*. New wasn't there that day and it's been claimed by Matlock that the late Mick Ronson sat in on guitar, although there's no documentary evidence to collaborate this.

In September 1979, Matlock and New departed to participate with Iggy Pop in his American and European tours with line-up 'B' effectively splitting. When the tour was over Matlock and New remained with Iggy to record his *Soldier* album.

SPECIAL DUTIES - The Punk Singles Collection.

In early 1980, New went off to play with **Generation X**. Meanwhile Matlock re-united with Danny Kustow and they formed **The Spectres** first proper line-up ('C'). Former **Tom Robinson Band** keyboardist Mark Ambler came in on keyboards, the Little Roosters' Graeme Potter on drums and Art Collins on sax. The band also included at various times Dolphin Taylor (also ex-**Tom Robinson Band**) and C.C. Smith (previously with Gloria Mundi). They began gigging live around London with a horn section added.

Their first single *This Strange Effect*, a cover of an old Ray Davies song, received little airplay after its release in May 1980 and passed largely unnoticed. The 'B' side *Getting Away With Murder* had been demoed back in 1979. It had also featured in their John Peel session of July 1979.

A Collins/Matlock composition *Stories* was released as their second 45 in October 1980. The song, a curious hybrid of styles, attracted favourable reviews, but again failed to chart. After supporting The Ramones at the Hammersmith Odeon they looked destined to sign with Arista. The deal fell through at the last minute when Matlock took exception to the label's insistence on choosing their next single.

Thereafter **The Spectres** began to drift. In late 1980, Kustow and Ambler quit. Mick Hanson was recruited as a replacement on guitar. The band continued to lose their way and eventually split in 1981.

Matlock went on to a number of further bands - The Subterraneans (with NME journalist Nick Kent), the Swingers, Hot Club (along with **Chelsea**'s James Stevenson), London Cowboys and Concrete Bullet Invisible (with former Doll By Doll mainman Jackie Leven). In the nineties, he contributed to Ian Hunter's *Dirty Laundry* and **Gene October**'s *Life And Struggle*. He also released a solo album with The Philistines, prior to achieving much more success with his Creation album, *Who's He When He's At Home* and a reunion album with **The Sex Pistols**.

As for **The Spectres** well *Stories* got a further airing in 1993 on *After The Anarchy* (Connoisseur Collection VSOP CD 188), a CD compilation of post-**Sex Pistols** material.

The Speed

Personnel incl:	NIGEL HAMILTON	drms	A

45:	Big City/All Day And All The Night (some PS)	(It IT 1) 1978

Some copies of this 45 came in picture sleeves and these are more expensive and collectable. The 45 is now quite hard to track down. They also contributed one cut, *She's All There* to the *Identity Parade* (TJM TJMLP 3) 1980 compilation.

Nigel Hamilton was also in Cobra and was later in **The Tearjerkers**

Speedball

| 45: | No Survivors/ | |
| | Is Somebody There? | (No Pap/Dirty Dick DD 1/2) 1979 |

This mod-revivalist act from Southend evolved out of a local punk band The Idiot, who didn't release any 45s but contributed *Ging Gang Gooly* to a compilation of local bands *Southend Rock* (Sonet SNTF 806) 1978. They were also known briefly as The Bright Boys before recording *No Survivors*, one of the first mod revival 45s. Their name was miscredited as **Speedball(s)** on the label because the local record shop which owned it preferred it that way. Some copies came in a printed sleeve, which was later withdrawn. The single is now quite collectable, copies with the withdrawn sleeve, more so.

Two of the band's members also spent several months in detention centres for burglary!

Speedometers

Personnel:	LEE DALLON	keyb'ds	A
	MARTIN FINLAY	gtr, vcls	A
	PAUL SPENCER	drms	A
	IAN TAYLOR	gtr, vcls	A
	ROBBIE WATSON	bs, vcls	A

| ALBUM: | 1(A) DAY IN THE LIGHT | (Acrobat ACRO 5) 1979 |

45s:	Disgrace/Work (PS)	(Mascot NILE 1) 1978
	Liverpool Ladies (PS)	(Mascot NILE 2) 1978
	Tonight Tonight/Day In The Lights (PS)	(Acrobat BAT 6) 1979

A power-pop band. *Tonight Tonight* contains some decent guitar work and quite strong vocals.

Spelling Mistakes

| EP: | 1 POPSTAR (Popstar/Mirrors/ | |
| | Rubber Duck/Urge) | (Stortbeat BEAT 7) 1979 |

An enthusiastic EP but the production is rather messy. The Stortbeat label was based in Harlow, Essex.

John Spencer's Louts

Personnel:	CHAS AMBLER	keyb'ds, drms	A
	JOHNNY G	gtr, drms, hrmnca	A
	JOHN SPENCER	gtr, vcls, keyb'ds	A
	DAVID THORNE	bs, banjo	A
	(SIAN DANIELS	vcls	A)
	(ANDY McDONALD	vcls, woodwind	A)
	(ADAM SKEAPING	cello	A)

SPEEDOMETERS - Tonight Tonight.

JOHN SPENCER'S LOUTS - Natural Man.

| ALBUM: | 1(A) THE LAST LP | (Beggars Banquet BEGA 3) 1978 |

45s:	Natural Man/My Old Lady (PS)	(Beggars Banquet BEG 10) 1978
	Crazy For My Lady/	
	Can't Buy My Soul (PS)	(Beggars Banquet BEG 12) 1978
	Natural Man/	
	Crazy For My Lady (PS)	(Beggars Banquet BEG 34) 1980

A popish outfit. *Natural Man* is a slow number notable for its gravel-throated vocals.

Mike Spenser and The Cannibals

Personnel:	PAUL BALBI	drms	A
	ZENON DE FLEUR	gtr, vcls	A
	JOHNNY GUITAR	gtr	A
	STEVE LEWINS	bs	A
	MIKE SPENSER	vcls	A

45s:	* Sometimes Good Guys/	
	Nothing Takes The Place	(Big Cock F-UK 1) 1978
	Nadine/You Can't/Sweet Little 16 (PS)	(Hit F-UK 2) 1978
	Pick 'N' Choose/	
	I Could See Right Through You (PS)	(Hit F-UK 3) 1979

NB: * This came in a printed paper bag sleeve.

The Cannibals were actually **The Bishops**, who'd started life as **The Count Bishops** but then abbreviated their name. **Mike Spenser** was their vocalist and they also recorded these three 45s as **Mike Spenser and The Cannibals**.

Mike Spenser continued to use **The Cannibals** name, releasing a plethora of garage/trash 45s and albums thoughout the eighties, but these are not really relevant to this book.

Spherical Objects

Personnel:	JOHN BISSET-SMITH	gtr, vcls	AB
	FREDERICK BURROWS	bs	AB
	ROGER HILTON	drms	AB
	DUNCAN PRESTBURY	keyb'ds	AB
	STEVE SOLAMAR	gtr, vcls, hrmnca	AB
	ROGER BLACKBURN	gtr	B
	MIKE RABBIT	gtr	B
	MIKE ZEE	bs	B

ALBUMS:	1(A) PAST AND PARCEL	(Object Music OBJ 001) 1978
	2(A) ELLIPTICAL OPTIMISM	(Object Music OBJ 004) 1979
	3(A) FURTHER ELLIPSES	(Object Music OBJ 012) 1980
	4(B) NO MAN'S LAND	(Object Music OBJ 016) 1981

45s:	The Kill/The Knot (PS)	(Object Music OM 01) 1978
	Seventies Romance/	
	Sweet Tooth (PS)	(Object Music OM 04) 1978

Spherical Objects hailed from Manchester playing on *Past And Parcel* rather simple, lightweight rock with Steve Solamar's rather irritating vocals their main distinguishing feature. Their first 'B' side *The Knot* features some rather cheesy organ which recalls the mid-sixties U.S. garage band sound.

On *Elliptical Optimism* Duncan Prestbury's swirling, bubblegum, organ is more prominent and the instrumentation is more interesting. The rather mannered, Ferryesque vocals are less aggressive on this album which veered between the good and the mediocre, but did represent a musical progression on its predecessor.

Further Ellipses veered more towards dance music with less guitar and more horns and synthesizer. The material is stronger on this and it's probably the best of the quartet.

No Man's Land, their final offering, represented a return to basics musically. It featured an expanded line-up, but gone were the horns and keyboards. In their place came guitar, bass and drums with periodic patches of Solamar's harmonica. It featured some appealing slow numbers and had some lovely moments, but the band's career passed unnoticed for most people.

SPHERICAL OBJECTS - The Kill.

Spider

Personnel incl: BILLY GREEN

45s:	Children Of The Street/	
	Down And Out (some PS)	(Alien ALIEN 14) 1980
	College Luv/Born To Be Wild (some PS)	(Alien ALIEN 16) 1980
	New Romance/Cross Fire (PS)	(Dreamland 2090 441) 1980
	Everything Is Alright/Shady Lady (PS)	(Dreamland DSLP 4) 1980
	Better Be Good To Me/I Love (PS)	(Dreamland DSLP 11) 1981
	All The Time/Feel Like A Man	(City NIK 7) 1981
	Do You Want To Die For England/	
	Animals	(Test Pressing TP 2) 1982

Originally a three-piece **Spider** were signed to Terri Hooley's Good Vibrations label. Their one and only release for them was *Dancin' In The Streets*, which appeared on the *Battle Of The Bands* (EP) (Good Vibrations GOT 7) 1978. The double 7" set also featured contributions from **The Idiots**, **The Outcasts** and **Rudi**. This was not 'the' *Dancin' In The Street* but a competent but typical fast-paced punkish song.

They went on to record on Alien, Dreamland, City and Test Pressing. The picture sleeve releases of their two 45s on Alien are now hard to track down and becoming expensive.

The Spiders

45:	Mony Mony/Who's The Other One (PS)	(Reds REDS 004) 1980

This band's sole 45 was a cover of Tommy James and The Shondells' sixties hit *Mony Mony*.

Spitfire Boys

Personnel:	BLISTER		
	(aka BUDGIE, aka PETER CLARK)	drms	A
	JONES (aka DAVE LITTLER)	gtr	A
	MAGGOT (aka PAUL RUTHERFORD)	vcls	A
	ZERO (aka PETE GRIFFITHS)	bs	A

45s:	British Refugee/Mein Kampf	(RK RK 1001) 1977
	Funtime/Transcendental Changing	(SRT SRTS 948) 1979

This 45 was originally issued in a plain sleeve with a push out centre. It was later re-issued in a picture sleeve with a solid centre. Both copies are now quite collectable. This is largely because Maggot went on to become vocalist for Frankie Goes To Hollywood. Budgie also went on to greater things. Firstly, with **The Slits** and then with **Siouxsie and The Banshees**.

Judging by the song titles on their first 45, they were heavily into Nazi chic though it's unclear whether they were for or against it as the lyrics are inaudible. The 'A' side benefitted from some fierce guitar playing.

Their second effort *Funtime* was third division buzzsaw punk with monotonous vocals.

Spizzenergi

Personnel:	MARK COALFIELD	keyb'ds	A
	PETE HYDE	gtr	A
	HERO SHIMA	drms	A
	JIM SOLAR	bs	A
	SPIZZ	vcls, gtr	A

45s:	Soldier Soldier/Virginia Plain (PS)	(Rough Trade RTSO 3) 1979
	Where's Captain Kirk?/	
	Amnesia (PS)	(Rough Trade RTSO 4) 1979
*	Mega City 3/Work (PS)	(Rough Trade RTSO 6) 1982
*	Jungle Fever/The Meaning (PS)	(Rough Trade RTSO 7) 1982

NB: * as **Spizzenergi 2**. Also relevant are two CDs, *Unhinged* (Damaged Goods DAMGOOD 36) 1994, which includes **Spizz Energi** material and *Spizz Not Dead Shock 1978 - 1988* (Cherry Red CDMRED 130) 1996.

Spizz formed **Spizzenergi** during 1979, after the demise of **Spizz Oil**. They are best remembered as the first band to top the newly-created indie chart, early in 1980, with the unusual single *Where's Captain Kirk?* for no less than seven weeks. This attracted a contract with a major label A&M, but as if to celebrate the milestone **Spizz** changed the band's name again to **Athletico Spizz Co** and then to **Athletico Spizz 80**.

After a spell as **Spizzles** they reverted back to **Spizzenergi 2** for two further 45s for Rough Trade, which are also listed above.

Unhinged is a sixteen-track, diverse compilation which features alternate mixes of offbeat songs like *Spock's Missing*, *Hot Desert* and the techno-dance number *Mega City 3*. There's also a cut from 1988 recorded with ex-**Secret Affair** vocalist Ian Page titled *Love Me Like A Rocket*.

SPIZZENERGI - Where's Captain Kirk?

Their classic *Where's Captain Kirk?* got further exposure on *Punk Lost And Found* (Shanachie SH 5705) 1996, *The Best Punk Album In The World.... Ever, Vol. 2* (2-CD) (Virgin VTDCD 79) 1996 and on the lavish 5-CD box set *1-2-3-4 - A History Of Punk And New Wave 1976 - 1979* (MCA/Universal MCD 60066) 1999. They also contributed two cuts *Virginia Plain* and *Cold City* to *Spiked* (Summit SUMCD 4094) 1997.

Spizzles

Personnel:	LU	gtr, piano	A
	C.D. SNARE	drms	A
	JIM SOLAR	bs, synth	A
	SPIZZ	vcls	A

ALBUM: 1(A) SPIKEY DREAM FLOWERS (A&M AMLE 68523) 1981

NB: The CD *Spizz Not Dead Shock 1978 - 1988* (Cherry Red CDMRED 130) 1996 includes material from this era.

45s:	Risk/Melancholy (PS)	(A&M AMS 8107) 1981
	Danger Of Living/Scared (PS)	(A&M AMS 8124) 1981

This was a later version of **Athletico Spizz 80** (previously Spizz 77, **Spizz Oil** and **Spizzenergi**). On *Spikey Dream Flowers* **The Spizzles** sing of robots and war games, but with little success. The best track is arguably *Melancholy*, which at least features some decent guitar work. After this, they changed names again to **Spizzenergi 2** and there were several further name changes - the one constant being the inclusion of **Spizz**, who continued gigging occasionally well into the nineties!

SPIZZLES - Spiky Dream Flowers.

Spizz Oil

Personnel:	FRANK GUEST	drms, piano	A
	PETE PETROL	lead gtr	A
	SPIZZ	vcls, gtr	A

EP: 1(A) THE PEEL SESSION (Cold City/6000 Crazy/ Pure Noise/Alien Language/Protect From Heat/ Platform 3/Switched Off) (Strange Fruit SFPS 022) 1987

45s:	6000 Crazy/1989/Fibre (PS)	(Rough Trade RTSO 1) 1979
	Cold City/Red And Black/Solarisation (Shun)/ Platform 3	(Rough Trade RTSO 2) 1979

NB: Also relevant is a CD *Spizz Not Dead Shock 1978 - 1988* (Cherry Red CDMRED 130) 1996, which includes material from this period.

Spizz was an interesting character. He made his live debut as a solo vocalist at Birmingham Barabarella's punk festival in August 1977. That October he linked with guitarist Pete O'Dowd (Pete Petrol) to form Spizz 77. The following year, with drummer Frank Guest added, **Spizz** had changed their name again to **Spizz Oil**. This incarnation recorded a session for John Peel on 7th August 1978, which was later issued on *The Peel Session* (EP) by Strange Fruit in 1987. It contained *6,000 Crazy* and *Cold City* their two best-known songs from their pre-**Spizzenergi** era. *6,000 Crazy* and *Pure Noise*, in particular, are quite experimental. After two singles for Rough Trade, Petrol left in 1979 and **Spizz** teamed up with a new group of musicians to form **Spizzenergi**.

Split Screens

45: Just Don't Try/(flip side by **Just Frank**) (Rok ROK III/IV) 1978

An Oxford band, who played at London venues like the Moonlight Club quite often. In addition to this split 45, they had *Just Don't Try* included on the now rare compilation *Odd Bods Mods And Sods* (Rok ROKLP 001) 1979, which has been reissued on CD (Captain Mod MODSKA CD 2) 1996. *Just Don't Try*, with its catchy guitar intro, leater resurfaced on *100% British Mod* (Captain Mod MODSKA DCD 8) 1998.

SPIZZ OIL - Peel Session.

Splodgenessabounds

Personnel:	MAX SPLODGE	vcls	A

ALBUM:	1(A)	SPLODGENESSABOUNDS	(Deram SML 1121) 1981
	2(A)	IN SEARCH OF SEVEN GOLDEN GUSSETS	(Razor RAZ 1) 1982

NB: (2) credited to **Splodge** and also issued on CD (Captain Oi AHOY CD 089) 1998. There's also a cassette compilation *Nightmare On Rude Street* (Receiver RRCD 148) 1991, *Live* (Receiver RRCD 237) 1998 and *I Don't Know* (Captain Oi! AHOY CD 130) 2000.

HCP

EP:	1(A)	COWPUNK MEDIUM (Cowpunk Medium/ Have You Got A Light Boy?/Morning Milky) (PS)	(Deram BUM 3) 1981	69

NB: (1) came with a free flexi, *Brown Paper Dub* (BUMP 3).

HCP

45s:	Simon Templar/Two Pints Of Lager And A Packet Of Crisps Please (PS)	(Deram BUM 1) 1980	7
	Two Little Boys/Horse (PS)	(Deram ROLF 1) 1980	26
+	Bicycle Seat/ Bicycle Seat (alt version) (PS)	(Deram BUM 2) 1980	-
+	The 12 Days Of Christmas	(Secret SHH 126) 1981	-
*	Mouth And Trousers/ In Search Of The Seven (PS)	(Razor RZS 102) 1982	-

NB: + Credited to Max Splodge. * Credited to Splodge.

Max Splodge was the central figure behind this band. The remaining members operated under various pseudonyms. Initially a joke band (and

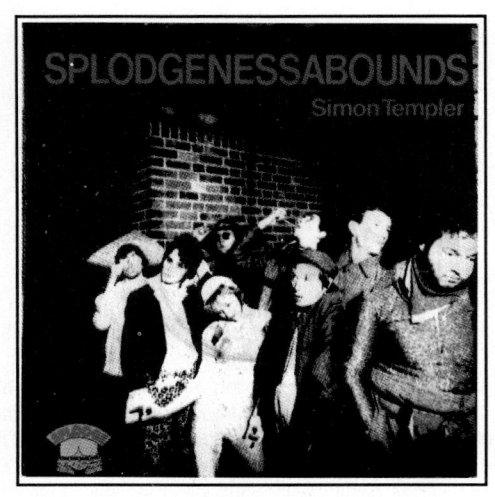

SPLODGENESSABOUNDS - Simon Templar.

not a very tasteful one at that) they are usually associated with the punk / new wave era. They are best remembered for *Two Pints Of Lager And A Packet Of Crips Please* (the most frequent pub order?) which actually gave them a Top 10 hit, spending eight weeks in the charts.

They enjoyed a further hit with their own interpretation of Rolf Harris' *Two Little Boys*, which also enjoyed a seven week chart stay.

Max Splodge with Desert Island Joe appeared on *Oi The Album* (EMI ZIT 1) 1980, (later reissued on CD (Captain Oi! AHOY CD 72) 1997 with *Isubeleeeene*. He returned on *Strength Through Oi!* (Decca) 1981 with the ridiculous *Isubaleene (Part 2)* and *We're Pathetique* as Splodge sought to establish the band as leaders of 'Punk Pathetique' movement, then went on to issue an amusing eponymous debut album before the group split in 1982.

Max Splodge then put together a new line-up and recorded the jokey *In Search Of The Seven Golden Gussets* album for Razor.

Self-styled leaders of the 'Punk Pathetique' movement **Splodgenessabounds** also appeared on *100% British Oi!* (Captain Oi! DCD 83) 1997 with *Pathetique*, one of their better songs.

Splodgenessabounds re-emerged in 2000 with a new album *I Don't Know* of fourteen cuts blending punk, jazz, reggae and even the odd ballad!

Two Pints Of Lager And A Packet Of Crisps has resurfaced on a few retrospective compilations, including *New Wave Archive* (Rialto RMCD 201) 1997 and *Punk, Vol. 2* (Music Club MCCD 027) 1991.

Phones Sportsman Band

EP: 1 I REALLY LOVE YOU (I Really Love You/Get Down And Get With It/I Woke Up This Morning/Wah Wah Track/The Olton) (Rather GEAR 9) 1980

Phones Sportsman whose real name was Dave Barrington is best known as a member of **Swell Maps**. This was a one-off solo venture.

The Spys

45: The Young Ones/Heavy Scene (PS) (No Bad NB 3) 1979

This seemingly obscure 1979 outfit was actually **XTC**.

The Squad

Personnel incl:	GUS CHAMBERS	vcls
	DANNY CUNNINGHAM	gtr
	TERRY HALL	vcls
	MARC HATWOOD	drms
	SAM McNULTY	bs

SPLODGE - Mouth And Trousers.

| 45s: | Red Alert/£8-A-Week (PS) | (Squad SQS 1) 1979 |
| | Millionaire/Brockhill Boys (PS) | (Squad SQS 3) 1979 |

This Coventry-based punk band underwent numerous line-up changes. Some contend that Terry Hall (later of The Specials) was once a member. They also contributed a cut *Flasher* to *Sent From Coventry* (Kathedral KATH 1) 1980. *£8-A-Week* and *Red Alert* later resurfaced on *Punk Rock Rarities, Vol. 2* (Anagram CD PUNK 83) 1996.

The Squares

Personnel:	BRIAN HOGAN		A
	PADDY HOGAN		A
	RAY RICHARDS		A
	TIM SLIM		A

45s:	No Fear/Nobody's Fool	(Sire SIR 4003) 1978
	This Is Airebeat/Stop Being A Boy	(Sire SIR 4011) 1979
	Carry Me Home/?	(Sire SIR 4029) 1979
	Buddy Holly/I May Be Bitter	(Airebeat ABT 4) 1980
	Buddy Holly/I May Be Bitter (PS)	(Hype TICK 1) 198?

A pop-punk trio who toured with **The Undertones**. *This Is Airebeat* is indeed airy and beaty pop.

Squeeze

Personnel: (up to 1986)	CHRIS DIFFORD	vcls, gtr	ABCDEF
	PAUL GUNN	drms	A
	JOOLS HOLLAND (JULIAN HOLLAND)	keyb'ds	ABC F
	GLENN TILBROOK	vcls, gtr	ABCDEF
	HARRY KAKOULLI	bs	B
	GILSON LAVIS	drms	BCDEF
	JOHN BENTLEY	bs	CDE
	PAUL CARRACK	keyb'ds	D
	DON SNOW	keyb'ds	E
	KEITH WILKINSON	bs	F

				HCP
ALBUMS: (up to 1986)	1(B)	SQUEEZE	(A&M AMLH 68465) 1978	-
	2(C)	COOL FOR CATS	(A&M AMLH 68503) 1979	45
	3(C)	ARGY BARGY	(A&M AMLH 64802) 1980	32
	4(D)	EAST SIDE STORY	(A&M AMLH 64854) 1981	19
	5(E)	SWEETS FROM A STRANGER	(A&M AMLH 64899) 1982	20
	6(-)	THE SINGLES - 45's AND UNDER	(A&M AMLH 68552) 1982	3
	7(F)	COSI FAN O TUTTI FRUITTI	(A&M AMA 5085) 1985	31

NB: (1) reissued at mid-price (A&M AMID 122) 1982 and on CD (A&M 5408062) 1998. (2) was originally available in different colour sleeves and on CD at mid-price (A&M CDMID 131) 1991 and again (A&M 5408042) 1998. (3) also on CD (A&M 5408032) 1998. (4) also issued on CD at mid-price (A&M CDMID 132) 1991 and again (A&M 5408052) 1998. (5) also issued on CD (A&M 5408072) 1998. (6) also issued on CD (A&M CDA 64922) 1984. (7) also issued on CD (A&M CDA 5085) 1985 and again (A&M 540 8022) 1998. There are also a number of relevant compilations, *Greatest Hits: Squeeze* (A&M 3971812) 1992, *Excess Moderation* (2-CD set) (A&M 5406512) 1996 and *Six Of One* (6-CD set) (A&M 5408012) 1997.

EP:	1(B) PACKET OF THREE (Cat On A Wall/Backtrack/ Nightride) (7" Red and blue photo PS) (Deptford Fun City DFC 01) 1977		

NB: There was also a 12" version with the same catalogue number in a plain pink die-cut sleeve. Only 500 were issued. The 7" was reissued in 1979.

				HCP
45s:	*	Take Me I'm Yours/No Disco Kid, No	(BTM SBT 107) 1977	-
(up to 1986)		Take Me I'm Yours/Night Nurse (7" PS)	(A&M AMS 7335) 1978	19
		Take Me I'm Yours/Night Nurse (12" PS)	(A&M AMSP 7335) 1978	-
	+	Bang Bang/All Fed Up (PS)	(A&M AMS 7360) 1978	49
	x	Goodbye Girl/Saints Alive (PS)	(A&M AMS 7398) 1978	63
	α	Cool For Cats/Model (PS)	(A&M AMS 7426) 1979	2
	β	Cool For Cats/Model (12" PS)	(A&M AMSP 7426) 1979	-
	χ	Up The Junction/It's So Dirty (PS)	(A&M AMS 7444) 1979	2
	δ	Slap And Tickle/All's Well (PS)	(A&M AMS 7466) 1979	24
	ε	Christmas Day/Going Crazy (PS)	(A&M AMS 7495) 1979	-
	φ	Another Nail In My Heart/Pretty Thing (PS)	(A&M AMS 7507) 1980	17
	γ	Pulling Mussels (From A Shell)/What The Butler Saw (PS)	(A&M AMS 7523) 1980	44
	η	Wrong Way	(Smash Hits) 1980	-
	ι	Is That Love/Trust	(A&M AMS 8129) 1981	35
	φ	Tempted/Yap Yap (PS)	(A&M AMS 8147) 1981	41
	ι	Labelled With Love/Squabs On Forty Fab	(A&M AMS 8166) 1981	4
	κ	Black Coffee In Bed/The Hurt (PS)	(A&M AMS 8219) 1982	51
	κ	When The Hangover Strikes/Elephant Girl (PS)	(A&M AMS 8237) 1982	-
		Annie Get Your Gun/Spanish Guitar (PS)	(A&M AMS 8259) 1982	43
		Last Time Forever/Suite From Five Strangers (PS)	(A&M AM 255) 1985	45
		Last Time Forever/Suite From Five Strangers (12", PS)	(A&M AMY 255) 1985	-
		No Place Like Home/The Fortnight Saga (PS)	(A&M AM 277) 1985	-
		No Place Like Home/The Fortnight Saga (12", PS)	(A&M AMY 277) 1985	-
		Heartbreaking World/Big Bens (PS)	(A&M AM 291) 1985	-
		Heartbreaking World/Big Bens/Tempted/By Your Side (12", PS)	(A&M AMY 291) 1985	-
		King George Street/Love's Crashing Ways (PS)	(A&M AM 306) 1986	-
		King George Street/Love's Crashing Ways/Up The Junction (12", PS)	(A&M AMY 306) 1986	-
Reissue:		Take Me I'm Yours/Up The Junction	(Old Gold OG 9364) 1983	-
		Cool For Cats/Labelled With Love	(Old Gold OG 9546) 1985	-

NB: * Release cancelled. + Some copies on green vinyl. x Some copies with 3D picture sleeve. α There were three other limited edition issues of this release; 100,000 copies in pale pink vinyl, 5,000 copies in brilliant pink vinyl and 1,000 copies in red vinyl. β This came in pale pink vinyl. χ Some copies in lilac vinyl. δ Some copies in red vinyl. ε Some copies in white vinyl. φ Some copies in clear vinyl. γ Some copies in red vinyl. η This was a green vinyl flexi release. ι A picture sleeve release was quickly withdrawn and the final record came without a picture sleeve. φ some copies came with a free 5" U.S. single *If I Didn't Love You*. κ There was also a picture disc version of this release.

Squeeze was conceived in March 1974 in Deptford, London when Chris Difford, who'd been born in London on 4th November 1954, met Glenn Tilbrook (also a Londoner, born on 31st August 1957) after Tilbrook answered Difford's advert seeking members for a new group in a music paper. With the recruitment of a boogie pianist Jools (Julian) Holland and drummer Paul Gunn, the line-up was completed. The band took its name from the title of a Velvet Underground album.

In 1976 they signed to Miles Copeland's BTM label and management company. Gunn was soon replaced on drums by former Mustard member Gilson Lavis. Then in January 1977, they recorded *Take Me I'm Yours* for BTM. After being scheduled for release it was then withdrawn. A further six months elapsed before they finally made it onto vinyl by virtue of a 7" *Packet Of Three* EP. This was produced by John Cale and appeared on the Deptford Fun City label. Their musical menu at the time was very much an amalgam of pub rock and new wave. There was also a limited edition 12" version of this EP. Only 500 copies of this were released.

This helped secure them a deal with A&M worldwide. They became A&M's first 'new wave' signing since **The Sex Pistols**.

Their debut 45 for A&M, *Take Me I'm Yours* had immediate appeal and took them into the Top 20, peaking at No. 19 during a nine week stay. However, their debut album, produced by Cale, failed to register significant sales to enter the charts. It's generally accepted now that the album was issued too early in their career. The album was inconsistent and the only stand out tracks were their previous 45, *Take Me I'm Yours* and their next one *Bang Bang*, which was the obvious choice for a follow-up. However, even this only managed five weeks in the charts, peaking at No. 49. Some copies of the 45 came on green vinyl.

To help promote the new album **Squeeze** toured the U.S.A. in Spring 1978, but they had to bill themselves as U.K. **Squeeze** so they were not confused with a U.S. outfit called Tight Squeeze. In August 1978, they promoted themselves to a wider audience by appearing at the Reading Festival. A further line-up change occured when bassist Harry Kakoulli left to go solo. His replacement was John Bentley.

In November 1978, a new 45 *Goodbye Girl* was released. Some copies came in a 3D picture sleeve. The song, which was included on their next album, spent just two weeks in the charts, peaking at No. 63.

It was really with the release of *Cool For Cats* the title track of their next album, in March 1979, that their career began to take off commercially. The 45 got to No. 2 and spent eleven weeks in the charts. To help publicise it the 45 was released in a wide range of different formats. See the discography for full details. It set the style for their arresting but often odd tunes on the album of the same name, produced by John Wood. This registered them in the album charts for the first time, climbing to No. 45. Aside from the title cut, it contained at least two other classic numbers. *Up The Junction* was a slice of working class consciousness that also got to No. 2 when subsequently released on 45. The rather sleazy, synthetic rocker *Slap And Tickle* was also noteworthy and climbed to No. 24 when subsequently selected for 45 release. However, their attempt to achieve a Christmas hit with the festive *Christmas Day* flopped.

In view of Wood's earlier production success he was again selected to produce *Argy Bargy*, released in February 1980. Previewed by the release of *Another Nail In My Heart*, which climbed to No. 17 during a nine week chart stay, the album built on their earlier intricate pop style and offered considerable diversity and often clever material. The catchy cleverness was typified on *Pulling Mussels (From A Shell)*, which became their next hit. It peaked at No. 44, spending six weeks in the charts. Also worthy of mention are the lighthearted *Farfisa Beat* and *If I Didn't Love You*. The album itself climbed to No. 32.

SQUEEZE - Squeeze.

Despite four U.S. tours and a mini-greatest hits EP, *6 Squeeze Songs Crammed Into One Ten Inch Record EP* **Squeeze** failed to make a significant commercial breakthrough there. When they returned to Britain after their fourth tour, Jools Holland decided to quit the band in August 1980. His replacement was Paul Carrack. The experienced Carrack, who'd been born in Sheffield in April 1951, had previously been with Ace, Frankie Miller and Roxy Music. Holland went on to form his own band Millionaires, but also began to launch what would become a very successful media career. After supporting **The Police** on tour he made a documentary about them for U.K. TV. One thing led to another and he became co-host of 'The Tube' between 1982-87. As most of you will recall, this was a classic music programme in this era. It was the start of a long and successful media career for Holland, who still comperes his own TV music show today.

The new line-up appeared with **Elvis Costello** at the Top Rank Club in Swansea on 30th November 1980 to play a benefit for the family of Welsh boxer Johnny Owen, who died from injuries acquired in an earlier World title bout. Over the coming months the band's links with **Elvis Costello** strengthened. In March 1981, Tilbrook linked up with **Costello** for a one-off 45 *From A Whisper To A Scream*. Then in May, the band's new album *East Side Story* was co-produced by **Costello** and Roger Bechirian. There was also one cut produced by **Dave Edmunds**. Again this was a very diverse collection, even more so than previous efforts. It ranged between soul, pop, rock, country and psychedelia, but lacked overall coherence. Still it was one of their finest moments, with a number of highlights. *Messed Around* veered into rockabilly territory, *Someone Else's Heart* was a sentimental Difford composition and *Mumbo Jumbo* catches the ear. The selection of 45 cuts from this album seem more arbitrary than previously. *Is That Love?* got to No. 35 during an eight week stay and the soul-flavoured *Tempted* reached No. 41, but perhaps more significantly gave them their first U.S. hit, peaking at No. 49. Paul Carrack handled the vocals on this song. The album proved their most successful, peaking at No. 19.

In October 1981, the non-album country-flavoured 45 *Labelled With Love* was released. Spending ten weeks in the charts and climbing to No. 4, it proved their most successful since *Up The Junction*. Shortly before the 45's release Carrack departed to join Carlene Carter's band. Former **Sinceros'** member Don Snow replaced him.

The new line-up's first single was *Black Coffee In Bed*. Both **Elvis Costello** and Paul Young assisted on the vocals. The 45, which also figured on their fifth album *Sweets For A Stranger*, was a modest hit. It got to No. 51, spending just four weeks in the chart.

The album got to No. 20, but spent nineteen fewer weeks in the charts than its predecessor. On this *I've Returned* stands out for Tilbrook's fresh and engaging vocals and some fine ringing guitar work. *When The Hangover Strikes*, a leisurely number, was culled for 45 release but failed to chart. A further cut, the Alan Tarney-produced *Annie Get Your Gun*, was then chosen and climbed to No. 43 during a four week chart stay.

The band's decision to split, announced in November 1982, came as little surprise. The inevitable compilation *The Singles - 45's And Under* followed and became by far their most commercially successful album. It spent twenty-nine weeks in the charts and peaked at No. 3. Their final live appearance was during the three-day Jamaica World Music Festival at the Bob Marley Performing Centre near Montego Bay in November 1982.

THE STADIUM DOGS - Easy Beat.

Take Me I'm Yours and *Bang Bang* were included on the sampler *No Wave* (A&M AMLE 68505) in 1979. The former also figured on *A History Of Punk, Vol. 2* (Virgin CDOVD 487) in 1997. *Take Me I'm Yours* resurfaced on *Teenage Kicks* (PolyGram TV 5253382) 1995 and on *1-2-3-4 - A History Of Punk And New Wave 1976 - 1979* (MCA/Universal MCD 60066) 1999, a 5-CD box set.

In the short-term Difford and Tilbrook continued as a duo with supporting musicians and continued to release material that sounded much like **Squeeze**. It was little surprise when they reformed **Squeeze** in 1985 and various line-ups of the band, continued to gig and record well into the nineties.

Jools Holland later achieved far greater fame as a TV music programme presenter.

Squire

Personnel:	STEVE BAKER	gtr	A
	ENZO ESPOSITO	bs, vcls	A
	ROSS DI'LANDA	drms	A
	TONY MEYNELL	gtr, vcls	A

ALBUMS:	1(A)	HITS FROM 3,000 YEARS AGO	(Hi-Lo LO 01) 1983
	2(A)	GET SMART	(Hi-Lo LO 02) 1983
	3(A)	THE SINGLES ALBUM	(Hi-Lo LO 03) 1985

NB: Most of their material is also contained on two CDs *Big Smashes* (Tangerine TANGCD 4) 1992 and *Get Ready To Go* (Tangerine TANGCD 7) 1994.

45s:	*	Get Ready To Go/	
		(track by **Coming Shortly**)	(Rok ROK 1/11) 1979
	#	Walking Down The King's Road/	
		It's A Mod Mod World	(I-Spy SEE 2) 1979
	+	The Face Of Youth Today/	
		I Know A Girl	(I-Spy SEE 4) 1979
		My Mind Goes Round In Circles/	
		Does Stephanie Know? (PS)	(Stage One STAGE 2) 1980
		No Time Tomorrow/Don't Cry To Me (PS)	(Hi-Lo HI 001) 1982
		Girl On A Train/	
		Every Trick In The Book (PS)	(Hi-Lo HI 002) 1982
		Every Trick In The Book/	
		Every Trick In The Book (instr.) (PS)	(Hi-Lo HI 003) 1983
		Every Trick In The Book/Every Trick In The	
		Book (Elastic Mix) (12", PS)	(Hi-Lo HIT 003) 1983
		Jesamine/When I Try, I Lie (PS)	(Hi-Lo HI 004) 1983
	x	The Young Idea/It's Getting Better	(Hi-Lo HI 005/SFL 2) 1984
	α	Does Stephanie Know?	(Hi-Lo LOX 1) 1985

NB: * Issued in a company sleeve. # Issued in a keyhole company sleeve. + Issued in a keyhole company sleeve with paper or plastic labels. x **Squire** fan club issue. α Flexidisc.

A Woking band, like **The Jam**, who had a considerable influence on Paul Weller. *Get Ready To Go*, released on Rok in May 1979 is usually considered to be the first mod revival single. Their next two singles were produced by **Secret Affair**'s Ian Page and David Cairns after they had signed to the I-Spy label.

They then switched to Hi-Lo. Their 1983 album *Hits From 3,000 Years Ago* is billed as Anthony Meynell and **Squire**. This comprised eleven demos and three live cuts. All fourteen cuts were penned by Meynell who sings on all but three. Much of it sounds straight out of 1965.

Get Smart! the same year contains a dozen new 'perfect pop' songs sung by Meynell. His brother plays drums and the duo are assisted by session horn and keyboard players.

The best place to check out their music now is on two Tangerine CDs. *Big Smasher* issued by Tangerine in 1992 spans their whole career from when they signed with Arista's I-Spy in 1979 to their demise in 1984. Included here are early 45s like *My Mind Goes Round In Circles* and *Walking Down The King's Road*, (which are essentially catchy pop tunes influenced by bands like The Beatles and The Byrds); *No Time Tomorrow*, (their most adventurous 45 - a voyage towards the world of psychedelia, with backward tracking and a delightful sparse sound) and a cover of Big Star's *September Gurls*.

Get Ready To Go followed in 1994. It featured the rest of their early singles, nine cuts from their *Hits From 3,000 Years Ago* album from 1980 and some previously unreleased cuts from 1982.

Squire also appeared on *Mods Mayday '79* (Bridge House BHLP 003) 1979 playing *B-A-B-Y Baby Love*, *Walking Down The Kings Road* and *Live Without Her Love*. They later figured on *Mods Mayday 2 - Modnight At The Bridge* (CD) (Receiver RRCD 228) 1997, which comprises outtakes from the night. They also contributed four songs to *It's A Mod Mod World - The Hi-Lo Compilation* (Antenna ANTENNA 2) 1997, which comprised mostly U.S. bands. Their excellent *Livin' In The City* with its strong chorus, vocals and guitar work can also be found on *100% British Mod* (Captain Mod MODSKA DCD 8) 1998.

Detour has also put out an archive 45 *The Place I Used To Live*.

The Stadium Dogs

Personnel:	PAUL COUSINO	bs, vcls	A
	PAUL GRIFFITHS	gtr, vcls	A
	JONATHAN PERKINS	keyb'ds	A
	KIRK THORN	gtr, vcls	A
	KEVIN WILKINSON	drms	A

ALBUM:	1(A)	WHAT'S NEXT	(Magnet MAG 5025) 1978
45:		Easy Beat/Android Rocker/ Media Withdrawal (PS)	(Audiogenics A 17) 1977
Reissue:		Easy Beat/Android Rocker/ Media Withdrawl (PS)	(Magnet MAG 114) 1978

A South Coast quintet who are best remembered for *Easy Beat*, which was quite an interesting 45 with a distinctive introduction. Originally issued on Audiogenics, it was later picked up and reissued by Magnet, along with a whole album of their material. The other two cuts on the 45 aren't worth needle time. In their better moments they sounded like a sort of new wave 10 CC.

Stage B

Personnel:	COLIN FLETCHER	bs	A
	DESSIE POTTER	gtr	A
	CHARLIE REILLEY	vcls	A
	OWEN HOWELL	drms	A

45:	Recall To Life/Light On The Hillside	(Shock SRS 502) 1980

Stage B were selected for a pilot run of BBC Northern Ireland's 'Green Rock' series, although it never got shown because of a technician's strike. They also recorded a single *Recall To Life* for Shock Rock Records, but it never took off and neither did they. Both sides of the single were also included on the compilation *Belfast* (Shock Rock SLR 007) 1980. This is very much third division new wave, but the flip side is the more interesting of the two songs.

Sta-Prest

45:	Schooldays/Tomorrow (PS)	(Avatar AAA 103) 1980

From Wickford in Essex, another band strongly influenced by **The Jam** but visually they sported a spiky punk image.

Starjets

Personnel:	PAUL BROWN	gtr	A
	LIAM L'ESTRANGE		AB
	JOHN MARTIN		AB
	TERRY SHARPE		AB
	BRUCE WOODLEY	lead vcls	A
	PAT GRIBBEN	gtr	B

ALBUM:	1(A)	(GOD BLESS) THE STARJETS	(Epic 83534) 1979

NB: (1) also issued on CD (Captain Oi! AHOY CD 99) 1999, with bonus cuts.

STIFF LITTLE FINGERS - Suspect Device.

		HCP
45s:	It Doesn't Really Matter/Schooldays	(Epic EPC 6968) 1979 -
	Run With The Pack/Watchout (PS)	(Epic EPC 7123) 1979 -
	Ten Years/One More Word (PS)	(Epic EPC 7417) 1979 -
	War Stories/Do The Rush (PS)	(Epic EPC 7770) 1979 51
	Schooldays/What A Life (PS)	(Epic EPC 7986) 1979 -
	Shiralee/Standby 19	(Epic EPC 8276) 1980 -

The **Starjets** set out gigging in 1977, mainly in drinking bars on the Fall's Road, Belfast. They were one of numerous bands in this era who sounded far better on stage than on record. Their lyrics often related stories about life in Ulster, and reflected the violence associated with life in the Province. However, unlike **Stiff Little Fingers**, their lyrics were not overtly political. They recorded six singles for Epic, but attained no commercial success. They also toured with **Stiff Little Fingers** in 1979. This tour did enable them to build up a loyal following on the campus circuit, but when in August of the same year their debut album *God Bless The Starjets* was released by Epic it did not live up to expectation. Full of fast-moving no-holes-barred punk rock it was badly produced. Some tracks like *Schooldays* and *Any Danger Love*, had some good guitar riffs and *Run With The Pack* was a little unusual - containing revving motor bikes, vocal falsettos and exhibiting a sort of rockabilly influence but, overall it was a disappointing album.

They suffered a setback in March 1980 when Paul Brown, the band's founder member, departed on account of musical differences. He was replaced by Pat Gribben, who had previously played with **The Jets**. At the end of the month they issued a single *Shiralee* which promised little, and by the summer of 1980, they had changed their name to Tango Brigade.

Steppes

Personnel:	DODD	bs	A
	DAVE HENDERSON	vcls	A
	MARK SUTHERLAND	gtr	A
	ANDY ROSS	gtr	A

45:	The Beat Drill/ (flip side by Fifty Fantastics)	(South Circular SGS 108) 1979

The **Steppes**, Fifty Fantastics whose *God's Got Religion* featured on the other side of this 45, along with **The Disco Zombies** were all one and the same band eminating from Andy Ross at Food Records.

Stiff Little Fingers

Personnel:	GORDON BLAIR	drms	A
	JAKE BURNS	vcls, lead gtr	ABCD
	HENRY CLUNEY	gtr	ABCD
	ALI McMORDIE	bs	ABCD
	BRIAN FALOON	drms	B
	JIM REILLY	drms	C
	BRIAN 'DOLPHIN' TAYLOR	drms	D

STIFF LITTLE FINGERS - Alternative Ulster.

ALBUMS: HCP
- 1(B) INFLAMMABLE MATERIAL (Rough Trade ROUGH 1) 1979 14
- 2(C) NOBODY'S HEROES (Chrysalis CHR 1270) 1980 8
- 3(C) HANX! (Chrysalis CHR 1300) 1980 9
- 4(C) GO FOR IT (Chrysalis CHR 1339) 1981 14
- 5(D) NOW THEN (Chrysalis CHR 1400) 1982 24
- 6(-) ALL THE BEST (dbl) (Chrysalis CTY 1414) 1983 19

NB: (1) reissued (EMI EMC 3554) 1989 and on CD (EMI CDP 7921052) 1989. (2) reissued (EMI EMC 3555) 1989 and on CD (EMI CDP 7921062) 1989. (3) reissued at mid-price on (EMI Fame FA 3215) 1989 and at mid-price on CD (EMI CDFA 3215) 1989. (4) reissued at mid-price on (EMI Fame FA 3216) 1989 and at mid-price on CD (EMI CDFA 3216) 1989 and again (Dojo DOJO CD 148) 1993. (5) also issued on CD (Fame CDFA 3306) 1994 and again on CD (EMI Gold CDGOLD 1090) 1997. (6) issued as a 2-CD set (Chrysalis CCD 1414) 1988 and again on CD (Chrysalis CDS 7977412) 1988. Also relevant are *The Peel Sessions Album* (Strange Fruit SFRLP 106) 1989, also on CD (SFRCD 106); *Stiff Little Fingers* (Strange Fruit SFRLP 1) 1989, also on CD (STRCD 1) 1989; *Live And Loud* (dbl) (Link LP 026) 1988, which came on green or black vinyl and CD (Link CD 026) 1989, but with a different sleeve to the record; *Live In Sweden* (Limited Edition EDT 3LP) 1989 in green vinyl and on CD (Ltd EDT 3CD) 1989; *Greatest Hits Live* (Link STR CD 010) 1991 and *Alternative Chartbusters* (Link AOK 103) 1991, *Fly The Flags - Live At Brixton Academy 27/10/1991* (Dojo DOJOCD 75) 1992; *Live In Concert* (Windsong WINCD 037) 1993; *Greatest Hits Live* (Dojo DOJOCD 110) 1993 and again with some different tracks (Original Masters SMMCD 538) 1999; *Stand Up And Shout* (PinHead PINCD 105) 1998; *Pure Fingers Live* (Snapper SMMCD 516) 1999; *And Best Of All / Hope Street* (2-CD set) (EMI 4988162) 1999; *Tin Soldiers* (Harry May MAYO CD 105) 1999; *Handheld And Rigital Digital* (CD & Video) (SLF VIDC9 991) 2000; and *Inspired (A Collection)* (2-CD set) (Recall SMDCD 276) 2000.

EPs: HCP
- 1(D) PAY £1.10 OR LESS (That's When Your Blood Bumps/Two Guitars Clash/Listen/Sad-Eyed People) (Chrysalis CHS 2580) 1982 33
- 2(B) THE PEEL SESSION EP (12.9.78) (Johnny Was/Law And Order/Barbed Wire Love/Suspect Device) (12" PS) (Strange Fruit SFPS 004) 1986 -

NB: (2) also issued on cassette (SFPSC 004) 1987 and on CD (SFPSCD 004) 1988.

45s: HCP
(up to 1983)
- * Suspect Device/Wasted Life (Rigid Digits SRD-1) 1978 -
- Alternative Ulster/78 rpm (PS) (Rough Trade RT 004) 1978 -
- + Suspect Device/Wasted Life (PS) (Rough Trade RT 006) 1979 -
- Gotta Getaway/Bloody Sunday (PS) (Rough Trade RT 015) 1979 -
- Straw Dogs/You Can't Say Crap On The Radio (PS) (Chrysalis CHS 2368) 1979 44
- At The Edge/Silly Encores: Running Bear/White Christmas (PS) (Chrysalis CHS 2406) 1980 15
- Nobody's Hero/Tin Soldiers (PS) (Chrysalis CHS 2424) 1980 36
- x Back To Front/Mr. Fire Coal-Man (PS) (Chrysalis CHS 2447) 1980 49
- Just Fade Away/Go For It/It Doesn't Make It Alright (live) (PS) (Chrysalis CHS 2510) 1981 47
- Silver Lining/Safe As Houses (PS) (Chrysalis CHS 2517) 1981 68
- α Listen/Two Guitars Clash (PS) (Chrysalis CHSDJ 2580) 1982 -
- β Excerpt From "Now Then"/(cut by Iggy Pop) (Chrysalis/Melody Maker no#) 1982 -
- Talk Back/Good For Nothing (PS) (Chrysalis CHS 2601) 1982 -
- Bits Of Kids/Stands To Reason (PS) (Chrysalis CHS 2637) 1982 73
- Bits Of Kids/Stands To Reason (12" PS) (Chrysalis CHS 12 2637) 1982 -
- The Price Of Admission/Touch And Go (PS) (Chrysalis CHS 2671) 1983 -

NB: * This was originally issued in a pressing of 500 with a handmade picture sleeve and a red label with catalogue number on the right hand side. It was repressed three months later in June 1978 with a different machine-cut picture sleeve and various coloured labels. + This was a reissue in the same sleeve. x This was a double 'A' side. α This was a jukebox issue. β This was a flexidisc which came free with 'Melody Maker'.

Arguably, the most interesting and controversial band to emerge from Northern Ireland's punk explosion was **Stiff Little Fingers**. The only band to sing consistently of Northern Ireland's troubles, some of **Stiff Little Fingers** songs made most political punk anthems sound empty. **Stiff Little Fingers** actually had something to get angry about! The group appeared to have been an outlet through which its members vented their pent up aggression. However, to their critics, **Stiff Little Fingers** were simply cashing in on the Troubles.

For Jake Burns (lead gtr, vcls), Henry Cluney (gtr), Ali McMordie (bs) and Brian Faloon (drms), **Stiff Little Fingers** had originally been formed as an escape route from their mundane lives in Ulster. Burns left school with sufficient 'A' level grades to enter a local polytechnic. He lasted there for just four months, spending five months on the dole, before becoming an accounts clerk - a job he stuck for just two weeks until **Stiff Little Fingers** were formed. As Burns told Melody Maker's Harry Doherty in an interview in March 1980:

"Personally, I'd had enough of Belfast. It's such an oppressive place. It's not so much the people but the tradition: get a job near your folks, get a house near your folks, don't leave the street. The atmosphere really got on my nerves."

Cluney, an early devotee of new wave and the founder-member of the band, had also been in the dole queue. Faloon was a telex operator and McMordie a disillusioned student.

It was in the autumn of 1977 when **Stiff Little Fingers** took to the road playing cover versions of punk classics like **The Sex Pistols**' *God Save The Queen* and **The Clash**'s *White Riot* and *Complete Control* at such venues as the Glenmachon Hotel in Hollywood, and the Trident Bar in Bangor.

Around the same time a couple of would-be rock journalists, Dave McCullough (later of Sounds) and Gavin Martin (later of NME) were producing a fanzine, which they called 'Alternative Ulster', dedicated to the musical, cultural and social 'alternatives' offered by Ulster. Terri Hooley had already planned to issue as a flexi-disc a song called *Alternative Ulster*

STIFF LITTLE FINGERS - Gotta Getaway.

STIFF LITTLE FINGERS - At The Edge.

given away with a future issue of the fanzine. However, this fell through. The band were intelligent enough to realise that they would never achieve wider recognition playing simply punk cover versions and sought guidance.

The launching pad for their career was their friendship with journalists, Colin McClelland, of the Sunday News and Gordon Ogilvie, who worked for the Daily Express in Northern Ireland. Both had been enticed by Jake to come and hear the band. Very quickly they developed a close friendship with the band and became their managerial team. It was Gordon Ogilvie who encouraged Jake Burns and the boys to write songs about life and their experiences in Belfast. Ogilvie soon began to write much of the group's material and inevitably allegations that he was using the band as a vehicle for his own political motivations followed. The precise level of his influence on Jake is difficult to gauge. Inevitably, the band denied that they were puppets on his string and always maintained that they held the power of veto over all decisions that affected the band.

Just twelve days later, **Stiff Little Fingers** returned to play Ogilvie two songs they had written about their experiences in Belfast:- *Suspect Device* and *Wasted Life*. For Jake Burns *Wasted Life* was a particularly personal song, which he had written about a mate of his, who had joined 'the organisation' and died under the wheels of a bus that he and a colleague had been trying to rob to boost the funds of 'the organisation'. Burn's mate had first been attracted to 'the organisation' when they had come around recruiting members, whilst the two of them were playing in the street. He had apparently turned to Burns and said "Fuck, I could be a soldier".

Wasted Life was a bitter tirade against the extremists who recruited people to die for pointless causes:

"I could be a soldier
Go out there and fight to save this land
Be a people's soldier
Paramilitary gun in hand
I won't be no soldier
I won't take no orders from no one
Stuff their fucking armies
Killing isn't my idea of fun"
(from *Wasted Life*)

Later in the song, Burns describes the extremists as "nothing but blind fascists". It was later rumoured that *Wasted Life* distorted the facts about Jake's mate who had left 'the organisation' by the time of his death. This may or may not have been the case - but the song had much wider application in any case.

Leaving aside for now, the possibility of more sinister implications behind McClelland and Ogilvie's involvement with the band, the two appear to have provided **Stiff Little Fingers** with the encouragement and impetus to boost their growing confidence, which supplemented their natural aggression. Ogilvie transformed their lyrics into more articulate forms and the choruses into short, punchy (if repetitive) slogans, which their audience could adopt and perhaps identify with.

Early in 1978 just 500 copies of *Suspect Device* were pressed on Rigid Digits Records. The band had to fold and glue the sleeves themselves. Ogilvie sent a copy to John Peel, who repeatedly played it on his radio programme. Soon the single was being distributed in Britain through Rough Trade. By the end of 1978 it had sold 25,000 copies! The band had promoted their first single by packaging it in a demo tape design to resemble an incendiary device. It was rumoured one record company actually had to ring them to ask for another copy as they'd thrown theirs into a bucket of water!

Other highs for **Stiff Little Fingers** in 1978 were their nationwide tour with **The Tom Robinson Band** and the release of their second Rigid Digit single *Alternative Ulster*. Burns described this in his early stage introductions as "a song about having nothing to do". It was produced by Ed Hollis, who had previously been manager and producer for **Eddie and The Hot Rods**. The song was really describing life in Belfast and directed at those who were bored and complained of nothing to do. **Stiff Little Fingers** had no solution to Belfast's problems, but their message was clear, 'Get off your arses and do something!', which after all was how **Stiff Little Fingers** would escape from Belfast! On 8th November 1978, it entered the Melody Maker Chart at No. 30.

Just a few days later drummer Brian Faloon left the band ostensibly because life on the road did not agree with, but shortly afterwards it became clear he planned to settle down and marry. His replacement, Jim Reilly, originally from Belfast was working with his uncle as a window cleaner in Sheffield before he saw **Stiff Little Fingers'** advertisement for a new drummer and promptly presented himself as an acceptable replacement.

1978 had also had its traumas. Island Records had enticed the group to London with the promise of a lucrative recording contract. The band had patiently marked time in a plush London hotel only to be told that they weren't wanted, when Managing Director, Chris Blackwell returned from a holiday in Jamaica. This undoubtedly left **Stiff Little Fingers** bitter and even more determined to prove themselves on their own. *Rough Trade* a track on their stunning debut album, *Imflammable Material* articulated their resentment.

"And you're sitting there in your London office
Snug and warm
And you think that you've won
Just remember this is just round one
We're gonna do it our way
We're gonna make it on our own"
(from *Rough Trade*)

After the Island episode, funds and morale were low. So when Rough Trade offered to distribute the band's own Rigid Digit's label it was accepted as a lifeline by the band.

1978 also saw **Stiff Little Fingers** quit Belfast and move to London, except for Cluney, who hated London and remained in Belfast, visiting London only when he had to. On the one hand this marked the attainment of one of their ambitions. But inevitably, too, it was depicted as a sell out. **Stiff Little Fingers** were regarded by some as writing and performing songs about politically sensitive troubles in Ulster from the relatively safety of London.

Nonetheless no one could dispute **Stiff Little Fingers** impact on the British rock scene by the end of the year. In John Peel's 'Festive 50' for 1978, *Suspect Device* had been voted No. 4 and *Alternative Ulster* No. 11. **Stiff Little Fingers** had also been voted the second best new band in Britain in an NME poll.

Their debut album, *Inflammable Material* released by Rough Trade in February 1979, produced by Geoff Travis and Mayo Thompson (who had reformed demented Texas psychedelics The Red Crayola), was highly acclaimed:-

"*Imflammable Material* is the classic punk record. A crushing contemporary, brutally inspired by blatant, bitter rebellion and frustration, that supplies neither questions or answers but consistently explodes *Fuck Off: Leave Me Alone* in the most scalding, dirty way since the set slogans, *Anarchy In The U.K.* and *White Riot* were laid to rest."
(Paul Morley, NME Feb 10th 1979)

Hearing it one is minded to remark that it may have made even greater impact had it come a year or eighteen months earlier. A series of pulsating punk-rock numbers were delivered at breakneck speed. The songs were full of anger and resentment and concentrated on expressing emotions and experiences of their upbringing in Belfast. Burn's raucous voice combined with the fiery, lashing guitars of Cluney and himself to create a barbaric, merciless, assault on the listener's senses. In addition to *Suspect Device*, *Rough Trade* and *Alternative Ulster*, the album contained a number of other poignant numbers. *White Noise* illustrated the group's repulsion towards racism, using the National Front's own language to parody the movement:-

"Ahmed is a Paki
Curry, coffee, queer
Ten to a bed
Flocking over here"
(from *White Noise*)

Unfortunately, the lyrics tended to be drowned in a wall of noise executed at breakneck speed and, as a result, the song was misinterpreted by some sectors of the public. One such misunderstanding led to Newcastle's Community Relations Officer's claiming that the record could cause "bitterness and hatred in the city". Such publicity, of course, merely brought **Stiff Little Fingers** to the attention of an even larger public.

State Of Emergency, a self-penned number, was a further appeal to Ulster's youth to breakaway from their no-win environment:-

"So please don't just sit there
Let's try to break out,
From all the hatred,
Suspicion and doubt
Try to change your life,
That is no life at all."
(from *State Of Emergency*)

Barbed Wire Love set a teenage romance against the background of the troubles in Northern Ireland. Other songs which were written about the band's personal experiences could equally have wider application. The message behind *No More Of That* was to stop letting people tell you what to do, although inevitably, given the tone of much of the remainder of the album, many interpreted it as a plea to put an end to sectarian killings on the streets of Belfast. Equally, Burns claimed that *Breakout* was written about his disillusionment whilst working (for two weeks) as an accounts clerk, although it, too, could be applied to the political situation in Northern Ireland. *Law And Order* was undoubtedly a bitter tirade against the brutality of the security forces. By contrast, *Johnny Was*, represented a welcome break from the relentless breakneck speed, high volume assault on the listener's senses. A **Clash**-influenced interpretation of a reggae tune, this eight minute epic featured some absorbing rhythm guitars and enabled Burns to demonstrate his vocal dexterity.

Although lyrically repetitive and limited in scope and variety, *Inflammable Material* had made **Stiff Little Fingers** a household name. In February 1979, it entered the album charts at No. 14. Although this proved its highest position it spent a total of nineteen weeks in the charts.

Spring 1979 saw **Stiff Little Fingers** headlining an extensive Rough Trade package tour with **Essential Logic** and **Robert Rental and The Normal**. On stage **Stiff Little Fingers** were dynamite. Frills, such as a fanfare to herald their arrival, together with an expensive light show and sound system, ensured this. Burns dressed in his leather jacket would prance around the stage hoarsely rasping out the band's slogans at breackneck speed accompanied by the brutal twin guitar riffs of Cluney and himself. Burns had readily admitted that on stage he underwent a complete personality change - naturally a shy, friendly man he became a leather-clad demon. The centre spot on stage would be reserved for McMordie, the most photogenic member of the band. To the right would be the chubby figure of Cluney grinding away with relentless power on his guitar - **Stiff Little Fingers** provided the sole outlet for this non-drinking, mild mannered individual. In the background would be the spectacle of Jimmy Reilly's explosive drumming. Meanwhile, the whole audience would invariably leap up and down in a frenzy to lyrics that were often drowned by instrumentation.

The nature of the pulsating punk they played, loaded with slogans and banner waving, perhaps made it inevitable that their concerts would attract the same unruly, mindless elements that had blighted **Sham 69**'s live appearances. Burns abruptly led the band offstage towards the end of a Hammersmith Palais concert on 5th August 1979, having first ordered the house-lights to be focused on the faces of the offenders. Later, on Sunday 2nd September 1979, when **Stiff Little Fingers** headlined a free concert in Brixton's Brockwell Park, as part of a Brixton Carnival Against Racism, which had been organised by Lambeth Borough Council, the gig was broken up when the stage was invaded and a crash barrier gave way.

May 1979 saw the issue of their third and final Rigid Digits/Rough Trade single *Gotta Gettaway*. The 'A' side expressed the band's feelings about leaving Belfast for London. The single also marked drummer Jim Reilly's debut on record. However, it was not a Top 20 hit.

The second half of 1979 saw another milestone in the development of the band, when they signed for Chrysalis. Ever since the chart success of *Inflammable Material* major record companies had been itching to sign the red hot Ulster punk band. Some saw **Stiff Little Fingers** signing for a major label as a further sellout, but for the band to achieve long-lasting major success it was a necessity. Even at this stage they were living on a modest budget, their signing to Chrysalis - for a reported advance of £30,000 - offered them financial security. However, Burns later contended that they could have signed to a number of other labels for more, for example, Pye offered them £100,000 and their own record company. Chrysalis were chosen because they promised the group almost total artistic freedom, including choice of singles, sleeves and 'B' sides as well as a high royalty. At the same time, of course, Chrysalis had the scale and size of operation necessary to promote **Stiff Little Fingers** throughout the world.

The autumn of 1979 saw the band embark on a fifteen date nationwide tour taking in such venues as Bristol's Locarno (7th October), Blackburn's St. George's Hall (9th October), Portsmouth's Locarno (11th October), Cardiff's Top Rank (14th October), Manchester's Polytechinic (16th October) and Aberdeen's Capitol (21st October). The tour enabled them to promote their debut single for Chrysalis, *Straw Dogs*, which had been released on 21st September 1979. A song about mercenaries, it was not the band's best single and received an indifferent reception by the rock press, but it did give them their chart debut reaching No. 44. Somehow the lyrics and music didn't quite blend together as effectively as on some of their earlier recordings. The 'B' side was apparently based on the reaction to Jake using the word 'crap' during an interview on Newcastle's Metro Radio.

The end of 1979 saw **Stiff Little Fingers** return to Belfast to headline a Christmas show at the city's Ulster Hall. One day earlier they had played at Dublin's Olympic. The band followed this up by announcing in January 1980 a twenty-three date tour itinerary to tie in with the 14th March 1980 release of their debut album for Chrysalis *Nobody's Heroes*. An NME preview of the album on 1st March 1980 remarked: "Where *Inflammable Material* was a frenzied expression of breathless escape, an outpouring of fresh energy mingled wiith stale disgust, *Nobody's Heroes* catches the band in a phase of growing self-awareness: still running, but allowing themselves a glance at how far they have come; still militant, but coming to terms with the realisation that like patriotism, anger isn't enough - foul realities require understanding as well as that; still in the realm of the political, but trying to deal sometimes with the more purely personal also." (Paul du Noyer, NME, 1st March 1980)

The album, although it showed signs of lyrical and musical diversification, was still almost exclusively a collection of pulsating punk numbers delivered at frantic speed. The lyrics, largely written by Ogilvie, were as direct and concise as the music. *Gotta Gettaway* provided a forceful opener, with

STIFF LITTLE FINGERS - Inflammable Material.

Burns' growling vocals and some demonic guitar riffs. The next track, *Wait And See* - a sort of autobiographical history of the group, which indicated their apprehension about the future - followed much the same format. The lyrics, which included a fond farewell to the band's original drummer, Brian Faloon, recounted how the band tried to get better gear despite their lack of money and how they'd hung on despite repeatedly being told that they were not good enough to make the big time. *Fly The Flag*, which contained some more barbarous guitar riffs, poured scorn over the "I'm Alright Jack" mentality. *At The Edge*, which was written about the things Jake's parents said to him (apparently quoting his dad's favourite cliches word for word) had, by the time of the album, surprisingly become the group's most successful single reaching No. 15 in the charts, during its nine week residency. The first side closed with the title track *Nobody's Heroes*, in which Burns emphatically rejects any quest for stardom or for fighting wrongs beyond his control.

Side Two showed some signs of greater musical diversity. *Bloody Dub*, the opening track, was a reggae-influenced instrumental, complete with grating guitar work and shattering glass - it was an interesting number but lacked melodic punch. Next came their different musical interpretation of The Specials' espistole against colour prejudice, *Doesn't Make It Right* - regarded by many as inferior to The Specials version, it was arguably one of the album's strongest tracks. *I Don't Like You* was nihilism taken to extreme - a stream of vindictive abuse delivered in **Stiff Little Fingers**' usual aggressive style.

"You are a scratch from the human race
You are a waste of a name
A waste of time and a waste of space
Looking at me, it's hard for me
Next to you
You've only one thing to say
I don't like you
(from *I Don't Like You*)

No Charge was most notable for some catchy guitar riffs and the side closed with *Tin Soldier* - a typically bitter tirade against those who recruited people to the army, this song was clearly applicable to the situation in their homeland of Northern Ireland.

Perhaps one of **Stiff Little Fingers**' strengths was that they always displayed an awareness of their own inadequacies: Jake Burns acknowledged this in an interview with Melody Maker's Harry Doherty (29th March 1980): "We still have a long way to go. We know that. I still think our records sounded wrong, indescribably wrong. They do not sound like a professional band. There's something not there. I don't like it. The new album has gone closer, but it is still not right." Another truth the band readily faced was that they could not continually sing about the troubles in Ulster - the inspiration behind their early songs - particularly now they were based in London. This perhaps inevitably meant that their music would be less angry in the future. *Nobody's Heroes* spent ten weeks in the album charts, peaking at No. 8.

However, the title track from the album *Nobody's Hero* was a minor hit, reaching No. 36 in May 1980 and their follow-up single, *Back To Front*, which was relatively disappointing, also climbed to No. 49 in the lower echelons of the chart in August of the same year.

Their next excursion into the album market was a live LP, *Hanx* released in September 1980. Jake Burns explained the reason for this to Melody Maker (September 1980): "*Hanx* is our way of saying thank you to the fans for the last year's support. We've always concentrated on being mainly a live band, and we think the album captures what it's like to see a gig on a good night." *Hanx* was recorded at Aylesbury Friars and London's Rainbow. It included live versions of *Nobody's Hero, Barbed Wire Love, Johnny Was, Wasted Love* and *Suspect Device*. The album climbed to No. 9 during a five week chart stay.

Stiff Little Fingers embarked on a lengthy U.K. tour, supported by **The Wall**, in April/May 1981, which kicked off at Belfast's Ulster Hall (21st April) and took in thirty venues. The tour tied in with the release of their latest album, *Go For It* and their rather ordinary 45, *Just Fade Away*, which had been released in late March.

1981 also saw **Stiff Little Fingers** appear in 'Iris In The Traffic' which was part of the BBC's 'Play For Today' series. Set in Ulster in 1978, when the band were struggling to break through, it featured Jake Burns making his acting debut and included the band performing. But musically things were

STIFF LITTLE FINGERS - All The Best.

not going so well. Many felt they had outgrown their audience and *Silver Lining*, their next 45, which addressed itself to the uneven distribution of wealth, also failed to chart. They played a one-off gig at London's Lyceum Ballroom in The Strand on Sunday 27th September and then departed for a three week French tour. The tour was to prove a farewell for their drummer, Jim Reilly, for once it was over he quit to return to Ireland and put together a new outfit. His replacement, Dolphin Taylor, had previously played with **The Tom Robinson Band**.

If 1981 had seen **Stiff Little Fingers** marking time, they started 1982 on a high note, embarking on a new tour, which commenced in Hull on 20th January, and encompassed eleven major venues and coincided with the issue of a new four-track Chrysalis EP, *One Pound Ten Or Less*. It was not well received. *Sad-Eyed People* was a catchy number, with some fine guitar work but the remaining material was well below par. Still it did climb to No. 33 in the charts. They played a one-off gig for Solidarity at North East London Polytechnic on 24th March, but were visibly beginning to loose their sparkle. Their April 1982 single, *Talk Back*, which marked a movement away from their early punkish aggression towards rather mundane rock, did nothing to reverse this trend.

A further U.K. tour ('The Out Of Our Skulls Tour') kicked off at Dunstable's Queensway Hall on 30th August. To coincide with this, a further 45, *Bits Of Kids*, was issued. This abrasive number was one of their better singles, but it only got to No. 73. In September *Now Then...* their fifth LP was issued. It contained eleven tracks and was their first new set for eighteen months. It included *Bits Of Kids* and a re-work of the 1970 Nicky Thomas reggae hit *Love Of The Common People*. Every album included a giant poster of the band. Again sales were disappointing. It climbed to No. 24 but only spent six weeks in the charts. They were featured in Channel Four's 'Whatever You Want' series, but overall 1982 had been a disappointing year for the band. What would 1983 hold for them?

Well Jake, it seems, had aready decided to quit. In mid-January 1983, **Stiff Little Fingers** announced that they were going their separate ways. Jake told NME that he thought *Now Then* was the best album the band had made. He added: "Unfortunately, I think it's also the best we would ever make, so I've decided to call it a day." The band would have been radically different without Jake and when Dolphin Talylor also decided to leave, the remaining three decided it would be hopeless to continue. Gordon Olgilvie told Melody Maker, "Obviously Jake's departure means the end of **Stiff Little Fingers** as we know it. I hope to continue writing songs with Jake and will back him in what he is going to do. And, if what Henry, Ali and I are working on plans out as well as we expect we hope to produce records, probably with an official change of name to simply SLF". Whilst Jake was announcing his intention to form a new band, McMordie, Cluney and Ogilvie were talking of returning to the studio to experiment with fresh ideas. As a farewell gesture, the band played two concerts, at Newcastle City Hall (5th February) and Glasgow Apollo (6th February); issued a farewell 45, *The Price Of Admission*, backed by *Touch And Go*, which was among the best and certainly most melodic they had made; and a double compilation LP *All The Best*, which featured the 'A' and 'B' sides of all their 45s. This rose to No. 19 in the album charts in February 1983, during a nine week stay.

After the band broke up in 1982, Jake Burns and Dolphin Taylor formed a short-lived group called Go West with ex-**Jam** member **Bruce Foxton**. When Go West split Dolphin joined **Spear Of Destiny**, Burns formed Big Wheel (with Steve Grantley (drms), Sean Martin (bs) and Nicky Muir (keyb'ds). They cut three 45s in both 7" and 12" formats. McMordie formed Fiction Groove and Cluney joined Fairground Attraction.

Jake Burns reformed the band in 1987 with Cluney, McMordie and Taylor. They recorded new, mostly live material. In 1991, ex-**Jam** member **Bruce Foxton** curtailed his solo career to replace McMordie in the band.

Stiff Little Fingers recorded four John Peel sessions in all. The first of these on 13th April 1978 comprised *Alternative Ulster, Wasted Life, Johnny Was* and *State Of Emergency*. It was not included on *The Peel Sessions Album* - the others all were. Despite this omission *The Peel Sessions* album included many of their finest moments like *Suspect Device, Law And Order, Straw Dogs, At The Edge* and *Nobody's Hero*.

Later, on 3rd March 1980 they recorded *Fly The Flag, At The Edge* and *Gotta Getaway* for Mike Reed. They also did one David Jensen session comprising *Sad-Eyed People, Listen, That's When Your Blood Bumps* and *Two Guitars Clash*.

Live In Concert released on Windsong in 1993 dates from 8th April 1981 and comprises eight cuts all from *Go For It!*, their third studio album. The bass is very low in the mix and the recording quality could certainly have been better, but it still captures a lot of the band's dynamism.

Tin Soldiers, a 1999 CD, concentrates on later material and is less relevant to this book. There are demo versions of three cuts from *Flags And Emblems*, a 1991 album for Essential, and three demos from *Unplugged*. The other ten tracks were recorded for Dojo's 1995 *Pure Fingers* CD, but not used.

Handheld & Rigital Digital will interest mostly the band's die-hard fans. Only available via the internet or mail-order, the package comprises a live CD, live video and colour booklet. It's a souvenir of their 'Hope Street' tour and both CD and video were recorded at Golders Green in 1999. There are renditions of old favourites like *Alternative Ulster, Suspect Device* and *At The Edge* and an unlisted encore version of *Johnny Was* is at the end of the video version of the show.

Stiff Little Fingers have also appeared on a number of compilations. You can also hear *Alternative Ulster* on *Wanna Buy A Bridge* (Rough Trade ROUGH 3) 1980, *The Best Punk Album In The World.... Ever, Vol. 1* (2-CD) (Virgin VTDCD 42) 1995, *Spiked* (EMI Gold CDGOLD 1057) 1996 and *The Best Punk Anthems.... Ever* (2-CD) (Virgin VTDCD 198) 1998, on the 5-CD box set, *1-2-3-4 - A History Of Punk And New Wave 1976 - 1979* (MCA/Universal MCD 6006) in 1999 and on *Something Better Change (Punk Junk)* (EMI OP 5237 7824) in 2000. *Johnny Was* also figured on *AZ DOR* (Celluloid CEL 2-006545) 1979. *Closed Groove* and *Barbed Wire Love* both got a further airing on *Backstage Pass* (Supermusic SVP 2001) 198?. *Law And Order* was also included on *Rock Against Racism's Greatest Hits* (RAR 1) 1980. *Suspect Device* resurfaced on *The Best Punk Album In The World.... Ever, Vol. 2* (2-CD) (Virgin VTDCD 79) 1996, *20 Of Another Kind, Vol. 1* (Polydor POLS 1006) 1979 and *25 Years Of Rough Trade Shops* (4-CD box set) (Mute CDSTUMM 191) 2001. Other compilation appearances have included *At The Edge* on *A History Of Punk, Vol. 2* (Virgin CDOVD 487) 1997, *Nobody's Hero* and *Alternative Ulster* on *Punk, Vol. 2* (Music Club MCCD 027) 1991 and on *Punk - The Worst Of Total Anarchy* (2-CD) (Disky SP 871952) 1996 and, finally, *Drowning* on *Wave (The Biggest New Wave Hits)* (3-CD set) (Disky HR 868442) 1996.

There's also a good retrospective CD compilation of their material, *Alternative Chartbusters* which came out in 1991. The most recent collection is *Inspired* a 2-CD set released in 2000.

Stiff Little Fingers had made a few excellent 45s, but their music lacked variety and following their move to London the firepower and zeal, for which they were reknowned in their early days, deserted them. They could hardly sing about Ulster from their London base and became a band without a cause. The failure of their music to progress left them with a rapidly diminishing audience... by the middle of 1982 the writing was well and truely on the wall for them. Nonetheless, for a while, in 1978 they were one of the hottest punk bands around.

The Stiffs

Personnel:			
IAN BARNES	gtr, vcls	ABCDEFG
PHIL HENDRIKS	vcls, gtr	ABCDEFG
TOMMY O'KANE	drms	AB D
MARK YOUNG	bs	A
JOHN McVITTIE	bs, vcls	B D
MICK ALDERSON	bs	C
JOHN MAYOR	drms, vcls	C EF
MARK HURLBUTT	bs, vcls	EF
JOHN WADE	gtr, vcls	F
MARK COLERIDGE	drms	G
STEVE FIELDING	bs	G

EP: 1(B) BROOKSIDE RIOT SQUAD (Standard English/ D.C. Rip/Brookside Riot Squad) (PS) (Dork UR 1) 1978

NB: There's also three CDs *Volume Control - Live* (Receiver RRCD 289 2) 2000, *The Punk Collection* (Captain Oi! AHOY CD 102) 1999 and *Stiffology 1981 - 88* (Angel Air SJPCD 062) 2001.

45s:
Inside Out/Kids On The Street (PS) (Dork UR 2) 1979
Inside Out/Kids On The Street (PS) (Zonophone Z 3) 1980
Volume Control/Nothing To Lose (PS) (Zonophone Z 14) 1981
Goodbye My Love/Roundabout (PS) (Stiff BUY 86) 1981
The Young Guitars/Yer Under Attack (12", PS) (Dark UR 7) 1985

The Stiffs first came together in Blackburn, Lancashire in 1976. Ian 'Strang' Barnes and Phil Hendriks were just fourteen year old school mates when they linked up with Tommy O'Kane and Mark Young to form a band. Their first gig followed in late 1977 with punk now in full flow. A few months later Mark Young was replaced by 'Big' John McVittie, who was a slightly more able bass player and could offer his parents' back garden for rehearsals. In 1978, they recorded a seven-cut demo and the best three cuts were released on the self-financed *Brookside Riot Squad* (EP) on the Dork imprint. Just 1,000 copies were pressed and most remained unsold as the band considered the record sub-standard and hid many of the copies beneath a bed, which caused it to become a collectors' item on account of its rarity. In fact *Brookside Riot Squad* and *Standard English* still sound reasonable today.

Their next release *Inside Out* backed by *Kids On The Street* in December 1979 marked a definite musical progression embodying more melody but power and energy too. The first 1,000 copies had the labels on the wrong sides, but the 45 attracted a lot of airplay from John Peel and went on to sell 5,000 copies becoming an indie chart hit. There was the inevitable Peel session on 14th February 1980. The band played five cuts; *Let's Activate, Brookside Riot Squad, Best Place In Town* and *Innocent Bystander*. As a consequence of all this *Inside Out* was reissued by EMI's Zonophone subsidiary early in 1980. In mid-1980, **The Stiffs** signed a long-term deal with EMI. Hedley Leyton became their manager, but their A&R man left soon after they signed the contract, which left the band a bit directionless. Several recordings were rejected because they weren't considered commercially viable. Eventually *Volume Control* and *Nothing To Lose* were released on a 45 and the latter track was a tongue-in-cheek jibe at the situation. The 45, with its heavy-metalish leanings, got lots of airplay but failed to chart. EMI put plans for a follow-up and album on hold and Hedley Leyton arranged for them to leave the label and negotiated a one-off 45 deal for them with Stiff Records. They were given the Glitter Band's seventies hit *Goodbye My Love* to cover. It met with mixed reviews but attracted national radio airplay. Despite this, and a national tour with the **UK Subs** and **Anti-Pasti** to coincide with its release, sales were not that great. By mid-1981, with the onset of 'New Romantics' and synthesizers, their sound was out of vogue. Disillusioned, they split up in June 1981.

There was a brief reformation in 1982 (line-up 'C'). They played a Peel session on 10th March comprising *Standing Ovation, Over The Balcony, Hook In Your Heart* and *Child's Play*. For this session ex-Mott The Hoople drummer Dale Griffin stood in for John Mayor.

Later, in 1985 there was a reunion (line-up 'D') and a recording session for a new 45 *The Young Guitars*. For this, John Mayor and Mark Hurlbutt were drafted in (line-up 'E') as O'Kane and McVittie were unavailable. This was a lively effort as was the flip side *Yer Under Attack* for which extra guitarist John Wade was added. This line-up also backed **Vicious Rumours** on their *Look Don't Touch* 12" single, which was co-written by Hendriks and released in the summer of 1985.

Between late 1986 and December 1988 (line-up 'G') played over 250 live 'Glam Punk' gigs across Europe. Mark Coleridge had previously played with Gary Glitter, **Afraid Of Mice** and Glass Torpedoes. They finally called it a day at Christmas 1988.

The Stiffs also figured on a couple of compilations:- *Yer Under Attack* can be heard on *User Friendly - North By North West* (SRT 6KL 866) and *Inside Out* and *Volume Control* resurfaced on *Zonophone Punk Singles Collection* (Anagram CDPUNK 97) 1997.

Captain Oi!'s *The Punk Collection* twenty-track CD features their singles (including relevant 'B' sides) and a number of unissued radio sessions. This is arse-kicking punk in the tradition of bands like **The Clash** and **Stiff Little Fingers**.

Volume Control - Live CD comprises a reformed line-up playing their old songs.

Stiffology 1981-88 included some previously unreleased material, most notably their Peel session from 1982 and a Griffin/Watts - produced track, *Best Place In Town*, along with demos, alternative mixes and amusing sleevenotes from Dale Griffin, who handled some of their production.

The Stilettos

45:	This Is The Way/Who Can It Be (PS)	(Ariola ARD 200) 1980	

A mod revival combo.

The Stingrays

Personnel:	CHRIS BOSTOCK	gtr	A
	RUSS MAINWARING	vcls, gtr	A
	PAUL MATTHEWS	bs	A
	SEAN McLUSKY	drms	A

This quartet contributed the promising fast-paced *Sound* to *Avon Calling - The Bristol Compilation* (Heartbeat HB 1) in 1979.

Stinky Toys

Personnel:	BRUNO CARONE	gtr	A
	ALBIN DERIAT	bs	A
	JACNO	gtr	A
	ELLI MEDEIROS	vcls	A
	HERVE ZENOUDA	drms	A

ALBUM:	1(A)	STINKY TOYS	(Polydor 2393 174) 1977

45:	Boozy Creed/Driver Blues (PS)	(Polydor 2056 630) 1977

A very marginal case for inclusion as this was a French punk band. I've mentioned them because they began gigging regularly in London in 1976, They also played on the second night of the 100 Club Punk Festival. Their records were substandard rock 'n' boogie not helped either by Elli Medeiros' vocals and they soon disintegrated.

The Stoat

Personnel:	GEORGE DECSY	drms	A
	RICHARD WALL	bs, vcls	A
	JOHN WATERS	gtr	A

45:	Office Girl/Little Jenny	(City NIK 1) 1977
	Up To You/Loving A Killer	(City NIK 3) 1978

The Stoat from South-west London were the first band to record on the City label. They also recorded a session for John Peel on 17th October 1978. This comprised *Tears Run Dry*, *No Way To Say Goodbye*, *Don't Say Nothing* and *Escorts*. *Office Girl* is an undistinguished song about a young executive luring a nubile typist behind the filing cabinet, accompanied by twanging guitars. Both sides of this 45 can also be heard on *Punk Rock Rarities, Vol. 1* (Anagram CDPUNK 63) in 1995. *Up To You*, penned by Wall and Waters, is another ordinary song. The flip side *Loving A Killer*, which they dedicated to Mary Bell, is much better with stronger vocals and guitar work.

The Stopouts

Personnel:	STEVE GRACE	vcls, gtr	A
	SUE JAMES	bs, vcls	A
	JOHN JONES	drms	A

45:	Strange Thoughts/Just For You (PS)	(Skeleton SKL 001) 1978

A short-lived band, which was more memorable for who was in it than its own product. Steve Grace had previously been in Nasty Pop. Sue James turned in a strong vocal performance on *Strange Thoughts*, which gave a nod and a wink in the direction of psychedelia.

Sue James later joined Dead Or Alive.

Stormtrooper

Personnel:	NIGEL HUTCHINGS	vcls	A
	MIKE LEE	drms	A
	JEFFREY PICCININI	bs	A
	JOHN PILKA	gtr	A

45:	* I'm A Mess/It's Not Me	(Solent SS 047) 1977

NB: * Some copies came in a plain stamped sleeve with an insert.

An obscure and now quite collectable punk era 45. Some copies came in a stamped plain sleeve with an insert and these are worth twice the price of the others. Reviewing this in NME Tony Parsons described it as "about as musical as the sound of a commuter getting shoved under a tube train during the rush hour".

Stormtrooper

45:	Pride Before A Fall/ Still Comin' Home (PS)	(Heartbeat BEAT 1) 1980

This later 45 was by a different band.

The Stowaways

Personnel:	MICK LISTER	vcls, gtr	A
	CLIFF ROWSWELL	drms	A
	RAY ROWSWELL	bs	A

45:	I Wanna Be Me/My Friends/ You'll Tie Me Down (PS)	(Supermusic SUP 27) 1979

A very rare and expensive mod-influenced single.

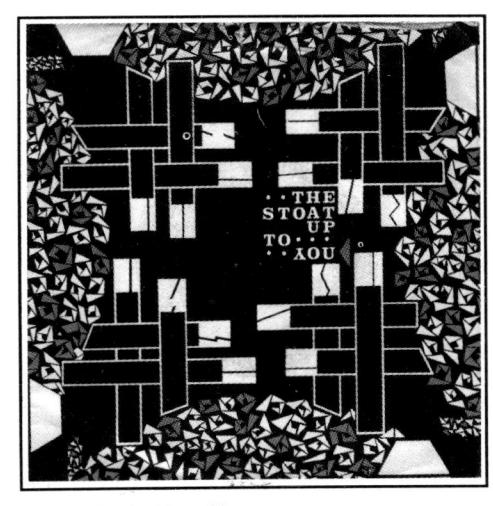

THE STOAT - Up to You.

Stranger Than Fiction

45s: Into The Void/Darkness (PS) (Ellie Jay EJSP 9301) 198?
Losing You/
You Don't Turn Me On Anymore (PS) (Ambergris AGM 1) 1981

From Wakefield in Yorkshire, **Stranger Than Fiction** first came to attention when they contributed the guitar driven *Immortal In Mirrors* to *Hicks From The Sticks* (Rockburgh Records ROC 111) in 1980.

The Strangeways

Personnel:
RINGO HIGGENBOTTEM drms A
BOB MARSDEN bs, vcls A
BARRY SMITH gtr, vcls A
ADA WILSON gtr, vcls A

45s: Show Her You Care/
You're On Your Own (PS) (Real ARE 2) 1978
All The Sounds Of Fear/Wasting Time (PS) (Real ARE 7) 1979

Fronted by **Ada Wilson**, who also released some solo recordings, **The Strangeways** were a new wave band from Wakefield. The rear sleeve of their second single included a photo from 'Quadrophenia' indicating that they hooked up with the mod revival in their later days. *Show Her You Care* is an O.K. but rather twee pop song.

THE STRANGLERS - Something Better Change.

The Stranglers

Personnel:
JET BLACK drms A
JJ BURNEL gtr A
HUGH CORNWELL bs A
DAVE GREENFIELD keyb'ds A

HCP

ALBUMS: 1(A) STRANGLERS IV - RATTUS NORVEGICUS
(up to   (United Artists UAG 30045) 1977 4
1986) 2(A) NO MORE HEROES (United Artists UAG 30200) 1977 2
3(A) BLACK AND WHITE (United Artists UAG 30222) 1978 2
4(A) STRANGLERS LIVE - X CERTIFICATE
      (United Artists UAG 30224) 1979 7
5(A) THE RAVEN (United Artists UAG 30262) 1979 4
6(A) THE MENINBLACK (Liberty LBG 30313) 1981 8
7(A) LA FOLIE (Liberty LBG 30342) 1981 11
8(A) THE COLLECTION 1977-1982 (compilation)
      (Liberty LBG 30353) 1982 12
9(A) FELINE (Epic EPC 25237) 1983 4
10(A) AURAL SCULPTURE (Epic EPC 26220) 1984 14
11(A) OFF THE BEATEN TRACK (Liberty LBG 5001) 1986 80
12(A) DREAMTIME (Epic EPC 26648) 1986 16

NB: (1) 10,000 copies came with a free 7" *Choosey Susie* / *Peasant In The Big Shitty* (live) (FREE 3) in a red picture sleeve. (1) reissued (Fame FA 3001) 1982 and issued on CD (Liberty C2 85), (EMI CDP 746 502 2) 1988, (Fame CDFA 3001) 1988 and EMI/Premier PRDFCD 5) 1996. (2) reissued (Fame FA 3190) 1987 and issued on CD (Fame CDFA 3190) 1988, (EMI CDP 746 613 2) 1988 and on CD (Fame CDFA 3190) 1988, (EMI CDP 746 613 2) 1988 and (EMI/Premier PRDFCD 6) 1996. (1) and (2) also issued on CD (EMI 7243 8 52266 2 5) 1996 and (EMI 7243 8 52265 2) 1996, both are with an extra bonus CD. 75,000 copies of (3) came with a free white vinyl 7" *Walk On By* / *Tits* / *Mean To Me* (FREE 9). It came in a die-cut sleeve and card insert, a few copies were mispressed on blue or biege vinyl. (3) reissued (Epic EPC 26439) 1986 and issued on CD (EMI C2 109) 1983 and (EMI CDP 790 596 2) 1988. (4) reissued in 1985 and issued on (CD) (EMI C2 110) 1988, (EMI CDP 790 597 2) 1988 and (EMI GOLD CDFA 3313) 1998. 20,000 copies of (5) came with a 3-D cover and inner sleeve. Some copies of (5) were mispressed and the 'B' side plays country and western music! (matrix no UAK 30263). (5) reissued (Fame FA 3131) 1988 and issued on CD (EMI CDP 746 615 2) 1987, (Harvest CZ 20) 1987, (Fame CDFA 3131) 1988 and (EMI 7466152) 1992. The CDs contain an extra cut *Bear Cage*. (6) reissued in 1985 and issued on CD (Fame CDFA 3208) 1988 and (Fame CDM 790 876 2) 1988. The CD version contains two extra cuts *Top Secret* and *Man In White*. (7) reissued (Fame FA 3083) 1983 and issued on CD (Liberty CZ 86) 1988, (Fame CDFA 3083) 1988, (Fame CDP 748 614 2) 1988 and (EMI GOLD CDFA 3083) 1988. Some copies of (8) came in a withdrawn 'dark' sleeve and these are now quite collectable. (8) reissued (Fame FA 3230) 1985 and issued on CD (Liberty CDP 746066 2) 1989, (Fame CDFA 3230) 1989, (EMI GOLD CDGOLD 1071) 1997 and (Disky DC 881872) 1998. (9) came with a bonus one-sided 7" *Aural Sculpture* (XPS 167) 1983 and initial copies of the cassette version contained a remix of *Midnight Summer Dream*. (9) reissued in 1986 and issued on CD as a CD set with *Aural Sculpture* and *Dreamtime* (Epic 4673952) 1990 and as a CD set with *Dreamtime* (Epic 4668352) with the addition of *Golden Brown* and by itself (Epic CDEPC 25237) 1992 and again (Epic 4844692) 1997. (10) reissued (Epic 4504881) 1987 and issued on CD (Epic CD 26220) 1988 and (Epic 4746762) 1997. (12) also issued on CD (Epic 26648) 1986 and again on vinyl (Epic 4633661) and CD (Epic 4633662) in 1989.

There are also several compilations and retrospective releases:- *Greatest Hits 1977 - 1990* (Epic 4675411) 1990 and on CD (Epic 4675412) 1990. This reached No. 4 and spent forty-seven weeks in the charts; *The Singles* (EMI EM 1314) 1989 and on CD (Liberty CDP 791 796 2) 1989; *Rarities* (Liberty CDP 791 072 2/CZ 141) 1988 (the CD versions have additional tracks *Rok It To The Moon*, *Shut Up*, *Old Codger*, *Yellowcake UF6*, *Vietnamerica* and *Love 30*); *The Early Years (Rare, Live And Unreleased)* (New Speak SPEAK 101) 1991 and on CD (New Speak SPEAKCD 101) 1992 and (Castle CLACD 401) 1994; *Live At The Hope And Anchor (22nd Nov 1977)* (EMI 7987892) 1991 and on CD (EMI CDGO 2033) 1992 and (Fame CDFA 3316) 1995; *The Old Testament - (The United Artists Studio Recordings 1977 - 1982)* (4-CD set) (EMI CDSTRANG 1) 1993; *Strangled - From Birth And Beyond* (SIS SISCD 001) 1994; *The Sessions* (Essential ESSCD 283) 1995; *The Hit Men (The Complete Singles 1977 - 1990)* (EMI CDEMC 3759) 1997; *The Masters* (Eagle EABCD 111) 1998; *Stranglers Archive (Live In London)* (Rialto RMCD 220) 1997; *Death & Night & Blood* (Receiver RRCD 187) 1994; *Access All Areas* (Blueprint SOF 001CD) 1998; *Saturday Night Sunday Morning* (Castle Communications ESSCD 194) 1993; *The Best Of The Epic Years* (Epic 487997-2) 1997; *Live At The Hammersmith Odeon '81* (EMI 7243 4 97773 2 3) 1999; and *Rare, Live And Unreleased* (Castle ESM CD 715) 1999.

HCP

EPs: 1(A) DON'T BRING HARRY (Don't Bring Harry/Wired/
Crabs (live)/In The Shadow (live)
    (United Artists STR 1) 1979 41
2(A) RADIO 1 SESSION (1982) (The Man They Love To
Hate/Nuclear Device/Genetix/Down In The Sewer)
    (Night Tracks) 1989 -

NB: (2) was originally recorded as a session for the David Jensen show.

HCP

45s: * (Get A) Grip (On Yourself)/
(up to London Lady (PS) (United Artists UP 36211) 1977 44
1986) + Peaches/Go Buddy Go (PS) (United Artists UP 36248) 1977 8
Something Better Change/
Straighten Out (PS) (United Artists UP 36277) 1977 9
x No More Heroes/
In The Shadows (PS) (United Artists UP 36300) 1977 8
Five Minutes/
Rok It To The Moon (PS) (United Artists UP 36350) 1978 11
Nice 'n' Sleazy/Shut Up (PS) (United Artists UP 36379) 1978 18
Walk On By/Old Codger/
Tank (PS) (United Artists 36429) 1978 21
Duchess/Fools Rush Out (PS) (United Artists BP 308) 1979 14
Nuclear Device (The Wizard Of Oz)/
Yellowcake UF6 (PS) (United Artists BP 318) 1979 36
Bear Cage/
Shah Shah A Go Go (PS) (United Artists BP 344) 1980 36
Bear Cage (Extended)/

THE STRANGLERS - STRANGLERS IV.

	Sha Sha A Go Go (12" PS)	(United Artists 12-BP 344) 1980 -	
	Who Wants The World/		
	The Meninblack (PS)	(United Artists BPX 355) 1980	39
	Thrown Away/Top Secret (PS)	(Liberty BP 383) 1981	42
	Just Like Nothing On Earth/		
	Man In White (PS)	(Liberty BP 393) 1981	-
	Let Me Introduce You To The Family/		
	Vietnamerica (PS)	(Liberty BP 405) 1981	42
#	Golden Brown/Love 30 (PS)	(Liberty BP 407) 1982	2
	La Folie/Waltzinblack (PS)	(Libery BP 410) 1982	47
	Strange Little Girl/Cruel Garden (PS)	(Liberty BP 412) 1982	7
	The European Female/		
	Savage Beast (PS)	(Epic EPC A 2893) 1983	9
	The European Female/		
	Savage Beast (picture disc)	(Epic EPCA 11-2893) 1983	-
	Midnight Summer Dream/		
	Vladimir And Olga (PS)	(Epic EPC A 3167) 1983	35
	Paradise/Pawsher (PS)	(Epic A 3387) 1983	48
	Paradise/Pawsher/Permission (12" PS)	(Epic TA 3387) 1983	-
α	Skin Deep/Here And Now (PS)	(Epic A 4738) 1981	15
	Skin Deep/Here And Now/		
	Vladimir And The Beast (12" PS)	(Epic A 12-4738) 1984	-
	No Mercy/In One Door (PS)	(Epic A 4921) 1984	37
β	No Mercy/in One Door (PS)	(Epic WA 4921) 1984	-
χ	No Mercy/In One Door//Hot Club (Riot Mix)/		
	Head On The Line (PS)	(Epic EPC GA 4921) 1985	-
	Let Me Down Easy/Achiles Heel (PS)	(Epic A 6045) 1985	48
δ	Let Me Down Easy (Extended)/Achiles Heel/		
	Place De Victories (instrumental)/Vladimir Goes To Heaven/		
	The Aura/Sculpture Manifesto (12" PS)		
		(Epic EPC QTA 6045) 1985	-
	Nice In Nice/		
	Since You Went Away (PS)	(Epic 650057) 1986	30
ε	Nice In Nice/Since You Went Away (PS)	(Epic WA) 1986	-
	Nice In Nice/		
	Since You Went Away (12", PS)	(Epic 650056) 1986	-
	Always The Sun/Norman Normal (PS)	(Epic SOLAR 1) 1986	30
ε	Always The Sun/Norman Normal (PS)	(Epic WA) 1986	-
	Always The Sun/Norman Normal/		
	Soul (12", PS)	(Epic SOLART 1) 1986	-
	Big In America/Dry Day (PS)	(Epic HUGE 1) 1986	48
ε	Big In America/Dry Day (PS)	(Epic WA) 1986	-
	Big In America/Dry Day/		
	Uptown (12", PS)	(Epic HUGET 1) 1986	-

NB: * Early copies appeared in a paper picture sleeve, later ones in a card picture sleeve. + Initial copies in a group picture sleeve with a 'blackmail' lettering were withdrawn and are now horrendously rare and expensive. These were replaced with a group picture sleeve. x Early copies had a 'wreath' design on the side with No More Heroes. # Some picture sleeves came with gold lettering, others with white. α 10,000 copies came in a 'skin feel' picture sleeve with a 'Skin Deep' tattoo. β This was an ear-shaped picture disc. χ This was a double pack with a gatefold picture sleeve. δ This was a limited edition 12" EP. ε This was a 7" shaped picture disc release.

The Stranglers are an immensely significant band in the context of this book. They not only pre-dated and survived the punk scene, but unlike **The Damned** and **Siouxsie and The Banshees** they survived into the nineties with their original line-up intact.

The roots of the band go back to the small Surrey village of Chiddingfold in the autumn of 1974. Jet Black (whose real name was Brian Duffy) had been born on 26th August 1943. A qualified carpenter, he'd also been involved in ice cream and wine business exploits, as well as pursuing his musical interests as a drummer. He was the quartet's oldest member and his drumming had jazz origins, which are partly accounted for by the era he grew up in.

Jean Jacques Burnel was born in London on 21st February 1952, but had French parents. He'd graduated from Bradford University with a history degree. His main musical achievement by this stage was to teach classical guitar.

Hugh Cornwell was also a London lad, born there on 28th August 1948. He'd attended a North London grammar school with a future star Richard Thompson, who'd taught him to play bass. They were in a school band Emil and The Detectives with son of Melody Maker jazz critic Max Jones (Nick) on drums. They played largely Buddy Holly and Everly Brothers covers. **Hugh Cornwell** went on to study chemistry at Bristol University and also spent 2 ½ years researching in Sweden. During this time he played in various amateur groups. Returning to Britain he worked briefly teaching biology at an 'A' level crammer in Guildford, but was dismissed for becoming too friendly with his pupils.

Dave Greenfield was the most experienced of the four musicians. He'd played in several groups since leaving school, initially as a guitarist and later on keyboards. He'd also had a spell in Hamburg.

As the Guildford Stranglers they played around the pub and club circuit during 1974. At this time the line-up was Black, **J.J. Burnel** and **Cornwell** plus a Swedish guitarist Hans Warmling who'd once been a member of Johnny Sox. By early 1975 the band had abbreviated their name to simply **The Stranglers**. Soon after Hans Warmling returned to Scandinavia they recruited Dave Greenfield as their keyboard player.

By the winter of 1975 **The Stranglers** had signed a management deal with a major London booking agency called the Albion. This secured them a support band slot at a number of London gigs. In the Autumn of 1976 they filled the support slot on Patti Smith's tour, which included gigs at major London venues like the Roundhouse and Hammersmith Odeon. They produced a demo cassette containing powerful versions of three of their best original numbers:- *Grip*, *Bitchin'* and *Go Buddy Go*. Then in October and November they embarked on their own U.K. tour using a former ice cream van belonging to Black as transport. They finally signed a record deal with United Artists in December 1976.

With Martin Rushent producing, their debut single *(Get A) Grip (On Yourself)* was released in February 1977. It had a very distinctive opening passage, repeated twice on the keyboards, before the vocals come in. The flip side *London Lady* was more uptempo with a number of short breaks of guitar, bass and drums. The 45 was an impressive start and reportedly sold 2,000 copies in the first week. Labelled as 'punk' it could expect little daytime airplay, so to get to No. 44 and spend four weeks in the charts was a good performance.

On 3rd March 1977, they recorded their first of two John Peel sessions. It comprised *Something Better Change*, *Hangin' Around*, *I Feel Like A Wog* and *Goodbye Toulouse*. All except for *I Feel Like A Wog* later appeared on their debut album (*I Feel Like A Wog* later figured on *No More Heroes*). *Something Better Change* from this session was later included on *Winter Of Discontent* (Strange Fruit SFRCD 204) 1990.

Their debut album, *Stranglers IV - Rattus Norvegicus* was released in April 1977. It was originally to be called *Dead On Arrival*. Early copies came with a free 7" single with *Choosey Suzie* on one side and a live recording of *Peasant In The Big Shitty* on the other. The album was notable for a strong Doors influence, but Lou Reed and J.J. Cale and shades of U.S. psychedelic punk groups were evident too. On side one keyboards and the rhythm section are very much to the fore on the opening cut *Sometimes*, which is also notable for its aggressive lyrics.

"Someday I'm gonna smack your face
Someday I'm gonna smack your face

Somebody's gonna call your bluff
Somebody's gonna treat you rough
You're way past your station
Beat you, honey, till you drop"
(from *Someday*)

It also has a lot of instrumentation. *Goodbye Toulouse* has an unusual organ intro which gives way to more fast-paced guitar. This is followed by *London Lady*, one of songs which led to the band being labelled as misogynists. The Doors' influence is particularly evident on the slow-paced *Princess Of The Streets*, a song about a lady **J.J. Burnel** had lived with for a while whilst at Earls Court in London. The side closes with the rather sinister *Hanging Around*. Side two opens with *Peaches*, one of **The Stranglers**' best known and finest songs. The lyrics are positively leering, the backing vocals menacing and the rhythm section is choppy.

"Strolling along minding my own business
Well there goes a girl and a half
She's got me going up and down
Walking on the beaches looking at the peaches"
(from *Peaches*)

This is a highly memorable number, but some found the lyrics offensive. It's followed by *(Get A) Grip (On Yourself)*, *Ugly*, which is possibly the weakest number on the album and ends with the lengthy *Down In The Sewer*. This opens with an instrumental passage, a good guitar riff, later joined by organ and bass. The lyrics basically describe existence down in the sewers. There's also an instrumental passage at the end which eventually builds into a climax, with a church-organ sound, speeds up and then ends with sounds of squeaking rodents and water running down a drain. Certainly an adventurous number. To help promote the album the band appeared on a Radio One 'In Concert' broadcast. They also headlined a punk package at the Roundhouse, which included **The Jam** and **Cherry Vanilla** on the bill. This all helped expose them to a wider audience. This was one of punk's finest albums and it enjoyed the commercial success it deserved. It spent a remarkable thirty-four weeks in the charts climbing to No. 4.

In spring 1977, they toured the continent and then the U.K. supported by punk band **London**. In May the excellent *Peaches* was issued as a 45 coupled with *Go Buddy Go*, a danceable rocker. Despite giving a cleaned-up version of the song to radio stations as a one-sided promo (United Artists FREE 4), *Peaches* got very little airplay with most stations plugging *Go Buddy Go* and it was this that they performed on 'Top Of The Pops'. The single spent fourteen weeks in the charts peaking at No. 8. The original picture sleeves for the 45 featured 'Blackmail' style lettering which some found offensive. So for a while the single was sold without a picture sleeve until a new design was issued. Copies with the original picture sleeve are now very collectable.

Their subsequent British tour was plagued with problems. The first gig had to be cancelled because **Hugh Cornwell** had flu. Some concerts were cancelled by the venues following trouble at other punk concerts and some were disrupted by violence. **J.J. Burnel** also narrowly avoided being called up for French military service.

In July 1977, a third 45 was issued *Something Better Change*. This mid-paced rocker with catchy organ and an aggressive vocal performance from **Cornwell** reached No. 9, spending a total of eight weeks in the charts. They followed this with another extensive European tour.

On 13th September 1977, they played a second session for John Peel. It featured *Dead Ringer*, *No More Heroes*, *Burning Up Time* and *Bring On The Nubiles*. All four songs appeared on their second album *No More Heroes*, which was released the following month. The title cut was released as a 45 in September. This was another of their finest moments. It starts with a few keyboard notes and a roll of the drums and then the lyrics complain about the lack of current heroes of the stature of Trotsky and Sancho Panza. The flip side *In The Shadows* was a slow menacing number. Early copies of the single sported a wreath design on the side with *No More Heroes* on. Promo copies only featured *No More Heroes* (United Artists FREE 8). *In The Shadows* wasn't included on the *No More Heroes* album but it did later emerge on *Black And White*. The 45 *No More Heroes* got to No. 8 and spent nine weeks in the charts.

The *No More Heroes* album was weaker musically overall than its predecessor, but lyrically it pulled no punches. Side one opened with *I Feel Like A Wog* which acted as advocate for those who are treated as inferior. *Bitching* is an undistinguished number. *Dead Ringer*'s opening chords

THE STRANGLERS - No More Heroes.

sound remarkably similar to those on *Peaches* - the song deals with a case of mistaken identity. *Dangenham Dave* dealt rather impassionately with the suicide of one of their stalwart fans. *Bring On The Nubiles* contained blatently sexist lyrics and the side closed with their earlier 45 *Something Better Change*. Side two opens with the title cut and finest moment on the album. This is followed by *Peasant In The Big Shitty*, a studio version this time. It opens with a beaty drum solo and then unnerving guitar joins in followed by expressive vocals but the rest of the song doesn't live up to the opening. *Burning Up Time* displays a similar vocal style to *Something Better Change*. *English Towns* is one of the weaker cuts and the lengthy finale *School Mam* doesn't achieve the standard of *Down In The Sewers* on their first album. Despite this, *No More Heroes* was still a fine second album. It spent nineteen weeks in the charts and got to No. 2.

On 22nd November **The Stranglers** played at London's Hope And Anchor as part of a three week festival. Live versions of *Straighten Out* and *Hanging Around* later appeared on the *Hope And Anchor Front Row Festival* album. A third number from this concert *In The Shadows* was later featured on the band's *Don't Bring Harry* EP.

In the winter of 1977/78 **The Stranglers** frequently appeared unpublicised at a number of smaller venues. This was possibly a ploy to avoid some of the violence and trouble which had plagued their previous U.K. tour.

In January 1978, a new 45 the rather messy *5 Minutes* was released. This was inspired by a rape that occured at one of J.J. Burnel's flats. It wasn't one of their better efforts - the backing, in particular, sounded rather cluttered. It still got to No. 11 during a nine week chart residency.

Early in 1978 the band toured America and Canada. In April, the excellent *Nice 'N' Sleazy* was issued as a 45. This was a catchy number with lots of riffing organ. On the flip was a short punk thrash *Shut Up*, which wasn't included on any albums. One of their best singles *Nice 'N' Sleazy* surprisingly only climbed to No. 18 during an eight week chart stay. They then toured Iceland, Scandinavia and the continent returning to Britain at the end of May for the release of their third album *Black And White*.

Black And White opens strongly with *Track*, which featured some appealing keyboards and came complete with the sound of explosions. This is followed by the excellent *Nice 'N' Sleazy*. *Outside Tokyo* is a slower number. *Sweden (All Quiet On The Eastern Front)* was a neatly structured ode;

"Let me tell you about Sweden
Only country where the clouds are interesting
Big brother says it's the place to go

Too much time to think
Too little to do
Too much time too little to do
Cos it's all quiet on the eastern front"
(from *Sweden (All Quiet On The Eastern Front)*)

Laura Logic plays saxophone on the undistinguished *Hey! (Rise Of The Robots)*. The side closes with *Toiler On The Sea*. This is a narrative song with a recurring tune. It commenced with an instrumental passage and the fade-out at the end featured synthesized waves. Incidentally there was also a Swedish language version of *In The Shadows* (United Artists UP 36459) backed by *In The Shadows*.

Side two of the album is weaker. *Curfew* has a nice reverberating intro, some good guitar/organ interplay and is another narrative song.

"The enemy has cut down all the power
London south of the Thames is invaded
Westminster is razed to the ground
The government has fled
The government has fled
The government has fled for Scotland today

It becomes black and white
Is it true what they say?
They turn the day into night
Black and white becomes

The government has fled into thin air
What's left of our troops has joined with the Scots
To form in defence across of the north
Stay in your homes
Stay in your homes
Be off the streets by nightfall."
(from *Curfew*)

Threatened has an unnerving intro, but *Do You Wanna* and *Death And Night And Blood (Yukio)* are rather ordinary. *In The Shadows* is a good song, a slow, menacing number with rumbling upfront bass and deadpan vocals. The album closes with *Enough Time*, which is a little unusual but which pales in comparison to say *Down In The Sewers* despiite the morse code segments superimposed on organ.

THE STRANGLERS - Black And White.

Early copies of *Black And White* came with a free 7" containing a cover of Bacharach-David's *Walk On By* (a Doors-style rework of Diane Warwick's old hit), *Tits* and *Mean To Me*. In the 'States, the album was pressed on grey marbled vinyl and the accompanying free 7" came on white vinyl. The cassette version of *Black And White* added *Mean To Me* to compensate for the lack of a 7". The album again performed well commercially, spending a total of eighteen weeks in the charts and peaking at No. 2.

In July 1978, *Walk On By* was released as the band's next single. As it was over six minutes long an edited verson was released as a promo for radio stations. It spent eight weeks in the charts and climbed to No. 21. In the autumn they appeared at a Battersea Park concert, where they were joined on stage by some strippers for *Nice 'N' Sleazy*.

A live album *Live (X Cert)* was released in March 1979. It was a good representation of their live sound and on stage banter. It climbed to No. 7 and spent ten weeks in the chart. In Japan it was released in a gatefold sleeve including a 45 containing *Choosey Susie* and their cover of Tommy James and The Shondells' *Mony Mony*. The package also included a lyric sheet and poster.

Soon after the live album **J.J. Burnel** released a solo album *Euroman Cometh* (United Artists UAG 30214). The band returned in August with a new 45, the more melodic *Duchess*. The otherwise unavailable *Fools Rush Out* was on the flip side. The 45 became their third consecutive one to spend eight weeks in the charts - this time climbing to No. 14. In August **The Stranglers** also topped the bill at a one night Loch Lomond festival in Scotland which included fireworks and searchlights. They also supported The Who at Wembley Stadium the same month, using the occasion to showcase seven tracks from their forthcoming album *The Raven*.

The Raven was issued in September 1979. The first 20,000 copies had a 3-D illustration on the front. Previously most of their material had dealt with human relationships, but this album revealed a new political consciousness with track titles like *Nuclear Device, Shah Shah A Go Go* and *Genetix*. The title cut is one of the strongest numbers and this is preceded by a pleasant short instrumental number *Baroque Bordello*, which sported some pleasant harpsichord-like keyboards. Also of note is *Don't Bring Me Down*, a slow drugs-related number which utilised a piano accompaniment as opposed to the synthesizers used on most other tracks. Their earlier melodic 45 *Duchess* was also included. The album got to No. 4 but enjoyed a shorter chart residency (just eight weeks) than its predecessors.

Collectors may want to track down an American issue of the *Duchess* 45, which has *The Raven* on the flip side (IRS IR 9018) 1980. In France, a French language version of *Don't Bring Harry* was also released around this time.

In October 1979, the band embarked on a further U.K. tour. The same month *Nuclear Device* was issued as a 45, backed by a non-album instrumental cut *Yellowcake UF6*. This spent four weeks in the charts peaking at No. 36. The same month **Hugh Cornwell** and Robert Williams released an album *Nosferatu* (United Artists UAG 30251) 1979. The following month a 45, a version of Cream's *White Room* was released backed by *Loves In A Lost Land* (United Artists BP 320) 1979. Indeed **Cornwell**'s interests had expanded well beyond **The Stranglers** by now. He was trying his hand at production. Early output from this had been a five cut demo from **The Pop Group** and an album for Leila and The Snakes.

In December 1979, a four track Christmas EP titled *Don't Bring Harry* was released. Aside from the title cut, it included the live version of *In The Shadows* from their earlier *Hope And Anchor* concert, a live version of **J.J. Burnel**'s *Crabs* and a cut from **Hugh Cornwell**'s recent album called *Wired*. A one-sided promo of *Don't Bring Harry* was also issued. The EP climbed to No. 41 in the charts. Collectors may be interested in a 12" EP released in Japan, which in addition to this material, also contained their earlier foreign language versions of *Don't Bring Harry* (in French) and *Sweden (All Quiet On The Eastern Front)* in Swedish.

In March 1980, *Bear Cage*, a new song, was coupled with *Shah Shah A Go Go* (from their *Raven* album) and released as a double 'A' side. The 12" had an extended version of *Bear Cage*. The 45 again stalled at No. 36, but spent five weeks in the chart. **Cornwell** also spent two months in jail following a drug bust, which meant a planned tour of India could not go ahead. He later related his experiences in prison in a short book 'Inside Information'.

Initial copies of the band's May 1979 single *Who Wants The World* (identifiable by a red corner to the sleeve) sold for just 75p. Despite this marketing ploy the 45, a strong one, only enjoyed a four week chart stay peaking at No. 39. Again collectors may be interested in a Japanese release on United Artists, which included these two songs on an EP along with *Shah Shah A Go Go* and both versions of *Bear Cage*.

In June 1979 they were in trouble again - accused of inciting a riot at a French university when the promoter had failed to provide a generator. The band suggested the angry audience should take out their displeasure on the university (not them). In the end they returned to Nice later that year with the French authorities clamering for jail sentences, but the matter was resolved by payment of fines. They toured Britain again in July and then went on to the 'States where they had recently severed their relationship with A&M switching to Miles Copeland's IRS label. IRS released an album *Stranglers IV* (IRS SP 70011) comprising a selection of tracks from *The Raven* and some singles. Inital copies contained an EP comprised of **Hugh**

Cornwell's *White Room* and **J.J. Burnel**'s *Do The European*, *Straighten Out* and *Choosey Susie*.

In February 1981, a new single *Thrown Away* was released backed by *Top Secret*. This was a minor hit, climbing to No. 4 during a four week chart stay. *Thrown Away* was on their forthcoming album *The Meninblack*, but *Top Secret* was one of the two tracks (the other being *Men In White*) that only made it onto the CD version.

The Meninblack was a concept album devised by **Hugh Cornwell**, which was released in February 1981. The Men In Black were supposed to be Extraterrestrials who silence people who had seen UFOs and other extraterrestrial activity to maintain their secrecy. The inner spread of the cover reproduces "The Last Supper" with the addition of one assassin. The album completely lacks **The Stranglers** usual thrust and energy. It contains lots of keyboards, synthesizers and special effects but overall is very disappointing. Although it got to No. 8 it spent only five weeks in the charts suggesting that only the band's fans bought it.

In November 1981, they released a further album *La Folie* and a single off it, *Let Me Introduce You To The Family*. The 45, which featured the otherwise unavailable *Vietnamerica* on the flip, could only climb to No. 42 and spent just three weeks in the charts. The album had two real highlights. The delightful *Golden Brown* with its waltzing harpsichord and **Cornwell**'s relaxed, gentle vocals was a very melodic song and a significant departure in style for the band. *Tramp* was also a strong number. Although *La Folie* only climbed to No. 11, it enjoyed eighteen weeks in the charts - the previous album to enjoy such a long chart residency had been *Black And White*.

In February 1982, they recorded a session for David Jensen. The four cuts comprised *The Man They Love To Hate*, *Nucleur Device*, *Genetix* and *Down In The Sewer*. They were later released as an EP on Night Tracks in 1989.

Golden Brown was a natural choice for 45 release in March 1982. An instrumental *Love 30* was put on the flip side. Early copies of the 45 had gold-coloured lettering on the sleeve. On later copies this was changed to white. It became their highest placed chart single climbing to No. 2 during a twelve week chart stay. A 12" version of the 45 was released in Germany.

In April *La Folie*, a slow number sung by **J.J. Burnel** in French was put out as a 45 backed by *Waltzinblack*. This spent just three weeks in the charts climbing to No. 47.

In July, *Strange Little Girl* another fine song in a similar vein to *Golden Brown* was released on 45. It climbed to No. 7 and spent nine weeks in the charts. The flip side *Cruel Garden* was another non-album cut.

In September, a compilation *The Collection 1977-82* was issued. It contained a selection of their better material and got to No. 12 during a sixteen week stay.

During 1982, **The Stranglers** were involved in various legal wrangles with EMI who'd taken over United Artists. By the end of the year they were able to sign to Epic and in November 1982 their first single on Epic was the melodic *European Female*. It was backed by *Savage Beast* and got to No. 9 spending eight weeks in the charts. A picture disc version was released in January 1983 to coincide with the release of their *Feline* album the same month. Initial copies came with a bonus one-sided 45 *Aural Sculpture*. This was included on the cassette version of the album. (The U.S. version of the album included *Golden Brown*). This album was their first to experiment with dance rhythms, but it included few outstanding songs. Aside from the title track, the better songs are *Paradise* and *Lets's Tango In Paris*. The album sold well, though, climbing to No. 4 and spending eleven weeks in the charts.

In February, *Midnight Summer Dream* was culled from the album as their next 45. A new song *Vladimir And Olga* was put out on the flip. It spent four weeks in the chart. Its best position was No. 35. Its release coincided with a new U.K. tour. A further cut *Paradise* was taken from the album in July with another new song *Pawsher* on the flip. The 12" version featured a second new track *Permission*. *Paradise* was in the charts for just three weeks and its best position was No. 48. **The Stranglers** played at Reading Festival in summer 1983 and also toured the continent that summer. They then took a long break and no new material was released until September 1984. During this quiet period for the band **J.J. Burnel** and Dave Greenfield released an album *Fire And Water* (Epic EPC 25707) in November 1983 and later, in 1984, a 45, *Rain & Dole & Tea / Consequences* (Epic EPC A 4076).

The Stranglers returned in September 1984 with the commercial 45 *Skin Deep*. Unusually for them this deployed backing vocals on the chorus and a piano accompaniment. It took them back into the Top 20, peaking at No. 15 during their seven weeks in the charts.

Their *Aural Sculptures* album followed in November. This was possibly their best album since their debut with a number of quality cuts. The album opens softly with *Ice Cream* but the mood soon changes with the introduction of punchy horns. An instrumental reprise is followed by *Skin Deep* and then *Let Me Down Easy*, which has a catchy chorus. *No Mercy* has a pleasing guitar riff. The side concludes with a 'progressive' sort of song *North Winds*. Side two is less impressive but *Punch And Judy* exudes some humorous lyrics, *Laughing* is a slow number with lots of synthesizers and the finale *Mad Hatter* combined jazzy vocals, xylophone and backing vocals. The album spent ten weeks in the charts climbing to No. 14.

Two singles were culled from *Aural Sculptures*. Firstly, in November to coincide with the album, *No Mercy*. A non-album cut *In One Door* was put on the flip. This got to No. 37 and spent seven weeks in the charts. It was followed, in February 1985, by *Let Me Down Easy*, again backed by a new song *Achilles Heel*. This just made the Top 50, reaching No. 48 in its four week stay.

In 1986, the *Off The Beaten Track* compilation was issued and this made the lower reaches of the chart. Later in the year a new album *Dreamtime* returned them to the Top 20, climbing to No. 16 during its six weeks chart stay. One of its cuts *Nice In Nice* was released as a taster single in August. Both this and the follow-up *Always The Sun*, released the same month as the album, climbed to No. 30 and coincidentally they both stayed five weeks in the chart. A third single from the album *Big In America* improved on this by a week, but its highest position was only No. 48.

There are a plethora of compilations and retrospective releases of their material, much of which is still available.

Their compilation appearances have included two live cuts *Straighten Out* and *Hanging Around* on the *Hope And Anchor Front Row Festival* (dbl) (Warner Bros K 66077) in 1978; *Peaches* and *(Get A) Grip (On Yourself)* on *The Best Punk Album In The World.... Ever, Vol. 1* (2-CD) (Virgin VTCD 42) 1995; *No More Heroes* and *Something Better Change* on *Vol. 2* (2-CD) (Virgin VTCD 79) 1996 of the same series; *Peaches* and *(Get A) Grip (On Yourself)* on *The Best Punk Anthems.... Ever* (2-CD) (Virgin VTDCD 198) and on *God Save The Punks* (2-CD) (Disky DOU 882552) 1998; *(Get A) Grip (On Yourself)* on *Burning Ambitions (A History Of Punk)* (Anagram CD BRED 3) in 1996. You'll also find *Peaches* on *A History Of Punk, Vol. 1* (Virgin CDOVD 486) 1997; *Something Better Change* on *Punk - The Worst Of Total Anarchy* (2-CD) (Disky SP 871952) 1996 and it also features on *Spiked* (EMI Gold CDGOLD 1057) 1996 along with *Hanging Around*. *No More Heroes* also figures on *The Sound Of The Suburbs* (Columbia 4888252) 1997 and on *Teenage Kicks* (PolyGram TV 525382) 1995. Finally, their new wave classic *Golden Brown* can also be heard on *New Wave Archive* (Rialto RMCD 201) 1997, *New Wave Classics* (2-CD) (Disky DOU 878282) 1998, *Wave (The Biggest New Wave Hits)* (3-CD set) (Disky HR 868442) 1996 and *Wave Romantics, Vol. 2* (SPV SPV 08438992) 1995, whilst you can also check out *Skin Deep* on *Wave Party* (Columbia

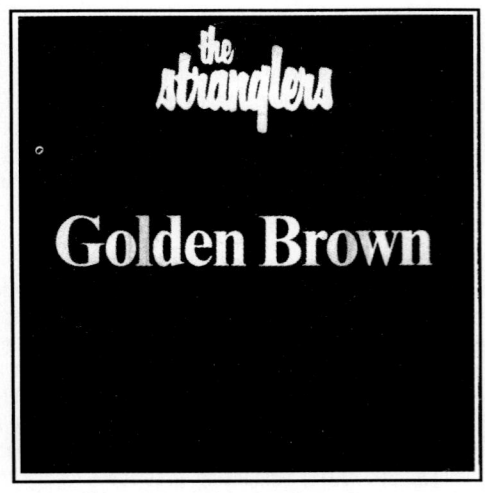

THE STRANGLERS - Golden Brown.

4758322) 1995. In 1999, *(Get A) Grip (On Yourself)* was included on the 5-CD box set *1-2-3-4 - A History Of Punk And New Wave 1976 - 1979* (MCA/Universal MCD 60066).

Rarities released in 1988 by EMI delves deeply into their back catalogue with (on side one) some interesting results. It includes the *Choosey Susie* freebie, the radio version of *Peaches*, both sides of the first **Celia and The Mutations** single, promo edits of *No More Heroes* and *Walk On By*, *Don't Bring Harry* sung in French and the Swedish language *Sweden*. The second side is less interesting, though, concentrating more on 'B' sides and 12" mixes.

The Early Years released by New Speak in 1991 includes two sets of early demos and ten live tracks, one of which dates back to 1975. Some of the live material had figured previously on their 1979 release *X-Cert Live* and on their 1988 release *All Day And All Of The Night*. The earlier session from 1974 comprises a version of their 1982 hit *Strange Little Girl* (which is little different from their later one) and two previously unreleased songs, *Wasted* and *My Young Dreams*, which are basically pretty slick keyboard-based pop. The 1976 demos feature versions of *Grip*, *Bitching* and *Go Buddy Go*. Again there's little significant difference between these versions and the later ones except that these earlier ones are a little slower. The live tracks on the collection feature **The Stranglers** performing nine songs from *Rattus Norvegicus* and *No More Heroes*. These are taken from a Hammersmith Odeon gig in 1976 when they were a support slot for Patti Smith. Finally, there's a live version of them playing *Princess Of The Street* at the Railway Tavern a year earlier. The sound quality of the live tracks is pretty good and helps to recreate some of the excitement of punk's earliest period. Given, though, that most of the material appears elsewhere this is only an essential artefact for the band's serious fans.

Live At The Hope And Anchor is a nineteen-cut live album which captures their entire set at the venue's Front Row Festival on 22nd November 1977. All of their songs of the time are included. The album opens with the sexist *Tits* (which later turned up on the free single which accompanied the *Black And White* album), then moves on to cover all their early favourites from *Rattus Norvegicus* and *No More Heroes*, then a couple of oddities in the form of *Choosie Susie* and *Mean To Me* were included for good measure. The recording is unedited so it's far from flawless but if you like that live and raw feel this could be for you.

The Old Testament - The U.A. Studio Recordings released in 1993 is a 4-CD set accompanied by a one hundred and twelve-page booklet written by Chris Twomey. On offer are all the band's United Artists album tracks and 'A' and 'B' sides - eighty-three songs in all. The booklet is well-written and contains a discography illustrated in colour.

Saturday Night Sunday Morning is a twelve-track live CD featuring Hugh Cornwell's last performance with the group at Alexandra Palace on Saturday 11th August 1990.

Strangled - From Birth And Beyond is a compilation CD sure to interest the band's fans. It compiles the several rare recordings which "Strangled" magazine (the mouthpiece of The Stranglers Information Service) has given away over the years in the form of free flexis or 7" vinyl. The CD also includes two outtakes from the *Stranglers In The Night* sessions, *Mr. Big* and *I'll Be Seeing You*.

THE STRANGLERS - Walk On By.

The Sessions, a 1995 release from Essential features two 1977 Peel Sessions of *Rattus Norvegicus* and *No More Heroes* material, plus a David Jensen session from 1982.

In 1996, EMI reissued *Rattus Norvegicus* on CD and supplied a bonus disc comprising *Choosey Susie* and *Go Buddy Go* (added to a live version of *Peasant In The Big Shitty*). *No More Heroes* was reissued too with a bonus disc which included a 'B' side *Straighten Out*.

The Hit Men is a 2-CD set, issued in 1997, which includes their numerous hits and selected album tracks.

In 1997 Epic released *The Best Of The Epic Years*. This covers **The Stranglers**' period as a pop act with Epic after their punk rock period with United Artists. Offered at 'a nice price' although the band were past their prime there is plenty of baroque, polished pop on offer in the form of *Always The Sun*, *Nice Is Nice* and *European Female*.

THE STRANGLERS - Five Minutes.

In 1999 EMI released *Live At The Hammersmith Odeon '81*. By this time their sound had softened markedly from their early punk edge and the concert contained none of their seventies hits. Instead on offer is the likes of *Golden Brown*, *Who Wants The World* and *Let Me Introduce You To The World*, which had a disco beat!

Rare, Live And Unreleased was a further CD release in 1999. This was originally released as *The Early Years* by Newspeak in 1992. It now has altered artwork but otherwise it's the same CD and its appeal will mainly be to fans of the band. It includes a good debut of *Grip*, some good **Hugh Cornwell** guitar on *Bitching* and big handclaps on *Go Buddy Go*. Some of the other cuts like *Wasted* and *My Young Dreams* are very MOR, but the slow version of *Princess Of The Streets* will appeal to some.

Something Better Change was the title cut of EMI's 2000 punk compilation.

As we leave the time frame of this book in 1986 **The Stranglers**, having long survived the punk era, had outlasted almost all of their contemporaries. Eleven Top 20 albums and twenty-five Top 50 singles to date, they were still going strong! Even when vocalist **Hugh Cornwell** finally departed in the summer of 1990 to develop a solo career they still carried on with a new vocalist Paul Roberts and ex-**Vibrator** John Ellis on guitar.

Straight Up

Personnel:		
	HIRONS	A
	HOWLETT	A
	MASON	A
	PELLING	A

45:	One Out All Out/	
	(this side by **Justin Case**)	(Rok ROK XX/XIX) 1980

This was the last release on Rok. The above four-piece line-up is not certain but based on songwriting credits. *One Out All Out* is a strong composition with a choppy guitar intro and Union put-down lyrics. You'll also find it as a bonus cut on the CD reissue of *Odd Bods Mods And Sods* (Captain Mod MODSKA CD 2) 1996 and on *100% British Mod* (Captain Mod MODSKA DCD 8) 1998.

Straps

Personnel:	JOHN GRANT		A
	DAVE REEVES		A
	JIM WALKER		A
	JOHN WERNER		A
	SIMON WERNER		A

ALBUM:	1(A)	THE STRAPS ALBUM	(Cyclops CYC 2) 1983

45:	Just Can't Take It Anymore/	
	New Age (PS)	(Donut DONUT 1) 1980
	Brixton/No Liquor (PS)	(Donut DONUT 3) 1982

The Straps like **Theatre Of Hate** grew out of the ashes of **The Pack**. They were also big mates of **The Damned**. Their debut 45 *Just Can't Take It Anymore* is punkabilly in style. The second 45 *Brixton* and their album is delivered in a more standard punk format.

The Streets

Personnel incl:	RICKY WALTIER	vcls	AB
	WILL JAMES	drms	B
	FRANKY JODI	bs	B
	BARRY SMITH	gtr	B

Fronted by vocalist Ricky Waltier **The Streets** were regulars on the punk circuit during 1977 and early 1978, but then split. Later in the year Ricky Waltier was gigging again with a new line-up ('B').

Their sole vinyl epitaph seems to have been *Sniper*, a lyrically repetitive but instrumentally promising contribution to *Farewell To The Roxy* (Lightning LIP 2) 1978 album, which was later reissued on CD (Captain Oi! AHOY CD 86) 1998.

Pete Stride and John Plain

Personnel:	JOHN PLAIN	gtr	A
	PETE STRIDE	gtr	A

ALBUM:	1(A)	NEW GUITARS IN TOWN	(Beggars Banquet BEGA 17) 1980

45:	Laugh At Me/	
	Jimmy Brown (PS)	(Beggars Banquet BEG 41) 1980

This project was a collaboration between **Pete Stride** (of **The Lurkers**) and 'Honest' John Plain (of **The Boys**). On this promising album, made after **The Lurkers** had temporarily split up in late 1979, they are assisted by Tony Bateman (bs) and Jack Black (drms) (also of **The Boys**).

THE STUKAS - Klean Living Kids.

Strike

This Oi! band first appeared on *Strength Thru' Oi!* (Decca) in 1981 with two songs *Gang Warfare* and *Skinhead*, which glorified skinhead culture. They contributed *Victim* to *Back On The Streets* (EP) (Secret SHH 138) 1983. The track, which is about street fighting, can also be heard on *Secret Records Punk Singles Collection, Vol. 1* (Anagram CDPUNK 13) 1993.

Strike

Personnel:	STEVEN DRAKE	drms	A
	PAUL KENNY	lead gtr	A
	NOEL RAFFERTY	gtr	A
	LORAY SPORT	bs	A
	LESLEY WHITTEN	vcls	A

A Northern Irish band from Belfast. They contributed *Radio Songs* and *Running Past* to the compilation *Belfast* (Shock Rock SLR 007) in 1980. *Radio Songs* is quite power-popish and *Running Past* exhibits quite an **Undertones** influence.

The Stripes

Personnel:	PAUL GUIDOTTI	drms	A
	VINCE SMITH	vcls, bs	A
	MICHAEL TODD	gtr, vcls	A

45:	One Step Ahead/	(Ellie Jay PINKO 1) 1982

The Stripes formed in Romford, Essex in 1980. They became a popular live attraction supporting bands like **The Chords**. They recorded a lot of demos but only the above 45 *One Step Ahead*, a mod-pop offering which is now one of the mod revivals rarest singles. It can also be heard on *100% British Mod* (Captain Mod MODSKA DCD 8) 1998.

Studio Sweethearts

Personnel:	HOWARD BATES	bs	A
	BILLY DUFFY	gtr	A
	PHIL ROLAND		A
	MIKE ROSSI	gtr	A

45:	I Believe/It Isn't Me	(DJM DJS 10915) 1979

This was basically **Slaughter and The Dogs**, who recorded this 45 for DJM using a new name **Studio Sweethearts** in their quest for more success. It didn't happen and they quickly reverted back to their original monicker. Later still they were known as simply Slaughter.

Billy Duffy had previously been in **The Nosebleeds**. He went on to greater fame with **The Cult**. Phil Roland had previously been in **Eater** and Mike Rossi was later in The Duellists.

The Stukas

Personnel:	KEVIN ALLEN	bs	A
	PAUL BROWN	vcls	A
	RAGGY LEWIS	gtr	A
	JOHN MACKIE	drms	A
	MICK SMITHERS	gtr	A

45s:	Klean Living Kids/Oh Little Girl (PS)	(Chiswick NS 21) 1977
	I'll Send You A Postcard/Dead Lazy/	
	Sport Sport	(Sonet SON 2134) 1978
	Washing Machine Boogie/Motorbike	(Sonet SON 2159) 1978

The Stukas were torn between two styles - new wave and power-pop. Great instrumentally, they were hampered by ineffectual vocals. *Klean Living Kids* can also be heard on the sampler *Long Shots Dead Certs And Odds On Favourites* (Chiswick CH 5) in 1978.

The Stukas, in addition to these three 45s, also recorded one session for John Peel on 24th January 1978. This comprised *Dead Lazy*, *Big Boy*, *Motorbike* and *Sport*. Lewis was later in **The Autographs**, who cut one 45 for RAK later in 1978.

Poly Styrene

Personnel:	POLY STYRENE (MARION ELLIOT)	vcls	A
with	RICHARD BAILEY	drms	A
	TED BUNTING	horns	A
	KUMA KARADA	bs	A
	DARYLL LEE QUE	perc	A
	KEVIN McALEA	keyb'ds	A
	G.T. MOORE	gtr	A
	RICHARD MOORE	gtr	A

ALBUM: 1 TRANSLUCENCE (Liberty/United Artists UAG 30320) 1980

NB: (1) also issued on CD (Receiver TTCD 128) 1990.

EP: 1 GODS AND GODESSES (Trick Of The Witch/ Paramatma/Sacred Temple/ Big Boys, Big Toys)   (Awesome AORT 7) 1986

NB: (1) was also released in 12" format.

45: Talk In Toytown/ Sub-Tropical (PS)   (Liberty/United Artists BP 370) 1980

After disbanding **X-Ray Spex**, **Poly Styrene** recorded a solo album *Translucence* in 1980 in a marketedly different easy listening style. Savaged at the time by the critics, it was in keeping with her emerging interest in mysticism. She joined the Spiritual Life and Krishna Consciousness Movement and continued to record at the temple's own recording studio and perform periodically at a very limited number of venues. She returned to the commercial world with an Eastern-influenced popish EP in 1986 *Gods And Godesses*, which attracted little interest.

SUB CULTURE - Loud And Clear EP.

Sub Culture

Personnel:	BEETER	vcls	A
	DEAN TYRELL	gtr	A
	MATT	drms	A
	PHIL	bs	A

EP: 1(A) LOUD AND CLEAR (Loud And Clear/Rogue Trooper/ University City)   (Essential ESS 002) 1983

A Cambridge-based Oi! quartet. Aside from this EP they also contributed *Stick Together* to the *Oi! Oi! That's Yer Lot!* (Secret SEC 5) 1983 compilation.

The three cuts from *The Loud And Clear* EP also got a further airing on *Oi! The Rarities, Vol. 1* (Captain Oi! AHOY LP 43) 1996. It's also on the CD version (AHOY CD 43) 1996. *Loud And Clear* has some distinctive guitar parts, but pretty routine vocals of this ilk. *Rogue Trooper* is a run-of-the-mill effort, but *Universal City* is more powerful with some biting lyrics. Overall, though, very much a second division Oi! band.

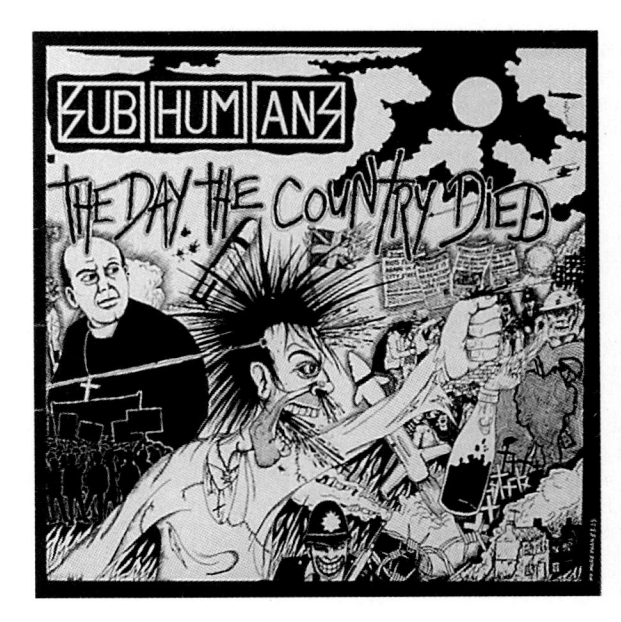

SUBHUMANS - The Day The Country Died.

Subhumans

Personnel:	BRUCE	gtr	A
(up to	DICK (RICHARD LUCAS)	vcls	A
1986)	GRANT	bs	A
	TROTSKY	drms	A

ALBUMS: 1(A) THE DAY THE COUNTRY DIED (Spiderleg SOL 9) 1982
(up to   2(A) TIME FLIES.... BUT AEROPLANES CRASH
1986)   (Bluurg FISH 6) 1983
        3(A) FROM THE CRADLE TO THE GRAVE
                     (Bluurg FISH 8) 1984
        4(A) WORLD'S APART (Bluurg FISH 12) 1985
        5(A) EP-LP   (Bluurg FISH 14) 1986

NB: (1) also issued on CD (Bluurg XLP 1CD) 1998. (2) also issued on CD (Bluurg FISH 25CD) 1998. (3) also issued on CD (Bluurg FISH 8CD) 1998. (4) also issued on CD (Bluurg FISH 12CD). (5) also issued on CD (Bluurg FISH 14CD) 1998.

EPs: 1(A) DEMOLITION WAR ( )   (Spider Leg SOB 1) 1981
      2(A) PARASITES (Parasites/Drugs Of Youth/ Animal Society/ Who's Gonna Fight) (PS)   (Spider Leg SPIDL 3) 1982
      3(A) REASONS FOR EXISTENCE (Big City/ Reasons For Existence/ Cancer Peroxide) (PS) (Spider Leg SPIDL 5) 1983
      4(A) RELIGIOUS WARS (Religious Wars/Love Is.../ Work Experience/ It's Gonna Get Worse) (PS) (Spider Leg SPIDL 7) 1983
      5(A) EVOLUTION (Evolution/So Much Money/ Germ/Not Me) (PS)   (Bluurg FISH 2) 1983
      6(A) WHEN THE BOMB DROPS (When The Bomb Drops/Rats/Joe Public/ Labels) (12", PS)   (Bluurg FISH 10) 1984

Subhumans were one of the best of the **Crass**-influenced anarcho-punk bands of the eighties. Their lyrics dealt with the familair issues for bands of this genre (anti-government, anti-police, human rights, vegetarianism) but they did so with humour. Most of the music on their debut album was thrash-based with its origins in both punk and hard rock. *Til The Pigs Come Round* typified the material on this album:-

"Oh what a great experience
My house is full of deviants
My dad is going mad downstairs
My brother has just dyed his hair

Chorus: We got punks and drunks
And thrills and pills

And lots of things
To make your head go round
It's fun fun fun fun fun fun
Til the pigs come round"
(from *Til The Pigs Come Round*)

From The Cradle To The Grave is a sort of punk concept album - the title track accounts for the whole of the second side. Side one has track titles like *Reality Is Waiting For A Bus*, *Wake Up Screaming* and *Adversity*.

"Just stay dead the advert said
The whole damn country died of boredom"
(from *Adversity*).

For a final album *29: 29 Split Vision* in 1987 Grant was replaced on bass by a guy called Phil. Some band members went on to form Citizens Fish, who were popular on the free festival circuit with their blend of punk and ska. Bluurg was Dick Lucas' own label and he continued to operate it well after **Subhumans**' demise.

Subs

45: Gimme Your Heart/Party Clothes (PS) (Stiff OFF 1) 1978

This short-lived four-piece punk project involved **Larry Wallis** who was earlier with underground bands like The Deviants and The Pink Fairies. *Gimme Your Heart* is a beaty fast-paced song with upfront vocals, but it lacks that extra something to distinguish it from the pack.

SUBS - Gimme Your Heart.

Substitute

45: The One/Look Sharp (some PS) (Ignition IR 2) 1979

This band's 45 came inside a striking 'union jack' sleeve. They are rumoured to have featured one or more members of **The Vibrators**.

Suburban Studs

Personnel: PAUL MORTON   bs   A
            KEITH OWEN   gtr   A
            STEVE POOL   drms   A
            EDDIE ZIPPS   vcls, gtr A

ALBUM: 1(A) SLAM   (Pogo POW 001) 1978

NB: (1) also issued on CD with additional tracks, *Slam (The Complete Suburban Studs Punk Collection)* (Anagram CD PUNK 21) 1993.

45s: * No Faith/Questions (PS)   (Pogo POG 001/LYN 44845) 1977
        I Hate School/Young Power (PS) (Pogo POG 002) 1978

NB: * This was originally issued with a sax break but this version was withdrawn.

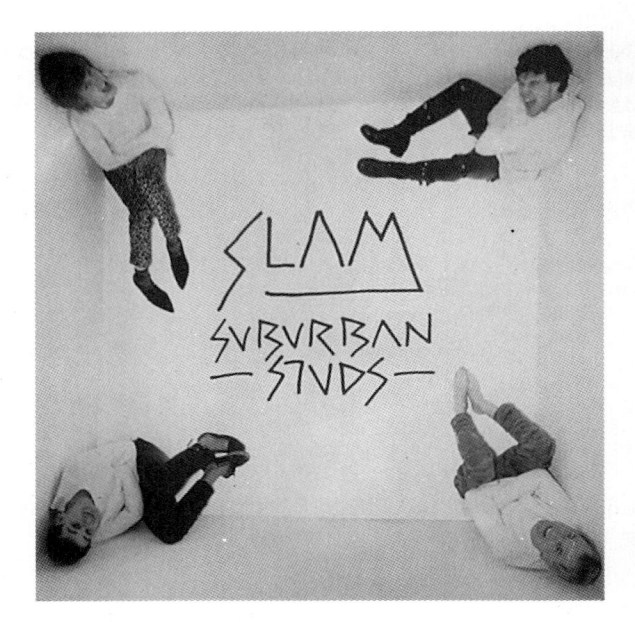

SUBURBAN STUDS - Slam.

This punk quartet formed in Birmingham in 1977. They were one of the earlier punk bands to gain a recording contract. The Pogo label was actually marketed by WEA, but between them they made a pretty poor job of marketing this band. They also played at London's seminal punk venue The Hope And Anchor and are captured there playing on the *Hope And Anchor Front Row Festival* (Warner Bros K 66077) 1978. They contribute their finest moment, the sparky *I Hate School*, to this double album. This was quite an improvement on their debut 45 *Faith* which had made little impression. This was originally issued with a sax break and then issued again without one.

They also recorded a John Peel session on 21st December 1977. This comprised *Suburban Studs*, *I Hate School*, *Necro* and *No Faith*.

Their album *Slam* included their singles, popular live numbers like *Bondage* and *Throbbing Lust* and also featured an energetic cover of The Who's *My Generation*. Much of their material, though, was routine punk and they faded into obscurity and disbanded before the decade was through. If you do want to check them out the Anagram CD compilation is your best bet and contains bonus tracks.

You can also hear *I Hate School* on *Punk And Disorderly, Vol. 2 (Further Charges)* (Anagram CDPUNK 22) 1993, *Punk Compilation* (Emporio EMPRCD 550) 1994 and on the 5-CD box set *1-2-3-4 - A History Of Punk And New Wave 1976 - 1979* (MCA/Universal 60066) 1999.

One final postscript in their story was a reformation in 1996 to appear in the 'Holidays In The Sun' Blackpool Punk Festival.

Subway Sect

Personnel: VIC GODARD   vcls   ABCDE
            PAUL MYERS   bs   ABC
            PAUL PACKHAM   drms   A
            ROBERT SIMMONS gtr   ABC
            MARK LAFF   drms   B
            ROB WARD   drms   CD
            STEVE ATKINSON keyb'ds D
            JOHNNY BRITTON gtr   DE
            COLIN SCOTT   bs   D
            TERRY CHIMES   drms   E
            CHIMES   bs   E

ALBUMS: 1(E) WHAT'S THE MATTER BOY? (MCA MCF 3070) 1980
        2(-) SONGS FOR SALE   (London SH 8549) 1982
        3(-) A RETROSPECTIVE (1977-81)
                                      (Rough Trade ROUGH 56) 1985
        4(-) HOLIDAY HYMN   (MCA/E1 01) 1985
        5(-) T.R.O.U.B.L.E.   (Rough Trade ROUGH 86) 1986

NB: (1) reissued (MCA MCL 1687) 1982 and on CD (Demon MAVCD 645) 1996 and again (Universal 844 973 2) 2000 with bonus cuts. (2) and (3) credited to Vic Godard and **Subway Sect**. (4) and (5) credited to Vic Godard. There is also a

Subway Sect (CD) *We Oppose All Rock 'n' Roll* (Overground OVER 53CD) 1996 and Vic Godard's *In Trouble Again* (Tugboat TUG 001CD) 1998. More recent is *20 Odd Years - The Story Of Vic Godard & The Subway Sect* (Motion PACECD 010) 1999.

45s:	Nobody's Scared/Don't Split It (PS)	(Braik BRS 01)	1978
*	Ambition/A Different Story (PS)	(Rough Trade RT 007)	1979
x	Split Up That Money/Out Of Touch	(Oddball/MCA 585)	1980
x	Stop That Girl (Instrumentally Scared)/ Vertical Integration (PS)	(Rough Trade RT 68)	1981
x	Stamp Of A Vamp/ Hey Now (I'm In Love)	(Club Left CLUB 1)	1981
x	Hey Now (I'm In Love)/ Just In Time (PS)	(London LON 005)	1982
x	Hey Now (I'm In Love)/Just In Time/ Mr. Bennett (10")	(London LONX 005)	1982
x	Hey Now (I'm In Love)/Just In Time/ Mr. Bennett (12")	(London LONT 005)	1982
+	Holiday Hymn/Nice On The Ice (PS)	(El Benelux EL 4)	1985
+	Holiday Hymn/Nice On The Ice/Stop The Girl/Ice On The Volcano/T.R.O.U.B.L.E. (12" PS)	(El Benelux EL 4T)	1985
Reissue:	# Ambition/Different Story/Chain Smoking/ Ambition (7")	(Overground OVER 45)	1996

NB: * This was initially issued in a yellow picture sleeve, then later in an orange one. x Credited to Vic Godard and **Subway Sect**. + credited to Vic Godard. # This was also issued as a CD single.

Subway Sect formed in London in July 1976. Vic Godard had been born and grown up in Barnes in South-west London. He'd befriended the other members in the original line-up - Simmons, Packham and Myers - at Sheen Secondary School in South-west London. They played some early rehearsals in the Hammersmith subway which they claimed inspired their name. Line-up 'A' made its proper live debut as part of the 100 Club Punk Festival on 20th September 1976.

They underwent a few line-up changes in their early months. First to leave was Paul Packham after just three months. Mark Laff came in as a replacement and this revised line-up toured supporting **The Clash** on their 'White Riot' tour. Soon after Laff too departed to join the recently formed **Generation X**. He was replaced on drums by Rob Ward. This new line-up ('C') undertook their own U.K. tour. In October 1977, they recorded the first of two John Peel sessions. Simmon's discordant guitar work was very much to the fore on tracks like *Chain Smoking* and *Parallel Lines*. Upon their return they released their debut 45, *Nobody's Scared* on Bernie Rhodes' Braik label (he was **The Clash**'s manager). To promote it, the band played a number of gigs with a French band called The Lous.

When *Nobody's Scared* made little impact Vic Godard ousted Myers and Simmons and put together a new line-up ('D'). In December 1978, this new line-up taped a second John Peel session. This included the punkish *Watching The Devil* and the soul-inspired *Stool Pigeon*. There was also a now legendary unreleased 1978 Subway Sect album. They supported **The Buzzcocks** on a national tour and signed to Rough Trade. A new 45, *Ambition* was released. Initial copies came in a yellow picture sleeve, an orange version was used for later ones. Despite improved marketing and promotion the 45 fared little better than their first effort. A German documentary "Punk In London 1977" featured **The Subway Sect** performing *Ambition* at rehearsals. Soon after Bernie Rhodes hired a London funk band as backing musicians **The Subway Sect** disintegrated due to lack of interest. Rhodes put together a new line-up, retaining Britton and adding ex-**Clash** drummer Terry Chimes and his brother, who played bass. Now operating under the moniker Vic Godard and **The Subway Sect**, this new line-up finally recorded the band's first album *What's The Matter Boy?*, which was released in April 1980. To help promote it, they appeared at the Music Machine supporting **Siouxsie and The Banshees**.

The album had its moments, notably a lovely ballad *Make Me Sad*, *Birth And Death* and a soul-pop number *Split Up The Money*, which was culled for 45 release. Later, in January 1981, Rough Trade issued the 45 *Stop That Girl*, on which the band was backed by The Black Arabs.

By now, though, Rhodes had decided to launch Godard as a solo artist. He issued Godard's jazzy *Stamp Of A Vamp* 45 on his own Club Left label and then secured a deal for him with Island. The fruit of this was was an album of mostly original '40s style crooner music paying homage to Godard's idol Cole Porter. It includes a cover of Porter's *Love For Sale*. This could hardly have been more different from the early punk rantings of **The Subway Sect**. But the album sounds sincere - some fine pop melodies are delivered in Godard's suave vocal style. One cut *Hey Now (I'm In Love)* was selected for 45 release, but like all the previous 45s Godard had been connected with it made little impact. The four jazz musicians Rhodes had drafted in for the *Love For Sale* project left to form Jo Boxers, after a tour supporting **Altered Images**.

In 1982, Godard began work on *T.R.O.U.B.L.E.* a swing-jazz album with Simon Booth (who was later in Working Week) for the new Blanco y Negro label recently formed by Geoff Travis and Mike Always. However the project was unfortunately shelved when its budget was largely swallowed up paying musicians and studio fees.

In 1985, Rough Trade released the compilation *A Retrospective (1977 - 81)*. This comprises **The Subway Sect**'s two sessions for John Peel and both sides of the *Nobody's Scared* 45. The same year, an uptempo number from the *T.R.O.U.B.L.E.* project *Holiday Hymn* was issued on a 45 in the Benelux countries. Then, in 1986, Rough Trade decided to release the *T.R.O.U.B.L.E.* album, which had spent three years in the can. It included new versions of earlier songs like *Out Of Touch* and *Chain Smoking* as well as poppier soul-jazz numbers like *Ice On A Volcano* and *Tidal Wave*. However, disillusioned with the fact the tapes weren't mixed, Godard had had enough. He retired from the music business to fulfil one of his ambitions - to work as a postman!

He did however, return to the music business in 1992. Godard and **The Subway Sect** have also cropped up on a number of compilations. The NME cassette *C-81* (Rough Tapes COPY 1) 1981 featured *Parallel Lines*; *Jive Wire* (NME 002) 1982 and *A Constant Source Of Interruption* (Rough Trade RCD 6004) 1990 both gave a further airing to *Stop That Girl*, *Pogo-A-Go-Go* (NME 021) 1985 included *Ambition*, *Viva Eight* (2-CD) contained a live version of *Talent To Follow* and **The Slits**' album *Bootleg Retrospective* (Rough Trade YY 3) 1980 included a version of *Sister Ray* with **The Subway Sect**. In 1999, *Ambition* was included on the 5-CD box set *1-2-3-4 - A History Of Punk And New Wave 1976 - 1979* (MCA/Universal MCD 60066) and again on *25 Years Of Rough Trade Shops* (4-CD box set) (Mute CDSTUMM 191) in 2001.

The Overground label reissued *Ambition* in 1996 on 7" and CD single with previously unreleased versions of *Chain Smoking* and *Ambition* included. The same year Demon reissued *What's The Matter Boy?* on CD.

We Oppose All Rock 'n' Roll, issued on Overground in 1996, is a remastered issue of their *Retrospective* album. It came with a bonus CD containing three early rarities (*Exit No Return*, *Parallel Lines* (alt version) and *Staying Out Of View*).

In 1998, Vic Godard's *In T.R.O.U.B.L.E Again* was re-vocalised, remixed and reissued on CD as it was never completed to his satisfaction back in 1982. Aside from a cover of Noel Coward's *20th Century Blues* and re-workings of *Holiday Hymn* and *Chainsmoking*, it comprised originals.

In 2000, Universal reissued their first album on CD remastered, with lively sleevenotes and the addition of the *Stop That Girl* 45 and their 1978 Peel session.

The definitive guide to Vic Godard's punk adventures and his swing days is the double CD *20 Odd Years - The Story Of Vic Godard and The Subway Sect*. It includes a number of songs from their unreleased 1978 album.

SUBWAY SECT - Ambition.

Nikki Sudden

Personnel:
HUGO BURNHAM (of GANG OF FOUR)		drms	A
JOHNNY RIVERS		keyb'ds	A
PHONES SPORTSMAN		bs	ABC
STEVE TAYTON		sax	A
NIKKI SUDDEN		vcls	ABCD
RICHARD EARL		gtr	B
EMPIRE (of TELEVISION PERSONALITIES)		drms	B
PAUL PARYRUS		bs	B
MARK LEMON		bs, vcls	D
TYLA		gtr	D
ANDY WICKETT		organ	D

CASS:	1(A)	BEAU GESTE	(Rather RATHER 10)	1983
ALBUMS:	1(B)	WAITING ON EGYPT	(Abstract ABT 003)	1982
(up to	2(B)	THE BIBLE BELT	(Ficknife SHARP 110)	1983
1986)	3(C)	JACOBITES	(Glass)	1984
	4(D)	ROBESPIERRE'S VELVET BASEMENT	(Glass)	1985
	5(-)	TEXAS	(Creation CRELP 012)	1986

NB: (3) and (4) credited to **Nikki Sudden** and Dave Kusworth. (3) also issued on CD (Regency Sound JANIDA 001) 1993. (4) also issued as a double CD (Regency Sound JANIDA 002) 1993.

EP:	1(C)	THE SHAME OF ANGELS	(Pawnhearts 174 701)	1984

NB: (1) credited to **Nikki Sudden** and Dave Kusworth.

45s:	Back To The Start/ Running On My Train (PS)	(Rather GEAR 11)	1981
	Channel Steamer/ Chelsea Embankment (PS)	(Abstract ABS 009)	1982

These were solo ventures of **Nikki Sudden**, who had first emerged as guitarist and vocalist with **Swell Maps**. He went on to enjoy several further, mostly short-lived projects, in the eighties and nineties.

Aside from the electric *Big Store*, *Jacobites* is a mixture of **Sudden** and Kusworth acoustic ballads delivered with quivering voices typified by the beauty of tracks like *Kings And Queens*.

Robespierre's Velvet Basement features bass/drums rhythm accompaniment and harmonica. Originally featuring twenty-four tracks they are more upbeat with a fuller sound than on the debut. The reissue on Regency Sound is on a double CD with ten bonus tracks:- *When The Rain Comes*, *Every Girl*, *Into My Arms*, *If I'm Crying*, *Country Girl*, *Sloth*, *Someone Who Cares*, *Before I Die*, *Pin Your Heart To Me* and *Road Of Broken Dreams*.

Sunset Boys

45:	Wreck My Bed/Tutti Frutti/Copy Cat (Blues)/ Wreck My Bed (Hippy Version) (PS)	(Gimp GIM 1234)	1979

A country punk duo from Croydon who were linked to **Maxim's Trash**.

THE SURPRISES - Jeremy Thorpe Is Innocent.

The Surprises

Personnel:
JANICE CONNOLLY		vcls	A
JOHN NESTER		bs, vcls	A
ROB PETERS		drms, perc, vcls	A
CONRAD SCHWARZ		lead vcls	A
JOHN WORMALD		gtr, vcls	A

45:	Jeremy Thorpe Is Innocent (We Know Who Did It)/ Flying Attack/Little Sir Echo (PS)	(Dead Dog DEAD 01) 1979

Records that take the piss out of politicians - great fun. Take a look at these lyrics, which are sung in a loose sort of punk format with a catchy and at times discordant introduction:-

"Jeremy Thorpe is innocent
Set up by some cunning punks
Caught in the house with his trousers down
Politics in a low-me-down
Oh Jeremy, Oh Jeremy, Oh Jeremy, Je-re-my
(We Know Who Did It You Know)

Harold Wilson is innocent
Mary knows that he ain't bent
Esso was a state and he was king
But he didn't know a sodding thing
Oh Harold, Oh Harold, Oh Harold, Harold....
(We know who did it you know)

The Queen did it, the Queen did it
She admitted to me that she did it
The Queen did it, the Queen did it
The Queen did it, the Queen did it
She admitted to me that she did it
And she is still Queen

Tricky Dicky is innocent
Didn't pay the CIA a cent
Robert Redford set it up
To make a film and earn a buck
Oh Tricky Dicky, Tricky Dicky
Oh Tricky Dicky, Tricky Dicky

The Queen did it, the Queen did it
She admitted to me that she did it
The Queen did it, the Queen did it
The Queen did it, the Queen did it
She admitted to me that she did it
And she is still Queen.
(from *Jeremy Thorpe Is Innocent*).

Don't recall hearing this one on the airwaves. The record was recorded in Birmingham. *Flying Attack* deals with an alien attack in a humourous way. The third cut, *Little Sir Echo* is a throwaway.

The Suspects

Personnel:
GERRY ADAMS		bs	A
DAVE ASGROVE		gtr, vcls	A
SARAH BARRY		keyb'ds	A
TONY HARRISON		drms	A
FRED TWIGG		lead gtr	A

CASS:	1(A)	LIVING IN STRAIGHT LINES	1983

The Suspects were **Dave Asgrove**'s band and definitely one of the best acts on the anarcho-punk circuit. This tape is certainly above-average for music of this genre. Some of the cuts also featured on compilations, such as *Bullshit Detector Two* on Crass Records. There's good guitar work and competent playing on this tape which was available from an address in Norwich.

The Suspects

Personnel:
PETE DAVIES		drms	A
BARRY FARMER		bs	A

	JOHNNY	vcls	A
	ANDY RIFF	gtr	A

The Suspects emerged out of the ashes of The Rotting Clits. They often supported **The UK Subs** and Pete Davies later joined them. **The Suspects** contributed *Nothing To Declare* to *Live At The Vortex, Vol. 1* (NEMS NEL 6013) 1978, which was later issued on CD (Anagram CDPUNK 68) 1995.

The Sussed

Personnel:	BILL FRANCIS	drms	A
	TOM FRANCIS	gtr	A
	BILL JOHNSTONE	bs	A
	OSCAR	vcls	A
	TONY PAINTING	gtr	A

45s:	I Like You/Tango/The Perv (PS)	(Shoestring LACE 002) 1979
*	I've Got Me A Parka/	
	Myself, Myself And I Repeated (PS)	(Graduate GRAD 7) 1980

NB: * Issued with paper labels, but reissued in 1986 with silver ones.

Essentially a pub-rock combo from Edgbaston in the Midlands but *I've Got Me A Parka*, as you can imagine, was popular with the mod revivalists. It's quite humourous, as one might expect. You'll also find it on CD on *100% British Mod* (Captain Mod MODSKA DCD 8) 1998 and on vinyl on *This Is Mod* (dbl) (Get Back GET 39) 1999.

Swell Maps

Personnel:	DAVE BARRINGTON		
	(PHONES SPORTSMAN)	vcls	A
	EPIC SOUNDTRACKS	drms, vcls	AB
	NIKKI SUDDEN		
	(NIKKI MATTRESS)	vcls, gtr, piano	AB
	BIGGLES BOOK	gtr	
	RICHARD EARL	vcls	B
	JOWE HEAD	bs, vcls	B
	JOHN 'GOLDEN'		
	COCKTRILL	vcls	

ALBUMS:	1(B)	A TRIP TO MARINEVILLE	
		(Rough Trade ROUGH 2/Rather TROY 1) 1979
	2(B)	SWELL MAPS IN 'JANE FROM OCCUPIED EUROPE'
		(Rough Trade ROUGH 15) 1980
	3(-)	WHATEVER HAPPENS NEXT... (dbl)
		(Rough Trade ROUGH 21) 1981
	4(-)	SWELL MAPS IN 'COLLISION TIME'
		(Rough Trade ROUGH 41) 1982
	5(-)	TRAIN OUT OF IT	(Antar ANTAR 4) 1987

NB: (1) originally issued with an inner sleeve and die-cut EP, *Loin Of The Surf, Doctor At Cake, Steven Does* and *Bronze And Baby Shoes* (GEAR FIVE). Reissued (Mute MAPS 1) 1990 and on CD (Mute CD MAPS 1) 1990, with eight extra tracks. (2) reissued (Mute MAPS 2) 1990 and on CD (Mute CD MAPS 2) 1990, with eight extra tracks. (5) reissued on CD (Mute CD MAPS 3) 1991, with eight extra tracks. (3) reissued on CD (Mute CD MAPS 4) 1991. There's also a U.S.-only double album *Collision Time Revisited* (Mute 7 71421-1) 1989, which was also available on CD (Mute 7 71421-2) 1989.

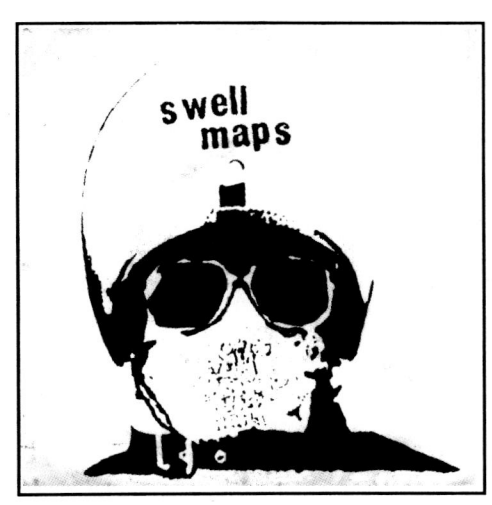

45s:	Read About Seymour/Ripped And Torn/	
	Black Velvet (PS)	(Rather GEAR ONE) 1978
	Dresden Style/Mystery Track/Ammunition Train/	
	Full Moon (Dub) (PS)	
		(Rough Trade RT 012/Rather GEAR 3) 1979
*	Real Shocker/English Verse/	
	Monologues (PS)	(Rough Trade RT 021/Rather GEAR 6) 1979
	Let's Build A Car/Big Maz In The Country/	
	... Then Poland (PS)	
		(Rough Trade RT 036/Rather GEAR 7) 1980
Reissue:	+Read About Seymour/Ripped And Torn/
	Black Velvet (PS)	
		(Rough Trade RT 010/Rather GEAR ONE MK 2) 1979
x	Dresden Style/Ammunition Train/
	Full Moon (Dub) (PS)
		(Rough Trade RT 012/Rather GEAR 3) 1980

NB: * Issued in picture sleeve with two different colours. + Reissue came with a different rear sleeve. x Reissue came with a different rear sleeve and a new vocal on *Dresden Style*.

An early inspiration on **Swell Maps** was Marc Bolan! Yes, back in 1972 **Epic Soundtracks**, **Nikki Sudden** and Dave Barrington got together to form a band in Solihull in the Midlands after watching Marc Bolan in action. In the next few years they underwent various line-up changes and used a number of different names. Eventually the line-up stabilised to Epic, Head, Earl and **Sudden**. The later double compilation *Whatever Happens Next...* includes songs from some of the tapes they recorded in these early days. Their name **Swell Maps** is taken from the charts surfers used to measure wave intensity.

Swell Maps recorded their *Read About Seymour* 45 on 14th September 1977 at Spaceward Studios in Cambridge, but it was not released until February 1978. In the meantime, they'd made their live debut on Boxing Day 1977 at Birmingham's Barbarellas. Only 2,000 copies of their 45 were pressed initially on their own Rather Records.

The 'A' side, penned by **Sudden**, started with an unorthodox two-chord riff which gave way to a savage guitar/drums assault, which suddenly halted and the whole experience lasted just 1'27". It attracted airplay from John Peel and became a 'Sounds' 'Single of the Week'. On the flip side *Ripped & Torn* has an usual introduction which gives way to a fast-paced rocker. The final track *Black Velvet* is another riffy fast-paced rocker.

In October 1978, they recorded their first of three sessions for John Peel. Aside from *Read About Seymour*, this included *Harmony In Your Bathroom, Full Moon In My Pocket, Blam* and *International Rescue*. The latter track was considered as a possible follow-up release, but they simply couldn't afford another DIY effort and it remained in the can until its inclusion as a bonus track on a CD reissue of their first album.

At the end of December 1978 they returned to the studio to record both sides of a follow-up 45 and most of their debut album. Another **Nikki Sudden** composition *Dresden Style* was released in February 1979 to critical acclaim. 14,000 copies were pressed and the 'B' side also contained a mystery track. When the 45 was reissued in mid-1980 the mystery track was deleted and the vocals redone. The rear sleeve also mentions that *Dresden Style* has been remixed.

Their debut album *A Trip To Marineville* was released in July 1979. It was housed in an eye-catching outer sleeve and the inner bag contained lyrics, full track details and a four-track EP. The album sold well on the indie market. Musically it was something of a hotch potch. The best track was *Midget Submarine*, which became one of their most popular songs. Overall, most of the **Nikki Sudden** compositions are pretty conventional in structure, but characterised by lots of distorted guitar and **Sudden**'s individualistic vocals. These dominate Side one, but there are also some brief piano instrumentals courtesy of **Epic Soundtracks**. Side two is dominated by tracks like *Gunboats* and *Adventuring Into Basketry*.

Shortly before the album was released, they recorded a second Peel session in May 1979. For this they were assisted by Lora Logic on saxophone and Josi Munns and Andy Beans on backing vocals. The whole session was later included in its entirety on *Whatever Happens Next*.

SWELL MAPS - Read About Seymour.

Among the content was *Bandits One Five*, which they never issued in completed studio form.

A third 45 *Real Shocks* was released in September 1979. This was both more melodic and more muted than their earlier 45s. The colours on the cover to the original issue were in wash tones. There was a later pressing which had them in solid tone.

Their fourth single, *Let's Build A Car*, released in January 1980 is usually considered a classic. It featured the band's characteristic ball-crunching, distorted guitars, punchy rhythm and wacky piano. It made the higher echelons of the indie charts. Collectors will be interested in the Japanese release of this 45 which came with a fold-out sleeve and is now quite collectable.

In March 1980, a final Peel session was recorded. It was broadcast on 1st April and comprised six tracks:- *Big Empty Field, Bleep And Booster Came Round For Tea, Secret Island, (Let's) Buy A Bridge, The Helicopter Spies* and *A Raincoat's Room*. Four of these previewed material from their next album *Jane From Occupied Europe*, which followed in July 1980. The two exceptions being *Bleep And Booster Came Round For Tea* and *A Raincoat's Room*. Overall, this album was stronger than their debut. **Sudden**'s more conventional rock songs were again successful and the instrumentals veered more towards free-form jazz but with discipline. One of the strongest tracks was the instrumental *Collision With A Frogman Vs The Mangrove Delta Plan*. This would prove to be their final studio effort as internal tensions had emerged during an earlier Italian tour in spring 1980. When they returned to the U.K. from this they announced their split.

In May 1981, Rough Trade issued the double compilation album *Whatever Happens Next*. This contained material from their collection of home recordings extending as far back as 1974. This is one for die-hard fans of the band, who may, on repeated listening, find it rewarding.

In May 1982, Rough Trade put out a compilation *Collision Time*. This featured most of their singles and some album tracks.

In April 1987, *Train Out Of It* was released on Antar. This comprised a collection of singles and previously unissued or obscure material. Then, in 1989, **Swell Maps** had a double retrospective album *Collision Time Revisited* issued on Mute in the U.S.A.. The following year Mute reissued their first two albums. The CD versions featured extra cuts.

The **Swell Maps** also collaborated in a number of interesting projects. In late 1978, they appeared as the AFV's on a five track **Steve Treatment** EP (see his entry for further details). They also appeared backing a couple of friends on **Cult Figures**' *Zip Nolan* 45, despite disclaimers to the contrary. **Nikki Sudden** also sang vocals (as Nikki Mapp) on two 45s by **Metrophase** (see entry for details). This project could have included other **Swell Maps** members too. See also **Phones Sportsman Band**, **Nikki Sudden** and **Epic Soundtracks** for details of other solo entries.

Swell Maps also made some interesting compilation appearances, particularly with 'What A Nice Way To Turn Seventeen Magazine' Edition No. 2 which came with an EP (Rather/Seventeen GEAR 17) 1984 included *Shoot The Angels* and *Elephant Flowers* as The Sad-Go-Round. Edition No. 3 came with an album (Rather/Seventeen RATHER 13) 1984 which featured *Big Empty Field No. 2* and *The Cave Dwellers* (the latter as The Sad-Go-Round). Finally, Edition No. 6 came with an album (Seventeen SEVENTEEN 06) 1986, which included an uncredited track *The Train Out Of It*.

Other compilation appearances included the instrumental *Secret Island* and *Amphitheatres* on the cassette *Hiding In The Hangar* (Cockpit) 1982; an alternate version of *International Rescue* on the cassette *Entertaining Albert* (Action Tapes PAINT IT 1) 1983 and *A Tribute To Ricky Dicky* (Flame/Rouska RUSH 003) 1986 included *Marshmallows* and *Harmony In Your Bathroom*. The **Nikki Sudden** 1983 cassette *Beau Geste* (Rather RATHER 10) featured The Swell Maps on *Shattered*. More recently, the lavish 5-CD box set *1-2-3-4 - A History Of Punk And New Wave 1976 - 1979* (MCA/Universal MCD 60066) 1999 gave further exposure to *Read About Seymour* and *Let's Build A Car* figured on the 4-CD box set *25 Years Of Rough Trade Shops* (Mute CDSTUMM 191) in 2001.

After the **Swell Maps**' demise **Nikki Sudden** had a solo career and also worked with members of the Waterboys, Birthday Party and R.E.M. at various times. **Epic Soundtracks** played with Crime and City Solution and recorded a solo single and a 12" with Jowe Head. He later drummed with These Immortal Souls. Jowe Head worked solo and played bass with **T.V. Personalities**. Richard Earl recorded a solo album and then quit the music business.

Swell Maps remain significant as pioneers in the U.K. new wave.

Swift Nick

An early eighties ranter whose scathing punk poem about and called *The Sun* can be found on *The Oi! Of Sex* (Syndicate SYNLP 4) 1984, which was later reissued on CD (Captain Oi! AHOY CD 23) 1994.

David Sylvian

				HCP
ALBUMS:	1	BRILLIANT TREES	(Virgin V 2290) 1984	4
(up to	2	GONE TO EARTH	(Virgin VDL 1) 1986	24
1986)				

NB: (1) later reissued (Virgin OVED 239) 1990 and also issued on CD (Virgin CDV 2290) 1994. (2) also issued on CD (CDVDL 1) 1992. Also relevant is a limited edition 5-CD set *Weatherbox* (Virgin DSCD 1) 1989.

				HCP
EP:	1	WORDS WITH THE SHAMEN (12", PS)		
(up to			(Virgin VS 835-12) 1985	72
1986)				

				HCP
45s:	#	Bamboo Houses/Bamboo Music (PS)	(Virgin VS 510) 1982	30
(up to	#	Bamboo Houses/Bamboo Music/		
1986)		(A&B Mixes) (12", PS)	(Virgin VS 510-12) 1982	-
	+	Forbidden Colours/		
		The Seed And The Sower (PS)	(Virgin VS 601) 1983	16
	+	Forbidden Colours/The Seed And The Sower/		
		Last Regrets (12", PS)	(Virgin VS 601-12) 1983	-
		Red Guitar/Forbidden Colours (PS)	(Virgin VS 633) 1984	17
		Red Guitar/		
		Forbidden Colours (12", PS)	(Virgin VS 633-12) 1984	-
		Red Guitar/		
		Forbidden Colours (pic. disc)	(Virgin VSY 633) 1984	-
	*	The Ink In The Well (Remix)/		
		Weathered Wall (Instrumental) (PS)	(Virgin VS 700) 1984	36
	*	The Ink In The Well/Weathered		
		Wall (Instrumental) (12", PS)	(Virgin VS 700-12) 1984	-
	x	Pulling Punches (7" Mix)/		
		Backwaters (Remix) (PS)	(Virgin VS 717) 1984	56
		Pulling Punches (7" Mix)/		
		Backwaters (Remix) (pic. disc)	(Virgin VSY 717) 1984	-
	x	Pulling Punches (Extended Mix)/		
		Backwaters (Remix) (12", PS)	(Virgin VS 717-12) 1984	-
		Taking The Veil/Answered Prayers (PS)	(Virgin VS 815) 1986	53
	α	Taking The Veil/Answered Prayers (PS)	(Virgin VSS 815) 1986	-
		Taking The Veil/		
		Answered Prayers (12", PS)	(Virgin VS 815-12) 1986	-
		Silver Moon/Gone To Earth (PS)	(Virgin VS 895) 1986	-
	+	Silver Moon/Gone To Earth (PS)	(Virgin VS 895) 1986	-
		Silver Moon/Gone To Earth (12", PS)	(Virgin VS 895-12) 1986	-

NB: # Credited to David Sylvain and Riuichi Sakamoto. + Credited to Sylvian Sakamoto. * Issued in a poster picture sleeve. x Came with three postcards. α This rectangular picture disc came in a stickered PVC sleeve.

David Sylvian was born as David Batt in Lewisham in South-east London on 23rd February 1958. He is best remembered as the vocalist with **Japan**, but his disagreements with **Mick Karn** hindered their progress when they were enjoying deserved success and when they split in 1982 he embarked on a solo career.

In 1982, he teamed up with Riuichi Sakamoto to record *Bamboo Houses*, which brought them a No. 30 hit spending four weeks in the chart. A follow-up *Forbidden Colours*, a beautiful song which was in the mould of **Japan**, spent eight weeks in the charts climbing to No. 16.

On *Brilliant Trees* Sylvian was assisted by ex-**Japan** members Steve Jansen and Richard Barbieri as well as Holger Czukay, Riuichi Sakamoto and Jon Hassell. The end result is similar to **Japan**'s later albums. Sales were very good, with the album climbing to No. 4 during a chart duration of fourteen weeks. Three singles *Red Guitar*, *The Ink In The Well* and *Pulling Punches* were culled from the album, charting at No's 17, 36 and 56 respectively.

Encouraged by the success of *Brilliant Trees* **Sylvian** headed to Tokyo in late 1984 where he worked with Seigen Ono and Riuichi Sakamoto again. He recorded an African-sounding tape entitled *Preparations For A Journey* with Ono. Then he spent eight days with Sakamoto working on "Steel Cathedrals", a lengthy soundtrack for a video film about Tokyo by a man called Yamaguchi.

Words With The Shamen was a **Sylvian**/Hassell collaboration, which Holger Czukay also assisted on. Musically something between pop music and avant-garde, it conjured up visions of the Sahara and Arabia. Part of this work was issued on a 12" EP in 1985, which spent a week at No. 72 in the chart. The complete work later appeared as a limited edition, numbered cassette, titled *Alchemy (An Index Of Possibilities)* (Virgin SLY 1) in 1985. It was later released on CD.

Fuelled on by growing self-confidence **Sylvian** recorded an extravagant double album *Gone To Earth*, which was released in August 1986. One disc was a rock album, which featured some scorching guitar-work by ex-progressive rockers Bill Nelson and Robert Fripp on tracks like *Before The Bullfight* and *Wave*. The title track *Gone To Earth* featured a strained rough vocal (in contrast to the smooth vocal style on the rest of the album) which is highlighted on the quirky pop song *Silver Moon* and the jazz ballad *Laughing And Forgetting*. The second disc contains tranquil instrumental material and titles like *The Healing Place*, *Answered Prayers* and *The Wooden Cross* had strong Christian leanings. For a double album sales were again quite good and the album reached No. 24, but only spent five weeks in the chart. Two singles were lifted from *Gone To Earth*, *Taking The Veil* and *Silver Moon*. The former enjoyed three weeks in the chart, climbing to No. 53. **Sylvian** collectors will want a 7" square picture disc of this release. *Silver Moon* was not a hit, a limited fold-out sleeve edition of this will interest collectors.

Sylvian continued to record well beyond the time frame of this book. In 1989, *Weatherbox* a 5-CD box set was released comprising *Brilliant Trees*, both discs of *Gone To Earth*, *Secrets Of The Beehive* (a 1987 album) and *Alchemy - An Index Of Possibilities*. It came in a custom box with a colour poster and fifty-six page booklet.

Syndicate

45: One Way Or Another/I Want To Be Somebody/
(two cuts by **Restricted Hours**) (PS)
(Stevenage/Rock Against Racism) 1979

This disc was released with a white label in a fold over picture sleeve. The group involved members of **The Astronauts**.

THE TABLE - Do The Standing Still.

THE TABLE - Sex Cells.

The System

A Wigan-based anarcho-punk band who released a live tape on the Rotting Bodies label in May 1983.

The Table

Personnel:	TONY BARNES	gtr, bs	ABC
	LEN LEWIS	drms, perc	AB
	MICKY O'CONNOR	gtr	A
	RUSSELL YOUNG	vcls, gtr, keyb'ds, bs	ABC
	KEVIN BANNON	gtr	B
	TIM COX	lead gtr, vcls	C
	RICHARD RAE	drms	C

45s: Do The Standing Still (Classics Illustrated)/
The Magical Melon Of The Tropics (PS)   (Virgin VS 176) 1977
Sex Cells/The Road Of Lyfe (PS)   (Chiswick NS 31) 1978

The Table formed in Cardiff out of the early seventies band John Stabber. Initially they were a duo comprising Russell Young and Tony Barnes and played at the 1974 Windsor Festival as Do You Want A Table. In 1976, with their name abbreviated to **The Table**, they were transformed into a quartet with the addition of Len Lewis and Micky O'Connor. They signed an agreement with Virgin which gave them free studio time but no advance. At this time they were intending to operate primarily as a studio outfit. Their first 45 on Virgin *Do The Standing Still* was quite catchy but too repetitive. It was also included on *Guillotine 10"* (Virgin VCL 5001) in 1978. The flip side *The Magical Melon Of The Tropics* culminates in quite an unusual instrumental jam. On the follow-up *Sex Cells*, the vocalist sings of his obsession with the idea of sex with school girls. This is much stronger than the first 45 and also has some good guitar segments. The flip side *The Road Of Lyfe* ends in mayhem, but of all four cuts only *Sex Cells* is a really good tune.

Do The Standing Still later resurfaced on the 5-CD box set *1-2-3-4 - A History Of Punk And New Wave 1976 - 1979* (MCA/Universal MCD 60066) in 1999.

The Tagmemics

45: Chimneys (Do The) Big Baby/
Take Your Brain Out For A Walk (PS)   (Index INDEX 003) 1980

This project included former members of **Art Attacks**.

Micky Take and The Take Ons

45: Bird Dog/The Price Of Living Is High   (Polydor 2058 969) 1978

This is a mickey take on Johnny Rotten and punk rock generally. Musically, it will be no surprise that it's not delivered in a punk style. This is someone playing under a pseudonym.

TALK TALK - The Party's Over.

Talk Talk

Personnel:
SIMON BRENNER	keyb'ds	A	
LEE HARRIS	drms	AB	
MARK HOLLIS	vcls, piano, gtr	AB	
PAUL WEBB	bs, vcls	AB	
TIM FRIESE-GREEN	keyb'ds	B	

			HCP
ALBUMS: 1(A)	THE PARTY'S OVER	(EMI EMC 3413) 1982	21
(up to 2(B)	IT'S MY LIFE	(EMI EMC 240002 1) 1984	35
1986) 3(B)	THE COLOUR OF SPRING	(EMI EMC 3506) 1986	8

NB: (1) reissued (EMI ATAK 65) 1985 and also issued on CD (EMI CDP 746 366 2) 1987 and (EMI Fame CDFA 3187) 1988. (2) reissued (EMI ATAK 116) 1989 and also issued on CD (EMI CDP 746 063 2) 1985. (3) reissued (EMI ATAK 145) 1990 and also issued on CD (EMI CDP 746 228 2) 1986 and again (EMI CZ 287) 1990. There are also a couple of relevant compilations; *Natural History (The Very Best Of Talk Talk)* (Parlophone PCSD 109) 1990, also on CD (Parlophone CDP 793 976 2) 1990, which got to No. 3; *The Very Best Of Talk Talk* (EMI CDADV 102) 1997; and *Asides And Besides* (2CD Set) (EMI CDEMC 3670) 1996 and (EMI 8548072) 1998.

			HCP
45s:	Mirror Man/Strike Up The Band (PS)	(EMI EMI 5265) 1982	-
(up to	Talk Talk/Talk Talk (Alt. Version) (PS)	(EMI EMI 5284) 1982	52
1986)	Talk Talk (Extended)/		
	Talk Talk (Alt. Version) (12", PS)	(EMI 12EMI 5284) 1982	-
	Today/It's So Serious (PS)	(EMI EMI 5314) 1982	14
	Today (Extended)/		
	It's So Serious (12", PS)	(EMI 12EMI 5314) 1982	-
	Talk Talk (Remix)/Mirror Man (PS)	(EMI EMI 5352) 1982	23
	Talk Talk (Remix)/		
	Talk Talk (BBC Version) (12", PS)	(EMI 12EMI 5352) 1982	-
	Talk Talk (Remix)/		
	Mirror Man (Picture disc)	(EMI EMIP 5352) 1982	-
	My Foolish Friend/		
	Call In The Nightboys (PS)	(EMI EMI 5373) 1983	57
	My Foolish Friend (Extended)/Call In The Nightboys/		
	My Foolish Friend (12", PS)	(EMI 12EMI 5373) 1983	-
	It's My Life/Does Caroline Know? (PS)	(EMI EMI 5443) 1984	46
	It's My Life (Extended)/Does Caroline Know?/		
	It's My Life (12", PS)	(EMI 12EMI 5443) 1984	-
	Such A Shame/		
	Again, A Game... Again (PS)	(EMI EMI 5433) 1984	49
	The Talk Talk Demos (Double 7" [EMI 5433 + PSR 467])		
	(poster sleeve)	(EMI EMID 5433) 1984	-
	Such A Shame (Extended)/Such A Shame/		
	Again, A Game... Again (12", PS)	(EMI 12EMI 5433) 1984	-
	Dum Dum Girl/Without You (PS)	(EMI EMI 5480) 1984	74
	Dum Dum Girl (Extended)/Such A Shame (Dub)/		
	Without You (Extended)/		
	Dum Dum Girl (U.S. 7" Mix) (12", PS)	(EMI 12EMI 5480) 1984	-
	Life Is What You Make It/It's Getting Late		
	In The Evening (PS)	(EMI EMI 5540) 1986	16
	Life Is What You Make It (Extended)/It's Getting Late		
	In The Evening (12", PS)	(EMI 12EMI 5540) 1986	-
	Life Is What You Make It (Extended)/It's Getting Late In The Evening/It's My Life/Does Caroline Know? (double 12", PS)	(EMI 12EMID 5540) 1986	-
	Life Is What You Make It (Extended Dance Mix)/		
	Life Is What You Make It (Early Mix)/It's Getting Late In The Evening (12", PS)	(EMI 12EMIX 5540) 1986	-
	Living In Another World/		
	For What It's Worth (PS)	(EMI EMI 5551) 1986	48
	Living In Another World/For What It's Worth (Shaped picture disc)	(EMI EMIP 5551) 1986	-
	Living in Another World (Extended)/		
	Living In Another World/		
	For What It's Worth (12", PS)	(EMI 12EMI 5551) 1986	-
	Living In Another World (U.S. Mix)/		
	Living In Another World (Album Version)/		
	For What It's Worth (12", PS)	(EMI 12EMIX 5551) 1986	-
	Give It Up/		
	Pictures Of Bernadette (PS)	(Parlophone R 6131) 1986	59
	Give It Up/Pictures Of Bernadette/Pictures Of Bernadette (Dance Mix)	(Parlophone 12R 6131) 1986	-
	I Don't Believe In You/		
	Does Caroline Know? (PS)	(Parlophone R 6144) 1986	-
	I Don't Believe In You/Does Caroline Know? (Live)/		
	Happiness Is Easy (12", PS)	(Parlophone 12R 6144) 1986	-

The pivotal figure in **Talk Talk** was Mark Hollis. Mark was born in Tottenham in 1955. His elder brother Ed was manager and producer for **Eddie and The Hotrods** and it was Mark's love of music that led him to drop out of his course in child psychology at Sussex University in 1977 to return to London and concentrate on writing songs.

Mark was briefly a roadie for **Eddie and The Hot Rods**, but then formed his own group **Reaction** whose sole 1978 45 *I Can't Resist* was a mod-influenced recording. In addition to the single the band also contributed an early version of *Talk Talk*, which Mark co-wrote with his brother Ed, to the *Streets* (Beggars Banquet BEGA 1) 1977 compilation the previous year.

The Reaction split up in 1979 and Mark Hollis spent the next couple of years concentrating on writing new material. In 1981 Island booked Hollis some demo time and to help out in the sessions Ed Hollis recruited Lee Harris (drms) and Paul Webb (bs). After Simon Brenner was added on keyboards the band became known as **Talk Talk**. After seeing their live debut David Jensen (a BBC DJ) invited the band to do a session on his show and about a month later the band were signed by EMI.

Talk Talk were essentially part of (though never wholeheartedly behind) the New Romantic movement. Indeed they supported **Duran Duran** on a national tour and even hired Colin Thurston (who had produced **Duran Duran**'s first album) to do the honours on their own debut album. Prior to this their first 45 *Mirror Man* had sold disappointingly and *Talk Talk* had only managed a highest chart placing of 52. It was their third single *Today* that took them into the Top 20, climbing to No. 14 during its thirteen weeks in the charts.

Their debut album *The Party's Over* included *Talk Talk* and *Today* and these were really its finest moments. Much of the other material was poorly arranged (dissatisfied with Thurston the band had seized control of production themselves halfway through the session) and an unimaginative barrage of synthesized music and drums. Still, in spite of this, the album made quite an impression spending twenty-five weeks in the charts and narrowly missing the Top 20. On the back of this success EMI issued a remixed version of *Talk Talk* and this fared better than the earlier version peaking at No. 23 during its ten week chart sojourn. Hollis also decided to move away from the band's synthesizer-based sound, which meant that Simon Brenner's days with the band were over. In March 1983, the non-album 45 *My Foolish Friend* gave them a further minor hit, rising to No. 57 during its three week chart stint.

Hollis spent the remainder of 1983 writing new songs. He also recruited Tim Friese-Greene, who'd initially worked as an engineer but later became a producer. Tim had already steered **Blue Zoo** into the charts and he was also a talented keyboard player. Although never officially a member of the group Friese-Greene formed a songwriting partnership with Hollis which proved most durable. They quickly co-wrote *It's My Life*, which was selected as the title track for the band's next album. Released as a single in January 1984, it only climbed to No. 46 but is usually considered to be one of the band's best songs and actually performed better commercially across the Atlantic. The album appeared the following month and was a vast improvement on their earlier effort. It included slower more pensive material like *Renee, Does Caroline Know?* and *Tomorrow Started*, although aside from the title cut the highlights included *Such A Shame*, *It's You* and another Hollis/Friese-Greene collaboration. Guitars also figured on one of their records for the first time, supplied by session man Robbie McIntosh. Despite all this the album failed to equal its predecessor in terms of sales, stalling at No. 35 and spending just eight weeks in the charts.

In March a second 45 *Such A Shame* was culled from the album. In addition to the usual 12" format with an extended 'A' side, as an additional marketing ploy, a double-pack 7" in a poster sleeve was released featuring a bonus single of three demos (*Talk Talk*, *Mirror Man* and *Candy*). It failed to work because the single failed to advance beyond No. 49 during its six-week chart stay and a third 45 from the album *Dum Dum* in June stalled at No. 74. Later in the year *It's My Mix*, a mini-album featuring extended or remixed versions of six of their more popular songs, was released in the 'States and Italy and this sold quite steadily as an import here in Britain.

The whole of 1985 was spent writing and recording. They returned in January 1986 with the excellent 45 *Life Is What You Make It*, which took them into the Top 20 for the first time for nearly four years, peaking at No. 16. It also secured them a successful appearance on 'Top Of The Pops'. Also of note is the haunting 'B' side *It's Getting Late In The Evening*. The 'A' side was arguably the stand-out track on their third album *The Colour Of Spring*. This abandoned their earlier synthesized sound for Hammond organ with Stevie Winwood performing the honours and a wide array of guests including David Rhodes (gtr), David Roach (sax) and Morris Pert (perc) were featured on the album, which climbed to No. 8 and spent an impressive twenty-one weeks in the charts, eventually going gold. Three further 45s - *Living In Another Word*, *Give It Up* and *I Don't Believe In You* - were taken from it. The first two became minor hits, peaking at No. 48 and 59 respectively. They embarked on a World Tour in Spring 1986 to promote the album.

Strangely, although *The Colour Of Spring* brought the group to the brink of international success, it would be another two-and-a-half years before they returned with another album *Spirit Of Eden*. This would prove their most demanding album to date. They had indeed progressed a long way from the rather lightweight synthetic pop outfit they had started out as.

Talk Talk can also be heard on *The Model* (Spectrum 5529182) 1997.

Natural History (The Very Best Of Talk Talk) is a twelve-track compilation which documents their development from virtual New Romantics to proponents of mood music.

Tanz Der Youth

Personnel:	ANDY COLQUHOUN	bs	A
	BRIAN JAMES	vcls, gtr	A
	TONY MOORE	keyb'ds, synth	A
	ALAN POWELL	drms	A

45:	I'm Sorry, I'm Sorry/Delay (PS)	(Radar ADA 19) 1978

A band of some pedigree this. Andy Colquhoun had been in **Warsaw Pakt**, James, who formed the band, was in **The Damned** and Powell came from Hawkwind. The name is German for "Dance of the Youth".

In addition to this 45, they recorded a session for John Peel which was broadcast on 9th August 1978. This comprised *I'm Sorry I'm Sorry*, *Why I Die*, *Mistaken* and *Delay*. *I'm Sorry, I'm Sorry* is a decent hard rock single with menace, wit and flair.

After their demise James went solo and he was later in Lords Of The New Church. Colquhoun later resurfaced in a reformed Deviants line-up.

Taxi Girl

Personnel:	JET BLACK	drms	A
	JEAN-JACQUES BURNEL	vcls	A
	DANIEL DARC	vcls	A
	NAPOLEAN GLOSS	drms, perc	A
	KEN NICOL	vcls	A
	PHILIPPE	bs	A
	JEFF SEOPARDIE	congas	A
	LAURENT SINCLAIR	keyb'ds	A
	VIVIENNE VOG	vcls	A
	MIRWAIS	gtr	A
	BILL ZORN	vcls	A

ALBUM:	1(A)	SEPPUKA	(Virgin 201 899) 1981

NB: There have been three albums *Cherchez Le Garcon* (Fan Club FC 040 CD) 1987, *Compilation* (Fan Club FC 049 CD) 1989 and *Quelque Part Dans Paris* (Fan Club FC 071 CD) 1990.

45s:	Cherchez Le Garcon/Jardin Chinois (PS)	(Vrgin VS 467) 1980
	Aussi Belle Qu'une Balle	(Play It Again Sam BIAS 15) 1986
	Aussie Belle Qu'une Balle (12")	(Play It Again Sam BIAS 16) 1986

Taxi Girl is most notable for the involvement of **Stranglers'**, **Jean-Jacques Burnel**, who produced the album, and Jet Black, the drummer. The album was quite pretentious and arty, but also rather dull. It is probably best forgotten.

Bram Tchaikovsky

Personnel:	KEITH BOYCE	drms	AB
	MICKY BROADBENT	vcls, bs, keyb'ds	AB
	BRAM TCHAIKOVSKY	vcls, gtr	AB
	DENIS FORBES	gtr	B

ALBUMS:	1(A)	STRANGE MAN, CHANGED MAN	(Radar 17) 1979
	2(B)	THE RUSSIANS ARE COMING	(Radar 26) 1980
	3(-)	FUNLAND	(Arista 1164) 1981

NB: (2) retitled as *Pressure* in the U.S.

45s:	Robber/Whiskey And Wine	(Radar SAM 96) 1977
	Sarah Smiles/Turn On The Light	(Criminal SWAG 3) 1979
	Lullaby Of Broadway/	
	Who Wants To Be A Criminal (PS)	(Criminal BRAM 58) 1979
	Girl Of My Dreams/Come Back	(Radar ADA 28) 1979
*	I'm The One That's Leaving/Amelia	(Radar ADA 37) 1979
	Let's Dance/Rock And Roll Cabaret (PS)	(Radar ADA 54) 1980
	Shall We Dance/Miracle Cure (PS)	(Arista ARIST 403) 1981
	Breaking Down The Walls Of Heartache/	
	Egyptian Mummies	(Arista ARIST 413) 1981

NB: * Picture disc.

Bram Tchaikovsky was formed by the **Motors'** ex-guitarist, bassist and vocalist. There's quite a lot of **Motors'** influence on *Strange Man, Changed Man*, which **Tchaikovsky** co-produced with ex-band mate **Nick Garvey**. The album has stood up to time well and the three 45 cuts, *Girl Of My*

BRAM TCHAIKOVSKY - Strange Man, Changed Man.

Dreams, *I'm The One That's Leaving* and *Sarah Smiles* all sound good today. One track that doesn't sound so good though is their cover of The Monkees' *I'm A Believer*.

The follow-up *The Russians Are Coming* was retitled as *Pressure* for the U.S. market in view of the Cold War. Unfortunately the songwriting is inconsistent on this one.

The band then underwent various line-up changes. Their final album *Funland* had few highlights, but there are a couple of good covers of *Breaking Down The Walls Of Heartache* and an old **Motors**' 'B' side *Soul Surrender*. The album was again produced by **Nick Garvey**.

T.D.A.

An obscure four-piece punk band from Kent. Their self titled *T.D.A.*, a raw punk shouter, was originally included on *Riotous Assembly* (Riot City ASSEMBLY 1) in 1982. It later got a further airing on *100% Hardcore Punk* (Captain Oi! AHOY DCD) in 1998.

THE TEARDROP EXPLODES - Treason.

The Teardrop Explodes

Personnel:			
JULIAN COPE	bs, vcls	ABCDEFG H
GARY DWYER	drms	ABCDEFG H
MICK FINKLER	gtr	ABC
PAUL SIMPSON	keyb'ds	A
GERARD QUINN	keyb'ds	B
DAVID BALFE	keyb'ds	CDE G H
ALAN GILL	gtr	D
TROY TATE	gtr, vcls	EFG
(ALFIE ALGIUS	bs	F)
(JEFF HAMMER	keyb'ds	F)
(RON FRANCOIS	bs	H)

HCP
ALBUMS: 1(D) KILIMANJARO (Mercury 6359 035) 1980 24
2(F) WILDER (Mercury 6359 056) 1981 29

NB: (1) repressed in March 1981 with a revised track listing, new sleeve, but the same catalogue number. (1) later reissued (Mercury PRICE 59) 1984. (1) reissued on CD (Mercury 836 897-2) 1989, again in 1996 and again (Mercury 5483222) 2000, with bonus tracks. (2) reissued on CD (Mercury 836 896-2) 1996 and again (Mercury 5482842) 2000, with bonus tracks. (1) and (2) reissued as a 2-CD set (Mercury 528 601-2) 1995. There's also *Everybody Wants To Shag The Teardrop Explodes* (Mercury 842 439-2) 1990 (CD), it was also available on vinyl (Mercury 842439-1) 1990 and got to No. 72 and *Piano* (Document DCD 4) 1990 (CD), which was also on vinyl (Document DLP 4).

HCP
45s: α Sleeping Gas/Camera Camera/Kirby Workers' Dream
  Fades (PS) (Zoo CAGE 003) 1979 -
  Bouncing Babies/
  All I Am Is Loving You (PS) (Zoo CAGE 005) 1979 -
  Treason (It's Just A Story)/
  Read It In Books (PS) (Zoo CAGE 008) 1980 -
  When I Dream/Kilimanjaro (PS) (Mercury TEAR 1) 1980 47
  Reward/
  Strange House In The Snow (PS) (Mercury TEAR 2) 1981 6
  Treason/Use Me (PS) (Mercury TEAR 3) 1981 18
  Treason/Traison/Use Me (12", PS) (Mercury TEAR 312) 1981 -
  Ha Ha I'm Drowning/
  Poppies In The Field (PS) (Mercury TEAR 4) 1981 -
* Ha Ha I'm Drowning/Poppies In The Field/
  Bouncing Babies/Read It In Books (Mercury TEAR 44) 1981 -
  Passionate Friend/
  Christ Versus Warhol (PS) (Mercury TEAR 5) 1981 25
  Passionate Friend/
  Christ Versus Warhol (12") (Mercury TEAR 512) 1981 -
  Colours Fly Away/Window Shopping For A New
  Crown Of Thorns (PS) (Mercury TEAR 6) 1981 54
  Colours Fly Away/East Of The Equator/
  Window Shopping For A New Crown
  Of Thorns (12", PS) (Mercury TEAR 612) 1981 -
  Tiny Children/
  Rachael Built A Steamboat (PS) (Mercury TEAR 7) 1982 44
+ Tiny Children/
  Rachael Built A Steamboat (Mercury TEAR 7G) 1982 -
  Tiny Children/Rachael Built A Steamboat/
  Sleeping Gas (live) (12", PS) (Mercury TEAR 712) 1982 -
  You Disappear From View/Suffocate (Mercury TEAR 8) 1983 41
* You Disappear From View/Suffocate/Ouch Monkey's/
  Soft Enough For You/
  The In-Psychlopedia (PS) (Mercury TEAR 88) 1983 -
  You Disappear From View/Suffocate (Baroque Version)/
  Ouch Monkey's/Soft Enough For You/The
  In-Psychlopedia (12", 33 rpm PS) (Mercury TEAR 812) 1983 -
  Reward/Treason (PS) (Mercury TEAR 9) 1985 -
  Reward (Remix)/Strange House In The Snow/
  Treason (Remix)/Use Me (12", PS) (Mercury TEAR 912) 1985 -

NB: α Issued in a red or blue picture sleeve. * Gatefold double pack. + Gatefold sleeve.

The Teardrop Explodes were at the forefront of the thriving Liverpool punk/new wave scene of the late seventies and early eighties, along with **Echo and The Bunnymen** and **Orchestral Manuvoeuvres In The Dark**. They formed in October 1978. The nucleus of the band was Julian Cope (bs, vcls) and Gary Dwyer (drms). Cope had been born on 21st October 1958 in Bargoed, Wales, but spent his childhood in Tamworth in the Midlands. He was attending teachers training college in Liverpool at the time and previously been in the Crucial Three with Michael Finkler and Paul Simpson, The Nova Mob and A Shallow Madness. Dwyer had previously been a roadie for another Liverpool band **Big In Japan**.

They played their first gig with Finkler and Simpson (line-up 'A') at Liverpool's Eric's, along with **Echo and The Bunnymen**, in November 1978. Soon afterwards they cut a three-track EP *Sleeping Gas*, which was released in February 1979 on Liverpool's Zoo Records. This was the city's top indie label at the time run by Bill Drummond and David Balfe. The EP

THE TEARDROP EXPLODES - Kilimanjaro (2nd version).

was issued in three different pressings. Initially it came in a red sleeve with folded sleeves along the edges, this was replaced by a blue cover, then finally a red one with the seams at the rear of the sleeve. Original copies are very hard to find and collectable because of Zoo's limited distribution at the time. The title track's experimentation with electronics lead some to categorise the band as part of the emerging electro-pop scene which was an error.

Their follow-up 45, *Bouncing Babies*, released in June 1979, set what would become a regular pattern of having a commercial pop tune on the 'A' side and an obscure, strange number on the flip, in this case *All I Am Is Loving You*.

By now Gerard Quinn had replaced Paul Simpson on keyboards. Simpson had departed to **The Wild Swans**. They went on to release a highly collectable 12" single for Zoo in 1982. A few months later Quinn himself departed to **The Wild Swans** and was replaced by David Balfe. Balfe had been co-managing **The Teardrop Explodes** with Zoo's Bill Drummond. Balfe had previously been in **Lori and The Chameleons**, **Big In Japan** and **Those Naughty Lumps**.

The Teardrop Explodes' third and final 45 for Zoo *Treason (It's Just A Story)*, was released in February 1980. This sold well and, along with a series of nationwide dates, helped them secure a deal with Phonogram's Mercury label. Its flip side is noteworthy for being co-written by Julian Cope and Ian McCulloch (of **Echo and The Bunnymen**). Both bands have subsequently recorded several versions of the song.

Shortly before signing for Phonogram in the summer of 1980 Finkler quit for academia. His replacement was Alan Gill from **Dalek I Love You**. The new line-up ('D') toured incessantly and enjoyed their first hit when their next single *When I Dream*, released in September 1980, became a minor hit. Although it only reached No. 47, it stayed in the charts for six weeks. The following month their first album *Kilimanjaro* was released. This won them considerable acclaim and spent a total of thirty-five weeks in the charts, although the highest position it reached was No. 24. The album was released twice in the U.K.. The original issue featured a colour picture of the band which was very poor and is generally regarded as one of the worst record sleeves. By the time of the second release, in March 1981, they enjoyed a Top Ten hit with their latest single *Reward*, which was their first to come in a Martyn Atkins sleeve. This got to No. 6 during a thirteen-week chart residency. So *Reward* was added to the track listing, which also featured a longer version of *When I Dream*. It also came in a new Martyn Atkins 'zebra' cover. Musically many of the songs had a childlike, dreamy quality. The brass and keyboard string arrangements recalled some of the sixties West Coast's finest moments. Some cuts like *Reward*, *Treason*, *When I Dream* and *Poppies In The Field* in particular, stand out.

When *Kilimanjaro* was issued in the 'States the track listing was changed again. The tracks were re-ordered, a re-mixed version of *Reward* was included and a new track *Suffocate* was added which didn't appear on any U.K. releases until after the band had split. This U.S.-only remixed version of *Reward* also appeared on a U.S. promo 12" along with *When I Dream* and *Ha, Ha I'm Drowning*.

For **The Teardrop Explodes**' next U.K. 45 it was decided to release a remixed version of *Treason* in April 1981. This got to No. 18 during an eight week chart stay. This time a Julian Cope solo cut was on the flip side.

In August 1981, two cuts *Ha, Ha, I'm Drowning* and *Poppies In The Field* were culled from the *Kilimanjaro* album for release on a 45, but Cope objected and the projected release was withdrawn. However, it remained available as an import in some shops. There was also a double-pack release of this 45 in a gatefold sleeve and an earlier Zoo 'A' side (*Bouncing Babies*) and 'B' side (*Read It In Books*). In its place *Passionate Friend* was released the following month. This was really a taster for their next album. In addition to their now characteristic brass passages, ex-**Shake** member Troy Tate had been added to the line-up and provided some delicate sitar. It brought the band a third Top 30 hit, climbing to No. 25 during a ten week chart stay.

Gill had returned to **Dalek I Love You** after the first album, but in addition to Tate, the band now included Alfie Agius on bass and Jeff Hammer on keyboards. This line-up recorded their second album *Wilder*, which was released in November 1981. This was a more consistent album musically. Among the finer tracks were *Bent Out Of Shape*, *Seven Views Of*

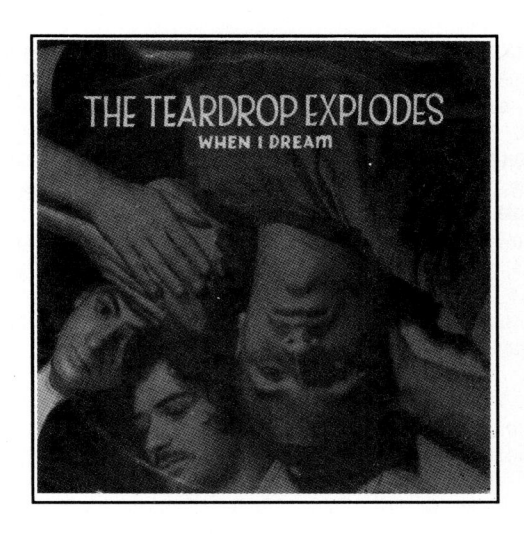

THE TEARDROP EXPLODES - When I Dream.

Jerusalem and *Colours Fly Away*. This latter one was also issued as a 45 to tie in with the album's release. The flip side *Window Shopping For A New Crown Of Thorns* sounds influenced by Nico. The 12" version featured an additional instrumental cut, *East Of The Equator*. The *Colours Fly Away* 45 peaked at No. 54, spending just three weeks in the chart. The *Wilder* album fared better, climbing to No. 29, although its chart residency of just six weeks contrasted markedly with the thirty-five weeks of *Kilimanjaro*.

There was a long gap before the band's next vinyl output *Tiny Children* in June 1982. For this Cope, Dwyer and Tate were rejoined by Balfe and bassist Ron Francois, who'd previously been in The Sinceros (**Lene Lovich**'s backing band). *Tiny Children*, a slow-organ based number attracted quite a lot of airplay but only became a minor hit. It peaked at No. 44 during a seven week stay. There was also a 12" version which contained a lengthy live version of *Sleeping Gas* from December 1981.

Towards the end of 1982, after incessant overseas touring, the band had slimmed down to a trio of Cope, Dwyer and Balfe. Commercially their fortunes were declining and with the three of them beginning to harbour individual ambitions, they collectively decided that the group had had its day. They split in November 1982, although a final 45 *You Disappear From View* was released in February 1983 and undeservedly rather neglected because they weren't around to promote it. Nonetheless, the 45 still spent three weeks in the chart peaking at No. 41. The flip side featured *Suffocate*, which had previously only been available on the U.S. version of *Kilimanjaro*. A double pack 45 was also issued with three tracks of a 33 rpm 7" disc. There was also a five-track 12" version of this release. This had a modified sleeve design and a different baroque recording of *Suffocate* with harpsichord and muted string backing.

After **The Teardrop Explodes**' demise Cope embarked on a solo career during the nineties, which explored his fascination for sixties pop/psychedelia and Kraut rock in particular, with varying degress of commercial success. Balfe formed a new management company and later set up the successful Food label. Cope also wrote 'Krautrocksampler - One Head's Guide To The Great Kosmische Musik - 1968 Onwards...'.

The 1982 compilation *To The Shores Of Lake Placid* (Zoo FOUR) included three early **Teardrop Explodes** songs - two of them; a version of *When I Dream* and *Take A Chance* (recorded for an early Peel session) are unavailable elsewhere. The compilation also features solo outings by Julian Cope as '**Whopper**' and **The Turquoise Swimming Pools** (who were David Balfe with assistance from Troy Tate and his producer Hugh Jones).

In 1990, a compilation album of previously unissued outtakes and other rarities titled *Everybody Wants To Shag The Teardrop Explodes* was issued. It even returned them to the charts for one week at No. 72. This was actually to have been their third album but was shelved when they split back in 1982. It includes their lacklustre *You Disappear From View* 45 as well as three of the other tracks which were featured in the single's original double pack format - *Soft Enough*, *The In-Psychopaedia* and *Ouch Monkeys*. Also included is *Strange House In The Snow* from a much earlier session and two new cuts *Metranil Vavin* and *Sex (Pussy Face)*, which both later resurfaced on Cope's *World Shut Your Mouth* album. There's also a dance number *Serious Danger*. If you've much interest in the band you'll want this but it's not up to the standard of *Kilimanjaro* and *Wilder*.

The title of their *Piano* compilation was taken from their sleeve illustration on the *Sleeping Gas* EP. It is not taken from the original master tapes but includes many of their finest moments. *Bouncing Babies*, *When I Dream* and *Read It In Books* (which Julian Cope co-wrote with **Echo and The Bunnymen**'s Ian McCulloch in their Crucial Three days) all feature. There are some experimental 'B' sides too - *Camera Camera* and the experimental *Kirkby Workers Dream Fades* from their debut 45 and *All I Am Is Loving You* (the out of tune flip side to *Bouncing Babies*, their second 45). Also included is their contribution to Zoo's final sampler *To The Shores Of Lake Placid*, a brief number called *Take A Chance* and their cover of *Kwalo Klobinski's Lullaby*, originally released under the pseudonym of **Whooper**.

In 1996, Fontana reissued *Kilimanjaro* and *Wilder* on CD at mid-price. The *Kilimanjaro* issue is in its second cover and track listing alongside the hit single *Reward*. The *Wilder* reissue is also in its second sleeve with Cope doing his impression of Bowie on the front of *Heroes* as opposed to its strikingly freaky original sleeve. Sadly, Fontana could have added sleeve-notes, photos of the original sleeves inside the booklets and bonus tracks inside these reissues, but they chose not to.

In 1997, they contributed *Reward* to the CD compilation *The Sound Of The Suburbs* (Columbia 488825 2) and to *Teenage Kicks* (PolyGram TV 5253382) 1995. You can also check out *Treason (It's Just A Story)* on *The Best Punk Album In The World.... Ever, Vol. 2* (2-CD) (Virgin VTDCD 79) 1996.

In 2000, their two albums were remastered and reissued by Mercury with bonus tracks. On *Kilimanjaro* these include *Reward* and a live nine-minute version of *Sleeping Gas*. The bonus cuts on *Wilder* include 'B' sides and some of the material from *Everybody Wants To Shag The Teardrop Explodes*.

The Teardrops

Personnel:	HELEN BARBROOK		A
	BOK BOK		A
	TONY FRIEL		A
	STEVE GARVEY	bs	A
	TREV WAY		A

ALBUM: 1(A) FINAL VINYL (Illuminated JAMS 2) 1980

EP: 1( ) LEAVE ME NO CHANCE (12", PS) (Bent BIGB 3) 1978

NB: (1) This EP came in a polythene bag.

45: Seeing Double/
Teardrops And Heartaches (PS) (TJM TJM 9) 1979

A Manchester-based band most notable in personnel terms for including former **Buzzcocks**' bassist Steve Garvey. Tony Friel had been an early member of **The Fall**. Musically, the band's main influences were **The Buzzcocks** and **Sex Pistols**. *Final Vinyl* has its moments but is ruined by unnecessary talking and noises which detracts from some of the music.

The Tearjerkers

Personnel:	NIGEL HAMILTON	drms	A
	HOWARD INGRAM	bs	A
	PAUL MAXWELL	vcls	A
	PAUL 'THE GROOVER' McLLWAINE	gtr	A
	BRIAN RAWSON	gtr	A

CASS: 1(A) TEARJERKERS (Gray GRC 1) 198?

45s: Love Affair/Bus Stop (PS) (Good Vibrations GOT 9) 1979
Murder Mystery/
Heart On The Line (PS) (Back Door DOOR 1) 1980

The Tearjerkers were regular performers at Belfast's Harp Bar, who did build up a loyal following in Northen Ireland, and were championed in a fanzine called 'Positive Reaction'. They recorded a single, *Love Affair* for Good Vibrations, secured a session for John Peel and eventually secured a recording contract with Back Door, a Phonogram subsidiary midway through 1979. However, like many of their colleagues, they failed to meet their new record company's expectations and faded from the scene after just one unsuccessful single *Murder Mystery* in 1980. They did also have three cuts on a U.S. Mercury compilation of Back Door releases.

Love Affair later resurfaced on *Good Vibrations: The Punk Singles Collection* (Anagram CD PUNK 36) 1994. It's quite commercial really and nearer to pop than punk.

Tea Set

Personnel:	CALLY	drms	A
	NICK EGAN	vcls	A
	NICK HAEFFNER	gtr	A
	DUNCAN STRINGER	gtr	A
	RON WEST	bs	A

EP: 1(A) CUPS AND SAUCERS (On Them/Sing Song/
Grey Starting/B52G) (World's Beat Series 003) 1978

NB: (1) This came with a stapled lyric book sleeve.

45s: * Parry Thomas/Tri-X Pan (PS) (Waldo's Beat PS 006) 1979
+ South Pacific/The Preacher (PS) (Demon D 1009) 1980
Keep On Running (Big Noise From The Jungle)/
Flaccid Pot (PS) (Mainly Modern STP 3) 1980

NB: * Came in a gatefold picture sleeve with a poster envelope. + Came in a fold-out picture sleeve with inserts.

The **Tea Set**'s final 45 *Keep On Running (Big Noise From The Jungle)* was produced by **Strangler** Hugh Cornwall.

The Teenage Filmstars

Personnel:	ED BALL	vcls	A
	PAUL DAMIEN	drms	A
	JOE FOSTER	gtr	A
	DAN TREACY	bs	A

45s: * (There's A) Cloud Over Liverpool/Sometimes Good Guys
Don't Follow Trends (PS) (Clockwork COR 002) 1979
The Odd Man Out/I Apologise (Wessex WEX 275) 1980
I Helped Patrick McGoohan Escape/
We're Not Sorry (PS) (Fab Listening FL 1) 1980

Reissue: The Odd Man Out/I Apologise (Blueprint BLU 2013) 1980

NB: * The first 150 copies came in foldout picture sleeves. All three of their 45s and four unreleased tracks by the band were later included on *1977 - 1980 - A Day In The Life Of Gilbert And George* (Rev-Ola CREV 005) 1992, also on CD.

100% BRITISH MOD compilation featuring The Teenage Filmstars.

After making an EP himself Ed Ball missed the comraderie of playing in a band so he put together **The Teenage Filmstars** with Dan Treacy, the co-founder of **Television Personalities**. Their first 45 *(There's A) Cloud Over Liverpool* was inspired by kitchen sink drama films and **Wire**'s *Outdoor Miner*. It was one of the best songs Ed Ball ever did. The flip was a play on a song by American garage punk band The Standells, *Sometimes Good Guys Don't Wear White*.

The follow-up *The Odd Man Out* was taken from a film title. Musically - the ska revivalish song was a bit of a cash-in on 2-Tone. Ed Ball got Pye to pay £3,000 for him to make the record at the Wessex production company and recording studio in Portsmouth. Initially 1,000 copies were released on Wessex, but then Pye took up the option and issued it on their Blueprint subsidiary.

Ed was a great fan of "The Prisoner", which explained the selection of *I Helped Patrick McGoohan Escape*. This humorous tribute to the TV series came with a guitar riff lifted straight out of The Spencer Davis Group's *Keep On Runnin'*. It was later recorded by his next band **The Times**.

The Final Countdown (Re-Elect The President NIXON 4) 1988 compilation gave a further airing to *The Odd Man Out*. More recently, a German 7" EP *Boys About Town* (Little Teddy LITE 736) 1995 includes *(There's A) Cloud Over Liverpool* live on K.U.S.F. radio, *Odd Man Out* and *I Apologise* can both be heard on *This Is Mod, Vol. 2* (Anagram CDMGRAM 101) 1996 and *I Apologise* also figured on *100% British Mod* (Captain Mod MODSKA DCD 8) 1998.

The Teenbeats

Personnel incl: HUGGY LEAVER   vcls

45s: I Can't Control Myself/I Never Win (PS)   (Safari SAFE 17) 1979
       Strength Of The Nation/
       I'm Gone Tomorrow (PS)   (Safari SAFE 19) 1979

A mod revival band from Hastings in Sussex, who had a strong reputation as a live band and a charismatic frontman in Huggy Leaver. They chose the old Troggs' hit *I Can't Control Myself* for their first release and also figured on the *Uppers On The South Downs* (Safari UPP 1) 1980 compilation. The follow-up *Strength Of The Nation* was quite anthemic. They had a good live reputation.

A projected third single on Red Shadow *Can't Dance (To The Music)* never saw the light of day and this five-piece were history soon into the start of the new decade.

Both sides of their second 45 later resurfaced on *This Is Mod, Vol. 5* (Anagram CDMGRAM 110) 1997.

The Television Personalities

Personnel:			
(up to	ED BALL	organ, vcls	ABC EFG
1986)	GERRARD BENNETT	drms	A
	JOHN BENNETT	bs	ABC
	JOE FOSTER	gtr	AB EFG
	DAN TREACY	vcls	ABCDEFG
	MARK 'EMPIRE' SHEPPARD		
	(of Swell Maps)	drms	BCDE
	BERNARD COOPER	bs	DE
	MARK FLUNDER	bs	F
	DAVE MUSKER	organ	FG
	JOWE HEAD	bs	G

ALBUMS: 1(C) AND DON'T THE KIDS JUST LOVE IT
(up to   (Rough Trade ROUGH 24) 1981
1986)   2(E) MUMMY YOU'RE NOT WATCHING ME
                                  (Whaam! WHAAM 3) 1982
         3(E) THEY COULD HAVE BEEN BIGGER
               THAN THE BEATLES   (Whaam! BIG 5) 1982
         4(-) TURN ON.... TUNE IN (unreleased) (Whaam BIG 10) 1983
         5(G) THE PAINTED WORD   (Illuminated JAMS 37) 1985

NB: (1) The first 1,000 copies came with an insert. (1) reissued in 1984 and again (Fire REFIRE 7) 1991. (2) was a limited edition of 3,500. The first 1,000 copies had an insert. (2) later reissued (Dreamworld BIG DREAM 1) 1986 and again (Fire REFIRE 8) 1991. (3) was a limited edition of 2,500 with a hand-painted sleeve. (3) later reissued (Dreamworld BIG DREAM 2) 1986 and again (Fire REFIRE 9) 1991. (5) originally scheduled for release in 1983 (Whaam! BIG 7), but later cancelled. Issued again (Fire REFIRE 10) 1991. There's also a CD compilation *Primetime 1981 - 1992* (Reactive REMCD 529) 1998; 12" EP *How I Learned To Love The Bomb* (Overground OVER 30) 1993 and *Chocolat Art (A Special Tribute To James Last)* (Pastell POWCD 2) 1993; There was also a cassette-only fan club issue *I Know Where Dan Treacy Lives (Live At Forum 20/9/84)* (Dreamworld HWDS 001) 1984.

EP: 1(A) WHERE'S BILL GRUNDY NOW? (Part-time Punks/
             Where's Bill Grundy Now?/Happy Families/Posing At
             The Roundhouse) (PS)   (Kings Road LYN 5976/7) 1978

NB: (1) The first 2,000 copies came with a hand-stamped label thereafter there were three different picture sleeve designs with white labels (LYN 5976/7). The EP was reissued (Rough Trade RT 033) 1979, with a different picture sleeve and printed labels.

45s: *   14th Floor/
(up to   Oxford Street W1 (PS)   (Teen '78 SRTS/CUS 77/089) 1978
1986)   Smashing Time/
            King And Country (PS)   (Rough Trade RT 051) 1980
            I Know Where Syd Barrett Lives/
            Arthur The Gardener (PS) (Rough Trade RT 063) 1981
        +   Three Wishes/Geoffrey Ingram/
            And Don't The Kids Just Love It (PS) (Whaam! WHAAM 4) 1982
        α   Biff Bang Pow!/A Picture Of Dorian Grey (one-sided flexidisc)
                (Creation Artefact 002/Lyntone LYN 13546) 1982
            A Sense Of Belonging/
            Paradise Estate (PS)   (Rough Trade RT 109) 1983
        β   How I Learnt To Love The Bomb/Then God Snaps His Fingers/
            Now You're Just Being Ridiculous (12", PS)
                                     (Dreamworld DREAM 4) 1986
        χ   How I Learnt To Love The Bomb/Grocer's Daughter/
            Girl Called Charity (7", PS) (Dreamworld DREAM 10) 1986
Reissue: # 14th Floor/Oxford Street W1 (PS) (Overground OVER 03) 1989

NB: * Copies came in various different picture sleeves. + Just 2,000 copies were pressed. They came in two different picture sleeve designs. α Some copies came with 'Communication Blur' fanzine. β Limited edition of 3,700. χ Limited edition of 1,000. # These came in numbered picture sleeves in yellow, black or white vinyl.

Television Personalities emerged out of the indie punk explosion of the early eighties, but as you will read, their influences and sound was different to the other bands. They were formed in Chelsea, London in 1976 by Edward Ball and Dan Treacy, who quickly recruited Joe Foster and two brothers John and Gerrard Bennett.

They were originally known as Teen 78, but as Dan Treacy was writing titles on the white test pressing labels of their first single *14th Floor* to send off to John Peel, he decided to put the line-up as Hughie Green, Bob Monkhouse and Bruce Forsyth just for a joke! In an interview with Record Collector's John Reed he explained how the name **Television Personalities** came to him as he was about the mail the record off to John Peel. He liked it and gave it repeated airplay. Now one of punk's major collectables, the record was issued in a number of different picture sleeves. Around 100 came on glossy art paper depicting a photo of a young Daniel Treacy sitting on Santa Claus' knee. Other versions had just writing on the sleeve. There was also a third version with a picture of Cilla Black and someone looking like the Queen riding a bike with Alan Price. Musically, we're talking a typical punk thrash, but the single has remained much in demand by

TV Personalities - I Know Where Syd Barrett Lives.

collectors. This prompted the reissue on Overground in 1989. This came in a newly designed picture sleeve and copies were pressed on yellow, white or black vinyl.

Spurred on Dan re-entered the studio on 26th August 1978 with Edward Ball on drums and backing vocals to record the *Where's Bill Grundy Now?* EP. The recording session cost just £22.50. The EP was released in November 1978 on the Kings Road record label that Bill and Treacy had recently set up. The first 2,000 copies featured a picture of a headless Reginauld Maudling MP on the front, track details on the back and the record labels hand-stamped by Dan. Later copies came in wrap around sleeve designs - the most common featured a picture of a punk in sunglasses with a letter from Gary Bushell (then with 'Sounds' on the back). The four-track single became a success largely due to the repeated airplay which John Peel gave to one of the tracks, *Part-Time Punks*. The cut was also featured on Rough Trade's U.S. sampler, *Wanna Buy A Bridge?* (Rough US 3) 1980. Collectors will also be interested in a very rare promo version of *Where's Bill Grundy Now?* with hand-stamped labels and individually typed lyrics/poetry on the sleeve.

Dan virtually retired on the profits from the EP, but was persuaded to return to the studio by Rough Trade's Geoff Travis to make some new recordings in January 1980. The final vinyl to result from this was a third 45, *Smashing Time*. The first 2,000 pressings came with an orange hula-hoop girl on one side of the label, while later pressings came in standard Rough Trade labels. Musically, this 45 was far removed from punk and the intro to the flip side *King Of Country* even recalled The Byrds' *Eight Miles High*.

In the summer of 1980 **Television Personalities** recorded their sole John Peel session. Then, in November, they embarked on their first European tour which included a residency in Berlin. Joe Foster recorded a solo single under the name **Missing Scientists** for Rough Trade shortly before leaving **Television Personalities** due to musical differences.

The first **Television Personalities** album *And Don't The Kids Just Love It*, released in January 1981, confirmed the band's transition from punk to sixties - influenced garage-pop, which had begun with their previous 45. One cut, the quaint *I Know Where Syd Barrett Lives* was culled for 45 release. There is also an extremely rare Japanese release of this 45 in a gatefold picture sleeve with a different picture sleeve which die-hard fans of the band will want to track down, if they can ever find a copy for sale. The album is now rare and collectable. It was reissued in 1984 and these copies are easier to obtain.

Early in 1981, Dan Treacy and Ed Ball set up a new record label called Whaam! after differences with Rough Trade. The first releases were a 45 by Ed Ball's new band **The Times** and by **Gifted Children** (a pseudonym project, see entry for details). Ed Ball rejoined **Television Personalities** on bass for live gigs between February-May 1981 and Joe Foster rejoined for two Berlin gigs with Nico. Come August 1981, with their *Syd Barrett* single in the Dutch charts, Ball was briefly back in the line-up again for a memorable Dutch tour.

Back in Britain, the band became a part of the mini psychedelic revival in the summer of 1981. They recorded their *Mummy You're Not Watching Me* album, which was released in January 1982. This is now rare and collectable, particularly with its original insert, which the first 1,000 copies contained. Musically, it utilises keyboards and basic studio effects to attempt to recreate the spacey psychedelia of bands like Pink Floyd. This works most successfully on *David Hockney Diaries*, but the low budget production makes the album only a partially successful venture. It also includes both sides of the **Gifted Children** 45. The album was reissued in 1986 on Dreamworld. In June 1982, *Three Wishes* (which later appeared on the *They Could Have Been Bigger Than The Beatles* album) was issued on a 45 with *Geoffrey Ingram* (from their first album) and the previously unreleased *And Don't The Kids Just Love It* (the title name of the first album). The 45 came in a wraparound sleeve design with a number of different variations of the lettering.

Later, in October 1982, 2,500 copies of *They Could Have Been Bigger Than The Beatles* were issued, with spray painted sleeves. This album contained their debut *14th Floor* 45, demos and out-takes, two covers of Creation's finest *Painter Man* and *Making Time* - a total of sixteen art rock tracks in all. *The Boy In The Paisley Shirt* particularly stood out on this album, which was also reissued in 1986 on Dreamworld. It received good reviews, particularly in Europe. Unfortunately Dan Treacy suffered a nervous breakdown which prevented them capitalising in the short-term on the album's success.

In the Autumn they took to the road again with new bassist Mark Flunder. Not long after Dan expanded the line-up to include Dave Musker (organ) and Joe Foster rejoined yet again on 12-string guitar. This line-up toured Italy, then with Flunder having been replaced by former **Swell Maps**' Jowe Head, headed for Germany in January 1983. When they returned Dan suffered a further nervous breakdown. This rendered the band impotent for most of the year.

Late in 1983 Dan entered the studio again with Joe Foster and some assistance from Mark Sheppard, who went on to play with **Robyn Hitchcock**. They planned to call it *And God Snaps His Fingers* and release it on Whaam! When Rough Trade got to hear it, they expressed a wish to release it and so two cuts *A Sense Of Belonging* and *Paradise Estate* were put out on a 45 to preview the forthcoming album. The cover depicted a photograph of a battered child, which soon led to controversy as the press denounced it as a publicity stunt. Rough Trade's distributors refused to handle it and so the label quickly deleted it. This led **Television Personalities** to sever their link with Rough Trade for good! It was January 1985 before the album finally appeared on Iluminated Records. It contained thirteen cuts - all originals - which ranged from psychedelia to haunting rock, which exuded a very melancholic mood. Overall, it was well worth waiting for and was selling well until disaster struck again. Illuminated Records went into receivership! Like their previous albums, this one has become a collectors item too.

After this latest disaster Joe Foster left due to "musical differences" again. Dave Musker departed, too, and the pair of them helped establish Alan McGee's Creation label. Foster released two of the first singles on the label as **Slaughter Joe**, while Musker joined The Jasmine Minks. Foster later went on to establish his own Kaleidoscope Sound label which spawned My Bloody Valentine among others.

Meanwhile, **Television Personalities** went out on the road again as a trio comprising Treacy, Head and a new drummer Jeff Bloom. They continued to gig and record for years but that's another story.

In 1985, Dan Treacy established a new label Dreamworld to issue old and in demand **Television Personalities** albums and other recordings. This is a cheaper way of picking up copies of *Mummy You're Not Watching Me* and *They Could Have Been Bigger Than The Beatles* which sell for half the price of the originals.

The 12" EP *How I Learned To Love The Bomb* compiles five tracks from two 7" and 12" singles issued during 1986. The evocatively titled songs were (apart from the title cuts) *She Was Only The Grocer's Daughter, A Girl Called Charity, Then God Snaps His Fingers* and *Now You're Just Being Ridiculous*.

Chocolat Art (A Special Tribute To James Last) is a CD issue of a 1984 gig. The twenty-two tracks include several diverse cover versions including *I'm Waiting For The Man, Louie Louie, Helter Skelter, I Can't Explain, See My Friends* and *Interstellar Overdrive*.

They've also been featured on a number of compilations:- *Three Wishes* was included on *Seeds 1: Pop* (Cherry Red BRED 74) 1987 on which it

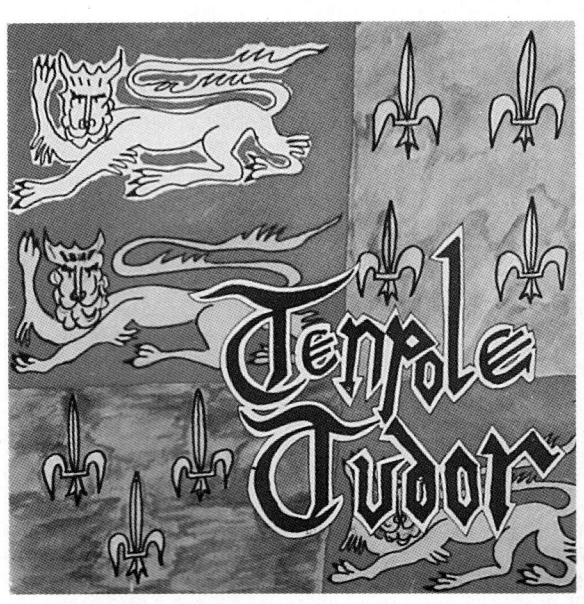

TENPOLE TUDOR - Eddie, Old Bob, Dick & Garry.

stands out from the other tracks and on *Alive At The Living Room* (Creation CRELP 001) 1984, which also featured *A Day In Heaven*. *All For Art... And Art For All* (Whaam! BIG 8) 1984 gave a further airing to *The Dream Inspires*, *Happy All The Time* and *My Favourite Films*. *Back To Vietnam* resurfaced on *Communicate!!!! Live At Thames Poly* (dble) (T.P.S.U. RECORD 0001) 1985. *Beyond The Wildwood - A Tribute To Syd Barrett* (Imaginary ILLUSION 001) 1987 featured their version of *Apples And Oranges*. The cassette compilation *Everlasting* (Rhythm BAIT 1) 1989 included *Just Me And My Desire*. *Let's Try Another Ideal Guest House* (Shelter SHELTER 2) 1987 included *Miracles Take Longer*. The CD-only sampler *15 Flaming Groovies* (Fire FIRE CD 19) 1989 included *Room At The Top Of The Stairs* and *My Hedonistic Tendencies* (the latter track was from the later 1990 album *Privilege*). Finally, *Part-time Punks* got a further airing on *1-2-3-4 - A History Of Punk And New Wave 1976-1979* (MCA/Universal MCD 60066), a 5-CD box set issued in 1999 and again on *25 Years Of Rough Trade Shops* (4-CD box set) (Mute CDSTUMM 191) in 2001.

Certainly one of the most-interesting bands to emerge from the new wave era it's no surprise that **Television Personalities** have become one of its most collectable bands.

The Tennis Shoes

Personnel:	JOHN BAYLEY	vcls, gtr, stylophone	A
	STEWART BOOTH	vcls	A
	KEN DAMPIER	vcls, gtr	A
	HOWARD EDGAR	bs	A
	BEVERLEY GLICK	vcls	A
	PETER HORNSBY	keyb'ds	A
	FIONA IMLAH	vcls	A
	COLIN P. MINCHIN	gtr	A
	GLENN MORRIS	drms	A

| 45: | Rolf Is Stranger Than Richard/ Medium Wave/So Large (PS) | (Bonaparte BONE 3) 1978 |

Tennis Shoes played a sort of rubbishy studentish type pop. Eminently forgettable.

Tenpole Tudor

Personnel:	DICK CRIPPEN	bs, vcls	A
	OLD BOB KINGSTON	gtr, vcls	A
	GARRY LONG	drms, vcls	A
	EDDIE TENPOLE	vcls	A
	(MUNCH UNIVERSE	gtr	A)

HCP

| ALBUMS: | 1(A) | EDDIE, OLD BOB, DICK & GARRY | (Stiff SEEZ 31) 1981 | 44 |
| | 2(A) | LET THE FOUR WINDS BLOW | (Stiff SEEZ 42) 1981 | - |

NB: (1) also issued on CD (Repertoire REP 4220-WY) 1991. (2) also issued on CD (Disky STIFFCD 12) 1994. There are also two CD compilations, *Wunderbar (The Best Of Tenpole Tudor)* (Dojo DOJOCD 76) 1992 and *Swords Of A Thousand Men* (2CD set) (Recall/Red Snapper SMDCD 144) 1997.

HCP

45s:	* Who Killed Bambi/Silly Thing (PS)	(Virgin VS 256) 1979	6
	* Rock Around The Clock/ The Great Rock 'n' Roll Swindle (PS)	(Virgin VS 290) 1979	21
	Real Fun/What's In A Word (PS)	(Korova KOW 4) 1980	-
	Three Bells In A Row/Fashion/ Rock 'n' Roll Music (PS)	(Stiff BUY 98) 1980	-
	Swords Of A Thousand Men/ Love And Food (PS)	(Stiff BUY 109) 1981	6
	Wunderbar/Tenpole 45 (PS)	(Stiff BUY 120) 1981	16
	Throwing My Baby Out With The Bathwater/ Conga Tribe (PS)	(Stiff BUY 129) 1981	49
	Let The Four Winds Blow/ Sea Of Thunder (PS)	(Stiff BUY 137) 1982	-

NB: * These were solo Eddie Tenpole 45s with **The Sex Pistols** on the flip side.

Eddie Tenpole was born in Scotland in 1955. He first came to prominence in the 1978 film 'The Great Rock 'n' Roll Swindle' singing *Who Killed Bambi* and *Rock Around The Clock*, which were both hit singles. He was a stand-in vocalist for **The Sex Pistols** after John Lydon left them. Then, in late 1979, he formed his own band **Tenpole Tudor**, who were based in London.

The band adopted a personna of drunken debauchery which was aided by Eddie's unique and wobbly vocals. Eddie usually appeared in a kilt. After an initial 45 for Korova, they signed to Stiff. Their three track 7" debut for Stiff, released in October 1980, included a cover of Chuck Berry's *Rock 'n' Roll Music*. It was the highly accessible pop-punk *Swords Of A Thousand Men* which broke them into the U.K. Top Ten. It climbed to No. 6 during a twelve-week chart residency. The same month, March 1981, a debut album *Eddie, Old Bob, Dick & Garry* was released. The stronger material on this tended to be the 45 releases - *Swords Of A Thousand Men* and *Wunderbar*. Their rock energy and good humour shine through and on the better tracks there are catchy melodies, although there are also real turkeys too. The album sold quite well, climbing to No. 44 and spending eight weeks in the charts.

Wunderbar, from their debut album, delivered a second significant hit, in August 1981, peaking at No. 16 and spending a total of nine weeks in the charts.

A further 45, *Throwing My Baby Out With The Bathwater* was released in October 1981, as a preview to a new album. The 45 spent five weeks in the charts climbing to No. 49. The album, *Let The Four Winds Blow* followed the following month. It experimented with pseudo-country, mock-funk and other styles, but it didn't sell as well. In February 1982, the title cut was issued as a 45 and when that flopped the group disbanded.

Some collectors may be interested in a Canadian-only release *Swords Of A Thousand Men*, which collected the best tracks from their two albums inside the artwork from the second one. More accessible, though, are two CD compilations *Wunderbar (The Best Of Tenpole Tudor)* and *Swords Of A Thousand Men*, a 2-CD set.

After their demise, SNP-supporter Eddie recorded a further 45 for Stiff *The Hayrick Song* in both 7" and 12" format. It didn't really sell and he went on to an acting career. As well as appearing in a lot of TV adverts, he was also in the film 'Absolute Beginners'. The Tudors went their own way also recording a 45 for Stiff - *Tied Up With Lou Cool* in February 1983. When this didn't register they drifted out of the music business. For a short while, though, **Tenpole Tudor** were quite fun.

Wunderbar (The Best Of Tenpole Tudor) as one would expect collects their best songs, including the title cut, *Swords Of A Thousand Men* and *Throwing My Baby Out With The Bath Water*.

The Swords Of A Thousand Men, issued by Recall/Red Snapper in 1997, is a two-CD set drawn from their two Stiff albums and 'B' sides. It highlights that none of their remaining material was up to the standard of their classic 'A' sides *Wunderbar*, *Swords Of A Thousand Men* and *Throwing My Baby Out With The Bath Water*, but it's pleasant enough.

Inevitably **Tenpole Tudor** have appeared on some various artists compilations, including *Wunderbar* on *New Wave Classics* (2-CD) (Disky DOU 878282) 1998 and *Swords Of A Thousand Men* on *Teenage Kicks* (PolyGram TV 2523382) 1995.

Terri and The Terrors

Personnel:	TERRI HOOLEY	vcls	A
	(GORDON BLAIR	bs	A)
	(RONNIE MATTHEWS	gtr	A)
	(BRIAN YOUNG	gtr	A)

| 45: | Laugh At Me/ Laugh At Me (Again) (Folded PS) | (Fresh FRESH 4) 1979 |

NB: The flip was credited to Terri and The My Ways.

Terri and The Terrors were actually Good Vibrations' owner Terri Hooley backed by Brian, Gordon and Ronnie from **Rudi** plus some members of another Northen Irish punk band **The Outcasts**. Their sole 45 was a cover of Sonny Bono's *Laugh At Me*. It begins with an extended vocal introduction which talks about 'setting those controls for the dark side of the moon' and asks 'is she really going out with him?'. Hooley then goes on to say 'I never thought I'd get to cut a record by myself but I've got something I want to say' before embarking on the 'song', which contains virtually spoken lyrics. A novelty item for sure. You can also check it out on *Good Vibrations: The Punk Singles Collection* (Anagram CD PUNK 36) 1994. The 45 was actually released on Fresh Records. There's an orchestral version of the song on the flip side credited to Terri and The My Ways.

The The

Personnel:	PETER 'Triash' ASHWORTH	drms	A
(up to	MATT JOHNSON	vcls, gtr	AB
1986)	TOM JOHNSTONE	bs	A
	KEITH LAWS	synth, drm machine	A

				HCP
ALBUMS:	1(B)	BURNING BLUE SOUL	(4AD CAD 113) 1981	-
(up to	2(C)	SOUL MINING	(Epic 25525) 1983	27
1986)	3(C)	INFECTED	(Epic 26770) 1986	14

NB: (1) credited to Matt Johnson. It was later repackaged and reissued in a different sleeve but with the same catalogue number and later on CD (4AD HAD 113CD) 1984. (2) initially issued with a 12" single containing *Perfect, Soup Of Mixed Emotions* and *Fruit Of The Heart* and later on CD (Epic CD 25525) 1987 with a bonus cut *Perfect* and again (Epic 4663372) 1990. The first 25,000 copies of (3) came with the 'Torture' sleeve and poster. Later copies have a different catalogue number (TA 3588). (3) later issued on CD (Epic CD 26770) 1987 with extra 12" mixes of *Sweet Bird Of Truth*, *Slow Train To Dawn* and *Infected*.

			HCP
45s:	Controversial Subject/Black And White (PS)	(4AD AD 10) 1980	-
(up to	Cold Spell Ahead/Hot Ice (PS)	(Some Bizzare BZS 4) 1981	-
1986)	Uncertain Smile/Three Orange Kisses From Kazan (PS)	(Epic EPC A 2787) 1982	68
*	Uncertain Smile/Three Orange Kisses From Kazan/ Waiting For The Upturn (12", PS)	(Epic EPC 13 2787) 1982	-
	Perfect/The Nature Of Virtue (PS)	(Epic EPC A 3119) 1983	-
	Perfect/ The Nature Of Virtue (12", PS)	(Epic EPC A 13 3119) 1983	-
	This Is The Day/ Mental Healing Process (PS)	(Epic A 3710) 1983	71
	This Is The Day/Mental Healing Process/Absolute Liberation/ Leap Into The Wind (7" double-pack, PS)	(Epic A 3710) 1983	-
	This Is The Day/I've Been Waiting For Tomorrow (All Of My Life) (12", PS)	(Epic TA 3710) 1983	-
+	Dumb As Death's Head (flexi)	(Melody Maker) 1983	-
	Uncertain Smile/ Dumb As Death's Head (PS)	(Epic A 3588) 1983	-
	Uncertain Smile/Soul Mining (12", PS)	(Epic TA 3588) 1983	-
x	Sweet Bird Of Truth/Harbour Lights/ Sleeping Juice (12", PS)	(Epic TRUTH 1) 1986	-
	Heartland/Born In The New S.A. (PS)	(Epic TRUTH 2) 1986	29
	Heartland/Born In The New S.A./ Flesh And Bones (12", PS)	(Epic TRUTH T2) 1986	-
	Heartland/Born In The New S.A./ Sweet Bird Of Truth (12", PS)	(Epic TRUTH Q2) 1986	-
α	Heartland/Born In The New S.A./Sweet Bird Of Truth/ Harbour Lights (Cassette)	(Epic TRUTH C2) 1986	-
	Heartland/Born In The New S.A./Flesh And Bones/ Perfect/Fruit Of The Heart (12" double-pack PS)	(Epic TRUTH D2) 1986	-
	Infected/Disturbed (PS)	(Epic TRUTH 3) 1986	48
β	Infected (Energy Mix)/ Disturbed (12", PS)	(Epic TRUTH T3) 1986	-
α	Infected (Skull Crusher Mix)/Disturbed/ Soul Mining/Sinking Feeling/Infected	(Epic TRUTH C3) 1986	-
	Infected/Infected (Energy Mix)/Disturbed/ Soul Mining (Remix)/ Sinking Feeling (12", double-pack, PS)	(Epic TRUTH D3) 1986	-

NB: * Some copies came on yellow vinyl. + This had *Jonathon* by The Sines on the reverse side. x This was a limited edition release of 7,500. α Cassette releases. β some copies came with a different uncensored picture sleeve.

The The were led and centred around the very private Matt Johnson who was sometimes dubed 'the Howard Hughes of Rock' because of his reclusive nature. He grew up in Loughton, Essex, but after leaving school at 16 moved up to London, where he worked for a music publisher. In the late seventies he met up with John Hyde and Colin Tucker forming a trio called **Plain Characters**, who released a few cult singles. They later formed a studio outfit **The Gadgets** whose music was based around a Wasp synthsizer and drum machine.

By 1979 Matt had also teamed up to write songs with Keith Laws. In time they were supplemented by Peter Ashworth on drums and Tom Johnstone on bass and became known as **The The**. A debut 45 *Controversial Subject* was issued in July 1980. Although all four members are listed on the sleeve (Ashworth under the pseudonym 'Triash') only Laws and Johnson actually played on the disc. Just 2,500 copies were pressed so it's now hard to track down.

With Laws rapidly losing interest in the project Matt Johnson recorded a solo album *Burning Blue Soul*, which was issued in August 1981 in a 'psychedelic eye' sleeve, which is now quite rare. The album was a meandering affair which had its moments but lacked any overall consistency. When two years later 4AD reissued the album, Johnson hated the original artwork so much that he got his then girlfriend Fiona Skinner to redesign both the inner and outer sleeve and sleevenotes were added.

Although Keith Laws played on the second The The 45 *Cold Spell Ahead* by the time of its release in September 1981 he had left the group.

By late 1981, the Some Bizzare label had achieved considerable chart success with **Soft Cell** and on the strength of this got **The The** signed by CBS/Epic. Initially they must have been disappointed when Johnson was so dissatisfied with his first project, an album called *Pornography Of Despair*, that he ensured it was never released.

This meant that **The The**'s eventual first release for Epic was an updated version of *Cold Spell Ahead*, which eventually transformed into *Uncertain Smile*. As well as the usual 7" and 12" formats there was also a limited edition 12" yellow vinyl version which has become collectable. The single, which was a minor hit peaking at No. 68 during its three week chart stay, helped establish **The The** as a cult band. The cut was also included on *Sounds Schizophrenia* (CBS/Sounds SS 10) 1983.

A further single *Perfect* followed in February 1983 but despite a favourable critical reception it failed to repeat their earlier chart success. They also enjoyed a five-night residency at The Marquee Club in Wardour Street.

In September *This Is The Day* returned them to the lower echelons of the charts, climbing to No. 71 during its three-week chart sojourn. In addition to the 7" and 12" releases there is also a double-pack which included tracks from the scrapped *Pornography Of Despair* album which are not available elsewhere and hence of particular interest to the band's fans.

The first **The The** album *Soul Mining* emerged in October 1983. Guesting with Matt Johnson on the record were Zeke Manyika (of Orange Juice), Jim Thirwell, **Thomas Leer** and Jools Holland. Early copies of the album came

THE THE - Infected.

THE THE - This Is The Day.

with a free 12" single featuring a re-recorded version of *Perfect* and two previously unreleased instrumentals *Soup Of Mixed Emotions* and *Fruits Of The Heart*. The highlights of the album were really the earlier singles *This Is The Day* and *Uncertain Smile*. Although it didn't get that much airplay it sold well reaching No. 27 during its five weeks in the charts. Collectors often prefer the cassette version of the album as it contains several bonus tracks.

1984 - 85 was a particularly quiet period for Matt Johnson, but one new **The The** recording *Flesh And Bones* appeared on *If You Can't Please Yourself, You Can't Please Your Soul* (EMI TAPE 1) 1985. When he returned in 1986, it was with a limited edition 12" single *Sweet Bird Of Truth*. The lyrics were controversial, dealing with the Middle Eastern crisis and the consequent lack of airplay condemned it to obscurity. Their next 45 *Heartland* was uncontroversial and released in no less than five different formats. It brought them their biggest hit so far, spending an impressive ten weeks in the charts and cracking the Top 30 at No. 29. Just two months later they were into controversy again as a result of the 'Masturbating Devil' cover to their next 45 and title track to their forthcoming album *Infected*. Many found the cover offensive and with record shops refusing to stock it and no airplay Epic quickly substituted an alternative sleeve. The single did pierce the Top 50, peaking at No. 48 during its five weeks in the charts.

When the *Infected* album was released in November 1986 (over three years after their previous album *Soul Mining*), it was well received, spending thirty weeks in the charts and rising to No. 14. It contained their previous three singles *Sweet Bird Of Truth*, *Heartland*, and *Infected* and also spawned further ones in 1987 - *Slow Train To Dawn*, which included a duet with Neneh Cherry, as well as a reissue of *Sweet Bird Of Truth*. To accompany the album "Infected - The Movie", a largely self-financed project filmed in places as diverse as The Bronx and The Amazon was released and premiered in a special edition of "The Tube" on Channel 4. It helped publicise the band to previously untapped audiences and their effective blend of often original and accessible music continued to ensure them a strong cult following for many years to come.

In their early days **The The** also contributed an untitled track to the futurist *Some Bizzarre Album* (Some Bizzare SBL 1) in 1981. Both sides of their debut 45 *Controversial Subject* and *Black And White* later resurfaced on *Natures Mortes* (4AD CAD 117CD) in 1997. You'll also find *Controversial Subject* on *A History Of Punk, Vol. 2* (Virgin CDOVD 487) 1997 and *This Is The Day* on *Wave Party* (Columbia 4758322) 1995.

Theatre Of Hate

Personnel:			
	KIRK BRANDON	vcls, gtr	ABCD
	LUKE RANDALL	drms	AB
	JONATHAN WERNER	bs	A
	SIMON WERNER	gtr	A
	STEVE GUTHRIE	gtr	B
	JAMIE STUART	bs	B
	BILLY DUFFY	bs	B
	JOHN BOY LENNARD	sax	CD
	NIGEL PRESTON	drms	CD
	STAN STAMMERS	bs	CD

HCP

ALBUMS:	1(B)	HE WHO DARES WINS - LIVE AT THE WAREHOUSE, LEEDS	(SS SSSSS 1P) 1981	-
	2(-)	LIVE AT THE LYCEUM (compilation)	(Straight Music TOH 1) 1981	-
	3(C)	WESTWORLD	(Burning Rome TOH 1) 1982	17
	4(-)	HE WHO DARES WINS - LIVE IN BERLIN	(SS SSSSS 2P) 1982	-
	5(-)	REVOLUTION (The Best Of...) (Compilation)	(Burning Rome TOH 2) 1984	67
	6(-)	REVOLUTION/HE WHO DARES WINS - LIVE IN BERLIN	(Burning Rome TOH 2C) 1984	-
	7(-)	ORIGINAL SIN LIVE	(Dojo DOJOLP 19) 1985	-

NB: (1) also issued on CD (Loma LOMACD 35) 1996. (2) was a cassette release. (3) reissued (Burning Rome BRR 010) 1991 on vinyl with a free 4-track EP and on CD with five bonus cuts. Later issued again on CD (Dojo DOJOCD 220) 1996 and (Snapper SMMCD 511) 1997. (6) was a double-play cassette. Also relevant are:- *Complete Singles Collection* (Cherry Red CDMGRAM 93) 1995; *He Who Dares I & II* (Dojo LOMA CD 35) 1996 is a reissue of (1) and (4) on CD; and *The Singles Collection* (Yeahh! YEAHH 2) 1999.

HCP

45s:	Original Sin/Legion (PS)	(SS SS 3) 1980 -
	Rebel Without A Brain/ My Own Invention (PS)	(Burning Rome BRR 1) 1981 -
	Nero/Incinerator (12", PS)	(Burning Rome BRR 1931) 1981 -
	Do You Believe In The Westworld?/ Propaganda (PS)	(Burning Rome BRR 2) 1981 40
	Do You Believe In The Westworld?/(Alt. Version)/ Propaganda/(Alt. Version)/Original Sin (Re-recording) (12", PS)	(Burning Rome BRR T2/2T) 1982 -
	The Hop/Conquistador (PS)	(Burning Rome BRR 3) 1982 70
*	Ghost Of Love (Live)	(Masterbag BAG 002) 1982 -
+	Poppies (Flexi)	(Vinyl V 17) 1982 -
	Eastworld/Assegai (PS)	(Burning Rome BRR 4) 1982 -
	Eastworld (Russian Roulette)/Poppies/ Assegai (Extended) (12", PS)	(Burning Rme BRR 4T) 1982 -
x	The Wake/Love Is A Ghost/Poppies/ Legion	(Bliss TOH 1EP) 1985 -
	The Hop/Conquistador/Do You Believe In The Westworld?/ Original Sin (12", PS)	(Burning Rome BRRT 1985) 1985 -

NB: * This flexi came free with 'Masterbag' magazine. + This flexi came free with the Dutch 'Vinyl' magazine. x This live EP was given away free with a 'Theatre Of Hate' T-Shirt!

Theatre Of Hate were formed by Kirk Brandon, who previously fronted a London-based band called **The Pack**, whose records are all highly collectable now. *He Who Dares Wins - Live At The Warehouse, Leeds*, *Live At The Lyceum* and *Live In Berlin* were all official bootlegs released to reduce the sale of over-priced illegal cassettes of the band live. Their studio album *Westworld* was produced by **The Clash**'s Mick Jones. This probably captures them at their best. Its better moments include *Do You Believe?* which dealt with the major world powers and the aftermath of a neutron bomb explosion, the haunting *Love Is A Ghost* and the unnerving *Do You Believe In The Westworld?*, which got to No. 40 when released as a 45. The album fared well commercially too. It climbed to No. 17 during its six weeks in the charts and had a decidedly punkish feel. The vinyl reissue of this album in 1991 came with a free 4-track EP containing *Original Sin*, *Legion* and two songs from their days as **The Pack**, *Heathen* and *Brave New Soldiers*. By contrast the CD version of the reissue includes previously unreleased versions of *Propaganda*, *Rebel Without A Brain*, *Incinerator* and *Legion* as well as a remix of *Nero*. All of these additional items are worth hearing, especially the hard to find and sought-after **Pack** 45, but it was a shame that you had to buy both the vinyl and CD reissue to get to hear all this extra material.

The band also appeared on two flexis. The first of these *Ghosts Of Love* was given away with 'Masterbag' magazine. The second *Poppies* was given away with a Dutch magazine 'Vinyl'.

He Who Dares Wins - Live In Berlin was produced by the band's manager Terry Razor. It had a very full rock sound and featured saxophone.

Brandon terminated **Theatre Of Hate** in September 1982, but regrouped with manager Terry Razor and Stan Stammers to form **Spear Of Destiny** in December 1982. Of the remaining members Lennard headed to Canada

THEATRE OF HATE - The Hop.

where he formed Diodes. Preston joined The Sex Gang Children and was later in **The Cult**.

In 1984, Burning Rome, which Brandon and Razor owned put out a 'Best Of' collection called *Revolution*. This included their finest moments and got to No. 67, spending three weeks in the charts.

Later in 1985, Dojo purchased a live tape of the band which was released as *Original Sin - Live*.

In 1993, Demon released *Ten Years After* which is what would have been their second album. It remained unreleased because the group split and later evolved into **Spear Of Destiny**. Many of the tracks on this album found their way onto **Spear Of Destiny**'s *Grapes Of Wrath* album, but they didn't all and the CD includes some previously unreleased takes, notably the eerie *The Man Who Tunes The Drums* and *The Grapes Of Wrath*, which make it of particular interest.

In 1996, Dojo reissued their two official live bootlegs - albums (1) and (4) in the discography - on one CD. The sound quality is slightly inferior on the Leeds set and there's also considerable duplication of material between the two sets, which makes the CD largely of archival value. Still it serves as a reminder that at its best their music could be both original and inspired.

The Singles Collection CD rounds up all the tracks the outfit released as singles and includes *Americanos* which would have been their final single had they not split in Autumn 1982. It is also graced with sleevenotes penned by Kirk Brandon himself and CDROM videos for *The Hop* and *Propaganda*, as well as the band's 'Top Of The Pops' appearance performing their No. 40 hit *Do You Believe In The Westworld?*.

Original Sin can also be heard on *Gothic Rock 2* (Jungle FREUD CD 051) 1995.

They Must Be Russians

ALBUM: 1 THEY MUST BE RUSSIANS   (First Floor FF 2) 1983

45: Psycho Analysis/(other side by Joe 9T
    and The Thunderbirds)   (Gemme JOE 9T/LYN 6526) 198?
    Devolution/Infatuation   (Box Office EBOF 4) 1984
    Devolution/Infatuation (12")   (Box Office EBOFT 4) 1984
    Red Square (12")   (Native NTV 7) 1986

A Sheffield band. In addition to the above, they contributed *Where Have I Seen You*, an appealing song with some delightful guitar moments, to *Hicks From The Sticks* (Rockburgh Records ROC 111) in 1980.

Thieves Like Us

Personnel incl: BARRON   A
                 MEREDITH   A
                 PARISH   A
                 STONOR   A

45s: Mind Made/Strike Out (PS)   (Earlobe ELS 1) 1980
     (Do It) For The Rest Of Your Life/Murder In New York/
     Touch Your Love (PS)   (PX 1093) 198?

One of the lesser-known mod revival bands. The *Mind Made* 45 isn't very good, but *(Do It) For The Rest Of Your Life* is well worth a spin.

This Heat

Personnel: CHARLES BULLEN   gtr, viola, vcls   A
            CHARLES HAYWARD   perc, keyb'ds, vcls A
            GARETH WILLIAMS   keyb'ds, gtr, bs, vcls A

ALBUMS: 1(A) THIS HEAT   (Piano THIS 1) 1979
        2(A) DECEIT   (Rough Trade ROUGH 26) 1981

NB: (1) reissued (HEAT 1) in 1988 and also issued on CD (Recommended HEAT 1CD) 1991. (2) also issued on CD (These HEAT 2 CD) 1992. There's also *Repeat* (These HEAT 6 CD) 1993. Both also available on vinyl. Also relevant is *Made Available: John Peel Sessions* (These 10 CD) 1996.

45: Health And Efficiency/Graphic/
     Varispeed (12", PS)   (Piano THIS 1201) 1980

This Heat was formed in 1976 when former Gong, **Raincoats** and Phil Manzanera's Quiet Sun member Charles Hayward linked up with Charles Bullen and Gareth Williams. **This Heat** soon developed into an experimental new wave act utilising tape loops and slick production tricks.

Their debut album features both live and studio cuts from their first two years. The conventional instruments (guitar, clarinet, drums, keyboards etc.) are interspersed with loops, phasing and overdubs in a way that is both adventurous but also emotionally withdrawn. This album was very experimental and combined furious atonal songs like *The Fall Of Saigon*, *Horizontal Hold* and *24 Track Loop* with quieter pieces.

The follow-up *Deceit* was more coherent and intelligent. There is also a tape *This Heat With Mario Boyer Diekauroh* released in France on the Tago Mago label in 1982. This featured tapes of studio sessions the band had in 1977/78 with the Ghanian drummer Mario Boyer.

Repeat consists of two reworked tracks from the past and a previously unissued percussion piece used to accompany a dance at Sadler's Wells. The lengthy revamped version of *24 Track Loop* had previously appeared on the Recommended Records Sampler as *Pool* in very similar forms. Interesting but likely to appeal mostly to fans of the band.

This Heat recorded two sessions for John Peel. The first broadcast on 22nd April 1977, comprised *Full Of Saigon*, *Not Waving But Drowning* and *Horizontal Hold*. The second consisted of *Makershift*, *Sitting*, *Basement Boy*, *Slither* and *Rimp Romp Ramp*. This was broadcast on 24th November 1977.

The *Made Available: John Peel Sessions* CD released in 1996 covers their two broadcasts for Peel in 1977. Now remastered *Horizontal Hold* sounds full of gothic drones, repetition and cross-rhythms - it is an excellent instrumental. *Makeshift Swahili* is similar, but there are also excursions into

THIEVES LIKE US - Mind Made.

THIS MORTAL COIL - Song To The Siren.

more serene, pieces like *Rimp Romp Ramp*, which draws on a wide source of sounds. This is a very interesting archive release.

This Mortal Coil

Personnel:	Various members of **Cocteau Twins**, Dead Can Dance, **Modern English**, Xmal Deutschland and other 4AD artists		A
			HCP
ALBUM: (up to 1986)	1(A) IT'LL ALL END IN TEARS	(4AD CAD 411) 1984	38

NB: (1) also issued on CD (CAD 411 CD) 1986.

			HCP
45s: (up to 1986)	Song To The Siren/ 16 Days (Reprise) (PS)	(4AD AD 310) 1983	66
	Song To The Siren/16 Days/ Gathering Dust (12", PS)	(4AD BAD 310) 1983	-
*	Kangaroo/It'll End In Tears (PS)	(4AD AD 410) 1984	-
	Come Here My Love/Drugs (10", PS)	(4AD BAD 410) 1986	-

NB: * This came in two different sleeve designs and label colours. 2,500 copies were pressed of each.

This was really a studio agglomeration created by Ivo Watts-Russell, co-owner of the Wandsworth-based 4AD label. They comprised members of **Cocteau Twins**, Dead Can Dance, **Modern English**, Xmal Deutschland and other 4AD artists. The album, which spent four weeks in the chart peaking at No. 38, mixes some instrumentals with vocal numbers. Pleasant but not exceptional, the album included cover versions of songs by some of Watts-Russell's favourite artists, including Tim Buckley, Roy Harper, Syd Barrett and Gene Clark. The first single *Song To The Siren* was also an excellent Tim Buckley cover. It was a minor hit, climbing to No. 66 during a two week chart sojourn.

They continued to record well beyond this book's time frame.

Those Helicopters

Personnel:	ANDREW BARNDEN	drms	A
	HARLAN COCKBURN	sax, gtr	A
	STEPHEN JOHN MAUGHAN	bs	A
	ALAN ROBINSON	vcls	A
	VINCENT WHITLOCK	keyb'ds	A
	ANDY WOOD	gtr	A

45s:	South Coast Towns/World Without Love/ Flash Benadette	(Bonaparte BONE 4) 1979
	Shark/Eskimo (PS)	(State Of The Art STATE 0000001) 1980
	Dr. Janov/ Technical Smack (PS)	(Lavender Sound LAVENDER 001) 1981

A band with good ideas, although their debut 45 *South Coast Towns*, whilst a good tune, was poorly produced with near inaudible vocals and didn't capture them at their best. *World Without Love* is an awful cover of the old Peter and Gordon No. 1. *Flash Bernadette* utilises lots of brass.

Those Naughty Lumps

Personnel:	MARTIN ARMADILLO	A
	P.M. HART	A
	TONY MITCHELL	A
	KEVIN WILKINSON	A
	PETER 'KID' YOUNGER	A

THOSE HELECOPTERS - South Coast Towns.

THIS MORTAL COIL - Kangaroo.

THOSE NAUGHTY LUMPS - Iggy Pop's Jacket.

EP:	1(A)	DOWN AT THE ZOO	(Open Eye OP-EP 1002) 1980
45:		Iggy Pop's Jacket/	
		Pure And Innocent (fold-out PS)	(Zoo CAGE 002) 1979

This oddly-named outfit formed in Liverpool in the summer of 1977. They soon secured a residency at the city's Havana Club but their vinyl debut didn't come until 1979, when they were among the first bands to have a record released on Bill Drummond's new indie label, Zoo Records. *Iggy Pop's Jacket* is quite an unusual and interesting song, which can also be heard on the sampler *To The Shores Of Lake Placid* (Zoo FOUR) 1982. The following year they recorded a four-track EP for another new Liverpool-based indie label Open Eye. Their progress was hampered by several personnel changes with only Hart and Wilkinson lasting the course from the original line-up. They soon faded from the scene. Only Younger remained in the music business, briefly surfacing with **Wah! Heat**.

The Threats

Personnel:	GOGS	gtr	A
	JAMO	vcls	A
	MEECHO	drms	A
	TIN	bs	A

EPs:	1(A)	GO TO HELL (Go To Hell/Afghanistan	
		Wasted) (PS)	(Rondelet ROUND 22) 1982
	2(A)	POLITICIANS AND MINISTERS (Politicians And Ministers/	
		Writing's On The Wall/	
		Deep End Depression) (PS)	(Rondelet ROUND 29) 1982

This short-lived punk four-piece came from Midlothian in Scotland. They signed to Rondelet and issued these two EPs in 1982 but then split. *Go To Hell* and *Politicians And Ministers* later resurfaced on *Rondelet Punk Singles Collection* (Anagram CDPUNK 49) in 1995, which was also issued in vinyl (Captain Oi! AHOY LP 513) 1996. You'll also find *Politicians And Ministers* on *100% Hardcore Punk* (Captain Oi! AHOY DCD 84) 1998.

Three Party Split

45s:	Dubious Parentage/Kandidate (PS)	(B&C CBS 16) 1979
	Insane/Totally Insane (PS)	(B&C BCS 19) 1979

Dubious Parentage is a satirical politico-punk record.

Throbbing Gristle

Personnel:	CHRIS CARTER	keyb'ds	A
	PETER CHRISTOPHERSON	effects	A
	GENESIS P. ORRIDGE	bs, clarinet	A
	COSEY FANNI TUTTI	gtr, vcls	A

ALBUMS: (up to 1986)	1(A)	THE SECOND ANNUAL REPORT OF THROBBING GRISTLE	(Industrial IR 0002) 1977
	2(A)	D.O.A. THE THIRD AND FINAL REPORT OF THROBBING GRISTLE	(Industrial IR 0004) 1978
	3(A)	BRING YOU 20 JAZZ FUNK GREATS	(Industrial IR 0008) 1979
	4(A)	HEATHEN EARTH	(Industrial IR 0009) 1980
	5(A)	A BOXED SET (5-LP Set)	(Fetish FX 1) 1981
	6(A)	FUNERAL IN BERLIN	(Zensor 01) 1981
	7(A)	MUSIC FROM THE DEATH FACTORY MAY '79	(Death 01) 1982
	8(A)	JOURNEY THROUGH A BODY	(Walter Ulbricht 001) 1982
	9(A)	ASSUME POWER FOCUS	(Power Focus 001) 1982
	10(A)	LIVE AT THE DEATH FACTORY, MAY '79	(T.G. 33033) 1982
	11(A)	THEE PSYCHICK SACRIFICE (Dbl)	(Karnage/Illuminated KILL 1) 1982
	12(A)	RAFTERS	(Italian EX 23) 1982
	13(A)	FUHRER DER MENSHEIT (10")	(American Photograph 1 JAP) 1983
	14(A)	MISSION IS TERMINATED/NICE TRACKS	(Expanded EX 39 LY2) 1983

THROBBING GRISTLE - Greatest Hits.

	15(A)	EDITIONS FRANKFURT - BERLIN	
			(Svensk Illuminated JAMS 31) 1983
	16(A)	IN THE SHADOW OF THE SUN	
			(Illuminated JAMS 35) 1984
	17(A)	ONCE UPON A TIME	(Casual Abandon CAS 1J) 1984
	18(A)	SPECIAL TREATMENT	(Mental Decay 01-1) 1984
	19(A)	SACRIFICE	(Castle Communications DOJOLP 29) 1986

NB: (1) was a limited edition of 785 copies. They came with a questionnaire, zerox strip and two stickers in a white heavy duty sleeve. (1) was reissued (Fetish FET 2001) 1978 as a limited edition of 2,000 in a T.G. 'lightning flash' sleeve with a questionnaire. (1) reissued again (Fetish FET 2001) 1979 in a glossy sleeve, then on Fetish in 1981 the whole album was re-cut with the music playing backwards, and again (Mute MIR 001) 1983. (1) later issued on CD (Mute TGCD 2) 1991 and (Grey Area TGCD 2) 1993. The first 1,000 copies of (2) came with a calendar and postcard. (2) issued again (Industrial IR 0004) 1979 - the D.J. Confusion Mix and the original mix (Mute MIR 002) 1983. (2) also issued on CD (Mute TGCD 3) 1991 and (Grey Area TGCD 3) 1993. The first 2,000 copies of (3) came with a black and white poster. (3) reissued (Mute MIR 003) 1983 and later issued on CD (Mute TGCD 4) 1991 and (Grey Area TGCD 4) 1993. (4) was issued in a gatefold sleeve, the first 785 copies on blue vinyl. It was later reissued (Mute MIR 004) 1983 and was later issued on CD (Mute TGCD 5) 1991 and (Grey Area TGCD 5). (5) was a box set with a 28-page booklet and badge. Only 5,000 were pressed. (7) was a limited edition of 50 copies. (8) was a limited edition of 1,000 copies. It was later issued on CD (Grey Area TGCD 8) 1993. (9) was a limited edition of 1,000 copies. It was also issued on CD (Paragoric PA 016CD) 1997 and again (Triple XXX TX 60010 CD) 1998. (10) was a picture disc 1,355 copies were pressed. (11) was a budget-priced double album. (14) comprised an album plus a 12" containing *Damura Sunrise* and *You Don't Know* and a 16-page booklet. (16) was a soundtrack. (17) later issued on CD (Jungle OBSESSCD 2) 1994. Other relevant CD releases are *TGCD 1* (Mute CD 1) 1986 which was accompanied by a booklet; *Mission Of Dead Souls* (Mute CDTG 6) 1991 and *Greatest Hits: Entertainment Through Pain* (Mute CDTG 7) 1991, which had been issued on Rough Trade's U.S. label in 1981 on vinyl and was widely available here. *Live - Volume 1* (Grey Area TGCD 10) 1993, *Live - Volume 2* (Grey Area TGCD 11) 1993, *Live - Volume 3* (Grey Area TGCD 12) 1993 and *Live - Volume 4* (Grey Area TGCD 13) 1993.

45s:	*	United/Zyklon B Zombie (PS)	(Industrial IR 0003) 1978
	+	We Hate You (Little Girls)/ Five Knuckle Shuffle (PS)	(Sordide Sentimentale SS 45001) 1979
	x	Subhuman/ Something Came Over Me (PS)	(Industrial IR 0013) 1980
	x	Adrenalin/ Distant Dreams (Part Two) (PS)	(Industrial IT 0015) 1980
		Discipline (Live)/ Discipline (Live) (12", PS)	(Fetish FET 006) 1981

NB: * This was remixed and reissued later in 1978, then again with an extended remixed flip side in 1980. 1,000 copies in white vinyl and 1,000 copies in clear vinyl. + This was a French release, a limited edition pressing of 1,560 copies in an A4 fold-out sleeve with inserts. It was later reissued in the U.S. (Adolescent AR TT 010) in 1981. x These 45s were issued in polythene camoflage bags. The 'A' side was recorded live in Berlin and the 'B' side live in Manchester.

Throbbing Gristle are the group most associated with Industrial Music, which was essentially an appendage of punk rock. It shared punk's antagonism to the mainstream, particularly its nihilism and noise, but it sounded entirely different to punk's three-chord format. Its origins lay in the experimentation of the Dadaists and Futurists and the electronic ventures of acts like Kraftwerk, Eno and David Bowie. The Industrial Music of **Throbbing Gristle** blended punk elements with electronic music and free-form improvisation. The electronically-treated music based on a combination of echo, phasing, reverb and tape manipulation was somehow alien to the ears and conjured up drab industrial landscapes as opposed to picturesque scenery.

Throbbing Gristle were formed in Manchester in September 1975. Their leader Genesis P. Orridge had previously been in punk group **The Pork Dukes**. They set up their own label Industrial Records which would be the pivot of the Industrial Music genre. In 1976, a cassette-only release limited to 50 copies was circulated to friends. *The Best Of Throbbing Gristle Volume II* is extremely rare today. The mono recording is reputed to be a superb example of their savage early sound. Its tracks included *Slug Bait, Very Friendly, We Hate You, Seers Of E* and *Dead Ed*. There was no Volume I!

Most of 1977 was spent setting up the Industrial Records label and working on a film 'After Cease To Exist'. This ten-minute movie came with a twenty-one minute soundtrack which made up one side of their debut album *2nd Annual Report*, released in November 1977. It was packaged to resemble an annual report coming in a plain white sleeve with a small sticker in the top right hand corner. They only had the finance to produce 785 copies. The other side of the album featured material from four live concerts and two studio tracks. The highlight was the menacing *Slug Bait*. Original copies of this album, which also included a questionnaire designed to give the band maximum information on the people who were buying the record, are now very rare and collectable. It has since been reissued a few times as detailed in the above discography.

In July 1978, **Throbbing Gristle** issued a 45 *United* in a black and white picture sleeve. This contrasted considerably with the earlier album. The 'A' side was a deliberately commercial synth-pop song, but on the flip was a three chord punk song. After the first 20,000 copies were sold the single was remixed and a remixed version of the 'B' side featured Cosey's guitar more up front in the mix.

United appeared on **Throbbing Gristle**'s next album *D.O.A. The Third And Final Report*, which appeared in December 1978, but the track had been speeded up to last just 16 seconds! This album had a full colour sleeve and was a more professional offering than their debut. Four tracks were live and each band member was given the opportunity to do a solo number. Of particular note were *Death Threats*, which consisted of messages left on the group's ansaphone, and *Hamburger Lady*, a true story about a woman burned from the waist up who was still alive. The first 1,000 copies sold by mail order included a black and white postcard of Cosey's niece Debbie and a calender. The initial pressing quickly sold out and a repress quickly organised. Of these 1,000 copies - the 'D.J. Confusion' ones were cut to convey the impression of having eight tracks of equal length, which of course wasn't the case at all.

During 1979 **Throbbing Gristle** played a number of concerts culminating in an appearance at London's YMCA. For this the band wore white in contrast to their usual black leather/military image. This seems to have represented a conscious attempt to change their image. This was sustained when Genesis P. Orridge posed with the group on a cliff top at Beachy Head clad in a 'Frank Sinatra' outfit for the cover photo of *20 Jazz Funk Greats* released in December 1979. Eah side opened with a jazz-funk track. The initial 2,000 copies contained a now sought-after black and white poster of the band. The atmosphere of *Jazz Funk Greats* is intentionally listless and loveless. The songs are sombre, full of grubby textures and isolated effects.

Earlier in the year a limited edition single (1,560 copies) *We Hate You (Little Girls) / Five Knuckle Struggle* was released in France on the Sordide Sentimentale label. Lavishly packaged in an A4 fold-out sleeve whose inserts included a collage, lyrics and text by J.P. Turmel. The 'A' side had originally appeared on their very first tape back in 1976. The 45 was later reissued on the San Francisco-based Adolescent label in 1981. The flip side was a studio recording dating from 1978.

The first 785 copies of *Heathen Earth* (the astute among you will notice this is the same number as their first album) came on blue vinyl. The cover photo features a dog's teeth and question from a Charles Manson song "Can the world be as sad as it seems?". There are no track listings on this album, which was issued in June 1980 in a gatefold sleeve. In September two double 'A' side 45s were issued simultaneously in camouflaged plastic

THROBBING GRISTLE - Heathen Earth.

covers and picture sleeves, *Subhuman / Something Came Over Me* and *Adrenalin / Distant Dreams*. *Subhuman* reverted back to the old style savage **Throbbing Gristle**. On the reverse was an instrumental from *Heaven Earth* with a vocal track added. *Adrenalin* veered towards techno-pop, while *Distant Dreams* was dominated by synthesizer and unlike their other material.

Behind the scene things were far from rosy with the band. On 18th August 1978 Cosey Fanni Tutti left Genesis P. Orridge and moved in with **Chris Carter**. Then, in May 1981, Orridge married his new girlfriend Paula. The band had played three dates in Germany in November 1980. They commenced 1981 with two London gigs, one of which was subsequently issued on a cassette by Rough Trade as *Psychic Rally In Heaven (Beyond Jazz Funk)*. They finally announced their split after playing two California dates in May 1981. This was done by mailing out black-bordered postcards with the message "The mission is terminated". Earlier that month their final single a 12" containing two recent live versions of *Discipline* taken from concerts in Manchester and Berlin was issued.

After their demise Peter Christopherson, Genesis P. Orridge and his girlfriend Paula formed Psychic TV. **Chris Carter** and Cosey Fanni Tutti operated as a duo sometimes known as **Creative Technology Institute**. Later, in 1984, Peter Christopherson ended his links with P. Orridge and formed Coil with former Psychic TV member Geoff Rushton.

There have been many retrospective releases of their material. The five-LP boxed set issued on Fetish in 1981 featured *D.O.A. The Third And Final Report*, *20 Jazz Funk Greats* and *Heathen Earth*, the 1981 reissue of *2nd Annual Report* on Fetish, which aside from being re-cut with the music played backwards also featured a chamber music ensemble on side two, and a previously unreleased recording of their final concert titled *Mission Of Dead Souls*. The same five albums were later reissued individually on Mute in 1983 in their original sleeves.

The U.S. compilation *Throbbing Gristle's Greatest Hits (Entertainment Through Pain)* was easily obtained here, collectors seek this out because some tracks were treated with minor amounts of reverb and echo. It was eventually released here on CD in 1991 by Mute. It's not really a 'best of' but contains a wide-ranging selection of their material. Also in 1991 Mute put out *Mission Of Dead Souls* on CD. This was taken from their final live concert in San Francisco, which certainly had its moments.

Journey Through A Body included some of their last ever recordings. *Assume Power Focus*, a limited edition of 1,000, was compiled from unused studio tapes by Geoff Rushton, later of Psychic TV. *Live At The Death Factory, May '79* was a picture disc presented in a plastic wallet in a limited edition of 1,355 copies and taken from a live concert. *The Psychic Sacrifice* was a budget-priced double album containing many of their favourites. It was later edited down to a single album *Sacrifice* in 1986. *Rafters* and *Funeral In Berlin* were both taken from late 1980 concerts and contained lots of recent material. The 10" mini-album *Fuhrer Der Mensheit* included some songs from *Funeral In Berlin*.

Mission Is Terminated is an album of Italian bands interspersed with snippets of **Throbbing Gristle**, **The Slits**' singer Ari Up, conversations with Genesis P. Orridge, Peter Christopherson and an extract from an early Psychic TV gig. Along with this album came a 45 r.p.m. 12" containing *You Don't Know* and *Damura Sunrise* and a sixteen-page booklet, which includes a long interview with Genesis P. Orridge and rare photos.

Editions Frankfurt-Berlin contains material from a German concert and like *Once Upon A Time* (which is also compiled from live concerts) is not one of their better efforts.

Many of **Throbbing Gristle**'s albums are now available on CD. Their first CD release *TG CD 1* on Mute in 1986 contained previously unreleased studio recordings from 1979. With it came a booklet in which the former members reminisced about their experiences with the band.

Four Volumes Of Live is a four-CD sampler which takes in the highlights of their October 1976 ICA performance, the Crypt concert (where Genesis P. Orridge behaved very strangely) and a concert at Oundle Public School.

They've also had a few compilation appearances. *United* was included on *Business Unusual* (Cherry Red ARED 2) 1978 and *25 Years Of Rough Trade Shops* (4-CD box set) (Mute CDSTUMM 191) 2001; whilst *The Last Testament* (Fetish FR 2011) 1983 included a re-edited recording of *Discipline* and *Distants Dreams* and *We Hate You (Little Girls)* both figured on *The Industrial Records Story 1976 - 1981* (Illuminated JAMS 39) 1984.

Be warned that **Throbbing Gristle**'s music is an acquired taste - certainly not for everybody. Despite that many of their records have become very collectable and their significance at the forefront of Industrial Music and their influence on acts like **Cabaret Voltaire**, Non, **23 Skidoo** and **Whitehouse** was considerable.

The Throbs

Personnel:	ANDY	bs	A
	JAMES	gtr	A
	STEVE	vcls	A
	TONY	drms	A

CASS: 1(A) SKATEBOARDS FROM HELL (Doomsday Tapes) 198?

This four-track cassette was sold for 20p, which went to help Greenpeace. It contained four tracks - *We Make Homebrew Not War*, *Burning Rain*, *I Love Una Stubbs* and *September*. The first two pursue a strong anti-nuclear theme, the third is an ode to TV actress Una Stubbs and *September* is an instrumental with good guitar playing, which is more experimental musically. The sound quality is very good for a D.I.Y. cassette. It was available from an address in Surrey.

The Throbs also contributed a cut *Happy But Not Ignorant* to *Punk Lives! - Let's Slam* (Rot SLAM 2) 1986. They came from Kingston-upon-Thames in South-west London and later went into fanzine production.

TIGHTS - Howard Hughes.

THE TIMES - I Helped Patrick McGoohan Escape.

Tickets

Personnel:	M.R. JAMES	synth	A
	JOHN B. McGEADY	bs, vcls	A
	ANDY SCOTT	drms	A
	KEN SCOTT	gtr, vcls	A

45: I'll Be Your Pin Up/
    Guess I'll Have To Sit Alone (PS)   (Bridgehouse BHS 3) 1979

This band also involved two members of **Wasted Youth**.

The Tigers

Personnel:	NICHOLAS COLA	keyb'ds, vcls	A
	PETE DOBSON	drms	A
	TONY JACKS	gtr, vcls	A
	ROSS McGEENEY	gtr, vcls	A
	NIC POTTER	bs	A

45s: * Kidding Stops/Big Expense, Small Income   (Strike KIK 1) 1979
     Promises Promises/Ska Trekkin' (PS)   (Strike KIK 3) 1980

NB: * This was issued in a die-cut sleeve.

Strike Records did a special promotion of **The Tigers** debut single by initially offering a copy of the title cut to their projected album *Savage Music* along with stickers and badges. The 45 was critically acclaimed in some quarters, but it never really took off. Although the album was released in the 'States by A&M and in Europe by WEA, it surprisingly didn't get a U.K. release.

Tights

Personnel:	ROBERT BANKS	gtr	A
	RICK MAYHEW	drms	A
	BARRY ISLAND	bs, keyb'ds	A
	MALCOLM ORGEE	vcls	A

45s: Bad Hearts/It/Cracked (PS)   (Cherry Red CHERRY 1) 1978
    * Howard Hughes/
      China's Eternal (PS)   (Cherry Red CHERRY 2) 1978

NB: * This was also issued on a cassette (Cherry Red CSP-CHERRY 2) 1978.

A Worcester band. Their debut 45 *Bad Hearts* came in a picture sleeve which featured a young girl bound by barbed wire. The vocals are good and accompanied by chainsaw buzz-guitar backing. *Howard Hughes* may well have been the first-ever U.K. cassette single. The band could also claim the first two releases on the Cherry Red label. As its title suggests *Howard Hughes* is about the millionaire recluse and it's played in a standard punk format with a brief but good instrumental segment. *China's Eternal* is much slower, with soft, almost spoken vocal segments and the guitars are joined by synthesizers. Produced by John Acock, the 45 was recorded at Millstream Studios, Cheltenham.

China's Eternal can also be heard on *Business Unusual* (Cherry Red ARED 2) in 1979, whilst both their 45s can be heard on *Cherry Red Punk Singles Collection* (Anagram CDPUNK 51) in 1995.

The Times

Personnel:	ED BALL	vcls	AB
(up to	PAUL DAMIEN	drms	A
1986)	JOHN EAST		AB
	RAY KENT	keyb'ds	AB
	SIMON SMITH	drms	B

ALBUMS:	1(A)	POP GOES ART!	(Whaam! BIG 01) 1982
(up to	2(A)	THIS IS LONDON	(Art Pop ART 19) 1983
1986)	3(A)	I HELPED PATRICK McGOOHAN ESCAPE	
		(6 track mini-LP)	(Art Pop No 1) 1983
	4(B)	HELLO EUROPE	(Art Pop ART 17) 1984
	5(B)	BLUE PERIOD (mini LP)	(Art Pop ARTPOP 2) 1985
	6(B)	ENJOY!	(Art Pop ART 15) 1986
	7(B)	UP AGAINST IT	(Art Pop ART 16) 1986

NB: (1) originally issued in a hand-sprayed sleeve. (1) reissued (Art Pop ART 20) in a hand-sprayed sleeve with a few magazine cuttings taped to a plain white cover. Reissued with a signed 'hand painted' picture disc in 1990, also on CD (Art Pop ART CD 20) 1990. (1) also issued on one CD with *Go! With The Times* (Pastell POW 3) 1985, a German-only vinyl release, which had been recorded in 1980. (2) originally issued on a white label with blue print. Later copies were on a black label with white print. (2) and (4) issued on one CD (Rev-Ola CREV 028CD) 1993. (3) also issued on CD (Rev-Ola CREV 006CD) 1992. There's also a compilation of Ed Ball material, *Pink Ball, Brown Ball, Red Ball* (Creation CRELP 073) 1991.

EP:	1(B)	BOYS ABOUT TOWN (David Jones (Is On His Way)/Victim 1960/Up Against It/ Song For Joe Orton) (12", PS)	(Art Pop POP 43DOZ) 1985

45s:		Red With Purple Flashes/	
(up to		Biff! Bang! Pow! (PS)	(Whaam! WHAAM 002) 1981
1986)	*	Here Come The Holidays/	
		Three Cheers For The Sun (PS)	(Art Pop POP 50) 1982
		I Helped Patrick McGoohan Escape/	
		Theme From "Danger Man" (PS)	(Art Pop POP 49) 1983
		Boys Brigade/Power Is Forever (PS)	(Art Pop POP 46) 1984
		Blue Fire/Where The Blue Begins (PS)	(Art Pop POP 45) 1984
		London Boys/(Where To Go) When The Sun Goes Down (PS)	(Unicorn PHZ 1) 1985

NB: * 'A' side credited to Joni Dee and **The Times**.

The Times metamorphosised out of **The Teenage Filmstars**', Ed Ball's previous band. Ball started a new label Whaam! with Dan Treacy in 1981. The first two releases were Dan's **Television Personalities**' project **The Gifted Children** and **The Times**' first 45 *Red With Purple Flashes*. This was a Creation-inspired pop art effort and the flip-side *Biff! Bang! Pow!*

THE TIMES - Theme From Dangerman.

THE TIMES - Blue Fire.

even took the title of one of their 'B' sides.

The sleeve to their first album *Pop Goes Art!* was issued in a hand-sprayed sleeve designed by Ed's brother Andrew. The album's full of short pop songs and instrumentals but there's also one extended track *This Is Tomorrow* which features some exhilarating psychedelic guitar work. In 1983, after a disagreement with Dan Treacy, Ed Ball launched his own Art Pop label. He reissued *Pop Goes Art* in a hand-painted sleeve with a few magazine cuttings taped to a plain white cover.

For their next 45, *Here Come The Holidays*, Ed Ball persuaded Joni Suckett, the female vocalist with **Fad Gadget** to sing vocals on this summery pop offering. This explains why the 'A' side is credited to Joni Dee and **The Times**.

They then re-recorded *I Helped Patrick McGoohan Escape* for Warner Brothers' *A Splash Of Colour* (WEA K 85415) 1982 compilation. In the mini-psychedelic revival of 1982 this was the compilation that fronted it all up. Warner Brothers didn't release the 45 in the end so it came out on Art Pop. The 45 had a version of the "Danger Man" theme on the flip. The six track mini-LP released in December 1983 in addition to these, included two songs from their earlier *This Is London* album (*Big Painting* and *Stranger Than Fiction*) as well as *All Systems Are Go!* and *Up Against It*.

The *This Is London* album came out in July 1983. Earlier copies have a white label with blue print, but later ones had a black label with white print. The album is about the seedier side of London. Sixties psych-pop was alive and well on cuts like *The Chimes Of Big Ben* and *Goodbye Piccadilly*. *Whatever Happened To Thamesbeat* veered towards the mod revival of the time and *Will Success Spoil Frank Summit* speculates on the fate of a Liverpool lad who moves down to London. The album used Linn drum machines that sound dated now.

Simon Smith, formerly of **Merton Parkas** and **Mood Six**, came in on drums for the *Hello Europe* album. They toured Europe to promote it but it didn't go down as well as their earlier efforts there. It did spawn two further singles, *Boys Brigade* and *Blue Fire*. Overall, though, *Hello Europe* was a disappointing funky bass and horn orientated album, which represented a change of musical direction.

The mini-album *Blue Period* was released in April 1985 in a blue sleeve, but a few copies came with a grey one. It also included *Blue Fire* and *Boys Brigade* from the album. Their next release was a four track 12" EP *Boys About Town* in October 1985. This partly explored Ball's interest in writer Joe Orton, hence the inclusion of *Song For Joe Orton*.

During 1985 Ball embarked on one of his most obscure projects - the Clockwork Orange tribute 45 which was credited to Edward Ball's L'Orange Mechanik, *Symphony/Intermezzo (Sprechstimme)/Scherzo* (Art Pop POP 44) 1985. It was an amalgam of pop and classical. Later, in 1989, he released a whole album of material *Edward Ball's L'Orange Mechanik* (Creation CRELP 055), which came with a free book of Edgar Allen Poe's poems.

We must leave our trip with Ed Ball and **The Times** in the mid-eighties, but he went on to record with **The Times** and many interesting spin off projects throughout the nineties, when he also recorded solo.

Aside from the appearance on *A Splash Of Colour*, **The Times** have appeared on a couple of other compilations. You can hear their version of *The Slider* on the 12" Marc Bolan tribute album *Lunacy Is Legend* (Barracuda BLUE 12 UTA 9) 1987. *Pensioners On Ecstasy* (Creation CRELP 082) 1990 also includes their *Wah! Kylie*.

Not really punk or new wave, strictly speaking **The Times** were a successful nostalgia act that successfully relived swinging Britain circa 1967.

Nick Toczecks Britanarchists

An Oi! ranter/poet who contributed *Stiff With A Quiff* to *The Oi! Of Sex* (Syndicate SYNLP 4) 1984, also reissued on CD (Captain Oi! AHOY CD 23) 1994. This is a powerful song with good guitar work.

Terry Tonik

45:	Just A Little Mod/		
	Smashed And Blocked (die-cut PS)		(Posh TOFF 1) 1980

Mark Brennan reveals in his sleevenotes that **Terry Tonik** was a pseudonym for Ian Harris, who wrote the popish *Just A Little Mod* back in 1969 but didn't record it until a decade later. Andy Powell (of Wishbone Ash) plays guitar on this disc. It is one of the most sought-after discs of this genre. Indeed a few copies came with a promotional A4 booklets. Expect to pay in excess of £100 for these. Both sides can also be heard on *This Is Mod, Vol. 2* (Anagram CDMGRAM 101) 1996, whilst *Just A Little Mod* later resurfaced on *100% British Mod* (Captain Mod MODSKA DCD 8) 1998.

The Tools

Personnel:	GEORGE GAMBLE	drms	A
	ROGER LLOYD-COOPER	gtr, vcls	A
	STUART MARTIN	bs	A
	JIMMY McCULLOUGH	gtr	A
	PETE VARIETY	vcls	A
45:	Gotta Make Some Money Somehow/		
	TV Eyes (PS)		(Oily SLICK 2) 1979

A one-off 45 on an Aberdeen-based label. Both sides were group compositions. By no means full-blooded punk, but the influence is there. The 'A' side has some nice guitar work courtesy of Jimmy McCullough. *TV Eyes* is quite R&B influenced.

Too Much

Personnel:	COLIN JOHN BATES	vcls	A
	DICK CONOLLY	bs	A
	DAVE MEW	drms	A
	RUSS SOLLOF	gtr	A
45s:	Who You Wanna Be/		
	Another Time Another Place		(Lightning GIL 513) 1978
	Kick Me One More Time/Be Mine/		
	It's Only For Me (gatefold PS)		(Lightning GIL 552) 1978

Both of these 45s are now rare and expensive. They also had a French-only release *Silex Pistols/Photo Photo* (Pat 00814575) in 1978. You can also hear *Who You Wanna Be* and *Kick Me One More Time* on *Lightning Records Punk Collection* (Anagram CDPUNK 79) 1996.

To The Finland Station

Personnel:	GARY FINCH	bs, vcls	AB
	JULIAN MacQUEEN	vcls, gtr	ABCDE
	STEPHEN PENFOLD	drms, bs	BCDEF
	CLAIRE MACAULEY	vcls, gtr	DEF
	KEVIN WIREMU	drms	EF
	ROD MACAULEY	gtr	F
CASS:	1(-) POLITICS ARE PRIOR TO THE VAGARIES		
	OF FASHION (comp.)		(Melodia) 1984
45:	Domino Theory (45 r.p.m.)/		
	Betrayal Pivotal Couples (33 r.p.m.)		(Melodia M3) 1981

Formed at the end of 1980, by Julian MacQueen and Gary Finch **To The Finland Station** was named after a book by Edmund Wilson about Lenin and the Russian Revolution. Stephen Penfold (drums) was recruited to complete the band. However, in this form, the band only did one gig before Finch quit. After an abortive six month search for a bass-player, the band bought a primitive drum machine and Penfold switched to bass.

Along with **A Popular History Of Signs**, they were founder members of the co-operative record label and promotions agency Melodia. Throughout 1981, the band gigged in and around London and towards the end of 1981, Claire Macauley (vocals and guitar), ex-**Leopards**, joined to fill out the sound. Also on recordings and at some gigs, Nigel Fonseca and Andy Minion (both saxophones) were also used. They released their first single *Domino Theory* on Melodia in January 1982. The single got great reviews and, in particular, the band became darlings of the left-wing alternative press, such as City Limits, The Leveller etc. MacQueen's idea for the band was politics and melody, in other words to wed a serious political lyric with a strong "catchy" melody. This was a deliberate contrast to the other "political" bands of the time, such as **The Gang Of Four**, **Pop Group** etc, whose hard political message tended to be matched with a tough abrasive sound.

Because of Melodia's hand-to-mouth existence, no funds were available to do a second single until the end of 1982. By this time Kevin Wiremu (drums), ex-**Leopards**, had replaced the drum machine. The second single was *Foreign Correspondent / Shouting At The World* but it was never released. MacQueen and Penfold, ever the perfectionists, blew the entire budget on recording it and remixing it several times. Before further funds

THE TOOLS - Gotta Make Some Money.

TO THE FINLAND STATION - Domino Theory.

THE TOURISTS - Blind Among The Flowers.

THE TOURISTS - The Loneliest Man In The World.

could be found, MacQueen quit in early 1983 to be the world's first Marxist country-and-western singer, forming the new country band Cut Loose. The band continued for a few months with Claire Macauley as lead singer and her brother Rod, ex-**Leopards**, joining on guitar before Penfold quit in the autumn of 1983 and the band disintegrated.

Melodia released a posthumous cassette compilation, the snappily titled *Politics Are Prior To The Vagaries Of Fashion* in 1984.

The Tourists

Personnel:	EDDY CHIN	bs	A
	PEET COOMBES	gtr, vcls	A
	ANNIE LENNOX	vcls	A
	DAVE STEWART	gtr	A
	JIM TOOMEY	drms	A

			HCP
ALBUMS: 1(A)	THE TOURISTS	(Logo LOGO 1018) 1979	72
2(A)	REALITY EFFECT	(Logo LOGO 1019) 1979	23
3(A)	LUMINOUS BASEMENT	(RCA RCALP 5001) 1980	75

NB: (1) reissued (RCA Int. INTK 5096) 1981. (3) came with a free yellow vinyl single, *From The Middle Room/Into The Future* (Free 5001). There's also a CD compilation *Greatest Hits* (Camden 74321523812) 1997.

			HCP
45s:	Blind Among The Flowers/		
	He Who Laughs Last (PS)	(Logo GO 350) 1979	52
	Blind Among The Flowers/He Who Laughs Last//		
	The Golden Lamp/		
	Wrecked (double pack, gatefold PS)	(Logo GO(D) 350) 1979	-
	The Loneliest Man In The World/		
	Don't Get Left Behind (PS)	(Logo GO 360) 1979	32
	The Loneliest Man In The World/		
	Don't Get Left Behind (picture disc)	(Logo GO(P) 360) 1979	-
	I Only Want To Be With You/		
	Summer Night (PS)	(Logo GO 370) 1979	4
	So Good To Be Back Home/		
	Circular Fever (PS)	(Logo TOUR 1) 1980	8
	Don't Say I Told You So/		
	Strange Sky (PS)	(RCA TOUR 2) 1980	40

The lynch pins of **The Tourists** were Scot Annie Lennox, who was born on 25th December 1954 in Aberdeen, Scotland and Dave Stewart, born on 9th September 1952 in Sunderland. Lennox was in London to study at the Royal Academy of Music, but having failed to complete the course she met Stewart in 1977 whilst working at Pippins, a restaurant in Hampstead, North London. Stewart had travelled down to London as a 15-year old stowaway in the back of a van belonging to Amazing Blondel after they'd gigged in Newcastle.

Stewart's first recording was with Brian Harrison as Harrison and Stewart on the local Multicord label in Sunderland. Back in 1973, Stewart was a member of Longdancer who recorded two albums *If It Was So Simple* and *Trailer For A Good Life*, which were put out on Elton John's Rocket label. See my earlier book 'The Tapestry Of Delights' for further details of Longdancer. Between the demise of Longdancer and meeting Annie Lennox, Dave Stewart worked as a record dealer in London's Swiss Cottage market for a while.

Linking up with Lennox and his best friend guitarist/vocalist Peet Coombes, Stewart formed **The Catch** during 1977 (see their entry for details).

With the addition of drummer Jim Toomey and bassist Eddie Chin, **The Catch** became **The Tourists**. They released a debut 45 *Blind Among The Flowers* in May 1979. This was an upbeat, pop-punk number, which became a minor hit peaking at No. 52 in the charts during a five week stay. In June 1979, a double pack 7" version of the 45 was issued. The two additional tracks were *The Golden Lamp* and *Wrecked*. An eponymous album was issued the same month. This included both sides of their first 45 and the delightful ballad *The Loneliest Man In The World*. Perhaps an unlikely choice for a pop-punk band it was quite a heart string puller and an ideal choice for their next 45, in August 1979. It spent seven weeks in the chart peaking at No. 32. All material on the album was all penned by Coombes. Most of it was sixties-influenced (á la Byrds, Mamas and The Papas etc.). There are quite a lot of duets between Annie Lennox and Peet Coombes. It's fair to say that the group added a little of their own interpretation to this music. The album spent one week in the charts at No. 72. The following month **The Tourists** made a successful appearance at the Reading Rock Festival.

A follow-up album *Reality Effect* was released in October 1979. Again all the songs were penned by Coombes (except for a cover of Dusty Springfield's *I Only Want To Be With You*). The version, little changed from the original, gave them their biggest hit. It reached No. 4 and spent a total of fourteen weeks in the charts. In January 1980, a self-penned cut from the album *So Good To Be Back Home* was culled for 45 release. This also became a Top 10 hit, peaking at No. 8 during a nine week chart stay. The album fared much better commercially than its predecessor. The musical format was very similar, but the group better known. *Reality Effect* spent sixteen weeks in the chart, climbing to No. 23.

In September 1980, **The Tourists** switched to RCA and released a new 45 *Don't Say I Told You So* to preview their *Luminous Basement* album released the following month. The 45s 'B' side, *Strange Sky* was a non-album cut. Neither the 45 (No. 40) or the album (No. 75) fared as well as their predecessors. The album did come with a free yellow vinyl single, *From The Middle Room / Into The Future*.

The Tourists disbanded whilst on a tour of Australia. Even after this Lennox and Stewart continued to work together. A jam session at Conny Plank's Cologne studio with members of DAF and Can on New Year's Eve recorded a new 45 and soon after a new group, the highly successful Eurythmics, was born. Later, in the nineties, both Lennox and Stewart embarked on solo ventures.

The 1997 *Greatest Hits* compilation is now the best means of accessing their music.

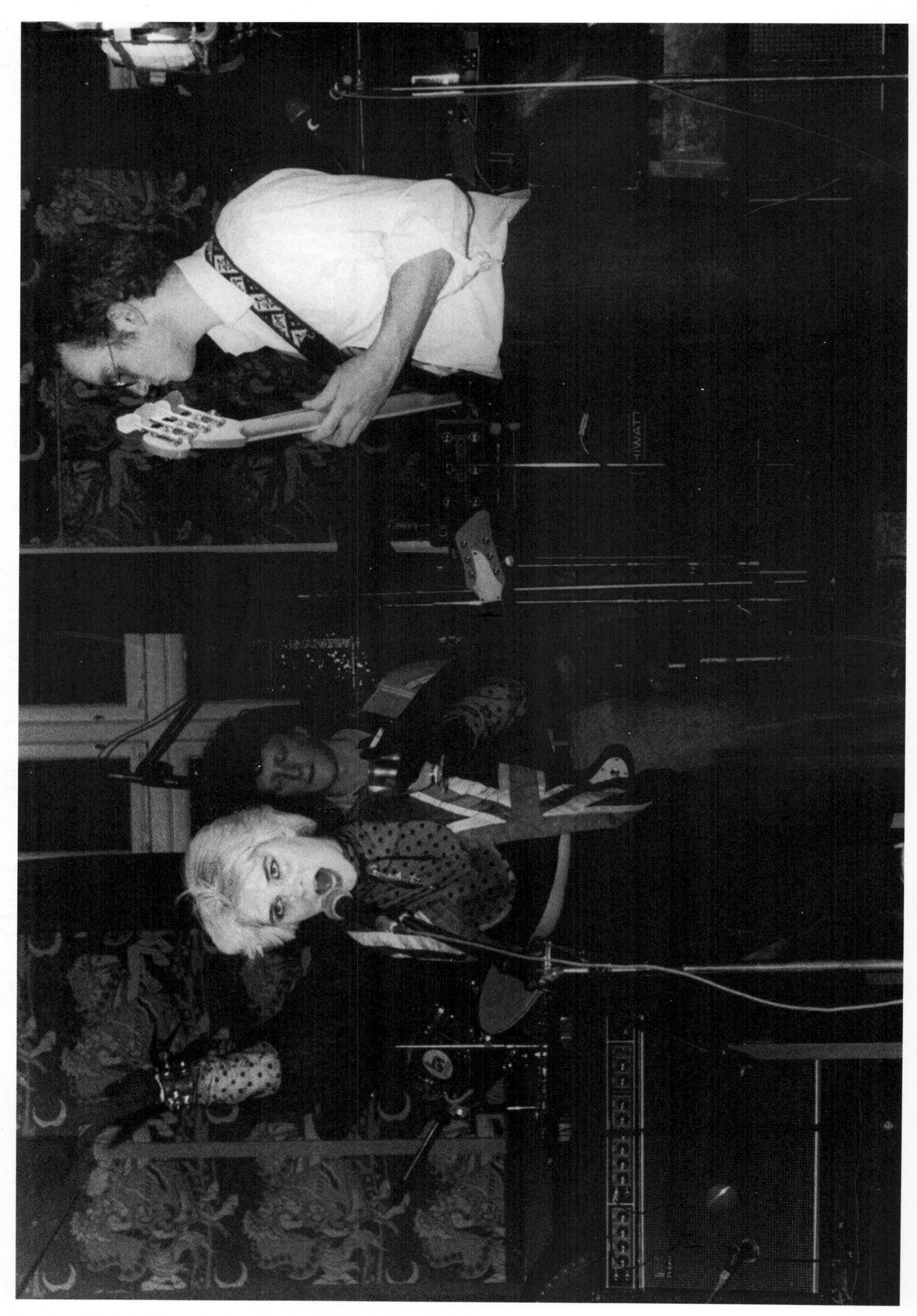

Toyah live at The Duke Of Lancaster, Barnet, London 1979. Photo: Steven Richards.

The Tours

45s:	Language School/Foreign Girls (PS)	(Tours T1) 1979
	Tourist Information/You Knew (PS)	(Virgin VS 307) 1979

A pop-punk band from Poole in Dorset. They were in the mould of **The Undertones** but lacked a vocalist of the stature of Feargal Sharkey. They also seem to have been influenced by Roxy Music.

Toyah

HCP

ALBUMS:	1	SHEEP FARMING IN BARNET	(Safari IC 064) 1979 -
(up to	2	THE BLUE MEANING	(Safari IEYA 666) 1980 40
1986)	3	TOYAH TOYAH TOYAH	(Safari LIVE 2) 1981 22
	4	ANTHEM	(Safari VOOR 1) 1981 2
	5	THE CHANGELING	(Safari VOOR 9) 1982 6
	6	WARRIOR ROCK - TOYAH ON TOUR	(Safari TNT 1) 1982 20
	7	LOVE IS THE LAW	(Safari VOOR 10) 1983 28
	8	TOYAH! TOYAH! TOYAH!	(K-Tel NE 1268) 1984 43
	9	MINX	(Portrait PRT 26415) 1985 24
	10	MAYHEM	(Safari VOOR 77) 1985 -
	11	THE LADY AND THE TIGER	(Editions EG EGED 44) 1986 -

NB: (1) also issued on CD (Great Expectations PIPCD 014) 1990. (2) also issued on CD (Great Expectations PIPCD 015) 1990. (3) also issued on CD (Great Expectations PIPCD 016) 1990. (4) also issued on CD (Safari VOORD 1) 1986 and again (Connoisseur EVSOP CD 263) 1999. (5) also issued on CD (Connoisseur EVSOP CD 264) 1999. (9) also included on CD (Epic CD 26415) 1985. Also relevant are *The Best Of Toyah* (Connoisseur Collection CSAPCD 115) 1994, *Looking Back* (Tring QED 065) 1996, *Live And More* (Connoisseur Collection CSAPCD 125) 1998 and *The Very Best Of Toyah* (Reactive REMCD 501) 1998.

HCP

EPs:	1	SHEEP FARMING IN BARNET (Neon Womb/ Indecision/Waiting/Our Movie /Vindication/ Dance) (PS)	(Safari SAP 1) 1979 -
	2	FOUR FROM TOYAH (It's A Mystery/War Boys/ Angels And Demons/ Revelations) (PS)	(Safari TOY 1) 1981 4
	3	FOUR MORE FROM TOYAH (Good Morning Universe/ Urban Tribesmen/In The Fairground/ The Furious Futures) (PS)	(Safari TOY 2) 1981 14

NB: (2) came with a flexidisc *Stand Proud* (FLX 215).

HCP

45s:	Victims Of The Riddle/	
(up to	Victims Of The Riddle (Vivisection) (PS)	(Safari SAFE 15) 1979 -
1986)	Bird In Flight/Tribal Look (PS)	(Safari SAFE 22) 1980 -
*	Ieya/The Helium Song (PS)	(Safari SAFE 28) 1981 48
	Danced/Ghosts/Neon Womb (PS)	(Safari SAFE 32) 1981 -
	I Want To Be Free/Walkie Talkie/ Allen	(Safari SAFE 34) 1981 8
*	Thunder In The Mountains/ Street Addict (PS)	(Safari SAFE 38) 1981 4
*	Brave New World/Warrior Rock (PS)	(Safari SAFE 45) 1981 21
	Be Loud Be Proud (Be Heard)/ Laughing With The Fools (PS)	(Safari SAFE 52) 1982 30
	Rebel Run/ To The Mountains High (PS)	(Safari SAFE 56) 1983 24
	The Vow/Explode (PS)	(Safari SAFE 58) 1983 50
	Line Of Symmetry	(Charisma CBEP 415) 1985 -
	Don't Fall In Love (I Said)/ Snow Covers The Kids (PS)	(Portrait A 6160) 1985 22
*	Soul Passing Through Soul/ All In A Rage (PS)	(Portrait A 6359) 1985 57
	Soul Passing Through Soul/ All In A Rage (12", PS)	(Portrait TA 6359) 1985 -
*	World In Action/Soldiers Of Fortune (PS)	(Portrait A 6545) 1985 -
	World In Action/ Soldiers Of Fortune (12", PS)	(Portrait TA 6545) 1985 -

NB: * Also issued as a picture disc.

TOYAH - Sheep Farming In Barnet.

Toyah (her full name is Toyah Ann Wilcox) was born at King's Heath, Birmingham on 18th May 1958. She carefully moulded herself as an identikit punk female singer having risen to some prominence via drama. In her youth she joined the Birmingham Old Rep Drama School and later worked as a mime artist for the Ballet Rambert.

She made her debut in a BBC TV play called 'Glitter', which also featured Noel Edmonds and Phil Daniels, singing in the band Bilbo Baggins. She played Emma in 'Tales From The Vienna Wood' and actor Ian Charleston took her to tea with Derek Jarman, who offered her the part of Mad in 'Jubilee'. Through this role she teamed up with **Adam Ant** and together with Eve Goddard the three of them formed a short-lived band called The Man Eaters.

Soon after **Toyah** formed her own group with Joel Bogen (gtr), Steve Bray (drms) (ex-**Boyfriends**), Pete Bush (keyb'ds) and Mark Henry (bs). She continued her acting career appearing in 'The Corn Is Green' with Katharine Hepburn and she also played the role of Monkey in 'Quadrophenia'.

Her band signed to Safari in 1979. A debut 45 *Victims Of The Riddle* was released. The follow-up *Bird In Flight* showcased her flamboyant vocal style. By this time Charlie Francis (who'd been in **Patrick Fitzgerald**'s backing group) had replaced Mark Henry on bass.

Her mini-album *Sheep Farming In Barnet* was released in 1979 while she was appearing in 'Quatermass'. Musically, it was full of punk enthusiasm and boisterousness but sounded rather a mish-mash. It contained six tracks in all:- *Neon Womb, Indecision, Waiting, Our Movie, Vindication* and *Dance*. This was later expanded into a full length album. It was a busy year for **Toyah** who hosted BBC Midlands' 'Look! Hear!' series and played a small role in 'Shoestring' along with several other acting parts.

A further album *The Blue Meaning* in 1980 brought her first chart success as it climbed to No. 40, spending four weeks in the charts. It was really her *Four From Toyah* (EP) in 1981 which broke her into the big time, particularly the repetitive lisp of *It's A Mystery*. This climbed to No. 4 in the singles chart, in which it spent fourteen weeks in all. The same year she enjoyed a No. 8 hit with *I Want To Be Free* during an eleven week chart sojourn. The nursery anthem appealed to a wide audience and most importantly many of the country's teenagers. She ended the year with the effervescent *Thunder In The Mountains* climbing to No. 4 during its nine week chart residency. She also had two more hit albums *Toyah Toyah Toyah* and *Anthem*, which reached No. 22 and No. 2 respectively. In 1990, her first three albums were reissued on CD by Great Expectations.

In 1982, **Toyah** reaped further chart success with the hypnotic *Ieya* (originally released the previous year) and the pulsating *Be Loud Be Proud (Be Heard)*, *The Changeling* was a No. 6 album, enjoying a twelve week chart residency. This was possibly her best album with *The Creepy Room* and *Angel And Me* two of its stand-out tracks. In 1999, both *Anthem* and *The Changeling* were reissued on CD by Connoisseur. *Anthem* included as bonus cuts the content of the *Four From Toyah* (EP) and the 'B' sides *Alien* and *Walkie Talkie*. The CD reissue of *The Changeling* also comes with bonus tracks - three of the four from the *Four More From Toyah* (EP) rather annoyingly omitting *The Furious (Futures)*.

Although she continued to record with Joel Bogen she dispensed with her band for future albums utilising session musicians instead. Further acting credits included roles in 'The Tempest' and the stage play 'Trafford Tanzi'. She enjoyed a Top 20 album with *Warrior Rock - Toyah On Tour* in 1982.

Toyah married ex-Giles, Giles and Fripp, King Crimson and Fripp and Eno guitarist Robert Fripp and became a buddhist. She continued to enjoy commercial success with two further hit singles - *Rebel Run* (No. 24) and *The Vow* (No. 50) - and an album *Love Is The Law*, which spent seven weeks in the charts peaking at No. 28, but it proved to be her last for Safari.

Her final hit album *Minx* came out on Portrait in 1985, but in 1987 she made further recordings for Editions E.G. Her final hit single was a cover version of Martha and The Muffins' *Echo Beach* in 1987. Her material has not aged well for the most part and it's probably no bad thing that in the nineties she concentrated on her career as a stage actress and TV producer.

The CD compilation *The Best Of Toyah* released on Connoisseur Collection in 1994 includes her catchy *It's A Mystery* along with most of her other singles. Alternatively, Reactive's 1998 CD collection *The Very Best Of Toyah* covers similar material, but utilises more album cuts.

TOY DOLLS - Everybody Jitterbug.

Toy Dolls

Personnel:	FLIP	bs	A
	HAPPY BOB	drms	A
	OLGA	lead vcls	A

				HCP
ALBUMS: 1(A)	DIG THAT GROOVE BABY	(Volume VOLP 1) 1983	-	
(up to 2(A)	A FAR OUT DISC	(Volume VOLP 2) 1985	71	
1986) 3(A)	SINGLES 1983-84	(Volume VOLM 020) 1986	-	

NB: (1) also issued on CD (Volume VOCD 1) 1988. (2) also issued on CD (Volume VOCD 002) 1988 and also on CD as *Dig That Groove Baby* (Receiver RRCD 166) 1993. (3) also on CD (Receiver RRCD 167) 1993. Compilations include *The Collection* (Castle CCSCD 335) 1992 and *Ten Years Of Toys* (Dojo DOJO LP 171) 1989; also on CD (Dojo DOJO CD 171) 1994. Also relevant is *On Stage In Stuttgart* (Receiver RRCD 278) 1999.

			HCP
45s: *	Tommy Kowey's Car/She Goes To Finos	(GBH SSM 005) 1981	-
(up to +	Tommy Kowey's Car/(She's A) Working Ticket/		
1986)	Everybody Jitterbug/Teenager In Love/		
	I've Got Asthma (PS)	(GRC GRC 104) 1981	-
	Everybody Jitterbug/		
	(She's A) Working Ticket (PS)	(Zonophone Z 31) 1982	-
	Nellie The Elephant/		
	Dig That Groovy Baby (PS)	(Volume VOL 3) 1983	4
	Cheerio And Toodle Pip/H.O. (PS)	(Volume VOL 5) 1983	-
	Alfie From The Bronx/Hanky Panky (PS)	(Volume VOL 7) 1983	-
	We're Mad/Deirdre's A Slag (PS)	(Volume VOL 10) 1984	-
	We're Mad/Deirdre's A Slag/		
	Rupert The Bear (12", PS)	(Volume VOLT 10) 1984	-
	She Goes To Finos/		
	Spiders In The Dressing Room (PS)	(Volume VOL 12) 1984	-
	She Goes To Finos/Spiders In The Dressing Room/		
	Come Back Jackie (12", PS)	(Volume VOLT 12) 1984	-
	James Bond Lives Down Our Street/		
	Olga I Cannot (PS)	(Volume VOL 17) 1984	-
	Geordies Gone To Jail/Idle Gossip (PS)	(Volume VOL 21) 1986	-

NB: * Only 500 copies pressed. This did not appear in a picture sleeve. + Issued in a yellow paper picture sleeve with an insert.

Hailing from Sunderland **Toy Dolls** were an Oi! trio centred around lead singer Olga. Numerous other bassists and drummers have passed through their ranks. Their two early 45s on GBH and GRC are now very rare and quite pricey to purchase. The same year they contributed *She Goes To Fino's* and *Deidre's A Slag* to *Strength Thru' Oi!* (Decca) in 1981. They played a sort of fun, fast-paced punk, with little taste or style. They enjoyed a rapid elevation to the national stage in December 1984 when their breakneck version of *Nellie The Elephant* rose to No. 4 in the charts, in which it enjoyed a total stay of twelve weeks.

They developed a dedicated cult following with songs like *Yul Bryner Was A Skinhead, Geordies Gone To Jail, Nowt Can Compare To Sunderland Fine-Fair* and *Deidre's A Slag* (which was actually an attack on 'Coronation Street's' Deirdre Barlow). Their second album *A Far Out Disc* spent a week in the charts at No. 71.

Many of their 'best' songs, including their rare debut 45 *Tommy Kowey's Car*, are included on *The Collection* CD released in 1992. They did severely damage their punk credibility by composing a new theme tune to the children's TV pop show 'Razamatazz'.

Singles 1983 - 1984 contains only seven tracks and has a short playing time of just under twenty-four minutes. *Ten Years Of Toys*, originally issued on vinyl in 1989 and then subsequently on CD in 1994, includes several of their early singles, including *Tommy Kowey's Car*, which is now a collector's item. They contributed *Everybody Jitterbug* to *Burning Ambition: A History Of Punk, Vol. 3* (Anagram CD PUNK 98) 1997. You'll also find their lighthearted *Everybody Jitterbug* and frantic *(She's A) Worky Ticket* on *Oi! The Singles Collection, Vol. 3* (Captain Oi! AHOY CD 67) 1997. *Everybody Jitterbug* is also on *The Zonophone Punk Singles Collection* (Anagram CDPUNK 97) 1997, whilst their hit single *Nellie The Elephant* got further exposure on *New Wave Archive* (Rialto RMCD 201), also in 1997.

On Stage In Stuttgart is taken from two German gigs in Stuttgart and Frankfurt. Unfortunately the packaging gives no details of dates. Most of their better-known songs are featured alongside amusing covers of *Sabre Dance* and the theme from *Raiders Of The Lost Ark*.

The Toys

EPs:	1( )	STILL DANCING (The Things I Say/	
		Blanket To Blanket/Pretty Girl/	
		Johnny Head In Air) (PS)	(Toys TOYS 2) 1979
	2( )	MY MIND WANDERS (My Mind Wanders/	
		The Girl On My Wall/Toytime/I'd Do	
		Anything For You) (PS)	(SRTS SRTS/79/CUS 345) 1979
45:		Go For The Police/I'm Alright	(Red Bus RBUS 54) 1980

A pop band from St. Albans who wrote some pretty sharp melodies.

The Trainspotters

45s:	High Rise/	
	Rock 'n' Roll Hall Of Fame (PS)	(Arista ARIST 290) 1979
	Unfaithful/Hiring The Hall	(Arista ARIST 320) 1979

The Trainspotters sound like a third division **Members** on *High Rise* which, as its title suggests, is a song about living in a tower block delivered in a three chord format.

The Transmitters

Personnel:
JIM CHASE	drms, keyb'ds		AB
VINCE CUTCLIFFE	gtr		A
SAM DODSON	bs, gtr, keyb'ds		AB
MIKEL LEE	gtr		A
JOHN QUINN	vcls		A
ROB CHAPMAN	keyb'ds, vcls		B
DAVE BABY	sax		B
JULIAN TREASURE	drms		B
SID WEELS	bs		B

ALBUMS: 1(A) 24 HOURS (Ebony EBY 1002) 1978
2(B) AND WE CALL THIS LEISURE TIME
(Heartbeat HB 4) 1982

CASS: 1(-) I JAX DUB (Eccentric EX 2 C50) 197?

EP: 1( ) STILL HUNTING FOR THE UGLY MAN (The Ugly Man/The One That Won The War/Free Trade/Curious) (12", PS) (Step Forward SF 1212) 1979

45s: Party/O.5. Alive (PS) (Ebony EYE 11) 1978
Nowhere Train/Uninvited Guest/
Persons Unknown (die-cut PS) (Ebony EYE 12) 1978

The Transmitters' vocalist Rob Chapman had previously been with **Glaxo Babies**, a Bristol quintet who some compared to The Residents in terms of their formless experimentation. It will therefore come as little surprise that **The Transmitters** from Ealing in West London trod a similar path. The lyrics are interesting, the music is minimalist, the overall sound is often on the brink of total weirdness. Interesting but demanding, with some similarities to **The Fall**. Seek out if you like experiemental music.

Trax

Personnel incl:
WILLIE ADAMSON	vcls	A
DEREK ARMSTRONG	bs	A
NOBBY MARTIN	keyb'ds	A

EP: 1(A) TRAX (Home/Losing Out/
Late Nite Call Out) (Lonely LONESOME ONE) 1979

Trax hailed from Dunfermline, but they never followed up this promising debut EP. Some dismissed them as **Skids** copyists and their keyboards are reminiscent of Barclay James Harvest.

Steve Treatment

EPs: 1 5-A-SIDED 45 (The Hippy-Posed Engrosement/
Hooked On A Trend/Negative Nights/
Taste Your Own Medecine/
Danger Zone) (Rather GEAR 2) 1978
2 Chosen To Go/Tempest Fashion Baby/
Cry In Alphabet Sharp/Change Of Plan/
Head Of A Raven (Backbone 2BHIT 2) 1979

NB: (2) credited to **Steve Treatment** and The Zodiac Fassion.

45: Heaven Knows/
Step Inside A Worn-Out Shoe (Backbone 2BHIT 1) 1979

On the *5-A-Sided 45* (EP), despite disclaimers to the contrary on the sleeve, the band described as the AFV's were in fact **The Swell Maps** playing under a pseudonym! They issued this on their own Rather label. It was critically acclaimed at the time.

The Trend

45: Teenage Crush/Cool Johnny (Trendy TREND 1) 1979

A home-produced effort. *Teenage Crush* is catchy and quite infectious with melodramatic vocals.

THE TRANSMITTERS - 24 Hours.

The Trokkoids

CASS: 1( ) CONFRONT THE VOID (THE THRINKY THRONG)
(Destroy Stewart Granger Records) 1979

A D.I.Y. album full of crafty electronics, harsh tape edits, indiscriminate feedback and dopey narration. This didn't have commercial distribution.

Troops Of Tomorrow

EP: 1( ) TROOPS OF TOMORROW (Just When You Thought It Was Quiet) (12") (Troops TROOPS 1) 1982

This was a spin-off project of **The Vibrators**.

Tubeway Army

Personnel:
PAUL GARDINER	bs		AB
GARY NUMAN (WEBB)	vcls, gtr, synth, keyb'ds		AB
JESS LIDYARD	drms		A
BARRY BENN	drms		B
SEAN BURKE	gtr		B

HCP
ALBUMS: 1(A) TUBEWAY ARMY (Beggars Banquet BEGA 4) 1978 14
2(A) REPLICAS (Beggars Banquet BEGA 7) 1979 1

NB: (1) Originally 5,000 copies were released in blue vinyl in a gatefold sleeve, some copies also had a badge. The second pressing came in a white stickered sleeve. (1) later reissued at budget price (Fame FA 3060) 1983. (1) reissued remastered on album and CD (Beggars Banquet BBL 4CD) 1998. (2) was originally issued with a large black and white poster. (2) issued on CD (MCI Original Masters MUSCD 509) 1995 and then remastered on album and CD (Beggars Banquet BBL 7CD) 1998. Also of relevance is *The Plan* (Beggars Banquet BEGA 55) 1985. This comprised early **Tubeway Army** demos. There was also a limited edition (4,800 copies) picture disc release of this album. The album got to No. 29. In 1985, a series of three vinyl EPs were also issued: *Tubeway Army, Vol. 1* (Beggars Banquet BEG 92 E) 1985 with an alternate mix of *That's Too Bad* on yellow vinyl; *Tubeway Army, Vol. 2* (Beggars Banquet BEG 123 E) 1985, issued on red or black vinyl; and *Tubeway Army, Vol. 3* (Beggars Banquet BEG 124E) 1985, issued on blue or black vinyl. There's also a cassette-only compilation, *Tubeway Army 1978/1979* (Beggars Banquet BEGC 7879) 1985.

HCP
45s: * That's Too Bad/
Oh! I Didn't Say (Beggars Banquet BEG 5) 1978 -
* Bombers/O.D. Receiver/
Blue Eyes (Beggars Banquet BEG 8) 1978 -
Down In The Park/Do You
Need The Service? (PS) (Beggars Banquet BEG 17) 1979 -
+ Down In The Park/Do You Need The Service?/I Nearly Married
A Human 2 (12", PS) (Beggars Banquet BEG 17T) 1979 -
x Are 'Friends' Electric/
We Are So Fragile (PS) (Beggars Banquet BEG 18) 1979 1

o   Are 'Friends' Electric/
    We Are So Fragile (12", PS)   (INT 126.501) 1979 -
α   That's Too Bad/Oh! Didn't I Say/Bombers/
    O.D. Receiver/Blue Eyes
    (double pack, gatefold PS)   (Beggars Banquet BACK 2) 1979 -

NB: * Limited edition of 4,000. + Limited edition of 5,000. x There was also a picture disc release (BEG 18 P). o This was a German 12" distributed in the U.K. by Beggars Banquet. α Some copies with a mispressed second disc omitted O.D. Receiver. There's also a Peel Session (Strange Fruit SFPS 32) 1987.

Gary Numan's real name was Gary Webb. He was born on 8th March 1958 in Hammersmith, London. In 1977, he formed a punk outfit called **Mean Street**. This proved to be a flop, so later in the year he decided to start afresh with Paul Gardiner (a friend who he'd played with in an outfit called The Lasers). The trio was completed by Gary's uncle Jess Lidyard. They called themselves **Tubeway Army** and negotiated a one-off deal with the Beggars Banquet label.

4,000 copies of *That's Too Bad* were pressed and released in February 1978. It was a punk-influenced guitar-orientated effort and sold quite well.

In July 1978, a follow-up *Bombers*, was released. Again 4,000 copies were pressed and this sold quite well. Gary is credited as songwriter under his early pseudonym Valerian on this album. The success of these two singles lead to a longer contract with Beggars Banquet. When outside commitments forced Jess Lidyard to leave the band, it expanded to a quartet with the addition of Barry Benn and Sean Burke. By now the band were gigging at some of London's top punk venues. This period of their history was later captured on a bootleg album and 45 called *Live At The Roxy*.

Whilst things appeared to be going well, Gary was increasingly bothered by the violence at gigs. He also wanted to play at bigger venues and bring synthesizers into **Tubeway Army**'s repertoire. This lead to a classic case of musical differences between members. By August 1978, both Benn and Burke had left. Gary also chose this time to change his name to **Numan**.

He used his new name on the band's eponymous album, *Tubeway Army*, which was released in August 1978. The first 5,000 copies were pressed in blue vinyl. Musically, guitars still dominated within a three minute post-punk structure, but the album also featured some primitive electronics. These became influential on other bands' recordings at the time. It is worth noticing that neither of their first two 45s appeared on the album.

During 1979 **Numan** came up with a new image for his change of musical style. One of his other talents was as a Sci-fi short story writer and he began to turn some of these into songs. His next 45 release *Down In The Park* was a case in point. It introduced a new haunting, synthesizer-based sound to his fans. He used the cover to introduce a new visual image - as a jet black clothed android with white blond hair. It was the first of his singles to be issued in a 12" format too. The 12" featured an extra cut, *I Nearly Married A Human 2*. *Down In The Park* was also included on *20 Of Another Kind, Vol. 2* (Polydor POLX 1) in 1979 and *Machines* (Virgin V 2177) in 1980.

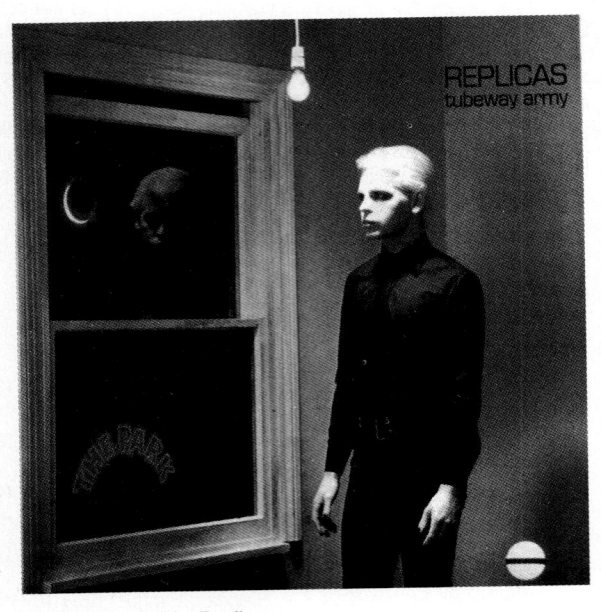

TUBEWAY ARMY - Replicas.

As you'll nearly all know it was *Are 'Friends' Electric?*, released in May 1979, that brought the band to the public eye. As a promotional gimmick, a limited picture disc release came out the following month. He used a Peel session and an appearance on 'The Old Grey Whistle Test' to help promote it. The record soon topped the charts, where it stayed for four weeks. It spent sixteen weeks in the charts in all. A couple of different release formats which may interest collectors. There was a 12" German picture sleeve distributed by Beggars Banquet and a three minute forty-five seconds edited version which appeared as a U.S. promo.

A new album, *Replicas* was released in June 1979. The album, which sounds dated now, seemed stunningly innovative at the time. Clinical synthesizer, coupled with deadpan vocals singing mostly sci-fi lyrics - this was a winner at the time. Their earlier *Are Friends Electric?* 45 was also included as the jewel in the crown. *Replicas* topped the album charts and spent a massive thirty-one weeks in them overall. This motivated Beggars Banquet to reissue their debut album in a white cover drawn by Garry Robson. This also spent ten weeks in the charts peaking at No. 14. Also, in June 1979, their first two 45s was issued in a double-pack format.

From hereon their records were credited to **Gary Numan** as opposed to **Tubeway Army**. See his entry for details. In 1981, *Are Friends Electric?* and *Down In The Park* were issued as a cassingle in a box (Beggars Banquet IT 418497). A year earlier a demo version of *Down In The Park* appeared on the soundtrack album *Times Square* (RSO 2685 145).

The Strange Fruit 1987 release captures the group just months away from their *Are Friends Electric?* hit. This three-track session from January 1979 includes two of their best numbers *Me I Disconnect From You* and *Down In The Park*.

In 1996, *Beggars Banquet - The Punk Singles Collection* (Anagram CDPUNK 73) gave a further airing to *That's Too Bad*, *Bombers* and *I Don't Need To Tell Her*.

Turquoise Swimming Pools

Personnel:	DAVID BALFE	keyb'ds	A
	HUGH JONES		A
	TROY TATE	gtr, vcls	A

The **Turquoise Swimming Pools** did not release any singles or albums in their own right, but they did contribute two cuts that were otherwise unreleased at the time to the superb compilation *To The Shores Of Lake Placid* (Zoo FOUR) 1982. David Balfe and Troy Tate were both members of **The Teardrop Explodes**, whilst Hugh Jones was Julian Cope's producer. *The Wind*, penned by David Balfe, is a pleasant popish song with prominent piano. *Burst Balloons* is similar in style (again written by Balfe), with agreeable vocals and backing. Both songs are well worth a listen.

TV 21

Personnel:	NEIL BALDWIN	bs	A
	STEVEN BROWN	perc	A
	DAVE HAMPTON	trumpet, vcls	A
	ALLY PALMER	gtr, vcls	A
	ALI PATERSON	drms	A
	NORMAN RODGER	gtr, vcls	A

ALBUM: 1(A) A THIN RED LINE   (Deram SML 1123) 1981

45s: Playing With Fire/
        Shattered By It All (foldout PS)   (Powbeat AAARGH! 1) 1980
        Ambition/Ticking Away/
        This Is Zero (foldout PS)   (Powbeat AAARGH! 2) 1980
        Snakes And Ladders/Artistic Licence/
        Ambition/Playing With Fire
        (double pack, PS)   (Deram DM 442/DMF 442) 1981
        Something's Wrong/
        The Hidden Voice (PS)   (Deram DM 447) 1981
        Something's Wrong/
        The Hidden Voice/On The Run (12", PS) (Deram DM 448) 1981
        On The Run/End Of A Dream (PS)   (Demon D 1004) 1981

A Scottish outfit who sounded a bit like **XTC** and have also been likened to **U2** and Haircut One Hundred on occasions. The vocals from singer

Norman Rodger are appealing. The music is essentially guitar orientated, but included trumpet and keyboards. Quite interesting.

25 Rifles

45:	World War 3/Revolution Blues/Hey Little/		
	Dance 'Bout Now (12")	(25 Rifles TFR+ 1)	1979

An obscure mod revival 45 which came in a stamped sleeve. The band came from Leeds, and their 12" was available by mail order.

23 Skidoo

Personnel:	FITZ HAAMAN	drms, vcls	A
	ALEX TURNBULL	bs, vcls	A
	J.C.M. TURNBULL	gtr, vcls	A

ALBUMS:	1(A)	SEVEN SONGS (Mini LP)	(Fetish FM 2008)	1982
	2(A)	THE CULLING IS COMING	(Operation Twilights)	1983
	3(A)	URBAN GAMELAN	(Illuminated JAMS 40)	1985

NB: (1) reissued (Illuminated JAMS 47) 1985. (1) reissued again on vinyl (Skidoo SKLP 02) 2000, also on CD (Skidoo SKCD 02) 2000. (2) reissued (Laylah LAY 23) 1988, also on CD (LAY 23CD) 1983. (2) reissued again on vinyl (Skidoo SKLP 03) 2000, also on CD (Skidoo SKCD 03) 2000. (3) reissued on vinyl (Skidoo SKLP 04) 2000, also on CD (Skidoo SKCD 04) 2000. Also relevant is *23 Skidoo* (dbl) (Virgin V 2912) 2000, also on CD (Virgin CDV 2912) 2000.

45s:	Ethics/Another Baby's Face (PS)	(Pineapple PULP 23)	1981
	Last Words/Last Words (Alt. Version)		
	(Promo only)	(Fetish FE 10)	1981
	The Gospel Comes To New Guinea/		
	Last Words (12", PS)	(Fetish FE 11)	1981
	Tearing Up The Plans/Just Like Everybody/		
	Gregouka (12", PS)	(Fetish FP 20)	1982
	Coup (Two Versions)/		
	In The Palace (12", PS)	(Illuminated ILL 2812)	1985
	Language	(Illuminated ILL 2812)	1985
	Ozze	(Illuminated ILL 5812)	1985
	Thought Of You	(Illuminated 12 LEV 72)	1986
	The Assassins With Soul	(Illuminated 12 LEV 72)	1986

23 Skidoo were chronologically one of the later Industrial Music bands. They played an aggressive brand of electro-funk but also experimented with tape-loops etc. Their early music was very similar to that of their friends **Cabaret Voltaire**, but **23 Skidoo** were less Western and more freeform in their appraoch.

Ironically their debut album *Seven Songs* listed eight tracks and contained nine. It was later reissued in 1985 with twelve tracks! It veers between

TV 21 - A Thin Red Line.

TWINK AND THE FAIRIES - Do It '77.

dancey tracks like *Vegas El Bandito*; African percussion as represented by the like of *Quiet Pillage* and soundscapes in the form of *Mary's Operation*.

One side of *The Culling Is Coming* utilises Balinese Gamelon instruments. The other side 'A Summer Rite' contained their own interpretation of urban decay recorded live at the first WOMAD festival in 1982.

The Tearing Up The Plans 12" included the Pipes Of Pan giving the disc an almost hypnotic quality.

Urban Gamelan was less cerebral and utilised CO2 cylinders and glass jugs. Another band which was an acquired taste! Their experimental nature guaranteed that they enjoyed no more than a cult following.

Twink and The Fairies

Personnel:	TWINK (JOHN ALDER)	drms, vcls	A
	RUSSEL HUNTER	drms	A
	PAUL RUDOLPH	gtr, vcls	A
	DUNCAN SANDERSON	bs, vcls	A

EP:	Do It '77/The Psychedelic Punkaroo/		
	Enter The Diamonds (12", PS)	(Chiswick SWT 26)	1978

Twink (John Alder) made this 12" EP with his old colleagues from The Pink Fairies. You can read about them and The Deviants (which Hunter and Rudolph had been in previously) in my earlier book 'The Tapestry Of Delights'.

This EP was **Twink**'s attempt at punk. He'd earlier been vocalist in the short-lived **Rings**. He's certainly done better things than this.

After this EP, **Twink and The Fairies** disbanded once agan when **Twink** moved to Belgium. Duncan Sanderson joined Lightning Raiders. **Twink** returned in 1986 with more solo recordings and reformed the Pink Fairies again in 1987.

Twist

Personnel:	STEVE CORDUNER	drms	A
	JIMMY EDWARDS	vcls	A
	PETER MARSH	gtr, vcls	A
	ANDY PASK	bs	A

ALBUM:	1(A)	THIS IS YOUR LIFE	(Polydor 2383 552)	1979

45s:	This Is Your Life/Life's A		
	Commercial Break (PS)	(Polydor 2059 156)	1979
	Ads/Rebound (PS)	(Polydor POSP 84)	1979

An obscure band who never attained the success they deserved. Pete Marsh had previously been in an easy listening band called Easy Street and later Blanket Of Secrecy. Andy Pask had been in **Landscape** and Steve Corduner was previously in Nasty Pop.

Elvis Costello and Steve Nieve guested on *This Is Your Life* and **Costello**'s influence in particular is evident from the good bouncy rock 'n' roll thereon.

Ads was co-produced by Pete Marsh, the dynamic element within the band, and Roger Bechirian. The lyrics are polished and deal with Marsh's persepective on the television watcher's mentality. This got further exposure on *20 Of Another Kind, Vol. 2* (Polydor POLX 1) in 1979.

2.3 (Children)

Personnel:	PAUL BOWER	gtr	A
	HAYDN BOYES-WESTON	drms	A
	PAUL SHAFT	bs	A

45:    All Time Low/Where To Now? (PS)(Fast Products FAST 2) 1978

A short-lived group who also contributed a cut to the *NMX: Live At Sheffield* (NMX) 1981 cassette compilation. *All Time Low* is an infectious, manic depression paean, which was an NME 'Single of the Week'. Both sides of the single were also included on the sampler *Fast Product* (Fast EMC 3312) in 1979. Their drummer Haydn Boyes - Weston was later with **Cabaret Voltaire**.

Sean Tyla (Gang)

Personnel:	MICHAEL DESMARAIS	drms	AB
	BRUCE IRVINE	gtr	AB
	DEKE LEONARD	gtr, vcls, keyb'ds	A
	PETER O'SULLIVAN	bs	A
	BRIAN TURRINGTON	bs	AB
	SEAN TYLVA	gtr, vcls	ABC
	KEN WHALEY	bs	B

ALBUMS:	1(A)	YACHTLESS	(Beserkley BSERK 11) 1977
	2(A)	MOONPROOF	(Beserkeley BESERK 16) 1978
	3(C)	JUST POPPED OUT	(Polydor 2391 463) 1980
	4(C)	REDNECK IN BABYLON	(Zilch RIEN 1) 1981

NB: (1) also issued on CD (Beserkley BECD 503) 1989. Some copies of (2) issued on yellow vinyl. There's also a **Tyla Gang** CD *Blow You Out* (Skydog 622392) 1997. (3) and (4) are credited to **Sean Tyla**.

45s:	Styrofoam/		
	Texas Chainsaw Massacre Boogie (PS)	(Stiff BUY 4) 1976	
	Dust On The Needle/Pool Hall Punk	(Beserkley BZZ 5) 1977	
	Tropical Love/		
	Walking The Dog-Live (PS)	(Beserkley BZZ 15) 1978	
*	Breakfast In Marin/Paradise Track &		
	English Electric	(Zilch ZILCH 1) 1978	
*	Landing Lights/Tonight &		
	English Electric (PS)	(Zilch ZILCH 7) 1979	

NB: * **Sean Tyla** solo singles.

Sean Tyla had previously played with highly-touted pub-rockers Ducks Deluxe, but like **Dave Edmunds**, **Nick Lowe** and others he got sucked into the whole punk/new wave scene. Indeed **Tyla Gang**'s 45 *Styrofoam* was the Stiff label's fourth release. Both sides of the 45 were also included on *Hits Greatest Stiffs* (Stiff FIST 1) in 1977. His band was also full of veterans of the seventies pub-rock scene and his albums are straight down the line, no-holes-barred, hard rockers with **Tyla**'s hoarse vocals. Solid, but unexceptional. *Yachtless* is full of driving guitar and upfront drumming and is the more energetic of the two **Tyla Gang** albums. *Moonproof* features more acoustic guitar and a subtler sound, but it still has plenty of drive.

The band are also captured live playing *Styrofoam* and *On The Street* on *Hope And Anchor Front Row Festival* (dbl) (Warner Bros K 66077) 1978.

After he disbanded the **Sean Tyla Gang**, Sean continued as a solo artist. He recorded *Just Popped Out* with a whole host of pub rock cronies and Joan Jett.

Typhoons

45:    Telstar/In Fae A Brothin' (PS)   (Bohemian BO 1) 1981

The **Typhoons** were a pseudonym used by **Ruts D.C.**.

UK Subs

Personnel:	NICKY GARRATT	lead gtr	ABCD
(up to	CHARLIE HARPER		
1986)	(DAVID CHARLES PEREZ)	vcls, gtr	ABCDEF
	LIONS	drms	A
	PAUL SLACK	bs	AB E
	PETER DAVIS	drms	B
	ALVIN GIBBS	bs	CD
	STEVE ROBERTS	drms	C
	KIM WYLIE	drms	D
	STEVE JONES	drms	E
	CAPTAIN SCARLETT	gtr	E
	RAB FAE BEITH	drms	F
	JOHN FALLON	gtr	F
	JEZZ MONCUR	bs	F

HCP

ALBUMS:	1(B)	ANOTHER KIND OF BLUES	(Gem GEMLP 100) 1979 21
(up to	2(B)	BRAND NEW AGE	(Gem GEMLP 106) 1980 18
1986)	3(B)	CRASH COURSE (live)	(Gem GEMLP 111) 1980 8
	4(C)	DIMINISHED RESPONSIBILITY	
			(Gem GEMLP 112) 1981 18
	5(D)	ENDANGERED SPECIES	(Abstract) 1982 -
	6(E)	FLOOD OF LIES	(Fallout FALLLP 018) 1983 -
	7(F)	GROSS OUT U.S.A. (live) (CD)	
			(Fallout FALLLP 031) 1985 -
	8(F)	HUNTINGDON BEACH	(UK Subs RFB LP 1) 1985 -
	9(-)	IN ACTION	(Red Flame RFB LP 2) 1986 -
	10(-)	SUBS STANDARDS	(Dojo DOJOLP 28) 1986 -
	11(-)	RAW MATERIAL	(Killerwatt KILP 2001) 1986 -

NB: (1) also issued on CD (Abstract AABCD 801) 1991, (Dojo DOJOCD 226) 1995 and *Another Kind Of Blues... Plus* (Diablo DIAB 862) 1998. (1) reissued again on CD (Captain Oi! AHOY CD 134) 2000 with bonus cuts. (2) also issued on CD (Abstract AABCD 802) 1991, (Dojo DOJOCD 228) 1995 with bonus cuts and again (Captain Oi! AHOY CD 136) 2000. (3) also issued on CD (Abstract AABCD 803) 1991, on CD (Dojo DOJO 229) 1995 with bonus cuts and again (Captain Oi! AHOY CD 140) 2000. (4) also issued on CD (Abstract AABCD 804) 1991 and on red vinyl. (4) reissued again on CD (Captain Oi! AHOY CD 143) 2000 with bonus cuts. (5) and (8) also issued on one CD (Dojo LOMACD 7) 1994. (5) reissued on red vinyl, 1,500 only (Link Classics CLINK 4) 198?. (6) also issued on CD with *Singles 1982-85* (Fallout FALLCD 18) 1995 and later as a single CD with seven bonus tracks (Captain Oi! AHOY CD 166) 2001. (8) also issued on CD (FM-Revolver REVXD 150) 1990 and again (Captain Oi! AHOY CD 114) 1999 with bonus cuts. (9) also issued on CD (Solid Inc. RNB 001) 1999. There have also been numerous compilations *Recorded 1979-81* (Abstract AABT 300) 1982 copies came in blue vinyl with a stencil, *In Action* (RFB RFLP 2) 1986, 5,000 copies only in green vinyl, also on CD (FM-Revolver REVXD 142) 1990; *Greatest Hits - Live In Paris*

UK Subs - Brand New Age.

(Released Emotions REM 005) 1990; *Europe Calling* (Released Emotions REM 12 CD) 1992; *Left For Dead, Alive In Hollywood* (CD) (Roir RE 412 CD) 1994; *The Peel Sessions (1978-79)* (Fallout FALLCD 53) 1997; *The Punk Singles Collection* (Anagram CD PUNK 66) 1995 and again (Captain Oi! AHOY LP 518) 1997; *Quintessentials* (Fallout FALLCD 054) 1997; *The Singles 1978-82* (Abstract AABT 800) 1991 and (Get Back GBR 001) 1993; *Scum Of The Earth - The Best Of The UK Subs* (Music Club MCCD 120) 1993; *UK Subs Box Set* (4CD) (Abstract SUBBOX 1) 1996; *Punk Rock Rarities* (CD) (Captain Oi! AHOY CD 93) 1998; *Warhead* (CD) (Harry May MAYO CD 107) 1999; *Sub Mission - The Best Of UK Subs 1982 - 98* (Fallout/Jungle Fall CD 055) 1999; *Left For Dead* (ROIR RUSCD 8256) 1999 and *Time Warp - Greatest Hits* (Anagram CDPUNK 120) 2001.

HCP

EPs:				
1(B)	SHE'S NOT THERE/KICKS (She's Not There/Kicks/Victim/The Same Thing) (PS)	(Gem GEMS 14)	1979	36
2(C)	KEEP RUNNIN' (Keep On Runnin' (Till You Burn)/Perfect Girl/Ice Age/Party In Paris (French Version))	(Gem GEMEP 45)	1981	-
3(D)	SHAKE UP THE CITY (Shake Up The City/Self Destruct/Police State/War Of The Roses) (PS)	(Abstract ABS 012)	1982	-
4(D)	LIVE AT GOSSIPS	(Chaos LIVE 009)	1982	-
5(E)	Magic/Private Army/The Spell/Multiple Minds/Primary Strength (12", PS)	(Fallout FALL 12024)	1984	-

NB: (1) Some copies on green vinyl. (2) Some copies on blue vinyl. (3) Some copies on red vinyl. (4) is a cassette EP.

HCP

45s:				
*	C.I.D./I Live In A Car/B.I.C. (PS)	(City NIK 5)	1978	-
+	Stranglehold/World War/Rockers (PS)	(Gem GEMS 5)	1979	26
x	Tomorrow's Girls/Scum Of The Earth/Telephone Numbers (PS)	(Gem GEMS 10)	1979	28
	C.I.D./I Live In A Car/B.I.C. (PS)	(Pinnacle PIN 22)	1979	-
o	Warhead/I'm Waiting For The Man/The Harper (PS)	(Gem GEMS 23)	1980	30
α	Teenage/Left For Dead/New York State Police (PS)	(Gem GEMS 30)	1980	32
β	Party In Paris/Fall Of The Empire (PS)	(Gem GEMS 42)	1980	37
χ	Keep On Runnin' (Till You Burn)/Perfect Girl (PS)	(Gem GEMS 45)	1980	41
	Countdown/Plan Of Action (PS)	(NEMS NEM 304)	1981	-
	Party In Paris	(Ramkup CAC 2)	1982	-
	Another Typical City/Still Life (PS)	(Fallout FALL 17)	1983	-
	Another Typical City/Still Life/Veronique (12")	(Fallout FALL 12017)	1983	-
δ	This Gun Says/Speak For Myself/Wanted	(Fallout FALL 36)	1985	-

NB: * Issued in clear, blue, green, orange and red vinyl. + Some copies on red vinyl. x Some copies on blue vinyl. o Some copies on brown vinyl. α Some copies on pink and orange vinyl. β Some copies on yellow vinyl. χ Some copies on blue vinyl. δ Issued on red and blue vinyl. ε One-sided fan club single, 500 copies only, no picture sleeve.

The driving force behind **The UK Subs** was veteran **Charlie Harper**. His real name was David Charles Perez. He was born on 25th April 1944, which meant he was 33 when he formed **The UK Subs** in London in 1977. **Harper** had spent some years gigging on the R&B circuit in various pubs and clubs as a vocalist and harmonica player. **Harper** was inspired by the sheer energy of punk and assembled Nick Garratt (gtr), Paul Slack (bs) and a drummer called Lions, initially as The Marauders. They soon changed names to **The UK Subs** (short for United Kingdom Subversives).

Musically they played raw and aggressive punk, although they were a first division as opposed to premier league act. Their vinyl debut came in April 1978 when they appeared on the *Farewell To The Roxy* (Lightning LIP 2) compilation. They contributed two live tracks, *I Live In A Car* and *Telephone Numbers*.

This helped secure them a one-off deal with the independent City label. The resulting 45 *C.I.D.* was released in a range of different coloured vinyls. They also built up a reputation as a powerful live act centred around **Charlie Harper**'s stage personna.

On 31st May 1978, they recorded their first of three sessions for John Peel. This comprised *I Couldn't Be You*, *Stranglehold*, *Tomorrow's Girls*, *Disease* and *C.I.D.*. A second session consisting of *Another Kind Of Blues*, *TV Blues*, *World War* and *All I Wanna Know* followed on 15th September 1978.

In the spring of 1979 they signed a deal with the RCA subsidiary Gem. Their first single for the label *Stranglehold* in June 1979 set the tone for the high energy fast-paced punk which typified their style. It became a significant hit for them, spending eight weeks in the charts and peaking at No. 26. Their third and final Peel session was recorded on 28th June 1979. It comprised *Crash Course*, *Killer*, *Emotional Blackmail*, *100* and *Lady Esquire*. In August 1979, they put out another 45 *Tomorrow's Girls*, which again made the Top 30, this time peaking at No. 28 during a six week stay.

Their first three singles were all included on their debut album *Another Kind Of Blues*, released in October 1979. This came on blue vinyl in a blue sleeve with a blue label, but there was no evidence of blues influence in their music. On offer was no-holes-barred full-blooded punk. This spent six weeks in the album charts, climbing to No. 21. Highlights on this album included *C.I.D.*, *Stranglehold*, *Tomorrow's Girls* and the brilliant *Live In A Car*. The CD reissue includes additional original single mixes and 'B' sides, making it a good introduction to the band's early years. The superb *C.I.D.* was also included on *Business Unusual* (Cherry Red ARED 2) in 1979.

The UK Subs also tried hard at reinterpreting other people's songs. They got to No. 36 in the singles charts with an EP on which the lead cut was a frantic punk-style re-appraisal of The Zombies' *She's Not There*, released in November 1979.

Their next 45, *Warhead*, which climbed to No. 30 and spent four weeks in the charts, included a cover of Velvet Underground's *I'm Waiting For The Man* on the flip. Their second album *Brand New Age*, released in April 1980 featured *Warhead* and spawned a further single *Teenage* (which brought them a further hit (No. 32) the following month). It also featured them singing the 'signature tune' *Emotional Blackmail* twice. The album built on their earlier commercial success climbing to No. 18 during a nine week chart stay. The CD reissue on Dojo came with bonus cuts. They bettered this later in the year when *Crash Course* (a live album) was released. This succeeded in capturing their chaotic, almost riotous rabble rousing stage act and frenetic audience participation. Climbing all the way to No. 8 during a six week chart stay, the album was the pinnacle of their achievement. It featured most of their finest songs to date. The CD reissue on Dojo came with bonus cuts.

In the autumn of 1980, Slack and Davis left the band. Former **Users** and **Hellions** member Alvin Gibbs came in on bass and Steve Roberts was their new drummer. This modified line-up enjoyed a No. 37 hit with *Party In Paris* in Autumn 1980. The hit also appeared on their *Diminished Responsibility* album, released in February 1981. This showed **Harper** and his colleagues' songwriting to have matured as the lyrics dealt with issues such as gangsters (*Gangster*), racism (*You Don't Belong*), rioting (*Confrontation*), Paris (*Party In Paris*) and urban decay. The album again sold well, climbing to No. 18 during a five week chart residency. Again the CD reissue on Dojo features bonus cuts. However, it proved to be their final hit album and *Keep On Runnin' (Till You Burn)*, released in April 1981, became their final hit single peaking at No. 41.

Before the year was out further personnel changes were forced on the band. Steve Roberts left to join **Cyanide** and later **Ligotage**. He was replaced on drums by Kim Wylie. Their new album *Endangered Species* showed a more sensitive side to their music, but by now the band, who were very much in **Sham 69** mould of punk were facing fierce competition from the emerging Oi! movement.

In late 1982, Garratt left to form Rebekka Frame and Gibbs joined **Urban Dogs**. **Charlie Harper** put together an entirely new band (line-up 'E') which included the returning Paul Slack. They cut an album, EP and 45 for Fallout. They failed to gain momentum commercially but the album *Flood Of Lies* did have some merit. It sported a great political cartoon of Maggie Thatcher on the front cover and marked a return to their aggressive style.

In late 1984, **Harper** again put together a new line-up ('F') which included former **Wall** and **Patrick Fitzgerald** drummer Rab Fae Beith. This was responsible for the live CD *Crash Course*, which successfully captured their raucous live style and included many of their old classics. Even this couldn't rekindle their earlier commercial success though as the world had moved on.

Greatest Hits - Live In Paris is compiled from concerts during their 1989 European tour. Hit singles like *Stranglehold*, *Warhead* and *Tomorrow's Girls* are included and the album culminates in versions of two Doors' songs, *Roadhouse Blues* and *Back Door Man*.

Europe Calling captures the **UK Subs** in Paris and Vienna. Their classic late seventies numbers figure but the collection also includes five new studio cuts. The sound quality and playing is adequate and the album, which concludes with a radio interview with **Charlie Harper**, will appeal mainly to the nostalgic.

Peel Sessions 1978 - 1979 compiles their three sessions for John Peel and the band sound pretty sparky at times too.

Europe Calling, put out in 1998, compiles live tracks.

Self Destruct, *Police State* and *War Of The Roses* all resurfaced on *Abstract Punk Singles Collection* (Anagram CDPUNK 52) in 1995. A year earlier *Another Typical City*, *Private Army*, *This Gun Says*, *Hey Santa* and *Jodie Foster* had all figured on *The Fallout Punk Singles Collection* (Anagram CDPUNK 30). Their other compilation appearances include *Stranglehold* on *Burning Ambitions (A History Of Punk)* (Anagram CDBRED 3) 1996; *C.I.D.* on *Burning Ambitions, Vol. 2* (Anagram CDPUNK 81) 1996 and on *1-2-3-4 - A History Of Punk And New Wave 1976 - 1979* (MCA/Universal MCD 60066) 1999, which is a 5-CD box set; *Warhead* on *Burning Ambitions, Vol. 3* (Anagram CDPUNK 98) 1997 and *Punk - The Worst Of Total Anarchy* (2-CD) (Disky SP 871952) 1996; *World War* on *New Wave Archive* (Rialto RMCD 201) 1997; *I Live In A Car* on *Punk - Live And Nasty* (Emporio EMPRCD 586) 1995 and *Police State* on *Punk And Disorderly, Vol. 3 (The Final Solution)* (Anagram CDPUNK 23) 1993.

Warhead, a 1999 CD, comprises live versions of many of their favourites along with a good selection of studio material. This includes all three tracks from their debut EP on City, *C.I.D.*, *Live In A Car* and *BIC*, along with later singles *Countdown* and *The Motivator*. The remaining material on this better than average collection comprises assorted album tracks.

Compiled by **Charlie Harper** himself *Sub Mission - The Best Of UK Subs 1982 - 98* compiles the cream of the band's releases between these dates. Listen out for *Police State* (originally on their 1982 *Shake Up The City* EP) - a fine slice of punk. Included with this release is an eighteen-track live bonus CD recorded at Bristol in 1991. Fans will also want to get *In Action (Tenth Anniversary)* a thirty-two track CD of a 1987 gig. All their best-known songs from their first decade are included and the sound quality is above-average, but sadly no sleevenotes are supplied.

Captain Oi! also reissued their eighth album *Huntingdon Beach* in 1999 with bonus cuts including their *This Gun Says* 45 and all four cuts from their rare *In Holland* EP.

Left For Dead (CD) (available in the U.K. as an U.S. import) is a reissue of a 1986 live cassette release. By the time it was recorded **Charlie Harper** was their only surviving original member. All of their finest moments are featured like the punk R&B of *C.I.D.* and *Stranglehold*. Some tracks have inappropriate metal guitar solos which seem misplaced given their punk ethos. This is primarily an album for their serious fans.

The Captain Oi! reissue of *Another Kind Of Blues* comes with the 45 versions of some of the tracks recorded for the album as bonus cuts, lyrics and two sets of sleevenotes by Mark Brennan and guitarist Nicky Garratt.

Captain Oi! reissued the Dojo CD reissue of *Brand New Age* with its ten bonus cuts in 2000 along with lyrics and sleevenotes by Mark Brennan and **UK Subs** guitarist Nicky Garratt. Similarly, the Captain Oi! CD issue of *Crash Course* reissued the earlier Dojo reissue by including the four songs recorded at the Lyceum in 1979 which were combined with the original GEM release as the 12" *For Export Only* with added sleevenotes from Mark Brennan and Nicky Garratt.

In 2001, Captain Oi! reissued *Flood Of Lies* (AHOY CD 166) along with seven bonus tracks which rounded-up everything recorded by line-up 'E' of the band, including both the 7" and 12" versions of *Another Typical City*. The same label issued *Time Warp - Greatest Hits* (Anagram CDPUNK 120) 2001, which comprises re-recordings of their previous classics, although these are no match for the originals.

Harper never allowed **The UK Subs** to die. They continued to produce albums and 45s throughout the eighties and into the nineties. They are more of a punk revival act nowadays - perhaps, not surprisingly they haven't rediscovered their earlier commercial success.

Ultra-Violent

Personnel:			
	ADRIAN BAILEY	vcls	A
	DUF	bs	A
	ANDREW GRIFFITHS	gtr	A
	JAZ	drms	A

EP: 1(A) CRIME FOR REVENGE (Crime For Revenge/Where Angel's Dare Not Tread/Dead Generation) (PS)
(Riot City RIOT 25) 1983

A brutal sounding punk band from Halifax. All three cuts on this are raw and raucous. There's some cutting guitar work on *Where Angels Dare Not Tread*. whilst *Crime For Revenge* and *Dead Generation* are literally frantic.

Crime For Revenge can also be heard on *Riot City Singles Collection, Vol. 1* (Anagram CDPUNK 15) 1997 and on *100% Hardcore Punk Rock* (Captain Oi! AHOY DCD 84) 1997. You'll also find *Dead Generation* on *Riot City Singles Collection, Vol. 2* (Anagram CDPUNK 55) 1995. Both of these singles collections were also issued on vinyl by Captain Oi! (AHOY DLP 503 and 511).

Ultravox!

Personnel: (up to 1986)			
	WARREN CANN	drms	ABC
	CHRIS CROSS (CHRIS ST. JOHN)	bs	ABCD
	BILLY CURRIE	violin, synth	ABCD
	JOHN FOXX (DENNIS LEIGH)	vcls	AB
	STEVE SHEARS	gtr	A
	ROBIN SIMON	gtr	B
	MIDGE URE	vcls, gtr	CD
	(MARK BRZEZICKI	drms	D)

				HCP
ALBUMS: (up to 1986)	1(A)	ULTRAVOX!	(Island ILPS 9449) 1977	-
	2(A)	HA! HA! HA!	(Island ILPS 9505) 1977	-
	3(B)	SYSTEMS OF ROMANCE	(Island ILPS 9555) 1978	-
	4(A/B)	THREE INTO ONE (compilation)		
			(Island ILPS 9614) 1980	
	5(C)	VIENNA	(Chrysalis CHR 1296) 1980	3
	6(C)	RAGE IN EDEN	(Chrysalis CDL 1338) 1981	4
	7(C)	QUARTET	(Chrysalis CDL 1394) 1982	6
	8(C)	MONUMENT - THE SOUNDTRACK		
			(Chrysalis CUX 1452) 1983	9
	9(C)	LAMENT	(Chrysalis CDL 1459) 1984	8
	10(-)	THE COLLECTION (compilation)	(Chrysalis UTV 1) 1985	2
	11(D)	U-VOX	(Chrysalis CDL 1545) 1986	9

NB: (1) issued in a gatefold sleeve and on CD (Island IMCD 146) 1992. (2) issued with 7" *Quirks/Modern Love* (live) (Island WIP 6417) and inner sleeve and on CD (Island IMCD 147) 1992. (3) also issued on CD (Island IMCD 149) 1992, now deleted. (4) reissued on vinyl in 1986 and issued on CD (Island IMCD 30) 1989. (5) issued on CD (Chrysalis CCD 1296) 1985 and again in 1994. (6) issued on CD (Chrysalis CPCD 1338) 1987 deleted in 1992 and again (EMI GOLD CDGOLD 1097) 1997. There was also a limited marble picture disc version of (7) (Chrysalis PCDL 1394). (7) also issued on CD (Chrysalis CCD 1394) 1988, deleted in 1992.

ULTRA-VIOLENT - Crime For Revenge EP.

ULTRAVOX! - The Thin Wall.

(8) also issued on CD (Chrysalis CCD 1452) 1986. (9) issued in a screen-printed sleeve. There was also a picture disc release of (9) (PCDL 1459) 1984. (9) also issued on CD (Chrysalis CCD 1459) 1984, deleted in 1992. (10) came with a bonus 12". Also issued on CD (Chrysalis CCD 1490) 1985. There are also some other CD compilations, *Dancing With Tears In My Eyes* (Music For Pleasure OLD GOLD 1078) 1997; *Rare, Vol. 1* (Chrysalis CDCHR 6053) 1993 and *Rare, Vol. 2* (Chrysalis CDCHR 6078) 1994 and finally there's a 3-CD set comprising their first three albums (Island 5241522) 1995.

EPs:	1(A)	RETRO (live) (The Wild, The Beautiful And The Damned/Young Savage/My Sex/ The Man Who Dies Everyday)	(Island IEP 8) 1977
	2(A)	THE PEEL SESSIONS (21.7.77)	(Stange Fruit SFPS) 1988

			HCP
45s: *α	Dangerous Rhythm/My Sex	(Island WIP 6375) 1977	-
(up to α	Young Savage/Slip Away (PS)	(Island WIP 6392) 1977	-
1986) α	Rockwrok/Hiroshima Mon Amour (PS)	(Island WIP 6404) 1977	-
	Slow Motion/Dislocation (PS)	(Island WIP 6454) 1978	-
+	Slow Motion/Dislocation (12", PS)	(Island 12WIP 6454) 1978	-
	Quiet Men/Cross Fade (PS)	(Island WIP 6459) 1978	-
x	Quiet Men/Cross Fade (12", PS)	(Island 12WIP 6459) 1978	-
o	Sleepwalk/Waiting (PS)	(Chrysalis CHS 2441) 1980	29
	Passing Strangers/ Sound On Sound (PS)	(Chrysalis CHS 2457) 1980	-
	Passing Strangers/ Sound On Sound (12", PS)	(Chrysalis CHS 12-2457) 1980	-
o	Vienna/Passionate Reply (PS)	(Chrysalis CHS 2481) 1980	2
	Vienna/Passionate Reply/ Herr X (12", PS)	(Chrysalis CHS 12-2481) 1980	-
o	Passing Strangers/ Face To Face (PS)	(Chrysalis CHS 2457) 1980	57
	Passing Strangers/Face To Face/ King's Lead Hat (12", PS)	(Chrysalis CHS 12-2457) 1980	-
	Slow Motion/Quiet Men (PS)	(Island WIP 6691) 1981	33
	Slow Motion/Dislocation//Quiet Men/Hiroshima Mon Amour (Remix) (double-pack)	(Island DWIP 6691) 1981	-
o	All Stood Still/Alles Klar (PS)	(Chrysalis CHS 2522) 1981	8
	All Stood Still/Alles Klar/ Keep Talking (12", PS)	(Chrysalis CHS 12-2522) 1981	-
	The Thin Wall/ I Never Wanted To Begin (PS)	(Chrysalis CHS 2549) 1981	14
	The Thin Wall/I Never Wanted To Begin (12", PS)	(Chrysalis CHS 12-2549) 1981	-
o	The Voice/Paths And Angels (PS)	(Chrysalis CHS 2559) 1981	16
o	The Voice/All Stood Still (live)/Paths And Angels/ Private Lives (live) (12", PS)	(Chrysalis CHS 12-2559) 1981	-
	The Voice (live)	(Fan Club) 1981	-
o	Reap The Wild Wind/ Hosanna (In Excelsis Deo) (PS)	(Chrysalis CHS 2639) 1982	12
	Reap The Wild Wind/Hosanna (In Excelsis Deo) (12", PS)	(Chrysalis CHS 12-2639) 182	-
o	Hymn/Monument (PS)	(Chrysalis CHS 2557) 1982	11
o	Hymn/Monument/ The Thin Wall (12", PS)	(Chrysalis CHS 12-2557) 1982	-
β	Visions In Blue/ Break Your Back (PS)	(Chrysalis CHS 2676) 1983	15
o	Visions In Blue/Break Your Back/ Reap The Wild Wind (12", PS)	(Chrysalis CHS 12-2676) 1983	-
oβ	We Came To Dance/Overlook (PS)	(Chrysalis VOX 1) 1985	18
o	We Came To Dance/ Overlook (12", PS)	(Chrysalis VOXX 1) 1983	-
o	One Small Day/Easterly (PS)	(Chrysalis VOX 2) 1984	27
	One Small Day/Easterly (12", PS)	(Chrysalis VOXX 2) 1984	-
o	Dancing With Tears In My Eyes/ Building (PS)	(Chrysalis UV 1) 1984	3
#o	Dancing With Tears In My Eyes/ Building (12", PS)	(Chrysalis UVX 1) 1984	-
o	Lament/Heart Of The Country (PS)	(Chrysalis UV 2) 1984	22
	Lament/Heart Of The Country/ Lament (instr) (12", PS)	(Chrysalis UVX 2) 1984	-
oβ	Love's Great Adventure/ White China (PS)	(Chrysalis UV 3) 1984	12
	Love's Great Adventure/ White China (12", PS)	(Chrysalis UVX 3) 1984	-
oβ	Same Old Story/3 (PS)	(Chrysalis UV 4) 1986	31
o	Same Old Story/3/All In One (12", PS)	(Chrysalis UVX 4) 1986	-
o	All Fall Down/Dreams (PS)	(Chrysalis UV 5) 1986	30
	All Fall Down (2 versions)/ Dreams (12", PS)	(Chrysalis UVX 5) 1986	-

NB: * Initially issued without a picture sleeve, but later copies came with one. α These first three **Ultravox** singles were reissued in July 1981. + Issued on translucent vinyl. x Issued on white vinyl. o Some copies on clear vinyl. β Also picture disc versions of this release. # Came in a gatefold picture sleeve with a poster.

Ultravox! formed in London in mid-1976 out of the ashes of the glam-influence Tiger Lily. **John Foxx** (whose real name was Dennis Leigh) was born in Chorley, Lancashire. He'd formed Tiger Lily back in 1973 with Chris St. John (who'd been born in London on 14th July 1952) on bass, Canadian Warren Cann on drums and Steve Shears on guitar. Tiger Lily were a Roxy Music - inspired outfit. Their first major gig was at London's Marquee Club in August 1973 supporting The Heavy Metal Kids. In October they added Yorkshireman Billy Currie on keyboards. In March 1975, they recorded Fats Waller's *Ain't Misbehavin'* with *Monkey Jive* on the flip for the Gull label. The 'A' side was recorded for an X-certificate film of the same name which flopped. This resulted in the record being withdrawn. Some copies did get out and those with picture sleeves are now quite collectable. The 45 was reissued, with a different picture sleeve in 1977 and then again in 1980, on Dead Good Records.

Basically, though, Tiger Lily didn't take off and, after choosing various names - The Zips, London Soundtrack, The Innocents and Fire Of London - during 1976, they finally settled for **Ultravox!** that July. In this new combo Chris St. John was known as Chris Cross. They signed to Island Records in July, contributing *The Wild, The Beautiful And The Damned* to the label's sampler that year. An unusual track with Bill Currie's electric violin it makes quite an impression on initial listening.

Their debut single *Dangerous Rhythm* was released in February 1977. They combined synthesizer with danceable new wave pop music. Quite an accessible record but it didn't attract enough attention to lead them into the charts. It was taken from their debut album *Ultravox!*, which was produced by Brian Eno, Steve Lillywhite and the group, which appeared the following month. The album was well received. It blended much of the roughness of punk with the synthesizer sound of groups like Kraftwerk. It included *The Wild, The Beautiful And The Damned*, which originally figured on the Island sampler, and *I Want To Be A Machine* and the minimalistic *My Sex* (the flip to their debut 45) also stand out.

Their follow-up single in May 1977 *Young Savage* is fast-paced and punkish in comparison to much of their debut album and much less interesting. A third single *Rockwrok* was released in October and as the title hints this was a tight straightforward rocker. Much more of the same was to be heard on its parent album *Ha! Ha! Ha!*, which appeared the same month. The album is notable for Billy Currie's superb electric violin playing and this is particularly so on *Hiroshima Mon Amour*. This album also comes with a free live 7" featuring *Quirks* and *Modern Love*.

The first three **Ultravox!** singles were all reissued in July 1981 after they became famous following the success of *Vienna*.

In February 1978, they released a four track live EP which contained some of their finest moments to date; *The Wild, The Beautiful And The Damned*, *Young Savage*, *My Sex* and *The Man Who Dies Everyday*. The same

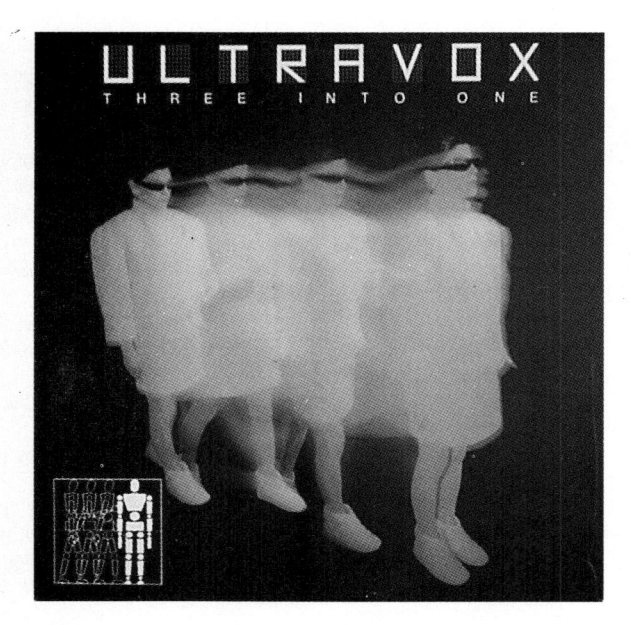

ULTRAVOX! - Three Into One.

month they travelled to West Germany to record with Conny Plank. Prior to this Steve Shears left to join Cowboys International. He was replaced by former Neu guitarist Robin Simon. In August **Ultravox!** played at the Reading Rock Festival, where they were second on the bill to **The Jam**. They also played five consecutive gigs at London's Marquee in an attempt to build up their credibility.

Their next album Systems Of Romance was produced by Conny Plank. There's little trace of any punkish influence here. On the album's highlights, which includes their 4th and 5th singles Slow Motion and Quiet Men and Just For A Moment, synthesized electro-pop is the order of the day, whilst the lyrics concentrate on a range of experiences. This is a good album but it failed to chart and the omens weren't looking good for the group. They played two last U.K. dates at London's Marquee club in late December and were dropped by Island in January 1979. After they signed off with some final gigs in the 'States **John Foxx** left to go solo when they returned to the U.K. in March. The remaining members put the project on hold whilst they searched for a new singer and guitarist. In this interim period they each pursued their own interests. Billy Currie went off to play with **Gary Numan**, Robin Simon played guitar for **Magazine**, where he remained, Chris Cross wrote songs for his brother and Warren Cann worked with New Zealand singer Zaine Griff.

Their prayers were finally answered when Glaswegian singer and guitarist **James 'Midge' Ure** was recruited to the band in April 1979. He'd played with Currie in **Visage** and had then gone on to Salvation, which became Slik, who found short-lived fame when they enjoyed a No. 1 with Forever And Ever. **Ure** left them in 1977, linking up with ex-**Sex Pistol** Glenn Matlock in **The Rich Kids**. It was from **Rich Kids** that **Ure** joined.

Having worked on new material for some months, the new line-up went on the road in November 1979. They played four gigs at Liverpool's Eric's in preparation for a U.S. tour, which they commenced in December. With **John Foxx** now enjoying chart success for the first time as a solo artist **Ultravox**, who had now dropped the exclamation mark from their name, signed to Chrysalis. They released their first single for their new label in June 1980. Sleepwalk, as its title suggests, had a hypnotic feel and inaugurated a new style for the band based around a more symphonic use of synthesizers. It gave them their first hit, climbing to No. 29 during an eleven week chart stay. In response to the band achieving success at last Island issued Three Into One, a compilation of songs (including all their 45 'A' sides) from their first three albums, but chart success still evaded **Ultravox** releases on Island.

In September 1980, Chrysalis released a second 45 Passing Strangers, from their forthcoming Vienna album, in both 7" and 12" formats. Initially, it did not chart but the album, released the following month, propelled them into stardom. Not only did it climb to No. 3, it also spent a stunning seventy-two weeks in the charts. The music was melodic, haunting, accessible and interesting - yes, all of these (in some cases all at once). It not only included Sleepwalk and Passing Strangers (which got to No. 57 during a four week chart residency when released as a 45), but the stunning title track, which got to No. 2 and was only kept off the top spot by one of the worst records ever made Joe Dolce's Shaddap You Face.

The album also became their first to chart Stateside (No. 164) and as late as June 1981 spawned a fourth and final hit when All Stood Still spent ten weeks in the charts peaking at No. 8. In the interim Island finally achieved some chart success with the band releasing the three-track EP Slow Motion, which spent a month in the charts and climbed to No. 33.

In August 1981, a new single The Thin Wall was released in both 7" and 12" formats. It had been recorded earlier in the year in West Germany with producer Conny Plank. The 45 brought them another hit climbing to No. 14 and spending eight weeks in the chart. It also featured on their next album Rage In Eden which was released the following month. This proved to be the final one produced by Conny Plank. Again it was excellent, featured complex synthesizer patterns which blended beautifully with the remaining instrumentation and Ure's now more operatic style vocals. The album sold well, spending a total of twenty-three weeks in the charts and peaking at No. 4.

In November 1981, a further 45 The Voice was culled from it. This gave them another Top 20 hit. It rose to No. 16 spending a total of twelve weeks in the charts.

The first part of 1982 saw **Midge Ure** pursuing a number of other directions. In June, he released a solo 45 for Chrysalis No Regrets, which climbed to No. 9. He also worked for **Visage** and undertook production duties for Steve Harley, Attrix and Modern Man.

In September a new 45 Reap The Wild Wind was released. This was taken from their forthcoming album Quartet, which was produced by George Martin, recorded in Montserrat and released the following month. The lyrics to many songs have religious overtones, **Ure**'s vocals are clear but the smooth synthesizer-dominated music is often backing rather than primary. Reap The Wild Wind rose to No. 12 during its nine weeks in the charts. It also gave them their first U.S. hit where it peaked at No. 71. The album, which possibly suffers from being a bit samey, sold well. In Britain it enjoyed thirty weeks in the charts, peaking at No. 6 and it also became their first U.S. hit album. It rose to No. 61 in the 'States. Three further 45s, Hymn, We Came To Dance and Visions In Blue were taken from the album. In Britain they reached No's 11, 15 and 18 respectively, but none of them were able to capitalise on the success of Reap The Wild Wind in the 'States, which remains their only U.S. hit single. Meanwhile **Ure** also continued his own exploits. After A Fashion, which he recorded with **Japan** bassist **Mick Karn** got to No. 39 in July.

The live Monument - The Soundtrack was released in October. It was the soundtrack to a concert videocassette which, featured, in addition to the title track, five of their best songs:- Reap The Wild Wind, The Voice, Vienna, Mine For Life and Hymn. It peaked at No. 9, spending fifteen weeks in the charts.

February 1984 saw the release of One Small Day. This was one of the finest singles, although this wasn't translated into record sales - as it only got to No. 27 spending six weeks in the charts. It previewed their next album Lament, which the band produced themselves. It certainly confirmed the quality of their smooth, sophisticated, synthesized sound and spawned

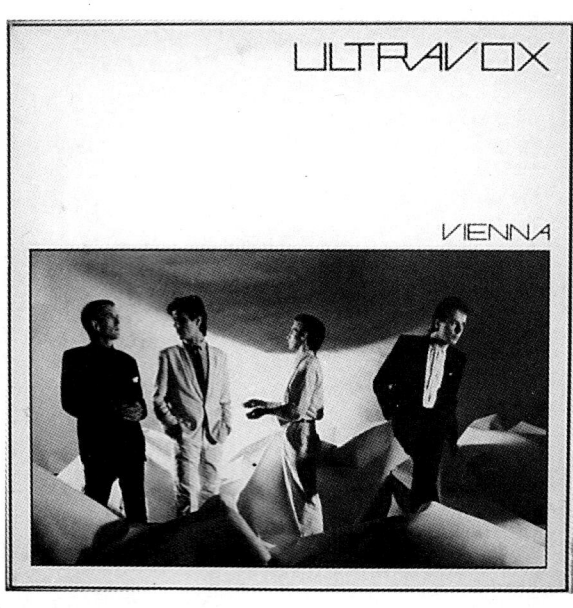

ULTRAVOX! - Vienna.

another major hit 45 with *Dancing With Tears In My Eyes*. Released the following month, this climbed to No. 3 and spent ten weeks in the charts. The album consolidated their success rising to No. 8 during a twenty-two-week chart stay. Then, in July, the title track was issued as a 45. Spending six weeks in the charts it climbed to No. 22.

By now, the release of a compilation was inevitable. *The Collection*, a fourteen-cut tour de force of their Chrysalis singles between 1980-84 did them justice, it was a fitting showcase for their talents. It climbed to No. 2 and spent fifty-three weeks in the charts. Their latest single *Love's Great Adventure* continued their success, rising to No. 12 during a nine week chart residency.

With Mark Brzezicki (of Big Country) now guesting on drums, after Warren Cann had departed to join Helden, they returned in 1986 with another Top Ten album *U-Vox* and two more minor hit singles, *Same Old Story* and *All Fall Down*, which climbed to No's 31 and 30 respectively.

The success of **Ure**'s solo album *The Gift* almost certainly served to hasten **Ultravox**'s demise. They eventually disbanded in 1987, although Currie and Simon formed U-Vox with Marcus O'Higgins on vocals the same year. In 1989, they played **Ultravox** songs on their tour. **Ultravox** did later reform in 1993, although not with **Midge Ure** who by then had established a successful solo career. He was replaced on vocals by Tony Fenelle.

Inevitably *Vienna* has appeared on a number of compilations, including *The Model* (Spectrum 5529182) 1997, *New Romantics* (EMI Gold CDGOLD 1041) 1996, *Wave Romantics, Vol. 2* (SPV SPV 08438992) and *New Wave Classics* (2-CD) (Disky DOU 878282) 1998, along with *Reap The Wild Wind*. You'll also find *All Stood Still* on *Wave (The Biggest New Wave Hits)* (3-CD set) (Disky HR 868442) 1996 and a slice of primitive **Ultravox** *Young Savage* got a further airing on the 5-CD box set *1-2-3-4 - A History Of Punk And New Wave 1976 - 1979* (MCA/Universal MCD 60066) in 1999.

Ultravox were unquestionably one of Britain's top bands of the early eighties, although they failed to conquer the 'States. They emerged as part of the new wave but soon mellowed into one of the most successful (in Britain) proponents of the New Romantic movement.

Undead

Personnel:		
	RICHARD DENNING	A
	MARTIN HAMM	A
	PHILLIP HAMM	A
	ALISTAIR SCARLETT	A
	DAVID SIMMONS	A

ALBUM:	1(A)	THE KILLING OF REALITY	(Riot City CITY 006) 1984
EP:	1(A)	VIOLENT VISIONS (Violent Visions/Dead Revolutions/ This Place Is Burning) (PS)	(Riot City RIOT 15) 1982
45:		It's Corruption/Undead (PS)	(Riot City RIOT 7) 1982

An eighties Oi!/punk band from Bristol, who formed in mid-1981. Back in 1982, they also contributed a cut called *Sanctuary* to *Riotous Assembly* (Riot City ASSEMBLY 1) and *This Place Is Burning* was included on *Life's A Riot And Then You Die* (Riot City CITY 009) in 1985. You can also check out *Undead* and *Dead Revolution* on *Riot City Singles Collection, Vol. 1* (Anagram CDPUNK 15) 1997 or on vinyl (Captain Oi! AHOY DLP 503) 199? and *It's Corruption* and *This Place Is Burning* also resurfaced on *Vol. 2* (Anagram CDPUNK 55) 1995 and on vinyl (Captain Oi! AHOY DLP 511) 1996 of the same series.

The Underdogs

Personnel:			
	MARTIN ALLCHURCH	bs, vcls	A
	BILL	drms, vcls	A
	COLIN LAWSON	gtr, vcls	A
	U.G.	vcls	A

EP:	1(A)	EAST OF DACHAU (East Of Dachau/ Johnny Go Home/ Dead Soldier) (PS)	(Riot City RIOT 26) 1983

The Underdogs seem to have come from Leeds and the title cut of their *East Of Dachau* EP is a strong punk-rocker.

"Are there Russians in Russia?
Are they really red?
Ein volk, ein reinch, ein führer
Black square instead of red"
(from *East Of Dachau*)

The flip side's not bad either. *Dead Soldier* starts with a drum roll and some storming guitar. The band were helped out on backing vocals by Ricky Fox of **The Expelled**, who also recorded on Riot City.

East Of Dachau was also included on *Life's A Riot And Then You Die* (Riot City CITY 009) in 1985. It resurfaced again on *Riot City Singles Collection, Vol. 1* (Anagram CDPUNK 15) 1997, whilst *Johnny Go Home* was included on *Vol. 2* (Anagram CDPUNK 55) 1995 of the series. Both of these Riot City collections were also issued on vinyl by Captain Oi! (AHOY DLP 503 and 511).

The Undertones

Personnel:			
	MIKE BRADLEY	bs	A
(up to	BILLY DOHERTY	drms	A
1986)	DAMIEN O'NEILL	gtr, bs	A
	JOHN O'NEILL	gtr	A
	FEARGAL SHARKEY	vcls	A

				HCP
ALBUMS:	1(A)	THE UNDERTONES	(Sire SRK 6071) 1979	13
(up to	2(A)	HYPNOTISED	(Sire SRK 6088) 1980	6
1986)	3(A)	THE POSITIVE TOUCH	(Ardeck ARD 103) 1981	17
	4(A)	THE SIN OF PRIDE	(Ardeck ARD 104) 1983	43
	5(A)	ALL WRAPPED UP (dble)	(Ardeck ARD 1654281/3) 1983	67
	6(A)	CHER O'BOWLIES: THE PICK OF THE UNDERTONES	(Ardeck EMS 1172) 1986	96

NB: (1) reissued (Sire SRK 6081) 1979 in October (the original release was in May) with the addition of their hit singles *Teenage Kicks* and *Get Over You*, the substitution of the 45 mix of *Here Comes The Summer* and a different cover design. (1) reissued again (Ardeck ARDM 1647391) 1983 and on CD (Fame CDFA 3188/CDM 752 023 2) 1990, now deleted, (Dojo DOJO CD 191) 1994 and (Essential ESMCD 484) 1997, with seven additional cuts. (1) reissued again (Essential ESMCD 831) 2000 with additional tracks. A limited number of (2) came with a cardboard mobile. (2) reissued (Ardeck ARDM 1647421) 1983 and issued on CD (Dojo DOJOCD 192) 1994 and (Essential ESMCD 486) 1997, with additional cuts. (2) reissued again (Essential ESMCD 832) 2000 with additional tracks. (3) also issued on CD (Dojo DOJOCD 193) 1994 and (Essential ESMCD 485) 1997, with additional tracks and again (Essential ESMCD 853) 2000 with bonus tracks. There are some collectable misspressings of (4) with different tracks *Bittersweet* and *Stand So Close*. (4) also issued on CD (Dojo DOJOCD 194) 1994 and (Essential ESCM 487) 1997, with additional tracks and again (Essential ESMCD 854) 2000 with bonus tracks. (6) also issued on CD (Fame CDP 746 365 2) 1987 and (Fame CDFA 3226) 1989. Also of interest is *Peel Sessions: Undertones* (Strange Fruit SFRLP 103) 1989, also on CD (SFRCD 103) 1989 and re-packaged in 1994. There's also some CD-only 'best ofs':- *The Best Of The Undertones: Teenage Kicks* (Castle Communications TVCD 121) 1993; *Teenage Kicks (The Best Of The Undertones)* (Rennaissance Collector Series CCDCD 808) 1997; *True Confessions (Singles A's And B's)* (2-CD set) (Essential ESDCD 788) 1999 and *The Singles Box*

THE UNDERDOGS - East Of Dachau EP.

THE UNDERTONES - Teenage Kick EP (inner).

Set (12-CD single set) (Essential ESFCD 893) 2000. There's also a various artists tribute album:- *Teenage Hits (A Tribute To The Undertones)* (Metrodome METRO 322) 2000.

HCP

EPs:	1(A)	TEENAGE KICKS (PS) (Teenage Kicks/		
(up to		Smarter Than U/True Confessions/		
1986)		Emergency Cases)	(Good Vibrations GOT 4) 1978	31
	2(A)	THE PEEL SESSIONS (PS) (21.1.79) (Listening In/		
		Family Entertainment/Here Comes The Summer/		
		Billy's Third) (12", PS)	(Strange Fruit SFPS 016) 1986	-

NB: Just 7,000 copies of (1) were issued in a poster sleeve. (1) reissued (Sire SIR 4007) 1978 in a far more professional picture sleeve and reissued as a 12" (Andeck 12ARDS 1) 1983 and again in a limited edition of 2,000 on green vinyl in a numbered poster picture sleeve (Dojo TONES 1) 1994. (2) also issued on CD (Strange Fruit SFPSCD 016) 1988.

HCP

45s:		Get Over You/Really Really/		
(up to		She Can Only Say No (PS)	(Sire SIR 4010) 1979	57
1986)	*	Jimmy Jimmy/Mars Bars (PS)	(Sire SIR 4015) 1979	16
	+	Here Comes The Summer/One Way Love/		
		Top Twenty (PS)	(Sire SIR 4022) 1979	34
	+	You've Got My Number (Why Don't Use It!)/		
		Let's Talk About Girls (PS)	(Sire SIR 4024) 1979	32
		My Perfect Cousin/Hard Luck (Again)/		
		I Don't Wanna See You Again (PS)	(Sire SIR 4038) 1980	9
	+	Wednesday Week/Told You So (PS)	(Sire SIR 4042) 1980	11
		It's Going To Happen!/		
		Fairly In The Money Now (PS)	(Ardeck ARDS 8) 1981	18
		Julie Ocean/Kiss In The Dark (PS)	(Ardeck ARDS 9) 1981	41
		Beautiful Friend/Life's Too Easy (PS)	(Ardeck ARDS 10) 1982	-
		The Love Parade/Like That (PS)	(Ardeck ARDS 11) 1983	-
		The Love Parade/Like That/You're Welcome/		
		Crisis Of Mine/		
		Family Entertainment (12", PS)	(Ardeck 12 ARDS 11) 1983	-
		Got To Have You Back/		
		Turning Blue (PS)	(Ardeck ARDS 12) 1983	-
		Got To Have You Back/Turning Blue/		
		Bye Bye Baby Blue (12", PS)	(Ardeck 12 ARDS 12) 1983	-
		Chain Of Love/Window Shopping		
		For New Clothes (PS)	(Ardeck ARDS 13) 1983	-
Reissues:		Teenage Kicks/Emergency Cases (PS)	(Ardeck ARDS 1) 1983	-
		Teenage Kicks/Smarter Than U/True Confessions/		
		Emergency Cases (12", PS)	(Ardeck 12 ARDS 1) 1983	-
		My Perfect Cousin/Hard Luck (Again)/I Don't Want		
		To See You Again	(Ardeck ARDS 6) 1983	-
		My Perfect Cousin/Hard Luck (Again)/I Don't Want		
		To See You Again	(Ardeck 12 ARDS 6) 1983	-

NB: * The original issue came in green vinyl with a plastic sleeve and tour dates insert. + Reissued in identical form to their original releases in April 1982.

'Perfect pop', 'dumb entertainment', 'utterly innocuous music', 'a sublime unity of pop and punk' - these are just some of the descriptions that have been applied to describe **The Undertones** - the most successful and probably the best band to emerge from Northern Ireland in this era. Their innocence, naivety and uncomplicated small town charm won the hearts of rock audiences throughout Britain. They were indeed a strange phenomena - their lyrics were almost juvenile, their music innocuous and yet the end result in noise, theme and delivery was some of the best rock music to come out of Northen Ireland or indeed Britain in this era.

All five of the band grew up not more than a mile away from one another on the Catholic side of Londonderry. Whereas part of the motivation behind the formation of **Stiff Little Fingers**, Northern Ireland's other top new wave band, was to get out of Belfast; **The Undertones**, in their early days at least, showed no such inclination to 'breakout' of 'Derry. Undoubtedly, the band's greatest asset was vocalist Feargal Sharkey, who grew up along with his three sisters and three brothers in a tiny two-bedroomed terrace house in the Rosemont district of 'Derry. Sharkey possessed a captivating, quivering high-pitched whine that won over the hearts of so many of Britain's record-buying public. Yet he had only a casual interest in music as a child, his main ambition had been to be an electrician or failing that to start a career in the civil service. It was at his mother's insistence that Feargal was entered for all sorts of local talent shows, indeed she even paid for him to have voice-training sessions.

The band was formed on the initiative of its guitarist, John O'Neill, who also became its main songwriter, his younger brother, Vincent and Billy Doherty, its drummer. However, the line-up lacked a vocalist and it was Billy Doherty, impressed by Sharkey's unusual and appealing voice, who persuaded his former classmate to join the band. So keen was Doherty to recruit Sharkey to the band that they apparently borrowed guitars and amplifiers from a mate, who they had to return them to the next day, in what was clearly a successful attempt to impress Sharkey with their professionalism! Sharkey, who was working as a trainee television repairer after a period on the dole and an unsuccessful attempt to get a job in local government, probably felt, too, that he had little to lose from the venture. The line-up was completed by John's Fellow guitarist brother, Damian, who brought an electric guitar (the others had been practising on acoustics) and bassist Mickey Bradley was drafted in to replace Vincent. The band was very much a by-product of the troubles in 'Derry - an outlet to amuse the five youngsters and compensate for the lack of entertainment in trouble-torn 'Derry. They brought their equipment from a mail-order firm, paying £1 a week over two years to clear the debt.

The state of music when **The Undertones** started playing in 'Derry (they played their first gig at a school concert on St. Patrick's Day, March 17th 1976) was such that groups either played cover version of Carpenters songs or re-workings of the heavy metal anthems of Thin Lizzy and the like. So it can't have been all that easy for the band when they started their own brand of new wave in venues like the Casbah in 'Derry. At first they were regarded as a joke. But they soldiered on and gradually built up an audience of loyal fans.

Perhaps one of the most important developments in their career came with the formation of Terri Hooley's Good Vibrations label in Belfast. Hooley was searching for promising local talent to put onto vinyl and for him **The Undertones**, particularly Sharkey's unique vocals were an attractive proposition. For **The Undertones** it enabled the fulfillment of what was then their ultimate ambition - to make a record! Prior to their contract with Hooley, this was a prospect that appeared unlikely as Chiswick, Stiff and Radar, had all rejected a demo tape recorded by the band that had included *Teenage Kicks* and *Get Over You*, which later became their first two hit singles.

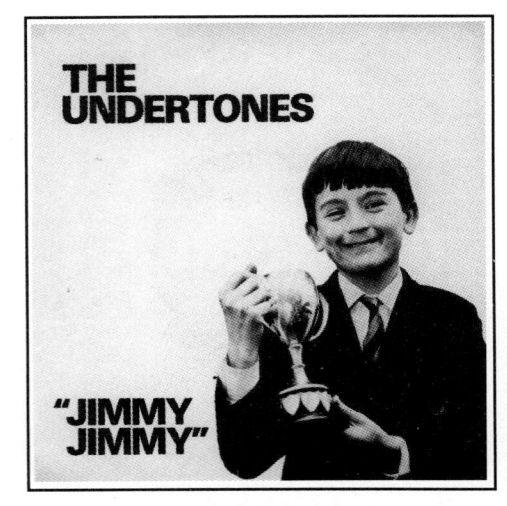

THE UNDERTONES - Jimmy Jimmy.

They recorded their *Teenage Kicks* EP for Good Vibrations on 16th June 1978, although it was not actually released until mid-September of the same year. Even then, success would have almost certainly eluded the band but for Billy Doherty's persistence in first writing to and then telephoning John Peel, at the BBC, to urge him to play their single on his influential late-night show. When Peel discovered it, he didn't just play it once, he played it time and time again. Indeed, he rapidly became the bands No. 1 fan. Peter Powell, then made the single his record of the week, ensuring that it received regular airplay to day time audiences. The record began to sell and major labels became interested. Prior to Peel's plugs, the band having fulfilled what they then perceived as their ultimate ambition - to make a record - had been on the verge of breaking up. Now Feargal Sharkey had negotiated them a £36,000 five year contract with Sire Records. Sire rapidly repressed the single and with the weight of their promotional machine behind it, *Teenage Kicks* rose to No. 31 in the charts during a six week stay, despite some derisory reviews in the U.K. rock press. This secured the band an appearance on 'Top of The Pops', on 22nd October 1978.

In retrospect *Teenage Kicks* was one of the classics of 1978. A perfect slice of punk with pop charm and some requisite powerful rhythm guitar. The other three tracks were more stereotypical three-chord British punk. The back cover of the Good Vibrations release featured some of the murkiest photos of a band to grace a picture sleeve alongside some classic 'Derry graffiti declaring "The Undertones are shit". History would prove otherwise.

On 16th October 1978, **The Undertones** recorded one of two sessions which were not included on their album/EP. This comprised *Get Over You*, *Top 20*, *She Can Say No* and *Male Model*.

Success had come to **The Undertones** so rapidly that, when they embarked on their first British tour with **The Rezilios** at the start of November 1978, they were still managerless. But not all went well for them as the support act on **The Rezillos** tour, which took the band for the first time to such venues as The Marquee (12th and 13th November), Birmingham Town Hall (29th Nov.), The City Hall, Newcastle (30th Nov.), the Free Trade Hall, Manchester (1st Dec.) and London Lyceum (3rd Dec.). Halfway through the tour **The Rezillos** split up and the band were forced to conclude what had by all account been a badly organised tour, by themselves. They fixed a number of gigs in their own right, playing at Camden's Electric Ballroom on 9th December supported by **The Valves** and **The Addix**, at the Nashville on 18th and 19th December supported by **The Squares** and at the Russell Club, Manchester, on the 21st December. A week prior to this, they had arranged a small number of gigs at The Pound, in Belfast, as well as a limited number of other venues, back in their beloved Ireland. The band were consistently well-received throughout the tour - Sharkey's transfixing, quivering vocals setting them apart from the hoards of otherwise similar new wave bands who were on the road at the time. However, on the tour, they developed a fervent dislike for touring that was to remain with them for the remainder of their career. They were homesick for their girlfriends and for 'Derry, where they had soon grown to enjoy the gigs they played.

In January 1979, **The Undertones** were voted the sixth best new group to emerge in 1978, in an NME poll (**Stiff Little Fingers** came second). On 27th January 1979, the band's second single, *Get Over You*, was issued. It received a derisory review in the NME which described it as 'pre-Immediate

THE UNDERTONES - You've Got My Number.

THE UNDERTONES - It's Going To Happen.

Faces R&B'. Like *Teenage Kicks*, it was a short punchy single made a little special by Feargal's vocals. It became a minor hit spending four weeks and reaching No. 57 in the U.K. charts. It was their first collaboration with Roger Bechirian. The harmonies bore some similarity to The Ramones and such comparisons also seem valid on the Billy Doherty-penned *Really Really*. **The Undertones** also had a track from their debut EP, *True Confessions*, included on Sire's compilation album, *The Sire Machine Turns You Up* (Sire SMP 1), which was also issued in January 1979. This helped expose them to a wider audience. The same year *Teenage Kicks* was included on the soundtrack to *That Summer!* (Spartan/Arista SPART 1088).

Jimmy Jimmy, the story of a young boy killed in Northern Ireland, was released by Sire Records on 20th April 1979. There was a limited edition issue version in green vinyl with a clear plastic sleeve. It was a tremendous and charming single - their most successful to date and put them back in the charts, eventually climbing to No. 16 during a ten week chart residency, to give them their first Top 20 hit.

On 27th April 1979, the band embarked on their most extensive tour yet, taking in venues as far apart as Aberdeen University (April 28th), The Village, Newport (May 11th), Liverpool's Eric's (May 12th), The Lyceum, London (May 20th), The Fiesta, Plymouth (May 29th), and Brighton Poly (June 2nd). The tour enabled them to promote their new single and their debut album *The Undertones*, which had been produced in London by Roger Bechirian. Acclaimed almost universally by the rock press, it was soon labelled as perfect pop. Undeniably their music was unadventurous and lacked imagination, yet it had a certain freshness and urgency, which made it infectious. The album contained thirteen brisk, animated songs, including their latest single *Jimmy, Jimmy*, the happy-go-lucky, *Here Comes The Summer*, a re-worked version of *True Confessions*, (from their debut EP), which relied on heavy percussion backbone and synthesizer beat, the powerful *Male Model* and *Jump Boys*. The lyrics were full of teenage obsessions about girls, doubts, loneliess and infatuation. They were direct and clear, but at the same time never intense. However, surprisingly, their first two singles *Teenage Kicks* and *Get Over You* were omitted from the original release. The album was widely acclaimed. In a warm and complimentary review, Paul Morley, writing in NME, on 5th May 1979, said:-

"**The Undertones** sing about doubt, loneliness, yearning, deceit and infatuation. Throughout this record they successfully explore and explain a convincing romantic Undertones world full of recognisable and graphic characters and delicately defined but trival complications. They are immaculate chronicles of private, primitive and tender times; they gloriously turn inadequacy into ecstacy."

Harry Doherty writing in Melody Maker likened the album to a Sten-gun, with the dip on repeat, with each of the tracks like a bullet, leaving the walls around the listener peppered with bullets by the end of side two. It climbed to No. 13 spending a total of twenty-one weeks in the charts.

On stage the band were in many ways the antithesis of a rock band. This was particularly so in the case of Sharkey, a scraggy figure who rushed around the stage gracelessly in scruffy, unfashionable apparel. Despite this, he had a definite charisma on stage and as a live attraction **The Undertones** were dynamite. Most of their concert audiences returned home ecstatic. Writing in Melody Maker on 12th May Steve Redmond, after a gig at Manchester wrote:-

THE UNDERTONES - Wednesday Week.

"**The Undertones** are surely the brightest, classiest pop band around at the moment - and boy, do they love success! Lead singer Feargal Sharkey laps up the adulation, demanding even more applause from his following but it would be wrong to suggest that he, or for that matter, any of the band, don't give in return".

Not everything was going smoothly, though. When the '**Tones** played at Guildford they were forced to leave the stage when a row broke out after they refused to let **Jimmy Pursey** and ex-**Sex Pistols**, Paul Cook and Steve Jones, gig with them. They later returned to the stage to find their equipment had been stolen.

Their next single, *Here Comes The Summer*, which reached No. 34 during a six week chart stint, was released at the end of July, to generally good reviews. It was a simple, catchy number, that rejoiced about the the fun of spending summer days on sandy beaches. The critics were now comparing **The Undertones** to The Small Faces. They were also a popular live attraction. They headlined at London's Marquee club between 1-4th August. Then, on Saturday 1st September 1979, they played at Edinburgh's 30,000 seater Royal Highland showground, along with Van Morrison and The Chieftains. This was some compensation for their disappointment at having to cancel a Northern Irish free festival at which the band were to have been joined by **The Clash**, **The Boys**, **Shake** and **The Moondogs**.

30th September saw the band embark on a new twenty-one date tour commencing at Bristol's Locarno. To coincide with this tour, their debut album was deleted, on 5th October, and replaced by a newly packaged album with the same title. In addition to the previous material, this album included their first two singles *Teenage Kicks* and *Get Over You*, and substituted the single mix of *Here Comes The Summer* for the album one. A further single, *You've Got My Number (Why Don't You Use It!)* was also issued at the same time. It wasn't one of their better ones, but contained some good guitar riffs, generated energy, and climbed to No. 32 in the charts on 20th October 1979. It spent a total of six weeks in the charts. The 'B' side was quite a successful re-work of U.S. garage band The Chocolate Watch Band's *Let's Talk About Girls*, that Lenny Kaye had included on his seminal *Nuggets* compilation.

If things were going well for the band on the mainland, back in Ulster their popularity seemed to have dwindled - probably a reaction against their departure from 'Derry to London. They were a subject of jest and missiles whilst recording an edition of 'Something Else' in Belfast, and ended their last song abruptly before leaving the stage. The programme, which featured sketches satirising Ulster-Sectarian attitudes and social mores, was broadcast on 20th January 1980.

Undeterred the band released a further single *My Perfect Cousin* on 28th March 1980 and then set off on a new twenty-seven date tour, supported by 'Derry colleagues **The Moondogs**, to tie in with the releaase of their second album *Hypnotized* on 18th April 1980. *My Perfect Cousin* which was one of their better singles, was written by Damian O'Neill and begged some comparison to The Kinks' *David Watts* insofar as it was a grudging song about the sort of wonderboy that other schoolkids are inevitably envious of:-

"His mother brought him a synthesizer
Got the Human League in to advise her
Now he's making lots of noise
Playing along with the art school boys"
(From *My Perfect Cousin*)

It reached No. 9 becoming the band's most successful single. It spent a total of ten weeks in the charts. The album, which was again produced by Roger Bechirian and was this time recorded in Holland and London, included a re-work of the old Drifters' song, *Under The Boardwalk*, along with fourteen self-penned compositions, including *My Perfect Cousin*. The opening track, *More Songs About Chocolate And Girls* contained the line "never too late to enjoy dumb entertainment" not only showing the band's wry humour by sending themselves up, but also their guile in pre-empting their critics. The title of the track was also, of course, a send up of The Talking Heads' *More Songs About Buildings And Food*. Other stand out cuts included *Wednesday Week*, a future 45, *Nine Times Out Of Ten*, which true to the band's formula was simple but appealing, with catchy guitar work and drumming, and *What's With Terry?* which illustrated just what a good guitar band they were. Predictably, too, the album contained a flush of songs about girls, complete with catchy guitar riffs and choruses - *Hypnotized*, *Tearproof*, *See That Girl* and *Girls That Don't Talk*. Overall, *Hypnotized* represented a consolidation on the simple pop formula of their first album. The ingredients were much the same, but the tunes were stronger.

Their next tour, which coincided with the release of their album, became known as the 'Humming' tour, and took place in three stages. The first began at Brighton's Top Rank on 23rd April 1980, and included nine other dates - the last two in Belfast. The second stage commenced at the Cambridge Corn Exchange on 9th May and involved a further nine dates, culminating at the Hammersmith Palais on 20th May. The third, seven-date stage kicked off at Sheffield's Top Rank on 28th May and ended at Newcastle's City Hall. The three stage tour was organised in a way that enabled the band to return to their girlfriends and families in 'Derry for short periods in between their life on the road. The band had always been united in their hatred of touring - primarily because it took them away from their girlfriends. In June of the same year the band set out on a month long tour of America, supporting **The Clash**. June also saw the release of a further single *Wednesday Week* taken from the *Hypnotized* album. A reflective pop ballad, displaying Feargal's magnificent vocals and John O'Neill's songwriting talents both to best effect, this was again one of the band's superior singles. It was a commercial success, too, reaching No. 11 in July 1980 during a nine week chart stay. **The Undertones** were now at the peak of their popularity.

On 9th December 1980, **The Undertones** completed their last of five sessions for John Peel. It comprised just three songs:- *The Positive Touch*, *You're Welcome* and *When Saturday Comes*.

Early in 1981, feeling that Sire's promotion of them had sometimes been found wanting, particularly on the Continent and in the 'States, where copies of their records were difficult to obtain, they signed a new deal with EMI which was conditional on them having their own Ardeck label, which was distributed by EMI. Ardeck promptly re-issued their first two albums and seven singles. In the spring they embarked on a new *Positive Touch* tour, accompanied by the Edinburgh band **TV21**. The thirty-nine date tour commenced at the Apollo, Glasgow on 25th April, and included two big London appearances at The Rainbow (on 21st May) and the Hammersmith Palais (24th May). The tour was a thundering success, with **The Undertones** getting rave reviews throughout. For Feargal, John and Billy,

THE UNDERTONES - Julie Ocean.

THE UNDERTONES - The Undertones.

their recent marriages seemed to have reduced the tension of touring.

Their next single release *It's Going To Happen!*, in April 1981, was superb. An urgent dynamic number, with a great tune. It gave them another U.K. hit reaching No. 18 and spending nine weeks in the charts. It was in many respects the furthest extension of their original sound. On the flip 'Tommy Tate and The Torpedoes' provided a jokey *Fairly In The Money Now*.

Their third album, *Positive Touch*, produced by Roger Bechirian, was issued in May 1981. It marked a considerable musical progression for the band, utilising keyboards, saxophone and trumpet, to give their sound a fuller flavour. It captured Feargal on top form, nowhere more so than on the yearning ballad, *Julie Ocean*, which is probably the album's highpoint, but also on other ballads like, *You're Welcome*, (the story of a grief stricken girlfriend awaiting her boyfriend's release from Long Kesh) and *Forever Paradise*, which was given tender vocal treatment by Sharkey. The title track, a pleasant, melodic number, *When Saturday Comes* was strongly rooted in the late '60s and the excellent *It's Going To Happen!* was also included. There was also a splattering of more typical **Undertones** songs, like *Boy Wonder*, *Life's Too Easy* and *His Good Looking Girlfriend*. Unlike their first two albums, it also contained comment on the situation in Ulster. Aside from *You're Welcome*, *Sigh And Explode*, was about the trepidation and uncertainty that existed beneath the surface in Ulster, and *Crisis Of Mine*, a John O'Neill composition, was written at the time of the first H Block Hunger strike and summarised the band's dilemma about whether the group should make public their views on the hunger strike. Sadly the greater complexity of their material reduced the immediacy of its appeal to their fans and the album's sales were disappointing. It only climbed to No. 17 and spent six weeks in the charts.

Their next 45, was a different and better mix of *Julie Ocean*, the sensitive John O'Neill ballad from *Positive Touch*, which was issued on 6th July 1981. This beautiful song was only a minor hit, but marked a diversification in style of the band's singles. They had no further single releases in 1981, but played at a major concert in Castlebar, County Mayo over the 1-2nd August weekend. *It's Going To Happen!* was included on a WEA compilation entitled *Life In The European Theatre*, which was realised in December 1981. The royalties from the album being donated to various anti-nuke groups, including CND and Friends Of The Earth.

On 26th August 1981, they recorded a session for Richard Skinner. This consisted of four songs:- *Song Number One*, *Bye-Bye Baby Blue*, *Just Like Romeo And Juliet* and *Beautiful Friend*.

Undeterred by the comparative failure of *Julie Ocean*, their February 1982 45, *Beautiful Friend*, was another rather offbeat number lacking their usual punchy melody, it was unsuccessful. The flip was a re-recorded version of *Life's Too Easy* from the *Positive Touch* LP.

Although they started work on a fourth studio album, most of the first half of 1982 was spent arranging for the construction of their own recording studio in 'Derry. This was Feargal's idea - the band had always been appalled by the lack of places to rehearse in the city - and whilst its primary aim was as a place for kids to practise, it was intended that any budding stars that emerged would be transferred to the band's new Ardeck label.

A one-off concert at Kilburn's National Ballroom on 16th August 1982 showed them to be as fresh and alert as ever. But when their next 45 *Love Parade*, a piece of '60s-styled organ-drenched psychedelia with Feargal at times sounding like David Surkamp (of Pavlov's Dog), emerged in October, it was hardly what their fans expected and again failed to chart. In retrospect, it was one of their more interesting singles and again underlined the increasing diversification of their music. A 12" version of the 45 was also issued, and included three additional live tracks.

Overall 1982 had been an extremely quiet year for the band. Could they recover from so long away from the public eye? Clearly 1983 would be a make or break year for the band.

The New Year started on an optimistic note. March saw the release of a new LP, *The Sin Of Pride*, as well as a 45, *Got To Have You Back*, an old Isley Brothers song taken from the album, which was issued in 7" and 12" format. A fast rocker with prominent keyboards, it lacked the catchy melodies usually associated with the band. The album, which was produced by Mike Hedges and the band, exhibited a considerable '60s soul influence, and was well received. The title cut was influenced by a Left Banke song called *Pretty Ballerina* and Sylvia and The Sapphires supplied back-up on many of the tracks. *Save Me* and *Untouchable* were '60s soul-influenced dance numbers. The opening track on side two, *Conscious*, was an effective blend of chiming guitars, dance beat and rich production. *Valentine's Treatment* provided a showcase for Sharkey's vocal dexterity and the album also featured two beautiful ballads, John O'Neill's *Soul Seven*, and the O'Neill brothers *Love Before Romance*, which both received suitably sensitive vocal treatment from Feargal Sharkey. The album also contained their earlier 45, *The Love Parade*, and a future one, *Chain Of Love*.

Whilst the album made a brief appearance at No. 43 in the charts during a five week stay, it did not become a major success in terms of sales. Were the band finding it hard to re-establish themselves after their lengthy silence? Feargal Sharkey told NME:

"I think we were right in doing what we did, because I think the LP is really good. And at the end of the day if the record's good we made the right decision, rather than just doing a rehash of *Jimmy Jimmy* 12 times, sticking it out and saying this is our new LP folks - rush out in your millions and buy it!"

Yet, despite a twenty-five date spring tour, which included a Hammersmith Odeon appearance, on which Liverpool band Cook Da Books provided the support; an appearance in the BBC's 'Sight And Sound In Concert' series, during March, and a further 45, *Chain Of Love* (taken from *The Sin Of Pride*), the band failed to recapture their earlier success. *Chain Of Love* was quite an original number, with some pleasant xenophone playing and Feargal in excellent vocal form, although many questioned whether it was a suitable 45 for the band. Of equal interest is the non-album flip side, *Window Shopping For New Clothes*, an harmonic '60s-influenced sound, which contained lyrics like:

THE UNDERTONES - Hypnotized.

"Intuition tells me
The kind of clothes to wear
But intuition can't help me
Become a self-made millionaire"
(from Window Shopping For New Clothes)

It seemed **The Undertones** were not destined to become millionaires. Early in June 1983 they announced their decision to go their separate ways. They played their final U.K. gig at Crystal Palace Football Ground on 4th June 1983, appeared at festivals in Toulouse and Brest in France, before returning to Dublin for their farewell appearance at the 17th July Festival. The band's statement, supposedly explaining their split, sounds like a complete pisstake:-

"We have felt in recent months that, being on the verge of international stardom with all the trappings of wealth and the restriction that such a predicament would bring was not too much of an attractive proposition. The thought of having to live in luxury in exotic tax havens, lazing by the pool drinking cocktails served by lightly clad females, flying the world in private jets, and the ultimate - being interviewed on Breakfast TV by Mike Smith - would ruin our ability to continue making such great records, and would eventually even affect our position as the world's number one live group".

So why had they split? Has there been conflict about the band's musical direction? Or, had differences of personality won the day? It seems not. The split almost certainly resulted from a realisation that the band had outlived its usefulness. Later, in October 1983, Feargal Sharkey told NME:-

"Sin Of Pride was the best thing I ever did with the group. So there was no musical differences or any of that rubbish. I had been thinking about it for ages but I hadn't the guts to do it. I kept thinking, next time will be better".

"It was getting to the stage of being a dodgy outfit like Gary Glitter, trundling the circuit hoping for another hit. We all wanted to be successful, but we couldn't accumulate our ideas in the right direction, we were holding each other back. One day I said I've had enough and the rest said so have we. And that was more or less that". Indeed their later material, particularly their experiemnts with Motown and psychedelia, showed the talents of the O'Neill brothers and Sharkey to have outgrown the playing and arranging skills of the band.

Shortly after the announcement, Ardeck set about making the band's back catalogue, including the Sire recordings, available. In October 1983, *My Perfect Cousin* was re-issued backed by *Hard Luck (Again)* and *Don't Wanna See You Again*. The first 5,000 copies came in a double-pack with a free three track 45 containing, *Here Comes The Summer*, *One Way Love* and *Top Twenty*. They also issued in November 1983, a double LP *All Wrapped Up*, which featured all their 45s including the flip sides. It reached No. 23 in the charts the following month and spent four weeks in the charts in all. EMI also issued a video EP cassette, fetauring all six of the band's promotional films.

So what is **The Undertones** place in pop history? Enjoying eight Top 50 hits between 1978-81 they were one of the best and most-loved groups of their ilk. They were less cynical than **The Buzzcocks** and less threatening than The Ramones, but musically better than both. As a live band they were superb. So why didn't they sell more records? Partly, because they never set themselves up as spokespersons for late '70s youth in the way that Paul Weller of **The Jam** did. Though lyrically they were often witty, they payed more attention to the feel and the sound of their songs, than their lyrical content. Bands like **The Clash** and **The Jam** sought to influence their audience through their lyrics, but **The Undertones**' prime consideration was to write good tunes. They were never fashionable or particular about their appearance, like **Duran Duran** were. This, together with their refusal to move from 'Derry and their self-efacing image, all helped to reduce their attractiveness to many of the more impressionable youths of the late '70s. Yet, given their personalities and background, it seems impossible to imagine that **The Undertones** could ever have been any different at this stage in their development. Their music alone will ensure that they are remembered as the best Northern Irish rock band from the late '70s and among the best bands from this era anywhere in the world.

In the band's immediate aftermath, John O'Neill and Bill Dohery remained in 'Derry. John set about writing songs for a new project and Bill got a job as a quantity surveyor with a 'Derry building company. Des O'Neill and Mickey Bradley travelled to London and began working on a new group, with black U.S. singer David Drumgold. Only Feargal was soon to return to

THE UNDERTONES - Sin Of Pride.

the limelight. Vince Clarke (ex-**Depeche Mode** and Yazoo) and G.C. Radcliffe, who had co-produced Yazoo's albums, were busy constructing a new project, The Assembly. They planned a series of releases, each featuring a different guest performer, and Feargal Sharkey was invited to be their first guest. The resulting 45, *Never Never* was issued in October 1983, in both 7" and 12" format. The 'A' side was well-suited to Feargal's vocal style. Entering the charts in mid-November 1983 it had climbed to No. 4 by early December. In what would otherwise have been a lean time for Feargal, The Assembly had enabled him to remain in the public eye, whilst he prepared to launch a new solo career, which was quite successful for a while.

The Peel Sessions album in 1989 contains twelve tracks from three sessions. Sadly, there is no version of *Teenage Kicks*, but plenty of their finer moments like *Here Comes The Summer* are included and there's even a cover of Gary Glitter's *Rock 'n' Roll*. This release was re-packaged again in 1994. In this case the re-packaging amounted to printing the photo of the band that appeared inside the original booklet on the cover of the new one.

The Best Of The Undertones: Teenage Kicks released in 1993 is a twenty-five track compilation containing many of their best moments.

Inevitably *Teenage Kicks* has resurfaced on a number of various artists compilations, including *The Best Punk Album In The World.... Ever, Vol. 1* (2-CD) (Virgin VTDCD 42) 1995, *The Best Punk Anthems.... Ever* (2-CD) (Virgin VTDCD 198) (which also features *Jimmy Jimmy*), *Burning Ambitions, Vol. 2* (Anagram CDPUNK 81) 1996, *The Sound Of The Suburbs* (Columbia 4888252) 1997 and on the five CD box set *1-2-3-4 - A History Of Punk And New Wave 1976 - 1979* (MCA/Universal MCD 60066) 1999. It also appears on *Teenage Kicks* (PolyGram TV 5253382) 1995 along with *My Perfect Cousin*, which can also be heard on *The Best Punk Album In The World.... Ever, Vol. 2* (Virgin VTDCD 79) 1996.

In 2000, their first four albums were remastered and reissued with appropriate 'B' sides, different mixes, additional outtakes and extensive sleevenotes with comments from guitarist John O'Neill.

Sharkey aside, the remaining **Undertones** came together to form That Petrol Emotion. There was talk of an **Undertones** reunion in 1993, but Feargal Sharkey, who was working in A&R for Polydor at the time, wasn't interested.

Untamed Youth

45:    Untamed Youth/Runnin' Wild (PS)   (Hardcore HAR 001) 1979

One of a number of mod revival acts from Essex. Dagenham was **Untamed Youth**'s home turf and this was their sole vinyl offering. Only 1,000 copies were pressed and the 45 is now very hard to find.

The Untouchables

45:	Keep On Walking/	
	Keep Your Distance (PS)	(Fried Egg EGG 11) 1981

A west country R&B band. *Keep On Walking* also resurfaced on *E(gg)clectic* (Fried Egg FRY 2), a 1981 label sampler.

The Unwanted

Personnel:	VINCE ELY	drms	A
	PAUL GARDNER	gtr	A
	OLLIE	vcls	AB
	DAVE LYNCH	gtr	B

ALBUM:	1( )	MESSAGE TO THE WORLD	(Raw RAWLP 103) 1978
45s:		Withdrawal/1978/Bleak Outlook (PS)	(Raw RAW 6) 1977
		Secret Police/These Boots Are Made For Walking (PS)	(Raw RAW 15) 1978
	*	Memory Man/Guns Of Love	(Raw RAW 30) 1978
Reissue:		Withdrawal/1978/Bleak Outlook (12")	(Raw RAWT 6) 1977

NB: * Unissued. The 12" reissue of *Withdrawal* did not come in a picture sleeve.

The Unwanted first came to the attention when they contributed one cut *Freedom* to *Live At The Roxy* (Harvest SHVL 4069) in 1977. This compilation was later reissued (Receiver RR 132) in 1991. *The Raw Records Punk Collection* (Anagram CDPUNK 14) 1983 features seven of their songs:- *Withdrawl, Bleak Outlook, 1984, Secret Police, These Boots Are Made For Walking, I'm Not Me* and *End Is Nigh*.

Vince Ely went on to join **The Psychedelic Furs**.

Uproar

Personnel:	BAZ	bs	A
	DAVE	gtr	A
	GOIC	drms	A
	STU	vcls	A

ALBUM:	1(A)	AND THE LORD SAID LET THERE BE UPROAR	
			(Lightbeat BTSLP 1) 1983
EPs:	1(A)	REBEL YOUTH (Rebel Youth/No War No More/ Fallen Angel/Victims) (PS)	(Beat The System RAW 1) 1982
	2(A)	DIE FOR ME (Better Off Dead/It's Not You/ Have A Good Laugh/ Dead Rockers) (PS)	(Beat The System RAW 2) 1983
	3(A)	NOTHING CAN STOP YOU (Nothing Can Stop You/ Your Empire/No Escape/Shoot To Kill) (PS)	
			(Volume VOL 9) 1983

This four-piece hailed from Peterlee in County Durham. They signed to Beat The System for whom they recorded the *Rebel Youth* and *Die For Me* EPs and the *And The Lord Said* album. They then switched to Volume Records for the *Nothing Can Stop You* (EP). Their final recording in 1985 was an album *Never Forgive* for the German label Underground Records.

Four of their cuts - *Die For Me, Better Off Dead, Rebel Youth* and *Victims* - can also be heard on *Beat The System Punk Singles Collection* (Anagram CDPUNK 61) 1995. *Rebel Youth* also got a further airing on *100% Hardcore Punk Rock* (Captain Oi! AHOY DCD 84) 1997.

The Upset

Personnel incl: ROLO McGINTY

45:	Hurt/Lift Off (PS)	(Upset UPSET 1) 1980

A D.I.Y. recording of the soul/beat revival genre. McGinty was later in The Kingdom and The Woodentops.

Urban Disturbance

45:	Wild Boys In Cortinas/(flip side by **V.I.P.s**) (Rok ROK V/VI) 1979

A Swindon band.

Urban Dogs

Personnel:	CHARLIE HARPER	vcls	AB
	KNOX	vcls, gtr, bs	AB
	TURKEY	drms, keyb'ds	B

ALBUMS:	1(A)	URBAN DOGS	(Fallout FALL LP 12) 1983
	2(B)	NO PEDIGREE	(Flicknife SHARP 032) 1985

NB: (1) There's also a cassette version with two extra tracks (Fallout FALL CLP 12) 1983. *The Best Of Charlie Harper & The Urban Dogs* (Captain Oi! AHOY CD 108) 1999 compiles their material and some of **Harper**'s solo material.

45s:	New Babarians/Speed Kills/ Cocaine (PS)	(Fallout FALL 008) 1982
	Limo Life/Warhead (PS)	(Fallout FALL 011) 1982

This was basically a short-lived collaboration between **UK Subs** vocalist **Charlie Harper** and **Vibrators**' guitarist **Knox**, plus a rhythm section formed in 1982. On offer is riotous punk. There's a strong Stooges and Iggy Pop influence aongside the early **Sex Pistols** and **Stranglers**. The eponymous album's highlights include a version of **The Vibrators**' *Into The Future* retitled *Sex Kick* and covers of Iggy Pop's *I Wanna Be Your Dog* and The New York Doll's *Human Being*. High energy, raucous, punk.

No Pedigree has a strong Iggy Pop influence too. *Lost In A Dream* is a great cut with superb garage-punk style keyboards. The same style is also evident on *The Word*. There's a good cover of Bobby 'Boris' Picket and The Crypt-Kickers' *Monster Mash*, but a less convincing one of John Lennon's *Cold Turkey*. One side two they try their hand at T. Rex's *Children Of The Revolution*. Overall, this is a good album.

The Best Of Charlie Harper & The Urban Dogs is an eighteen-track compilation of his solo singles and cuts from his solo album *Stolen Property*, as well as the two **Urban Dogs** 45s and cuts from their two albums. So far as **The Urban Dogs** material is concerned, highlights include their covers of *Cocaine* and *I Wanna Be Your Dog* and their own stomping *Wanna Wound*.

Two of their songs - *New Barbarians* and *Limo Life* - can also be heard on *The Fallout Punk Singles Collection* (Anagram CDPUNK 30) in 1994.

URBAN DOGS - No Pedigree.

Midge Ure

			HCP
ALBUM: (up to 1986)	1 THE GIFT	(Chrysalis CHR 1508) 1985	2

NB: (1) also issued on CD (Chrysalis CCD 1508) 1993 and again (EMI Gold CDGOLD 1045) 1996. Also relevant is *If I Was (The Best Of Midge Ure And Ultravox)* (Chrysalis CDCHR 1987) 1993.

			HCP
45s: (up to 1986)	Can't Even Touch You/ I Can't Be Anyone (PS)	(Chrysalis) 1982	-
	No Regrets/Mood Music (PS)	(Chrysalis CHS 2618) 1982	9
	No Regrets/Mood Music (12")	(Chrysalis CHS 122618) 1982	-
*	After A Fashion/Textures (PS)	(Musicfest FEST 1) 1983	39
*	After A Fashion/Textures (12")	(Musicfest FESTX 1) 1983	-
+	If I Was/Piano (PS)	(Chrysalis URE 1) 1985	1
+	If I Was/Piano/ The Man Who Sold The World (12")	(Chrysalis UREX 1) 1985	-
+x	That Certain Smile/The Gift (PS)	(Chrysalis URE 2) 1985	28
+	That Certain Smile/The Gift (12")	(Chrysalis UREX 2) 1985	-
	That Certain Smile/The Gift/ That Certain Smile (instr.)/ Fade To Grey (double 12")	(Chrysalis UREX 2) 1985	-
+	Wastelands/The Chieftain (PS)	(Chrysalis URE 3) 1986	46
+	Wastelands/The Chieftain/ Dancer (12")	(Chrysalis UREX 3) 1986	-
+	Call Of The Wild/ When The Wind Blows (PS)	(Chrysalis URE 4) 1986	27
o+	Call Of The Wild/When The Wind Blows/ After A Fashion (12")	(Chrysalis UREX 4) 1986	-

NB: * Credited to **Midge Ure and Mick Karn**. + Some copies issued on clear vinyl. x There was also a picture disc 7" release. o *After A Fashion* on this 12" release credited to **Midge Ure and Mick Karn**.

Midge Ure was born James Ure on 10th October 1953 in Glasgow, Scotland. His roster of bands comprised **Visage**, whom he left to join Salvation, who later became Slik, who enjoyed a No. 1 with *Forever And Ever*. He left Slik in 1977, teaming up with former **Sex Pistol** Glenn Matlock in **The Rich Kids**, who arguably failed to fulfill their promise.

Ure finally achieved long-term stardom when he joined **Ultravox** in April 1979 and re-invigorated the band. By 1982, though, he was already pursuing a number of extra-curricular activities. His second solo 45 for Chrysalis *No Regrets* spent ten weeks in the charts, peaking at No. 9. He also worked for **Visage** and as a producer for Steve Harley, Attrix and Modern Man. The following year he recorded another single *After A Fashion* with **Japan**'s bassist **Mick Karn**. This was also a minor hit, climbing to No. 39 during a four week chart stint.

In December 1984, Ure was a key player in Band Aid's No. 1 hit *Do They Know It's Christmas?*, which made No. 1 again when it was re-released in 1989.

Ure broke big as a solo artist in 1985. His single *If I Was* topped the U.K. chart and the album it was culled from *The Gift* rose to No. 2, spending fifteen weeks in the chart. The album contained a laid back cover of Jethro Tull's 1969 hit *Living In The Past*. The album, which spawned two further hits with *That Certain Smile* (No. 28) and *Wastelands* (No. 46), could easily have been mistaken for **Ultravox** with its blend of synth-rock and exploratory instrumentals. Its success undoubtedly hastened their demise, which came in 1987, although there were various reformations.

Ure went on to enjoy a pretty successful solo career. You'll also find *After A Fashion*, which he recorded with **Japan**'s **Mick Karn**, on *New Romantics* (EMI Gold CDGOLD 1041) 1996.

The Users

Personnel:	ANDREW BOR	drms	AB
	CHRIS 'PANIC' FREE	gtr	AB
	JAMES HAIGHT	vcls	AB
	BOB KWOK	bs	A
	ALVIN GIBBS	bs	B

45s:	Sick Of You/(I'm) In Love With Today (PS)	(Raw RAW 1) 1977
	Sick Of You/(I'm) In Love With Today (12")	(Raw RAWT 1) 1977
*	Warped 45: Kicks In Style/ Dead On Arrival (PS)	(War WARP 1) 1978

NB: * This was a numbered limited edition of 5,000.

The Users formed as a trio - Bor, Free and Haight - in Cambridge in 1977. Their debut *Sick Of You* was pure speed-punk released on Raw Records in August that year. They also featured on two compilations, *(I'm) In Love With Today* can also be heard on *Raw Deal* (Raw RAWLP 1) 1977 (reissued in 1979) and *Sick Of You* and *(I'm) In Love With Today* resurfaced on *Oh! No It's More From Raw* (Raw RAWLP 2) 1978. In 1978, they switched to War for *Kicks In Style* and in the summer recruited a fourth member, bassist Alvin Gibbs.

This enhanced line-up continued to gig and recorded an album with **Sex Pistols**' soundman Dave Goodman on the mixing board. It remained in the can and Gibbs quit. The others attempted unsuccessfully to relaunch themselves as a 'mod' revival band before disbanding. Gibbs was later in **Brains** (with Brian James, the ex-**Damned** guitarist). He went on to play with **UK Subs** and also played with Iggy Pop, the book 'Neighbourhood Threats. On Tour With Iggy Pop' relays his experiences in this era.

In 1993, *Sick Of You* and *(I'm) In Love With Today* got a further airing on *The Raw Records Punk Collection* (Anagram CDPUNK 14). **The Users** also contributed *Kicks In Style* and *Dead On Arrival* to *Punk Rock Rarities, Vol. 2* (Anagram CDPUNK 83) 1996 and *Sick Of You* got a further airing on the 5-CD box set *1-2-3-4 - A History Of Punk And New Wave 1976 - 1979* (MCA/Universal MCD 60066) in 1999.

U2

Personnel:	BONO (PAUL HEWSON)	vcls	A
	ADAM CLAYTON	bs	A
	THE EDGE (DAVID EVANS)	gtr, keyb'ds	A
	LARRY (LAURENCE) MULLEN	drms	A

U2 live at The Electric Ballroom, London 7th December 1979. Photo: Steven Richards.

ALBUMS:	1(A)	BOY	(Island ILPS 9646) 1980	HCP 52
(up to	2(A)	OCTOBER	(Island ILPS 9680) 1981	11
1986)	3(A)	WAR	(Island ILPS 9733) 1983	1
	4(A)	UNDER A BLOOD RED SKY - LIVE	(Island IMA 3) 1983	2
	5(A)	THE UNFORGETTABLE FIRE	(Island U2 5) 1984	1
	6(A)	WIDE AWAKE IN AMERICA	(ISSP 22) 1985	11

NB: (1) reissued on vinyl (Island ILPM 9646) 1995 and on CD (Island CID 110) 1986 and later at mid-price (Island IMCD 211) 1995. (2) also issued on CD (Island CID 111) 1986 and later at mid-price (Island IMCD 223) 1996, with different back cover artwork. (1) and (2) were also available in a '1 + 1' cassette format in a cigarette style card box (Island ICT 9646) and (Island ICT 9680), respectively. There was also a picture disc release of (3) (PILPS 9733). Counterfeits also exist of this but they are detectable from having a ILPS catalogue number. (3) also issued on CD (Island CID 112) 1985 with pink cover lettering and reissued at mid-price (Island IMCD 141) 1991 with red cover lettering. (4) also issued on CD (Island CID 113) 1986. (5) reissued on vinyl (ILPM 2087) 1996 and also issued on CD (Island CID 102) 1985, (DCC 102) 1993 and at mid-price with slightly different artwork (Island IMCD 236) 1996. (6) also issued on CD (Island IMCD 75) 1989. Also relevant are:- *The Best Of U2 1980 - 1990* (Island CIDU 211) 1998. There are also four various artists tribute albums *Zoovenir (A Tribute To U2)* (Tribute TR 025CD) 1998, *We Will Follow (A Tribute To U2)* (Cleopatra CLEO 5962) 1999, *A Tribute To U2* (Cleopatra CLEO 0596) 1999 and *We Will Follow (A Tribute To U2)* (Anagram CDMGRAM 124) 1999.

45s:				HCP
(up to	*	U2: THREE (Out Of Control/Stories For The Boys/ Boy-Girl) (PS)	(CBS CBS 7951) 1979	-
1986)	+	U2: THREE (Out Of Contol/Stories For The Boys/ Boy-Girl) (12", PS)	(CBS CBS 12-7951) 1979	-
	#	Another Day/ Twilight (Demo Version) (PS)	(CBS CBS 8306) 1980	-
		11 O'Clock Tick Tock/Tough (PS)	(Island WIP 6601) 1980	-
		A Day Without Me/ Things To Make And Do (PS)	(Island WIP 6630) 1980	-
		I Will Follow/Boy-Girl (live) (PS)	(Island WIP 6656) 1980	-
		Fire/J.Swallo (PS)	(Island WIP 6679) 1981	35
		Fire/J.Swallo/11 O'Clock Tick Tock (live)/ The Ocean (live)/Cry/The Electric Co. (live) (7", double pack, PS)	(Island UWIP 6679) 1981	-
		Gloria/I Will Follow (live) (PS)	(Island WIP 6733) 1981	55
		A Celebration/Trash, Trampoline And The Party Girl (PS)	(Island WIP 6770) 1982	47
	o	New Year's Day/Treasure (Whatever Happened To Pete The Chop) (PS)	(Island WIP 6848) 1983	10
		New Year's Day/Treasure (Whatever Happened To Pete The Chop)/Fire (live)/I Threw A Brick Through A Window (live)/A Day Without Me (live) (7", double pack, PS)	(Island UWIP 6848) 1983	-
		New Year's Day/Treasure (Whatever Happened To Pete The Chop)/Fire (live)/I Threw A Brick Through A Window (live)/A Day Without Me (live) (12", PS)	(Island 12 WIP 6848) 1983	-
		Two Hearts Beat As One/ Endless Deep (PS)	(Island IS 109) 1983	18
		Two Hearts Beat As One/Endless Deep/ New Year's Day (U.S. Remix)/Two Hearts Beat As One (U.S. Remix) (7", double pack, PS)	(Island ISD 109) 1983	-
		Two Hearts Beat As One (Club Mix)/ New Year's Day (U.S. Remix)/Two Hearts Beat As One (U.S. Remix) (12", PS)	(Island 12IS 109) 1983	-
		Pride (In The Name Of Love)/ Boomerang 2 (Vocal) (PS)	(Island IS 202) 1984	3
	α	Pride (In The Name Of Love)/ Boomerang 2 (Vocal) (PS)	(Island ISP 202) 1984	-
		Pride (In The Name Of Love)/4th July/ Boomerang 1 (instr.) / Boomerang 2 (vocal) (double pack, gatefold sleeve, PS)	(Island ISD 202) 1984	-
		Pride (In The Name Of Love)/4th July/ Boomerang 1/Boomerang 2/ A Celebration (cassette)	(Island CIS 202) 1984	-
		Pride (In The Name Of Love)/4th July/ Boomerang 1/ Boomerang 2 (12", white PS)	(Island 12IS 202) 1984	-
		Pride (In The Name Of Love)/4th July/ Boomerang 1/Boomerang 2/ 11 O'Clock Tick Tock (Full Length Version)/ Touch (12", blue PS)	(Island 12IX 202) 1984	-
		The Unforgettable Fire/A Sort Of Homecoming (live) ('4 Portraits' PS)	(Island IS 220) 1985	6
		The Unforgettable Fire/A Sort Of Homecoming (live)/ Love Comes Tumbling/Sixty Seconds In Kingdom Come/ The Three Sunrises (7" double pack 'Larry Mullen Jr' gatefold PS)	(Island ISD 220) 1985	-
		The Unforgettable Fire/A Sort Of Homecoming (live) (PS) (logo-shaped picture disc)	(Island ISP 220) 1985	-
		The Three Sunrises/The Unforgettable Fire/ A Sort Of Homecoming (live)/Love Comes Tumbling/ Bass Trap (12")	(Island 12IS 220) 1985	-

U2 - Boy.

NB: * An Irish-only release originally on black vinyl. Later copies appeared on white, orange or yellow vinyl in the eighties. There were also mispressings on brown vinyl. + An Irish-only 1,000 only 12" release in an orange CBS sleeve with a numbered sticker. There was a reissue in 1981 in a black sleeve and slightly different label. In 1985 there was an Irish-only cassette version of this release (CBS 40-7951). # An Irish-only release originally on black vinyl. Later versions in the eighties appeared on white, yellow or orange vinyl. Copies of the three Irish-only 7" singles were made available in the 4x7" pack, *4 U2 Play* (CBS PAC 1) 1982. o Some copies of WIP 6848 were mispressed with a Martha Reeves track and a Motown label. These are quite collectable. α This was a picture disc release.

U2 were formed in Dublin, Ireland in 1977 as a school boy band featuring Bono (Paul Hewson), who was born in Dublin on 10th May 1960, The Edge (David Evans), who was born in Wales on 8th August 1961, Adam Clayton and Larry Mullen junior. These four, together with Dick Evans, had originally formed as Feedback in 1976, in response to a note Mullen had left on a school notice board. In these days they were mostly a covers band. They changed name to The Hype and finally settled on **U2** after Evans departed to form **The Virgin Prunes**. It was around this time that Paul Hewson adopted the name Bono, which he took from a billboard he'd seen advertising a hearing aid retailer Bono Vox.

The band started gigging around the clubs and pubs of Dublin and soon got noticed. At the Limerick Civic Week they won a talent contest sponsored by Guinness, whilst they were still in their last year at school. This secured them £500 and the opportunity to audition for CBS Ireland at the Keystone Studios. With Paul McGuiness having become their manager, they got to support **The Stranglers** and The Greedy Bastards on tour.

The Limerick contest adjudicator, A&R man Jackie Hayden arranged for them to record some demos at the Windmill Lane studios in Dublin. This lead to a deal with CBS Ireland. The U.K. CBS operation did not take up the option on the deal. They continued to establish a fan base in Ireland aided by an RTE Radio 2 Irish demo session tape broadcast and finally released their first single in September 1979. *U2 Three* comprised three cuts; *Out Of Control*, *Stories For The Boys* and *Boy-Girl*. *Out Of Control* attracted considerable airplay as a lightish, popish song on the country's national radio show. On the 'B' side was *Stories For The Boys* (a smoother version of this was later re-recorded for their *Boy* album) and *Boy-Girl*, which later re-appeared in a live format on the flip to a later 45 *I Will Follow*. The single go to No. 17 in Ireland but CBS U.K. still decided not to release it. Inevitably it is now quite collectable in all its various formats; besides the 7", there was also a limited edition 12" release of just 1,000 copies. This came in an orange CBS custom sleeve with a sticker indicating the copy of the numbered edition you owned and displaying the RRP of just £1.49! The single was reissued on 7" during the early eighties on various shades of colour vinyl as part of the *4 U2* pack as well as on cassette. The three tracks were produced by the band with assistance from Chris de Whalley.

Just before Christmas 1980 **U2** came to London, playing at various clubs in a whistestop tour. Back in Ireland, a second 45 was released in February 1980 *Another Day*. A popish new wave style recording it failed to make the Irish charts. The flip side *Twilight* was recorded in about 15 minutes and sounds like it. A better version was later recorded for their *Boy* album. They followed this in May 1980 with *11 O'Clock Tick Tock*, which became their first 45 to be released in Britain, too, on Island. Having toured Ireland in March, they arrived in Britain in May to coincide with the release of the single. The 'A' side wasn't included on their debut album, nor was the flip side *Touch*. However, the latter was subsequently featured on the second 12" release of the *Pride* single in 1984. It is worth noting that *11 O'Clock Tick Tock* was produced by Martin Hannett, best known for his work with **Joy Division**. *11 O'Clock...*, a haunting brooding song was included on the tribute compilation to the late producer *Martin* (Factory FACD 325), which is the song's only appearance on CD. The flip side *Touch* was a relatively simplistic, almost naive sort of song.

In August 1980, *A Day Without Me* was released. This would later appear on their *Boy* album. If the 'A' side was a perversely jolly song, given that it's subject matter was suicide, the instrumental flip side *Things To Make And Do*, notable for the chiming guitar work of The Edge, was lighter in tone. Packaged in a striking picture sleeve showing the reversed image of a deserted railway station the single sold quite well, but not well enough to chart. To help promote it Island prepared a special promo version, of the 45 - a special one-sided disc with an 'A' label, which is now very collectable. Hardcore **U2** fans may want to track down a version of the 45 released in Holland. In addition, there is a French 45 with *A Day Without Me* on the 'A' side and *I Will Follow* (their next U.K. 'A' side) on the flip.

Prior to the release of *I Will Follow*, which became something of a **U2** anthem, the band played a sell-out concert at London's Marquee Club on 22nd September 1980. *I Will Follow*, released the following month, also features on their *Boy* album. The vibrant, soaring number was released around the world and got lots of airplay in the U.S.. Despite this, it surprisingly failed to chart in Britain. On its flipside was the non-album live version of *Boy-Girl*. This had previously only been available in studio format on their Irish only *U2: Three* release.

Their debut album *Boy* was released in November 1980. To help promote it, they played as support on a Talking Heads U.K. tour during December. Produced by Steve Lillywhite the boy featured on the front cover was Peter, a brother of **Virgin Prunes**' vocalist Guggi. The album included their earlier 45s *I Will Follow* and *A Day Without Me*; re-recorded versions of *Out Of Control* and *Stories Of Boys* from their Irish-only *U2: Three* release and of *Twilight* (their second 45 'B' side). Best of the new material are *An Cat Dubh* and *Into The Heart*. Certainly it's an impressive debut, The Edge's guitarwork particularly catches the ears, but the rhythm section play nice and tight and Bono's vocals are powerful and emotional without ever becoming histrionic. The British test pressing of this album comprised two one-sided discs and is very collectable. The album brought them their first chart success. Ironically this came in the U.S. where it climbed to No. 63 in March 1981, after they'd undertaken a highly acclaimed U.S. tour the previous month. The album belatededly reached No. 52 in the U.K. in August 1981, during a thirty-one week chart occupation.

During the first half of 1981 they followed a hectic touring schedule, touring mainland Europe in February before embarking on a three-month stint in the U.S. from March-May. In between they recorded a new 45 *Fire*, which gave them their first U.K. hit when it was released in July, peaking at No. 35. It featured a choir-led introduction and was a pounding number. The flip *J. Swalle* is a drifting, evocative song. There is also a limited edition double pack release, which features four live tracks as well recorded from a Boston gig in March 1981 during their U.S. tour.

The follow-up 45 *Gloria* was a new song *not* a cover of the Van Morrison classic. On the flip side was a live version of *I Will Follow* recorded at London's Marquee Club in November 1980. There is also a Dutch release of this song featuring the studio 'A' side and a live 'B' side recorded at Hattem, Holland in early 1982 in a different picture sleeve. This is one of the most collectable **U2** releases. *Gloria* reached No. 55 during a four week chart stay.

Their second album again produced by Lillywhite, *October* was released in October 1981. Much of the album displayed the energy and sparkiness of punk and post-punk music that had originally inspired the band. Its stronger tracks include *Gloria, I Fall Down* and *Is That All?* The title track and *Scarlet* introduced a softer, more melodic side to their work. In the U.K. *Octobre* climbed to No. 11 (a significant advance on their debut effort, as they were becoming better known) and spent forty-one weeks in the charts. It got to No. 104 in the 'States.

A Celebration released in March 1982, was a heads-down rocker with a Beatles-inspired riff and revved-up guitar. It's the rarest of all their regular 45s because it was never featured on an album and was also deleted after just six months! The 'B' side *Trash, Trampoline And The Party Girl* also appears on their later live album *Under A Blood Red Sky* and remained part of their live repertoire under a shortened title *Party Girl* for much longer than the 'A' side. The powerful, but not particularly commercial 45 stalled at No. 47, spending just four weeks in the charts. There's a collectable Japanese release of this song with *Fire* on the reverse side.

On 17th March 1982, **U2** played a highly successful St. Patrick's Day gig at the Ritz in New York, but much of the year was spent recording new material at the Windmill Lane Studios in Dublin, their long-term professional base.

During a concert in Belfast, Northen Ireland, in October 1982 Bono introduced a new song into their act *Sunday Bloody Sunday*. Penned by The Edge its lyrics carried a powerful "peace in Ireland" message which became a live focus for the band during the following years.

In February 1983, *New Year's Day*, a powerful piano-driven song inspired by Polish Solidarity leader Lech Walesa promoted by a Snow-bound video, brought then their first big hit. It spent eight weeks in the charts peaking at No. 10. Along with *Sunday Bloody Sunday*, it featured on their phenomenally successful album *War*, released the same month. It combined love songs like *Two Hearts Beat As One* and *Drowning Man* with political protest numbers like *Seconds, The Refugee* and, of course, *Sunday Bloody Sunday*. Bizarrely, the album featured Kid Creole's Coconuts on backing vocals. The album entered the U.K. charts at No. 1 and spent a staggering one-hundred and forty-three weeks in the charts. It also reached No. 12 in the U.S., where *New Year's Day* became their first hit single, climbing to No. 53 in May. They'd embarked on a new U.S. tour in April and their performances won widespread critical acclaim and large crowds. On 28th May they took part in a three day U.S. festival.

Meanwhile *Two Hearts Beat As One*, a danced-tinged rocker was culled from *War* for 45 release in April 1983. The remixes on the double pack and 12" editions by Francois Kervorkian are essential listening for fans of the band. The 45 got to No. 18 here and spent five weeks in the charts.

Drawing on their rapidly growing reputation as a live band **U2** released a live mini-album *Under A Blood Red Sky* in November 1983, simultaneously with a video of the same title. The title, incidentally, was taken from the lyrics to their *New Year's Day* song. It featured eight dynamic live versions

U2 - October.

of songs from their first three albums recorded in Boston, Massachusetts; West Germany and at the Red Rocks festival in Colorado. It reached No. 2 in the U.K., spending a phenomenal two-hundred and one weeks in the charts and also got to No. 28 in the 'States, where *I Will Follow* belatedly reached No. 81 in the charts in January 1984. All of this rendered *Under A Blood Red Sky* the most successful live album ever.

In July 1984, Bono sang *Blowing In The Wind* with Bob Dylan at the latter's concert at Ireland's Slane Castle. The following month **U2** established their own Mothers Records to showcase the recordings of (mostly Irish) unsigned artists.

Their next studio release *Pride (In The Name Of Love)* appeared in September 1984. A powerhouse number dedicated to Reverend Martin Luther King it is widely acknowledged as one of their finest moments. No fewer than six different formats of this release appeared in the shops. Of these the 7" picture disc has become one of the band's most treasured collectables. See the discography for details of all the different formats. The 45 got to No. 3, spending eleven weeks in the charts. In the U.S. it peaked at No. 33. It previewed their latest album *The Unforgettable Fire*, which they got Brian Eno (and his collaborator Daniel Lanois) to produce. Lyrically it was largely a celebration of Martin Luther King and personal heroism. Other highs aside from *Pride...* were *A Sort Of Homecoming*, *Wire* and the title track, which all appeared on side one. The same standard is not maintained on side two and notable on *Elvis Presley And America*. In Britain, the album topped the charts and spent an incredible one-hundred and twenty-seven weeks in them overall. In the 'States it got to No. 12.

The band's stature was confirmed when Bono contributed a vocal part to Band Aid's *Do They Know It's Christmas?* on 25th November and Adam Clayson played bass on the disc.

In January 1985, **U2** embarked on their first U.S. arenas tour following an extremely successful tour of Europe. In May *The Unforgettable Fire* was released as a 45 and climbed to No. 6 during a six week chart residency. This time four different formats were used - there is plenty to interest the collector. The double-pack artwork differs from the 7" and 12". Hardest to find is the shaped picture disc. This had a limited run of just 2,000 and was released *after* the 45 had dropped out of the charts.

On 22nd June 1985, **U2** headlined the U.K.'s Milton Keynes Bowl. Then, on 13th July, they played at the Live-Aid at Wembley Stadium. In May *Wide Awake In America*, a live studio five-track collection was released. The title track was the only new cut. It is notable for a stunning eight-minute live version of *Bad*. Available as an import album in Britain it reached No. 11 and spent sixteen weeks in the charts. In the 'States it was released as an EP and climbed to No. 37.

U2 also made a few compilation appearances in their early days. *Stories For Boys* figured on an Irish-only *Just For Kicks* (Kick KK 1) 1980 compilation, which is now very hard to find. *Dancin' Master* (NME 001) the first of NME's special offer cassettes included a live version of *An Cat Dubh*, taken from the live Boston tapes from 1981. There's also a U.S. radio album set *Two Sides Live* (WBMS) from this period, which is now an expensive purchase. Even more expensive is *King Biscuit Flower Hour* (KBFH) 1981, a U.S. radio album set which includes another of **U2**'s Boston gigs intermixed with tracks by Devo. Finally, a version of *Gloria* featured on a cassette compilation *Wheel To Wheel* (Island ICT 4005) 1981.

So as we leave them at the end of 1985 **U2** had progressed a long way from their new wave roots in Dublin to become one of the world's most successful stadium rock acts.

The Valves

Personnel:	G. DAIR	drms	A
	RONNIE MacKINNON	gtr	A
	DEE ROBOT	vcls	A
	GORDON SCOTT	bs	A

45s:	Robot Love/For Adolfs Only (PS)	(Zoom ZUM 1) 1977
	Tarzan Of The Kings Road/	
	Ain't No Surf In Portobello (PS)	(Zoom ZUM 3) 1978
	I Don't Mean Nothing At All/	
	Lina Vindalco (PS)	(Albion DEL 3) 1979

THE VAPORS - Turning Japanese.

The rather strange *Robot Love* was the first release on Edinburgh's Zoom label. This was probably a Scottish group. *It Don't Mean Nothing At All* has a great opening and neatly suspended backing vocals but is nothing special.

The Vandells

Personnel:	DAVE BARNARD	bs	A
	STEWART GREEN	drms	A
	ANTHONY MAYBERRY	gtr	A
	DEAN MORIARTY	piano, organ	A
	MARCUS VANDELL	vcls	A

45:	Ruby Toot/I See Everything (PS)	(Loose End L1) 1980

Another of the South Coast's mod revival bands. Although this was their sole 45, they also contributed *Bank Holiday* and *Another Girl* to *Vaultage '79 (Two Sides Of Brighton)* (Attrix RB 08), a local Brighton compilation. Given the importance of Bank Holidays in mod symbolism, it's no surprise that someone wrote a song about them, so this Brighton band did. *Bank Holiday* subsequently resurfaced on *Vaultage Punk Collection* (Anagram CDPUNK 101) 1997 and on *100% British Mod* (Captain Mod MODSKA DCD 8) 1998. Mark Brennan reveals in his sleevenotes to the later that **The Vandells** recorded an album's worth of material which remains unreleased.

Cherry Vanilla

Personnel incl:	CHERRY	vcls	A

ALBUMS:	1(A)	BAD GIRL	(RCA PL 25122) 1978
	2(A)	VENUS DE VINYL	(RCA PL 25217) 1979

45s:	The Punk/Foxy Bitch	(RCA PB 5053) 1977
	Moonlight/Mr. Spider	(RCA PB 5145) 1979

Although American, **Cherry Vanilla** was an important part of Britain's punk scene for a brief while in the late seventies. Originally from New York she had once worked as David Bowie's publicist. She relocated to Britain when she decided to establish a recording career. Back in the 'States she had contributed to *Live At Max's, Kansas City* (Ram 1213) in 1976. This album was reissued (CBS 82670) in 1978. On this she was backed by the New York-based Backstreet Boys.

In Britain, she worked with guitarist/songwriter Louis Lepore and various back-up players. She was often supported by **The Police** for live work.

Both her albums are pretty good, if inconsistent. *Bad Girl* is pretty direct with *Foxy Bitch* and *I Know How To Hook* among the highlights.

Venus De Vinyl is subtler, containing some cleverly arranged and varied music with sensitive lyrics.

The Vapors

Personnel:	EDWARD BAZALGETTE	gtr	A
	DAVE FENTON	gtr, vcls	A
	HOWARD SMITH	drms	A
	STEVE SMITH	bs	A

ALBUMS: HCP
    1(A) NEW CLEAR DAYS (United Artists UAG 30300) 1980 44
    2(A) MAGNETS   (Liberty LBG 30324) 1981 -

NB: (1) also issued on CD (Captain Mod MODSKA CD 11) 2000 and (2) also issued on CD (Captain Mod MODSKA CD 12) 2000. There's also a compilation *Turning Japanese (The Best Of The Vapors)* (EMI GOLD CDGO 2071) 1996.

45s: HCP
Prisoners/Sunstroke (PS)   (United Artists BP 321) 1979 -
Turning Japanese/
Here Comes The Judge   (United Artists BP 334) 1980 3
News At Ten/Wasted/
Talk Talk (PS)   (United Artists BP 345) 1980 44
Waiting For The Weekend/
Billy (PS)   (United Artists BP 367) 1980 -
Spiders/Galleries For Guns (PS)   (United Artists BP 385) 1981 -
Jimmie Jones/Daylight Titans (PS)   (Liberty BP 401) 1981 44

The Vapors hailed from Guildford, Surrey, where they formed in April 1979. A mod-influenced band they were managed by **Jam** bassist **Bruce Foxton** and Paul Weller's father John. Bruce had originally seen them playing at a pub called Scratches, just outside Godalming in Surrey. Their first national exposure came when they supported **The Jam** on their 'Setting Sons' U.K. tour. **Foxton** was also instrumental in securing them London gigs and a Peel session.

They were signed by United Artists in September 1979 and their debut 45 *Prisoners* followed in October. Their big breakthrough came with the extremely catchy *Turning Japanese* the following spring. Not only did it climb to No. 3 in the U.K. charts in which it spent thirteen weeks in total, it also got to No. 36 in the U.S.A. and was a massive international hit, for example, reaching No. 1 in Australia. In a sense this early commercial success proved their ultimate downfall. They could never equal its commercial success or shake off the commercial image they were labelled with of a consequence of its success.

In the 'States there was considerable speculation that the song was about wanking or more specifically the oriental-looking facial contortions one pulls at the point of climax. Dave Fenton, who wrote the song, simply describes it as a love song, but was more ambivalent about its meaning in interviews in the 'States at the time.

Their debut album, whilst dominated by the single, contained a few other focussed pop-punk offerings. It spent six weeks in the album charts peaking at No. 44. Coincidentally it also spawned a further hit, *News At Ten*, which also stalled at No. 44.

Their next album *Magnets* showcased their singer David Fenton's emerging political consciousness in some of his songs. Whilst it produced a further hit - *Jimmie Jones* (which incredibly also stalled at No. 44 during its six week chart residency) - the album itself made little impact at all. Still labelled as **Jam** clones **The Vapors** saw the writing on the wall and split before the end of 1981.

Guitarist Ed Bazalgette went on to join the BBC as a film editor. Howard Smith ended up at the PRS. Steve Smith briefly joined Shoot Dispute, who were initally sponsored by **Bruce Foxton**, they supported him on live gigs during his brief solo career. Dave Fenton went into electronic music - he recorded a solo single and fronted various bands called Vapor Corporation none of whom made it onto vinyl.

Both of their original albums have recently been reissued on CD with bonus cuts rounding up their non-album releases. They are accompanied by booklets which contain lyrics, single covers and excellent sleevenotes by Mark Brennan.

Inevitably, *Turning Japanese* has resurfaced on a number of compilations including *The Sound Of The Suburbs* (Columbia 4888252) 1997, *Spiked* (EMI Gold CDGOLD 1057) 1996, *Teenage Kicks* (PolyGram TV 5253382) 1995 and *Wave (The Biggest New Wave Hits)* (3-CD set) (Disky HR 868442) 1996.

Varicose Veins

EP: 1   INCREDIBLE (Geographical Problems/
             Just Because)   (Warped WARP 1) 1978

Just 200 copies of this EP were pressed. It didn't come in a picture sleeve. It was sold by mail-order only, making it a very rare and expensive punk artefact nowadays.

Various Artists

Personnel:	JONJO	vcls, gtr	A
	JOHN LANGLEY	drms	A
	WILLIAM KELLY STAIR	bs	A

45:   Original Mixed Up Kid/Unofficial Secrets (Fried Egg EGG 9) 1981

NB: There's also a CD compilation *The Complete Works* (Sugar Shack FOD 019) 2000.

A Bristol new wave band, although their vinyl debut, *Own Up* on *Avon Calling - The Bristol Compilation* (Heartbeat HB 1) in 1979 was much more R&B flavoured.

Elvis Costello was a clear influence on their new wave music. They recorded a fast-paced upbeat 45 *Original Mixed-Up Kid* for Fried Egg, which is melodic and very accessible. The flip side *Unofficial Secrets* has a **Police**-influenced rhythm and is pretty good too, making this arguably the best single released on the label. You can also check out both sides on *E(gg)clectic* (Fried Egg FRY 2) in 1981.

The Complete Works, a nineteen-track compilation, rounds up all their output. John Langley, their drummer, later resurfaced in Blue Aeroplanes with his brother Gerard.

The Varukers

Personnel:	BRAINS	drms
	BRUCE	gtr
	GEORGE	bs
	TONY	vcls

ALBUMS: 1( ) BLOODSUCKERS   (Riot City CITY 005) 1983
              2( ) LIVE IN HOLLAND   (Rot DUTCH 001) 1985
              3( ) PREPARE FOR THE ATTACK   (Rot ATTACK 001) 1986

NB: (1) and (3) reissued on one CD (Anagram CDPUNK 56) 1995. Also of relevance are: *Deadly Games* (Abstract AABT 806 CD) 1992, *Live In Leeds* (Retch RRCD 002) 1998, also on vinyl (Data KICKBACK 001) 1999, *The Singles 1981 - 85* (Anagram CDPUNK 74) 1996 and *The Best Of The Varukers* (Anagram CDPUNK 110) 1999.

EPs: 1( ) DON'T WANNA BE A VICTIM (I Don't Wanna Be A
                   Victim/No Masters, No Slaves/Dance Till
                   Your Head) (PS)   (Tempest/Inferno HELL 4) 1982

THE VARUKERS -

2( )	ANOTHER RELIGION ANOTHER WAR (Another Religion Another War/No Escape/Condemned To Death/ The Last War/Who Pays?/Neglected/Deadly Games/ Seek Shelter In Hell) (12", PS)	(Riot City RIOT 31) 1983
3( )	MASSACRED MILLIONS (Massacred Millions/Will They Never Learn/Thatcher's Fortress/ The Bomb Blast) (12", PS)	(Rot ASS 16) 1984

NB: (1) credited to The Verukas.

45s:	Protest And Survive/No Scapegoat/Soldier Boy/ Never Again (PS)	(Tempest/Inferno HELL 1) 1981
	Die For The Government/ All Systems Fall (PS)	(Riot City RIOT 27) 1983
	Led To The Slaughter/The End Is Nigh/ Your Dead (PS)	(Riot City RIOT 29) 1983

The band specialised in fast-paced, noisy, third generation punk. Their hometown was Leamington Spa. Along with **Chaos UK** and **Disorder** they were at the forefront of the U.K. hardcore movement, which later developed into thrash metal. They underwent numerous line-up changes and just one of them is listed above. They had a very uncompromising style and their *Blood Suckers* album in particular remains a classic of the hardcore genre. They signed to Rot for subsequent albums *Prepare For Attack* and *Live In Holland*. They have continued to tour and record until the present day. Releases have included *Still Bollox And Still Hear* (We Bite WB 1136 LP/CD) 1995 and *Murder* (We Bite WB 1165 LP/CD) 1995, *Live In Leeds 1984* has been issued on Retch (RRCD 002) 1998 and *Data* (KICKBACK 001) 1999. *Deadly Games* is a twenty-seven track history of the band which takes in many of their indie label 45 releases like *The End Is Nigh*, *Led To The Slaughter* and of course the title cut.

Back in 1985 *Die For Your Government* figured on *Life's A Riot And Then You Die* (Riot City CITY 009). More recently, *Die For Your Government* and *Led To The Slaughter* have resurfaced on *Riot City Singles Collection, Vol. 1* (Anagram CDPUNK 15) 1997, whilst *Vol. 2* (Anagram CDPUNK 55) 1995 has featured *All Systems Fall* and *End Is Nigh*. Both of these last two compilations have also been issued on vinyl by Captain Oi! (AHOY DLP 503 and 511). *Massacred Millions, Will They Never Learn* and *Killed By Man's Own Hands* also figure on *Rot Records Punk Singles Collection* (Anagram CDPUNK 40) 1994.

V.D.U.'s - Don't Cry For Me.

V.D.U.'s

Personnel:	MICHELLE ARCHER	vcls	A
	ANDY BATES	bs	A
	PAUL DEWEY	gtr	A
	JEF HARVEY	vcls	A
	STEVE PATTERSON	drms	A

45:	Don't Cry For Me/Little White Line/ Holiday Romances (PS)	(Thin Sliced TSR 1) 1980

A one-off new wave 45. **The V.D.U.'s** dominant feature, certainly on *Don't Cry For Me*, is Michelle Archer's distinctive vocals. *Little White Line* is rather nondescript. *Holiday Romances* has a distinctive guitar intro and is quite riffy at times.

Venom

An Oi! group from Wales who contributed *Where's Dock Green?* to *Back On The Streets* (EP), which is translated to 'Where the fuck's the police' on the disc. It got a further airing on *Secret Records Punk Singles Collection, Vol. 2* (Anagram CDPUNK 60) in 1995.

Vermillion (and The Aces)

Personnel:	KENNY ALTON	gtr	A
	PETE DAVIES	drms	A
	FRITZ	bs	A
	VERMILLION SANDS	vcls	AB
	CHARLIE CASEY	bs	B
	NOEL MARTIN	drms, vcls	B
	STEVE TANNET	vcls, gtr	B

45s:	Angry Young Women/Nymphomania/ Wild Boys (PS)	(Illegal ILM 0010) 1978
*	The Letter/I Like Motorcycles (PS)	(Illegal ILS 0015) 1979

NB: * With The Aces.

Line-up 'A' played on the first 45 and line-up 'B' on the second with The Aces, who were formerly in **Menace**. This second 45 was produced by Mick Farren.

The Vibrators

Personnel: (up to 1986)	KNOX (IAN CARNOCHAN)	vcls, gtr	ABCD	G
	EDDIE (JOHN EDWARDS)	drms	ABCDEF	G
	PAT COLLIER	bs	A	G
	JOHN ELLIS	drms	AB	G
	GARY TIBBS	bs	B	
	DAVE BIRCH	gtr	C	
	DON SNOW	keyb'ds	C	
	BEN BRIERLY	bs	D	
	GREG VAN COOK	gtr	DEF	
	KIP	vcls	E	
	IAN WOODCOCK	bs	E	
	PHIL RAM (aka BIRDMAN)	gtr	E	
	ADRIAN WYATT	gtr	F	

				HCP
ALBUMS:	1(A)	PURE MANIA	(Epic EPC 82097) 1977	49
(up to	2(B)	V 2	(Epic EPC 82495) 1978	33
1986)	3(A)	GUILTY	(Anagram GRAM 002) 1982	-
	4(A)	ALASKA 127	(Ram RAM LP 001) 1984	-
	5(A)	FIFTH AMENDMENT	(Ram CHPLP 002) 1985	-
	6(A)	VIBRATORS LIVE	(Revolver REV LP 85) 1986	-

NB: (2) reissued on CD (Rewind/EPIC 49338 2) 1999. (3) and (4) reissued on one CD (Anagram CDPUNK 16) 1993. (5) reissued on one CD (Anagram CD PUNK 34) 1994 along with *Recharged* (from 1988). Also relevant are *Live At The Marquee 1977* (Released Emotions REM 018) 1993, also on CD; *BBC Live In Concert (1977): Vibrators/The Boys* (Windsong WIND CD 036) 1993; *Demos '76 '77* (Dojo DOLE CD 102) 1994; and *Live At The Marquee 1977* (Dojo DOLE CD 110) 1996. There are also a few compilations featuring material from this era:- *Batteries Included* (CBS Embassy CBS 31840) 1980, which was re-recorded as *Power Of Money* (Anagram GRAM 52) 1993, which was later repackaged as *The Best Of The Vibrators* (Anagram CD PUNK 43) 1995; *Independent Punk Singles Collection* (Anagram CD PUNK 76) 1996; an acoustic compilation *Unpunked* (Vibrators VIBES 001) 1996; a CD *Public Enemy Number 1* (Harry May MAYO CD 106) 1999; *The BBC Punk Sessions* (Captain Oi! AHOY CD 135) 2000; *Noise Boys* (Receiver RRCD 291 2) 2000 and *The Best Of 25 Years Of Pure Mania* (2-CD) (Epic 500631 2) 2001.

			HCP
45s:	We Vibrate/Whips And Furs	(Rak RAK 245) 1976	-
(up to +	Pogo Dancing/The Pose	(Rak RAK 246) 1976	-
1986) x	Bad Time/No Heart	(Rak RAK 253) 1977	-
	Baby, Baby/Into The Future (PS)	(Epic SEPC 5302) 1977	-
	London Girls (live)/ Stiff Little Fingers (live) (PS)	(Epic SEPC 5565) 1977	-
	Automatic Lover/Destroy (PS)	(Epic SEPC 6137) 1978	35
	Judy Says (Knock You In The Head)/		

Pure Mania (PS)	(Epic SEPC 6393)	1978 70
Gimme Some Lovin'/ Power Cry (live) (PS)	(Rat Race RAT 2)	1980 -
o Disco In Mosco/Take A Chance (PS)	(Rat Race RAT 4)	1980 -
Baby, Baby (new version)/ Dragnet (PS)	(Anagram ANA 4)	1982 -
Guilty/Hang Ten	(Anagram ANA 8)	1983 -
M.X. America/Shadow Of Love (PS)	(Ram RAM 7005)	1983 -
Flying Home/Flash Flash Flash/ M.X. America (12")	(Ram RAM 70077)	1984 -
Flying Home/ Punish Me With Kisses (PS)	(Carrerre CAR 329)	1984 -
Flying Home/Punish Me With Kisses/ M.X. America (12")	(Carrere CART 329)	1984 -
Baby Blue Eyes/ Amphetamine Blue (PS)	(Carrere CAR 338)	1984 -
Baby Blue Eyes/Amphetamine Blue/ Flying Home (12, some PS)	(Carrere CART 338)	1984 -
Blown Away By Love/ The Demolishers (PS)	(Ram CHP 7011)	1985 -
Blown Away By Love/The Demolishers/ Stil Not Over You (12")	(Ram 12CHP 7011)	1985 -

NB: + 'B' side with Chris Spedding. x Unreleased, one-sided test pressing. o The picture sleeve came with various coloured writing.

The Vibrators formed in London in February 1976. **Knox** (real name Ian Carnochan) had been in the music business for some while - playing mostly in R&B bands during the sixties and seventies. He also had a short stint in an Irish showband and a brief spell in a Teddy boy outfit. After that particular band he formed Despair with a couple of his cousins. It was with them that *Whips And Furs* and *She's Bringing You Down* - both later **Vibrators**' favourites were written. By Christmas 1975, he'd decided Despair would only lead to more of the same. So he formed **The Vibrators** the following February with Pat Collier and John Ellis.

The Vibrators played their first concert supporting **The Stranglers** at Hornsey College Of Art in March 1976. Their repertoire at this time comprised mostly R&B. They had a residency at the Lord Nelson, a down-at-heel pub rock venue on the Holloway Road, for a while.

Their first big break came when they played on the second night of the 100 Club Punk festival in September 1976 with session guitarist Chris Spedding. **The Damned** were on the same bill. After this, they were associated with the emerging punk rock scene and toured Britain quite extensively. On 28th October 1976, they played their first of three sessions for John Peel. It comprised *Dance To The Music*, *We Vibrate*, *Jenny Jenny*, *I'm Gonna Be Your Nazi Baby* and *Sweet Sweetheart*. They returned on 4th January 1977 to record a Peel session with guitarist Chris Spedding. This comprised *Pogo Dancing*, *Hurt By Love*, *Motor Bikin'*, *Get Out Of My Pagoda* and *Misunderstood*. Chris Spedding linked them up with Mickie Most, who arranged for them to record a couple of singles for release by Rak. The first, *We Vibrate*, was a Pat Collier composition. The second, *Pogo Dancing*, was recorded with Chris Spedding. A third single *Bad Time* was recorded, but not released because they switched labels to Epic/CBS. Indeed a live **Vibrators** song was included on a *Sounds Of CBS* album the following year.

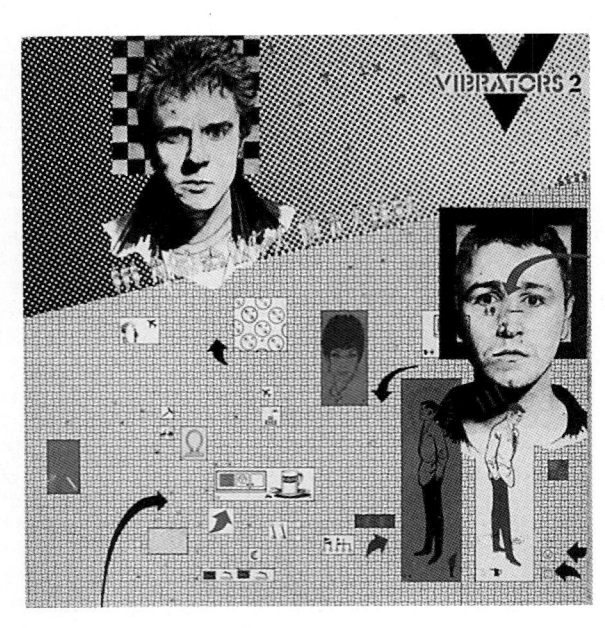

Their first new recording for Epic was a love ballad *Baby Baby*. Their debut album *Pure Mania*, produced by Robin Mayhew, followed shortly after in June. This was a high energy punk album, which sold well enough to spend five weeks in the charts, peaking at No. 49. The album is generally accepted to be one of punk's finest. The same month, a further Peel session was broadcast comprising *Petrol*, *Keep It Clean*, *Baby Baby*, *London Girls* and *She's Bringing You Down*.

To help promote *Pure Mania*, they toured Britain supporting Ian Hunter and the Continent. When they returned Pat Collier left to form **The Boyfriends**. He was replaced by Gary Tibbs.

The new line-up set about recording a second album *V2*. This time Vic Maile handled production. The album was recorded during the period when they briefly switched their base to Berlin. Again the album fared pretty well. It climbed to No. 33 during a two week chart residency. A hit single *Automatic Lover* (No. 35) was culled from it. It spent a total of five weeks in the charts. Other strong cuts include *Flying Duck Theory*, *Destroy*, *Wake Up* and the finale *Troops Of Tomorrow*, which has an extended intro and uses distorted vocals in places. They played their final Peel session in March 1978. It consisted of *Automatic Lover*, *Troops Of Tomorrow*, *Destroy* and *Fall In Love*.

Just when things seemed to be progressing steadily the band's foundations were rocked by the departure of John Ellis to form Rapid Eye Movement, although he went on to work with Peter Gabriel and Gary Tibbs, who joined Roxy Music in November 1978, and later played with **Adam and The Ants**. Both had tired of touring. Don Snow (keyb'ds, sax) and Dave Birch (gtr) briefly joined. This new line-up recorded what turned out to be their second and last hit single *Judy Says (Knock You In The Head)*. It got to No. 70, spending three weeks in the chart.

Feeling the band was now too 'safe' **Knox** sacked Snow and Birch and replaced them with Marianne Faithful's husband Ben Brierly (bs) and former **Electric Chairs**' member Greg Van Cook (gtr). This proved a short-lived configuration with the band appearing to mark time musically, **Knox** himself decided to quit. Surprisingly, this didn't sound the death knell for the band. Eddie and Greg soldiered on, initially with ex-**Eater** Ian Woodcock (bs) and a new vocalist called Kip. A later conglomeration including Phil Ram (aka Birdman) (gtr) and Adrian Wyatt (gtr) recorded two 45s for Rat Race in 1980. The second of these *Disco In Mosco* was later covered by German outfit Die Toten Hosen on their own *Learning English, Vol. 1* (Charisma 91823) 1991. The band finally split up in late 1980. **Knox** recorded with Charie Harper of the **UK Subs** as **The Urban Dogs**.

Knox, meanwhile, released an album *Plutonium Express* for Razor in 1983. Then he linked up with former members of Hanoi Rocks to form Fallen Angels. Pat Collier started his own Alaska 127 studio during the early eighties. It became a launch pad for a new generation of punk bands. Brimming with new enthusiasm it was now Collier who put the original **Vibrators** line-up back in the studio. The resulting album *Guilty* was released by Anagram. More routine, melodic rock than full blooded punk, the album was sufficiently good enough to relaunch their career. Further similar albums followed - *Alaska 127*, *Fifth Amendment* and, in January 1986, *Vibrators Live*. By then Pat Collier had returned to his studio to be replaced by Noel Thomson.

The original vinyl compilation was *Batteries Included*, but Anagram released *Best Of The Vibrators* and *Independent Punk Singles Collection* in the mid-nineties.

There are now plenty of compilations including their early material to choose from as well as some live material from the punk era. *The Power Of Money (The Best Of The Vibrators)* features songs specially re-recorded for this album by their 1992 line-up (which by then included just two original members). The material is substantial and mostly melodic but lacked the quirkiness of some of their more adventurous contemporaries. *Automatic Lover* and *Judy Says* are enjoyable moments of punk-pop and *Every Day I Die A Little* demonstrated that they could perform an emotive ballad effectively.

Live At The Marquee 1977 is a punchy set which conveys a sense of urgency and aggression and should appeal to their fans. They also shared

THE VIBRATORS - V 2.

a *BBC Radio 1 Live In Concert* CD with **The Boys** which included many of their better moments.

The Independent Punk Singles Collection is what it purports to be. *Disco In Moscow* and *MX America* still catch the ear.

The Vibrators have also figured on a number of various artists singles compilations, including the following:- *Automatic Lover* on *A History Of Punk, Vol. 1* (Virgin CDOVD 486) 1997 and *Teenage Kicks* (PolyGram TV 5253382) 1995; *Judy Says* and *London Girls* on *Spiked* (Summit SUMCD 4094) 1997; *Dragnet* on *Punk And Disorderly, Vol. 3 (The Final Solution)* (Anagram CDPUNK 23) 1993; *Baby Baby, Dragnet, Guilty* and *Hang Ten* on *Anagram Punk Singles Collection* (Anagram CDPUNK 37) 1994; *Troops Of Tomorrow* on *Holidays In The Sun, Vol. 1* (Anagram HITS 01) 1999; and *Baby Baby Punk Compilation* (Emporio EMPRCD 550) 1994 and on the lavish 5-CD box set *1-2-3-4 - A History Of Punk And New Wave 1976 - 1979* (MCA/Universal MCD 60066) in 1999.

Public Enemy Number 1, a 1979 CD, includes eight 'demo' versions of tracks later recorded for Epic for inclusion on their first two albums. Some of these 'demos', especially *Public Enemy Number 1*, are noticeably different from the versions which eventually appeared on the albums. The remaining eight cuts date from a 1977 Marquee gig which was originally released on CD by Released Emotions in 1991, but collectors will note that instead of *She's Bringing You Down* a rogue track by psychobilly outfit Demented Are Go called *Frenzied Beat* turns up as track eight.

The BBC Punk Sessions released in 2000 comprises their three Peel sessions from 1976 - 78 and nine cuts from 1978 which comprised their second 'In Concert' session recorded at the Paris Theatre.

Noise Boys (CD) compiles a series of outtakes from four separate sessions recorded between 1978 and 1980 and is really for completists only.

The Best Of: 25 Years Of Pure Mania is a thirty-eight track double CD collection compiling their three years with Epic between 1977-80. The first disc comprises their early singles, including their debut *We Vibrate* (which was actually released on RAK) alongside the most popular material from their two Epic albums *Pure Mania* and *V2*. On the second is a live concert from The Marquee in 1977, which had been released earlier by Released Emotions. This version has been remixed and is punchier, although the number of cuts has been reduced from nineteen to fifteen.

The Vibrators are one of the few punk bands from the class of '76 still on the road. Over a quarter of a century they've recorded a series of quality albums and CDs. They deserve all the success they can get.

Vice Creems

Personnel:	NIGEL BIRCHALL	gtr	A
	MARTIN GODFREY	drms	A
	COLIN KEINCH	gtr	AB
	CHRIS LUGMAYER	bs	A
	KRIS NEEDS	vcls	AB
	MICHAEL BLAIR	gtr	B
	NICHOLAS KHAN	drms	B
	ANTHONY ROSS	bs	B

45s:	Won't You Be My Girl?/01-01-212 (PS)	(Tiger GRRRR 1) 1978
	Danger Love/Like A Tiger (PS)	(Zig Zag ZZ22 001) 1979

Kris Needs, the vocalist with **Vice Creems**, was also a journalist with 'Zig Zag' magazine. Their first 45 came in a gatefold sleeve in 1978. They also contributed a cut called *No Passion* to *Aylesbury Goes Flaccid* (Flaccid FLAC 1), while *01-01-212* also featured on *Business Unusual* (Cherry Red ARED 2) in 1979.

Vice Squad

Personnel:	SHANE BALDWIN	drms	AB
	DAVE BATEMAN	gtr	AB
	BEKI BONDAGE (REBECCA BONS)	lead vcls	A
	MARK HAMBLY	bs	AB
	LIA	lead vcls	B
	SOOTY	gtr	B

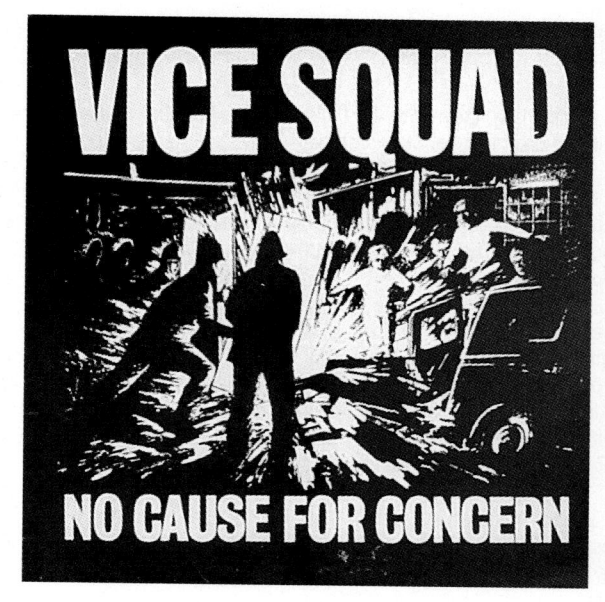

VICE SQUAD - No Cause For Concern.

HCP

ALBUMS: (up to 1986)	1(A)	NO CAUSE FOR CONCERN	(Zonophone ZEM 103) 1981 32
	2(A)	STAND STRONG STAND PROUD	(Zonophone ZEM 104) 1982 47
	3(B)	SHOT AWAY	(Anagram LPGRAM 14) 1984 -

NB: (1) issued on CD (Dojo DOJOCD 167) 1994 with two extra tracks, *(So) What For The 80's* and *Sterile*. (1) also reissued on CD (Captain Oi! AHOY CD 153) 2000 with extra cuts. (2) issued on CD (Dojo DOJOCD 170) 1993 with four extra tracks. (2) also reissued on CD (Captain Oi! AHOY CD 156) 2000 with extra cuts. (3) issued on CD (Anagram CDPUNK 28) 1993 with six bonus cuts. Also relevant are *The BBC Sessions* (Anagram CDPUNK 99) 1997, also on vinyl (Get Back GET 28/29 LP) 1998, *Punk Singles Collection* (Anagram CDPUNK 89) 1997 and *The Rarities 1979 - 1985* (Captain Oi! AHOY CD 123) 1999.

EPs:	1(A)	SINGLES (12")	(Riot City RIOT 12 1/2) 1982
	2(A)	EVIL (flexidisc)	(Vice Squad Fan Club) 198?

HCP

45s: (up to 1986)	*	Last Rockers/Living On Dreams/Latex Love (PS)	(Riot City RIOT 1) 1980 -
		Resurrection/Young Blood/Hurricane (PS)	(Riot City RIOT 2) 1981 -
		Out Of Reach/Sterile/Out Of Reach (PS)	(Zonophone Z26) 1982 68
		Rock 'n' Roll Massacre/Stand Strong And Proud/Tomorrow (PS)	(Zonophone Z30) 1982 -
		Black Sheep/New Blood (PS)	(Anagram ANA 16) 1983 -
		Black Sheep/New Blood/The Pledge (12", PS)	(Anagram 12 ANA 16) 1983 -
		You'll Never Know/What's Going On (PS)	(Anagram ANA 22) 1984 -
		You'll Never Know/What's Going On/The Times They Are A Changin' (12", PS)	(Anagram 12 ANA 22) 1984 -
		Teenage Rampage/High Spirits (PS)	(Anagram ANA 26) 1985 -

NB: * This release came with a poster.

Vice Squad were one of the most successful of the second generation of punk bands. Their music was powerful, their lyrics bitter and in Beki Bondage (real name Rebecca Bond) their lead vocalist, they had a real vocal talent and focus for the group. She was also promoted as one of punk's leading sex symbols.

They formed in Bristol in 1979 from an amalgamation of two local teenage bands, TV Brakes and The Contingent. Their vinyl debut came when they contributed *Nothing* to *Avon Calling - The Bristol Compilation* (Heartbeat HB 1) in 1979. This caught Beki in good form. They gigged for some months without attracting a record deal and consequently decided to set up their own Riot City label. Their first single *Last Rockers* was released in December 1980. After a follow-up 45 *Resurrection*, both **Vice Squad** and their label were signed up by EMI Zonophone. Their *No Cause For Concern* album was released and it achieved respectable sales, spending five weeks in the album charts and peaking at No. 32. The 1994 CD reissue of this on Dojo adds two extra cuts, *(So) What For The 80's* and *Sterile*.

A few months later they achieved their only hit when *Out Of Reach* spent a week in the charts at No. 68 in February 1982.

Their second album *Stand Strong Stand Proud* fared pretty well too. Like their debut it spent five weeks in the charts, but this time they only achieved No. 47. The 1994 CD reissue of *Stand Strong Stand Proud* adds four bonus cuts.

The real problem was that they didn't achieve a significant commercial breakthrough with their 45s. When EMI realised they weren't going to make the money they envisaged out of the band, relations soured and the band were dropped. As a result of this Bondage decided to strike out on her own in 1983. She formed a new group **Ligotage** and recorded a new 45 *Crime And Passion*, but it made little impact and the group soon fizzled out.

Vice Squad, meanwhile, recorded a third album *Shot Away* and three singles with a new girl vocalist called Lia and a second guitarist Sooty before splitting in 1985.

Back in 1982, they also contributed *Cowards* and *It's A Sell Out* to *Riotous Assembly* (Riot City ASSEMBLY 1). Then three years later *Last Rockers* and *Resurrection* figured on *Life's A Riot And Then You Die* (Riot City CITY 009). **Vice Squad** also contributed *Last Rockers* and *Young Blood* to *Riot City: The Punk Singles Collection* (Anagram CDPUNK 15) 1997 and *Living On Dreams* and *Humane* to *Vol. 2* of the same series (Anagram CDPUNK 55) 1995. Both of these compilations were also issued on vinyl by Captain Oi! *Take It Or Leave It* resurfaced on *Spiked* (Summit SUMCD 4094) 1997; *Out Of Reach*, *Stand Strong Stand Proud* and *Citizen* all got a further airing on *The Zonophone Punk Singles Collection* (Anagram CDPUNK 97) 1997 and *Last Rockers* also figured on *Burning Ambitions (A History Of Punk)* (Anagram CDBRED 3) 1996. Yes, wait for it! There's still more. They contributed three cuts; *Black Sheep*, *You'll Never Know* and *Teenage Rampage* to *Anagram Records Punk Singles Collection* (Anagram CDPUNK 37) 1994; *Stand Strong Stand Proud* got a further airing on *Punk, Vol. 2* (Music Club MCCD 027) 1991 and *Punk - The Worst Of Total Anarchy* (2-CD) (Disky SP 871952) 1996; and, finally, you can also check out *Resurrection* on *Punk And Disorderly, Vol. 2 (Further Charges)* (Anagram CDPUNK 22) 1993.

The Rarities 1979 - 1985 features tracks from demo sessions and the band's first live gig in 1979. Much of the material is unimpressive and unimaginative. There's a poor live cover of **The Sex Pistols**' *Belsen Was A Gas*. Only of note is a cut recorded in a garage in 1977 by pre-**Vice Squad** combo TV Brakes and two tracks by post-**Vice Squad** combo **Sweet Revenge**.

Vice Versa

Personnel: STEPHEN SNGLETON   A
             DAVID SYDENHAM   A
             MARK WHITE   A

EP: 1(A)   MUSIC 4 (New Girls Neutrons/Science-Fact/Riot Squad/
             Camille) (PS)   (Neutron NT 001/PX 1092) 1979

VICE VERSA - Music 4 EP.

This Sheffield trio's fusion of drum-machine driven electronics and northern soul as displayed at their 'Futurama' appearance was exciting, but Singleton and White traded all this in for a career with ABC.

The above EP came in a poster picture sleeve and comprised short structured songs. Interesting and experimental, this is certainly worth a spin.

Sid Vicious

                                                                    HCP
ALBUM: 1   SID SINGS (live)   (Virgin V 2114) 1979 30

NB: (1) also issued on CD (Virgin OVED 85) 1988, (Virgin CDV 2144) 1989 and again (Virgin VJCP 68058) 1999. There's also *Sid Dead Live* (Anagram CDPUNK 86) 1997, *Live At Max's 1978* (Get Back GET 57) 2000 on vinyl, *Sid Vicious Live* (Ritchie RITCHIE 1) 1987 on vinyl, also on CD (Dressed To Kill REDTX 123) 1999.

45:       Naked/I'm Ashamed   (Wonderful WO 73) 1979

Sid Vicious (real name John Ritchie) was born on 10th May 1957. He was the original drummer in **Siouxsie and The Banshees**, but left in February 1977 to become bassist and sing some vocals in **The Sex Pistols**, when Glen Matlock left to form **Rich Kids**.

Fuller details of **Sid Vicious'** career appear in the **Sex Pistols** entry. These 'solo' efforts were released after his death from a drug overdose while he was awaiting trial for the murder of his girlfriend Nancy Spungen.

On *Sid Sings*, a live record taken from a New York party gig he is joined by ex-New York Doll Jerry Nolan's band The Nolans for a well-below-par performance of punk standards. The album spent eight weeks in the charts peaking at No. 30.

Sid also resurfaced on *Punk-The Worst Of Total Anarchy* (2-CD) (Disky SP 871952) 1996 singing his version of *My Way*, which can also be heard on *The Best Punk Album In The World.... Ever, Vol. 1* (2-CD) (Virgin VTDCD 42) 1995 and on *The Best Punk Anthems.... Ever* (2-CD) (Virgin VTDCD 198) 1998.

Sid Dead Live is a seventeen-track compilation featuring highlights from the debut album he recorded in September 1978, whilst he was living in New York with his girlfriend Nancy Spungen. He played a few local gigs with a pick-up group comprising Steve Dier, Jerry Nolan, Arthur Kane and Mick Jones, who were in town mixing *Give 'Em Enough Rope*. On offer here is a pretty shambolic run through of songs like *Search And Destroy*, *I Wanna Be Your Dog*, *Something Else*, *Stepping Stone*, *Belsen Was A Gas* and a truncated version of *My Way*. In 2000 the same material was issued on vinyl as *Live At Max's 1978*.

Vicious Rumours

Personnel: JOHN COUPE   bs   A
              JOHN MUNDY   vcls   A
              DANNY SHOOBERT   drms   A

ALBUMS: 1(A) ANYTIME DAY OR NIGHT   (Oi OIR 5) 1986
(up to 2(A) THE SICKEST MEN IN TOWN   (Link LP 022) 1987
1987)

NB: (1) also issued on CD (Captain Oi! AHOY CD 20) 1994 with two bonus cuts. (2) also issued on CD (Captain Oi! AHOY CD 26) 1995 with six bonus cuts. There's also a compilation, *The Best Of Vicious Rumours* (Captain Oi! AHOY CD 125) 1999.

45:       Rita/Nighthawk   (Dork UR BOB 5) 1984

A yobbish Oi! trio who formed in Bexleyheath, Kent in 1979, but whose vinyl debut didn't come to light until they contributed *This Is Your Loife* to the *Son Of Oi!* (Syndicate SYNLP 3) 1983 compilation, which was later issued on CD (Captain Oi! AHOY CD 9) 1993. By then, they had established themselves as a popular attraction on the Oi! live circuit and appeared on later compilations like *Oi! Of Sex* (Syndicate SYNLP 4) 1984, to which they contributed *Vicious Rumours* and *Take The Blame*. This compilation was also later issued on CD (Captain Oi! AHOY CD 23) 1994. Their vocalist John Mundy was at this time distinctive for a rather fetching

Mohican hairstyle. Their first album was released in 1986 and brought an element of cockney humour to the second wave of British Oi!, even if the music was somewhat lacking. The title cut was also included on the CD compilation *The Best Of Oi! Records* (Captain Oi! AHOY CD 38) 1995, which compiled tracks from the Oi! labels seventeen albums. The debut album *Anytime Day Or Night* has also been reissued on CD with two bonus cuts *Nobodys Fool* and *Hangover*, which originally appeared on *This Is Oi!* (Oi! OIR 004) 1986, which was later issued on CD (Captain Oi! AHOY CD 6) 1993. They appeared on more Oi! compilations on Link before releasing their second album *The Sickest Men In Town*, which was reissued by Mark Brennan's Captain Oi! label in 1994 with six bonus cuts.

Vicious Rumours disbanded in 1988. *The Best Of Vicious Rumours* (CD) on Captain Oi! is a twenty-track selection rounding up cuts from their two albums and their contributions to compilations like *Son Of Oi!* and *This Is Oi!*. They can also be heard playing *Anytime Day Or Night* on *100% British Oi!* (Captain Oi! AHOY DCD 83) 1997.

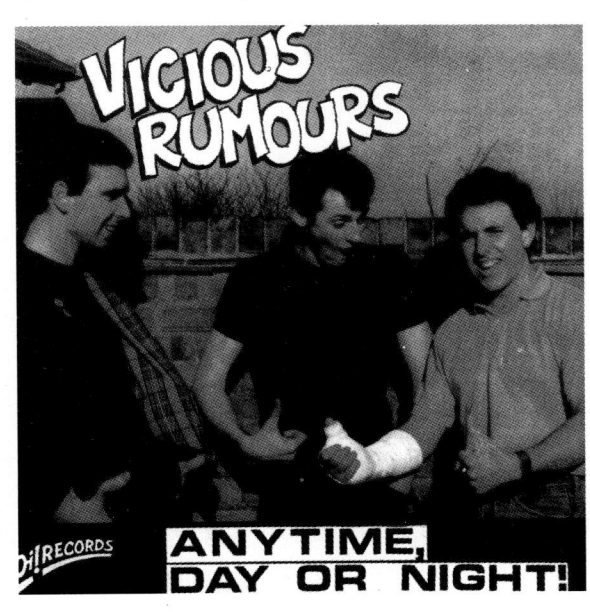

VICIOUS RUMOURS - Anytime Day Or Night.

Vicious White Kids

Personnel:	GLEN MATLOCK	bs	A
	STEVE NEW	gtr	A
	RAT SCABIES		A
	SID VICIOUS		A

This was a 'fun' group which comprised **The Rich Kids'** Glen Matlock and Steve New (whilst they were waiting for their *Ghost Of Princes In Towers* album to be released), Rat Scabies (of **The Damned**) and **Sid Vicious**. They played a one-off gig on 15th August 1978 at London's Electric Ballroom in Camden Town, as a leaving present for Sid and his girlfriend Nancy Spungen, who were due to fly to New York the next day. They also have a cut *C'mon Everybody* on *Punk - Live And Nasty* (Emporio EMPRCD 586) in 1995.

Victim

Personnel:	JEFF BEATTIE	drms	A
	COLIN CAMPBELL	vcls, gtr	A
	WES GRAHAM	bs	A
	KEN MATTHEWS	gtr	A

EP:	1(A)	THE VICTIM	(TJM TJM 13) 1979

NB: (1) This remains unreleased.

45s:	*	Strange Things By Night/ Mixed Up World (PS)	(Good Vibrations GOT 2) 1978
		Why Are Fire Engines Red/I Need You (PS)	(TJM TJM 14) 1979
		The Teen Age/Junior Criminals/ Hung On To Yourself (PS)	(TJM TJM 15) 1980
Reissue:		The Teen Age/Junior Criminals/ Hung On To Yourself (PS)	(Illuminated ILL 1) 1980

NB: * Released in a wraparound pcture sleeve.

Victim were a group of **Jam**-like clones, who did produce one well-received single *Strange Thing By Night*. It had a very distinctive guitar introduction but then developed into a fairly routine punk fayre. They split up shortly after this was released. Some of the band then teamed up with former members of **The Androids**, a short-lived hard core heavy metal/punk outfit, in another short-lived venture, **Emergency**, who never really got going. All three, however, were regulars at The Harp Bar. **Victim** later re-formed with some new personnel, a new set and image and made for Manchester, where they issued further singles for TJM, and became a hard core pub band. *The Teen Age* was actually produced by **The Damned**'s Rat Scabies, but their self-titled EP was never released.

Strange Thing By Night later resurfaced on *Good Vibrations: The Punk Singles Collection* (Anagram CD PUNK 36) 1994. Five of their cuts - *Why Are Fire Engines Red*, *I Need You*, *Teenage Victim*, *Junior Criminals* and *Hang On To Yourself* - can also be heard on *Rabid / TJM Punk Singles Collection* (Receiver RRCD 227) 1996.

Victimize

Personnel incl:	ROMAN JUGG	A
	BRYAN MERRICK	A

45s:	*	Baby Buyer/Hi Rising Failure (PS)	(I.M.E. IME 1) 1979
	+	Wh?r? Did Th? Mon?y Go (PS)	(I.M.E. IME 2) 1980

NB: * Only 2,000 pressed. + Only 500 pressed.

A four-piece including Roman Jugg and Bryan Merrick, who were later in **The Damned**. These two 45s are now hard to find and quite expensive if you do. *Wh?r? Did Th? Mon?y Go* is punkish with good guitar and vocals.

They later became known as Missing Men. Roman Jugg later married one of the dancers from Dr. and The Medics.

The Violators

Personnel:	ANDY	gtr	A
	LOUISE	vcls	A
	MATCHI	bs	A
	SEAN	vcls	A
	TONY	drms	A

ALBUM:	1(A)	DIE WITH DIGNITY	(No Future 1201 26) 1983

EPs:	1(A)	SUMMER OF '81 (12", PS)	(No Future 12 Oi! 26) 1983
	2(A)	THERE A GUITAR BURNING (There's A Guitar Burning/Life On The Red Line) (12", PS)	(No Future 12 Oi! 27) 1983

45s:	Gangland/The Fugitive (PS)	(No Future Oi! 9) 1982
	Summer Of '81/ Live Fast Die Young (PS)	(No Future Oi! 19) 1982
	Life On The Red Line/ Crossing The Sangsara (PS)	(Future FS 2) 1983
Reissue:	Gangland/The Fugitive	(Future FS 1) 1982

THE VIOLATORS - Gangland.

An early eighties Oi! punk band. Musically, they amalgamate elements of heavy metal with punk. So on offer on *Die With Dignity* is fast punk death screech. Along with the title cut come tracks like *Summer Of '81* and *Government Stinks*. Their third 45 wasn't very punkish at all. One reviewer likened it to a **U2** demo before the hook line was added.

The band can also be found on a number of compilations. *Gangland*, *Summer Of '81* and *Die With Dignity* all resurfaced on *No Future - The Punk Singles Collection* (dbl) (Captain Oi! AHOY DLP 508) 1996. *The Fugitive*, *Live Fast Die Young* and *Pointless Slaughter* can all be heard on *No Future - The Punk Singles Collection, Vol. 2* (dbl) (Captain Oi! AHOY DLP 512) 1996. Alternatively, the same six tracks can be found on CD *The History Of No Future* (Anagram CDPUNK 111) 1999. You'll also find *Gangland* on *Punk And Disorderly, Vol. 2 (Further Charges)* (Anagram CD PUNK 22) 1993, whilst *Summer Of '81* got further exposure on *Punk And Disorderly, Vol. 3 (The Final Solution)* (Anagram CD PUNK 23) 1993 and *Punk Compilation* (Emporio EMPRCD 550) 1994.

The Vipers live at the Electric Ballroom, London 19th October 1979. Photo: Steven Richards.

Vipers

Personnel incl: PAUL BOYLE — gtr, vcls
GEORGE SWEENEY — gtr

45: I've Got You/No Such Thing (PS) (Mulligan LUNS 718) 1978

A promising 45 by a Southern Irish band. On *I've Got You* there's lots of slamming guitars and a strident piano sequence bubbling beneath them. The flip *No Such Thing* is simple, with sawing rhythms and venomous vocals from Paul Boyle.

V.I.P.s

Personnel:			
JED DMOCHOWSKI	vcls	A
GUY MORLEY	gtr	A
ANDREW PRICE	bs	A
PAUL SHUREY	drms	A

V.I.P.'s - Causing Complications.

EP: 1( ) MUSIC FOR FUNSTERS (I'm Perfect/I Believe/
Boys Of The City) (Bust SOL 3) 1978

45s: Just Can't Let You Go/
(flip side by **Urban Disturbance**) (Rok ROK V/VI) 1979
Causing Compilcations/Run Run Belinda/
Love Is A Golden World (PS) (Gem GEMS 25) 1980
The Quarter Moon/
Hippy Hippy Shake (PS) (Gem GEMS 39) 1980
I Need Somebody To Love (Could It Be You?)/
One More Chance//Stuttgart Special/Who Knows/
Janine (double pack PS) (Gem GEMS 39) 1980
Things Aren't What They Used To Be/
I Thought You Were My Friend (PS) (Gem GEMS 47) 1980

NB: There's also a CD compilation, *Beat Crazy! The Best Of The V.I.P.s* (Tangerine TANG CD 12) 1997.

The V.I.P.s, from Warwick blended Merseybeat with new wave power pop. Their debut D.I.Y. pop EP *Music For Funsters* is pretty shambolic. The following year they recorded *Just Can't Let You Go*, a punky number for Rok, before signing to Gem for a series of quirky, sixties-influenced pop ditties. They finally called it quits in early 1983. *Need Somebody To Love*, *Stuttgart Special*, *Who Knows* and *Janine* can all be found on *This Is Mod, Vol. 2* (Anagram CDMGRAM 101) 1996 and *Just Can't Let You Go*, a pleasant mod-pop ditty got a further airing on *100% British Mod* (Captain Mod MODSKA DCD 8) 1998. All their material (except the one side for Rok) is collected on Tangerine's colourful seventeen-track collection.

The Virgin Prunes

Personnel:			
(up to 1986)	DIK EVANS	gtr	ABC
	GAVIN FRIDAY		
	(FIONAN HANVEY)	vcls	ABCD
	GUGGI (DEREK ROWEN)	vcls	ABC
	POD (ANTHONY MURPHY)	drms	A D
	STRONGMAN (TREVOR ROWEN)	bs	ABCD
	HAA-LACKA BINTTI	keyb'ds, perc	B
	MARY O'NELLON	perc, gtr	CD
	(DAVE-ID BUSARAS SCOTT		
	(DAVID WATSON)	vcls	ABCD)

ALBUMS: 1(C) IF I DIE, I DIE (Rough Trade ROUGH 49) 1982
(up to 2(C) HERESIE (Invitational Suicide INV 0500) 1982
1986) 3(C) A NEW FORM OF BEAUTY PARTS 1-4 (dbl)
(Italian Records EX 41) 1982
4(D) OVER THE RAINBOW (Baby Records BABY 002) 1985
5(D) THE MOON LOOKED DOWN AND LAUGHED
(Baby Records BABY 005) 1986

NB: (1) issued on CD (Rough Trade ROUGH CD 49) 1990 and again (New Rose NR 452043) 1994. (2) is a 10" box set containing two 10" discs and five booklets. The second disc is from a live performance at the Rex Club, Paris, in June 1982. (2) reissued (Baby Records BABY 011) 1983 and later on CD (New Rose 422475) 1994. The sleeve to (3) makes reference to the fact that this double album was supposed to be a five-part project. (4) is an album of rarities and previously unavailable tracks. The exception being *Jigsawmen - Tallama* which was different to the original flexidisc version. (2) and (4) also issued on one CD (Baby Records BABY CD 002) 1986. (5) also issued on CD (Baby Records BABY CD 005) 1986. (5) later reissued on CD (New Rose 422474) 1994 with a new cover. Also relevant is *Greatest Hits* (Burning Airlines PILOT 007) 1997.

CASS:	1(C)	A NEW FORM OF BEAUTY PART IV (Din Glorious/ Din Glorious)	(Rough Tapes COPY 007) 1982

NB: (1) issued on CD (New Rose NR 452042) 1994.

EPs: (up to 1986)	1(B)	TWENTY TENS (Twenty Tens/Revenge/The Children Are Crying/In The Greylight)	(Baby BABY 001) 1981
	2(B)	A NEW FORM OF BEAUTY (7", 10", 12" box set)	(Rough Trade RT 089-091) 1981
45s: (up to 1986)	*	Moments Of Mine (Despite Straight Lines)/ In The Greylight, War	(Rough Trade RT 072) 1981
		A New Form Of Beauty Part One: Sandpaper Lullaby/ Sleep/Fantasy Dreams (PS)	(Rough Trade RT 089) 1981
		A New Form Of Beauty Part Two: Come To Daddy/Sweet Home (Under White Clouds)/ Sad World (10", PS)	(Rough Trade RT 090) 1981
		A New Form Of Beauty Part Three: The Beast (Seven Bastards Suck)/The Slow Children (Abbagal)/ Brain Damage/ No Birds To Fly (12", PS)	(Rough Trade RT 091) 1981
		Beast/The Slow Children	(Rough Trade RT 99) 1982
		Pagan Lovesong/ Dave-Id Is Dead (PS)	(Rough Trade RT 106) 1982
		Pagan Lovesong (Vibe Akimbo)/ Pagan Lovesong/ Dave-Id Is Dead (12", PS)	(Rough Trade 12 RT 106) 1982
		(What Shall We Do When) Baby Turns Blue/ Yeo (PS)	(Rough Trade RT 119) 1982
		(What Shall We Do When) Baby Turns Blue/ Yeo/Chance Of A Lifetime (12", PS)	(Rough Trade RTT 119) 1982
		Love Lasts Forever/ True Life Story (PS)	(Baby Records BABY 003) 1986
		Love Lasts Forever/Lovelornalimbo/"I Like The Way You're Frightened" (12", PS)	(Baby Records BABY 004) 1986

NB: * This was first issued in a blue picture sleeve with insert and later in a black picture sleeve with no insert.

This unusual Dublin performance-art and avant-garde musical ensemble was formed in 1976. Their inspiration was the punk/new wave phenomenon in the U.K.. A community had been formed in Dublin called The Village and Fionan Hanvey (who used the pseudonym Gavin Friday in **The Virgin Prunes**) was invited by Paul Hewson (later to become Bono of **U2**) to join a group of arty Dublin youths. By the end of 1977 the band was formed comprising Dik Evans (brother of **U2**'s The Edge), Gavin Friday, Guggi (Derek Rowen), Dave-Id Busaras Scott (David Watson), Pod (Anthony Murphy) and Strongman (Trevor Rowen).

Their early gigs were as much performance events as music gigs. By the early eighties they had developed a strong cult following in Dublin and the surrounding area. Their first release was a self-financed four-track EP called *Twenty Tens* in 1981. It attracted enough attention for them to be signed by Rough Trade. During the remainder of the year they recorded four singles for the London-based label. The first was *Moments Of Mine (Despite Straight Lines)*, the remainder were a three part sequel *A New Form Of Beauty*, initially released as 7", 10" and 12" singles and then available as a box set.

Pod was the first band member to leave due to their disaffected religious stance. Haa-Lácka Bintti joined briefly on keyboards and percussion in 1981, but then Mary O'Nellon came in on drums.

The cassette *A New Form Of Beauty 4* released on Rough Trade in 1982 included extracts from a performance at their "A New Form Of Beauty 5" exhibition at the Douglas Hyde Gallery, Trinity College, Dublin on 8th November 1981.

Their first album proper was *If I Die, I Die* in 1982. Produced by Colin Newman formerly of **Wire**, the album covers a wide range of music from fragile pop (*Ballad Of The Man*) to more complex and challenging extended compositions like *Bau-dachong* and *Caucasian Walk*. At the same time a mixed studio/live album *Heresy* was released as a 10" box set. This contained two 10" discs and five booklets. The second disc was from a live performance at the Rex Club, Paris, in June 1982. The whole project seemed designed to emphasise that the performance-art aspect of the group hadn't been totally neglected. There was also a double album *A New Form Of Beauty Parts 1-4*. The sleevenotes indicate that this was originally intended to be a seven-part project.

By 1984, both Guggi and Dik Evans had become disenchanted with the music industry and quit. Pod rejoined as drummer and O'Nellon switched to guitar.

In 1985, they released an album of rarities and previously unavailable tracks, one of which *Jigsawmentollama* had previously appeared in slightly different format on a flexidisc, on their own Baby Records.

The Moon Looked Down And Laughed, produced by **Soft Cell**'s Dave Ball, comprised largely ballads and melodic pop, representing a significant change in musical direction. The record-buying public didn't respond to this more commercial project and Gavin Friday quit to embark on a solo career. There was a live album *The Hidden Lie*, which was recorded in Paris on 6th June 1986 whilst he was still with the band, released in 1987.

Strongman and O'Nellon recorded further albums - *Lite Fantastik* (1988) and *Nada* (1989) - as The Prunes, but these were pale imitations of their earlier efforts.

In 1988, *Heresie* was re-released in a cardboard gatefold sleeve with notes from Strongman and O'Nellon on Rough Trade. The first pressings were in clear vinyl and erroneously listed *Pagan Lovesong* twice on Disc 2.

In 1991, Rough Trade reissued ....*If I Die, I Die*, but they used the 12" version of *Baby Turns Blue* by mistake and *Ulakanakulot/Decline And Fall* was mastered too slowly. These errors were later corrected when it was reissued by New Rose in 1994, with a cover photo which was slightly different to the original version. Other CD reissues on New Rose were *A New Form Of Beauty* and *Heresie*.

The Virgin Prunes have appeared on a number of (often obscure) compilations over the years. *Song*, from a performance at the Project Arts Centre, Dublin, on 25th April 1981 was included on a limited edition (230 copies) cassette *Endzeit* (Power Focus 003/Data 0012) in 1981; *Third Secret* appeared on *Perspectives And Distortions* (Cherry Red Records BRED 15) 1981; *Red Nettle* featured on the *C81* NME cassette released in 1981; *Pagan Lovesong* has appeared on no less than four compilations:- *Gothic Rock* (LP) (Jungle FREUD 38) 1992, *The Indie Scene 1982* (CD) (Connoisseur's Choice IBM CD) 1982 in the U.K. and, abroad, *Compilation* (LP) (Rough Trade Deutschland RTD 5) and *Selezione Rough Trade* (LP) (Base/Rough Trade, Italy RT 011); *Baby Turns Blue* has appeared on two, *A To Z Of Irish Rock* (CD) (Solid Records) 1992 and *Gothic Rock 2* (LP) (Jungle FREUD 051) 1995, also on CD (FREUD CD 051) 1995; *In The Greylight* resurfaced on *The Indie Scene 1981* (CD) (Connoisseur's Choice

THE VIRGIN PRUNES - The Moon Looked Down And Laughed.

IBM CD 81) and *Walls Of Jericho* got a further airing on *New Wave Club Class X 3* (LP) (Antler Subway AS 5070), also on CD. Abroad *Decline And Fall* was included on *Requiem* (LP) (Japan Record/Rough Trade 35JC-104) 1984 and, in Holland, *Mad Bird In The Wood* figured on *Dokument (Ten Highlights In The History Of Popular Music)* (Vinyl Records RR9940) 1982. Finally, a slightly different version of *Jigsaw Mentallama* to the one on their *Over The Rainbow* album came as a flexidisc with Vinyl magazine in December 1981.

The Virgin Prunes were unique, their performances were usually a mixture of theatrical performance, surrealist art, rock 'n' roll and punk aggression. They could both alienate and intrigue an audience. Working in the same post-punk experimental forum as bands like **The Pop Group**, **The Fall**, **Throbbing Gristle** and **Public Image Limited**, they went on to influence a number of subsequent Gothic bands.

Visage

Personnel:			
	BARRY ADAMSON	bs	A
	BILEY CURRIE	violin	A
	RUSTY EGAN	drms	AB
	DAVE FORMULA	keyb'ds	A
	JOHN McGEOGH	gtr	A
	STEVE STRANGE	vcls	AB
	MIDGE URE	gtr	A
	ANDY BARNETT		B
	GARY BARNACLE		B
	PETE BARNACLE		B

				HCP
ALBUMS:	1(A)	VISAGE	(Polydor 2490 157) 1980	13
	2(B)	THE ANVIL	(Polydor POLD 5060) 1982	6
	3(-)	FADE TO GREY - THE SINGLES COLLECTION		
			(Polydor VCS 1) 1983	38
	4(B)	BEAT BOY	(Polydor POLH 12) 1984	79

NB: (1) also issued on CD (Polydor 8000292) 1991 and (One Way OW 34518) 1997. (2) also issued on CD (One Way OW 34518) 1997. There was also a Dance Mix Promo version of (3). (3) also issued on CD (Polydor 5210532) 1996. (4) also issued on CD (8230522) 1988. There's also a compilation *The Damned Don't Cry* (Spectrum Music 544 381-2) 2000.

			HCP
45s:	Tar/Frequency 7 (PS)	(Radar ADA 48) 1979	-
	Fade To Grey/The Steps	(Polydor POSP 194) 1980	8
	Mind Of A Toy/We Move (PS)	(Polydor POSP 236) 1981	13
*	Visage (Remix)/Second Steps	(Polydor POSP 293) 1981	21
	Damned Don't Cry/Motivation	(Polydor POSP 390) 1982	11
x	Night Train/I'm Still Searching	(Polydor POSP 441) 1982	12
x	Pleasure Boys/The Anvil	(Polydor POSP 523) 1982	44
#	Pleasure Boys (Dance Mix)/		
	The Anvil (Dance Mix) (12")	(Polydor POSPX 523) 1982	-
@	Der Amboss (12" promo only)	(Polydor POSPV 523) 1982	-
	Love Glove/She's A Machine (PS)	(Polydor POSP 691) 1984	54
	Love Glove/She's A Machine (12")	(Polydor POSPX 691) 1984	-
	Beat Boy/		
	Beat Boy (alt. version) (PS)	(Polydor POSP 709) 1984	-
Reissues:	Fade To Grey/Mind Of A Toy	(Old Gold OG 9580) 1986	
	Damned Don't Cry/Night Train	(Old Gold OG 9778) 1987	
	Fade To Grey/Night Train	(Old Gold OG 4050) 1988	
	Mind Of A Toy/Damned Don't Cry	(Old Gold OG 4052) 1988	
	Mind Of A Toy/We Move (Dance Mix)/		
	Frequency 7 (Dance Mix)/		
	Mind Of A Toy (Video) (CD Video)	(Polydor 080 012-2) 1988	-

NB: * This came in 'Mirror', 'Cowboy' or 'Melting Face' sleeves. x There were also picture disc versions of these releases (POSPP 441 and POSPP 523). # Only 800 copies were released. @ This came in a stickered plain black sleeve and labels.

Visage were initially started as a part-time group centered around punk/new wave cult figure Steve Strange. **Visage** included a talented array of musicians with **Midge Ure** and Billy Currie from **Ultravox**, Rusty Egan, who'd been drummer in **The Rich Kids** and Dave Formula of **Magazine**.

Their early albums made quite an impact. Their eponymous debut climbed to No. 13 and spent a very credible twenty-nine weeks in the chart. It also produced three hit singles:- *Fade To Grey* (No. 8), *Mind Of A Toy* (No. 13) and *Visage* (No. 21). *The Anvil* built on this success, climbing to No. 6 during a sixteen week chart sojourn. It also contained two more hit singles; *Damned Don't Cry* (No. 11) and *Night Train* (No. 12).

They played a sort of dance-orientated music with lots of guitars and synthesizers which soom became associated with the New Romantic movement. If you do want to investigate their music *Fade To Grey - The Singles Collection* is a good bet. This includes their finest moments - *Night Train*, *Pleasure Boys* and *We Move*. It also includes an otherwise unreleased version of *In The Year 2525*. This album enjoyed eleven weeks in the chart, peaking at No. 38.

Beat Boy was recorded by a modified line-up ('B'), and was rockier than their previous efforts. Its eight long tracks are rather repetitive and a little tedious in places. It sold reasonably well climbing to No. 79 during its two weeks in the chart.

The Damned Don't Cry (CD) compilation at over 77 minutes is good value. Their first 'B' side *Frequency 7* was a big success at New York's Roxy Club and is now cited as an early example of techno-rock.

The Visitors

Personnel:			
	COLIN CRAIGIE	vcls, gtr	A
	ALAN LAING	drms	A
	DEREK McVAY	vcls, bs	A
	JOHN McVAY	vcls, keyb'ds	A

45s:	Take It Or Leave It/No Compromise	(NRG SRT5/NRG 002) 1978
	Electric Heat/Moth/On Line (PS)	(Deep Cuts DEEP 1) 1979
*	Empty Rooms/	
	Orcadian Visitors (PS)	(Departure RAPTURE 1) 1980
*	Compatability/Poet's End (PS)	(Rational RATE 2) 1981

NB: * issued in a fold-over picture sleeve.

VISAGE - Visage.

THE VISITORS - Electric Heat.

The first 45, which didn't come in a picture sleeve, is now hard to find and quite expensive if you do come across a copy. *Electric Heat* released on the Edinburgh Deep Cuts label is excellent. Recorded at Cargo sixteen track studios in Rochdale, the single has both a futuristic and sinister feel. The group look very young from the photo on the picture sleeve.

The Vitamins

The Vitamins' sole vinyl excursion seems to have been the one cut *Newtown* they contributed to *Vaultage '78 (Two Sides Of Brighton)* (Attrix RB 03) in 1978, which is a decent pop-punkish effort.

Vivabeat

45:	Man From China/On Patrol (PS)	(Charisma CD 346)	1979

This one-off 45 features lots of electronics and is in **Human League**, **Gary Numan** and **Ultravox** territory.

Von Trapp Family

Personnel:	CYKE BANCROFT	alto sax	A
	MARK FINN	bs	A
	RAY FLORES	drms	A
	KEVIN ROGERS	vcls	A
	NICK SALOMAN	gtr, harmonium	A
	CHRIS WHITAKER	gtr, vcls	A

45:	Brand New Thrill/Dreaming Again/ No Reflexes (PS)	(Woronzow W 001)	1980

The **Von Trapp Family** were the first act to record on the Woronzow label. They featured Nick Saloman, who is better known as the man behind The Bevis Frond and the 45 was produced by Bari Watts. *Brand New Thrill* later resurfaced on *Woronzoid* (Woronzow WOO 10) 1989.

V2

Personnel:	B'DALE	drms	A
	JONATHAN E	vcls	A
	REV P.P. SMYTHE	gtr	A
	STAN THE MAN	bs	A

45s: *	Speed Freak/Nothing To Do/ That's It	(Bent SMALL BENT 1)	1978
	Man In The Box/ When The World Isn't There (12", PS)	(TJM TJM 1)	1979
+	Is Anybody Out There	(TJM TJM 6)	1979

NB: * Only 800 issued, later on red vinyl. + Unissued. There's also a CD *V2 (Anthology)* (Overground OVER 55CD) 1996.

A Manchester band. Originally just 800 copies of *Speed Freak* were issued. It was later reissued on red vinyl. In addition to the above **V2** contributed two cuts, *Overture* and *City Creatures* to *Identity Parade* (TJM TJMLP 1) 1979, a label sampler. *Man In The Box* is a confident and edgy tune by this glamboy beat group. *Man In The Box* and *When The World Isn't There* later turned up on *Rabid/TJM Punk Singles Collection* (Receiver RRCD 227) in 1996.

The Vye

Personnel:	DAVID ALBONE	drms	A
	RICHARD EAGER	lead gtr	A
	DALE HARGREAVES	gtr, vcls	A
	SIMON HOLLIS	bs	A
	ANDREW TILLISON	keyb'ds, vcls	A

45:	Five Hours 'Til Tonight/Right Girl, Wrong Time/ Til Dawn (PS)	(Dead Good DEAD 8)	1980

In addition to this 45 **The Vye** also contributed *King's New Clothes* to the compilation *499 2139* (Rocket DIAL 1) 1979. This sounds quite derivative of the mid-sixties but with keyboards added.

Wah!

Personnel:	KING BLUFF	keyb'ds, synth	A
	PAUL BARLOW	drms	AB
	CARL WASHINGTON	bs	ABC
	PETE WYLIE	vcls, gtr	ABC
	HENRY PRIESTMAN	keyb'ds	B
	CHARLIE GRIFFITHS	synth	C
	CHRIS JOYCE	drms	C
	JAY NAUGHTON	piano	C
	THE SAPPHIRES	backing vcls	C

ALBUM:	1(A)	NAH-POO = THE ART OF BLUFF		HCP
			(Eternal CLASSIC 1)	1981 33

45s:		Forget The Down!/ The Checkmate Syndrome (PS)	(Eternal SLATE 1)	HCP 1981 -
	+	Some Say/Forget The Down (PS)	(Eternal SIMEY 1)	1981 -
	*	Remember/A Crack Is A Crack (PS)	(Eternal ZAZU 1)	1982 -
		The Story Of The Blues/Talkin' Blues (PS)	(Eternal JF 1)	1982 3
		The Story Of The Blues/Talkin' Blues/ Seven Minutes To Midnight (Live) (12", PS)	(Eternal JFX)	1982 -
		Hope (I Wish You'd Believe Me)/ Sleep (PS)	(Eternal X 9880)	1982 37
		Hope (I Wish You'd Believe Me)/Sleep/ You Can't Put Your Arms Around A Memory/ Year Of Decision/Lespwash (12", PS)	(Eternal X 9880)	1982 -

NB: + This was also issued as a 12". * This was credited to Shambeko! Say Wah.

This was a later version of Pete Wylie's Liverpool-based **Wah! Heat**. See that entry for details of their early days. It was after abbreviating their name to **Wah!** and signing to WEA's Eternal subsidiary that they broke through commercially.

On their debut album *Nah-Poo = The Art Of Bluff* it's Wylie's melodramatic vocals on tracks like *The Death Of Wah* and *Seven Minutes To Midnight* that catches the ear. The album enjoyed five weeks in the chart peaking at No. 33. After this, former It's Immaterial drummer Henry Priestman replaced Bluff on keyboards and two further singles were released. The second of these *Remember* was credited to Shambeko! Say Wah.

During the summer of 1982 Wylie and Washington reconfigured the band again putting together a new line-up 'C'. This included ex-**Durutti Column** drummer Chris Joyce. This achieved even greater commercial success with *The Story Of The Blues* climbing to No. 3 during a twelve week chart residency and *Hope (I Wish You'd Believe Me)* also made the Top 40, climbing to No. 37 during a five week residency. Both were also available in 12" format with additional cuts. For *The Story Of The Blues* they drew on a Spector-like 'wall of sound' style.

After these two 'hit' 45s they changed name again to **The Mighty Wah**.

VON TRAPP FAMILY - Brand New Thrill.

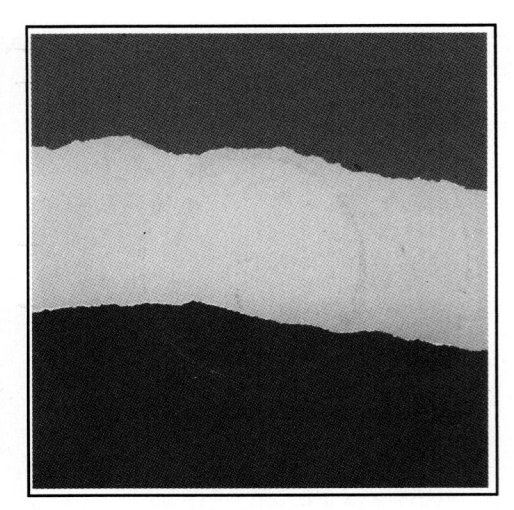

WAH! HEAT - Seven Minutes To Midnight.

Wah! Heat

Personnel:	ROB 'JONIE' JONES	drms	A
	PETE WYLIE	vcls, gtr	AB
	PETE YOUNGER	bs	A
	KING BLUFF	keyb'ds, synth	B
	JOE MUSKER	drms	B
	COLIN REDMOND	gtr	B
	CARL WASHINGTON	bs	B

45s: * Better Scream/(Hey Disco) Joe (PS) (Inevitable INEV 001) 1980
Seven Minutes To Midnight/
Don't Step On The Cracks (PS) (Inevitable INEV 004) 1980

NB: * Issued in a wraparound picture sleeve housed in a polythene bag.

Wah! Heat was the third in a trio of groups (the other two being **Echo and The Bunnymen** and **Teardrop Explodes**) who spearheaded Liverpool's doomy post-punk scene. The band was formed in early 1979 by Pete Wylie, who at one time had played together with the frontmen of the other two bands (Ian McCulloch and Julian Cope) in The Crucial Three. Not surprisingly that was a short-lived affair because the talents and egos of the three of them were too big to contain within the same group. Rob Jones had previously been in Crash Course, whilst Pete Younger's previous band was **Those Naughty Lumps**.

In January 1980 they issued *Better Scream* on an indie label in a wraparound picture sleeve which was contained within a polythene bag. After this Wylie dispensed with the services of Jones and Younger to put together a new line-up ('B'). Jones went on to play for The High Five and his replacement Joe Musker had been with Dead Or Alive. On tour guitarist Colin Redmond was added to this line-up. Their debut single's flip side *(Hey Disco) Joe* also figured on *Hicks From The Sticks* (Rockburgh Records ROC 111) that year.

This new line-up recorded a second indie single *Seven Minutes To Midnight* in November before signing to WEA subsidiary label Eternal and abbreviating their name to simply **Wah!**. At this point former It's Immaterial drummer Paul Barlow replaced Joe Musker.

The Wall

Personnel:	RAD RAE BEITH	drms	ABCD
	ANDY GRIFFITHS	bs	ABCD
	IAN LOWERY	vcls	A
	NICK WARD	gtr	ABC
	KELLY	vcls	BC
	HEED	gtr	CD

ALBUMS: 1(B) PERSONAL TROUBLES AND PUBLIC ISSUES
  (Fresh LP 2) 1981
2(D) DIRGES AND ANTHEMS (Polydor POLS 1048) 1982

NB: There's also a CD compilation *The Punk Collection* (Captain Oi! AHOY CD 95) 1998.

EP: 1(D) DAY TRIPPER (Day Tripper/Animal Grip/
  When I'm Dancing/Castles) (PS) (No Future Oi! 21) 1983

45s: New Way/Suckers/
Uniforms (PS) (Small Wonder SMALL 13) 1979
Kiss The Mirror/Exchange (PS) (Small Wonder SMALL 21) 1979
Ghetto/Another New Day (PS) (Fresh FRESH 17) 1980
Hobby For A Day/Redeemer/8334 (PS) (Fresh FRESH 27) 1981
Remembrance/Hsi Nao/
Hooligan Nights (Polydor POSP 260) 1981
Epitaph/Rewind/New Rebel (Polydor POSP 365) 1981

The Wall formed in Sunderland in late 1977. They got their first break when they were signed by the Walthamstow, London-based Small Wonder label in 1979. Two 45s - *New Way* and *Kiss The Mirror* - were released and the second one made quite an impression in the indie chart. By now, their original vocalist Ian Lowery had left. His replacement Kelly had previously been with **Ruefrex**.

They switched to Fresh Records in 1980 for their debut album *Personal Troubles And Public Issues*. Each subject was allocated one side of the album. The end result is quite successful; crisply produced with good clear vocals, intelligent lyrics and powerful guitar work.

Following this a new guitarist Heed joined and the band temporarily became a quintet. Soon after Kelly and Ward both left and **The Wall** continued as a trio. The new line-up signed to a major label, Polydor, and released a second album *Dirges And Anthems*. This was accompanied by a three track bonus 45. A more refined approach is taken on this album with saxophone, acoustic guitar and the occasional reggae rhythm. The powerful guitars of its predecessor were toned down. Whatever, the band and label didn't see eye to eye and **The Wall**'s major label liaison proved short-lived. *Hobby For A Day* later resurfaced on *Fresh Records Punk Singles Collection* (Anagram CDPUNK 32) 1994.

The Wall returned once more on the Oi-orientated No Future label to record a four cut 45, which included a revved up version of The Beatles' *Day Tripper*. After this made little impact, they called it a day. *The Punk Collection* issued by Captain Oi! compiles singles and some album tracks.

New Way and *Exchange* both got fresh exposure on *Small Wonder Punk Singles Collection, Vol. 1* (Anagram CDPUNK 29) 1994 and *Vol. 2* (Anagram CDPUNK 70) 1996 included *Suckers* and *Uniforms*. Their version of *Day Tripper* can also be heard on *No Future - The Punk Singles Collection* (dbl) (Captain Oi! AHOY DLP 508) 1996 and *When I'm Dancin'* also appeared on *Vol. 2* (Captain Oi! AHOY DLP 512) 1996 of the same series. Alternatively, if you prefer CDs, both songs are on the 2-CD set *The History Of No Future* (Anagram CDPUNK 111) 1999. Finally, *Hobby For A Day* resurfaced on *Punk And Disorderly, Vol. 2 (Further Charges)* (Anagram CDPUNK 22) 1993.

Ian Lowery later fronted **Ski Patrol**.

THE WALL - Personal Troubles And Public Issues.

Larry Wallis

45:	Police Car/On Parole (PS)	(Stiff BUY 22)	1977

NB: Some copies came with a picture sleeve, others with a die-cut company sleeve.

Larry Wallis, like **Nick Lowe** and **Dave Edmunds**, benefitted from the punk and new wave explosion, but had been involved in the music scene since the late sixties. Initially, he was singer and guitarist with The Entire Sioux Nation before joining biker band Shagrat, which soon evolved into The Pink Fairies' first line-up. **Wallis** then left The 'Fairies, but rejoined them in late 1972, following brief spells in Blodwyn Pig and UFO. He played on The Fairies hard rock-orientated *Kings Of Oblivion* and was with them in their free festival heyday of 1973. Whilst The Fairies were in limbo during 1974 - 75 he took a slot in Lemmy's Motorhead. He recorded a solo album *Parole* for United Artists in 1975 (although it was not released until 1979). When he was edged out of Motorhead he rekindled The Pink Fairies again, but they split in 1977.

In the punk and new wave era **Wallis** became an in-house producer for Jake Riviera's new Stiff label. He worked with **The Adverts** and **Members** among others and recorded the buoyant *Police Car* 45 for them in November 1977. He was also on the Live Stiff's package tour and contributed *Police Car* to the resulting album *Stiff Live Stiffs* (Stiff GET 1) 1978. His finest moment of the punk and new wave era *Police Car* was recently included on *1-2-3-4 - A History Of Punk And New Wave, 1976 - 1979* (MCA/Universal MCD 60066), a 5-CD box set issued in 1999.

In 1978, he produced Mick Farren's *Vampire's Stole My Lunch Money* album, then in the early eighties he formed his own band The Death Commandos Of Love. In 1987, he was involved in yet another Pink Fairies reunion and the resulting album *Kill 'Em And Eat 'Em* and a handful of live gigs. Larry's a true hardy annual.

Wanderers

Personnel:	STIV BATORS	vcls	A
	RICK GOLDSTEIN	drms	A
	DAVE PARSONS	gtr, vcls	A
	DAVID TREGANNA	bs, vcls	A

ALBUM:	1(A)	THE ONLY LOVERS LEFT ALIVE	
		(Polydor POLS 1028)	1981

NB: (1) also issued on CD (Captain Oi! AHOY CD 141) 2000.

45s:	Ready To Snap/Beyond The Law	(Polydor POSP 239)	1981
	The Times They Are A-Changin'/ Little Bit Frightening	(Polydor POSP 284)	1981

Bringing together former Dead Boy Stiv Bators and **Sham 69** members (Ricky Goldstein, Dave Parsons and David Treganni), this actually started life as a **Sham 69** project. When Jimmy Pursey left, his replacement was Stiv Bators. For contractual reasons **Sham 69**'s name could not be used and a different name the **Wanderers** was used. As a result the album failed to attract the attention it deserved. It comprised well-produced, decent rock and is notable for a brave rockified version of Bob Dylan's *The Times They Are A-Changin'*, which was also released as a 45.

After they split in late '81, Treganna and Bators went on to form the far more successful Lords Of The New Church. **The Wanderers** were left as a small footnote in the history of punk, but the Captain Oi! reissue of their album with extensive sleevenotes is welcome.

The Wardens

Personnel:	EMBRYS BAIRD	bs, vcls	A
	PETER CUFF	drms	A
	BARRY SMALE	lead vcls	A
	NEIL WILMOT	gtr	A

45:	Do So Well/Lust Like This	(Snu Peas TIC 001)	1979

A Brighton band who also appeared on *499 2139* (Rocket DIAL 1) 1979 playing *Tricky Girls*, a fast-paced song with some good guitar work.

Wargasm

Personnel:	ADDIE	gtr	A
	DAFFY (PAUL ARMSTRONG)	vcls	A
	ALAN MURRELL	drms	A
	WANKER	bs	A

CASS:	1(A)	TIME FOR A WANK (mini LP)	1981

A hard hitting fun anarcho politico band whose mini-album was only released on tape.

The Warm

ALBUM:	1( )	NOVA VAGA	(Warm PFLP 201) 1979
EP:	1( )	THE DEMO TAPES (It's The Kooler/ Teenage Space Queen/Crazy Daisy Lady/ Maybe Baby/Gonna Luv U)	(Warm SMS 001/2001/2) 1978

NB: (1) This appeared in a double pack format.

45s:	It's The Kooler/Teenage Space Queen (PS)	(Warm 2001) 1978
	Crazy Daisy Lady/Maybe Baby/ Gonna Luv U (PS)	(Warm 2002) 1978
	Floosie/Chewing Gum Sue/Bye Bye It's The Blues/ Sometimes (PS)	(Warm 2003) 1978
	Shanty Town/?	(Warm 2007) 1978

Musically we're talking garage-punk. The *Floosie* 45 was a two chord thrash so bad in its execution that it's perversely enjoyable.

The Demo Tapes (EP) retailed at 99p and featured two singles in a double sleeve with a photo of the young Mae West on the front.

Warm Jets

Personnel incl: DAVE CAIRNS

45s:	Big City Boy/Mr. Natural (PS)	(RSO RSO 47)	1979
	Sticky Jack/Shell Shock (PS)	(Bridgehouse BHS 1)	1981

The Warm Jets are notable for including ex-members of Cockney Rebel as well as Dave Cairns. He'd been in **Arms and Legs** and **New Hearts** and was later the impetus behind **Secret Affair**.

The Warriors

Personnel:	CHARLIE DUGGAN	gtr	A
	JOHN FISHER	drms	A
	ARTHUR KITCHENER	bs	A
	ROI PEARCE	vcls	A

After the demise of **Last Resort** Duggan, Kitchener and Pearce formed **The Warriors** and ex-**Gonads**, **Combat 84** and **Business** member John Fisher was drafted in on drums to make up the four-piece. They contributed *Horror Show* to *Oi! Oi! That's Yer Lot* (Secret SEC 5) in 1983. This competent effort later got a further airing on the CD *100% British Oi!* (Captain Oi! AHOY DCD 83) in 1997. *Here To Stay* and *Warriors (Come Out To Play)* also figured on *Trouble On The Terraces - 16 Classic Football Anthems* (Step-1 STEP 91) 1996.

They later contributed *Wicked Women* to the *United Skins* (Boots & Braces SKREW LP 1) 1982 compilation, but split when Roi Pearce departed for the **4-Skins**.

Later in 1994, Arthur Kitchener reformed the band with original **Last Resort** vocalist Saxby on vocals. This modified line-up recorded two albums on Step-1.

WARSAW PAKT - Needle Time.

Warsaw Pakt

Personnel:	ANDY COLQUHOIN	gtr	A
	JIMMY COULL	vcls	A
	LUCAS FOX	drms	A
	ANDY McCONNELL	gtr	A
	CHRIS UNDERHILL	bs	A
	JOHN WALKER	gtr	A

ALBUM: 1(A) NEEDLE TIME   (Island ILPS 9515) 1978

NB: (1) This album came in a numbered stamped mailer picture sleeve with an insert. Reissued on CD (Captain Trip CTCD 238) 1999.

CASS: 1(A) SEE YOU IN COURT   (Stuff Central) 1979

45: * Safe And Warm/Sick And Tired   (Island PAKT 1) 1978

NB: * A few of these 45s came in picture sleeves.

A London-based thrash punk band who created a bit of a stir when their album appeared in local shops within 24 hours of the start of its recording. It sounded like it too. The record was packaged in a mailing envelope covered with stickers and rubber stamps. The album's insert includes a log of the 21 hours it took to complete the package.

Needle Time is basically a live set without an audience. Guitarist Andy McConnell is the dominant force on the album and every other track is co-credited to him. It kicks off with a fast-paced cover of The Who's *It's Not True*, which is an amalgam of power chords, jangle and heavy metal/blues licks. On side two *Nosebleed* features some interesting chord changes and the band conjure up an effective, tight sound on tracks like *Believe Me Honey*, *Lorraine* and *Safe And Warm*.

The band prospered in the punk era from the groundswell of energy and activity, but were neither young nor punks. They were old pro's given a new lease of life.

Lucas Fox had previously been in Motorhead. He went on to play in **Sisterhood**. Andy Colquhoin was later in **Tanz der Youth** and The Deviants.

The Wasps

Personnel:	JESSE LYNN-DEAN	vcls	ABCD
	DEL MAY	gtr	A
	JOHN RICH	drms	ABC
	STEVE WOLLASTON	bs	AB
	GARY WELLMAN	gtr	BC
	STEVE DOMINIC	bs	C
	NEIL FITCH	gtr	D
	TIAM GRANT	drms	D
	DAVE OWEN	bs	D

45s:	Teenage Treats/		
	She Made More Magic (PS)	(4-Play FOUR 001)	1977
*	Can't Wait 'Til '78/Bunch Of Stiffs (PS)	(NEMS NES 115)	1977
	Rubber Cars/This Time (PS)	(RCA PB 5137)	1978

NB: * The 'B' side was credited to **Mean Street**.

This Walthamstow-based band emerged in mid-1977 and soon became a popular act at London punk venues like the Vortex and the Roxy. By the time of their debut 45 on 4-Play in November 1977 Gary Wellman had replaced original member Del May on guitar. The following month, with clubs like the Roxy and CBGB's already having put out compilations, the Vortex decided to do the same. *Live At The Vortex* (NEMS NEL 6013) 1977 featured mostly second division, unsigned punk bands and **The Wasps** punk rallying cry *Can't Wait 'Til '78* was included along with *Waiting For The Man*. The former with Lynn-Dean's spoken introduction is an excellent period piece. It was later released as a single with *Bunch Of Stiffs* by **Mean Street** on the flip. *Teenage Treats* was a good single with a great guitar riff and fine singing.

By the time of a February 1978 Peel session Steve Dominic had taken over from Wollaston on bass.

In 1979, **The Wasps** secured a major label deal with RCA. In February 1979, *Rubber Car* was released (but it sounded pure '77). It was recorded by line-up 'B'. Some of the other original members challenged the use of the name and RCA withdrew the single and dumped the band.

They recorded a second Peel session before splitting in 1978.

Wollaston formed New Age group Sadhana. Wellman tried his hand at a solo career. Rich resurfaced in R&B combo No Dice. Lynn-Dean recorded a solo 45 *Do It* for Creole in 1979 and then returned to France.

You can also check out *Can't Wait 'Til '78* on the 5-CD box set *1-2-3-4 - A History Of Punk And New Wave 1976 - 1979* (MCA/Universal 60066) 1999.

The Wasps remain a short-lived second string punk band but one well worth hearing.

Wasted Youth

Personnel:	ROCCO BARKER	A
	NICK LOW	A
	DARREN MURPHY	A
	ANDY SCOTT	A
	KEN SCOTT	A

ALBUMS:	1(A)	WILD AND WONDERFUL CRIES		
(up to			(Bridge House BHLP 006)	1981
1986)	2(A)	FROM THE INNER DEPTHS	(VC VCLP)	1985

45s:	Jealousy/Baby (PS)	(Bridge House BHS 5)	1981
(up to	I'll Remember You/		
1986)	My Friends Are Dead (PS)	(Bridge House BHS 10)	1981
	Rebecca's Room/		
	Things Never Seem The Same (PS)	(Fresh FRESH 30)	1981
	Rebecca's Room/Things Never Seem		
	The Same (PS)	(Bridge House BHS 12)	1982
	Wildlife/Games (PS)	(Bridge House BHS 13)	1982

A London band who signed to Bridge House Records, which operated from the now legendary pub in Canning Town. Musically influenced by psychedelia, punk, and Lou Reed, they developed their own unique style. *Jealousy* was a well-received debut. *Rebecca's Room*, produced by Martin Hannett veered towards new romanticism. It can also be heard on *Fresh Records Punk Singles Collection* (Anagram CDPUNK 32) 1994.

Wasted Youth continued well beyond this book's timespan. Their guitarist Rocco went on to play in Flesh for Lulu. Darren Murphy later had a dance label and ran the TTL pressing plant.

Wasteland

EP:	1( )	WANT NOT (Our Radio Nation Burns/Oh No!/		
		Bombsite Baby) (PS)	(Ellie Jay/Disaster EJSP 9261)	1979

| 45: | Friends, Romans, Countrymen/ Leave Me Alone (PS) | (Invicta INV 014) 1980 |

Wasteland came from Kent and originally set out as a punk outfit called Infested, although they had no recorded output under this name. By 1979 they had changed name to **Wasteland** and latched onto the mod revival movement. Just 2,000 copies of the EP and 1,000 copies of the 45 were issued and as a consequence both are hard to find now. The EP was available by mail-order only from Disaster records in Canterbury.

Water Pistols

Personnel:	ANDREW
	CHARLES
	SIMON
	TERRENCE

| 45: | Gimme That Punk Junk/Soft Punk (PS) | (State STATE 38) 1976 |

This lighthearted disc was an 'NME Single of the Week' in January 1977.

"Of all the chains that I hang on my nose
I like the one that hangs down to my toes....
I slashed my brother Ben Sherman to bits
I am determined to have punk rock hits.....
My best friend Sooty I like him a lot
I can't stand Sweep he's not into punk rock....
I like to swear and smash up Dinky toys
Throw hymn books in church and make lots of noise....
Come to my room
Smash all my trains
Rip up my comics
And break all my prams....
I am a rebel and Simon's my name
My mum thinks I'm crazy I drive her insane
I know two chords and I sing out of tune
If punk rock lasts I will make a fortune...."
(from *Gimme That Punk Junk*).

Way Out

This mod revival band contribute two cuts, *This Working Way* and *Just The Girl* to *This Is Mod, Vol. 3 (Diamond Collection)* (Anagram CDMGRAM 106) 1996.

The What

Personnel:	DAVE ALUCARD	bs	A
	MICK TAYLOR	vcls, gtr	A
	PHIL TROTSKY	drms	A

| EP: | 1(A) | EAST COAST KIDS (East Coast Kids/What Is The Cure/ Anything Goes) (PS) | (Humber Records HREP 4) 198? |

An obscure mod revival combo whose EP was issued in a photocopied picture sleeve. Alucard and Taylor wrote *East Coast Kids*, a sixties influenced disc, which can also be heard on *100% British Mod* (Captain Mod MODSKA DCD 8) 1998.

Where's Lisse

| Personnel incl: | JOHN NOVAK | vcls | A |

| EP: | 1(A) | WHERE'S LISSE | (Glass) 1982 |

| 45s: | Talk Takes Too Long/ You Stole My Gun | (Glass GLASS 008) 1981 |
| | Tutorial Single | (Glass GLASS 014) 1982 |

A four-piece whose plus points included John Novak's resilient vocals and some decent melodies, although some of their instrumentation is a bit rudimentary.

White Boy

| Personnel: | MR. OTT | vcls | A |
| | JAKE WHIPP | gtr | A |

| EP: | 1(A) | SPASTIC (I'm So Straight/Electric Suicide/ Little Idiots/Just An Old Fart) (PS) | (Doodley Squat Records) 1977 |

A two man father and son team. The thirty-five year old Mr. Ott crones whilst his nineteen year old son retreads a few Hendrix licks on guitar!

White Door

| ALBUM: | 1 | WINDOWS | (Clay CLAYLP 7) 1983 |

45s:	Windows/In Heaven (PS)	(Clay CLAY 26) 1983
	Jerusalem/Americana	(Clay CLAY 30) 1983
	Flame In My Heart/ Behind The White Door (PS)	(Clay CLAY 37) 1984
	Flame In My Heart/ Behind The White Door (12", PS)	(Clay CLAY 37) 1984

This is a synth-pop trio basically comprising two synthesizers and a vocalist along with some guests. The ethereal vocals blend beautifully with the dancey instrumental backing making **White Door** a better-than-average example of this genre.

White Heat

Personnel:	SIMON BOSWELL	keyb'ds	A
	JOHN EARLE	sax	A
	ALAN FISH	gtr	A
	COLIN ROBERTS	bs	A
	JOHN ROBERTS	drms	A
	BOB SMEATON	vcls	A
	BRYAN YOUNGER	gtr	A

| ALBUM: | 1(A) | IN THE ZERO HOUR | (Valium VALP 101) 1982 |

45s:	Nervous Breakdown/Sammy Sez (PS)	(Valium VAL 1) 1980
	Finished With The Fashions/ Ordinary Joe (PS)	(Valium VAL 02) 1980
	City Beat/It's No Use (Young Ones) (PS)	(Valium VAL 03) 1981

A mod-influenced band of the early eighties.

Whitehouse

| Personnel incl: | WILLIAM BENNETT | A |

ALBUMS/CASSETTES:
| 1(A) | BIRTHDEATH EXPERIENCE | (Come Org. WDC 881004) 1980 |
| 2(A) | TOTAL SEX | (Come Org WDC 881005) 1980 |

WHITE DOOR - Jerusalem.

3(A)	ERECTOR	(Come Org WDC 881007)	1980
4(A)	DEDICATED TO PETER KÜRTEN, SADIST AND MASS SLAYER	(Come Org WDC 881010)	1981
5(A)	GREAT WHITE DEATH	(Come Org WDC 8810??)	1981
6(A)	BÜCHENWALD	(Come Org WDC 881013)	1981
7(A)	NEW BRITAIN	(Come Org WDC 881017)	1981
8(A)	LIVE ACTION 1	(Come Org. WDC 881020)	1981
9(A)	LIVE ACTION 2	(Come Org WDC 881022)	1981
10(A)	PSYCHOPATHIA SEXUALIS	(Come Org WDC 881027)	198?
11(A)	RIGHT TO KILL - DEDICATED TO DENNIS ANDREW NEILSEN	(Come Org WDC 883033)	198?
12(A)	150 MURDEROUS PASSIONS	(Come Org WDC 8830??)	198?
13(A)	RADIO INTERVIEWS/LIVE ACTION 9 U.S.A. VOL. 1	(Come Org WDC 883044)	198?
14(A)	LIVE ACTION 13 U.S.A. VOL. III	(Come Org WDC 883046)	198?
15(A)	LIVE ACTION 14 U.S.A. VOL IV	(Come Org. WDC 883047)	198?
16(A)	LIVE ACTION 15/LIVE ACTION 16 U.S.A. VOL. V	(Come Org WDC 883048)	198?
17(A)	LIVE ACTION 20 U.S.A. VOL. VI	(Come Org WDC 883049)	198?
18(A)	LIVE ACTION 22/LIVE ACTION 23	(Come Org WDC 883050)	198?
19(A)	U.S.A. REHEARSAL	(Come Org WDC 883052)	198?
20(A)	LIVE ACTION 24/LIVE ACTION 25	(Come Org WDC 883053)	198?
21(A)	LIVE ACTION 26	(Come Org WDC 883055)	198?
22(A)	CREAM OF THE SECOND COMING (Dbl)	(Susan Lawly 1)	198?

NB: (2) also issued on CD (Susan Lawly SLCD 009) 1994. (3) issued on different coloured vinyls. Some copies of (4) also issued on coloured vinyl and some in custom sleeves. (4) also issued on CD (Susan Lawly SLCD 013) 1996. (5) also issued on CD (Susan Lawly SLCD 017) 1996. (6) also issued on CD (Susan Lawly SLCD 014) 1996. (7) also issued on CD (Susan Lawly SLCD 015) 1996. (8), (9), (13) - (21) are all cassettes. (10) was issued in clear or black vinyl. (12) was recorded with **Nurse With Wound**. Other **Whitehouse** CDs were *Quality Time* (Susan Lawly SLCD 012) 1996, *Thank Your Lucky Stars* (Susan Lawly SLCD 018) 1997 and *Worthless* (Susan Lawly SLCD 020) 1998.

Led by former **Essential Logic** member and guitarist William Bennett **Whitehouse** were part of the Industrial Music Scene which developed as one of the post punk genres. They were heavily influenced by **Throbbing Gristle** and originally known as **Come**. They became notorious for producing some of the most unnerving and disturbing electronic music ever made. The lyrics, in so far as they were audible, dealt with themes such as death, murder, sexual perversion and fascist ideology. With songs which idolised murders like Peter Sutcliffe and Peter Kürten, even Rough Trade, one of the most experimental labels around, decided not to handle their records.

Total Sex is a good introduction to their music and the CD issue includes two bonus cuts *Foreplay* and *Her Entry*. Both have previously figured on the United Dairies compilation *Hoisting The Black Flag*.

Erector is generally considered to be one of their most effective albums and features *Shitfun*, one of their legendary songs, and the totally deranged *Socratisation Day*.

Bückenwald is a misanthrope's paradise, full of tortuous passages of sadistically high-pitched squeals and deep internal pulses. This is the ideal music to accompany stories and headlines of death and disaster.

Great White Death contains some of the band's more memorable material - *Ass-Destroyer, Rapemaker, You Don't Have To Say Please, I'm Comin Up Your Ass* and *My Cock's On Fire*. The CD reissue on Susan Lawly in 1997 comes re-mastered with a full fourteen-minute version of the latter song and a high-gloss twelve-page booklet with lyrics.

Whitehouse also contributed extensively to *Anthology 1: Come Organisation Archives 1979 - 1981* (Susan Lawly SLCD 019) 1998.

Whitehouse were arguably the most extreme and uncompromising of the Industrial Music bands and like all of these genre, were very much an acquired taste.

The White SS

45:	Mercy Killing/ I'm Not The One (live) (PS)	(White SS CIA 72)	1978

This is now a very rare and quite expensive and collectable punk single but the people behind it remain a mystery. There are lyric sheets setting out their political opinions, which are intended to be right wing but just seem muddled. It seems they favour euthanasia (usually considered a libertarian cause), but condemn pornography. The singer boasts *I'm gonna shock you from your complacency*, but the record is a damp squid.

Whooper

This was actually a pseudonym for **Teardrop Explodes**' Julian Cope. He contributed one cut *Kwalo Klobinsky's Lullaby* on the compilation *To The Shores Of Lake Placid* (Zoo FOUR) 1982. This is a very sensitive, delicate song with a haunting aura which in common with all the cuts on the compilation is worth a listen.

The Wild Beasts

45s:	Minimum Maximum/Another Noun (PS)	(Fried Egg EGG 2)	1979
	Last One Of The Boys/ We're Only Monsters (PS)	(Ring Piece CVS 886)	1980
	Life Is A Bum/Mary Lou/The Limit (PS)	(Warped BEND 1)	1981

A west country band. *Minimum Maximum* is a straight-forward pop-orientated song. You'll also find it on the compilation *E(gg)clectic* (Fried Egg FRY 2), released in 1981.

The Wild Swans

Personnel incl: PAUL SIMPSON
GERALD QUINN

45s:	* The Revolutionary Spirit/God Forbid	(Zoo CAGE 009)	1982
	+ The Revolutionary Spirit/ God Forbid (12", PS)	(Zoo CAGE 009)	1982

NB: * This 7" version, which came with a stamped white label and no picture sleeve was unissued, but a few copies do exist. + Some copies of this came with 'The Lament Of Icarus' painting on the top right of the front sleeve. These were quickly withdrawn.

Paul Simpson had been in the first **Teardrop Explodes** line-up and before that in The Crucial Three and A Shallow Madness. **The Wild Swans** 45 is one of the most collectable release on the Zoo label. Quinn had replaced Simpson briefly in **The Teardrop Explodes** before heading for **The Wild Swans** himself.

Ada Wilson

45s:	In The Quiet Of My Room/ I'm In Control Here (PS)	(Ellie Jay EJSP 9288)	1979
	* In The Quiet Of My Room/ I'm In Control Here	(Barn BARN 012)	1980
	+ Head In The Clouds/ It Doesn't Have To Be	(Rockburgh ROCS 224)	1980
	In The Quiet Of My Room (New Version)/ In The Quiet Of My Room (PS)	(Thin Sliced TSR 5)	1985

NB: * This was a reissue of the 45 on Ellie Jay but without a picture sleeve. + This was recorded with Keeping Dark.

Ada Wilson came from Wakefield in Yorkshire and also recorded with **The Strangeways**. *Head In The Clouds* got a further airing on *Hicks From The Sticks* (Rockburgh Records ROC 111) in 1980. It's a new wavish pop song.

The Wimps

EP:	1( ) HAMBURGER RADIO (Can I Walk You Home Carolina/Hamburger Radio/New Girl At School/ Modern Girl) (PS)	(Sniff SNORT 1)	1979

45:	At The Discotheque/Blind Minds/ Gonna Loose (PS)		(Sniff SNORT 2)	1979

The Wimps sing on these records of their love for schoolgirls, McDonalds and power pop nostalgia.

Wire

| Personnel: (up to 1986) | BRUCE GILBERT ROBERT GOTOBED (MARK FELD) GRAHAM LEWIS COLIN NEWMAN MIKE THORNE | gtr, vcls, synth drms, perc bs, vcls, synth vcls, gtr, keyb'ds keyb'ds | AB AB AB AB B |

				HCP
ALBUMS: (up to 1986)	1(A) 2(B) 3(A) 4(A) 5(A) 6(A)	PINK FLAG CHAIRS MISSING 154 DOCUMENT AND EYEWITNESS: ELECTRIC BALLROOM (live from 1979) WIRE PLAY POP (mini-album) IN THE PINK (live)	(Harvest SHSP 4076) 1977 - (Harvest SHSP 4093) 1978 48 (Harvest SHSP 4105) 1979 39 (Rough Trade ROUGH 29) 1981 - (Pink Label PINKY 7) 1986 - (Dojo DOJOLP 36) 1986 -

NB: (1) came with an inner lyric bag. (1) also issued on CD (Harvest CD HAR 1) 1987 with one additional track *Options R* and again (EMI CDGO 2063) 1994. The first 10,000 copies of (2), which came with an inner lyric bag, were printed on lilac vinyl. (2) also issued on CD (Harvest CD HAR 2) 1987, with three additional tracks, *Go Ahead*, *Former Airline* and *A Question Of Degree* and again (EMI CDGO 2065) 1994. A limited number of copies of (3) came with a free 7" EP comprising *Song I/Get Down (Parts 1 And II)/Let's Panic Later/Small Electric Piece* (PSR 444) and all contained an inner lyric bag. (3) also issued on CD (Harvest CD HAR 3) 1997, with three additional tracks *Get Down (Parts 1 & II)*, *Let's Panic Later* and *Small Electric Piece*, and again (EMI CDGO 2064) 1994. (1), (2) and (3) also issued as a 3-CD set (EMI 5283572) 2000. (4) came with a free 12" EP *Live At Notre Dame Hall*. It comprised *Underwater Experiences*, *Go Ahead*, *Ally In Exile*, *Relationship*, *Our Swimmer*, *Witness To The Fact*, *2 People In A Room* and *Heartbeat*. (4) reissued in 1984 and on CD (Mute 9 61079-2) in 1991. There's also a 'best of' from this period *On Returning (Wire 1977-1979)* (Harvest CDP 792 535 2) 1989, which was reissued in 1996 and again in 2000. Once available but now deleted is *Peel Sessions: Wire Vol. 2* (Strange Fruit SFRCD 108) 1990 also on vinyl (SFRLP 108) 1990. An alternative compilation is *Behind The Curtain* (EMI CDGO 2066) 1995. There's also a tribute CD *Whore (Various Artists Play Wire)* (WMO 002CD) 2000.

| EPs: | (1) 2(A) | 154 (12", PS five track white label sampler) SNAKEDRILL (A Serious Of Snakes/Drill/ Advantage In Height/ Up To The Sun) (12", PS) | (Harvest SPSLP 299) 1979 (Mute 12 MUTE 53) 1986 |

			HCP
45s: (up to 1986)		Mannequin/Feeling Called Love/ 12 XU (PS) Mannequin/Feeling Called Love/ 12 XU (12", PS) I Am The Fly/Ex-Lion Tamer (PS) Dot Dash/Options R (PS) Outdoor Miner/ Practice Makes Perfect (PS) Outdoor Miner/ Practice Makes Perfect (PS) A Question Of Degree/ Former Airline (PS) Map Ref 41° In 93° W/ Go Ahead (PS) Our Swimmer/ Midnight Bahnhof Cafe (PS) Crazy About Love/Second Length/ Catapult 30 (12", PS)	(Harvest HAR 5144) 1977 - (Harvest HAR 5144) 1977 - (Harvest HAR 5151) 1978 - (Harvest HAR 5161) 1978 - (Harvest HAR 5172) 1979 51 (Harvest HAR 5172) 1979 - (Harvest HAR 5187) 1979 - (Harvest HAR 5192) 1979 - (Rough Trade RTO 79) 1981 - (Rough Trade RTO 123) 1983 -
	* x		

NB: * Pressed on white vinyl. x This came in two different sleeve colours.

Wire were one of the most adventurous bands to emerge in the late seventies. Their early music was minimalist but in the early eighties their non-conformist avant-garde music combined *both* art and anger, often with a futuristic sound, which gave it an unique feel.

Wire first got together in October 1976. They comprised Bruce Gilbert (born in Watford on 18th May 1946), Robert Gotobed (whose real name was Mark Feld and as such had entered the world in Leicester in 1951), Graham Lewis (born in Grantham, Lincolnshire on 22nd February 1953) and finally, **Colin Newman** (born in Salisbury on 16th September 1954). Prior to his days in **Wire** Robert Gotobed had been in a group called Snakes along with **Nick Garvey** who later resurfaced in **The Motors**. Gotobed can be heard playing a version of The Flamin' Groovies *Teenage Head* (Dynamite 45-006) with The Snakes, which was released on a Dutch-based label. With *Lights Out* on the reverse this 45 is now pretty rare. After The Snakes Gotobed spent a while with the **Art Attacks**, but this was prior to their recording phase.

Wire's first vinyl appearance came in April 1977 when they appeared at the Roxy for two nights and their contributions *12XU* and *Lowdown* were included on *The Roxy London WC2* (Harvest SHVL 4069) 1977. This album was later reissued (Receiver RR 132) 1991. The speed thrash of *12XU* and the menacing *Lowdown* (the only slow cut on the album) stand out. They also established their blank and expressionless live style (which didn't go down well with some audiences) from the outset.

In the race to sign up new punk bands **Wire** were recruited to EMI's Harvest label. In September 1977, they recorded some demos with EMI's Mike Thorne producing. One of these *Culture Vutures* didn't appear on vinyl until tapes of the Peel sessions were released in 1987.

They briefly toured Britain and returned to produce a strong and edgy 45 *Mannequin* in November. It was quickly deleted, but this and a re-recorded version of *12XU* appeared on their debut album *Pink Flag*, released the same month. This was quite unlike any other punk album to date. Firstly, it contained no less than twenty-one tracks and none of them was more than three minutes long. Musically it comprised from the opening cut *Reuters* onwards twenty-one short sharp shocks of variety and imagination, although the overall images were cold and bleak and the guitar assaults frequently brutal. This was an excellent debut album and a fine testament to Mike Thorne's skills as a producer.

They followed this with a superb second single *I Am The Fly* in February 1978. This starts with an unnervingly discordant opening guitar section. When the vocals join in they are punkish and quite catchy, but it's really the guitar work which catches the ear. It deserved to be a hit, but wasn't. After two spring tours, they began work on a second album.

In June 1978, a third single, the uptempo *Dot Dash* was released, with *Options R* on the flip side. The single was quickly deleted and surprisingly neither cut was included on their forthcoming album *Chairs Missing*. However, both sides of the 45 were included on *The Rare Stuff* (EMI SHSM 2028). *Dot Dash* was later featured on NME's *Pogo A Go-Go* (NME 021) 1986 cassette, which was only available by mail-order from NME. *Options R* was later added to the CD issue of *Pink Flag* in 1987.

June 1978 also marked the debut at London's Lyceum of producer Mike Thorne on keyboards, which freed up **Colin Newman** for extra guitar duties and helped give the band a fuller sound. After touring the 'States, they

WIRE - Chairs Missing.

Wire live at The Electric Ballroom, London 29th February 1980. Photo: Steven Richards.

returned to Britain in September to tour and promote their *Chairs Missing* album released the same month. The first 10,000 copies were printed on lilac vinyl and the album came in another starkly-designed sleeve. Bruce Gilbert and Graham Lewis designed all their Harvest sleeves. The band had matured considerably on this album. Gilbert's relentless guitar thrash had been replaced by a carefully textured sound, which also incorporated Thorne's keyboards and synthesizers. This immediately becomes apparent on the opening cut *Practice Makes Perfect* which opens and closes with some delightfully discordant and unnerving guitar work. It also broke the four minute barrier, by just six seconds! Their greater sophistication is apparent, too, on the second cut *French Film Blurred*. This is followed by *Another The Letter*. Lasting just one minute six seconds this has a catchy electro-pop style introduction and a very abrupt ending. *Men 2nd* is a weaker cut, but *Marooned* opens with a great guitar riff and is a slow-paced, rather intense number. *Sand In My Joints* is a fast-paced punk thrash as is *Being Sucked In Again*. The side closes with *Heartbeat*, one of the tracks which breaks the three minute barrier. *Mercy* opens side two with a superb, atmospheric guitar introduction - clocking in at five minutes forty-six seconds it's the longest track on the album and gives them time to develop. Next up at just one minute forty-six seconds is *Outdoor Miner* with an appealing guitar intro and more melodic than most of their output this was selected as their next 45 and released in January 1979. EMI felt that the 45 version was too short so a middle eight piano section was added. As an additional marketing ploy, some copies were pressed on white vinyl and naturally these are now more collectable than the standard black vinyl issue. The promotional push worked, *Outdoor Miner* brought them their only hit of the punk era. It enjoyed a three week chart residency, peaking at No. 51. It's followed by their excellent earlier second 45 *I Am The Fly* and then another of their finest moments - the weird, discordant, almost psychedelic, *I Feel Mysterious Today*. After two slower numbers *From The Nursery* and *Used To*, the album concludes with the fast-paced punk thrash of *Too Late*, which also breaks the four minute barrier. *Chairs Missing* was a superbly consistent album and one of the most creative of the punk/new wave era. It also took **Wire** into the album chart for the first time, spending one week at No. 48 in October 1978.

Wire gigged in Britain in February 1979 and then supported Roxy Music on a European tour that spring. Returning to Britain for more gigs they played songs that were so new they weren't even included on their forthcoming album *154*. The album was preceded by a non-album 45 coupling *A Question Of Degree* and *Former Airline* in June. This is now sought-after and not too expensive.

154 was released in September 1979. Originally, the album came shrink-wrapped with a free four-track EP in a plain black sleeve. Each band member wrote and produced one track on the EP - the best was Lewis' *Let's Panic Later*. The whole EP was included on the cassette version of the album (TCSHSP 405). There was also a five-track 12" sampler EP of the album, which included two of its finest moments; *Map Ref 41 N 93 W* and *I Should Have Known Better*. White label test pressings of this are by some way the rarest and most expensive **Wire** artifacts, but beware of counterfeits! *154* is another superb album. Compared to their earlier efforts the music is subtler and smoother but it's still a superbly consistent effort. Listen out for *Once Is Enough* a generally chaotic song with a decidedly weird and unnerving introduction. Interesting! Other highlights worth hearing include *Indirect Enquiries*, *40 Versions*, *The Other Window* and *A Touching Display*, which is more commercially focused with good guitar work. Another classic new wave album, this is recommended. Despite its unconventional approach the album spent a week in the charts at No. 39, which was the highest chart placing **Wire** achieved.

In November 1979, **Wire** performed *People In A Room* at the Jeanetta Cochran Theatre, Holborn, in collaboration with the Central School Of Art. In the first half of the evening each **Wire** member delivered a solo composition. In the second half they performed as a group.

It was now apparent that the four individuals who composed **Wire** felt that they had taken the band as far as they could. They split up in 1980 after a final live gig at London's Electric Ballroom. This was naturally recorded and made up most of *Document And Eyewitness*, released by Rough Trade in July 1981. Free with the record came an additional 12" featuring seven live cuts recorded at London's Notre Dame Hall and a version of *Heartbeat* (originally on *Chairs Missing*) from a live concert at Montreal in Canada. The album, incidentally, featured largely new compositions, although they weren't as good as those on their previous two studio albums. To coincide with the album's release Rough Trade issued two cuts, *Our Swimmer* and *Midnight Bahnhof Cafe* (recorded two years earlier) on a 45. Then, in 1983, they released in collaboration with the BBC, the 12" *Crazy About Love*, originally recorded for the John Peel Show back in 1979.

After **Wire**'s demise **Colin Newman** recorded as a solo artist. His first album *A-Z* is thought to have featured material originally intended for a fourth **Wire** album. Gilbert and Lewis worked as a duo which developed into **Dome** (see entry for more details). Gotobed went on to session work (playing with **Newman** among others) and then joined **Fad Gadget**.

Wire reformed in 1984, after **Colin Newman** contacted Lewis and Gilbert upon returning from India. They gigged in June previewing mostly new material some of which featured on the *Snakedrill* 12"-only album, which was released in November 1986. Further recordings followed but these fall

WIRE - 154.

outside the time span of this book. There have also been some compilations like the mini-album *Wire Play Pop* and *On Returning (1977-79)*. This collection compiled and annotated by Jon Savage draws all its material from their first three albums. The opening cut is *1.2.X.U.* (taken from their vinyl debut on *The Roxy, London WC2*), there are eight tracks in all from *Pink Flag* representing their early punk days and the remaining material comes from *Chairs Missing* and *154*. An excellent collection.

The Peel Sessions Album from 1990 comprises their three Peel sessions and accurately traces their progression from three chord short sharp shockers to a highly experimental and avant-garde combo as captured in their third Peel session, which comprised just one exploratory fifteen-minute cut *Crazy About Love*.

Behind The Curtain: Early Versions 1977 & 1978 is a thirty-one track collection of material from their early days. It includes six cuts from their April Fools Day '77 Roxy Club appearance.

In 1997, a live version of **Wire**'s *1.2.X.U.* was included on *New Wave Archive* (Rialto RMCD 201). *I Am The Fly* can also be heard on *The Best Punk Album In The World.... Ever, Vol. 1* (2-CD) (Virgin VTDCD 42) 1995 and *Outdoor Miner* appeared on *Vol. 2* (2-CD) (Virgin VTDCD 79) in 1996. Both *I Am The Fly* and *Outdoor Miner* also figure on *The Best Punk Anthems... Ever* (2-CD) (Virgin VTDCD 198) 1998. You can also check out *12XU* on *Burning Ambitions (A History Of Punk)* (Anagram CDBRED 3) 1996 and *Outdoor Miner* appears on *Spiked* (EMI Gold CDGOLD 1057) 1996. Finally, *Mannequin* was included on *A History Of Punk, Vol. 2* (Virgin CDOVD 487) 1997 and on the 5-CD box set *1-2-3-4 - A History Of Punk And New Wave 1976 - 1979* (MCA/Universal MCD 60066) in 1999.

During the nineties the reformed **Wire** dropped the 'e' becoming Wir, but they never made a further commercial breakthrough. In 1995, Elastica utilised a riff from *3 Girl Rhumba* for their worldwide hit *Connection*. **Newman** went on to work for singer and guitarist Justine Frischman.

Wire were one of the most inventive and interesting bands to emerge from the punk/new wave era. Their first three albums are recommended, particularly the second one *Chairs Missing*.

Wolfboys!!

Personnel:	JASPER BERLIN	gtr, vcls	A
	MARTIN FIEBER	gtr, vcls	A
	CLIVE GRONOW	lead vcls	A
	TERRY HAGGERTY	bs	A
	MARK IRVING	drms	A

This band's sole vinyl offering seems to have been *Feelin' Hard* on the compilation *499 2139* (Rocket DIAL 1) 1979. This features some discordant guitar snippets and vocals which recall the style of **Albertos Y Los Trios Paranoias**.

Wolfgang Press

Personnel:	MICHAEL ALLEN	vcls, bs	A
	MARK COX	keyb'ds	A
	ANDREW GRAY	drms	A

ALBUMS: (up to 1986)	1(A)	THE BURDEN OF MULES	(4AD CAD 308) 1983
	2(A)	LEGENDARY WOLFGANG PRESS AND OTHER TALL STORIES	(4AD CAD 514) 1985
	3(A)	STANDING UP STRAIGHT	(4AD CAD 606) 1986

NB: (2) also issued on CD (4AD CAD 514CD) 1987 and again (4AD GAD 514CD) 1998. (3) also issued on CD (4AD CAD 606CD) 1987 and again (4AD GAD 606CD) 1998.

EPs: (up to 1986)	1(A)	SCARECROW (Desire/Respect/Ecstasy) (12")	(4AD BAD 409) 1984
	2(A)	WATER (Tremble (My Girl Doesn't)/My Way/ The Deep Briny/Fire-Eater) (12")	(4AD BAD 502) 1985
	3(A)	SWEATBOX (Sweatbox/Muted/Heart Of Stone/ I'm Coming Home (Mama)) (12", PS)	(4AD BAD 506) 1985

NB: (1-3) later compiled onto one compilation *The Legendary Wolfgang Press And Other Tall Stories* (4AD CAD 514) 1986, also on CD (4AD CAD 514 CD) 1987.

45:	Kings Of Soul (Crowned Mix)/(De-Throned Mix)/ (7" Mix) (12")	(4AD no #) 1983

NB: This was a promo-only release. Only 50 copies were pressed. It had the same tracks on each side and didn't come in a picture sleeve.

London's **Wolfgang Press** were one of the more challenging and adventurous bands to emerge in th post-punk era.

The Burden Of Mules, released in an Alberto Ricci record cover, is a dark and gloomy recording.

They then recorded a trio of EPs with **Cocteau Twin** Robin Guthrie producing. The first *Scarecrow* is a well-produced blend of guitars, synthesizers and percussion supporting Allen's almost spoken vocals. In a more lighthearted moment it included a cover of Otis Redding's *Respect*.

On *Water* they use a much more minimalist backing whilst Allen's vocal style is more ballad-orientated.

Sweatbox was the most musically sophisticated of the three EPs, which with some songs remixed and/or edited from the original format, were compiled in 1986 onto *The Legendary Wolfgang Press And Other Tall Stories*.

Woody and The Splinters

Personnel:	JOHN CRAMPTON	gtr, vcls	A
	IAN JARVIS	drms	A
	ROB McROBERT	bs	A

A Brighton area band who contributed two cuts to *Vaultage '79 (Another Two Sides Of Brighton)*. Both *I Want You To Be My Girl* and *I Must Be Mad* are promising, pacey pop-punkers. The former was later included on *Vaultage Punk Collection* (Anagram CDPUNK 101) 1997.

The Work

Personnel incl:	TIM HODGKINSON	vcls
	CATHERINE JAUNIAUX	vcls

ALBUM: (up to 1986)	1(A)	SLOW CRIMES	(Recommended) 1982

NB: (1) also issued on CD (Megaphone 001) 1992 and again (Woof WOOF 003) 1995.

45:	*	I Hate America/Fingers And Toes/ Duty (PS)	(Woof WOOF 2) 1981

NB: * Issued in clear vinyl.

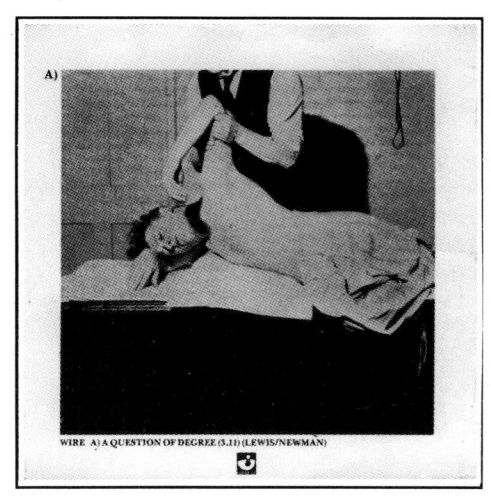

WIRE - A Question Of Degree.

A post-punk act from the Henry Cow stable. Fronted by Tim Hodgkinson, whose vocals weren't always the most tuneful, **The Work** utilised imaginative arrangements and adventurous musicianship on their album and 45. They included some members of **The Art Bears**. On *Slow Crimes* Hodgkinson's histrionic vocals and the wailings of part-time supporting vocalist Catherine Jauniaux ensure plenty of aggression on cuts like *I Hate America*, *Do It* and *Maggot Song*.

Wreckless Eric

Personnel:			
	JOHN BROWN	bs	A
	ERIC	vcls, gtr	ABC
	COLIN FLETCHER	lead gtr	A
	WALTER MACON	gtr	A
	DAVE OTWAY	drms	AB
	STEVE CURRIE	bs	B
	JOHN GLYN	sax	B
	STEVE GOLDING	drms	B
	DAVE WHITTON	drms	B
	MALCOLM BRADY	gtr	C
	JOHN BROWN	bs	C
	MALCOLM MORLEY	gtr	C
	PETE SOLLEY	keyb'ds	C
	GLER WADE	drms	C

				HCP
ALBUMS:	1(B)	WRECKLESS ERIC	(Stiff SEEZ 6) 1978	46
	2(C)	THE WONDERFULL WORLD OF WRECKLESS ERIC	(Stiff SEEZ 9) 1978	-
	3(-)	BIG SMASH (dbl) (compilation)	(Stiff SEEZ 21) 1980	30

NB: (1) was a 10" album, some copies were issued on brown vinyl (SEEZ B6) and also issued on CD (Repertoire REP 4217-WY) 1991. (2) issued in black vinyl, but there were also some copies in green vinyl (SEEZ B9) and some in picture disc format with an insert (SEEZ P9). (3) also issued on CD (Disky STIFFCD 13) 1994.

45s:	Whole Wide World/Semaphore Signals (PS)	(Stiff BUY 16) 1977
*	Reconnez Cherie/Rags And Tatters (PS)	(Stiff BUY 25) 1978
	Take The Cash/Girlfriend (PS)	(Stiff BUY 34) 1978
	Crying, Waiting, Hoping/ I Wish It Would Rain (PS)	(Stiff BUY 40) 1978
	Hit And Miss Judy/ Let's Go To The Pictures (PS)	(Stiff BUY 49) 1979
+	Hit And Miss Judy/Let's Go To The Pictures/ I Need A Situation (12", PS)	(Stiff S12 BUY 49) 1979
	A Pop Song/Reconnez Cherie (PS)	(Stiff BUY 64) 1980
	Broken Doll/I Need A Situation (PS)	(Stiff BUY 75) 1980
	Broken Doll/I Need A Situation/ A Little Bit More (12", PS)	(Stiff S12 BUY 75) 1980

NB: * Issued on yellow vinyl. + Issued on orange vinyl in a die-cut picture sleeve.

Wreckless Eric's real name was Eric Goulden and he was born in Newhaven, Sussex in 1954. He emerged out of London's pub-rock scene in 1976 to be one of the first acts signed by David Robinson's new Stiff Records. Like label-mates **Elvis Costello** and **Nick Lowe** he became closely associated with the punk movement, although his music wasn't strictly-speaking punk rock. He was part of the legendary Stiff's live U.K. tour-by-train in October 1977 along with label-mates **Elvis Costello**, **Nick Lowe**, **Ian Dury and The Blockheads** and **Larry Wallis**. He appeared on the compilation *A Bunch Of Stiff Records* (Stiff SEEZ 2) 1977.

Prior to this in August 1977 with line-up 'A' he released his first 45 *Whole Wide World* - the first in a series of tuneful 45s which surprisingly failed to chart. This also figured on his first John Peel session, which was broadcast on 11th October 1977, along with *Semaphore Signals* (the flip side of the 45), *Personal Hygiene*, *Rags And Tatters* and *Reconnez Cherie*. Two of the tracks, *Semaphore Signals* and *Reconnez Cherie*, also appeared as his contribution from the 1977 Stiff tour to *Live Stiff Live* (Stiff GET 1) 1978, the compilation to commemorate the tour. **Ian Dury** was part of his backing band The New Rockets.

Reconnez Cherie, another excellent tune which showcased his inventiveness as a songwriter, was released as a 45 in February 1978, but again failed to chart. This was surprising given the relatively high profile that Stiff's various promotional activities had given him.

His 10" album *Wreckless Eric*, which appeared on brown vinyl in March 1978, was recorded with a new band (line-up 'B'). This was more successful appearing in the chart for one week at No. 46. This included *Whole Wide World* and *Reconnez Cherie*, with its flip side *Rags And Tatters*, but not *Semaphore Signals*. The 1991 CD reissue of this album on Repertoire came with three bonus cuts, two of which were versions of Devo's *Be Stiff*. However, *Semaphore Signals* was featured in his second and final Peel session broadcast on 8th March 1978, along with three other cuts from the album; *Grown Ups*, *Waxworks* and *Brain Thieves*.

In September 1978, he contributed the title track to *Be Stiff* (Stiff ODD 2), a promo-only compilation from a Stiff 1978 tour. He also contributed *Semaphore Signals* and *I Wish It Would Rain* to *Can't Start Dancin'* (Stiff/Sounds 3) 1978. He then worked with a new band (line-up 'C') to produce *The Wonderful World Of Wreckless Eric*. Released in October, this album was also available in green vinyl and picture disc format. *Take The Cash* was culled for 45 release the same month, but failed to chart. Later, in December, the two cover versions on the album of Buddy Holly's *Crying, Waiting And Hoping* and The Temptations' *I Wish It Would Rain* were issued on one 45 but these fared little better. Overall, though, the album is an enjoyable listen.

In 1979, *Whole Wide World* figured on the soundtrack *That Summer!* (Spartan/Arista SPART 1088). It later resurfaced on *The Best Punk Album In The World.... Ever, Vol. 2* (2-CD) (Virgin VTDCD 79) in 1996.

Following further commercially unsuccessful 45s, *Hit And Miss Judy* and *A Pop Song*, Stiff decided to smooth out **Wreckless Eric**'s endearing rough edges in one last attempt for commercial success. The result was the double album set *Big Smash*. The first album contained decidedly more commercially-orientated material with *Good Conversation* the stand out track. The second album comprised material from his first two albums and some 45s. This had been issued as a single album titled *The Whole Wide World* in the 'States and the title cut, produced and mostly played by **Nick Lowe** probably remains his finest number.

He recorded a couple of sessions for Mike Read in 1980. The first broadcast on 17th March featured *It'll Soon Be The Weekend*, *Out Of The Blue*, *Broken Doll* and *A Pop Song*, tracks which all appeared among the album of new material on Big Smash. The second session broadcast on 29th December comprised two of his classics *Whole Wide World* and *Reconnez Cherie*, along with *I Saw Her Standing There* and *Feelings*.

Stiff's marketing ploy did pay off because *Big Smash* spent four weeks in the charts, peaking at No. 30 and was by some way his best-selling album.

Two 45s, *A Pop Song* and *Broken Doll* were taken from *Big Smash*, but neither charted.

Wreckless Eric retired from the music business for a while in the early eighties, but he returned in 1984 to form Captains Of Industry with ex-**Ian Dury and The Blockheads** members Mickey Gallagher and Norman Watt-Roy, Baz Murphy (organ) and ex-**Piranhas** drummer David Adland. Later, in 1986, he formed the Len Bright Combo with ex-Milkshakes Bruce Brand and Russ Wilkins. He returned to work as **Wreckless Eric** from

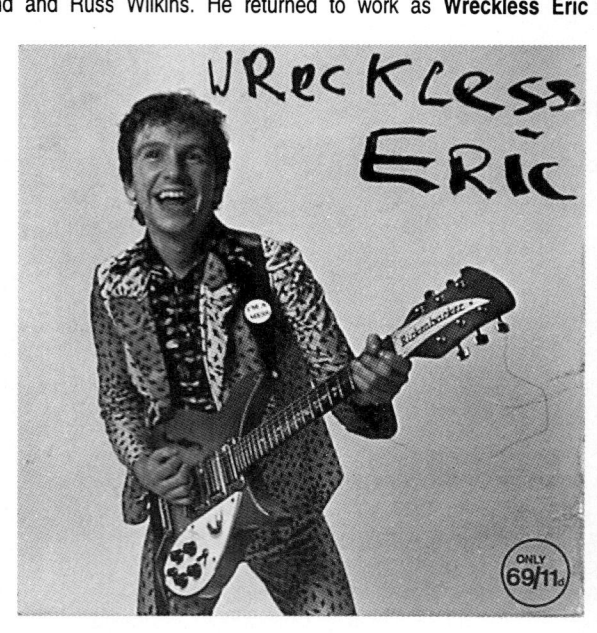

WRECKLESS ERIC - Wreckless Eric 10".

1988 onwards. In these latter years he worked a lot on the Continent, particularly France. He still plays regularly in Britain and on the Continent to the present day.

In 1991, he joined German band Die Toten Hosen making a guest appearance on their version of *Whole Wide World* on their album *Learning English, Vol. 1*. Later in 1999, *Whole Wide World* figured on *1-2-3-4 - A History Of Punk And New Wave 1976 - 1979* (MCA/Universal MCD 60066), a 5-CD box set compilation.

Wreckless Eric was a refreshing, unique and original talent in the punk/new wave era. He didn't achieve the commercial success his talent merited but his live act was popular and entertaining making him a significant part of the new wave scene.

The X-Certs

Personnel:	CLIVE ARNOLD	gtr, vcls	A
	SIMON JUSTICE	gtr, vcls	A
	PHIL LOVERING	bs	A
	NEIL MACKIE	drms	A

The X-Certs contributed the promising pop-punkish *Anthem* to *Avon Calling - The Bristol Compilation* (Heartbeat HB 1) in 1979. They also had a cut called *Blue Movies* on *4 Alternatives* (EP) (Heartbeat PULSE 4) in 1979 too.

X-Certs

45s:	Feeling The Groove (PS)	(Zama) 1979
	Together/Untogether (PS)	(Recreational PLAY 1) 1981

A three-piece band from Coventry who were signed initially by the Midlands-based Zama label. Their second 45 came with a lyric insert.

X-Cretas

An eighties punk band from Kent. They contributed two cuts *Familiarity* and *It's Our Life* to *Wet Dreams* (Rot ASS 4). On *It's Our Life*, in particular the lyrics, which are barely decipherable, fail to fit with the music and both cuts are substandard.

X-Dreamysts

Personnel:	ROE BUTCHER	vcls, bs	A
	JOHN DOHERTY	gtr	A
	BRIAN MOFFATT	drms	A
	VEL WALLIS	vcls	A

ALBUM:	1(A)	X-DREAMYSTS	(Polydor 2442 181) 1980

45s:	Right Way Home/	
	Dance Away Love (PS)	(Good Vibrations GOT 5) 1978
	Bad News/Money Talks (PS)	(Polydor 2059 129) 1979
	I Don't Wanna Go/Silly Games (PS)	(Polydor 2059 235) 1980
	Stay The Way You Are/	
	Race Against Time (PS)	(Polydor 2059 252) 1980

The X-Dreamysts came out of Coleraine, a little town in Co. Derry. They formed in 1977, but as early as 1975 the four members had been playing with a number of local bands. Originally known as The Flying Squad, they set out playing cover versions of country music classics by the likes of The Byrds, Buffalo Springfield and Gram Parsons. This proved sufficiently popular with their audiences to enable them to buy their own equipment. By the summer of 1977, they started writing their own material, their first self-penned number being *City Girl* written by Vel Wallis. They then recorded a single for Good Vibrations, *Right Way Home* (which sounded a little like **Eddie and The Hot Rods** and sold 10,000 copies). When Good Vibrations signed a distribution deal with Polydor, the **X-Dreamysts** were quickly snapped up and recorded three singles for them. The first *Bad News/Money Talks* was released on 22nd June 1979. But this and subsequent recordings, an album and two 45s, showed their relationship with Polydor to be just as disasterous as country-mates **Protex**'s had been.

They recorded a session for John Peel, which was broadcast on 10th January 1980. It comprised *I Don't Wanna Go* (a Polydor 45), *Pardoned City*, *One In Every Crowd* and *Reality Blues*.

Bad News, their debut 45 for Polydor, also figured on *20 Of Another Kind, Vol. 2* (Polydor POLX 1) 1979. *Dance Away Lover*, the flip side to their Good Vibrations 45, later figured on *Good Vibrations - The Punk Singles Collection* (Anagram CD PUNK 36) 1994. It's a pretty decent punk offering with strong vocals and competent guitar.

The **X-Dreamysts** were essentially a mainstream rock outfit, who played and sang imaginatively a collection of original material. Their association with Good Vibrations had ensured that they also appealed to new wave audiences, but they were not exceptional and split up early in the eighties.

X-E-Cutors

45:	Too Far To Look Inside My Head/	
	(other side by **X-Films**)	(Rok ROK XIII/XIV) 1980

This split single came in a die-cut company sleeve. *Too Far To Look Inside My Head* is lighthearted and quite rocky. It was subsequently included as a bonus cut on Captain Mod's CD reissue of the Rok Records compilation *Odd Bods Mods And Sods* (Captain Mod MODSKA CD 2) 1996.

X-Films

45:	After My Blood/	
	(other side by **X-E-Cutors**)	(Rok ROK XIII/XIV) 1980

This split single was issued in a die-cut company sleeve. *After My Blood* is rather mediocre. You'll also find it as a bonus track on Captain Mod's CD reissue of the Rok Records compilation *Odds Bods Mods And Sods* (Captain Mod MODSKA CD 2) 1996.

X-Ray Spex

Personnel:	PAUL DEAN	bs	ABC
	B.P. HURDING	drms	ABC
	LORA LOGIC (SUSAN WHITBY)	sax	A
	JAK 'AIRPORT' STAFFORD	gtr	ABC
	POLY STYRENE (MARION ELLIOT)	vcls	ABC
	STEVE 'RUDI' THOMPSON	sax	B
	JOHN GLIN	sax	C

			HCP
ALBUM:	1(B)	GERM FREE ADOLESCENTS	
		(EMI International INS 3023) 1978	30

NB: (1) was originally issued with a lyric inner sleeve. It was re-issued in the nineties with the same catalogue number on orange vinyl. (1) also issued on CD

X-RAY SPEX - Germ Free Adolescents LP.

(Virgin CDVM) 1992 with both sides of their Virgin 45 added. Other relevant CDs are *Live At The Roxy Club* (Receiver RRLP 140) 1991, also on CD (Receiver RRCD 140) 1993 and three compilations *Obsessed With You* (Receiver RRLP 145) 1991, also on CD (Receiver RRCD 145) 1991; *Germfree Adolescents* (Virgin CDVM 9001) 1991 and *Non-Genetically Engineered* (Burning Airlines PILOT 057) 2000.

HCP

45s:			
	Oh Bondage, Up Yours!/		
	I Am A Cliche (some PS)	(Virgin VS 189)	1977 -
	Oh Bondage, Up Yours!/		
	I Am A Cliche (12")	(Virgin VS 189-12)	1977 -
*	The Day The World Turned Day-Glo/		
	I Am A Poseur (PS)	(EMI International INT 553)	1978 23
+	Identity/Let's Submerge (PS)	(EMI International INT 563)	1978 24
	Germ Free Adolescents/		
	Age (PS)	(EMI International INT 573)	1978 19
x	Highly Inflammable/		
	Warrior In Woolworths (PS)	(EMI International INT 583)	1979 45

NB: * The first 15,000 copies were on orange vinyl. + Initial copies came on pink vinyl. x Inital copies came on red vinyl.

The central figure in **X-Ray Spex** was undoubtedly **Poly Styrene**. Her real name was Marion Elliot and she grew up in Brixton, South London. As many of you may know she left school at 15 and got a job selling sweets in Woolworths. She then trained as a clothes buyer (an experience that later had a considerable bearing on the songs and visual image of **X-Ray Spex** later), but jacked in a conventional lifestyle to hitch-hike around Britain. In the summer of 1976 she had an unsuccessful pop single *Silly Billy* for GTO. It was after seeing **The Sex Pistols** at the Pier Pavilion at Hastings that she then hit on the idea of setting up her own band. The inspiration for her own name **Poly Styrene** came from the 'Yellow Pages'. She then advertised for musicians and Paul Dean, B.P. Hurding, Jack Stafford and Susan Whitby were duly recruited. At **Poly Styrene**'s instigation Susan adopted the name **Laura Logic**.

X-Ray Spex got an amazing early break! In only their second live gig (at London's Roxy Club) they were recorded performing a raw early version of *Oh Bondage, Up Yours!*. The track appeared on *The Roxy, London, WC2* (Harvest SHSP 4069) 1977, which was reissued ten years later in 1987, and quickly propelled the group to quite a wide audience. It also became a punk catch phrase and one of the classic singles of 1977, after the band were signed by Virgin. Perhaps, surprisingly, it wasn't a hit but it is an essential ingredient of any punk collection.

"Bind me tie me chain me to the wall
I wanna be a slave to you all
Oh, bondage! Up yours!
Oh, bondage! No more!
Oh, bondage! Up yours!
Oh, bondage! No more!
Chain store chain smoke
I consume you all
Chain gang chain mail
I don't think at all
Trash me crash me beat me till I fall
I wanna be a victim for you all
Oh, bondage! Up yours!

X-RAY SPEX - Oh Bondage, Up Yours!

X-RAY SPEX - The Day The World Turned Day-Glo.

Oh, bondage! No more!
Oh, bondage! Up yours!
Oh, bondage! NO MORE!
(from *Oh, Bondage! Up Yours!*)

X-Ray Spex's success at The Roxy had secured them a Sunday residency at 'The Man In The Moon' on the Kings Road, where they were supported by **The Unwanted**. Meanwhile **Poly Styrene**, a plump woman who wore a brace on her teeth, drew on her training experience as a clothes buyer to become a punk icon whose colourful clothes and individualism made her shine out like a beacon even at the height of the punk era.

Surprisingly, Virgin let **X-Ray Spex** go, but their manager Falcon Stuart negotiated them an attractive contract with EMI, who were keen to get into the punk scene, having sacked **The Sex Pistols**.

When the group was formed **Lora Logic** was still studying at the City Of London School For Girls. After ten months she had to leave to concentrate on her exams, although there is speculation that she was pushed. Rudi Thompson was drafted in as her replacement on sax.

X-Ray Spex were recorded playing a live version of *Let's Submerge* at the Hope and Anchor in late 1977. The recording was later included on *The Hope And Anchor Front Row Festival* (Warner Bros K 66077), which was released in March 1978. The same month the band's first of two Peel sessions went out over the airwaves on 6th March 1978. It previewed *Identity* (a future 45), and three other cuts, which like *Identity* would later appear on their album. These were:- *Genetic Engineering*, *Art-I-Ficial* and *I Am A Poseur*.

The band's first single for EMI followed in April. *The Day The World Turned Day-Glo* was quite commercial, including a funky brass section. The first 15,000 copies were pressed on orange vinyl. The song's immediate appeal brought success. It spent seven weeks in the charts, peaking at No. 23.

"I clambered over mounds and mounds of polystyrene foam
Then fell into a swimming pool filled with Fairy Snow
And watched the world turn Day-Glo, you know, you know
The world turned Day-Glo, you know
I wrenched the nylon curtains back as far as they would go
Then peered through perspex window panes at the acrylic road
I drove my polypropylene car on wheels of sponge
Then pulled into a Wimpy Bar to have a rubber bun
The X-rays were penetrating through the latex breeze
Synthetic fibre see-thru leaves fell down from rayon trees
The day the world turned Day-Glo, you know, you know
The world turned Day-Glo, you know, you know
The world turned Day-Glo, you know? OH -OH!
(from *The Day The World Turned Day-Glo*)

X-Ray Spex were now hot property. They'd played six weeks at C.B.G.B.'s in New York in late March and then returned for a U.K. tour which culminated in an appearance at the Anti-Nazi League Rally in Victoria Park at the end of April. Their next 45 *Identity*, released in July, had been written back in 1977. The lyrics responded to 'punks' doing things journalists told them to like smashing mirrors:-

"Identity
Is the crisis
Can't you see
Identity identity
When you look in the mirror
Do you see yourself
Do you see yourself
On the TV screen
Do you see yourself
In the magazine
When you see yourself
Does it make you scream
When you look in the mirror
Do you smash it quick
Do you take the glass
And slash your wrists
Did you do it for fame
Did you do it in a fit
Did you do it before
You read about it"
(*Identity*)

Initial copies came on pink vinyl. This was a full-blooded punk song and it did quite well. It enjoyed ten weeks in the charts, peaking at No. 24.

Their album *Germ Free Adolescents* was released in November. In fact the title cut was put out on a 45 as a taster the previous month. It was in marked contrast to their earlier punkish style, with a synthesizer dominated sound. The subject matter, also an advert for personal hygiene, was a little unusual:-

"I know your antiseptic
Your deodorant smells nice
I'd like to get to know you
But your deep frozen like ice
He's a germ free adolescent
Cleanliness is her obsession
Cleans her teeth ten times a day
Scrub away, scrub away, scrub away
The S.R. way...
You may get to touch her
If your gloves are sterilised
Rinse your mouth out with Listerine
Blow disinfectant in her eyes
Her phobia is infection
She needs one to survive
It's built in protection
Without fear she'd give up and die"
(*Germ Free Adolescents*)

This became their most successful single, climbing into the Top 20 to No. 19 during an eleven week chart residency.

The album didn't contain much new material, which is perhaps a weakness. It included both sides of their first two 45s for EMI, as well as the title cut which had just been released on 45. Of the new material; *Obsessed With You*, *I Can't Do Anything*, *I Live Off You* and *Plastic Bag* all dated from their 1977 Roxy era. The latter was their longest cut, at just under five

X-RAY SPEX - Identity.

X-RAY SPEX - Germ Free Adolescents 7".

minutes. The lyrics are both triumphant and self-effacing:-

"1977 and we are going mad
It's 1977 and we've seen too many ad's
1977 and we're gonna show them all
That apathy's a drag
My mind is like a plastic bag
That corresponds to all those ads
It sucks up all the rubbish
That is fed in through by ear
I eat Kleenex for breakfast
And use soft hygienic Weetabix
To dry my tears"
(from *Plastic Bag*)

This pounding punk screamer stands out on the album alongside their three 45 cuts, the beaty punker *I Can't Do Anything* and the riffy *Warrior In Woolworths*, which was played in a different seventies guitar-driven style. The album, now a significant punk collectable, fared well spending fourteen weeks in the charts and peaking at No. 30.

Poly Styrene was clearly becoming bored by life as a pop artist and it turned out the band's U.K. tour of November and December 1978 would be their last. On 13th November their second and final Peel concert went out over the airwaves to help promote their album. It comprised *Germ-Free Adolescents* and *Warrior In Woolworths* as well as *Age* (an experimental song on which **Poly Styrene** utilised a different vocal style). This had appeared on the flip side of the *Germ Free Adolescent* 45. Film from a concert in Liverpool during the tour was used for an 'Omnibus' documentary "Who is Poly Styrene?". This went out in January 1978 and showed them recording what would turn out to be their final single *Highly Inflammable*. This was released in April 1979 and what with its references to Peter Pan and Tinkerbell was likened to a nursery rhyme. It was certainly their most commercial single. The content sugggested they were running out of ideas. *Warrior In Woolworths*, from their album, appeared on the flip. It was also the least successful of their four EMI singles, rising to No. 45 during its four weeks in the charts.

X-Ray Spex also appeared on some other compilations. Their debut 45 *Oh Bondage, Up Yours!* appeared on *Dead On Arrival* (Virgin VD 2508) 1978, which was pressed on luminous vinyl, *Guillotine 10"* (Virgin VCL 5001) in 1978 and on *Rock Against Racism's Greatest Hits* (RAR/Virgin RAR 1) 1980. It was also compiled again, in 1999, on the lavish 5-CD box set, *1-2-3-4 - A History Of Punk And New Wave 1976 - 1979* (MCA/Universal MCD 60066). Other compilation appearances include *Identity* on *The Best Punk Album In The World.... Ever, Vol. 1* (2-CD) (Virgin VTDCD 42) 1995; *The Best Punk Anthems.... Ever* (2-CD) (Virgin VTDCD 198) 1998 and it's on *God Save The Punks* (2-CD) (Disky DOU 882552) 1998, which also includes *Oh Bondage Up Yours!* as does *Burning Ambition (A History Of Punk)* (Anagram CDBRED 3) 1996. *The Day The World Turned Day-Glo* can also be found on *The Best Punk Album In The World.... Ever, Vol. 2* (2-CD) (Virgin VTDCD 79) 1996; *A History Of Punk, Vol. 1* (Virgin CDOVD 486) 1997; *Holidays In The Sun, Vol. 1* (Anagram HITS 01) 1999 and on *Punk - The Worst Of Total Anarchy* (2-CD) (Disky SP 871952) 1996. Finally, *Germfree Adolescents* can also be heard on *Teenage Kicks* (PolyGram TV 5253382) 1995.

X-RAY SPEX - Highly Inflammable.

In recent years there has been a CD of them *Live At The Roxy Club* and two compilations *Obsessed With You* and *Germfree Adolescents*. The *Germfree Adolescents* compilation takes the original album and adds a few single cuts, including the seminal *Oh Bondage Up Yours!*, meaning that (aside from a couple of live tracks on compilations) their entire vinyl output is here.

After their demise **Poly Styrene** recorded a solo album and 45 and returned in 1986 with a four track EP. **Laura Logic** formed **Essential Logic** and made somo solo recordings. Jak 'Airport' Stafford and Paul Dean formed Airport and Dean. Steve 'Rudi' Thompson departed to join **The Boys** and was replaced on sax by John Glin in the band's twilight days.

X-Ray Spex's career was brief but colourful. *Germ Free Adolescents* certainly ranks among one of the finest albums of the punk era and let's salute one of punk's finest bands.

XS Discharge

45s: Across The Border/
Frustration (PS)   (Groucho Marxist COMMUNIQUE 3) 1980
Life's A Wank (PS)   (Groucho Marxist WH 3) 1980

In addition to these 45s **XS Discharge** contributed one cut *Lifted* to a compilation EP, *Ha! Ha! Funny Plois (Paisley Rock Against Racism)* (Groucho Marxist Co-operative COMMUNIQUE 2) 1980.

XS Energy

45s: * Eighteen/Jenny's Alright/Horroscope!   (World WRECK 1) 1978
Use You/Imaginary (PS)   (Dead Good DEAD 3) 1979

NB: * Originally issued in numbered foldover yellow or green picture sleeves with stamped white labels. This was later reissued (Dead Good DEAD 1) 1979 in two different formats. One the 'National Souvenir Issue' came with a different foldover picture sleeve and stamped white labels. Some copies came without a picture sleeve in a stamped white sleeve with yellow printed labels.

A Lincoln punk band.

XTC

Personnel:
TERRY CHAMBERS   drms   ABC
COLIN MOULDING   bs, vcls   ABCDE
ANDY PARTRIDGE   gtr, vcls   ABCDE
JOHNATHAN PERKINS keyb'ds   A
BARRY ANDREWS   keyb'ds   B
DAVE GREGORY   synth, gtr   CDE
IAN GREGORY   drms   E
(PETER PHIPPS)   drms   D

HCP

ALBUMS: 1(B) WHITE MUSIC   (Virgin V 2095) 1978 38
(up to   2(B) GO 2   (Virgin V 2108) 1978 21
1986)   3(C) DRUMS AND WIRES   (Virgin V 2129) 1979 34
         4(C) BLACK SEA   (Virgin V 2173) 1980 16
         5(C) ENGLISH SETTLEMENT (dbl) (Virgin V 2223) 1982 5
         6(-) WAXWORKS (compilation)   (Virgin V 2251) 1982 54
         7(D) MUMMER   (Virgin V 2264) 1983 51
         8(D) THE BIG EXPRESS   (Virgin V 2325) 1984 38
         9(E) SKYLARKING   (Virgin V 2399) 1986 90

NB: (1) reissued at mid-price (Virgin OVED 60) 1984 and issued on CD (Virgin CDV 2095) 1988 with seven additional cuts; *Science Friction, She's So Square, Dance Band, Hang On To The Night, Heatwave, Traffic Light Rock* and *Instant Tunes*. The first 15,000 copies of (2) came with the *Go+* 12" EP comprising *Dance With Me Germany, Beat The Bible, A Dictionary Of Modern Marriage, Clap Clap Clap, We Kill The Beast* and an insert. (2) reissued at mid-price (Virgin OVED 61) 1984 and issued on CD (Virgin CDV 2108) 1987 with one additional track *Are You Receiving Me*. The first 15,000 copies of (3) came with a free 7" *Chain Of Command/Limelight* and a gatefold insert. (3) reissued at mid-price (Virgin OVED 113) 1986 and issued on CD (Virgin CDV 2129) 1987 with two additional cuts, *Limelight* and *Chain Of Command*. Initial copies of (4) came in a green paper outer sleeve with a lyric insert. (4) reissued at mid-price (Virgin OVED 83) 1986 and also issued on CD (Virgin CDV 2173) 1987 with three additional cuts, *Smokeless Zone, Don't Lose Your Temper* and *The Somambulist*. Initial copies of (5) came in a textured sleeve. (5) also issued on CD (Virgin CDV 2223) 198? without *Leisure* and *Down In The Cockpit*. (6) was a compilation of 'A' sides. The first 50,000 copies also came with a free compilation of 'B' sides *Beeswax. Beeswax* was later reissued at mid-price (Virgin OVED 9) 1983 in its own right. (7) reissued at mid-price (Virgin OVED 142) 1986 and on CD (Virgin CDV 2264) 1987 with the addition of six tracks; *Frost Circus, Jump, Toys, Procession Towards Learning Land* and *Desert Island*. Initial copies of (8) came in a circular sleeve and inner bag. (8) reissued at mid-price (Virgin OVED 182) 1988 and also issued on CD (Virgin CDV 2325) 1987 with three additional cuts, *Red Brick Dream Washaway* and *Blue Overall*. Initial copies of (9) had an embossed sleeve and inner bag. Also relevant are:- *The Compact XTC - The Singles 1978 - 1985* (CD) (Virgin CDV 2251) 1986; *Explode Together (The Dub Experiments 1978 -80)* (CD) (Virgin CDOVD 308) 1990; *Rag And Bone Buffet* (CD) (Virgin CDOVD 311) 1990, which comprises rarities and out-takes and *Fossil Fuel (The XTC Singles Collection 1977 - 1992)* (CD) (Virgin CDVD 2811) 1986. Also of interest may be *A Testimonial Dinner (A Tribute To XTC)* (Cooking Vinyl COOKCD 145) 1998, which is a various artists tribute to **XTC**, *Live In Concert 1980* (Windsong WINCD 026) 199 and *Transistor Blast: The Best Of The BBC Sessions* (4-CD set) (Cooking Vinyl COOKCD 152) 1999.

EP: 1(B) 3-D (Science Friction/She's So Square/
          Dance Band) (12")   (Virgin VS 188-12) 1977

HCP

45s: * Science Friction/
(up to   She's So Square (some PS) (Virgin VS 188) 1977 -
1986)   Statue Of Liberty/
         Hang On To The Night (PS) (Virgin VS 201) 1978 -
         This Is Pop?/Heatwave (PS) (Virgin VS 209) 1978 -
         Are You Receiving Me/
         Instant Tunes (PS)   (Virgin VS 231) 1978 -
      + Life Begins At The Hop/
         Home Safari (PS)   (Virgin VS 259) 1979 54

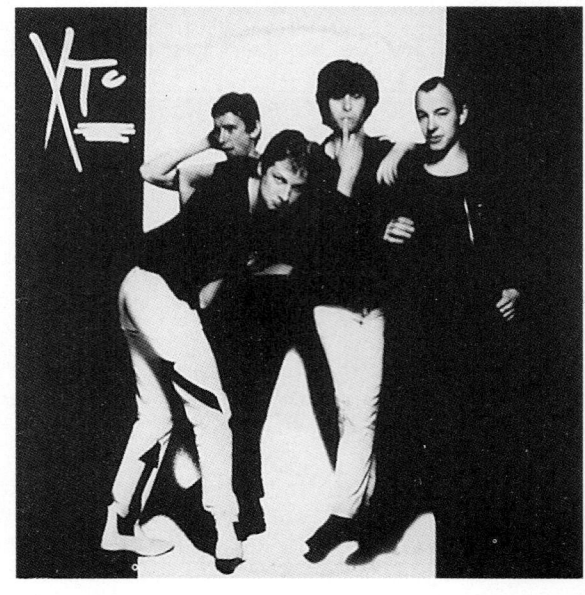

XTC - White Music.

#	Making Plans For Nigel/Bushman President (HSS 2)/ Pulsing, Pulsing (PS)	(Virgin VS 282)	1979	17
o	Ten Feet Tall/ (other side by **The Skids**)	(Smash Hits HIT 002)	1980	-
	Wait Till Your Boat Goes Down/ Ten Feet Tall (U.S. version) (PS)	(Virgin VS 322)	1980	-
	Generals And Majors/ Don't Lose Your Temper (PS)	(Virgin VS 365)	1980	32
	Generals And Majors/Don't Lose Your Temper/ Smokeless Zone/ The Somnambulist (double pack)	(Virgin VS 365)	1980	-
	Towers Of London/ Set Myself On Fire (live) (PS)	(Virgin VS 372)	1980	31
	Towers Of London/Set Myself On Fire (live)/ Battery Brides (live)/ Scissor Man (double pack)	(Virgin VS 372)	1980	-
	Take This Town/ (other side by **The Ruts**) (PS)	(RSO RSO 71)	1981	-
α	Sgt. Rock (Is Going To Help Me)/ Living Through Another Cuba (live)/ Generals And Majors (live) (PS)	(Virgin VS 384)	1981	16
	Respectable Street/Strange Tales, Strange Tails/ Officer Blue (PS)	(Virgin VS 407)	1981	-
β	Senses Working Overtime/Blame The Weather/ Tissue Tigers (The Arguers) (PS)	(Virgin VS 462)	1982	10
	Senses Working Overtime/Egyptian Solution (Homo Safari Series No. 3)/Blame The Weather/ Tissue Tigers (The Arguers) (12", PS)	(Virgin VS 462-12)	1982	-
χ	Looking For Footprints	(Lyntone LYN 11032)	1982	-
	Ball And Chain/Punch And Judy/Heaven Is Paved With Broken Glass (PS)	(Virgin VS 482)	1982	58
	Ball And Chain/Heaven Is Paved With Broken Glass/Punch And Judy/ Cockpit Dance Mixture (12", PS)	(Virgin VS 482-12)	1982	-
δ	No Thugs In The House/Chain Of Command/ Limelight/Over Rusty Water (PS)	(Virgin VS 490)	1982	-
	Great Fire/Gold (some PS)	(Virgin VS 553)	1983	-
	Great Fire/Gold/Frost Circus (Homo Safari Series No. 5)/Procession Towards Learning (Homo Safari Series No. 6) (12", PS)	(Virgin VS 533-12)	1983	-
	Wonderland/Jump (PS)	(Virgin VS 606)	1983	-
	Wonderland/Jump (picture disc)	(Virgin VSY 606)	1983	-
	Love On A Farmboy's Wages/In Loving Memory Of A Name (PS)	(Virgin VS 613)	1983	50
φ	Love On A Farmboy's Wages/In Loving Memory Of A Name/Desert Island/Toys	(Virgin VS 613)	1983	-
	Love On A Farmboy's Wages/Burning With Optimism's Flames (live)/English Roundabout (live)/ Cut It Out (live) (12", PS)	(Virgin VS 613-12)	1983	-
γ	All You Pretty Girls/ Washaway (some PS)	(Virgin VS 709)	1984	55
	All You Pretty Girls/Washaway/ Red Brick Dream (12", PS)	(Virgin VS 709-12)	1984	-
η	This World Over/Blue Overall (PS)	(Virgin VS 721)	1984	-
	This World Over/ Blue Overall (12", PS)	(Virgin VS 721-12)	1984	-
	Wake Up/Take This Town/Mantis On Parole (Home Safari Series No. 4) (PS)	(Virgin VS 746)	1985	-
	Wake Up/Take This Town/Mantis On Parole/ Home Safari Service No. 4/Making Plans For Nigel/ Sgt. Rock (Is Going To Help Me)/ Senses Working Overtime (12", PS)	(Virgin VS 746-12)	1985	-
	Grass/Dear God (PS)	(Virgin VS 882)	1986	-
	Grass/Extrovert/Dear God (12", PS)	(Virgin VS 882-12)	1986	-

NB: * Unreleased, some copies came in picture sleeves. These are mega-rarities. + The first 30,000 copies came in clear vinyl with a PVC sleeve and insert. # Initially copies came with a game-board picture sleeve and playing pieces. o 33 rpm red flexidisc. α The first 20,000 copies came in a poster picture sleeve with a stickered PVC sleeve. β This was initially released in a fold out poster picture sleeve. χ This was a flexi disc which came free with 'Flexipop' magazine, issue 16 on red, blue, green or yellow vinyl. δ Some copies came in a 9" die-cut gatefold picture sleeve. φ Double-pack. γ Outer die-cut picture sleeve. η Copies came with postcards.

The origins of **XTC** go as far back as 1967 when Dave Gregory (later to be their guitarist) formed a school band which gradually became known as The Pink Warmth. The psychedelic combo played at various youth clubs around Swindon and it was at one of these that Dave met with Andy Partridge, who'd started learning to play the guitar. Andy (who'd been born on 11th December 1953) was fifteen at the time. They became close friends but didn't actually team up in the same band until 1979.

Meanwhile, in the early seventies Andy met Colin Moulding, whom he encouraged to learn to play guitar and through Colin, Terry Chambers joined on drums. This trio was supplemented for a short while by the addition of Steve Philips on guitar. When they had developed themselves sufficiently to play live gigs they were billed as the Helium Kidz. At this stage they were a typical mid-seventies guitar/keyboar combo, but with psychedelic leanings.

By 1976, with a new breed guitar bands emerging, they underwent a change of name and image to **XTC**, inspired by a Jimmy Durante film. Their initial organist Jonathan Perkins had been replaced by Barry Andrews, previously of **King Crimson**. They became a local attraction in Swindon gigging at 'The Affair' before transferring up to the London Club scene. They soon established themselves as part of the bourgeoning new wave scene.

XTC - Making Plans For Nigel.

XTC also recorded two sessions for John Peel during 1977. The first broadcast on 24th June comprised *She's So Square*, *Crosswires*, *Radios In Motion* and *Science Friction*. The second, which went out on the airwaves on 26th September 1977, consisted of *Into The Atom Age*, *I'm Bugged*, *Heatwave 2* and *Dance Band*.

After earlier auditions for CBS Records they were signed by Virgin. A debut 45 *Science Friction* was produced by John Leckie and released together with a limited edition picture sleeve in October 1977. This is now very hard to find and you can expect to pay in excess of £100 for pristine copies in their limited edition picture sleeves.

A 12" edition *3-D EP* with *Science Friction*, *She's So Square* and *Dance Band* was kept on Virgin's catalogue for longer and is easier to locate. The French and German pressings of this one are particularly rare and collectable.

On 25th October 1977, a session recorded for Dave Lee Travis and comprising *She's So Square*, *Dance Band*, *Heatwave 2* and *Science Friction*, was broadcast.

Their second single *Statue Of Liberty* released in January confirmed that their high-octane organ-driven pop was totally different to that of their contemporaries. A fact underscored by their debut album *White Music*, which was critically acclaimed. Aside from a cover version of Bob Dylan's *All Along The Watchtower* it contained well-crafted and often hyperactive material typified by songs like *Statue Of Liberty*, *Spinning Top*, *Radios In Motion* and *This Is Pop?*. The subsequent CD release of this contained seven additional tracks, including the three from their *3-D EP* and *Traffic Light Rock*. A live version of this last-mentioned song had appeared on a freebie disc with 'Record Mirror' in December 1977. The disc also featured material from Tangerine Dream, **The Motors** and U-Roy. Early copies of the *White Music* album had the title printed in white on a white background. They came in a standard Virgin black inner bag. The album, which had only taken a week to record, was critically acclaimed and gave them their first chart success. It spent four weeks in the chart, peaking at No. 38.

A second Dave Lee Travis session comprising *Statue Of Liberty*, *Radios In Motion*, *This Is Pop?* and *Into The Atom Age* (which are all on *White Music*) was broadcast on 7th February 1978.

The group embarked on a European tour supported by Talking Heads. Virgin, meanwhile, released *This Is Pop?* as a further 45 from the band.

They returned to Abbey Road studios in August to work on a second album *Go 2*, which was released two months later. The first 15,000 copies also contained a bonus five track 12" EP featuring dub remixes as well as a two-sided gatefold insert with a map of Swindon. The material on the album, mostly penned by Partridge, ranged from jerky to menacing and again confirmed their own unique style. Again the album sold well, peaking at No. 2, although only spending three weeks in the charts. Overseas pressings of the album didn't contain the bonus 12" EP. Instead, they contained an extra cut *Are You Receiving Me?*, which wasn't included on the U.K. pressings. When the album was subsequently issued on CD in Britain in 1987 *Are You Receiving Me?* was included as well as the bonus EP. The song was also selected for the next 45 release in late October 1978.

The following month, on 23rd November 1978, **XTC**'s third and final Peel session was broadcast. It featured four tracks *Mekanic Dancing*, *The Rhythm*, *New Town Animal In A Furnished Cage* and *Super Thief* (all on their *Go 2* album).

XTC toured the 'States to promote their new album, again with Talking Heads, for a ten-date programme. When they returned Barry Andrews announced that he was leaving the band. This is thought to be because of the inclusion of only two of his compositions on *Go 2*. He linked up with Robert Fripp to form The League Of Gentlemen and also recorded several singles for Virgin before finally settling in Shriekback. Back in Swindon Andy Partridge contacted his old mate Dave Gregory and asked him to join the band. The new line-up taped a session for Andy Peebles, which was broadcast a few days later. They also began work on a new single *Life Begins At The Hop*, which was the first written by their bassist Colin Moulding. It had a bizarre instrumental *Homo Safari* (the first in a series of six instrumentals) on the flip-side. The song's fast-paced sixties flavour brought them their first 45 hit, climbing to No. 54 and spending a total of four weeks in the charts. It also secured them an appearance on 'Top Of The Pops', which helped to bring them to the attention of a wider audience. The first 50,000 copies of the single, which was released in May 1979, came on clear vinyl inside a plastic printed sleeve with a gatefold insert.

After a short U.K. tour the band reconvened at the new Townhouse studios. This marks the beginning of their big drum sound as they worked on a new album. In July, they toured Australia, New Zealand and Japan extensively as their reputation grew.

Their third album, *Drums And Wires*, was released in August. The first 20,000 copies contained a free 7" single combining *Chain Of Command* with *Limelight* . There was also an insert containing the lyrics to all their albums so far. U.S. copies of the freebie 45 featured a third cut, *Day In Day Out*. The music on this album with tracks like *Making Plans For Nigel*, *Real By Real* and *Scissor Man* was more commercial but still intelligent. It spent seven weeks in the chart, peaking at No. 34. It subsequently climbed to No. 176 in the 'States.

Making Plans For Nigel, the **XTC** song that probably just about everyone who knows anything about music remembers, was released as a 45 at Virgin's instigation in September 1979. It was accompanied by two non-album tracks, *Bushman President (Homo Safari Series No. 2)* and *Pulsing, Pulsing*. The first 20,000 copies came in a game-board sleeve, which could be folded out, along with cardboard playing pieces. The immediate appeal of the song helped make the band a household name. It became their first Top 20 hit, spending a total of eleven weeks in the charts and climbing to No. 17. They also toured incessantly in this period and were a very popular live attraction.

An Andy Partridge composition *Wait Till Your Boat Goes Down* was selected as their next 45, along with a re-recorded version of *Ten Feet Tall* from *Drums And Wires* with Phil Weinman producing. This did not chart.

In February 1980, a solo album had been released by Andy Partridge, the mid-price *Take Away (The Lure Of Salvage)*. For this Patridge took the multi-track recordings of the previous two albums, reprocessed some of the songs electronically and re-built them with new effects and some new lyrics. Released under the name Mr. Partridge the album did not chart but was interesting.

Their next 45, released in August 1980, was a double 'A' side *Generals And Majors / Don't Lose Your Temper*. Early copies were also available as a double pack backed with two non-LP cuts, *Smokeless Zone* and *The Somnambulist*. This returned them to the charts, where it spent eight weeks peaking at No. 32.

They interrupted the European leg of a world tour to participate in a BBC recording session about the band. This was later broadcast as "XTC At The Manor" on BBC 2 in October 1980. In the broadcast a song called *Towers Of London* was heavily featured and this was rapidly released as a 45. It brought them another hit, climbing to No. 31 during a five week chart stay. Again, a double-pack version of this release was available, which in addition to a live recording of *Set Myself On Fire* on the flip, contained a bonus 7" including *Scissor Man* (from a John Peel session) and *Battery Brides*, another live cut.

Their fourth album *Black Sea*, released in September 1980, is generally thought to be one of their best. Its highlights included *Generals And Majors*, *Towers Of London*, *Respectable Street* and *Sgt. Rock (Is Going To Help Me)*. Certainly it was one of their most successful commercially and their first to reach the Top 20. It got to No. 6 in the U.K. during a seven week chart residency. It later rose to the No. 41 slot in the U.S..

The following month an interesting **XTC** rarity appeared. A 45 by The Colonels, which paired *Too Many Cooks In The Kitchen* with *I Need Protection*. This was made by Colin Moulding (the Colonel) and Terry Chambers. The band, meanwhile, contributed *Take This Town* to the soundtrack of the movie "Times Square", which also featured contributions from other U.K. punk and new wave bands. *Take This Town* was also released a 45, coupled with **The Ruts**' *Babylon's Burning*.

In January 1981, *Sgt. Rock (Is Going To Help Me)* was also issued as a single from *Black Sea*. This was another of their songs that people tend to remember. Initial pressings came with a fold-out poster sleeve. Additional interest was created through the inclusion of live versions of *Living Through Another Cuba* and *Generals And Majors* on the flip. This single again sold well, rising to No. 16 during a nine week U.K. chart stay to give them their highest placed hit to date.

1981 was a year of considerable touring which took the band as far afield as the United States and Venezuela, the Middle East, South-East Asia and Australia in the course of the year. They also performed for the last time in England at Cardiff on 2nd June. A final 45 *Respectable Street* was culled from the *Black Sea* album with two new songs, *Strange Tales, Strange Tails* and *Officer Blue*, on the flip. Released in March 1981, this did not chart.

At the end of 1981 they returned to the studio to work on a new album. *Senses Working Overtime* was released in January 1982 as a taster 45, with *Blame The Weather* and *Tissue Tigers* on the flip. Early copies came in a poster sleeve. The 'A' side has a Beatlesque chorus and some distinctive guitar work. Scaling the charts to No. 10 it became their only Top 10 hit and spent nine weeks in the charts. It was also their first, since

XTC - English Settlement.

1977, to appear in 12" format too. The double album *English Settlement* followed in February. It was more experimental than their previous efforts covering a range of different styles. The album, produced by Hugh Padgham was pruned in several foreign countries and only released as a single album initially. This was soon rectified as several good tracks got omitted, consequently these abridged foreign versions of the album are quite collectable. It was also their best-selling album, climbing to No. 5 and spending eleven weeks in the charts. It subsequently reached No. 48 in the U.S.A. in May.

Ball And Chain was the next album cut selected for 45 release. There was also a 12" edition which included an additional cut - a remix of *Down In The Cockpit* (from the album) titled *Cockpit Dance Mixture*. It spent four weeks in the charts peaking at No. 58.

During a 1982 World Tour Andy Partridge collapsed on stage in Paris on 18th March from exhaustion. In April, he collapsed again on the U.S. leg of the tour. The tour had to be cancelled and what amounted to a nervous breakdown for Partridge cast considerable doubt over the future of the group. This doubt increased when Terry Chambers, who was not enamoured with the group's material and restless at the prospect of little live work, decided to emigrate to Australia. Their latest 45, *No Thugs In Our House* (taken from *English Settlement*), released in May 1982, also failed to sell in significant quantities.

It seems Virgin expected the group to fold because they released a singles collection in November titled *Waxworks*. This included all their 'A' sides (except for *Respectable Street*) and was accompanied by a free album of their 'B' sides (*Beeswax*), which was sold separately. (This included a different version of *Heaven Is Paved With Broken Glass*). The compilation spent three weeks in the charts, peaking at No. 54.

It is a measure of their resilience that **XTC** did survive. Ex-Glitter band drummer Peter Phipps, who knew Dave Gregory, filled in on recordings for their next album. Initially Virgin were reluctant to release it feeling that it lacked an outstanding track. When Andy Partridge wrote a new song called *Great Fire* they agreed. Backed by *Gold* it was issued in April 1983. There was also a 12" version with two additional tracks, *Frost Circus* and *Procession Towards Learning Land*, which were part of the "Homo Safari" instrumental series. However, the single failed to chart, as did the next effort *Wonderland*, backed by *Jump*, which was issued in July 1983. Initially this 45 was released as a limited edition picture disc which is now quite collectable.

Great Fire and *Wonderland* were both included on *Murmur*, which Virgin eventually released in August 1983. When it was later issued on CD in 1987 a number of additional tracks, mostly 'B' sides from the last few releases were added. The album was varied but not particularly commercial. It climbed to No. 51 during a four week chart residency. A further cut, Partridge's rustic *Love On A Farmboy's Wages* was culled from *Murmur* and released in September. Initial copies appeared as a double-pack with two extra cuts, *Desert Island* and *Toys*. There was also a 12" variation with three songs on the flip - *Burning With Optimism's Flames*, *English Roundabout* and *Cut It Out* (a different version of their earlier *Scissor Man* - which had been taped in May 1981 at London's Hammersmith Odeon). This fared better than their most recent efforts. It returned the band to the charts, climbing to No. 50 during a four week chart stay.

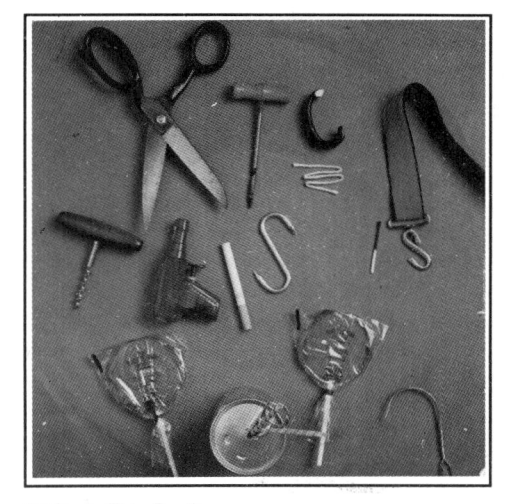

XTC - Is This Pop?

XTC - Waxworks.

XTC concluded the year with a Christmas song *Thanks For Christmas/ Countdown To Christmas Partytime* (Virgin VS 642) recorded under a pseudonym, The Three Wise Men. Very few copies got as far as the shops and it was quickly deleted. It's therefore quite collectable but not an expensive item yet.

In 1984, they started working on a new album. As a taster, a new 45 *All You Pretty Girls* was released in September in a limited edition die-cut sleeve. It contained an appealing chorus and had obvious commercial appeal. It gave them another minor U.K. hit, climbing to No. 55 and spending five weeks in the chart. The 12" version contained an additional cut *Red Brick Dream*.

The next album *The Big Express* followed in October. dealing with disgruntled songs about life in the big city or glorifying the alternative on *The Everyday Stuff Of A Small Town* it leaned musically in a sort of blues-pop direction. It only enjoyed a two week chart tenure, but it did reach No. 38, which was higher than their two previous albums. It also spawned a second 45 *This World Over* backed with *Blue Overall*, a non-album cut although it did figure on the later CD issue of the album in 1987. A 12" version has an extended rendition of the 'A' side but neither charted.

Now desperate for another hit Virgin issued *Wake Up* from the album. On the flip side were *Take This Town* and *Mantis On Parole (Homo Safari Series No. 2)*. As an additional marketing ploy the 12" version included three of their earlier hits *Making Plans For Nigel*, *Sgt. Rock* and *Senses Working Overtime*. However, the single didn't sell well enough to make the charts.

Most of you will know that the Dukes Of Stratosphear recordings were made by **XTC** under a pseudonym. Andy Partridge had always wanted to make a psychedelic recording and their mini-album *25 O'Clock* (Virgin WOW1) 1985 was a superb slice of sixties pop psychedelia. For a piece of self-indulgence this was incredibly good. Stand out tracks like *My Love Explodes* and *The Mole From The Ministry* are full of flower-pop vocals, fuzztone guitar and swirling keyboards and sound straight out of 1967. They were also issued on a Virgin 45. Their album *Psonic Psunspot* (Virgin V 2440) 1987 was also a sixties style pop effort with some psychedelic influences. It's fairly lightweight though and not nearly as good as the mini-album. The first 5,000 copies of *Psonic Psunspot* (VP 2440) came on multi-coloured vinyl. A 45 *You're A Good Man Albert Brown/Vanishing Girl* (Virgin VS 982) 1987 was taken from the album. There was also a 12" version (VS 98212) which included both their 45s. If you want the Duke Of Stratosphear recordings on CD then you need *Chips From The Chocolate Fireball* (Virgin COMCD 11) 1989, which included *25 O'Clock* and *Psonic Psunspot*, as well as an inner booklet. After *Psonic Psunspot* the Dukes Of Stratosphear became defunct - Andy and his colleagues felt they had taken the project as far as they could.

In 1986, **XTC** worked with Todd Rungren on a new album *Skylarking*. This exuded a definite sixties pop influence too. A 45, *Grass* was released in August in both 7" and 12" format and the album followed in October. Initial copies came in an embossed sleeve and inner bag. Here we must leave **XTC** but they continued on beyond the time frame of this book.

Inevitably given the length of time they have been around **XTC** have appeared on a number of compilations:- *Hope And Anchor Frontline Festival* (dbl) (WEA K 66077) 1978, which was issued on blue vinyl included live versions of *I'm Bugged* and *Science Friction*; *Guillotine* (Virgin VCL 5001) 1978, which was a 10" release with a poster, included a studio version of *Traffic Light Rock*; *DOA - Dead On Arrival* (Virgin VD 2508) 1978, issued on luminous vinyl with a poster insert, featured *Radios In Motion*; *Cash Cows* (Virgin MILK 1) included *Respectable Street*, a live version of which can also be heard on the double album *Urrgh! A Music War* (A&M AMLX 64692) 1981; *Machines* (Virgin V 2177) 1980 included *The Somnambulist*; you'll also find *Life In The European Theatre* (WEA K 58412) 1982 and *She's Having A Baby* (IRS 6211) 1988 included a remixed version of *Happy Families*. There's also the compilation *Half Pounder*, available to 'Record Mirror' readers, which included *Radios In Motion*. More recently, *Are You Receiving Me?* resurfaced on *A Post Punk Primer* (Virgin CDOVD 498) 1997; *Generals And Majors* got a further airing on *Teenage Kicks* (PolyGram TV 525382) 1995 and *Dear God* featured on *Wave (The Biggest New Wave Hits)* (3-CD set) (Disky HR 868442) 1996.

There are also a number of compilations to interest the collector:- *The Compact XTC - The Singles 1978 - 1985* (CD); *Fossil Fuel (XTC Singles Collection 1977-1992)* (CD), *Explode Together (The Dub Experiments 1978 - 1980)* (CD), which included Andy Partridge's solo album *Take Away (The Lure Of Salvage)* and **XTC**'s experimental *Go+* EP and *Rag And Bone Buffet*, which consisted of rarities and outtakes. The material on this is very diverse ranging from ambient (*Over Rusty Water*), wild rock (*Strange Tales, Strange Tails*), songs with interesting chord changes (*Ten Feet Tall*) and *The World Is Full Of Angry Young Men* veered towards soul. Collectors may also want to track down a various artists tribute album to **XTC** called *A Testimonial Dinner*.

Live In Concert 1980 is assembled from a set taped in December 1980 for BBC Radio's 'In Concert' series. It concentrates on the punk-popper's liveliest early material featuring songs like *This Is Pop, Generals And Majors, Life Begins At The Hop, Making Plans For Nigel* and *Towers Of London*.

Transistor Blast is a 4-CD set, budget-priced and cheaply-packaged which generally concentrates on their earlier material. There are two CDs of BBC studio sessions covering the years between 1977 and 1989. A lot of this material had been released previously, but it's still good to see them in this extended format. The material on the third CD was taped at two 'BBC Radio One In Concert' shows during 1978/79 and the fourth documents a hot gig at the Hammersmith Palais on 22nd December 1980 with Andy Partridge championing a dose of the 'flu to turn in a fine performance.

Science Friction, arguably one of their finest, can also be heard on *1-2-3-4 - A History Of Punk And New Wave 1976 - 1979* (MCA/Universal MCD 60066), a 5-CD box set released in 1999.

XTC travelled a long way in their long distinguished career from their punk/new wave beginnings. They've produced a handful of classic pop singles, experimented with psychedelia as The Dukes Of Stratosphear and have undoubtedly been one of the most innovative and durable acts to emerge from the punk/new wave era.

Xtract

Personnel:	KARL	gtr	A
	KIP	drms	A
	ROD	bs	A
	HARVEY WARRANT	vcls	A

EP:	1(A)	BLAME IT ON THE YOUTH (Blame It On The Youth/ War Heroes/ Iron Lady (Boys In Blue) (PS)	(Pax PAX 10) 1983

In addition to this EP this Lancashire band contributed tracks to various compilations including *Punk's Dead - Nah Mate The Smell Is Jus Summink In Yer Underpants* (12") (Pax PAX 7) 1982, *Bollox To The Gonads Here's The Testicles* (Pax PAX 14) 1983 and *Religious As Hell* (Rot HELL 036) 1986. More recently they contributed *Aftermath, Blame It On The Youth* and *War Heroes* to *Pax Records Punk Collection* (Anagram CDPUNK 75) 1996.

THE YACHTS - The Yachts.

The Yachts

Personnel:	BOB BELLIS	drms	ABCD
	J.J. CAMPBELL	vcls	A
	MARTIN DEMPSEY	bs	AB
	HENRY PRIESTMAN	vcls, keyb'ds	ABCD
	MARTIN J. WATSON	gtr, vcls	ABCD
	MICK SHINER	bs	C
	GLYN HAVARD	bs	D

ALBUMS:	1(B)	THE YACHTS	(Radar RAD 19) 1979
	2(C)	WITHOUT RADAR	(Radar RAD 27) 1980

NB: (1) came with a live 7" *Suffice To Say/On And On* (PS) (Sam 98).

45s:	Suffice To Say/ Freedom Is A Heavy Wine (PS)	(Stiff BUY 19) 1977
*	Look Back In Love (Not In Anger)/ I Can't Stay Long (PS)	(Radar ADA 23) 1978
	Yachting Type/Hypnotising Lies (PS)	(Radar ADA 25) 1978
+	Love You, Love You/Crazy People (PS)	(Radar ADA 36) 1979
	Box Zoz/Permanent Damage (live) (PS)	(Radar ADA 42) 1979
	Now I'm Spoken For/Secret Agent (PS)	(Radar ADA 49) 1979
	There's A Ghost In My House/Revelry/ The Yachting Type (PS)	(Radar ADA 52) 1980
	IOU/24 Hours From Tulsa (PS)	(Radar ADA 57) 1980
	A Fool Like You/Dubmarine (PS)	(Demon D 1005) 1981

NB: * Issued on blue vinyl. + Issued on orange vinyl.

XTC - Beeswax.

The Yachts formed in Liverpool in April 1977. The five art students were originally known as Albert Dock and The Codfish Warriors. They gigged locally and eventually caught the eye playing a support slot for **Elvis Costello** at Eric's. This led to a one-off 45 deal on Eric's Stiff label. The resulting single, the snappy *Suffice To Say* appeared in September 1977. They also played as **Chuddy Nuddies** in this era (see entry for details).

The Stiff single helped raise their profile and they played some of the London venues. However, before the year was out, they switched to the new Radar label, whose roster also included **Elvis Costello** and **Nick Lowe**. They also became a quartet with Campbell leaving and Priestman becoming their vocalist and frontman. Radar released a string of singles by **The Yachts**, which were mostly favourably received, but none of them sold well enough to chart. Arguably their 45 for Stiff was their best. One of their later efforts for Radar was a cover of R. Dean Taylor's *There's A Ghost In The House*. Lyrically, much of their material was in the usual boy/girl realm but with humour. Musically, they ranged from sixties influenced rock with cheesy organ to fast-paced punk-cum-power-pop.

The Yachts recorded two sessions for John Peel. The first, broadcast on 24th October 1978, comprised *Mantovani's Hits*, *Yachting Types*, *Look Back In Love* and *Then And Now*. The latter also figured in their second session, which went out on 2nd July 1979, along with *Love You Love You*, *In A Second* and *March Of The Moderaters*.

They recorded their first album, produced by Richard Gottleib, whilst on a U.S. tour. In January 1980, Dempsey departed to **Pink Military** with Mick Shiner replacing him on bass. This new line-up ('C') recorded a second album *Without Radar*, which they promoted on a European tour as support to The Who. By now Radar was in dire straits financially, which hindered their promotional activities. When the label collapsed they switched to the new Demon label for a final 45. By now Havard had replaced Shiner on bass. Havard was previously with **The Edge**. After they split in late 1981 Priestman joined It's Immaterial (who also included Campbell and Dempsey) but he went on to greater fame with The Christians in 1987.

Suffice To Say later resurfaced on the 5-CD box set *1-2-3-4 - A History Of Punk And New Wave 1976 - 1979* (MCA/Universal MCD 60066) in 1999.

The Yobs

Personnel:	JACK BLACK	drms	A B
	MATT DANGERFIELD	bs	A B
	JOHN PLAIN	gtr	A B
	KID REID	vcls, gtr	A B
	CASINO STEEL	keyb'ds	A
	RUDI	keyb'ds	B

ALBUM: 1( ) CHRISTMAS ALBUM (Safari RUDE 1) 1980

NB: (1) later reissued (Great Expectations PIPLP 006) 1990, also on CD (PIPCD 006) and later on CD (Captain Oi! AHOYCD 157) 2000, with their Christmas singles as bonus tracks. There's also *Christmas, Vol. 2* (Receiver RRLP 153) 1991, also on CD (Receiver RRCD 153) 1991.

THE YOBS - Christmas Album.

45s:	Run Rudolph Run/The Worm Song (PS)	(NMS NES 114) 1977
	Silent Night/Stille Nacht (PS)	(Yob YOB 79) 1978
	Rub-A-Dum-Dum/Another Christmas (PS)	(Safari YULE 1) 1981
	Yobs On 45/ The Ballad Of Warrington (PS)	(Fresh FRESH 41) 1982

The Yobs were **The Boys**' alter ego. See **The Boys** entry for more details of the personnel involved. **The Yobs** released tongue-in-cheek singles at Christmas-time. They began in 1977 with a cover of Chuck Berry's *Run Rudolph Run*, in a sleeve that pictured Nazi Rudolph Hess. On the flip side was the amusing *Worm Song*. They followed this in 1978 with a bizarre rendition of *Silent Night*. In 1979, Safari released an entire album of **Yobs**' material. Among the tracks featured were their punkish interpretations of *Jingle Bells*, *Auld Lang Syne*, *12 Days Of Christmas*, *White Christmas*, *We Wish You A Merry Christmas* and *May The God Lord Bless And Keep You*. This is mostly pretty good fun.

Their take on *Silent Night* appears as a bonus cut on the 1999 Captain Oi! CD reissue of **The Boys**' *Alternative Chartbusters* album.

The Young Bucks

Personnel:	STEVE BROOKES	bs	A
	ARCHIE BROWN	vcls	A
	PAT RAFFERTY	organ	A
	TONY WADSWORTH	gtr	A
	TOM WILDER	drms	A

45: Get Your Feet Back On The Ground/ Cold, Cold Morning (PS) (Blueport BLU 1) 1977

A Newcastle band whose 45 had plenty of keyboards and drums and some enterprising sax on the flip side. There's room for improvement in the vocals, but otherwise a promising effort. They often played as a support band to **Penetration** up in Newcastle. Their London debut was at the Hope and Anchor but they failed to break through on the London scene.

YOUNG MARBLE GIANTS - Colossal Youth.

Young Marble Giants

Personnel:	PHILIP MOXHAM	bs	A
	STUART MOXHAM	gtr, keyb'ds	A
	ALISON STATTON	vcls	A

ALBUM: 1(A) COLOSSAL YOUTH (Rough Trade ROUGH 8) 1980

NB: (1) also issued on CD (Rough Trade ROUGH LCD 8) 1990 and again (Les Disques Du Crepuscule TW1 984-2) 1994. Also relevant is *Salad Days* (Vinyl Japan ASKCD 113) 2000.

EPs: 1(A) FINAL DAY (Final Day/Radio Silents/Cakewalking/ (Uncredited 4th Track) (PS) (Rough Trade RT 043) 1980

2(A)	TESTCARD (Click Talk/Zebra Tracks/Sporting Life/ This Way/Posed By Models/ The Clock) (PS)		(Rough Trade RT 059) 1981

Hailing from Cardiff, the Moxham brothers and singer Alison Stratton produced an album *Colossal Youth* whose air of calm and serenity is usually cited as evidence that Rough trade's product wasn't confined to simply aggressive guitar-led acts. With Stratton's gentle vocals and a soft accompaniment of bass, organ and beat box with few overdubs they were able to create an enchanting minimalistic sort of music which will appeal to some.

There are some nonsensical lyrics and infectious tunes on cuts like *Choci Loni* and *Salad Days*. The 1990 mid-price CD issue of the album by Rough Trade also added the six tracks from their 1981 EP *Testcard*, whilst the CD reissue of the album on Les Disques Du Crepuscule includes as bonus tracks their *Final Day* EP and an obscure cut *Ode To Booker T*, which had previously only figured on the *Is The War Over* compilation.

Final Day resurfaced on the 4-CD box set *25 Years Of Rough Trade Shops* (Mute CDSTUMM 191) in 2001.

Stratton later formed Weekend, who went on to record a number of albums. Stuart Moxham went on to record an album as **Gist**, with some assistance from his brother Philip.

The Young Ones

Personnel incl:	MARTIN BROAD	drms	A
	RICHARD BULL	gtr	A
	JOHN HOLLIDAY	bs	A
	PAUL LEWIS	vcls	A

45:	Rock 'n' Roll Radio/Little Bit Of Loving	(Virgin VS 205) 1978

A raw but promising band who emerged on the London club and pub circuit during 1978. They played easy-listening pop-punk. Their sounds were enjoyable but lacked punch. They toured the U.K. with **The Boomtown Rats** and later became **The Reputations**, a mod revival combo.

The Zeros

Personnel:	STEVE COTTON	bs	A
	PHIL GAYLOR	drms	A
	STEVE GODFREY	gtr	A

45:	Hungry/Radio Fun	(Small Wonder SMALL 2) 1977

Like many other groups in the punk era **The Zeros** made their vinyl debut on Walthamstowe's Small Wonder label in November 1977. The same month they recorded a session for John Peel, which was broadcast on 30th November 1977. This featured *Nice Girls*, *Hungry*, *Solid State* and *Easy Way Out*, three of which don't appear to have made it onto vinyl.

Hungry originally appeared on *Streets* (Beggars Banquet BEGA 1) 1997 and later resurfaced on *Small Wonder Punk Singles Collection, Vol. 1* (Anagram CDPUNK 29) 1994 and *Vol. 2* (Anagram CDPUNK 70) 1996 included *Radio Fun*.

The Zeros

45:	What's Wrong With A Pop Group/ (track by Action Replay)	(Rok ROK XV/XVI) 1979

This is a different band to the one which recorded on Small Wonder in 1977. The Rok 45 is more mod than punk influenced. It was later included as a bonus cut on *Odd Bods Mods And Sods* (Captain Mod MODSKA CD 2), a reissue of an earlier Rok compilation.

Zero Zero

45:	Chinese Boys/ Coupe De Ville Dawn (PS)	(Interference INT 001) 1979

This D.I.Y. 45 was available through Small Wonder, Step Forward and Rough Trade.

The Zones

Personnel:	WILLY GARDNER	vcls, gtr	A
	KENNY HYSLOP	drms	A
	BILLY McISAAC	vcls, keyb'ds	A
	RUSSELL WEBB	bs	A

ALBUM:	1(A)	UNDER INFLUENCE	(Arista SMART 1095) 1979

NB: (1) This album appeared in four different covers.

45s:	Stuck With You/No Angels (PS)	(Zoom ZUM 4) 1978
	Sign Of The Times/Away From It All	(Arista ARIST 205) 1978
	Looking To The Future/ Do It All Again (PS)	(Arista ARIST 265) 1979
	Mourning Star/Under Influence (PS)	(Arista ARIST 286) 1979

The Zones were one of the very few punk era acts who evolved out of a successful pre-punk era band. The act in question was Slik, who enjoyed a U.K. No. 1 in January 1976 with *Forever And Ever* and a No. 24 with *Requiem* in May 1976. Both records had spent nine weeks in the charts. With the onset of punk Slik refocused their glam-pop style and changed name to **PVC 2**. Under this moniker, the Glasgow-based outfit recorded a 45 for the new Edinburgh indie label Zoom. The disc in question was *Put You In The Picture*. The name change can't have helped the band get wider exposure and the single failed to put **PVC 2** in the picture. Once this became apparent **PVC 2**'s lead vocalist and guitarist quit. **Midge Ure** had headed for London to team up with former **Sex Pistols** guitarist Glen Matlock in his new band **The Rich Kids**. The three remaining members - Hyslop, McIsaac and Webb - recruited ex-Hot Valves vocalist Willie Gardner and made the full transition to punk, renaming themselves as **The Zones**.

The Zones first disc was a Russell Webb composition *Stuck With You*. It came out on Zoom and they toured as a support act to **The Clash** to help promote it. A few months later the Zoom label was sold to Arista and with good song-writing skills and the clout of a major label behind them a breakthrough was on the cards.

The Zones toured incessantly during 1978. They also recorded two sessions for John Peel. The first, *Sign Of The Times*, *Away From It All*, *No Sense Of Humour* and *Tough At The Bottom* was broadcast on 23rd May. A second; comprising *It's Only Fashion*, *The End*, *Anything Goes* and *Deadly Dolls* followed on 22nd September.

THE ZONES - Under Influence.

Sign Of The Times, their second 45, was produced by Graeme Douglas with grandiose Spectorian noises and synthesized guitar solos.

Looking To The Future is a slow sub-reggae tune.

They played a variety of material on an album *Under Influence*, which was consistent in the sense of having no weak cuts but nothing stood out either. Despite the promotional weight of Arista, none of their three 45s sold well enough to chart.

By November 1979, **The Zones** had become disillusioned and split. Russell Webb joined **The Skids** and a little over a year later Kenny Hyslop teamed up with him there too. Hyslop went on to play with **Simple Minds** for a while too.

Zorro

Personnel incl: DAVE SMITH vcls

EP: 1 'ARRODS DON'T SELL 'EM ('Arrods Don't Sell 'Em/Soldier Boy/ Starlight) (some PS) (Bridgehouse BHEP 1) 1979

An East Anglian band. *Soldier Boy* was a **Bethnal** song. At their live gigs they played almost exclusively non-originals.

THE ZSOUNDS - The Curse Of Zsounds.

The Zsounds

Personnel: STEVE LAKE vcls, bs A
JOSEF PORTAR drms A
LAURENCE WOOD gtr A

ALBUM: 1(A) THE CURSE OF ZSOUNDS (Rough Trade ROUGH 31) 1981

NB: (1) Also issued on CD (Rugger Bugger GAP 014/SEEP 006) 1994 and as a double album (Lazy Dog SEEP 006) 1995 on import from Greece.

EP: 1(A) LA VACHE QUI RIT (Not So Brace NSB 001) 1982
NB: (1) This came with a poster.

45s: * Can't Cheat Karma/War/Subvert (PS) (Crass 4219844/3) 1981
Demystification/
Great White Hunter (PS) (Rough Trade RT 069) 1981
Dancing/True Love (PS) (Rough Trade RT 094) 1982
More Trouble Coming Every Day/
Knife (PS) (Rough Trade RT 098) 1982
+ Menáge (12.59) (Recommended RR 14.15) 198?

NB: * This was issued in a gatefold picture sleeve with a poster. + This was a one-sided disc in a fold-out sleeve inside a PVC sleeve.

The Zsounds came from Oxford and played above average pop-punk, with some appealing hooks. They are probably best remembered for their fine Crass label 45 *Subvert*:-

"If you get a job
You can be an agent
You can work for revolution
In your place of employment"
(from *Subvert*)

The lyrics were sung to an accompanying descending riff built around a fast-paced major/minor chord sequence and some jangling guitar.

Their album was a minor anarcho-punk classic with lyrics dealing with the usual preoccupations of government, war and oppression. The music ranges from synth-pop to post-punk rantings and is recommended listening. The CD reissue on Rugger Bugger in 1994 is augmented by their five singles and a glossy eighteen-page booklet. The double album release was available on Greek import. One disc was a straightforward reissue of their 1981 Rough Trade album. The second disc featured their five singles.

They also contributed a cut *This Land* to *Holidays In The Sun, Vol. 2* (Anagram HITS 02) 1999.

PLAY DEAD - The First Flower.

CONFLICT - Increase The Pressure.

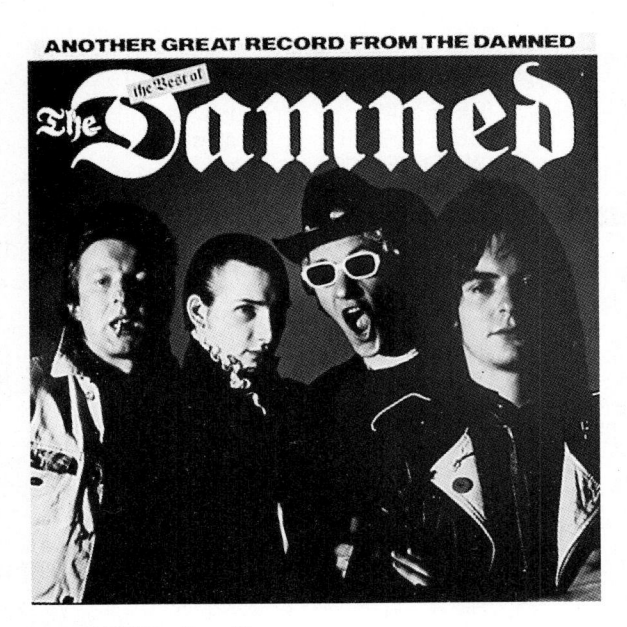

THE DAMNED - Best Of.

THE DAMNED - Captains Birthday Party.

BAUHAUS - She's In Parties.

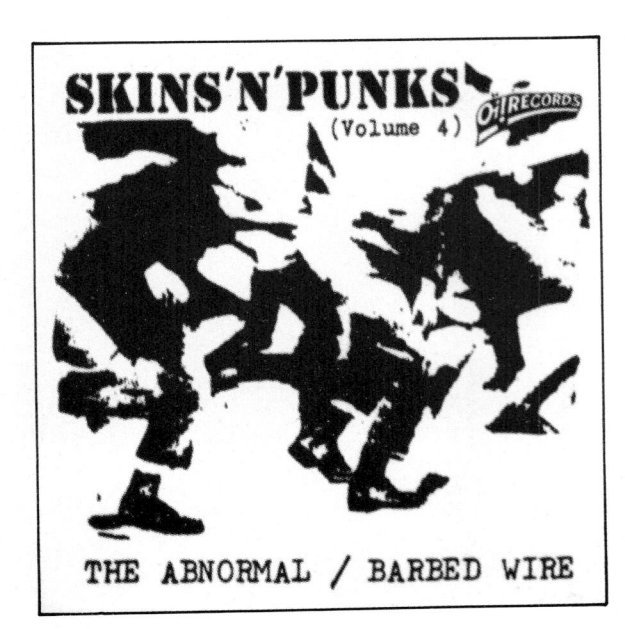

THE OUTPATIENTS - New Japanese Hairstyles.

SKINS 'N' PUNKS VOL. 4.

EATER - Get Your Yo-Yo's Out.

A SELECTION OF VINYL COMPILATIONS

NB: Artists in bold appear as entries in this book.

AVON CALLING.

Absurd Take Away (Absurd TAKE 1) 1980

Angels With Dirty Faces (No Future MPUNK 8) 1983

Avon Calling: The Bristol Compilation
(Heartbeat HB 1) 1979
SIDE ONE: **Glaxo Babies** - *It's Irrational*; **Europeans** - *On The Continent*; **Private Dicks** - *Green Is In The Red*; **Moskow** - *Too Much Commotion*; **Essential Bop** - *Chronicle*; **Directors** - *What You've Got*; Various Artists - *Own Up*. SIDE TWO: **Sneak Preview** - *Slugweird*; **Stingrays** - *Sound*; **X-Certs** - *Anthem*; **Apartment** - *The Alternative*; **Numbers** - *Cross-Slide*; **Vice Squad** - *Nothing*; **Stereo Models** - *Move Fast - Stay Ahead*; **Double Vision** - *My Dead Mother*.

Aylesbury Goes Flacid (Flaccid FLAC 1) 1978
SIDE ONE: **Vice Creems** - *No Passion*; Speedos - *She's A Shocker*; Man Ezeke - *Brixton Reggae Rock*; Peter Out and The Faders - *Need You (Oh Yeah)*; Robins - *Stuck On You*; Haircuts - *Do You Remember L-L-Longwick*; **Wild Willy Barrett** - *Nigel Pringle*; SIDE TWO: Clumsy - *Help Yourself*; Anal Surgeons - *Wide Boy*; Smiffy - *Ain't It Good To Be Alive*; Abbott - *Roll Me Up*; Ken Liversausage - *Gooseberry Puss*; **Robert and The Remoulds** - *L.A.G.O.C.O.*; Redwood - *Just Another Weakend*.

Back On The Streets (EP) (Secret SHH 138) 1982
SIDE ONE: **Venom** - *Where's Dock Green?*; **Victim** - *The Strike*. SIDE TWO: **East End Badoes** - *The Way It's Got To Be*; **Skin Disease** - *I'm Thick*; **Angela Rippon's Bum** - *Fight For Your Lives*.

Banquet Of Steel (Aardvark STEAL 2) 1980

Battle Of The Bands (2x7") (Good Vibrations GOT 7) 1978
DISC ONE: **Outcasts** - *The Cops Are Comin'*; **Rudi** - *Overcome By Fumes*. DISC TWO: **Idiots** - *Parents*; **Spider** - *Dancin' In The Street*.

Belfast (Shock Rock SLR 007) 1980
SIDE ONE: **Stage B** - *Recall To Life*; **Strike** - *Radio Songs*; **Ex-Producers** - *The System Is Here*; **Ezy Meat** - *Sexy Lady*; **Reflex Action** - *Spies*. SIDE TWO: **Strike** - *Running Past*; **Reflex Action** - *Recession*; **Stage B** - *Light On The Hillside*; **Ezy Meat** - *Soho Escapade*; **Ex-Producers** - *Behind The Door*.

Belfast Rocks (Rip Off ROLP 1) 1978

Be Stiff (Tour '78 Official Release) (Stiff ODD 2) 1978

Be Stiff Route '78 (Stiff DEAL 1) 1978

Best Of Rot - End Of An Era (2-LP) 198?

Beyond The Groove (Polydor) 1980

Bollocks To Christmas (EP) (Secret SHH 126) 1981
SIDE ONE: **Business** - *Step Into Christmas*; **Gonads** - *(I'm Dreaming Of A) White Christmas*; SIDE TWO: **4-Skins** - *Merry Christmas Everybody*; Max Splodge - *The 12 Days Of Christmas*.

Bollox To The Gonads Here's The Testicles
(Pax PAX 14) 1983
SIDE ONE: **Mau Maus** - *Just Another Day*; Savage Circle - *Don't Do It*; Legion Of Parasites - *Dying World*; **Anti-System** - *Schoolboy*; P.S.A. - *Yankee*; **Xtract** - *Waiting For The Genocide*; Crude SS - *Ingenskola*; Repulsive Alien - *Say And Do*; **Riot Squad** - *Police Power*; Savage Circle - *We Don't Have To*; Subversion - *God's A Fairytale*; **Skeptix** - *Traitor*; P.S.A. - *Nuclear Peace*; **Mau Maus** - *Running With The Pack*; Instigators - *Monkey Man*.

Britannia Waives The Rules (Secret SHH 136-12) 198?
SIDE ONE: **Exploited** - *Y.O.P.* SIDE TWO: **Chron Gen** - *Clouded Eyes*; **Infa-Riot** - *Feel The Race*.

Business Unusual (Cherry Red ARED 2) 1979
SIDE ONE: **UK Subs** - *CID*; **Leyton Buzzards** - *19 And Mad*; **Outcasts** - *Just Another Teenage Rebel*; **Dave Goodman and Friends** - *Justifiable Homicide*; **Outsiders** - *Consequences*; **Record Players** - *MOR*; **Vice Creems** - *01-01-212*; Dole - *New Wave Love*. SIDE TWO: Tights - *China's Eternal*; **Skunks** - *Good From The Bad*; **Thomas Leer** - *Private Plane*; **Robert Rental** - *ACC*; **Throbbing Gristle** - *United*; **Cabaret Voltaire** - *Do The Mussolini (Headkick)*.

A Bunch Of Stiff Records (Stiff SEEZ 2) 1977

BRITTANIA WAIVES THE RULES.

CAN'T START DANCIN'.

Can't Start Dancin' (Stiff/Sounds 3) 1978
SIDE ONE: **Ian Dury and The Blockheads** - *Sex Drugs And Rock & Roll*; **Ian Dury and The Blockheads** - *Razzle In My Pocket*; Mickey Jupp - *Making Friends*; Mickey Jupp - *You Made A Fool Out Of Me*; Jona Lewie - *Denny Laine's Valet*; Jona Lewie - *I'll Get By In Pittsburgh*; **Wreckless Eric** - *Semaphore Signals*. SIDE TWO: **Wreckless Eric** - *I Wish It Would Rain*; Rachel Sweet - *I'll Watch The News*; Rachel Sweet - *Cuckoo Clock*; **Lene Lovich** - *Monkey Talk*; Lene Lovich - *Momentary Breakdown*; The Rumour - *All Fall Down*; The Rumour - *Loving You Is Far Too Easy*.

CARRY ON Oi!

Carry On Oi! (Secret SEC 2) 1981
SIDE ONE: Garry Johnson - *United*; J.J. All Stars - *Dambusters March*; **Business** - *Suburban Rebels*; **Infa-Riot** - *Each Dawn I Die*; **The Partisans** - *Arms Race*; **Ejected** - *East End Kids*; **Peter and The Test Tube Babies** - *Transvestite*; **Blitz** - *Nation On Fire*; **Last Resort** - *King On The Jungle*. SIDE TWO: **Gonads** - *Tuckers Ruckers Ain't No Suckers*; **4 Skins** - *Evil*; **The Business** - *Product*; **Red Alert** - *SPG*; Oi! The Comrade? - *Guvnors Man*; **Peter and The Test Tube Babies** - *Maniac*; **Ejected** - *What Am I Gonna Do?*; **Partisans** - *No U Turns*; **Blitz** - *Youth*; Oi! The Choir - *Walk On*.

NB: Reissued on vinyl (Step-1 STEPLP 018) 1998 and on CD (Step-1 STEPCD 018) 1998. Also issued on CD with one bonus track **Red Alert** - *We've Got The Power* (Captain Oi! AHOY CD 119) 1999 and again on vinyl (Get Back GET 42) 1999.

Cash Cows (Virgin MILK 1) 1980
SIDE ONE: **XTC** - *Respectable Street*; **Human League** - *The Black Hit Of Space*; Mike Oldfield - *Sheba*; **Japan** - *Ain't That Peculiar*; **Ruts** - *West One (Shine On Me)*; **Skids** - *Arena*. SIDE TWO: **Professionals** - *Kick Down The Doors*; **Flying Lizards** - *Hands 2 Take*; **Fingerprintz** - *Yes Eyes*; Captain Beefheart and The Magic Band - *Dirty Blue Gene*; Gillan - *Are You Sure*; Kevin Coyne - *Taking On The World*; **Public Image Ltd.** - *Attack*.

The Class Of '81 (Upper Class CHIN 1) 1981

A Country Fit For Heroes, Vol. 1 (12") (No Future Oi! 3) 1982

A Country Fit For Heroes, Vol. 2 (No Future Oi! 23) 1983
NB: *Vol. 1* and *Vol. 2* reissued on CD (Captain Oi! AHOY CD 15) 1994. See CD section for track listing.

The Crap Stops Here (Rabid/Absurd LAST 1) 1980
SIDE ONE: **Slaughter and The Dogs** - *Cranked Up Really High*; **Slaughter and The Dogs** - *The Bitch*; **Nosebleeds** - *Ain't Bin To No Music School*; **John Cooper Clarke** - *Psycle Sluts Part 1 & 2*; **John Cooper Clarke** - *Bronze Adonis*; **Gyro** - *Central Detention Centre*; **Gyro** - *Purple And Red*; SIDE TWO: **Jilted John** - *Jilted John*; **Out** - *Who Is Innocent?*; **Out** - *Linda's Just A Statue*; **Jilted John** - *Mrs. Pickering*; **Chris Sievey** - *Last*; **Freshies** - *Yesterday/Tomorrow*; **Ed Banger** - *Kinnel Tommy*; Prime Time Suckers - *Wing Wang*.

The Cutting Edge (Razor RAZ 16) 1985

Daffodils To The Daffodils, Here's The Daffodils (Pax PAX 19) 1984
SIDE ONE: **Mau Maus** - *Facts Of War*; Onslaught - *Black Horse Of Famine*; Destrucktions - *Trade Union*; Unjust - *In Shape*; Noncens - *The Battle Field*; Destrucktions - *Who's Got The Power*; Unjust - *No Justice*; Morbid Humour - *Give Us This Day*; Noncens - *Give Us A Future*; Leitmotiv - *Living In A Tin*; SIDE TWO: No Control - *Suicide*; Leitmotiv - *Silent Run*; **Demob** - *No Room For You*; Unjust - *Ivan's Revenge*; Onslaught - *Shadow Of Death*; Noncens - *Black And White*; Unjust - *Rather Off Dead*; Morbid Humour - *Oh My God (Part 1)*; Morbid Humour - *Oh My God (Part 2)*.

D.O.A. Dead On Arrival (Virgin VD 2508) 1978

Defiant Pose (Illegal ILP 011) 1983
SIDE ONE: Lords Of The New Church - *Holy War*; Cramps - *Drug Train*; Alarm - *Marching On*; Crown Of Thorns - *Gone Are The Days*; Wall Of Voodoo - *On Interstate 15*; Fall - *Fiery Jack*; Cosmetics - *The Crack*; SIDE TWO: Chelsea - *Evacuate*; **Chron Gen** - *Reality*; **Business** - *Loud Proud 'n' Punk*; **Major Accident** - *Mr. Nobody*; **Manace** - *Insane Society*; **Cortinas** - *Fascist Dictator*; **Sham 69** - *Red London*; **Models** - *Freeze*; **Circle Jerks** - *Political Stu*.

CASH COWS.

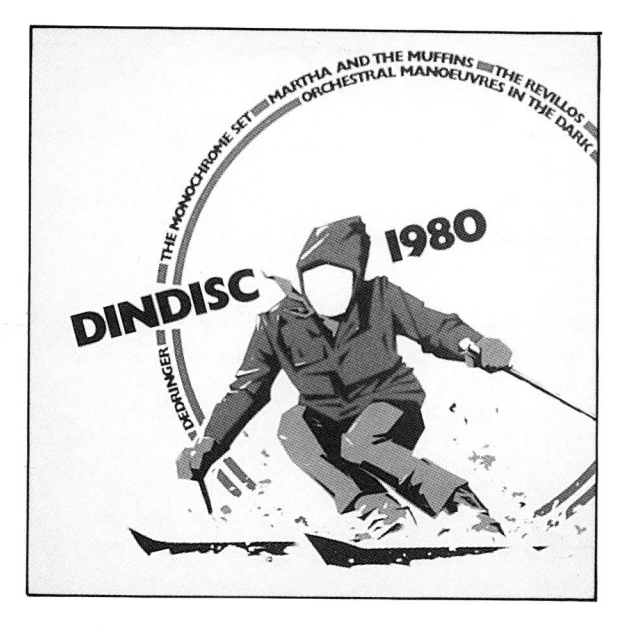

DINDISC 1980.

A Diamond Hidden In The Mouth Of A Corpse (JGPS 035) 1985

Dindisc 1980 (DinDisc DONE 1) 1980
SIDE ONE: Martha and The Muffins - *Echo Beach*; Martha and The Muffins - *Suburban Dream*; **Monochrome Set** - *405 Lines*; **Monochrome Set** - *Apocalypso*; Dedringer - *Sunday Drivers*. **SIDE TWO:** Revillos - *Hungry For Love*; **The Revillos** - *On The Beach*; **Orchestral Manoeuvres In The Dark** - *Waiting For The Man*; **Orchestral Manoeuvres In The Dark** - *Messages*; **Orchestral Manoeuvres In The Dark** - *Electricity*.

NB: Came with free 20" x 20" game.

Earcom 2 (Fast Products FAST 9B) 1979

Earcom 3 (Fast Products FAST 9C) 1979

East (Dead Good GOOD 1) 1980
NB: Includes two cuts by **B-Movie**.

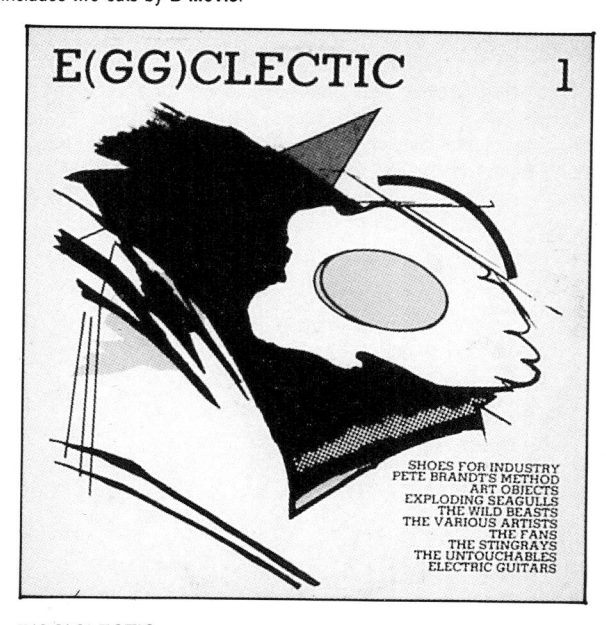

E(GG)CLECTIC.

E(gg)clectic (Fried Egg FRY 2) 1981
SIDE ONE: Shoes For Industry - *Jerusalem*; Pete Brandt's Method - *Positive Thinking*; **Art Objects** - *Hard Objects*; **Exploding Seagulls** - *Johnny Runs For Paregoric*; **Wild Beasts** - *Minimum Maximum*; **Shoes For Industry** - *Invasion Of The French Boyfriends*; **SIDE TWO: Various Artists** - *Original Mixed Up Kid*; **Fans** - *Following You*; **Stingrays** - *Exceptions*; **Various Artists** - *Unofficial Secrets*; **Untouchables** - *Keep On Walking*; **Electric Guitars** - *Continental Shelf*.

A Factory Sample (Factory FAC 2) 1978
Joy Division - *Digital* and *Glass*; **Durrutti Column** - *Thin Ice (Detail)* and *No Communication*; John Dowie - *Acne*, *Idiot* and *Hitler's Liver*; **Cabaret Voltaire** - *Baader Meinhof* and *Sex In Secret*.

Farewell To The Roxy (Lightning LIP 2) 1978
NB: Also issued on CD (Captain Oi! AHOY CD 86) 1998.
SIDE ONE: Blitz - *Strange Boy*; **Acme Sewage Co.** - *Smile And Wave Goodbye*; **Billy Karloff and The Goats** - *Relics From The Past*; **U.K. Subs** - *I Live In A Car*, **U.K. Subs** - *Telephone Numbers*; **Tickets** - *Get Yourself Killed*; **Red Lights** - *Never Wanna Leave*. **SIDE TWO: XL 5** - *Here Comes The Knife*; **Jets** - *TV Drink*; **Streets** - *Sniper*; **Plastix** - *Tough On You*; **Bears** - *Fun Fun Fun*; **Open Sore** - *Vertigo*; **Crabs** - *Lullabies Lie*.

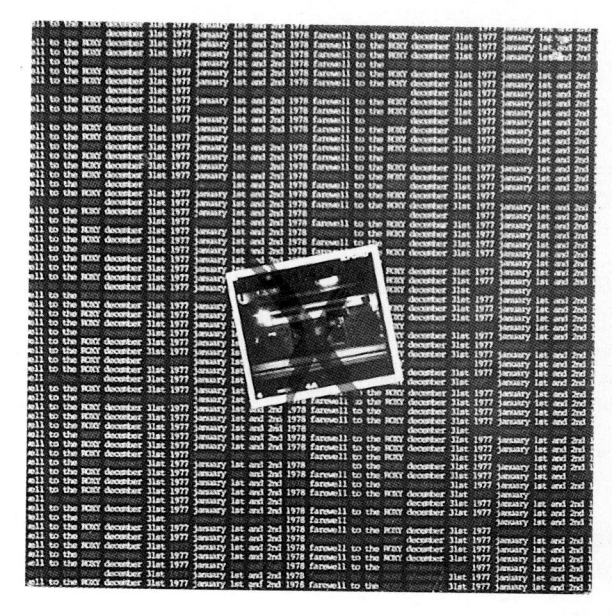

FAREWELL TO THE ROXY.

Fast Product (Fast EMC 3312) 1979
SIDE ONE: Mekons - *Never Been In A Riot*; **Mekons** - *Heart And Soul*; **Mekons** - *32 Weeks*; **Scars** - *Adultery*; **Scars** - *Horrorshow*; **Human League** - *Being Boiled*; **Human League** - *Circus Of Death*. **SIDE TWO: 2.3** - *All Time Low*; **2.3** - *Where To Now?*; **Gang Of Four** - *Love Like Anthrax*; **Gang Of Four** - *Armalite Rifle*; **Gang Of Four** - *Damaged Goods*; **Mekons** - *I'll Have To Dance Then (On My Own)*; **Mekons** - *Where Were You?*.

First Edition (Editions ED EGED 15) 1982
(Features **Adam and The Ants'** *Deutscher Girls* and *Plastic Surgery*)

499 2139.

4 ALTERNATIVES (EP).

4 Alternatives (EP) (Heartbeat PULSE 4) 1979
SIDE ONE: **Numbers** - *Alternative Suicide;* **X-Certs** - *Blue Movies;* SIDE TWO: **Joe Public** - *Hotel Rooms;* **48 Hours** - *Back To Ireland.*

499 2139 (Rocket DIAL 1) 1979
SIDE ONE: **Act** - *Sure Fire;* **Lambrettas** - *Go Steady;* **Classics** - *Audio Audio;* **Malcolm Practice** - *Kicking Up A Fuss;* **Escalators** - *Carscape;* **Vye** - *King's New Clothes;* **Wolfboys!!** - *Feelin' Hard.* SIDE TWO: **Malcolm Practice** - *Sex Object;* **Wardens** - *Tricky Girls;* **Brick Wall Band** - *Distant Drums;* **Les Elite** - *Career Girls;* **Reafer** - *Green Glass Green;* **Sinister** - *Alice In Wonderland;* **Act** - *Stop The Beat.*

**Fools Gold -
Chiswick Chartbusters, Vol. 1** (Chiswick CH 2) 1977
SIDE ONE: **101'ers** - *Keys To Your Heart;* **Count Bishops** - *Teenage Letter;* **Gorillas** - *She's My Gal;* **Little Bob Story** - *I'm Crying;* **Count Bishops** - *Train Train;* **Gorillas** - *Gorilla Got Me;* SIDE TWO: **Radio Stars** - *Dirty Pictures;* **Gorillas** - *Gatecrasher;* **Rocky Sharpe and The Razors** - *Drip Drop;* **Little Bob Story** - *Baby Don't Cry;* **Count Bishops** - *Route 66;* **Rocky Sharpe and The Razors** - *So Hard To Laugh.*

A Fresh Selection (Fresh FRESH LP 8) 1981
SIDE ONE: **Dumb Blondes** - *Sorrow;* **Cuddly Toys** - *Someone's Crying;* **Igloos** - *Octopus;* **Family Fodder** - *Savoir Faire;* **Cuddly Toys** - *Madman;* **Wilko Johnson** - *Back In The Night;* **Bernie Torme** - *All Day And All Of The Night;* SIDE TWO: **UK Decay** - *Unwind;* **Manufactured Romance** - *Time Of My Life;* **Dark** - *Hawaii Five O;* **Wall** - *Ghetto;* **J.C.'s Mainmen** - *Earbending;* **Menace** - *The Young Ones;* **Art Attacks** - *Punk Rock Stars.*

Guillotine 10" (Virgin VCL 5001) 1978
SIDE ONE: **The Motors** - *You Beat The Hell Outta Me;* **Penetration** - *Don't Dictate;* **The Table** - *Do The Standing Still (Classics Illustrated);* **Avant Gardener** - *Strange Gurl In Clothes.* SIDE TWO: **XTC** - *Traffic Light Rock;* **Roky Erickson** - *Bermuda;* **Poet and The Roots** - *All Wi Doin' Is Defendin';* **X-Ray Spex** - *Oh Bondage Up Yours!.*

Have A Rotten Christmas (Rot ASS 18) 1984
SIDE ONE: **Animal Farm** - *So Sad;* **Varukers** - *State Enemy;* **No Choice** - *Immunity;* **Skeptix** - *War Drum;* **Resistance 77** - *Banned From The Welfare;* **Enemy** - *Images;* SIDE TWO: **Riot Squad** - *10 Years Time;* **No Choice** - *Underground;* **Skeptix** - *Return To Hell;* **Paranoia** - *1984;* **Animal Farm** - *Who Is The Enemy?.*

Have A Rotten Christmas, Vol. 2 (Rot ASS 22) 1985
SIDE ONE: **Xtract** - *Lies;* **Rattus** - *Will Evil Win?;* **No Choice** - *No Money;* **Varukers** - *Will They Never Learn?;* **Existenz** - *Stupid Girl;* **Skeptix** - *Another Day;* SIDE TWO: **English Dogs** - *Incisor;* **Xtract** - *Dead Hero;* **Existenz** - *Human Killer;* **No Choice** - *Watzwar;* **Rattus** - *Kukaan Ei Voi Toistaan Auttaa.*

Heat From The Street (Charisma CLASS 8) 1981

Hell Comes To Your House (Riot City REAGAN 1) 1982

Heroes And Cowards (Stiff SEE 20) 1978
(Features **The Adverts'** *One Chord Wonders* and *Quickstep*)

Hicks From The Sticks (Rockburgh ROC 111) 1980
SIDE ONE: **Airkraft** - *Move In Rhythm;* **Expelaires** - *Sympathy (Don't Be Taken In);* **Clock DVA** - *You're Without Sound;* **Music For Pleasure** - *The Human Factor;* **Nightmares In Wax** - *Shangri-La;* **Ada Wilson** and **Keeping Dark** - *Head In The Clouds;* **Modern Eon** - *Choreography;* **Medium Medium** - *Them Or Me;* SIDE TWO: **Radio 5** - *True Colours;* **They Must Be Russians** - *Where Have I Seen You;* **Section 25** - *After-Image;* **Art Failure** - *Gimmick;* **I'm So Hollow** - *I Don't Know;* **Wah! Heat** - *Hey Disco Joe;* **Stranger Than Fiction** - *Immortal In Minors;* **Distributors** - *TV Me.*

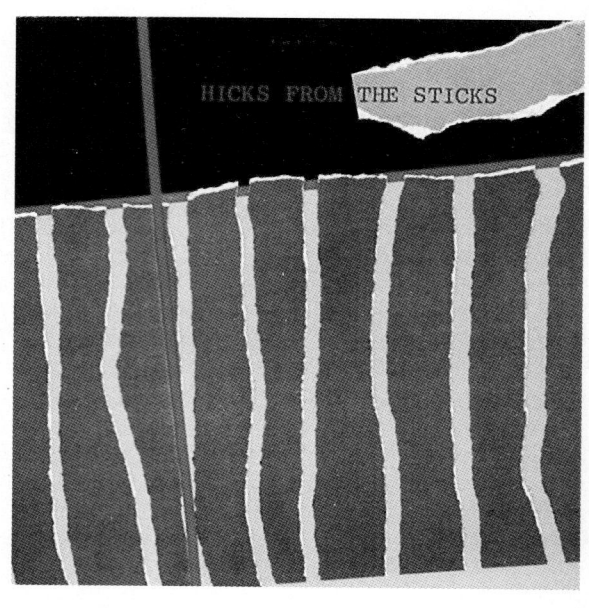

HICKS FROM THE STICKS.

Hits - Greatest Stiffs (Stiff FIST 1) 1977
SIDE ONE: **Nick Lowe** - *Heart Of The City;* **Pink Fairies** - *Between The Lines;* **Roogalator** - *Cincinnatti Fatback;* **Tyla Gang** - *Styrofoam;* **Tyla Gang** - *Texas Chainsaw Massacre.* SIDE TWO: **Lew Lewis** - *Caravan Man;* **Damned** - *Help;* **Richard Hell** - *You Gotta Lose;* **Plummet Airlines** - *This Is The World;* **Motorhead** - *Leavin' Here;* **Elvis Costello** - *Radio Sweetheart.*

HITS - GREATEST STIFFS.

Hope And Anchor Front Row Festival (2-LP) (Warner Bros K 66077) 1978

SIDE ONE: Wilko Johnson Band - *Dr. Feelgood*; **Stranglers** - *Straighten Out*; **Tyla Gang** - *Styrofoam*; Pirates - *Don't München*; Steve Gibbons Band - *Speed Kills*; **XTC** - *I'm Bugged*; **Suburban Studs** - *I Hate School*. SIDE TWO: **Pleasers** - *Billy*; **XTC** - *Science Friction*; Dire Straits - *Eastbound Train*; Burlesque - *Bizz Fizz*; **X-Ray Spex** - *Let's Submerge*; **999** - *Crazy*. SIDE THREE: **Saints** - *Demolition Girl*; **999** - *Quite Disappointing*; **Only Ones** - *Creatures Of Doom*; Pirates - *Gibson Martin Fender*; Steel Pulse - *Sound Check*; Roogalator - *Zero Hero*. SIDE FOUR: Philip Rambow - *Underground Romance*; **Pleasers** - *Rock & Roll Radio*; **Tyla Gang** - *On The Street*; Steve Gibbons Band - *Johnny Cool*; Wilko Johnson Band - *Twenty Yards Behind*; **Stranglers** - *Hanging Around*.

Hybrid Kids (Cherry Red) 1979

If You Can't Please Yourself, You Can't Please Your Soul (Some Bizzare ET 260663-1) 1985

The Industrial Records Story (Illuminated JAMS 39) 1984

Jubilee Cert X Soundtrack (EG/Polydor 2302079) 1978

SIDE ONE: Adam and The Ants - *Deutscher Girls*; **Wayne County and The Electric Chairs** - *Paranoia Paradise*; **Chelsea** - *Right To Work*; **Maneaters** - *Nine To Five*; **Adam and The Ants** - *Plastic Surgery*. SIDE TWO: **Suzi Pinns** - *Rule Britannia*; **Suzi Pinns** - *Jerusalem*; Amilcar - *Wargasm In Pornotopia*; Brian Eno - *Slow Water*, Brian Eno - *Dover Beach*.

NB: Reissued on CD (Caroline EGCD 34) 1996.

A Kick Up The Arse, Vol. 1 (Rot ASS 21) 1985

SIDE ONE: **Cult Maniax** - *Cities*; Butcher - *Leave Alive*; Last Rites - *Oi Oi Oi*; **External Menace** - *Coalition Blues*; Picture Frame Seduction - *3 2 1 Go*; **Reality** - *To Know Her*; **Expelled** - *Cider*. SIDE TWO: **External Menace** - *Vietnam*; **Cult Maniax** - *Drugs*; **Expelled** - *Violent Minds*; Last Rites - *Addict*; **Reality** - *Ballad Of Mad Harry*; Butcher - *Time Will Tell*; Picture Frame Seduction - *My Mate Sulphate*.

The Label Sofa (The Label TRLP 002) 1979

NB: Also issued as a 'translumar defractor' 3D picture disc in a stickered PVC sleeve.

Labels Unlimited - The Second Cherry Red Collection (Cherry Red ARED 4) 1979

SIDE ONE: **Rudi** - *Big Time*; **Girlschool** - *Take It All Away*; **Those Naughty Lumps** - *Iggy Pop's Jacket*; **Spizz Oil** - *Cold City*; **Llygod Ffyrning** - *N.C.B.*; **Newtown Neurotics** - *Hypocrite*; **Crisis** - *Holocaust*; Scissor Fits - *I Don't Want To Work For British Airways*. SIDE TWO: **Shapes** - *Wot's For Lunch Mum?*; **Piranhas** - *Jilly*; Staa Marx - *Pleasant Valley Sunday*; **Glaxo Babies** - *Who Killed Bruce Lee?*; **Poison Girls** - *Closed Shop*; I Jog and The Tracksuits - *Red Box*; **AK Process** - *After All Love*; **Second Layer** - *Metal Sheet*.

The Last Testament (Festish FR 2011) 1983

Let's Get Pissed It's Xmas (Rot CULT 001) 1987

SIDE ONE: Bristles - *Coming Back*; Riot Squad - *Hate The Law*; Drongos For Europe - *Can't Afford To Fall*; Oi Polloi - *Silent Minority*; Terveet Kadet - *City And Stars*; Existenz - *Man Of His Own*; Crude SS - *Forced Values*; **Paranoia** - *Robots*. SIDE TWO: Terveet Kadet - *Outsider*; Drongos For Europe - *Dresden*; Oi Polloi - *Boot Down The Doors*; Crude SS - *Sick Pleasure*; Bristles - *Lonely*; **Riot Squad** - *Hidden Fear*; Existenz - *Good Time*.

Let's Get Pissed, It's Xmas Vol. 2 (Rot CULT 002) 1987

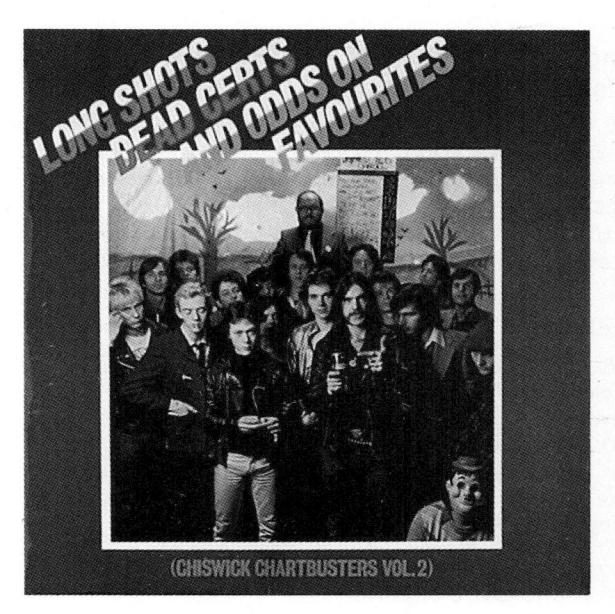

LONG SHOTS, DEAD CERTS AND ODDS ON FAVOURITES - CHISWICK CHARTBUSTERS.

Life's A Riot And Then You Die (Riot City CITY 009) 1985

Vice Squad - *Last Rockers*; **Abrasive Wheels** - *Vicious Circle*; **Chaos UK** - *4 Minute Warning*; **Chaotic Dischord** - *Never Trust A Friend*; **Court Martial** - *Got To Get Out*; Ejected - *Have You Got 10p?*; **Undead** - *This Place Is Burning*; **Expelled** - *Make It Alone*; **Vice Squad** - *Resurrection*; **Emergency** - *Points Of View*; **Abrasive Wheels** - *Burn 'Em Down*; **Underdogs** - *East Of Dachau*; **Chaotic Dischord** - *Don't Throw It All Away*; **Resistance '77** - *Nuclear Attack*; **Mayhem** - *Gentle Murder*; **Varukers** - *Die For Your Government*.

Live At The Roxy (Harvest SHSP 4069) 1977

NB: Reissued with extra tracks as *Live From The Roxy* (Essential ESMCD 772).

Live At The Vortex, Vol. 1 (NEMS NEL 6013) 1978

SIDE ONE: **Wasps** - *Can't Wait Til '78*; **Mean Street** - *Bunch Of Stiffs*; **Neo** - *Small Lives*; **Wasps** - *Waiting For My Man*; Bernie Torme - *Living For Kicks*; **Art Attacks** - *Animal Bondage*. SIDE TWO: Bernie Torme - *Streetfighter*; **Art Attacks** - *Frankenstein's Heartbeat*; **Neo** - *Tell Me The Truth*; **Suspects** - *Nothing To Declare*; **Maniacs** - *You Don't Break My Heart*; **Maniacs** - *I Ain't Gonna Be History*.

NB: Reissued on CD (Anagram CDPUNK 68) 1995.

MACHINES.

Long Shots, Dead Certs And Odds On Favourites - Chiswick Chartbusters (Chiswick CH 5) 1978
SIDE ONE: **Radiators From Space** - *Television Screen*; **Skrewdriver** - *Anti-Social*; **Johnny Moped** - *No-One*; **Radiators From Space** - *Enemies*; **Skrewdriver** - *You're So Dumb*; Motorhead - *Motorhead*. SIDE TWO: **Radio Stars** - *No Russians In Space*; **Rings** - *I Wanna Be Free*; Jeff Hill - *I Want You To Dance With Me*; **Count Bishops** - *Baby You're Wrong*; **Amazorblades** - *Common Truth*; **Stukas** - *Klean Living Kids*.

Machines (Virgin V 2177) 1980
SIDE ONE: **O.M.D.** - *Messages*; **Silicon Teens** - *Memphis Tennessee*; **Tubeway Army** - *Down In The Park*; **Human League** - *Being Boiled*; **Thomas Leer** - *Private Plane*; **Dalek II** - *Dalek I Love You (Destiny)*. SIDE TWO: **John Foxx** - *Underpass*; **Henry Badowski** - *Making Love With My Wife*; **Fad Gadget** - *Ricky's Hand*; **Public Image Ltd.** - *Pied Piper*; Karel Halka - *The Eyes Have It*; **Gary Numan** - *Aircrash Bureau*; **XTC** - *The Somnambulist*.

A Manchester Collection (Object Music OBJ 003) 1979

Manchester - So Much To Answer For
(Strange Fruit SFRLP 20) 1990

MODS MAYDAY '79.

Mods Mayday '79 (Bridge House BHLP 003) 1979
SIDE ONE: **Secret Affair** - *Time For Action*; **Secret Affair** - *Let Your Heart Dance*; **Beggar** - *Don't Throw Your Life Away*; **Small Hours** - *Hanging In The Balance*; **Mods** - *Tonight's The Night*; **Mods** - *Let Me Be The One*; **Squire** - *B-A-B-Y Baby Love*; **Small Hours** - *Midnight To Six*. SIDE TWO: **Beggar** - *Broadway Show*; **Beggar** - *All Night*; **Mods** - *Love Only Me*; **Squire** - *Walking Down The King's Road*; **Squire** - *Live Without Her Love*; **Secret Affair** - *I'm Not Free (But I'm Cheap)*; **Small Hours** - *End Of The Night*.

NB: Reissued on CD (Dojo DOJOCD 5) 1994.

The Moonlight Tapes (Danceville DANCE 1) 1980
SIDE ONE: **Sore Throat** - *Complex*; **Members** - *Rat Up A Drainpipe*; Lightning Raiders - *Views*; Local Operator - *Law And Order*. SIDE TWO: **Edge** - *Next In Line*; Q.T.'s - *Shaftesbury Avenue*; School Bullies - *Lookin' For Another*; **Passions** - *Why Me*; Soul Boys - *Red Sun*; Kameras - *Return Of The Ice Age*.

New Electric Warriors (Logo MOGO 4011) 1980

New Wave (Vertigo 6300 902) 1977
SIDE ONE: **Ramones** - *Judy Is A Punk*; **Dead Boys** - *Sonic Reducer*; Patti Smith - *Piss Factory*; New York Dolls - *Personality Crisis*; Runaways - *Hollywood*; Skyhooks - *Horror Movie*; Richard Hell and The Void-oids - *Love Comes In Spurts*; Little Bob Story - *All Or Nothing*. SIDE TWO: The **Boomtown Rats** - *Looking After No. 1*; Talking Heads - *Love Goes To Building On Fire*; **The Damned** - *New Rose*; Ramones - *Suzy Is A Headbanger*; Dead Boys - *All This And More*; Flamin' Groovies - *Shake Some Action*; Runaways - *Cherry Bomb*; New York Dolls - *Who Are The Mystery Girls?*.

No Future - The Punk Singles Collection (2-LP)
(Captain Oi! AHOY DLP 508) 1996
SIDE ONE: **Blitz** - *Someone's Gonna Die Tonight*; **Blitz** - *Attack*; **The Partisans** - *Police Story*; **Blitzkrieg** - *The Future Must Be Ours*; **Peter and The Test Tube Babies** - *Banned From The Pubs*; **Peter and The Test Tube Babies** - *Peacehaven Wild Kids*; **Red Alert** - *In Britain*; **Red Alert** - *Murder Missile*. SIDE TWO: **Blitz** - *Never Surrender*; **Attak** - *Today's Generation*; **Blitzkrieg** - *Lest We Forget*; **Violators** - *Gangland*; **Insane** - *El Salvador*; **Channel 3** - *I've Got A Gun*; **The Partisans** - *17 Years Of Hell*; **The Partisans** - *The Power And The Greed*. SIDE THREE: **Red Alert** - *Take No Prisoners*; **The Samples** - *Dead Hero*; **Peter and The Test Tube Babies** - *Run Like Hell*; **Blitz** - *Warriors*; **Attak** - *Murder In The Subway*; **Crux** - *Keep On Running*; **Crash** - *Religion*; **Violators** - *Summer Of '81*. SIDE FOUR: **Red Alert** - *City Invasion*; **Wall** - *Day Tripper*; **Blood** - *Megalomania*; **A.B.H.** - *Wanna Riot*; **Rose Of Victory** - *Suffragette City*; **Screaming Dead** - *Night Creatures*; **Violators** - *Die With Dignity*; **Red Alert** - *There's A Guitar Burning*.

NO FUTURE - THE PUNK SINGLES COLLECTION, VOL. 2.

No Future - The Punk Singles Collection, Vol. 2 (2-LP) (Captain Oi! AHOY DLP 512) 1996
SIDE ONE: **Blitz** - *Fight To Live*; **Blitz** - *45 Revolutions*; **Partisans** - *Killing Machine*; **Crux** - *C.I.A.*; **Peter and The Test Tube Babies** - *Moped Lads*; **Red Alert** - *Screaming At The Nation*; **Blitz** - *Razors In The Night*; **Attak** - *Hell*. SIDE TWO: **Attak** - *No Escape*; **Blitzkrieg** - *Abuse Of Power*; **Violators** - *The Fugitive*; **Insane** - *Chinese Rocks*; **Channel 3** - *Manzanar And Mannequin*; **Partisans** - *Bastards In Blue*; **Red Alert** - *Empire Of Crime*; **Red Alert** - *Sell Out*. SIDE THREE: **Samples** - *Fire Another Round*; **Peter and The Test Tube Babies** - *Up Yer Bum*; **Blitz** - *Youth*; **Attak** - *Future Dreams*; **Crash** - *Fight For Your Life*; **Crux** - *Streets At Night*; **Violators** - *Live Fast Die Young*; **Red Alert** - *Negative Reaction*. SIDE FOUR: **Wall** - *When I'm Dancin'*; **Blood** - *Calling The Shots*; **Blood** - *Parasite In Paradise*; **On Parole** - *Condemned*; **Rose Of Victory** - *Overdrive*; **Screaming Dead** - *Angel Of Death*; **Violators** - *Pointless Slaughter*; **Red Alert** - *All The Way To Glory*.

NB: There are also two CD compilations: *No Future - The Singles, Collection, Vol. 1* (Anagram CDPUNK 11) 1994 and *No Future - The Singles Collection, Vol. 2* (Anagram CDPUNK 54) 1995 containing the same material as their vinyl counterparts.

No Wave (A&M AMLE 68505) 1979
SIDE ONE: Secret - *Going Down Again*; **Joe Jackson** - *Is She Really Going Out With Him?*; **Police** - *Roxanne*; **Klark Kent** - *Don't Care*; David Kubinec - *Love In The First Degree*; Bobby Henry - *Head Case*; **Squeeze** -

Take Me, I'm Yours; Dickies - You Drive Me Ape. **SIDE TWO:** Secret - Lucky Lizard; **Squeeze** - Bang Bang; David Kubinec - Line Shooter; **Shrink** - Valid Or Void; **Klark Kent** - Office Girls; **Joe Jackson** - Sunday Papers; **The Police** - Can't Stand Losing You; Dickies - Hideous.

Objectivity (Object Music OBJ 006) 1980

Odd Bods, Mods And Sods (Rok ROK LP 001) 1979
SIDE ONE: V.I.P.'s - Can't Believe It's True; **Squire** - Livin' In The City; **Split Screens** - Know What I Want; **Clerks** - No Good For Me; **Justin Case** - Statik Motion; **Urban Disturbance** - Wild Boys In Cortinas; **SIDE TWO: V.I.P.'s** - Just Can't Let You Go; **Squire** - Get Ready To Go; **Split Screens** - Just Don't Try; **Just Frank** - You; **Clerks** - When The Lights Go Out.

NB: Reissued on CD with extra material (Captain Mod MODSKA CD 2) 1996.

Oh No It's More From Raw (Raw Records RAWL 2) 1978
SIDE ONE: Unwanted - Withdrawel/1984; **Users** - Sick Of You; **Hammersmith Gorillas** - Leavin' Home; **Some Chicken** - Blood On The Wall; **Gorillas** - It's My Life; **Soft Boys** - Hear My Brane; **SIDE TWO: Killjoys** - Johnny Won't Get To Heaven; **Hammersmith Gorillas** - You Really Got Me; **Users** - I'm In Love With Today; **Some Chicken** - New Religion; Downliners Sect - Showbiz; **Killjoys** - Naive.

Oi! Against Racism (Havin' A Laugh HAL LP 004) 198?
SIDE ONE: Angelic Upstarts - Kids On The Street (live); Nabat - Nati Per Niente; **Oppressed** - Sleeping With The Enemy; Skacha - Enganados; N.N. All Stars - Classe Operaia; Brickwall United - Open Their Eyes; Klaxon - eSSe TiOeRrelA; **Red Alert** - One Flag. **SIDE TWO: Attila The Stockbroker** - This Is Free Europe; Stage Bottles - We've Got To Fight; Klasse Kriminale - C'era Un Giovane Che Disse...; Templars - Never Fade Away; **Red London** - Children Of War; Drunken Nuns - I Reietti Sono Tornati; **Sham 69** - If The Kids Are United (live).

Oi! Chartbusters, Vol. 1 (Link LP 03) 1987
NB: See CD section for track listing. Reissued in 1990 with **The Oppressed** track replaced by a track by **The Strike**.

Oi! Chartbusters, Vol. 2 (Street Link LP 016) 1987
NB: See CD section for track listing. Later pressing had grey instead of blue covers. Repressed on Black Link. White label test pressings were made.

NO WAVE.

Oi! AGAINST RACISM.

Oi! Chartbusters, Vol. 3 (Street Link LP 034) 1988

Oi! Chartbusters, Vol. 4 (Street Link LP 054) 1988

Oi! Chartbusters, Vol. 5 (Street Link LP 081) 1989

Oi! Chartbusters, Vol. 6 (Street Link LP 127) 1990

Oi! Glorious Oi! (Street Link LP 023) 1987
NB: Repressed on Black Link.

The Oi! Of Sex (Syndicate SYN LP 4) 1984
SIDE ONE: Prole - We'll Never Say Die; **Cock Sparrer** - The Sun Says; **Gonads** - S.E.7 Dole Day; **Burial** - Old Man's Poison; **Vicious Rumours** - Vicious Rumours; **Jimmy Mack** - Zombie Mind Eaters; **Rat Patrol** - Rat Trap; **Crossed Hammers** - Here We Go; **Swift Nick** - The Sun. **SIDE TWO: Burial** - Friday Night; **Prole** - Destination Room 101; **Orgasm Guerillas** - Frankie Goes To Pot; **Little Dave** - Being Short; **Nick Toczecks Britanarchists** - Stiff With A Quiff; **Vicious Rumours** - Take The Blame; **ABH** - Don't Mess With The SAS; **Dogsbody** - Murder; **Garry Johnson** - If Looks Could Kill.

NB: Also issued again on vinyl (Street Link LP 036) 1988 and on CD (Captain Oi! AHOY CD 23) 1994.

Oi! Oi! That's Yer Lot! (Secret SEC 5) 1982
SIDE ONE (Punk Side): Business - Real Enemy; **Five O** - Dr. Crippens; **Oppressed** - White Flag; **Sub-Culture** - Stick Together; **Crux** - Liddle Towers; **Warriors** - Horror Show; **Attak** - Big Brother; **Black Flag** - Revenge. **SIDE TWO (Drunk Side):** Arthur and The Afters - Arthur's Theme; Frankie and The Flames - On Yer Bike; Magnificent Gonads - Getting Pissed; **Attila The Stokebroker** - Willie Whitelaw's Willie; Judge Dread - The Belle Of Snodland Town; Skin Graft - Oi! Oi! Music; **Attila The Stockbroker** - Away Day; Coming Blood - Such Fun.

NB: Later reissued (Street Link LP 068) 1989, (Roadrunner RR 9945) 1989 and (Get Back GET 46) 2000 with one bonus cut Back On The Street.

Oi! That's What I Call Music (Street Link LP 038) 1988

Oi! The Album (EMI ZIT 1) 1980
SIDE ONE: Cockney Rejects - Oi, Oi, Oi; **Peter and The Test Tube Babies** - (Wanna) Rob A Bank; **4-Skins** - Wonderful World; Postmen - Have A Cigar; **Exploited** - Daily News; Terrible Twins - Generation Of Scars; **Angelic Upstarts** - Guns For The Afghan Rebels; **Cock Sparrer** - Sunday Stripper. **SIDE TWO: Angelic Upstarts** - Last Night Another

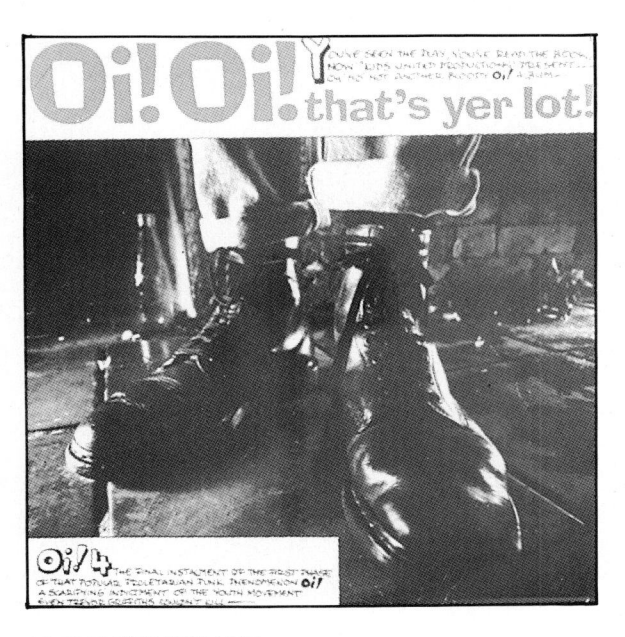

Oi! Oi! THAT'S YER LOT!

Soldier, **4-Skins** - *Chaos*; **Cockney Rejects** - *Here We Go Again*; Max Splodge and Desert Island Joe - *Isabeleeeene*; Postmen - *Beardsmen*; **Slaughter and The Dogs** - *Where Have All The Bootboys Gone?*; Barney and The Rubbles - *Bootboys*; **Peter and The Test Tube Babies** - *Intensive Care*; **Exploited** - *I Still Believe In Anarchy*.

NB: Also issued on CD (Captain Oi! AHOY CD 72) 1997 and on vinyl (Captain Oi! AHOY LP 72) 1998.

Oi! The Main Event (Link LP 041) 1988

Oi!... The Picture Disc (Street Link LP 014) 1987

Oi!... The Picture Disc, Vol. 2 (Street Link LP 037) 1988

Oi! The Resurrection (Link LP 01) 1987

NB: See CD section for track listing.

The Only Alternative (Rondelet ABOUT 10) 1982

Perspectives And Distortions (Cherry Red BRED 15) 1981

Pillows And Prayers (Cherry Red Z RED 41) 1982

SIDE ONE: **Five Or Six** - *Portrait*; **Monochrome Set** - *Eine Symphonie Des Grauens*; **Thomas Leer** - *All About You*; Tracey Thorn - *Plain Sailing*; Ben Watt - *Some Things Don't Matter*; Kevin Coyne - *Love In Your Heart*;

PILLOWS AND PRAYERS.

Piero Milesi - *Modi 2 (Extract)*; Joe Crow - *Compulsion*. SIDE TWO: Marine Girls - *Lazy Ways*; Felt - *My Face Is On Fire*; Eyeless In Gaza - *No Noise*; Passage - *Xoyo*; Everything But The Girl - *On My Mind*; **Attila The Stockbroker** - *A Bang And A Wimpey*; The Misunderstood - *I Unseen*; **Nightingales** - *Don't Blink*; Quentin Crisp - *Stop The Music For A Minute*.

NB: Reissued on CD (Cherry Red CDMRED 41) 1996.

Pressages (4AD BAD 11) 1980

Prototypes (Blueprint BLUSP 1) 1979

Punk And Disorderly: New Wave 1976-1981 (Telstar STAR 2520) 1991. (Also on CD TCD 2520 and MC STAC 2520)

SIDE ONE: **Undertones** - *Teenage Kicks*; **Elvis Costello and The Attractions** - *Pump It Up*; **Ian Dury** - *Sex And Drugs And Rock & Roll*; **Damned** - *Neat Neat Neat*; **Bow Wow Wow** - *C30, C60, C90 Go*; **Stiff Little Fingers** - *Alternative Ulster*; **Sham 69** - *Hersham Boys*; **999** - *Emergency*; **Stranglers** - *No More Heroes*. SIDE TWO: **Jam** - *The Eton Rifles*; **Adverts** - *Gary Gilmore's Eyes*; **Boomtown Rats** - *She's So Modern*; Blondie - *Rip Her To Shred's*; **Buzzcocks** - *Orgasm Addict*; **Original Pistols** - *Pretty Vacant*; **Tenpole Tudor** - *Swords Of A Thousand Men*; Department S - *Is Vic There?*; **Jilted John** - *Jilted John*.

PUNK AND DISORDERLY.

Punk And Disorderly - Further Charges (Anagram GRAM 001) 1982

SIDE ONE: **G.B.H.** - *Sick Boy*; **Expelled** - *Dreaming*; **Insane** - *El Salvador*; **One Way System** - *Stab The Judge*; **Court Martial** - *Gotta Get Out*; **Action Pact** - *London Bouncers*; **Dark** - *The Masque*; **Violators** - *Gangland*. SIDE TWO: **Channel 3** - *I've Got A Gun*; **Abrasive Wheels** - *Vicious Circle*; **Enemy** - *Fallen Hero*; **Riot/Clone** - *Death To Humanity*; **Wall** - *Hobby For A Day*; **Disorder** - *More Than Fights*; Erazerhead - *Shellshock*; **Vice Squad** - *Resurrection*.

NB: Reissued on CD (Anagram CDPUNK 22) 1993.

Punk And Disorderly III - The Final Solution (Anagram GRAM 005) 1983

SIDE ONE: **Abrasive Wheels** - *Burn 'Em Down*; **One Way System** - *Give Us A Future*; **Newtown Neurotics** - *Kick Out The Tories*; **U.K. Subs** - *Police State*; **The Destructors** - *Jailbait*; **Expelled** - *Government Policy*; **Samples** - *Dead Hero*; **Angelic Upstarts** - *Woman In Disguise*. SIDE TWO: **Adicts** - *Viva La Revolution*; **The Vibrators** - *Dragnet*; **Exploited** - *Computers Don't Blunder*; **Urban Dogs** - *New Barbarians*; **Ejected** - *Have You Got 10p?*; **Chron Gen** - *Outlaw*; **Action Pact** - *Suicide Bag*; **Violators** - *Summer Of '81*.

NB: Reissued on CD (Anagram CD PUNK 23) 1993.

PUNK AND DISORDERLY - FURTHER CHARGES.

Punk Lives! - Let's Slam (Rot SLAM 002) 1986
SIDE ONE: Anihilated - *Inferno*; Stone The Crowz - *Suffer Children*; Rattus - *Naytelma*; **Political Asylum** - *Cats Eyes*; **Rabid** - *Bloody Road To Glory*; Poison Justice - *Rebellious City*; **SIDE TWO: Political Asylum** - *Flight Of Fancy*; **Throbs** - *Happy But Ignorant*; Poison Justice - *Life To It's End*; **Rabid** - *Black Cat*; Stone The Crowz - *Friendship*; **Anihilated** - *40 Dumb Animals*.

Punk Lives - Let's Slam 2 (Rot SLAM 003) 1987
SIDE ONE: Jive Turkey - *Giro Day*; Sad Society - *Contaminate*; Atrox - *Seeing Blind Dead*; **Disturbed** - *Presidents Dead*; Perjury - *Spend Spend Spend*; Rejected - *Boys In Blue*; **SIDE TWO:** Atrox - *Protest With Action*; Sad Society - *Don't Say*; Jive Turkey - *Never Say Goodbye Johnny Ray*; Perjury - *One Too Many*; **Disturbed** - *Ridicule*; Rejected - *Rape*.

Punks Not Dead - Nah Mate The Smell Is Jus Summink In Yer Underpants (12") (Pax PAX 7) 1982
SIDE ONE: Mau Maus - *Give Us A Future*; **Xtract** - *War Heroes*; **Anti-System** - *Man's World*; **Mania** - *Power To The People*; Xpozez - *Factory Fodder*; Septic Psychos - *Not Wanted*; **SIDE TWO: Anti-System** - *Breakout*; **Xtract** - *Aftermath*; Septic Psychos - *The Thatcher*; Xpozez - *No Respect*; **Mau Maus** - *Clampdown*; **Mania** - *Stick Together*.

Quality Of Life (Fast) 1978

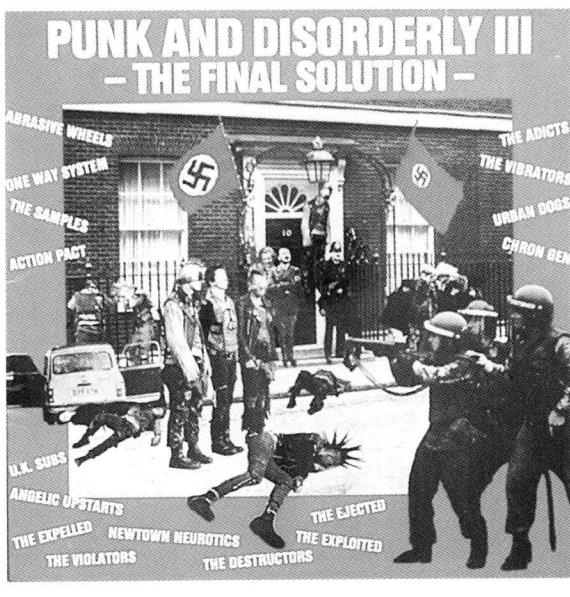

PUNK AND DISORDERLY III - THE FINAL SOLUTION.

PUNKS NOT DEAD - NAH MATE THE SMELL IS JUS SUMMINK IN YER UNDERPANTS.

The Rare Stuff (EMI SHSM 2028) 1979
SIDE ONE: Saints - *River Deep Mountain High*; **Wire** - *Dot Dash*; **Banned** - *Him Or Me*; **Flys** - *E.C.4*; **Rich Kids** - *Only Arsenic*; **Flys** - *Love And A Molotov Cocktail*; **Banned** - *You Dirty Rat*; **Saints** - *One Way Street*. **SIDE TWO: Saints** - *Lipstick On Your Collar*; **Saints** - *Demolition Girl*; **Wire** - *Options R*; **Flys** - *Can I Crash Here?*; **Flys** - *Civilization*; **Banned** - *C.P.G.J.'s*; **Banned** - *Little Girl*; Shirts - *Cyrinda*.

Raw Deal (Raw RAWLP 1) 1977
SIDE ONE: Users - *(I'm) In Love With Today*; **Acme Sewage Co.** - *I Don't Need You*; **G.T.'s** - *Millionaire*; Bloodclots - *Louie Louie (live)*; **Sick Things** - *Bondage Boy*; **Psycho's** - *Soul Train*. **SIDE TWO: Sick Things** - *Kids On The Street*; **Killjoys** - *At Night*; **Psycho's** - *Young British And White*; **Acme Sewage Co.** - *I Can See You*; **G.T.'s** - *Move On*; Zhain - *Get Ready*.

Razor Sharp Cuts (Razor RAZ 12) 1984
SIDE ONE: Adicts - *Chinese Takeaway*; Splodge - *Pilchard Freak*; **Cock Sparrer** - *Chip On Your Shoulder (live)*; **Newtown Neurotics** - *The Mess*; Brothers Gonad - *Lager Top*; Knox - *Goin' Uptown*; **Red London** - *Soul Train*; **Chron Gen** - *Too Much Talk*; **SIDE TWO: Newtown Neurotics** - *Living With Unemployment*; **Red London** - *This Is England (Part 2)*; **Cock Sparrer** - *Close Down*; Splodge - *Mouth N Trousers*; Knox - *Streetheart*; **Chron Gen** - *Puppets Of War*; **Angelic Upstarts** - *Progress*; **Adicts** - *Joker In The Pack*.

THE RARE STUFF.

RAW DEAL.

Recommended Sampler (Recommended 104) 1982

Riot City Singles Collection, Vol. 1 (2-LP)
(Captain Oi! AHOY DLP 503) 1996
NB: See CD section for track listing.

Riot City Singles Collection, Vol. 2 (2-LP)
(Captain Oi! AHOY DLP 511) 1996
NB: See CD section for track listing.

Riotous Assembly (Riot City ASSEMBLY 1) 1982
Vice Squad - *Cowards*; Organised Chaos - *Mary Whitehouse*; **Abrasive Wheels** - *Criminal Youth*; **Court Martial** - *Your War*; **Chaos UK** - *Sensless Conflict*; Dead Katss - *Fun Wars*; **Resistance 77** - *Bricks In Brixton*; Havoc - *Where Does Your Money Go*; Vice Squad - *It's A Sell Out*; Mayhem - *Psycho*; Expelled - *Blown Away*; **TDA** - *TDA*; **Undead** - *Sanctuary*; Lunatic Fringe - *British Man*; **Chaotik Dischord** - *Accident*.

Rondelet Punk Singles Collection
(Captain Oi! AHOY LP 513) 1996
NB: See CD section for track listing.

Room To Move (EP) (Energy NRG 1) 1980

Rot In Hell 1977 (Rot ASS 15) 1985
SIDE ONE: Out Of Order - *Annihilator*; Overdose - *The Fugitive*; Filth - *Emmerdale Farm*; No Concern - *Shall We Shan't We*; **Varukers** - *The Bomb Blast*; Constant State - *I Can See Through You*; **Oi Polloi** - *Thugs In Uniform*; XXX - *Buy N Roll*; D.O.S. - *Fighting Factions*; Freshly - *Fry, Bleed - Liar*; SIDE TWO: **Resistance 77** - *The Jokes On Me*; Overdose - *One More Time*; Out Of Order - *Lynching Party*; Angry Rats - *New Clear War*; **Oi Polloi** - *Never Give In*; No Concern - *Enough Is Enough*; Bleed - *Up In The Morning*; XXX - *We Rule OK*; Constant State - *So This Is Transilvania*; Freshly - *Born Under Stars*; D.O.S. - *D.O.S.*.

The Secret Life Of Punks (Secret SEC 10) 1982
SIDE ONE: Exploited - *Dogs Of War*; 4-Skins - *One Law For Them*; Infa Riot - *Kids Of The 80s*; Partisans - *No U Turns*; Business - *Employers Black List*; **Gonads** - *I Lost My Love To A U.K. Sub*; **Blitz** - *Youth*. SIDE TWO: Business - *Harry May*; Chron Gen - *Jet Boy Jet Girl*; Last Resort - *King Of The Jungle*; **Peter and The Test Tube Babies** - *Maniac*; Infa Riot - *Catch 22*; 4-Skins - *Yesterday's Heroes*; Exploited - *Army Life*.
NB: Later reissued (Link LP 078) 1989.

**Secret Records
(The Best And The Rest)** (Get Back GET 12) 1999.
SIDE ONE: Infa Riot - *Kids Of The 80's*; 4-Skins - *One Law For Them*; Business - *Harry May*; Business - *National Insurance Blacklist*; Exploited - *Dead Cities*; Exploited - *Hitler's In The Charts Again*; Exploited - *Class War*; Exploited - *Alternative*; 4-Skins - *Yesterday's Heroes*; 4-Skins - *Justice*; 4-Skins - *Get Out Of My Life*. SIDE TWO: Infa Riot - *The Winner*; Business - *Smash The Discos*; Business - *Dayo*; 4-Skins - *Norman*; Business - *Last Train To Clapham Junction*; Business - *Tell Us The Truth*; Business - *Do They Owe Us A Living?*; Exploited - *Crashed Out*; Exploited - *What You Gonna Do?*; Chron Gen - *Jet Boy Jet Girl*; Chron Gen - *Abortions*.
NB: Also issued on CD.

Secret Records Punk Singles Collection, Vol. 1 (Captain Oi! AHOY LP 504) 1996
NB: See CD section for track listing.

Secret Records Punk Singles Collection, Vol. 2 (Captain Oi! AHOY LP 507) 1996
NB: See CD section for track listing.

Sent From Coventry (with booklet) (Kathedral KATH 1) 1980
SIDE ONE: Wild Boys - *We're Only Monsters*; Clique - *Mother's Never Know*; End - *Panic In The Night*; Mix - *With You*; Machine - *Character Change*; Urge - *Nuclear Terrorist*; SIDE TWO: Protege - *Protection*; Solid Action - *Message From A Loner*; Wild Boys - *Lorraine*; **Squad** - *Flasher*; Homicide - *Armageddon*; Riot Act - *Sirens*; V. Babies - *Donna Blitzen*.

Shake To Date (Albion/Shake SHAKE 1) 1981

Short Circuit: Live At The Electric Circus (Virgin VCL 5003) 1977
SIDE ONE: **Fall** - *Stepping Out*; **John Cooper Clarke** - *(You Never See A Nipple In The) Daily Express*; **Joy Division** - *At A Later Date*; **Drones** - *Persecution Complex*. SIDE TWO: Steel Pulse - *Makka Splaff*; **John Cooper Clarke** - *I Married A Monster From Outer Space*; **Fall** - *Last Orders*; **Buzzcocks** - *Time's Up*.

The Sire Machine Turns You Up (Sire SMP 1) 1978
SIDE ONE: Ramones - *Ramona*; Paley Brothers - *Come Out And Play*; Richard Hell and The Voidoids - *You Gotta Lose*; Martha Velez - *Get Up Stand Up*; DMZ - *Mighty Idy*; Dead Boys - *Ain't It Fun*; **Undertones** - *True Confessions*. SIDE TWO: Flamin' Groovies - *You Tore Me Down*; Squares - *Magic Love*; Patti Smith - *Hey Joe*; Radio Birdman - *Hand Of Law*; Tuff Darts - *Who's Been Sleeping Here*; Richard Hell and The Voidoids - *Blank Generation*; Rezillos - *(My Baby Does) Good Sculptures*.

THE SIRE MACHINE TURNS YOU UP

Small Wonder Punk Singles Collection (2-LP) (Captain Oi! AHOY DLP 514) 1996
NB: See CD section for track listing.

Some Bizzare Album (Some Bizzare BZLP 1) 1981
SIDE ONE: Illustration - *Tidal Flow*; **Depeche Mode** - *Photographic*; **The The** - *The The*; B Movie - *Moles*; **Jell** - *I Dare Say It Will Hurt A Little*; Blah Blah Blah - *Central Park*. SIDE TWO: **Blancmange** - *Sad Day*; **Soft Cell** - *The Girl With The Patent Leather Face*; Neu Electrikk - *Lust Of Berlin*; **Naked Lunch** - *La Femme*; **Fast Set** - *King Of The Rumbling Spires*; Loved One - *Observations*.

Something Better Change (Punk Junk) (EMI OP 5237 7824) 2000

Son Of Oi! (Syndicate SYN LP 3) 1983
ARTHUR'S SIDE: **Cock Sparrer** - *Chip On My Shoulder (live)*; Kraut - *Onwards*; **Prole!!** - *Generation Landslide*; **Garry Johnson** - *The Young Conservatives*; Paranoid Pictures - *Tomorrow's Whirl*; **Gonads** - *Jobs Not Jails*; Clockwork Destruction - *Violent Playground*; Phil Sexton and Mick Turpin - *Joe Public*; Alaska Cowboys - *Herpes In Seatle*; **Gary and The Gonads** - *Lager Top Blues*; Terry McCann - *Made In England*; Mick Turpin - *6.27 To London*. TERRY'S SIDE: The OrGaSM GUeriLAs - *Sing Something Swindle*; **Attila/Newtown Neurotics** - *Andy Is A Corporalist/Mindless Version*; **4-Skins** - *On The Streets*; **Garry Johnson** - *Boy About Town*; **Business (R.I.P.)** - *Out In The Cold*; Maniac Youth - *Make Mine Molotov*; **Angelic Upstarts** - *I Understand (live)*; Oi! The Robot - *Manifesto!*; Phil Sexton - *Top Of The Pops*; **Vicious Rumours** - *This Is Your Loife*; L.O.L.S. Choir - *Jerusalem*; Oxo's Midnight Stumblers - *Beano*.

NB: Reissued on vinyl (Link LP 030) 1988 and on CD (Captain Oi! AHOY CD 9) 1993.

SON OF Oi!

The Southend Connection (Waterfront Records WF 045) 1989
SIDE ONE: Engineers - *Ace Of Spades*; Boz and The Bozmen - *Creepy John*; **Records** - *You Changed The Lock*; Pete Zear - *Tomorrow's World*. SIDE TWO: Rent Party - *Walk That Mess*; Micky Jupp - *The Road*; Kursaal Flyers - *My Sugar Turns To Alcohol*; Famous Potatoes - *Hold That Critter Down*.

Stiffs Live Stiffs (Stiff GET 1) 1978
SIDE ONE: **Nick Lowe**'s Last Chicken In The Shop - *I Knew The Bride*; **Nick Lowe**'s Last Chicken In The Shop - *Let's Eat*; **Wreckless Eric**'s New Rockets - *Semaphore Signals*; **Wreckless Eric**'s New Rockets - *Reconnez Cherie*; Larry Wallis' Psychedelic Rowdies - *Police Car*. SIDE TWO: **Elvis Costello and The Attractions** - *I Just Don't Know What To Do With Myself*; **Elvis Costello and The Attractions** - *Miracle Man*; **Ian Dury and The Blockheads** - *Billericay Dickie*; **Ian Dury and The Blockheads** - *Wake Up And Make Love With Me*; All - *Sex Drugs Rock & Roll And Chaos*.

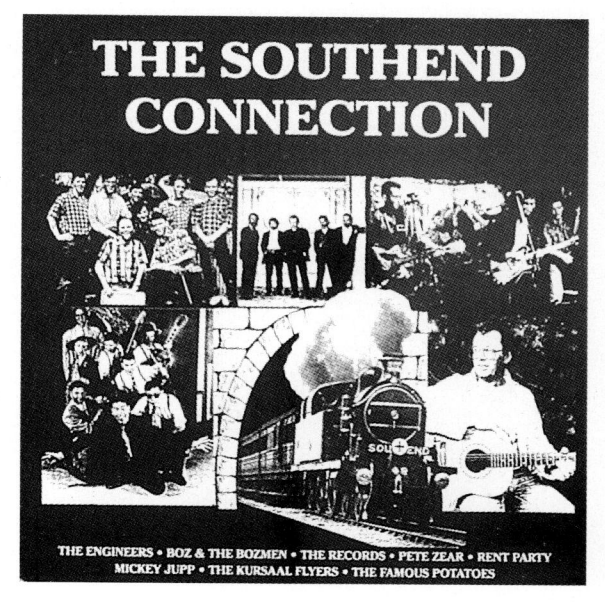

THE SOUTHEND CONNECTION.

Streets (Beggars Banquet BEGA 1) 1977
SIDE ONE: Doll - *Trash*; **Members** - *Fear On The Streets*; **Lurkers** - *Be My Prisoner*; Arthur Comics? - *Isgodaman*; **Art Attacks** - *Arabs In 'Arrads*; Dogs - *19*; **Reaction** - *Talk Talk Talk Talk*; Cane - *College Girls*. SIDE TWO: **Slaughter and The Dogs** - *Cranked Up Really High*; **Nosebleeds** - *Ain't Bin To No Music School*; **Drones** - *Lookalikes*; **Zeros** - *Hungry*; **Pork Dukes** - *Bend And Flush*; **Exile** - *Disaster Movie*; **Drive** - *Jerkin*; John Cooper Clarke - *Innocents*; Tractor - *No More Rock N Roll*.

Street To Street - A Liverpool Album (Open Eye OE LP 501) 1979

Street To Street - A Liverpool Album Vol. 2 (Open Eye OE LP 502) 1981

Strength Thru Oi! (Decca) 1981
SIDE ONE: **Garry Johnson** - *National Service*; **4-Skins** - *1984*; **Strike** - *Gang Warfare*; **Infa Riot** - *Riot Riot*; **Garry Johnson** - *Dead End Yobs*; **Last Resort** - *Working Class Kids*; **Criminal Class** - *Blood On The Streets*; **Toy Dolls** - *She Goes To Fino's*; Barney Rubble - *Best Years Of Our Lives*; **Cock Sparrer** - *Taken For A Ride (We Think You Don't)*; **Infa Riot** - *We Outnumber You*; **Garry Johnson** - *The New Face Of Rock 'n' Roll*; SIDE TWO: Barney Rubble - *Beans*; Splodge - *We're Pathétique*; **4-Skins** - *Sorry*; **Cock Sparrer** - *Running Riot*; **Last Resort** - *Johnny Barden*; Splodge - *Isubaleene (Part 2)*; **Criminal Class** - *Running Away*; **Strike** - *Skinhead*; **Toy Dolls** - *Deidre's A Slag*; Shaven Heads - *Harbour Mafia Mantra (An Acapella Delight)*.

NB: Later issued on Wonderful World (WOW LP 3).

That Summer! (Soundtrack) (Spartan/Arista SPART 1088) 1979
SIDE ONE: **Ian Dury and The Blockheads** - *Sex And Drugs And Rock & Roll*; Mink De Ville - *Spanish Stroll*; **Elvis Costello** - *(I Don't Want To Go To) Chelsea*; **Boomtown Rats** - *She's So Modern*; **Zones** - *New Life*; **Only Ones** - *Another Girl, Another Planet*; **Wreckless Eric** - *Whole Wide World*; Patti Smith Group - *Because The Night*. SIDE TWO: **Boomtown Rats** - *Kicks*; Ramones - *Rockaway Beach*; **Undertones** - *Teenage Kicks*; **Eddie and The Hot Rods** - *Do Anything You Wanna Do*; **Ian Dury and The Blockheads** - *What A Waste*; **Nick Lowe** - *I Love The Sound Of Breaking Glass*; **Elvis Costello** - *Watching The Detectives*; Richard Hell and The Voidoids - *Blank Generation*.

They Only Come Out At Night (Clay CLAYLP 17) 1985

THIS IS MOD.

This Is Mod (2-LP) (Get Back GET 39) 1999
SIDE ONE: **The Circles** - *Opening Up*; **The Killermeters** - *Why Should It Happen To Me*; **The Nips** - *Happy Song*; **The Amber Squad** - *Can We Go Dancing*; **The Deadbeats** - *Choose You*. SIDE TWO: **The Letters** - *Nobody Loves Me*; **The Odds** - *Saturday Night*; **The Purple Hearts** - *Gun Of Life*; **Long Tall Shorty** - *What's Going On*; **The Cigarettes** - *Can't Sleep At Night*. SIDE THREE: **Small World** - *Stupidity Street*; **The Nips** - *Nobody To Love*; **The Accidents** - *Blood Splattered With Guitars*; **The Amber Squad** - *I Can't Put My Finger On You*; **Sema 4** - *Even If I Know*. SIDE FOUR: The Untouchables UK - *Protect Your Love*; **The Scene** - *Looking For Love*; **Long Tall Shorty** - *On The Streets Again*; **The Rage** - *Looking For You*; **The Sussed** - *I've Got Me Parka*.

This Is Oi! (Oi OIR 004) 1986
NB: See CD section for track list.

Total Anarchy (Beat The System ANARCHY 1) 1982
SIDE ONE: **External Menace** - *What The Hell*; **One Way System** - *Riot Torn City*; **Uproar** - *Soldier Boy*; **Anti-Social** - *Your Choice*; **Fits** - *I Hate*; **Chaotic Youth** - *Out Of Order*; **Death Sentence** - *Die A Hero*; SIDE TWO: **One Way System** - *Me And You*; **Chaotic Youth** - *Don't Take Their Shit*; **Death Sentence** - *Death Sentence*; **Fits** - *Lights*; **Uproar** - *Boring Senseless Violence*; **Anti-Social** - *Screw You*; **External Menace** - *External Menace*.

Total Noise #1 (EP) (Total Noise TOT 1) 1982
SIDE ONE: **Business** - *Loud Proud And Punk*; **Blitz** - *Voice Of A Generation*; SIDE TWO: **The Gonads** - *TNT*; **Dead Generation** - *Francine*.

To The Shores Of Lake Placid (Zoo FOUR) 1982
SIDE ONE: **Big In Japan** - *Society For Cutting Up Men*; **Those Naughty Lumps** - *Iggy Pop's Jacket*; **The Teardrop Explodes** - *When I Dream*; **Echo and The Bunnymen** - *Pictures On My Wall*; **Echo and The Bunnymen** - *Read It In Books*; **Lori and The Chameleons** - *Lonely Spy*; **The Turquoise Swimming Pools** - *The Winds*. SIDE TWO: **Whopper** - *Kwalo Klobinsky's Lullaby*; **Dalek (I Love You)** - *A Suicide*; **The Turquoise Swimming Pools** - *Burst Balloons*; **The Teardrop Explodes** - *Camera Camera*; **Big In Japan** - *Suicide A Go Go*; **Echo and The Bunnymen** - *Villiers Terrace*; **The Teardrop Explodes** - *Take A Chance*.

A Trip To The Dentist (Skeleton SKL LP 1) 1980
(A Liverpool compilation featuring **Afraid Of Mice**)

TOTAL NOISE #1 (EP).

Trouble On The Terraces - 16 Classic Football Anthems (Step-1 STEP LP 91) 1996
ONSIDE: **Cock Sparrer** - *Trouble On The Terraces*; **Business** - *Saturday's Heroes*; **Infa Riot** - *Bootboys*; **Oppressed** - *We're The Hooligans*; **4-Skins** - *Saturday*; **Gonads** - *Tuckers Ruckers*; **Angelic Upstarts** - *Blood On The Terraces*; **Warriors** - *Here To Stay*. OFFSIDE: **Cock Sparrer** - *Runnin' Riot*; **Business** - *Handball*; **Infa Riot** - *Riot Riot*; **4-Skins** - *ACAB*; **Section 5** - *Every Saturday*; **Argy Bargy** - *Read All About It*; **Last Resort** - *Resort Bootboys*; **Warriors** - *Warriors (Come Out To Play)*.

20 Of Another Kind (Polydor POLS 1006) 1979
SIDE ONE: **Plastic Bertrand** - *Ca Plane Pour Moi*; **Jam** - *In The City*; **Skids** - *Sweet Suburbia*; **Otway and Barratt** - *Beware Of The Flowers ('Cos I'm Sure They're Going To Get You Yeh!)*; **Sham 69** - *Borstal Breakout*; **Cure** - *Killing An Arab*; **Stiff Little Fingers** - *Suspect Device*; **Adverts** - *Gary Gilmore's Eyes*; **Generation X** - *Ready Steady Go*; **999** - *Homicide*; SIDE TWO: **Stranglers** - *No More Heroes*; **Boys** - *The First Time*; **Patrik Fitzgerald** - *Irrelevant Battles*; **Sham 69** - *If The Kids Are United*; **Jolt** - *No Excuses*; **Otway and Barratt** - *Really Free*; **Heartbreakers** - *Born Too Loose*; **999** - *Emergency*; **Lurkers** - *I'm On Heat*; **Jam** - *'A' Bomb In Wardour Street*.

20 Of Another Kind, Vol. 2 (Polydor POLX-1) 1979
SIDE ONE: **Jam** - *Strange Town*; **Tubeway Army** - *Down In The Park*; **Cure** - *Boys Don't Cry*; **Twist** - *Ads*; **Chords** - *Now It's Gone*; **Sham 69** - *No Entry*; **Patrik Fitzgerald** - *All Sewn Up*; **Protex** - *I Can't Cope*; **Invaders** - *Best Thing I Ever Did (New Future)*; **Purple Hearts** - *Millions Like Us*. SIDE TWO: **Sham 69** - *Hersham Boys*; **Lurkers** - *Out In The Dark*; **Twist** - *This Is Your Life*; **Headboys** - *The Shape Of Things To

TROUBLE ON THE TERRACES - 16 CLASSIC FOOTBALL ANTHEMS.

20 OF ANOTHER KIND, VOL. 2.

Come; **Jam** - *The Butterfly Collector*; **Patrik Fitzgerald** - *Improve Myself*; **Invaders** - *Girls In Action*; **Carpettes** - *Lost Love*; **Xdreamysts** - *Bad News*; **Gary Numan** - *Tracks*.

Two Ninety Nine (Rot ASS 10) 1984
SIDE ONE: **Animal Farm** - *Model Soldier*; Killroy - *Red Alert*; Naked Prey - *Bone Orchard*; **Mania** - *We Don't Need You*; Clampdown - *Use Your Brain*; Sick Vicars - *Zombie Nation*; Radio Nine - *Desperation Times*; Patrol - *Don't Criticise*; **Enemy** - *Last But Not Least (live)*; SIDE TWO: Patrol - *S.S. Officer*; Clampdown - *Murder And Maim*; **Resistance 77** - *Russia*; Those Obnoxious Types - *I'm Glad I'm Sick*; Radio Nine - *Where Are They Now?*; **Mania** - *Shoulder To Shoulder*; Naked Prey - *Call Of The Reaper*; Sick Vicars - *Shattered Mirror*; **Paranoia** - *Dead Man's Dreams*.

Unzipping The Abstract (Manchester Musicians Collective) 1980

Uppers On The South Downs (Safari UPP 1) 1980

Vaultage '78 (Two Sides Of Brighton) (Attrix RB 03) 1978
SIDE ONE: **Nicky and The Dots** - *Girl Gets Nervous*; **Nicky and The Dots** - *I Find That Really Suprises Me*; **Nicky and The Dots** - *Wrong Street*; **Dodgems** - *I Don't Care*; **Devil's Dykes** - *Fruitless*; **Devil's Dykes** - *Plastic Flowers*; **Peter and The Test Tube Babies** - *Elvis Is Dead*. SIDE TWO: **Parrots** - *Larger Than Life*; **Parrots** - *Vicious Circles*; **Vitamins** - *Newtown*; **Dodgems** - *Lord Lucan Is Missing*; **Piranhas** - *Tension*; **Piranhas** - *Virginity*; **Piranhas** - *I Don't Want My Body*.

Vaultage '79 (Attrix RB 08) 1979
SIDE ONE: **Vandells** - *Bank Holiday*; **Vandells** - *Another Girl*; **Chefs** - *You Get Everywhere*; **Chefs** - *Food*; **Golinski Brothers** - *Bloody*; **Golinski Brothers** - *Too Scared*; SIDE TWO: **Lillettes** - *Hey Operator*; **Lillettes** - *Nervous Wreck*; **Ijax All Stars** - *Sounchek*; **Ijax All Stars** - *Reggaed Rumble*; **Woody and The Splinters** - *I Want You To Be My Girl*; **Woody and The Splinters** - *I Must Be Mad*.

Vaultage '80 (Attrix RB 11) 1980
SIDE ONE: Birds With Ears - *Head In My Bag*; Objeks - *Negative Conversation*; Emma Sharpe - *Motorway*; **Reward System** - *Extradition*; Hollow Men - *Never Again*; Idrenes - *Red Gold And Green*; Dick Damage and The Dilemma - *Do The Winklepicker*; SIDE TWO: Red Squares - *The Russians Are Coming*; Mockingbirds - *Money*; Exclusives - *Sinking Gondola*; April and The Fools - *You Do*; Ammonites - *Blue Lagoon*; Bright Girls - *Hidden From History*; Life Size Models - *Have You Seen My Friend*.

Voices, Notes And Noise (Recommended RM 01) 198?

VAULTAGE '78.

Wanna Buy A Bridge? (Rough Trade 053) 1980
NB: This album was marketed in the 'States.

Wargasm (Pax PAX 4) 1982
SIDE ONE: **Danse Society** - *Continent*; **Flux Of Pink Indians** - *Tapioca Sunrise*; Canker Opera - *White Coffins*; Dead Kennedys - *Kinky Sex Makes The World Go Round*; Rat Scabies - *I Hate War*; SIDE TWO: **Poison Girls** - *Statement*; Captain Sensible - *Hey Jo*; **Mau Maus** - *The Kill*; **Angelic Upstarts** - *Victory For Poland*; **System** - *Their Decisions*; **Infa Riot** - *Power*; Quite Unnerving - *Wargasm*.

We Couldn't Agree On A Title (Integrated Circuit) 1981

Wet Dreams (Rot ASS 4) 1984
SIDE ONE: **Riot Squad** - *Unite And Fight*; **Breakout** - *Waste Away*; **Paranoia** - *Shattered Glass*; **Clockwork Soldiers** - *Hit And Run*; **Christianity B.C.** - *Trinity*; **X-Cretas** - *Familiarity*; **Resistance 77** - *Communist Cunt*; **Dead Man's Shadow** - *Flower In The Gun*; SIDE TWO: **X-Cretas** - *It's Our Life*; **Riot Squad** - *Friday Night Hero*; **Paranoia** - *Disillusion*; **Resistance 77** - *Send In The SAS*; **Christianity B.C.** - *What A Shame*; **External Menace** - *Shocktrooper*; **Clockwork Soldiers** - *Dream*.

What A Nice Way To Turn Seventeen No. 3 (Rather RATHER 13) 1984

VAULTAGE '79.

What You See Is What You Are (Deptford Fun City DLP 02) 1978
SIDE ONE: **Alternative TV** - *Action Time Vision*; **Alternative TV** - *Going Round In Circles*; **Alternative TV** - *Fellow Sufferer*; **Alternative TV** - *Splitting In Two*. SIDE TWO: Here and Now - *What You See... Is What You Are*; Here and Now - *Dog In Hell*; Here and Now - *Addicted*.

Where The Hell Is Leicester (S&T) 1980
(A local Leicester compilation featuring **The Amber Squad**).

WNW6 - Moonlight Radio (Armageddon MOON 1) 1981
SIDE ONE: Out On Blue Six - *Examples*; Room - *Chat Shows*; Dr. Mix and The Remix - *Heat*; **Chefs** - *Locked Out*; **Artery** - *Into The Garden*; Academy One - *Heaven*; SIDE TWO: Icarus - *Tower Block Kid*; Pinkies - *Cartoon*; Flying Club - *Next Two Minutes*; Flying Club - *Keep Still Keep Quiet*; **Patrik Fitzgerald** Group - *Breathing's Painful*; Decorators - *Twilight View*.

World War 3 (Rot WW 001) 1987

Special thanks to Mark Brennan for help in compiling this section.

WET DREAMS.

Oi! SINGLES COLLECTION, VOL. 4.

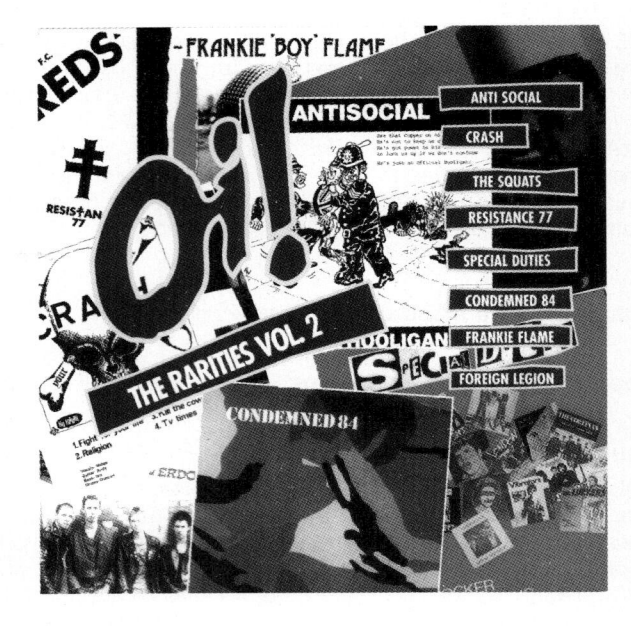

Oi! THE RARITIES VOL. 2.

FLICKNIFE PUNK SINGLES COLLECTION.

ABSTRACT PUNK SINGLES COLLECTION.

A SELECTION OF CD COMPILATIONS

NB: Artists in bold appear as entries in this book.

1-2-3-4 - A History Of Punk And New Wave (1976-79) (5-CD) (MCA/Universal MCD 60066) 1999

DISC ONE: **Clash** - *Complete Control*; **Sex Pistols** - *Anarchy In The UK*; **Damned** - *New Rose*; Ramones - *The Blitzkrieg Bop*; **Lurkers** - *Shadow*; **Eater** - *Thinkin' Of The USA*; **Nosebleeds** - *Ain't Bin To No Music School*; **Sham 69** - *Borstal Breakout*; **Suburban Studs** - *I Hate School*; **Menace** - *G.L.C.*; **Adverts** - *One Chord Wonders*; **Chelsea** - *Right To Work*; **Killjoys** - *Johnny Won't Get To Heaven*; **Drones** - *Bone Idol*; **Slaughter and The Dogs** - *Where Have All The Boot Boys Gone*; **UK Subs** - *C.I.D.*; **Wasps** - *Can't Wait 'Till '78*; **Subway Sect** - *Ambition*; **Saints** - *(I'm) Stranded*; **Buzzcocks** - *Orgasm Addict*. DISC TWO: **Jam** - *In The City*; **Generation X** - *Your Generation*; **Boys** - *First Time*; **Stranglers** - *(Get A) Grip (On Yourself)*; **Penetration** - *Don't Dictate*; **Ruts** - *In A Rut*; **Rudi** - *Big Time*; **Protex** - *Don't Ring Me Up*; **Outcasts** - *Just Another Teenage Rebel*; **Members** - *Solitary Confinement*; **999** - *Emergency*; **Leyton Buzzards** - *19 And Mad*; **Not Sensibles** - *I'm In Love With Margaret Thatcher*; **Riff Raff** - *Romford Girls*; **Users** - *Sick Of You*; **Nips** - *Gabrielle*; **Mekons** - *Where Were You?*; **Angelic Upstarts** - *Murder Of Liddle Towers*; **X Ray Spex** - *Oh Bondage Up Yours!*; **Skids** - *Sweet Suburbia*; **Radiators From Space** - *Television Screen*; **Stiff Little Fingers** - *Alternative Ulster*; **Undertones** - *Teenage Kicks*. DISC THREE: **Eddie and The Hot Rods** - *Teenage Depression*; **Rich Kids** - *Rich Kids*; **Vibrators** - *Baby Baby*; **Yachts** - *Suffice To Say*; Jonathan Richman and The Modern Lovers - *Roadrunner*; **Klark Kent** - *Don't Care*; **Radio Stars** - *Nervous Wreck*; **Tom Robinson Band** - *Up Against The Wall*; **Nick Lowe** - *So It Goes*; **Larry Wallis** - *Police Car*; **Johnny Moped** - *Hard Lovin' Man*; **Flys** - *Love And A Molotov Cocktail*; **Spizzenergi** - *Where's Captain Kirk?*; Dead Boys - *Sonic Reducer*; Dictators - *Search & Destroy*; Heartbreakers - *Born To Lose*; Pere Ubu - *The Modern Dance*; **Electric Chairs** - *Fuck Off*; Dead Kennedys - *California Uber Alles*. DISC FOUR: Richard Hell and The Voidoids - *(I Belong To The) Blank Generation*; **Cure** - *10:15 Saturday Night*; Blondie - *Rip Her To Shreds*; **Rezillos** - *I Can't Stand My Baby*; **Snatch** - *All I Want*; **Boomtown Rats** - *Looking After No. 1*; **Squeeze** - *Take Me I'm Yours*; **Ian Dury and The Blockheads** - *Sex And Drugs And Rock & Roll*; Mink Deville - *Spanish Stroll*; **Joe Jackson** - *Is She Really Going Out With Him?*; **Wreckless Eric** - *Whole Wide World*; **Television Personalities** - *Part-Time Punks*; **Patrik Fitzgerald** - *Safety Pin Stuck In My Heart*; Johnny Thunders - *You Can't Put Your Arm Round A Memory*; **John Cooper Clarke** - *Psycle Sluts (Part 1)*; **Jilted John** - *Jilted John*; **Albertos Y Los Trios Paranoias** - *Kill*; The Dickies - *Paranoid*. DISC FIVE: **Public Image Ltd** - *Public Image*; **Joy Division** - *Warsaw*; **Siouxsie and The Banshees** - *The Staircase (Mystery)*; **Gang Of Four** - *Damaged Goods*; **Au Pairs** - *You*; **Alternative TV** - *How Much Longer*; **Swell Maps** - *Read About Seymour*; **Adam and The Ants** - *Young Parisians*; **Monochrome Set** - *The Monochrome Set*; **Pop Group** - *We Are All Prostitutes*; **Slits** - *Typical Girls*; **Wire** - *Mannequin*; **Magazine** - *Shot By Both Sides*; **XTC** - *Science Friction*; **Table** - *Do The Standing Still*; **Only Ones** - *Another Girl, Another Planet*; **Ultravox!** - *Young Savage*; **Punishment Of Luxury** - *Puppet Life*; Devo - *Jocko Homo*; Television - *Marquee Moon*.

100% British Mod (2-CD) (Captain Mod MODSKACD 008) 1998

Accidents - *Blood Splattered With Guitars*; **Aces** - *One Way Street*; **Amber Squad** - *Can We Go Dancing*; **Blue Movies** - *Mary Jane*; **Cigarettes** - *They're Back Again*; **Circles** - *Circles*; **Clerks** - *When The Lights Go Out*; **Clueless** - *No Vacancies*; **Crooks** - *Modern Boys*; **Deadbeats** - *Choose You*; **Directions** - *Three Bands Tonight*; **Exits** - *Fashion Plague*; **Fast Cars** - *Kids Just Wanna Dance*; **Just Frank** - *You*; **Justin Case** - *Statik Motion*; **Killermeters** - *Why Should It Happen To Me*; **Letters** - *Nobody Loves Me*; **Long Tall Shorty** - *1970's Boy*; **Media** - *Back On The Beach Again*; **Name** - *Fuck Art Let's Dance*; **Nightriders** - *I Saw Her With Another Guy*; **Odds** - *Saturday Night*; **Purple Hearts** - *Plane Crash*; **Reputations** - *I Believe You*; **Run 229** - *Soho*; **Same** - *Wild About You*; **Scene** - *Hey Girl*; **Scoop** - *You Can Do It*; **Sema 4** - *Sema 4 Messages*; **Small World** - *First Impressions*; **Split Screen** - *Know What I Want*; **Squire** - *Livin' In The City*; **Straight Up** - *One Out All Out*; **Stripes** - *One Step Ahead*; **Sussed** - *I've Got Me Parka*; **Teenage Film Stars** - *I Apologise*; **Terry Tonik** - *Just A Little Mod*; **Vandells** - *Bank Holiday*; **VIP's** - *Just Can't Let You Go*; **What** - *East Coast Kids*.

100% BRITISH Oi!.

100% British Oi! (2-CD) (Captain Oi! AHOY CD 083) 1998

ABH - *Don't Mess With The SAS*; **Angelic Upstarts** - *Victory In Poland*; **Anti-Establishment** - *1980's*; **Anti-Social** - *Official Hooligan*; **Attak** - *Today's Generation*; **Barbed Wire** - *Age That Didn't Care*; **Blitz** - *Warriors*; **Blood** - *Such Fun*; **Burial** - *Friday Night*; **Business** - *Product*; **Cockney Rejects** - *Beginning Of The End*; **Cock Sparrer** - *Chip On My Shoulder*; **Combat 84** - *Poseur*; **Condemned 84** - *Oi! Ain't Dead*; **Crack** - *Going Out*; **Criminal Class** - *Fighting The System*; **Crux** - *CIA*; **Ejected** - *Have You Got 10p*; **Five O** - *Dr. Crippens*; **4-Skins** - *Sorry*; **Gonads** - *Jobs Not Jails*; **Guttersnipes** - *Addicted To Love*; **Infa Riot** - *Riot Riot*; **Intensive Care** - *Ghost Town*; **Last Resort** - *Resort Bootboys*; **Menace** - *Screwed Up*; **Menace** - *White Flag*; **Partisans** - *17 Years Of Hell*; **Peter and The Test Tube Babies** - *Up Yer Bum*; **Prole** - *Generation Landslide*; **Red Alert** - *Take No Prisoners*; **Section 5** - *For The Love Of Oi!*; **Sham 69** - *Borstal Breakout*; **Skin Deep** - *Football Violence*; **Slaughter and The Dogs** - *Situations*; **Splodgenessabounds** - *Pathetique*; **Strike** - *Skinhead*; **Subculture** - *Loud And Clear*; **Vicious Rumours** - *Anytime Day Or Night*; **Warriors** - *Horror Show*.

100% Hardcore Punk (2-CD) (Captain Oi! AHOY DCD 84) 1998

DISC ONE: **Abrasive Wheels** - *The Army Song*; **Abrasive Wheels** - *Shout It Out*; Anthrax - *They've Got It All Wrong*; **Blitz** - *Never Surrender*; **Blitzkrieg** - *The Future Must Be Ours*; **The Blood** - *Meglomania*; **Broken Bones** - *Decapitated*; **Chaos UK** - *Four Minute Warning*; **Chaos UK** - *No Security*; **Chaotic Discord** - *Fuck Religion Fuck Politics*; **Discharge** - *Decontrol*; **Disorder** - *Rampton Song*; **Disorder** - *Complete Disorder*; **English Dogs** - *Psycho Killer*; **English Dogs** - *Ultimate Sacrifice*; **The Exploited** - *Dead Cities*; **The Exploited** - *Rival Leaders*; **External Menace** - *No Views*; **The Fits** - *Too Many Rules*; **G.B.H.** - *Sick Boy*. DISC TWO: **The Insane** - *Dead And Gone*; **Mau Maus** - *Society's Rejects*; **Mau Maus** - *Just Another Day*; **Mayhem** - *Psycho*; **Oi Polloi** - *Thugs In Uniform*; **One Way System** - *No Return*; **One Way System** - *Give Us A Future*; **The Partisans** - *Police Story*; **The Partisans** - *No U Turns*; **Resistance 77** - *Nuclear Attack*; **Riot Squad** - *Society's Fodder*; **Riot Squad** - *Lost Cause*; **Skeptix** - *Traitor*; **Special Duties** - *Violent Youth*; **T.D.A.** - *T.D.A.*; **The Threats** - *Politicians & Ministers*; **Ultra Violent** - *Crime For Revenge*; **Uproar** - *Rebel Youth*; **The Varukers** - *Die For Your Government*; **The Varukers** - *Led To The Slaughter*.

100% Punk (Telstar Arena TAECD 4107) 1999

Blondie - *Hanging On The Telephone*; **Psychedelic Furs** - *Pretty In Pink*; **Ian Dury** - *What A Waste*; **Stranglers** - *No More Heroes*; **Ian Dury** - *Sheena Is A Punk Rocker*; **Buzzcocks** - *Ever Fallen In Love*; **Stiff Little Fingers** - *Alternative Ulster*; **Generation X** - *Your Generation*; **Only Ones** - *Another Girl Another Planet*; **Undertones** - *Teenage Kicks*; **Sham 69** - *If

The Kids Are United; **Dead Kennedys** - *Holiday In Cambodia*; **Adicts** - *Love Sucks*; **Adverts** - *Bored Teenagers*; **John Cooper Clarke** - *Beesley Street*; **Television** - *Marquee Moon*.

25 Years Of Rough Trade Shops
(4-CD Box Set) (Mute CDSTUMM 191) 2001

DISC ONE: **Pere Ubu** - *30 Seconds Over Tokyo*; **Buzzcocks** - *Boredom*; **Congos** - *Fisherman*; **Cabaret Voltaire** - *Nag Nag Nag*; **The Normal** - *T.V.O.D.*; **Stiff Little Fingers** - *Suspect Device*; **Throbbing Gristle** - *United*; **Subway Sect** - *Ambition*; **Television Personalities** - *Part-Time Punks*; **Raincoats** - *Fairytale In The Supermarket*; **Crass** - *Reality Asylum*; **Joy Division** - *Transmission*; **Go-Betweens** - *People Say*; **Swell Maps** - *Let's Build A Car*; **Young Marble Giants** - *Final Day*; **Fall** - *How I Wrote 'Elephant Man'*; **Birthday Party** - *Mr. Clarinet*. DISC TWO: **...And The Native Hipsters** - *There Goes Concorde Again*; **Scritti Politti** - *The Sweetest Girl*; **Robert Wyatt** - *Shipbuilding*; **Foetus** - *Gums Bleed*; **Smiths** - *Hand In Glove*; **Cocteau Twins** - *Sugar Hiccup*; **Einstürzende Neubauten** - *Krieg In Den Stadten*; **Nick Cave and The Bad Seeds** - *Tupelo*; **Talking Heads** - *Road To Nowhere*; **Sonic Youth** - *Death Valley '69*; **Tackhead** - *Hard Left*; **Lee 'Scratch' Perry and Dub Syndicate** - *Jungle*; **Sugarcubes** - *Birthday*.

NB: Discs 3 and 4 not relevant to this book.

Abstract Punk Singles Collection
(Anagram CDPUNK 52) 1995

Gymslips - *48 Crash*; **Gymslips** - *Big Sister*; **Gymslips** - *Robot Man*; **U.K. Subs** - *Self Destruct*; **U.K. Subs** - *Police State*; **U.K. Subs** - *War Of The Roses*; **New Model Army** - *Vengence*; **Outcasts** - *Nowhere To Run*; **Joolz** - *Denise*; **AWOL** - *Three Johns*; **New Model Army** - *Great Expectations*; **New Model Army** - *Price*; **Hagar The Womb** - *Armchair*; **Gymslips** - *Evil Eye*; **Gymslips** - *Drink Problem*; **Downbeats** - *Daddy's Been Working*; **Redskins** - *Lean On Me*; **Redskins** - *Unionise*; **Newtown Neurotics** - *Kick Out The Tories*; **Newtown Neurotics** - *Mindless Violence*.

ANAGRAM PUNK SINGLES COLLECTION.

Anagram Punk Singles Collection
(Anagram CDPUNK 37) 1994

One Way System - *Give Us A Future*; **One Way System** - *Just Another Hero*; **Pressure** - *You Talk We Talk*; **Angelic Upstarts** - *Woman In Disguise*; **Angelic Upstarts** - *Lust For Glory*; **Vibrators** - *Baby Baby*; **Vibrators** - *Dragnet*; **One Way System** - *Jerusalem*; **Pressure** - *Pressure*; **Angelic Upstarts** - *Solidarity*; **Angelic Upstarts** - *Five Flew Over The Cuckoo's Nest*; **Vibrators** - *Guilty*; **Vibrators** - *Hang Ten*; **One Way System** - *Cum On Feel The Noise*; **One Way System** - *Breakin' In*; **Outcasts** - *Nowhere Left To Run*; **Angelic Upstarts** - *Not Just A Name*; **One Way System** - *This Is The Age*; **Vice Squad** - *Black Sheep*; **One Way System** - *Children Of The Night*; **Vice Squad** - *You'll Never Know*; **Furyo** - *Legacy*; **Vice Squad** - *Teenage Rampage*.

The Beat Generation And The Angry Young Men
(Captain Mod MODSKA CD 3) 1997

Long Tall Shorty - *That's What I Want*; **Small Hours** - *Underground*; **Purple Hearts** - *I'll Make You Mine*; **Les Elite** - *Frustration*; **Long Tall Shorty** - *I Do*; **Merton Parkas** - *Dangerous Man*; **Les Elite** - *Get A Job*; **Directions** - *Weekend Dancers*; **Purple Hearts** - *Concrete Mixer*; **Les Elite** - *Career Girl*; **Long Tall Shorty** - *All By Myself*; **Directions** - *It May Be Too Late*; **Merton Parkas** - *You Say You Will*; **Small Hours** - *The Kid*; **Purple Hearts** - *Hazy Darkness*.

Beat The System Punk Singles Collection
(Anagram CDPUNK 61) 1995

One Way System - *Stab The Judge*; **One Way System** - *Riot Torn City*; **External Menace** - *Youth Of Today*; **External Menace** - *Someday*; **Uproar** - *Die For Me*; **Uproar** - *Better Off Dead*; **Chaotic Youth** - *Sad Society*; **Chaotic Youth** - *No Future UK*; **Fits** - *I Hate*; **Fits** - *Time Is Right*; **Anti-Social** - *Official Hooligan*; **External Menace** - *No Views*; **External Menace** - *Poor Excuse*; **Anti-Social** - *Backstreet Boys*; **Death Sentence** - *Death Sentence*; **Anti-Social** - *Too Many People*; **Uproar** - *Rebel Youth*; **Uproar** - *Victims*; **Post Mortem** - *IRA*; **Post Mortem** - *Day By Day*; **One Way System** - *Me And You*; **Chaotic Youth** - *Arms Race*; **Death Sentence** - *Victims Of War*; **Fits** - *Listen To Me*.

BEAT THE SYSTEM PUNK SINGLES COLLECTION.

The Beggars Banquet Punk Collection
(Anagram CDPUNK 73) 1996

Lurkers - *Shadow*; **Lurkers** - *Freak Show*; **Doll** - *Don't Tango On My Heart*; **Doll** - *Trash*; **Tubeway Army** - *That's Too Bad*; **Lurkers** - *Ain't Got A Clue*; **Tubeway Army** - *Bombers*; **Tubeway Army** - *I Don't Need To Tell Her*; **Doll** - *Desire Me*; **Lurkers** - *Just 13*; **Lurkers** - *Out In The Dark*; **Doll** - *Cinderella With A Husky Smile*; **Carpettes** - *I Don't Mean It*; **Lurkers** - *New Guitar In Town*; **Doll** - *You Used To Be My Hero*; **Carpettes** - *Johnny Won't Hurt Me*; **Carpettes** - *Nothing Ever Changes*; **Carpettes** - *Last Lone Ranger*; **Stride, Pete & John Plain** - *Laugh At Me*; **Ivor Biggun** - *Winkers Song*.

The Best Of Oi! Records
(Captain Oi! AHOY CD 38) 1995

Oppressed - *Joe Hawkins*; **Section 5** - *We Won't Change*; **Condemned 84** - *Survive*; **Oi! Polloi** - *Skinhead*; **Vicious Rumours** - *Anytime Day Or Night*; **Barbed Wire** - *The Age That Didn't Care*; **Last Rough Cause** - *My Life*; **Society's Rejects** - *United We Stand*; **Betrayed** - *United Oi!*; **Magnificent** - *Coming On Strong*; **Glory** - *Clockwork Land*; **Abnormal** - *New Generation*; **Barbed Wire** - *Don't Let The Bastards Beat You*; **Oppressed** - *Victims*; **Last Stand** - *Approved Cuts*; **Press** - *It's Not What I Want*; **Radicts** - *Kids Of The Nation*; **Winston & The Churchills** - *Why Do You?*.

The Best Of Punk
(Select SELCD 577) 2001

Damned - *Neat Neat Neat*; **Vibrators** - *Automatic Lover*; **Jilted John** - *Jilted John*; **Sham 69** - *If The Kids Are United*; **The Runaways** - *Black Leather*; **Jonathan Richman** - *Roadrunner*; **Damned** - *Disguise*; **Stranglers**

- *Peaches* (live); Dead Kennedys - *California Uber Alles*; **Damned** - *Lovely Money*; **Sham 69** - *Hersham Boys*; Jonathan Richman - *Egyptian Reggae*; **Damned** - *I Think I'm Wonderful*; **Sham 69** - *Hurry Up Harry*; **Vice Squad** - *Teenage Rampage*; Dead Kennedys - *Holiday In Cambodia*; **Patrick Fitzgerald** - *Safety Pin Stuck In My Heart*.

The Best Punk Album In The World... Ever, Vol. 1
(2-CD)　　　　　　　　　　　　　　　(Virgin VTDCD 42) 1995

Sex Pistols - *Anarchy In The UK*; **Buzzcocks** - *Ever Fallen In Love*; **Undertones** - *Teenage Kicks*; **Skids** - *Into The Valley*; **Damned** - *New Rose*; **Ruts** - *Babylon's Burning*; Ramones - *Sheena Is A Punk Rocker*; **Members** - *Sound Of The Suburbs*; **Jam** - *All Around The World*; **Only Ones** - *Another Girl Another Planet*; Iggy Pop - *Passenger*; **XTC** - *Making Plans For Nigel*; **Stranglers** - *Peaches*; **Ian Dury and The Blockheads** - *Sex And Drugs And Rock & Roll*; **Chelsea** - *(I Don't Want To Go To) Chelsea*; Blondie - *Denis*; **Tom Robinson Band** - *2-4-6-8 Motorway*; Dr. Feelgood - *Milk And Alcohol*; **Boomtown Rats** - *Looking After No. 1*; **Adam and The Ants** - *Deutscher Girls*; **Siouxsie and The Banshees** - *Christine*; **X-Ray Spex** - *Identity*; **Bow Wow Wow** - *C30 C60 C90 Go*; **Public Image Ltd.** - *Public Image*; **Sid Vicious** - *My Way*; **Sex Pistols** - *God Save The Queen*; **Damned** - *Neat Neat Neat*; **Adverts** - *Gary Gilmore's Eyes*; **Rezillos** - *Top Of The Pops*; **Motors** - *Dancing The Night Away*; **Buzzcocks** - *What Do I Get?*; **Jilted John** - *Jilted John*; **Wire** - *I Am The Fly*; Devo - *Mongoloid*; Jonathan Richman and The Modern Lovers - *Roadrunner*; Tubes - *White Punks On Dope*; Richard Hell and The Voidoids - *Blank Generation*; Television - *Marquee Moon*; Talking Heads - *Psycho Killer*; **Pretenders** - *Stop Your Sobbing*; **Joe Jackson** - *Is She Really Going Out With Him?*; **Generation X** - *Ready Steady Go*; **Stranglers** - *(Get A) Grip (On Yourself)*; **Magazine** - *Shot By Both Sides*; **Stiff Little Fingers** - *Alternative Ulster*; **Killing Joke** - *Eighties*; **Flying Lizards** - *Money*; **John Cooper Clarke** - *Kung Fu International*.

The Best Punk Album In The World... Ever, Vol. 2
(2-CD)　　　　　　　　　　　　　　　(Virgin VTDCD 79) 1996

Sex Pistols - *Pretty Vacant*; Iggy Pop - *Lust For Life*; **Stranglers** - *No More Heroes*; **Siouxsie and The Banshees** - *Hong Kong Garden*; **Spizze nergi 2** - *Where's Captain Kirk?*; **Buzzcocks** - *Orgasm Addict*; **Eddie and The Hot Rods** - *Do Anything You Want To Do*; **Jam** - *Eton Rifles*; **Undertones** - *My Perfect Cousin*; Blondie - *Hanging On The Telephone*; **Saints** - *This Perfect Day*; **Ruts** - *Staring At The Rude Boys*; **X-Ray Spex** - *Day The World Turned Day-glo*; **Generation X** - *King Rocker*; **Bow Wow Wow** - *I Want Candy*; **Adam and The Ants** - *Kings Of The Wild Frontier*; **B-52's** - *Rock Lobster*; **Elvis Costello and The Attractions** - *Pump It Up*; **Ian Dury and The Blockheads** - *Sweet Gene Vincent*; **Nick Lowe** - *So It Goes*; Mink Deville - *Spanish Stroll*; **Pretenders** - *Brass In Pocket*; **Psychedelic Furs** - *Pretty In Pink*; **Boomtown Rats** - *Rat Trap*; **Sex Pistols** - *Holiday In The Sun*; **Stranglers** - *Something Better Change*; **Sham 69** - *If The Kids Are United*; **Vapors** - *Turning Japanese*; **Buzzcocks** - *I Don't Mind*; **Penetration** - *Don't Dictate*; **Skids** - *Saints Are Coming*; Dr. Feelgood - *She Does It Right*; Richard Hell and The Voidoids - *Love Comes In Spurts*; Dead Boys - *Sonic Reducer*; Patti Smith Group - *Rock 'n'*

THE BEGGARS BANQUET PUNK SINGLES COLLECTION.

THE BEST OF Oi! RECORDS.

Roll Nigger; **Stiff Little Fingers** - *Suspect Device*; **Damned** - *Smash It Up*; Tubes - *Don't Touch Me There*; Flamin' Groovies - *Shake Some Action*; **Banned** - *Little Girl*; **Wreckless Eric** - *Whole Wide World*; **Teardrop Explodes** - *Treason (It's Just A Story)*; **Wire** - *Outdoor Miner*; Devo - *Satisfaction*; **Public Image Ltd.** - *Death Disco*; **Joy Division** - *Love Will Tear Us Apart*; **John Cooper Clarke** - *Beasley Street*.

The Best Punk Anthems... Ever
(2-CD)　　　　　　　　　　　　　　　(Virgin VTDCD 198) 1998

Members - *Sound Of The Suburbs*; **Tom Robinson Band** - *2-4-6-8 Motorway*; **Jam** - *Eton Rifles*; **Jilted John** - *Jilted John*; **Eddie and The Hot Rods** - *Do Anything You Wanna Do*; **Damned** - *New Rose*; **Sham 69** - *If The Kids Are United*; **Undertones** - *Teenage Kicks*; Iggy Pop - *Lust For Life*; **Skids** - *Into The Valley*; **Ian Dury and The Blockheads** - *Sex And Drugs And Rock & Roll*; **Buzzcocks** - *Orgasm Addict*; **Wire** - *I Am The Fly*; Richard Hell and The Voidoids - *Blank Generation*; **Magazine** - *Shot By Both Sides*; Dr. Feelgood - *Milk And Alcohol*; Devo - *Mongoloid*; **999** - *Emergency*; **Wire** - *Outdoor Miner*; **Rezillos** - *Top Of The Pops*; **Flying Lizards** - *Money*; **Buzzcocks** - *Ever Fallen In Love*; Blondie - *Hanging On The Telephone*; **Stranglers** - *Peaches*; **Bow Wow Wow** - *C30 C60 C90 Go*; **Stiff Little Fingers** - *Alternative Ulster*; **Sid Vicious** - *My Way*; Ramones - *Sheena Is A Punk Rocker*; **John Cooper Clarke** - *Kung Fu International*; **Damned** - *Neat Neat Neat*; **Adverts** - *Gary Gilmore's Eyes*; **XTC** - *Making Plans For Nigel*; **Undertones** - *Jimmy Jimmy*; **Vapors** - *Turning Japanese*; **Motors** - *Dancing The Night Away*; **Skids** - *Saints Are Coming*; **Public Image Ltd.** - *Public Image*; **Stranglers** - *(Get A) Grip (On Yourself)*; **Penetration** - *Don't Dictate*; **X-Ray Spex** - *Identity*; **Elvis Costello and The Attractions** - *(I Don't Want To Go To) Chelsea*; Iggy Pop - *Passenger*; **Sex Pistols** - *God Save The Queen*; **Only Ones** - *Another Girl, Another Planet*; **Ruts** - *Babylon's Burning*; Television - *Marquee Moon*; Jonathan Richmond's Modern Lovers - *Roadrunner*.

Bollocks To Christmas　　　　　(Dojo DOJOCD 204) 1994

Bad Manners - *Christmas Time Again*; Frank Sidebottom - *Christmas Is Really Fantastic*; **Business** - *Step Into Christmas*; **Anti-Nowhere League** - *Snowman*; Frantic Flintstones - *Blue Christmas*; **4-Skins** - *Merry Christmas Everybody*; Frank Sidebottom - *O Come All Ye Faithful (Adeste Fidelis)*; Judge Dread - *Jingle Bells*; **U.K. Subs** - *Hey Santa*; **Splodge** - *Twelve Days Of Christmas*; Alien Sex Fiend - *Stuff The Turkey*; **Yobs** - *Another Christmas*; Frank Sidebottom - *I Wish It Could Be Christmas*; Macc Lads - *Jingle Bells*; Judge Dread - *Christmas In Dreadland*; Hot Knives - *Turkey Stomp*; Frantic Flintstones - *Santa Bring My Baby Back*; **U.K. Subs** - *Auld Lang Syne*; **Yobs** - *C-h-r-i-s-t-m-a-s*; **Gonads** - *White Christmas*; **Business** - *Drinking And Driving*; Frank Sidebottom - *Christmas Medley*; **Stiff Little Fingers** - *White Christmas* (live).

British Punk Rock 1977　　　　(Anagram CDPUNK 500) 1998

Alternative TV - *How Much Longer*; **Carpettes** - *Radio Wunderbar*; **Cock Sparrer** - *Running Riot*; Oroonies - *Corgi Crap*; **Eater** - *Thinking Of The USA*; **Killjoys** - *Johnny Won't Get To Heaven*; **Menace** - *Insane Society*;

Puncture - *Mucky Pup*; **Blitzkrieg Bop** - *Let's Go*; **Suburban Studs** - *Questions*; **Unwanted** - *Withdrawal*; **Vibrators** - *Baby Baby (I Know You're A Lady)*; **Depressions** - *Living On Dreams*; **Users** - *Sick Of You*; **Maniacs** - *Chelsea '77*; **Zeros** - *Hungry*; **Snivelling Shits** - *I Can't Come*; **Cane** - *College Girls*; **999** - *Nasty Nasty*; **Wasps** - *Can't Wait Until '78*.

Burning Ambitions
(A History Of Punk)   (Anagram CDBRED 3) 1996

Buzzcocks - *Boredom*; **Fall** - *Bingo Masters Breakout*; **Wire** - *12XU*; **Alternative TV** - *Life*; **101'ers** - *Keys To Your Heart*; **999** - *I'm Alive*; **Adverts** - *Gary Gilmore's Eyes*; **Stranglers** - *(Get A) Grip (On Yourself)*; **Vibrators** - *Baby Baby*; **X-Ray Spex** - *Oh Bondage Up Yours!*; **Saints** - *I'm Stranded*; Johnny Thunders and The Heartbreakers - *Chinese Rocks*; **Damned** - *Love Song*; **Ruts** - *In A Rut*; **U.K. Subs** - *Strangehold*; **Cockney Rejects** - *Flares And Slippers*; **Killing Joke** - *Wait*; Dead Kennedys - *Holiday In Cambodia*; **Vice Squad** - *Last Rockers*; **Anti-Pasti** - *Someone's Gonna Die*; **GBH** - *City Baby Attacked By Rats*; **Attila The Stockbroker** - *Russians In The DHSS*. **Angelic Upstarts** - *Lust For Glory*.

Burning Ambitions, Vol. 2
(A History Of Punk)   (Anagram CDPUNK 81) 1996

Hollywood Brats - *Then He Kissed Me*; **Boys** - *I Don't Care*; **Eater** - *Thinkin' Of The USA*; **Patrik Fitzgerald** - *Safety Pin Stuck In My Heart*; **Vibrators** - *Automatic Lover*; **Alternative TV** - *Action Time Vision*; **Angelic Upstarts** - *Murder Of Liddle Towers*; **U.K. Subs** - *CID*; **Cockney Rejects** - *Police Car*; **Undertones** - *Teenage Kicks*; **Fall** - *Totally Wired*; Dead Kennedys - *Kill The Poor*; **Exploited** - *Exploited Barmy Army*; **Anti-Nowhere League** - *So What*; **Partisans** - *Seventeen Years Of Hell*; **One Way System** - *Stab The Judge*; **Peter and The Test Tube Babies** - *Run Like Hell*; **Business** - *Smash The Discos*; **Blitz** - *Warriors*; **Damned** - *Dozen Girls*; **Violators** - *Summer Of '81*; **Blood** - *Meglomania*; **New Model Army** - *Vengeance*; **New Model Army** - *You'll Never Know*.

Burning Ambitions, Vol. 3   (Anagram CDPUNK 98) 1997

Sham 69 - *If The Kids Are United*; **U.K. Subs** - *Warhead*; **Cockney Rejects** - *Greatest Cockney Rip Off*; **Anti-Pasti** - *Another Dead Soldier*; **Discharge** - *Decontrol*; Dead Kennedys - *Too Drunk To Fuck*; **Peter and The Test Tube Babies** - *Transvestite*; **Disorder** - *Rampton Song*; **Chron Gen** - *Puppets Of War*; **Anti-Nowhere League** - *Let's Break The Law*; **G.B.H.** - *No Survivors*; **G.B.H.** - *Stand Strong Stand Proud*; **Toy Dolls** - *Everybody Jitterbug*; **Adicts** - *Viva La Revolution*; **Abrasive Wheels** - *Burn 'Em Down*; **One Way System** - *Jerusalem*; **Chaos UK** - *Farmyard Boogie*; **Varukers** - *Die For Your Government*; **Chaotic Dischord** - *Fuck Religion, Fuck Politics, Fuck The Lot Of You*; **Broken Bones** - *Decapitated*.

Carry On Oi!   (Captain Oi! AHOY CD 119) 1999

Garry Johnston - *United*; J.J. All Stars - *Dambusters March*; **Business** - *Suburban Rebels*; **Infa Riot** - *Each Dawn I Die*; **Partisans** - *Arms Race*; **Ejected** - *East End Kids*; **Peter and The Test Tube Babies** - *Transvestite*;

CHERRY RED PUNK SINGLES COLLECTION.

Blitz - *Nation On Fire*; **Gonads** - *Tuckers Ruckers Ain't No Suckers*; **4-Skins** - *Evil*; **Business** - *Product*; **Red Alert** - *SPG*; Oi! The Comrade - *Guvnor's Man*; **Peter and The Test Tube Babies** - *Maniac*; **Ejected** - *What Am I Gonna Do?*; **Partisans** - *No U Turns*; **Blitz** - *Youth*; Oi! The Chrous - *Walk On*. Bonus track: **Red Alert** - *We've Got The Power*.

NB: Originally issued on vinyl (Secret SEC 2) 1981.

Cherry Red Punk Singles
Collection   (Anagram CDPUNK 51) 1995

Tights - *Bad Hearts*; **Tights** - *Cracked*; **Tights** - *Howard Hughes*; **Tights** - *China's Eternal*; Destroy All Monsters - *Bored*; Destroy All Monsters - *You're Gonna Die*; **Hollywood Brats** - *Then He Kissed Me*; **Hollywood Brats** - *Sick On You*; Destroy All Monsters - *November 22nd 1963*; Destroy All Monsters - *Meet The Creeper*; The Runaways - *Right Now*; The Runaways - *Black Leather*; Destroy All Monsters - *Nobody Knows*; Destroy All Monsters - *What Do I Get*; Dead Kennedys - *Holiday In Cambodia*; Dead Kennedys - *Police Truck*; Dead Kennedys - *Kill The Poor*; Dead Kennedys - *In Sight*; Dead Kennedys - *Too Drunk To Fuck*; Dead Kennedys - *Prey*.

The Chiswick Sampler
(Good Clean Fun)   (Chiswick CDWIKX 162) 1995

Count Bishops - *Beautiful Delilah*; **101'ers** - *Sweet Revenge*; **Gorillas** - *Gatecrasher*; **Johnny Moped** - *Groovy Ruby*; **Radiators From Space** - *Enemies*; **Whirlwind** - *Tear It Up*; **Whirlwind** - *Teenage Cutie*; Motorhead - *Train Kept A Rollin'*; **Bishops** - *I Want Candy*; **Radio Stars** - *Radio Stars*; **Radio Stars** - *Buy Chiswick Records*; **Damned** - *Smash It Up*; **Riff Raff** - *Romford Girls*; **Johnny and The Self-Abusers** - *Dead Vandals*; Rocky Sharpe and The Replays - *Come On Let's Go*; **Sniff 'n' The Tears** - *Driver's Seat*; **Sniff 'n' The Tears** - *Poison Pen Mail*; **Radiators** - *Let's Talk About The Weather*; Disguise - *There's A Boy On Our Street*; Albania - *Addicts Of The First Night*; 2-2 - *Swim The Indian Ocean*; Motordamn - *Over The Top*.

The Chiswick Story (2-CD)   (Chiswick CDWIK 2 100) 1992

Count Bishops - *Route 66*; **Count Bishops** - *Teenage Letter*; **Count Bishops** - *Train Train*; **101'ers** - *Keys To Your Heart*; **Gorillas** - *She's My Gal*; **Gorillas** - *Gorilla Got Me*; Rocky Sharpe and The Razors - *Drip Drop*; Little Bob Story - *I'm Crying*; **Radio Stars** - *Dirty Pictures*; **Radio Stars** - *No Russians In Russia*; **Radio Stars** - *Nervous Wreck*; **Radio Stars** - *Real Me*; **Radiators From Space** - *Television Screen*; Motorhead - *Motorhead*; **Rings** - *I Wanna Be Free*; **Johnny Moped** - *No One*; **Johnny Moped** - *Darling Let's Have Another Baby*; **Johnny Moped** - *Little Queenie*; Jeff Hill - *I Want You To Dance With Me*; **Amazorblades** - *Common Truth*; **Johnny and The Self-Abusers** - *Saints And Sinners*; Whirlwind - *Hang Loose (I've Gotta Rock)*; **Whirlwind** - *I Only Wish (That I'd Been Told)*; **Whirlwind** - *Heaven Knows*; **Radiators** - *Million Dollar Hero*; **Radiators** - *Dancing Years*; **Riff Raff** - *Cosmonaut*; **Bishops** - *I Want Candy*; **Drug Addix** - *Gay Boys In Bondage*; Rocky Sharpe and The Replays - *Rama Lama Ding Dong*; Rocky Sharpe and The Replays - *Imagination*; Rocky Sharpe and The Replays - *Shout Shout (Knock Yourself Out)*; Rocky Sharpe and The Replays - *Heart*; **Sniff 'n' The Tears** - *Driver's Seat*; Disguise - *Hey Baby*; Dan Kelleher - *I Couldn't Help But Cry*; Stickshifts - *Automobile*; **Damned** - *Love Song*; **Damned** - *Smash It Up*; **Nips** - *Gabrielle*; Red Beans and Rice - *That Driving Beat*; Textones - *I Can't Fight It*; Albania - *Albania (Are You All Mine)*; Albania - *Go Go Go*; TV Smith's Explorer's - *Tomahawk Cruise*; Terry Woods - *Tennessee Stud*; Meteors - *Radioactive Kid*; 2-2 - *Insufficient Data*; 2-2 - *Kwagayo*; Roddy Radiation and Tearjerkers - *Desire*; Jakko - *Grab What You Can (Biez Co Mozesz)*.

A Country Fit For Heroes
Vol. 1 & 2   (Captain Oi! AHOY CD 15) 1994

Blitzkreig - *The Future Must Be Ours*; **Violators** - *Die With Dignity*; **Violators** - *Government Stinks*; Hostile Youth - *Fight Back*; **The Samples** - *Government Downfall*; **One Way System** - *Jerusalem*; **Attak** - *Blue Patrol*; **Crux** - *CIA*; Distortion - *Action Man*; Pseudo Sadists - *Power Schemes*; **Chaotic Youth** - *Whose Bomb*; **Patrol** - *Unknown Soldiers*; **Patrol** - *Nurse Nurse*; **Mania** - *Blood Money*; Government Lies - *Did He Or Didn't He*; **On Parole** - *Condemned*; **Criminal Damage** - *Criminal Crew*; **ABH** - *Country Boy Rocker*; **ABH** - *Wanna Riot*; Cadaverous Clan - *Snow Blindness*; **Impact** - *Storm Trooper Tactics*; **Intensive Care** - *Fight And Die*; **Intensive Care** - *Ghost Town*.

NB: Originally issued seperately on vinyl (No Future Oi! 3 and 23 respectively) 1982/1983.

A COUNTRY FIT FOR HEROES VOL. 1 & 2.

The Countdown Compilation
(Captain Mod MODSKA CD 6) 1997

Makin Time - *Only Time Will Tell*; The Combine - *Dreams Come True*; The Alljacks - *Guilty*; The Co-Stars - *Not Ready For Love*; The Kick - *Stuck On The Edge Of A Blade*; Stupidity - *Bend Don't Break*; **The Times** - *Whatever Happened To Thames Beat*; **The Gents** - *The Faker*; The Moment - *Sticks And Stones*; The Scene - *Inside Out (For Your Love)*; Fast Eddie - *I Don't Need No Doctor*; The Jetset - *Wednesday Girl*. Bonus tracks:- The Kick - *I Can't Let Go*; The Kick - *Armchair Politician*; Fast Eddie - *My Babe*; Fast Eddie - *Help Me*; Fast Eddie - *Sweet Sensations*.

The Fallout Punk Singles Collection
(Anagram CDPUNK 30) 1994

Enemy - *Fallen Hero*; Adicts - *Viva La Revolution*; Action Pact - *Suicide Bag*; Enemy - *Punk's Alive*; Rabid - *Jubilee*; Urban Dogs - *New Barbarians*; Action Pact - *People*; Urban Dogs - *Limo Life*; Enemy - *Last Rites*; Action Pact - *London Bouncers*; U.K. Subs - *Another Typical City*; Action Pact - *Question Of Choice*; Broken Bones - *Decapitated*; Fallen Angels - *Amphetamine Blues*; U.K. Subs - *Private Army*; Broken Bones - *Cruxifix*; Action Pact - *Yet Another Dole Queue Song*; Fallen Angels - *Inner Planet Love*; Action Pact - *Coctail Credibility*; Broken Bones - *Through My Eyes*; U.K. Subs - *This Gun Says*; Adicts - *Champs Elysees*; Broken Bones - *Never Say Die*; U.K. Subs - *Hey Santa*; U.K. Subs - *Jodie Foster*.

Farewell To The Roxy
(Captain Oi! AHOY CD 86) 1998

Blitz - *Strange Boy*; Acme Sewage Co. - *Smile And Wave Goodbye*; Billy Karloff and The Goats - *Relics From The Past*; U.K. Subs - *I Live In A*

THE FALLOUT PUNK SINGLES COLLECTION.

THE GOOD VIBRATIONS PUNK SINGLES COLLECTION.

Car; **U.K. Subs** - *Telephone Numbers*; **Tickets** - *Get Yourself Killed*; **Red Lights** - *Never Wanna Leave*; **XL5** - *Here Comes The Knife*; **Jets** - *TV Drink*; **Streets** - *Sniper*; **Plastix** - *Tough On You*; **Bears** - *Fun Fun Fun*; **Open Sore** - *Vertigo*; **Crabs** - *Lullabies Lie*.

NB: Originally issued on vinyl (Lightning LIP 2) 1978.

Fresh Records Punk Singles Collection
(Anagram CDPUNK 32) 1994

Dark - *My Friends*; **Dark** - *John Wayne*; **Dark** - *Einstein's Brain*; **Dark** - *On The Wires*; **Dark** - *Masque*; **Art Attacks** - *Punk Rock Stars*; **Art Attacks** - *Rat City*; **Cuddly Toys** - *Madman*; **Cuddly Toys** - *Astral Joe*; **Cuddly Toys** - *Someone's Crying*; **Cuddly Toys** - *It's A Shame*; **Dark** - *Hawaii Five-O*; **Menace** - *Young One's*; **Family Fodder** - *Debbie Harry*; **Manufactured Romance** - *I've Had The Time Of My Life*; **Wall** - *Hobby For A Day*; **J.C.'s Mainmen** - *Earbending*; **Play Dead** - *Poison Takes A Hold*; **Wasted Youth** - *Rebecca's Room*; **Chron Gen** - *Puppets Of War*; **Play Dead** - *TV Eye*.

God Save The Punks (2-CD)
(Disky DOU 882552) 1998

Sex Pistols - *Pretty Vacant*; **Blondie** - *Denis*; **Generation X** - *Valley Of The Dolls*; **Banned** - *Little Girl*; **Penetration** - *Danger Signs*; **Public Image Ltd.** - *Death Disco*; **Magazine** - *Shot By Both Sides*; **X-Ray Spex** - *Identity*; **Ruts** - *Staring At The Rude Boys*; **999** - *Homicide*; Red Hot Chilli Peppers - *Punk Rock Classic*; **Discharge** - *Decontrol*; Ramones - *Substitute*; **Stranglers** - *Peaches*; **Sid Vicious** - *Born To Lose*; **Fischer Z** - *Limbo*; **Skids** - *Saints Are Coming*; Blondie - *Hanging On The Telephone*; **Public Image Ltd.** - *Public Image*; **X-Ray Spex** - *Oh Bondage Up Yours!*; Bad Brains - *Banned In DC*; **G.B.H.** - *No Survivors*; **Discharge** - *Never Again*; Ramones - *Surf City*; **Stranglers** - *(Get A) Grip (On Yourself)*; Red Hot Chilli Peppers - *Millionaires Against Hunger*; **999** - *Emergency*; **Saints** - *This Perfect Day*; **Buzzcocks** - *Everybody's Happy Nowadays*; **Sex Pistols** - *No One Is Innocent*.

God Save The Queen (20 Years Of Punk) (3-CD Set)
(Dressed To Kill KITOFF 50) 1997

The Good Vibrations Punk Singles Collection
(Anagram CDPUNK 36) 1994

Rudi - *Big Time*; **Victim** - *Strange Thing By Night*; **Outcasts** - *Love Is For Sops*; **Undertones** - *Smarter Than U*; **X Dreamysts** - *Dance Away Lover*; **Protex** - *Don't Ring Me Up*; **Protex** - *Listening In*; **Idiots** - *Parents*; **Spider** - *Dancin' In The Street*; **Outcasts** - *The Cops Are Comin'*; **Rudi** - *Overcome By Fumes*; **Ruefrex** - *Cross The Line*; **Tearjerkers** - *Love Affair*; **Moondogs** - *Ya Don't Do Ya*; **Rudi** - *I Spy*; **Shapes** - *Airline Disaster*; **Outcasts** - *Self Conscious Over You*; **Outcasts** - *Love You For Never*; **Bankrobbers** - *On My Mind*; **Bears** - *Decisions*; **Jets** - *Original Terminal*; **Shock Treatment** - *Belfast Telegraph*; **Lids** - *I Don't Want You*; **Androids** - *Bondage In Belfast*; **Terri and The Terrors** - *Laugh At Me*.

The Greatest Punk Album Of All Time
(6-CD Set)   (Dressed To Kill REDTK 110) 1999.

Dead Kennedys - *Holiday In Cambodia*; **Vice Squad** - *Black Sheep*; **Anti-Nowhere League** - *I Hate People*; **999** - *Homicide*; Johnny Thunders - *Chinese Rocks (live)*; **Sham 69** - *Borstal Breakout*; **Chaotic Dischord** - *Fuck Religion Fuck Politics Fuck The Lot Of You*; **Chaos UK** - *Four Minute Warning*; **Red London** - *CND*; **Adicts** - *Bad Boy*; **Menace** - *GLC*; **Alternative TV** - *How Much Longer*; **Blitz** - *Warrior*; **Stiff Little Fingers** - *Listen*; **Exploited** - *Alternative*; **Exploited** - *Babylon's Burning*; **Slaughter and The Dogs** - *White Light White Heat*; **Damned** - *Disco Man*; **Stranglers** - *Go Buddy Go*; **Anti-Pasti** - *Another Dead*; **Stiff Little Fingers** - *Suspect Device*; **GBH** - *Catch*; **Chelsea** - *Evacuate*; **Chron Gen** - *Jet Boy Jet Girl*; **Adicts** - *Joker In The Pack*; **Eater** - *Thinking Of The USA*; **Drones** - *Bone Idol*; **Suburban Studs** - *No Faith*; Dead Kennedys - *Kill The Poor*; **Peter and The Test Tube Babies** - *Up Yer Bum*; Resurrection Experience - *Do What I Do*; **Sham 69** - *Hurry Up Harry*; Electric Sex Circus - *Spanner Badge*; **Adicts** - *Chinese Takeaway*; **Damned** - *Help*; **Patrick Fitzgerald** - *All My Friends Are Dead*; **UK Subs** - *I Live In A Car*; **Splodge** - *Tough Shit Wilson*; **Ruts** - *In A Rut*; **Eddie and The Hot Rods** - *Teenage Depression*; **Sex Pistols** - *Anarchy In The UK*; **Lurkers** - *New Guitar In Town*; **Chelsea** - *Right To Work*; **Stranglers** - *Peaches*; **Adverts** - *No Time To Be 21*; **Chron Gen** - *Misadventure*; **Damned** - *New Rose*; Electric Sex Circus - *Cut Your Head Off*; **Newtown Neurotics** - *Mess*; **Angelic Upstarts** - *Machine Gun Kelly*; **One Way System** - *Cum On Feel The Noize*; **Vibrators** - *Baby Baby (I Know You're A Lady)*; **Angelic Upstarts** - *Upstart*; **Varukers** - *Massacred Millions*; **Special Duties** - *Bullshit Crass*; **Lurkers** - *Just Thirteen*; **Cockney Rejects** - *Flares And Slippers*; Morgans - *Tommy*; **Sham 69** - *If The Kids Are United*; **Boys** - *I Don't Care*; **Ex-Pistols** - *Land Of Hope And Glory*; **Mekons** - *Fight The Cuts*; **Redskins** - *Unionize*; Billy Bragg - *It Stays Here*; **Penetration** - *Don't Dictate*; **Poison Girls** - *Old Tart*; Three Johns - *Death Of The European*; **New Model Army** - *Spirit Of The Falklands*; Joolz - *Paved With Gold*; Morgans - *Atishoo*; Dead Kennedys - *Chemical Warfare*; **Angelic Upstarts** - *Murder Of Liddle Towers*; **Patrick Fitzgerald** - *Irrelevant Battles*; **Stiff Little Fingers** - *Suspect Device*; **Chelsea** - *Right To Work*; **Chaos UK** - *Selfish Few*; **Chaos UK** - *Fuck Religion Fuck Politics Fuck The Lot Of You*; **Chaotic Dischord** - *Hitler's In The Charts Again*; **999** - *Bye Bye England*; **Sex Pistols** - *Submission*; **Spizz** - *Soldier Soldier*; **Notsensibles** - *I'm In Love With Margaret Thatcher*; **Menace** - *GLC*; **Red London** - *CND*; MC5 - *Kick Out The Jams*; **Violators** - *Government Stinks*; **Sham 69** - *If The Kids Are United*; **Damned** - *Gun Fury*; Tom Robinson - *Glad To Be Gay 1994*; Billy Bragg - *Between The Wars*; **UK Subs** - *Fascist Regime*; **Anti-Nowhere League** - *Streets Of London*; **Stiff Little Fingers** - *Alternative Ulster*; **Angelic Upstarts** - *Solidarity*; **Poison Girls** - *Persons Unknown*; Three Johns - *Fruit Flies*; **Newtown Neurotics** - *Living With Unemployment*; **Anti-Pasti** - *No Government*; Captain Sensible - *Smash It Up*; **Sex Pistols** - *Anarchy In The UK*; **Exploited** - *Class War*; **Varukers** - *Protest And Survive*; **Threats** - *Politicians And Ministers*; **Riot Squad** - *Fuck The Tories*; **Adicts** - *How Sad*; **Sham 69** - *Borstal Breakout*; **Fall** - *Rowche Rumble*; **Ruts** - *Babylon's Burning*; Iggy & The Stooges - *I Got Nothing*; **Au Pairs** - *America*; **Chron Gen** - *Fiasco*; **Boys** - *Cop Cars*; **Stranglers** - *Peasant In The Big Shitty*; **Cortinas** - *Fascist Dictator*; **Redskins** - *Red Strike The Blues*; **Theatre Of Hate** - *Do You Believe In The Westworld*; **Vice Squad** - *Stand Strong Stand Proud (live)*; **New Model Army** - *Vengeance*; **Ruts** - *In A Rut*.

The History Of No Future
(2-CD)   (Anagram CDPUNK 111) 1999

DISC ONE: **Blitz** - *Someone's Gonna Die Tonight*; **Partisans** - *Police Story*; **Blitzkrieg** - *The Future Must Be Ours*; **Peter and The Test Tube Babies** - *Banned From The Pubs*; **Red Alert** - *In Britain*; **Blitz** - *Never Surrender*; **Attak** - *Today's Generation*; **Blitzkrieg** - *Lest We Forget*; **Violators** - *Gangland*; **Insane** - *El Salvador*; **Channel 3** - *I've Got A Gun*; **Partisans** - *17 Years Of Hell*; **Red Alert** - *Take No Prisoners*; **Samples** - *Dead Hero*; **Peter and The Test Tube Babies** - *Run Like Hell*; **Blitz** - *Warriors*; **Attak** - *Murder In The Subway*; **Crux** - *Keep On Running*; **Violators** - *Summer Of '81*; **Red Alert** - *City Invasion*; **Wall** - *Day Tripper*; **Blood** - *Megalomania*; **A.B.H.** - *Wanna Riot*; **Rose Of Victory** - *Suffragette City*; **Screaming Dead** - *Night Creatures*; **Violators** - *Die With Dignity*; **Red Alert** - *There's A Guitar Burning*; DISC TWO: **Blitz** - *Fight To Live*; **Partisans** - *Killing Machine*; **Crux** - *C.L.A.*; **Peter and The Test Tube Babies** - *Moped Lads*; **Red Alert** - *Screaming At The Nation*; **Blitz** - *Razors In The Night*; **Attak** - *Hell*; **Blitzkrieg** - *Abuse Of Power*; **Violators** - *The Fugitive*; **Insane** - *Chinese Rocks*; **Channel 3** - *Manzanar And Mannequin*; **Partisans** - *Bastards In Blue*; **Red Alert** - *Empire Of Crime*; **Samples** - *Fire Another Round*; **Peter and The Test Tube Babies** - *Up Yer Bum*; **Blitz** - *Youth*; **Attak** - *Future Dreams*; **Crash** - *Fight For Your Life*; **Violators** - *Live Fast Die Young*; **Red Alert** - *Negative Reaction*; **Wall** - *When I'm Dancin'*; **Blood** - *Calling The Shots*; **On Parole** - *Condemned*; **Rose Of Victory** - *Overdrive*; **Screaming Dead** - *Angel Of Death*; **Violators** - *Pointless Slaughter*; **Red Alert** - *All The Way To Glory*.

A History Of Punk, Vol. 1   (Virgin CDOVD 486) 1997

Sex Pistols - *God Save The Queen*; **Ian Dury and The Blockheads** - *Sex And Drugs And Rock & Roll*; **Generation X** - *King Rocker*; **Magazine** - *Shot By Both Sides*; **X-Ray Spex** - *Day The World Turned Day-Glo*; **Rich Kids** - *Rich Kids*; **Damned** - *Love Song*; **Penetration** - *Don't Dictate*; **Skids** - *Into The Valley*; **Vibrators** - *Automatic Lover*; **Stranglers** - *Peaches*; **Ruts** - *Babylon's Burning*; Devo - *Satisfaction (Can't Get No)*; **Slits** - *Typical Girls*; **Buzzcocks** - *Ever Fallen In Love*; Dead Kennedys - *Kill The Poor*; **Jilted John** - *Jilted John*; **Sham 69** - *Hersham Boys*; **Eddie and The Hot Rods** - *Do Anything You Wanna Do*; **Jam** - *Eton Rifles*.

A History Of Punk, Vol. 2   (Virgin CDOVD 487) 1997

Adam and The Ants - *Deutscher Girls*; **Members** - *Sound Of The Suburbs*; **Squeeze** - *Take Me I'm Yours*; **Public Image Ltd.** - *Public Image*; **Stiff Little Fingers** - *At The Edge*; **Jam** - *All Around The World*; **Damned** - *I Just Can't Be Happy Today*; **Passions** - *I'm In Love With A German Film Star*; **Simple Minds** - *Life In A Day*; **The The** - *Controversial Subject*; **Wire** - *Mannequin*; Sweet Rachel - *Baby Let's Play House*; Sweet Rachel - *Nellie The Elephant*; Dickies - *Banana Splits*; **Lena Lovich** - *Lucky Number*; **Exploited** -*Dead Cities*; **Fall** - *Cruisers Creek*; **Flying Lizards** - *Money*; **Motors** - *Airport*; XTC - *Science Friction*.

A History Of Punk (2-CD)   (Receiver RDPCD 011) 1998

Holidays In The Sun, Vol. 1   (HITS 01) 1999

Slaughter and The Dogs - *Where Have All The Bootboys Gone*; **The Drones** - *Persecution Complex*; **Notsensibles** - *I'm In Love With Margaret Thatcher*; **X-Ray Spex** - *The Day The World Turned Dayglo*; **Anti-Nowhere League** - *So What*; **Chron Gen** - *Outlaw*; **The Vibrators** - *Troops Of Tomorrow*; Hanx - *Alternative Ulster*; **Eater** - *Thinking Of The USA*; **Spizzenergi** - *Where's Captain Kirk?*; T.V. Smith - *Gary Gilmore's Eyes*; Erase Today - *Changes*; **Special Duties** - *Colchester Council*; **One Way System** - *Jackie Was A Junkie*; Funeral Dress - *Nightmares*; **Major Accident** - *Worst Enemy*; **External Menace** - *Rude Awakening*; Sic Boy Federation - *Do You Wanna Be A Sic Boy*; Mere Dead Men - *Designer*; **Blood** - *Waste Of Flesh And Bone*; V2 - *I Feel Alright*;

Holidays In The Sun, Vol. 2   (HITS 02) 1999

B-Bang Cider - *Vision*; **Lurkers** - *I'm On Heat*; **Suburban Studs** - *No Faith*; USSR - *John Lennon Is Dead*; **Radio Stars** - *Blame It On The Young*; **Zounds** - *This Land*; **Crack** - *Don't Just Sit There*; **999** - *Nasty*

LIGHTNING RECORDS PUNK SINGLES COLLECTION.

LIVE AT THE VORTEX.

Nasty; **Alternative TV** - *Splitting In Two*; **Carpettes** - *Nothing Ever Changes*; **Buzzcocks** - *Boredom*; **Sham 69** - *Junkie*; Capo Regime - *Same Old Story*; **Proles** - *Stereo Love*; **English Dogs** - *I've Got A Gun*; **Splodgenessabounds** - *Two Little Boys*; Krill - *Don't Look In The Freezer*; Casualties - *Casualties*; Walking Abortions - *Vision Red*; Public Toys - *Do What You Wanna Do*; Stains - *Freeloader*; **Salford Jets** - *Who You Lookin' At*; Eddie Mooney and **V2** - *Man In The Box*; **G.B.H.** - *Pretty Vacant*.

In Goth Daze (Anagram CDMGRAM 89) 1998

Specimen - *Hex*; Nico - *Vegas*; Alien Sex Fiend - *Psychotic Louie Louie*; Bone Orchard - *Kicking Up The Sawdust*; Alien Sex Fiend - *Can't Stop Smoking*; Specimen - *Sharp Teeth Pretty Teeth*; Zero Lacreche - *Last Year's Wife*; In Excelsis - *Carnivale Of The Gullible*; Play Dead - *Tenant*; **Red Lorry Yellow Lorry** - *Beating My Head*; Ritual - *Mind Disease*; Screaming Dead - *Creatures Of The Night*; Specimen - *Hole*; Skeletal Family - *Alone She Cries*; Furyo - *Legacy*; Bauhaus - *18*; 1919 - *Caged 19*; **Red Lorry Yellow Lorry** - *Hollow Eyes*; Skeletal Family - *So Sure*;

Jubilee (Caroline EGCD 34) 1996

Adam and The Ants - *Deutscher Girls*; **Adam and The Ants** - *Plastic Surgery*; **Wayne County and The Electric Chairs** - *Paranoia Blues*; **Chelsea** - *Right To Work*; **Maneaters** - *Nine To Five*; **Suzi Pinns** - *Rule Britannia*; Amilcar - *Wargasm In Pornotopia*; Brian Eno - *Slow Water*; Brian Eno - *Dover Beach*.

NB: Originally issued on vinyl (EG/Polydor 2302079) 1978.

Lightning Records Punk Collection (Anagram CDPUNK 79) 1996

Jet Bronx and The Forbidden - *Ain't Doin' Nuthin'*; **Mirrors** - *Cure For Cancer*; **Jerks** - *Get Your Woofing Dog Off Me*; **Blitzkrieg Bop** - *Let's Go*; Martin and The Brownshirts - *Taxi Driver*; Elton Motello - *Jet Boy Jet Girl*; **Fruit Eating Bears** - *Chevy Heavy*; **Dirty Dogs** - *Let Go Of My Hands*; **Horror Comic** - *I Don't Mind*; **Too Much** - *Who You Wanna Be*; **Nerves** - *TV Adverts*; Cane - *D.K. Dance*; Cane - *College Girls*; Neville Wanker and The Punters - *Boys On The Dole*; **Mirrors** - *Dark Glasses*; **Nasty Media** - *Spiked Copy*; **Blitzkrieg Bop** - *U.F.O.*; **Krypton Tunes** - *All In Jail*; **Jerks** - *Cool*; **Too Much** - *Kick Me One More Time*; **Open Sore** - *Vertigo (live)*; **Crabs** - *Lullabies Lie (live)*.

Live At The Roxy (Thunderbolt CDTB 011) 1995

NB: Contains the same content as *Farewell To The Roxy* - see that entry for track list.

Live From The Roxy (Essential ESMCD 772) 19??

Slaughter and The Dogs - *Runaway*; **Slaughter and The Dogs** - *Boston Babies*; **Sham 69** - *Rip Off*; **Sham 69** - *Borstal Breakout*; **Wire** - *Just Don't Care*; **Wire** - *TV*; **Adverts** - *Bored Teenagers*; **Adverts** - *Gary Gilmore's Eyes*; **Boys** - *Living In The City*; **Boys** - *Sabre Dance*; **Boys** - *Sick On You*; **X-Ray Spex** - *I Am A Cliché*; **Buzzcocks** - *Orgasm Addict*; **Buzzcocks** - *Breakdown*; **Buzzcocks** - *Love Battery*; **UK Subs** - *World War*; **UK Subs** - *I Couldn't Be With You*; **Damned** - *Smash It Up*; **Damned** - *Neat Neat Neat*.

NB: Originally issued on vinyl, but with fewer tracks (Harvest SHSP 4069) 1977.

Live At The Vortex (Anagram CDPUNK 68) 1995

Wasps - *Can't Wait Till '78*; **Wasps** - *Waiting For My Man*; **Mean Street** - *Bunch Of Stiffs*; **Neo** - *Small Lives*; **Neo** - *Tell Me The Truth*; Bernie Torme - *Living For Kicks*; Bernie Torme - *Streetfighter*; **Art Attacks** - *Animal Bondage*; **Art Attacks** - *Frankenstein's Heartbeat*; **Suspects** - *Nothing To Declare*; **Maniacs** - *You Don't Break My Heart*; **Maniacs** - *I Ain't Gonna Be History*.

NB: Originally issued on vinyl (NEMS NEL 6103) 1978.

Live Stiffs (Diablo DIAB 851) 1997

Nick Lowe - *I Knew The Bride*; **Nick Lowe** - *Let's Eat*; **Wreckless Eric** - *Semaphore Signals*; **Wreckless Eric** - *Reconnez Cherie*; **Larry Wallis** - *Police Car*; **Elvis Costello** - *I Just Don't Know What To Do With Myself*; **Elvis Costello** - *Miracle Man*; **Ian Dury and The Blockheads** - *Wake Up And Make Love With Me*; **Ian Dury and The Blockheads** - *Billericay Dickie*; **Ian Dury and The Blockheads** - *Sex And Drugs And Rock & Roll And Chaos*.

NB: Originally issued on vinyl as *Stiffs Live Stiffs* (Stiff GET 1) 1978.

The Model (Spectrum 5529182) 1997

Duran Duran - *Girls On Film*; **Spandau Ballet** - *Chant No. 1*; **Visage** - *Fade To Grey*; Kraftwerk - *Model*; Heaven 17 - *Temptation*; **OMD** - *Enola Gay*; **New Order** - *Blue Monday*; **Classix Nouveaux** - *Is It A Dream*; Thomas Dolby - *Hyperactive*; **Ultravox** - *Vienna*; Tears For Fears - *Mad World*; Hazel O'Connor - *Will You*; Kate Bush - *Babooshka*; **Human League** - *Love Action*; ABC - *Poison Arrow*; **Talk Talk** - *Talk Talk*; **Blancmange** - *Living On The Ceiling*; Blondie - *Rapture*; **Japan** - *Ghosts*; **Midge Ure** - *No Regrets*.

Mods Mayday '79 (Dojo DOJOCD 5) 1994

Secret Affair - *Time For Action*; **Secret Affair** - *Let Your Heart Dance*; **Beggar** - *Don't Throw Your Life Away*; **Small Hours** - *Hanging In The Balance*; **Mods** - *Tonight's The Night*; **Mods** - *Let Me Be The One*; **Squire** - *B-a-by Baby Love*; **Small Hours** - *Midnight To Six*; **Beggar** - *Broadway Show*; **Beggar** - *All Night*; **Mods** - *Love Only Me*; **Squire** - *Walking Down The King's Road*; **Squire** - *Live Without Her Love*; **Secret Affair** - *I'm Not Free (But I'm Cheap)*; **Small Hours** - *End Of The Night*.

NB: Originally issued on vinyl (Bridge House BHLP 003) 1979.

Mods Mayday, Vol. 2 (Receiver RRCD 228) 1996

Merton Parkas - *Tears Of A Clown*; **Merton Parkas** - *When Will It Be*; **Merton Parkas** - *Plastic Smile*; **Merton Parkas** - *I Don't Want To Know You*; **Merton Parkas** - *Silent People*; **Merton Parkas** - *Tell Me What I Say*; **Squire** - *It's A Mod Mod World*; **Squire** - *The Face Of Youth Today*; **Squire** - *I've Got You On My Mind*; **Small Hours** - *Underground*; **Small Hours** - *The Mess*; **Small Hours** - *Can't Do Without You*; **Small Hours** - *By The Light*; **Beggar** - *Friday Night*; **Beggar** - *Doing Alright As I Am*.

More Tea Vicar, Vol. 1 (Rhythm Vicar PREACH 015CD) 1999

Vice Squad - *Can't Buy Back The Dead*; **Vice Squad** - *Westend Stars*; **Red Alert** - *Money Whore*; **Red Alert** - *For Valour*; Anti Flag - *You Gotta Die For Your Government*; Anti Flag - *Drink Drunk Punch*; **Vice Squad** - *Out Of Reach*; **Vice Squad** - *Resurrection*; Degeneration - *Police State One*; Degeneration - *Degenerate Army*; Merricks - *Scream*; Gundog - *Nation On Fire*; Glueball - *Chainsaw Part One*; Glueball - *Fuck You*; Extreme Noise Terror - *Bullshit Propaganda*; Extreme Noise Terror - *Cruelty To Carnivores*; Filthkick - *Crime Without A Name*; Filthkick - *Between The Lines*.

More Tea Vicar, Vol. 2 (Rhythm Vicar PREACH 024CD) 2000

Red Alert - *Money Whore*; **Red Alert** - *For Valour*; Snap Her - *I Wanna Beavis You*; Snap Her - *Sex Change*; **Cockney Rejects** - *Bad Man*;

NO FUTURE - THE SINGLES COLLECTION, VOL. 1.

Cockney Rejects - *Fighting In The Streets*; Real McKenzies - *Stone Of The Kings*; Real McKenzies - *Bastards*; Anti Flag - *Safe Tonight*; Anti Flag - *Police State USA*; Raw Noise - *Final Void*; Raw Noise - *Terror Continues*; Raw Power - *State Oppression*; Raw Power - *Alter Your Brain*; Glueball - *No I No You*; Glueball - *Speed Slave*.

Natures Mortes (4AD CAD 117CD) 1997

Birthday Party - *Mr. Clarinet*; Psychotik Tanks - *Let's Have A Party*; **Rema Rema** - *Feedback Song*; **In Camera** - *Die Laughing*; **Bauhaus** - *Rose Garden Funeral Of Sores*; **Mass** - *You And I*; **Cupol** - *Like This For Ages*; **Modern English** - *Gathering Dust*; Sort Sol - *Marble Station*; **The The** - *Controversial Subject*; Past Seven Days - *Raindance*; **Dif Juz** - *Re:*; CVO - *Sargaso Sea*; Past Seven Days - *So Many Others*; Last Dance - *Malignant Love*; **The The** - *Black And White*.

New Romantics (EMI Gold CDGOLD 1041) 1996

Spandau Ballet - *Chant No. 1*; **Duran Duran** - *Girls On Film*; Heaven 17 - *Fascist Groove Thang*; **Japan** - *Quiet Life*; Our Daughters Wedding - *Lawnchairs*; China Crisis - *African And White*; **Ultravox** - *Vienna*; Kraftwerk - *Model*; **OMD** - *Messages*; Devo - *Whip It*; **Human League** - *Empire State Human*; **Illustrated Man** - *Head Over Heels*; **John Foxx** - *Underpass*; **Classix Nouveaux** - *Is It A Dream*; Midge Ure and Mick Karn - *After A Fashion*.

New Wave Archive (Rialto RMCD 201) 1997

Stranglers - *Golden Brown*; **Sex Pistols** - *God Save The Queen*; **Toy Dolls** - *Nellie The Elephant*; **Adverts** - *Gary Gilmore's Eyes*; **Sham 69** - *If The Kids Are United*; **Slaughter and The Dogs** - *Where Have All The Boot Boys Gone*; Dickies - *Banana Splits*; **Buzzcocks** - *Boredom*; **Wire** - *12XU*; **X-Ray Spex** - *Oh Bondage Up Yours!*; **U.K. Subs** - *World War*; **Splodgenessabounds** - *Two Pints Of Lager*, **Damned** - *New Rose*; New York Dolls - *Personality Crisis*; **Boys** - *Babylon's Burning*; **Eddie and The Hot Rods** - *Do Anything You Wanna Do*; **Revillos** - *Graveyard Groove*; **Jilted John** - *Jilted John*; **Jilted John** - *Seventeen*.

New Wave Classics (2-CD) (Disky DOU 878282) 1998

Public Image Ltd. - *This Is Not A Love Song*; **Killing Joke** - *Love Like Blood*; Thomas Dolby - *She Blinded Me With Science*; China Crisis - *Christian*; **A Flock Of Seagulls** - *I Ran*; EMF - *Unbelievable*; Heaven 17 - *Trouble*; **Stranglers** - *Golden Brown*; Culture Club - *War Song*; **Ultravox** - *Reap The Wild Wind*; Fun Boy Three and Bananarama - *Really Saying Something*; Selecter - *On My Radio*; **New Model Army** - *No Rest*; Morrissey - *Suedehead*; **Fischer Z** - *Worker*; **A Flock Of Seagulls** - *Wishing*; **Ultravox** - *Vienna*; Kate Bush - *Cloudbursting*; **Tenpole Tudor** - *Wunderbar*; Billy Idol - *White Wedding*; **Lena Lovich** - *Lucky Number*; Talking Heads - *Psycho Killer*; China Crisis - *Black Man Ray*; Heaven 17 - *Penthouse And Pavement*; Look - *I Am The Beat*; **Duran Duran** - *Girls On Film*; Thomas Dolby - *Hyperactive*; Komtur - *Hans Von Stoffein*; **Ian Dury and The Blockheads** - *Hit Me With Your Rhythm Stick*.

New Wave Danger (3-CD set) (Dressed To Kill DTKBOX 80) 1998

No Future - The Singles Collection, Vol. 1 (Anagram CDPUNK 11) 1994

NB: Also issued on vinyl (Captain Oi! AHOY DLP 508) 1996. See vinyl section for track list.

No Future - The Singles Collection, Vol. 2 (Anagram CDPUNK 54) 1995

NB: Also issued on vinyl (Captain Oi! AHOY DLP 512) 1996. See vinyl section for track list.

Odd Bods Mods & Sods (Captain Mod MODSKA CD 2) 1996

V.I.P.'s - *Can't Believe It's True*; **Squire** - *Livin' In The City*; **Split Screens** - *Know What I Want*; **Justin Case** - *No Good For Me*; **Urban Disturbance** - *Wild Boys In Cortinas*; **V.I.P.'s** - *Just Can't Let You Go*; **Squire** - *Get Ready To Go*; **Split Screens** - *Just Don't Try*; **Just Frank** - *You*; **Clerks** - *When The Lights Go Out*. Bonus Tracks:- **Coming Shortly** - *Doing The Flail*; **Hazard** - *Gotta Change My Life*; **Blue Movies** - *Mary Jane*; **X-E-Cutors** - *Too Far To Look Inside My Head*; **X-Films** - *After My Blood*; **Zeros** - *What's Wrong With A Pop Group*; **Action Replay** - *Decisions*; **Innocent Bystanders** - *Where Is Johnny*; **Debutantes** - *Man In The Street*; **Justin Case** - *TV*; **Straight Up** - *One Out All Out*.

NB: Expanded reissue of Rok (ROKLP 001) 1979.

Oi! Chartbusters, Vol. 1 (Harry May MAYOCD 501) 2000

Sham 69 - *Give A Dog A Bone*; **Infa Riot** - *Riot Riot*; **Accident** - *Borstal Breakout*; **Business** - *Get Out Of My House*; **Splodgenessabounds** - *Two Little Boys*; **Blood** - *Such Fun*; **Cockney Rejects** - *Motorhead*; **Exploited** - *Daily News*; **Blitz** - *4Q*; **Combat 84** - *Poseur*; **Cock Sparrer** - *Run For Cover*; **4-Skins** - *Plastic Gangsters*; **Angelic Upstarts** - *Leave Me Alone*; **Last Resort** - *Held Hostage*.

NB: Originally issued on vinyl (Link LP 03) 1987.

Oi! Chartbusters, Vol. 2 (Harry May MAYO CD 502) 2000

Menace - *GLC*; **Strike** - *Mania*; **Infa Riot** - *Five Minute Fashions*; **Business** - *Suburban Rebels (live)*; **Splodgenessabounds** - *Two Pints Of Lager*; **Blood** - *Stark Raving Normal*; **Cockney Rejects** - *Police Car*; **Partisans** - *Blind Ambition*; **Blitz** - *Time Bomb*; **Combat 84** - *Rapist*; **Cock Sparrer** - *Running Riot (live)*; **4-Skins** - *Clockwork Skinhead*; **Angelic Upstarts** - *Liddle Towers*; **Last Resort** - *Violence In Our Minds*.

NB: Originally issued on vinyl (Street Link LP 016) 1987.

Oi! FUCKIN' Oi!.

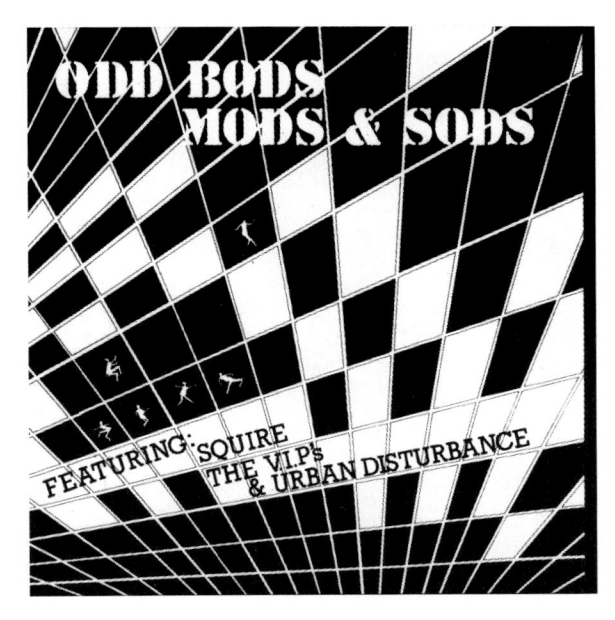

ODD BODS, MODS AND SODS.

Oi Chartbusters, Vol. 1 and 2   (Step-1 STEPCD 011) 1998

Menace - *GLC*; **Strike** - *Mania*; **Infa Riot** - *Five Minute Fashion*; **Business** - *Suburban Rebels*; **Splodgenessabounds** - *Two Pints Of Lager*; **Blood** - *Stark Raving Normal*; **Cockney Rejects** - *Police Car*; **Partisans** - *Blind Ambition*; **Blitz** - *Time Bomb*; **Combat '84** - *Rapist*; **Cock Sparrer** - *Runnin' Riot*; **4-Skins** - *Clockwork Skinhead*; **Angelic Upstarts** - *Murder Of Liddle Towers*; **Last Resort** - *Violence In Our Minds*; **Sham 69** - *Give A Dog A Bone (live)*; **Infa Riot** - *Riot Riot*; **Accident** - *Borstal Breakout*; **Business** - *Get Outta My 'Ouse*; **Splodgenessabounds** - *Two Little Boys*; **Blood** - *Such Fun*; **Cockney Rejects** - *Motorhead*; **Exploited** - *Daily News*; **Blitz** - *4Q*; **Combat 84** - *Poseur*; **Cock Sparrer** - *Run For Cover*; **4-Skins** - *Plastic Gangsters*; **Angelic Upstarts** - *Leave Me Alone*; **Last Resort** - *Held Hostage*.

Oi! Fuckin' Oi!   (Harry May MAYO CD 110) 1999

4-Skins - *One Law For Them*; **Cock Sparrer** - *England Belongs To Me*; **Last Resort** - *Working Class Kids*; **Business** - *Harry May*; **Blitz** - *Warriors*; **Partisans** - *Blind Ambition*; **Cockney Rejects** - *Greatest Cockney Rip Off*; **Blood** - *Stark Raving Normal*; **Menace** - *I'm Civilised*; **Infa Riot** - *Kids Of The 80's*; **Peter and The Test Tube Babies** - *Maniac*; **Gonads** - *Tuckers Ruckers Ain't No Suckers*; **Red Alert** - *SPG*; **Crack** - *Don't Just Sit There*; **The Oppressed** - *White Flag*; **Angelic Upstarts** - *Murder Of Liddle Towers*.

The Oi! Of Sex   (Captain Oi! AHOY CD 23) 1994

Prole - *We'll Never Say Die*; **Cock Sparrer** - *The Sun Says*; **Gonads** - *SE7 Dole Day*; **Burial** - *Old Man's Poison*; **Vicious Rumours** - *Vicious Rumours*; **Jimmy Mack** - *Zombie Mind Eaters*; **Rat Patrol** - *Rat Trap*; **Crossed Hammers** - *Here We Go*; **Swift Nick** - *The Sun*; **Burial** - *Friday Night*; **Prole** - *Destination Room 101*; **Orgasm Guerillas** - *Frankie Goes To Pot*; **Little Dave** - *Being Short*; **Nick Toczeck's Britainarchists** - *Stiff With A Quiff*; **Vicious Rumours** - *Take The Blame*; **ABH** - *Don't Mess With The SAS*; **Dogsbody** - *Murder*; **Garry Johnson** - *If Looks Could Kill*.

NB: Originally issued on vinyl (Syndicate SYNLP 4) 1984.

Oi! The Album   (Captain Oi! AHOY CD 72) 1997

Cockney Rejects - *Oi Oi Oi*; **Peter and The Test Tube Babies** - *Rob A Bank (Wanna)*; **4-Skins** - *Wonderful World*; **Postmen** - *Have A Cigar*; **Exploited** - *Daily News*; Terrible Twins - *Generation Of Scars*; **Angelic Upstarts** - *Guns For The Afghan Rebels*; **Cock Sparrer** - *Sunday Stripper*; **Angelic Upstarts** - *Last Night Another Soldier*; **4-Skins** - *Chaos*; **Cockney Rejects** - *Here We Go Again*; **Max Splodge & Desert Island Joe** - *Isubeleeeene*; Postmen - *Beardsmen*; **Slaughter and The Dogs** - *Cranked Up Really High*; Barney and The Rubbles - *Bootboys*; **Peter and The Test Tube Babies** - *Intensive Care*; **Exploited** - *I Still Believe In Anarchy*.

NB: Originally issued on vinyl (EMI ZIT 1) 1980.

THE Oi! OF SEX.

Oi! The Demos   (Captain Oi! AHOY CD 81) 1997

Crack - *I Want You*; **ABH** - *999*; Distortion - *War Hero*; **Case** - *By The Way*; **Angelic Upstarts** - *Listen To The Silence*; **Sub-Culture** - *In My Time*; **The Burial** - *Backstreet Child*; **Anti-Establishment** - *House Of The Rising Sun*; Terrible Twins - *Surfin' Dream*; **Case** - *Crazy Town*; **ABH** - *Teenage Oppression*; **Crux** - *Liddle Towers*; Distortion - *Chaos Is*; **Angelic Upstarts** - *She Don't Cry Anymore*; **The Burial** - *I Can't Forget*; **Foreign Legion** - *Perfect Society*; **Case** - *Criminal Ways*; **Skin Deep** - *Never Change*; Postmen - *Navy*; **Cockney Rejects** - *In The Underworld (live)*.

Oi! The Rarities, Vol. 1   (Captain Oi! AHOY CD 43) 1995

Sub Culture - *Loud And Clear*; **Anti-Social** - *Backstreet Boys*; **Crux** - *Keep On Running*; **Red Alert** - *Border Guards*; **Case** - *Smiling My Life Away*; **Last Rough Cause** - *My Life*; **Anti-Establishment** - *1980's*; **Criminal Class** - *Soldier*; **Sub Culture** - *Rogue Trooper*; **Anti-Social** - *Your Choice*; **Crux** - *Streets At Night*; **Red Alert** - *Third And Final*; **Case** - *Oh*; **Anti-Establishment** - *Mechanical Man*; **Criminal Class** - *Fighting The System*; **Sub Culture** - *University City*; **Anti-Social** - *New Punks*; **Crux** - *Brighton Front*; **Red Alert** - *Sell Out*; **Case** - *Criminal Ways*; **Anti-Social** - *Screw U*; **Crux** - *I'll Die With My Boots On*; **Red Alert** - *District Boredom*; **Last Rough Cause** - *The Violent Few*.

NB: Also issued on vinyl (Captain Oi! AHOY LP 43) 1998.

Oi! The Rarities, Vol. 2   (Captain Oi! AHOY CD 46) 1995

Crash - *Fight For Your Life*; **Anti-Social** - *Battle Scarred Skinheads*; **Squats** - *Chaos In Nijmegen*; **Special Duties** - *Punk Rocker*; **Condemned 84** - *Oi! Ain't Dead*; **Resistance 77** - *You Reds*; **Frankie Flame** - *Dick*

Oi! THE RARITIES VOL. 1.

Oi! THE RARITIES VOL. 3.

Barton; **Foreign Legion** - *Message From Nowhere*; **Crash** - *Religion*; **Anti-Social** - *Official Hooligan*; **Squats** - *Shut Yer Bleedin Head*; **Special Duties** - *Too Much Talkin*; **Condemned 84** - *Under Her Thumb*; **Resistance 77** - *Young And Wrong*; **Frankie Flame** - *Bloodshot Eyes*; **Foreign Legion** - *Trenchline*; **Crash** - *Kill The Cow*; **Anti-Social** - *Sewer Rat*; **Squats** - *We Hate School*; **Condemned 84** - *Follow The Leader*; **Crash** - *TV Times*; **Squats** - *City Cowboys*; **Condemned 84** - *The Nutter*; **Squats** - *Ravensbruck*.

NB: Also issued on vinyl (Captain Oi! AHOY LP 46) 1998.

Oi! The Rarities, Vol. 3　　　(Captain Oi! AHOY CD 53) 1995
Guttersnipes - *Addicted To Love*; **Skin Deep** - *Football Violence*; **Condemned 84** - *Boots Go Marching In*; **Partisans** - *Blind Ambition*; **Crowbar** - *Hippie Punks*; **Optimists** - *Mull Of Kintyre*; **Samples** - *Vendetta*; **Intensive Care** - *Cowards*; **Guttersnipes** - *Loves Young Dream*; **Skin Deep** - *Boots On His Feet*; **Condemned 84** - *Up Yours*; **Partisans** - *Come Clean*; **Crowbar** - *White Riot*; **Optimists** - *The Plumber Song*; **Samples** - *Computer Future*; **Intensive Care** - *Class Of 84*; **Skin Deep** - *Count The Dead*; **Condemned 84** - *We Will Never Die*; **Partisans** - *Change*; **Samples** - *Rabies*; **Intensive Care** - *Organised Crime*; **Condemned 84** - *Kick Down The Doors*.

NB: Also issued on vinyl (Captain Oi! AHOY LP 053) 1998.

Oi! The Rarities, Vol. 4　　　(Captain Oi! AHOY CD 58) 1996
Crack - *Don't You Ever Let Me Down*; **Intensive Care** - *The Hypocrite*; **Special Duties** - *Violent Society*; **Red London** - *This Is England*; **Demob** - *No Room For You*; **Intensive Care** - *As Sober As A Judge*; **Splodge** -

Oi! THE RARITIES VOL. 4.

Oi! THE RARITIES VOL. 5.

Mouth And Trousers; **Anti-Establishment** - *No Trust*; **Distorted Truth** - *Party Political Bullshit*; **Crack** - *I Can't Take It*; **Intensive Care** - *Points Of View*; **Special Duties** - *Colchester Council*; **Red London** - *Soul Train*; **Demob** - *Think Straight*; **Intensive Care** - *Rebels*; **Splodge** - *The Seven Golden Gussets*; **Anti-Establishment** - *Future Girl*; **Distorted Truth** - *Fallout*; **Intensive Care** - *Exocet UK*; **Red London** - *Revolution Times*; **Demob** - *New Breed*; **Intensive Care** - *Rubberman*.

Oi! The Rarities, Vol. 5　　　(Captain Oi! AHOY CD 62) 1996
Crack - *Going Out*; **Demob** - *Anti-Police*; **Indecent Exposure** - *Riots*; **Combat 84** - *Poseur*; **Anti-Establishment** - *Anti-Men*; **Crack** - *The Troops Have Landed*; **Gonads** - *TNT*; **Dead Generation** - *Francine*; **Combat 84** - *Skinhead*; **The Infas** - *Sound And Fury*; **Crack** - *I Caught You Out*; **Demob** - *Teenage Adolescence*; **Indecent Exposure** - *A Matter Of Time*; **Combat 84** - *Violence*; **Anti-Establishment** - *Misunderstood*; **Crack** - *All Or Nothing*; **Blitz** - *Voice Of A Generation*; **Infas** - *Triffic Spiff Ya O.K.*; **Combat 84** - *Combat 84*.

Oi! The Resurrection　　　(Harry May MAYOCD 516) 2001
4-Skins - *Yesterday's Heroes*; **Vicious Rumours** - *Pull You Through*; **Skin Deep** - *Self Respect*; **Menace** - *I'm Civilised*; **Renegade** - *Revenge*; **Condemned 84** - *No Way In*; **Business** - *Mortgage Mentality*; **Cockney Rejects** - *I Wanna Be A Star*; **Section 5** - *For The Love Of Oi!*; **Magnificent** - *Heat Of The Street*; **Accident** - *Crazy*; **Strike** - *Hungry Gun*; **Intensive Care** - *Framed*; **Last Resort** - *Soul Boys*.

NB: Originally issued on vinyl (Link LP 01) 1987.

Oi! The Singles Collection, Vol. 1　　　(Captain Oi! AHOY CD 60) 1996
4-Skins - *One Law For Them*; **4-Skins** - *Brave New World*; **Business** - *Harry May*; **Business** - *National Insurance Blacklist*; **Cock Sparrer** - *England Belongs To Me*; **Cock Sparrer** - *Argy Bargy*; **Oppressed** - *Work Together*; **Oppressed** - *Victims*; **Blitz** - *Never Surrender*; **Blitz** - *Razors In The Night*; **Partisans** - *Police Story*; **Infa Riot** - *Kids Of The '80s*; **Infa Riot** - *Still Out Of Order*; **One Way System** - *Give Us A Future*; **One Way System** - *Just Another Hero*; **Major Accident** - *Mr. Nobody*; **Major Accident** - *That's You*; **Red Alert** - *In Britain*; **Red Alert** - *Screaming At The Nation*; **Red Alert** - *Murder Missile*.

Oi! The Singles Collection, Vol. 2　　　(Captain Oi! AHOY CD 63) 1996
Sham 69 - *Borstal Breakout*; **Sham 69** - *Hey Little Rich Boy*; **Menace** - *Screwed Up*; **Menace** - *Insane Society*; **Angelic Upstarts** - *The Murder Of Liddle Towers*; **Angelic Upstarts** - *Police Oppression*; **Cockney Rejects** - *Flares 'N' Slippers*; **Cockney Rejects** - *Police Car*; **Cockney Rejects** - *I Wanna Be A Star*; **Last Resort** - *Violence In Our Minds*; **Last Resort** - *Held Hostage*; **Last Resort** - *Soul Boys*; **Peter and The Test Tube Babies** - *Banned From The Pubs*; **Peter and The Test Tube Babies** - *Moped Lads*; **Peter and The Test Tube Babies** - *Peacehaven Wild Kids*; **Blood** -

Oi! THE SINGLES VOL. 1.

Meglomania; **Blood** - *Parasite In Paradise*; **Blood** - *Calling The Shots*; **Ejected** - *Have You Got 10p?*; **Ejected** - *Class Of '82*; **Ejected** - *One Of The Boys*.

Oi! The Singles Collection, Vol. 3   (Captain Oi! AHOY CD 67) 1997

Sham 69 - *Angels With Dirty Faces*; **Sham 69** - *The Cockney Kids Are Innocent*; **Cockney Rejects** - *I'm Not A Fool*; **Cockney Rejects** - *East End*; **Angelic Upstarts** - *Last Night Another Soldier*; **Angelic Upstarts** - *The Man Who Came In From The Beano*; **Toy Dolls** - *Everybody Jitterbug*; **Toy Dolls** - *(She's A) Worky Ticket*; **Business** - *Smash The Discos*; **Business** - *Dayo*; **4-Skins** - *Yesterday's Heroes*; **4-Skins** - *Justice*; **4-Skins** - *Get Out Of My Life*; **Blitz** - *Warriors*; **Blitz** - *Youth (Different Version)*; **Oppressed** - *Urban Soldiers*; **Oppressed** - *Ultra Violence*; **Oppressed** - *Run From You*.

Oi! The Singles Collection, Vol. 4   (Captain Oi! AHOY CD 71) 1997

Slaughter and The Dogs - *Cranked Up Really High*; **Slaughter and The Dogs** - *The Bitch*; **Menace** - *I Need Nothing*; **Menace** - *Electrocutioner*; **Cockney Rejects** - *Bad Man*; **Cockney Rejects** - *The New Song*; **Angelic Upstarts** - *England*; **Angelic Upstarts** - *Stick's Diary*; **The Partisans** - *17 Years Of Hell*; **The Partisans** - *The Power And The Greed*; **The Partisans** - *Bastards In Blue*; **Infa Riot** - *The Winner*; **Infa Riot** - *School's Out*; **One Way System** - *Jerusalem*; **One Way System** - *Jackie Was A Junkie*; **The Blood** - *Stark Raving Normal*; **The Blood** - *Mesrine*.

Oi! THE SINGLES VOL. 2.

Oi! THE SINGLES VOL. 3.

Oi! The Tin   (Can Can CANCAN 002CD) 1997

Cockney Rejects - *Oi Oi Oi*; **Sham 69** - *What Have We Got*; **Menace** - *GLC*; **4-Skins** - *One Law For Them*; **Last Resort** - *Working Class Kids*; **Business** - *Harry May*; **Angelic Upstarts** - *2 Million Voices*; **Angelic Upstarts** - *Kids Of The '80s*; **Cock Sparrer** - *England Belongs To Me*; **Red Alert** - *In Britain*; **4-Skins** - *Evil*; **Blitz** - *Someone's Gonna Die*; **Partisans** - *Police Story*; **Gonads** - *Tucker's Ruckers Ain't No Suckers*; **Last Resort** - *Violence In Our Minds*; **Peter and The Test Tube Babies** - *Banned From Pubs*; **Sham 69** - *Borstal Breakout*; **Cockney Rejects** - *We Can Do Anything*; **Ejected** - *East End Kids*; **Angelic Upstarts** - *England*.

Oi! This Is England (3-CD set)   (Dressed To Kill REDTK 107) 1999

Menace - *GLC*; **Strike** - *Mania*; **Infa Riot** - *Five Minute Fashion*; **Business** - *Suburban Rebels*; **Splodgenessabounds** - *Two Pints Of Lager*; **Blood** - *Stark Raving Normal*; **Cockney Rejects** - *Police Car*; **Partisans** - *Blind Ambition*; **Blitz** - *Time Bomb*; **Combat 84** - *Rapist*; **Cock Sparrer** - *Running Riot*; **4-Skins** - *Clockwork Skinhead*; **Angelic Upstarts** - *Murder Of Liddle Towers*; **Last Resort** - *Murder In Our Minds*; **Sham 69** - *Give A Dog A Bone*; **Infa Riot** - *Riot Riot*; **Accident** - *Borstal Breakout*; **Business** - *Get Outta My 'Ouse*; **Splodgenessabounds** - *Two Little Boys*; **Blood** - *Such Fun*; **Cockney Rejects** - *Motorhead*; **Exploited** - *Daily News*; **Blitz** - *4Q*; **Combat 84** - *Poseur*; **Cock Sparrer** - *Run For Cover*; **4-Skins** - *Plastic Gangsters*; **Angelic Upstarts** - *Leave Me Alone*; **Last Resort** - *Held Hostage*; **Gonads** - *Joys Of Oi*; **Menace** - *Last Years Youth*; **Accident** - *Blitzkrieg Bop*; **Blood** - *Napalm Job*; **Sham 69** - *Tell Us The Truth*; **Splodgenessabounds** - *Wiffy Woman*; **Partisans** - *Change*; **Business** - *Outlaw*; **Chron Gen** - *Living Next Door To Alice*; **Blitz** - *Youth*; **Ruts** - *Babylon's Burning*; **Combat 84** - *F82123*; **Angelic Upstarts** - *Never Return To Hell*; **Cock Sparrer** - *Teenage Heart*; **Partisans** - *Come Clean*; **Business** - *Product*; **Case** - *Smiling My Life Away*; Section 5 - *Street Rock 'N' Roll*; **Gonads** - *Gonads Theme*; **Infa Riot** - *Emergency*; **Splodgenessabounds** - *Delirious*; **Angelic Upstarts** - *When Will They Learn*; **Accident** - *Garageland*; **Blitz** - *Escape*; **Blood** - *Dead Generation*; **Blood** - *Gestapo Khazi*; **Vice Squad** - *Stand Strong Stand Proud*; **Frankie and The Flames** - *On Yer Bike*; **Crack** - *You Kept Me Waiting*; **Angelic Upstarts** - *I Won't Pay For Liberty*; **Criminal Class** - *Soldier*; **Sham 69** - *Cockney Kids Are Innocent*; **Infa Riot** - *Schools Out*; **Slaughter and The Dogs** - *Where Have All The Boot Boys Gone*; **Gonads** - *Eat The Rich*; **Business** - *Chasing Rainbows*; **One Way System** - *Stab The Judge*; **Peter and The Test Tube Babies** - *Transvestite*; **Exploited** - *Computers Don't Blunder*; **4-Skins** - *Summer Holiday*; **Blood** - *Stark Raving Normal*; **Slaughter and The Dogs** - *Twist And Turn*; **Angelic Upstarts** - *Brighton Bomb*; **Business** - *Disco Girls*; **Case** - *Oh*; Section 5 - *Every Saturday*; **Last Resort** - *Eight Pounds A Week*; **Lurkers** - *I'm On Heat*; **Peter and The Test Tube Babies** - *Jinx*; **Crack** - *Cum On Feel The Noize*; **Cockney Rejects** - *It Will Only Ever Be*; **Frankie and The Flames** - *Dick Barton*.

Pax Records Punk Collection   (Anagram CDPUNK 75) 1996

Infa Riot - *Power*; **Angelic Upstarts** - *Victory In Poland*; **Mau Maus** - *Society's Rejects*; **Mau Maus** - *Social System*; **X-Tract** - *Aftermath*; **Mania** -

PAX RECORDS PUNK COLLECTION.

Stick Together; **Mau Maus** - *No Concern*; **Mau Maus** - *Clampdown*; **X-Tract** - *Blame It On The Youth*; **X-Tract** - *War Heroes*; **Anti-System** - *Government Lies*; **Anti-System** - *Schoolboy*; **Mau Maus** - *Just Another Day*; **Mau Maus** - *Running With The Pack*; **Riot Squad** - *Police Power*; **Skeptix** - *Traitor*; **Exploited** - *Rival Leaders*; **Exploited** - *Army Style*; **Exploited** - *Singalongabushell*; **Demob** - *No Room For You*.

Pillows And Prayers (A Cherry Red Compilation 1982 -1983) (Cherry Red CDMRED 41) 1996

Five Or Six - *Portrait*; **Monochrome Set** - *Eine Symphonie Des Grauns*; **Thomas Leer** - *All About You*; Tracey Thorn - *Plain Sailing*; Ben Watt - *Some Things Don't Matter*; Kevin Coyne - *Love In Your Heart*; Pierro Milesi - *Modi 2*; Joe Crow - *Compulsion*; Marine Girls - *Lazy Ways*; Felt - *My Face Is On Fire*; Eyeless In Gaza - *No Noise*; Passage - *Xoyo*; Everything But The Girl - *On My Mind*; **Attila The Stockbroker** - *Bang And A Wimpey*; Misunderstood - *I Unseen*; **Nightingales** - *Don't Blink*; Quentin Crisp - *Stop The Music For A Minute*.

NB: Originally issued on vinyl (Cherry Red Z RED 41) 1982.

A Post Punk Primer (Virgin CDOVD 498) 1997

Japan - *Gentlemen Take Polaroids*; **Killing Joke** - *Requiem*; **Magazine** - *Song From The Floorboards*; Devo - *Peek A Boo*; **Monochrome Set** - *Monochrome Set*; **Howard Devoto** - *Cold Imagination*; **Public Image Ltd.** - *Albatross*; **XTC** - *Are You Receiving Me?*; Jah Wobble - *Betrayal*; Andy Partridge - *Commerciality*; **Human League** - *Empire State Human*; Tom Verlaine - *Five Miles Of You*; **Spear Of Destiny** - *Never Take Me Alive*; Robert Quine - *Pick Up*.

Pretty Vacant (Castle Pie PIESD 026) 1999

Sex Pistols - *Pretty Vacant*; **Sham 69** - *If The Kids Are United*; **Adverts** - *Bored Teenagers*; **X-Ray Spex** - *I'm A Cliche*; Johnny Thunders and The Heartbreakers - *Personality Crisis*; **Lurkers** - *Shut Out The Light*; **Johnny Moped** - *Hard Loving Man*; **UK Subs** - *Telephone Numbers*; **Slaughter and The Dogs** - *Where Have All The Boot Boys Gone*; **Gene October** - *Born To Keep On Running*; **Stranglers** - *Raven*; Dummies - *One Hit Wonder*; **Ruts** - *Something That I Said*; **Buzzcocks** - *Fast Cars*; **999** - *Feeling Alright With The Crew*.

Punk (Music Club MCCD 015) 1991

Buzzcocks - *What Do I Get?*; **Sex Pistols** - *EMI*; New York Dolls - *Personality Crisis*; **Sham 69** - *Angels With Dirty Faces*; Johnny Thunders - *Born To Lose*; **Adverts** - *Bored Teenagers*; New York Dolls - *Looking For A Kiss*; **Sham 69** - *Rip Off*; Johnny Thunders - *One Track Mind*; **Slaughter and The Dogs** - *Boston Babies*; **Sex Pistols** - *Pretty Vacant*; **Adverts** - *No Time To Be 21*; **Discharge** - *Hear Nothing, See Nothing, Say Nothing*; **Boys** - *Brickfield Nights*; **Buzzcocks** - *Time's Up*.

Punk, Vol. 2 (Music Club MCCD 027) 1991

Sex Pistols - *Anarchy In The UK*; **Ruts** - *Babylon's Burning*; **Stiff Little Fingers** - *Nobody's Hero*; **Sham 69** - *Borstal Breakout*; **Exploited** - *Dead Cities*; **Lurkers** - *Ain't Got A Clue*; **Peter and The Test Tube Babies** - *Maniac*; **999** - *Feeling Alright With The Crew*; **Adicts** - *Chinese Take Away*; **Chelsea** - *Right To Work*; **Sex Pistols** - *Holidays In The Sun*; **Stiff Little Fingers** - *Alternative Ulster*; **Splodgenessabounds** - *Two Pints Of Lager*; **Vice Squad** - *Stand Strong, Stand Proud*; **Ruts** - *Something That I Said*; **Anti-Nowhere League** - *I Hate People*; **Angelic Upstarts** - *Teenage Warning*; **Cockney Rejects** - *Flares 'N' Slippers*; **Exploited** - *Punk's Not Dead*; **Blitz** - *Warriors*.

Punk (3-CD Set) (Music Club MCBX 017) 1994

Punk - Live And Nasty (Emporio EMPRCD 586) 1995

U.K. Subs - *I Live In A Car*; **Damned** - *In A Rut*; **Sham 69** - *White Riot*; **Ruts** - *Babylon's Burning*; **GBH** - *I Am The Hunted*; **Sex Pistols** - *Submission*; **Adverts** - *No Time To Be 21*; **Buzzcocks** - *What Do I Get?*; Dickies - *Nights In White Satin*; **Slaughter and The Dogs** - *Runaway*; Eater - *Don't Need It*; **Boys** - *New Guitar In Town*; **Vicious White Kids** - *C'mon Everybody*; **Johnny Moped** - *Hard Loving Man*; **Chelsea** - *Urban Kids*; **Lurkers** - *Wolf At The Door*.

Punk - The Worst Of Total Anarchy (2-CD) (Disky SP 871952) 1996

Sex Pistols - *Anarchy In The U.K.*; **Sham 69** - *Hersham Boys*; Red Hot Chilli Peppers - *Catholic School Girls Rule*; Plasmatics - *Butcher Baby*; **Generation X** - *King Rocker*; **Adverts** - *Gary Gilmore's Eyes*; **Buzzcocks** - *Ever Fallen In Love*; **Stiff Little Fingers** - *Nobody's Hero*; **Bow Wow Wow** - *C30 C60 C90 Go*; **999** - *Nasty Nasty*; Johnny Thunders and The Heartbreakers - *Born To Lose*; **Ruts** - *Babylon's Burning*; **GBH** - *No Survivors*; **Lurkers** - *Heroin It's All Over*; **No Dice** - *Come Dancing*; **Sid Vicious** - *My Way*; Red Hot Chilli Peppers - *Get Up And Jump*; **Sex Pistols** - *God Save The Queen*; **Buzzcocks** - *Love You More*; **Members** - *Sound Of The Suburbs*; **999** - *Homicide*; Ramones - *Sheena Is A Punk Rocker*; **Stranglers** - *Something Better Change*; **Discharge** - *Never Again*; **U.K. Subs** - *Warhead*; **Vice Squad** - *Stand Strong, Stand Proud*; Plasmatics - *Tight Black Pants*; **Cockney Rejects** - *Badman*; **No Dice** - *Why Sugar*; **X-Ray Spex** - *Day The World Turned Day-Glo*; **Angelic Upstarts** - *Kids On The Streets*; **Adverts** - *No Time To Be 21*.

Punk Alert (Emporio EMPRCD 678) 1997

Punk And Disorderly (Abstract AABT 100CD) 1994

Punk And Disorderly (The Best Of Punk & Disorderly) (Cleopatra CLP 9824) 1996

Punk And Disorderly (4-CD Set) (Summit SUMBX 4012) 1998

Punk And Disorderly, Vol. 2 (Further Charges) (Anagram CDPUNK 22) 1993

GBH - *Sick Boy*; **Expelled** - *Dreaming*; **Insane** - *El Salvador*; **One Way System** - *Stab The Judge*; **Court Martial** - *Gotta Get Out*; **Action Pact** - *London Bouncers*; **Dark** - *Masque*; **Violators** - *Gangland*; **Channel 3** - *I've Got A Gun*; **Abrasive Wheels** - *Vicious Circle*; **Enemy** - *Fallen Hero*; **Riot** - *Death To Humanity*; **Wall** - *Hobby For A Day*; **Disorder** - *More Than Fights*; Erazerhead - *Shellshock*; **Vice Squad** - *Resurrection*; **Alternative TV** - *How Much Longer*; **Drones** - *Corgi Crap*; **Suburban Studs** - *I Hate School*; **Peter and The Test Tube Babies** - *Run Like Hell*.

NB: Originally issued on vinyl (Anagram GRAM 001) 1982.

Punk And Disorderly, Vol. 3 (The Final Solution) (Anagram CD PUNK 23) 1993

Abrasive Wheels - *Burn 'Em Down*; **One Way System** - *Give Us A Future*; **Newtown Neurotics** - *Kick Out The Tories*; **U.K. Subs** - *Police State*; **Destructor** - *Jailbait*; **Expelled** - *Government Policy*; **Samples** - *Dead Hero*; **Angelic Upstarts** - *Woman In Disguise*; **Adicts** - *Viva La Revolution*; **Vibrators** - *Dragnet*; **Exploited** - *Computers Don't Blunder*;

Urban Dogs - *New Barbarians*; **Ejected** - *Have You Got 10p?*; **Chron Gen** - *Outlaw*; **Action Pact** - *Suicide Bag*; **Violators** - *Summer Of '81*.
NB: Originally issued on vinyl (Anagram GRAM 005) 1983.

Punk And Nasty (2-CD)   (Emporio DEMPCD 010) 1996

Punk Chartbusters, Vol. 1   (Wolverine WRR 028) 1996

Punk City Rockers (4-CD Set)   (Castle MBSCD 440) 1995
(Reissued Castle Pulse (PBXCD 426) 1998)

UK Subs - *Motivator*; **Business** - *Blind Justice*; **Angelic Upstarts** - *I Won't Pay For Liberty*; **Anti-Nowhere League** - *We're The League*; **Vibrators** - *24 Hour People*; **AB's** - *Concrete Hits Bones*; **Exploited** - *Army Life*; **Blood** - *Done Some Brain Cells Last Night*; **Gonads** - *Punk City Rockers*; **999** - *Let's Face It (live)*; **Cockney Rejects** - *Man's Life In The Army*; Guitar Gangsters - *Gotta Get Out Of Here*; **Infa Riot** - *Emergency*; **Lurkers** - *I'm On Heat (live)*; **Defects** - *Defected Breakdown*; **Defects** - *No U Turns*; **Crack** - *Don't You Ever Let Me Down*; **Blitz** - *Killing Dream*; **Anti-Nowhere League** - *Streets Of London*; **Exploited** - *I Believe In Anarchy*; **Cockney Rejects** - *Dead Generation*; Guitar Gangsters - *Long Division*; **Vibrators** - *Feel Alright*; **Infa Riot** - *Five Minute Fashion*; **Angelic Upstarts** - *Never 'Ad Nothin' (live)*; **Magnificent** - *You're The Best*; **Partisans** - *Time Was Right*; **Stiff Little Fingers** - *At The Edge*; **Crack** - *Going Out*; **Lurkers** - *Lucky John*; **Barbed Wire** - *In The Ghetto*; **Ejected** - *What Am I Gonna Do*; **999** - *Lust Power And Money (live)*; **Business** - *Loud Proud And Punk*; **Maniacs** - *Ain't No Legend*; **UK Subs** - *Teenage (live)*; **Cockney Rejects** - *Greatest Cockney Ripoff*; **Lurkers** - *Going Monkee Again*; **Stiff Little Fingers** - *Silver Lining (live)*; **UK Subs** - *Combat Zone*; **Angelic Upstarts** - *Never Return To Hell*; **Crack** - *Glory Boys*; **Anti-Nowhere League** - *Out On The Wasteland*; **Maniacs** - *Chelsea 77*; **Exploited** - *Yop*; **Business** - *H Bomb*; **999** - *Inside Out (live)*; **Attack** - *Big Brother*; **Vibrators** - *Flying Duck Theory*; **Blood** - *Degenerate*; **AB's** - *Sweetest Kiss*; Guitar Gangsters - *It Must Be Physical*; **Special Duties** - *Violent Society*; **Blitz** - *Warrior*; **Adicts** - *Joker In The Pack (live)*; **Chelsea** - *High Rise Living (live)*; **Ruts** - *H Eyes (live)*; **Adverts** - *Bored Teenagers (live)*; **999** - *Biggest Prize In Sport*; **Slaughter and The Dogs** - *Cranked Up Really High (live)*; **Vice Squad** - *Coward (live)*; **Exploited** - *Cop Cars*; **Chelsea** - *Decide (live)*; **Ruts** - *I Ain't Sophisticated (live)*; **Adverts** - *New Boys (live)*; **Slaughter and The Dogs** - *Johnny T (live)*; **Adicts** - *Steam Roller (live)*; **Vice Squad** - *Out Of Reach*; **Anti-Nowhere League** - *I Hate People (live)*; **Vice Squad** - *EMI (live)*; **Chelsea** - *Come On*; **Adicts** - *How Sad (live)*.

Punk Compilation   (Emporio EMPRCD 550) 1994

Violators - *Summer Of '81*; Erazerhead - *Shellshock*; **Chaos U.K.** - *Four Minute Warning*; **Disorder** - *Complete Disorder*; **Hollywood Brats** - *When He Kissed Me*; Johnny Thunders - *Chinese Rocks*; **Buzzcocks FOC** - *Tomorrow's Sunset*; **Angelic Upstarts** - *Women In Disguise*; **Vibrators** - *Baby Baby*; **999** - *Black Flowers For The Bride*; **999** - *Teenage Rampage*; **Chaotic Dischord** - *Great Rock And Roll Swindle*; Xpozez - *1,000*

PUNK ROCK RARITIES, VOL. 1.

PUNK ROCK RARITIES, VOL. 2.

Marching Feet; **Blitz** - *Razors In The Night*; **Saints** - *Follow The Leader*; **Drones** - *Bone Idol*; **Suburban Studs** - *I Hate School*; **ATV** - *Action Time Vision*; **Peter and The Test Tube Babies** - *Run Like Hell*; **Tights** - *Bad Hearts*; **Adicts** - *Love Sucks*; **One Way System** - *Give Us A Break*; **Partisans** - *17 Years Of Hell*; **Channel 3** - *I've Got A Gun*; **Eater** - *Outside View*.

Punk Generation (4-CD Set)   (Castle MBSCD 419) 1995

Punk Lives   (TrueTrax TRTCD 146) 1995

Punk Lost And Found   (Shanachie SH 5705) 1996

Johnny and The Self-Abusers - *Saints And Sinners*; **Generation X** - *Shakin' All Over*; **Professionals** - *Justifiable Homicide*; **101'ers** - *Keys To Your Heart*; **Spizzenergi** - *Where's Captain Kirk?*; **Freshies** - *I'm In Love With The Girl On The Manchester Megastore Checkout*; **Radiators From Space** - *Television Screen*; **Killjoys** - *Johnny Won't Go To Heaven*; **Snivelling Shits** - *Terminal Stupid*; **Eater** - *Waiting For The Man*; **Soft Boys** - *(I Want To Be An) Anglepoise Lamp*; **Nips** - *Gabrielle*; **Generation X** - *New Order*; **Damned** - *Smash It Up*; Billy Bragg - *Cosmonaut*.

Punkorama, Vol. 1   (Epitaph E 864482) 1994

Punkorama, Vol. 2   (Epitaph 64842) 1996

Punk Rock Losers   (Al's ALBR 1) 1997

Punk Rock Rarities, Vol. 1   (Anagram CDPUNK 63) 1995

Bears - *On Me*; **Mutants** - *Hard Time*; **Mutants** - *Schoolteacher*; **Mutants** - *Lady*; **Stoat** - *Office Girl*; **Stoat** - *Little Jenny*; **Billy Karloff** - *Crazy Paving*; **Billy Karloff** - *Backstreet Billy*; **Embryo** - *I'm Different*; **Embryo** - *You Know He Did*; **Rivals** - *Here Comes The Night*; **Rivals** - *Both Sides*; **Murder Inc.** - *Sound So False*; **Murder Inc.** - *Polythene Dream*; **Murder Inc.** - *Nobody Cares*; **Jump Squad** - *Lord Of The Dance*; **Jump Squad** - *Debt*; **Charge** - *Kings Cross*; **Charge** - *Brave New World*; **Charge** - *God's Kids*.

Punk Rock Rarities, Vol. 2   (Anagram CDPUNK 83) 1996

Users - *Kicks In Style*; **Users** - *Dead On Arrival*; **Maniacs** - *Chelsea '77*; **Maniacs** - *I Ain't No Legend*; **Art Attacks** - *I Am A Dalek*; **Art Attacks** - *Neutron Bomb*; **Dole** - *New Wave Love*; **Satans Rats** - *You Make Me Sick*; **Satans Rats** - *Louise*; **Front** - *System*; **Front** - *Queen's Mafia*; **Dyaks** - *Gutter Kids*; **Dyaks** - *It's A Game*; **Squad** - *Eight Pounds A Week*; **Squad** - *Red Alert*; **Shove** - *Raise The Roof Tonight*; **Shove** - *Violence*; **Shove** - *Pigs*; **Shove** - *Nutters Of York*; **Satellites** - *Vietnam*; **Satellites** - *Lucy Is A Prostitute*; **Satellites** - *I Fell In Love With A Lesbian*.

Punks From The Underground (Skydog 622432) 1997

Punks Undercover (Cleopatra CLP 9930) 1997

The Punk, The Bad And The Ugly (Cleopatra CLP 9959) 1997

Rabid/TJM Punk Singles Collection (Receiver RRCD 227) 1996

Slaughter and The Dogs - *Cranked Up Really High*; **Slaughter and The Dogs** - *Bitch*; **Nosebleeds** - *Ain't Been To No Music School*; **Nosebleeds** - *Fascist Pigs*; **John Cooper Clarke** - *Innocents*; **John Cooper Clarke** - *Suspended Sentence*; **John Cooper Clarke** - *Psycle Sluts*; **Gyro** - *Central Detention Centre*; **Jilted John** - *Jilted John*; **Ed Banger** - *Kinnel Tommy*; **Out** - *Who Is Innocent?*; **V2** - *Man In The Box*; **V2** - *When The World Isn't There*; **Distractions** - *It Doesn't Bother Me*; **Slaughter and The Dogs** - *It's Alright*; **Slaughter and The Dogs** - *Edgar Allen Poe*; **Slaughter and The Dogs** - *Twist And Turn*; **Slaughter and The Dogs** - *UFO*; **Frantic Elevators** - *Voice In The Dark*; **Pathetix** - *Love In Decay*; **Victim** - *Why Are Fire Engines Red*; **Victim** - *I Need You*; **Victim** - *Teenage Victim*; **Victim** - *Junior Criminals*; **Victim** - *Hang On To Yourself*.

The Raw Records Punk Collection (Anagram CDPUNK 14) 1993

Users - *Sick Of You*; **Users** - *I'm In Love With Today*; **Killjoys** - *Johnny Won't Go To Heaven*; **Killjoys** - *Naive*; **Unwanted** - *Withdrawal*; **Unwanted** - *Bleak Outlook*; **Unwanted** - *1984*; **Some Chicken** - *New Religion*; **Some Chicken** - *Blood On The Wall*; **Lockjaw** - *Radio Call Sign*; **Lockjaw** - *Young Ones*; **Some Chicken** - *Arabian Daze*; **Some Chicken** - *Number Seven*; **Gorillas** - *It's My Life*; **Gorillas** - *My Son's Alive*; **Unwanted** - *Secret Police*; **Unwanted** - *These Boots Are Made For Walking*; **Lockjaw** - *Journalist Jive*; **Unwanted** - *I'm Not Me*; **Unwanted** - *End Is Nigh*; **Sick Things** - *Bondage Boy*; **Sick Things** - *Kids On The Streets*; **Psycho's** - *So Young*; **Psycho's** - *Straight Jacket*; **Killjoys** - *At Night*; **Acme Sewage Co.** - *I Wish You Dead*; **Acme Sewage Co.** - *I Don't Need You*; **GT's** - *Millionaire*; **Psycho's** - *Young British And White*; **Acme Sewage Co.** - *I Can See You*.

Riot City Singles Collection, Vol. 1 (Anagram CDPUNK 15) 1997

Vice Squad - *Last Rockers*; **Vice Squad** - *Young Blood*; **Insane** - *Politics*; **Abrasive Wheels** - *Vicious Circle*; **Court Martial** - *Gotta Get Out*; **Chaos UK** - *Four Minute Warning*; **Undead** - *Undead*; **Expelled** - *Dreaming*; **Abrasive Wheels** - *Army Song*; **Chaotic Dischord** - *Fuck The World*; **Court Martial** - *No Solution*; **Chaos UK** - *No Security*; **Mayhem** - *Dogsbody*; **Ejected** - *Have You Got 10p?*; **Undead** - *Dead Revolution*; **Abrasive Wheels** - *Burn 'Em Down*; **Expelled** - *Make It Alone*; **Resistance 77** - *Nottingham Problem*; **Ejected** - *Fast 'n' Loud*; **No Choice** - *Cream Of The Crop*; **Emergency** - *Points Of View*; **Chaotic Dischord** - *Never Trust

RIOT CITY SINGLES COLLECTION, VOL. 1.

RONDELET PUNK SINGLES COLLECTION.

A Friend; **Sex Aids** - *Back On The Piss Again*; **Mayhem** - *Gentle Murder*; **Ultraviolent** - *Crime For Revenge*; **Underdogs** - *East Of Dachau*; **Varukers** - *Die For Your Government*; **Ejected** - *Russians*; **Varukers** - *Led To The Slaughter*; **Chaotic Dischord** - *Cliff*.

NB: Also issued on vinyl (Captain Oi! AHOY DLP 503) 1996.

Riot City Singles Collection, Vol. 2 (Anagram CDPUNK 55) 1995

Vice Squad - *Living On Dreams*; **Vice Squad** - *Humane*; **Insane** - *Dead And Gone*; **Abrasive Wheels** - *Voice Of Youth*; **Court Martial** - *Fight For Your Life*; **Chaos UK** - *Kill Your Baby*; **Undead** - *It's Corruption*; **Expelled** - *What Justice*; **Abrasive Wheels** - *Juvenile*; **Chaotic Dischord** - *Too Late*; **Court Martial** - *Too Late*; **Chaos UK** - *What About A Future*; **Mayhem** - *Street Fight*; **Ejected** - *Class Of '82*; **Undead** - *This Place Is Burning*; **Abrasive Wheels** - *Urban Rebel*; **Expelled** - *Government Policy*; **Resistance 77** - *Join The Army*; **Ejected** - *I Don't Care*; **No Choice** - *Sadist Dream*; **Emergency** - *City Fun*; **Chaotic Dischord** - *Pop Stars*; **Sex Aids** - *We Are The Road Crew*; **Mayhem** - *(Your Face Fits) Lie And Die*; **Ultraviolent** - *Dead Generation*; **Underdogs** - *Johnny Go Home*; **Varukers** - *All Systems Fail*; **Ejected** - *Twenty Four Years*; **Varukers** - *End Is Nigh*.

NB: Also issued on vinyl (Captain Oi! AHOY DLP 511) 1996.

Rondelet Punk Singles Collection (Anagram CDPUNK 49) 1995

Anti-Pasti - *No Government*; **Anti-Pasti** - *Two Years Too Late*; **Anti-Pasti** - *Another Dead Soldier*; **Anti-Pasti** - *Six Guns*; **Fits** - *Burial*; **Special Duties** - *Violent Society*; **Special Duties** - *Colchester Council*; **Dead Man's Shadow** - *Bomb Scare*; **Dead Man's Shadow** - *Another Hiroshima*; **Anti-Pasti** - *East To The West*; **Membranes** - *Muscles*; **Special Duties** - *Police State*; **Threats** - *Go To Hell*; **Riot Squad** - *Fuck The Tories*; **Riot Squad** - *We Are The Riot Squad*; **Special Duties** - *Bullshit Crass*; **Riot Squad** - *Riot In The City*; **Anti-Pasti** - *Caution In The Wind*; **Dead Man's Shadows** - *Flower In The Gun*; **Membranes** - *High Street Yanks*; **Threats** - *Politicians And Ministers*; **Fits** - *Last Laugh*.

NB: Also issued on vinyl (Captain Oi! AHOY LP 513) 1996.

Rot Records Punk Singles Collection (Anagram CDPUNK 40) 1994

Riot Squad - *Lost Cause*; **Riot Squad** - *I'm OK Fuck You*; **Riot Squad** - *There Ain't No Solution*; **Clockwork Soldiers** - *Wet Dreams*; **Dead Man's Shadow** - *Flowers In The Gun*; **Resistance 77** - *Enemy*; **Animal Farm** - *Model Soldier*; **Paranoia** - *Shattered Glass*; **Enemy** - *Last But Not Least*; **Patrol** - *Don't Criticise*; **Resistance 77** - *Russia*; **Riot Squad** - *Hate The Law*; **Varukers** - *Massacred Millions*; **Varukers** - *Will They Never Learn*; **English Dogs** - *Incisor*; **Oi Polloi** - *Boot Down The Door*; **Skeptix** - *Return To Hell*; **Rattus** - *Evil Will Win*; **English Dogs** - *Forward Into Battle*;

ROT RECORDS PUNK SINGLES COLLECTION.

Varukers - *Killed By My Mans Own Hands*; **Rabid** - *Bloody Road To Glory*; **Rejected** - *Boys In Blue*; **Expelled** - *Cider*; **Cult Maniax** - *Cities*.

Secret Records Punk Singles Collection Vol. 1
(Anagram CDPUNK 13) 1993

Exploited - *Dogs Of War*; **Exploited** - *Army Life*; **Exploited** - *Exploited Barmy Army*; **Infa Riot** - *Kids Of The 80's*; **4-Skins** - *One Law For Them*; **Exploited** - *Dead Cities*; **Business** - *Harry May*; **4-Skins** - *Yesterday's Heroes*; **Chron Gen** - *Jet Boy Jet Girl*; **Chron Gen** - *Attack Exploited*; **Gonads** - *I Lost My Love To A U.K. Sub*; **Gonads** - *Punk City Rockers*; **Business** - *Smash The Discos*; **Business** - *H-Bomb*; **Exploited** - *TOP*; **Exploited** - *Computers Don't Blunder*; **Exploited** - *Troops Of Tomorrow*; **Infa Riot** - *Feel The Rage*; **Chron Gen** - *Clouded Eyes*; **Chron Gen** - *Outlaw*; **Strike** - *Victim*; **4-Skins** - *Low Life*; **4-Skins** - *Seems To Me*.

NB: Also issued on vinyl (Captain Oi! AHOY LP 507) 1996.

Secret Records Punk Singles Collection Vol. 2
(Anagram CDPUNK 60) 1995

Exploited - *Blown To Bits*; **Exploited** - *Fuck The Mods*; **Exploited** - *I Believe In Anarchy*; **Exploited** - *Hitler's In The Charts Again*; **Exploited** - *Alternative*; **Exploited** - *Addiction*; **4-Skins** - *Brave New World*; **4-Skins** - *Justice*; **Business** - *Employers Blacklist*; **Business** - *Disco Girls*; **Chron Gen** - *Subway Sadist*; **Chron Gen** - *Behind Closed Doors*; **Chron Gen** - *Disco Tech*; **Gonads** - *Punk Rock Will Never Die*; **Gonads** - *Got Any Wriggly's John*; **Gonads** - *She Can't Whip Me*; **Infa Riot** - *School's Out*; **Angela Rippon's Bum** - *Fight For Your Life*; **Skin Disease** - *I'm Thick*; **Venom** - *Where's Dock Green*; **East End Badoes** - *Way It's Got To Be*.

NB: Also issued on vinyl (Captain Oi! AHOY LP 507) 1996.

The Skinhead Tin
(Harry May CAN CAN 004CD) 2000

4-Skins - *Clockwork Skinhead*; Bad Manners - *Skinhead Girl*; Skoidats - *Saturday Skins*; Judge Dread - *Bring Back The Skins*; **Last Resort** - *Skinheads In Stapress*; Loafers - *Skinhead*; Skoidats - *Skinhead Revolt*; Section 5 - *Skins Will Never Die*; Intensified - *Skinhead Train*; Judge Dread - *Skinhead*; Fatskins - *American Skins*; **Combat 84** - *Skinhead*; Busters All Stars - *Skinhead Love Affair*; **Anti-Social** - *Battle Scarred Skinheads*; Section 5 - *Skinhead Girl*; Judge Dread and The Originals - *Skinhead Moonstomp*; **Condemned 84** - *Skinhead (live)*; Laurel Aitken - *Skinhead Train (live)*; Verona with Bad Manners - *Skinhead Boy*; **Last Resort** - *Oi! Oi! Skinhead*.

Small Wonder Punk Singles Collection, Vol. 1
(Anagram CDPUNK 29) 1994

Puncture - *Mucky Pup*; **Zeros** - *Hungry*; **Carpettes** - *Radio Wunderbar*; **Patrick Fitzgerald** - *Safety Pin Stuck In My Heart*; **Menace** - *GLC*; **Patrick Fitzgerald** - *Buy Me Sell Me*; **Leyton Buzzards** - *Nineteen And Mad*; **Punishment Of Luxury** - *Puppet Life*; **Carpettes** - *Small Wonder*; **Demon Preachers** - *Little Miss Perfect*; **Nicky and The Dots** - *Never Been So Stuck*; **Wall** - *New Way*; **Molesters** - *Disco Love*; **Cravats** - *The End*; **Menace** - *Last Year's Youth*; **Murder The Disturbed** - *DNA*; **Molesters** - *End Of Civilisation*; **Cockney Rejects** - *Flares 'N' Slippers*; **Fatal Microbes** - *Violence Grows*; **Wall** - *Exchange*; **English Sub-Titles** - *Time Tunnel*; **Proles** - *Soft Ground*; **Cravats** - *Precinct*; **Cravats** - *You're Driving Me*; **Cravats** - *Off The Beach*; **Anthrax** - *They've Got It All Wrong*.

NB: There's also a vinyl compilation (Captain Oi! AHOY DLP 514) 1996.

Small Wonder Punk Singles Collection, Vol. 2
(Anagram CDPUNK 70) 1996

Puncture - *Can't Play Rock 'n' Roll*; **Zeros** - *Radio Fun*; **Carpettes** - *How About Me And You*; **Patrick Fitzgerald** - *Set Me Free*; **Menace** - *I'm Civilised*; **Patrick Fitzgerald** - *Little Rippers*; **Patrick Fitzgerald** - *Irrelevant Battles*; **Leyton Buzzards** - *Youthanasia*; **Punishment Of Luxury** - *Demon*; **Carpettes** - *2NE1*; **Nicky and The Dots** - *Linoleum Walk*; **Wall** - *Suckers*; **Wall** - *Uniforms*; **Cravats** - *Burning Bridges*; **Cravats** - *I Am The Dreg*; **Molesters** - *Commuter Man*; **Menace** - *Carry No Banners*; **Murder The Disturbed** - *Walking Corpses*; **Molesters** - *Girl Behind The Curtain*; **Cockney Rejects** - *Police Car*; **Fatal Microbes** - *Beautiful Picture*; **English Sub-Titles** - *Sweat*; **Proles** - *SMK*; **Anthrax** - *What Will Tomorrow*.

Son Of Oi!
(Captain Oi! AHOY CD 9) 1993

Cock Sparrer - *Chip On My Shoulder (live)*; Kraut - *Onwards*; **Prole** - *Generation Landslide*; **Garry Johnson** - *The Young Conservatives*; Paranoid Pictures - *Tomorrow's Whirl*; **Gonads** - *Jobs Not Jails*; **Clockwork Destruction** - *Violent Playground*; Phil Sexton, Mick Turpin - *Joe Public*; Alaska Cowboys - *Herpes In Seattle*; **Garry and The Gonads** - *Lager Top Blues*; Terry McCann - *Made In England*; Mick Turpin - *6.27 To London*; **Orgasm Guerillas** - *Sing Something Swindle*; **Attila and The Newtown Neurotics** - *Andy Is A Corporatist-Mindless Version*; **4-Skins** - *On The Streets*; **Garry Johnson** - *Boy About Town*; **Business** - *Out In The Cold*; Maniac Youth - *Make Mine Molotov*; **Angelic Upstarts** - *I Understand (live)*; Oi! The Robot - *Manifest Oi!*; Phil Sexton - *Top Of The Pops*; **Vicious Rumours** - *This Is Your Loife*; L.O.L.S Choir - *Jerusalem*; **Oxo's Midnight Stumblers** - *Beano*.

NB: Originally issued on vinyl (Syndicate SYNLP 3) 1983.

The Sound Of The Suburbs
(Columbia 4888252) 1997

Jam - *Eton Rifles*; **Adam and The Ants** - *Ant Music*; **Buzzcocks** - *Ever Fallen In Love*; **Only Ones** - *Another Girl Another Planet*; **Undertones** - *Teenage Kicks*; Martha and The Muffins - *Echo Beach*; **Altered Images** - *Happy Birthday*; Elvis Costello - *Oliver's Army*; **Tom Robinson Band** - *2-4-6-8 Motorway*; **Ian Dury and The Blockheads** - *Hit Me With Your Rhythm Stick*; Blondie - *Call Me*; **Teardrop Explodes** - *Reward*; **Boomtown Rats** - *I Don't Like Mondays*; **Psychedelic Furs** - *Pretty In Pink*; **Stranglers** - *No More Heroes*; **Vapors** - *Turning Japanese*; **Eddie and The Hot Rods** - *Do Anything You Wanna Do*; **Members** - *Sound Of The Suburbs*.

SECRET RECORDS PUNK SINGLES COLLECTION, VOL. 2.

Spiked (EMI Gold CDGOLD 1057) 1996
Stranglers - *Something Better Change*; **Ruts** - *Babylon's Burning*; **Buzzcocks** - *Ever Fallen In Love*; **Skids** - *Sweet Suburbia*; **Stiff Little Fingers** - *Alternative Ulster*; **Vapors** - *Turning Japanese*; Talking Heads - *Wild Wild Life*; **Magazine** - *Shot By Both Sides*; **Penetration** - *Don't Dictate*; **Generation X** - *King Rocker*; **999** - *Emergency*; **Wire** - *Outdoor Miner*; **Tom Robinson Band** - *Glad To Be Gay*; **Buzzcocks** - *What Do I Get?*; **Cockney Rejects** - *I'm Not A Fool*; Ramones - *Sheena Is A Punk Rocker*; **Stiff Little Fingers** - *Suspect Device*; **Stranglers** - *Hanging Around*.

Spiked (Summit SUMCD 4094) 1997
Vibrators - *Judy Says*; **Vibrators** - *London Girls*; **999** - *Inside Out*; **999** - *English Wipeout*; **Lurkers** - *Ain't Got A Clue*; **Lurkers** - *Solitaire*; **Angelic Upstarts** - *42nd Street*; **Angelic Upstarts** - *Burglar*; **Spizzenergi** - *Virginia Plain*; **Spizzenergi** - *Cold City*; **Eddie and The Hot Rods** - *Teenage Depression*; **Eddie and The Hot Rods** - *Quit This Town*; Johnny Thunders - *Stepping Stone*; **Johnny Thunders** - *Too Much Junkie Business*; **Suburban Studs** - *No Faith*; **Vice Squad** - *Take It Or Leave It*; **Blitz** - *We Are The Boys*; **Anti-Pasti** - *Two Years Too Late*; **Peter and The Test Tube Babies** - *Peacehaven Wild Kids*.

Teenage Kicks (PolyGram TV 5253382) 1995
Sex Pistols - *Pretty Vacant*; **Jam** - *Going Underground*; **Undertones** - *My Perfect Cousin*; **Eddie and The Hot Rods** - *Do Anything You Wanna Do*; **Sham 69** - *If The Kids Are United*; **Elvis Costello and The Attractions** - *Pump It Up*; **Stranglers** - *No More Heroes*; **Boomtown Rats** - *She's So Modern*; **Ian Dury and The Blockheads** - *Hit Me With Your Rhythm Stick*; **Buzzcocks** - *Ever Fallen In Love*; **Skids** - *Working For The Yankee Dollar*; **Vapors** - *Turning Japanese*; **Generation X** - *King Rocker*; **X-Ray Spex** - *Germ Free Adolescents*; **Ian Dury and The Blockheads** - *What A Waste*; **Department S** - *Is Vic There*; **Bow Wow Wow** - *Go Wild In The Country*; Hazel O'Connor - *Eighth Day*; **Vibrators** - *Automatic Lover*; **Lena Lovich** - *Lucky Number*; **Rich Kids** - *Rich Kids*; **Jam** - *Start*; **Undertones** - *Teenage Kicks*; Blondie - *Hanging On The Telephone*; **Pretenders** - *Brass In Pocket*; **Motors** - *Airport*; **Squeeze** - *Take Me, I'm Yours*; **Police** - *Can't Stand Losing You*; Split Enz - *I Got You*; **Psychedelic Furs** - *Pretty In Pink*; **Tom Robinson** - *2-4-6-8 Motorway*; Cheap Trick - *I Want You To Want Me*; Flamin' Groovies - *Shake Some Action*; **Tenpole Tudor** - *Swords Of A Thousand Men*; **Jags** - *Back Of My Hand*; Cars - *My Best Friend's Girl*; Knack - *My Sharona*; **Secret Affair** - *Time For Action*; **XTC** - *Generals And Majors*; **Teardrop Explodes** - *Reward*; Buggles - *Clean Clean*; Dr. Feelgood - *Roxette*; Graham Parker - *Hey Lord Don't Ask Me Questions*; Mink Deville - *Spanish Stroll*; Jonathan Richman - *Roadrunner*; Iggy Pop - *Real Wild Child*.

This Is Mod, Vol. 1
(Rarities 1979-81) (Anagram CDMGRAM 98) 1995
Circles - *Opening Up*; **Circles** - *Billy*; **Amber Squad** - *We Can Go Dancing*; **Amber Squad** - *You Should See What I Do To You In My Dreams*; **Cigarettes** - *Can't Sleep At Night*; **Cigarettes** - *It's The Only Way To Live*; **Cigarettes** - *All We Want Is Your Money*; **Cigarettes** - *I've Forgotten My Number*; **Cigarettes** - *They're Back Again*; **Deadbeats** - *Choose You*; **Deadbeats** - *Julie's New Boyfriend*; **Deadbeats** - *Oh No*; **Letters** - *Nobody Loves Me*; **Letters** - *Don't Want You Back*; **Nips** - *Happy Song*; **Nips** - *Nobody To Love*; **Odds** - *Saturday Night*; **Odds** - *Not Another Love Song*; **Circles** - *Circles*; **Circles** - *Summer Nights*.

This Is Mod, Vol. 2 (Anagram CDMGRAM 101) 1996
Killermeters - *Twisted Wheel*; **Killermeters** - *SX 225*; **Purple Hearts** - *Plane Crash*; **Purple Hearts** - *Scooby Doo*; **Purple Hearts** - *Gun Of Life*; **Exits** - *Fashion Plague*; **Exits** - *Cheam*; **VIP's** - *Need Somebody To Love*; **VIP's** - *Stuttgart Special*; **VIP's** - *Who Knows*; **VIP's** - *Janine*; **Crooks** - *Modern Boys*; **Crooks** - *Beat Goes On*; **Same** - *Wild About You*; **Same** - *Movements*; **Crooks** - *All The Time In The World*; **Crooks** - *Bangin' My Head*; **Teenage Film Stars** - *Odd Man Out*; **Teenage Film Stars** - *I Apologise*; **Terry Tonik** - *Just A Little Mod*; **Terry Tonik** - *Smashed And Blocked*.

This Is Mod, Vol. 3
(Diamond Collection) (Anagram CDMGRAM 106) 1996
Scene - *Looking For Love*; **Scene** - *Let Me Know*; **Long Tall Shorty** - *On The Streets Again*; **Long Tall Shorty** - *I Fought The Law*; **Long Tall Shorty** - *Promises*; **Scene** - *Something That You Said*; **Scene** - *Stop Go*; **Moment** - *In This Town*; **Long Tall Shorty** - *What's Going On*; **Long Tall Shorty** - *Steppin' Stone*; **Long Tall Shorty** - *Win Or Lose*; **Long Tall Shorty** - *England*; **Moment** - *One Two They Fly*; **Scene** - *Good Lovin'*; **Scene** - *2 Plus 2 What's Music*; B-Team - *All I Ever Wanted*; B-Team - *Bad Day*; **Way Out** - *This Working Way*; **Way Out** - *Just The Girl*; **Rage** - *Looking For You*; **Rage** - *Come On Now*; **Rage** - *Hallelujah*.

This Is Mod, Vol. 4
(Modities) (Anagram CDMGRAM 107) 1996
Accidents - *Blood Splattered With Guitars*; **Accidents** - *Curtains For You*; **Directions** - *Three Bands Tonite*; **Directions** - *On The Train*; **Lambrettas** - *Go Steady*; **Lambrettas** - *Cortinas*; **Lambrettas** - *Listen Listen Listen*; **Nightriders** - *I Saw Her With Another Guy*; **Nightriders** - *London Town*; **Merton Parkas** - *Flat 19*; **Merton Parkas** - *Band Of Gold*; **Onlookers** - *You And I*; **Onlookers** - *Understand*; **Onlookers** - *Julia*; **Reputations** - *I Believe You*; **Reputations** - *Breaking Communications*; **Reputations** - *All Day And All Of The Night*; **Reputations** - *They Think I Don't See Them*; Untouchables (U.K.) - *Protect Your Love*; Untouchables (U.K.) - *Sister Salvation*.

This Is Mod, Vol. 5 (Anagram CDMGRAM 110) 1997
Amber Squad - *I Can't Put My Finger On You*; **Amber Squad** - *Tell You A Lie*; **Killermeters** - *Why Should It Happen To Me*; **Killermeters** - *Cardiac Arrest*; **Graduates** - *If You Want It*; **Graduates** - *Hey Young Girl*; **Aces** - *One Way Street*; **Small World** - *First Impressions*; **Small World** - *Stupidity Street*; **Small World** - *Tomorrow Never Comes*; **Long Tall Shorty** - *Win Or Lose*; **Long Tall Shorty** - *Ain't Done Wrong*; **Sema 4** - *Even If I Know*; **Sema 4** - *Sema 4 Messages*; **Sema 4** - *Actors All*; **Sema 4** - *Do You Know Your Friends*; **Purple Hearts** - *My Life's A Jigsaw*; **Purple Hearts** - *Guy Who Made Her A Star*; **Purple Hearts** - *Just To Please You*; **Teenbeats** - *Strength Of The Nation*; **Teenbeats** - *If I'm Gone Tomorrow*.

This Is Oi! (Captain Oi! AHOY CD 6) 1993
The Oppressed - *Work Together*; **Vicious Rumours** - *Nobody's Fool*; **Section 5** - *Dance Dance Dance*; **The Radicts** - *Kids Of The Nation*; **Feckin Ejits** - *The Picket Song*; **Barbed Wire** - *Nazi Britain (Fuck Off)*; **Condemned 84** - *Jimmy Davey*; **Society's Rejects** - *It's Your Life*; **Oi Polloi** - *Minority Authority*; **Barbed Wire** - *No Hope*; **Condemned 84** - *Teenage Slag*; **Society's Rejects** - *Politician*; **Oi Polloi** - *Skinhead*; **Feckin Ejits** - *Ejits Party*; **Section 5** - *Ghost Town*; **The Oppressed** - *Victims*; **The Radicts** - *Revolution City*; **Vicious Rumours** - *Hangover*.

NB: Originally issued on vinyl (Oi! OIR 004) 1986.

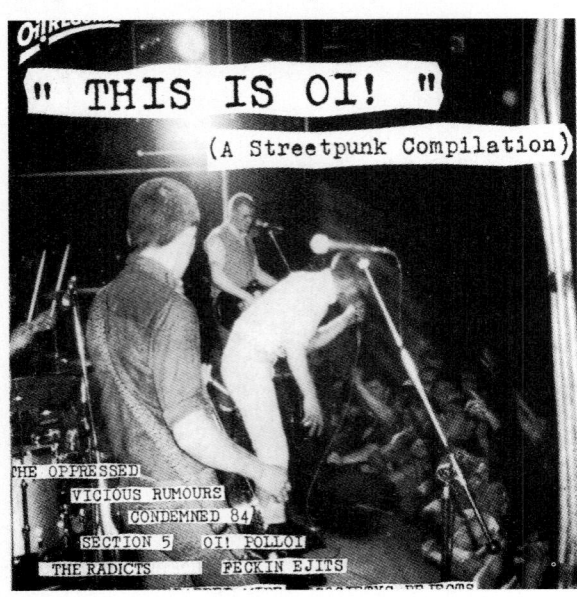

THIS IS Oi!.

THE ZONOPHONE PUNK SINGLES COLLECTION.

The Ultimate Punk Box Set
(3-CD set) (Receiver RRBCD 607) 1999

Sex Pistols - *God Save The Queen*; **Sham 69** - *Angels With Dirty Faces (live)*; **Bow Wow Wow** - *Go Wild In The Country (live)*; **Toy Dolls** - *Nellie The Elephant*; **Adverts** - *One Chord Wonders*; Dickies - *Banana Splits*; **X-Ray Spex** - *Oh Bondage Up Yours! (live)*; **Splodgenessabounds** - *Two Pints Of Lager And A Packet Of Crisps Please*; **Eddie and The Hot Rods** - *Do Anything You Wanna Do (live)*; **Ruts** - *Babylon's Burning (live)*; **Stranglers** - *Something Better Change*; Regents - *7 Teen*; **Jilted John** - *Jilted John*; **Fall** - *Chislers*; Bad Manners - *My Girl Lollipop (live)*; New York Dolls - *Personality Crisis*; **Slaughter and The Dogs** - *Angels Of The Night*; **Vibrators** - *Automatic Lover (live)*; **999** - *Emergency*; **Buzzcocks** - *Boredom*; **Wire** - *Lowdown (live)*; **Johnny Moped** - *Hard Loving Man (live)*; **Eater** - *Don't Need It (live)*; Johnny Thunders and The Heartbreakers - *Chinese Rocks (live)*; **Boys** - *Independent Girl (live)*; **UK Subs** - *World War (live)*; **Yobs** - *Senseless Lass*; Gaye Bikers On Acid - *Watch That Roundabout Ben*; **Chelsea** - *I'm On Fire*; **Lurkers** - *Take Me Back To Babylon*; **John Cooper Clarke** - *Psycle Sluts (Part 1)*; **Theatre Of Hate** - *Do You Believe In The Westworld*; **Discharge** - *Nightmare Continues (live)*; **V2** - *Man In A Box*; **Anti-Nowhere League** - *So What (live)*; Extreme Noise Terror - *System Shit*; **Nosebleeds** - *Fascist Pigs*; **Chaos UK** - *Month Of Sundays*; **Killjoys** - *This Is Not Love*; Stupids - *Slumber Party Massacre*; Ripcord - *Abuse*; Mick Hucknell and **The Frantic Elevators** - *Voice In The Dark*; **English Dogs** - *Cranked Up Really High*; Civilised Society - *Violence Sucks*; **Abrasive Wheels** - *Sonic Omen*; Spermbirds - *Something To Prove*; **GBH** - *City Baby Attacked By Rats*; Doctor and The Crippens - *Garden Centre Murders*; **Sore Throat** - *Channel Zero Reality*; **Play Dead** - *Holy Holy*.

Vaultage Punk Collection (Anagram CDPUNK 101) 1997

Piranhas - *Jilly*; **Piranhas** - *Virginity*; **Piranhas** - *Tension*; **Nicky and The Dots** - *Girls Get Nervous*; **Nicky and The Dots** - *Wrong Street*; **Dodgems** - *Lord Lucan Is Missing*; **Peter and The Test Tube Babies** - *Elvis Is Dead*; **Vandells** - *Bank Holidays*; **Golinski Brothers** - *Bloody*; **Lillettes** - *Nervous Wreck*; **Lillettes** - *Hey Operator*; **Woody and The Splinters** - *I Want You To Be My Girl*; **Chefs** - *Sweetie*; **Chefs** - *Thrush*; **Piranhas** - *Happy Families*; **Chefs** - *24 Hours*; **Chefs** - *Let's Make U*; Exclusives - *Sinking Gondola*; **Reward System** - *Extradition*.

Wave (The Biggest New Wave Hits)
(3-CD Set) (Disky HR 868442) 1996

Spandau Ballet - *To Cut A Long Story Short*; Billy Idol - *White Wedding*; Fischer Z - *So Long*; Scritti Politti - *Asylum In Jerusalem*; **Penetration** - *Don't Dictate*; Korgis - *Everybody's Gotta Learn Sometime*; **A Flock Of Seagulls** - *Wishing If I Had A Photograph Of You*; **Ultravox** - *All Stood Still*; Dwight Twilly - *Girls*; Thomas Dolby - *She Blinded Me With Science*; China Crisis - *Wishful Thinking*; **Stranglers** - *Golden Brown*; **Ian Dury and The Blockheads** - *Hit Me With Your Rhythm Stick*; Knack - *My Sharona*; Billy Idol - *Hot In The City*; Fun Boy Three - *Telephone Always Ring*; **Killing Joke** - *Love Like Blood*; **A Flock Of Seagulls** - *I Ran*; **XTC** - *Dear God*; **Spandau Ballet** - *Chant No. 1*; Pete Wylie - *Sinful*; **Ian Dury and The Blockheads** - *Reasons To Be Cheerful*; Talking Heads - *Slippery People*; Talking Heads - *Love Of The Common People*; **Stiff Little Fingers** - *Drowning*; Mobiles - *Drowning In Berlin*; Kajagoogoo - *Big Apple*; Kajagoogoo - *Independence Day*; Heaven 17 - *Temptation*; **Spandau Ballet** - *Musclebound*; Thomas Dolby - *Hyperactive*; Feargal Sharkey - *Good Heart*; Fra Lippo Lippi - *Shouldn't Have To Be Like That*; **Gang Of Four** - *At Home He's A Tourist*; Frazier Chorus - *Dream Kitchen*; Martha & The Muffins - *Echo Beach*; **Fischer Z** - *Worker*; **Vapors** - *Turning Japanese*; **Comsat Angels** - *Day One*; **Flying Lizards** - *Money*; Culture Club - *Church Of The Poison Mind*; **Ian Dury** - *Sex And Drugs And Rock 'n' Roll*; Talking Heads - *Psycho Killer*.

Wave Party (Columbia 4758322) 1995

Adam Ant - *Goody Two Shoes*; Fiction Factory - *Feels Like Heaven*; **The The** - *This Is The Day*; **Stranglers** - *Skin Deep*; **Psychedelic Furs** - *Pretty In Pink*; Fruer - *Doot Doot*; Men At Work - *Who Can It Be Now*; Dead Or Alive - *You Spin Me Round*; **Altered Images** - *Don't Talk To Me About Love*; Romantics - *Talking In Your Sleep*; Deacon Blue - *Real Gone Kid*; **Spear Of Destiny** - *Wheel*; Godfathers - *Birth, School, Work, Death*; **Psychedelic Furs** - *Heaven*; **Spandau Ballet** - *Be Free With Your Love*; Nits - *Dutch Mountains*.

Wave Romantics, Vol. 2 (SPV SPV 08438992) 1995

Nick Cave - *Do You Love Me*; **New Model Army** - *Green And Grey*; **Stranglers** - *Golden Brown*; Iggy Pop - *Beside You*; **Ultravox** - *Vienna*.

The Zonophone Punk Singles Collection (Anagram CDPUNK 97) 1997

Cockney Rejects - *The Greatest Cockney Rip Off*; **Stiffs** - *Inside Out*; **Cockney Rejects** - *I'm Forever Blowing Bubbles*; **Cockney Rejects** - *We Can Do Anything*; **Cockney Rejects** - *We Are The Firm*; **Angelic Upstarts** - *Last Night Another Soldier*; **Angelic Upstarts** - *England*; **Stiffs** - *Volume Control*; **Honey Bane** - *Turn Me On Turn Me Off*; **Angelic Upstarts** - *Kids On The Street*; **Angelic Upstarts** - *I Understand*; **Cockney Rejects** - *Easy Life*; **Cockney Rejects** - *On The Streets Again*; **Honey Bane** - *Jimmy (Listen To Me)*; **Angelic Upstarts** - *Different Strokes*; **Angelic Upstarts** - *Never Say Die*; **Vice Squad** - *Out Of Reach*; **Vice Squad** - *Stand Strong, Stand Proud*; **Toy Dolls** - *Everybody Jitterbug*; **Vice Squad** - *Citizen*.

Special thanks to Mark Brennan for help in compiling this section.

THE CIRCLES - Opening Up.

LAST STAND - Boston Callin'.

REDS - Do Anything You Wanna Do.

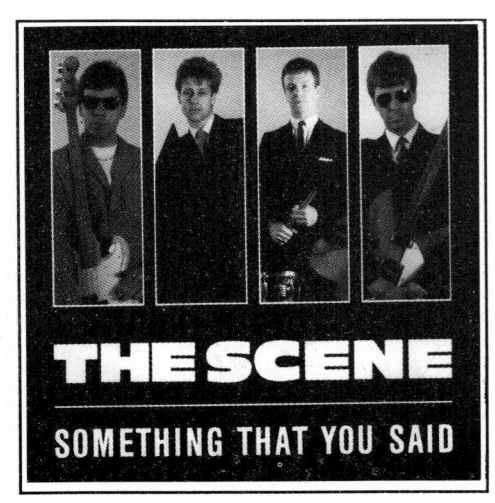

THE SCENE - Something That You Said.

KRONSTADT UPRISING - The Unknown Revolution.

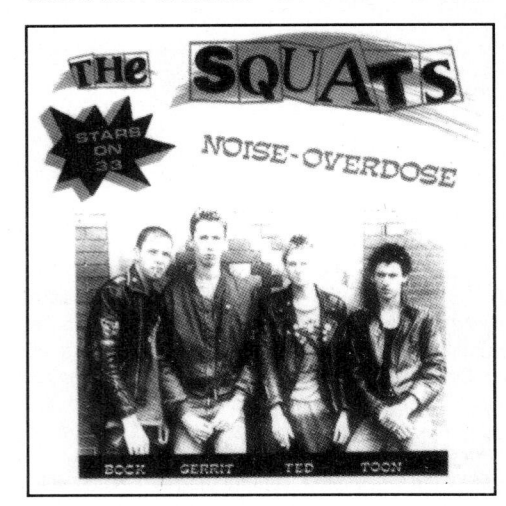

THE SQUATS - Noise-Overdose.

CRACK - Battle Of The Bands.

BACK TO ZERO - Your Side Of Heaven.

SOME IMPORTANT PUNK, NEW WAVE AND Oi LABELS.

Absurd (Manchester)

Singles:

Cat. No.	Artist	Titles		Year
ABSURD 1	Blah Blah Blah	In The Army/Why Diddle?	PS	1979
ABSURD 2	Eddie Fiction	UFO Part 2/UFO Part 1	PS	1979
ABSURD 3	48 Chairs	Snap It Around/Psycle Sluts	PS	1979
ABSURD 4	Gerry & The Holograms	Gerry & The Holograms/Increased Resistance	PS	1979
ABSURD 5	Gerry & The Holograms	The Emperor's New Music	PS	1979
ABSURD 6	The Mothmen	Does It Matter Irene?/Please Let Go	PS	1979
ABSURD 7	Cairo	I Like Bluebeat/(Version)	PS	1980
ABSURD 8	NAAFI Sandwich	Slice One/Slice Two	PS	1980
ABSURD 9	Not Reissued			
ABSURD 10	Bet Lynch's Legs	Riders In The Sky/High Noon	PS	1980
ABSURD 11	Bet Lynch's Legs	Some Like It Hot/Some Don't	PS	1980
ASK 15	Cairo	Movie Stars/Cuthbert's Birthday Treat	PS	1980

LP

LAST 2	Slaughter and The Dogs	Live Slaughter Rabid Dogs		1980

Anagram (London, Cherry Red subsidiary)

7" Singles (* indicates vinyl & CD release):

Cat. No.	Artist	Titles		Year
ANA 1	One Way System	Give Us A Future/Just Another Hero	PS	1982
ANA 3	Angelic Upstarts	Woman In Disguise / Lust For Glory	PS	1982
ANA 4	The Vibrators	Baby Baby/Dragnet	PS	1982
ANA 5	One Way System	Jerusalem/Jackie Was A Junkie	PS	1982
ANA 7	Angelic Upstarts	Solidarity/Five Flew Over The Cuckoo's Nest	PS	1982
ANA 8	The Vibrators	Guilty / Hang Ten	PS	1983
ANA 9	One Way System	Cum On Feel The Noize/Breakin' In	PS	1983
ANA 10	Turkey Bones and The Wild Dogs	Goldfish/Zoology	PS	1983
* ANA 11	Alien Sex Fiend	Ignore The Machine/The Gun At The End Of My Gun	PS	1983
ANA 12	The Outcasts	Nowhere Left To Run/The Runnings Over Time To Play	PS	1983
ANA 13	Angelic Upstarts	Not Just A Name/The Leech	PS	1983
ANA 14	One Way System	This Is The Age/Into The Fires	PS	1983
ANA 15	Alien Sex Fiend	Lips Can't Go/Drive My Rocket (Up Uranus)	PS	1983
ANA 16	Vice Squad	Black Sheep/New Blood	PS	1983
ANA 17	Tempest	Montezuma/ABC	PS	198?
ANA 18	Alien Sex Fiend RIP	(Blue Crumb Truck)/New Christian Music	PS	1984
ANA 19	One Way System	VISIONS OF ANGELS EP: Children Of The Night/Down/Shine Again	PS	1984
ANA 20	Sunglasses After Dark	Morbid Silence/Let's Go	PS	1984
ANA 21	Longpig	Why Do People Find Each Other Strange?Darkboy	PS	1984
ANA 22	Vice Squad	You'll Never Know/What's Going On?	PS	1984
ANA 23	Alien Sex Fiend	Dead And Buried/Attack!!	PS	1984
ANA 25	Alien Sex Fiend Est	Trip To The Moon	PS	198?
ANA 26	Vice Squad	Teenage Rampage/High Spirits	PS	1985
ANA 27	Sweet	Sixteens/Action	PS	1984
ANA 28	Sweet	IT'S... THE SWEET MIX	PS	1985
ANA 29	Sweet	SWEET 2th - Wigwam-Willy mix/Teen-Action mix	PS	1985
ANA 32	Alien Sex Fiend	Smells Like.../Buggin' Me	PS	1986
ANA 33	Alien Sex Fiend	Hurricane Fighter Plane/It Lives Again	PS	198?
ANA 34	Alien Sex Fiend	The Impossible Mission/Brain (Is In My Cupboard)	PS	1987
ANA 35	Meteors	Go Buddy Go/You Crack Me Up	PS	1987
ANA 36	ATV	My Baby's Laughing	PS	1987
ANA 38	Alien Sex Fiend	Here Cum Germs/Ravi Mix	PS	1987
ANA 39	Meteors	Don't Touch The Bang Bang Fruit/Dateless Nites	PS	1987
ANA 40	Alien Sex Fiend	Stuff The Turkey/They All Call Me Crazee	PS	1987
ANA 43	The Meteors	Raw Hide	PS	1988
ANA 44	Taboo	Number 6/Hypnotique	PS	198?
ANA 50	The Purple Helmets	Brand New Cadillac/Under The Sun	PS	198?
* ANA 55	Kirk Brandon's 10:51	Children Of The Damned/Satellite/*At Her Majesty's Request (*extra track on CD)	PS	1987
CDANA 56	Alien Sex Fiend	INFERNO THE MIXES Inferno/Planet 2/Echoes	PS	198?

10" Singles:

Cat. No.	Artist	Titles		Year
ANA 18	Alien Sex Fiend	R.I.P./New Christian Music/Crazee	PS	1984

11" Singles:

Cat. No.	Artist	Titles		Year
ANA 25	Alien Sex Fiend	E.S.T. (Trip To The Moon)/Boneshaker Baby/I Am A Product (Live)	PS	198?

12" Singles:

Cat. No.	Artist	Titles		Year
12 ANA 02	Pressure	You Talk We Talk/Shoot		1982
12 ANA 03	Angelic Upstarts	Woman In Disguise/Lust For Glory/42nd Street		1982
12 ANA 06	Pressure	Pressure/Sixteen Seconds/Check It Out		1982
12 ANA 07	Angelic Upstarts	Solidarity/Five Flew Over The Cuckoo's Nest/Dollars And Pounds/Don't Stop		1983
* 12 ANA 11	Alien Sex Fiend	Ignore The Machine/The Gurl At The End Of My Gun/I'm Not Mad		1983
S ANA 11	Alien Sex Fiend	Ignore The Machine (Special Electrode Mix by Sanny X) / The Gurl At The End Of My Gun/Ignore The Dub		1983
12 ANA 12	The Outcasts	Nowhere Left To Run/The Running's Over Time To Pray/ Nowhere (Instrumental)/Ruby	PS	1983
12 ANA 13	Angelic Upstarts	Not Just A Name/The Leech/Leave Me Alone/ Liddle Towers/White Riot		1983
12 ANA 15	Alien Sex Fiend	Lips Can't Go (Dance Mix)/Toytown Mix/ Drive My Rocket (Up Uranus)/30 Second Coma	PS	1983
12 ANA 16	Vice Squad	Black Sheep/New Blood/The Pledge		1983
12 ANA 17	Tempest	Montezuma/The Calm Before/ABC (Extended)		198?
12 ANA 18	Alien Sex Fiend	R.I.P. Blue Crumb Truck/R.I.P. New Dub Truck/New Christian Music		1984
12 ANA 19	One Way System	VISIONS OF ANGELS EP: Out Of Mind/Children Of The Night/ Shine Again		1984
12 ANA 20	Sunglasses After Dark	Morbid Silence/Let's Go/Untamed Culture/Hell – Hag Shuffle		1984
12 ANA 21	Longpig	Why Do People Find Each Other Strange?/Darkboy/ Primitive Sensibility		1984
12 ANA 22	Vice Squad	You'll Never Know / What's Going On? / The Times They Are A' Changing		1984
12 ANA 23	Alien Sex Fiend	Dead And Buried/Attack!!/Ignore The Machine... Dub		1984
12 ANA 24	Furyo	FURIOSO E.P.: Legacy / King Of Hearts /Cavalcade		1984
12 ANA 27	Sweet	Sixteens / Action / Teenage Rampage		1984
12 ANA 28	Sweet	IT'S.... SWEET MIX		1985
12 ANA 29	Sweet	Sweet 2th The Wigwam-Willy Mix / The Teen Action Mix		1985
12 ANA 30	Alien Sex Fiend	I'm Doing Time In A Maximum Security Twilight Home / I'm Doing Time / In And Out Of My Mind / Backward Beaver		1985
12 ANA 31	The Meteors	Surf City / The Edge / Johnny's Here		1986
12 ANA 32	Alien Sex Fiend	Smells Like... (Shit Mix #1) / Buggin' Me / Smells Like...(Plip Plox Mix #2)		1986
12 ANA 33	Alien Sex Fiend	Hurricane Fighter Plane / Hurricane Fighter Dub / It Lived Again / It Lives Again (again)		198?
12 ANA 34	Alien Sex Fiend	The Impossible Mission / My Brain Is In The Cupboard - Above The Kitchen Sink / The Impossible Mission #2		1987
12 ANA 35	Meteors	Go Buddy Go (The Wonkey Donkey Mix) / Wildkat Ways / You Crack Me Up		1987
12 ANA 37	Silver Chapter	Debbie / PEPSI / Neon Queen / UFO		1987
12 ANA 38	Alien Sex Fiend	Here Cum Germs / Camel Camel / Here Cum Germs		1987
12 ANA 39	Meteors	Don't Touch The Bang Bang Fruit / Dateless Nites / Corpse Grinder		1987
12 ANA 40	Alien Sex Fiend	Stuff The Turkey / Stuff The Turkey (Bootiful Dub #1) / They All Call Me Crazee / Crazier Still		1987
12 ANA 41	Meteors	Somebody Put Something In My Drink / Fire Fire / Bad Moon Rising		1988
12 ANA 42	Dynamic Duo	Batman Theme (Where Are Batman and Robin) / Batman Theme (Utility Bop) / Batman Theme (Gotham Gothic) (Eggstacy)		1988
12 ANA 43	Meteors	Raw Hide / Little Red Riding Hood / Surfin' On The Planet Zorch		1988
12 ANA 44	Taboo	Number 6 / Hypnotique		198?
12 ANA 45	Alien Sex Fiend	Bun Ho! (Cranium mix) / Silver Machine / Satisfaction / Bun Ho! (Time Gentlemen Please)		198?
* 12 ANA 46	Alien Sex Fiend	Haunted House / Haunted House (dub)		198?
12 ANAD 47	Stud Puppet Joy	(So Keep It Up) / Joy (It Is Up)		198?
12 ANAD 48	Blue World	Hello Darling / Little Ivan's Blue World		198?
12 ANA 50	Purple Helmets	Brand New Cadillac / Under The Sun / Baby		198?
12 ANA 51	Meteors	Please Don't Touch / Disneyland / My Kinda Rockin'		198?
* 12 ANA 52	Alien Sex Fiend	Now I'm Feeling Zombiefied / Psyche Out Zombie Dub / B.I.M. / *Ain't Got Time To Bleed Dub * extra track on CD		198?
* 12 ANA 53	Alien Sex Fiend	I Walk The Line / Schools Out / Here She Comes / Can't Stop Smoking		198?
* 12 ANA 54	Alien Sex Fiend	Magic / Mrs. Fiend Goes To Outer Space... / Comatose - The Ultra Mix		198?

Albums:

Cat. No.	Artist	Titles	Year
* GRAM 38	Alien Sex Fiend	Another Planet	1988
GRAM 39	Various	Graveyard Stomp	198?
GRAM 40	A.T.V.	Splitting In Two	1989
* GRAM 41	Alien Sex Fiend	Too Much Acid? (Double Live Album)	1989
* GRAM 42	Purple Helmets	Rise Again	1989
GRAM 43	Meteors	Undead Unfriendly And Unstoppable	1990
* GRAM 44	Joolz	Hex	1990
* GRAM 45	Meteors	Live Styles Of The Sick And Shameless (Live)	1990
* GRAM 46	Alien Sex Fiend	Curse	1990
* GRAM 47	Pigface	Gub	1991
CDMGRAM 48	Chaos UK	Total Chaos	1991
CDMGRAM 49	Disorder	The Complete Disorder	1991
CDMGRAM 50	Channel 3	I've Got A Gun / After The Lights Go Out	1991
* GRAM 51	Alien Sex Fiend	Open Head Surgery	1992
CDGRAM 52	The Vibrators	The Power Of Money (Best Of Compilation)	1992
CDMGRAM 53	Hawkwind	Mighty Hawkwind Classics 1980-85	1992
CDMGRAM 54	Hawkwind	This Is Hawkwind Do Not Panic	1992
CDMGRAM 55	Robert Calvert	Freq Revisited	1992
CDMGRAM 56	Various	Travellers Aid Trust	1992
CDMGRAM 57	Hawkwind	Zones	199?
CDMGRAM 59	Various	Frenchy Scissorhands (The Best Of Flicknife Records)	199?
* GRAM 60	Alien Sex Fiend	The Altered States Of America	1993
CDMGRAM 61	Hawkwind	Best Of Friends & Relations	1993
CDMGRAM 62	Barracudas	Two Sides Of A Coin	1993
CDMGRAM 63	The Runaways	And Now The Runaways	1993
CDMGRAM 64	Various	Burning Ambitions - (A History Of Punk) - Part 2	1993
CDMGRAM 65	Frantic Flintstones	Jamboree	1993
CDMGRAM 66	Meteors	Best Of...	1993
CDMGRAM 67	Only Ones	Remains	1993
CDGRAM 68	Adicts	27	1993
CDMGRAM 69	Alien Sex Fiend	The Legendary Batcave Tapes	1993
CDGRAM 70	Johnny Thunders	Chinese Rocks-The Ultimate Live Collection	1993
CDGRAM 71	999	You Us It	1993
CDGRAM 72	Sharks	Recreational Killer	1993
CDMGRAM 73	England's Glory	The Legendary Lost Album	1994
CDMGRAM 74	Steve Diggle and Flag Of Convenience	Best Of...	1994
CDMGRAM 75	Skeletal Family	Best Of	1994
CDMGRAM 76	The Mekons	The Mekons	1994
CDMGRAM 77	Long Tall Texans	Aces And Eights	1994
CDMGRAM 78	Guiter Gangsters	Power Chords For England	1994
CDMGRAM 79	Various	Night Of The Living Pussies	1994
* GRAM 80	Alien Sex Fiend	Inferno	1994
CDMGRAM 81	Hula	Best Of Hula	1994
CDMGRAM 82	The Essence	Dancing In The Rain (Best Of...)	1994
CDMGRAM 83	Blyth Power	10 Years Inside The Horse	1994
CDMGRAM 84	Divine	Born To Be Cheap	1994
CDMGRAM 85	Nico	Heroine	1994
CDGRAM 86	Frantic Flintstones	Enjoy Yourself	1994
CDGRAM 87	Paul Fenech	Daddy's Hammer	199?
CDMGRAM 88	Long Tall Texans	Texas Beat (Best Of)	199?
CDMGRAM 89	Various	In Goth Daze	199?
CDGRAM 90	Thee Waltons	Get Out Yer Vegetables	1995
CDMGRAM 91	Hawkwind Friends and Relations	The Rarities	1995
CDGRAM 92	Kirk Brandon	Stone In The Rain	1995
CDMGRAM 93	Theatre Of Hate	Singles Collection	1995
CDMGRAM 94	Hawkwind	Independence Day Volumes 1 & 2	1995
CDMGRAM 95	The Essence	Purity	1995
CDMGRAM 96	The Essence	A Monument Of Trust	1995
CDMGRAM 97	Snake Corps	Spice (Best Of)	1995
CDMGRAM 98	Various	This Is Mod Volume 1	1995
CDMGRAM 99	Alien Sex Fiend	The Singles 1983-1995	1995
CDMGRAM 100	Sharks	Colour My Flesh	199?
CDMGRAM 101	Various	This Is Mod Vol. 2	1996
CDMGRAM 102	Alternative TV	Vibing Up The Senile Man / What You See Is What You Are	1996
CDMGRAM 103	The Essence	Ecstasy / Nothing Lasts Forever	1996
CDMGRAM 104	Sad Lovers and Giants	From E-Mail To Eternity (The Best Of S.L.A.G.S.)	1996
CDMGRAM 105	Hawkwind Friends And Relations	Cosmic Travellers	1996

Catalog	Artist	Title	Notes	Year
CDMGRAM 106	Various	This Is Mod Vol. 3 - The Diamond Collection		1996
CDMGRAM 107	Various	This Is Mod Vol. 4 – Modities		1996
CDMGRAM 108	Eddie and The Hotrods	Doing Anything They Want To Do		1996
CDMGRAM 109	Chaos UK	The Morning After The Night Before		1997
CDMGRAM 110	Various	This Is Mod Volume 5		1997
CDMGRAM 111	The Merton Parkas	The Complete Mod Collection		1997
CDMGRAM 112	The Membranes	The Best Of The Membranes		1997
CDMGRAM 113	UK Subs	Riot		1997
CDMGRAM 114	The Vibrators	French Lessons with Correction		1997
CDMGRAM 115	The Piranhas	The Piranhas		1997
CDMGRAM 116	Various	This Is Mod Vol. 6		1997
CDMGRAM 117	Johnny Thunders	Belfast Rocks		1997
CDMGRAM 118	Disorder	Sliced Punx On Meathooks		1998
CDMGRAM 119	The Boys	Power Cut		1998
CDGRAM 120	Alien Sex Fiend	Fiends At The Controls - Vol. 1 & 2	(2-CD)	1999
CDMGRAM 121	Various	Goth Oddity - A Tribute To David Bowie		1999
CDMGRAM 122	Brian Connolly's Sweet	Greatest Hits Remixed		1999
CDMGRAM 123	The Meteors	The Meteors Vs The World		1999
CDMGRAM 124	Various	We Wil Follow - A Tribute To U2		1999
CDMGRAM 125	Various	Party O' The Times - A Tribute To Prince		2000
CDMGRAM 126	Various	A Tribute To Led Zeppelin - The Song Remains Remixed		2000
CDMGRAM 127	Various	Appetite For Reconstruction - A Tribute To Guns and Roses		2000
CDMGRAM 128	Various	The Blackest Album 2 - An Industrial Tribute To Metallica		2000
CDMGRAM 129	Various	Darken My Fire - A Gothic Tribute To The Doors		2000
CDMGRAM 130	Various	We Will Rock You - A Tribute To Queen		2000
CDMGRAM 131	Various	Virgin Voices - A Tribute To Madonna		2000
CDMGRAM 132	P. Paul Fenech	Screaming In The 10th Key		2000
CDMGRAM 133	Various	Songs Of Change - A Tribute to the Scorpions		2000
CDMGRAM 134	Various	Ghost Town - A Tribute To The Specials		2000
CDMGRAM 135	Various	Voodoo Dejah - A Tribute To Dread Zeppelin		2000
CDMGRAM 136	Various	Covered In Nails - A Tribute To The Nine Inch Nails		2000
CDMGRAM 138	Various	Cherub Rock - A Tribute To The Smashing Pumpkins		2000
CDMGRAM 139	Various	Smells Like Bleach - A Tribute To Nirvana		
CDMGRAM 140	Various	A Punk Tribute To Metallica		2000
CDMGRAM 141	Various	Just Can't Get Enough - A Tribute To Depeche Mode		2000
CDPUNK 01	Blitz	Voice Of A Generation		1989
CDPUNK 02	Channel 3	I've Got A Gun / After The Lights Go Out		1989
CDPUNK 03	Peter and The Test Tube Babies	Pissed And Proud		1989
CDPUNK 04	Partisans	Police Story		1989
CDPUNK 10	Eater	The Compleat Eater		1993
CDPUNK 11	Various	No Future Singles Collection		1993
CDPUNK 12	Chaos UK	Enough To Make You Sick The Chipping Sodbury Bonfire Tape		1993
CDPUNK 13	Various	Secret Records Punk Singles Collection		1993
CDPUNK 14	Various	Raw Records Punk Singles Collection		1993
CDPUNK 15	Various	Riot City Punk Singles Collection		1993
CDPUNK 16	Vibrators	Guilty/Alaska 127		1993
CDPUNK 17	Angelic Upstarts	Reason Why?		1993
CDPUNK 18	The Exploited	Live And Loud		1993
CDPUNK 19	Disorder	Under The Scalpel Blade / One Day Son All This Will Be Yourz		1993
CDPUNK 20	Drones	Further Temptation		1993
CDPUNK 21	Suburban Studs	Slam - The Complete Studs Collection		1993
CDPUNK 22	Various	Punk And Disorderly - Further Charges		1993
CDPUNK 23	Various	Punk And Disorderly - The Final Solution		1993
CDPUNK 24	A.T.V.	The Image Has Cracked - The ATV Collection		1993
CDPUNK 25	Blitz	The Complete Singles Collection		1993
CDPUNK 26	Chaos UK	Total Chaos		1994
CDPUNK 27	Chaotic Dischord	Their Greatest Fuckin Hits		1994
CDPUNK 28	Vice Squad	Shot Away		1994
CDPUNK 29	Various	Small Wonder Punk Singles Collection		1994
CDPUNK 30	Various	Fallout Punk Singles Collection		1994
CDPUNK 31	Patrik Fitzgerald	The Very Best Of Patrik Fitzgerald		1994
CDPUNK 32	Various	Fresh Records Punk Singles Collection		1994
CDPUNK 33	The Adicts	The Complete Adicts Singles Collection		1994
CDPUNK 34	The Vibrators	Fifth Amendment / Recharged		1994
CDPUNK 35	Raped	The Complete Raped Collection		1994
CDPUNK 36	Various	Good Vibrations Punk Singles Collection		1994
CDPUNK 37	Various	Anagram Punk Singles Collection		1994
CDPUNK 38	The Notsensibles	Instant Punk Classics		1994
CDPUNK 39	Disorder	Live In Oslo / Violent World		1994

Catalog	Artist	Title	Year
CDPUNK 40	Various	Rot Records Punk Singles Collection	1994
CDPUNK 41	Riot City	The Complete Punk Collection	1995
CDPUNK 42	Various	Flicknife Records Punk Collection	1995
CDPUNK 43	The Vibrators	The Best Of The Vibrators	1995
CDPUNK 44	Anti-Nowhere League	Complete Singles Collection	1995
CDPUNK 45	Various	Razor Records Punk Collection	1995
CDPUNK 46	Disorder	Complete Disorder	1995
CDPUNK 47	Uk/Dk	Original Soundtrack	1995
CDPUNK 48	Anti-Pasti	The Last Call	1995
CDPUNK 49	Rondelet Records	Punk Singles Collection	1995
CDPUNK 50	One Way System	The Best Of	1995
CDPUNK 51	Cherry Red Records	Punk Singles Collection	1995
CDPUNK 52	Abstract Records	Punk Singles Collection	1995
CDPUNK 53	Anti-Pasti	Caution In The Wind	1995
CDPUNK 54	No Future Volume 2	Punk Singles Collection	1995
CDPUNK 55	Riot City Volume 2	Punk Singles Collection	1995
CDPUNK 56	Varukers	Prepare For The Attack / Bloodsucker	1995
CDPUNK 57	The Business	The Business Singles Collection	1995
CDPUNK 58	Vibrators	Meltdown/Vicious Circle	1995
CDPUNK 59	Angelic Upstarts	The Independent Punk Singles	1995
CDPUNK 60	Secret Records Volume 2	Punk Singles Collection	1995
CDPUNK 61	Beat The System	Punk Singles Collection	1995
CDPUNK 62	Outcasts	Punk Singles Collection	1995
CDPUNK 63	Various	Punk Rock Rarities Volume 1	1995
CDPUNK 64	Peter and The Test Tube Babies	Complete Singles Collection	1995
CDPUNK 65	Chaos UK	Flogging The Corpse	1995
CDPUNK 66	UK Subs / Urban Dogs	Punk Singles Collection	1995
CDPUNK 67	999	The Biggest Prize in Sport	1995
CDPUNK 68	Various	Live at the Vortex	1995
CDPUNK 69	The Lurkers	Powerjive / King Of The Mountain	1995
CDPUNK 70	Small Wonder	Punk Singles Collection Volume 2	1996
CDPUNK 71	Chaos UK	Short Sharp Shock	1996
CDPUNK 72	Chaotic Dischord	Fuck Religion Fuck Politics Fuck The Lot Of You / Don't Throw It All Away	1996
CDPUNK 73	Various	Beggars Banquet Punk Singles Collection	1996
CDPUNK 74	Varukers	Punk Singles Collection	1996
CDPUNK 75	Various	Pax Records Punk Singles Collection	1996
CDPUNK 76	Vibrators	The Independent Punk Singles Collection	1996
CDPUNK 77	Rudi	Big Time - The Best Of Rudi	1996
CDPUNK 78	999	The Albion Punk Singles Collection	1996
CDPUNK 79	Various	Lightning Punk Singles Collection	1996
CDPUNK 80	Carpettes	The Punk Collection	1996
CDPUNK 81	Various	Burning Ambitions - (A History Of Punk) - Part 2	1996
CDPUNK 82	G.B.H.	Live In Los Angeles	1996
CDPUNK 83	Various	Punk Rock Rarities Volume 2	1996
CDPUNK 84	Chaotic Dischord	Goat Fuckin' Virgin Killerz From Hell / Very Fucking Bad	1996
CDPUNK 85	The Boys	Complete Punk Singles Collection	1996
CDPUNK 88	Sid Vicious	Sid Dead Live	1997
CDPUNK 87	Adicts	27	1997
CDPUNK 88	Disorder	The Rest Home For Senile Old Punks Proudly Presents.... Disorder	1997
CDPUNK 89	Vice Squad	The Complete Punk Singles Collection	1997
CDPUNK 90	Cockney Rejects	The Punk Singles Collection	1997
CDPUNK 91	Newtown Neurotics	Punk Singles Collection	1997
CDPUNK 92	999	You Us It (Pic Disc)	1997
CDPUNK 93	999	Live At The Nashville	1997
CDPUNK 94	Lurkers	Beggars Banquet Singles Collection	1997
CDPUNK 95	Adverts	Punk Singles Collection	1997
CDPUNK 96	Guitar Gangsters	Power Chords For England	1997
CDPUNK 97	Various	Zonophone Punk Singles Collection	1997
CDPUNK 98	Various	Burning Ambitions Volume 3	1997
CDPUNK 99	Vice Squad	The BBC Sessions	1997
CDPUNK 101	Various	Attrix Records Collection	199?
CDPUNK 102	The Adverts	Cast Of Thousands	1998
CDPUNK 103	Chaos UK	Radioactive Earslaughter / 100% Two Fingers In The Air Punk Rock	1998
CDPUNK 104	Blitz	The Very Best Of Blitz	1998
CDPUNK 105	The Adicts	The Very Best Of The Adicts	1998
CDPUNK 106	Anti-Pasti	The Punk Singles Collection	1998
CDPUNK 107	The Adverts	The Best Of The Adverts	1998
CDPUNK 108	Chaos UK	The Best Of...	1998
CDPUNK 109	Disorder	The Best Of...	1998

Cat. No.	Artist	Titles		Year
CDPUNK 110	Varukers	Best Of...		1999
CDPUNK 111	Various	History Of No Future		1999
CDPUNK 112	The Boys	The Very Best Of The Boys		1999
CDPUNK 113	Cockney Rejects	The Very Best Of The Cockney Rejects		1999
CDPUNK 114	Blitz	The No Future Years	(2-CD)	2000
CDPUNK 116	Vice Squad	The Very Best Of Vice Squad		2000
CDPUNK 117	Disorder	Sliced Punx On Meathooks		2000
CDPUNK 118	Sham 69	If The Kids Are United		2000
CDPUNK 119	Chaos UK	Chaos In Japan		2000

Double Albums:

Cat. No.	Artist	Titles
DGRAM 001	Various	Punk And Disorderly 2 & 3
K LO 1	Various	Grime Of The Century (Contains Punk And Disorderly 11213 GRAM 006 / DRED 3)
WINDSONG 02	Alien Sex Fiend	ASF Box

Armageddon (UK Catalogue, Anglo-American label)

7" Singles:

Cat. No.	Artist	Titles		Year
AS 002	Soft Boys	Kingdom Of Love/Vegetable Man	PS	1980
AS 003	Jad Fair	The Zombies Of Mora-Tau		1980
AS 004	Kimberley Rew	Stomping All Over The World/Nothing's Going To Change Your Life / Fighting Somebody's War	PS	1980
AS 005	Soft Boys	I Wanna Destroy You/I'm An Old Pervert	PS	1980
AS 007	Thomas Dolby	Urges / Leipzig	PS	1981
AS 008	Robyn Hitchcock	The Man Who Invented Himself / Dancing On God's Thumb	PS	1981
AS 009	Half Japanese	Spy / I Know How It Feels... Bad / My Knowledge Was Wrong	PS	1981
AS 012	Kimberley Rew (with dB's)	My Baby Does Her Hairdo Long/Fishing	PS	1981
AS 013	Blurt	The Fish Needs A Bike / This Is My Royal Wedding Souvenir	PS	1981
AS 014	Kevin Dunn and The Regiment Of Women	Oktyabrina / 20,000 Years In Sing Sing	PS	1981
AS 015	Adrian Munsey	Main Theme		1981
AS 017	Firmament and The Elements	The Festival Of Frothy Muggament / Maxence Cup	PS	1981
AS 029	Soft Boys	Only The Stones Remain / The Asking Tree	PS	1981

EPs:

Cat. No.	Artist	Titles		Year
AEP 002	Soft Boys	Near The Soft Boys	PS	1980
AEP 003	Jad Fair	Zombies Of Mora Tau		1980
AEP 12004	Pylon		(10", 45 rpm)	1981
AEP 12005	Method Actors	Rhythms Of You	(Seven Song 10" EP)	1981

Three Album, Box Set:

Cat. No.	Artist	Titles	Year
ABOX 1	Half Japanese	Half Gentlemen, Not Beasts	1981

Albums

Cat. No.	Artist	Titles	Year
ARM 1	Soft Boys	Underwater Moonlight	1980
ARM 2	Last Words	Famous	1981
ARM 3	Kevin Dunn and The Regiment Of Women	The Judgment Of Paris	1981
ARM 4	Robyn Hitchcock	Black Snake Diamond Role	1981
ARM 5	Pylon	Gyrate	1981
ARM 6	Blurt	Blurt In Berlin	1981
ARM 7	Half Japanese	Loud	1981
ARM 8	Danny Addler	Gusha Gusha Music	1981
ARM 9	Midnight Rags	Werewolf Of London	1981
ARM 10	Ron Cuccia	Music From The Big Tomato	1981
ARM 12	Swimming Pool Q's	The Deep End	1981
HEDON 1-2	Plummet Airlines	On Stoney Ground	1981
HEDON 4	Radio Free Europe	Laugh On Cue	1981

Attrix (Brighton)

Various Formats:

Cat. No.	Artist	Titles	Year
RB 01	Attrix	Hard Times / Lost Lenore	1979
RB 02	Various	Cassette / Fanzine	1979

Cat. No.	Artist	Titles	Year
RB 03	Various	Vaultage 78	1979
RB 04	The Piranhas	Jilly / Coloured Music	1980
RB 05	Johnny and Executives	Terror In The Parking Lot / Shy Little Girl / Never Go Home / I Got Rabies	1980
RB 06	The Piranhas	Yap Yap Yap / Happy Families	1980
RB 07	The Dodgems	Hard Shoulder / Science Fiction	1980
RB 08	Various	Vaultage 79	1980
RB 09	The Piranhas	The Piranhas LP Not Released	
RB 10	The Chefs	Sweetie / Thrush / Records And Tea / Someone I Know	1980
RB 11	Various	Vaultage 80	1980
RB 12	Birds With Ears	Youth In Asia LP	1981
RB 13	The Chefs	24 Hours / Let's Make Up / Someone I Know	1981
RB 14	The Parrots	The Parrots EP: Photography Song / Home Sweet Home / Serious Thing / Breaking Up New Sound	198?

Beat The System (Blackpool)

Singles:

Cat. No.	Artist	Titles	Year
FIT 1	The Fits	You Said We'd Never Make It EP: Listen To Me / Odd Bod Mod / Bad Dream	1982
FIT 2	Anti-Social	With Another Punk EP: To Many People / Lets Have Some Fun	1982
MENACE 1	External Menace	Youth Of Today EP: Youth Of Today / Don't Conform / Main St. Riot / Someday	1982
MENACE 2	External Menace	No Views EP: No Views / We Wanna Know / Poor Excuse / Escape From Hell	1982
WAY 1	One Way System	Stab The Judge EP: Stab The Judge / Riot Torn City / Me And You	1982
DEATH 1	Death Sentence	Death And Pure Destruction EP: Death And Pure Destruction / Die A Hero / Victims Of War / Death Sentence	1982
SOCIAL 1	Anti-Social	Made In England EP: Backstreet Boys / Your Choice / New Punks / Screw U	1982
BTS 2	Anti-Social	Official Hooligan EP: Battle Scarred Skinheads / Sewer Rat / Official Hooligan	1982
YOUTH 1	Chaotic Youth	Sad Society EP: Sad Society / No Future UK / Tip Off / Arms Race	1982
RAW 1	Uproar	Rebel Youth EP: Rebel Youth / No War No More / Fallen Angel / Victims	1982
RAW 2	Uproar	Die For Me EP: Better Off Dead / It's Not You / Have A Good Laugh / Dead Rockers	1983
POST 1	Post Mortem	Post Mortem EP: Day By Day / IRA / 48 Crash / Can The Can	1983

Albums:

Cat. No.	Artist	Titles	Year
BTSLP 1	Various Artists	Total Anarchy	198?
BTSLP 2	Uproar	And The Lord Said Let There Be Uproar	198?

Beggars Banquet (London)

7" Singles (the first 70):

Cat. No.	Artist	Titles	Year
BEG 1	Lurkers	Shadow/Low Story Free Admission single	1977
BEG 2	Lurkers	Freak Show/Mass Media Believer	1977
BEG 3	Johnny G	Call Me Bwana/Suzi Was a Girl From Greenford	1978
BEG 4	Doll	Don't Tango On My Heart/Trash	1978
BEG 5	Tubeway Army	That's Too Bad/Oh Didn't I Say	1978
BEG 7	Johnny G	Hippy's Graveyard/Miles And Miles	1978
BEG 8	Tubeway Army	Bombers/Blue Eyes/O.D. Receiver	1978
BEG 11	Doll	Desire Me/TV Addict Some with bonus disc	
BEG 13	Johnny G	Everybody Goes Cruisin' On Saturday Night/Sick 'n' Tired/Highway Shoes/ You Can't Catch Every Train	1978
BEG 14	Lurkers	Just 13/	1978
BEG 15	Duffo	Give Me Back My Brain/Duff Records	1979
BEG 16	Johnny G	Golden Years/Permanent Stranger	1979
BEG 17	Tubeway Army	Down In The Park/Do You Need Service	1979
BEG 17T	Tubeway Army	Down In The Park/Do You Need Service/I Nearly Married A Human 12"	1979
BEG 18	Tubeway Army	Are "Friends" Electric/We Are Fragile	1979
BEG 19	Lurkers	Out In The Dark/Suzie	1979
BEG 20	Duffo	Tower Of Madness/I'm A Genius	1979
BEG 21	Heartbreakers	Get Off The Phone/I Wanna Be Loved	1979
BEG 22	Merton Parkas	You Need Wheels/I Don't Want To Know You	1979
BEG 23	Gary Numan	Cars/Asylum	1979
BEG 24	Rentals	I've Got A Crush On You/New York	1979
BEG 25	Merton Parkas	Plastic Smile/Man With The Disguise	1979
BEG 26	Doll	Cinderella With A Husky Voice/Because Now	1979
BEG 27	Carpettes	I Didn't Mean It/Easy Way Out	1979
BEG 28	Lurkers	New Guitar In Town/Pick Me Up	1979
BEG 29	Gary Numan	Complex / Bombers (live)	1979

Cat. No.	Artist	Titles		Year
BEG 30	Merton Parkas	Give It To Me Now/Band Of Gold		1979
BEG 31	Doll	You Used To Be My Hero/Zero Heroes		1980
BEG 32	Carpettes	Johnny Won't Hurt You/Frustration Paradise		1980
BEG 33	Shox	No Turning Back/Lying Here		1980
BEG 34	John Spencer	Natural Man/Crazy For My Lady		1980
BEG 35	Gary Numan	We Are Glass/Trois Gymnopedies (1st Movement)		1980
BEG 36	Chrome	New Age/Information		1980
BEG 37	Bauhaus	Dark Entries/(untitled)	(also on 4.A.D)	1980
BEG 39	Cockney 'n' Westerns	She's No Angel/Had Me A Real Good Time		1980
BEG 40	Johnny G	Night After Night/Old Soldiers		1980
BEG 41	Pete Stride & John Plain	Laugh At Me/Jimmy Brown		1980
BEG 42	Andde Leek	Move On (In Your Maserati)/Rubin Decides		1980
BEG 43	Merton Parkas	Put Me In The Picture/In The Midnight Hour		1980
BEG 44	Johnny G	Blue Suede Shoes/Highway Shoes		1980
BEG 45	Spirit	We've Got a Lot to Learn/Fish Fry Road		1980
BEG 46	Gary Numan	I Die, You Die/Down In The Park		1980
BEG 48	Colin Newman	B/Classic Remains/Alone On The Piano		1980
BEG 49	Carpettes	The Last Lone Ranger/Love So Strong/Fan Club		1980
BEG 50	Gary Numan	This Wreckage/Photograph		1980
BEG 51	Freez	Southern Freez /		1981
BEG 52	Colin Newman	Inventory/This Picture		1981
BEG 53	Jason Black	I'm Walking Alone/Good Good Lovin'		1981
BEG 54	Bauhaus	Kick In The Eye/Satori	(54T = 12")	1981
BEG 55	Freez	Flying High, Part 1/Flying High, Part 2	(55T = 12")	1981
BEG 56	Spirit	Turn To The Right/Potatoland Theme		1981
BEG 59	Bauhaus	Passion Of Lovers/1-2-3-4		1981
BEG 60	Morrissey/Mullen	Do Like You/Badness		1981
BEG 61	Paul Gardiner	Stormtrooper In Drag/Night Talk	(61T = 12")	1981
BEG 62	Gary Numan	She's Got Claws/I Sing Rain	(62T = 12")	1981
BEG 63	Morrissey/Mullen	Stay Awhile/Mercy Mercy		1981
BEG 65	Johnny G	Alone With Her Tonight/I Just Want To Sing The Blues		1981
BEG 66	Freez	Anti-Freez	(66T, 12")	1981
BEG 67	Johnny G.	G Beat/Leave Me Alone		1981
BEG 68	Gary Numan	Love Needs No Disguise/Take Me Home	(68T, 12")	1981
BEG 70	Gary Numan	Music For Chameleons/Noise Noise		1982

Albums (the first 30):

Cat. No.	Artist	Titles	Year
BEGA 1	Various	Streets	1978
BEGA 2	Lurkers	Fulham Fallout	1978
BEGA 3	John Spencer	The Last LP	1978
BEGA 4	Tubeway Army	Tubeway Army	1978
BEGA 5	Duffo	Duffo	1978
BEGA 6	Johnny G.	Sharp And Natural	1978
BEGA 7	Tubeway Army	Replicas	1979
BEGA 8	Lurkers	God's Lonely Men	1979
BEGA 9	Heartbreakers	Live At Max's Kansas City	1979
BEGA 10	Gary Numan	The Pleasure Principle	1979
BEGA 11	Merton Parkas	Face In The Crowd	1979
BEGA 12	Doll	Listen To The Silence	1979
BEGA 14	Carpettes	Frustration Paradise	1979
BEGA 15	Chrome	Red Explosion	1979
BEGA 16	Johnny G.	G-Beat	1979
BEGA 19	Gary Numan	Telekon	1980
BEGA 20	Colin Newman	A-Z	1980
BEGA 21	Carpettes	Fight Among Yourselves	1980
BEGA 22	Freez	Southern Freez	1981
BEGA 23	Spirit	Potato Land	1981
BEGA 24	Gary Numan	Living Ornaments '79	1981
BEGA 25	Gary Numan	Living Ornaments '80	1981
BEGA 27	Morrissey Mullen	Badness	1981
BEGA 28	Gary Numan	Dance	1981
BEGA 29	Bauhaus	Mask	1981
BEGA 30	Johnny G.	Water Into Wine	1981

Box Set:

Cat. No.	Artist	Titles	Year
BOX 1	Gary Numan	Living Ornaments '79 + Living Ornaments '80	1981

Cat. No.	Artist	Titles	Year		
BACK 1	Lurkers	Shadow/Love Story/Freak Show / Mass Media Believer	(Reissue, double pack)	1979
BACK 2	Tubeway Army	That's Too Bad/Oh Didn't I Say/Bombers/Blue Eyes/O.D. Receiver	(Reissue, double pack)	1979
BACK 3	Lurkers	I Don 't Need to Tell Her/Pills/Just 13/Countdown	(double pack)	1979

Captain Oi! (High Wycombe)

CDs:

Cat. No.	Artist	Titles	Year
AHOY CD 1	Last Resort	Skinhead Anthems	1993
AHOY CD 2	The Business	Welcome To The Real World	1993
AHOY CD 3	The 4-Skins	The Good The Bad The 4 Skins	1993
AHOY CD 4	Cock Sparrer	Shock Troops	1993
AHOY CD 5	The Oppressed	Oi! Oi! Music	1993
AHOY CD 6	Various	This Is Oi!	1993
AHOY CD 7	The Business	Suburban Rebels	1993
AHOY CD 8	The 4-Skins	A Fistful Of 4-Skins	1993
AHOY CD 9	Various	Son Of Oi!	1993
AHOY CD 10	Infa Riot	Still Out Of Order	1993
AHOY CD 11	The Crack	In Search Of The Crack	1993
AHOY CD 12	Red Alert	We've Got The Power	1993
AHOY CD 13	The Business	Saturday's Heroes	1994
AHOY CD 14	One Way System	All Systems Go	1994
AHOY CD 15	Various	A Country Fit For Heroes 1 & 2	1994
AHOY CD 16	Major Accident	Clockwork Heroes	1994
AHOY CD 17	Menace	GLC – Best Of	1994
AHOY CD 18	Chron Gen	Best Of Chron Gen	1994
AHOY CD 19	The Business	Singalongabusiness	1994
AHOY CD 20	Vicious Rumours	Anytime Day Or Night	1994
AHOY CD 21	One Way System	Writing On The Wall	1994
AHOY CD 22	Attak	Zombies	1994
AHOY CD 23	Various	The Oi! Of Sex	1994
AHOY CD 24	The Ejected	A Touch Of Class	1994
AHOY CD 25	Abrasive Wheels	When The Punks Go...	1994
AHOY CD 26	Vicious Rumours	Sickest Men In Town	1994
AHOY CD 27	Major Accident	Massacred Melodies + A Clockwork Legion	1994
AHOY CD 28	Erazerhead	Shellshocked – Best Of	1994
AHOY CD 29	The Defects	Defective Breakdown	1994
AHOY CD 30	The Magnificent	Hit And Run	1994
AHOY CD 31	Resistance 77	Thoroughbred Men	1994
AHOY CD 32	Action Pact	Punk Singles Collection	1995
AHOY CD 33	The Enemy	Gateway To Hell	1995
AHOY CD 34	The Ejected	Spirit Of Rebellion	1995
AHOY CD 35	Special Duties	77 In 82	1995
AHOY CD 36	Cock Sparrer	Rarities	1995
AHOY CD 37	Section 5	We Won't Change	1995
AHOY CD 38	Various	The Best Of Oi! Records	1995
AHOY CD 39	Barbed Wire	The Age That Didn't Care	1995
AHOY CD 40	The Dark	The Best Of The Dark	1995
AHOY CD 41	The Fits	The Fits Punk Collection	1995
AHOY CD 42	The Oppressed	Fatal Blow + Dead & Buried	1995
AHOY CD 43	Various	Oi! The Rarities Vol. 1	1995
AHOY CD 44	Anti-Social	Battle Scarred Skinheads – The Best Of Anti Social	1995
AHOY CD 45	Red Alert	Oi! Singles Collection	1995
AHOY CD 46	Various	Oi! The Rarities Vol. 2	1995
AHOY CD 47	Abrasive Wheels	Black Leather Girl	1995
AHOY CD 48	English Dogs	Mad Punx And English Dogs + Invasion Of The Porky Men	1995
AHOY CD 49	Infa Riot	Sound And Fury	1995
AHOY CD 50	Slaughter and The Dogs	Cranked Up Really High	1995
AHOY CD 51	Abrasive Wheels	The Punk Singles Collection	1995
AHOY CD 52	External Menace	Pure Punk Rock!	1995
AHOY CD 53	Various	Oi! The Rarities Vol. 3	1995
AHOY CD 54	The Guttersnipes	The Poor Dress Up	1996
AHOY CD 55	Section 5	The Best Of	1996
AHOY CD 56	Major Accident	The Clockwork Demos	1996
AHOY CD 57	Cock Sparrer	Running Riot In 84	1996
AHOY CD 58	Various	Oi! The Rarities Vol. 4	1996
AHOY CD 59	Action Pact	Mercury Theatre On Air + Survival Of The Fattest	1996

AHOY CD 60	Various	Oi! The Singles Collection Vol. 1	1996
AHOY CD 61	Mau Maus	Complete Mau Maus Punk Singles Collection	1996
AHOY CD 62	Various	Oi! The Rarities Vol. 5	1996
AHOY CD 63	Various	Oi! The Singles Collection Vol. 2	1996
AHOY CD 64	Cyanide	The Punk Rock Collection	1996
AHOY CD 65	The Carpettes	Frustration Paradise + Fight Amongst Yourselves	1996
AHOY CD 66	The Depressions	The Punk Rock Collection	1997
AHOY CD 67	Various	Oi! The Singles Collection Vol. 3	1997
AHOY CD 68	The Outcasts	Blood And Thunder	1997
AHOY CD 69	The Crack	All Cracked Up	1997
AHOY CD 70	The Partisans	The Time Was Right	1997
AHOY CD 71	Various	Oi! The Singles Collection Vol. 4	1997
AHOY CD 72	Various	Oi! The Album	1997
AHOY CD 73	The Lurkers	Fulham Fallout	1997
AHOY CD 74	The Lurkers	God's Lonely Men	1997
AHOY CD 75	Special Duties	77 In 97	1997
AHOY CD 76	Klasse Kriminalle	The Best Of	1997
AHOY CD 77	London	The Punk Rock Collection	1997
AHOY CD 78	Anti-Establishment	The Oi! Collection	1997
AHOY CD 79	Crux / The Samples	The Oi! Collection	1997
AHOY CD 80	Angelic Upstarts	Rarities	1997
AHOY CD 81	Various	Oi! The Demos	1997
AHOY CD 82	The Resort	1989	1997
AHOY DCD 83	Various	100% British Oi! (dbl)	1997
AHOY DCD 84	Various	100% Hardcore Punk (dbl)	1998
AHOY CD 85	ABH/Subculture	The Oi! Collection	1998
AHOY CD 86	Various	Farewell To The Roxy	1998
AHOY CD 87	Angelic Upstarts	Last Tango In Moscow	1998
AHOY CD 88	The Adicts	Sound Of Music + Smart Alex	1998
AHOY CD 89	Splodge	In Search Of The Seven Golden Gussetts	1998
AHOY CD 90	Guitar Gangsters	Prohibition + Money With Menaces	1998
AHOY CD 91	Chelsea	Chelsea	1998
AHOY CD 92	Chelsea	Alternative Hits	1998
AHOY CD 93	U.K. Subs	Punk Rock Rarities	1998
AHOY CD 94	Chelsea	Evacuate	1998
AHOY CD 95	The Wall	The Punk Collection	1998
AHOY CD 96	The Skeptix	Pure Punk Rock	1998
AHOY CD 97	U.K. Subs	Endangered Species	1998
AHOY CD 98	Chelsea	Punk Singles Collection 77-82	1998
AHOY CD 99	The Starjets	God Save The Starjets – The Punk Collection	1999
AHOY CD 101	The Boys	The Boys	1999
AHOY CD 102	The Stiffs	The Punk Collection	1999
AHOY CD 103	The Partisans	The Best Of The Partisans	1999
AHOY CD 104	The Boys	Alternative Chartbusters	1999
AHOY CD 105	The Expelled	A Punk Collection	1999
AHOY CD 106	Chelsea	Punk Rock Rarities	1999
AHOY CD 107	Red Alert	Rarities	1999
AHOY CD 108	Charlie Harper and New Barbarians	The Urban Dogs – The Best Of	1999
AHOY CD 109	The Crack	The Best Of The Crack	1999
AHOY CD 110	Intensive Care	The Oi! Collection	1999
AHOY CD 111	The Drones	Sorted	1999
AHOY CD 112	The Ejected	The Best Of The Ejected	1999
AHOY CD 113	The Boys	To Hell With The Boys	1999
AHOY CD 114	U.K. Subs	Huntingdon Beach	1999
AHOY CD 115	The Gonads	Oi! Back And Barking	1999
AHOY CD 116	Angelic Upstarts	Blood On The Terraces	1999
AHOY CD 117	The Boys	Boys Only	1999
AHOY CD 118	Special Duties	The Punk Singles Collection	1999
AHOY CD 119	Various	Carry On Oi!	1999
AHOY CD 120	The Boys	Punk Rock Rarities	1999
AHOY CD 121	Angelic Upstarts	The EMI Punk Years	1999
AHOY CD 122	Cockney Rejects	The Power And The Glory	1999
AHOY CD 123	Vice Squad	Punk Rock Rarities	1999
AHOY CD 124	The Gymslips	Rockin With The Renees	1999
AHOY CD 125	Vicious Rumours	The Best Of	1999
AHOY CD 126	Blitzkrieg/Insane	The Punk Collection	1999
AHOY CD 127	The Saints	Eternally Yours	1999
AHOY CD 128	The 4-Skins	Singles And Rarities	1999
AHOY CD 129	The Saints	I'm Stranded	1999

Cat. No.	Artist	Title	Year
AHOY CD 130	Splodgenessabounds	I Don't Know	2000
AHOY CD 131	Slaughter and The Dogs	Do It Dog Style	2000
AHOY CD 132	Eddie and The Hot Rods	Teenage Depression	2000
AHOY CD 133	Eddie and The Hot Rods	Life On The Line	2000
AHOY CD 134	U.K. Subs	Another Kind Of Blues	2000
AHOY CD 135	The Vibrators	The BBC Punk Sessions	2000
AHOY CD 136	U.K. Subs	Brand New Age	2000
AHOY CD 137	The Lurkers	BBC Punk Sessions	2000
AHOY CD 138	Angelic Upstarts	BBC Punk Sessions	2000
AHOY CD 139	Sham 69	The Rarities 77-80	2000
AHOY CD 140	U.K. Subs	Crash Course	2000
AHOY CD 141	The Wanderers	Only Lovers Left Alive	2000
AHOY CD 142	Slaughter and The Dogs	Bite Back	2000
AHOY CD 143	U.K. Subs	Diminished Responsibilty	2000
AHOY CD 144	The Boys	To Original Hell With + Odds 'N' Sods	2000
AHOY CD 145	Guitar Gangsters	Road To Reality	2000
AHOY CD 146	Red Alert	The Best Of	2000
AHOY CD 147	999	999	2000
AHOY CD 148	999	Separates	2000
AHOY CD 149	The Dickies	Incredible Shrinking Dickies	2000
AHOY CD 150	The Dickies	Dawn Of The Dickies	2000
AHOY CD 151	Stiff Little Fingers	Go For It	2000
AHOY CD 152	Stiff Little Fingers	Now Then	2000
AHOY CD 153	Vice Squad	No Cause For Concern	2000
AHOY CD 154	Slaughter and The Dogs	The Punk Singles Collection	2000
AHOY CD 155	Criminal Class	Blood On The Streets – The Criminal Class Oi! Collection	2000
AHOY CD 156	Vice Squad	Stand Strong Stand Proud	2000
AHOY CD 157	The Yobs	The Christmas Album	2000
AHOY CD 158	Angelic Upstarts	Two Million Voices	2001
AHOY CD 159	Chelsea	BBC Punk Sessions 77-80	2001
AHOY CD 160	The Exploited	Punk Singles And Rarities 80-83	2001
AHOY CD 161	Blitz	Punk Singles And Rarities 80-83	2001
AHOY CD 162	Anti-Nowhere League	Punk Singles And Rarities 80-84	2001
AHOY CD 164	Instant Agony	The Punk Collection	2001
AHOY CD 166	U.K.Subs	Flood Of Lies	2001
AHOY CD 167	U.K.Subs	Japan Today	2001
AHOY CD 168	The Oppressed	Oi! Singles And Rarities	2001
AHOY CD 169	Resistance 77	Retaliate First	2001
AHOY CD 170	Splodgenessabounds	The Artful Splodger	2001
AHOY CD 171	Menace	Crisis	2001
AHOY CD 172	The Skids	Days In Europa	2001
AHOY CD 173	The Revillos	Rev Up	2001
AHOY CD 174	Penetration	Coming Up For Air	2001

LPs:

Cat. No.	Artist	Titles	
AHOY LP 1	Last Resort	Skinhead Anthems	1996
AHOY LP 3	The 4-Skins	The Good The Bad And The 4 Skins	1996
AHOY LP 4	Cock Sparrer	Shock Troops	1996
AHOY LP 5	The Oppressed	Oi! Oi! Music	1996
AHOY LP 8	The 4-Skins	A Fistful Of	1996
AHOY LP 10	Infa Riot	Still Out Of Order	1996
AHOY LP 12	Red Alert	We've Got The Power	1996
AHOY LP 14	One Way System	All Systems Go	1996
AHOY LP 16	Major Accident	Clockwork Heroes	1996
AHOY LP 17	Menace	GLC - The Best Of Menace	1996
AHOY LP 21	One Way System	Writing On The Wall	1996
AHOY LP 24	The Ejected	A Touch Of Class	1996
AHOY LP 25	Abrasive Wheels	When The Punks Go Marching In	1996
AHOY LP 35	Special Duties	77 In 82	1996
AHOY LP 42	The Oppressed	Fatal Blow / Dead And Buried	1996
AHOY LP 43	Various Oi!	Oi! The Rarities Vol.1	1996
AHOY LP 44	Anti Social	Battle Scarred Skinheads - The Best Of Anti Social	1996
AHOY LP 46	Various Oi!	Oi! The Rarities Vol.2	1996
AHOY LP 50	Slaughter and The Dogs	Cranked Up Really High	1996
AHOY LP 51	Abrasive Wheels	Punk Singles Collection	1996
AHOY LP 53	Various Oi!	Oi! The Rarities Vol.3	1996
AHOY LP 57	Cock Sparrer	Runnin Riot In 84	1996
AHOY LP 72	Various Oi!	Oi! The Album	1996

Cat. No.	Artist	Titles		Year
AHOY LP 73	The Lurkers	Fulham Fallout		1996
AHOY LP 75	Special Duties	'77 In '97		1996
AHOY LP 131	Slaughter and The Dogs	Do It Dog Style		2000
AHOY LP 149	The Dickies	Incredible Shrinking Dickies		2000
AHOY LP 150	The Dickies	Dawn Of The Dickies		2000
AHOY LP 501	Chaos UK	Chaos UK LP		1996
AHOY LP 502	Chaos UK	The Singles		1996
AHOY DLP 503	Various Punk	Riot City Punk Singles Collection Vol. 1		1996
AHOY LP 504	Various Punk	Secret Records Punk Singles Collection Vol. 1		1996
AHOY LP 505	Blitz	Complete Blitz Punk Singles Collection		1996
AHOY LP 506	Riot Squad	Complete Riot Squad Punk Collection		1996
AHOY LP 507	Various Punk	Secret Records Punk Singles Collection Vol. 2		1996
AHOY DLP 508	Various Punk	No Future Punk Singles Collection Vol.1		1996
AHOY LP 509	Chaos UK	Enough To Make You Sick / Chipping Sodbury Bonfire Tapes		1996
AHOY LP 510	Angelic Upstarts	The Independent Punk Singles Collection		1996
AHOY DLP 511	Various Punk	Riot City Punk Singles Collection Vol.2		1996
AHOY DLP 512	Various Punk	No Future Punk Singles Collection Vol.2		1996
AHOY LP 513	Various Punk	Rondelet Punk Singles Collection		1996
AHOY DLP 514	Various Punk	Small Wonder Punk Singles Collection		1996
AHOY DLP 515	The Adicts	Complete Adicts Punk Singles Collection		1996
AHOY LP 516	One Way System	The Best Of One Way System		1996
AHOY LP 517	The Varukers	The Punk Singles 1981-85		1996
AHOY LP 518	Uk Subs	The Punk Singles Collection		1996
AHOY LP 519	The Boys	The Boys		1998
AHOY LP 520	The Boys	Alternative Chartbusters		1998

Picture Disc LPs:

Cat. No.	Artist	Titles		
AHOY PD 1	Last Resort	Skinhead Anthems		2001
AHOY PD 72	Various Oi!	Oi! The Album		2001
AHOY PD 149	The Dickies	Incredible Shrinking Dickies		2001
AHOY PD 150	The Dickies	Dawn Of The Dickies		2001
AHOY PD 521	The Exploited	Punks Not Dead		2001
AHOY PD 522	The Exploited	Troops Of Tomorrow		2001

Captain Mod (High Wycombe)

CDs:

Cat. No.	Artist	Titles		Year
MODSKA CD 1	The Crooks	Just Released		1996
MODSKA CD 2	Various	Odd Bods Mods And Sods		1996
MODSKA CD 3	Various	The Beat Generation And Angry Young Men		1996
MODSKA CD 4	The Ska-dows	Ska'd For Life		1997
MODSKA CD 5	Long Tall Shorty	1970's Boy		1997
MODSKA CD 6	Various	5-4-3-2-1 Go! – The Countdown Compilation		1997
MODSKA DCD 7	Various	100% British Ska	(dbl)	1998
MODSKA DCD 8	Various	100% British Mod	(dbl)	1998
MODSKA CD 9	Bad Manners	Mental Notes		1999
MODSKA CD 10	The Chords	So Far Away		2000
MODSKA CD 11	The Vapors	New Clear Days		2001
MODSKA CD 12	The Vapors	Magnets		2001
MODSKA CD 14	Secret Affair	Glory Boys		2001
MODSKA CD 15	Secret Affair	Behind Closed Doors		2001
MODSKA CD 16	Secret Affair	Business As Usual		2001
MODSKA CD 17	The Selector	Too Much Pressure		2001
MODSKA CD 18	The Selector	Celebrate The Bullet		2001
COLU CD 1	Special Duties	Wembley! Wembley! (Here We Come)		
KILLIE CD 1	The Chosen / Last Years Men	Glory Glory Kilmarnock F.C.		
RHINO CD 1	Millwall FC& Supporters	Let 'Em Come		

Chiswick (London)

Singles:

Cat. No.	Artist	Titles		Year
SW 1	Count Bishops	Speedball EP	7", 1st 1,000 in glossy PS	1975
S 2	Vince Taylor	Brand New Cadillac/Pledging My Love	7"	1976
S 3	101'ers	Keys To Your Heart/5 Star Rock & Roll Petrol	7"	1976
S 4	Gorillas	She's My Gal/Why Wait Until Tomorrow	7"	1976

Cat. No.	Artist	Titles		Year
S 5	Count Bishops	Train Train/Takin' It Easy	7"	1976
SW 6	Rocky Sharpe	Rocky Sharpe And The Razors	7"	1976
SW 7	Little Bob Story	Little Bob Story EP	7"	1976
S 8	Gorillas	Gatecrasher/Gorilla Got Me	7"	1977
S 9	Radio Stars	Dirty Pictures/Sail Away	7"	1977
S 10	Radiators From Space	Television Screen/Love Detective	7"	1977
S 11	Skrewdriver	You're So Dumb/Better Off Crazy	7"	1977
S 12	Count Bishops	Baby You're Wrong/Stay Free	7"	1977
S 13	Motorhead	Motorhead/City Kids	7", also on 12" [NS 13]	1977
S 14	Rings	I Wanna Be Free/Automobile	7"	1977
S 15	Johnny Moped	No-One/Incendiary Device	7"	1977

NB: Several of the above were later reissued with an 'NS' prefix.

Cat. No.	Artist	Titles		Year
NS 16	Jeff Hill	I Want You To Dance With Me/Feel Like Lovin' You	7"	1977
SW 17	Radio Stars	Stop It EP	7"	1977
NS 18	Skrewdriver	Anti-Social/18th Nervous Breakdown		1977
NS 19	Radiators From Space	Enemies/Psychotic Reaction	7"	1977
NS 20	Amazorblades	Common Truth/Messaround	7"	1977
NS 21	Stukas	Klean Living Kid/Oh Little Girl	7"	1977
NS 22	Johnny and The Self-Abusers	Saints And Sinners	7"	1977
NS 23	Radio Stars	Nervous Wreck/Horrible Breath	7", also numbered 12" [NS 23]	1977
NS 24	Radiators From Space	Prison Bars/Teenager In Love	(unissued, labels only!)	
NS 25	Whirlwind	Hang Loose/Together Forever	7"	1978
SWT 26	Twink	Twink EP	12"	1978
NS 27	Johnny Moped	Darling Let's Have Another Baby/Something Else/It Really Digs	7"	1978
NS 28	Skrewdriver	Streetfight/Unbeliever	7", unissued, white labels only	
NS 29	The Radiators	Million Dollar Hero/Prison Bars	7"	1978
SW 30	The Jook	The Jook EP	7"	1978

Albums:

Cat. No.	Artist	Titles		Year
CH 1/WIK 1	Count Bishops	Count Bishops		1977
WIK 2	Motorhead	Motorhead		1977
CH 3	Skrewdriver	All Screwed Up	Mini-LP, 12 tracks, 45rpm, 3 different colour sleeves [also issued as a 15-track German LP, WIK 3]	1977
WIK 4	Radiators From Space	TV Tube Heart		1977
WIK 5	Radio Stars	Songs For Swinging Lovers	Shinkwrapped with free single, "No Russians In Russia"/"Dirty Pictures" (PROMO 2, no PS)	1977
WIK 6	Little Bob Story	Off The Rails		1977
WIK 7	Whirlwind	Blowin' Up A Storm	10"	1978
WIK 8	Johnny Moped	Cycledelic	Some copies with "Basically, The Originally Johnny Moped Tape" 7" (PROMO 3)	1978
WIK 9	Sniff 'n' Tears	Fickle Heart	(unissued)	
WIK 10	Matchbox	Setting The Woods On Fire		1978

Clay (Stoke-on-Trent)

Singles:

Cat. No.	Artist	Titles			Year
CLAY 1	Discharge	Realities Of War/They Declare It/But After The Gig/Society's Victim		PS	1980
CLAY 2	Plastiic Idols	Adventure/Remix		PS	1980
CLAY 3	Discharge	Fight Back/War's No Fairytale/Always Restrictions/You Take Part In Creating The System/Religious Instigates		PS	1980
CLAY 4	Demon	Liar/Wild Woman	(red vinyl!)	PS	1980
CLAY 5	Discharge	Decontrol/It's No TV Sketch/Tomorrow Belongs To Us		PS	1980
CLAY 6	Discharge	Never Again/Death Dealers/Two Monstrous Nuclear Stock Piles		PS	1981
CLAY 7	Dave Edge	New World/?		PS	198?
CLAY 8	G.B.H.	No Survivors/Self Destruct/Big Women		PS	1982
CLAY 9	Zanti Misfitz	Kidz Songs/Alice Liddel's Bad Trip		PS	1982
CLAY 10	White Door	Way Of The World/The Extra		PS	1982
CLAY 11	G.B.H.	Sick Boy/Slit Your Own Throat/Am I Dead Yet		PS	1982
CLAY 12	The Lurkers	This Dirty Town/Wolf At The Door			1982
CLAY 13	Zanti Misfitz	Love Ends At 8/Invasion Of The Electric Deathman		PS	1982
CLAY 14	Discharge	State Violence State Control/Doomsday		PS	1982
* CLAY 15	White Order	Kings Of The Orient/?		PS	1982
CLAY 16	G.B.H.	Give Me The Fire/Man Trap	(picture disc)	PS	1982
CLAY 17	The Lurkers	Drag You Out/Heroin It's All Over	(picture disc)	PS	1982
CLAY 18	The Killboys	This Is Not Love/In Your Light		PS	198?

Cat. No.	Artist	Titles		Year
* CLAY 19	Lowlife	Logic And Lust/The Animal Nightclub	PS	198?
CLAY 20	Peter Anthony	Song For Fescon/?	PS	198?
CLAY 21	The Lurkers	Frankenstein Again/One Man's Meat	PS	1983
CLAY 22	G.B.H.	Catch 23/Hellhole	PS	1983
* CLAY 23	White Door	Love Breakdown/Breakdown (inst.)	PS	1983
CLAY 24	Abrasive Wheels	Jailhouse Rock/Sonic Omen	PS	1983
CLAY 25	Demon	The Plague/The Only Sane Man	PS	1983
CLAY 26	White Door	Windows/In Heaven	PS	1983
* CLAY 27	Sex Gang Children	Mauritia Mayer/Children's Prayer	PS	1983
CLAY 28	Abrasive Wheels	Banner Of Hope/Law Of The Jungle	PS	1983
CLAY 29	Discharge	Price Of Silence/Born To Die In The Gutter	PS	1983
CLAY 30	White Door	Jerusalem/Americana	PS	1984
* CLAY 31	Play Dead	Break/Bloodstains/Pleasure	PS	1984
CLAY 32	The Lurkers	Let's Dance Now/Midnight Hour	PS	1984
* CLAY 33	Abrasive Wheels	The Prisoner/Christianne/Black Leather Girl	PS	1984
* CLAY 34	Discharge	The More I See/Protest And Survive/(Extended Version)	PS	1984
* CLAY 35	Play Dead	Isabel/Solace	PS	1984
* CLAY 36	G.B.H.	Do What You Do/Four Men/Children Of Dust	PS	1984
* CLAY 37	White Door	Flame In My Heart/Behind The White Door		1984
CLAY 38	Sharks In Italy	Time/Dancing		1984
* CLAY 39	Veil	Maniken/Dreams Endowed/Panic		1984
* CLAY 40	Play Dead	Conspiracy/Silent Conspiracy		1984
* CLAY 41	Demon	Wonderland/Blackheath/Nowhere To Run		1984
* CLAY 42	Play Dead	Sacrosanct/Pale Fire		198?
* CLAY 43	Discharge	Ignorance/No Compromise/(Extended Version)		1985
* CLAY 44	Rebel Christening	Tribal Eye/Desire And Glory		1985
CLAY 45	Veil	Thirst/Sway		1986
CLAY 46	Sharks In Italy	Precious/Could You Be Loved		1985
CLAY 47	Performance	Wish I Was Free Again/Version		1985
CLAY 48	Demon	Tonight The Herd Is Back/Hurricane/Night Of The Demon/ Don't Break The Circle (dbl 7")		1988
* CLAY 49	Climax Blues Band	Couldn't Get It Right/The Deceiver		1988

Plate 12" Series:

Cat. No.	Artist	Titles		Year
PLATE 1	Product	Style Wars EP - Tracks unknown	PS	198?
PLATE 2	Discharge	Why/Visions Of War/Does The System Work/A Look At Tomorrow/ Maimed + Slaughtered/Mania For Conquest/Ain't No Feeble Bastard/ Is This To Be (12" EP)	PS	1981
PLATE 3	G.B.H.	Race Against Time/Knife Edge/Lycanthropy/Necrophilia/ Sick Boy/State Executioner/Dead On Arrival/Generals/Freaks (CD)	PS	1984
PLATE 4	Zanti Misfitz	Heroes Are Go EP - Tracks unknown	PS	198?
PLATE 5	Discharge	Warning/Where There's A Will/In Defence Of Our Future/ Anger Burning	PS	198?
PLATE 6	English Dogs	Mad Punx And English Dogs EP - Tracks unknown	PS	198?
PLATE 7	The Lurkers	Final Vinyl - Frankenstein Again/Shut Out The Light/ Let's Dance Now/Midnight Hour/By The Heart	PS	1984
PLATE 8	Demon	Heart Of Our Time/Blackheath Pt's 1 + 2/High Clamber/The Plague/ The Link Pt's 1 + 2	PS	1985
PLATE 9	Excalibur	Hot For Love/Early In The Morning/Come On And Rock/ Deaths Door	PS	1985

* = Released on 12".

Albums:

Cat. No.	Artist	Titles		Year
CLAY LP 2	Grace	Grace Live		1982
CLAY LP 3	Discharge	Hear Nothing See Nothing Say Nothing		1982
CLAY LP 4	G.B.H.	City Baby Attacked By Rats		1982
CLAY LP 5	G.B.H.	Leather, Bristles, No Survivors And Sick Boys		1981
CLAY LP 6	Demon	The Plague	(pic disc)	1983
CLAY LP 7	White Door	Windows		1983
CLAY LP 8	G.B.H.	City Baby's Revenge		1983
CLAY LP 9	Abrasive Wheels	Black Leather Girl		1984
CLAY LP 10	English Dogs	Invasion Of The Porky Men		1984
CLAY LP 11	Play Dead	From The Promised Land		1984
CLAY LP 12	Discharge	Never Again		1984
CLAY LP 13	Reggae Nomix	Reggae Nomix		1984
CLAY LP 14	Veil	Surrender		1985
CLAY LP 15	Demon	British Standard		1985

Cat. No.	Artist	Titles		Year
CLAY LP 16	Play Dead	Into The Fire		1985
CLAY LP 17	Various Artists	They Only Come Out At Night		1985
CLAY LP 18	Demon	Heart Of Our Time		1985
CLAY LP 19	Discharge	Grave New World		1986
CLAY LP 20	Play Dead	Singles 82-85		1986
CLAY LP 21	G.B.H.	Clay Years 81-84		1987
CLAY LP 22	Demon	The Unexpected Guest		1987
CLAY LP 23	Demon	Breakout	(also on CD, 1988)	1987
CLAY LP 24	Discharge	1980-86		1986
CLAY LP 25	Demon	Night Of The Demon		1988
CLAY LP 26	Climax Blues Band	Drastic Steps	(also on CD)	1988

Deptford Fun City (London)

7" Singles:

Cat. No.	Artist	Titles		Year
DFC 01	Squeeze	Packet Of Three EP	PS, also 12"	1977
DFC 02	Alternative TV	How Much Longer/You Bastard	PS	1977
DFC 03	Jools Holland	Boogie Woogie 78 EP	PS	1978
DFC 04	Alternative TV	Life After Life/Life After Dub	PS	1978
DFC 07	Alternative TV	Action Time Vision/Another Coke (live)	PS	1978
DFC 11	Henry Badowski	Baby Sign Here With Me/Making Love With My Wife (Released with A&M)	PS	1979

Albums:

Cat. No.	Artist	Titles		Year
DLP 01	Alternative TV	The Image Has Cracked		1978
DLP 02	Alternative TV/Here and Now	What You See Is What You Are		1978
DLP 03	Alternative TV	Vibing Up The Senile Man (Part One)		1978
DLP 04	Good Missionaries	Fire from Heaven		1979
DLP 05	Alternative TV	Action Time Vision	Sampler album	1980
DLP 06	Mark Perry	Snappy Turns		1980

Din Disc (London, Virgin Records subsidiary)

7" Singles (the first 40):

Cat. No.	Artist	Titles		Year
DIN 1	Revillos	Where's The Boy For Me?/The Fiend	PS, Snatzo/DinDisc	1979
DIN 2	Orchestral Manoeuvres In The Dark	Electricity/Almost (reissue of Factory record)	PS,	1979
DIN 3	Brian Brain	Brother's Famous/Brian's Sister Sue	PS	1979
DIN 3	Duggie Campbell	Enough To Make You Mine/Steamin'	PS	1979
DIN 4	Martha and The Muffins	Cheesies And Gum/Insect Love	PS	1979
DIN 5	Revillos	Motor Bike Beat / No Such Luck	PS Snatzo/DinDisc	1979
DIN 6	OMD	Red Frame White Light/I Betray My Friends	PS Also 12", DIN 6-12	1980
DIN 8	Bardi Blaise	Trans-Siberian Express Competition Slide	PS	1980
DIN 9	Martha and The Muffins	Echo Beach/Teddy the Dink	PS	1980
DIN 10	Dedringer	Sunday Drivers/We Don't Mind	PS	1980
DIN 11	Dedringer	Maxine/Innocent Till Proven Guilty PS with bonus 45: Took A Long Time/We Don't Mind	(doublepack)	1981
DIN 12	Dedringer	Direct Line/She's Not Ready	PS	1981
DIN 15	OMD	Messages/Taking Sides Again	PS	1980
DINZ 16	Revillos	Scuba Scuba/Scuba Boy Bop	PS	1980
DIN 17	Martha and The Muffins	Saigon/Copacabana	PS	1980
DIN 18	Monochrome Set	Strange Boutique/Surfing SW12	PS	1980
DINZ 20	Revillos	Hungry For Love/Voodoo 2	PS	1980
DIN 22	OMD	Enola Gay/Annex (also 12" DIN 22-12)	PS	1980
DIN 23	Monochrome Set	405 Lines/Goodbye Joe	PS	1980
DIN 24	OMD	Souvenir/Motion And Heart/Secret Heart (also 10" DIN 24-10)	PS	1981
DIN 26	Monochrome Set	Apocalypso/Fiasce Bongo	PS	1980
DIN 27	Martha and The Muffins	Was Ezo/Trance And Dance	PS	1981
DIN 30	Modern Eon	Euthenics/Cardinal Sides	(tri-gatefold PS)	1981
DIN 31	Modern Eon	Child's Play/Visionary	PS	1980
DIN 32	Martha Ladly	Finlandia/Tasmania	PS	1981
DIN 33	Nash The Slash	Novel Romance/In A Glass Eye	PS	1981
DIN 34	Martha and The Muffins	Women Around The World/22 In Cincinnati	PS	1981
DIN 35	Modern Eon	Mechanic/Splash	PS	1981
DIN 36	OMD	Joan Of Arc/Romance Of The Telescope	PS	1981

Cat. No.	Artist	Titles		Year
DIN 37	Hot Gossip	Criminal World	PS, Also DIN 37-12, 12"	1981
DIN 38	Hot Gossip	Soul Warfare/Soul Warfare (instrumental) PS, Also DIN 38-12, 12"		1981
DIN 40	OMD	Maid Of Orleans/Navigation	PS	1982
DIN 40-12	OMD	Maid Of Orleans/Navigation/Experiments In Vertical Take Off	PS, 12"	1982

Albums (the first 12):

Cat. No.	Artist	Titles	Year
DID 1	Martha and The Muffins	Metro Music	1979
DID 2	OMD	Orchestral Manoeuvres In The Dark	1980
DID 3	Revillos	Rev Up	1980
DID 4	Monochrome Set	The Strange Boutique	1980
DID 5	Martha and The Muffins	Trance And Dance	1980
DID 6	OMD	Organisation	1980
DID 8	Monochrome Set	Love Zombies	1980
DID 9	Nash The Slash	Children Of The Night	1981
DID 10	Martha and The Muffins	This Is The Ice Age	1981
DID 11	Modern Eon	Fiction Tales	1981
DID 12	OMD	Architecture And Morality	1981

Disorder Records

Various Formats:

Cat. No.	Artist	Titles	Year
ORDER 1	Disorder	Complete Disorder / Today's World / Violent Crime / Insane Youth	1981
ORDER 2	Disorder	Distortion To Deafness EP: You've Got To Be Someone / Daily Life / More Than Fights	1981
ORDER 4	Disorder	Mental Disorder EP: Bullshit Everyone / Rampton Song / Provocated War / 3 Blind Mice / Buy I Gurt Pint	1983
12 ORDER 3	Disorder	Perdition 12" EP: Stagnation / Life / Out Of Order / Condemned / Media / Suicide Children / Preachers / Rembranse Day	1982
12 ORDER 5	Disorder	1st three 7" EP's	1983

Do It (London, distributed by Virgin)

7" and 12" Singles and EPs:

Cat. No.	Artist	Titles		Year
DUN 1	Method	Kings On The Corner/Dynamo	PS	197?
DUN 2	Roogalator	Zero Hour/Sweet Mama Kundalini	PS	1978
DUN 3	Comic Romance	Cry Myself To Sleep/Cowboys And Indians	PS	197?
DUN 4	M	Moderne Man/Satisfy Your Life	PS	197?
DUN 5	Nick Plytas	Your Dream Is a Daydream/Johnny Runaway	PS	197?
DUNIT 7	Again Again	The Way We Were EP	PS	197?
DUN 8	Adam and The Ants	Zerox/ Whip In My Valise	PS	1979
DUNIT 9	Mataya Clifford	Living Wild/Buzz Buzz	PS	19??
DUNIT 10	Adam and The Ants	Ant Music EP (Car Trouble/You're So Physical / Pie/Friends)	PS	1980
DUN 11	Yello	Bimbo/T Splash	PS	198?
DUN 13	Yello	Bostitch (remix, with dubs)/She's Got A Gun (alternate version)	PS	1981
DUN 13	Yello	Bostitch/Downtown Samba/Daily Disco	PS, 12"	1982
DUN 14	Mothmen	Temptation/People People	PS	1981
DUN 15	Donnie Mayor	Can't Wait Till The Summer/Holiday Theme	PS	1981
DUN 16	Anthony More	World Service/Driving Girls	PS	1981
DUN 17	Everest The Hard Way	Tightrope/When You're Young	PS, Also 12"	1982
DUN 18	Yello	She's Got a Gun/Bluehead	PS	1982
DUN 1812	Yello	She's Got a Gun/Bluehead/ Everything Is Young And There Is No Reason	PS, 12"	1982
DUN 19	Mothmen	Wadada/As They Are	PS	1982
DUN 20	Adam and The Ants	Friends/Kick/Physical (alternate version)	PS	1982
DUNIT 20	Adam and The Ants	Friends/Kick/Physical (alternate version)/ Cartrouble, Parts 1 and 2 (alternate versions)	PS, 12"	1982

Albums:

Cat. No.	Artist	Titles	Year
RIDE 1	Roogalator	Play It By Ear	1977
RIDE 2	Danny Adler	The Danny Adler Story	1978
RIDE 3	Adam and The Ants	Dirk Wears White Sox	1979
RIDE 7	Anthony More	Flying Doesn't Help	1981
RIDE 8	Yello	Claro Que Si	1981
RIDE 9	Mothmen	One Black Dot	1982

Eric's (Liverpool)

7" Singles and Albums:

Cat. No.	Artist	Titles		Year
ERIC'S 001	Holly	Yankee Rose/Treasure Island/Desperate Dan	PS	1979
ERIC'S 002	Pink Military	Spellbound/Blood And Lipstick/Clowntown/I Cry	PS	1979
ERIC'S 003	(same as 001)			1979
ERIC'S 004	Pink Military	Do Animals Believe in God?	Album, with Virgin Records	1980
ERIC'S 005	Pink Military	Did You See Her?/Everyday	PS, with Virgin Records	1980
ERIC'S 006	Frantic Elevators	You Know What You Told Me/Production Prevention	PS	1980
ERIC'S 007	Holly	Hobo Joe/Stars Of The Bars	PS	1980
ERIC'S 008	Various	Jukebox At Eric's	Compilation LP	1980

F-Beat (London)

7" Singles (the first 21):

Cat. No.	Artist	Titles		Year
XX 1	Elvis Costello	I Can't Stand Up For Falling Down/Girls Talk	PS	1980
XX 2	Clive Langer and The Boxes	Splash/Hullo	PS	1980
XX 3	Elvis Costello	High Fidelity/Getting Mighty Crowded	PS	1980
XX 3T	Elvis Costello	High Fidelity/Getting Mighty Crowded/Clowntime Is Over (alternate version)	PS, 12"	1980
XX 4	Clive Langer and The Boxes	It's All Over Now/Lovely Evening	PS	1980
XX 5	Elvis Costello	New Amsterdam/Dr. Luther's Assistant	PS	1980
XX 5E	Elvis Costello	New Amsterdam/Dr. Luther's Assistant/Ghost Train/Just A Memory	PS, 7" EP	1980
XX 7	Attractions	Single Girl/Slow Patience	PS	1980
XX 8	Carlene Carter and Dave Edmunds	Baby Ride Easy/Too Bad About Sandy		1980
XX 9	Rockpile	Wrong Way/Now And Always	PS	1980
XX 12	Elvis Costello	Clubland/Clean Money/Hoover Factory	PS	1980
XX 14	Elvis Costello	From A Whisper To A Scream/Luxembourg	PS	1981
XX 17	Elvis Costello	A Good Year For The Roses/Your Angel Steps Out Of Heaven	PS	1981
XX 18	Carlene Carter	Oh How Happy/Billy	PS	1981
XX 19	Elvis Costello	Sweet Dreams/Psycho (live)	PS	1981
XX 20	Nick Lowe	Burning/Zulu Kiss	PS	1982
XX 21	Elvis Costello	I'm Your Toy (live)/Cry Cry Cry/Wondering		1982
XX 21T	Elvis Costello	I'm Your Toy (live)/My Shoes Keep Walking Back To You/Blues Keep Calling/Honky Tonk	PS, 12"	1982

Albums:

Cat. No.	Artist	Titles	Year
XX LP 1	Elvis Costello	Get Happy	1980
XX LP 2	Clive Langer and The Boxes	Splash	1980
XX LP 6	Elvis Costello	Ten Bloody Mary's And Ten How's Your Fathers	1980
XX LP 7	Rockpile	Seconds Of Pleasure	1980
XX LP 11	Elvis Costello	Trust	1981
XX LP 13	Elvis Costello	Almost Blue	1981
XX LP 14	Nick Lowe	Nick The Knife	1982
XX LP 17	Elvis Costello	Imperial Bedroom	1982
XX LP 18	Nick Lowe	The Abominable Snowman	1983
XX LP 19	Elvis Costello	Punch The Clock	1983

Factory (Manchester, later run by Rough Trade/Pinnacle)

7" and 12" Singles and Albums:

Cat. No.	Artist	Titles		Year
FAC 2	Various Artists	A Factory Sample (dbl. EP, silver gatefold sleeve, with stickers, PS)		1978
FAC 5	A Certain Ratio	All Night Party/The Thin Boys	(ltd. ed. 5000, PS)	1979
FAC 6	Orchestral Manoeuvres In The Dark	Electricity/Almost	(ltd. ed. 5000, braille PS)	1979
FACT 10	Joy Division	Unknown Pleasures	LP	1979
FAC 11	X-O-Dus	English Black Boys/See Them A-Come	PS, 12"	1979
FAC 12	Distractions	Time Goes By So Slow/Pillow Fight	PS	1979
FAC 13	Joy Division	Transmission/Novelty	PS	1979
FAC 13.12	Joy Division	Transmission/Novelty	PS, 12"	1980
FACT 14	Durutti Column	The Return Of The Durutti Column	(LP, sand paper sleeve, free 'Testoard Flexi" [FACT 14C])	1980
FACT 14	Durutti Column	The Return Of The Durutti Column	LP	1980
FACT 14C	Martin Hannett	First Aspect Of The Same Thing/Second Aspect Of The Same Thing (flexidisc)		1980
FAC 16	A Certain Ratio	The Graveyard And The Ballroom	(cassette, first 400 in orange purse with insert)	1979

Cat. No.	Artist	Title	Format	Year
FAC 16	A Certain Ratio	The Graveyard And The Ballroom	(cassette, various colours, with insert)	1979
FAC 17	Crawling Chaos	Sex Machine/Berlin	PS	1980
FAC 18	Section 25	Girls Don't Count/Knew Noise/Up To You	PS	1980
FAC 18-12	Section 25	Girls Don't Count/Knew Noise/Up To You	PS, 12"	1980
FACTUS 2	Joy Division	She's Lost Control/Atmosphere	PS, 12"	1980
FAC 19	John Dowie	Hard To Be An Egg/Mind Sketch	(white vinyl, yellow label, feather on clear sleeve)	1981
FAC 22	A Certain Ratio	Flight/Blown Away/And Then Again	PS, 12"	1980
FAC 23	Joy Division	Love Will Tear Us Apart/These Days/Love Will Tear Us Apart (Again)	PS	1980
FAC 23-12	Joy Division	Love Will Tear Us Apart/These Days/Love Will Tear Us Apart (Again)	12"	1980
FAC 24	Various Artists	A Factory Quartet	dbl. LP	1980
FACT 25	Joy Division	Closer	LP	1980
FAC 28	Joy Division	Komakino/Incubation/(Untitled)	flexi	1980
FAC 29	Names	Night Shift/I Wish I Could Speak Your Language	PS	1981
FACT 30	Sex Pistols	The Heyday	(Cassette, satin pouch with Xmas card)	1981
FAC 31	Minny Pops	Dolphin Spurt/Goddess	PS	1981
FAC 32	Crispy Ambulance	Unsightly And Serene	10" single, PS	1981
FAC 33	New Order	Ceremony/In A Lonely Place	Embossed PS	1981
FAC 33T	New Order	Ceremony/In A Lonely Place	Green PS, 12"	1981
FAC 33T	New Order	Ceremony/In A Lonely Place	Cream/Blue PS, 12", initially with remix	1981
FAC 34	E.S.G.	You're No Good/Ufo/Moody	PS	1981
FAC 35	A Certain Ratio	To Each ...	LP	1981
FAC 39	Tunnel Vision	Watching The Hydroplanes/Morbid Fear	PS, ltd. ed. clear vinyl	1981
FACT 40	Joy Division	Still	dbl. LP. initially in cloth sleeve	1981
FAC 41	Stockholm Monsters	Fairy Tales/Death Is Slowly Coming	gold lettering on mock-leather PS, various colours	1982
FAC 42	A Certain Ratio	The Double 12"	gatefold PS	1982
FAC 43	Royal Family and The Poor	Art On 45/Dream Domination	PS, 12"	1982
FACT 44	Durutti Column	LC	LP	1981
FACT 45	Section 25	Always Now	LP	1981
FAC 48	Kevin Hewick	Ophelia's Drinking Song; Cathy's Clown/He Holds You Tighter	PS	1982
FAC 49	Swamp Children	Honey/Little Voices	PS, 12"	1981
FACT 50	New Order	Movement	LP	1981
FAC 51B	New Order	Hacienda Club Xmas Flexi	free flexi	1982
FAC 52	A Certain Ratio	Waterline/Funaezakea	12", PS	1981
FAC 53	New Order	Everything's Gone Green/Procession	various PS	1981
FAC 55	A Certain Ratio	Sextet	LP	1982
FAC 57	Minny Pops	Secret Story/Island	PS	1982
FAC 58	Stockholm Monsters	Happy Ever After/Soft Babies	PS	1982
FAC 59	52nd Street	Look Into My Eyes/Express	PS	1982
FACT 60	Wake	Harmony	mini-LP	1983
FAC 62	A Certain Ratio	Knife Slits Water/Tumba Rumba	PS	1982
FAC 62-12	A Certain Ratio	Knife Slits Water/Kether Hot Knives	12", PS	1982
FAC 63	New Order	Temptation/Hurt	PS	1982
FAC 63-12	New Order	Temptation/Hurt	12", PS	1982
FAC 64	Durutti Column	I Get Along Without You Very Well/Prayer	PS	1982
FAC 65	A Certain Ratio	I'd Like To See You Again	LP	1982
FAC 66-12	Section 25	The Beast/Sakura/Sakura (Matrix Mix)/Trident	12", PS	1983
FAC 67	Quando Quango	Tingle/So Exciting	12", PS	1982
FAC 68	Section 25	Back To Wonder/Beating Heart	PS	1983
FACT 70	Swamp Children	So Hot	LP	1983
FAC 72	A Certain Ratio	I Need Someone Tonight/Don't You Worry 'Bout A Thing	PS	1983
FAC 72-12	A Certain Ratio	I Need Someone Tonight/Don't You Worry 'Bout A Thing	12", PS	1983
FAC 73	New Order	Blue Monday/The Beach	12", various PS: perforated/whole gloss/matt outer, some with black/silver inner	1983
FACT 74	Durutti Column	Another Setting	LP	1983
FACT 75	New Order	Power, Corruption And Lies	LP	1983
FAC 78	James	Jimone (Single)	PS	1983
FAC 79	Quando Quango	Love Tempo/Love Tempo (Remix)	12", PS	1983
FACT 80	Stockholm Monsters	Almer Mater	LP	1984
FAC 82-12	Cabaret Voltaire	Yashar/Yashar (Version)	12", PS	1983
FACT 84	Durutti Column	Without Mercy	LP	1984
FAC 87-12	Kalima	The Smiling Hour/Fly Away	12", PS	1983
FAC 88	Wake	Talk About The Past/Everybody Works So Hard	PS	1984
FAC 88-12	Wake	Talk About The Past/Everybody Works So Hard	12", PS	1984
FACT 90	Section 25	From The Hip	LP	1984
FAC 92	Marcel King	Keep On Dancing/Reach For Love	12", PS	1984
FAC 93	New Order	Confusion/Confused Beats/Confusion (Inst.)/(Rough Mix)	12", PS	1983
FAC 95	Royal Family and The Poor		LP	198?
FAC 96	Ad Infinitum	Telstar/Telstar In A Piano Bar	PS	1984
FAC 97	Streelife	Act On Instinct/(Mix Version)	12", PS	1984

Cat. No.	Artist	Titles			Year
FACT 100	New Order	Low Life		LP	1985
FAC 102	Quando Quango	Atom Rock/Triangle		12", PS	1984
FAC 103	New Order	Thieves Like Us/Lonesome Tonight		12", PS	1984
FAC 106	Life	Tell Me/Tell Me Theme		PS	1984
FAC 107	Stockholm Monsters	All At Once/National Pastime		PS	1984
FAC 108	Section 25	Looking From A Hilltop/(Remix Version)		PS	1984
FAC 108-12	Section 25	Looking From A Hilltop/(Remix Version)		12", PS	1984

Fallout

Various Formats:

Cat. No.	Artist	Titles			Year
FALL 001	The Enemy	Fallen Hero/Tomorrow's Warning/Prisoner Of War		PS	1982
FALL 002	The Adicts	Viva La Revolution/Steamroller/Numbers		PS	1982
FALL 003	Action Pact	Suicide Bag/Stanwell/Blue Blood		PS	1982
FALL 004	The Enemy	Punk's Alive/Twist And Turn/Picadilly Sidetracks		PS	1982
FALL 005	The Dark	The Living End	Live Mini-LP		1982
FALL 006	The Adicts	Songs Of Praise	LP		1982
FALL 007	The Rabid	Blood Road To Glory EP:- Jubilee/Glory Of War/Police Victim/Crisis 82			1982
FALL 008	Urban Dogs	New Barbarians/Speed Kills/Cocaine		PS	1982
FALL 009	Rabid	Bring Out Your Dead	Mini-LP		1982
FALL 010	Action Pact	People/Times Must Change/Sixties Flix		PS	1983
FALL 011	Urban Dogs	Limo Life/Warhead		PS	1982
FALL 012	Urban Dogs	Urban Dogs	LP		1983
FALL 013	Action Pact	Mercury Theatre: On Air	LP		1983
FALL 014	The Enemy	Last Rites/Why Not		PS	1983
FALL 015	The Enemy	Gateway To Hell	LP		1983
FALL 016	Action Pact	London Bouncers/Gothic Party Time/New Kings Girl/ The Cruelist Thief	(also 12")	PS	1983
FALL 017	U.K. Subs	Another Typical City/Still Life/Veronique	(also 12")	PS	1983
FALL 018	U.K. Subs	Flood Of Lies	LP	(later on CD)	1983
FALL 019	Action Pact	Question Of Choice/Hook Line And Sinker/Suss Of The Swiss		PS	1983
FALL 020	Broken Bones	Decapitated/Problem/Liquidated Brains		PS	1983
FALL 021	The Adicts	This Is Your Life	LP		1984
FALL 022	Fallen Angels	Amphetamine Blues/He's A Rebel		PS	1984
FALL 023	Fallen Angels	Fallen Angels	LP		1984
FALL 024	U.K. Subs	Magic EP:- Private Army/The Spell/Multiple Minos/Primary Strength		12", PS	1984
FALL 025	Broken Bones	Crucifix/Fight The Good Fight/I.O.U.	(also 12")	PS	1984
FALL 026	Action Pact	Yet Another Dole Queue Song/Rockaway Beach/1974/ Rock & Roll Pt. 2	(also 12")	PS	1984
FALL 12 027	Fallen Angels	Inner Planet Love/Precious Heart	Mini-LP	PS	1984
FALL 028	Broken Bones	DEM Bones	LP		1984
FALL 029	Action Pact	Cocktail Credibility/Consumer Madness		PS	1984
FALL 030	Action Pact	Survival Of The Fattest	LP		1984
FALL 031	U.K. Subs	Gross Out USA	LP	(later on CD)	1985
FALL 032	Various Artists	God Bless America	LP	Compilation	1985
FALL 033	Not Released				
FALL 034	Broken Bones	Seeing Through My Eyes//Point Of Agony/It's Like/Decapitated Pt. 2/ Death Is Imminent		PS	1985
FALL 035	Not Released				
FALL 036	U.K. Subs	This Gun Says/Speak For Myself/Wanted		PS	1985
FALL 037	Not Released				
FALL 038	The Adicts	Bar Room Bop:- Champ Elysees/Sound Of Music/ Who Spilt My Beer/Cowboys	(also 12")	PS	1985
FALL 12 039	Broken Bones	Never Say Die/10,s Or A Dime/Gotta Get Out Of Here		12", PS	1986
FALL 040	Various Artists	Radioactive	LP	(singles compilation)	
FALL 041	Broken Bones	F.O.A.D.	LP		1987
FALL 042	The Adicts	Fifth Overture	LP		1987
FALL 043	Broken Bones	Decapitated	LP		1987
FALL 044	U.K. Subs	Hey Santa/Captain Scarlet/Thunderbiird/Street Legal		PS	1987
FALL 045	U.K. Subs	Japan Today	LP	(later on CD)	1987
FALL 046	The Adicts	Rockers In Rags	LP		1990
FALL 047	U.K. Subs	Killing Time	LP	(also on CD)	1989
FALL 048	U.K. Subs	Mad Cow Fever	LP	(also on CD)	1991
FALL 049	U.K. Subs	Live In Croatia	(Free CD with 050)		1991
FALL 050	U.K. Subs	Normal Service Resumed	LP	(also on CD)	1993
FALL 051	U.K. Subs	Jodie Foster/Here Comes Alex/Another Cuba		PS	1997

Compilation and discography Mark Brennan. Special thanks to Alan Hauser.

Fetish (London)

7" Singles:

Cat. No.	Artist	Titles			Year
FE 001	L.O.K.	Funhouse/Starlet Love/Tell Me		PS	1979
FE 002	WKGB	Non-Stop/Ultramarine		PS	1979
FE 003	Bongos	Telephoto Lens/Glow In The Dark		PS	1980
FE 004	Snatch	Shopping for Clothes/Joey/Red Army		PS	1980
FE 005	Bongos	In The Congo / Mambo Sun		PS	1981
FE 006	Throbbing Gristle	Discipline/Discipline (Two different live takes)		12", PS	1981
FE 007	Bush Tetras	Boom/Das Ah Riot		PS	1981
FE 008	Clock DVA	4 Hours/Sensorium		PS	1981
FE 009	Bongos	Bulrushes/Automatic Doors		PS	1982
FE 12	Stephen Mallinder	Temperature Drop/Cool Down		PS	1981
FE 14	Perry Haines	What's What/What's Funk	(also 12")	PS	1981
FE 16-EP	Bush Tetras	Rituals EP		12", PS	1982

Albums

Cat. No.	Artist	Titles		Year
FR 2001	Throbbing Gristle	Second Annual Report		1977
FR 2002	Clock DVA	Thirst		1981
FR 2003	8-Eyed Spy	8-Eyed Spy		1981
FR 2004	Bongos	The Bongos		1981
FR 1	Various	Shake, Rattle, And Roll		198?
FM 2009	Bongos	Time And The River	Mini-LP	1982

Fiction (London)

7" Singles (12" singles same, but with prefic FICSX):

Cat. No.	Artist	Titles			Year
FICS 001	Cure	Killing An Arab/10:15 Saturday Night	PS. Also SMALL 11 (see Small Wonder)		1979
FICS 002	Cure	Boys Don't Cry/Plastic Passion		PS	1979
FICS 003	Purple Hearts	Millions Like Us/Beat That!		PS	1979
FICS 004	Back To Zero	Your Side Of Heaven/Back To Back		PS	1979
FICS 005	Cure	Jumping Someone Else's Train/I'm Cold		PS	1979
FICS 006	Cult Hero	I'm A Cult Hero/I Dig You		PS	1979
FICS 007	Purple Hearts	Frustration/Extraordinary Sensation		PS	1979
FICS 008	Passions	Hunted/Oh No, It's You		PS	1979
FICS 009	Purple Hearts	Jimmy/What Am I		PS	1980
FICS 010	Cure	A Forest/Another Journey	(also 12")	PS	1980
FICS 012	Cure	Primary/Descent	(also 12")	PS	1981
FICS 013	Associates	A/Would I... Bounce Back	(also 12")	PS	1981
FICS 014	Cure	Charlotte Sometimes/Splintered In The Head		PS	1981

Albums:

Cat. No.	Artist	Titles	Year
FIX 1	Cure	Three Imaginary Boys	1979
FIX 3	Passions	Michael and Miranda	1980
FIX 6	Cure	Faith	1981

Fresh (London)

7" Singles:

Cat. No.	Artist	Titles		Year
FRESH 1	Family Fodder	Playing Golf With My Flesh Crawling/My Baby Takes Valium	PS	1981
FRESH 2	Dark	My Friends/John Wayne	PS	1981
FRESH 3	Art Attacks	Punk Rock Stars/Rat City/First And Last	PS	1981
FRESH 4	Terry Hooley and The Terrors	Laugh At Me/Terry Hooley And My Ways: Laugh At Me	PS	1981
FRESH 5	Second Layer	Flesh As Property EP (Courts Or Wars/Metal Sheet/Germany)	PS	1981
FRESH 6	Metrophase	In Black/Neobeauty/Cold Rebellion	PS	1981
FRESH 7	Bernie Torme Band	All Day And All Of The Night/What's Next	PS	1981
FRESH 8	Family Fodder	Warm/Desire	PS	1981
FRESH 10	Cuddly Toys	Madman/Join The Girls	PS	1981
FRESH 11	Four Kings	Loving You Is No Disgrace/Disgraceful Version	PS	1981
FRESH 12	U.K. Decay	For My Country/Unwind Tonight	PS	1981
FRESH 13	Dark	Hawaii Five-O Theme/Don't Look Now	PS	1981
FRESH 14	Menace	The Young Ones/Tomorrow's World/Live For Today	PS	1981
FRESH 15	Family Fodder	Deborah Harry/Deborah Harry (version)	PS	1981

Cat. No.	Artist	Titles		Year
FRESH 16	Manufactured Romance	Time Of My Life/Room To Breathe	PS	1981
FRESH 17	Wall	Ghetto/Another New Day/Mercury	PS	1981
FRESH 18	They Must Be Russians	Don't Try To Cure Yourself/The Truth About Kanga Parts/Air To Breathe	PS	1981
FRESH 19	Big Hair	Puppet On A String/Lies	PS	1981
FRESH 21	Dumb Blondes	Strange Love/Sorrow	PS	1981
FRESH 22	Family Fodder	Savoir Faire/Carnal Knowledge	PS	1981
FRESH 24	Dark	Einstein's Brain/Muzak	PS	1981
FRESH 25	Cuddly Toys	Someone's Crying/Bring On The Ravers/Dancing Glass (instrumental)/Broken Mirrors/Slide	PS	1981
FRESH 26	U.K. Decay	Unexpected Guests/Dresden	PS	1981
FRESH 27	Wall	Hobby For A Day/Redeemer/8334	PS	1981
FRESH 28	J.C.'s Mainmen	Casual Trousers/Earbending	PS	1981
FRESH 29	Play Dead	Poison Takes A Hold/Introduction	PS	1981
FRESH 30	Wasted Youth	Rebecca's Room/Things Never Seem The Same As They Did	PS	1981
FRESH 34	Beasts In Cages	My Coo Ca Choo/Sandcastles	PS	1981
FRESH 35	Dark	In The Wires/Shattered Glass	PS	1981
FRESH 37	Family Fodder	Schizophrenia Parts 1 And 2	PS, 12" cat. no. 37/12	1981
FRESH 38	Play Dead	TV Eye/Final Epitaph	PS	1981
FRESH 39	Cuddly Toys	It's a Shame/Fall Down	PS	1982
FRESH 40	Levi Dexter and The Ripchords	I Get So Excited/Other Side Of Midnight	PS	1982
FRESH 46	Dark	Masque/War Zone	PS	1982
FRESH NBP 1	Nancy Peppers	I Believe/Where Did We Go Wrong	PS	1982

Albums:

Cat. No.	Artist	Titles	Year
FRESH LP 1	Cuddly Toys	Guillotine Theatre	1981
FRESH LP 3	Family Fodder	Monkey Banana Kitchen	1981
FRESH LP 4	Wilko Johnson	Ice On Motorway	1981

Fried Egg

7" Singles:

Cat. No.	Artist	Titles		Year
EGG 1	Shoes For Industry	Can't Help It/Laugh Beat	PS	1979
EGG 2	Wild Beasts	Minimum Maximum/Another Noun	PS	1979
EGG 3	The Fans	Givin' Me That Look/Stay The Night/He'll Have To Go	PS	1979
EGG 4	Shoes For Industry	Spend/Sheepdog Trials Inna Babylon	PS	1981
EGG 7	Art Objects	Hard Objects/Bibliotheque/Fit Of Pique	PS	1981
EGG 8	Exploding Seagulls	Johnny Runs To The Cinema/Take Me To The Cinema	PS	1981
EGG 9	Various Artists	Original Mixed Up Kid/Unofficial Secrets	PS	1981
EGG 10	The Fans	You Don't Live Here/Following You	PS	1981
EGG 11	The Untouchables	Keep On Walking/Keep Your Distance	PS	1981
EGG 12	Electric Guitars	Health/Continental Shelf	PS	1981

Albums:

Cat. No.	Artist	Titles	Year
FRY 1	Shoes For Industry	Talk Like A Whelk	1981
FRY 2	Various Artists	E(gg)clectic	1981

Get Back (Italy)

Albums:

Cat. No.	Artist	Titles		Year
GET 6	The Drones	Further Temptations	(2-LP)	1996
GET 7	Anti-Pasti	The Last Call		1996
GET 8	Menace	G.L.C. The Final Vinyl		1996
GET 9	Chron Gen	Chronic Generation		199?
GET 10	Various Artists	No Future, The Best And The Rest		1997
GET 11	Various Artists	Riot City		1997
GET 12	Various Artists	Secret Records (The Best And The Rest)	(LP/CD)	1997
GET 13	Penetration	The Early Years		1997
GET 14	Blitz	All Out Attack		1997
GET 15	The Partisans	Police Story		1997
GET 16	Attak	Zombies		1997
GET 17	Abrasive Wheels	When The Punks Go Marchin' In		1997
GET 18	The Fits	Too Many Rules	(LP/CD)	1997
GET 19	Red Alert	Rebels In Society	(LP/CD)	1997

Cat. No.	Artist	Titles		Year
GET 20	Special Duties	Distorted Truth	(LP/CD)	1997
GET 21	One Way System	Gutterbox	(3-LP Boxset)	1997
GET 22	Dead Man's Shadow	The 4 P's	(LP/CD)	1997
GET 23	Threats	Wasted	(LP/CD)	1997
GET 24	The Adverts	The Complete Peel Sessions	(2-LP)	1997
GET 25	The Drones	The Attic Tapes 75-82		1997
GET 26	Alternative TV	The Image Has Cracked		1998
GET 27	Eater	The Album		1998
GET 28	The Varukers	Bloodsuckers		1998
GET 29	Vice Squad	BBC Sessions		1998
GET 30	The Adverts	Singles Collection		1998
GET 31	Destroy All Monsters	Destroy All Monsters		1998
GET 32	Jayne County	Goddess Of Wet Dreams		1998
GET 33	The Stooges	Rubber		1998
GET 34	Lydia Lunch	Widowspeak	(2-LP)	1998
GET 35	The Boys	The Boys		1998
GET 36	Sham 69	Tell Us The Truth		1998
GET 37	Disorder	Complete Disorder		1998
GET 38	Chelsea	Chelsea		1999
GET 39	Various Artists	This Is Mod	(2-LP)	1999
GET 40	Raped	Complete Recordings		1999
GET 41	The Partisans	The Time Was Right		1999
GET 42	Various Artists	Carry On Oi!		1999
GET 43	The 4-Skins	Low Life		1999
GET 44	The 4-Skins	From Chaos To 1984		1999
GET 45	The Maniacs	Ain't No Legend		1999
GET 46	Various Artists	Oi! Oi! That's Yer Lot		1999
GET 47	Hollywood Brats	Hollywood Brats		1999
GET 48	Chaos UK	Total Chaos		1999
GET 49	Johnny Thunders	Chinese Rocks		1999
GET 50	The Varukers	The Punk Singles 1981-1985		2000
GET 51	The Boys	To Hell With The Boys		2000
GET 52	The Boys	Boys Only		2000
GET 53	The Boys	Alternative Chartbusters		2000
GET 54	Pere Ubu	The Modern Dance		2000
GET 55	Johnny Thunders	Born To Loose		2000
GET 56	Sex Pistols	Burton-On-Trent Recordings		2000
GET 57	Sid Vicious	Live At Max's 1978		2000
GET 58	Pere Ubu	Dub Housing		2000
GET 59	Pere Ubu	New Picnic Time		2000
GET 60	New York Dolls	Actress: Birth Of The New York Dolls	(LP/CD)	2000
GET 61	UK Subs	Live At The Roxy		2000
GET 62	Iggy Pop	Nuggets	(2-LP)	2000
GET 63	Eddie and The Hot Rods	Doing Anything They Wanna Do		2000
GET 65	The Vibrators	Independent Punk Singles Collection	(2-LP)	2000
GET 66	The Modern Lovers	The Modern Lovers		2000
GET 67	Jonathan Richman and The Modern Lovers	Jonathan Richman and The Modern Lovers		2000
GET 68	Nico	Heroine		2000
GET 69	Joy Division	Preston 28th February 1980		2000
GET 70	Anti-Pasti	Caution In The Wind		2000
GET 71	Blitz	The Complete Singles Collection		2000
GET 72	Various Artists	This Is Mod Vol. 2		2000
GET 73	Pere Ubu	Terminal Tower		2001
GET 74	Buzzcocks	Beating Hearts (Manchester 1978)	(2-LP)	2001
GET 211	One Way System	All Systems Go		2001
GET 212	One Way System	Writing On The Wall		2001

Good Vibrations (Belfast, Northern Ireland)

Singles:

Cat. No.	Artist	Titles		Year
GOT 1	Rudi	Big Time / Number 1	PS	1978
GOT 2	Victim	Strange Thing By Night / Mixed Up World	PS	1978
GOT 3	The Outcasts	Just Another Teenage Rebel / Love Is For Sops	PS	1978
GOT 4	The Undertones	Teenage Kicks / Smarter Than You / True Confessions / Emergency Cases	PS	1978
GOT 5	X-Dreamysts	Right Way Home / Dance Away Love	PS	1978

Cat. No.	Artist	Titles		Year
GOT 6	Protex	Don't Ring Me Up / Your Attention / Listening In	PS	1978
GOT 7	Battle Of The Bands	The Outcasts -The Cops Are Comin' / Rudi — Overcome By Fumes / The Idiots- Parents / Spider -Dancin' In The Street	2 x 7", PS	1978
GOT 8	Ruefrex	One By One / Cross The Line / Don't Panic	PS	1980
GOT 9	The Tearjerkers	Love Affair / Bus Stop	PS	1979
GOT 10	The Moondogs	Ya Don't Do Ya / She's Nineteen	PS	1979
GOT 11	Tee Vees	Doctor Headlove / War Machine	PS	1979
GOT 12	Rudi	I Spy EP:- I Spy / Sometimes / Ripped In Two / Genuine Reply	PS	1979
GOT 13	The Shapes	Airline Disasters / Blast Off	PS	1979
GOT 14	P.B.R. Streetgang	Big Day	One sided flexi disc	
GOT 15	Andy White	Six String Street / Travelling Circus	PS	1979
GOT 16	The Kameras	Artificial Joy	Not Released	
GOT 17	The Outcasts	Self Conscious Over You / Love You For Never	PS	1979
GOT 18	The Bankrobbers	On My Mind / All Night	PS	1979

Good Vibrations International

Singles:

Cat. No.	Artist	Titles		Year
GVI 1	The Bears	Insane / Decisions	PS	1979
GVI 2	The Jets	Original Terminal / Iceburn	PS	1979
GVI 3	Static Routines	Rock 'n' Roll Circus / Sheet Music	PS	1979
GVI 4	Not Released			
GVI 5	Strange Movements	Dancing In The Ghetto / Amuse Yourself	PS	1979

Albums:

Cat. No.	Artist	Titles	Year
BIG 1	The Outcasts	Self Conscious Over You	1979
BIG 2	Not Released		
BIG 3	The Nerves	Notre Demo	1981

Harry May

CDs:

Cat. No.	Artist	Titles	Year
MAYOCD 101	Blitz	Warriors	1999
MAYOCD 102	Cockney Rejects	Greatest Cockney Rip Off	1999
MAYOCD 103	The 4-Skins	Clockwork Skinhead	1999
MAYOCD 104	Infa Riot	In For A Riot	1999
MAYOCD 105	Stiff Little Fingers	Tin Soldiers	1999
MAYOCD 106	The Vibrators	Public Enemy No. 1	1999
MAYOCD 107	UK Subs	Warhead	1999
MAYOCD 108	Demented Are Go	Satan's Rejects	1999
MAYOCD 109	The Selecter	Too Much Pressure	1999
MAYOCD 110	Various Artists	Oi! Fuckin' Oi!	1999
MAYOCD 111	Last Resort	King Of The Jungle	1999
MAYOCD 112	Cock Sparrer	Chip On My Shoulder	1999
MAYOCD 113	The Boys	Sick On You	1999
MAYOCD 114	The Lurkers	Ain't Got A Clue	1999
MAYOCD 115	The Macc Lads	Gods Gift To Women	1999
MAYOCD 116	Angelic Upstarts	Never Ad Nothing	1999
MAYOCD 117	The Adicts	Joker In The Pack	1999
MAYOCD 118	Bad Manners	Special Brew	1999
MAYOCD 119	Guana Batz	Can't Take The Pressure	1999
MAYOCD 120	Various Artists	In The Mood For Ska	1999
MAYOCD 121	Red Alert	Border Guards	2001
MAYOCD 123	The Skatalites	Guns Of Navarone	2001
MAYOCD 124	King Kurt	Alcoholic Rat	2001
MAYOCD 125	Various Artists	A Proper Fucking Punk Album	2001
MAYOCD 500	The Exploited	Live On Stage	2001
MAYOCD 501	Various Artists	Oi! Chartbusters Vol. 1	2000
MAYOCD 502	Various Artists	Oi! Chartbusters Vol. 2	2000
MAYOCD 503	4-Skins	From Chaos To 1984	2000
MAYOCD 504	Anti-Nowhere League	Live In Yugoslavia	2000
MAYOCD 505	Angelic Upstarts	Lost And Found	2000
MAYOCD 513	Various Artists	Stomping At The Klub Foot	2000
MAYOCD 516	Various Artists	Oi! The Resurrection	2000
MAYOCD 517	The Macc Lads	The Beer Necessities	2000

Cat. No.	Artist	Titles		Year
CAN CAN 001CD	Bad Manners	Can Can		1997
CAN CAN 002CD	Various Artists	Oi! The Tin		1997
CAN CAN 003CD	Last Resort	Violence In Our Minds		1997
CAN CAN 004CD	Various Artists	The Skinhead Tin		1997
CAN CAN 005CD	Cockney Rejects	Oi! Oi! Oi!		1997
CAN CAN 006CD	The 4-Skins	One Law For Them		1997
CAN CAN 007CD	Cock Sparrer	England Belongs		1997
CAN CAN 008CD	The Exploited	Dead Cities		2000
CAN CAN 009CD	The Ruts	In A Can		2000
CAN CAN 010CD	Judge Dread	Judge Dread's Big Tin		2000
CAN CAN 011CD	The Business	Harry May		2000
CAN CAN 012CD	Anti-Nowhere League	So What		2000
AWOL 1	The Oppressed	Noise EP:- Cum On Feel The Noise/Mama Weer All Crazee Now/Gudbuy T'Jane	PS	
AWOL 2	The Last Resort	Violence In Our Minds EP:- Violence In Our Minds/Held Hostage/Soul Boys/Eight Pounds A Week	PS	
AWOL 3	Cock Sparrer	England Belongs To Me/Argy Bargy	PS	

Heartbeat (Bristol)

7" Singles:

Cat. No.	Artist	Titles		Year
PULSE 2	Europeans	Europeans/Voices	PS	1979
12 PULSE 3	Glaxo Babies	This Is Your Life EP (This Is Your Life/Stay Awake/Because Of You/Who Killed Bruce Lee?)	PS	1979
PULSE 4	Various	Alternatives EP (The Numbers: Alternative Suicide/X-Certs: Blue Movies/Joe Public: Hotel Rooms/48 Hours: Back To Ireland)	PS	1979
PULSE 5	Glaxo Babies	Christine Keeler/Nova Bossanova	PS	1979
PULSE 6	Private Dicks	She Said Go/Private Dicks	PS	1979
PULSE 7	Apartment	The Car/Winter	PS	1980
PULSE 8	Glaxo Babies	Shake (The Foundations)/She Went To Pieces	PS	1980
PULSE 9	Letters	Nobody Loves Me/Don't Want You Back	PS	1979
PULSE 10	Art Objects	Showing Off To Impress The Girls/Our Silver Sister	PS	1980
PULSE 11	Final Eclipse	Birdsong/New Dawn	PS	1980

Albums:

Cat. No.	Artist	Titles	Year
HB 1	Various	Avon Calling—The Bristol Compilation	1979
HB 2	Glaxo Babies	Nine Months To The Disco	1980
HBM 3	Glaxo Babies	Put Me On The Guest List	1980
HB 4	Transmitters	And We Call This Leisure Time	1981
HB 5	Art Objects	Bagpipe Music	1981

I-Spy (London, distributed by Arista)

Singles:

Cat. No.	Artist	Titles		Year
SEE 1	Secret Affair	Time ForAction/Soho Strut	PS	1979
SEE 2	Squire	Walking Down The Kings Road/It's A Mod, Mod, Mod World	PS	1979
SEE 3	Secret Affair	Let Your Heart Dance/Sorry Wrong Number	PS	1979
SEE 4	Squire	The Face Of Youth Today/I Know A Girl	PS	1979
SEE 5	Secret Affair	My World/So Cool	PS	1980
SEE 6	Laurel Atkin	Rudy Got Married/Honey Come Back To Me	PS	1980
SEE 8	Secret Affair	Sounds Of Confusion/Take It Or Leave It	PS	1980
SEE 10	Secret Affair	Do You Know/Dance Master	PS	1981
SEE 11	Secret Affair	Lost In The Night (Mack The Knife)/The Big Beat	PS	1982

Albums:

Cat. No.	Artist	Titles	Year
I-SPY 1	Secret Affair	Glory Boys	1979
I-SPY 2	Secret Affair	Behind Closed Doors	1980
I-SPY 3	Secret Affair	Business As Usual	1982

Illegal (London)

7" Singles:

Cat. No.	Artist	Titles		Year
IL 001	Police	Fallout/Nothing Achieving	PS	1977 (reissued 1980)

Cat. No.	Artist	Titles		Year
IL 002	Wayne County and The Electric Chairs	Stuck On You/Paranoia Paradise/The Last Time	PS	1977
IL 003	John Cale	Animal Justice/Hedda Gabbler	PS	1977
IL 004	Menace	Screwed Up/Insane Society	PS	1977
IL 005	Wayne County and The Electric Chairs	What You Got/Thunder When She Walks	PS	1977
IL 006	John Cale	Jack The Ripper In The Moulin Rouge/ Memphis	(unissued, test pressings only)	1977
IL 007	Spirit	Nature's Way/Stone Free	PS	1977
IL 008	Menace	I Need Nothing/Electrocutioner	PS	1978
IL 009	Johnny Curious and The Strangers	In Tune/Road To Cheltenham/Jennifer/Pissheadville	PS	1978
ILS 010	Vermillion	Angry Young Women/Nymphomania/Wild Boys	PS	1978
ILS 011	Lines	White Night/Barbican	PS	1979
ILS 012	Kim Fowley	In My Garage/Rubber Rainbow	PS	1979
ILS 013	Cramps	Gravest Hits EP (Human Fly/The Way I Walk/Domino/Surfin Board / Lonesome Town)	PS	1979
ILS 014	Root Boy Slim and Sex Change Band	Dare To Be Fat/World War III	PS	1979
ILS 015	Vermillion and The Aces	I Like Motorcycles/The Letter	PS	1979
ILS 016	Mick Dorey and The Sirens	Paranoia Station/Jacqueline Foster	PS	1979
ILS 017	Cramps	Fever/Garbageman	PS	1979
ILS 018	Skafish	Disgracing The Family Name/Work Song	PS	1980
ILS 019	Split Enz	I See Red/Give It A Whirl/Hermit McDermitt	PS	1980
ILS 020	Skafish	Obsessions Of You/Sink Or Swim	PS	1980
ILS 021	Cramps	Drug Train/Love Me/I Can't Hardly Stand It	PS	1980
ILS 022	Skafish	Maybe One Time/No Liberation Here	PS	1980
ILS 023	Patrick D. Martin	Computer Datin'/Police Paranoia	PS	1981
ILS 025	Renaissance	Fairies Living At The Bottom/Remember	PS	1981
ILS 027	Renaissance	Bonjour Swansong/ Ukraine Ways	PS	1982
ILS 028	Lords Of The New Church	New Church/Livin' On Livin'	PS	1982
ILS 029	The Cosmetics	The Crack / ?	PS	1982
ILS 030	Lords Of The New Church	Open Your Eyes/Girls Girls Girls	PS	1982
ILS 031	Wall Of Voodoo	Interstate 15/There's Nothing On The Side	PS	1982
ILS 032	The Alarm	Marching On/Across The Border/Lie Of The Land	PS	1982
ILS 033	Lords Of The New Church	Russian Roulette/Young Don't Cry	PS	1982
ILS 034	Gene October	Suffering In The Land/Suffering Dub	PS	1983
ILS 035	Crown Of Thorns	Kingdom Come/Gone Are The Days	PS	1983
ILS 036	Wall Of Voodoo	Mexican Radio/Call Of The West	PS	1984

Albums:

Cat. No.	Artist	Titles		Year
ILP 001	Spirit	Spirit Live		1977
ILP 002	Kim Fowley	Sunset Boulevard		1978
ILP 003	Root Boy Slim and Sex Change Band	Root Boy Slim and The Sex Change Band		1979
ILP 004	Root Boy Slim and Sex Change Band	Zoom		1979
ILP 005	Cramps	Songs The Lord Taught Us		1980
ILP 006	Various	Doing Time On Vinyl	sampler	19??
ILP 007	Skafish	Skafish		1979
ILP 008	Renaissance	Camera Camera		1981
ILP 009	Lords Of The New Church	Lords Of The New Church		1982
ILP 010	Wall Of Voodoo	Call Of The West		1982
ILP 011	Various Artists	Defiant Pose		1983
ILP 012	Cramps	Off The Bone		1983
ILP 013				
ILP 014	Yip Yip Coyote	Yip Yip Coyote		1984
ILP 015				
ILP 016	Lords Of The New Church	Killer Lords		
ILP 017	Various	Athens Ga - Inside Out		
ILP 018				
ILP 019				
ILP 020	Shok Paris	Steel And Sunlight		1988
ILP 021	Lords Of The New Church	Live At The Spit		1988
ILP 022	Wall Of Voodoo	Ugly Americans		1988
ILP 023	Balancing Act	Three Squares And A Roof		1988
ILP 024	Chelsea	Backtrax		1988
ILP 025				
ILP 026	Bears	Rise And Shine		1988
ILP 027	Seducer	Too Much Ain't Enough		1988
ILP 028				
ILP 029	Let's Active	Every Dog Has Its Day		1989
ILP 030	Billy Currie	Transportation		1989
ILP 031	Steve Hunter	The Deacon		1989

Cat. No.	Artist	Titles		Year
ILP 032	Jimmy Z	Anytime Anyplace		1989
ILP 033	Various	Guitar Speak		1989
ILP 034	Various	No Speak Sampler		1989
ILP 035	Gary Numan	Metal Rhythm		1989
ILP 036	Stewart Copeland	Equalizer		1989
ILP 037	Pete Haycock	Guitar And Son		1989
ILP 038	William Orbit	Strange Cargo		1989
ILP 039	Wishbone Ash	Nouveau Calls		1989

Industrial (London, distributed by Rough Trade)

Various Formats:

Cat. No.	Artist	Titles		Year
IR 0001	Throbbing Gristle	Best Of Volume II	(private cassette, 50 copies only)	1976
IR 00012	Throbbing Gristle	2nd Annual Report	LP, 785 only, white heavy duty sleeve, with questionnaire, xerox strip and two stickers	1977
IR 0003	Throbbing Gristle	United/Zyklon B Zombie	7", (re-pressed, 1,000 white vinyl, 1,000 clear vinyl IR 0003/U, 1979; later with extended B-side and 'Memorial Issue' in matrix, 1980)	1978
IR 0004	Throbbing Gristle	D.O.A. The Third And Final Report	LP (mail-order version includes postcard and calendar, later 'DJ confusion' copy with banded tracks, 1979)	1978
IR 0005	Monte Cazazza	To Mom On Mother's Day/Candy Man	7", with insert, 2,500 only	1979
IR 0006	The Leather Nun	Slow Death EP		1979
IR 0007	Thomas Leer/Robert Rental	The Bridge	LP	1979
IR 0008	Throbbing Gristle	20 Jazz Funk Greats	LP (1st 2,000 with B&W poster)	1979
IR 0009	Throbbing Gristle	Heathen Earth	LP (gatefold sleeve, 1st 785 on blue vinyl)	1980
IR 0010	Monte Cazazza	Something For Nobody EP		1980
IR 0011	SPK	Meat Processing Section: Slogun/Mekano	7", labels list "Slogan"/"Factory", with insert, as Surgical Penis Klinik	1980
IR 0012	Elizabeth Welch	Stormy Weather/Ya're Blase	7"	1980
IR 0013	Throbbing Gristle	Subhuman/Something Came Over Me	7", in polythene camouflage bag	1980
IR 0014	Dorothy	I Confess/Softness	7"	1980
IR 0015	Throbbing Gristle	Adrenalin/Distant Dreams (Part 2)	7", in polythene camouflage bag	1980
IR 0016	William S. Burroughs	Nothing Here Now But The Recordings	LP	1980
IRVC 1	Throbbing Gristle	Heathen Earth	Video	1980
IRVC 2	Throbbing Gristle	Live At Oundle Public School	Video	1980

Kathedral Records

Album:

Cat. No.	Artist	Title	Year
KATH 1	Various Artists	Sent From Coventry	1980

Lightning Records - The Punk Discography

Singles:

Cat. No.	Artist	Titles		Year
LIG 501	Jet Bronx and The Forbidden	Ain't Doin Nuthin' / I Can't Stand It	PS	
GIL 503	The Mirrors	Cure For Cancer / Nice Vice	PS	1978
GIL 504	Blitzkrieg Bop	Let's Go / Life Is Just A So So / Mental Case	PS	1978
GIL 507	Martin and The Brownshirts	Taxi Driver / Boring	PS	1978
LIG 508	Elton Motello	Jet Boy Jet Girl / Pogo Pogo	PS	1978
GIL 509	Fruit Eating Bears	Chevy Heavy / Fifties Cowboy	PS	1978
GIL 511	Dirty Dogs	Let's Go On My Hands / Shouldn't Do It / Gonna Quit / Guitar In My Hand	PS	1978
GIL 512	Horror Conic	I Don't Mind / England 77	PS	1978
GIL 513	Too Much	Who You Wanna Be / Another Time Another Place	PS	1978
GIL 520	The Nerves	TV Adverts / Sex Education	PS	1978
LIG 525	Jet Bronx and The Forbidden	Rock 'N' Roll Romance / On The Wall	PS	1978
GIL 531	Cane	Dice / Suburban Guerrilla / D.K. Dance	PS	1978
GIL 534	Snifters	I Like Boys / Baby Punker	PS	1978
GIL 536	Neville Wanker and The Punters	Boys On The Dole / Sing A Little Song For The Boys..	PS	1978
GIL 540	The Mirrors	Dark Glasses / 999	PS	1978
GIL 542	Nasty Media	Spiked Copy / Winter / The Ripper / John Peel	PS	1978
GIL 543	Blitzkrieg Bop	U.F.O. / Viva Bobby Joe	PS	1979

GIL 546	Krypton Tunes	Limited Vision / Jail	PS	1978
GIL 549	The Jerks	Cool / Jerkin	PS	1978
GIL 552	Too Much	Be Mine / Kick Me One More Time / It's Only For Me	(gatefold, PS)	1978

Underground Records:

| URA 1 | The Jerks | Get Your Woofing Dog Off Me / Hold My Hand | PS | 1978 |

Plus Mod Release:

| GIL 519 | The Exits | The Fashion Plague / Cheam | PS | 1978 |

Album:

Cat. No.	Artist	Titles		Year
LIP 2	Various Artists	Farewell To The Roxy		1978

Link

White Link Albums:

Cat. No.	Artist	Titles		Year
LP 01	Various	Oi! The Ressurection	Compilation	1987
LP 02	4-Skins	Wonderful World Of		1987
LP 03	Various	Oi! Chartbusters Vol. 1	Compilation	1987
LP 04	Sham 69	Live And Loud		1987

Blue Link Albums:

Cat. No.	Artist	Titles		Year
LP 05	Cock Sparrer	Live And Loud		1987
LP 06	The Meteors	Live And Loud		1987
LP 07	Bad Manners	Live And Loud		1987
LP 08	Section 5	For The Love Of Oi!		1987
LP 09	Cockney Rejects	Live And Loud		1987
LP 010	The Adicts	Live And Loud		1987
LP 011	Various	The Sound Of Oi!	Compilation	1987
LP 012	Accident	Crazy		1987
LP 013	The Ruts	Live And Loud		1987
LP 014	Various	Oi!.. The Picture Disc	Compilation	1987
LP 015	4-Skins	A Few Skins More. Vol. 1	Dble	1987
LP 016	Various	Oi! Chartbusters Vol. 2	Compilation	1987
LP 017	Last Resort/Combat 84	Death Or Glory	Split Album	1987
LP 018	The Exploited	Live And Loud		1987
LP 019	Angelic Upstarts	Blood On The Terraces		1987
LP 020	Anti-Heroes	That's Right		1987
LP 021	4-Skins	A Few Skins More, Vol. 2	Dble	1987
LP 022	Vicious Rumours	Sickest Men In Town		1987
LP 023	Various	Oi! Glorious Oi!	Compilation	1987
LP 024	The Blood/The Gonads	Full Time Result	Split Album	1987
LP 025	Sham 69	Live And Loud, Vol. 2		1988
LP 026	Stiff Little Fingers	Live And Loud	Dble	1988
LP 027	The Magnificent	Hit And Run		1988
LP 028	Various	Beat Of The Street	Sampler	1988
LP 029	Blitz	Blitzed.. An All Out Attack		1988
LP 030	Various	Son Of Oi!	Compilation	1988

Black Link Albums:

Cat. No.	Artist	Titles		Year
LP 031	Section 5	Street Rock 'n' Roll		1988
LP 032	Cock Sparrer	Runnin' Riot		1988
LP 033	The Partisans	The Time Was Right		1988
LP 034	Various	Oi! Chartbusters Vol. 3	Compilation	1988
LP 035	The Business	Welcome To The Real World		1988
LP 036	Various	The Oi! Of Sex	Compilation	1988
LP 037	Various	Oi! The Picture Disc Vol. 2	Compilation	1988
LP 038	Various	Oi! That's What I Call Music	Compilation	1988
LP 039	The Glory	We Are What We Are		1988
LP 040	Angelic Upstarts	Live And Loud		1988
LP 041	Various	Oi! The Main Event	Compilation	1988
LP 042	Splodgenessabounds	Live And Loud		1988
LP 043	The Business	Suburban Rebels		1988
LP 044	Major Accident	Tortured Tunes		1988
LP 045	The Last Resort	Kings Of The Jungle		1988

LP 046	The Business	Smash The Discos		1988
LP 047	The Heavy Metal Kids	Live And Loud		1988
LP 048	Chaotic Dischord	You've Got To Be Obscene To Be Heard		1988
LP 049	The Gonads	Live And Loud		1988
LP 050	Vice Squad	Live And Loud		1988
MLP 051	Frantic Flintstones	Rockin' Out	Mini LP	1988
LP 052	Infa Riot	Live And Loud		1988
LP 053	Various	Underground Rockers	Compilation	1988
LP 054	Various	Oi! Chartbusters Vol. 4	Compilation	1988
LP 055	Various	A Guaranteed Mug Free Zone	Sampler	1988
LP 056	Close Shave	Oi! Kinnock Give Us Back Our Rose		1988
LP 057	Various	The U.S. Of Oi!		1988
LP 058	The Coffin Nails	A Fistfull Of Burgers		1988
LP 059	Anti-Heroes	Don't Tread On Me		1988
LP 060	The Deltas	Tuffer Than Tuff		1988
MLP 061	Combat 84	The Charge Of The 7th Cavalry		1989
MLP 062	The Nitros	Nightshades		1988
LP 063	Sex Pistols	Live And Loud	Also cassette MC 063	1989
LP 064	The Business	Loud Proud And Punk – Live		1989
LP 065	The Exploited	Punk's Not Dead		1989
LP 066	The Exploited	Troops Of Tomorrow		1989
LP 067	Various	Carry On Oi!	Compilation	1989
LP 068	Various	Oi! Oi! That's Yer Lot	Compilation	1989
MLP 069	The Polecats	Live And Rockin'		1989
LP 070	Condemned 84	Live And Loud		1989
LP 071	The Kicker Boys	Kicker Boys		1989
LP 072	The Frantic Flintstones	Not Christmas Album		1989
LP 073	The Crack	In Search Of		1989
MLP 074	Some Kinda Earthquake	Devastating	Mini LP	1989
MLP 075	Sham 69	Sham's Last Stand	Mini LP	1989
LP 076	Guttersnipe Army	Never Die		1989
LP 077	Various	Katz Keep Rockin'	Compilation	1989
LP 078	Various	The Secret Life Of Punks	Compilation	1989
LP 079	Infa Riot	Still Out Of Order		1989
LP 080	Boz and The Bozmen	Dress In Dead Men's Suits		1989
LP 081	Various	Oi! Chartusters Vol. 5	Compilation	1989
LP 082	The Batfinks	Wazzed 'n' Blasted		1989
LP 083				
MLP 084	Demented Are Go	The Day The Earth Spat Blood	Mini LP	1989
LP 085	The Gonads	The Revenge Of		1989
LP 086	Moonstomp	They Never See		1989
MLP 087	The Lurkers	King Of The Mountain	Mini LP	1989
LP 088	The Resort	1989	White label test pressings were made.	1989
LP 089	Various	Rockin' At The Take Two	Compilation	1989
LP 090	4-Skins	Live And Loud		1989
LP 091	The Turnpike Cruisers	Drive Drive Drive		1989
LP 092	Slaughter and The Dogs	The Slaughterhouse Tapes		1989
LP 093	The Radiacs	Hellraiser		1989
LP 094	Various	Underground Rockers Vol. 2	Compilation	1989
LP 095	Various	Pop Oi!	Compilation	1989
LP 096	The Deltas	Live And Rockin'		1989
LP 097	The Business	Live And Loud		1989
LP 098	The Frantic Flintstones	Live And Rockin'		1989
LP 099	Sugar Puff Demons	Falling From Grace	Lyric sheet with first 1,000	1989
MLP 100	The AB's	Mentalenema	Mini LP	1989
MLP 101	The Tailgators	Live And Rockin'	Mini LP	1989
MLP 102	Rockin' Rockett 88	I'm Coming Home	Mini LP. Insert with first 1,000	1989
LP 103	The Lurkers	Live And Loud		1989
LP 104	Dark Streets	Scared Stiff		1989
LP 105	Guitar Gangsters	Prohbition		1989
LP 106	King Kurt	Live And Rockin'		1989
LP 107	999	Live And Loud		1989
LP 108	Peter and The Test Tube Babies	Live And Loud		1989
LP 109	The Frantic Flintstones	The Nightmare Continues... Demonic Verses... Chuck's Revenge		1989
LP 110	The Cropdusters	If The Sober Go To Heaven		1989
LP 111	Various	Katz Keep Rockin' Vol. 2	Compilation	1989
LP 112				
LP 113	Stage Fright	Island Of The Lost Souls		1989

Cat. No.	Artist	Title	Notes	Year
LP 114	Various	New York Hardcore – Where The Wild Ones Are Compilation. Insert with first 3,000.		1989
LP 115	The Business	Saturday's Heroes		1990
LP 116	Demented Are Go	Live And Rockin'		1990
LP 117	Close Shave	Hard As Nails		1990
LP 118	The Coffin Nails	Live And Rockin'		1990
LP 119	Section 5	The Way We Were		1990
LP 120	The Anti-Nowhere League	Live And Loud		1990
LP 121	Distorted Truth	Smashed Hits	Lyric sheet with first 1,500	1990
LP 122	The Batfinks	Live And Rockin'		1990
LP 123	Various	Rockin' At The Take Two Vol. 2	Compilation	1990
LP 124	The Termites	Overload		1990
LP 125	999	The Cellblock Tapes		1990
LP 126	The Tailgators	The Tailgators		1990
LP 127	Various	Oi! Chartbusters Vol. 6	Compilation	1990
LP 128	The Radiacs	Live And Rockin'		1990
LP 129	The Frantic Flintstones	Schlachtof Boogie Woogie		1990
LP 130	Various	Oi! Oi! Oi!	Compilation	1990
LP 131	Rantanplan	Two Worlds At Once		1990
LP 132	Not Released			
LP 133	King Kurt	Destination Demoland		1990
LP 140	Angelic Upstarts	Lost And Found		1990
LP 141	Cock Sparrer	Shock Troops		1990

Mute (London, distributed by Rough Trade) (Early releases)

7" Singles:

Cat. No.	Artist	Titles		Year
MUTE 001	The Normal	T.VO.D./Warm Leatherette	PS	1978
MUTE 002	Fad Gadget	Back to Nature/The Box	PS	1979
MUTE 003	Silicon Teens	Memphis, Tennessee/Let's Dance	PS	1979
MUTE 004	Silicon Teens	Judy In Disguise/Chip 'n' Roll	PS	1979
MUTE 005	Deutsch Amerikanische Freundschaft (D.A.F.)	Kebab Traume/Gezalt	PS	1980
MUTE 006	Fad Gadget	Rickey's Hand/Hand Shake	PS	1980
MUTE 007	Non	Sound Tracks 1-3/Mode Of Infection/Knife Ladder/Can't I Look Straight/Flasheards	PS, eight-track EP with two holes	1980
MUTE 008	Silicon Teens	Sun Flight/Just Like Eddie	PS	1980
MUTE 009	Fad Gadget	Fireside Favourite/Insecticide	PS	1980
MUTE 010	Robert Rental	Double Heart/On Location	PS	1980
MUTE 011	Deutsch Amerikanische Freundschaft (D.A.F.)	Der Rauber Un der Prinz/Tanz Mit Mer	PS	1980
MUTE 012	Fad Gadget	Make Room/Lady Shave	PS	1981
MUTE 013	Depeche Mode	Dreaming of Me/Ice Machine	PS	1981
MUTE 014	Depeche Mode	New Life/Shout!	PS, also 12"	1981
MUTE 015	Non	Rise	12", three-tracks	1981
MUTE 016	Depeche Mode	Just Can't Get Enough/Any Second Now	PS, also 12"	1981
MUTE 017	Fad Gadget	Saturday Night Special/Swallow It Live	PS	1981
MUTE 018	Depeche Mode	See You/Now This Is Fun	PS, also 12"	1982
MUTE 020	Yazoo	Only You/Situation	PS	1982
MUTE 021	Fad Gadget	King of the Flies/Plain Clothes	PS	1982

Albums:

Cat. No.	Artist	Titles	Year
STUMM 1	Deutsch Amerikanische Freundschaft (D.A.F.)	Die Kleinen Und Die Bosen	1980
STUMM 2	Silicon Teens	Music for Parties	1980
STUMM 3	Fad Gadget	Fireside Favourites	1980
STUMM 4	Boyd Rice	Boyd Rice	1981
STUMM 5	Depeche Mode	Speak And Spell	1981
STUMM 6	Fad Gadget	Incontinent	1981
STUMM 8	Fad Gadget	Under The Flag	1982

New Hormones (Manchester)

Various Formats:

Cat. No.	Artist	Titles		Year
ORG 1	Buzzcocks	Spiral Scratch EP: Breakdown / Time's Up / Boredom/ Friends Of Mine	PS, 7"	1977 (reissued 1979)
ORG 3	The Tiller Boys	Big Noise From The Jungle EP: Big Noise From The Jungle/ Statues And Pyramids/What Me Worry	7", PS	1979
ORG 4	Ludus	The Visit EP: Lullaby Cheat/Unveil/Sightseeing/ I Can't Swim, I Have Nightmares	12", PS	1980
ORG 5	Decorators	Twilight View/Reflections	PS	1980
ORG 6	Eric Random	That's What I Like About Me	12", PS four-track mini-album	1980
ORG 7	Dislocation Dance	It's So Difficult/Familiar View/Birthday Outlook/Perfectly In Control	7" EP, PS	1980
ORG 8	Ludus	My Cherry Is In Sherry/Anatomy Is Not Destiny	PS	1981
ORG 9	Diagram Brothers	Bricks/Postal Bargains	PS	1981
ORG 10	Dislocation Dance	Slip the Disc EP	PS	1981
ORG 11	Eric Random	Dow Chemical Company/Skin Deep	PS	1981
ORG 12	Ludus	Patient /Mother's Hour	PS	1981
CAT 1	Ludus	Pickpocket	LP	1981
CAT 2	C.P. Lee Mystery Guild	Radio Sweat	LP	1981
ORG 20	Ludus	Danger Came Smiling	LP	1982
ORG 18	Eric Random Meets Bedlamites	Earthbound Ghost Needs	LP	1982

No Future

7" and 12" Singles:

Cat. No.	Artist	Titles		Year
Oi! 1	Blitz	Somone's Gonna Die/Attack/Fight To Live/45 Revolutions		1982
Oi! 2	The Partisans	Police Story/Killing Machine		1982
Oi! 3	Various	A Country Fit For Heroes	12"	1982
Oi! 4	Peter and The Test Tube Babies	Banned From The Pubs/Moped Lads/Peacehaven Wild Kids		1982
Oi! 5	Red Alert	In Britain/Murder Missile/Screaming At The Nation		1982
Oi! 6	Blitz	Never Surrender/Razors In The Night		1982
Oi! 7	Attak	Today's Generation/Hell/No Escape		1982
Oi! 8	Blitzkrieg	Lest We Forget/Abuse Of Power/Destruction Warfare/Heroes		1982
Oi! 9	The Violators	Gangland/The Fugitive		1982
Oi! 10	The Insane	El Salvador/Chinese Rocks		1982
Oi! 11	Channel 3	I've Got A Gun/Manzanar/Mannequin		1982
Oi! 12	The Partisans	17 Years Of Hell/The Power And The Greed/Bastards In Blue		1982
Oi! 13	Red Alert	Take No Prisoners/Empire Of Crime/Sell Out		1982
Oi! 14	The Samples	Dead Hero/Fire Another Round/Suspicion		1982
Oi! 15	Peter and The Test Tube Babies	Run Like Hell/Up Yer Bum		1982
Oi! 16	Blitz	Warriors/Youth		1982
Oi! 17	Attak	Murder In The Subway/Future Dreams		1982
Oi! 18	Crux/Crash	Keep On Running/Streets At Night/Brighton Front/I'll Die With My Boots On/ Fight For Your Life/Religion/Kill The Cow/TV Times		1982
Oi! 19	The Violators	Summer Of '81/Live Fast Die Young		1983
Oi! 20	Red Alert	City Invasion/Negative Reaction		1983
Oi! 21	The Wall	Day Tripper/Ceremony/Industrial Nightmare /Growing Up/Hall Of/Miracles/ When I'm Dancing/Animal Grip/Castles/Spirit Dance/Funhouse		1983
Oi! 22	The Blood	Megalomania/Calling The Shots/Parasite In Paradise		1983
Oi! 23	Various	A Country Fit For Heroes, Vol. 2	Sampler	1983
Oi! 24	Rose Of Victory	Suffragette City/Overdrive		1983
Oi! 25	Screaming Dead	Night Creatures/Angel Of Death/Necroania		1983
Oi! 26	The Violators	Gangland/The Fugitive/Summer Of '81/Live Fast Die Young/Die With Dignity/ Government Stinks		1983
Oi! 27	Red Alert	There's A Guitar Burning/The Dust Has Settled/Tranquility/All The Way To Glory/ The Revolution Will/Come/Cast Iron's Crusade		1983

Albums:

Cat. No.	Artist	Titles	Year
PUNK 1	Blitz	Voice Of A Generation	1982
PUNK 2	Channel 3	I've Got A Gun	1982
PUNK 3	Peter and The Test Tube Babies	Pissed And Proud	1983
PUNK 4	The Partisans	The Partisans	1983
PUNK 5	Red Alert	We've Got The Power	1983
PUNK 6	Attak	Zombies	1983
PUNK 7	Channel 3	After The Lights Go Out	1983

| PUNK 8 | Various | Angels With Dirty Faces | Compilation | 1983 |
| PUNK 9 | Various | There Is No Future | Compilation | 1984 |

Not Very Nice Records

Albums:

Cat. No.	Artist	Titles	Year
GRR 1	Chaotic Dischord	Now That's What I Call	1985
GRR 2	Chaotic Dischord	Goat Fucking Virgin Killerz From Hell	1986
GRR 3	Chaotic Dischord	Very Fucking Bad	1988

Oi! Records

CDs:

Cat. No.	Artist	Titles		Year
OIR 001	Complete Control	Brick Blood 'n' Guts In 1985		1985
OIR 002	Section 5	We Won't Change		1985
OIR 003	Condemned 84	Battle Scarred		1986
OIR 004	Various	This Is Oi!	Sampler	1986
OIR 005	Vicious Rumours	Any Time Day Or Night		1986
OIR 006	Barbed Wire	The Age That Didn't Care		1986
OIR 007	Last Rough Cause/Society's Rejects	Skins 'n' Punks Vol. 1		1986
OIR 008	Oi! Polloi/The Betrayed	Skins 'n' Punks Vol. 2		1987
OIR 009	The Glory/The Magnificent	Skins 'n' Punks Vol. 3		1987
OIR 010	The Abnormal/Barbed Wire	Skins 'n' Punks Vol. 4		1987
OIR 011	Oi Polloi	Unite And Win		1987
OIR 012	The Oppressed	Dead And Buried		1988
OIR 013	Last Stand	Boston Callin'		1989
OIR 014	The Slaggers	On Yer Toez		1989
OIR 015	The Radicts/The Press	Skins 'n' Punks Vol. 5		1989
OIR 016	Winston and The Churchills	Brewing Since 1983		1990
OPLP 1	The Oppressed	Oi! Oi! Music		1984

Overground (Brighton)

Various Formats:

Cat. No.	Artist	Titles		Year
OVER 01	Satan's Rats	Year Of The Rats/Louise	7" 1,000 only [600 yellow vinyl, 400 white vinyl; also 25 numbered gold vinyl w/l test pressings)	1989
OVER 02	Satan's Rats	In My Love For You/Facade	7", 1,000 only [600 yellow vinyl, 400 white; also 25 no'd gold vinyl w/l test pressings)	1989
OVER 03	TV Personalities	14th Floor/Oxford Street W1	7", no'd PS 600 yellow vinyl, 400 white; 1,000 black vinyl w/ different back on PS	1989
OVER 04	The Soft Boys	The Face Of Death/The Yodelling Hoover	7", 1,000 only [600 yellow vinyl, 400 white]; also 15 gold v. test pressing	1989
OVER 05	The Soft Boys	Raw Cuts	6-track CD, 1,000 only	1989
OVER 06	The Pastels	Songs For Children EP: Heavens Above!/Tea Time Tales/Something Going On [Demo]/Until Morning Comes [Demo]	7"; 2,604 blue vinyl, 840 black, 201 clear, 157 green	1989
OVER 07	The Adolescents	The Adolescents	LP, red vinyl, 900 only	1989
OVER 05	Personality Crisis	Creatures For A While	LP, red vinyl, 1,000 only	1990
OVER 09	Personality Crisis	Twighlight's Last Gleaming/The Jam (live)	7", 1,000 only	1990
OVER 10	The Soft Boys	Raw Cuts	mini-LP, 1,000 only	1990
OVER 11	The Neon Boys	Time EP: (Don't Die/Time/That's All I Know (Right Now)/Love Comes In Spurts)	7", purple vinyl, 2,000 only	1990
OVER 11	The Neon Boys	Time EP	12" test pressing, 20 only	1990
OVER 12	The Dickies	Just Say Yes/Ayatollah You So	7", with lyric sheet, 3,000 only [1,000 mauve vinyl, 1,000 blue, 1,000 white]	1990
OVER 12	The Dickies	Just Say Yes/Ayatollah You So	7", black vinyl test pressing, 50 only	1990
OVER 12CD	The Dickies	Just Say Yes/Ayatollah You So/Dead Heat	CD	1990
OVER 13	TV Personalities	I Know Where Syd Barrett Lives/Arthur The Gardener	7", 2,000 only	1990
OVER 14	Satan's Rats	You Make Me Sick	7", clear vinyl, 567 only	1990
OVER 15	TV Personalities	Silly Girl	7", unissued, 100 test pressings only	
OVER 16CD	The Long Ryders	Metallic B.O.	CD, light brown sleeve, 700 only reissued jointly with Prima [SID 001] in different dark brown sleeve	1990
OVER 17	The Dickies	Roadkill	'tour' flexidisc, 5,000 only	1990

Cat. No.	Artist	Titles		Year
OVER 18	The Pooh Sticks	John Peel Sessions	LP, 2,000 only	1991
OVER 19	The Neon Boys/ Richard Hell and Voidoids (Part III)	That's All I Know (Right Now)/Love Comes In Spurts/High Heeled Wheels/ Don't Die/Time	12", last 2 tracks by Richard Hell & Voidoids (Part III), clear vinyl, 2,000 only	1991
OVER 19CD	The Neon Boys Etc.	That's All I Know (Right Now)	CD, 2,000 only	1991
OVER 20	TV Personalities	Three Wishes/Geoffrey Ingram/And Don't The Kids Just Love It	7", 2,000 only	1991
OVER 21	TV Personalities	Camping In France	live LP; CD adds 3 bonus tracks: "Happy All The Time", "Girl On A Motorcycle" and "Just Call Me Jack"; OVER 21CD	1991
OVER 22	The Undead	Evening Of Desire/Attitude/Slave To Fashion/My Kinda Town	12" 1,500 only	1992
OVER 23	TV Personalities	Smashing Time EP: Smashing Time/King And Country/ Three Cheers For Simon	7", 2,000 only	1992
OVER 24	Richard Hell	Three New Songs EP: The Night Is Coming On/ Baby Huey (Baby Do You Wanna Dance?)/Frank Sinatra	7", 134 yellow, 2,800 black	1992
OVER 24CD	Richard Hell	Three New Songs	CD, 3,000 only	1992
OVER 25	TV Personalities	Part-Time Punks EP: Part Time Punks/Where's Bill Grundy Now?/ Happy Families/Posing At The Roundhouse	7", 2,200 only	1992
OVER 26	Fastbacks/Gas Huffer	Lose/King Of Hubcaps	7", large centre joint release with Steve Priest Fan Club SPFC 4502; pink vinyl, 2,000 only	1992
OVER 27	TV Personalities	Favourite Films/The Dream Inspires/Happy All The Time	7", 2,000 only	1992
OVER 28CD	Various	Communicate!!!! Live At Thames Poly	CD, 1,000 only	1992
OVER 29	Alternative TV Live 1978	CD, joint release with Feel Good All Over FGAO 16		1993
OVER 30	TV Personalities	How I Learned To Love The Bomb EP: How I Learned To Love The Bomb/Now You're Just Being Ridiculous/The God Snaps His Fingers/ A Girl Called Charity/ She Was Only The Grocer's Daughter	12", 2,000 only,	1992 (CD issued 1994)
OVER 3ICD	Mighty Lemon Drops	All The Way (Live In Cincinnati)	CD, 1,600 only	1993
OVER 32	The Undead	There's A Riot In Tompkins Square/Put Your Clothes Back On (live)/ I Want You Dead (live)	7", 1,400 only	1993
OVER 33CD	Crime	San Francisco's Doomed	CD, joint release with Solar Lodge Doomed Two	1994
OVER 34	TV Personalities	A Sense Of Belonging/Baby's Turning Blue	7", 2,000 only	1994
OVER 35CD	Jowe Head	Unhinged	CD	1994
OVER 36/ OVER 36CD	Richard Hell	Another World/Blank Generation/Love Comes In Spurts	7" (2,000 only) and CD (1,500 only)	1994
OVER 37CD	Proles	Stereo Love	CD	1994
OVER 38	TV Personalities	The Prettiest Girl In The World EP: The Prettiest Girl In The World/ Miracles Take Longer/If That's What Love Is/Apples And Oranges	7", 2,000 only	1994
OVER 39CD	Alternative TV	My Life As A Child Star	CD	1994
OVER 4OCD	The June Brides	For Better Or Worse (1983-86)	CD	1995
OVER 41	TV Personalities	I Was A Mod Before You Was A Mod	LP/CD	1995
OVER 42	Thee Headcoatees	The Sound Of The Baskervilles	LP/CD	1995

(Courtesy of Record Collector)

Pax (Sheffield)

Various Formats:

Cat. No.	Artist	Titles		Year
PAX 1	Various	Five Miles To Midnight	12", PS	1981
PAX 2	Danse Society	There Is No Shame In Death: There Is No Shame In Death / Dolphins / These Frayed Edges	12", PS	1981
PAX 3	Stunt Kites	Lebensraum	12", PS	198?
PAX 4	Various	Wargasm Compilation	LP	1982
PAX 5	Danse Society	We're So Happy: Woman's Own / We're So Happy / Continent / Belief	12", PS	1982
PAX 6	Mau Maus	Society's Rejects: Society's Rejects / Secret Society / Images / Social System / The Kill / Leaders / Crisis / The Oath	7", PS	1982
PAX 7	Various	Punk's Dead - Nah Mate The Smell Is Jus Summink In Yer Underpants	12", PS	1982
PAX 8	Mau Maus	No Concern: No Concern / Clampdown / Why Do We Suffer	7", PS	1982
PAX 9	UV Pop	Just A Game / No Song Tomorrow	7", PS	1982
PAX 10	Xtract	Blame It On The Youth: Blame It On The Youth / War Heroes / Iron Lady / Boys In Blue	7", PS	1983
PAX 11	Anti System	Defence Of The Realm: Animal Welfare / No Leader To Choose / Service - 1000 Rifles / Government Lies / Bomb Threat	7", PS	1983

Cat. No.	Artist	Titles		Year
PAX 12	Mau Maus	Facts Of War: Facts Of War / Just Another Day / Unforgotten / Religious Rights / Running With The Pack	7", PS	1983
PAX 13	NOT ISSUED			
PAX 14	Various	Bollox To The Gonads Here's The Testicles	Compilation LP	1983
PAX 15	The Exploited	Rival Leaders: Rival Leaders / Army Style / Singalongabushell	7", PS	1983
PAX 16	Mau Maus	Live At The Marples	LP	1984
PAX 17	Leitmotiv	Silent Run / Living In A Tin	7", PS	1984
PAX 18	The Exploited	Let's Start A War	LP	1984
PAX 19	Various	Daffodils To The Daffodils, Here's The Daffodils	Compilation LP	1984
PAX 20	Mau Maus	Running With The Pack	LP	1984

Picasso Records

Singles:

Cat. No.	Artist	Titles	Year
PIKT 001	Angelic Upstarts	Machine Gun Kelly / Paint It In Red / There's A Drink In It	1985

Albums:

Cat. No.	Artist	Titles	Year
P1K 001	Nan	Friday 13th	198?
P1K 002	Chron Gen	Nowhere To Run	1985
P1K 003	Chelsea	Live And Well	1985
P1K 004	Angelic Upstarts	Last Tango In Moscow	1985
P1K 005	Ligotage	Forgive And Forget	1985
HCLP 001M	Chron Gen	Live At The Waldorf	1985

Rabid (Manchester)

Singles:

Cat. No.	Artist	Titles		Year
TOSH 101	Slaughter and The Dogs	Cranked Up Really High / The Bitch	PS 1st pressing, blue labels, later cream plastic labels	1977
TOSH 101	Slaughter and The Dogs	Cranked Up Really High / The Bitch	PS 2nd pressing, b&w paper labels	1977
TOSH 102	The Nosebleeds	Ain't Bin To No Music School / Fascist Pigs	PS	1977
TOSH 103	John Cooper Clarke	Innocents / Suspended Sentence / Psycle Sluts Parts 1 & 2	orange foldout PS, green labels; later blue foldout PS with blue labels; 'French' pressing with photocopied PS	1978
TOSH 104	Gyro	Central Detention Centre/Purple And Red	PS	1978
TOSH 105	Jilted John	Jilted John / Going Steady	PS	1978
TOSH 106	Ed Banger	Kinnel Tommy / Baby Was A Baby	PS	1978
TOSH 107	Gordon The Moron	De Do Dough Don't Be Dough / (Version)	12", unissued	1978
TOSH 108	unissued			
TOSH 109	Chris Sievey	Baiser / Last	PS	1979
TOSH 110	Tim Green	Who Can Tell / Keep Me With You	PS	1979
TOSH 111	Gordon The Moron	Fit For Nothing / Sold On You	PS	1979
TOSH 112	unissued			
TOSH 113	The Out	Who Is Innocent / Linda's Just A Statue	PS	1979

Associated Singles:

Cat. No.	Artist	Titles		Year
EMI Int. INT 570	Ed Banger	Kinnel Tommy/Baby Was A Baby	PS reissue	1978
EMI Int. INT 567	Jilted John	Jilted John / Going Steady	PS reissue	1978
Virgin VS 308	The Out	Who Is Innocent / Linda's Just A Statue	PS reissue	1979

Albums:

Cat. No.	Artist	Titles		Year
HAT 23	Slaughter and The Dogs	Live Slaughter Rabid Dogs	LP, white sleeve with sticker	1977
NOZE 1	John Cooper Clarke	Ou Est La Maison De Fromage?	LP	1980
LAST 1	Various	The Crap Stops Here	LP, label also lists Absurd	1980

Radar (London)

Singles:

Cat. No.	Artist	Titles		Year
ADA 1	Nick Lowe	I Love The Sound Of Breaking Glass/They Called It Rock	PS	1978
ADA 2	Profits	I'm A Hog For You Baby/What I Want	PS	1978
ADA 3	Elvis Costello and The Attractions	(I Don't Want To Go To) Chelsea / You Belong To Me	PS	1978

Cat. No.	Artist	Titles	Notes		Year
ADA 4	Iggy Pop/James Williamson	Kill City/I Got Nuthin'		PS	1978
ADA 5	La Dusseldorf	La Dusseldorf/Silver Cloud	Released on LP only	PS	1978
ADA 6	Pezband	On And On/I'm Leavin'		PS	1978
ADA 7	Andy Arthurs	I Can Detect You (For 100,000 Miles)/ I Am A Machine	Promo only; commercial release on TDS label		1978
ADA 8	Soft Boys	(I Want To Be An) Angelpoise Lamp/Fat Man's Son		PS	1978
ADA 9	Good Rats	Mr. Mechanic/Victory In Space		PS	1978
ADA 10	Elvis Costello and The Attractions	Pump It Up/Big Tears		PS	1978
ADA 11	Steroids	In The Colonies/Sha La La Loo Lay		PS	1978
ADA 12	Nick Lowe	Little Hitler/Cruel to Be Kind		PS	1978
ADA 13	13th Floor Elevators	You're Gonna Miss Me/Tried To Hide		PS	1978
ADA 14	Shadows Of Knight	Gloria/Oh Yeah		PS	1978
ADA 15	Ray Campi and His Rockabilly Rebels	Teenage Boogie/Rockabilly Rebel		PS	1978
ADA 16	Electric Prunes	I Had Too Much To Dream (Last Night)/Luvin'		PS	1978
ADA 17	Count Five	Psychotic Reaction/They're Gonna Get You		PS	1978
ADA 18	Bette Bright and The Illuminations	My Boyfriend's Back/Hold On, I'm Comin'		PS	1978
ADA 19	Tanz Der Youth	I'm Sorry, I'm Sorry/Dealy		PS	1978
ADA 20	Metal Urbain	Hysteric Connective/Pas Poubelle		PS	1978
ADA 21	Bette Bright	Captain Of Your Ship/Those Greedy Eyes		PS	1978
ADA 22	Red Krayola	Wives In Orbit/Yik Yak		PS	1978
ADA 23	Yachts	Look Back In Love (Not In Anger)/I Can't Stay Long		PS	1978
ADA 24	Elvis Costello and The Attractions	Radio Radio/Tiny Steps		PS	1978
ADA 25	Yachts	Yachting Types/Hypnotising Lies		PS	1978
ADA 26	Nick Lowe	American Squirm/ (What's So Funny 'Bout) Peace, Love And Understanding		PS	1978
ADA 27	Neon	Don't Eat Bricks/Hanging Off An "O"		PS	1979
ADA 28	Brain Tchaikovsky	Girl Of My Dreams/Come Back		PS	1979
ADA 29	The Pop Group	She Is Beyond Good And Evil/3:38		PS	1979
ADA 30	Richard Hell and The Voidoids	Kid With The Replaceable Head/I'm Your Man		PS	1979
ADA 31	Elvis Costello and The Attractions	Oliver's Army/My Funny Valentine		PS	1979
ADA 32	Elvis Costello and The Attractions	Accidents Will Happen/My Funny Valentine		PS Holland only	1979
ADA 35	Elvis Costello and The Attractions	Accidents Will Happen/Talking In The Dark / Wednesday Week		PS	1979
ADA 36	Yachts	Love You, Love You/Hazy People		PS	1979
ADA 37	Bram Tchaikovsky	I'm The One That's Leaving/Amelia		PS	1979
ADA 40	Sussex	Treat Me Kind/What's The Point	Also 40C, green vinyl	PS	1979
ADA 41	Wayne Kramer	The Harder They Come/East Side Girl		PS	1979
ADA 42	Yachts	Box 202/Permanent Damage		PS	1979
ADA 43	Nick Lowe	Cruel to Be Kind/Endless Grey Ribbon		PS	1979
ADA 44	Inmates	Dirty Water/Danger Zone		PS	1979
ADA 46	999	Found Out Too Late/Lie, Lie, Lie		Withdrawn	
ADA 47	Inmates	Walk/Talkin' Woman		PS	1979
ADA 48	Visage	Tar/Frequency 7		Withdrawn	
ADA 49	Yachts	Now I'm Spoken For/Secret Agents		PS	1979
ADA 50	Inmates	Love Got Me/If Time Would Turn Backwards		PS	1980

NB: The following singles were released following Radar's absorption into WEA.

Cat. No.	Artist	Titles			Year
ADA 52	Yachts	There's A Ghost In My House/Revelry/Yachting Type		PS	1980
ADA 53	Inmates	Three Time Loser/If I Could Turn Time Backwards		PS	1980
ADA 54	Bram Tchaikovsky	Let's Dance/Rock 'n' Roll Cabaret		PS	1980
ADA 56	Bram Tchaikovsky	Pressure/Mr. President		PS	1980
ADA 57	Yachts	I.O.U./24 Hours From Tulsa		PS	1980
ADA 62	D.J. Kane	Lately Things Get Screwed Up All The Time/Wrong Condition		PS	1980
ADA 63	Inmates	heartbeat/Tallahassee Lassie		PS	1980

Albums:

Cat. No.	Artist	Titles		Year
RAD 1	Nick Lowe	Jesus Of Cool (Pure Pop For Now People)		1978
RAD 2	Iggy Pop/James Williamson	Kill City		1978
RAD 3	Elvis Costello and The Attractions	This Year's Model	Issued with free single, SAM 83	1978
RAD 4	National Lampoon	That's Not Funny, That's Sick		1978
RAD 5	Good Rats	From Rats To Riches		1978
RAD 6	Pezband	Laughing In The Dark		1978
RAD 7	La Dusseldorf	La Dusseldorf		1978
RAD 9	Ray Campi and His Rockabilly Rebels	Wildcat Shakeout	issued with free single, SAM 86	1979
RAD 10	La Duddeldorf	Viva		1979
RAD 11	Shadows of Knight	Gloria		1979
RAD 12	Red Krayola	The Parable of Arable Land		1978
RAD 13	13th Floor Elevators	The Psychedelic Sounds Of The 13th Floor Elevators		1978
RAD 14	Elvis Costello and The Attractions	Armed Forces		1979

Cat. No.	Artist	Titles		Year
RAD 15	13th Floor Elevators	Easter Everywhere		1979
RAD 16	Red Krayola	God Bless The Red Krayola		1979
RAD 17	Bram Tchaikovsky	Strange Man, Changed Man		1979
RAD 18	Red Krayola	Soldier Talk		1979
RAD 19	Yachts	S.O.S.		1979
RAD 20	The Pop Group	Y		1979

Promo Singles:

Cat. No.	Artist	Titles		Year
SAM 83	Elvis Costello and The Attractions	Neat Neat Neat/Stranger In The House	Free with album, RAD 3	1978
SAM 86	Ray Campi and His Rockabilly Rebels	Caterpillar/Play It Cool	Free with album, RAD 9	1979
SAM 88	Various	13th Floor Elevators - She Lives (In A Time Of Her Own); Red Krayola - Pink Stainless Tail; Golden Dawn – Starvation; Lost and Found - There Would Be No Doubt		1978
SFI-347	Various	Red Krayola - Hurricane Fighter Plane; 13th Floor Elevators – Reverberation	Flexi-disc	1978

EPs:

Cat. No.	Artist	Titles		Year
RDR 1	Pere Ubu	Datapanik In The Year Zero	12"	1978
RDR 2	Clive Langer and The Boxes	I Want The Whole World	12"	1978

Rat Race (London)

7" Singles:

Cat. No.	Artist	Titles	Year
RAT 1	John Ellis	Babies In Jars/Photostadt	1980
RAT 2	Vibrators	Gimme Some Lovin'/Power Cry	1980
RAT 3	Almost Brothers	You'll Never Make It/You Give Me The Creeps	1980
RAT 4	Vibrators	Disco In Mosco/Take A Chance	1980
RAT 5	Greg Bright	I'm A Believer/Sweet In The Leyden Jar	1980
RAT 6	John Ellis	Hit Man/Hollow Graham	1980
RAT 7	Almost Brothers	Don't Pass The Buck/ Theme For A Lonely American Private Detective In Paris	1981
RAT 8	Almost Brothers	Bum's Rush/Where The Wind Sighs	1981
RAT 9	Almost Brothers	Actions/Saxophone/Don't Hold Your Breath/And The Day After EP	1982

Rather (London, distributed by Rough Trade)

7" Singles:

Cat. No.	Artist	Titles		Year
GEAR ONE	Swell Maps	Read About Seymour/Black Velvet/ Ripped And Torn	Also Rough Trade RT010	1978
GEAR TWO	Steve Treatment	5-A-Sided 45: The Hippy Posed Engrosement/Hooked On A Trend/ Negative Nights/Taste Your Own Medecine/Danger Zone		1978
GEAR THREE	Swell Maps	Dresden Style/Ammunition Train/ Full Moon	Also Rough Trade RT012	1979
GEAR 4	Cult Figures	Zip Nolan/P. W. T./Zip Dub	Also Rough Trade RT 020	1979
GEAR 5	Swell Maps	Loin Of The Surf/Doctor At Cake/Steve Does/ Bronze And Baby Shoes	Free with the album below	1979
GEAR SIX	Swell Maps	Real Shocks/Monologues/ An English Verse	Also Rough Trade RT 021	1979
GEAR 7	Swell Maps	Let's Build A Car/Big Mac/Then Poland	Also Rough Trade RT 036	1980
GEAR 8	Cult Figures	I Remember/Almost A Love Song/Laura Kate		1980
GEAR 9	Phones Sportsman Band	I Really Love You/Get Down And Get With It/I Woke Up This Morning/ Wah Wah Track/The Olton		1980
GEAR 11	Nikki Sudden	Back To The Start/Running On My Train		1981

Albums:

Cat. No.	Artist	Titles		Year
TROY 1	Swell Maps	A Trip to Marineville	Also Rough Trade ROUGH 2	1979
RATHER 10	Nikki Sudden	Beau Geste		1983
RATHER 13	What A Nice Way To Turn Seventeen No. 3			1984
GEAR 17	What A Nice Way To Turn Seventeen No. 2			1984

Raw (Cambridge)

7" Singles:

Cat. No.	Artist	Titles		Year
RAW 1	Users	Sick Of You/I'm In Love With Today	PS	1977
RAW 2	The Hammersmith Gorillas	You Really Got Me/Leaving Home	PS	1977
RAW 3	Kiljoys	Johnny Won't Get To Heaven/Naive	PS	1977
RAW 4	Creation	Making Time/Painter Man	PS	1977
RAW 5	The Soft Boys	Give It To The Soft Boys EP: (Wading Through A Ventilator/ The Face Of Death/Hear My Brane)	PS	1977
RAW 6	The Unwanted	Withdrawal 1978/Bleak Outlook	PS	1977
RAW 7	Some Chicken	New Religion/Blood On The Wall	PS	1977
RAW 8	Lockjaw	Radio Call Sign/The Young Ones	PS	1977
RAW 9	Matchbox	Troublesome Bay/R 'n R Boogie	PS	1978
RAW 10	Downliners Sect	Showbiz/Killing Me	PS	1977
RAW 11	Riot Rockers	Tennessee Saturday Night/Some Kinda Earthquake	PS	1978
RAW 12	Danny Wild and The Wildcats	Mean Evil Daddy/Old Bill Boogie	PS	1978
RAW 13	Some Chicken	Arabian Daze/No. 7	PS	1978
RAW 14	The Gorillas	It's My Life/My Son's Alive	PS	1978
RAW 15	The Unwanted	Secret Police/These Boots Are Made For Walking	PS	1978
RAW 16	The Eyes	I Like It/Once Ain't Enough	PS	1978
RAW 17	Some Chicken	Arabian Daze/No. 7 Same as RAW 13	PS	1978
RAW 18	Salt	Cobra's Melody EP: (Keep Your Mother Worrying/All Wired Up/ Key To The Highway/Cobra's Melody)	PS	1978
RAW 19	Lockjaw	Journalist Jive/I'm A Virgin/A Doonga Doonga	PS	1978
RAW 21	Mystery Train	The Sun Story/A Song For Gene	PS	1979
RAW 25	Troggs	Just A Little Too Much/The True Troggs Tapes?	PS	1979
RAW 26	Gorillas	Message To The World/Outta My Brain	PS	1979
RAW 27	Faron's Flamingoes	Bring It On Home To Me/C'mon Everybody	PS	1979
RAW 29	Eyes	Once In A Lifetime/Hello Love You	PS	1979
RAW 31	The Now	Into The 1980s/Nine O'Clock	PS	1979
RAW 35	Ersatz	Motor Body Love/Gimme A Reason	PS	1979
RAW 36	Leonard Vice	I've Got Spots/		1979

NB: 1, 6, 12, 13, and 17 were also issued as 12", singles to celebrate the label's first anniversary in 1978 (Prefix RAWT).

Albums:

Cat. No.	Artist	Titles		Year
RAWL 1	Various	Raw Deal	Compilation	1977
RAWL 2	Various	(Oh No, It's) More from Raw	Anniversary album	1978
RAWL 3	Various	Raw Rockabilly	Also as 10", prefix: TRAWL	1978
RWLP 101	Matchbox	Setting The Woods On Fire	Released through Chiswick	1978
RWLP 102	Danny Wild and The Wildcats	Wild In The Country		1978
RWLP 103	Gorillas	Message To The World		1978
RWLP 104	Various	The Mersey Survivors	Compilation	1978
RWLP 105	Karl Terry and The Cruisers	Cruisin'		1978
RWLP 106	Downliners Sect	Showbiz		1979

Razor

Singles:

Cat. No.	Artist	Titles		Year
RAZ 101	The Adicts	Chinese Takeaway / You'll Never Walk Alone	PS	1982
RAZ 102	Splodge	Mouth And Trousers / In Search Of The Seven Golden Gussets	PS	1982
RAZ 103	The Brothers Gonad	Delilah / Lager Top / Sandra / My Grandma	PS	198?
RAZ 104	The Adicts	Bad Boy / Shake Rattle Bang Your Head	PS	1983
RAZ 105	Red London	This Is England / Soul Train / Revolution Tapes	PS	1983
RAZ 106	David Fenton	Fresh Air / Buried In Snow	PS	1983
RAZ 107	Newtown Neurotics	Blitzkrieg Bop / Hypocrite / I Remember You	PS	1983
RAZ 108	Long Tall Texans	Saints And Sinners / Poison / Right First Time / Who's Sorry Now	PS	1987
RAZ 109	Long Tall Texans	Should I Stay Or Should I Go / Indians (live) / Should I Stay Or Should I Go (live)	PS	1988
RAZ 110	Tin Gods	Cosmetics / Little Caesers / Motorway Drive / Burning Down The Temples	PS	1988
RAZ 111	Tattooed Love Boys	Why Waltz When You Can Rock 'N' Roll / Long Version		198?
RAZ 112	Long Tall Texans	Get Back Wet Back / Somethin's Cookin' / Get Your Teeth Out Of My Jugular / Alamo Mix		198?
RAZ 113	Dirty Strangers	Thrill Of The Thrill / Kick And Run		198?
RAZ 114	The Zombies	Time Of The Season / She's Not There / This Could Be Our Year		198?
RAZ 115	The Highliners	Benny Hill Boogie / Surfer Jones		198?

Albums:

Cat. No.	Artist	Titles		Year
RAZ 1	Splodge	In Search Of The Seven Golden Gussets		1982
RAZ 2	The Adicts	Sound Of Music		1982
RAZ 3	Vardis	The Lions Share		1983
RAZ 4	Various	Ballroom Blitz	Compilation	1983
RAZ 5	Not Released			
RAZ 6	Newtown Neurotics	Beggars Can Be Choosers		1983
RAZ 7	Knox	Plutonium Express		1983
RAZ 8	Not Released			
RAZ 9	Cock Sparrer	Shock Troops		1983
RAZ 10	Red London	This Is England		1983
RAZ 11	Accept	Metal Masters		1984
RAZ 12	Various	Razor Sharp Cuts	Compilation	1984
RAZ 13	Purple Hearts	Head On Collision Time		1985
RAZ 14	The Lambrettas	Kick Start		1985
RAZ 15	The Adicts	Smart Alex		1985
RAZ 16	Various Artists	The Cutting Edge	Compilation	1985
RAZ 17	Bryn Gregory and The Co-Stars	The Beat Goes On		1986
RAZ 18	Menace	GLC RIP		1986
RAZ 19	Purple Hearts	Popish Frenzy		1986
RAZ 20	Chron Gen	Chronic Generation		1986
RAZ 21	The Saints	Best Of The Saints		1986
RAZ 22	The Purple Gang	Granny Takes A Trip		1986
RAZ 23	Long Tall Texans	Sodbusters		1987
RAZ 24	Mink Deville	Cabretta		1987
RAZ 25	Flying Padovanis	They Call Me Crazy		1987
RAZ 26	Cock Sparrer	True Grit		1987
RAZ 27	The Sect	Voice Of Reason		1987
RAZ 28	Long Tall Texans	Los Me Boleros		1987
RAZ 29	The Grip	Be Yourself		1988
RAZ 30	Not Released			
RAZ 31	Angelic Upstarts	Last Tango In Moscow		1988
RAZ 32	Angelic Upstarts	Live In Yugoslavia		1988
RAZ 33	Angelic Upstarts	Bootlegs And Rarities		1988
RAZ 34	The Zombies	Meet The Zombies		1988
RAZ 35	Steve Gibbons Band	Down In The Bunker		1988
RAZ 36	The Midniters	Easy Money		1988
RAZ 37	Long Tall Texans	Saturnalia		1989
RAZ 38	Uncle Sam	Heaven Or Hollywood		1989
RAZ 39	Dumpys Rusty Nuts	Firkin Well Live		1989
RAZ 40	Not Released			
RAZ 41	The Zombies	Five Live Zombies		1989
RAZ 42	The Guttersnipes	The Poor Dress Up		1990
RAZ 43	Not Released			
RAZ 44	Long Tall Texans	Five Beans In A Wheel		1989
RAZ 45	The Highliners	Bound For Glory		1989
RAZ 46	The Grip	Be Yourself		1989
RAZ 47	Last Of The Teenage Idols	Satellite Head Gone Soft		1990
RAZ 48	Feline Groove	Feline Groove		1990

Real Records (London) (Early releases)

7" Singles:

Cat. No.	Artist	Titles		Year
ARE 1	Johnny Thunders	Dead Or Alive/Downtown	PS	1978
ARE 2	Strangeways	Come on Boys (Show Her You Care)/You're On Your Own	PS	1978
ARE 3	Johnny Thunders	You Can't Put Your Arm Around A Memory/Hurtin'	Blue vinyl, PS	1978
ARE 6	Pretenders	Stop Your Sobbin'/The Wait		1978
ARE 7	Strangeways	All The Sounds Of Fear/Wasting Time	PS	1979
ARE 9	Pretenders	Kid/Tattooes Love Boys	PS	1979
ARE 11	Pretenders	Brass In Pocket/Swinging London/Nervous But Shy	PS	1979
ARE 12	Pretenders	Talk Of The Town/Cuban Slide	PS	1980
ARE 13	Moondogs	Who's Gonna Tell Mary/Overcaring Parents	PS	1981
ARE 15	Pretenders	Message Of Love/Porcelain	PS	1980
ARE 16	Moondogs	Imposter/Baby Snatcher	PS	1981
ARE 17	Pretenders	Day After Day/In The Sticks	PS	1981
ARET 17	Pretenders	Day After Day/In The Sticks	12", PS	1981

Cat. No.	Artist	Titles		Year
ARE 18	Pretenders	I Go To Sleep/English Roses (live)	PS	1981
ARET 18	Pretenders	I Go To Sleep/English Roses (live)/ Louie, Louie (live)	12", PS	1981

Albums:

Cat. No.	Artist	Titles	Year
RAL 1	Johnny Thunders	So Alone	1978
RAL 3	The Pretenders	The Pretenders	1979

Red Rhino (York)

Various Formats:

Cat. No.	Artist	Titles		Year
RED 01	The Odds	Saturday Night/Not Another Love Song	PS	1980
RED 02	Akrylykz	Smart Boy/Spyderman	PS	1980
RED 03	Dead Beats	Choose You/Julie's New Boyfriend	PS	1980
RED 05	The Distributors	Lean On Me/Never Never	PS	1981
RED 06	Rhythm Clicks	Short Time/Lies Don't Talk/Chains	PS	1981
RED 07	Mekons	Snow/Another One Time	PS	1981
RED 08	Normil Hawaians	Gala Failed EP: Party Party/Levels Of Water/Obedience/The Return/ Sang Sang	PS	1981
RED 09	Distributors	Get Rid Of These Things/Wages For Lovers	PS	1981
RED 10	Soul On Ice	Underwater/Splintered Lens/Breathless	PS	198?
RED 12	Soviet France	Ritual	LP	198?
RED 13	Time In Motion	Quiet Type/Stay With You	PS	1982
RED 14	1919	Caged/After The Fall	PS	1982
RED 15	Xpozez	1000 Marching Feet	PS	1982
RED 16	Nod and Friends	Dad/Daz	PS	1982
RED 17	Steve Dixon	Candy Blues/Candy Ina Babylon/Friction And Sheets	PS	1982
RED 18	Hula	Black Pop Workout EP	PS	1982
RED 19	Time In Motion	I Wanna Be Your Telephone Exchange	PS	1982
RED 20	Red Lorry Yellow Lorry	Beating My Head/I'm Still Waiting	PS	1982
RED 21	Darkness and Jive	Hooked On You/Tarzan	PS	1982
RED 22	1919	Repulsion	PS	1982
RED 23	Soviet France	Norsche	LP	198?
RED 24	Soul On Ice	Widescreen/The Voice		198?
RED 25	1919	Machine	LP	1983
RED 26	Zoot and The Roots	I Ate The Little Red Rooster/Ronnie Get Your Gun		1983
RED 27	Darkness and Jive	Furnace/Guys And Dolls		1983
RED 28	Red Lorry Yellow Lorry	Take It All/Happy	PS	1983
RED 30	See You In Vegas	The Day The World Caught Fire/Work/Dirty Harry On The Falls Road	PS	1983
RED 31	The Tronics	Wild Cat Rock/Tonight	PS	1983
RED 33	Punilux	Hold Me (Never Mould Me)/Golden Corsets	PS	1983
RED 34	Punilux	Seven	LP	1983
RED 35	Hula	Cut From Inside	LP	1983
RED 36	Skeletal Family	The Night/Waiting Here	PS	1983
RED 37	Pulp	Everybody's Probem/There Was...	PS	1983
RED 38	Native Europe	Searching For An Orchestration	LP	1983
RED 39	Red Lorry Yellow Lorry	He's Read/See The Fire	PS	1983
RED 40	Soviet France	Mohnomische	LP	198?
RED 41	Skeletal Family	She Cries Alone/The Wind Blows/Eternal		1984
RED 42	Skeletal Family	Recollect	LP	1984
RED 43	Skeletal Family	So Sure/Trees/Batman/Lies		1984
RED 44	Skeletal Family	Burning Oil	LP	1984
RED 45	Soviet France	Elstre	LP	1984
RED 46	Neville Luxury	Feels Like Dancing	LP	1984
RED 47	Hula	(No-One Leaves The) Fever Car		1984
RED 48	Red Lorry Yellow Lorry	This Today EP (This Today/Beating My Head/He's Read/ Take It All/See The Fire)		1984
RED 49	Red Lorry Yellow Lorry	Monkey's On Juice/Push/Silence		1984
RED 50	Red Lorry Yellow Lorry	Talk About The Weather	LP	1984
RED 52	Red Lorry Yellow Lorry	Hollow Eyes/Feel A Piece		1984
RED 53	Hula	Murmur	LP	1984
RED 54	Skeletal Family	Promised Land/Stand By Me/Just A Friend		1984
RED 55	Red Lorry Yellow Lorry	Chance/Generation		1984
RED 56	Hula	Get The Habit		198?
RED 57	Skeletal Family	Futile Combat	LP	1985
RED 58	Soviet France	Popular Soviet Songs	LP	1985
RED 59	Skeletal Family	Together Burning	LP	1985

Cat. No.	Artist	Titles		Year
RED 60	Red Lorry Yellow Lorry	Spinning Round/Hold Yourself Down		1985
RED 62	Hula	Walk On Stalks Of Shattered Glass	PS	1985
RED 63	Hula	One Thousand Hours 2-LP		1986
RED 64	Hula	Freeze Out		1986
RED 65	Red Lorry Yellow Lorry	Paint Your Wagon LP		1986
RED 66	Red Lorry Yellow Lorry	Walking On Your Hands/Which Side/Jipp (Instrumental Mix)		1986
RED 67	Soviet France	Gesture Signal Threat LP		1986
RED 68	Soviet France	A Flock Of Rotations LP		1986
RED 71	Hula	Shadowland LP		1986
RED 72	Hula	Black Wall Blue	PS	1986
RED 73	Red Lorry Yellow Lorry	Cut Down/Running Fever/Pushed Me		1986
RED 74	Hula	Poison (Night Mix)		1987
RED 75	Hula	Voice		1987
RED 76	Red Lorry Yellow Lorry	Crawling Mantra/Hang Man/All The Same/Shout At The Sky		1987
RED 79	The Creepers	Brute/Lucky		1987
RED 80	Hula	Cut Me Loose		1987
RED 82	The Creepers	Rock 'n' Roll Liquorice LP		1987
RED 83	Hula	Threshold LP		1987
RED 85	Hula	Cut From Inside LP		1987
RED 86	Red Lorry Yellow Lorry	Smashed Hits LP		1987
RED 87	Rhythm Sisters	Road To Roundhay Pier LP		1987
RED 88	Various Artists	Til Things Are Better - A Tribute To Johnny Cash	LP	198?
RED 90	Horseland	Love Dies Again/An Understanding		198?
RED 91	Soviet France	Shouting At The Ground LP		198?
RED 92	Rhythm Sisters	American Boys		198?
RED 133	Red Army Choir	Schizophrenic / Movie Men / Simon		198?

Revenge Records

Single:

Cat. No.	Artist	Titles	Year
RR 1	Sweet Revenge	Flowers In The City / Great Big Kiss / Nothing Ever Goes The Way It's Planned	198?

(Vice Squad without Beki or Lia)

Riot City Records (Bristol)

7" Singles:

Cat. No.	Artist	Titles		Year
RIOT 1	Vice Squad	Last Rockers EP: Last Rockers / Living On Dreams / Latex Love	PS	1980
RIOT 2	Vice Squad	Resurrection EP: Resurrection / Young Blood / Humane	PS	1981
RIOT 3	The Insane	Politics / Dead And Gone / Last Day	PS	1981
RIOT 4	Abrasive Wheels	Vicious Circle EP: Vicious Circle / Attack / Voice Of Youth	PS	1981
RIOT 5	Court Martial	Gotta Get Out EP: Gotta Get Out / Fight For Your Life / Young Offender	PS	1982
RIOT 6	Chaos UK	Burning Britain EP: Four Minute Warning / Kill Your Baby / Army / Victimised	PS	1982
RIOT 7	Undead	It's Corruption / Undead	PS	1982
RIOT 8	The Expelled	No Life No Future EP: No Life No Future / Dreaming / What Justice	PS	1982
RIOT 9	Abrasive Wheels	ABW EP: Army Song / Juvenile / So Slow	PS	1982
RIOT 10	Chaotic Dischord	Fuck The World EP: Fuck The World / You're Gonna Die / Sold Out To The GPO	PS	1982
RIOT 11	Court Martial	No Solution EP: No Solution / Too Late / Take Control	PS	1982
RIOT 12	Chaos UK	Loud Political And Uncompromising EP: No Security / What About A Future / Hypocrite	PS	1982
RIOT 13	Mayhem	Gentle Murder EP: Dogsbody / Street Fight / Patriots / Blood Money	PS	1982
RIOT 14	The Ejected	Have You Got 10p? / Class Of '82 / One Of The Boys	PS	1982
RIOT 15	Undead	Violent Visions / Dead Revolution / This Place Is Burning	PS	1982
RIOT 16	Abrasive Wheels	Burn'Em Down / Urban Rebel	PS	1982
RIOT 17	The Expelled	Government Policy / Make It Alone	PS	1982
RIOT 18	Resistance 77	Nowhere To Play EP: Nottingham Problem / Join The Army / Collars And Ties / Nuclear Attack	PS	1982
RIOT 19	The Ejected	Noise For The Boys EP: Fast 'N' Loud / I Don't Care / What Happened In Brighton	PS	1982
RIOT 20	No Choice	Sadist Dream / Nuclear Disaster / Cream Of The Crop	PS	1983
RIOT 21	Emergency	Points Of View / City Fun / Does Anybody Realise	PS	1983
RIOT 22	Chaotic Dischord	Never Trust A Friend / Popstars / Are Students Safe	PS	1983
RIOT 23	Sex Aids	Back On The Piss Again / The Amazing Mr. Michael Hogarth / Road Crew	PS	1983

Cat. No.	Artist	Titles		Year
RIOT 24	Mayhem	Pulling Puppets Strings EP: Gentle Murder / Your Face Fits / Clean Cut	PS	1983
RIOT 25	Ultra Violent	Crime For Revenge / Dead Generation / Where Angels Fear To Tread	PS	1983
RIOT 26	The Underdogs	East Of Dachau / Johnny Go Home / Dead Soldier	PS	1983
RIOT 27	The Varukers	Die For Your Government / All Systems Fail	PS	1983
RIOT 28	The Ejected	Press The Button EP: Russians / 24 Years / In The City	PS	1983
RIOT 29	The Varukers	Led To The Slaughter / The End Is Nigh / You're Dead	PS	1983

12" singles

Cat. No.	Artist	Titles		Year
12 RIOT 1/2	Vice Squad	Last Rockers / Resurrection	6 track 12" with both singles on	1981
12 RIOT 30	Chaotic Dischord	Don't Throw It All Away: Great Rock 'N' Roll Swindle / Don't Throw It All Away / Stab Your Back / Sausage Beans And Chips / Who Killed Et (I Killed The Fucker!) / 22 Hole Doc.Martens / Anarchy In Woolworths / Batcave Benders Meet The Alien Durex Machine		1983
12 RIOT 31	The Varukers	Another Religion Another War: Another Religion Another War / No Escape / Condemned To Death / The Last War / Who Pays? / Neglected / Deadly Games / Seek Shelter In Hell		1984
12 RIOT 32	Chaos UK	The Singles	This is their two singles plus one track from "Riotous Assembly"	1984

Albums:

Cat. No.	Artist	Titles		Year
ASSEMBLY 1	Various	Riotous Assembly	Compilation	1982
CITY 001	Abrasive Wheels	When The Punks Go Marching In		1982
CITY 002	Chaos UK	Chaos UK LP		1983
CITY 003	The Ejected	A Touch Of Class		1983
CITY 004	Chaotic Dischord	Fuck Politics Fuck Religion Fuck The Lot Of You		1983
CITY 005	The Varukers	Bloodsuckers		1983
CITY 006	Undead	The Killing Of Reality		1984
CITY 007	The Ejected	Spirit Of Rebellion		1984
CITY 008	Chaotic Dischord	Live In New York		1984
CITY 009	Various	Life's A Riot And Then You Die	Compilation	1985
REAGAN 1	Various	Hell Comes To Your House	Compilation	1982

Rok

Various Formats:

Cat. No.	Artist	Titles		Year
ROK I/II	Squire: Get Ready To Go / Coming Shortly: Doing The Flat			1979
ROK III/IV	Just Frank: You / Split Screens: Just Don't Cry			1979
ROK V/VI	The V.I.P.'s: Can't Let You Go / Urban Disturbance: Wild Boys In Cortinas			1980
ROK VII/VIII	The Clerks: No Good For Me / Hazard: Gotta Change My Life			1980
ROK IX/X	Blue Movies: Mary Jane / The Noise: Criminal			1980
ROK XI/XII	Synchonised Mesh: October Friday / EF Band: Another Day Gone			1980
ROK XIII/XIV	X-E-Cutors: Too Far To Look Inside My Head / X-Films: After My Blood			1980
ROK XV/XVI	The Zeros: What's Wrong With A Pop Group / Action Replay: Decisions			1979
ROK XVII/XVIII	Innocent Bystanders: Where Is Johnny / Debutantes: Man In The Street			1980
ROK XIX/XX	Justin Case: TV / Straight Up: One Out All Out			1980
ROK LP 1	Various Artists	Odds, Bods, Mods And Sods	Compilation	1979

Rondelet Records

Albums:

Cat. No.	Artist	Titles		Year
ABOUT 1	Witchfynde	Give 'Em Hell		1980
ABOUT 2	Witchfynde	Stagefright		1980
ABOUT 3	Brooklyn	You Never Know What You'll Find		1980
ABOUT 4	Gaskin	End Of The World		1981
ABOUT 5	Anti-Pasti	The Last Call		1981
ABOUT 6	The Fits	You're Nothing You're Nowhere		1982
ABOUT 7	Anti-Pasti	Caution In The Wind		1982
ABOUT 8	Gaskin	No Way Out		1982
ABOUT 9	Special Duties	77 In 82		1982
ABOUT 10	Various	The Only Alternative	Compilation	1982
ABOUT 11	Wibbley Brothers	Go Weird		1982
ABOUT 12	Heritage	Remorse Code		198?
ABOUT 13	Anti-Pasti	Anti-Pasti Singles Collection		1983

Singles:

Cat. No.	Artist	Titles		Year
ROUND 1	Witchfynde	Give 'Em Hell / Gettin' Heavy	PS	1979
ROUND 2	Anti-Pasti	1980 / Something New / No Government/Two Years Too Late	PS	1980
ROUND 3	Brooklyn	I Wanna Be A Detective / Two Wheels	PS	1980
ROUND 4	Witchfynde	In The Stars / Wake Up Screaming	PS	1980
ROUND 5	Anti-Pasti	Let Them Free / Hell / Another Dead Soldier	PS	1981
ROUND 6	Brooklyn	Hollywood / Late Again	PS	1981
ROUND 7	Gaskin	I'm No Fool / Sweet Dream Maker	PS	1981
ROUND 8	Heritage	Strange Place To Be / Misunderstood	PS	1981
ROUND 9	Wibbley Brothers	First Aid / No More Canoeing / Barnstormer / Farming In A Babylon	PS	1981
ROUND 10	Anti-Pasti	Six Guns / Now's The Time / Call The Army	PS	1981
ROUND 11	Guy Jackson	Radio One / Metal Fatigue	PS	1981
ROUND 12	Stilts	Waiting For A Miracle / People And Buildings	PS	198?
ROUND 13	The Fits	Burial / Straps	PS	1982
ROUND 14	Justin Fashanu	Do It 'Cos You Like It / Heaven On Earth	PS	1982
ROUND 15	Special Duties	Violent Society /It Ain't Our Fault / Colchester Council	PS	1982
ROUND 16	Dead Man's Shadow	Bomb Scare / Another Hiroshima / Fighting For Reality	PS	1982
ROUND 17	Catwax Axe Co.	Wax Walk / Jumbo Jet	PS	1982
ROUND 18	Anti-Pasti	East To The West / Burn In Your Own Flames	PS	1982
ROUND 19	The Membranes	Muscles / All Roads Lead To Norway / Great Mistake / Entertaining Friends	PS	1982
ROUND 20	Special Duties	Police State / We Gotta Fight / Special Duties / It Just Ain't Me	PS	1982
ROUND 21	Gaskin	Mony Mony / Queen Of Flames	PS	1982
ROUND 22	Threats	Go To Hell/ Afghanistan / Wasted	PS	1982
ROUND 23	Riot Squad	Fuck The Tories / We Are The Riot Squad / Civil Destruction	PS	1982
ROUND 24	Special Duties	Bullshit Crass / You're Doing Yourself No Good	PS	1982
ROUND 25	Riot Squad	Riot In The City / Why Should We / Religion Doesn't Mean A Thing	PS	1982
ROUND 26	Anti-Pasti	Caution In The Wind /Blind Faith/Last Train To Nowhere	PS	1982
ROUND 27	Dead Man's Shadow	Flower In The Gun / The Last Cowboy	PS	1982
ROUND 28	The Membranes	Pinstripe Hype / The Hitch / High St Yanks / Funny Old World / Man From Moscow	PS	1982
ROUND 29	The Threats	Politicians And Ministers / Writing On The Wall / Dead End Depression Can't Stop Me / 1980's / Underground Army	PS	1982
ROUND 30	The Fits	Last Laugh / Different Ways / Nothing To Prove	PS	1982
ROUND 31	Soft As Ghosts	Mystified / Facets Of Life	PS	1983

Rot Records (Mansfield)

Various Formats:

Cat. No.	Artist	Titles			Year
ASS 1	Riot Squad	Lost Cause / Suspicion / Unite And Fight / Police Power		PS	1983
ASS 2	Riot Squad	I'm OK Fuck You /Societies Fodder / In The Future / Friday Night Hero		PS	1983
ASS 3	Riot Squad	There Ain't No Solution / Government Schemes		PS	1984
ASS 4	Various	Wet Dreams	LP	Compilation	1984
ASS 5	Clockwork Soldiers	Wet Dreams / Suicide / In The Name Of Science		PS	1984
ASS 6	Resistance 77	Viva La Resistance (EP) - Enemy / Will They Survive / Russia / Advance Factory Units		PS	1984
ASS 7	Animal Farm	Model Soldier / John And Julie		PS	1984
ASS 8	Paranoia	Dead Man's Dreams / Man In Black		PS	1984
ASS 9	The Enemy	Last But Not Least / Images (Live)		PS	1984
ASS 10	Various	Two Ninety Nine	LP	Compilation	1984
ASS 11	Paranoia	Shattered Glass	LP		1984
ASS 12	The Enemy	Last But Not Least	LP		1984
ASS 13	Riot Squad	No Potential Threat	LP		1984
ASS 14	Resistance 77	Thoroughbred Men	LP		1984
ASS 15	Various	Rot In Hell 1977	LP	Compilation	1984
ASS 16	The Varukers	Massacred Millions: Massacred Millions / Will They Never Learn / Thatcher's Fortress/The Bomb Blast	12" EP	PS	1984
ASS 17	English Dogs	To The Ends Of The Earth: Ambassador Of Fire / The Chase Is On / Incisor / Survival Of The Fittest	12" EP	PS	1984
ASS 18	Various	Have A Rotten Christmas	LP	Compilation	1984
ASS 19	Not Released				
ASS 20	English Dogs	Forward Into Battle	LP		1985
ASS 21	Various	Kick Up The Arse	LP	Compilation	1985
ASS 22	Various	Have A Rotten Christmas Vol 2	LP	Compilation	1985
ATTACK 001	The Varukers	Prepare For The Attack	LP		1986

Cat. No.	Artist	Title	Format	Type	Year
CULT 001	Various	Lets Get Pissed It's Xmas	LP	Compilation	1987
CULT 002	Various	Lets Get Pissed It's Xmas Vol. 2	LP	Compilation	1987
DUTCH 001	The Varukers	Live In Holland LP			198?
HELL 036	Various	Religious As Hell	LP	Compilation	1986
HOLEIN 001	Various	What You Doing With That Hole In Your Head	LP		198?
SLAM 002	Various	Punk Lives Lets Slam	LP	Compilation	1986
SLAM 003	Various	Punk Lives Lets Slam 2	LP	Compilation	1987
WW 001	Various	World War 3	LP	Compilation	1987
AWS 001	Various	Best Of Rot - End Of An Era	dble LP	Compilation	198?
PFS ONE	Picture Frame Seduction	Hand And The Rider	LP		1985

Rough Trade (London)

7" Singles (the first 100):

Cat. No.	Artist	Titles			Year
RT 001	Metal Urbain	Paris Maquis/Cle De Contact	Co-release with Radar	PS	1978
RT 002	Augustus Pablo	Pablo Meets Mr. Bassie/ Mr. Bassie Special	Co-release with Rockers Records, no PS		1978
RT 003	Cabaret Voltaire	Extended Play EP: Headkick (Do The Mussolini)/Talkover/ Here She Comes/The Set Up		PS	1978
RT 004	Stiff Little Fingers	Alternative Ulster/'78 Revolutions	Co-release with Rigid Digits, PS		1978
RT 005	The Monochrome Set	He's Frank/Alphaville		PS	1978
RT 006	Stiff Little Fingers	Suspect Device/Wasted Life	Co-release with Rigid Digits, PS		1978
RT 007	Subway Sect	Ambition/A Different Story		PS	1978
RT 008	Electric Eels	Agitated/Cyclotron		PS	1979
RT 009	Kleenex	Ain't You/Hedi's Head	Co-release with Sunrise. Fold-out poster sleeve		1978
RT 010	Swell Maps	Read About Seymour/Ripped And Torn/ Black Velvet	Co-release with Rather (RT/GEAR 1 (MK. 2)) PS		1978
RT 011	File Under Pop	Heathrow/Corrugate/Heathrow SLB		PS	1979
RT 012	Swell Maps	Dresden Style/Ammunition Train/ Full Moon (Dub)	Co-release with Rather (RT/GEAR 3), some with booklet	PS	1979
RT 013	Raincoats	Fairytale In A Supermarket/In Love/Adventures Close To Home		PS	1979
RT 014	Kleenex	You/U		PS	1979
RT 015	Stiff Little Fingers	Gotta Getaway/Bloody Sunday	Co-release with Rigid Digits, PS		1979
RT 016	Metal Boys	Sweet Marilyn/Fugue For A Darkening Island		PS	1979
RT 017	Doctor Mix	No Fun/No Fun (Version)		no PS	1979
RT 018	Cabaret Voltaire	Nag Nag Nag/Is That Me (Finding Someone At The Door Again?)		PS	1979
RT 019	The Monochrome Set	Einesymphonie Des Grauens/Lester Leaps In		PS	1979
RT 020	Cult Figures	Zip Nolan (Highway Patrolman)/Playing With Toys/ Zip Dub	Co-release with Rather (RT/GEAR 4), folded PS		1979
RT 021	Swell Maps	Real Shocks/Monologues/English Verse	Co-release with Rather (RT/GEAR 6) PS		1979
RT 022	The Last Words	Animal World/No Music In The World Today		PS	1979
RT 023	The Pop Group	We Are All Prostitutes/Amnesty International Report On British Army Torture Of Irish Prisoners		PS	1979
RT 024	The Feelies	Raised Eyebrows/Fa Ce La		PS	1979
RT 025	The Pack	King Of Kings/Number 12		PS	1979
RT 026T	The Red Crayola	Micro-Chips And Fish/The Story So Far 12"		PS	1979
RT 027T	Scritti Politti	4 A-Sides EP: Doubt Beat/Bibbly 0 Tek/Pa's/Confidence		12", PS	1979
RT 028	The Monochrome Set	The Monochrome Set/Mr. Bizarro		PS	1979
RT 029	Essential Logic	Flora Force/Popcorn Boy (Waddle Ya Do?)		PS	1979
RT 030	The Plastics	Copy/Robot		PS	1979
RT 031	Delta 5	Mind Your Own Business/Now That You've Gone		PS	1979
RT 032	Dr. Mix and The Remix	I Can't Control Myself/(Version)		PS	1979
RT 033	TV Personalities	Where's Bill Grundy Now Ep: Part-Time Punks/Where's Bill Grundy Now?/ Happy Families/Posing At The Roundhouse		PS	1979
RT 034	Scritti Politti	Work In Progress EP: Scritlock's Door/ Opec-Immac/Messthetics/Hegemony	Co-release with St. Pancras Records (RT/SCRIT 21), in plastic sleeve w/ insert, PS		1979
RT 035	Cabaret Voltaire	Silent Command/Chance Versus Causality		PS	1979
RT 036	Swell Maps	Let's Build A Car/Big Maz In The Country/ Then Poland	Co-release with Rather (RT/GEAR 71), PS		1980
RT 037	Robert Wyatt	Arauco/Guantanamera		PS	1980
RT 038T	Cabaret Voltaire	Three Mantras: Western Mantra/Eastern Mantra		12", 33rpm, PS	1980
RT 039	The Slits/The Pop Group	In The Beginning There Was Rhythm/ Where There's A Way	Co-release with Y Records (RT/Y1), PS Dble. A-side, one side each, budget price release		1980

RT 040	The Prefects	Going Through The Motions/Things In General	Co-release with Vindaloo (RT/UGH 2), PS	1980
RT 041	Delta 5	You/Anticipation	PS	1980
RT 042	The Prats	1990's Pop EP: Disco Pope/Nothing/TV Set/Nobody Noticed	PS	1980
RT 043	Young Marble Giants	Final Day/Radio Silents/Cakewalking	PS	1980
RT 044	The Slits	Man Next Door/(Version)	Co-release with Y Records (RT/Y4) PS	1980
RT 045	James 'Blood' Ulmer	Are You Glad To Be In America?/T.V. Blues	PS	1980
RT 046	Robert Wyatt/Peter Blackman	Stalin Wasn't Stalling/Stalingrad	One side each PS	1981
RT 047	Liliput	Split/Die Matrosen	PS	1980
RT 048	The Fall	How I Wrote 'Elastic Man'/City Hobgoblins	PS	1980
RT 049	Pere Ubu	Final Solution/My Dark Ages	PS	1980
RT 050	Essential Logic	Eugene/Tame The Neighbours	PS	1980
RT 051	T.V. Personalities	Smashing Time/King And Country	PS	1980
RT 052	Robert Wyatt	At Last I Am Free/Strange Fruit	PS	1981
RT 053	Essential Logic	Music Is A Better Noise/Moontown	PS	1981
RT 054	The Red Craydla	Born In Flames/The Sword Of God	PS	1980
RT 055	Girls At Our Best!	Politics/It's Fashion	Co-release with Rather (RT/RR 2), PS	1980
RT 056	The Fall	Totally Wired/Putta Block	PS	1980
RT 057	Missing Scientists	Big City, Bright Lights/Discotheque X	PS	1980
RT 058	The Gist	This Is Love/Yanks	PS	1980
RT 059	Young Marble Giants	Testcard EP: Clicktalk/Zebra Trucks/Sporting Life/This Way/Posed By Models/The Clock	PS	1981
RT 060	Cabaret Voltaire	Seconds Too Late/Control Addict	PS	1980
RT 061	Delta 5	Try/Colour	PS	1980
RT 062	Liliput	Eiseger Wind/When The Cat's Away, Then The Mice Will Play	PS	1981
RT 063	TV Personalities	I Know Where Syd Barrett Lives/Arthur The Gardener	PS	1980
RT 064T	Furious Pig	I Don't Like Your Face/Johnny So Long/The Kind Mother	12"	1981
RT 065	Blue Orchids	The Flood/Disney Boys	PS	1980
RT 066	Pere Ubu	Not Happy/Lonesome Cowboy Dave	PS	1981
RT 067	Blue Orchids	Work/The House That Faded Out	PS	1981
RT 068	Vic Godard and Subway Sect	Stop That Girl/Instrumentally Scared/Vertical Integration	Co-release with Oddball Records, PS	1981
RT 069	Zounds	Demystification/Great White Hunter	PS	1981
RT 070	Mark Beer	Pretty / Per (Version)	PS	1981
RT 071	The Fall	Slates: Middle Mass/An Older Lover Etc./Prole Art Threat/Fit And Working Again/Slates Slags Etc./Leave The Capitol	10", 33rpm maxi single PS	1981
RT 072	Virgin Prunes	In The Greylight/War/Moments And Mine/Despite Straight Lines	PS	1981
RT 073	The Red Crayola	An Old Man's Dream/The Milkmaid	PS	1981
RT 074	Essential Logic	Fanfare In The Garden/The Captain	PS	1981
RT 075	The Nightingales	Idiot Strength/Seconds	PS	1981
RT 076	Tan Tan	Theme From A Summer Place/Princess	PS	1981
RT 076T	Tan Tan	Theme From A Summer Place/Princess	12", PS	1981
RT 077	Panther Burns	Train Kept A-Rolling/Red Headed Woman	Co-release with Frenzi Records, PS	1981
RT 078	The Red Crayola	Days Of Future Pilots/Ratman The Rat Catcher	Scheduled but not released	
RT 079	Wire	Our Swimmer/Midnight Bahnhof Cafe	PS	1981
RT 080	The Prats	General Davis/Alliance	PS	1981
RT 081	R. Wyatt and Dishari	Grass/Trade Union	One side each PS	1981
RT 082	Jackie Mittoo	These Eyes/Wall Street	PS	1981
RT 083	Bunny Wailer	Riding/Rise And Shine	Co-release with Solomon Records (RT/SM 007) PS	1981
RT 084	Epic Soundtracks	Jelly Babies/A 3-Acre Floor/Pop In Packets	PS	1981
RT 085	The Gist	Love At First Sight/Light Aircraft	PS	1982
RT 086	DNA	A Taste Of DNA EP	12", PS	1981
RT 087	Lora Logic	Wonderful Offer/Stereo	PS	1981
RT 087T	Lora Logic	Wonderful Offer/Stereo/Rather Than Repeat	12", PS	1981
RT 088	David Gamson	Sugar, Sugar/Honey, Honey	PS	1981
RT 088T	David Gamson	Sugar, Sugar/Honey, Honey	12", PS	1981
RT 089	Virgin Prunes	Sandpaper Lullaby/Sleep/Fantasy Dreams	PS	1981
RT 090T	Virgin Prunes	Come To Daddy/Sweet Home Under White Clouds/Sad World	10", PS	1981
RT 091	Scritti Politti	The 'Sweetest Girl'/Lions After Slumber	PS	1981
RT 091T	Scritti Politti	The 'Sweetest Girl' (Ext)/Lions After Slumber (Different Mix)	12", PS	1981
RT 092	Martin Pig	Lovely Rita Meter Maid/Somebody Loves You	PS	1982
RT 093	The Raincoats	Running Away/No-One's Little Girl	PS	1982
RT 094	Zounds	Dancing/True Love	PS	1982
RT 095	Cabaret Voltaire	Jazz The Glass/Burnt To The Ground	PS	1981
RT 096T	Cabaret Voltaire	Eddie's Out/Walls Of Jericho	12", initial batch incl pink vinyl edition of RT 095 PS	1981
RT 097	Weekend	The View From Her Room/Leaves Of Spring	PS	1982

Cat. No.	Artist	Titles		Year
RT 097T	Weekend	The View From Her Room/Leaves Of Spring	12", PS	1982
RT 098	Zounds	More Trouble Coming Every Day/Knife	PS	1982
RT 099T	Virgin Prunes	The Beast (Seven Bastard Suck)/The Slow Children (Abbagal)/Brain Damage/No Birds To Fly	12", PS	1982
RT 100	Mighty Diamonds	Pastakouchie/Party Time	PS	1982

Albums (the first 45):

Cat. No.	Artist	Titles		Year
ROUGH 1	Stiff Little Fingers	Inflammable Material		1979
ROUGH 2	Swell Maps	A Trip to Marineville	Also Rather TROY 1	1979
ROUGH 3	Raincoats	The Raincoats		1979
ROUGH 4	Cabaret Voltaire	Mix Up		1979
ROUGH 5	Essential Logic	Beat Rhythm News		1979
ROUGH 6	Doctor Mix and The Remix	Wall Of Noise		1979
ROUGH 7	Cabaret Voltaire	Live At The YMCA		1980
ROUGH 8	Young Marble Giants	Colossal Youth		1980
ROUGH 9	The Pop Group	For How Much Longer Do We Tolerate Mass Murder		1980
ROUGH 10	Fall	Totale's Turns (live)		1980
ROUGH 11	Cabaret Voltaire	The Voice Of America		1980
ROUGH 12	The Pop Group	We Are Time		1980
ROUGH 13	Raincoats	Odyshape		1980
ROUGH 14	Pere Ubu	The Art of Walking		1980
ROUGH 15	Swell Maps	Jane From Occupied Europe		1980
ROUGH 16	James "Blood" Ulmer	Are You Glad To Be In?		1980
ROUGH 18	Fall	Grotesque (After The Gramme)		1980
ROUGH 19	Red Crayola	Kangaroo		1981
ROUGH 20	Scritti Politti	Songs To Remember		1981
ROUGH 21	Swell Maps	Whatever Happens Next		1981
ROUGH 23	Pere Ubu	360 Degrees of Simulated Stereo		1981
ROUGH 24	Television Personalities	And Don't The Kids Just Love It		1981
ROUGH 25	Gist	Embrace The Herd		1981
ROUGH 26	This Heat	Deceit		1981
ROUGH 27	Cabaret Voltaire	Red Mecca		1981
ROUGH 28	Lora Logic	Pedigree Chum		1981
ROUGH 29	Wire	Document And Eyewitness		1981
ROUGH 31	Zounds	The Curse Of Zounds		1981
ROUGH 33	Pere Ubu	Song Of The Boiling Man		1981
ROUGH 35	Robert Wyatt	Nothing Can Stop Us		1982
ROUGH 36	Blue Orchids	Greatest Hits		1981
ROUGH 37	Various	Soweto Compilation		1981
ROUGH 38	Mighty Diamonds	Changes		1981
ROUGH 40	Robert Wyatt	The Animals Film		1982
ROUGH 41	Swell Maps	Collision Time		1982
ROUGH 42	Cabaret Voltaire	2 X 12"		1982
ROUGH 43	Lilliput	Lilliput		1982
ROUGH 45	Go-Betweens	Send Me A Lullaby		1982

7" Singles:

Cat. No.	Artist	Titles		Year
RTSO 1	Spizzoil	6,000 Crazy/1989/Fibre	PS	1979
RTSO 2	Spizzoil	Cold City/Red And Black/Solarisation/Platform 3	PS	1979
RTSO 3	Spizzenergi	Soldier's Soldier/Virginia Plain	PS	1979
RTSO 4	Spizzenergi	Where's Captain Kirk?/Amnesia	PS	1979
RTSO 5	Athletico Spizz '80	No Room/Spock's Missing	PS	1979
RTSO 6	Spizzenergi 2	Mega Gity 3/Work	PS	1982
RTSO 7	Spizzenergi 2	Jungle Fever/The Meaning	PS	1982
Disque Bleu BLI	Monochrome Set	He's Frank (Slight Return)/Silicon Carne/Fallout	PS	1979
Cells SELL ONE	Essential Logic	Aerosol Burns/World Friction	PS	1979
ISAU 1024	Angelic Upstarts	The Murder of Liddle Towers/Police Oppression	PS	1979
RT GOT 1	Protex	Don't Ring Me Up/Attention/Listening In	PS	1979

Safari (London)

7" Singles (the first few):

Cat. No.	Artist	Titles		Year
SAFE 1	Electric Chairs	Eddie And Sheena/Rock 'n 'Roll CleopatraPS	1978	
SAFE 3	Chanter Sisters	Na Na hey Hey (Kiss Him Goodbye)/When The Lights Go Out	PS	1978
SAFE 4	Playmate	Last Dance/Oriental Explosion	PS	1978

Cat. No.	Artist	Titles		Year
SAFE 5	Richard Clayderman	Ballade Pour Adeline (piano and orchestra)/		
		Ballade Pour Adeline (piano solo)	PS	1978
SAFE 6	George Dekker	Reggae Star/Reggae Jah	PS	1978
SAFE 7	Dennis O'Brien	Talk/Malibu Bay	PS	1978
SAFE 8	Roy Mason Apps	Everytime We Say Goodbye/Pearl	PS	1978
SAFE 9	Wayne County and The Electric Chairs	Trying To Get On The Road/Evil-Minded Mama	PS	1978
SAFE 10	Chanter Sisters	Can't Stop Dancing/Back On The Radio	PS	1978
SAFE 11	Cheetah	Pressure Drop/Don't Stop Making Love	PS	1978
SAFE 12	Bill Barclay	Burns Night Fever/Guinness Book Of Records	PS	1978
SAFE 13	Wayne County and The Electric Chairs	Berlin/Waiting For The Marines	PS	1978
SAFE 14	Glenn Hughes	I Found A Woman/L.A. Cut Off	PS	1978
SAFE 15	Toyah	Victims Of The Riddle/Victims Of The Riddle (Vivisection)	PS	1979
SAFE 16	The Man	Hey You (Get Out Of My Bed)/Tomcat	PS	1979
SAFE 17	Teenbeats	I Can't Control Myself/I'll Never Win	PS	1979
SAFE 18	Electric Chairs	So Many Ways/J'Attends Les Marines	PS	1979
SAFE 19	Teenbeats	Strength Of The Nation/If I'm Gone Tomorrow	PS	1979
SAFE 20	Bill Barclay	Hey Jimmy/I'm Gonna See A Lady Tonight	PS	1979
SAFE 21	Boys	Kamikaze/Bad Days	PS	1979
SAFE 22	Toyah	Bird In Flight/Tribal Look	PS	1980
SAFE 23	Boys	Terminal Love/I Love Me	PS	1980
SAFE 24	Gary Holton	Ruby (Don't Take Your Love To Town)/Listen/Love Is Young	PS	1980
SAFE 29	Blood Donor	Dr. Who/Soap Box Blues	PS	1980
SAFE 30	Purple Hearts	My Life's A Jigsaw/Just To Please You/		
		The Guy Who Made Her A Star	PS	1980
SAFE 31	Boys	Weekend/Cool	PS	1980
SAFE 33	Boys	Let It Rain/Lucy	PS	1980
SAFE 34	Toyah	I Want To Be Free/Walkie Talkie/Alien	PS	1981
SAFE 35	George Dekker	Atlantic Road (The Prophecy)/The Other Side Of Atlantic Road	PS	1981
SAFE 36	Erogenous Zones	Say It's Not So/War Games	PS	1981
SAFE 37	Dave Atkins	Acquaintances/Lavinia	PS	1981
SAFE 38	Toyah	Thunder In The Mountain/Street Addict		
		Also picture disc (SAFEP 38) and 12" (SAFEL 38)	PS	1981
SAFE 39	Weapon of Peace	Jah Love/West Park	PS	1981
SAFE 42	Weapon of Peace	Foul Play/Travelling Fever	Also 12", PS	1982

EPs:

Cat. No.	Artist	Titles		Year
SAFEP 1	Various	From The Butterfly Ball EP: Love Is All/Sitting In A Dream/Little Chalk Blue/		
		Homeward	PS	19??
SAP 1	Toyah	Sheep Farming In Barnet EP: Neon Womb/Indecision/Waiting/Our Movie/Danced/		
		Last Goodbye	PS	1980
SAP 2	Genocide	Images Of Delusion: Images Of Delusion/Pre-Set Future/Last Day On Earth/		
		Plastic People In Stereo		1979
TOY 1	Toyah	Four From Toyah EP: It's A Mystery/Warboys/Angels And Demons/		
		Revelation	PS	1981
TOY 2	Toyah	Four More from Toyah EP	PS	1981
WC 2	Wayne County and The Electric Chairs	Blatantly Offensive EP: Fuck Off/Night Time/Toilet Love/		
		Mean Muthafuckin Man	PS	1978
YULE 1	Yobs	Rub-A-Dum-Dum/Another Christmas Yobs = Boys	PS	1981

Albums (the first few):

Cat. No.	Artist	Titles		Year
1-2 BOYS	Boys	To Hell With The Boys		1979
GOOD 1	Wayne County and The Electric Chairs	Storm The Gates Of Heaven		1978
GOOD 2	Wayne County and The Electric Chairs	Things Your Mother Never Told You		1979
LIVE 2	Toyah	Toyah, Toyah, Toyah		1981
LONG 1	Wayne County and The Electric Chairs	Electric Chairs		1978
RUDE 1	Yobs	The Yobs' Christmas Album		1980
UPP 1	Various	Uppers On The South Downs	Compilation	1980
VOOR 1	Toyah	Anthem		1981

Secret Records

Singles:

Cat. No.	Artist	Titles		Year
SHH 101	Brain Brain	They've Got Me In A Bottle / I Get Pain	PS	1978
SHH 102	Temporary Title	Tell Him / Motorway	PS	1978
SHH 103	The Civilians	America / In Search Of Pleasure	PS	197?
SHH 104	The Fallout Club	Falling Years / The Beat Boys	PS	1979

Cat. No.	Artist	Titles		Format	Year
SHH 105	Brian Brain	Another Million Miles / Personality Counts		PS	1979
SHH 106	Baby Patrol	Fusion Fusion / Turn It Down		PS	1979
SHH 107	Zoe Nichols	Rubber Ball / With A Little Love		PS	1980
SHH 108	Voice	Sign Your Name / Going Home		PS	1980
SHH 109	Brain Brain	Culture EP: Fun People / At Home He's A Tourist / Working In A Farmyard In A White Suit / Careeing		PS	1980
SHH 110	The Exploited	Dogs Of War / Blown To Bits		PS	1981
SHH 111	Mandingo	Mr.Oh Ah Man / Dub Version		PS	1981
SHH 112	The Exploited	Army Life / Crashed Out / Fuck The Mods		PS	1981
SHH 113	The Exploited	Exploited Barmy Army / I Believe In Anarchy / What You Gonna Do		PS	1981
SHH 114	Lovely Previn	From A To B / Tower Of Strength		PS	1981
SHH 115	The Voice	She's Leaving / Going Home		PS	1981
SHH 116	Temporary Title	Cheon Sam / Pyjama Song		PS	1981
SHH 117	Infa Riot	Kids Of The 80's / Still Out Of Order		PS	1981
SHH 118	Paul Dupre	Northern Lights / Sight And Sound		PS	1981
SHH 119	Brian Brain	Jive Jive / Hello To The Working Class		PS	1981
SHH 120	The Exploited	Dead Cities / Hitler's In The Charts Again / Class War		PS	1981
SHH 121	Keith and Jeff Chegwin	More To Love / Night After Night		PS	1981
SHH 122	The Klones	Disco Rhythm / Metal Man		PS	1981
SHH 123	The Business	Harry May / Employers Black List		PS	1981
SHH 124	Lovely Previn	I'll Never Get Over You / Cheat		PS	1981
SHH 125	The 4 Skins	Yesterday's Heroes / Justice / Get Out Of My Life		PS	1981
SHH 126	Various	Bollocks To Christmas EP: The Business - Bollocks To Christmas / The Gonads – White Xmas / The 4 Skins – Merry Christmas Everybody / Max Splodge - 12 Days Of Xmas	Compilation	PS	1981
SHH 127	Polka Dots	Rosemary / Don't Love Me At All		PS	1981
SHH 128	Not Released				
SHH 129	Chron Gen	Jet Boy Jet Girl / Abortions / Subway Sadist		PS	1982
SHH 130	The Exploited	Attack / Alternative		PS	1982
SHH 131	The Gonads	Pure Punk For Row People EP: Sandra Bigg / I Lost My Love To A UK Sub / Annie's Song / Punk Rock Will Never Die / Got Any Wriggly's John		PS	1982
SHH 132	The Business	Smash The Discos / Dayo / Disco Girls		PS	1982
SHH 133	Infa Riot	The Winner / Schools Out		PS	1982
SHH 134	The Gonads	Peace Artists EP: Punk City Rockers / SLAG / She Can't Whip Me / Gonads Anthem		PS	1982
SHH 135	Lovely Previn	Wasted Love / Down On The Farm		PS	
SHH 136	Various	Britannia Waives The Rules: The Exploited - Y.O.P. / Infa Riot - Feel The Rage / Chron Gen - Clouded Eyes	Compilation	12", PS	1982
SHH 137	Twisted Sister	Ruff Cuts EP: Shoot 'Em Down / Under The Blade / What You Don't Know / Leader Of The Pack		PS	1982
SHH 138	Various	Back On The Streets EP: Skin Disease - I'm Thick / Angela Rippon's Bum - Fight For Your Lives / Venom — Where's Dock Green / The Strike - Victims / East End Badoes - The Way It's Gonna Be		Compilation PS	1982
SHH 139	Chron Gen	Outlaw / Behind Closed Doors / Disco Tech		PS	1982
SHH 140	The Exploited	Computers Don't Blunder /Addiction		PS	1982
SHH 141	The 4-Skins	Low Life / Bread Or Blood		PS	1982
SHH 142	Brian Brain	Funky Zoo / Flies		PS	198?
SHH 143	Dog Dog Dog	Take The Fever / Skin Deep		PS	198?
SHH 144	Plastic Gangsters	Plastic Gangsters / Sretsgnag Citslap			1983
SHH 145	The Exploited	Troops Of Tomorrow / (Radio Edit)		PS	1983
SHH 146	Dinah Rod and The Drains	Somebodys In My Drain / Some Bodies Pt's 1,2,3 & 4	also 12" (SHH 146-12)	PS	1983
SHH 147	The Papers	The Only One I See Is Me / Reggae On The Rocks		Not Released	
SHH 148	The Dossers	Red Night / Punk Rocker / Running Running / Armada		PS	1983
SHH 149	The 4-Skins	Seems To Me / Norman		Not Released	
SHH 150	The Business	Out Of Business EP: H-Bomb / Last Train To Clapham Junction / Tell Us The Truth / Law And Order / Do They Owe Us A Living		Not Released	
CF 101	The 4-Skins	One Law For Them / Brave New World		PS	1981
FREEBIE 1	Chron Gen	Living Next Door To Alice / Ripper / Puppets Of War		PS	1982

Albums:

Cat. No.	Artist	Titles			Year
SEC 1	The Exploited	Punk's Not Dead			1981
SEC 2	Various	Carry On Oi!	Compilation		1981
SEC 3	Chron Gen	Chronic Generation			1982
SEC 4	The 4-Skins	The Good The Bad The 4-Skins			1982
SEC 5	Various	Oi! Oi! That's Yer lot	Compilation		1982
SEC 6	Lovely Previn	Shatterproof			1982

Cat. No.	Artist	Titles		Year
SEC 7	Infa Riot	Still Out Of Order		1982
SEC 8	The Exploited	Troops Of Tomorrow		1982
SEC 9	Twisted Sister	Under The Blade		1982
SEC 10	Various Artists	Secret Life Of Punks	Compilation	1982
SEC 11	The Business	Suburban Rebels		1983
BRAIN 1	Brian Brain	Unexpected Noises		198?

Sensible (Edinburgh)

7" Singles:

Cat. No.	Artist	Titles		Year
FAB 1	Rezillos	Can't Stand My Baby/I Wanna Be Your Man	PS	1977
FAB 2	Rezillos	Flying Saucer Attack/(My Baby Does) Good Sculptures	PS	1977
FAB 3	Neon	Bottles/I'm Only Little/Anytime, Anyplace, Anywhere	PS	197?

Small Wonder (London)

7" Singles and EPs:

Cat. No.	Artist	Titles		Year
SMALL 1	Puncture	Mucky Pup/Can't Rock 'n' Roll	PS	1977
SMALL 2	Zeros	Hungry/Radio Fun	PS	1977
SMALL 3	Carpettes	Radio Wunderbar EP: How About Me And You/Help I'm Trapped/Radio Wunderbar/Cream Of The Youth	PS	1977
SMALL 4	Patrik Fitzgerald	Safety Pin In Your Heart EP: Banging And Shouting/Safety Pin Stuck In My Heart/Work Rest Play Reggae/Set Me Free/Optimism/Reggae	PS	1977
SMALL 5	Menace	GLC/I'm Civilized	PS	1977
SMALL 6	Patrik Fitzgerald	Buy Me, Sell Me/Little Dippers/Trendy/The Backstreet Boys	PS	1977
SMALL 7	Leyton Buzzards	19 And Mad/Villain/Youthanasia	PS	1978
SMALL 8	Punishment Of Luxury	Puppet Life/The Demon	PS	1978
SMALL 9	Carpettes	Small Wonder/2 N.E. 1	PS	1978
SMALL 10	Demon Preacher	Little Miss Perfect/Perfect Dub	PS	1978
SMALL 11	Cure	Killing An Arab/10.15	PS	1978
SMALL 12	Nicky and The Dots	Never Been So Stuck/Linoleum Walk	PS	1979
SMALL 13	Wall	New Way/Suckers/Uniforms	PS	1979
SMALL 14	Molesters	Commuter Man/Disco Love	PS	1979
SMALL 15	Cravats	The End/Burning Bridges/I Hate The Universe	PS	1979
SMALL 16	Menace	Last Year's Youth/Carry No Banners	PS	1979
SMALL 17	Murder The Disturbed	DNA/Walking Corpses/The Ultimate System	PS	1979
SMALL 18	Molesters	The End Of Civilisation/Girl Behind The Curtain	PS	1979
SMALL 19	Cockney Rejects	Flares 'n' Slippers/Police Car/I Wanna Be A Star	PS	1979
SMALL 20	Fatal Microbes	Violence Grows/Beautiful Pictures/Cry Baby	PS	1979
SMALL 21	Wall	Exchange/Kiss The Mirror	PS	1979
SMALL 22	English Subtitles	Time Tunnel/Sweat/Reconstruction	PS	1979
SMALL 23	Proles	Soft Ground/S.M.K.	PS	1979
SMALL 24	Cravats	Precinct/Who's In Here With Me	PS	1980
SMALL 25		You're Driving Me/I Am The Dreg	PS	1980

EPs:

Cat. No.	Artist	Titles	7" and 12"	PS	Year
WEENY 1	Patrik Fitzgerald	Paranoid Ward	12"	PS	1978
WEENY 2	Crass	Feeding The 5,000	12"	PS	1979
WEENY 3	Fatal Microbes	Fatal Microbes Meet The Poison Girls	12"	PS	1979
WEENY 4	Poison Girls	Hex	12"	PS	1979
TEENY 1	Frank Sumatra	Story So Far EP	EP; alias for Family Fodder, PS		1979
TEENY 2	Bauhaus	Bela Lugosi's Dead	12"	PS	1979

Album:

Cat. No.	Artist	Titles	Year
CRAVAT1	Cravat	Cravats In Toytown	1980

Step Forward (London)

Singles:

Cat. No.	Artist	Titles		Year
SF 1	Cortinas	Fascist Dictator/Television Families	PS	1977
SF 2	Chelsea	Right To Work/The Loner	PS	1977
SF 3	Models	Freeze/Man Of The Year	PS	1977

Cat. No.	Artist	Titles		Year
SF 4	Sham 69	I Don't Wanna/Ulster/Red London	PS, also 12"	1977
SF 5	Chelsea	High Rise Living/No Admission	PS	1977
SF 6	Cortinas	Defiant Pose/Independence	PS, also 12"	1978
SF 7	The Fall	Bingo Master's Break Out EP: Psycho Mafia/Bingo Master/Repetition	PS	1978
SF 8	Chelsea	Urban Kids/No Flowers	PS	1978
SF 9	The Fall	It's The New Thing/Various Times	PS	1978
SF 10	Lemon Kittens	Spoonfed And Writhing EP: Shakin'All Over/This Kind Of Dying/Morbo Talk/Bookburner/ Whom Do I Have To Ask?/C'halet D'Amout/Not A Mirror	PS	1979
SF 11	The Fall	Rowche Rumble/In My Area	PS	1979
SF 1212	Transmitters	The Ugly Man/The One That Won The War/Free Trade/Curious	12", PS	1979
SF 13	The Fall	Fiery Jack/2nd Dark Age/Psykick Dance Hall No. 2	PS	1980
SF 14	Chelsea	No-One's Coming Outside/What Would You Do	PS	1980
SF 15	Chelsea	Look At The Outside/Don't Get Me Wrong	PS	1980
SF 16	Chelsea	No Escape/Decide	PS	1980
SF 17	Chelsea	Rockin' Horse/Years Away	PS	1981
SF 18	Chelsea	Freemans/ID Parade/How Do You Know?	PS	1981
SF 19	Chron Gen	Reality/Subway Sadist	PS	1981
SF 20	Chelsea	Evacuate/New Era	PS	1981
SF 21	Chelsea	War Across The Nation/High Rise Living	PS	1982
SF 22	Chelsea	Stand Out/Last Drink	PS	1982
SF 23	Major Accident	Mr. Nobody/That's You	PS	1983

Albums:

Cat. No.	Artist	Titles	Year
SFLP 1	The Fall	Live at the Witch Trials	1979
SFLP 2	Chelsea	Chelsea	1979
SFLP 3	Sods	Minutes To Go	1979
SFLP 4	The Fall	Dragnet	1979
SFLP 5	Chelsea	Alternative Hits	1981
SFLP 7	Chelsea	Evacuate	1982
SFLP 8			
SFLP 9	Major Accident	Massacred Melodies	1982
SFLP 10	Chelsea	Just For The Record	1985

Stiff (London)

Singles:

Cat. No.	Artist	Titles		Year
BUY 1	Nick Lowe	So It Goes/Heart Of The City	PS	1976
BUY 2	Pink Fairies	Between The Lines/Spoiling For A Fight	PS	1976
BUY 3	Roogalator	Cincinnati Fatback/All Aboard	PS	1976
BUY 4	Tyla Gang	Styrofoam/Texas Chainsaw Massacre Boogie	PS	1976
BUY 5	Lew Lewis	Caravan Man/Boogie On The Streets	PS	1976
BUY 6	Damned	New Rose/Help	PS	1976
BUY 7	Richard Hell and The Voidoids	Another World/Blank Generation/You Gotta Lose	PS	1976
BUY 8	Plummet Airlines	Silver Shirt/This Is The World	PS	1976
BUY 9	Motorhead	Leavin' Here/White Line Fever	Never released, in box set	
BUY 10	Damned	Neat Neat Neat/Stab You Back/Singalonga Scabies	PS	1977
BUY 11	Elvis Costello	Less Than Zero/Radio Sweetheart	PS	1977
BUY 12	Max Wall	England's Glory/Dream Tobacco	PS	1977
BUY 13	Adverts	One Chord Wonders/Quick Step	PS	1977
BUY 14	Elvis Costello	Alison/Welcome To The Working Week	PS	1977
BUY 15	Elvis Costello	Red Shoes/Mystery Dance	PS	1977
BUY 16	Wreckless Eric	Whole Wide World/Semaphore Signals	PS	1977
BUY 17	Ian Dury	Sex And Drugs And Rock & Roll/Razzle In My Pocket	PS	1977
BUY 18	Damned	Problem Child/You Take My Money	PS	1977
BUY 19	Yachts	Suffice To Say/Freedom Is A Heady Wine	PS	1977
BUY 20	Elvis Costello	Watching The Detectives/Blame It On Cain/Mystery Dance	PS	1977

NB: BUY 1-10 and 11-20 were each available as limited edition boxed sets from Stiff, original picture sleeves but new pressings.

BUY 21	Nick Lowe	Halfway To Paradise/I Don't Want The Night To End	PS	1977
BUY 22	Larry Wallis	Police Car/On Parole	PS	1977
BUY 23	Ian Dury and The Blockheads	Sweet Gene Vincent/You're More Than Fair	PS	1977
BUY 24	Damned	Don't Cry Wolf/One Way Love	PS	1977
BUY 25	Wreckless Eric	Reconnez Cheri/Rags And Tatters	PS	1978
BUY 26	Jane Aire and The Belvederes	Yankee Wheels/Nasty. . Nice	PS	1978
BUY 27	Ian Dury	What A Waste!/Wake Up And Make Love To Me	PS	1978
BUY 28	Box Tops	Cry Like A Baby/The Letter	PS	1978
BUY 29	Humphrey Ocean	Whoops A Daisy/Davey Crockett	PS	1978

BUY 30	Jona Lewie	The Baby She's On The Street/Denny Laine's Valet	PS	1978
BUY 31	Just Water	Singing In The Rain/Witness To The Crime	PS	1978
BUY 32	Lene Lovich	I-Think We're Alone Now/Lucky Number	PS	1978
BUY 33	Wazmo Nariz	Tele-Tele-Telephone/Wacker Drive Also 12" (NAZ 1)	PS	1978
BUY 34	Wreckless Eric	Take The Cash/Girlfriend	PS	1978
BUY 35	Lene Lovich	Home/Lucky Number	Not issued	
BUY 36	MickyJupp	Old Rockin'Roller/Spy	PS	1978
BUY 37	Jona Lewie	Hallelujah Europa/	Not issued	
BUY 38	Ian Dury and The	Blockheads Hit Me With Your Rhythm Stick/There Ain't Half Been Some Clever Bastards	Also 12", PS	1978
BUY 39	Rachel Sweet	B-A -B-Y/Suspended Animation	PS	1978
BUY 40	Wreckless Eric	Crying, Waiting, Hoping/I Wish It Would Rain	PS	1978
BUY 41	Binky Baker	Toe Knee Black Burn/Rainy Day In Brighton	PS	1978
BUY 42	Lene Lovich	Lucky Number/Home Also 12", with Lucky Number (version), PS		1979
BUY 43	Rumour	Frozen Years/All Fall Down	PS	1979
BUY 44	Rachel Sweet	I Go To Pieces/Who Does Lisa Like?	PS	1979
BUY 45	Rumour	Emotional Traffic/Hard Enough To Show Also red, amber, and green vinyl editions. Also 12"	PS	1979
BUY 46	Lene Lovich	Say When/One Lonely Heart Also 12"	PS	1979
BUY 47	Kirsty MacColl	They Don't Know/Turn My Motor On	PS	1979
BUY 48	Lew Lewis Reformer	Win Or Lose/Photo Finish	PS	1979
BUY 49	Wreckless Eric	Hit And Miss Judy/Let's Go To The Pictures	Also orange 12", PS	1979
BUY 50	Ian Dury	Reasons To Be Cheerful, Part 3/Common As Muck	Also 12", PS	1979
BUY 51	Angie	Peppermint Lump/Breakfast In Naples	PS	1979
BUY 52	45's	Couldn't Believe A Word/Lonesome Lane	PS	1979
BUY 53	Lene Lovich	Bird Song/Trixi	PS	1979
BUYIT 53	Lene Lovich	Bird Song/Trixi/Too Tender	12", PS	1979
BUY 54	Duplicates	I Want To Make You Very Happy/Call Of The Faithful	PS	1979
BUY 55	Rachel Sweet	Baby, Let's Play House/Wildwood Saloon	PS	1979
BUY 56	Madness	One Step Beyond/Mistakes	56S, in Spanish, PS	1979
BUYIT 56	Madness	One Step Beyond/Mistakes/Nutty Theme	12", PS	1979
BUY 57	Kirsty MacColl	You Caught Me Out/	Not issued	1979
BUY 58	Michael O'Brien	Made In Germany/The Queen Likes Pop	PS	1979
BUY 59	Pointed Sticks	Out Of Luck/What Do You Want Me To Do?/Somebody's Mom	Also 12"	1979
BUY 60	GT's	Boys Have Feelings Too/Be Careful	PS	1979
BUY 61	Jona Lewie	God Bless Whoever Made You/Feeling Stupid	PS	1979
BUY 62	Madness	My Girl/Stepping Into Line	Also 12", PS	1980
BUY 63	Lene Lovich	Angels/The Fly	Also 12", PS	1980
BUY 64	Wreckless Eric	A Pop Song/Reconnez Cherie	PS	1980
BUY 65	Feelies	Everybody's Got Something to Hide/Original Love	PS	1980
BUY 66	Dirty Looks	Lie To Me/Rosario's Ashes	PS	1980
BUY 67	Rachel Sweet	Fool's Gold/I Got A Reason	PS	1980
BUY 68	Lew Lewis	"1:30, 2:30, 3:30"/The Mood I'm In	PS	1980
BUY 69	Lene Lovich	What Will I Do Without You/Joan (and) Monkey Talk/The Night/Too Tender (To Touch)/You Can't Kill Me	Double 45 set, PS	1980
BUY 70	Desmond Dekker	Israelites/Why Fight	Also 10", PS	1980
BUY 71	Madness	Work, Rest And Play EP: Night Boat To Cairo/Deceives The Eye/The Young And The Old/Don't Quote Me On That	PS	1980
BUY 72	Graham Parker	Stupefaction/Women In Charge	Also 12", PS	1980
BUY 73	Jona Lewie	You'll Always Find Me In The Kitchen At Parties/Bureaucrat	PS	1980
BUY 74	Any Trouble	Yesterday's Love/Nice Girls	PS	1980
BUY 75	Wreckless Eric	Broken Doll/I Need A Situation	PS	1980
BUY 76	Plasmatics	Butcher Baby/Tight Black Pants	Also 12", PS	1980
BUY 77	Dirty Looks	Let Go/Accept Me	PS	1980
BUY 78	Go Go's	We Got The Beat/How Much More	PS	1980
BUY 79	Any Trouble	Second Choice/Name Of The Game/Bible Belt	PS	1980
BUY 80	Rachel Sweet	Spellbound/Lovers' Lane	PS	1980
BUY 81	Rumour	My Little Red Book/Name And Number	PS	1980
BUY 82	Graham Parker	Love Without Greed/Mercury Poisoning	PS	1980
BUY 83	Otis Watkins	You Talk Too Much/If You're Ready To Rock	PS	1980
BUY 84	Madness	Baggy Trousers/The Business	PS	1980
BUY 85	Jona Lewie	Big Shot - Momentarily/I'll Get By In Pittsburgh	Also 5" (BUY 585), PS	1980
BUY 86	Stiffs	Goodbye My Love/Magic Roundabout	PS	1980
BUY 87	Desmond Dekker	Please Don't Bend/Workout (groove version)	PS	1980
BUY 88	Joe "King" Carrasco and The Crowns	Buena/Tuff Enuff	PS	1980
BUY 89	Dirty Looks	Tailin' You/Automatic Pilot	PS	1980
BUY 90	Ian Dury and The Blockheads	I Want To Be Straight/That's Not All He Wants To Say	Also 12", PS	1980
BUY 91	Plasmatics	Monkey Suit/Squirm (live)	Red/yellow vinyl, PS	1981

Cat. No.	Artist	Titles		Year
BUY 92	Rumour	I Don't Want The Night To End/Pyramids	PS	1981
BUY 93	Mexicano	Trial By Television/Jamaican Child	Also 12", PS	1981
BUY 94	Any Trouble	No Idea/Girls Are Always Right	PS	1981
BUY 95	Equators	Baby Come Back/Georgie	PS	1980
BUY 96	Not issued			
BUY 97	Lene Lovich	New Toy/Cat's Away	Also 12", PS	1981
BUY 98	Tenpole Tudor	3 Bells In A Row/Fashion/Rock And Roll Music	PS	1981
BUY 99	Elmo and Patsy	Grandma Got Run Over By A Reindeer/Christmas	PS	1980
BUY 100	Ian Dury and The Blockheads	Superman's Big Sister/You'll See Glimpses	Also 12", PS	1980
BUY 101	John Otway	Green Green Grass Of Home/Wednesday Club	PS	1980
BUY 102	Madness	Embarassment/Crying Shame	PS	1980
BUY 103	Nigel Dixon	Thunderbird/Someone's On The Loose	PS	1981
BUY 104	Jona Lewie	Stop The Cavalry/Laughing Tonight	PS	1980
BUY 105	Desmond Dekker	Many Rivers To Cross/Pickney Gal	PS	1980
BUY 106	London Cast Of "Oklahoma"	Oklahoma/Oh, What a Beautiful Morning	PS	1980
BUY 107	Not issued			
BUY 108	Madness	The Return Of The Los Palmas 7/That's The Way To Do It	Also 12", PS	1981
BUY 109	Tenpole Tudor	The Swords Of A Thousand Men/Love And Food	PS	1981
BUY 110	Jona Lewie	Louise (We Get It Right)/It Will Never Go Wrong	Also 12", PS	1981
BUY 111	Lonesome Tone	Mum, Dad, Love, Hate And Elvis/	Not issued	
BUY 112	Madness	Grey Day/Memories Also ZBUY, cassette	PS	1981
BUY 113	Equators	If You Need Me/So What's New	PS	1981
BUYIT 113	Equators	If You Need Me/Feelin' High/Rankin' Discipline	12", PS	1981
BUY 114	Bubba Lou and The Highballs	Love All Over the Place /	Not issued	
BUY 115	John Otway	Turning Point/Too Much Air, Not Enough Oxygen	PS	1981
BUY 116	Not issued			
BUY 117	Belle Stars	Hiawatha/Big Blonde	PS	1981
BUY 118	Department S	Going Left Right/She's Expecting You	PS	1981
BUYIT 118	Department S	Going Left Right/She's Expecting You/Is Vic There?	12", PS	1981
BUY 119	Any Trouble	Trouble With Love/She'll Belong To Me	PS	1981
BUY 120	Tenpole Tudor	Wunderbar/ Tenpole 45	PS	1981
BUY 121	Sprout Head Uprising	Throw Some Water In/Nothing To Sing	PS	1981
BUY 122	Jona Lewie	Shaggy Raggy/Shaggy Raggied	PS	1981
BUY 123	Belle Stars	Slick Trick/Take Another Look	PS	1981
BUY 124	Alvin Stardust	Pretend/Goose Bumps	PS	1981
BUY 125	Billy Bremner	Loud Music In Cars/The Price Is Right	PS	1981
BUY 126	Madness	Shut Up/A Town With No Name	PS	1981
BUY 127	Not issued			
BUY 128	Department S	I Want/Monte Carlo Or Bust	PS	1981
BUY 129	Tenpole Tudor	Throwing My Baby Out With The Bath Water/Conga Tribe	PS	1981
BUY 130	Belle Stars	Another Latin Love Song/Stop Now/Having A Good Time/Miss World	PS	1981
BUY 131	Jona Lewie	Re-arranging Deck Chairs On The Titanic/I'll Be Home	PS	1981
BUY 132	Alvin Stardust	Wonderful Time Up There/Love You So Much	PS	1981
BUY 133	Cory Band and Gwalia Singers	Stop The Cavalry/Longest Day	PS	1981
BUY 134	Madness	It Must Be Love/Shadow On The House	PS	1981
BUY 135	Ian Dury and The Blockheads	What A Waste/Wake Up And Make Love With Me	Reissue	1981
BUY 136	The Dancing Did	Lost Platoon/Human Chicken	PS	1981
BUY 137	Tenpole Tudor	Let The Four Winds Blow/Sea Of Thunder	PS	1982
BUY 138	Pookiesnakenburger	Just One Cornetto/Turkish Bath	PS	1982
BUY 139	Jone Lewie	I Think I'll Get My Hair Cut/What Have I Done	PS	1982
BUY 140	Madness	Cardiac Arrest/In The City	PS	1982
BUY 141	Not issued			
BUY 142	Alvin Stardust	Weekend/Butterflies	PS	1982
BUY 143	Billy Bremner	Laughter Turns To Tears/Tired And Emotional	PS	1982
BUY 144	Desmond Dekker	Book Of Rules/Allamanna	PS	1982
BUY 145	Astronauts	I'm Your Astronaut/Commander Incredible	PS	1982
BUY 146	Madness	House Of Fun/Don't Look Back	PS	1982
BUY 147	Jane Aire	I Close My Eyes And Count To Ten/Heart Of The City	PS	1982
BUY 148	Electric Guitars	Language Problems/Night Bears	PS	1982
BUY 149	Lene Lovich	Lucky Number/New Toy	PS	1982
BUY 150	Belle Stars	Iko Iko/The Reason	PS	1982

UK singles; (prefixes as noted):

Cat. No.	Artist	Titles		Year
BLO 1	Wilko Johnson	Oh Lonesome Me/Beauty	PS	19??
BOY 1	Devo	Satisfaction/		
		Sloppy 7" and 12", Boojie Boy Records (Stiff distribution)	PS	1978
BOY 2	Devo	Be Stiff/Social Fools Also lemon or clear vinyl	PS	1978

Cat. No.	Artist	Titles			Year
BROKEN 1	Dave Stewart, with Colin Blunstone	What Becomes Of The Brokenhearted/There Is No Reward		PS	1981
BROKEN 2	Dave Stewart, with Barbara Gaskin	It's My Party/Waiting In The Wings		PS	1981
CLAP 1	Thunderbolts	Dust On My Needle/Something Else		PS	198?
DAMNED 1	Damned	Stretcher Case Baby/Sick Of Being Sick	Given away at the Marquee Club in London		1977
DEA/SUK 1	Wayne Kramer	Ramblin' Rose/Get Some	Stiffwick/Chistiff (special Stiff/Chiswick cooperative release)	PS	1977
DEV 1	Devo	Mongoloid/Jocko Homo	Boojie Boy Records, 7" and 12"		1978
FREEBIE 1	Ian Dury	Sex And Drugs And Rock & Roll/Two Steep Hills/England's Glory		Pressed for NME	1977
FREEBIE 2	Various	Excerpts From Stiffs Greatest Hits		Promo only	1978
GFR 001	Mickey Jupp	Don't Talk To Me/Funk In My Trunk		PS	1981
HORN 1	Davey Payne	Saxophone Man/Foggy Day In London		PS	1979
LEW 1	Lew Lewis	Lucky Seven/Night Talk			1978
LOT 1	Johnnie Allan	Promised Land	Oval Records (Stiff distribution)		
	Pete Fowler	One Heart One Song			1978
MAX 1	Various	Commemorates Dave Robinson's Wedding			1979
RUM 1	Rumour	Frozen Years/All Fall Down		Promo only	1979
UPP 1	Mickey Jupp's Legend	My Typewriter/Nature's Radio		Promo only	19??
WED 1	Nick Jones and Ian MacRae	Ballad of Lady Di/Three Minutes Silence			1981

Albums:

Cat. No.	Artist	Titles			Year
SEEZ 0	Various	Heroes And Cowards	Compilation, Italy; No UK release		1978
SEEZ 1	Damned	Damned, Damned, Damned			1977
SEEZ 2	Various	A Bunch Of Stiffs	Compilation		1977
SEEZ 3	Elvis Costello	My Aim Is True			1977
SEEZ 4	Ian Dury and The Blockheads	New Boots And Panties			1977
SEEZ 5	Damned	Music For Pleasure			1977
SEEZ 6	Wreckless Eric	Wreckless Eric		12" and 10" versions	1978
SEEZ 7	Lene Lovich	Stateless		Also as pic disc	1978
SEEZ 8	Jona Lewie	On The Other Hand There's A Fist		Also as pic disc	1978
SEEZ 9	Wreckless Eric	The Wonderful World Of Wreckless Eric		Also as pic disc	1978
SEEZ 10	Mickey Jupp	Juppanese		Also as pic disc	1978
SEEZ 11	Jane Aire and The Belvedere's			Never released	
SEEZ 12	Rachel Sweet	Fool Around		Also as pic disc	1978
SEEZ 13	Rumour	Frogs, Sprouts, Clogs And Krauts			1979
SEEZ 14	Ian Dury	Do It Yourself			1979
SEEZ 16	Lew Lewis	Save The Wail			1979
SEEZ 17	Madness	One Step Beyond			1979
SEEZ 18	Rachel Sweet	Protect The Innocent			1980
SEEZ 19	Lene Lovich	Flex			1980
SEEZ 20	Feelies	Crazy Rhythms			1980
SEEZ 21	Wreckless Eric	Big Smash			1980
SEEZ 22	Dirty Looks	Dirty Looks			1980
SEEZ 23	Graham Parker	The Up Escalator			1980
SEEZ 24	Plasmatics	New Hope For The Wretched			1980
SEEZ 25	Any Trouble	Where Are All The Nice Girls?			1980
SEEZ 26	Desmond Dekker	Black And Dekker			1980
SEEZ 27	Rumour	Purity Of Essence			1980
SEEZ 28	Joe "King" Carrasco And The Crowns	Joe 'King' Carrasco			1980
SEEZ 29	Madness	Absolutely			1980
SEEZ 30	Ian Dury and The Blockheads	Laughter			1980
SEEZ 31	Tenpole Tudor	Eddie, Old Bob, Dick, And Gary			1981
SEEZ 32	Not issued				
SEEZ 33	Not issued				
SEEZ 34	Not issued				
SEEZ 35	Equators	Hot			1981
SEEZ 36	Desmond Dekker	Compass Point			1981
SEEZ 37	Any Trouble	Wheels In Motion			1981
SEEZ 38	Dirty Looks	Turn It Up			1981
SEEZ 39	Madness	Seven			1981
SEEZ 40	Jona Lewie	Heart Skips A Beat			1981
SEEZ 41	Ian Dury	Juke Box Dury			1981
SEEZ 42	Tenpole Tudor	Let The Four Winds Blow			1981

(UK albums; prefixes as noted):

Cat. No.	Artist	Titles			Year
DEAL 1	Various	Be Stiff Route '78	Dealer album with 16p booklet and package with biographies, etc.		1978
FIST 1	Various	Hits Greatest Stiffs	Compilation of singles		1977

Cat. No.	Artist	Titles		Year
FREEB 3	Various	Wonderful Time Out There	Compilation of singles	1981
GET 1	Various	Stiffs Live Stiff	Compilation	1978
GET 2	Mickey Jupp	Legend		1978
GET 3	Various	Akron Compilation	Compilation	1978
GOMM 1	Ian Gomm	Fomm With The Wind	Includes interview	197?
HIT TV 1	Madness	Complete Madness	Greatest hits	1982
JAH 1	Jah Bunny	Dubs International	Reggae	198?
JE 36103	Ian Gomm	Gomm With The Wind	Reissue	198?
LENE 1	Lene Lovich		Interview album	198?
MAIL 1	UK Subs	Live	12" EP	19??
ODD 1	Devo	Be Stiff	Mini-album	1978
ODD 2	Various	Be Stiff (Tour '78 Official Release)	Compilation, promo only	1978
SON 1	Various	Son Of Stiff Tour	Compilation, sampler	197?
SOUNDS 3	Various	Can't Start Dancin'	Obtained with coupons clipped from Sounds	1979
TNT 1	Mickey Dread	World War III	Reggae	1980
TRUBZ 1	Any Trouble	Live At The Venue		1980

EPs:

Cat. No.	Artist	Titles		Year
LAST 1	Nick Lowe	Bowi	PS	1977
LAST 2	Alberto Y Los Trios Paranoias	Snuff Rock: Kill/Gobbing On Life/Snuffin' Like That/Snuffin' In A Babylon	PS	1977
LAST 3	Wreckless Eric	Piccadilly Menial	Not released	
LAST 4	Mick Farren and The Deviants	Screwed Up	PS	1978
LAST 5	Sports	Who Listens To The Radio/Step By Step/So Obvious/Suspicious Mind	PS	1979

Stiff/One Off

7" Singles:

Cat. No.	Artist	Titles		Year
OFF 1	Subs	Gimme Your Heart/Party Clothes	PS	1978
OFF 2	Ernie Graham	Romeo And The Lonely Girl/Only Time Will Tell	PS	1978
OFF 3	Members	Solitary Confinement/Rat Up A Drainpipe	PS	1978
OFF 4	Realists	I've Got A Heart/Living In The City	PS	1978

Odd-size records, size and prefix as noted:

Cat. No.	Artist	Titles		Year
CROWN 1	Joe "King" Carrasco and The Crowns	Buena	10" 78rpm	1980
ERIC 1	Wreckless Eric	Six tracks from Big Smash	10" 33rpm	1980
SMUT 1	Dirty Looks	Six tracks	10" 33rpm	1980

Stiff-America

Albums:

Cat. No.	Artist	Titles		Year
USE 1	Wreckless Eric	Whole Wide World	Compilation	1979
USE 2	Ian Dury	New Boots And Panties		1979
USE 3	Various	The Last Compilation Album... Until The Next One	Compilation	1980
USE 4	Feelies	Crazy Rhythms		1980
USE 5	John Otway	Deep Thought		1980
USE 6	Any Trouble	Where Are All The Nice Girls?		1980
USE 8	Jona Lewie	On The Other Hand There's A Fist		1981
USE 9	Plasmatics	New Hope For The Wretched		1981
WOW 11	Plasmatics	Beyond The Valley Of 1984		1981
USE 13	Any Trouble	Wheels In Motion		1981
USE 14	Rough Trade	Avoid Freud		198?
USE 17	Ian Dury and The Blockheads	Juke Box Dury		1982

The Label (London)

Singles:

Cat. No.	Artist	Titles		Year
TLR 001	Eater	Outside View/You	PS	1977
TLR 002	Peko and Naka	Ageso Na Omae/Yamete	PS	1977
TLR 003	Eater	Thinking Of The USA/Space Dreamin'/Michael's Monetary System	PS	1977
TLR 004	Eater	Lock It Up/Jeepster	Also 12", PS	1977
TLR 005	Front	System/Queen's Mafia	PS	1978

Cat. No.	Artist	Titles		Year
TLR 006	Bombers	I'm A Liar, Babe/2230 AD	PS	1978
TLR 007	Eater	Get Your Yo-Yo's Out EP: Debutantes' Ball/No More	Also 12", (live), PS	1978
TLR 008	Dave Goodman and Friends	Justifiable Homicide/Take Down Your Fences	Red vinyl, PS	1978
TLR 009	Eater	What She Wants She Needs/Reach For The Sky	PS	1978
TLR 010	Cash Pussies	99% Is Shit/Cash Flow	PS	1979
TLR 011	Nick Wellings and The Section	You Better Move On/Punk Funk	PS	1979

Albums:

Cat. No.	Artist	Titles		Year
TLR LP 001	Eater	The Album		1978
TLR LP 002	Various	The Label Sofa	Compilation	1979

United Dairies

Run by John Fothergill and Steve Stapleton this label concentrated in the post-punk era on groups they found interesting and different. Their first thirteen releases are set out below:-

Cat. No.	Artist	Titles		Year
UD 001	Nurse With Wound	Chance Meeting On A Disecting Table...		1979
UD 002	Lemon Kittens	We Buy A Hammer For Daddy		1980
UD 003	Nurse With Wound	To The Quiet Men From A Tiny Girl		1980
UD 004	Nurse With Wound	Merzbild Schwet		1980
UD 005	Bombay Ducks	Dance Music		198?
UD 006	Various	Hoisting The Black Flag	Compilation	1981
UD 007	Lemon Kittens	Cake Beast	12" EP	1981
UD 008	Nurse With Wound	Insect And Individual Silenced		1981
UD 009	The 150 Murderous Passions			198?
UD 010	Musique Concret	Bringing Up Baby		198?
UD 011	Operating Theatre	Rapid Eye Movement		198?
UD 012	Various	An Afflicted Man's Musica Box	Compilation	1985
UD 013	Nurse With Wound	Homotopy To Marie		1985

NB: All releases are albums except UD 007.

Zonophone

Singles:

Cat. No.	Artist	Titles		Year
Z 1	Gang Of Four	Outside The Trains Don't Run On Time / He'd Send In The Army	PS	1980
Z 2	Cockney Rejects	Greatest Cockney Rip Off / Hate Of The City	PS	1980
Z 3	The Stiffs	Inside Out / Kids On The Street	PS	1980
Z 4	Cockney Rejects	I'm Forever Blowing Bubbles / West Side Boys	PS	1980
Z 5	The Barracudas	Summer Fun / Chevy Baby	PS	1980
Z 6	Cockney Rejects	We Can Do Anything / 15 Nights	PS	1980
Z 7	Angelic Upstarts	Last Night Another Soldier / Man Who Came In From The Beano	PS	1980
Z 8	The Barracudas	His Last Summer / Barracuda Waver / Surfers Are Back	PS	1980
Z 9	Not Released (Was to have been Cockney Rejects "Oi! Oi! Oi!" / "War On The Terraces")			
Z 10	Cockney Rejects	We Are The Firm / War On The Terraces	PS	1980
Z 11	The Barracudas	1965 Again / Rendezvous	PS	1980
Z 12	Angelic Upstarts	England / Sticks Diary	PS	1980
Z 13	Lip Service	Ruby / Jimmy Brown	PS	1981
Z 14	The Stiffs	Volume Control / Nothing To Lose	PS	1981
Z 15	Honey Bane	Turn Me On Turn Me Off / In Dreams / T'aint Nobodys Business / Negative Exposure	PS	1981
Z 16	Angelic Upstarts	Kids On The Street / The Sun Never Shines	PS	1981
Z 17	The Barracudas	I Can't Pretend / The KGB (Made A Man Out Of Me)	PS	1981
Z 18	Not Released			
Z 19	Honey Bane	Baby Love / Mass Production	PS	1981
Z 20	Cockney Rejects	Easy Life / Motorhead / Hang 'Em High	PS	1981
Z 21	Cockney Rejects	On The Streets Again / Lomdob	PS	1981
Z 22	Angelic Upstarts	I Understand / Never Come Back	PS	1981
Z 23	Honey Bane	Jimmy (Listen To Me) / Negative Exposure / Jimmy (Listen To Me)	PS	1981
Z 24	Bumble and The Beez	Fools / Working Class	PS	1981
Z 25	Angelic Upstarts	Different Strokes / Different Dub	PS	1981
Z 26	Vice Squad	Out Of Reach / Sterile / (So What) For The Eighties	PS	1982
Z 27	Bumble and The Beez	The Room Above / Blowzing	PS	1982
Z 28	Angelic Upstarts	Never Say Die / We Defy You	PS	1982
Z 29	Not Released			
Z 30	Vice Squad	Stand Strong, Stand Proud / Tomorrow's Soldier / Darkest Hour / Rock 'N' Roll Massacre	PS	1982

Cat. No.	Artist	Titles		Year
Z 31	Toy Dolls	Everybody Jitterbug / She's A Worky Ticket	PS	1982
Z 32	Honey Bane	Wish I Could Be Me / Childhood Prince	PS	1982
Z 33	Not Released			
Z 34	Vice Squad	Citizen / Scarred For Life / Faceless Men	PS	198?
Z 35	John Dark	Sillouette / Sillouette (Instr)	PS	198?
Z 36	Honey Bane	Dizzy Dreamers / I O's Burning /Ongoing Situation	PS	198?
Z 37	Bumble and The Beez	My Life / Signing On	PS	1986
Z 38	Cargo	Holding On For Love /It's Your Love	PS	1986
Z 39	Frank Sidebottom	The Popular Medley EP	PS	1985
Z 40	Frank Sidebottom	Oh Blimey It's Christmas / Oliver's Army / Christmas In Australia	PS	1985
Z 41	Frank Sidebottom	I'm The Urban Spaceman / Oh Supermum / Sci Fi Medley / Space Is Ace	PS	1986

Zoo (Liverpool)

45s:

Cat. No.	Artist	Titles		Year
CAGE 001	Big In Japan	From Y To Z And Never Again EP: Nothing Special/Suicide A Go Go/ Taxi Cindy And The Barbi Dolls	PS	1978
CAGE 002	Those Naughty Lumps	Iggy Pop's Jacket/Pure And Innocent	PS	1979
CAGE 003	The Teardrop Explodes	Sleeping Gas/Camera Camera/Kirkby' Workers' Dream Fades	PS	1979
CAGE 004	Echo and The Bunnymen	The Pictures On My Wall/Read It In Books	PS	1979
CAGE 005	The Teardrop Explodes	Bouncing Babies/All I Am Is Loving You	PS	1979
CAGE 006	Lori and The Chameleons	Touch/Love By The Ganges	PS, later on Sire	1979
CAGE 007	Expelaires	To See You/Frequency	PS	1979
CAGE 008	The Teardrop Explodes	Treason (It's Just A Story)/Read It In Books	PS	1980
CAGE 009	Wild Swans	Revolutionary Spirit/God Forbid	Also 12"	1982

Album:

Cat. No.	Artist	Titles	Year
FOUR	Various	To The Shores Of Lake Placid Sampler (Issued with a gatefold sleeve and four-page booklet)	1982

Zoom (Edinburgh)

Singles:

Cat. No.	Artist	Titles		Year
ZUM 1	The Valves	Robot Love/For Adolfs Only	PS	1977
ZUM 2	PVC2	Put You In The Picture/Pain/Deranged, Demented And Free	PS	1977
ZUM 3	The Valves	Tarzan Of The King's Road/Ain't No Surf	PS	1977
ZUM 4	The Zones	Stuck With You/We're No Angels	PS	1978
ZUM 5	Mike Heron	Sold On Your Love/Portland Rose	PS	1978
ZUM 6	The Questions	Some Other Guy/Rock & Roll Ain't Dead	PS	1978
ZUM 7	Nightshift	Love Is Blind/She Makes Me Love Her	PS	1978
ZUM 8	The Questions	Can't Get Over You/Answers	PS	1979
ZUM 9	Nightshift	Jet Set/Bad Dreams	PS	1979
ZUM 10	Simple Minds	Life In A Day/Special Love	PS	1979
ZUM 11	Simple Minds	Chelsea Girl/Garden Of Hate	PS	1979
ZUM 12	London Zoo	Receiving End/London Zoo	PS	1979
ZUM 13	Tony Pilley	Off The Hook/Mummy And Daddy (release cancelled)		
ZUM 14	The Cheetahs	Radioactive/The Only One/Minefield	PS	1979

Album:

Cat. No.	Artist	Titles	Year
ZULP 1	Simple Minds	Life In A Day	1979

Special thanks to Mark Brennan for help with Attrix, Beat The System, Captain Oi!, Captain Mod, Clay, Disorder, Fallout, Good Vibrations, Illegal, Lightning, Link, Pax, Razor, Riot City, Rondelet, Rot, Secret, Step Forward and Zonophone. Thanks also to Record Collector, an important source for many of these, along with assorted label catalogues.

Index:

a

A.B.H.	19
The Abnormal	19
Abrasive Wheels	19 - 20
The Accelerators	20
The Accidents	20 - 21
Accidents On East Lancs	21
Accursed	21
The Aces	21
Acme Sewage Co	21
The Act	21
Actifed	21
Action Pact	22 - 23
Action Replay	23
Adam and The Ants	23 - 26
Addix	26
The Adicts	26 - 27
A.D. 1984	27
Advertising	27
The Adverts	27 - 28
Afflicted	28
Afraid Of Mice	28
After Dark	29
Airkraft	29
Aka and Charlatans	29
AK Process	29
Akrylykz	29
The Alarm	29 - 31
Albertos Y Los Trios Paranoias	31
Aliens	31
The Allies	31
Altered Images	31 - 33
Alternative TV	33 - 35
The Alternators	35
Amazorblades	35
The Amber Squad	35
American Echoes	35
Anarcho-Punk Cassette Compilations	35 - 36
The Androids	36
Androids Of Mu	36
And The Native Hipsters	36
Angela Rippon's Bum	36
Angelic Upstarts	36 - 39
Angel Street	39
Anihilated	39
Animal Farm	39
Anthrax	39
Anti-Establishment	39 - 40
The Anti-Nowhere League	40 - 41
Anti-Pasti	41
Anti-Social	41
Anti-Social	41 - 42
Anti System	42
Any Trouble	42 - 43
The Apartment	43
Architects Of Disaster	43
Arms and Legs	43
Art Attacks	43
The Art Bears	43 - 44
Artery	44
Art Failure	44
Article 58	44
Art Objects	44
Dave Asgrove Band	44
Athletico Spizz 80	44 - 45
Attak	45
Attic	45
Attila The Stockbroker	45 - 46
The Attractions	46
Attrix	46
Auntiepus	46
The Au Pairs	46 - 47
Aural Exciters	47
The Autographs	47
Avant Gardener(s)	47

b

Henry Badowski	47
Back To Zero	47
The Balloons	47 - 48
Honey Bane	48
Ed Banger	48
Bankrobbers	48
The Banned	48 - 49
Barbed Wire	49
Wild Willy Barrett	49
Bauhaus	49 - 51
The Bears	51
The Bearz	51
Bee Bee Cee	51
Mark Beer	51
B.E.F. (British Electric Foundation)	52
Beggar	52
Berlin Blondes	52
Bethnal	52
Bet Lynch's Legs	53
The Betrayed	53
Big In Japan	53
The Bishops	53
Bitch	54
Blah Blah Blah	54
Blancmange	54 - 55
Blanks	55
Blitz	55 - 56
Blitz	56
The Blitz Brothers	56
Blitzkrieg	56 - 57
Blitzkrieg Bop	57
Blood	57 - 58
The Bloodclots	58
The Bloomsbury Set	58
Blue Movies	58
Blue Nile	58
Blue Orchids	58
Blunt Instrument	58
Blurt	59
B-Movie	59
Bodies	59
The Bollock Brothers	59 - 60
The Bombers	60
Books	60
The Boomtown Rats	60 - 62
Bow Wow Wow	62 - 63
The Box	63
The Boyfriends	63
The Boys	63 - 64
Brakes	64 - 65
Breakout	65
Brent Ford and The Nylons	65
Brian Brain	65
Brick Wall Band	65
Brilliant	65
Broken Bones	66
The Brothers Gonad	66
B-Team	66
Bullets	66
The Burial	66
Jean-Jacques Burnel	66 - 67
The Business	67 - 69
Buzzards	69
The Buzzcocks	69 - 71

c

Cabaret Voltaire	71 - 73
Jo Callis	73
Camera Obscura	74
Andy Cameron	74
Cardiac Arrest	74
The Cardiacs	74
The Carpettes	74 - 75
Chris Carter	75
Case	75
The Cash Pussies	75
The Catch	75
Ceila and The Mutations	75
A Certain Ratio	76 - 77
Chaos UK	77 - 78
Chaotic Dischord	78
Chaotic Youth	78
Charge	78 - 79
Charlie Parkas	79
The Chefs	79
The Cheetahs	79
Chelsea	79 - 80
The Chords	80
Chris and Cosey/ Creative Technology Institute	80 - 81
Christian Death	81
Christianity B.C.	81
Chron Gen	81
Chuddy Nuddies	81
The Cigarettes	81 - 82
The Circles	82
Clapham South Escalators	82
The Clash	82 - 86
The Classics	86
Classix Nouveaux	86 - 87
Alan Clayson and The Argonauts	87
The Clerks	87
Clock DVA	87 - 88
Clockwork Soldiers	88
The Clues	88
Cobra	88
Cockney 'n' Westerns	88
The Cockney Rejects	88 - 89
Cock Sparrer	89 - 90
The Cocteau Twins	90 - 91
Color Tapes	91
Combat 84	91 - 92
Coming Shortly	92
Comsat Angels	92 - 93
The Condemned	93
Condemned 84	93
Conflict	94
John Cooper Clarke	94 - 95
Hugh Cornwell	95
The Cortinas	95
Elvis Costello and The Attractions	95 - 99
The Count Bishops	99
Wayne County and The Electric Chairs	99 - 100
Court Martial	100 - 101
The Coventry Automatics	101
The Crabs	101
Crack	101 - 102
Crash	102
Crass	102 - 103
The Cravats	103
Craze	103
The Creatures	103 - 104
Criminal Class	104
Crisis	104
Crispy Ambulance	104
The Crooks	104 - 105
Crossed Hammers	105
Crowbar	105
Crux	105
Cuban Heels	105 - 106
Cuddly Toys	106
The Cult	106 - 107
Cult Figures	107
Cult Hero	107
Cult Maniax	107 - 108
Cupol	108
The Cure	108 - 111
Cyanide	111
The Cybermen	111

d

Dagaband	111
Dalek (Dalek I Love You)	111 - 112
Dalek O.K.	112
Dali's Car	112
The Damned	112 - 116
The Dancing Did	116
Danse Society	116
Dark	116 - 117
The Dazzlers	117
The D.C. 10's	117
The Deadbeats	117
Dead Generation	117
Dead Fingers Talk	117
Dead Man's Shadow	117
Deadly Toys	118
Death Cult	118
Death Sentence	118
Debutantes	118
Defects	118
Delta 5	118 - 119
Demob	119
Demon Preachers	119
Depeche Mode	119 - 121
The Depressions	122
The Desperate Bicycles	122 - 123
The Destructors (V)	123
The Details	123
The Detonators	123
Devil's Dykes	123
Howard Devoto	123
Diagram Brothers	123
Dials	124
Die Electro Eels	124
Dif Juz	124
The Direct Hits	124
The Directions	124
The Directors	125
Discharge	125
Disco Zombies	125 - 126
Disorder	126
Distractions	126
The Distributors	126
Disruptors	127
The Disturbed	127
The Dodgems	127
Dogsbody	127
The Doodlebugs	127
The Dole	127
The Doll	127 - 128
Dome	128
The Donkees	128
The Donkeys	128
The Door and The Window	128
Double Vision	128
Dregs	128
Drinking Electricity	128 - 129
Drive	129
The Drones	129
The Drug Addix	129
Dry Rib	130

Artist	Pages
The Duplicates	130
Duran Duran	130 - 131
Durutti Column	132 - 133
Ian Dury (and The Blockheads)	133 - 135
Dyaks	135

e

Artist	Pages
Earthbound	135
East End Badoes	135
Eater	135 - 136
Echo and The Bunnymen	136 - 137
Eddie and The Hot Rods	137 - 139
The Edge	139
Dave Edmunds	139 - 141
The Ejected	141
Electric Guitars	141
Electro Tunes	142
Embryo	142
Emergency	142
Empire	142
The Enemy	142 - 143
English Dogs	143
English Sub-Titles	143
The Escalators	143
Essential Bop	143 - 144
Essential Logic	144
Ethel The Frog	144
Europeans	144
The Exile	144
The Exits	144 - 145
Expelaires	145
The Expelled	145
The Ex-Pistols	146
Exploding Seagulls	146
The Exploited	146 - 147
Ex-Producers	147
External Menace	147
Ezy Meat	147

f

Artist	Pages
The 4-Skins	147 - 149
Fad Gadget	149
The Fall	149 - 152
Fallen Angels	152
Fan Club	152
The Fans	152
Fashion (Music)	152 - 153
Fast Cars	153
Fast Set	153
The Fatal Microbes	153
The Feckin' Ejits	153 - 154
The Feelies	154
Graham Fellows	154
Fenzyx	154
Alex Fergusson	154
Eddie Fiction	154
File Under Pop	154
Fingerprintz	154 - 155
Fire Engines	155
The First Steps	155
Fischer Z	155 - 156
Fish Turned Human	156
The Fits	156 - 157
Patrick Fitzgerald	157
Five O	157
Five Or Six	158
The Fix	158
The Fixx	158
Flag Of Convenience	158
The Flirts	159
A Flock Of Seagulls	159

Artist	Pages
Flux Of Pink Indians	159 - 160
The Flying Lizards	160
Fly On The Wall	160
The Flys	160 - 161
Ford Workers On Strike	161
Foreign Legion	162
Foreign Press	162
Foreign Press	162
48 Chairs	162
48 Hours	162
John Foxx	162 - 163
Bruce Foxton	163
Frankie Flame	163
The Frantic Elevators	164
The Freshmen	164
The Freshies	164 - 165
The Front	165
Fruit Eating Bears	165
Fun Four	165

g

Artist	Pages
Johnny G	165 - 166
The Gadgets	166
Gaffa	166
Gang Of Four	166 - 167
Gangsters	167
Gardez Darkx	168
Paul Gardiner	168
Nick Garvey	168
The Gas	168
GBH	168 - 169
Gene Loves Jezebel	169
Generation X	170 - 171
Genocide	171
The Gents	171
Gerry and The Holograms	171
The Gifted Children	171 - 172
Girls At Our Best	172
Girlschool	172 - 173
Girl Skwadd	173
Gist	173
Glass Torpedoes	173
Glaxo Babies	173 - 174
The Glory	174
The Glove	174
Vic Godard and The Subway Sect	174
Golinski Brothers	174
The Gonads	174 - 175
Dave Goodman and Friends	175
The Good Missionaries	175
Gordon and Julie	175
Gordon The Moron	176
The Gorillas	176
The Graduate	176
The Graduates	176
Grow-Up	176
The G.T.'s	176
The Gymslips	176 - 177
Gyro	177

h

Artist	Pages
Paul Haig	177
Hambi and The Dance	177
The Hammersmith Gorillas	178
Happy Family	178
Charlie Harper	178
Hazard	178
Headache	178
The Headboys	178
Headhunters	178
The Heartbeats	178

Artist	Pages
Helsinki 5 Below	179
Heroes	179
Robyn Hitchcock (and The Egyptians)	179 - 180
Holly	181
The Hollywood Brats	181
Homosexuals	181
Horrorcomic	181
Hot Water	181
Human League	181 - 183

i

Artist	Pages
Icon A.D.	184
Icons Of Filth	184
The Idiots	184
Ijax All Stars	184
Illustration	184
I'm So Hollow	184
In Camera	184
The Incredible Kidda Band	184
Indecent Exposure	184 - 185
The Industrials	185
Infa Riot	185 - 186
Inner City Unit	186
Innocent Bystanders	186
Insane	186 - 187
Instant Automations	187
Intensive Care	187
Intra Vein	187
Intro	187
Invaders	187
I.Q. Zero	187

j

Artist	Pages
Joe Jackson	188 - 189
The Jags	189
The Jam	189 - 193
Japan	193 - 195
JC's Mainman	195
Jell	196
The Jerks	196
The Jets	196
Joe Public	196
Jilted John	196
Johnny and The Self-Abusers	196
Garry Johnson	196
The Jolt	197
Josef K	197
Joy De Vivre	197
Joy Division	197 - 200
The Jump	200
Jump Squad	200
The Junco Partners	200
Just Frank	200
Justin Case	200

k

Artist	Pages
Harry Kakoulli	200
Billy Karloff	200 - 201
Karma Sutra	201
Mick Karn	201
Klark Kent	201
The Kidz Next Door	201
The Killermeters	201 - 202
Killing Joke	202 - 203
The Killjoys	203
King	204
Kleenex	204
The K9's	204

Artist	Pages
Knox	204
Kronstadt Uprising	204 - 205
Krypton Tunes	205

l

Artist	Pages
The Lambrettas	205
Landscape	205 - 206
Last Resort	206 - 207
Last Resort	207
Last Rough Cause	207
The Last Stand	207
The Last Words	208
Thomas Leer	208
Lemon Kittens	208 - 209
The Leopards	209
Le Ritz	209
Les Elite	209
The Letters	209
The Leyton Buzzards	209 - 210
Ligotage	210
The Lillettes	210
Lip Moves	210
Little Dave	210
Llygod Ffyrnig	210 - 211
Local Heroes SW9	211
Lockjaw	211
London	211
London SS	211
Long Tall Shorty	211 - 212
Lori and The Chameleons	212
The Loved One	212
Lene Lovich	212 - 213
Nick Lowe	213 - 214
The Low Numbers	214 - 215
Ludus	215
The Lurkers	215 - 216

m

Artist	Pages
Machines	216
Jimmy Mack	216
Mad Virgins	216
Magazine	216 - 218
Magic Michael	218
Major Accident	219 - 220
Malcolm Practice	220
The Man-Eaters	220
The Maniacs	220
Bob Manton	220
Manufactured Romance	220
Martin and The Brownshirts	220
Mass	220
Mau Maus	220 - 221
Maxim's Trash	221
Mayhem	221
Malcolm McLaren	221 - 222
The Meanies	222
Mean Street	222
The Media	222
Medium Medium	222
The Mekons	222 - 223
The Members	223 - 224
The Membranes	224 - 225
The Men	225
Menace	225 - 226
The Merton Parkas	226
Metrophase	226
Midnight Rags	227
Mighty Wah	227
Steve Miro and Eyes	227
The Mirrors	227
Missing Presumed Dead	227 - 228

The Mob	228	**o**		Pork Dukes	282	Kimberley Rew	304
M.O.D.	228			The Portraits	282	Rewsrd System	304
Mod 79	228	Phil Oakey and Giorgio Moroder	253	Post Mortem	282	Ambrose Reynolds	304 - 305
The Models	228	The Obtainers/Mag-Spys	253 - 254	Pragvec	282	The Rezillos	305 - 306
The Modernaires	228	Occasionally David	254	Predator	282	Rhabstallion	306
Modern English	228 - 229	Occult Chemistry	254	The Pretenders	282 - 284	Rhesus Negative	306
Modern Eon	229 - 230	Gene October	254	Private Dicks	284	Rhythm Of Life	306
Modern Man	230	The Odds	254	Private Sector	284	The Ribs	306
The Mo-dettes	230	The Offs	254	The Professionals	284 - 285	The Rich Kids	306 - 307
The Mods	230	Oi! Polloi	254	Prole	285	Riff Raff	307
The Mods	230 - 231	O-Level	254	The Proles	285	Rikki	
The Molesters	231	Omega Tribe	254 - 255	Protex	285 - 286	and The Last Days Of Earth	307 - 308
Moment	231	101'ers	255	Pseudo Existors	286	Rikki and The Numbers	308
The Monitors	231	One Way System	255 - 256	The Psychedelic Furs	286 - 287	The Rings	308
The Monochrome Set	231 - 233	The Onlookers	256	Psychos	287	Riot/Clone	308
The Mood	233	The Only Ones	256 - 257	Psykyk Volts	287	Riot Squad	308 - 309
The Moodists	233	Open Sore	257 - 258	Public Image Ltd.	287 - 289	Riot Squad	309
Mood Six	233 - 234	The Oppressed	258 - 259	Public Zone	289	The Rip Chords	309
The Moors Murderers	234	The Optimists	259	Pulp	289	The Rivals	309
Johnny Moped	234	Orange Disaster	259	Puncture	289	The Rivits	309
Moskow	234	Orchestral Manoeuvres		Punishment Of Luxury	290	Robert and The Remoulds	309
The Most	234	In The Dark	259 - 262	The Punkettes	290	Tom Robinson Band	309 - 311
Elton Motello	234 - 235	The Orgasm Guerrillas	262	Pure Hell	290	Rose Of Victory	312
The Mothmen	235	Original Mirrors	262	The Purple Hearts	290 - 291	The Rowdies	312
Motor Boys Motor	235	The Others	262	Jimmy Pursey	291	Johnny Rubbish	312
The Motors	235 - 236	John Otway		PVC 2	291	Barney Rubble	312
MP's	236	and Wild Willy Barrett	262 - 263			Rudi	312
Murder Inc.	236	Ouida and The Numbers	263			Rudimentary Peni	312 - 313
Murder The Disturbed	236	The Out	263	**q**		Ruefrex	313
Pauline Murray and The Girls	236 - 237	The Outcasts	263 - 265			Run 229	313
Pauline Murray and The Storm	237	The Outpatients	265	The Quads	291	Rus	313
Music For Pleasure	237	The Outsiders	265	The Questions	291	The Ruts	314 - 315
The Mutants	237						
Mystere Five's	237						
Mystery Girls	237	**p**		**r**		**s**	
		The Pack	265	Rabid	292	Sabre Jets	315
		The Pack	266	The Radiators	292	Sad Lovers and Giants	315
n		Pale Fountains	266	The Radiators From Space	292	The Saints	316 - 317
NAAFI Sandwich	238	The Panik	266	Radio 5	293	Salford Jets	317
Naked 1981	238	Paranoia	266 - 267	Radio Stars	293 - 294	The Same	317
Naked Lunch	238	The Parrots	267	The Rage	294	The Samples	317 - 318
The Name	238	The Partisans	267 - 268	The Raincoats	294 - 295	Satan's Rats	318
Nash The Slash	238	The Passengers	268	Eric Random	295	The Satelites	318
Nasty Media	238	The Passions	268 - 269	The Raped	295	The Scabs	318
Naughtiest Girl Was A Monitor	238	The Pathetix	269	Rat Patrol	295	Scars	318
Nazis Against Facism	238	Penetration	269 - 271	Reacta	296	The Scene	319
The Negatives	238	Perfect Zebras	271	The Reaction	296	The Scene	319
Neo	239	Mark Perry	271 - 272	The Reactors	296	The Scene	319
Neon	239	Peter		Reafer	296	Schoolgirl Bitch	319
Neon Hearts	239	and The Test Tube Babies	272	The Realists	296	The Scoop	319
The Nerves	239	The Photos	273	Reality	296	Scritti Politti	319 - 320
The New Hearts	239	The Physicals	273	The Record Players	296	Second Layer	320
Colin Newman	239 - 240	The Pigs	273	The Records	296 - 297	Secret Affair	320 - 321
New Model Army	240 - 241	Pink Industry	273 - 274	Red Alert	297 - 299	Section 25	321 - 322
New Order	241 - 244	Pink Military	274	Red Balune	299	Sema 4	322
Newtown Neurotics	244	Suzi Pinns	274	Redbeat	299	The Senate	322
Nicky and The Dots	244	Pin Point	274	Red Lights	299	Will Sergeant	322 - 323
Nightingales	244 - 245	The Piranhas	274	Red London	299 - 300	17	323
Nightmares In Wax	245	Placebo	274 - 275	Red Lorry Yellow Lorry	300	Sex Aids	323
The Nightriders	245 - 246	Plain Characters	275	Red Rage	300	The Sex Pistols	323 - 328
999	246 - 247	Plastic Bertrand	275	Redskins	300 - 301	Shake	328 - 329
Nipple Erectors	247	Plastix	275	The Reducers	301	Sham 69	329 - 331
The Nips	247 - 248	Play Dead	275 - 276	The Reflections	301	The Shapes	331
No Choice	248	The Pleasers	276	Reflex Action	302	Steve Sharp and The Cleancuts	331
No Entry Band	248	Plugs	276	Rema-Rema	302	Shock Treatment	331
The Normal	248	Plummet Airlines	276	Robert Rental (and The Normal)	302	Shoes For Industry	332
Norman and The Hooligans	248	Pneumonia	276	The Reputations	302	The Shove	332
The Normil Hawaiians	248	Poems	276	The Resistance	302	Shox	332
The Nosebleeds	249	Poison Girls	276 - 277	Resistance 77	302 - 303	Shrink	332
Notsensibles	249	The Police	277 - 279	The Resistors	303	The Sick Things	332
The Now	249	Political Asylum	279 - 280	Restricted Hours	303	Chris Sievey	332
Gary Numan	249 - 253	The Pop Group	280 - 281	The Retreads	303 - 304	Silent Noise	332
The Numbers	253	The Pop Rivets	281	Revenge	304	The Silicon Teens	333
Nurse With Wound	253	A Popular History Of Signs	281	The Revillos	304	Simple Minds	333 - 335

Entry	Page
Sinister	335
Siouxsie and The Banshees	335 - 339
The Sisterhood	339 - 340
The Sisters Of Mercy	340
Six Minute War	340
Skeletal Family	340 - 341
Skeptix	341
The Skids	340 - 343
Skin Deep	343
Skin Disease	343
Ski Patrol	343 - 344
Skrewdriver	344
The Skunks	344
Slaughter and The Dogs	344 - 345
Slime	345
The Slits	345 - 347
Smack	347
Small Hours	347
Small World	347
Smart Alec	347
The Smirks	347
Snatch	347
Sneak Preview	348
Sniff 'N' The Tears	348
The Snivelling Shits	348 - 349
Social Disease	349
Social Security	349
Society's Rejects	349
The Soft Boys	349 - 351
Soft Cell	352 - 353
The Softies	353
Some Chicken	354
Sonic Git	354
Sore Throat	354
The Sound	354
Epic Soundtracks	354
The Southern Death Cult	354
Spandau Ballet	355 - 357
Spear Of Destiny	357 - 358
Special Duties	358 - 360
The Spectres	360
The Speed	360
Speedball	361
Speedometers	361
Spelling Mistakes	361
John Spencer's Louts	361
Mike Spenser and The Cannibals	361
Spherical Objects	361 - 362
Spider	362
The Spiders	362
Spitfire Boys	362
Spizzenergi	362 - 363
Spizzles	363
Spizz Oil	363
Split Screens	363
Splodgenessabounds	363 - 364
Phones Sportsman Band	364
The Spys	364
The Squad	364
The Squares	364
Squeeze	364 - 366
Squire	366 - 367
The Stadium Dogs	367
Stage B	367
Sta-Prest	367
Starjets	367
Steppes	367
Stiff Little Fingers	367 - 372
The Stiffs	372 - 373
The Stilettos	373
The Stingrays	373
Stinky Toys	373
The Stoat	373
The Stopouts	373
Stormtrooper	373
Stormtrooper	373
The Stowaways	373
Stranger Than Fiction	374
The Strangeways	374
The Stranglers	374 - 379
Straight Up	379 - 380
Straps	380
The Streets	380
Strike	380
Strike	380
The Stripes	380
Studio Sweethearts	380
The Stukkas	380 - 381
Poly Styrene	381
Sub Culture	381
Subhumans	381 - 382
Subs	382
Substitute	382
Suburban Studs	382
Subway Sect	382 - 383
Nikki Sudden	384
Sunset Boys	384
The Surprises	384
The Suspects	384
The Suspects	384 - 385
The Sussed	385
Swell Maps	385 - 386
Swift Nick	386
David Sylvian	386 - 387
Syndicate	387
The System	387

t

Entry	Page
The Table	387
The Tagmemics	387
Micky Take and The Take Ons	387
Talk Talk	388 - 389
Tanz Der Youth	389
Taxi Girl	389
Bram Tchaikovsky	389 - 390
T.D.A.	390
The Teardrop Explodes	390 - 392
The Teardrops	392
The Tearjerkers	392
Tea Set	392
The Teenage Filmstars	392 - 393
The Teenbeats	393
The Television Personalities	393 - 395
The Tennis Shoes	395
Tenpole Tudor	395
Terri and The Terrors	395 - 396
The The	396 - 397
Theatre Of Hate	397 - 398
They Must Be Russians	398
Thieves Like Us	398
This Heat	398 - 399
This Mortal Coil	399
Those Helicopters	399
Those Naughty Lumps	399 - 400
The Threats	400
Three Party Split	400
Throbbing Gristle	400 - 402
The Throbs	402
Tickets	402
The Tigers	402
Tights	402 - 403
The Times	403 - 404
Nick Toczecks Britanarchists	404
Terry Tonik	404
The Tools	404
Too Much	404
To The Finland Station	404 - 405
The Tourists	405
The Tours	406
Toyah	406 - 407
Toy Dolls	407
The Toys	407
The Trainspotters	407
The Transmitters	409
Trax	409
Steve Treatment	409
The Trend	409
The Trokkoids	409
Troops Of Tomorrow	409
Tubeway Army	409 - 410
Turquoise Swimming Pools	410
TV 21	410 - 411
25 Rifles	411
23 Skidoo	411
Twink and The Fairies	411
Twist	411 - 412
2.3 (Children)	412
Sean Tyla (Gang)	412
Typhoons	412

u

Entry	Page
UK Subs	412 - 414
Ultra-Violent	414
Ulktravox!	414 - 417
Undead	417
The Underdogs	417
The Undertones	417 - 422
Untamed Youth	422
The Untouchables	423
The Unwanted	423
Uproar	423
The Upset	423
Urban Disturbance	423
Urban Dogs	423
Midge Ure	424
The Users	424
U2	424 - 427

v

Entry	Page
The Valves	427
The Vandells	427
Cherry Vanilla	427
The Vapors	428
Varicose Veins	428
Various Artists	428
The Varukers	428 - 429
V.D.U.'s	429
Venom	429
Vermillion (and The Aces)	429
The Vibrators	429 - 431
Vice Creems	431
Vice Squad	431 - 432
Vice Versa	432
Sid Vicious	432
Vicious Rumours	432 - 433
Vicious White Kids	433
Victim	433
Victimize	433
The Violators	433 - 434
Vipers	434
V.I.P.'s	434
The Virgin Prunes	434 - 436
Visage	436
The Visitors	436 - 437
The Vitamins	437
Vivabeat	437
Von Trapp Family	437
V2	437
Vye	437

w

Entry	Page
Wah!	437
Wah! Heat	437 - 438
The Wall	438
Larry Wallis	439
Wanderers	439
The Wardens	439
Wargasm	439
The Warm	439
Warm Jets	439
The Warriors	439
Warsaw Pakt	440
The Wasps	440
Wasted Youth	440
Wasteland	440 - 441
Water Pistols	441
Way Out	441
The What	441
Where's Lisse	441
White Boy	441
White Door	441
White Heat	441
Whitehouse	441 - 442
The White SS	442
Whooper	442
The Wild Beasts	442
The Wild Swans	442
Ada Wilson	442
The Wimps	442 - 443
Wire	443 - 445
Wolfboys!	445
Wolfgang Press	445
Woody and The Splinters	445
The Work	445 - 446
Wreckless Eric	446 - 447

x

Entry	Page
X-Certs	447
X-Cretas	447
X-Dreamysts	447
X-E-Cutors	447
X-Films	447
X-Ray Spex	447 - 450
XS Discharge	450
XS Energy	450
XTC	450 - 454
Xtract	454

y

Entry	Page
The Yachts	454 - 455
The Yobs	455
The Young Bucks	455
Young Marble Giants	455 - 456
The Young Ones	456

z

Entry	Page
The Zeros	456
The Zeros	456
Zero Zero	456
The Zones	456 - 457
Zorro	457
The Zsounds	457

THE TAPESTRY OF DELIGHTS
3RD EDITION

The 3rd Edition includes:-

* The original 600 page text.

* A new 90 page section containing around 1,000 new entries and / or updates to existing entries with lots of illustrations.

* An expanded section on relevant sixties and early seventies compilations/ soundtracks.

* An updated index incorporating all entries in the update section.

Price: £32.50
(Plus £4.50 P&P UK)
(£6.50 Air Mail Europe and Surface Mail Overseas.)

A vastly expanded 734 page guide with full discographies - Personnel details - Reissue information - Comment on artistes - Compilation listings - Rarity Scale - Over 3,200 entries - Profusely illustrated including 12 pages of full colour.

Alternatively... if you already own Tapestry Of Delights you can buy the new 128 page section only perfect bound with the full colour cover for £6.50 (Plus £2.00 P&P UK, £3.50 Air Mail Europe and Surface Mail Overseas).

To purchase books send a cheque payable to Borderline Productions. Payment must be in sterling. We regret we cannot accept credit card payments.

BORDERLINE PRODUCTIONS
Print House, Sedgley Street, Wolverhampton, WV2 3AJ, England.
Tel: +44 (0)1902 450505. Fax: +44 (0) 1902 450980.

Fuzz, Acid and Flowers
4th Edition

The 4th Edition includes:-

* The original 403 page text.

* A new 163 page section containing over 1,400 new entries and / or updates to existing entries with lots of illustrations.

* A vastly expanded section on relevant sixties and early seventies compilations / soundtracks.

* Details of lots of recent retrospective compilations.

Price: £28.00
(Plus £4.50 P&P UK)
(£6.50 Air Mail Europe and Surface Mail Overseas.)

A vastly expanded 568 page guide to American Garage, Psychedelic and Hippie Rock (1964-75). Discographies - Personnel details - Comment - Compilation listings - Rarity scale. Profusely illustrated, including 8 pages of full colour.

Alternatively... if you already own Fuzz Acid And Flowers you can buy the update section, perfect bound with the full colour cover for £8.00 (Plus £2.00 P&P UK, £3.50 AirMail Europe and Surface Mail Overseas).

To purchase books send a cheque payable to Borderline Productions. Payment must be in sterling. We regret we cannot accept credit card payments.

BORDERLINE PRODUCTIONS

Print House, Sedgley Street, Wolverhampton, WV2 3AJ, England.
Tel: +44 (0)1902 450505. Fax: +44 (0) 1902 450980.

Dreams Fantasies and Nightmares

Price: £28.00
(Plus £4.50 P&P UK)
(£6.50 Air Mail Europe and Surface Mail Overseas.)

This is your opportunity to buy the third in our series of publications aimed to provide detailed encyclopaedic guides to the rock and pop music of the golden era from the early sixties to mid-seventies. 'Fuzz, Acid and Flowers' provided a comprehensive guide to the garage, psychedelic and hippie rock of the USA. 'Tapestry Of Delights' dealt with a wide range of musical genres in the UK during this era. 'Dreams, Fantasies and Nightmares' branches out to cover rock, pop, beat, folk, folk-rock, blues-rock, psychedelia, flower-pop, garage, progressive rock and more from Canada and Australasia in this era. It also provides a general introduction to Latin American beat, psychedelia, garage and progressive rock.

Each section includes an A-Z listing of the artistes with discographies, personnel details and, for most entries, comment on the music. Details of relevant sixties and early seventies compilations and recent retrospective compilations are also included.

The book is profusely illustrated throughout with black and white illustrations and there is also a 12-page colour section.

To purchase books send a cheque payable to Borderline Productions. Payment must be in sterling.
We regret we cannot accept credit card payments.

BORDERLINE PRODUCTIONS
Print House, Sedgley Street, Wolverhampton, WV2 3AJ, England.
Tel: +44 (0)1902 450505. Fax: +44 (0) 1902 450980.

SCENTED GARDENS OF THE MIND

A COMPREHENSIVE GUIDE TO THE GOLDEN ERA OF PROGRESSIVE ROCK (1968 - 1980) IN MORE THAN 20 EUROPEAN COUNTRIES.

This superb book provides a comprehensive guide to progressive rock and related music genres in more than 20 European countries. It perfectly complements our earlier publication 'Cosmic Dreams At Play', which was a guide to German progressive and electronic rock. Most entries contain personnel details and discographies and a description of the music. Containing 552 pages, the book is profusely illustrated with a colour section in the centre. There is currently no similar English language encyclopaedic guide to the music of all these countries.

Price: £25.00
(Plus £5.00 P&P UK)
(£7.00 Air Mail Europe and Surface Mail Overseas.)

AN AMERICAN ROCK HISTORY

PART FIVE - THE MIDWEST (C)

MINNESOTA AND WISCONSIN (1960 - 1997)

This latest volume in this excellent series for record collectors and music fans contains discographies and histories of over 1,750 bands and artistes from Minnesota and Wisconsin, as well as details of personnel line-ups. The book includes 16 pages of illustrations of which 8 are in full colour.

Price £24.95 UK (plus £4.00 P&P)
(£5.50 Air Mail Europe and Surface Mail Oversea)

To purchase books send a cheque payable to Borderline Productions. Payment must be in sterling. We regret we cannot accept credit card payments.

BORDERLINE PRODUCTIONS
Print House, Sedgley Street, Wolverhampton, WV2 3AJ, England.
Tel: +44 (0)1902 450505. Fax: +44 (0) 1902 450980.